The Norton Introduction to

LITERATURE

SIXTH EDITION

The Norton Introduction to
LITERATURE

SIXTH EDITION

Carl E. Bain

Jerome Beaty

J. Paul Hunter

W • W • NORTON & COMPANY • NEW YORK • LONDON

Composition by Maple-Vail.
Manufacturing by R. R. Donnelley & Sons.

Cover illustration: Wayne Thiebaud, *Apartment Hill*. Courtesy the Nelson-Atkins Museum of
Art, Kansas City, Missouri (Purchase: Acquired with the assistance of the Friends Art).

Library of Congress Cataloging-in-Publication Data

The Norton introduction to literature / [edited by] Carl E. Bain,
Jerome Beaty, J. Paul Hunter. — 6th ed.
p. cm.
Includes indexes.
1. Literature — Collections. I. Bain, Carl E. II. Beaty, Jerome
III. Hunter, J. Paul
PN6014.N67 1994b

808 — dc20

94-42758

ISBN 0-393-96665-8

W. W. Norton & Company, Inc., 500 Fifth Avenue, New York, N.Y. 10110
W. W. Norton & Company Ltd., 10 Coptic Street, London WC1A 1PU

3 4 5 6 7 8 9 0

CONTENTS

FICTION

Fiction: Reading, Responding, Writing   3

Understanding the Text   18

v

POETRY

Poetry: Reading, Responding, Writing 651

Understanding the Text   675

WRITING ABOUT LITERATURE

FOREWORD TO THE
SIXTH EDITION

Reading is action. Even though it is often done quietly and alone, reading is a profoundly social activity, and a vigorous and demanding one. There is nothing passive about reading; it requires attention, energy, an act of will. Texts have the potential for meaning, implication, response, and result; but the reader must activate them, give them life, and turn them from quiet print into a lively interplay of ideas and feelings. Reading makes things happen, usually in the mind and imagination, but sometimes in the larger world as well, for the process of reading involves not just the consciousness of the self but an awareness of the other—what is beyond the self. Reading doesn't just happen to you; you have to **do** it, and doing it involves decision, reaching out, discovery, awareness. Reading is an act of power, and learning how to get the most out of its possibilities can be an invigorating activity. For all its association with quietness, solitude, and the sedentary life, reading involves—at its deepest level—action and interaction.

Through six editions, *The Norton Introduction to Literature* has been committed to helping students learn to read and enjoy literature. This edition, like those before it, offers many different ways of building and reinforcing the skills of reading; in addition to studying literature in terms of its elements, our book emphasizes reading works in different contexts—authorial, historical, and cultural. We have strengthened our offering of texts in contextual groups in this edition with the addition of four new chapters: to fiction, "Culture as Contexts: Border Stories" and "Literary Form as Context: The Short Short Story"; to poetry, "The Author's Work in Context: Adrienne Rich"; and to drama, "The Author's Work as Context: Anton Chekhov." Also, we have strengthened the connection between reading and writing at several points throughout the book. The introductory chapters to each genre—fiction, poetry, drama—first treat the reading experience generally, then work to involve students in examining their own responses as a first step toward writing about literature. New student papers, roughly three for each genre, offer a variety of responses to selected writing suggestions. And as in previous editions, we have provided many new selections.

But the Sixth Edition remains more than a grab-bag of good things to read. The book offers in a single volume a complete course in reading and writing about literature. It is both an anthology and a textbook—a teaching anthology—for the indispensable course in which college student and college teacher begin to read literature, and to write about it, seriously together.

The works are arranged in order to introduce a reader to the study of literature. Each genre is approached in three logical steps. Fiction, for example, is introduced by *Fiction: Reading, Responding, Writing* which treats the purpose and nature of fiction, the reading experience, and the first steps one takes to begin writing about fiction. This is followed by the seven-chapter section called *Understanding the Text*, in which stories are analyzed by questions of craft, the so-called elements of fiction; this section ends with a chapter entitled "The Whole Text," which makes use of all or most of the analytical aids offered in the previous chapters, putting them together to see the work as a whole. The third section, *Exploring Contexts*, suggests some ways of seeing a work of literature interacting with its temporal and cultural contexts and reaching out beyond the page.

The sections on reading, analyzing, and placing the work in context are followed, in each genre, by guidance in taking that final and extremely difficult step—evaluation. *Evaluating Poetry*, for example, discusses how one would go about assessing the merits of two poems, not to offer definitive judgments, a litmus test, or even a checklist or formula, but to show how one goes about bringing to consciousness, defining, modifying, articulating, and negotiating one's judgments about a work of literature.

Ending each genre, *Reading More* _____ is a reservoir of additional examples, for independent study or a different approach. The book's arrangement seeks to facilitate the reader's movement from narrower to broader questions, mirroring the way people read—wanting to learn more as they experience more.

We offer a full section on *Writing about Literature*. In it we deal both with the writing process as applied to literary works—choosing a topic, gathering evidence, developing an argument, and so forth—and with the varieties of a reader's written responses, from copying and paraphrasing to analysis and interpretation: we explore not merely the hows, but the whats and whys as well.

In this section we also offer a discussion of critical approaches, designed to provide the student with a basic overview of contemporary critical theory, as well as an introduction to its terminology.

The Sixth Edition includes 52 stories, 17 of which are new; 389 poems, 100 of which are new; and 18 plays, 5 of which are new.

In fiction, we have added new stories by Rudolfo Anaya, Margaret Atwood, Toni Cade Bambara, Charles Baxter, Angela Carter, Denise Chávez, Kate Chopin, Julio Cortázar, Richard Dokey, Ernest Hemingway, Ha Jin, Yasunari Kawabata, Margaret Laurence, Reginald McKnight, Guy Vanderhaeghe, Eudora Welty, and Lynna Williams.

The poetry section has been similarly infused with selections familiar and fresh, with newly included works by Ai, Elizabeth Alexander, Agha Shahid Ali, Anna Laetitia Barbauld, April Bernard, Earle Birney, Elizabeth Bishop, Louise Bogan, Roo Borson, Emily Brontë, Gwendolyn Brooks, Mary, Lady Chudleigh, Judith Ortiz Cofer, Wendy Cope, Hart Crane, H. D., T. S. Eliot, Louise Erdrich, Carolyn Forché, John Gay, Louise Glück, Thomas Gray, Barbara Howes, Erica Jong, Archibald Lampman, Irving Layton, Edna St. Vincent Millay, Marianne Moore, Erin Mouré, Susan Musgrave, Ricardo Pau-Llosa, Katherine Philips, Alberto Alvaro Ríos, Sir Charles G. D. Roberts, Muriel Rukeyser, Duncan Campbell Scott, Richard Snyder, Derek Walcott, Edmund Waller, and Walt Whitman.

New selections to the drama section include Anton Chekhov's *The Cherry*

Orchard, Caryl Churchill's *Top Girls,* Marsha Norman's *Getting Out,* Bernard Shaw's *Pygmalion,* and Sophocles' *Antigone.*

Certain editorial procedures that proved their usefulness in earlier editions have been retained. First of all, the works are annotated, as is customary in Norton anthologies; the notes are informational and not interpretative, for the aim is to help readers understand and appreciate the work, not to dictate a meaning or a response. In order to avoid giving the impression that all literature was written at the same time, we have noted at the right margin after each selection the date of first book publication (or, when preceded by a *p,* first periodical publication or, when the date appears at the left margin, the year of composition).

In all our work on this edition we have been guided by teachers in other English departments and in our own, by students who wrote us as the authors of the textbook they were using, and by those who were able to approach us after class as their teachers: we hope that with such help we have been able to offer you a solid and stimulating introduction to the experience of literature.

Acknowledgments We would like to thank our teachers, for their example in the love of literature and in the art of sharing that love; our students, for their patience as we are learning from them to be better teachers of literature; our wives and children, for their understanding when the work of preparing this text made us seem less than perfectly loving husbands and fathers.

We would also like to thank our colleagues, many of whom have taught our book and evaluated our efforts, for their constant encouragement and enlightenment. Of our colleagues at Emory University and the University of Chicago, we would like especially to thank Jim Boyle, John Bugge, Louis Corrigan, William B. Dillingham, Larry Eby, Mark Sanders, Ron Schuchard, Deborah Sitter, John Sitter, Sally Wolff King and Emily Wright (Emory) and Jonathan Martin, Robert von Hallberg, Michelle Hawley, Anne Elizabeth Murdy, Janel Mueller, Vicky Olwell, Richard Strier, and John Wright (Chicago). For their help in selecting papers by student writers, we would like to thank Geneva Ballard, Theresa Budniakiewicz, Rebecca S. Ries, and Avantika Rohatgi, of Indiana University — Purdue University at Indianapolis, and Thomas Miller, Tilly Warnock, Lisa-Anne Culp, Loren Goodman, Brendan McBryde, and Ruthe Thompson, at the University of Arizona. We also thank the students whose papers we include: Daniel Bronson, Geoffrey Clement, Teri Garrity, Meaghan E. Parker, Sara Rosen, Sherry Schnake, Kimberly Smith, Thaddeus Smith, Jeanette Sperhac, and Caryl Zook. For their work on the *Instructor's Guide,* we thank Gayla McGlamery and Bryan Crockett, Loyola College in Baltimore.

And we thank also Elizabeth Alkagond, Columbia College; M. Allen, Bakersfield College; Marjorie Allen, LaSalle University; Preston Allen, Miami-Dade Community College; Sally Allen, North Georgia College; Bruce Anawalt, Washington State University; Anne Andrews, Mississippi State University; Charles Angel, Bridgewater State College; Booker Anthony, Fayetteville State University; Robert Arledge, Southern University at New Orleans; Michael Atkinson, University of Cincinnati; Janet Auten, American University; Sylvia Baer,

Gloucester County College; Raymond Bailey, Bishop State Community College; Lee Baker, High Point College; Harold Bakst, Minneapolis Community College; Nancy Barendse, Christopher Newport College; Chris Barkley, Palomar College; Linda Barlow, Fayetteville State University; William Barnette, Prestonsburg Community College; Dr. Barney, Citrus College; E. Barnton, California State University, Bakersfield; Harry E. Batty, University of Maine; Shawn Beaty, Hokkaido University; Nancy Beers, Temple University; Linda Bensel-Meyers, University of Tennessee, Knoxville; Lawrence Berkoben, California State University; Tracey Besmark, Ashland Community College; Barbara Bird, St. Petersburg Community College; Lillian Bisson, Marymount College; Clark Blaise, University of Iowa; T. E. Blom, University of British Columbia; Roy L. Bond, University of Texas at Dallas; Steven Bouler, Tuskegee University; Veleda Boyd, Tarleton State University; Helen Bridge, Chabot College; Sandra Brim, North Georgia College; Loretta Brister, Tarleton State University; Patrick Broderick, Santa Rosa Junior College; Robert Brophy, California State University, Long Beach; Theresa Brown, Tufts University; William Brown, Philadelphia College of Textiles and Science; Virginia Brumbach, Eastfield College; C. Bryant, Colby College; Edward Burns, William Paterson College of New Jersey; Daniel Cahill, University of Northern Iowa; Martha Campbell, St. Petersburg Community College at Tarpon Springs; William Campbell, Monroe Community College; D. Cano, Santa Monica Community College; Nathan Carb, Rowan College of New Jersey; Roger Carlstrom, Yakima Valley Community College; Martha Carpentier, Seton Hall University; Anne Carr, Southeast Community College; Conrad Carroll, Northern Kentucky University; Gisela Casines, Florida International University; Ahwadhesh Chaudhary, Texas College; Dr. Clark, Citrus College; John Clower, Indiana University–Purdue University at Indianapolis; Steven Cole, Temple University; Cindy Collins, Fullerton College; Kathleen Collins, Creighton University; Marianne Conroy, McGill University; Pat Conner, Memphis State University; Martha Cook, Longwood College; Holly Cordova, Contra Costa College; Susan Cornett, St. Petersburg Community College at Tarpon Springs; Brian Corrigan, North Georgia College; Betty Corum, Owensboro Community College; Beverly Cotton, Cerritos College; Delmar Crisp, Wesleyan College; Virginia Critchlow, Monroe Community College; Carol Cunningham-Ruiz, Bakersfield College; Lennett Daigle, North Georgia College; Christopher Dark, Tarleton State University; Vivian Davis, Eastfield College; Hugh Dawson, University of San Francisco; Martha Day, Richard Bland College; George Diamond, Moravian College; Helen DiBona, North Carolina Central University; Sister Mary Colleen Dillon, Thomas More College; Marvin Diogenes, University of Arizona; Frank Dobson, Indiana University–Purdue University at Indianapolis; Minna Doskow, Rowan College of New Jersey; Donald Dowdey, Virginia Wesleyan College; Bonnie Duncan, Upper Iowa University; Timothy Dykstal, Auburn University; Wayne Eason, University of North Carolina at Charlotte; Paula Eckard, University of North Carolina at Charlotte; Mary Eiser, Kauai Community College; Marianne Eismann, Wake Forest University; Joyce Ellis, North Carolina Central University; Reed Ellis, St. John's Community College; Peggy Endel, Florida International University; James Erickson, Wichita State University; Dessagene Ewing, Delaware County Community College; Jim Ewing, North Georgia College; Sasha Feinstein, Indiana University; Charles Feldstein, Florida Community College at Jacksonville; Norman Feltes, York University; Jean Fields, Lindenwood College; Mildred Flynn, South Dakota University; Eileen Foley, University of Maine; Dolores Formicella, Delaware County Community College; Elsa Ann Gaines, North Georgia College; Dennis Gaitner, Frostburg State University; Reloy Garcia, Creighton University; Joseph Glaser, Western Kentucky University; Andrea Glebe, University of Nevada; Karen Gleeman, Normandale Community College; C. Golliher, Victor Valley College; Douglas Gordon, Christopher Newport College; Donna Gormly, Eastfield College; Kathryn Graham, Virginia Polytechnic Institute and State University; Pat Gregory, Community College of Philadelphia; Ann Grigsby, University of New Mexico; Alan Grob, Rice University; Lynda Haas, Hillsborough Community College; Florence Halle, Memphis State University; Jerry Harris, Western Oregon State College; Sydney Harrison, Manatee Community College; Joan Hartman, William Patterson College; Charles Hatten, Bellarmine College; Bruce Henderson, Fullerton College; Nancy Henry, SUNY at Binghamton; David Hernandez, Eastfield College; Robert Herzog, Monroe Community College; Laura Higgs, Clemson University; David Hill, SUNY College at Oswego; Robert Hipkiss, California State University; David Hoegberg, Indiana University–Purdue University at Indianapolis; Eartha Holley, Delaware State University; R. C. Hoover, Wenatchee Valley College; Roger Horn, Charles County Community College; L. C. Howard, Skyline College; Erlene Hubly, University of Northern Iowa; William Hudson, Radford University; David Hufford, Iowa Western Community College; Deirdre Hughes, Fullerton College; Dr. Humphrey, Citrus College; Kathryn Montgomery Hunter, Northwestern University School of Medicine; Lisa Hunter, University of Wisconsin Medical School; P. Hunter, Los Angeles Valley College; Edelina Huntley, Appalachian State University; Robert Huntley, Washington and Lee University; Sharon Irvin, Florida Institute of Technology; Sylvia Iskander, University of Southwestern Louisiana; Eleanor James, Montgomery County Community College; Anne Johnson, Jacksonville State University; Christopher Johnson, Missouri Valley College; Craig Johnson, Hillsborough Community College; Darryl Johnson, St. Cloud State University; Dolores Johnson, Seattle University; Karen Johnson, Indiana University–Purdue University at Indianapolis; Dr. Jones, Citrus College; Grace Jones, Owensboro Community College; Walter Kalaidjian, St. Cloud State University; Frank Kastor, Wichita State University; E. Kenney, Colby College; Don King, Central Washington University; Andrew Kirk, University of California, Davis; John Klijinski, Idaho State University; William Klink, Charles County Community College; Michael Krasny, San Francisco State University; Anne Krause, Yakima Valley Community College; Harold Kuglemass, Onondaga Community College; Stuart Kurland, Muhlenberg College; Donald Lawler, East Carolina University; Lynn Lewis, Memphis State University; Vincent J. Liesenfeld, University of Oklahoma; Jun Liu, California State University, Los Angeles; Travis Livingston, Tarleton State University; Lillian Liwag-Sutcliffe, Old Dominion University; Mary Lowe-Evans, University of West Florida; Michael Lund, Longwood College; Kathleen Lyons, Bellarmine College; Thomas Mack, University of South Carolina; Patricia MacVaugh, Lehigh County Community College; Emory Maiden, Appalachian State University; Christina Malcolmson, Bates College; Dexter Marks, Jersey City State College; William Martin, Tarleton State University; Frank Mason, University of South Florida; Pam Mathis, North Arkansas Community College; Laura May, St. Petersburg Community College; Katherine Maynard, Rider College; R. McAllister, Victor Valley College; Kathleen McCloy, Shoreline Community College; Betty J. McCommas, Ouachita Baptist University; Clare McDonnell, Neumann College; Frank McLaughlin, Ramapo College; Thomas McLaughlin, Appalachian State University; William McMahon, Western Kentucky University; Terrence McNally, Northern Kentucky University; Alan McNarie, University of Hawaii; Nyan McNeill, Foothill College; Jay Meek, University of North Dakota; Ivan Melada, University of New Mexico; Donna Melancon, Xavier University; Linda Merions, LaSalle University; Darlene Mettler, Wesleyan College; R. Metzger, Los Angeles Valley College; Brian Michaels, Diane Middlebrook (Stanford University) St. John's Community College; Daniel Miller, Northern Kentucky University; George Miller, University of Delaware; Ron Miller, University of West Florida; Leslie Mittelman, California State University, Long Beach; Rosa Mizerski, West Valley College; Rosemary Moffett, Elizabethtown Community College; Warren Moore, Loyola College; Mike Moran, University of Georgia; Dean Morgan, Olympic College; William Morgan, Illinois State University; William Morris, University of South Florida; Sharon Morrow, University of Southern Indiana; Renate Muendel, West Chester University; Gordon Mundell, University of Nebraska; David Murdoch, Rochester Institute of Technology; Carol Murphy, Roanoke College; Thomas Murray, Trenton State College; Joseph Nacca, Community College of Finger Lakes; Joseph Nasser, Rochester Institute of Technology; Mary Neil, Eastfield College; Kay Nelson, St. Cloud University; Dorothy Newman, Southern University; Lee Nicholson, Modesto Junior College; Mimi Nicholson, University of Southern Indiana; Elizabeth Nollen, West Chester University; Dale Norris, Des Moines Community College; Robert Ochsner, University of Maryland at Baltimore; Sarah Oglesby, Madisonville Community College; Francis Olley, Saint Joseph's University; Ann Olson, Central Washington University; Regina Oost, Wesleyan College; Mildred Orenstein, Drexel University; Kathleen O'Shea, Monroe Community College; Thornton Penfield, Southern University; Christopher Penna, University of Delaware; Rita Perkins, Camden County College; Donald Peterson, City College of San Francisco; Steven Phelan, Rollins College; Randall Popken, Tarleton State University; Robert Post, University of Washington; Pamela Postma, University of North Carolina at Greensboro; Linda Ray Pratt, University of Nebraska; Ross Primm, Columbia College; Richard Quaintance, Rutgers University; James Randall, Coe College; Rosemary Raynal, Davidson College; Mary Rea, Indiana University–Purdue University at Indianapolis; Thomas Redshaw, University of St. Thomas; Ron Reed, Hazard Community College; Donna Reiss, Tidewater Community College; Alan Richardson, Boston College; Ann Richey, Virginia

Polytechnic Institute and State University; Joan Richmond, Tarleton State University; Harold Ridley, LeMoyne College; Leonard Roberts, Northampton Area Community College; Douglas Robinson, University of Mississippi; J. Robinson, Victor Valley College; Beate Rodewald, Palm Beach Atlantic College; Ruben Rodriguez, Tarleton State University; Owen Rogal, St. Ambrose University; Eva Rosenn, Wesleyan College; William Rossiter, Flathead Valley College; Connie Rothwell, University of North Carolina; Don Rud, Texas Tech University; Don Russ, Kennesaw State College; Charles J. Rzepka, Boston University; Christina Savage, Long Beach City College; Vicki Scannell, Pierce College; Paul Schacht, SUNY College at Geneseo; Steven Scherwatzky, Merrimack College; Marie Schiebold, Skyline College; Ronald Schleifer, University of Oklahoma; Linda Schmidt, Iowa Western Community College; Roger Schmidt, Idaho State College; Michael Schoenecke, Texas Tech University; Jane Schultz, Indiana University–Purdue University at Indianapolis; Lucille Schultz, University of Cincinnati; Carolyn Segal, Lehigh University; JoAnn Seiple, University of North Carolina; Bill Senior, Broward Community College; Pat Shalter, Reading Area Community College; Lewis Sheffler, Missouri Valley College; Richard Siciliano, Charles County Community College; Odette Sims, Modesto Junior College; Judy Jo Small, North Carolina State University; Louise Smith, University of Massachusetts; Peter Smith, Wesleyan College; Stephen Smith, LaSalle University; Thomas Sonith, Widener University; B. Spears, Victor Valley College; Dr. Spencer, California State University, Bakersfield; Rich Sprouse, North Georgia College; Ann Spurlock, Mississippi State University; David Stacey, Missouri Valley College; Nancy Stahl, Indiana University–Purdue University at Indianapolis; Jamie Steckelberg, University of North Dakota; James Stick, Des Moines Community College; Bruce Stillians, University of Hawaii; McKay Sundwall, East Carolina University; Kathryn Swanson, Augsburg College; John Taylor, College of Marin; Judith Taylor, Northern Kentucky University; David Thibodaux, University of Southwestern Louisiana; Victor Thompson, Thomas Nelson Community College; Charles Thornbury, College of St. Benedict; Mike Thro, Tidewater Community College; Kathleen Tickner, Brevard Community College; Edna Troiano, Charles County Community College; Gail Tubbs, Washington College; Richard Turner, Indiana University–Purdue University at Indianapolis; Teresa Tweet, Augustana College; D. Unrue, University of Nevada; Margaret Vail, Xavier University; Diana Valdina, Cayuga County Community College; Kenneth Vandover, Lincoln University; Eleanor Vassal, St. Petersburg Community College; Tim Viator, North Georgia College; Richard Victor, Saddleback College; Jeanne Walker, University of Delaware; Cynthia Wall, University of Virginia; Leslie Wallace, DeAnza College; W. Wallis, Los Angeles Valley College; R. Warkentin, California State University, Dominguez Hills; David Weekes, Eastern Washington University; Edwin Weihe, Seattle University; Ronald Wendling, Saint Joseph's University; Agnes Whitsel, Mercer University; Keith Wicker, Henderson Community College; Inga Wiehl, Yakima Valley College; Waller Wigginton, Idaho State University; Arthur Williams, Louisiana School for Mathematics, Science and the Arts; Jack Williams, California State University; James Wilson, University of Southwestern Louisiana;

Sharon Wilson, Fort Hays State University; Sandra Witt, University of Northern Iowa; Susan Wolstenholme, Cayuga County Community College; Strohn Woodward, University of Maine; James Wyatt, Lindsey Wilson College; Linda Yakle, St. Petersburg Community College; and Dr. Zounes, Los Angeles Valley College.

We would like to thank our friends at W. W. Norton & Company, especially the late John Benedict and the late Barry Wade, to whom we dedicate this revision, and also Allen Clawson, Carol Hollar-Zwick, Kate Lovelady, John Mardirosian, Fred McFarland, Diane O'Connor, Nancy Palmquist, David Sutter, Ann Tappert, and Candace Watt.

J.B., J.P.H.

The Norton Introduction to

LITERATURE

SIXTH EDITION

FICTION

∇ ∇ ∇

Fiction: Reading, Responding, Writing

SPENCER HOLST

The Zebra Storyteller

Once upon a time there was a Siamese cat who pretended to be a lion and spoke inappropriate Zebraic.

That language is whinnied by the race of striped horses in Africa.

Here now: An innocent zebra is walking in a jungle and approaching from another direction is the little cat; they meet.

"Hello there!" says the Siamese cat in perfectly pronounced Zebraic. "It certainly is a pleasant day, isn't it? The sun is shining, the birds are singing, isn't the world a lovely place to live today!"

The zebra is so astonished at hearing a Siamese cat speaking like a zebra,   5
why—he's just fit to be tied.

So the little cat quickly ties him up, kills him, and drags the better parts of the carcass back to his den.

The cat successfully hunted zebras many months in this manner, dining on filet mignon of zebra every night, and from the better hides he made bow neckties and wide belts after the fashion of the decadent princes of the Old Siamese court.

He began boasting to his friends he was a lion, and he gave them as proof the fact that he hunted zebras.

The delicate noses of the zebras told them there was really no lion in the neighborhood. The zebra deaths caused many to avoid the region. Superstitious, they decided the woods were haunted by the ghost of a lion.

3

10   One day the storyteller of the zebras was ambling, and through his mind ran plots for stories to amuse the other zebras, when suddenly his eyes brightened, and he said, "That's it! I'll tell a story about a Siamese cat who learns to speak our language! What an idea! That'll make 'em laugh!"

Just then the Siamese cat appeared before him, and said, "Hello there! Pleasant day today, isn't it!"

The zebra storyteller wasn't fit to be tied at hearing a cat speaking his language, because he'd been thinking about that very thing.

He took a good look at the cat, and he didn't know why, but there was something about his looks he didn't like, so he kicked him with a hoof and killed him.

That is the function of the storyteller.

1971

T he Zebra Storyteller" suggests that the purpose of stories is to prepare us for the unexpected. Though the storyteller thinks he is just spinning stories out of his own imagination in order to amuse, his stories prove to be practical. When the extraordinary occurs—like a Siamese cat speaking Zebraic—the storyteller is prepared because he has already imagined it, and he alone is able to protect his tribe against the unheard-of.

Other storytellers make the function of fiction less extraordinary. According to them, fiction enables readers to avoid projecting false hopes and fears (such as the zebras' superstitious belief that they are being preyed on by the ghost of a lion) and shows them what they can actually expect in their everyday lives, so that they can prepare themselves. In George Eliot's novel *Adam Bede*, Hetty Sorrel is being paid admiring attention by the young squire, and she dreams of elopement, marriage, all sorts of vague pleasures. She does not dream that she will be seduced, made pregnant, abandoned. Her imagination has not been trained to project any "narrative" other than her dreams: "Hetty had never read a novel," George Eliot tells us, "[so] how could she find a shape for her expectations?"

We are all storytellers, then, of one stripe or another. Whenever we plan the future or ponder a decision, we are telling stories—projecting expectations through narrative. Whether we tell stories or read them, we are educating our imaginations, either extending our mental experience in the actual, as Hetty might have done by reading novels, or preparing ourselves for the extraordinary and unexpected, like the zebra storyteller.

The actual and the extraordinary suggest two different uses readers make of fiction. Sometimes we want to read about people like ourselves, or about places, experiences, and ideas that are familiar and agreeable. Most of us initially prefer American literature and twentieth-century literature to literature remote in time or place. Indeed, stories must somehow be related to our own lives before we can find them intellectually or emotionally meaningful. No matter what our literary experience and taste, most of us relate in a special way to stories about people like us, experiences like our own, and especially to a story that mentions our hometown or neighborhood or the name of the street that we used to walk along on our way to school. No one would deny that one of the many things that fiction may be "for" is learning about ourselves and the world around us.

But occasionally the last thing we want is a story about people like ourselves, experiences like those of our everyday lives, and places and times like here and now. On such occasions we want (or are accused of wanting) to escape. If fiction must be relevant enough to relate meaningfully to us, it must also be "irrelevant," different, strange—as strange, perhaps, as a Siamese cat speaking Zebraic. It must take us out of ourselves, out of the confining vision of our own eyes, which is conditioned by our own background and experience, and show us that there are ways of looking at the world other than our own. So, in addition to many stories about approximately our own time and place, this collection includes a sprinkling of stories written in the last century, a few written in vastly different cultures, and a few written about worlds that have not existed or do not (yet) exist.

What a story shows us or teaches us we may call its **message**—an objective, universal truth that we were unaware of before reading the story. We gradually learn, however, that stories tell us not so much what life means as what it's like. Rather than abstract or "objective" truths, stories deal with perceptions. These perceptions may be translated into messages, but we soon discover that the messages boil down to things like "There's good and bad in everybody," "Hurting people is wrong," and "Everything is not what it seems"—messages we do not need Western Union, much less Western literature, to deliver. Indeed, we do not have to agree with what a story says or shows so long as we are convinced that if we had *those* eyes and were *there*, this is what we might see.

Whenever we can say yes, we are convinced, then we have been able to go beyond the limitations of our own vision, our own past and conditions. We are able to see a new world, or the same old world in a new way. And by recognizing that we can see things differently, we realize that things we used to think were fixed, objective entities "out there," were fixed only in our perceptions. Or, as is too often the case, we realize that we have been accepting things at face value; we have been perceiving what habit and convention have told us is "really there." Stories, then, may awaken us to look at things for ourselves. For example, we "know" a table top is square, but in a story we may be told it is diamond-shaped. We understand that if we were to look at the table top from a certain angle it would appear diamond-shaped. But doesn't that mean that the table top is square only when we look at it from a certain angle? How often do we look at a table top from that angle? We look again, and we recognize that though we've always "known" a table top is a square, we may have never actually *seen* it as one. The story has not only allowed us to see reality from another angle, but it has helped us to sharpen our own vision, our own experience.

In the story that follows, both the eighteen-year-old narrator and Jack are storytellers: each projects a future. The story, however, remains in the present, so we cannot tell which projection is right. Like the characters, we are more or less in the middle of our own lives. Though they may not get to know the future, both Jack and the narrator learn through their storytelling that more than one scenario of the future can be projected. Even if we think the narrator as naive as George Eliot's Hetty, projecting a dream rather than a possible reality, she has now at least "read Jack's novel," so she knows there are alternative futures. And so do we.

ELIZABETH TALLENT

No One's a Mystery

For my eighteenth birthday Jack gave me a five-year diary with a latch and a little key, light as a dime. I was sitting beside him scratching at the lock, which didn't seem to want to work, when he thought he saw his wife's Cadillac in the distance, coming toward us. He pushed me down onto the dirty floor of the pickup and kept one hand on my head while I inhaled the musk of his cigarettes in the dashboard ashtray and sang along with Rosanne Cash on the tape deck. We'd been drinking tequila and the bottle was between his legs, resting up against his crotch, where the seam of his Levi's was bleached linen-white, though the Levi's were nearly new. I don't know why his Levi's always bleached like that, along the seams and at the knees. In a curve of cloth his zipper glinted, gold.

"It's her," he said. "She keeps the lights on in the daytime. I can't think of a single habit in a woman that irritates me more than that." When he saw that I was going to stay still he took his hand from my head and ran it through his own dark hair.

"Why does she?" I said.

"She thinks it's safer. Why does she need to be safer? She's driving exactly fifty-five miles an hour. She believes in those signs: 'Speed Monitored by Air-craft.' It doesn't matter that you can look up and see that the sky is empty."

"She'll see your lips move, Jack. She'll know you're talking to someone."

"She'll think I'm singing along with the radio."

He didn't lift his head, just raised the fingers in salute while the pressure of his palm steadied the wheel, and I heard the Cadillac honk twice, musically; he was driving easily eighty miles an hour. I studied his boots. The elk heads stitched into the leather were bearded with frayed thread, the toes were scuffed, and there was a compact wedge of muddy manure between the heel and the sole—the same boots he'd been wearing for the two years I'd known him. On the tape deck Rosanne Cash sang, "Nobody's into me, no one's a mystery."

"Do you think she's getting famous because of who her daddy is or for her-self?" Jack said.

"There are about a hundred pop tops on the floor, did you know that? Some little kid could cut a bare foot on one of these, Jack."

"No little kids get into this truck except for you."

"How come you let it get so dirty?"

" 'How come,' " he mocked. "You even sound like a kid. You can get back into the seat now, if you want. She's not going to look over her shoulder and see you."

"How do you know?"

"I just know," he said. "Like I know I'm going to get meat loaf for supper. It's in the air. Like I know what you'll be writing in that diary."

"What will I be writing?" I knelt on my side of the seat and craned around to look at the butterfly of dust printed on my jeans. Outside the window Wyo-ming was dazzling in the heat. The wheat was fawn and yellow and parted smoothly by the thin dirt road. I could smell the water in the irrigation ditches hidden in the wheat.

"Tonight you'll write, 'I love Jack. This is my birthday present from him. I can't imagine anybody loving anybody more than I love Jack.' "

"I can't."

"In a year you'll write, 'I wonder what I ever really saw in Jack. I wonder why I spent so many days just riding around in his pickup. It's true he taught me something about sex. It's true there wasn't ever much else to do in Cheyenne.' "

"I won't write that."

"In two years you'll write, 'I wonder what that old guy's name was, the one with the curly hair and the filthy dirty pickup truck and time on his hands.' "

"I won't write that."

"No?"

"Tonight I'll write, 'I love Jack. This is my birthday present from him. I can't imagine anybody loving anybody more than I love Jack.' "

"No, you can't," he said. "You can't imagine it."

"In a year I'll write, 'Jack should be home any minute now. The table's set— my grandmother's linen and her old silver and the yellow candles left over from the wedding—but I don't know if I can wait until after the trout à la Navarra to make love to him.' "

"It must have been a fast divorce."

"In two years I'll write, 'Jack should be home by now. Little Jack is hungry for his supper. He said his first word today besides "Mama" and "Papa." He said "kaka." ' "

Jack laughed. "He was probably trying to finger-paint with kaka on the bathroom wall when you heard him say it."

"In three years I'll write, 'My nipples are a little sore from nursing Eliza Rosamund.' "

"Rosamund. Every little girl should have a middle name she hates."

" 'Her breath smells like vanilla and her eyes are just Jack's color of blue.' "

"That's nice," Jack said.

"So, which one do you like?"

"I like yours," he said. "But I believe mine."

"It doesn't matter. I believe mine."

"Not in your heart of hearts, you don't."

"You're wrong."

"I'm not wrong," he said. "And her breath would smell like your milk, and it's kind of a bittersweet smell, if you want to know the truth."

1985

Since Jack and the narrator are not zebras but people you may think of as real, maybe even people somewhat like yourself, you may feel in a position to take sides. One of the pleasures of reading and one of the ways of penetrating the meaning and effectiveness of stories is through your emotional responses, which often begin with your rooting for, identifying with, admiring, or despising one character or the other. Our wishes and fears, our expectations and emotions, and the kind of world we imagine that the characters inhabit make up the major register of our emotional responses to fiction. And one of the first moves from reading to writing about fiction may well involve this "partisanship."

Some of your emotional responses to a story will come from your own first- or second-hand experience. You may have been in a situation somewhat like that in "No One's a Mystery" (as the narrator, the wife, or Jack), and who you were in the triangle may have something to do with how you respond to the story. Or, if you are a cat-lover with four Siamese kittens, you may not be able fully to identify with the zebra storyteller.

There are two views emphasized in "No One's a Mystery," two main characters you might identify or side with. How do you feel about the narrator? You may think she's a fool for getting involved with a married man, or immoral, and so perhaps you feel bitter about her projections of a married life with Jack, and believe they will never come true. Or you may identify with her, and find her dreams poignant (if hopeless) or uplifting (if you think they might come true), while Jack may be viewed as either realistic or cynical. An early paper in a literature course may have you defend the projections into the future of Jack or the narrator. You may wish to argue that both are wrong, both right, or that the truth lies somewhere in between. Or you may argue for the story's third character, the wife, who, though not embodied, may nevertheless elicit your sympathy. Try writing down your view of a story like this in essay form before discussing it with others. You will then have a record of your uninfluenced, unchallenged view. Later, you may be surprised to find that some of your class-mates do not agree with you. But in discussing or arguing for your views you may discover not only that there are reasonable differences of opinion, but that what one believes about the future beyond the story reveals something about that person. A second paper may be either an argument with someone else's position or a composite or new view based on your discussion and exchange with classmates. And you may want to look at what you learned about yourself from your arguments about the story.

These ideas for papers are meant to be more than suggested writing assign-ments. They also suggest one *way* of writing about literature and are meant to show that writing about a story is not some special or arcane art but just a some-what more formal, responsible, committed way of talking about what you have read. Think of the last time you saw a movie with a friend and left the theater discussing the film. If you were to put such responses down on paper, look at them carefully, think about them a bit, and try to make your views or responses convincing, you've taken the first step toward writing about literature. You could even call it literary criticism.

Writing about the characters and events in stories as if they were real peo-ple and real happenings, and writing about your responses to and opinions about them, is only one kind of writing about literature. You can only write such a paper *after* you have read the whole story and formed an opinion, and your "argument" will involve going back to the story seeking out details to sup-port your position, and, perhaps, situating where you are coming from in terms of personal experience, moral or religious views, and so on. But reading a story is not just something to argue or even think about after you have read it. It is first of all an experience—made up of thoughts and feelings—that happens *while you are in the very act of reading.*

One of the things most of us do when we are actively engaged in reading a story is to anticipate or interpret: what will happen next? what kind of person is a given character? how is the world of the story related to the world as I know it? what kind of a story is it? will it end happily or not? You will notice two aspects to such anticipation. One involves our experience, direct or indirect, in the world, and may be thought of as referential or representational; that is, we take the nouns to refer to real things—the word *table* calls up a more or less concrete image of a table—and from the words describing characters we imagine more or less real people and their actions and choices as potentially if not actually real. We have discussed "No One's a Mystery" as if the narrator and Jack were real people living in the real world, specifically Wyoming. The other aspect is literary. We pay attention to the words themselves, to their sounds, their connotations, their relation to other words that look or sound like them, and not just to what they denote—tables or Cadillacs or jewels. Stories can even play with these referential and literary aspects of words, surprising us by shifting from one aspect to another. The zebra who did not tell stories was astonished, and the words say "he's just fit to be tied." This is a common figure of speech, and we do not expect to take the words "seriously" or referentially. We are surprised, then, when the story does: "So the little cat quickly ties him up. . . ."

We are aware that a story is a story and that telling a story involves certain conventions—for example, stories are generally written in the past tense, though we like to imagine them as happening in a kind of present, with the end not yet known. Different kinds of stories, too, have their own conventions: fairy tales and sometimes other fantasies, like "The Zebra Storyteller," begin with "Once upon a time"; in ghost stories and certain other scary stories there is almost always a beautiful young woman threatened by danger; these stories, adventure stories, and comic stories almost always end happily, and so on.

Anticipation begins at the beginning—or even earlier. As soon as we read the title of the story that follows, "The Jewelry," we start: will it be lost? stolen? inherited? Our anticipation is channeled by first- or second-hand life experience—how we think jewelry functions in "the real world." Notice that this anticipation is triggered by the title. Life experiences do not come with titles to guide us, but our reading experience tells us that titles are significant, worth paying attention to if we are to anticipate and understand. Perhaps not as early as our reading of the title, but soon, we begin to anticipate a shape or configuration of the entire story. Based on our own real experiences and what we've read, we project a vague shape early on, frequently adjusting it as we proceed through the story, but always connected to it as we read on. With the first sentence of "The Jewelry"—"Having met the girl one evening, at the house of the office-superintendent, M. Lantin became enveloped in love as in a net"—we begin casting our own net. The story will involve love. What do we know or believe about love? about different kinds of love? about the possible outcomes of falling in love? What is the connection between love and jewelry? We are not yet prepared to define that connection, but we may have tentative expectations about it. Though the first sentence may be summarized in "real" or experiential terms as "M. Lantin has fallen (deeply) in love," the precise *words* in the sentence that describe falling in love are "became enveloped in love as in a net." Does this merely emphasize how deeply he has fallen in love or is there something uncomfortable, painful, even ominous about the words—note, about the *words*—"enveloped as in a net"? How we anticipate and interpret what the story "means" or "says about life" will be conditioned throughout by our life experience, by such literary "devices" as the title, by the precise words of the story, and by our experience with kinds of stories and what usually happens and eventuates in such stories. We must remain tentative in our expectations, however, and alert to changes and modifications; for example, when the fourth paragraph of this story concludes with "and [he] married her," we must abandon the love-and-courtship story we anticipated and imagine an entirely new set of possibilities.

GUY DE MAUPASSANT

The Jewelry[1]

Having met the girl one evening, at the house of the office-superintendent, M. Lantin became enveloped in love as in a net.

She was the daughter of a country-tutor, who had been dead for several years. Afterward she had come to Paris with her mother, who made regular visits to several bourgeois families of the neighborhood, in hopes of being able to get her daughter married. They were poor and respectable, quiet and gentle. The young girl seemed to be the very ideal of that pure good woman to whom every young man dreams of entrusting his future. Her modest beauty had a charm of angelic shyness; and the slight smile that always dwelt about her lips seemed a reflection of her heart.

Everybody sang her praises; all who knew her kept saying: "The man who gets her will be lucky. No one could find a nicer girl than that."

M. Lantin, who was then chief clerk in the office of the Minister of the Interior, with a salary of 3,500 francs a year,[2] demanded her hand, and married her.

1. Translated by Lafcadio Hearn.   2. A midlevel bureaucratic wage, perhaps about $25,000–$30,000 today.

He was unutterably happy with her. She ruled his home with an economy so adroit that they really seemed to live in luxury. It would be impossible to conceive of any attentions, tendernesses, playful caresses which she did not lavish upon her husband; and such was the charm of her person that, six years after he married her, he loved her even more than he did the first day.

There were only two points upon which he ever found fault with her—her love of the theater, and her passion for false jewelry.

Her lady-friends (she was acquainted with the wives of several small office holders) were always bringing her tickets for the theaters; whenever there was a performance that made a sensation, she always had her *loge* secured, even for first performances; and she would drag her husband with her to all these entertainments, which used to tire him horribly after his day's work. So at last he begged her to go to the theater with some lady-acquaintances who would consent to see her home afterward. She refused for quite a while—thinking it would not look very well to go out thus unaccompanied by her husband. But finally she yielded, just to please him; and he felt infinitely grateful to her therefor.

Now this passion for the theater at last evoked in her the desire of dress. It was true that her toilette remained simple, always in good taste, but modest; and her sweet grace, her irresistible grace, ever smiling and shy, seemed to take fresh charm from the simplicity of her robes. But she got into the habit of suspending in her pretty ears two big cut pebbles, fashioned in imitation of diamonds; and she wore necklaces of false pearls, bracelets of false gold, and haircombs studded with paste-imitations of precious stones.

Her husband, who felt shocked by this love of tinsel and show, would often say—"My dear, when one has not the means to afford real jewelry, one should appear adorned with one's natural beauty and grace only—and these gifts are the rarest of jewels."

But she would smile sweetly and answer: "What does it matter? I like those things—that is my little whim. I know you are right; but one can't make oneself over again. I've always loved jewelry so much!"

And then she would roll the pearls of the necklaces between her fingers, and make the facets of the cut crystals flash in the light, repeating: "Now look at them—see how well the work is done. You would swear it was real jewelry."

He would then smile in his turn, and declare to her: "You have the tastes of a regular Gypsy."

Sometimes, in the evening, when they were having a chat by the fire, she would rise and fetch the morocco box in which she kept her "stock" (as M. Lantin called it)—would put it on the tea-table, and begin to examine the false jewelry with passionate delight, as if she experienced some secret and mysterious sensations of pleasure in their contemplation; and she would insist on putting one of the necklaces round her husband's neck, and laugh till she couldn't laugh any more, crying out: "Oh! how funny you look!" Then she would rush into his arms, and kiss him furiously.

One winter's night, after she had been to the Opera, she came home chilled through, and trembling. Next day she had a bad cough. Eight days after that, she died of pneumonia.

Lantin was very nearly following her into the tomb. His despair was so fright- 15
ful that in one single month his hair turned white. He wept from morning till
night, feeling his heart torn by inexpressible suffering—ever haunted by the
memory of her, by the smile, by the voice, by all the charm of the dead woman.

Time did not assuage his grief. Often during office hours his fellow-clerks
went off to a corner to chat about this or that topic of the day—his cheeks might
have been seen to swell up all of a sudden, his nose wrinkle, his eyes fill with
water—he would pull a frightful face, and begin to sob.

He had kept his dead companion's room just in the order she had left it, and
he used to lock himself up in it every evening to think about her—all the furniture, and even all her dresses, remained in the same place they had been on the
last day of her life.

But life became hard for him. His salary, which, in his wife's hands, had
amply sufficed for all household needs, now proved scarcely sufficient to supply
his own few wants. And he asked himself in astonishment how she had managed
always to furnish him with excellent wines and with delicate eating which he
could not now afford at all with his scanty means.

He got a little into debt, like men obliged to live by their wits. At last one
morning that he happened to find himself without a cent in his pocket, and a
whole week to wait before he could draw his monthly salary, he thought of
selling something; and almost immediately it occurred to him to sell his wife's
"stock"—for he had always borne a secret grudge against the flash-jewelry that
used to annoy him so much in former days. The mere sight of it, day after day,
somewhat spoiled the sad pleasure of thinking of his darling.

He tried a long time to make a choice among the heap of trinkets she had 20
left behind her—for up to the very last day of her life she had kept obstinately
buying them, bringing home some new thing almost every night—and finally
he resolved to take the big pearl necklace which she used to like the best of all,
and which he thought ought certainly to be worth six or eight francs, as it was
really very nicely mounted for an imitation necklace.

He put it in his pocket, and walked toward the office, following the boule-
vards, and looking for some jewelry-store on the way, where he could enter with
confidence.

Finally he saw a place and went in; feeling a little ashamed of thus exposing
his misery, and of trying to sell such a trifling object.

"Sir," he said to the jeweler, "please tell me what this is worth."

The jeweler took the necklace, examined it, weighed it, took up a magnifying
glass, called his clerk, talked to him in whispers, put down the necklace on the
counter, and drew back a little bit to judge of its effect at a distance.

M. Lantin, feeling very much embarrassed by all these ceremonies, opened 25
his mouth and began to declare—"Oh! I know it can't be worth much" . . .
when the jeweler interrupted him saying:

"Well, sir, that is worth between twelve and fifteen thousand francs; but I
cannot buy it unless you can let me know exactly how you came by it."

The widower's eyes opened enormously, and he stood gaping—unable to
understand. Then after a while he stammered out: "You said? . . . Are you sure?"

The jeweler, misconstruing the cause of this astonishment, replied in a dry tone—"Go elsewhere if you like, and see if you can get any more for it. The very most I would give for it is fifteen thousand. Come back and see me again, if you can't do better."

M. Lantin, feeling perfectly idiotic, took his necklace and departed; obeying a confused desire to find himself alone and to get a chance to think.

But the moment he found himself in the street again, he began to laugh, and he muttered to himself: "The fool!—oh! what a fool; If I had only taken him at his word. Well, well!—a jeweler who can't tell paste from real jewelry!"

30

And he entered another jewelry-store, at the corner of the Rue de la Paix. The moment the jeweler set eyes on the necklace, he examined—"Hello! I know that necklace well—it was sold here!"

M. Lantin, very nervous, asked:

"What's it worth?"

"Sir, I sold it for twenty-five thousand francs. I am willing to buy it back again for eighteen thousand—if you can prove to me satisfactorily, according to legal presciptions, how you came into possession of it"—This time, M. Lantin was simply paralyzed with astonishment. He said: "Well . . . but please look at it again, sir. I always thought until now that it was . . . was false."

The jeweler said:

35

"Will you give me your name, sir?"

"Certainly. My name is Lantin; I am employed at the office of the Minister of the Interior. I live at No. 16, Rue des Martyrs."

The merchant opened the register, looked, and said: "Yes; this necklace was sent to the address of Madame Lantin, 16 Rue des Martyrs, on July 20th, 1876."

And the two men looked into each other's eyes—the clerk wild with surprise; the jeweler suspecting he had a thief before him.

The jeweler resumed:

40

"Will you be kind enough to leave this article here for twenty-four hours only—I'll give you a receipt."

M. Lantin stuttered: "Yes-ah! certainly." And he went out folding up the receipt, which he put in his pocket.

Then he crossed the street, went the wrong way, found out his mistake, returned by way of the Tuileries, crossed the Seine, found out he had taken the wrong road again, and went back to the Champs-Elysées without being able to get one clear idea into his head. He tried to reason, to understand. His wife could never have bought so valuable an object as that. Certainly not. But then, it must have been a present! . . . A present from whom? What for?

He stopped and stood stock-still in the middle of the avenue.

A horrible suspicion swept across his mind. . . . She? . . . But then all those other pieces of jewelry must have been presents also! . . . Then it seemed to him that the ground was heaving under his feet; that a tree, right in front of him, was falling toward him; he thrust out his arms instinctively, and fell senseless.

45

He recovered his consciousness again in a drug-store to which some bystanders had carried him. He had them lead him home, and he locked himself into his room.

Until nightfall he cried without stopping, biting his handkerchief to keep himself from screaming out. Then, completely worn out with grief and fatigue, he went to bed, and slept a leaden sleep.

A ray of sunshine awakened him, and he rose and dressed himself slowly to go to the office. It was hard to have to work after such a shock. Then he reflected that he might be able to excuse himself to the superintendent, and he wrote to him. Then he remembered he would have to go back to the jeweler's; and shame made his face purple. He remained thinking a long time. Still he could not leave the necklace there; he put on his coat and went out.

It was a fine day; the sky extended all blue over the city, and seemed to make it smile. Strollers were walking aimlessly about, with their hands in their pockets.

Lantin thought as he watched them passing: "How lucky the men are who have fortunes! With money a man can even shake off grief—you can go where you please—travel—amuse yourself! Oh! if I were only rich!"

He suddenly discovered he was hungry—not having eaten anything since the evening before. But his pockets were empty; and he remembered the necklace. Eighteen thousand francs! Eighteen thousand francs!—that was a sum—that was!

He made his way to the Rue de la Paix and began to walk backward and forward on the sidewalk in front of the store. Eighteen thousand francs! Twenty times he started to go in; but shame always kept him back.

Still he was hungry—very hungry—and had not a cent. He made one brusque resolve, and crossed the street almost at a run, so as not to let himself have time to think over the matter; and he rushed into the jeweler's.

As soon as he saw him, the merchant hurried forward, and offered him a chair with smiling politeness. Even the clerks came forward to stare at Lantin, with gaiety in their eyes and smiles about their lips.

The jeweler said: "Sir, I made inquiries; and if you are still so disposed, I am ready to pay you down the price I offered you."

The clerk stammered: "Why, yes—sir, certainly."

The jeweler took from a drawer eighteen big bills,[3] counted them, and held them out to Lantin, who signed a little receipt, and thrust the money feverishly into his pocket.

Then, as he was on the point of leaving, he turned to the ever-smiling merchant, and said, lowering his eyes: "I have some—I have some other jewelry, which came to me in the same—from the same inheritance. Would you purchase them also from me?"

The merchant bowed, and answered: "Why, certainly, sir—certainly. . . ." One of the clerks rushed out to laugh at his ease; another kept blowing his nose as hard as he could.

Lantin, impassive, flushed and serious, said: "I will bring them to you." And he hired a cab to get the jewelry.

When he returned to the store, an hour later, he had not yet breakfasted.

3. French paper money varies in size; the larger the bill, the larger the denomination.

50

55

60

They examined the jewelry—piece by piece—putting a value on each. Nearly all had been purchased from that very house.

Lantin, now, disputed estimates made, got angry, insisted on seeing the books, and talked louder and louder the higher the estimates grew.

The big diamond earrings were worth 20,000 francs; the bracelets, 35,000; the brooches, rings and medallions, 16,000; a set of emeralds and sapphires, 14,000; solitaire, suspended to a gold neckchain, 40,000; the total value being estimated at 196,000 francs.

The merchant observed with mischievous good nature: "The person who owned these must have put all her savings into jewelry."

Lantin answered with gravity: "Perhaps that is as good a way of saving money as any other." And he went off, after having agreed with the merchant that an expert should make a counter-estimate for him the next day.

When he found himself in the street again, he looked at the Column Vendôme[4] with the desire to climb it, as if it were a May pole. He felt jolly enough to play leapfrog over the Emperor's head—up there in the blue sky.

He breakfasted at Voisin's[5] restaurant, and ordered wine at 20 francs a bottle.

Then he hired a cab and drove out to the Bois.[6] He looked at the carriages passing with a sort of contempt, and a wild desire to yell out to the passers-by: "I am rich, too—I am! I have 200,000 francs!"

The recollection of the office suddenly came back to him. He drove there, walked right into the superintendent's private room, and said: "Sir, I come to give you my resignation. I have just come into a fortune of *three* hundred thousand francs." Then he shook hands all round with his fellow-clerks; and told them all about his plans for a new career. Then he went to dinner at the Café Anglais.

Finding himself seated at the same table with a man who seemed to him quite genteel, he could not resist the itching desire to tell him, with a certain air of coquetry, that he had just inherited a fortune of *four* hundred thousand francs.

For the first time in his life he went to the theater without feeling bored by the performance; and he passed the night in revelry and debauch.

Six months after he married again. His second wife was the most upright of spouses, but had a terrible temper. She made his life very miserable.

1883

Stories are not always written. Ballads and even epics were sung, plays are still acted out on the stage, and most cultures have or had oral storytellers. Writing, however, makes a difference. Oral or dramatic "readings" or performances are communal, the responses tend to be uniform (though there's always the person in the audience who laughs at the wrong time), and their purpose is

4. Famous column with a statue of Napoleon at the top.   5. Like the Café Anglais below, a well-known and high-priced restaurant.   6. Large Parisian park where the rich took their outings.

more overtly to move or persuade the group or community. They have a closer relation to classical rhetoric, political speeches, or concerts than written narrative does. We read, usually, alone, most of the time silently, and if there are—and there usually are—emotions, they are deeply personal, not shared. There is a tendency, then, in literary criticism, and in reading for and discussing literature in class, to stress interpretation, the "ideas" in literary texts, or the formal structures, and to slight somewhat the emotional or affective aspect of our essentially solitary literary experience. But though it may be difficult to develop the vocabulary needed to talk about literature—we have to get beyond "I liked it" and "I didn't like it"—we must never forget the deeply stirring response that literature engenders and the differences in kinds and depths of response that different works stimulate.

▼ ▼ ▼

QUESTIONS

1. What specific words or phrases in the first two paragraphs of "The Jewelry" alert you to the possibility that all may not be as it seems? How are these expectations or fears allayed in the next few paragraphs? What new fears or expectations are aroused very soon thereafter?

2. Since the story is called "The Jewelry" and life does not come wrapped in such convenient titles, you may come to suspect the truth before M. Lantin. How does your attitude toward him change?

WRITING SUGGESTIONS

1. Copy "The Zebra Storyteller." Exchange papers with a classmate. Carefully proofread each other's papers. Can you believe you could have made errors in simple copying?

2. Stop "The Zebra Storyteller" after paragraph 5 (". . . fit to be tied") and, in five to ten paragraphs, write your own ending.

3. Write a parody or imitation of "No One's a Mystery" giving it the same title as another recent song.

4. Write a two- or three-page scene of Jack (from "No One's a Mystery") and his wife at home.

5. Write an "off-stage" scene that shows how Lantin's first wife got one or more pieces of the jewelry.

Understanding
the Text

1 PLOT

n "The Zebra Storyteller" you can see the skeleton of the typical short
story **plot** or **plot structure**. Plot simply means the arrangement of the
action, an imagined event or a series of such events.

Action usually involves **conflict**, a struggle between opposing forces, and it
often falls into something like the same five parts that we find in a play: exposition, rising action, turning point (or climax), falling action, conclusion. The
conflict in this little tale is between the Siamese cat and the zebras, especially
the zebra storyteller. The first part of the action, called the **exposition**, introduces the characters, situation, and, usually, time and place. The exposition
here is achieved in three sentences: the time is "once upon a," the place
Africa, the characters a Siamese cat who speaks Zebraic and an innocent
zebra, and the situation their meeting. We then enter the second part of the
plot, the **rising action**: events that complicate the situation and intensify or
complicate the conflict or introduce new ones. The first event here is the meeting between an innocent zebra and the Zebraic-speaking cat. That initial conflict of zebra and cat is over in a hurry—the zebra who is "fit to be tied" is tied
up and eaten. Complications build with the cat's continuing success in killing
zebras, and the zebras' growing fears and consequent superstitious belief that
the ghost of a lion haunts the region preying on zebras. The **turning point** or
climax of the action is the third part of the story, the appearance of the zebra
storyteller: until now the cat has had it all his way, but his luck is about to
change. From this point on the complications that grew in the first part of the
story are untangled—the zebra storyteller, for example, is not surprised when

18

he meets a Siamese cat speaking Zebraic, "because he'd been thinking about that very thing"; this is the fourth part of the story, the reverse movement or **falling action**. The story ends at the fifth part, the **conclusion**: the point at which the situation that was destablized at the beginning of the story (when the Zebraic-speaking cat appeared) becomes stable once more: Africa is once again free of cats speaking the language of zebras.

This typical arrangement of the action of a story is not just a formula for composing a narrative or for critical analysis; it also has its emotional and intellectual effect on your responses as reader. The exposition invites you to immediately begin building images of the time and place of the action, the people, the situation, and the issues involved, and even to identify with or root for one or more of the participants. You choose to be on the side of the zebras or the Siamese cat (though your choice is guided by the language and details of the story: the cat speaks "inappropriate" Zebraic, the zebra is introduced as "innocent"). As the situation becomes more complicated during the rising action, you are led to be increasingly concerned with how "your" zebras, the "good guys," are going to get out of the increasingly bad situation (the cat eating more and more zebras), or, if the complications of the rising action are positive (as in the marriage and prosperity and happiness of M. Lantin in "The Jewelry"), you become more and more concerned about what is going to happen to turn things around (for even if you do not know about turning points in narrative, you know that sometimes things in stories and even in real life—knock on wood—seem too good to be true or too good to last). Consciously or unconsciously you become involved in the story, trying to anticipate how the complications will unravel, how everything will come out.

Another aspect of structure that affects you the reader is the order in which the events are told. In life, actions occur one after the other, sequentially. Most stories grant this sequential unfolding of life's events but many do not describe events chronologically. When historical order is disturbed, a plot is created. "The king died and then the queen died," to use one critic's example, is not a plot, for it has not been "tampered with." "The queen died after the king died" includes the same historical events, but the order in which they are reported has been changed. The reader of the first sentence focuses on the king first; the reader of the second sentence focuses on the queen. While essentially the same thing has been said, the difference in focus and emphasis changes the effect and, in the broadest sense, the meaning as well. The **history** has been structured into plot.

The ordering of events, then, provides stories with structure and plot, and has its consequences in effect and meaning. The first opportunity for **structur-**

ing a story is at the beginning, and beginnings are consequently particularly sensitive and important. Why does a story begin where it does? No event (at least since the Big Bang) is a true beginning; your own life story begins before you were born and even before you were conceived. So to begin a story the author has to make a **selection**, to indicate that for the purposes of this story the beginning is a given point rather than any other. "Having met the girl one evening, at the house of the office-superintendent, M. Lantin became enveloped in love as in a net." That first sentence of "The Jewelry" seems a perfectly natural and "innocent" way to begin a story that will involve Lantin and his wife. But why not begin with a slightly modified paragraph 5: "M. Lantin was perfectly happy in his marriage"? or with paragraph 9, inserting a new first sentence: "M. Lantin was perfectly happy with his wife and smiled at her two little faults: her love of the theater, and her passion for false jewelry. He felt shocked by . . ."? After all, this last sentence would immediately introduce the jewelry that gives the story its title. Or the story could begin with the death of the girl's father, her move with her mother to Paris, and so on. (Note that she is never given a name, just "the girl" first, then "his wife.") These are the earliest events mentioned in the exposition, and so in the unstructured history they would come first. In searching for a reason for Maupassant's beginning, we might look at what we learn and what is emphasized in the beginning as it now stands: the class of Lantin and his income; the girl's beauty, modesty, respectability, poverty, and her mother's search for a husband for her; Lantin's falling in love as if into a "net." It might be useful to consider on your own or in an assigned essay how the details in these first eight paragraphs affect your reading, responding, and understanding of the people, events, and "meaning" of the story. Or you might want to explain why John Cheever's "The Country Husband," in this chapter, begins, "To begin at the beginning, the airplane from Minneapolis in which Francis Weed was traveling East ran into heavy weather," rather than with, say, paragraph 11, when the Weeds are preparing to go out on the evening on which Francis meets the baby-sitter; or even, with a few adjustments, with paragraph 15, when the baby-sitter opens the door and Francis sees her for the first time, for it is with their encounter that the story seems truly to begin.

The point at which a story ends is also a sensitive and meaningful aspect of its structure. A typical beginning—first sentence (Lantin meets the girl) or first **discriminated occasion** (the first encounter of a zebra with the Zebraic-speaking cat)—destabilizes the history; something happens that changes the ordinary life of one or more characters and sets off a new course of events, the story. A typical ending either reestablishes the old order (no more cats eating zebras, no more romantic escapades for Francis Weed) or establishes a new one (Lantin remarried). Endings, like beginnings, affect the reader and suggest meaning. And like beginnings, they are arbitrary structures that interrupt history, for all stories (or more precisely, histories) about individuals end the same way, as Margaret Atwood somewhat cynically suggests in "Happy Endings": *"John and Mary die. John and Mary die. John and Mary die."* That is only true, of course, if you equate the story with the history, for the history not only extends backward as far as you can see but also forward to the end of the lives of those in the story. (And why not the lives of their children, grandchildren, and so on?) Not all stories end with the deaths of the characters who interest us; in fact, of the stories in this and the introductory chapters only Atwood's ends with the deaths of both its major characters, while "The Zebra Storyteller" ends with the death of the Zebraic-speaking cat. Where a story ends goes a long way to determining how it affects us and what we make of it. "The Zebra Storyteller" ends with the triumph of the zebra over the Siamese cat, leaving us with the feeling that good guys win, and with a moral that leads us to the "point" or meaning of the story. "No One's a Mystery" leaves us without an answer and pushes us back into our own experiences and beliefs to judge who is right and who is wrong about the couple's future.

All questions about the effect or meaning of beginnings and endings follow from an assumption that we must now recognize: that there are reasons for the structures of the narrative, indeed, that in a short story, in part because of its brevity, everything must "count." One writer has said that if there is a gun on the wall at the beginning of a story, it must be fired by the end. The relevance of events or details is not limited, however, merely to future action, events in the plot, for most seem to have relevance in other ways. In paragraph 9 of "The Country Husband," for example, Francis Weed listens to "the evening sounds of Shady Hill." These include a door slamming, the sound of someone cutting grass—which do not lead to events but may establish the nature of the suburban setting—and the sound of someone playing (badly) Beethoven's "Moonlight Sonata," which may on the one hand, because of the nature of the piece, reinforce Weed's thoughtful or dreamy mood or introduce "romance" into the story, and on the other hand, because of the petulant and self-pitying performance, show why Weed is dissatisfied with the shallowness of his suburban neighbors, and perhaps suburban life. Notice the "may" and the "perhaps" in the previous sentence. The relevancy of a detail to a story is not always as simple and incontrovertible as the inevitable shooting of the gun. Though you ought to be alert as to how the details function in affecting you or contributing to your visualization or understanding of the people, incidents, and issues of the story, there is not necessarily a precise answer to the question of how a detail functions. In Cheever's story, why does Mr. Nixon shout "Varmints! Rascals! . . . . Avaunt and quit my sight!" at the squirrels? What does it add? What would be lost without it? You may see the effects and implications differently from your classmates; indeed you may not have chosen this detail to interrogate at all. These differences of selection and explanation may shed light on why readers respond to, understand, and judge stories differently.

Structuring a story is not just a matter of choosing where to begin or end it, or of choosing or inventing affective and meaningful details, but also of ordering all the events in between. Sometimes, as Atwood says, the plot is "just one thing after another, a what and a what and a what." Even when that is the case, sometimes the reader is forced to think back to prior events. In a detective story, for example, the crime has usually been committed before the story begins, in the history and not in the plot. At the end, when the detective explains "who done it," you must think back not only to the crime, but to all the hints or clues that you have been given. In such a story we expect the ending to explain what happened earlier; in "A Rose for Emily," however, and similar stories, there is an ending that forces us to reinterpret many of the details that went before, though while reading we did not realize reinterpretation would be necessary, so the ending is a surprise not only in what it tells us but in the fact that we did not know there was anything that we had not been told. Sometimes, however, the story moves back; that is, instead of making you think of earlier events, it actually breaks into its own order, reaches back into the history, and presents or dramatizes a scene that happened before the fictional present. In "Sonny's Blues," for example, there is such a replay or **flashback** (or rather a series of flashbacks). There is a very brief scene from the past triggered by the word "safe" (par. 79), the narrator recalling his father's words, which then leads to a specific dramatized scene—the last time the narrator talked to his mother. This is followed by another scene—the narrator's conversation with Sonny after their mother's funeral. This scene of course follows the previous one but in terms of where the story began (the fictional present) it is in the past, and therefore is in fact a flashback. Nor does the story return to the fictional present for some time—"I read about Sonny's trouble in the spring. Little Grace died in the fall . . ." (par. 177)—when Sonny has been living with the narrator for two weeks, and it proceeds from that point to the end.

One reason for structuring the history into plot is to engage the reader's attention, to make the reader read on. This can be done not only by arousing the reader's expectations of what will happen next but also by generating **curiosity**—the desire to know what is happening or has happened. It is the sheer power of curiosity, for example, that keeps us reading intensely when we know as little as Watson or Sherlock Holmes himself at the beginning of a story or "case." But it is not only the detective story that plays upon our curiosity. "Sonny's Blues" begins, "I read about it in the paper . . . ," and that "it" without antecedent is repeated seven times in the first paragraph and first two sentences of the second paragraph. Read those first two paragraphs and stop. If you try at this point to examine what is going on in your mind, you more than likely will find that you are asking yourself what "it" might refer to, and you will more than likely have framed for yourself several possible answers. It may be in part for this reason that Baldwin begins how and where he does, getting you engaged in the story, so that you will read on. Even a title, such as "The Zebra Storyteller," "A Very Old Man with Enormous Wings," or "The Rocking-Horse Winner," can make us curious enough to pick up a story; after that, it's up to the story to keep us engaged.

Perhaps stronger than curiosity is **suspense**—that particular kind of expectation involving anticipation of and doubt about what is going to happen next (as differentiated from expectations about what a character is like, what the theme is or how it will develop, and so on). Even in reading a little fable like "The Zebra Storyteller" our minds are—or should be—at work: a cat speaking Zebraic is killing zebras; the zebra storyteller thinking of plots comes up with the idea of a story in which a cat speaking Zebraic is killing zebras: "What an idea! That'll make 'em laugh!" he tells himself. Then he meets the cat—what will happen next? How many possibilities did you or can you anticipate? Even though you now know the ending, you could go back to this point in the story and, recalling your expectations, reconstruct or reinvent the rest of the story.

Sometimes the suspense is generated and defined not so much by what happens within the story as it is by what we expect from stories. In "The Jewelry," for example, when Lantin's wife dies so early in the story, we know this is not the end; something is going to happen or be revealed because there are several pages left and stories do not go on unless something is going to happen. But what? Lantin grieves so intensely, locks himself in her room . . . will her ghost return? He is going bankrupt, he looks over his wife's jewelry, and when he goes to sell a piece he finds it is not mere costume jewelry, but real. How much sooner than Lantin himself do you realize the source of the jewelry? There is a certain satisfaction in seeing the truth before he does. But *then* what do you expect to happen next? Do you anticipate his debauching? How did you expect the story to end?

If you were to pause just before reading the final paragraph of the Maupassant story and consciously explore your expectations, you would see that these are based on both fictional and actual conventions—indeed, most of us would probably assume the story could have ended with the word "debauch," without the final brief paragraph, and that the story would end with the irony of Lantin's getting pleasure out of his having been betrayed. We can accept this even within our conventional moral terms—he may get bitter pleasures for a time, but he will soon tire of such pleasures or be undone by them.

The final paragraph, however, if it does not contradict, deepens the irony: now he has a truly "upright" wife—and he is miserable. Our conventional expectations that morality brings happiness, that infidelity and debauchery lead to various kinds of ruin, are wrenched into question. He has tired of debauchery, but is he better off leading a moral life? Is the world amoral—or even immoral? Do good guys finish last? We do not have to believe this, but to read the story fully we need to call our perhaps more optimistic and conventional views into question.

In order to keep you engaged and alert, a story must make you ask questions about what will happen or what will be revealed next. To respond fully to a story you must be alert to the signals and guess along with the author. One way of seeing whether and how your mind is engaged in your reading is to pause at crucial points in the story and consciously explore what you think is coming. In "No One's a Mystery" the story does the pausing and the conscious specification of what might happen next for you—it gives two versions of what might happen and then the story ends, without resolution. (Though not without point; for to suggest that both naivete and cynicism are merely attitudes, and that neither is an infallible clue to the future, is an insight and a challenge, even if it is not, strictly speaking, a resolution.) At least in one aspect, fiction is a guessing game.

Like all guessing games, from quiz shows to philosophy, the plot game in fiction has certain guidelines. A well-structured plot will play fair with you, offering at appropriate points all the necessary indications or clues to what will happen next, not just springing new and essential information on you at the last minute ("Meanwhile, unknown to our hero, the Marines were just on the other side of the hill . . ."). It is this playing fair that makes the ending of a well-structured story satisfying or, when you look back on it, inevitable. Most stories also offer a number of reasonable but false signals (red herrings) to get you off the scent, so that in a well-structured story the ending, though inevitable, is also surprising. And though there is usually an overarching action from beginning to end, in many stories there are layers of expectation or suspense, so that as soon as one question is answered another comes forth to replace it, keeping you in doubt as to the final outcome.

Unlike most guessing games, however, the reward is not for the right guess—anticipating the outcome before the final paragraph—but for the number of guesses, right *and* wrong, that you make, the number of signals you respond to. If you are misled by none of the false signals in the early pages of a story—by Sonny's friend saying, " 'Listen. They'll let him out and then it'll just start all over again' " (par. 36), for example—you may be closer to being "right," but you have missed many of the implications of the story. But, more important, you have missed the pleasure of *learning* the "truth" a story has to offer, and you know how much less meaningful it is to be told something than to learn for yourself, through your own experience. Fiction is a way of transmitting not just perception but experience.

Though plot is the structuring of events, an event can be an outcome or consequence as well as a happening, and the expectation, surprise, and perception surrounding plot structure can involve meaning as well as action, as we have seen in the worldview suggested by the ending of "The Jewelry." Maupassant's ending upsets our conventional thinking about human conduct and morality. The ending of "The Country Husband" may upset your expectations based on the conventions of storytelling. We usually expect some kind of dramatic change, some revelation. Here we may expect Francis to run off with the baby-sitter and have a violent confrontation with Clayton Thomas. (Many students seem to be on the side of Francis and Anne—until they are asked to identify Francis not with themselves or with story heroes but, say, with their own fathers!) Cheever says, in effect, not only that life is not like that, but that stories should not be like that. Though expectations based on social, moral, or literary conventions that support the ordinary are not so consciously aroused as are those aroused by action and adventure—the kind of expectation described by the term *suspense*—their fulfillment, modification, or contradiction is a significant aim and effect of many stories. Fiction is in part a guessing game, but it is not merely a game. Many stories seek to give new insights into human perception, experience, meaning, or at least to challenge our more or less unconsciously held beliefs. They strive to tell truths—new, subjective truths, but truths—even though they "lie" about the actuality of the people and events represented. But first they have to get your attention, and one way is by arousing your curiosity and exciting your anticipation. That is one of the primary functions of plot. Alertness to signals, anticipating what is to come next, and remembering what has been said and signaled earlier are essential to fully appreciating and understanding stories and their structures. That is how you should function as a reader of plot.

▼   ▼ ▼

MARGARET ATWOOD

Happy Endings

John and Mary meet.
What happens next?
If you want a happy ending, try A.

A.   John and Mary fall in love and get married. They both have worthwhile and remunerative jobs which they find stimulating and challenging. They buy a charming house. Real estate values go up. Eventually, when they can afford live-in help, they have two children, to whom they are devoted. The children turn out well. John and Mary have a stimulating and challenging sex life and worthwhile friends. They go on fun vacations together. They retire. They both have hobbies which they find stimulating and challenging. Eventually they die. This is the end of the story.

5   B.   Mary falls in love with John but John doesn't fall in love with Mary. He merely uses her body for selfish pleasure and ego gratification of a tepid kind. He comes to her apartment twice a week and she cooks him dinner, you'll notice that he doesn't even consider her worth the price of a dinner out, and after he's eaten the dinner he fucks her and after that he falls asleep, while she does the dishes so he won't think she's untidy, having all those dirty dishes lying around, and puts on fresh lipstick so she'll look good when he wakes up, but when he wakes up he doesn't even notice, he puts on his socks and his shorts and his pants and his shirt and his tie and his shoes, the reverse order from the one in which he took them off. He doesn't take off Mary's clothes, she takes them off herself, she acts as if she's dying for it every time, not because she likes sex exactly, she doesn't, but she wants John to think she does because if they do it often enough surely he'll get used to her, he'll come to depend on her and they will get married, but John goes out the door with hardly so much as a good-night and three days later he turns up at six o'clock and they do the whole thing over again.

        Mary gets run-down. Crying is bad for your face, everyone knows that and so does Mary but she can't stop. People at work notice. Her friends tell her John is a rat, a pig, a dog, he isn't good enough for her, but she can't believe it. Inside John, she thinks, is another John, who is much nicer. This other John will emerge like a butterfly from a cocoon, a Jack from a box, a pit from a prune, if the first John is only squeezed enough.

        One evening John complains about the food. He has never complained about the food before. Mary is hurt.

        Her friends tell her they've seen him in a restaurant with another woman, whose name is Madge. It's not even Madge that finally gets to

Mary: it's the restaurant. John has never taken Mary to a restaurant. Mary collects all the sleeping pills and aspirins she can find, and takes them and a half a bottle of sherry. You can see what kind of a woman she is by the fact that it's not even whiskey. She leaves a note for John. She hopes he'll discover her and get her to the hospital in time and repent and then they can get married, but this fails to happen and she dies.

John marries Madge and everything continues as in A.

C. John, who is an older man, falls in love with Mary, and Mary, who is only twenty-two, feels sorry for him because he's worried about his hair falling out. She sleeps with him even though she's not in love with him. She met him at work. She's in love with someone called James, who is twenty-two also and not yet ready to settle down.

John on the contrary settled down long ago: this is what is bothering him. John has a steady, respectable job and is getting ahead in his field, but Mary isn't impressed by him, she's impressed by James, who has a motorcycle and a fabulous record collection. But James is often away on his motorcycle, being free. Freedom isn't the same for girls, so in the meantime Mary spends Thursday evenings with John. Thursdays are the only days John can get away.

John is married to a woman called Madge and they have two children, a charming house which they bought just before the real estate values went up, and hobbies which they find stimulating and challenging, when they have the time. John tells Mary how important she is to him, but of course he can't leave his wife because a commitment is a commitment. He goes on about this more than is necessary and Mary finds it boring, but older men can keep it up longer so on the whole she has a fairly good time.

One day James breezes in on his motorcycle with some top-grade California hybrid and James and Mary get higher than you'd believe possible and they climb into bed. Everything becomes very underwater, but along comes John, who has a key to Mary's apartment. He finds them stoned and entwined. He's hardly in any position to be jealous, considering Madge, but nevertheless he's overcome with despair. Finally he's middle-aged, in two years he'll be bald as an egg and he can't stand it. He purchases a handgun, saying he needs it for target practice—this is the thin part of the plot, but it can be dealt with later—and shoots the two of them and himself.

Madge, after a suitable period of mourning, marries an understanding man called Fred and everything continues as in A, but under different names.

D. Fred and Madge have no problems. They get along exceptionally well and are good at working out any little difficulties that may arise. But their charming house is by the seashore and one day a giant tidal wave approaches. Real estate values go down. The rest of the story is about what caused the tidal wave and how they escape from it. They do, though thousands drown, but Fred and Madge are virtuous and lucky. Finally on high ground they clasp each other, wet and dripping and grateful, and continue as in A.

E. Yes, but Fred has a bad heart. The rest of the story is about how kind and understanding they both are until Fred dies. Then Madge devotes herself to charity work until the end of A. If you like, it can be "Madge," "cancer," "guilty and confused," and "bird watching."

F. If you think this is all too bourgeois, make John a revolutionary and Mary a counterespionage agent and see how far that gets you. Remember, this is Canada. You'll still end up with A, though in between you may get a lustful brawling saga of passionate involvement, a chronicle of our times, sort of.

You'll have to face it, the endings are the same however you slice it. Don't be deluded by any other endings, they're all fake, either deliberately fake, with malicious intent to deceive, or just motivated by excessive optimism if not by downright sentimentality.

The only authentic ending is the one provided here:
John and Mary die. John and Mary die. John and Mary die.

So much for endings. Beginnings are always more fun. True connoisseurs, however, are known to favor the stretch in between, since it's the hardest to do anything with.

That's about all that can be said for plots, which anyway are just one thing after another, a what and a what and a what.

Now try How and Why.

1983

JOHN CHEEVER

The Country Husband

To begin at the beginning, the airplane from Minneapolis in which Francis Weed was traveling East ran into heavy weather. The sky had been a hazy blue, with the clouds below the plane lying so close together that nothing could be seen of the earth. The mist began to form outside the windows, and they flew into a white cloud of such density that it reflected the exhaust fires. The color of the cloud darkened to gray, and the plane began to rock. Francis had been in heavy weather before, but he had never been shaken up so much. The man in the seat beside him pulled a flask out of his pocket and took a drink. Francis smiled at his neighbor, but the man looked away; he wasn't sharing his pain killer with anyone. The plane began to drop and flounder wildly. A child was crying. The air in the cabin was overheated and stale, and Francis' left foot went to sleep. He read a little from a paper book that he had bought at the airport, but the violence of the storm divided his attention. It was black outside the ports. The exhaust fires blazed and shed sparks in the dark, and, inside, the shaded lights, the stuffiness, and the window curtains gave the cabin an atmosphere of intense and misplaced domesticity. Then the light flickered and went out. "You know what I've always wanted to do?" the man beside Francis said suddenly. "I've always wanted to buy a farm in New Hampshire and raise beef cattle." The stewardess announced that they were going to make an emergency landing. All but the children saw in their minds the spreading wings of the Angel of Death. The pilot could be heard singing faintly, "I've got sixpence, jolly, jolly sixpence. I've got sixpence to last me all my life . . ."[1] There was no other sound.

The loud groaning of the hydraulic valves swallowed up the pilot's song, and there was a shrieking high in the air, like automobile brakes, and the plane hit flat on its belly in a cornfield and shook them so violently that an old man up forward howled, "Me kidneys! Me kidneys!" The stewardess flung open the door, and someone opened an emergency door at the back, letting in the sweet noise of their continuing mortality—the idle splash and smell of a heavy rain. Anxious for their lives, they filed out of the doors and scattered over the cornfield in all directions, praying that the thread would hold. It did. Nothing happened. When it was clear that the plane would not burn or explode, the crew and the steward-ess gathered the passengers together and led them to the shelter of a barn. They were not far from Philadelphia, and in a little while a string of taxis took them into the city. "It's just like the Marne,[2]" someone said, but there was surprisingly little relaxation of that suspiciousness with which many Americans regard their fellow travelers.

In Philadelphia, Francis Weed got a train to New York. At the end of that journey, he crossed the city and caught just as it was about to pull out the commuting train that he took five nights a week to his home in Shady Hill.

He sat with Trace Bearden. "You know, I was in that plane that just crashed outside Philadelphia," he said. "We came down in a field . . ." He had traveled faster than the newspapers or the rain, and the weather in New York was sunny and mild. It was a day in late September, as fragrant and shapely as an apple. Trace listened to the story, but how could he get excited? Francis had no powers that would let him re-create a brush with death—particularly in the atmosphere of a commuting train, journeying through a sunny countryside where already, in the slum gardens, there were signs of harvest. Trace picked up his newspaper, and Francis was left alone with his thoughts. He said good night to Trace on the platform at Shady Hill and drove in his secondhand Volkswagen up to the Blenhollow neighborhood, where he lived.

The Weeds' Dutch Colonial house was larger than it appeared to be from the driveway. The living room was spacious and divided like Gaul,[3] into three parts. Around an ell to the left as one entered from the vestibule was the long

5

1. Song popular with Allied troops in World War II.   2. On September 8, 1914, over 1,000 Paris taxicabs were requisitioned to move troops to the Marne River to halt the encircling Germans.   3. Ancient France (Gaul) is so described by Julius Caesar in *The Gallic War*.

table, laid for six, with candles and a bowl of fruit in the center. The sounds and smells that came from the open kitchen door were appetizing, for Julia Weed was a good cook. The largest part of the living room centered on a fireplace. On the right were some bookshelves and a piano. The room was polished and tranquil, and from the windows that opened to the west there was some late-summer sunlight, brilliant and as clear as water. Nothing here was neglected; nothing had not been burnished. It was not the kind of household where, after prying open a stuck cigarette box, you would find an old shirt button and a tarnished nickel. The hearth was swept, the roses on the piano were reflected in the polish of the broad top, and there was an album of Schubert waltzes on the rack. Louisa Weed, a pretty girl of nine, was looking out the western windows. Her young brother Henry was standing beside her. Her still younger brother, Toby, was studying the figures of some tonsured monks drinking beer on the polished brass of the woodbox. Francis, taking off his hat and putting down his paper, was not consciously pleased with the scene; he was not that reflective. It was his element, his creation, and he returned to it with that sense of lightness and strength with which any creature returns to his home. "Hi, everybody," he said. "The plane from Minneapolis . . ."

Nine times out of ten, Francis would be greeted with affection, but tonight the children are absorbed in their own antagonisms. Francis had not finished his sentence about the plane crash before Henry plants a kick in Louisa's behind. Louisa swings around, saying, *Damn you!*" Francis makes the mistake of scolding Louisa for bad language before he punishes Henry. Now Louisa turns on her father and accuses him of favoritism. Henry is always right; she is persecuted and lonely; her lot is hopeless. Francis turns to his son, but the son has justification for the kick—she hit him first; she hit him on the ear, which is dangerous. Louisa agrees with this passionately. She hit him on the ear, and she *meant* to hit him on the ear, because he messed up her china collection. Henry says that this is a lie. Little Toby turns away from the woodbox to throw in some evidence for Louisa. Henry claps his hand over little Toby's mouth. Francis separates the two boys but accidentally pushes Toby into the woodbox. Toby begins to cry. Louisa is already crying. Just then, Julia Weed comes into that part of the room where the table is laid. She is a pretty, intelligent woman, and the white in her hair is premature. She does not seem to notice the fracas. "Hello, darling," she says serenely to Francis. "Wash your hands, everyone. Dinner is ready." She strikes a match and lights the six candles in this vale of tears.[4]

This simple announcement, like the war cries of the Scottish chieftains, only refreshes the ferocity of the combatants. Louisa gives Henry a blow on the shoulder. Henry, although he seldom cries, has pitched nine innings and is tired. He bursts into tears. Little Toby discovers a splinter in his hand and begins to howl. Francis says loudly that he has been in a plane crash and that he is tired. Julia appears again from the kitchen and, still ignoring the chaos, asks Francis to go upstairs and tell Helen that everything is ready. Francis is happy to go; it is like

---

4. Common figurative reference to earthly life (vale is valley), though here the tears are literal.

getting back to headquarters company.[5] He is planning to tell his oldest daughter about the airplane crash, but Helen is lying on her bed reading a *True Romance* magazine, and the first thing Francis does is to take the magazine from her hand and remind Helen that he has forbidden her to buy it. She did not buy it, Helen replies. It was given to her by her best friend, Bessie Black. Everybody reads *True Romance*. Bessie Black's father reads *True Romance*. There isn't a girl in Helen's class who doesn't read *True Romance*. Francis expresses his detestation of the magazine and then tells her that dinner is ready—although from the sounds downstairs it doesn't seem so. Helen follows him down the stairs. Julia has seated herself in the candlelight and spread a napkin over her lap. Neither Louisa nor Henry has come to the table. Little Toby is still howling, lying face down on the floor. Francis speaks to him gently: "Daddy was in a plane crash this afternoon, Toby. Don't you want to hear about it?" Toby goes on crying. "If you don't come to the table now, Toby," Francis says, "I'll have to send you to bed without any supper." The little boy rises, gives him a cutting look, flies up the stairs to his bedroom, and slams the door. "Oh, dear," Julia says, and starts to go after him. Francis says that she will spoil him. Julia says that Toby is ten pounds underweight and has to be encouraged to eat. Winter is coming, and he will spend the cold months in bed unless he has his dinner. Julia goes upstairs. Francis sits down at the table with Helen. Helen is suffering from the dismal feeling of having read too intently on a fine day, and she gives her father and the room a jaded look. She doesn't understand about the plane crash, because there wasn't a drop of rain in Shady Hill.

Julia returns with Toby, and they all sit down and are served. "Do I have to look at that big, fat slob?" Henry says, of Louisa. Everybody but Toby enters into this skirmish, and it rages up and down the table for five minutes. Toward the end, Henry puts his napkin over his head and, trying to eat that way, spills spinach all over his shirt. Francis asks Julia if the children couldn't have their dinner earlier. Julia's guns are loaded for this. She can't cook two dinners and lay two tables. She paints with lightning strokes that panorama of drudgery in which her youth, her beauty, and her wit have been lost. Francis says that he must be understood; he was nearly killed in an airplane crash, and he doesn't like to come home every night to a battlefield. Now Julia is deeply concerned. Her voice trembles. He doesn't come home every night to a battlefield. The accusation is stupid and mean. Everything was tranquil until he arrived. She stops speaking, puts down her knife and fork, and looks into her plate as if it is a gulf. She begins to cry. "Poor Mummy!" Toby says, and when Julia gets up from the table, drying her tears with a napkin, Toby goes to her side. "Poor Mummy," he says. "Poor Mummy!" And they climb the stairs together. The other children drift away from the battlefield, and Francis goes into the back garden for a cigarette and some air.

It was a pleasant garden, with walks and flower beds and places to sit. The sunset had nearly burned out, but there was still plenty of light. Put into a

---

5. That is, like escaping from combat to relative safety behind the lines.

thoughtful mood by the crash and the battle, Francis listened to the evening sounds of Shady Hill. "Varmints! Rascals!" old Mr. Nixon shouted to the squirrels in his bird-feeding station. "Avaunt and quit my sight!" A door slammed. Someone was cutting grass. Then Donald Goslin, who lived at the corner, began to play the "Moonlight Sonata."[6] He did this nearly every night. He threw the tempo out the window and played it *rubato*[7] from beginning to end, like an outpouring of tearful petulance, lonesomeness, and self-pity—of everything it was Beethoven's greatness not to know. The music rang up and down the street beneath the trees like an appeal for love, for tenderness, aimed at some lovely housemaid—some fresh-faced, homesick girl from Galway, looking at old snapshots in her third-floor room. "Here, Jupiter, here, Jupiter," Francis called to the Mercers' retriever. Jupiter crashed through the tomato vines with the remains of a felt hat in his mouth.

10   Jupiter was an anomaly. His retrieving instincts and his high spirits were out of place in Shady Hill. He was as black as coal, with a long, alert, intelligent, rakehell face. His eyes gleamed with mischief, and he held his head high. It was the fierce, heavily collared dog's head that appears in heraldry, in tapestry, and that used to appear on umbrella handles and walking sticks. Jupiter went where he pleased, ransacking wastebaskets, clotheslines, garbage pails, and shoe bags. He broke up garden parties and tennis matches, and got mixed up in the processional at Christ Church on Sunday, barking at the men in red dresses.[8] He crashed through old Mr. Nixon's rose garden two or three times a day, cutting a wide swath through the Condesa de Sastagos,[9] and as soon as Donald Goslin lighted his barbecue fire on Thursday nights, Jupiter would get the scent. Nothing the Goslins did could drive him away. Sticks and stones and rude commands only moved him to the edge of the terrace, where he remained, with his gallant and heraldic muzzle, waiting for Donald Goslin to turn his back and reach for the salt. Then he would spring onto the terrace, lift the steak lightly off the fire, and run away with the Goslins' dinner. Jupiter's days were numbered. The Wrightsons' German gardener or the Farquarsons' cook would soon poison him. Even old Mr. Nixon might put some arsenic in the garbage that Jupiter loved. "Here, Jupiter, Jupiter!" Francis called, but the dog pranced off, shaking the hat in his white teeth. Looking at the windows of his house, Francis saw that Julia had come down and was blowing out the candles.

Julia and Francis Weed went out a great deal. Julia was well liked and gregarious, and her love of parties sprang from a most natural dread of chaos and loneliness. She went through the morning mail with real anxiety, looking for invitations, and she usually found some, but she was insatiable, and if she had gone out seven nights a week, it would not have cured her of a reflective look—the look of someone who hears distant music—for she would always suppose that there was a more brilliant party somewhere else. Francis limited her to two

---

6. Beethoven's *Sonata Quasi una Fantasia* (1802), a famous and frequently sentimentalized piano composition.   7. With intentional deviations from strict tempo.   8. Probably the choir. 9. Rather uncommon yellow and red roses difficult to grow.

week-night parties, putting a flexible interpretation on Friday, and rode through the weekend like a dory in a gale. The day after the airplane crash, the Weeds were to have dinner with the Farquarsons.

Francis got home late from town, and Julia got the sitter while he dressed, and then hurried him out of the house. The party was small and pleasant, and Francis settled down to enjoy himself. A new maid passed the drinks. Her hair was dark, and her face was round and pale and seemed familiar to Francis. He had not developed his memory as a sentimental faculty. Wood smoke, lilac, and other such perfumes did not stir him, and his memory was something like his appendix—a vestigial repository. It was not his limitation at all to be unable to escape the past; it was perhaps his limitation that he had escaped it so successfully. He might have seen the maid at other parties, he might have seen her taking a walk on Sunday afternoons, but in either case he would not be searching his memory now. Her face was, in a wonderful way, a moon face—Norman or Irish—but it was not beautiful enough to account for his feeling that he had seen her before, in circumstances that he ought to be able to remember. He asked Nellie Farquarson who she was. Nellie said that the maid had come through an agency, and that her home was Trénon, in Normandy—a small place with a church and a restaurant that Nellie had once visited. While Nellie talked on about her travels abroad, Francis realized where he had seen the woman before. It had been at the end of the war. He had left a replacement depot with some other men and taken a three-day pass in Trénon. On their second day, they had walked out to a crossroads to see the public chastisement of a young woman who had lived with the German commandant during the Occupation.

It was a cool morning in the fall. The sky was overcast, and poured down onto the dirt crossroads a very discouraging light. They were on high land and could see how like one another the shapes of the clouds and the hills were as they stretched off toward the sea. The prisoner arrived sitting on a three-legged stool in a farm cart. She stood by the cart while the Mayor read the accusation and the sentence. Her head was bent and her face was set in that empty half smile behind which the whipped soul is suspended. When the Mayor was finished, she undid her hair and let it fall across her back. A little man with a gray mustache cut off her hair with shears and dropped it on the ground. Then, with a bowl of soapy water and a straight razor, he shaved her skull clean. A woman approached and began to undo the fastenings of her clothes, but the prisoner pushed her aside and undressed herself. When she pulled her chemise over her head and threw it on the ground, she was naked. The women jeered; the men were still. There was no change in the falseness or the plaintiveness of the prisoner's smile. The cold wind made her white skin rough and hardened the nipples of her breasts. The jeering ended gradually, put down by the recognition of their common humanity. One woman spat on her, but some inviolable grandeur in her nakedness lasted through the ordeal. When the crowd was quiet, she turned—she had begun to cry—and, with nothing on but a pair of worn black shoes and stockings, walked down the dirt road alone away from the village. The round white face had aged a little, but there was no question but that the maid who passed his cocktails and later served Francis his dinner was the woman who had been punished at the crossroads.

The war seemed now so distant and that world where the cost of partisanship had been death or torture so long ago. Francis had lost track of the men who had been with him in Vésey. He could not count on Julia's discretion. He could not tell anyone. And if he had told the story now, at the dinner table, it would have been a social as well as a human error. The people in the Farquarsons' living room seemed united in their tacit claim that there had been no past, no war—that there was no danger or trouble in the world. In the recorded history of human arrangements, this extraordinary meeting would have fallen into place, but the atmosphere of Shady Hill made the memory unseemly and impolite. The prisoner withdrew after passing the coffee, but the encounter left Francis feeling languid; it had opened his memory and his senses, and left them dilated. Julia went into the house. Francis stayed in the car to take the sitter home.

15 Expecting to see Mrs. Henlein, the old lady who usually stayed with the children, he was surprised when a young girl opened the door and came out onto the lighted stoop. She stayed in the light to count her textbooks. She was frowning and beautiful. Now, the world is full of beautiful young girls, but Francis saw here the difference between beauty and perfection. All those endearing flaws, moles, birthmarks, and healed wounds were missing, and he experienced in his consciousness that moment when music breaks glass, and felt a pang of recognition as strange, deep and wonderful as anything in his life. It hung from her frown, from an impalpable darkness in her face—a look that impressed him as a direct appeal for love. When she had counted her books, she came down the steps and opened the car door. In the light, he saw that her cheeks were wet. She got in and shut the door.

"You're new," Francis said.

"Yes. Mrs. Henlein is sick. I'm Anne Murchison."

"Did the children give you any trouble?"

"Oh, no, no." She turned and smiled at him unhappily in the dim dashboard light. Her light hair caught on the collar of her jacket, and she shook her head to set it loose.

20 "You've been crying."

"Yes."

"I hope it was nothing that happened in our house."

"No, no, it was nothing that happened in your house." Her voice was bleak. "It's no secret. Everybody in the village knows. Daddy's an alcoholic, and he just called me from some saloon and gave me a piece of his mind. He thinks I'm immoral. He called just before Mrs. Weed came back."

"I'm sorry."

25 "Oh, Lord!" She gasped and began to cry. She turned toward Francis, and he took her in his arms and let her cry on his shoulder. She shook in his embrace, and this movement accentuated his sense of the fineness of her flesh and bone. The layers of their clothing felt thin, and when her shuddering began to diminish, it was so much like a paroxysm of love that Francis lost his head

and pulled her roughly against him. She drew away. "I live on Belleview Avenue," she said. "You go down Lansing Street to the railroad bridge."

"All right." He started the car.

"You turn left at that traffic light. . . . Now you turn right here and go straight on toward the tracks."

The road Francis took brought him out of his own neighborhood, across the tracks, and toward the river, to a street where the near-poor lived, in houses whose peaked gables and trimmings of wooden lace conveyed the purest feelings of pride and romance, although the houses themselves could not have offered much privacy or comfort, they were all so small. The street was dark, and, stirred by the grace and beauty of the troubled girl, he seemed, in turning into it, to have come into the deepest part of some submerged memory. In the distance, he saw a porch light burning. It was the only one, and she said that the house with the light was where she lived. When he stopped the car, he could see beyond the porch light into a dimly lighted hallway with an old-fashioned clothes tree. "Well, here we are," he said, conscious that a young man would have said something different.

She did not move her hands from the books, where they were folded, and she turned and faced him. There were tears of lust in his eyes. Determinedly—not sadly—he opened the door on his side and walked around to open hers. He took her free hand, letting his fingers in between hers, climbed at her side the two concrete steps, and went up a narrow walk through a front garden where dahlias, marigolds, and roses—things that had withstood the light frosts—still bloomed, and made a bittersweet smell in the night air. At the steps, she freed her hand and then turned and kissed him swiftly. Then she crossed the porch and shut the door. The porch light went out, then the light in the hall. A second later, a light went on upstairs at the side of the house, shining into a tree that was still covered with leaves. It took her only a few minutes to undress and get into bed, and then the house was dark.

Julia was asleep when Francis got home. He opened a second window and got into bed to shut his eyes on that night, but as soon as they were shut—as soon as he had dropped off to sleep—the girl entered his mind, moving with perfect freedom through its shut doors and filling chamber after chamber with her light, her perfume, and the music of her voice. He was crossing the Atlantic with her on the old *Mauretania*[1] and, later, living with her in Paris. When he woke from his dream, he got up and smoked a cigarette at the open window. Getting back into bed, he cast around in his mind for something he desired to do that would injure no one, and he thought of skiing. Up through the dimness in his mind rose the image of a mountain deep in snow. It was late in the day. Wherever his eyes looked, he saw broad and heartening things. Over his shoulder, there was a snow-filled valley, rising into wooded hills where the trees dimmed the whiteness like a sparse coat of hair. The cold deadened all sound but the loud, iron clanking of the lift machinery. The light on the trails was

30

1. The original *Mauretania* (1907–1935), sister ship of the *Lusitania*, which was sunk by the Germans in 1915, was the most famous transatlantic liner of its day.

blue, and it was harder than it had been a minute or two earlier to pick the turns, harder to judge—now that the snow was all deep blue—the crust, the ice, the bare spots, and the deep piles of dry powder. Down the mountain he swung, matching his speed against the contours of a slope that had been formed in the first ice age, seeking with ardor some simplicity of feeling and circumstance. Night fell then, and he drank a Martini with some old friend in a dirty country bar.

In the morning, Francis' snow-covered mountain was gone, and he was left with his vivid memories of Paris and the *Mauretania*. He had been bitten gravely. He washed his body, shaved his jaws, drank his coffee, and missed the seventy-thirty-one. The train pulled out just as he brought his car to the station, and the longing he felt for the coaches as they drew stubbornly away from him reminded him of the humors of love. He waited for the eight-two, on what was now an empty platform. It was a clear morning; the morning seemed thrown like a gleaming bridge of light over his mixed affairs. His spirits were feverish and high. The image of the girl seemed to put him into a relationship to the world that was mysterious and enthralling. Cars were beginning to fill up the parking lot, and he noticed that those that had driven down from the high land above Shady Hill were white with hoarfrost. This first clear sign of autumn thrilled him. An express train—a night train from Buffalo or Albany—came down the tracks between the platforms, and he saw that the roofs of the foremost cars were covered with a skin of ice. Struck by the miraculous physicalness of everything, he smiled at the passengers in the dining car, who could be seen eating eggs and wiping their mouths with napkins as they traveled. The sleeping-car compartments, with their soiled bed linen, trailed through the fresh morning like a string of rooming-house windows. Then he saw an extraordinary thing; at one of the bedroom windows sat an unclothed woman of exceptional beauty, combing her golden hair. She passed like an apparition through Shady Hill, combing and combing her hair, and Francis followed her with his eyes until she was out of sight. Then old Mrs. Wrightson joined him on the platform and began to talk.

"Well, I guess you must be surprised to see me here the third morning in a row," she said, "but because of my window curtains I'm becoming a regular commuter. The curtains I bought on Monday I returned on Tuesday, and the curtains I bought Tuesday I'm returning today. On Monday, I got exactly what I wanted—it's a wool tapestry with roses and birds—but when I got them home, I found they were the wrong length. Well, I exchanged them yesterday, and when I got them home, I found they were still the wrong length. Now I'm praying to high heaven that the decorator will have them in the right length, because you know my house, you *know* my living-room windows, and you can imagine what a problem they present. I don't know what to do with them."

"I know what to do with them," Francis said.

"What?"

"Paint them black on the inside, and shut up."

There was a gasp from Mrs. Wrightson, and Francis looked down at her to be sure that she knew he meant to be rude. She turned and walked away from him, so damaged in spirit that she limped. A wonderful feeling enveloped him, as if light were being shaken about him, and he thought again of Venus combing and combing her hair as she drifted through the Bronx. The realization of how many years had passed since he had enjoyed being deliberately impolite sobered him. Among his friends and neighbors, there were brilliant and gifted people—he saw that—but many of them, also, were bores and fools, and he had made the mistake of listening to them all with equal attention. He had confused a lack of discrimination with Christian love, and the confusion seemed general and destructive. He was grateful to the girl for this bracing sensation of independence. Birds were singing—cardinals and the last of the robins. The sky shone like enamel. Even the smell of ink from his morning paper honed his appetite for life, and the world that was spread out around him was plainly a paradise.

If Francis had believed in some hierarchy of love—in spirits armed with hunting bows, in the capriciousness of Venus and Eros[2]—or even in magical potions, philters, and stews, in scapulae and quarters of the moon,[3] it might have explained his susceptibility and his feverish high spirits. The autumnal loves of middle age are well publicized, and he guessed that he was face to face with one of these, but there was not a trace of autumn in what he felt. He wanted to sport in the green woods, scratch where he itched, and drink from the same cup.

His secretary, Miss Rainey, was late that morning—she went to a psychiatrist three mornings a week—and when she came in, Francis wondered what advice a psychiatrist would have for him. But the girl promised to bring back into his life something like the sound of music. The realization that this music might lead him straight to a trial for statutory rape at the country courthouse collapsed his happiness. The photograph of his four children laughing into the camera on the beach at Gay Head reproached him. On the letterhead of his firm there was a drawing of the Laocoön,[4] and the figure of the priest and his sons in the coils of the snake appeared to him to have the deepest meaning.

He had lunch with Pinky Trabert. At a conversational level, the mores of his friends were robust and elastic, but he knew that the moral card house would come down on them all—on Julia and the children as well—if he got caught taking advantage of a baby-sitter. Looking back over the recent history of Shady Hill for some precedent, he found there was none. There was no turpitude; there had not been a divorce since he lived there; there had not even been a breath of scandal. Things seemed arranged with more propriety even than in the Kingdom of Heaven. After leaving Pinky, Francis went to a jeweler's and bought the girl a bracelet. How happy this clandestine purchase made him, how stuffy and comical the jeweler's clerks seemed, how sweet the women who passed at his back smelled! On Fifth Avenue, passing Atlas with his shoulders

2. The Roman name for the goddess of love (Greek *Aphrodite*) and the Greek name for her son (Roman *Cupid*).   3. Love-inducing and predictive magic. *Scapulae*: shoulderblades or bones of the back.   4. Famous Greek statue, described here, now in the Vatican museum; the "meaning" for Weed seems to reside in the physical struggle, not in the legend (in which the priest and his sons were punished for warning the Trojans about the wooden horse).

bent under the weight of the world,[5] Francis thought of the strenuousness of containing his physicalness within the patterns he had chosen.

He did not know when he would see the girl next. He had the bracelet in his inside pocket when he got home. Opening the door of his house, he found her in the hall. Her back was to him, and she turned when she heard the door close. Her smile was open and loving. Her perfection stunned him like a fine day—a day after a thunderstorm. He seized her and covered her lips with his, and she struggled but she did not have to struggle for long, because just then little Gertrude Flannery appeared from somewhere and said, "Oh, Mr. Weed . . ."

Gertrude was a stray. She had been born with a taste for exploration, and she did not have it in her to center her life with her affectionate parents. People who did not know the Flannerys concluded from Gertrude's behavior that she was the child of a bitterly divided family, where drunken quarrels were the rule. This was not true. The fact that little Gertrude's clothing was ragged and thin was her own triumph over her mother's struggle to dress her warmly and neatly. Garrulous, skinny, and unwashed, she drifted from house to house around the Blenhollow neighborhood, forming and breaking alliances based on an attachment to babies, animals, children her own age, adolescents, and sometimes adults. Opening your front door in the morning, you would find Gertrude sitting on your stoop. Going into the bathroom to shave, you would find Gertrude using the toilet. Looking into your son's crib, you would find it empty, and, looking further, you would find that Gertrude had pushed him in his baby carriage into the next village. She was helpful, pervasive, honest, hungry, and loyal. She never went home of her own choice. When the time to go arrived, she was indifferent to all its signs. "Go home, Gertrude," people could be heard saying in one house or another, night after night. "Go home, Gertrude. It's time for you to go home now, Gertrude." "You had better go home and get your supper, Gertrude." "I told you to go home twenty minutes ago, Gertrude." "Your mother will be worrying about you, Gertrude." "Go home, Gertrude, go home."

There are times when the lines around the human eye seem like shelves of eroded stone and when the staring eye itself strikes us with such a wilderness of animal feeling that we are at a loss. The look Francis gave the little girl was ugly and queer, and it frightened her. He reached into his pockets—his hands were shaking—and took out a quarter. "Go home, Gertrude, go home, and don't tell anyone, Gertrude. Don't—" He choked and ran into the living room as Julia called down to him from upstairs to hurry and dress.

The thought that he would drive Anne Murchison home later that night ran like a golden thread through the events of the party that Francis and Julia went to, and he laughed uproariously at dull jokes, dried a tear when Mabel Mercer told him about the death of her kitten, and stretched, yawned, sighed, and grunted like any other man with a rendezvous at the back of his mind. The bracelet was in his pocket. As he sat talking, the smell of grass was in his nose,

5. In Greek legend the Titan Atlas supported the heavens on his shoulders but has come to be depicted as bearing the globe; the statue is at Rockefeller Center.

and he was wondering where he would park the car. Nobody lived in the old Parker mansion, and the driveway was used as a lovers' lane. Townsend Street was a dead end, and he could park there, beyond the last house. The old lane that used to connect Elm Street to the riverbanks was overgrown, but he had walked there with his children, and he could drive his car deep enough into the brushwoods to be concealed.

The Weeds were the last to leave the party, and their host and hostess spoke of their own married happiness while they all four stood in the hallway saying good night. "She's my girl," their host said, squeezing his wife. "She's my blue sky. After sixteen years, I still bite her shoulders. She makes me feel like Hannibal crossing the Alps.[6]"

The Weeds drove home in silence. Francis brought the car up the driveway and sat still, with the motor running. "You can put the car in the garage," Julia said as she got out. "I told the Murchison girl she could leave at eleven. Someone drove her home." She shut the door, and Francis sat in the dark. He would be spared nothing then, it seemed, that a fool was not spared: ravening lewdness, jealousy, this hurt to his feelings that put tears in his eyes, even scorn—for he could see clearly the image he now presented, his arms spread over the steering wheel and his head buried in them for love.

Francis had been a dedicated Boy Scout when he was young, and, remembering the precepts of his youth, he left his office early the next afternoon and played some round-robin squash, but, with his body toned up by exercise and a shower, he realized that he might better have stayed at his desk. It was a frosty night when he got home. The air smelled sharply of change. When he stepped into the house, he sensed an unusual stir. The children were in their best clothes, and when Julia came down, she was wearing a lavender dress and her diamond sunburst. She explained the stir: Mr. Hubber was coming at seven to take their photograph for the Christmas card. She had put out Francis' blue suit and a tie with some color in it, because the picture was going to be in color this year. Julia was lighthearted at the thought of being photographed for Christmas. It was the kind of ceremony she enjoyed.

Francis went upstairs to change his clothes. He was tired from the day's work and tired with longing, and sitting on the edge of the bed had the effect of deepening his weariness. He thought of Anne Murchison, and the physical need to express himself, instead of being restrained by the pink lamps of Julia's dressing table, engulfed him. He went to Julia's desk, took a piece of writing paper, and began to write on it. "Dear Anne, I love you, I love you, I love you . . ." No one would see the letter, and he used no restraint. He used phrases like "heavenly bliss," and "love nest." He salivated, sighed, and trembled. When Julia called him to come down, the abyss between his fantasy and the practical world opened so wide that he felt it affected the muscles of his heart.

Julia and the children were on the stoop, and the photographer and his

45

6. The Carthaginian general (274–183 B.C.) attacked the Romans from the rear by crossing the Alps, considered impregnable, with the use of elephants.

assistant had set up a double battery of floodlights to show the family and the architectural beauty of the entrance to their house. People who had come home on a late train slowed their cars to see the Weeds being photographed for their Christmas card. A few waved and called to the family. It took half an hour of smiling and wetting their lips before Mr. Hubber was satisfied. The heat of the lights made an unfresh smell in the frosty air, and when they were turned off, they lingered on the retina of Francis' eyes.

Later that night, while Francis and Julia were drinking their coffee in the living room, the doorbell rang. Julia answered the door and let in Clayton Thomas. He had come to pay for some theatre tickets that she had given his mother some time ago, and that Helen Thomas had scrupulously insisted on paying for, though Julia had asked her not to. Julia invited him in to have a cup of coffee. "I won't have any coffee," Clayton said, "but I will come in for a minute." He followed her into the living room, said good evening to Francis, and sat awkwardly in a chair.

Clayton's father had been killed in the war, and the young man's father-lessness surrounded him like an element. This may have been conspicuous in Shady Hill because the Thomases were the only family that lacked a piece; all the other marriages were intact and productive. Clayton was in his second or third year of college, and he and his mother lived alone in a large house, which she hoped to sell. Clayton had once made some trouble. Years ago, he had stolen some money and run away; he had got to California before they caught up with him. He was tall and homely, wore hornrimmed glasses, and spoke in a deep voice.

"When do you go back to college, Clayton?" Francis asked.

"I'm not going back," Clayton said. "Mother doesn't have the money, and there's no sense in all this pretense. I'm going to get a job, and if we sell the house, we'll take an apartment in New York."

"Won't you miss Shady Hill?" Julia asked.

"No," Clayton said. "I don't like it."

"Why not?" Francis asked.

"Well, there's a lot here I don't approve of," Clayton said gravely. "Things like the club dances. Last Saturday night, I looked in toward the end and saw Mr. Granner trying to put Mrs. Minot into the trophy case. They were both drunk. I disapprove of so much drinking."

"It was Saturday night," Francis said.

"And all the dovecotes are phony," Clayton said. "And the way people clutter up their lives. I've thought about it a lot, and what seems to me to be really wrong with Shady Hill is that it doesn't have any future. So much energy is spent in perpetuating the place—in keeping out undesirables, and so forth—that the only idea of the future anyone has is just more and more commuting trains and more parties. I don't think that's healthy. I think people ought to be able to dream big dreams about the future. I think people ought to be able to dream great dreams."

"It's too bad you couldn't continue with college," Julia said.

"I want to go to divinity school," Clayton said.

"What's your church?" Francis asked.

"Unitarian, Theosophist, Transcendentalist, Humanist,"[7] Clayton said.

"Wasn't Emerson a transcendentalist?" Julia asked.

"I mean the English transcendentalists," Clayton said. "All the American transcendentalists were goops."

"What kind of job do you expect to get?" Francis asked.

"Well, I'd like to work for a publisher," Clayton said, "but everyone tells me there's nothing doing. But it's the kind of thing I'm interested in. I'm writing a long verse play about good and evil. Uncle Charlie might get me into a bank, and that would be good for me. I need the discipline. I have a long way to go in forming my character. I have some terrible habits. I talk too much. I think I ought to take vows of silence. I ought to try not to speak for a week, and discipline myself. I've thought of making a retreat at one of the Episcopalian monasteries, but I don't like Trinitarianism."

"Do you have any girl friends?" Francis asked.

"I'm engaged to be married," Clayton said. "Of course, I'm not old enough or rich enough to have my engagement observed or respected or anything, but I bought a simulated emerald for Anne Murchison with the money I made cutting lawns this summer. We're going to be married as soon as she finishes school."

Francis recoiled at the mention of the girl's name. Then a dingy light seemed to emanate from his spirit, showing everything—Julia, the boy, the chairs—in their true colorlessness. It was like a bitter turn of the weather.

"We're going to have a large family," Clayton said. "Her father's a terrible rummy, and I've had my hard times, and we want to have lots of children. Oh, she's wonderful, Mr. and Mrs. Weed, and we have so much in common. We like all the same things. We sent out the same Christmas card last year without planning it, and we both have an allergy to tomatoes, and our eyebrows grow together in the middle. Well, goodnight."

Julia went to the door with him. When she returned, Francis said that Clayton was lazy, irresponsible, affected, and smelly. Julia said that Francis seemed to be getting intolerant; the Thomas boy was young and should be given a chance. Julia had noticed other cases where Francis had been short-tempered. "Mrs. Wrightson has asked everyone in Shady Hill to her anniversary party but us," she said.

"I'm sorry, Julia."

"Do you know why they didn't ask us?"

"Why?"

"Because you insulted Mrs. Wrightson."

"Then you know about it?"

"June Masterson told me. She was standing behind you."

Julia walked in front of the sofa with a small step that expressed, Francis knew, a feeling of anger.

65

70

75

7. All are deviations from orthodox Christianity and tend to be more man- than God-oriented, though their differences hardly seem reconcilable; the American transcendentalists (see below) tended to change the emphasis from the study of thought to belief in "intuition."

"I did insult Mrs. Wrightson, Julia, and I meant to. I've never liked her parties, and I'm glad she's dropped us."

"What about Helen?"

"How does Helen come into this?"

"Mrs. Wrightson's the one who decides who goes to the assemblies."

"You mean she can keep Helen from going to the dances?"

"Yes."

"I hadn't thought of that."

"Oh. I knew you hadn't thought of it," Julia cried, thrusting hiltdeep into this chink of his armor. "And it makes me furious to see this kind of stupid thoughtlessness wreck everyone's happiness."

"I don't think I've wrecked anyone's happiness."

"Mrs. Wrightson runs Shady Hill and has run it for the last forty years. I don't know what makes you think that in a community like this you can indulge every impulse you have to be insulting, vulgar, and offensive."

"I have very good manners," Francis said, trying to give the evening a turn toward the light.

"Damn you, Francis Weed!" Julia cried, and the spit of her words struck him in the face. "I've worked hard for the social position we enjoy in this place, and I won't stand by and see you wreck it. You must have understood when you settled here that you couldn't expect to live like a bear in a cave."

"I've got to express my likes and dislikes."

"You can conceal your dislikes. You don't have to meet everything head on, like a child. Unless you're anxious to be a social leper. It's no accident that we get asked out a great deal! It's no accident that Helen has so many friends. How would you like to spend your Saturday nights at the movies? How would you like to spend your Sunday raking up dead leaves? How would you like it if your daughter spent the assembly nights sitting at her window, listening to the music from the club? How would you like it—" He did something then that was, after all, not so unaccountable, since her words seemed to raise up between them a wall so deadening that he gagged. He struck her full in the face. She staggered and then, a moment later, seemed composed. She went up the stairs to their room. She didn't slam the door. When Francis followed, a few minutes later, he found her packing a suitcase.

"Julia, I'm very sorry."

"It doesn't matter," she said. She was crying.

"Where do you think you're going?"

"I don't know. I just looked at a timetable. There's an eleven-sixteen into New York. I'll take that."

"You can't go, Julia."

"I can't stay. I know that."

"I'm sorry about Mrs. Wrightson, Julia, and I'm—"

"It doesn't matter about Mrs. Wrightson. That isn't the trouble."

"What is the trouble?"

"You don't love me."

"I do love you, Julia."

"No, you don't."

"Julia, I do love you, and I would like to be as we were—sweet and bawdy and dark—but now there are so many people."

"You hate me."

"I don't hate you, Julia."

"You have no idea of how much you hate me. I think it's subconscious. You don't realize the cruel things you've done."

"What cruel things, Julia?"

"The cruel acts your subconscious drives you to in order to express your hatred of me."

"What, Julia?"

"I've never complained."

"Tell me."

"You don't know what you're doing."

"Tell me."

"Your clothes."

"What do you mean?"

"I mean the way you leave your dirty clothes around in order to express your subconscious hatred of me."

"I don't understand."

"I mean your dirty socks and your dirty pajamas and your dirty underwear and your dirty shirts!" She rose from kneeling by the suitcase and faced him, her eyes blazing and her voice ringing with emotion. "I'm talking about the fact that you've never learned to hang up anything. You just leave your clothes all over the floor where they drop, in order to humiliate me. You do it on purpose!" She fell on the bed, sobbing.

"Julia, darling!" he said, but when she felt his hand on her shoulder she got up.

"Leave me alone," she said. "I have to go." She brushed past him to the closet and came back with a dress. "I'm not taking any of the things you've given me," she said. "I'm leaving my pearls and the fur jacket."

"Oh, Julia!" Her figure, so helpless in its self-deceptions, bent over the suitcase made him nearly sick with pity. She did not understand how desolate her life would be without him. She didn't understand the hours that working women have to keep. She didn't understand that most of her friendships existed within the framework of their marriage, and that without this she would find herself alone. She didn't understand about travel, about hotels, about money. "Julia, I can't let you go! What you don't understand, Julia, is that you've come to be dependent on me."

She tossed her head back and covered her face with her hands. "Did you say that I was dependent on you?" she asked. "Is that what you said? And who is it that tells you what time to get up in the morning and when to go to bed at night? Who is it that prepares your meals and picks up your dirty clothes and invites your friends to dinner? If it weren't for me, your neckties would be greasy and your clothing would be full of moth holes. You were alone when I met you, Francis Weed, and you'll be alone when I leave. When Mother asked you for a list to send out invitations to our wedding, how many names did you have to give her? Fourteen!"

"Cleveland wasn't my home, Julia."

"And how many of your friends came to the church? Two!"

"Cleveland wasn't my home, Julia."

"Since I'm not taking the fur jacket," she said quietly, "you'd better put it back into storage. There's an insurance policy on the pearls that comes due in January. The name of the laundry and maid's telephone number—all those things are in my desk. I hope you won't drink too much, Francis. I hope that nothing bad will happen to you. If you do get into serious trouble, you can call me."

"Oh, my darling, I can't let you go!" Francis said. "I can't let you go, Julia!" He took her in his arms.

"I guess I'd better stay and take care of you for a little while longer," she said.

Riding to work in the morning, Francis saw the girl walk down the aisle of the coach. He was surprised; he hadn't realized that the school she went to was in the city, but she was carrying books, she seemed to be going to school. His surprise delayed his reaction, but then he got up clumsily and stepped into the aisle. Several people had come between them, but he could see her ahead of him, waiting for someone to open the car door, and then, as the train swerved, putting out her hand to support herself as she crossed the platform into the next car. He followed her through that car and halfway through another before calling her name—"Anne! Anne!"—but she didn't turn. He followed her into still another car, and she sat down in an aisle seat. Coming up to her, all his feelings warm and bent in her direction, he put his hand on the back of her seat—even this touch warmed him—and leaning down to speak to her, he saw that it was not Anne. It was an older woman wearing glasses. He went on deliberately into another car, his face red with embarrassment and the much deeper feeling of having his good sense challenged; for if he couldn't tell one person from another, what evidence was there that his life with Julia and the children had as much reality as his dreams of iniquity in Paris or the litter, the grass smell, and the cave-shaped trees in Lovers' Lane.

Late that afternoon, Julia called to remind Francis that they were going out for dinner. A few minutes later, Trace Bearden called. "Look, fellar," Trace said. "I'm calling for Mrs. Thomas. You know? Clayton, that boy of hers, doesn't seem able to get a job, and I wondered if you could help. If you'd call Charlie Bell—I know he's indebted to you—and say a good word for the kid, I think Charlie would—"

"Trace, I hate to say this," Francis said, "but I don't feel that I can do anything for that boy. The kid's worthless. I know it's a harsh thing to say, but it's a fact. Any kindness done for him would backfire in everybody's face. He's just a worthless kid, Trace, and there's nothing else to be done about it. Even if we got him a job, he wouldn't be able to keep it for a week. I know that to be a fact. It's an awful thing, Trace, and I know it is, but instead of recommending that kid, I'd feel obligated to warn people against him—people who knew his father and would naturally want to step in and do something. I'd feel obliged to warn them. He's a thief . . ."

The moment this conversation was finished, Miss Rainey came in and stood by his desk. "I'm not going to be able to work for you any more, Mr. Weed," she said. "I can stay until the seventeenth if you need me, but I've been offered a whirlwind of a job, and I'd like to leave as soon as possible."

She went out, leaving him to face alone the wickedness of what he had done to the Thomas boy. His children in their photograph laughed and laughed, glazed with all the bright colors of summer, and he remembered that they had met a bagpiper on the beach that day and he had paid the piper a dollar to play them a battle song of the Black Watch.[8] The girl would be at the house when he got home. He would spend another evening among his kind neighbors, picking and choosing dead-end streets, cart tracks, and the driveways of abandoned houses. There was nothing to mitigate his feeling—nothing that laughter or a game of softball with the children would change—and, thinking back over the plane crash, the Farquarsons' new maid, and Anne Murchison's difficulties with her drunken father, he wondered how he could have avoided arriving at just where he was. He was in trouble. He had been lost once in his life, coming back from a trout stream in the north woods, and he had now the same bleak realization that no amount of cheerfulness or hopefulness or valor or perseverance could help him find, in the gathering dark, the path that he'd lost. He smelled the forest. The feeling of bleakness was intolerable, and he saw clearly that he had reached the point where he would have to make a choice.

He could go to a psychiatrist, like Miss Rainey; he could go to church and confess his lusts; he could go to a Danish-massage parlor[9] in the West Seventies that had been recommended by a salesman; he could rape the girl or trust that he would somehow be prevented from doing this; or he could get drunk. It was his life, his boat, and, like every other man, he was made to be the father of thousands, and what harm could there be in a tryst that would make them both feel more kindly toward the world? This was the wrong train of thought, and he came back to the first, the psychiatrist. He had the telephone number of Miss Rainey's doctor, and he called and asked for an immediate appointment. He was insistent with the doctor's secretary—it was his manner in business—and when she said that the doctor's schedule was full for the next few weeks, Francis demanded an appointment that day and was told to come at five.

The psychiatrist's office was in a building that was used mostly by doctors and dentists, and the hallways were filled with the candy smell of mouthwash and memories of pain. Francis' character had been formed upon a series of private resolves—resolves about cleanliness, about going off the high diving board or repeating any other feat that challenged his courage, about punctuality, honesty, and virtue. To abdicate the perfect loneliness in which he had made his most vital decisions shattered his concept of character and left him now in a

135

---

8. Originally a British Highland regiment that became a line regiment and distinguished itself in battle.   9. Sometimes fronts for houses of prostitution.

condition that felt like shock. He was stupefied. The scene for his *miserere mei Deus*[1] was, like the waiting room of so many doctor's offices, a crude token gesture toward the sweets of domestic bliss: a place arranged with antiques, coffee tables, potted plants, and etchings of snow-covered bridges and geese in flight, although there were no children, no marriage bed, no stove, even, in this travesty of a house, where no one had ever spent the night and where the curtained windows looked straight onto a dark air shaft. Francis gave his name and address to a secretary and then saw, at the side of the room, a policeman moving toward him. "Hold it, hold it," the policeman said. "Don't move. Keep your hands where they are."

"I think it's all right, Officer," the secretary began. "I think it will be —"

"Let's make sure," the policeman said, and he began to slap Francis' clothes, looking for what — pistols, knives, an icepick? Finding nothing, he went off and the secretary began a nervous apology: "When you called on the telephone, Mr. Weed, you seemed very excited, and one of the doctor's patients has been threatening his life, and we have to be careful. If you want to go in now?" Francis pushed open a door connected to an electrical chime, and in the doctor's lair sat down heavily, blew his nose into a handkerchief, searched in his pockets for cigarettes, for matches, for something, and said hoarsely, with tears in his eyes, "I'm in love, Dr. Herzog."

140   It is a week or ten days later in Shady Hill. The seven-fourteen has come and gone, and here and there dinner is finished and the dishes are in the dishwashing machine. The village hangs, morally and economically, from a thread; but it hangs by its thread in the evening light. Donald Goslin has begun to worry the "Moonlight Sonata" again. *Marcato ma sempre pianissimo!*[2] He seems to be wringing out a wet bath towel, but the housemaid does not heed him. She is writing a letter to Arthur Godfrey.[3] In the cellar of his house, Francis Weed is building a coffee table. Dr. Herzog recommends woodwork as a therapy, and Francis finds some true consolation in the simple arithmetic involved and in the holy smell of new wood. Francis is happy. Upstairs, little Toby is crying, because he is tired. He puts off his cowboy hat, gloves, and fringed jacket, unbuckles the belt studded with gold and rubies, the silver bullets and holsters, slips off his suspenders, his checked shirt, and Levi's, and sits on the edge of his bed to pull off his high boots. Leaving this equipment in a heap, he goes to the closet and takes his space suit off a nail. It is a struggle for him to get into the long tights, but he succeeds. He loops the magic cape over his shoulders and, climbing onto the footboard of his bed, he spreads his arms and flies the short distance to the floor, landing with a thump that is audible to everyone in the house but himself.

"Go home, Gertrude, go home," Mrs. Masterson says. "I told you to go home an hour ago, Gertrude. It's way past your suppertime, and your mother will be

1. Have mercy upon me, O God; first words of 51st Psalm.   2. Stressed but always very softly.   3. At the time of the story, host of a daytime radio program especially popular with housewives.

worried. Go home!" A door on the Babcocks' terrace flies open, and out comes Mrs. Babcock without any clothes on, pursued by a naked husband. (Their children are away at boarding school, and their terrace is screened by a hedge.) Over the terrace they go and in at the kitchen door, as passionate and handsome a nymph and satyr as you will find on any wall in Venice. Cutting the last of the roses in her garden, Julia hears old Mr. Nixon shouting at the squirrels in his bird-feeding station. "Rapscallions! Varmints! Avaunt and quit my sight!" A miserable cat wanders into the garden, sunk in spiritual and physical discomfort. Tied to its head is a small straw hat—a doll's hat—and it is securely buttoned into a doll's dress, from the skirts of which protrudes its long, hairy tail. As it walks, it shakes its feet, as if it had fallen into water.

"Here, pussy, pussy, pussy!" Julia calls.

"Here, pussy, here, poor pussy!" But the cat gives her a skeptical look and stumbles away in its skirts. The last to come is Jupiter. He prances through the tomato vines, holding in his generous mouth the remains of an evening slipper. Then it is dark; it is a night where kings in golden suits ride elephants over the mountains.[4]

1958

JAMES BALDWIN

Sonny's Blues

I read about it in the paper, in the subway, on my way to work. I read it, and I couldn't believe it, and I read it again. Then perhaps I just stared at it, at the newsprint spelling out his name, spelling out the story. I stared at it in the swinging lights of the subway car, and in the faces and bodies of the people, and in my own face, trapped in the darkness which roared outside.

It was not to be believed and I kept telling myself that, as I walked from the subway station to the high school. And at the same time I couldn't doubt it. I was scared, scared for Sonny. He became real to me again. A great block of ice got settled in my belly and kept melting there slowly all day long, while I taught my classes algebra. It was a special kind of ice. It kept melting, sending trickles of ice water all up and down my veins, but it never got less. Sometimes it hardened and seemed to expand until I felt my guts were going to come spilling out or that I was going to choke or scream. This would always be at a moment when I was remembering some specific thing Sonny had once said or done.

When he was about as old as the boys in my classes his face had been bright and open, there was a lot of copper in it; and he'd had wonderfully direct brown

4. See Sinclair Lewis, *Main Street* (1920), in which the protagonist finds the small town of Gopher Prairie stifling and leaves with her son for Washington, D.C., where, she tells him, " 'We're going to find elephants with golden howdahs from which peep young maharanees with necklaces of rubies. . . .' "

eyes, and great gentleness and privacy. I wondered what he looked like now. He had been picked up, the evening before, in a raid on an apartment downtown, for peddling and using heroin.

I couldn't believe it: but what I mean by that is that I couldn't find any room for it anywhere inside me. I had kept it outside me for a long time. I hadn't wanted to know. I had had suspicions, but I didn't name them, I kept putting them away. I told myself that Sonny was wild, but he wasn't crazy. And he'd always been a good boy, he hadn't ever turned hard or evil or disrespectful, the way kids can, so quick, so quick, especially in Harlem. I didn't want to believe that I'd ever see my brother going down, coming to nothing, all that light in his face gone out, in the condition I'd already seen so many others. Yet it had happened and here I was, talking about algebra to a lot of boys who might, every one of them for all I knew, be popping off needles every time they went to the head.[1] Maybe it did more for them than algebra could.

5   I was sure that the first time Sonny had ever had horse,[2] he couldn't have been much older than these boys were now. These boys, now, were living as we'd been living then, they were growing up with a rush and their heads bumped abruptly against the low ceiling of their actual possibilities. They were filled with rage. All they really knew were two darknesses, the darkness of their lives, which was now closing in on them, and the darkness of the movies, which had blinded them to that other darkness, and in which they now, vindictively, dreamed, at once more together than they were at any other time, and more alone.

When the last bell rang, the last class ended, I let out my breath. It seemed I'd been holding it for all that time. My clothes were wet—I may have looked as though I'd been sitting in a steam bath, all dressed up, all afternoon. I sat alone in the classroom a long time. I listened to the boys outside, downstairs, shouting and cursing and laughing. Their laughter struck me for perhaps the first time. It was not the joyous laughter which—God knows why—one associates with children. It was mocking and insular, its intent was to denigrate. It was disenchanted, and in this, also, lay the authority of their curses. Perhaps I was listening to them because I was thinking about my brother and in them I heard my brother. And myself.

One boy was whistling a tune, at once very complicated and very simple, it seemed to be pouring out of him as though he were a bird, and it sounded very cool and moving through all that harsh, bright air, only just holding its own through all those other sounds.

I stood up and walked over to the window and looked down into the courtyard. It was the beginning of the spring and the sap was rising in the boys. A teacher passed through them every now and again, quickly, as though he or she couldn't wait to get out of that courtyard, to get those boys out of their sight and off their minds. I started collecting my stuff. I thought I'd better get home and talk to Isabel.

The courtyard was almost deserted by the time I got downstairs. I saw this

1. Lavatory.   2. Heroin.

boy standing in the shadow of a doorway, looking just like Sonny. I almost called his name. Then I saw that it wasn't Sonny, but somebody we used to know, a boy from around our block. He'd been Sonny's friend. He'd never been mine, having been too young for me, and, anyway, I'd never liked him. And now, even though he was a grown-up man, he still hung around that block, still spent hours on the street corners, was always high and raggy. I used to run into him from time to time and he'd often work around to asking me for a quarter or fifty cents. He always had some real good excuse, too, and I always gave it to him. I don't know why.

But now, abruptly, I hated him. I couldn't stand the way he looked at me, partly like a dog, partly like a cunning child. I wanted to ask him what the hell he was doing in the school courtyard.

He sort of shuffled over to me, and he said, "I see you got the papers. So you already know about it."

"You mean about Sonny? Yes, I already know about it. How come they didn't get you?"

He grinned. It made him repulsive and it also brought to mind what he'd looked like as a kid. "I wasn't there. I stay away from them people."

"Good for you." I offered him a cigarette and I watched him through the smoke. "You come all the way down here just to tell me about Sonny?"

"That's right." He was sort of shaking his head and his eyes looked strange, as though they were about to cross. The bright sun deadened his damp dark brown skin and it made his eyes look yellow and showed up the dirt in his kinked hair. He smelled funky. I moved a little away from him and I said, "Well, thanks. But I already know about it and I got to get home."

"I'll walk you a little ways," he said. We started walking. There were a couple of kids still loitering in the courtyard and one of them said goodnight to me and looked strangely at the boy beside me.

"What're you going to do?" he asked me. "I mean, about Sonny?"

"Look. I haven't seen Sonny for over a year, I'm not sure I'm going to do anything. Anyway, what the hell can I do?"

"That's right," he said quickly, "ain't nothing you can do. Can't much help old Sonny no more, I guess."

It was what I was thinking and so it seemed to me he had no right to say it.

"I'm surprised at Sonny, though," he went on—he had a funny way of talking, he looked straight ahead as though he were talking to himself—"I thought Sonny was a smart boy, I thought he was too smart to get hung."

"I guess he thought so too," I said sharply, "and that's how he got hung. And how about you? You're pretty goddamn smart, I bet."

Then he looked directly at me, just for a minute. "I ain't smart," he said. "If I was smart, I'd have reached for a pistol a long time ago."

"Look. Don't tell me your sad story, if it was up to me, I'd give you one." Then I felt guilty—guilty, probably, for never having supposed that the poor bastard had a story of his own, much less a sad one, and I asked, quickly, "What's going to happen to him now?"

He didn't answer this. He was off by himself some place.

"Funny thing," he said, and from his tone we might have been discussing the quickest way to get to Brooklyn, "when I saw the papers this morning, the first thing I asked myself was if I had anything to do with it. I felt sort of responsible."

I began to listen more carefully. The subway station was on the corner, just before us, and I stopped. He stopped, too. We were in front of a bar and he ducked slightly, peering in, but whoever he was looking for didn't seem to be there. The juke box was blasting away with something black and bouncy and I half watched the barmaid as she danced her way from the juke box to her place behind the bar. And I watched her face as she laughingly responded to something someone said to her, still keeping time to the music. When she smiled one saw the little girl, one sensed the doomed, still-struggling woman beneath the battered face of the semi-whore.

"I never *give* Sonny nothing," the boy said finally, "but a long time ago I come to school high and Sonny asked me how it felt." He paused, I couldn't bear to watch him, I watched the barmaid, and I listened to the music which seemed to be causing the pavement to shake. "I told him it felt great." The music stopped, the barmaid paused and watched the juke box until the music began again. "It did."

All this was carrying me some place I didn't want to go. I certainly didn't want to know how it felt. It filled everything, the people, the houses, the music, the dark, quicksilver barmaid, with menace; and this menace was their reality.

30 "What's going to happen to him now?" I asked again.

"They'll send him away some place and they'll try to cure him." He shook his head. "Maybe he'll even think he's kicked the habit. Then they'll let him loose"—he gestured, throwing his cigarette into the gutter. "That's all."

"What do you mean, that's *all?*"

But I knew what he meant.

"I *mean*, that's *all*." He turned his head and looked at me, pulling down the corners of his mouth. "Don't you know what I mean?" he asked, softly.

35 "How the hell *would* I know what you mean?" I almost whispered it, I don't know why.

"That's right," he said to the air, "how would *he* know what I mean?" He turned toward me again, patient and calm, and yet I somehow felt him shaking, shaking as though he were going to fall apart. I felt that ice in my guts again, the dread I'd felt all afternoon; and again I watched the barmaid, moving about the bar, washing glasses, and singing. "Listen. They'll let him out and then it'll just start all over again. That's what I mean."

"You mean—they'll let him out. And then he'll just start working his way back in again. You mean he'll never kick the habit. Is that what you mean?"

"That's right," he said, cheerfully. "*You* see what I mean."

"Tell me," I said at last, "why does he want to die? He must want to die, he's killing himself, why does he want to die?"

40 He looked at me in surprise. He licked his lips. "He don't want to die. He wants to live. Don't nobody want to die, ever."

Then I wanted to ask him—too many things. He could not have answered, or if he had, I could not have borne the answers. I started walking. "Well, I guess it's none of my business."

"It's going to be rough on old Sonny," he said. We reached the subway station. "This is your station?" he asked. I nodded. I took one step down. "Damn!" he said, suddenly. I looked up at him. He grinned again. "Damn it if I didn't leave all my money home. You ain't got a dollar on you, have you? Just for a couple of days, is all."

All at once something inside gave and threatened to come pouring out of me. I didn't hate him any more. I felt that in another moment I'd start crying like a child.

"Sure," I said. "Don't sweat." I looked in my wallet and didn't have a dollar, I only had a five. "Here," I said. "That hold you?"

He didn't look at it—he didn't want to look at it. A terrible, closed look came over his face, as though he were keeping the number on the bill a secret from him and me. "Thanks," he said, and now he was dying to see me go. "Don't worry about Sonny. Maybe I'll write him or something."

"Sure," I said. "You do that. So long."

"Be seeing you," he said. I went on down the steps.

And I didn't write Sonny or send him anything for a long time. When I finally did, it was just after my little girl died, and he wrote me back a letter which made me feel like a bastard.

Here's what he said:

Dear brother,

You don't know how much I needed to hear from you. I wanted to write you many a time but I dug how much I must have hurt you and so I didn't write. But now I feel like a man who's been trying to climb up out of some deep, real deep and funky hole and just saw the sun up there, outside. I got to get outside.

I can't tell you much about how I got here. I mean I don't know how to tell you. I guess I was afraid of something or I was trying to escape from something and you know I have never been very strong in the head (smile). I'm glad Mama and Daddy are dead and can't see what's happened to their son and I swear if I'd known what I was doing I would never have hurt you so, you and a lot of other fine people who were nice to me and who believed in me.

I don't want you to think it had anything to do with me being a musician. It's more than that. Or maybe less than that. I can't get anything straight in my head down here and I try not to think about what's going to happen to me when I get outside again. Sometime I think I'm going to flip and never get outside and sometime I think I'll come straight back. I tell you one thing, though, I'd rather blow my brains out than go through this again. But that's what they all say, so they tell me. If I tell you when I'm coming to New York and if you could meet me, I sure would appreciate it. Give my love to Isabel and the kids and I was sure sorry to hear about little Gracie. I wish I could be like Mama and say the Lord's will be done, but I don't know it seems to me that trouble is the one thing that never does get stopped and I don't know what good it does to blame it on the Lord. But maybe it does some good if you believe it.

Your brother,
Sonny

Then I kept in constant touch with him and I sent him whatever I could and I went to meet him when he came back to New York. When I saw him many things I thought I had forgotten came flooding back to me. This was because I had begun, finally, to wonder about Sonny, about the life that Sonny lived inside. This life, whatever it was, had made him older and thinner and it had deepened the distant stillness in which he had always moved. He looked very unlike my baby brother. Yet, when he smiled, when we shook hands, the baby brother I'd never known looked out from the depths of his private life, like an animal waiting to be coaxed into the light.

"How you been keeping?" he asked me.

"All right. And you?"

"Just fine." He was smiling all over his face. "It's good to see you again."

"It's good to see you."

The seven years' difference in our ages lay between us like a chasm: I wondered if these years would ever operate between us as a bridge. I was remembering, and it made it hard to catch my breath, that I had been there when he was born; and I had heard the first words he had ever spoken. When he started to walk, he walked from our mother straight to me. I caught him just before he fell when he took the first steps he ever took in this world.

"How's Isabel?"

"Just fine. She's dying to see you."

"And the boys?"

"They're fine, too. They're anxious to see their uncle."

"Oh, come on. You know they don't remember me."

"Are you kidding? Of course they remember you."

He grinned again. We got into a taxi. We had a lot to say to each other, far too much to know how to begin.

As the taxi began to move, I asked, "You still want to go to India?"

He laughed. "You still remember that. Hell, no. This place is Indian enough for me."

"It used to belong to them," I said.

And he laughed again. "They damn sure knew what they were doing when they got rid of it."

Years ago, when he was around fourteen, he'd been all hipped on the idea of going to India. He read books about people sitting on rocks, naked, in all kinds of weather, but mostly bad, naturally, and walking barefoot through hot coals and arriving at wisdom. I used to say that it sounded to me as though they were getting away from wisdom as fast as they could. I think he sort of looked down on me for that.

"Do you mind," he asked, "if we have the driver drive alongside the park? On the west side—I haven't seen the city in so long."

"Of course not," I said. I was afraid that I might sound as though I were humoring him, but I hoped he wouldn't take it that way.

So we drove along, between the green of the park and the stony, lifeless elegance of hotels and apartment buildings, toward the vivid, killing streets of our childhood. These streets hadn't changed, though housing projects jutted up out of them now like rocks in the middle of a boiling sea. Most of the houses in which we had grown up had vanished, as had the stores from which we had stolen, the basements in which we had first tried sex, the rooftops from which we had hurled tin cans and bricks. But houses exactly like the houses of our past yet dominated the landscape, boys exactly like the boys we once had been found themselves smothering in these houses, came down into the streets for light and air and found themselves encircled by disaster. Some escaped the trap, most didn't. Those who got out always left something of themselves behind, as some animals amputate a leg and leave it in the trap. It might be said, perhaps, that I had escaped, after all, I was a school teacher; or that Sonny had, he hadn't lived in Harlem for years. Yet, as the cab moved uptown through streets which seemed, with a rush, to darken with dark people, and as I covertly studied Sonny's face, it came to me that what we both were seeking through our separate cab windows was that part of ourselves which had been left behind. It's always at the hour of trouble and confrontation that the missing member aches.

We hit 110th Street and started rolling up Lenox Avenue. And I'd known this avenue all my life, but it seemed to me again, as it had seemed on the day I'd first heard about Sonny's trouble, filled with a hidden menace which was its very breath of life.

"We almost there," said Sonny.

"Almost." We were both too nervous to say anything more.

We live in a housing project. It hasn't been up long. A few days after it was up it seemed uninhabitably new, now, of course, it's already rundown. It looks like a parody of the good, clean, faceless life—God knows the people who live in it do their best to make it a parody. The beat-looking grass lying around isn't enough to make their lives green, the hedges will never hold out the streets, and they know it. The big windows fool no one, they aren't big enough to make space out of no space. They don't bother with the windows, they watch the TV screen instead. The playground is most popular with the children who don't play at jacks, or skip rope, or roller skate, or swing, and they can be found in it after dark. We moved in partly because it's not too far from where I teach, and partly for the kids; but it's really just like the houses in which Sonny and I grew up. The same things happen, they'll have the same things to remember. The moment Sonny and I started into the house I had the feeling that I was simply bringing him back into the danger he had almost died trying to escape.

Sonny has never been talkative. So I don't know why I was sure he'd be dying to talk to me when supper was over the first night. Everything went fine, the oldest boy remembered him, and the youngest boy liked him, and Sonny had remembered to bring something for each of them; and Isabel, who is really much nicer than I am, more open and giving, had gone to a lot of trouble about dinner and was genuinely glad to see him. And she's always been able to tease Sonny in a way that I haven't. It was nice to see her face so vivid again and to hear her laugh and watch her make Sonny laugh. She wasn't, or, anyway, she didn't seem to be, at all uneasy or embarrassed. She chatted as though there were no subject which had to be avoided and she got Sonny past his first, faint stiffness. And thank God she was there, for I was filled with that icy dread again.

75

Everything I did seemed awkward to me, and everything I said sounded freighted with hidden meaning. I was trying to remember everything I'd heard about dope addiction and I couldn't help watching Sonny for signs. I wasn't doing it out of malice. I was trying to find out something about my brother. I was dying to hear him tell me he was safe.

"Safe!" my father grunted, whenever Mama suggested trying to move to a neighborhood which might be safer for children. "Safe, hell! Ain't no place safe for kids, nor nobody."

80   He always went on like this, but he wasn't, ever, really as bad as he sounded, not even on weekends, when he got drunk. As a matter of fact, he was always on the lookout for "something a little better," but he died before he found it. He died suddenly, during a drunken weekend in the middle of the war, when Sonny was fifteen. He and Sonny hadn't ever got on too well. And this was partly because Sonny was the apple of his father's eye. It was because he loved Sonny so much and was frightened for him, that he was always fighting with him. It doesn't do any good to fight with Sonny. Sonny just moves back, inside himself, where he can't be reached. But the principal reason that they never hit it off is that they were so much alike. Daddy was big and rough and loud-talking, just the opposite of Sonny, but they both had—that same privacy.

Mama tried to tell me something about this, just after Daddy died. I was home on leave from the army.

This was the last time I ever saw my mother alive. Just the same, this picture gets all mixed up in my mind with pictures I had of her when she was younger. The way I always see her is the way she used to be on a Sunday afternoon, say, when the old folks were talking after the big Sunday dinner. I always see her wearing pale blue. She'd be sitting on the sofa. And my father would be sitting in the easy chair, not far from her. And the living room would be full of church folks and relatives. There they sit, in chairs all around the living room, and the night is creeping up outside, but nobody knows it yet. You can see the darkness growing against the windowpanes and you hear the street noises every now and again, or maybe the jangling beat of a tambourine from one of the churches close by, but it's real quiet in the room. For a moment nobody's talking, but every face looks darkening, like the sky outside. And my mother rocks a little from the waist, and my father's eyes are closed. Everyone is looking at something a child can't see. For a minute they've forgotten the children. Maybe a kid is lying on the rug, half asleep. Maybe somebody's got a kid in his lap and is absent-mindedly stroking the kid's head. Maybe there's a kid, quiet and big-eyed, curled up in a big chair in the corner. The silence, the darkness coming, and the darkness in the faces frighten the child obscurely. He hopes that the hand which strokes his forehead will never stop—will never die. He hopes that there will never come a time when the old folks won't be sitting around the living room, talking about where they've come from, and what they've seen, and what's happened to them and their kinfolk.

But something deep and watchful in the child knows that this is bound to end, is already ending. In a moment someone will get up and turn on the light.

Then the old folks will remember the children and they won't talk any more that day. And when light fills the room, the child is filled with darkness. He knows that every time this happens he's moved just a little closer to that darkness outside. The darkness outside is what the old folks have been talking about. It's what they've come from. It's what they endure. The child knows that they won't talk any more because if he knows too much about what's happened to *them*, he'll know too much too soon, about what's going to happen to *him*.

The last time I talked to my mother, I remember I was restless. I wanted to get out and see Isabel. We weren't married then and we had a lot to straighten out between us.

There Mama sat, in black, by the window. She was humming an old church song, *Lord, you brought me from a long ways off.* Sonny was out somewhere. Mama kept watching the streets.

"I don't know," she said, "if I'll ever see you again, after you go off from here. But I hope you'll remember the things I tried to teach you."

"Don't talk like that," I said, and smiled. "You'll be here a long time yet."

She smiled, too, but she said nothing. She was quiet for a long time. And I said, "Mama, don't you worry about nothing. I'll be writing all the time, and you be getting the checks. . . ."

"I want to talk to you about your brother," she said, suddenly. "If anything happens to me he ain't going to have nobody to look out for him."

"Mama," I said, "ain't nothing going to happen to you *or* Sonny. Sonny's all right. He's a good boy and he's got good sense."

"It ain't a question of his being a good boy," Mama said, "nor of his having good sense. It ain't only the bad ones, nor yet the dumb ones that gets sucked under." She stopped, looking at me. "Your Daddy once had a brother," she said, and she smiled in a way that made me feel she was in pain. "You didn't never know that, did you?"

"No," I said, "I never knew that," and I watched her face.

"Oh, yes," she said, "your Daddy had a brother." She looked out of the window again. "I know you never saw your Daddy cry. But *I* did—many a time, through all these years."

I asked her, "What happened to his brother? How come nobody's ever talked about him?"

This was the first time I ever saw my mother look old.

"His brother got killed," she said, "when he was just a little younger than you are now. I knew him. He was a fine boy. He was maybe a little full of the devil, but he didn't mean nobody no harm."

Then she stopped and the room was silent, exactly as it had sometimes been on those Sunday afternoons. Mama kept looking out into the streets.

"He used to have a job in the mill," she said, "and, like all young folks, he just liked to perform on Saturday nights. Saturday nights, him and your father would drift around to different places, go to dances and things like that, or just sit around with people they knew, and your father's brother would sing, he had a fine voice, and play along with himself on his guitar. Well, this particular Saturday night, him and your father was coming home from some place, and

85

90

95

they were both a little drunk and there was a moon that night, it was bright like day. Your father's brother was feeling kind of good, and he was whistling to himself, and he had his guitar slung over his shoulder. They was coming down a hill and beneath them was a road that turned off from the highway. Well, your father's brother, being always kind of frisky, decided to run down this hill, and he did, with that guitar banging and clanging behind him, and he ran across the road, and he was making water behind a tree. And your father was sort of amused at him and he was still coming down the hill, kind of slow. Then he heard a car motor and that same minute his brother stepped from behind the tree, into the road, in the moonlight. And he started to cross the road. And your father started to run down the hill, he says he don't know why. This car was full of white men. They was all drunk, and when they seen your father's brother they let out a great whoop and holler and they aimed the car straight at him. They was having fun, they just wanted to scare him, the way they do sometimes, you know. But they was drunk. And I guess the boy, being drunk, too, and scared, kind of lost his head. By the time he jumped it was too late. Your father says he heard his brother scream when the car rolled over him, and he heard the wood of that guitar when it give, and he heard them strings go flying, and he heard them white men shouting, and the car kept on a-going and it ain't stopped till this day. And, time your father got down the hill, his brother weren't nothing but blood and pulp."

Tears were gleaming on my mother's face. There wasn't anything I could say.

"He never mentioned it," she said, "because I never let him mention it before you children. Your Daddy was like a crazy man that night and for many a night thereafter. He says he never in his life seen anything as dark as that road after the lights of that car had gone away. Weren't nothing, weren't nobody on that road, just your Daddy and his brother and that busted guitar. Oh, yes. Your Daddy never did really get right again. Till the day he died he weren't sure but that every white man he saw was the man that killed his brother."

She stopped and took out her handkerchief and dried her eyes and looked at me.

"I ain't telling you all this," she said, "to make you scared or bitter or to make you hate nobody. I'm telling you this because you got a brother. And the world ain't changed."

I guess I didn't want to believe this. I guess she saw this in my face. She turned away from me, toward the window again, searching those streets.

"But I praise my Redeemer," she said at last, "that He called your Daddy home before me. I ain't saying it to throw no flowers at myself, but, I declare, it keeps me from feeling too cast down to know I helped your father get safely through this world. Your father always acted like he was the roughest, strongest man on earth. And everybody took him to be like that. But if he hadn't had me there—to see his tears!"

She was crying again. Still, I couldn't move. I said, "Lord, Lord, Mama, I didn't know it was like that."

"Oh, honey," she said, "there's a lot that you don't know. But you are going to find out." She stood up from the window and came over to me. "You got to hold on to your brother," she said, "and don't let him fall, no matter what it looks like is happening to him and no matter how evil you gets with him. You going to be evil with him many a time. But don't you forget what I told you, you hear?"

"I won't forget," I said. "Don't you worry, I won't forget. I won't let nothing happen to Sonny."

My mother smiled as though she was amused at something she saw in my face. Then, "You may not be able to stop nothing from happening. But you got to let him know you's *there*."

Two days later I was married, and then I was gone. And I had a lot of things on my mind and I pretty well forgot my promise to Mama until I got shipped home on a special furlough for her funeral.

And, after the funeral, with just Sonny and me alone in the empty kitchen, I tried to find out something about him.

"What do you want to do?" I asked him.

"I'm going to be a musician," he said.

For he had graduated, in the time I had been away, from dancing to the juke box to finding out who was playing what, and what they were doing with it, and he had bought himself a set of drums.

"You mean, you want to be a drummer?" I somehow had the feeling that being a drummer might be all right for other people but not for my brother Sonny.

"I don't think," he said, looking at me very gravely, "that I'll ever be a good drummer. But I think I can play a piano."

I frowned. I'd never played the role of the oldest brother quite so seriously before, had scarcely ever, in fact, *asked* Sonny a damn thing. I sensed myself in the presence of something I didn't really know how to handle, didn't understand. So I made my frown a little deeper as I asked: "What kind of musician do you want to be?"

He grinned. "How many kinds do you think there are?"

"Be *serious*," I said.

He laughed, throwing his head back, and then looked at me. "I *am* serious."

"Well, then, for Christ's sake, stop kidding around and answer a serious question. I mean, do you want to be a concert pianist, you want to play classical music and all that, or—or what?" Long before I finished he was laughing again. "For Christ's *sake*, Sonny!"

He sobered, but with difficulty. "I'm sorry. But you sound so—*scared!*" and he was off again.

"Well, you may think it's funny now, baby, but it's not going to be so funny when you have to make your living at it, let me tell you *that*." I was furious because I knew he was laughing at me and I didn't know why.

"No," he said, very sober now, and afraid, perhaps, that he'd hurt me, "I don't want to be a classical pianist. That isn't what interests me. I mean"—he paused, looking hard at me, as though his eyes would help me to understand, and then gestured helplessly, as though perhaps his hand would help—"I mean,

I'll have a lot of studying to do, and I'll have to study *everything,* but, I mean, I want to play *with*—jazz musicians." He stopped. "I want to play jazz," he said.

Well, the word had never before sounded as heavy, as real, as it sounded that afternoon in Sonny's mouth. I just looked at him and I was probably frowning a real frown by this time. I simply couldn't see why on earth he'd want to spend his time hanging around nightclubs, clowning around on bandstands, while people pushed each other around a dance floor. It seemed—beneath him, somehow. I had never thought about it before, had never been forced to, but I suppose I had always put jazz musicians in a class with what Daddy called "good-time people."

125   "Are you *serious?*"

"Hell, *yes,* I'm serious."

He looked more helpless than ever, and annoyed, and deeply hurt.

I suggested, helpfully: "You mean—like Louis Armstrong?"

His face closed as though I'd struck him. "No. I'm not talking about none of that old-time, down home crap."

130   "Well, look, Sonny, I'm sorry, don't get mad. I just don't altogether get it, that's all. Name somebody—you know, a jazz musician you admire."

"Bird."

"Who?"

"Bird! Charlie Parker!³ Don't they teach you nothing in the goddamn army?"

I lit a cigarette. I was surprised and then a little amused to discover that I was trembling. "I've been out of touch," I said. "You'll have to be patient with me. Now. Who's this Parker character?"

135   "He's just one of the greatest jazz musicians alive," said Sonny, sullenly, his hands in his pockets, his back to me. "Maybe *the* greatest," he added, bitterly, "that's probably why *you* never heard of him."

"All right," I said, "I'm ignorant. I'm sorry. I'll go out and buy all the cat's records right away, all right?"

"It don't," said Sonny, with dignity, "make any difference to me. I don't care what you listen to. Don't do me no favors."

I was beginning to realize that I'd never seen him so upset before. With another part of my mind I was thinking that this would probably turn out to be one of those things kids go through and that I shouldn't make it seem important by pushing it too hard. Still, I didn't think it would do any harm to ask: "Doesn't all this take a lot of time? Can you make a living at it?"

He turned back to me and half leaned, half sat, on the kitchen table. "Everything takes time," he said, "and—well, yes, sure, I can make a living at it. But what I don't seem to be able to make you understand is that it's the only thing I want to do."

140   "Well, Sonny," I said gently, "you know people can't always do exactly what they *want* to do—"

---

3. Charlie ("Bird") Parker (1920–1955), brilliant saxophonist and innovator of jazz; working in New York in the mid-1940s, he developed, with Dizzy Gillespie and others, the style of jazz called "bebop." He was a narcotics addict.

"No, I don't know that," said Sonny, surprising me. "I think people *ought* to do what they want to do, what else are they alive for?"

"You getting to be a big boy," I said desperately, "it's time you started thinking about your future."

"I'm thinking about my future," said Sonny, grimly. "I think about it all the time."

I gave up. I decided, if he didn't change his mind, that we could always talk about it later. "In the meantime," I said, "you got to finish school." We had already decided that he'd have to move in with Isabel and her folks. I knew this wasn't the ideal arrangement because Isabel's folks are inclined to be dicty[4] and they hadn't especially wanted Isabel to marry me. But I didn't know what else to do. "And we have to get you fixed up at Isabel's."

There was a long silence. He moved from the kitchen table to the window. "That's a terrible idea. You know it yourself."

"Do you have a *better* idea?"

He just walked up and down the kitchen for a minute. He was as tall as I was. He had started to shave. I suddenly had the feeling that I didn't know him at all.

He stopped at the kitchen table and picked up my cigarettes. Looking at me with a kind of mocking, amused defiance, he put one between his lips. "You mind?"

"You smoking already?"

He lit the cigarette and nodded, watching me through the smoke. "I just wanted to see if I'd have the courage to smoke in front of you." He grinned and blew a great cloud of smoke to the ceiling. "It was easy." He looked at my face. "Come on, now. I bet you was smoking at my age, tell the truth."

I didn't say anything but the truth was on my face, and he laughed. But now there was something very strained in his laugh. "Sure. And I bet that ain't all you was doing."

He was frightening me a little. "Cut the crap," I said. "We already decided that you was going to go and live at Isabel's. Now what's got into you all of a sudden?"

"*You* decided it," he pointed out. "*I* didn't decide nothing." He stopped in front of me, leaning against the stove, arms loosely folded. "Look, brother. I don't want to stay in Harlem no more, I really don't." He was very earnest. He looked at me, then over toward the kitchen window. There was something in his eyes I'd never seen before, some thoughtfulness, some worry all his own. He rubbed the muscle of one arm. "It's time I was getting out of here."

"Where do you want to *go*, Sonny?"

"I want to join the army. Or the navy, I don't care. If I say I'm old enough, they'll believe me."

Then I got mad. It was because I was so scared. "You must be crazy. You goddamn fool, what the hell do you want to go and join the *army* for?"

"I just told you. To get out of Harlem."

4. Snobbish, bossy.

145

150

155

"Sonny, you haven't even finished *school*. And if you really want to be a musician, how do you expect to study if you're in the *army?*"

He looked at me, trapped, and in anguish. "There's ways. I might be able to work out some kind of deal. Anyway, I'll have the G.I. Bill when I come out."

160   "*If* you come out." We stared at each other. "Sonny, please. Be reasonable. I know the setup is far from perfect. But we got to do the best we can."

"I ain't learning nothing in school," he said. "Even when I go." He turned away from me and opened the window and threw his cigarette out into the narrow alley. I watched his back. "At least, I ain't learning nothing you'd want me to learn." He slammed the window so hard I thought the glass would fly out, and turned back to me. "And I'm sick of the stink of these garbage cans!"

"Sonny," I said, "I know how you feel. But if you don't finish school now, you're going to be sorry later that you didn't." I grabbed him by the shoulders. "And you only got another year. It ain't so bad. And I'll come back and I swear I'll help you do *whatever* you want to do. Just try to put up with it till I come back. Will you please do that? For me?"

He didn't answer and he wouldn't look at me.

"Sonny. You hear me?"

165   He pulled away. "I hear you. But you never hear anything *I* say."

I didn't know what to say to that. He looked out of the window and then back at me. "OK," he said, and sighed. "I'll try."

Then I said, trying to cheer him up a little, "They got a piano at Isabel's. You can practice on it."

And as a matter of fact, it did cheer him up for a minute. "That's right," he said to himself. "I forgot that." His face relaxed a little. But the worry, the thoughtfulness, played on it still, the way shadows play on a face which is staring into the fire.

But I thought I'd never hear the end of that piano. At first, Isabel would write me, saying how nice it was that Sonny was so serious about his music and how, as soon as he came in from school, or wherever he had been when he was supposed to be at school, he went straight to that piano and stayed there until suppertime. And, after supper, he went back to that piano and stayed there until everybody went to bed. He was at the piano all day Saturday and all day Sunday. Then he bought a record player and started playing records. He'd play one record over and over again, all day long sometimes, and he'd improvise along with it on the piano. Or he'd play one section of the record, one chord, one change, one progression, then he'd do it on the piano. Then back to the record. Then back to the piano.

170   Well, I really don't know how they stood it. Isabel finally confessed that it wasn't like living with a person at all, it was like living with sound. And the sound didn't make any sense to her, didn't make any sense to any of them — naturally. They began, in a way, to be afflicted by this presence that was living in their home. It was as though Sonny were some sort of god, or monster. He moved in an atmosphere which wasn't like theirs at all. They fed him and he ate, he washed himself, he walked in and out of their door; he certainly wasn't

nasty or unpleasant or rude, Sonny isn't any of those things; but it was as though he were all wrapped up in some cloud, some fire, some vision all his own; and there wasn't any way to reach him.

At the same time, he wasn't really a man yet, he was still a child, and they had to watch out for him in all kinds of ways. They certainly couldn't throw him out. Neither did they dare to make a great scene about that piano because even they dimly sensed, as I sensed, from so many thousands of miles away, that Sonny was at that piano playing for his life.

But he hadn't been going to school. One day a letter came from the school board and Isabel's mother got it—there had, apparently, been other letters but Sonny had torn them up. This day, when Sonny came in, Isabel's mother showed him the letter and asked where he'd been spending his time. And she finally got it out of him that he'd been down in Greenwich Village, with musicians and other characters, in a white girl's apartment. And this scared her and she started to scream at him and what came up, once she began—though she denies it to this day—was what sacrifices they were making to give Sonny a decent home and how little he appreciated it.

Sonny didn't play the piano that day. By evening, Isabel's mother had calmed down but then there was the old man to deal with, and Isabel herself. Isabel says she did her best to be calm but she broke down and started crying. She says she just watched Sonny's face. She could tell, by watching him, what was happening with him. And what was happening was that they penetrated his cloud, they had reached him. Even if their fingers had been a thousand times more gentle than human fingers ever are, he could hardly help feeling that they had stripped him naked and were spitting on that nakedness. For he also had to see that his presence, that music, which was life or death to him, had been torture for them and that they had endured it, not at all for his sake, but only for mine. And Sonny couldn't take that. He can take it a little better today than he could then but he's still not very good at it and, frankly, I don't know anybody who is.

The silence of the next few days must have been louder than the sound of all the music ever played since time began. One morning, before she went to work, Isabel was in his room for something and she suddenly realized that all of his records were gone. And she knew for certain that he was gone. And he was. He went as far as the navy would carry him. He finally sent me a postcard from some place in Greece and that was the first I knew that Sonny was still alive. I didn't see him any more until we were both back in New York and the war had long been over.

He was a man by then, of course, but I wasn't willing to see it. He came by the house from time to time, but we fought almost every time we met. I didn't like the way he carried himself, loose and dreamlike all the time, and I didn't like his friends, and his music seemed to be merely an excuse for the life he led. It sounded just that weird and disordered.

Then we had a fight, a pretty awful fight, and I didn't see him for months. By and by I looked him up, where he was living, in a furnished room in the Village, and I tried to make it up. But there were lots of other people in the room and Sonny just lay on his bed, and he wouldn't come downstairs with me,

175

and he treated these other people as though they were his family and I weren't. So I got mad and then he got mad, and then I told him that he might just as well be dead as live the way he was living. Then he stood up and he told me not to worry about him any more in life, that he *was* dead as far as I was concerned. Then he pushed me to the door and the other people looked on as though nothing were happening, and he slammed the door behind me. I stood in the hallway, staring at the door. I heard somebody laugh in the room and then the tears came to my eyes. I started down the steps, whistling to keep from crying, I kept whistling to myself, *You going to need me, baby, one of these cold, rainy days.*

I read about Sonny's trouble in the spring. Little Grace died in the fall. She was a beautiful little girl. But she only lived a little over two years. She died of polio and she suffered. She had a slight fever for a couple of days, but it didn't seem like anything and we just kept her in bed. And we would certainly have called the doctor, but the fever dropped, she seemed to be all right. So we thought it had just been a cold. Then, one day, she was up, playing, Isabel was in the kitchen fixing lunch for the two boys when they'd come in from school, and she heard Grace fall down in the living room. When you have a lot of children you don't always start running when one of them falls, unless they start screaming or something. And, this time, Gracie was quiet. Yet, Isabel says that when she heard that *thump* and then that silence, something happened to her to make her afraid. And she ran to the living room and there was little Grace on the floor, all twisted up, and the reason she hadn't screamed was that she couldn't get her breath. And when she did scream, it was the worst sound, Isabel says, that she'd ever heard in all her life, and she still hears it sometimes in her dreams. Isabel will sometimes wake me up with a low, moaning, strangling sound and I have to be quick to awaken her and hold her to me and where Isabel is weeping against me seems a mortal wound.

I think I may have written Sonny the very day that little Grace was buried. I was sitting in the living room in the dark, by myself, and I suddenly thought of Sonny. My trouble made his real.

One Saturday afternoon, when Sonny had been living with us, or anyway, been in our house, for nearly two weeks, I found myself wandering aimlessly about the living room, drinking from a can of beer, and trying to work up courage to search Sonny's room. He was out, he was usually out whenever I was home, and Isabel had taken the children to see their grandparents. Suddenly I was standing still in front of the living room window, watching Seventh Avenue. The idea of searching Sonny's room made me still. I scarcely dared to admit to myself what I'd be searching for. I didn't know what I'd do if I found it. Or if I didn't.

On the sidewalk across from me, near the entrance to a barbecue joint, some people were holding an old-fashioned revival meeting. The barbecue cook, wearing a dirty white apron, his conked[5] hair reddish and metallic in the pale sun, and a cigarette between his lips, stood in the doorway, watching them. Kids

5. Processed: straightened and greased.

and older people paused in their errands and stood there, along with some older men and a couple of very tough-looking women who watched everything that happened on the avenue, as though they owned it, or were maybe owned by it. Well, they were watching this, too. The revival was being carried on by three sisters in black, and a brother. All they had were their voices and their Bibles and a tambourine. The brother was testifying[6] and while he testified two of the sisters stood together, seeming to say, amen, and the third sister walked around with the tambourine outstretched and a couple of people dropped coins into it. Then the brother's testimony ended and the sister who had been taking up the collection dumped the coins into her palm and transferred them to the pocket of her long black robe. Then she raised both hands, striking the tambourine against the air, and then against one hand, and she started to sing. And the two other sisters and the brother joined in.

It was strange, suddenly, to watch, though I had been seeing these meetings all my life. So, of course, had everybody else down there. Yet, they paused and watched and listened and I stood still at the window. " 'Tis the old ship of Zion," they sang, and the sister with the tambourine kept a steady, jangling beat, "it has rescued many a thousand!" Not a soul under the sound of their voices was hearing this song for the first time, not one of them had been rescued. Nor had they seen much in the way of rescue work being done around them. Neither did they especially believe in the holiness of the three sisters and the brother, they knew too much about them, knew where they lived, and how. The woman with the tambourine, whose voice dominated the air, whose face was bright with joy, was divided by very little from the woman who stood watching her, a cigarette between her heavy, chapped lips, her hair a cuckoo's nest, her face scarred and swollen from many beatings, and her black eyes glittering like coal. Perhaps they both knew this, which was why, when, as rarely, they addressed each other, they addressed each other as Sister. As the singing filled the air the watching, listening faces underwent a change, the eyes focusing on something within; the music seemed to soothe a poison out of them; and time seemed, nearly, to fall away from the sullen, belligerent, battered faces, as though they were fleeing back to their first condition, while dreaming of their last. The barbecue cook half shook his head and smiled, and dropped his cigarette and disappeared into his joint. A man fumbled in his pockets for change and stood holding it in his hand impatiently, as though he had just remembered a pressing appointment further up the avenue. He looked furious. Then I saw Sonny, standing on the edge of the crowd. He was carrying a wide, flat notebook with a green cover, and it made him look, from where I was standing, almost like a schoolboy. The coppery sun brought out the copper in his skin, he was very faintly smiling, standing very still. Then the singing stopped, the tambourine turned into a collection plate again. The furious man dropped in his coins and vanished, so did a couple of the women, and Sonny dropped some change in the plate, looking directly at the woman with a little smile. He started across the avenue, toward the house. He has a slow, loping walk, something like the way Harlem hipsters

6. Publicly professing belief.

walk, only he's imposed on this his own half-beat. I had never really noticed it before.

I stayed at the window, both relieved and apprehensive. As Sonny disappeared from my sight, they began singing again. And they were still singing when his key turned in the lock.

"Hey," he said.

"Hey, yourself. You want some beer?"

185 "No. Well, maybe." But he came up to the window and stood beside me, looking out. "What a warm voice," he said.

They were singing *If I could only hear my mother pray again!*

"Yes," I said, "and she can sure beat that tambourine."

"But what a terrible song," he said, and laughed. He dropped his notebook on the sofa and disappeared into the kitchen. "Where's Isabel and the kids?"

"I think they went to see their grandparents. You hungry?"

190 "No." He came back into the living room with his can of beer. "You want to come some place with me tonight?"

I sensed, I don't know how, that I couldn't possibly say no. "Sure. Where?"

He sat down on the sofa and picked up his notebook and started leafing through it. "I'm going to sit in with some fellows in a joint in the Village."

"You mean, you're going to play, tonight?"

"That's right." He took a swallow of his beer and moved back to the window. He gave me a sidelong look. "If you can stand it."

195 "I'll try," I said.

He smiled to himself and we both watched as the meeting across the way broke up. The three sisters and the brother, heads bowed, were singing *God be with you till we meet again.* The faces around them were very quiet. Then the song ended. The small crowd dispersed. We watched the three women and the lone man walk slowly up the avenue.

"When she was singing before," said Sonny, abruptly, "her voice reminded me for a minute of what heroin feels like sometimes—when it's in your veins. It makes you feel sort of warm and cool at the same time. And distant. And— and sure." He sipped his beer, very deliberately not looking at me. I watched his face. "It makes you feel—in control. Sometimes you've got to have that feeling."

"Do you?" I sat down slowly in the easy chair.

"Sometimes." He went to the sofa and picked up his notebook again. "Some people do."

200 "In order," I asked, "to play?" And my voice was very ugly, full of contempt and anger.

"Well"—he looked at me with great, troubled eyes, as though, in fact, he hoped his eyes would tell me things he could never otherwise say—"they *think* so. And *if* they think so—!"

"And what do *you* think?" I asked.

He sat on the sofa and put his can of beer on the floor. "I don't know," he said, and I couldn't be sure if he were answering my question or pursuing his thoughts. His face didn't tell me. "It's not so much to *play.* It's to *stand* it, to be able to make it at all. On any level." He frowned and smiled: "In order to keep from shaking to pieces."

"But these friends of yours," I said, "they seem to shake themselves to pieces pretty goddamn fast."

"Maybe." He played with the notebook. And something told me that I should curb my tongue, that Sonny was doing his best to talk, that I should listen. "But of course you only know the ones that've gone to pieces. Some don't—or at least they haven't *yet* and that's just about all *any* of us can say." He paused. "And then there are some who just live, really, in hell, and they know it and they see what's happening and they go right on. I don't know." He sighed, dropped the notebook, folded his arms. "Some guys, you can tell from the way they play, they on something *all* the time. And you can see that, well, it makes something real for them. But of course," he picked up his beer from the floor and sipped it and put the can down again, "they *want* to, too, you've got to see that. Even some of them that say they don't—*some*, not all."

"And what about you?" I asked—I couldn't help it. "What about you? Do *you* want to?"

He stood up and walked to the window and I remained silent for a long time. Then he sighed. "Me," he said. Then: "While I was downstairs before, on my way here, listening to that woman sing, it struck me all of a sudden how much suffering she must have had to go through—to sing like that. It's *repulsive* to think you have to suffer that much."

I said: "But there's no way not to suffer—is there, Sonny?"

"I believe not," he said and smiled, "but that's never stopped anyone from trying." He looked at me. "Has it?" I realized, with this mocking look, that there stood between us, forever, beyond the power of time or forgiveness, the fact that I had held silence—so long!—when he had needed human speech to help him. He turned back to the window. "No, there's no way not to suffer. But you try all kinds of ways to keep from drowning in it, to keep on top of it, and to make it seem—well, like *you*. Like you did something, all right, and now you're suffering for it. You know?" I said nothing. "Well you know," he said, impatiently, "why *do* people suffer? Maybe it's better to do something to give it a reason, *any* reason."

"But we just agreed," I said, "that there's no way not to suffer. Isn't it better, then, just to—take it?"

"But nobody just takes it," Sonny cried, "that's what I'm telling you! Everybody tries not to. You're just hung up on the *way* some people try—it's not *your* way!"

The hair on my face began to itch, my face felt wet. "That's not true," I said, "that's not true. I don't give a damn what other people do, I don't even care how they suffer. I just care how *you* suffer." And he looked at me. "Please believe me," I said, "I don't want to see you—die—trying not to suffer."

"I won't," he said flatly, "die trying not to suffer. At least, not any faster than anybody else."

"But there's no need," I said, trying to laugh, "is there? in killing yourself."

215   I wanted to say more, but I couldn't. I wanted to talk about will power and how life could be—well, beautiful. I wanted to say that it was all within; but was it? or, rather, wasn't that exactly the trouble? And I wanted to promise that I would never fail him again. But it would all have sounded—empty words and lies.

So I made the promise to myself and prayed that I would keep it.

"It's terrible sometimes, inside," he said, "that's what's the trouble. You walk these streets, black and funky and cold, and there's not really a living ass to talk to, and there's nothing shaking, and there's no way of getting it out—that storm inside. You can't talk it and you can't make love with it, and when you finally try to get with it and play it, you realize *nobody's* listening. So *you've* got to listen. You got to find a way to listen."

And then he walked away from the window and sat on the sofa again, as though all the wind had suddenly been knocked out of him. "Sometimes you'll do *anything* to play, even cut your mother's throat." He laughed and looked at me. "Or your brother's." Then he sobered. "Or your own." Then: "Don't worry. I'm all right now and I think I'll *be* all right. But I can't forget—where I've been. I don't mean just the physical place I've been, I mean where I've *been*. And *what* I've been."

"What have you been, Sonny?" I asked.

220   He smiled—but sat sideways on the sofa, his elbow resting on the back, his fingers playing with his mouth and chin, not looking at me. "I've been something I didn't recognize, didn't know I could be. Didn't know anybody could be." He stopped, looking inward, looking helplessly young, looking old. "I'm not talking about it now because I feel *guilty* or anything like that—maybe it would be better if I did, I don't know. Anyway, I can't really talk about it. Not to you, not to anybody," and now he turned and faced me. "Sometimes, you know, and it was actually when I was most *out* of the world, I felt that I was in it, that I was *with* it, really, and I could play or I didn't really have to *play*, it just came out of me, it was there. And I don't know how I played, thinking about it now, but I know I did awful things, those times, sometimes, to people. Or it wasn't that I *did* anything to them—it was that they weren't real." He picked up the beer can; it was empty; he rolled it between his palms: "And other times—well, I needed a fix, I needed to find a place to lean, I needed to clear a space to *listen*—and I couldn't find it, and I—went crazy, I did terrible things to *me*, I was terrible *for* me." He began pressing the beer can between his hands, I watched the metal begin to give. It glittered, as he played with it like a knife, and I was afraid he would cut himself, but I said nothing. "Oh well. I can never tell you. I was all by myself at the bottom of something, stinking and sweating and crying and shaking, and I smelled it, you know? *my* stink, and I thought I'd die if I couldn't get away from it and yet, all the same, I knew that everything I was doing was just locking me in with it. And I didn't know," he paused, still flattening the beer can, "I didn't know, I still *don't* know, something kept telling me that maybe it was good to smell your own stink, but I didn't think that *that* was what I'd been trying to do—and—who can stand it?" and he abruptly dropped the ruined beer can, looking at me with a small, still smile, and then rose, walking

to the window as though it were the lodestone rock. I watched his face, he watched the avenue. "I couldn't tell you when Mama died—but the reason I wanted to leave Harlem so bad was to get away from drugs. And then, when I ran away, that's what I was running from—really. When I came back, nothing had changed, I hadn't changed, I was just—older." And he stopped, drumming with his fingers on the windowpane. The sun had vanished, soon darkness would fall. I watched his face. "It can come again," he said, almost as though speaking to himself. Then he turned to me. "It can come again," he repeated. "I just want you to know that."

"All right," I said, at last. "So it can come again. All right."

He smiled, but the smile was sorrowful. "I had to try to tell you," he said.

"Yes," I said. "I understand that."

"You're my brother," he said, looking straight at me, and not smiling at all.

"Yes," I repeated, "yes. I understand that."   225

He turned back to the window, looking out. "All that hatred down there," he said, "all that hatred and misery and love. It's a wonder it doesn't blow the avenue apart."

We went to the only nightclub on a short, dark street, downtown. We squeezed through the narrow, chattering, jampacked bar to the entrance of the big room, where the bandstand was. And we stood there for a moment, for the lights were very dim in this room and we couldn't see. Then, "Hello, boy," said the voice and an enormous black man, much older than Sonny or myself, erupted out of all that atmospheric lighting and put an arm around Sonny's shoulder. "I been sitting right here," he said, "waiting for you."

He had a big voice, too, and heads in the darkness turned toward us.

Sonny grinned and pulled a little away, and said, "Creole, this is my brother. I told you about him."

Creole shook my hand. "I'm glad to meet you, son," he said, and it was clear   230
that he was glad to meet me there, for Sonny's sake. And he smiled, "You got a real musician in your family," and he took his arm from Sonny's shoulder and slapped him, lightly, affectionately, with the back of his hand.

"Well. Now I've heard it all," said a voice behind us. This was another musician, and a friend of Sonny's, a coal-black, cheerful-looking man, built close to the ground. He immediately began confiding to me, at the top of his lungs, the most terrible things about Sonny, his teeth gleaming like a lighthouse and his laugh coming up out of him like the beginning of an earthquake. And it turned out that everyone at the bar knew Sonny, or almost everyone; some were musicians, working there, or nearby, or not working, some were simply hangers-on, and some were there to hear Sonny play. I was introduced to all of them and they were all very polite to me. Yet, it was clear that, for them, I was only Sonny's brother. Here, I was in Sonny's world. Or, rather: his kingdom. Here, it was not even a question that his veins bore royal blood.

They were going to play soon and Creole installed me, by myself, at a table in a dark corner. Then I watched them, Creole, and the little black man, and Sonny, and the others, while they horsed around, standing just below the bandstand. The light from the bandstand spilled just a little short of them and, watching them laughing and gesturing and moving about, I had the feeling that they, nevertheless, were being most careful not to step into that circle of light too suddenly; that if they moved into the light too suddenly, without thinking, they would perish in flame. Then, while I watched, one of them, the small black man, moved into the light and crossed the bandstand and started fooling around with his drums. Then—being funny and being, also, extremely ceremonious—Creole took Sonny by the arm and led him to the piano. A woman's voice called Sonny's name and a few hands started clapping. And Sonny, also being funny and being ceremonious, and so touched, I think, that he could have cried, but neither hiding it nor showing it, riding it like a man, grinned, and put both hands to his heart and bowed from the waist.

Creole then went to the bass fiddle and a lean, very bright-skinned brown man jumped up on the bandstand and picked up his horn. So there they were, and the atmosphere on the bandstand and in the room began to change and tighten. Someone stepped up to the microphone and announced them. Then there were all kinds of murmurs. Some people at the bar shushed others. The waitress ran around, frantically getting in the last orders, guys and chicks got closer to each other, and the lights on the bandstand, on the quartet, turned to a kind of indigo. Then they all looked different there. Creole looked about him for the last time, as though he were making certain that all his chickens were in the coop, and then he—jumped and struck the fiddle. And there they were.

All I know about music is that not many people ever really hear it. And even then, on the rare occasions when something opens within, and the music enters, what we mainly hear, or hear corroborated, are personal, private, vanishing evocations. But the man who creates the music is hearing something else, is dealing with the roar rising from the void and imposing order on it as it hits the air. What is evoked in him, then, is of another order, more terrible because it has no words, and triumphant, too, for that same reason. And his triumph, when he triumphs, is ours. I just watched Sonny's face. His face was troubled, he was working hard, but he wasn't with it. And I had the feeling that, in a way, everyone on the bandstand was waiting for him, both waiting for him and pushing him along. But as I began to watch Creole, I realized that it was Creole who held them all back. He had them on a short rein. Up there, keeping the beat with his whole body, wailing on the fiddle, with his eyes half closed, he was listening to everything, but he was listening to Sonny. He was having a dialogue with Sonny. He wanted Sonny to leave the shoreline and strike out for the deep water. He was Sonny's witness that deep water and drowning were not the same thing—he had been there, and he knew. And he wanted Sonny to know. He was waiting for Sonny to do the things on the keys which would let Creole know that Sonny was in the water.

235   And, while Creole listened, Sonny moved, deep within, exactly like someone in torment. I had never before thought of how awful the relationship must be between the musician and his instrument. He has to fill it, this instrument, with the breath of life, his own. He has to make it do what he wants it to do. And a piano is just a piano. It's made out of so much wood and wires and little ham-

mers and big ones, and ivory. While there's only so much you can do with it, the only way to find this out is to try; to try and make it do everything.

And Sonny hadn't been near a piano for over a year. And he wasn't on much better terms with his life, not the life that stretched before him now. He and the piano stammered, started one way, got scared, stopped; started another way, panicked, marked time, started again; then seemed to have found a direction, panicked again, got stuck. And the face I saw on Sonny I'd never seen before. Everything had been burned out of it, and, at the same time, things usually hidden were being burned in, by the fire and fury of the battle which was occurring in him up there.

Yet, watching Creole's face as they neared the end of the first set, I had the feeling that something had happened, something I hadn't heard. Then they finished, there was scattered applause, and then, without an instant's warning, Creole started into something else, it was almost sardonic, it was *Am I Blue*.[7] And, as though he commanded, Sonny began to play. Something began to happen. And Creole let out the reins. The dry, low, black man said something awful on the drums, Creole answered, and the drums talked back. Then the horn insisted, sweet and high, slightly detached perhaps, and Creole listened, commenting now and then, dry, and driving, beautiful and calm and old. Then they all came together again, and Sonny was part of the family again. I could tell this from his face. He seemed to have found, right there beneath his fingers, a damn brand-new piano. It seemed that he couldn't get over it. Then, for a while, just being happy with Sonny, they seemed to be agreeing with him that brand-new pianos certainly were a gas.

Then Creole stepped forward to remind them that what they were playing was the blues. He hit something in all of them, he hit something in me, myself, and the music tightened and deepened, apprehension began to beat the air. Creole began to tell us what the blues were all about. They were not about anything very new. He and his boys up there were keeping it new, at the risk of ruin, destruction, madness, and death, in order to find new ways to make us listen. For, while the tale of how we suffer, and how we are delighted, and how we may triumph is never new, it always must be heard. There isn't any other tale to tell, it's the only light we've got in all this darkness.

And this tale, according to that face, that body, those strong hands on those strings, has another aspect in every country, and a new depth in every generation. Listen, Creole seemed to be saying, listen. Now these are Sonny's blues. He made the little black man on the drums know it, and the bright, brown man on the horn. Creole wasn't trying any longer to get Sonny in the water. He was wishing him Godspeed. Then he stepped back, very slowly, filling the air with the immense suggestion that Sonny speak for himself.

Then they all gathered around Sonny and Sonny played. Every now and again one of them seemed to say, amen. Sonny's fingers filled the air with life, his life. But that life contained so many others. And Sonny went all the way back, he really began with the spare, flat statement of the opening phrase of the

240

---

7. A favorite jazz standard, brilliantly recorded by Billie Holiday.

song. Then he began to make it his. It was very beautiful because it wasn't hurried and it was no longer a lament. I seemed to hear with what burning he had made it his, and what burning we had yet to make it ours, how we could cease lamenting. Freedom lurked around us and I understood, at last, that he could help us to be free if we would listen, that he would never be free until we did. Yet, there was no battle in his face now, I heard what he had gone through, and would continue to go through until he came to rest in earth. He had made it his: that long line, of which we knew only Mama and Daddy. And he was giving it back, as everything must be given back, so that, passing through death, it can live forever. I saw my mother's face again, and felt, for the first time, how the stones of the road she had walked on must have bruised her feet. I saw the moonlit road where my father's brother died. And it brought something else back to me, and carried me past it, I saw my little girl again and felt Isabel's tears again, and I felt my own tears begin to rise. And I was yet aware that this was only a moment, that the world waited outside, as hungry as a tiger, and that trouble stretched above us, longer than the sky.

Then it was over. Creole and Sonny let out their breath, both soaking wet, and grinning. There was a lot of applause and some of it was real. In the dark, the girl came by and I asked her to take drinks to the bandstand. There was a long pause, while they talked up there in the indigo light and after awhile I saw the girl put a Scotch and milk on top of the piano for Sonny. He didn't seem to notice it, but just before they started playing again, he sipped from it and looked toward me, and nodded. Then he put it back on top of the piano. For me, then, as they began to play again, it glowed and shook above my brother's head like the very cup of trembling.[8]

1957

8. See Isaiah 51:17, 22–23: "Awake, awake, stand up, O Jerusalem, which hast drunk at the hand of the Lord the cup of his fury; thou hast drunken the dregs of the cup of trembling, and wrung them out. . . . Behold, I have taken out of thine hand the cup of trembling, even the dregs of the cup of my fury; thou shalt no more drink it again: But I will put it into the hand of them that afflict thee; . . ."

PLOT A Glossary

action: an imagined event or series of events (an event may be verbal as well as physical, so that saying something or telling a story within the story may be an event)

climax: see *turning point*

conclusion: the fifth part of the structure, the point at which the situation that was destabilized at the beginning of the story becomes stable once more

conflict: a struggle between opposing forces, such as between two people, a person and something in nature or society, or even between two drives, impulses, or parts of the self

curiosity: the desire to know what is happening or has happened

discriminated occasion: the first specific event in a story, more usually in the form of a specific scene than in summary

expectation: the anticipation of what is to happen next (see *suspense*), what a character is like or how he or she will develop, what the theme or meaning of the story will prove to be, and so on

exposition: that part of the structure that sets the scene, introduces and identifies characters, establishes the situation at the beginning of the narrative, though additional exposition is often scattered throughout the story

falling action: the fourth part of plot structure, in which the complications of the rising action are untangled

flashback: structuring device whereby a scene from the fictional past is inserted into the fictional present or dramatized out of order

history: the imaginary people, places, chronologically arranged events that we assume exist in the world of the author's imagination, a world from which he or she chooses and arranges or rearranges the story elements

plot/plot structure: the arrangement of the action

red herring: a false lead, something that misdirects expectations

rising action: the second of the five parts of plot structure, in which events complicate the situation that existed at the beginning of a work, intensifying the conflict or introducing new conflict

selection: the process by which authors leave out some things that seem to be important to the story and include some things that do not seem very important

structuring: the arrangement or rearrangement of the elements in the history

suspense: the expectation of and doubt about what is going to happen next

turning point or **climax:** the third part of plot structure, the point at which the action stops rising and begins falling or reversing

QUESTIONS

1. We are advised by Margaret Atwood that if we want a happy ending to try her sketch A; does it have a happy ending? What does she claim is the only authentic ending for a story? What is the difference between the way Atwood uses the word "plot" and the way it is used in the introduction to this chapter?

2. Rearrange the incidents in "The Country Husband" in chronological order. The structured story begins, "To begin at the beginning . . ." and tells about the near-crash of Francis's plane. Why is that the beginning? What is it the beginning of? Describe the location, appearance, and socioeconomic make-up of Shady Hill. Why is the dog Jupiter "an anomaly" (par. 10)? Why do Clayton Thomas and Anne also not "belong"? Who wins the struggle between Francis Weed and Shady Hill?

3. The opening scene of "Sonny's Blues" is not the first incident in Sonny and his brother's relationship; why does the story begin here? Does this story have a "happy ending"? According to Atwood, Baldwin should, in all honesty, carry on with the story until both Sonny and his brother die; why does Baldwin's story end here?

4. In "Sonny's Blues," how is the first-person narrator, the person telling the story, identified or characterized in the first sentence? in the first paragraph? in the first couple pages? in the story as a whole?

WRITING SUGGESTIONS

1. Choose one of Atwood's "stories" (or conflate two or three) and write a scene or two illustrating the How or the Why.

2. Compare the treatment of marital infidelity in Cheever and Tallent's "No One's a Mystery," Maupassant's "The Jewelry," or one or more of the sketches in "Happy Endings."

3. Write a story or a sketch or outline of a story centering on the same situation in "The Country Husband" but set in the 1990s, and in a place you know.

4. Rearrange the episodes in "Sonny's Blues" as they would appear in the hypothetical history—that is, in chronological order. Pick the three or four changes that seem to you most important. Describe the difference in effect and significance that Baldwin has achieved with his structuring or rearrangement.

2 POINT OF VIEW

S tructuring involves more than plot, more than the ordering of events; selection involves more than the choosing or inventing of incidents. What would "Sonny's Blues" be like seen through the eyes of Sonny? What incidents might he choose to tell? In what order might he arrange them? And what does it do to "The Cask of Amontillado" when we realize, at the end, that it is being told by Montresor fifty years after the event and that his last—probably dying—words, referring to Fortunato, are, "*In pace requiescat*"? Why is he telling the story now? What additional resonance do his final words have?

Who is telling us the story—whose words are we reading? Where does this person stand in relation to what is going on in the story? In drama, events appear before us directly. In narrative, someone is always *between* us and the events—a viewer, a speaker, or both. Narrative, unlike drama, is always mediated. The way a story is mediated is a key element in fictional structure. This mediation involves both the angle of vision—the point from which the people, events, and other details are viewed—and also the words of the story lying between us and the history. The viewing aspect is called the **focus,** and the verbal aspect the **voice.** Both are generally lumped together in the term **point of view.**

Focus acts much as a movie camera does, choosing what we can look at and the angle at which we can view it, framing, proportioning, emphasizing— even distorting. Plot is a structure that places us in a time relationship to the history; focus places us in a spatial relationship.

We must pay careful attention to the focus at any given point in a story. Is it fixed or mobile? Does it stay at more or less the same angle to, and at the same distance from, the characters and action, or does it move around or in and out? In the first three and a half paragraphs of "An Occurrence at Owl Creek Bridge," for example, we seem to be seeing through the lens of a camera that can swing left or right, up or down, but that stays pretty much at the same angle and distance from the bridge. By the middle of the fourth paragraph, however, we're inside the mind of the man who's about to be hanged: "The arrangement commended itself to his judgment. . . . He looked a moment. . . . A piece of dancing driftwood caught his attention. . . . How slowly it appeared to move!" From now on we are inside the condemned man's head. The focus is more limited in scope—for almost all the rest of the

73

story we can see and hear only what he sees and hears. But because the focus is internal as well as limited, we can also know what he thinks. This limited, internal focus is usually called the **centered** or **central consciousness.**

The centered consciousness has been perhaps the most popular focus in fiction for the past hundred years—through most of the history of the modern short story, in fact—and its tightly controlled range and concentration on a single individual seem particularly suited for the short form. During much of this period, fiction, both long and short, has been in one sense realistic—that is, treating the everyday and the natural. It has become increasingly clear, however, that the apparently real is not necessarily what "is" but what is *perceived by* the senses and mind of the individual. (This is sometimes called **psychological realism.**) The centered consciousness, in which things, people, and events are narrated as if perceived through the filter of an individual character's consciousness, has therefore seemed the more realistic way to tell a story. It is a comfortable focus for readers, too. On the one hand, they can identify with someone whose thoughts and perception they share, even if the character is fallible, like Lantin in "The Jewelry." We can identify with point of view in a story told in the first person ("I"), too, but we are too close at times. We cannot escape. The camera cannot pull back as it can in a third-person story.

First-person stories, like "The Cask of Amontillado," are always limited too, and almost always get inside the speaker's mind, though Montresor hides his plans from us. While they cannot withdraw spatially from the narrator, they almost always are withdrawn temporally; that is, the "I" telling the story is older than the "I" experiencing the events. The narrator of Poe's story, for example, is telling what happened fifty years earlier.

The psychological realism gained by having a limited narrator exacts a price from the reader. If we don't hold the author (or the story) responsible for the absolute truth, validity, accuracy, and opinions of the focal character—if he or she is just telling us what he or she thinks, feels, sees—we must accept the possibility that the narrator's vision may be **unreliable.** At a significant point in "Owl Creek Bridge," for example, you will find that the camera pulls back from Peyton Farquhar and we are made to recognize to what extent his consciousness is a reliable witness to what has been going on. The history here is only an occurrence; the limited point of view structures the mere occurrence into a story.

When the point of view is limited, whether to a first-person narrator or to a centered consciousness, it is tied to that individual. When he or she leaves the room, the camera must go too, and if we are to know what happens in the room when the focal character is gone, some means of bringing the information to that character must be devised, such as a letter or a report by another character. The camera may pull back out of the character's mind or even, as in "Owl Creek Bridge," above and away from the character, but it does not generally jump around. An unlimited point of view permits such freedom. In "The Zebra Storyteller" we are with the first zebra (who is killed) when he meets a cat speaking Zebraic and are told he is "astonished." We learn that the zebras can smell no lion and so "decided the woods were haunted by the ghost of a lion," and we get inside the mind of the storyteller and "hear" him speaking to himself. Throughout, the story seems free to see matter from one focus or another and even to dip inside a character's mind.

There are no laws governing point of view in fiction, but there is a general feeling that once a point of view is chosen that ought to be the law for that story. The movement of the focus at the beginning of "An Occurrence at Owl Creek Bridge" is not a jump but a narrowing down: the panorama at the beginning of the story, apparently from the point of view and in the voice of a distant observer, is adjusted and then we settle in, which is not an uncommon device (note how many movies used to begin with a panoramic shot of a town and gradually focused on a house or room). When toward the end of the story the "camera" moves back and away from Peyton Farquhar, we find there has been another reason for the panoramic shot at the beginning. There has been no jumping around and the narrowing and widening seem to be justifiable and meaningful. There are stories in this anthology—"The Most Dangerous Game," "Barn Burning," and "The Lame Shall Enter First," for example—in which the point of view does shift—or jump—from a previously established centered consciousness. Whether these are "flaws" must be judged in each case in terms of function: is the shift merely a narrative convenience or manipulation or is it consistent with or does it contribute to the significance or vision of the story?

Focus and voice often coincide; that is why they are commonly lumped together as point of view. There is no discrepancy that I can see (or hear) between the viewing and the telling in "The Cask of Amontillado," for example. But sometimes there is a discrepancy. Like the focus, the voice in "Owl Creek Bridge" at the beginning of the story is not centered in Peyton Farquhar, but even when the focus narrows on him the voice telling the story is not his; note, for example, "As these thoughts, *which have here to be set down in words*, were flashed into the doomed man's brain" (emphasis added). The discrepancy may prepare a careful reader for later developments in the story.

I have used the common term **narrator** in the usual way—to mean the person who tells the story. You will have noticed that often the narrator really is a

person in the story, like Montresor, the narrator in "The Cask of Amontillado."
But how about the narrator in "Owl Creek Bridge"? Who is it who sets down
Farquhar's words and can say things that Farquhar is not thinking, such as,
"Death is a dignitary who, when he comes announced, is to be received with
formal manifestations of respect, even by those most familiar with him. In the
code of military etiquette silence and fixity are forms of deference" (par. 2).
Where is the speaker standing? What kind of person is this narrator?

Is Ambrose Bierce the narrator? Where the narrator plays some role in the
story we are less likely to identify him or her with the author; where the narrator is an unidentified voice we often tend to do so. To say that Bierce is the narrator of "Owl Creek Bridge" is not necessarily wrong, but it can be misleading.
We can dig up a few facts about the author's life and read them into the story,
or, worse, read the character or detail of the story into the author's life. It is
more prudent, therefore, especially on the basis of a single story, not to speak
of the author but of the author's **persona,** the voice or figure of the author who
tells and structures the story, who may or may not resemble in nature or values
the actual person of the author. Mary Anne Evans wrote novels under the
name of George Eliot; her first-person narrator speaks of "himself." That male
narrator may be a good example of the persona or representative that most
authors construct to "write" their stories.

We say *write* the stories. The narrator of "Owl Creek Bridge" has to "set
down in words" what Farquhar is thinking. But just as poets write of singing
their songs (poems), so we often speak of telling a story, and we speak of a narrator, which means a teller. There are stories, usually with first-person narra-
tors, that make much of the convention of oral storytelling—Louise Erdrich's
"Love Medicine" for example. "The Cask of Amontillado" is more subtly
"oral." It even has an **auditor,** someone other than the reader—that is, a character or characters within the fiction—to whom the "speech" is addressed. The
"You" in the second sentence is no more you the reader than the "I" is Poe.
He is a silent character within the fiction, here one whose identity or role can,
with some thought, be identified.

We are used to thinking of a story in terms of its plot, so that to summarize
a story usually means giving a plot summary. But if you shift focus and voice
you will often find that though the history has not changed, the story has. You
might want to test this out by rewriting "The Cask of Amontillado" in the voice
and focus of the auditor, or "The Country Husband" in the voice and focus of
Anne, the baby sitter, or Francis Weed's wife.

Just as Margaret Atwood's "Happy Endings" is a story about plot-structure,
so "Blow-Up," whose narrator, Michel/I, is appropriately a photographer, seems

to be about focus as a means of structuring (and understanding) an event. Because it is a written story, Michel needs a voice, words, but they are chiefly means of describing the visual images, and these become clearer (if they do) not so much from the words as from the enhancement of the details through the enlargement (blowing up) of the photograph.

Point of view has been discussed here largely as a matter of structure, as having a role in creating the story and making it this story and no other. This structuring also engenders meaning and effect. What is the effect, for example, of having such a scoundrel as Montresor tell the story of "The Cask of Amontillado" in the first person? How do we feel about him during the story? Whose side are we on? Do we admire his cleverness or wit? Would we if the story were told from some other point of view? We can talk about how without the shift of the focus to Farquhar Bierce would not have a story, but what is the effect of the surprise ending of that story? How surprising is it? Do we feel cheated? Do we admire the cleverness of the telling? In some says there might be a story in "Blow-Up" without Michel the photographer, but not only would its structure be vastly different, but its current effect—mystery, puzzlement, curiosity, suspense—would be lost. "Sonny's Blues" should be the brother's story, for the outward action, the incidents, chiefly involve him, but the point of view is Sonny's and the meaning for us is the meaning for him. By sharing the experience with him, we must ask whether he/we has/have done the right thing. What do we learn? What do we feel? Much of what a story means, much of its effect upon us depends on the eyes through which it is seen and on the voice that tells it to us.

▼ ▼ ▼

EDGAR ALLAN POE

The Cask of Amontillado

The thousand injuries of Fortunato I had borne as I best could, but when he ventured upon insult I vowed revenge. You, who so well know the nature of my soul, will not suppose, however, that I gave utterance to a threat. *At length* I would be avenged; this was a point definitively settled—but the very definitiveness with which it was resolved precluded the idea of risk. I must not only punish but punish with impunity. A wrong is unredressed when retribution overtakes its redresser. It is equally unredressed when the avenger fails to make himself felt as such to him who has done the wrong.

It must be understood that neither by word nor deed had I given Fortunato cause to doubt my good will. I continued, as was my wont, to smile in his face, and he did not perceive that my smile *now* was at the thought of his immolation.

He had a weak point—this Fortunato—although in other regards he was a man to be respected and even feared. He prided himself upon his connoisseurship in wine. Few Italians have the true virtuoso spirit. For the most part their enthusiasm is adopted to suit the time and opportunity, to practice imposture upon the British and Austrian *millionaires*. In painting and gemmary, Fortunato, like his countrymen, was a quack, but in the matter of old wines he was sincere. In this respect I did not differ from him materially;—I was skilful in the Italian vintages myself, and bought largely whenever I could.

It was about dusk, one evening during the supreme madness of the carnival season, that I encountered my friend. He accosted me with excessive warmth, for he had been drinking much. The man wore motley. He had on a tight-fitting parti-striped dress, and his head was surmounted by the conical cap and bells. I was so pleased to see him that I should never have done wringing his hand.

5   I said to him—"My dear Fortunato, you are luckily met. How remarkably well you are looking to-day. But I have received a pipe[1] of what passes for Amontillado, and I have my doubts."

"How?" said he. "Amontillado? A pipe? Impossible! And in the middle of the carnival!"

"I have my doubts," I replied; "and I was silly enough to pay the full Amontillado price without consulting you in the matter. You were not to be found, and I was fearful of losing a bargain."

"Amontillado!"

"I have my doubts."

10   "Amontillado!"

"And I must satisfy them."

"Amontillado!"

"As you are engaged, I am on my way to Luchresi. If any one has a critical turn it is he. He will tell me——"

"Luchresi cannot tell Amontillado from Sherry."

15   "And yet some fools will have it that his taste is a match for your own."

"Come, let us go."

"Whither?"

"To your vaults."

"My friend, no; I will not impose upon your good nature. I perceive you have an engagement. Luchresi——"

20   "I have no engagement;—come."

"My friend, no. It is not the engagement, but the severe cold with which I perceive you are afflicted. The vaults are insufferably damp. They are encrusted with nitre."

"Let us go, nevertheless. The cold is merely nothing. Amontillado! You have been imposed upon. And as for Luchresi, he cannot distinguish Sherry from Amontillado."

---

1. A cask holding 126 gallons.

Thus speaking, Fortunato possessed himself of my arm; and putting on a mask of black silk and drawing a *roquelaire*[2] closely about my person, I suffered him to hurry me to my palazzo.

There were no attendants at home; they had absconded to make merry in honour of the time. I had told them that I should not return until the morning, and had given them explicit orders not to stir from the house. These orders were sufficient, I well knew, to insure their immediate disappearance, one and all, as soon as my back was turned.

I took from their sconces two flambeaux, and giving one to Fortunato, bowed him through several suites of rooms to the archway that led into the vaults. I passed down a long and winding staircase, requesting him to be cautious as he followed. We came at length to the foot of the descent, and stood together upon the damp ground of the catacombs of the Montresors.

The gait of my friend was unsteady, and the bells upon his cap jingled as he strode.

"The pipe," said he.

"It is farther on," said I; "but observe the white web-work which gleams from these cavern walls."

He turned towards me, and looked into my eyes with two filmy orbs that distilled the rheum of intoxication.

"Nitre?" he asked, at length.

"Nitre," I replied. "How long have you had that cough?"

"Ugh! ugh! ugh!—ugh! ugh! ugh!—ugh! ugh! ugh!—ugh! ugh! ugh!—ugh! ugh! ugh!"

My poor friend found it impossible to reply for many minutes.

"It is nothing," he said, at last.

"Come," I said, with decision, "we will go back; your health is precious. You are rich, respected, admired, beloved; you are happy, as once I was. You are a man to be missed. For me it is no matter. We will go back; you will be ill, and I cannot be responsible. Besides, there is Luchresi——"

"Enough," he said; "the cough is a mere nothing; it will not kill me. I shall not die of a cough."

"True—true," I replied; "and, indeed, I had no intention of alarming you unneccessarily—but you should use all proper caution. A draught of this Medoc[3] will defend us from the damps."

Here I knocked off the neck of a bottle which I drew from a long row of its fellows that lay upon the mould.

"Drink," I said, presenting him the wine.

He raised it to his lips with a leer. He paused and nodded to me familiarly, while his bells jingled.

"I drink," he said, "to the buried that repose around us."

"And I to your long life."

He again took my arm, and we proceeded.

"These vaults," he said, "are extensive."

---

2. Roquelaure: man's heavy, knee-length cloak.   3. Like De Grâve (below), a French wine.

45 "The Montresors," I replied, "were a great and numerous family."
"I forget your arms."
"A huge human foot d'or,[4] in a field azure; the foot crushes a serpent rampant whose fangs are imbedded in the heel."
"And the motto?"
"*Nemo me impune lacessit.*"[5]
50 "Good!" he said.
The wine sparkled in his eyes and the bells jingled. My own fancy grew warm with the Medoc. We had passed through long walls of piled skeletons, with casks and puncheons intermingling, into the inmost recesses of the catacombs. I paused again, and this time I made bold to seize Fortunato by an arm above the elbow.
"The nitre!" I said; "see, it increases. It hangs like moss upon the vaults. We are below the river's bed. The drops of moisture trickle among the bones. Come, we will go back ere it is too late. Your cough——"
"It is nothing," he said; "let us go on. But first, another draught of the Medoc."
I broke and reached him a flaçon of De Grâve. He emptied it at a breath. His eyes flashed with a fierce light. He laughed and threw the bottle upwards with a gesticulation I did not understand.
55 I looked at him in surprise. He repeated the movement—a grotesque one.
"You do not comprehend?" he said.
"Not I," I replied.
"Then you are not of the brotherhood."
"How?"
60 "You are not of the masons."[6]
"Yes, yes," I said; "yes, yes."
"You? Impossible! A mason?"
"A mason," I replied.
"A sign," he said, "a sign."
65 "It is this," I answered producing from beneath the folds of my *roquelaire* a trowel.
"You jest," he exclaimed, recoiling a few paces. "But let us proceed to the Amontillado."
"Be it so," I said, replacing the tool beneath the cloak and again offering him my arm. He leaned upon it heavily. We continued our route in search of the Amontillado. We passed through a range of low arches, descended, passed on, and descending again, arrived at a deep crypt, in which the foulness of the air caused our flambeaux rather to glow than flame.
At the most remote end of the crypt there appeared another less spacious. Its walls had been lined with human remains, piled to the vault overhead, in the fashion of the great catacombs of Paris. Three sides of this interior crypt were still ornamented in this manner. From the fourth side the bones had been

4. Of gold. 5. "No one provokes me with impunity." 6. Masons or Freemasons, an international secret society condemned by the Catholic Church. Montresor means by mason one who builds with stone, brick, etc.

thrown down, and lay promiscuously upon the earth, forming at one point a mound of some size. Within the wall thus exposed by the displacing of the bones, we perceived a still interior crypt or recess, in depth about four feet, in width three, in height six or seven. It seemed to have been constructed for no especial use within itself, but formed merely the interval between two of the colossal supports of the roof of the catacombs, and was backed by one of their circumscribing walls of solid granite.

It was in vain that Fortunato, uplifting his dull torch, endeavoured to pry into the depth of the recess. Its termination the feeble light did not enable us to see.

"Proceed," I said; "herein is the Amontillado. As for Luchresi——" 70

"He is an ignoramus," interrupted my friend, as he stepped unsteadily forward, while I followed immediately at his heels. In an instant he had reached the extremity of the niche, and finding his progress arrested by the rock, stood stupidly bewildered. A moment more and I had fettered him to the granite. In its surface were two iron staples, distant from each other about two feet, horizontally. From one of these depended a short chain, from the other a padlock. Throwing the links about his waist, it was but the work of a few seconds to secure it. He was too much astounded to resist. Withdrawing the key I stepped back from the recess.

"Pass your hand," I said, "over the wall; you cannot help feeling the nitre. Indeed, it is *very* damp. Once more let me *implore* you to return. No? Then I must positively leave you. But I will first render you all the little attentions in my power."

"The Amontillado!" ejaculated my friend, not yet recovered from his astonishment.

"True," I replied; "the Amontillado."

As I said these words I busied myself among the pile of bones of which I 75 have before spoken. Throwing them aside, I soon uncovered a quantity of building stone and mortar. With these materials and with the aid of my trowel, I began vigorously to wall up the entrance of the niche.

I had scarcely laid the first tier of the masonry when I discovered that the intoxication of Fortunato had in great measure worn off. The earliest indication I had of this was a low moaning cry from the depth of the recess. It was *not* the cry of a drunken man. There was then a long and obstinate silence. I laid the second tier, and the third, and the fourth; and then I heard the furious vibration of the chain. The noise lasted for several minutes, during which, that I might hearken to it with the more satisfaction, I ceased my labours and sat down upon the bones. When at last the clanking subsided, I resumed the trowel, and finished without interruption the fifth, the sixth, and the seventh tier. The wall was now nearly upon a level with my breast. I again paused, and holding the flambeaux over the mason-work, threw a few feeble rays upon the figure within.

A succession of loud and shrill screams, bursting suddenly from the throat of the chained form, seemed to thrust me violently back. For a brief moment I hesitated, I trembled. Unsheathing my rapier, I began to grope with it about the recess; but the thought of an instant reassured me. I placed my hand upon the solid fabric of the catacombs and felt satisfied. I reapproached the wall. I replied to the yells of him who clamoured. I re-echoed, I aided, I surpassed them in volume and in strength. I did this, and the clamourer grew still.

It was now midnight, and my task was drawing to a close. I had completed the eighth, the ninth and the tenth tier. I had finished a portion of the last and the eleventh; there remained but a single stone to be fitted and plastered in. I struggled with its weight; I placed it partially in its destined position. But now there came from out the niche a low laugh that erected the hairs upon my head. It was succeeded by a sad voice, which I had difficulty in recognizing as that of the noble Fortunato. The voice said—

"Ha! ha! ha!—he! he! he!—a very good joke, indeed—an excellent jest. We will have many a rich laugh about it at the palazzo—he! he! he!—over our wine—he! he! he!"

"The Amontillado!" I said.

"He! he! he!—he! he! he!—yes, the Amontillado. But is it not getting late? Will not they be awaiting us at the palazzo—the Lady Fortunato and the rest? Let us be gone."

"Yes," I said, "let us be gone."

"For the love of God, Montresor!"

"Yes," I said, "for the love of God!"

But to these words I hearkened in vain for a reply. I grew impatient. I called aloud—

"Fortunato!"

No answer. I called again—

"Fortunato!"

No answer still. I thrust a torch through the remaining aperture and let it fall within. There came forth in return only a jingling of the bells. My heart grew sick; it was the dampness of the catacombs that made it so. I hastened to make an end of my labour. I forced the last stone into its position; I plastered it up. Against the new masonry I re-erected the old rampart of bones. For the half of a century no mortal has disturbed them. *In pace requiescat!*[7]

1846

AMBROSE BIERCE

An Occurrence at Owl Creek Bridge

I

A man stood upon a railroad bridge in Northern Alabama, looking down into the swift waters twenty feet below. The man's hands were behind his back, the wrists bound with a cord. A rope loosely encircled his neck. It was attached to a

7. May he rest in peace!

stout cross-timber above his head, and the slack fell to the level of his knees. Some loose boards laid upon the sleepers supporting the metals of the railway supplied a footing for him and his executioners—two private soldiers of the Federal army, directed by a sergeant, who in civil life may have been a deputy sheriff. At a short remove upon the same temporary platform was an officer in the uniform of his rank, armed. He was a captain. A sentinel at each end of the bridge stood with his rifle in the position known as "support," that is to say, vertical in front of the left shoulder, the hammer resting on the forearm thrown straight across the chest—a formal and unnatural position, enforcing an erect carriage of the body. It did not appear to be the duty of these two men to know what was occurring at the centre of the bridge; they merely blockaded the two ends of the foot plank which traversed it.

Beyond one of the sentinels nobody was in sight; the railroad ran straight away into a forest for a hundred yards, then, curving, was lost to view. Doubtless there was an outpost further along. The other bank of the stream was open ground—a gentle acclivity crowned with a stockade of vertical tree trunks, loopholed for rifles, with a single embrasure through which protruded the muzzle of a brass cannon commanding the bridge. Midway of the slope between bridge and fort were the spectators—a single company of infantry in line, at "parade rest," the butts of the rifles on the ground, the barrels inclining slightly backward against the right shoulder, the hands crossed upon the stock. A lieutenant stood at the right of the line, the point of his sword upon the ground, his left hand resting upon his right. Excepting the group of four at the centre of the bridge not a man moved. The company faced the bridge, staring stonily, motionless. The sentinels, facing the banks of the stream, might have been statues to adorn the bridge. The captain stood with folded arms, silent, observing the work of his subordinates but making no sign. Death is a dignitary who, when he comes announced, is to be received with formal manifestations of respect, even by those most familiar with him. In the code of military etiquette silence and fixity are forms of deference.

The man who was engaged in being hanged was apparently about thirty-five years of age. He was a civilian, if one might judge from his dress, which was that of a planter. His features were good—a straight nose, firm mouth, broad forehead, from which his long, dark hair was combed straight back, falling behind his ears to the collar of his well-fitting frock coat. He wore a moustache and pointed beard, but no whiskers; his eyes were large and dark grey and had a kindly expression which one would hardly have expected in one whose neck was in the hemp. Evidently this was no vulgar assassin. The liberal military code makes provision for hanging many kinds of people, and gentlemen are not excluded.

The preparations being complete, the two private soldiers stepped aside and each drew away the plank upon which he had been standing. The sergeant turned to the captain, saluted and placed himself immediately behind that officer, who in turn moved apart one pace. These movements left the condemned man and the sergeant standing on the two ends of the same plank, which spanned three of the cross-ties of the bridge. The end upon which the civilian stood almost, but not quite, reached a fourth. This plank had been held in place by the weight of the captain; it was now held by that of the sergeant. At a signal from the former, the latter would step aside, the plank would tilt and the condemned man go down between two ties. The arrangement commended itself to his judgment as simple and effective. His face had not been covered nor his eyes bandaged. He looked a moment at his "unsteadfast footing," then let his gaze wander to the swirling water of the stream racing madly beneath his feet. A piece of dancing driftwood caught his attention and his eyes followed it down the current. How slowly it appeared to move! What a sluggish stream!

He closed his eyes in order to fix his last thoughts upon his wife and children. The water, touched to gold by the early sun, the brooding mists under the banks at some distance down the stream, the fort, the soldiers, the piece of drift—all had distracted him. And now he became conscious of a new disturbance. Striking through the thought of his dear ones was a sound which he could neither ignore nor understand, a sharp, distinct, metallic percussion like the stroke of a blacksmith's hammer upon the anvil; it had the same ringing quality. He wondered what it was, and whether immeasurably distant or near by—it seemed both. Its recurrence was regular, but as slow as the tolling of a death knell. He awaited each stroke with impatience and—he knew not why—apprehension. The intervals of silence grew progressively longer, the delays became maddening. With their greater infrequency the sounds increased in strength and sharpness. They hurt his ear like the thrust of a knife; he feared he would shriek. What he heard was the ticking of his watch.

He unclosed his eyes and saw again the water below him. "If I could free my hands," he thought, "I might throw off the noose and spring into the stream. By diving I could evade the bullets, and, swimming vigorously, reach the bank, take to the woods, and get away home. My home, thank God, is as yet outside their lines; my wife and little ones are still beyond the invader's farthest advance."

As these thoughts, which have here to be set down in words, were flashed into the doomed man's brain rather than evolved from it, the captain nodded to the sergeant. The sergeant stepped aside.

II

Peyton Farquhar was a well-to-do planter, of an old and highly-respected Alabama family. Being a slave owner, and, like other slave owners, a politician, he was naturally an original secessionist and ardently devoted to the Southern cause. Circumstances of an imperious nature which it is unnecessary to relate here, had prevented him from taking service with the gallant army which had fought the disastrous campaigns ending with the fall of Corinth,[1] and he chafed under the inglorious restraint, longing for the release of his energies, the larger life of the soldier, the opportunity for distinction. That opportunity, he felt, would come, as it comes to all in war time. Meanwhile he did what he could. No service was too humble for him to perform in aid of the South, no adventure too perilous for him to undertake if consistent with the character of a civilian

---

1. Corinth, Mississippi, captured by General Ulysses S. Grant in April 1862.

who was at heart a soldier, and who in good faith and without too much qualification assented to at least a part of the frankly villainous dictum that all is fair
in love and war.

One evening while Farquhar and his wife were sitting on a rustic bench near
the entrance to his grounds, a grey-clad soldier rode up to the gate and asked for
a drink of water. Mrs. Farquhar was only too happy to serve him with her own
white hands. While she was gone to fetch the water, her husband approached
the dusty horseman and inquired eagerly for news from the front.

"The Yanks are repairing the railroads," said the man, "and are getting ready   10
for another advance. They have reached the Owl Creek bridge, put it in order,
and built a stockade on the other bank. The commandant has issued an order,
which is posted everywhere, declaring that any civilian caught interfering with
the railroad, its bridges, tunnels, or trains, will be summarily hanged. I saw the
order."

"How far is it to the Owl Creek bridge?" Farquhar asked.

"About thirty miles."

"Is there no force on this side the creek?"

"Only a picket post half a mile out, on the railroad, and a single sentinel at
this end of the bridge."

"Suppose a man—a civilian and student of hanging—should elude the   15
picket post and perhaps get the better of the sentinel," said Farquhar, smiling,
"what could he accomplish?"

The soldier reflected. "I was there a month ago," he replied. "I observed that
the flood of last winter had lodged a great quantity of driftwood against
the wooden pier at this end of the bridge. It is now dry and would burn like
tow."

The lady had now brought the water, which the soldier drank. He thanked
her ceremoniously, bowed to her husband, and rode away. An hour later, after
nightfall, he repassed the plantation, going northward in the direction from
which he had come. He was a Federal scout.

III

As Peyton Farquhar fell straight downward through the bridge, he lost consciousness and was as one already dead. From this state he was awakened—ages
later, it seemed to him—by the pain of a sharp pressure upon his throat, followed
by a sense of suffocation. Keen, poignant agonies seemed to shoot from his neck
downward through every fibre of his body and limbs. These pains appeared to
flash along well-defined lines of ramification, and to beat with an inconceivably
rapid periodicity. They seemed like streams of pulsating fire heating him to an
intolerable temperature. As to his head, he was conscious of nothing but a feeling of fullness—of congestion. These sensations were unaccompanied by
thought. The intellectual part of his nature was already effaced; he had power
only to feel, and feeling was torment. He was conscious of motion. Encompassed in a luminous cloud, of which he was now merely the fiery heart, without
material substance, he swung through unthinkable arcs of oscillation, like a vast
pendulum. Then all at once, with terrible suddenness, the light about him shot

upward with the noise of a loud plash; a frightful roaring was in his ears, and all was cold and dark. The power of thought was restored; he knew that the rope had broken and he had fallen into the stream. There was no additional strangulation; the noose about his neck was already suffocating him, and kept the water from his lungs. To die of hanging at the bottom of a river!—the idea seemed to him ludicrous. He opened his eyes in the blackness and saw above him a gleam of light, but how distant, how inaccessible! He was still sinking, for the light became fainter and fainter until it was a mere glimmer. Then it began to grow and brighten, and he knew that he was rising toward the surface—knew it with reluctance, for he was now very comfortable. "To be hanged and drowned," he thought, "that is not so bad; but I do not wish to be shot. No; I will not be shot; that is not fair."

He was not conscious of an effort, but a sharp pain in his wrist apprised him that he was trying to free his hands. He gave the struggle his attention, as an idler might observe the feat of a juggler, without interest in the outcome. What splendid effort!—what magnificent, what superhuman strength! Ah, that was a fine endeavour! Bravo! The cord fell away; his arms parted and floated upward, the hands dimly seen on each side in the growing light. He watched them with a new interest as first one and then the other pounced upon the noose at his neck. They tore it away and thrust it fiercely aside, its undulations resembling those of a water-snake. "Put it back, put it back!" He thought he shouted these words to his hands, for the undoing of the noose had been succeeded by the direst pang which he had yet experienced. His neck ached horribly; his brain was on fire; his heart, which had been fluttering faintly, gave a great leap, trying to force itself out at his mouth. His whole body was racked and wrenched with an insupportable anguish! But his disobedient hands gave no heed to the command. They beat the water vigorously with quick, downward strokes, forcing him to the surface. He felt his head emerge; his eyes were blinded by the sunlight; his chest expanded convulsively, and with a supreme and crowning agony his lungs engulfed a great draught of air, which instantly he expelled in a shriek!

He was now in full possession of his physical senses. They were, indeed, preternaturally keen and alert. Something in the awful disturbance of his organic system had so exalted and refined them that they made record of things never before perceived. He felt the ripples upon his face and heard their separate sounds as they struck. He looked at the forest on the bank of the stream, saw the individual trees, the leaves and the veining of each leaf—the very insects upon them, the locusts, the brilliant-bodied flies, the grey spiders stretching their webs from twig to twig. He noted the prismatic colors in all the dewdrops upon a million blades of grass. The humming of the gnats that danced above the eddies of the stream, the beating of the dragon flies' wings, the strokes of the water spiders' legs, like oars which had lifted their boat—all these made audible music. A fish slid along beneath his eyes and he heard the rush of its body parting the water.

He had come to the surface facing down the stream; in a moment the visible world seemed to wheel slowly round, himself the pivotal point, and he saw the bridge, the fort, the soldiers upon the bridge, the captain, the sergeant, the two privates, his executioners. They were in silhouette against the blue sky. They shouted and gesticulated, pointing at him; the captain had drawn his pistol, but did not fire; the others were unarmed. Their movements were grotesque and horrible, their forms gigantic.

Suddenly he heard a sharp report and something struck the water smartly within a few inches of his head, spattering his face with spray. He heard a second report, and saw one of the sentinels with his rifle at his shoulder, a light cloud of blue smoke rising from the muzzle. The man in the water saw the eye of the man on the bridge gazing into his own through the sights of the rifle. He observed that it was a grey eye, and remembered having read that grey eyes were keenest and that all famous marksmen had them. Nevertheless, this one had missed.

A counter swirl had caught Farquhar and turned him half round; he was again looking into the forest on the bank opposite the fort. The sound of a clear, high voice in a monotonous singsong now rang out behind him and came across the water with a distinctness that pierced and subdued all other sounds, even the beating of the ripples in his ears. Although no soldier, he had frequented camps enough to know the dread significance of that deliberate, drawling, aspirated chant; the lieutenant on shore was taking a part in the morning's work. How coldly and pitilessly—with what an even, calm intonation, presaging and enforcing tranquillity in the men—with what accurately-measured intervals fell those cruel words:

"Attention, company. . . . Shoulder arms. . . . Ready. . . . Aim. . . . Fire."

Farquhar dived—dived as deeply as he could. The water roared in his ears like the voice of Niagara, yet he heard the dulled thunder of the volley, and rising again toward the surface, met shining bits of metal, singularly flattened, oscillating slowly downward. Some of them touched him on the face and hands, then fell away, continuing their descent. One lodged between his collar and neck; it was uncomfortably warm, and he snatched it out.

As he rose to the surface, gasping for breath, he saw that he had been a long time under water; he was perceptibly farther down stream—nearer to safety. The soldiers had almost finished reloading; the metal ramrods flashed all at once in the sunshine as they were drawn from the barrels, turned in the air, and thrust into their sockets. The two sentinels fired again, independently and ineffectually.

The hunted man saw all this over his shoulder; he was now swimming vigorously with the current. His brain was as energetic as his arms and legs; he thought with the rapidity of lightning.

"The officer," he reasoned, "will not make that martinet's error a second time. It is as easy to dodge a volley as a single shot. He has probably already given the command to fire at will. God help me, I cannot dodge them all!"

An appalling plash within two yards of him, followed by a loud rushing sound, *diminuendo*, which seemed to travel back through the air to the fort and died in an explosion which stirred the very river to its deeps! A rising sheet of water, which curved over him, fell down upon him, blinded him, strangled him! The cannon had taken a hand in the game. As he shook his head free from the commotion of the smitten water, he heard the deflected shot humming through the air ahead, and in an instant it was cracking and smashing the branches in the forest beyond.

30   "They will not do that again," he thought; "the next time they will use a charge of grape. I must keep my eye upon the gun; the smoke will apprise me—the report arrives too late; it lags behind the missile. It is a good gun."

Suddenly he felt himself whirled round and round—spinning like a top. The water, the banks, the forest, the now distant bridge, fort and men—all were commingled and blurred. Objects were represented by their colors only; circular horizontal streaks of color—that was all he saw. He had been caught in a vortex and was being whirled on with a velocity of advance and gyration which made him giddy and sick. In a few moments he was flung upon the gravel at the foot of the left bank of the stream—the southern bank—and behind a projecting point which concealed him from his enemies. The sudden arrest of his motion, the abrasion of one of his hands on the gravel, restored him and he wept with delight. He dug his fingers into the sand, threw it over himself in handfuls and audibly blessed it. It looked like gold, like diamonds, rubies, emeralds; he could think of nothing beautiful which it did not resemble. The trees upon the bank were giant garden plants; he noted a definite order in their arrangement, inhaled the fragrance of their blooms. A strange, roseate light shone through the spaces among their trunks, and the wind made in their branches the music of æolian harps. He had no wish to perfect his escape, was content to remain in that enchanting spot until retaken.

A whizz and rattle of grapeshot among the branches high above his head roused him from his dream. The baffled cannoneer had fired him a random farewell. He sprang to his feet, rushed up the sloping bank, and plunged into the forest.

All that day he travelled, laying his course by the rounding sun. The forest seemed interminable; nowhere did he discover a break in it, not even a wood-man's road. He had not known that he lived in so wild a region. There was something uncanny in the revelation.

By nightfall he was fatigued, footsore, famishing. The thought of his wife and children urged him on. At last he found a road which led him in what he knew to be the right direction. It was as wide and straight as a city street, yet it seemed untravelled. No fields bordered it, no dwelling anywhere. Not so much as the barking of a dog suggested human habitation. The black bodies of the great trees formed a straight wall on both sides, terminating on the horizon in a point, like a diagram in a lesson in perspective. Overhead, as he looked up through this rift in the wood, shone great golden stars looking unfamiliar and grouped in strange constellations. He was sure they were arranged in some order which had a secret and malign significance. The wood on either side was full of singular noises, among which—once, twice, and again—he distinctly heard whispers in an unknown tongue.

35   His neck was in pain, and, lifting his hand to it, he found it horribly swollen. He knew that it had a circle of black where the rope had bruised it. His eyes felt congested; he could no longer close them. His tongue was swollen with thirst;

he relieved its fever by thrusting it forward from between his teeth into the cool air. How softly the turf had carpeted the untravelled avenue! He could no longer feel the roadway beneath his feet!

Doubtless, despite his suffering, he fell asleep while walking, for now he sees another scene—perhaps he has merely recovered from a delirium. He stands at the gate of his own home. All is as he left it, and all bright and beautiful in the morning sunshine. He must have travelled the entire night. As he pushes open the gate and passes up the wide white walk, he sees a flutter of female garments; his wife, looking fresh and cool and sweet, steps down from the verandah to meet him. At the bottom of the steps she stands waiting, with a smile of ineffable joy, an attitude of matchless grace and dignity. Ah, how beautiful she is! He springs forward with extended arms. As he is about to clasp her, he feels a stunning blow upon the back of the neck; a blinding white light blazes all about him, with a sound like the shock of a cannon—then all is darkness and silence!

Peyton Farquhar was dead; his body, with a broken neck, swung gently from side to side beneath the timbers of the Owl Creek bridge.

1891

JULIO CORTÁZAR

Blow-Up[1]

It'll never be known how this has to be told, in the first person or in the second, using the third person plural or continually inventing modes that will serve for nothing. If one might say: I will see the moon rose, or: we hurt me at the back of my eyes, and especially: you the blond woman was the clouds that race before my your his our yours their faces. What the hell.

Seated ready to tell it, if one might go to drink a bock over there, and the typewriter continue by itself (because I use the machine), that would be perfection. And that's not just a manner of speaking. Perfection, yes, because here is the aperture which must be counted also as a machine (of another sort, a Contax 1.1.2) and it is possible that one machine may know more about another machine than I, you, she—the blond—and the clouds. But I have the dumb luck to know that if I go this Remington will sit turned to stone on top of the table with the air of being twice as quiet that mobile things have when they are not moving. So, I have to write. One of us all has to write, if this is going to get told. Better that it be me who am dead, for I'm less compromised than the rest; I who see only the clouds and can think without being distracted, write without being distracted (there goes another, with a grey edge) and remember without being distracted, I who am dead (and I'm alive, I'm not trying to fool anybody, you'll see when we get to the moment, because I have to begin some way and I've begun with this period, the last one back, the one at the beginning, which in the end is the best of the periods when you want to tell something).

1. Translated by Paul Blackburn.

All of a sudden I wonder why I have to tell this, but if one begins to wonder why he does all he does do, if one wonders why he accepts an invitation to lunch (now a pigeon's flying by and it seems to me a sparrow), or why when someone has told us a good joke immediately there starts up something like a tickling in the stomach and we are not at peace until we've gone into the office across the hall and told the joke over again; then it feels good immediately, one is fine, happy, and can get back to work. For I imagine that no one has explained this, that really the best thing is to put aside all decorum and tell it, because, after all's done, nobody is ashamed of breathing or of putting on his shoes; they're things that you do, and when something weird happens, when you find a spider in your shoe or if you take a breath and feel like a broken window, then you have to tell what's happening, tell it to the guys at the office or to the doctor. Oh, doctor, every time I take a breath . . . Always tell it, always get rid of that tickle in the stomach that bothers you.

And now that we're finally going to tell it, let's put things a little bit in order, we'd be walking down the staircase in this house as far as Sunday, November 7, just a month back. One goes down five floors and stands then in the Sunday in the sun one would not have suspected of Paris in November, with a large appetite to walk around, to see things, to take photos (because we were photographers, I'm a photographer). I know that the most difficult thing is going to be finding a way to tell it, and I'm not afraid of repeating myself. It's going to be difficult because nobody really knows who it is telling it, if I am I or what actually occurred or what I'm seeing (clouds, and once in a while a pigeon) or if, simply, I'm telling a truth which is only my truth, and then is the truth only for my stomach, for this impulse to go running out and to finish up in some manner with, this, whatever it is.

We're going to tell it slowly, what happens in the middle of what I'm writing is coming already. If they replace me, if, so soon, I don't know what to say, if the clouds stop coming and something else starts (because it's impossible that this keep coming, clouds passing continually and occasionally a pigeon), if something out of all this . . . And after the "if" what am I going to put if I'm going to close the sentence structure correctly? But if I begin to ask questions, I'll never tell anything, maybe to tell would be like an answer, at least for someone who's reading it.

Roberto Michel, French-Chilean, translator and in his spare time an amateur photographer, left number 11, rue Monsieur-le-Prince Sunday November 7 of the current year (now there're two small ones passing, with silver linings). He had spent three weeks working on the French version of a treatise on challenges and appeals by José Norberto Allende, professor at the University of Santiago. It's rare that there's wind in Paris, and even less seldom a wind like this that swirled around corners and rose up to whip at old wooden venetian blinds behind which astonished ladies commented variously on how unreliable the weather had been these last few years. But the sun was out also, riding the wind and friend of the cats, so there was nothing that would keep me from taking a walk along the docks of the Seine and taking photos of the Conservatoire and Sainte-Chapelle. It was hardly ten o'clock, and I figured that by eleven the light would be good, the best you can get in the fall; to kill some time I detoured around by the Isle Saint-Louis and started to walk along the quai d'Anjou, I stared for a bit at the hôtel de Lauzun, I recited bits from Apollinaire[2] which always get into my head whenever I pass in front of the hôtel de Lauzun (and at that I ought to be remembering the other poet, but Michel is an obstinate beggar), and when the wind stopped all at once and the sun came out at least twice as hard (I mean warmer, but really it's the same thing), I sat down on the parapet and felt terribly happy in the Sunday morning.

One of the many ways of contesting level-zero, and one of the best, is to take photographs, an activity in which one should start becoming an adept very early in life, teach it to children since it requires discipline, aesthetic education, a good eye and steady fingers. I'm not talking about waylaying the lie like any old reporter, snapping the stupid silhouette of the VIP leaving number 10 Downing Street,[3] but in all ways when one is walking about with a camera, one has almost a duty to be attentive, to not lose that abrupt and happy rebound of sun's rays off an old stone, or the pigtails-flying run of a small girl going home with a loaf of bread or a bottle of milk. Michel knew that the photographer always worked as a permutation of his personal way of seeing the world as other than the camera insidiously imposed upon it (now a large cloud is going by, almost black), but he lacked no confidence in himself, knowing that he had only to go out without the Contax to recover the keynote of distraction, the sight without a frame around it, light without the diaphragm aperture or $\frac{1}{250}$ sec. Right now (what a word, *now*, what a dumb lie) I was able to sit quietly on the railing overlooking the river watching the red and black motorboats passing below without it occurring to me to think photographically of the scenes, nothing more than letting myself go in the letting go of objects, running immobile in the stream of time. And then the wind was not blowing.

After, I wandered down the quai de Bourbon until getting to the end of the isle where the intimate square was (intimate because it was small, not that it was hidden, it offered its whole breast to the river and the sky), I enjoyed it, a lot. Nothing there but a couple and, of course, pigeons; maybe even some of those which are flying past now so that I'm seeing them. A leap up and I settled on the wall, and let myself turn about and be caught and fixed by the sun, giving it my face and ears and hands (I kept my gloves in my pocket). I had no desire to shoot pictures, and lit a cigarette to be doing something; I think it was that moment when the match was about to touch the tobacco that I saw the young boy for the first time.

What I'd thought was a couple seemed much more now a boy with his mother, although at the same time I realized that it was not a kid and his mother, and that it was a couple in the sense that we always allegate to couples when we see them leaning up against the parapets or embracing on the benches in the squares. As I had nothing else to do, I had more than enough time to wonder

2. Guillaume Apollinaire (1880–1918), avant-garde French poet who experimented with typographical and calligraphic outrageousness as well as unusual verbal associations. 3. Residence of the British Prime Minister.

why the boy was so nervous, like a young colt or a hare, sticking his hands into his pockets, taking them out immediately, one after the other, running his fingers through his hair, changing his stance, and especially why was he afraid, well, you could guess that from every gesture, a fear suffocated by his shyness, an impulse to step backwards which he telegraphed, his body standing as if it were on the edge of flight, holding itself back in a final, pitiful decorum.

10   All this was so clear, ten feet away—and we were alone against the parapet at the tip of the island—that at the beginning the boy's fright didn't let me see the blond very well. Now, thinking back on it, I see her much better at that first second when I read her face (she'd turned around suddenly, swinging like a metal weathercock, and the eyes, the eyes were there), when I vaguely understood what might have been occurring to the boy and figured it would be worth the trouble to stay and watch (the wind was blowing their words away and they were speaking in a low murmur). I think that I know how to look, if it's something I know, and also that every looking oozes with mendacity, because it's that which expels us furthest outside ourselves, without the least guarantee, whereas to smell, or (but Michel rambles on to himself easily enough, there's no need to let him harangue on this way). In any case, if the likely inaccuracy can be seen beforehand, it becomes possible again to look; perhaps it suffices to choose between looking and the reality looked at, to strip things of all their unnecessary clothing. And surely all that is difficult besides.

    As for the boy I remember the image before his actual body (that will clear itself up later), while now I am sure that I remember the woman's body much better than the image. She was thin and willowy, two unfair words to describe what she was, and was wearing an almost-black fur coat, almost long, almost handsome. All the morning's wind (now it was hardly a breeze and it wasn't cold) had blown through her blond hair which pared away her white, bleak face—two unfair words—and put the world at her feet and horribly alone in the front of her dark eyes, her eyes fell on things like two eagles, two leaps into nothingness, two puffs of green slime. I'm not describing anything, it's more a matter of trying to understand it. And I said two puffs of green slime.

    Let's be fair, the boy was well enough dressed and was sporting yellow gloves which I would have sworn belonged to his older brother, a student of law or sociology; it was pleasant to see the fingers of the gloves sticking out of his jacket pocket. For a long time I didn't see his face, barely a profile, not stupid—a terrified bird, a Fra Filippo[4] angel, rice pudding with milk—and the back of an adolescent who wants to take up judo and has had a scuffle or two in defense of an idea or his sister. Turning fourteen, perhaps fifteen, one would guess that he was dressed and fed by his parents but without a nickel in his pocket, having to debate with his buddies before making up his mind to buy a coffee, a cognac, a pack of cigarettes. He'd walk through the streets thinking of the girls in his class, about how good it would be to go to the movies and see the latest film, or to buy novels or neckties or bottles of liquor with green and white labels on them. At home (it would be a respectable home, lunch at noon and romantic land-

---

4. Fra Filippo Lippi (1406?–1469), Florentine painter of the early Renaissance.

scapes on the walls, with a dark entryway and a mahogany umbrella stand inside the door) there'd be the slow rain of time, for studying, for being mama's hope, for looking like dad, for writing to his aunt in Avignon. So that there was a lot of walking the streets, the whole of the river for him (but without a nickel) and the mysterious city of fifteen-year-olds with its signs in doorways, its terrifying cats, a paper of fried potatoes for thirty francs, the pornographic magazine folded four ways, a solitude like the emptiness of his pockets, the eagerness for so much that was incomprehensible but illumined by a total love, by the availability analogous to the wind and the streets.

This biography was of the boy and of any boy whatsoever, but this particular one now, you could see he was insular, surrounded solely by the blond's presence as she continued talking with him. (I'm tired of insisting, but two long ragged ones just went by. That morning I don't think I looked at the sky once, because what was happening with the boy and the woman appeared so soon I could do nothing but look at them and wait, look at them and . . .) To cut it short, the boy was agitated and one could guess without too much trouble what had just occurred a few minutes before, at most half-an-hour. The boy had come onto the tip of the island, seen the woman and thought her marvelous. The woman was waiting for that because she was there waiting for that, or maybe the boy arrived before her and she saw him from one of the balconies or from a car and got out to meet him, starting the conversation with whatever, from the beginning she was sure that he was going to be afraid and want to run off, and that, naturally, he'd stay, stiff and sullen, pretending experience and the pleasure of the adventure. The rest was easy because it was happening ten feet away from me, and anyone could have gauged the stages of the game, the derisive, competitive fencing; its major attraction was not that it was happening but in foreseeing its denouement. The boy would try to end it by pretending a date, an obligation, whatever, and would go stumbling off disconcerted, wishing he were walking with some assurance, but naked under the mocking glance which would follow him until he was out of sight. Or rather, he would stay there, fascinated or simply incapable of taking the initiative, and the woman would begin to touch his face gently, muss his hair, still talking to him voicelessly, and soon would take him by the arm to lead him off, unless he, with an uneasiness beginning to tinge the edge of desire, even his stake in the adventure, would rouse himself to put his arm around her waist and to kiss her. Any of this could have happened, though it did not, and perversely Michel waited, sitting on the railing, making the settings almost without looking at the camera, ready to take a picturesque shot of a corner of the island with an uncommon couple talking and looking at one another.

Strange how the scene (almost nothing: two figures there mismatched in their youth) was taking on a disquieting aura. I thought it was I imposing it, and that my photo, if I shot it, would reconstitute things in their true stupidity. I would have liked to know what he was thinking, a man in a grey hat sitting at the wheel of a car parked on the dock which led up to the footbridge, and whether he was reading the paper or asleep. I had just discovered him because people inside a parked car have a tendency to disappear, they get lost in that wretched, private cage stripped of the beauty that motion and danger give it. And nevertheless, the car had been there the whole time, forming part (or deforming that part) of the isle. A car: like saying a lighted streetlamp, a park bench. Never like saying wind, sunlight, those elements always new to the skin and the eyes, and also the boy and the woman, unique, put there to change the island, to show it to me in another way. Finally, it may have been that the man with the newspaper also became aware of what was happening and would, like me, feel that malicious sensation of waiting for everything to happen. Now the woman had swung around smoothly, putting the young boy between herself and the wall, I saw them almost in profile, and he was taller, though not much taller, and yet she dominated him, it seemed like she was hovering over him (her laugh, all at once, a whip of feathers), crushing him just by being there, smiling, one hand taking a stroll through the air. Why wait any longer? Aperture at sixteen, a sighting which would not include the horrible black car, but yes, that tree, necessary to break up too much grey space . . .

15   I raised the camera, pretended to study a focus which did not include them, and waited and watched closely, sure that I would finally catch the revealing expression, one that would sum it all up, life that is rhythmed by movement but which a stiff image destroys, taking time in cross section, if we do not choose the essential imperceptible fraction of it. I did not have to wait long. The woman was getting on with the job of handcuffing the boy smoothly, stripping from him what was left of his freedom a hair at a time, in an incredibly slow and delicious torture. I imagined the possible endings (now a small fluffy cloud appears, almost alone in the sky), I saw their arrival at the house (a basement apartment probably, which she would have filled with large cushions and cats) and conjectured the boy's terror and his desperate decision to play it cool and to be led off pretending there was nothing new in it for him. Closing my eyes, if I did in fact close my eyes, I set the scene: the teasing kisses, the woman mildly repelling the hands which were trying to undress her, like in novels, on a bed that would have a lilac-colored comforter, on the other hand she taking off his clothes, plainly mother and son under a milky yellow light, and everything would end up as usual, perhaps, but maybe everything would go otherwise, and the initiation of the adolescent would not happen, she would not let it happen, after a long prologue wherein the awkwardnesses, the exasperating caresses, the running of hands over bodies would be resolved in who knows what, in a separate and solitary pleasure, in a petulant denial mixed with the art of tiring and disconcerting so much poor innocence. It might go like that, it might very well go like that; that woman was not looking for the boy as a lover, and at the same time she was dominating him toward some end impossible to understand if you do not imagine it as a cruel game, the desire to desire without satisfaction, to excite herself for someone else, someone who in no way could be that kid.

Michel is guilty of making literature, of indulging in fabricated unrealities. Nothing pleases him more than to imagine exceptions to the rule, individuals outside the species, not-always-repugnant monsters. But that woman invited speculation, perhaps giving clues enough for the fantasy to hit the bullseye.

Before she left, and now that she would fill my imaginings for several days, for I'm given to ruminating, I decided not to lose a moment more. I got it all into the view-finder (with the tree, the railing, the eleven-o'clock sun) and took the shot. In time to realize that they both had noticed and stood there looking at me, the boy surprised and as though questioning, but she was irritated, her face and body flat-footedly hostile, feeling robbed, ignominiously recorded on a small chemical image.

I might be able to tell it in much greater detail but it's not worth the trouble. The woman said that no one had the right to take a picture without permission, and demanded that I had her over the film. All this in a dry, clear voice with a good Parisian accent, which rose in color and tone with every phrase. For my part, it hardly mattered whether she got the roll of film or not, but anyone who knows me will tell you, if you want anything from me, ask nicely. With the result that I restricted myself to formulating the opinion that not only was photography in public places not prohibited, but it was looked upon with decided favor, both private and official. And while that was getting said, I noticed on the sly how the boy was falling back, sort of actively backing up though without moving, and all at once (it seemed almost incredible) he turned and broke into a run, the poor kid, thinking that he was walking off and in fact in full flight, running past the side of the car, disappearing like a gossamer filament of angel-spit in the morning air.

But filaments of angel-spittle are also called devil-spit, and Michel had to endure rather particular curses, to hear himself called meddler and imbecile, taking great pains meanwhile to smile and to abate with simple movements of his head such a hard sell. As I was beginning to get tired, I heard the car door slam. The man in the grey hat was there, looking at us. It was only at that point that I realized he was playing a part in the comedy.

He began to walk toward us, carrying in his hand the paper he had been pretending to read. What I remember best is the grimace that twisted his mouth askew, it covered his face with wrinkles, changed somewhat both in location and shape because his lips trembled and the grimace went from one side of his mouth to the other as though it were on wheels, independent and involuntary. But the rest stayed fixed, a flour-powdered clown or bloodless man, dull dry skin, eyes deepset, the nostrils black and prominently visible, blacker than the eyebrows or hair or the black necktie. Walking cautiously as though the pavement hurt his feet; I saw patent-leather shoes with such thin soles that he must have felt every roughness in the pavement. I don't know why I got down off the railing, nor very well why I decided to not give them the photo, to refuse that demand in which I guessed at their fear and cowardice. The clown and the woman consulted one another in silence: we made a perfect and unbearable triangle, something I felt compelled to break with a crack of a whip. I laughed in their faces and began to walk off, a little more slowly, I imagine, than the boy. At the level of the first houses, beside the iron footbridge, I turned around to look at them. They were not moving, but the man had dropped his newspaper; it seemed to me that the woman, her back to the parapet, ran her hands over the stone with the classical and absurd gesture of someone pursued looking for a way out.

20   What happened after that happened here, almost just now, in a room on the fifth floor. Several days went by before Michel developed the photos he'd taken on Sunday; his shots of the Conservatoire and of Sainte-Chapelle were all they should be. Then he found two or three proof-shots he'd forgotten, a poor attempt to catch a cat perched astonishingly on the roof of a rambling public urinal, and also the shot of the blond and the kid. The negative was so good that he made an enlargement; the enlargement was so good that he made one very much larger, almost the size of a poster. It did not occur to him (now one wonders and wonders) that only the shots of the Conservatoire were worth so much work. Of the whole series, the snapshot of the tip of the island was the only one which interested him; he tacked up the enlargement on one wall of the room, and the first day he spent some time looking at it and remembering, that gloomy operation of comparing the memory with the gone reality; a frozen memory, like any photo, where nothing is missing, not even, and especially, nothingness, the true solidifier of the scene. There was the woman, there was the boy, the tree rigid above their heads, the sky as sharp as the stone of the parapet, clouds and stones melded into a single substance and inseparable (now one with sharp edges is going by, like a thunderhead). The first two days I accepted what I had done, from the photo itself to the enlargement on the wall, and didn't even question that every once in a while I would interrupt my translation of José Norberto Allende's treatise to encounter once more the woman's face, the dark splotches on the railing. I'm such a jerk; it had never occurred to me that when we look at a photo from the front, the eyes reproduce exactly the position and the vision of the lens; it's these things that are taken for granted and it never occurs to anyone to think about them. From my chair, with the typewriter directly in front of me, I looked at the photo ten feet away, and then it occurred to me that I had hung it exactly at the point of view of the lens. It looked very good that way; no doubt, it was the best way to appreciate a photo, though the angle from the diagonal doubtless has its pleasures and might even divulge different aspects. Every few minutes, for example when I was unable to find the way to say in good French what José Norberto Allende was saying in very good Spanish, I raised my eyes and looked at the photo; sometimes the woman would catch my eye, sometimes the boy, sometimes the pavement where a dry leaf had fallen admirably situated to heighten a lateral section. Then I rested a bit from my labors, and I enclosed myself again happily in that morning in which the photo was drenched, I recalled ironically the angry picture of the woman demanding I give her the photograph, the boy's pathetic and ridiculous flight, the entrance on the scene of the man with the white face. Basically, I was satisfied with myself; my part had not been too brilliant, and since the French have been given the gift of the sharp response, I did not see very well why I'd chosen to leave without a complete demonstration of the rights, privileges and prerogatives of citizens. The important thing, the really important thing was having helped the kid to escape in time (this in case my theorizing was correct, which was not sufficiently proven, but the running away itself seemed to show it so). Out of

plain meddling, I had given him the opportunity finally to take advantage of his fright to do something useful; now he would be regretting it, feeling his honor impaired, his manhood diminished. That was better than the attentions of a woman capable of looking as she had looked at him on that island. Michel is something of a puritan at times, he believes that one should not seduce someone from a position of strength. In the last analysis, taking that photo had been a good act.

Well, it wasn't because of the good act that I looked at it between paragraphs while I was working. At that moment I didn't know the reason, the reason I had tacked the enlargement onto the wall; maybe all fatal acts happen that way, and that is the condition of their fulfillment. I don't think the almost-furtive trembling of the leaves on the tree alarmed me, I was working on a sentence and rounded it out successfully. Habits are like immense herbariums, in the end an enlargement of 32×28 looks like a movie screen, where, on the tip of the island, a woman is speaking with a boy and a tree is shaking its dry leaves over their heads.

But her hands were just too much. I had just translated: "In that case, the second key resides in the intrinsic nature of difficulties which societies . . ."— when I saw the woman's hand beginning to stir slowly, finger by finger. There was nothing left of me, a phrase in French which I would never have to finish, a typewriter on the floor, a chair that squeaked and shook, fog. The kid had ducked his head like boxers do when they've done all they can and are waiting for the final blow to fall; he had turned up the collar of his overcoat and seemed more a prisoner than ever, the perfect victim helping promote the catastrophe. Now the woman was talking into his ear, and her hand opened again to lay itself against his cheekbone, to caress and caress it, burning it, taking her time. The kid was less startled than he was suspicious, once or twice he poked his head over the woman's shoulder and she continued talking, saying something that made him look back every few minutes toward that area where Michel knew the car was parked and the man in the grey hat, carefully eliminated from the photo but present in the boy's eyes (how doubt that now) in the words of the woman, in the woman's hands, in the vicarious presence of the woman. When I saw the man come up, stop near them and look at them, his hands in his pockets and a stance somewhere between disgusted and demanding, the master who is about to whistle in his dog after a frolic in the square, I understood, if that was to understand, what had to happen now, what had to have happened then, what would have to happen at that moment, among these people, just where I had poked my nose in to upset an established order, interfering inno- cently in that which had not happened, but which was now going to happen, now was going to be fulfilled. And what I had imagined earlier was much less horrible than the reality, that woman, who was not there by herself, she was not caressing or propositioning or encouraging for her own pleasure, to lead the angel away with his tousled hair and play the tease with his terror and his eager grace. The real boss was waiting there, smiling petulantly, already certain of the business; he was not the first to send a woman in the vanguard, to bring him the prisoners manacled with flowers. The rest of it would be so simple, the car, some house or another, drinks, stimulating engravings, tardy tears, the awakening in hell. And there was nothing I could do, this time I could do absolutely nothing. My strength had been a photograph, that, there, where they were taking their revenge on me, demonstrating clearly what was going to happen. The photo had been taken, the time had run out, gone; we were so far from one another, the abusive act had certainly already taken place, the tears already shed, and the rest conjecture and sorrow. All at once the order was inverted, they were alive, moving, they were deciding and had decided, they were going to their future; and I on this side, prisoner of another time, in a room on the fifth floor, to not know who they were, that woman, that man, and that boy, to be only the lens of my camera, something fixed, rigid, incapable of intervention. It was horrible, their mocking me, deciding it before my impotent eye, mocking me, for the boy again was looking at the flour-faced clown and I had to accept the fact that he was going to say yes, that the proposition carried money with it or a gimmick, and I couldn't yell for him to run, or even open the road to him again with a new photo, a small and almost meek intervention which would ruin the framework of drool and perfume. Everything was going to resolve itself right there, at that moment; there was like an immense silence which had nothing to do with physical silence. It was stretching it out, setting itself up. I think I screamed, I screamed terribly, and that at that exact second I realized that I was beginning to move toward them, four inches, a step, another step, the tree swung its branches rhythmically in the foreground, a place where the railing was tarnished emerged from the frame, the woman's face turned toward me as though surprised, was enlarging, and then I turned a bit, I mean that the camera turned a little, and without losing sight of the woman, I began to close in on the man who was looking at me with the black holes he had in place of eyes, surprised and angered both, he looked, wanting to nail me onto the air, and at that instant I happened to see something like a large bird outside the focus that was flying in a single swoop in front of the picture, and I leaned up against the wall of my room and was happy because the boy had just managed to escape, I saw him running off, in focus again, sprinting with his hair flying in the wind, learning finally to fly across the island, to arrive at the footbridge, return to the city. For the second time he'd escaped them, for the second time I was helping him to escape, returning him to his precarious paradise. Out of breath, I stood in front of them; no need to step closer, the game was played out. Of the woman you could see just maybe a shoulder and a bit of the hair, brutally cut off by the frame of the picture; but the man was directly center, his mouth half open, you could see a shaking black tongue, and he lifted his hands slowly, bringing them into the foreground, an instant still in perfect focus, and then all of him a lump that blotted out the island, the tree, and I shut my eyes, I didn't want to see any more, and I covered my face and broke into tears like an idiot.

Now there's a big white cloud, as on all these days, all this untellable time. What remains to be said is always a cloud, two clouds, or long hours of a sky perfectly clear, a very clean, clear rectangle tacked up with pins on the wall of my room. That was what I saw when I opened my eyes and dried them with my fingers: the clear sky, and then a cloud that drifted in from the left, passed gracefully and slowly across and disappeared on the right. And then another, and for a change sometimes, everything gets grey, all one enormous cloud, and suddenly the splotches of rain cracking down, for a long spell you can see it raining over the picture, like a spell of weeping reversed, and little by little, the frame becomes clear, perhaps the sun comes out, and again the clouds begin to come, two at a time, three at a time. And the pigeons once in a while, and a sparrow or two.

1956

▼ ▼ ▼

POINT OF VIEW A Glossary

auditor: someone other than the reader—a character within the fiction—to whom the story or "speech" is addressed

centered (central) consciousness: a limited point of view, one tied to a single character throughout the story, often revealing his or her inner thoughts but unable to read the thoughts of others

focus: the point from which people, events, and other details in a story are viewed. See *point of view*

limited point of view or **limited focus:** a perspective pinned to a single character, whether first-person or a third-person centered consciousness, so that we cannot know for sure what is going on in the minds of other characters; when the focal character leaves the room in a story we must go too and cannot know what is going on while our "eyes" or "camera" is gone. A variation on this, which generally has no name and is often lumped with the *omniscient point of view,* is the point of view that can wander like a camera from one character to another and close in or move back but cannot (or at least does not) get inside anyone's head, does not present from the inside any character's thoughts

narrator: the person who tells the story

omniscient point of view: see *unlimited focus*

persona: the voice or figure of the author who tells and structures the story, and who may or may not share the values of the actual person of the author

point of view: focus; the point from which people, events, and other details in a story are viewed. This term is sometimes used to include both focus and voice

psychological realism: a modification of the concept of realism, or telling it like it is, which recognizes that what is real to the individual is that which he or she perceives. It is the ground for the use of the centered consciousness, or the first-person narrator, since both of these present reality only as something perceived by the focal character

unlimited focus or **omniscient point of view:** a perspective that can be seen from one character's view, then another's, then another's, or can be moved in or out of any character at any time

unreliable narrator: a speaker or voice whose vision or version of the details of the story are consciously or unconsciously deceiving; such a narrator's version is usually subtly undermined by details in the story or the reader's general knowledge of facts outside the story; if, for example, the narrator were to tell you that Columbus was Spanish, and that he discovered America in the fourteenth century when his ship *The Golden Hind* landed on the coast of Florida near present-day Gainesville, you might not trust other things he tells you

voice: the acknowledged or unacknowledged source of the words of the story; the "speaker;" the "person" telling the story

QUESTIONS

1. Who is the auditor, the "You," addressed in the first paragraph of "The Cask of Amontillado"? (You may want to wait until you have finished the last sentence of the story before answering.) When is the story being told? Why? How does your knowledge of the auditor and the occasion influence the story's effect?

2. Looking back over "An Occurrence at Owl Creek Bridge," how many of Peyton Farquhar's sensory perceptions can you reinterpret now that you know what must have been really happening?

3. Summarize, as best you can, the problem the narrator of "Blow-Up" has in deciding how the story is to be told. Why does he say a typewriter would be the best narrator? Who is the narrator? Is Roberto Michel (par. 6) the same "one" who goes down five floors that Sunday in paragraph 4? In paragraph 6, sentence 2, Michel is "He," but after two sentences of description, there is a shift to "I"; what is the effect of such shifting on you as reader (besides impatience or puzzlement)?

4. Near the end of paragraph 11, the narrator of "Blow-Up" says, "I'm not describing anything, it's more a matter of trying to understand it." How do the two differ? In what way may they relate to both the reader's taking in of what is read and his or her attempt to understand it? How does the distinction justify Michel's imagining the boy's life and home (paragraph 12), his foreseeing what is going to happen next in paragraphs 13 and 15? To what extent is the distinction modified by Michel's revision of his understanding of the scene in paragraph 22? How is the narrator's statement about understanding in paragraph 11 related to his statement in paragraph 16 that "Michel is guilty of making literature, of indulging in fabricating realities," and why the word "guilty"?

5. Why is the word "now" in paragraph 7 of "Blow-Up" "a dumb lie"? How do you understand all the parenthetical remarks about clouds? From whose focus are the clouds seen? The final paragraph centers on the clouds and sky. What is the effect? How do you understand the significance of this attention? In what way(s) is it a suitable ending?

WRITING SUGGESTIONS

1. Write a parody of "The Cask of Amontillado" set in modern times, perhaps on a college campus ("A Barrel of Bud"?).

2. Write a "pre-text" narrating the "thousand injuries" and the insult that triggered Montresor's revenge, or sketch several possibilities for such a pre-text narrated from various points of view.

3. What would the effect be if "Blow-Up" were told "straight," from the simple first-person point of view? (Use specific details from the story in your analysis. You may want to duplicate several paragraphs and "edit," omitting all deviations from first-person narration.)

3 CHARACTERIZATION

I n a good many stories the narrator is a disembodied offstage voice, without an identity or a personal history, without influence on the action, without qualities other than those that a voice and style may suggest. So it is in some of the earlier stories in this volume—"The Zebra Storyteller," "No One's a Mystery," "The Jewelry," "An Occurrence at Owl Creek Bridge." Poe's narrator, however, not only tells us the story but has a part in the action as well; without him we not only would not know the story, but neither would there be a story. He looks back into his past; he is there in the story, speaking, listening, reacting. In addition to being the narrator, he is a **character:** someone who acts, appears, or is referred to as playing a part in a work.

The most common term for the character with the leading male role is **hero,** the "good guy" who opposes the **villain,** or "bad guy." The leading female character is the **heroine.** Heroes and heroines are usually larger than life, stronger or better than most human beings, almost godlike (and there's even a brand of heroes nowadays so close to being godlike that they are called superheroes). In most modern fiction, however, the leading character is much more ordinary, more like the rest of us. Such a character is called the **anti-hero,** not because he opposes the hero but because he is not like a hero in stature or perfection. An older and more neutral term than hero for the leading character, a term that does not imply either the presence or absence of outstanding virtue (and with the added advantage of referring equally to male and female), is **protagonist,** whose opponent is the **antagonist.** You might get into long and pointless arguments by calling Lantin or Montresor a hero, but either is his story's protagonist.

The **major characters** are those we see more of over a longer period of time; we learn more about them, and we think of them as more complex and frequently therefore more "realistic" than the **minor characters,** the figures who fill out the story. These major characters can grow and change, as Lantin does and as Judith does in Doris Lessing's "Our Friend Judith"; by the end of these stories both protagonists have acted unpredictably based on what we learned earlier in the story about them and their past actions. Characters who can thus "surprise convincingly," an influential critic says, are **round characters.** Because Tallent's and Poe's characters are not very complex and do not change in surprising ways, they are called **flat.** But we must be careful not to let terms like *flat* and *round* turn into value judgments. Because flat characters are less complex than round ones it is easy to assume they are artistically inferior; we need only to think of the characters of Charles Dickens, almost all of whom are flat, to realize that this is not always true.

The terms *flat* and *round*, like the terms *hero* and *antihero*, are not absolute or precise. They designate extremes or tendencies, not pigeonholes. Is Poe's Montresor entirely flat? Is Shakespeare's Falstaff? Charlie Chaplin's Little Tramp? Little Orphan Annie? Are all these characters equally flat? We will probably agree that Baldwin's Sonny is a round character, but what about Cortázar's Michel? Cheever's Francis Weed? Are they all equally round? Our answers are less important than our looking carefully at these characters to see what we know about each of them, to what degree they can be summed up in a phrase or a sentence; to discover how we learned what we know about them and how our judgment has been controlled by the story; to think about and perhaps judge the assumptions about human motivation, behavior, and nature that underlie the character and his or her characterization. Flat and round are useful as categories but are even more useful as tools of investigation, as ways of focusing our attention and sharpening our perception.

Though most of Dickens's flat characters are highly individualized, not to say unique, some, like Fagin, the avaricious Jewish moneylender, are **stereotypes**: characters based on conscious or unconscious cultural assumptions that sex, age, ethnic or national identification, occupation, marital status, and so on are predictably accompanied by certain character traits, actions, even values.

The stereotype may be very useful in creating a round character, one who can surprise convincingly: Judith, according to a Canadian woman, is "one of your typical English spinsters." Judith, however, acts in ways that deny the limitations of the stereotype. A stereotype is, after all, only a quick—and somewhat superficial—form of classification, and classification is a common first step in definitions. One of the chief ways we have of describing or defining is by placing the thing to be defined in a category or class and then distinguishing it from the other members of that class. A good deal of **characterization**—the art, craft, method of presentation, or creation of fictional personages—involves a similar process. Characters are almost inevitably identified by category—by sex, age, nationality, occupation, and so on. We learn that the narrator of "Why I Live at the P.O." is a woman, relatively young, who lives in a small town in Mississippi.

Paradoxically, the more groups a character is placed in, the more individual he or she becomes. Fenstad's mother, for example, is an old woman, a protective and critical mother, two separate but closely related stereotypes that categorize her, but she is also a social, political, and intellectual radical, which significantly individualizes her within the various categories into which she fits.

Not all generalizations involve cultural stereotypes, of course. Some may involve generalized character traits that the story or narrator defines for us (and that we must accept unless events in the story prove otherwise). Physical characteristics also serve as categories. As with stereotypes, when physical characteristics are multiplied, the result is more and more particularizing or individualizing. The detailed physical description of Judith makes it possible to visualize her rather fully, almost to recognize her as an individual:

> Judith is tall, small-breasted, slender. Her light brown hair is parted in the centre and cut straight around her neck. A high straight forehead, straight nose, and full grave mouth are setting for her eyes, which are green, large and prominent. Her lids are very white, fringed with gold, and moulded close over the eyeball. . . . (par. 7)

There are many other ways in which a character is characterized and individualized besides stereotyping and "destereotyping," and besides classifying and particularizing by physical description. In most cases we see what characters do and hear what they say; we sometimes learn what they think, and what other people think or say about them; we often know what kind of clothes they wear, what and how much they own, treasure, or covet; we may be told about their childhood, parents, or some parts of their past. We learn about Eudora Welty's "Sister" from her age, sex, and where she lives. We learn a good deal more from the way she talks to her family and they to her, how she decides what she owns, and what she chooses to take with her when she moves.

Though characterization is gradual, taking place sequentially through the story, it is not, as it may seem natural to assume, entirely cumulative. We do not begin with an empty space called Judith or Francis Weed or Sonny and fill it gradually by adding physical traits, habitual actions, ways of speaking, and so on. Our imaginations do not work that way. Rather, just as at each point in the action we project some sort of configuration of how the story will come out or what the world of the story will be like or mean, so we project a more or less complete image of each character at the point at which the he or she is first mentioned or appears. This image is based on the initial reference in the text, our reading, and life experiences and associations (Don't you have an image of a Herb? a Maude? a spinster?). The next time the character is mentioned, or when he or she speaks or acts, we do not so much "adjust" our first impression as we project a new image (just as in the plot we project a new series of developments and a new outcome). There may be some carryover, but we do not in

the course of the story put the character together like a Mr. Potato Head.
Instead, we overlay one image on the other, and though the final image may
be the most enduring, the early images do not all disappear: our view of the
character is multidimensional, flickering, like a time-lapse photograph. Perhaps that is why it is rare that any actor in a film based on a novel or story
matches the way we imagined that character if we have read the book or story
first—our imagination has not one image but rather a sequence of images associated with that character. It is also why some of us feel that seeing the film
before reading the book hobbles the imagination. A particular character's physical attributes, for example, may not be described in a novel until after that character has been involved in some incident; the reader may then need to adjust
his earlier vision of that character, which is not an option for the viewer of a
film. It is thus the reader, rather than a casting director, who finalizes a character in his or her own imagination.

For no matter how many methods of characterization are employed, at
some point the definition of the individual stops. No matter how individualized the character may be, he or she remains a member of a number of
groups, and we make certain assumptions about that character based on our
fixed or stereotyped notions of those groups. To destroy a stereotype, a story
must introduce a stereotype to destroy. And somehow the destereotyped character, no matter how particularized, remains to some degree representative. If
Judith turns out to be not as prudish and prissy as the stereotype of the English
spinster has led us to believe, we may well conclude that the stereotype is false
and that Judith is more representative of the real English spinster than the stereotype is. Indeed, this tendency to generalize from the particulars of a story
extends beyond cultural groups, sometimes to human character at large: if
Sonny can change his ways after years of habitual conduct, then human character, the story might seem to say, is not permanently fixed at birth, in infancy,
childhood, ever.

One of the reasons it is so difficult to discuss character is precisely that the
principles of definition and evaluation of fictional characters (not of their characterizations, the way they are presented) are the same as those we use for real
people, an area of violent controversy and confusion. The very term *character*,
when it refers not to a fictional personage but to a combination of qualities in
a human being, is somewhat ambiguous. It usually has moral overtones, often
favorable (a man of character); it is sometimes neutral but evaluative (character reference). Judgment about character (not characterization, remember) usually involves moral terms like *good* and *bad* and *strong* and *weak*. **Personality**
usually implies that which distinguishes or individualizes a person, and the

judgment called for is not so much moral as social—*pleasing* or *displeasing*. An older term, **nature** (it is in one's nature to be so or do such), usually implies something inherent or inborn, something fixed and thus predictable. The **existential character** implies the opposite; that is, whatever our past, our conditioning, our pattern or previous behavior, we can, by choice, by free will, change all that right this minute, as Sonny does.

Fictional characters thus frequently seem to be part of the history that lies behind the story or beyond the story as part of our own world, to exist in a reality that is detachable from the words and events of the story in which they appear. We feel we might recognize Tom Jones, Jane Eyre, or Sherlock Holmes on the street, and we might be able to anticipate what they would say or do in *our* world, outside the story. Fictional characters are neither real nor detachable, of course, and they exist only in the words of the works in which they are presented. We must not forget the distinction between the character and the characterization, the method by which he or she is presented; so we must be careful to distinguish the *good character*, meaning someone whom, if real, we would consider virtuous, and the *good characterization*, meaning a fictional person who, no matter what his or her morality or behavior, is well presented.

We must recognize that characters are not finally detachable—that they have roles, functions, limitations, and their very existence in the context of the story; we must not confuse fictional characters with real people, or character with characterization. This is not to say, however, that we may not learn about real people from characters in fiction or learn to understand fictional characters in part from what we know about real people. For real people too exist in a context of other people and other elements, their history and geography and their "narrator," the one who is representing them—that is, *you*. Indeed, it may be worth paying particular attention to how stories create the images of people and what those images assume about human character precisely because this process and these assumptions are so similar to the way we get to know and understand real people. For we are all artists representing reality to ourselves. If we study the art of characterization we may become better artists, able to enrich both our reading and our lives.

The Grace Paley story that ends this chapter is here as a reminder that the elements of fiction are abstractions, useful for analysis but not truly separable. In that story, for example, the narrator's father tells her to tell a simple story, and her first attempt is pure plot or incident. But he says she's left everything out—what her protagonist looks like, what her parents were like—circumstances and character. She tries again, and this time her version is heavy on character of both the fictional woman and her son. Now the father challenges, then praises, the ending. The narrator says the end is not the end, the woman's character is not fixed, but what we have called existential—she can change. Throughout plot, or action, and character are fused. As Henry James has said,

> What is character but the determination of incident? What is incident but the illustration of character? . . . It is an incident for a woman to stand up with her hand resting on a table and look at you in a certain way; or if it is not an incident I think it will be hard to say what it is. At the same time it is an expression of character. If you say you don't see it, . . . this is exactly what the artist who has reasons of his own for thinking he *does* see it undertakes to show you.

▾ ▾ ▾

EUDORA WELTY

Why I Live at the P.O.

I was getting along fine with Mama, Papa-Daddy, and Uncle Rondo until my sister Stella-Rondo just separated from her husband and came back home again. Mr. Whitaker! Of course I went with Mr. Whitaker first, when he first appeared here in China Grove, taking "Pose Yourself" photos, and Stella-Rondo broke us up. Told him I was one-sided. Bigger on one side than the other, which is a deliberate, calculated falsehood: I'm the same. Stella-Rondo is exactly twelve months to the day younger than I am and for that reason she's spoiled.

She's always had anything in the world she wanted and then she'd throw it away. Papa-Daddy give her this gorgeous Add-a-Pearl necklace when she was eight years old and she threw it away playing baseball when she was nine, with only two pearls.

So as soon as she got married and moved away from home the first thing she did was separate! From Mr. Whitaker! This photographer with the popeyes she said she trusted. Came home from one of those towns up in Illinois and to our complete surprise brought this child of two.

Mama said she like to make her drop dead for a second. "Here you had this marvelous blonde child and never so much as wrote your mother a word about it," says Mama. "I'm thoroughly ashamed of you." But of course she wasn't.

Stella-Rondo just calmly takes off this *hat,* I wish you could see it. She says, "Why, Mama, Shirley-T.'s adopted, I can prove it."

"How?" says Mama, but all I says was, "H'm!" There I was over the hot stove, trying to stretch two chickens over five people and a completely unexpected child into the bargain without one moment's notice.

"What do you mean—'H'm'?" says Stella-Rondo, and Mama says, "I heard that, Sister."

I said that oh, I didn't mean a thing, only that whoever Shirley-T. was, she was the spit-image of Papa-Daddy if he'd cut off his beard, which of course he'd never do in the world. Papa-Daddy's Mama's papa and sulks.

Stella-Rondo got furious! She said, "Sister, I don't need to tell you you got a lot of nerve and always did have and I'll thank you to make no future reference to my adopted child whatsoever."

"Very well," I said. "Very well, very well. Of course I noticed at once she looks like Mr. Whitaker's side too. That frown. She looks like a cross between Mr. Whitaker and Papa-Daddy."

"Well, all I can say is she isn't."

"She looks exactly like Shirley Temple to me," says Mama, but Shirley-T. just ran away from her.

So the first thing Stella-Rondo did at the table was turn Papa-Daddy against me.

"Papa-Daddy," she says. He was trying to cut up his meat. "Papa-Daddy!" I was taken completely by surprise. Papa-Daddy is about a million years old and's got this long-long beard. "Papa-Daddy, Sister says she fails to understand why you don't cut off your beard."

So Papa-Daddy l-a-y-s down his knife and fork! He's real rich. Mama says he is, she says he isn't. So he says, "Have I heard correctly? You don't understand why I don't cut off my beard?"

"Why," I says, "Papa-Daddy, of course I understand, I did not say any such a thing, the idea!"

He says, "Hussy!"

I says, "Papa-Daddy, you know I wouldn't any more want you to cut off your beard than the man in the moon. It was the farthest thing from my mind! Stella-Rondo sat there and made that up while she was eating breast of chicken."

But he says, "So the postmistress fails to understand why I don't cut off my beard. Which job I got you through my influence with the government. 'Bird's nest'—is that what you call it?"

Not that it isn't the next to smallest P.O. in the entire state of Mississippi.

I says, "Oh, Papa-Daddy," I says, "I didn't say any such a thing, I never dreamed it was a bird's nest, I have always been grateful though this is the next to smallest P.O. in the state of Mississippi, and I do not enjoy being referred to as a hussy by my own grandfather."

But Stella-Rondo says, "Yes, you did say it too. Anybody in the world could of heard you, that had ears."

"Stop right there," says Mama, looking at me.

So I pulled my napkin straight back through the napkin ring and left the table.

As soon as I was out of the room Mama says, "Call her back, or she'll starve to death," but Papa-Daddy says, "This is the beard I started growing on the Coast when I was fifteen years old." He would of gone on till nightfall if Shirley-T. hadn't lost the Milky Way she ate in Cairo.

So Papa-Daddy says, "I am going out and lie in the hammock, and you can all sit here and remember my words: I'll never cut off my beard as long as I live, even one inch, and I don't appreciate it in you at all." Passed right by me in the hall and went straight out and got in the hammock.

It would be a holiday. It wasn't five minutes before Uncle Rondo suddenly appeared in the hall in one of Stella-Rondo's flesh-colored kimonos, all cut on the bias, like something Mr. Whitaker probably thought was gorgeous.

"Uncle Rondo!" I says. "I didn't know who that was! Where are you going?"

"Sister," he says, "get out of my way, I'm poisoned."

"If you're poisoned stay away from Papa-Daddy," I says. "Keep out of the hammock. Papa-Daddy will certainly beat you on the head if you come within forty miles of him. He thinks I deliberately said he ought to cut off his beard after he got me the P.O., and I've told him and told him and told him, and he acts like he just don't hear me. Papa-Daddy must of gone stone deaf."

"He picked a fine day to do it then," says Uncle Rondo, and before you could say "Jack Robinson" flew out in the yard.

What he'd really done, he'd drunk another bottle of that prescription. He does it every single Fourth of July as sure as shooting, and it's horribly expensive. Then he falls over in the hammock and snores. So he insisted on zigzagging right on out to the hammock, looking like a half-wit.

Papa-Daddy woke with this horrible yell and right there without moving an inch he tried to turn Uncle Rondo against me. I heard every word he said. Oh, he told Uncle Rondo I didn't learn to read till I was eight years old and he didn't see how in the world I ever got the mail put up at the P.O., much less read it all, and he said if Uncle Rondo could only fathom the lengths he had gone to get me that job! And he said on the other hand he thought Stella-Rondo had a brilliant mind and deserved credit for getting out of town. All the time he was just lying there swinging as pretty as you please and looping out his beard, and poor Uncle Rondo was *pleading* with him to slow down the hammock, it was making him as dizzy as a witch to watch it. But that's what Papa-Daddy likes about a hammock. So Uncle Rondo was too dizzy to get turned against me for the time being. He's Mama's only brother and is a good case of a one-track mind. Ask anybody. A certified pharmacist.

Just then I heard Stella-Rondo raising the upstairs window. While she was married she got this peculiar idea that it's cooler with the windows shut and locked. So she has to raise the window before she can make a soul hear her outdoors.

So she raises the window and says, "*Oh!*" You would have thought she was mortally wounded.

Uncle Rondo and Papa-Daddy didn't even look up, but kept right on with what they were doing. I had to laugh.

I flew up the stairs and threw the door open! I says, "What in the wide world's the matter, Stella-Rondo? You mortally wounded?"

"No," she says, "I am not mortally wounded but I wish you would do me the favor of looking out that window there and telling me what you see."

So I shade my eyes and look out the window.

"I see the front yard," I says.

"Don't you see any human beings?"

"I see Uncle Rondo trying to run Papa-Daddy out of the hammock," I says. "Nothing more. Naturally, it's so suffocating-hot in the house, with all the windows shut and locked, everybody who cares to stay in their right mind will have to go out and get in the hammock before the Fourth of July is over."

"Don't you notice anything different about Uncle Rondo?" asks Stella-Rondo.

"Why, no, except he's got on some terrible-looking flesh-colored contraption I wouldn't be found dead in, is all I can see," I says.

"Never mind, you won't be found dead in it, because it happens to be part of my trousseau, and Mr. Whitaker took several dozen photographs of me in it," says Stella-Rondo. "What on earth could uncle Rondo *mean* by wearing part of my trousseau out in the broad open daylight without saying so much as 'Kiss my foot,' *knowing* I only got home this morning after my separation and hung my negligee up on the bathroom door, just as nervous as I could be?"

"I'm sure I don't know, and what do you expect me to do about it?" I says. "Jump out the window?"

"No, I expect nothing of the kind. I simply declare that Uncle Rondo looks like a fool in it, that's all," she says. "It makes me sick to my stomach."

"Well, he looks as good as he can," I says. "As good as anybody in reason could." I stood up for Uncle Rondo, please remember. And I said to Stella-Rondo, "I think I would do well not to criticize so freely if I were you and came home with a two-year-old child I had never said a word about, and no explanation whatever about my separation."

"I asked you the instant I entered this house not to refer one more time to my adopted child, and you gave me your word of honor you would not," was all Stella-Rondo would say, and started pulling out every one of her eyebrows with some cheap Kress tweezers.

So I merely slammed the door behind me and went down and made some green-tomato pickle. Somebody had to do it. Of course Mama had turned both the Negroes loose; she always said no earthly power could hold one anyway on the Fourth of July, so she wouldn't even try. It turned out that Jaypan fell in the lake and came within a very narrow limit of drowning.

So Mama trots in. Lifts up the lid and says, "H'm! Not very good for your Uncle Rondo in his precarious condition, I must say. Or poor little adopted Shirley-T. Shame on you!"

That made me tired. I says, "Well, Stella-Rondo had better thank her lucky stars it was her instead of me came trotting in with that very peculiar-looking child. Now if it had been me that trotted in from Illinois and brought a peculiar-looking child or two, I shudder to think of the reception I'd of got, much less controlled the diet of an entire family."

"But you must remember, Sister, that you were never married to Mr. Whitaker in the first place and didn't go up to Illinois to live," says Mama, shaking a spoon in my face. "If you had I would of been just as overjoyed to see you and your little adopted girl as I was to see Stella-Rondo, when you wound up with your separation and came on back home."

"You would not," I says.

55   "Don't contradict me, I would," says Mama.

But I said she couldn't convince me though she talked till she was blue in the face. Then I said, "Besides, you know as well as I do that that child is not adopted."

"She most certainly is adopted," says Mama, stiff as a poker.

I says, "Why, Mama, Stella-Rondo had her just as sure as anything in this world, and just too stuck up to admit it."

"Why, Sister," said Mama. "Here I thought we were going to have a pleasant Fourth of July, and you start right out not believing a word your own baby sister tells you!"

60   "Just like Cousin Annie Flo. Went to her grave denying the facts of life," I reminded Mama.

"I told you if you ever mentioned Annie Flo's name I'd slap your face," says Mama, and slaps my face.

"All right, you wait and see," I says.

"I," says Mama, "*I* prefer to take my children's word for anything when it's humanly possible." You ought to see Mama, she weighs two hundred pounds and has real tiny feet.

Just then something perfectly horrible occurred to me.

65   "Mama," I says, "can that child talk?" I simply had to whisper! "Mama, I wonder if that child can be—you know—in any way? Do you realize?" I says, "that she hasn't spoke one single, solitary word to a human being up to this minute? This is the way she looks," I says, and I looked like this.

Well, Mama and I just stood there and stared at each other. It was horrible!

"I remember well that Joe Whitaker frequently drank like a fish," says Mama. "I believed to my soul he drank *chemicals*." And without another word she marches to the foot of the stairs and calls Stella-Rondo.

"Stella-Rondo? O-o-o-o-o! Stella-Rondo!"

"What?" says Stella-Rondo from upstairs. Not even the grace to get up off the bed.

70   "Can that child of yours talk?" asks Mama.

Stella-Rondo says, "Can she what?"

"Talk! Talk!" says Mama. "Burdyburdyburdyburdy!"

So Stella-Rondo yells back, "Who says she can't talk?"

"Sister says so," says Mama.

75   "You didn't have to tell me, I know whose word of honor don't mean a thing in this house," says Stella-Rondo.

And in a minute the loudest Yankee voice I ever heard in my life yells out, "OE'm Pop-OE the Sailor-r-r-r Ma-a-an!" and then somebody jumps up and down in the upstairs hall. In another second the house would of fallen down.

"Not only talks, she can tap-dance!" calls Stella-Rondo. "Which is more than some people I won't name can do."

"Why, the little precious darling thing!" Mama says, so surprised. "Just as smart as she can be!" Starts talking baby talk right there. Then she turns on me. "Sister, you ought to be thoroughly ashamed! Run upstairs this instant and apologize to Stella-Rondo and Shirley-T."

"Apologize for what?" I says. "I merely wondered if the child was normal, that's all. Now that she's proved she is, why, I have nothing further to say."

But Mama just turned on her heel and flew out, furious. She ran right upstairs and hugged the baby. She believed it was adopted. Stella-Rondo hadn't done a thing but turn her against me from upstairs while I stood there helpless over the hot stove. So that made Mama, Papa-Daddy, and the baby all on Stella-Rondo's side.

Next, Uncle Rondo.

I must say that Uncle Rondo has been marvelous to me at various times in the past and I was completely unprepared to be made to jump out of my skin, the way it turned out. Once Stella-Rondo did something perfectly horrible to him—broke a chain letter from Flanders Field—and he took the radio back he had given her and gave it to me. Stella-Rondo was furious! For six months we all had to call her Stella instead of Stella-Rondo, or she wouldn't answer. I always thought Uncle Rondo had all the brains of the entire family. Another time he sent me to Mammoth Cave with all expenses paid.

But this would be the day he was drinking that prescription, the Fourth of July.

So at supper Stella-Rondo speaks up and says she thinks Uncle Rondo ought to try to eat a little something. So finally Uncle Rondo said he would try a little cold biscuits and ketchup, but that was all. So *she* brought it to him.

"Do you think it wise to disport with ketchup in Stella-Rondo's flesh-colored kimono?" I says. Trying to be considerate! If Stella-Rondo couldn't watch out for her trousseau, somebody had to.

"Any objections?" asks Uncle Rondo, just about to pour out all of the ketchup.

"Don't mind what she says, Uncle Rondo," says Stella-Rondo. "Sister has been devoting this solid afternoon to sneering out my bedroom window at the way you look."

"What's that?" says Uncle Rondo. Uncle Rondo has got the most terrible temper in the world. Anything is liable to make him tear the house down if it comes at the wrong time.

So Stella-Rondo says, "Sister says, 'Uncle Rondo certainly does look like a fool in that pink kimono!' "

Do you remember who it was really said that?

Uncle Rondo spills out all the ketchup and jumps out of his chair and tears off the kimono and throws it down on the dirty floor and puts his foot on it. It had to be sent all the way to Jackson to the cleaners and re-pleated.

"So that's your opinion of your Uncle Rondo, is it?" he says. "I look like a fool, do I? Well, that's the last straw. A whole day in this house with nothing to do, and then to hear you come out with a remark like that behind my back!"

"I didn't say any such of a thing, Uncle Rondo," I says, "and I'm not saying who did, either. Why, I think you look all right. Just try to take care of yourself and not talk and eat at the same time," I says. "I think you better go lie down."

"Lie down my foot," says Uncle Rondo. I ought to of known by that he was fixing to do something perfectly horrible.

95 So he didn't do anything that night in the precarious state he was in—just played Casino with Mama and Stella-Rondo and Shirley-T. and gave Shirley-T. a nickel with a head on both sides. It tickled her nearly to death, and she called him "Papa." But at 6:30 A.M. the next morning, he threw a whole five-cent package of some unsold one-inch firecrackers from the store as hard as he could into my bedroom and they every one went off. Not one bad one in the string. Anybody else, there'd be one that wouldn't go off.

Well, I'm just terribly susceptible to noise of any kind, the doctor has always told me I was the most sensitive person he had ever seen in his whole life, and I was simply prostrated. I couldn't eat! People tell me they heard it as far as the cemetery, and old Aunt Jep Patterson, that had been holding her own so good, thought it was Judgment Day and she was going to meet her whole family. It's usually so quiet here.

And I'll tell you it didn't take me any longer than a minute to make up my mind what to do. There I was with the whole entire house on Stella-Rondo's side and turned against me. If I have anything at all I have pride.

So I just decided I'd go straight down to the P.O. There's plenty of room there in the back, I says to myself.

Well! I made no bones about letting the family catch on to what I was up to. I didn't try to conceal it.

100 The first thing they knew, I marched in where they were all playing Old Maid and pulled the electric oscillating fan out by the plug, and everything got real hot. Next I snatched the pillow I'd done the needlepoint on right off the davenport from behind Papa-Daddy. He went "Ugh!" I beat Stella-Rondo up the stairs and finally found my charm bracelet in her bureau drawer under a picture of Nelson Eddy.[1]

"So that's the way the land lies," says Uncle Rondo. There he was, piecing on the ham. "Well, Sister, I'll be glad to donate my army cot if you got any place to set it up, providing you'll leave right this minute and let me get some peace." Uncle Rondo was in France.

"Thank you kindly for the cot and 'peace' is hardly the word I would select if I had to resort to firecrackers at 6:30 A.M. in a young girl's bedroom," I says to him. "And as to where I intend to go, you seem to forget my position as postmistress of China Grove, Mississippi," I says. "I've always got the P.O."

Well, that made them all sit up and take notice.

I went out front and started digging up some four-o'clocks to plant around the P.O.

105 "Ah-ah-ah!" says Mama, raising the window. "Those happen to be my four-o'clocks. Everything planted in that star is mine. I've never known you to make anything grow in your life."

"Very well," I says. "But I take the fern. Even you, Mama, can't stand there

---

1. Nelson Eddy (1901–1967), opera singer who enjoyed phenomenal popularity in the 1930s and 1940s when he costarred in several film musicals with Jeanette MacDonald. The two were known as "America's Singing Sweethearts."

and deny that I'm the one watered that fern. And I happen to know where I can send in a box top and get a packet of one thousand mixed seeds, no two the same kind, free."

"Oh, where?" Mama wants to know.

But I says, "Too late. You 'tend to your house, and I'll 'tend to mine. You hear things like that all the time if you know how to listen to the radio. Perfectly marvelous offers. Get anything you want free."

So I hope to tell you I marched in and got that radio, and they could of all bit a nail in two, especially Stella-Rondo, that it used to belong to, and she well knew she couldn't get it back, I'd sue for it like a shot. And I very politely took the sewing-machine motor I helped pay the most on to give Mama for Christmas back in 1929, and a good big calendar, with the first-aid remedies on it. The thermometer and the Hawaiian ukulele certainly were rightfully mine, and I stood on the step-ladder and got all my watermelon-rind preserves and every fruit and vegetable I'd put up, every jar. Then I began to pull the tacks out of the bluebird wall vases on the archway to the dining room.

"Who told you you could have those, Miss Priss?" says Mama, fanning as hard as she could.

"I bought 'em and I'll keep track of 'em," I says. "I'll tack 'em up one on each side of the post-office window, and you can see 'em when you come to ask me for your mail, if you're so dead to see 'em."

"Not I! I'll never darken the door to that post office again if I live to be a hundred," Mama says. "Ungrateful child! After all the money we spent on you at the Normal.[2]"

"Me either," says Stella-Rondo. "You can just let my mail lie there and *rot*, for all I care. I'll never come and relieve you of a single, solitary piece."

"I should worry," I says. "And who you think's going to sit down and write you all those big fat letters and postcards, by the way? Mr. Whitaker? Just because he was the only man ever dropped down in China Grove and you got him—unfairly—is he going to sit down and write you a lengthy correspondence after you come home giving no rhyme nor reason whatsoever for your separation and no explanation for the presence of that child? I may not have your brilliant mind, but I fail to see it."

So Mama says, "Sister, I've told you a thousand times that Stella-Rondo simply got homesick, and this child is far too big to be hers," and she says, "Now, why don't you just sit down and play Casino?"

Then Shirley-T. sticks out her tongue at me in this perfectly horrible way. She has no more manners than the man in the moon. I told her she was going to cross her eyes like that some day and they'd stick.

"It's too late to stop me now," I says. "You should have tried that yesterday. I'm going to the P.O. and the only way you can possibly see me is to visit me there."

So Papa-Daddy says, "You'll never catch me setting foot in that post office,

2. I.e., normal school (teachers college).

even if I should take a notion into my head to write a letter some place." He says, "I won't have you reachin' out of that little old window with a pair of shears and cuttin' off any beard of mine. I'm too smart for you!"

"We all are," says Stella-Rondo.

120 But I said, "If you're so smart, where's Mr. Whitaker?"

So then Uncle Rondo says, "I'll thank you from now on to stop reading all the orders I get on postcards and telling everybody in China Grove what you think is the matter with them," but I says, "I draw my own conclusions and will continue in the future to draw them." I says, "If people want to write their innermost secrets on penny postcards, there's nothing in the wide world you can do about it, Uncle Rondo."

"And if you think we'll ever *write* another postcard you're sadly mistaken," says Mama.

"Cutting off your nose to spite your face then," I says. "But if you're all determined to have no more to do with the U.S. mail, think of this: What will Stella-Rondo do now, if she wants to tell Mr. Whitaker to come after her?"

"Wah!" says Stella-Rondo. I knew she'd cry. She had a conniption fit right there in the kitchen.

125 "It will be interesting to see how long she holds out," I says. "And now—I am leaving."

"Good-bye," says Uncle Rondo.

"Oh, I declare," says Mama, "to think that a family of mine should quarrel on the Fourth of July, or the day after, over Stella-Rondo leaving old Mr. Whitaker and having the sweetest little adopted child! It looks like we'd all be glad!"

"Wah!" says Stella-Rondo, and has a fresh conniption fit.

"He left *her*—you mark my words," I says. "That's Mr. Whitaker. I know Mr. Whitaker. After all, I knew him first. I said from the beginning he'd up and leave her. I foretold every single thing that's happened."

130 "Where did he go?" asks Mama.

"Probably to the North Pole, if he knows what's good for him," I says.

But Stella-Rondo just bawled and wouldn't say another word. She flew to her room and slammed the door.

"Now look what you've gone and done, Sister," says Mama. "You go apologize."

"I haven't the time, I'm leaving," I says.

135 "Well, what are you waiting around for?" asks Uncle Rondo.

So I just picked up the kitchen clock and marched off, without saying, "Kiss my foot," or anything, and never did tell Stella-Rondo good-bye.

There was a girl going along on a little wagon right in front.

"Girl," I says, "come help me haul these things down the hill, I'm going to live in the post office."

Took her nine trips in her express wagon. Uncle Rondo came out on the porch and threw her a nickel.

140 And that's the last I've laid eyes on any of my family or my family laid eyes on me for five solid days and nights. Stella-Rondo may be telling the most horri-

ble tales in the world about Mr. Whitaker, but I haven't heard them. As I tell everybody, I draw my own conclusions.

But oh, I like it here. It's ideal, as I've been saying. You see, I've got everything cater-cornered, the way I like it. Hear the radio? All the war news. Radio, sewing machine, book ends, ironing board and that great big piano lamp—peace, that's what I like. Butter-bean vines planted all along the front where the strings are.

Of course, there's not much mail. My family are naturally the main people in China Grove, and if they prefer to vanish from the face of the earth, for all the mail they get or the mail they write, why, I'm not going to open my mouth. Some of the folks here in town are taking up for me and some turned against me. I know which is which. There are always people who will quit buying stamps just to get on the right side of Papa-Daddy.

But here I am, and here I'll stay. I want the world to know I'm happy.

And if Stella-Rondo should come to me this minute, on bended knees, and *attempt* to explain the incidents of her life with Mr. Whitaker, I'd simply put my fingers in both my ears and refuse to listen.

1941

CHARLES BAXTER

Fenstad's Mother

On Sunday morning after communion Fenstad drove across town to visit his mother. Behind the wheel, he exhaled with his hand flat in front of his mouth to determine if the wine on his breath could be detected. He didn't think so. Fenstad's mother was a lifelong social progressive who was amused by her son's churchgoing, and, wine or no wine, she could guess where he had been. She had spent her life in the company of rebels and deviationists, and she recognized all their styles.

Passing a frozen pond in the city park, Fenstad slowed down to watch the skaters, many of whom he knew by name and skating style. From a distance they were dots of color ready for flight, frictionless. To express grief on skates seemed almost impossible, and Fenstad liked that. He parked his car on a residential block and took out his skates from the back seat, where he kept them all winter. With his fingertips he touched the wooden blade guards, thinking of the time. He checked his watch; he had fifteen minutes.

Out on the ice, still wearing his churchy Sunday-morning suit, tie, and over-coat, but now circling the outside edge of the pond with his bare hands in his overcoat pockets, Fenstad admired the overcast sky and luxuriated in the brittle cold. He was active and alert in winter but felt sleepy throughout the summer. He passed a little girl in a pink jacket, pushing a tiny chair over the ice. He waved to his friend Ann, an off-duty cop, practicing her twirls. He waved to other friends. Without exception they waved back. As usual, he was impressed by the way skates improved human character.

Twenty minutes later, in the doorway of her apartment, his mother said, "Your cheeks are red." She glanced down at his trousers, damp with melted snow. "You've been skating." She kissed him on the cheek and turned to walk into her living room. "Skating after church? Isn't that some sort of doctrinal error?"

5   "It's just happiness," Fenstad said. Quickly he checked her apartment for any signs of memory loss or depression. He found none and immediately felt relief. The apartment smelled of soap and Lysol, the signs of an old woman who wouldn't tolerate nonsense. Out on her coffee table, as usual, were the letters she was writing to her congressman and to political dictators around the globe. Fenstad's mother pleaded for enlightened behavior and berated the dictators for their bad political habits.

She grasped the arm of the sofa and let herself down slowly. Only then did she smile. "How's your soul, Harry?" she asked. "What's the news?"

He smiled back and smoothed his hair. Martin Luther King's eyes locked into his from the framed picture on the wall opposite him. In the picture King was shaking hands with Fenstad's mother, the two of them surrounded by smiling faces. "My soul's okay, Ma," he said. "It's a hard project. I'm always working on it." He reached down for a chocolate-chunk cookie from a box on top of the television. "Who brought you these?"

"Your daughter Sharon. She came to see me on Friday." Fenstad's mother tilted her head at him. "You *want* to be a good person, but she's the real article. Goodness comes to her without any effort at all. She says you have a new girlfriend. A pharmacist this time. Susan, is it?" Fenstad nodded. "Harry, why does your generation always have to find the right person? Why can't you learn to live with the wrong person? Sooner or later everyone's wrong. Love isn't the most important thing, Harry, far from it. Why can't you see that? I still don't comprehend why you couldn't live with Eleanor." Eleanor was Fenstad's ex-wife. They had been divorced for a decade, but Fenstad's mother hoped for a reconciliation.

"Come on, Ma," Fenstad said. "Over and done with, gone and gone." He took another cookie.

10   "You live with somebody so that you're living with *somebody*, and then you go out and do the work of the world. I don't understand all this pickiness about lovers. In a pinch anybody'll do, Harry, believe me."

On the side table was a picture of her late husband, Fenstad's mild, middle-of-the-road father. Fenstad glanced at the picture and let the silence hang between them before asking, "How are you, Ma?"

"I'm all right." She leaned back in the sofa, whose springs made a strange, almost human groan. "I want to get out. I spend too much time in this place in January. You should expand my horizons. Take me somewhere."

"Come to my composition class," Fenstad said. "I'll pick you up at dinnertime on Tuesday. Eat early."

"They'll notice me," she said, squinting. "I'm too old."

15   "I'll introduce you," her son said. "You'll fit right in."

Fenstad wrote brochures in the publicity department of a computer company during the day, and taught an extension English-composition class at the downtown campus of the state university two nights a week. He didn't need the money; he taught the class because he liked teaching strangers and because he enjoyed the sense of hope that classrooms held for him. This hopefulness and didacticism he had picked up from his mother.

On Tuesday night she was standing at the door of the retirement apartment building, dressed in a dark blue overcoat—her best. Her stylishness was belied slightly by a pair of old fuzzy red earmuffs. Inside the car Fenstad noticed that she had put on perfume, unusual for her. Leaning back, she gazed out contentedly at the nighttime lights.

"Who's in this group of students?" she asked. "Working-class people, I hope. Those are the ones you should be teaching. Anything else is just a career."

"Oh, they work, all right." He looked at his mother and saw, as they passed under a streetlight, a combination of sadness and delicacy in her face. Her usual mask of tough optimism seemed to be deserting her. He braked at a red light and said, "I have a hairdresser and a garage mechanic and a housewife, a Mrs. Nelson, and three guys who're sanitation workers. Plenty of others. One guy you'll really like is a young black man with glasses who sits in the back row and reads *Workers' Vanguard* and Bakunin[1] during class. He's brilliant. I don't know why he didn't test out of this class. His name's York Follette, and he's—"

"I want to meet him," she said quickly. She scowled at the moonlit snow. "A man with ideas. People like that have gone out of my life." She looked over at her son. "What I hate about being my age is how *nice* everyone tries to be. I was never nice, but now everybody is pelting me with sugar cubes." She opened her window an inch and let the cold air blow over her, ruffling her stiff gray hair.

When they arrived at the school, snow had started to fall, and at the other end of the parking lot a police car's flashing light beamed long crimson rays through the dense flakes. Fenstad's mother walked deliberately toward the door, shaking her head mistrustfully at the building and the police. Approaching the steps, she took her son's hand. "I liked the columns on the old buildings," she said, "the old university buildings, I mean. I liked Greek Revival better than this Modernist-bunker stuff." Inside, she blinked in the light at the smooth, waxed linoleum floors and cement-block walls. She held up her hand to shade her eyes. Fenstad took her elbow to guide her over the snow melting in puddles in the entryway. "I never asked you what you're teaching tonight."

"Logic," Fenstad said.

"Ah." She smiled and nodded. "Dialectics!"

"Not quite. Just logic."

She shrugged. She was looking at the clumps of students standing in the

20

25

1. *Workers' Vanguard* was an anarchist magazine published from 1932 to 1939 in New York. Its founders set out to "Americanize" the doctrines of Mikhail Bakunin (1814–1876), an anarchist and Russian revolutionary whose quarrel with Karl Marx split the European revolutionary movement apart, and to reform American society on the basis of industrial syndicates and decentralized communes.

glare of the hallway, drinking coffee from paper cups and smoking cigarettes in the general conversational din. She wasn't used to such noise: she stopped in the middle of the corridor underneath a wall clock and stared happily in no particular direction. With her eyes shut she breathed in the close air, smelling of wet overcoats and smoke, and Fenstad remembered how much his mother had always liked smoke-filled rooms, where ideas fought each other, and where some of those ideas died.

"Come on," he said, taking her hand again. Inside Fenstad's classroom six people sat in the angular postures of pre-boredom. York Follette was already in the back row, his copy of *Workers' Vanguard* shielding his face. Fenstad's mother headed straight for him and sat down in the desk next to his. Fenstad saw them shake hands, and in two minutes they were talking in low, rushed murmurs. He saw York Follette laugh quietly and nod. What was it that blacks saw and appreciated in his mother? They had always liked her—written to her, called her, checked up on her—and Fenstad wondered if they recognized something in his mother that he himself had never been able to see.

At seven thirty-five most of the students had arrived and were talking to each other vigorously, as if they didn't want Fenstad to start and thought they could delay him. He stared at them, and when they wouldn't quiet down, he made himself rigid and said, "Good evening. We have a guest tonight." Immediately the class grew silent. He held his arm out straight, indicating with a flick of his hand the old woman in the back row. "My mother," he said. "Clara Fenstad." For the first time all semester his students appeared to be paying attention: they turned around collectively and looked at Fenstad's mother, who smiled and waved. A few of the students began to applaud; others joined in. The applause was quiet but apparently genuine. Fenstad's mother brought herself slowly to her feet and made a suggestion of a bow. Two of the students sitting in front of her turned around and began to talk to her. At the front of the class Fenstad started his lecture on logic, but his mother wouldn't quiet down. This was a class for adults. They were free to do as they liked.

Lowering his head and facing the blackboard, Fenstad reviewed problems in logic, following point by point the outline set down by the textbook: *post hoc* fallacies, false authorities, begging the question, circular reasoning, *ad hominem* arguments, all the rest. Explaining these problems, his back turned, he heard sighs of boredom, boldly expressed. Occasionally he glanced at the back of the room. His mother was watching him carefully, and her face was expressing all the complexity of dismay. Dismay radiated from her. Her disappointment wasn't personal, because his mother didn't think that people as individuals were at fault for what they did. As usual, her disappointed hope was located in history and in the way people agreed with already existing histories.

She was angry with him for collaborating with grammar. She would call it unconsciously installed authority. Then she would find other names for it.

30 "All right," he said loudly, trying to make eye contact with someone in the room besides his mother, "let's try some examples. Can anyone tell me what, if anything, is wrong with the following sentence? 'I, like most people, have a unique problem.' "

The three sanitation workers, in the third row, began to laugh. Fenstad caught himself glowering and singled out the middle one.

"Yes, it is funny, isn't it?"

The man in the middle smirked and looked at the floor. "I was just thinking of my unique problem."

"Right," Fenstad said. "But what's wrong with saying, 'I, like most people, have a unique problem'?"

"Solving it?" This was Mrs. Nelson, who sat by the window so that she could gaze at the tree outside, lit by a streetlight. All through class she looked at the tree as if it were a lover. 35

"Solving what?"

"Solving the problem you have. What is the problem?"

"That's actually not what I'm getting at," Fenstad said. "Although it's a good *related* point. I'm asking what might be wrong logically with that sentence."

"It depends," Harold Ronson said. He worked in a service station and sometimes came to class wearing his work shirt with his name tag, HAROLD, stitched into it. "It depends on what your problem is. You haven't told us your problem."

"No," Fenstad said, "my problem is *not* the problem." He thought of Alice in Wonderland and felt, physically, as if he himself were getting small. "Let's try this again. What might be wrong with saying that most people have a unique problem?" 40

"You shouldn't be so critical," Timothy Melville said. "You should look on the bright side, if possible."

"What?"

"He's right," Mrs. Nelson said. "Most people have unique problems, but many people do their best to help themselves, such as taking night classes or working at meditation."

"No doubt that's true," Fenstad said. "But why can't most people have a unique problem?"

"Oh, I disagree," Mrs. Nelson said, still looking at her tree. Fenstad glanced at it and saw that it was crested with snow. It *was* beautiful. No wonder she looked at it. "I believe that most people do have unique problems. They just shouldn't talk about them all the time." 45

"Can anyone," Fenstad asked, looking at the back wall and hoping to see something there that was not wall, "can anyone give me an example of a unique problem?"

"Divorce," Barb Kjellerud said. She sat near the door and knitted during class. She answered questions without looking up. "Divorce is unique."

"No, it isn't!" Fenstad said, failing in the crucial moment to control his voice. He and his mother exchanged glances. In his mother's face for a split second was the history of her compassionate, ambivalent attention to him. "Divorce is not unique." He waited to calm himself. "It's everywhere. Now try again. Give me a unique problem."

Silence. "This is a trick question," Arlene Hubbly said. "I'm sure it's a trick question."

"Not necessarily. Does anyone know what *unique* means?" 50

"One of a kind," York Follette said, gazing at Fenstad with dry amusement. Sometimes he took pity on Fenstad and helped him out of jams. Fenstad's mother smiled and nodded.

"Right," Fenstad crowed, racing toward the blackboard as if he were about to write something. "So let's try again. Give me a unique problem."

"You give *us* a unique problem," one of the sanitation workers said. Fenstad didn't know whether he'd been given a statement or a command. He decided to treat it as a command.

"All right," he said. He stopped and looked down at his shoes. Maybe it *was* a trick question. He thought for ten seconds. Problem after problem presented itself to him. He thought of poverty, of the assaults on the earth, of the awful complexities of love. "I can't think of one," Fenstad said. His hands went into his pockets.

"That's because problems aren't personal," Fenstad's mother said from the back of the room. "They're collective." She waited while several students in the class sat up and nodded. "And people must work together on their solutions." She talked for another two minutes, taking the subject out of logic and putting it neatly in politics, where she knew it belonged.

The snow had stopped by the time the class was over. Fenstad took his mother's arm and escorted her to the car. After letting her down on the passenger side and starting the engine, he began to clear the front windshield. He didn't have a scraper and had forgotten his gloves, so he was using his bare hands. When he brushed the snow away on his mother's side, she looked out at him, surprised, a terribly aged Sleeping Beauty awakened against her will.

Once the car had warmed up, she was in a gruff mood and repositioned herself under the seat belt while making quiet but aggressive remarks. The sight of the new snow didn't seem to calm her. "Logic," she said at last. "That wasn't logic. Those are just rhetorical tactics. It's filler and drudgery."

"I don't want to discuss it now."

"All right. I'm sorry. Let's talk about something more pleasant."

They rode together in silence. Then she began to shake her head. "Don't take me home," she said. "I want to have a spot of tea somewhere before I go back. A nice place where they serve tea, all right?"

He parked outside an all-night restaurant with huge front plate-glass windows; it was called Country Bob's. He held his mother's elbow from the car to the door. At the door, looking back to make sure that he had turned off his headlights, he saw his tracks and his mother's in the snow. His were separate footprints, but hers formed two long lines.

Inside, at the table, she sipped her tea and gazed at her son for a long time. "Thanks for the adventure, Harry. I do appreciate it. What're you doing in class next week? Oh, I remember. How-to papers. That should be interesting."

"Want to come?"

"Very much. I'll keep quiet next time, if you want me to."

Fenstad shook his head. "It's okay. It's fun having you along. You can say whatever you want. The students loved you. I knew you'd be a sensation, and you were. They'd probably rather have you teaching the class than me."

He noticed that his mother was watching something going on behind him, and Fenstad turned around in the booth so that he could see what it was. At first all he saw was a woman, a young woman with long hair wet from snow and hanging in clumps, talking in the aisle to two young men, both of whom were nodding at her. Then she moved on to the next table. She spoke softly. Fenstad couldn't hear her words, but he saw the solitary customer to whom she was speaking shake his head once, keeping his eyes down. Then the woman saw Fenstad and his mother. In a moment she was standing in front of them.

She wore two green plaid flannel shirts and a thin torn jacket. Like Fenstad, she wore no gloves. Her jeans were patched, and she gave off a strong smell, something like hay, Fenstad thought, mixed with tar and sweat. He looked down at her feet and saw that she was wearing penny loafers with no socks. Coins, old pennies, were in both shoes; the leather was wet and cracked. He looked in the woman's face. Under a hat that seemed to collapse on either side of her head, the woman's face was thin and chalk-white except for the fatigue lines under her eyes. The eyes themselves were bright blue, beautiful, and crazy. To Fenstad, she looked desperate, percolating slightly with insanity, and he was about to say so to his mother when the woman bent down toward him and said, "Mister, can you spare any money?"

Involuntarily, Fenstad looked toward the kitchen, hoping that the manager would spot this person and take her away. When he looked back again, his mother was taking her blue coat off, wriggling in the booth to free her arms from the sleeves. Stopping and starting again, she appeared to be stuck inside the coat; then she lifted herself up, trying to stand, and with a quick, quiet groan slipped the coat off. She reached down and folded the coat over and held it toward the woman. "Here," she said. "Here's my coat. Take it before my son stops me."

"Mother, you can't." Fenstad reached forward to grab the coat, but his mother pulled it away from him.

When Fenstad looked back at the woman, her mouth was open, showing several gray teeth. Her hands were outstretched, and he understood, after a moment, that this was a posture of refusal, a gesture saying no, and that the woman wasn't used to it and did it awkwardly. Fenstad's mother was standing and trying to push the coat toward the woman, not toward her hands but lower, at waist level, and she was saying, "Here, here, here, here." The sound, like a human birdcall, frightened Fenstad, and he stood up quickly, reached for his wallet, and removed the first two bills he could find, two twenties. He grabbed the woman's chapped, ungloved left hand.

"Take these," he said, putting the two bills in her icy palm, "for the love of God, and please go."

He was close to her face. Tonight he would pray for her. For a moment the woman's expression was vacant. His mother was still pushing the coat at her, and the woman was unsteadily bracing herself. The woman's mouth was open, and her stagnant-water breath washed over him. "I know you," she said. "You're my little baby cousin."

"Go away, please," Fenstad said. He pushed at her. She turned, clutching his money. He reached around to put his hands on his mother's shoulders. "Ma," he said, "she's gone now. Mother, sit down. I gave her money for a coat." His mother fell down on her side of the booth, and her blue coat rolled over on the bench beside her, showing the label and the shiny inner lining. When he looked up, the woman who had been begging had disappeared, though he could still smell her odor, an essence of wretchedness.

"Excuse me, Harry," his mother said. "I have to go to the bathroom."

She rose and walked toward the front of the restaurant, turned a corner, and was out of sight. Fenstad sat and tried to collect himself. When the waiter came, a boy with an earring and red hair in a flattop, Fenstad just shook his head and said, "More tea." He realized that his mother hadn't taken off her earmuffs, and the image of his mother in the ladies' room with her earmuffs on gave him a fit of uneasiness. After getting up from the booth and following the path that his mother had taken, he stood outside the ladies'-room door and, when no one came in or out, he knocked. He waited for a decent interval. Still hearing no answer, he opened the door.

His mother was standing with her arms down on either side of the first sink. She was holding herself there, her eyes following the hot water as it poured from the tap around the bright porcelain sink down into the drain, and she looked furious. Fenstad touched her and she snapped toward him.

"Your logic!" she said.

He opened the door for her and helped her back to the booth. The second cup of tea had been served, and Fenstad's mother sipped it in silence. They did not converse. When she had finished, she said, "All right. I do feel better now. Let's go."

At the curb in front of her apartment building he leaned forward and kissed her on the cheek. "Pick me up next Tuesday," she said. "I want to go back to that class." He nodded. He watched as she made her way past the security guard at the front desk; then he put his car into drive and started home.

That night he skated in the dark for an hour with his friend, Susan, the pharmacist. She was an excellent skater; they had met on the ice. She kept late hours and, like Fenstad, enjoyed skating at night. She listened attentively to his story about his mother and the woman in the restaurant. To his great relief she recommended no course of action. She listened. She didn't believe in giving advice, even when asked.

The following Tuesday, Fenstad's mother was again in the back row next to York Follette. One of the fluorescent lights overhead was flickering, which gave the room, Fenstad thought, a sinister quality, like a debtors' prison or a refuge for the homeless. He'd been thinking about such people for the entire week. For seven days now he had caught whiffs of the woman's breath in the air, and one morning, Friday, he thought he caught a touch of the rotten-celery smell on his own breath, after a particularly difficult sales meeting.

Tonight was how-to night. The students were expected to stand at the front of the class and read their papers, instructing their peers and answering questions if necessary. Starting off, and reading her paper in a frightened monotone, Mrs. Nelson told the class how to bake a cheese soufflé. Arlene Hubbly's paper was about mushroom hunting. Fenstad was put off by the introduction. "The advantage to mushrooms," Arlene Hubbly read, "is that they are delicious. The disadvantage to mushrooms is that they can make you sick, even die." But then she explained how to recognize the common shaggymane by its cylindrical cap and dark tufts; she drew a model on the board. She warned the class against the *Clitocybe illudens*, the Jack-o'-Lantern. "Never eat a mushroom like this one or *any* mushroom that glows in the dark. Take heed!" she said, fixing her gaze on the class. Fenstad saw his mother taking rapid notes. Harold Ronson, the mechanic, reading his own prose painfully and slowly, told the class how to get rust spots out of their automobiles. Again Fenstad noticed his mother taking notes. York Follette told the class about the proper procedures for laying down attic insulation and how to know when enough was enough, so that a homeowner wouldn't be robbed blind, as he put it, by the salesmen, in whose ranks he had once counted himself.

Barb Kjellerud had brought along a cassette player, and told the class that her hobby was ballroom dancing; she would instruct them in the basic waltz. She pushed the play button on the tape machine, and "Tales from the Vienna Woods" came booming out. To the accompaniment of the music she read her paper, illustrating, as she went, how the steps were to be performed. She danced alone in front of them, doing so with flair. Her blond hair swayed as she danced, Fenstad noticed. She looked a bit like a contestant in a beauty contest who had too much personality to win. She explained to the men the necessity of leading. Someone had to lead, she said, and tradition had given this responsibility to the male. Fenstad heard his mother snicker.

When Barb Kjellerud asked for volunteers, Fenstad's mother raised her hand. She said she knew how to waltz and would help out. At the front of the class she made a counterclockwise motion with her hand, and for the next minute, sitting at the back of the room, Fenstad watched his mother and one of the sanitation workers waltzing under the flickering fluorescent lights.

"What a wonderful class," Fenstad's mother said on the way home. "I hope you're paying attention to what they tell you."

Fenstad nodded. "Tea?" he asked.

She shook her head. "Where're you going after you drop me off?"

"Skating," he said. "I usually go skating. I have a date."

"With the pharmacist? In the dark?"

"We both like it, Ma." As he drove, he made an all-purpose gesture. "The moon and the stars," he said simply.

When he left her off, he felt unsettled. He considered, as a point of courtesy, staying with her a few minutes, but by the time he had this idea he was already away from the building and was headed down the street.

He and Susan were out on the ice together, skating in large circles, when Susan pointed to a solitary figure sitting on a park bench near the lake's edge. The sky had cleared; the moon gave everything a cold, fine-edged clarity. When Fenstad followed the line of Susan's finger, he saw at once that the figure on the bench was his mother. He realized it simply because of the way she sat there, drawn into herself, attentive even in the winter dark. He skated through the uncleared snow over the ice until he was standing close enough to speak to her. "Mother," he said, "what are you doing here?"

She was bundled up, a thick woolen cap drawn over her head, and two scarves covering much of her face. He could see little other than the two lenses of her glasses facing him in the dark. "I wanted to see you two," she told him. "I thought you'd look happy, and you did. I like to watch happiness. I always have."

"How can you see us? We're so far away."

"That's how I saw you."

This made no sense to him, so he asked, "How'd you get here?"

"I took a cab. That part was easy."

"Aren't you freezing?"

"I don't know. I don't know if I'm freezing or not."

He and Susan took her back to her apartment as soon as they could get their boots on. In the car Mrs. Fenstad insisted on asking Susan what kind of safety procedures were used to ensure that drugs weren't smuggled out of pharmacies and sold illegally, but she didn't appear to listen to the answer, and by the time they reached her building, she seemed to be falling asleep. They helped her up to her apartment. Susan thought that they should give her a warm bath before putting her into bed, and, together, they did. She did not protest. She didn't even seem to notice them as they guided her in and out of the bathtub.

Fenstad feared that his mother would catch some lung infection, and it turned out to be bronchitis, which kept her in her apartment for the first three weeks of February, until her cough went down. Fenstad came by every other day to see how she was, and one Tuesday, after work, he went up to her floor and heard piano music: an old recording, which sounded much-played, of the brightest and fastest jazz piano he had ever heard—music of superhuman brilliance. He swung open the door to her apartment and saw York Follette sitting near his mother's bed. On the bedside table was a small tape player, from which the music poured into the room.

Fenstad's mother was leaning back against the pillow, smiling, her eyes closed.

Follette turned toward Fenstad. He had been talking softly. He motioned toward the tape machine and said, "Art Tatum.[2] It's a cut called 'Battery Bounce.' Your mother's never heard it."

"Jazz, Harry," Fenstad's mother said, her eyes still closed, not needing to see her son. "York is explaining to me about Art Tatum and jazz. Next week he's

_____

2. Art Tatum (1910–1956), jazz pianist renowned for his harmonic imagination and extravagant virtuosity.

going to try something more progressive on me." Now his mother opened her eyes. "Have you ever heard such music before, Harry?"

They were both looking at him. "No," he said, "I never heard anything like it."

"This is my unique problem, Harry." Fenstad's mother coughed and then waited to recover her breath. "I never heard enough jazz." She smiled. "What glimpses!" she said at last. 105

After she recovered, he often found her listening to the tape machine that York Follette had given her. She liked to hear the Oscar Peterson[3] Trio as the sun set and the lights of evening came on. She now often mentioned glimpses. Back at home, every night, Fenstad spoke about his mother in his prayers of remembrance and thanksgiving, even though he knew she would disapprove.

1990

DORIS LESSING

Our Friend Judith

I stopped inviting Judith to meet people when a Canadian woman remarked, with the satisfied fervour of one who has at last pinned a label on a rare specimen: "She is, of course, one of your typical English spinsters."

This was a few weeks after an American sociologist, having elicited from Judith the facts that she was fortyish, unmarried, and living alone, had enquired of me: "I suppose she has given up?" "Given up what?" I asked; and the subsequent discussion was unrewarding.

Judith did not easily come to parties. She would come after pressure, not so much—one felt—to do one a favour, but in order to correct what she believed to be a defect in her character. "I really ought to enjoy meeting new people more than I do," she said once. We reverted to an earlier pattern of our friendship: odd evenings together, an occasional visit to the cinema, or she would telephone to say: "I'm on my way past you to the British Museum. Would you care for a cup of coffee with me? I have twenty minutes to spare."

It is characteristic of Judith that the word "spinster," used of her, provoked fascinated speculation about other people. There are my aunts, for instance: aged seventy-odd, both unmarried, one an ex-missionary from China, one a retired matron of a famous London hospital. These two old ladies live together under the shadow of the cathedral in a country town. They devote much time to the Church, to good causes, to letter writing with friends all over the world, to the grandchildren and the great-grandchildren of relatives. It would be a mistake, however, on entering a house in which nothing has been moved for fifty years, to diagnose a condition of fossilised late-Victorian integrity. They read

3. Oscar Peterson (b. 1925), jazz pianist and composer, greatly influenced by Tatum.

every book review in the *Observer* or the *Times*,[1] so that I recently got a letter from Aunt Rose enquiring whether I did not think that the author of *On the Road*[2] was not—perhaps?—exaggerating his difficulties. They know a good deal about music, and write letters of encouragement to young composers they feel are being neglected—"You must understand that anything new and original takes time to be understood." Well-informed and critical Tories, they are as likely to dispatch telegrams of protest to the Home Secretary[3] as letters of support. These ladies, my aunts Emily and Rose, are surely what is meant by the phrase "English spinster." And yet, once the connection has been pointed out, there is no doubt that Judith and they are spiritual cousins, if not sisters. Therefore it follows that one's pitying admiration for women who have supported manless and uncomforted lives needs a certain modification?

One will, of course, never know; and I feel now that it is entirely my fault that I shall never know. I had been Judith's friend for upward of five years before the incident occurred which I involuntarily thought of—stupidly enough—as the first time Judith's mask slipped.

A mutual friend, Betty, had been given a cast-off Dior[4] dress. She was too short for it. Also she said: "It's not a dress for a married woman with three children and a talent for cooking. I don't know why not, but it isn't." Judith was the right build. Therefore one evening the three of us met by appointment in Judith's bedroom, with the dress. Neither Betty nor I was surprised at the renewed discovery that Judith was beautiful. We had both often caught each other, and ourselves, in moments of envy when Judith's calm and severe face, her undemonstratively perfect body, succeeded in making everyone else in a room or a street look cheap.

Judith is tall, small-breasted, slender. Her light brown hair is parted in the centre and cut straight around her neck. A high straight forehead, straight nose, a full grave mouth are setting for her eyes, which are green, large and prominent. Her lids are very white, fringed with gold, and moulded close over the eyeball, so that in profile she has the look of a staring gilded mask. The dress was of dark green glistening stuff, cut straight, with a sort of loose tunic. It opened simply at the throat. In it Judith could of course evoke nothing but classical images. Diana, perhaps, back from the hunt, in a relaxed moment? A rather intellectual wood nymph who had opted for an afternoon in the British Museum Reading Room? Something like that. Neither Betty nor I said a word, since Judith was examining herself in a long mirror, and must know she looked magnificent.

Slowly she drew off the dress and laid it aside. Slowly she put on the old cord skirt and woollen blouse she had taken off. She must have surprised a resigned glance between us, for she then remarked, with the smallest of mocking smiles: "One surely ought to stay in character, wouldn't you say?" She added,

---

1. Prestigious London newspapers representing roughly the younger, more liberal establishment and the Establishment proper, respectively. 2. Jack Kerouac (1922–1969), a leading writer of the Beat Generation, 1950s forerunners of the hippies. Kerouac heroes felt themselves completely cut off from and victimized by American society. 3. Head of the British government department responsible for domestic matters. 4. Famous French designer of high fashions.

reading the words out of some invisible book, written not by her, since it was a very vulgar book, but perhaps by one of us: "It does everything *for* me, I must admit."

"After seeing you in it," Betty cried out, defying her, "I can't bear for anyone else to have it. I shall simply put it away." Judith shrugged, rather irritated. In the shapeless skirt and blouse, and without makeup, she stood smiling at us, a woman at whom forty-nine out of fifty people would not look twice.

A second revelatory incident occurred soon after. Betty telephoned me to say that Judith had a kitten. Did I know that Judith adored cats? "No, but of course she would," I said.

Betty lived in the same street as Judith and saw more of her than I did. I was kept posted about the growth and habits of the cat and its effect on Judith's life. She remarked for instance that she felt it was good for her to have a tie and some responsibility. But no sooner was the cat out of kittenhood than all the neighbours complained. It was a tomcat, ungelded, and making every night hideous. Finally the landlord said that either the cat or Judith must go, unless she was prepared to have the cat "fixed."[5] Judith wore herself out trying to find some person, anywhere in Britain, who would be prepared to take the cat. This person would, however, have to sign a written statement not to have the cat "fixed." When Judith took the cat to the vet to be killed, Betty told me she cried for twenty-four hours.

"She didn't think of compromising? After all, perhaps the cat might have preferred to live, if given the choice?"

"Is it likely I'd have the nerve to say anything so sloppy to Judith? It's the nature of a male cat to rampage lustfully about, and therefore it would be morally wrong for Judith to have the cat fixed, simply to suit her own convenience."

"She said that?"

"She wouldn't have to *say* it, surely?"

A third incident was when she allowed a visiting young American, living in Paris, the friend of a friend and scarcely known to her, to use her flat while she visited her parents over Christmas. The young man and his friends lived it up for ten days of alcohol and sex and marijuana, and when Judith came back it took a week to get the place clean again and the furniture mended. She telephoned twice to Paris, the first time to say that he was a disgusting young thug and if he knew what was good for him he would keep out of her way in the future; the second time to apologise for losing her temper. "I had a choice either to let someone use my flat, or to leave it empty. But having chosen that you should have it, it was clearly an unwarrantable infringement of your liberty to make any conditions at all. I do most sincerely ask your pardon." The moral aspects of the matter having been made clear, she was irritated rather than not to receive letters of apology from him—fulsome, embarrassed, but above all, baffled.

It was the note of curiosity in the letters—he even suggested coming over to

5. Gelded, castrated.

get to know her better—that irritated her most. "What do you suppose he means?" she said to me. "He lived in my flat for ten days. One would have thought that should be enough, wouldn't you?"

The facts about Judith, then, are all in the open, unconcealed, and plain to anyone who cares to study them; or, as it became plain she feels, to anyone with the intelligence to interpret them.

She has lived for the last twenty years in a small two-roomed flat high over a busy West London street. The flat is shabby and badly heated. The furniture is old, was never anything but ugly, is now frankly rickety and fraying. She has an income of two hundred pounds[6] a year from a dead uncle. She lives on this and what she earns from her poetry, and from lecturing on poetry to night classes and extramural university classes.

She does not smoke or drink, and eats very little, from preference, not self-discipline.

She studied poetry and biology at Oxford, with distinction.

She is a Castlewell. That is, she is a member of one of the academic upper-middleclass families, which have been producing for centuries a steady supply of brilliant but sound men and women who are the backbone of the arts and sciences in Britain. She is on cool good terms with her family, who respect her and leave her alone.

She goes on long walking tours, by herself, in such places as Exmoor or West Scotland.

Every three or four years she publishes a volume of poems.

The walls of her flat are completely lined with books. They are scientific, classical and historical; there is a great deal of poetry and some drama. There is not one novel. When Judith says: "Of course I don't read novels," this does not mean that novels have no place, or a small place, in literature; or that people should not read novels; but that it must be obvious she can't be expected to read novels.

I had been visiting her flat for years before I noticed two long shelves of books, under a window, each shelf filled with the works of a single writer. The two writers are not, to put it at the mildest, the kind one would associate with Judith. They are mild, reminiscent, vague and whimsical. Typical English *belles-lettres*, in fact, and by definition abhorrent to her. Not one of the books in the two shelves has been read; some of the pages are still uncut. Yet each book is inscribed or dedicated to her: gratefully, admiringly, sentimentally and, more than once, amorously. In short, it is open to anyone who cares to examine these two shelves, and to work out dates, to conclude that Judith from the age of fifteen to twenty-five had been the beloved young companion of one elderly literary gentleman, and from twenty-five to thirty-five the inspiration of another.

During all that time she had produced her own poetry, and the sort of poetry, it is quite safe to deduce, not at all likely to be admired by her two admirers. Her poems are always cool and intellectual; that is their form, which is contra-

6. About one-third or even one-half of a subsistence income.

dicted or supported by a gravely sensuous texture. They are poems to read often; one has to, to understand them.

I did not ask Judith a direct question about these two eminent but rather fusty lovers. Not because she would not have answered, or because she would have found the question impertinent, but because such questions are clearly unnecessary. Having those two shelves of books where they are, and books she could not conceivably care for, for their own sake, is publicly giving credit where credit is due. I can imagine her thinking the thing over, and deciding it was only fair, or perhaps honest, to place the books there; and this despite the fact that she would not care at all for the same attention be paid to her. There is something almost contemptuous in it. For she certainly despises people who feel they need attention.

For instance, more than once a new emerging wave of "modern" young poets have discovered her as the only "modern" poet among their despised and well-credited elders. This is because, since she began writing at fifteen, her poems have been full of scientific, mechanical and chemical imagery. This is how she thinks, or feels.

More than once has a young poet hastened to her flat, to claim her as an ally, only to find her totally and by instinct unmoved by words like "modern," "new," "contemporary." He has been outraged and wounded by her principle, so deeply rooted as to be unconscious, and to need no expression but a contemptuous shrug of the shoulders, that publicity seeking or to want critical attention is despicable. It goes without saying that there is perhaps one critic in the world she has any time for. He has sulked off, leaving her on her shelf, which she takes it for granted is her proper place, to be read by an appreciative minority.

Meanwhile she gives her lectures, walks alone through London, writes her poems, and is seen sometimes at a concert or a play with a middleaged professor of Greek, who has a wife and two children.

Betty and I had speculated about this professor, with such remarks as: Surely she must sometimes be lonely? Hasn't she ever wanted to marry? What about that awful moment when one comes in from somewhere at night to an empty flat?

It happened recently that Betty's husband was on a business trip, her children visiting, and she was unable to stand the empty house. She asked Judith for a refuge until her own home filled again.

Afterwards Betty rang me up to report: "Four of the five nights Professor Adams came in about ten or so."

"Was Judith embarrassed?"

"Would you expect her to be?"

"Well, if not embarrassed, at least conscious there was a situation?"

"No, not at all. But I must say I don't think he's good enough for her. He can't possibly understand her. He calls her Judy."

"Good God."

"Yes. But I was wondering. Suppose the other two called her Judy—'little Judy'—imagine it! Isn't it awful? But it does rather throw a light on Judith?"

"It's rather touching."

"I suppose it's touching. But *I* was embarrassed—oh, not because of the situation. Because of how she was, with him. 'Judy, is there another cup of tea in that pot?' And she, rather daughterly and demure, pouring him one."

"Well yes, I can see how you felt."

"Three of the nights he went to her bedroom with her—very casual about it, because she was being. But he was not there in the mornings. So I asked her. You know how it is when you ask her a question. As if you've been having long conversations on that very subject for years and years, and she is merely continuing where you left off last. So when she says something surprising, one feels such a fool to be surprised?"

45   "Yes. And then?"

"I asked her if she was sorry not to have children. She said yes, but one couldn't have everything."

"One can't have everything, she said?"

"Quite clearly feeling she *has* nearly everything. She said she thought it was a pity, because she would have brought up children very well."

"When you come to think of it, she would, too."

50   "I asked about marriage, but she said on the whole the role of a mistress suited her better."

"She used the word 'mistress'?"

"You must admit it's the accurate word."

"I suppose so."

"And then she said that while she liked intimacy and sex and everything, she enjoyed waking up in the morning alone and *her own person.*"

55   "Yes, *of course.*"

"Of course. But now she's bothered because the professor would like to marry her. Or he feels he ought. At least, he's getting all guilty and obsessive about it. She says she doesn't see the point of divorce, and anyway, surely it would be very hard on his poor old wife after all these years, particularly after bringing up two children so satisfactorily. She talks about his wife as if she's a kind of nice old charwoman, and it wouldn't be *fair* to sack her, you know. Anyway. What with one thing and another. Judith's going off to Italy soon in order *to collect herself.*"

"But how's she going to pay for it?"

"Luckily the Third Programme's[7] commissioning her to do some arty programmes. They offered her a choice of The Cid—El Thid[8] you know—and the Borgias. Well, the Borghese, then. And Judith settled for the Borgias."

"The Borgias," I said, *"Judith?"*

60   "Yes, quite. I said that too, in that tone of voice. She saw my point. She says the epic is right up her street, whereas the Renaissance has never been on her wave length. Obviously it couldn't be, all the magnificence and cruelty and *dirt.*

---

7. British Broadcasting Corporation public radio service (and now also television channel) specializing in classical music, literature and plays, lectures, etc.   8. Castilian, standard Spanish, pronunciation of El Cid (rhymes with *steed*), the title of an 11th-century soldier-hero and hero of many works of literature.

But of course chivalry and a high moral code and all those idiotically noble goings-on are right on her wave length."

"Is the money the same?"

"Yes. But is it likely Judith would let money decide? No, she said that one should always choose something new, that isn't up one's street. Well, because it's better for her character, and so on, to get herself unsettled by the Renaissance. She didn't say *that*, of course."

"Of course not."

Judith went to Florence; and for some months postcards informed us tersely of her doings. Then Betty decided she must go by herself for a holiday. She had been appalled by the discovery that if her husband was away for a night she couldn't sleep; and when he went to Australia for three weeks, she stopped living until he came back. She had discussed this with him, and he had agreed that if she really felt the situation to be serious, he would despatch her by air, to Italy, in order to recover her self-respect. As she put it.

I got this letter from her: "It's no use, I'm coming home. I might have known. Better face it, once you're really married you're not fit for man nor beast. And if you remember what I used to be like! *Well!* I moped around Milan. I sunbathed in Venice, then I thought my tan was surely worth something, so I was on the point of starting an affair with another lonely soul, but I lost heart, and went to Florence to see Judith. She wasn't there. She'd gone to the Italian Riviera. I had nothing better to do, so I followed her. When I saw the place I wanted to laugh, it's so much not Judith, you know, all those palms and umbrellas and gaiety at all costs and ever such an ornamental blue sea. Judith is in an enormous stone room up on the hillside above the sea, with grape vines all over the place. You should see her, she's got beautiful. It seems for the last fifteen years she's been going to Soho[9] every Saturday morning to buy food at an Italian shop. I must have looked surprised, because she explained she liked Soho. I suppose because all that dreary vice and nudes and prostitutes and everything prove how right she is to be as she is? She told the people in the shop she was going to Italy, and the *signora*[1] said, what a coincidence, she was going back to Italy too, and she did hope an old friend like Miss Castlewell would visit her there. Judith said to me: 'I felt lacking, when she used the word friend. Our relations have always been formal. Can you understand it?' she said to me. 'For fifteen years,' I said to her. She said: 'I think I must feel it's a kind of imposition, don't you know, expecting people to feel friendship for one.' *Well.* I said: 'You ought to understand it, because you're like that yourself.' 'Am I?' she said. 'Well, think about it,' I said. But I could see she didn't want to think about it. Anyway, she's here, and I've spent a week with her. The widow Maria Rineiri inherited her mother's house, so she came home, from Soho. On the ground floor is a tatty little *rosticceria*[2] patronised by the neighbours. They are all working people. This isn't tourist country, up on the hill. The widow lives above the shop with her little

65

9. A section of London roughly equivalent to Greenwich Village in New York—foreign restaurants and groceries, haunt of writers, painters, etc.—but in recent years increasingly known for prostitutes and pornography. 1. Proprietress. 2. Grill.

boy, a nasty little brat of about ten. Say what you like, the English are the only people who know how to bring up children, I don't care if that's insular. Judith's room is at the back, with a balcony. Underneath her room is the barber's shop, and the barber is Luigi Rineiri, the widow's younger brother. Yes, I was keeping him until the last. He is about forty, tall dark handsome, a great *bull*, but rather a sweet fatherly bull. He has cut Judith's hair and made it lighter. Now it looks like a sort of gold helmet. Judith is all brown. The widow Rineiri has made her a white dress and a green dress. They fit, for a change. When Judith walks down the street to the lower town, all the Italian males take one look at the golden girl and melt in their own oil like ice cream. Judith takes all this in her stride. She sort of acknowledges the homage. Then she strolls into the sea and vanishes into the foam. She swims five miles every day. *Naturally.* I haven't asked Judith whether she has collected herself, because you can see she hasn't. The widow Rineiri is matchmaking. When I noticed this I wanted to laugh, but luckily I didn't because Judith asked me, really wanting to know: 'Can you see me married to an Italian barber?' (Not being snobbish, but stating the position, so to speak.) 'Well yes,' I said, 'you're the only women I know who I can see married to an Italian barber.' Because it wouldn't matter who she married, she'd always be her *own person.* 'At any rate, for a time,' I said. At which she said, asperously,[3] 'You can use phrases like for a time in England but not in Italy.' Did you ever see England, at least London, as the home of licence, liberty and free love? No, neither did I, but of course she's right. Married to Luigi it would be the family, the neighbours, the church and the *bambini.*[4] All the same she's thinking about it, believe it or not. Here she's quite different, all relaxed and free. She's melting in the attention she gets. The widow mothers her and makes her coffee all the time, and listens to a lot of good advice about how to bring up that nasty brat of hers. Unluckily she doesn't take it. Luigi is crazy for her. At mealtimes she goes to the *trattoria*[5] in the upper square and all the workmen treat her like a goddess. Well, a film star then. I said to her, you're mad to come home. For one thing her rent is ten bob[6] a week, and you eat *pasta* and drink red wine till you bust for about one and sixpence. No, she said, it would be nothing but self-indulgence to stay. Why? I said. She said, she's got nothing to stay for. (Ho ho.) And besides, she's done her research on the Borghese, though so far she can't see her way to an honest presentation of the facts. What made these people tick? she wants to know. And so she's only staying because of the cat. I forgot to mention the cat. This is a town of cats. The Italians here love their cats. I wanted to feed a stray cat at the table, but the waiter said no; and after lunch, all the waiters came with trays crammed with leftover food and stray cats came from everywhere to eat. And at dark when the tourists go in to feed and the beach is empty—you know how empty and forlorn a beach is at dusk?—well cats appear from everywhere. The beach seems to move, then you see it's cats. They go stalking along the thin inch of grey water at the edge of the sea, shaking their paws crossly at each step, snatching at the dead little fish, and throwing them with their mouths up on to

3. Sharply, harshly. 4. Children. 5. Inexpensive restaurant. 6. Shillings. There are 20 shillings to the pound; *one and sixpence* below is one and a half shillings.

the dry stand. Then they scamper after them. You've never seen such a snarling and fighting. At dawn when the fishing boats come in to the empty beach, the cats are there in dozens. The fisherman throw them bits of fish. The cats snarl and fight over it. Judith gets up early and goes down to watch. Sometimes Luigi goes too, being tolerant. Because what he really likes is to join the evening promenade with Judith on his arm around and around the square of the upper town. Showing her off. Can you *see* Judith? But she does it. Being tolerant. But she smiles and enjoys the attention she gets, there's no doubt about it.

"She has a cat in her room. It's a kitten really, but it's pregnant. Judith says she can't leave until the kittens are born. The cat is too young to have kittens. Imagine Judith. She sits on her bed in that great stone room, with her bare feet on the stone floor, and watches the cat, and tries to work out why a healthy uninhibited Italian cat always fed on the best from the *rosticceria* should be neurotic. Because it is. When it sees Judith watching it gets nervous and starts licking at the roots of its tail. But Judith goes on watching, and says about Italy that the reason why the English love the Italians is because the Italians make the English feel superior. They have no discipline. And that's a despicable reason for one nation to love another. Then she talks about Luigi and says he has no sense of guilt, but a sense of sin; whereas she has no sense of sin but she has guilt. I haven't asked her if this has been an insuperable barrier, because judging from how she looks, it hasn't. She says she would rather have a sense of sin, because sin can be atoned for, and if she understood sin, perhaps she would be more at home with the Renaissance. Luigi is very healthy, she says, and not neurotic. He is a Catholic of course. He doesn't mind that she's an atheist. His mother has explained to him that the English are all pagans, but good people at heart. I suppose he thinks a few smart sessions with the local priest would set Judith on the right path for good and all. Meanwhile the cat walks nervously around the room, stopping to lick, and when it can't stand Judith watching it another second, it rolls over on the floor, with its paws tucked up, and rolls up its eyes, and Judith scratches its lumpy pregnant stomach and tells it to relax. It makes *me* nervous to see her, it's not like her, I don't know why. Then Luigi shouts up from the barber's shop, then he comes up and stands at the door laughing, and Judith laughs, and the widow says: Children, enjoy yourselves. And off they go, walking down to the town eating ice cream. The cat follows them. It won't let Judith out of its sight, like a dog. When she swims miles out to sea, the cat hides under a beach hut until she comes back. Then she carries it back up the hill, because that nasty little boy chases it. *Well.* I'm coming home tomorrow thank God, to my dear old Billy, I was mad ever to leave him. There is something about Judith and Italy that has upset me, I don't know what. The point is, what on earth can Judith and Luigi *talk* about? Nothing. How can they? And of course it doesn't matter. So I turn out to be a prude as well. See you next week."

It was my turn for a dose of the sun, so I didn't see Betty. On my way back from Rome I stopped off in Judith's resort and walked up through narrow streets to the upper town, where, in the square with the vine-covered *trattoria* at the corner, was a house with ROSTICCERIA written in black paint on a cracked wooden board over a low door. There was a door curtain of red beads, and flies settled on the beads. I opened the beads with my hands and looked into a small dark room with a stone counter. Loops of salami hung from metal hooks. A glass bell covered some plates of cooked meats. There were flies on the salami and on the glass bell. A few tins on the wooden shelves, a couple of pale loaves, some wine casks and an open case of sticky pale green grapes covered with fruit flies seemed to be the only stock. A single wooden table with two chairs stood in a corner, and two workmen sat there, eating lumps of sausage and bread. Through another bead curtain at the back came a short, smoothly fat, slender-limbed woman with greying hair. I asked for Miss Castlewell, and her face changed. She said in an offended, offhand way: "Miss Castlewell left last week." She took a white cloth from under the counter, and flicked at the flies on the glass bell. "I'm a friend of hers," I said, and she said: Si,[7] and put her hands palm down on the counter and looked at me, expressionless. The workmen got up, gulped down the last of their wine, nodded and went. She ciao'd[8] them; and looked back at me. Then, since I didn't go, she called: "Luigi!" A shout came from the back room, there was a rattle of beads, and in came first a wiry sharp-faced boy, and then Luigi. He was tall, heavy-shouldered, and his black rough hair was like a cap, pulled low over his brows. He looked good-natured, but at the moment uneasy. His sister said something, and he stood beside her, an ally, and confirmed: "Miss Castlewell went away." I was on the point of giving up, when through the bead curtain that screened off a dazzling light eased a thin tabby cat. It was ugly and it walked uncomfortably, with its back quarters bunched up. The child suddenly let out a "Sssss" through his teeth, and the cat froze. Luigi said something sharp to the child, and something encouraging to the cat, which sat down, looked straight in front of it, then began frantically licking at its flanks. "Miss Castlewell was offended with us," said Mrs. Rineiri suddenly, and with dignity. "She left early one morning. We did not expect her to go." I said: "Perhaps she had to go home and finish some work."

Mrs. Rineiri shrugged, then sighed. Then she exchanged a hard look with her brother. Clearly the subject had been discussed, and closed forever.

"I've known Judith a long time," I said, trying to find the right note. "She's a remarkable woman. She's a poet." But there was no response to this at all. Meanwhile the child, with a fixed bared-teeth grin, was staring at the cat, narrowing his eyes. Suddenly he let out another "Sssssss" and added a short high yelp. The cat shot backwards, hit the wall, tried desperately to claw its way up the wall, came to its senses and again sat down and began its urgent, undirected licking at its fur. This time Luigi cuffed the child, who yelped in earnest, and then ran out into the street past the cat. Now that the way was clear the cat shot across the floor, up onto the counter, and bounded past Luigi's shoulder and straight through the bead curtain into the barber's shop, where it landed with a thud.

"Judith was sorry when she left us," said Mrs. Rineiri uncertainly. "She was crying."

"I'm sure she was."

7. "Yes."   8. Said goodbye to.

"And so," said Mrs. Rineiri, with finality, laying her hands down again, and looking past me at the bead curtain. That was the end. Luigi nodded brusquely at me, and went into the back. I said goodbye to Mrs. Rineiri and walked back to the lower town. In the square I saw the child, sitting on the running board of a lorry[9] parked outside the *trattoria*, drawing in the dust with his bare toes, and directing in front of him a blank, unhappy stare.

I had to go through Florence, so I went to the address Judith had been at. No, Miss Castlewell had not been back. Her papers and books were still here. Would I take them back with me to England? I made a great parcel and brought them back to England.

I telephoned Judith and she said she had already written for the papers to be sent, but it was kind of me to bring them. There had seemed to be no point, she said, in returning to Florence.

"Shall I bring them over?"

"I would be very grateful, of course."

Judith's flat was chilly, and she wore a bunchy sage-green woollen dress. Her hair was still a soft gold helmet, but she looked pale and rather pinched. She stood with her back to a single bar of electric fire—lit because I demanded it— with her legs apart and her arms folded. She contemplated me.

"I went to the Rineiris' house."

"Oh. Did you?"

"They seemed to miss you."

She said nothing.

"I saw the cat too."

"Oh. Oh, I suppose you and Betty discussed it?" This was with a small unfriendly smile.

"Well, Judith, you must see we were likely to?"

She gave this her consideration and said: "I don't understand why people discuss other people. Oh—I'm not criticising you. But I don't see why you are so interested. I don't understand human behaviour and I'm not particularly interested."

"I think you should write to the Rineiris."

"I wrote and thanked them, of course."

"I don't mean that."

"You and Betty have worked it out?"

"Yes, we talked about it. We thought we should talk to you, so you should write to the Rineiris."

"Why?"

"For one thing, they are both very fond of you."

"Fond," she said smiling.

"Judith, I've never in my life felt such an atmosphere of being let down."

Judith considered this. "When something happens that shows one there is really a complete gulf in understanding, what is there to say?"

9. Truck.

75

80

85

90

95

"It could scarcely have been a complete gulf in understanding. I suppose you are going to say we are being interfering?"

Judith showed distaste. "That is a very stupid word. And it's a stupid idea. No one can interfere with me if I don't let them. No, it's that I don't understand people. I don't understand why you or Betty should care. Or why the Rineiris should, for that matter," she added with the small tight smile.

"Judith!"

"If you've behaved stupidly, there's no point in going on. You put an end to it."

100 "What happened? Was it the cat?"

"Yes, I suppose so. But it's not important." She looked at me, saw my ironical face, and said: "The cat was too young to have kittens. That is all there was to it."

"Have it your way. But that is obviously not all there is to it."

"What upsets me is that I don't understand at all why I was so upset then."

"What happened? Or don't you want to talk about it?"

105 "I don't give a damn whether I talk about it or not. You really do say the most extraordinary things, you and Betty. If you want to know, I'll tell you. What does it matter?"

"I would like to know, of course."

"*Of course!*" she said. "In your place I wouldn't care. Well, I think the essence of the thing was that I must have had the wrong attitude to that cat. Cats are supposed to be independent. They are supposed to go off by themselves to have their kittens. This one didn't. It was climbing up on to my bed all one night and crying for attention. I don't like cats on my bed. In the morning I saw she was in pain. I stayed with her all that day. Then Luigi—he's the brother, you know."

"Yes."

"Did Betty mention him? Luigi came up to say it was time I went for a swim. He said the cat should look after itself. I blame myself very much. That's what happens when you submerge yourself in somebody else."

110 Her look at me was now defiant; and her body showed both defensiveness and aggression. "Yes. It's true. I've always been afraid of it. And in the last few weeks I've behaved badly. It's because I let it happen."

"Well, go on."

"I left the cat and swam. It was late, so it was only for a few minutes. When I came out of the sea the cat had followed me and had had a kitten on the beach. That little beast Michele—the son, you know?—well, he always teased the poor thing, and now he had frightened her off the kitten. It was dead, though. He held it up by the tail and waved it at me as I came out of the sea. I told him to bury it. He scooped two inches of sand away and pushed the kitten in—on the beach, where people are all day. So I buried it properly. He had run off. He was chasing the poor cat. She was terrified and running up the town. I ran too. I caught Michele and I was so angry I hit him. I don't believe in hitting children. I've been feeling beastly about it ever since."

"You were angry."

"It's no excuse. I would never have believed myself capable of hitting a child. I hit him very hard. He went off, crying. The poor cat had got under a big lorry parked in the square. Then she screamed. And then a most remarkable thing happened. She screamed just once, and all at once cats just materialised. One minute there was just one cat, lying under a lorry, and the next, dozens of cats. They sat in a big circle around the lorry, all quite still, and watched my poor cat."

"Rather moving," I said.

"Why?"

"There is no evidence one way or the other," I said in inverted commas, "that the cats were there out of concern for a friend in trouble."

"No," she said energetically. "There isn't. It might have been curiosity. Or anything. How do we know? However, I crawled under the lorry. There were two paws sticking out of the cat's back end. The kitten was the wrong way round. It was stuck. I held the cat down with one hand and I pulled the kitten out with the other." She held out her long white hands. They were still covered with fading scars and scratches. "She bit and yelled, but the kitten was alive. She left the kitten and crawled across the square into the house. Then all the cats got up and walked away. It was the most extraordinary thing I've ever seen. They vanished again. One minute they were all there, and then they had vanished. I went after the cat, with the kitten. Poor little thing, it was covered with dust— being wet, don't you know. The cat was on my bed. There was another kitten coming, but it got stuck too. So when she screamed and screamed I just pulled it out. The kittens began to suck. One kitten was very big. It was a nice fat black kitten. It must have hurt her. But she suddenly bit out—snapped, don't you know, like a reflex action, at the back of the kitten's head. It died, just like that. Extraordinary, isn't it?" she said, blinking hard, her lips quivering. "She was its mother, but she killed it. Then she ran off the bed and went downstairs into the shop under the counter. I called to Luigi. You know, he's Mrs. Rineiri's brother."

"Yes, I know."

"He said she was too young, and she was badly frightened and very hurt. He took the alive kitten to her but she got up and walked away. She didn't want it. Then Luigi told me not to look. But I followed him. He held the kitten by the tail and he banged it against the wall twice. Then he dropped it into the rubbish heap. He moved aside some rubbish with his toe, and put the kitten there and pushed rubbish over it. Then Luigi said the cat should be destroyed. He said she was badly hurt and it would always hurt her to have kittens."

"He hasn't destroyed her. She's still alive. But it looks to me as if he were right."

"Yes, I expect he was."

"What upset you—that he killed the kitten?"

"Oh no, I expect the cat would if he hadn't. But that isn't the point, is it?"

"What is the point?"

"I don't think I really know." She had been speaking breathlessly, and fast. Now she said slowly: "It's not a question of right or wrong, is it? Why should it be? It's a question of what one is. That night Luigi wanted to go promenading with me. For him, that was *that*. Something had to be done, and he'd done it. But I felt ill. He was very nice to me. He's a very good person," she said, defiantly.

"Yes, he looks it."

"That night I couldn't sleep. I was blaming myself. I should never have left the cat to go swimming. Well, and then I decided to leave the next day. And I did. And that's all. The whole thing was a mistake, from start to finish."

"Going to Italy at all?"

130 "Oh, to go for a holiday would have been all right."

"You've done all that work for nothing? You mean you aren't going to make use of all that research?"

"No. It was a mistake."

"Why don't you leave it a few weeks and see how things are then?"

"Why?"

135 "You might feel differently about it."

"What an extraordinary thing to say. Why should I? Oh, you mean, time passing, healing wounds—that sort of thing? What an extraordinary idea. It's always seemed to me an extraordinary idea. No, right from the beginning I've felt ill at ease with the whole business, not myself at all."

"Rather irrationally, I should have said."

Judith considered this, very seriously. She frowned while she thought it over. Then she said: "But if one cannot rely on what one feels, what can one rely on?"

"On what one thinks, I should have expected you to say."

140 "Should you? Why? Really, you people are all very strange. I don't under-stand you." She turned off the electric fire, and her face closed up. She smiled, friendly and distant, and said: "I don't really see any point at all in discussing it."

                                                                    1963

GRACE PALEY

A Conversation with My Father

My father is eighty-six years old and in bed. His heart, that bloody motor, is equally old and will not do certain jobs any more. It still floods his head with brainy light. But it won't let his legs carry the weight of his body around the house. Despite my metaphors, this muscle failure is not due to his old heart, he says, but to a potassium shortage. Sitting on one pillow, leaning on three, he offers last-minute advice and makes a request.

"I would like you to write a simple story just once more," he says, "the kind de Maupassant wrote, or Chekhov, the kind you used to write. Just recognizable people and then write down what happened to them next."

I say, "Yes, why not? That's possible." I want to please him, though I don't remember writing that way. I *would* like to try to tell such a story, if he means the kind that begins: "There was a woman . . ." followed by plot, the absolute line between two points which I've always despised. Not for literary reasons, but because it takes all hope away. Everyone, real or invented, deserves the open destiny of life.

Finally I thought of a story that had been happening for a couple of years right across the street. I wrote it down, then read it aloud. "Pa," I said, "how about this? Do you mean something like this?"

> Once in my time there was a woman and she had a son. They lived nicely, in a   5
> small apartment in Manhattan. This boy at about fifteen became a junkie, which is
> not unusual in our neighborhood. In order to maintain her close friendship with
> him, she became a junkie too. She said it was part of the youth culture, with which
> she felt very much at home. After a while, for a number of reasons, the boy gave it
> all up and left the city and his mother in disgust. Hopeless and alone, she grieved.
> We all visit her.

"O.K., Pa, that's it," I said, "an unadorned and miserable tale."

"But that's not what I mean," my father said. "You misunderstood me on purpose. You know there's a lot more to it. You know that. You left everything out. Turgenev[1] wouldn't do that. Chekhov wouldn't do that. There are in fact Russian writers you never heard of, you don't have an inkling of, as good as anyone, who can write a plain ordinary story, who would not leave out what you have left out. I object not to facts but to people sitting in trees talking senselessly, voices from who knows where . . ."

"Forget that one, Pa, what have I left out now? In this one?"

"Her looks, for instance."

"Oh. Quite handsome, I think. Yes."   10

"Her hair?"

"Dark, with heavy braids, as though she were a girl or a foreigner."

"What were her parents like, her stock? That she became such a person. It's interesting, you know."

"From out of town. Professional people. The first to be divorced in their county. How's that? Enough?" I asked.

"With you, it's all a joke," he said. "What about the boy's father. Why didn't   15
you mention him? Who was he? Or was the boy born out of wedlock?"

"Yes," I said. "He was born out of wedlock."

"For Godsakes, doesn't anyone in your stories get married? Doesn't anyone have the time to run down to City Hall before they jump into bed?"

"No," I said. "In real life, yes. But in my stories, no."

"Why do you answer me like that?"

"Oh, Pa, this is a simple story about a smart woman who came to N.Y.C.   20
full of interest love trust excitement very up to date, and about her son, what a

---

1. Ivan Sergevich Turgenev (1818–1883); his best-known novel, *Fathers and Sons,* deals with the conflict between generations.

hard time she had in this world. Married or not, it's of small consequence."

"It is of great consequence," he said.

"O.K.," I said.

"O.K. O.K. yourself," he said, "but listen. I believe you that she's good-looking, but I don't think she was so smart."

"That's true," I said. "Actually that's the trouble with stories. People start out fantastic. You think they're extraordinary, but it turns out as the work goes along, they're just average with a good education. Sometimes the other way around, the person's a kind of dumb innocent, but he outwits you and you can't even think of an ending good enough."

25 "What do you do then?" he asked. He had been a doctor for a couple of decades and then an artist for a couple of decades and he's still interested in details, craft, technique.

"Well, you just have to let the story lie around till some agreement can be reached between you and the stubborn hero."

"Aren't you talking silly, now?" he asked. "Start again," he said. "It so happens I'm not going out this evening. Tell the story again. See what you can do this time."

"O.K.," I said. "But it's not a five-minute job." Second attempt:

> Once, across the street from us, there was a fine handsome woman, our neighbor. She had a son whom she loved because she'd known him since birth (in helpless chubby infancy, and in the wrestling, hugging ages, seven to ten, as well as earlier and later). This boy, when he fell into the fist of adolescence, became a junkie. He was not a hopeless one. He was in fact hopeful, an ideologue and successful converter. With his busy brilliance, he wrote persuasive articles for his high-school newspaper. Seeking a wider audience, using important connections, he drummed into Lower Manhattan newsstand distribution a periodical called *Oh! Golden Horse!*[2]
>
> 30 In order to keep him from feeling guilty (because guilt is the stony heart of nine tenths of all clinically diagnosed cancers in America today, she said), and because she had always believed in giving bad habits room at home where one could keep an eye on them, she too became a junkie. Her kitchen was famous for a while—a center for intellectual addicts who knew what they were doing. A few felt artistic like Coleridge and others were scientific and revolutionary like Leary.[3] Although she was often high herself, certain good mothering reflexes remained, and she saw to it that there was lots of orange juice around and honey and milk and vitamin pills. However, she never cooked anything but chili, and that no more than once a week. She explained, when we talked to her, seriously, with neighborly concern, that it was her part in the youth culture and she would rather be with the young, it was an honor, than with her own generation.
>
> One week, while nodding[4] through an Antonioni[5] film, this boy was severely jabbed by the elbow of a stern and proselytizing girl, sitting beside him. She offered

2. "Horse" is a slang term for heroin.   3. Samuel Taylor Coleridge (1772–1834), English Romantic poet, wrote his allegedly unfinished poem *Kubla Khan* in an opium dream. Timothy Leary (b. 1920), American psychologist who promoted the use of psychedelic drugs.   4. A slang term referring to the narcotic effect of heroin.   5. Michelangelo Antonioni (b. 1912), Italian director (*Blow-Up*, *Zabriskie Point*).

immediate apricots and nuts for his sugar level, spoke to him sharply, and took him home.

She had heard of him and his work and she herself published, edited, and wrote a competitive journal called *Man Does Live By Bread Alone*. In the organic heat of her continuous presence he could not help but become interested once more in his muscles, his arteries, and nerve connections. In fact he began to love them, treasure them, praise them with funny little songs in *Man Does Live* . . .

> *the fingers of my flesh transcend*
> *my transcendental soul*
> *the tightness in my shoulders end*
> *my teeth have made me whole*

To the mouth of his head (that glory of will and determination) he brought hard apples, nuts, wheat germ, and soybean oil. He said to his old friends, From now on, I guess I'll keep my wits about me. I'm going on the natch. He said he was about to begin a spiritual deep-breathing journey. How about you too, Mom? he asked kindly.

His conversion was so radiant, splendid, that neighborhood kids his age began to say that he had never been a real addict at all, only a journalist along for the smell of the story. The mother tried several times to give up what had become without her son and his friends a lonely habit. This effort only brought it to supportable levels. The boy and his girl took their electronic mimeograph and moved to the bushy edge of another borough. They were very strict. They said they would not see her again until she had been off drugs for sixty days.

At home alone in the evening, weeping, the mother read and reread the seven issues of *Oh! Golden Horse!* They seemed to her as truthful as ever. We often crossed the street to visit and console. But if we mentioned any of our children who were at college or in the hospital or dropouts at home, she would cry out, My baby! My baby! and burst into terrible, face-scarring, time-consuming tears. The End.
35

First my father was silent, then he said, "Number One: You have a nice sense of humor. Number Two: I see you can't tell a plain story. So don't waste time." Then he said sadly, "Number Three: I suppose that means she was alone, she was left like that, his mother. Alone. Probably sick?"

I said, "Yes."

"Poor woman. Poor girl, to be born in a time of fools, to live among fools. The end. The end. You were right to put that down. The end."

I didn't want to argue, but I had to say, "Well, it is not necessarily the end, Pa."

"Yes," he said, "what a tragedy. The end of a person."
40

"No, Pa," I begged him. "It doesn't have to be. She's only about forty. She could be a hundred different things in this world as time goes on. A teacher or a social worker. An ex-junkie! Sometimes it's better than having a master's in education."

"Jokes," he said. "As a writer that's your main trouble. You don't want to recognize it. Tragedy! Plain tragedy! Historical tragedy! No hope. The end."

"Oh, Pa," I said. "She could change."

"In your own life, too, you have to look it in the face." He took a couple of nitroglycerin.[6] "Turn to five," he said, pointing to the dial on the oxygen tank.

---

6. Medicine for certain heart conditions.

He inserted the tubes into his nostrils and breathed deep. He closed his eyes and said, "No."

I had promised the family to always let him have the last word when arguing, but in this case I had a different responsibility. That woman lives across the street. She's my knowledge and my invention. I'm sorry for her. I'm not going to leave her there in that house crying. (Actually neither would Life, which unlike me has no pity.)

Therefore: She did change. Of course her son never came home again. But right now, she's the receptionist in a storefront community clinic in the East Village. Most of the customers are young people, some old friends. The head doctor said to her, "If we only had three people in this clinic with your experiences . . ."

"The doctor said that?" My father took the oxygen tubes out of his nostrils and said, "Jokes. Jokes again."

"No, Pa, it could really happen that way, it's a funny world nowadays."

"No," he said. "Truth first. She will slide back. A person must have character. She does not."

"No, Pa," I said. "That's it. She's got a job. Forget it. She's in that storefront working."

"How long will it be?" he asked. "Tragedy! You too. When will you look it in the face?"

1974

▼ ▼ ▼

CHARACTERIZATION A Glossary

antagonist: a neutral term for a character who opposes the leading male or female character; see *hero / heroine* and *protagonist*

antihero: a leading character who is not, like a "hero," perfect or even outstanding but is rather ordinary and representative of the more or less average person

character: (1) a fictional personage; (2) a combination of a person's qualities, especially moral qualities, so that such terms as "good" and "bad," "strong" and "weak," often apply. See *personality* and *nature*

characterization: the fictional or artistic presentation of a fictional personage; terms like "a good character" can, then, be ambiguous—they may mean that the personage is virtuous, or that he or she is well presented whatever his or her characteristics or moral qualities

existential character: a person real or fictional who, whatever his or her past or conditioning, can change by an act of will

flat character: fictional character, often but not always a minor character, who is relatively simple, who is presented as having rather few, though sometimes dominant, traits, and who thus does not change much in the course of a story. See *round character*

hero / heroine: the leading male / female character, usually larger than life, sometimes almost godlike. See *antihero, protagonist,* and *villain*

major characters: those characters whom we see and learn about the most

minor characters: those figures who fill out the story

nature: as it refers to a person—"it is his [or her] nature"—a rather old term suggesting something inborn, inherent, fixed, and thus predictable. See *character, personality*

personality: that which distinguishes or individualizes a person; its qualities are judged not so much in terms of their moral value, as in "character," but as to whether they are "pleasing" or "unpleasing"

protagonist: the main character in a work, who may be male or female, heroic or not heroic; thus the most neutral term. See *hero / heroine, antihero,* and *antagonist*

round character: a complex character, often a major character, who can grow and change and "surprise convincingly"—that is, act in a way that you did not expect from what had gone before but now accept as possible, even probable, and "realistic"

stereotype: a characterization based on conscious or unconscious assumptions that some one aspect, such as gender, age, ethnic or national identity, religion, occupation, marital status, determines what humans are like, and so is accompanied by certain traits, actions, and even values

villain: the one who opposes the hero and heroine, the "bad guy"; see *antagonist* and *hero*

QUESTIONS

1. What image do you have of Sister, the narrator of "Why I Live at the P.O.," after the first ten paragraphs? How do paragraphs 37–49 sharpen, confirm, modify, expand, or change your image? paragraphs 63–68, 94–95? 99 and 108–10? 128–30? 136–38? Is she reliable? Compare paragraphs 8 and 14, and paragraphs 47 and 89, but remember that all the words of the story are Sister's. What is the effect of the contradictions on your view of the characters? on your expectations? on your response to the story? When in relation to the time of the actions is Sister telling this story? When would you date actions of the story? based on what evidence?

2. How would you describe the relationship between Harry Fenstad and his mother? What signs are there that he loves her? What evidence is there that he is concerned about her aging? How would you describe her attitude toward him? What signs are there of affection, admiration? There are, in the course of the story, two specific differences of opinion between Fenstad and his mother—her views of love, marriage, and his relationship to his first wife (pars. 8–11), and the scene with the homeless woman (pars. 66–73)—as well as differences that might be described broadly as political (pars. 55 and 58). What is the effect on these differences on your view of their characters? Whose side are you on? To what extent do your own political beliefs influence your judgment of the characters? To what extent may it be said that Fenstad's mother's viewing everything politically and his viewing everything in personal or "liberal humanistic" terms (find examples of both) suggest a difference in their questions?

3. Because we are told the story of "Our Friend Judith" by a friend, we never get to know Judith from the inside and are never very close to the action. This seems to have the effect of lessening the suspense and perhaps even our interest in or feelings for Judith. What is gained by this focus and voice? How does it change the meaning of the story? The friend says she blundered and lost her opportunity to find out what Judith and her life were really like. How did she lose the opportunity? Was it really a blunder? Could she have found out what she wanted to know if she had not "blundered"? What is the friend "really" like?

WRITING SUGGESTIONS

1. In paragraph 63 of "Why I Live at the P.O.," after Mama says that she prefers to believe her children, the narrator tells us that Mama weighs two hundred pounds and has small feet. What is the effect of this peculiar shift from one sentence to the next? What does it contribute to your image of Sister? Find several more such non sequiturs and analyze their effect. Write a brief essay on the relationship between style and humor in "Why I Live at the P.O."

2. Trace your views of the character of Fenstad's mother from the first paragraph to the final scene, following both changes and consistencies.

3. Write an analysis of the character of the narrator of "Our Friend Judith." Base your interpretation solidly on specific passages, incidents, and attitudes in the story.

4. Write for or against one of these two interpretations of Judith's character. Or show why neither is satisfactory:

   a. Judith seems to be cool, intellectual, and respectable, but she's really fiery and passionate; she's hypocritical, since she lives one kind of life in the open and another in secret.

   b. Judith is her own woman. She does not need a man to lean on or depend on, but has her own full life, her profession, and does her own thing in her own way, the way men are praised for doing but women often condemned for doing.

5. Imagine a discussion / argument between Margaret Atwood and Grace Paley about writing stories, and especially about how to end them.

4 SETTING

A ll stories, like all individuals, are embedded in a context or setting—a time and place. The time can be contemporary ("No One's a Mystery") or historical ("The Cask of Amontillado") or even mythically vague ("The Zebra Storyteller"). It can be very limited, only a few minutes elapsing ("No One's a Mystery") or some years ("Sonny's Blues"). The place can be rather fixed and interior ("A Conversation with My Father") or varied ("Our Friend Judith"). It can be foreign ("The Cask of Amontillado") or American ("The Country Husband") or tied to a region ("A Rose for Emily" and the South) or a locale ("Sonny's Blues" and Harlem). Just as character and plot are so closely interrelated as to be ultimately indistinguishable (see Chapter 3), so too are character, plot, and setting. Paradoxically, to see this interpenetration, we must think of them first as separable elements. The individuals in the stories are embedded in the specific context, and the more we know of the setting, and of the relationship of the character to the setting, the more likely we are to understand the character and the story.

Even in a spare story like "No One's a Mystery" the interaction or interrelation of setting, character, and plot is important and revealing. The eighteen-year-old narrator and Jack, her lover, are in his dirty pickup truck on the highway. His wife approaches in her Cadillac—with the lights on even though it's daytime, a habit he hates. The vehicles they drive and their condition tell you a good deal about Jack, his wife, and their relationship. The significance of Jack's driving a pickup (and of the muddy manure on his boots) is modulated by the almost casually dropped information that they are in Wyoming, in or near Cheyenne.

Place or setting is seldom insignificant or unrelated to a larger historical context. "The Jewelry" is set in Paris in the late 1870s. Quite naturally, you might say, since it was written by a Frenchman in the early 1880s; he's just writing about his own time and place. True enough, but the cynicism, the somewhat bitter irony of the story set among the bourgeoisie and the bureaucracy, owes a good deal of its tone to the recent (1870–71) defeat of France and the siege and occupation of Paris by the Prussian Bismarck. (France paid Germany a billion dollars in reparations, an unheard-of amount in those days, and did so, to the world's astonishment, in just three years. Might this have something to do with the emphasis on money in the story?) The interaction of tone and times, setting and situation, are fused in this story in a way that would scarcely be possible in another context. Money, adultery, and high living are not unknown in our society, but try rewriting this story by setting it in New York in the 1990s.

John Cheever's "The Country Husband" is set in the early to middle 1950s, in my time and close enough to yours so that you know the important things about the period—Elvis, Marilyn, all that. World War II seems distant, but not too distant: a man in midlife crisis served in the army during that time. It is set in suburban New York, not too remote or exotic a setting, since it has many of the qualities of the suburbs of any medium-sized to large city in the 1990s. Yet the story is still somewhat of a period piece. The myth of the calm, undisturbed, comfortable good life—peace and plenty in the suburbs after the decades of Depression and war, the milieu of "Leave It to Beaver" and "Father Knows Best"—still prevailed. Airplane accidents and alcoholic fathers and memories of war were banned. And it seemed, at certain times, boring, almost unbearably so. All the excitement, all the romance of life, was gone, kept away by rows of white picket fences. Yes, we have suburbs like Shady Hill, but not many of the wives stay at home like Julia Weed and we no longer believe they are fenced off from the problems and promises of the Big City. The setting of this 1958 story makes of Francis a "weed" and though there are still crabgrass and dandelions in some of our finest neighborhoods, he and history would be difficult to transplant.

"The Country Husband" is, despite its relative modernity, an historical story. Its time, place, and historical setting interact with its narrative. Some stories are more overtly historical, and their milieu—or the stereotypes associated with it—are more obviously significant than those in Cheever's tale. The protagonist and the plot of "The Cask of Amontillado" are Machiavellian (characterized by subtle or unscrupulous cunning; after the Italian Renaissance politician and writer Niccolò Machiavelli, 1460–1527), and the story is set in Italy during the Renaissance. The Puritan goodman Brown lives in the reign of King William (1689–1702) in Salem, Massachusetts, where in 1692 the famous witch trials were held—what better place and time for a story whose subject is a witches' meeting and whose theme has to do with man's natural depravity? An *English* "spinster" seems (or seemed) much more prudish and virginal than just any old spinster, Italian lovers more sensual than Anglo-Saxon ones, and in "Our Friend Judith" testing those conventions is, virtually, the story.

In some stories setting, even when appropriate and natural, can symbolize whole ways of life or value systems. In "The Lady with the Dog," Yalta with its fruit, seashore, and semitropical climate exemplifies a more passionate, pleasurable, exciting life than the cold and cloudy, bureaucratic, intellectually rarefied air and routine of Moscow. Faulkner's "A Rose for Emily" is set in the deep South (Jefferson, Mississippi) in the years between, roughly, 1880 and the 1920s. Those are the years when the Civil War and the postwar Reconstruction were over and the resegregated South was nostalgic for the mythic antebellum values of gentility and gallantry. Emily is almost a symbol of the culture, its myths, and its reality.

Jing-Mei Woo, the narrator of "A Pair of Tickets," explores the relation of place, heritage, and ethnic identity. Living in San Francisco she had, at fifteen, "vigorously denied that I had any Chinese whatsoever below my skin" (par. 2), but at thirty-six, as she crosses the border from Hong Kong into China, she finds that she is "becoming Chinese." In Guangzhou, however, she discovers that within the vast change of place and cultures, in the modern world, at least among the privileged, there is a homogeneity: though men and women are working without safety belts or helmets on a scaffold made of bamboo held together with plastic strips, the hotel she is taken to "looks like a grander version of the Hyatt Regency." There are "shopping arcades and restaurants all encased in granite and glass," and in the rooms color television, a wet bar, Coke Classic, M & M's, Johnnie Walker Red, and so on. Her father's family circumvents her plan to have a Chinese feast and they dine on hamburgers, french fries, apple pie à la mode, delivered by room service. In the modern city of Shanghai, meeting her twin half-sisters for the first time, she finds she is Chinese not because of place or face, but because of "blood." But within this story is another story, her mother's story, with another setting in time and conditions. Fleeing from Kweilin and the advance of the Japanese army in 1944, Jing-Mei's mother was forced by overwhelming circumstances to abandon her twin babies. Jing-Mei can now explain a good deal about her own past, about her mother and their relationship, from the story of her actions and the historical circumstances of the war.

If one of the functions of literature is to engender the sympathetic understanding of others and of other subjective visions of the world, setting—the time and place in which the fictional characters and action are embedded—is an essential element.

WILLIAM FAULKNER

A Rose for Emily

I

When Miss Emily Grierson died, our whole town went to her funeral: the men through a sort of respectful affection for a fallen monument, the women mostly out of curiosity to see the inside of her house, which no one save an old manservant—a combined gardener and cook—had seen in at least ten years.

It was a big, squarish frame house that had once been white, decorated with cupolas and spires and scrolled balconies in the heavily lightsome style of the seventies, set on what had once been our most select street. But garages and cotton gins had encroached and obliterated even the august names of that neighborhood; only Miss Emily's house was left, lifting its stubborn and coquettish decay above the cotton wagons and the gasoline pumps—an eyesore among eyesores. And now Miss Emily had gone to join the representatives of those august names where they lay in the cedar-bemused cemetery among the ranked and anonymous graves of Union and Confederate soldiers who fell at the battle of Jefferson.

Alive, Miss Emily had been a tradition, a duty, and a care; a sort of hereditary obligation upon the town, dating from that day in 1894 when Colonel Sartoris, the mayor—he who fathered the edict that no Negro woman should appear on the streets without an apron—remitted her taxes, the dispensation dating from the death of her father on into perpetuity. Not that Miss Emily would have accepted charity. Colonel Sartoris invented an involved tale to the effect that Miss Emily's father had loaned money to the town, which the town, as a matter of business, preferred this way of repaying. Only a man of Colonel Sartoris' generation and thought could have invented it, and only a woman could have believed it.

When the next generation, with its more modern ideas, became mayors and aldermen, this arrangement created some little dissatisfaction. On the first of the year they mailed her a tax notice. February came, and there was no reply. They wrote her a formal letter, asking her to call at the sheriff's office at her convenience. A week later the mayor wrote her himself, offering to call or to send his car for her, and received in reply a note on paper of an archaic shape, in a thin, flowing calligraphy in faded ink, to the effect that she no longer went out at all. The tax notice was also enclosed, without comment.

They called a special meeting of the Board of Aldermen. A deputation waited upon her, knocked at the door through which no visitor had passed since she ceased giving china-painting lessons eight or ten years earlier. They were admitted by the old Negro into a dim hall from which a stairway mounted into still more shadow. It smelled of dust and disuse—a close, dank smell. The Negro led them into the parlor. It was furnished in heavy, leather-covered furniture.

5

When the Negro opened the blinds of one window, a faint dust rose sluggishly about their thighs, spinning with slow motes in the single sun-ray. On a tarnished gilt easel before the fireplace stood a crayon portrait of Miss Emily's father.

They rose when she entered—a small, fat woman in black, with a thin gold chain descending to her waist and vanishing into her belt, leaning on an ebony cane with a tarnished gold head. Her skeleton was small and spare; perhaps that was why what would have been merely plumpness in another was obesity in her. She looked bloated, like a body long submerged in motionless water, and of that pallid hue. Her eyes, lost in the fatty ridges of her face, looked like two small pieces of coal pressed into a lump of dough as they moved from one face to another while the visitors stated their errand.

She did not ask them to sit. She just stood in the door and listened quietly until the spokesman came to a stumbling halt. Then they could hear the invisible watch ticking at the end of the gold chain.

Her voice was dry and cold. "I have no taxes in Jefferson. Colonel Sartoris explained it to me. Perhaps one of you can gain access to the city records and satisfy yourselves."

"But we have. We are the city authorities, Miss Emily. Didn't you get a notice from the sheriff, signed by him?"

"I received a paper, yes," Miss Emily said. "Perhaps he considers himself the sheriff. . . . I have no taxes in Jefferson."

"But there is nothing on the books to show that, you see. We must go by the—"

"See Colonel Sartoris. I have no taxes in Jefferson."

"But, Miss Emily—"

"See Colonel Sartoris." (Colonel Sartoris had been dead almost ten years.) "I have no taxes in Jefferson. Tobe!" The Negro appeared. "Show these gentlemen out."

II

So she vanquished them, horse and foot, just as she had vanquished their fathers thirty years before about the smell. That was two years after her father's death and a short time after her sweetheart—the one we believed would marry her— had deserted her. After her father's death she went out very little; after her sweetheart went away, people hardly saw her at all. A few of the ladies had the temerity to call, but were not received, and the only sign of life about the place was the Negro man—a young man then—going in and out with a market basket.

"Just as if a man—any man—could keep a kitchen properly," the ladies said; so they were not surprised when the smell developed. It was another link between the gross, teeming world and the high and mighty Griersons.

A neighbor, a woman, complained to the mayor, Judge Stevens, eighty years old.

"But what will you have me do about it, madam?" he said.

"Why, send her word to stop it," the woman said. "Isn't there a law?"

"I'm sure that won't be necessary," Judge Stevens said. "It's probably just 20
a snake or a rat that nigger of hers killed in the yard. I'll speak to him about
it."

The next day he received two more complaints, one from a man who came
in diffident deprecation. "We really must do something about it, Judge. I'd be
the last one in the world to bother Miss Emily, but we've got to do something."
That night the Board of Aldermen met—three gray-beards and one younger
man, a member of the rising generation.

"It's simple enough," he said. "Send her word to have her place cleaned up.
Give her a certain time to do it in, and if she don't . . ."

"Dammit, sir," Judge Stevens said, "will you accuse a lady to her face of
smelling bad?"

So the next night, after midnight, four men crossed Miss Emily's lawn and
slunk about the house like burglars, sniffing along the base of the brickwork and
at the cellar openings while one of them performed a regular sowing motion
with his hand out of a sack slung from his shoulder. They broke open the cellar
door and sprinkled lime there, and in all the outbuildings. As they recrossed the
lawn, a window that had been dark was lighted and Miss Emily sat in it, the
light behind her, and her upright torso motionless as that of an idol. They crept
quietly across the lawn and into the shadow of the locusts that lined the street.
After a week or two the smell went away.

That was when people had begun to feel really sorry for her. People in our 25
town, remembering how old lady Wyatt, her great-aunt, had gone completely
crazy at last, believed that the Griersons held themselves a little too high for
what they really were. None of the young men were quite good enough for Miss
Emily and such. We had long thought of them as a tableau; Miss Emily a
slender figure in white in the background, her father a spraddled silhouette in
the foreground, his back to her and clutching a horsewhip, the two of them
framed by the back-flung front door. So when she got to be thirty and was still
single, we were not pleased exactly, but vindicated; even with insanity in the
family she wouldn't have turned down all of her chances if they had really
materialized.

When her father died, it got about that the house was all that was left to her;
and in a way, people were glad. At last they could pity Miss Emily. Being left
alone, and a pauper, she had become humanized. Now she too would know the
old thrill and the old despair of a penny more or less.

The day after his death all the ladies prepared to call at the house and offer
condolence and aid, as is our custom. Miss Emily met them at the door, dressed
as usual and with no trace of grief on her face. She told them that her father
was not dead. She did that for three days, with the ministers calling on her, and
the doctors, trying to persuade her to let them dispose of the body. Just as they
were about to resort to law and force, she broke down, and they buried her father
quickly.

We did not say she was crazy then. We believed she had to do that. We
remembered all the young men her father had driven away, and we knew that

with nothing left, she would have to cling to that which had robbed her, as people will.

III

She was sick for a long time. When we saw her again, her hair was cut short, making her look like a girl, with a vague resemblance to those angels in colored church windows—sort of tragic and serene.

30   The town had just let the contracts for paving the sidewalks, and in the summer after her father's death they began to work. The construction company came with niggers and mules and machinery, and a foreman named Homer Barron, a Yankee—a big, dark, ready man, with a big voice and eyes lighter than his face. The little boys would follow in groups to hear him cuss the niggers, and the niggers singing in time to the rise and fall of picks. Pretty soon he knew everybody in town. Whenever you heard a lot of laughing anywhere about the square, Homer Barron would be in the center of the group. Presently we began to see him and Miss Emily on Sunday afternoons driving in the yellow-wheeled buggy and the matched team of bays from the livery stable.

At first we were glad that Miss Emily would have an interest, because the ladies all said, "Of course a Grierson would not think seriously of a Northerner, a day laborer." But there were still others, older people, who said that even grief could not cause a real lady to forget *noblesse oblige*—without calling it *noblesse oblige*. They just said, "Poor Emily. Her kinsfolk should come to her." She had some kin in Alabama; but years ago her father had fallen out with them over the estate of old lady Wyatt, the crazy woman, and there was no communication between the two families. They had not even been represented at the funeral.

And as soon as the old people said, "Poor Emily," the whispering began. "Do you suppose it's really so?" they said to one another. "Of course it is. What else could . . . " This behind their hands; rustling of craned silk and satin behind jalousies closed upon the sun of Sunday afternoon as the thin, swift clop-clop-clop of the matched team passed: "Poor Emily."

She carried her head high enough—even when we believed that she was fallen. It was as if she demanded more than ever the recognition of her dignity as the last Grierson; as if it had wanted that touch of earthiness to reaffirm her imperviousness. Like when she bought the rat poison, the arsenic. That was over a year after they had begun to say "Poor Emily," and while the two female cousins were visiting her.

"I want some poison," she said to the druggist. She was over thirty then, still a slight woman, though thinner than usual, with cold, haughty black eyes in a face the flesh of which was strained across the temples and about the eyesockets as you imagine a lighthouse-keeper's face ought to look. "I want some poison," she said.

35   "Yes, Miss Emily. What kind? For rats and such? I'd recom—"

"I want the best you have. I don't care what kind."

The druggist named several. "They'll kill anything up to an elephant. But what you want is—"

"Arsenic," Miss Emily said. "Is that a good one?"

"Is . . . arsenic? Yes ma'am. But what you want—"

"I want arsenic."

The druggist looked down at her. She looked back at him, erect, her face like a strained flag. "Why, of course," the druggist said. "If that's what you want. But the law requires you to tell what you are going to use it for."

Miss Emily just stared at him, her head tilted back in order to look him eye for eye, until he looked away and went and got the arsenic and wrapped it up. The Negro delivery boy brought her the package; the druggist didn't come back. When she opened the package at home there was written on the box, under the skull and bones: "For rats."

IV

So the next day we all said, "She will kill herself"; and we said it would be the best thing. When she had first begun to be seen with Homer Barron, we had said, "She will marry him." Then we said, "She will persuade him yet," because Homer himself had remarked—he liked men, and it was known that he drank with the younger men in the Elk's Club—that he was not a marrying man. Later we said, "Poor Emily," behind the jalousies as they passed on Sunday afternoon in the glittering buggy, Miss Emily with her head high and Homer Barron with his hat cocked and a cigar in his teeth, reins and whip in a yellow glove.

Then some of the ladies began to say that it was a disgrace to the town and a bad example to the young people. The men did not want to interfere, but at last the ladies forced the Baptist minister—Miss Emily's people were Episcopal—to call upon her. He would never divulge what happened during that interview, but he refused to go back again. The next Sunday they again drove about the streets, and the following day the minister's wife wrote to Miss Emily's relations in Alabama.

So she had blood-kin under her roof again and we sat back to watch developments. At first nothing happened. Then we were sure that they were to be married. We learned that Miss Emily had been to the jeweler's and ordered a man's toilet set in silver, with the letters H. B. on each piece. Two days later we learned that she had bought a complete outfit of men's clothing, including a nightshirt, and we said, "They are married." We were really glad. We were glad because the two female cousins were even more Grierson than Miss Emily had ever been.

So we were not surprised when Homer Barron—the streets had been finished some time since—was gone. We were a little disappointed that there was not a public blowing-off, but we believed that he had gone on to prepare for Miss Emily's coming, or to give her a chance to get rid of the cousins. (By that time it was a cabal, and we were all Miss Emily's allies to help circumvent the cousins.) Sure enough, after another week they departed. And, as we had expected all along, within three days Homer Barron was back in town. A neighbor saw the Negro man admit him at the kitchen door at dusk one evening.

And that was the last we saw of Homer Barron. And of Miss Emily for some time. The Negro man went in and out with the market basket, but the front door remained closed. Now and then we would see her at a window for a moment, as the men did that night when they sprinkled the lime, but for almost six months she did not appear on the streets. Then we knew that this was to be expected too; as if that quality of her father which had thwarted her woman's life so many times had been too virulent and too furious to die.

When we next saw Miss Emily, she had grown fat and her hair was turning gray. During the next few years it grew grayer and grayer until it attained an even pepper-and-salt iron-gray, when it ceased turning. Up to the day of her death at seventy-four it was still that vigorous iron-gray, like the hair of an active man.

From that time on her front door remained closed, save for a period of six or seven years, when she was about forty, during which she gave lessons in china-painting. She fitted up a studio in one of the downstairs rooms, where the daughters and grand-daughters of Colonel Sartoris' contemporaries were sent to her with the same regularity and in the same spirit that they were sent on Sundays with a twenty-five cent piece for the collection plate. Meanwhile her taxes had been remitted.

50

Then the newer generation became the backbone and the spirit of the town, and the painting pupils grew up and fell away and did not send their children to her with boxes of color and tedious brushes and pictures cut from the ladies' magazines. The front door closed upon the last one and remained closed for good. When the town got free postal delivery Miss Emily alone refused to let them fasten the metal numbers above her door and attach a mailbox to it. She would not listen to them.

Daily, monthly, yearly we watched the Negro grow grayer and more stooped, going in and out with the market basket. Each December we sent her a tax notice, which would be returned by the post office a week later, unclaimed. Now and then we would see her in one of the downstairs windows—she had evidently shut up the top floor of the house—like the carven torso of an idol in a niche, looking or not looking at us, we could never tell which. Thus she passed from generation to generation—dear, inescapable, impervious, tranquil, and perverse.

And so she died. Fell ill in the house filled with dust and shadows, with only a doddering Negro man to wait on her. We did not even know she was sick; we had long since given up trying to get any information from the Negro. He talked to no one, probably not even to her, for his voice had grown harsh and rusty, as if from disuse.

She died in one of the downstairs rooms, in a heavy walnut bed with a curtain, her gray head propped on a pillow yellow and moldy with age and lack of sunlight.

V

The Negro met the first of the ladies at the front door and let them in, with their hushed, sibilant voices and their quick, curious glances, and then he disappeared. He walked right through the house and out the back and was not seen again.

The two female cousins came at once. They held the funeral on the second day, with the town coming to look at Miss Emily beneath a mass of bought flowers, with the crayon face of her father musing profoundly above the bier and the ladies sibilant and macabre; and the very old men—some in their brushed Confederate uniforms—on the porch and the lawn, talking of Miss Emily as if she had been a contemporary of theirs, believing that they had danced with her and courted her perhaps, confusing time with its mathematical progression, as the old do, to whom all the past is not a diminishing road, but, instead, a huge meadow which no winter ever quite touches, divided from them now by the narrow bottleneck of the most recent decade of years.

Already we knew that there was one room in that region above stairs which no one had seen in forty years, and which would have to be forced. They waited until Miss Emily was decently in the ground before they opened it.

The violence of breaking down the door seemed to fill this room with pervading dust. A thin, acrid pall as of the tomb seemed to lie everywhere upon this room decked and furnished as for a bridal: upon the valance curtains of faded rose color, upon the rose-shaded lights, upon the dressing table, upon the delicate array of crystal and the man's toilet things backed with tarnished silver, silver so tarnished that the monogram was obscured. Among them lay a collar and tie, as if they had just been removed, which, lifted, left upon the surface a pale crescent in the dust. Upon a chair hung the suit, carefully folded; beneath it the two mute shoes and the discarded socks.

The man himself lay in the bed.

For a long while we just stood there, looking down at the profound and fleshless grin. The body had apparently once lain in the attitude of an embrace, but now the long sleep that outlasts love, that conquers even the grimace of love, had cuckolded him. What was left of him, rotted beneath what was left of the nightshirt, had become inextricable from the bed in which he lay; and upon him and upon the pillow beside him lay that even coating of the patient and biding dust.

Then we noticed that in the second pillow was the indentation of a head. One of us lifted something from it, and leaning forward, that faint and invisible dust dry and acrid in the nostrils, we saw a long strand of iron-gray hair.

1931

AMY TAN

A Pair of Tickets

The minute our train leaves the Hong Kong border and enters Shenzhen, China, I feel different. I can feel the skin on my forehead tingling, my blood rushing through a new course, my bones aching with a familiar old pain. And I think, My mother was right. I am becoming Chinese.

"Cannot be helped," my mother said when I was fifteen and had vigorously denied that I had any Chinese whatsoever below my skin. I was a sophomore at

Galileo High in San Francisco, and all my Caucasian friends agreed: I was about as Chinese as they were. But my mother had studied at a famous nursing school in Shanghai, and she said she knew all about genetics. So there was no doubt in her mind, whether I agreed or not: Once you are born Chinese, you cannot help but feel and think Chinese.

"Someday you will see," said my mother. "It's in your blood, waiting to be let go."

And when she said this, I saw myself transforming like a werewolf, a mutant tag of DNA suddenly triggered, replicating itself insidiously into a *syndrome*, a cluster of telltale Chinese behaviors, all those things my mother did to embarrass me — haggling with store owners, pecking her mouth with a toothpick in public, being color-blind to the fact that lemon yellow and pale pink are not good combinations for winter clothes.

5   But today I realize I've never really known what it means to be Chinese. I am thirty-six years old. My mother is dead and I am on a train, carrying with me her dreams of coming home. I am going to China.

We are going to Guangzhou, my seventy-two-year-old father, Canning Woo, and I, where we will visit his aunt, whom he has not seen since he was ten years old. And I don't know whether it's the prospect of seeing his aunt or if it's because he's back in China, but now he looks like he's a young boy, so innocent and happy I want to button his sweater and pat his head. We are sitting across from each other, separated by a little table with two cold cups of tea. For the first time I can ever remember, my father has tears in his eyes, and all he is seeing out the train window is a sectioned field of yellow, green, and brown, a narrow canal flanking the tracks, low rising hills, and three people in blue jackets riding an ox-driven cart on this early October morning. And I can't help myself. I also have misty eyes, as if I had seen this a long, long time ago, and had almost forgotten.

In less than three hours, we will be in Guangzhou, which my guidebook tells me is how one properly refers to Canton these days. It seems all the cities I have heard of, except Shanghai, have changed their spellings. I think they are saying China has changed in other ways as well. Chungking is Chongqing. And Kweilin is Guilin. I have looked these names up, because after we see my father's aunt in Guangzhou, we will catch a plane to Shanghai, where I will meet my two half-sisters for the first time.

They are my mother's twin daughters from her first marriage, little babies she was forced to abandon on a road as she was fleeing Kweilin for Chungking in 1944. That was all my mother had told me about these daughters, so they had remained babies in my mind, all these years, sitting on the side of a road, listening to bombs whistling in the distance while sucking their patient red thumbs.

And it was only this year that someone found them and wrote with this joyful news. A letter came from Shanghai, addressed to my mother. When I first heard about this, that they were alive, I imagined my identical sisters transforming from little babies into six-year-old girls. In my mind, they were seated next to each other at a table, taking turns with the fountain pen. One would write a neat row of characters: *Dearest Mama. We are alive.* She would brush back her wispy bangs and hand the other sister the pen, and she would write: *Come get us. Please hurry.*

Of course they could not know that my mother had died three months before, suddenly, when a blood vessel in her brain burst. One minute she was talking to my father, complaining about the tenants upstairs, scheming how to evict them under the pretense that relatives from China were moving in. The next minute she was holding her head, her eyes squeezed shut, groping for the sofa, and then crumpling softly to the floor with fluttering hands.

So my father had been the first one to open the letter, a long letter it turned out. And they did call her Mama. They said they always revered her as their true mother. They kept a framed picture of her. They told her about their life, from the time my mother last saw them on the road leaving Kweilin to when they were finally found.

And the letter had broken my father's heart so much—these daughters calling my mother from another life he never knew—that he gave the letter to my mother's old friend Auntie Lindo and asked her to write back and tell my sisters, in the gentlest way possible, that my mother was dead.

But instead Auntie Lindo took the letter to the Joy Luck Club and discussed with Auntie Ying and Auntie An-mei what should be done, because they had known for many years about my mother's search for her twin daughters, her endless hope. Auntie Lindo and the others cried over this double tragedy, of losing my mother three months before, and now again. And so they couldn't help but think of some miracle, some possible way of reviving her from the dead, so my mother could fulfill her dream.

So this is what they wrote to my sisters in Shanghai: "Dearest Daughters, I too have never forgotten you in my memory or in my heart. I never gave up hope that we would see each other again in a joyous reunion. I am only sorry it has been too long. I want to tell you everything about my life since I last saw you. I want to tell you this when our family comes to see you in China. . . ." They signed it with my mother's name.

It wasn't until all this had been done that they first told me about my sisters, the letter they received, the one they wrote back.

"They'll think she's coming, then," I murmured. And I had imagined my sisters now being ten or eleven, jumping up and down, holding hands, their pigtails bouncing, excited that their mother—*their* mother—was coming, whereas my mother was dead.

"How can you say she is not coming in a letter?" said Auntie Lindo. "She is their mother. She is your mother. You must be the one to tell them. All these years, they have been dreaming of her." And I thought she was right.

But then I started dreaming, too, of my mother and my sisters and how it would be if I arrived in Shanghai. All these years, while they waited to be found, I had lived with my mother and then had lost her. I imagined seeing my sisters at the airport. They would be standing on their tiptoes, looking anxiously, scanning from one dark head to another as we got off the plane. And I would recognize them instantly, their faces with the identical worried look.

"*Jyejye, Jyejye*. Sister, Sister. We are here," I saw myself saying in my poor version of Chinese.

"Where is Mama?" they would say, and look around, still smiling, two flushed and eager faces. "Is she hiding?" And this would have been like my mother, to stand behind just a bit, to tease a little and make people's patience pull a little on their hearts. I would shake my head and tell my sisters she was not hiding.

"Oh, that must be Mama, no?" one of my sisters would whisper excitedly, pointing to another small woman completely engulfed in a tower of presents. And that, too, would have been like my mother, to bring mountains of gifts, food, and toys for children—all bought on sale—shunning thanks, saying the gifts were nothing, and later turning the labels over to show my sisters, "Calvin Klein, 100% wool."

I imagined myself starting to say, "Sisters, I am sorry, I have come alone . . ." and before I could tell them—they could see it in my face—they were wailing, pulling their hair, their lips twisted in pain, as they ran away from me. And then I saw myself getting back on the plane and coming home.

After I had dreamed this scene many times—watching their despair turn from horror into anger—I begged Auntie Lindo to write another letter. And at first she refused.

"How can I say she is dead? I cannot write this," said Auntie Lindo with a stubborn look.

"But it's cruel to have them believe she's coming on the plane," I said. "When they see it's just me, they'll hate me."

"Hate you? Cannot be." She was scowling. "You are their own sister, their only family."

"You don't understand," I protested.

"What I don't understand?" she said.

And I whispered. "They'll think I'm responsible, that she died because I didn't appreciate her."

And Auntie Lindo looked satisfied and sad at the same time, as if this were true and I had finally realized it. She sat down for an hour, and when she stood up she handed me a two-page letter. She had tears in her eyes. I realized that the very thing I had feared, she had done. So even if she had written the news of my mother's death in English, I wouldn't have had the heart to read it.

"Thank you," I whispered.

The landscape has become gray, filled with low flat cement buildings, old factories, and then tracks and more tracks filled with trains like ours passing by in the opposite direction. I see platforms crowded with people wearing drab Western clothes, with spots of bright colors: little children wearing pink and yellow, red and peach. And there are soldiers in olive green and red, and old ladies in gray tops and pants that stop mid-calf. We are in Guangzhou.

Before the train even comes to a stop, people are bringing down their belongings from above their seats. For a moment there is a dangerous shower of heavy suitcases laden with gifts to relatives, half-broken boxes wrapped in miles of string to keep the contents from spilling out, plastic bags filled with yarn and vegetables and packages of dried mushrooms, and camera cases. And then we are caught in a stream of people rushing, shoving, pushing us along, until we find ourselves in one of a dozen lines waiting to go through customs. I feel as if I were getting on a number 30 Stockton bus in San Francisco. I am in China, I remind myself. And somehow the crowds don't bother me. It feels right. I start pushing too.

I take out the declaration forms and my passport. "Woo," it says at the top, and below that, "June May," who was born in "California, U.S.A.," in 1951. I wonder if the customs people will question whether I'm the same person as in the passport photo. In this picture, my chin-length hair is swept back and artfully styled. I am wearing false eyelashes, eye shadow, and lip liner. My cheeks are hollowed out by bronze blusher. But I had not expected the heat in October. And now my hair hangs limp with the humidity. I wear no makeup; in Hong Kong my mascara had melted into dark circles and everything else had felt like layers of grease. So today my face is plain, unadorned except for a thin mist of shiny sweat on my forehead and nose.

Even without makeup, I could never pass for true Chinese. I stand five-foot-six, and my head pokes above the crowd so that I am eye level only with other tourists. My mother once told me my height came from my grandfather, who was a northerner, and may have even had some Mongol blood. "This is what your grandmother once told me," explained my mother. "But now it is too late to ask her. They are all dead, your grandparents, your uncles, and their wives and children, all killed in the war, when a bomb fell on our house. So many generations in one instant."

She had said this so matter-of-factly that I thought she had long since gotten over any grief she had. And then I wondered how she knew they were all dead.

"Maybe they left the house before the bomb fell," I suggested.

"No," said my mother. "Our whole family is gone. It is just you and I."

"But how do you know? Some of them could have escaped."

"Cannot be," said my mother, this time almost angrily. And then her frown was washed over by a puzzled blank look, and she began to talk as if she were trying to remember where she had misplaced something. "I went back to that house. I kept looking up to where the house used to be. And it wasn't a house, just the sky. And below, underneath my feet, were four stories of burnt bricks and wood, all the life of our house. Then off to the side I saw things blown into the yard, nothing valuable. There was a bed someone used to sleep in, really just a metal frame twisted up at one corner. And a book, I don't know what kind, because every page had turned black. And I saw a teacup which was unbroken but filled with ashes. And then I found my doll, with her hands and legs broken, her hair burned off. . . . When I was a little girl, I had cried for that doll, seeing it all alone in the store window, and my mother had bought it for me. It was an American doll with yellow hair. It could turn its legs and arms. The eyes moved up and down. And when I married and left my family home, I gave the doll to

35

40

my youngest niece, because she was like me. She cried if that doll was not with her always. Do you see? If she was in the house with that doll, her parents were there, and so everybody was there, waiting together, because that's how our family was."

The woman in the customs booth stares at my documents, then glances at me briefly, and with two quick movements stamps everything and sternly nods me along. And soon my father and I find ourselves in a large area filled with thousands of people and suitcases. I feel lost and my father looks helpless.

"Excuse me," I say to a man who looks like an American. "Can you tell me where I can get a taxi?" He mumbles something that sounds Swedish or Dutch.

"Syau Yen! Syau Yen!" I hear a piercing voice shout from behind me. An old woman in a yellow knit beret is holding up a pink plastic bag filled with wrapped trinkets. I guess she is trying to sell us something. But my father is staring down at this tiny sparrow of a woman, squinting into her eyes. And then his eyes widen, his face opens up and he smiles like a pleased little boy.

"Aiyi! Aiyi!"—Auntie Auntie!—he says softly.

45   "Syau Yen!" coos my great-aunt. I think it's funny she has just called my father "Little Wild Goose." It must be his baby milk name, the name used to discourage ghosts from stealing children.

They clasp each other's hands—they do not hug—and hold on like this, taking turns saying, "Look at you! You are so old. Look how old you've become!" They are both crying openly, laughing at the same time, and I bite my lip, trying not to cry. I'm afraid to feel their joy. Because I am thinking how different our arrival in Shanghai will be tomorrow, how awkward it will feel.

Now Aiyi beams and points to a Polaroid picture of my father. My father had wisely sent pictures when he wrote and said we were coming. See how smart she was, she seems to intone as she compares the picture to my father. In the letter, my father had said we would call her from the hotel once we arrived, so this is a surprise, that they've come to meet us. I wonder if my sisters will be at the airport.

It is only then that I remember the camera. I had meant to take a picture of my father and his aunt the moment they met. It's not too late.

"Here, stand together over here," I say, holding up the Polaroid. The camera flashes and I hand them the snapshot. Aiyi and my father still stand close together, each of them holding a corner of the picture, watching as their images begin to form. They are almost reverentially quiet. Aiyi is only five years older than my father, which makes her around seventy-seven. But she looks ancient, shrunken, a mummified relic. Her thin hair is pure white, her teeth are brown with decay. So much for stories of Chinese women looking young forever, I think to myself.

50   Now Aiyi is crooning to me: "Jandale." So big already. She looks up at me, at my full height, and then peers into her pink plastic bag—her gifts to us, I have figured out—as if she is wondering what she will give to me, now that I am so old and big. And then she grabs my elbow with her sharp pincerlike grasp and turns me around. A man and a woman in their fifties are shaking hands

with my father, everybody smiling and saying, "Ah! Ah!" They are Aiyi's oldest son and his wife, and standing next to them are four other people, around my age, and a little girl who's around ten. The introductions go by so fast, all I know is that one of them is Aiyi's grandson, with his wife, and the other is her granddaughter, with her husband. And the little girl is Lili, Aiyi's great-granddaughter.

Aiyi and my father speak the Mandarin dialect from their childhood, but the rest of the family speaks only the Cantonese of their village. I understand only Mandarin but can't speak it that well. So Aiyi and my father gossip unrestrained in Mandarin, exchanging news about people from their old village. And they stop only occasionally to talk to the rest of us, sometimes in Cantonese, sometimes in English.

"Oh, it is as I suspected," says my father, turning to me. "He died last summer." And I already understood this. I just don't know who this person, Li Gong, is. I feel as if I were in the United Nations and the translators had run amok.

"Hello," I say to the little girl. "My name is Jing-mei." But the little girl squirms to look away, causing her parents to laugh with embarrassment. I try to think of Cantonese words I can say to her, stuff I learned from friends in Chinatown, but all I can think of are swear words, terms for bodily functions, and short phrases like "tastes good," "tastes like garbage," and "she's really ugly." And then I have another plan: I hold up the Polaroid camera, beckoning Lili with my finger. She immediately jumps forward, places one hand on her hip in the manner of a fashion model, juts out her chest, and flashes me a toothy smile. As soon as I take the picture she is standing next to me, jumping and giggling every few seconds as she watches herself appear on the greenish film.

By the time we hail taxis for the ride to the hotel, Lili is holding tight onto my hand, pulling me along.

In the taxi, Aiyi talks nonstop, so I have no chance to ask her about the different sights we are passing by.

"You wrote and said you would come only for one day," says Aiyi to my father in an agitated tone. "One day! How can you see your family in one day! Toishan is many hours' drive from Guangzhou. And this idea to call us when you arrive. This is nonsense. We have no telephone."

My heart races a little. I wonder if Auntie Lindo told my sisters we would call from the hotel in Shanghai?

Aiyi continues to scold my father. "I was so beside myself, ask my son, almost turned heaven and earth upside down trying to think of a way! So we decided the best was for us to take the bus from Toishan and come into Guangzhou — meet you right from the start."

And now I am holding my breath as the taxi driver dodges between trucks and buses, honking his horn constantly. We seem to be on some sort of long freeway overpass, like a bridge above the city. I can see row after row of apartments, each floor cluttered with laundry hanging out to dry on the balcony. We pass a public bus, with people jammed in so tight their faces are nearly wedged against the window. Then I see the skyline of what must be downtown Guangzhou. From a distance, it looks like a major American city, with highrises and construction going on everywhere. As we slow down in the more congested part of the city, I see scores of little shops, dark inside, lined with counters and shelves. And then there is a building, its front laced with scaffolding made of bamboo poles held together with plastic strips. Men and women are standing on narrow platforms, scraping the sides, working without safety straps or helmets. Oh, would OSHA[1] have a field day here, I think.

60   Aiyi's shrill voice rises up again: "So it is a shame you can't see our village, our house. My sons have been quite successful, selling our vegetables in the free market. We had enough these last few years to build a big house, three stories, all of new brick, big enough for our whole family and then some. And every year, the money is even better. You Americans aren't the only ones who know how to get rich!"

The taxi stops and I assume we've arrived, but then I peer out at what looks like a grander version of the Hyatt Regency. "This is communist China?" I wonder out loud. And then I shake my head toward my father. "This must be the wrong hotel." I quickly pull out our itinerary, travel tickets, and reservations. I had explicitly instructed my travel agent to choose something inexpensive, in the thirty-to-forty-dollar range. I'm sure of this. And there it says on our itinerary: Garden Hotel, Huanshi Dong Lu. Well, our travel agent had better be prepared to eat the extra, that's all I have to say.

The hotel is magnificent. A bellboy complete with uniform and sharp-creased cap jumps forward and begins to carry our bags into the lobby. Inside, the hotel looks like an orgy of shopping arcades and restaurants all encased in granite and glass. And rather than be impressed, I am worried about the expense, as well as the appearance it must give Aiyi, that we rich Americans cannot be without our luxuries even for one night.

But when I step up to the reservation desk, ready to haggle over this booking mistake, it is confirmed. Our rooms are prepaid, thirty-four dollars each. I feel sheepish, and Aiyi and the others seem delighted by our temporary surroundings. Lili is looking wide-eyed at an arcade filled with video games.

Our whole family crowds into one elevator, and the bellboy waves, saying he will meet us on the eighteenth floor. As soon as the elevator door shuts, everybody becomes very quiet, and when the door finally opens again, everybody talks at once in what sounds like relieved voices. I have the feeling Aiyi and the others have never been on such a long elevator ride.

65   Our rooms are next to each other and are identical. The rugs, drapes, bedspreads are all in shades of taupe. There's a color television with remote-control panels built into the lamp table between the two twin beds. The bathroom has marble walls and floors. I find a built-in wet bar with a small refrigerator stocked with Heineken beer, Coke Classic, and Seven-Up, mini-bottles of Johnnie Walker Red, Bacardi rum, and Smirnoff vodka, and packets of M & M's, honey-roasted cashews, and Cadbury chocolate bars. And again I say out loud, "This is communist China?"

My father comes into my room. "They decided we should just stay here and

1. Occupational Safety and Health Administration.

visit," he says, shrugging his shoulders. "They say, Less trouble that way. More time to talk."

"What about dinner?" I ask. I have been envisioning my first real Chinese feast for many days already, a big banquet with one of those soups steaming out of a carved winter melon, chicken wrapped in clay, Peking duck, the works.

My father walks over and picks up a room service book next to a *Travel & Leisure* magazine. He flips through the pages quickly and then points to the menu. "This is what they want," says my father.

So it's decided. We are going to dine tonight in our rooms, with our family, sharing hamburgers, french fries, and apple pie à la mode.

Aiyi and her family are browsing the shops while we clean up. After a hot ride on the train, I'm eager for a shower and cooler clothes.

The hotel has provided little packets of shampoo which, upon opening, I discover is the consistency and color of hoisin sauce.[2] This is more like it, I think. This is China. And I rub some in my damp hair.

Standing in the shower, I realize this is the first time I've been by myself in what seems like days. But instead of feeling relieved, I feel forlorn. I think about what my mother said, about activating my genes and becoming Chinese. And I wonder what she meant.

Right after my mother died, I asked myself a lot of things, things that couldn't be answered, to force myself to grieve more. It seemed as if I wanted to sustain my grief, to assure myself that I had cared deeply enough.

But now I ask the questions mostly because I want to know the answers. What was that pork stuff she used to make that had the texture of sawdust? What were the names of the uncles who died in Shanghai? What had she dreamt all these years about her other daughters? All the times when she got mad at me, was she really thinking about them? Did she wish I were they? Did she regret that I wasn't?

• • •

At one o'clock in the morning, I awake to tapping sounds on the window. I must have dozed off and now I feel my body uncramping itself. I'm sitting on the floor, leaning against one of the twin beds. Lili is lying next to me. The others are asleep, too, sprawled out on the beds and floor. Aiyi is seated at a little table, looking very sleepy. And my father is staring out the window, tapping his fingers on the glass. The last time I listened my father was telling Aiyi about his life since he last saw her. How he had gone to Yenching University, later got a post with a newspaper in Chungking, met my mother there, a young widow. How they later fled together to Shanghai to try to find my mother's family house, but there was nothing there. And then they traveled eventually to Canton and then to Hong Kong, then Haiphong and finally to San Francisco. . . .

"Suyuan didn't tell me she was trying all these years to find her daughters," he is now saying in a quiet voice. "Naturally, I did not discuss her daughters

70

75

2. Sweet brownish-red sauce made from soybeans, flour, sugar, water, spices, garlic, and chili.

with her. I thought she was ashamed she had left them behind."

"Where did she leave them?" asks Aiyi. "How were they found?"

I am wide awake now. Although I have heard parts of this story from my mother's friends.

"It happened when the Japanese took over Kweilin," says my father.

80 "Japanese in Kweilin?" says Aiyi. "That was never the case. Couldn't be. The Japanese never came to Kweilin."

"Yes, that is what the newspapers reported. I know this because I was working for the news bureau at the time. The Kuomintang[3] often told us what we could say and could not say. But we knew the Japanese had come into Kwangsi Province. We had sources who told us how they had captured the Wuchang-Canton railway. How they were coming overland, making very fast progress, marching toward the provincial capital."

Aiyi looks astonished. "If people did not know this, how could Suyuan know the Japanese were coming?"

"An officer of the Kuomintang secretly warned her," explains my father. "Suyuan's husband also was an officer and everybody knew that officers and their families would be the first to be killed. So she gathered a few possessions and, in the middle of the night, she picked up her daughters and fled on foot. The babies were not even one year old."

"How could she give up those babies!" sighs Aiyi. "Twin girls. We have never had such luck in our family." And then she yawns again.

85 "What were they named?" she asks. I listen carefully. I had been planning on using just the familiar "Sister" to address them both. But now I want to know how to pronounce their names.

"They have their father's surname, Wang," says my father. "And their given names are Chwun Yu and Chwun Hwa."

"What do the names mean?" I ask.

"Ah." My father draws imaginary characters on the window. "One means 'Spring Rain,' the other 'Spring Flower,' " he explains in English, "because they born in the spring, and of course rain come before flower, same order these girls are born. Your mother like a poet, don't you think?"

I nod my head. I see Aiyi nod her head forward, too. But it falls forward and stays there. She is breathing deeply, noisily. She is asleep.

90 "And what does Ma's name mean?" I whisper.

" 'Suyuan,' " he says, writing more invisible characters on the glass. "The way she write it in Chinese, it mean 'Long-Cherished Wish.' Quite a fancy name, not so ordinary like flower name. See this first character, it means something like 'Forever Never Forgotten.' But there is another way to write 'Suyuan.' Sound exactly the same, but the meaning is opposite." His finger creates the brushstrokes of another character. "The first part look the same: 'Never Forgotten.' But the last part add to first part make the whole word mean 'Long-Held Grudge.' Your mother get angry with me, I tell her her name should be Grudge."

---

3. National People's Party, led by Generalissimo Chiang Kai-shek (1887–1975).

My father is looking at me, moist-eyed. "See, I pretty clever, too, hah?"

I nod, wishing I could find some way to comfort him. "And what about my name," I ask, "what does 'Jing-mei' mean?"

"Your name also special," he says. I wonder if any name in Chinese is not something special. " 'Jing' like excellent *jing*. Not just good, it's something pure, essential, the best quality. *Jing* is good leftover stuff when you take impurities out of something like gold, or rice, or salt. So what is left—just pure essence. And 'Mei,' this is common *mei*, as in *meimei*, 'younger sister.' "

I think about this. My mother's long-cherished wish. Me, the younger sister who was supposed to be the essence of the others. I feed myself with the old grief, wondering how disappointed my mother must have been. Tiny Aiyi stirs suddenly, her head rolls and then falls back, her mouth opens as if to answer my question. She grunts in her sleep, tucking her body more closely into the chair.

"So why did she abandon those babies on the road?" I need to know, because now I feel abandoned too.

"Long time I wondered this myself," says my father. "But then I read that letter from her daughters in Shanghai now, and I talk to Auntie Lindo, all the others. And then I knew. No shame in what she done. None."

"What happened?"

"Your mother running away—" begins my father.

"No, tell me in Chinese," I interrupt. "Really, I can understand."

He begins to talk, still standing at the window, looking into the night.

• • •

After fleeing Kweilin, your mother walked for several days trying to find a main road. Her thought was to catch a ride on a truck or wagon, to catch enough rides until she reached Chungking, where her husband was stationed.

She had sewn money and jewelry into the lining of her dress, enough, she thought, to barter rides all the way. If I am lucky, she thought, I will not have to trade the heavy gold bracelet and jade ring. These were things from her mother, your grandmother.

By the third day, she had traded nothing. The roads were filled with people, everybody running and begging for rides from passing trucks. The trucks rushed by, afraid to stop. So your mother found no rides, only the start of dysentery pains in her stomach.

Her shoulders ached from the two babies swinging from scarf slings. Blisters grew on the palms from holding two leather suitcases. And then the blisters burst and began to bleed. After a while, she left the suitcases behind, keeping only the food and a few clothes. And later she also dropped the bags of wheat flour and rice and kept walking like this for many miles, singing songs to her little girls, until she was delirious with pain and fever.

Finally, there was not one more step left in her body. She didn't have the strength to carry those babies any further. She slumped to the ground. She knew she would die of her sickness, or perhaps from thirst, from starvation, or from the Japanese, who she was sure were marching right behind her.

She took the babies out of the slings and sat them on the side of the road, then lay down next to them. You babies are so good, she said, so quiet. They smiled back, reaching their chubby hands for her, wanting to be picked up again. And then she knew she could not bear to watch her babies die with her.

She saw a family with three young children in a cart going by. "Take my babies, I beg you," she cried to them. But they stared back with empty eyes and never stopped.

She saw another person pass and called out again. This time a man turned around, and he had such a terrible expression—your mother said it looked like death itself—she shivered and looked away.

When the road grew quiet, she tore open the lining of her dress, and stuffed jewelry under the shirt of one baby and money under the other. She reached into her pocket and drew out the photos of her family, the picture of her father and mother, the picture of herself and her husband on their wedding day. And she wrote on the back of each the names of the babies and this same message: "Please care for these babies with the money and valuables provided. When it is safe to come, if you bring them to Shanghai, 9 Weichang Lu, the Li family will be glad to give you a generous reward. Li Suyuan and Wang Fuchi."

And then she touched each baby's cheek and told her not to cry. She would go down the road to find them some food and would be back. And without looking back, she walked down the road, stumbling and crying, thinking only of this last hope, that her daughters would be found by a kindhearted person who would care for them. She would not allow herself to imagine anything else.

She did not remember how far she walked, which direction she went, when she fainted, or how she was found. When she awoke, she was in the back of a bouncing truck with several other sick people, all moaning. And she began to scream, thinking she was now on a journey to Buddhist hell. But the face of an American missionary lady bent over her and smiled, talking to her in a soothing language she did not understand. And yet she could somehow understand. She had been saved for no good reason, and it was now too late to go back and save her babies.

When she arrived in Chungking, she learned her husband had died two weeks before. She told me later she laughed when the officers told her this news, she was so delirious with madness and disease. To come so far, to lose so much and to find nothing.

I met her in a hospital. She was lying on a cot, hardly able to move, her dysentery had drained her so thin. I had come in for my foot, my missing toe, which was cut off by a piece of falling rubble. She was talking to herself, mumbling.

"Look at these clothes," she said, and I saw she had on a rather unusual dress for wartime. It was silk satin, quite dirty, but there was no doubt it was a beautiful dress.

"Look at this face," she said, and I saw her dusty face and hollow cheeks, her eyes shining black. "Do you see my foolish hope?"

"I thought I had lost everything, except these two things," she murmured. "And I wondered which I would lose next. Clothes or hope? Hope or clothes?"

"But now, see here, look what is happening," she said, laughing, as if all her prayers had been answered. And she was pulling hair out of her head as easily as one lifts new wheat from wet soil.

It was an old peasant woman who found them. "How could I resist?" the peasant woman later told your sisters when they were older. They were still sitting obediently near where your mother had left them, looking like little fairy queens waiting for their sedan to arrive.

The woman, Mei Ching, and her husband, Mei Han, lived in a stone cave. There were thousands of hidden caves like that in and around Kweilin so secret that the people remained hidden even after the war ended. The Meis would come out of their cave every few days and forage for food supplies left on the road, and sometimes they would see something that they both agreed was a tragedy to leave behind. So one day they took back to their cave a delicately painted set of rice bowls, another day a little footstool with a velvet cushion and two new wedding blankets. And once, it was your sisters.

They were pious people, Muslims, who believed the twin babies were a sign of double luck, and they were sure of this when, later in the evening, they discovered how valuable the babies were. She and her husband had never seen rings and bracelets like those. And while they admired the pictures, knowing the babies came from a good family, neither of them could read or write. It was not until many months later that Mei Ching found someone who could read the writing on the back. By then, she loved these baby girls like her own.

In 1952 Mei Han, the husband, died. The twins already eight years old, and Mei Ching now decided it was time to find your sisters' true family.

She showed the girls the picture of their mother and told them they had been born into a great family and she would take them back to see their true mother and grandparents. Mei Ching told them about the reward, but she swore she would refuse it. She loved these girls so much, she only wanted them to have what they were entitled to—a better life, a fine house, educated ways. Maybe the family would let her stay on as the girls' amah. Yes, she was certain they would insist.

Of course, when she found the place at 9 Weichang Lu, in the old French Concession, it was something completely different. It was the site of a factory building, recently constructed, and none of the workers knew what had become of the family whose house had burned down on that spot.

Mei Ching could not have known, of course, that your mother and I, her new husband, had already returned to that same place in 1945 in hopes of finding both her family and her daughters.

Your mother and I stayed in China until 1947. We went to many different cities—back to Kweilin, to Changsha, as far south as Kunming. She was always looking out of one corner of her eye for twin babies, then little girls. Later we went to Hong Kong, and when we finally left in 1949 for the United States, I think she was even looking for them on the boat. But when we arrived, she no longer talked about them. I thought, At last, they have died in her heart.

When letters could be openly exchanged between China and the United States, she wrote immediately to old friends in Shanghai and Kweilin. I did not know she did this. Auntie Lindo told me. But of course, by then, all the street names had changed. Some people had died, others had moved away. So it took many years to find a contact. And when she did find an old schoolmate's address and wrote asking her to look for her daughters, her friend wrote back and said this was impossible, like looking for a needle on the bottom of the ocean. How did she know her daughters were in Shanghai and not somewhere else in China? The friend, of course, did not ask, How do you know your daughters are still alive?

So her schoolmate did not look. Finding babies lost during the war was a matter of foolish imagination, and she had no time for that.

But every year, your mother wrote to different people. And this last year, I think she got a big idea in her head, to go to China and find them herself. I remember she told me, "Canning, we should go, before it is too late, before we are too old." And I told her we were already too old, it was already too late.

I just thought she wanted to be a tourist! I didn't know she wanted to go and look for her daughters. So when I said it was too late, that must have put a terrible thought in her head that her daughters might be dead. And I think this possibility grew bigger and bigger in her head, until it killed her.

Maybe it was your mother's dead spirit who guided her Shanghai schoolmate to find her daughters. Because after your mother died, the schoolmate saw your sisters, by chance, while shopping for shoes at the Number One Department Store on Nanjing Dong Road. She said it was like a dream, seeing these two women who looked so much alike, moving down the stairs together. There was something about their facial expressions that reminded the schoolmate of your mother.

She quickly walked over to them and called their names, which of course, they did not recognize at first, because Mei Ching had changed their names. But your mother's friend was so sure, she persisted. "Are you not Wang Chwun Yu and Wang Chwun Hwa?" she asked them. And then these double-image women became very excited, because they remembered the names written on the back of an old photo, a photo of a young man and woman they still honored, as their much-loved first parents, who had died and become spirit ghosts still roaming the earth looking for them.

* * *

At the airport, I am exhausted. I could not sleep last night. Aiyi had followed me into my room at three in the morning, and she instantly fell asleep on one of the twin beds, snoring with the might of a lumberjack. I lay awake thinking about my mother's story, realizing how much I have never known about her, grieving that my sisters and I had both lost her.

And now at the airport, after shaking hands with everybody, waving good-bye, I think about all the different ways we leave people in this world. Cheerily waving good-bye to some at airports, knowing we'll never see each other again. Leaving others on the side of the road, hoping that we will. Finding my mother in my father's story and saying good-bye before I have a chance to know her better.

Aiyi smiles at me as we wait for our gate to be called. She is so old. I put one 135
arm around her and one arm around Lili. They are the same size, it seems. And
then it's time. As we wave good-bye one more time and enter the waiting area,
I get the sense I am going from one funeral to another. In my hand I'm clutching a pair of tickets to Shanghai. In two hours we'll be there.

The plane takes off. I close my eyes. How can I describe to them in my
broken Chinese about our mother's life? Where should I begin?

"Wake up, we're here," says my father. And I awake with my heart pounding
in my throat. I look out the window and we're already on the runway. It's gray
outside.

And now I'm walking down the steps of the plane, onto the tarmac and
toward the building. If only, I think, if only my mother had lived long enough
to be the one walking toward them. I am so nervous I cannot feel my feet. I am
just moving somehow.

Somebody shouts, "She's arrived!" And then I see her. Her short hair. Her
small body. And that same look on her face. She has the back of her hand
pressed hard against her mouth. She is crying as though she had gone through
a terrible ordeal and were happy it is over.

And I know it's not my mother, yet it is the same look she had when I was five 140
and had disappeared all afternoon, for such a long time, that she was convinced I
was dead. And when I miraculously appeared, sleepy-eyed, crawling from underneath my bed, she wept and laughed, biting the back of her hand to make sure
it was true.

And now I see her again, two of her, waving, and in one hand there is a
photo, the Polaroid I sent them. As soon as I get beyond the gate, we run toward
each other, all three of us embracing, all hesitations and expectations forgotten.

"Mama, Mama," we all murmur, as if she is among us.

My sisters look at me, proudly. "*Meimei jandale*," says one sister proudly to
the other. "Little Sister has grown up." I look at their faces again and I see no
trace of my mother in them. Yet they still look familiar. And now I also see what
part of me is Chinese. It is so obvious. It is my family. It is in our blood. After
all these years, it can finally be let go.

My sisters and I stand, arms around each other, laughing and wiping the
tears from each other's eyes. The flash of the Polaroid goes off and my father
hands me the snapshot. My sisters and I watch quietly together, eager to see
what develops.

The gray-green surface changes to the bright colors of our three images, 145
sharpening and deepening all at once. And although we don't speak, I know we
all see it: Together we look like our mother. Her same eyes, her same mouth,
open in surprise to see, at last, her long-cherished wish.

1989

ANTON CHEKHOV

The Lady with the Dog[1]

I

People were telling one another that a newcomer had been seen on the promenade—a lady with a dog. Dmitry Dmitrich Gurov had been a fortnight in Yalta,[2] and was accustomed to its ways, and he, too, had begun to take an interest in fresh arrivals. From his seat in Vernet's outdoor café, he caught sight of a young woman in a toque, passing along the promenade; she was fair and not very tall; after her trotted a white Pomeranian.

Later he encountered her in the municipal park and in the square several times a day. She was always alone, wearing the same toque, and the Pomeranian always trotted at her side. Nobody knew who she was, and people referred to her simply as "the lady with the dog."

"If she's here without her husband, and without any friends," thought Gurov, "it wouldn't be a bad idea to make her acquaintance."

He was not yet forty but had a twelve-year-old daughter and two sons in high school. He had been talked into marrying in his third year at college, and his wife now looked nearly twice as old as he did. She was a tall woman with dark eyebrows, erect, dignified, imposing, and, as she said of herself, a "thinker." She was a great reader, omitted the "hard sign"[3] at the end of words in her letters, and called her husband "Dimitry" instead of Dmitry; and though he secretly considered her shallow, narrow-minded, and dowdy, he stood in awe of her, and disliked being at home. He had first begun deceiving her long ago and he was now constantly unfaithful to her, and this was no doubt why he spoke slightingly of women, to whom he referred as *the lower race*.

He considered that the ample lessons he had received from bitter experience entitled him to call them whatever he liked, but without this "lower race" he could not have existed a single day. He was bored and ill-at-ease in the company of men, with whom he was always cold and reserved, but felt quite at home among women, and knew exactly what to say to them, and how to behave; he could even be silent in their company without feeling the slightest awkwardness. There was an elusive charm in his appearance and disposition which attracted women and caught their sympathies. He knew this and was himself attracted to them by some invisible force.

Repeated and bitter experience had taught him that every fresh intimacy, while at first introducing such pleasant variety into everyday life, and offering itself as a charming, light adventure, inevitably developed, among decent people (especially in Moscow, where they are so irresolute and slow to move), into a problem of excessive complication leading to an intolerably irksome situation.

1. Translated by Ivy Litvinov.   2. Russian city on the Black Sea; a resort for southern vacations.
3. Conventional sign that was used following consonants; to omit it was then "progressive."

But every time he encountered an attractive woman he forgot all about this experience, the desire for life surged up in him, and everything suddenly seemed simple and amusing.

One evening, then, while he was dining at the restaurant in the park, the lady in the toque came strolling up and took a seat at a neighboring table. Her expression, gait, dress, coiffure, all told him that she was from the upper classes, that she was married, that she was in Yalta for the first time, alone and bored. . . . The accounts of the laxity of morals among visitors to Yalta are greatly exaggerated, and he paid no heed to them, knowing that for the most part they were invented by people who would gladly have transgressed themselves, had they known how to set about it. But when the lady sat down at a neighboring table a few yards away from him, these stories of easy conquests, of excursions to the mountains, came back to him, and the seductive idea of a brisk transitory liaison, an affair with a woman whose very name he did not know, suddenly took possession of his mind.

He snapped his fingers at the Pomeranian and, when it trotted up to him, shook his forefinger at it. The Pomeranian growled. Gurov shook his finger again.

The lady glanced at him and instantly lowered her eyes.

"He doesn't bite," she said, and blushed.

"May I give him a bone?" he asked, and on her nod of consent added in friendly tones: "Have you been long in Yalta?"

"About five days."

"And I am dragging out my second week here."

Neither spoke for a few minutes.

"The days pass quickly, and yet one is so bored here," she said, not looking at him.

"It's the thing to say it's boring here. People never complain of boredom in godforsaken holes like Belyev or Zhizdra, but when they get here it's: 'Oh, the dullness! Oh, the dust!' You'd think they'd come from Granada[4] to say the least."

She laughed. Then they both went on eating in silence, like complete strangers. But after dinner they left the restaurant together, and embarked upon the light, jesting talk of people free and contented, for whom it is all the same where they go, or what they talk about. They strolled along, remarking on the strange light over the sea. The water was a warm, tender purple, the moonlight lay on its surface in a golden strip. They said how close it was, after the hot day. Gurov told her he was from Moscow, had a degree in literature but worked in a bank; that he had at one time trained himself to sing in a private opera company, but had given up the idea; that he owned two houses in Moscow. . . . And from her he learned that she had grown up in Petersburg, but had gotten married in the town of S., where she had been living two years, that she would stay another month in Yalta, and that perhaps her husband, who also needed a rest, would join her. She was quite unable to explain whether her husband was a member of the province council, or on the board of the *zemstvo*,[5] and was greatly

4. Romantic city in southern Spain.   5. An elective provincial council.

amused at herself for this. Further, Gurov learned that her name was Anna Sergeyevna.

Back in his own room he thought about her, and felt sure he would meet her the next day. It was inevitable. As he went to bed he reminded himself that only a very short time ago she had been a schoolgirl, like his own daughter, learning her lessons; he remembered how much there was of shyness and constraint in her laughter, in her way of conversing with a stranger—it was probably the first time in her life that she found herself alone, and in a situation in which men could follow her and watch her, and speak to her, all the time with a secret aim she could not fail to divine. He recalled her slender, delicate neck, her fine gray eyes.

"And yet there's something pathetic about her," he thought to himself as he fell asleep.

II

A week had passed since the beginning of their acquaintance. It was a holiday. Indoors it was stuffy, but the dust rose in clouds out of doors, and people's hats blew off. It was a parching day and Gurov kept going to the outdoor café for fruit drinks and ices to offer Anna Sergeyevna. The heat was overpowering.

In the evening, when the wind had dropped, they walked to the pier to see the steamer come in. There were a great many people strolling about the landing-place; some, bunches of flowers in their hands, were meeting friends. Two peculiarities of the smart Yalta crowd stood out distinctly—the elderly ladies all tried to dress very youthfully, and there seemed to be an inordinate number of generals about.

Owing to the roughness of the sea the steamer arrived late, after the sun had gone down, and it had to maneuver for some time before it could get alongside the pier. Anna Sergeyevna scanned the steamer and passengers through her lorgnette, as if looking for someone she knew, and when she turned to Gurov her eyes were glistening. She talked a great deal, firing off abrupt questions and forgetting immediately what it was she had wanted to know. Then she lost her lorgnette in the crush.

The smart crowd began dispersing, features could no longer be made out, the wind had quite dropped, and Gurov and Anna Sergeyevna stood there as if waiting for someone else to come off the steamer. Anna Sergeyevna had fallen silent, every now and then smelling her flowers, but not looking at Gurov.

"It's turning out a fine evening," he said. "What shall we do? We might go for a drive."

She made no reply.

He looked steadily at her and suddenly took her in his arms and kissed her lips, and the fragrance and dampness of the flowers closed round him, but the next moment he looked behind him in alarm—had anyone seen them?

"Let's go to your room," he murmured.

And they walked off together, very quickly.

Her room was stuffy and smelt of some scent she had bought in the Japanese shop. Gurov looked at her, thinking to himself: "How full of strange encounters life is!" He could remember carefree, good-natured women who were exhilarated by love-making and grateful to him for the happiness he gave them, however short-lived; and there had been others—his wife among them—whose caresses were insincere, affected, hysterical, mixed up with a great deal of quite unnecessary talk, and whose expression seemed to say that all this was not just love-making or passion, but something much more significant; then there had been two or three beautiful, cold women, over whose features flitted a predatory expression, betraying a determination to wring from life more than it could give, women no longer in their first youth, capricious, irrational, despotic, brainless, and when Gurov had cooled to these, their beauty aroused in him nothing but repulsion, and the lace trimming on their underclothes reminded him of fish-scales.

But here the timidity and awkwardness of youth and inexperience were still apparent; and there was a feeling of embarrassment in the atmosphere, as if someone had just knocked at the door. Anna Sergeyevna, "the lady with the dog," seemed to regard the affair as something very special, very serious, as if she had become a fallen woman, an attitude he found odd and disconcerting. Her features lengthened and drooped, and her long hair hung mournfully on either side of her face. She assumed a pose of dismal meditation, like a repentant sinner in some classical painting.

"It isn't right," she said. "You will never respect me anymore."

On the table was a watermelon. Gurov cut himself a slice from it and began slowly eating it. At least half an hour passed in silence.

Anna Sergeyevna was very touching, revealing the purity of a decent, naïve woman who had seen very little of life. The solitary candle burning on the table scarcely lit up her face, but it was obvious that her heart was heavy.

"Why should I stop respecting you?" asked Gurov. "You don't know what you're saying."

"May God forgive me!" she exclaimed, and her eyes filled with tears. "It's terrible."

"No need to seek to justify yourself."

"How can I justify myself? I'm a wicked, fallen woman, I despise myself and have not the least thought of self-justification. It isn't my husband I have deceived, it's myself. And not only now, I have been deceiving myself for ever so long. My husband is no doubt an honest, worthy man, but he's a flunky. I don't know what it is he does at his office, but I know he's a flunky. I was only twenty when I married him, and I was devoured by curiosity, I wanted something higher. I told myself that there must be a different kind of life I wanted to live, to live. . . . I was burning with curiosity . . . you'll never understand that, but I swear to God I could no longer control myself, nothing could hold me back, I told my husband I was ill, and I came here. . . . And I started going about like one possessed, like a madwoman . . . and now I have become an ordinary, worthless woman, and everyone has a right to despise me."

Gurov listened to her, bored to death. The naïve accents, the remorse, all was so unexpected, so out of place. But for the tears in her eyes, she might have been jesting or play-acting.

"I don't understand," he said gently. "What is it you want?"

She hid her face against his breast and pressed closer to him.

"Do believe me, I implore you to believe me," she said. "I love all that is honest and pure in life, vice is revolting to me, I don't know what I'm doing. The common people say they are snared by the Devil. And now I can say that I have been snared by the Devil, too."

"Come, come," he murmured.

He gazed into her fixed, terrified eyes, kissed her, and soothed her with gentle affectionate words, and gradually she calmed down and regained her cheerfulness. Soon they were laughing together again.

When, a little later, they went out, there was not a soul on the promenade, the town and its cypresses looked dead, but the sea was still roaring as it dashed against the beach. A solitary fishing-boat tossed on the waves, its lamp blinking sleepily.

They found a carriage and drove to Oreanda.

"I discovered your name in the hall, just now," said Gurov, "written up on the board. Von Diederitz. Is your husband a German?"

"No. His grandfather was, I think, but he belongs to the Orthodox Church himself."

When they got out of the carriage at Oreanda they sat down on a bench not far from the church, and looked down at the sea, without talking. Yalta could be dimly discerned through the morning mist, and white clouds rested motionless on the summits of the mountains. Not a leaf stirred, the grasshoppers chirruped, and the monotonous hollow roar of the sea came up to them, speaking of peace, of the eternal sleep lying in wait for us all. The sea had roared like this long before there was any Yalta or Oreanda, it was roaring now, and it would go on roaring, just as indifferently and hollowly, when we had passed away. And it may be that in this continuity, this utter indifference to the life and death of each of us lies hidden the pledge of our eternal salvation, of the continuous movement of life on earth, of the continuous movement toward perfection.

Side by side with a young woman, who looked so exquisite in the early light, soothed and enchanted by the sight of all this magical beauty—sea, mountains, clouds and the vast expanse of the sky—Gurov told himself that, when you came to think of it, everything in the world is beautiful really, everything but our own thoughts and actions, when we lose sight of the higher aims of life, and of our dignity as human beings.

Someone approached them—a watchman, probably—looked at them and went away. And there was something mysterious and beautiful even in this. The steamer from Feodosia could be seen coming towards the pier, lit up by the dawn, its lamps out.

"There's dew on the grass," said Anna Sergeyevna, breaking the silence.

"Yes. Time to go home."

They went back to the town.

After this they met every day at noon on the promenade, lunching and dining together, going for walks, and admiring the sea. She complained of sleep lessness, of palpitations, asked the same questions over and over again, alternately surrendering to jealousy and the fear that he did not really respect her. And often, when there was nobody in sight in the square or the park, he would draw her to him and kiss her passionately. The utter idleness, these kisses in broad daylight, accompanied by furtive glances and the fear of discovery, the heat, the smell of the sea, and the idle, smart, well-fed people continually crossing their field of vision, seemed to have given him a new lease on life. He told Anna Sergeyevna she was beautiful and seductive, made love to her with impetuous passion, and never left her side, while she was always pensive, always trying to force from him the admission that he did not respect her, that he did not love her a bit, and considered her just an ordinary woman. Almost every night they drove out of town, to Oreanda, the waterfall, or some other beauty-spot. And these excursions were invariably a success, each contributing fresh impressions of majestic beauty.

All this time they kept expecting her husband to arrive. But a letter came in which he told his wife that he was having trouble with his eyes, and implored her to come home as soon as possible. Anna Sergeyevna made hasty preparations for leaving. 55

"It's a good thing I'm going," she said to Gurov. "It's the intervention of fate."

She left Yalta in a carriage, and he went with her as far as the railway station. The drive took nearly a whole day. When she got into the express train, after the second bell had been rung, she said:

"Let me have one more look at you. . . . One last look. That's right."

She did not weep, but was mournful, and seemed ill, the muscles of her cheeks twitching.

"I shall think of you . . . I shall think of you all the time," she said. "God 60 bless you! Think kindly of me. We are parting forever, it must be so, because we ought never to have met. Good-bye—God bless you."

The train steamed rapidly out of the station, its lights soon disappearing, and a minute later even the sound it made was silenced, as if everything were conspiring to bring this sweet oblivion, this madness, to an end as quickly as possible. And Gurov, standing alone on the platform and gazing into the dark distance, listened to the shrilling of the grasshoppers and the humming of the telegraph wires, with a feeling that he had only just awakened. And he told himself that this had been just one more of the many adventures in his life, and that it, too, was over, leaving nothing but a memory. . . . He was moved and sad, and felt a slight remorse. After all, this young woman whom he would never again see had not been really happy with him. He had been friendly and affectionate with her, but in his whole behaviour, in the tones of his voice, in his very caresses, there had been a shade of irony, the insulting indulgence of the fortunate male, who was, moreover, almost twice her age. She had insisted in calling him good, remarkable, high-minded. Evidently he had appeared to her different from his real self, in a word he had involuntarily deceived her. . . .

There was an autumnal feeling in the air, and the evening was chilly.

"It's time for me to be going north, too," thought Gurov, as he walked away from the platform. "High time!"

III

When he got back to Moscow it was beginning to look like winter; the stoves were heated every day, and it was still dark when the children got up to go to school and drank their tea, so that the nurse had to light the lamp for a short time. Frost had set in. When the first snow falls, and one goes for one's first sleigh-ride, it is pleasant to see the white ground, the white roofs; one breathes freely and lightly, and remembers the days of one's youth. The ancient lime-trees and birches, white with hoarfrost, have a good-natured look, they are closer to the heart than cypresses and palms, and beneath their branches one is no longer haunted by the memory of mountains and the sea.

Gurov had always lived in Moscow, and he returned to Moscow on a fine frosty day, and when he put on his fur-lined overcoat and thick gloves, and sauntered down Petrovka Street, and when, on Saturday evening, he heard the church bells ringing, his recent journey and the places he had visited lost their charm for him. He became gradually immersed in Moscow life, reading with avidity three newspapers a day, while declaring he never read Moscow newspapers on principle. Once more he was caught up in a whirl of restaurants, clubs, banquets, and celebrations, once more glowed with the flattering consciousness that well-known lawyers and actors came to his house, that he played cards in the Medical Club opposite a professor. He could once again eat a whole serving of Moscow Fish Stew served in a pan.

He had believed that in a month's time Anna Sergeyevna would be nothing but a vague memory, and that hereafter, with her wistful smile, she would only occasionally appear to him in dreams, like others before her. But the month was now well over and winter was in full swing, and all was as clear in his memory as if he had parted with Anna Sergeyevna only the day before. And his recollections grew ever more insistent. When the voices of his children at their lessons reached him in his study through the evening stillness, when he heard a song, or the sounds of a music-box in a restaurant, when the wind howled in the chimney, it all came back to him: early morning on the pier, the misty mountains, the steamer from Feodosia, the kisses. He would pace up and down his room for a long time, smiling at his memories, and then memory turned into dreaming, and what had happened mingled in his imagination with what was going to happen. Anna Sergeyevna did not come to him in his dreams, she accompanied him everywhere, like his shadow, following him everywhere he went. When he closed his eyes, she seemed to stand before him in the flesh, still lovelier, younger, tenderer than she had really been, and looking back, he saw himself, too, as better than he had been in Yalta. In the evenings she looked out at him from the bookshelves, the fireplace, the corner, he could hear her breathing, the sweet rustle of her skirts. In the streets he followed women with his eyes, to see if there were any like her. . . .

He began to feel an overwhelming desire to share his memories with someone. But he could not speak of his love at home, and outside his home who was there for him to confide in? Not the tenants living in his house, and certainly not his colleagues at the bank. And what was there to tell? Was it love that he had felt? Had there been anything exquisite, poetic, anything instructive or even amusing about his relations with Anna Sergeyevna? He had to content himself with uttering vague generalizations about love and women, and nobody guessed what he meant, though his wife's dark eyebrows twitched as she said:

"The role of a coxcomb doesn't suit you a bit, Dimitry."

One evening, leaving the Medical Club with one of his card-partners, a government official, he could not refrain from remarking:

"If you only knew what a charming woman I met in Yalta!"

The official got into his sleigh, and just before driving off, turned and called out:

"Dmitry Dmitrich!"

"Yes?"

"You were quite right, you know—the sturgeon was just a *leetle* off."

These words, in themselves so commonplace, for some reason infuriated Gurov, seemed to him humiliating, gross. What savage manners, what people! What wasted evenings, what tedious, empty days! Frantic card-playing, gluttony, drunkenness, perpetual talk always about the same thing. The greater part of one's time and energy went on business that was no use to anyone, and on discussing the same thing over and over again, and there was nothing to show for it all but a stunted wingless existence and a round of trivialities, and there was nowhere to escape to, you might as well be in a madhouse or a convict settlement.

Gurov lay awake all night, raging, and went about the whole of the next day with a headache. He slept badly on the succeeding nights, too, sitting up in bed, thinking, or pacing the floor of his room. He was sick of his children, sick of the bank, felt not the slightest desire to go anywhere or talk about anything.

When the Christmas holidays came, he packed his things, telling his wife he had to go to Petersburg in the interests of a certain young man, and set off for the town of S. To what end? He hardly knew himself. He only knew that he must see Anna Sergeyevna, must speak to her, arrange a meeting, if possible.

He arrived at S. in the morning and engaged the best suite in the hotel, which had a carpet of gray military frieze, and a dusty ink-pot on the table, surmounted by a headless rider, holding his hat in his raised hand. The hall porter told him what he wanted to know: von Diederitz had a house of his own in Staro-Goncharnaya Street. It wasn't far from the hotel, he lived on a grand scale, luxuriously, kept carriage-horses, the whole town knew him. The hall porter pronounced the name "Drideritz."

Gurov strolled over to Staro-Goncharnaya Street and discovered the house. In front of it was a long gray fence with inverted nails hammered into the tops of the palings.

"A fence like that is enough to make anyone want to run away," thought Gurov, looking at the windows of the house and the fence.

He reasoned that since it was a holiday, Anna's husband would probably be at home. In any case it would be tactless to embarrass her by calling at the house. And a note might fall into the hands of the husband, and bring about catastrophe. The best thing would be to wait about on the chance of seeing her. And he walked up and down the street, hovering in the vicinity of the fence, watching for his chance. A beggar entered the gate, only to be attacked by dogs, then, an hour later, the faint, vague sounds of a piano reached his ears. That would be Anna Sergeyevna playing. Suddenly the front door opened and an old woman came out, followed by a familiar white Pomeranian. Gurov tried to call to it, but his heart beat violently, and in his agitation he could not remember its name.

He walked on, hating the gray fence more and more, and now ready to tell himself irately that Anna Sergeyevna had forgotten him, had already, perhaps, found distraction in another—what could be more natural in a young woman who had to look at this accursed fence from morning to night? He went back to his hotel and sat on the sofa in his suite for some time, not knowing what to do, then he ordered dinner, and after dinner, had a long sleep.

"What a foolish, restless business," he thought, waking up and looking towards the dark windowpanes. It was evening by now. "Well, I've had my sleep out. And what am I to do in the night?"

He sat up in bed, covered by the cheap gray quilt, which reminded him of a hospital blanket, and in his vexation he fell to taunting himself.

85   "You and your lady with a dog . . . there's adventure for you! See what you get for your pains."

On his arrival at the station that morning he had noticed a poster announcing in enormous letters the first performance at the local theatre of *The Geisha*.[6] Remembering this, he got up and made for the theatre.

"It's highly probable that she goes to first nights," he told himself.

The theatre was full. It was a typical provincial theatre, with a mist collecting over the chandeliers, and the crowd in the gallery fidgeting noisily. In the first row of the stalls[7] the local dandies stood waiting for the curtain to go up, their hands clasped behind them. There, in the front seat of the governor's box, sat the governor's daughter, wearing a boa, the governor himself hiding modestly behind the drapes, so that only his hands were visible. The curtain stirred, the orchestra took a long time tuning up their instruments. Gurov's eyes roamed eagerly over the audience as they filed in and occupied their seats.

Anna Sergeyevna came in, too. She seated herself in the third row of the stalls, and when Gurov's glance fell on her, his heart seemed to stop, and he knew in a flash that the whole world contained no one nearer or dearer to him, no one more important to his happiness. This little woman, lost in the provincial crowd, in no way remarkable, holding a silly lorgnette in her hand, now filled his whole life, was his grief, his joy, all that he desired. Lulled by the sounds coming from the wretched orchestra, with its feeble, amateurish violinists, he thought how beautiful she was . . . thought and dreamed. . . .

6. Operetta by Sidney Jones (1861–1946) that toured eastern Europe in 1898–99.   7. Seats at the front of a theater, near the stage and separated from nearby seats by a railing.

Anna Sergeyevna was accompanied by a tall, round-shouldered young man   90
with small whiskers, who nodded at every step before taking the seat beside her
and seemed to be continually bowing to someone. This must be her husband,
whom, in a fit of bitterness, at Yalta, she had called a "flunky." And there really
was something of a lackey's servility in his lanky figure, his side-whiskers, and
the little bald spot on the top of his head. And he smiled sweetly, and the badge
of some scientific society gleaming in his buttonhole was like the number on a
footman's livery.

The husband went out to smoke in the first interval, and she was left alone
in her seat. Gurov, who had taken a seat in the stalls, went up to her and said in
a trembling voice, with a forced smile: "How d'you do?"

She glanced up at him and turned pale, then looked at him again in alarm,
unable to believe her eyes, squeezing her fan and lorgnette in one hand, evidently struggling to overcome a feeling of faintness. Neither of them said a word.
She sat there, and he stood beside her, disconcerted by her embarrassment, and
not daring to sit down. The violins and flutes sang out as they were tuned, and
there was a tense sensation in the atmosphere, as if they were being watched
from all the boxes. At last she got up and moved rapidly towards one of the exits.
He followed her and they wandered aimlessly along corridors, up and down
stairs; figures flashed by in the uniforms of legal officials, high-school teachers
and civil servants, all wearing badges; ladies, coats hanging from pegs flashed
by; there was a sharp draft, bringing with it an odor of cigarette butts. And Gurov,
whose heart was beating violently, thought:

"What on earth are all these people, this orchestra for? . . ."

The next minute he suddenly remembered how, after seeing Anna Sergeyevna off that evening at the station, he had told himself that all was over, and
they would never meet again. And how far away the end seemed to be now!

She stopped on a dark narrow staircase over which was a notice bearing the   95
inscription "To the upper circle."

"How you frightened me!" she said, breathing heavily, still pale and half-
stunned. "Oh, how you frightened me! I'm almost dead! Why did you come?
Oh, why?"

"But, Anna," he said, in low, hasty tones. "But, Anna. . . . Try to understand
. . . do try. . . ."

She cast him a glance of fear, entreaty, love, and then gazed at him steadily,
as if to fix his features firmly in her memory.

"I've been so unhappy," she continued, taking no notice of his words. "I
could think of nothing but you the whole time, I lived on the thoughts of you.
I tried to forget—why, oh, why did you come?"

On the landing above them were two schoolboys, smoking and looking   100
down, but Gurov did not care, and, drawing Anna Sergeyevna towards him,
began kissing her face, her lips, her hands.

"What are you doing, oh, what are you doing?" she said in horror, drawing
back. "We have both gone mad. Go away this very night, this moment. . . . By
all that is sacred, I implore you. . . . Somebody is coming."

Someone was ascending the stairs.

"You must go away," went on Anna Sergeyevna in a whisper. "D'you hear me, Dmitry Dmitrich? I'll come to you in Moscow. I have never been happy, I am unhappy now, and I shall never be happy—never! Do not make me suffer still more! I will come to you in Moscow, I swear it! And now we must part! My dear one, my kind one, my darling, we must part."

She pressed his hand and hurried down the stairs, looking back at him continually, and her eyes showed that she was in truth unhappy. Gurov stood where he was for a short time, listening, and when all was quiet, went to look for his coat, and left the theatre.

IV

105 And Anna Sergeyevna began going to Moscow to see him. Every two or three months she left the town of S., telling her husband that she was going to consult a specialist on female diseases, and her husband believed her and did not believe her. In Moscow she always stayed at the Slavyanski Bazaar, sending a man in a red cap to Gurov the moment she arrived. Gurov went to her, and no one in Moscow knew anything about it.

One winter morning he went to see her as usual (the messenger had been to him the evening before, but had not found him at home). His daughter was with him, for her school was on the way and he thought he might as well see her to it.

"It is forty degrees," said Gurov to his daughter, "and yet it is snowing. You see it is only above freezing close to the ground, the temperature in the upper layers of the atmosphere is quite different."

"Why doesn't it ever thunder in winter, Papa?"

He explained this, too. As he was speaking, he kept reminding himself that he was going to a rendezvous and that not a living soul knew about it, or, probably, ever would. He led a double life—one in public, in the sight of all whom it concerned, full of conventional truth and conventional deception, exactly like the lives of his friends and acquaintances, and another which flowed in secret. And, owing to some strange, possibly quite accidental chain of circumstances, everything that was important, interesting, essential, everything about which he was sincere and never deceived himself, everything that composed the kernel of his life, went on in secret, while everything that was false in him, everything that composed the husk in which he hid himself and the truth which was in him— his work at the bank, discussions at the club, his "lower race," his attendance at anniversary celebrations with his wife—was on the surface. He began to judge others by himself, no longer believing what he saw, and always assuming that the real, the only interesting life of every individual goes on as under cover of night, secretly. Every individual existence revolves around mystery, and perhaps that is the chief reason that all cultivated individuals insisted so strongly on the respect due to personal secrets.

110 After leaving his daughter at the door of her school Gurov set off for the Slavyanski Bazaar. Taking off his overcoat in the lobby, he went upstairs and knocked softly on the door. Anna Sergeyevna, wearing the gray dress he liked most, exhausted by her journey and by suspense, had been expecting him since

the evening before. She was pale and looked at him without smiling, but was in his arms almost before he was fairly in the room. Their kiss was lingering, prolonged, as if they had not met for years.

"Well, how are you?" he asked. "Anything new?"

"Wait, I'll tell you in a minute. . . . . . I can't. . . ."

She could not speak, because she was crying. Turning away, she held her handkerchief to her eyes.

"I'll wait till she's had her cry out," he thought, and sank into a chair.

He rang for tea, and a little later, while he was drinking it, she was still standing there, her face to the window. She wept from emotion, from her bitter consciousness of the sadness of their life; they could only see one another in secret, hiding from people, as if they were thieves. Was not their life a broken one?

"Don't cry," he said.

It was quite obvious to him that this love of theirs would not soon come to an end, and that no one could say when this end would be. Anna Sergeyevna loved him ever more fondly, worshipped him, and there would have been no point in telling her that one day it must end. Indeed, she would not have believed him.

He moved over and took her by the shoulders, intending to caress her, to make a joke, but suddenly he caught sight of himself in the looking-glass.

His hair was already beginning to turn gray. It struck him as strange that he should have aged so much in the last few years, have lost so much of his looks. The shoulders on which his hands lay were warm and quivering. He felt a pity for this life, still so warm and exquisite, but probably soon to fade and droop like his own. Why did she love him so? Women had always believed him different from what he really was, had loved in him not himself but the man their imagination pictured him, a man they had sought for eagerly all their lives. And afterwards when they discovered their mistake, they went on loving him just the same. And not one of them had ever been happy with him. Time had passed, he had met one woman after another, become intimate with each, parted with each, but had never loved. There had been all sorts of things between them, but never love.

And only now, when he was gray-haired, had he fallen in love properly, thoroughly, for the first time in his life.

He and Anna Sergeyevna loved one another as people who are very close and intimate, as husband and wife, as dear friends love one another. It seemd to them that fate had intended them for one another, and they could not understand why she should have a husband, and he a wife. They were like two migrating birds, the male and the female, who had been caught and put into separate cages. They forgave one another all that they were ashamed of in the past and in the present, and felt that this love of theirs had changed them both.

Formerly, in moments of melancholy, he had consoled himself by the first argument that came into his head, but now arguments were nothing to him, he felt profound pity, desired to be sincere, tender.

"Stop crying, my dearest," he said. "You've had your cry, now stop. . . . Now let us have a talk, let us try and think what we are to do."

Then they discussed their situation for a long time, trying to think how they could get rid of the necessity for hiding, deception, living in different towns, being so long without meeting. How were they to shake off these intolerable fetters?

"How? How?" he repeated, clutching his head. "How?"

And it seemed to them that they were within an inch of arriving at a decision, and that then a new, beautiful life would begin. And they both realized that the end was still far, far away, and that the hardest, the most complicated part was only just beginning.

1899

▼ ▼ ▼

QUESTIONS

1. What is there in the second paragraph of "A Rose for Emily" that suggests the speaker is not just casually spinning a yarn about a weird lady but sees some more general meaning in the tale? What might that meaning be? What might it have to do with the setting in time and place? In what ways may the manipulation of historical time relate to that more general meaning?

2. The mother of Jing-mei Woo, in "A Pair of Tickets," told her that being Chinese is a matter of genetics and she finds that that is true. What is the role of place and time (history), then, in this story?

3. Yalta, where "The Lady with the Dog" opens, is a resort on the Black Sea; Moscow, where Gurov lives, is described at the beginning of section III. To what extent do the settings relate to the events and emotions of the story? How do other details—such as the watermelon in II (Yalta) and the slightly "off" sturgeon in III (Moscow)—relate to the settings and the attitudes and feelings associated with the places? Which are conventionally assumed to be more real, the feelings we have on holiday or those in our everyday lives? How is this convention related to our expectations about the outcome of the story? to the meaning of the story?

WRITING SUGGESTIONS

1. Write an outline of "A Rose for Emily" arranging the events in chronological order and dating them as precisely as possible. Then write a three-para-

graph analysis of why the story is structured—the chronology rearranged—as it is.

2. Compare the use of episodes from World War II in "The Country Husband" and "A Pair of Tickets."

3. Write a personal narrative about a visit to a place important in your family history that you had never visited before and how you felt about your relation to that place; or about an episode that made you recognize or affirm your ethnic identity or heritage.

4. Write a fifth section of "The Lady with the Dog."

5 SYMBOLS

One of the chief devices for bridging the gap between the writer's vision and the reader's is the **symbol**, commonly defined as something that stands for something else: a flower, for example, may be seen as a symbol of a particular state. Symbols are generally **figurative;** that is, they compare or put together two *unlike* things. While a senator may represent a state, he represents it *literally*: the state is a governmental unit, and the senator is a member of the government. But the flower has nothing to do with government, and so represents the state only figuratively.

But why speak of anything in terms of something else? Why should snakes commonly be symbolic of evil? Sure, some snakes are poisonous, but for some people so are bees, and a lot of snakes are not only harmless but actually helpful ecologically. (In Kipling's *The Jungle Book* the python Ka, while frightening, is on the side of Law and Order.) Through repeated use over the centuries, the snake has become a traditional symbol of Evil—not just danger, sneakiness, and repulsiveness, but theological, absolute Evil. Had Peyton Farquhar, in "An Occurrence at Owl Creek Bridge," been confronted by a snake when he was thrown ashore, we would not necessarily have said, "Aha—snake, symbol of Evil," though that potential meaning might have hovered around the incident and sent us looking backward and forward in the story for supporting evidence that this snake was being used symbolically. However, when we discover that the stranger in "Young Goodman Brown" has a walking stick upon which is carved the image of a snake, we are much more likely to find it such a symbol because of other, related potential symbols or meanings in the context: the term *goodman*, used throughout the story, suggests the distinct possibility that Brown (how common a name) stands for more than a "mere" individual young man. Brown's bride is named Faith—a common name among the early Puritans, but together with *goodman* suggesting symbolic possibilities. Then, just before the stranger with the walking stick appears, Brown says, "What if the devil himself should be at my very elbow!"

A single item, even something as traditionally fraught with meaning as a snake or a rose, becomes a symbol only when its potentially symbolic meaning is confirmed by something else in the story, just as a point needs a second point to define a line. Multiple symbols, potential symbols, direct and indirect hints such as Brown's mention of the devil: these are among the ways in which details may be identified as symbols (for interpreting symbols is relatively easy once you know what is and what probably is not a symbol).

One form of what may be called an indirect hint is repetition. That an "old maid" like Judith should have a cat seems so ordinary it borders on the trite. But when she chooses to have her male cat put to death rather than neutered, it is likely to make some of us sit up and take notice. This choice may suggest something about the unconventional in her character, but we probably don't think of the cat as itself representing anything. What happens, though, when there appears another cat, a female this time, whose sex life calls forth strange behavior on Judith's part? And when the killing of a kitten interrupts Judith's affair with Luigi? It is difficult to say when or if the literal cats shade off into symbols, for they remain so solidly cats in the story. All we can say for sure is that cats become more important in reading and understanding this story than, say, the cask of Amontillado does in the Poe story. The cask remains a thing pure and simple. Repetition, then, calls attention to details and may alert us to potential symbolic overtones, but it does not necessarily turn a thing into a symbol; so long as we get the suggestions of significance, however, agreeing on exactly what—or when—something may be called a symbol is not important.

Direct hints may take the form of explicit statements. (Authors are not so anxious to hide their meanings as some readers are prone to believe.) We also may be alerted to the fact that something is standing for something else when it does not by itself seem to make literal sense. It does not take us long to realize that "Young Goodman Brown" is not entirely as realistic a story as "Sonny's Blues" or "The Lady with the Dog." When things do not seem explicable in terms of everyday reality, we often look beyond them for some meaning. Roses are real enough, but neither Faulkner's narrator nor anyone else in the story gives Emily a real rose. What, then, does the rose in the title "A Rose for Emily" suggest?

We must remember, however, that symbols do not exist solely for the transmission of a meaning we can paraphrase; they do not disappear from the story, our memory, or our response once their "meaning" has been sucked out of them, any more than Emily ceases to exist as an individual after we recognize her representative or universal nature. Faith's pink ribbons and Judith's cats are objects in their stories, whatever meanings or suggestions of meanings they give rise to.

As I have often implied and occasionally said, few symbols can be exhausted, translated into an abstract phrase or equivalent: the "something else" that the "something" stands for is ultimately elusive. After you have read

Ann Beattie's "Janus," try to paraphrase just what the bowl stands for. Or explain with certainty what Faith's pink ribbon symbolizes in "Young Goodman Brown." It is not that the bowl and the ribbon mean nothing but that they mean so many things that no single equivalence will do; even an abstract statement seems to reduce rather than fully explain the significance to the reader.

When a figure is expressed as an explicit comparison, often signaled by *like* or *as*, it is called a **simile**: "eyes as blue as the sky"; "the baby brother I'd never known looked out from the depths of his private life, like an animal waiting to be coaxed into the light" ("Sonny's Blues"). An implicit comparison or identification of one thing with another unlike itself, without a verbal signal but just seeming to say "A *is* B," is called a **metaphor**: "His heart, that bloody motor" ("A Conversation with My Father"); "What I hate about being my age is how *nice* everyone tries to be. . . . everybody is pelting me with sugar cubes" ("Fenstad's Mother"). Sometimes all figures are loosely referred to as metaphors.

An **allegory** is like a metaphor in that one thing (usually nonrational, abstract, religious) is implicitly spoken of in terms of something that is concrete and usually sensuous (perceptible by the senses), but the comparison in allegory is extended to include a whole work or a large portion of a work. *The Pilgrim's Progress* is probably the most famous prose allegory in English; its central character is named Christian; he was born in the City of Destruction and sets out for the Celestial City, passes through the Slough of Despond and Vanity Fair, meets men named Pliable and Obstinate, and so on.

When an entire story, like "Young Goodman Brown," is symbolic, it is sometimes called a **myth**. *Myth* originally meant a story of communal origin that provided an explanation or religious interpretation of man, nature, the universe, and the relation between them. When used by one culture to describe the stories of another culture, the word usually implies that the stories are false: we speak of classical myths, but Christians do not speak of Christian myth. We also apply the term *myth* now to stories by individuals, sophisticated authors, but often there is still the implication that the mythic story relates to a communal or group experience, whereas a symbolic story may be more personal or private. It is hard to draw the line firmly: "Young Goodman Brown" seems to have clearly national, American implications, and "A Rose for Emily" seems to encapsulate something about the southern culture of seventy to a hundred years ago, but is "The Loons" personally symbolic or mythic? A plot or character element that recurs in cultural or cross-cultural myths, such as images of the devil, as in "Young Goodman Brown," is now widely called an **archetype**.

A symbol can be as brief and local as a metaphor or as extended as an allegory. Like an allegory it usually speaks in concrete terms of the non- or superrational, the abstract, that which is not immediately perceived by the senses. Though some allegories can be complex, with paraphrasable equivalences, allegory usually implies one-to-one relationships (as do the names from *The Pilgrim's Progress*), and literary symbols usually have highly complex or even inexpressible equivalences, as in "Janus." "Janus" is complexly symbolic in that there are areas of meaning or implication that cannot be rendered in other terms or conveniently separated from the particulars of the story. The ultimate unparaphrasable nature of most symbolic images or stories is not vagueness but richness, not disorder but complexity.

▼   ▼   ▼

NATHANIEL HAWTHORNE

Young Goodman Brown

Young goodman Brown came forth, at sunset, into the street of Salem village,[1] but put his head back, after crossing the threshold, to exchange a parting kiss with his young wife. And Faith, as the wife was aptly named, thrust her own pretty head into the street, letting the wind play with the pink ribbons of her cap, while she called to goodman Brown.

"Dearest heart," whispered she, softly and rather sadly, when her lips were close to his ear, "pr'y thee, put off your journey until sunrise, and sleep in your own bed to-night. A lone woman is troubled with such dreams and such thoughts, that she's afeard of herself, sometimes. Pray, tarry with me this night, dear husband, of all nights in the year!"

"My love and my Faith," replied young goodman Brown, "of all nights in the year, this one night must I tarry away from thee. My journey, as thou callest it, forth and back again, must needs be done 'twixt now and sunrise. What, my sweet, pretty wife, dost thou doubt me already, and we but three months married!"

"Then, God bless you!" said Faith, with the pink ribbons, "and may you find all well, when you come back."

"Amen!" cried goodman Brown. "Say thy prayers, dear Faith, and go to bed at dusk, and no harm will come to thee."

So they parted; and the young man pursued his way, until, being about to turn the corner by the meeting-house, he looked back, and saw the head of Faith still peeping after him, with a melancholy air, in spite of her pink ribbons.

"Poor little Faith!" thought he, for his heart smote him. "What a wretch am I, to leave her on such an errand! She talks of dreams, too. Methought, as she spoke, there was trouble in her face, as if a dream had warned her what work is to be done to-night. But, no, no! 't would kill her to think it. Well; she's a blessed

5

1. Salem, Massachusetts, Hawthorne's birthplace (1804), was the scene of the famous witch trials of 1692; *goodman:* husband, master of household.

angel on earth; and after this one night, I'll cling to her skirts and follow her to Heaven."

With this excellent resolve for the future, goodman Brown felt himself justified in making more haste on his present evil purpose. He had taken a dreary road, darkened by all the gloomiest trees of the forest, which barely stood aside to let the narrow path creep through, and closed immediately behind. It was all as lonely as could be; and there is this peculiarity in such a solitude, that the traveler knows not who may be concealed by the innumerable trunks and the thick boughs overhead; so that, with lonely footsteps, he may yet be passing through an unseen multitude.

"There may be a devilish Indian behind every tree," said goodman Brown, to himself; and he glanced fearfully behind him, as he added, "What if the devil himself should be at my very elbow!"

His head being turned back, he passed a crook of the road, and looking forward again, beheld the figure of a man, in grave and decent attire, seated at the foot of an old tree. He arose, at goodman Brown's approach, and walked onward, side by side with him.

"You are late, goodman Brown," said he. "The clock of the Old South was striking as I came through Boston; and that is full fifteen minutes agone."

"Faith kept me back awhile," replied the young man, with a tremor in his voice, caused by the sudden appearance of his companion, though not wholly unexpected.

It was now deep dusk in the forest, and deepest in that part of it where these two were journeying. As nearly as could be discerned, the second traveler was about fifty years old, apparently in the same rank of life as goodman Brown, and bearing a considerable resemblance to him, though perhaps more in expression than features. Still, they might have been taken for father and son. And yet, though the elder person was as simply clad as the younger, and as simple in manner too, he had an indescribable air of one who knew the world, and would not have felt abashed at the governor's dinner-table, or in king William's[2] court, were it possible that his affairs should call him thither. But the only thing about him, that could be fixed upon as remarkable, was his staff, which bore the likeness of a great black snake, so curiously wrought, that it might almost be seen to twist and wriggle itself, like a living serpent. This, of course, must have been an ocular deception, assisted by the uncertain light.

"Come, goodman Brown!" cried his fellow-traveler, "this is a dull pace for the beginning of a journey. Take my staff, if you are so soon weary."

"Friend," said the other, exchanging his slow pace for a full stop, "having kept covenant by meeting thee here, it is my purpose now to return whence I came. I have scruples, touching the matter thou wot'st of."

"Sayest thou so?" replied he of the serpent, smiling apart. "Let us walk on, nevertheless, reasoning as we go, and if I convince thee not, thou shalt turn back. We are but a little way in the forest, yet."

---

2. William III (1650–1702), ruler of England from 1689 to 1702, until 1694 jointly with his wife, Mary II.

"Too far, too far!" exclaimed the goodman, unconsciously resuming his walk. "My father never went into the woods on such an errand, nor his father before him. We have been a race of honest men and good Christians, since the days of the martyrs. And shall I be the first of the name of Brown, that ever took this path, and kept"—

"Such company, thou wouldst say," observed the elder person, interpreting his pause. "Good, goodman Brown! I have been as well acquainted with your family as with ever a one among the Puritans; and that's no trifle to say. I helped your grandfather, the constable, when he lashed the Quaker woman so smartly through the streets of Salem. And it was I that brought your father a pitch-pine knot, kindled at my own hearth, to set fire to an Indian village, in king Philip's[3] war. They were my good friends, both; and many a pleasant walk have we had along this path, and returned merrily after midnight. I would fain be friends with you, for their sake."

"If it be as thou sayest," replied goodman Brown, "I marvel they never spoke of these matters. Or, verily, I marvel not, seeing that the least rumor of the sort would have driven them from New-England. We are a people of prayer, and good works, to boot, and abide no such wickedness."

"Wickedness or not," said the traveler with the twisted staff, "I have a very general acquaintance here in New-England. The deacons of many a church have drunk the communion wine with me; the selectmen, of divers towns, make me their chairman; and a majority of the Great and General Court are firm supporters of my interest. The governor and I, too—but these are state-secrets."

"Can this be so!" cried goodman Brown, with a stare of amazement at his undisturbed companion. "Howbeit, I have nothing to do with the governor and council; they have their own ways, and are no rule for a simple husbandman, like me. But, were I to go on with thee, how should I meet the eye of that good old man, our minister, at Salem village? Oh, his voice would make me tremble, both Sabbath-day and lecture-day[4]!"

Thus far, the elder traveler had listened with due gravity, but now burst into a fit of irrepressible mirth, shaking himself so violently, that his snake-like staff actually seemed to wriggle in sympathy.

"Ha! ha! ha!" shouted he, again and again; then composing himself, "Well, go on, goodman Brown, go on; but, pr'y thee, don't kill me with laughing!"

"Well, then, to end the matter at once," said goodman Brown, considerably nettled, "there is my wife, Faith. It would break her dear little heart; and I'd rather break my own!"

"Nay, if that be the case," answered the other, "e'en[5] go thy ways, goodman Brown. I would not, for twenty old women like the one hobbling before us, that Faith should come to any harm."

As he spoke, he pointed his staff at a female figure on the path, in whom goodman Brown recognized a very pious and exemplary dame, who had taught

20

25

---

3. Metacom or Metacomet, chief of the Wampanoag Indians, known as King Philip, led a war against the New England colonists in 1675–76 that devastated many frontier communities.
4. The day—in the New England colonies usually a Thursday—appointed for an informal sermon.
5. Just.

him his catechism, in youth, and was still his moral and spiritual adviser, jointly with the minister and deacon Gookin.

"A marvel, truly, that goody[6] Cloyse should be so far in the wilderness, at night-fall!" said he. "But, with your leave, friend, I shall take a cut through the woods, until we have left this Christian woman behind. Being a stranger to you, she might ask whom I was consorting with, and whither I was going."

"Be it so," said his fellow-traveler. "Betake you to the woods, and let me keep the path."

Accordingly, the young man turned aside, but took care to watch his companion, who advanced softly along the road, until he had come within a staff's length of the old dame. She, meanwhile, was making the best of her way, with singular speed for so aged a woman, and mumbling some indistinct words, a prayer, doubtless, as she went. The traveler put forth his staff, and touched her withered neck with what seemed the serpent's tail.

30   "The devil!" screamed the pious old lady.

"Then goody Cloyse knows her old friend?" observed the traveler, confronting her, and leaning on his writhing stick.

"Ah, forsooth, and is it your worship, indeed?" cried the good dame. "Yea, truly is it, and in the very image of my old gossip, goodman Brown, the grandfather of the silly fellow that now is. But, would your worship believe it? my broomstick hath strangely disappeared, stolen, as I suspect, by that unhanged witch, goody Cory, and that, too, when I was all anointed with the juice of smallage and cinque-foil and wolf's-bane[7]"—

"Mingled with fine wheat and the fat of a new-born babe," said the shape of old goodman Brown.

"Ah, your worship knows the receipt," cried the old lady, cackling aloud. "So, as I was saying, being all ready for the meeting, and no horse to ride on, I made up my mind to foot it; for they tell me, there is a nice young man to be taken into communion to-night. But now your good worship will lend me your arm, and we shall be there in a twinkling."

35   "That can hardly be," answered her friend. "I may not spare you my arm, goody Cloyse, but here is my staff, if you will."

So saying, he threw it down at her feet, where, perhaps, it assumed life, being one of the rods which its owner had formerly lent to the Egyptian Magi.[8] Of this fact, however, goodman Brown could not take cognizance. He had cast up his eyes in astonishment, and looking down again, beheld neither goody Cloyse nor the serpentine staff, but his fellow-traveler alone, who waited for him as calmly as if nothing had happened.

"That old woman taught me my catechism!" said the young man; and there was a world of meaning in this simple comment.

They continued to walk onward, while the elder traveler exhorted his companion to make good speed and persevere in the path, discoursing so aptly, that

6. Short for "goodwife" or housewife.   7. Plants traditionally associated with witchcraft.   8. Exodus 7:8–12. The Lord instructs Moses to have his prophet Aaron throw down his rod before the Pharaoh, whereupon it will be turned into a serpent. The Pharaoh has his magicians (magi) do likewise, "but Aaron's rod swallowed up their rods."

his arguments seemed rather to spring up in the bosom of his auditor, than to be suggested by himself. As they went, he plucked a branch of maple, to serve for a walking-stick, and began to strip it of the twigs and little boughs, which were wet with evening dew. The moment his fingers touched them, they became strangely withered and dried up, as with a week's sunshine. Thus the pair proceeded, at a good free pace, until suddenly, in a gloomy hollow of the road, goodman Brown sat himself down on the stump of a tree, and refused to go any farther.

"Friend," said he, stubbornly, "my mind is made up. Not another step will I budge on this errand. What if a wretched old woman do choose to go to the devil, when I thought she was going to Heaven! Is that any reason why I should quit my dear Faith, and go after her?"

"You will think better of this, by-and-by," said his acquaintance, composedly. "Sit here and rest yourself awhile; and when you feel like moving again, there is my staff to help you along." 40

Without more words, he threw his companion the maple stick, and was as speedily out of sight, as if he had vanished into the deepening gloom. The young man sat a few moments, by the roadside, applauding himself greatly, and thinking with how clear a conscience he should meet the minister, in his morning-walk, nor shrink from the eye of good old deacon Gookin. And what calm sleep would be his, that very night, which was to have been spent so wickedly, but purely and sweetly now, in the arms of Faith! Amidst these pleasant and praiseworthy meditations, goodman Brown heard the tramp of horses along the road, and deemed it advisable to conceal himself within the verge of the forest, conscious of the guilty purpose that had brought him thither, though now so happily turned from it.

On came the hoof-tramps and the voices of the riders, two grave old voices, conversing soberly as they drew near. These mingled sounds appeared to pass along the road, within a few yards of the young man's hiding-place; but owing, doubtless, to the depth of the gloom, at that particular spot, neither the travelers nor their steeds were visible. Though their figures brushed the small boughs by the way-side, it could not be seen that they intercepted, even for a moment, the faint gleam from the strip of bright sky, athwart which they must have passed. Goodman Brown alternately crouched and stood on tip-toe, pulling aside the branches, and thrusting forth his head as far as he durst, without discerning so much as a shadow. It vexed him the more, because he could have sworn, were such a thing possible, that he recognized the voices of the minister and deacon Gookin, jogging along quietly, as they were wont to do, when bound to some ordination or ecclesiastical council. While yet within hearing, one of the riders stopped to pluck a switch.

"Of the two, reverend Sir," said the voice like the deacon's, "I had rather miss an ordination-dinner than to-night's meeting. They tell me that some of our community are to be here from Falmouth[9] and beyond, and others from Connecticut and Rhode-Island; besides several of the Indian powows, who, after

9. A port in extreme southern Massachusetts; Salem is in northern Massachusetts.

their fashion, know almost as much deviltry as the best of us. Moreover, there is a goodly young woman to be taken into communion."

"Mighty well, deacon Gookin!" replied the solemn old tones of the minister. "Spur up, or we shall be late. Nothing can be done, you know, until I get on the ground."

45   The hoofs clattered again, and the voices, talking so strangely in the empty air, passed on through the forest, where no church had ever been gathered, nor solitary Christian prayed. Whither, then, could these holy men be journeying, so deep into the heathen wilderness? Young goodman Brown caught hold of a tree, for support, being ready to sink down on the ground, faint and overburthened with the heavy sickness of his heart. He looked up to the sky, doubting whether there really was a Heaven above him. Yet, there was the blue arch, and the stars brightening in it.

"With Heaven above, and Faith below, I will yet stand firm against the devil!" cried goodman Brown.

While he still gazed upward, into the deep arch of the firmament, and had lifted his hands to pray, a cloud, though no wind was stirring, hurried across the zenith, and hid the brightening stars. The blue sky was still visible, except directly overhead, where this black mass of cloud was sweeping swiftly northward. Aloft in the air, as if from the depths of the cloud, came a confused and doubtful sound of voices. Once, the listener fancied that he could distinguish the accents of town's-people of his own, men and women, both pious and ungodly, many of whom he had met at the communion-table, and had seen others rioting at the tavern. The next moment, so indistinct were the sounds, he doubted whether he had heard aught but the murmur of the old forest, whispering without a wind. Then came a stronger swell of those familiar tones, heard daily in the sunshine, at Salem village, but never, until now, from a cloud of night. There was one voice, of a young woman, uttering lamentations, yet with an uncertain sorrow, and entreating for some favor, which, perhaps, it would grieve her to obtain. And all the unseen multitude, both saints and sinners, seemed to encourage her onward.

"Faith!" shouted goodman Brown, in a voice of agony and desperation; and the echoes of the forest mocked him, crying—"Faith! Faith!" as if bewildered wretches were seeking her, all through the wilderness.

The cry of grief, rage, and terror, was yet piercing the night, when the unhappy husband held his breath for a response. There was a scream, drowned immediately in a louder murmur of voices, fading into far-off laughter, as the dark cloud swept away, leaving the clear and silent sky above goodman Brown. But something fluttered lightly down through the air, and caught on the branch of a tree. The young man seized it, and beheld a pink ribbon.

50   "My Faith is gone!" cried he, after one stupefied moment. "There is no good on earth; and sin is but a name. Come, devil! for to thee is this world given."

And maddened with despair, so that he laughed loud and long, did goodman Brown grasp his staff and set forth again, at such a rate, that he seemed to fly along the forest-path, rather than to walk or run. The road grew wilder and drearier, and more faintly traced, and vanished at length, leaving him in the heart of the dark wilderness, still rushing onward, with the instinct that guides mortal man to evil. The whole forest was peopled with frightful sounds; the creaking of the trees, the howling of wild beasts, and the yell of Indians; while, sometimes, the wind tolled like a distant church-bell, and sometimes gave a broad roar around the traveler, as if all Nature were laughing him to scorn. But he was himself the chief horror of the scene, and shrank not from its other horrors.

"Ha! ha! ha!" roared goodman Brown, when the wind laughed at him. "Let us hear which will laugh loudest! Think not to frighten me with your deviltry! Come witch, come wizard, come Indian powow, come devil himself! and here come goodman Brown. You may as well fear him as he fear you!"

In truth, all through the haunted forest, there could be nothing more frightful than the figure of goodman Brown. On he flew, among the black pines, brandishing his staff with frenzied gestures, now giving vent to an inspiration of horrid blasphemy, and now shouting forth such laughter, as set all the echoes of the forest laughing like demons around him. The fiend in his own shape is less hideous, than when he rages in the breast of man. Thus sped the demoniac on his course, until, quivering among the trees, he saw a red light before him, as when the felled trunks and branches of a clearing have been set on fire, and throw up their lurid blaze against the sky, at the hour of midnight. He paused, in a lull of the tempest that had driven him onward, and heard the swell of what seemed a hymn, rolling solemnly from a distance, with the weight of many voices. He knew the tune; it was a familiar one in the choir of the village meeting-house. The verse died heavily away, and was lengthened by a chorus, not of human voices, but of all the sounds of the benighted wilderness, pealing in awful harmony together. Goodman Brown cried out; and his cry was lost to his own ear, by its unison with the cry of the desert.

In the interval of silence, he stole forward, until the light glared full upon his eyes. At one extremity of an open space, hemmed in by the dark wall of the forest, arose a rock, bearing some rude, natural resemblance either to an altar or a pulpit, and surrounded by four blazing pines, their tops a flame, their stems untouched, like candles at an evening meeting. The mass of foliage, that had overgrown the summit of the rock, was all on fire, blazing high into the night, and fitfully illuminating the whole field. Each pendent twig and leafy festoon was in a blaze. As the red light arose and fell, a numerous congregation alternately shone forth, then disappeared in shadow, and again grew, as it were, out of the darkness, peopling the heart of the solitary woods at once.

"A grave and dark-clad company!" quoth goodman Brown.

In truth, they were such. Among them, quivering to-and-fro, between gloom and splendor, appeared faces that would be seen, next day, at the council-board of the province, and others which, Sabbath after Sabbath, looked devoutly heavenward, and benignantly over the crowded pews, from the holiest pulpits in the land. Some affirm, that the lady of the governor was there. At least, there were high dames well known to her, and wives of honored husbands, and widows, a great multitude, and ancient maidens, all of excellent repute, and fair young girls, who trembled, lest their mothers should espy them. Either the sudden

55

gleams of light, flashing over the obscure field, bedazzled goodman Brown, or he recognized a score of the church-members of Salem village, famous for their especial sanctity. Good old deacon Gookin had arrived, and waited at the skirts of that venerable saint, his revered pastor. But, irreverently consorting with these grave, reputable, and pious people, these elders of the church, these chaste dames and dewy virgins, there were men of dissolute lives and women of spotted fame, wretches given over to all mean and filthy vice, and suspected even of horrid crimes. It was strange to see, that the good shrank not from the wicked, nor were the sinners abashed by the saints. Scattered, also, among their pale-faced enemies, were the Indian priests, or powows, who had often scared their native forest with more hideous incantations than any known to English witch-craft.

"But, where is Faith?" thought goodman Brown; and, as hope came into his heart, he trembled.

Another verse of the hymn arose, a slow and solemn strain, such as the pious love, but joined to words which expressed all that our nature can conceive of sin, and darkly hinted at far more. Unfathomable to mere mortals is the lore of fiends. Verse after verse was sung, and still the chorus of the desert swelled between, like the deepest tone of a mighty organ. And, with the final peal of that dreadful anthem, there came a sound, as if the roaring wind, the rushing streams, the howling beasts, and every other voice of the unconverted wilderness, were mingling and according with the voice of guilty man, in homage to the prince of all. The four blazing pines threw up a loftier flame, and obscurely discovered shapes and visages of horror on the smoke-wreaths, above the impious assembly. At the same moment, the fire on the rock shot redly forth, and formed a glowing arch above its base, where now appeared a figure. With reverence be it spoken, the apparition bore no slight similitude, both in garb and manner, to some grave divine of the New-England churches.

"Bring forth the converts!" cried a voice, that echoed through the field and rolled into the forest.

At the word, goodman Brown stept forth from the shadow of the trees, and approached the congregation, with whom he felt a loathful brotherhood, by the sympathy of all that was wicked in his heart. He could have well nigh sworn, that the shape of his own dead father beckoned him to advance, looking downward from a smoke-wreath, while a woman, with dim features of despair, threw out her hand to warn him back. Was it his mother? But he had no power to retreat one step, nor to resist, even in thought, when the minister and good old deacon Gookin, seized his arms, and led him to the blazing rock. Thither came also the slender form of a veiled female, led between goody Cloyse, that pious teacher of the catechism, and Martha Carrier, who had received the devil's promise to be queen of hell. A rampant hag was she! And there stood the proselytes, beneath the canopy of fire.

"Welcome, my children," said the dark figure, "to the communion of your race! Ye have found, thus young, your nature and your destiny. My children, look behind you!"

They turned; and flashing forth, as it were, in a sheet of flame, the fiend-worshippers were seen; the smile of welcome gleamed darkly on every visage.

"There," resumed the sable form, "are all whom ye have reverenced from youth. Ye deemed them holier than yourselves, and shrank from your own sin, contrasting it with their lives of righteousness, and prayerful aspirations heaven-ward. Yet, here are they all, in my worshipping assembly! This night it shall be granted you to know their secret deeds; how hoary-bearded elders of the church have whispered wanton words to the young maids of their households; how many a woman, eager for widow's weeds, has given her husband a drink at bed-time, and let him sleep his last sleep in her bosom; how beardless youths have made haste to inherit their fathers' wealth; and how fair damsels—blush not, sweet ones!—have dug little graves in the garden, and bidden me, the sole guest, to an infant's funeral. By the sympathy of your human hearts for sin, ye shall scent out all the places—whether in church, bed-chamber, street, field, or for-est—where crime has been committed, and shall exult to behold the whole earth one stain of guilt, one mighty blood-spot. Far more than this! It shall be yours to penetrate, in every bosom, the deep mystery of sin, the fountain of all wicked arts, and which, inexhaustibly supplies more evil impulses than human power—than my power, at its utmost!—can make manifest in deeds. And now, my children, look upon each other."

They did so; and, by the blaze of the hell-kindled torches, the wretched man beheld his Faith, and the wife her husband, trembling before that unhallowed altar.

"Lo! there ye stand, my children," said the figure, in a deep and solemn tone, almost sad, with its despairing awfulness, as if his once angelic nature could yet mourn for our miserable race. "Depending upon one another's hearts, ye had still hoped, that virtue were not all a dream. Now are ye undeceived! Evil is the nature of mankind. Evil must be your only happiness. Welcome, again, my children, to the communion of your race!"

"Welcome!" repeated the fiend-worshippers, in one cry of despair and tri-umph.

And there they stood, the only pair, as it seemed, who were yet hesitating on the verge of wickedness, in this dark world. A basin was hollowed, naturally, in the rock. Did it contain water, reddened by the lurid light? or was it blood? or, perchance, a liquid flame? Herein did the Shape of Evil dip his hand, and prepare to lay the mark of baptism upon their foreheads, that they might be partakers of the mystery of sin, more conscious of the secret guilt of others, both in deed and thought, than they could now be of their own. The husband cast one look at his pale wife, and Faith at him. What polluted wretches would the next glance shew them to each other, shuddering alike at what they disclosed and what they saw!

"Faith! Faith!" cried the husband. "Look up to Heaven, and resist the Wicked One!"

Whether Faith obeyed, he knew not. Hardly had he spoken, when he found himself amid calm night and solitude, listening to a roar of the wind, which

65

died heavily away through the forest. He staggered against the rock and felt it chill and damp, while a hanging twig, that had been all on fire, besprinkled his cheek with the coldest dew.

70   The next morning, young goodman Brown came slowly into the street of Salem village, staring around him like a bewildered man. The good old minister was taking a walk along the graveyard, to get an appetite for breakfast and meditate his sermon, and bestowed a blessing, as he passed, on goodman Brown. He shrank from the venerable saint, as if to avoid an anathema. Old deacon Gookin was at domestic worship, and the holy words of his prayer were heard through the open window. "What God doth the wizard pray to?" quoth goodman Brown. Goody Cloyse, that excellent old Christian, stood in the early sunshine, at her own lattice, catechising a little girl, who had brought her a pint of morning's milk. Goodman Brown snatched away the child, as from the grasp of the fiend himself. Turning the corner by the meeting-house, he spied the head of Faith, with the pink ribbons, gazing anxiously forth, and bursting into such joy at sight of him, that she skipt along the street, and almost kissed her husband before the whole village. But, goodman Brown looked sternly and sadly into her face, and passed on without a greeting.

Had goodman Brown fallen asleep in the forest, and only dreamed a wild dream of a witch-meeting?

Be it so, if you will. But, alas! it was a dream of evil omen for young goodman Brown. A stern, a sad, a darkly meditative, a distrustful, if not a desperate man, did he become, from the night of that fearful dream. On the Sabbath-day, when the congregation were singing a holy psalm, he could not listen, because an anthem of sin rushed loudly upon his ear, and drowned all the blessed strain. When the minister spoke from the pulpit, with power and fervid eloquence, and, with his hand on the open bible, of the sacred truths of our religion, and of saint-like lives and triumphant deaths, and of future bliss or misery unutterable, then did goodman Brown turn pale, dreading, lest the roof should thunder down upon the gray blasphemer and his hearers. Often, awakening suddenly at midnight, he shrank from the bosom of Faith, and at morning or eventide, when the family knelt down at prayer, he scowled, and muttered to himself, and gazed sternly at his wife, and turned away. And when he had lived long, and was borne to his grave, a hoary corpse, followed by Faith, an aged woman, and children and grandchildren, a goodly procession, besides neighbors, not a few, they carved no hopeful verse upon his tomb-stone; for his dying hour was gloom.

1835

MARGARET LAURENCE

The Loons

Just below Manawaka, where the Wachakwa River ran brown and noisy over the pebbles, the scrub oak and grey-green willow and chokecherry bushes grew in a dense thicket. In a clearing at the centre of the thicket stood the Tonnerre family's shack. The basis of this dwelling was a small square cabin made of poplar poles and chinked with mud, which had been built by Jules Tonnerre some fifty years before, when he came back from Batoche[1] with a bullet in his thigh, the year that Riel was hung and the voices of the Metis entered their long silence.[2] Jules had only intended to stay the winter in the Wachakwa Valley, but the family was still there in the thirties, when I was a child. As the Tonnerres had increased, their settlement had been added to, until the clearing at the foot of the town hill was a chaos of lean-tos, wooden packing cases, warped lumber, discarded car tyres, ramshackle chicken coops, tangled strands of barbed wire and rusty tin cans.

The Tonnerres were French halfbreeds, and among themselves they spoke a *patois* that was neither Cree nor French. Their English was broken and full of obscenities. They did not belong among the Cree of the Galloping Mountain reservation, further north, and they did not belong among the Scots-Irish and Ukrainians of Manawaka, either. They were, as my Grandmother MacLeod would have put it, neither flesh, fowl, nor good salt herring. When their men were not working at odd jobs or as section hands on the c.p.r.[3] they lived on relief. In the summers, one of the Tonnerre youngsters, with a face that seemed totally unfamiliar with laughter, would knock at the doors of the town's brick houses and offer for sale a lard-pail full of bruised wild strawberries, and if he got as much as a quarter he would grab the coin and run before the customer had time to change her mind. Sometimes old Jules, or his son Lazarus, would get mixed up in a Saturday-night brawl, and would hit out at whoever was nearest or howl drunkenly among the offended shoppers on Main Street, and then the Mountie would put them for the night in the barred cell underneath the Court House, and the next morning they would be quiet again.

Piquette Tonnerre, the daughter of Lazarus, was in my class at school. She was older than I, but she had failed several grades, perhaps because her attendance had always been sporadic and her interest in schoolwork negligible. Part of the reason she had missed a lot of school was that she had had tuberculosis of the bone, and had once spent many months in hospital. I knew this because my father was the doctor who had looked after her. Her sickness was almost the only thing I knew about her, however. Otherwise, she existed for me only as a vaguely embarrassed presence, with her hoarse voice and her clumsy limping walk and her grimy cotton dresses that were always miles too long. I was neither friendly nor unfriendly towards her. She dwelt and moved somewhere within my scope of vision, but I did not actually notice her very much until that peculiar summer when I was eleven.

"I don't know what to do about that kid," my father said at dinner one evening. "Piquette Tonnerre, I mean. The damn bone's flared up again. I've had her in hospital for quite a while now, and it's under control all right, but I hate like the dickens to send her home again."

1. In Saskatchewan, where in 1885 a battle of the Northwest Rebellion was fought.　2. Louis Riel (1844–1885), leader of the Metis, a people of mixed white and native Canadian blood.　3. Canadian Pacific Railway.

"Couldn't you explain to her mother that she has to rest a lot?" my mother said.

"The mother's not there," my father replied. "She took off a few years back. Can't say I blame her. Piquette cooks for them, and she says Lazarus would never do anything for himself as long as she's there. Anyway, I don't think she'd take much care of herself, once she got back. She's only thirteen, after all. Beth, I was thinking—what about taking her up to Diamond Lake with us this summer? A couple of months rest would give that bone a much better chance."

My mother looked stunned.

"But Ewen—what about Roddie and Vanessa?"

"She's not contagious," my father said. "And it would be company for Vanessa."

"Oh dear," my mother said in distress, "I'll bet anything she has nits in her hair."

"For Pete's sake," my father said crossly, "do you think Matron would let her stay in the hospital for all this time like that? Don't be silly, Beth."

Grandmother MacLeod, her delicately featured face as rigid as a cameo, now brought her mauve-veined hands together as though she were about to begin prayer.

"Ewen, if that halfbreed youngster comes along to Diamond Lake, I'm not going," she announced. "I'll go to Morag's for the summer."

I had trouble in stifling my urge to laugh, for my mother brightened visibly and quickly tried to hide it. If it came to a choice between Grandmother Mac-Leod and Piquette, Piquette would win hands down, nits or not.

"It might be quite nice for you, at that," she mused. "You haven't seen Morag for over a year, and you might enjoy being in the city for a while. Well, Ewen dear, you do what you think best. If you think it would do Piquette some good, then we'll be glad to have her, as long as she behaves herself."

So it happened that several weeks later, when we all piled into my father's old Nash, surrounded by suitcases and boxes of provisions and toys for my ten-month-old brother, Piquette was with us and Grandmother MacLeod, miraculously, was not. My father would only be staying at the cottage for a couple of weeks, for he had to get back to his practice, but the rest of us would stay at Diamond Lake until the end of August.

Our cottage was not named, as many were, "Dew Drop Inn" or "Bide-a-Wee," or "Bonnie Doon." The sign on the roadway bore in austere letters only our name, MacLeod. It was not a large cottage, but it was on the lakefront. You could look out the windows and see, through the filigree of the spruce trees, the water glistening greenly as the sun caught it. All around the cottage were ferns, and sharp-branched raspberry bushes, and moss that had grown over fallen tree trunks. If you looked carefully among the weeds and grass, you could find wild strawberry plants which were in white flower now and in another month would bear fruit, the fragrant globes hanging like miniature scarlet lanterns on the thin hairy stems. The two grey squirrels were still there, gossiping at us from the tall spruce beside the cottage, and by the end of the summer they would again be tame enough to take pieces of crust from my hands. The broad moose antlers that hung above the back door were a little more bleached and fissured after the winter, but otherwise everything was the same. I raced joyfully around my kingdom, greeting all the places I had not seen for a year. My brother, Roderick, who had not been born when we were here last summer, sat on the car rug in the sunshine and examined a brown spruce cone, meticulously turning it round and round in his small and curious hands. My mother and father toted the luggage from car to cottage, exclaiming over how well the place had wintered, no broken windows, thank goodness, no apparent damage from storm-felled branches or snow.

Only after I had finished looking around did I notice Piquette. She was sitting on the swing, her lame leg held stiffly out, and her other foot scuffing the ground as she swung slowly back and forth. Her long hair hung black and straight around her shoulders, and her broad coarse-featured face bore no expression—it was blank, as though she no longer dwelt within her own skull, as though she had gone elsewhere. I approached her very hesitantly.

"Want to come and play?"

Piquette looked at me with a sudden flash of scorn.

"I ain't a kid," she said.

Wounded, I stamped angrily away, swearing I would not speak to her for the rest of the summer. In the days that followed, however, Piquette began to interest me, and I began to want to interest her. My reasons did not appear bizarre to me. Unlikely as it may seem, I had only just realised that the Tonnerre family, whom I had always heard called halfbreeds, were actually Indians, or as near as made no difference. My acquaintance with Indians was not extensive. I did not remember ever having seen a real Indian, and my new awareness that Piquette sprang from the people of Big Bear and Poundmaker, of Tecumseh, of the Iroquois who had eaten Father Brébeuf's[4] heart—all this gave her an instant attraction in my eyes. I was devoted reader of Pauline Johnson[5] at this age, and sometimes would orate aloud and in an exalted voice, *West Wind, blow from your prairie nest; Blow from the mountains, blow from the west*—and so on. It seemed to me that Piquette must be in some way a daughter of the forest, a kind of junior prophetess of the wilds, who might impart to me, if I took the right approach, some of the secrets which she undoubtedly knew—where the whippoorwill made her nest, how the coyote reared her young, or whatever it was that it said in Hiawatha.[6]

I set about gaining Piquette's trust. She was not allowed to go swimming, with her bad leg, but I managed to lure her down to the beach—or rather, she came because there was nothing else to do. The water was always icy, for the lake was fed by springs, but I swam like a dog, thrashing my arms and legs around at such speed and with such an output of energy that I never grew cold.

4. Father Brebeuf, 17th-century Jesuit missionary. *Tecumseh:* Shawnee chief who fought on the side of the British in the War of 1812. *Big Bear, Poundmaker:* Cree chiefs and supporters of Riel. 5. Native Canadian author.　6. The eponymous hero of Henry Wadsworth Longfellow's *The Song of Hiawatha* (1854–55) learns similar—though not identical—"secrets" (III, 145–58).

Finally, when I had enough, I came out and sat beside Piquette on the sand. When she saw me approaching, her hand squashed flat the sand castle she had been building, and she looked at me sullenly, without speaking.

"Do you like this place?" I asked, after a while, intending to lead on from there into the question of forest lore.

Piquette shrugged. "It's okay. Good as anywhere."

"I love it," I said. "We come here every summer."

"So what?" Her voice was distant, and I glanced at her uncertainly, wondering what I could have said wrong.

"Do you want to come for a walk?" I asked her. "We wouldn't need to go far. If you walk just around the point there, you come to a bay where great big reeds grow in the water, and all kinds of fish hang around there. Want to? Come on."

She shook her head.

"Your dad said I ain't supposed to do no more walking than I got to." I tried another line.

"I bet you know a lot about the woods and all that, eh?" I began respectfully.

Piquette looked at me from her large dark unsmiling eyes.

"I don't know what in hell you're talkin' about," she replied. "You nuts or somethin'? If you mean where my old man, and me, and all them live, you better shut up, by Jesus, you hear?"

I was startled and my feelings were hurt, but I had a kind of dogged perseverance. I ignored her rebuff.

"You know something, Piquette? There's loons here, on this lake. You can see their nests just up the shore there, behind those logs. At night, you can hear them even from the cottage, but it's better to listen from the beach. My dad says we should listen and try to remember how they sound, because in a few years when more cottages are built at Diamond Lake and more people come in, the loons will go away."

Piquette was picking up stones and snail shells and then dropping them again.

"Who gives a good goddamn?" she said.

It became increasingly obvious that, as an Indian, Piquette was a dead loss. That evening I went out by myself, scrambling through the bushes that overhung the steep path, my feet slipping on the fallen spruce needles that covered the ground. When I reached the shore, I walked along the firm damp sand to the small pier that my father had built, and sat down there. I heard someone else crashing through the undergrowth and the bracken, and for a moment I thought Piquette had changed her mind, but it turned out to be my father. He sat beside me on the pier and we waited, without speaking.

At night the lake was like black glass with a streak of amber which was the path of the moon. All around, the spruce trees grew tall and close-set, branches blackly sharp against the sky, which was lightened by a cold flickering of stars. Then the loons began their calling. They rose like phantom birds from the nests on the shore, and flew out onto the dark still surface of the water.

No one can ever describe that ululating sound, the crying of the loons, and no one who has heard it can ever forget it. Plaintive, and yet with a quality of chilling mockery, those voices belonged to a world separated by aeons from our neat world of summer cottages and the lighted lamps of home.

"They must have sounded just like that," my father remarked, "before any person ever set foot here."

Then he laughed. "You could say the same, of course, about sparrows, or chipmunks, but somehow it only strikes you that way with the loons."

"I know," I said.

Neither of us suspected that this would be the last time we would ever sit here together on the shore, listening. We stayed for perhaps half an hour, and then we went back to the cottage. My mother was reading beside the fireplace. Piquette was looking at the burning birch log, and not doing anything.

"You should have come along," I said, although in fact I was glad she had not. 45

"Not me," Piquette said. "You wouldn' catch me walkin' way down there jus' for a bunch of squawkin' birds."

Piquette and I remained ill at ease with one another. I felt I had somehow failed my father, but I did not know what was the matter, nor why she would not or could not respond when I suggested exploring the woods or playing house. I thought it was probably her slow and difficult walking that held her back. She stayed most of the time in the cottage with my mother, helping her with the dishes or with Roddie, but hardly ever talking. Then the Duncans arrived at their cottage, and I spent my days with Mavis, who was my best friend. I could not reach Piquette at all, and I soon lost interest in trying. But all that summer she remained as both a reproach and a mystery to me.

That winter my father died of pneumonia, after less than a week's illness. For some time I saw nothing around me, being completely immersed in my own pain and my mother's. When I looked outward once more, I scarcely noticed that Piquette Tonnerre was no longer at school. I do not remember seeing her at all until four years later, one Saturday night when Mavis and I were having Cokes in the Regal Café. The jukebox was booming like tuneful thunder, and beside it, leaning lightly on its chrome and its rainbow glass, was a girl.

Piquette must have been seventeen then, although she looked about twenty. I stared at her, astounded that anyone could have changed so much. Her face, so stolid and expressionless before, was animated now with a gaiety that was almost violent. She laughed and talked very loudly with the boys around her. Her lipstick was bright carmine, and her hair was cut short and frizzily permed. She had not been pretty as a child, and she was not pretty now, for her features were still heavy and blunt. But her dark and slightly slanted eyes were beautiful, and her skin-tight skirt and orange sweater displayed to enviable advantage a soft and slender body.

She saw me, and walked over. She teetered a little, but it was not due to her once-tubercular leg, for her limp was almost gone. 50

"Hi, Vanessa." Her voice had the same hoarseness. "Long time no see, eh?"

"Hi," I said. "Where've you been keeping yourself, Piquette?"

"Oh, I been around," she said. "I been away almost two years now. Been all over the place—Winnipeg, Regina, Saskatoon. Jesus, what I could tell you! I come back this summer, but I ain't stayin'. You kids goin' to the dance?"

"No," I said abruptly, for this was a sore point with me. I was fifteen, and thought I was old enough to go to the Saturday-night dances at the Flamingo. My mother, however, thought otherwise.

55 "Y'oughta come," Piquette said. "I never miss one. It's just about the on'y thing in this jerkwater town that's any fun. Boy, you couldn' catch me stayin' here. I don' give a shit about this place. It stinks."

She sat down beside me, and I caught the harsh over-sweetness of her perfume.

"Listen, you wanna know something, Vanessa?" she confided, her voice only slightly blurred. "Your dad was the only person in Manawaka that ever done anything good to me."

I nodded speechlessly. I was certain she was speaking the truth. I knew a little more than I had that summer at Diamond Lake, but I could not reach her now any more than I had then. I was ashamed, ashamed of my own timidity, the frightened tendency to look the other way. Yet I felt no real warmth towards her—I only felt that I ought to, because of that distant summer and because my father had hoped she would be company for me, or perhaps that I would be for her, but it had not happened that way. At this moment, meeting her again, I had to admit that she repelled and embarrassed me, and I could not help despising the self-pity in her voice. I wished she would go away. I did not want to see her. I did not know what to say to her. It seemed that we had nothing to say to one another.

"I'll tell you something else," Piquette went on. "All the old bitches an' biddies in this town will sure be surprised. I'm gettin' married this fall—my boyfriend, he's an English fella, works in the stockyards in the city there, a very tall guy, got blond wavy hair. Gee, is he ever handsome. Got this real classy name. Alvin Gerald Cummings—some handle, eh? They call him Al."

60 For the merest instant, then, I saw her. I really did see her, for the first and only time in all the years we had both lived in the same town. Her defiant face, momentarily, became unguarded and unmasked, and in her eyes there was a terrifying hope.

"Gee, Piquette—" I burst out awkwardly, "that's swell. That's really wonderful. Congratulations—good luck—I hope you'll be happy—"

As I mouthed the conventional phrases, I could only guess how great her need must have been, that she had been forced to seek the very things she so bitterly rejected.

When I was eighteen, I left Manawaka and went away to college. At the end of my first year, I came back home for the summer. I spent the first few days in talking non-stop with my mother, as we exchanged all the news that somehow had not found its way into letters—what had happened in my life and what had happened here in Manawaka while I was away. My mother searched her memory for events that concerned people I knew.

"Did I ever write you about Piquette Tonnerre, Vanessa?" she asked one morning.

"No, I don't think so," I replied. "Last I heard of her, she was going to marry some guy in the city. Is she still there?"

My mother looked perturbed, and it was a moment before she spoke, as though she did not know how to express what she had to tell and wished she did not need to try.

"She's dead," she said at last. Then, as I stared at her, "Oh, Vanessa, when it happened, I couldn't help thinking of her as she was that summer—so sullen and gauche and badly dressed. I couldn't help wondering if we could have done something more at that time—but what could we do? She used to be around in the cottage there with me all day, and honestly it was all I could do to get a word out of her. She didn't even talk to your father very much, although I think she liked him in her way."

"What happened?" I asked.

"Either her husband left her, or she left him," my mother said. "I don't know which. Anyway, she came back here with two youngsters, both only babies—they must have been born very close together. She kept house, I guess, for Lazarus and her brothers, down in the valley there, in the old Tonnerre place. I used to see her on the street sometimes, but she never spoke to me. She'd put on an awful lot of weight, and she looked a mess, to tell you the truth, a real slattern, dressed any old how. She was up in court a couple of times—drunk and disorderly, of course. One Saturday night last winter, during the coldest weather, Piquette was alone in the shack with the children. The Tonnerres made home brew all the time, so I've heard, and Lazarus said later she'd been drinking most of the day when he and the boys went out that evening. They had an old wood-stove there—you know the kind, with exposed pipes. The shack caught fire. Piquette didn't get out, and neither did the children."

I did not say anything. As so often with Piquette, there did not seem to be anything to say. There was a kind of silence around the image in my mind of the fire and the snow, and I wished I could put from my memory the look that I had seen once in Piquette's eyes.

I went up to Diamond Lake for a few days that summer, with Mavis and her family. The MacLeod cottage had been sold after my father's death, and I did not even go to look at it, not wanting to witness my long-ago kingdom possessed now by strangers. But one evening I went down to the shore by myself.

The small pier which my father had built was gone, and in its place there was a large and solid pier built by the government, for Galloping Mountain was now a national park, and Diamond Lake had been re-named Lake Wapakata, for it was felt that an Indian name would have a greater appeal to tourists. The one store had become several dozen, and the settlement had all the attributes of a flourishing resort—hotels, dance-hall, cafés with neon signs, the penetrating odours of potato chips and hot dogs.

I sat on the government pier and looked out across the water. At night the lake at least was the same as it had always been, darkly shining and bearing within its black glass the streak of amber that was the path of the moon. There was no wind that evening, and everything was quiet all around me. It seemed too quiet, and then I realized that the loons were no longer here. I listened for some time, to make sure, but never once did I hear that long-drawn call, half mocking and half plaintive, spearing through the stillness across the lake.

I did not know what had happened to the birds. Perhaps they had gone away to some far place of belonging. Perhaps they had been unable to find such a place, and had simply died out, having ceased to care any longer whether they lived or not.

I remembered how Piquette had scorned to come along, when my father and I sat there and listened to the lake birds. It seemed to me now that in some unconscious and totally unrecognized way, Piquette might have been the only one, after all, who had heard the crying of the loons.

1966

ANN BEATTIE

Janus

The bowl was perfect. Perhaps it was not what you'd select if you faced a shelf of bowls, and not the sort of thing that would inevitably attract a lot of attention at a crafts fair, yet it had real presence. It was as predictably admired as a mutt who has no reason to suspect he might be funny. Just such a dog, in fact, was often brought out (and in) along with the bowl.

Andrea was a real estate agent, and when she thought that some prospective buyers might be dog lovers, she would drop off her dog at the same time she placed the bowl in the house that was up for sale. She would put a dish of water in the kitchen for Mondo, take his squeaking plastic frog out of her purse and drop it on the floor. He would pounce delightedly, just as he did every day at home, batting around his favorite toy. The bowl usually sat on a coffee table, though recently she had displayed it on top of a pine blanket chest and on a lacquered table. It was once placed on a cherry table beneath a Bonnard[1] still life, where it held its own.

Everyone who has purchased a house or who has wanted to sell a house must be familiar with some of the tricks used to convince a buyer that the house is quite special: a fire in the fireplace in early evening; jonquils in a pitcher on the kitchen counter, where no one ordinarily has space to put flowers; perhaps the slight aroma of spring, made by a single drop of scent vaporizing from a lamp bulb.

The wonderful thing about the bowl, Andrea thought, was that it was both subtle and noticeable—a paradox of a bowl. Its glaze was the color of cream and seemed to glow no matter what light it was placed in. There were a few bits of color in it—tiny geometric flashes—and some of these were tinged with flecks

1. Pierre Bonnard (1867–1947), French painter.

of silver. They were as mysterious as cells seen under a microscope; it was diffi-cult not to study them, because they shimmered, flashing for a split second, and then resumed their shape. Something about the colors and their random placement suggested motion. People who liked country furniture always com-mented on the bowl, but then it turned out that people who felt comfortable with Biedermeier[2] loved it just as much. But the bowl was not at all ostentatious, or even so noticeable that anyone would suspect that it had been put in place deliberately. They might notice the height of the ceiling on first entering a room, and only when their eye moved down from that, or away from the refrac-tion of sunlight on a pale wall, would they see the bowl. Then they would go immediately to it and comment. Yet they always faltered when they tried to say something. Perhaps it was because they were in the house for a serious reason, not to notice some object.

Once, Andrea got a call from a woman who had not put in an offer on a house she had shown her. That bowl, she said—would it be possible to find out where the owners had bought that beautiful bowl? Andrea pretended that she did not know what the woman was referring to. A bowl, somewhere in the house? Oh, on a table under the window. Yes, she would ask, of course. She let a couple of days pass, then called back to say that the bowl had been a present and the people did not know where it had been purchased.

When the bowl was not being taken from house to house, it sat on Andrea's coffee table at home. She didn't keep it carefully wrapped (although she trans-ported it that way, in a box); she kept it on the table, because she liked to see it. It was large enough so that it didn't seem fragile, or particularly vulnerable if anyone sideswiped the table or Mondo blundered into it at play. She had asked her husband to please not drop his house key in it. It was meant to be empty.

When her husband first noticed the bowl, he had peered into it and smiled briefly. He always urged her to buy things she liked. In recent years, both of them had acquired many things to make up for all the lean years when they were graduate students, but now that they had been comfortable for quite a while, the pleasure of new possessions dwindled. Her husband had pronounced the bowl "pretty," and he had turned away without picking it up to examine it. He had no more interest in the bowl than she had in his new Leica.[3]

She was sure that the bowl brought her luck. Bids were often put in on houses where she had displayed the bowl. Sometimes the owners, who were always asked to be away or to step outside when the house was being shown, didn't even know that the bowl had been in their house. Once—she could not imagine how—she left it behind, and then she was so afraid that something might have happened to it that she rushed back to the house and sighed with relief when the woman owner opened the door. The bowl, Andrea explained— she had purchased a bowl and set it on the chest for safekeeping while she toured the house with the prospective buyers, and she . . . She felt like rushing past the frowning woman and seizing her bowl. The owner stepped aside, and it was only when Andrea ran to the chest that the lady glanced at her a little

5

2. Mid-19th-century heavy, stuffed German furniture.   3. An expensive German camera.

strangely. In the few seconds before Andrea picked up the bowl, she realized that the owner must have just seen that it had been perfectly placed, that the sunlight struck the bluer part of it. Her pitcher had been moved to the far side of the chest, and the bowl predominated. All the way home, Andrea wondered how she could have left the bowl behind. It was like leaving a friend at an outing—just walking off. Sometimes there were stories in the paper about families forgetting a child somewhere and driving to the next city. Andrea had only gone a mile down the road before she remembered.

In time, she dreamed of the bowl. Twice, in a waking dream—early in the morning, between sleep and a last nap before rising—she had a clear vision of it. It came into sharp focus and startled her for a moment—the same bowl she looked at every day.

10   She had a very profitable year selling real estate. Word spread, and she had more clients than she felt comfortable with. She had the foolish thought that if only the bowl were an animate object she could thank it. There were times when she wanted to talk to her husband about the bowl. He was a stockbroker, and sometimes told people that he was fortunate to be married to a woman who had such a fine aesthetic sense and yet could also function in the real world. They were a lot alike, really—they had agreed on that. They were both quiet people—reflective, slow to make value judgments, but almost intractable once they had come to a conclusion. They both liked details, but while ironies attracted her, he was more impatient and dismissive when matters became many sided or unclear. But they both knew this; it was the kind of thing they could talk about when they were alone in the car together, coming home from a party or after a weekend with friends. But she never talked to him about the bowl. When they were at dinner, exchanging their news of the day, or while they lay in bed at night listening to the stereo and murmuring sleepy disconnections, she was often tempted to come right out and say that she thought that the bowl in the living room, the cream-colored bowl, was responsible for her success. But she didn't say it. She couldn't begin to explain it. Sometimes in the morning, she would look at him and feel guilty that she had such a constant secret.

Could it be that she had some deeper connection with the bowl—a relationship of some kind? She corrected her thinking: how could she imagine such a thing, when she was a human being and it was a bowl? It was ridiculous. Just think of how people lived together and loved each other . . . But was that always so clear, always a relationship? She was confused by these thoughts, but they remained in her mind. There was something within her now, something real, that she never talked about.

The bowl was a mystery, even to her. It was frustrating, because her involvement with the bowl contained a steady sense of unrequited good fortune; it would have been easier to respond if some sort of demand were made in return. But that only happened in fairy tales. The bowl was just a bowl. She did not believe that for one second. What she believed was that it was something she loved.

In the past, she had sometimes talked to her husband about a new property she was about to buy or sell—confiding some clever strategy she had devised to persuade owners who seemed ready to sell. Now she stopped doing that, for all her strategies involved the bowl. She became more deliberate with the bowl, and more possessive. She put it in houses only when no one was there, and removed it when she left the house. Instead of just moving a pitcher or a dish, she would remove all the other objects from a table. She had to force herself to handle them carefully, because she didn't really care about them. She just wanted them out of sight.

She wondered how the situation would end. As with a lover, there was no exact scenario of how matters would come to a close. Anxiety became the operative force. It would be irrelevant if the lover rushed into someone else's arms, or wrote her a note and departed to another city. The horror was the possibility of the disappearance. That was what mattered.

She would get up at night and look at the bowl. It never occurred to her that she might break it. She washed and dried it without anxiety, and she moved it often, from coffee table to mahogany corner table or wherever, without fearing an accident. It was clear that she would not be the one who would do anything to the bowl. The bowl was only handled by her, set safely on one surface or another; it was not very likely that anyone would break it. A bowl was a poor conductor of electricity: it would not be hit by lightning. Yet the idea of damage persisted. She did not think beyond that—to what her life would be without the bowl. She only continued to fear that some accident would happen. Why not, in a world where people set plants where they did not belong, so that visitors touring a house would be fooled into thinking that dark corners got sunlight— a world full of tricks?

She had first seen the bowl several years earlier, at a crafts fair she had visited half in secret, with her lover. He had urged her to buy the bowl. She didn't *need* any more things, she told him. But she had been drawn to the bowl, and they had lingered near it. Then she went on to the next booth, and he came up behind her, tapping the rim against her shoulder as she ran her fingers over a wood carving. "You're still insisting that I buy that?" she said. "No," he said. "I bought it for you." He had bought her other things before this—things she liked more, at first—the child's ebony-and-turquoise ring that fitted her little finger; the wooden box, long and thin, beautifully dovetailed, that she used to hold paper clips; the soft gray sweater with a pouch pocket. It was his idea that when he could not be there to hold her hand she could hold her own—clasp her hands inside the lone pocket that stretched across the front. But in time she became more attached to the bowl than to any of his other presents. She tried to talk herself out of it. She owned other things that were more striking or valuable. It wasn't an object whose beauty jumped out at you; a lot of people must have passed it by before the two of them saw it that day.

Her lover had said that she was always too slow to know what she really loved. Why continue with her life the way it was? Why be two-faced, he asked her. He had made the first move toward her. When she would not decide in his favor, would not change her life and come to him, he asked her what made her think she could have it both ways. And then he made the last move and left. It

15

was a decision meant to break her will, to shatter her intransigent ideas about honoring previous commitments.

Time passed. Alone in the living room at night, she often looked at the bowl sitting on the table, still and safe, unilluminated. In its way, it was perfect: the world cut in half, deep and smoothly empty. Near the rim, even in dim light, the eye moved toward one small flash of blue, a vanishing point on the horizon.

1986

▼   ▼   ▼

SYMBOLS A Glossary

allegory: as in *metaphor*, one thing (usually nonrational, abstract, religious) is implicitly spoken of in terms of something concrete, usually sensuous, but in an allegory the comparison is extended to include an entire work or large portion of a work

archetype: a plot or character element that recurs in cultural or cross-cultural myths

figurative: nonliteral; implicitly or explicitly representative of something in terms of some other unlike thing that seems to be similar or analogous

metaphor: an implicit comparison or identification of one thing with another unlike itself without the use of a verbal signal

myth: like allegory, myth usually is symbolic and extensive, including an entire work or story; though it no longer is necessarily specific to or pervasive in a single culture—individual authors may now be said to create myths—there is still a sense that myth is communal or cultural, while the symbolic can often be private or personal

simile: a figure that explicitly expresses comparison, often signaled by *like* or *as*

symbol: a person, place, thing, event, or pattern in a literary work that designates itself and at the same time figuratively represents or "stands for" something else. Often the thing or idea represented is more abstract, general, non- or superrational; the symbol more concrete and particular

QUESTIONS

1. Why does goodman Brown go to a witches' meeting?
2. Why does Faith Brown, his wife, wear pink ribbons?
3. In what way are the Tonnerres stereotyped in the first two paragraphs of "The Loons"? How do you explain young Piquette's behavior toward the narrator? How has Piquette changed when Vanessa sees her at seventeen? How has Piquette changed again at eighteen? Is this a reversion to the white American stereotype of Native Americans / Canadians? How does the story of Piquette's life modify the stereotype?
4. What do the loons represent to young Vanessa and her father? What does the disappearance of the loons mean to Vanessa?
5. In reading "Janus," what impression do you get of Andrea—and her attachment to the bowl—in the first half of the story? What expectations—if any—are aroused by that first half? What does it mean to you that Andrea thought the bowl was meant to be half empty (par. 6)? What other qualities of the bowl seem to suggest something about Andrea or her life? In paragraph 14, Andrea wonders how the situation would end. This probably makes some readers, perhaps most, think about how this story is going to end. How does it? Where did Andrea get the bowl? How significant is that? Why is the story called "Janus"?

WRITING SUGGESTIONS

1. Write a parody of "Young Goodman Brown" or an imitation, perhaps in the style of Stephen King or Anne Rice.
2. Write an analysis of the symbolism used in one of the stories in *Fiction: Reading, Responding, Writing* or in one of the stories in the first three chapters of this textbook.
3. Write an essay in which you define and then argue for or against the proposition that neither the narrator nor her father but only Piquette had really "heard the crying of the loons" (par. 76).
4. Paraphrase several possible meanings of the bowl in "Janus," argue for one or explain how the symbol of the bowl may be both meaningful and yet elude any possible paraphrase of its meaning.

STUDENT WRITING

Geoffrey Clement's essay on "Sonny's Blues" (from Chapter 1) responds to the second writing suggestion, above. In it, he deftly traces the symbolism and the thematic and evaluative force of images of water in its solid (ice), liquid, and gaseous (steam, boiling) states in the story.

The Struggle to Surface

in the Water of "Sonny's Blues"

Geoffrey Clement

In "Sonny's Blues," James Baldwin employs water as a symbol that enables him to concentrate more clearly on the lack of and the crucial need for a real sense of communication among members of society. As Baldwin captures the intensity of Sonny's and his brother's struggles to understand their situation, he vividly depicts a society that seeks to swallow up the souls of its inhabitants and gradually to drown them spiritually. Thus, Baldwin illustrates quite clearly his sense of the hopelessness in man's plight. In portraying the struggle of street life in Harlem, he uses water in its opposite forms-- frozen water and boiling water--and toward the end of the story, as Sonny's and his brother's revelations help to resolve the conflict, the water becomes calm.

Initially, and as a result of Sonny's arrest, Sonny's brother gradually realizes that he has not fulfilled his promise and that his feelings of love for his brother have certainly gone unexpressed, if indeed they exist. As a result, he feels physically the coldness that has permeated his emotional life: "It was a special kind of ice. It kept melting, sending trickles of ice water all up and down my veins, but it never got less. Sometimes it hardened and seemed to expand . . ." (par. 2). So the ice represents his guilt and his fears, both of which will lessen little. Although he learns to adapt to these feelings, they occasionally resurface. Upon Sonny's return from prison, for example, his brother thinks, "and thank God she [his wife] was there, for I was filled with that icy dread again. Everything I did seemed awkward to me, and everything I said sounded freighted with hidden meaning. . . . I was dying to hear him tell me he was safe" (par. 78). In addition to this guilt, Sonny's brother experiences much of the same emotional turmoil that Sonny has endured. In this passage in particular, he is seeking reassurance that there is a way to survive their imprisonment without having to feel the pain Sonny felt. Baldwin not only uses ice to show the brother's disappointment in his failures as a brother but also to point to the brother's own struggle for security, identity, and communication.

As Sonny's brother begins to realize that within him there has grown a heart hardened and haunted by the cold darkness of Harlem's streets, he also begins to recognize many of the realities that his brother has faced and that he too must eventually face. Sonny's brother is spiritually walking through "the vivid, killing streets of our childhood. These streets hadn't changed, though housing projects jutted up out of them now like rocks in the middle of a boiling sea" (par. 73). Here, Baldwin paints an almost hellish picture of pain and suffering, of emotional torment and fears, and of spiritual drowning and isolation, all of which slowly become real in the mind of Sonny's brother. He begins to feel for the first time in his life the depth of his denial of his brother. Tragically, he finds that when he is ready to reach out to help Sonny, he cannot, for he is even more lost and confused than Sonny himself. Sonny's brother wants desperately to save Sonny from the inevitable struggle, yet he learns from Sonny that "the storm inside" (par. 217) will pass over only with the constant expression of love. Clearly, the process of revelation is a very dramatic one, since Sonny's brother comes to understand Sonny's need for a giving, communicating, responsible relationship, a commitment filled with careful listening, compassion, and understanding. Sonny does not believe he can make his brother understand his experiences with drugs: "I can never tell you. I was all by myself at the bottom of something . . . and I thought I'd die if I couldn't get away from it and yet, all the same, I knew that everything I was doing was just locking me in with it" (par. 220). Once his brother grasps the importance of listening with love and understanding, however, Sonny is finally able to reach out.

Toward the end of the story, the ice and the boiling sea come together, and there is peace; Sonny is able to reach out, and he starts to swim in the calmer water. Now, he finds freedom in expressing his struggles through his music, while at the same time alerting his audience to the lessons he has learned. Creole "wanted Sonny to leave the shoreline and strike out for the deep water. He was Sonny's witness that deep water and drowning were not the same thing" (par. 234). As Sonny ventures further and further into his own understanding of life's struggles, he tries, his brother tells us, "to find new ways to make us listen. For, while the tale of how we suffer, and how we are delighted, and how we may triumph is never new, it always must be heard. . . . it's the only light we've got in all this darkness" (par. 238). In a powerful way, Sonny taught the audience to listen: "Freedom lurked around us and I understood, at last, that he could help us be free if we would listen, that we would never be

free until we did" (par. 240). The boiling rage
of the streets and the coldness within his heart
are reconciled as the brother finally witnesses
"Sonny's world" (par. 231). Finally, he
recognizes that Sonny has found the strength of
knowing that he has discovered in music the
outlet through which he can express himself and
warn others of his mistakes. He sends up to the
bandstand not water, not ice, but Scotch and
milk. Sonny sips it in a sort of communion and
puts it back on top of the piano, where "it
glowed and shook above [his] head like the very
cup of trembling" (par. 241).

Thoughout his story, Baldwin stresses the lack
of companionship to try to manipulate the
reader's emotions. Playing on the contrasts
between forms of water, he draws parallels to the
theme of emotional conflict within the minds of
Sonny and his brother. While the sea is calmer
toward the end, there is still a sense of rage,
because only in the expression of his struggle is
Sonny able to find meaning, satisfaction, and
forgiveness for his brother. The streets,
society's common ground, still try to isolate its
members as each person individually struggles to
reach the surface. But if the struggler can find
a listening helper, which Sonny finds in his
brother, then he will reach the surface and
breathe the fulfilling breath of love. The cup of
trembling will be taken out of the struggler's

hand, the Bible tells us, and will be put "into
the hand of them that afflict thee" (p. 70n.).
Light gracefully touches and penetrates the
surface of the water, and the cup of trembling
is still.

6 THEME

f you ask what a story is "about," an author is likely to answer by telling you the **subject**. Indeed, many authors tell you the subject in their titles: "An Occurrence at Owl Creek Bridge," "Her First Ball." Though a subject is always concrete, it may be stated at somewhat greater length than the few words of a title: "a man's thoughts as he faces execution for spying during the Civil War" ("Owl Creek Bridge"); "a young girl's excitement at her first grown-up dance and an incident that temporarily depresses her" ("Her First Ball").

A friend might be more likely to tell you what a story is about by giving you a summary of the action: "This weird Southern lady is jilted by a Yankee. She kills him and sleeps with his corpse. There's a smell around the house before too long, but nobody knows about the murder until she dies." (We sometimes call this a **plot summary,** but you will notice that this summary describes the history, the events, in more or less chronological order, while the plot arranges or structures the history differently; in "A Rose for Emily," remember, we do not figure out there's been a murder and certainly don't know about Emily's sleeping with the corpse until the end of the story, though of course the jilting, murder, and so on happen in the order described in the summary of the history.)

Your teacher may well explain a story by summarizing its **theme.** Some refer to the central idea, the thesis, or even the message of the story, and that is roughly what we mean by theme: a generalization or abstraction from the story. Thus, the subject of "Young Goodman Brown" may be said to be a coven (witches' meeting) or, more fully, "a young colonial New England husband is driven mad by finding everyone he thought good and pure attending a witches' meeting." The theme may be "everyone partakes of evil," or, more succinctly, "the Fall." There are, as you can see, degrees of generalization and abstraction; subject (a young man finds that everyone is evil) shades off into theme, which itself can be more or less general and abstract.

Discussions of literature in or out of class sometimes seem to suggest that stories exist for their themes, that we read only to get the "point" or message. But most themes, you must admit, are somewhat less than earth-shattering. That all men and women are evil may be debatable, but it certainly isn't news. That not all unmarried women (even English women) of a certain age are prudish, dried up, and repressed—an apparent theme of "Our Friend Judith"—is rather widely recognized, something we scarcely need a dozen or so pages of fiction to find out. No wonder, then, that some of our more skeptical friends contend that stories are only elaborate ways of "saying something simple," that literature is a game in which authors hide their meanings under shells of words. Of course, reading a dozen or so pages of a story like "Our Friend Judith" can be enjoyable. Could it be that we really read fiction for fun, and all our talk about themes is just hiding from our Puritan natures the fact that we are goofing off?

I don't believe that articulating the theme of a story is either the purpose of or the excuse for reading fiction, or that authors hide their meanings like Easter eggs. In order to relate his or her unique vision of reality to an absent and unknown reader, a writer must find a way of communicating—some common ground on which to meet the various unique individuals who will read the story. Common experiences, common assumptions, common language, and commonplaces offer such ground. Readers reach out from their own subjective worlds toward that new and different vision of the author with the help of the common elements (the general), and especially through the commonplaces of theme, bringing back the particulars and generalizations of the story to their own reading and living experience. In "Janus," the reader sees a successful suburban real estate agent who is married to a stockbroker but who has lost her lover, a man she truly loved, because she could not or would not decide to leave her husband; a woman whose world is "perfect," but cut in half and empty, like the beloved bowl her lover picked out for her and gave her. Generalizing, the reader may conclude that what the story says (its theme) is that life, or a full or happy life, is more than convention and material success, that love is more important than comfort and "perfection." Though the reader's own situation and choices may be considerably different from those of the protagonist in Beattie's story, he or she may be led by the story to ponder what is truly important and valuable in life, what "the perfect life" consists in, thereby coming to a greater understanding of the story—and, whether he or she agrees with the conclusions of the story or not, to a fuller understanding of the issues and theme of the story.

The significance of any story is modified to some extent by the reader's experience of books and life. You should not reduce every story to the dimensions of what you already know and feel, but you should reach out to the story and bring it back to you as an addition to and modification of your own experience. To make a story yours, to make it more than a yarn about a woman who sells real estate and has been unfaithful to her stockbroker husband and was left by her lover because she would not get a divorce, requires translating it somehow into terms that, while not necessarily psychological or moral pre-

cepts, alter or broaden to some degree your own vision of yourself, others, life
in general.

When I discussed symbols, I said that even while a symbol suggests the
meaning beyond the particulars of the fiction, it remains a detail in the fictional world—the snakelike staff of the stranger in "Young Goodman Brown"
remains a staff, Judith's cats remain cats. Some critics would say that this is
true also of theme and that theme is related to the story as integrally as symbolic meaning is to detail; that is, rather than "Young Goodman Brown" telling us something we did not know before, its theme and its story modify each
other. The theme as I've stated it relates to spiritual evil, the kind of evil suggested by the snake and Satan figures. But this theme is not entirely portable—
it cannot be taken out of the story and used as substitute for what the story
"means"—nor can it, without qualification, be used to explain all the significant details in the story. The facts that Brown is a newlywed, that Faith wears
pink (coquettish?) ribbons, and that she, whom Brown thought so pure and
innocent, shows up at the meeting of witches and sinners, suggest a more specific kind of evil than the spiritual or theological evil suggested by the snake
and Satan: moral or, even more specifically, sexual evil. This means we must
modify our definition of the theme. But how? What does the story imply about
the relationship of sex and evil? Is all sex evil? Is Original Sin sexual? Some
details—the snake, the Satanic guide—suggest a theme, other details modify it;
still others—Brown's behavior after the night of the witches' meeting—may
modify it further, so that the theme, though an approximate version of it may
be abstracted from the story, remains embedded in it, ultimately inseparable
from the details of plot, character, setting, and symbol.

A statement that can do justice to all the complexity and all the particulars
of the story is not likely to take the simple form of a **message.** Indeed, it is the
complex particularity of literature, its ultimate irreducibility, that makes critics
and teachers reject message (which suggests a simple packaged statement) as a
suitable term even for the paraphrasable thematic content of a story.

"Young Goodman Brown" is an allegorical story whose details do function
as symbols with paraphrasable meanings, yet even its theme refuses to be
reduced to a simple statement. "How Much Land Does a Man Need?" is a **parable,** a short fiction that illustrates an explicit moral lesson. That lesson, the
theme, is implied by the title. (And here the devil appears not only, at times, in
disguise, but also in his proper person.) Even so, Tolstoy's story is not without
complexity. How do you account for the first section of the story? Does your
paraphrase of the theme accommodate the conversation between the sisters
there? "Her First Ball" is not allegorical and neither is it parabolic. Though

realistic, however, it is a short, rather simple story that seems to have a simple theme overtly enunciated by one of the characters: Leila's elderly partner. But the scene with the elderly partner is not the end of the story. Leila goes on to dance with a young partner and seems to forget the man's "message." What is the story "saying"? Is her forgetting "bad"? Or "sad"? Or "good"? The specifics of the story modify and enrich all the generalizations we can abstract from it, while these themes and questions, if we recognize them, modify and enrich our reading, our experience of the story.

I realize I may have been talking as if a theme or themes spring out at the reader, while to some of you my inferences of themes may seem like pulling rabbits out of hats. "How Much Land Does a Man Need?" does not involve much of a trick: the title asks the question that, once answered, suggests the theme. But neither is too much conjuring needed to infer the theme of "Young Goodman Brown": I derived the theme of theological evil from the symbols (the snake-staff, Satan figure, names) and I tested physical details—like pink ribbons and the narrative situation (the three-month marriage)—that had sexual implications against the theme to see if I would have to modify my paraphrase. In "Her First Ball" a character raises a general issue that is tested by subsequent events in the story and modified by them.

There are, of course, other ways that details suggest generalizations or meaning, and other ways to abstract meaning from detail. Aided by footnotes, perhaps, you likely noticed the historical and biblical **allusions**—references to history, the Bible, sometimes literature, paintings, and so on—in "Young Good-man Brown." The scene is Salem in the time of King William—that is, about the time of the Salem witch trials—and the stranger's serpentine staff is related to those of the Pharoah's Egyptian magi, which turn to snakes. So allusion as well as symbols, plot, focus and voice, and character are elements that contribute to and must be accounted for in paraphrasing a theme. That is why theme is important, and why it comes last in a discussion of the elements of fiction.

But remember, the theme is an inadequate abstraction from the story; the story and its details do not disappear or lose significance once distilled into theme, nor could you reconstruct a story merely from its paraphrased theme. Indeed, theme and story, history and structure, do not so much interact, are not so much interrelated, as they are fused, inseparable.

▼　▼　▼

LEO TOLSTOY

How Much Land Does a Man Need?[1]

I

An elder sister came to visit her younger sister in the country. The elder was married to a tradesman in town, the younger to a peasant in the village. As the sisters sat over their tea talking, the elder began to boast of the advantages of town life: saying how comfortably they lived there, how well they dressed, what fine clothes her children wore, what good things they ate and drank, and how she went to the theatre, promenades, and entertainments.

The younger sister was piqued, and in turn disparaged the life of a tradesman, and stood up for that of a peasant.

"I would not change my way of life for yours," said she. "We may live roughly, but at least we are free from anxiety. You live in better style than we do, but though you often earn more than you need, you are very likely to lose all you have. You know the proverb, 'Loss and gain are brothers twain.' It often happens that people who are wealthy one day are begging their bread the next. Our way is safer. Though a peasant's life is not a fat one, it is a long one. We shall never grow rich, but we shall always have enough to eat."

The elder sister said sneeringly:

5   "Enough? Yes, if you like to share with the pigs and the calves! What do you know of elegance or manners! However much your goodman may slave, you will die as you are living—on a dung heap—and your children the same."

"Well, what of that?" replied the younger. "Of course our work is rough and coarse. But, on the other hand, it is sure, and we need not bow to anyone. But you, in your towns, are surrounded by temptations; to-day all may be right, but to-morrow the Evil One may tempt your husband with cards, wine, or women, and all will go to ruin. Don't such things happen often enough?"

Pahóm, the master of the house, was lying on the top of the stove and he listened to the women's chatter.

"It is perfectly true," thought he. "Busy as we are from childhood tilling mother earth, we peasants have no time to let any nonsense settle in our heads. Our only trouble is that we haven't land enough. If I had plenty of land, I shouldn't fear the Devil himself!"

The women finished their tea, chatted a while about dress, and then cleared away the tea-things and lay down to sleep.

10   But the Devil had been sitting behind the stove, and had heard all that was said. He was pleased that the peasant's wife had led her husband into boasting,

---

1. Translated by Louise and Aylmer Maude.

and that he had said that if he had plenty of land he would not fear the Devil himself.

"All right," thought the Devil. "We will have a tussle. I'll give you land enough; and by means of that land I will get you into my power."

II

Close to the village there lived a lady, a small landowner who had an estate of about three hundred acres. She had always lived on good terms with the peasants until she engaged as her steward an old soldier, who took to burdening the people with fines. However careful Pahóm tried to be, it happened again and again that now a horse of his got among the lady's oats, now a cow strayed into her garden, now his calves found their way into her meadows—and he always had to pay a fine.

Pahóm paid up, but grumbled and, going home in a temper, was rough with his family. All through that summer, Pahóm had much trouble because of this steward, and he was even glad when winter came and the cattle had to be stabled. Though he grudged the fodder when they could no longer graze on the pasture-land, at least he was free from anxiety about them.

In the winter the news got about that the lady was going to sell her land and that the keeper of the inn on the high road was bargaining for it. When the peasants heard this they were very much alarmed.

"Well," thought they, "if the innkeeper gets the land, he will worry us with fines worse than the lady's steward. We all depend on that estate."

So the peasants went on behalf of their Commune, and asked the lady not to sell the land to the innkeeper, offering her a better price for it themselves. The lady agreed to let them have it. Then the peasants tried to arrange for the Commune to buy the whole estate, so that it might be held by them all in common. They met twice to discuss it, but could not settle the matter; the Evil One sowed discord among them and they could not agree. So they decided to buy the land individually, each according to his means; and the lady agreed to this plan as she had to the other.

Presently Pahóm heard that a neighbor of his was buying fifty acres, and that the lady had consented to accept one half in cash and to wait a year for the other half. Pahóm felt envious.

"Look at that," thought he, "the land is all being sold, and I shall get none of it." So he spoke to his wife.

"Other people are buying," said he, "and we must also buy twenty acres or so. Life is becoming impossible. That steward is simply crushing us with his fines."

So they put their heads together and considered how they could manage to buy it. They had one hundred rúbles laid by. They sold a colt and one half of their bees, hired out one of their sons as a laborer and took his wages in advance; borrowed the rest from a brother-in-law, and so scraped together half the purchase money.

Having done this, Pahóm chose out a farm of forty acres, some of it wooded, and went to the lady to bargain for it. They came to an agreement, and he shook hands with her upon it and paid her a deposit in advance. Then they went to town and signed the deeds; he paying half the price down, and undertaking to pay the remainder within two years.

So now Pahóm had land of his own. He borrowed seed, and sowed it on the land he had bought. The harvest was a good one, and within a year he had managed to pay off his debts both to the lady and to his brother-in-law. So he became a landowner, ploughing and sowing his own land, making hay on his own land, cutting his own trees, and feeding his cattle on his own pasture. When he went out to plough his fields, or to look at his growing corn, or at his grass-meadows, his heart would fill with joy. The grass that grew and the flowers that bloomed there seemed to him unlike any that grew elsewhere. Formerly, when he had passed by that land, it had appeared the same as any other land, but now it seemed quite different.

III

So Pahóm was well-contented, and everything would have been right if the neighboring peasants would only not have trespassed on his corn-fields and meadows. He appealed to them most civilly, but they still went on: now the Communal herdsmen would let the village cows stray into his meadows, then horses from the night pasture would get among his corn. Pahóm turned them out again, and forgave their owners, and for a long time he forbore to prosecute any one. But at last he lost patience and complained to the District Court. He knew it was the peasants' want of land, and no evil intent on their part, that caused the trouble, but he thought:

"I cannot go on overlooking it or they will destroy all I have. They must be taught a lesson."

So he had them up, gave them one lesson, and then another, and two or three of the peasants were fined. After a time Pahóm's neighbors began to bear him a grudge for this, and would now and then let their cattle on to his land on purpose. One peasant even got into Pahóm's wood at night and cut down five young lime trees for their bark. Pahóm passing through the wood one day noticed something white. He came nearer and saw the stripped trunks lying on the ground, and close by stood the stumps where the trees had been. Pahóm was furious.

"If he had only cut one here and there it would have been bad enough," thought Pahóm, "but the rascal has actually cut down a whole clump. If I could only find out who did this, I would pay him out."

He racked his brain as to who it could be. Finally he decided: "It must be Simon—no one else could have done it." So he went to Simon's homestead to have a look round, but he found nothing, and only had an angry scene. However, he now felt more certain than ever that Simon had done it, and he lodged a complaint. Simon was summoned. The case was tried, and retried, and at the end of it all Simon was acquitted, there being no evidence against him. Pahóm felt still more aggrieved, and let his anger loose upon the Elder and the Judges.

"You let thieves grease your palms," said he. "If you were honest folk yourselves you would not let a thief go free."

So Pahóm quarrelled with the Judges and with his neighbors. Threats to burn his building began to be uttered. So though Pahóm had more land, his place in the Commune was much worse than before.

About this time a rumor got about that many people were moving to new parts.

"There's no need for me to leave my land," thought Pahóm. "But some of the others might leave our village and then there would be more room for us. I would take over their land myself and make my estate a bit bigger. I could then live more at ease. As it is, I am still too cramped to be comfortable."

One day Pahóm was sitting at home when a peasant, passing through the village, happened to call in. He was allowed to stay the night, and supper was given him. Pahóm had a talk with this peasant and asked him where he came from. The stranger answered that he came from beyond the Vólga, where he had been working. One word led to another, and the man went on to say that many people were settling in those parts. He told how some people from his village had settled there. They had joined the Commune, and had had twenty-five acres per man granted them. The land was so good, he said, that the rye sown on it grew as high as a horse, and so thick that five cuts of a sickle made a sheaf. One peasant, he said, had brought nothing with him but his bare hands, and now he had six horses and two cows of his own.

Pahóm's heart kindled with desire. He thought:

"Why should I suffer in this narrow hole, if one can live so well elsewhere? I will sell my land and my homestead here, and with the money I will start afresh over there and get everything new. In this crowded place one is always having trouble. But I must first go and find out all about it myself."

Towards summer he got ready and started. He went down the Vólga on a steamer to Samára, then walked another three hundred miles on foot, and at last reached the place. It was just as the stranger had said. The peasants had plenty of land: every man had twenty-five acres of Communal land given him for his use, and any one who had money could buy, besides, at a rúble an acre as much good freehold land as he wanted.

Having found out all he wished to know, Pahóm returned home as autumn came on, and began selling off his belongings. He sold his land at a profit, sold his homestead and all his cattle, and withdrew from membership in the Commune. He only waited till the spring, and then started with his family for the new settlement.

IV

As soon as Pahóm and his family reached their new abode, he applied for admission into the Commune of a large village. He stood treat to the Elders and obtained the necessary documents. Five shares of Communal land were given him for his own and his sons' use: that is to say—125 acres (not all together, but in different fields) besides the use of the Communal pasture. Pahóm put up the buildings he needed, and bought cattle. Of the Communal land alone he had three times as much as at his former home, and the land was good corn-land. He was ten times better off than he had been. He had plenty of arable land and pasturage, and could keep as many head of cattle as he liked.

At first, in the bustle of building and settling down, Pahóm was pleased with it all, but when he got used to it he began to think that even here he had not enough land. The first year, he sowed wheat on his share of the Communal land and had a good crop. He wanted to go on sowing wheat, but had not enough Communal land for the purpose, and what he had already used was not available; for in those parts wheat is only sown on virgin soil or on fallow land. It is sown for one or two years, and then the land lies fallow till it is again overgrown with prairie grass. There were many who wanted such land and there was not enough for all; so that people quarreled about it. Those who were better off wanted it for growing wheat, and those who were poor wanted it to let to dealers, so that they might raise money to pay their taxes. Pahóm wanted to sow more wheat, so he rented land from a dealer for a year. He sowed much wheat and had a fine crop, but the land was too far from the village—the wheat had to be carted more than ten miles. After a time Pahóm noticed that some peasant-dealers were living on separate farms and were growing wealthy; and he thought: "If I were to buy some freehold land and have a homestead on it, it would be a different thing altogether. Then it would all be nice and compact."

The question of buying freehold land recurred to him again and again.

He went on in the same way for three years, renting land and sowing wheat. The seasons turned out well and the crops were good, so that he began to lay money by. He might have gone on living contentedly, but he grew tired of having to rent other people's land every year, and having to scramble for it. Wherever there was good land to be had, the peasants would rush for it and it was taken up at once, so that unless you were sharp about it you got none. It happened in the third year that he and a dealer together rented a piece of pasture-land from some peasants; and they had already ploughed it up, when there was some dispute and the peasants went to law about it, and things fell out so that the labor was all lost.

"If it were my own land," thought Pahóm, "I should be independent, and there would not be all this unpleasantness."

So Pahóm began looking out for land which he could buy; and he came across a peasant who had bought thirteen hundred acres, but having got into difficulties was willing to sell again cheap. Pahóm bargained and haggled with him, and at last they settled the price at 1,500 rúbles, part in cash and part to be paid later. They had all but clinched the matter when a passing dealer happened to stop at Pahóm's one day to get a feed for his horses. He drank tea with Pahóm and they had a talk. The dealer said that he was just returning from the land of the Bashkírs,[2] far away, where he had bought thirteen thousand acres of

2. Extreme eastern European Russia, extending southwest from the Ural Mountains; the land is chiefly steppes with fertile meadows in the valleys.

land, all for 1,000 rúbles. Pahóm questioned him further, and the tradesman said:

"All one need do is to make friends with the chiefs. I gave away one hundred rúbles' worth of silk robes and carpets, besides a case of tea, and I gave wine to those who would drink it; and I got the land for less than a penny an acre." And he showed Pahóm the title-deeds, saying:

"The land lies near a river, and the whole prairie is virgin soil."

Pahóm plied him with questions, and the tradesman said:

"There is more land there than you could cover if you walked a year, and it all belongs to the Bashkírs. They are as simple as sheep, and land can be got almost for nothing."

"There now," thought Pahóm, "with my one thousand rúbles, why should I get only thirteen hundred acres, and saddle myself with a debt besides? If I take it out there, I can get more than ten times as much for the money."

V

Pahóm inquired how to get to the place, and as soon as the tradesman had left him, he prepared to go there himself. He left his wife to look after the homestead, and started on his journey taking his man with him. They stopped at a town on their way and bought a case of tea, some wine, and other presents, as the tradesman had advised. On and on they went until they had gone more than three hundred miles, and on the seventh day they came to a place where the Bashkírs had pitched their tents. It was all just as the tradesman had said. The people lived on the steppes, by a river, in felt-covered tents. They neither tilled the ground, nor ate bread. Their cattle and horses grazed in herds on the steppe. The colts were tethered behind the tents, and the mares were driven to them twice a day. The mares were milked, and from the milk kumiss was made. It was the women who prepared kumiss, and they also made cheese. As far as the men were concerned, drinking kumiss and tea, eating mutton, and playing on their pipes, was all they cared about. They were all stout and merry, and all the summer long they never thought of doing any work. They were quite ignorant, and knew no Russian, but were good-natured enough.

As soon as they saw Pahóm, they came out of their tents and gathered round their visitor. An interpreter was found, and Pahóm told them he had come about some land. The Bashkírs seemed very glad; they took Pahóm and led him into one of the best tents, where they made him sit on some down cushions placed on a carpet, while they sat around him. They gave him some tea and kumiss, and had a sheep killed, and gave him mutton to eat. Pahóm took presents out of his cart and distributed them among the Bashkírs, and divided the tea amongst them. The Bashkírs were delighted. They talked a great deal among themselves, and then told the interpreter to translate.

"They wish to tell you," said the interpreter, "that they like you, and that it is our custom to do all we can to please a guest and to repay him for his gifts. You have given us presents, now tell us which of the things we possess please you best, that we may present them to you."

"What pleases me best here," answered Pahóm, "is your land. Our land is crowded and the soil is exhausted; but you have plenty of land and it is good land. I never saw the like of it."

The interpreter translated. The Bashkírs talked among themselves for a while. Pahóm could not understand what they were saying, but saw that they were much amused and that they shouted and laughed. Then they were silent and looked at Pahóm while the interpreter said:

"They wish me to tell you that in return for your presents they will gladly give you as much land as you want. You have only to point it out with your hand and it is yours."

The Bashkírs talked again for a while and began to dispute. Pahóm asked what they were disputing about, and the interpreter told him that some of them thought they ought to ask their Chief about the land and not act in his absence, while others thought there was no need to wait for his return.

VI

While the Bashkírs were disputing, a man in a large fox-fur cap appeared on the scene. They all became silent and rose to their feet. The interpreter said, "This is our Chief himself."

Pahóm immediately fetched the best dressing-gown and five pounds of tea, and offered these to the Chief. The Chief accepted them, and seated himself in the place of honor. The Bashkírs at once began telling him something. The Chief listened for a while, then made a sign with his head for them to be silent, and addressing himself to Pahóm, said in Russian:

"Well, let it be so. Choose whatever piece of land you like; we have plenty of it."

"How can I take as much as I like?" thought Pahóm. "I must get a deed to make it secure, or else they may say, 'It is yours,' and afterwards may take it away again."

"Thank you for your kind words," he said aloud. "You have much land, and I only want a little. But I should like to be sure which bit is mine. Could it not be measured and made over to me? Life and death are in God's hands. You good people give it to me, but your children might wish to take it away again."

"You are quite right," said the Chief. "We will make it over to you."

"I heard that a dealer had been here," continued Pahóm, "and that you gave him a little land, too, and signed title-deeds to that effect. I should like to have it done in the same way."

The Chief understood.

"Yes," replied he, "that can be done quite easily. We have a scribe, and we will go to town with you and have the deed properly sealed."

"And what will be the price?" asked Pahóm.

"Our price is always the same: one thousand rúbles a day."

Pahóm did not understand.

"A day? What measure is that? How many acres would that be?"

"We do not know how to reckon it out," said the Chief. "We sell it by the day. As much as you can go round on your feet in a day is yours, and the price is one thousand rúbles a day."

Pahóm was surprised.

"But in a day you can get round a large tract of land," he said. 70

The Chief laughed.

"It will all be yours!" said he. "But there is one condition: If you don't return on the same day to the spot whence you started, your money is lost."

"But how am I to mark the way that I have gone?"

"Why, we shall go to any spot you like, and stay there. You must start from 75 that spot and make your round, taking a spade with you. Wherever you think necessary, make a mark. At every turning, dig a hole and pile up the turf; then afterwards we will go round with a plough from hole to hole. You may make as large a circuit as you please, but before the sun sets you must return to the place you started from. All the land you cover will be yours."

Pahóm was delighted. It was decided to start early next morning. They talked a while, and after drinking some more kumiss and eating some more mutton, they had tea again, and then the night came on. They gave Pahóm a feather-bed to sleep on, and the Bashkírs dispersed for the night, promising to assemble the next morning at daybreak and ride out before sunrise to the appointed spot.

VII

Pahóm lay on the feather-bed, but could not sleep. He kept thinking about the land.

"What a large tract I will mark off!" thought he. "I can easily do thirty-five miles in a day. The days are long now, and within a circuit of thirty-five miles what a lot of land there will be! I will sell the poorer land, or let it to peasants, but I'll pick out the best and farm it. I will buy two oxteams, and hire two more laborers. About a hundred and fifty acres shall be plough-land, and I will pasture cattle on the rest."

Pahóm lay awake all night, and dozed off only just before dawn. Hardly were his eyes closed when he had a dream. He thought he was lying in that same tent and heard somebody chuckling outside. He wondered who it could be, and rose and went out, and he saw the Bashkír Chief sitting in front of the tent holding his sides and rolling about with laughter. Going nearer to the Chief, Pahóm asked: "What are you laughing at?" But he saw that it was no longer the Chief, but the dealer who had recently stopped at his house and had told him about the land. Just as Pahóm was going to ask, "Have you been here long?" he saw that it was not the dealer, but the peasant who had come up from the Vólga, long ago, to Pahóm's old home. Then he saw that it was not the peasant either, but the Devil himself with hoofs and horns, sitting there and chuckling, and before him lay a man barefoot, prostrate on the ground, with only trousers and a shirt on. And Pahóm dreamt that he looked more attentively to see what sort of a man it was that was lying there, and he saw that the man was dead, and that it was himself! He awoke horror-struck.

"What things one does dream," thought he. 80

Looking round he saw through the open door that the dawn was breaking.

"It's time to wake them up," thought he. "We ought to be starting."

He got up, roused his man (who was sleeping in his cart), bade him harness; and went to call the Bashkírs.

"It's time to go to the steppe to measure the land," he said.

85   The Bashkírs rose and assembled, and the Chief came too. Then they began drinking kumiss again, and offered Pahóm some tea, but he would not wait.

"If we are to go, let us go. It is high time," said he.

VIII

The Bashkírs got ready and they all started: some mounted on horses, and some in carts. Pahóm drove in his own small cart with his servant and took a spade with him. When they reached the steppe, the morning red was beginning to kindle. They ascended a hillock (called by the Bashkírs a *shikhan*) and dismounting from their carts and their horses, gathered in one spot. The Chief came up to Pahóm and stretching out his arms towards the plain:

"See," said he, "all this, as far as your eye can reach, is ours. You may have any part of it you like."

Pahóm's eyes glistened: it was all virgin soil, as flat as the palm of your hand, as black as the seed of a poppy, and in the hollows different kinds of grasses grew breast high.

90   The Chief took off his fox-fur cap, placed it on the ground and said:

"This will be the mark. Start from here, and return here again. All the land you go round shall be yours."

Pahóm took out his money and put it on the cap. Then he took off his outer coat, remaining in his sleeveless under-coat. He unfastened his girdle and tied it tight below his stomach, put a little bag of bread into the breast of his coat, and tying a flask of water to his girdle, he drew up the tops of his boots, took the spade from his man, and stood ready to start. He considered for some moments which way he had better go—it was tempting everywhere.

"No matter," he concluded, "I will go towards the rising sun."

He turned his face to the east, stretched himself, and waited for the sun to appear above the rim.

95   "I must lose no time," he thought, "and it is easier walking while it is still cool."

The sun's rays had hardly flashed above the horizon, before Pahóm, carrying the spade over his shoulder, went down into the steppe.

Pahóm started walking neither slowly nor quickly. After having gone a thousand yards he stopped, dug a hole, and placed pieces of turf one on another to make it more visible. Then he went on; and now that he had walked off his stiffness he quickened his pace. After a while he dug another hole.

Pahóm looked back. The hillock could be distinctly seen in the sunlight, with the people on it, and the glittering tires of the cart-wheels. At a rough guess Pahóm concluded that he had walked three miles. It was growing warmer; he took off his under-coat, flung it across his shoulder, and went on again. It had grown quite warm now; he looked at the sun, it was time to think of breakfast.

"The first shift is done, but there are four in a day, and it is too soon yet to turn. but I will just take off my boots," said he to himself.

He sat down, took off his boots, stuck them into his girdle, and went on. It was easy walking now.

"I will go on for another three miles," thought he, "and then turn to the left. This spot is so fine, that it would be a pity to lose it. The further one goes, the better the land seems."

He went straight on for a while, and when he looked round, the hillock was scarcely visible and the people on it looked like black ants, and he could just see something glistening there in the sun.

"Ah," thought Pahóm, "I have gone far enough in this direction, it is time to turn. Besides I am in a regular sweat, and very thirsty."

He stopped, dug a large hole, and heaped up pieces of turf. Next he untied his flask, had a drink, and then turned sharply to the left. He went on and on; the grass was high, and it was very hot.

Pahóm began to grow tired: he looked at the sun and saw that it was noon.

"Well," he thought, "I must have a rest."

He sat down, and ate some bread and drank some water; but he did not lie down, thinking that if he did he might fall asleep. After sitting a little while, he went on again. At first he walked easily: the food had strengthened him; but it had become terribly hot and he felt sleepy, still he went on, thinking: "An hour to suffer, a life-time to live."

He went a long way in this direction also, and was about to turn to the left again, when he perceived a damp hollow: "It would be a pity to leave that out," he thought. "Flax would do well there." So he went on past the hollow, and dug a hole on the other side of it before then turned the corner. Pahóm looked towards the hillock. The heat made the air hazy: it seemed to be quivering, and through the haze the people on the hillock could scarcely be seen.

"Ah!" thought Pahóm, "I have made the sides too long; I must make this one shorter." And he went along the third side, stepping faster. He looked at the sun: it was nearly half-way to the horizon, and he had not yet done two miles of the third side of the square. He was still ten miles from the goal.

"No," he thought, "though it will make my land lop-sided, I must hurry back in a straight line now. I might go too far, and as it is I have a great deal of land."

So Pahóm hurriedly dug a hole, and turned straight towards the hillock.

IX

Pahóm went straight towards the hillock, but he now walked with difficulty. He was done up with the heat, his bare feet were cut and bruised, and his legs began to fail. He longed to rest, but it was impossible if he meant to get back before sunset. The sun waits for no man, and it was sinking lower and lower.

"Oh dear," he thought, "if only I have not blundered trying for too much! What if I am too late?"

He looked towards the hillock and at the sun. He was still far from his goal, and the sun was already near the rim.

115   Pahóm walked on and on; it was very hard walking but he went quicker and quicker. He pressed on, but was still far from the place. He began running, threw away his coat, his boots, his flask, and his cap, and kept only the spade which he used as a support.

"What shall I do," he thought again, "I have grasped too much and ruined the whole affair. I can't get there before the sun sets."

And this fear made him still more breathless. Pahóm went on running, his soaking shirt and trousers stuck to him and his mouth was parched. His breast was working like a blacksmith's bellows, his heart was beating like a hammer, and his legs were giving way as if they did not belong to him. Pahóm was seized with terror lest he should die of the strain.

Though afraid of death, he could not stop. "After having run all that way they will call me a fool if I stop now," thought he. And he ran on and on, and drew near and heard the Bashkírs yelling and shouting to him, and their cries inflamed his heart still more. He gathered his last strength and ran on.

The sun was close to the rim, and cloaked in mist looked large, and red as blood. Now, yes now, it was about to set! The sun was quite low, but he was also quite near his aim. Pahóm could already see the people on the hillock waving their arms to hurry him up. He could see the fox-fur cap on the ground and the money on it, and the Chief sitting on the ground holding his sides. And Pahóm remembered his dream.

120   "There is plenty of land," thought he, "but will God let me live on it? I have lost my life, I have lost my life! I shall never reach that spot!"

Pahóm looked at the sun, which had reached the earth: one side of it had already disappeared. With all his remaining strength he rushed on, bending his body forward so that his legs could hardly follow fast enough to keep him from falling. Just as he reached the hillock it suddenly grew dark. He looked up—the sun had already set! He gave a cry: "All my labor has been in vain," thought he, and was about to stop, but he heard the Bashkírs still shouting, and remembered that though to him, from below, the sun seemed to have set, they on the hillock could still see it. He took a long breath and ran up the hillock. It was still light there. He reached the top and saw the cap. Before it sat the Chief laughing and holding his sides. Again Pahóm remembered his dream, and he uttered a cry: his legs gave way beneath him, he fell forward and reached the cap with his hands.

"Ah, that's a fine fellow!" exclaimed the Chief. "He has gained much land!"

Pahóm's servant came running up and tried to raise him, but he saw that blood was flowing from his mouth. Pahóm was dead!

The Bashkírs clicked their tongues to show their pity.

125   His servant picked up the spade and dug a grave long enough for Pahóm to lie in, and buried him in it. Six feet from his head to his heels was all he needed.

1886

KATHERINE MANSFIELD

Her First Ball

Exactly when the ball began Leila would have found it hard to say. Perhaps her first real partner was the cab. It did not matter that she shared the cab with the Sheridan girls and their brother. She sat back in her own little corner of it, and the bolster on which her hand rested felt like the sleeve of an unknown young man's dress suit; and away they bowled, past waltzing lampposts and houses and fences and trees.

"Have you really never been to a ball before, Leila? But, my child, how too weird—" cried the Sheridan girls.

"Our nearest neighbor was fifteen miles," said Leila softly, gently opening and shutting her fan.

Oh, dear, how hard it was to be indifferent like the others! She tried not to smile too much; she tried not to care. But every single thing was so new and exciting . . . Meg's tuberoses, Jose's long loop of amber, Laura's little dark head, pushing above her white fur like a flower through snow. She would remember for ever. It even gave her a pang to see her cousin Laurie throw away the wisps of tissue paper he pulled from the fastening of his new gloves. She would like to have kept those wisps as a keepsake, as a remembrance. Laurie leaned forward and put his hand on Laura's knee.

"Look here, darling," he said. "The third and the ninth as usual, Twig?"   5

Oh, how marvellous to have a brother! In her excitement Leila felt that if there had been time, if it hadn't been impossible, she couldn't have helped crying because she was an only child, and no brother had ever said "Twig?" to her; no sister would ever say, as Meg said to Jose that moment, "I've never known your hair go up more successfully than it has tonight!"

But, of course, there was no time. They were at the drill hall already; there were cabs in front of them and cabs behind. The road was bright on either side with moving fan-like lights, and on the pavement gay couples seemed to float through the air; little satin shoes chased each other like birds.

"Hold on to me, Leila; you'll get lost," said Laura.

"Come on, girls, let's make a dash for it," said Laurie.

Leila put two fingers on Laura's pink velvet cloak, and they were somehow   10
lifted past the big gold lantern, carried along the passage, and pushed into the little room marked "Ladies." Here the crowd was so great there was hardly space to take off their things; the noise was deafening. Two benches on either side were stacked high with wraps. Two old women in white aprons ran up and down tossing fresh armfuls. And everybody was pressing forward trying to get at the little dressing table and mirror at the far end.

A great quivering jet of gas lighted the ladies' room. It couldn't wait; it was dancing already. When the door opened again and there came a burst of tuning from the drill hall, it leaped almost to the ceiling.

Dark girls, fair girls were patting their hair, tying ribbons again, tucking handkerchiefs down the front of their bodices, smoothing marble-white gloves. And because they were all laughing it seemed to Leila that they were all lovely.

"Aren't there any invisible hairpins?" cried a voice. "How most extraordinary! I can't see a single invisible hairpin."

"Powder my back, there's a darling," cried some one else.

"But I must have a needle and cotton. I've torn simply miles and miles of the frill," wailed a third.

Then, "Pass them along, pass them along!" The straw basket of programs was tossed from arm to arm. Darling little pink-and-silver programs, with pink pencils and fluffy tassels. Leila's fingers shook as she took one out of the basket. She wanted to ask someone, "Am I meant to have one too?" but she had just time to read: "Waltz 3. *Two, Two in a Canoe.* Polka 4. *Making the Feathers Fly,*" when Meg cried, "Ready, Leila?" and they pressed their way through the crush in the passage towards the big double doors of the drill hall.

Dancing had not begun yet, but the band had stopped tuning, and the noise was so great it seemed that when it did begin to play it would never be heard. Leila, pressing close to Meg, looking over Meg's shoulder, felt that even the little quivering colored flags strung across the ceiling were talking. She quite forgot to be shy; she forgot how in the middle of dressing she had sat down on the bed with one shoe off and one shoe on and begged her mother to ring up her cousins and say she couldn't go after all. And the rush of longing she had had to be sitting on the veranda of their forsaken upcountry home, listening to the baby owls crying "More pork" in the moonlight, was changed to a rush of joy so sweet that it was hard to bear alone. She clutched her fan, and, gazing at the gleaming, golden floor, the azaleas, the lanterns, the stage at one end with its red carpet and gilt chairs and the band in a corner, she thought breathlessly, "How heavenly; how simply heavenly!"

All the girls stood grouped together at one side of the doors, the men at the other, and the chaperones in dark dresses, smiling rather foolishly, walked with little careful steps over the polished floor towards the stage.

"This is my little country cousin Leila. Be nice to her. Find her partners; she's under my wing," said Meg, going up to one girl after another.

Strange faces smiled at Leila—sweetly, vaguely. Strange voices answered, "Of course, my dear." But Leila felt the girls didn't really see her. They were looking towards the men. Why didn't the men begin? What were they waiting for? There they stood, smoothing their gloves, patting their glossy hair and smiling among themselves. Then, quite suddenly, as if they had only just made up their minds that that was what they had to do, the men came gliding over the parquet. There was a joyful flutter among the girls. A tall, fair man flew up to Meg, seized her program, scribbled something; Meg passed him on to Leila. "May I have the pleasure?" He ducked and smiled. There came a dark man wearing an eyeglass, then cousin Laurie with a friend, and Laura with a little freckled fellow whose tie was crooked. Then quite an old man—fat, with a big bald patch on his head—took her program and murmured, "Let me see, let me see!" And he was a long time comparing his program, which looked black with names, with hers. It seemed to give him so much trouble that Leila was ashamed. "Oh, please don't bother," she said eagerly. But instead of replying the fat man wrote something, glanced at her again. "Do I remember this bright little face?" he said softly. "Is it known to me of yore?" At that moment the band began playing; the fat man disappeared. He was tossed away on a great wave of music that came flying over the gleaming floor, breaking the groups up into couples, scattering them, sending them spinning. . . .

Leila had learned to dance at boarding school. Every Saturday afternoon the boarders were hurried off to a little corrugated iron mission hall where Miss Eccles (of London) held her "select" classes. But the difference between that dusty-smelling hall—with calico texts on the walls, the poor terrified little woman in a brown velvet toque with rabbit's ears thumping the cold piano, Miss Eccles poking the girls' feet with her long white wand—and this was so tremendous that Leila was sure if her partner didn't come and she had to listen to that marvelous music and to watch the others sliding, gliding over the golden floor, she would die at least, or faint, or lift her arms and fly out of one of those dark windows that showed the stars.

"Ours, I think—" Some one bowed, smiled, and offered her his arm; she hadn't to die after all. Some one's hand pressed her waist, and she floated away like a flower that is tossed into a pool.

"Quite a good floor, isn't it?" drawled a faint voice close to her ear.

"I think it's most beautifully slippery," said Leila.

"Pardon!" The faint voice sounded surprised. Leila said it again. And there was a tiny pause before the voice echoed. "Oh, quite!" and she was swung round again.   25

He steered so beautifully. That was the great difference between dancing with girls and men, Leila decided. Girls banged into each other, and stamped on each other's feet; the girl who was gentleman always clutched you so.

The azaleas were separate flowers no longer; they were pink and white flags streaming by.

"Were you at the Bells' last week?" the voice came again. It sounded tired. Leila wondered whether she ought to ask him if he would like to stop.

"No, this is my first dance," said she.

Her partner gave a little gasping laugh. "Oh, I say," he protested.   30

"Yes, it is really the first dance I've ever been to." Leila was most fervent. It was such a relief to be able to tell somebody. "You see, I've lived in the country all my life up until now. . . ."

At that moment the music stopped, and they went to sit on two chairs against the wall. Leila tucked her pink satin feet under and fanned herself, while she blissfully watched the other couples passing and disappearing through the swing doors.

"Enjoying yourself, Leila?" asked Jose, nodding her golden head.

Laura passed and gave her the faintest little wink; it made Leila wonder for a moment whether she was quite grown up after all. Certainly her partner did not say very much. He coughed, tucked his handkerchief away, pulled down his waistcoat, took a minute thread off his sleeve. But it didn't matter. Almost immediately the band started, and her second partner seemed to spring from the ceiling.

35 "Floor's not bad," said the new voice. Did one always begin with the floor? And then, "Were you at the Neaves' on Tuesday?" And again Leila explained. Perhaps it was a little strange that her partners were not more interested. For it was thrilling. Her first ball! she was only at the beginning of everything. It seemed to her that she had never known what the night was like before. Up till now it had been dark, silent, beautiful very often—oh, yes—but mournful somehow. Solemn. And now it would never be like that again—it had opened dazzling bright.

"Care for an ice?" said her partner. And they went through the swing doors, down the passage, to the supper room. Her cheeks burned, she was fearfully thirsty. How sweet the ices looked on little glass plates, and how cold the frosted spoon was, iced too! And when they came back to the hall there was the fat man waiting for her by the door. It gave her quite a shock again to see how old he was; he ought to have been on the stage with the fathers and mothers. And when Leila compared him with her other partners he looked shabby. His waistcoat was creased, there was a button off his glove, his coat looked as if it was dusty with French chalk.

"Come along, little lady," said the fat man. He scarcely troubled to clasp her, and they moved away so gently, it was more like walking than dancing. But he said not a word about the floor. "Your first dance, isn't it?" he murmured.

"How *did* you know?"

"Ah," said the fat man, "that's what it is to be old!" He wheezed faintly as he steered her past an awkward couple. "You see, I've been doing this kind of thing for the last thirty years."

40 "Thirty years?" cried Leila. Twelve years before she was born!

"It hardly bears thinking about, does it?" said the fat man gloomily. Leila looked at his bald head, and she felt quite sorry for him.

"I think it's marvelous to be still going on," she said kindly.

"Kind little lady," said the fat man, and he pressed her a little closer, and hummed a bar of the waltz. "Of course," he said, "you can't hope to last anything like as long as that. No-o," said the fat man, "long before that you'll be sitting up there on the stage, looking on, in your nice black velvet. And these pretty arms will have turned into little short fat ones, and you'll beat time with such a different kind of fan—a black bony one." The fat man seemed to shudder. "And you'll smile away like the poor old dears up there, and point to your daughter, and tell the elderly lady next to you how some dreadful man tried to kiss her at the club ball. And your heart will ache, ache"—the fat man squeezed her closer still, as if he really was sorry for that poor heart—"because no one wants to kiss you now. And you'll say how unpleasant these polished floors are to walk on, how dangerous they are. Eh, Mademoiselle Twinkletoes?" said the fat man softly.

Leila gave a light little laugh, but she did not feel like laughing. Was it—could it all be true? It sounded terribly true. Was this first ball only the beginning of her last ball after all? At that the music seemed to change; it sounded sad, sad it rose upon a great sigh. Oh, how quickly things changed! Why didn't happiness last for ever? For ever wasn't a bit too long.

"I want to stop," she said in a breathless voice. The fat man led her to the door.

"No," she said. "I won't go outside. I won't sit down. I'll just stand here, thank you." She leaned against the wall, tapping with her foot, pulling up her gloves and trying to smile. But deep inside her a little girl threw her pinafore over her head and sobbed. Why had he spoiled it all?

"I say, you know," said the fat man, "you mustn't take me seriously, little lady."

"As if I should!" said Leila, tossing her small dark head and sucking her underlip. . . .

Again the couples paraded. The swing doors opened and shut. Now new music was given out by the bandmaster. But Leila didn't want to dance any more. She wanted to be home, or sitting on the veranda listening to those baby owls. When she looked through the dark windows at the stars, they had long beams like wings. . . .

But presently a soft, melting, ravishing tune began, and a young man with curly hair bowed before her. She would have to dance, out of politeness, until she could find Meg. Very stiffly she walked into the middle; very haughtily she put her hand on his sleeve. But in one minute, in one turn, her feet glided, glided. The lights, the azaleas, the dresses, the pink faces, the velvet chairs, all became one beautiful flying wheel. And when her next partner bumped her into the fat man and he said, "Par*don*," she smiled at him more radiantly than ever. She didn't even recognize him again.

1922

ANGELA CARTER

A Souvenir of Japan

When I went outside to see if he was coming home, some children dressed ready for bed in cotton nightgowns were playing with sparklers in the vacant lot on the corner. When the sparks fell down in beards of stars, the smiling children cooed softly. Their pleasure was very pure because it was so restrained. An old woman said: "And so they pestered their father until he bought them fireworks." In their language, fireworks are called *hannabi*, which means "flower fire." All through summer, every evening, you can see all kinds of fireworks, from the humblest to the most elaborate, and once we rode the train out of Shinjuku for an hour to watch one of the public displays which are held over rivers so that the dark water multiplies the reflections.

By the time we arrived at our destination, night had already fallen. We were in the suburbs. Many families were on their way to enjoy the fireworks. Their mothers had scrubbed and dressed up the smallest children to celebrate the treat. The little girls were especially immaculate in pink and white cotton kimonos tied with fluffy sashes like swatches of candy floss. Their hair had been most beautifully brushed, arranged in sleek, twin bunches and decorated with twists of gold and silver thread. These children were all on their best behavior, because they were staying up late, and held their parents' hands with a charming propriety. We followed the family parties until we came to some fields by the river and saw, high in the air, fireworks already opening out like variegated parasols. They were visible from far away and, as we took the path that led through the fields towards their source, they seemed to occupy more and more of the sky.

Along the path were stalls where shirtless cooks with sweatbands round their heads roasted corncobs and cuttlefish over charcoal. We bought cuttlefish on skewers and ate them as we walked along. They had been basted with soy sauce and were very good. There were also stalls selling goldfish in plastic bags and others for big balloons with rabbit ears. It was like a fairground—but such a well-ordered fair! Even the patrolling policemen carried colored paper lanterns instead of torches.[1] Everything was altogether quietly festive. Ice-cream sellers wandered among the crowd, ringing handbells. Their boxes of wares smoked with cold and they called out in plaintive voices, "Icy, icy, icy cream!" When young lovers dispersed discreetly down the tracks in the sedge, the shadowy, indefatigable salesmen pursued them with bells, lamps and mournful cries.

By now, a great many people were walking towards the fireworks but their steps fell so softly and they chatted in such gentle voices there was no more noise than a warm, continual, murmurous humming, the cozy sound of shared happiness, and the night filled with a muted, bourgeois yet authentic magic. Above our heads, the fireworks hung dissolving earrings on the night. Soon we lay down in a stubbled field to watch the fireworks. But, as I expected, he very quickly grew restive.

5   "Are you happy?" he asked. "Are you sure you're happy?" I was watching the fireworks and did not reply at first although I knew how bored he was and, if he was himself enjoying anything, it was only the idea of my pleasure—or, rather, the idea that he enjoyed my pleasure, since this would be a proof of love. I became guilty and suggested we return to the heart of the city. We fought a silent battle of self-abnegation and I won it, for I had the stronger character. Yet the last thing in the world that I wanted was to leave the scintillating river and the gentle crowd. But I knew his real desire was to return and so return we did, although I do not know if it was worth my small victory of selflessness to bear his remorse at cutting short my pleasure, even if to engineer this remorse had, at some subterranean level, been the whole object of the outing.

Nevertheless, as the slow train nosed back into the thickets of neon, his natural liveliness returned. He could not lose his old habit of walking through the streets with a sense of expectation, as if a fateful encounter might be just around the corner, for, the longer one stayed out, the longer something remarkable might happen and, even if nothing ever did, the chance of it appeased the sweet ache of his boredom for a little while. Besides, his duty by me was done. He had taken me out for the evening and now he wanted to be rid of me. Or so

---

1. Flashlights (British).

I saw it. The word for wife, *okusan*, means the person who occupies the inner room and rarely, if ever, comes out of it. Since I often appeared to be his wife, I was frequently subjected to this treatment, though I fought against it bitterly.

But I usually found myself waiting for him to come home knowing, with a certain resentment, that he would not; and that he would not even telephone me to tell me he would be late, either, for he was far too guilty to do so. I had nothing better to do than to watch the neighborhood children light their sparklers and giggle; the old woman stood beside me and I knew she disapproved of me. The entire street politely disapproved of me. Perhaps they thought I was contributing to the delinquency of a juvenile for he was obviously younger than I. The old woman's back was bowed almost to a circle from carrying, when he was a baby, the father who now supervised the domestic fireworks in his evening *déshabillé* of loose, white, crepe drawers, naked to the waist. Her face had the seamed reserve of the old in this country. It was a neighborhood poignantly rich in old ladies.

At the corner shop, they put an old lady outside on an upturned beer crate each morning, to air. I think she must have been the household grandmother. She was so old she had lapsed almost entirely into a somnolent plant life. She was of neither more nor less significance to herself or to the world than the pot of morning glories which blossomed beside her and perhaps she had less significance than the flowers, which would fade before lunch was ready. They kept her very clean. They covered her pale cotton kimono with a spotless pinafore trimmed with coarse lace and she never dirtied it because she did not move. Now and then, a child came out to comb her hair. Her consciousness was quite beclouded by time and, when I passed by, her rheumy eyes settled upon me always with the same, vague, disinterested wonder, like that of an Eskimo watching a train. When she whispered, *Irrasyaimase*, the shopkeeper's word of welcome, in the ghostliest of whispers, like the rustle of a paper bag, I saw her teeth were rimmed with gold.

The children lit sparklers under a mouse-colored sky and, because of the pollution in the atmosphere, the moon was mauve. The cicadas throbbed and shrieked in the backyards. When I think of this city, I shall always remember the cicadas who whirr relentlessly all through the summer nights, rising to a piercing crescendo in the subfusc dawn. I have heard cicadas even in the busiest streets, though they thrive best in the back alleys, where they ceaselessly emit that scarcely tolerable susurration which is like a shrill intensification of extreme heat.

A year before, on such a throbbing, voluptuous, platitudinous, subtropical night, we had been walking down one of these shady streets together, in and out of the shadows of the willow trees, looking for somewhere to make love. Morning glories climbed the lattices which screened the low, wooden houses, but the darkness hid the tender colors of these flowers, which the Japanese prize because they fade so quickly. He soon found a hotel, for the city is hospitable to lovers. We were shown into a room like a paper box. It contained nothing but a mattress spread on the floor. We lay down immediately and began to kiss one another. Then a maid soundlessly opened the sliding door and, stepping out of her slip-

10

pers, crept in on stockinged feet, breathing apologies. She carried a tray which contained two cups of tea and a plate of candies. She put the tray down on the matted floor beside us and backed, bowing and apologizing, from the room while our uninterrupted kiss continued. He started to unfasten my shirt and then she came back again. This time, she carried an armful of towels. I was stripped stark naked when she returned for a third time to bring the receipt for his money. She was clearly a most respectable woman and, if she was embarrassed, she did not show it by a single word or gesture.

I learned his name was Taro. In a toy store, I saw one of those books for children with pictures which are cunningly made of paper cut-outs so that, when you turn the page, the picture springs up in the three stylized dimensions of a backdrop in Kabuki. It was the story of Momotaro, who was born from a peach. Before my eyes, the paper peach split open and there was the baby, where the stone should have been. He, too, had the inhuman sweetness of a child born from something other than a mother, a passive, cruel sweetness I did not immediately understand, for it was that of the repressed masochism which, in my country, is usually confined to women.

Sometimes he seemed to possess a curiously unearthly quality when he perched upon the mattress with his knees drawn up beneath his chin in the attitude of a pixie on a doorknocker. At these times, his face seemed somehow both too flat and too large for his elegant body which had such curious, androgynous grace with its svelte, elongated spine, wide shoulders and unusually well developed pectorals, almost like the breasts of a girl approaching puberty. There was a subtle lack of alignment between face and body and he seemed almost goblin, as if he might have borrowed another person's head, as Japanese goblins do, in order to perform some devious trick. These impressions of a weird visitor were fleeting yet haunting. Sometimes, it was possible for me to believe he had practiced an enchantment upon me, as foxes in this country may, for, here, a fox can masquerade as human and at the best of times the high cheekbones gave to his face the aspect of a mask.

His hair was so heavy his neck drooped under its weight and was of a black so deep it turned purple in sunlight. His mouth also was purplish and his blunt, bee-stung lips those of Gauguin's Tahitians. The touch of his skin was as smooth as water as it flows through the fingers. His eyelids were retractable, like those of a cat, and sometimes disappeared completely. I should have liked to have had him embalmed and been able to keep him beside me in a glass coffin, so that I could watch him all the time and he would not have been able to get away from me.

As they say, Japan is a man's country. When I first came to Tokyo, cloth carps fluttered from poles in the gardens of the families fortunate enough to have borne boy children, for it was the time of the annual festival, Boys Day. At least they do not disguise the situation. At least one knows where one is. Our polarity was publicly acknowledged and socially sanctioned. As an example of the use of the word *dewa*, which occasionally means, as far as I can gather, "in," I once found in a textbook a sentence which, when translated, read: "In a society where men dominate, they value women only as the object of men's passions."

If the only conjunction possible to us was that of the death-defying double-somersault of love, it is, perhaps, a better thing to be valued only as an object of passion than never to be valued at all. I had never been so absolutely the mysterious other. I had become a kind of phoenix, a fabulous beast; I was an outlandish jewel. He found me, I think, inexpressibly exotic. But I often felt like a female impersonator in Japan.

In the department store there was a rack of dresses labeled: "For Young and Cute Girls Only." When I looked at them, I felt as gross as Glumdalclitch.[2] I wore men's sandals because they were the only kind that fitted me and, even so, I had to take the largest size. My pink cheeks, blue eyes and blatant yellow hair made of me, in the visual orchestration of this city in which all heads were dark, eyes brown and skin monotone, an instrument which played upon an alien scale. In a sober harmony of subtle plucked instruments and wistful flutes, I blared. I proclaimed myself like in a perpetual fanfare. He was so delicately put together that I thought his skeleton must have the airy elegance of a bird's and I was sometimes afraid that I might smash him. He told me that when he was in bed with me, he felt like a small boat upon a wide, stormy sea.

We pitched our tent in the most unlikely surroundings. We were living in a room furnished only by passion amongst homes of the most astounding respectability. The sounds around us were the swish of brooms upon *tatami* matting and the clatter of demotic Japanese. On all the window ledges, prim flowers bloomed in pots. Every morning, the washing came out on the balconies at seven. Early one morning, I saw a man washing the leaves of his tree. Quilts and mattresses went out to air at eight. The sunlight lay thick enough on these unpaved alleys to lay the dust and somebody always seemed to be practicing Chopin in one or another of the flimsy houses, so lightly glued together from plywood it seemed they were sustained only by willpower. Once I was at home, however, it was as if I occupied the inner room and he did not expect me to go out of it, although it was I who paid the rent.

Yet, when he was away from me, he spent much of the time savoring the most annihilating remorse. But this remorse or regret was the stuff of life to him and out he would go again the next night, or, if I had been particularly angry, he would wait until the night after that. And, even if he fully intended to come back early and had promised me he would do so, circumstances always somehow denied him and once more he would contrive to miss the last train. He and his friends spent their nights in a desultory progression from coffee shop to bar to *pachinko* parlor to coffee shop again, with the radiant aimlessness of the pure existential hero. They were connoisseurs of boredom. They savored the various bouquets of the subtly differentiated boredoms which rose from the long, wasted hours at the dead end of night. When it was time for the first train in the morning, he would go back to the mysteriously deserted, Piranesi[3] perspectives of the station, discolored by dawn, exquisitely tortured by the notion—which

2. In Jonathan Swift's *Gulliver's Travels*, Glumdalclitch is a giantess of Brobdingnag. She is Gulliver's nurse and, though only nine years old, is nearly 40 feet tall.   3. Giambattista Piranesi (1720–1778), Italian printmaker famous for exaggerated (oversized), dramatic, mysterious, almost dreamlike prints of Roman architecture and ruins.

probably contained within it a damped-down spark of hope—that, this time, he might have done something irreparable.

I speak as if he had no secrets from me. Well, then, you must realize that I was suffering from love and I knew him as intimately as I knew my own image in a mirror. In other words, I knew him only in relation to myself. Yet, on those terms, I knew him perfectly. At times, I thought I was inventing him as I went along, however, so you will have to take my word for it that we existed. But I do not want to paint our circumstantial portraits so that we both emerge with enough well-rounded, spuriously detailed actuality that you are forced to believe in us. I do not want to practice such sleight of hand. You must be content only with glimpses of our outlines, as if you had caught sight of our reflections in the looking-glass of somebody else's house as you passed by the window. His name was not Taro. I only called him Taro so that I could use the conceit of the peach boy, because it seemed appropriate.

Speaking of mirrors, the Japanese have a great respect for them and, in old-fashioned inns, one often finds them hooded with fabric covers when not in use. He said: "Mirrors make a room uncozy." I am sure there is more to it than that although they love to be cozy. One must love coziness if one is to live so close together. But, as if in celebration of the thing they feared, they seemed to have made the entire city into a cold hall of mirrors which continually proliferated whole galleries of constantly changing appearances, all marvelous but none tangible. If they did not lock up the real looking-glasses, it would be hard to tell what was real and what was not. Even buildings one had taken for substantial had a trick of disappearing overnight. One morning, we woke to find the house next door reduced to nothing but a heap of sticks and a pile of newspapers neatly tied with string, left out for the garbage collector.

20   I would not say that he seemed to me to possess the same kind of insubstantiality although his departure usually seemed imminent, until I realized he was as erratic but as inevitable as the weather. If you plan to come and live in Japan, you must be sure you are stoical enough to endure the weather. No, it was not insubstantiality; it was a rhetoric valid only on its own terms. When I listened to his protestations, I was prepared to believe he believed in them, although I knew perfectly well they meant nothing. And that isn't fair. When he made them, he believed in them implicitly. Then, he was utterly consumed by conviction. But his dedication was primarily to the idea of himself in love. This idea seemed to him magnificent, even sublime. He was prepared to die for it, as one of Baudelaire's dandies[4] might have been prepared to kill himself in order to preserve himself in the condition of a work of art, for he wanted to make this experience a masterpiece of experience which absolutely transcended the everyday. And this would annihilate the effects of the cruel drug, boredom, to which he was addicted although, perhaps, the element of boredom which is implicit in an affair so isolated from the real world was its principal appeal for him. But I had

---

4. Charles Baudelaire (1821–1867), 19th-century French writer who lived a life of excess and debauchery, and took such a lifestyle, the life of a "dandy," as a theme for his infamous poetic work, *Les fleurs du mal (The Flowers of Evil)* (1857).

no means of knowing how far his conviction would take him. And I used to turn over in my mind from time to time the question: how far does a pretense of feeling, maintained with absolute conviction, become authentic?

This country has elevated hypocrisy to the level of the highest style. To look at a samurai, you would not know him for a murderer, or a geisha for a whore. The magnificence of such objects hardly pertains to the human. They live only in a world of icons and there they participate in rituals which transmute life itself to a series of grand gestures, as moving as they are absurd. It was as if they all thought, if we believe in something hard enough, it will come true and, lo and behold! they had and it did. Our street was in essence a slum but, in appearance, it was a little enclave of harmonious quiet and, *mirabile dictu*, it was the appearance which was the reality, because they all behaved so well, kept everything so clean and lived with such rigorous civility. What terrible discipline it takes to live harmoniously. They had crushed all their vigor in order to live harmoniously and now they had the wistful beauty of flowers pressed dry in an enormous book.

But repression does not necessarily give birth only to severe beauties. In its programmed interstices, monstrous passions bloom. They torture trees to make them look more like the formal notion of a tree. They paint amazing pictures on their skins with awl and gouge, sponging away the blood as they go; a tattooed man is a walking masterpiece of remembered pain. They boast the most passionate puppets in the world who mimic love suicides in a stylized fashion, for here there is no such comfortable formula as "happy ever after." And, when I remembered the finale of the puppet tragedies, how the wooden lovers cut their throats together, I felt the beginnings of unease, as if the hieratic imagery of the country might overwhelm me, for his boredom had reached such a degree that he was insulated against everything except the irritation of anguish. If he valued me as an object of passion, he had reduced the word to its root, which derives from the Latin, *patior*, I suffer. He valued me as an instrument which would cause him pain.

So we lived under a disoriented moon which was as angry a purple as if the sky had bruised its eye, and, if we made certain genuine intersections, these only took place in darkness. His contagious conviction that our love was unique and desperate infected me with an anxious sickness; soon we would learn to treat one another with the circumspect tenderness of comrades who are amputees, for we were surrounded by the most moving images of evanescence, fireworks, morning glories, the old, children. But the most moving of these images were the intangible reflections of ourselves we saw in one another's eyes, reflections of nothing but appearances, in a city dedicated to seeming, and, try as we might to possess the essence of each other's otherness, we would inevitably fail.

1974

▾ ▾ ▾

THEME A Glossary

allusion: reference in a story to history, the Bible, literature, painting, music, and so on, that suggests the meaning or generalized relevance of details in the story

message: a misleading term for *theme*, or the central idea or statement of a story, misleading because it suggests a simple, packaged statement that preexists and for the simple communication of which the story is written

parable: a short fiction that illustrates an explicit moral lesson

plot summary: a description of the arrangement of the action in the order in which it actually appears in a story; the term is popularly used to mean the description of the history, or chronological order, of the action as it would have appeared in reality. It is important to indicate exactly in which sense you are using the term

subject: the concrete and literal description of what a story is about

theme: a generalized, abstract paraphrase of the inferred central or dominant idea of a story

QUESTIONS

1. How much land *does* a man—or woman—need? What do you mean by "need"?

2. Leila, in "Her First Ball," soon shakes off the gloomy thoughts offered her by her older partner. Is she just an empty-headed girl too shallow to think of serious things, or is she just young and healthy, enjoying life?

3. "A Souvenir of Japan" is at once, a love story, an analysis of Japanese culture as seen by an outsider, and a questioning of the nature of feelings and perception—are they "real" or constructed? The third sentence of the story sets up its subtleties, twists, paradoxes: "[The children's] pleasure was very pure because it was so restrained." Go through the story and find several instances of such arresting, puzzling statements. How does paragraph 18, in which the narrator analyzes how she is telling the story, relate to the theme? How do the fireworks of the first paragraph relate to the theme?

WRITING SUGGESTIONS

1. Compare Hawthorne's and Tolstoy's devils, their disguises, and how they function, and analyze what these figures imply about God and virtue in the two stories.

2. Land works well as a symbol of material wealth and as a symbol of the vanity of human wishes, the inevitable end of life, and therefore of the need for spiritual values. "How Many BMWs Does a Man Need" does not quite make it (but you could try a parody along those lines). Can you find a contemporary symbol that can work the way land does for Tolstoy? If you can, write an imitation or parody, calling it, perhaps, "How Much ——— Does a Person Need?"

3. Rewrite "Her First Ball" using another focus and voice.

4. Write a narrative or an essay on one of the provocative phrases or sentences in "A Souvenir of Japan," such as "he . . . had the inhuman sweetness of a child born from something other than a mother, a passive, cruel sweetness I did not immediately understand, for it was that of the repressed maochism which, in my country, is usually confined to women" (par. 11); "how far does a pretense of feeling, maintained with absolute conviction, become authentic?" (par. 20); "soon we would learn to treat one another with the circumspect tenderness of comrades who are amputees" (par. 23).

7 THE WHOLE TEXT

> I feel that discussing story-writing in terms of plot, character,
> and theme is like trying to describe the expression on a face by
> saying where the eyes, nose, and mouth are.
> — FLANNERY O'CONNOR, "Writing Short Stories"

Plot, point of view, character, symbol, and theme are useful concepts. But they do not really exist as discrete parts or constituents of a finished work. In "How Much Land Does a Man Need?", for example, Pahóm's greed is a constituent both of his character and of the story's theme.

Analyzing a story means breaking it down into pieces we can handle. Analyzing may require talking or writing about a story in terms of its "elements," but we must remain aware of the arbitrariness of those distinctions and of the inextricable, organic integrity of the story itself. As you read the stories that follow in this chapter, apply all that you have learned about the history, the structure, and the elements of fiction, but be especially alert as to how the elements interact. Notice how after taking it apart in order to analyze it, we can put the story back together.

JOSEPH CONRAD

The Secret Sharer

I

On my right hand there were lines of fishing-stakes resembling a mysterious system of half-submerged bamboo fences, incomprehensible in its division of the domain of tropical fishes, and crazy[1] of aspect as if abandoned for ever by some nomad tribe of fishermen now gone to the other end of the ocean; for there was no sign of human habitation as far as the eye could reach. To the left a group of barren islets, suggesting ruins of stone walls, towers, and blockhouses, had its foundations set in a blue sea that itself looked solid, so still and stable did it lie below my feet; even the track of light from the westering sun shone smoothly, without that animated glitter which tells of an imperceptible ripple.

1. Irregular, rickety.

And when I turned my head to take a parting glance at the tug which had just left us anchored outside the bar, I saw the straight line of the flat shore joined to the stable sea, edge to edge, with a perfect and unmarked closeness, in one leveled floor half brown, half blue under the enormous dome of the sky. Corresponding in their insignificance to the islets of the sea, two small clumps of trees, one on each side of the only fault in the impeccable joint, marked the mouth of the river Meinam[2] we had just left on the first preparatory stage of our homeward journey; and, far back on the inland level, a larger and loftier mass, the grove surrounding the great Paknam pagoda, was the only thing on which the eye could rest from the vain task of exploring the monotonous sweep of the horizon. Here and there gleams as of a few scattered pieces of silver marked the windings of the great river; and on the nearest of them, just within the bar, the tug steaming right into the land became lost to my sight, hull and funnel and masts, as though the impassive earth had swallowed her up without an effort, without a tremor. My eye followed the light cloud of her smoke, now here, now there, above the plain, according to the devious curves of the stream, but always fainter and farther away, till I lost it at last behind the mitre-shaped hill of the great pagoda. And then I was left alone with my ship, anchored at the head of the Gulf of Siam.

She floated at the starting-point of a long journey, very still in an immense stillness, the shadows of her spars flung far to the eastward by the setting sun. At that moment I was alone on her decks. There was not a sound in her—and around us nothing moved, nothing lived, not a canoe on the water, not a bird in the air, not a cloud in the sky. In this breathless pause at the threshold of a long passage we seemed to be measuring our fitness for a long and arduous enterprise, the appointed task of both our existences to be carried out, far from all human eyes, with only sky and sea for spectators and for judges.

There must have been some glare in the air to interfere with one's sight, because it was only just before the sun left us that my roaming eyes made out beyond the highest ridge of the principal islet of the group something which did away with the solemnity of perfect solitude. The tide of darkness flowed on swiftly; and with tropical suddenness a swarm of stars came out above the shadowy earth, while I lingered yet, my hand resting lightly on my ship's rail as if on the shoulder of a trusted friend. But, with all that multitude of celestial bodies staring down at one, the comfort of quiet communion with her was gone for good. And there were also disturbing sounds by this time—voices, footsteps forward; the steward flitted along the main deck, a busily ministering spirit; a handbell tinkled urgently under the poop deck. . . .

I found my two officers waiting for me near the supper table, in the lighted cuddy. We sat down at once, and as I helped the chief mate, I said:

"Are you aware that there is a ship anchored inside the islands? I saw her mast-heads above the ridge as the sun went down."

He raised sharply his simple face, overcharged by a terrible growth of

5

2. The Menan (Chao Phraya) runs through Bangkok, Thailand, into the Gulf of Siam. The Paknam Pagoda stands at the mouth of the river.

whisker, and emitted his usual ejaculations, "Bless my soul, sir! You don't say so!"

My second mate was a round-cheeked, silent young man, grave beyond his years, I thought; but as our eyes happened to meet I detected a slight quiver on his lips. I looked down at once. It was not my part to encourage sneering on board my ship. It must be said, too, that I knew very little of my officers. In consequence of certain events of no particular significance, except to myself, I had been appointed to the command only a fortnight before. Neither did I know much of the hands forward. All these people had been together for eighteen months or so, and my position was that of the only stranger on board. I mention this because it has some bearing on what is to follow. But what I felt most was my being a stranger to the ship; and if all the truth must be told, I was somewhat of a stranger to myself. The youngest man on board (barring the second mate), and untried as yet by a position of the fullest responsibility, I was willing to take the adequacy of the others for granted. They had simply to be equal to their tasks; but I wondered how far I should turn out faithful to that ideal conception of one's own personality every man sets up for himself secretly.

Meantime the chief mate, with an almost visible effect of collaboration on the part of his round eyes and frightful whiskers, was trying to evolve a theory of the anchored ship. His dominant trait was to take all things into earnest consideration. He was of a painstaking turn of mind. As he used to say, he "liked to account to himself" for practically everything that came in his way, down to a miserable scorpion he had found in his cabin a week before. The why and the wherefore of that scorpion—how it got on board and came to select his room rather than the pantry (which was a dark place and more what a scorpion would be partial to), and how on earth it managed to drown itself in the inkwell of his writing-desk—had exercised him infinitely. The ship within the islands was much more easily accounted for; and just as we were about to rise from table he made his pronouncement. She was, he doubted not, a ship from home lately arrived. Probably she drew too much water to cross the bar except at the top of spring tides. Therefore she went into that natural harbor to wait for a few days in preference to remaining in an open roadstead.

"That's so," confirmed the second mate suddenly, in his slightly hoarse voice. "She draws over twenty feet. She's the Liverpool ship *Sephora* with a cargo of coal. Hundred and twenty-three days from Cardiff."

We looked at him in surprise.

"The tugboat skipper told me when he come on board for your letters, sir," explained the young man. "He expects to take her up the river the day after tomorrow."

After thus overwhelming us with the extent of his information he slipped out of the cabin. The mate observed regretfully that he "could not account for that young fellow's whims." What prevented him telling us all about it at once, he wanted to know.

I detained him as he was making a move. For the last two days the crew had had plenty of hard work, and the night before they had very little sleep. I felt painfully that I—a stranger—was doing something unusual when I directed him to let all hands turn in without setting an anchor-watch.[3] I proposed to keep on deck myself till one o'clock or thereabouts. I would get the second mate to relieve me at that hour.

"He will turn out the cook and the steward at four," I concluded, "and then give you a call. Of course at the slightest sign of any sort of wind we'll have the hands up and make a start at once."

He concealed his astonishment. "Very well, sir." Outside the cuddy he put his head in the second mate's door to inform him of my unheard-of caprice to take a five hours' anchor-watch on myself. I heard the other raise his voice incredulously—"What? The captain himself?" Then a few more murmurs, a door closed, then another. A few moments later I went on deck.

My strangeness, which had made me sleepless, had prompted that unconventional arrangement, as if I had expected in those solitary hours of the night to get on terms with the ship of which I knew nothing, manned by men of whom I knew very little more. Fast alongside a wharf, littered like any ship in port with a tangle of unrelated things, invaded by unrelated shore people, I had hardly seen her yet properly. Now, as she lay cleared for sea, the stretch of her main deck seemed to me very fine under the stars. Very fine, very roomy for her size, and very inviting. I descended the poop and paced the waist, my mind picturing to myself the coming passage through the Malay Archipelago, down the Indian Ocean, and up the Atlantic. All its phases were familiar enough to me, every characteristic, all the alternatives which were likely to face me on the high seas—everything! . . . except the novel responsibility of command. But I took heart from the reasonable thought that the ship was like other ships, the men like other men, and that the sea was not likely to keep any special surprises expressly for my discomfiture.

Arrived at that comforting conclusion, I bethought myself of a cigar and went below to get it. All was still down there. Everybody at the after end of the ship was sleeping profoundly. I came out again on the quarter-deck, agreeably at ease in my sleeping suit on that warm, breathless night, barefooted, a glowing cigar in my teeth, and, going forward, I was met by the profound silence of the fore end of the ship. Only as I passed the door of the forecastle I heard a deep, quiet, trustful sigh of some sleeper inside. And suddenly I rejoiced in the great security of the sea as compared with the unrest of the land, in my choice of that untempted life presenting no disquieting problems, invested with an elementary moral beauty by the absolute straightforwardness of its appeal and by the singleness of its purpose.

The riding-light[4] in the fore-rigging burned with a clear, untroubled, as if symbolic, flame, confident and bright in the mysterious shades of the night. Passing on my way aft along the other side of the ship, I observed that the rope side-ladder, put over, no doubt, for the master of the tug when he came to fetch away our letters, had not been hauled in as it should have been. I became annoyed at this, for exactitude in small matters is the very soul of discipline.

---

3. A detachment of seamen kept on deck while the ship lies at anchor.   4. Special light displayed by ship while ("riding") at anchor.

Then I reflected that I had myself peremptorily dismissed my officers from duty, and by my own act had prevented the anchor-watch being formally set and things properly attended to. I asked myself whether it was wise ever to interfere with the established routine of duties even from the kindest of motives. My action might have made me appear eccentric. Goodness only knew how that absurdly whiskered mate would "account" for my conduct, and what the whole ship thought of that informality of their new captain. I was vexed with myself.

Not from compunction certainly, but, as it were mechanically, I proceeded to get the ladder in myself. Now a side-ladder of that sort is a light affair and comes in easily, yet my vigorous tug, which should have brought it flying on board, merely recoiled upon my body in a totally unexpected jerk. What the devil! . . . I was so astounded by the immovableness of that ladder that I remained stockstill, trying to account for it to myself like that imbecile mate of mine. In the end, of course, I put my head over the rail.

20   The side of the ship made an opaque belt of shadow on the darkling glassy shimmer of the sea. But I saw at once something elongated and pale floating very close to the ladder. Before I could form a guess a faint flash of phosphorescent light, which seemed to issue suddenly from the naked body of a man, flickered in the sleeping water with the elusive, silent play of summer lightning in a night sky. With a gasp I saw revealed to my stare a pair of feet, the long legs, a broad livid back immersed right up to the neck in a greenish cadaverous glow. One hand, awash, clutched the bottom rung of the ladder. He was complete but for the head. A headless corpse! The cigar dropped out of my gaping mouth with a tiny plop and a short hiss quite audible in the absolute stillness of all things under heaven. At that I suppose he raised up his face, a dimly pale oval in the shadow of the ship's side. But even then I could only barely make out down there the shape of his black-haired head. However, it was enough for the horrid, frost-bound sensation which had gripped me about the chest to pass off. The moment of vain exclamations was past too. I only climbed on the spare spar and leaned over the rail as far as I could, to bring my eyes nearer to that mystery floating alongside.

As he hung by the ladder, like a resting swimmer, the sea-lightning played about his limbs at every stir; and he appeared in it ghastly, silvery, fish-like. He remained as mute as a fish, too. He made no motion to get out of the water, either. It was inconceivable that he should not attempt to come on board, and strangely troubling to suspect that perhaps he did not want to. And my first words were prompted by just that troubled incertitude.

"What's the matter?" I asked in my ordinary tone, speaking down to the face upturned exactly under mine.

"Cramp," it answered, no louder. Then slightly anxious, "I say, no need to call any one."

25   "I was not going to," I said.

"Are you alone on deck?"

"Yes."

I had somehow the impression that he was on the point of letting go the ladder to swim away beyond my ken—mysterious as he came. But, for the moment, this being appearing as if he had risen from the bottom of the sea (it was certainly the nearest land to the ship) wanted only to know the time. I told him. And he, down there, tentatively:

"I suppose your captain's turned in?"   30

"I am sure he isn't," I said.

He seemed to struggle with himself, for I heard something like the low, bitter murmur of doubt. "What's the good?" His next words came out with a hesitating effort.

"Look here, my man. Could you call him out quietly?"

I thought the time had come to declare myself.

"*I* am the captain."

I heard a "By Jove!" whispered at the level of the water. The phosphores-   35
cence flashed in the swirl of the water all about his limbs, his other hand seized the ladder.

"My name's Leggatt."

The voice was calm and resolute. A good voice. The self-possession of that man had somehow induced a corresponding state in myself. It was very quietly that I remarked:

"You must be a good swimmer."

"Yes. I've been in the water practically since nine o'clock. The question for me now is whether I am to let go this ladder and go on swimming till I sink from exhaustion or—to come on board here."

I felt this was no mere formula of desperate speech, but a real alternative in   40
the view of a strong soul. I should have gathered from this that he was young; indeed, it is only the young who are ever confronted by such clear issues. But at the time it was pure intuition on my part. A mysterious communication was established already between us two—in the face of that silent, darkened tropical sea. I was young, too; young enough to make no comment. The man in the water began suddenly to climb up the ladder, and I hastened away from the rail to fetch some clothes.

Before entering the cabin I stood still, listening in the lobby at the foot of the stairs. A faint snore came through the closed door of the chief mate's room. The second mate's door was on the hook, but the darkness in there was abso-lutely soundless. He, too, was young and could sleep like a stone. Remained the steward, but he was not likely to wake up before he was called. I got a sleeping suit out of my room, and, coming back on deck, saw the naked man from the sea sitting on the main-hatch, glimmering white in the darkness, his elbows on his knees and his head in his hands. In a moment he had concealed his damp body in a sleeping suit of the same gray-stripe pattern as the one I was wearing, and followed me like my double on the poop. Together we moved right aft, barefooted, silent.

"What is it?" I asked in a deadened voice, taking the lighted lamp out of the binnacle, and raising it to his face.

"An ugly business."

He had rather regular features; a good mouth; light eyes under somewhat heavy, dark eyebrows; a smooth, square forehead; no growth on his cheeks; a small, brown mustache, and a well-shaped, round chin. His expression was concentrated, meditative, under the inspecting light of the lamp I held up to his face; such as a man thinking hard in solitude might wear. My sleeping suit was just right for his size. A well-knit young fellow of twenty-five at most. He caught his lower lip with the edge of white, even teeth.

45   "Yes," I said, replacing the lamp in the binnacle. The warm, heavy tropical night closed upon his head again.

    "There's a ship over there," he murmured.

    "Yes, I know. The *Sephora*. Did you know of us?"

    "Hadn't the slightest idea. I am the mate of her—" He paused and corrected himself. "I should say I *was*."

    "Aha! Something wrong?"

50   "Yes. Very wrong indeed. I've killed a man."

    "What do you mean? Just now?"

    "No, on the passage. Weeks ago. Thirty-nine south. When I say a man—"

    "Fit of temper," I suggested confidently.

    The shadowy, dark head, like mine, seemed to nod imperceptibly above the ghostly gray of my sleeping suit. It was, in the night, as though I had been faced by my own reflection in the depths of a sombre and immense mirror.

55   "A pretty thing to have to own up to for a Conway[5] boy," murmured my double distinctly.

    "You're a Conway boy?"

    "I am," he said, as if startled. Then, slowly . . . "Perhaps you too . . ."

    It was so; but being a couple of years older I had left before he joined. After a quick interchange of dates a silence fell; and I thought suddenly of my absurd mate with his terrific whiskers and the "Bless my soul—you don't say so" type of intellect. My double gave me an inkling of his thoughts by saying:

    "My father's a parson in Norfolk. Do you see me before a judge and jury on that charge? For myself I can't see the necessity. There are fellows that an angel from heaven—And I am not that. He was one of those creatures that are just simmering all the time with a silly sort of wickedness. Miserable devils that have no business to live at all. He wouldn't do his duty and wouldn't let anybody else do theirs. But what's the good of talking! You know well enough the sort of ill-conditioned snarling cur . . ."

60   He appealed to me as if our experiences had been as identical as our clothes. And I knew well enough the pestiferous danger of such a character where there are no means of legal repression. And I knew well enough also that my double there was no homicidal ruffian. I did not think of asking him for details, and he told me the story roughly in brusque, disconnected sentences. I needed no more. I saw it all going on as though I were myself inside that other sleeping suit.

    "It happened while we were setting a reefed foresail, at dusk. Reefed foresail! You understand the sort of weather. The only sail we had left to keep the ship running; so you may guess what it had been like for days. Anxious sort of job,

---

5. The wooden battleship *Conway*, which was used to train young officers for the Royal Navy and merchant service.

that. He gave me some of his cursed insolence at the sheet.[6] I tell you I was overdone with this terrific weather that seemed to have no end to it. Terrific, I tell you—and a deep ship. I believe the fellow himself was half crazed with funk. It was no time for gentlemanly reproof, so I turned round and felled him like an ox. He up and at me. We closed just as an awful sea made for the ship. All hands saw it coming and took to the rigging, but I had him by the throat, and went on shaking him like a rat, the men above us yelling. 'Look out! Look out!' Then a crash as if the sky had fallen on my head. They say that for over ten minutes hardly anything was to be seen of the ship—just the three masts and a bit of the forecastle head and of the poop all awash driving along in a smother of foam. It was a miracle that they found us, jammed together behind the forebits. It's clear that I meant business, because I was holding him by the throat still when they picked us up. He was black in the face. It was too much for them. It seems they rushed us aft together, gripped as we were, screaming 'Murder!' like a lot of lunatics, and broke into the cuddy. And the ship running for her life, touch and go all the time, any minute her last in a sea fit to turn your hair gray only a-looking at it. I understand that the skipper, too, started raving like the rest of them. The man had been deprived of sleep for more than a week, and to have this spring on him at the height of a furious gale nearly drove him out of his mind. I wonder they didn't fling me overboard after getting the carcass of their precious shipmate out of my fingers. They had rather a job to separate us, I've been told. A sufficiently fierce story to make an old judge and a respectable jury sit up a bit. The first thing I heard when I came to myself was the maddening howling of that endless gale, and on that the voice of the old man. He was hanging on to my bunk, staring into my face out of his sou'wester.

"'Mr. Leggatt, you have killed a man. You can act no longer as chief mate of this ship.'"

His care to subdue his voice made it sound monotonous. He rested a hand on the end of the skylight to steady himself with, and all that time did not stir a limb, so far as I could see. "Nice little tale for a quiet tea party," he concluded in the same tone.

One of my hands, too, rested on the end of the skylight; neither did I stir a limb, so far as I knew. We stood less than a foot from each other. It occurred to me that if old "Bless my soul—you don't say so" were to put his head up the companion and catch sight of us, he would think he was seeing double, or imagine himself come upon a scene of weird witchcraft: the strange captain having a quiet confabulation by the wheel with his own gray ghost. I became very much concerned to prevent anything of the sort. I heard the other's soothing undertone:

"My father's a parson in Norfolk," it said. Evidently he had forgotten he had told me this important fact before. Truly a nice little tale.

"You had better slip down into my stateroom now," I said, moving off stealthily. My double followed my movements; our bare feet made no sound; I let him

65

6. Rope or chain attached to lower corner of sail used for shortening or slackening it.

in, closed the door with care, and, after giving a call to the second mate, returned on deck for my relief.

"Not much sign of any wind yet," I remarked when he approached.

"No, sir. Not much," he assented sleepily in his hoarse voice, with just enough deference, no more, and barely suppressing a yawn.

"Well, that's all you have to look out for. You have got your orders."

"Yes, sir."

I paced a turn or two on the poop and saw him take up his position face forward with his elbow in the ratlines of the mizzen-rigging before I went below. The mate's faint snoring was still going on peacefully. The cuddy lamp was burning over the table on which stood a vase with flowers, a polite attention from the ship's provision merchant — the last flowers we should see for the next three months at the very least. Two bunches of bananas hung from the beam symmetrically, one on each side of the rudder-casing. Everything was as before in the ship — except that two of her captain's sleeping suits were simultaneously in use, one motionless in the cuddy, the other keeping very still in the captain's stateroom.

It must be explained here that my cabin had the form of the capital letter L, the door being within the angle and opening into the short part of the letter. A couch was to the left, the bedplace to the right; my writing-desk and the chronometers' table faced the door. But any one opening it, unless he stepped right inside, had no view of what I call the long (or vertical) part of the letter. It contained some lockers surmounted by a bookcase; and a few clothes, a thick jacket or two, caps, oilskin coat, and such-like, hung on hooks. There was at the bottom of that part a door opening into my bathroom, which could be entered also directly from the saloon. But that way was never used.

The mysterious arrival had discovered the advantage of this particular shape. Entering my room, lighted strongly by a big bulkhead lamp swung on gimbals above my writing-desk, I did not see him anywhere till he stepped out quietly from behind the coats hung in the recessed part.

"I heard somebody moving about, and went in there at once," he whispered. I, too, spoke under my breath.

"Nobody is likely to come in here without knocking and getting permission."

He nodded. His face was thin and the sunburn faded, as though he had been ill. And no wonder. He had been, I heard presently, kept under arrest in his cabin for nearly nine weeks. But there was nothing sickly in his eyes or in his expression. He was not a bit like me, really; yet, as we stood leaning over my bedplace, whispering side by side, with our dark heads together and our backs to the door, anybody bold enough to open it stealthily would have been treated to the uncanny sight of a double captain busy talking in whispers with his other self.

"But all this doesn't tell me how you came to hang on to our side-ladder," I inquired, in the hardly audible murmurs we used, after he had told me something more of the proceedings on board the *Sephora* once the bad weather was over.

"When we sighted Java Head[7] I had had time to think all those matters out several times over. I had six weeks of doing nothing else, and with only an hour or so every evening for a tramp on the quarterdeck."

He whispered, his arms folded on the side of my bedplace, staring through the open port. And I could imagine perfectly the manner of this thinking out— a stubborn if not a steadfast operation; something of which I should have been perfectly incapable.

80

"I reckoned it would be dark before we closed with the land," he continued, so low that I had to strain my hearing, near as we were to each other, shoulder touching shoulder almost. "So I asked to speak to the old man. He always seemed very sick when he came to see me—as if he could not look me in the face. You know, that foresail saved the ship. She was too deep to have run long under bare poles. And it was I that managed to set it for him. Anyway, he came. When I had him in my cabin—he stood by the door looking at me as if I had the halter round my neck already—I asked him right away to leave my cabin door unlocked at night while the ship was going through Sunda Straits. There would be the Java coast within two or three miles, off Anjer Point. I wanted nothing more. I've had a prize for swimming my second year in the Conway."

"I can believe it," I breathed out.

"God only knows why they locked me in every night. To see some of their faces you'd have thought they were afraid I'd go about at night strangling people. Am I a murdering brute? Do I look it? By Jove! if I had been he wouldn't have trusted himself like that into my room. You'll say I might have chucked him aside and bolted out, there and then—it was dark already. Well, no. And for the same reason I wouldn't think of trying to smash the door. There would have been a rush to stop me at the noise, and I did not mean to get into a confounded scrimmage. Somebody else might have got killed—for I would not have broken out only to get chucked back, and I did not want any more of that work. He refused, looking more sick than ever. He was afraid of the men, and also of that old second mate of his who had been sailing with him for years—a gray-headed old humbug; and his steward, too, had been with him devil knows how long— seventeen years or more—a dogmatic sort of loafer who hated me like poison, just because I was the chief mate. No chief mate ever made more than one voyage in the *Sephora*, you know. Those two old chaps ran the ship. Devil only knows what the skipper wasn't afraid of (all his nerve went to pieces altogether in that hellish spell of bad weather we had)—of what the law would do to him— of his wife, perhaps. Oh yes! she's on board. Though I don't think she would have meddled. She would have been only too glad to have me out of the ship in any way. The 'brand of Cain'[8] business, don't you see? That's all right. I was ready enough to go off wandering on the face of the earth—and that was price enough to pay for an Abel of that sort. Anyhow, he wouldn't listen to me. 'This

7. A famous landmark for clipper ships engaged in the China trade on the western end of Java, the southern entrance to the Sunda Straits mentioned below; the killing thus took place some 1,500 miles south of the present scene. 8. Genesis 4:14–15.

thing must take its course. I represent the law here.' He was shaking like a leaf. 'So you won't?' 'No!' 'Then I hope you will be able to sleep on that," I said, and turned my back on him. 'I wonder that *you* can,' cries he, and locks the door.

"Well, after that, I couldn't. Not very well. That was three weeks ago. We have had a slow passage through the Java Sea; drifted about Carimata[9] for ten days. When we anchored here they thought, I suppose, it was all right. The nearest land (and that's five miles) is the ship's destination; the consul would soon set about catching me; and there would have been no object in bolting to these islets there. I don't suppose there's a drop of water on them. I don't know how it was, but tonight that steward, after bringing me my supper, went out to let me eat it, and left the door unlocked. And I ate it—all there was, too. After I had finished I strolled out on the quarterdeck. I don't know that I meant to do anything. A breath of fresh air was all I wanted, I believe. Then a sudden temptation came over me. I kicked off my slippers and was in the water before I had made up my mind fairly. Somebody heard the splash and they raised an awful hullabaloo. 'He's gone! Lower the boats! He's committed suicide! No, he's swimming.' Certainly I was swimming. It's not easy for a swimmer like me to commit suicide by drowning. I landed on the nearest islet before the boat left the ship's side. I heard them pulling about in the dark, hailing, and so on, but after a bit they gave up. Everything quieted down and the anchorage became as still as death. I sat down on a stone and began to think. I felt certain they would start searching for me at daylight. There was no place to hide on those stony things—and if there had been, what would have been the good? But now I was clear of that ship I was not going back. So after a while I took off all my clothes, tied them up in a bundle with a stone inside, and dropped them in the deep water on the outer side of that islet. That was suicide enough for me. Let them think what they liked, but I didn't mean to drown myself. I meant to swim till I sank—but that's not the same thing. I struck out for another of these little islands, and it was from that one that I first saw your riding-light. Something to swim for. I went on easily, and on the way I came upon a flat rock a foot or two above water. In the daytime, I dare say, you might make it out with a glass from your poop. I scrambled up on it and rested myself for a bit. Then I made another start. That last spell must have been over a mile."

85   His whisper was getting fainter and fainter, and all the time he stared straight out through the porthole, in which there was not even a star to be seen. I had not interrupted him. There was something that made comment impossible, in his narrative, or perhaps in himself; a sort of feeling, a quality, which I can't find a name for. And when he ceased, all I found was a futile whisper, "So you swam for our light?"

"Yes—straight for it. It was something to swim for. I couldn't see any stars low down because the coast was in the way, and I couldn't see the land, either. The water was like glass. One might have been swimming in a confounded thousand feet deep cistern with no place for scrambling out anywhere; but what

---

9. The Karimata Islands in the straits between Borneo and Sumatra, some 300 miles northeast of the Sunda Straits.

I didn't like was the notion of swimming round and round like a crazed bullock before I gave out; and as I didn't mean to go back . . . No. Do you see me being hauled back, stark naked, off one of these little islands by the scruff of the neck and fighting like a wild beast? Somebody would have got killed for certain, and I did not want any of that. So I went on. Then your ladder—"

"Why didn't you hail the ship?" I asked, a little louder.

He touched my shoulder lightly. Lazy footsteps came right over our heads and stopped. The second mate had crossed from the other side of the poop and might have been hanging over the rail, for all we knew.

"He couldn't hear us talking—could he?" My double breathed into my very ear anxiously.

His anxiety was an answer, a sufficient answer, to the question I had put to him. An answer containing all the difficulty of that situation. I closed the port- hole quietly, to make sure. A louder word might have been overheard.

"Who's that?" he whispered then.

"My second mate. But I don't know much more of the fellow than you do."

And I told him a little about myself. I had been appointed to take charge while I least expected anything of the sort, not quite a fortnight ago. I didn't know either the ship or the people. Hadn't had the time in port to look about me or size anybody up. And as to the crew, all they knew was that I was appointed to take the ship home. For the rest, I was almost as much of a stranger on board as himself, I said. And at the moment I felt it most acutely. I felt that it would take very little to make me a suspect person in the eyes of the ship's company.

He had turned about meantime; and we, the two strangers in the ship, faced each other in identical attitudes.

"Your ladder—" he murmured, after a silence. "Who'd have thought of find- ing a ladder hanging over at night in a ship anchored out here! I felt just then a very unpleasant faintness. After the life I've been leading for nine weeks, any- body would have got out of condition. I wasn't capable of swimming round as far as your rudder-chains. And, lo and behold! there was a ladder to get hold of. After I gripped it I said to myself, 'What's the good?' When I saw a man's head looking over I thought I would swim away presently and leave him shouting— in whatever language it was. I didn't mind being looked at. I—I liked it. And then you speaking to me so quietly—as if you had expected me—made me hold on a little longer. It had been a confounded lonely time—I don't mean while swimming. I was glad to talk a little to somebody that didn't belong to the *Seph- ora*. As to asking for the captain, that was a mere impulse. It could have been no use, with all the ship knowing about me and the other people pretty certain to be round here in the morning. I don't know—I wanted to be seen, to talk with somebody, before I went on. I don't know what I would have said. . . . 'Fine night, isn't it?' or something of the sort."

"Do you think they will be round here presently?" I asked, with some incre- dulity.

"Quite likely," he said faintly.

He looked extremely haggard all of a sudden. His head rolled on his shoul- ders.

90

95

"H'm. We shall see then. Meantime get into that bed," I whispered. "Want help? There."

100   It was a rather high bedplace with a set of drawers underneath. This amazing swimmer really needed the lift I gave him by seizing his leg. He tumbled in, rolled over on his back, and flung one arm across his eyes. And then, with his face nearly hidden, he must have looked exactly as I used to look in that bed. I gazed upon my other self for a while before drawing across carefully the two green serge curtains which ran on a brass rod. I thought for a moment of pinning them together for greater safety, but I sat down on the couch, and once there I felt unwilling to rise and hunt for a pin. I would do it in a moment. I was extremely tired, in a peculiarly intimate way, by the strain of stealthiness, by the effort of whispering, and the general secrecy of this excitement. It was three o'clock by now, and I had been on my feet since nine, but I was not sleepy; I could not have gone to sleep. I sat there, fagged out, looking at the curtains, trying to clear my mind of the confused sensation of being in two places at once, and greatly bothered by an exasperating knocking in my head. It was a relief to discover suddenly that it was not in my head at all, but on the outside of the door. Before I could collect myself, the words "Come in" were out of my mouth, and the steward entered with a tray, bringing in my morning coffee. I had slept, after all, and I was so frightened that I shouted, "This way! I am here, steward," as though he had been miles away. He put down the tray on the table next the couch and only then said, very quietly, "I can see you are here, sir." I felt him give me a keen look, but I dared not meet his eyes just then. He must have wondered why I had drawn the curtains of my bed before going to sleep on the couch. He went out, hooking the door open as usual.

        I heard the crew washing decks above me. I knew I would have been told at once if there had been any wind. Calm, I thought, and I was doubly vexed. Indeed, I felt dual more than ever. The steward reappeared suddenly in the doorway. I jumped up from the couch so quickly that he gave a start.

        "What do you want here?"

        "Close your port, sir—they are washing decks."

        "It is closed," I said, reddening.

105   "Very well, sir." But he did not move from the doorway and returned my stare in an extraordinary, equivocal manner for a time. Then his eyes, wavered, all his expression changed, and in a voice unusually gentle, almost coaxingly.

        "May I come in to take the empty cup away, sir?"

        "Of course!" I turned my back on him while he popped in and out. Then I unhooked and closed the door and even pushed the bolt. This sort of thing could not go on very long. The cabin was as hot as an oven, too. I took a peep at my double, and discovered that he had not moved; his arm was still over his eyes; but his chest heaved, his hair was wet, his chin glistened with perspiration. I reached over him and opened the port.

        "I must show myself on deck," I reflected.

        Of course, theoretically, I could do what I liked, with no one to say nay to me within the whole circle of the horizon; but to lock my cabin door and take the key away I did not dare. Directly I put my head out of the companion I saw the group of my two officers, the second mate barefooted, the chief mate in long india-rubber boots, near the break of the poop, and the steward half-way down the poop ladder talking to them eagerly. He happened to catch sight of me and dived, the second ran down on the main deck shouting some order or other, and the chief mate came to meet me, touching his cap.

There was a sort of curiosity in his eye that I did not like. I don't know whether the steward had told them that I was "queer" only, or downright drunk, but I know the man meant to have a good look at me. I watched him coming with a smile which, as he got into point-blank range, took effect and froze his very whiskers. I did not give him time to open his lips.

"Square the yards by lifts and braces before the hands go to breakfast."

It was the first particular order I had given on board that ship; and I stayed on deck to see it executed too. I had felt the need of asserting myself without loss of time. That sneering young cub got taken down a peg or two on that occasion, and I also seized the opportunity of having a good look at the face of every foremast man as they filed past me to go to the after braces. At breakfast time, eating nothing myself, I presided with such frigid dignity that the two mates were only too glad to escape from the cabin as soon as decency permitted; and all the time the dual working of my mind distracted me almost to the point of insanity. I was constantly watching myself, my secret self, as dependent on my actions as my own personality, sleeping in that bed, behind that door which faced me as I sat at the head of the table. It was very much like being mad, only it was worse, because one was aware of it.

I had to shake him for a solid minute, but when at last he opened his eyes it was in the full possession of his senses, with an inquiring look.

"All's well so far," I whispered. "Now you must vanish into the bathroom."

He did so, as noiseless as a ghost, and I then rang for the steward, and facing him boldly, directed him to tidy up my stateroom while I was having my bath — "and be quick about it." As my tone admitted of no excuses, he said, "Yes, sir," and ran off to fetch his dustpan and brushes. I took a bath and did most of my dressing, splashing, and whistling softly for the steward's edification, while the secret sharer of my life stood drawn bolt upright in that little space, his face looking very sunken in daylight, his eyelids lowered under the stern, dark line of his eyebrows drawn together by a slight frown.

When I left him there to go back to my room the steward was finishing dusting. I sent for the mate and engaged him in some insignificant conversation. It was, as it were, trifling with the terrific character of his whiskers; but my object was to give him an opportunity for a good look at my cabin. And then I could at last shut, with a clear conscience, the door of my stateroom and get my double back into the recessed part. There was nothing else for it. He had to sit still on a small folding stool, half smothered by the heavy coats hanging there. We listened to the steward going into the bathroom out of the saloon, filling the water-bottles there, scrubbing the bath, setting things to rights, whisk, bang, clatter — out again into the saloon — turn the key — click. Such was my scheme for keeping my second self invisible. Nothing better could be contrived under the circumstances. And there we sat: I at my writing-desk ready to appear busy with

110

115

some papers, he behind me, out of sight of the door. It would not have been prudent to talk in daytime; and I could not have stood the excitement of that queer sense of whispering to myself. Now and then, glancing over my shoulder, I saw him far back there, sitting rigidly on the low stool, his bare feet close together, his arms folded, his head hanging on his breast—and perfectly still. Anybody would have taken him for me.

I was fascinated by it myself. Every moment I had to glance over my shoulder. I was looking at him when a voice outside the door said:

"Beg pardon, sir."

"Well!" . . . I kept my eyes on him, and so when the voice outside the door announced, "There's a ship's boat coming our way, sir," I saw him give a start—the first movement he had made for hours. But he did not raise his bowed head.

"All right. Get the ladder over."

I hesitated. Should I whisper something to him? But what? His immobility seemed to have been never disturbed. What could I tell him he did not know already? . . . Finally I went on deck.

II

The skipper of the *Spehora* had a thin, red whisker all round his face, and the sort of complexion that goes with hair of that color; also the particular, rather smeary shade of blue in the eyes. He was not exactly a showy figure; his shoulders were high, his stature but middling—one leg slightly more bandy than the other. He shook hands, looking vaguely around. A spiritless tenacity was his main characteristic, I judged. I behaved with a politeness which seemed to disconcert him. Perhaps he was shy. He mumbled to me as if he were ashamed of what he was saying; gave his name (it was something like Archbold—but at this distance of years I hardly am sure), his ship's name, and a few other particulars of that sort, in the manner of a criminal making a reluctant and doleful confession. He had had terrible weather on the passage out—terrible—terrible—wife aboard, too.

By this time we were seated in the cabin and the steward brought in a tray with a bottle and glasses. "Thanks! No." Never took liquor. Would have some water, though. He drank two tumblerfuls. Terrible thirsty work. Ever since daylight had been exploring the islands round his ship.

"What was that for—fun?" I asked with an appearance of polite interest.

"No!" He sighed. "Painful duty."

As he persisted in his mumbling and I wanted my double to hear every word, I hit upon the notion of informing him that I regretted to say I was hard of hearing.

"Such a young man too!" he nodded, keeping his smeary, blue, unintelligent eyes fastened upon me. "What was the cause of it—some disease?" he inquired, without the least sympathy and as if he thought that, if so, I'd got no more than I deserved.

"Yes; disease," I admitted in a cheerful tone which seemed to shock him. But my point was gained, because he had to raise his voice to give me his tale.

It is not worth while to record that version. It was just over two months since all this had happened, and he had thought so much about it that he seemed completely muddled as to its bearings, but still immensely impressed.

"What would you think of such a thing happening on board your own ship? I've had the *Sephora* for these fifteen years. I am a well-known shipmaster."

He was densely distressed—and perhaps I should have sympathized with him if I had been able to detach my mental vision from the unsuspected sharer of my cabin as though he were my second self. There he was on the other side of the bulkhead, four or five feet from us, no more, as we sat in the saloon. I looked politely at Captain Archbold (if that was his name), but it was the other I saw, in a gray sleeping suit, seated on a low stool, his bare feet close together, his arms folded, and every word said between us falling into the ears of his dark head bowed on his chest. 130

"I have been at sea now, man and boy, for seven and thirty years, and I've never heard of such a thing happening in an English ship. And that it should be my ship. Wife on board, too."

I was hardly listening to him.

"Don't you think," I said, "that the heavy sea which, you told me, came aboard just then might have killed the man? I have seen the sheer weight of a sea kill a man very neatly, by simply breaking his neck."

"Good God!" he uttered impressively, fixing his smeary blue eyes on me. "The sea! No man killed by the sea ever looked like that." He seemed positively scandalized at my suggestion. And as I gazed at him, certainly not prepared for anything original on his part, he advanced his head close to mine and thrust his tongue out at me so suddenly that I couldn't help starting back.

After scoring over my calmness in this graphic way he nodded wisely. If I had seen the sight, he assured me, I would never forget it as long as I lived. The weather was too bad to give the corpse a proper sea burial. So next day at dawn they took it up on the poop, covering its face with a bit of bunting; he read a short prayer, and then, just as it was, in its oilskins and long boots, they launched it amongst those mountainous seas that seemed ready every moment to swallow up the ship herself and the terrified lives on board of her. 135

"That reefed foresail saved you," I threw in.

"Under God—it did," he exclaimed fervently. "It was by a special mercy, I firmly believe, that it stood some of those hurricane squalls."

"It was the setting of that sail which—" I began.

"God's own hand in it," he interrupted me. "Nothing less could have done it. I don't mind telling you that I hardly dared give the order. It seemed impossible that we could touch anything without losing it, and then our last hope would have been gone."

The terror of that gale was on him yet. I let him go on for a bit, then said casually—as if returning to a minor subject: 140

"You were very anxious to give up your mate to the shore people, I believe?"

He was. To the law. His obscure tenacity on that point had in it something incomprehensible and a little awful; something, as it were, mystical, quite apart from his anxiety that he should not be suspected of "countenancing any doings of that sort." Seven and thirty virtuous years at sea, of which over twenty of immaculate command, and the last fifteen in the *Sephora*, seemed to have laid him under some pitiless obligation.

"And you know," he went on, groping shamefacedly amongst his feelings, "I did not engage that young fellow. His people had some interest with my owners. I was in a way forced to take him on. He looked very smart, very gentlemanly, and all that. But do you know—I never liked him, somehow. I am a plain man. You see, he wasn't exactly the sort for the chief mate of a ship like the *Sephora*."

I had become so connected in thoughts and impressions with the secret sharer of my cabin that I felt as if I, personally, were being given to understand that I, too, was not the sort that would have done for the chief mate of a ship like the *Sephora*. I had no doubt of it in my mind.

145 "Not at all the style of man. You understand," he insisted superfluously, looking hard at me.

I smiled urbanely. He seemed at a loss for a while.

"I suppose I must report a suicide."

"Beg pardon?"

"Sui-cide! That's what I'll have to write to my owners directly I get in."

150 "Unless you manage to recover him before tomorrow," I assented dispassionately. . . . "I mean, alive."

He mumbled something which I really did not catch, and I turned my ear to him in a puzzled manner. He fairly bawled:

"The land—I say, the mainland is at least seven miles off my anchorage."

"About that."

My lack of excitement, of curiosity, of surprise, of any sort of pronounced interest, began to arouse his distrust. But except for the felicitous pretense of deafness I had not tried to pretend anything. I had felt utterly incapable of playing the part of ignorance properly, and therefore was afraid to try. It is also certain that he had brought some ready-made suspicions with him, and that he viewed my politeness as a strange and unnatural phenomenon. And yet how else could I have received him? Not heartily! That was impossible for psychological reasons, which I need not state here. My only object was to keep off his inquiries. Surlily? Yes, but surliness might have provoked a point-blank question. From its novelty to him and from its nature, punctilious courtesy was the manner best calculated to restrain the man. But there was the danger of his breaking through my defense bluntly. I could not, I think, have met him by a direct lie, also for psychological (not moral) reasons. If he had only known how afraid I was of his putting my feeling of identity with the other to the test! But, strangely enough (I thought of it only afterward), I believe that he was not a little disconcerted by the reverse side of that weird situation, by something in me that reminded him of the man he was seeking—suggested a mysterious similitude to the young fellow he had distrusted and disliked from the first.

155 However that might have been the silence was not very prolonged. He took another oblique step.

"I reckon I had no more than a two-mile pull to your ship. Not a bit more."

"And quite enough, too, in this awful heat," I said.

Another pause full of mistrust followed. Necessity, they say, is mother of invention, but fear, too, is not barren of ingenious suggestions. And I was afraid he would ask me point-blank for news of my other self.

"Nice little saloon, isn't it?" I remarked, as if noticing for the first time the way his eyes roamed from one closed door to the other. "And very well fitted out, too. Here, for instance," I continued, reaching over the back of my seat negligently and flinging the door open, "is my bathroom."

He made an eager movement, but hardly gave it a glance. I got up, shut the door of the bathroom, and invited him to have a look round, as if I were very proud of my accommodation. He had to rise and be shown round, but he went through the business without any raptures whatever.

"And now we'll have a look at my stateroom," I declared, in a voice as loud as I dared to make it, crossing the cabin to the starboard side with purposely heavy steps.

He followed me in and gazed around. My intelligent double had vanished. I played my part.

"Very convenient—isn't it?"

"Very nice. Very comf . . ." He didn't finish, and went out brusquely as if to escape from some unrighteous wiles of mine. But it was not to be. I had been too frightened not to feel vengeful; I felt I had him on the run, and I meant to keep him on the run. My polite insistence must have had something menacing in it, because he gave in suddenly. And I did not let him off a single item: mates' rooms, pantry, storerooms, the very sail-locker, which was also under the poop— he had to look into them all. When at last I showed him out on the quarter- deck he drew a long, spiritless sigh, and mumbled dismally that he must really be going back to his ship now. I desired my mate, who had joined us, to see to the captain's boat.

The man of whiskers gave a blast on the whistle which he used to wear hanging round his neck, and yelled, "*Sephora's* away!" My double down there in my cabin must have heard, and certainly could not feel more relieved than I. Four fellows came running out from somewhere forward and went over the side, while my own men, appearing on deck too, lined the rail. I escorted my visitor to the gangway ceremoniously, and nearly overdid it. He was a tenacious beast. On the very ladder he lingered, and in that unique, guiltily conscientious manner of sticking to the point:

"I say . . . you . . . you don't think that—"

I covered his voice loudly.

"Certainly not. . . . I am delighted. Goodbye."

I had an idea of what he meant to say, and just saved myself by the privilege of defective hearing. He was too shaken generally to insist, but my mate, close witness of that parting, looked mystified and his face took on a thoughtful cast. As I did not want to appear as if I wished to avoid all communication with my officers, he had the opportunity to address me.

"Seems a very nice man. His boat's crew told our chaps a very extraordinary story, if what I am told by the steward is true. I suppose you had it from the captain, sir?"

160

165

170

"Yes. I had a story from the captain."

"A very horrible affair—isn't it, sir?"

"It is."

"Beats all these tales we hear about murders in Yankee ships."

175 "I don't think it beats them. I don't think it resembles them in the least."

"Bless my soul—you don't say so! But of course I've no acquaintance whatever with American ships, not I, so I couldn't go against your knowledge. It's horrible enough for me. . . . But the queerest part is that those fellows seemed to have some idea the man was hidden aboard here. They had really. Did you ever hear of such a thing?"

"Preposterous—isn't it?"

We were walking to and fro athwart the quarter-deck. No one of the crew forward could be seen (the day was Sunday), and the mate pursued:

"There was some little dispute about it. Our chaps took offense. 'As if we would harbor a thing like that,' they said. 'Wouldn't you like to look for him in our coal-hole?' Quite a tiff. But they made it up in the end. I suppose he did drown himself. Don't you, sir?"

180 "I don't suppose anything."

"You have no doubt in the matter, sir?"

"None whatever."

I left him suddenly. I felt I was producing a bad impression, but with my double down there it was most trying to be on deck. And it was almost as trying to be below. Altogether a nerve-trying situation. But on the whole I felt less torn in two when I was with him. There was no one in the whole ship whom I dared take into my confidence. Since the hands had got to know his story, it would have been impossible to pass him off for any one else, and an accidental discovery was to be dreaded now more than ever. . . .

The steward being engaged in laying the table for dinner, we could talk only with our eyes when I first went down. Later in the afternoon we had a cautious try at whispering. The Sunday quietness of the ship was against us; the stillness of air and water around her was against us; the elements, the men were against us—everything was against us in our secret partnership; time itself—for this could not go on for ever. The very trust in Providence was, I supposed, denied to his guilt. Shall I confess that this thought cast me down very much? And as to the chapter of accidents which counts for so much in the book of success, I could only hope that it was closed. For what favorable accident could be expected?

185 "Did you hear everything?" were my first words as soon as we took up our position side by side, leaning over my bedplace.

He had. And the proof of it was his earnest whisper, "The man told you he hardly dared to give the order."

I understood the reference to be to that saving foresail.

"Yes. He was afraid of it being lost in the setting."

"I assure you he never gave the order. He may think he did, but he never gave it. He stood there with me on the break of the poop after the maintopsail blew away, and whimpered about our last hope—positively whimpered about it and nothing else—and the night coming on! To hear one's skipper go on like that in such weather was enough to drive any fellow out of his mind. It worked me up into a sort of desperation. I just took it into my own hands and went away from him, boiling, and—But what's the use telling you? *You* know! . . . Do you think that if I had not been pretty fierce with them I should have got the men to do anything? Not it! The boss'en[1] perhaps? Perhaps! It wasn't a heavy sea—it was a sea gone mad! I suppose the end of the world will be something like that; and a man may have the heart to see it coming once and be done with it—but to have to face it day after day . . . I don't blame anybody. I was precious little better than the rest. Only—I was an officer of that old coal-wagon, anyhow. . . ."

"I quite understand," I conveyed that sincere assurance into his ear. He was out of breath with whispering; I could hear him pant slightly. It was all very simple. The same strung-up force which had given twenty-four men a chance, at least, for their lives had, in a sort of recoil, crushed an unworthy mutinous existence.

But I had no leisure to weigh the merits of the matter—footsteps in the saloon, a heavy knock. "There's enough wind to get under way with, sir." Here was the call of a new claim upon my thoughts and even upon my feelings.

"Turn the hands up," I cried through the door. "I'll be on deck directly."

I was going out to make the acquaintance of my ship. Before I left the cabin our eyes met—the eyes of the only two strangers on board. I pointed to the recessed part where the little camp-stool awaited him and laid my finger on my lips. He made a gesture—somewhat vague—a little mysterious, accompanied by a faint smile, as if of regret.

This is not the place to enlarge upon the sensations of a man who feels for the first time a ship move under his feet to his own independent word. In my case they were not unalloyed. I was not wholly alone with my command; for there was that stranger in my cabin. Or, rather, I was not completely and wholly with her. Part of me was absent. That mental feeling of being in two places at once affected me physically as if the mood of secrecy had penetrated my very soul. Before an hour had elapsed since the ship had begun to move, having occasion to ask the mate (he stood by my side) to take a compass bearing of the Pagoda, I caught myself reaching up to his ear in whispers. I say I caught myself, but enough had escaped to startle the man. I can't describe it otherwise than by saying that he shied. A grave, preoccupied manner, as though he were in possession of some perplexing intelligence, did not leave him henceforth. A little later I moved away from the rail to look at the compass with such a stealthy gait that the helmsman noticed it—and I could not help noticing the unusual roundness of his eyes. These are trifling instances, though it's to no commander's advantage to be suspected of ludicrous eccentricities. But I was also more seriously affected. There are to a seaman certain words, gestures, that should in given conditions come as naturally, as instinctively, as the winking of a menaced eye. A certain order should spring on to his lips without thinking; a certain sign should get itself made, so to speak, without reflection. But all unconscious alert-

190

---

1. *Bosun* or *boatswain*, petty officer in charge of deck crew and of rigging.

ness had abandoned me. I had to make an effort of will to recall myself back (from the cabin) to the conditions of the moment. I felt that I was appearing an irresolute commander to those people who were watching me more or less critically.

195   And, besides, there were the scares. On the second day out, for instance, coming off the deck in the afternoon (I had straw slippers on my bare feet) I stopped at the open pantry door and spoke to the steward. He was doing something there with his back to me. At the sound of my voice he nearly jumped out of his skin, as the saying is, and incidentally broke a cup.

"What on earth's the matter with you?" I asked, astonished.

He was extremely confused. "Beg your pardon, sir. I made sure you were in your cabin."

"You see I wasn't."

"No, sir. I could have sworn I had heard you moving in there not a moment ago. It's most extraordinary . . . very sorry, sir."

200   I passed on with an inward shudder. I was so identified with my secret double that I did not even mention the fact in those scanty, fearful whispers we exchanged. I suppose he had made some slight noise of some kind or other. It would have been miraculous if he hadn't at one time or another. And yet, haggard as he appeared, he looked always perfectly self-controlled, more than calm—almost invulnerable. On my suggestion he remained almost entirely in the bathroom, which, upon the whole, was the safest place. There could be really no shadow of an excuse for any one ever wanting to go in there, once the steward had done with it. It was a very tiny place. Sometimes he reclined on the floor, his legs bent, his head sustained on one elbow. At others I would find him on the camp-stool, sitting in his gray sleeping suit and with his cropped dark hair like a patient, unmoved convict. At night I would smuggle him into my bedplace, and we would whisper together, with the regular footfalls of the officer of the watch passing and repassing over our heads. It was an infinitely miserable time. It was lucky that some tins of fine preserves were stowed in a locker in my stateroom; hard bread I could always get hold of; and so he lived on stewed chicken, pâté de foie gras, asparagus, cooked oysters, sardines—on all sorts of abominable sham-delicacies out of tins. My early morning coffee he always drank; and it was all I dared do for him in that respect.

Every day there was the horrible maneuvering to go through so that my room and then the bathroom should be done in the usual way. I came to hate the sight of the steward, to abhor the voice of that harmless man. I felt that it was he who would bring on the disaster of discovery. It hung like a sword over our heads.

The fourth day out, I think (we were then working down the east side of the Gulf of Siam, tack for tack,[2] in light winds and smooth water)—the fourth day, I say, of this miserable juggling with the unavoidable, as we sat at our evening meal, that man, whose slightest movement I dreaded, after putting down the dishes ran up on deck busily. This could not be dangerous. Presently he came

---

2. By a series of shiftings back and forth of sails.

down again; and then it appeared that he had remembered a coat of mine which I had thrown over a rail to dry after having been wetted in a shower which had passed over the ship in the afternoon. Sitting stolidly at the head of the table I became terrified at the sight of the garment on his arm. Of course he made for my door. There was no time to lose.

"Steward!" I thundered. My nerves were so shaken that I could not govern my voice and conceal my agitation. This was the sort of thing that made my terrifically whiskered mate tap his forehead with his forefinger. I had detected him using that gesture while talking on deck with a confidential air to the carpenter. It was too far to hear a word, but I had no doubt that this pantomime could only refer to the strange new captain.

"Yes, sir," the pale-faced steward turned resignedly to me. It was this maddening course of being shouted at, checked without rhyme or reason, arbitrarily chased out of my cabin, suddenly called into it, sent flying out of his pantry on incomprehensible errands, that accounted for the growing wretchedness of his expression.

"Where are you going with that coat?"   205

"To your room, sir."

"Is there another shower coming?"

"I'm sure I don't know, sir. Shall I go up again and see, sir?"

"No! never mind."

My object was attained, as of course my other self in there would have heard   210
everything that passed. During this interlude my two officers never raised their eyes off their respective plates; but the lip of that confounded cub, the second mate, quivered visibly.

I expected the steward to hook my coat on and come out at once. He was very slow about it; but I dominated my nervousness sufficiently not to shout after him. Suddenly I became aware (it could be heard plainly enough) that the fellow for some reason or other was opening the door of the bathroom. It was the end. The place was literally not big enough to swing a cat in. My voice died in my throat and I went stony all over. I expected to hear a yell of surprise and terror, and made a movement, but had not the strength to get on my legs. Everything remained still. Had my second self taken the poor wretch by the throat? I don't know what I could have done next moment if I had not seen the steward come out of my room, close the door, and then stand quietly by the sideboard.

"Saved," I thought. "But, no! Lost! Gone! He was gone!"

I laid my knife and fork down and leaned back in my chair. My head swam. After a while, when sufficiently recovered to speak in a steady voice, I instructed my mate to put the ship round at eight o'clock himself.

"I won't come on deck," I went on. "I think I'll turn in, and unless the wind shifts I don't want to be disturbed before midnight. I feel a bit seedy."

"You did look middling bad a little while ago," the chief mate remarked   215
without showing any great concern.

They both went out, and I stared at the steward clearing the table. There was nothing to be read on that wretched man's face. But why did he avoid my eyes? I asked myself. Then I thought I should like to hear the sound of his voice.

"Steward!"

"Sir!" Startled as usual.

"Where did you hang up that coat?"

220   "In the bathroom, sir." The usual anxious tone. "It's not quite dry yet, sir."

For some time longer I sat in the cuddy. Had my double vanished as he had come? But of his coming there was an explanation, whereas his disappearance would be inexplicable. . . . I went slowly into my dark room, shut the door, lighted the lamp, and for a time dared not turn round. When at last I did I saw him standing bolt upright in the narrow recessed part. It would not be true to say I had a shock, but an irresistible doubt of his bodily existence flitted through my mind. Can it be, I asked myself, that he is not visible to other eyes than mine? It was like being haunted. Motionless, with a grave face, he raised his hands slightly at me in a gesture which meant clearly, "Heavens! what a narrow escape!" Narrow indeed. I think I had come creeping quietly as near insanity as any man who has not actually gone over the border. That gesture restrained me, so to speak.

The mate with the terrific whiskers was now putting the ship on the other tack. In the moment of profound silence which follows upon the hands going to their stations I heard on the poop his raised voice: "Hard alee!"[3] and the distant shout of the order repeated on the main deck. The sails, in that light breeze, made but a faint fluttering noise. It ceased. The ship was coming round slowly; I held my breath in the renewed stillness of expectation; one wouldn't have thought that there was a single living soul on her decks. A sudden brisk shout, "Mainsail haul!" broke the spell, and in the noisy cries and rush overhead of the men running away with the main brace we two, down in my cabin, came together in our usual position by the bedplace.

He did not wait for my question. "I heard him fumbling here and just managed to squat myself down in the bath," he whispered to me. "The fellow only opened the door and put his arm in to hang the coat up. All the same. . . ."

"I never thought of that," I whispered back, even more appalled than before at the closeness of the shave, and marveling at that something unyielding in his character which was carrying him through so finely. There was no agitation in his whisper. Whoever was being driven distracted, it was not he. He was sane. And the proof of his sanity was continued when he took up the whispering again.

225   "It would never do for me to come to life again."

It was something that a ghost might have said. But what he was alluding to was his old captain's reluctant admission of the theory of suicide. It would obviously serve his turn — if I had understood at all the view which seemed to govern the unalterable purpose of his action.

"You must maroon me as soon as ever you can get amongst these islands off the Cambodje[4] shore," he went on.

"Maroon you! We are not living in a boy's adventure tale," I protested. His scornful whispering took me up.

"We aren't indeed! There's nothing of a boy's tale in this. But there's nothing

---

3. I.e., put the helm all the way over to the side away from the wind.   4. Cambodian.

else for it. I want no more. You don't suppose I am afraid of what can be done to me? Prison or gallows or whatever they may please. But you don't see me coming back to explain such things to an old fellow in a wig and twelve respectable tradesmen, do you? What can they know whether I am guilty or not—or of *what* I am guilty, either? That's my affair. What does the Bible say? 'Driven off the face of the earth.'[5] Very well. I am off the face of the earth now. As I came at night so I shall go."

"Impossible!" I murmured. "You can't."

"Can't? . . . . Not naked like a soul on the Day of Judgment. I shall freeze on to this sleeping suit. The Last Day is not yet—and . . . you have understood thoroughly. Didn't you?"

I felt suddenly ashamed of myself. I may say truly that I understood—and my hesitation in letting that man swim away from my ship's side had been a mere sham sentiment, a sort of cowardice.

"It can't be done now till next night," I breathed out. "The ship is on the offshore tack and the wind may fail us."

"As long as I know that you understand," he whispered. "But of course you do. It's a great satisfaction to have got somebody to understand. You seem to have been there on purpose." And in the same whisper, as if we two whenever we talked had to say things to each other which were not fit for the world to hear, he added, "It's very wonderful."

We remained side by side talking in our secret way—but sometimes silent or just exchanging a whispered word or two at long intervals. And as usual he stared through the port. A breath of wind came now and again into our faces. The ship might have been moored in dock, so gently and on an even keel she slipped through the water, that did not murmur even at our passage, shadowy and silent like a phantom sea.

At midnight I went on deck, and to my mate's great surprise put the ship round on the other tack. His terrible whiskers flitted round me in silent criticism. I certainly should not have done it if it had been only a question of getting out of that sleepy gulf as quickly as possible. I believe he told the second mate, who relieved him, that it was a great want of judgment. The other only yawned. That intolerable cub shuffled about so sleepily and lolled against the rails in such a slack, improper fashion that I came down on him sharply.

"Aren't you properly awake yet?"

"Yes, sir! I am awake."

"Well, then, be good enough to hold yourself as if you were. And keep a look out. If there's any current we'll be closing with some islands long before daylight."

The east side of the gulf is fringed with islands, some solitary, others in groups. On the blue background of the high coast they seem to float on silvery patches of calm water, arid and gray, or dark green and rounded like clumps of evergreen bushes, with the larger ones, a mile or two long, showing the outlines of ridges, ribs of gray rock under the dank mantle of matted leafage. Unknown

230

235

240

5. Genesis 4:14.

to trade, to travel, almost to geography, the manner of life they harbor is an unsolved secret. There must be villages—settlements of fishermen at least—on the largest of them, and some communication with the world is probably kept up by native craft. But all that forenoon, as we headed for them, fanned along by the faintest of breezes, I saw no sign of man or canoe in the field of the telescope I kept on pointing at the scattered group.

At noon I gave no orders for a change of course, and the mate's whiskers became much concerned and seemed to be offering themselves unduly to my notice. At last I said:

"I am going to stand right in. Quite in—as far as I can take her."

The stare of extreme surprise imparted an air of ferocity also to his eyes, and he looked truly terrific for a moment.

"We're not doing well in the middle of the gulf," I continued casually. "I am going to look for the land breezes tonight."

"Bless my soul! Do you mean, sir, in the dark amongst the lot of all them islands and reefs and shoals?"

"Well, if there are any regular land breezes at all on this coast one must get close inshore to find them—mustn't one?"

"Bless my soul!" he exclaimed again under his breath. All that afternoon he wore a dreamy, comtemplative appearance which in him was a mark of perplexity. After dinner I went into my stateroom as if I meant to take some rest. There we two bent our dark heads over a half-unrolled chart lying on my bed.

"There," I said. "It's got to be Koh-ring.[6] I've been looking at it ever since sunrise. It has got two hills and a low point. It must be inhabited. And on the coast opposite there is what looks like the mouth of a biggish river—with some town, no doubt, not far up. It's the best chance for you that I can see."

"Anything. Koh-ring let it be."

He looked thoughtfully at the chart as if surveying chances and distances from a lofty height—and following with his eyes his own figure wandering on the blank land of Cochin-China, and then passing off that piece of paper clean out of sight into uncharted regions. And it was as if the ship had two captains to plan her course for her. I had been so worried and restless running up and down that I had not had the patience to dress that day. I had remained in my sleeping suit, with straw slippers and a soft floppy hat. The closeness of the heat in the gulf had been most oppressive, and the crew were used to see me wandering in that airy attire.

"She will clear the south point as she heads now," I whispered into his ear. "Goodness only knows when, though—but certainly after dark. I'll edge her in to half a mile, as far as I may be able to judge in the dark . . ."

"Be careful," he murmured warningly—and I realized suddenly that all my future, the only future for which I was fit, would perhaps go irretrievably to pieces in any mishap to my first command.

I could not stop a moment longer in the room. I motioned him to get out of

---

6. *Koh* or *Ko* means *island*; there are a large number of islands with that prefix at the head of the Gulf of Siam, but not, apparently, a Koh-ring.

sight and made my way on the poop. That unplayful cub had the watch. I walked up and down for a while thinking things out, then beckoned him over.

"Send a couple of hands to open the two quarter-deck ports," I said mildly.

He actually had the impudence, or else so forgot himself in his wonder at such an incomprehensible order, as to repeat:

"Open the quarter-deck ports! What for, sir?"

"The only reason you need concern yourself about is because I tell you to do so. Have them opened wide and fastened properly."

He reddened and went off, but I believe made some jeering remark to the carpenter as to the sensible practice of ventilating a ship's quarter-deck. I know he popped into the mate's cabin to impart the fact to him, because the whiskers came on deck, as it were by chance, and stole glances at me from below—for signs of lunacy or drunkenness, I suppose.

A little before supper, feeling more restless than ever, I rejoined, for a moment, my second self. And to find him sitting so quietly was surprising, like something against nature, inhuman.

I developed my plan in a hurried whisper.

"I shall stand in as close as I dare and then put her round. I shall presently find means to smuggle you out of here into the sail-locker, which communicates with the lobby. But there is an opening, a sort of square for hauling the sails out, which gives straight on the quarterdeck and which is never closed in fine weather, so as to give air to the sails. When the ship's way is deadened in stays[7] and all the hands are aft at the main braces you shall have a clear road to slip out and get overboard through the open quarter-deck port. I've had them both fastened up. Use a rope's end to lower yourself into the water so as to avoid a splash—you know. It could be heard and cause some beastly complication."

He kept silent for a while, then whispered, "I understand."

"I won't be there to see you go," I began with an effort. "The rest . . . I only hope I have understood too."

"You have. From first to last"—and for the first time there seemed to be a faltering, something strained in his whisper. He caught hold of my arm, but the ringing of the supper bell made me start. He didn't though; he only released his grip.

After supper I didn't come below again till well past eight o'clock. The faint, steady breeze was loaded with dew; and the wet, darkened sails held all there was of propelling power in it. The night, clear and starry, sparkled darkly, and the opaque, lightless patches shifting slowly amongst the low stars were the drifting islets. On the port bow there was a big one more distant and shadowily imposing by the great space of sky it eclipsed.

On opening the door I had a back view of my very own self looking at a chart. He had come out of the recess and was standing near the table.

"Quite dark enough," I whispered.

He stepped back and leaned against my bed with a level, quiet glance. I sat

---

7. When the ship's forward motion is slowed or stopped while its head is being turned toward the wind for the purpose of shifting the sail

on the couch. We had nothing to say to each other. Over our heads the officer of the watch moved here and there. Then I heard him move quickly. I knew what that meant. He was making for the companion; and presently his voice was outside my door.

"We are drawing in pretty fast, sir. Land looks rather close."

"Very well," I answered. "I am coming on deck directly."

I waited till he was gone out of the cuddy, then rose. My double moved too. The time had come to exchange our last whispers, for neither of us was ever to hear each other's natural voice.

"Look here!" I opened a drawer and took out three sovereigns. "Take this, anyhow. I've got six and I'd give you the lot, only I must keep a little money to buy some fruit and vegetables for the crew from native boats as we go through Sunda Straits."

He shook his head.

"Take it," I urged him, whispering desperately. "No one can tell what . . ."

He smiled and slapped meaningly the only pocket of the sleeping jacket. It was not safe, certainly. But I produced a large old silk handkerchief of mine, and tying the three pieces of gold in a corner, pressed it on him. He was touched, I suppose, because he took it at last and tied it quickly round his waist under the jacket, on his bare skin.

Our eyes met; several seconds elapsed, till, our glances still mingled, I extended my hand and turned the lamp out. Then I passed through the cuddy, leaving the door of my room wide open. . . . "Steward!"

He was still lingering in the pantry in the greatness of his zeal, giving a rub-up to a plated cruet stand the last thing before going to bed. Being careful not to wake up the mate, whose room was opposite, I spoke in an undertone.

He looked round anxiously. "Sir!"

"Can you get me a little hot water from the galley?"

"I am afraid, sir, the galley fire's been out for some time now."

"Go and see."

He fled up the stairs.

"Now," I whispered loudly into the saloon—too loudly, perhaps, but I was afraid I couldn't make a sound. He was by my side in an instant—the double captain slipped past the stairs—through a tiny dark passage . . . a sliding door. We were in the sail-locker, scrambling on our knees over the sails. A sudden thought struck me. I saw myself wandering barefooted, bareheaded, the sun beating on my dark poll. I snatched off my floppy hat and tried hurriedly in the dark to ram it on my other self. He dodged and fended off silently. I wonder what he thought had come to me before he understood and suddenly desisted. Our hands met gropingly, lingered united in a steady, motionless clasp for a second. . . . No word was breathed by either of us when they separated.

I was standing quietly by the pantry door when the steward returned.

"Sorry, sir. Kettle barely warm. Shall I light the spirit-lamp?"

"Never mind."

I came out on deck slowly. It was now a matter of conscience to shave the land as close as possible—for now he must go overboard whenever the ship was put in stays. Must! There could be no going back for him. After a moment I walked over to leeward and my heart flew into my mouth at the nearness of the land on the bow. Under any other circumstances I would not have held on a minute longer. The second mate had followed me anxiously.

I looked on till I felt I could command my voice.

"She will weather," I said then in a quiet tone.

"Are you going to try that, sir?" he stammered out incredulously.

I took no notice of him and raised my tone just enough to be heard by the helmsman.

"Keep her good full."[8]

"Good full, sir."

The wind fanned my cheek, the sails slept, the world was silent. The strain of watching the dark loom of the land grow bigger and denser was too much for me. I had to shut my eyes—because the ship must go closer. She must! The stillness was intolerable. Were we standing still?

When I opened my eyes the second view started my heart with a thump. The black southern hill of Koh-ring seemed to hang right over the ship like a towering fragment of the everlasting night. On that enormous mass of blackness there was not a gleam to be seen, not a sound to be heard. It was gliding irresistibly towards us and yet seemed already within reach of the hand. I saw the vague figures of the watch grouped in the waist, gazing in awed silence.

"Are you going on, sir?" inquired an unsteady voice at my elbow.

I ignored it. I had to go on.

"Keep her full. Don't check her way. That won't do now," I said warningly.

"I can't see the sails very well," the helmsman answered me, in strange, quavering tones.

Was she close enough? Already she was, I won't say in the shadow of the land, but in the very blackness of it, already swallowed up as it were, gone too close to be recalled, gone from me altogether.

"Give the mate a call," I said to the young man who stood at my elbow as still as death. "And turn all hands up."

My tone had a borrowed loudness reverberated from the height of the land. Several voices cried out together, "We are all on deck, sir."

Then stillness again, with the great shadow gliding closer, towering higher, without a light, without a sound. Such a hush had fallen on the ship that she might have been a bark of the dead floating in slowly under the very gate of Erebus.

"My God! Where are we?"

It was the mate moaning at my elbow. He was thunderstruck, and as it were deprived of the moral support of his whiskers. He clapped his hands and absolutely cried out, "Lost!"

"Be quiet," I said sternly.

He lowered his tone, but I saw the shadowy gesture of his despair. "What are we doing here?"

290

295

300

305

8. I.e., keep the ship's sails filled with wind.

"Looking for the land wind."

He made as if to tear his hair, and addressed me recklessly.

"She will never get out. You have done it, sir. I knew it'd end in something like this. She will never weather, and you are too close now to stay. She'll drift ashore before she's round. O my God!"

I caught his arm as he was raising it to batter his poor devoted head, and shook it violently.

"She's ashore already," he wailed, trying to tear himself away.

"Is she? . . . Keep good full there!"

"Good full, sir," cried the helmsman in a frightened, thin, childlike voice.

I hadn't let go the mate's arm and went on shaking it. "Ready about,[9] do you hear? You go forward"—shake—"and stop there"—shake—"and hold your noise"—shake—"and see these head-sheets properly overhauled"—shake, shake—shake.

And all the time I dared not look towards the land lest my heart should fail me. I released my grip at last and he ran forward as if fleeing for dear life.

I wondered what my double there in the sail-locker thought of this commotion. He was able to hear everything—and perhaps he was able to understand why, on my conscience, it had to be thus close—no less. My first order "Hard alee!" re-echoed ominously under the towering shadow of Koh-ring as if I had shouted in a mountain gorge. And then I watched the land intently. In that smooth water and light wind it was impossible to feel the ship coming-to.[1] No! I could not feel her. And my second self was making now ready to slip out and lower himself overboard. Perhaps he was gone already. . . ?

The great black mass brooding over our very mast-heads began to pivot away from the ship's side silently. And now I forgot the secret stranger ready to depart, and remembered only that I was a total stranger to the ship. I did not know her. Would she do it? How was she to be handled?

I swung the mainyard and waited helplessly. She was perhaps stopped, and her very fate hung in the balance, with the black mass of Koh-ring like the gate of the everlasting night towering over her taffrail. What would she do now? Had she way on her[2] yet? I stepped to the side swiftly, and on the shadowy water I could see nothing except a faint phosphorescent flash revealing the glassy smoothness of the sleeping surface. It was impossible to tell—and I had not learned yet the feel of my ship. Was she moving? What I needed was something easily seen, a piece of paper, which I could throw overboard and watch. I had nothing on me. To run down for it I didn't dare. There was no time. All at once my strained, yearning stare distinguished a white object floating within a yard of the ship's side—white, on the black water. A phosphorescent flash passed under it. What was that thing? . . . I recognized my own floppy hat. It must have fallen off his head . . . and he didn't bother. Now I had what I wanted—the saving mark for my eyes. But I hardly thought of my other self, now gone from the

9. I.e., be ready to shift the sails (tack). The head-sheets, below, are the lines attached to the sails of the forward mast, and to overhaul is to slacken a rope by pulling it in the opposite direction to that used in hoisting a sail and thus loosening the blocks.   1. Coming to a standstill.   2. Was she moving?

ship, to be hidden for ever from all friendly faces, to be a fugitive and a vagabond on the earth, with no brand of the curse on his sane forehead to stay a slaying hand . . . too proud to explain.

And I watched the hat—the expression of my sudden pity for his mere flesh. It had been meant to save his homeless head from the dangers of the sun. And now—behold—it was saving the ship, by serving me for a mark to help out the ignorance of my strangeness. Ha! It was drifting forward, warning me just in time that the ship had gathered sternway.   320

"Shift the helm," I said in a low voice to the seaman standing still like a statue.

The man's eyes glistened wildly in the binnacle light as he jumped round to the other side and spun round the wheel.

I walked to the break of the poop. On the overshadowed deck all hands stood by the forebraces waiting for my order. The stars ahead seemed to be gliding from right to left. And all was so still in the world that I heard the quiet remark, "She's round," passed in a tone of intense relief between two seamen.

"Let go and haul."

The foreyards ran round with a great noise, amidst cheery cries. And now   325
the frightful whiskers made themselves heard giving various orders. Already the ship was drawing ahead. And I was alone with her. Nothing! no one in the world should stand now between us, throwing a shadow on the way of silent knowledge and mute affection; the perfect communion of a seaman with his first command.

Walking to the taffrail, I was in time to make out, on the very edge of a darkness thrown by a towering black mass like the very gateway of Erebus—yes, I was in time to catch an evanescent glimpse of my white hat left behind to mark the spot where the secret sharer of my cabin and of my thoughts, as though he were my second self, had lowered himself into the water to take his punishment: a free man, a proud swimmer striking out for a new destiny.

1912

The first paragraph of the story clearly functions as exposition, especially in describing the setting, the place and time of day. Its last sentence suggests something of the situation—the speaker is alone with *his* ship. It also establishes the focus and voice. In the description of the scene in the Gulf of Siam, there are some words that, though appropriate, are not necessarily inevitable. These are words that might not be used by just any narrator or in just any circumstances and so may characterize the speaker or his situation. In the first sentence alone you may notice "mysterious," "incomprehensible," even "crazy," which, though it deals with the physical irregularity of the fences, also suggests the irrational. These words arouse suspense and so further the plot, but they may also suggest something of the theme. And, since another speaker would be likely to see things somewhat differently and use different words, his choices may also characterize the speaker. Some of the details of the paragraph may also be symbolic.

1. How does the second paragraph further advance the description of setting, of situation, of theme? Are any of the details here symbolic or potentially symbolic? The last sentence of this paragraph seems to relate directly to theme, though it may also help characterize the narrator. There are many such sentences in the story—an example might be "And suddenly I rejoiced in the great security of the sea . . ." (par. 17). Collect five or six such sentences and see how they relate not only to theme but to other elements.

2. How does paragraph 7 characterize the second mate, explain the narrator's situation, and further arouse suspense and further define the theme?

3. How does the description of the episode with the scorpion (par. 8) characterize the chief mate, and, when looked back upon later, further the plot and suspense? How does the chief mate's propensity for logical explanations relate to the theme?

4. How does the "unconventional arrangement" of the narrator-captain's standing the first anchor-watch relate to his character? to the plot? to the theme(s)?

5. When the narrator notices that the rope side-ladder has not been hauled in, he blames himself for having disturbed the ship's routine and conjectures about how he will look in the eyes of the officers and crew and how his conduct will be "accounted" for by the chief mate. All this relates to the characters of the two men, the plot or suspense, and the theme. It is just then that "the secret sharer" appears at the very end of that same ladder. Is he, then, in some way symbolic? If so, how? In the light of all that follows, is it good or bad to break the rules? Does following or breaking rules seem to have anything to do with being a captain? Explain.

6. What is the effect of paragraph 20, in which "something elongated and pale" appears at the bottom of the ladder? How many elements are involved in that description (including the first sentence of the next paragraph)?

7. When Leggatt is aboard and dressed in the captain's sleeping suit, he is described as looking like the captain's "double." That, plus Leggatt's arriving from the sea naked, looking like a fish, being phosphorescent and oblong, together with the title of the story, and the narrator's seeing his first command as a test, has led a substantial number of critics and other readers to view these details as Freudian symbols and to attribute to this story a Freudian, or at least a psychological, theme. Make out the best case you can for such a reading of the story. What happens to the specifics of the situation, the characters, the plot? Which details are symbolic in your version and which are not? Now

make out the best case *against* such a reading. If you are so committed to one position or the other that you cannot see how there can be another side, pair yourself off with someone else in the class who has made the best counterargument.

8. When Leggatt tells his story there is a shift in the focus and voice. How does this story within a story function in the plot of "The Secret Sharer"? How does it help define the character of Leggatt? How does it relate to the theme of "the double" in the larger story?

9. Why does the captain hide Leggatt rather than turn him in? How do all the elements of the story contribute to your answering this question?

10. The captain of the *Sephora* tells his version of Leggatt's crime, but the narrator says, "It is not worth while to record that version. It was just over two months since all this had happened, and . . . he seemed completely muddled . . ." (par. 128). Yet the narrator is telling his and Leggatt's story at a "distance of years," and there is a bit of Archbold's story in the paragraphs that follow. Write a fuller (two- or three-page) version of how the *Sephora* captain would tell the story. How does this shift in focus and voice affect the plot? the characterization of the captain of the *Sephora*? of Leggatt? of the narrator of "The Secret Sharer"? the theme?

11. Archbold believes Leggatt was too gentlemanly to be chief mate of the *Sephora*, and the narrator, so identified now with Leggatt, thinks Archbold would not consider the narrator himself a suitable chief mate (much less captain). How would you analyze this notion in terms of focus? character? symbol? theme?

12. There seems to be a turn in the story after Archbold leaves: ironically, Leggatt seems more of a burden to the narrator, who now seems to see himself in his role as captain: "I was not wholly alone with my command; for there was that stranger in my cabin. . . . Part of me was absent" (par. 194). What is the effect of this feeling of split identity on the plot? How does it relate to focus? The whole story can be read as the initiation of the narrator into leadership or captaincy. How does Leggatt figure in that initiation theme? How does his character relate to it? Is he a symbol? If you think he is, of what is he a symbol? How do the final episode and final two paragraphs of the story relate to this portion of the plot, this view of Leggatt, this theme? Can you imagine this story—the story of a new captain taking over command of a strange ship, with mates not of his own choosing and not of his own "kind," of the strained relations between the new captain and the other officers, of his routine and unroutine orders, of his emotional state, and of his first daring act of seamanship, of all this—without any mention of, or presence of, or story of, a Leggatt, a secret

sharer? Write a brief synopsis of such a story. Is there some way in which you might still call it "The Secret Sharer"? Who has the secret and with whom does he share it?

13. How does the captain's giving Leggatt his hat figure in the plot? What does it suggest about the narrator's character and feelings? Of what, if anything, might it be a symbol?

14. Write a sequel to "The Secret Sharer" about what happens to Leggatt after he leaves the ship, using as much evidence as you can from the elements and details of Conrad's story but with a new focus and voice.

The story that follows is funnier than, but just as serious as, "The Secret Sharer." It is the title story, or chapter, of a work that calls itself a novel but can also be seen as a collection of related but separable stories (indeed, many of the chapters were first published separately as stories, and a new edition of *Love Medicine* adds four new stories or chapters and rearranges the original sequence). Reading the whole novel or collection may enrich your understanding and enjoyment of the parts but this story is, as you will see, quite wonderful, enjoyable, and understandable by itself. It is a somewhat unfamiliar world you will be entering; though nearer to us in time and space, it is perhaps even stranger than the world of "The Secret Sharer." Stop reading after paragraph 18, look at item 1 below (p. 294), and get your bearings.

LOUISE ERDRICH

Love Medicine

I never really done much with my life, I suppose. I never had a television. Grandma Kashpaw had one inside her apartment at the Senior Citizens, so I used to go there and watch my favorite shows. For a while she used to call me the biggest waste on the reservation and hark back to how she saved me from my own mother, who wanted to tie me in a potato sack and throw me in a slough. Sure, I was grateful to Grandma Kashpaw for saving me like that, for raising me, but gratitude gets old. After a while, stale. I had to stop thanking her. One day I told her I had paid her back in full by staying at her beck and call. I'd do anything for Grandma. She knew that. Besides, I took care of Grandpa like nobody else could, on account of what a handful he'd gotten to be.

But that was nothing. I know the tricks of mind and body inside out without ever having trained for it, because I got the touch. It's a thing you got to be born with. I got secrets in my hands that nobody ever knew to ask. Take Grandma Kashpaw with her tired veins all knotted up in her legs like clumps of blue snails. I take my fingers and I snap them on the knots. The medicine flows out of me. The touch. I run my fingers up the maps of those rivers of veins or I knock very gentle above their hearts or I make a circling motion on their stomachs, and it helps them. They feel much better. Some women pay me five dollars.

I couldn't do the touch for Grandpa, though. He was a hard nut. You know, some people fall right through the hole in their lives. It's invisible, but they come to it after time, never knowing where. There is this woman here, Lulu Lamartine, who always had a thing for Grandpa. She loved him since she was a girl and always said he was a genius. Now she says that his mind got so full it exploded.

How can I doubt that? I know the feeling when your mental power builds up too far. I always used to say that's why the Indians got drunk. Even statistically we're the smartest people on the earth. Anyhow with Grandpa I couldn't hardly believe it, because all my youth he stood out as a hero to me. When he started getting toward second childhood he went through different moods. He would stand in the woods and cry at the top of his shirt. It scared me, scared everyone, Grandma worst of all.

Yet he was so smart—do you believe it?—that he *knew* he was getting foolish. 5

He said so. He told me that December I failed school and come back on the train to Hoopdance. I didn't have nowhere else to go. He picked me up there and he said it straight out: "I'm getting into my second childhood." And then he said something else I still remember: "I been chosen for it. I couldn't say no." So I figure that a man so smart all his life—tribal chairman and the star of movies and even pictured in the statehouse and on cans of snuff—would know what he's doing by saying yes. I think he was called to second childhood like anybody else gets a call for the priesthood or the army or whatever. So I really did not listen too hard when the doctor said this was some kind of disease old people got eating too much sugar. You just can't tell me that a man who went to Washington and gave them bureaucrats what for could lose his mind from eating too much Milky Way. No, he put second childhood on himself.

Behind those songs he sings out in the middle of Mass, and back of those stories that everybody knows by heart, Grandpa is thinking hard about life. I know the feeling. Sometimes I'll throw up a smokescreen to think behind. I'll hitch up to Winnipeg and play the Space Invaders for six hours, but all the time there and back I will be thinking some fairly deep thoughts that surprise even me, and I'm used to it. As for him, if it was just the thoughts there wouldn't be no problem. Smokescreen is what irritates the social structure, see, and Grandpa has done things that just distract people to the point they want to throw him in the cookie jar where they keep the mentally insane. He's far from that, I know for sure, but even Grandma had trouble keeping her patience once he started sneaking off to Lamartine's place. He's not supposed to have his candy, and Lulu feeds it to him. That's *one* of the reasons why he goes.

Grandma tried to get me to put the touch on Grandpa soon after he began stepping out. I didn't want to, but before Grandma started telling me again what a bad state my bare behind was in when she first took me home, I thought I should at least pretend.

I put my hands on either side of Grandpa's head. You wouldn't look at him and say he was crazy. He's a fine figure of a man, as Lamartine would say, with all his hair and half his teeth, a beak like a hawk, and cheeks like the blades of a hatchet. They put his picture on all the tourist guides to North Dakota and even copied his face for artistic paintings. I guess you could call him a monument all of himself. He started grinning when I put my hands on his templates, and I knew right then he knew how come I touched him. I knew the smokescreen was going to fall.

And I was right: just for a moment it fell.

"Let's pitch whoopee," he said across my shoulder to Grandma.

They don't use that expression much around here anymore, but for damn sure it must have meant something. It got her goat right quick.

She threw my hands off his head herself and stood in front of him, overmatching him pound for pound, and taller too, for she had a growth spurt in middle age while he had shrunk, so now the length and breadth of her surpassed him. She glared up and spoke her piece into his face about how he was off at all hours tomcatting and chasing Lamartine again and making a damn old fool of himself.

"And you got no more whoopee to pitch anymore anyhow!" she yelled at last, surprising me so my jaw just dropped, for us kids all had pretended for so long that those rustling sounds we heard from their side of the room at night never happened. She sure had pretended it, up till now, anyway. I saw that tears were in her eyes. And that's when I saw how much grief and love she felt for him. And it gave me a real shock to the system. You see I thought love got easier over the years so it didn't hurt so bad when it hurt, or feel so good when it felt good. I thought it smoothed out and old people hardly noticed it. I thought it curled up and died, I guess. Now I saw it rear up like a whip and lash.

She loved him. She was jealous. She mourned him like the dead.

And he just smiled into the air, trapped in the seams of his mind.

So I didn't know what to do. I was in a laundry then. They was like parents to me, the way they had took me home and reared me. I could see her point for wanting to get him back the way he was so at least she could argue with him, sleep with him, not be shamed out by Lamartine. She'd always love him. That hit me like a ton of bricks. For one whole day I felt this odd feeling that cramped my hands. When you have the touch, that's where longing gets you. I never loved like that. It made me feel all inspired to see them fight, and I wanted to go out and find a woman who I would love until one of us died or went crazy. But I'm not like that really. From time to time I heal a person all up good inside, however when it comes to the long shot I doubt that I got staying power.

And you need that, staying power, going out to love somebody. I knew this quality was not going to jump on me with no effort. So I turned my thoughts back to Grandma and Grandpa. I felt her side of it with my hands and my tangled guts, and I felt his side of it within the stretch of my mentality. He had gone out to lunch one day and never came back. He was fishing in the middle of Lake Turcot. And there was big thoughts on his line, and he kept throwing them back for even bigger ones that would explain to him, say, the meaning of how we got here and why we have to leave so soon. All in all, I could not see myself treating Grandpa with the touch, bringing him back, when the real part of him had chose to be off thinking somewhere. It was only the rest of him that stayed around causing trouble, after all, and we could handle most of it without any problem.

Besides, it was hard to argue with his reasons for doing some things. Take Holy Mass. I used to go there just every so often, when I got frustrated mostly, because even though I know the Higher Power dwells everyplace, there's something very calming about the cool greenish inside of our mission. Or so I thought, anyway. Grandpa was the one who stripped off my delusions in this matter, for it was he who busted right through what Father Upsala calls the sacred serenity of the place.

We filed in that time. Me and Grandpa. We sat down in our pews. Then the rosary got started up pre-Mass and that's when Grandpa filled up his chest and opened his mouth and belted out them words.

HAIL MARIE FULL OF GRACE.

He had a powerful set of lungs.

And he kept on like that. He did not let up. He hollered and he yelled them prayers, and I guess people was used to him by now, because they only muttered theirs and did not quit and gawk like I did. I was getting red-faced, I admit. I give him the elbow once or twice, but that wasn't nothing to him. He kept on. He shrieked to heaven and he pleaded like a movie actor and he pounded his chest like Tarzan in the Lord I Am Not Worthies. I thought he might hurt himself. Then after a while I guess I got used to it, and that's when I wondered: how come?

So afterwards I out and asked him. "How come? How come you yelled?"

"God don't hear me otherwise," said Grandpa Kashpaw.

I sweat. I broke right into a little cold sweat at my hairline because I knew this was perfectly right and for years not one damn other person had noticed it. God's been going deaf. Since the Old Testament, God's been deafening up on us. I read, see. Besides the dictionary, which I'm constantly in use of, I had this Bible once. I read it. I found there was discrepancies between then and now. It struck me. Here God used to raineth bread from clouds, smite the Phillipines, sling fire down on red-light districts where people got stabbed. He even appeared in person every once in a while. God used to pay attention, is what I'm saying.

Now there's your God in the Old Testament and there is Chippewa Gods as well. Indian Gods, good and bad, like tricky Nanabozho or the water monster, Missepeshu, who lives over in Lake Turcot. That water monster was the last God I ever heard to appear. It had a weakness for young girls and grabbed one of the Blues off her rowboat. She got to shore all right, but only after this monster had its way with her. She's an old lady now. Old Lady Blue. She still won't let her family fish that lake.

Our Gods aren't perfect, is what I'm saying, but at least they come around. They'll do a favor if you ask them right. You don't have to yell. But you do have to know, like I said, how to ask in the right way. That makes problems, because to ask proper was an art that was lost to the Chippewas once the Catholics

20

25

gained ground. Even now, I have to wonder if Higher Power turned it back, if we got to yell, or if we just don't speak its language.

I looked around me. How else could I explain what all I had seen in my short life—King smashing his fist in things, Gordie drinking himself down to the Bismarck hospitals, or Aunt June left by a white man to wander off in the snow. How else to explain the times my touch don't work, and farther back, to the oldtime Indians who was swept away in the outright germ warfare and dirty-dog killing of the whites. In those times, us Indians was so much kindlier than now.

30   We took them in.

Oh yes, I'm bitter as an old cutworm just thinking of how they done to us and doing still.

So Grandpa Kashpaw just opened my eyes a little there. Was there any sense relying on a God whose ears was stopped? Just like the government? I says then, right off, maybe we got nothing but ourselves. And that's not much, just person-ally speaking. I know I don't got the cold hard potatoes it takes to understand everything. Still, there's things I'd like to do. For instance, I'd like to help some people like my Grandpa and Grandma Kashpaw get back some happiness within the tail ends of their lives.

I told you once before I couldn't see my way clear to putting the direct touch on Grandpa's mind, and I kept my moral there, but something soon happened to make me think a little bit of mental adjustment wouldn't do him and the rest of us no harm.

It was after we saw him one afternoon in the sunshine courtyard of the Senior Citizens with Lulu Lamartine. Grandpa used to like to dig there. He had his little dandelion fork out, and he was prying up them dandelions right and left while Lamartine watched him.

35   "He's scratching up the dirt, all right," said Grandma, watching Lamartine watch Grandpa out the window.

Now Lamartine was about half the considerable size of Grandma, but you would never think of sizes anyway. They were different in an even more notice-able way. It was the difference between a house fixed up with paint and picky fence, and a house left to weather away into the soft earth, is what I'm saying. Lamartine was jacked up, latticed, shuttered, and vinyl sided, while Grandma sagged and bulged on her slipped foundations and let her hair go the silver gray of rain-dried lumber. Right now, she eyed the Lamartine's pert flowery dress with such a look it despaired me. I knew what this could lead to with Grandma. Alternating tongue storms and rock-hard silences was hard on a man, even one who didn't notice, like Grandpa. So I went fetching him.

But he was gone when I popped through the little screen door that led out on the courtyard. There was nobody out there either, to point which way they went. Just the dandelion fork quibbling upright in the ground. That gave me an idea. I snookered over to the Lamartine's door and I listened in first, then knocked. But nobody. So I went walking through the lounges and around the card tables. Still nobody. Finally it was my touch that led me to the laundry room. I cracked the door. I went in. There they were. And he was really loving her up good, boy, and she was going hell for leather. Sheets was flapping on the lines above, and washcloths, pillowcases, shirts was also flying through the air, for they was trying to clear out a place for themselves in a high-heaped but shallow laundry cart. The washers and dryers was all on, chock full of quarters, shaking and moaning. I couldn't hear what Grandpa and the Lamartine was billing and cooing, and they couldn't hear me.

I didn't know what to do, so I went inside and shut the door.

The Lamartine wore a big curly light-brown wig. Looked like one of them squeaky little white-people dogs. Poodles they call them. Anyway, that wig is what saved us from the worse. For I could hardly shout and tell them I was in there, no more could I try and grab him. I was trapped where I was. There was nothing I could really do but hold the door shut. I was scared of somebody else upsetting in and really getting an eyeful. Turned out though, in the heat of the clinch, as I was trying to avert my eyes you see, the Lamartine's curly wig jumped off her head. And if you ever been in the midst of something and had a big change like that occur in the someone, you can't help know how it devastates your basic urges. Not only that, but her wig was almost with a life of its own. Grandpa's eyes were bugging at the change already, and swear to God if the thing didn't rear up and pop him in the face like it was going to start something. He scrambled up, Grandpa did, and the Lamartine jumped up after him all addled looking. They just stared at each other, huffing and puffing, with quizzical expression. The surprise seemed to drive all sense completely out of Grandpa's mind.

"The letter was what started the fire," he said. "I never would have done it." 40

"What letter?" said the Lamartine. She was stiff-necked now, and elegant, even bald, like some alien queen. I gave her back the wig. The Lamartine replaced it on her head, and whenever I saw her after that, I couldn't help thinking of her bald, with special powers, as if from another planet.

"That was a close call," I said to Grandpa after she had left.

But I think he had already forgot the incident. He just stood there all quiet and thoughtful. You really wouldn't think he was crazy. He looked like he was just about to say something important, explaining himself. He said something, all right, but it didn't have nothing to do with anything that made sense.

He wondered where the heck he put his dandelion fork. That's when I decided about the mental adjustment.

Now what was mostly our problem was not so much that he was not all there, 45 but that what was there of him often hankered after Lamartine. If we could put a stop to that, I thought, we might be getting someplace. But here, see, my touch was of no use. For what could I snap my fingers at to make him faithful to Grandma? Like the quality of staying power, this faithfulness was invisible. I know it's something that you got to acquire, but I never known where from. Maybe there's no rhyme or reason to it, like my getting the touch, and then again maybe it's a kind of magic.

It was Grandma Kashpaw who thought of it in the end. She knows things. Although she will not admit she has a scrap of Indian blood in her, there's no doubt in my mind she's got some Chippewa. How else would you explain the way she'll be sitting there, in front of her TV story, rocking in her armchair and suddenly she turns on me, her brown eyes hard as lake-bed flint.

"Lipsha Morrissey," she'll say, "you went out last night and got drunk."

How did she know that? I'll hardly remember it myself. Then she'll say she just had a feeling or ache in the scar of her hand or a creak in her shoulder. She is constantly being told things by little aggravations in her joints or by her household appliances. One time she told Gordie never to ride with a crazy Lamartine boy. She had seen something in the polished-up tin of her bread toaster. So he didn't. Sure enough, the time came we heard how Lyman and Henry went out of control in their car, ending up in the river. Lyman swam to the top, but Henry never made it.

Thanks to Grandma's toaster, Gordie was probably spared.

Someplace in the blood Grandma Kashpaw knows things. She also remembers things, I found. She keeps things filed away. She's got a memory like them video games that don't forget your score. One reason she remembers so many details about the trouble I gave her in early life is so she can flash back her total when she needs to.

Like now. Take the love medicine. I don't know where she remembered that from. It came tumbling from her mind like an asteroid off the corner of the screen.

Of course she starts out by mentioning the time I had this accident in church and did she leave me there with wet overhalls? No she didn't. And ain't I glad? Yes I am. Now what you want now, Grandma?

But when she mentions them love medicines, I feel my back prickle at the danger. These love medicines is something of an old Chippewa specialty. No other tribe has got them down so well. But love medicines is not for the layman to handle. You don't just go out and get one without paying for it. Before you get one, even, you should go through one hell of a lot of mental condensation. You got to think it over. Choose the right one. You could really mess up your life grinding up the wrong little thing.

So anyhow, I said to Grandma I'd give this love medicine some thought. I knew the best thing was to go ask a specialist like Old Man Pillager, who lives up in a tangle of bush and never shows himself. But the truth is I was afraid of him, like everyone else. He was known for putting the twisted mouth on people, seizing up their hearts. Old Man Pillager was serious business, and I have always thought it best to steer clear of that whenever I could. That's why I took the powers in my own hands. That's why I did what I could.

I put my whole mentality to it, nothing held back. After a while I started to remember things I'd heard gossiped over.

I heard of this person once who carried a charm of seeds that looked like baby pearls. They was attracted to a metal knife, which made them powerful. But I didn't know where them seeds grew. Another love charm I heard about I couldn't go along with, because how was I suppose to catch frogs in the act, which it required. Them little creatures is slippery and fast. And then the powerfullest of all, the most extreme, involved nail clips and such. I wasn't anywhere near asking Grandma to provide me all the little body bits that this last love recipe called for. I went walking around for days just trying to think up something that would work.

Well I got it. If it hadn't been the early fall of the year, I never would have got it. But I was sitting underneath a tree one day down near the school just watching people's feet go by when something tells me, look up! Look up! So I look up, and I see two honkers, Canada geese, the kind with little masks on their faces, a bird what mates for life. I see them flying right over my head naturally preparing to land in some slough on the reservation, which they certainly won't get off of alive.

It hits me, anyway. Them geese, they mate for life. And I think to myself, just what if I went out and got a pair? And just what if I fed some part—say the goose heart—of the female to Grandma and Grandpa ate the other heart? Wouldn't that work? Maybe it's all invisible, and then maybe again it's magic. Love is a stony road. We know that for sure. If it's true that the higher feelings of devotion get lodged in the heart like people say, then we'd be home free. If not, eating goose heart couldn't harm nobody anyway. I thought it was worth my effort, and Grandma Kashpaw thought so, too. She had always known a good idea when she heard one. She borrowed me Grandpa's gun.

So I went out to this particular slough, maybe the exact same slough I never got thrown in by my mother, thanks to Grandma Kashpaw, and I hunched down in a good comfortable pile of rushes. I got my gun loaded up. I ate a few of these soft baloney sandwiches Grandma made me for lunch. And then I waited. The cattails blown back and forth above my head. Them stringy blue herons was spearing up their prey. The thing I know how to do best in this world, the thing I been training for all my life, is to wait. Sitting there and sitting there was no hardship on me. I got to thinking about some funny things that happened. There was this one time that Lulu Lamartine's little blue tweety bird, a paraclete, I guess you'd call it, flown up inside her dress and got lost within there. I recalled her running out into the hallway trying to yell something, shaking. She was doing a right good jig there, cutting the rug for sure, and the thing is it *never* flown out. To this day people speculate where it went. They fear she might perhaps of crushed it in her corsets. It sure hasn't ever yet been seen alive. I thought of funny things for a while, but then I used them up, and strange things that happened started weaseling their way into my mind.

I got to thinking quite naturally of the Lamartine's cousin named Wristwatch. I never knew what his real name was. They called him Wristwatch because he got his father's broken wristwatch as a young boy when his father passed on. Never in his whole life did Wristwatch take his father's watch off. He didn't care if it worked, although after a while he got sensitive when people asked what time it was, teasing him. He often put it to his ear like he was listening to the tick. But it was broken for good and forever, people said so, at least that's what they thought.

Well I saw Wristwatch smoking in his pickup one afternoon and by nine that evening he was dead.

He died sitting at the Lamartine's table, too. As she told it, Wristwatch had

60

just eaten himself a good-size dinner and she said would he take seconds on the hot dish when he fell over to the floor. They turnt him over. He was gone. But here's the strange thing: when the Senior Citizen's orderly took the pulse he noticed that the wristwatch Wristwatch wore was now working. The moment he died the wristwatch started keeping perfect time. They buried him with the watch still ticking on his arm.

I got to thinking. What if some gravediggers dug up Wristwatch's casket in two hundred years and that watch was still going? I thought what question they would ask and it was this: Whose hand wound it?

I started shaking like a piece of grass at just the thought.

65   Not to get off the subject or nothing. I was still hunkered in the slough. It was passing late into the afternoon and still no honkers had touched down. Now I don't need to tell you that the waiting did not get to me, it was the chill. The rushes was very soft, but damp. I was getting cold and debating to leave, when they landed. Two geese swimming here and there as big as life, looking deep into each other's little pinhole eyes. Just the ones I was looking for. So I lifted Grandpa's gun to my shoulder and I aimed perfectly, and *blam! Blam!* I delivered two accurate shots. But the thing is, them shots missed. I couldn't hardly believe it. Whether it was that the stock had warped or the barrel got bent someways, I don't quite know, but anyway them geese flown off into the dim sky, and Lipsha Morrissey was left there in the rushes with evening fallen and his two cold hands empty. He had before him just the prospect of another day of bone-cracking chill in them rushes, and the thought of it got him depressed.

Now it isn't my style, in no way, to get depressed.

So I said to myself, Lipsha Morrissey, you're a happy S.O.B. who could be covered up with weeds by now down at the bottom of this slough, but instead you're alive to tell the tale. You might have problems in life, but you still got the touch. You got the power, Lipsha Morrissey. Can't argue that. So put your mind to it and figure out how not to be depressed.

I took my advice. I put my mind to it. But I never saw at the time how my thoughts led me astray toward a tragic outcome none could have known. I ignored all the danger, all the limits, for I was tired of sitting in the slough and my feet were numb. My face was aching. I was chilled, so I played with fire. I told myself love medicine was simple. I told myself the old superstitions was just that—strange beliefs. I told myself to take the ten dollars Mary MacDonald had paid me for putting the touch on her arthritis joint, and the other five I hadn't spent yet from winning bingo last Thursday. I told myself to go down to the Red Owl store.

And here is what I did that made the medicine backfire. I took an evil short-cut. I looked at birds that was dead and froze.

70   All right. So now I guess you will say, "Slap a malpractice suit on Lipsha Morrissey."

I heard of those suits. I used to think it was a color clothing quack doctors had to wear so you could tell them from the good ones. Now I know better that it's law.

As I walked back from the Red Owl with the rock-hard, heavy turkeys, I argued to myself about malpractice. I thought of faith. I thought to myself that faith could be called belief against the odds and whether or not there's any proof. How does that sound? I thought how we might have to yell to be heard by Higher Power, but that's not saying it's not *there*. And that is faith for you. It's belief even when the goods don't deliver. Higher Power makes promises we all know they can't back up, but anybody ever go and slap an old malpractice suit on God? Or the U.S. government? No they don't. Faith might be stupid, but it gets us through. So what I'm heading at is this. I finally convinced myself that the real actual power to the love medicine was not the goose heart itself but the faith in the cure.

I didn't believe it, I knew it was wrong, but by then I had waded so far into my lie I was stuck there. And then I went one step further.

The next day, I cleaned the hearts away from the paper packages of gizzards inside the turkeys. Then I wrapped them hearts with a clean hankie and brung them both to get blessed up at the mission. I wanted to get official blessings from the priest, but when Father answered the door to the rectory, wiping his hands on a little towel, I could tell he was a busy man.

"Booshoo,[1] Father," I said. "I got a slight request to make of you this afternoon." 75

"What is it?" he said.

"Would you bless this package?" I held out the hankie with the hearts tied inside it.

He looked at the package, questioning it.

"It's turkey hearts," I honestly had to reply.

A look of annoyance crossed his face. 80

"Why don't you bring this matter over to Sister Martin," he said. "I have duties."

And so, although the blessing wouldn't be as powerful, I went over to the Sisters with the package.

I rung the bell, and they brought Sister Martin to the door. I had her as a music teacher, but I was always so shy then. I never talked out loud. Now, I had grown taller than Sister Martin. Looking down, I saw that she was not feeling up to snuff. Brown circles hung under her eyes.

"What's the matter?" she said, not noticing who I was.

"Remember me, Sister?" 85

She squinted up at me.

"Oh yes," she said after a moment. "I'm sorry, you're the youngest of the Kashpaws. Gordie's brother."

Her face warmed up.

"Lipsha," I said, "that's my name."

"Well, Lipsha," she said, smiling broad at me now, "what can I do for you?" 90

They always said she was the kindest-hearted of the Sisters up the hill, and

1. *Bonjour*, French for "good day."

she was. She brought me back into their own kitchen and made me take a big yellow wedge of cake and a glass of milk.

"Now tell me," she said, nodding at my package. "What have you got wrapped up so carefully in those handkerchiefs?"

Like before, I answered honestly.

"Ah," said Sister Martin. "Turkey hearts." She waited.

95 "I hoped you could bless them."

She waited some more, smiling with her eyes. Kindhearted though she was, I began to sweat. A person could not pull the wool down over Sister Martin. I stumbled through my mind for an explanation, quick, that wouldn't scare her off.

"They're a present," I said, "for Saint Kateri's statue."

"She's not a saint yet."

"I know," I stuttered on, "in the hopes they will crown her."

100 "Lipsha," she said, "I never heard of such a thing."

So I told her. "Well the truth is," I said, "it's a kind of medicine."

"For what?"

"Love."

"Oh Lipsha," she said after a moment, "you don't need any medicine. I'm sure any girl would like you exactly the way you are."

105 I just sat there. I felt miserable, caught in my pack of lies.

"Tell you what," she said, seeing how bad I felt, "my blessing won't make any difference anyway. But there is something you can do."

I looked up at her hopeless.

"Just be yourself."

I looked down at my plate. I knew I wasn't much to brag about right then, and I shortly became even less. For as I walked out the door I stuck my fingers in the cup of holy water that was sacred from their touches. I put my fingers in and blessed the hearts, quick, with my own hand.

110 I went back to Grandma and sat down in her little kitchen at the Senior Citizens. I unwrapped them hearts on the table, and her hard agate eyes went soft. She said she wasn't even going to cook those hearts up but eat them raw so their power would go down strong as possible.

I couldn't hardly watch when she munched hers. Now that's true love. I was worried about how she would get Grandpa to eat his, but she told me she'd think of something and don't worry. So I did not. I was supposed to hide off in her bedroom while she put dinner on a plate for Grandpa and fixed up the heart so he'd eat it. I caught a glint of the plate she was making for him. She put that heart smack on a piece of lettuce like in a restaurant and then attached to it a little heap of boiled peas.

He sat down. I was listening in the next room.

She said, "Why don't you have some mash potato?" So he had some mash potato. Then she gave him a little piece of boiled meat. He ate that. Then she said, "Why you didn't never touch your salad yet. See that heart? I'm feeding you it because the doctor said your blood needs building up."

I couldn't help it, at that point I peeked through a crack in the door.

I saw Grandpa picking at that heart on his plate with a certain look. He 115
didn't look appetized at all, is what I'm saying. I doubted our plan was going to
work. Grandma was getting worried, too. She told him one more time, loudly,
that he had to eat that heart.

"Swallow it down," she said. "You'll hardly notice it."

He just looked at her straight on. The way he looked at her made me think
I was going to see the smokescreen drop a second time, and sure enough it
happened.

"What you want me to eat this for so bad?" he asked her uncannily.

Now Grandma knew the jig was up. She knew that he knew she was working
medicine. He put his fork down. He rolled the heart around his saucer plate.

"I don't want to eat this," he said to Grandma. "It don't look good." 120

"Why it's fresh grade-A," she told him. "One hundred percent."

He didn't ask percent what, but his eyes took on an even more warier look.

"Just go on and try it," she said, taking the salt shaker up in her hand. She
was getting annoyed. "Not tasty enough? You want me to salt it for you?" She
waved the shaker over his plate.

"All right, skinny white girl!" She had got Grandpa mad. Oopsy-daisy, he
popped the heart into his mouth. I was about to yawn loudly and come out of
the bedroom. I was about ready for this crash of wills to be over, when I saw he
was still up to his old tricks. First he rolled it into one side of his cheek.
"Mmmmm," he said. Then he rolled it into the other side of his cheek.
"Mmmmmmm," again. Then he stuck his tongue out with the heart on it and
put it back, and there was no time to react. He had pulled Grandma's leg once
too far. Her goat was got. She was so mad she hopped up quick as a wink and
slugged him between the shoulderblades to make him swallow.

Only thing is, he choked. 125

He choked real bad. A person can choke to death. You ever sit down at a
restaurant table and up above you there is a list of instructions what to do if
something slides down the wrong pipe? It sure makes you chew slow, that's for
damn sure. When Grandpa fell off his chair better believe me that little graphic
illustrated poster fled into my mind. I jumped out the bedroom. I done everything within my power that I could do to unlodge what was choking him. I
squeezed underneath his ribcage. I socked him in the back. I was desperate. But
here's the factor of decision: he wasn't choking on the heart alone. There was
more to it than that. It was other things that choked him as well. It didn't seem
like he wanted to struggle or fight. Death came and tapped his chest, so he went
just like that. I'm sorry all through my body at what I done to him with that
heart, and there's those who will say Lipsha Morrissey is just excusing himself
off the hook by giving song and dance about how Grandpa gave up.

Maybe I can't admit what I did. My touch had gone worthless, that is true.
But here is what I seen while he lay in my arms.

You hear a person's life will flash before their eyes when they're in danger.
It was him in danger, not me, but it was *his* life come over me. I saw him dying,
and it was like someone pulled the shade down in a room. His eyes clouded

over and squeezed shut, but just before that I looked in. He was still fishing in
the middle of Lake Turcot. Big thoughts was on his line and he had half a case
of beer in the boat. He waved at me, grinned, and then the bobber went under.

Grandma had gone out of the room crying for help. I bunched my force up
in my hands and I held him. I was so wound up I couldn't even breathe. All the
moments he had spent with me, all the times he had hoisted me on his shoulders or pointed into the leaves was concentrated in that moment. Time was
flashing back and forth like a pinball machine. Lights blinked and balls hopped
and rubber bands chirped, until suddenly I realized the last ball had gone down
the drain and there was nothing. I felt his force leaving him, flowing out of
Grandpa never to return. I felt his mind weakening. The bobber going under in
the lake. And I felt the touch retreat back into the darkness inside my body,
from where it came.

130   One time, long ago, both of us were fishing together. We caught a big old
snapper what started towing us around like it was a motor. "This here fishline is
pretty damn good," Grandpa said. "Let's keep this turtle on and see where he
takes us." So we rode along behind that turtle, watching as from time to time it
surfaced. The thing was just about the size of a washtub. It took us all around
the lake twice, and as it was traveling, Grandpa said something as a joke. "Lipsha," he said, "we are glad your mother didn't want you because we was always
looking for a boy like you who would tow us around the lake."

"I ain't no snapper. Snappers is so stupid they stay alive when their head's
chopped off," I said.

"That ain't stupidity," said Grandpa. "Their brain's just in their heart, like
yours is."

When I looked up, I knew the fuse had blown between my heart and my
mind and that a terrible understanding was to be given.

Grandma got back into the room and I saw her stumble. And then she went
down too. It was like a house you can't hardly believe has stood so long, through
years of record weather, suddenly goes down in the worst yet. It makes sense, is
what I'm saying, but you still can't hardly believe it. You think a person you
know has got through death and illness and being broke and living on commodity rice will get through anything. Then they fold and you see how fragile were
the stones that underpinned them. You see how instantly the ground can shift
you thought was solid. You see the stop signs and the yellow dividing markers of
roads you traveled and all the instructions you had played according to vanish.
You see how all the everyday things you counted on was just a dream you had
been having by which you run your whole life. She had been over me, like a
sheer overhang of rock dividing Lipsha Morrissey from outer space. And now
she went underneath. It was as though the banks gave way on the shores of Lake
Turcot, and where Grandpa's passing was just the bobber swallowed under by
his biggest thought, her fall was the house and the rock under it sliding after,
sending half the lake splashing up to the clouds.

135   Where there was nothing.

You play them games never knowing what you see. When I fell into the dream alongside of both of them I saw that the dominions I had defended myself from anciently was but delusions of the screen. Blips of light. And I was scot-free now, whistling through space.

I don't know how I come back. I don't know from where. They was slapping my face when I arrived back at Senior Citizens and they was oxygenating her. I saw her chest move, almost unwilling. She sighed the way she would when somebody bothered her in the middle of a row of beads she was counting. I think it irritated her to no end that they brought her back. I knew from the way she looked after they took the mask off, she was not going to forgive them disturbing her restful peace. Nor was she forgiving Lipsha Morrissey. She had been stepping out onto the road of death, she told the children later at the funeral. I asked was there any stop signs or dividing markers on that road, but she clamped her lips in a vise the way she always done when she was mad.

Which didn't bother me. I knew when things had cleared out she wouldn't have no choice. I was not going to speculate where the blame was put for Grandpa's death. We was in it together. She had slugged him between the shoulders. My touch had failed him, never to return.

All the blood children and the took-ins, like me, came home from Minneapolis and Chicago, where they had relocated years ago. They stayed with friends on the reservation or with Aurelia or slept on Grandma's floor. They were struck down with grief and bereavement to be sure, every one of them. At the funeral I sat down in the back of the church with Albertine. She had gotten all skinny and ragged haired from cramming all her years of study into two or three. She had decided that to be a nurse was not enough for her so she was going to be a doctor. But the way she was straining her mind didn't look too hopeful. Her eyes were bloodshot from driving and crying. She took my hand. From the back we watched all the children and the mourners as they hunched over their prayers, their hands stuffed full of Kleenex. It was someplace in that long sad service that my vision shifted. I began to see things different, more clear. The family kneeling down turned to rocks in a field. It struck me how strong and reliable grief was, and death. Until the end of time, death would be our rock.

So I had perspective on it all, for death gives you that. All the Kashpaw children had done various things to me in their lives—shared their folks with me, loaned me cash, beat me up in secret—and I decided, because of death, then and there I'd call it quits. If I ever saw King again, I'd shake his hand. Forgiving somebody else made the whole thing easier to bear.

Everybody saw Grandpa off into the next world. And then the Kashpaws had to get back to their jobs, which was numerous and impressive. I had a few beers with them and I went back to Grandma, who had sort of got lost in the shuffle of everybody being sad about Grandpa and glad to see one another.

Zelda had sat beside her the whole time and was sitting with her now. I wanted to talk to Grandma, say how sorry I was, that it wasn't her fault, but only mine. I would have, but Zelda gave me one of her looks of strict warning as if to say, "I'll take care of Grandma. Don't horn in on the women."

If only Zelda knew, I thought, the sad realities would change her. But of course I couldn't tell the dark truth.

It was evening, late. Grandma's light was on underneath a crack in the door. About a week had passed since we buried Grandpa. I knocked first but there wasn't no answer, so I went right in. The door was unlocked. She was there but she didn't notice me at first. Her hands were tied up in her rosary, and her gaze was fully absorbed in the easy chair opposite her, the one that had always been Grandpa's favorite. I stood there, staring with her, at the little green nubs in the cloth and plastic armrest covers and the sad little hair-tonic stain he had made on the white doily where he laid his head. For the life of me I couldn't figure what she was staring at. Thin space. Then she turned.

145   "He ain't gone yet,' she said.

Remember that chill I luckily didn't get from waiting in the slough? I got it now. I felt it start from the very center of me, where fear hides, waiting to attack. It spiraled outward so that in minutes my fingers and teeth were shaking and clattering. I knew she told the truth. She seen Grandpa. Whether or not he had been there is not the point. She had *seen* him, and that meant anybody else could see him, too. Not only that but, as is usually the case with these here ghosts, he had a certain uneasy reason to come back. And of course Grandma Kashpaw had scanned it out.

I sat down. We sat together on the couch watching his chair out of the corner of our eyes. She had found him sitting in his chair when she walked in the door.

"It's the love medicine, my Lipsha," she said. "It was stronger than we thought. He came back even after death to claim me to his side."

I was afraid. "We shouldn't have tampered with it," I said. She agreed. For a while we sat still. I don't know what she thought, but my head felt screwed on backward. I couldn't accurately consider the situation, so I told Grandma to go to bed. I would sleep on the couch keeping my eye on Grandpa's chair. Maybe he would come back and maybe he wouldn't. I guess I feared the one as much as the other, but I got to thinking, see, as I lay there in darkness, that perhaps even through my terrible mistakes some good might come. If Grandpa did come back, I thought he'd return in his right mind. I could talk with him. I could tell him it was all my fault for playing with power I did not understand. Maybe he'd forgive me and rest in peace. I hoped this. I calmed myself and waited for him all night.

150   He fooled me though. He knew what I was waiting for, and it wasn't what he was looking to hear. Come dawn I heard a blood-splitting cry from the bedroom and I rushed in there. Grandma turnt the lights on. She was sitting on the edge of the bed and her face looked harsh, pinched-up, gray.

"He was here," she said. "He came and laid down next to me in bed. And he touched me."

Her heart broke down. She cried. His touch was so cold. She laid back in bed after a while, as it was morning, and I went to the couch. As I lay there, falling asleep, I suddenly felt Grandpa's presence and the barrier between us like a swollen river. I felt how I had wronged him. How awful was the place where I had sent him. Behind the wall of death, he'd watched the living eat and cry and get drunk. He was lonesome, but I understood he meant no harm.

"Go back," I said to the dark, afraid and yet full of pity. "You got to be with your own kind now," I said. I felt him retreating, like a sigh, growing less. I felt his spirit as it shrunk back through the walls, the blinds, the brick courtyard of Senior Citizens. "Look up Aunt June," I whispered as he left.

I slept late the next morning, a good hard sleep allowing the sun to rise and warm the earth. It was past noon when I awoke. There is nothing, to my mind, like a long sleep to make those hard decisions that you neglect under stress of wakefulness. Soon as I woke up that morning, I saw exactly what I'd say to Grandma. I had gotten humble in the past week, not just losing the touch but getting jolted into the understanding that would prey on me from here on out. Your life feels different on you, once you greet death and understand your heart's position. You wear your life like a garment from the mission bundle sale ever after—lightly because you realize you never paid nothing for it, cherishing because you know you won't ever come by such a bargain again. Also you have the feeling someone wore it before you and someone will after. I can't explain that, not yet, but I'm putting my mind to it.

"Grandma," I said, "I got to be honest about the love medicine."   155

She listened. I knew from then on she would be listening to me the way I had listened to her before. I told her about the turkey hearts and how I had them blessed. I told her what I used as love medicine was purely a fake, and then I said to her what my understanding brought me.

"Love medicine ain't what brings him back to you, Grandma. No, it's something else. He loved you over time and distance, but he went off so quick he never got the chance to tell you how he loves you, how he doesn't blame you, how he understands. It's true feeling, not no magic. No supermarket heart could have brung him back."

She looked at me. She was seeing the years and days I had no way of knowing, and she didn't believe me. I could tell this. Yet a look came on her face. It was like the look of mothers drinking sweetness from their children's eyes. It was tenderness.

"Lipsha," she said, "you was always my favorite."

She took the beads off the bedpost, where she kept them to say at night, and   160 she told me to put out my hand. When I did this, she shut the beads inside of my fist and held them there a long minute, tight, so my hand hurt. I almost cried when she did this. I don't really know why. Tears shot up behind my eyelids, and yet it was nothing. I didn't understand, except her hand was so strong, squeezing mine.

The earth was full of life and there were dandelions growing out the window, thick as thieves, already seeded, fat as big yellow plungers. She let my hand go. I got up. "I'll go out and dig a few dandelions," I told her.

Outside, the sun was hot and heavy as a hand on my back. I felt it flow down my arms, out my fingers, arrowing through the ends of the fork into the earth.

With every root I prized up there was return, as if I was kin to its secret lesson. The touch got stronger as I worked through the grassy afternoon. Uncurling from me like a seed out of the blackness where I was lost, the touch spread. The spiked leaves full of bitter mother's milk. A buried root. A nuisance people dig up and throw in the sun to wither. A globe of frail seeds that's indestructible.

1982

---

1. In the first dramatized scene, Lipsha, the narrator, at Grandma Kashpaw's request, tries to "put the touch" on Grandpa. By this time, some seventeen or eighteen paragraphs into the story, focus and voice and the setting and situation have been established; you should be getting a good idea of Lipsha's character, and you should be forming some fairly definite expectations about the plot, and, with the help of the title, you should have some glimmers about the developing theme. Write down what you have observed of the structure and elements of the story and what you expect to happen. As you read on, note how your expectations are fulfilled or modified: in what ways are these surprises or changes in expectations related to plot? character? theme? how do they define the world of the fiction? differ from your prior view of the world? To what extent are they convincing?

2. Voice is a dominant element in this story, and it is in large measure through Lipsha's voice that we infer his character. His language is ungrammatical—the story opens with "I never really *done* much . . ." and is full of phrases like "I don't got"—and his malapropisms (ludicrous misuse of words)—"templates" for "temples," "laundry" for "quandary," and "Phillipines" for "Philistines"—tend to undercut his apparent confidence in his literary skills ("Besides the dictionary, which I'm constantly in use of, I had this Bible once. I read it." [par. 26]). His limitations, skillfully indicated, extend to his somewhat naive view of reality—or causality: for example, his version of why Grandpa has symptoms of senility, his "thoughtful" acceptance of Grandpa's illuminating insight that God is going deaf. These errors, attitudes, and views, however, are endearing and often quite funny. Some of them will turn out, in strange ways, to seem almost wise. His kindness and good nature show through the errors and naivete, and he is capable of insights that, though naive and tender, are not ludicrous: "I thought love got easier over the years so it didn't hurt so bad when it hurt, or feel so good when it felt good" (par. 14); "From time to time I heal a person all up good inside, however when it comes to the long shot I doubt I got staying power. / And you need that, staying power, going out to love

somebody" (pars. 17 and 18). His voice reveals character and theme, and his character is instrumental in this plot. A challenging topic for a paper might be to show not only how the theme is presented in this story through a character who is not well educated or intellectually profound, but how the character's very limitations contribute meaning and force to that theme.

3. How is "love medicine" related to the plot? to Grandma's and Lipsha's characters? to theme? In what way(s) may it be considered a symbol?

4. Lipsha tells the stories of Lulu's "tweety bird" that disappeared up her dress and of Wristwatch, whose broken watch started keeping time after its owner dropped dead. He then says, "Not to get off the subject or nothing" (par. 65). Are these stories off the subject? How do they arouse expectations? How do they function in the plot? What do they tell you of Lipsha's character? of the nature of the people on the reservation? Are they related to the theme? if so, how? When he thinks of Wristwatch's grave being dug up in two hundred years, the watch still running, and the diggers asking, "Whose hand wound it?" he says he "started shaking like a piece of grass at just the thought" (par. 64). Is it with awe and fear or with laughter? Do you find it awesome or funny? If there is a difference between how you feel and how you believe Lipsha feels, what is the effect? What is the relationship of this difference to plot, character, voice, and the other elements of the story? How is this episode related to the "subject" he does not mean to be getting off of when the story continues: for example, he says he fires two "accurate" shots at the geese but the shots miss; how does this affect your view of his "reliability" and thus your reading of character? plot? theme? How does it affect your reading of his glance forward, "I never saw at the time how my thoughts led me astray toward a tragic outcome none could have known" (par. 68)? There is a death involved. Is it "tragic"? How do you respond to it? He says he took "an evil shortcut" in practicing love medicine: does that mean that he has discovered that the old beliefs are not "superstitions" or "strange" as he thought at the time?

5. Toward the end of the story, Lipsha tells Grandma that it was not "love medicine" that brought Grandpa's ghost back to her but love itself, not magic but feeling. Grandma looks at him tenderly and says, " 'Lipsha, . . . you was always my favorite' " (par. 159). Explain this passage in terms of the plot (but be sure to remember Lulu); in terms of Lipsha's character; in terms of Grandma's; in terms of theme (and you might even want to think of "love medicine" as symbol).

Like "Love Medicine," "The Watcher" is also told in the first person and is funny and serious. Charlie is only eleven when the incidents occur, but the voice is that of an older Charlie. His language, like Lipsha's, is the chief source of the humor, but his is not ungrammatical or sprinkled with malapropisms; rather, it is sophisticated, wry, and a bit sardonic. It fits the serious aspects of the story, which is not, as in "Love Medicine," about love. Just as you did in reading "Love Medicine," you might stop at an early point in the story (here I suggest paragraph 27) and take stock of your responses thus far, your attitude toward the narrator, and what, if anything, you are anticipating.

GUY VANDERHAEGHE

The Watcher

I suppose it was having a bad chest that turned me into an observer, a watcher, at an early age.

"Charlie has my chest," my mother often informed friends. "A real weakness there," she would add significantly, thumping her own wishbone soundly.

I suppose I had. Family lore had me narrowly escaping death from pneumonia at the age of four. It seems I spent an entire Sunday in delirium, soaking the sheets. Dr. Carlyle was off at the reservoir rowing in his little skiff and couldn't be reached—something for which my mother illogically refused to forgive him. She was a woman who nursed and tenaciously held dark grudges. Forever after that incident the doctor was slightlingly and coldly dismissed in conversation as a "man who betrayed the public's trust."

Following that spell of pneumonia, I regularly suffered from bouts of bronchitis, which often landed me in hospital in Fortune, forty miles away. Compared with the oxygen tent and the whacking great needles that were buried in my skinny rump there, being invalided at home was a piece of cake. Coughing and hacking, I would leaf through catalogues and read comic books until my head swam with print-fatigue. My diet was largely of my own whimsical choosing—hot chocolate and graham wafers were supplemented by sticky sweet coughdrops, which I downed one after the another until my stomach could take no more, revolted, and tossed up the whole mess.

5   With the first signs of improvement in my condition my mother moved her baby to the living-room chesterfield, where she and the radio could keep me company. The electric kettle followed me and was soon burbling in the corner, jetting steam into the air to keep my lungs moist and pliable. Because I was neither quite sick nor quite well, these were the best days of my illnesses. My stay at home hadn't yet made me bored and restless, my chest no longer hurt when I breathed, and that loose pocket of rattling phlegm meant I didn't have to worry about going back to school just yet. So I luxuriated in this steamy equatorial climate, tended by a doting mother as if I were a rare tropical orchid.

My parents didn't own a television and so my curiosity and attention were focused on my surroundings during my illnesses. I tried to squeeze every bit of juice out of them. Sooner than most children I learned that if you kept quiet and still and didn't insist on drawing attention to yourself as many kids did, adults were inclined to regard you as being one with the furniture, as significant and sentient as a hassock. By keeping mum I was treated to illuminating glances into an adult world of conventional miseries and scandals.

I wasn't sure at the age of six what a miscarriage was, but I knew that Ida Thompson had had one and that now her plumbing was buggered. And watching old lady Kuznetzky hang her washing, through a living-room window trickling with condensed kettle steam, I was able to confirm for myself the rumour that the old girl eschewed panties. As she bent over to rummage in her laundry basket I caught a brief glimpse of huge, white buttocks that shimmered in the pale spring sunshine.

I also soon knew (how I don't remember exactly) that Norma Ruggs had business with the Liquor Board Store when she shuffled by our window every day at exactly 10:50 a.m. She was always at the store door at 11:00 when they unlocked and opened up for business. At 11:15 she trudged home again, a pint of ice cream in one hand, a brown paper bag disguising a bottle of fortified wine in the other, and her blotchy complexion painted a high colour of shame.

"Poor old girl," my mother would say whenever she caught sight of Norma passing by in her shabby coat and sloppy man's overshoes. They had been in high school together, and Norma had been class brain and valedictorian. She had been an obliging, dutiful girl and still was. For the wine wasn't Norma's — the ice cream was her only vice. The booze was her husband's, a vet who had come back from the war badly crippled.

All this careful study of adults may have made me old before my time. In any case it seemed to mark me in some recognizable way as being "different" or "queer for a kid." When I went to live with my grandmother in July of 1959 she spotted it right away. Of course, she was only stating the obvious when she declared me skinny and delicate, but she also noted in her vinegary voice that my eyes had a bad habit of never letting her go, and that I was the worst case of little pitchers having big ears that she had ever come across.

I ended up at my grandmother's because in May of that year my mother's bad chest finally caught up with her, much to her and everyone else's surprise. It had been pretty generally agreed by all her acquaintances that Mabel Bradley's defects in that regard were largely imagined. Not so. A government-sponsored X-ray programme discovered tuberculosis, and she was packed off, pale and drawn with worry, for a stay in the sanatorium at Fort Qu'Appelle.

For roughly a month, until the school year ended, my father took charge of me and the house. He was a desolate, lanky, drooping weed of a man who had married late in life but nevertheless had been easily domesticated. I didn't like him much.

My father was badly wrenched by my mother's sickness and absence. He scrawled her long, untidy letters with a stub of gnawed pencil, and once he got shut of me, visited her every weekend. He was a soft and sentimental man whose

10

eyes ran to water at the drop of a hat, or more accurately, death of a cat. Unlike his mother, my Grandma Bradley, he hadn't a scrap of flint or hard-headed common sense in him.

But then neither had any of his many brothers and sisters. It was as if the old girl had unflinchingly withheld the genetic code for responsibility and practicality from her pin-headed offspring. Life for her children was a series of thundering defeats, whirlwind calamities, or, at best, hurried strategic retreats. Businesses crashed and marriages failed, for they had—my father excepted—a taste for the unstable in partners marital and fiscal.

My mother saw no redeeming qualities in any of them. By and large they drank too much, talked too loudly, and raised ill-mannered children—monsters of depravity whose rudeness provided my mother with endless illustrations of what she feared I might become. "You're eating just like a pig," she would say, "exactly like your cousin Elvin." Or to my father, "You're neglecting the belt. He's starting to get as lippy as that little snot Muriel."

And in the midst, in the very eye of this familial cyclone of mishap and discontent, stood Grandma Bradley, as firm as a rock. Troubles of all kinds were laid on her doorstep. When my cousin Criselda suddenly turned big-tummied at sixteen and it proved difficult to ascertain with any exactitude the father, or even point a finger of general blame in the direction of a putative sire, she was shipped off to Grandma Bradley until she delivered. Uncle Ernie dried out on Grandma's farm and Uncle Ed hid there from several people he had sold prefab, assemble-yourself, crop-duster airplanes to.

So it was only family tradition that I should be deposited there. When domestic duties finally overwhelmed him, and I complained too loudly about fried-egg sandwiches for dinner *again*, my father left the bacon rinds hardening and curling grotesquely on unwashed plates, the slut's wool eddying along the floor in the currents of a draft, and drove the one hundred and fifty miles to the farm, *right then and there*.

My father, a dangerous man behind the wheel, took any extended trip seriously, believing the highways to be narrow, unnavigable ribbons of carnage. This trip loomed so dangerously in his mind that, rather than tear a hand from the wheel, or an eye from the road, he had me, *chronic sufferer of lung disorders*, light his cigarettes and place them carefully in his dry lips. My mother would have killed him.

"You'll love it at Grandma's," he kept saying unconvincingly, "you'll have a real boy's summer on the farm. It'll build you up, the chores and all that. And good fun too. You don't know it now, but you are living the best days of your life right now. What I wouldn't give to be a kid again. You'll love it there. There's chickens and *everything*."

It wasn't exactly a lie. There were chickens. But the *everything*—as broad and overwhelming and suggestive of possibilities as my father tried to make it sound—didn't cover much. It certainly didn't comprehend a pony or a dog as I had hoped, chickens being the only livestock on the place.

It turned out that my grandmother, although she had spent most of her life on that particular piece of ground and eventually died there, didn't care much for the farm and was entirely out of sympathy with most varieties of animal life. She did keep chickens for the eggs, although she admitted that her spirits lifted considerably in the fall when it came time to butcher the hens.

Her flock was a garrulous, scraggly crew that spent their days having dust baths in the front yard, hiding their eggs, and, fleet and ferocious as hunting cheetahs, running down scuttling lizards which they trampled and pecked to death while their shiny, expressionless eyes shifted dizzily in their stupid heads. The only one of these birds I felt any compassion for was Stanley the rooster, a bedraggled male who spent his days tethered to a stake by a piece of bailer twine looped around his leg. Poor Stanley crowed heart-rendingly in his captivity: his comb drooped pathetically, and he was utterly crestfallen as he lecherously eyed his bantam beauties daintily scavenging. Grandma kept him in this unnatural bondage to prevent him fertilizing the eggs and producing blood spots in the yolks. Being a finicky eater I approved this policy, but nevertheless felt some guilt over Stanley.

No, the old Bradley homestead, all that encompassed by my father's *everything*, wasn't very impressive. The two-storey house, though big and solid, needed paint and shingles. A track had been worn in the kitchen linoleum clean through to the floorboards and a long rent in the screen door had been stitched shut with waxed thread. The yard was little more than a tangle of thigh-high ragweed and sowthistle to which the chickens repaired for shade. A windbreak of spruce on the north side of the house was dying from lack of water and the competition from Scotch thistle. The evergreens were no longer green; their sere needles fell away from the branches at the touch of a hand.

The abandoned barn out back was flanked by two mountainous rotted piles of manure which I remember sprouting button mushrooms after every warm soaker of a rain. That pile of shit was the only useful thing in a yard full of junk: wrecked cars, old wagon wheels, collapsing sheds. The barn itself was mightily decayed. The paint had been stripped from its planks by rain, hail, and dry, blistering winds, and the roof sagged like a tired nag's back. For a small boy it was an ominous place on a summer day. The air was still and dark and heavy with heat. At the sound of footsteps rats squeaked and scrabbled in the empty mangers, and the sparrows which had spattered the rafters white with their dung whirred about and fluted ghostly cries.

In 1959 Grandma Bradley would have been sixty-nine, which made her a child of the gay nineties—although the supposed gaiety of that age didn't seem to have made much impress upon the development of her character. Physically she was an imposing woman. Easily six feet tall, she carried a hundred and eighty pounds on her generous frame without prompting speculation as to what she had against girdles. She could touch the floor effortlessly with the flat of her palms and pack an eighty-pound sack of chicken feed on her shoulder. She dyed her hair auburn in defiance of local mores, and never went to town to play bridge, whist, or canasta without wearing a hat and getting dressed to the teeth. Grandma loved card games of all varieties and considered anyone who didn't a mental defective.

25

A cigarette always smouldered in her trap. She smoked sixty a day and rolled them as thin as knitting needles in an effort at economy. These cigarettes were so wispy and delicate they tended to get lost between her swollen fingers.

And above all she believed in plain speaking. She let me know that as my father's maroon Meteor pulled out of the yard while we stood waving goodbye on the front steps.

"Let's get things straight from the beginning," she said without taking her eyes off the car as it bumped toward the grid road. "I don't chew my words twice. If you're like any of the rest of them I've had here, you've been raised as wild as a goddamn Indian. Not one of my grandchildren have been brought up to mind. Well, you'll mind around here. I don't jaw and blow hot air to jaw and blow hot air. I belted your father when he needed it, and make no mistake I'll belt you. Is that understood?"

"Yes," I said with a sinking feeling as I watched my father's car disappear down the road, swaying from side to side as its suspension was buffeted by pot-holes.

30 "These bloody bugs are eating me alive," she said, slapping her arm. "I'm going in."

I trailed after her as she slopped back into the house in a pair of badly mauled, laceless sneakers. The house was filled with a half-light that changed its texture with every room. The venetian blinds were drawn in the parlour and some flies carved Immelmanns in the dark air that smelled of cellar damp. Others battered their bullet bodies *tip-tap, tip-tap* against the window-panes.

In the kitchen my grandmother put the kettle on the stove to boil for tea. After she had lit one of her matchstick smokes, she inquired through a blue haze if I was hungry.

"People aren't supposed to smoke around me," I informed her. "Because of my chest. Dad can't even smoke in our house."

"That so?" she said genially. Her cheeks collapsed as she drew on her butt. I had a hint there, if I'd only known it, of how she'd look in her coffin. "You won't like it here then," she said. "I smoke all the time."

35 I tried a few unconvincing coughs. I was ignored. She didn't respond to the same signals as my mother.

"My mother has a bad chest, too," I said. "She's in a TB sanatorium."

"So I heard," my grandmother said, getting up to fetch the whistling kettle. "Oh, I suspect she'll be as right as rain in no time with a little rest. TB isn't what it used to be. Not with all these new drugs." She considered. "That's not to say though that your father'll ever hear the end of it. Mabel was always a silly little shit that way."

I almost fell off my chair. I had never thought I'd live to hear the day my mother was called a silly little shit.

"Drink tea?" asked Grandma Bradley, pouring boiling water into a brown teapot.

40 I shook my head.

"How old are you anyway?" she asked.

"Eleven."

"You're old enough then," she said, taking down a cup from the shelf. "Tea gets the kidneys moving and carries off the poisons in the blood. That's why all the Chinese live to be so old. They all live to be a hundred."

"I don't know if my mother would like it," I said. "Me drinking tea."

"You worry a lot for a kid," she said, "don't you?"

I didn't know how to answer that. It wasn't a question I had ever considered. I tried to shift the conversation.

"What's there for a kid to do around here?" I said in an unnaturally inquisitive voice.

"Well, we could play cribbage."

"I don't know how to play cribbage."

She was genuinely shocked. "What!" she exclaimed. "Why, you're eleven years old! Your father could count a cribbage hand when he was five. I taught all my kids to."

"I never learned how," I said. "We don't even have a deck of cards at our house. My father hates cards. Says he had too much of them as a boy."

At this my grandmother arched her eyebrows. "Is that a fact? Well, hoity-toity."

"So, since I don't play cards," I continued in a strained manner I imagined was polite, "what could I do—I mean, for fun?"

"Make your own fun," she said. "I never considered fun such a problem. Use your imagination. Take a broomstick and make like Nimrod."

"Who's Nimrod?" I asked.

"Pig ignorant," she said under her breath, and then louder, directly to me, "Ask me no questions and I'll tell you no lies. Drink your tea."

And that, for the time being, was that.

It's all very well to tell someone to make their own fun. It's the making of it that is the problem. In a short time I was a very bored kid. There was no one to play with, no horses to ride, no gun to shoot gophers, no dog for company. There was nothing to read except the *Country Guide* and *Western Producer*. There was nothing or nobody interesting to watch. I went through my grandmother's drawers but found nothing as surprising there as I had discovered in my parents'.

Most days it was so hot that the very idea of fun boiled out of me and evaporated. I moped and dragged myself listlessly around the house in the loose-jointed, water-boned way kids have when they can't stand anything, not even their precious selves.

On my better days I tried to take up with Stanley the rooster. Scant chance of that. Tremors of panic ran through his body at my approach. He tugged desperately on the twine until he jerked his free leg out from under himself and collapsed in the dust, his heart bumping the tiny crimson scallops of his breast feathers, the black pellets of his eyes glistening, all the while shitting copiously. Finally, in the last extremes of chicken terror, he would allow me to stroke his yellow beak and finger his comb.

I felt sorry for the captive Stanley and several times tried to take him for a walk, to give him a chance to take the air and broaden his limited horizons. But this prospect alarmed him so much that I was always forced to return him to his stake in disgust while he fluttered, squawked and flopped.

So fun was a commodity in short supply. That is, until something interesting turned up during the first week of August. Grandma Bradley was dredging little watering canals with a hoe among the corn stalks on a bright blue Monday morning, and I was shelling peas into a colander on the front stoop, when a black car nosed diffidently up the road and into the yard. Then it stopped a good twenty yards short of the house as if its occupants weren't sure of their welcome. After some time, the doors opened and a man and woman got carefully out.

The woman wore turquoise-blue pedal-pushers, a sloppy black turtleneck sweater, and a gash of scarlet lipstick swiped across her white, vivid face. This was my father's youngest sister, Aunt Evelyn.

The man took her gently and courteously by the elbow and balanced her as she edged up the front yard in her high heels, careful to avoid turning an ankle on a loose stone, or in an old tyre track.

65   The thing which immediately struck me about the man was his beard—the first I had ever seen. Beards weren't popular in 1959—not in our part of the world. His was a randy, jutting, little goat's-beard that would have looked wicked on any other face but his. He was very tall and his considerable height was accented by a lack of corresponding breadth to his body. He appeared to have been racked and stretched against his will into an exceptional and unnatural anatomy. As he walked and talked animatedly, his free hand fluttered in front of my aunt. It sailed, twirled and gambolled on the air. Like a butterfly enticing a child, it seemed to lead her hypnotized across a yard fraught with perils for city-shod feet.

My grandmother laid down her hoe and called sharply to her daughter.

"Evvie!" she called. "Over here, Evvie!"

At the sound of her mother's voice my aunt's head snapped around and she began to wave jerkily and stiffly, striving to maintain a tottering balance on her high-heeled shoes. It wasn't hard to see that there was something not quite right with her. By the time my grandmother and I reached the pair, Aunt Evelyn was in tears, sobbing hollowly and jamming the heel of her palm into her front teeth.

The man was speaking calmly to her. "Control. Control. Deep, steady breaths. Think sea. Control. Control. Control. Think sea, Evelyn. Deep. Deep. Deep," he muttered.

70   "What the hell is the matter, Evelyn?" my grandmother asked sharply. "And who is *he*?"

"Evelyn is a little upset," the man said, keeping his attention focused on my aunt. "She's having one of her anxiety attacks. If you'd just give us a moment we'll clear this up. She's got to learn to handle stressful situations." He inclined his head in a priestly manner and said, "Be with the sea, Evelyn. Deep. Deep. Sink in the sea."

"It's her damn nerves again," said my grandmother.

"Yes," the man said benignly, with a smile of blinding condescension. "Sort of."

"She's been as nervous as a cut cat all her life," said my grandmother, mostly to herself.

"Momma," said Evelyn, weeping. "Momma."

"Slide beneath the waves, Evelyn. Down, down, down to the beautiful pearls," the man chanted softly. This was really something.

My grandmother took Aunt Evelyn by her free elbow, shook it, and said sharply, "Evelyn, shut up!" Then she began to drag her briskly toward the house. For a moment the man looked as if he had it in mind to protest, but in the end he meekly acted as a flanking escort for Aunt Evelyn as she was marched into the house. When I tried to follow, my grandmother gave me one of her looks and said definitely, "You find something to do out here."

I did. I waited a few minutes and then duck-walked my way under the parlour window. There I squatted with my knobby shoulder blades pressed against the siding and the sun beating into my face.

My grandmother obviously hadn't wasted any time with the social niceties. They were fairly into it.

"Lovers?" said my grandmother. "Is that what it's called now? Shack-up, you mean."

"Oh, Momma," said Evelyn, and she was crying, "it's all right. We're going to get married."

"You believe that?" said my grandmother. "You believe that geek is going to marry you?"

"Thompson," said the geek, "my name is Thompson, Robert Thompson, and we'll marry as soon as I get my divorce. Although Lord only knows when that'll be."

"That's right," said my grandmother, "Lord only knows." Then to her daughter, "You got another one. A real prize off the midway, didn't you? Evelyn, you're a certifiable lunatic."

"I didn't expect this," said Thompson. "We came here because Evelyn has had a bad time of it recently. She hasn't been eating or sleeping properly and consequently she's got herself run down. She finds it difficult to control her emotions, don't you, darling?"

I thought I heard a mild yes.

"So," said Thompson, continuing, "we decided Evelyn needs some peace and quiet before I go back to school in September."

"School," said my grandmother. "Don't tell me you're some kind of teacher?" She seemed stunned by the very idea.

"No," said Aunt Evelyn, and there was a tremor of pride in her voice that testified to her amazement that she had been capable of landing such a rare and remarkable fish. "Not a teacher. Robert's a graduate student of American Literature at the University of British Columbia."

"Hoity-toity," said Grandmother. "A graduate student. A graduate student of American Literature."

"Doctoral programme," said Robert.

"And did you ever ask yourself, Evelyn, what the hell this genius is doing with you? Or is it just the same old problem with you—elevator panties? Some guy comes along and pushes the button. Up, down. Up, down."

The image this created in my mind made me squeeze my knees together deliciously and stifle a giggle.

"Mother," said Evelyn, continuing to bawl.

95 "Guys like this don't marry barmaids," said my grandmother.

"Cocktail hostess," corrected Evelyn. "I'm a cocktail hostess."

"You don't have to make any excuses, dear," said Thompson pompously. "Remember what I told you. You're past the age of being judged."

"What the hell is that supposed to mean?" said my grandmother. "And by the way, don't start handing out orders in my house. You won't be around long enough to make them stick."

"That remains to be seen," said Thompson.

100 "Let's go, Robert," said Evelyn nervously.

"Go on upstairs, Evelyn. I want to talk to your mother."

"You don't have to go anywhere," said my grandmother. "You can stay put."

"Evelyn, go upstairs." There was a pause and then I heard the sound of a chair creaking, then footsteps.

"Well," said my grandmother at last, "round one. Now for round two—get the hell out of my house."

105 "Can't do that."

"Why the hell not?"

"It's very difficult to explain," he said.

"Try."

"As you can see for yourself, Evelyn isn't well. She is very highly strung at the moment. I believe she is on the verge of a profound personality adjustment, a breakthrough." He paused dramatically. "Or breakdown."

110 "It's times like this that I wished I had a dog on the place to run off undesirables."

"The way I read it," said Thompson, unperturbed, "is that at the moment two people bulk very large in Evelyn's life. You and me. She needs the support and love of us both. You're not doing your share."

"I ought to slap your face."

"She has come home to try to get a hold of herself. We have to bury our dislikes for the moment. She needs to be handled very carefully."

"You make her sound like a trained bear. *Handled.* What that girl needs is a good talking to, and I am perfectly capable of giving her that."

115 "No, Mrs. Bradley," Thompson said firmly in that maddeningly self-assured tone of his. "If you don't mind me saying so, I think that's part of her problem. It's important now for you to just let Evelyn *be.*"

"Get out of my house," said my grandmother, at the end of her tether.

"I know it's difficult for you to understand," he said smoothly, "but if you understood the psychology of this you would see it's impossible for me to go; or for that matter, for Evelyn to go. If I leave she'll feel *I've* abandoned her. It can't be done. We're faced with a real psychological balancing act here."

"Now I've heard everything," said my grandmother. "Are you telling me you'd have the gall to move into a house where you're not wanted and just . . . just *stay there?*"

"Yes," said Thompson. "And I think you'll find me quite stubborn on this particular point."

"My God," said my grandmother. I could tell by her tone of voice that she had never come across anyone like Mr. Thompson before. At a loss for a suitable reply, she simply reiterated, "My God."

"I'm going upstairs now," said Thompson. "Maybe you could get the boy to bring in our bags while I see how Evelyn is doing. The car isn't locked." The second time he spoke his voice came from further away; I imagined him paused in the doorway. "Mrs. Bradley, please let's make this stay pleasant for Evelyn's sake."

She didn't bother answering him.

When I barged into the house some time later with conspicuous noisiness, I found my grandmother standing at the bottom of the stairs staring up the steps. "Well, I'll be damned," she said under her breath. "I've never seen anything like that. Goddamn freak." She even repeated it several times under her breath. "Goddamn freak. Goddamn freak."

Who could blame me if, after a boring summer, I felt my chest tighten with anticipation. Adults could be immensely interesting and entertaining if you knew what to watch for.

At first things were disappointingly quiet. Aunt Evelyn seldom set forth outside the door of the room she and her man inhabited by squatters' right. There was an argument, short and sharp, between Thompson and Grandmother over this. The professor claimed no one had any business prying into what Evelyn did up there. She was an adult and had the right to her privacy and her own thoughts. My grandmother claimed *she* had a right to know what was going on up there, even if nobody else thought she did.

I could have satisfied her curiosity on that point. Not much was going on up there. Several squints through the keyhole had revealed Aunt Evelyn lolling about the bedspread in a blue housecoat, eating soda crackers and sardines, and reading a stack of movie magazines she had me lug out of the trunk of the car.

Food, you see, was beginning to become something of a problem for our young lovers. Grandma rather pointedly set only three places for meals, and Evelyn, out of loyalty to her boyfriend, couldn't very well sit down and break bread with us. Not that Thompson didn't take such things in his stride. He sauntered casually and conspicuously about the house as if he owned it, even going so far as to poke his head in the fridge and rummage in it like some pale, hairless bear. At times like that my grandmother was capable of looking through him as if he didn't exist.

On the second day of his stay Thompson took up with me, which was all right as far as I was concerned. I had no objection. Why he decided to do this I'm not sure exactly. Perhaps he was looking for some kind of an ally, no matter how weak. Most likely he wanted to get under the old lady's skin. Or maybe he just couldn't bear not having anyone to tell how wonderful he was. Thompson was that kind of a guy.

I was certainly let in on the secret. He was a remarkable fellow. He dwelt at great length on those things which made him such an extraordinary human being. I may have gotten the order of precedence all wrong, but if I remember correctly there were three things which made Thompson very special and different from all the other people I would ever meet, no matter how long or hard I lived.

First, he was going to write a book about a poet called Allen Ginsberg[1] which was going to knock the socks off everybody who counted. It turned out he had actually met this Ginsberg the summer before in San Francisco and asked him if he could write a book about him and Ginsberg had said, Sure, why the hell not? The way Thompson described what it would be like when he published this book left me with the impression that he was going to spend most of the rest of his life riding around on people's shoulders and being cheered by a multitude of admirers.

Second, he confessed to knowing a tremendous amount about what made other people tick and how to adjust their mainsprings when they went kaflooey. He knew all this because at one time his own mainspring had gotten a little out of sorts. But now he was a fully integrated personality with a highly creative mind and a strong intuitive sense. That's why he was so much help to Aunt Evelyn in her time of troubles.

Third, he was a Buddhist.

The only one of these things which impressed me at the time was the bit about being a Buddhist. However, I was confused, because in the *Picture Book of the World's Great Religions* which we had at home, all the Buddhists were bald, and Thompson had a hell of a lot of hair, more than I had ever seen on a man. But even though he wasn't bald, he had an idol. A little bronze statue with the whimsical smile and slightly crossed eyes which he identified as Padmasambhava.[2] He told me that it was a Tibetan antique he had bought in San Francisco as an object of veneration and an aid to his meditations. I asked him what a meditation was and he offered to teach me one. So I learned to recite with great seriousness and flexible intonation one of his Tibetan meditations, while my grandmother glared across her quintessentially Western parlour with unbelieving eyes.

I could soon deliver. "A king must go when his time has come. His wealth, his friends and his relatives cannot go with him. Wherever men go, wherever they stay, the effect of their past acts follows them like a shadow. Those who are in the grip of desire, the grip of existence, the grip of ignorance, move helplessly round through the spheres of life, as men or gods or as wretches in the lower regions."

Not that an eleven-year-old could make much of any of *that*.

1. American poet (b. 1926) whose epic poem *Howl* (1956) is a significant product of the Beat movement.   2. Legendary Buddhist mystic who introduced Tantric Buddhism to Tibet. His followers emphasize Tantric ritual, worship, and yoga.

Which is not to say that even an eleven-year-old could be fooled by Robert Thompson. In his stubbornness, egoism and blindness he was transparently un-Buddhalike. To watch him and my grandmother snarl and snap their teeth over that poor, dry bone, Evelyn, was evidence enough of how firmly bound we all are to the wretched wheel of life and its stumbling desires.

No, even his most effective weapon, his cool benevolence, that patina of patience and forbearance which Thompson displayed to Grandmother, could crack.

One windy day when he had coaxed Aunt Evelyn out for a walk I followed them at a distance. They passed the windbreak of spruce, and at the sagging barbed-wire fence he gallantly manipulated the wires while my aunt floundered over them in an impractical dress and crinoline. It was the kind of dippy thing she would decide to wear on a hike.

Thompson strode along through the rippling grass like a wading heron, his baggy pant-legs flapping and billowing in the wind. My aunt moved along gingerly behind him, one hand modestly pinning down her wind-teased dress in the front, the other hand plastering the back of it to her behind.

It was only when they stopped and faced each other that I realized that all the time they had been traversing the field they had been arguing. A certain vaguely communicated agitation in the attitude of her figure, the way his arm stabbed at the featureless wash of sky, implied a dispute. She turned toward the house and he caught her by the arm and jerked it. In a fifties calendar fantasy her dress lifted in the wind, exposing her panties. I sank in the grass until their seed tassels trembled against my chin. I wasn't going to miss watching this for the world.

She snapped and twisted on the end of his arm like a fish on a line. Her head was flung back in an exaggerated, antique display of despair; her head rolled grotesquely from side to side as if her neck were broken.

Suddenly Thompson began striking awkwardly at her exposed buttocks and thighs with the flat of his hand. The long, gangly arm slashed like a flail as she scampered around him, the radius of her escape limited by the distance of their linked arms.

From where I knelt in the grass I could hear nothing. I was too far off. As far as I was concerned there were no cries and no pleading. The whole scene, as I remember it, was shorn of any of the personal idiosyncrasies which manifest themselves in violence. It appeared a simple case of retribution.

That night, for the first time, my aunt came down to supper and claimed her place at the table with queenly graciousness. She wore shorts, too, for the first time, and gave a fine display of mottled, discoloured thighs which reminded me of bruised fruit. She made sure, almost as if by accident, that my grandmother had a good hard look at them.

Right out of the blue my grandmother said, "I don't want you hanging around that man any more. You stay away from him."

"Why?" I asked rather sulkily. He was the only company I had. Since my aunt's arrival Grandmother had paid no attention to me whatsoever.

It was late afternoon and we were sitting on the porch watching Evelyn squeal as she swung in the tyre swing Thompson had rigged up for me in the barn. He had thrown a length of stray rope over the runner for the sliding door and hung a tyre from it. I hadn't the heart to tell him I was too old for tyre swings.

Aunt Evelyn seemed to be enjoying it though. She was screaming and girlishly kicking up her legs. Thompson couldn't be seen. He was deep in the settled darkness of the barn, pushing her back and forth. She disappeared and reappeared according to the arc which she travelled through. Into the barn, out in the sun. Light, darkness. Light, darkness.

Grandma ignored my question. "Goddamn freak," she said, scratching a match on the porch rail and lighting one of her rollies. "Wait and see, he'll get his wagon fixed."

150 "Aunt Evelyn likes him," I noted pleasantly, just to stir things up a bit.

"Your Aunt Evelyn's screws are loose," she said sourly. "And he's the son of a bitch who owns the screwdriver that loosened them."

"He must be an awful smart fellow to be studying to be a professor at a university," I commented. It was the last dig I could chance.

"One thing I know for sure," snapped my grandmother. "He isn't smart enough to lift the toilet seat when he pees. There's evidence enough for that."

After hearing that, I took to leaving a few conspicuous droplets of my own as a matter of course on each visit. Every little bit might help things along.

155 I stood in his doorway and watched Thompson meditate. And don't think that, drenched in *satori*[3] as he was, he didn't know it. He put on quite a performance sitting on the floor in his underpants. When he came out of his trance he pretended to be surprised to see me. While he dressed we struck up a conversation.

"You know, Charlie," he said while he put on his sandals (I'd never seen a grown man wear sandals in my entire life), "you remind me of my little Padmasambhava," he said, nodding to the idol squatting on his dresser. "For a while, you know, I thought it was the smile, but it isn't. It's the eyes."

"Its eyes are crossed," I said, none too flattered at the comparison.

"No they're not," he said good-naturedly. He tucked his shirt-tail into his pants. "The artist, the maker of that image, set them fairly close together to suggest—aesthetically speaking—the intensity of inner vision, its concentration." He picked up the idol and, looking at it, said, "These are very watchful eyes, very knowing eyes. Your eyes are something like that. From your eyes I could tell you're an intelligent boy." He paused, set Padma-sambhava back on the dresser, and asked. "Are you?"

I shrugged.

160 "Don't be afraid to say if you are," he said. "False modesty can be as corrupting as vanity. It took me twenty-five years to learn that."

3. A state of enlightenment in Buddhism, achieved by intensive meditation.

"I usually get all A's on my report card," I volunteered.

"Well, that's something," he said, looking around the room for his belt. He picked a sweater off a chair and peered under it. "Then you see what's going on around here, don't you?" he asked. "You see what your grandmother is mistakenly trying to do?"

I nodded.

"That's right," he said. "You're a smart boy." He sat down on the bed. "Come here."

I went over to him. He took hold of me by the arms and looked into my eyes with all the sincerity he could muster. "You know, being intelligent means responsibilities. It means doing something worth while with your life. For instance, have you given any thought as to what you would like to be when you grow up?"

"A spy," I said.

The silly bugger laughed.

It was the persistent, rhythmic thud that first woke me, and once wakened, I picked up the undercurrent of muted clamour, of stifled struggle. The noise seeped through the beaverboard wall of the adjoining bedroom into my own, a storm of hectic urgency and violence. The floorboards of the old house squeaked; I heard what sounded like a strangled curse and moan, then a fleshy, meaty concussion which I took to be a slap. Was he killing her at last? Choking her with the silent, poisonous care necessary to escape detection?

I remembered Thompson's arm flashing frenziedly in the sunlight. My aunt's discoloured thighs. My heart creaked in my chest with fear. And after killing her? Would the madman stop? Or would he do us all in, one by one?

I got out of bed on unsteady legs. The muffled commotion was growing louder, more distinct. I padded into the hallway. The door to their bedroom was partially open, and a light showed. Terror made me feel hollow; the pit of my stomach ached.

They were both naked, something which I hadn't expected, and which came as quite a shock. What was perhaps even more shocking was the fact that they seemed not only oblivious of me, but of each other as well. She was slung around so that her head was propped on a pillow resting on the footboard of the bed. One smooth leg was draped over the edge of the bed and her heel was beating time on the floorboards (the thud which woke me) as accompaniment to Thompson's plunging body and the soft, liquid grunts of expelled air which he made with every lunge. One of her hands gripped the footboard and her knuckles were white with strain.

I watched until the critical moment, right through the growing frenzy and ardour. They groaned and panted and heaved and shuddered and didn't know themselves. At the very last he lifted his bony, hatchet face with the jutting beard to the ceiling and closed his eyes; for a moment I thought he was praying as his lips moved soundlessly. But then he began to whimper and his mouth fell open and he looked stupider and weaker than any human being I had ever seen before in my life.

"Like pigs at the trough," my grandmother said at breakfast. "With the boy up there too."

My aunt turned a deep red, and then flushed again so violently that her thin lips appeared to turn blue.

175 I kept my head down and went on shovelling porridge. Thompson still wasn't invited to the table. He was leaning against the kitchen counter, his bony legs crossed at the ankles, eating an apple he had helped himself to.

"He didn't hear anything," my aunt said uncertainly. She whispered conspiratorially across the table to Grandmother. "Not at that hour. He'd been asleep for hours."

I thought it wise, even though it meant drawing attention to myself, to establish my ignorance. "Hear what?" I inquired innocently.

"It wouldn't do any harm if he had," said Thompson, calmly biting and chewing the temptress's fruit.

"You wouldn't see it, would you?" said Grandma Bradley. "It wouldn't matter to you what he heard? You'd think that was manly."

180 "Manly has nothing to do with it. Doesn't enter into it," said Thompson in that cool way he had. "It's a fact of life, something he'll have to find out about sooner or later."

Aunt Evelyn began to cry. "Nobody is ever pleased with me," she spluttered. "I'm going crazy trying to please you both. I can't do it." She began to pull nervously at her hair. "He made me," she said finally in a confessional, humble tone to her mother.

"Evelyn," said my grandmother, "you have a place here. I would never send you away. I want you here. But he has to go. I want him to go. If he is going to rub my nose in it that way he has to go. I won't have that man under my roof."

"Evelyn isn't apologizing for anything," Thompson said. "And she isn't running away either. You can't force her to choose. It isn't healthy or fair."

"There have been other ones before you," said Grandma. "This isn't anything new for Evelyn."

185 "Momma!"

"I'm aware of that," he said stiffly, and his face vibrated with the effort to smile. "Provincial mores have never held much water with me. I like to think I'm above all that."

Suddenly my grandmother spotted me. "What are you gawking at!" she shouted. "Get on out of here!"

I didn't budge an inch.

"Leave him alone," said Thompson.

190 "You'll be out of here within a week," said Grandmother. "I swear."

"No," he said smiling. "When I'm ready."

"You'll go home and go with your tail between your legs. Last night was the last straw," she said. And by God you could tell she meant it.

Thompson gave her his beatific Buddha-grin and shook his head from side to side, very, very slowly.

A thunderstorm was brewing. The sky was a stew of dark, swollen clouds and a strange apple-green light. The temperature stood in the mid-nineties, not a breath of breeze stirred, my skin crawled and my head pounded above my eyes and through the bridge of my nose. There wasn't a thing to do except sit on the bottom step of the porch, keep from picking up a sliver in your ass, and scratch the dirt with a stick. My grandmother had put her hat on and driven into town on some unexplained business. Thompson and my aunt were upstairs in their bedroom, sunk in a stuporous, sweaty afternoon's sleep.

Like my aunt and Thompson, all the chickens had gone to roost to wait for rain. The desertion of his harem had thrown the rooster into a flap. Stanley trotted neurotically around his tethering post, stopping every few circuits to beat his bedraggled pinions and crow lustily in masculine outrage. I watched him for a bit without much curiosity, and then climbed off the step and walked toward him, listlessly dragging my stick in my trail.

"Here Stanley, Stanley," I called, not entirely sure how to summon a rooster, or instil in him confidence and friendliness.

I did neither. My approach only further unhinged Stanley. His stride lengthened, the tempo of his pace increased, and his head began to dart abruptly from side to side in furtive despair. Finally, in a last desperate attempt to escape, Stanley upset himself trying to fly. He landed in a heap of disarranged, stiff, glistening feathers. I put my foot on his string and pinned him to the ground.

"Nice pretty, pretty Stanley," I said coaxingly, adopting the tone that a neighbour used with her budgie, since I wasn't sure how one talked to a bird. I slowly extended my thumb to stroke his bright-red neck feathers. Darting angrily, he struck the ball of my thumb with a snappish peck and simultaneously hit my wrist with his heel spur. He didn't hurt me, but he did startle me badly. So badly I gave a little yelp. Which made me feel foolish and more than a little cowardly.

"You son of a bitch," I said, reaching down slowly and staring into one unblinking glassy eye in which I could see my face looming larger and larger. I caught the rooster's legs and held them firmly together. Stanley crowed defiantly and showed me his wicked little tongue.

"Now, Stanley," I said, "relax, I'm just going to stroke you. I'm just going to stroke you. I'm just going to pet Stanley."

No deal. He struck furiously again with a snake-like agility, and bounded in my hand, wings beating his poultry smell into my face. A real fighting cock at last. Maybe it was the weather. Perhaps his rooster pride and patience would suffer no more indignities.

The heat, the sultry menace of the gathering storm, made me feel prickly, edgy. I flicked my middle finger smartly against his tiny chicken skull, hard enough to rattle his pea-sized brain. "You like that, buster?" I asked him, and snapped him another one for good measure. He struck back again, his comb red, crested, and rubbery with fury.

I was angry myself. I turned him upside down and left him dangling, his wings drumming against the legs of my jeans. Then I righted him abruptly; he looked dishevelled, seedy and dazed.

"OK, Stanley," I said, feeling the intoxication of power. "I'm boss here, and you behave." There was a gleeful edge to my voice, which surprised me a little.

I realized I was hoping this confrontation would escalate. Wishing that he would provoke me into something.

205 Strange images came into my head: the bruises on my aunt's legs; Thompson's face drained of life, lifted like an empty receptacle toward the ceiling, waiting to be filled, the tendons of his neck stark and rigid with anticipation.

I was filled with anxiety, the heat seemed to stretch me, to tug at my nerves and my skin. Two drops of sweat, as large and perfectly formed as tears, rolled out of my hairline and splashed on to the rubber toes of my runners.

"Easy, Stanley," I breathed to him, "easy," and my hand crept deliberately towards him. This time he pecked me in such a way, directly on the knuckle, that it actually hurt. I took up my stick and rapped him on the beak curtly, the prim admonishment of a schoolmarm. I didn't hit him very hard, but it was hard enough to split the length of his beak with a narrow crack. The beak fissured like the nib of a fountain pen. Stanley squawked, opened and closed his beak spasmodically, bewildered by the pain. A bright jewel of blood bubbled out of the split and gathered to a trembling bead.

"There," I said excitedly, "now you've done it. How are you going to eat with a broken beak? You can't eat anything with a broken beak. You'll starve, you stupid goddamn chicken."

A wind that smelled of rain had sprung up. It ruffled his feathers until they moved with a barely discernible crackle.

210 "Poor Stanley," I said, and at last, numbed by the pain, he allowed me to stroke the gloss of his lacquer feathers.

I wasn't strong enough or practised enough to do a clean and efficient job of wringing his neck, but I succeeded in finishing him off after two clumsy attempts. Then because I wanted to leave the impression that a skunk had made off with him, I punched a couple of holes in his breast with my jack knife and tried to dribble some blood on the ground. Poor Stanley produced only a few meagre spots; this corpse refused to bleed in the presence of its murderer. I scattered a handful of his feathers on the ground and buried him in the larger of the two manure piles beside the barn.

"I don't think any skunk got that rooster," my grandmother said suspiciously, nudging at a feather with the toe of her boot until, finally disturbed, it was wafted away by the breeze.

Something squeezed my heart. How did she know?

"Skunks hunt at night," she said. "Must have been somebody's barn cat."

215 "You come along with me," my grandmother said. She was standing in front of the full-length hall mirror, settling on her hat, a deadly-looking hat pin poised above her skull. "We'll go into town and you can buy a comic book at the drugstore."

It was Friday and Friday was shopping day. But Grandma didn't wheel her battered De Soto to the kerb in front of the Brite Spot Grocery, she parked it in front of Maynard & Pritchard, Barristers and Solicitors.

"What are we doing here?" I asked.

Grandma was fumbling nervously with her purse. Small-town people don't like to be seen going to the lawyer's. "Come along with me. Hurry up."

"Why do I have to come?"

"Because I don't want you making a spectacle of yourself for the half-wits and loungers to gawk at," she said. "Let's not give them too much to wonder about." 220

Maynard & Pritchard, Barristers and Solicitors, smelled of wax and varnish and probity. My grandmother was shown into an office with a frosted pane of glass in the door and neat gilt lettering that announced it was occupied by D. F. Maynard, QC. I was ordered to occupy a hard chair, which I did, battering my heels on the rungs briskly enough to annoy the secretary into telling me to stop it.

My grandmother wasn't closeted long with her Queen's Counsel before the door opened and he glided after her into the passageway. Lawyer Maynard was the neatest man I had ever seen in my life. His suit fit him like a glove.

"The best I can do," he said, "is send him a registered letter telling him to remove himself from the premises, but it all comes to the same thing. If that doesn't scare him off, you'll have to have recourse to the police. That's all there is to it. I told you that yesterday and you haven't told me anything new today, Edith, that would make me change my mind. Just let him know you won't put up with him any more."

"No police," she said. "I don't want the police digging in my family's business and Evelyn giving one of her grand performances for some baby-skinned constable straight out of the depot. All I need is to get her away from him for a little while, then I could tune her in. I could get through to her in no time at all."

"Well," said Maynard, shrugging, "we could try the letter, but I don't think 225 it would do any good. He has the status of a guest in your home; just tell him to go."

My grandmother was showing signs of exasperation. "But he *doesn't* go. That's the point. I've told him and told him. But he *won't*."

"Mrs. Bradley," said the lawyer emphatically, "Edith, as a friend, don't waste your time. The police."

"I'm through wasting my time," she said.

Pulling away from the lawyer's office, my grandmother began a spirited conversation with herself. A wisp of hair had escaped from under her hat, and the dye winked a metallic red light as it jiggled up and down in the hot sunshine.

"I've told him and told him. But he won't listen. The goddamn freak thinks 230 we're involved in a christly debating society. He thinks I don't mean business. But I mean business. I do. There's more than one way to skin a cat or scratch a dog's ass. We'll take the wheels off his little red wagon and see how she pulls."

"What about my comic book?" I said, as we drove past the Rexall.

"Shut up."

Grandma drove the De Soto to the edge of town and stopped it at the Ogdens' place. It was a service station, or rather had been until the BA company had taken out their pumps and yanked the franchise, or whatever you call it, on the two brothers. Since then everything had gone steadily downhill. Cracks in the window-panes had been taped with masking tape, and the roof had been patched with flattened tin cans and old licence plates. The building itself was surrounded by an acre of wrecks, sulking hulks rotten with rust, the guts of their upholstery spilled and gnawed by rats and mice.

But the Ogden brothers still carried on a business after a fashion. They stripped their wrecks for parts and were reputed to be decent enough mechanics whenever they were sober enough to turn a wrench or thread a bolt. People brought work to them whenever they couldn't avoid it, and the rest of the year gave them a wide berth.

235 The Ogdens were famous for two things: their meanness and their profligacy as breeders. The place was always aswarm with kids who never seemed to wear pants except in the most severe weather, and tottered about the premises, their legs smeared with grease, shit, or various combinations of both.

"Wait here," my grandmother said, slamming the car door loudly enough to bring the two brothers out of their shop. Through the open door I saw a motor suspended on an intricate system of chains and pulleys.

The Ogdens stood with their hands in the pockets of their bib overalls while my grandmother talked to them. They were quite a sight. They didn't have a dozen teeth in their heads between them, even though the oldest brother couldn't have been more than forty. They just stood there, one sucking on a cigarette, the other on a Coke. Neither one moved or changed his expression, except once, when a tow-headed youngster piddled too close to Grandma. He was lazily and casually slapped on the side of the head by the nearest brother and ran away screaming, his stream cavorting wildly in front of him.

At last, their business concluded, the boys walked my grandmother back to the car.

"You'll get to that soon?" she said, sliding behind the wheel.

240 "Tomorrow all right?" said one. His words sounded all slack and chewed, issuing from his shrunken, old man's mouth.

"The sooner the better. I want that seen to, Bert."

"What seen to?" I asked.

"Bert and his brother Elwood are going to fix that rattle that's been plaguing me."

"Sure thing," said Elwood. "Nothing but clear sailing."

245 "What rattle?" I said.

"What rattle? What rattle? The one in the glove compartment," she said, banging it with the heel of her hand. "That rattle. You hear it?"

Thompson could get very edgy some days. "I should be working on my dissertation," he said, coiled in the big chair. "I shouldn't be wasting my time in this shit-hole. I should be working!"

"So why aren't you?" said Evelyn. She was spool knitting. That and reading movie magazines were the only things she ever did.

"How the christ do I work without a library? You see a goddamn library within a hundred miles of this place?"

"Why do you need a library?" she said calmly. "Can't you write?"

"Write?" he said, looking at the ceiling. "Write, she says. What the hell do you know about it? What the hell do *you* know about it?"

"I can't see why you can't write."

"Before you write, you research. That's what you do, you *research*."

"So bite my head off. It wasn't my idea to come here."

"It wasn't me that lost my goddamn job. How the hell were we supposed to pay the rent?"

"You could have got a job."

"I'm a student. Anyway, I told you, if I get a job my wife gets her hooks into me for support. I'll starve to death before I support that bitch."

"We could go back."

"How many times does it have to be explained to you? I don't get my scholarship cheque until the first of September. We happen to be broke. Absolutely. In fact, you're going to have to hit the old lady up for gas and eating money to get back to the coast. We're stuck here. Get that into your empty fucking head. The Lord Buddha might have been able to subsist on a single bean a day; I can't."

My grandmother came into the room. The conversation stopped.

"Do you think," she said to Thompson, "I could ask you to do me a favour?"

"Why, Mrs. Bradley," he said, smiling, "whatever do you mean?"

"I was wondering whether you could take my car into town to Ogdens' to get it fixed."

"Oh," said Thompson. "I don't know where it is. I don't think I'm your man."

"Ask anyone where it is. They can tell you. It isn't hard to find."

"Why would you ask me to do you a favour, Mrs. Bradley?" inquired Thompson complacently. Hearing his voice was like listening to someone drag their nails down a blackboard.

"Well, you can be goddamn sure I wouldn't," said Grandma, trying to keep a hold of herself, "except that I'm right in the middle of doing my pickling and canning. I thought you might be willing to move your lazy carcass to do something around here. Every time I turn around I seem to be falling over those legs of yours." She looked at the limbs in question as if she would like to dock them somewhere in the vicinity of the knee.

"No, I don't think I can," said Thompson easily, stroking his goat beard. "And why the hell can't you?"

"Oh, let's just say I don't trust you, Mrs. Bradley. I don't like to leave you alone with Evelyn. Lord knows what ideas you might put in her head."

"Or take out."

"That's right. Or take out," said Thompson with satisfaction. "You can't imagine the trouble it took me to get them in there." He turned to Evelyn. "She can't imagine the trouble, can she, dear?"

Evelyn threw her spool knitting on the floor and walked out of the room.

"Evelyn's mad and I'm glad," shouted Thompson at her back. "And I know how to tease her!"

"Charlie, come here," said Grandma. I went over to her. She took me firmly by the shoulder. "From now on," said my grandma, "my family is off limits to you. I don't want to see you talking to Charlie here, or to come within sniffing distance of Evelyn."

"What do you think of that idea, Charlie?" said Thompson. "Are you still my friend or what?"

I gave him a wink my grandma couldn't see. He thought that was great; he laughed like a madman. "Superb," he said. "Superb. There's no flies on Charlie. What a diplomat."

"What the hell is the matter with you, Mr. Beatnik?"[4] asked Grandma, annoyed beyond bearing. "What's so goddamn funny?"

"Ha, ha!" roared Thompson. "What a charming notion! Me a beatnik!"

280   Grandma Bradley held the mouthpiece of the phone very close to her lips as she spoke into it. "No, it can't be brought in. You'll have to come out here to do the job."

She listened with an intent expression on her face. Spotting me pretending to look in the fridge, she waved me out of the kitchen with her hand. I dragged myself out and stood quietly in the hallway.

"This is a party line," she said, "remember that."

Another pause while she listened.

"OK," she said and hung up.

285   I spent some of my happiest hours squatting in the corn patch. I was completely hidden in there; even when I stood, the maturing stalks reached a foot or more above my head. It was a good place. On the hottest days it was relatively cool in that thicket of green where the shade was dark and deep and the leaves rustled and scraped and sawed drily overhead.

Nobody ever thought to look for me there. They could bellow their bloody lungs out for me and I could just sit and watch them getting uglier and uglier about it all. There was some satisfaction in that. I'd just reach up and pluck myself a cob. I loved raw corn. The newly formed kernels were tiny, pale pearls of sweetness that gushed juice. I'd munch and munch and smile and smile and think, why don't you drop dead?

It was my secret place, my sanctuary, where I couldn't be found or touched by them. But all the same, if I didn't let them intrude on me—that didn't mean I didn't want to keep tabs on things.

At the time I was watching Thompson stealing peas at the other end of the garden. He was like some primitive man who lived in a gathering culture. My grandma kept him so hungry he was constantly prowling for food: digging in cupboards, rifling the refrigerator, scrounging in the garden.

Clad only in Bermuda shorts he was a sorry sight. His bones threatened to rupture his skin and jut out every which way. He sported a scrub-board chest with two old pennies for nipples, and a wispy garland of hair decorated his

4. A derisive term for adherents to the 1950's Beat movement, a social and literary rebellion against "square" conventions.

sunken breastbone. His legs looked particularly rackety; all gristle, knobs and sinew.

We both heard the truck at the same time. It came bucking up the approach, spurting gravel behind it. Thompson turned around, shaded his eyes and peered at it. He wasn't much interested. He couldn't get very curious about the natives.

The truck stopped and a man stepped out on to the runningboard of the '51 IHC. He gazed around him, obviously looking for something or someone. This character had a blue handkerchief sprinkled with white polka dots tied in a triangle over his face. Exactly like an outlaw in an Audie Murphy[5] Western. A genuine goddamn Jesse James.

He soon spotted Thompson standing half-naked in the garden, staring stupidly at this strange sight, his mouth bulging with peas. The outlaw ducked his head back into the cab of the truck, said something to the driver, and pointed. The driver then stepped out on to his runningboard and, standing on tippy-toe, peered over the roof of the cab at Thompson. He too wore a handkerchief tied over his mug, but his was red.

Then they both got down from the truck and began to walk very quickly toward Thompson with long, menacing strides.

"Fellows?" said Thompson.

At the sound of his voice the two men broke into a stiff-legged trot, and the one with the red handkerchief, while still moving, stooped down smoothly and snatched up the hoe that lay at the edge of the garden.

"What the hell is going on here, boys?" said Thompson, his voice pitched high with concern.

The man with the blue mask reached Thompson first. One long arm, a dirty clutch of fingers on its end, snaked out and caught him by the hair and jerked his head down. Then he kicked him in the pit of the stomach with his work boots.

"OK, fucker," he shouted, "too fucking smart to take a fucking hint?" and he punched him on the side of the face with several short, snapping blows that actually tore Thompson's head out of his grip. Thompson toppled over clumsily and fell in the dirt. "Get fucking lost," Blue Mask said more quietly.

"Evelyn!" yelled Thompson to the house. "Jesus Christ, Evelyn!"

I crouched lower in the corn patch and began to tremble. I was certain they were going to kill him.

"Shut up," said the man with the hoe. He glanced at the blade for a second, considered, then rotated the handle in his hands and hit Thompson a quick chop on the head with the blunt side. "Shut your fucking yap," he repeated.

"Evelyn! Evelyn! Oh God!" hollered Thompson, "I'm being murdered! For God's sake, somebody help me!" The side of his face was slick with blood.

"I told you shut up, cock sucker," said Red Mask, and kicked him in the ribs several times. Thompson groaned and hugged himself in the dust.

5. World War II's most decorated GI, Murphy (1924–1971) went on to star in low-budget Western films as a baby-faced hero.

"Now you get lost, fucker," said the one with the hoe, "because if you don't stop bothering nice people we'll drive a spike in your skull."

305   "Somebody help me!" Thompson yelled at the house.

"Nobody there is going to help you," Blue Mask said. "You're all on your own, smart arse."

"You bastards," said Thompson, and spat ineffectually in their direction.

For his defiance he got struck a couple of chopping blows with the hoe. The last one skittered off his collar-bone with a sickening crunch.

"That's enough," said Red Mask, catching the handle of the hoe. "Come on."

310   The two sauntered back toward the truck, laughing. They weren't in any hurry to get out of there. Thompson lay on his side staring at their retreating backs. His face was wet with tears and blood.

The man with the red mask looked back over his shoulder and wiggled his ass at Thompson in an implausible imitation of effeminacy. "Was it worth it, tiger?" he shouted. "Getting your ashes hauled don't come cheap, do it?"

This set them off again. Passing me they pulled off their masks and stuffed them in their pockets. They didn't have to worry about Thompson when they had their backs to him; he couldn't see their faces. But I could. No surprise. They were the Ogden boys.

When the truck pulled out of the yard, its gears grinding, I burst out of my hiding place and ran to Thompson, who had got to his knees and was trying to stop the flow of blood from his scalp with his fingers. He was crying. Another first for Thompson. He was the first man I'd seen cry. It made me uncomfortable. "The sons of bitches broke my ribs," he said, panting with shallow breaths. "God, I hope they didn't puncture a lung."

"Can you walk?" I asked.

315   "Don't think I don't know who's behind this," he said, getting carefully to his feet. His face was white. "You saw them," he said. "You saw their faces from the corn patch. We got the bastards."

He leaned a little on me as we made our way to the house. The front door was locked. We knocked. No answer. "Let me in, you old bitch!" shouted Thompson.

"Evelyn, open the goddamn door!" Silence. I couldn't hear a thing move in the house. It was as if they were all dead in there. It frightened me.

He started to kick the door. A panel splintered. "Open this door! Let me in, you old slut, or I'll kill you!"

Nothing.

320   "You better go," I said nervously. I didn't like this one little bit. "Those guys might come back and kill you."

"Evelyn!" he bellowed. "Evelyn!"

He kept it up for a good five minutes, alternately hammering and kicking the door, pleading with and threatening the occupants. By the end of that time he was sweating with exertion and pain. He went slowly down the steps, sobbing, beaten. "You saw them," he said, "we have the bastards dead to rights."

He winced when he eased his bare flesh on to the hot seat-covers of the car.

"I'll be back," he said, starting the motor of the car. "This isn't the end of this."

When Grandma was sure he had gone, the front door was unlocked and I was let in. I noticed my grandmother's hands trembled a touch when she lit her cigarette.

"You can't stay away from him, can you?" she said testily.

"You didn't have to do that," I said. "He was hurt. You ought to have let him in."

"I ought to have poisoned him a week ago. And don't talk about things you don't know anything about."

"Sometimes," I said, "all of you get on my nerves."

"Kids don't have nerves. Adults have nerves. They're the only ones entitled to them. And don't think I care a plugged nickel what does, or doesn't, get on your nerves."

"Where's Aunt Evelyn?"

"Your Aunt Evelyn is taken care of," she replied.

"Why wouldn't she come to the door?"

"She had her own road to Damascus.[6] She has seen the light. Everything has been straightened out," she said. "Everything is back to normal."

He looked foolish huddled in the back of the police car later that evening. When the sun began to dip, the temperature dropped rapidly, and he was obviously cold dressed only in his Bermuda shorts. Thompson sat all hunched up to relieve the strain on his ribs, his hands pressed between his knees, shivering.

My grandmother and the constable spoke quietly by the car for some time; occasionally Thompson poked his head out the car window and said something. By the look on the constable's face when he spoke to Thompson, it was obvious he didn't care for him too much. Thompson had that kind of effect on people. Several times during the course of the discussion the constable glanced my way.

I edged a little closer so I could hear what they were saying.

"He's mad as a hatter," said my grandmother. "I don't know anything about two men. If you ask me, all this had something to do with drugs. My daughter says that this man takes drugs. He's some kind of beatnik."

"Christ," said Thompson, drawing his knees up as if to scrunch himself into a smaller, less noticeable package, "the woman is insane."

"One thing at a time, Mrs. Bradley," said the RCMP constable.

"My daughter is finished with him," she said. "He beats her, you know. I want him kept off my property."

"I want to speak to Evelyn," Thompson said. He looked bedraggled and frightened. "Evelyn and I will leave this minute if this woman wants. But I've got to talk to Evelyn."

"My daughter doesn't want to see you, mister. She's finished with you," said

6. According to biblical legend, Saul (later Paul), was on his way to Damascus to subdue the Christians there when he was stopped by a vision of Jesus. He was temporarily blinded, and his conversion was immediate.

Grandma Bradley, shifting her weight from side to side. She turned her attention to the constable. "He beats her," she said, "bruises all over her. Can you imagine?"

345   "The boy knows," said Thompson desperately. "He saw them. How many times do I have to tell you?" He piped his voice to me. "Didn't you, Charlie? You saw them, didn't you?"

"Charlie?" said my grandmother. This was news to her.

I stood very still.

"Come here, son," said the constable.

I walked slowly over to them.

350   "Did you see the faces of the men?" the constable asked, putting a hand on my shoulder. "Do you know the men? Are they from around here?"

"How would he know?" said my grandmother. "He's a stranger."

"He knows them. At least he saw them," said Thompson. "My little Padmasambhava never misses a trick," he said, trying to jolly me. "You see everything, don't you, Charlie? You remember everything, don't you?"

I looked at my grandmother, who stood so calmly and commandingly, waiting.

"Hey, don't look to her for the answers," said Thompson nervously. "Don't be afraid of her. You remember everything, don't you?"

355   He had no business begging me. I had watched their game from the sidelines long enough to know the rules. At one time he had imagined himself a winner. And now he was asking me to save him, to take a risk, when I was more completely in her clutches than he would ever be. He forgot I was a child. I depended on her.

Thompson, I saw, was powerless. He couldn't protect me. God, I remembered more than he dreamed. I remembered how his lips had moved soundlessly, his face pleading with the ceiling, his face blotted of everything but abject urgency. Praying to a simpering, cross-eyed idol. His arm flashing as he struck my aunt's bare legs. Crawling in the dirt, covered with blood.

He had taught me that "Those who are in the grip of desire, the grip of existence, the grip of ignorance, move helplessly round through the spheres of life, as men or gods or as wretches in the lower regions." Well, he was helpless now. But he insisted on fighting back and hurting the rest of us. The weak ones like Evelyn and me.

I thought of Stanley the rooster and how it had felt when the tendons separated, the gristle parted and the bones crunched under my twisting hands.

"I don't know what he's talking about," I said to the constable softly. "I didn't see anybody."

360   "Clear out," said my grandmother triumphantly. "Beat it."

"You dirty little son of a bitch," he said to me. "You mean little bugger."

He didn't understand much. He had forced me into the game, and now that I was a player and no longer a watcher he didn't like it. The thing was that I was good at the game. But he, being a loser, couldn't appreciate that.

Then suddenly he said, "Evelyn." He pointed to the upstairs window of the house and tried to get out of the back seat of the police car. But of course he couldn't. They take the handles off the back doors. Nobody can get out unless they are let out.

"Goddamn it!" he shouted. "Let me out! She's waving to me! She wants me!"

I admit that the figure was hard to make out at that distance. But any damn fool could see she was only waving goodbye.

1982

QUESTIONS

1. What is the focus of the narration? the voice? What expectations of plot, theme, character are aroused by the first fifteen or eighteen paragraphs? What are your early interpretations of the title? Trace "watching" through the story and its relation to character, plot, and theme.

2. For some time the narrator summarizes his childhood and gives brief character sketches of members of his family. How would you describe the narrator's characterizations—are they jovial? sympathetic? loving? critical? sardonic? nasty? What do you think of the narrator during these early (twenty to thirty) paragraphs? Does your view of him change in the course of the story? If so, how many times, in what ways, and when? How does the narrator's character relate to the incidents of the story (plot) and theme?

3. Though there is a brief scene with the father in paragraphs 18 and 19, the first lengthy, fully discriminated scene takes place in paragraphs 28 to 57. How does the scene contribute to the picture of the setting? characterization? theme?

4. It is not until paragraph 62 that "something interesting turned up"—the arrival of Aunt Evelyn and Robert Thompson. Did the first sixty-plus paragraphs hold your interest despite the absence of incident? If so, how? What expectations, if any, did those first paragraphs engender? What expectations or curiosity is aroused by the new arrivals? How does it contribute to the characterization of the narrator (Charlie)? Grandma Bradley? What are your first responses to and opinions of Aunt Evelyn? Thompson? What is the tone of the scene? What conflict is building? Whose side are you on in the ensuing argument? Why? Whose side is the narrator on? How do you know?

5. How does the narrator know what Evelyn does during the day? How does he know that Thompson beats her? What resemblance does Thompson see between Charlie and Padma-sambhava? Why does Charlie think Thompson a "silly bugger" when he laughs at what Charlie tells him he wants to be when

he grows up (par. 167)? How is this related to Thompson's character? Charlie's situation? the theme?

6. On the evening of the day Thompson whipped Evelyn, why does she come down to dinner in shorts (par. 144)? What does that tell you about her character? about Thompson? What expectations are aroused? In paragraphs 190 and 191, Grandma says Thompson will be out of the house in a week, but he says he won't. Who do you think will prove to be right? Why? What did you expect Grandma to do to get rid of Thompson? How was your expectation related to the characters? to plot? to theme?

7. How does paragraph 194 contribute to setting? expectations? characterization? How is the scene between Charlie and Stanley that follows related to details earlier in the story? What is the effect of the scene on the characterization of Charlie? on the theme? Is Stanley a symbol? Explain, by indicating what you mean by "symbol" and, if you think he is a symbol, what it is he symbolizes.

8. How is paragraph 355 related to plot? Charlie's character? theme?

9. How many previous scenes and details are echoed or brought to bear on the final scene (paragraphs 336 to the end of story)? How does that scene derive from and impinge upon the characterization of Charlie? How does it bring out, reinforce, or define the theme?

WRITING SUGGESTIONS

1. Show how the discussion of "The Country Husband" or "Sonny's Blues" in the chapter on plot would be modified and expanded by writing a essay on the whole text of the story.

2. Write a brief analytical essay on "The Secret Sharer" in terms of symbol or "Love Medicine" in terms of theme. How does the discussion of theme in this chapter's student essay differ from your treatment of an isolated element in one of these two stories?

3. Write an essay on the whole text of "The Real Thing," "The Yellow Wallpaper," or "A Hunger Artist" (all stories in *Reading More Fiction*).

STUDENT WRITING

Daniel Bronson's paper is a whole-text response to one of the earlier stories in the text, "A Rose for Emily." In his paper, Daniel traces the theme of resistance to change in the story, which he supports with examples from the text.

"Like the Sand of the Hourglass . . ."

Daniel Bronson

The year 1865 saw the end of the Civil War between the Union and the Confederacy, and saw the beginning of a "New South." With the many changes pressed upon the South, the so-called "Old South" could no longer exist. For example, people could not own slaves as they had in the past, and they couldn't survive anymore simply by belonging to a family with an "august name." These changes didn't happen overnight however; they took many years to occur. In William Faulkner's "A Rose for Emily," we are shown the transition from Old South to New South as it takes place in the little town of Jefferson, and we see how Miss Emily Grierson, survivor of the Old South, resists these changes.

Jefferson was once inhabited by many well-off families who were members of the Old South's aristocratic class. As time, and the

323

Reconstruction, marched on, these families slowly disappeared. Eventually, the last true living legacy of the Old South in Jefferson was Miss Emily Grierson. She had been raised to be a Southern Belle, an upstanding member of society, and she clung to her world of the Old South. She kept a black servant, Tobe, who did everything for her, just as if he were a slave, and she lived in "a big, squarish frame house that had once been white, decorated with cupolas and spires and scrolled balconies in the heavily lightsome style of the seventies, set on what had once been our most select street" (par. 2). With the infiltration of the New South, however, "garages and cotton gins . . . encroached and obliterated even the august names of that neighborhood" (par. 2). Yet the house remained, "lifting its stubborn and coquettish decay above the cotton wagons and the gasoline pumps," just as its willful inhabitant "carried her head high . . . even when we believed that she was fallen" (par. 33).

The house was all that Miss Emily really had left after her father died. When he passed away, Miss Emily spent three days denying his death and not letting the doctors and ministers dispose of the body. Though it is not told first in the story, this was the first time Miss Emily had rejected the truth in order to retain her world of the past: a world in which other members of the Old South, such as Colonel Sartoris, lived on after they too had died.

Colonel Sartoris also represented the Old South, and he protected Emily when her father died. As mayor of Jefferson at the time, he remitted her taxes, and since no aristocratic woman such as Miss Emily could possibly lower herself to accept charity, came up with a story of how her father had loaned money to Jefferson and this was how Miss Emily was to be repaid. "Only a man of Colonel Sartoris' generation and thought could have invented it, and only a woman could have believed it" (par. 3). So when Miss Emily was later approached by members of the generation of city authorities who wanted her taxes, she held onto the past and told them repeatedly to see Colonel Sartoris, even though he had been dead for almost ten years. Furthermore, when city authorities asked her whether or not she received "a notice from the sheriff, signed by him," she remarks, "Perhaps he considers himself the sheriff" (pars. 9, 10). Obviously, Miss Emily didn't accept that whoever was the new sheriff was really the sheriff. As far as she was concerned, the sheriff was still the same person it was several years ago.

We are shown not only the government of the Old South Jefferson, when it sided with Miss Emily, and the government of the New South Jefferson, when it was against Miss Emily, but we also catch a glimpse of Jefferson's government when it was still under transition. About two years after her father's death, a smell developed around Miss Emily's house. The "member of the rising generation" on the Board of Aldermen said that the solution to the problem was " 'simple enough. . . . Send her word to have her place cleaned up. Give her a certain time to do it in, and if she don't . . . .' " At that point the remaining Old South revealed itself when the eighty-year-old mayor, Judge Stevens, irately asked, "will you accuse a lady to her face of smelling bad?" (pars. 22, 23). It is apparent that though there were some old-timers left, just as Jefferson changed, so did its people.

Members of the Old South were very honorable, graceful and above all, dignified. They had great respect for each other and for each other's feelings, and were quick to help one another whenever possible. Most importantly however, they always retained their dignity, no matter what. Miss Emily preserved her world of the Old South by hanging on to her dignity. It was because her dignity was so essential to her that a major conflict arose when Miss Emily met Homer Barron. Homer was a personification of Reconstruction and was Miss Emily's opposite in every way. He was a Yankee, a solicializer, a member of the vulgar, haphazard post-war generation, and "a day laborer," having been hired to build Jefferson's sidewalks and thereby contribute to the urbanization of the town.

When opposites attracted however, Miss Emily put her dignity on the line and was seen "on Sunday afternoons driving in the yellow-wheeled buggy and the matched team of bays from the livery stable" with Homer (par. 30). The ladies of the town said, "'Of course a Grierson would not think seriously of a Northerner,'" and the "older people," those of the Old South, "said that even grief could not cause a real lady to forget *noblesse oblige*--without calling it *noblesse oblige*." (par. 31). As time passed, Homer and Miss Emily were seen again and again, until finally, "some of the ladies began to say that it was a disgrace to the town and a bad example to the young people. The men did not want to interfere, but at last the ladies forced the Baptist minister . . . to call upon her" (par. 44). Then "the minister's wife wrote to Miss Emily's relations in Alabama" (par. 44). When they arrived, Miss Emily realized she had to do something to preserve her dignity and pride that kept her Old South alive.

Her choices were few: marry Homer, or separate from him completely. At first it appeared that Miss Emily and Homer were either married or getting ready to be married, for she "ordered a man's toilet set in silver, with the letters H.B. on each piece" and she "bought a complete outfit of men's clothing, including a nightshirt" (par. 45). Unfortunately, while this may have kept her reputation from being tarnished as far as the New South people were concerned, it was still not enough for Miss Emily's Old South dignity. It demanded that she never demean herself to being married to a Northerner. Therefore, in order to keep Homer, but not what he was or what he stood for, Miss Emily killed him, then kept him in a bed where she could be with him when she chose without "compromising her dignity." This violence and necrophilia reflect her wish to hold onto the South's dead past as well as her own and the price she pays to do so.

Miss Emily retained her sense of her dignity and her private version of the world of the Old South for the rest of her life. She was a "monument," "a tradition, a duty, and a care" (pars. 1, 3). Living secluded, she surrounded herself as best as she could by locking herself in her old house with only her memories and her black servant. When she died, she did so in dignity, "in a heavy walnut bed with a curtain, her gray head propped on a pillow" (par. 53). With her death went her Old South world as well, leaving behind only "the very old men--some in their brushed Confederate uniforms" to remind the New South of the past (par. 55) and to offer a rose of remembrance and respect for Emily.

▾ ▾ ▾

Exploring Contexts

8 THE AUTHOR'S WORK AS CONTEXT: D. H. LAWRENCE AND FLANNERY O'CONNOR

E ven if it were desirable to read a story as a thing in itself, separate from everything else we had ever read or seen and from everything else the author had written, this is in practice impossible. We can *first* look into Chapman's Homer or Faulkner's fiction only once. After we read a second and then a third story by an author, we begin to recognize the voice and have a sense of familiarity, as we would with a growing acquaintance. Each story is part of the author's entire body of work—the **canon**—which, taken together, forms something like a huge single entity, a vision, a world, a "superwork."

The author's voice and vision soon create in us certain expectations—of action, structure, characterization, world view, language. We come to expect short sentences from Hemingway, long ones from Faulkner, a certain amount of violence from both. We are not surprised if a Conrad story is set in Africa or Asia or aboard ship, but we are surprised if a Faulkner story takes place outside Mississippi (his portion of which, we soon learn, he calls Yoknapatawpha).

When we find an author's vision attractive or challenging, we naturally want to find out more about it, reading not only the literary works in the canon but the author's nonfictional prose—essays, letters, anything we can find that promises a fuller or clearer view of that unique way of looking at the world.

Such knowledge is helpful—within limits. D. H. Lawrence warned us to trust the tale and not the teller. A statement of beliefs or of intentions is not necessarily the same as what a given work may show or achieve; and, on the other hand, writers often embody in their art what they cannot articulate, what indeed may not be expressible, in discursive prose.

In this chapter we will look briefly but closely at the work of two writers, D. H. Lawrence and Flannery O'Connor. We will look both at differences between works by the same writer and at similarities.

The two short stories and brief selections from Lawrence's letters and criticism in this chapter are meant to make you feel more at home (and interested) in Lawrence's world and to raise questions about the relationship of the individual work to an author's work as a whole. Of course, a couple of short stories and a few pages of nonfiction alone cannot adequately represent the career of a writer who was a novelist, poet, critic, and essayist as well as short-story writer, nor can two stories represent the richness and variety of the fifty or more that he published over many years. However, as the stories come from different decades, they do represent somewhat the continuities and changes during his career. "Odour of Chrysanthemums" is characteristically set in the coal-mining region of his native English Midlands, the scene of many of his novels, including three of the most famous, which also span his career—*Sons and Lovers* (1913), *The Rainbow* (1915), and *Lady Chatterly's Lover* (1928). Though we have included brief excerpts from "Nottingham and the Mining Countryside" and from his "Autobiographical Sketch" (and the selection from "Women Are So Cocksure" may seem related to "Odour of Chrysanthemums" in another respect), there is no way in so few selections to represent both Lawrence's emphasis on the Midlands and the scope of his settings—his stories take place all over Western Europe, in the Americas, and in Australia. The London setting of "The Rocking-Horse Winner" only faintly indicates Lawrence's growing cosmopolitanism socially as well as geographically. It also suggests, though superficially, his developing interest in the superreal and the mythic—concerns most fully developed in *The Plumed Serpent* (1926) and *The Man Who Died* (1929)—and his movement in content and style away from nineteenth-century notions of realism.

It may be useful to see the first story here (one of Lawrence's very first stories) through the eyes of its first "professional" reader as he remembers the experience. Not long before World War I, a young woman sent to Ford Madox Ford, then editor of *The English Review*, three poems and a short story written by a schoolmaster friend of hers, the then-unknown D. H. Lawrence. Ford read the story first and, he recalls, knew immediately that he had a genius on his hands, "a big one." The very title, "Odour of Chrysanthemums," Ford noted, "makes an impact on the mind," indicates that the writer is observant (not many people realize that chrysanthemums have an odor), and sets the dark autumnal tone of the story. From the very first sentence, Ford goes on to say,

> . . . you know that this fellow with the power of observation is going to write whatever he writes about from the inside. The "Number 4" shows that. He will be the sort of fellow who knows that for the sort of people who work about engines, engines have a sort of individuality. He had to give the engine the personality of a number. . . . "With seven full wagons". . . . The "seven" is good. The ordinary careless writer would say "some small wagons." This man knows what he wants. He sees the scene of his story exactly. He has an authoritative mind.
>
> "It appeared round the corner with loud threats of speed." . . . Good writing; slightly, but not *too* arresting. . . . "But the colt that it startled from among the gorse . . . out-distanced it at a canter." Good again. This fellow does not "state." He doesn't say: "It was coming slowly," or—what would have been a little better—"at seven miles an hour." Because even "seven miles an hour" means nothing definite for the untrained mind. It might mean something for a trainer or pedestrian racers. The imaginative writer writes for all humanity; he does not limit his desired readers to specialists. . . . But anyone knows that an engine that makes a great deal of noise and yet cannot overtake a colt at a canter must be a ludicrously ineffective machine. We know then that this fellow knows his job.
>
> . . . . [T]his man knows. He knows how to open a story with a sentence of the right cadence for holding the attention. He knows how to construct a paragraph. He knows the life he is writing about. . . . You can trust him for the rest. . . .

—from "Before the Wars," *Selected Memories, The Bodley Head Ford Madox Ford* (London, 1962), I, 322–23

In that strange and strangely different story, "The Rocking-Horse Winner," written at the other end of Lawrence's career and published posthumously in 1932, you will find the same precision of detail and the same "inside view," in the first description of Paul's riding the horse, for example; in the description of the horse's "lowered face" ("Its red mouth was slightly open, its big eye was wide and glassy-bright" [par. 42]); and in the precise accounting of the races, the odds, the money.

Ford read "Odour of Chrysanthemums" outside the context available to us. He did not know anything of the author and had read nothing else by him. Ford was an excellent editor (as well as writer) and to his credit spotted Lawrence's genius, a genius quite different from his own. Lawrence's mastery of detail made Ford trust him, but what he trusted him for seems to have been knowledge of the "other ninety-nine hundredths" of the population, the working class. An English writer of genius with knowledge of the working class was no doubt rare and notable in those prewar days, and Lawrence's early works are full of details of the lives of miners and their families. But Lawrence, we now know, considered not class but the man-woman relationship the "great relationship of humanity," all others being subsidiary. Because we know that, know of Lawrence's notoriety for describing sexual relations, know his later works in which sexual relations are the major or basic concern—and perhaps because of the emphasis on sex in our own time—in reading "Odour of Chrysanthemums" we focus our attention less on the picture of the working class than on the strange relationship between the Bateses. The class element is still in the story, but the context of Lawrence's other works and utterances highlights this other human relationship.

Though Ford stressed Lawrence's power of observation in terms of the outside of things, he does say that "this fellow . . . is going to write whatever he writes about from the inside." It is not just Lawrence's powers of observation but his penetration to the inside of his characters' beings, to the shockingly original but convincing motives and feelings he finds there, and his insight into relationships, particularly love relationships, that mark his best work. Unfortunately, there is not space here to represent his more positive, fully developed, and explicit incarnations of man-woman love, found particularly in his novels *Women in Love* (1920) and *Lady Chatterley's Lover*. We can briefly indicate, however, what woman-man love is not in "Odour of Chrysanthemums":

> Was this what it all meant—utter, intact separateness, obscured by heat of living? . . . There had been nothing between them, and yet they had come together, exchanging their nakedness repeatedly. Each time he had taken her, they had been two isolated beings, far apart as now [when he was dead]. . . . I have been fighting a husband who did not exist. *He* existed all the time . . . apart all the while, living as she never lived, feeling as she never felt.
>
> (par. 218)

and what parent-child love is by what it is not in "The Rocking-Horse Winner":

> . . . when her children were present, she always felt the center of her heart go hard. This troubled her, and in her manner she was all the more gentle and anxious for her children, as if she loved them very much. Only she herself knew that at the center of her heart was a hard little place that could not feel love, no, not for anybody. Everybody else said of her: "She is such a good mother. She adores her children." Only she herself, and her children themselves, knew it was not so.
>
> (par. 1)

In this chapter we have also included two of Flannery O'Connor's stories, both from her posthumous volume, *Everything That Rises Must Converge*, and so representative at least of the final years of her brief career. (She died at thirty-nine, having published some thirty-one stories, two novels, essays, and reviews.) The title story of that final volume is perhaps the more characteristic, for O'Connor frequently turned her piercingly accurate vision on the middle-aged and elderly, especially women, and on southern culture. Both these stories center, as many of her others do, on a sudden revelation of a truth about the self, shedding a new and unflattering light on one's attitudes, behaviors, beliefs. The exposure often involves snobbery, racism, or self-righteousness, often in false religious or falsely humanistic form. The first two are exemplified in "Everything That Rises Must Converge," self-righteousness and the falsely humanistic in "The Lame Shall Enter First." Her settings and situations are not so varied as Lawrence's, her world is narrower, and her focus fiercely concentrated. Like Lawrence, however, O'Connor has a keen eye for realistic detail and for her characters' self-deception. Violence is often in or near the surface of her fiction; as in Faulkner, it is used to shake up the reader and make him or her look beyond the conventional and the ordinary into a kind of truth, often an uncomfortable truth that lies within. Though O'Connor is a deeply religious and serious writer, her stories are replete with irony and wit, and are sometimes downright funny. Indeed, as you will see, she is not above using comic pratfalls seriously.

The central, sometimes obsessive concerns and assumptions that permeate an author's work not only relate the individual stories to each other, mutually illuminating and enriching them, but they also serve as the author's trademark. It is not difficult to recognize or even parody a story by Lawrence or O'Connor.

Embodying these larger concerns and underlying such larger structures as plot, focus, and voice are the basic characteristics of the author's language, such as **diction,** the choice and use of words; sentence structure; **rhetorical tropes,** figures of thought and speech; **imagery;** and **rhythm**—in other words, the author's **style.**

Perhaps because of the uniqueness of style, the vocabulary for discussing stylistic elements is not very precise or accessible. We can broadly characterize diction as **formal** ("The Cask of Amontillado") or informal (most of the stories in this collection), and within the broad term **informal** we can identify a level of language that approximates the speech of ordinary people and call it **colloquial** ("Why I Live at the P.O."). But to characterize precisely an author's diction so that it adequately describes his or her work and marks it off from the work of contemporaries is a very difficult task indeed. We can note Faulkner's long sentences, but it is hard to get much definition in the stylistic fingerprint of an author merely by measuring the lengths of sentences or tabulating connectives (though these qualities no doubt do subliminally contribute to the effect of the works on readers and do help to identify the author).

Diction and sentence structure contribute to the **tone** of a work, or the implied attitude or stance of the author toward the characters and events, an aspect somewhat analogous to tone of voice. When what is being said and the tone are consistent, it is difficult to separate one from the other; when there seems to be a discrepancy we have some words that are useful to describe the difference. If the language seems exaggerated, we call it **overstatement** or **hyperbole.** Sometimes it will be the narrator, sometimes a character, who uses language so intensive or exaggerated that we must read it at a discount, as it were, and judge the speaker's accuracy or honesty in the process. When Julian's mother, in "Everything That Rises Must Converge," says, " 'I've always had a great deal of respect for my colored friends. . . . I'd do anything in the world for them . . .' " (par. 32), we know she protests too much, that she is exaggerating, and we see her racism through or underneath her language. When Sister in "Why I Live at the P.O." says, ". . . I do not enjoy being referred to as a hussy by my own grandfather," we know that she means to express her dislike of being called a hussy much more forcefully than she does. She is indulging in a bit of obvious **understatement** or **litotes.** When a word or expression carries not only its literal meaning, but a different meaning for the speaker as well, we have an example of **verbal irony.** When Fortunato says, "I shall not die of a cough," Montresor's "True—true" may seem reassuring but we learn later in the story why it is both accurate and ominous. There are also nonverbal forms of irony, the most common of which is **dramatic irony,** in which a character holds a position or has an expectation that is reversed or fulfilled in an unexpected way. Knowing her husband's habit of drinking himself into unconsciousness, Elizabeth Bates expects him to be brought home like a log. How is her expectation fulfilled? She had also said bitterly, "But he needn't come rolling in here in his pit-dirt, for *I* won't wash him," and yet she does. Why is her determination altered? As you read through, or look back over "Odour of Chrysanthemums," watch for other reversed or unexpectedly fulfilled expectations.

Another, highly emphasized element of style is **imagery.** In its broadest sense imagery includes any sensory detail or evocation in a work. Note how much more imagery in that sense we find in "Fenstad's Mother" than in, say, "The Zebra Storyteller." Imagery in this broad sense, however, is so prevalent in literature that it would take exhaustive statistics to differentiate styles by counting the number of sensory elements per hundred or thousand words, categorizing the images as primarily visual, tactile, etc. In a more restricted sense imagery refers to figurative language (see Chapter 5 on symbols), particularly that which defines an abstraction or any emotional or psychological state with a sensory comparison. The opening paragraph of "Odour of Chrysanthemums" illustrates the broader definition of imagery, and this passage from later in the same story may represent the figurative sense: "Life with its smoky burning gone from him, had left him apart. . . . In her womb was ice of fear. . . ."

We might say that if an author's vision gives us his or her profile, the style gives us a fingerprint—though the fingerprint is unique and definitive, it is also harder to come by than a glimpse of a profile. Ultimately, however, vision and style are less distinguishable from each other than the profile-fingerprint image suggests. For vision and style, just like history and structure, do more than interact: they are inextricably fused or compounded. Let us look back at the Ford passage. He says this of "the gorse, which still flickered indistinctly in the raw afternoon" (though he misquotes it slightly and rather loosely calls it a phrase):

> . . .Good too, distinctly good. This is the just-sufficient observation of Nature that gives you, in a single phrase, landscape, time of day, weather, season.

Is this vision or style? The observation of Nature is clearly vision, but expressing that vision economically, tautly, is style. The two merge.

Whatever else this passage is, it is vintage, typical Lawrence. Perhaps it would take more than just these ten words, but surely in a paragraph or two we know we're in the fictional world that he perceived and that he embodied in his stories, novels, and poems in a language of his own created out of that language we share.

▼   ▼   ▼

D. H. LAWRENCE

Odour of Chrysanthemums

I

The small locomotive engine, Number 4, came clanking, stumbling down from Selston with seven full waggons. It appeared round the corner with loud threats of speed, but the colt that it startled from among the gorse, which still flickered indistinctly in the raw afternoon, outdistanced it at a canter. A woman, walking up the railway line to Underwood, drew back into the hedge, held her basket aside, and watched the footplate of the engine advancing. The trucks thumped heavily past, one by one, with slow inevitable movement, as she stood insignificantly trapped between the jolting black waggons and the hedge; then they curved away towards the coppice where the withered oak leaves dropped noiselessly, while the birds, pulling at the scarlet hips beside the track, made off into the dusk that had already crept into the spinney. In the open, the smoke from the engine sank and cleaved to the rough grass. The fields were dreary and forsaken, and in the marshy strip that led to the whimsey, a reedy pit-pond, the fowls had already abandoned their run among the alders, to roost in the tarred fowl-house. The pit-bank loomed up beyond the pond, flames like red sores licking its ashy sides, in the afternoon's stagnant light. Just beyond rose the tapering chimneys and the clumsy black headstocks of Brinsley Colliery. The two wheels were spinning fast up against the sky, and the winding-engine rapped out its little spasms. The miners were being turned up.

The engine whistled as it came into the wide bay of railway lines beside the colliery, where rows of trucks stood in harbour.

Miners, single, trailing and in groups, passed like shadows diverging home. At the edge of the ribbed level of sidings squat a low cottage, three steps down from the cinder track. A large bony vine clutched at the house, as if to claw down the tiled roof. Round the bricked yard grew a few wintry primroses. Beyond, the long garden sloped down to a bush-covered brook course. There were some twiggy apple trees, winter-crack trees, and ragged cabbages. Beside the path hung dishevelled pink chrysanthemums, like pink cloths hung on bushes. A woman came stooping out of the felt-covered fowl-house, half-way down the garden. She closed and padlocked the door, then drew herself erect, having brushed some bits from her white apron.

She was a tall woman of imperious mien, handsome, with definite black eyebrows. Her smooth black hair was parted exactly. For a few moments she stood steadily watching the miners as they passed along the railway: then she turned towards the brook course. Her face was calm and set, her mouth was closed with disillusionment. After a moment she called:

5 "John!" There was no answer. She waited, and then said distinctly:

"Where are you?"

"Here!" replied a child's sulky voice from among the bushes. The woman looked piercingly through the dusk.

"Are you at that brook?" she asked sternly.

For answer the child showed himself before the raspberry-canes that rose like whips. He was a small, sturdy boy of five. He stood quite still, defiantly.

10 "Oh!" said the mother, conciliated. "I thought you were down at that wet brook—and you remember what I told you—"

The boy did not move or answer.

"Come, come on in," she said more gently, "it's getting dark. There's your grandfather's engine coming down the line!"

The lad advanced slowly, with resentful, taciturn movement. He was dressed in trousers and waistcoat of cloth that was too thick and hard for the size of the garments. They were evidently cut down from a man's clothes.

As they went slowly towards the house he tore at the ragged wisps of chrysanthemums and dropped the petals in handfuls along the path.

"Don't do that—it does look nasty," said his mother. He refrained, and she, 15
suddenly pitiful, broke off a twig with three or four wan flowers and held them
against her face. When mother and son reached the yard her hand hesitated,
and instead of laying the flower aside, she pushed it in her apron-band. The
mother and son stood at the foot of the three steps looking across the bay of lines
at the passing home of the miners. The trundle of the small train was imminent.
Suddenly the engine loomed past the house and came to a stop opposite the
gate.

The engine-driver, a short man with round grey beard, leaned out of the cab
high above the woman.

"Have you got a cup of tea?" he said in a cheery, hearty fashion.[1]

It was her father. She went in, saying she would mash.[1] Directly, she
returned.

"I didn't come to see you on Sunday," began the little grey-bearded man.

"I didn't expect you," said his daughter. 20

The engine-driver winced; then, reassuming his cheery, airy manner, he
said:

"Oh, have you heard then? Well, and what do you think——?"

"I think it is soon enough," she replied.

At her brief censure the little man made an impatient gesture, and said coaxingly, yet with dangerous coldness:

"Well, what's a man to do? It's no sort of life for a man of my years, to sit at 25
my own hearth like a stranger. And if I'm going to marry again it may as well be
soon as late—what does it matter to anybody?"

The woman did not reply, but turned and went into the house. The man in
the engine-cab stood assertive, till she returned with a cup of tea and a piece of
bread and butter on a plate. She went up the steps and stood near the footplate
of the hissing engine.

"You needn't 'a' brought me bread an' butter," said her father. "But a cup of
tea"—he sipped appreciatively—"it's very nice." He sipped for a moment or two,
then: "I hear as Walter's got another bout on," he said.

"When hasn't he?" said the woman bitterly.

"I heered tell of him in the 'Lord Nelson'[2] braggin' as he was going to spend
that b—— afore he went: half a sovereign[3] that was."

"When?" asked the woman. 30

"A' Sat'day night—I know that's true."

"Very likely," she laughed bitterly. "He gives me twenty-three shillings."

"Aye, it's a nice thing, when a man can do nothing with his money but make
a beast of himself!" said the grey-whiskered man. The woman turned her head
away. Her father swallowed the last of his tea and handed her the cup.

"Aye," he sighed, wiping his mouth. "It's a settler, it is——"

---

1. Prepare (tea).   **2.** A public house, pub.   **3.** A sovereign was about half a week's wage; there
are 20 shillings (see below) to the pound.

35 He put his hand on the lever. The little engine strained and groaned, and the train rumbled towards the crossing. The woman again looked across the metals. Darkness was settling over the spaces of the railway and trucks: the miners, in grey sombre groups, were still passing home. The winding-engine pulsed hurriedly, with brief pauses. Elizabeth Bates looked at the dreary flow of men, then she went indoors. Her husband did not come.

The kitchen was small and full of firelight; red coals piled glowing up the chimney mouth. All the life of the room seemed in the white, warm hearth and the steel fender reflecting the red fire. The cloth was laid for tea; cups glinted in the shadows. At the back, where the lowest stairs protruded into the room, the boy sat struggling with a knife and a piece of white wood. He was almost hidden in the shadow. It was half-past four. They had but to await the father's coming to begin tea. As the mother watched her son's sullen little struggle with the wood, she saw herself in his silence and pertinacity; she saw the father in her child's indifference to all but himself. She seemed to be occupied by her husband. He had probably gone past his home, slunk past his own door, to drink before he came in, while his dinner spoiled and wasted in waiting. She glanced at the clock, then took the potatoes to strain them in the yard. The garden and fields beyond the brook were closed in uncertain darkness. When she rose with the saucepan, leaving the drain steaming into the night behind her, she saw the yellow lamps were lit along the high road that went up the hill away beyond the space of the railway lines and the field.

Then again she watched the men trooping home, fewer now and fewer.

Indoors the fire was sinking and the room was dark red. The woman put her saucepan on the hob, and set a batter pudding near the mouth of the oven. Then she stood unmoving. Directly, gratefully, came quick young steps to the door. Someone hung on the latch a moment, then a little girl entered and began pulling off her outdoor things, dragging a mass of curls, just ripening from gold to brown, over her eyes with her hat.

Her mother chid her for coming late from school, and said she would have to keep her at home the dark winter days.

40 "Why, mother, it's hardly a bit dark yet. The lamp's not lighted, and my father's not home."

"No, he isn't. But it's a quarter to five! Did you see anything of him?"

The child became serious. She looked at her mother with large, wistful blue eyes.

"No, mother, I've never seen him. Why? Has he come up an' gone past, to Old Brinsley? He hasn't, mother, 'cos I never saw him."

"He'd watch that," said the mother bitterly, "he'd take care as you didn't see him. But you may depend upon it, he's seated in the 'Prince o' Wales.' He wouldn't be this late."

45 The girl looked at her mother piteously.

"Let's have our teas, mother, should we?" said she.

The mother called John to table. She opened the door once more and looked out across the darkness of the lines. All was deserted: she could not hear the winding-engines.

"Perhaps," she said to herself, "he's stopped to get some ripping[4] done."

They sat down to tea. John, at the end of the table near the door, was almost lost in the darkness. Their faces were hidden from each other. The girl crouched against the fender slowly moving a thick piece of bread before the fire. The lad, his face a dusky mark on the shadow, sat watching her who was transfigured in the red glow.

"I do think it's beautiful to look in the fire," said the child.

50

"Do you?" said her mother. "Why?"

"It's so red, and full of little caves—and it feels so nice, and you can fair smell it."

"It'll want mending directly," replied her mother, "and then if your father comes he'll carry on and say there never is a fire when a man comes home sweating from the pit.—A public-house is always warm enough."

There was silence till the boy said complainingly: "Make haste, our Annie."

"Well, I am doing! I can't make the fire do it no faster, can I?"

55

"She keeps wafflin'[5] it about so's to make 'er slow," grumbled the boy.

"Don't have such an evil imagination, child," replied the mother.

Soon the room was busy in the darkness with the crisp sound of crunching. The mother ate very little. She drank her tea determinedly, and sat thinking. When she rose her anger was evident in the stern unbending of her head. She looked at the pudding in the fender, and broke out:

"It is a scandalous thing as a man can't even come home to his dinner! If it's crozzled[6] up to a cinder I don't see why I should care. Past his very door he goes to get to a public-house, and here I sit with his dinner waiting for him——"

She went out. As she dropped piece after piece of coal on the red fire, the shadows fell on the walls, till the room was almost in total darkness.

60

"I canna see," grumbled the invisible John. In spite of herself, the mother laughed.

"You know the way to your mouth," she said. She set the dustpan outside the door. When she came again like a shadow on the hearth, the lad repeated, complaining sulkily:

"I canna see."

"Good gracious!" cried the mother irritably, "you're as bad as your father if it's a bit dusk!"

Nevertheless she took a paper spill from a sheaf on the mantelpiece and proceeded to light the lamp that hung from the ceiling in the middle of the room. As she reached up, her figure displayed itself just rounding with maternity.

65

"Oh, mother——!" exclaimed the girl.

"What?" said the woman, suspended in the act of putting the lamp-glass over the flame. The copper reflector shone handsomely on her, as she stood with uplifted arm, turning to face her daughter:

"You've got a flower in your apron!" said the child, in a little rapture at this unusual event.

4. Coal-mining term for taking down the roof of an underground road in order to make it higher.
5. Waving.   6. Shriveled.

"Goodness me!" exclaimed the woman, relieved. "One would think the house was afire." She replaced the glass and waited a moment before turning up the wick. A pale shadow was seen floating vaguely on the floor.

70 "Let me smell!" said the child, still rapturously, coming forward and putting her face to her mother's waist.

"Go along, silly!" said the mother, turning up the lamp. The light revealed their suspense so that the woman felt it almost unbearable. Annie was still bending at her waist. Irritably, the mother took the flowers out from her apron-band.

"Oh, mother—don't take them out!" Annie cried, catching her hand and trying to replace the sprig.

"Such nonsense!" said the mother, turning away. The child put the pale chrysanthemums to her lips, murmuring:

"Don't they smell beautiful!"

75 Her mother gave a short laugh.

"No," she said, "not to me. It was chrysanthemums when I married him, and chrysanthemums when you were born, and the first time they ever brought him home drunk, he'd got brown chrysanthemums in his button-hole."

She looked at the children. Their eyes and their parted lips were wondering. The mother sat rocking in silence for some time. Then she looked at the clock.

"Twenty minutes to six!" In a tone of fine bitter carelessness she continued: "Eh, he'll not come now till they bring him. There he'll stick! But he needn't come rolling in here in his pit-dirt, for I won't wash him. He can lie on the floor—— Eh, what a fool I've been, what a fool! And this is what I came here for, to this dirty hole, rats and all, for him to slink past his very door. Twice last week—he's begun now——"

She silenced herself, and rose to clear the table.

80 While for an hour or more the children played, subduedly intent, fertile of imagination, united in fear of the mother's wrath, and in dread of their father's home-coming, Mrs. Bates sat in her rocking-chair making a "singlet" of thick cream-coloured flannel, which gave a dull wounded sound as she tore off the grey edge. She worked at her sewing with energy, listening to the children, and her anger wearied itself, lay down to rest, opening its eyes from time to time and steadily watching, its ears raised to listen. Sometimes even her anger quailed and shrank, and the mother suspended her sewing, tracing the footsteps that thudded along the sleepers outside; she would lift her head sharply to bid the children "hush," but she recovered herself in time, and the footsteps went past the gate, and the children were not flung out of their playworld.

But at last Annie sighed, and gave in. She glanced at her waggon of slippers, and loathed the game. She turned plaintively to her mother.

"Mother!"—but she was inarticulate.

John crept out like a frog from under the sofa. His mother glanced up.

"Yes," she said, "just look at those shirtsleeves!"

85 The boy held them out to survey them, saying nothing. Then somebody called in a hoarse voice away down the line, and suspense bristled in the room, till two people had gone by outside, talking.

"It is time for bed," said the mother.

"My father hasn't come," wailed Annie plaintively. But her mother was primed with courage.

"Never mind. They'll bring him when he does come—like a log." She meant there would be no scene. "And he may sleep on the floor till he wakes himself. I know he'll not go to work tomorrow after this!"

The children had their hands and faces wiped with a flannel.[7] They were very quiet. When they had put on their nightdresses, they said their prayers, the boy mumbling. The mother looked down at them, at the brown silken bush of intertwining curls in the nape of the girl's neck, at the little black head of the lad, and her heart burst with anger at their father who caused all three such distress. The children hid their faces in her skirts for comfort.

When Mrs. Bates came down, the room was strangely empty, with a tension of expectancy. She took up her sewing and stitched for some time without raising her head. Meantime her anger was tinged with fear.

II

The clock struck eight and she rose suddenly, dropping her sewing on her chair. She went to the stairfoot door, opened it, listening. Then she went out, locking the door behind her.

Something scuffled in the yard, and she started though she knew it was only the rats with which the place was overrun. The night was very dark. In the great bay of railway lines, bulked with trucks, there was no trace of light, only away back she could see a few yellow lamps at the pit-top, and the red smear of the burning pit-bank on the night. She hurried along the edge of the track, then, crossing the converging lines, came to the stile by the white gates, whence she emerged on the road. Then the fear which had led her shrank. People were walking up to New Brinsley; she saw the lights in the houses; twenty yards further on were the broad windows of the "Prince of Wales," very warm and bright, and the loud voices of men could be heard distinctly. What a fool she had been to imagine that anything had happened to him! He was merely drinking over there at the "Prince of Wales." She faltered. She had never yet been to fetch him, and she never would go. So she continued her walk towards the long straggling line of houses, standing blank on the highway. She entered a passage between the dwellings.

"Mr. Rigley?—Yes! Did you want him? No, he's not in at this minute."

The raw-boned woman leaned forward from her dark scullery and peered at the other, upon whom fell a dim light through the blind of the kitchen window.

"Is it Mrs. Bates?" she asked in a tone tinged with respect.

"Yes. I wondered if your Master was at home. Mine hasn't come yet."

" 'Asn't 'e! Oh, Jack's been 'ome an 'ad 'is dinner an' gone out. 'E's just gone for 'alf an hour afore bedtime. Did you call at the 'Prince of Wales'?"

"No——"

"No, you didn't like——! It's not very nice." The other woman was indulgent.

90

95

7. Washrag.

There was an awkward pause. "Jack never said nothink about—about your Mes-
ter," she said.

"No!—I expect he's stuck in there!"

Elizabeth Bates said this bitterly, and with recklessness. She knew that the
woman across the yard was standing at her door listening, but she did not care.
As she turned:

"Stop a minute! I'll just go an' ask Jack if 'e knows anythink," said Mrs.
Rigley.

"Oh, no—I wouldn't like to put—!"

"Yes, I will, if you will just step inside an' see as th' childer doesn't come
downstairs and set theirselves afire."

Elizabeth Bates, murmuring a remonstrance, stepped inside. The other
woman apologized for the state of the room.

The kitchen needed apology. There were little frocks and trousers and childish undergarments on the squab[8] and on the floor, and a litter of playthings
everywhere. On the black American cloth[9] of the table were pieces of bread and
cake, crusts, slops, and a teapot with cold tea.

"Eh, ours is just as bad," said Elizabeth Bates, looking at the woman, not at
the house. Mrs. Rigley put a shawl over her head and hurried out, saying:

"I shanna be a minute."

The other sat, noting with faint disapproval the general untidiness of the
room. Then she fell to counting the shoes of various sizes scattered over the
floor. There were twelve. She sighed and said to herself, "No wonder!"—glancing at the litter. There came the scratching of two pairs of feet on the yard, and
the Rigleys entered. Elizabeth Bates rose. Rigley was a big man, with very large
bones. His head looked particularly bony. Across his temple was a blue scar,
caused by a wound got in the pit, a wound in which the coal-dust remained
blue like tattooing.

"'Asna 'e come whoam yit?" asked the man, without any form of greeting,
but with deference and sympathy. "I couldna say wheer he is—'e's non ower
theer!"—he jerked his head to signify the "Prince of Wales."

"'E's 'appen[1] gone up to th' 'Yew,' " said Mrs. Rigley.

There was another pause. Rigley had evidently something to get off his
mind:

"Ah left 'im finishin' a stint," he began. "Loose-all[2] 'ad bin gone about ten
minutes when we com'n away, an' I shouted, 'Are ter comin', Walt?' an' 'e said
'Go on, Ah shanna be but a 'ef a minnit,' so we com'n ter th' bottom, me an'
Browers, thinkin' as 'e wor just behint, an' 'ud come up i' th' next bantle[3]——"

He stood perplexed, as if answering a charge of deserting his mate. Elizabeth
Bates, now again certain of disaster, hastened to reassure him:

"I expect 'e's gone up to th' 'Yew Tree,' as you say. It's not the first time. I've
fretted myself into a fever before now. He'll come home when they carry him."

"Ay, isn't it too bad!" deplored the other woman.

8. Sofa.   9. Enameled oilcloth.   1. Perhaps.   2. Signal to quit work and come to the surface.   3. An open seat or car of the lift or elevator that takes the miners to the surface.

"I'll just step up to Dick's an' see if 'e *is* theer," offered the man, afraid of appearing alarmed, afraid of taking liberties.

"Oh, I wouldn't think of bothering you that far," said Elizabeth Bates, with emphasis, but he knew she was glad of his offer.

As they stumbled up the entry, Elizabeth Bates heard Rigley's wife run across the yard and open her neighbour's door. At this, suddenly all the blood in her body seemed to switch away from her heart.

"Mind!" warned Rigley. "Ah've said many a time as Ah'd fill up them ruts in this entry, sumb'dy 'll be breakin' their legs yit."

She recovered herself and walked quickly along with the miner.

"I don't like leaving the children in bed, and nobody in the house," she said.

"No, you dunna!" he replied courteously. They were soon at the gate of the cottage.

"Well, I shanna be many minnits. Dunna you be frettin' now, 'e'll be all right," said the butty.[4]

"Thank you very much, Mr. Rigley," she replied.

"You're welcome!" he stammered, moving away. "I shanna be many minnits."

The house was quiet. Elizabeth Bates took off her hat and shawl, and rolled back the rug. When she had finished, she sat down. It was a few minutes past nine. She was startled by the rapid chuff of the winding-engine at the pit, and the sharp whirr of the brakes on the rope as it descended. Again she felt the painful sweep of her blood, and she put her hand to her side, saying aloud, "Good gracious!—it's only the nine o'clock deputy going down," rebuking herself.

She sat still, listening. Half an hour of this, and she was wearied out.

"What am I working up like this for?" she said pitiably to herself, "I s'll only be doing myself some damage."

She took out her sewing again.

At a quarter to ten there were footsteps. One person! She watched for the door to open. It was an elderly woman, in a black bonnet and a black woollen shawl—his mother. She was about sixty years old, pale, with blue eyes, and her face all wrinkled and lamentable. She shut the door and turned to her daughter-in-law peevishly.

"Eh, Lizzie, whatever shall we do, whatever shall we do!" she cried.

Elizabeth drew back a little, sharply.

"What is it, mother?" she said.

The elder woman seated herself on the sofa.

"I don't know, child, I can't tell you!"—she shook her head slowly. Elizabeth sat watching her, anxious and vexed.

"I don't know," replied the grandmother, sighing very deeply. "There's no end to my troubles, there isn't. The things I've gone through, I'm sure it's enough ——!" She wept without wiping her eyes, the tears running.

"But, mother," interrupted Elizabeth, "what do you mean? What is it?"

4. Buddy, fellow worker.

The grandmother slowly wiped her eyes. The fountains of her tears were stopped by Elizabeth's directness. She wiped her eyes slowly.

"Poor child! Eh, you poor thing!" she moaned. "I don't know what we're going to do, I don't—and you as you are—it's a thing, it is indeed!"

Elizabeth waited.

"Is he dead?" she asked, and at the words her heart swung violently, though she felt a slight flush of shame at the ultimate extravagance of the question. Her words sufficiently frightened the old lady, almost brought her to herself.

"Don't say so, Elizabeth! We'll hope it's not as bad as that; no, may the Lord spare us that, Elizabeth. Jack Rigley came just as I was sittin' down to a glass afore going to bed, an' 'e said, ' 'Appen you'll go down th' line, Mrs. Bates. Walt's had an accident. 'Appen you'll go an' sit wi' 'er till we can get him home.' I hadn't time to ask him a word afore he was gone. An' I put my bonnet on an' come straight down, Lizzie. I thought to myself, 'Eh, that poor blessed child, if anybody should come an' tell her of a sudden, there's no knowin'; what'll 'appen to 'er.' You mustn't let it upset you, Lizzie—or you know what to expect. How long is it, six months—or is it five, Lizzie? Ay!"—the old woman shook her head—"time slips on, it slips on! Ay!"

Elizabeth's thoughts were busy elsewhere. If he was killed—would she be able to manage on the little pension and what she could earn?—she counted up rapidly. If he was hurt—they wouldn't take him to the hospital—how tiresome he would be to nurse!—but perhaps she'd be able to get him away from the drink and his hateful ways. She would—while he was ill. The tears offered to come to her eyes at the picture. But what sentimental luxury was this she was beginning?—She turned to consider the children. At any rate she was absolutely necessary for them. They were her business.

"Ay!" repeated the old woman, "it seems but a week or two since he brought me his first wages. Ay—he was a good lad, Elizabeth, he was, in his way. I don't know why he got to be such a trouble, I don't. He was a happy lad at home, only full of spirits. But there's no mistake he's been a handful of trouble, he has! I hope the Lord'll spare him to mend his ways. I hope so, I hope so. You've had a sight o' trouble with him, Elizabeth, you have indeed. But he was a jolly enough lad wi' me, he was, I can assure you. I don't know how it is. . . ."

The old woman continued to muse aloud, a monotonous irritating sound, while Elizabeth thought concentratedly, startled once, when she heard the winding-engine chuff quickly, and the brakes skirr with a shriek. Then she heard the engine more slowly, and the brakes made no sound. The old woman did not notice. Elizabeth waited in suspense. The mother-in-law talked, with lapses into silence.

"But he wasn't your son, Lizzie, an' it makes a difference. Whatever he was, I remember him when he was little, an' I learned to understand him and to make allowances. You've got to make allowances for them—"

It was half-past ten, and the old woman was saying: "But it's trouble from beginning to end; you're never too old for trouble, never too old for that——" when the gate banged back, and there were heavy feet on the steps.

"I'll go, Lizzie, let me go," cried the old woman, rising. But Elizabeth was at the door. It was a man in pit-clothes.

"They're bringin' 'im, Missis," he said. Elizabeth's heart halted a moment. Then it surged on again, almost suffocating her.

"Is he—is it bad?" she asked.

The man turned away, looking at the darkness:

"The doctor says 'e'd been dead hours. 'E saw 'im i' th' lamp-cabin."

The old woman, who stood just behind Elizabeth, dropped into a chair and folded her hands, crying: "Oh, my boy, my boy!"

"Hush!" said Elizabeth, with a sharp twitch of a frown. "Be still, mother, don't waken th' children: I wouldn't have them down for anything!"

The old woman moaned softly, rocking herself. The man was drawing away. Elizabeth took a step forward.

"How was it?" she asked.

"Well, I couldn't say for sure," the man replied, very ill at ease. " 'E wor finishin' a stint an' th' butties 'ad gone, an' a lot o' stuff come down atop 'n 'im."

"And crushed him?" cried the widow, with a shudder.

"No," said the man, "it fell at th' back of 'im. 'E wor under th' face, an' it niver touched 'im. It shut 'im in. It seems 'e wor smothered."

Elizabeth shrank back. She heard the old woman behind her cry:

"What?—what did 'e say it was?"

The man replied, more loudly: " 'E wor smothered!"

Then the old woman wailed aloud, and this relieved Elizabeth.

"Oh, mother," she said, putting her hands on the old woman, "don't waken th' children, don't waken th' children."

She wept a little, unknowing, while the old mother rocked herself and moaned. Elizabeth remembered that they were bringing him home, and she must be ready. "They'll lay him in the parlour," she said to herself, standing a moment pale and perplexed.

Then she lighted a candle and went into the tiny room. The air was cold and damp, but she could not make a fire, there was no fireplace. She set down the candle and looked round. The candlelight glittered on the lustre-glasses,[5] on the two vases that held some of the pink chrysanthemums, and on the dark mahogany. There was a cold, deathly smell of chrysanthemums in the room. Elizabeth stood looking at the flowers. She turned away, and calculated whether there would be room to lay him on the floor, between the couch and the chiffonier. She pushed the chairs aside. There would be room to lay him down and to step round him. Then she fetched the old red tablecloth, and another old cloth, spreading them down to save her bit of carpet. She shivered on leaving the parlour; so, from the dresser-drawer she took a clean shirt and put it at the fire to air. All the time her mother-in-law was rocking herself in the chair and moaning.

5. Glass pendants around the edge of an ornamental vase.

"You'll have to move from there, mother," said Elizabeth. "They'll be bringing him in. Come in the rocker."

The old mother rose mechanically, and seated herself by the fire, continuing
to lament. Elizabeth went into the pantry for another candle, and there, in the
little penthouse[6] under the naked tiles, she heard them coming. She stood still
in the pantry doorway, listening. She heard them pass the end of the house,
and come awkwardly down the three steps, a jumble of shuffling footsteps and
muttering voices. The old woman was silent. The men were in the yard.

170   Then Elizabeth heard Matthews, the manager of the pit, say: "You go in
first, Jim. Mind!"

The door came open, and the two women saw a collier backing into the
room, holding one end of a stretcher, on which they could see the nailed pit-
boots of the dead man. The two carriers halted, the man at the head stooping to
the lintel of the door.

"Wheer will you have him?" asked the manager, a short, white-bearded man.

Elizabeth roused herself and came from the pantry carrying the unlighted
candle.

"In the parlour," she said.

175   "In there, Jim!" pointed the manager, and the carriers backed round into the
tiny room. The coat with which they had covered the body fell off as they awkwardly turned through the two doorways, and the women saw their man, naked
to the waist, lying stripped for work. The old woman began to moan in a low
voice of horror.

"Lay th' stretcher at th' side," snapped the manager, "an' put 'im on th'
cloths. Mind now, mind! Look you now——!"

One of the men had knocked off a vase of chrysanthemums. He stared awkwardly, then they set down the stretcher. Elizabeth did not look at her husband.
As soon as she could get in the room, she went and picked up the broken vase
and the flowers.

"Wait a minute!" she said.

The three men waited in silence while she mopped up the water with a
duster.

180   "Eh, what a job, what a job, to be sure!" the manager was saying, rubbing
his brow with trouble and perplexity. "Never knew such a thing in my life,
never! He'd no business to ha' been left. I never knew such a thing in my life!
Fell over him clean as a whistle, an' shut him in. Not four foot of space, there
wasn't—yet it scarce bruised him."

He looked down at the dead man, lying prone, half naked, all grimed with
coal-dust.

"''Sphyxiated,' the doctor said. It *is* the most terrible job I've ever known.
Seems as if it was done o' purpose. Clean over him, an' shut 'im in, like a
mouse-trap"—he made a sharp, descending gesture with his hand.

The colliers standing by jerked aside their heads in hopeless comment.

The horror of the thing bristled upon them all.

6. Structure, usually with a sloping roof, attached to house.

Then they heard the girl's voice upstairs calling shrilly: "Mother, mother— 185
who is it? Mother, who is it?"

Elizabeth hurried to the foot of the stairs and opened the door:

"Go to sleep!" she commanded sharply. "What are you shouting about? Go
to sleep at once—there's nothing——"

Then she began to mount the stairs. They could hear her on the boards, and
on the plaster floor of the little bedroom. They could hear her distinctly:

"What's the matter now?—what's the matter with you, silly thing?"—her
voice was much agitated, with an unreal gentleness.

"I thought it was some men come," said the plaintive voice of the child. 190
"Has he come?"

"Yes, they've brought him. There's nothing to make a fuss about. Go to sleep
now, like a good child."

They could hear her voice in the bedroom, they waited whilst she covered
the children under the bedclothes.

"Is he drunk?" asked the girl, timidly, faintly.

"No! No—he's not! He's—he's asleep."

"Is he asleep downstairs?" 195

"Yes—and don't make a noise."

There was silence for a moment, then the men heard the frightened child
again:

"What's that noise?"

"It's nothing, I tell you, what are you bothering for?"

The noise was the grandmother moaning. She was oblivious of everything, 200
sitting on her chair rocking and moaning. The manager put his hand on her
arm and bade her "Sh-sh!!"

The old woman opened her eyes and looked at him. She was shocked by
this interruption, and seemed to wonder.

"What time is it?"—the plaintive thin voice of the child, sinking back unhappily into sleep, asked this last question.

"Ten o'clock," answered the mother more softly. Then she must have bent
down and kissed the children.

Matthews beckoned to the men to come away. They put on their caps, and
took up the stretcher. Stepping over the body, they tiptoed out of the house.
None of them spoke till they were far from the wakeful children.

When Elizabeth came down she found her mother alone on the parlour 205
floor, leaning over the dead man, the tears dropping on him.

"We must lay him out," the wife said. She put on the kettle, then returning
knelt at the feet, and began to unfasten the knotted leather laces. The room was
clammy and dim with only one candle, so that she had to bend her face almost
to the floor. At last she got off the heavy boots and put them away.

"You must help me now," she whispered to the old woman. Together they
stripped the man.

When they arose, saw him lying in the naïve dignity of death, the women
stood arrested in fear and respect. For a few moments they remained still, looking down, the old mother whimpering. Elizabeth felt countermanded. She saw

him, how utterly inviolable he lay in himself. She had nothing to do with him. She could not accept it. Stooping, she laid her hand on him, in claim. He was still warm, for the mine was hot where he had died. His mother had his face between her hands, and was murmuring incoherently. The old tears fell in succession as drops from wet leaves; the mother was not weeping, merely her tears flowed. Elizabeth embraced the body of her husband, with cheek and lips. She seemed to be listening, inquiring, trying to get some connection. But she could not. She was driven away. He was impregnable.

She rose, went into the kitchen, where she poured warm water into a bowl, brought soap and flannel and a soft towel.

210   "I must wash him," she said.

Then the old mother rose stiffly, and watched Elizabeth as she carefully washed his face, carefully brushing the big blonde moustache from his mouth with the flannel. She was afraid with a bottomless fear, so she ministered to him. The old woman, jealous, said:

"Let me wipe him!"—and she kneeled on the other side drying slowly as Elizabeth washed, her big black bonnet sometimes brushing the dark head of her daughter. They worked thus in silence for a long time. They never forgot it was death, and the touch of the man's dead body gave them strange emotions, different in each of the women; a great dread possessed them both, the mother felt the lie was given to her womb, she was denied; the wife felt the utter isolation of the human soul, the child within her was a weight apart from her.

At last it was finished. He was a man of handsome body, and his face showed no traces of drink. He was blonde, full-fleshed, with fine limbs. But he was dead.

"Bless him," whispered his mother, looking always at his face, and speaking out of sheer terror. "Dear lad—bless him!" She spoke in a faint sibilant ecstasy of fear and mother love.

215   Elizabeth sank down again to the floor, and put her face against his neck, and trembled and shuddered. But she had to draw away again. He was dead, and her living flesh had no place against his. A great dread and weariness held her: she was so unavailing. Her life was gone like this.

"White as milk he is, clear as a twelve-month baby, bless him, the darling!" the old mother murmured to herself. "Not a mark on him, clear and clean and white, beautiful as ever a child was made," she murmured with pride. Elizabeth kept her face hidden.

"He went peaceful, Lizzie—peaceful as sleep. Isn't he beautiful, the lamb? Ay—he must ha' made his peace, Lizzie. 'Appen he made it all right, Lizzie, shut in there. He'd have time. He wouldn't look like this if he hadn't made his peace. The lamb, the dear lamb. Eh, but he had a hearty laugh. I loved to hear it. He had the heartiest laugh, Lizzie, as a lad——"

Elizabeth looked up. The man's mouth was fallen back, slightly open under the cover of the moustache. The eyes, half shut, did not show glazed in the obscurity. Life with its smoky burning gone from him, had left him apart and utterly alien to her. And she knew what a stranger he was to her. In her womb was ice of fear, because of this separate stranger with whom she had been living as one flesh. Was this what it all meant—utter, intact separateness, obscured by heat of living? In dread she turned her face away. The fact was too deadly. There had been nothing between them, and yet they had come together, exchanging their nakedness repeatedly. Each time he had taken her, they had been two isolated beings, far apart as now. He was no more responsible than she. The child was like ice in her womb. For as she looked at the dead man, her mind, cold and detached, said clearly: "Who am I? What have I been doing? I have been fighting a husband who did not exist. *He* existed all the time. What wrong have I done? What was that I have been living with? There lies the reality, this man."—And her soul died in her for fear: she knew she had never seen him, he had never seen her, they had met in the dark and had fought in the dark, not knowing whom they met nor whom they fought. And now she saw, and turned silent in seeing. For she had been wrong. She had said he was something he was not; she had felt familiar with him. Whereas he was apart all the while, living as she never lived, feeling as she never felt.

In fear and shame she looked at his naked body, that she had known falsely. And he was the father of her children. Her soul was torn from her body and stood apart. She looked at his naked body and was ashamed, as if she had denied it. After all, it was itself. It seemed awful to her. She looked at his face, and she turned her own face to the wall. For his look was other than hers, his way was not her way. She had denied him what he was—she saw it now. She had refused him as himself.—And this had been her life, and his life.—She was grateful to death, which restored the truth. And she knew she was not dead.

And all the while her heart was bursting with grief and pity for him. What had he suffered? What stretch of horror for this helpless man! She was rigid with agony. She had not been able to help him. He had been cruelly injured, this naked man, this other being, and she could make no reparation. There were the children—but the children belonged to life. This dead man had nothing to do with them. He and she were only channels through which life had flowed to issue in the children. She was a mother—but how awful she knew it now to have been a wife. And he, dead now, how awful he must have felt it to be a husband. She felt that in her next world he would be a stranger to her. If they met there, in the beyond, they would only be ashamed of what had been before. The children had come, for some mysterious reason, out of both of them. But the children did not unite them. Now he was dead, she knew how eternally he was apart from her, how eternally he had nothing more to do with her. She saw this episode of her life closed. They had denied each other in life. Now he had withdrawn. An anguish came over her. It was finished then: it had become hopeless between them long before he died. Yet he had been her husband. But how little!

"Have you got his shirt, 'Lizabeth?"

Elizabeth turned without answering, though she strove to weep and behave as her mother-in-law expected. But she could not, she was silenced. She went into the kitchen and returned with the garment.

"It is aired," she said, grasping the cotton shirt here and there to try. She was almost ashamed to handle him; what right had she or anyone to lay hands on him; but her touch was humble on his body. It was hard work to clothe him.

220

He was so heavy and inert. A terrible dread gripped her all the while: that he could be so heavy and utterly inert, unresponsive, apart. The horror of the distance between them was almost too much for her—it was so infinite a gap she must look across.

At last it was finished. They covered him with a sheet and left him lying, with his face bound. And she fastened the door of the little parlour, lest the children should see what was lying there. Then, with peace sunk heavy on her heart, she went about making tidy the kitchen. She knew she submitted to life, which was her immediate master. But from death, her ultimate master, she winced with fear and shame.

1914

D. H. LAWRENCE

The Rocking-Horse Winner

There was a woman who was beautiful, who started with all the advantages, yet she had no luck. She married for love, and the love turned to dust. She had bonny children, yet she felt they had been thrust upon her, and she could not love them. They looked at her coldly, as if they were finding fault with her. And hurriedly she felt she must cover up some fault in herself. Yet what it was that she must cover up she never knew. Nevertheless, when her children were present, she always felt the centre of her heart go hard. This troubled her, and in her manner she was all the more gentle and anxious for her children, as if she loved them very much. Only she herself knew that at the centre of her heart was a hard little place that could not feel love, no, not for anybody. Everybody else said of her: "She is such a good mother. She adores her children." Only she herself, and her children themselves, knew it was not so. They read it in each other's eyes.

There were a boy and two little girls. They lived in a pleasant house, with a garden, and they had discreet servants, and felt themselves superior to anyone in the neighbourhood.

Although they lived in style, they felt always an anxiety in the house. There was never enough money. The mother had a small income, and the father had a small income, but not nearly enough for the social position which they had to keep up. The father went in to town to some office. But though he had good prospects, these prospects never materialized. There was always the grinding sense of the shortage of money, though the style was always kept up.

At last the mother said: "I will see if *I* can't make something." But she did not know where to begin. She racked her brains, and tried this thing and the other, but could not find anything successful. The failure made deep lines come into her face. Her children were growing up, they would have to go to school. There must be more money, there must be more money. The father, who was always very handsome and expensive in his tastes, seemed as if he never *would* be able to do anything worth doing. And the mother, who had a great belief in herself, did not succeed any better, and her tastes were just as expensive.

And so the house came to be haunted by the unspoken phrase: *There must be more money! There must be more money!* The children could hear it all the time, though nobody said it aloud. They heard it at Christmas, when the expensive and splendid toys filled the nursery. Behind the shining modern rocking-horse, behind the smart doll's-house, a voice would start whispering: "There *must* be more money! There *must* be more money!" And the children would stop playing, to listen for a moment. They would look into each other's eyes, to see if they had all heard. And each one saw in the eyes of the other two that they too had heard. "There *must* be more money! There *must* be more money!"

It came whispering from the springs of the still-swaying rocking-horse, and even the horse, bending his wooden, champing head, heard it. The big doll, sitting so pink and smirking in her new pram,[1] could hear it quite plainly, and seemed to be smirking all the more self-consciously because of it. The foolish puppy, too, that took the place of the teddy-bear, he was looking so extraordinarily foolish for no other reason but that he heard the secret whisper all over the house: "There *must* be more money!"

Yet nobody ever said it aloud. The whisper was everywhere, and therefore no one spoke it. Just as no one ever says: "We are breathing!" in spite of the fact that breath is coming and going all the time.

"Mother," said the boy Paul one day, "why don't we keep a car of our own? Why do we always use uncle's, or else a taxi?"

"Because we're the poor members of the family," said the mother.

"But why *are* we, mother?"

"Well—I suppose," she said slowly and bitterly, "it's because your father has no luck."

The boy was silent for some time.

"Is luck money, mother?" he asked rather timidly.

"No, Paul. Not quite. It's what causes you to have money."

"Oh!" said Paul vaguely. "I thought when Uncle Oscar said *filthy lucker*, it meant money."

"*Filthy lucre* does mean money," said the mother. "But it's lucre, not luck."

"Oh!" said the boy. "Then what *is* luck, mother?"

"It's what causes you to have money. If you're lucky you have money. That's why it's better to be born lucky than rich. If you're rich, you may lose your money. But if you're lucky, you will always get more money."

"Oh! Will you? And is father not lucky?"

"Very unlucky, I should say," she said bitterly.

The boy watched her with unsure eyes.

"Why?" he asked.

"I don't know. Nobody ever knows why one person is lucky and another unlucky."

"Don't they? Nobody at all? Does *nobody* know?"

"Perhaps God. But He never tells."

---

1. Baby carriage.

"He ought to, then. And aren't you lucky either, mother?"

"I can't be, if I married an unlucky husband."

"But by yourself, aren't you?"

"I used to think I was, before I married. Now I think I am very unlucky indeed."

30 "Why?"

"Well—never mind! Perhaps I'm not really," she said.

The child looked at her, to see if she meant it. But he saw, by the lines of her mouth, that she was only trying to hide something from him.

"Well, anyhow," he said stoutly, "I'm a lucky person."

"Why?" said his mother, with a sudden laugh.

35 He stared at her. He didn't even know why he had said it.

"God told me," he asserted, brazening it out.

"I hope He did, dear!" she said, again with a laugh, but rather bitter.

"He did, mother!"

"Excellent!" said the mother, using one of her husband's exclamations.

40 The boy saw she did not believe him; or, rather, that she paid no attention to his assertion. This angered him somewhat, and made him want to compel her attention.

He went off by himself, vaguely, in a childish way, seeking for the clue to "luck." Absorbed, taking no heed of other people, he went about with a sort of stealth, seeking inwardly for luck. He wanted luck, he wanted it, he wanted it. When the two girls were playing dolls in the nursery, he would sit on his big rocking-horse, charging madly into space, with a frenzy that made the little girls peer at him uneasily. Wildly the horse careered, the waving dark hair of the boy tossed, his eyes had a strange glare in them. The little girls dared not speak to him.

When he had ridden to the end of his mad little journey, he climbed down and stood in front of his rocking-horse, staring fixedly into its lowered face. Its red mouth was slightly open, its big eye was wide and glassy-bright.

"Now!" he would silently command the snorting steed. "Now, take me to where there is luck! Now take me!"

And he would slash the horse on the neck with the little whip he had asked Uncle Oscar for. He *knew* the horse could take him to where there was luck, if only he forced it. So he would mount again, and start on his furious ride, hoping at last to get there. He knew he could get there.

45 "You'll break your horse, Paul!" said the nurse.

"He's always riding like that! I wish he'd leave off!" said his elder sister Joan.

But he only glared down on them in silence. Nurse gave him up. She could make nothing of him. Anyhow he was growing beyond her.

One day his mother and his Uncle Oscar came in when he was on one of his furious rides. He did not speak to them.

"Hallo, you young jockey! Riding a winner?" said his uncle.

50 "Aren't you growing too big for a rocking-horse? You're not a very little boy any longer, you know," said his mother.

But Paul only gave a blue glare from his big, rather close-set eyes. He would speak to nobody when he was in full tilt. His mother watched him with an anxious expression on her face.

At last he suddenly stopped forcing his horse into the mechanical gallop, and slid down.

"Well, I got there!" he announced fiercely, his blue eyes still flaring, and his sturdy long legs straddling apart.

"Where did you get to?" asked his mother.

"Where I wanted to go," he flared back at her.

"That's right, son!" said Uncle Oscar. "Don't you stop till you get there. What's the horse's name?"

"He doesn't have a name," said the boy.

"Gets on without all right?" asked the uncle.

"Well, he has different names. He was called Sansovino last week."

"Sansovino, eh? Won the Ascot.[2] How did you know his name?"

"He always talks about horse-races with Bassett," said Joan.

The uncle was delighted to find that his small nephew was posted with all the racing news. Bassett, the young gardener, who had been wounded in the left foot in the war[3] and had got his present job through Oscar Cresswell, whose batman he had been, was a perfect blade of the "turf."[4] He lived in the racing events, and the small boy lived with him.

Oscar Cresswell got it all from Bassett.

"Master Paul comes and asks me, so I can't do more than tell him, sir," said Bassett, his face terribly serious, as if he were speaking of religious matters.

"And does he ever put anything on a horse he fancies?"

"Well—I don't want to give him away—he's a young sport, a fine sport, sir. Would you mind asking him himself? He sort of takes a pleasure in it, and perhaps he'd feel I was giving him away, sir, if you don't mind."

Bassett was serious as a church.

The uncle went back to his nephew and took him off for a ride in the car.

"Say, Paul, old man, do you ever put anything on a horse?" the uncle asked.

The boy watched the handsome man closely.

"Why, do you think I oughtn't to?" he parried.

"Not a bit of it! I thought perhaps you might give me a tip for the Lincoln."

The car sped on into the country, going down to Uncle Oscar's place in Hampshire.

"Honour bright?" said the nephew.

"Honour bright, son!" said the uncle.

"Well, then, Daffodil."

"Daffodil! I doubt it, sonny. What about Mirza?"

"I only know the winner," said the boy. "That's Daffodil."

"Daffodil, eh?"

2. A race run at a course of that name in Berkshire. Other races mentioned in the story are Lincolnshire Handicap, then run at Lincoln Downs; the St. Leger Stakes, run at Doncaster; the Grand National Steeplechase, run at Aintree, the most famous steeplechase in the world; the famous Derby, a mile-and-a-half race for three-year-olds run at Epsom Downs.   3. World War I, 1914–18.   4. Dashing young horseplayer. *Batman:* British officer's orderly.

80 There was a pause. Daffodil was an obscure horse comparatively.

"Uncle!"

"Yes, son?"

"You won't let it go any further, will you? I promised Bassett."

"Bassett be damned, old man! What's he got to do with it?"

85 "We're partners. We've been partners from the first. Uncle, he lent me my first five shillings, which I lost. I promised him, honour bright, it was only between me and him; only you gave me that ten-shilling note I started winning with, so I thought you were lucky. You won't let it go any further, will you?"

The boy gazed at his uncle from those big, hot, blue eyes, set rather close together. The uncle stirred and laughed uneasily.

"Right you are, son! I'll keep your tip private. Daffodil, eh? How much are you putting on him?"

"All except twenty pounds," said the boy. "I keep that in reserve."

The uncle thought it a good joke.

90 "You keep twenty pounds in reserve, do you, you young romancer? What are you betting, then?"

"I'm betting three hundred," said the boy, gravely. "But it's between you and me, Uncle Oscar! Honour bright?"

The uncle burst into a roar of laughter.

"It's between you and me all right, you young Nat Gould,[5] he said, laughing. "But where's your three hundred?"

"Bassett keeps it for me. We're partners."

95 "You are, are you! And what is Bassett putting on Daffodil?"

"He won't go quite as high as I do, I expect. Perhaps he'll go a hundred and fifty."

"What, pennies?" laughed the uncle.

"Pounds," said the child, with a surprised look at his uncle. "Bassett keeps a bigger reserve than I do."

Between wonder and amusement Uncle Oscar was silent. He pursued the matter no further, but he determined to take his nephew with him to the Lincoln races.

100 "Now, son," he said, "I'm putting twenty on Mirza, and I'll put five for you on any horse you fancy. What's your pick?"

"Daffodil, uncle."

"No, not the fiver on Daffodil!"

"I should if it was my own fiver," said the child.

"Good! Good! Right you are! A fiver for me and a fiver for you on Daffodil."

105 The child had never been to a race-meeting before, and his eyes were blue fire. He pursed his mouth tight, and watched. A Frenchman just in front had put his money on Lancelot. Wild with excitement, he flayed his arms up and down, yelling "*Lancelot! Lancelot!*" in his French accent.

Daffodil came in first, Lancelot second, Mirza third. The child, flushed and

5. Nathaniel Gould (1857–1919), novelist and journalist whose writings in both genres concerned horse-racing.

with eyes blazing, was curiously serene. His uncle brought him four five-pound notes, four to one.

"What am I to do with these?" he cried, waving them before the boy's eyes.

"I suppose we'll talk to Bassett," said the boy. "I expect I have fifteen hundred now; and twenty in reserve; and this twenty."

His uncle studied him for some moments.

"Look here, son!" he said. "You're not serious about Bassett and that fifteen hundred, are you?"

"Yes, I am. But it's between you and me, uncle. Honour bright!"

"Honour bright all right, son! But I must talk to Bassett."

"If you'd like to be a partner, uncle, with Bassett and me, we could all be partners. Only, you'd have to promise, honour bright, uncle, not to let it go beyond us three. Bassett and I are lucky, and you must be lucky, because it was your ten shillings I started winning with. . . ."

Uncle Oscar took both Bassett and Paul into Richmond Park for an afternoon, and there they talked.

"It's like this, you see, sir," Bassett said. "Master Paul would get me talking about racing events, spinning yarns, you know, sir. And he was always keen on knowing if I'd made or if I'd lost. It's about a year since, now, that I put five shillings on Blush of Dawn for him—and we lost. Then the luck turned, with the ten shillings he had from you, that we put on Singhalese. And since that time, it's been pretty steady, all things considering. What do you say, Master Paul?"

"We're all right when we're sure," said Paul. "It's when we're not quite sure that we go down."

"Oh, but we're careful then," said Bassett.

"But when are you *sure*?" smiled Uncle Oscar.

"It's Master Paul, sir," said Bassett, in a secret, religious voice. "It's as if he had it from heaven. Like Daffodil, now, for the Lincoln. That was as sure as eggs."

"Did you put anything on Daffodil?" asked Oscar Cresswell.

"Yes, sir. I made my bit."

"And my nephew?"

Bassett was obstinately silent, looking at Paul.

"I made twelve hundred, didn't I, Bassett? I told uncle I was putting three hundred on Daffodil."

"That's right," said Bassett, nodding.

"But where's the money?" asked the uncle.

"I keep it safe locked up, sir. Master Paul he can have it any minute he likes to ask for it."

"What, fifteen hundred pounds?"

"And twenty! And *forty*, that is, with the twenty he made on the course."

"It's amazing!" said the uncle.

"If Master Paul offers you to be partners, sir, I would, if I were you; if you'll excuse me," said Bassett.

Oscar Cresswell thought about it.

"I'll see the money," he said.

They drove home again, and sure enough, Bassett came round to the garden-house with fifteen hundred pounds in notes. The twenty pounds reserve was left with Joe Glee, in the Turf Commission deposit.

135 "You see, it's all right, uncle, when I'm *sure!* Then we go strong, for all we're worth. Don't we, Bassett?"

"We do that, Master Paul."

"And when are you sure?" said the uncle, laughing.

"Oh, well, sometimes I'm *absolutely* sure, like about Daffodil," said the boy; "and sometimes I have an idea; and sometimes I haven't even an idea, have I, Bassett? Then we're careful, because we mostly go down."

"You do, do you! And when you're sure, like about Daffodil, what makes you sure, sonny?"

140 "Oh, well, I don't know," said the boy uneasily. "I'm sure, you know, uncle; that's all."

"It's as if he had it from heaven, sir," Bassett reiterated.

"I should say so!" said the uncle.

But he became a partner. And when the Leger was coming on, Paul was "sure" about Lively Spark, which was a quite inconsiderable horse. The boy insisted on putting a thousand on the horse, Bassett went for five hundred, and Oscar Cresswell two hundred. Lively Spark came in first, and the betting had been ten to one against him. Paul had made ten thousand.

"You see," he said, "I was absolutely sure of him."

145 Even Oscar Cresswell had cleared two thousand.

"Look here, son," he said, "this sort of thing makes me nervous."

"It needn't, uncle! Perhaps I shan't be sure again for a long time."

"But what are you going to do with your money?" asked the uncle.

"Of course," said the boy, "I started it for mother. She said she had no luck, because father is unlucky, so I thought if I was lucky, it might stop whispering."

150 "What might stop whispering?"

"Our house. I *hate* our house for whispering."

"What does it whisper?"

"Why—why"—the boy fidgeted—"why, I don't know. But it's always short of money, you know, uncle."

"I know it, son, I know it."

155 "You know people send mother writs, don't you, uncle?"

"I'm afraid I do," said the uncle.

"And then the house whispers, like people laughing at you behind your back. It's awful, that is! I thought if I was lucky . . ."

"You might stop it," added the uncle.

The boy watched him with big blue eyes, that had an uncanny cold fire in them, and he said never a word.

160 "Well, then!" said the uncle. "What are we doing?"

"I shouldn't like mother to know I was lucky," said the boy.

"Why not, son?"

"She'd stop me."

"I don't think she would."

"Oh!"—and the boy writhed in an odd way—"I *don't* want her to know, uncle." 165

"All right, son! We'll manage it without her knowing."

They managed it very easily. Paul, at the other's suggestion, handed over five thousand pounds to his uncle, who deposited it with the family lawyer, who was then to inform Paul's mother that a relative had put five thousand pounds into his hands, which sum was to be paid out a thousand pounds at a time, on the mother's birthday, for the next five years.

"So she'll have a birthday present of a thousand pounds for five successive years," said Uncle Oscar. "I hope it won't make it all the harder for her later."

Paul's mother had her birthday in November. The house had been "whispering" worse than ever lately, and, even in spite of his luck, Paul could not bear up against it. He was very anxious to see the effect of the birthday letter, telling his mother about the thousand pounds.

When there were no visitors, Paul now took his meals with his parents, as he 170 was beyond the nursery control. His mother went into town nearly every day. She had discovered that she had an odd knack of sketching furs and dress materials, so she worked secretly in the studio of a friend who was the chief "artist" for the leading drapers. She drew the figures of ladies in furs and ladies in silk and sequins for the newspaper advertisements. This young woman artist earned several thousand pounds a year, but Paul's mother only made several hundreds, and she was again dissatisfied. She so wanted to be first in something, and she did not succeed, even in making sketches for drapery advertisements.

She was down to breakfast on the morning of her birthday. Paul watched her face as she read her letters. He knew the lawyer's letter. As his mother read it, her face hardened and became more expressionless. Than a cold, determined look came on her mouth. She hid the letter under the pile of others, and said not a word about it.

"Didn't you have anything nice in the post for your birthday, mother?" said Paul.

"Quite moderately nice," she said, her voice cold and absent.

She went away to town without saying more.

But in the afternoon Uncle Oscar appeared. He said Paul's mother had had 175 a long interview with the lawyer, asking if the whole five thousand could not be advanced at once, as she was in debt.

"What do you think, uncle?" said the boy.

"I leave it to you, son."

"Oh, let her have it, then! We can get some more with the other," said the boy.

"A bird in the hand is worth two in the bush, laddie!" said Uncle Oscar.

"But I'm sure to *know* for the Grand National; or the Lincolnshire; or else 180 the Derby. I'm sure to know for *one* of them," said Paul.

So Uncle Oscar signed the agreement, and Paul's mother touched the whole five thousand. Then something very curious happened. The voices in the house suddenly went mad, like a chorus of frogs on a spring evening. There were certain new furnishings, and Paul had a tutor. He was *really* going to Eton, his father's school, in the following autumn. There were flowers in the winter, and a blossoming of the luxury Paul's mother had been used to. And yet the voices in the house, behind the sprays of mimosa and almond blossom, and from under the piles of iridescent cushions, simply trilled and screamed in a sort of ecstasy: "There *must* be more money! Oh-h-h; there *must* be more money Oh, now, now-w! Now-w-w—there *must* be more money!—more than ever! More than ever!"

It frightened Paul terribly. He studied away at his Latin and Greek with his tutors. But his intense hours were spent with Bassett. The Grand National had gone by: he had not "known," and had lost a hundred pounds. Summer was at hand. He was in agony for the Lincoln. But even for the Lincoln he didn't "know," and he lost fifty pounds. He became wild-eyed and strange, as if something were going to explode in him.

"Let it alone, son! Don't you bother about it!" urged Uncle Oscar. But it was as if the boy couldn't really hear what his uncle was saying.

"I've got to know for the Derby! I've got to know for the Derby!" the child reiterated, his big blue eyes blazing with a sort of madness.

185 His mother noticed how overwrought he was.

"You'd better go to the seaside. Wouldn't you like to go now to the seaside, instead of waiting? I think you'd better," she said, looking down at him anxiously, her heart curiously heavy because of him.

But the child lifted his uncanny blue eyes.

"I couldn't possibly go before the Derby, mother!" he said. "I couldn't possibly!"

"Why not?" she said, her voice becoming heavy when she was opposed. "Why not? You can still go from the seaside to see the Derby with your Uncle Oscar, if that's what you wish. No need for you to wait here. Besides, I think you care too much about these races. It's a bad sign. My family has been a gambling family, and you won't know till you grow up how much damage it has done. But it has done damage. I shall have to send Bassett away, and ask Uncle Oscar not to talk racing to you, unless you promise to be reasonable about it; go away to the seaside and forget it. You're all nerves!"

190 "I'll do what you like, mother, so long as you don't send me away till after the Derby," the boy said.

"Send you away from where? Just from this house?"

"Yes," he said, gazing at her.

"Why, you curious child, what makes you care about this house so much, suddenly? I never knew you loved it."

He gazed at her without speaking. He had a secret within a secret, something he had not divulged, even to Bassett or to his Uncle Oscar.

195 But his mother, after standing undecided and a little bit sullen for some moments, said:

"Very well, then! Don't go to the seaside till after the Derby, if you don't wish it. But promise me you won't let your nerves go to pieces. Promise you won't think so much about horse-racing and events, as you call them!"

"Oh, no," said the boy casually. "I won't think much about them, mother. You needn't worry. I wouldn't worry, mother, if I were you."

"If you were me and I were you," said his mother, "I wonder what we *should* do!"

"But you know you needn't worry, mother, don't you?" the boy repeated.

"I should be awfully glad to know it," she said wearily. 200

"Oh, well, you *can*, you know. I mean, you *ought* to know you needn't worry," he insisted.

"Ought I? Then I'll see about it," she said.

Paul's secret of secrets was his wooden horse, that which had no name. Since he was emancipated from a nurse and a nursery-governess, he had had his rocking-horse removed to his own bedroom at the top of the house.

"Surely, you're too big for a rocking-horse!" his mother had remonstrated.

"Well, you see, mother, till I can have a *real* horse, I like to have *some* sort 205
of animal about," had been his quaint answer.

"Do you feel he keeps you company?" she laughed.

"Oh, yes! He's very good, he always keeps me company, when I'm there," said Paul.

So the horse, rather shabby, stood in an arrested prance in the boy's bedroom.

The Derby was drawing near, and the boy grew more and more tense. He hardly heard what was spoken to him, he was very frail, and his eyes were really uncanny. His mother had sudden strange seizures of uneasiness about him. Sometimes, for half-an-hour, she would feel a sudden anxiety about him that was almost anguish. She wanted to rush to him at once, and know he was safe.

Two nights before the Derby, she was at a big party in town, when one of 210
her rushes of anxiety about her boy, her first-born, gripped her heart till she could hardly speak. She fought with the feeling, might and main, for she believed in common-sense. But it was too strong. She had to leave the dance and go downstairs to telephone to the country. The children's nursery-governess was terribly surprised and startled at being rung up in the night.

"Are the children all right, Miss Wilmot?"

"Oh, yes, they are quite all right."

"Master Paul? Is he all right?"

"He went to bed as right as a trivet. Shall I run up and look at him?"

"No," said Paul's mother reluctantly. "No! Don't trouble. It's all right. Don't 215
sit up. We shall be home fairly soon." She did not want her son's privacy intruded upon.

"Very good," said the governess.

It was about one o'clock when Paul's mother and father drove up to their house. All was still. Paul's mother went to her room and slipped off her white fur cloak. She had told her maid not to wait up for her. She heard her husband downstairs, mixing a whisky-and-soda.

And then, because of the strange anxiety at her heart, she stole upstairs to her son's room. Noiselessly she went along the upper corridor. Was there a faint noise? What was it?

She stood, with arrested muscles, outside his door, listening. There was a strange, heavy, and yet not loud noise. Her heart stood still. It was a soundless noise, yet rushing and powerful. Something huge, in violent, hushed motion. What was it? What in God's name was it? She ought to know. She felt that she knew the noise. She knew what it was.

Yet she could not place it. She couldn't say what it was. And on and on it went, like a madness.

Softly, frozen with anxiety and fear, she turned the door-handle.

The room was dark. Yet in the space near the window, she heard and saw something plunging to and fro. She gazed in fear and amazement.

Then suddenly she switched on the light, and saw her son, in his green pyjamas, madly surging on the rocking-horse. The blaze of light suddenly lit him up, as he urged the wooden horse, and lit her up, as she stood, blonde, in her dress of pale green and crystal, in the doorway.

"Paul!" she cried. "Whatever are you doing?"

"It's Malabar!" he screamed, in a powerful, strange voice. "It's Malabar!"

His eyes blazed at her for one strange and senseless second, as he ceased urging his wooden horse. Then he fell with a crash to the ground, and she, all her tormented motherhood flooding upon her, rushed to gather him up.

But he was unconscious, and unconscious he remained, with some brain-fever. He talked and tossed, and his mother sat stonily by his side.

"Malabar! It's Malabar! Bassett, Bassett, I *know*! It's Malabar!"

So the child cried, trying to get up and urge the rocking-horse that gave him his inspiration.

"What does he mean by Malabar?" asked the heart-frozen mother.

"I don't know," said the father stonily.

"What does he mean by Malabar?" she asked her brother Oscar.

"It's one of the horses running for the Derby," was the answer.

And, in spite of himself, Oscar Cresswell spoke to Bassett, and himself put a thousand on Malabar: at fourteen to one.

The third day of the illness was critical: they were waiting for a change. The boy, with his rather long, curly hair, was tossing ceaselessly on the pillow. He neither slept nor regained consciousness, and his eyes were like blue stones. His mother sat, feeling her heart had gone, turned actually into a stone.

In the evening, Oscar Cresswell did not come, but Bassett sent a message, saying could he come up for one moment, just one moment? Paul's mother was very angry at the intrusion, but on second thought she agreed. The boy was the same. Perhaps Bassett might bring him to consciousness.

The gardener, a shortish fellow with a little brown moustache, and sharp little brown eyes, tip-toed into the room, touched his imaginary cap to Paul's mother, and stole to the bedside, staring with glittering, smallish eyes, at the tossing, dying child.

"Master Paul!" he whispered. "Master Paul! Malabar came in first all right, a clean win. I did as you told me. You've made over seventy thousand pounds, you have; you've got over eighty thousand. Malabar came in all right, Master Paul."

"Malabar! Malabar! Did I say Malabar, mother? Did I say Malabar? Do you think I'm lucky, mother? I knew Malabar, didn't I? Over eighty thousand pounds! I call that lucky, don't you, mother? Over eighty thousand pounds! I knew, didn't I know I knew! Malabar came in all right. If I ride my horse till I'm sure, then I tell you, Bassett, you can go as high as you like. Did you go for all you were worth, Bassett?"

"I went a thousand on it, Master Paul."

"I never told you, mother, that if I can ride my horse, and *get there*, then I'm absolutely sure—oh absolutely! Mother, did I ever tell you? I *am* lucky!"

"No, you never did," said the mother.

But the boy died in the night.

And even as he lay dead, his mother heard her brother's voice saying to her: "My God, Hester, you're eighty-odd thousand to the good, and a poor devil of a son to the bad. But, poor devil, poor devil, he's best gone out of a life where he rides his rocking-horse to find a winner."

240

1932

D. H. LAWRENCE

Passages from Essays and Letters

from "Nottingham and the Mining Countryside"

I was born . . . in Eastwood, a mining village of some three thousand souls, about eight miles from Nottingham. . . . It is hilly country. . . . To me it seemed, and still seems, an extremely beautiful countryside, just between the red sandstone and the oak-trees of Nottingham, and the cold limestone, the ash-trees, the stone fences of Derbyshire. To me, as a child and a young man, it was still the old England of the forest and agricultural past; there were no motorcars, the mines were, in a sense, an accident in the landscape, and Robin Hood and his merry men were not very far away.

. . . The people lived almost entirely by instinct, men of my father's age could not really read. And the pit did not mechanize men. . . . My father loved the pit. He was hurt badly, more than once, but he would never stay away. He loved the contact, the intimacy, as men in the war loved the intense male comradeship of the dark days.

Now the colliers had also an instinct for beauty. The colliers' wives had not. The colliers were deeply alive, instinctively. But they had no daytime ambition, and no daytime intellect. They avoided, really, the rational aspect of life. . . . They didn't even care very profoundly about wages. It was the women, naturally, who nagged on this score. . . . The collier went to the pub and drank in order to continue the intimacy with his mates.

. . . Life for him did not consist of facts, but in a flow. Very often he loved his garden. And very often he had a genuine love of the beauty of flowers. . . .

. . . Most women love flowers as possessions, and as trimmings. They can't look at a flower, and wonder a moment, and pass on. If they see a flower that arrests their attention, they must at once pick it, pluck it. Possession! A possession! Something added on to *me!*

from *"Love"*

. . . the love between a man and a woman . . . is dual. It is the melting into pure communion, and it is the friction of sheer sensuality, both. In pure communion I become whole in love. And in pure, fierce passion of sensuality, I am burned into essentiality. I am driven from the matrix unto sheer separate distinction. I become my single self, inviolable and unique, as the gems were perhaps once driven into themselves out of the confusion of earths. . . .

from *"Women Are So Cocksure"*

. . . [My mother] was convinced . . . that a man ought not to drink beer. This conviction developed from the fact, naturally, that my father drank beer. He sometimes drank too much. He sometimes boozed away the money necessary for the young family: When my father came in tipsy, she saw scarlet.

from *"Art and Morality"*

Apples are always apples! says Vox Populi, Vox Dei.[1]

Sometimes they're sin, sometimes they're a knock on the head, sometimes they're a bellyache, sometimes they're part of a pie, sometimes they're sauce for a goose. . . .

What art has got to do, and will go on doing, is to reveal things in their different relationships. That is to say, you've got to see in the apples the bellyache. Sir Isaac's knock on the cranium, the vast, moist wall through which the insect bores to lay her eggs in the middle, and the untasted, unknown quality which Eve saw hanging on a tree.

from *"Morality and the Novel"*

The business of art is to reveal the relation between man and his circumambient universe, at the living moment. As mankind is always struggling in the toils of old relationships, art is always ahead of the "times," which themselves are always far in the rear of the living moment.

When van Gogh paints sunflowers, he reveals, or achieves, the vivid relation between himself, as man, and the sunflowers, as sunflower, at that quick moment of time. His painting does not represent the sunflower itself. We shall

---

1. The voice of the people [is] the voice of God.

never know what the sunflower itself is. And the camera will *visualize* the sunflower far more perfectly than van Gogh can.

The vision on the canvas is a third thing, utterly intangible and inexplicable, the offspring of the sunflower itself and van Gogh himself. . . .

. . . The novel is the highest example of subtle interrelatedness that man has discovered. Everything is true in its own time, place, and circumstance, and untrue outside of its own place, time, circumstance. If you try to nail anything down, in the novel, either it kills the novel, or the novel gets up and walks away with the nail.

. . . Love is a great emotion. But if you set out to write a novel, and you yourself are in the throes of the great predilection for love, love as the supreme, the only emotion worth living for, then you will write an immoral novel.

Because *no* emotion is supreme, or exclusively worth living for. *All* emotions go to the achieving of a living relationship between a human being and the other human being or creature or thing he becomes purely related to. All emotions, including love and hate, and rage and tenderness, go to the adjusting of the oscillating, unestablished balance between two people who amount to anything . . .

A new relation, a new relatedness hurts somewhat in the attaining; and will always hurt. So life will always hurt. . . .

Each time we strive to a new relation, with anyone or anything, it is bound to hurt somewhat. Because it means the struggle with and the displacing of old connections, and this is never pleasant. And, moreover, between living things at least, an adjustment means also a fight, for each party, inevitably, must "seek its own" in the other, and be denied. When, in the two parties, each of them seeks his own, her own, absolutely, then it is a fight to the death. And this is true of the thing called "passion . . ."

The great relationship for humanity will always be the relation between man and woman. The relation between man and man, woman and woman, parent and child, will always be subsidiary.

And the relation between man and woman will change forever, and will forever be the new central clue to human life. It is the *relation itself* which is the quick and the central clue to life, not the man, nor the woman, nor the children that result from the relationship, as a contingency.

from "Why the Novel Matters"

We have curious ideas of ourselves. We think of ourselves as a body with a spirit in it, or a body with a soul in it, or a body with a mind in it. . . .

It is a funny sort of superstition. Why should I look at my hand, as it so cleverly writes these words, and decide that it is a mere nothing compared to the mind that directs it? Why should I imagine that there is a *me* which is more *me* than my hand is? Since my hand is absolutely alive, me alive . . .

And that's what you learn, when you're a novelist. And that's what you are liable *not* to know, if you're a parson, or a philosopher, or a scientist, or a stupid person.

Now I absolutely flatly deny that I am a soul, or a body, or a mind, or an intelligence, or a brain, or a nervous system, or a bunch of glands, or any of the rest of these bits of me. The whole is greater than the part. And therefore, I, who am man alive, am greater than my soul, or spirit, or body, or mind, or consciousness, or anything else that is merely a part of me. I am man a man, and alive. I am man alive, and as long as I can, I intend to go on being man alive.

For this reason I am a novelist. And being a novelist, I consider myself superior to the saint, the scientist, the philosopher, and the poet, who are all great masters of different bits of man alive, but never get the whole [thing] . . .

We should ask for no absolutes, or absolute. . . . There is no absolute good, there is nothing absolutely right. All things flow and change, and even change is not absolute. . . .

. . . If the one I love remains unchanged and unchanging, I shall cease to love her. It is only because she changes and startles me into change and defies my inertia, and is herself staggered in her inertia by my changing, that I can continue to love her. If she stayed put, I might as well love the pepper-pot . . .

In life, there is right and wrong, good and bad, all the time. But what is right in one case is wrong in another. And in the novel you see one man becoming a corpse, because of his so-called goodness, another going dead because of his so-called wickedness. Right and wrong is an instinct: but an instinct of the whole consciousness in a man, bodily, mental, spiritual at once. And only in the novel are *all* things given full play, or at least, they may be given full play, when we realize that life itself, and not inert safety, is the reason for living. For out of the full play of all things emerges the only thing that is anything, the wholeness of a man, the wholeness of a woman, man alive, and live woman.

from "Autobiographical Sketch"

They ask me; "Did you find it very hard to get on and to become a success?" And I have to admit that if I can be said to have got on, and if I can be called a success, then I *did not* find it hard.

I never starved in a garret, nor waited in anguish for the post to bring me an answer from editor or publisher, nor did I struggle in sweat and blood to bring forth mighty works, nor did I ever wake up and find myself famous.

. . . My father was a collier, and only a collier, nothing praise-worthy about him. He wasn't even respectable, in so far as he got drunk rather frequently, never went near a chapel, and was usually rather rude to his little immediate bosses at the pit . . .

My mother was, I suppose, superior. She came from town, and belonged really to the lower bourgeoisie. She spoke King's English, without an accent, and never in her life could even imitate a sentence of the dialect which my father spoke, and which we children spoke out of doors . . .

. . . I have *wanted* to feel truly friendly with some, at least, of my fellow-men. Yet I have never quite succeeded. Whether I got on *in* the world is a question; but I certainly don't get on very well *with* the world. And whether I am a worldly success or not I really don't know. But I feel, somehow, not much of a human success.

By which I mean that I don't feel there is any very cordial or fundamental contact between me and society, or me and other people. There is a breach. And my contact is with something that is nonhuman, nonvocal . . .

[Why?] The answer, as far as I can see, has something to do with class. Class makes a gulf, across which all the best human flow is lost. It is not exactly the triumph of the middle classes that has made the deadness, but the triumph of the middle-class *thing*.

As a man from the working class, I feel that the middle class cut off some of my vital vibration when I am with them. I admit them charming and educated and good people often enough. *But they just stop some part of me from working.* . . .

Then why don't I live with my working people? Because their vibration is limited in another direction. They are narrow, but still fairly deep and passionate, whereas the middle class is broad and shallow and passionless . . .

I cannot make the transfer from my own class into the middle class. I cannot, not for anything in the world, forfeit my passional consciousness and my old blood-affinity with my fellow-men and the animals and the land, for that other thin, spurious mental conceit which is all that is left of the mental consciousness once it has made itself exclusive.

from the Letters

TO A. W. MCLEOD, 26 APRIL 1913

I am so sure that only through a readjustment between men and women, and a making free and healthy of this sex, will she [England] get out of her present atrophy. Oh, Lord, and if I don't "subdue my art to a metaphysic," as somebody very beautifully said of Hardy, I do write because I want folk—English folk—to alter, and have more sense.

TO A. W. MCLEOD, 2 JUNE 1914

I think the only re-sourcing of art, revivifying it, is to make it more the joint work of man and woman. I think *the* one thing to do, is for men to have courage to draw nearer to women, expose themselves to them, and be altered by them; and for women to accept and admit men. That is the start—by bringing themselves together, men and women—revealing themselves to each other, gaining great blind knowledge and suffering and joy, which it will take a big further lapse of civilization to exploit and work out. Because the source of all life and knowledge is in man and woman, and the source of all living is in the interchange and the meeting and mingling of these two: man-life and woman-life, man-knowledge and woman-knowledge, man-being and woman-being.

TO J. B. PINKER, 16 DECEMBER 1915

... Tell Arnold Bennett[2] that all rules of construction hold good only for novels which are copies of other novels. A book which is not a copy of other books has its own construction, and what he calls faults, he being an old imitator, I call characteristics.

TO ROLF GARDINER, 9 AUGUST 1924

What we need is to smash a few big holes in European suburbanity, let in a little real fresh air.

TO LADY OTTOLINE MORRELL, 5 FEBRUARY 1929

... Don't you think it's nonsense when Murry says that my world is not the ordinary man's world and that I am a sort of animal with a sixth sense? Seems to me more likely he's a sort of animal with only four senses—the real sense of touch missing. They all seem determined to make a freak of me—to save their own short-failings, and make them "normal."

▼   ▼   ▼

FLANNERY O'CONNOR
The Lame Shall Enter First

Sheppard sat on a stool at the bar that divided the kitchen in half, eating his cereal out of the individual pasteboard box it came in. He ate mechanically, his eyes on the child, who was wandering from cabinet to cabinet in the panelled kitchen, collecting the ingredients for his breakfast. He was a stocky blond boy of ten. Sheppard kept his intense blue eyes fixed on him. The boy's future was written in his face. He would be a banker. No, worse. He would operate a small loan company. All he wanted for the child was that he be good and unselfish and neither seemed likely. Sheppard was a young man whose hair was already white. It stood up like a narrow brush halo over his pink sensitive face.

The boy approached the bar with the jar of peanut butter under his arm, a plate with a quarter of a small chocolate cake on it in one hand and the ketchup bottle in the other. He did not appear to notice his father. He climbed up on the stool and began to spread peanut butter on the cake. He had very large

2. An early 20th-century novelist (1867–1931) whose major works—*The Old Wives' Tale* (1908) and *The Clayhanger Trilogy* (1910–15)—treat the middle classes in the pottery country of the English Midlands in a naturalistic manner (usually criticizing the money-grubbing, social-climbing selfishness of the society). In his later years he more or less turned into a hack, though a clever one, and it is to Bennett as a very popular, successful hack that Lawrence is referring.

round ears that leaned away from his head and seemed to pull his eyes slightly too far apart. His shirt was green but so faded that the cowboy charging across the front of it was only a shadow.

"Norton," Sheppard said, "I saw Rufus Johnson yesterday. Do you know what he was doing?"

The child looked at him with a kind of half attention, his eyes forward but not yet engaged. They were a paler blue than his father's as if they might have faded like the shirt; one of them listed, almost imperceptibly, toward the outer rim.

"He was in an alley," Sheppard said, "and he had his hand in a garbage can. He was trying to get something to eat out of it." He paused to let this soak in. "He was hungry," he finished, and tried to pierce the child's conscience with his gaze.

The boy picked up the piece of chocolate cake and began to gnaw it from one corner.

"Norton," Sheppard said, "do you have any idea what it means to share?"

A flicker of attention. "Some of it's yours," Norton said.

"Some of it's *his*," Sheppard said heavily. It was hopeless. Almost any fault would have been preferable to selfishness—a violent temper, even a tendency to lie.

The child turned the bottle of ketchup upside down and began thumping ketchup onto the cake.

Sheppard's look of pain increased. "You are ten and Rufus Johnson is fourteen," he said. "Yet I'm sure your shirts would fit Rufus." Rufus Johnson was a boy he had been trying to help at the reformatory for the past year. He had been released two months ago. "When he was in the reformatory, he looked pretty good, but when I saw him yesterday, he was skin and bones. He hasn't been eating cake with peanut butter on it for breakfast."

The child paused. "It's stale," he said. "That's why I have to put stuff on it."

Sheppard turned his face to the window at the end of the bar. The side lawn, green and even, sloped fifty feet or so down to a small suburban wood. When his wife was living, they had often eaten outside, even breakfast, on the grass. He had never noticed then that the child was selfish. "Listen to me," he said, turning back to him, "look at me and listen."

The boy looked at him. At least his eyes were forward.

"I gave Rufus a key to this house when he left the reformatory—to show my confidence in him and so he would have a place he could come to and feel welcome any time. He didn't use it, but I think he'll use it now because he's seen me and he's hungry. And if he doesn't use it, I'm going out and find him and bring him here. I can't see a child eating out of garbage cans."

The boy frowned. It was dawning upon him that something of his was threatened.

Sheppard's mouth stretched in disgust. "Rufus's father died before he was born," he said. "His mother is in the state penitentiary. He was raised by his grandfather in a shack without water or electricity and the old man beat him every day. How would you like to belong to a family like that?"

"I don't know," the child said lamely.

"Well, you might think about it sometime," Sheppard said.

20   Sheppard was City Recreational Director. On Saturdays he worked at the reformatory as a counselor, receiving nothing for it but the satisfaction of knowing he was helping boys no one else cared about. Johnson was the most intelligent boy he had worked with and the most deprived.

Norton turned what was left of the cake over as if he no longer wanted it.

"Maybe he won't come," the child said and his eyes brightened slightly.

"Think of everything you have that he doesn't!" Sheppard said. "Suppose you had to root in garbage cans for food? Suppose you had a huge swollen foot and one side of you dropped lower than the other when you walked?"

The boy looked blank, obviously unable to imagine such a thing.

25   "You have a healthy body," Sheppard said, "a good home. You've never been taught anything but the truth. Your daddy gives you everything you need and want. You don't have a grandfather who beats you. And your mother is not in the state penitentiary."

The child pushed his plate away. Sheppard groaned aloud.

A knot of flesh appeared below the boy's suddenly distorted mouth. His face became a mass of lumps with slits for eyes. "If she was in the penitentiary," he began in a kind of racking bellow, "I could go to seeeeee her." Tears rolled down his face and the ketchup dribbled on his chin. He looked as if he had been hit in the mouth. He abandoned himself and howled.

Sheppard sat helpless and miserable, like a man lashed by some elemental force of nature. This was not a normal grief. It was all part of his selfishness. She had been dead for over a year and a child's grief should not last so long. "You're going on eleven years old," he said reproachfully.

The child began an agonizing high-pitched heaving noise.

30   "If you stop thinking about yourself and think what you can do for somebody else," Sheppard said, "then you'll stop missing your mother."

The boy was silent but his shoulders continued to shake. Then his face collapsed and he began to howl again.

"Don't you think I'm lonely without her too?" Sheppard said. "Don't you think I miss her at all? I do, but I'm not sitting around moping. I'm busy helping other people. When do you see me just sitting around thinking about my troubles?"

The boy slumped as if he were exhausted but fresh tears streaked his face.

"What are you going to do today?" Sheppard asked, to get his mind on something else.

35   The child ran his arm across his eyes. "Sell seeds," he mumbled.

Always selling something. He had four quart jars full of nickels and dimes he had saved and he took them out of his closet every few days and counted them. "What are you selling seeds for?"

"To win a prize."

"What's the prize?"

"A thousand dollars."

40   "And what would you do if you had a thousand dollars?"

"Keep it," the child said and wiped his nose on his shoulder.

"I feel sure you would," Sheppard said. "Listen," he said and lowered his voice to an almost pleading tone, "suppose by some chance you did win a thousand dollars. Wouldn't you like to spend it on children less fortunate than yourself? Wouldn't you like to give some swings and trapezes to the orphanage? Wouldn't you like to buy poor Rufus Johnson a new shoe?"

The boy began to back away from the bar. Then suddenly he leaned forward and hung with his mouth open over his plate. Sheppard groaned again. Everything came up, the cake, the peanut butter, the ketchup—a limp sweet batter. He hung over it gagging, more came, and he waited with his mouth open over the plate as if he expected his heart to come up next.

"It's all right," Sheppard said, "it's all right. You couldn't help it. Wipe your mouth and go lie down."

The child hung there a moment longer. Then he raised his face and looked blindly at his father.

"Go on," Sheppard said. "Go on and lie down."

The boy pulled up the end of his t-shirt and smeared his mouth with it. Then he climbed down off the stool and wandered out of the kitchen.

Sheppard sat there staring at the puddle of half-digested food. The sour odor reached him and he drew back. His gorge rose. He got up and carried the plate to the sink and turned the water on it and watched grimly as the mess ran down the drain. Johnson's sad thin hand rooted in garbage cans for food while his own child, selfish, unresponsive, greedy, had so much that he threw it up. He cut off the faucet with a thrust of his fist. Johnson had a capacity for real response and had been deprived of everything from birth; Norton was average or below and had had every advantage.

He went back to the bar to finish his breakfast. The cereal was soggy in the cardboard box but he paid no attention to what he was eating. Johnson was worth any amount of effort because he had the potential. He had seen it from the time the boy had limped in for his first interview.

Sheppard's office at the reformatory was a narrow closet with one window and a small table and two chairs in it. He had never been inside a confessional but he thought it must be the same kind of operation he had here, except that he explained, he did not absolve. His credentials were less dubious than a priest's; he had been trained for what he was doing.

When Johnson came in for his first interview, he had been reading over the boy's record—senseless destruction, windows smashed, city trash boxes set afire, tires slashed—the kind of thing he found where boys had been transplanted abruptly from the country to the city as this one had. He came to Johnson's I. Q. score. It was 140. He raised his eyes eagerly.

The boy sat slumped on the edge of his chair, his arms hanging between his thighs. The light from the window fell on his face. His eyes, steel-colored and very still, were trained narrowly forward. His thin dark hair hung in a flat forelock across the side of his forehead, not carelessly like a boy's, but fiercely like an old man's. A kind of fanatic intelligence was palpable in his face.

Sheppard smiled to diminish the distance between them.

The boy's expression did not soften. He leaned back in his chair and lifted a monstrous club foot to his knee. The foot was in a heavy black battered shoe with a sole four or five inches thick. The leather parted from it in one place and the end of an empty sock protruded like a gray tongue from a severed head. The case was clear to Sheppard instantly. His mischief was compensation for the foot.

55 "Well Rufus," he said, "I see by the record here that you don't have but a year to serve. What do you plan to do when you get out?"

"I don't make no plans," the boy said. His eyes shifted indifferently to something outside the window behind Sheppard in the far distance.

"Maybe you ought to," Sheppard said and smiled.

Johnson continued to gaze beyond him.

"I want to see you make the most of your intelligence," Sheppard said. "What's most important to you? Let's talk about what's important to *you*." His eyes dropped involuntarily to the foot.

60 "Study it and git your fill," the boy drawled.

Sheppard reddened. The black deformed mass swelled before his eyes. He ignored the remark and the leer the boy was giving him. "Rufus," he said, "you've got into a lot of senseless trouble but I think when you understand why you do these things, you'll be less inclined to do them." He smiled. They had so few friends, saw so few pleasant faces, that half his effectiveness came from nothing more than smiling at them. "There are a lot of things about yourself that I think I can explain to you," he said.

Johnson looked at him stonily. "I ain't asked for no explanation," he said. "I already know why I do what I do."

"Well good!" Sheppard said. "Suppose you tell me what's made you do the things you've done?"

A black sheen appeared in the boy's eyes. "Satan," he said. "He has me in his power."

65 Sheppard looked at him steadily. There was no indication on the boy's face that he had said this to be funny. The line of his thin mouth was set with pride. Sheppard's eyes hardened. He felt a momentary dull despair as if he were faced with some elemental warping of nature that had happened too long ago to be corrected now. This boy's questions about life had been answered by signs nailed on the pine trees: DOES SATAN HAVE YOU IN HIS POWER? REPENT OR BURN IN HELL. JESUS SAVES. He would know the Bible with or without reading it. His despair gave way to outrage. "Rubbish!" he snorted. "We're living in the space age! You're too smart to give me an answer like that."

Johnson's mouth twisted slightly. His look was contemptuous but amused. There was a glint of challenge in his eyes.

Sheppard scrutinized his face. Where there was intelligence anything was possible. He smiled again, a smile that was like an invitation to the boy to come into a school room with all its windows thrown open to the light. "Rufus," he said, "I'm going to arrange for you to have a conference with me once a week. Maybe there's an explanation for your explanation. Maybe I can explain your devil to you."

After that he had talked to Johnson every Saturday for the rest of the year. He talked at random, the kind of talk the boy would never have heard before. He talked a little above him to give him something to reach for. He roamed from simple psychology and the dodges of the human mind to astronomy and the space capsules that were whirling around the earth faster than the speed of sound and would soon encircle the stars. Instinctively he concentrated on the stars. He wanted to give the boy something to reach for besides his neighbor's goods. He wanted to stretch his horizons. He wanted him to *see* the universe, to see that the darkest parts of it could be penetrated. He would have given anything to be able to put a telescope in Johnson's hands.

Johnson said little and what he did say, for the sake of his pride, was in dissent or senseless contradiction, with the clubfoot raised always to his knee like a weapon ready for use, but Sheppard was not deceived. He watched his eyes and every week he saw something in them crumble. From the boy's face, hard but shocked, braced against the light that was ravaging him, he could see that he was hitting dead center.

Johnson was free now to live out of garbage cans and rediscover his old ignorance. The injustice of it was infuriating. He had been sent back to the grandfather; the old man's imbecility could only be imagined. Perhaps the boy had by now run away from him. The idea of getting custody of Johnson had occurred to Sheppard before, but the fact of the grandfather had stood in the way. Nothing excited him so much as thinking what he could do for such a boy. First he would have him fitted for a new orthopedic shoe. His back was thrown out of line every time he took a step. Then he would encourage him in some particular intellectual interest. He thought of the telescope. He could buy a second-hand one and they could set it up in the attic window. He sat for almost ten minutes thinking what he could do if he had Johnson here with him. What was wasted on Norton would cause Johnson to flourish. Yesterday when he had seen him with his hand in the garbage can, he had waved and started forward. Johnson had seen him, paused a split-second, then vanished with the swiftness of a rat, but not before Sheppard had seen his expression change. Something had kindled in the boy's eyes, he was sure of it, some memory of the lost light.

He got up and threw the cereal box in the garbage. Before he left the house, he looked into Norton's room to be sure he was not still sick. The child was sitting cross-legged on his bed. He had emptied the quart jars of change into one large pile in front of him, and was sorting it out by nickels and dimes and quarters.

That afternoon Norton was alone in the house, squatting on the floor of his room arranging packages of flower seeds in rows around himself. Rain slashed against the window panes and rattled in the gutters. The room had grown dark but every few minutes it was lit by silent lightning and the seed packages showed up gaily on the floor. He squatted motionless like a large pale frog in the midst of this potential garden. All at once his eyes became alert. Without warning the rain had stopped. The silence was heavy as if the downpour had been hushed by violence. He remained motionless, only his eyes turning.

70

Into the silence came the distinct click of a key turning in the front door lock. The sound was a very deliberate one. It drew attention to itself and held it as if it were controlled more by a mind than by a hand. The child leapt up and got into the closet.

The footsteps began to move in the hall. They were deliberate and irregular, a light and then a heavy one, then a silence as if the visitor had paused to listen himself or to examine something. In a minute the kitchen door screeked. The footsteps crossed the kitchen to the refrigerator. The closet wall and the kitchen wall were the same. Norton stood with his ear pressed against it. The refrigerator door opened. There was a prolonged silence.

75 He took off his shoes and then tiptoed out of the closet and stepped over the seed packages. In the middle of the room, he stopped and remained where he was, rigid. A thin bony-face boy in a wet black suit stood in his door, blocking his escape. His hair was flattened to his skull by the rain. He stood there like an irate drenched crow. His look went through the child like a pin and paralyzed him. Then his eyes began to move over everything in the room—the unmade bed, the dirty curtains on the one large window, a photograph of a wide-faced young woman that stood up in the clutter on top of the dresser.

The child's tongue suddenly went wild. "He's been expecting you, he's going to give you a new shoe because you have to eat out of garbage cans!" he said in a kind of mouse-like shriek.

"I eat out of garbage cans," the boy said slowly with a beady stare, "because I like to eat out of garbage cans. See?"

The child nodded.

"And I got ways of getting my own shoe. See?"

80 The child nodded, mesmerized.

The boy limped in and sat down on the bed. He arranged a pillow behind him and stretched his short leg out so that the big black shoe rested conspicuously on a fold of the sheet.

Norton's gaze settled on it and remained immobile. The sole was as thick as a brick.

Johnson wiggled it slightly and smiled. "If I kick somebody *once* with this," he said, "it learns them not to mess with me."

The child nodded.

85 "Go in the kitchen," Johnson said, "and make me a sandwich with some of that rye bread and ham and bring me a glass of milk."

Norton went off like a mechanical toy, pushed in the right direction. He made a large greasy sandwich with ham hanging out the sides of it and poured out a glass of milk. Then he returned to the room with the glass of milk in one hand and the sandwich in the other.

Johnson was leaning back regally against the pillow. "Thanks, waiter," he said and took the sandwich.

Norton stood by the side of the bed, holding the glass.

The boy tore into the sandwich and ate steadily until he finished it. Then he took the glass of milk. He held it with both hands like a child and when he lowered it for breath, there was a rim of milk around his mouth. He handed

Norton the empty glass. "Go get me one of them oranges in there, waiter," he said hoarsely.

Norton went to the kitchen and returned with the orange. Johnson peeled it with his fingers and let the peeling drop in the bed. He ate it slowly, spitting the seeds out in front of him. When he finished, he wiped his hands on the sheet and gave Norton a long appraising stare. He appeared to have been softened by the service. "You're his kid all right," he said. "You got the same stupid face."

The child stood there stolidly as if he had not heard.

"He don't know his left hand from his right," Johnson said with a hoarse pleasure in his voice.

The child cast his eyes a little to the side of the boy's face and looked fixedly at the wall.

"Yaketty yaketty yak," Johnson said, "and never says a thing."

The child's upper lip lifted slightly but he didn't say anything.

"Gas," Johnson said. "Gas."

The child's face began to have a wary look of belligerence. He backed away slightly as if he were prepared to retreat instantly. "He's good," he mumbled. "He helps people."

"Good!" Johnson said savagely. He thrust his head forward. "Listen here," he hissed, "I don't care if he's good or not. He ain't *right!*"

Norton looked stunned.

The screen door in the kitchen banged and someone entered. Johnson sat forward instantly. "Is that him?" he said.

"It's the cook," Norton said. "She comes in the afternoon."

Johnson got up and limped into the hall and stood in the kitchen door and Norton followed him.

The colored girl was at the closet taking off a bright red raincoat. She was a tall light-yellow girl with a mouth like a large rose that had darkened and wilted. Her hair was dressed in tiers on top of her head and leaned to the side like the Tower of Pisa.

Johnson made a noise through his teeth. "Well look at Aunt Jemima," he said.

The girl paused and trained an insolent gaze on them. They might have been dust on the floor.

"Come on," Johnson said, "let's see what all you got besides a nigger." He opened the first door to his right in the hall and looked into a pink-tiled bathroom. "A pink can!" he murmured.

He turned a comical face to the child. "Does he sit on that?"

"It's for company," Norton said, "but he sits on it sometimes."

"He ought to empty his head in it," Johnson said.

The door was open to the next room. It was the room Sheppard had slept in since his wife died. An ascetic-looking iron bed stood on the bare floor. A heap of Little League baseball uniforms was piled in one corner. Papers were scattered over a large roll-top desk and held down in various places by his pipes. Johnson stood looking into the room silently. He wrinkled his nose. "Guess who?" he said.

The door to the next room was closed but Johnson opened it and thrust his head into the semi-darkness within. The shades were down and the air was close with a faint scent of perfume in it. There was a wide antique bed and a mammoth dresser whose mirror glinted in the half light. Johnson snapped the light switch by the door and crossed the room to the mirror and peered into it. A silver comb and brush lay on the linen runner. He picked up the comb and began to run it through his hair. He combed it straight down on his forehead. Then he swept it to the side, Hitler fashion.

"Leave her comb alone!" the child said. He stood in the door, pale and breathing heavily as if he were watching sacrilege in a holy place.

Johnson put the comb down and picked up the brush and gave his hair a swipe with it.

"She's dead," the child said.

115 "I ain't afraid of dead people's things," Johnson said. He opened the top drawer and slid his hand in.

"Take your big fat dirty hands off my mother's clothes!" the child said in a high suffocated voice.

"Keep your shirt on, sweetheart," Johnson murmured. He pulled up a wrinkled red polka dot blouse and dropped it back. Then he pulled out a green silk kerchief and whirled it over his head and let it float to the floor. His hand continued to plow deep into the drawer. After a moment it came up gripping a faded corset with four dangling metal supporters. "Thisyer must be her saddle," he observed.

He lifted it gingerly and shook it. Then he fastened it around his waist and jumped up and down, making the metal supporters dance. He began to snap his fingers and turn his hips from side to side. "Gonter rock, rattle and roll," he sang. "Gonter rock, rattle and roll. Can't please that woman, to save my doggone soul." He began to move around, stamping the good foot down and slinging the heavy one to the side. He danced out the door, past the stricken child and down the hall toward the kitchen.

A half hour later Sheppard came home. He dropped his raincoat on a chair in the hall and came as far as the parlor door and stopped. His face was suddenly transformed. It shone with pleasure. Johnson sat, a dark figure, in a high-backed pink upholstered chair. The wall behind him was lined with books from floor to ceiling. He was reading one. Sheppard's eyes narrowed. It was a volume of the Encyclopedia Britannica. He was so engrossed in it that he did not look up. Sheppard held his breath. This was the perfect setting for the boy. He had to keep him here. He had to manage it somehow.

120 "Rufus!" he said, "it's good to see you boy!" and he bounded forward with his arm outstretched.

Johnson looked up, his face blank. "Oh hello," he said. He ignored the hand as long as he was able but when Sheppard did not withdraw it, he grudgingly shook it.

Sheppard was prepared for this kind of reaction. It was part of Johnson's make-up never to show enthusiasm.

"How are things?" he said. "How's your grandfather treating you?" He sat down on the edge of the sofa.

"He dropped dead," the boy said indifferently.

"You don't mean it!" Sheppard cried. He got up and sat down on the coffee table nearer the boy.   125

"Naw," Johnson said, "he ain't dropped dead. I wisht he had."

"Well where is he?" Sheppard muttered.

"He's gone with a remnant to the hills," Johnson said. "Him and some others. They're going to bury some Bibles in a cave and take two of different kinds of animals and all like that. Like Noah. Only this time it's going to be fire, not flood."

Sheppard's mouth stretched wryly. "I see," he said. Then he said, "In other words the old fool has abandoned you?"

"He ain't no fool," the boy said in an indignant tone.   130

"Has he abandoned you or not?" Sheppard asked impatiently.

The boy shrugged.

"Where's your probation officer?"

"I ain't supposed to keep up with him," Johnson said. "He's supposed to keep up with me."

Sheppard laughed. "Wait a minute," he said. He got up and went into the   135
hall and got his raincoat off the chair and took it to the hall closet to hang it up. He had to give himself time to think, to decide how he could ask the boy so that he would stay. He couldn't force him to stay. It would have to be voluntary. Johnson pretended not to like him. That was only to uphold his pride, but he would have to ask him in such a way that his pride could still be upheld. He opened the closet door and took out a hanger. An old gray winter coat of his wife's still hung there. He pushed it aside but it didn't move. He pulled it open roughly and winced as if he had seen the larva inside a cocoon. Norton stood in it, his face swollen and pale, with a drugged look of misery on it. Sheppard stared at him. Suddenly he was confronted with a possibility. "Get out of there," he said. He caught him by the shoulder and propelled him firmly into the parlor and over to the pink chair where Johnson was sitting with the encyclopedia in his lap. He was going to risk everything in one blow.

"Rufus," he said, "I've got a problem. I need your help."

Johnson looked up suspiciously.

"Listen," Sheppard said, "we need another boy in the house." There was a genuine desperation in his voice. "Norton here has never had to divide anything in his life. He doesn't know what it means to share. And I need somebody to teach him. How about helping me out? Stay here for a while with us, Rufus. I need your help." The excitement in his voice made it thin.

The child suddenly came to life. His face swelled with fury. "He went in her room and used her comb!" he screamed, yanking Sheppard's arm. "He put on her corset and danced with Leola, he . . ."

"Stop this!" Sheppard said sharply. "Is tattling all you're capable of? I'm not   140
asking you for a report on Rufus's conduct. I'm asking you to make him welcome here. Do you understand?

"You see how it is?" he asked, turning to Johnson.

Norton kicked the leg of the pink chair viciously, just missing Johnson's swollen foot. Sheppard yanked him back.

"He said you weren't nothing but gas!" the child shrieked.

A sly look of pleasure crossed Johnson's face.

145 Sheppard was not put back. These insults were part of the boy's defensive mechanism. "What about it, Rufus?" he said. "Will you stay with us for a while?"

Johnson looked straight in front of him and said nothing. He smiled slightly and appeared to gaze upon some vision of the future that pleased him. "I don't care," he said and turned a page of the encyclopedia. "I can stand anywhere."

"Wonderful." Sheppard said. "Wonderful."

"He said," the child said in a throaty whisper, "you didn't know your left hand from your right."

150 There was a silence.

Johnson wet his finger and turned another page of the encyclopedia.

"I have something to say to both of you," Sheppard said in a voice without inflection. His eyes moved from one to the other of them and he spoke slowly as if what he was saying he would say only once and it behooved them to listen. "If it made any difference to me what Rufus thinks of me," he said, "then I wouldn't be asking him here. Rufus is going to help me out and I'm going to help him out and we're both going to help you out. I'd simply be selfish if I let what Rufus thinks of me interfere with what I can do for Rufus. If I can help a person, all I want is to do it. I'm above and beyond simple pettiness."

Neither of them made a sound. Norton stared at the chair cushion. Johnson peered closer at some fine print in the encyclopedia. Sheppard was looking at the tops of their heads. He smiled. After all, he had won. The boy was staying. He reached out and ruffled Norton's hair and slapped Johnson on the shoulder. "Now you fellows sit here and get acquainted," he said gaily and started toward the door. "I'm going to see what Leola left us for supper."

When he was gone, Johnson raised his head and looked at Norton. The child looked back at him bleakly. "God, kid," Johnson said in a cracked voice, "how do you stand it?" His face was stiff with outrage. "He thinks he's Jesus Christ!"

II

155 Sheppard's attic was a large unfinished room with exposed beams and no electric light. They had set the telescope up on a tripod in one of the dormer windows. It pointed now toward the dark sky where a sliver of moon, as fragile as an egg shell, had just emerged from behind a cloud with a brilliant silver edge. Inside, a kerosene lantern set on a trunk cast their shadows upward and tangled them, wavering slightly, in the joints overhead. Sheppard was sitting on a packing box, looking through the telescope, and Johnson was at his elbow, waiting to get at it. Sheppard had bought it for fifteen dollars two days before at a pawn shop.

"Quit hoggin it," Johnson said.

Sheppard got up and Johnson slid onto the box and put his eye to the instrument.

Sheppard sat down on a straight chair a few feet away. His face was flushed with pleasure. This much of his dream was a reality. Within a week he had made it possible for this boy's vision to pass through a slender channel to the stars. He looked at Johnson's bent back with complete satisfaction. The boy had on one of Norton's plaid shirts and some new khaki trousers he had bought him. The shoe would be ready next week. He had taken him to the brace shop the day after he came and had him fitted for a new shoe. Johnson was as touchy about the foot as if it were a sacred object. His face had been glum while the clerk, a young man with a bright pink bald head, measured the foot with his profane hands. The shoe was going to make the greatest difference in the boy's attitude. Even a child with normal feet was in love with the world after he had got a new pair of shoes. When Norton got a new pair, he walked around for days with his eyes on his feet.

Sheppard glanced across the room at the child. He was sitting on the floor against a trunk, trussed up in a rope he had found and wound around his legs from his ankles to his knees. He appeared so far away that Sheppard might have been looking at him through the wrong end of the telescope. He had had to whip him only once since Johnson had been with them—the first night when Norton had realized that Johnson was going to sleep in his mother's bed. He did not believe in whipping children, particularly in anger. In this case, he had done both and with good results. He had had no more trouble with Norton.

The child hadn't shown any positive generosity toward Johnson but what he couldn't help, he appeared to be resigned to. In the mornings Sheppard sent the two of them to the Y swimming pool, gave them money to get their lunch at the cafeteria and instructed them to meet him in the park in the afternoon to watch his Little League baseball practice. Every afternoon they had arrived at the park, shambling, silent, their faces closed each on his own thoughts as if neither were aware of the other's existence. At least he could be thankful there were no fights.

Norton showed no interest in the telescope. "Don't you want to get up and look through the telescope, Norton?" he said. It irritated him that the child showed no intellectual curiosity whatsoever. "Rufus is going to be way ahead of you."

Norton leaned forward absently and looked at Johnson's back.

Johnson turned around from the instrument. His face had begun to fill out again. The look of outrage had retreated from his hollow cheeks and was shored up now in the caves of his eyes, like a fugitive from Sheppard's kindness. "Don't waste your valuable time, kid," he said. "You seen the moon once, you seen it."

Sheppard was amused by these sudden turns of perversity. The boy resisted whatever he suspected was meant for his improvement and contrived when he was vitally interested in something to leave the impression he was bored. Sheppard was not deceived. Secretly Johnson was learning what he wanted him to learn—that his benefactor was impervious to insult and that there were no cracks in his armor of kindness and patience where a successful shaft could be

160

driven. "Some day you may go to the moon," he said. "In ten years men will probably be making round trips there on schedule. Why you boys may be spacemen. Astronauts!"

"Astro-nuts," Johnson said.

165   "Nuts or nauts," Sheppard said, "it's perfectly possible that you, Rufus Johnson, will go to the moon."

Something in the depths of Johnson's eyes stirred. All day his humor had been glum. "I ain't going to the moon and get there alive," he said, "and when I die I'm going to hell."

"It's at least possible to get to the moon," Sheppard said dryly. The best way to handle this kind of thing was with gentle ridicule. "We can see it. We know it's there. Nobody has given any reliable evidence there's a hell."

"The Bible has give the evidence," Johnson said darkly, "and if you die and go there you burn forever."

170   The child leaned forward.

"Whoever says it ain't a hell," Johnson said, "is contradicting Jesus. The dead are judged and the wicked are damned. They weep and gnash their teeth while they burn," he continued, "and it's everlasting darkness."

The child's mouth opened. His eyes appeared to grow hollow.

"Satan runs it," Johnson said.

Norton lurched up and took a hobbled step toward Sheppard. "Is she there?" he said in a loud voice. "Is she there burning up?" He kicked the rope off his feet. "Is she on fire?"

175   "Oh my God," Sheppard muttered. "No no," he said, "of course she isn't. Rufus is mistaken. Your mother isn't anywhere. She's not unhappy. She just isn't." His lot would have been easier if when his wife died he had told Norton she had gone to heaven and that some day he would see her again, but he could not allow himself to bring him up on a lie.

Norton's face began to twist. A knot formed in his chin.

"Listen," Sheppard said quickly and pulled the child to him, "your mother's spirit lives on in other people and it'll live on in you if you're good and generous like she was."

The child's pale eyes hardened in disbelief.

Sheppard's pity turned to revulsion. The boy would rather she be in hell than nowhere. "Do you understand?" he said. "She doesn't exist." He put his hand on the child's shoulder. "That's all I have to give you," he said in a softer, exasperated tone, "the truth."

180   Instead of howling, the boy wrenched himself away and caught Johnson by the sleeve. "Is she there, Rufus?" he said "Is she there, burning up?"

Johnson's eyes glittered. "Well," he said, "she is if she was evil. Was she a whore?"

"Your mother was not a whore," Sheppard said sharply. He had the sensation of driving a car without brakes. "Now let's have no more of this foolishness. We were talking about the moon."

"Did she believe in Jesus?" Johnson asked.

Norton looked blank. After a second he said, "Yes," as if he saw that this was necessary. "She did," he said. "All the time."

"She did not," Sheppard muttered.   185

"She did all the time," Norton said. "I heard her say she did all the time."

"She's saved," Johnson said.

The child still looked puzzled. "Where?" he said. "Where is she at?"

"On high," Johnson said.

"Where's that?" Norton gasped.   190

"It's in the sky somewhere," Johnson said, "but you got to be dead to get there. You can't go in no space ship." There was a narrow gleam in his eyes now like a beam holding steady on its target.

"Man's going to the moon," Sheppard said grimly, "is very much like the first fish crawling out of the water onto land billions and billions of years ago. He didn't have an earth suit. He had to grow his adjustments inside. He developed lungs."

"When I'm dead will I go to hell or where she is?" Norton asked.

"Right now you'd go where she is," Johnson said, "but if you live long enough, you'll go to hell."

Sheppard rose abruptly and picked up the lantern. "Close the window,   195
Rufus," he said. "It's time we went to bed."

On the way down the attic stairs he heard Johnson say in a loud whisper behind him, "I'll tell you all about it tomorrow, kid, when Himself has cleared out."

The next day when the boys came to the ball park, he watched them as they came from behind the bleachers and around the edge of the field. Johnson's hand was on Norton's shoulder, his head bent toward the younger boy's ear, and on the child's face there was a look of complete confidence, of dawning light. Sheppard's grimace hardened. This would be Johnson's way of trying to annoy him. But he would not be annoyed. Norton was not bright enough to be damaged much. He gazed at the child's dull absorbed little face. Why try to make him superior? Heaven and hell were for the mediocre, and he was that if he was anything.

The two boys came into the bleachers and sat down about ten feet away, facing him, but neither gave him any sign of recognition. He cast a glance behind him where the Little Leaguers were spread out in the field. Then he started for the bleachers. The hiss of Johnson's voice stopped as he approached.

"What have you fellows been doing today?" he asked genially.

"He's been telling me . . ." Norton started.   200

Johnson pushed the child in the ribs with his elbow. "We ain't been doing nothing," he said. His face appeared to be covered with a blank glaze but through it a look of complicity was blazoned forth insolently.

Sheppard felt his face grow warm, but he said nothing. A child in a Little League uniform had followed him and was nudging him in the back of the leg with a bat. He turned and put his arm around the boy's neck and went with him back to the game.

That night when he went to the attic to join the boys at the telescope, he found Norton there alone. He was sitting on the packing box, hunched over, looking intently through the instrument. Johnson was not there.

"Where's Rufus?" Sheppard asked.

"I said where's Rufus?" he said louder.

"Gone somewhere," the child said without turning around.

"Gone where?" Sheppard asked.

"He just said he was going somewhere. He said he was fed up looking at stars."

"I see," Sheppard said glumly. He turned and went back down the stairs. He searched the house without finding Johnson. Then he went to the living room and sat down. Yesterday he had been convinced of his success with the boy. Today he faced the possibility that he was failing with him. He had been overlenient, too concerned to have Johnson like him. He felt a twinge of guilt. What difference did it make if Johnson liked him or not? What was that to him? When the boy came in, they would have a few things understood. As long as you stay here there'll be no going out at night by yourself, do you understand?

I don't have to stay here. It ain't nothing to me staying here.

Oh my God, he thought. He could not bring it to that. He would have to be firm but not make an issue of it. He picked up the evening paper. Kindness and patience were always called for but he had not been firm enough. He sat holding the paper but not reading it. The boy would not respect him unless he showed firmness. The doorbell rang and he went to answer it. He opened it and stepped back, with a pained disappointed face.

A large dour policeman stood on the stoop, holding Johnson by the elbow. At the curb a patrol car waited. Johnson looked very white. His jaw was thrust forward as if to keep from trembling.

"We brought him here first because he raised such a fit," the policeman said, "but now that you've seen him, we're going to take him to the station and ask him a few questions."

"What happened?" Sheppard muttered.

"A house around the corner from here," the policeman said. "A real smash job, dishes broken all over the floor, furniture turned upside down . . ."

"I didn't have a thing to do with it!" Johnson said. "I was walking along minding my own bidnis when this cop came up and grabbed me."

Sheppard looked at the boy grimly. He made no effort to soften his expression.

Johnson flushed. "I was just walking along," he muttered, but with no conviction in his voice.

"Come on, bud," the policeman said.

"You ain't going to let him take me, are you?" Johnson said. "You believe me, don't you?" There was an appeal in his voice that Sheppard had not heard there before.

This was crucial. The boy would have to learn that he could not be protected when he was guilty. "You'll have to go with him, Rufus," he said.

"You're going to let him take me and I tell you I ain't done a thing?" Johnson said shrilly.

Sheppard's face became harder as his sense of injury grew. The boy had failed him even before he had had a chance to give him the shoe. They were to have got it tomorrow. All his regret turned suddenly on the shoe; his irritation at the sight of Johnson doubled.

"You made out like you had all this confidence in me," the boy mumbled.

"I did have," Sheppard said. His face was wooden. 225

Johnson turned away with the policeman but before he moved, a gleam of pure hatred flashed toward Sheppard from the pits of his eyes.

Sheppard stood in the door and watched them get into the patrol car and drive away. He summoned his compassion. He would go to the station tomorrow and see what he could do about getting him out of trouble. The night in jail would not hurt him and the experience would teach him that he could not treat with impunity someone who had shown him nothing but kindness. Then they would go get the shoe and perhaps after a night in jail it would mean even more to the boy.

The next morning at eight o'clock the police sergeant called and told him he could come pick Johnson up. "We booked a nigger on that charge," he said. "Your boy didn't have nothing to do with it."

Sheppard was at the station in ten minutes, his face hot with shame. Johnson sat slouched on a bench in a drab outer office, reading a police magazine. There was no one else in the room. Sheppard sat down beside him and put his hand tentatively on his shoulder.

The boy glanced up—his lip curled—and back to the magazine. 230

Sheppard felt physically sick. The ugliness of what he had done bore in upon him with a sudden dull intensity. He had failed him at just the point where he might have turned him once and for all in the right direction. "Rufus," he said, "I apologize. I was wrong and you were right. I misjudged you."

The boy continued to read.

"I'm sorry."

The boy wet his finger and turned a page.

Sheppard braced himself. "I was a fool, Rufus," he said. 235

Johnson's mouth slid slightly to the side. He shrugged without raising his head from the magazine.

"Will you forget it, this time?" Sheppard said. "It won't happen again."

The boy looked up. His eyes were bright and unfriendly. "I'll forget it," he said, "but you better remember it." He got up and stalked toward the door. In the middle of the room he turned and jerked his arm at Sheppard and Sheppard jumped up and followed him as if the boy had yanked an invisible leash.

"Your shoe," he said eagerly, "today is the day to get your shoe!" Thank God for the shoe!

But when they went to the brace shop, they found that the shoe had been 240 made two sizes too small and a new one would not be ready for another ten days. Johnson's temper improved at once. The clerk had obviously made a mistake in the measurements but the boy insisted the foot had grown. He left the shop with a pleased expression, as if, in expanding, the foot had acted on some inspiration of its own. Sheppard's face was haggard.

After this he redoubled his efforts. Since Johnson had lost interest in the telescope, he bought a microscope and a box of prepared slides. If he couldn't impress the boy with immensity, he would try the infinitesimal. For two nights Johnson appeared absorbed in the new instrument, then he abruptly lost interest in it, but he seemed content to sit in the living room in the evening and read the encyclopedia. He devoured the encyclopedia as he devoured his dinner, steadily and without dint to his appetite. Each subject appeared to enter his head, be ravaged, and thrown out. Nothing pleased Sheppard more than to see the boy slouched on the sofa, his mouth shut, reading. After they had spent two or three evenings like this, he began to recover his vision. His confidence returned. He knew that some day he would be proud of Johnson.

On Thursday night Sheppard attended a city council meeting. He dropped the boys off at a movie on his way and picked them up on his way back. When they reached home, an automobile with a single red eye above its windshield was waiting in front of the house. Sheppard's lights as he turned into the driveway illuminated two dour faces in the car.

"The cops!" Johnson said. "Some nigger has broke in somewhere and they've come for me again."

"We'll see about that," Sheppard muttered. He stopped the car in the driveway and switched off the lights. "You boys go in the house and go to bed," he said. "I'll handle this."

245 He got out and strode toward the squad car. He thrust his head in the window. The two policemen were looking at him with silent knowledgeable faces. "A house on the corner of Shelton and Mills," the one in the driver's seat said. "It looks like a train run through it."

"He was in the picture show downtown," Sheppard said. "My boy was with him. He had nothing to do with the other one and he had nothing to do with this one. I'll be responsible."

"If I was you," the one nearest him said, "I wouldn't be responsible for any little bastard like him."

"I said I'd be responsible," Sheppard repeated coldly. "You people made a mistake the last time. Don't make another."

The policemen looked at each other. "It ain't our funeral," the one in the driver's seat said, and turned the key in the ignition.

250 Sheppard went in the house and sat down in the living room in the dark. He did not suspect Johnson and he did not want the boy to think he did. If Johnson thought he suspected him again, he would lose everything. But he wanted to know if his alibi was airtight. He thought of going to Norton's room and asking him if Johnson had left the movie. But that would be worse. Johnson would know what he was doing and would be incensed. He decided to ask Johnson himself. He would be direct. He went over in his mind what he was going to say and then he got up and went to the boy's door.

It was open as if he had been expected but Johnson was in bed. Just enough light came in from the hall for Sheppard to see his shape under the sheet. He came in and stood at the foot of the bed. "They've gone," he said. "I told them you had nothing to do with it and that I'd be responsible."

There was a muttered "Yeah," from the pillow.

Sheppard hesitated. "Rufus," he said, "you didn't leave the movie for anything at all, did you?"

"You make out like you got all this confidence in me!" a sudden outraged voice cried, "and you ain't got any! You don't trust me no more now than you did then!" The voice, disembodied, seemed to come more surely from the depths of Johnson than when his face was visible. It was a cry of reproach, edged slightly with contempt.

"I do have confidence in you," Sheppard said intensely. "I have every confidence in you. I believe in you and I trust you completely."

"You got your eye on me all the time," the voice said sullenly. "When you get through asking me a bunch of questions, you're going across the hall and ask Norton a bunch of them."

"I have no intention of asking Norton anything and never did," Sheppard said gently. "And I don't suspect you at all. You could hardly have got from the picture show downtown and out here to break in a house and back to the picture show in the time you had."

"That's why you believe me!" the boy cried, "—because you think I couldn't have done it."

"No, no!" Sheppard said. "I believe you because I believe you've got the brains and the guts not to get in trouble again. I believe you know yourself well enough now to know that you don't have to do such things. I believe that you can make anything of yourself that you set your mind to."

Johnson sat up. A faint light shone on his forehead but the rest of his face was invisible. "And I could have broke in there if I'd wanted to in the time I had," he said.

"But I know you didn't," Sheppard said. "There's not the least trace of doubt in my mind."

There was a silence. Johnson lay back down. Then the voice, low and hoarse, as if it were being forced out with difficulty, said, "You don't want to steal and smash up things when you've got everything you want already."

Sheppard caught his breath. The boy was thanking him! He was thanking him! There was gratitude in his voice. There was appreciation. He stood there, smiling foolishly in the dark, trying to hold the moment in suspension. Involuntarily he took a step toward the pillow and stretched out his hand and touched Johnson's forehead. It was cold and dry like rusty iron.

"I understand. Good night, son," he said and turned quickly and left the room. He closed the door behind him and stood there, overcome with emotion.

Across the hall Norton's door was open. The child lay on the bed on his side, looking into the light from the hall.

After this, the road with Johnson would be smooth.

Norton sat up and beckoned to him.

He saw the child but after the first instant, he did not let his eyes focus directly on him. He could not go in and talk to Norton without breaking Johnson's trust. He hesitated, but remained where he was a moment as if he saw nothing. Tomorrow was the day they were to go back for the shoe. It would be a climax to the good feeling between them. He turned quickly and went back into his own room.

The child sat for some time looking at the spot where his father had stood. Finally his gaze became aimless and he lay back down.

270   The next day Johnson was glum and silent as if he were ashamed that he had revealed himself. His eyes had a hooded look. He seemed to have retired within himself and there to be going through some crisis of determination. Sheppard could not get to the brace shop quickly enough. He left Norton at home because he did not want his attention divided. He wanted to be free to observe Johnson's reaction minutely. The boy did not seem pleased or even interested in the prospect of the shoe, but when it became an actuality, certainly then he would be moved.

The brace shop was a small concrete warehouse lined and stacked with the equipment of affliction. Wheel chairs and walkers covered most of the floor. The walls were hung with every kind of crutch and brace. Artificial limbs were stacked on the shelves, legs and arms and hands, claws and hooks, straps and human harnesses and unidentifiable instruments for unnamed deformities. In a small clearing in the middle of the room there was a row of yellow plastic-cushioned chairs and a shoe-fitting stool. Johnson slouched down in one of the chairs and set his foot up on the stool and sat with his eyes on it moodily. What was roughly the toe had broken open again and he had patched it with a piece of canvas; another place he had patched with what appeared to be the tongue of the original shoe. The two sides were laced with twine.

There was an excited flush on Sheppard's face; his heart was beating unnaturally fast.

The clerk appeared from the back of the shop with the new shoe under his arm. "Got her right this time!" he said. He straddled the shoe-fitting stool and held the shoe up, smiling as if he had produced it by magic.

It was a black slick shapeless object, shining hideously. It looked like a blunt weapon, highly polished.

275   Johnson gazed at it darkly.

"With this shoe," the clerk said, "you won't know you're walking. You'll think you're riding!" He bent his bright pink bald head and began gingerly to unlace the twine. He removed the old shoe as if he were skinning an animal still half alive. His expression was strained. The unsheathed mass of foot in the dirty sock made Sheppard feel queasy. He turned his eyes away until the new shoe was on. The clerk laced it up rapidly. "Now stand up and walk around," he said, "and see if that ain't power glide." He winked at Sheppard. "In that shoe," he said, "he won't know he don't have a normal foot."

Sheppard's face was bright with pleasure.

Johnson stood up and walked a few yards away. He walked stiffly with almost no dip in his short side. He stood for a moment, rigid, with his back to them.

"Wonderful!" Sheppard said. "Wonderful." It was as if he had given the boy a new spine.

280   Johnson turned around. His mouth was set in a thin icy line. He came back to the seat and removed the shoe. He put his foot in the old one and began lacing it up.

"You want to take it home and see if it suits you first?" the clerk murmured.

"No," Johnson said. "I ain't going to wear it at all."

"What's wrong with it?" Sheppard said, his voice rising.

"I don't need no new shoe," Johnson said. "And when I do, I got ways of getting my own." His face was stony but there was a glint of triumph in his eyes.

"Boy," the clerk said, "is your trouble in your foot or in your head?"

"Go soak your skull," Johnson said. "Your brains are on fire."

The clerk rose glumly but with dignity and asked Sheppard what he wanted done with the shoe, which he dangled dispiritedly by the lace.

Sheppard's face was a dark angry red. He was staring straight in front of him at a leather corset with an artificial arm attached.

The clerk asked him again.

"Wrap it up," Sheppard muttered. He turned his eyes to Johnson. "He's not mature enough for it yet," he said. "I had thought he was less of a child."

The boy leered. "You been wrong before," he said.

That night they sat in the living room and read as usual. Sheppard kept himself glumly entrenched behind the Sunday New York *Times*. He wanted to recover his good humor, but every time he thought of the rejected shoe, he felt a new charge of irritation. He did not trust himself even to look at Johnson. He realized that the boy had refused the shoe because he was insecure. Johnson had been frightened by his own gratitude. He didn't know what to make of the new self he was becoming conscious of. He understood that something he had been was threatened and he was facing himself and his possibilities for the first time. He was questioning his identity. Grudgingly, Sheppard felt a slight return of sympathy for the boy. In a few minutes, he lowered his paper and looked at him.

Johnson was sitting on the sofa, gazing over the top of the encyclopedia. His expression was trancelike. He might have been listening to something far away. Sheppard watched him intently but the boy continued to listen, and did not turn his head. The poor kid is lost, Sheppard thought. Here he had sat all evening, sullenly reading the paper, and had not said a word to break the tension. "Rufus," he said.

Johnson continued to sit, stock-still, listening.

"Rufus," Sheppard said in a slow hypnotic voice, "you can be anything in the world you want to be. You can be a scientist or an architect or an engineer or whatever you set your mind to, and whatever you set your mind to be, you can be the best of its kind." He imagined his voice penetrating to the boy in the black caverns of his psyche. Johnson leaned forward but his eyes did not turn. On the street a car door closed. There was a silence. Then a sudden blast from the door bell.

Sheppard jumped up and went to the door and opened it. The same policeman who had come before stood there. The patrol car waited at the curb.

"Lemme see that boy," he said.

Sheppard scowled and stood aside. "He's been here all evening," he said. "I can vouch for it."

The policeman walked into the living room. Johnson appeared engrossed in his book. After a second he looked up with an annoyed expression, like a great man interrupted at his work.

300 "What was that you were looking at in that kitchen window over on Winter Avenue about a half hour ago, bud?" the policeman asked.

"Stop persecuting this boy!" Sheppard said. "I'll vouch for the fact he was here. I was here with him."

"You heard him," Johnson said. "I been here all the time."

"It ain't everybody makes tracks like you," the policeman said and eyed the clubfoot.

"They couldn't be his tracks," Sheppard growled, infuriated. "He's been here all the time. You're wasting your own time and you're wasting ours." He felt the *ours* seal his solidarity with the boy. "I'm sick of this," he said. "You people are too damn lazy to go out and find whoever is doing these things. You come here automatically."

305 The policeman ignored this and continued looking through Johnson. His eyes were small and alert in his fleshy face. Finally he turned toward the door. "We'll get him sooner or later," he said, "with his head in a window and his tail out."

Sheppard followed him to the door and slammed it behind him. His spirits were soaring. This was exactly what he had needed. He returned with an expectant face.

Johnson had put the book down and was sitting there, looking at him slyly. "Thanks," he said.

Sheppard stopped. The boy's expression was predatory. He was openly leering.

"You ain't such a bad liar yourself," he said.

310 "Liar?" Sheppard murmured. Could the boy have left and come back? He felt himself sicken. Then a rush of anger sent him forward. "Did you leave?" he said furiously. "I didn't see you leave."

The boy only smiled.

"You went up in the attic to see Norton," Sheppard said.

"Naw," Johnson said, "that kid is crazy. He don't want to do nothing but look through that stinking telescope."

"I don't want to hear about Norton," Sheppard said harshly. "Where were you?"

315 "I was sitting on that pink can by my ownself," Johnson said. "There wasn't no witnesses."

Sheppard took out his handkerchief and wiped his forehead. He managed to smile.

Johnson rolled his eyes. "You don't believe in me," he said. His voice was cracked the way it had been in the dark room two nights before. "You make out like you got all this confidence in me but you ain't got any. When things get hot, you'll fade like the rest of them." The crack became exaggerated, comic. The mockery in it was blatant. "You don't believe in me. You ain't got no confidence," he wailed. "And you ain't any smarter than that cop. All that about tracks—that was a trap. There wasn't any tracks. That whole place is concreted in the back and my feet were dry."

Sheppard slowly put the handkerchief back in his pocket. He dropped down on the sofa and gazed at the rug beneath his feet. The boy's clubfoot was set within the circle of his vision. The pieced-together shoe appeared to grin at him with Johnson's own face. He caught hold of the edge of the sofa cushion and his knuckles turned white. A chill of hatred shook him. He hated the shoe, hated the foot, hated the boy. His face paled. Hatred choked him. He was aghast at himself.

He caught the boy's shoulder and gripped it fiercely as if to keep himself from falling. "Listen," he said, "you looked in that window to embarrass me. That was all you wanted—to shake my resolve to help you, but my resolve isn't shaken. I'm stronger than you are. I'm stronger than you are and I'm going to save you. The good will triumph."

"Not when it ain't true," the boy said. "Not when it ain't right." 320

"My resolve isn't shaken," Sheppard repeated. "I'm going to save you."

Johnson's look became sly again. "You ain't going to save me," he said. "You're going to tell me to leave this house. I did those other two jobs too—the first one as well as the one I done when I was supposed to be in the picture show."

"I'm not going to tell you to leave," Sheppard said. His voice was toneless, mechanical. "I'm going to save you."

Johnson thrust his head forward. "Save yourself," he hissed. "Nobody can save me but Jesus."

Sheppard laughed curtly. "You don't deceive me," he said. "I flushed that 325 out of your head in the reformatory. I saved you from that, at least."

The muscles in Johnson's face stiffened. A look of such repulsion hardened on his face that Sheppard drew back. The boy's eyes were like distorting mirrors in which he saw himself made hideous and grotesque. "I'll show you," Johnson whispered. He rose abruptly and started headlong for the door as if he could not get out of Sheppard's sight quick enough, but it was the door to the back hall he went through, not the front door. Sheppard turned on the sofa and looked behind him where the boy had disappeared. He heard the door to his room slam. He was not leaving. The intensity had gone out of Sheppard's eyes. They looked flat and lifeless as if the shock of the boy's revelation were only now reaching the center of his consciousness. "If he would only leave," he murmured. "If he would only leave now of his own accord."

The next morning Johnson appeared at the breakfast table in the grandfather's suit he had come in. Sheppard pretended not to notice but one look told him what he already knew, that he was trapped, that there could be nothing now but a battle of nerves and that Johnson would win it. He wished he had never laid eyes on the boy. The failure of his compassion numbed him. He got out of the house as soon as he could and all day he dreaded to go home in the evening. He had a faint hope that the boy might be gone when he returned. The grandfather's suit might have meant he was leaving. The hope grew in the afternoon. When he came home and opened the front door, his heart was pounding.

He stopped in the hall and looked silently into the living room. His expectant expression faded. His face seemed suddenly as old as his white hair. The two boys were sitting close together on the sofa, reading the same book. Norton's cheek rested against the sleeve of Johnson's black suit. Johnson's finger moved under the lines they were reading. The elder brother and the younger. Sheppard looked woodenly at this scene for almost a minute. Then he walked into the room and took off his coat and dropped it on a chair. Neither boy noticed him. He went on to the kitchen.

Leola left the supper on the stove every afternoon before she left and he put it on the table. His head ached and his nerves were taut. He sat down on the kitchen stool and remained there, sunk in his depression. He wondered if he could infuriate Johnson enough to make him leave of his own accord. Last night what had enraged him was the Jesus business. It might enrage Johnson, but it depressed him. Why not simply tell the boy to go? Admit defeat. The thought of facing Johnson again sickened him. The boy looked at him as if he were the guilty one, as if he were a moral leper. He knew without conceit that he was a good man, that he had nothing to reproach himself with. His feelings about Johnson now were involuntary. He would like to feel compassion for him. He would like to be able to help him. He longed for the time when there would be no one but himself and Norton in the house, when the child's simple selfishness would be all he had to contend with, and his own loneliness.

330 He got up and took three serving dishes off the shelf and took them to the stove. Absently he began pouring the butterbeans and the hash into the dishes. When the food was on the table, he called them in.

They brought the book with them. Norton pushed his place setting around to the same side of the table as Johnson's and moved his chair next to Johnson's chair. They sat down and put the book between them. It was a black book with red edges.

"What's that you're reading?" Sheppard asked, sitting down.

"The Holy Bible," Johnson said.

God give me strength, Sheppard said under his breath.

335 "We lifted it from a ten cent store," Johnson said.

"We?" Sheppard muttered. He turned and glared at Norton. The child's face was bright and there was an excited sheen to his eyes. The change that had come over the boy struck him for the first time. He looked alert. He had on a blue plaid shirt and his eyes were a brighter blue than he had ever seen them before. There was a strange new life in him, the sign of new and more rugged vices. "So now you steal?" he said, glowering. "You haven't learned to be generous but you have learned to steal."

"No he ain't," Johnson said. "I was the one lifted it. He only watched. He can't sully himself. It don't make any difference about me. I'm going to hell anyway."

Sheppard held his tongue.

"Unless," Johnson said, "I repent."

340 "Repent, Rufus," Norton said in a pleading voice. "Repent, hear? You don't want to go to hell."

"Stop talking this nonsense," Sheppard said, looking sharply at the child.

"If I do repent, I'll be a preacher," Johnson said. "If you're going to do it, it's no sense in doing it halfway."

"What are you going to be, Norton," Sheppard asked in a brittle voice, "a preacher too?"

There was a glitter of wild pleasure in the child's eyes. "A space man!" he shouted.

"Wonderful," Sheppard said bitterly.   345

"Those space ships ain't going to do you any good unless you believe in Jesus," Johnson said. He wet his finger and began to leaf through the pages of the Bible. "I'll read you where it says so," he said.

Sheppard leaned forward and said in a low furious voice, "Put that Bible up, Rufus, and eat your dinner."

Johnson continued searching for the passage.

"Put that Bible up!" Sheppard shouted.

The boy stopped and looked up. His expression was startled but pleased.   350

"That book is something for you to hide behind," Sheppard said. "It's for cowards, people who are afraid to stand on their own feet and figure things out for themselves."

Johnson's eyes snapped. He backed his chair a little way from the table. "Satan has you in his power," he said. "Not only me. You too."

Sheppard reached across the table to grab the book but Johnson snatched it and put it in his lap.

Sheppard laughed. "You don't believe in that book and you know you don't believe in it!"

"I believe it!" Johnson said. "You don't know what I believe and what I   355
don't."

Sheppard shook his head. "You don't believe it. You're too intelligent."

"I ain't too intelligent," the boy muttered. "You don't know nothing about me. Even if I didn't believe it, it would still be true."

"You don't believe it!" Sheppard said. His face was a taunt.

"I believe it!" Johnson said breathlessly. "I'll show you I believe it!" He opened the book in his lap and tore out a page of it and thrust it into his mouth. He fixed his eyes on Sheppard. His jaws worked furiously and the paper crackled as he chewed it.

"Stop this," Sheppard said in a dry, burnt-out voice. "Stop it."   360

The boy raised the Bible and tore out a page with his teeth and began grinding it in his mouth, his eyes burning.

Sheppard reached across the table and knocked the book out of his hand. "Leave the table," he said coldly.

Johnson swallowed what was in his mouth. His eyes widened as if a vision of splendor were opening up before him. "I've eaten it!" he breathed. "I've eaten it like Ezekiel and it was honey to my mouth!"[1]

"Leave this table," Sheppard said. His hands were clenched beside his plate.

---

1. Ezekiel 3:1–3. The Lord in a vision told Ezekiel to eat a roll and go speak to the captive Israelites; when he ate "it was in my mouth as honey for sweetness."

365   "I've eaten it!" the boy cried. Wonder transformed his face. "I've eaten it like Ezekiel and I don't want none of your food after it nor no more ever."

     "Go then," Sheppard said softly. "Go. Go."

     The boy rose and picked up the Bible and started toward the hall with it. At the door he paused, a small black figure on the threshold of some dark apocalypse. "The devil has you in his power," he said in a jubilant voice and disappeared.

     After supper Sheppard sat in the living room alone. Johnson had left the house but he could not believe that the boy had simply gone. The first feeling of release had passed. He felt dull and cold as at the onset of an illness and dread had settled in him like a fog. Just to leave would be too anticlimactic an end for Johnson's taste; he would return and try to prove something. He might come back a week later and set fire to the place. Nothing seemed too outrageous now.

     He picked up the paper and tried to read. In a moment he threw it down and got up and went into the hall and listened. He might be hiding in the attic. He went to the attic door and opened it.

370   The lantern was lit, casting a dim light on the stairs. He didn't hear anything. "Norton," he called, "are you up there?" There was no answer. He mounted the narrow stairs to see.

     Amid the strange vine-like shadows cast by the lantern, Norton sat with his eye to the telescope. "Norton," Sheppard said, "do you know where Rufus went?"

     The child's back was to him. He was sitting hunched, intent, his large ears directly above his shoulders. Suddenly he waved his hand and crouched closer to the telescope as if he could not get near enough to what he saw.

     "Norton!" Sheppard said in a loud voice.

     The child didn't move.

375   "Norton!" Sheppard shouted.

     Norton started. He turned around. There was an unnatural brightness about his eyes. After a moment he seemed to see that it was Sheppard. "I've found her!" he said breathlessly.

     "Found who?" Sheppard said.

     "Mamma!"

     Sheppard steadied himself in the door way. The jungle of shadows around the child thickened.

380   "Come and look!" he cried. He wiped his sweaty face on the tail of his plaid shirt and then put his eye back to the telescope. His back became fixed in a rigid intensity. All at once he waved again.

     "Norton," Sheppard said, "you don't see anything in the telescope but star clusters. Now you've had enough of that for one night. You'd better go to bed. Do you know where Rufus is?"

     "She's there!" he cried, not turning around from the telescope. "She waved at me!"

"I want you in bed in fifteen minutes," Sheppard said. After a moment he said, "Do you hear me, Norton?"

The child began to wave frantically.

"I mean what I say," Sheppard said. "I'm going to call in fifteen minutes and see if you're in bed."

He went down the steps again and returned to the parlor. He went to the front door and cast a cursory glance out. The sky was crowded with the stars he had been fool enough to think Johnson could reach. Somewhere in the small wood behind the house, a bull frog sounded a low hollow note. He went back to his chair and sat a few minutes. He decided to go to bed. He put his hands on the arms of the chair and leaned forward and heard, like the first shrill note of a disaster warning, the siren of a police car, moving slowly into the neighborhood and nearer until it subsided with a moan outside the house.

He felt a cold weight on his shoulders as if an icy cloak had been thrown about him. He went to the door and opened it.

Two policemen were coming up the walk with a dark snarling Johnson between them, handcuffed to each. A reporter jogged alongside and another policeman waited in the patrol car.

"Here's your boy," the dourest of the policemen said. "Didn't I tell you we'd get him?"

Johnson jerked his arm down savagely. "I was waitin for you!" he said. "You wouldn't have got me if I hadn't of wanted to get caught. It was my idea." He was addressing the policemen but leering at Sheppard.

Sheppard looked at him coldly.

"Why did you want to get caught?" the reporter asked, running around to get beside Johnson. "Why did you deliberately want to get caught?"

The question and the sight of Sheppard seemed to throw the boy into a fury. "To show up that big tin Jesus!" he hissed and kicked his leg out at Sheppard. "He thinks he's God. I'd rather be in the reformatory than in his house, I'd rather be in the pen! The Devil has him in his power. He don't know his left hand from his right, he don't have as much sense as his crazy kid!" He paused and then swept on to his fantastic conclusion. "He made suggestions to me!"

Sheppard's face blanched. He caught hold of the door facing.

"Suggestions?" the reporter said eagerly, "what kind of suggestion?"

"Immor'l suggestions!" Johnson said. "What kind of suggestions do you think? But I ain't having none of it, I'm a Christian, I'm . . ."

Sheppard's face was tight with pain. "He knows that's not true," he said in a shaken voice. "He knows he's lying. I did everything I knew how for him. I did more for him than I did for my own child. I hoped to save him and I failed, but it was an honorable failure. I have nothing to reproach myself with. I made no suggestions to him."

"Do you remember the suggestions?" the reporter asked. "Can you tell us exactly what he said?"

"He's a dirty atheist," Johnson said. "He said there wasn't no hell."

400 "Well, they seen each other now," one of the policemen said with a knowing sigh. "Let's us go."

"Wait," Sheppard said. He came down one step and fixed his eyes on Johnson's eyes in a last desperate effort to save himself. "Tell the truth, Rufus," he said. "You don't want to perpetrate this lie. You're not evil, you're mortally confused. You don't have to make up for that foot, you don't have to . . ."

Johnson hurled himself forward. "Listen at him!" he screamed. "I lie and steal because I'm good at it! My foot don't have a thing to do with it! The lame shall enter first! The halt'll be gathered together. When I get ready to be saved, Jesus'll save me, not that lying stinking atheist, not that . . ."

"That'll be enough out of you," the policeman said and yanked him back. "We just wanted you to see we got him," he said to Sheppard, and the two of them turned around and dragged Johnson away, half turned and screaming back at Sheppard.

"The lame'll carry off the prey!" he screeched, but his voice was muffled inside the car. The reporter scrambled into the front seat with the driver and slammed the door and the siren wailed into the darkness.

405 Sheppard remained there, bent slightly like a man who has been shot but continues to stand. After a minute he turned and went back in the house and sat down in the chair he had left. He closed his eyes on a picture of Johnson in a circle of reporters at the police station, elaborating his lies. "I have nothing to reproach myself with," he murmured. His every action had been selfless, his one aim had been to save Johnson for some decent kind of service, he had not spared himself, he had sacrificed his reputation, he had done more for Johnson than he had done for his own child. Foulness hung about him like an odor in the air, so close that it seemed to come from his own breath. "I have nothing to reproach myself with," he repeated. His voice sounded dry and harsh. "I did more for him than I did for my own child." He was swept with a sudden panic. He heard the boy's jubilant voice. Satan has you in his power.

"I have nothing to reproach myself with," he began again. "I did more for him than I did for my own child." He heard his voice as if it were the voice of his accuser. He repeated the sentence silently.

Slowly his face drained of color. It became almost gray beneath the white halo of his hair. The sentence echoed in his mind, each syllable like a dull blow. His mouth twisted and he closed his eyes against the revelation. Norton's face rose before him, empty, forlorn, his left eye listing almost imperceptibly toward the outer rim as if it could not bear a full view of grief. His heart constricted with a repulsion for himself so clear and intense that he gasped for breath. He had stuffed his own emptiness with good works like a glutton. He had ignored his own child to feed his vision of himself. He saw the clear-eyed Devil, the sounder of hearts, leering at him from the eyes of Johnson. His image of himself shrivelled until everything was black before him. He sat there paralyzed, aghast.

He saw Norton at the telescope, all back and ears, saw his arm shoot up and wave frantically. A rush of agonizing love for the child rushed over him like a transfusion of life. The little boy's face appeared to him transformed; the image of his salvation; all light. He groaned with joy. He would make everything up to him. He would never let him suffer again. He would be mother and father. He jumped up and ran to his room, to kiss him, to tell him that he loved him, that he would never fail him again.

The light was on in Norton's room but the bed was empty. He turned and dashed up the attic stairs and at the top reeled back like a man on the edge of a pit. The tripod had fallen and the telescope lay on the floor. A few feet over it, the child hung in the jungle of shadows, just below the beam from which he had launched his flight into space.

1965

FLANNERY O'CONNOR

Everything That Rises Must Converge

Her doctor had told Julian's mother that she must lose twenty pounds on account of her blood pressure, so on Wednesday nights Julian had to take her downtown on the bus for a reducing class at the Y. The reducing class was designed for working girls over fifty, who weighed from 165 to 200 pounds. His mother was one of the slimmer ones, but she said ladies did not tell their age or weight. She would not ride the buses by herself at night since they had been integrated, and because the reducing class was one of her few pleasures, necessary for her health, and *free*, she said Julian could at least put himself out to take her, considering all she did for him. Julian did not like to consider all she did for him, but every Wednesday night he braced himself and took her.

She was almost ready to go, standing before the hall mirror, putting on her hat, while he, his hands behind him, appeared pinned to the door frame, waiting like Saint Sebastian for the arrows to begin piercing him.[1] The hat was new and had cost her seven dollars and a half. She kept saying, "Maybe I shouldn't have paid that for it. No, I shouldn't have. I'll take it off and return it tomorrow. I shouldn't have bought it."

Julian raised his eyes to heaven. "Yes, you should have bought it," he said. "Put it on and let's go." It was a hideous hat. A purple velvet flap came down on one side of it and stood up on the other; the rest of it was green and looked like a cushion with the stuffing out. He decided it was less comical than jaunty and pathetic. Everything that gave her pleasure was small and depressed him.

She lifted the hat one more time and set it down slowly on top of her head. Two wings of gray hair protruded on either side of her florid face, but her eyes, sky-blue, were as innocent and untouched by experience as they must have been when she was ten. Were it not that she was a widow who had struggled fiercely to feed and clothe and put him through school and who was supporting him

---

1. Discovered to be a Christian, Sebastian, Roman commander in Milan, was tied to a tree, shot with arrows, and left for dead. (He recovered but when he reasserted his faith he was clubbed to death.)

still, "until he got on his feet," she might have been a little girl that he had to take to town.

5 "It's all right, it's all right," he said. "Let's go." He opened the door himself and started down the walk to get her going. The sky was a dying violet and the houses stood out darkly against it, bulbous liver-colored monstrosities of a uniform ugliness though no two were alike. Since this had been a fashionable neighborhood forty years ago, his mother persisted in thinking they did well to have an apartment in it. Each house had a narrow collar of dirt around it in which sat, usually, a grubby child. Julian walked with his hands in his pockets, his head down and thrust forward and his eyes glazed with the determination to make himself completely numb during the time he would be sacrificed to her pleasure.

The door closed and he turned to find the dumpy figure, surmounted by the atrocious hat, coming toward him. "Well," she said, "you only live once and paying a little more for it, I at least won't meet myself coming and going."

"Some day I'll start making money," Julian said gloomily—he knew he never would—"and you can have one of those jokes whenever you take the fit." But first they would move. He visualized a place where the nearest neighbors would be three miles away on either side.

"I think you're doing fine," she said, drawing on her gloves. "You've only been out of school a year. Rome wasn't built in a day."

She was one of the few members of the Y reducing class who arrived in hat and gloves and who had a son who had been to college. "It takes time," she said, "and the world is in such a mess. This hat looked better on me than any of the others, though when she brought it out I said, 'Take that thing back. I wouldn't have it on my head,' and she said, 'Now wait till you see it on,' and when she put it on me, I said, 'We-ull,' and she said, 'If you ask me, that hat does something for you and you do something for the hat, and besides,' she said, 'with that hat, you won't meet yourself coming and going.'"

10 Julian thought he could have stood his lot better if she had been selfish, if she had been an old hag who drank and screamed at him. He walked along, saturated in depression, as if in the midst of his martyrdom he had lost his faith. Catching sight of his long, hopeless, irritated face, she stopped suddenly with a grief-stricken look, and pulled back on his arm. "Wait on me," she said. "I'm going back to the house and take this thing off and tomorrow I'm going to return it. I was out of my head. I can pay the gas bill with that seven-fifty."

He caught her arm in a vicious grip. "You are not going to take it back," he said. "I like it."

"Well," she said, "I don't think I ought . . ."

"Shut up and enjoy it," he muttered, more depressed than ever.

"With the world in the mess it's in," she said, "it's a wonder we can enjoy anything. I tell you, the bottom rail is on the top."

15 Julian sighed.

"Of course," she said, "if you know who are you, you can go anywhere." She said this every time he took her to the reducing class. "Most of them in it are not our kind of people," she said, "but I can be gracious to anybody. I know who I am."

"They don't give a damn for your graciousness," Julian said savagely. "Knowing who you are is good for one generation only. You haven't the foggiest idea where you stand now or who you are."

She stopped and allowed her eyes to flash at him. "I most certainly do know who I am," she said, "and if you don't know who you are, I'm ashamed of you."

"Oh hell," Julian said.

"Your great-grandfather was a former governor of this state," she said. "Your grandfather was a prosperous land-owner. Your grandmother was a Godhigh."   20

"Will you look around you," he said tensely, "and see where you are now?" and he swept his arm jerkily out to indicate the neighborhood, which the growing darkness at least made less dingy.

"You remain what you are," she said. "Your great-grandfather had a plantation and two hundred slaves."

"There are no more slaves," he said irritably.

"They were better off when they were," she said. He groaned to see that she was off on that topic. She rolled onto it every few days like a train on an open track. He knew every stop, every junction, every swamp along the way, and knew the exact point at which her conclusion would roll majestically into the station: "It's ridiculous. It's simply not realistic. They should rise, yes, but on their own side of the fence."

"Let's skip it," Julian said.   25

"The ones I feel sorry for," she said, "are the ones that are half white. They're tragic."

"Will you skip it?"

"Suppose we were half white. We would certainly have mixed feelings."

"I have mixed feelings now," he groaned.

"Well let's talk about something pleasant," she said. "I remember going to   30
Grandpa's when I was a little girl. Then the house had double stairways that went up to what was really the second floor—all the cooking was done on the first. I used to like to stay down in the kitchen on account of the way the walls smelled. I would sit with my nose pressed against the plaster and take deep breaths. Actually the place belonged to the Godhighs but your grandfather Chestny paid the mortgage and saved it for them. They were in reduced circumstances," she said, "but reduced or not, they never forgot who they were."

"Doubtless that decayed mansion reminded them," Julian muttered. He never spoke of it without contempt or thought of it without longing. He had seen it once when he was a child before it had been sold. The double stairways had rotted and been torn down. Negroes were living in it. But it remained in his mind as his mother had known it. It appeared in his dreams regularly. He would stand on the wide porch, listening to the rustle of oak leaves, then wander through the high-ceilinged hall into the parlor that opened onto it and gaze at the worn rugs and faded draperies. It occurred to him that it was he, not she, who could have appreciated it. He preferred its threadbare elegance to anything he could name and it was because of it that all the neighborhoods they had lived in had been a torment to him—whereas she had hardly known the difference. She called her insensitivity "being adjustable."

"And I remember the old darky who was my nurse, Caroline. There was no better person in the world. I've always had a great respect for my colored friends," she said. "I'd do anything in the world for them and they'd . . ."

"Will you for God's sake get off that subject?" Julian said. When he got on a bus by himself, he made it a point to sit down beside a Negro, in reparation as it were for his mother's sins.

"You're mighty touchy tonight," she said. "Do you feel all right?"

"Yes I feel all right," he said. "Now lay off."

35   She pursed her lips. "Well, you certainly are in a vile humor," she observed. "I just won't speak to you at all."

They had reached the bus stop. There was no bus in sight and Julian, his hands still jammed in his pockets and his head thrust forward, scowled down the empty street. The frustration of having to wait on the bus as well as ride on it began to creep up his neck like a hot hand. The presence of his mother was borne in upon him as she gave a pained sigh. He looked at her bleakly. She was holding herself very erect under the preposterous hat, wearing it like a banner of her imaginary dignity. There was in him an evil urge to break her spirit. He suddenly unloosened his tie and pulled it off and put it in his pocket.

She stiffened. "Why must you look like *that* when you take me to town?" she said. "Why must you deliberately embarrass me?"

"If you'll never learn where you are," he said, "you can at least learn where I am."

40   "You look like a—thug," she said.

"Then I must be one," he murmured.

"I'll just go home," she said. "I will not bother you. If you can't do a little thing like that for me . . ."

Rolling his eyes upward, he put his tie back on. "Restored to my class," he muttered. He thrust his face toward her and hissed, "True culture is in the mind, the *mind*," he said, and tapped his head, "the mind."

"It's in the heart," she said, "and in how you do things and how you do things is because of who you *are*."

45   "Nobody in the damn bus cares who you are."

"I care who I am," she said icily.

The lighted bus appeared on top of the next hill and as it approached, they moved out into the street to meet it. He put his hand under her elbow and hoisted her up on the creaking step. She entered with a little smile, as if she were going into a drawing room where everyone had been waiting for her. While he put in the tokens, she sat down on one of the broad front seats for three which faced the aisle. A thin woman with protruding teeth and long yellow hair was sitting on the end of it. His mother moved up beside her and left room for Julian beside herself. He sat down and looked at the floor across the aisle where a pair of thin feet in red and white canvas sandals were planted.

His mother immediately began a general conversation meant to attract anyone who felt like talking. "Can it get any hotter?" she said and removed from her purse a folding fan, black with a Japanese scene on it, which she began to flutter before her.

"I reckon it might could," the woman with the protruding teeth said, "but I know for a fact my apartment couldn't get no hotter."

"It must get the afternoon sun," his mother said. She sat forward and looked up and down the bus. It was half filled. Everybody was white. "I see we have the bus to ourselves," she said. Julian cringed. 50

"For a change," said the woman across the aisle, the owner of the red and white canvas sandals. "I come on one the other day and they were thick as fleas—up front and all through."

"The world is in a mess everywhere," his mother said. "I don't know how we've let it get in this fix."

"What gets my goat is all those boys from good families stealing automobile tires," the woman with the protruding teeth said. "I told my boy, I said you may not be rich but you been raised right and if I ever catch you in any such mess, they can send you on to the reformatory. Be exactly where you belong."

"Training tells," his mother said. "Is your boy in high school?"

"Ninth grade," the woman said.

"My son just finished college last year. He wants to write but he's selling 55 typewriters until he gets started," his mother said.

The woman leaned forward and peered at Julian. He threw her such a malevolent look that she subsided against the seat. On the floor across the aisle there was an abandoned newspaper. He got up and got it and opened it out in front of him. His mother discreetly continued the conversation in a lower tone but the woman across the aisle said in a loud voice, "Well that's nice. Selling typewriters is close to writing. He can go right from one to the other."

"I tell him," his mother said, "that Rome wasn't built in a day."

Behind the newspaper Julian was withdrawing into the inner compartment of his mind where he spent most of his time. This was a kind of mental bubble in which he established himself when he could not bear to be a part of what was going on around him. From it he could see out and judge but in it he was safe from any kind of penetration from without. It was the only place where he felt free of the general idiocy of his fellows. His mother had never entered it but from it he could see her with absolute clarity.

The old lady was clever enough and he thought that if she had started from 60 any of the right premises, more might have been expected of her. She lived according to the laws of her own fantasy world, outside of which he had never seen her set foot. The law of it was to sacrifice herself for him after she had first created the necessity to do so by making a mess of things. If he had permitted her sacrifices, it was only because her lack of foresight had made them necessary. All of her life had been a struggle to act like a Chestny without the Chestny goods, and to give him everything she thought a Chestny ought to have; but since, said she, it was fun to struggle, why complain? And when you had won, as she had won, what fun to look back on the hard times! He could not forgive her that she had enjoyed the struggle and that she thought *she* had won.

What she meant when she said she had won was that she had brought him up successfully and had sent him to college and that he had turned out so well — good looking (her teeth had gone unfilled so that his could be straightened), intelligent (he realized he was too intelligent to be a success), and with a future ahead of him (there was of course no future ahead of him). She excused his gloominess on the grounds that he was still growing up and his radical ideas on his lack of practical experience. She said he didn't yet know a thing about "life," that he hadn't even entered the real world—when already he was as disenchanted with it as a man of fifty.

The further irony of all this was that in spite of her, he had turned out so well. In spite of going to only a third-rate college, he had, on his own initiative, come out with a first-rate education; in spite of growing up dominated by a small mind, he had ended up with a large one; in spite of all her foolish views, he was free of prejudice and unafraid to face facts. Most miraculous of all, instead of being blinded by love for her as she was for him, he had cut himself emotionally free of her and could see her with complete objectivity. He was not dominated by his mother.

The bus stopped with a sudden jerk and shook him from his meditation. A woman from the back lurched forward with little steps and barely escaped falling in his newspaper as she righted herself. She got off and a large Negro got on. Julian kept his paper lowered to watch. It gave him a certain satisfaction to see injustice in daily operation. It confirmed his view that with a few exceptions there was no one worth knowing within a radius of three hundred miles. The Negro was well dressed and carried a briefcase. He looked around and then sat down on the other end of the seat where the woman with the red and white canvas sandals was sitting. He immediately unfolded a newspaper and obscured himself behind it. Julian's mother's elbow at once prodded insistently into his ribs. "Now you see why I won't ride on these buses by myself," she whispered.

The woman with the red and white canvas sandals had risen at the same time the Negro sat down and had gone further back in the bus and taken the seat of the woman who had got off. His mother leaned forward and cast her an approving look.

Julian rose, crossed the aisle, and sat down in the place of the woman with the canvas sandals. From this position, he looked serenely across at his mother. Her face had turned an angry red. He stared at her, making his eyes the eyes of a stranger. He felt his tension suddenly lift as if he had openly declared war on her.

He would have liked to get in conversation with the Negro and to talk with him about art or politics or any subject that would be above the comprehension of those around them, but the man remained entrenched behind his paper. He was either ignoring the change of seating or had never noticed it. There was no way for Julian to convey his sympathy.

His mother kept her eyes fixed reproachfully on his face. The woman with the protruding teeth was looking at him avidly as if he were a type of monster new to her.

"Do you have a light?" he asked the Negro.

Without looking away from his paper, the man reached in his pocket and handed him a packet of matches.

"Thanks," Julian said. For a moment he held the matches foolishly. A NO SMOKING sign looked down upon him from over the door. This alone would not have deterred him; he had no cigarettes. He had quit smoking some months before because he could not afford it. "Sorry," he muttered and handed back the matches. The Negro lowered the paper and gave him an annoyed look. He took the matches and raised the paper again.

His mother continued to gaze at him but she did not take advantage of his momentary discomfort. Her eyes retained their battered look. Her face seemed to be unnaturally red, as if her blood pressure had risen. Julian allowed no glimmer of sympathy to show on his face. Having got the advantage, he wanted desperately to keep it and carry it through. He would have liked to teach her a lesson that would last her a while, but there seemed no way to continue the point. The Negro refused to come out from behind his paper.

Julian folded his arms and looked stolidly before him, facing her but as if he did not see her, as if he had ceased to recognize her existence. He visualized a scene in which, the bus having reached their stop, he would remain in his seat and when she said, "Aren't you going to get off?" he would look at her as a stranger who had rashly addressed him. The corner they got off on was usually deserted, but it was well lighted and it would not hurt her to walk by herself the four blocks to the Y. He decided to wait until the time came and then decide whether or not he would let her get off by herself. He would have to be at the Y at ten to bring her back, but he could leave her wondering if he was going to show up. There was no reason for her to think she could always depend on him.

He retired again into the high-ceilinged room sparsely settled with large pieces of antique furniture. His soul expanded momentarily but then he became aware of his mother across from him and the vision shriveled. He studied her coldly. Her feet in little pumps dangled like a child's and did not quite reach the floor. She was training on him an exaggerated look of reproach. He felt completely detached from her. At that moment he could with pleasure have slapped her as he would have slapped a particularly obnoxious child in his charge.

He began to imagine various unlikely ways by which he could teach her a lesson. He might make friends with some distinguished Negro professor or lawyer and bring him home to spend the evening. He would be entirely justified but her blood pressure would rise to 300. He could not push her to the extent of making her have a stroke, and moreover, he had never been successful at making any Negro friends. He had tried to strike up an acquaintance on the bus with some of the better types, with ones that looked like professors or ministers or lawyers. One morning he had sat down next to a distinguished-looking dark brown man who had answered his questions with a sonorous solemnity but who had turned out to be an undertaker. Another day he had sat down beside a cigar-smoking Negro with a diamond ring on his finger, but after a few stilted pleasantries, the Negro had rung the buzzer and risen, slipping two lottery tickets into Julian's hand as he climbed over him to leave.

70

75 He imagined his mother lying desperately ill and his being able to secure only a Negro doctor for her. He toyed with that idea for a few minutes and then dropped it for a momentary vision of himself participating as a sympathizer in a sit-in demonstration. This was possible but he did not linger with it. Instead, he approached the ultimate horror. He brought home a beautiful suspiciously Negroid woman. Prepare yourself, he said. There is nothing you can do about it. This is the woman I've chosen. She's intelligent, dignified, even good, and she's suffered and she hasn't thought it *fun*. Now persecute us, go ahead and persecute us. Drive her out of here, but remember, you're driving me too. His eyes were narrowed and through the indignation he had generated, he saw his mother across the aisle, purple-faced, shrunken to the dwarf-like proportions of her moral nature, sitting like a mummy beneath the ridiculous banner of her hat.

He was tilted out of his fantasy again as the bus stopped. The door opened with a sucking hiss and out of the dark a large, gaily dressed, sullen-looking colored woman got on with a little boy. The child, who might have been four, had on a short plaid suit and a Tyrolean hat with a blue feather in it. Julian hoped that he would sit down beside him and that the woman would push in beside his mother. He could think of no better arrangement.

As she waited for her tokens, the woman was surveying the seating possibilities—he hoped with the idea of sitting where she was least wanted. There was something familiar-looking about her but Julian could not place what it was. She was a giant of a woman. Her face was set not only to meet opposition but to seek it out. The downward tilt of her large lower lip was like a warning sign: DON'T TAMPER WITH ME. Her bulging figure was encased in a green crepe dress and her feet overflowed in red shoes. She had on a hideous hat. A purple velvet flap came down on one side of it and stood up on the other; the rest of it was green and looked like a cushion with the stuffing out. She carried a mammoth red pocketbook that bulged throughout as if it were stuffed with rocks.

To Julian's disappointment, the little boy climbed up on the empty seat beside his mother. His mother lumped all children, black and white, into the common category, "cute," and she thought little Negroes were on the whole cuter than little white children. She smiled at the little boy as he climbed on the seat.

Meanwhile the woman was bearing down upon the empty seat beside Julian. To his annoyance, she squeezed herself into it. He saw his mother's face change as the woman settled herself next to him and he realized with satisfaction that this was more objectionable to her than it was to him. Her face seemed almost gray and there was a look of dull recognition in her eyes, as if suddenly she had sickened at some awful confrontation. Julian saw that it was because she and the woman had, in a sense, swapped sons. Though his mother would not realize the symbolic significance of this, she would feel it. His amusement showed plainly on his face.

80 The woman next to him muttered something unintelligible to herself. He was conscious of a kind of bristling next to him, a muted growling like that of an angry cat. He could not see anything but the red pocketbook upright on the

bulging green thighs. He visualized the woman as she had stood waiting for her tokens—the ponderous figure, rising from the red shoes upward over the solid hips, the mammoth bosom, the haughty face, to the green and purple hat.

His eyes widened.

The vision of the two hats, identical, broke upon him with the radiance of a brilliant sunrise. His face was suddenly lit with joy. He could not believe that Fate had thrust upon his mother such a lesson. He gave a loud chuckle so that she would look at him and see that he saw. She turned her eyes on him slowly. The blue in them seemed to have turned a bruised purple. For a moment he had an uncomfortable sense of her innocence, but it lasted only a second before principle rescued him. Justice entitled him to laugh. His grin hardened until it said to her as plainly as if he were saying aloud: Your punishment exactly fits your pettiness. This should teach you a permanent lesson.

Her eyes shifted to the woman. She seemed unable to bear looking at him and to find the woman preferable. He became conscious again of the bristling presence at his side. The woman was rumbling like a volcano about to become active. His mother's mouth began to twitch slightly at one corner. With a sinking heart, he saw incipient signs of recovery on her face and realized that this was going to strike her suddenly as funny and was going to be no lesson at all. She kept her eyes on the woman and an amused smile came over her face as if the woman were a monkey that had stolen her hat. The little Negro was looking up at her with large fascinated eyes. He had been trying to attract her attention for some time.

"Carver!" the woman said suddenly. "Come heah!"

When he saw that the spotlight was on him at last, Carver drew his feet up and turned himself toward Julian's mother and giggled.

85

"Carver!" the woman said. "You heah me? Come heah!"

Carver slid down from the seat but remained squatting with his back against the base of it, his head turned slyly around toward Julian's mother, who was smiling at him. The woman reached a hand across the aisle and snatched him to her. He righted himself and hung backwards on her knees, grinning at Julian's mother. "Isn't he cute?" Julian's mother said to the woman with the protruding teeth.

"I reckon he is," the woman said without conviction.

The Negress yanked him upright but he eased out of her grip and shot across the aisle and scrambled, giggling wildly, onto the seat beside his love.

"I think he likes me," Julian's mother said, and smiled at the woman. It was the smile she used when she was being particularly gracious to an inferior. Julian saw everything was lost. The lesson had rolled off her like rain on a roof.

90

The woman stood up and yanked the little boy off the seat as if she were snatching him from contagion. Julian could feel the rage in her at having no weapon like his mother's smile. She gave the child a sharp slap across his leg. He howled once and then thrust his head into her stomach and kicked his feet against her shins. "Behave," she said vehemently.

The bus stopped and the Negro who had been reading the newspaper got off. The woman moved over and set the little boy down with a thump between herself and Julian. She held him firmly by the knee. In a moment he put his hands in front of his face and peeped at Julian's mother through his fingers.

"I see yoooooooo!" she said and put her hand in front of her face and peeped at him.

The woman slapped his hand down. "Quit yo' foolishness," she said, "before I knock the living Jesus out of you!"

95   Julian was thankful that the next stop was theirs. He reached up and pulled the cord. The woman reached up and pulled it at the same time. Oh my God, he thought. He had the terrible intuition that when they got off the bus together, his mother would open her purse and give the little boy a nickel. The gesture would be as natural to her as breathing. The bus stopped and the woman got up and lunged to the front, dragging the child, who wished to stay on, after her. Julian and his mother got up and followed. As they neared the door, Julian tried to relieve her of her pocketbook.

"No," she murmured, "I want to give the little boy a nickel."

"No!" Julian hissed. "No!"

She smiled down at the child and opened her bag. The bus door opened and the woman picked him up by the arm and descended with him, hanging at her hip. Once in the street she set him down and shook him.

Julian's mother had to close her purse while she got down the bus step but as soon as her feet were on the ground, she opened it again and began to rummage inside. "I can't find but a penny," she whispered, "but it looks like a new one."

100   "Don't do it!" Julian said fiercely between his teeth. There was a streetlight on the corner and she hurried to get under it so that she could better see into her pocketbook. The woman was heading off rapidly down the street with the child still hanging backward on her hand.

"Oh little boy!" Julian's mother called and took a few quick steps and caught up with them just beyond the lamppost. "Here's a bright new penny for you," and she held out the coin, which shone bronze in the dim light.

The huge woman turned and for a moment stood, her shoulders lifted and her face frozen with frustrated rage, and stared at Julian's mother. Then all at once she seemed to explode like a piece of machinery that had been given one ounce of pressure too much. Julian saw the black fist swing out with the red pocketbook. He shut his eyes and cringed as he heard the woman shout, "He don't take nobody's pennies!" When he opened his eyes, the woman was disappearing down the street with the little boy staring wide-eyed over her shoulder. Julian's mother was sitting on the sidewalk.

"I told you not to do that," Julian said angrily. "I told you not to do that!"

He stood over her for a minute, gritting his teeth. Her legs were stretched out in front of her and her hat was on her lap. He squatted down and looked her in the face. It was totally expressionless. "You got exactly what you deserved," he said. "Now get up."

105   He picked up her pocketbook and put what had fallen out back in it. He picked the hat up off her lap. The penny caught his eye on the sidewalk and he picked that up and let it drop before her eyes into the purse. Then he stood up

and leaned over and held his hands out to pull her up. She remained immobile. He sighed. Rising above them on either side were black apartment buildings, marked with irregular rectangles of light. At the end of the block a man came out of a door and walked off in the opposite direction. "All right," he said, "suppose somebody happens by and wants to know why you're sitting on the sidewalk?"

She took the hand and, breathing hard, pulled heavily up on it and then stood for a moment, swaying slightly as if the spots of light in the darkness were circling around her. Her eyes, shadowed and confused, finally settled on his face. He did not try to conceal his irritation. "I hope this teaches you a lesson," he said. She leaned forward and her eyes raked his face. She seemed trying to determine his identity. Then, as if she found nothing familiar about him, she started off with a headlong movement in the wrong direction.

"Aren't you going on to the Y?" he asked.

"Home," she muttered.

"Well, are we walking?"

For answer she kept going. Julian followed along, his hands behind him. He saw no reason to let the lesson she had had go without backing it up with an explanation of its meaning. She might as well be made to understand what had happened to her. "Don't think that was just an uppity Negro woman," he said. "That was the whole colored race which will no longer take your condescending pennies. That was your black double. She can wear the same hat as you, and to be sure," he added gratuitously (because he thought it was funny), "it looked better on her than it did on you. What all this means," he said, "is that the old world is gone. The old manners are obsolete and your graciousness is not worth a damn." He thought bitterly of the house that had been lost for him. "You aren't who you think you are," he said.

She continued to plow ahead, paying no attention to him. Her hair had come undone on one side. She dropped her pocketbook and took no notice. He stooped and picked it up and handed it to her but she did not take it.

"You needn't act as if the world had come to an end," he said, "because it hasn't. From now on you've got to live in a new world and face a few realities for a change. Buck up," he said, "it won't kill you."

She was breathing fast.

"Let's wait on the bus," he said.

"Home," she said thickly.

"I hate to see you behave like this," he said. "Just like a child. I should be able to expect more of you." He decided to stop where he was and make her stop and wait for a bus. "I'm not going any farther," he said stopping. "We're going on the bus."

She continued to go on as if she had not heard him. He took a few steps and caught her arm and stopped her. He looked into her face and caught his breath. He was looking into a face he had never seen before. "Tell Grandpa to come get me," she said.

He stared, stricken.

"Tell Caroline to come get me," she said.

Stunned, he let her go and she lurched forward again, walking as if one leg were shorter than the other. A tide of darkness seemed to be sweeping her from him. "Mother!" he cried. "Darling, sweetheart, wait!" Crumpling, she fell to the pavement. He dashed forward and fell at her side, crying, "Mamma, Mamma!" He turned her over. Her face was fiercely distorted. One eye, large and staring, moved slightly to the left as if it had become unmoored. The other remained fixed on him, raked his face again, found nothing and closed.

"Wait here, wait here!" he cried and jumped up and began to run for help toward a cluster of lights he saw in the distance ahead of him. "Help, help!" he shouted, but his voice was thin, scarcely a thread of sound. The lights drifted farther away the faster he ran and his feet moved numbly as if they carried him nowhere. The tide of darkness seemed to sweep him back to her, postponing from moment to moment his entry into the world of guilt and sorrow.

1965

FLANNERY O'CONNOR

Passages from Essays and Letters

from *"The Fiction Writer and His Country"*

. . . when I look at stories I have written I find that they are, for the most part, about people who are poor, who are afflicted in both mind and body, who have little—or at best a distorted—sense of spiritual purpose, and whose actions do not apparently give the reader a great assurance of the joy of life.

Yet how is this? For I am no disbeliever in spiritual purpose and no vague believer. I see from the standpoint of Christian orthodoxy. This means that for me the meaning of life is centered in our Redemption by Christ and what I see in the world I see in its relation to that.

Some may blame preoccupation with the grotesque on the fact that here we have a Southern writer and that this is just the type of imagination that Southern life fosters. . . . I find it hard to believe that what is observable behavior in one section can be entirely without parallel in another. At least, of late, Southern writers have had the opportunity of pointing out that none of us invented Elvis Presley and that that youth is himself probably less an occasion for concern than his popularity, which is not restricted to the Southern part of the country.

When you can assume that your audience holds the same beliefs you do, you can relax a little and use more normal means of talking to it; when you have to assume that it does not, then you have to make your vision apparent by shock—to the hard of hearing you shout, and for the almost-blind you draw large and startling figures.

from "The Grotesque in Southern Fiction"

All novelists are fundamentally seekers and describers of the real, but the realism of each novelist will depend on his view of the ultimate reaches of reality. . . . If the novelist is in tune with this [modern scientific] spirit, if he believes that actions are predetermined by psychic make-up or the economic situation or some other determinable factor, then he will be concerned above all with an accurate reproduction of the things that most immediately concern man, with the natural forces that he feels control his destiny. . . .

On the other hand, if the writer believes that our life is and will remain essentially mysterious, . . . then what he sees on the surface will be of interest to him only as he can go through it into an experience of mystery itself. . . . [F]or this kind of writer, the meaning of a story does not begin except at a depth where adequate motivation and adequate psychology and the various determinations have been exhausted. Such a writer will be interested in what we don't understand rather than in what we do.

from "The Nature and Aim of Fiction"[1]

. . . The beginning of human knowledge is through the senses, and the fiction writer begins where human perception begins. He appeals through the senses, and you cannot appeal to the senses with abstractions. . . . [F]iction is so very much an incarnational art.

Now the word *symbol* scares a good many people off, just as the word *art* does. They seem to feel that a symbol is some mysterious thing put in arbitrarily by the writer to frighten the common reader—sort of a literary Masonic grip that is only for the initiated. They seem to think that it is a way of saying something that you aren't actually saying, and so . . . they approach it as if it were a problem in algebra. Find *x*. And when they do find or think they find this abstraction, *x*, then they go off with an elaborate sense of satisfaction and the notion that they have "understood" the story. . . .

I think for the fiction writer himself, symbols are something he uses simply as a matter of course. You might say that these are details that, while having their essential place in the literal level of the story, operate in depth as well as on the surface, increasing the story in every direction.

People have a habit of saying, "What is the theme of your story?" and they expect you to give them a statement. . . . And when they've got a statement . . . , they go off happy and feel it is no longer necessary to read the story. . . . , but for the fiction writer himself the whole story is the meaning, because it is an experience, not an abstraction.

1. These selections and those that follow (from "Writing Short Stories") are composites, edited from O'Connor manuscripts by Sally and Robert Fitzgerald in *Mystery and Manners*.

from *"Writing Short Stories"*

. . . A story is a complete dramatic action—and in good stories, the characters are shown through the action and the action is controlled through the characters, and the result of this is meaning that derives from the whole presented experience.

. . . Nothing essential to the main experience can be left out of a short story. All the action has to be satisfactorily accounted for in terms of motivation, and there has to be a beginning, a middle, and an end, though not necessarily in that order.

. . . I prefer to talk about the meaning in a story rather than the theme of a story. People talk about the theme of a story as if the theme were like the string that a sack of chicken feed is tied with. They think that if you can pick out the theme, the way you pick the right thread in the chicken-feed sack, you can rip the story open and feed the chickens. But this is not the way meaning works in fiction.

When you can state the theme of a story, when you can separate it from the story itself, then you can be sure the story is not a very good one. The meaning of a story has to be embodied in it, has to be made concrete in it. A story is a way to say something that can't be said any other way, and it takes every word in the story to say what the meaning is. You tell a story because a statement would be inadequate.

An idiom characterizes a society, and when you ignore the idiom, you are very likely ignoring the whole social fabric that could make a meaningful character. You can't cut characters off from their society and say much about them as individuals. You can't say anything meaningful about the mystery of a personality unless you put that personality in a believable and significant social context.

from *"On Her Own Work"*

In most English classes the short story has become a kind of literary specimen to be dissected. Every time a story of mine appears in a Freshman anthology, I have a vision of it, with its little organs laid open, like a frog in a bottle.

I realize that a certain amount of this what-is-the-significance has to go on, but I think something has gone wrong in the process when, for so many students, the story becomes simply a problem to be solved, something which you evaporate to get Instant Enlightenment.

A story isn't any good unless it successfully resists paraphrase, unless it hangs on and expands in the mind. Properly, you analyze to enjoy, but it's equally true that to analyze with any discrimination, you have to have enjoyed already, and I think that the best reason to hear a story read is that it should stimulate that primary enjoyment.

I often ask myself what makes a story work, and what makes it hold up as a story, and I have decided that it is probably some action, some gesture of a character that is unlike any other in the story, one which indicates where the real heart of the story lies. This would have to be an action or a gesture which was both totally right and totally unexpected; it would have to be one that was both in character and beyond character; it would have to suggest both the world and eternity. The action or gesture I'm talking about would have to be on the anagogical level, that is, the level which has to do with the Divine life and our participation in it. It would be a gesture that transcended any neat allegory that might have been intended or any pat moral categories a reader could make. It would be a gesture which somehow made contact with mystery.

. . . in my own stories I have found that violence is strangely capable of returning my characters to reality and preparing them to accept their moment of grace . . .

We hear many complaints about the prevalence of violence in modern fiction, and it is always assumed that this violence is a bad thing and meant to be an end in itself. With the serious writer, violence is never an end in itself. It is the extreme situation that best reveals what we are essentially . . .

from "Novelist and Believer"

. . . Great fiction . . . is not simply an imitation of feeling. The good novelist not only finds a symbol for feeling, he finds a symbol and a way of lodging it which tells the intelligent reader whether this feeling is adequate or inadequate, whether it is moral or immoral, whether it is good or evil. And his theology, even in its most remote reaches, will have a direct bearing on this.

. . . The artist penetrates the concrete world in order to find at its depths the image of its source, the image of ultimate reality. This in no way hinders his perception of evil but rather sharpens it, for only when the natural world is seen as good does evil become intelligible as a destructive force and a necessary result of our freedom.

from the Letters

TO A PROFESSOR OF ENGLISH, 28 MARCH 1961

The meaning of a story should go on expanding for the reader the more he thinks about it, but meaning cannot be captured in an interpretation. If teachers are in the habit of approaching a story as if it were a research problem for which any answer is believable so long as it is not obvious, then I think students will never learn to enjoy fiction. Too much interpretation is certainly worse than too little, and where feeling for a story is absent, theory will not supply it.

TO LOUISE AND TOM GOSSETT, 10 APRIL 1961

I have just read a review of my book [*The Violent Bear It Away*], long and damming [*sic*], which says it don't give us hope and courage and that all novels should give us hope and courage. I think if the novel is to give us virtue the selection of hope and courage is rather arbitrary—why not charity, peace, patience, joy, benignity, long-suffering and fear of the Lord? Or faith? The fact of the matter is that the modern mind opposes courage to faith. It also demands that the novel provide us with gifts that only religion can give. I don't think the novel can offend against the truth, but I think its truths are more particular than general. But this is a large subject and I ain't no aesthetician.

TO ROSLYN BARNES, 17 JUNE 1961

Can you tell me if the statement: "everything that rises must converge" is a true proposition in physics? I can easily see its moral, historical and evolutionary significance, but I want to know if it is also a correct physical statement.

TO "A", 22 JULY 1961

I had a story that I had written a first draft sort of on and Caroline thought as usual that it wasn't dramatic enough (and she was right) and told me all the things that I tell you when I read one of yours. She did think the structure was good and the situation. All I got to do is write the story. This one is called "The Lame Shall Enter First."

TO "A", 16 SEPTEMBER 1961

The thing I am writing now is surely going to convince Jack [the author John Hawkes] that I am of the Devil's party. It is out of hand right now but I am hoping I can bring it into line. It is a composite of all the eccentricities of my writing and for this reason may not be any good, maybe almost a parody. But what you start, you ought to carry through and if it is no good, I don't have to publish it. I am thinking of changing the title to "The Lame Will Carry Off the Prey."

TO JOHN HAWKES, 28 NOVEMBER 1961

You haven't convinced me that I write with the Devil's will or belong in the romantic tradition and I'm prepared to argue some more with you on this if I can remember where we left off at. I think the reason we can't agree on this is because there is a difference in our two devils. My Devil has a name, a history and a definite plan. His name is Lucifer, he's a fallen angel, his sin is pride, and his aim is the destruction of the Divine plan. Now I judge that your Devil is co-equal to God, not his creature: that pride is his virtue not his sin; and that his aim is not to destroy the Divine plan because there isn't any Divine plan to destroy. My Devil is objective and yours is subjective. You say one becomes "evil" when one leaves the herd. I say that depends entirely on what the herd is doing.

TO "A", 9 DECEMBER 1961

Some friends of mine in Texas wrote me that a friend of theirs went into a bookstore looking for a paperback copy of A *Good Man*. The clerk said, "We don't have that one but we have another by that author, called *The Bear That Ran Away With It*. I foresee the trouble I am going to have with "Everything That Rises Must Converge"—"Every Rabbit That Rises Is a Sage."

TO CECIL DAWKINS, 6 SEPTEMBER 1962

About the story ["The Lame Shall Enter First"] I certainly agree that it don't work and have never felt that it did, but in heaven's name where do you get the idea that Sheppard represents Freud? Freud never entered my mind and looking back over it, I can't make him fit now. The story is about a man who thought he was good and thought he was doing good when he wasn't. Freud was a great one, wasn't he, for bringing home to people the fact that they weren't what they thought they were, so if Freud were in this, which he is not, he would certainly be on the other side of the fence from Shepp. The story doesn't work because I don't know, don't sympathize, don't like Mr. Sheppard in the way that I know and like most of my other characters. This is a story, not a statement. I think you ought to look for simpler explanations of why things don't work and not mess around with philosophical ideas where they haven't been intended or don't apply. There's nothing in the story that could possibly suggest that Sheppard represents Freud. This is some theory of which you are possessed. I am wondering if this kind of theorizing could be what is interfering with your getting going on some writing. Don't mix up thought-knowledge with felt-knowledge. If Sheppard represents anything here, it is, as he realizes at the end of the story, the empty man who fills up his emptiness with good works.

TO "A", 3 NOVEMBER 1962

. . . In that story of mine ["The Lame Shall Enter First"] . . . the little boy wouldn't have been looking for his mother if she hadn't been a good one when she was alive. This of course could be debated, but it's nowhere suggested in the story that she wasn't a good one.

TO MARION MONTGOMERY, 16 JUNE 1963

I never wrote and thanked you for innerducing me at Georgia or for the copy of *The Sermon of Introduction*, but I liked them. They made up for my present lack of popularity with the *Atlanta Journal-Constitution* book page, that alert sheet of Sunday criticism. Did you ever see their mention of "Everything That Rises Must Converge"? Unsigned. I suspect somebody from Atlanta U. did it.

TO "A", 1 SEPTEMBER 1963

The topical is poison. I got away with it in "Everything That Rises" but only because I say a plague on everybody's house as far as the race business goes.

▼ ▼ ▼

THE AUTHOR'S WORK AS CONTEXT A Glossary

canon: an author's entire body of work

colloquial diction: level of language or vocabulary that is *informal* in that it is the language of ordinary people but tends to imitate or suggest ordinary spoken rather than written language

diction: choice of words; often generally characterized as *formal, informal,* or *colloquial*; an aspect of *style*

dramatic irony: the unexpected fulfillment or reversal of a character's expectations

formal diction: large, sophisticated, and traditional vocabulary

hyperbole: see *overstatement*

imagery: broadly thought of, the visual descriptions, or even any sensory impressions generated, in a work, but more narrowly and usually, the figurative language, including *metaphors, similes, analogies* (see *Symbols: A Glossary,* p. 210); an aspect of *style*

informal diction: level of language or vocabulary that characterizes the written language of ordinary people

litotes: see *understatement*

overstatement or **hyperbole:** language that is so intense or exaggerated it must be read "at a discount," as meaning less than it literally states

rhetorical tropes: figures of thought or speech; part of *style*

rhythm: the pattern of sound pulsations in the voice as one reads (or as the sound is imagined in the mind); an aspect of *style*

style: the basic characteristics of the language of an author (or an age); while sometimes considered the manner as opposed to the matter, as "ornament," it is now more often seen as organic or fused, with the substance, manner, and matter being as closely related as body and soul; indeed, much recent criticism suggests that there is no "meaning" prior to language, that to think or mean is to think or mean in language itself

tone: the implied attitude or stance of the author toward the characters and events, somewhat like "tone of voice"

understatement or **litotes:** language that obviously underrates something or portrays it as lesser than it is usually thought to be

verbal irony: a word or expression that carries not only its literal meaning but for the speaker has a different, sometimes even an opposite, meaning

QUESTIONS

1. What sensory details do you find in the opening paragraph of "Odour of Chrysanthemums"? later in the story? What expectations are aroused by the opening paragraph? When do you first begin to suspect that Walter Bates is not off drinking somewhere?

2. In what ways might the opening of "The Rocking-Horse Winner" prepare you for the surreal or supernatural events later in the story?

3. If you did not know that "Odour of Chrysanthemums" and "The Rocking-Horse Winner" were by the same author, what internal evidence (elements, views, language within the story) might suggest it? How does "The Rocking-Horse Winner" of 1932 differ from the 1914 story "Odour of Chrysanthemums"?

4. How does Sheppard explain why Norton throws up ("The Lame Shall Enter First," par. 48)? Why do you think Norton throws up (other than his putting peanut butter and ketchup on his cake!)?

5 . What internal evidence is there that "The Lame Shall Enter First" and "Everything That Rises Must Converge" are by the same author?

WRITING SUGGESTIONS

1. Describe the continuity and the change or development in Lawrence's work, assuming those two stories are typical of that work and time of publication.

2. Briefly retell the story of "Everything That Rises Must Converge" from the point of view, perhaps even in the voice, of the African-American woman who is wearing "*the* hat."

3. Compare the function of money in "The Rocking-Horse Winner" and "The Lame Shall Enter First."

9 CULTURE AS CONTEXT: BORDER STORIES

Over the past two hundred years, the meaning of the word "culture" has changed from "enabling growth" (as in agri*culture*), to the arts or familiarity with the arts ("high culture," "a cultured person"), to a whole way of life ("Japanese culture"). In everyday use it sometimes is associated with "race," though it is usually distinguished from race in that culture is social rather than biological, learned from other members of the group or from experience rather than inherited through the genes (as "race," narrowly defined, is). Its current use is transitional and a sort of stopgap response to modern life: while it was used for a time to designate "primitive" groups (tribes) and their way of life, then applied to present-day national groups, it has been complicated by the worldwide spread of knowledge, experience, and interdependence of both material culture—clothing (jeans), tools, appliances, means of travel (cars and jets), and communication (television, computers, "the information highway")—and cultural ideas, like social and political organization (democracy, for example) or economic organization (such as the market economy), or tastes (like "American" popular music).

Often for the individual, the family, or larger groups, there is or seems to be a clash between the traditional culture of the group that has been passed on for generations or centuries and the practical pressures of survival (culture developed as a means of survival) in the modern world. As a result, we have developed the term "multiculturalism," whose definition and evaluation are intellectual and emotional battlegrounds.

As Americans, we tend to think ours is the only multicultural society and ours the only struggle to define what that means or should mean. We have become more and more conscious of how questionable the term "American culture" is or was, more and more aware that it represents not something clear and "natural," but the power structure of the nation. (This is not just a matter of race and gender: for some time "American" meant Northeastern, Christian [even Protestant], and at least second-generation.) In our new awareness we have taken what we used to consider "subcultures" into account, often with hyphens—African-American, Asian-American, and so on—though, of course, we are all immigrants (even Native Americans apparently came to this continent across the Bering Straits or some earlier bridge from Asia).

Multiculturalism implies rejection of the older idea of assimilation, of America as "melting pot," which meant, in effect, "Reject your group's culture and adopt ours" (that is, the culture of the majority or of those in power). But for some, multiculturalism strongly implies separatism as well, almost an adversarial stance toward other "subcultures," a last-ditch effort to retain the culture of the homeland or place of origin. So there is developing—influenced, interestingly, by forces in Eastern Europe after the breakup of the Soviet Union—what some call "transculturalism," a retention of something of the original, learned culture blended with other cultures and modern experience or "American" culture.

Whatever the outcome, it seems safe to say that our notions of "American" and of "culture" are in flux, even as world culture is in flux. (Notice, for example, that when June May gets to China—in "A Pair of Tickets"—her family takes her to a hotel much like a Hyatt Regency and orders hamburgers, french fries, and apple pie à la mode.) If culture is a means of survival and trans- or multiculturalism is the nature of contemporary culture, for survival's sake we must be aware not only of our own heritage but of that of others and of all our experiences of the here and now.

In this chapter this fluctuating cultural condition is represented by stories of Chicano/a experience, for Chicano culture is demonstrably, if not uniquely, a complex, fluctuating culture. Chicanos are not only Mexican Americans who speak traditional Spanish and recent English; they also combine Native American and Spanish (and thus Catholic) history and experience. But Chicanos live in the United States, most often (but far from always) near the Mexican border. This border position—geographical, linguistic, ethnic, cultural— is both unique, and, paradoxically, typical. We all live on the cultural border.

Rudolfo Anaya's "The Water People" delineates a religious borderline in Chicano culture that parallels the mixed Native American and Spanish "blood" or heritage, a border that runs between ancient native religions rooted in the natural world—a religion "moderns" may think of as legend or magic— and the Catholicism brought to the New World by the Spanish, now long a part of Chicano experience. These seemingly opposing visions of the world are variously negotiated but seldom ignored in Chicano culture. Here Ultima—a "good witch," who practices magic and herbal curing but goes to the Catholic church—suggests to Tony in a dream that these religious traditions, like Tony's divided blood or heritage, are part of one "great cycle that binds us all."

Juan Sánchez, in Richard Dokey's story, moves from Mexico to Mexicali and then almost four hundred miles north of the border to Twin Pines in the

Sierra Nevada mountains east of Stockton, seeking cooler, healthier air. His son, Jésus—born "miraculously" after the deaths of two earlier children and Juan's tubes having been tied—now grown, has a job in the Stockton cannery and brags to his father about the cannery's "greatness" and its "marvelous machines." His values are clearly not those of his father. He is proud of his room, though his father sees only its soiled bed and walls, the bare light bulb, the smell; proud of his "entertainment," a shabby pool hall and a movie house that leaves his father "beyond disappointment." A geographical, generational, and cultural border has been crossed, and Juan longs for Mexico, the home he had left with such hopes.

In "The Last of the Menu Girls" there are geographical and cultural borders as well, largely implicitly but explicitly in the Juan María section where the issue of illegal immigration is raised. Despite the specific location, the names, and the occasional Spanish phrases, this trenchant yet engaging story of "How I Spent My Summer Vacation" could have been set in any pocket of American culture, because the vibrant Chicano culture, though unique, is in its fluctuation and complexity typical of most modern American cultures.

▼ ▼ ▼

RUDOLFO ANAYA

The Water People

"Hey Toni-eeeeee. Huloooooo Antonioforous!"

A voice called.

At first I thought I was dreaming. I was fishing, and sitting on a rock; the sun beating on my back had made me sleepy. I had been thinking how Ultima's medicine had cured my uncle and how he was well and could work again. I had been thinking how the medicine of the doctors and of the priest had failed. In my mind I could not understand how the power of God could fail. But it had.

"Toni-eeeeee!" the voice called again.

5   I opened my eyes and peered into the green brush of the river. Silently, like a deer, the figure of Cico emerged. He was barefoot, he made no noise. He moved to the rock and squatted in front of me. I guess it was then that he decided to trust me with the secret of the golden carp.

"Cico?" I said. He nodded his dark, freckled face.

"Samuel told you about the golden carp," he said.

"Yes," I replied.

"Have you ever fished for carp?" he asked. "Here in the river, or anywhere?"

10   "No," I shook my head. I felt as if I was making a solemn oath.

"Do you want to see the golden carp?" he whispered.

"I have hoped to see him all summer," I said breathlessly.

"Do you believe the golden carp is a god?" he asked.

The commandment of the Lord said, Thou shalt have no other gods before me . . .

I could not lie. I knew he would find the lie in my eyes if I did. But maybe there were other gods? Why had the power of God failed to cure my uncle?

"I am a Catholic," I stuttered, "I can believe only in the God of the church—" I looked down. I was sorry because now he would not take me to see the golden carp. For a long time Cico did not speak.

"At least you are truthful, Tony," he said. He stood up. The quiet waters of the river washed gently southward. "We have never taken a non-believer to see him," he said solemnly.

"But I want to believe," I looked up and pleaded, "it's just that I have to believe in Him." I pointed across the river to where the cross of the church showed above the tree tops.

"Perhaps—" he mused for a long time. "Will you make an oath?" he asked.

"Yes," I answered. But the commandment said, Thou shalt not take the Lord's name in vain.

"Swear by the cross of the church that you will never hunt or kill a carp." He pointed to the cross. I had never sworn on the cross before. I knew that if you broke your oath it was the biggest sin a man could commit, because God was witness to the swearing on his name. But I would keep my promise! I would never break my oath!

"I swear," I said.

"Come!" Cico was off, wading across the river. I followed. I had waded across that river many times, but I never felt an urgency like today. I was excited about seeing the magical golden carp.

"The golden carp will be swimming down the creek today," Cico whispered. We scrambled up the bank and through the thick brush. We climbed the steep hill to the town and headed towards the school. I never came up this street to go to school and so the houses were not familiar to me. We paused at one place.

"Do you know who lives there?" Cico pointed at a green arbor. There was a fence with green vines on it, and many trees. Every house in town had trees, but I had never seen a place so green. It was thick like some of the jungles I saw in the movies in town.

"No," I said. We drew closer and peered through the dense curtain of green that surrounded a small adobe hut.

"Narciso," Cico whispered.

Narciso had been on the bridge the night Lupito was murdered. He had tried to reason with the men; he had tried to save Lupito's life. He had been called a drunk.

"My father and my mother know him," I said. I could not take my eyes from the garden that surrounded the small house. Every kind of fruit and vegetable I knew seemed to grow in the garden, and there was even more abundance here than on my uncles' farms.

30   "I know," Cico said, "they are from the llano[1]—"

"I have never seen such a place," I whispered. Even the air of the garden was sweet to smell.

"The garden of Narciso," Cico said with reverence, "is envied by all—Would you like to taste its fruits?"

"We can't," I said. It was a sin to take anything without permission.

"Narciso is my friend," Cico said. He reached through the green wall and a secret latch opened an ivy-laden door. We walked into the garden. Cico closed the door behind him and said, "Narciso is in jail. The sheriff found him drunk."

35   I was fascinated by the garden. I forgot about seeing the golden carp. The air was cool and clear, not dusty and hot like the street. Somewhere I heard the sound of gurgling water.

"Somewhere here there is a spring," Cico said, "I don't know where. That is what makes the garden so green. That and the magic of Narciso—"

I was bewildered by the garden. Everywhere I looked there were fruit-laden trees and rows and rows of vegetables. I knew the earth was fruitful because I had seen my uncles make it bear in abundance; but I never realized it could be like this! The ground was soft to walk on. The fragrance of sun-dazzling flowers was deep, and soft, and beautiful.

"The garden of Narciso," I whispered.

"Narciso is my friend," Cico intoned. He pulled some carrots from the soft, dark earth and we sat down to eat.

40   "I cannot," I said. It was silent and peaceful in the garden. I felt that someone was watching us.

"It is all right," Cico said.

And although I did not feel good about it, I ate the golden carrot. I had never eaten anything sweeter or juicier in my life.

"Why does Narciso drink?" I asked.

"To forget," Cico answered.

45   "Does he know about the golden carp?" I asked.

"The magic people all know about the coming day of the golden carp," Cico answered. His bright eyes twinkled. "Do you know how Narciso plants?" he asked.

"No," I answered. I had always thought farmers were sober men. I could not imagine a drunk man planting and reaping such fruits!

"By the light of the moon," Cico whispered.

"Like my uncles, the Lunas—"

50   "In the spring Narciso gets drunk," Cico continued. "He stays drunk until the bad blood of spring is washed away. Then the moon of planting comes over the elm trees and shines on the horde of last year's seeds—It is then that he gathers the seeds and plants. He dances as he plants, and he sings. He scatters the seeds by moonlight, and they fall and grow—The garden is like Narciso, it is drunk."

---

1. Plains. The Llano Estacado (or enclosed plain) stretches from Roswell, southeast New Mexico, to Lubbock, west Texas.

"My father knows Narciso," I said. The story Cico had told me was fascinating. It seemed that the more I knew about people the more I knew about the strange magic hidden in their hearts.

"In this town, everybody knows everybody," Cico said.

"Do you know everyone?" I asked.

"Uh-huh," he nodded.

"You know Jasón's Indian?"   55

"Yes."

"Do you know Ultima?" I asked.

"I know about her cure," he said. "It was good. Come on now, let's be on our way. The golden carp will be swimming soon—"

We slipped out of the coolness of the garden into the hot, dusty street. On the east side of the school building was a barren playground with a basketball goal. The gang was playing basketball in the hot sun.

"Does the gang know about the golden carp?" I asked as we approached the   60
group.

"Only Samuel," Cico said, "only Samuel can be trusted."

"Why do you trust me?" I asked. He paused and looked at me.

"Because you are a fisherman," he said. "There are no rules on who we trust, Tony, there is just a feeling. The Indian told Samuel the story; Narciso told me; now we tell you. I have a feeling someone, maybe Ultima, would have told you. We all share—"

"Hey!" Ernie called, "you guys want to play!" They ran towards us.

"Nah," Cico said. He turned away. He did not face them.   65

"Hi, Tony," they greeted me.

"Hey, you guys headed for Blue Lake? Let's go swimming," Florence suggested.

"It's too hot to play," Horse griped. He was dripping with sweat.

"Hey, Tony, is it true what they say? Is there a bruja at your house?" Ernie asked.

"¡A bruja!" "¡Chingada!" "¡A la veca!"[2]   70

"No," I said simply.

"My father said she cursed someone and three days later that person changed into a frog—"

"Hey! Is that the old lady that goes to church with your family!" Bones shrieked.

"Let's go," Cico said.

"Knock it off, you guys, are we going to play or not!" Red pleaded. Ernie   75
spun the basketball on his finger. He was standing close to me and grinning as the ball spun.

"Hey, Tony, can you make the ball disappear?" He laughed. The others laughed too.

"Hey, Tony, do some magic!" Horse threw a hold around my neck and locked me into his half-nelson.

2. Common obscenities. *Bruja:* witch.

"Yeah!" Ernie shouted in my face. I did not know why he hated me.

"Leave him alone, Horse," Red said.

80 "Stay out of it, Red," Ernie shouted, "you're a Protestant. You don't know about the brujas!"

"They turn to owls and fly at night," Abel shouted.

"You have to kill them with a bullet marked with a cross," Lloyd added. "It's the law."

"Do magic," Horse grunted in my ear. His half-nelson was tight now. My stomach felt sick.

"Voodoo!" Ernie spun the ball in my face.

85 "Okay!" I cried. It must have scared Horse because he let loose and jumped back. They were all still, watching me.

The heat and what I had heard made me sick. I bent over, wretched and vomited. The yellow froth and juice of the carrots splattered at their feet.

"Jesuschriss!" "¡Chingada!" "¡Puta!" "¡A la madre!"[3]

"Come on," Cico said. We took advantage of their surprise and ran. We were over the hill, past the last few houses, and at Blue Lake before they recovered from the astonishment I saw in their faces. We stopped to rest and laugh.

"That was great, Tony," Cico gasped, "that really put Ernie in his place—"

90 "Yeah," I nodded. I felt better after vomiting and running. I felt better about taking the carrots, but I did not feel good about what they had said about Ultima.

"Why are they like that?" I asked Cico. We skirted Blue Lake and worked our way through the tall, golden grass to the creek.

"I don't know," Cico answered, "except that people, grown-ups and kids, seem to want to hurt each other—and it's worse when they're in a group."

We walked on in silence. I had never been this far before so the land interested me. I knew that the waters of El Rito flowed from springs in the dark hills. I knew that those hills cradled the mysterious Hidden Lakes, but I had never been there. The creek flowed around the town, crossed beneath the bridge to El Puerto, then turned towards the river. There was a small reservoir there, and where the water emptied into the river the watercress grew thick and green. Ultima and I had visited the place in search of roots and herbs.

The water of El Rito was clear and clean. It was not muddy like the water of the river. We followed the footpath along the creek until we came to a thicket of brush and trees. The trail skirted around the bosque.

95 Cico paused and looked around. He pretended to be removing a splinter from his foot, but he was cautiously scanning the trail and the grass around us. I was sure we were alone; the last people we had seen were the swimmers at the Blue Lake a few miles back. Cico pointed to the path.

"The fishermen follow the trail around the brush," he whispered, "they hit the creek again just below the pond that's hidden in here." He squirmed into the thicket on hands and knees, and I followed. After a while we could stand up again and follow the creek to a place where an old beaver dam made a large pond.

3. Common obscenities.

It was a beautiful spot. The pond was dark and clear, and the water trickled and gurgled over the top of the dam. There was plenty of grass along the bank, and on all sides the tall brush and trees rose to shut off the world.

Cico pointed. "The golden carp will come through there." The cool waters of the creek came out of a dark, shadowy grotto of overhanging thicket, then flowed about thirty feet before they entered the large pond. Cico reached into a clump of grass and brought out a long, thin salt cedar branch with a spear at the end. The razor-sharp steel glistened in the sun. The other end of the spear had a nylon cord attached to it for retrieving.

"I fish for the black bass of the pond," Cico said. He took a position on a high clump of grass at the edge of the bank and motioned for me to sit by the bank, but away from him.

"How can you see him?" I asked. The waters of the pool were clear and pure, but dark from their depth and shadows of the surrounding brush. The sun was crystaline white in the clear, blue sky, but still there was the darkness of shadows in this sacred spot.

"The golden carp will scare him up," Cico whispered. "The black bass thinks he can be king of the fish, but all he wants is to eat them. The black bass is a killer. But the real king is the golden carp, Tony. He does not eat his own kind—"

Cico's eyes remained glued on the dark waters. His body was motionless, like a spring awaiting release. We had been whispering since we arrived at the pond, why I didn't know, except that it was just one of those places where one can communicate only in whispers, like church.

We sat for a long time, waiting for the golden carp. It was very pleasant to sit in the warm sunshine and watch the pure waters drift by. The drone of the summer insects and grasshoppers made me sleepy. The lush green of the grass was cool, and beneath the grass was the dark earth, patient, waiting . . . .

To the northeast two hawks circled endlessly in the clear sky. There must be something dead on the road to Tucumcari,[4] I thought.

Then the golden carp came. Cico pointed and I turned to where the stream came out of the dark grotto of overhanging tree branches. At first I thought I must be dreaming. I had expected to see a carp the size of a river carp, perhaps a little bigger and slightly orange instead of brown. I rubbed my eyes and watched in astonishment.

"Behold the golden carp, Lord of the waters—" I turned and saw Cico standing, his spear held across his chest as if in acknowledgment of the presence of a ruler.

The huge, beautiful form glided through the blue waters. I could not believe its size. It was bigger than me! And bright orange! The sunlight glistened off his golden scales. He glided down the creek with a couple of small carp following, but they were like minnows compared to him.

"The golden carp," I whispered in awe. I could not have been more entranced if I had seen the Virgin, or God Himself. The golden carp had seen

---

4. City in east-central New Mexico.

me. It made a wide sweep, its back making ripples in the dark water. I could have reached out into the water and touched the holy fish!

"He knows you are a friend," Cico whispered.

Then the golden carp swam by Cico and disappeared into the darkness of the pond. I felt my body trembling as I saw the bright golden form disappear. I knew I had witnessed a miraculous thing, the appearance of a pagan god, a thing as miraculous as the curing of my uncle Lucas. And I thought, the power of God failed where Ultima's worked; and then a sudden illumination of beauty and understanding flashed through my mind. This is what I had expected God to do at my first holy communion! If God was witness to my beholding of the golden carp then I had sinned! I clasped my hands and was about to pray to the heavens when the waters of the pond exploded.

I turned in time to see Cico hurl his spear at the monstrous black bass that had broken the surface of the waters. The evil mouth of the black bass was open and red. Its eyes were glazed with hate as it hung in the air surrounded by churning water and a million diamond droplets of water. The spear whistled through the air, but the aim was low. The huge tail swished and contemptuously flipped it aside. Then the black form dropped into the foaming waters.

"Missed," Cico groaned. He retrieved his line slowly.

I nodded my head. "I can't believe what I have seen," I heard myself say, "are all the fish that big here—"

"No," Cico smiled, "they catch two and three pounders below the beaver dam, the black bass must weigh close to twenty—" He threw his spear and line behind the clump of grass and came to sit by me. "Come on, let's put our feet in the water. The golden carp will be returning—"

"Are you sorry you missed?" I asked as we slid our feet into the cool water.

"No," Cico said, "it's just a game."

The orange of the golden carp appeared at the edge of the pond. As he came out of the darkness of the pond the sun caught his shiny scales and the light reflected orange and yellow and red. He swam very close to our feet. His body was round and smooth in the clear water. We watched in silence at the beauty and grandeur of the great fish. Out of the corners of my eyes I saw Cico hold his hand to his breast as the golden carp glided by. Then with a switch of his powerful tail the golden carp disappeared into the shadowy water under the thicket.

I shook my head. "What will happen to the golden carp?"

"What do you mean?" Cico asked.

"There are many men who fish here—"

Cico smiled. "They can't see him, Tony, they can't see him. I know every man from Guadalupe[5] who fishes, and there ain't a one who has ever mentioned seeing the golden carp. So I guess the grown-ups can't see him—"

"The Indian, Narciso, Ultima—"

"They're different, Tony. Like Samuel, and me, and you—"

"I see," I said. I did not know what that difference was, but I did feel a strange

5. County in east-central New Mexico, west of Tucumcari.

brotherhood with Cico. We shared a secret that would always bind us.

"Where does the golden carp go?" I asked and nodded upstream.

"He swims upstream to the lakes of the mermaid, the Hidden Lakes—"

"The mermaid?" I questioned him.

"There are two deep, hidden lakes up in the hills," he continued, "they feed the creek. Some people say those lakes have no bottom. There's good fishing, but very few people go there. There's something strange about those lakes, like they are haunted. There's a strange power, it seems to watch you—"

"Like the *presence* of the river?" I asked softly. Cico looked at me and nodded.

"You've felt it," he said.

"Yes."

"Then you understand. But this thing at the lakes is stronger, or maybe not stronger, it just seems to want you more. The time I was there—I climbed to one of the overhanging cliffs, and I just sat there, watching the fish in the clear water—I didn't know about the power then, I was just thinking how good the fishing would be, when I began to hear strange music. It came from far away. It was a low, lonely murmuring, maybe like something a sad girl would sing. I looked around, but I was alone. I looked over the ledge of the cliff and the singing seemed to be coming from the water, and it seemed to be calling me—"

I was spellbound with Cico's whispered story. If I had not seen the golden carp perhaps I would not have believed him. But I had seen too much today to doubt him.

"I swear, Tony, the music was pulling me into the dark waters below! The only thing that saved me from plunging into the lake was the golden carp. He appeared and the music stopped. Only then could I tear myself away from that place. Man, I ran! Oh how I ran! I had never been afraid before, but I was afraid then. And it wasn't that the singing was evil, it was just that it called for me to join it. One more step and I'da stepped over the ledge and drowned in the waters of the lake—"

I waited a long time before I asked the next question. I waited for him to finish reliving his experience. "Did you see the mermaid?"

"No," he answered.

"Who is she?" I whispered.

"No one knows. A deserted woman—or just the wind singing around the edges of those cliffs. No one really knows. It just calls people to it—"

"Who?"

He looked at me carefully. His eyes were clear and bright, like Ultima's, and there were lines of age already showing.

"Last summer the mermaid took a shepherd. He was a man from Méjico, new here and working for a ranch beyond the hills. He had not heard the story about the lakes. He brought his sheep to water there, and he heard the singing. He made it back to town and even swore that he had seen the mermaid. He said it was a woman, resting on the water and singing a lonely song. She was half woman and half fish—He said the song made him want to wade out to the middle of the lake to help her, but his fear had made him run. He told everyone the story, but no one believed him. He ended up getting drunk in town and swearing he would prove his story by going back to the lakes and bringing back the mer-woman. He never returned. A week later the flock was found near the lakes. He had vanished—"

"Do you think the mermaid took him?" I asked.

"I don't know, Tony," Cico said and knit his brow, "there's a lot of things I don't know. But never go to the Hidden Lakes alone, Tony, never. It's not safe."

I nodded that I would honor his warning. "It is so strange," I said, "the things that happen. The things that I have seen, or heard about."

145 "Yes," he agreed.

"These things of the water, the mermaid, the golden carp. They are strange. There is so much water around the town, the river, the creek, the lakes—"

Cico leaned back and stared into the bright sky. "This whole land was once covered by a sea, a long time ago—"

"My name means sea," I pondered aloud.

"Hey, that's right," he said, "Márez means sea, it means you came from the ocean, Tony Márez arisen from the sea—"

150 "My father says our blood is restless, like the sea—"

"That is beautiful," he said. He laughed. "You know, this land belonged to the fish before it belonged to us. I have no doubt about the prophecy of the golden carp. He will come to rule again!"

"What do you mean?" I asked.

"What do I mean?" Cico asked quizzically. "I mean that the golden carp will come to rule again. Didn't Samuel tell you?"

"No," I shook my head.

155 "Well he told you about the people who killed the carp of the river and were punished by being turned into fish themselves. After that happened, many years later, a new people came to live in this valley. And they were no better than the first inhabitants, in fact they were worse. They sinned a lot, they sinned against each other, and they sinned against the legends they knew. And so the golden carp sent them a prophecy. He said that the sins of the people would weigh so heavy upon the land that in the end the whole town would collapse and be swallowed by water—"

I must have whistled in exclamation and sighed.

"Tony," Cico said, "this whole town is sitting over a deep, underground lake! Everybody knows that. Look." He drew on the sand with a stick. "Here's the river. The creek flows up here and curves into the river. The Hidden Lakes complete the other border. See?"

I nodded. The town was surrounded by water. It was frightening to know that! "The whole town!" I whispered in amazement.

"Yup," Cico said, "the whole town. The golden carp has warned us that the land cannot take the weight of the sins—the land will finally sink!"

"But you live in town!" I exclaimed.

160 He smiled and stood up. "The golden carp is my god, Tony. He will rule the new waters. I will be happy to be with my god—"

It was unbelievable, and yet it made a wild kind of sense! All the pieces fitted!

"Do the people of the town know?" I asked anxiously.

"They know," he nodded, "and they keep on sinning."

"But it's not fair to those who don't sin!" I countered.

"Tony," Cico said softly, "all men sin."

I had no answer to that. My own mother had said that losing your innocence and becoming a man was learning to sin. I felt weak and powerless in the knowledge of the impending doom.

"When will it happen?" I asked.

"No one knows," Cico answered. "It could be today, tomorrow, a week, a hundred years—but it will happen."

"What can we do?" I asked. I heard my voice tremble.

"Sin against no one," Cico answered.

I walked away from that haven which held the pond and the swimming waters of the golden carp feeling a great weight in my heart. I was saddened by what I had learned. I had seen beauty, but the beauty had burdened me with responsibility. Cico wanted to fish at the dam, but I was not in the mood for it. I thanked him for letting me see the golden carp, crossed the river, and trudged up the hill homeward.

I thought about telling everyone in town to stop their sinning, or drown and die. But they would not believe me. How could I preach to the whole town, I was only a boy. They would not listen. They would say I was crazy, or bewitched by Ultima's magic.

I went home and thought about what I had seen and the story Cico told. I went to Ultima and told her the story. She said nothing. She only smiled. It was as if she knew the story and found nothing fantastic or impending in it. "I would have told you the story myself," she nodded wisely, "but it is better that you hear the legend from someone your own age . . ."

"Am I to believe the story?" I asked. I was worried.

"Antonio," she said calmly and placed her hand on my shoulder, "I cannot tell you what to believe. Your father and your mother can tell you, because you are their blood, but I cannot. As you grow into manhood you must find your own truths—"

That night in my dreams I walked by the shore of a great lake. A bewitching melody filled the air. It was the song of the mer-woman! I looked into the dark depths of the lake and saw the golden carp, and all around him were the people he had saved. On the bleached shores of the lake the carcasses of sinners rotted.

Then a huge golden moon came down from the heavens and settled on the surface of the calm waters. I looked towards the enchanting light, expecting to see the Virgin of Guadalupe, but in her place I saw my mother!

Mother, I cried, you are saved! We are all saved!

Yes, my Antonio, she smiled, we who were baptized in the water of the moon which was made holy by our Holy Mother the Church are saved.

Lies! my father shouted, Antonio was not baptized in the holy water of the moon, but in the salt water of the sea!

165

170

175

180

I turned and saw him standing on the corpse-strewn shore. I felt a searing pain spread through my body.

Oh please tell me which is the water that runs through my veins, I moaned; oh please tell me which is the water that washes my burning eyes!

It is the sweet water of the moon, my mother crooned softly, it is the water the Church chooses to make holy and place in its font. It is the water of your baptism.

185 *Lies, lies, my father laughed, through your body runs the salt water of the oceans. It is that water which makes you Márez and not Luna. It is the water that binds you to the pagan god of Cico, the golden carp!*

Oh, I cried, please tell me. The agony of pain was more than I could bear. The excruciating pain broke and I sweated blood.

There was a howling wind as the moon rose and its powers pulled at the still waters of the lake. Thunder split the air and the lightning bursts illuminated the churning, frothy tempest. The ghosts stood and walked upon the shore.

The lake seemed to respond with rage and fury. It cracked with the laughter of madness as it inflicted death upon the people. I thought the end had come to everything. The cosmic struggle of the two forces would destroy everything!

The doom which Cico had predicted was upon us! I clasped my hands and knelt to pray. The terrifying end was near. Then I heard a voice speak above the sound of the storm. I looked up and saw Ultima.

190 *Cease! she cried to the raging powers, and the power from the heavens and the power from the earth obeyed her. The storm abated.*

Stand, Antonio, she commanded, and I stood. You both know, she spoke to my father and my mother, that the sweet water of the moon which falls as rain is the same water that gathers into rivers and flows to fill the seas. Without the waters of the moon to replenish the oceans there would be no oceans. And the same salt waters of the oceans are drawn by the sun to the heavens, and in turn become again the waters of the moon. Without the sun there would be no waters formed to slake the dark earth's thirst.

The waters are one, Antonio. I looked into her bright, clear eyes and understood her truth.

You have been seeing only parts, she finished, and not looking beyond into the great cycle that binds us all.

Then there was peace in my dreams and I could rest.

1972

RICHARD DOKEY

Sánchez

That summer the son of Juan Sánchez went to work for the Flotill Cannery in Stockton. Juan drove with him to the valley in the old Ford.

While they drove, the boy, whose name was Jesús, told him of the greatness of the cannery, of the great aluminum buildings, the marvelous machines, and the belts of cans that never stopped running. He told him of the building on one side of the road where the cans were made and how the cans ran in a metal tube across the road to the cannery. He described the food machines, the sanitary precautions. He laughed when he spoke of the labeling. His voice was serious about the money.

When they got to Stockton, Jesús directed him to the central district of town, the skid row where the boy was to live while he worked for the Flotill. It was a cheap hotel on Center Street. The room smelled. There was a table with one chair. The floor was stained like the floor of a public urinal and the bed was soiled, as were the walls. There were no drapes on the windows. A pall spread out from the single light bulb overhead that was worked with a length of grimy string.

"I will not stay much in the room," Jesús said, seeing his father's face. "It is only for sleep. I will be working overtime, too. There is also the entertainment."

Jesús led him from the room and they went out into the street. Next to the hotel there was a vacant lot where a building had stood. The hole which was left had that recent, peculiar look of uprootedness. There were the remains of the foundation, the broken flooring, and the cracked bricks of tired red to which the gray blotches of mortar clung like dried phlegm. But the ground had not yet taken on the opaqueness of wear that the air and sun give it. It gleamed dully in the light and held to itself where it had been torn, as earth does behind a plow. Juan studied the hole for a time; then they walked up Center Street to Main, passing other empty lots, and then moved east toward Hunter Street. At the corner of Hunter and Main a wrecking crew was at work. An iron ball was suspended from the end of a cable and a tall machine swung the ball up and back and then whipped it forward against the building. The ball was very thick-looking, and when it struck the wall the building trembled, spurted dust, and seemed to cringe inward. The vertical lines of the building had gone awry. Juan shook each time the iron struck the wall.

"They are tearing down the old buildings," Jesús explained. "Redevelopment," he pronounced. "Even my building is to go someday."

Juan looked at his son. "And what of the men?" he asked. "Where do the men go when there are no buildings?"

Jesús, who was a head taller than his father, looked down at him and then shrugged in that Mexican way, the head descending and cocking while the shoulders rise as though on puppet strings. "¿Quien sabe?"[1]

"And the large building there?" Juan said, looking across the rows of parked cars in Hunter Square. "The one whose roof rubs the sky. Of what significance?"

"That is the new courthouse," Jesús said.

"There are no curtains on the windows."

"They do not put curtains on such windows," Jesús explained.

"No," sighed Juan, "that is true."

They walked north on Hunter past the new Bank of America and entered an

---

1. "Who knows?"

old building. They stood to one side of the entrance. Jesús smiled proudly and inhaled the stale air.

"This is the entertainment," he said.

Juan looked about. A bar was at his immediate left, and a bald man in a soiled apron stood behind it. Beyond the bar there were many thick-wooded tables covered with green material. Men crouched over them and cone-shaped lights hung low from the ceiling casting broad cones of light downward upon the men and tables. Smoke drifted and rolled in the light and pursued the men when they moved quickly. There was the breaking noise of balls striking together, the hard wooden rattle of the cues in the racks upon the wall, the humming slither of the scoring disks along the loose wires overhead, the explosive cursing of the men. The room was warm and dirty. Juan shook his head.

"I have become proficient at the game," Jesús said.

"This is the entertainment," Juan said, still moving his head.

Jesús turned and walked outside. Juan followed. The boy pointed across the parked cars past the courthouse to a marquee on Main Street. "There are also motion pictures," Jesús said.

Juan had seen a movie as a young man working in the fields near Fresno. He had understood no English then. He sat with his friends in the leather seats that had gum under the arms and watched the images move upon the white canvas. The images were dressed in expensive clothes. There was laughing and dancing. One of the men did kissing with two very beautiful women, taking turns with each when the other was absent. This had embarrassed Juan, the embracing and unhesitating submission of the women with so many unfamiliar people to watch. Juan loved his wife, was very tender and gentle with her before she died. He never went to another motion picture, even after he had learned English, and this kept him from the Spanish films as well.

"We will go to the cannery now," Jesús said, taking his father's arm. "I will show you the machines."

Juan permitted himself to be led away, and they moved back past the bank to where the men were destroying the building. A ragged hole, like a wound, had been opened in the wall. Juan stopped and watched. The iron ball came forward tearing at the hole, enlarging it, exposing the empty interior space that had once been a room. The floor of the room teetered at a precarious angle. The wood was splintered and very dry in the noon light.

"I do not think I will go to the cannery," Juan said.

The boy looked at his father like a child who has made a toy out of string and bottle caps only to have it ignored.

"But it is honorable work," Jesús said, suspecting his father. "And it pays well."

"Honor," Juan said. "Honor is a serious matter. It is not a question of honor. You are a man now. All that is needed is a room and a job at the Flotill. Your father is tired, that is all."

"You are disappointed," Jesús said, hanging his head.

"No," Juan said. "I am beyond disappointment. You are my son. Now you have a place in the world. You have the Flotill."

Nothing more was said, and they walked to the car. Juan got in behind the wheel. Jesús stood beside the door, his arms at his sides, the fingers spread. Juan looked up at him. The boy's eyes were big.

"You are my son," Juan said, "and I love you. Do not have disappointment. I am not of the Flotill. Seeing the machines would make it worse. You understand, niño?"[2]

"Sí, Papa," Jesús said. He put a hand on his father's shoulder.

"It is a strange world, niñito," Juan said.

"I will earn money. I will buy a red car and visit you. All in Twin Pines will be envious of the son of Sánchez, and they will say that Juan Sánchez has a son of purpose."

"Of course, Jesús mío," Juan said. He bent and placed his lips against the boy's hand. "I will look for the bright car. I will write regardless." He smiled, showing yellowed teeth. "Goodbye, querido," he said. He started the car, raced the engine once too high, and drove off up the street.

When Juan Sánchez returned to Twin Pines, he drove the old Ford to the top of Bear Mountain and pushed it over. He then proceeded systematically to burn all that was of importance to him, all that was of nostalgic value, and all else that meant nothing in itself, like the extra chest of drawers he had kept after his wife's death, the small table in the bedroom, and the faded mahogany stand in which he kept his pipe and tobacco and which sat next to the stuffed chair in the front room. He broke all the dishes, cups, plates, discarded all the cooking and eating utensils in the same way. The fire rose in the blue wind carrying dust wafers of ash in quick, breathless spirals and then released them in a panoply of diluted smoke, from which they drifted and spun and fell like burnt snow. The forks, knives, and spoons became very black with a flaky crust of oxidized metal. Then Juan burned his clothing, all that was unnecessary, and the smoke dampened and took on a thick smell. Finally he threw his wife's rosary into the flames. It was a cheap one, made of wood, and disappeared immediately. He went into his room then and lay down on the bed. He went to sleep.

When he woke, it was dark and cool. He stepped outside, urinated, and then returned, shutting the door. The darkness was like a mammoth held breath, and he felt very awake listening to the beating of his heart. He would not be able to sleep now, and so he lay awake thinking.

He thought of his village in Mexico, the baked white clay of the small houses spread like little forts against the stillness of the bare mountains, the men with their great wide hats, their wide, white pants, and their naked, brown-skinned feet, splayed against the fine dust of the road. He saw the village cistern and the women all so big and slow, always with child, enervated by the earth and the unbearable sun, the enervation passing into their very wombs like the acceptance, slow, silent blood. The men walked bent as though carrying the air or sky, slept against the buildings in the shade like old dogs, ate dry, hot food that dried them inside and seemed to bake the moisture from the flesh, so that the men and women while still young had faces like eroded fields and fingers like

---

2. Son. Niñito: dear son. Querido: dear one.

30

35

stringy, empty stream beds. It was a hard land. It took the life of his father and mother before he was twelve and the life of his aunt, with whom he then lived, before he was sixteen.

When he was seventeen he went to Mexicali because he had heard much of America and the money to be obtained there. They took him in a truck with other men to work in the fields around Bakersfield, then in the fields near Fresno. On his return to Mexicali he met La Belleza, as he came to call her: loveliness. He married her when he was nineteen and she only fifteen. The following year she had a baby girl. It was stillborn and the birth almost killed her, for the doctor said the passage was oversmall. The doctor cautioned him (warned him, really) La Belleza could not have children and live, and he went outside into the moonlight and wept.

He had heard much of the liveliness of the Sierra Nevada above what was called the Mother Lode, and because he feared the land, believed almost that it possessed the power to kill him—as it had killed his mother and father, his aunt, was, in fact, slow killing so many of his people—he wanted to run away from it to the high white cold of the California mountains, where he believed his heart would grow, his blood run and, perhaps, the passage of La Belleza might open. Two years later he was taken in the trucks to Stockton in the San Joaquin Valley to pick tomatoes, and he saw the Sierra Nevada above the Mother Lode.

It was from a distance, of course, and in the summer, so that there was no snow. But when he returned he told La Belleza about the blueness of the mountains in the warm, still dawn, the extension of them, the aristocracy of their unmoving height, and that they were only fifty miles away from where he had stood.

He worked very hard now and saved his money. He took La Belleza back to his village, where he owned the white clay house of his father. It was cheaper to live there while he waited, fearing the sun, the dust, and the dry, airless silence, for the money to accumulate. That fall La Belleza became pregnant again by an accident of passion and the pregnancy was very difficult. In the fifth month the doctor—who was an atheist—said that the baby would have to be taken or else the mother would die. The village priest, a very loud, dramatic man—an educated man who took pleasure in striking a pose—proclaimed the wrath of God in the face of such sacrilege. It was the child who must live, the priest cried. The pregnancy must go on. There was the immortal soul of the child to consider. But Juan decided for the atheist doctor, who did take the child. La Belleza lost much blood. At one point her heart had stopped beating. When the child was torn from its mother and Juan saw that it was a boy, he ran out of the clay house of his father and up the dusty road straight into a hideous red moon. He cursed the earth, the sky. He cursed his village, himself, the soulless indifference of the burnt mountains. He cursed God.

Juan was very afraid now, and though it cost more money, he had himself tied by the atheist doctor so that he could never again put the life of La Belleza in danger, for the next time, he knew with certainty, would kill her.

The following summer he went again on the trucks to the San Joaquin Valley. The mountains were still there, high and blue in the quiet dawn, turned to a milky pastel by the heat swirls and haze of midday. Sometimes at night he stepped outside the shacks in which the men were housed and faced the darkness. It was tragic to be so close to what you wanted, he would think, and be unable to possess it. So strong was the feeling in him, particularly during the hot, windless evenings, that he sometimes went with the other men into Stockton, where he stood on the street corners of skid row and talked, though he did not get drunk on cheap wine or go to the whores, as did the other men. Nor did he fight.

They rode in old tilted trucks covered with canvas and sat on rude benches staring out over the slats of the tail gate. The white glare of headlights crawled up and lay upon them, waiting to pass. They stared over the whiteness. When the lights swept out and by, the glass of the side windows shone. Behind the windows sometimes there would be the ghost flash of an upturned face, before the darkness clamped shut. Also, if one of the men had a relative who lived in the area, there was the opportunity to ride in a car.

He had done so once. He had watched the headlights of the car pale, then whiten the back of one of the trucks. He saw the faces of the men turned outward and the looks on the faces that seemed to float upon the whiteness of the light. The men sat forward, arms on knees, and looked over the glare into the darkness. After that he always rode in the trucks. 45

When he returned to his village after that season's harvest, he knew they could wait no longer. He purchased a dress of silk for La Belleza and in a secondhand store bought an American suit for himself. He had worked hard, sold his father's house, saved all his money, and on a bright day in early September they crossed the border at Mexicali and caught the Greyhound for Fresno.

Juan got up from his bed to go outside. He stood looking up at the stars. The stars were pinned to the darkness, uttering little flickering cries of light, and as always he was moved by the nearness and profusion of their agony. His mother had told him the stars were a kind of purgatory in which souls burned in cold, silent repentance. He had wondered after her death if the earth too were not a star burning in loneliness, and he could never look at them later without thinking this and believing that the earth must be the brightest of all stars. He walked over to the remains of the fire. A dull heat came from the ashes and a column of limp smoke rose and then bent against the night wind. He studied the ashes for a time and then looked over the tall pine shapes to the southern sky. It was there all right. He could feel the dry char of its heat, that deeper, dryer burning. He imagined it, of course. But it was there nevertheless. He went back into the cabin and lay down, but now his thoughts were only of La Belleza and the beautiful Sierra Nevada.

From Fresno all the way up the long valley to Stockton they had been full with pride and expectation. They had purchased oranges and chocolate bars and they ate them laughing. The other people on the bus looked at them, shook their heads, and slept or read magazines. He and La Belleza gazed out the window at the land.

In Stockton they were helped by a man named Eugenio Mendez. Juan had met him while picking tomatoes in the delta. Eugenio had eight children and a very fat but very kind and tolerant wife named Anilla. He had helped them find a cheap room off Center Street, where they stayed while determining their next course of action. Eugenio had access to a car, and it was he who drove them finally to the mountains.

50   It was a day like no other day in his life: to be sitting in the car with La Belleza, to be in this moving car with his Belleza heading straight toward the high, lovely mountains. The car traveled from the flatness of the valley into the rolling brown swells of the foothills, where hundreds of deciduous and evergreen oaks grew, their puffball shapes like still pictures of exploding holiday rockets, only green, but spreading up and out and then around and down in nearly perfect canopies. At Jackson the road turned and began an immediate, constant climb upward.

It was as though his dream about it had materialized. He had never seen so many trees, great with dignity: pines that had gray bark twisted and stringy like hemp; others whose bark resembled dry, flat ginger cookies fastened with black glue about a drum, and others whose bark pulled easily away; and those called redwoods, standing stiff and tall, amber-hued with straight rolls of bark as thick as his fist, flinging out high above great arms of green. And the earth, rich red, as though the blood of scores of Indians had just flowed there and dried. Dark patches of shadow stunned with light, blue flowers, orange flowers, birds, even deer. They saw them all on that first day.

"¿A dónde vamos?" Eugenio had asked. "Where are we going?"

"Bellísima," Juan replied. "Into much loveliness."

They did not reach Twin Pines that day. But on their return a week later they inquired in Jackson about the opportunity of buying land or a house in the mountains. The man, though surprised, told them of the sawmill town of Twin Pines, where there were houses for sale.

55   Their continued luck on that day precipitated the feeling in Juan that it was indeed the materialization of a dream. He had been able in all those years to save two thousand dollars, and a man had a small shack for sale at the far edge of town. He looked carefully at Juan, at La Belleza and Eugenio and said "One thousand dollars," believing they could never begin to possess such a sum. When Juan handed him the money, the man was so struck that he made out a bill of sale. Juan Sanchez and his wife had their home in the Sierra.

When Juan saw the cabin close up, he knew the man had stolen their money. It was small, the roof slanted to one side, the door would not close evenly. The cabin was gradually falling downhill. But it was theirs and he could, with work, repair it. Hurriedly they drove back to Jackson, rented a truck, bought some cheap furniture and hauled it back to the cabin. When they had moved in, Juan brought forth a bottle of whiskey and for the first time in his life proceeded to get truly drunk.

Juan was very happy with La Belleza. She accepted his philosophy completely, understood his need, made it her own. In spite of the people of the town, they created a peculiar kind of joy. And anyway Juan had knowledge about the people.

Twin Pines had been founded, he learned, by one Benjamin Carter, who lived with his daughter in a magnificent house on the hill overlooking town. This Benjamin Carter was a very wealthy man. He had come to the mountains thirty years before to save his marriage, for he had been poor once and loved when he was poor, but then he grew very rich because of oil discovered on his father's Ohio farm and he went away to the city and became incapable of love in the pursuit of money and power. When he at last married the woman whom he had loved, a barrier had grown between them, for Ben Carter had changed but the woman had not. Then the woman became ill and Ben Carter promised her he would take her West, all the way West away from the city so that it could be as it had been in the beginning of their love. But the woman was with child. And so Ben Carter rushed to the California mountains, bought a thousand acres of land, and hurried to build his house before the rain and snows came. He hired many men and the house was completed, except for the interior work and the furnishings. All that winter men he had hired worked in the snow to finish the house while Ben Carter waited with his wife in the city. When it was early spring they set out for California, Ben Carter, his wife, and the doctor, who strongly advised against the rough train trip and the still rougher climb by horse and wagon from Jackson to the house. But the woman wanted the child born properly, so they went. The baby came the evening of their arrival at the house, and the woman died all night having it. It was this Ben Carter who lived with that daughter now in the great house on the hill, possessing her to the point, it was said about his madness, that he had murdered a young man who had shown interest in her.

Juan learned all this from a Mexican servant who had worked at the great house from the beginning, and when he told the story to La Belleza she wept because of its sadness. It was a tragedy of love, she explained, and Juan—soaring to the heights of his imagination—believed that the town, all one hundred souls, had somehow been infected with the tragedy, as they were touched by the shadow of the house itself, which crept directly up the highway each night when the sun set. This was why they left dead chickens and fish on the porch of the cabin or dumped garbage into the yard. He believed he understood something profound and so did nothing about these incidents, which, after all, might have been the pranks of boys. He did not want the infection to touch him, nor the deeper infection of their prejudice because he was Mexican. He was not indifferent. He was simply too much in love with La Belleza and the Sierra Nevada. Finally the incidents stopped.

Now the life of Juan Sánchez entered its most beautiful time. When the first snows fell he became delirious, running through the pines, shouting, rolling on the ground, catching the flakes in his open mouth, bringing them in his cupped hands to rub in the hair of La Belleza, who stood in the doorway of their cabin laughing at him. He danced, made up a song about snowflakes falling on a desert and then a prayer which he addressed to the Virgin of Snowflakes. That night while the snow fluttered like wings against the bedroom window, he celebrated the coming of the whiteness with La Belleza.

He understood that first year in the mountains that love was an enlargement of himself, that it enabled him to be somehow more than he had ever been

60

before, as though certain pores of his senses had only just been opened. Whereas before he had desired the Sierra Nevada for its beauty and contrast to his harsh fatherland, now he came to acquire a love for it, and he loved it as he loved La Belleza; he loved it as a woman. Also in that year he came to realize that there was a fear or dread about such love. It was more a feeling than anything else, something which reached thought now and then, particularly in those last moments before sleep. It was an absolutely minor thing. The primary knowledge was of the manner in which this love seemed to assimilate everything, rejecting all that would not yield. This love was a kind of blindness.

That summer Juan left La Belleza at times to pick the crops of the San Joaquin Valley. He had become good friends with the servant of the big house and this man had access to the owner's car, which he always drove down the mountain in a reckless but confident manner. After that summer Juan planned also to buy a car, not out of material desire, but simply because he believed this man would one day kill himself, and also because he did not wish to be dependent.

He worked in the walnuts near the town of Linden and again in the tomatoes of the rich delta. He wanted very much to have La Belleza with him, but that would have meant more money and a hotel room in the skid row, and that was impossible because of the pimps and whores, the drunks and criminals and the general despair, which the police always tapped at periodic intervals, as one does a vat of fermenting wine. The skid row was a place his love could not assimilate, but he could not ignore it because so many of his people were lost there. He stayed in the labor camps, which were also bad because of what the men did with themselves, but they were tolerable. He worked hard and as often as he could and gazed at the mountains, which he could always see clearly in the morning light. When tomato season was over he returned to La Belleza.

Though the town would never accept them as equals, it came that summer to tolerate their presence. La Belleza made straw baskets which she sold to the townspeople and which were desired for their beauty and intricacy of design. Juan carved animals, a skill he had acquired from his father, and these were also sold. The activity succeeded so well that Juan took a box of these things to Jackson, where they were readily purchased. The following spring he was able to buy the Ford.

65   Juan acquired another understanding that second year in the mountains. It was, he believed, that love, his love, was the single greatness of which he was capable, the thing which ennobled him and gave him honor. Love, he became convinced, was his only ability, the one success he had accomplished in a world of insignificance. It was a simple thing, after all, made so painfully simple each time he went to the valley to work with his face toward the ground, every time he saw the men in the fields and listened to their talk and watched them drive off to the skid row at night. After he had acquired this knowledge, the nights he had to spend away from La Belleza were occupied by a new kind of loneliness, as though a part of his body had been separated from the whole. He began also to understand something more of the fear or dread that seemed to trail behind love.

It happened late in the sixth year of their marriage. It was impossible, of course, and he spent many hours at the fire in their cabin telling La Belleza of the impossibility, for the doctor had assured him that all had been well tied. He had conducted himself on the basis of that assumption. But doctors can be wrong. Doctors can make mistakes. La Belleza was with child.

For the first five months the pregnancy was not difficult, and he came almost to believe that indeed the passage of La Belleza would open. He prayed to God. He prayed to the earth and sky. He prayed to the soul of his mother. But after the fifth month the true sickness began and he discarded prayer completely in favor of blasphemy. There was no God and never could be God in the face of such sickness, such unbelievable human sickness. Even when he had her removed to the hospital in Stockton, the doctors could not stop it, but it continued so terribly that he believed that La Belleza carried sickness itself in her womb.

After seven months the doctors decided to take the child. They brought La Belleza into a room with lights and instruments. They worked on her for a long time and she died there under the lights with the doctors cursing and perspiring above the large wound of her pain. They did not tell him of the child, which they had cleaned and placed in an incubator, until the next day. That night he sat in the Ford and tried to see it all, but he could only remember the eyes of La Belleza in the vortex of pain. They were of an almost eerie calmness. They had possessed calmness, as one possesses the truth. Toward morning he slumped sideways on the seat and went to sleep.

So he put her body away in the red earth of the town cemetery beyond the cabin. The pines came together overhead and in the heat of midday a shadow sprinkled with spires of light lay upon the ground so that the earth was cool and clean to smell. He did not even think of taking her back to Mexico, since, from the very beginning she had always been part of that dream he had dreamed. Now she would be always in the Sierra Nevada, with the orange and blue flowers, the quiet, deep whiteness of winter, and all that he ever was or could be was with her.

But he did not think these last thoughts then, as he did now. He had simply performed them out of instinct for their necessity, as he had performed the years of labor while waiting for the infant Jesús to grow to manhood. Jesús. Why had he named the boy Jesús? That, perhaps, had been instinct too. He had stayed after La Belleza's death for the boy, to be with him until manhood, to show him the loveliness of the Sierra Nevada, to instruct him toward true manhood. But Jesús. Ah, Jesús. Jesús the American. Jesús of the Flotill. Jesús understood nothing. Jesús, he believed, was forever lost to knowledge. That day with Jesús had been his own liberation.

For a truth had come upon him after the years of waiting, the ultimate truth that he understood only because La Belleza had passed through his life. Love was beauty, La Belleza and the Sierra Nevada, a kind of created or made thing. But there was another kind of love, a very profound, embracing love that he had felt of late blowing across the mountains from the south and that, he knew now, had always been there from the beginning of his life, disguised in the sun and

70

wind. In this love there was blood and earth and, yes, even God, some kind of god, at least the power of a god. This love wanted him for its own. He understood it, that it had permitted him to have La Belleza and that without it there could have been no Belleza.

Juan placed an arm over his eyes and turned to face the wall. The old bed sighed. An image went off in his head and he remembered vividly the lovely body of La Belleza. In that instant the sound that loving had produced with the bed was alive in him like a forgotten melody, and his body seemed to swell and press against the ceiling. It was particularly cruel because it was so sudden, so intense, and came from so deep within him that he knew it must all still be alive somewhere, and that was the cruelest part of all. He wept softly and held the arm across his eyes.

In the dark morning the people of the town were awakened by the blaze of fire that was the house of Juan Sánchez. Believing that he had perished in the flames, several of the townspeople placed a marker next to the grave of his wife with his name on it. But, of course, on that score they were mistaken. Juan Sánchez had simply gone home.

1981

DENISE CHÁVEZ

The Last of the Menu Girls

NAME: Rocío Esquibel
AGE: Seventeen
PREVIOUS EXPERIENCE WITH THE SICK AND DYING: My Great Aunt
    Eutilia
PRESENT EMPLOYMENT: Work-study aide at Altavista Memorial

I never wanted to be a nurse. My mother's aunt died in our house, seventy-seven years old and crying in her metal crib: "Put a pillow on the floor. I can jump," she cried. "Go on, let me jump. I want to get away from here, far away."

Eutilia's mattress was covered with chipped clothlike sheaves of yellowed plastic. She wet herself, was a small child, undependable, helpless. She was an old lady with a broken hip, dying without having gotten down from that rented bed. Her blankets were sewn by my mother: corduroy patches, bright yellows, blues and greens, and still she wanted to jump!

"Turn her over, turn her over, turn her, wait a minute, wait—turn . . ."

Eutilia faced the wall. It was plastered white. The foamed, concrete turnings of some workman's trowel revealed daydreams: people's faces, white clouds, phantom pianos slowly playing half lost melodies, "Las Mañanitas," "Cielito Lindo,"[1] songs formulated in expectation, dissolved into confusion. Eutilia's

---

1. Literally, "Little Mornings," traditionally sung to a girl on her 15th birthday; familiar song, "Beautiful Little Sky," in which a girl's eyes are compared to the sky.

blurred faces, far off tunes faded into the white walls, into jagged, broken waves.

I never wanted to be a nurse, ever. All that gore and blood and grief. I was not as squeamish as my sister Mercy, who could not stand to put her hands into a sinkful of dirty dishes filled with floating food—wet bread, stringy vegetables and bits of softened meat. Still, I didn't like the touch, the smells. How could I? When I touched my mother's feet, I looked away, held my nose with one hand, the other with finger laced along her toes, pulling and popping them into place. "It really helps my arthritis, baby—you don't know. Pull my toes, I'll give you a dollar, find my girdle, and I'll give you two. Ouch. Ouch. Not so hard. There, that's good. Look at my feet. You see the veins? Look at them. Aren't they ugly? And up here, look where I had the operations . . . ugly, they stripped them and still they hurt me."

She rubbed her battered flesh wistfully, placed a delicate and lovely hand on her right thigh. Mother said proudly, truthfully, "I still have lovely thighs."

PREVIOUS EXPERIENCE WITH THE SICK AND DYING: Let me think . . .

Great Aunt Eutilia came to live with us one summer and seven months later she died in my father's old study, the walls lined with books, whatever answers were there—unread.

Great Aunt Eutilia smelled like the mercilessly sick. At first, a vague, softened aroma of tiredness and spilled food. And later, the full-blown emptyings of the dying: gas, putrefaction and fetid lucidity. Her body poured out long, held-back odors. She wet her diapers and sheets and knocked over medicines and glasses of tepid water, leaving in the air an unpleasant smell.

I danced around her bed in my dreams, naked, smiling, jubilant. It was an exultant adolescent dance for my dying aunt. It was necessary, compulsive. It was a primitive dance, a full moon offering that led me slithering into her room with breasts naked and oily at thirteen . . .

No one home but me.

Led me to her room, my father's refuge, those halcyon days now that he was gone—and all that remained were dusty books, cast iron bookends, reminders of the spaces he filled. Down the steps I leaped into Eutilia's faded and foggy consciousness where I whirled and danced and sang: I am your flesh and my mother's flesh and you are . . . are . . . Eutilia stared at me. I turned away.

I danced around Eutilia's bed. I hugged the screen door, my breasts indented in the meshed wire. In the darkness Eutilia moaned, my body wet, her body dry. Steamy we were, and full of prayers.

Could I have absolved your dying by my life? Could I have lessened your agony with my spirit-filled dance in the deep darkness? The blue fan stirred, then whipped nonstop the solid air; little razors sliced through consciousness and prodded the sick and dying woman, whose whitened eyes screeched: Ay! Ay! Let me jump, put a pillow, I want to go away . . . let me . . . let me . . .

10

15   One day while playing "Cielito Lindo" on the piano in the living room, Eutilia got up and fell to the side of the piano stool. Her foot caught on the rug, "¡Ay! ¡Ay! ¡Ay! ¡Ay! Canta y no llores . . ."[2]

All requests were silenced. Eutilia rested in her tattered hospital gown, having shredded it to pieces. She was surrounded by little white strips of raveled cloth. Uncle Toño, her babysitter, after watching the evening news, found her naked and in a bed of cloth. She stared at the ceiling, having played the piano far into the night. She listened to sounds coming from around the back of her head. Just listened. Just looked. Just shredded. Shredded the rented gown, shredded it. When the lady of the house returned and asked how was she, meaning, does she breathe, Toño answered, "Fine."

Christ on his crucifix! He'd never gone into the room to check on her. Later, when they found her, Toño cried, his cousin laughed. They hugged each other, then cried, then laughed, then cried. Eutilia's fingers never rested. They played beautiful tunes. She was a little girl in tatters in her metal bed with sideboards that went up and down, up and down . . .

The young girls danced they played they danced they filled out forms.

PREVIOUS EMPLOYMENT: None.

      There was always a first job, as there was the first summer of the very first boyfriend. That was the summer of our first swamp cooler. The heat bore down and congealed sweat. It made rivulets trace the body's meridian and, before it stopped, was wiped away, never quite dismissed.

20   On the tops of the neighbors' houses old swamp coolers, with their jerky grating and droning moans, strained to ease the southern implacabilities. Whrr whrr cough whrr.

Regino Suárez climbed up and down the roof, first forgetting his hammer and then the cooler filter. His boy, Eliterio, stood at the bottom of the steps that led to the sun deck and squinted dumbly at the blazing sun. For several days Regino tramped over my dark purple bedroom. I had shut the curtains to both father and son and rested in violet contemplation of my first boyfriend.

Regino stomped his way to the other side of the house where Eutilia lay in her metal crib, trying to sleep, her weary eyes uncomprehending. The noise was upsetting, she could not play. The small blue fan wheezed freshness. Regino hammered and paced then climbed down. When lunchtime came, a carload of fat daughters drove Regino and the handsome son away.

If Eutilia could have read a book, it would have been the *Bible*, or maybe her novena to the Santo Niño de Atocha,[3] he was her boy . . .

PREVIOUS EXPERIENCE WITH THE SICK AND DYING:

      This question reminds me of a story my mother told me about a very old woman, Doña Mercedes, who was dying of cancer. Doña Mercedes lived with

---

2. "Sing and don't cry."   3. Prayer to the Saint Niño, the holy child of Atocha.

her daughter, Corina, who was my mother's friend. The old woman lay in bed, day after day, moaning and crying softly, not actually crying out, but whimpering in a sad, hopeless way. "Don't move me," she begged when her daughter tried to change the sheets or bathe her. Every day this ordeal of maintenance became worse. It was a painful thing and full of dread for the old woman, the once fastidious and upright Doña Mercedes. She had been a lady, straight and imposing, and with a headful of rich dark hair. Her ancestors were from Spain. "You mustn't move me, Corina," Doña Mercedes pleaded, "never, please. Leave me alone, mi'jita,⁴" and so the daughter acquiesced. Cleaning around her tortured flesh and delicately wiping where they could, the two women attended to Doña Mercedes. She died in the daytime, as she had wanted.

When the young women went to lift the old lady from her death bed, they struggled to pull her from the sheets; and, when finally they turned her on her side, they saw huge gaping holes in her back where the cancer had eaten through the flesh. The sheets were stained, the bedsores lost in a red wash of bloody pus. Doña Mercedes' cancer had eaten its way through her back and onto those sheets. "Don't move me, please don't move me," she had cried.

The two young women stuffed piles of shredded disinfected rags soaked in Lysol into Doña Mercedes' chest cavity, filling it, and horrified, with cloths over their mouths, said the prayers for the dead. Everyone remembered her as tall and straight and very Spanish.

PRESENT EMPLOYMENT: Work-study aide at Altavista Memorial Hospital

I never wanted to be a nurse. Never. The smells. The pain. What was I to do then, working in a hospital, in that place of white women, whiter men with square faces? I had no skills. Once in the seventh grade I'd gotten a penmanship award. Swirling R's in boredom, the ABC's ad infinitum. Instead of dipping chocolate cones at the Dairy Queen next door to the hospital, I found myself a frightened girl in a black skirt and white blouse standing near the stairwell to the cafeteria.

I stared up at a painting of a dark-haired woman in a stiff nurse's cap and grey tunic, tending to men in old fashioned service uniforms. There was a beauty in that woman's face whoever she was. I saw myself in her, helping all of mankind, forgetting and absolving all my own sick, my own dying, especially relatives, all of them so far away, removed. I never wanted to be like Great Aunt Eutilia, or Doña Mercedes with the holes in her back, or my mother, her scarred legs, her whitened thighs.

MR. SMITH

Mr. Smith sat at his desk surrounded by requisition forms. He looked up to me with glassy eyes like filmy paperweights.
MOTHER OF GOD, MR. SMITH WAS A WALLEYED HUNCHBACK!

4. My "darling daughter."

"Mr. Smith, I'm Rocío Esquibel, the work-study student from the university and I was sent down here to talk to you about my job."

"Down here, down here," he laughed, as if it were a private joke. "Oh, yes, you must be the new girl. Menus," he mumbled. "Now just have a seat and we'll see what we can do. Would you like some iced tea?"

It was nine o'clock in the morning, too early for tea. "No, well, yes, that would be nice."

"It's good tea, everyone likes it. Here, I'll get you some." Mr. Smith got up, more hunchbacked than I'd imagined. He tiptoed out of the room whispering, "Tea, got to get this girl some tea."

35   There was a bit of the gruesome Golom[5] in him, a bit of the twisted spider in the dark. Was I to work for this gnome? I wanted to rescue souls, not play attendant to this crippled, dried up specimen, this cartilaginous insect with his misshapen head and eyes that peered out to me like the marbled eyes of statues one sees in museums. History preserves its freaks. God, was my job to do the same? No, never!

I faced Dietary Awards, Degrees in Food Management, menus for Low Salt and Fluids; the word Jello leaped out at every turn. I touched the walls. They were moist, never having seen the light.

In my dreams, Mr. Smith was encased in green Jello; his formaldehyde breath reminded me of other smells—decaying, saddened dead things; my great aunt, biology class in high school, my friend Dolores Casaus. Each of us held a tray with a dead frog pinned in place, served to us by a tall stoop-shouldered Viking turned farmer, our biology teacher Mr. Franke, pink-eyed, half blind. Dolores and I cut into the chest cavity and explored that small universe of dead cold fibers. Dolores stopped at the frog's stomach, then squeezed out its last meal, a green mash, spinach-colored, a viscous fluid—that was all that remained in that miniaturized, unresponding organ, all that was left of potential life.

Before Eutilia died she ate a little, mostly drank juice through bent and dripping hospital straws. The straws littered the floor where she'd knocked them over in her wild frenzy to escape. "Dioooooooos," she cried in that shrill voice. "Dios mío, Diosito, por favor. Ay, I won't tell your mamá, just help me get away . . . Diosito de mi vida . . . Diosito de mi corazón . . . agua, agua . . . por favor, por favor . . ."[6]

Mr. Smith returned with my iced tea.

40   "Sugar?"

Sugar, yes, sugar. Lots of it. Was I to spend all summer in this smelly cage? What was I to do? What? And for whom? I had no business here. It was summertime and my life stretched out magically in front of me: there was my boyfriend, my freedom. Senior year had been the happiest of my life; was it to change?

"Anytime you want to come down and get a glass of tea, you go right ahead.

---

5. In Jewish legend a man created by mystic rites.   6. "My God, oh, loving God, please. . . .
Loving God of my life . . . Loving God of my heart . . . water, water . . . please, please."

We always have it on hand. Everyone likes my tea," he said with pride.

"About the job?" I asked.

Mr. Smith handed me a pile of green forms. They were menus.

In the center of the menu was listed the day of the week, and to the left and coming down in a neat order were the three meals, breakfast, lunch and dinner. Each menu had various choices for each meal.

LUNCH:

☐ Salisbury Steak	☐ Mashed potatoes and gravy
☐ Fish sticks	☐ Macaroni and cheese
☐ Enchiladas	☐ Broccoli and onions
☐ Rice almondine	

Drinks	*Dessert*
☐ Coffee	☐ Jello
☐ Tea	☐ Carrot cake
☐ 7-Up	☐ Ice Cream, vanilla
☐ Other	

"Here you see a menu for Friday, listing the three meals. Let's take lunch. You have a choice of Salisbury steak, enchiladas, they're really good, Trini makes them, she's been working for me for twenty years. Her son George Jr. works for me, too, probably his kids one day." At this possibility, Mr. Smith laughed at himself. "Oh, and fish sticks. You a . . . ?"

"Our Lady of the Holy Scapular."

"Sometimes I'll get a menu back with a thank you written on the side, 'Thanks for the liver, it was real good', or 'I haven't had rice pudding since I was a boy.' Makes me feel good to know we've made our patients happy."

Mr. Smith paused, reflecting on the positive aspects of his job.

"Mind you, these menus are only for people on regular diets, not everybody, but a lot of people. I take care of the other special diets, that doesn't concern you. I have a girl working for me now, Arlene Rutschman. You know . . ."

My mind raced forward, backward. Arlene Rutschman, the Arlene from Holy Scapular, Arlene of the soft voice, the limp mannerisms, the plain, too goodly face, Arlene, president of Our Lady's Sodality, in her white and navy blue beanie, her bobby socks and horn-rimmed glasses, the Arlene of the school dances with her perpetual escort, Bennie Lara, the toothy better-than-no-date date, the Arlene of the high grades, the muscular, yet turned-in legs, the curly unattractive hair, *that* Arlene, the dud?

"Yes, I know her."

"Good!"

"We went to school together."

"Wonderful!"

"She works here?"

"Oh, she's a nice girl. She'll help you, show you what to do, how to distribute the menus."

"Distribute the menus?"

"Now you just sit there, drink your tea and tell me about yourself."

This was the first of many conversations with Mr. Smith, the hunchbacked dietician, a man who was never anything but kind to me.

"Hey," he said proudly, "these are my kids. Norma and Bardwell. Norma's in Junior High, majoring in boys, and Bardwell is graduating from the Military Institute."

"Bardwell. That's an unusual name," I said as I stared at a series of 5 x 7's on Mr. Smith's desk.

"Bardwell, well, that was my father's name. Bardwell B. Smith. The Bard, they called him!" At this he chuckled to himself, myopically recalling his father, tracing with his strange eyes patterns of living flesh and bone.

"He used to recite."

The children looked fairly normal. Norma was slight, with a broad toothy smile. Bardwell, or Bobby, as he was called, was not unhandsome in his uniform, if it weren't for one ragged, splayed ear that slightly cupped forward, as if listening to something.

Mr. Smith's image was nowhere in sight. "Camera shy," he said. To the right of Mr. Smith's desk hung a plastic gold framed prayer beginning with the words: "Oh Lord of Pots and Pans." To the left, near a dried out water-cooler was a sign, "Bless This Mess."

Over the weeks I began to know something of Mr. Smith's convoluted life, its anchorings. His wife and children came to life, and Mr. Smith acquired a name: Marion, and a vague disconcerting sexuality. It was upsetting for me to imagine him fathering Norma and Bardwell. I stared into the framed glossies full of disbelief. Who was Mrs. Smith? What was she like?

Eutilia never had any children. She'd been married to José Esparza, a good man, a handsome man. They ran a store in Agua Tibia. They prospered, until one day, early in the morning, about three a.m., several men from El Otro Lado[7] called out to them in the house. "Don José, wake up! We need to buy supplies." Eutilia was afraid, said, "No, José, don't let them in." He told her, "Woman, what are we here for?" And she said, "But at this hour, José? At this hour?" Don José let them into the store. The two men came in carrying two sacks, one that was empty, and another that they said was full of money. They went through the store, picking out hats, clothing, tins of corned beef, and stuffing them into the empty sack. "So many things, José," Eutilia whispered, "*too* many things!" "Oh no," one man replied, "we have the money, don't you trust us, José?" "Cómo no, compadre,"[8] he replied easily. "We need the goods, don't be afraid, compadre." "Too many things, too many things," Eutilia sighed, huddled in the darkness in her robe. She was a small woman, with the body of a little girl. Eutilia looked at José, and it was then that they both knew. When the two men had loaded up, they turned to Don José, took out a gun, which was hidden in a sack, and said, "So sorry, compadre, but you know . . . stay there, don't follow

---

7. The other side (of the border, i.e. Mexico).   8. "Why not, friend."

us." Eutilia hugged the darkness, saying nothing for the longest time. José was a handsome man, but dumb.

The village children made fun of José Esparza, laughed at him and pinned notes and pieces of paper to his pants. "Tonto, tonto"[9] and "I am a fool." He never saw these notes, wondered why they laughed.

"I've brought you a gift, a bag of rocks"; all fathers have said that to their children. Except Don José Esparza. He had no children, despite his looks. "At times a monkey can do better than a prince," la comadre[1] Lucaya used to say to anyone who would listen.

The bodies of patients twisted and moaned and cried out, and cursed, but for the two of us in that basement world, all was quiet save for the occasional clinking of an iced tea glass and the sporadic sound of Mr. Smith clearing his throat.

"There's no hurry," Mr. Smith always said. "Now you just take your time. Always in a hurry. A young person like you."

ARLENE RUTSCHMAN

"You're so lucky that you can speak Spanish," Arlene intoned. She stood tiptoes, held her breath, then knocked gently on the patient's door. No sound. A swifter knock. "I could never remember what a turnip was," she said.

"Whatjawant?" a voice bellowed.

"I'm the menu girl; can I take your order?"

Arlene's high tremulous little girl's voice trailed off, "Good morning, Mr. Samaniego! What'll it be? No, it's not today you leave, tomorrow, after lunch. Your wife is coming to get you. So, what'll it be for your third-to-the-last meal? Now we got poached or fried eggs. Poached. P-o-a-c-h-e-d. That's like a little hard in the middle, but a little soft on the outside. Firm. No, not like scrambled. Different. Okay, you want scrambled. Juice? We got grape or orange. You like grape? Two grape. And some coffee, black."

A tall Anglo man, gaunt and yellowed like an old newspaper, his eyes rubbed black like an old raccoon's, ranged the hallway. The man talked quietly to himself and smoked numbers of cigarettes as he weaved between attendants with half-filled urinals and lugubrious I.V.'s. He reminded me of my father's friends, angular Anglos in their late fifties, men with names like Bud or Earl, men who owned garages or steak houses, men with firm hairy arms, clear blue eyes and tattoos from the war.

"That's Mr. Ellis, 206." Arlene whispered, "jaundice."

"Oh," I said, curiously contemptuous and nervous at the same time, unhappy and reeling from the phrase, "I'm the menu girl!" How'd I ever manage to get such a dumb job? At least the Candy Stripers wore a cute uniform, and they got to do fun things like deliver flowers and candy.

"Here comes Mrs. Samaniego. The wife."

---

9. "Stupid, stupid."   1. Daughter's godmother.

"Mr. Ellis's wife?" I said, with concern.

"No, Mr. Samaniego's wife, Donelda." Arlene pointed to a wizened and giggly old woman who was sneaking by the information desk, past the silver-haired volunteer, several squirmy grandchildren in tow. Visiting hours began at two p.m., but Donelda Samaniego had come early to beat the rush. From the hallway, Arlene and I heard loud smacks, much kidding and general merriment. The room smelled of tamales.

85   "Old Mr. Phillips in 304, that's the Medical Floor, he gets his cath[2] at eleven, so don't go ask him about his menu then. It upsets his stomach."

Mrs. Daniels in 210 told Arlene weakly, "Honey, yes, you, honey, who's the other girl? Who is she? You'll just have to come back later, I don't feel good. I'm a dying woman, can't you see that?" When we came back an hour later, Mrs. Daniels was asleep, snoring loudly.

Mrs. Gustafson, a sad wet-eyed, well-dressed woman in her late sixties, dismissed us from the shade of drawn curtains as her husband, G.P. "Gus" Gustafson, the judge, took long and fitful naps only to wake up again, then go back to sleep, beginning once more his inexorable round of disappearances.

"Yesterday I weighed myself in the hall and I'm getting fat. Oh, and you're so thin."

"The hips," I said, "the hips."

"You know, you remind me of that painting," Arlene said, thoughtfully.

90   "Which?"

"Not which, who. The one in the stairwell. Florence Nightingale, she looks like you."

"That's who that is!"

"The eyes."

"She does?"

95   "The eyes."

"The eyes?"

"And the hair."

"The eyes and the hair? Maybe the hair, but not the eyes."

"Yes."

100   "I don't think so."

"Oh yes! Every time I look at it."

"Me?"

Arlene and I sat talking at our table in the cafeteria, that later was to become *my* table. It faced the dining room. From that vantage point I could see everything and not be seen.

We talked, two friends almost, if only she weren't so, so, little girlish with ribbons. Arlene was still dating Bennie and was majoring in either home ec or biology. They seemed the same in my mind: babies, menus and frogs. Loathsome, unpleasant things.

105   It was there, in the coolness of the cafeteria, in that respite from the green forms, at our special table, drinking tea, laughing with Arlene, that I, still shy,

---

2. Catheter.

still judgmental, still wondering and still afraid, under the influence of caffeine, decided to stick it out. I would not quit the job.

"How's Mr. Prieto in 200?"

"He left yesterday, but he'll be coming back. He's dying."

"Did you see old Mr. Carter? They strapped him to the wheelchair finally."

"It was about time. He kept falling over."

"Mrs. Domínguez went to bland."[3]

"She was doing so well."

"You think so? She couldn't hardly chew. She kept choking."

"And that grouch, what's her name, the head nurse, Stevens in 214 . . ."

"She's the head nurse? I didn't know that—god, I filled out her menu for her . . . she was sleeping and I . . . no wonder she was mad . . . how did I know she was the head nurse?"

"It's okay. She's going home or coming back, I can't remember which. Esperanza González is gonna be in charge."

"She was real mad."

"Forget it, it's okay."

"The woman will never forgive me, I'll lose my job," I sighed.

I walked home past the Dairy Queen. It took five minutes at the most. I stopped midway at the ditch's edge, where the earth rose and where there was a concrete embankment on which to sit. To some this was the quiet place, where neighborhood lovers met on summer nights to kiss, and where older couples paused between their evening walks to rest. It was also the talking place, where all the neighbor kids discussed life while eating hot fudge sundae with nuts. The bench was large; four could sit on it comfortably. It faced an open field in the middle of which stood a huge apricot tree. Lastly, the bench was a stopping place, the "throne," we called it. We took off hot shoes and dipped our cramped feet into the cool ditch water, as we sat facing the southern sun at the quiet talking place, at our thrones, not thinking anything, eyes closed, but sun. The great red velvet sun.

One night I dreamt of food, wading through hallways of food, inside some dark evil stomach. My boyfriend waved to me from the ditch's bank. I sat on the throne, ran alongside his car, a blue Ford, in which he sat, on clear plastic seat covers, with that hungry Church-of-Christ smile of his. He drove away, and when he returned, the car was small and I was too big to get inside.

Eutilia stirred. She was tired. She did not recognize anyone. I danced around the bed, crossed myself, en el nombre del padre, del hijo y del espíritu santo,[4] crossed forehead, chin and breast, begged for forgiveness even as I danced.

And on waking, I remembered. *Nabos. Turnips.* But of course.

It seemed right to me to be working in a hospital, to be helping people, and yet: why was I only a menu girl? Once a menu was completed, another would

---

3. Bland diet.   4. In the name of the Father, of the Son, and of the Holy Ghost.

take its place and the next day another. It was a never ending round of food and more food. I thought of Judge Gustafson.

When Arlene took a short vacation to the Luray Caverns, I became the official menu girl. That week was the happiest of my entire summer.

125   That week I fell in love.

ELIZABETH RAINEY

130   Elizabeth Rainey, Room 240, was in for a D and C.[5] I didn't know what a D and C was, but I knew it was mysterious and to me, of course, this meant it had to do with sex. Elizabeth Rainey was propped up in bed with many pillows, a soft blue, homemade quilt at the foot of her bed. Her cheeks were flushed, her red lips quivering. She looked fragile, and yet her face betrayed a harsh indelicate bitterness. She wore a creme-colored gown on which her loose hair fell about her like a cape. She was a beautiful woman, full-bodied, with the translucent beauty certain women have in the midst of sorrow—clear and unadorned, her eyes bright with inexplicable and self-contained suffering.

She cried out to me rudely, as if I personally had offended her. "What do you want? Can't you see I want to be alone. Now close the door and go away! Go away!"

"I'm here to get your menu." I could not bring myself to say, I'm the menu girl.

"Go away, go away, I don't want anything. I don't want to eat. Close the door!"

Elizabeth Rainey pulled her face away from me and turned to the wall, and, with deep and self-punishing exasperation, grit her teeth, and from the depths of her self-loathing a small inarticulate cry escaped—"Oooooh."

I ran out, frightened by her pain, yet excited somehow. She was so beautiful and so alone. I wanted in my little girl's way to hold her, hold her tight and in my woman's way never to feel her pain, ever, whatever it was.

"Go away, go away," she said, her trembling mouth rimmed with pain, "go away!"

She didn't want to eat, told me to go away. How many people yelled to me to go away that summer, have yelled since then, countless people, of all ages, sick people, really sick people, dying people, people who were well and still rudely tied into their needs for privacy and space, affronted by these constant impositions from, of all people, the menu girl!

"Move over and move out, would you? Go away! Leave me alone!"

135   And yet, of everyone who told me to go away, it was this woman in her solitary anguish who touched me the most deeply. How could I, age seventeen, not knowing love, how could I presume to reach out to this young woman in her sorrow, touch her and say, "I know, I understand."

Instead, I shrank back into myself and trembled behind the door. I never went back into her room. How could I? It was too terrible a vision, for in her I

---

5. Dilation and curettage; expanding and cleaning the uterus by scraping.

saw myself, all life, all suffering. What I saw both chilled and burned me. I stood long in that darkened doorway, confused in the presence of human pain. I wanted to reach out . . . I wanted to . . . I wanted to . . . But *how?*

As long as I live I will carry Elizabeth Rainey's image with me: in a creme-colored gown she is propped up, her hair fanning pillows in a room full of deep sweet acrid and overspent flowers. Oh, I may have been that summer girl, but yes, I knew, I understood. I would have danced for her, Eutilia, had I but dared.

DOLORES CASAUS

Dolores of the frog entrails episode, who'd played my sister Ismene in the world literature class play,[6] was now a nurse's aide on the surgical floor, changing sheets, giving enemas and taking rectal temperatures.

It was she who taught me how to take blood pressure, wrapping the cuff around the arm, counting the seconds and then multiplying beats. As a friend, she was rude, impudent, delightful; as an aide, most dedicated. One day for an experiment, with me as a guinea pig, she took the blood pressure of my right leg. That day I hobbled around the hospital, the leg cramped and weak. In high school Dolores had been my double, my confidante and the best Ouija board partner I ever had. When we set our fingers to the board, the dial raced and spun, flinging out letters—notes from the long dead, the crying out. Together we contacted la Llorona[7] and would have unraveled *that* mystery if Sister Esperidiana hadn't caught us in the religion room during lunchtime communing with that distressed spirit who had so much to tell!

Dolores was engaged. She had a hope chest. She wasn't going to college because she had to work, and her two sisters-in-law, the Nurses González and González—Esperanza, male, and Bertha, female, were her supervisors.

As a favor to Dolores, González the Elder, Esperanza would often give her a left-over tray of "regular" food, the patient having checked out or on to other resting grounds. Usually I'd have gone home after the ritualistic glass of tea but one day, out of boredom perhaps, most likely out of curiosity, I hung around the surgical floor talking to Dolores, my only friend in all the hospital. I clung to her sense of wonder, her sense of the ludicrous, to her humor in the face of order, for even in that environment of restriction, I felt her still probing the whys and wherefores of science, looking for vestiges of irregularity with immense childlike curiosity.

The day of the left-over meal found Dolores and me in the laundry room, sandwiched between bins of feces and urine stained sheets to be laundered. There were also dripping urinals waiting to be washed. Hunched over a tray of fried chicken, mashed potatoes and gravy, lima beans and vanilla ice cream, we devoured crusty morsels of Mr. Smith's fried chicken breasts. The food was good. We fought over the ice cream. I resolved to try a few more meals before the summer ended, perhaps in a more pleasant atmosphere.

140

6. The Greek tragedy *Antigone*, by Sophocles. Dolores played Ismene, the weaker sister of Antigone, played by Rocío.   7. The Weeper, a dead woman's ghost, folklore.

That day, I lingered at the hospital longer than usual. I helped Dolores with Francisca Pacheco, turning the old woman on her side as we fitted the sheet on the mattress. "Cuidado, no me toquen,"[8] she cried. When Dolores took her temperature rectally, I left the room, but returned just as quickly, ashamed of my timidity. I was always the passing menu girl, too afraid to linger, too unwilling to see, too busy with summer illusions. Every day I raced to finish the daily menus, punching in my time card, greeting the beginning of what I considered to be my *real* day outside those long and smelly corridors where food and illness intermingled, leaving a sweet thick air of exasperation in my lungs. The "ooooh" of Elizabeth Rainey's anxious flesh.

The "ay ay ay" of Great Aunt Eutilia's phantom cries awaited me in my father's room. On the wall the portrait of his hero Napoleon hung, shielded by white sheets. The sun was too bright that summer for delicate fading eyes, the heat too oppressive. The blue fan raced to bring freshness to that acrid tomb full of ghosts.

I walked home slowly, not stopping at the quiet place. Compadre Regino Suárez was on the roof. The cooler leaked. Impatient with Regino and his hearty wave, his habit of never doing any job thoroughly, I remembered that I'd forgotten my daily iced tea. The sun was hot. All I wanted was to rest in the cool darkness of my purple room.

The inside of the house smelled of burnt food and lemons. My mother had left something on the stove again. To counteract the burnt smell she'd placed lemons all over the house. Lemons filled ashtrays and bowls, they lay solidly on tables and rested in hot corners. I looked in the direction of Eutilia's room. Quiet. She was sleeping. She'd been dead five years but, still, the room was hers. She was sleeping peacefully. I smelled the cleansing bitterness of lemons.

MRS. DANIELS

When I entered rooms and saw sick, dying women in their forties, I always remembered room 210, Mrs. Daniels, the mother of my cousin's future wife.

Mrs. Daniels usually lay in bed, whimpering like a little dog, moaning to her husband, who always stood nearby, holding her hand, saying softly, "Now, Martha, Martha. The little girl only wants to get your order."

"Send her away, goddammit!"

On those days that Mr. Daniels was absent, Mrs. Daniels whined for me to go away. "Leave me alone, can't you see I'm dying" she said and looked toward the wall. She looked so pale, sick, near death to me, but somehow I knew, not really having imagined death without the dying, not having felt the outrage and loathing, I knew and saw her outbursts for what they really were: deep hurts, deep distresses. I saw her need to release them, to fling them at others, dribbling pain / anguish / abuse, trickling away those vast torrential feelings of sorrow and hate and fear, letting them fall wherever they would, on whomever they might. I was her white wall. I was her whipping girl upon whom she spilled her dark-

8. "Watch out, don't touch me."

ened ashes. She cried out obscenely to me, sending me reeling from her room, that room of loathing and dread. That room anxious with worms.

Who of us has not heard the angry choked words of crying people, listened, not wanting to hear, then shut our ears, said enough, I don't want to. Who has not seen the fearful tear-streamed faces, known the blank eyes and felt the holding back, and, like smiling thoughtless children, said: "I was in the next room, I couldn't help hearing, I heard, I saw, you didn't know, did you? I know."

We rolled up the pain, assigned it a shelf, placed it in the hardened place, along with a certain self-congratulatory sense of wonder at the world's unfortunates like Mrs. Daniels. We were embarrassed to be alive.

JUAN MARIA / THE NOSE

"Cómo se dice[9] when was the last time you had a bowel movement?" Nurse Luciano asked. She was from Yonkers, a bright newlywed. Erminia, the ward secretary, a tall thin horsey woman with a postured Juárez hairdo of exaggerated sausage ringlets, replied through chapped lips, "Oh, who cares, he's sleeping."

"He's from México, huh?" Luciano said with interest.

"An illegal alien," Rosario retorted. She was Erminia's sister, the superintendent's secretary, with the look of a badly scarred bulldog. She'd stopped by to invite Erminia to join her for lunch.

"So where'd it happen?" Luciano asked.

"At the Guadalajara Bar on Main Street," Erminia answered, moistening her purple lips nervously. It was a habit of hers.

"Hey, I remember when we used to walk home from school. You remember, Rocío?" Dolores asked, "We'd try to throw each other through the swinging doors. It was real noisy in there."

"Father O'Kelley said drink was the defilement of men, the undoing of staunch, god-fearing women," I said.

"Our father has one now and then," Rosario replied, "that doesn't mean anything. It's because he was one of those aliens."

"Those kind of problems are bad around here I heard," Luciano said, "people sneaking across the border and all."

"Hell, you don't know the half of it," Nurse González said as she came up to the desk where we all stood facing the hallway. "It's an epidemic."

"I don't know, my mother always had maids, and they were all real nice except the one who stole her wedding rings. We had to track her all the way to Piedras Negras[1] and even then she wouldn't give them up," Erminia interjected.

"Still, it doesn't seem human the way they're treated at times."

"Some of them, they ain't human."

"Still, he was drunk, he wasn't full aware."

"Full aware, my ass," retorted Esperanza angrily, "he had enough money to buy booze. If that's not aware, I don't know what aware is. Ain't my goddam

---

9. "How do you say . . ."   1. Mexican town on the Texas border.

fault the bastard got into a fight and someone bit his nose off. Ain't *my* fault he's
here and *we* gotta take care of him. Christ! If *that* isn't aware, I don't know what
aware is!"

Esperanza González, head surgical floor nurse, the short but highly
respected Esperanza of no esperanzas,[2] the Esperanza of the short-bobbed hair,
the husky deferential voice, the commands, the no-nonsense orders and brisk-
ness, Esperanza the future sister-in-law of Dolores, my only friend, Esperanza
the dyke, who was later killed in a car accident on the way to somewhere, said:
"Now get back to work all of you, we're just here to clean up the mess."

Later when Esperanza was killed my aunt said, "How nice. In the paper they
called her lover her sister. How nice!"

170   "Hey, Erminia, lunch?" asked Rosario, almost sheepishly. "You hungry?"

"Coming, Rosario," yelled Erminia from the back office where she was getting her purse. "Coming!"

"God, I'm starving," Rosario said, "can you hear my stomach?"

"Go check Mr. Carter's cath, Dolores, will you?" said Esperanza in a softer
tone.

"Well, I don't know, I just don't know," Luciano pondered. "It doesn't seem
human, does it? I mean how in the world could anyone in their right mind bite
off another person's nose? How? You know it, González, you're a tough rooster.
If I didn't know you so well already, you'd scare the hell out of me. How long
you been a nurse?"

175   "Too long, Luciano. Look, I ain't a new bride, that's liable to make a person
soft. Me, I just clean up the mess."

"Luciano, what you know about people could be put on the head of a pin.
You just leave these alien problems to those of us who were brought up around
here and know what's going on. Me, I don't feel one bit sorry for that bastard,"
Esperanza said firmly. "Christ, Luciano, what do you expect, he don't speak no
Engleesh!"

"His name is Juan María Mejía," I ventured.

Luciano laughed. Esperanza laughed. Dolores went off to Mr. Carter's room,
and Rosario chatted noisily with Erminia as they walked toward the cafeteria.

"Hey, Rosario," Luciano called out, "what happened to the rings?"

180   It was enchilada day. Trini was very busy.

Juan María the Nose was sleeping in the hallway; all the other beds were
filled. His hospital gown was awry, the grey sheet folded through sleep-deadened
limbs. His hands were tightly clenched. The hospital screen barely concealed
his twisted private sleep of legs akimbo, moist armpits and groin. It was a sleep
of sleeping off, of hard drunken wanderings, with dreams of a bar, dreams of a
fight. He slept the way little boys sleep, carelessly half exposed. I stared at him.

Esperanza complained and muttered under her breath, railing at the Anglo
sons of bitches and at all the lousy wetbacks, at everyone, male and female,
goddamn them and their messes. Esperanza was dark and squat, pura india[3]
tortured by her very face. Briskly, she ordered Dolores and now me about. I had

---

2. Hope of no hopes.   **3.** Pure Indian. Slang for ugly woman.

graduated overnight, as if in a hazy dream, to assistant, but unofficial, ward
secretary.

I stared across the hallway to Juan María the Nose. He faced the wall, a
dangling I.V. at the foot of the bed. Esperanza González, R.N., looked at me.

"Well, and *who* are you?"

"I'm the menu, I mean, I *was* the menu . . ." I stammered. "I'm helping   185
Erminia."

"So get me some cigarettes. Camels. I'll pay you tomorrow when I get paid."

Yes, it was really González, male, who ran the hospital.

Arlene returned from the Luray Caverns with a stalactite charm bracelet for
me. She announced to Mr. Smith and me that she'd gotten a job with an insurance company.

"I'll miss you, Rocío."

"Me, too, Arlene." God knows it was the truth. I'd come to depend on her,   190
our talks over tea. No one ever complimented me like she did.

"You never get angry, do you?" she said admiringly.

"Rarely," I said. But inside, I was always angry.

"What do you want to do?"

"Want to do?"

"Yeah."   195

I want to be someone else, somewhere else, someone important and responsible and sexy. I want to be sexy.

"I don't know. I'm going to major in drama."

"You're sweet," she said. "Everyone likes you. It's in your nature. You're the
Florence Nightingale of Altavista Memorial, that's it!"

"Oh God, Arlene, I don't want to be a nurse, *ever!* I can't take the smells. No
one in our family can stand smells."

"You look like that painting. I always did think it looked like you . . ."   200

"You did?"

"Yeah."

"Come on, you're making me sick, Arlene."

"Everyone likes you."

"Well . . ."   205

"So keep in touch. I'll see you at the University."

"Home ec?"

"Biology."

We hugged.

The weeks progressed. My hours at the hospital grew. I was allowed to check   210
in patients, to take their blood pressures and temperatures. I flipped through the
patients' charts, memorizing names, room numbers, types of diet. I fingered the
doctors' reports with reverence. Perhaps someday I would begin to write in them
as Erminia did: "2:15 p.m., Mrs. Daniels, pulse normal, temp normal, Dr. Blasse
checked patient, treatment on schedule, medication given to quiet patient."

One day I received a call at the ward desk. It was Mr. Smith.

"Ms. Esquibel? Rocío? This is Mr. Smith, you know, down in the cafeteria."

"Yes, Mr. Smith! How are you? Is there anything I can do? Are you getting the menus okay? I'm leaving them on top of your desk."

"I've been talking to Nurse González, surgical; she says they need you there full time to fill in and could I do without you?"

215 "Oh, I can do both jobs; it doesn't take that long, Mr. Smith."

"No, we're going by a new system. Rather, it's the old system. The aides will take the menu orders like they used to before Arlene came. So, you come down and see me, Rocío, have a glass of iced tea. I never see you any more since you moved up in the world. Yeah, I guess you're the last of the menu girls."

The summer passed. June, July, August, my birth month. There were serious days, hurried admissions, feverish errands, quick notes jotted in the doctor's charts. I began to work Saturdays. In my eagerness to "advance," I unwittingly had created more work for myself, work I really wasn't skilled to do.

My heart reached out to every person, dragged itself through the hallways with the patients, cried when they did, laughed when they did. I had no business in the job. I was too emotional.

Now when I walked into a room I knew the patient's history, the cause of illness. I began to study individual cases with great attention, turning to a copy of *The Family Physician*, which had its place among my father's old books in his abandoned study.

220 Gone were the idle hours of sitting in the cafeteria, leisurely drinking iced tea, gone were the removed reflections of the outsider.

My walks home were measured, pensive. I hid in my room those long hot nights, nights full of wrestling, injured dreams. Nothing seemed enough.

Before I knew it, it was the end of August, close to that autumnal time of setting out. My new life was about to begin. I had made that awesome leap into myself that steamy summer of illness and dread—confronting at every turn, the flesh, its lingering cries.

"Ay, Ay, Ay, Ay, Canta y no llores! Porque cantando se alegran, Cielito Lindo, los corazones . . ."[4] The little thin voice of an old woman sang from one of the back rooms. She pumped the gold pedals with fast furious and fervant feet, she smiled to the wall, its faces, she danced on the ceiling.

Let me jump.

225 "Goodbye, Dolores, it was fun."

"I'll miss you, Rocío! But you know, gotta save some money. I'll get back to school someday, maybe."

"What's wrong, Erminia? You mad?" I asked.

"I thought you were gonna stay and help me out here on the floor."

"Goddamn right!" complained Esperanza. "Someone told me this was your last day, so why didn't you tell me? Why'd I train you for, so you could leave us? To go to school? What for? So you can get those damned food stamps? It's a

---

4. "Sing and don't cry! Because singing brightens the heart; Beautiful Little Sky."

disgrace all those wetbacks and healthy college students getting our hard earned tax money. Makes me sick. Christ!" Esperanza shook her head with disgust.

"Hey, Erminia, you tell Rosario goodbye for me and Mrs. Luciano, too," I said sadly.

"Yeah, okay. They'll be here tomorrow," she answered tonelessly. I wanted to believe she was sad.

"I gotta say goodbye to Mr. Smith," I said, as I moved away.

"Make him come up and get some sun," González snickered. "Hell no, better not, he might get sunstroke and who'd fix my fried chicken?"

I climbed down the steps to the basement, past the cafeteria, past my special table, and into Mr. Smith's office, where he sat, adding numbers.

"Miss Esquibel, Rocío!"

"This is my last day, Mr. Smith. I wanted to come down and thank you. I'm sorry about . . ."

"Oh no, it worked out all right. It's nothing."

Did I see, from the corner of my eye, a set of Friday's menus he himself was tabulating—salisbury steak, macaroni and cheese . . .

"We'll miss you, Rocío. You were an excellent menu girl."

"It's been a wonderful summer."

"Do you want some tea?"

"No, I really don't have the time."

"I'll get . . ."

"No, thank you, Mr. Smith, I *really* have to go, but thanks. It's really good tea."

I extended my hand, and for the first time, we touched. Mr. Smith's eyes seemed fogged, distracted. He stood up and hobbled closer to my side. I took his grave cold hand, shook it softly, and turned to the moist walls. When I closed the door, I saw him in front of me, framed in paper, the darkness of that quiet room. Bless this mess.

Eutilia's voice echoed in the small room. Goodbye. Goodbye. And let me jump.

I turned away from the faces, the voices, now gone: Father O'Kelley, Elizabeth Rainey, Mrs. Luciano, Arlene Rutschman, Mrs. Daniels, Juan María the Nose, Mr. Samaniego and Donelda, his wife, their grandchildren, Mr. Carter, Earl Ellis, Dolores Casaus, Erminia and her sister, the bulldog. Esperanza González, Francisca Pacheco, Elweena Twinbaum, the silver-haired volunteer whose name I'd learned the week before I left Altavista Memorial. I'd made a list on a menu of all the people I'd worked with. To remember. It seemed right.

From the distance I heard Marion Smith's high voice: "Now you come back and see us!"

Above the stairs the painting of Florence Nightingale stared solidly into weary soldiers' eyes. Her look encompassed all the great unspeakable sufferings of every war. I thought of Arlene typing insurance premiums.

Farther away, from behind and around my head, I heard the irregular but joyful strains of "Cielito Lindo" played on a phantom piano by a disembodied

230

235

240

245

250

but now peaceful voice that sang with great quivering emotion: De la sierra morena, Cielito Lindo . . . viene bajando . . .[5]

Regino fixed the cooler. I started school. Later that year I was in a car accident. I crashed into a brick wall at the cemetery. I walked to Dolores' house, holding my bleeding face in my hands. Dolores and her father argued all the way to the hospital. I sat quietly in the back seat. It was a lovely morning. So clear. When I woke up I was on the surgical floor. Everyone knew me. I had so many flowers in the room I could hardly breathe. My older sister, Ronelia, thought I'd lost part of my nose in the accident and she returned to the cemetery to look for it. It wasn't there.

Mr. Smith came to see me once. I started to cry.

"Oh no, no, no, now don't you do that, Rocío. You want some tea?"

No one took my menu order. I guess that system had finally died out. I ate the food, whatever it was, walked the hallways in my grey hospital gown slit in the back, railed at the well-being of others, cursed myself for being so stupid. I only wanted to be taken home, down the street, past the quiet-talking place, a block away, near the Dairy Queen, to the darkness of my purple room.

255   It was time.

PREVIOUS EMPLOYMENT: Altavista Memorial Hospital
SUPERVISORS: Mr. Marion Smith, Dietician, and Miss Esperanza González,
     R.N., Surgical Floor.
DATES: June 1966 to August 1966
IN A FEW SENTENCES GIVE A BRIEF DESCRIPTION OF YOUR JOB:
     As Ward Secretary, I was responsible for . . . let me think . . .

                                                                          1986

▼ ▼ ▼

QUESTIONS

1. Why did Juan Sánchez want to leave his native village in Mexico? Why did he choose the Sierra Nevada above Stockton as his new home? How does the central district of Stockton appear to Juan? to Jesús? to you?

2. What element of Western religion and legend—classical as well as Christian—do you find in Cico's story of the golden carp? What religious overtones are there in Narciso's garden? How does the incident of Tony's harassment by his school friends relate to the religious and cultural themes of the story?

3. How did you feel about Mr. Smith when he was first introduced in "The Last of the Menu Girls"? What role did you expect him to play? How did your response to him change during the story? What is a "menu girl"? What signifi-

5. From the dark highlands, Beautiful Little Sky . . . you are coming down.

cance do you find in the fact that Rocío is the "last" of them? How do the Mexican Americans in the story feel about illegal immigration? Did you find the story depressing? uplifting? educational? what? Are you moved by stories that deal with sorrow, death, disease? Do you seek them out? avoid them? read them reluctantly, only when assigned or highly recommended? Did you see *Philadelphia*? Did you avoid seeing it? Why (or why not)?

WRITING SUGGESTIONS

1. Write a personal narrative centering on an incident or situation that involved your "mixed" heritage (even if that "mixture" is made up of ethnic ingredients as close as Mexican and Guatemalan, English and Scots, Blackfoot and Sioux, Italian and Irish). If you have had no such experience, search out members of your family or friends who may have, interview them, and write a narrative based on their experience.

2. Research the history of one of your ethnic strains and write a report of the "mixing" of that heritage over the centuries; e.g., the invasion of Russia and the Ukraine by Mongolians, of France by Germanic tribes, etc.

3. Using specific textual passages to support your position, write an essay on "Sánchez" about Jésus's parentage and the implication of his name; or, write about whether Juan going "home" means (1) he went back to Mexico, or (2) he committed suicide.

4. Write (a) an analytical character sketch of Rocío Esquibel ("The Last of the Menu Girls"), documenting it with specific references to and passages from the text, or (b) an account of what Rocío learned that summer, indicating as specifically as possible how her experience was affected by each of the patients and each of her friends at the hospital.

10 LITERARY KIND AS CONTEXT: INITIATION STORIES

Themes are useful for grouping stories together for comparison, both to highlight similarities and to reveal differences in history and structure and so to discover the uniqueness of the work. Types of characters—stereotypes—are useful for the same purpose: to show both the common qualities and the unique combination of qualities in a particular character in a story. Though all grouping and classification, used poorly, can blur distinctions and make all members of a group seem the same, when used well they do not blur but bring into focus the individuality of each member or being.

Literary criticism lacks the specific and agreed-on system of classification of biology, so that its terms are not so fixed as *phylum, genus, species*. In general, we use the term **genre** for the largest commonly agreed-on categories: fiction, poetry, drama. When I'm trying to be consistent, I use the term **subgenre** for the divisions of fiction—novel, novella, short story, and so on. A **kind** is a species or subcategory within a subgenre.

One kind of short story, so common that some maintain it is not a kind but is equivalent to the subgenre short story itself, is the **initiation** story, in which a character—often but not always a child or young person—first learns a significant truth about the universe, reality, society, people, himself or herself. Such a subject tends to dictate the main outlines of the story's action: it begins with the protagonist in a state of innocence or mistaken belief (exposition); it leads up to the moment of illumination or the discovery of the truth (rising action to climax or turning point), and ends usually with some indication of the result of that discovery (falling action to conclusion). This kind is particularly suitable to a short story because it lends itself to brief treatment: the illumination is more or less sudden—there is no need for lengthy development, for multiple scenes or settings, for much time to pass, for too many complications of action or a large cast of characters—yet it can encapsulate a whole life or important segment of a life and wide-ranging, significant themes.

If you've been reading this anthology from the beginning, you have already run into a number of initiation stories, and you may have some idea of what sorts of truths their protagonists discover. Young goodman Brown discovers the universality of evil in human beings. The captain in "The Secret Sharer" discovers that someone very much like him, virtually his double and therefore

probably he himself, is not only capable of murder but may, under certain circumstances and in his capacity as a captain or leader, consciously choose murder as the lesser of evils. Leila ("Her First Ball") comes across the truth that
youth is fleeting (you cannot say she really learns it, since by the end of that
very short story she has forgotten it). We have also seen that one may retreat
from the truth physically or psychologically, as does Brown, or remain
unchanged or revert to one's former state, as Leila does.

Since to the young all things seem possible—one can be a doctor, novelist,
tennis star, saint, and swinger, serially or simultaneously—many of the truths
learned in initiation stories have to do with limitation. The girl in "Boys and
Girls" learns that she is "only a girl." Sometimes the child learns the difference
between romance and reality, as does the boy in "Araby" or between words and
reality in the adult world, as Hazel does in "Gorilla, My Love."

Sometimes, the initiation takes place as an unscheduled event, as in
"Araby." At other times there is a ritual or **rite of passage**, such as a formal
entry into society ("Her First Ball"). What do we usually think of as the purpose of a debut? How does the society intend to induct its new member? As
you read "Her First Ball," think about these questions and watch how Leila's
debut fulfills its ritual role, how it differs from it, and how it may induct Leila
into society more truly than intended.

By the time you finish this chapter you should have some idea of the variations possible within the initiation story, and as you look back to such stories as
"Sonny's Blues," "The Country Husband," "How Much Land Does a Man
Need?", "Her First Ball," "Odour of Chrysanthemums," and many of the others, you should have a still better idea of the range of stories in this kind.
Adults may be initiated as well as children and adolescents; the truths may be
bitter or pleasing, cosmic, social, psychological; the initiates may change forever, retreat, shrug off what they have learned. By seeing all these stories as
part of the large group of initiation stories you may the more readily notice the
differences in the protagonists, the learning experiences, and the results of the
initiations on the protagonists, whether they are permanent or temporary, life-
denying or life-enhancing. You may, in other words, have gone a long way
toward defining the unique vision of the story, its precise and individual illumination of reality. And that's the function of classification in the first place.

▼ ▼ ▼

JAMES JOYCE

Araby

North Richmond Street, being blind,[1] was a quiet street except at the hour when the Christian Brothers' School set the boys free. An uninhabited house of two storeys stood at the blind end, detached from its neighbours in a square ground. The other houses of the street, conscious of decent lives within them, gazed at one another with brown imperturbable faces.

The former tenant of our house, a priest, had died in the back drawing-room. Air, musty from having been long enclosed, hung in all the rooms, and the waste room behind the kitchen was littered with old useless papers. Among these I found a few paper-covered books, the pages of which were curled and damp: *The Abbot*, by Walter Scott, *The Devout Communicant* and *The Memoirs of Vidocq*.[2] I liked the last best because its leaves were yellow. The wild garden behind the house contained a central apple tree and a few straggling bushes, under one of which I found the late tenant's rusty bicycle-pump. He had been a very charitable priest; in his will he had left all his money to institutions and the furniture of his house to his sister.

When the short days of winter came, dusk fell before we had well eaten our dinners. When we met in the street the houses had grown sombre. The space of sky above us was the colour of ever-changing violet and towards it the lamps of the street lifted their feeble lanterns. The cold air stung us and we played till our bodies glowed. Our shouts echoed in the silent street. The career of our play brought us through the dark muddy lanes behind the houses, where we ran the gauntlet of the rough tribes from the cottages, to the back doors of the dark dripping gardens where odours arose from the ashpits,[3] to the dark odorous stables where a coachman smoothed and combed the horse or shook music from the buckled harness. When we returned to the street, light from the kitchen windows had filled the areas. If my uncle was seen turning the corner, we hid in the shadow until we had seen him safely housed. Or if Mangan's sister came out on the doorstep to call her brother in to his tea, we watched her from our shadow peer up and down the street. We waited to see whether she would remain or go in and, if she remained, we left our shadow and walked up to Mangan's steps resignedly. She was waiting for us, her figure defined by the light from the half-opened door. Her brother always teased her before he obeyed, and I stood by the railings looking at her. Her dress swung as she moved her body, and the soft rope of her hair tossed from side to side.

1. Dead-end street.   2. The 1820 novel by Sir Walter Scott (1771–1834) is a romance about the Catholic Mary, Queen of Scots (1542–1587), who was beheaded; a Catholic religious tract: *The Devout Communicant: or Pious Meditations and Aspirations for the Three Days Before and Three Days After Receiving the Holy Eucharist* (1813); the "memoirs" were probably *not* written by François Vidocq (1775–1857), a French criminal who became chief of detectives and who died poor and disgraced for his part in a crime that he solved.   3. Where fireplace ashes were dumped.

Every morning I lay on the floor in the front parlour watching her door. The blind was pulled down to within an inch of the sash so that I could not be seen. When she came out on the doorstep my heart leaped. I ran to the hall, seized my books and followed her. I kept her brown figure always in my eye and, when we came near the point at which our ways diverged, I quickened my pace and passed her. This happened morning after morning. I had never spoken to her, except for a few casual words, and yet her name was like a summons to all my foolish blood.

Her image accompanied me even in places the most hostile to romance. On Saturday evenings when my aunt went marketing I had to go to carry some of the parcels. We walked through the flaring streets, jostled by drunken men and bargaining women, amid the curses of labourers, the shrill litanies of shop-boys who stood on guard by the barrels of pigs' cheeks, the nasal chanting of street-singers, who sang a *come-all-you* about O'Donovan Rossa,[4] or a ballad about the troubles in our native land. These noises converged in a single sensation of life for me: I imagined that I bore my chalice safely through a throng of foes. Her name sprang to my lips at moments in strange prayers and praises which I myself did not understand. My eyes were often full of tears (I could not tell why) and at times a flood from my heart seemed to pour itself out into my bosom. I thought little of the future. I did not know whether I would ever speak to her or not or, if I spoke to her, how I would tell her of my confused adoration. But my body was like a harp and her words and gestures were like fingers running upon the wires.

One evening I went into the back drawing-room in which the priest had died. It was a dark rainy evening and there was no sound in the house. Through one of the broken panes I heard the rain impinge upon the earth, the fine incessant needles of water playing in the sodden beds. Some distant lamp or lighted window gleamed below me. I was thankful that I could see so little. All my senses seemed to desire to veil themselves and, feeling that I was about to slip from them, I pressed the palms of my hands together until they trembled, murmuring: "*O love! O love!*" many times.

At last she spoke to me. When she addressed the first words to me I was so confused that I did not know what to answer. She asked me was I going to *Araby.*[5] I forgot whether I answered yes or no. It would be a splendid bazaar, she said; she would love to go.

"And why can't you?" I asked.

While she spoke she turned a silver bracelet round and round her wrist. She could not go, she said, because there would be a retreat that week in her convent. Her brother and two other boys were fighting for their caps and I was alone at the railings. She held one of the spikes, bowing her head towards me. The light from the lamp opposite our door caught the white curve of her neck, lit up

5

---

4. Jeremiah O'Donovan (1831–1915) was a militant Irish nationalist who fought on despite terms in prison and banishment. *Come-all-you:* A song, of which there were many, which began "Come, all you Irishmen." **5.** A bazaar billed as a "Grand Oriental Fête," Dublin, May 1894.

her hair that rested there and, falling, lit up the hand upon the railing. It fell over one side of her dress and caught the white border of a petticoat, just visible as she stood at ease.

10   "It's well for you," she said.

"If I go," I said. "I will bring you something."

What innumerable follies laid waste my waking and sleeping thoughts after that evening! I wished to annihilate the tedious intervening days. I chafed against the work of school. At night in my bedroom and by day in the classroom her image came between me and the page I strove to read. The syllables of the word *Araby* were called to me through the silence in which my soul luxuriated and cast an Eastern enchantment over me. I asked for leave to go to the bazaar on Saturday night. My aunt was surprised and hoped it was not some Freemason[6] affair. I answered few questions in class. I watched my master's face pass from amiability to sternness; he hoped I was not beginning to idle. I could not call my wandering thoughts together. I had hardly any patience with the serious work of life which, now that it stood between me and my desire, seemed to me child's play, ugly monotonous child's play.

On Saturday morning I reminded my uncle that I wished to go to the bazaar in the evening. He was fussing at the hallstand, looking for the hat-brush, and answered me curtly:

"Yes, boy, I know."

15   As he was in the hall I could not go into the front parlour and lie at the window. I left the house in bad humour and walked slowly towards the school. The air was pitilessly raw and already my heart misgave me.

When I came home to dinner my uncle had not yet been home. Still it was early. I sat staring at the clock for some time and, when its ticking began to irritate me, I left the room. I mounted the staircase and gained the upper part of the house. The high, cold, empty, gloomy rooms liberated me and I went from room to room singing. From the front window I saw my companions playing below in the street. Their cries reached me weakened and indistinct and, leaning my forehead against the cool glass, I looked over at the dark house where she lived. I may have stood there for an hour, seeing nothing but a brown-clad figure cast by my imagination, touched discreetly by the lamplight at the curved neck, at the hand upon the railings and at the border below the dress.

When I came downstairs again I found Mrs. Mercer sitting at the fire. She was an old, garrulous woman, a pawnbroker's widow, who collected used stamps for some pious purpose. I had to endure the gossip of the tea-table. The meal was prolonged beyond an hour and still my uncle did not come. Mrs. Mercer stood up to go: she was sorry she couldn't wait any longer, but it was after eight o'clock and she did not like to be out late, as the night air was bad for her. When she had gone I began to walk up and down the room, clenching my fists. My aunt said:

"I'm afraid you may put off your bazaar for this night of Our Lord."

At nine o'clock I heard my uncle's latchkey in the hall door. I heard him

---

6. The Masons, or Freemasons, were considered enemies of the Catholics.

talking to himself and heard the hallstand rocking when it had received the weight of his overcoat. I could interpret these signs. When he was midway through his dinner I asked him to give me the money to go to the bazaar. He had forgotten.

"The people are in bed and after their first sleep now," he said.

I did not smile. My aunt said to him energetically:

"Can't you give him the money and let him go? You've kept him late enough as it is."

My uncle said he was very sorry he had forgotten. He said he believed in the old saying: "All work and no play makes Jack a dull boy." He asked me where I was going and, when I had told him a second time, he asked me did I know *The Arab's Farewell to his Steed*.[7] When I left the kitchen he was about to recite the opening lines of the piece to my aunt.

I held a florin[8] tightly in my hand as I strode down Buckingham Street towards the station. The sight of the streets thronged with buyers and glaring with gas recalled to me the purpose of my journey. I took my seat in a third-class carriage of a deserted train. After an intolerable delay the train moved out of the station slowly. It crept onward among ruinous houses and over the twinkling river. At Westland Row Station a crowd of people pressed to the carriage doors; but the porters moved them back, saying that it was a special train for the bazaar. I remained alone in the bare carriage. In a few minutes the train drew up beside an improvised wooden platform. I passed out on to the road and saw by the lighted dial of a clock that it was ten minutes to ten. In front of me was a large building which displayed the magical name.

I could not find any sixpenny entrance and, fearing that the bazaar would be closed, I passed in quickly through a turnstile, handing a shilling to a weary-looking man. I found myself in a big hall girdled at half its height by a gallery. Nearly all the stalls were closed and the greater part of the hall was in darkness. I recognized a silence like that which pervades a church after a service. I walked into the centre of the bazaar timidly. A few people were gathered about the stalls which were still open. Before a curtain, over which the words *Café Chantant*[9] were written in coloured lamps, two men were counting money on a salver. I listened to the fall of the coins.

Remembering with difficulty why I had come I went over to one of the stalls and examined porcelain vases and flowered tea-sets. At the door of the stall a young lady was talking and laughing with two young gentlemen. I remarked their English accents and listened vaguely to their conversation.

"O, I never said such a thing!"

"O, but you did!"

"O, but I didn't!"

"Didn't she say that?"

"Yes. I heard her."

7. Or *The Arab's Farewell to His Horse*, sentimental 19th-century poem by Caroline Norton. The speaker has sold the horse.   8. Two-shilling piece; thus four times the "sixpenny entrance" fee. 9. Café with music.

"O, there's a . . . fib!"

Observing me, the young lady came over and asked me did I wish to buy anything. The tone of her voice was not encouraging; she seemed to have spoken to me out of a sense of duty. I looked humbly at the great jars that stood like eastern guards at either side of the dark entrance to the stall and murmured:

"No, thank you."

35   The young lady changed the position of one of the vases and went back to the two young men. They began to talk of the same subject. Once or twice the young lady glanced at me over her shoulder.

I lingered before her stall, though I knew my stay was useless, to make my interest in her wares seem the more real. Then I turned away slowly and walked down the middle of the bazaar. I allowed the two pennies to fall against the sixpence in my pocket. I heard a voice call from one end of the gallery that the light was out. The upper part of the hall was now completely dark.

Gazing up into the darkness I saw myself as a creature driven and derided by vanity; and my eyes burned with anguish and anger.

1914

TONI CADE BAMBARA

Gorilla, My Love

That was the year Hunca Bubba changed his name. Not a change up, but a change back, since Jefferson Winston Vale was the name in the first place. Which was news to me cause he'd been my Hunca Bubba my whole lifetime, since I couldn't manage Uncle to save my life. So far as I was concerned it was a change completely to somethin soundin very geographical weatherlike to me, like somethin you'd find in a almanac. Or somethin you'd run across when you sittin in the navigator seat with a wet thumb on the map crinkly in your lap, watchin the roads and signs so when Granddaddy Vale say "Which way, Scout," you got sense enough to say take the next exit or take a left or whatever it is. Not that Scout's my name. Just the name Granddaddy call whoever sittin in the navigator seat. Which is usually me cause I don't feature sittin in the back with the pecans. Now, you figure pecans all right to be sittin with. If you thinks so, that's your business. But they dusty sometime and make you cough. And they got a way of slidin around and dippin down sudden, like maybe a rat in the buckets. So if you scary like me, you sleep with the lights on and blame it on Baby Jason and, so as not to waste good electric, you study the maps. And that's how come I'm in the navigator seat most times and get to be called Scout.

So Hunca Bubba in the back with the pecans and Baby Jason, and he in love. And we got to hear all this stuff about this woman he in love with and all. Which really ain't enough to keep the mind alive, though Baby Jason got no better sense than to give his undivided attention and keep grabbin at the photograph which is just a picture of some skinny woman in a countrified dress with her hand shot up to her face like she shame fore cameras. But there's a movie house in the background which I ax about. Cause I am a movie freak from way back, even though it do get me in trouble sometime.

Like when me and Big Brood and Baby Jason was on our own last Easter and couldn't go to the Dorset cause we'd seen all the Three Stooges they was. And the RKO Hamilton was closed readying up for the Easter Pageant that night. And the West End, the Regun and the Sunset was too far, less we had grownups with us which we didn't. So we walk up Amsterdam Avenue to the Washington and *Gorilla, My Love* playin, they say, which suit me just fine, though the "my love" part kinda drag Big Brood some. As for Baby Jason, shoot, like Granddaddy say, he'd follow me into the fiery furnace if I say come on. So we go in and get three bags of Havmore potato chips which not only are the best potato chips but the best bags for blowin up and bustin real loud so the matron come trottin down the aisle with her chunky self, flashin that flashlight dead in your eye so you can give her some lip, and if she answer back and you already finish seein the show anyway, why then you just turn the place out. Which I love to do, no lie. With Baby Jason kickin at the seat in front, egging me on, and Big Brood mumblin bout what fiercesome things we goin do. Which means me. Like when the big boys come up on us talkin bout Lemme a nickel. It's me that hide the money. Or when the bad boys in the park take Big Brood's Spaudeen[1] way from him. It's me that jump on they back and fight awhile. And it's me that turns out the show if the matron get too salty.

So the movie come on and right away it's this churchy music and clearly not about no gorilla. Bout Jesus. And I am ready to kill, not cause I got anything gainst Jesus. Just that when you fixed to watch a gorilla picture you don't wanna get messed around with Sunday School stuff. So I am mad. Besides, we see this raggedy old brown film *King of Kings*[2] every year and enough's enough. Grownups figure they can treat you just anyhow. Which burns me up. There I am, my feet up and my Havmore potato chips really salty and crispy and two jawbreakers in my lap and the money safe in my shoe from the big boys, and there comes this Jesus stuff. So we all go wild. Yellin, booin, stompin and carrying on. Really to wake the man in the booth up there who musta went to sleep and put on the wrong reels. But no, cause he holler down to shut up and then he turn the sound up so we really gotta holler like crazy to even hear ourselves good. And the matron ropes off the children section and flashes her light all over the place and we yell some more and some kids slip under the rope and run up and down the aisle just to show it take more than some dusty ole velvet rope to tie us down. And I'm flingin the kid in front of me's popcorn. And Baby Jason kickin seats. And it's really somethin. Then here come the big and bad matron, the one they let out in case of emergency. And she totin that flashlight like she gonna use it on somebody. This here the colored matron Brandy and her friends call Thunderbuns. She do not play. She do not smile. So we shut up and watch the simple ass picture.

1. Probably refers to "Spaldeen," the small rubber ball made by the Spalding company and used for stick-ball.   2. Although there is a 1961 version of the film, this probably refers to the silent-movie version made in the 1920s.

5   Which is not so simple as it is stupid. Cause I realized that just about anybody in my family is better than this god they always talkin about. My daddy wouldn't stand for nobody treatin any of us that way. My mama specially. And I can just see it now, Big Brood up there on the cross talkin bout Forgive them Daddy cause they don't know what they doin. And my Mama say Get on down from there you big fool, whatcha think this is, playtime? And my Daddy yellin to Granddaddy to get him a ladder cause Big Brood actin the fool, his mother side of the family showin up. And my mama and her sister Daisy jumpin on them Romans beatin them with they pocketbooks. And Hunca Bubba tellin them folks on they knees they better get out the way and go get some help or they goin to get trampled on. And Granddaddy Vale sayin Leave the boy alone, if that's what he wants to do with his life we ain't got nothin to say about it. Then Aunt Daisy givin him a taste of that pocketbook, fussin bout what a damn fool old man Granddaddy is. Then everybody jumpin in his chest like the time Uncle Clayton went in the army and come back with only one leg and Granddaddy say somethin stupid about that's life. And by this time Big Brood off the cross and in the park playin handball or skully[3] or somethin. And the family in the kitchen throwin dishes at each other, screamin bout if you hadn't done this I wouldn't had to do that. And me in the parlor trying to do my arithmetic yellin Shut it off.

    Which is what I was yellin all by myself which make me a sittin target for Thunderbuns. But when I yell We want our money back, that gets everybody in chorus. And the movie windin up with this heavenly cloud music and the smart-ass up there in his hole in the wall turns up the sound again to drown us out. Then there comes Bugs Bunny which we already seen so we know we been had. No gorilla my nuthin. And Big Brood say Awwww sheeet, we goin to see the manager and get our money back. And I know from this we business. So I brush the potato chips out of my hair which is where Baby Jason like to put em, and I march myself up the aisle to deal with the manager who is a crook in the first place for lyin out there sayin *Gorilla, My Love* playin. And I never did like the man cause he oily and pasty at the same time like the bad guy in the serial, the one that got a hideout behind a push-button bookcase and play "Moonlight Sonata"[4] with gloves on. I knock on the door and I am furious. And I am alone, too. Cause Big Brood suddenly got to go so bad even though my mama told us bout goin in them nasty bathrooms. And I hear him sigh like he disgusted when he get to the door and see only a little kid there. And now I'm really furious cause I get so tired grownups messin over kids cause they little and can't take em to court. What is it, he say to me like I lost my mittens or wet myself or am somebody's retarded child. When in reality I am the smartest kid P.S. 186 ever had in its whole lifetime and you can ax anybody. Even them teachers that don't like me cause I won't sing them Southern songs or back off when they tell me my questions are out of order. And cause my Mama come up there in a minute

---

3. A basketball game that tests shooting skill and can be played alone or as a contest between two people.   4. Popular name for Beethoven's 14th Sonata. The man who plays this song with gloves on refers to the ever-creepy *Phantom of the Opera*.

when them teachers start playin the dozens[5] behind colored folks. She stalks in with her hat pulled down bad and that Persian lamb coat draped back over one hip on account of she got her fist planted there so she can talk that talk which gets us all hypnotized, and teacher be comin undone cause she know this could be her job and her behind cause Mama got pull with the Board and bad by her own self anyhow.

So I kick the door open wider and just walk right by him and sit down and tell the man about himself and that I want my money back and that goes for Baby Jason and Big Brood too. And he still trying to shuffle me out the door even though I'm sittin which shows him for the fool he is. Just like them teachers do fore they realize Mama like a stone on that spot and ain't backin up. So he ain't gettin up off the money. So I was forced to leave, takin the matches from under his ashtray, and set a fire under the candy stand, which closed the raggedy ole Washington down for a week. My Daddy had the suspect it was me cause Big Brood got a big mouth. But I explained right quick what the whole thing was about and I figured it was even-steven. Cause if you say Gorilla, My Love, you supposed to mean it. Just like when you say you goin to give me a party on my birthday, you gotta mean it. And if you say me and Baby Jason can go South pecan haulin with Granddaddy Vale, you better not be comin up with no stuff about the weather look uncertain or did you mop the bathroom or any other trickified business. I mean even gangsters in the movies say My word is my bond. So don't nobody get away with nothin far as I'm concerned. So Daddy put his belt back on. Cause that's the way I was raised. Like my Mama say in one of them situations when I won't back down, Okay Badbird, you right. Your point is well-taken. Not that Badbird my name, just what she say when she tired arguin and know I'm right. And Aunt Jo, who is the hardest head in the family and worse even than Aunt Daisy, she say, You absolutely right Miss Muffin, which also ain't my real name but the name she gave me one time when I got some medicine shot in my behind and wouldn't get up off her pillows for nothin. And even Granddaddy Vale—who got no memory to speak of, so sometime you can just plain lie to him, if you want to be like that—he say, Well if that's what I said, then that's it. But this name business was different they said. It wasn't like Hunca Bubba had gone back on his word or anything. Just that he was thinkin bout gettin married and was usin his real name now. Which ain't the way I saw it at all.

So there I am in the navigator seat. And I turned to him and just plain ole ax him. I mean I come right on out with it. No sense goin all around that barn the old folks talk about. And like my mama say, Hazel—which is my real name and what she remembers to call me when she bein serious—when you got somethin on your mind, speak up and let the chips fall where they may. And if anybody don't like it, tell em to come see your mama. And Daddy look up from the paper and say, You hear your Mama good, Hazel. And tell em to come see me first. Like that. That's how I was raised.

---

5. Ritualized game or contest in which two participants exchange insults directed against each other's relatives.

So I turn clear round in the navigator seat and say, "Look here, Hunca Bubba or Jefferson Windsong Vale or whatever your name is, you gonna marry this girl?"

"Sure am," he say, all grins.

And I say, "Member that time you was baby-sittin me when we lived at four-o-nine and there was this big snow and Mama and Daddy got held up in the country so you had to stay for two days?"

And he say, "Sure do."

"Well. You remember how you told me I was the cutest thing that ever walked the earth?"

"Oh, you were real cute when you were little," he say, which is supposed to be funny. I am not laughin.

"Well. You remember what you said?"

And Granddaddy Vale squintin over the wheel and axin Which way, Scout. But Scout is busy and don't care if we all get lost for days.

"Watcha mean, Peaches?"

"My name is Hazel. And what I mean is you said you were going to marry *me* when I grew up. You were going to wait. That's what I mean, my dear Uncle Jefferson." And he don't say nuthin. Just look at me real strange like he never saw me before in life. Like he lost in some weird town in the middle of night and lookin for directions and there's no one to ask. Like it was me that messed up the maps and turned the road posts round. "Well, you said it, didn't you?" And Baby Jason lookin back and forth like we playin ping-pong. Only I ain't playin. I'm hurtin and I can hear that I am screamin. And Granddaddy Vale mumblin how we never gonna get to where we goin if I don't turn around and take my navigator job serious.

"Well, for cryin out loud, Hazel, you just a little girl. And I was just teasin."

" 'And I was just teasin,' " I say back just how he said it so he can hear what a terrible thing it is. Then I don't say nuthin. And he don't say nuthin. And Baby Jason don't say nuthin nohow. Then Granddaddy Vale speak up. "Look here, Precious, it was Hunca Bubba what told you them things. This here, Jefferson Winston Vale." And Hunca Bubba say, "That's right. That was somebody else. I'm a new somebody."

"You a lyin dawg," I say, when I meant to say treacherous dog, but just couldn't get hold of the word. It slipped away from me. And I'm crying and crumplin down in the seat and just don't care. And Granddaddy say to hush and steps on the gas. And I'm losin my bearins and don't even know where to look on the map cause I can't see for cryin. And Baby Jason cryin too. Cause he is my blood brother and understands that we must stick together or be forever lost, what with grown-ups playin change-up and turnin you round every which way so bad. And don't even say they sorry.

1972

ALICE MUNRO

Boys and Girls

My father was a fox farmer. That is, he raised silver foxes, in pens; and in the fall and early winter, when their fur was prime, he killed them and skinned them and sold their pelts to the Hudson's Bay Company or the Montreal Fur Traders. These companies supplied us with heroic calendars to hang, one on each side of the kitchen door. Against a background of cold blue sky and black pine forests and treacherous northern rivers, plumed adventurers planted the flags of England or of France; magnificent savages bent their backs to the portage.

For several weeks before Christmas, my father worked after supper in the cellar of our house. The cellar was white-washed, and lit by a hundred-watt bulb over the worktable. My brother Laird and I sat on the top step and watched. My father removed the pelt inside-out from the body of the fox, which looked surprisingly small, mean and rat-like, deprived of its arrogant weight of fur. The naked, slippery bodies were collected in a sack and buried at the dump. One time the hired man, Henry Bailey, had taken a swipe at me with this sack, saying, "Christmas present!" My mother thought that was not funny. In fact she disliked the whole pelting operation—that was what the killing, skinning, and preparation of the furs was called—and wished it did not have to take place in the house. There was the smell. After the pelt had been stretched inside-out on a long board my father scraped away delicately, removing the little clotted webs of blood vessels, the bubbles of fat; the smell of blood and animal fat, with the strong primitive odour of the fox itself, penetrated all parts of the house. I found it reassuringly seasonal, like the smell of oranges and pine needles.

Henry Bailey suffered from bronchial troubles. He would cough and cough until his narrow face turned scarlet, and his light blue, derisive eyes filled up with tears; then he took the lid off the stove, and, standing well back, shot out a great clot of phlegm—hsss—straight into the heart of the flames. We admired him for this performance and for his ability to make his stomach growl at will, and for his laughter, which was full of high whistlings and gurglings and involved the whole faulty machinery of his chest. It was sometimes hard to tell what he was laughing at, and always possible that it might be us.

After we had been sent to bed we could still smell fox and still hear Henry's laugh, but these things, reminders of the warm, safe, brightly lit downstairs world, seemed lost and diminished, floating on the stale cold air upstairs. We were afraid at night in the winter. We were not afraid of *outside* though this was the time of year when snowdrifts curled around our house like sleeping whales and the wind harassed us all night, coming up from the buried fields, the frozen swamp, with its old bugbear chorus of threats and misery. We were afraid of *inside*, the room where we slept. At this time the upstairs of our house was not finished. A brick chimney went up one wall. In the middle of the floor was a square hole, with a wooden railing around it; that was where the stairs came up.

On the other side of the stairwell were the things that nobody had any use for any more—a soldiery roll of linoleum, standing on end, a wicker baby carriage, a fern basket, china jugs and basins with cracks in them, a picture of the Battle of Balaclava,[1] very sad to look at. I had told Laird, as soon as he was old enough to understand such things, that bats and skeletons lived over there; whenever a man escaped from the county jail, twenty miles away, I imagined that he had somehow let himself in the window and was hiding behind the linoleum. But we had rules to keep us safe. When the light was on, we were safe as long as we did not step off the square of worn carpet which defined our bedroom-space; when the light was off no place was safe but the beds themselves. I had to turn out the light kneeling on the end of my bed, and stretching as far as I could to reach the cord.

5   In the dark we lay on our beds, our narrow life rafts, and fixed our eyes on the faint light coming up the stairwell, and sang songs. Laird sang "Jingle Bells," which he would sing any time, whether it was Christmas or not, and I sang "Danny Boy." I loved the sound of my own voice, frail and supplicating, rising in the dark. We could make out the tall frosted shapes of the windows now, gloomy and white. When I came to the part, *When I am dead, as dead I well may be*—a fit of shivering caused not by the cold sheets but by pleasurable emotion almost silenced me. *You'll kneel and say, an Ave there above me*—What was an Ave? Every day I forgot to find out.

Laird went straight from singing to sleep. I could hear his long, satisfied, bubbly breaths. Now for the time that remained to me, the most perfectly private and perhaps the best time of the whole day, I arranged myself tightly under the covers and went on with one of the stories I was telling myself from night to night. These stories were about myself, when I had grown a little older; they took place in a world that was recognizably mine, yet one that presented opportunities for courage, boldness and self-sacrifice, as mine never did. I rescued people from a bombed building (it discouraged me that the real war had gone on so far away from Jubilee). I shot two rabid wolves who were menacing the schoolyard (the teachers cowered terrified at my back). I rode a fine horse spiritedly down the main street of Jubilee, acknowledging the townspeople's gratitude for some yet-to-be-worked-out piece of heroism (nobody ever rode a horse there, except King Billy in the Orangemen's Day[2] parade). There was always riding and shooting in these stories, though I had only been on a horse twice—bareback because we did not own a saddle—and the second time I had slid right around and dropped under the horse's feet; it had stepped placidly over me. I really was learning to shoot, but I could not hit anything yet, not even tin cans on fence posts.

Alive, the foxes inhabited a world my father made for them. It was surrounded by a high guard fence, like a medieval town, with a gate that was pad-

1. An indecisive Crimean War battle fought on October 25, 1854.   2. The Orange Society is an Irish Protestant group named after William of Orange, who, as King William III of England, defeated the Catholic James II. The Society sponsors an annual procession on July 12 to commemorate the victory of William III at the Battle of the Boyne (1690).

locked at night. Along the streets of this town were ranged large, sturdy pens. Each of them had a real door that a man could go through, a wooden ramp along the wire, for the foxes to run up and down on, and a kennel—something like a clothes chest with airholes—where they slept and stayed in winter and had their young. There were feeding and watering dishes attached to the wire in such a way that they could be emptied and cleaned from the outside. The dishes were made of old tin cans, and the ramps and kennels of odds and ends of old lumber. Everything was tidy and ingenious; my father was tirelessly inventive and his favourite book in the world was *Robinson Crusoe*.[3] He had fitted a tin drum on a wheelbarrow, for bringing water down to the pens. This was my job in summer, when the foxes had to have water twice a day. Between nine and ten o'clock in the morning, and again after supper, I filled the drum at the pump and trundled it down through the barnyard to the pens, where I parked it, and filled my watering can and went along the streets. Laird came too, with his little cream and green gardening can, filled too full and knocking against his legs and slopping water on his canvas shoes. I had the real watering can, my father's, though I could only carry it three-quarters full.

The foxes all had names, which were printed on a tin plate and hung beside their doors. They were not named when they were born, but when they survived the first year's pelting and were added to the breeding stock. Those my father had named were called names like Prince, Bob, Wally and Betty. Those I had named were called Star or Turk, or Maureen or Diana. Laird named one Maud after a hired girl we had when he was little, one Harold after a boy at school, and one Mexico, he did not say why.

Naming them did not make pets out of them, or anything like it. Nobody but my father ever went into the pens, and he had twice had blood-poisoning from bites. When I was bringing them their water they prowled up and down on the paths they had made inside their pens, barking seldom—they saved that for nighttime, when they might get up a chorus of community frenzy—but always watching me, their eyes burning, clear gold, in their pointed, malevolent faces. They were beautiful for their delicate legs and heavy, aristocratic tails and the bright fur sprinkled on dark down their backs—which gave them their name—but especially for their faces, drawn exquisitely sharp in pure hostility, and their golden eyes.

Besides carrying water I helped my father when he cut the long grass, and the lamb's quarter and flowering money-musk, that grew between the pens. He cut with the scythe and I raked into piles. Then he took a pitchfork and threw fresh-cut grass all over the top of the pens, to keep the foxes cooler and shade their coats, which were browned by too much sun. My father did not talk to me unless it was about the job we were doing. In this he was quite different from my mother, who, if she was feeling cheerful, would tell me all sorts of things— the name of a dog she had had when she was a little girl, the names of boys she had gone out with later on when she was grown up, and what certain dresses of

10

3. Novel (1719) by Daniel Defoe about a man shipwrecked on a desert island; it goes into great detail about his ingenious contraptions.

hers had looked like—she could not imagine now what had become of them. Whatever thoughts and stories my father had were private, and I was shy of him and would never ask him questions. Nevertheless I worked willingly under his eyes, and with a feeling of pride. One time a feed salesman came down into the pens to talk to him and my father said, "Like to have you meet my new hired man." I turned away and raked furiously, red in the face with pleasure.

"Could of fooled me," said the salesman. "I thought it was only a girl."

After the grass was cut, it seemed suddenly much later in the year. I walked on stubble in the earlier evening, aware of the reddening skies, the entering silences, of fall. When I wheeled the tank out of the gate and put the padlock on, it was almost dark. One night at this time I saw my mother and father standing talking on the little rise of ground we called the gangway, in front of the barn. My father had just come from the meathouse; he had his stiff bloody apron on, and a pail of cut-up meat in his hand.

It was an odd thing to see my mother down at the barn. She did not often come out of the house unless it was to do something—hang out the wash or dig potatoes in the garden. She looked out of place, with her bare lumpy legs, not touched by the sun, her apron still on and damp across the stomach from the supper dishes. Her hair was tied up in a kerchief, wisps of it falling out. She would tie her hair up like this in the morning, saying she did not have time to do it properly, and it would stay tied up all day. It was true, too; she really did not have time. These days our back porch was piled with baskets of peaches and grapes and pears, bought in town, and onions and tomatoes and cucumbers grown at home, all waiting to be made into jelly and jam and preserves, pickles and chili sauce. In the kitchen there was a fire in the stove all day, jars clinked in boiling water, sometimes a cheesecloth bag was strung on a pole between two chairs, straining blue-black grape pulp for jelly. I was given jobs to do and I would sit at the table peeling peaches that had been soaked in the hot water, or cutting up onions, my eyes smarting and streaming. As soon as I was done I ran out of the house, trying to get out of earshot before my mother thought of what she wanted me to do next. I hated the hot dark kitchen in summer, the green blinds and the flypapers, the same old oilcloth table and wavy mirror and bumpy linoleum. My mother was too tired and preoccupied to talk to me, she had no heart to tell about the Normal School Graduation Dance; sweat trickled over her face and she was always counting under her breath, pointing at jars, dumping cups of sugar. It seemed to me that work in the house was endless, dreary and peculiarly depressing; work done out of doors, and in my father's service, was ritualistically important.

I wheeled the tank up to the barn, where it was kept, and I heard my mother saying, "Wait till Laird gets a little bigger, then you'll have a real help."

What my father said I did not hear. I was pleased by the way he stood listening, politely as he would to a salesman or a stranger, but with an air of wanting to get on with his real work. I felt my mother had no business down here and I wanted him to feel the same way. What did she mean about Laird? He was no help to anybody. Where was he now? Swinging himself sick on the swing, going around in circles, or trying to catch caterpillars. He never once stayed with me till I was finished.

"And then I can use her more in the house," I heard my mother say. She had a dead-quiet, regretful way of talking about me that always made me uneasy. "I just get my back turned and she runs off. It's not like I had a girl in the family at all."

I went and sat on a feed bag in the corner of the barn, not wanting to appear when this conversation was going on. My mother, I felt, was not to be trusted. She was kinder than my father and more easily fooled, but you could not depend on her, and the real reasons for the things she said and did were not to be known. She loved me, and she sat up late at night making a dress of the difficult style I wanted, for me to wear when school started, but she was also my enemy. She was always plotting. She was plotting now to get me to stay in the house more, although she knew I hated it (*because* she knew I hated it) and keep me from working for my father. It seemed to me she would do this simply out of perversity, and to try her power. It did not occur to me that she could be lonely, or jealous. No grown-up could be; they were too fortunate. I sat and kicked my heels monotonously against a feedbag, raising dust, and did not come out till she was gone.

At any rate, I did not expect my father to pay any attention to what she said. Who could imagine Laird doing my work—Laird remembering the padlock and cleaning out the watering-dishes with a leaf on the end of a stick, or even wheeling the tank without it tumbling over? It showed how little my mother knew about the way things really were.

I have forgotten to say what the foxes were fed. My father's bloody apron reminded me. They were fed horsemeat. At this time most farmers still kept horses, and when a horse got too old to work, or broke a leg or got down and would not get up, as they sometimes did, the owner would call my father, and he and Henry went out to the farm in the truck. Usually they shot and butchered the horse there, paying the farmer from five to twelve dollars. If they had already too much meat on hand, they would bring the horse back alive, and keep it for a few days or weeks in our stable, until the meat was needed. After the war the farmers were buying tractors and gradually getting rid of horses altogether, so it sometimes happened that we got a good healthy horse, that there was just no use for any more. If this happened in the winter we might keep the horse in our stable till spring, for we had plenty of hay and if there was a lot of snow—and the plow did not always get our road cleared—it was convenient to be able to go to town with a horse and cutter.[4]

The winter I was eleven years old we had two horses in the stable. We did not know what names they had had before, so we called them Mack and Flora. Mack was an old black workhorse, sooty and indifferent. Flora was a sorrel mare, a driver. We took them both out in the cutter. Mack was slow and easy to handle.

20

4. A small, light sleigh.

Flora was given to fits of violent alarm, veering at cars and even at other horses, but we loved her speed and high-stepping, her general air of gallantry and abandon. On Saturdays we went down to the stable and as soon as we opened the door on its cosy, animal-smelling darkness Flora threw up her head, rolled her eyes, whinnied despairingly and pulled herself through a crisis of nerves on the spot. It was not safe to go into her stall; she would kick.

This winter also I began to hear a great deal more on the theme my mother had sounded when she had been talking in front of the barn. I no longer felt safe. It seemed that in the minds of the people around me there was a steady undercurrent of thought, not to be deflected, on this one subject. The word *girl* had formerly seemed to me innocent and unburdened, like the world *child*; now it appeared that it was no such thing. A girl was not, as I had supposed, simply what I was; it was what I had to become. It was a definition, always touched with emphasis, with reproach and disappointment. Also it was a joke on me. Once Laird and I were fighting, and for the first time ever I had to use all my strength against him; even so, he caught and pinned my arm for a moment, really hurting me. Henry saw this, and laughed, saying, "Oh, that there Laird's gonna show you, one of these days!" Laird was getting a lot bigger. But I was getting bigger too.

My grandmother came to stay with us for a few weeks and I heard other things. "Girls don't slam doors like that." "Girls keep their knees together when they sit down." And worse still, when I asked some questions, "That's none of girls' business." I continued to slam the doors and sit as awkwardly as possible, thinking that by such measures I kept myself free.

When spring came, the horses were let out in the barnyard. Mack stood against the barn wall trying to scratch his neck and haunches, but Flora trotted up and down and reared at the fences, clattering her hooves against the rails. Snow drifts dwindled quickly, revealing the hard grey and brown earth, the familiar rise and fall of the ground, plain and bare after the fantastic landscape of winter. There was a great feeling of opening-out, of release. We just wore rubbers now, over our shoes; our feet felt ridiculously light. One Saturday we went out to the stable and found all the doors open, letting in the unaccustomed sunlight and fresh air. Henry was there, just idling around looking at his collection of calendars which were tacked up behind the stalls in a part of the stable my mother had probably never seen.

"Come to say goodbye to your old friend Mack?" Henry said. "Here, you give him a taste of oats." He poured some oats into Laird's cupped hands and Laird went to feed Mack. Mack's teeth were in bad shape. He ate very slowly, patiently shifting the oats around in his mouth, trying to find a stump of a molar to grind it on. "Poor old Mack," said Henry mournfully. "When a horse's teeth's gone, he's gone. That's about the way."

"Are you going to shoot him today?" I said. Mack and Flora had been in the stable so long I had almost forgotten they were going to be shot.

Henry didn't answer me. Instead he started to sing in a high, trembly, mocking-sorrowful voice, *Oh, there's no more work, for poor Uncle Ned, he's gone* where the good darkies go.[5] Mack's thick, blackish tongue worked diligently at Laird's hand. I went out before the song was ended and sat down on the gangway.

I had never seen them shoot a horse, but I knew where it was done. Last summer Laird and I had come upon a horse's entrails before they were buried. We had thought it was a big black snake, coiled up in the sun. That was around in the field that ran up beside the barn. I thought that if we went inside the barn, and found a wide crack or knothole to look through we would be able to see them do it. It was not something I wanted to see; just the same, if a thing really happened, it was better to see it, and know.

My father came down from the house, carrying the gun.

"What are you doing here?" he said.

"Nothing."

"Go on up and play around the house."

He sent Laird out of the stable. I said to Laird, "Do you want to see them shoot Mack?" and without waiting for an answer led him around to the front door of the barn, opened it carefully, and went in. "Be quiet or they'll hear us," I said. We could hear Henry and my father talking in the stable, then the heavy, shuffling steps of Mack being backed out of his stall.

In the loft it was cold and dark. Thin, crisscrossed beams of sunlight fell through the cracks. The hay was low. It was a rolling country, hills and hollows, slipping under our feet. About four feet up was a beam going around the walls. We piled hay up in one corner and I boosted Laird up and hoisted myself. The beam was not very wide; we crept along it with our hands flat on the barn walls. There were plenty of knotholes, and I found one that gave me the view I wanted—a corner of the barnyard, the gate, part of the field. Laird did not have a knothole and began to complain.

I showed him a widened crack between two boards. "Be quiet and wait. If they hear you you'll get us in trouble."

My father came in sight carrying the gun. Henry was leading Mack by the halter. He dropped it and took out his cigarette papers and tobacco; he rolled cigarettes for my father and himself. While this was going on Mack nosed around in the old, dead grass along the fence. Then my father opened the gate and they took Mack through. Henry led Mack way from the path to a patch of ground and they talked together, not loud enough for us to hear. Mack again began searching for a mouthful of fresh grass, which was not to be found. My father walked away in a straight line, and stopped short at a distance which seemed to suit him. Henry was walking away from Mack too, but sideways, still negligently holding on to the halter. My father raised the gun and Mack looked up as if he had noticed something and my father shot him.

Mack did not collapse at once but swayed, lurched sideways and fell, first on his side; then he rolled over on his back and, amazingly, kicked his legs for a few seconds in the air. At this Henry laughed, as if Mack had done a trick for

30

35

5. Lines from the Stephen Foster song "Old Uncle Ned."

him. Laird, who had drawn a long, groaning breath of surprise when the shot was fired, said out loud, "He's not dead." And it seemed to me it might be true. But his legs stopped, he rolled on his side again, his muscles quivered and sank. The two men walked over and looked at him in a businesslike way; they bent down and examined his forehead where the bullet had gone in, and now I saw his blood on the brown grass.

"Now they just skin him and cut him up," I said. "Let's go." My legs were a little shaky and I jumped gratefully down into the hay. "Now you've seen how they shoot a horse," I said in a congratulatory way, as if I had seen it many times before. "Let's see if any barn cat's had kittens in the hay." Laird jumped. He seemed young and obedient again. Suddenly I remembered how, when he was little, I had brought him into the barn and told him to climb the ladder to the top beam. That was in the spring, too, when the hay was low. I had done it out of a need for excitement, a desire for something to happen so that I could tell about it. He was wearing a little bulky brown and white checked coat, made down from one of mine. He went all the way up, just as I told him, and sat down on the top beam with the hay far below him on one side, and the barn floor and some old machinery on the other. Then I ran screaming to my father, "Laird's up on the top beam!" My father came, my mother came, my father went up the ladder talking very quietly and brought Laird down under his arm, at which my mother leaned against the ladder and began to cry. They said to me, "Why weren't you watching him?" but nobody ever knew the truth. Laird did not know enough to tell. But whenever I saw the brown and white checked coat hanging in the closet, or at the bottom of the rag bag, which was where it ended up, I felt a weight in my stomach, the sadness of unexorcized guilt.

I looked at Laird who did not even remember this, and I did not like the look on this thin, winter-pale face. His expression was not frightened or upset, but remote, concentrating. "Listen," I said, in an unusually bright and friendly voice, "you aren't going to tell, are you?"

"No," he said absently.

"Promise."

"Promise," he said. I grabbed the hand behind his back to make sure he was not crossing his fingers. Even so, he might have a nightmare; it might come out that way. I decided I had better work hard to get all thoughts of what he had seen out of his mind—which, it seemed to me, could not hold very many things at a time. I got some money I had saved and that afternoon we went into Jubilee and saw a show, with Judy Canova,[6] at which we both laughed a great deal. After that I thought it would be all right.

Two weeks later I knew they were going to shoot Flora. I knew from the night before, when I heard my mother ask if the hay was holding out all right, and my father said, "Well, after to-morrow there'll just be the cow, and we should be able to put her out to grass in another week." So I knew it was Flora's turn in the morning.

This time I didn't think of watching it. That was something to see just one

6. American comedian best known for her yodeling in hillbilly movies of the 1940s.

time. I had not thought about it very often since, but sometimes when I was busy, working at school, or standing in front of the mirror combing my hair and wondering if I would be pretty when I grew up, the whole scene would flash into my mind: I would see the easy, practised way my father raised the gun, and hear Henry laughing when Mack kicked his legs in the air. I did not have any great feeling of horror and opposition, such as a city child might have had; I was too used to seeing the death of animals as a necessity by which we lived. Yet I felt a little ashamed, and there was a new wariness, a sense of holding-off, in my attitude to my father and his work.

It was a fine day, and we were going around the yard picking up tree branches that had been torn off in winter storms. This was something we had been told to do, and also we wanted to use them to make a teepee. We heard Flora whinny, and then my father's voice and Henry's shouting, and we ran down to the barnyard to see what was going on.

The stable door was open. Henry had just brought Flora out, and she had broken away from him. She was running free in the barnyard, from one end to the other. We climbed up on the fence. It was exciting to see her running, whinnying, going up on her hind legs, prancing and threatening like a horse in a Western movie, an unbroken ranch horse, though she was just an old driver, an old sorrel mare. My father and Henry ran after her and tried to grab the dangling halter. They tried to work her into a corner, and they had almost succeeded when she made a run between them, wild-eyed, and disappeared around the corner of the barn. We heard the rails clatter down as she got over the fence, and Henry yelled, "She's into the field now!"

That meant she was in the long L-shaped field that ran up by the house. If she got around the center, heading towards the lane, the gate was open; the truck had been driven into the field this morning. My father shouted to me, because I was on the other side of the fence, nearest the lane, "Go shut the gate!"

I could run very fast. I ran across the garden, past the tree where our swing was hung, and jumped across a ditch into the lane. There was the open gate. She had not got out, I could not see her up on the road; she must have run to the other end of the field. The gate was heavy. I lifted it out of the gravel and carried it across the roadway. I had it half-way across when she came in sight, galloping straight towards me. There was just time to get the chain on. Laird came scrambling through the ditch to help me.

Instead of shutting the gate, I opened it as wide as I could. I did not make any decision to do this, it was just what I did. Flora never slowed down; she galloped straight past me, and Laird jumped up and down, yelling, "Shut it, shut it!" even after it was too late. My father and Henry appeared in the field a moment too late to see what I had done. They only saw Flora heading for the township road. They would think I had not got there in time.

They did not waste any time asking about it. They went back to the barn and got the gun and the knives they used, and put these in the truck; then they turned the truck around and came bouncing up the field toward us. Laird called to them, "Let me go too, let me go too!" and Henry stopped the truck

45

and they took him in. I shut the gate after they were all gone.

I supposed Laird would tell. I wondered what would happen to me. I had never disobeyed my father before, and I could not understand why I had done it. Flora would not really get away. They would catch up with her in the truck. Or if they did not catch her this morning somebody would see her and telephone us this afternoon or tomorrow. There was no wild country here for her to run to, only farms. What was more, my father had paid for her, we needed the meat to feed the foxes, we needed the foxes to make our living. All I had done was make more work for my father who worked hard enough already. And when my father found out about it he was not going to trust me any more; he would know that I was not entirely on his side. I was on Flora's side, and that made me no use to anybody, not even to her. Just the same, I did not regret it; when she came running at me and I held the gate open, that was the only thing I could do.

I went back to the house, and my mother said, "What's all the commotion?" I told her that Flora had kicked down the fence and got away. "Your poor father," she said, "now he'll have to go chasing over the countryside. Well, there isn't any use planning dinner before one." She put up the ironing board. I wanted to tell her, but thought better of it and went upstairs and sat on my bed.

Lately I had been trying to make my part of the room fancy, spreading the bed with old lace curtains, and fixing myself a dressing-table with some leftovers of cretonne for a skirt. I planned to put up some kind of barricade between my bed and Laird's, to keep my section separate from his. In the sunlight, the lace curtains were just dusty rags. We did not sing at night any more. One night when I was singing Laird said, "You sound silly," and I went right on but the next night I did not start. There was not so much need to anyway, we were no longer afraid. We knew it was just old furniture over there, old jumble and confusion. We did not keep to the rules. I still stayed awake after Laird was asleep and told myself stories, but even in these stories something different was happening, mysterious alterations took place. A story might start off in the old way, with a spectacular danger, a fire or wild animals, and for a while I might rescue people; then things would change around, and instead, somebody would be rescuing me. It might be a boy from our class at school, or even Mr. Campbell, our teacher, who tickled girls under the arms. And at this point the story concerned itself at great length with what I looked like—how long my hair was, and what kind of dress I had on; by the time I had these details worked out the real excitement of the story was lost.

It was later than one o'clock when the truck came back. The tarpaulin was over the back, which meant there was meat in it. My mother had to heat dinner up all over again. Henry and my father had changed from their bloody overalls into ordinary working overalls in the barn, and they washed their arms and necks and faces at the sink, and splashed water on their hair and combed it. Laird lifted his arm to show off a streak of blood. "We shot old Flora," he said, "and cut her up in fifty pieces."

"Well I don't want to hear about it," my mother said. "And don't come to my table like that."

My father made him go and wash the blood off.   55

We sat down and my father said grace and Henry pasted his chewing-gum on the end of his fork, the way he always did; when he took it off he would have us admire the pattern. We began to pass the bowls of steaming, overcooked vegetables. Laird looked across the table at me and said proudly, distinctly, "Anyway it was her fault Flora got away."

"What?" my father said.

"She could of shut the gate and she didn't. She just open' it up and Flora run out."

"Is that right?" my father said.

Everybody at the table was looking at me. I nodded, swallowing food with   60
great difficulty. To my shame, tears flooded my eyes.

My father made a curt sound of disgust. "What did you do that for?"

I did not answer. I put down my fork and waited to be sent from the table, still not looking up.

But this did not happen. For some time nobody said anything, then Laird said matter-of-factly, "She's crying."

"Never mind," my father said. He spoke with resignation, even good humour, the words which absolved and dismissed me for good. "She's only a girl," he said.

I didn't protest that, even in my heart. Maybe it was true.   65

                                                                      1968

▼ ▼ ▼

LITERARY KIND AS CONTEXT A Glossary

genre: the largest category for classifying literature—fiction, poetry, drama

initiation story: a *kind* of short story in which a character—often but not always a child or young person—first learns a significant, usually life-changing truth about the universe, society, people, himself or herself

kind: a species or subcategory within a *subgenre; initiation stories* are a subcategory of the subgenre short story

rite of passage: a ritual or ceremony marking an individual's passing from one stage or state to a more advanced one, or an event in one's life that seems to have such significance; a formal initiation

subgenre: division within the category of a *genre;* novel, novella, and short story are subgenres of the genre fiction

QUESTIONS

1. What does the title literally denote in the story "Araby"? What does it suggest? How do both its denotative and connotative meanings function in the story?

2. What is the point of view (focus) in "Araby"? Are the words of the story the boy's? How does the difference between focus and voice define the nature of the initiation in the story?

3. What is the nature of the initiation in "Boys and Girls"? in "Gorilla, My Love"? How are the two initiation experiences similar? How do they differ?

4. The phrase "only a girl" appears twice in Alice Munro's story. How do the contexts differ? How do the implications of the phrase differ at each appearance (that is, what does it mean or suggest each time)?

WRITING SUGGESTIONS

1. Compare the use of the theme of romance-of-childhood versus realism-of-maturity in "Araby" and "Boys and Girls."

2. Using "Gorilla, My Love" as a model, write a personal narrative in which you describe an initiation in your own life, or a fictional event.

3. Find a pattern of words or images that recurs throughout one of the stories in this chapter. Relate the pattern to the story's theme, citing evidence from the story.

STUDENT WRITING

Teri Garrity's paper is one student's response to the third writing assignment. Teri discovered a pattern of blindness and light in "Araby," and, in her paper, relates the pattern to the larger theme of appearance and reality in the story. She substantiates her thesis by using concrete examples from the story.

To See the Light

Teri Garrity

Many times we encounter something or someone who appears to be more important to us than anything else. Often we lose track of those things that really are most worthy. Occasionally, we hurt others or ourselves in the process of discovering which things are of greatest significance in our lives. One of the main themes in James Joyce's story "Araby" seems to involve such a blindness to reality. From the blindness of North Richmond Street to the blindness of the boy during his maturation, Joyce effectively illustrates the complexities of a boy's rough transition into adulthood and the confusing feelings that accompany the transition. From these blindnesses, Joyce concludes the story with the boy's painful insight into reality.

Part of the transition from childhood to adulthood involves encountering new feelings. One

of the deepest of these feelings is that of love
and relationships. As the boy in the story
matures, his feelings are not an exception.
Although he believes his love is true, it is
actually blind. That is, his love for Mangan's
sister is purely physical. The first picture the
reader is given of her describes ". . . her figure
defined by the light from the half-opened door"
(par. 3). This image of the girl reappears
throughout the story. Consequently, the boy seems
to be blind to all except the aura of light that
accompanies her appearance. Furthermore, because
he has never communicated with the girl, the
boy's attraction is superficial. Each description
of her is similar to the following: "Her dress
swung as she moved her body, and the soft rope of
her hair tossed from side to side" (par. 3). The
reader is given only physical descriptions of
Mangan's sister; thus, he is able to infer the
boy's confusion between real and ideal love. In
contrast, although the boy seems to be completely
obsessed with the girl, he does not wish for her
to know. For instance, he watches her out the
window each day, but pulls the blind "down to
within an inch of the sash so that I could not be
seen" (par. 4). Even though he does not realize
his own blindness, he seems to want the girl to
be blind to his feelings. It is apparent, then,
that the boy does not understand, or see, that
there is more to a real love relationship than
physical attraction. His blindness to this fact

leads him to be blind about the most important things in life.

As the boy's desire becomes stronger, he begins to lose sight of the more "serious work of life" (par. 12). That is, he becomes blind to everything but the girl he adores. He "chafed against the work of school" (par. 12), and "answered few questions in class" (par. 12). He completely disregards these important duties since they "stood between me and my desire," and thus, "seemed to me child's play, ugly monotonous child's play" (par. 12). Although these serious things appear to him to be "child's play," it is, in fact, his obsessive infatuation that is childish. His inability to see this, or his blindness, causes him to also become blind to the reality that he is, indeed, still a child. He is no longer interested in his companions, and their cries become "weakened and indistinct" (par. 16). The thoughts that once occupied his mind, such as playing and shouting, are replaced with images of a blind obsession. His inability to see this reality causes him a great deal of confusion. He refers to his "confused adoration," and how he, "didn't understand," and "could not tell why" (par. 5). Although he cannot interpret these feelings, they seem to reveal that he is blind to his thoughts, to his future, and to reality.

Perhaps the worst part of the boy's blindness to reality is the fact that it results in self-deception. Because of his intense admiration for the girl, he views her as a "single sensation of life" (par. 5), and he imagines that his "body was like a harp and her words and gestures were like fingers running upon the wires" (par. 5). The girl does seem to be playing him like a musical instrument: she seems to be able to manipulate him in any way. He is under her complete control. He gives up everything he has and deceives himself into thinking that he has a relationship with her. Moreover, he becomes so obsessed with presenting her a gift from Araby that he also becomes blind to the fact that she is interested in the gift, not in him.

Although he is unaware of it, the boy seems to be slowly realizing that his love is, indeed, blind. He once observes that, "Some distant lamp or lighted window gleamed below me. I was thankful that I could see so little" (par. 6). This distant lamp seems to symbolize the realization (that he would soon encounter) of his false adoration. Moreover, his reference to blindness, or thankfulness that he could not see much, is his way of avoiding the painful truth of reality. However, the boy inevitably encounters this painful realization at Araby. When he comes upon the busy bazaar, he remembers "with difficulty" (par. 26), why he is there. The busy street seems to trigger his realization that he has so long been blind to the complexity and confusion associated with his infatuation. The final determinant in his realization is the conversation between the trio at the bazaar. He recognizes the triviality of the conversation and manages to relate it to his love. After examining the "great jars that stood like eastern guards at either side of the dark entrance" (par. 33), the boy utters, "No thank you" (par. 34). This seems to reveal that he has begun to overcome his blindness and realize the truth of the relationship. In addition, the fact that the salesclerk changes the position of one of the jars could represent an elimination of the "guards" and an opening of the dark tunnel into a light one. That is, it symbolizes an elimination of the boy's blindness.

As the boy leaves the bazaar, he sees the truth: "Gazing up into the darkness, I saw myself as a creature driven and derided by vanity; and my eyes burned with anguish and anger" (par. 37). This feeling symbolizes his complete realization of his self-deceit and the shame he has succumbed to. He is overcome with anger that he let his emotions control him and cause him to be blind to all else. This pattern of blindness--from the notion of real love to the important things in life to his self-deception--suggests that he is, in fact, involved in a conflict between appearance and reality. The boy's realization of the conflict is not only a painful cure for his blindness, but it is also a large step in the direction of adulthood.

11 FORM AS CONTEXT: THE SHORT SHORT STORY

The short short story, a story of about two thousand words or less, though it has been around for a long time, has rather suddenly become quite popular. There have been many attempts to explain this phenomenon, explanations ranging from the shrinking attention span "caused" by television, to the hurried, fragmented nature of modern life, to our disenchantment with lengthy explanations of behavior by psychologists, politicians, and novelists. There have also been attempts to define the form generically. Its boundaries have been those of the anecdote, the vignette, the parable, the poem, the short story proper, yet all these borders have been contested.

Length is not just an aspect of form, however; it also contributes significantly to a story's effect and to your consequent response. You rarely read a full-length novel in a single sitting, so not only is there a momentary recapitulation in your mind as you pick up the narrative again—something like the excerpts from the previous episode in a television miniseries—but you have lived another period of your life outside of the narrative. When you sit down to read again you are not exactly the same repository of experiences as when you put the book down, and not only are you at a different point in your life, your mood may have drastically changed as well. The novel has advantages, however, in its duration and in the times of your readings and departures: you are likely to recall the characters, scenes, and incidents, in one order or another, in more or less accurate detail, from time to time during the period you are away from the text. The novel thereby gets a texture, layers of memories and views from different angles, that is rarely obtained by a short story, and never by a short short story. You usually read a short story in a single sitting, and though it has an immediate and concentrated impact and you pause a moment and savor its emotional and intellectual effect, you can rarely recall it in all its detail; yet rarely too do you immediately begin at the beginning and read it through once again. The effect of the short short story is stronger; even if the after-effect is of the same duration (and it often is longer, because its economy has left so much out that you have to supply a great deal yourself), it is stronger compared to the length of time of your reading. You can remember, if not all, at least almost all the details. Yet it is not uncommon for strongly impressed readers to immediately read the story again. So the differences between novels, short stories, and short short stories are not merely their formal length, but the different way you read and respond to them.

On a personal note: though I can read four or five short short stories in the time it takes me to read a short story, I find it unsatisfactory to read four or five short short stories in a row. Their effects are so strong and so concentrated that reading several overcharges my response system. I rehearse the story in my mind, recalling its details, often its words, and try to fill in the details the story's conciseness can only imply. So I'd advise taking a break, perhaps at least an hour, between reading each of the stories in this chapter. And when one of these stories affects you, you may want to write an account of your emotive and intellectual responses, what you recall, and what you force yourself to supply.

The stories in this chapter represent a sampling of short short stories the editors found emotionally or intellectually moving, stories that reverberated in the mind long after the story ended. (And note that there are other stories in the anthology that fit the definition: "The Zebra Storyteller," "No One's a Mystery," "Happy Endings," and hovering around or just over the border, "The Cask of Amontillado," "A Conversation with My Father," "Her First Ball," and "Araby".)

They also represent the limits and the variety of the form. Chopin's and Hemingway's stories share the ironic reversal that perhaps come from Maupassant, but Chopin's is, as its title suggests, limited to an hour of fictional time, while Hemingway's spans years, defying any unity or constricting of time the brevity of the narrative might lead you to expect. Jamaica Kincaid's "Girl" does not seem so much to span time as to compact it: the story is largely the words of mother to daughter (with two brief responses by the daughter). The near-monologue does not take place at one moment, however; rather, we can infer (there are no internal time-indicators) — in part from the repetition, in part from our memories of our own childhood — that its instructions were repeated time and time again over the years the girl was growing up. "A Very Old Man with Enormous Wings" represents the many short short tales that are fantasies — written in a literary mode involving the consciously unreal — about places, societies, or beings that never existed, do not exist, or do not yet exist, or with qualities that are beyond or counter to the ordinary or commonsensical. Often such fantasies tease us with the possibilities of allegory but are more than likely symbolic — untranslatable into "messages" or ordinary "meaning." They exist on their own terms, representing certain aspects of human experience in fantasy more precisely than might be done in discursive prose, scientific formulas, graphs, charts. I've saved the best for last. Is Yasunari Kawabata's "The Grasshopper and the Bell Cricket" a novel of fewer than fifteen hundred words, or is it an expanded haiku? All that you have learned of history and structure, focus and voice, characterization, symbol, and theme are needed to articulate the breadth and delicacy of this superb short short story.

▼   ▼   ▼

KATE CHOPIN

The Story of an Hour

Knowing that Mrs. Mallard was afflicted with a heart trouble, great care was taken to break to her as gently as possible the news of her husband's death.

It was her sister Josephine who told her, in broken sentences; veiled hints that revealed in half concealing. Her husband's friend Richards was there, too, near her. It was he who had been in the newspaper office when intelligence of the railroad disaster was received, with Brently Mallard's name leading the list of "killed." He had only taken the time to assure himself of its truth by a second telegram, and had hastened to forestall any less careful, less tender friend in bearing the sad message.

She did not hear the story as many women have heard the same, with a paralyzed inability to accept its significance. She wept at once, with sudden, wild abandonment, in her sister's arms. When the storm of grief had spent itself she went away to her room alone. She would have no one follow her.

There stood, facing the open window, a comfortable, roomy armchair. Into this she sank, pressed down by a physical exhaustion that haunted her body and seemed to reach into her soul.

5   She could see in the open square before her house the tops of trees that were all aquiver with the new spring life. The delicious breath of rain was in the air. In the street below a peddler was crying his wares. The notes of a distant song which some one was singing reached her faintly, and countless sparrows were twittering in the eaves.

There were patches of blue sky showing here and there through the clouds that had met and piled one above the other in the west facing her window.

She sat with her head thrown back upon the cushion of the chair, quite motionless, except when a sob came up into her throat and shook her, as a child who has cried itself to sleep continues to sob in its dreams.

She was young, with a fair, calm face, whose lines bespoke repression and even a certain strength. But now there was a dull stare in her eyes, whose gaze was fixed away off yonder on one of those patches of blue sky. It was not a glance of reflection, but rather indicated a suspension of intelligent thought.

There was something coming to her and she was waiting for it, fearfully. What was it? She did not know; it was too subtle and elusive to name. But she felt it, creeping out of the sky, reaching toward her through the sounds, the scents, the color that filled the air.

Now her bosom rose and fell tumultuously. She was beginning to recognize 10 this thing that was approaching to possess her, and she was striving to beat it back with her will—as powerless as her two white slender hands would have been.

When she abandoned herself a little whispered word escaped her slightly parted lips. She said it over and over under her breath: "free, free, free!" The vacant stare and the look of terror that had followed it went from her eyes. They stayed keen and bright. Her pulses beat fast, and the coursing blood warmed and relaxed every inch of her body.

She did not stop to ask if it were or were not a monstrous joy that held her. A clear and exalted perception enabled her to dismiss the suggestion as trivial.

She knew that she would weep again when she saw the kind, tender hands folded in death; the face that had never looked save with love upon her, fixed and gray and dead. But she saw beyond that bitter moment a long procession of years to come that would belong to her absolutely. And she opened and spread her arms out to them in welcome.

There would be no one to live for her during those coming years; she would live for herself. There would be no powerful will bending hers in that blind persistence with which men and women believe they have a right to impose a private will upon a fellow-creature. A kind intention or a cruel intention made the act seem no less a crime as she looked upon it in that brief moment of illumination.

And yet she had loved him—sometimes. Often she had not. What did it 15 matter! What could love, the unsolved mystery, count for in face of this possession of self-assertion which she suddenly recognized as the strongest impulse of her being!

"Free! Body and soul free!" she kept whispering.

Josephine was kneeling before the closed door with her lips to the keyhole, imploring for admission. "Louise, open the door! I beg; open the door—you will make yourself ill. What are you doing, Louise? For heaven's sake open the door."

"Go away. I am not making myself ill." No; she was drinking in a very elixir of life through that open window.

Her fancy was running riot along those days ahead of her. Spring days, and summer days, and all sorts of days that would be her own. She breathed a quick prayer that life might be long. It was only yesterday she had thought with a shudder that life might be long.

She arose at length and opened the door to her sister's importunities. There 20 was a feverish triumph in her eyes, and she carried herself unwittingly like a goddess of Victory. She clasped her sister's waist, and together they descended the stairs. Richards stood waiting for them at the bottom.

Some one was opening the front door with a latchkey. It was Brently Mallard who entered, a little travel-stained, composedly carrying his grip-sack and umbrella. He had been far from the scene of accident, and did not even know there had been one. He stood amazed at Josephine's piercing cry; at Richards' quick motion to screen him from the view of his wife.

But Richards was too late.

When the doctors came they said she had died of heart disease—of joy that kills.

1891

ERNEST HEMINGWAY

A Very Short Story

One hot evening in Padua they carried him up onto the roof and he could look out over the top of the town. There were chimney swifts in the sky. After a while it got dark and the searchlights came out. The others went down and took the bottles with them. He and Luz could hear them below on the balcony. Luz sat on the bed. She was cool and fresh in the hot night.

Luz stayed on night duty for three months. They were glad to let her. When they operated on him she prepared him for the operating table; and they had a joke about friend or enema. He went under the anesthetic holding tight on to himself so he would not blab about anything during the silly, talky time. After he got on crutches he used to take the temperatures so Luz would not have to get up from the bed. There were only a few patients, and they all knew about it. They all liked Luz. As he walked back along the halls he thought of Luz in his bed.

Before he went back to the front they went into the Duomo[1] and prayed. It was dim and quiet, and there were other people praying. They wanted to get married, but there was not enough time for the banns, and neither of them had birth certificates. They felt as though they were married, but they wanted everyone to know about it, and to make it so they could not lose it.

Luz wrote him many letters that he never got until after the armistice. Fifteen came in a bunch to the front and he sorted them by the dates and read them all straight through. They were all about the hospital, and how much she loved him, and how it was impossible to get along without him, and how terrible it was missing him at night.

5   After the armistice they agreed he should go home to get a job so they might be married. Luz would not come home until he had a good job and could come to New York to meet her. It was understood he would not drink, and he did not want to see his friends or anyone in the States. Only to get a job and be married. On the train from Padua to Milan they quarreled about her not being willing to come home at once. When they had to say goodbye, in the station at Milan, they kissed goodbye, but were not finished with the quarrel. He felt sick about saying goodbye like that.

He went to America on a boat from Genoa. Luz went back to Pordenone to

1. Cathedral

open a hospital. It was lonely and rainy there, and there was a battalion of arditi quartered in the town. Living in the muddy, rainy town in the winter, the major of the battalion made love to Luz, and she had never known Italians before, and finally wrote to the States that theirs had been only a boy and girl affair. She was sorry, and she knew he would probably not be able to understand, but might someday forgive her, and be grateful to her, and she expected, absolutely unexpectedly, to be married in the spring. She loved him as always, but she realized now it was only a boy and girl love. She hoped he would have a great career and believed in him absolutely. She knew it was for the best.

The major did not marry her in the spring, or any other time. Luz never got an answer to the letter to Chicago about it. A short time after he contracted gonorrhea from a salesgirl in a loop[2] department store while riding in a taxicab through Lincoln Park.

1925

GABRIEL GARCÍA MÁRQUEZ

A Very Old Man with Enormous Wings[1]

A TALE FOR CHILDREN

On the third day of rain they had killed so many crabs inside the house that Pelayo had to cross his drenched courtyard and throw them into the sea, because the newborn child had a temperature all night and they thought it was due to the stench. The world had been sad since Tuesday. Sea and sky were a single ash-gray thing and the sands of the beach, which on March nights glimmered like powdered light, had become a stew of mud and rotten shellfish. The light was so weak at noon that when Pelayo was coming back to the house after throwing away the crabs, it was hard for him to see what it was that was moving and groaning in the rear of the courtyard. He had to go very close to see that it was an old man, a very old man, lying face down in the mud, who, in spite of his tremendous efforts, couldn't get up, impeded by his enormous wings.

Frightened by that nightmare, Pelayo ran to get Elisenda, his wife, who was putting compresses on the sick child, and he took her to the rear of the courtyard. They both looked at the fallen body with mute stupor. He was dressed like a ragpicker. There were only a few faded hairs left on his bald skull and very few teeth in his mouth, and his pitiful condition of a drenched great-grandfather had taken away any sense of grandeur he might have had. His huge buzzard wings, dirty and half-plucked, were forever entangled in the mud. They looked at him so long and so closely that Pelayo and Elisenda very soon overcame their surprise and in the end found him familiar. Then they dared speak to him, and he answered in an incomprehensible dialect with a strong sailor's voice. That

2. Chicago business and shopping district.   1. Translated by Gregory Rabassa.

was how they skipped over the inconvenience of the wings and quite intelligently concluded that he was a lonely castaway from some foreign ship wrecked by the storm. And yet, they called in a neighbor woman who knew everything about life and death to see him, and all she needed was one look to show them their mistake.

"He's an angel," she told them. "He must have been coming for the child, but the poor fellow is so old that the rain knocked him down."

On the following day everyone knew that a flesh-and-blood angel was held captive in Pelayo's house. Against the judgment of the wise neighbor woman, for whom angels in those times were the fugitive survivors of a celestial conspiracy, they did not have the heart to club him to death. Pelayo watched over him all afternoon from the kitchen, armed with his bailiff's club, and before going to bed he dragged him out of the mud and locked him up with the hens in the wire chicken coop. In the middle of the night, when the rain stopped, Pelayo and Elisenda were still killing crabs. A short time afterward the child woke up without a fever and with a desire to eat. Then they felt magnanimous and decided to put the angel on a raft with fresh water and provisions for three days and leave him to his fate on the high seas. But when they went out into the courtyard with the first light of dawn, they found the whole neighborhood in front of the chicken coop having fun with the angel, without the slightest reverence, tossing him things to eat through the openings in the wire as if he weren't a supernatural creature but a circus animal.

5   Father Gonzaga arrived before seven o'clock, alarmed at the strange news. By that time onlookers less frivolous than those at dawn had already arrived and they were making all kinds of conjectures concerning the captive's future. The simplest among them thought that he should be named mayor of the world. Others of sterner mind felt that he should be promoted to the rank of five-star general in order to win all wars. Some visionaries hoped that he could be put to stud in order to implant on earth a race of winged wise men who could take charge of the universe. But Father Gonzaga, before becoming a priest, had been a robust woodcutter. Standing by the wire, he reviewed his catechism in an instant and asked them to open the door so that he could take a close look at that pitiful man who looked more like a huge decrepit hen among the fascinated chickens. He was lying in a corner drying his open wings in the sunlight among the fruit peels and breakfast leftovers that the early risers had thrown him. Alien to the impertinences of the world, he only lifted his antiquarian eyes and murmured something in his dialect when Father Gonzaga went into the chicken coop and said good morning to him in Latin. The parish priest had his first suspicion of an imposter when he saw that he did not understand the language of God or know how to greet His ministers. Then he noticed that seen close up he was much too human: he had an unbearable smell of the outdoors, the back side of his wings was strewn with parasites and his main feathers had been mistreated by terrestrial winds, and nothing about him measured up to the proud dignity of angels. Then he came out of the chicken coop and in a brief sermon warned the curious against the risks of being ingenuous. He reminded them that the devil had the bad habit of making use of carnival tricks in order

to confuse the unwary. He argued that if wings were not the essential element in determining the difference between a hawk and an airplane, they were even less so in the recognition of angels. Nevertheless, he promised to write a letter to his bishop so that the latter would write to his primate so that the latter would write to the Supreme Pontiff in order to get the final verdict from the highest courts.

His prudence fell on sterile hearts. The news of the captive angel spread with such rapidity that after a few hours the courtyard had the bustle of a market-place and they had to call in troops with fixed bayonets to disperse the mob that was about to knock the house down. Elisenda, her spine all twisted from sweeping up so much marketplace trash, then got the idea of fencing in the yard and charging five cents admission to see the angel.

The curious came from far away. A traveling carnival arrived with a flying acrobat who buzzed over the crowd several times, but no one paid any attention to him because his wings were not those of an angel but, rather, those of a sidereal bat. The most unfortunate invalids on earth came in search of health: a poor woman who since childhood had been counting her heartbeats and had run out of numbers; a Portuguese man who couldn't sleep because the noise of the stars disturbed him; a sleepwalker who got up at night to undo the things he had done while awake; and many others with less serious ailments. In the midst of that shipwreck disorder that made the earth tremble, Pelayo and Elisenda were happy with fatigue, for in less than a week they had crammed their rooms with money and the line of pilgrims waiting their turn to enter still reached beyond the horizon.

The angel was the only one who took no part in his own act. He spent his time trying to get comfortable in his borrowed nest, befuddled by the hellish heat of the oil lamps and sacramental candles that had been placed along the wire. At first they tried to make him eat some mothballs, which, according to the wisdom of the wise neighbor woman, were the food prescribed for angels. But he turned them down, just as he turned down the papal lunches[2] that the penitents brought him, and they never found out whether it was because he was an angel or because he was an old man that in the end he ate nothing but eggplant mush. His only supernatural virtue seemed to be patience. Especially during the first days, when the hens pecked at him, searching for the stellar parasites that proliferated in his wings, and the cripples pulled out feathers to touch their defective parts with, and even the most merciful threw stones at him, trying to get him to rise so they could see him standing. The only time they succeeded in arousing him was when they burned his side with an iron for branding steers, for he had been motionless for so many hours that they thought he was dead. He awoke with a start, ranting in his hermetic language and with tears in his eyes, and he flapped his wings a couple of times, which brought on a whirlwind of chicken dung and lunar dust and a gale of panic that did not seem to be of this world. Although many thought that his reaction had been one not of rage but of pain, from then on they were careful not to annoy him,

2. Choice, extremely expensive meals.

because the majority understood that his passivity was not that of a hero taking his ease but that of a cataclysm in repose.

Father Gonzaga held back the crowd's frivolity with formulas of maidservant inspiration while awaiting the arrival of a final judgment on the nature of the captive. But the mail from Rome showed no sense of urgency. They spent their time finding out if the prisoner had a navel, if his dialect had any connection with Aramaic, how many times he could fit on the head of a pin, or whether he wasn't just a Norwegian with wings. Those meager letters might have come and gone until the end of time if a providential event had not put an end to the priest's tribulations.

It so happened that during those days, among so many other carnival attractions, there arrived in town the traveling show of the woman who had been changed into a spider for having disobeyed her parents. The admission to see her was not only less than the admission to see the angel, but people were permitted to ask her all manner of questions about her absurd state and to examine her up and down so that no one would ever doubt the truth of her horror. She was a frightful tarantula the size of a ram and with the head of a sad maiden. What was most heart-rending, however, was not her outlandish shape but the sincere affliction with which she recounted the details of her misfortune. While still practically a child she had sneaked out of her parents' house to go to a dance, and while she was coming back through the woods after having danced all night without permission, a fearful thunderclap rent the sky in two and through the crack came the lightning bolt of brimstone that changed her into a spider. Her only nourishment came from the meatballs that charitable souls chose to toss into her mouth. A spectacle like that, full of so much human truth and with such a fearful lesson, was bound to defeat without even trying that of a haughty angel who scarcely deigned to look at mortals. Besides, the few miracles attributed to the angel showed a certain mental disorder, like the blind man who didn't recover his sight but grew three new teeth, or the paralytic who didn't get to walk but almost won the lottery, and the leper whose sores sprouted sunflowers. Those consolation miracles, which were more like mocking fun, had already ruined the angel's reputation when the woman who had been changed into a spider finally crushed him completely. That was how Father Gonzaga was cured forever of his insomnia and Pelayo's courtyard went back to being as empty as during the time it had rained for three days and crabs walked through the bedrooms.

The owners of the house had no reason to lament. With the money they saved they built a two-story mansion with balconies and gardens and high netting so that crabs wouldn't get in during the winter, and with iron bars on the windows so that angels wouldn't get in. Pelayo also set up a rabbit warren close to town and gave up his job as bailiff for good, and Elisenda bought some satin pumps with high heels and many dresses of iridescent silk, the kind worn on Sunday by the most desirable women in those times. The chicken coop was the only thing that didn't receive any attention. If they washed it down with creolin[3]

---

3. A disinfectant.

and burned tears of myrrh inside it every so often, it was not in homage to the angel but to drive away the dungheap stench that still hung everywhere like a ghost and was turning the new house into an old one. At first, when the child learned to walk, they were careful that he not get too close to the chicken coop. But then they began to lose their fears and got used to the smell, and before the child got his second teeth he'd gone inside the chicken coop to play, where the wires were falling apart. The angel was no less standoffish with him than with other mortals, but he tolerated the most ingenious infamies with the patience of a dog who had no illusions. They both came down with chicken pox at the same time. The doctor who took care of the child couldn't resist the temptation to listen to the angel's heart, and he found so much whistling in the heart and so many sounds in his kidneys that it seemed impossible for him to be alive. What surprised him most, however, was the logic of his wings. They seemed so natural on that completely human organism that he couldn't understand why other men didn't have them too.

When the child began school it had been some time since the sun and rain had caused the collapse of the chicken coop. The angel went dragging himself about here and there like a stray dying man. They would drive him out of the bedroom with a broom and a moment later find him in the kitchen. He seemed to be in so many places at the same time that they grew to think that he'd been duplicated, that he was reproducing himself all through the house, and the exasperated and unhinged Elisenda shouted that it was awful living in that hell full of angels. He could scarcely eat and his antiquarian eyes had also become so foggy that he went about bumping into posts. All he had left were the bare cannulae of his last feathers. Pelayo threw a blanket over him and extended him the charity of letting him sleep in the shed, and only then did they notice that he had a temperature at night, and was delirious with the tongue twisters of an old Norwegian. That was one of the few times they became alarmed, for they thought he was going to die and not even the wise neighbor woman had been able to tell them what to do with dead angels.

And yet he not only survived his worst winter, but seemed improved with the first sunny days. He remained motionless for several days in the farthest corner of the courtyard, where no one would see him, and at the beginning of December some large, stiff feathers began to grow on his wings, the feathers of a scarecrow, which looked more like another misfortune of decrepitude. But he must have known the reason for those changes, for he was quite careful that no one should notice them, that no one should hear the sea chanteys that he sometimes sang under the stars. One morning Elisenda was cutting some bunches of onions for lunch when a wind that seemed to come from the high seas blew into the kitchen. Then she went to the window and caught the angel in his first attempts at flight. They were so clumsy that his fingernails opened a furrow in the vegetable patch and he was on the point of knocking the shed down with the ungainly flapping that slipped on the light and couldn't get a grip on the air. But he did manage to gain altitude. Elisenda let out a sign of relief, for herself and for him, when she saw him pass over the last houses, holding himself up in some way with the risky flapping of a senile vulture. She kept watching him even when she was through cutting the onions and she kept on watching until it was no longer possible for her to see him, because then he was no longer an annoyance in her life but an imaginary dot on the horizon of the sea.

1968

JAMAICA KINCAID

Girl

Wash the white clothes on Monday and put them on the stone heap; wash the color clothes on Tuesday and put them on the clothesline to dry; don't walk barehead in the hot sun; cook pumpkin fritters in very hot sweet oil; soak your little cloths right after you take them off; when buying cotton to make yourself a nice blouse, be sure that it doesn't have gum on it, because that way it won't hold up well after a wash; soak salt fish overnight before you cook it; is it true that you sing benna[1] in Sunday school?; always eat your food in such a way that it won't turn someone else's stomach; on Sundays try to walk like a lady and not like the slut you are so bent on becoming; don't sing benna in Sunday school; you mustn't speak to wharf-rat boys, not even to give directions; don't eat fruits on the street—flies will follow you; *but I don't sing benna on Sundays at all and never in Sunday school*; this is how to sew on a button; this is how to make a buttonhole for the button you have just sewed on; this is how to hem a dress when you see the hem coming down and so to prevent yourself from looking like the slut I know you are so bent on becoming; this is how you iron your father's khaki shirt so that it doesn't have a crease; this is how you iron your father's khaki pants so that they don't have a crease; this is how you grow okra— far from the house, because okra tree harbors red ants; when you are growing dasheen, make sure it gets plenty of water or else it makes your throat itch when you are eating it; this is how you sweep a corner; this is how you sweep a whole house; this is how you sweep a yard; this is how you smile to someone you don't like too much; this is how you smile to someone you don't like at all; this is how you smile to someone you like completely; this is how you set a table for tea; this is how you set a table for dinner; this is how you set a table for dinner with an important guest; this is how you set a table for lunch; this is how you set a table for breakfast; this is how to behave in the presence of men who don't know you very well, and this way they won't recognize immediately the slut I have warned you against becoming; be sure to wash every day, even if it is with your own spit; don't squat down to play marbles—you are not a boy, you know; don't pick people's flowers—you might catch something; don't throw stones at black-birds, because it might not be a blackbird at all; this is how to make a bread pudding; this is how to make doukona[2]; this is how to make pepper pot; this is how to make a good medicine for a cold; this is how to make a good medicine

1. Sing popular music, calypso.   2. A spicy pudding, often made from plantain and wrapped in a plantain or banana leaf.

to throw away a child before it even becomes a child; this is how to catch a fish; this is how to throw back a fish you don't like, and that way something bad won't fall on you; this is how to bully a man; this is how a man bullies you; this is how to love a man, and if this doesn't work there are other ways, and if they don't work don't feel too bad about giving up; this is how to spit up in the air if you feel like it, and this is how to move quick so that it doesn't fall on you; this is how to make ends meet; always squeeze bread to make sure it's fresh; *but what if the baker won't let me feel the bread?*; you mean to say that after all you are really going to be the kind of woman who the baker won't let near the bread?

1983

YASUNARI KAWABATA

The Grasshopper and the Bell Cricket[1]

Walking along the tile-roofed wall of the university, I turned aside and approached the upper school. Behind the white board fence of the school playground, from a dusky clump of bushes under the black cherry trees, an insect's voice could be heard. Walking more slowly and listening to that voice, and furthermore reluctant to part with it, I turned right so as not to leave the playground behind. When I turned to the left, the fence gave way to an embankment planted with orange trees. At the corner, I exclaimed with surprise. My eyes gleaming at what they saw up ahead, I hurried forward with short steps.

At the base of the embankment was a bobbing cluster of beautiful varicolored lanterns, such as one might see at a festival in a remote country village. Without going any farther, I knew that it was a group of children on an insect chase among the bushes of the embankment. There were about twenty lanterns. Not only were there crimson, pink, indigo, green, purple, and yellow lanterns, but one lantern glowed with five colors at once. There were even some little red store-bought lanterns. But most of the lanterns were beautiful square ones which the children had made themselves with love and care. The bobbing lanterns, the coming together of children on this lonely slope—surely it was a scene from a fairy tale?

One of the neighborhood children had heard an insect sing on this slope one night. Buying a red lantern, he had come back the next night to find the insect. The night after that, there was another child. This new child could not buy a lantern. Cutting out the back and front of a small carton and papering it, he placed a candle on the bottom and fastened a string to the top. The number of children grew to five, and then to seven. They learned how to color the paper that they stretched over the windows of the cutout cartons, and to draw pictures on it. Then these wise child-artists, cutting out round, three-cornered, and lozenge leaf shapes in the cartons, coloring each little window a different color, with circles and diamonds, red and green, made a single and whole decorative

1. Translated by Lane Dunlop.

pattern. The child with the red lantern discarded it as a tasteless object that could be bought at a store. The child who had made his own lantern threw it away because the design was too simple. The pattern of light that one had had in hand the night before was unsatisfying the morning after. Each day, with cardboard, paper, brush, scissors, penknife, and glue, the children made new lanterns out of their hearts and minds. Look at my lantern! Be the most unusually beautiful! And each night, they had gone out on their insect hunts. These were the twenty children and their beautiful lanterns that I now saw before me.

Wide-eyed, I loitered near them. Not only did the square lanterns have old-fashioned patterns and flower shapes, but the names of the children who had made them were cut out in squared letters of the syllabary. Different from the painted-over red lanterns, others (made of thick cutout cardboard) had their designs drawn onto the paper windows, so that the candle's light seemed to emanate from the form and color of the design itself. The lanterns brought out the shadows of the bushes like dark light. The children crouched eagerly on the slope wherever they heard an insect's voice.

"Does anyone want a grasshopper?" A boy, who had been peering into a bush about thirty feet away from the other children, suddenly straightened up and shouted.

"Yes! Give it to me!" Six or seven children came running up. Crowding behind the boy who had found the grasshopper, they peered into the bush. Brushing away their outstretched hands and spreading out his arms, the boy stood as if guarding the bush where the insect was. Waving the lantern in his right hand, he called again to the other children.

"Does anyone want a grasshopper? A grasshopper!"

"I do! I do!" Four or five more children came running up. It seemed you could not catch a more precious insect than a grasshopper. The boy called out a third time.

"Doesn't anyone want a grasshopper?"

Two or three more children came over.

"Yes. I want it."

It was a girl, who just now had come up behind the boy who'd discovered the insect. Lightly turning his body, the boy gracefully bent forward. Shifting the lantern to his left hand, he reached his right hand into the bush.

"It's a grasshopper."

"Yes. I'd like to have it."

The boy quickly stood up. As if to say "Here!" he thrust out his fist that held the insect at the girl. She, slipping her left wrist under the string of her lantern, enclosed the boy's fist with both hands. The boy quietly opened his fist. The insect was transferred to between the girl's thumb and index finger.

"Oh! It's not a grasshopper. It's a bell cricket." The girl's eyes shone as she looked at the small brown insect.

"It's a bell cricket! It's a bell cricket!" The children echoed in an envious chorus.

"It's a bell cricket. It's a bell cricket."

Glancing with her bright intelligent eyes at the boy who had given her the cricket, the girl opened the little insect cage hanging at her side and released the cricket in it.

"It's a bell cricket."

"Oh, it's a bell cricket," the boy who'd captured it muttered. Holding up the insect cage close to his eyes, he looked inside it. By the light of his beautiful many-colored lantern, also held up at eye level, he glanced at the girl's face.

Oh, I thought. I felt slightly jealous of the boy, and sheepish. How silly of me not to have understood his actions until now! Then I caught my breath in surprise. Look! It was something on the girl's breast which neither the boy who had given her the cricket, nor she who had accepted it, nor the children who were looking at them noticed.

In the faint greenish light that fell on the girl's breast, wasn't the name "Fujio" clearly discernible? The boy's lantern, which he held up alongside the girl's insect cage, inscribed his name, cut out in the green papered aperture, onto her white cotton kimono. The girl's lantern, which dangled loosely from her wrist, did not project its pattern so clearly, but still one could make out, in a trembling patch of red on the boy's waist, the name "Kiyoko." This chance interplay of red and green—if it was chance or play—neither Fujio nor Kiyoko knew about.

Even if they remembered forever that Fujio had given her the cricket and that Kiyoko had accepted it, not even in dreams would Fujio ever know that his name had been written in green on Kiyoko's breast or that Kiyoko's name had been inscribed in red on his waist, nor would Kiyoko ever know that Fujio's name had been inscribed in green on her breast or that her own name had been written in red on Fujio's waist.

Fujio! Even when you have become a young man, laugh with pleasure at a girl's delight when, told that it's a grasshopper, she is given a bell cricket; laugh with affection at a girl's chagrin when, told that it's a bell cricket, she is given a grasshopper.

Even if you have the wit to look by yourself in a bush away from the other children, there are not many bell crickets in the world. Probably you will find a girl like a grasshopper whom you think is a bell cricket.

And finally, to your clouded, wounded heart, even a true bell cricket will seem like a grasshopper. Should that day come, when it seems to you that the world is only full of grasshoppers, I will think it a pity that you have no way to remember tonight's play of light, when your name was written in green by your beautiful lantern on a girl's breast.

1988

▼ ▼ ▼

QUESTIONS

1. How do the details in paragraphs 5–10 in "The Story of an Hour" prepare for the reversal that comes in paragraph 11? Did you find the turn surprising? convincing?

2. What details in the first four paragraphs of "A Very Short Story" make the characters' love seem real and convincing? There is a reversal in the sixth paragraph that makes this story's effect something like that of "The Story of an Hour." What is the effect of the final paragraph?

3. What humorous elements do you find in "A Very Old Man with Enormous Wings"? How do they function? Is the old man a symbol? If so, does he "stand for" something you can name or paraphrase? If you cannot say what he stands for, how can he be a symbol? If we do not read this story symbolically, how can we deal with its fantastic elements? take the story seriously as "literature"?

4. What images of the characters of the girl and her mother emerge from your reading of "Girl"? How are those images created?

5. What does the narrator contribute to the meaning and effect of "The Grasshopper and the Bell Cricket"? (Try to imagine the story without him.) What is the effect of the relatively lengthy description of the varied lanterns? To what extent are the meanings of "grasshopper" and "bell cricket" paraphrasable? What is the tone, effect, and meaning of the last two paragraphs?

WRITING SUGGESTIONS

1. Write a personal essay either about grief and its complexities or about another experience in which an initial and expected emotion gave way to something like its opposite.

2. Compare the ending of "A Very Short Story" to that of "The Jewelry."

3. Write a personal essay called "Boy" or "Another Girl" that deals with the oft-repeated and multiple instructions, advice, and commands of a parent (not necessarily a mother).

4. The introduction to the chapter suggests that all you have learned about the elements of fiction may be, perhaps must be, brought to bear on Kawabata's story. Write an analysis of this story as if for the earlier chapter called "The Whole Text."

Evaluating Fiction

To evaluate a work of literature—to determine its worth or quality—is one of the most fundamental, significant, and difficult activities in literary study. It is impossible to dodge such questions as "Is this story good?" "Is it great?" "Is it better than that one? . . . that other one?" "Is it worth reading? studying?" It is equally impossible to answer such questions definitively, for all time and for all readers.

It is, however, usually possible to answer the question, "Do you like this story?" and often possible to answer "Do you like this one more than or less than that other?" Whether you like a story or not when you first read it is therefore probably the proper place to *begin*. But it is a dangerous place to *stop* the process of evaluation. If our appreciation and understanding of literature is to grow, and if we are not content simply to accept without question the authority of "those who know best," we must learn to isolate, analyze, and articulate what it is *we* like about a story and to search out in our minds and experience the reasons *we* like it. We must listen to other readers' responses too, responses that may reinforce our own, may show us things to appreciate in the story that we missed, or may challenge the viability of our reasons, if not that of our responses.

Let us begin by reading a story together. Let's see how we like it, and what we can say about it.

RICHARD CONNELL

The Most Dangerous Game

"Off there to the right—somewhere—is a large island," said Whitney. "It's rather a mystery—"

"What island is it?" Rainsford asked.

"The old charts call it 'Ship-Trap Island,' " Whitney replied. "A suggestive name, isn't it? Sailors have a curious dread of the place. I don't know why. Some superstition—"

"Can't see it," remarked Rainsford, trying to peer through the dank tropical night that was palpable as it pressed its thick warm blackness in upon the yacht.

5 "You've good eyes," said Whitney, with a laugh, "and I've seen you pick off a moose moving in the brown fall bush at four hundred yards, but even you can't see four miles or so through a moonless Caribbean night."

"Nor four yards," admitted Rainsford. "Ugh! It's like moist black velvet."

"It will be light in Rio," promised Whitney. "We should make it in a few days. I hope the jaguar guns have come from Purdey's. We should have some good hunting up the Amazon. Great sport, hunting."

"The best sport in the world," agreed Rainsford.

"For the hunter," amended Whitney. "Not for the jaguar."

10 "Don't talk rot, Whitney," said Rainsford. "You're a big-game hunter, not a philosopher. Who cares how a jaguar feels?"

"Perhaps the jaguar does," observed Whitney.

"Bah! They've no understanding."

"Even so, I rather think they understand one thing—fear. The fear of pain and the fear of death."

"Nonsense," laughed Rainsford. "This hot weather is making you soft, Whitney. Be a realist. The world is made up of two classes—the hunters and the huntees. Luckily, you and I are hunters. Do you think we've passed that island yet?"

15 "I can't tell in the dark. I hope so."

"Why?" asked Rainsford.

"The place has a reputation—a bad one."

"Cannibals?" suggested Rainsford.

"Hardly. Even cannibals wouldn't live in such a God-forsaken place. But it's gotten into sailor lore, somehow. Didn't you notice that the crew's nerves seemed a bit jumpy today?"

20 "They were a bit strange, now you mention it. Even Captain Nielsen—"

"Yes, even that tough-minded old Swede, who'd go up to the devil himself and ask him for a light. Those fishy blue eyes held a look I never saw there before. All I could get out of him was: 'This place has an evil name among seafaring men, sir.' Then he said to me, very gravely: 'Don't you feel anything?'— as if the air about us was actually poisonous. Now, you mustn't laugh when I tell you this—I did feel something like a sudden chill.

"There was no breeze. The sea was as flat as a plate-glass window. We were drawing near the island then. What I felt was a—a mental chill; a sort of sudden dread."

"Pure imagination," said Rainsford. "One superstitious sailor can taint the whole ship's company with his fear."

"Maybe. But sometimes I think sailors have an extra sense that tells them when they are in danger. Sometimes I think evil is a tangible thing—with wave lengths, just as sound and light have. An evil place can, so to speak, broadcast vibrations of evil. Anyhow, I'm glad we're getting out of this zone. Well, I think I'll turn in now, Rainsford."

"I'm not sleepy," said Rainsford. "I'm going to smoke another pipe up on the after deck." 25

"Good night, then, Rainsford. See you at breakfast."

"Right. Good night, Whitney."

There was no sound in the night as Rainsford sat there, but the muffled throb of the engine that drove the yacht swiftly through the darkness, and the swish and ripple of the wash of the propeller.

Rainsford, reclining in a steamer chair, indolently puffed on his favorite brier. The sensuous drowsiness of the night was on him. "It's so dark," he thought, "that I could sleep without closing my eyes; the night would be my eyelids—"

An abrupt sound startled him. Off to the right he heard it, and his ears, expert in such matters, could not be mistaken. Again he heard the sound, and again. Somewhere, off in the blackness, some one had fired a gun three times. 30

Rainsford sprang up and moved quickly to the rail, mystified. He strained his eyes in the direction from which the reports had come, but it was like trying to see through a blanket. He leaped upon the rail and balanced himself there, to get greater elevation; his pipe, striking a rope, was knocked from his mouth. He lunged for it; a short, hoarse cry came from his lips as he realized he had reached too far and had lost his balance. The cry was pinched off short as the bloodwarm waters of the Caribbean Sea closed over his head.

He struggled up to the surface and tried to cry out, but the wash from the speeding yacht slapped him in the face and the salt water in his open mouth made him gag and strangle. Desperately he struck out with strong strokes after the receding lights of the yacht, but he stopped before he had swum fifty feet. A certain cool-headedness had come to him; it was not the first time he had been in a tight place. There was a chance that his cries could be heard by some one aboard the yacht, but that chance was slender, and grew more slender as the yacht raced on. He wrestled himself out of his clothes, and shouted with all his power. The lights of the yacht became faint and ever-vanishing fireflies; then they were blotted out entirely by the night.

Rainsford remembered the shots. They had come from the right, and doggedly he swam in that direction, swimming with slow, deliberate strokes, conserving his strength. For a seemingly endless time he fought the sea. He began to count his strokes; he could do possibly a hundred more and then—

Rainsford heard a sound. It came out of the darkness, a high screaming sound, the sound of an animal in an extremity of anguish and terror.

He did not recognize the animal that made the sound; he did not try to; with fresh vitality he swam toward the sound. He heard it again; then it was cut short by another noise, crisp, staccato. 35

"Pistol shot," muttered Rainsford, swimming on.

Ten minutes of determined effort brought another sound to his ears—the most welcome he had ever heard—the muttering and growling of the sea breaking on a rocky shore. He was almost on the rocks before he saw them; on a night less calm he would have been shattered against them. With his remaining strength he dragged himself from the swirling waters. Jagged crags appeared to jut into the opaqueness; he forced himself upward, hand over hand. Gasping, his hands raw, he reached a flat place at the top. Dense jungle came down to the very edge of the cliffs. What perils that tangle of trees and underbrush might hold for him did not concern Rainsford just then. All he knew was that he was safe from his enemy, the sea, and that utter weariness was on him. He flung himself down at the jungle edge and tumbled headlong into the deepest sleep of his life.

When he opened his eyes he knew from the position of the sun that it was late in the afternoon. Sleep had given him new vigor; a sharp hunger was picking at him. He looked about him, almost cheerfully.

"Where there are pistol shots, there are men. Where there are men, there is food," he thought. But what kind of men, he wondered, in so forbidding a place? An unbroken front of snarled and ragged jungle fringed the shore.

40 He saw no sign of a trail through the closely knit web of weeds and trees; it was easier to go along the shore, and Rainsford floundered along by the water. Not far from where he had landed, he stopped.

Some wounded thing, by the evidence a large animal, had thrashed about in the underbrush; the jungle weeds were crushed down and the moss was lacerated; one patch of weeds was stained crimson. A small, glittering object not far away caught Rainsford's eye and he picked it up. It was an empty cartridge.

"A twenty-two," he remarked. "That's odd. It must have been a fairly large animal too. The hunter had his nerve with him to tackle it with a light gun. It's clear that the brute put up a fight. I suppose the first three shots I heard was when the hunter flushed his quarry and wounded it. The last shot was when he trailed it here and finished it."

He examined the ground closely and found what he had hoped to find—the print of hunting boots. They pointed along the cliff in the direction he had been going. Eagerly, he hurried along, now slipping on a rotten log or a loose stone, but making headway; night was beginning to settle down on the island.

Bleak darkness was blacking out the sea and jungle when Rainsford sighted the lights. He came upon them as he turned a crook in the coast line, and his first thought was that he had come upon a village, for there were many lights. But as he forged along he saw to his great astonishment that all the lights were in one enormous building—a lofty structure with pointed towers plunging upward into the gloom. His eyes made out the shadowy outlines of a palatial château; it was set on a high bluff, and on three sides of it cliffs dived down to where the sea licked greedy lips in the shadows.

45 "Mirage," thought Rainsford. But it was no mirage, he found, when he opened the tall spiked iron gate. The stone steps were real enough; the massive door with a leering gargoyle for a knocker was real enough; yet about it all hung an air of unreality.

He lifted the knocker, and it creaked up stiffly, as if it had never before been used. He let it fall, and it startled him with its booming loudness. He thought he heard steps within; the door remained closed. Again Rainsford lifted the heavy knocker, and let it fall. The door opened then, opened as suddenly as if it were on a spring, and Rainsford stood blinking in the river of glaring gold light that poured out. The first thing Rainsford's eyes discerned was the largest man Rainsford had ever seen—a gigantic creature, solidly made and blackbearded to the waist. In his hand the man held a long-barreled revolver, and he was pointing it straight at Rainsford's heart.

Out of the snarl of beard two small eyes regarded Rainsford.

"Don't be alarmed," said Rainsford, with a smile which he hoped was disarming. "I'm no robber. I fell off a yacht. My name is Sanger Rainsford of New York City."

The menacing look in the eyes did not change. The revolver pointed as rigidly as if the giant were a statue. He gave no sign that he understood Rainsford's words, or that he had even heard them. He was dressed in uniform, a black uniform trimmed with gray astrakhan.

"I'm Sanger Rainsford of New York," Rainsford began again. "I fell off a yacht. I am hungry."

The man's only answer was to raise with his thumb the hammer of his revolver. Then Rainsford saw the man's free hand go to his forehead in a military salute, and he saw him click his heels together and stand at attention. Another man was coming down the broad marble steps, an erect, slender man in evening clothes. He advanced to Rainsford and held out his hand.

In a cultivated voice marked by a slight accent that gave it added precision and deliberateness, he said: "It is a very great pleasure and honor to welcome Mr. Sanger Rainsford, the celebrated hunter, to my home."

Automatically Rainsford shook the man's hand.

"I've read your book about hunting snow leopards in Tibet, you see" explained the man. "I am General Zaroff."

Rainsford's first impression was that the man was singularly handsome; his second was that there was an original, almost bizarre quality about the general's face. He was a tall man past middle age, for his hair was a vivid white; but his thick eyebrows and pointed military mustache were as black as the night from which Rainsford had come. His eyes, too, were black and very bright. He had high cheek bones, a sharp-cut nose, a spare, dark face, the face of a man used to giving orders, the face of an aristocrat. Turning to the giant in uniform, the general made a sign. The giant put away his pistol, saluted, withdrew.

"Ivan is an incredibly strong fellow," remarked the general, "but he has the misfortune to be deaf and dumb. A simple fellow, but, I'm afraid, like all his race, a bit of a savage."

"Is he Russian?"

"He is a Cossack," said the general, and his smile showed red lips and pointed teeth. "So am I."

"Come," he said, "we shouldn't be chatting here. We can talk later. Now you want clothes, food, rest. You shall have them. This is a most restful spot."

Ivan had reappeared, and the general spoke to him with lips that moved but gave forth no sound.

"Follow Ivan, if you please, Mr. Rainsford," said the general. "I was about to have my dinner when you came. I'll wait for you. You'll find that my clothes will fit you, I think."

It was to a huge, beam-ceilinged bedroom with a canopied bed big enough for six men that Rainsford followed the silent giant. Ivan laid out an evening suit, and Rainsford, as he put it on, noticed that it came from a London tailor who ordinarily cut and sewed for none below the rank of duke.

The dining room to which Ivan conducted him was in many ways remarkable. There was a medieval magnificence about it; it suggested a baronial hall of feudal times with its oaken panels, its high ceiling, its vast refectory table where twoscore men could sit down to eat. About the hall were the mounted heads of many animals—lions, tigers, elephants, moose, bears; larger or more perfect specimens Rainsford had never seen. At the great table the general was sitting, alone.

"You'll have a cocktail, Mr. Rainsford," he suggested. The cocktail was surpassingly good; and, Rainsford noted, the table appointments were of the finest—the linen, the crystal, the silver, the china.

65 They were eating *borsch*, the rich, red soup with whipped cream so dear to Russian palates. Half apologetically General Zaroff said: "We do our best to preserve the amenities of civilization here. Please forgive any lapses. We are well off the beaten track, you know. Do you think the champagne has suffered from its long ocean trip?"

"Not in the least," declared Rainsford. He was finding the general a most thoughtful and affable host, a true cosmopolite. But there was one small trait of the general's that made Rainsford uncomfortable. Whenever he looked up from his plate he found the general studying him, appraising him narrowly.

"Perhaps," said General Zaroff, "you were surprised that I recognized your name. You see, I read all books on hunting published in English, French, and Russian. I have but one passion in my life, Mr. Rainsford, and it is the hunt."

"You have some wonderful heads here," said Rainsford as he ate a particularly well cooked filet mignon. "That Cape buffalo is the largest I ever saw."

"Oh, that fellow. Yes, he was a monster."

70 "Did he charge you?"

"Hurled me against a tree," said the general. "Fractured my skull. But I got the brute."

"I've always thought," said Rainsford, "that the Cape buffalo is the most dangerous of all big game."

For a moment the general did not reply; he was smiling his curious red-lipped smile. Then he said slowly: "No. You are wrong, sir. The Cape buffalo is not the most dangerous big game." He sipped his wine. "Here in my preserve on this island," he said in the same slow tone, "I hunt more dangerous game."

Rainsford expressed his surprise. "Is there big game on this island?"

75 The general nodded. "The biggest."

"Really?"

"Oh, it isn't here naturally, of course. I have to stock the island."

"What have you imported, general?" Rainsford asked. "Tigers?"

The general smiled. "No," he said. "Hunting tigers ceased to interest me some years ago. I exhausted their possibilities, you see. No thrill left in tigers, no real danger. I live for danger, Mr. Rainsford."

The general took from his pocket a gold cigarette case and offered his guest a long black cigarette with a silver tip; it was perfumed and gave off a smell like incense.

"We will have some capital hunting, you and I," said the general. "I shall be most glad to have your society."

"But what game—" began Rainsford.

"I'll tell you," said the general. "You will be amused, I know. I think I may say, in all modesty, that I have done a rare thing. I have invented a new sensation. May I pour you another glass of port, Mr. Rainsford?"

"Thank you, general."

The general filled both glasses, and said: "God makes some men poets. Some He makes kings, some beggars. Me He made a hunter. My hand was made for the trigger, my father said. He was a very rich man with a quarter of a million acres in the Crimea, and he was an ardent sportsman. When I was only five years old he gave me a little gun, specially made in Moscow for me, to shoot sparrows with. When I shot some of his prize turkeys with it, he did not punish me; he complimented me on my marksmanship. I killed my first bear in the Caucasus when I was ten. My whole life has been one prolonged hunt. I went into the army—it was expected of noblemen's sons—and for a time commanded a division of Cossack cavalry, but my real interest was always the hunt. I have hunted every kind of game in every land. It would be impossible for me to tell you how many animals I have killed."

The general puffed at his cigarette.

"After the debacle in Russia[1] I left the country, for it was imprudent for an officer of the Czar to stay there. Many noble Russians lost everything. I, luckily, had invested heavily in American securities, so I shall never have to open a tea room in Monte Carlo or drive a taxi in Paris. Naturally, I continued to hunt—grizzlies in your Rockies, crocodiles in the Ganges, rhinoceroses in East Africa. It was in Africa that the Cape buffalo hit me and laid me up for six months. As soon as I recovered I started for the Amazon to hunt jaguars, for I had heard they were unusually cunning. They weren't." The Cossack sighed. "They were no match at all for a hunter with his wits about him, and a high-powered rifle. I was bitterly disappointed. I was lying in my tent with a splitting headache one night when a terrible thought pushed its way into my mind. Hunting was beginning to bore me! And hunting, remember, had been my life. I have heard that in America business men often go to pieces when they give up the business that has been their life."

"Yes, that's so," said Rainsford.

The general smiled. "I had no wish to go to pieces," he said. "I must do something. Now, mine is an analytical mind, Mr. Rainsford. Doubtless that is why I enjoy the problems of the chase."

1. The Revolution of 1917, which overthrew the Czar and prepared the way for Communist rule.

90   "No doubt, General Zaroff."

"So," continued the general, "I asked myself why the hunt no longer fascinated me. You are much younger than I am, Mr. Rainsford, and have not hunted as much, but you perhaps can guess the answer."

"What was it?"

"Simply this: hunting had ceased to be what you call 'a sporting proposition.' It had become too easy. I always got my quarry. Always. There is no greater bore than perfection."

The general lit a fresh cigarette.

95   "No animal had a chance with me any more. That is no boast; it is a mathematical certainty. The animal had nothing but his legs and his instinct. Instinct is no match for reason. When I thought of this it was a tragic moment for me, I can tell you."

Rainsford leaned across the table, absorbed in what his host was saying.

"It came to me as an inspiration what I must do," the general went on.

"And that was?"

The general smiled the quiet smile of one who had faced an obstacle and surmounted it with success. "I had to invent a new animal to hunt," he said.

100   "A new animal? You're joking."

"Not at all," said the general. "I never joke about hunting. I needed a new animal. I found one. So I bought this island, built this house, and here I do my hunting. The island is perfect for my purposes—there are jungles with a maze of trails in them, hills, swamps—"

"But the animal, General Zaroff?"

"Oh," said the general, "it supplies me with the most exciting hunting in the world. No other hunting compares with it for an instant. Every day I hunt, and I never grow bored now, for I have a quarry with which I can match my wits."

Rainsford's bewilderment showed in his face.

105   "I wanted the ideal animal to hunt," explained the general. "So I said: 'What are the attributes of an ideal quarry?' And the answer was, of course: 'It must have courage, cunning, and, above all, it must be able to reason.'"

"But no animal can reason," objected Rainsford.

"My dear fellow," said the general, "there is one that can."

"But you can't mean—" gasped Rainsford.

"And why not?"

110   "I can't believe you are serious, General Zaroff. This is a grisly joke."

"Why should I not be serious? I am speaking of hunting."

"Hunting? Good God, General Zaroff, what you speak of is murder."

The general laughed with entire good nature. He regarded Rainsford quizzically. "I refuse to believe that so modern and civilized a young man as you seem to be harbors romantic ideas about the value of human life. Surely your experiences in the war—"

"Did not make me condone cold-blooded murder," finished Rainsford stiffly.

115   Laughter shook the general. "How extraordinarily droll you are!" he said. "One does not expect nowadays to find a young man of the educated class, even in America, with such a naïve, and, if I may say so, mid-Victorian point of view.

It's like finding a snuff-box in a limousine. Ah, well, doubtless you had Puritan ancestors. So many Americans appear to have had. I'll wager you'll forget your notions when you go hunting with me. You've a genuine new thrill in store for you, Mr. Rainsford."

"Thank you, I'm a hunter, not a murderer."

"Dear me," said the general, quite unruffled, "again that unpleasant word. But I think I can show you that your scruples are quite ill founded."

"Yes?"

"Life is for the strong, to be lived by the strong, and, if need be, taken by the strong. The weak of the world were put here to give the strong pleasure. I am strong. Why should I not use my gift? If I wish to hunt, why should I not? I hunt the scum of the earth—sailors from tramp ships—lascars, blacks, Chinese, whites, mongrels—a thoroughbred horse or hound is worth more than a score of them."

"But they are men," said Rainsford hotly.   120

"Precisely," said the general. "That is why I use them. It gives me pleasure. They can reason, after a fashion. So they are dangerous."

"But where do you get them?"

The general's left eyelid fluttered down in a wink. "This island is called Ship-Trap," he answered. "Sometimes an angry god of the high seas sends them to me. Sometimes, when Providence is not so kind, I help Providence a bit. Come to the window with me."

Rainsford went to the window and looked out toward the sea.

"Watch! Out there!" exclaimed the general, pointing into the night. Rains-   125
ford's eyes saw only blackness, and then, as the general pressed a button, far out to sea Rainsford saw the flash of lights.

The general chuckled. "They indicate a channel," he said, "where there's none: giant rocks with razor edges crouch like a sea monster with wide-open jaws. They can crush a ship as easily as I crush this nut." He dropped a walnut on the hardwood floor and brought his heel grinding down on it. "Oh, yes," he said, casually, as if in answer to a question, "I have electricity. We try to be civilized here."

"Civilized? And you shoot down men?"

A trace of anger was in the general's black eyes, but it was there for but a second, and he said, in his most pleasant manner: "Dear me, what a righteous young man you are! I assure you I do not do the thing you suggest. That would be barbarous. I treat these visitors with every consideration. They get plenty of good food and exercise. They get into splendid physical condition. You shall see for yourself tomorrow."

"What do you mean?"

"We'll visit my training school," smiled the general. "It's in the cellar. I have   130
about a dozen pupils down there now. They're from the Spanish bark San Lucar that had the bad luck to go on the rocks out there. A very inferior lot, I regret to say. Poor specimens and more accustomed to the deck than to the jungle."

He raised his hand, and Ivan, who served as waiter, brought thick Turkish coffee. Rainsford, with an effort, held his tongue in check.

"It's a game, you see," pursued the general blandly. "I suggest to one of them that we go hunting. I give him a supply of food and an excellent hunting knife. I give him three hours' start. I am to follow, armed only with a pistol of the smallest caliber and range. If my quarry eludes me for three whole days, he wins the game. If I find him"—the general smiled—"he loses."

"Suppose he refuses to be hunted?"

"Oh," said the general, "I give him his option, of course. He need not play that game if he doesn't wish to. If he does not wish to hunt, I turn him over to Ivan. Ivan once had the honor of serving as official knouter to the Great White Czar,[2] and he has his own ideas of sport. Invariably, Mr. Rainsford, invariably they choose the hunt."

135   "And if they win?"

The smile on the general's face widened. "To date I have not lost," he said.

Then he added, hastily: "I don't wish you to think me a braggart, Mr. Rainsford. Many of them afford only the most elementary sort of problem. Occasionally I strike a tartar. One almost did win. I eventually had to use the dogs."

"The dogs?"

"This way, please. I'll show you."

140   The general steered Rainsford to a window. The lights from the windows sent a flickering illumination that made grotesque patterns on the courtyard below, and Rainsford could see moving about there a dozen or so huge black shapes; as they turned toward him, their eyes glittered greenly.

"A rather good lot, I think," observed the general. "They are let out at seven every night. If anyone should try to get into my house—or out of it—something extremely regrettable would occur to him." He hummed a snatch of song from the Folies Bergère.[3]

"And now," said the general, "I want to show you my new collection of heads. Will you come with me to the library?"

"I hope," said Rainsford, "that you will excuse me tonight, General Zaroff. I'm really not feeling at all well."

"Ah, indeed?" the general inquired solicitously. "Well, I suppose that's only natural, after your long swim. You need a good, restful night's sleep. Tomorrow you'll feel like a new man, I'll wager. Then we'll hunt, eh? I've one rather promising prospect—"

145   Rainsford was hurrying from the room.

"Sorry you can't go with me tonight," called the general. "I expect rather fair sport—a big, strong black. He looks resourceful—Well, good night, Mr. Rainsford; I hope you have a good night's rest."

The bed was good, and the pajamas of the softest silk, and he was tired in every fiber of his being, but nevertheless Rainsford could not quiet his brain with the opiate of sleep. He lay, eyes wide open. Once he thought he heard stealthy steps in the corridor outside his room. He sought to throw open the

2. Probably Nicholas II (1868–1918), who was overthrown by the Revolution and executed; "White" designates those opposed to the Communists, or "Reds."   3. Paris theater and music hall.

door; it would not open. He went to the window and looked out. His room was high up in one of the towers. The lights of the château were out now; and it was dark and silent, but there was a fragment of sallow moon, and by its wan light he could see, dimly, the courtyard; there, weaving in and out in the pattern of shadow, were black, noiseless forms; the hounds heard him at the window and looked up, expectantly, with their green eyes. Rainsford went back to bed and lay down. By many methods he tried to put himself to sleep. He had achieved a doze when, just as morning began to come, he heard, far off in the jungle, the faint report of a pistol.

General Zaroff did not appear until luncheon. He was dressed faultlessly in the tweeds of a country squire. He was solicitous about the state of Rainsford's health.

"As for me," sighed the general, "I do not feel so well. I am worried, Mr. Rainsford. Last night I detected traces of my old complaint."

To Rainsford's questioning glance the general said: "Ennui. Boredom." 150

Then, taking a second helping of *crêpes suzette*, the general explained: "The hunting was not good last night. The fellow lost his head. He made a straight trail that offered no problems at all. That's the trouble with these sailors; they have dull brains to begin with, and they do not know how to get about in the woods. They do excessively stupid and obvious things. It's most annoying. Will you have another glass of Chablis, Mr. Rainsford?"

"General," said Rainsford firmly, "I wish to leave this island at once."

The general raised his thickets of eyebrows; he seemed hurt. "But, my dear fellow," the general protested, "you've only just come. You've had no hunting—"

"I wish to go today," said Rainsford. He saw the dead black eyes of the general on him, studying him. General Zaroff's face suddenly brightened.

He filled Rainsford's glass with venerable Chablis from a dusty bottle. 155

"Tonight," said the general, "we will hunt—you and I."

Rainsford shook his head. "No, general," he said, "I will not hunt."

The general shrugged his shoulders and delicately ate a hothouse grape. "As you wish, my friend," he said. "The choice rests entirely with you. But may I not venture to suggest that you will find my idea of sport more diverting than Ivan's?"

He nodded toward the corner to where the giant stood, scowling, his thick arms crossed on his hogshead of a chest.

"You don't mean—" cried Rainsford. 160

"My dear fellow," said the general, "have I not told you I always mean what I say about hunting? This is really an inspiration. I drink to a foeman worthy of my steel—at last."

The general raised his glass, but Rainsford sat staring at him.

"You'll find this game worth playing," the general said enthusiastically. "Your brain against mine. Your woodcraft against mine. Your strength and stamina against mine. Outdoor chess! And the stake is not without value, eh?"

"And if I win—" began Rainsford huskily.

165 "I'll cheerfully acknowledge myself defeated if I do not find you by midnight of the third day," said General Zaroff. "My sloop will place you on the mainland near a town."

The general read what Rainsford was thinking.

"Oh, you can trust me," said the Cossack. "I will give you my word as a gentleman and a sportsman. Of course you, in turn, must agree to say nothing of your visit here."

"I'll agree to nothing of the kind," said Rainsford.

"Oh," said the general, "in that case—But why discuss that now? Three days hence we can discuss it over a bottle of Veuve Cliquot,[4] unless—"

170 The general sipped his wine.

Then a businesslike air animated him. "Ivan," he said to Rainsford, "will supply you with hunting clothes, food, a knife. I suggest you wear moccasins; they leave a poorer trail. I suggest too that you avoid the big swamp in the southeast corner of the island. We call it Death Swamp. There's quicksand there. One foolish fellow tried it. The deplorable part of it was that Lazarus followed him. You can imagine my feelings, Mr. Rainsford. I loved Lazarus; he was the finest hound in my pack. Well, I must beg you to excuse me now. I always take a siesta after lunch. You'll hardly have time for a nap, I fear. You'll want to start, no doubt. I shall not follow till dusk. Hunting at night is so much more exciting than by day, don't you think? Au revoir, Mr. Rainsford, au revoir."

General Zaroff, with a deep, courtly bow, strolled from the room.

From another door came Ivan. Under one arm he carried khaki hunting clothes, a haversack of food, a leather sheath containing a long-bladed hunting knife; his right hand rested on a cocked revolver thrust in the crimson sash about his waist. . . .

Rainsford had fought his way through the bush for two hours. "I must keep my nerve. I must keep my nerve," he said through tight teeth.

175 He had not been entirely clear-headed when the château gates snapped shut behind him. His whole idea at first was to put distance between himself and General Zaroff, and, to this end, he had plunged along, spurred on by the sharp rowels of something very like panic. Now he had got a grip on himself, had stopped, and was taking stock of himself and the situation.

He saw that straight flight was futile; inevitably it would bring him face to face with the sea. He was in a picture with a frame of water, and his operations, clearly, must take place within that frame.

"I'll give him a trail to follow," muttered Rainsford, and he struck off from the rude paths he had been following into the trackless wilderness. He executed a series of intricate loops; he doubled on his trail again and again, recalling all the lore of the fox hunt, and all the dodges of the fox. Night found him leg-weary, with hands and face lashed by the branches, on a thickly wooded ridge. He knew it would be insane to blunder on through the dark, even if he had the strength. His need for rest was imperative and he thought: "I have played the

4. A fine champagne; Chablis, above, is a very dry white Burgundy table wine.

fox, now I must play the cat of the fable."[5] A big tree with a thick trunk and outspread branches was nearby, and, taking care to leave not the slightest mark, he climbed up into the crotch, and stretching out on one of the broad limbs, after a fashion, rested. Rest brought him new confidence and almost a feeling of security. Even so zealous a hunter as General Zaroff could not trace him there, he told himself; only the devil himself could follow that complicated trail through the jungle after dark. But, perhaps, the general was a devil—

An apprehensive night crawled slowly by like a wounded snake, and sleep did not visit Rainsford, although the silence of a dead world was on the jungle. Toward morning when a dingy gray was varnishing the sky, the cry of some startled bird focused Rainsford's attention in that direction. Something was coming through the bush, coming slowly, carefully, coming by the same winding way Rainsford had come. He flattened himself down on the limb, and through a screen of leaves almost as thick as tapestry, he watched. The thing that was approaching was a man.

It was General Zaroff. He made his way along with his eyes fixed in utmost concentration on the ground before him. He paused, almost beneath the tree, dropped to his knees and studied the ground. Rainsford's impulse was to hurl himself down like a panther, but he saw that the general's right hand held something metallic—a small automatic pistol.

The hunter shook his head several times, as if he were puzzled. Then he straightened up and took from his case one of his black cigarettes; its pungent incense-like smoke floated up to Rainsford's nostrils.

Rainsford held his breath. The general's eyes had left the ground and were traveling inch by inch up the tree. Rainsford froze there, every muscle tensed for a spring. But the sharp eyes of the hunter stopped before they reached the limb where Rainsford lay; a smile spread over his brown face. Very deliberately he blew a smoke ring into the air; then he turned his back on the tree and walked carelessly away, back along the trail he had come. The swish of the underbrush against his hunting boots grew fainter and fainter.

The pent-up air burst hotly from Rainsford's lungs. His first thought made him feel sick and numb. The general could follow a trail through the woods at night; he could follow an extremely difficult trail; he must have uncanny powers; only by the merest chance had the Cossack failed to see his quarry.

Rainsford's second thought was even more terrible. It sent a shudder of cold horror through his whole being. Why had the general smiled? Why had he turned back?

Rainsford did not want to believe what his reason told him was true, but the truth was as evident as the sun that had by now pushed through the morning mists. The general was playing with him! The general was saving him for another day's sport! The Cossack was the cat; he was the mouse.[6] Then it was that Rainsford knew the full meaning of terror.

180

5. The fox boasts of his many tricks to elude the hounds; the cat responds he knows only one—to climb the nearest tree—but that this is worth more than all the fox's tricks.   6. A cat, sure of his prey, plays with a mouse before killing him.

185   "I will not lose my nerve. I will not."

He slid down the tree, and struck off again into the woods. His face was set and he forced the machinery of his mind to function. Three hundred yards from his hiding place he stopped where a huge dead tree leaned precariously on a smaller, living one. Throwing off his sack of food, Rainsford took his knife from its sheath and began to work with all his energy.

The job was finished at last, and he threw himself down behind a fallen log a hundred feet away. He did not have to wait long. The cat was coming again to play with the mouse.

Following the trail with the sureness of a bloodhound, came General Zaroff. Nothing escaped those searching black eyes, no crushed blade of grass, no bent twig, no mark, no matter how faint, in the moss. So intent was the Cossack on his stalking that he was upon the thing Rainsford had made before he saw it. His foot touched the protruding bough that was the trigger. Even as he touched it, the general sensed his danger and leaped back with the agility of an ape. But he was not quite quick enough; the dead tree, delicately adjusted to rest on the cut living one, crashed down and struck the general a glancing blow on the shoulder as it fell; but for his alertness, he must have been smashed beneath it. He staggered, but he did not fall; nor did he drop his revolver. He stood there, rubbing his injured shoulder, and Rainsford, with fear again gripping his heart, heard the general's mocking laugh ring through the jungle.

"Rainsford," called the general, "if you are within sound of my voice, as I suppose you are, let me congratulate you. Not many men know how to make a Malay man-catcher. Luckily, for me, I too have hunted in Malacca. You are proving interesting, Mr. Rainsford. I am going now to have my wound dressed; it's only a slight one. But I shall be back. I shall be back."

190   When the general, nursing his bruised shoulder, had gone, Rainsford took up his flight again. It was flight now, a desperate, hopeless flight, that carried him on for some hours. Dusk came, then darkness, and still he pressed on. The ground grew softer under his moccasins; the vegetation grew ranker, denser; insects bit him savagely. Then, as he stepped forward, his foot sank into the ooze. He tried to wrench it back, but the muck sucked viciously at his foot as if it were a giant leech. With a violent effort, he tore his foot loose. He knew where he was now. Death Swamp and its quicksand.

His hands were tight closed as if his nerve were something tangible that someone in the darkness was trying to tear from his grip. The softness of the earth had given him an idea. He stepped back from the quicksand a dozen feet or so and, like some huge prehistoric beaver, he began to dig.

Rainsford had dug himself in in France[7] when a second's delay meant death. That had been a placid pastime compared to his digging now. The pit grew deeper; when it was above his shoulders, he climbed out and from some hard saplings cut stakes and sharpened them to a fine point. These stakes he planted in the bottom of the pit with the points sticking up. With flying fingers he wove

---

7. During World War I he had quickly dug a hole or trench to shelter himself from exploding shells, bullets, etc.

a rough carpet of weeds and branches and with it he covered the mouth of the pit. Then, wet with sweat and aching with tiredness, he crouched behind the stump of a lightning-charred tree.

He knew his pursuer was coming; he heard the padding sound of feet on the soft earth, and the night breeze brought him the perfume of the general's cigarette. It seemed to Rainsford that the general was coming with unusual swiftness; he was not feeling his way along, foot by foot. Rainsford, crouching there, could not see the general, nor could he see the pit. He lived a year in a minute. Then he felt an impulse to cry aloud with joy, for he heard the sharp crackle of the breaking branches as the cover of the pit gave way; he heard the sharp scream of pain as the pointed stakes found their mark. He leaped up from his place of concealment. Then he cowered back. Three feet from the pit a man was standing, with an electric torch in his hand.

"You've done well, Rainsford," the voice of the general called. "Your Burmese tiger pit has claimed one of my best dogs. Again you score. I think, Mr. Rainsford, I'll see what you can do against my whole pack. I'm going home for a rest now. Thank you for a most amusing evening."

At daybreak Rainsford, lying near the swamp, was awakened by a sound that made him know that he had new things to learn about fear. It was a distant sound, faint and wavering, but he knew it. It was the baying of a pack of hounds.

Rainsford knew he could do one of two things. He could stay where he was and wait. That was suicide. He could flee. That was postponing the inevitable. For a moment he stood there, thinking. An idea that held a wild chance came to him, and, tightening his belt, he headed away from the swamp.

The baying of the hounds drew nearer, then still nearer, nearer, ever nearer. On a ridge Rainsford climbed a tree. Down a watercourse, not a quarter of a mile away, he could see the bush moving. Straining his eyes, he saw the lean figure of General Zaroff; just ahead of him Rainsford made out another figure whose wide shoulders surged through the tall jungle weeds; it was the giant Ivan, and he seemed pulled forward by some unseen force; Rainsford knew that Ivan must be holding the pack in leash.

They would be on him any minute now. His mind worked frantically. He thought of a native trick he had learned in Uganda. He slid down the tree. He caught hold of a springy young sapling and to it he fastened his hunting knife, with the blade pointing down the trail; with a bit of wild grapevine he tied back the sapling. Then he ran for his life. The hounds raised their voices as they hit the fresh scent. Rainsford knew now how an animal at bay feels.

He had to stop to get his breath. The baying of the hounds stopped abruptly, and Rainsford's heart stopped too. They must have reached the knife.

He shinnied excitedly up a tree and looked back. His pursuers had stopped. But the hope that was in Rainsford's brain when he climbed died, for he saw in the shallow valley that General Zaroff was still on his feet. But Ivan was not. The knife, driven by the recoil of the springing tree, had not wholly failed.

Rainsford had hardly tumbled to the ground when the pack took up the cry again.

"Nerve, nerve, nerve!" he panted, as he dashed along. A blue gap showed between the trees dead ahead. Ever nearer drew the hounds. Rainsford forced himself on toward that gap. He reached it. It was the shore of the sea. Across a cove he could see the gloomy gray stone of the château. Twenty feet below him the sea rumbled and hissed. Rainsford hesitated. He heard the hounds. Then he leaped far out into the sea. . . .

When the general and his pack reached the place by the sea, the Cossack stopped. For some minutes he stood regarding the blue-green expanse of water. He shrugged his shoulders. Then he sat down, took a drink of brandy from a silver flask, lit a perfumed cigarette, and hummed a bit from "Madame Butterfly."[8]

General Zaroff had an exceedingly good dinner in his great paneled dining hall that evening. With it he had a bottle of Pol Roger and half a bottle of Chambertin.[9] Two slight annoyances kept him from perfect enjoyment. One was the thought that it would be difficult to replace Ivan; the other was that his quarry had escaped him; of course the American hadn't played the game—so thought the general as he tasted his after-dinner liqueur. In his library he read, to soothe himself, from the works of Marcus Aurelius.[1] At ten he went up to his bedroom. He was deliciously tired, he said to himself, as he locked himself in. There was a little moonlight so, before turning on his light, he went to the window and looked down at the courtyard. He could see the great hounds, and he called: "Better luck another time," to them. Then he switched on the light.

205   A man, who had been hiding in the curtains of the bed, was standing there.

"Rainsford!" screamed the general. "How in God's name did you get here?"

"Swam," said Rainsford. "I found it quicker than walking through the jungle."

The general sucked in his breath and smiled. "I congratulate you," he said. "You have won the game."

Rainsford did not smile. "I am still a beast at bay," he said, in a low, hoarse voice. "Get ready, General Zaroff."

210   The general made one of his deepest bows. "I see," he said. "Splendid! One of us is to furnish a repast for the hounds. The other will sleep in this very excellent bed. On guard, Rainsford. . . ."

He had never slept in a better bed, Rainsford decided.

1924

A good many readers like "The Most Dangerous Game." In classes I teach it is often a favorite, or even *the* favorite. Yet other readers have urged me to

8. Opera (1904) by Giacomo Puccini (1858–1924).   9. Pol Roger is champagne, Chambertin is a highly esteemed red Burgundy wine.   1. Roman emperor (A.D. 161–180), Stoic philosopher, writer, and humanitarian.

drop this story from the anthology because it is "unworthy," not really Literature. Is this simply ignorance on the one hand or snobbery on the other?

Here are two brief papers, somewhat like those a student might write in class, the first supporting "The Most Dangerous Game," the second responding to the first.

Why "The Most Dangerous Game" Is Good Literature

Thaddeus Smith

"The Most Dangerous Game" by Richard Connell is exciting. Things happen in it, and you want to read on because you want to find out what will happen next and how it will come out. Too often the things we need to read for class are boring, nothing happens, or, if something does happen, it happens inside somebody's head. But here things happen outside; I mean, there's real action.

Not only is there action, but that action is important, a real life-and-death struggle. This story is not just about whether somebody used the wrong fork or had a good time or didn't have a good time at a party.

The good guy wins, the story ends happily, and when you finish reading it, you feel good about things. Sometimes in class I think only real downers are supposed to be good stories, like life always has to be full of gloom and doom. Now all of us die sooner or later, of course, but that's only the end, a minute or a month or something, and there's all the rest of the time when we're not dead and not really in the process of dying. That's life, and that's what a good story should be about.

"The Most Dangerous Game" is fun to read. Sometimes I think that what are supposed to be the "good" stories are the ones I don't like. But popular stories can be good: there have been several movies made of "The Most Dangerous Game" and several stories adapted from it with just a few things changed. But, I'm told, the world of literature isn't a democracy--you don't vote for what's Literature. When I say I like Stephen King--and I'm sure not the only one, because he sells lots and lots of books--teachers or English majors say wait fifty years and see if his stuff is still around.

Well, "The Most Dangerous Game" is over sixty-five years old, older than at least three-quarters of the stories in this anthology, so it's stood the test of time, whatever that is.

Why "The Most Dangerous Game"
Is Not Good Literature

Sara Rosen

Though "The Most Dangerous Game" may be "a good read," at least the first time through, and I have nothing against someone reading it or even liking it in its way, I don't think it ought to

be in *The Norton Introduction to Literature*. Being
in the anthology gives it a status it does not
deserve. It makes it the subject of serious study
by college students, and college students ought
to be engaged in more challenging and thought-
provoking reading material, even if outside of
class they are reading Stephen King and the likes
of "The Most Dangerous Game."

Though it's true that a life-and-death
struggle is important—for the person involved--it
has no relevance for us, no outreach: it does not
relate to our experience nor does it really
illuminate anything about our experience or the
way we look at life. I don't mean that a worthy
story must have a "message," necessarily, but it
should have a "theme," something that explores a
significant area of human experience and
understanding.

I admit that there is something like suspense
in Connell's story, but that is not enough.
There's nothing wrong with suspense in itself--
expectations of one sort or another are part of
every good work--but here the suspense is
manipulated at the price of consistency. Note how
we're seeing things from Rainsford's perspective
(not through his eyes and mind exactly, not in
the first person, but over his shoulder) until
near the end when he leaps into the sea. At that
point, when we're supposed to want most to know
what happens next, there's the more or less

artificial suspense added by three dots and a
break on the page, and then we're not with
Rainsford but Zaroff, just to make us wonder if
Rainsford did indeed die. It's a cheap trick.
Besides, don't we know from the beginning that in
this kind of story the hero never dies, so isn't
the suspense really phony? What's wrong with
stories like this is the unrealistic, wish-
fulfilling way it looks at reality: it tells us
that good guys always finish first; they win
because they're good.

While good guys do sometimes finish first, and
plenty of good stories end happily, more or less,
like "Sonny Blues," and "The Secret Sharer," life
is not always like that, and this victory seems a
little too easy.

Finally, Rainsford has no "character"; he's
just a good guy because he's an American and his
life is threatened by a bad guy who's a Russian;
and the bad guy is just a bad guy, with no
redeeming human qualities--it's all about guys in
white hats versus guys in black hats.

These are not polished and conclusive arguments, of course. Had the
writer of the first paper read the response, he might have had more to say.
About the alleged absence of theme in "The Most Dangerous Game," for
example:

There is a theme in Connell's story. It is a
very important one, one that you have to think

about, and that some people will agree with,
though it is not a theme that you necessarily
have to agree with in order to appreciate the
story. Notice it is set just after the Russian
Revolution, and Zaroff (the "son of the czar") is
a cruel aristocrat from the czarist regime who
believes in power, believes that might-makes-
right, and believes some people are better than
others and have a right to do what they will with
their "inferiors," even kill them for pleasure.
Rainsford at the beginning is a hunter/exploiter,
never thinking what the "inferior" beast, the
hunted, feels like. Having been put in the place
of the hunted he will no doubt learn to have more
reverence for life, more sympathy for the
underdog.

The opponent, hearing this contention that there is a significant theme in the story, might well respond that the theme as described is too pat, and that it is presented through too convenient (as well as unbelievable) a situation, too much of a set-up.

This, then, is only one example of the kinds of arguments readers can use to support their judgments. We need to go on from there to consider what we read for ("a good read," "an illumination of human life and experience"), and what we mean by "the reader," the one judging the story to be "good."

Let us assume for the moment that "the readers" can be represented roughly by the people in this class—you, those who agree you about stories, and those who, though they are more or less like you, do not always agree with you. We said earlier that if our appreciation and understanding of literature is to grow, and if we are not to merely accept what those considered "authorities" say is good or great, we must learn to isolate, analyze, and articulate what *we* like (or dislike) in a story. And, we said, we must listen to those with other responses as they articulate their reasons.

Now for the test. The next story is by a Nobel laureate and much revered writer, William Faulkner, and this is one of his most admired stories. It has some of the same attractive qualities as "The Most Dangerous Game"—conflict, action, suspense—but there are those who find it critically flawed. Regardless of which side we are on, we must take seriously both those who have reservations and questions and the author's and the story's established reputation. But first, we must read it.

WILLIAM FAULKNER

Barn Burning

The store in which the Justice of the Peace's court was sitting smelled of cheese. The boy, crouched on his nail keg at the back of the crowded room, knew he smelled cheese, and more: from where he sat he could see the ranked shelves close-packed with the solid, squat, dynamic shapes of tin cans whose labels his stomach read, not from the lettering which meant nothing to his mind but from the scarlet devils and the silver curve of fish—this, the cheese which he knew he smelled and the hermetic meat which his intestines believed he smelled coming in intermittent gusts momentary and brief between the other constant one, the smell and sense just a little of fear because mostly of despair and grief, the old fierce pull of blood. He could not see the table where the Justice sat and before which his father and his father's enemy (*our enemy* he thought in that despair; *ourn! mine and hisn both! He's my father!*) stood, but he could hear them, the two of them that is, because his father had said no word yet:

"But what proof have you, Mr. Harris?"

"I told you. The hog got into my corn. I caught it up and sent it back to him. He had no fence that would hold it. I told him so, warned him. The next time I put the hog in my pen. When he came to get it I gave him enough wire to patch up his pen. The next time I put the hog up and kept it. I rode down to his house and saw the wire I gave him still rolled on to the spool in his yard. I told him he could have the hog when he paid me a dollar pound fee. That evening a nigger came with the dollar and got the hog. He was a strange nigger. He said, 'He say to tell you wood and hay kin burn.' I said, 'What?' 'That whut he say to tell you,' the nigger said. 'Wood and hay kin burn.' That night my barn burned. I got the stock out but I lost the barn."

"Where is the nigger? Have you got him?"

"He was a strange nigger, I tell you. I don't know what became of him."

"But that's not proof. Don't you see that's not proof?"

"Get that boy up here. He knows." For a moment the boy thought too that the man meant his older brother until Harris said, "Not him. The little one. The boy," and, crouching, small for his age, small and wiry like his father, in patched and faded jeans even too small for him, with straight, uncombed, brown hair and eyes gray and wild as storm scud, he saw the men between himself and the table part and become a lane of grim faces, at the end of which he saw the Justice, a shabby, collarless, graying man in spectacles, beckoning him. He felt no floor under his bare feet; he seemed to walk beneath the palpable weight of the grim turning faces. His father, stiff in his black Sunday coat donned not for the trial but for the moving, did not even look at him. *He aims for me to lie,* he thought, again with that frantic grief and despair. *And I will have to do hit.*

"What's your name, boy?" the Justice said.

"Colonel Sartoris Snopes," the boy whispered.

"Hey?" the Justice said. "Talk louder. Colonel Sartoris? I reckon anybody named for Colonel Sartoris in this country can't help but tell the truth, can they?" The boy said nothing. *Enemy! Enemy!* he thought; for a moment he could not even see, could not see that the Justice's face was kindly nor discern that his voice was troubled when he spoke to the man named Harris: "Do you want me to question this boy?" But he could hear, and during those subsequent long seconds while there was absolutely no sound in the crowded little room save that of quiet and intent breathing it was as if he had swung outward at the end of a grape vine, over a ravine, and at the top of the swing had been caught in a prolonged instant of mesmerized gravity, weightless in time.

"No!" Harris said violently, explosively. "Damnation! Send him out of here!" Now time, the fluid world, rushed beneath him again, the voices coming to him again through the smell of cheese and sealed meat, the fear and despair and the old grief of blood:

"This case is closed. I can't find against you, Snopes, but I can give you advice. Leave this country and don't come back to it."

His father spoke for the first time, his voice cold and harsh, level, without emphasis: "I aim to. I don't figure to stay in a country among people who . . ." he said something unprintable and vile, addressed to no one.

"That'll do," the Justice said. "Take your wagon and get out of this country before dark. Case dismissed."

His father turned, and he followed the stiff black coat, the wiry figure walking a little stiffly from where a Confederate provost's man's[1] musket ball had taken him in the heel on a stolen horse thirty years ago, followed the two backs now, since his older brother had appeared from somewhere in the crowd, no taller than the father but thicker, chewing tobacco steadily, between the two lines of grim-faced men and out of the store and across the worn gallery and down the sagging steps and among the dogs and half-grown boys in the mild May dust, where as he passed a voice hissed:

"Barn burner!"

Again he could not see, whirling; there was a face in a red haze, moonlike, bigger than the full moon, the owner of it half again his size, he leaping in the red haze toward the face, feeling no blow, feeling no shock when his head struck the earth, scrabbling up and leaping again, feeling no blow this time either and tasting no blood, scrabbling up to see the other boy in full flight and himself already leaping into pursuit as his father's hand jerked him back, the harsh, cold voice speaking above him: "Go get in the wagon."

It stood in a grove of locusts and mulberries across the road. His two hulking sisters in their Sunday dresses and his mother and her sister in calico and sun-

1. Military policeman.

bonnets were already in it, sitting on and among the sorry residue of the dozen and more movings which even the boy could remember—the battered stove, the broken beds and chairs, the clock inlaid with mother-of-pearl, which would not run, stopped at some fourteen minutes past two o'clock of a dead and forgotten day and time, which had been his mother's dowry. She was crying, though when she saw him she drew her sleeve across her face and began to descend from the wagon. "Get back," the father said.

"He's hurt. I got to get some water and wash his . . ."

"Get back in the wagon," his father said. He got in too, over the tail-gate. His father mounted to the seat where the older brother already sat and struck the gaunt mules two savage blows with the peeled willow, but without heat. It was not even sadistic; it was exactly that same quality which in later years would cause his descendants to overrun the engine before putting a motor car into motion, striking and reining back in the same movement. The wagon went on, the store with its quiet crowd of grimly watching men dropped behind; a curve in the road hid it. *Forever* he thought. *Maybe he's done satisfied now, now that he has* . . . stopping himself, not to say it aloud even to himself. His mother's hand touched his shoulder.

"Does hit hurt?" she said.

"Naw," he said. "Hit don't hurt. Lemme be."

"Can't you wipe some of the blood off before hit dries?"

"I'll wash to-night," he said. "Lemme be, I tell you."

The wagon went on. He did not know where they were going. None of them ever did or ever asked, because it was always somewhere, always a house of sorts waiting for them a day or two days or even three days away. Likely his father had already arranged to make a crop on another farm before he . . . Again he had to stop himself. He (the father) always did. There was something about his wolf-like independence and even courage when the advantage was at least neutral which impressed strangers, as if they got from his latent ravening ferocity not so much a sense of dependability as a feeling that his ferocious conviction in the rightness of his own actions would be of advantage to all whose interest lay with his.

That night they camped, in a grove of oaks and beeches where a spring ran. The nights were still cool and they had a fire against it, of a rail lifted from a nearby fence and cut into lengths—a small fire, neat, niggard almost, a shrewd fire; such fires were his father's habit and custom always, even in freezing weather. Older, the boy might have remarked this and wondered why not a big one; why should not a man who had not only seen the waste and extravagance of war, but who had in his blood an inherent voracious prodigality with material not his own, have burned everything in sight? Then he might have gone a step farther and thought that that was the reason: that niggard blaze was the living fruit of nights passed during those four years in the woods hiding from all men, blue or gray,[2] with his strings of horses (captured horses, he called them). And older still, he might have divined the true reason: that the element of fire spoke

---

2. The colors of the Union and Confederate Civil War (1861–65) uniforms, respectively.

to some deep mainspring of his father's being, as the element of steel or of powder spoke to other men, as the one weapon for the preservation of integrity, else breath were not worth the breathing, and hence to be regarded with respect and used with discretion.

But he did not think this now and he had seen those same niggard blazes all his life. He merely ate his supper beside it and was already half asleep over his iron plate when his father called him, and once more he followed the stiff back, the stiff and ruthless limp, up the slope and on to the starlit road where, turning, he could see his father against the stars but without face or depth—a shape black, flat, and bloodless as though cut from tin in the iron folds of the frockcoat which had not been made for him, the voice harsh like tin and without heat like tin:

"You were fixing to tell them. You would have told him." He didn't answer. His father struck him with the flat of his hand on the side of the head, hard but without heat, exactly as he had struck the two mules at the store, exactly as he would strike either of them with any stick in order to kill a horse fly, his voice still without heat or anger: "You're getting to be a man. You got to learn. You got to learn to stick to your own blood or you ain't going to have any blood to stick to you. Do you think either of them, any man there this morning, would? Don't you know all they wanted was a chance to get at me because they knew I had them beat? Eh?" Later, twenty years later, he was to tell himself, "If I had said they wanted only truth, justice, he would have hit me again." But now he said nothing. He was not crying. He just stood there. "Answer me," his father said.

"Yes," he whispered. His father turned.

"Get on to bed. We'll be there tomorrow."   30

Tomorrow they were there. In the early afternoon the wagon stopped before a paintless two-room house identical almost with the dozen others it had stopped before even in the boy's ten years, and again, as on the other dozen occasions, his mother and aunt got down and began to unload the wagon, although his two sisters and his father and brother had not moved.

"Likely hit ain't fitten for hawgs," one of the sisters said.

"Nevertheless, fit it will and you'll hog it and like it," his father said. "Get out of them chairs and help your Ma unload."

The two sisters got down, big, bovine, in a flutter of cheap ribbons; one of them drew from the jumbled wagon bed a battered lantern, the other a worn broom. His father handed the reins to the older son and began to climb stiffly over the wheel. "When they get unloaded, take the team to the barn and feed them." Then he said, and at first the boy thought he was still speaking to his brother: "Come with me."

"Me?" he said.   35

"Yes," his father said. "You."

"Abner," his mother said. His father paused and looked back—the harsh level stare beneath the shaggy, graying, irascible brows.

"I reckon I'll have a word with the man that aims to begin to-morrow owning me body and soul for the next eight months."

They went back up the road. A week ago—or before last night, that is—he would have asked where they were going, but not now. His father had struck him before last night but never before had he paused afterward to explain why; it was as if the blow and the following calm, outrageous voice still rang, repercussed, divulging nothing to him save the terrible handicap of being young, the light weight of his few years, just heavy enough to prevent his soaring free of the world as it seemed to be ordered but not heavy enough to keep him footed solid in it, to resist it and try to change the course of its events.

40

Presently he could see the grove of oaks and cedars and the other flowering trees and shrubs, where the house would be, though not the house yet. They walked beside a fence massed with honeysuckle and Cherokee roses and came to a gate swinging open between two brick pillars, and now, beyond a sweep of drive, he saw the house for the first time and at that instant he forgot his father and the terror and despair both, and even when he remembered his father again (who had not stopped) the terror and despair did not return. Because, for all the twelve movings, they had sojourned until now in a poor country, a land of small farms and fields and houses, and he had never seen a house like this before. *Hit's big as a courthouse* he thought quietly, with a surge of peace and joy whose reason he could not have thought into words, being too young for that: *They are safe from him. People whose lives are a part of this peace and dignity are beyond his touch, he no more to them than a buzzing wasp: capable of stinging for a little moment but that's all; the spell of this peace and dignity rendering even the barns and stable and cribs which belong to it impervious to the puny flames he might contrive* . . . this, the peace and joy, ebbing for an instant as he looked again at the stiff black back, the stiff and implacable limp of the figure which was not dwarfed by the house, for the reason that it had never looked big anywhere and which now, against the serene columned backdrop, had more than ever that impervious quality of something cut ruthlessly from tin, depthless, as though, sidewise to the sun, it would cast no shadow. Watching him, the boy remarked the absolutely undeviating course which his father held and saw the stiff foot come squarely down in a pile of fresh droppings where a horse had stood in the drive and which his father could have avoided by a simple change of stride. But it ebbed only for a moment, though he could not have thought this into words either, walking on in the spell of the house, which he could even want but without envy, without sorrow, certainly never with that ravening and jealous rage which unknown to him walked in the ironlike black coat before him: *Maybe he will feel it too. Maybe it will even change him now from what maybe he couldn't help but be.*

They crossed the portico. Now he could hear his father's stiff foot as it came down on the boards with clocklike finality, a sound out of all proportion to the displacement of the body it bore and which was not dwarfed either by the white door before it, as though it had attained to a sort of vicious and ravening minimum not to be dwarfed by anything—the flat, wide, black hat, the formal coat of broadcloth which had once been black but which had now that friction-glazed greenish cast of the bodies of old house flies, the lifted sleeve which was too large, the lifted hand like a curled claw. The door opened so promptly that the boy knew the Negro must have been watching them all the time, an old man with neat grizzled hair, in a linen jacket, who stood barring the door with his body, saying, "Wipe yo foots, white man, fo you come in here. Major ain't home nohow."

"Get out of my way, nigger," his father said, without heat too, flinging the door back and the Negro also and entering, his hat still on his head. And now the boy saw the prints of the stiff foot on the doorjamb and saw them appear on the pale rug behind the machinelike deliberation of the foot which seemed to bear (or transmit) twice the weight which the body compassed. The Negro was shouting "Miss Lula! Miss Lula!" somewhere behind them, then the boy, deluged as though by a warm wave by a suave turn of carpeted stair and a pendant glitter of chandeliers and a mute gleam of gold frames, heard the swift feet and saw her too, a lady—perhaps he had never seen her like before either—in a gray, smooth gown with lace at the throat and an apron tied at the waist and the sleeves turned back, wiping cake or biscuit dough from her hands with a towel as she came up the hall, looking not at his father at all but at the tracks on the blond rug with an expression of incredulous amazement.

"I tried," the Negro cried. "I tole him to . . ."

"Will you please go away?" she said in a shaking voice. "Major de Spain is not at home. Will you please go away?"

His father had not spoken again. He did not speak again. He did not even look at her. He just stood stiff in the center of the rug, in his hat, the shaggy iron-gray brows twitching slightly above the pebble-colored eyes as he appeared to examine the house with brief deliberation. Then with the same deliberation he turned; the boy watched him pivot on the good leg and saw the stiff foot drag round the arc of the turning, leaving a final long and fading smear. His father never looked at it, he never once looked down at the rug. The Negro held the door. It closed behind them, upon the hysteric and indistinguishable woman-wail. His father stopped at the top of the steps and scraped his boot clean on the edge of it. At the gate he stopped again. He stood for a moment, planted stiffly on the stiff foot, looking back at the house. "Pretty and white, ain't it?" he said. "That's sweat. Nigger sweat. Maybe it ain't white enough yet to suit him. Maybe he wants to mix some white sweat with it."

Two hours later the boy was chopping wood behind the house within which his mother and aunt and the two sisters (the mother and aunt, not the two girls, he knew that; even at this distance and muffled by walls the flat loud voices of the two girls emanated an incorrigible idle inertia) were setting up the stove to prepare a meal, when he heard the hooves and saw the linen-clad man on a fine sorrel mare, whom he recognized even before he saw the rolled rug in front of the Negro youth following on a fat bay carriage horse—a suffused, angry face vanishing, still at full gallop, beyond the corner of the house where his father and brother were sitting in the two tilted chairs; and a moment later, almost before he could have put the axe down, he heard the hooves again and watched the sorrel mare go back out of the yard, already galloping again. Then his father began to shout one of the sisters' names, who presently emerged backward from the kitchen door dragging the rolled rug along the ground by one end while the

45

other sister walked behind it.

"If you ain't going to tote, go on and set up the wash pot," the first said.

"You, Sarty!" the second shouted. "Set up the wash pot!" His father appeared at the door, framed against that shabbiness, as he had been against that other bland perfection, impervious to either, the mother's anxious face at his shoulder. "Go on," the father said. "Pick it up." The two sisters stooped, broad, lethargic; stooping, they presented an incredible expanse of pale cloth and a flutter of tawdry ribbons.

50 "If I thought enough of a rug to have to git hit all the way from France I wouldn't keep hit where folks coming in would have to tromp on hit," the first said. They raised the rug.

"Abner," the mother said. "Let me do it."

"You go back and git dinner," his father said. "I'll tend to this."

From the woodpile through the rest of the afternoon the boy watched them, the rug spread flat in the dust beside the bubbling wash-pot, the two sisters stooping over it with that profound and lethargic reluctance, while the father stood over them in turn, implacable and grim, driving them though never raising his voice again. He could smell the harsh homemade lye they were using; he saw his mother come to the door once and look toward them with an expression not anxious now but very like despair; he saw his father turn, and he fell to with the axe and saw from the corner of his eye his father raise from the ground a flattish fragment of field stone and examine it and return to the pot, and this time his mother actually spoke: "Abner. Abner. Please don't. Please, Abner."

Then he was done too. It was dusk; the whippoorwills had already begun. He could smell coffee from the room where they would presently eat the cold food remaining from the mid-afternoon meal, though when he entered the house he realized they were having coffee again probably because there was a fire on the hearth, before which the rug now lay spread over the backs of the two chairs. The tracks of his father's foot were gone. Where they had been were now long, water-cloudy scoriations resembling the sporadic course of a Lilliputian mowing machine.

55 It still hung there while they ate the cold food and then went to bed, scattered without order or claim up and down the two rooms, his mother in one bed, where his father would later lie, the older brother in the other, himself, the aunt, and the two sisters on pallets on the floor. But his father was not in bed yet. The last thing the boy remembered was the depthless, harsh silhouette of the hat and coat bending over the rug and it seemed to him that he had not even closed his eyes when the silhouette was standing over him, the fire almost dead behind it, the stiff foot prodding him awake. "Catch up the mule," his father said.

When he returned with the mule his father was standing in the black door, the rolled rug over his shoulder. "Ain't you going to ride?" he said.

"No. Give me your foot."

He bent his knee into his father's hand, the wiry, surprising power flowed smoothly, rising, he rising with it, on to the mule's bare back (they had owned a saddle once; the boy could remember it though not when or where) and with the same effortlessness his father swung the rug up in front of him. Now in the starlight they retraced the afternoon's path, up the dusty road rife with honeysuckle, through the gate and up the black tunnel of the drive to the lightless house, where he sat on the mule and felt the rough warp of the rug drag across his thighs and vanish.

"Don't you want me to help?" he whispered. His father did not answer and now he heard again that stiff foot striking the hollow portico with that wooden and clocklike deliberation, that outrageous overstatement of the weight it carried. The rug, hunched, not flung (the boy could tell that even in the darkness) from his father's shoulder struck the angle of wall and floor with a sound unbelievably loud, thunderous, then the foot again, unhurried and enormous; a light came on in the house and the boy sat, tense, breathing steadily and quietly and just a little fast, though the foot itself did not increase its beat at all, descending the steps now; now the boy could see him.

"Don't you want to ride now?" he whispered. "We kin both ride now," the light within the house altering now, flaring up and sinking. *He's coming down the stairs now,* he thought. He had already ridden the mule up beside the horse block; presently his father was up behind him and he doubled the reins over and slashed the mule across the neck, but before the animal could begin to trot the hard, thin arm came round him, the hard, knotted hand jerking the mule back to a walk.

In the first red rays of the sun they were in the lot, putting plow gear on the mules. This time the sorrel mare was in the lot before he heard it at all, the rider collarless and even bareheaded, trembling, speaking in a shaking voice as the woman in the house had done, his father merely looking up once before stooping again to the hame he was buckling, so that the man on the mare spoke to his stooping back:

"You must realize you have ruined that rug. Wasn't there anybody here, any of your women . . ." he ceased, shaking, the boy watching him, the older brother leaning now in the stable door, chewing, blinking slowly and steadily at nothing apparently. "It cost a hundred dollars. But you never had a hundred dollars. You never will. So I'm going to charge you twenty bushels of corn against your crop. I'll add it in your contract and when you come to the commissary you can sign it. That won't keep Mrs. de Spain quiet but maybe it will teach you to wipe your feet off before you enter her house again."

Then he was gone. The boy looked at his father, who still had not spoken or even looked up again, who was now adjusting the logger-head in the hame.

"Pap," he said. His father looked at him—the inscrutable face, the shaggy brows beneath which the gray eyes glinted coldly. Suddenly the boy went toward him, fast, stopping as suddenly. "You done the best you could!" he cried. "If he wanted hit done different why didn't he wait and tell you how? He won't git no twenty bushels! He won't git none! We'll gether hit and hide hit! I kin watch . . ."

"Did you put the cutter back in that straight stock like I told you?"

"No, sir," he said.

"Then go do it."

60

65

That was Wednesday. During the rest of that week he worked steadily, at what was within his scope and some which was beyond it, with an industry that did not need to be driven nor even commanded twice; he had this from his mother, with the difference that some at least of what he did he liked to do, such as splitting wood with the half-size axe which his mother and aunt had earned, or saved money somehow, to present him with at Christmas. In company with the two older women (and on one afternoon, even one of the sisters), he built pens for the shoat and the cow which were a part of his father's contract with the landlord, and one afternoon, his father being absent, gone somewhere on one of the mules, he went to the field.

They were running a middle buster[3] now, his brother holding the plow straight while he handled the reins, and walking beside the straining mule, the rich black soil shearing cool and damp against his bare ankles, he thought *Maybe this is the end of it. Maybe even that twenty bushels that seems hard to have to pay for just a rug will be a cheap price for him to stop forever and always from being what he used to be*; thinking, dreaming now, so that his brother had to speak sharply to him to mind the mule: *Maybe he even won't collect the twenty bushels. Maybe it will all add up and balance and vanish—corn, rug, fire; the terror and grief, the being pulled two ways like between two teams of horses— gone, done with for ever and ever.*

Then it was Saturday; he looked up from beneath the mule he was harnessing and saw his father in the black coat and hat. "Not that," his father said. "The wagon gear." And then, two hours later, sitting in the wagon bed behind his father and brother on the seat, the wagon accomplished a final curve, and he saw the weathered paintless store with its tattered tobacco- and patent-medicine posters and the tethered wagons and saddle animals below the gallery. He mounted the gnawed steps behind his father and brother, and there again was the lane of quiet, watching faces for the three of them to walk through. He saw the man in spectacles sitting at the plank table and he did not need to be told this was a Justice of the Peace; he sent one glare of fierce, exultant, partisan defiance at the man in collar and cravat now, whom he had seen but twice before in his life, and that on a galloping horse, who now wore on his face an expression not of rage but of amazed unbelief which the boy could not have known was at the incredible circumstance of being sued by one of his own tenants, and came and stood against his father and cried at the Justice: "He ain't done it! He ain't burnt . . ."

"Go back to the wagon," his father said.

"Burnt?" the Justice said. "Do I understand this rug was burned too?"

"Does anybody here claim it was?" his father said. "Go back to the wagon." But he did not, he merely retreated to the rear of the room, crowded as that other had been, but not to sit down this time, instead, to stand pressing among the motionless bodies, listening to the voices:

"And you claim twenty bushels of corn is too high for the damage you did to the rug?"

---

3. A double moldboard plow that throws a ridge of earth both ways.

70

"He brought the rug to me and said he wanted the tracks washed out of it. I
washed the tracks out and took the rug back to him."

"But you didn't carry the rug back to him in the same condition it was in
before you made the tracks on it."

His father did not answer, and now for perhaps half a minute there was no
sound at all save that of breathing, the faint, steady suspiration of complete and
intent listening.

"You decline to answer that, Mr. Snopes?" Again his father did not answer.
"I'm going to find against you, Mr. Snopes. I'm going to find that you were
responsible for the injury to Major de Spain's rug and hold you liable for it. But
twenty bushels of corn seems a little high for a man in your circumstances to
have to pay. Major de Spain claims it cost a hundred dollars. October corn will
be worth about fifty cents. I figure that if Major de Spain can stand a ninety-five
dollar loss on something he paid cash for, you can stand a five-dollar loss you
haven't earned yet. I hold you in damages to Major de Spain to the amount of
ten bushels of corn over and above your contract with him, to be paid to him
out of your crop at gathering time. Court adjourned."

It had taken no time hardly, the morning was but half begun. He thought
they would return home and perhaps back to the field, since they were late, far
behind all other farmers. But instead his father passed on behind the wagon,
merely indicating with his hand for the older brother to follow with it, and
crossed the road toward the blacksmith shop opposite, pressing on after his
father, overtaking him, speaking, whispering up at the harsh, calm face beneath
the weathered hat: "He won't git no ten bushels neither. He won't git one. We'll
. . ." until his father glanced for an instant down at him, the face absolutely
calm, the grizzled eyebrows tangled above the cold eyes, the voice almost pleasant, almost gentle:

"You think so? Well, we'll wait till October anyway."

The matter of the wagon—the setting of a spoke or two and the tightening
of the tires—did not take long either, the business of the tires accomplished by
driving the wagon into the spring branch behind the shop and letting it stand
there, the mules nuzzling into the water from time to time, and the boy on the
seat with the idle reins, looking up the slope and through the sooty tunnel of
the shed where the slow hammer rang and where his father sat on an upended
cypress bolt, easily, either talking or listening, still sitting there when the boy
brought the dripping wagon up out of the branch and halted it before the door.

"Take them on to the shade and hitch," his father said. He did so and
returned. His father and the smith and a third man squatting on his heels inside
the door were talking, about crops and animals; the boy, squatting too in the
ammoniac dust and hoof-parings and scales of rust, heard his father tell a long
and unhurried story out of the time before the birth of the older brother even
when he had been a professional horsetrader. And then his father came up
beside him where he stood before a tattered last year's circus poster on the other
side of the store, gazing rapt and quiet at the scarlet horses, the incredible pois-
ings and convolutions of tulle and tights and the painted leers of comedians,
and said, "It's time to eat."

But not at home. Squatting beside his brother against the front wall, he watched his father emerge from the store and produce from a paper sack a segment of cheese and divide it carefully and deliberately into three with his pocket knife and produce crackers from the same sack. They all three squatted on the gallery and ate, slowly, without talking; then in the store again, they drank from a tin dipper tepid water smelling of the cedar bucket and of living beech trees. And still they did not go home. It was a horse lot this time, a tall rail fence upon and along which men stood and sat and out of which one by one horses were led, to be walked and trotted and then cantered back and forth along the road while the slow swapping and buying went on and the sun began to slant westward, they—the three of them—watching and listening, the older brother with his muddy eyes and his steady, inevitable tobacco, the father commenting now and then on certain of the animals, to no one in particular.

It was after sundown when they reached home. They ate supper by lamplight, then, sitting on the doorstep, the boy watched the night fully accomplish, listening to the whippoorwills and the frogs, when he heard his mother's voice: "Abner! No! No! Oh, God. Oh, God. Abner!" and he rose, whirled, and saw the altered light through the door where a candle stub now burned in a bottle neck on the table and his father, still in the hat and coat, at once formal and burlesque as though dressed carefully for some shabby and ceremonial violence, emptying the reservoir of the lamp back into the five-gallon kerosene can from which it had been filled, while the mother tugged at his arm until he shifted the lamp to the other hand and flung her back, not savagely or viciously, just hard, into the wall, her hands flung out against the wall for balance, her mouth open and in her face the same quality of hopeless despair as had been in her voice. Then his father saw him standing in the door.

85   "Go to the barn and get that can of oil we were oiling the wagon with," he said. The boy did not move. Then he could speak.

"What . . ." he cried. "What are you . . ."

"Go get that oil," his father said. "Go."

Then he was moving, running, outside the house, toward the stable: this the old habit, the old blood which he had not been permitted to choose for himself, which had been bequeathed him willy nilly and which had run for so long (and who knew where, battening on what of outrage and savagery and lust) before it came to him. *I could keep on*, he thought. *I could run on and on and never look back, never need to see his face again. Only I can't. I can't*, the rusted can in his hand now, the liquid sploshing in it as he ran back to the house and into it, into the sound of his mother's weeping in the next room, and handed the can to his father.

"Ain't you going to even send a nigger?" he cried. "At least you sent a nigger before!"

90   This time his father didn't strike him. The hand came even faster than the blow had, the same hand which had set the can on the table with almost excruciating care flashing from the can toward him too quick for him to follow it, gripping him by the back of his shirt and on to tiptoe before he had seen it quit the can, the face stooping at him in breathless and frozen ferocity, the cold,

dead voice speaking over him to the older brother, who leaned against the table, chewing with that steady, curious, sidewise motion of cows:

"Empty the can into the big one and go on. I'll catch up with you."

"Better tie him up to the bedpost," the brother said.

"Do like I told you," the father said. Then the boy was moving, his bunched shirt and the hard, bony hand between his shoulder-blades, his toes just touching the floor, across the room and into the other one, past the sisters sitting with spread heavy thighs in the two chairs over the cold hearth, and to where his mother and aunt sat side by side on the bed, the aunt's arms about his mother's shoulders.

"Hold him," the father said. The aunt made a startled movement. "Not you," the father said. "Lennie. Take hold of him. I want to see you do it." His mother took him by the wrist. "You'll hold him better than that. If he gets loose don't you know what he is going to do? He will go up yonder." He jerked his head toward the road. "Maybe I'd better tie him."

"I'll hold him," his mother whispered.   95

"See you do then." Then his father was gone, the stiff foot heavy and measured upon the boards, ceasing at last.

Then he began to struggle. His mother caught him in both arms, he jerking and wrenching at them. He would be stronger in the end, he knew that. But he had no time to wait for it. "Lemme go!" he cried. "I don't want to have to hit you!"

"Let him go!" the aunt said. "If he don't go, before God, I am going up there myself!"

"Don't you see I can't?" his mother cried. "Sarty! Sarty! No! No! Help me, Lizzie!"

Then he was free. His aunt grasped at him but it was too late. He whirled,   100
running, his mother stumbled forward on to her knees behind him, crying to the nearer sister: "Catch him, Net! Catch him!" But that was too late too, the sister (the sisters were twins, born at the same time, yet either of them now gave the impression of being, encompassing as much living meat and volume and weight as any other two of the family) not yet having begun to rise from the chair, her head, face, alone merely turned, presenting to him in the flying instant an astonishing expanse of young female features untroubled by any surprise even, wearing only an expression of bovine interest. Then he was out of the room, out of the house, in the mild dust of the starlit road and the heavy rifeness of honeysuckle, the pale ribbon unspooling with terrific slowness under his running feet, reaching the gate at last and turning in, running, his heart and lungs drumming, on up the drive toward the lighted house, the lighted door. He did not knock, he burst in, sobbing for breath, incapable for the moment of speech; he saw the astonished face of the Negro in the linen jacket without knowing when the Negro had appeared.

"De Spain!" he cried, panted. "Where's . . ." then he saw the white man too emerging from a white door down the hall. "Barn!" he cried. "Barn!"

"What?" the white man said. "Barn?"

"Yes!" the boy cried. "Barn!"

"Catch him!" the white man shouted.

105 But it was too late this time too. The Negro grasped his shirt, but the entire sleeve, rotten with washing, carried away, and he was out that door too and in the drive again, and had actually never ceased to run even while he was screaming into the white man's face.

Behind him the white man was shouting, "My horse! Fetch my horse!" and he thought for an instant of cutting across the park and climbing the fence into the road, but he did not know the park nor how high the vine-massed fence might be and he dared not risk it. So he ran on down the drive, blood and breath roaring; presently he was in the road again though he could not see it. He could not hear either: the galloping mare was almost upon him before he heard her, and even then he held his course, as if the very urgency of his wild grief and need must in a moment more find his wings, waiting until the ultimate instant to hurl himself aside and into the weed-choked roadside ditch as the horse thundered past and on, for an instant in furious silhouette against the stars, the tranquil early summer night sky which, even before the shape of the horse and rider vanished, stained abruptly and violently upward: a long, swirling roar incredible and soundless, blotting the stars, and he springing up and into the road again, running again, knowing it was too late yet still running even after he heard the shot and, an instant later, two shots, pausing now without knowing he had ceased to run, crying "Pap! Pap!", running again before he knew he had begun to run, stumbling, tripping over something and scrabbling up again without ceasing to run, looking backward over his shoulder at the glare as he got up, running on among the invisible trees, panting, sobbing, "Father! Father!"

At midnight he was sitting on the crest of a hill. He did not know it was midnight and he did not know how far he had come. But there was no glare behind him now and he sat now, his back toward what he had called home for four days anyhow, his face toward the dark woods which he would enter when breath was strong again, small, shaking steadily in the chill darkness, hugging himself into the remainder of his thin, rotten shirt, the grief and despair now no longer terror and fear but just grief and despair. *Father. My father*, he thought. "He was brave!" he cried suddenly, aloud but not loud, no more than a whisper: "He was! He was in the war! He was in Colonel Sartoris' cav'ry!" not knowing that his father had gone to that war a private in the fine old European sense, wearing no uniform, admitting the authority of and giving fidelity to no man or army or flag, going to war as Malbrouck[4] himself did: for booty—it meant nothing and less than nothing to him if it were enemy booty or his own.

The slow constellations wheeled on. It would be dawn and then sun-up after a while and he would be hungry. But that would be to-morrow and now he was only cold, and walking would cure that. His breathing was easier now and he decided to get up and go on, and then he found that he had been asleep because he knew it was almost dawn, the night almost over. He could tell that from the whippoorwills. They were everywhere now among the dark trees below him,

---

4. The duke of Marlborough (1650–1722), an English general whose name became distorted as Malbrough and Malbrouch in English and French popular songs celebrating his exploits.

constant and inflectioned and ceaseless, so that, as the instant for giving over to the day birds drew nearer and nearer, there was no interval at all between them. He got up. He was a little stiff, but walking would cure that too as it would the cold, and soon there would be the sun. He went on down the hill, toward the dark woods within which the liquid silver voices of the birds called unceasing— the rapid and urgent beating of the urgent and quiring heart of the late spring night. He did not look back.

1939

The reservations I hear most often can be summarized as three "charges":

1. Faulkner's style is bad. His sentences are often too long and complicated, vague, unnecessarily wordy, and sometimes hard to read.

2. The structure of the story seems almost haphazard: it wanders off the subject or out of focus.

3. The reasons the story gives—and insists upon—for people acting the way they do are unrealistic and shallow.

Can a story with a dubious style, form, theme, and vision of human actions and motives be good, much less great? Should I, must I, like it, or at least recognize its "literary value"?

Let us see a few examples of what those who find the story flawed might isolate, analyze, and articulate. We can begin with Faulkner's awkward and obscure style and pick out an early sentence—the second sentence of the story—as evidence:

The boy, crouched on his nail keg at the back of the crowded room, knew he smelled cheese, and more: from where he sat he could see the ranked shelves close-packed with the solid, squat, dynamic shapes of tin cans whose labels his stomach read, not from the lettering which meant nothing to his mind but from the scarlet devils and the silver curve of fish—this, the cheese which he knew he smelled and the hermetic meat which his intestines believed he smelled coming in intermittent gusts momentary and brief between the other constant one, the smell and sense just a little of fear because mostly of despair and grief, the old fierce pull of blood.

Even those who do not mind taking some pains in reading will probably acknowledge that this sentence is not immediately clear. The chief problem is how to relate the final phrase "the old fierce pull of blood" to the rest of the sentence, and so to discover what the sentence as a whole means. After a little work, you may decide that what the sentence says is that there is not only the smell of cheese and the imagined smell of canned meat but also the smell of despair and grief and even some smell of fear; and that despair, grief, and fear are in the boy's "blood," that is, inherited, in his genes. We still cannot be sure whether this implies that acquired traits or experiences are hereditary or whether "blood" means something else, and we still cannot be sure whether the smell of fear is imaginary—like the smell of the meat in the cans—or real—like the smell of the cheese (perhaps the smell of the sweat that comes with fear, or the odor some say fear gives off). But even if we have been successful in our unraveling of the meaning, what is the value of a sentence that has to be worked over so much and whose meaning even then is doubtful?

Now as to the matter of form. One reason "The Most Dangerous Game" is just a slick adventure story, some people say, is that everything in it is manipulated to heighten suspense. But if we criticize Connell for shifting focus for his own purposes, what can we say about the shifting of the focus in "Barn Burning"? One such shift occurs when the narrator is explaining why the man who burns other people's barns lights only a small neat fire when it is for his own use:

> Older, the boy might have remarked this and wondered why not a big one; why should not a man who had not only seen the waste and extravagance of war, but who had in his blood an inherent voracious prodigality with material not his own, have burned everything in sight? Then he might have gone a step farther and thought that that was the reason: that niggard blaze was the living fruit of nights passed during those four years in the woods hiding from all men, blue or gray, with his strings of horses (captured horses, he called them). And older still, he might have divined the true reason: that the element of fire spoke to some deep mainspring of his father's being, as the element of steel or of powder spoke to other men, as the one weapon for the preservation of integrity, else breath were not worth the breathing, and hence to be regarded with respect and used with discretion.

Is it okay to shift the focus temporally like this because the purpose of the shift is not "merely" to enhance the suspense but to clarify the meaning, to reveal "the true reason"?

Besides shifting to a time outside the story's present, sometimes the focus moves away from the boy's consciousness, which, like Rainsford's in "The Most Dangerous Game," dominates the rest of the story. When the father climbs aboard the wagon and immediately starts hitting the mules with a willow switch, the narrator comments,

> It was not even sadistic; it was exactly the same quality which in later years would cause his descendants to overrun the engine before putting a motor car into motion, striking and reining back in the same movement.

The time moves backward as well as forward and it always seems to do so in order to clarify or emphasize the meaning or illustrate the concept of "blood"—inborn, inherited habits or feelings. So, when his father tells him to get a can of oil the boy knows will be used to burn still another barn, despite the boy's repugnance at the act, he does it:

> Then he was moving, running, outside the house, toward the stable: this the old habit, the old blood which he had not been permitted to choose for himself, which had been bequeathed him willy nilly and which had run for so long (and who knew where, battening on what of outrage and savagery and lust) before it came to him. *I could keep on,* he thought. *I could run on and on and never look back, never need to see his face again. Only I can't. I can't,* . . .

This passage leads us directly into the third reservation or question, that having to do with the story's vision of the springs of human action. Can we accept that such habits, such capacities or incapacities, are bred into the "blood"? Can we even accept that this is a concept to be taken seriously, even if we cannot accept it? And if it is a serious concept, to what does it lead? to genetic determinism of one kind or another? to justifying "class"? to racism?

And, to go back to the earlier passage about the fire: what does it mean that "the element of fire spoke to some deep mainspring of his father's being, as the element of steel or powder spoke to other men"? And how is it that fire, swords, guns—violence—can be weapons "for the preservation of integrity," without which life is not worth living? What "integrity" is the father so intent on preserving? And what kind of "discretion" does the father show in his use of fire? What makes whether we accept the meaning of this passage crucial is that it is not embedded in the fiction, as part of the action and thoughts of the characters—the boy, let us say—but it is separated from them by the shift in focus and by the flat statement that we are being given the "true reason"; so it has the authority of the story / author and we either have to believe it or discount the whole vision of the story.

And if we look beneath the surface of these "true reasons" and the "pull of blood" and look at the events of the story itself, we begin to suspect a "hidden agenda," an ideology that determines what the characters are seen to do and why.

Why is it that the boy overcomes or betrays the "pull of blood" only when the "aristocratic" Major de Spain's barn is to be burned? Is the blood of the highborn somehow more valuable than that of the low? (Though a Snopes, the boy's first name is that of the aristocrat Colonel Sartoris.) Is some blood better than others? some loyalties better than others? Or is property a higher good than blood?

The selection of certain key passages or incidents, the analysis and interpretation of the text, can be used to directly confront these critical comments and questions, as well as to explore other, more positive areas of the story and its accomplishment. And the objections themselves can be examined in terms of what unspoken assumptions they make about what makes a story good, and what agendas they hide.

The long second sentence of "Barn Burning" does indeed put extraordinary emphasis on "blood." The concept here embodied in the word "blood" can stand such emphasis, even demands it, for "blood" is one of the forces that conflict within the boy. Therefore the sentence, though it may seem difficult, really gives ready access to the meaning of the story by calling attention to one of its key elements. Part of its length, too, consists in magnificent particularizing detail, the kind that convinces you that the author knows what he is talking about, and really "sees" the scene. (See the comments Ford Madox Ford makes on the first sentence in "Odour of Chrysanthemums"; you can make the same kind of analysis of this sentence.) The density of detail is also necessary in realizing (making real) the boy's sensations. The detail and the focus of the sentence also indicate where the significant action of the story is to take place—that is, inside the boy—and so we are made to understand and perhaps feel with him. Finally, the move from the smell of cheese to the "smell" of canned meat, to that of fear, is crucial: the smell of cheese is real. The smell of meat is inside the can and though it cannot actually be smelled while the can is intact it is real and is there. So what this suggests is that the boy's sensory imagination does not falsify, it just penetrates into things beyond the immediate present sense perceptions. This gives reality to the smell of despair, grief, fear—not necessarily real to the senses, but really there beneath the surface, real to the imagination. What the sentence does, then, is open up our notions of reality to include not just what the senses tell us, but what the imagination can sense. And since it does so through sensory images that gradually shade off into the imaginative, we are not just told that the imaginative is valid but we are made to feel that this is so. Thus the sentence that seemed unnecessarily long, complex, and difficult turns out to be functional. It does what no short sentence or series of sentences would be likely to manage.

Complexity, even obscurity, is not in all cases "bad"—as the criticism of the sentence seemed to assume. The literary value of language and detail does not necessarily follow rules of usage but questions of function—whether they work to create, reveal, intensify, the meaning and effect of the story.

Before going on to address the issue of the structure or theme of "Barn Burning," it may be appropriate to suggest that it is precisely in this merging of the physical and the imaginative, moral or psychological, that one of the strengths of the story—and of Faulkner—lies. The force that opposes blood, we soon learn, is the boy's sense of right and wrong. His father is accused of maliciously burning down Mr. Harris's barn. The boy knows his father is guilty. But when Harris demands the boy be called before the judge, the boy knows that because his ties to his father are those of "blood," he must lie. When the judge asks if Harris really wants the boy questioned there is a pause. For a boy,

> . . . it was as if he had swung outward at the end of a grape vine, over a ravine, and at the top of the swing had been caught in a prolonged instant of mesmerized gravity, weightless in time.

Most readers would acknowledge the appropriateness of the image both to the feeling of suspense and to the experience of the boy, and the intervention of the image suspends the meaning and imitates the boy's suspense. When Harris says the boy does not have to testify, "the smell of cheese and sealed meat, the fear and despair and the old grief of blood" return to the boy's consciousness. The importance and meaning of fear, despair, and grief in the "blood" is now a little clearer.

Faulkner's complexity, "idiosyncrasies" (what some call "flaws"), and difficulty (sometimes called "obscurity") usually come from this interpenetration of imagination and sensory reality or other things that we usually keep separate, like past and present. Each episode, character, detail, is saturated with the full world of his fiction, and its function seems to be primarily to embody that world rather than to further the plot or make a statement. The present is informed by the past and informs the future. Characters (Major de Spain) and names (Colonel Sartoris) that are minor or casual here are central elsewhere in Faulkner's canon, like actors in a repertory theater. The fiction is all one seamless, interconnected, timeless world. The interpenetration of community and generations is essential to the vision.

This gives both a smaller and larger role to the concept of "blood." "Blood" alone—inherited traits, customs, motives—does not determine behavior, but it is one of the multitude of communal and traditional forces that condition behavior. Though "blood" can explain many acts and impulses, its force does not eliminate free will. The boy does, after all, choose to warn the Major of his father's intention, chooses morality over blood. To claim that it was only Major de Spain's class or property that moved the boy to consider betraying his father is to ignore the fact that the story opens with his being on the verge of doing so in the Harris case. The father's crimes went well beyond the destruction of property; indeed it was the primacy of property over principles in his scheme of values that led him to serve neither North nor South but Mammon (by being a nonpartisan horse thief) during the Civil War.

Explaining the function of what may at first have seemed defects does not close the discussion about the merits of a work or the nature and function of literature. The discussion of the value of "Barn Burning" does not necessarily end here.

Until now, we have depersonalized the evaluations, assuming that the pros and cons are intellectual positions that have little or nothing to do with an individual reader, and that the "evidence" is always in the story. But already we have seen that some of the response to Faulkner is ideological, based on social or political values that have little to do with whether the focus shifts or the sentences are too long. We must admit that not all evidence of value is "on the page"; some beauty is in the eyes of the beholder. Let us keep in mind to be aware of our own responses and try at the same time to account for those responses in terms of both the narrative strategies and our own prejudices or predispositions.

BHARATI MUKHERJEE

The Management of Grief

A woman I don't know is boiling tea the Indian way in my kitchen. There are a lot of women I don't know in my kitchen, whispering, and moving tactfully. They open doors, rummage through the pantry, and try not to ask me where things are kept. They remind me of when my sons were small, on Mother's Day or when Vikram and I were tired, and they would make big, sloppy omelets. I would lie in bed pretending I didn't hear them.

Dr. Sharma, the treasurer of the Indo-Canada Society, pulls me into the hallway. He wants to know if I am worried about money. His wife, who has just come up from the basement with a tray of empty cups and glasses, scolds him. "Don't bother Mrs. Bhave with mundane details." She looks so monstrously pregnant her baby must be days overdue. I tell her she shouldn't be carrying heavy things. "Shaila," she says, smiling, "this is the fifth." Then she grabs a teenager by his shirttails. He slips his Walkman off his head. He has to be one of her four children, they have the same domed and dented foreheads. "What's the official word now?" she demands. The boy slips the headphones back on. "They're acting evasive, Ma. They're saying it could be an accident or a terrorist bomb."

All morning, the boys have been muttering, Sikh Bomb, Sikh Bomb. The men, not using the word, bow their heads in agreement. Mrs. Sharma touches her forehead at such a word. At least they've stopped talking about space debris and Russian lasers.

Two radios are going in the dining room. They are tuned to different stations. Someone must have brought the radios down from my boys' bedrooms. I haven't gone into their rooms since Kusum came running across the front lawn in her bathrobe. She looked so funny, I was laughing when I opened the door.

The big TV in the den is being whizzed through American networks and cable channels.

"Damn!" some man swears bitterly. "How can these preachers carry on like nothing's happened?" I want to tell him we're not that important. You look at the audience, and at the preacher in his blue robe with his beautiful white hair, the potted palm trees under a blue sky, and you know they care about nothing.

The phone rings and rings. Dr. Sharma's taken charge. "We're with her," he keeps saying. "Yes, yes, the doctor has given calming pills. Yes, yes, pills are having necessary effect." I wonder if pills alone explain this calm. Not peace, just a deadening quiet. I was always controlled, but never repressed. Sound can reach me, but my body is tensed, ready to scream. I hear their voices all around me. I hear my boys and Vikram cry, "Mommy, Shaila!" and their screams insulate me, like headphones.

The woman boiling water tells her story again and again. "I got the news first. My cousin called from Halifax before six A.M., can you imagine? He'd gotten up for prayers and his son was studying for medical exams and he heard on a rock channel that something had happened to a plane. They said first it had disappeared from the radar, like a giant eraser just reached out. His father called me, so I said to him, what do you mean, 'something bad'? You mean a hijacking? And he said, *behn*,[1] there is no confirmation of anything yet, but check with your neighbors because a lot of them must be on that plane. So I called poor Kusum straightaway. I knew Kusum's husband and daughter were booked to go yesterday."

Kusum lives across the street from me. She and Satish had moved in less than a month ago. They said they needed a bigger place. All these people, the Sharmas and friends from the Indo-Canada Society had been there for the housewarming. Satish and Kusum made homemade tandoori on their big gas grill and even the white neighbors piled their plates high with that luridly red, charred, juicy chicken. Their younger daughter had danced, and even our boys had broken away from the Stanley Cup telecast to put in a reluctant appearance. Everyone took pictures for their albums and for the community newspapers — another of our families had made it big in Toronto — and now I wonder how many of those happy faces are gone. "Why does God give us so much if all along He intends to take it away?" Kusum asks me.

I nod. We sit on carpeted stairs, holding hands like children. "I never once told him that I loved him," I say. I was too much the well brought up woman. I was so well brought up I never felt comfortable calling my husband by his first name.

1. No.

"It's all right," Kusum says. "He knew. My husband knew. They felt it. Modern young girls have to say it because what they feel is fake."

Kusum's daughter, Pam, runs in with an overnight case. Pam's in her McDonald's uniform. "Mummy! You have to get dressed!" Panic makes her cranky. "A reporter's on his way here."

"Why?"

"You want to talk to him in your bathrobe?" She starts to brush her mother's long hair. She's the daughter who's always in trouble. She dates Canadian boys and hangs out in the mall, shopping for tight sweaters. The younger one, the goody-goody one according to Pam, the one with a voice so sweet that when she sang *bhajans*[2] for Ethiopian relief even a frugal man like my husband wrote out a hundred dollar check, *she* was on that plane. *She* was going to spend July and August with grandparents because Pam wouldn't go. Pam said she'd rather waitress at McDonald's. "If it's a choice between Bombay and Wonderland, I'm picking Wonderland," she'd said.

15   "Leave me alone," Kusum yells. "You know what I want to do? If I didn't have to look after you now, I'd hang myself."

Pam's young face goes blotchy with pain. "Thanks," she says, "don't let me stop you."

"Hush," pregnant Mrs. Sharma scolds Pam. "Leave your mother alone. Mr. Sharma will tackle the reporters and fill out the forms. He'll say what has to be said."

Pam stands her ground. "You think I don't know what Mummy's thinking? *Why her?* that's what. That's sick! Mummy wishes my little sister were alive and I were dead."

Kusum's hand in mine is trembly hot. We continue to sit on the stairs.

20   She calls before she arrives, wondering if there's anything I need. Her name is Judith Templeton and she's an appointee of the provincial government. "Multiculturalism?" I ask, and she says, "partially," but that her mandate is bigger. "I've been told you knew many of the people on the flight," she says. "Perhaps if you'd agree to help us reach the others. . . ?"

She gives me time at least to put on tea water and pick up the mess in the front room. I have a few *samosas*[3] from Kusum's housewarming that I could fry up, but then I think, why prolong this visit?

Judith Templeton is much younger than she sounded. She wears a blue suit with a white blouse and a polka dot tie. Her blond hair is cut short, her only jewelry is pearl drop earrings. Her briefcase is new and expensive looking, a gleaming cordovan leather. She sits with it across her lap. When she looks out the front windows onto the street, her contact lenses seem to float in front of her light blue eyes.

"What sort of help do you want from me?" I ask. She has refused the tea, out of politeness, but I insist, along with some slightly stale biscuits.

2. Hymns.   3. Fried turnovers filled with meat or vegetable mixtures.

"I have no experience," she admits. "That is, I have an MSW and I've worked in liaison with accident victims, but I mean I have no experience with a tragedy of this scale—"

"Who could?" I ask.   25

"—and with the complications of culture, language, and customs. Someone mentioned that Mrs. Bhave is a pillar—because you've taken it more calmly."

At this, perhaps, I frown, for she reaches forward, almost to take my hand. "I hope you understand my meaning, Mrs. Bhave. There are hundreds of people in Metro directly affected, like you, and some of them speak no English. There are some widows who've never handled money or gone on a bus, and there are old parents who still haven't eaten or gone outside their bedrooms. Some houses and apartments have been looted. Some wives are still hysterical. Some husbands are in shock and profound depression. We want to help, but our hands are tied in so many ways. We have to distribute money to some people, and there are legal documents—these things can be done. We have interpreters, but we don't always have the human touch, or maybe the right human touch. We don't want to make mistakes, Mrs. Bhave, and that's why we'd like to ask you to help us."

"More mistakes, you mean," I say.

"Police matters are not in my hands," she answers.

"Nothing I can do will make any difference," I say. "We must all grieve in   30
our own way."

"But you are coping very well. All the people said, Mrs. Bhave is the strongest person of all. Perhaps if the others could see you, talk with you, it would help them."

"By the standards of the people you call hysterical, I am behaving very oddly and very badly, Miss Templeton." I want to say to her, *I wish I could scream, starve, walk into Lake Ontario, jump from a bridge.* "They would not see me as a model. I do not see myself as a model."

I am a freak. No one who has ever known me would think of me reacting this way. This terrible calm will not go away.

She asks me if she may call again, after I get back from a long trip that we all must make. "Of course," I say. "Feel free to call, anytime."

Four days later, I find Kusum squatting on a rock overlooking a bay in Ire-   35
land. It isn't a big rock, but it juts sharply out over water. This is as close as we'll ever get to them. June breezes balloon out her sari and unpin her knee-length hair. She has the bewildered look of a sea creature whom the tides have stranded.

It's been one hundred hours since Kusum came stumbling and screaming across my lawn. Waiting around the hospital, we've heard many stories. The police, the diplomats, they tell us things thinking that we're strong, that knowledge is helpful to the grieving, and maybe it is. Some, I know, prefer ignorance, or their own versions. The plane broke into two, they say. Unconsciousness was instantaneous. No one suffered. My boys must have just finished their breakfasts.

They loved eating on planes, they loved the smallness of plates, knives, and forks. Last year they saved the airline salt and pepper shakers. Half an hour more and they would have made it to Heathrow.

Kusum says that we can't escape our fate. She says that all those people — our husbands, my boys, her girl with the nightingale voice, all those Hindus, Christians, Sikhs, Muslims, Parsis, and atheists on that plane — were fated to die together off this beautiful bay. She learned this from a swami in Toronto.

I have my Valium.

Six of us "relatives" — two widows and four widowers — choose to spend the day today by the waters instead of sitting in a hospital room and scanning photographs of the dead. That's what they call us now: relatives. I've looked through twenty-seven photos in two days. They're very kind to us, the Irish are very understanding. Sometimes understanding means freeing a tourist bus for this trip to the bay, so we can pretend to spy our loved ones through the glassiness of waves or in sunspeckled cloud shapes.

40   I could die here, too, and be content.

"What is that, out there?" She's standing and flapping her hands and for a moment I see a head shape bobbing in the waves. She's standing in the water, I, on the boulder. The tide is low, and a round, black, headsized rock has just risen from the waves. She returns, her sari end dripping and ruined and her face is a twisted remnant of hope, the way mine was a hundred hours ago, still laughing but inwardly knowing that nothing but the ultimate tragedy could bring two women together at six o'clock on a Sunday morning. I watch her face sag into blankness.

"That water felt warm, Shaila," she says at length.

"You can't," I say. "We have to wait for our turn to come."

I haven't eaten in four days, haven't brushed my teeth.

45   "I know," she says. "I tell myself I have no right to grieve. They are in a better place than we are. My swami says I should be thrilled for them. My swami says depression is a sign of our selfishness."

Maybe I'm selfish. Selfishly I break away from Kusum and run, sandals slapping against stones, to the water's edge. What if my boys aren't lying pinned under the debris? What if they aren't stuck a mile below that innocent blue chop? What if, given the strong currents. . . .

Now I've ruined my sari, one of my best. Kusum has joined me, knee-deep in water that feels to me like a swimming pool. I could settle in the water, and my husband would take my hand and the boys would slap water in my face just to see me scream.

"Do you remember what good swimmers my boys were, Kusum?"

"I saw the medals," she says.

50   One of the widowers, Dr. Ranganathan from Montreal, walks out to us, carrying his shoes in one hand. He's an electrical engineer. Someone at the hotel mentioned his work is famous around the world, something about the place where physics and electricity come together. He has lost a huge family, something indescribable. "With some luck," Dr. Ranganathan suggests to me, " a good swimmer could make it safely to some island. It is quite possible that

there may be many, many microscopic islets scattered around."

"You're not just saying that?" I tell Dr. Ranganathan about Vinod, my elder son. Last year he took diving as well.

"It's a parent's duty to hope," he says. "It is foolish to rule out possibilities that have not been tested. I myself have not surrendered hope."

Kusum is sobbing once again. "Dear lady," he says, laying his free hand on her arm, and she calms down.

"Vinod is how old?" he asks me. He's very careful, as we all are. *Is*, not was.

"Fourteen. Yesterday he was fourteen. His father and uncle were going to take him down to the Taj and give him a big birthday party. I couldn't go with them because I couldn't get two weeks off from my stupid job in June." I process bills for a travel agent. June is a big travel month.

Dr. Ranganathan whips the pockets of his suit jacked inside out. Squashed roses, in darkening shades of pink, float on the water. He tore the roses off creepers in somebody's garden. He didn't ask anyone if he could pluck the roses, but now there's been an article about it in the local papers. When you see an Indian person, it says, please give him or her flowers.

"A strong youth of fourteen," he says, "can very likely pull to safety a younger one."

My sons, though four years apart, were very close. Vinod wouldn't let Mithun drown. *Electrical engineering*, I think, foolishly perhaps: this man knows important secrets of the universe, things closed to me. Relief spins me lightheaded. No wonder my boys' photographs haven't turned up in the gallery of photos of the recovered dead. "Such pretty roses," I say.

"My wife loved pink roses. Every Friday I had to bring a bunch home. I used to say, why? After twenty-odd years of marriage you're still needing proof positive of my love?" He has identified his wife and three of his children. Then others from Montreal, the lucky ones, intact families with no survivors. He chuckles as he wades back to shore. Then he swings around to ask me a question. "Mrs. Bhave, you are wanting to throw in some roses for your loved ones? I have two big ones left."

But I have other things to float: Vinod's pocket calculator; a half-painted model B-52 for my Mithun. They'd want them on their island. And for my husband? For him I let fall into the calm, glassy waters a poem I wrote in the hospital yesterday. Finally he'll know my feelings for him.

"Don't tumble, the rocks are slippery," Dr. Ranganathan cautions. He holds out a hand for me to grab.

Then it's time to get back on the bus, time to rush back to our waiting posts on hospital benches.

Kusum is one of the lucky ones. The lucky ones flew here, identified in multiplicate their loved ones, then will fly to India with the bodies for proper ceremonies. Satish is one of the few males who surfaced. The photos of faces we saw on the walls in an office at Heathrow and here in the hospital are mostly of women. Women have more body fat, a nun said to me matter-of-factly. They float better.

Today I was stopped by a young sailor on the street. He had loaded bodies,
he'd gone into the water when—he checks my face for signs of strength—when
the sharks were first spotted. I don't blush, and he breaks down. "It's all right," I
say. "Thank you." I had heard about the sharks from Dr. Ranganathan. In his
orderly mind, science brings understanding, it holds no terror. It is the shark's
duty. For every deer there is a hunter, for every fish a fisherman.

65   The Irish are not shy; they rush to me and give me hugs and some are crying.
I cannot imagine reactions like that on the streets of Toronto. Just strangers, and
I am touched. Some carry flowers with them and give them to any Indian they
see.

    After lunch, a policeman I have gotten to know quite well catches hold of
me. He says he thinks he has a match for Vinod. I explain what a good swimmer
Vinod is.

    "You want me with you when you look at photos?" Dr. Ranganathan walks
ahead of me into the picture gallery. In these matters, he is a scientist, and I am
grateful. It is a new perspective. "They have performed miracles," he says. "We
are indebted to them."

    The first day or two the policemen showed us relatives only one picture at a
time; now they're in a hurry, they're eager to lay out the possibles, and even the
probables.

    The face on the photo is of a boy much like Vinod; the same intelligent
eyes, the same thick brows dipping into a V. But this boy's features, even his
cheeks, are puffier, wider, mushier.

70   "No." My gaze is pulled by other pictures. There are five other boys who
look like Vinod.

    The nun assigned to console me rubs the first picture with a fingertip.
"When they've been in the water for a while, love, they look a little heavier."
The bones under the skin are broken, they said on the first day—try to adjust
your memories. It's important.

    "It's not him. I'm his mother. I'd know."

    "I know this one!" Dr. Ranganathan cries out suddenly from the back of the
gallery. "And this one!" I think he senses that I don't want to find my boys.
"They are the Kutty brothers. They were also from Montreal." I don't mean to
be crying. On the contrary, I am ecstatic. My suitcase in the hotel is packed
heavy with dry clothes for my boys.

    The policeman starts to cry. "I am so sorry, I am so sorry, ma'am. I really
thought we had a match."

75   With the nun ahead of us and the policeman behind, we, the unlucky ones
without our children's bodies, file out of the makeshift gallery.

    From Ireland most of us go on to India. Kusum and I take the same direct
flight to Bombay, so I can help her clear customs quickly. But we have to argue
with a man in uniform. He has large boils on his face. The boils swell and glow
with sweat as we argue with him. He wants Kusum to wait in line and he refuses
to take authority because his boss is on a tea break. But Kusum won't let her

coffins out of sight, and I shan't desert her though I know that my parents, elderly and diabetic, must be waiting in a stuffy car in a scorching lot.

"You bastard!" I scream at the man with the popping boils. Other passengers press closer. "You think we're smuggling contraband in those coffins!"

Once upon a time we were well brought up women; we were dutiful wives who kept our heads veiled, our voices shy and sweet.

In India, I become, once again, an only child of rich, ailing parents. Old friends of the family come to pay their respects. Some are Sikh, and inwardly, involuntarily, I cringe. My parents are progressive people; they do not blame communities for a few individuals.

In Canada it is a different story now.   80

"Stay longer," my mother pleads. "Canada is a cold place. Why would you want to be all by yourself?" I stay.

Three months pass. Then another.

"Vikram wouldn't have wanted you to give up things!" they protest. They call my husband by the name he was born with. In Toronto he'd changed to Vik so the men he worked with at his office would find his name as easy as Rod or Chris. "You know, the dead aren't cut off from us!"

My grandmother, the spoiled daughter of a rich *zamindar*[4], shaved her head with rusty razor blades when she was widowed at sixteen. My grandfather died of childhood diabetes when he was nineteen, and she saw herself as the harbinger of bad luck. My mother grew up without parents, raised indifferently by an uncle, while her true mother slept in a hut behind the main estate house and took her food with the servants. She grew up a rationalist. My parents abhor mindless mortification.

The zamindar's daughter kept stubborn faith in Vedic rituals; my parents   85
rebelled. I am trapped between two modes of knowledge. At thirty-six, I am too old to start over and too young to give up. Like my husband's spirit, I flutter between worlds.

Courting aphasia, we travel. We travel with our phalanx of servants and poor relatives. To hill stations and to beach resorts. We play contract bridge in dusty gymkhana clubs. We ride stubby ponies up crumbly mountain trails. At tea dances, we let ourselves be twirled twice round the ballroom. We hit the holy spots we hadn't made time for before. In Varanasi, Kalighat, Rishikesh, Hardwar, astrologers and palmists seek me out and for a fee offer me cosmic consolations.

Already the widowers among us are being shown new bride candidates. They cannot resist the call of custom, the authority of their parents and older brothers. They must marry; it is the duty of a man to look after a wife. The new wives will be young widows with children, destitute but of good family. They will make loving wives, but the men will shun them. I've had calls from the men over crackling Indian telephone lines. "Save me," they say, these substantial, edu-

4. Landowner.

cated, successful men of forty. "My parents are arranging a marriage for me." In a month they will have buried one family and returned to Canada with a new bride and partial family.

I am comparatively lucky. No one here thinks of arranging a husband for an unlucky widow.

Then, on the third day of the sixth month into this odyssey, in an abandoned temple in a tiny Himalayan village, as I make my offering of flowers and sweetmeats to the god of a tribe of animists, my husband descends to me. He is squatting next to a scrawny *sadhu* in moth-eaten robes. Vikram wears the vanilla suit he wore the last time I hugged him. The *sadhu* tosses petals on a butter-fed flame, reciting Sanskrit mantras and sweeps his face of flies. My husband takes my hands in his.

90   *You're beautiful,* he starts. Then, *What are you doing here?*

Shall I stay? I ask. He only smiles, but already the image is fading. *You must finish alone what we started together.* No seaweed wreathes his mouth. He speaks too fast just as he used to when we were an envied family in our pink split-level. He is gone.

In the windowless altar room, smoky with joss sticks and clarified butter lamps, a sweaty hand gropes for my blouse. I do not shriek. The *sadhu* arranges his robe. The lamps hiss and sputter out.

When we come out of the temple, my mother says, "Did you feel something weird in there?"

My mother has no patience with ghosts, prophetic dreams, holy men, and cults.

95   "No," I lie. "Nothing."

But she knows that she's lost me. She knows that in days I shall be leaving.

Kusum's put her house up for sale. She wants to live in an ashram in Hardwar. Moving to Hardwar was her swami's idea. Her swami runs two ashrams, the one in Hardwar and another here in Toronto.

"Don't run away," I tell her.

"I'm not running away," she says. "I'm pursuing inner peace. You think you or that Ranganathan fellow are better off?"

100   Pam's left for California. She wants to do some modelling, she says. She says when she comes into her share of the insurance money she'll open a yoga-cum-aerobics studio in Hollywood. She sends me postcards so naughty I daren't leave them on the coffee table. Her mother has withdrawn from her and the world.

The rest of us don't lose touch, that's the point. Talk is all we have, says Dr. Ranganathan, who has also resisted his relatives and returned to Montreal and to his job, alone. He says, whom better to talk with than other relatives? We've been melted down and recast as a new tribe.

He calls me twice a week from Montreal. Every Wednesday night and every Saturday afternoon. He is changing jobs, going to Ottawa. But Ottawa is over a hundred miles away, and he is forced to drive two hundred and twenty miles a day. He can't bring himself to sell his house. The house is a temple, he says; the king-sized bed in the master bedroom is a shrine. He sleeps on a folding cot. A devotee.

There are still some hysterical relatives. Judith Templeton's list of those needing help and those who've "accepted" is in nearly perfect balance. Acceptance means you speak of your family in the past tense and you make active plans for moving ahead with your life. There are courses at Seneca and Ryerson[5] we could be taking. Her gleaming leather briefcase is full of college catalogues and lists of cultural societies that need our help. She has done impressive work, I tell her.

"In the textbooks on grief management," she replies—I am her confidante, I realize, one of the few whose grief has not sprung bizarre obsessions—"there are stages to pass through: rejection, depression, acceptance, reconstruction." She has compiled a chart and finds that six months after the tragedy, none of us still reject reality, but only a handful are reconstructing. "Depressed Acceptance" is the plateau we've reached. Remarriage is a major step in reconstruction (though she's a little surprised, even shocked, over *how* quickly some of the men have taken on new families). Selling one's house and changing jobs and cities is healthy.

How do I tell Judith Templeton that my family surrounds me, and that like creatures in epics, they've changed shapes? She sees me as calm and accepting but worries that I have no job, no career. My closest friends are worse off than I. I cannot tell her my days, even my nights, are thrilling.

She asks me to help with families she can't reach at all. An elderly couple in Agincourt whose sons were killed just weeks after they had brought their parents over from a village in Punjab. From their names, I know they are Sikh. Judith Templeton and a translator have visited them twice with offers of money for air fare to Ireland, with bank forms, power-of-attorney forms, but they have refused to sign, or to leave their tiny apartment. Their sons' money is frozen in the bank. Their sons' investment apartments have been trashed by tenants, the furnishings sold off. The parents fear that anything they sign or any money they receive will end the company's or the country's obligations to them. They fear they are selling their sons for two airline tickets to a place they've never seen.

The high-rise apartment is a tower of Indians and West Indians, with a sprinkling of Orientals. The nearest bus stop kiosk is lined with women in saris. Boys practice cricket in the parking lot. Inside the building, even I wince a bit from the ferocity of onion fumes, the distinctive and immediate Indianness of frying *ghee*, but Judith Templeton maintains a steady flow of information. These poor old people are in imminent danger of losing their place and all their services.

I say to her, "They are Sikh. They will not open up to a Hindu woman." And what I want to add is, as much as I try not to, I stiffen now at the sight of

5. Seneca College of Applied Arts and Technology, in Willowdale; Ryerson Polytechnical Institute, Toronto.

beards and turbans. I remember a time when we all trusted each other in this new country, it was only the new country we worried about.

The two rooms are dark and stuffy. The lights are off, and an oil lamp sputters on the coffee table. The bent old lady has let us in, and her husband is wrapping a white turban over his oiled, hip-length hair. She immediately goes to the kitchen, and I hear the most familiar sound of an Indian home, tap water hitting and filling a teapot.

110 They have not paid their utility bills, out of fear and the inability to write a check. The telephone is gone; electricity and gas and water are soon to follow. They have told Judith their sons will provide. They are good boys, and they have always earned and looked after their parents.

We converse a bit in Hindi. They do not ask about the crash and I wonder if I should bring it up. If they think I am here merely as a translator, then they may feel insulted. There are thousands of Punjabi-speakers, Sikhs, in Toronto to do a better job. And so I say to the old lady, "I too have lost my sons, and my husband, in the crash."

Her eyes immediately fill with tears. The man mutters a few words which sound like a blessing. "God provides and God takes away," he says.

I want to say, but only men destroy and give back nothing. "My boys and my husband are not coming back," I say. "We have to understand that."

Now the old woman responds. "But who is to say? Man alone does not decide these things." To this her husband adds his agreement.

115 Judith asks about the bank papers, the release forms. With a stroke of the pen, they will have a provincial trustee to pay their bills, invest their money, send them a monthly pension.

"Do you know this woman?" I ask them.

The man raises his hand from the table, turns it over and seems to regard each finger separately before he answers. "This young lady is always coming here, we make tea for her and she leaves papers for us to sign." His eyes scan a pile of papers in the corner of the room. "Soon we will be out of tea, then will she go away?"

The old lady adds, "I have asked my neighbors and no one else gets *angrezi*[6] visitors. What have we done?"

"It's her job," I try to explain. "The government is worried. Soon you will have no place to stay, no lights, no gas, no water."

120 "Government will get its money. Tell her not to worry, we are honorable people."

I try to explain the government wishes to give money, not take. He raises his hand. "Let them take," he says. "We are accustomed to that. That is no problem."

"We are strong people," says the wife. "Tell her that."

"Who needs all this machinery?" demands the husband. "It is unhealthy, the bright lights, the cold air on a hot day, the cold food, the four gas rings. God will provide, not government."

---

6. English, Anglo.

"When our boys return," the mother says. Her husband sucks his teeth. "Enough talk," he says.

Judith breaks in. "Have you convinced them?" The snaps on her cordovan briefcase go off like firecrackers in that quiet apartment. She lays the sheaf of legal papers on the coffee table. "If they can't write their names, an X will do— I've told them that."

Now the old lady has shuffled to the kitchen and soon emerges with a pot of tea and two cups. "I think my bladder will go first on a job like this," Judith says to me, smiling. "If only there was some way of reaching them. Please thank her for the tea. Tell her she's very kind."

I nod in Judith's direction and tell them in Hindi, "She thanks you for the tea. She thinks you are being very hospitable but she doesn't have the slightest idea what it means."

I want to say, humor her. I want to say, my boys and my husband are with me too, more than ever. I look in the old man's eyes and I can read his stubborn, peasant's message: *I have protected this woman as best I can. She is the only person I have left. Give to me or take from me what you will, but I will not sign for it. I will not pretend that I accept.*

In the car, Judith says, "You see what I'm up against? I'm sure they're lovely people, but their stubbornness and ignorance are driving me crazy. They think signing a paper is signing their sons' death warrants, don't they?"

I am looking out the window. I want to say, *In our culture, it is a parent's duty to hope.*

"Now Shaila, this next woman is a real mess. She cries day and night, and she refuses all medical help. We may have to—"

"—Let me out at the subway," I say.

"I beg your pardon?" I can feel those blue eyes staring at me.

It would not be like her to disobey. She merely disapproves, and slows at a corner to let me out. Her voice is plaintive. "Is there anything I said? Anything I did?"

I could answer her suddenly in a dozen ways, but I choose not to. "Shaila? Let's talk about it," I hear, then slam the door.

A wife and mother begins her new life in a new country, and that life is cut short. Yet her husband tells her: Complete what we have started. We, who stayed out of politics and came halfway around the world to avoid religious and political feuding have been the first in the New World to die from it. I no longer know what we started, nor how to complete it. I write letters to the editors of local papers and to members of Parliament. Now at least they admit it was a bomb. One MP answers back, with sympathy, but with a challenge. You want to make a difference? Work on a campaign. Work on mine. Politicize the Indian voter.

My husband's old lawyer helps me set up a trust. Vikram was a saver and a careful investor. He had saved the boys' boarding school and college fees. I sell the pink house at four times what we paid for it and take a small apartment downtown. I am looking for a charity to support.

We are deep in the Toronto winter, gray skies, icy pavements. I stay indoors, watching television. I have tried to assess my situation, how best to live my life, to complete what we began so many years ago. Kusum has written me from Hardwar that her life is now serene. She has seen Satish and has heard her daughter sing again. Kusum was on a pilgrimage, passing through a village when she heard a young girl's voice, singing one of her daughter's favorite *bhajans*. She followed the music through the squalor of a Himalayan village, to a hut where a young girl, an exact replica of her daughter, was fanning coals under the kitchen fire. When she appeared, the girl cried out, "Ma!" and ran away. What did I think of that?

I think I can only envy her.

140   Pam didn't make it to California, but writes me from Vancouver. She works in a department store, giving make-up hints to Indian and Oriental girls. Dr. Ranganathan has given up his commute, given up his house and job, and accepted an academic position in Texas where no one knows his story and he has vowed not to tell it. He calls me now once a week.

I wait, I listen, and I pray, but Vikram has not returned to me. The voices and the shapes and the nights filled with visions ended abruptly several weeks ago.

I take it as a sign.

One rare, beautiful, sunny day last week, returning from a small errand on Yonge Street, I was walking through the park from the subway to my apartment. I live equidistant from the Ontario Houses of Parliament and the University of Toronto. The day was not cold, but something in the bare trees caught my attention. I looked up from the gravel, into the branches and the clear blue sky beyond. I thought I heard the rustling of larger forms, and I waited a moment for voices. Nothing.

"What?" I asked.

145   Then as I stood in the path looking north to Queen's Park and west to the university, I heard the voices of my family one last time. *Your time has come,* they said. *Go, be brave.*

I do not know where this voyage I have begun will end. I do not know which direction I will take. I dropped the package on a park bench and started walking.

1988

Let us begin a reader-oriented discussion of this story, by thinking of ourselves first as a general reader reading the opening of this story for the first time:

A woman I don't know is boiling tea the Indian way in my kitchen. There are a lot of women I don't know in my kitchen, whispering, and moving tactfully. They open doors, rummage through the pantry, and try not to ask me where things are kept. They remind me of when my sons were small, on Mother's Day or when Vikram and I were tired, and they would make big, sloppy omelets. I would lie in bed pretending I didn't hear them.

We are plunged immediately into the mind of an "I" whose identity we do not know, in a setting specified only as in or near a kitchen, and in a situation about which we know nothing. There is no exposition, no explanation. The more familiar past tense of most stories is absent; we are thrust into a narrative present without known precedent or purpose. The uncertainty makes us look at every word and detail for clues: "my kitchen" and "my sons . . . on Mother's Day" soon identifies the narrator as a mature female.

At this point, whether we find this indirection and uncertainty annoying or engaging (for making us work to figure out what is going on), we may ask a question or two not about the story but about ourselves. The first two stories in this chapter were not only written by men but were almost entirely about men. (No women appear in "The Most Dangerous Game" and the mother, aunt, and daughter in "Barn Burning" are peripheral.) "The Management of Grief" is not only written by a woman but tells the story through the consciousness of a woman, a strong and intelligent woman. On the other hand, this woman is a mother, somewhat older than most college students. The boy in "Barn Burning," though younger than you, is living through a part of life you have already lived through and so know something about first-hand. How much does the age of the central character have to do not just with your understanding, but with your feelings, your affective response to what you are reading?

The name "Vikram" in the first paragraph for many of us suggests little except foreignness, but "Dr. Sharma, the treasurer of the Indo-Canada Society" (par. 2), tells us enough about the cultural setting for the moment. In the ensuing conversation we learn the name of the narrator—Shaila Bhave—and learn that there has been an accident, perhaps a terrorist bombing, which may explain what seems to be the confusion of the opening scene.

The bomb, the next sentence tells us, may have been a Sikh bomb, and in the eighth paragraph we learn that it was a passenger plane that was, or might have been, bombed. What is a Sikh? Why would a Sikh bomb a plane full of people? Does the average American read this story with the same attitudes and emotions as the average Canadian? Indian? Sikh?

This is not to say that an eighteen-year-old male of Polish descent living in Cleveland cannot read this story with strong emotions and with deep sympathy for and understanding of Shaila Bhave and her tragedy. But would his responses be the same in nature and intensity as those of a middle-aged Indian woman living in Toronto or Vancouver?

For Indians, Sikhs, and some Canadians, this incident (which seems to be based on an actual disaster) is also likely to be controversial, even though the story itself does not concentrate on assessing blame or the political tensions or causes involved. Whether or not a story takes sides, touching on an issue that readers recognize as controversial inevitably affects how those readers evaluate the story. This does not necessarily mean that all Sikhs or all Indians hold one view. People often disagree with their own government's or community's actions—as many Americans did during the Vietnam war. The point is not that controversial stories are bad or that considering the politics or ideology of a work in evaluating it is bad. But we need to recognize the ideological or political factor in our assessment, to acknowledge who and where we are, where we are coming from, when we say, "This story is good" or "That story is lousy."

Evaluating a story, then, means reading carefully (and widely), learning as much as we can about the elements of fiction and of narrative strategies, and articulating our analyses; being honest about our own responses and feeling responsible for articulating them as clearly and convincingly as possible; taking our opinions seriously but listening with attention and an open mind to the judgments and reasoning of other readers. It requires as well some examination and knowledge of ourselves, of what in ourselves conditions our responses to fiction, and a willingness to look at what underlies our judgments and how we might learn and grow. Assessing the value of a story is difficult and a firm evaluation elusive in part because it means examining more than words on a page, it means examining so many ideas, beliefs, and feelings we take for granted. It means examining and, to a degree, evaluating our outer world and inner selves.

Reading More Fiction

HENRY JAMES

The Real Thing

I

When the porter's wife, who used to answer the house-bell, announced "A gentleman and a lady, sir" I had, as I often had in those days—the wish being father to the thought—an immediate vision of sitters. Sitters my visitors in this case proved to be; but not in the sense I should have preferred. There was nothing at first however to indicate that they mightn't have come for a portrait. The gentleman, a man of fifty, very high and very straight, with a moustache slightly grizzled and a dark grey walking-coat admirably fitted, both of which I noted professionally—I don't mean as a barber or yet as a tailor—would have struck me as a celebrity if celebrities often were striking. It was a truth of which I had for some time been conscious that a figure with a good deal of frontage was, as one might say, almost never a public institution. A glance at the lady helped to remind me of this paradoxical law: she also looked too distinguished to be a "personality." Moreover one would scarcely come across two variations together.

Neither of the pair immediately spoke—they only prolonged the preliminary gaze suggesting that each wished to give the other a chance. They were visibly shy; they stood there letting me take them in—which, as I afterwards perceived, was the most practical thing they could have done. In this way their embarrassment served their cause. I had seen people painfully reluctant to mention that they desired anything so gross as to be represented on canvas; but the scruples of my new friends appeared almost insurmountable. Yet the gentleman might have said "I should like a portrait of my wife," and the lady might have said "I should like a portrait of my husband." Perhaps they weren't husband and wife—this naturally would make the matter more delicate. Perhaps they wished to be done together—in which case they ought to have brought a third person to break the news.

"We come from Mr. Rivet," the lady finally said with a dim smile that had the effect of a moist sponge passed over a "sunk"[1] piece of painting, as well as of a vague allusion to vanished beauty. She was as tall and straight, in her degree, as her companion, and with ten years less to carry. She looked as sad as a woman could look whose face was not charged with expression; that is her tinted oval mask showed waste as an exposed surface shows friction. The hand of time had played over her freely, but to an effect of elimination. She was slim and stiff, and so well-dressed, in dark blue cloth, with lappets and pockets and buttons, that it was clear she employed the same tailor as her husband. The couple had an indefinable air of prosperous thrift—they evidently got a good deal of luxury for their money. If I was to be one of their luxuries it would behove me to consider my terms.

"Ah, Claude Rivet recommended me?" I echoed; and I added that it was very kind of him, though I could reflect that, as he only painted landscape, this wasn't a sacrifice.

The lady looked very hard at the gentleman, and the gentleman looked round the room. Then staring at the floor a moment and stroking his moustache, he rested his pleasant eyes on me with the remark: "He said you were the right one."

"I try to be, when people want to sit."

"Yes, we should like to," said the lady anxiously.

"Do you mean together?"

My visitors exchanged a glance. "If you could do anything with *me* I suppose it would be double," the gentleman stammered.

"Oh yes, there's naturally a higher charge for two figures than for one."

"We should like to make it pay," the husband confessed.

"That's very good of you," I returned, appreciating so unwonted a sympathy—for I supposed he meant pay the artist.

A sense of strangeness seemed to draw on the lady.

"We mean for the illustrations—Mr. Rivet said you might put one in."

"Put in—an illustration?" I was equally confused.

"Sketch her off, you know," said the gentleman, colouring.

It was only then that I understood the service Claude Rivet had rendered me; he had told them how I worked in black-and-white, for magazines, for story-books, for sketches of contemporary life, and consequently had copious employment for models. These things were true, but it was not less true—I may confess it now; whether because the aspiration was to lead to everything or to nothing I leave the reader to guess—that I couldn't get the honours, to say nothing of the emoluments, of a great painter of portraits out of my head. My "illustrations" were my pot-boilers; I looked to a different branch of art—far and away the most interesting it had always seemed to me—to perpetuate my fame. There was no

1. When colors lose their brilliance after they have dried on the canvas, they have "sunk in."

shame in looking to it also to make my fortune; but that fortune was by so much further from being made from the moment my visitors wished to be "done" for nothing. I was disappointed; for in the pictorial sense I had immediately *seen* them. I had seized their type—I had already settled what I would do with it. Something that wouldn't absolutely have pleased them, I afterwards reflected.

"Ah you're—you're—a—?" I began as soon as I had mastered my surprise. I couldn't bring out the dingy word "models": it seemed so little to fit the case.

"We haven't had much practice," said the lady.

"We've got to *do* something, and we've thought that an artist in your line might perhaps make something of us," her husband threw off. He further mentioned that they didn't know many artists and that they had gone first, on the off-chance—he painted views of course, but sometimes put in figures; perhaps I remembered—to Mr. Rivet, whom they had met a few years before at a place in Norfolk where he was sketching.

"We used to sketch a little ourselves," the lady hinted.

"It's very awkward, but we absolutely *must* do something," her husband went on.

"Of course we're not so *very* young," she admitted with a wan smile.

With the remark that I might as well know something more about them the husband had handed me a card extracted from a neat new pocket-book—their appurtenances were all of the freshest—and inscribed with the words "Major Monarch." Impressive as these words were they didn't carry my knowledge much further; but my visitor presently added: "I've left the army and we've had the misfortune to lose our money. In fact our means are dreadfully small."

"It's awfully trying—a regular strain," said Mrs. Monarch.

They evidently wished to be discreet—to take care not to swagger because they were gentlefolk. I felt them willing to recognise this as something of a drawback, at the same time that I guessed at an underlying sense—their consolation in adversity—that they *had* their points. They certainly had; but these advantages struck me as preponderantly social; such for instance as would help to make a drawing-room look well. However, a drawing-room was always, or ought to be, a picture.

In consequence of his wife's allusion to their age Major Monarch observed: "Naturally it's more for the figure that we thought of going in. We can still hold ourselves up." On the instant I saw that the figure was indeed their strong point. His "naturally" didn't sound vain, but it lighted up the question. "*She* has the best one," he continued, nodding at his wife with a pleasant after-dinner absence of circumlocution. I could only reply, as if we were in fact sitting over our wine, that this didn't prevent his own from being very good; which led him in turn to make answer: "We thought that if you ever have to do people like us we might be something like it. *She* particularly—for a lady in a book, you know."

I was so amused by them that, to get more of it, I did my best to take their point of view; and though it was an embarrassment to find myself appraising physically, as if they were animals on hire or useful blacks, a pair whom I should have expected to meet only in one of the relations in which criticism is tacit, I

20

25

looked at Mrs. Monarch judicially enough to be able to exclaim after a moment with conviction: "Oh yes, a lady in a book!" She was singularly like a bad illustration.

"We'll stand up, if you like," said the Major; and he raised himself before me with a really grand air.

30   I could take his measure at a glance—he was six feet two and a perfect gentleman. It would have paid any club in process of formation and in want of a stamp to engage him at a salary to stand in the principal window. What struck me at once was that in coming to me they had rather missed their vocation; they could surely have been turned to better account for advertising purposes. I couldn't of course see the thing in detail, but I could see them make somebody's fortune—I don't mean their own. There was something in them for a waistcoat-maker, an hotel-keeper or a soap-vendor. I could imagine "We always use it" pinned on their bosoms with the greatest effect; I had a vision of the brilliancy with which they would launch a table d'hôte.

Mrs. Monarch sat still, not from pride but from shyness, and presently her husband said to her; "Get up, my dear, and show how smart you are." She obeyed, but she had no need to get up to show it. She walked to the end of the studio and then came back blushing, her fluttered eyes on the partner of her appeal. I was reminded of an incident I had accidentally had a glimpse of in Paris being with a friend there, a dramatist about to produce a play, when an actress came to him to ask to be entrusted with a part. She went through her paces before him, walked up and down as Mrs. Monarch was doing. Mrs. Monarch did it quite as well, but I abstained from applauding. It was very odd to see such people apply for such poor pay. She looked as if she had ten thousand a year. Her husband had used the word that described her: she was in the London current jargon essentially and typically "smart." Her figure was, in the same order of ideas, conspicuously and irreproachably "good." For a woman of her age her waist was surprisingly small; her elbow moreover had the orthodox crook. She held her head at the conventional angle, but why did she come to *me*? She ought to have tried on jackets at a big shop. I feared my visitors were not only destitute but "artistic"—which would be a great complication. When she sat down again I thanked her, observing that what a draughtsman most valued in his model was the faculty of keeping quiet.

"Oh *she* can keep quiet," said Major Monarch. Then he added jocosely: "I've always kept her quiet."

"I'm not a nasty fidget, am I?" It was going to wring tears from me, I felt, the way she hid her head, ostrich-like, in the other's broad bosom.

The owner of this expanse addressed his answer to me. "Perhaps it isn't out of place to mention—because we ought to be quite business-like, oughtn't we?—that when I married her she was known as the Beautiful Statue."

35   "Oh dear!" said Mrs. Monarch ruefully.

"Of course I should want a certain amount of expression," I rejoined.

"Of *course*!"—and I had never heard such unanimity.

"And then I suppose you know that you'll get awfully tired."

"Oh we *never* get tired!" they eagerly cried.

"Have you had any kind of practice?"

They hesitated—they looked at each other. "We've been photographed— *immensely*," said Mrs. Monarch.

"She means the fellows have asked us themselves," added the Major.

"I see—because you're so good-looking."

"I don't know what they thought, but they were always after us."

"We always got our photographs for nothing," smiled Mrs. Monarch.

"We might have brought some, my dear," her husband remarked.

"I'm not sure we have any left. We've given quantities away," she explained to me.

"With our autographs and that sort of thing," said the Major.

"Are they to be got in the shops?" I enquired as a harmless pleasantry.

"Oh yes, *hers*—they used to be."

"Not now," said Mrs. Monarch with her eyes on the floor.

II

I could fancy the "sort of thing" they put on the presentation copies of their photographs, and I was sure they wrote a beautiful hand. It was odd how quickly I was sure of everything that concerned them. If they were now so poor as to have to earn shillings and pence they could never have had much of a margin. Their good looks had been their capital, and they had good-humouredly made the most of the career that this resource marked out for them. It was in their faces, the blankness, the deep intellectual repose of the twenty years of country-house visiting that had given them pleasant intonations. I could see the sunny drawing-rooms, sprinkled with periodicals she didn't read, in which Mrs. Monarch had continuously sat; I could see the wet shrubberies in which she had walked, equipped to admiration for either exercise. I could see the rich covers[2] the Major had helped to shoot and the wonderful garments in which, late at night, he repaired to the smoking-room to talk about them. I could imagine their leggings and waterproofs, their knowing tweeds and rugs, their rolls of sticks and cases of tackle and neat umbrellas; and I could evoke the exact appearance of their servants and the compact variety of their luggage on the platforms of country stations.

They gave small tips, but they were liked; they didn't do anything themselves, but they were welcome. They looked so well everywhere; they gratified the general relish for stature, complexion and "form." They knew it without fatuity or vulgarity, and they respected themselves in consequence. They weren't superficial; they were thorough and kept themselves up—it had been their line. People with such a taste for activity had to have some line. I could feel how even in a dull house they could have been counted on for the joy of life. At present something had happened—it didn't matter what, their little income had grown less, it had grown least—and they had to do something for pocket-money. Their friends could like them, I made out, without liking to support them. There was

---

2. Flocks of game birds.

something about them that represented credit—their clothes, their manners, their type; but if credit is a large empty pocket in which an occasional chink reverberates, the chink at least must be audible. What they wanted of me was to help to make it so. Fortunately they had no children—I soon divined that. They would also perhaps wish our relations to be kept secret: this was why it was "for the figure"— the reproduction of the face would betray them.

I liked them—I felt, quite as their friends must have done—they were so simple; and I had no objection to them if they would suit. But somehow with all their perfections I didn't easily believe in them. After all they were amateurs, and the ruling passion of my life was the detestation of the amateur. Combined with this was another perversity—an innate preference for the represented subject over the real one: the defect of the real one was so apt to be a lack of representation. I liked things that appeared; then one was sure. Whether they *were* or not was a subordinate and almost always a profitless question. There were other considerations, the first of which was that I already had two or three recruits in use, notably a young person with big feet, in alpaca, from Kilburn, who for a couple of years had come to me regularly for my illustrations and with whom I was still—perhaps ignobly—satisfied. I frankly explained to my visitors how the case stood, but they had taken more precautions than I supposed. They had reasoned out their opportunity, for Claude Rivet had told them of the projected *édition de luxe* of one of the writers of our day—the rarest of the novelists—who, long neglected by the multitudinous vulgar and dearly prized by the attentive (need I mention Philip Vincent?) had had the happy fortune of seeing, late in life, the dawn and then the full light of a higher criticism; an estimate in which on the part of the public there was something really of expiation. The edition preparing, planned by a publisher of taste, was practically an act of high reparation; the wood-cuts with which it was to be enriched were the homage of English art to one of the most independent representatives of English letters. Major and Mrs. Monarch confessed to me they had hoped I might be able to work *them* into my branch of the enterprise. They knew I was to do the first of the books, "Rutland Ramsay," but I had to make clear to them that my participation in the rest of the affair—this first book was to be a test—must depend on the satisfaction I should give. If this should be limited my employers would drop me with scarce common forms. It was therefore a crisis for me, and naturally I was making special preparations, looking about for new people, should they be necessary, and securing the best types. I admitted however that I should like to settle down to two or three good models who would do for everything.

55   "Should we have often to—a—put on special clothes?" Mrs. Monarch timidly demanded.

"Dear yes—that's half the business."

"And should we be expected to supply our own costumes?"

"Oh no; I've got a lot of things. A painter's models put on—or put off—anything he likes."

"And you mean—a—the same?"

60   "The same?"

Mrs. Monarch looked at her husband again.

"Oh she was just wondering," he explained, "if the costumes are in *general* use." I had to confess that they were, and I mentioned further that some of them—I had a lot of genuine greasy last-century things—had served their time, a hundred years ago, on living world-stained men and women; on figures not perhaps so far removed, in that vanished world, from *their* type, the Monarchs', *quoi!*[3] of a breeched and bewigged age. "We'll put on anything that *fits*," said the Major.

"Oh I arrange that—they fit in the pictures."

"I'm afraid I should do better for the modern books. I'd come as you like," said Mrs. Monarch.

"She has got a lot of clothes at home: they might do for contemporary life," her husband continued. 65

"Oh I can fancy scenes in which you'd be quite natural." And indeed I could see the slipshod rearrangements of stale properties—the stories I tried to produce pictures for without the exasperation of reading them—whose sandy tracts the good lady might help to people. But I had to return to the fact that for this sort of work—the daily mechanical grind—I was already equipped: the people I was working with were fully adequate.

"We only thought we might be more like *some* characters," said Mrs. Monarch mildly, getting up.

Her husband also rose; he stood looking at me with a dim wistfulness that was touching in so fine a man.

"Wouldn't it be rather a pull sometimes to have—a—to have—?" He hung fire; he wanted me to help him by phrasing what he meant. But I couldn't—I didn't know. So he brought it out awkwardly: "The *real* thing; a gentleman, you know, or a lady." I was quite ready to give a general assent—I admitted that there was a great deal in that. This encouraged Major Monarch to say, following up his appeal with an unacted gulp: "It's awfully hard—we've tried everything." The gulp was communicative; it proved too much for his wife. Before I knew it Mrs. Monarch had dropped again upon a divan and burst into tears. Her husband sat down beside her, holding one of her hands; whereupon she quickly dried her eyes with the other, while I felt embarrassed as she looked up at me. "There isn't a confounded job I haven't applied for—waited for—prayed for. You can fancy we'd be pretty bad first. Secretaryships and that sort of thing? You might as well ask for a peerage. I'd be *anything*—I'm strong; a messenger or a coalheaver. I'd put on a gold-laced cap and open carriage-doors in front of the haberdasher's; I'd hang about a station to carry portmanteaux; I'd be a postman. But they won't *look* at you; there are thousands as good as yourself already on the ground. *Gentlemen*, poor beggars, who've drunk their wine, who've kept their hunters!"

I was as reassuring as I knew how to be, and my visitors were presently on their feet again while, for the experiment, we agreed on an hour. We were discussing it when the door opened and Miss Churm came in with a wet umbrella. Miss Churm had to take the omnibus to Maida Vale and then walk 70

3. Whatever.

half a mile. She looked a trifle blowsy and slightly splashed. I scarcely ever saw her come in without thinking fresh how odd it was that, being so little in herself, she should yet be so much in others. She was a meagre little Miss Churm, but was such an ample heroine of romance. She was only a freckled cockney, but she could represent everything, from a fine lady to a shepherdess; she had the faculty as she might have had a fine voice or long hair. She couldn't spell and she loved beer, but she had two or three "points," and practice, and a knack, and mother-wit, and a whimsical sensibility, and a love of the theatre, and seven sisters, and not an ounce of respect, especially for the *h*.[4] The first thing my visitors saw was that her umbrella was wet, and in their spotless perfection they visibly winced at it. The rain had come on since their arrival.

"I'm all in a soak; there *was* a mess of people in the 'bus. I wish you lived near a stytion," said Miss Churm. I requested her to get ready as quickly as possible, and she passed into the room in which she always changed her dress. But before going out she asked me what she was to get into this time.

"It's the Russian princess, don't you know?" I answered; "the one with the 'golden eyes,' in black velvet, for the long thing in the *Cheapside*."

"Golden eyes? I *say!*" cried Miss Churm, while my companions watched her with intensity as she withdrew. She always arranged herself, when she was late, before I could turn around; and I kept my visitors a little on purpose, so that they might get an idea, from seeing her, what would be expected of themselves. I mentioned that she was quite my notion of an excellent model—she was really very clever.

"Do you think she looks like a Russian princess?" Major Monarch asked with lurking alarm.

"When I make her, yes."

"Oh if you have to *make* her—!" he reasoned, not without point.

"That's the most you can ask. There are so many who are not makeable."

"Well now, *here's* a lady"—and with a persuasive smile he passed his arm into his wife's—"who's already made!"

"Oh I'm not a Russian princess," Mrs. Monarch protested a little coldly. I could see she had known some and didn't like them. There at once was a complication of a kind I never had to fear with Miss Churm.

This young lady came back in black velvet—the gown was rather rusty and very low on her lean shoulders—and with a Japanese fan in her red hands. I reminded her that in the scene I was doing she had to look over some one's head. "I forget whose it is; but it doesn't matter. Just look over a head."

"I'd rather look over a stove," said Miss Churm; and she took her station near the fire. She fell into position, settled herself into a tall attitude, gave a certain backward inclination to her head and a certain forward droop to her fan, and looked, at least to my prejudiced sense, distinguished and charming, foreign and dangerous. We left her looking so while I went downstairs with Major and Mrs. Monarch.

"I believe I could come about as near it as that," said Mrs. Monarch.

---

4. Working-class Londoners, especially in the East End (cockneys), drop *h*'s 'orribly.

"Oh, you think she's shabby, but you must allow for the alchemy of art."

However, they went off with an evident increase of comfort founded on their demonstrable advantage in being the real thing. I could fancy them shuddering over Miss Churm. She was very droll about them when I went back, for I told her what they wanted.

"Well, if *she* can sit I'll tyke to bookkeeping," said my model.

"She's very ladylike," I replied as an innocent form of aggravation.

"So much the worse for *you*. That means she can't turn round."

"She'll do for the fashionable novels."

"Oh yes, she'll *do* for them!" my model humorously declared. "Ain't they bad enough without her?" I had often sociably denounced them to Miss Churm.

III

It was for the elucidation of a mystery in one of these works that I first tried Mrs. Monarch. Her husband came with her, to be useful if necessary—it was sufficiently clear that as a general thing he would prefer to come with her. At first I wondered if this were for "propriety's" sake—if he were going to be jealous and meddling. The idea was too tiresome, and if it had been confirmed it would speedily have brought our acquaintance to a close. But I soon saw there was nothing in it and that if he accompanied Mrs. Monarch it was—in addition to the chance of being wanted—simply because he had nothing else to do. When they were separate his occupation was gone and they never *had* been separate. I judged rightly that in their awkward situation their close union was their main comfort and that this union had no weak spot. It was a real marriage, an encouragement to the hesitating, a nut for pessimists to crack. Their address was humble—I remember afterwards thinking it had been the only thing about them that was really professional—and I could fancy the lamentable lodgings in which the Major would have been left alone. He could sit there more or less grimly with his wife—he couldn't sit there anyhow without her.

He had too much tact to try and make himself agreeable when he couldn't be useful; so when I was too absorbed in my work to talk he simply sat and waited. But I liked to hear him talk—it made my work, when not interrupting it, less mechanical, less special. To listen to him was to combine the excitement of going out with the economy of staying at home. There was only one hindrance—that I seemed not to know any of the people this brilliant couple had known. I think he wondered extremely, during the term of our intercourse, whom the deuce I *did* know. He hadn't a stray sixpence of an idea to fumble for, so we didn't spin it very fine; we confined ourselves to questions of leather and even of liquor—saddlers and breeches-makers and how to get excellent claret cheap—and matters like "good trains" and the habits of small game. His lore on these last subjects was astonishing—he managed to interweave the station-master with the ornithologist. When he couldn't talk about greater things he could talk cheerfully about smaller, and since I couldn't accompany him into reminiscences of the fashionable world he could lower the conversation without a visible effort to my level.

One day when my young lady happened to be present with my other sitters—she even dropped in, when it was convenient, for a chat—I asked her to be so good as to lend a hand in getting tea, a service with which she was familiar and which was one of a class that, living as I did in a small way, with slender domestic resources, I often appealed to my models to render. They liked to lay hands on my property, to break the sitting, and sometimes the china—it made them feel Bohemian. The next time I saw Miss Churm after this incident she surprised me greatly by making a scene about it—she accused me of having wished to humiliate her. She hadn't resented the outrage at the time, but had seemed obliging and amused, enjoying the comedy of asking Mrs. Monarch, who sat vague and silent, whether she would have cream and sugar, and putting an exaggerated simper into the question. She had tried intonations—as if she too wished to pass for the real thing—till I was afraid my other visitors would take offence.

Oh they were determined not to do this, and their touching patience was the measure of their great need. They would sit by the hour, uncomplaining, till I was ready to use them; they would come back on the chance of being wanted and would walk away cheerfully if it failed. I used to go to the door with them to see in what magnificent order they retreated. I tried to find other employment for them—I introduced them to several artists. But they didn't "take," for reasons I could appreciate, and I became rather anxiously aware that after such disappointments they fell back upon me with a heavier weight. They did me the honor to think me most *their* form. They weren't romantic enough for the painters, and in those days there were few serious workers in black-and-white. Besides, they had an eye to the great job I had mentioned to them—they had secretly set their hearts on supplying the right essence for my pictorial vindication of our fine novelist. They knew that for this undertaking I should want no costume-effects, none of the frippery of past ages—that it was a case in which everything would be contemporary and satirical and presumably genteel. If I could work them into it their future would be assured, for the labour would of course be long and the occupation steady.

One day Mrs. Monarch came without her husband—she explained his absence by his having had to go to the City.[8] While she sat there in her usual relaxed majesty there came at the door a knock which I immediately recognised as the subdued appeal of a model out of work. It was followed by the entrance of a young man whom I at once saw to be a foreigner and who proved in fact an Italian acquainted with no English word but my name, which he uttered in a way that made it seem to include all others. I hadn't then visited his country, nor was I proficient in his tongue; but as he was not so meanly constituted—what Italian is?—as to depend only on that member for expression he conveyed to me, in familiar but graceful mimicry, that he was in search of exactly the employment in which the lady before me was engaged. I was not struck with him at first, and while I continued to draw I dropped few signs of interest or encouragement. He stood his ground however—not importunately, but with a

8. Financial and legal center of London.

dumb dog-like fidelity in his eyes that amounted to innocent impudence, the manner of a devoted servant—he might have been in the house for years—unjustly suspected. Suddenly it struck me that this very attitude and expression made a picture; whereupon I told him to sit down and wait till I should be free. There was another picture in the way he obeyed me, and I observed as I worked that there were others still in the way he looked wonderingly, with his head thrown back, about the high studio. He might have been crossing himself in Saint Peter's. Before I finished I said to myself "The fellow's a bankrupt orange-monger, but a treasure."

When Mrs. Monarch withdrew he passed across the room like a flash to open the door for her, standing there with the rapt pure gaze of the young Dante spellbound by the young Beatrice.[9] As I never insisted, in such situations, on the blankness of the British domestic, I reflected that he had the making of a servant—and I needed one, but couldn't pay him to be only that—as well as of a model; in short I resolved to adopt my bright adventurer if he would agree to officiate in the double capacity. He jumped at my offer, and in the event my rashness—for I had really known nothing about him—wasn't brought home to me. He proved a sympathetic though a desultory ministrant, and had in a wonderful degree the *sentiment de la pose*.[1] It was uncultivated, instinctive, a part of the happy instinct that had guided him to my door and helped him to spell out my name on the card nailed to it. He had had no other introduction to me than a guess, from the shape of my high north window, seen outside, that my place was a studio and that as a studio it would contain an artist. He had wandered to England in search of fortune, like other itinerants, and had embarked, with a partner and a small green hand-cart, on the sale of penny ices. The ices had melted away and the partner had dissolved in their train. My young man wore tight yellow trousers with reddish stripes and his name was Oronte. He was sallow but fair, and when I put him into some old clothes of my own he looked like an Englishman. He was as good as Miss Churm, who could look, when requested, like an Italian.

IV

I thought Mrs. Monarch's face slightly convulsed when, on her coming back with her husband, she found Oronte installed. It was strange to have to recognise in a scrap of a lazzarone[2] a competitor to her magnificent Major. It was she who scented danger first, for the Major was anecdotally unconscious. But Oronte gave us tea, with a hundred eager confusions—he had never been concerned in so queer a process—and I think she thought better of me for having at last an "establishment." They saw a couple of drawings that I had made of the establishment, and Mrs. Monarch hinted that it never would have struck her he had sat for them. "Now the drawings you make from *us*, they look exactly like us," she reminded me, smiling in triumph; and I recognized that this was indeed just their defect. When I drew the Monarchs I couldn't anyhow get away from them—get into the character I wanted to represent; and I hadn't the least desire my model should be discoverable in my picture. Miss Churm never was, and Mrs. Monarch thought I hid her, very properly, because she was vulgar; whereas if she was lost it was only as the dead who go to heaven are lost—in the gain of an angel the more.

By this time I had got a certain start with "Rutland Ramsay," the first novel in the great projected series; that is I had produced a dozen drawings, several with the help of the Major and his wife, and I had sent them in for approval. My understanding with the publishers, as I have already hinted, had been that I was to be left to do my work, in this particular case, as I liked, with the whole book committed to me; but my connexion with the rest of the series was only contingent. There were moments when, frankly, it *was* a comfort to have the real thing under one's hand; for there were characters in "Rutland Ramsay" that were very much like it. There were people presumably as erect as the Major and women of as good a fashion as Mrs. Monarch. There was a great deal of country-house life—treated, it is true, in a fine fanciful ironical generalised way—and there was a considerable implication of knickerbockers and kilts. There were certain things I had to settle at the outset; such things for instance as the exact appearance of the hero and the particular bloom and figure of the heroine. The author of course gave me a lead, but there was a margin for interpretation. I took the Monarchs into my confidence, I told them frankly what I was about, I mentioned my embarrassments and alternatives. "Oh take *him!*" Mrs. Monarch murmured sweetly, looking at her husband; and "What could you want better than my wife?" the Major enquired with the comfortable candour that now prevailed between us.

I wasn't obliged to answer these remarks—I was only obliged to place my sitters. I wasn't easy in mind, and I postponed a little timidly perhaps the solving of my question. The book was a large canvas, the other figures were numerous, and I worked off at first some of the episodes in which the hero and the heroine were not concerned. When once I had set *them* up I should have to stick to them—I couldn't make my young man seven feet high in one place and five feet nine in another. I inclined on the whole to the latter measurement, though the Major more than once reminded me that *he* looked about as young as any one. It was indeed quite possible to arrange him, for the figure, so that it would have been difficult to detect his age. After the spontaneous Oronte had been with me a month, and after I had given him to understand several times over that his native exuberance would presently constitute an insurmountable barrier to our further intercourse, I waked to a sense of his heroic capacity. He was only five feet seven, but the remaining inches were latent. I tried him almost secretly at first, for I was really rather afraid of the judgment my other models would pass on such a choice. If they regarded Miss Churm as little better than a snare what would they think of the representation by a person so little the real thing as an Italian street-vendor of a protagonist formed by a public school?

If I went a little in fear of them it wasn't because they bullied me, because they had got an oppressive foothold, but because in their really pathetic decorum and mysteriously permanent newness they counted on me so intensely. I was therefore very glad when Jack Hawley came home: he was always of such good counsel. He painted badly himself, but there was no one like him for putting his finger on the place. He had been absent from England for a year; he had been somewhere—I don't remember where—to get a fresh eye. I was in a good deal of dread of any such organ, but we were old friends; he had been away for months and a sense of emptiness was creeping into my life. I hadn't dodged a missile for a year.

He came back with a fresh eye, but with the same old black velvet blouse, and the first evening he spent in my studio we smoked cigarettes till the small hours. He had done no work himself, he had only got the eye; so the field was clear for the production of my little things. He wanted to see what I had produced for the *Cheapside*, but he was disappointed in the exhibition. That at least seemed the meaning of two or three comprehensive groans which, as he lounged on my big divan, his leg folded under him, looking at my latest drawings, issued from his lips with the smoke of the cigarette. 105

"What's the matter with you?" I asked.

"What's the matter with *you?*"

"Nothing save that I'm mystified."

"You are indeed. You're quite off the hinge. What's the meaning of this new fad?" And he tossed me, with visible irreverence, a drawing in which I happened to have depicted both my elegant models. I asked if he didn't think it good, and he replied that it struck him as execrable, given the sort of thing I had always represented myself to him as wishing to arrive at; but I let that pass—I was so anxious to see exactly what he meant. The two figures in the picture looked colossal, but I supposed this was *not* what he meant, inasmuch as, for aught he knew the contrary, I might have been trying for some such effect. I maintained that I was working exactly in the same way as when he last had done me the honour to tell me I might do something some day. "Well, there's a screw loose somewhere," he answered; "wait a bit and I'll discover it." I depended upon him to do so: where else was the fresh eye? But he produced at last nothing more luminous than "I don't know—I don't like your types." This was lame for a critic who had never consented to discuss with me anything but the question of execution, the direction of strokes and the mystery of values.

"In the drawings you've been looking at I think my types are very handsome." 110

"Oh they won't do!"

"I've been working with new models."

"I see you have. *They* won't do."

"Are you very sure of that?"

"Absolutely—they're stupid." 115

"You mean *I* am—for I ought to get round that."

"You *can't*—with such people. Who are they?"

I told him, so far as was necessary, and he concluded heartlessly: "Ce sont des gens qu'il faut mettre à la porte."[3]

"You've never seen them; they're awfully good"—I flew to their defence.

"Not seen them? Why all this recent work of yours drops to pieces with them. It's all I want to see of them."

"No one else has said anything against it—the *Cheapside* people are pleased."

"Everyone else is an ass, and the *Cheapside* people the biggest asses of all. Come, don't pretend at this time of day to have pretty illusions about the public, especially about publishers and editors. It's not for *such* animals you work—it's for those who know, *coloro che sanno;*[4] so keep straight for *me* if you can't keep straight for yourself. There was a certain sort of thing you used to try for—and a very good thing it was. But this twaddle isn't *in* it." When I talked with Hawley later about "Rutland Ramsay" and its possible successors he declared that I must get back into my boat again or I should go to the bottom. His voice in short was the voice of warning.

I noted the warning, but I didn't turn my friends out of doors. They bored me a good deal; but the very fact that they bored me admonished me not to sacrifice them—if there was anything to be done with them—simply to irritation. As I look back at this phase they seem to me to have pervaded my life not a little. I have a vision of them as most of the time in my studio, seated against the wall on an old velvet bench to be out of the way, and resembling the while a pair of patient courtiers in a royal ante-chamber. I'm convinced that during the coldest weeks of the winter they held their ground because it saved them fire. Their newness was losing its gloss, and it was impossible not to feel them objects of charity. Whenever Miss Churm arrived they went away, and after I was fairly launched in "Rutland Ramsay" Miss Churm arrived pretty often. They managed to express to me tacitly that they supposed I wanted her for the low life of the book, and I let them suppose it, since they had attempted to study the work—it was lying about the studio—without discovering that it dealt only with the highest circles. They had dipped into the most brilliant of our novelists without deciphering many passages. I still took an hour from them, now and again, in spite of Jack Hawley's warning: it would be time enough to dismiss them, if dismissal should be necessary, when the rigour of the season was over. Hawley had made their acquaintance—he had met them at my fireside—and thought them a ridiculous pair. Learning that he was a painter they tried to approach him, to show him too that they were the real thing; but he looked at them, across the big room, as if they were miles away: they were a compendium of everything he most objected to in the social system of his country. Such people as that, all convention and patent-leather, with ejaculations that stopped conversation, had no business in a studio. A studio was a place to learn to see, and how could you see through a pair of feather-beds?

3. "That kind of person should be shown the door."   4. Dante, *The Divine Comedy*, "The Inferno," 4:131: actually, *color che sanno*—"those who know."

The main inconvenience I suffered at their hands was that at first I was shy of letting it break upon them that my artful little servant had begun to sit to me for "Rutland Ramsay." They knew I had been odd enough—they were prepared by this time to allow oddity to artists—to pick a foreign vagabond out of the streets when I might have had a person with whiskers and credentials, but it was some time before they learned how high I rated his accomplishments. They found him in an attitude more than once, but they never doubted I was doing him as an organ-grinder. There were several things they never guessed, and one of them was that for a striking scene in the novel, in which a footman briefly figured, it occurred to me to make use of Major Monarch as the menial. I kept putting this off, I didn't like to ask him to don the livery—besides the difficulty of finding a livery to fit him. At last, one day late in the winter, when I was at work on the despised Oronte, who caught one's idea on the wing, and was in the glow of feeling myself go very straight, they came in, the Major and his wife, with their society laugh about nothing (there was less and less to laugh at); came on like country-callers—they always reminded me of that—who have walked across the park after church and are presently persuaded to stay to luncheon. Luncheon was over, but they could stay to tea—I knew they wanted it. The fit was on me, however, and I couldn't let my ardour cool and my work wait, with the fading daylight, while my model prepared it. So I asked Mrs. Monarch if she would mind laying it out—a request which for an instant brought all the blood to her face. Her eyes were on her husband's for a second, and some mute telegraphy passed between them. Their folly was over the next instant; his cheerful shrewdness put an end to it. So far from pitying their wounded pride, I must add, I was moved to give it as complete a lesson as I could. They bustled about together and got out the cups and saucers and made the kettle boil. I know they felt as if they were waiting on my servant, and when the tea was prepared I said: "He'll have a cup, please—he's tired." Mrs. Monarch brought him one where he stood, and he took it from her, as if he had been a gentleman at a party squeezing a crush-hat with an elbow.

Then it came over me that she had made a great effort for me—made it with a kind of nobleness—and that I owed her a compensation. Each time I saw her after this I wondered what the compensation could be. I couldn't go on doing the wrong thing to oblige them. Oh it *was* the wrong thing, the stamp of the work for which they sat—Hawley was not the only person to say it now. I sent in a large number of the drawings I had made for "Rutland Ramsay," and I received a warning that was more to the point than Hawley's. The artistic adviser of the house for which I was working was of opinion that many of my illustrations were not what had been looked for. Most of these illustrations were the subjects in which the Monarchs had figured. Without going into the question of what *had* been looked for, I had to face the fact that at this rate I shouldn't get the other books to do. I hurled myself in despair on Miss Churm—I put her through all her paces. I not only adopted Oronte publicly as my hero, but one morning when the Major looked in to see if I didn't require him to finish a *Cheapside* figure for which he had begun to sit the week before, I told him I

125

had changed my mind—I'd do the drawing from my man. At this my visitor turned pale and stood looking at me. "Is *he* your idea of an English gentleman?" he asked.

I was disappointed, I was nervous, I wanted to get on with my work; so I replied with irritation: "Oh my dear Major—I can't be ruined for *you!*" . . .

It was a horrid speech, but he stood another moment—after which, without a word, he quitted the studio. I drew a long breath, for I said to myself that I shouldn't see him again. I hadn't told him definitely that I was in danger of having my work rejected, but I was vexed at his not having felt the catastrophe in the air, read with me the moral of our fruitless collaboration, the lesson that in the deceptive atmosphere of art even the highest respectability may fail of being plastic.

I didn't owe my friends money, but I did see them again. They reappeared together three days later, and, given all the other facts, there was something tragic in that one. It was a clear proof they could find nothing else in life to do. They had threshed the matter out in a dismal conference—they had digested the bad news that they were not in for the series. If they weren't useful to me even for the *Cheapside* their function seemed difficult to determine, and I could only judge at first that they had come, forgivingly, decorously, to take a last leave. This made me rejoice in secret that I had little leisure for a scene; for I had placed both my other models in position together and I was pegging away at a drawing from which I hoped to derive glory. It had been suggested by the passage in which Rutland Ramsay, drawing up a chair to Artemisia's piano-stool, says extraordinary things to her while she ostensibly fingers out a difficult piece of music. I had done Miss Churm at the piano before—it was an attitude in which she knew how to take on an absolutely poetic grace. I wished the two figures to "compose" together with intensity, and my little Italian had entered perfectly into my conception. The pair were vividly before me, the piano had been pulled out; it was a charming show of blended youth and murmured love, which I had only to catch and keep. My visitors stood and looked at it, and I was friendly to them over my shoulder.

They made no response, but I was used to silent company and went on with my work, only a little disconcerted—even though exhilarated by the sense that *this* was at least the ideal thing—at not having got rid of them after all. Presently I heard Mrs. Monarch's sweet voice beside or rather above me: "I wish her hair were a little better done." I looked up and she was staring with a strange fixedness at Miss Churm, whose back was turned to her. "Do you mind my just touching it?" she went on—a question which made me spring up for an instant as with the instinctive fear that she might do the young lady a harm. But she quieted me with a glance I shall never forget—I confess I should like to have been able to paint *that*—and went for a moment to my model. She spoke to her softly, laying a hand on her shoulder and bending over her; and as the girl, understanding, gratefully assented, she disposed her rough curls, with a few quick passes, in such a way as to make Miss Churm's head twice as charming. It was one of the most heroic personal services I've ever seen rendered. Then Mrs. Monarch turned away with a low sigh and, looking about her as if for something to do, stooped to the floor with a noble humility and picked up a dirty rag that had dropped out of my paint-box.

The Major meanwhile had also been looking for something to do, and, wandering to the other end of the studio, saw before him my breakfast-things neglected, unremoved. "I say, can't I be useful *here?*" he called out to me with an irrepressible quaver. I assented with a laugh that I fear was awkward, and for the next ten minutes, while I worked, I heard the light clatter of china and the tinkle of spoons and glass. Mrs. Monarch assisted her husband—they washed up my crockery, they put it away. They wandered off into my little scullery, and I afterwards found that they had cleaned my knives and that my slender stock of plate had an unprecedented surface. When it came over me, the latent eloquence of what they were doing, I confess that my drawing was blurred for a moment—the picture swam. They had accepted their failure, but they couldn't accept their fate. They had bowed their heads in bewilderment to the perverse and cruel law in virtue of which the real thing could be so much less precious than the unreal; but they didn't want to starve. If my servants were my models, then my models might be my servants. They would reverse the parts—the others would sit for the ladies and gentlemen and *they* would do the work. They would still be in the studio—it was an intense dumb appeal to me not to turn them out. "Take us on," they wanted to say—"we'll do *anything*."

My pencil dropped from my hand; my sitting was spoiled and I got rid of my sitters, who were also evidently rather mystified and awestruck. Then, alone with the Major and his wife I had a most uncomfortable moment. He put their prayer into a single sentence: "I say, you know—just let *us* do for you, can't you?" I couldn't—it was dreadful to see them emptying my slops; but I pretended I could, to oblige them, for about a week. Then I gave them a sum of money to go away, and I never saw them again. I obtained the remaining books, but my friend Hawley repeats that Major and Mrs. Monarch did me a permanent harm, got me into false ways. If it be true I'm content to have paid the price—for the memory.

1892, 1909

CHARLOTTE PERKINS GILMAN

The Yellow Wallpaper

It is very seldom that mere ordinary people like John and myself secure ancestral halls for the summer.

A colonial mansion, a hereditary estate, I would say a haunted house, and reach the height of romantic felicity—but that would be asking too much of fate!

Still I will proudly declare that there is something queer about it.

Else, why should it be let so cheaply? And why have stood so long untenanted?

John laughs at me, of course, but one expects that in marriage.

John is practical in the extreme. He has no patience with faith, an intense horror of superstition, and he scoffs openly at any talk of things not to be felt and seen and put down in figures.

John is a physician, and *perhaps*—(I would not say it to a living soul, of course, but this is dead paper and a great relief to my mind—) *perhaps* that is one reason I do not get well faster.

You see he does not believe I am sick!

And what can one do?

If a physician of high standing, and one's own husband, assures friends and relatives that there is really nothing the matter with one but temporary nervous depression—a slight hysterical tendency—what is one to do?

My brother is also a physician, and also of high standing, and he says the same thing.

So I take phosphates or phosphites—whichever it is, and tonics, and journeys, and air, and exercise, and am absolutely forbidden to "work" until I am well again.

Personally, I disagree with their ideas.

Personally, I believe that congenial work, with excitement and change, would do me good.

But what is one to do?

I did write for a while in spite of them; but it *does* exhaust me a good deal— having to be so sly about it, or else meet with heavy opposition.

I sometimes fancy that in my condition if I had less opposition and more society and stimulus—but John says the very worst thing I can do is to think about my condition, and I confess it always makes me feel bad.

So I will let it alone and talk about the house.

The most beautiful place! It is quite alone, standing well back from the road, quite three miles from the village. It makes me think of English places that you read about, for there are hedges and walls and gates that lock, and lots of separate little houses for the gardeners and people.

There is a *delicious* garden! I never saw such a garden—large and shady, full of box-bordered paths, and lined with long grape-covered arbors with seats under them.

There were greenhouses, too, but they are all broken now.

There was some legal trouble, I believe, something about the heirs and co-heirs; anyhow, the place has been empty for years.

That spoils my ghostliness, I am afraid, but I don't care—there is something strange about the house—I can feel it.

I even said so to John one moonlight evening, but he said what I felt was a *draught,* and shut the window.

I get unreasonably angry with John sometimes. I'm sure I never used to be so sensitive. I think it is due to this nervous condition.

But John says if I feel so, I shall neglect proper self-control; so I take pains to control myself—before him, at least, and that makes me very tired.

I don't like our room a bit. I wanted one downstairs that opened on the piazza and had roses all over the window, and such pretty old-fashioned chintz hangings! but John would not hear of it.

He said there was only one window and not room for two beds, and no near room for him if he took another.

He is very careful and loving, and hardly lets me stir without special direction.

I have a schedule prescription for each hour in the day; he takes all care from me, and so I feel basely ungrateful not to value it more.

He said we came here solely on my account, that I was to have perfect rest and all the air I could get. "Your exercise depends on your strength, my dear," said he, "and your food somewhat on your appetite; but air you can absorb all the time." So we took the nursery at the top of the house.

It is a big, airy room, the whole floor nearly, with windows that look all ways, and air and sunshine galore. It was nursery first and then playroom and gymnasium, I should judge; for the windows are barred for little children, and there are rings and things in the walls.

The paint and paper look as if a boys' school had used it. It is stripped off—the paper—in great patches all around the head of my bed, about as far as I can reach, and in a great place on the other side of the room low down. I never saw a worse paper in my life.

One of those sprawling flamboyant patterns committing every artistic sin.

It is dull enough to confuse the eye in following, pronounced enough to constantly irritate and provoke study, and when you follow the lame uncertain curves for a little distance they suddenly commit suicide—plunge off at outrageous angles, destroy themselves in unheard of contradictions.

The color is repellant, almost revolting; a smouldering unclean yellow, strangely faded by the slow-turning sunlight.

It is a dull yet lurid orange in some places, a sickly sulphur tint in others.

No wonder the children hated it! I should hate it myself if I had to live in this room long.

There comes John, and I must put this away,—he hates to have me write a word.

We have been here two weeks, and I haven't felt like writing before, since that first day.

I am sitting by the window now, up in this atrocious nursery, and there is nothing to hinder my writing as much as I please, save lack of strength.

John is away all day, and even some nights when his cases are serious.

I am glad my case is not serious!

But these nervous troubles are dreadfully depressing.

John does not know how much I really suffer. He knows there is no *reason* to suffer, and that satisfies him.

Of course it is only nervousness. It does weigh on me so not to do my duty in any way!

I mean to be such a help to John, such a real rest and comfort, and here I am a comparative burden already!

Nobody would believe what an effort it is to do what little I am able,—to dress and entertain, and order things.

It is fortunate Mary is so good with the baby. Such a dear baby!

And yet I *cannot* be with him, it makes me so nervous.

I suppose John never was nervous in his life. He laughs at me so about this wallpaper!

At first he meant to repaper the room, but afterwards he said that I was letting it get the better of me, and that nothing was worse for a nervous patient than to give way to such fancies.

He said that after the wallpaper was changed it would be the heavy bedstead, and then the barred windows, and then that gate at the head of the stairs, and so on.

"You know the place is doing you good," he said, "and really, dear, I don't care to renovate the house just for a three months' rental."

"Then do let us go downstairs," I said, "there are such pretty rooms there."

Then he took me in his arms and called me a blessed little goose, and said he would go down cellar, if I wished, and have it whitewashed into the bargain.

But he is right enough about the beds and windows and things.

It is an airy and comfortable room as any one need wish, and, of course, I would not be so silly as to make him uncomfortable just for a whim.

I'm really getting quite fond of the big room, all but that horrid paper.

Out of one window I can see the garden, those mysterious deep-shaded arbors, the riotous old-fashioned flowers, and bushes and gnarly trees.

Out of another I get a lovely view of the bay and a little private wharf belonging to the estate. There is a beautiful shaded lane that runs down there from the house. I always fancy I see people walking in these numerous paths and arbors, but John has cautioned me not to give way to fancy in the least. He says that with my imaginative power and habit of story-making, a nervous weakness like mine is sure to lead to all manner of excited fancies, and that I ought to use my will and good sense to check the tendency. So I try.

I think sometimes that if I were only well enough to write a little it would relieve the press of ideas and rest me.

But I find I get pretty tired when I try.

It is so discouraging not to have any advice and companionship about my work. When I get really well, John says we will ask Cousin Henry and Julia down for a long visit; but he says he would as soon put fireworks in my pillowcase as to let me have those stimulating people about now.

I wish I could get well faster.

But I must not think about that. This paper looks to me as if it *knew* what a vicious influence it had!

There is a recurrent spot where the pattern lolls like a broken neck and two bulbous eyes stare at you upside down.

I get positively angry with the impertinence of it and the everlastingness. Up and down and sideways they crawl, and those absurd, unblinking eyes are everywhere. There is one place where two breadths didn't match, and the eyes go all up and down the line, one a little higher than the other.

I never saw so much expression in an inanimate thing before, and we all know how much expression they have! I used to lie awake as a child and get more entertainment and terror out of blank walls and plain furniture than most children could find in a toy-store.

I remember what a kindly wink the knobs of our big, old bureau used to have, and there was one chair that always seemed like a strong friend.

I used to feel that if any of the other things looked too fierce I could always hop into that chair and be safe.

The furniture in this room is no worse than inharmonious, however, for we had to bring it all from downstairs. I suppose when this was used as a playroom they had to take the nursery things out, and no wonder! I never saw such ravages as the children have made here.

The wallpaper, as I said before, is torn off in spots, and it sticketh closer than a brother—they must have had perseverance as well as hatred.

Then the floor is scratched and gouged and splintered, the plaster itself is dug out here and there, and this great heavy bed which is all we found in the room, looks as if it had been through the wars.

But I don't mind it a bit—only the paper.

There comes John's sister. Such a dear girl as she is, and so careful of me! I must not let her find me writing.

She is a perfect and enthusiastic housekeeper, and hopes for no better profession. I verily believe she thinks it is the writing which made me sick!

But I can write when she is out, and see her a long way off from these windows.

There is one that commands the road, a lovely shaded winding road, and one that just looks off over the country. A lovely country, too, full of great elms and velvet meadows.

This wallpaper has a kind of sub-pattern in a different shade, a particularly irritating one, for you can only see it in certain lights, and not clearly then.

But in the places where it isn't faded and where the sun is just so—I can see a strange, provoking, formless sort of figure, that seems to skulk about behind that silly and conspicuous front design.

There's sister on the stairs!

Well, the Fourth of July is over! The people are all gone and I am tired out. John thought it might do me good to see a little company, so we just had mother and Nellie and the children down for a week.

Of course I didn't do a thing. Jennie sees to everything now.

But it tired me all the same.

John says if I don't pick up faster he shall send me to Weir Mitchell[1] in the fall.

But I don't want to go there at all. I had a friend who was in his hands once, and she says he is just like John and my brother, only more so!

---

1. Silas Weir Mitchell (1829–1914), American physician, novelist, and specialist in nerve disorders, popularized the "rest cure."

Besides, it is such an undertaking to go so far.

I don't feel as if it was worth while to turn my hand over for anything, and I'm getting dreadfully fretful and querulous.

90   I cry at nothing, and cry most of the time.

Of course I don't when John is here, or anybody else, but when I am alone.

And I am alone a good deal just now. John is kept in town very often by serious cases, and Jennie is good and lets me alone when I want her to.

So I walk a little in the garden or down that lovely lane, sit on the porch under the roses, and lie down up here a good deal.

I'm getting really fond of the room in spite of the wallpaper. Perhaps *because* of the wallpaper.

95   It dwells in my mind so!

I lie here on this great immovable bed—it is nailed down, I believe—and follow that pattern about by the hour. It is as good as gymnastics, I assure you. I start, we'll say, at the bottom, down in the corner over there where it has not been touched, and I determine for the thousandth time that I *will* follow that pointless pattern to some sort of conclusion.

I know a little of the principle of design, and I know this thing was not arranged on any laws of radiation, or alternation, or repetition, or symmetry, or anything else that I ever heard of.

It is repeated, of course, by the breadths, but not otherwise.

Looked at in one way each breadth stands alone, the bloated curves and flourishes—a kind of "debased Romanesque" with *delirium tremens*—go waddling up and down in isolated columns of fatuity.

100   But, on the other hand, they connect diagonally, and the sprawling outlines run off in great slanting waves of optic horror, like a lot of wallowing seaweeds in full chase.

The whole thing goes horizontally, too, at least it seems so, and I exhaust myself in trying to distinguish the order of its going in that direction.

They have used a horizontal breadth for a frieze, and that adds wonderfully to the confusion.

There is one end of the room where it is almost intact, and there, when the crosslights fade and the low sun shines directly upon it, I can almost fancy radiation after all,—the interminable grotesque seem to form around a common center and rush off in headlong plunges of equal distraction.

It makes me tired to follow it. I will take a nap I guess.

105   I don't know why I should write this.

I don't want to.

I don't feel able.

And I know John would think it absurd. But I *must* say what I feel and think in some way—it is such a relief!

But the effort is getting to be greater than the relief.

110   Half the time now I am awfully lazy, and lie down ever so much.

John says I mustn't lose my strength, and has me take cod liver oil and lots of tonics and things, to say nothing of ale and wine and rare meat.

Dear John! He loves me very dearly, and hates to have me sick. I tried to have a real earnest reasonable talk with him the other day, and tell him how I wish he would let me go and make a visit to Cousin Henry and Julia.

But he said I wasn't able to go, nor able to stand it after I got there; and I did not make out a very good case for myself, for I was crying before I had finished.

It is getting to be a great effort for me to think straight. Just this nervous weakness I suppose.

And dear John gathered me up in his arms, and just carried me upstairs and laid me on the bed, and sat by me and read to me till it tired my head. 115

He said I was his darling and his comfort and all he had, and that I must take care of myself for his sake, and keep well.

He says no one but myself can help me out of it, that I must use my will and self-control and not let any silly fancies run away with me.

There's one comfort, the baby is well and happy, and does not have to occupy this nursery with the horrid wallpaper.

If we had not used it, that blessed child would have! What a fortunate escape! Why, I wouldn't have a child of mine, an impressionable little thing, live in such a room for worlds.

I never thought of it before, but it is lucky that John kept me here after all, I 120 can stand it so much easier than a baby, you see.

Of course I never mention it to them any more—I am too wise,—but I keep watch of it all the same.

There are things in that paper that nobody knows but me, or ever will.

Behind that outside pattern the dim shapes get clearer every day.

It is always the same shape, only very numerous.

And it is like a woman stooping down and creeping about behind that pat- 125 tern. I don't like it a bit. I wonder—I begin to think—I wish John would take me away from here!

It is so hard to talk with John about my case, because he is so wise, and because he loves me so.

But I tried it last night.

It was moonlight. The moon shines in all around just as the sun does.

I hate to see it sometimes, it creeps so slowly, and always comes in by one window or another.

John was asleep and I hated to waken him, so I kept still and watched the 130 moonlight on that undulating wallpaper till I felt creepy.

The faint figure behind seemed to shake the pattern, just as if she wanted to get out.

I got up softly and went to feel and see if the paper *did* move, and when I came back John was awake.

"What is it, little girl?" he said. "Don't go walking about like that—you'll get cold."

I thought it was a good time to talk, so I told him that I really was not gaining here, and that I wished he would take me away.

135   "Why, darling!" said he, "our lease will be up in three weeks, and I can't see how to leave before.

"The repairs are not done at home, and I cannot possibly leave town just now. Of course if you were in any danger, I could and would, but you really are better, dear, whether you can see it or not. I am a doctor, dear, and I know. You are gaining flesh and color, your appetite is better, I feel really much easier about you."

"I don't weigh a bit more," said I, "nor as much; and my appetite may be better in the evening when you are here, but it is worse in the morning when you are away!"

"Bless her little heart!" said he with a big hug, "she shall be as sick as she pleases! But now let's improve the shining hours by going to sleep, and talk about it in the morning!"

"And you won't go away?" I asked gloomily.

140   "Why, how can I, dear? It is only three weeks more and then we will take a nice little trip of a few days while Jennie is getting the house ready. Really dear you are better!"

"Better in body perhaps—" I began, and stopped short, for he sat up straight and looked at me with such a stern, reproachful look that I could not say another word.

"My darling," said he, "I beg of you, for my sake and for our child's sake, as well as for your own, that you will never for one instant let that idea enter your mind! There is nothing so dangerous, so fascinating, to a temperament like yours. It is a false and foolish fancy. Can you not trust me as a physician when I tell you so?"

So of course I said no more on that score, and we went to sleep before long. He thought I was asleep first, but I wasn't, and lay there for hours trying to decide whether that front pattern and the back pattern really did move together or separately.

On a pattern like this, by daylight, there is a lack of sequence, a defiance of law, that is a constant irritant to a normal mind.

145   The color is hideous enough, and unreliable enough, and infuriating enough, but the pattern is torturing.

You think you have mastered it, but just as you get well underway in following, it turns a back-somersault and there you are. It slaps you in the face, knocks you down, and tramples upon you. It is like a bad dream.

The outside pattern is a florid arabesque, reminding one of a fungus. If you can imagine a toadstool in joints, an interminable string of toadstools, budding and sprouting in endless convolutions—why, that is something like it.

That is, sometimes!

There is one marked peculiarity about this paper, a thing nobody seems to notice but myself, and that is that it changes as the light changes.

150   When the sun shoots in through the east window—I always watch for that first long, straight ray—it changes so quickly that I never can quite believe it.

That is why I watch it always.

By moonlight—the moon shines in all night when there is a moon—I wouldn't know it was the same paper.

At night in any kind of light, in twilight, candlelight, lamplight, and worst of all by moonlight, it becomes bars! The outside pattern I mean, and the woman behind it is as plain as can be.

I didn't realize for a long time what the thing was that showed behind, that dim sub-pattern, but now I am quite sure it is a woman.

By daylight she is subdued, quiet. I fancy it is the pattern that keeps her so still. It is so puzzling. It keeps me quiet by the hour. 155

I lie down ever so much now. John says it is good for me, and to sleep all I can.

Indeed he started the habit by making me lie down for an hour after each meal.

It is a very bad habit I am convinced, for you see I don't sleep.

And that cultivates deceit, for I don't tell them I'm awake—O no!

The fact is I am getting a little afraid of John. 160

He seems very queer sometimes, and even Jennie has an inexplicable look.

It strikes me occasionally, just as a scientific hypothesis,—that perhaps it is the paper!

I have watched John when he did not know I was looking, and come into the room suddenly on the most innocent excuses, and I've caught him several times *looking at the paper!* And Jennie too. I caught Jennie with her hand on it once.

She didn't know I was in the room, and when I asked her in a quiet, a very quiet voice, with the most restrained manner possible, what she was doing with the paper—she turned around as if she had been caught stealing, and looked quite angry—asked me why I should frighten her so!

Then she said that the paper stained everything it touched, that she had found yellow smooches on all my clothes and John's, and she wished we would be more careful! 165

Did not that sound innocent? But I know she was studying that pattern, and I am determined that nobody shall find it out but myself!

Life is very much more exciting now than it used to be. You see I have something more to expect, to look forward to, to watch. I really do eat better, and am more quiet than I was.

John is so pleased to see me improve! He laughed a little the other day, and said I seemed to be flourishing in spite of my wallpaper.

I turned it off with a laugh. I had no intention of telling him it was *because* of the wallpaper—he would make fun of me. He might even want to take me away.

I don't want to leave now until I have found it out. There is a week more, and I think that will be enough. 170

I'm feeling ever so much better! I don't sleep much at night, for it is so interesting to watch developments; but I sleep a good deal in the daytime.

In the daytime it is tiresome and perplexing.

There are always new shoots on the fungus, and new shades of yellow all over it. I cannot keep count of them, though I have tried conscientiously.

It is the strangest yellow, that wallpaper! It makes me think of all the yellow things I ever saw—not beautiful ones like buttercups, but old foul, bad yellow things.

175 But there is something else about that paper—the smell! I noticed it the moment we came into the room, but with so much air and sun it was not bad. Now we have had a week of fog and rain, and whether the windows are open or not, the smell is here.

It creeps all over the house.

I find it hovering in the dining-room, skulking in the parlor, hiding in the hall, lying in wait for me on the stairs.

It gets into my hair.

Even when I go to ride, if I turn my head suddenly and surprise it—there is that smell!

180 Such a peculiar odor, too! I have spent hours in trying to analyze it, to find what it smelled like.

It is not bad—at first, and very gentle, but quite the subtlest, most enduring odor I ever met.

In this damp weather it is awful, I wake up in the night and find it hanging over me.

It used to disturb me at first. I thought seriously of burning the house—to reach the smell.

But now I am used to it. The only thing I can think of that it is like is the color of the paper! A yellow smell.

185 There is a very funny mark on this wall, low down, near the mopboard. A streak that runs round the room. It goes behind every piece of furniture, except the bed, a long, straight, even smooch, as if it had been rubbed over and over.

I wonder how it was done and who did it, and what they did it for. Round and round and round—round and round and round—it makes me dizzy!

I really have discovered something at last.

Through watching so much at night, when it changes so, I have finally found out.

The front pattern does move—and no wonder! The woman behind shakes it!

190 Sometimes I think there are a great many women behind, and sometimes only one, and she crawls around fast, and her crawling shakes it all over.

Then in the very bright spots she keeps still, and in the very shady spots she just takes hold of the bars and shakes them hard.

And she is all the time trying to climb through. But nobody could climb through that pattern—it strangles so; I think that is why it has so many heads.

They get through, and then the pattern strangles them off and turns them upside down, and makes their eyes white!

If those heads were covered or taken off it would not be half so bad.

I think that woman gets out in the daytime! 195

And I'll tell you why—privately—I've seen her!

I can see her out of every one of my windows!

It is the same woman, I know, for she is always creeping, and most women do not creep by daylight.

I see her in that long shaded lane, creeping up and down. I see her in those 200 dark grape arbors, creeping all around the garden.

I see her on that long road under the trees, creeping along, and when a carriage comes she hides under the blackberry vines.

I don't blame her a bit. It must be very humiliating to be caught creeping by daylight!

I always lock the door when I creep by daylight. I can't do it at night, for I know John would suspect something at once.

And John is so queer now, that I don't want to irritate him. I wish he would take another room! Besides, I don't want anybody to get that woman out at night but myself.

I often wonder if I could see her out of all the windows at once.

But, turn as fast as I can, I can only see out of one at one time. 205

And though I always see her, she *may* be able to creep faster than I can turn!

I have watched her sometimes away off in the open country, creeping as fast as a cloud shadow in a high wind.

If only that top pattern could be gotten off from the under one! I mean to try it, little by little.

I have found out another funny thing, but I shan't tell it this time! It does not do to trust people too much.

There are only two more days to get this paper off, and I believe John is 210 beginning to notice. I don't like the look in his eyes.

And I heard him ask Jennie a lot of professional questions about me. She had a very good report to give.

She said I slept a good deal in the daytime.

John knows I don't sleep very well at night, for all I'm so quiet!

He asked me all sorts of questions, too, and pretended to be very loving and kind.

As if I couldn't see through him! 215

Still, I don't wonder he acts so, sleeping under this paper for three months.

It only interests me, but I feel sure John and Jennie are secretly affected by it.

Hurrah! This is the last day, but it is enough. John to stay in town over night, and won't be out until this evening.

Jennie wanted to sleep with me—the sly thing! but I told her I should undoubtedly rest better for a night all alone.

That was clever, for really I wasn't alone a bit! As soon as it was moonlight and that poor thing began to crawl and shake the pattern, I got up and ran to help her.

I pulled and she shook, I shook and she pulled, and before morning we had peeled off yards of that paper.

A strip about as high as my head and half around the room.

And then when the sun came and that awful pattern began to laugh at me, I declared I would finish it to-day!

We go away to-morrow, and they are moving all my furniture down again to leave things as they were before.

Jennie looked at the wall in amazement, but I told her merrily that I did it out of pure spite at the vicious thing.

She laughed and said she wouldn't mind doing it herself, but I must not get tired.

How she betrayed herself that time!

But I am here, and no person touches this paper but me,—not *alive!*

She tried to get me out of the room—it was too patent! But I said it was so quiet and empty and clean now that I believed I would lie down again and sleep all I could; and not to wake me even for dinner—I would call when I woke.

So now she is gone, and the servants are gone, and the things are gone, and there is nothing left but that great bedstead nailed down, with the canvas mattress we found on it.

We shall sleep downstairs to-night, and take the boat home to-morrow.

I quite enjoy the room, now it is bare again.

How those children did tear about here!

This bedstead is fairly gnawed!

But I must get to work.

I have locked the door and thrown the key down into the front path.

I don't want to go out, and I don't want to have anybody come in, till John comes.

I want to astonish him.

I've got a rope up here that even Jennie did not find. If that woman does get out, and tries to get away, I can tie her!

But I forgot I could not reach far without anything to stand on!

This bed will *not* move!

I tried to lift and push it until I was lame, and then I got so angry I bit off a little piece at one corner—but it hurt my teeth.

Then I peeled off all the paper I could reach standing on the floor. It sticks horribly and the pattern just enjoys it! All those strangled heads and bulbous eyes and waddling fungus growths just shriek with derision!

I am getting angry enough to do something desperate. To jump out of the window would be admirable exercise, but the bars are too strong even to try.

Besides I wouldn't do it. Of course not. I know well enough that a step like that is improper and might be misconstrued.

I don't like to *look* out of the windows even—there are so many of those creeping women, and they creep so fast.

I wonder if they all come out of that wallpaper as I did?

But I am securely fastened now by my well-hidden rope—you don't get *me* out in the road there!

I suppose I shall have to get back behind the pattern when it comes night, and that is hard!

It is so pleasant to be out in this great room and creep around as I please!   250

I don't want to go outside. I won't, even if Jennie asks me to.

For outside you have to creep on the ground, and everything is green instead of yellow.

But here I can creep smoothly on the floor, and my shoulder just fits in that long smooch around the wall, so I cannot lose my way.

Why there's John at the door!

It is no use, young man, you can't open it!   255

How he does call and pound!

Now he's crying for an axe.

It would be a shame to break down that beautiful door!

"John dear!" said I in the gentlest voice, "the key is down by the front steps, under a plantain leaf!"

That silenced him for a few moments.   260

Then he said—very quietly indeed, "Open the door, my darling!"

"I can't," said I. "The key is down by the front door under a plantain leaf!"

And then I said it again, several times, very gently and slowly, and said it so often that he had to go and see, and he got it of course, and came in. He stopped short by the door.

"What is the matter?" he cried. "For God's sake, what are you doing!"

I kept on creeping just the same, but I looked at him over my shoulder.   265

"I've got out at last," said I, "in spite of you and Jane? And I've pulled off most of the paper, so you can't put me back!"

Now why should that man have fainted? But he did, and right across my path by the wall, so that I had to creep over him every time!

1892

FRANZ KAFKA

A Hunger Artist[1]

During these last decades the interest in professional fasting has markedly diminished. It used to pay very well to stage such great performances under one's own management, but today that is quite impossible. We live in a different world now. At one time the whole town took a lively interest in the hunger artist; from day to day of his fast the excitement mounted; everybody wanted to see

1. Translated by Edwin and Willa Muir.

him at least once a day; there were people who bought season tickets for the last few days and sat from morning till night in front of his small barred cage; even in the nighttime there were visiting hours, when the whole effect was heightened by torch flares; on fine days the cage was set out in the open air, and then it was the children's special treat to see the hunger artist; for their elders he was often just a joke that happened to be in fashion, but the children stood openmouthed, holding each other's hands for greater security, marveling at him as he sat there pallid in black tights, with his ribs sticking out so prominently, not even on a seat but down among straw on the ground, sometimes giving a courteous nod, answering questions with a constrained smile, or perhaps stretching an arm through the bars so that one might feel how thin it was, and then again withdrawing deep into himself, paying no attention to anyone or anything, not even to the all-important striking of the clock that was the only piece of furniture in his cage, but merely staring into vacancy with half shut eyes, now and then taking a sip from a tiny glass of water to moisten his lips.

Besides casual onlookers there were also relays of permanent watchers selected by the public, usually butchers, strangely enough, and it was their task to watch the hunger artist day and night, three of them at a time, in case he should have some secret recourse to nourishment. This was nothing but a formality, instituted to reassure the masses, for the initiates knew well enough that during his fast the artist would never in any circumstances, not even under forcible compulsion, swallow the smallest morsel of food: the honor of his profession forbade it. Not every watcher, of course, was capable of understanding this, there were often groups of night watchers who were very lax in carrying out their duties and deliberately huddled together in a retired corner to play cards with great absorption, obviously intending to give the hunger artist the chance of a little refreshment, which they supposed he could draw from some private hoard. Nothing annoyed the artist more than such watchers; they made him miserable; they made his fast seem unendurable; sometimes he mastered his feebleness sufficiently to sing during their watch for as long as he could keep going, to show them how unjust their suspicions were. But that was of little use; they only wondered at his cleverness in being able to fill his mouth even while singing. Much more to his taste were the watchers who sat close up to the bars, who were not content with the dim night lighting of the hall but focused him in the full glare of the electric pocket torch given them by the impresario. The harsh light did not trouble him at all, in any case he could never sleep properly, and he could always drowse a little, whatever the light, at any hour, even when the hall was thronged with noisy onlookers. He was quite happy at the prospect of spending a sleepless night with such watchers; he was ready to exchange jokes with them, to tell them stories out of his nomadic life, anything at all to keep them awake and demonstrate to them again that he had no eatables in his cage and that he was fasting as not one of them could fast. But his happiest moment was when the morning came and an enormous breakfast was brought them, at his expense, on which they flung themselves with the keen appetite of healthy men after a weary night of wakefulness. Of course there were people who argued that this breakfast was an unfair attempt to bribe the watchers, but that was going rather too far, and when they were invited to take on a night's vigil without a breakfast, merely for the sake of the cause, they made themselves scarce, although they stuck stubbornly to their suspicions.

Such suspicions, anyhow, were a necessary accompaniment to the profession of fasting. No one could possibly watch the hunger artist continuously, day and night, and so no one could produce first-hand evidence that the fast had really been rigorous and continuous; only the artist himself could know that, he was therefore bound to be the sole completely satisfied spectator of his own fast. Yet for other reasons he was never satisfied; it was not perhaps mere fasting that had brought him to such skeleton thinness that many people had regretfully to keep away from his exhibitions, because the sight of him was too much for them, perhaps it was dissatisfaction with himself that had worn him down. For he alone knew, what no other initiate knew, how easy it was to fast. It was the easiest thing in the world. He made no secret of this, yet people did not believe him, at the best they set him down as modest, most of them, however, thought he was out for publicity or else was some kind of cheat who found it easy to fast because he had discovered a way of making it easy, and then had the impudence to admit the fact, more or less. He had to put up with all that, and in the course of time had got used to it, but his inner dissatisfaction always rankled, and never yet, after any term of fasting—this must be granted to his credit—had he left the cage of his own free will. The longest period of fasting was fixed by his impresario at forty days, beyond that term he was not allowed to go, not even in great cities, and there was good reason for it, too. Experience had proved that for about forty days the interest of the public could be stimulated by a steadily increasing pressure of advertisement, but after that the town began to lose interest, sympathetic support began notably to fall off; there were of course local variations as between one town and another or one country and another, but as a general rule forty days marked the limit. So on the fortieth day the flower-bedecked cage was opened, enthusiastic spectators filled the hall, a military band played, two doctors entered the cage to measure the results of the fast, which were announced through a megaphone, and finally two young ladies appeared, blissful at having been selected for the honor, to help the hunger artist down the few steps leading to a small table on which was spread a carefully chosen invalid repast. And at this very moment the artist always turned stubborn. True, he would entrust his bony arms to the outstretched helping hands of the ladies bending over him, but stand up he would not. Why stop fasting at this particular moment, after forty days of it? He had held out for a long time, an illimitably long time; why stop now, when he was in his best fasting form, or rather, not yet quite in his best fasting form? Why should he be cheated of the fame he would get for fasting longer, for being not only the record hunger artist of all time, which presumably he was already, but for beating his own record by a performance beyond human imagination, since he felt that there were no limits to his capacity for fasting? His public pretended to admire him so much, why should it have so little patience with him; if he could endure fasting longer, why shouldn't the public endure it? Besides, he was tired, he was comfortable sitting in the straw, and now he was supposed to lift himself to his full height and go down to a meal the very thought of which gave him a nausea that only the presence of the ladies kept him from betraying, and even that with an effort. And he looked up into the eyes of the ladies who were apparently so friendly and in reality so cruel, and shook his head, which felt too heavy on its strengthless neck. But then there happened yet again what always happened. The impresario came forward, without a word—for the band made speech impossible—lifted his arms in the air above the artist, as if inviting Heaven to look down upon its creature here in the straw, this suffering martyr, which indeed he was, although in quite another sense; grasped him round the emaciated waist, with exaggerated caution, so that the frail condition he was in might be appreciated; and committed him to the care of the blenching ladies, not without secretly giving him a shaking so that his legs and body tottered and swayed. The artist now submitted completely; his head lolled on his breast as if it had landed there by chance; his body was hollowed out; his legs in a spasm of self-preservation clung close to each other at the knees, yet scraped on the ground as if it were not really solid ground, as if they were only trying to find solid ground; and the whole weight of his body, a feather-weight after all, relapsed onto one of the ladies, who, looking round for help and panting a little—this post of honor was not at all what she had expected it to be—first stretched her neck as far as she could to keep her face at least free from contact with the artist, when finding this impossible, and her more fortunate companion not coming to her aid but merely holding extended on her own trembling hand the little bunch of knucklebones that was the artist's, to the great delight of the spectators burst into tears and had to be replaced by an attendant who had long been stationed in readiness. Then came the food, a little of which the impresario managed to get between the artist's lips, while he sat in a kind of half-fainting trance, to the accompaniment of cheerful patter designed to distract the public's attention from the artist's condition; after that, a toast was drunk to the public, supposedly prompted by a whisper from the artist in the impresario's ear; the band confirmed it with a mighty flourish, the spectators melted away, and no one had any cause to be dissatisfied with the proceedings, no one except the hunger artist himself, he only, as always.

So he lived for many years, with small regular intervals of recuperation, in visible glory, honored by the world, yet in spite of that troubled in spirit, and all the more troubled because no one would take his trouble seriously. What comfort could he possibly need? What more could he possibly wish for? And if some good-natured person, feeling sorry for him, tried to console him by pointing out that his melancholy was probably caused by fasting, it could happen, especially when he had been fasting for some time, that he reacted with an outburst of fury and to the general alarm began to shake the bars of his cage like a wild animal. Yet the impresario had a way of punishing these outbreaks which he rather enjoyed putting into operation. He would apologize publicly for the artist's behavior, which was only to be excused, he admitted, because of the irritability caused by fasting; a condition hardly to be understood by well-fed people; then by natural transition he went on to mention the artist's equally incomprehensible boast that he could fast for much longer than he was doing; he praised the high ambition, the good will, the great self-denial undoubtedly implicit in such a statement; and then quite simply countered it by bringing out photographs, which were also on sale to the public, showing the artist on the fortieth day of a fast lying in bed almost dead from exhaustion. This perversion of the truth, familiar to the artist though it was, always unnerved him afresh and proved too much for him. What was a consequence of the premature ending of his fast was here presented as the cause of it! To fight against this lack of understanding, against a whole world of non-understanding, was impossible. Time and again in good faith he stood by the bars listening to the impresario, but as soon as the photographs appeared he always let go and sank with a groan back on to his straw, and the reassured public could once more come close and gaze at him.

A few years later when the witnesses of such scenes called them to mind, they often failed to understand themselves at all. For meanwhile the aforementioned change in public interest had set in; it seemed to happen almost overnight; there may have been profound causes for it, but who was going to bother about that; at any rate the pampered hunger artist suddenly found himself deserted one fine day by the amusement seekers, who went streaming past him to other more favored attractions. For the last time the impresario hurried him over half Europe to discover whether the old interest might still survive here and there; all in vain; everywhere, as if by secret agreement, a positive revulsion from professional fasting was in evidence. Of course it could not really have sprung up so suddenly as all that, and many premonitory symptoms which had not been sufficiently remarked or suppressed during the rush and glitter of success now came retrospectively to mind, but it was now too late to take any countermeasures. Fasting would surely come into fashion again at some future date, yet that was no comfort for those living in the present. What, then, was the hunger artist to do? He had been applauded by thousands in his time and could hardly come down to showing himself in a street booth at village fairs, and as for adopting another profession, he was not only too old for that but too fanatically devoted to fasting. So he took leave of the impresario, his partner in an unparalleled career, and hired himself to a large circus; in order to spare his own feelings he avoided reading the conditions of his contract.

A large circus with its enormous traffic in replacing and recruiting men, animals and apparatus can always find a use for people at any time, even for a hunger artist, provided of course that he does not ask too much, and in this particular case anyhow it was not only the artist who was taken on but his famous and long-known name as well, indeed considering the peculiar nature of his performance, which was not impaired by advancing age, it could not be objected that here was an artist past his prime, no longer at the height of his professional skill, seeking a refuge in some quiet corner of a circus; on the contrary, the hunger artist averred that he could fast as well as ever, which was entirely credible, he even alleged that if he were allowed to fast as he liked, and this was at once promised him without more ado, he could astound the world by establishing a record never yet achieved, a statement which certainly provoked a smile among the other professionals, since it left out of account the change in public opinion, which the hunger artist in his zeal conveniently forgot.

He had not, however, actually lost his sense of the real situation and took it as a matter of course that he and his cage should be stationed, not in the middle of the ring as a main attraction, but outside, near the animal cages, on a site that was after all easily accessible. Large and gaily painted placards made a frame for the cage and announced what was to be seen inside it. When the public came thronging out in the intervals to see the animals, they could hardly avoid passing the hunger artist's cage and stopping there for a moment, perhaps they might even have stayed longer had not those pressing behind them in the narrow gangway, who did not understand why they should be held up on their way toward the excitements of the menagerie, made it impossible for anyone to stand gazing quietly for any length of time. And that was the reason why the hunger artist, who had of course been looking forward to these visiting hours as the main achievement of his life, began instead to shrink from them. At first he could hardly wait for the intervals; it was exhilarating to watch the crowds come streaming his way, until only too soon—not even the most obstinate self-deception, clung to almost consciously, could hold out against the fact—the conviction was borne in upon him that these people, most of them, to judge from their actions, again and again, without exception, were all on their way to the menagerie. And the first sight of them from the distance remained the best. For when they reached his cage he was at once deafened by the storm of shouting and abuse that arose from the two contending factions, which renewed themselves continuously, of those who wanted to stop and stare at him—he soon began to dislike them more than the others—not out of real interest but only out of obstinate self-assertiveness, and those who wanted to go straight on to the animals. When the first great rush was past, the stragglers came along, and these, whom nothing could have prevented from stopping to look at him as long as they had breath, raced past with long strides, hardly even glancing at him, in their haste to get to the menagerie in time. And all too rarely did it happen that he had a stroke of luck, when some father of a family fetched up before him with his children, pointed a finger at the hunger artist and explained at length what the phenomenon meant, telling stories of earlier years when he himself had watched similar but much more thrilling performances, and the children, still rather uncomprehending, since neither inside nor outside school had they been sufficiently prepared for this lesson—what did they care about fasting?— yet showed by the brightness of their intent eyes that new and better times might be coming. Perhaps, said the hunger artist to himself many a time, things would be a little better if his cage were set not quite so near the menagerie. That made it too easy for people to make their choice, to say nothing of what he suffered from the stench of the menagerie, the animals' restlessness by night, the carrying past of raw lumps of flesh for the beasts of prey, the roaring at feeding times, which depressed him continually. But he did not dare to lodge a complaint with the management; after all, he had the animals to thank for the troops of people who passed his cage, among whom there might always be one here and there to take an interest in him, and who could tell where they might seclude him if he called attention to his existence and thereby to the fact that, strictly speaking, he was only an impediment on the way to the menagerie.

A small impediment, to be sure, one that grew steadily less. People grew familiar with the strange idea that they could be expected, in times like these, to take an interest in a hunger artist, and with this familiarity the verdict went out against him. He might fast as much as he could, and he did so; but nothing could save him now, people passed him by. Just try to explain to anyone the art of fasting! Anyone who has no feeling for it cannot be made to understand it. The fine placards grew dirty and illegible, they were torn down; the little notice board telling the number of fast days achieved, which at first was changed carefully every day, had long stayed at the same figure, for after the first few weeks even this small task seemed pointless to the staff; and so the artist simply fasted on and on, as he had once dreamed of doing, and it was no trouble to him, just as he had always foretold, but no one counted the days, no one, not even the artist himself, knew what records he was already breaking, and his heart grew heavy. And when once in a time some leisurely passer-by stopped, made merry over the old figure on the board and spoke of swindling, that was in its way the stupidest lie ever invented by indifference and inborn malice, since it was not the hunger artist who was cheating; he was working honestly, but the world was cheating him of his reward.

Many more days went by, however, and that too came to an end. An overseer's eye fell on the cage one day and he asked the attendants why this perfectly good cage should be left standing there unused with dirty straw inside it; nobody knew, until one man, helped out by the notice board, remembered about the hunger artist. They poked into the straw with sticks and found him in it. "Are you still fasting?" asked the overseer. "When on earth do you mean to stop?" "Forgive me, everybody," whispered the hunger artist; only the overseer, who had his ear to the bars, understood him. "Of course," said the overseer, and tapped his forehead with a finger to let the attendants know what state the man was in, "we forgive you." "I always wanted you to admire my fasting," said the hunger artist. "We do admire it," said the overseer, affably. "But you shouldn't admire it," said the hunger artist. "Well, then we don't admire it," said the overseer, "but why shouldn't we admire it?" "Because I have to fast, I can't help it," said the hunger artist. "What a fellow you are," said the overseer, "and why can't you help it?" "Because," said the hunger artist, lifting his head a little and speaking, with his lips pursed, as if for a kiss, right into the overseer's ear, so that no syllable might be lost, "because I couldn't find the food I liked. If I had found it, believe me, I should have made no fuss and stuffed myself like you or anyone else." These were his last words, but in his dimming eyes remained the firm though no longer proud persuasion that he was still continuing to fast.

"Well, clear this out now!" said the overseer, and they buried the hunger artist, straw and all. Into the cage they put a young panther. Even the most insensitive felt it refreshing to see this wild creature leaping around the cage that had so long been dreary. The panther was all right. The food he liked was brought him without hesitation by the attendants; he seemed not even to miss his freedom; his noble body, furnished almost to the bursting point with all that it needed, seemed to carry freedom around with it too; somewhere in his jaws it

10

seemed to lurk; and the joy of life streamed with such ardent passion from his throat that for the onlookers it was not easy to stand the shock of it. But they braced themselves, crowded round the cage, and did not want ever to move away.

1924

MORDECAI RICHLER

The Summer My Grandmother Was
Supposed to Die

Dr. Katzman discovered the gangrene on one of his monthly visits. "She won't last a month," he said.

He repeated that the second month, the third, and the fourth, and now she lay dying in the heat of the back bedroom.

"If only she'd die," my mother said. "Oh, God, why doesn't she die? God in heaven, what's she holding on for?"

The summer my grandmother was supposed to die we did not chip in with the Breenbaums to take a cottage in the Laurentians.[1] It wouldn't have been practical. The old lady couldn't be moved, the nurse came daily and the doctor twice a week, and so it seemed best to stay in the city and wait for her to die or, as my mother said, pass away. It was a hot summer, her bedroom was just behind the kitchen, and when we sat down to eat we could smell her. The dressings on my grandmother's left leg had to be changed several times a day and, according to Dr. Katzman, her condition was hopeless. "It's in the hands of the Almighty," he said.

5 "It won't be long now," my father said, "and she'll be better off, if you know what I mean."

"Please," my mother said.

A nurse came every day from the Royal Victorian Order. She arrived punctually at noon and at five to twelve I'd join the rest of the boys under the outside staircase to look up her dress as she climbed to our second-story flat. Miss Monohan favored lacy pink panties and that was better than waiting under the stairs for Cousin Bessie, for instance. She wore enormous cotton bloomers, rain or shine.

I was sent out to play as often as possible, because my mother felt it was not good for me to see somebody dying. Usually I'd just roam the scorched streets shooting the breeze. There was Arty, Gas sometimes, Hershey, Stan, and me. We talked about everything from A to Z.

"Why is it," Arty wanted to know, "that Tarzan never shits?"

10 "Dick Tracy too."

1. Mountains in eastern Canada between Hudson Bay and the St. Lawrence River.

"Or Wonder Woman."

"She's a dame."

"So?"

"Jees, wouldn't it be something if Superman crapped in the sky? He could just be flying over Waverly Street when, whamo, Mr. Rabinovitch catches it right in the kisser."

Mr. Rabinovitch was our Hebrew teacher.

"But there's Tarzan," Arty insisted, "in the jungle, week in and week out, and never once does he need to go to the toilet. It's not real, that's all."

Arty told me, "Before your grandma dies she's going to roll her eyes and gurgle. That's what they call the death-rattle."

"Aw, you know everything. Big shot."

"I *read* it, you jerk," Arty said, whacking me one, "in Perry Mason."

Home again I'd find my mother weeping.

"She's dying by inches," she said to my father one stifling night, "and none of them even come to see her. Oh, such children! They should only rot in hell."

"They're not behaving right. It's certainly not according to Hoyle," my father said.

"When I think of all the money and effort that went into making a rabbi out of Israel—the way Mother doted on him—and for what? Oh, what's the world coming to? God."

"It's not right."

Dr. Katzman was amazed. "I never believed she'd last this long. Really, it must be will-power alone that keeps her going. And your excellent care."

"I want her to die, Doctor. That's not my mother in the back room. It's an animal. I want her to please please die."

"Hush. You don't mean it. You're tired." And Dr. Katzman gave my father some pills for my mother to take. "A remarkable woman," he said. "A born nurse."

At night in bed my brother Harvey and I used to talk about our grandmother. "After she dies," I said, "her hair will go on growing for another twenty-four hours."

"Sez who?"

"Arty. It's a scientific fact. Do you think Uncle Lou will come from New York for the funeral?"

"Sure."

"Boy, that means another fiver for me. You too."

"You shouldn't say things like that, kiddo, or *her ghost will come back to haunt you.*"

"Well," I said, "I'll be able to go to her funeral, anyway. I'm not too young any more."

I was only six years old when my grandfather died, and I wasn't allowed to go to his funeral.

I have only one memory of my grandfather. Once he called me into his study, set me down on his lap, and made a drawing of a horse for me. On the horse he drew a rider. While I watched and giggled he gave the rider a beard and the round fur-trimmed cap of a rabbi.

My grandfather was a Zaddik,[2] one of the Righteous, and I've been told that to study Talmud with him had been a rare pleasure. I wasn't allowed to go to his funeral, but years after I was shown the telegrams of condolence that had come from Eire and Poland and Israel and even Japan. My grandfather had written many books: a translation of the Zohar into modern Hebrew — some twenty years' work — and lots of slender volumes of sermons, chassidic tales, and rabbinical commentaries. His books had been published in Warsaw and later in New York. He had been famous.

"At the funeral," my mother told me, "they had to have six motorcycle policemen to control the crowds. It was such a heat that twelve women fainted — and I'm *not* counting Mrs. Waxman from upstairs. With her, you know, *anything* to fall into a man's arms. Even Pinsky's. And did I tell you that there was even a French-Canadian priest there?"

"No kidding?"

"The priest was a real big *knacker*.[3] A bishop maybe. He used to study with the *zeyda*.[4] The *zeyda* was some personality, you know. Spiritual and worldly-wise at the same time. Such personalities they don't make any more. Today, rabbis and peanuts are the same size."

But, according to my father, the *zeyda* (his father-in-law) hadn't been as famous as all that. "There are things I could say," he told me. "There was another side to him."

My grandfather had come from generations and generations of rabbis, his youngest son was a rabbi, but none of his grandchildren would be one. My brother Harvey was going to be a dentist and at the time, 1937, I was interested in flying and my cousin Jerry was already a communist. I once heard Jerry say, "Our grandpappy wasn't all he was cracked up to be." When the men at the kosher bakeries went out on strike he spoke up against them on the streets where they were picketing and in the *shule*.[5] It was of no consequence to him that they were grossly underpaid. His superstitious followers had to have bread. "Grand-pappy," Jerry said, "was a prize reactionary."

A week after my grandfather died my grandmother suffered a stroke. Her right side was completely paralyzed. She couldn't speak. At first, it's true, my grandmother could say a few words and move her right hand enough to write her name in Hebrew. Her name was Malka. But her condition soon began to deteriorate.

My grandmother had six children and seven stepchildren, for my grandfather had been married before. His first wife had died in the old country. Two years later he had married my grandmother, the only daughter of the richest man in the village, and their marriage had been a singularly happy one. My grand-mother had been a beautiful girl. She had also been a wise, resourceful, and

---

2. "Righteous man" in Hebrew.   3. Big shot.   4. Grandfather.   5. Synagogue.

patient wife. Qualities, I fear, indispensable to life with a Zaddik. For the synagogue had paid my grandfather no stipulated salary and much of the money he had picked up here and there he had habitually distributed among rabbinical students, needy immigrants, and widows. A vice, and such it was to his hard-pressed family, which made him as unreliable a provider as a drunkard. And indeed, to carry the analogy further, my grandmother had had to make many hurried trips to the pawnbroker with her jewelry. Not all of it had been redeemed, either. But her children had been looked after. The youngest, her favorite, was a rabbi in Boston, the eldest was the actor-manager of a Yiddish theater in New York, and another was a lawyer. One daughter lived in Toronto, two in Montreal. My mother was the youngest daughter, and when my grandmother had her stroke there was a family meeting and it was decided that my mother would take care of her. This was my father's fault. All the other husbands spoke up — they protested their wives had too much work, they could never manage it — but my father detested quarrels, and he was silent. So my grandmother came to stay with us.

Her bedroom, the back bedroom, had actually been promised to me for my seventh birthday. But all that was forgotten now, and I had to go on sharing a bedroom with my brother Harvey. So naturally I was resentful when each morning before I left for school my mother said, "Go in and kiss the *baba*[6] good-bye."

All the same I'd go into the bedroom and kiss my grandmother hastily. She'd say "Bouyo-bouyo," for that was the only sound she could make. And after school it was, "Go in and tell the *baba* you're home."

"I'm home, *baba*."

"Bouyo-bouyo."

During those first hopeful months — "Twenty years ago who would have thought there'd be a cure for diabetes?" my father asked; "where there's life there's hope, you know" — she'd smile at me and try to speak, her eyes charged with effort. And even later there were times when she pressed my head urgently to her bosom with her surprisingly strong left arm. But as her illness dragged on and on and she became a condition in the house, something beyond hope or reproach, like the leaky icebox, there was less recognition and more ritual in those kisses. I came to dread her room. A clutter of sticky medicine bottles and the cracked toilet chair beside the bed; glazed but imploring eyes and a feeble smile, the wet slap of her lips against my cheeks. I flinched from her touch. After two years of it I protested to my mother. "Look what's the use of telling her I'm going or I'm here. She doesn't even recognize me any more."

"Don't be fresh. She's your grandmother."

My uncle who was in the theater in New York sent money regularly to help support my grandmother and, for the first few months, so did the other children. But once the initial and sustaining excitement had passed and it became likely that my grandmother might linger in her invalid condition for two or maybe even three more years, the checks began to drop off, and the children seldom

45

50

6. Grandma.

women on the parochial school board. The change reflected on my father. Not
only did his temper improve, but he stopped going to Tansky's every other night,
and began to come home early from work. Life at home had never been so rich.
But my grandmother's name was never mentioned. The back bedroom
remained empty and I continued to share a room with Harvey. I couldn't see
the point and so one evening I said, "Look, why don't I move into the back
bedroom?"

80   My father glared at me across the table.

"But it's empty like."

My mother left the table. And the next afternoon she put on her best dress
and coat and new spring hat.

"Where are you going?" my father asked.

"To see my mother."

85   "Don't go looking for trouble."

"It's been a month. Maybe they're not treating her right."

"They're experts."

"Did you think I was never going to visit her? I'm not inhuman, you know."

"All right, go," he said.

90   But after she'd gone my father went to the window and said, "Son-of-a-bitch."

Harvey and I sat outside on the steps watching the cars go by. My father sat
on the balcony above, cracking peanuts. It was six o'clock, maybe later, when
the ambulance turned the corner, slowed down, and parked right in front of the
house.

"Son-of-a-bitch," my father said. "I knew it."

My mother got out first, her eyes red and swollen, and hurried upstairs to
make my grandmother's bed.

"I'm sorry, Sam, I had to do it."

95   "You'll get sick again, that's what."

"You think she doesn't recognize people. From the moment she saw me she
cried and cried. Oh, it was terrible."

"They're experts there. They know how to handle her better than you do."

"Experts? Expert murderers you mean. She's got bedsores, Sam. Those dirty
little Irish nurses they don't change her linen often enough, they hate her. She
must have lost twenty pounds there."

"Another month and you'll be flat on your back again."

100   "Sam, what could I do? Please Sam."

"She'll outlive all of us. Even Muttel.[2] I'm going out for a walk."

She was back and I was to blame.

My father became a regular at Tansky's Cigar & Soda again and every morning I had to go in and kiss my grandmother. She began to look like a man. Little
hairs had sprouted on her chin, she had a spiky gray mustache and, of course,
she was practically bald. This near-baldness, I guess, sprang from the fact that
she had been shaving her head ever since she had married my grandfather the

2. The narrator's Yiddish name; could be the equivalent of Mordecai.

rabbi.[3] My grandmother had four different wigs, but she had not worn one since the first year of her illness. She wore a little pink cap instead. And so, as before, she said, "bouyo-bouyo," to everything.

Once more uncles and aunts sent five-dollar bills, though erratically, to help pay for my grandmother's support. Elderly people, former followers of my grandfather, came to inquire after the old lady's health. They sat in the back bedroom with her for hours, leaning on their canes, talking to themselves, rocking, always rocking to and fro. "The Holy Shakers," my father called them, and Harvey and I avoided them, because they always wanted to pinch our cheeks, give us a dash of snuff and laugh when we sneezed, or offer us a sticky old candy from a little brown bag with innumerable creases in it. When the visit was done the old people would unfailingly sit in the kitchen with my mother for another hour, watching her make lockshen[4] or bake bread. My mother always served them lemon tea and they would talk about my grandfather, recalling his books, his sayings, and his charitable deeds.

And so another two years passed, with no significant change in my grandmother's condition. But fatigue, bad temper, and even morbidity enveloped my mother again. She fought with her brothers and sisters and once, when I stepped into the living room, I found her sitting with her head in her hands, and she looked up at me with such anguish that I was frightened.

"What did I do now?" I asked.

"If, God forbid, I had a stroke, would you send me to the Old People's Home?"

"Don't be a joke. Of course not."

"I hope that never in my life do I have to count on my children for anything."

The summer my grandmother was supposed to die, the seventh year of her illness, my brother took a job as a shipper and he kept me awake at night with stories about the factory. "What we do, see, is clear out the middle of a huge pile of lengths of material. That makes for a kind of secret cave. A hideout. Well, then you coax one of the *shiksas*[5] inside and hi-diddle-diddle."

One night Harvey waited until I had fallen asleep and then he wrapped himself in a white sheet, crept up to my bed, and shouted, "Bouyo-bouyo."

I hit him. He shouted.

"Children. Children, please," my mother called. "I must get some rest."

As my grandmother's condition worsened—from day to day we didn't know when she'd die—I was often sent out to eat at my aunt's or at my other grandmother's house. I was hardly ever at home. On Saturday mornings I'd get together with the other guys and we'd walk all the way past the mountain to Eaton's, which was our favorite department store for riding up and down escalators and stealing.

In those days they let boys into the left-field bleachers free during the week and we spent many an afternoon at the ball park. The Montreal Royals, part of

105

110

115

---

3. Married Orthodox Jewish women customarily shave their heads or cover their hair.   4. Noodles.   5. Gentile girls.

the Dodger farm system, was some ball club too. There was Jackie Robinson and Roy Campanella, Honest John Gabbard, Chuck Connors, and Kermit Kitman was our hero. It used to kill us to see that crafty little hebe[6] running around there with all those tall dumb *goyim*.[7] "Hey, Kitman," we'd yell. "Hey, hey, shohead,[8] if your father knew you played ball on *shabus*[9]—" Kitman, unfortunately, was all field and no hit. He never made the majors. "There goes Kermit Kitman," we'd yell, after he'd gone down swinging again, "the first Jewish strikeout king of the International League." This we usually followed up by bellowing some choice imprecations in Yiddish.

It was after one of these games, on a Friday afternoon, that I came home to find a small crowd gathered in front of the house.

"That's the grandson."

"Poor kid."

Old people stood silent and expressionless across the street staring at our front door. A taxi pulled up and my aunt hurried out, hiding her face in her hands.

"After so many years," somebody said.

"And probably next year they'll discover a cure. Isn't that *always* the case?"

I took the stairs two at a time. The flat was full. Uncles and aunts from my father's side of the family, odd old people, Dr. Katzman, Harvey, neighbors, were all standing around and talking in hushed voices in the living room. I found my father in the kitchen, getting out the apricot brandy. "Your grandmother's dead," he said.

"She didn't suffer," somebody said. "She passed away in her sleep."

"A merciful death."

"Where's Maw?"

"In the bedroom with . . . you'd better not go in," my father said.

"I want to see her."

My mother's face was long with grief. She wore a black shawl, and glared down at a knot of handkerchief clutched in a fist that had been cracked by washing soda. "Don't come in here," she said.

Several bearded, round-shouldered men in black shiny coats stood round the bed. I couldn't see my grandmother.

"Your grandmother's dead."

"Daddy told me."

"Go and wash your face and comb your hair. You'll have to get your own supper."

"O.K."

"One minute. The *baba* left some jewelry. The ring is for Harvey's wife and the necklace is for yours."

"Who's getting married?"

"Better go and wash your face. And remember behind the ears, Muttel."

Telegrams were sent, long-distance calls were made, and all through the

6. Hebrew, Jew.   7. Gentiles.   8. Possibly *shorn-head*(?), referring to the short hair or crew cut of an athlete, in contrast to traditional long locks of Orthodox Jews(?).   9. Sabbath.

evening relatives and neighbors came and went like swarms of fish when crumbs have been dropped into the water.

"When my father died," my mother said, "they had to have *six* motorcycle policemen to control the crowds. Twelve people fainted, such a heat . . ."

The man from the funeral parlor came.

"There goes the only Jewish businessman in town," my Uncle Harry said, "who wishes all his customers were Germans."

"This is no time for jokes."

"Listen, life goes on."

My cousin Jerry had begun to use a cigarette holder. "Everyone's going to be sickeningly sentimental," he said. "Soon the religious mumbo-jumbo starts. I can hardly wait."

Tomorrow was the Sabbath and so, according to the law, my grandmother couldn't be buried until Sunday. She would have to lie on the floor all night. Two old grizzly women in white came to move and wash the body and a professional mourner arrived to sit up and pray for her.

"I don't trust his face," my mother said. "He'll fall asleep. You watch him, Sam."

"A fat lot of good prayers will do her now."

"Will you just watch him, please."

"I'll watch him, I'll watch him." My father was livid about my Uncle Harry. "The way he's gone after that apricot brandy you'd think that guy never saw a bottle in his life before."

Harvey and I were sent to bed, but we couldn't sleep. My aunt was sobbing over the body in the living room—"That dirty hypocrite," my mother said— there was the old man praying, coughing, and spitting into his handkerchief each time he woke; and hushed voices and whimpering from the kitchen, where my father and mother sat. Harvey was in a good mood, he let me have a few puffs of his cigarette.

"Well, kiddo, this is our last night together. Tomorrow you can take over the back bedroom."

"*Are you crazy?*"

"You always wanted it for yourself."

"She died in there, bud. You think I'm going to sleep in there?"

"Good night. Happy dreams, kiddo."

"Hey, let's talk some more."

Harvey told me a ghost story. "Did you know that when they hang a man," he said, "the last thing that happens is that he has an orgasm?"

"A what?"

"Forget it. I forgot you were still in kindergarten."

"I know plenty. Don't worry."

"At the funeral they're going to open her coffin to throw dirt in her face. It's supposed to be earth from Eretz.[1] They open it and you're going to have to look." Harvey stood up on his bed, holding his hands over his head like claws.

---

1. Eretz Yisrael, the Land of Israel.

He made a hideous face. "Bouyo-bouyo. Who's that sleeping in my bed? Woo-woo."

My uncle who was in the theater, the rabbi, and my aunt from Toronto, all came to Montreal for the funeral. Dr. Katzman came too.

"As long as she was alive," my mother said, "he couldn't even send five dollars a month. Some son! What a rabbi! I don't want him in my house, Sam. I can't bear the sight of him."

"You don't mean a word of that and you know it," Dr. Katzman said.

"Maybe you'd better give her a sedative," the rabbi said.

165 "Sam. Sam, will you say something, please."

My father stepped up to the rabbi, his face flushed. "I'll tell you this straight to your face, Israel," he said. "You've gone down in my estimation."

"Really," the rabbi said, smiling a little.

My father's face burned a deeper red. "Year by year," he said, "your stock has gone down with me."

And my mother began to weep bitterly, helplessly, without control. She was led unwillingly to bed. While my father tried his best to comfort her, as he said consoling things, Dr. Katzman plunged a needle into her arm. "There we are," he said.

170 I went to sit in the sun on the outside stairs with Arty. "I'm going to the funeral," I said.

"I couldn't go anyway."

Arty was descended from the tribe of high priests and so was not allowed to be in the presence of a dead body. I was descended from the Yisroelis.[2]

"The lowest of the low," Arty said.

"Aw."

175 My uncle, the rabbi, and Dr. Katzman stepped into the sun to light cigarettes.

"It's remarkable that she held out for so long," Dr. Katzman said.

"Remarkable?" my uncle said. "It's written that if a man has been married twice he will spend as much time with his first wife in heaven as he did on earth. My father, may he rest in peace, was married to his first wife for seven years and my mother, may she rest in peace, has managed to keep alive for seven years. Today in heaven she will be able to join my father, may he rest in peace."

Dr. Katzman shook his head, he pursed his lips. "It's amazing," he said. "The mysteries of the human heart. Astonishing."

My father hurried outside. "Dr. Katzman, please. It's my wife. Maybe the injection wasn't strong enough? She just doesn't stop crying. It's like a tap. Could you come please?"

180 "Excuse me," Dr. Katzman said to my uncle.

"Of course."

My uncle approached Arty and me.

"Well, boys," he said, "what would you like to be when you grow up?"

1961

2. The lowest of the three categories into which the Jewish people are traditionally divided.

BOBBIE ANN MASON

Shiloh

Leroy Moffitt's wife, Norma Jean, is working on her pectorals. She lifts three-pound dumbbells to warm up, then progresses to a twenty-pound barbell. Standing with her legs apart, she reminds Leroy of Wonder Woman.

"I'd give anything if I could just get these muscles to where they're real hard," says Norma Jean. "Feel this arm. It's not as hard as the other one."

"That's 'cause you're right-handed," says Leroy, dodging as she swings the barbell in an arc.

"Do you think so?"

"Sure."

Leroy is a truckdriver. He injured his leg in a highway accident four months ago, and his physical therapy, which involves weights and a pulley, prompted Norma Jean to try building herself up. Now she is attending a body-building class. Leroy has been collecting temporary disability since his tractor-trailer jack-knifed in Missouri, badly twisting his left leg in its socket. He has a steel pin in his hip. He will probably not be able to drive his rig again. It sits in the backyard, like a gigantic bird that has flown home to roost. Leroy has been home in Kentucky for three months, and his leg is almost healed, but the accident frightened him and he does not want to drive any more long hauls. He is not sure what to do next. In the meantime, he makes things from craft kits. He started by building a miniature log cabin from notched Popsicle sticks. He varnished it and placed it on the TV set, where it remains. It reminds him of a rustic Nativity scene. Then he tried string art (sailing ships on black velvet), a macramé owl kit, a snap-together B-17 Flying Fortress,[1] and a lamp made out of a model truck, with a light fixture screwed in the top of the cab. At first the kits were diversions, something to kill time, but now he is thinking about building a full-scale log house from a kit. It would be considerably cheaper than building a regular house, and besides, Leroy has grown to appreciate how things are put together. He has begun to realize that in all the years he was on the road he never took time to examine anything. He was always flying past scenery.

"They won't let you build a log cabin in any of the new subdivisions," Norma Jean tells him.

"They will if I tell them it's for you," he says, teasing her. Ever since they were married, he has promised Norma Jean he would build her a new home one day. They have always rented, and the house they live in is small and nondescript. It does not even feel like a home, Leroy realizes now.

Norma Jean works at the Rexall drugstore, and she has acquired an amazing amount of information about cosmetics. When she explains to Leroy the three stages of complexion care, involving creams, toners, and moisturizers, he thinks happily of other petroleum products—axle grease, diesel fuel. This is a connec-

5

1. World War II bomber.

the plants, informing Norma Jean when a plant is droopy or yellow. Mabel calls the plants "flowers," although there are never any blooms. She always notices if Norma Jean's laundry is piling up. Mabel is a short, overweight woman whose tight, brown-dyed curls look more like a wig than the actual wig she sometimes wears. Today she has brought Norma Jean an off-white dust ruffle she made for the bed; Mabel works in a custom-upholstery shop.

"This is the tenth one I made this year," Mabel says. "I got started and couldn't stop."

"It's real pretty," says Norma Jean.

30   "Now we can hide things under the bed," says Leroy, who gets along with his mother-in-law primarily by joking with her. Mabel has never really forgiven him for disgracing her by getting Norma Jean pregnant. When the baby died, she said that fate was mocking her.

"What's that thing?" Mabel says to Leroy in a loud voice, pointing to a tangle of yarn on a piece of canvas.

Leroy holds it up for Mabel to see. "It's my needlepoint," he explains. "This is a *Star Trek* pillow cover."

"That's what a woman would do," says Mabel. "Great day in the morning!"

"All the big football players on TV do it," he says.

35   "Why, Leroy, you're always trying to fool me. I don't believe you for one minute. You don't know what to do with yourself—that's the whole trouble. Sewing!"

"I'm aiming to build us a log house," says Leroy. "Soon as my plans come."

"Like *heck* you are," says Norma Jean. She takes Leroy's needlepoint and shoves it into a drawer. "You have to find a job first. Nobody can afford to build now anyway."

Mabel straightens her girdle and says, "I still think before you get tied down y'all ought to take a little run to Shiloh."

"One of these days, Mama," Norma Jean says impatiently.

40   Mabel is talking about Shiloh, Tennessee. For the past few years, she has been urging Leroy and Norma Jean to visit the Civil War battleground there.[4] Mabel went there on her honeymoon—the only real trip she ever took. Her husband died of a perforated ulcer when Norma Jean was ten, but Mabel, who was accepted into the United Daughters of the Confederacy in 1975, is still preoccupied with going back to Shiloh.

"I've been to kingdom come and back in that truck out yonder," Leroy says to Mabel, "but we never yet set foot in that battleground. Ain't that something? How did I miss it?"

"It's not even that far," Mabel says.

After Mabel leaves, Norma Jean reads to Leroy from a list she has made. "Thing you could do," she announces. "You could get a job as a guard at Union Carbide, where they'd let you set on a stool. You could get on at the lumberyard.

---

4. Where, in April 1862, more than 23,000 troops of the North and South, one-quarter of those who fought there, died. This was the first real indication of how bitter and bloody the war was to be. General Ulysses S. Grant, when reinforcements arrived, drove the Confederate forces, which had gained an initial victory by a surprise attack, back to their base in Corinth, Mississippi.

You could do a little carpenter work, if you want to build so bad. You could—"

"I can't do something where I'd have to stand up all day."

"You ought to try standing up all day behind a cosmetics counter. It's amazing that I have strong feet, coming from two parents that never had strong feet at all." At the moment Norma Jean is holding on to the kitchen counter, raising her knees one at a time as she talks. She is wearing two-pound ankle weights.

"Don't worry," says Leroy. "I'll do something."

"You could truck calves to slaughter for somebody. You wouldn't have to drive any big old truck for that."

"I'm going to build you this house," says Leroy. "I want to make you a real home."

"I don't want to live in any log cabin."

"It's not a cabin. It's a house."

"I don't care. It looks like a cabin."

"You and me together could lift those logs. It's just like lifting weights."

Norma Jean doesn't answer. Under her breath, she is counting. Now she is marching through the kitchen. She is doing goose steps.

Before his accident, when Leroy came home he used to stay in the house with Norma Jean, watching TV in bed and playing cards. She would cook fried chicken, picnic ham, chocolate pie—all his favorites. Now he is home alone much of the time. In the mornings, Norma Jean disappears, leaving a cooling place in the bed. She eats a cereal called Body Buddies, and she leaves the bowl on the table, with soggy tan balls floating in a milk puddle. He sees things about Norma Jean that he never realized before. When she chops onions, she stares off into a corner, as if she can't bear to look. She puts on her house slippers almost precisely at nine o'clock every evening and nudges her jogging shoes under the couch. She saves bread heels for the birds. Leroy watches the birds at the feeder. He notices the peculiar way goldfinches fly past the window. They close their wings, then fall, then spread their wings to catch and lift themselves. He wonders if they close their eyes when they fall. Norma Jean closes her eyes when they are in bed. She wants the lights turned out. Even then, he is sure she closes her eyes.

He goes for long drives around town. He tends to drive a car rather carelessly. Power steering and an automatic shift make a car feel so small and inconsequential that his body is hardly involved in the driving process. His injured leg stretches out comfortably. Once or twice he has almost hit something, but even the prospect of an accident seems minor in a car. He cruises the new subdivisions, feeling like a criminal rehearsing for a robbery. Norma Jean is probably right about a log house being inappropriate here in the new subdivisions. All the houses look grand and complicated. They depress him.

One day when Leroy comes home from a drive he finds Norma Jean in tears. She is in the kitchen making a potato and mushroom-soup casserole, with grated-cheese topping. She is crying because her mother caught her smoking.

"I didn't hear her coming. I was standing here puffing away pretty as you please," Norma Jean says, wiping her eyes.

"I knew it would happen sooner or later," says Leroy, putting his arm around her.

"She don't know the meaning of the word 'knock,' " says Norma Jean. "It's a wonder she hadn't caught me years ago."

60 "Think of it this way," Leroy says. "What if she caught me with a joint?"

"You better not let her!" Norma Jean shrieks. "I'm warning you, Leroy Moffitt!"

"I'm just kidding. Here, play me a tune. That'll help you relax."

Norma Jean puts the casserole in the oven and sets the timer. Then she plays a ragtime tune, with horns and banjo, as Leroy lights up a joint and lies on the couch, laughing to himself about Mabel's catching him at it. He thinks of Stevie Hamilton—a doctor's son pushing grass. Everything is funny. The whole town seems crazy and small. He is reminded of Virgil Mathis, a boastful policeman Leroy used to shoot pool with. Virgil recently led a drug bust in a back room at a bowling alley, where he seized ten thousand dollars' worth of marijuana. The newspaper had a picture of him holding up the bags of grass and grinning widely. Right now, Leroy can imagine Virgil breaking down the door and arresting him with a lungful of smoke. Virgil would probably have been alerted to the scene because of all the racket Norma Jean is making. Now she sounds like a hard-rock band. Norma Jean is terrific. When she switches to a latin-rhythm version of "Sunshine Superman," Leroy hums along. Norma Jean's foot goes up and down, up and down.

"Well, what do you think?" Leroy says, when Norma Jean pauses to search through her music.

65 "What do I think about what?"

His mind has gone blank. Then he says, "I'll sell my rig and build us a house." That wasn't what he wanted to say. He wanted to know what she thought—what she *really* thought—about them.

"Don't start in on that again," says Norma Jean. She begins playing "Who'll Be the Next in Line?"

Leroy used to tell hitchhikers his whole life story—about his travels, his hometown, the baby. He would end with a question: "Well, what do you think?" It was just a rhetorical question. In time, he had the feeling that he'd been telling the same story over and over to the same hitchhikers. He quit talking to hitchhikers when he realized how his voice sounded—whining and self-pitying, like some teenage-tragedy song. Now Leroy has the sudden impulse to tell Norma Jean about himself, as if he had just met her. They have known each other so long they have forgotten a lot about each other. They could become reacquainted. But when the oven timer goes off and she runs to the kitchen, he forgets why he wants to do this.

The next day, Mabel drops by. It is Saturday and Norma Jean is cleaning. Leroy is studying the plans of his log house, which have finally come in the mail. He has them spread out on the table—big sheets of stiff blue paper, with diagrams and numbers printed in white. While Norma Jean runs the vacuum, Mabel drinks coffee. She sets her coffee cup on a blueprint.

"I'm just waiting for time to pass," she says to Leroy, drumming her fingers on the table.　　　　　　　　　　　　　　　　　　　　　　　　　　70

As soon as Norma Jean switches off the vacuum, Mabel says in a loud voice, "Did you hear about the datsun dog that killed the baby?"

Norma Jean says, "The word is 'dachshund.'"

"They put the dog on trial. It chewed the baby's legs off. The mother was in the next room all the time." She raises her voice. "They thought it was neglect."

Norma Jean is holding her ears. Leroy manages to open the refrigerator and get some Diet Pepsi to offer Mabel. Mabel still has some coffee and she waves away the Pepsi.

"Datsuns are like that," Mabel says. "They're jealous dogs. They'll tear a　　75 place to pieces if you don't keep an eye on them."

"You better watch out what you're saying, Mabel," says Leroy.

"Well, facts is facts."

Leroy looks out the window at his rig. It is like a huge piece of furniture gathering dust in the backyard. Pretty soon it will be an antique. He hears the vacuum cleaner. Norma Jean seems to be cleaning the living room rug again.

Later, she says to Leroy, "She just said that about the baby because she caught me smoking. She's trying to pay me back."

"What are you talking about?" Leroy says, nervously shuffling blueprints.　　80

"You know good and well," Norma Jean says. She is sitting in a kitchen chair with her feet up and her arms wrapped around her knees. She looks small and helpless. She says, "The very idea, her bringing up a subject like that! Saying it was neglect."

"She didn't mean that," Leroy says.

"She might not have *thought* she meant it. She always says things like that. You don't know how she goes on."

"But she didn't really mean it. She was just talking."

Leroy opens a king-sized bottle of beer and pours it into two glasses, dividing　　85 it carefully. He hands a glass to Norma Jean and she takes it from him mechanically. For a long time, they sit by the kitchen window watching the birds at the feeder.

Something is happening. Norma Jean is going to night school. She has graduated from her six-week body-building course and now she is taking an adult-education course in composition at Paducah Community College. She spends her evenings outlining paragraphs.

"First you have a topic sentence," she explains to Leroy. "Then you divide it up. Your secondary topic has to be connected to your primary topic."

To Leroy, this sounds intimidating. "I never was any good in English," he says.

"It makes a lot of sense."

"What are you doing this for, anyhow?"　　　　　　　　　　　　　　　　90

She shrugs. "It's something to do." She stands up and lifts her dumbbells a few times.

"Driving a rig, nobody cared about my English."

"I'm not criticizing your English."

Norma Jean used to say, "If I lose ten minutes' sleep, I just drag all day."
Now she stays up late, writing compositions. She got a B on her first paper—a
how-to theme on soup-based casseroles. Recently Norma Jean has been cooking
unusual foods—tacos, lasagna, Bombay chicken. She doesn't play the organ
anymore, though her second paper was called "Why Music Is Important to Me."
She sits at the kitchen table, concentrating on her outlines, while Leroy plays
with his log house plans, practicing with a set of Lincoln Logs. The thought of
getting a truckload of notched, numbered logs scares him, and he wants to be
prepared. As he and Norma Jean work together at the kitchen table, Leroy has
the hopeful thought that they are sharing something, but he knows he is a fool
to think this. Norma Jean is miles away. He knows he is going to lose her. Like
Mabel, he is just waiting for time to pass.

95   One day, Mabel is there before Norma Jean gets home from work, and Leroy
finds himself confiding in her. Mabel, he realizes, must know Norma Jean better
than he does.

"I don't know what's got into that girl," Mabel says. "She used to go to bed
with the chickens. Now you say she's up all hours. Plus her a-smoking. I like to
died."

"I want to make her this beautiful home," Leroy says, indicating the Lincoln
Logs. "I don't think she even wants it. Maybe she was happier with me gone."

"She don't know what to make of you, coming home like this."

"Is that it?"

100   Mabel takes the roof off his Lincoln Log cabin. "You couldn't get *me* in a
log cabin," she says. "I was raised in one. It's no picnic, let me tell you."

"They're different now," says Leroy.

"I tell you what," Mabel says, smiling oddly at Leroy.

"What?"

"Take her on down to Shiloh. Y'all need to get out together, stir a little. Her
brain's all balled up over them books."

105   Leroy can see traces of Norma Jean's features in her mother's face. Mabel's
face has the texture of crinkled cotton, but suddenly she looks pretty. It occurs
to Leroy that Mabel has been hinting all along that she wants them to take her
with them to Shiloh.

"Let's all go to Shiloh," he says. "You and me and her. Come Sunday."

Mabel throws up her hands in protest. "Oh, no, not me. Young folks want to
be by theirselves."

When Norma Jean comes in with groceries, Leroy says excitedly, "Your
mama here's been dying to go to Shiloh for thirty-five years. It's about time we
went, don't you think?"

"I'm not going to butt in on anybody's second honeymoon," Mabel says.

110   "Who's going on a honeymoon, for Christ's sake?" Norma Jean says loudly.

"I never raised no daughter of mine to talk that-a-way," Mabel says.

"You ain't seen nothing yet," says Norma Jean. She starts putting away boxes
and cans, slamming cabinet doors.

"There's a log cabin at Shiloh." Mabel says, "It was there during the battle. There's bullet holes in it."

"When are you going to *shut up* about Shiloh, Mama?" asks Norma Jean.

"I always thought Shiloh was the prettiest place, so full of history," Mabel 115 goes on. "I just hoped y'all could see it once before I die, so you could tell me about it." Later, she whispers to Leroy, "You do what I said. A little change is what she needs."

"Your name means 'the king,' " Norma Jean says to Leroy that evening. He is trying to get her to go to Shiloh, and she is reading a book about another century.

"Well, I reckon I ought to be right proud."

"I guess so."

"Am I still king around here?"

Norma Jean flexes her biceps and feels them for hardness. "I'm not fooling 120 around with anybody, if that's what you mean," she says.

"Would you tell me if you were?"

"I don't know."

"What does *your* name mean?"

"It was Marilyn Monroe's real name."

"No kidding!" 125

"Norma comes from the Normans. They were invaders," she says. She closes her book and looks hard at Leroy. "I'll go to Shiloh with you if you'll stop staring at me."

On Sunday, Norma Jean packs a picnic and they go to Shiloh. To Leroy's relief, Mabel says she does not want to come with them. Norma Jean drives, and Leroy, sitting beside her, feels like some boring hitchhiker she has picked up. He tries some conversation, but she answers him in monosyllables. At Shiloh, she drives aimlessly through the park, past bluffs and trails and steep ravines. Shiloh is an immense place, and Leroy cannot see it as a battleground. It is not what he expected. He thought it would look like a golf course. Monuments are everywhere, showing through the thick clusters of trees. Norma Jean passes the log cabin Mabel mentioned. It is surrounded by tourists looking for bullet holes.

"That's not the kind of log house I've got in mind," says Leroy apologetically.

"I know *that*."

"This is a pretty place. Your mama was right." 130

"It's O.K.," says Norma Jean. "Well, we've seen it. I hope she's satisfied."

They burst out laughing together.

At the park museum, a movie on Shiloh is shown every half hour, but they decide that they don't want to see it. They buy a souvenir Confederate flag for Mabel, and then they find a picnic spot near the cemetery. Norma Jean has brought a picnic cooler, with pimiento sandwiches, soft drinks, and Yodels. Leroy eats a sandwich and then smokes a joint, hiding it behind the picnic cooler. Norma Jean has quit smoking altogether. She is picking cake crumbs from the cellophane wrapper, like a fussy bird.

Leroy says, "So the boys in gray ended up in Corinth. The Union soldiers zapped 'em finally. April 7, 1862."

135   They both know that he doesn't know any history. He is just talking about some of the historical plaques they have read. He feels awkward, like a boy on a date with an older girl. They are still just making conversation.

"Corinth is where Mama eloped to," says Norma Jean.

They sit in silence and stare at the cemetery for the Union dead and, beyond, at a tall cluster of trees. Campers are parked nearby, bumper to bumper, and small children in bright clothing are cavorting and squealing. Norma Jean wads up the cake wrapper and squeezes it tightly in her hand. Without looking at Leroy, she says, "I want to leave you."

Leroy takes a bottle of Coke out of the cooler and flips off the cap. He holds the bottle poised near his mouth but cannot remember to take a drink. Finally he says, "No, you don't."

"Yes, I do."

140   "I won't let you."

"You can't stop me."

"Don't do me that way."

Leroy knows Norma Jean will have her own way. "Didn't I promise to be home from now on?" he says.

"In some ways, a woman prefers a man who wanders," says Norma Jean. "That sounds crazy, I know."

145   "You're not crazy."

Leroy remembers to drink from his Coke. Then he says, "Yes, you *are* crazy. You and me could start all over again. Right back at the beginning."

"We *have* started all over again," says Norma Jean. "And this is how it turned out."

"What did I do wrong?"

"Nothing."

150   "Is this one of those women's lib things?" Leroy asks.

"Don't be funny."

The cemetery, a green slope dotted with white markers, looks like a subdivision site. Leroy is trying to comprehend that his marriage is breaking up, but for some reason he is wondering about white slabs in a graveyard.

"Everything was fine till Mama caught me smoking," says Norma Jean, standing up. "That set something off."

"What are you talking about?"

155   "She won't leave me alone—*you* won't leave me alone." Norma Jean seems to be crying, but she is looking away from him. "I feel eighteen again. I can't face that all over again." She starts walking away. "No, it *wasn't* fine. I don't know what I'm saying. Forget it."

Leroy takes a lungful of smoke and closes his eyes as Norma Jean's words sink in. He tries to focus on the fact that thirty-five hundred soldiers died on the grounds around him. He can only think of that war as a board game with plastic soldiers. Leroy almost smiles, as he compares the Confederates' daring attack on the Union camps and Virgil Mathis's raid on the bowling alley. General Grant, drunk and furious, shoved the Southerners back to Corinth, where Mabel and Jet Beasley were married years later, when Mabel was still thin and good-looking. The next day, Mabel and Jet visited the battleground, and then Norma Jean was born, and then she married Leroy and they had a baby, which they lost, and now Leroy and Norma Jean are here at the same battleground. Leroy knows he is leaving out a lot. He is leaving out the insides of history. History was always just names and dates to him. It occurs to him that building a house out of logs is similarly empty—too simple. And the real inner workings of a marriage, like most of history, have escaped him. Now he sees that building a log house is the dumbest idea he could have had. It was clumsy of him to think Norma Jean would want a log house. It was a crazy idea. He'll have to think of something else, quickly. He will wad the blueprints into tight balls and fling them into the lake. Then he'll get moving again. He opens his eyes. Norma Jean has moved away and is walking through the cemetery, following a serpentine brick path.

Leroy gets up to follow his wife, but his good leg is asleep and his bad leg still hurts him. Norma Jean is far away, walking rapidly toward the bluff by the river, and he tries to hobble toward her. Some children run past him, screaming noisily. Norma Jean has reached the bluff, and she is looking out over the Tennessee River. Now she turns toward Leroy and waves her arms. Is she beckoning to him? She seems to be doing an exercise for her chest muscles. The sky is unusually pale—the color of the dust ruffle Mabel made for their bed.

1982

RICHARD FORD

Great Falls

This is not a happy story. I warn you.

My father was a man named Jack Russell, and when I was a young boy in my early teens, we lived with my mother in a house to the east of Great Falls, Montana, near the small town of Highwood and the Highwood Mountains and the Missouri River. It is a flat, treeless benchland there, all of it used for wheat farming, though my father was never a farmer, but was brought up near Tacoma, Washington, in a family that worked for Boeing.

He—my father—had been an Air Force sergeant and had taken his discharge in Great Falls. And instead of going home to Tacoma, where my mother wanted to go, he had taken a civilian's job with the Air Force, working on planes, which was what he liked to do. And he had rented the house out of town from a farmer who did not want it left standing empty.

The house itself is gone now—I have been to the spot. But the double row of Russian olive trees and two of the outbuildings are still standing in the milkweeds. It was a plain, two-story house with a porch on the front and no place for the cars. At the time, I rode the school bus to Great Falls every morning, and my father drove in while my mother stayed home.

5   My mother was a tall pretty woman, thin, with black hair and slightly sharp features that made her seem to smile when she wasn't smiling. She had grown up in Wallace, Idaho, and gone to college a year in Spokane, then moved out to the coast, which is where she met Jack Russell. She was two years older than he was, and married him, she said to me, because he was young and wonderful looking, and because she thought they could leave the sticks and see the world together—which I suppose they did for a while. That was the life she wanted, even before she knew much about wanting anything else or about the future.

When my father wasn't working on airplanes, he was going hunting or fishing, two things he could do as well as anyone. He had learned to fish, he said, in Iceland, and to hunt ducks up on the DEW line—stations he had visited in the Air Force. And during the time of this—it was 1960—he began to take me with him on what he called his "expeditions." I thought even then, with as little as I knew, that these were opportunities other boys would dream of having but probably never would. And I don't think that I was wrong in that.

It is a true thing that my father did not know limits. In the spring, when we would go east to the Judith River Basin and camp up on the banks, he would catch a hundred fish in a weekend, and sometimes more than that. It was all he did from morning until night, and it was never hard for him. He used yellow corn kernels stacked onto a #4 snelled hook, and he would rattle this rig-up along the bottom of a deep pool below a split-shot sinker, and catch fish. And most of the time, because he knew the Judith River and knew how to feel his bait down deep, he would catch fish of good size.

It was the same with ducks, the other thing he liked. When the northern birds were down, usually by mid-October, he would take me and we would build a cattail and wheatstraw blind on one of the tule ponds or sloughs he knew about down the Missouri, where the water was shallow enough to wade. We would set out his decoys to the leeward side of our blind, and he would sprinkle corn on a hunger-line from the decoys to where we were. In the evenings when he came home from the base, we would go and sit out in the blind until the roosting fights came and put down among the decoys—there was never calling involved. And after a while, sometimes it would be an hour and full dark, the ducks would find the corn, and the whole raft of them—sixty, sometimes—would swim in to us. At the moment he judged they were close enough, my father would say to me, "Shine, Jackie," and I would stand and shine a seal-beam car light out onto the pond, and he would stand up beside me and shoot all the ducks that were there, on the water if he could, but flying and getting up as well. He owned a Model 11 Remington with a long-tube magazine that would hold ten shells, and with that many, and shooting straight over the surface rather than down onto it, he could kill or wound thirty ducks in twenty seconds' time. I remember distinctly the report of that gun and the flash of it over the water into the dark air, one shot after another, not even so fast, but measured in a way to hit as many as he could.

What my father did with the ducks he killed, and the fish, too, was sell them. It was against the law then to sell wild game, and it is against the law now. And though he kept some for us, most he would take—his fish laid on ice, or his ducks still wet and bagged in the burlap corn sacks—down to the Great Northern Hotel, which was still open then on Second Street in Great Falls, and sell them to the Negro caterer who bought them for his wealthy customers and for the dining car passengers who came through. We would drive in my father's Plymouth to the back of the hotel—always this was after dark—to a concrete loading ramp and lighted door that were close enough to the yards that I could sometimes see passenger trains waiting at the station, their car lights yellow and warm inside, the passengers dressed in suits, all bound for someplace far away from Montana—Milwaukee or Chicago or New York City, unimaginable places to me, a boy fourteen years old, with my father in the cold dark selling illegal game.

The caterer was a tall, stooped-back man in a white jacket, who my father called "Professor Ducks" or "Professor Fish," and the Professor referred to my father as "Sarge." He paid a quarter per pound for trout, a dime for whitefish, a dollar for a mallard duck, two for a speckle or a blue goose, and four dollars for a Canada. I have been with my father when he took away a hundred dollars for fish he'd caught and, in the fall, more than that for ducks and geese. When he had sold game in that way, we would drive out 10th Avenue and stop at a bar called The Mermaid which was by the air base, and he would drink with some friends he knew there, and they would laugh about hunting and fishing while I played pinball and wasted money in the jukebox.

It was on such a night as this that the unhappy things came about. It was in late October. I remember the time because Halloween had not been yet, and in the windows of the houses that I passed every day on the bus to Great Falls, people had put pumpkin lanterns, and set scarecrows in their yards in chairs.

My father and I had been shooting ducks in a slough on the Smith River, upstream from where it enters on the Missouri. He had killed thirty ducks, and we'd driven them down to the Great Northern and sold them there, though my father had kept two back in his corn sack. And when we had driven away, he suddenly said, "Jackie, let's us go back home tonight. Who cares about those hard-dicks at The Mermaid. I'll cook these ducks on the grill. We'll do something different tonight." He smiled at me in an odd way. This was not a thing he usually said, or the way he usually talked. He liked The Mermaid, and my mother—as far as I knew—didn't mind it if he went there.

"That sounds good," I said.

"We'll surprise your mother," he said. "We'll make her happy."

We drove out past the air base on Highway 87, past where there were planes taking off into the night. The darkness was dotted by the green and red beacons, and the tower light swept the sky and trapped planes as they disappeared over the flat landscape toward Canada or Alaska and the Pacific.

"Boy-oh-boy," my father said—just out of the dark. I looked at him and his eyes were narrow, and he seemed to be thinking about something. "You know, Jackie" he said, "your mother said something to me once I've never forgotten.

She said, 'Nobody dies of a broken heart.' This was somewhat before you were born. We were living down in Texas and we'd had some big blow-up, and that was the idea she had. I don't know why." He shook his head.

He ran his hand under the seat, found a half-pint bottle of whiskey, and held it up to the lights of the car behind us to see what there was left of it. He unscrewed the cap and took a drink, then held the bottle out to me. "Have a drink, son," he said. "Something oughta be good in life." And I felt that something was wrong. Not because of the whiskey, which I had drunk before and he had reason to know about, but because of some sound in his voice, something I didn't recognize and did not know the importance of, though I was certain it was important.

I took a drink and gave the bottle back to him, holding the whiskey in my mouth until it stopped burning and I could swallow it a little at a time. When we turned out the road to Highwood, the lights of Great Falls sank below the horizon, and I could see the small white lights of farms, burning at wide distances in the dark.

"What do you worry about, Jackie," my father said. "Do you worry about girls? Do you worry about your future sex life? Is that some of it?" He glanced at me, then back at the road.

"I don't worry about that," I said.

"Well, what then?" my father said. "What else is there?"

"I worry if you're going to die before I do," I said, though I hated saying that, "or if Mother is. That worries me."

"It'd be a miracle if we didn't," my father said, with the half-pint held in the same hand he held the steering wheel. I had seen him drive that way before. "Things pass too fast in your life, Jackie. Don't worry about that. If I were you, I'd worry we might not." He smiled at me, and it was not the worried, nervous smile from before, but a smile that meant he was pleased. And I don't remember him ever smiling at me that way again.

We drove on out behind the town of Highwood and onto the flat field roads toward our house. I could see, out on the prairie, a moving light where the farmer who rented our house to us was disking his field for winter wheat. "He's waited too late with that business," my father said and took a drink, then threw the bottle right out the window. "He'll lose that," he said, "the cold'll kill it." I did not answer him, but what I thought was that my father knew nothing about farming, and if he was right it would be an accident. He knew about planes and hunting game, and that seemed all to me.

"I want to respect your privacy," he said then, for no reason at all that I understood. I am not even certain he said it, only that it is in my memory that way. I don't know what he was thinking of. Just words. But I said to him, I remember well, "It's all right. Thank you."

We did not go straight out the Geraldine Road to our house. Instead my father went down another mile and turned, went a mile and turned back again so that we came home from the other direction. "I want to stop and listen now," he said. "The geese should be in the stubble." We stopped and he cut the lights and engine, and we opened the car windows and listened. It was eight o'clock at night and it was getting colder, though it was dry. But I could hear nothing, just the sound of air moving lightly through the cut field, and not a goose sound. Though I could smell the whiskey on my father's breath and on mine, could hear the motor ticking, could hear him breathe, hear the sound we made sitting side by side on the car seat, our clothes, our feet, almost our hearts beating. And I could see out in the night the yellow lights of our house, shining through the olive trees south of us like a ship on the sea. "I hear them, by God," my father said, his head stuck out the window. "But they're high up. They won't stop here now, Jackie. They're high flyers, those boys. Long gone geese."

There was a car parked off the road, down the line of wind-break trees, beside a steel thresher the farmer had left there to rust. You could see moonlight off the taillight chrome. It was a Pontiac, a two-door hard-top. My father said nothing about it and I didn't either, though I think now for different reasons.

The floodlight was on over the side door of our house and lights were on inside, upstairs and down. My mother had a pumpkin on the front porch, and the wind chime she had hung by the door was tinkling. My dog, Major, came out of the quonset shed and stood in the car lights when we drove up.

"Let's see what's happening here," my father said, opening the door and stepping out quickly. He looked at me inside the car, and his eyes were wide and his mouth drawn tight.

We walked in the side door and up the basement steps into the kitchen, and a man was standing there—a man I had never seen before, a young man with blond hair, who might've been twenty or twenty-five. He was tall and was wearing a short-sleeved shirt and beige slacks with pleats. He was on the other side of the breakfast table, his fingertips just touching the wooden tabletop. His blue eyes were on my father, who was dressed in hunting clothes.

"Hello," my father said.

"Hello," the young man said, and nothing else. And for some reason I looked at his arms, which were long and pale. They looked like a young man's arms, like my arms. His short sleeves had each been neatly rolled up, and I could see the bottom of a small green tattoo edging out from underneath. There was a glass of whiskey on the table, but no bottle.

"What's your name?" my father said, standing in the kitchen under the bright ceiling light. He sounded like he might be going to laugh.

"Woody," the young man said and cleared his throat. He looked at me, then he touched the glass of whiskey, just the rim of the glass. He wasn't nervous, I could tell that. He did not seem to be afraid of anything.

"Woody," my father said and looked at the glass of whiskey. He looked at me, then sighed and shook his head. "Where's Mrs. Russell, Woody? I guess you aren't robbing my house, are you?"

Woody smiled. "No," he said. "Upstairs. I think she went upstairs."

"Good," my father said, "that's a good place." And he walked straight out of the room, but came back and stood in the doorway. "Jackie, you and Woody

30

35

step outside and wait on me. Just stay there and I'll come out." He looked at Woody then in a way I would not have liked him to look at me, a look that meant he was studying Woody. "I guess that's your car," he said.

"That Pontiac." Woody nodded.

"Okay. Right," my father said. Then he went out again and up the stairs. At that moment the phone started to ring in the living room, and I heard my mother say, "Who's that?" And my father say, "It's me. It's Jack." And I decided I wouldn't go answer the phone. Woody looked at me, and I understood he wasn't sure what to do. Run, maybe. But he didn't have run in him. Though I thought he would probably do what I said if I would say it.

40   "Let's just go outside," I said.

And he said, "All right."

Woody and I walked outside and stood in the light of the floodlamp above the side door. I had on my wool jacket, but Woody was cold and stood with his hands in him pockets, and his arms bare, moving from foot to foot. Inside, the phone was ringing again. Once I looked up and saw my mother come to the window and look down at Woody and me. Woody didn't look up or see her, but I did. I waved at her, and she waved back at me and smiled. She was wearing a powder-blue dress. In another minute the phone stopped ringing.

Woody took a cigarette out of his shirt pocket and lit it. Smoke shot through his nose into the cold air, and he sniffed, looked around the ground and threw his match on the gravel. His blond hair was combed backwards and neat on the sides, and I could smell his aftershave on him, a sweet, lemon smell. And for the first time I noticed his shoes. They were twotones, black with white tops and black laces. They stuck out below his baggy pants and were long and polished and shiny, as if he had been planning on a big occasion. They looked like shoes some country singer would wear, or a salesman. He was handsome, but only like someone you would see beside you in a dime store and not notice again.

"I like it out here," Woody said, his head down, looking at his shoes. "Nothing to bother you. I bet you'd see Chicago if the world was flat. The Great Plains commence here."

45   "I don't know," I said.

Woody looked up at me, cupping his smoke with one hand. "Do you play football?"

"No," I said. I thought about asking him something about my mother. But I had no idea what it would be.

"I *have* been drinking," Woody said, "but I'm not drunk now."

The wind rose then, and from behind the house I could hear Major bark once from far away, and I could smell the irrigation ditch, hear it hiss in the field. It ran down from Highwood Creek to the Missouri, twenty miles away. It was nothing Woody knew about, nothing he could hear or smell. He knew nothing about anything that was here. I heard my father say the words, "That's a real joke," from inside the house, then the sound of a drawer being opened and shut, and a door closing. Then nothing else.

50   Woody turned and looked into the dark toward where the glow of Great Falls rose on the horizon, and we both could see the flashing lights of a plane low-

ering to land there. "I once passed my brother in the Los Angeles airport and didn't even recognize him," Woody said, staring into the night. "He recognized *me*, though. He said, 'Hey, bro, are you mad at me, or what?' I wasn't mad at him. We both had to laugh."

Woody turned and looked at the house. His hands were still in his pockets, his cigarette clenched between his teeth, his arms taut. They were, I saw, bigger, stronger arms than I had thought. A vein went down the front of each of them. I wondered what Woody knew that I didn't. Not about my mother—I didn't know anything about that and didn't want to—but about a lot of things, about the life out in the dark, about coming out here, about airports, even about me. He and I were not so far apart in age, I knew that. But Woody was one thing, and I was another. And I wondered how I would ever get to be like him, since it didn't necessarily seem so bad a thing to be.

"Did you know your mother was married before?" Woody said.

"Yes," I said. "I knew that."

"It happens to all of them, now," he said. "They can't wait to get divorced."

Woody dropped his cigarette into the gravel and toed it out with his black-and-white shoe. He looked up at me and smiled the way he had inside the house, a smile that said he knew something he wouldn't tell, a smile to make you feel bad because you weren't Woody and never could be.

It was then that my father came out of the house. He still had on his plaid hunting coat and his wool cap, but his face was as white as snow, as white as I have ever seen a human being's face to be. It was odd. I had the feeling that he might've fallen inside, because he looked roughed up, as though he had hurt himself somehow.

My mother came out the door behind him and stood in the floodlight at the top of the steps. She was wearing the powder-blue dress I'd seen through the window, a dress I had never seen her wear before, though she was also wearing a car coat and carrying a suitcase. She looked at me and shook her head in a way that only I was supposed to notice, as if it was not a good idea to talk now.

My father had his hands in his pockets, and he walked right up to Woody. He did not even look at me. "What do you do for a living?" he said, and he was very close to Woody. His coat was close enough to touch Woody's shirt.

"I'm in the Air Force," Woody said. He looked at me and then at my father. He could tell my father was excited.

"Is this your day off, then?" my father said. He moved even closer to Woody, his hands still in his pockets. He pushed Woody with his chest, and Woody seemed willing to let my father push him.

"No," he said, shaking his head.

I looked at my mother. She was just standing, watching. It was as if someone had given her an order, and she was obeying it. She did not smile at me, though I thought she was thinking about me, which made me feel strange.

"What's the matter with you?" my father said into Woody's face, right into his face—his voice tight, as if it had gotten hard for him to talk. "Whatever in the world is the matter with you? Don't you understand something?" My father took a revolver pistol out of his coat and put it up under Woody's chin, into the

55

60

soft pocket behind the bone, so that Woody's whole face rose, but his arms stayed at his sides, his hands open. "I don't know what to do with you," my father said. "I don't have any idea what to do with you. I just don't." Though I thought that what he wanted to do was hold Woody there just like that until something important took place, or until he could simply forget about all this.

My father pulled the hammer back on the pistol and raised it tighter under Woody's chin, breathing into Woody's face—my mother in the light with her suitcase, watching them, and me watching them. A half a minute must've gone by.

And then my mother said, "Jack, let's stop now. Let's just stop."

My father stared into Woody's face as if he wanted Woody to consider doing something—moving or turning around or anything on his own to stop this—that my father would then put a stop to. My father's eyes grew narrowed, and his teeth were gritted together, his lips snarling up to resemble a smile. "You're crazy, aren't you?" he said. "You're a goddamned crazy man. Are you in love with her, too? Are you, crazy man? Are you? Do you say you love her? Say you love her! Say you love her so I can blow your fucking brains in the sky."

"All right," Woody said. "No. It's all right."

"He doesn't love me, Jack. For God's sake," my mother said. She seemed so calm. She shook her head at me again. I do not think she thought my father would shoot Woody. And I don't think Woody thought so. Nobody did, I think, except my father himself. But I think he did, and was trying to find out how to.

My father turned suddenly and glared at my mother, his eyes shiny and moving, but with the gun still on Woody's skin. I think he was afraid, afraid he was doing this wrong and could mess all of it up and make matters worse without accomplishing anything.

"You're leaving," he yelled at her. "That's why you're packed. Get out. Go on."

"Jackie has to be at school in the morning," my mother said in just her normal voice. And without another word to any one of us, she walked out of the floodlamp light carrying her bag, turned the corner at the front porch steps and disappeared toward the olive trees that ran in rows back into the wheat.

My father looked back at me where I was standing in the gravel, as if he expected to see me go with my mother toward Woody's car. But I hadn't thought about that—though later I would. Later I would think I should have gone with her, and that things between them might've been different. But that isn't how it happened.

"You're sure you're going to get away now, aren't you, mister?" my father said into Woody's face. He was crazy himself, then. Anyone would've been. Everything must have seemed out of hand to him.

"I'd like to," Woody said. "I'd like to get away from here."

"And I'd like to think of some way to hurt you," my father said and blinked his eyes. "I feel helpless about it." We all heard the door to Woody's car close in the dark. "Do you think that I'm a fool?" my father said.

"No," Woody said. "I don't think that."

"Do you think you're important?"

"No," Woody said. "I'm not."

My father blinked again. He seemed to be becoming someone else at that 80
moment, someone I didn't know. "Where are you from?"

And Woody closed his eyes. He breathed in, then out, a long sigh. I was as
if this was somehow the hardest part, something he hadn't expected to be asked
to say.

"Chicago," Woody said. "A suburb of there."

"Are your parents alive?" my father said, all the time with his blue magnum
pistol pushed under Woody's chin.

"Yes," Woody said. "Yessir."

"That's too bad," my father said. "Too bad they have to know what you are. 85
I'm sure you stopped meaning anything to them a long time ago. I'm sure they
both wish you were dead. You didn't know that. But I know it. I can't help them
out, though. Somebody else'll have to kill you. I don't want to have to think
about you anymore. I guess that's it."

My father brought the gun down to his side and stood looking at Woody. He
did not back away, just stood, waiting for what I don't know to happen. Woody
stood a moment, then he cut his eyes at me uncomfortably. And I know that I
looked down. That's all I could do. Though I remember wondering if Woody's
heart was broken and what any of this meant to him. Not to me, or my mother,
or my father. But to him, since he seemed to be the one left out somehow, the
one who would be lonely soon, the one who had done something he would
someday wish he hadn't and would have no one to tell him that it was all right,
that they forgave him, that these things happen in the world.

Woody took a step back, looked at my father and at me again as if he
intended to speak, then stepped aside and walked away toward the front of our
house, where the wind chime made a noise in the new cold air.

My father looked at me, his big pistol in his hand. "Does this seem stupid to
you?" he said. "All this? Yelling and threatening and going nuts? I wouldn't
blame you if it did. You shouldn't even see this. I'm sorry. I don't know what to
do now."

"It'll be all right," I said. And I walked out to the road. Woody's car started
up behind the olive trees. I stood and watched it back out, its red taillights
clouded by exhaust. I could see their two heads inside, with the headlights shining behind them. When they got into the road, Woody touched his brakes, and
for a moment I could see that they were talking, their heads turned toward each
other, nodding. Woody's head and my mother's. They sat that way for a few
seconds, then drove slowly off. And I wondered what they had to say to each
other, something important enough that they had to stop right at that moment
and say it. Did she say, *I love you?* Did she say, *This is not what I expected to
happen?* Did she say, *This is what I've wanted all along?* and did he say, *I'm sorry
for all this,* or *I'm glad,* or *None of this matters to me?* These are not the kinds of
things you can know if you were not there. And I was not there and did not want
to be. It did not seem like I should be there. I heard the door slam when my

father went inside, and I turned back from the road where I could still see their taillights disappearing, and went back into the house where I was to be alone with my father.

90   Things seldom end in one event. In the morning I went to school on the bus as usual, and my father drove in to the air base in his car. We had not said very much about all that had happened. Harsh words, in a sense, are all alike. You can make them up yourself and be right. I think we both believed that we were in a fog we couldn't see through yet, though in a while, maybe not even a long while, we would see lights and know something.

In my third-period class that day a messenger brought a note for me that said I was excused from school at noon, and I should meet my mother at a motel down 10th Avenue South—a place not so far from my school—and we would eat lunch together.

It was a gray day in Great Falls that day. The leaves were off the trees and the mountains to the east of town were obscured by a low sky. The night before had been cold and clear, but today it seemed as if it would rain. It was the beginning of winter in earnest. In a few days there would be snow everywhere.

The motel where my mother was staying was called the Tropicana, and was beside the city golf course. There was a neon parrot on the sign out front, and the cabins made a U shape behind a little white office building. Only a couple of cars were parked in front of cabins, and no car was in front of my mother's cabin. I wondered if Woody would be here, or if he was at the air base. I wondered if my father would see him there, and what they would say.

I walked back to cabin 9. The door was open, though a DO NOT DISTURB sign was hung on the knob outside. I looked through the screen and saw my mother sitting on the bed alone. The television was on, but she was looking at me. She was wearing the powder-blue dress she had had on the night before. She was smiling at me, and I liked the way she looked at that moment, through the screen, in shadows. Her features did not seem as sharp as they had before. She looked comfortable where she was, and I felt like we were going to get along, no matter what had happened, and that I wasn't mad at her—that I had never been mad at her.

95   She sat forward and turned the television off. "Come in, Jackie," she said, and I opened the screen door and came inside. "It's the height of grandeur in here, isn't it?" My mother looked around the room. Her suitcase was open on the floor by the bathroom door, which I could see through and out the window onto the golf course, where three men were playing under the milky sky. "Privacy can be a burden, sometimes," she said, and reached down and put on her highheeled shoes. "I didn't sleep very well last night, did you?"

"No," I said, though I had slept all night. I wanted to ask her where Woody was, but it occurred to me at that moment that he was gone now and wouldn't be back, that she wasn't thinking in terms of him and didn't care where he was or ever would be.

"I'd like a nice compliment from you," she said. "Do you have one of those to spend?"

"Yes," I said. "I'm glad to see you."

"That's a nice one," she said and nodded. She had both her shoes on now. "Would you like to go have lunch? We can walk across the street to the cafeteria. You can get hot food."

"No" I said. "I'm not really hungry now." 100

"That's okay," she said and smiled at me again. And, as I said before, I liked the way she looked. She looked pretty in a way I didn't remember seeing her, as if something that had had a hold on her had let her go, and she could be different about things. Even about me.

"Sometimes, you know," she said, "I'll think about something I did. Just anything. Years ago in Idaho, or last week, even. And it's as if I'd read it. Like a story. Isn't that strange?"

"Yes," I said. And it did seem strange to me because I was certain then what the difference was between what had happened and what hadn't, and knew I always would be.

"Sometimes," she said, and she folded her hands in her lap and stared out the little side window of her cabin at the parking lot and the curving row of other cabins. "Sometimes I even have a moment when I completely forget what life's like. Just altogether." She smiled. "That's not so bad, finally. Maybe it's a disease I have. Do you think I'm just sick and I'll get well?"

"No. I don't know," I said. "Maybe. I hope so." I looked out the bathroom 105 window and saw the three men walking down the golf course fairway carrying golf clubs.

"I'm not very good at sharing things right now," my mother said. "I'm sorry." She cleared her throat, and then she didn't say anything for almost a minute while I stood there. "I *will* answer anything you'd like me to answer, though. Just ask me anything, and I'll answer it the truth, whether I want to or not. Okay? I will. You don't even have to trust me. That's not a big issue with us. We're both grown-ups now."

And I said, "Were you ever married before?"

My mother looked at me strangely. Her eyes got small, and for a moment she looked the way I was used to seeing her—sharp-faced, her mouth set and taut. "No," she said. "Who told you that? That isn't true. I never was. Did Jack say that to you? Did your father say that? That's an awful thing to say. I haven't been that bad."

"He didn't say that," I said.

"Oh, of course he did," my mother said. "He doesn't know just to let things 110 go when they're bad enough."

"I wanted to know that," I said. "I just thought about it. It doesn't matter."

"No, it doesn't," my mother said. "I could've been married eight times. I'm just sorry he said that to you. He's not generous sometimes."

"He didn't say that," I said. But I'd said it enough, and I didn't care if she believed me or didn't. It was true that trust was not a big issue between us then. And in any event, I know now that the whole truth of anything is an idea that stops existing finally.

"Is that all you want to know, then?" my mother said. She seemed mad, but not at me, I didn't think. Just at things in general. And I sympathized with her. "Your life's your own business, Jackie," she said. "Sometimes it scares you to death it's so much your own business. You just want to run."

"I guess so," I said.

"I'd like a less domestic life, is all." She looked at me, but I didn't say anything. I didn't see what she meant by that, though I knew there was nothing I could say to change the way her life would be from then on. And I kept quiet.

In a while we walked across 10th Avenue and ate lunch in the cafeteria. When she paid for the meal I saw that she had my father's silver-dollar money clip in her purse and that there was money in it. And I understood that he had been to see her already that day, and no one cared if I knew it. We were all of us on our own in this.

When we walked out onto the street, it was colder and the wind was blowing. Car exhausts were invisible and some drivers had their lights on, though it was only two o'clock in the afternoon. My mother had called a taxi, and we stood and waited for it. I didn't know where she was going, but I wasn't going with her.

"Your father won't let me come back," she said, standing on the curb. It was just a fact to her, not that she hoped I would talk to him or stand up for her or take her part. But I did wish then that I had never let her go the night before. Things can be fixed by staying; but to go out into the night and not come back hazards life, and everything can get out of hand.

My mother's taxi came. She kissed me and hugged me very hard, then got inside the cab in her powder-blue dress and high heels and her car coat. I smelled her perfume on my cheeks as I stood watching her. "I used to be afraid of more things than I am now," she said, looking up at me, and smiled. "I've got a knot in my stomach, of all things." And she closed the cab door, waved at me, and rode away.

I walked back toward my school. I thought I could take the bus home if I got there by three. I walked a long way down 10th Avenue to Second Street, beside the Missouri River, then over to town. I walked by the Great Northern Hotel, where my father had sold ducks and geese and fish of all kinds. There were no passenger trains in the yard and the loading dock looked small. Garbage cans were lined along the edge of it, and the door was closed and locked.

As I walked toward school I thought to myself that my life had turned suddenly, and that I might not know exactly how or which way for possibly a long time. Maybe, in fact, I might never know. It was a thing that happened to you— I knew that—and it had happened to me in this way now. And as I walked on up the cold street that afternoon in Great Falls, the questions I asked myself were these: why wouldn't my father let my mother come back? Why would Woody stand in the cold with me outside my house and risk being killed? Why would he say my mother had been married before, if she hadn't been? And my mother herself—why would she do what she did? In five years my father had gone off to Ely, Nevada, to ride out the oil strike there, and been killed by accident. And in the years since then I have seen my mother from time to time—in one place or another, with one man or other—and I can say, at least, that we know each other. But I have never known the answer to these questions, have never asked anyone their answers. Though possibly it—the answer—is simple: it is just low-life, some coldness in us all, some helplessness that causes us to misunderstand life when it is pure and plain, makes our existence seem like a border between two nothings, and makes us no more or less than animals who meet on the road—watchful, unforgiving, without patience or desire.

1987

LYNNA WILLIAMS

Personal Testimony

The last night of church camp, 1963, and I am sitting in the front row of the junior mixed-voice choir looking out on the crowd in the big sanctuary tent. The tent glows, green and white and unexpected, in the Oklahoma night; our choir director, Dr. Bledsoe, has schooled us in the sudden crescendos needed to compete with the sounds cars make when their drivers cut the corner after a night at the bars on Highway 10 and see the tent rising out of the plain for the first time. The tent is new to Faith Camp this year, a gift to God and the Southern Baptist Convention from the owner of a small circus who repented, and then retired, in nearby Oklahoma City. It is widely rumored among the campers that Mr. Talliferro came to Jesus late in life, after having what my mother would call Life Experiences. Now he walks through camp with the unfailing good humor of a man who, after years of begging hardscrabble farmers to forsake their fields for an afternoon of elephants and acrobats, has finally found a real draw: his weekly talks to the senior boys on "Sin and the Circus" incorporate a standing-room-only question-and-answer period, and no one ever leaves early.

Although I know I will never be allowed in the tent to hear one of Mr. Talliferro's talks—I will not be twelve forever, but I will always be a girl—I am encouraged by his late arrival into our Fellowship of Believers. I will take my time, too, I think: first I will go to high school, to college, to bed with a boy, to New York. (I think of those last two items as one since, as little as I know about sex, I do know it is not something I will ever be able to do in the same time zone as my mother.) Then when I'm fifty-two or so and have had, like Mr. Talliferro, sufficient Life Experiences, I'll move back to west Texas and repent.

Normally, thoughts of that touching—and distant—scene of repentance are how I entertain myself during evening worship service. But tonight I am unable to work up any enthusiasm for the vision of myself sweeping into my hometown to Be Forgiven. For once my thoughts are entirely on the worship service ahead.

My place in the choir is in the middle of six other girls from my father's church in Fort Worth; we are dressed alike in white lace-trimmed wash-and-wear blouses from J. C. Penney and modest navy pedal pushers that stop exactly three inches from our white socks and tennis shoes. We are also alike in having mothers who regard travel irons as an essential accessory to Christian Young Womanhood; our matching outfits are, therefore, neatly ironed.

At least their outfits are. I have been coming to this camp in the southwestern equivalent of the Sahara Desert for six years now, and I know that when it is a hundred degrees at sunset, cotton wilts. When I used my iron I did the front of my blouse and the pants, so I wouldn't stand out, and trusted that anyone standing behind me would think I was wrinkled from the heat.

Last summer, or the summer before, when I was still riding the line that separates good girls from bad, this small deception would have bothered me. This year I am twelve and a criminal. Moral niceties are lost on me. I am singing "Just as I Am" with the choir and I have three hundred dollars in my white Bible, folded and taped over John 3:16.

Since camp started three weeks ago, I have operated a business in the arts and crafts cabin in the break between afternoon Bible study and segregated (boys only / girls only) swimming. The senior boys, the same ones who are learning critical new information from Mr. Talliferro every week, are paying me to write the personal testimonies we are all expected to give at evening worship service.

We do not dwell on personal motivation in my family. When my brother, David, and I sin, it is the deed my parents talk about, not mitigating circumstances, and the deed they punish. This careful emphasis on what we do, never on why we do it, has affected David and me differently. He is a good boy, endlessly kind and cheerful and responsible, but his heroes are not the men my father followed into the ministry. David gives God and our father every outward sign of respect, but he worships Clarence Darrow[1] and the law. At fifteen, he has been my defense lawyer for years.

While David wants to defend the world, I am only interested in defending myself. I know exactly why I have started the testimony business: I am doing it to get back at my father. I am doing it because I am adopted.

Even though I assure my customers with every sale that we will not get caught, I never write a testimony without imagining public exposure of my wrongdoing. The scene is so familiar to me that I do not have to close my eyes to see it: the summons to the camp director's office and the door closing behind me; the shocked faces of other campers when the news leaks out; the Baptist Academy girls who comb their hair and go in pairs, bravely, to offer my brother comfort; the automatic rotation of my name to the top of everyone's prayer list. I spend hours imagining the small details of my shame, always leading to the moment when my father, called from Fort Worth to take me home, arrives at camp.

That will be my moment. I have done something so terrible that even my father will not be able to keep it a secret. I am doing this because of my father's secrets.

We had only been home from church for a few minutes; it was my ninth birthday, and when my father called me to come downstairs to his study, I was

1. Clarence Darrow (1857–1938) was the lawyer who defended biology teacher John Scopes in the 1925 "monkey trial" in Dayton, Tennessee.

still wearing the dress my mother had made for the occasion, pink dotted swiss with a white satin sash. David came out of his room to ask me what I had done this time—he likes to be prepared for court—but I told him not to worry, that I was wholly innocent of any crime in the weeks just before my birthday. At the bottom of the stairs I saw my mother walk out of the study and knew I was right not to be concerned: in matters of discipline my mother and father never work alone. At the door it came to me: my father was going to tell me I was old enough to go with him now and then to churches in other cities. David had been to Atlanta and New Orleans and a dozen little Texas towns; my turn had finally come.

My father was standing by the window. At the sound of my patent-leather shoes sliding across the hardwood floor, he turned and motioned for me to sit on the sofa. He cleared his throat; it was a sermon noise I had heard hundreds of times, and I knew that he had prepared whatever he was going to say.

All thoughts of ordering room-service hamburgers in an Atlanta hotel left me—prepared remarks meant we were dealing with life or death or salvation—and I wished for my mother and David. My father said, "This is hard for your mother; she wanted to be here, but it upsets her so, we thought I should talk to you alone." We had left any territory I knew, and I sat up straight to listen, as though I were still in church.

My father, still talking, took my hands in his; after a moment I recognized the weight of his Baylor[2] ring against my skin as something from my old life, the one in which I had woken up that morning a nine-year-old, dressed for church in my birthday dress, and come home.

My father talked and talked and talked; I stopped listening. I had grown up singing about the power of blood. I required no lengthy explanation of what it meant to be adopted. It meant I was not my father's child. It meant I was a secret, even from myself.

In the three years since that day in my father's study, I have realized, of course, that I am not my mother's child, either. But I have never believed that she was responsible for the lie about my birth. It is my father I blame. I am not allowed to talk about my adoption outside my family ("It would only hurt your mother," my father says. "Do you want to hurt your mother?"). Although I am universally regarded by the women of our church as a Child Who Wouldn't Know a Rule If One Reached Up and Bit Her in the Face, I do keep this one. My stomach hurts when I even think about telling anyone, but it hurts, too, when I think about having another mother and father somewhere. When the pain is enough to make me cry, I try to talk to my parents about it, but my mother's face changes even before I can get the first question out, and my father always follows her out of the room. "You're our child," he says when he returns. "We love you, and you're ours."

I let him hug me, but I am thinking that I have never heard my father tell a lie before. I am not his child. Not in the way David is, not in the way I believed

15

2. Baylor University, located in Waco, Texas.

I was. Later I remember that lie and decide that all the secrecy is for my father's benefit, that he is ashamed to tell the world that I am not his child because he is ashamed of me. I think about the Ford my father bought in Dallas three years ago; it has never run right, but he will not take it back. I think about that when I am sitting in my bunk with a flashlight, writing testimonies to the power of God's love.

My father is one reason I am handcrafting Christian testimonies while my bunkmates are making place mats from Popsicle sticks. There is another reason: I'm good at it.

Nothing else has changed. I remain Right Fielder for Life in the daily softball games. The sincerity of my belief in Jesus is perennially suspect among the most pious, and most popular, campers. And I am still the only girl who, in six years of regular attendance, has failed to advance even one step in Girls' Auxiliary. (Other, younger girls have made it all the way to Queen Regent with Scepter, while I remain a perpetual Lady-in-Waiting.) Until this year, only the strength of my family connections has kept me from sinking as low in the camp hierarchy as Cassie Mosley, who lisps and wears colorful native costumes that her missionary parents send from Africa.

20   I arrived at camp this summer as I do every year, resigned and braced to endure but buoyed by a fantasy life that I believe is unrivaled among twelve-year-old Baptist girls. But on our second night here, the promise of fish sticks and carrot salad hanging in the air, Bobby Dunn came and stood behind me in the cafeteria line.

Bobby Dunn, blond, ambitious, and in love with Jesus, is Faith Camp's standard for male perfection. He is David's friend, but he has spoken to me only once, on the baseball field last year, when he suggested that my unhealthy fear of the ball was really a failure to trust God's plan for my life. Since that day I have taken some comfort in noticing that Bobby Dunn follows the Scripture reading by moving his finger along the text.

Feeling him next to me, I took a breath, wondering if Bobby, like other campers in other years, had decided to attempt to bring me to a better understanding of what it means to serve Jesus. But he was already talking, congratulating me on my testimony at evening worship service the night before. (I speak publicly at camp twice every summer, the exact number required by some mysterious formula that allows me to be left alone the rest of the time.)

"You put it just right," he said. "Now me, I know what I want to say, but it comes out all wrong. I've prayed about it, and it seems to be God wants me to do better."

He looked at me hard, and I realized it was my turn to say something. Nothing came to me, though, since I agreed with him completely. He does suffer from what my saintly brother, after one particularly gruesome revival meeting, took to calling Jesus Jaw, a malady that makes it impossible for the devoted to say what they mean and sit down. Finally I said what my mother says to the ladies seeking comfort in the Dorcas Bible class: "Can I help?" Before I could take it back, Bobby Dunn had me by the hand and was pulling me across the cafeteria to a table in the far corner.

The idea of my writing testimonies for other campers—a sort of ghostwriting service for Jesus, as Bobby Dunn saw it—was Bobby's, but before we got up from the table, I had refined it and made it mine. The next afternoon in the arts and crafts cabin I made my first sale: five dollars for a two-minute testimony detailing how God gave Michael Bush the strength to stop swearing. Bobby was shocked when the money changed hands—I could see him thinking, Temple. Money-lenders. Jee-sus!—but Michael Bush is the son of an Austin car dealer, and he quoted his earthly father's scripture: "You get what you pay for."

Michael, who made me a professional writer with money he earned polishing used station wagons, is a sweet, slow-talking athlete from Bishop Military School. He'd been dateless for months and was convinced it was because the Baptist Academy girls had heard that he has a tendency to take the Lord's name in vain on difficult fourth downs. After his testimony that night, Michael left the tent with Patsy Lewis, but he waved good night to me.

For an underground business, I have as much word-of-mouth trade from the senior boys as I can handle. I estimate that my volume is second only to that of the snack stand that sells snow cones. Like the snow-cone stand, I have high prices and limited hours of operation. I arrive at the arts and crafts cabin every day at 2:00 P.M., carrying half-finished pot holders from the day before, and senior boys drift in and out for the next twenty minutes. I talk to each customer, take notes, and deliver the finished product by 5:00 P.M. the next day. My prices start at five dollars for words only and go up to twenty dollars for words and concept.

Bobby Dunn has appointed himself my sales force; he recruits customers who he thinks need my services and gives each one a talk about the need for secrecy. Bobby will not accept money from me as payment—he reminds me hourly that he is doing this for Jesus—but he is glad to be thanked in testimonies.

By the beginning of the second week of camp, our director, Reverend Stewart, and the camp counselors were openly rejoicing about the power of the Spirit at work, as reflected in the moving personal testimonies being given night after night. Bobby Dunn has been testifying every other night and smiling at me at breakfast every morning. Patsy Lewis has taught me how to set my hair on big rollers, and I let it dry while I sit up writing testimonies. I have a perfect pageboy, a white Bible bulging with five-dollar bills, and I am popular. There are times when I forget my father.

On this last night of camp I am still at large. But although I have not been caught, I have decided I am not cut out to be a small business. There is the question of good help, for one thing. Bobby Dunn is no good for detail work—clearly, the less he knows about how my mind works, the better—and so I have turned to Missy Tucker. Missy loves Jesus and her father and disapproves of everything about me. I love her because she truly believes I can be saved and, until that happens, is willing to get into almost any trouble I can think of, provided I do not try to stop her from quoting the appropriate Scripture. Even so, she resisted being drawn into the testimony business for more than a week, giving in only after I sank low enough to introduce her to Bobby Dunn and point out that she would be able to apply her cut to the high cost of braces.

The truth is, the business needs Missy. I am no better a disciple of the Palmer Handwriting Method than I am of Christ or of my mother's standards of behavior. No one can read my writing. Missy has won the penmanship medal at E. M. Morrow Elementary School so many times there is talk that it will be retired when we go off to junior high in the fall. When she's done writing, my testimonies look like poems.

The value of Missy's cursive writing skills, however, is offset by the ways in which she manifests herself as a True Believer. I can tolerate the Scripture quoting, but her fears are something else. I am afraid of snakes and of not being asked to pledge my mother's sorority at Baylor, both standard fears in Cabin A. Missy is terrified of Eastern religions.

Her father, a religion professor at a small Baptist college, has two passions: world religions and big-game hunting. In our neighborhood, where not rotating the tires on the family Ford on a schedule is considered eccentric, Dr. Tucker wears a safari jacket to class and greets everyone the same way: "Hi, wallaby." Missy is not allowed to be afraid of the dead animals in her father's den, but a pronounced sensitivity to Oriental mysticism is thought to be acceptable in a young girl.

Unless I watch her, Missy cannot be trusted to resist inserting a paragraph into every testimony in which the speaker thanks the Lord Jesus for not having allowed him or her to be born a Buddhist. I tell Missy repeatedly that if every member of the camp baseball team suddenly begins to compare and contrast Zen and the tenets of Southern Baptist fundamentalism in his three-minute testimony, someone—even in this trusting place—is going to start to wonder.

She says she sees my point but keeps arguing for more "spiritual" content in the testimonies, a position in which she is enthusiastically supported by Bobby Dunn. Missy and Bobby have fallen in love; Bobby asked her to wear his friendship ring two nights ago, using his own words. What is art to me is faith—and now love—to Missy, and we are not as close as we were three weeks ago.

I am a success, but a lonely one, since there is no one I can talk to about either my success or my feelings. My brother, David, who normally can be counted on to protect me from myself and others, has only vague, Christian concern for me these days. He has fallen in love with Denise Meeker, universally regarded as the most spiritually developed girl in camp history, and he is talking about following my father into the ministry. I believe that when Denise goes home to Corpus Christi, David will remember law school, but in the meantime he is no comfort to me.

Now, from my place in the front row of the choir, I know that I will not have to worry about a going-out-of-business sale. What I have secretly wished for all summer is about to happen. I am going to get caught.

Ten minutes ago, during Reverend Stewart's introduction of visitors from the pulpit, I looked out at the crowd in the tent and saw my father walking down the center aisle. As I watched, he stopped every few rows to shake hands and say hello, as casual and full of good humor as if this were his church on a Sunday morning. He is a handsome man, and when he stopped at the pew near the front where David is sitting, I was struck by how much my father and brother look alike, their dark heads together as they smiled and hugged. I think of David as belonging to me, not to my father, but there was an unmistakable sameness in their movements that caught me by surprise, and my eyes filled with tears. Suddenly David pointed toward the choir, at me, and my father nodded his head and continued walking toward the front of the tent. I knew he had seen me, and I concentrated on looking straight ahead as he mounted the stairs to the stage and took a seat to the left of the altar. Reverend Stewart introduced him as the special guest preacher for the last night of camp, and for an instant I let myself believe that was the only reason he had come. He would preach and we would go home together tomorrow. Everything would be all right.

I hear a choked-off sound from my left and know without turning to look that it is Missy, about to cry. She has seen my father, too, and I touch her hand to remind her that no one will believe she was at fault. Because of me, teachers have been patiently writing "easily led" and "cries often" on Missy's report cards for years, and she is still considered a good girl. She won't get braces this year, I think, but she will be all right.

In the next moment two things happen at once. Missy starts to cry, really cry, and my father turns in his seat, looks at me, and then away. It is then that I realize that Missy has decided, without telling me, that straight teeth are not worth eternal damnation. She and Bobby Dunn have confessed, and my father has been called. Now, as he sits with his Bible in his hands and his head bowed, his profile shows none of the cheer of a moment before, and none of the success-ful-Baptist-preacher expressions I can identify. He does not look spiritual or joy-ful or weighted down by the burden of God's expectations. He looks furious.

There are more announcements than I ever remember hearing on the last night of camp: prayer lists, final volleyball standings, bus departure times, a Lottie Moon Stewardship Award for Denise Meeker. After each item, I forget I have no reason to expect Jesus to help me and I pray for one more; I know that as soon as the last announcement is read, Reverend Stewart will call for a time of personal testimonies before my father's sermon.

Even with my head down I can see Bobby Dunn sinking lower into a center pew and, next to him, Tim Bailey leaning forward, wanting to be first at the microphone. Tim is another of the Bishop School jocks, and he has combed his hair and put on Sunday clothes. In his left hand he is holding my masterwork, reproduced on three-by-five cards. He paid me twenty-five dollars for it — the most I have ever charged — and it is the best piece of my career. The script calls for Tim to talk movingly about meeting God in a car-truck accident near Galveston, when he was ten. In a dramatic touch of which I am especially proud, he seems to imply that God was driving the truck.

40

Tim, I know, is doing this to impress a Baptist Academy girl who has told him she will go to her cotillion alone before she goes with a boy who doesn't know Jesus as his personal Lord and Savior. He is gripping the notecards as if they were Didi Thornton, and for the first time in a lifetime full of Bible verses, I see an application to my daily living. I truly am about to reap what I have sown.

The announcements end, and Reverend Stewart calls for testimonies. As Tim Bailey rises, so does my father. As he straightens up, he turns again to look at me, and this time he makes a gesture toward the pulpit. It is a mock-gallant motion, the kind I have seen him make to let my mother go first at miniature golf. For an instant that simple reminder that I am not an evil mutant—I have a family that plays miniature golf—makes me think again that everything will be all right. Then I realize what my father is telling me. Tim Bailey will never get to the pulpit to give my testimony. My father will get there first, will tell the worshipers in the packed tent his sorrow and regret over the misdeeds of his little girl. *His little girl.* He is going to do what I have never imagined in all my fantasies about this moment. He is going to forgive me.

45   Without knowing exactly how it has happened, I am standing up, half running from the choir seats to the pulpit. I get there first, before either my father or Tim, and before Reverend Stewart can even say my name, I give my personal testimony.

I begin by admitting what I have been doing for the past three weeks. I talk about being gripped by hate, unable to appreciate the love of my wonderful parents or of Jesus. I talk about making money from other campers who, in their honest desire to honor the Lord, became trapped in my web of wrongdoing.

Bobby Dunn is crying. To his left I can see Mr. Talliferro; something in his face, intent and unsmiling, makes me relax: I am a Draw. Everyone is with me now. I can hear Missy behind me, still sobbing into her hymnal, and to prove I can make it work, I talk about realizing how blessed I am to have been born within easy reach of God's healing love. I could have been born a Buddhist, I say, and the gratifying gasps from the audience make me certain I can say anything I want now.

For an instant I lose control and begin quoting poetry instead of Scripture. There is a shaky moment when all I can remember is bits of "Stopping by Woods on a Snowy Evening,"[3] but I manage to tie the verses back to a point about Christian choices. The puzzled looks on some faces give way to shouts of "Amen!" and as I look out at the rows of people in the green-and-white-striped tent I know I have won. I have written the best testimony anyone at camp has ever given.

I feel, rather than see, my father come to stand beside me, but I do not stop. As I have heard him do hundreds of times, I ask the choir to sing an invitational hymn and begin singing with them, "Softly and tenderly, Jesus is calling, calling to you and to me. Come home, come home. Ye who are weary, come home."

3. A poem by the American poet Robert Frost (1874–1963).

My father never does give a sermon.   50

While the hymn is still being sung, Bobby Dunn moves from his pew to the stage, and others follow. They hug me; they say they understand; they say they forgive me. As each one moves on to my father, I can hear him thanking them for their concern and saying, yes, he knows they will be praying for the family.

By ten o'clock, the last knot of worshipers has left the tent, and my father and I are alone on the stage. He is looking at me without speaking; there is no expression on his face that I have seen before. "Daddy," I surprise myself by saying. Daddy is a baby name that I have not used since my ninth birthday. My father raises his left hand and slaps me, hard, on my right cheek. He catches me as I start to fall, and we sit down together on the steps leading from the altar. He uses his handkerchief to clean blood from underneath my eye, where his Baylor ring has opened the skin. As he works the white square of cloth carefully around my face, I hear a sound I have never heard before, and I realize my father is crying. I am crying, too, and the mixture of tears and blood on my face makes it impossible to see him clearly. I reach for him anyway and am only a little surprised when he is there.

1992

REGINALD McKNIGHT

Into Night

At two-thirty in the afternoon last Tuesday, just like every day, Sandman got to be as restless as a ghost. Didn't he nor I nor his mama know why he got this way. It mighta had something to do with two-thirty being the time that *Cartoon Tyme* went off the air. That meant to Sandman they wasn't nothing on the box till six in the evening, when *Gimme a Break* come on. Sandman liked that show a whole bunch 'cause it have this big ol' fat woman on it who look like my daughter Erlene and who holler like everybody she talking to a mile away. From two-thirty on, wasn't nothing on but news, game shows, and soaps, programs a five-year-old cain't stand. But I know that didn't have all that much to do with why my grandchild got as fidgety as he did most every day. Most likely it had to do with the fact that his big sister, Tanika, was fend[1] to arrive home from school before long. And little Tanika had what I call a unnatural ability for knowing if Sandman done been in her room, messing with her things, which he did most every day.

Don't know what it was about that boy. Seem like he just couldn't break hisself away from going up to her room. Been doing that since Pauline, my daughter, and her husband, Ricardo, moved me in with them last winter. Didn't know what it was. The child has plenty of his own toys and things. He like to drive his mama and his sister and his daddy insane every day with his constant

1. About.

going up to her room and messing with her things. Even though things have changed since Tuesday last, I still think they should put the boy in preschool, like they done Tanika, but they won't. Pauline say, "Mama, they ain't nothing they can teach him at that school that I cain't teach him at home." Course she say it a whole lot prettier and fancier than that, 'cause of all the education she's had, but that's basically what she said. I know she get irritated with me sometimes, and I hates to interfere and get in the way, but I see what I see, and I know what I know. The boy don't mean no harm. When they first brung me here last winter, after Paul passed, I thought they wanted me to help with the chi'ren, and this big ol' house, but it seem like granmas is better seen and not heard. Seem like all they want me to do is sit around the house and crochet and look thankful I got family. Lord, I coulda did that back in Shreveport. Didn't need to come up here.

Now, the "crime of crimes," as far as Tanika was concerned, was "even breathing" on her model aero-planes. Ricardo fond of saying that Tanika is "uncanny" at remembering exactly where she set each and every model she had displayed round her room. But Sandman loves the models as much as his sister do, and he show his love for 'em by playing with 'em. But sometimes he break 'em, too. After a while, though, he got used to Tanika's temper, I suppose, even though the girl can explode like a bone-dry radiator when she want to, and even though she take forever to cool back down. He got used to, too, with her always screaming 'bout how her models is not toys and how "ab-so-loot-ly nooo-body" under nine years old is allowed in her room. That girl can screech and squeak, shake that one itty-bitty fist in his face, threaten the boy with "fis' soup and knuckle samwiches" till she near 'bout blue in the face. But Sandman steady[2] been in her room and steady play with her models. And ol' Sandman'll stand up in fronta Tanika like a deacon stand up before the altar to receive holy reprimand. He stand tall as he can in front of her and try not to look too bored or too sassy. The boy'll stay cool as ice cream, little as he is, nodding every now and then, but not saying a word. Now, before Tuesday, however, when Tanika'd be in a 'specially nasty mood she'd smack Sandman upside his head. And just like any sinner ought to fear one of the Lord's crackly lightning bolts, Sandman was afred of his sister's hurricane swings and lightning knuckles. But things been pretty calm since Tuesday last, like I said.

Well, the light from the T.V. shrunk down to a tiny dot and faded away. I was sitting up in the living room with him, at the time, and I looked up from my crocheting and watched him watch hisself get up from his Cap'n Starheart Official Star Command T.V. cushion, and glide on out the living room. Looked to me, at first, he was going down to the basement where his mama's studio at, but I said, "Uh-uh, baby, Mama's busy. Whyn't you stay up here with Granmama. You hungry?" He said he wasn't hungry.

5   "Well," I said, "I think you ought to go out'n play in the back, or you can take a nap, then."

He didn't say nothing for about a minute, just stood there, standing on the

---

2. Loosely, "always."

side of his shoes like he always do, so I said, "Baby, don't stand that way, you'll ruin your shoes. You wanna go out?" But he said he didn't wanna go out, said he wanted to take a nap. Well, I knew something was up. Ain't seen many five-year-old boys ask for a nap, but I said, "All right. You want me to go up with you and pat your back?" and he shook his head no, and went on up the stairs. I knew what he was gonna do. He was gonna go right straight up them stairs and go right on into Tanika's room. Don't know who he thought he was fooling. This an old house, and when it's quiet here, you can hear every creak and croak them steps and them floorboards make. Once somebody up on the landing, ain't but a half dozen or so sounds you gonna hear: If it's Sandman's room you gonna hear, "Grunt-grunt"—that's to the right. If it's Tanika's room it's gon' be, "Grunt-grunt-o-gruncha?" The bathroom say, "Grunt-grunt-o-pop," or "Grunt-grunt-o-squeak-pop," depending on whether you step on the doorsill or not. The rooms on the left, mine's and the master bedroom, have their own way, too. Didn't even have to get out my chair to know Sandman went up them twelve steps, and instead of going to his room: "Grunt-grunt," I heard, "Grunt" . . . and a long pause, and then . . . "grunt," and then a long, long, long pause, and then—he was sneaking, see—"o-gruncha?" I just had to laugh. And then right when I was thinking 'bout going up after him, Pauline hollered from downstairs, "Mama? Where Sandman at?" See, only a mama could have that kind of feeling that her child ain't up to no good. "Oh, he upstairs," I yelled back. "Napping."

She was quiet for a little bit, then she said, "Would you check on him for me, please?"

"All right, honey," I said. And I tiptoed up them dozen steps, thinking I'd peep at him in his sister's room for a bit before picking his narrow behind up and putting him in his own room. He just love Tanika's room and Tanika's things, but I myself can't stand it. Don't like the smell. Smells like model glue, strawberry talcum powder, and doll plastic. Child must have a thousand dolls in that room, and every one of 'em different. Different colors, different doll tricks, different sizes and shapes. But I'll tell you one thing: ain't never seen the girl play with a one. Most every one a them dolls was sent to her by her and Sandman's granmama who live in Tennessee. That woman just cain't stand the idea a my grandbaby being interested in model planes. Ricardo's mother got a little . . . money, see, and she like everybody to know it, so every chance she get she send Tanika some kinda doll. Don't matter what occasion it is, Christmas, Easter, Tanika's birthday, Sandman's birthday, good report card, bad report card, no report card, or "just for being a sweet thing," don't make no never mind. Woman like to make me spit up. The child got an army a dolls, a legion a dolls that cry, belch, sing, snore, pee, drink, get diaper rash, walk, blink, crawl. But Tanika, bless her heart, won't touch 'em.

If you's to walk into her room on any day, you wouldn't see a one of these dolls. But you can smell 'em. They crammed into her closet, stacked under her bed. Ain't but two or three of 'em ever even been removed from they boxes. Ricardo call Tanika's bedroom "the bone yard," and even joked about buying a plastic wreath to hang on her door. But Pauline didn't find that funny at all. Said Ricardo's sense of humor is morbid. Her and her fancy words—but I agree with her. Talk like that will only give the babies bad dreams.

10   Well, I opened up Tanika's door just a tee-nine-chee bit and peeked in, and Lord, what did I see. Lord, it made me put my hand to my chest, and made my eyes bug out, and made my breathing like to stop. I seen Sandman standing in the middle of Tanika's room spinning round slow like somebody dancing by hisself, and flying round and round was one of Tanika's aero-planes going round and round the room. I didn't mean to speak so loud, but I hollered, "Sandman!" and the boy jecked his head my way and the plane went zing and smacked right into the door. I jumped back. Well, before I could collect myself and open the door, I heard Pauline's footsteps on the stairs and she saying in her shrieky-high voice, "What's going on up there? What's that boy doing?" I opened up the door just as Pauline got up the stairs. "Paul," I was fend to say, but Pauline said, "Maxwell Sanders Harris! Boy, what'd I tell you about playing in your sister's room?" Pauline very light skinned like her daddy, and when she get upset like she was then, she get this maroon blush on her face, look just like a butterfly. Her daddy, Paul, used to color up the very same way, and so do Tanika. I'll tell you what, when they get to wearing that maroon butterfly, you better look out. "Huh, boy?" Pauline said. "What'd I say?"

"Not to," Sandman said.

"Then why'd you do it, huh?"

Sandman didn't say nothing, and I felt just turrible for the child. He stood there, as he always do on the side of his feet, with his hands behind his back, and his forehead creased, his eyes looking all worried. Like to make me cry. Had on his little suspenders, his little blue jeans a size or two too big. Big head, little scrawny neck. I just felt turrible, looking at that boy, and I said, "Paul, now you got work to do, honey. Let me talk to him."

"Mama, I been talking to this child enough to make my head spin. I'm damn sick and tired of him defying me. Damn sick and tired of it."

15   "Ain't no reason to cuss me, girl," I said. "I'm your—"

"Mind your bidness—boy, get to your room."

Sandman is usually a well-behaved child, but for some reason he didn't budge. Instead, he looked at my feet and he said, "Mama, that plane flew by itself." Then quick as you could blink, *whap!* Pauline slapped his face. "Oww!" he said, real slow and long. He opened his mouth wide and his eyes got big, and tears filled up his eyes. He put his hand on his face where Pauline'd hit and tears was just rolling, but he didn't make no crying sounds at all. Then again he said, "Oww."

"What'd I tell you about lying?" Pauline said.

"Pauline!" I said.

"Get to your room, boy!"

Whap! She hit him again.

"Pauline!"

And Sandman hunched over and he looked like he couldn't believe what his mama was doing. He opened his mouth wide and saliva was dripping in a long string from his mouth and there was that silent crying for a long, long time. You know how chi'ren be when they gots to rear up they breath before they starts to really let loose. That's just what Sandman did. And Lord-a-mighty he did let loose. Loud. Then he walked past us and went to his room, still all hunched over, still with his hand on his face, just wailing and wailing and wailing. "Shut up that crying," Pauline said. Then she turned to me and the butterfly was like to fly off her face, it was so hot and red. "What you got to say, Mama. Huh? What you got to say?"

And I looked at the boy walk into his room, then I looked at the aero-plane on the floor of Tanika's room, and I seen the fishing line tied to it, and I understood why it looked like the plane'd been flying. See, some of Tanika's models is on chrome stands, and some of 'em hangs from fishing lines from the ceiling. Ricardo give her the line, you understand. Apparently, what happened was the boy'd found something long to smack the plane with and make it fly in a circle like it did. But it was going so fast, I told myself, I couldn't see the line at first. But there it was, just as plain as day, tied onto the aero-plane, and at the other end of the line was the thumbtack that had held the line in the ceiling. I felt foolish, 'cause I was fend to tell Pauline that the plane did too fly. Seen it with my very own eyes, I was gonna say. But looked like I was wrong, so I didn't know what to say about that. The sound a Sandman's crying made me hurt in my chest and in my throat. Don't know why it upset me so. Ain't like I've never heard chi'ren cry before. And I really didn't wanna interfere with how my grown daughter raise her chi'ren. I might be her mama, but I'm a guest in this house. I got to respects what they say and do. Pauline is a good and strong woman, and I'm so proud of what she's done and what she's got. The child's got statues standing, and pictures hanging, in museums in Detroit and California and New York City, and here in Pittsburgh. Sometimes she take me down into her studio in the basement and show me what she working on. The stuff she do is so pretty, all them loud African colors, like a store full of jaw-breakers. Like to make your mouth water. I got to admit I don't care for everything she do, and I think she ought to put some more clothes on some of those women she paint and draw, and not make their faces look so cross, but I guess she know what she doing, and I guess I don't. But the one she working on now, the one she shown me a day or two ago, she call *The Vanishing Blue*,[3] which she tell me is about that Middle Passing,[4] I believe it is, when the white folks took our people from Africa. Well, it's all done in blue dots, like a million tiny blue dots, this one picture, see. Blues so light they nearly white, to blues so dark, they nearly black. And its animals and birds and trees, and it all look like you seeing down from way, way up in the air. Like you done passed from this life, and you looking down on everything. That one I like, and I understand it. But even if I don't understand or don't like something, I don't say anything. No, sir, I don't. She grown, and it's her life. Besides, she got them two fine chi'ren and a good husband who she tell me is the best optometrist in town. They got a nice house. They got two nice cars. And they been so good to me.

3. Refers to the disappearing horizon as seen from the stern of a ship.   4. Middle Passage is the term used to describe the transporting of Africans by ship to the Americas for the purpose of selling them into slavery.

20 But I had to say something. I mean, she was standing there in front of me, huffing and puffing with her hands on her hips, and her butterfly a-burning. She looked so tired, had beeswax under her fingernails, and what looked like charcoal on her cheek, a rope a that dreadful Rooster, Rasta, Roster hair, or whatever you calls it, hanging down over one eye. One wrong word might make things worse, I was thinking, and like I say, I didn't want to interfere, but when you looks at it the way a five-year-old do, that plane was flying. So I said, "It's my fault, baby. I was supposed to be watching him, and I wasn't. Don't be too hard on him."

"Mama," she said, and then she pointed her finger at me, which she know I don't like, "I have told him and told him and told him—"

"I know—"

"—to stay out of his sister's room. And I'm sick of it. And you know good and well you raised me to despise lying. Now, you got anything else to say?"

"No."

25 "Good." And she spun around and went. Sounded like a herd a buffalo going down them steps. Then I heard her holler up the stairs, "And, Mama, please leave that mess he made right where it is, till Ricardo and Tani get home. And Maxwell, boy, don't you let me hear you fooling around up there. You get your butt into that bed and stay quiet."

Well I did leave the "mess" where it was. I didn't feel like doing anything no how. Sandman was still in his room, gasping and whooping like his room didn't have no air in it. I shut his door, then went on into my own room and closed my door, too. I could still hear him a little bit. I wanted to go into his room and hold him a spell, but that was for his mama to do. If she'd come back upstairs for some reason, and seen me doing that, why, I think she'd a got upset all over again. Didn't know what to do with myself, so I just kicked off my shoes, pulled off my glasses, untucked my blouse, unfastened the top button of my pants, and laid down on my bed.

Just before my eyes got heavy, I heard a sound that said, "Doomp, d-doom doomp. Doomp, d-doom doomp," kinda like the way that Sergeant Joe Friday[5] music go. I knew it was Sandman fiddling around with something, and I got up and out my room in my stocking feet, stood outside the door to his room, and listened. He was talking to hisself, real quiet like. And the sound said, "Doomp, d-doom doomp." Got down on my knees and looked through the keyhole. Sandman was sitting on his toy box, his chin resting in his hands, bouncing his heels off the side of the toy box. "Doomp, d-doom doomp." Then he hopped down off the box, th'ew it open, and started digging through it. After a good deal of digging and searching and looking, he took out this little rubber super-hero doll—didn't know what its name was, only ones I know is Superman, Batman, and that Starheart fella he so crazy about, but this one I didn't know; besides, I couldn't see it all that well no how, since I didn't have my glasses on.

5. Sergeant Joe Friday, played by Jack Webb, was the head detective on *Dragnet*, the popular 1950s television series. The theme music that accompanied the capture and conviction of the criminal was always the ominous single notes: "Doomp, de-doom doomp. Doomp, de-doom doomp, doo!"

Well now, he closed the lid on the box, and stood the doll up on its feets, and backed up a few steps from the box. I could just barely see the doll's head poking up over Sandman's shoulder. What is he doing? I asked myself. Then he pointed his finger at the doll, and said in the loudest whisper he could, "Fly, Spiderman!" Well, I be dogged, I was thinking. Maybe he can too, make things fly. "Fly, Spiderman!" he said again. Almost made me laugh out loud. Then the boy said, "Shazzam!" and then when that didn't work, he said, "Eeeeagle Power!" then, "By the Power of Greeey-skuuull," "Up, up, and awaaaay," and "Spaaaace Ghooost!"[6] and his voice kept getting louder and louder, till I knew I better go on in there and tell him to hesh up before his mama come up and peel his behind. I stood up, and Lord did my knees argue with me. Used to be only on cloudy days when my arthur-itis trouble me, but since I come up here, it seem like just about a daily thing.

Well, I took ahold of the doorknob, and just as I twisted it, I heard Sandman holler, "Tired-ass punk," and I heard him th'ow the doll against the wall. It tickled me; I just had to laugh. But soon's I opened the door, I heard Pauline running back up the stairs. Reckon she wasn't in her studio at all, but in the kitchen, and since Sandman's room is right smack over the kitchen, she musta heard every sound he was making.

Well, she pushed right on past me without so much as a how do, and slammed the door shut, and I heard *whap! whap!* and it started up all over again. Lord-a-mighty it was a ugly sound. I just couldn't bear to hear it. I couldn't stand there two seconds. I went to my room and closed the door, laid on my bed, pressed the heels of my hands over my ears, but I could hear every sound. I heard the boy crying, and I heard Pauline barking just like a dog. "You little bastard, what'd I tell you? Huh? Huh?" Heard the sound of hangers sliding back and forth on the rod in Sandman's closet. Knew she was looking for a belt. She found one, too, 'cause I heard every one of them strokes. Every single one. And every now and then I heard that boy say things like, "Mama? Mama? I love you. I love you," and I heard hard things hitting the floor and I knew they was heels or elbows or knees or noggin. I knew the boy was burning up, scared, in a devil wind of hurt. I knew Pauline was hurting, too, blind, sick, dizzy, excited, and hurting her ownself. But I knew, also, that she didn't know it. I heard, "What I say?" and "black bastard" and "skin you alive" and "don't you dare raise your hand to me." I heard "please" and "sorry" and "didn't mean to" and "forgot to" and "love you, Mama, love you." But I knew Mama couldn't hear a thing but that hissing sound you hear, and blood and heat and ice and nightmares and howling, and the fire on her very own skin—heard it, *heard* it, not seen it— heard the flame tips of memory, and right behind it I heard the hurt of every single one a my babies, Erlene and Justine, Peter, Paul, Mark, and Juline, Pearline and John, Samuel and Pauline. Pauline. I heard my hands on Pauline, my leather on Pauline, switch, cord, ruler, hanger, towel, wet and heavy. And I

30

6. "Fly Spiderman!", "Shazzam!", "Eagle Power!", "By the Power of Greyskull," "Up, up, and away," and "Space Ghost" are powerful utterances employed by the cartoon superheroes Spiderman, Captain Marvel, Masters of the Universe, Superman, and Space Ghost.

heard me, too, my own screams, and my brothers and sisters, my mama, papa, aunts, and uncles and on back, and on back. All that sickening hissing fire. Heard it quivering in my belly, and balling up in my throat . . . . and on back and on back. I put my pillow over my head and heard my tears soak into it. Generations and generations of slaves and slavekeepers I heard. I couldn't escape that sound, and I couldn't understand why it was only now I was hearing just how turrible it is. I heard burning crosses and natureless men, women split open like pigs' knuckles, heard the pain of vanishing blue jungles and dry red soil, black long-tooth cats that creep in the night, white long-neck birds that could fill up a blue blue sky. All vanishing into endless ocean and ships full of stink and death. I heard the weight of a thousand leagues of water on my back, heard the howl of a million lost spirits black and white, and black and red, and black and blue. Then just black, so black I couldn't hear nothing no more, nor see, nor breathe, nor move. I wisht I coulda helped that boy, but I couldn't move.

Well, let me see can I go on. Let me get my mind right.

Naturally, Tanika had a hissy fit. Her voice poked me outta my sleep like Paul's skinny elbow used to. Didn't leave my room just then, but I knew her caramelly skin was lit up with the butterfly, them wingtips touching her temple to temple. "But Daddy," I heard her say, "that was my favorite plane."

They were in her bedroom. I could tell.

35 "Seem like to me," said her father, "that whichever model your brother break is your favorite." He talk kinda pretty, too, when he ain't too upset, so I cain't say it exactly the way he did. "You ever notice that?" he said.

"Well, I guess . . . . I like 'em all the same. They all my favorites. That's why I builds 'em."

Then Ricardo said back, "Uh-huh." Then his voice changed a notch. "Maybe we *ought* to put a lock on her door till ol' Sandman old enough to do like he ast."

"But Daddy, he is old enough. He five. He be in school next year."

"No," said Pauline. "I will not abide locks on these chi'ren's doors. Naw-aw. No."

40 "Awright, Pauline, calm down." And Ricardo's voice changed back. "I know he five, babygirl, but that's still young. You just got to learn patience. Let's just be patient for now. Now, it might make you happy if I tear his little seater-end up—"

"Yes it would!"

"Don't you backtalk your father, girl."

"—but since your mother already done that, I don't see no reason to. We all done seen enough of that around this house."

"You the one to talk, man."

45 "Hey, I didn't say I'm some kinda saint. I said 'we.' 'We.' "

They was all of 'em quiet for a spell. Then Ricardo said, "Patience, babygirl. You got to learn patience. And it's only one way to learn patience." And then he was quiet for a real long time. "How?" said Tanika. Then I heard Ricardo carry his big self down the stairs. He was chuckling. "How?" Tanika said, and Ricardo laughed a little harder. "How?" Tanika said. "Daddy, how?" Ricardo just laughed, and I heard Tanika following him, and it sound like she smacked him on the behind. "Dad-dy!" she said. I had to smile.

I heard Pauline close Tanika's door and open up Sandman's. Heard her switch on the light and close the door. The only thing I could hear her say was, "You hungry, baby?" and I knew she'd be sitting him on her lap, and wrapping her arms around him. Knew she be rocking him and cooing to him. And her voice be like a warm wind full of spices. She might look him over careful, thinking 'bout, "Maybe I ought to put some Mercurochrome right there, and a little bit back here, too, maybe." She cain't believe what she done, you see. Cain't even remember all of it, really. I knew Sandman be trembling inside, just like a day-old puppy tremble when it find itself too far from its mama's belly and teats. Then it be like he feel the sun rising in his stomach, and maybe he cry a little bit, and say he sorry, and Mama will feel her heart ease into twos and fours and eights, breaking real slow and silent, and she'll cry some too. Try to make him smile, she will, by saying things like, "You knows you a little hellion, boy. But you know Mama love her little rascal." And when she see him smile, her heart'll ease itself from eights to fours to twos and she'll thank Jesus that cain't nobody forgive and forget like a child. She'll get down on her knees and thank Jesus.

But I was sitting there asking myself, What if, after all that holding, after they done eaten and talked and everybody in bed, and Sandman laying there in the dark, what things'll be going through his head when it look like everything back to normal? For my daughter may believe that chi'ren forget, but I know better now. What'll he be thinking? Did I make that plane fly? Was it magic? Is Tanika a witch? Is that why I ain't never allowed to touch them planes? Maybe the whole family is witches—Tanika, Mama, Daddy, Granmama. Maybe late at night they all shrink down to the size of crickets, get inside them planes, and fly to China and New York and Disneyland. Why don't they take me? Maybe they hate me. Maybe they kill if I keep messing with them planes. 'Cause Mama say, "I'ma kill you, boy. I swear I'ma kill you, you don't do as I say." Did I make it fly? Or was it Daddy's fishing line made it fly?

Well, I guess that plane musta flew, all right, 'cause that night, last Tuesday night, we all seen something I don't think we'll ever forget. This is what happened:

I passed on dinner that evening. Just couldn't see sitting down with 'em and getting in their way. Wanted 'em to be just they own family that night. I went to bed, but I couldn't sleep. I tossed and turned in that bed, and it squeaked and squawked, and just about drove me outta my mind. It was a warm night and clear for a night in Pittsburgh, and I went to the window, got down on my knees to pray. I felt like I had to pray against all them sounds I'd heard in my sleep that afternoon, all that pain that been burned into my skin and found its way out my very own hands. Generations and generations. But I couldn't find no words. I looked out that window, and I watched that empty night sky. Never had noticed how big the sky is before, even though I'm in my seventy-seventh year,

50

and seen maybe ten, twenty, thirty thousand such skies. Never noticed how deep it was neither. The very idea of a endless sky made me dizzy, I tell you the truth. I cletched on to the windowsill like I was afred I might fall up and up and up, and keep on falling. I set there a long time on my knees like that, till my arthur-itis started fussing, till the sky turned from dark blue like one of Sandman's cleary marbles to black as a skillet. The clouds was almost invisible. Sky got deeper. Stars began to bleed out from the darkness. It was a glory to behold. "Thank you, Lord," I said. "Thank you." I don't know why I said that.

Next thing I heard was Tanika's elbow voice, poking me outta my sleep once more. "What you doing in my room, boy?" I heard her say. I pulled myself off the cool floor, and my knees and ankles couldn't slow me down none. Not really. Mothers is like that when they hear a child's voice in the night. Don't nothing slow 'em, not arthur-itis, or flu, or migraine, or dropsy. I heard heels and toes hit the floor, robes being pulled on, lights snapped on, doors open. Then Tanika said, "What? You want what?" And just as I was stepping into her room Sandman said, "Granmama, Tani won't teach me to fly her planes." He had a plane in his hand, and it looked like Tanika didn't know it till I did, 'cause her sleepish eyes got big and she screamed, "My Thunderbolt!" Just then Pauline stepped up behind me and her voice cut acrost the room. She said, "What the hell is going on here?" and just about this time Tanika was duking up a storm. Her lips was pushed up into her mouth, nostrils flaring. She chopped at Sandman, and chopped again, had the blind look in her eyes, and knew she heard the hiss. I could hear it. I could hear in that child's head like they was vipers from down below. Pauline was fend to push me out the way, but all in a second I'd grabbed her by her sleeve and hollered, "Tanika, put your hand down, girl! Put it down right this second!"

"Mama, just—"

But I said, "No." I heard that turrible, turrible hissing I know so well and I thought it was me who was gonna start chopping with my hands or with a belt or a shoe or anything else in reach, but it didn't feel like it should have. Didn't burn and build up, like it should have, yet I knew I heard that hissing. I know I did. Then we all turned back to the landing when we heard Ricardo say, "Lookit Sandman!" And when we looked from Ricardo to his son we seen that aero-plane in his hand, and the propeller on that thing was spinning like I don't know what, was just hissing, louder and louder, till you couldn't no longer call it a hiss no more, but a buzz. And wasn't too long before we seen that every aero-plane in that room was buzzing. And the spirit was in me, and I moved across the room on the balls of my feet, like I was Tanika's age. "It's a blessing, chi'ren," I said. "We being blessed." The planes on they chrome stands was buzzing. The planes on the ceiling was buzzing, going round and round on them fishing lines. I went to the window and seen the sky was back to being dark blue again. Didn't have no idea I was asleep that long. Anyway, I opened up the window, pulled up the screen, and put my hand out to Sandman. "Go ahead, Sandman. Go on ahead. It's a blessing. We being blessed." So my grandson walked up to me, and I rested my hand on his head, moved him closer to the window. "Go on, baby," I said. "It's a blessing." Then I turned back to look at the others. Ricardo had his hands in his robe pockets and was looking half crossy-eyed with sleep, half joyful in the presence of the Power, like he didn't know up from down. But Tanika and Pauline, well, they looked like twins to each other, all small and grayish. They eyes was big, but they didn't seem to be looking at anything in particular, and didn't look cross or scared or nothing, and they didn't have no butterflies on 'em neither. Just stood there, the tall twin behind the short one, a big right hand hooking fingers betwixt the fingers of a little right hand. I looked back down at my grandson, and I said, "Go on, baby."

Well Sandman just opened his hand and let that plane go and it floated off just like I knew it would, and I closed my eyes and listened to them tiny engines. I felt everybody move on up behind me. I felt Pauline's arm slip round my shoulder. Lord, Lord, all them little planes just fanning up tiny breezes all around us. A body'd have to carry a *pe*can for a heart not to be moved by all that. I do believe he would. So me and Sandman, Tanika and Ricardo, and my baby Pauline, well, one by one, we let them things fly into the night. They looked like little dots, little ink dots, in that blue sky. And they sounded like a million honeybees.

They sounded just like a million honeybees. 55

1992

HA JIN

In Broad Daylight

While I was eating corn cake and jellyfish at lunch, our gate was thrown open and Bare Hips hopped in. His large wooden pistol was stuck partly inside the waist of his blue shorts. "White Cat," he called me by my nickname, "hurry, let's go. They caught Old Whore at her home. They're going to take her through the streets this afternoon."

"Really?" I put down my bowl, which was almost empty, and rushed to the inner room for my undershirt and sandals. "I'll be back in a second."

"Bare Hips, did you say they'll parade Mu Ying today?" I heard Grandma ask in her husky voice.

"Yes, all the kids on our street have left for her house. I came to tell White Cat." He paused. "Hey, White Cat, hurry up!"

"Coming," I cried out, still looking for my sandals. 5

"Good, good!" Grandma said to Bare Hips, while flapping at flies with her large palm-leaf fan. "They should burn the bitch on Heaven Lamp like they did in the old days."

"Come, let's go," Bare Hips said to me the moment I was back. He turned to the door; I picked up my wooden scimitar and followed him.

"Put on your shoes, dear." Grandma stretched out her fan to stop me.

"No time for that, Grandma. I've got to be quick, or I'll miss something and won't be able to tell you the whole story when I get back."

We dashed into the street while Grandma was shouting behind us. "Come 10 back. Take the rubber shoes with you."

We charged toward Mu Ying's home on Eternal Way, waving our weapons above our heads. Grandma was crippled and never came out of our small yard. That was why I had to tell her about what was going on outside. But she knew Mu Ying well, just as all the old women in our town knew Mu well and hated her. Whenever they heard that she had a man in her home again, these women would say, "This time they ought to burn Old Whore on Heaven Lamp."

What they referred to was the old way of punishing an adulteress. Though they had lived in New China for almost two decades, some ancient notions still stuck in their heads. Grandma told me about many of the executions in the old days that she had seen with her own eyes. Officials used to have the criminals of adultery executed in two different ways. They beheaded the man. He was tied to a stake on the platform at the marketplace. At the first blare of horns, a masked headsman ascended the platform holding a broad ax before his chest; at the second blare of horns, the headsman approached the criminal and raised the ax over his head; at the third blare of horns, the head was lopped off and fell to the ground. If the man's family members were waiting beneath the platform, his head would be picked up to be buried together with his body; if no family member was nearby, dogs would carry the head away and chase each other around until they ate up the flesh and returned for the body.

Unlike the man, the woman involved was executed on Heaven Lamp. She was hung naked upside down above a wood fire whose flames could barely touch her scalp. And two men flogged her away with whips made of bulls' penises. Meanwhile she screamed for help and the whole town could hear her. Since the fire merely scorched her head, it took at least half a day for her to stop shrieking and a day and a night to die completely. People used to believe that the way of punishment was justified by Heaven, so the fire was called Heaven Lamp. But that was an old custom; nobody believed they would burn Mu Ying in that way.

Mu's home, a small granite house with cement tiles built a year before, was next to East Wind Inn on the northern side of Eternal Way. When we entered that street, Bare Hips and I couldn't help looking around tremulously, because that area was the territory of the children living there. Two of the fiercest boys, who would kill without having second thoughts, ruled that part of our town. Whenever a boy from another street wandered into Eternal Way, they'd capture him and beat him up. Of course we did the same thing; if we caught one of them in our territory, we'd at least confiscate whatever he had with him: grasshopper cages, slingshots, bottle caps, marbles, cartridge cases, and so on. We would also make him call every one of us "Father" or "Grandfather." But today hundreds of children and grown-ups were pouring into Eternal Way; two dozen urchins on that street surely couldn't hold their ground. Besides, they had already adopted a truce, since they were more eager to see the Red Guards[1] drag Mu Ying out of her den.

1. A national student organization sponsored by Mao Zedong as an instrument to start and develop the Great Proletarian Cultural Revolution (1966–76).

When we arrived, Mu was being brought out through a large crowd at the front gate. Inside her yard there were three rows of colorful washing hung on iron wires, and there was also a grape trellis. Seven or eight children were in there, plucking off grapes and eating them. Two Red Guards held Mu Ying by the arms, and the other Red Guards, about twenty of them, followed behind. They were all from Dalian City and wore home-made army uniforms. God knew how they came to know that there was a bad woman in our town. Though people hated Mu and called her names, no one would rough her up. Those Red Guards were strangers, so they wouldn't mind doing it.

Surprisingly, Mu looked rather calm; she neither protested nor said a word. The two Red Guards let go of her arms, and she followed them quietly into West Street. We all moved with them. Some children ran several paces ahead to look back at her.

Mu wore a sky-blue dress, which made her different from the other women who always wore jackets and pants suitable for honest work. In fact, even we small boys could tell that she was really handsome, perhaps the best looking woman of her age in our town. Though in her fifties, she didn't have a single gray hair; she was a little plump, but because of her long legs and arms she appeared rather queenly. While most of the women had sallow faces, hers looked white and healthy like fresh milk.

Skipping in front of the crowd, Bare Hips turned around and cried out at her, "Shameless Old Whore!"

She glanced at him, her round eyes flashing; the purple wart beside her left nostril grew darker. Grandma had assured me that Mu's wart was not a beauty-wart but a tear-wart. This meant that her life would be soaked in tears.

We knew where we were going, to White Mansion, which was our classroom building, the only two-storied house in the town. As we came to the end of West Street, a short man ran out from a street corner, panting for breath and holding a sickle. He was Meng Su, Mu Ying's husband, who sold bean jelly in summer and sugar-coated haws in winter at the marketplace. He paused in front of the large crowd, as though having forgotten why he had rushed over. He turned his head around to look back; there was nobody behind him. After a short moment he moved close, rather carefully.

"Please let her go," he begged the Red Guards. "Comrade Red Guards, it's all my fault. Please let her go." He put the sickle under his arm and held his hands together before his chest.

"Get out of the way!" commanded a tall young man, who must have been the leader.

"Please don't take her away. It's my fault. I haven't disciplined her well. Please give her a chance to be a new person. I promise, she won't do it again."

The crowd stopped to circle about. "What's your class status?" a square-faced young woman asked in a sharp voice.

"Poor peasant," Meng replied, his small eyes tearful and his cupped ears twitching a little. "Please let her go, sister. Have mercy on us! I'm kneeling down to you if you let her go." Before he was able to fall on his knees, two young men held him back. Tears were rolling down his dark fleshy cheeks, and his gray head began waving about. The sickle was taken away from him.

"Shut up," the tall leader yelled and slapped him across the face. "She's a snake. We traveled a hundred and fifty *li* to come here to wipe out poisonous snakes and worms. If you don't stop interfering, we'll parade you with her together. Do you want to join her?"

Silence. Meng covered his face with his large hands as though feeling dizzy.

A man in the crowd said aloud, "If you can share the bed with her, why can't you share the street?"

Many of the grown-ups laughed. "Take him, take him too!" someone told the Red Guards. Meng looked scared, sobbing quietly.

30 His wife stared at him without saying a word. Her teeth were clenched; a faint smile passed the corners of her mouth. Meng seemed to wince under her stare. The two Red Guards let his arms go, and he stepped aside, watching his wife and the crowd move toward the school.

Of Meng Su people in our town had different opinions. Some said he was a born cuckold who didn't mind his wife's sleeping with any man as long as she could bring money home. Some believed he was a good-tempered man who had stayed with his wife mainly for their children's sake; they forgot that the three children had grown up long before and were working in big cities far away. Some thought he didn't leave his wife because he had no choice—no woman would marry such a dwarf. Grandma, for some reason, seemed to respect Meng. She told me that Mu Ying had once been raped by a group of Russian soldiers under Northern Bridge and was left on the river bank afterwards. That night her husband sneaked there and carried her back. He looked after her for a whole winter till she recovered. "Old Whore doesn't deserve that good-hearted man," Grandma would say. "She's heartless and knows only how to sell her thighs."

We entered the school's playground where about two hundred people had already gathered. "Hey, White Cat and Bare Hips," Big Shrimp called us, waving his claws. Many boys from our street were there too. We went to join them.

The Red Guards took Mu to the front entrance of the building. Two tables had been placed between the stone lions that crouched on each side of the entrance. On one of the tables stood a tall paper hat with the big black characters on its side: "Down with Old Bitch!"

A young man in glasses raised his bony hand and started to address us, "Folks, we've gathered here today to denounce Mu Ying, who is a demon in this town."

35 "Down with Bourgeois Demons!" a slim woman Red Guard shouted. We raised our fists and repeated the slogan.

"Down with Old Bitch Mu Ying," a middle-aged man cried out with both hands in the air. He was an active revolutionary in our commune. Again we shouted, in louder voices.

The nearsighted man went on, "First, Mu Ying must confess her crime. We must see her attitude toward her own crime. Then we'll make the punishment fit both her crime and her attitude. All right, folks?"

"Right," some voices replied from the crowd.

"Mu Ying," he turned to the criminal, "you must confess everything. It's up to you now."

She was forced to stand on a bench. Staying below the steps, we had to raise   40
our heads to see her face.

The questioning began. "Why do you seduce men and paralyze their revolutionary will with your bourgeois poison?" the tall leader asked in a solemn voice.

"I've never invited any man to my home, have I?" she said rather calmly.
Her husband was standing at the front of the crowd, listening to her without
showing any emotion, as though having lost his mind.

"Then why did they go to your house and not to others' houses?"

"They wanted to sleep with me," she replied.

"Shameless!" Several women hissed in the crowd.   45

"A true whore!"

"Scratch her!"

"Rip apart her filthy mouth!"

"Sisters," she spoke aloud. "All right, it was wrong to sleep with them. But
you all know what it feels like when you want a man, don't you? Don't you once
in a while have that feeling in your bones?" Contemptuously, she looked at the
few withered middle-aged women standing in the front row, then closed her
eyes. "Oh, you want that real man to have you in his arms and let him touch
every part of your body. For that man alone you want to blossom into a woman,
a real woman—"

"Take this, you Fox Spirit!" A stout young fellow struck her on the side with   50
a fist like a sledgehammer. The heavy blow silenced her at once. She held her
sides with both hands, gasping for breath.

"You're wrong, Mu Ying," Bare Hips's mother spoke from the front of the
crowd, her forefinger pointing upward at Mu. "You have your own man, who
doesn't lack an arm or a leg. It's wrong to have others' men and more wrong to
pocket their money."

"I have my own man?" Mu glanced at her husband and smirked. She
straightened up and said, "My man is nothing. He is no good, I mean in bed.
He always comes before I feel anything."

All the adults burst out laughing. "What's that? What's so funny?" Big
Shrimp asked Bare Hips.

"You didn't get it?" Bare Hips said impatiently. "You don't know anything
about what happens between a man and a woman. It means that whenever she
doesn't want him to come close to her he comes. Bad timing."

"It doesn't sound like that," I said.   55

Before we could argue, a large bottle of ink smashed on Mu's head and
knocked her off the bench. Prone on the cement terrace, she broke into swearing and blubbering. "Oh, damn your ancestors! Whoever hit me will be
childless!" Her left hand was rubbing her head. "Oh Lord of Heaven, they treat
their grandma like this!"

"Serves you right!"

"A cheap weasel."

"Even a knife on her throat can't stop her."

"A pig is born to eat slop!"   60

When they put her back up on the bench, she became another person—her shoulders covered with black stains, and a red line trickling down her left temple. The scorching sun was blazing down on her as though all the black parts on her body were about to burn up. Still moaning, she turned her eyes to the spot where her husband had been standing a few minutes before. But he was no longer there.

"Down with Old Whore!" a farmer shouted in the crowd. We all followed him in one voice. She began trembling slightly.

The tall leader said to us, "In order to get rid of her counterrevolutionary airs, first, we're going to cut her hair." With a wave of his hand, he summoned the Red Guards behind him. Four men moved forward and held her down. The square-faced woman raised a large pair of scissors and thrust them into the mass of the dark hair.

"Don't, don't, please. Help, help! I'll do whatever you want me to—"

65 "Cut!" someone yelled.

"Shave her head bald!"

The woman Red Guard applied the scissors skillfully. After four or five strokes, Mu's head looked like the tail of a molting hen. She started blubbering again, her nose running and her teeth chattering.

A breeze came and swept away the fluffy curls from the terrace and scattered them on the sandy ground. It was so hot that some people took out fans, waving them continuously. The crowd stank of sweat.

Wooooo, wooooo, woo, woo. That was the train coming from Sand County at 3:30. It was a freight train, whose young drivers would toot the steam horn whenever they saw a young woman in a field beneath the track.

70 The questioning continued. "How many men have you slept with these years?" the nearsighted man asked.

"Three."

"She's lying," a woman in the crowd cried out.

"I told the truth, sister." She wiped off the tears from her cheeks with the back of her hand.

"Who are they?" the young man asked again. "Tell us more about them."

75 "An officer from the Little Dragon Mountain, and—"

"How many times did he come to your house?"

"I can't remember. Probably twenty."

"What's his name?"

"I don't know. He told me he was a big officer."

80 "Did you take money from him?"

"Yes."

"How much for each time?"

"Twenty *yuan*."

"How much altogether?"

85 "Probably five hundred."

"Comrades and Revolutionary Masses," the young man turned to us, "how shall we handle this parasite that sucked blood out of a revolutionary officer?"

"Quarter her with four horses!" an old woman yelled.

"Burn her on Heaven Lamp!"

"Poop on her face!" a small fat girl shouted, her hand raised like a tiny pistol with the thumb cocked up and the forefinger aimed at Mu. Some grown-ups snickered.

Then a pair of old cloth-shoes, a symbol for a promiscuous woman, were passed to the front. The slim young woman took the shoes and tied them together with the laces. She climbed on a table and was about to hang the shoes around Mu's neck. Mu elbowed the woman aside and knocked the shoes to the ground. The stout young fellow picked up the shoes, and jumped twice to slap her on the cheeks with the soles. "You're so stubborn. Do you want to change yourself or not?" he asked.

"Yes, I do," she replied meekly and dared not stir a bit. Meanwhile the shoes were being hung around her neck.

"Now she looks like a real whore," a woman commented.

"Sing us a tune, Sis," a farmer demanded.

"Comrades," the man in glasses resumed, "let us continue the denunciation." He turned to Mu and asked, "Who are the other men?"

"A farmer from Apple Village."

"How many times with him?"

"Once."

"Liar!"

"She's lying!"

"Give her one on the mouth!"

The young man raised his hands to calm the crowd down and questioned her again, "How much did you take from him?"

"Eighty *yuan*."

"One night?"

"Yes."

"Tell us more about it. How can you make us believe you?"

"That old fellow came to town to sell piglets. He sold a whole litter for eighty, and I got the money."

"Why did you charge him more than the officer?"

"No, I didn't. He did it four times in one night."

Some people were smiling and whispering to each other. A woman said that old man must have been a widower or never married.

"What's his name?" the young man went on.

"No idea."

"Was he rich or poor?"

"Poor."

"Comrades," the young man addressed us, "here we have a poor peasant who worked with his sow for a whole year and got only a litter of piglets. That money is the salt and oil money for his family, but this snake swallowed the money with one gulp. What shall we do with her?"

"Kill her!"

"Break her skull!"

"Beat the piss out of her!"

A few farmers began to move forward to the steps, waving their fists or rubbing their hands.

"Hold," a woman Red Guard with a huge Chairman Mao badge on her chest spoke in a commanding voice. "The Great Leader has instructed us: 'For our struggle we need words but not force.' Comrades, we can easily wipe her out with words. Force doesn't solve ideological problems." What she said restrained those enraged farmers, who remained in the crowd.

Wooo, woo, wooo, wooooooooooo, an engine screamed in the south. It was strange, because the drivers of the four o'clock train were a bunch of old men who seldom blew the horn.

"Who is the third man?" the nearsighted man continued to question Mu.

"A Red Guard."

The crowd broke into laughter. Some women asked the Red Guards to give her another bottle of ink. "Mu Ying, you're responsible for your own words," the young man said in a serious voice.

"I told you the truth."

"What's his name?"

"I don't know. He led the propaganda team that passed here last month."

"How many times did you sleep with him?"

"Once."

"How much did you make out of him?"

"None. That stingy dog wouldn't pay a cent. He said he was the worker who should be paid."

"So you were outsmarted by him?"

Some men in the crowd guffawed. Mu wiped her nose with her thumb, and at once she wore a thick mustache. "I taught him a lesson, though," she said.

"How?"

"I tweaked his ears, gave him a bleeding nose, and kicked him out. I told him never come back."

People began talking to each other. Some said that she was a strong woman who knew what was hers. Some said the Red Guard was no good; if you got something you had to pay for it. A few women declared that the rascal deserved such a treatment.

"Dear Revolutionary Masses," the tall leader started to speak. "We all have heard the crime Mu Ying committed. She lured one of our officers and one of our poor peasants into the evil water, and she beat a Red Guard black and blue. Shall we let her go home without punishment or shall we teach her an unforgettable lesson so that she won't do it again?"

"Teach her a lesson!" some voices cried out in unison.

"Then we're going to parade her through the streets."

Two Red Guards pulled Mu off the bench, and another picked up the tall hat. "Brothers and sisters," she begged, "please let me off just for once. Don't, don't! I promise I'll correct my fault. I'll be a new person. Help! Oh, help!"

It was no use resisting; within seconds the huge hat was firmly planted on her head. They also hung a big placard between the cloth-shoes lying against her chest. The words on the placard read:

I am a Broken Shoe
My Crime Deserves Death

They put a gong in her hands and ordered her to strike it when she announced the words written on the inner side of the gong.

My pals and I followed the crowd, feeling rather tired. Boys from East Street were wilder; they threw stones at Mu's back. One stone struck the back of her head and blood dropped on her neck. But they were stopped immediately by the Red Guards, because a stone missed Mu and hit a man on the shoulder. Old people, who couldn't follow us, were standing on chairs and windowsills with pipes and towels in their hands. We were going to parade her through every street. It would take several hours to finish the whole thing, as the procession would stop for a short while at every street corner.

Bong, Mu struck the gong and declared, "I am an evil monster."

"Louder!"

Dong, bong—"I have stolen men. I stink for a thousand years." 145

When we were coming out of the marketplace, Cross Eyes emerged from a narrow lane. He grasped my wrist and Bare Hips's arm and said, "Someone is dead at the train station. Come, let's go there and have a look." The word "dead" at once roused us. We, half a dozen boys, set out running to the train station.

The dead man was Meng Su. A crowd had gathered at the railroad a hundred meters east of the station house. A few men were examining the rail that was stained with blood and studded with bits of flesh. One man paced along the darker part of the rail and announced that the train had dragged Meng at least twenty meters.

Beneath the track, Meng's headless body lay in a ditch. One of his feet was missing, and the whitish shinbone stuck out several inches long. There were so many openings on his body that he looked like a large piece of fresh meat on the counter in the butcher's. Beyond him, ten paces away, a big straw hat remained on the ground. We were told that his head was under the hat.

Bare Hips and I went down the slope to have a glimpse at the head. Other boys dared not take a peep. We two looked at each other, asking with our eyes who should raise the straw hat. I held out my wooden scimitar and lifted the rim of the hat a little with the sword. A swarm of bluebottles charged out, droning like provoked wasps. We bent over to peek at the head. Two long teeth pierced through the upper lip. An eyeball was missing. The gray hair was no longer perceivable, as it was covered with mud and dirt. The open mouth filled with purplish mucus. A tiny lizard skipped, sliding away into the grass.

"Oh!" Bare Hips began vomiting. Sorghum gruel mixed with bits of string beans splashed on a yellowish boulder. "Leave it alone, White Cat." 150

We lingered at the station, listening to different versions of the accident. Some people said that Meng had gotten drunk and dropped asleep on the track. Some said he hadn't slept at all but laughed hysterically walking in the middle of the track toward the coming train. Some said he had not drunk a drop, as he had spoken with tears in his eyes to a few persons he had run into on his way to the station. In any case, he was dead, torn to pieces.

That evening when I was coming home, I heard Mu Ying groaning in the smoky twilight. "Take me home. Oh, help me. Who can help me? Where are you? Why don't you come and carry me home?"

She was lying at the bus stop, alone.

1993

POETRY

POETRY

▼ ▼ ▼

Poetry: Reading, Responding, Writing

f you're already a reader of poetry, you know: poetry reading is not just an intellectual and bookish activity; it is about feeling. Reading poetry well means responding to it: if you respond on a feeling level, you are likely to read more accurately, with deeper understanding, and with greater pleasure. And, conversely, if you read poetry accurately, and with attention to detail, you will almost certainly respond—or learn how to respond—to it on an emotional level. Reading poetry involves conscious articulation through language, and reading and responding come to be, for experienced readers of poetry, very nearly one. But those who teach poetry—and there are a lot of us, almost all enthusiasts about both poetry as a subject and reading as a craft—have discovered something else: writing about poetry helps both the reading and the responding processes. Responding involves remembering and reflecting as well. As you recall your own past and make associations between things in the text and things you already know and feel, you will not only respond more fully to a particular poem, but improve your reading skills more generally. Your knowledge and life experience informs your reading of what is before you, and allows you to connect things within the text—events, images, words, sounds—so that meanings and feelings develop and accumulate. Prior learning creates expectations: of pattern, repetition, association, or causality. Reflecting on the text—and on expectations produced by themes and ideas in the text—re-creates old feelings but directs them in new, often unusual ways. Poems, even when they are about things we have no experience of, connect to things we do know and order our memories, thoughts, and feelings in new and newly challenging ways.

A course in reading poetry can help you to be a better, more fully sensitive and responsive person: that's the larger goal. But the more immediate goal—and the route to the larger one—is to make you a better reader of texts and a more precise and careful writer yourself. Close attention to one text makes you appreciate, and understand, textuality and its possibilities more generally.

READING   Poems, perhaps even more than other texts, can sharpen your reading skills because they tend to be so compact, so fully dependent on concise expressions of feeling. In poems, ideas and feelings are packed tightly into just a few lines. The experiences of life are very concentrated here, and meanings emerge quickly, word by word. Poems often show us the very process of putting feelings into a language that can be shared with others—to *say* feelings in a communicable way. Poetry can be intellectual too, explaining and exploring ideas, but its focus is more often on how people feel than how they think. Poems work out a sharable language for feeling, and one of poetry's most insistent virtues involves its attempt to express the inexpressible. How can anyone, for example, put into words what it means to be in love? or how it feels to lose someone one cares about? Poetry tries, and it often captures exactly the shade of emotion that feels just right to a reader. No single poem can be said to express all the things that love or death feels like, or means, but one of the joys of experiencing poetry occurs when we read a poem and want to say, "Yes, that is just what it is like; I know exactly what that line means but I've never been able to express it so well." Poetry can be the voice of our feelings even when our minds are speechless with grief or joy. Reading is no substitute for living, but it can make living more abundant and more available.

Here are two poems that talk about the sincerity and depth of love between two people. Each is written as if it were spoken by one person to his or her lover, and each is definite and powerful about the intensity and quality of love; but the poems work in quite different ways—the first one asserting the strength and depth of love, the second implying intense feeling by reminiscing about events in the relationship between the two people.

ELIZABETH BARRETT BROWNING

How Do I Love Thee?

How do I love thee? Let me count the ways.
I love thee to the depth and breadth and height
My soul can reach, when feeling out of sight

For the ends of Being and ideal Grace.
I love thee to the level of every day's
Most quiet need, by sun and candlelight.
I love thee freely, as men strive for Right;
I love thee purely, as they turn from Praise;
I love thee with the passion put to use
In my old griefs, and with my childhood's faith.
I love thee with a love I seemed to lose
With my lost saints—I love thee with the breath,
Smiles, tears of all my life!—and, if God choose,
I shall but love thee better after death.

  5

  10

1850

JAROLD RAMSEY

The Tally Stick

Here from the start, from our first of days, look:
I have carved our lives in secret on this stick
of mountain mahogany the length of your arms
outstretched, the wood clear red, so hard and rare.
It is time to touch and handle what we know we share.

  5

Near the butt, this intricate notch where the grains
converge and join: it is our wedding.
I can read it through with a thumb and tell you now
who danced, who made up the songs, who meant us joy.
These little arrowheads along the grain,
they are the births of our children. See,
they make a kind of design with these heavy crosses,
the deaths of our parents, the loss of friends.

  10

Over it all as it goes, of course, I
have chiseled Events, History—random
hashmarks cut against the swirling grain.
See, here is the Year the World Went Wrong,
we thought, and here the days the Great Men fell.
The lengthening runes of our lives run through it all.

  15

See, our tally stick is whittled nearly end to end;
delicate as scrimshaw, it would not bear you up.
Regrets have polished it, hand over hand.
Yet let us take it up, and as our fingers
like children leading on a trail cry back
our unforgotten wonders, sign after sign,
we will talk softly as of ordinary matters,
and in one another's blameless eyes go blind.

  20

  25

p. 1977

The first poem is direct, but fairly abstract. It lists several ways in which the poet feels love and connects them to some noble ideas of higher obligations—to justice (line 7), for example, and to spiritual aspiration (lines 2–4). It suggests a wide range of things that love can mean and notices a variety of emotions. It is an ardent statement of feeling and asserts a permanence that will extend even beyond death. It contains admirable thoughts and memorable phrases that many lovers would like to hear said to themselves. What it does not do is say very much about what the relationship between the two lovers is like on an everyday basis, what experiences they have had together, what distinguishes their relationship from that of other devoted or ideal lovers. Its appeal is to our general sense of what love is like and how intense feelings can be; it does not offer everyday details. Love may differ from person to person and even from moment to moment, and so can poems about love.

"The Tally Stick" is much more concrete. The whole poem concentrates on a single object that, like "How Do I Love Thee?," "counts" or "tallies" the ways in which this couple love one another. This stick stands for their love and becomes a kind of physical reminder of it: its natural features—the notches and arrowheads and cross marks (lines 6, 10, and 12) along with the marks carved on it (lines 15–16, 20–21)—indicate events in the story of the relationship. (We could say that the stick *symbolizes* their love; later on, we will look at a number of terms like this that can be used to make it easier to talk about some aspects of poems, but for now it is enough to notice that the stick serves the lovers as a reminder of some specific details of their love.) It is a special kind of reminder to them because its language is "secret" (line 2), something they can share privately (except that we as readers of the poem are sort of looking over their shoulders, not intruding but sharing their secret). The poet interprets the particular features of the stick as standing for particular events—their wedding and the births of their children, for example—and carves marks into it as reminders of other events (lines 15ff.). The stick itself becomes a very personal object, and in the last stanza of the poem it is as if we watch the lovers touching the stick together and reminiscing over it, gradually dissolving into their emotions and each other as they recall the "unforgotten wonders" (line 25) of their lives together.

Both poems are powerful statements of feelings, each in its own way. Various readers will respond differently to each poem; the effect these poems have on their readers will lead some to prefer one and some the other. Personal preference does not mean that objective standards for poetry cannot be found (some poems are better than others, and later we will look in detail at features that help us to evaluate poems), but we need have no preconceived standard that all poetry must be one thing or another or work in one particular way. Some good poems are quite abstract, others quite specific. Any poem that helps us to articulate and clarify human feelings and ideas has a legitimate claim on us as readers.

Both "How Do I Love Thee?" and "The Tally Stick" are written as if they were addressed to the partner in the love relationship, and both talk directly about the intensity of the love. The poem below talks only indirectly about the quality and intensity of love. It is written as if it were a letter from a woman to her husband who has gone on a long journey on business. It directly expresses how much she misses him and indirectly suggests how much she cares about him.

EZRA POUND

The River-Merchant's Wife: A Letter

(after Rihaku[1])

While my hair was still cut straight across my forehead
I played about the front gate, pulling flowers.
You came by on bamboo stilts, playing horse,
You walked about my seat, playing with blue plums.
And we went on living in the village of Chokan: 5
Two small people, without dislike or suspicion.

At fourteen I married My Lord you.
I never laughed, being bashful.
Lowering my head, I looked at the wall.
Called to, a thousand times, I never looked back.   10

At fifteen I stopped scowling,
I desired my dust to be mingled with yours
For ever and for ever and for ever.
Why should I climb the look out?

At sixteen you departed,   15
You went into far Ku-to-yen, by the river of swirling eddies,
And you have been gone five months.
The monkeys make sorrowful noise overhead.

You dragged your feet when you went out.
By the gate now, the moss is grown, the different mosses,   20
Too deep to clear them away!

1. The Japanese name for Li Po, an eighth-century Chinese poet. Pound's poem is a loose paraphrase of Li Po's.

The leaves fall early this autumn, in wind.
The paired butterflies are already yellow with August
Over the grass in the West garden;
25   They hurt me. I grow older.
If you are coming down through the narrows of the river Kiang,
Please let me know beforehand,
And I will come out to meet you
        As far as Cho-fu-Sa.   1915

The "letter" tells us only a few facts about the nameless merchant's wife: that she is about sixteen and a half years old, that she married at fourteen and fell in love with her husband a year later, that she is now very lonely. About their relationship we know only that they were childhood playmates in a small Chinese village, that their marriage originally was not a matter of personal choice, and that the husband unwillingly went away on a long journey five months ago. But the words tell us a great deal about how the young wife feels, and the simplicity of her language suggests her sincere and deep longing. The daily noises she hears seem "sorrowful" (line 18), and she worries about the dangers of the far-away place where her husband is, thinking of it in terms of its perilous "river of swirling eddies" (line 16). She thinks of how moss has grown up over the unused gate, and more time seems to her to have passed than actually has (lines 22–25). Nostalgically she remembers their innocent childhood, when they played together without deeper love or commitment (lines 1–6), and contrasts that with her later satisfaction in their love (lines 11–14) and with her present anxiety, loneliness, and desire. We do not need to know the details of the geography of the river Kiang or how far Cho-fu-Sa is to sense that her wish to see him is very strong, that her desire is powerful enough to make her venture beyond the ordinary geographical bounds of her existence so that their reunion will come sooner. The closest she comes to a direct statement about her love is her statement that she desired that her dust be mingled with his "For ever and for ever and for ever" (lines 12–13). But her single-minded vision of the world, her perception of even the beauty of nature as only a record of her husband's absence and the passage of time, and her plain, apparently uncalculated language about her rejection of other suitors and her shutting out of the rest of the world all show her to be committed, desirous, nearly desperate for his presence. In a different sense, she has also counted the ways that she loves her man.

Here is another poem about marriage, equally about dependency but with a very different set of attitudes and feelings.

MARY, LADY CHUDLEIGH

To the Ladies

Wife and servant are the same,
But only differ in the name:
For when that fatal knot is tied,
Which nothing, nothing can divide,
When she the word *Obey* has said,   5
And man by law supreme has made,
Then all that's kind is laid aside,
And nothing left but state and pride.
Fierce as an eastern prince he grows,
And all his innate rigor shows: 10
Then but to look, to laugh, or speak,
Will the nuptial contract break.
Like mutes, she signs alone must make,
And never any freedom take,
But still be governed by a nod,   15
And fear her husband as her god:
Him still must serve, him still obey,
And nothing act, and nothing say,
But what her haughty lord thinks fit,
Who, with the power, has all the wit.   20
Then shun, oh! shun that wretched state,
And all the fawning flatterers hate.
Value yourselves, and men despise:
You must be proud, if you'll be wise.   1703

This poem is addressed directly to a specific audience, and presence
becomes as abhorrent here as absence does in the previous poem. Marriage
here is an oppressor and the husband the personification of oppression; the
poem blurs distinctions between discourses, insisting that "Wife" and "servant"
mean the same thing because they testify to parallel relationships of mastery
and obedience. Unlike the river-merchant's wife in the previous poem, this
speaker is angry and feels betrayed by events; rather than speak of her own specific experiences and feelings, she tries to arouse feelings in an audience she
counts on to recognize a repeated pattern and habit of marital experience.

Poems can be about the meaning of a relationship or about disappointment
just as easily as about emotional fulfillment, and poets are often very good at
suggesting the contradictions and uncertainties in relationships. Like other people, poets often find love quaint or downright funny, too, mainly because it

involves human beings who, however serious their intentions and concerns, are often inept, uncertain, and self-contradictory—in short, human. Showing us ourselves as others see us is one of the more useful tasks that poems perform, but the poems that result can be just as entertaining and pleasurable as they are educational. Here is a poem that imagines a very strange scene, a kind of fantasy of what happens when we *think* too much about sex or love, and it is likely to leave us laughing, whether or not we take it seriously as a statement of human anxiety and of the tendency to intellectualize too much.

TOM WAYMAN

Wayman in Love

At last Wayman gets the girl into bed.
He is locked in one of those embraces
so passionate his left arm is asleep
when suddenly he is bumped in the back.
"Excuse me," a voice mutters, thick with German.   5
Wayman and the girl sit up astounded
as a furry gentleman in boots and a frock coat
climbs in under the covers.

"My name is Doktor Marx," the intruder announces
settling his neck comfortably on the pillow.   10
"I'm here to consider for you the cost of a kiss."
He pulls out a notepad. "Let's see now,
we have the price of the mattress, this room must be rented,
your time off work, groceries for two,
medical fees in case of accidents . . ."   15

"Look," Wayman says,
"couldn't we do this later?"
The philosopher sighs, and continues: "You are affected too, Miss.
If you are not working, you are going to resent
your dependent position. This will influence   20
I assure you, your most intimate moments . . ."

"Doctor, please," Wayman says. "All we want
is to be left alone."
But another beard, more nattily dressed,
is also getting into the bed.   25
There is a shifting and heaving of bodies
as everyone wriggles out room for themselves.
"I want you to meet a friend from Vienna,"
Marx says. "This is Doktor Freud."

The newcomer straightens his glasses,⁣   30
peers at Wayman and the girl.
"I can see," he begins,
"that you two have problems . . ."   1973

RESPONDING   The poems we have looked at so far all describe, though in quite different ways, feelings associated with loving or being attached to someone and the expression—either physical or verbal—of those feelings. Watching how poems work out a language for feeling can help us to work out a language for our own feelings, but the process is also reciprocal: being conscious of feelings we already have can lead us into poems more surely and with more satisfaction. Readers with a strong romantic bent—and with strong yearnings or positive memories of desire—will be likely to find "The Tally Stick" and "The River-Merchant's Wife: A Letter" easy to respond to and like, while those more skeptical of human institutions and male habits will find not only the anger but the formulation of argument in "To the Ladies" attractive.

Poems can be about all kinds of experiences, and not all the things we find in them will replicate (or even relate to) experiences we may have individually had. But sharing through language will often enable us to get in touch with feelings—of love or anger, fear or confidence—we did not know we had. The next few poems involve another, far less pleasant set of feelings than those usually generated by love, but even here, where our experience may be limited, we are able to respond, to feel the tug of emotions within us that we may not be fully aware of. In the following poem, a father struggles to understand and control his grief over the death of a seven-year-old son. We don't have to be a father or to have lost a loved-one to be aware of—and even share—the speaker's pain because our own experiences will have given us some idea of what such a loss would feel like. And the words and strategies of the poem may alert us to expectations that our previous experiences with death may activate.

BEN JONSON

On My First Son

Farewell, thou child of my right hand,² and joy;
My sin was too much hope of thee, loved boy:

---

2. A literal translation of the son's name, Benjamin.

Seven years thou wert lent to me, and I thee pay,
Exacted by thy fate, on the just[3] day.
O could I lose all father now! for why
Will man lament the state he should envý,
To have so soon 'scaped world's and flesh's rage,
And, if no other misery, yet age?
Rest in soft peace, and asked, say, "Here doth lie
Ben Jonson his[4] best piece of poetry."
For whose sake henceforth all his vows be such
As what he loves may never like too much.   1616

This poem's attempts to rationalize the boy's death are quite conventional. Although the father tries to be comforted by pious thoughts, his feelings keep showing through. The poem's beginning—with its formal "farewell" and the rather distant-sounding address to the dead boy ("child of my right hand")—cannot be sustained for long: both of the first two lines end with bursts of emotion. It is as if the father is trying to explain the death to himself and to keep his emotions under control, but cannot quite manage it. Even the punctuation suggests the way his feelings compete with conventional attempts to put the death into some sort of perspective that will soften the grief, and the comma near the end of each of the first two lines marks a pause that cannot quite hold back the overflowing emotion. But finally the only "idea" that the poem supports is that the father wishes he did not feel so intensely; in the fifth line he fairly blurts that he wishes he could lose his fatherly emotions, and in the final lines he resolves never again to "like" so much that he can be this deeply hurt. Philosophy and religion offer their useful counsels in this poem, but they prove far less powerful than feeling. Rather than drawing some kind of moral about what death means, the poem presents the actuality of feeling as inevitable and nearly all-consuming.

The poem that follows similarly tries to suppress the rawness of feelings about the death of a loved one, but here the survivor is haunted by memories of his wife when he sees a physical object—a vacuum cleaner—that he associates with her.

HOWARD NEMEROV

The Vacuum

The house is so quiet now
The vacuum cleaner sulks in the corner closet,

---

3. Exact; the son died on his seventh birthday, in 1603.   4. Ben Jonson's (a common Renaissance form of the possessive).

Its bag limp as a stopped lung, its mouth
Grinning into the floor, maybe at my
Slovenly life, my dog-dead youth.   5

I've lived this way long enough,
But when my old woman died her soul
Went into that vacuum cleaner, and I can't bear
To see the bag swell like a belly, eating the dust
And the woolen mice, and begin to howl   10

Because there is old filth everywhere
She used to crawl, in the corner and under the stair.
I know now how life is cheap as dirt,
And still the hungry, angry heart
Hangs on and howls, biting at air.   1955   15

The poem is about a vacuum in the husband's life, but the title refers most
obviously to the vacuum cleaner that, like the tally stick we looked at earlier,
seems to stand for many of the things that were once important in the life he
had together with his wife. The cleaner is a reminder of the dead wife ("my
old woman," line 7) because of her devotion to cleanliness. But to the surviving husband buried in the filth of his life it seems as if the machine has
become almost human, a kind of ghost of her: it "sulks" (line 2), it has lungs
and a mouth (line 3), and it seems to grin, making fun of what has become of
him. He "can't bear" (line 8) to see it in action because it then seems too
much alive, too much a reminder of her life. The poem records his paralysis,
his inability to do more than discover that life is "cheap as dirt" without her
ordering and cleansing presence for him. At the end it is *his* angry heart that
acts like the haunting machine, howling and biting at air as if he has merged
with her spirit and the physical object that memorializes her. This poem puts a
strong emphasis on the stillness of death and the way it makes things seem to
stop; it captures in words the hurt, the anger, the inability to understand, the
vacuum that remains when a loved one dies and leaves a vacant space. But
here we do not see the body or hear a direct good-bye to the dead person;
rather we encounter the feeling that lingers and won't go away, recalled
through memory by an especially significant object, a mere thing but one that
has been personalized to the point of becoming nearly human in itself. (The
event described here is, by the way, fictional; the poet's wife did not in fact die.
Like a dramatist or writer of fiction, the poet may simply *imagine* an event in
order to analyze and articulate how such an event might feel in certain circumstances.)

Here is another poem about the death of a loved one:

SHARON OLDS

The Glass

I think of it with wonder now,
the glass of mucus that stood on the table
next to my father all weekend. The cancer
is growing fast in his throat now,
5   and as it grows it sends out pus like the
sun sending out flares, those pouring
tongues. So my father has to gargle, hack,
spit a mouth full of thick stuff
into the glass every ten minutes or so,
10   scraping the rim up his lower lip to
get the last bit off his skin, then he
sets the glass down on the table and it
sits there, like a glass of beer foam,
shiny and faintly golden, he gurgles and
15   coughs and reaches for it again and
gets the heavy sputum out,
full of bubbles and moving around like yeast—
he is like some god producing food from his own mouth.
He himself can eat nothing anymore,
20   just a swallow of milk sometimes,
cut with water, and even then it
can't always get past the tumor,
and the next time the saliva comes up it's
chalkish and ropey, he has to roll it in his
25   throat to form it and get it up and dis-
gorge the elliptical globule into the cup—
and the wonder to me is that it did not disgust me,
that glass of phlegm that stood there all day and
filled slowly with compound globes and I'd
30   empty it and it would fill again and
shimmer there on the table until the
room seemed to turn around it
in an orderly way, a model of the solar system
turning around the gold sun,
35   my father the dark earth that used to
lie at the center of the universe
now turning with the rest of us
around the bright glass of spit
on the table, these last mouthfuls.   1990

Like "The Vacuum," "The Glass" reflects on a loved one through unconventional images, material objects that suggest pain and unpleasantness rather

than joy and love. The "glass" of the title is not a mirror that reflects a beautiful face, not a crafted objet d'art, but rather a simple tumbler, and it is full of mucus—not a very appealing object. The loved one, the father of the person who is speaking the poem, is dying of cancer, and the indicators of his condition are painfully detailed. The sights and sounds are disgusting rather than pleasant; the body fluids are pus and spit, and the human sounds are gargling, gurgling, and hacking. It is almost as if the poem tries to create a picture as ugly as possible, for the father's physical struggle just to swallow and spit is chronicled moment by painful moment. "[T]he wonder to me," says the daughter who views the daily struggle and records it for us in the poem, "is that it did not disgust me" (line 27), and the poem transforms the central object of disgust ("that glass of phlegm," line 28) into something that stands for the daughter's love and the father's ability to accept it even in his deteriorating condition. The daughter's act of staying and emptying the glass represents not only fortitude and loyalty but the steadying influence of stability and predictability. She begins to see the glass itself—its regular filling and emptying of life and coming death—as a kind of center around which human activity revolves "in an orderly way" (line 33). The father, once the center of the family's universe, now seems to move with the others "around" (line 38) the fact of death as represented by the glass. It is an awful picture—awful in its details, awful in its implications of loss—but it is also beautiful in its own way. The poem shows that life and love can be portrayed, explained, and imprinted on our memories by even the most unattractive events, objects, and words.

Sometimes poems are a way of confronting feelings. Sometimes they explore feelings in detail and try to intellectualize or rationalize them. At other times, poems generate responses by recalling an experience many years in the past. In the following two poems, for example, memories of childhood provide perspective on two very different kinds of events. In the first, written as if the person speaking the poem were in the fifth grade, a child's sense of death is portrayed through her exploration of a photograph that makes her grandfather's earlier presence vivid to her memory—a memory that lingers primarily through smell and touch. In the second poem, another childhood memory— this time of overshoes—takes an adult almost physically back into childhood. As you read the two poems, keep track of (or perhaps even jot down) your responses. How much of your feeling is due to your own past experiences? In which specific places? What family photographs do you remember most vividly? What feelings did they invoke that make them so memorable? How are your memories different from those expressed in "Fifth Grade Autobiography"? in "The Fury of Overshoes"? Which feelings expressed in each poem are similar to your own? Where do your feelings differ most strongly? How would you articulate your responses to memories differently? In what ways does an awareness of your similar—and different—experiences and feelings make you a better reader of the poem?

RITA DOVE

Fifth Grade Autobiography

I was four in this photograph fishing
with my grandparents at a lake in Michigan.
My brother squats in poison ivy.
His Davy Crockett cap
5   sits squared on his head so the raccoon tail
flounces down the back of his sailor suit.

My grandfather sits to the far right
in a folding chair,
and I know his left hand is on
10   the tobacco in his pants pocket
because I used to wrap it for him
every Christmas. Grandmother's hips
bulge from the brush, she's leaning
into the ice chest, sun through the trees
15   printing her dress with soft
luminous paws.

I am staring jealously at my brother;
the day before he rode his first horse, alone.
I was strapped in a basket
20   behind my grandfather.
He smelled of lemons. He's died—

but I remember his hands.   1989

ANNE SEXTON

The Fury of Overshoes

They sit in a row
outside the kindergarten,
black, red, brown, all
with those brass buckles.
5   Remember when you couldn't
buckle your own

overshoe
or tie your own
shoe
or cut your own meat   10
and the tears
running down like mud
because you fell off your
tricycle?
Remember, big fish,   15
when you couldn't swim
and simply slipped under
like a stone frog?
The world wasn't
yours.   20
It belonged to
the big people.
Under your bed
sat the wolf
and he made a shadow   25
when cars passed by
at night.
They made you give up
your nightlight
and your teddy   30
and your thumb.
Oh overshoes,
don't you
remember me,
pushing you up and down   35
in the winter snow?
Oh thumb,
I want a drink,
it is dark,
where are the big people,   40
when will I get there,
taking giant steps
all day,
each day
and thinking   45
nothing of it?   1974

There is much more going on in the poems that we have glanced at than
we have taken time to consider, but even the quickest look at these poems suggests something of the range of feelings that poems can offer—the depth of
feeling, the clarity, the experience that may be articulately and precisely
shared. Not all poems are as accessible as those we've looked at so far, and

even the ones that are accessible usually yield themselves to us more readily and more completely if we approach them systematically by developing specific reading habits and skills—just as someone learning to play tennis systematically learns the rules, the techniques, the things to watch out for that are distinctive to the pleasures and hazards of that skill or craft. It helps if you develop a sense of what to expect, and the chapters that follow will help you to an understanding of the things that poets can do—and thus of what poems can do for you.

But knowing what to expect isn't everything, and I have one bit of advice to offer every prospective reader of poetry before going any further: Be open. Be open to new experience, be open to new feelings, be open to new ideas. Every poem in the world is a potential new experience, and no matter how sophisticated you become, you can still be surprised (and delighted) by new poems—and by rereading old ones. Good poems bear many, many rereadings, and often one discovers something new with every new reading. Be willing to let poems surprise you when you come to them; let them come on their own terms, let them be themselves. If you are open to poetry, you are open to much that the world can offer you.

No one can give you a method that will offer you total experience of all poems. But because many characteristics of an individual poem are characteristics that one poem shares with other poems, there are guidelines that can prompt you to ask the right questions. The chapters that follow will help you in detail with a variety of problems, but meanwhile here is a checklist of some things to remember:

1. *Read the syntax literally.* What the words say literally in normal sentences is only a starting point, but it is the place to start. Not all poems use normal prose syntax, but most of them do, and you can save yourself embarrassment by paraphrasing accurately (that is, rephrasing what the poem literally says, in plain prose) and not simply free-associating from an isolated word or phrase.

2. *Articulate for yourself what the title, subject, and situation make you expect.* Poets often use false leads and try to surprise you by doing shocking things, but defining expectation lets you be conscious of where you are when you begin.

3. *Identify the poem's situation.* What is said is often conditioned by where it is said and by whom. Identifying the speaker and his or her place in the situation puts what he or she says in perspective.

4. *Find out what is implied by the traditions behind the poem.* Verse forms,

poetic kinds, and metrical patterns all have a frame of reference, traditions of the way they are usually used and for what. For example, the anapest (two unstressed syllables followed by a stressed one, as in the word "Tennessee") is usually used for comic poems, and when poets use it "straight" they are aware of their "departure" and are probably making a point by doing it.

5. *Bother the reference librarian.* Look up anything you don't understand: an unfamiliar word (or an ordinary word used in an unfamiliar way), a place, a person, a myth, an idea—anything the poem uses. When you can't find what you need or don't know where to look, ask for help.

6. *Remember that poems exist in time, and times change.* Not only the meanings of words, but whole ways of looking at the universe vary in different ages. Consciousness of time works two ways: your knowledge of history provides a context for reading the poem, and the poem's use of a word or idea may modify your notion of a particular age.

7. *Take a poem on its own terms.* Adjust to the poem; don't make the poem adjust to you. Be prepared to hear things you do not want to hear. Not all poems are about your ideas, nor will they always present emotions you want to feel. But be tolerant and listen to the poem's ideas, not only to your desire to revise them for yourself.

8. *Be willing to be surprised.* Things often happen in poems that turn them around. A poem may seem to suggest one thing at first, then persuade you of its opposite, or at least of a significant qualification or variation.

9. *Assume there is a reason for everything.* Poets do make mistakes, but in poems that show some degree of verbal control it is usually safest to assume that the poet chose each word carefully; if the choice seems peculiar to us, it is often *we* who are missing something. Try to account for everything in a poem and see what kind of sense you can make of it. Poets make choices; try to figure out a coherent pattern that explains the text as it stands.

10. *Argue.* Discussion usually results in clarification and keeps you from being too dependent on personal biases and preoccupations that sometimes mislead even the best readers. Talking a poem over with someone else (especially someone very different) can expand your perspective.

WRITING ABOUT POEMS   If you have been keeping notes on your personal responses to the poems you've read, you have already taken an important step toward writing about them. There are many different ways to write about poems, just as there are many different things to say. (The chapter in the back of the book on *Writing About Literature* suggests many different kinds of topics.) But all writing begins from a clear sense of the poem itself and your responses to it, so the first steps (long before formally sitting down to write) are to read the poem over several times and keep notes on the things that strike you and the questions that remain.

Formulating a clear series of questions will usually help lead you to an appropriate approach to the poem and to a good topic. Learning to ask the right questions can save you a lot of time. Some questions—the kinds of questions implied in the ten guidelines for reading listed above (pp. 666–67)—are basic and more or less apply to all poems. But each poem makes demands of its own, too, because of its distinctive way of going about its business, so you will usually want to make a list of what seem to you the crucial questions for that poem. Here are—just to give you an example—some questions that could be useful in leading you to a paper topic on the first of the poems printed at the end of this chapter.

1. How does the title affect your reading of and response to the poem?
2. What is the poem about?
3. What makes the poem interesting to read?
4. Who is the speaker? What role does the speaker have in the poem?
5. What effect does the poem have on you as a reader? Do you think the poet intended to have such an effect?
6. What is distinctive about the poet's use of language? Which words especially contribute to the poem's effect?

What *is* poetry? Let your definition be cumulative as you read more and more poems. No dictionary definition will cover all that you find, and it is better to discover for yourself poetry's many ingredients, its many effects, its many ways of acting. What can it do for you? Wait and see. Begin to add up its effects after you have read carefully—after you have studied and reread—a hundred or so poems; that will be a beginning, and you will be able to add to that total as long as you continue to read new poems or reread old ones.

▼   ▼   ▼

WILLIAM SHAKESPEARE

[Let me not to the marriage of true minds]

Let me not to the marriage of true minds
Admit impediments.[5] Love is not love
Which alters when it alteration finds,
Or bends with the remover to remove:
Oh, no! it is an ever-fixéd mark,   5
That looks on tempests and is never shaken;
It is the star to every wandering bark,
Whose worth's unknown, although his height be taken.[6]
Love's not Time's fool, though rosy lips and cheeks
Within his bending sickle's compass come;   10
Love alters not with his brief hours and weeks,
But bears it out even to the edge of doom.
If this be error and upon me proved,
I never writ, nor no man ever loved.

1609

ANNE BRADSTREET

To My Dear and Loving Husband

If ever two were one, then surely we.
If ever man were loved by wife, then thee;
If ever wife was happy in a man,
Compare with me ye women if you can.
I prize thy love more than whole mines of gold,   5
Or all the riches that the East doth hold.
My love is such that rivers cannot quench,
Nor aught but love from thee give recompense.
Thy love is such I can no way repay;
The heavens reward thee manifold, I pray.   10
Then while we live, in love let's so persever,
That when we live no more we may live ever.

1678

---

5. The Marriage Service contains this address to the witnesses: "If any of you know cause or just impediments why these persons should not be joined together. . . ."   6. I.e., measuring the altitude of stars (for purposes of navigation) is not a measurement of value.

EDNA ST. VINCENT MILLAY

[I, being born a woman and distressed]

I, being born a woman and distressed
By all the needs and notions of my kind,
Am urged by your propinquity to find
Your person fair, and feel a certain zest
5   To bear your body's weight upon my breast:
So subtly is the fume of life designed,
To clarify the pulse and cloud the mind,
And leave me once again undone, possessed.
Think not for this, however, the poor treason
10   Of my stout blood against my staggering brain,
I shall remember you with love, or season
My scorn with pity,—let me make it plain:
I find this frenzy insufficient reason
For conversation when we meet again.   1923

GALWAY KINNELL

After Making Love We Hear Footsteps

For I can snore like a bullhorn
or play loud music
or sit up talking with any reasonably sober Irishman
and Fergus will only sink deeper
5   into his dreamless sleep, which goes by all in one flash,
but let there be that heavy breathing
or a stifled come-cry anywhere in the house
and he will wrench himself awake
and make for it on the run—as now, we lie together,
10   after making love, quiet, touching along the length of our bodies,
familiar touch of the long-married,
and he appears—in his baseball pajamas, it happens,
the neck opening so small
he has to screw them on, which one day may make him wonder
15   about the mental capacity of baseball players—
and says, "Are you loving and snuggling? May I join?"
He flops down between us and hugs us and snuggles himself to sleep,
his face gleaming with satisfaction at being this very child.

In the half darkness we look at each other
20   and smile
and touch arms across his little, startlingly muscled body—
this one whom habit of memory propels to the ground of his making,

sleeper only the mortal sounds can sing awake,
this blessing love gives again into our arms.   1980

LI-YOUNG LEE

Persimmons

In sixth grade Mrs. Walker
slapped the back of my head
and made me stand in the corner
for not knowing the difference
between *persimmon* and *precision*.   5
How to choose

persimmons. This is precision.
Ripe ones are soft and brown-spotted.
Sniff the bottoms. The sweet one
will be fragrant. How to eat: 10
put the knife away, lay down newspaper.
Peel the skin tenderly, not to tear the meat.
Chew the skin, suck it,
and swallow. Now, eat
the meat of the fruit,   15
so sweet,
all of it, to the heart.

Donna undresses, her stomach is white.
In the yard, dewy and shivering
with crickets, we lie naked,   20
face-up, face-down.
I teach her Chinese.
Crickets: *chiu chiu.* Dew: I've forgotten.
Naked: I've forgotten.
Ni, wo: you and me.   25
I part her legs,
remember to tell her
she is beautiful as the moon.

Other words
that got me into trouble were   30
fight and *fright, wren* and *yarn.*
Fight was what I did when I was frightened,
fright was what I felt when I was fighting.
Wrens are small, plain birds,
yarn is what one knits with.   35
Wrens are soft as yarn.
My mother made birds out of yarn.

I loved to watch her tie the stuff;
a bird, a rabbit, a wee man.

40 Mrs. Walker brought a persimmon to class
and cut it up
so everyone could taste
a *Chinese apple.* Knowing
it wasn't ripe or sweet, I didn't eat
45 but watched the other faces.

My mother said every persimmon has a sun
inside, something golden, glowing,
warm as my face.

Once, in the cellar, I found two wrapped in newspaper,
50 forgotten and not yet ripe.
I took them and set both on my bedroom windowsill,
where each morning a cardinal
sang, *The sun, the sun.*

Finally understanding
55 he was going blind,
my father sat up all one night
waiting for a song, a ghost.
I gave him the persimmons,
swelled, heavy as sadness,
60 and sweet as love.

This year, in the muddy lighting
of my parents' cellar, I rummage, looking
for something I lost.
My father sits on the tired, wooden stairs,
65 black cane between his knees,
hand over hand, gripping the handle.

He's so happy that I've come home.
I ask how his eyes are, a stupid question.
All gone, he answers.

70 Under some blankets, I find a box.
Inside the box I find three scrolls.
I sit beside him and untie
three paintings by my father:
Hibiscus leaf and a white flower.
75 Two cats preening.
Two persimmons, so full they want to drop from the cloth.

He raises both hands to touch the cloth,
asks, *Which is this?*

This is persimmons, Father.

Oh, the feel of the wolftail on the silk,   80
the strength, the tense
precision in the wrist.
I painted them hundreds of times
eyes closed. These I painted blind.
Some things never leave a person: 85
scent of the hair of one you love,
the texture of persimmons,
in your palm, the ripe weight.   1986

AUDRE LORDE

Recreation

Coming together
it is easier to work
after our bodies
meet
paper and pen   5
neither care nor profit
whether we write or not
but as your body moves
under my hands
charged and waiting   10
we cut the leash
you create me against your thighs
hilly with images
moving through our word countries
my body   15
writes into your flesh
the poem
you make of me

Touching you I catch midnight
as moon fires set in my throat   20
I love you flesh into blossom
I made you
and take you made
into me.   1978

ERIN MOURÉ

Thirteen Years

I am in a daydream of my uncle,
his shirt out at his daughter's wedding,

white scoop of the shirt-tail bobbing
on the dance floor & him in it, no,
his drunk friend pawing me, it was *his* shirt dangling,
I forgot this
my youngest cousin in his dress pants downing straight whisky,
& me too, tying tin cans to his sister's car.
The sour taste of it. Drink this, he said.

I am wondering how we live at all
or if we do.
The puppy we grew up with came from the same uncle's farm.
His shirt-tail beneath his suit jacket, dancing.
The friend of the family touching my new chest.
They told me not to say so.
I'll drive you to the motel, he said, his breath close.
No. Be nice to him, they said, & waved me off from the table.
I was so scared.
Everyone had been drinking. Including me. Thirteen years old.
Who the hell did my cousin marry.
I tell you.   1988

▼   ▼   ▼

QUESTIONS

1. Did you notice that "To the Ladies" was written in 1703? Were you at all surprised by your response to it when you read it? If not, does the date of publication modify your response? Why?

2. How did you respond to "Thirteen Years"? What message is the speaker trying to get across to us? How does she feel about herself and her relatives as she recounts this adolescent experience?

WRITING SUGGESTIONS

1. Jot down your responses to all of the marriage poems at the beginning of this chapter. Which one most accurately expresses your ideal of a good marriage? Why do you think so? What does your choice say about you?

2. Choose one of the poems on death, and write a letter to the grieving relative (the speaker) in which you offer condolences and comfort.

∇ ∇ ∇

Understanding
the Text

1 TONE

P oetry is full of surprises. Poems express anger or outrage just as effectively as love or sadness, and good poems can be written about going to a rock concert or having lunch or cutting the lawn, as well as about making love or gazing at a cloudless sky or smelling flowers. Even poems on "predictable" subjects can surprise us with unpredicted attitudes, unusual events, or a sudden twist. Knowing that a poem is about some particular subject—love, for example, or death—may give us a general idea of what to expect, but it never tells us altogether what we will find in a particular poem. Responding to a poem fully means being open to the poem and its surprises, being willing to let the poem guide us to its own stances, feelings, and ideas. Letting a poem speak to us means being willing to listen to *how* the poem says what it says—hearing the tone of voice implied in the way the words are spoken.

The following two poems—one about death and one about love—express rather different ideas and feelings from the poems we have read so far.

MARGE PIERCY

Barbie Doll

This girlchild was born as usual
and presented dolls that did pee-pee
and miniature GE stoves and irons

and wee lipsticks the color of cherry candy.
Then in the magic of puberty, a classmate said:
You have a great big nose and fat legs.

She was healthy, tested intelligent,
possessed strong arms and back,
abundant sexual drive and manual dexterity.
She went to and fro apologizing.
Everyone saw a fat nose on thick legs.

She was advised to play coy,
exhorted to come on hearty,
exercise, diet, smile and wheedle.
Her good nature wore out
like a fan belt.
So she cut off her nose and her legs
and offered them up.

In the casket displayed on satin she lay
with the undertaker's cosmetics painted on,
a turned-up putty nose,
dressed in a pink and white nightie.
Doesn't she look pretty? everyone said.
Consummation at last.
To every woman a happy ending.

1973

W. D. SNODGRASS

Leaving the Motel

Outside, the last kids holler
Near the pool: they'll stay the night.
Pick up the towels; fold your collar
Out of sight.

Check: is the second bed
Unrumpled, as agreed?
Landlords have to think ahead
In case of need,

Too. Keep things straight: don't take
The matches, the wrong keyrings—
We've nowhere we could keep a keepsake—
Ashtrays, combs, things

That sooner or later others
Would accidentally find.
Check: take nothing of one another's
And leave behind

Your license number only,
Which they won't care to trace;
We've paid. Still, should such things get lonely,
Leave in their vase   20

An aspirin to preserve
Our lilacs, the wayside flowers
We've gathered and must leave to serve
A few more hours;

That's all. We can't tell when   25
We'll come back, can't press claims,
We would no doubt have other rooms then,
Or other names.   1968

The first poem has the strong note of sadness that characterizes many death
poems, but its emphasis is not on the girl's death but on the disappointments
in her life. The only "scene" in the poem (lines 19–23) portrays the unnamed
girl at rest in her casket, but the still body in the casket contrasts not with vitality but with frustration and anxiety: her life since puberty (lines 5–6) had been
full of apologies and attempts to change her physical appearance and emotional makeup. The rest she achieves in death is not, however, a triumph,
despite what people say (line 23). Although the poem's last two words are
"happy ending," this girl without a name has died in embarrassment and without fulfillment, and the final lines are ironic, meaning the opposite of what
they say. The cheerful comments at the end lack force and truth because of
what we already know; we understand them as ironic because they underline
how unhappy the girl was and how false her cosmeticized corpse is to the sad
truth of her life.

The poem's concern is to suggest the falsity and destructiveness of those
standards of female beauty that have led to the tragedy of the girl's life. In an
important sense, the poem is not really *about* death at all in spite of the fact
that the girl's death and her repaired corpse are central to it. As the title suggests, the poem dramatizes how standardized, commercialized notions of femi-
ninity and prettiness can be painful and destructive to those whose bodies do
not precisely fit the conformist models, and the poem attacks vigorously those
conventional standards and the widespread, unthinking acceptance of them.

"Leaving the Motel" similarly goes in quite a different direction from many
poems on the subject of love. Instead of expressing assurance about how love
lasts and endures, or about the sincerity and depth of affection, this poem
describes a parting of lovers after a brief sexual encounter. But it does not
emphasize sexuality or eroticism in the meeting of the nameless lovers (we see

them only as they prepare to leave), nor does it suggest why or how they have found each other, or what either of them is like as a person. Its focus is on how careful they must be not to get caught, how exact and calculating they must be in their planning, how finite and limited their encounter must be, how sealed off this encounter is from the rest of their lives. The poem relates the tiny details the lovers must think of, the agreements they must observe, and the ritual checklist of their duties ("Check . . . Keep things straight . . . Check . . . ," lines 5, 9, 15). Affection and sentiment have their small place in the poem (notice the care for the flowers, lines 19–24, and the thought of "pressing claims," line 26), but the emphasis is on temporariness, uncertainty, and limits. The poem is about an illicit, perhaps adulterous, sexual encounter, but there is no sex in the poem, only a kind of archeological record of lust.

Labeling a poem as a "love poem" or a "death poem" is primarily a matter of convenience; such categories indicate the **subject** of a poem or the event or **topic** it chooses to engage. But as the poems we have been looking at suggest, poems that may be loosely called love poems or death poems may differ widely from one another, express totally different attitudes or ideas, and concentrate on very different aspects of the subject. The main advantages of grouping poems in this way for study is that a reader can become conscious of individual differences: a reading of two poems side by side may suggest how each is distinctive in what it has to say and how it says it.

What a poem has to say is often called its **theme,** the kind of statement it makes about its subject. We could say, for example, that the theme of "Leaving the Motel" is that illicit love is secretive, careful, transitory, and short on emotion and sentiment, or that secret sexual encounters tend to be brief, calculated, and characterized by restrained and insecure feelings. The theme of a poem may be expressed in several different ways, and poems often have more than one theme. "Barbie Doll" suggests that commercialized standards destroy human values; that rigid and idealized notions of normality cripple those who are different; that people are easily and tragically led to accept evaluations thrust upon them by others; that American consumers tend to be conformists, easily influenced in their outlook by advertising and by commercial products; that children who do not conform to middle-class standards and notions don't have a chance. The poem implies each of these statements, and all are quite central to it. But none of these statements individually nor all of them together would fully express or explain the poem itself. To state the themes in such a brief and abstract way—though it may be helpful in clarifying what the poem does and does not say—never does justice to the experience of the poem, the way it works on us as readers, the way we respond. Poems affect us in all sorts of ways—emotional and psychological as well as rational—and often a poem's dramatization of a story, an event, or a moment bypasses our rational responses and affects us far more deeply than a clear and logical argument would.

Sometimes poems express feelings directly and quite simply:

LINDA PASTAN

love poem

I want to write you
a love poem as headlong
as our creek
after thaw
when we stand   5
on its dangerous
banks and watch it carry
with it every twig
every dry leaf and branch
in its path   10
every scruple
when we see it
so swollen
with runoff
that even as we watch   15
we must grab
each other
and step back
we must grab each
other or   20
get our shoes
soaked we must
grab each other   1988

The directness and simplicity of this poem suggest how the art and craft of poems work. The poem expresses the desire to write a love poem even as the love poem itself begins to proceed; the desire and the resultant poem exist side by side, and in reading the poem we seem to watch the poet's creative process at work in developing appropriate metaphors and means of expression. The poem must be "headlong" (line 2), to match the power of a love that needs to be compared to the irresistible forces of nature. The poem should, like the love it expresses and the swollen creek it describes, sweep everything along, and it should represent (and reproduce) the sense of watching that the lovers have when they observe natural processes at work. The poem, like the action it represents, has to suggest to readers the kind of desire that grabbing each other means to the lovers.

The lovers in this poem seem, at least to themselves, to own the world they observe, in fact they are controlled by it. The creek on whose banks they stand is "our creek" (line 3), but what they observe as they watch its rising currents requires them ("must," lines 16, 19, 22) to "grab each other" over and over again. It is as if their love is part of nature itself, which subjects them to forces larger than themselves. Everything—twigs, leaves, branches, scruples—is carried along by the powerful currents after the "thaw" (line 4), and the poem replicates the repeated action of the lovers as if to power along observant readers just as the lovers are powered along by what they see. But the poem (and their love) admits dangers too; it is the fact of danger that propels the lovers to each other. The poem suggests that love provides a kind of haven, but the haven hardly involves passivity or peace; instead, it requires the kind of grabbing that means activity and boldness and deep passion. Love here is no quiet or simple matter even if the expression of it in poems can be direct and based on a simple observation of experience. The "love poem" itself—linked as it is with the headlong currents of the creek from which the lovers are protecting themselves—even represents that which is beyond love and that therefore both threatens it and at the same time makes it happen. The power of poetry is thus affirmed at the center of the poem, but what poetry is about (love and life) is suggested to be more important. Poetry makes things happen but is not itself a substitute for life, just a means to make it more energetic and meaningful.

Poems, then, differ widely from one another even when they share a common subject. And the subjects of poetry also vary widely. It isn't true that there are certain "poetic" subjects and that there are others that aren't appropriate to poetry. Any human activity, thought, or feeling can be the subject of poetry. Poetry often deals with beauty and the softer, more attractive human emotions, but it can deal with ugliness and less attractive human conduct as well, for poetry seeks to represent human beings and human events, showing us ourselves not only as we would like to be but as we are. Good poetry gets written about all kinds of topics, in all kinds of forms, with all kinds of attitudes. Here, for example, is a poem about a prison inmate—and about the conflict between individual and societal values.

ETHERIDGE KNIGHT

Hard Rock Returns to Prison from the Hospital for the Criminal Insane

Hard Rock was "known not to take no shit
From nobody," and he had the scars to prove it:
Split purple lips, lumped ears, welts above
His yellow eyes, and one long scar that cut
Across his temple and plowed through a thick   5
Canopy of kinky hair.

The WORD was that Hard Rock wasn't a mean nigger
Anymore, that the doctors had bored a hole in his head,
Cut out part of his brain, and shot electricity
Through the rest. When they brought Hard Rock back,   10
Handcuffed and chained, he was turned loose,
Like a freshly gelded stallion, to try his new status.
And we all waited and watched, like indians at a corral,
To see if the WORD was true.

As we waited we wrapped ourselves in the cloak   15
Of his exploits: "Man, the last time, it took eight
Screws to put him in the Hole."[1] "Yeah, remember when he
Smacked the captain with his dinner tray?" "He set
The record for time in the Hole—67 straight days!"
"Ol Hard Rock! man, that's one crazy nigger."   20
And then the jewel of a myth that Hard Rock had once bit
A screw on the thumb and poisoned him with syphilitic spit.

The testing came, to see if Hard Rock was really tame.
A hillbilly called him a black son of a bitch
And didn't lose his teeth, a screw who knew Hard Rock   25
From before shook him down and barked in his face.
And Hard Rock did *nothing*. Just grinned and looked silly,
His eyes empty like knot holes in a fence.

And even after we discovered that it took Hard Rock
Exactly 3 minutes to tell you his first name,   30
We told ourselves that he had just wised up,
Was being cool; but we could not fool ourselves for long,
And we turned away, our eyes on the ground. Crushed.
He had been our Destroyer, the doer of things
We dreamed of doing but could not bring ourselves to do, 35
The fears of years, like a biting whip,
Had cut grooves too deeply across our backs.

                                                    1968

---

1. Solitary confinement. *Screws:* guards.

The picture of Hard Rock as a kind of hero to other prison inmates is established early in the poem through a retelling of the legends circulated about him; the straightforward chronology of the poem sets up the mystery of how he will react after his "treatment" in the hospital. The poem identifies with those who wait; they are hopeful that Hard Rock's spirit has not been broken by surgery or shock treatments, and the lines crawl almost to a stop with disappointment in stanza 4. The *"nothing"* (line 27) of Hard Rock's response to teasing and taunting and the emptiness of his eyes ("like knot holes in a fence," line 28) reduce the heroic hopes and illusions to despair. The final stanza recounts the observers' attempts to reinterpret, to hang onto hope that their symbol of heroism could stand up against the best efforts to tame him, but the spirit has gone out of the hero-worshipers too, and the poem records them as beaten, conformed, deprived of their spirit as Hard Rock has been of his. The poem records the despair of the hopeless, and it protests against the cruel exercise of power that can curb even as rebellious a figure as Hard Rock.

The following poem is equally full of anger and disappointment, but it expresses its attitudes in a very different way.

WILLIAM BLAKE

London

I wander through each chartered street,
Near where the chartered Thames does flow,
And mark in every face I meet
Marks of weakness, marks of woe.

5   In every cry of every man,
In every Infant's cry of fear,
In every voice, in every ban,
The mind-forged manacles I hear.

How the Chimney-sweeper's cry
10   Every black'ning Church appalls;
And the hapless Soldier's sigh
Runs in blood down Palace walls.

But most through midnight streets I hear
How the youthful Harlot's curse
15   Blasts the new-born Infant's tear,
And blights with plagues the Marriage hearse.   1794

The poem gives a strong sense of how London feels to this particular observer; it is cluttered, constricting, oppressive. The wordplay here articulates and connects the strong emotions he associates with London experiences. The repeated words—"every," for example, or "cry"—intensify the sense of total despair in the city and weld connections between things not necessarily related—the cries of street vendors, for example, with the cries for help. The twice-used word "chartered" implies strong feelings too. The streets, instead of seeming alive with people or bustling with movement, are rigidly, coldly determined, controlled, cramped. Likewise the river seems as if it were planned, programmed, laid out by an oppressor. In actual fact, the course of the Thames had been altered (slightly) by the government before Blake's time, but most important is the word's emotional force, the sense it projects of constriction and artificiality: the person speaking experiences London as if human artifice had totally altered nature. Moreover, according to the poem, people are victimized, "marked" by their confrontations with urbanness and the power of institutions: the "Soldier's sigh" that "runs in blood down Palace walls" vividly suggests, through a metaphor that visually depicts the speaker's feelings, both the powerlessness of the individual and the callousness of power. The "description" of the city has clearly become, by now, a subjective, highly emotional, and vivid expression of how the speaker feels about London and what it represents to him.

Another thing about "London": at first it looks like an account of a personal experience, as if the speaker is describing and interpreting as he goes along: "I wander through each chartered street." But soon it is clear that he is describing many wanderings, putting together impressions from many walks, re-creating a typical walk—which shows him "every" person in the streets, allows him to generalize about the churches being "appalled" (literally, made white) by the cry of the representative Chimney-sweeper, and leads to his conclusions about soldiers, prostitutes, and infants. What we are given is not a personal record of an event, but a representation of it, as it seems in retrospect—not a story, not a narrative or chronological account of events, but a dramatization of self that compresses many experiences into one.

"London" is somber in spite of the poet's playfulness with words. Wordplay may be witty and funny if it calls attention to its own cleverness, but here it involves the discovery of unsuspected (but meaningful) connections between things. The term **tone** is used to describe the attitude a poem takes toward its subject and theme. If the theme of a poem is *what* the poem says, the tone involves *how* one says it. The tone of "London" is sad, despairing, and angry; reading "London" aloud, one would try to show in one's voice the strong feelings that the poem expresses, just as one would try to reproduce tenderness and caring and passion in reading aloud "The Tally Stick" or "How Do I Love Thee?"

The following two poems involve animals, although both of them place their final emphasis on what human beings are like: the animal in each case is only the means to the end of exploring human nature. The poems share a common assumption that animal behavior may appear to reflect human habits and conduct and may reveal much about ourselves, and in each case the character central to the poem is revealed to be surprisingly unlike the way she thinks of herself. But the poems are very different from one another. Read each poem aloud, and try to imagine what each main character is like. What tones of voice do you use to help express the character of the killer in the first poem? What demands on your voice does the second poem make?

MAXINE KUMIN

Woodchucks

Gassing the woodchucks didn't turn out right.
The knockout bomb from the Feed and Grain Exchange
was featured as merciful, quick at the bone
and the case we had against them was airtight,
both exits shoehorned shut with puddingstone,[2]
but they had a sub-sub-basement out of range.

Next morning they turned up again, no worse
for the cyanide than we for our cigarettes
and state-store Scotch, all of us up to scratch.
They brought down the marigolds as a matter of course
and then took over the vegetable patch
nipping the broccoli shoots, beheading the carrots.

The food from our mouths, I said, righteously thrilling
to the feel of the .22, the bullets' neat noses.
I, a lapsed pacifist fallen from grace
puffed with Darwinian pieties for killing,
now drew a bead on the littlest woodchuck's face.
He died down in the everbearing roses.

Ten minutes later I dropped the mother. She
flipflopped in the air and fell, her needle teeth
still hooked in a leaf of early Swiss chard.
Another baby next. O one-two-three
the murderer inside me rose up hard,
the hawkeye killer came on stage forthwith.

There's one chuck left. Old wily fellow, he keeps
me cocked and ready day after day after day.

2. A mixture of cement, pebbles, and gravel.

All night I hunt his humped-up form. I dream
I sight along the barrel in my sleep.
If only they'd all consented to die unseen
gassed underground the quiet Nazi way.   30

                                                                1972

ADRIENNE RICH

Aunt Jennifer's Tigers

Aunt Jennifer's tigers prance across a screen,
Bright topaz denizens of a world of green.
They do not fear the men beneath the tree;
They pace in sleek chivalric certainty.

Aunt Jennifer's fingers fluttering through her wool   5
Find even the ivory needle hard to pull.
The massive weight of Uncle's wedding band
Sits heavily upon Aunt Jennifer's hand.

When Aunt is dead, her terrified hands will lie
Still ringed with ordeals she was mastered by.   10
The tigers in the panel that she made
Will go on prancing, proud and unafraid.   1951

If you read "Woodchucks" aloud, how would your tone of voice change
from beginning to end? What tone would you use to read the ending? How
does the hunter feel about her increasing attraction to violence? Why does the
poem begin by calling the gassing of the woodchucks "merciful" and end by
describing it as "the quiet Nazi way"? What names does the hunter call herself? How does the name-calling affect your feelings about her? Exactly when
does the hunter begin to *enjoy* the feel of the gun and the idea of killing? How
does the poet make that clear?

Why are tigers a particularly appropriate contrast to the quiet and subdued
manner of Aunt Jennifer? What words used to describe the tigers seem particularly significant? In what ways is the tiger an opposite of Aunt Jennifer? In what
ways does it externalize her secrets? Why are Aunt Jennifer's hands described
as "terrified"? What clues does the poem give about why Aunt Jennifer is so
afraid? How does the poem make you feel about Aunt Jennifer? about her
tigers? about her life? How would you describe the tone of the poem? How
does the poet feel about Aunt Jennifer?

Twenty years after writing "Aunt Jennifer's Tigers," Adrienne Rich said this
about the poem:

In writing this poem, composed and apparently cool as it is, I thought I was creating a portrait of an imaginary woman. But this woman suffers from the opposition of her imagination, worked out in tapestry, and her life style, "ringed with ordeals she was mastered by." It was important to me that Aunt Jennifer was a person as distinct from myself as possible—distanced by the formalism of the poem, by its objective, observant tone—even by putting the woman in a different generation. In those years formalism was part of the strategy—like asbestos gloves, it allowed me to handle materials I couldn't pick up bare-handed.[3]

Not often do we have such an explicit comment on a poem by its author, and we don't actually have to have it to understand and experience the force of the poem (although such a statement may clarify why the author chose particular modes of presentation and how the poem fits into the author's own patterns of thinking and growing). Most poems contain within them what we need to know in order to tap the human and artistic resources they offer us.

Subject, theme, and tone: each of these categories gives us a way to begin considering poems and showing how one poem differs from another. Comparing poems on the same subject, or with a similar theme or tone, can lead to a clearer understanding of each individual poem and can refine our responses to the subtleties of individual differences. The title of a poem ("Leaving the Motel," for example) or the way the poem first introduces its subject often can give us a sense of what to expect, but we need to be open to surprise too. No two poems are going to be exactly alike in their effect on us; the variety of possible poems multiplies when you think of all the possible themes and tones that can be explored within any single subject. Varieties of feeling often coincide with varieties of thinking, and readers open to the pleasures of the unexpected may find themselves learning, growing, becoming more sensitive to ideas and human issues as well as more articulate about feelings and thoughts they already have.

▼   ▼   ▼

ALAN DUGAN

Elegy

I know but will not tell
you, Aunt Irene, why there
are soapsuds in the whiskey:

3. From "When We Dead Awaken: Writing as Re-Vision," a talk given in December 1971 at the Women's Forum of the Modern Language Association.

Uncle Robert had to have
a drink while shaving. May   5
there be no bloodshed in your house
this morning of my father's death
and no unkept appearance
in the living, since he has
to wear the rouge and lipstick   10
of your ceremony, mother,
for the first and last time:
father, hello and goodbye.   1963

DOROTHY PARKER

Comment

Oh, life is a glorious cycle of song,
A medley of extemporanea;
And love is a thing that can never go wrong;
And I am Marie of Rumania.   1926

SIR WALTER RALEGH

The Author's Epitaph, Made By Himself

Even such is time, which takes in trust
Our youth, our joys, and all we have,
And pays us but with age and dust,
Who in the dark and silent grave
When we have wandered all our ways   5
Shuts up the story of our days,
And from which earth, and grave, and dust
The Lord shall raise me up, I trust.   1628

CAROLYN FORCHÉ

Reunion

Just as he changes himself, in the end eternity changes him.
— MALLARMÉ

On the phonograph, the voice
of a woman already dead for three

decades, singing of a man
who could make her do anything.
On the table, two fragile
5   glasses of black wine,
a bottle wrapped in its towel.
It is that room, the one
we took in every city, it is
as I remember: the bed, a block
10   of moonlight and pillows.
My fingernails, pecks of light
on your thighs.
The stink of the fire escape.
The wet butts of cigarettes
15   you crushed one after another.
How I watched the morning come
as you slept, more my son
than a man ten years older.
How my breasts feel, years
20   later, the tongues swishing
in my dress, some yours, some
left by other men.
Since then, I have always
wakened first, I have learned
25   to leave a bed without being
seen and have stood
at the washbasins, wiping oil
and salt from my skin,
staring at the cupped water
30   in my two hands.
I have kept everything
you whispered to me then.
I can remember it now as I see you
again, how much tenderness we could
35   wedge between a stairwell
and a police lock, or as it was,
as it still is, in the voice
of a woman singing of a man
40   who could make her do anything.   1981

APHRA BEHN

On Her Loving Two Equally

I

How strong does my passion flow,
Divided equally twixt[4] two?
Damon had ne'er subdued my heart
Had not Alexis took his part;
Nor could Alexis powerful prove,   5
Without my Damon's aid, to gain my love.

II

When my Alexis present is,
Then I for Damon sigh and mourn;
But when Alexis I do miss,
Damon gains nothing but my scorn.   10
But if it chance they both are by,
For both alike I languish, sigh, and die.

III

Cure then, thou mighty wingéd god,[5]
This restless fever in my blood;
One golden-pointed dart take back: 15
But which, O Cupid, wilt thou take?
If Damon's, all my hopes are crossed;
Or that of my Alexis, I am lost.   1684

ROBERT HAYDEN

Those Winter Sundays

Sundays too my father got up early
and put his clothes on in the blueblack cold,
then with cracked hands that ached
from labor in the weekday weather made
banked fires blaze. No one ever thanked him.   5

I'd wake and hear the cold splintering, breaking.
When the rooms were warm, he'd call,
and slowly I would rise and dress,
fearing the chronic angers of that house,

---

4. Between. **5.** Cupid, who, according to myth, shot darts of lead and of gold at the hearts of
lovers, corresponding to false love and true love, respectively.

10   Speaking indifferently to him,
who had driven out the cold
and polished my good shoes as well.
What did I know, what did I know
of love's austere and lonely offices?

1966

SYLVIA PLATH

Daddy

You do not do, you do not do
Any more, black shoe
In which I have lived like a foot
For thirty years, poor and white,
5   Barely daring to breathe or Achoo.

Daddy, I have had to kill you.
You died before I had time—
Marble-heavy, a bag full of God,
Ghastly statue with one gray toe
10   Big as a Frisco seal

And a head in the freakish Atlantic
Where it pours bean green over blue
In the waters off beautiful Nauset.[6]
I used to pray to recover you.
15   Ach, du.[7]

In the German tongue, in the Polish town
Scraped flat by the roller
Of wars, wars, wars.
But the name of the town is common.
20   My Polack friend

Says there are a dozen or two.
So I never could tell where you
Put your foot, your root,
I never could talk to you.
25   The tongue stuck in my jaw.

It stuck in a barb wire snare.
Ich, ich, ich, ich,
I could hardly speak.
I thought every German was you.
30   And the language obscene

---

6. An inlet on Cape Cod.   **7.** "Oh, you" in German. Plath often portrays herself as Jewish and her oppressors as German. *Ich* (below): German for "I."   **8.** Sites of World War II German death

An engine, an engine
Chuffing me off like a Jew.
A Jew to Dachau, Auschwitz, Belsen.[8]
I began to talk like a Jew.
I think I may well be a Jew.   35

The snows of the Tyrol,[9] the clear beer of Vienna
Are not very pure or true.
With my gypsy-ancestress and my weird luck
And my Taroc[1] pack and my Taroc pack
I may be a bit of a Jew.   40

I have always been scared of *you*,
With your Luftwaffe,[2] your gobbledygoo.
And your neat moustache
And your Aryan eye, bright blue.
Panzer-man, panzer-man, O You—   45

Not God but a swastika
So black no sky could squeak through.
Every woman adores a Fascist,
The boot in the face, the brute
Brute heart of a brute like you.   50

You stand at the blackboard, daddy,
In the picture I have of you,
A cleft in your chin instead of your foot
But no less a devil for that, no not
Any less the black man who   55

Bit my pretty red heart in two.
I was ten when they buried you.
At twenty I tried to die
And get back, back, back to you.
I thought even the bones would do   60

But they pulled me out of the sack,
And they stuck me together with glue.
And then I knew what to do.
I made a model of you,
A man in black with a Meinkampf[3] look   65

And a love of the rack and the screw.
And I said I do, I do.
So daddy, I'm finally through.
The black telephone's off at the root,
The voices just can't worm through.   70

camps.   9. Alpine region in Austria and northern Italy. The snow there is, legendarily, as pure as
the beer is clear in Vienna.   1. Tarot, playing cards used mainly for fortune-telling.   2. German air force.   3. The title of Adolf Hitler's autobiography and manifesto (1925–27); German for
"my struggle."

If I've killed one man, I've killed two—
The vampire who said he was you
And drank my blood for a year,
Seven years, if you want to know.
Daddy, you can lie back now.

There's a stake in your fat black heart
And the villagers never liked you.
They are dancing and stamping on you.
They always *knew* it was you.
Daddy, daddy, you bastard, I'm through.

1966

SUSAN MUSGRAVE

You Didn't Fit

for my father

You wouldn't fit in your coffin
but to me it was no surprise.
All your life you had never fit in
anywhere; you saw no reason to
begin fitting now.

When I was little I remember
a sheriff coming. You were
taken to court because your
false teeth didn't fit and you
wouldn't pay the dentist. It was
your third set, you said none of them
fit properly. I was afraid then
that something would take you from me
as it has done now: death
with a bright face and teeth that
fit perfectly.

A human smile that shuts me out.
The Court, I remember, returned
your teeth, now marked an exhibit.
You were dismissed with costs—
I never understood. The teeth were
terrible. We liked you better
without them.

We didn't fit, either, into your
life or your loneliness, though you

tried, and we did too. Once
I wanted to marry you, and then left;
I'm still the child who won't fit
into the arms of anyone, but is
always reaching.   30

I was awkward for years, my bones
didn't fit in my body but stuck out
like my heart—people used to comment
on it. They said I was very good
at office parties where you took me   35
and let others do the talking—the
crude jokes, the corny men—I saw
how they hurt you and I loved you
harder than ever.

Because neither of us fit. Later you   40
blamed me, said "You must fit in,"
but I didn't and I still think
it made you secretly happy.

Like I am now: you won't fit in your
coffin. My mother, after a life   45
of it, says, "This is the last straw."
And it is. We're all clutching.   1985

JONATHAN SWIFT

A Description of a City Shower

    Careful observers may foretell the hour
(By sure prognostics) when to dread a shower:
While rain depends,[4] the pensive cat gives o'er
Her frolics, and pursues her tail no more
Returning home at night, you'll find the sink[5]   5
Strike your offended sense with double stink.
If you be wise, then go not far to dine;
You'll spend in coach hire more than save in wine.
A coming shower your shooting corns presage,
Old achés throb, your hollow tooth will rage.   10
Sauntering in coffeehouse is Dulman[6] seen;
He damns the climate and complains of spleen.
    Meanwhile the South, rising with dabbled wings,
A sable cloud athwart the welkin flings,
That swilled more liquor than it could contain,   15
And, like a drunkard, gives it up again.

---

4. Impends, is imminent.　　**5.** Sewer.　　**6.** A type name (from "dull man").

Brisk Susan whips her linen from the rope,
While the first drizzling shower is borne aslope:
Such is that sprinkling which some careless quean[7]
20 Flirts on you from her mop, but not so clean:
You fly, invoke the gods; then turning, stop
To rail; she singing, still whirls on her mop.
Not yet the dust had shunned the unequal strife,
But, aided by the wind, fought still for life,
25 And wafted with its foe by violent gust,
'Twas doubtful which was rain and which was dust.
Ah! where must needy poet seek for aid,
When dust and rain at once his coat invade?
Sole coat, where dust cemented by the rain
30 Erects the nap, and leaves a mingled stain.
      Now in contiguous drops the flood comes down,
Threatening with deluge this devoted town.
To shops in crowds the daggled females fly,
Pretend to cheapen[8] goods, but nothing buy.
35 The Templar spruce, while every spout's abroach,[9]
Stays till 'tis fair, yet seems to call a coach.
The tucked-up sempstress walks with hasty strides,
While streams run down her oiled umbrella's sides.
Here various kinds, by various fortunes led,
40 Commence acquaintance underneath a shed.
Triumphant Tories and desponding Whigs
Forget their feuds, and join to save their wigs.
Boxed in a chair the beau impatient sits,
While spouts run clattering o'er the roof by fits,
45 And ever and anon with frightful din
The leather sounds; he trembles from within.
So when Troy chairmen bore the wooden steed,
Pregnant with Greeks impatient to be freed
(Those bully Greeks, who, as the moderns do,
50 Instead of paying chairmen, run them through),[1]
Laocoön struck the outside with his spear,
And each imprisoned hero quaked for fear[2]
      Now from all parts the swelling kennels[3] flow,
And bear their trophies with them as they go:
55 Filth of all hues and odors seem to tell
What street they sailed from, by their sight and smell.
They, as each torrent drives with rapid force,
From Smithfield or St. Pulchre's shape their course,
And in huge confluence joined at Snow Hill ridge,

7. Wench, slut.   8. Bargain for. *Daggled*: spattered with mud.   9. Pouring out water. *The Templar*: a young man studying law.   1. Run them through with swords.   2. *The Aeneid*, II, 40–53.   3. Open gutters in the middle of the street.

Fall from the conduit prone to Holborn Bridge.[4]   60
Sweepings from butchers' stalls, dung, guts, and blood,
Drowned puppies, stinking sprats[5] all drenched in mud,
Dead cats, and turnip tops, come tumbling down the flood.   1710

THOMAS GRAY

Elegy Written in a Country Churchyard

The curfew tolls the knell of parting day,
    The lowing herd wind slowly o'er the lea,
The plowman homeward plods his weary way,
    And leaves the world to darkness and to me.

Now fades the glimmering landscape on the sight,   5
    And all the air a solemn stillness holds,
Save where the beetle wheels his droning flight,
    And drowsy tinklings lull the distant folds;

Save that from yonder ivy-mantled tower
    The moping owl does to the moon complain   10
Of such, as wandering near her secret bower,
    Molest her ancient solitary reign.

Beneath those rugged elms, that yew tree's shade,
    Where heaves the turf in many a moldering heap,
Each in his narrow cell forever laid,   15
    The rude[6] forefathers of the hamlet sleep.

The breezy call of incense-breathing Morn,
    The swallow twittering from the straw-built shed,
The cock's shrill clarion, or the echoing horn,[7]
    No more shall rouse them from their lowly bed.   20

For them no more the blazing hearth shall burn,
    Or busy housewife ply her evening care;
No children run to lisp their sire's return,
    Or climb his knees the envied kiss to share.

Oft did the harvest to their sickle yield,   25
    Their furrow oft the stubborn glebe[8] has broke;
How jocund did they drive their team afield!
    How bowed the woods beneath their sturdy stroke!

Let not Ambition mock their useful toil,
    Their homely joys, and destiny obscure;   30

4. *Smithfield:* site of cattle and sheep markets at the foot of Snow Hill. *St. Pulchre's:* church of St.
Sepulchre. Holborn Conduit drained into a foul-smelling sewer at Holborn Bridge.   5. Small
herrings.   6. Unlearned.   7. The hunter's horn.   8. Soil.

Nor Grandeur hear with a disdainful smile
   The short and simple annals of the poor.

The boast of heraldry,[9] the pomp of power,
   And all that beauty, all that wealth e'er gave,
35   Awaits alike the inevitable hour.
   The paths of glory lead but to the grave.

Nor you, ye proud, impute to these the fault,
   If Memory o'er their tomb no trophies[1] raise,
Where through the long-drawn aisle and fretted[2] vault
40   The pealing anthem swells the note of praise

Can storied urn or animated[3] bust
   Back to its mansion call the fleeting breath?
Can Honor's voice provoke the silent dust,
   Or Flattery soothe the dull cold ear of Death?

45 Perhaps in this neglected spot is laid
   Some heart once pregnant with celestial fire;
Hands that the rod of empire might have swayed,
   Or waked to ecstasy the living lyre.

But Knowledge to their eyes her ample page
50   Rich with the spoils of time did ne'er unroll;
Chill Penury repressed their noble rage,
   And froze the genial current of the soul.

Full many a gem of purest ray serene,
   The dark unfathomed caves of ocean bear:
55 Full many a flower is born to blush unseen,
   And waste its sweetness on the desert air.

Some village Hampden,[4] that with dauntless breast
   The little tyrant of his fields withstood;
Some mute inglorious Milton here may rest,
60   Some Cromwell guiltless of his country's blood.

The applause of listening senates to command,
   The threats of pain and ruin to despise,
To scatter plenty o'er a smiling land,
   And read their history in a nation's eyes,

65   Their lot forbade: nor circumscribed alone
   Their growing virtues, but their crimes confined;
Forbade to wade through slaughter to a throne,
   And shut the gates of mercy on mankind,

---

9. Noble birth.   **1.** An ornamental or symbolic group of figures depicting the achievements of the deceased.   **2.** Decorated with intersecting lines in relief.   **3.** Lifelike. *Storied urn:* a funeral urn with an epitaph or pictured story inscribed on it.   **4.** John Hampden (1594–1643), who, both as a private citizen and as a member of Parliament, zealously defended the rights of the people against the autocratic policies of Charles I.

The struggling pangs of conscious truth to hide,
   To quench the blushes of ingenuous shame,   70
Or heap the shrine of Luxury and Pride
   With incense kindled at the Muse's flame.

Far from the madding crowd's ignoble strife,
   Their sober wishes never learned to stray;
Along the cool sequestered vale of life   75
   They kept the noiseless tenor of their way.

Yet even these bones from insult to protect
   Some frail memorial still erected nigh,
With uncouth rhymes and shapeless sculpture decked,[5]
   Implores the passing tribute of a sigh.   80

Their name, their years, spelt by the unlettered Muse,
   The place of fame and elegy supply:
And many a holy text around she strews,
   That teach the rustic moralist to die.

For who to dumb Forgetfulness a prey,   85
   This pleasing anxious being e'er resigned,
Left the warm precincts of the cheerful day,
   Nor cast one longing lingering look behind?

On some fond breast the parting soul relies,
   Some pious drops the closing eye requires;   90
Even from the tomb the voice of Nature cries,
   Even in our ashes live their wonted fires.

For thee, who mindful of the unhonored dead
   Dost in these lines their artless tale relate;
If chance, by lonely contemplation led,   95
   Some kindred spirit shall inquire thy fate,

Haply some hoary-headed swain may say,
   "Oft have we seen him at the peep of dawn
Brushing with hasty steps the dews away
   To meet the sun upon the upland lawn.   100

"There at the foot of yonder nodding beech
   That wreathes its old fantastic roots so high,
His listless length at noontide would he stretch,
   And pore upon the brook that babbles by.

"Hard by yon wood, now smiling as in scorn,   105
   Muttering his wayward fancies he would rove,
Now drooping, woeful wan, like one forlorn,
   Or crazed with care, or crossed in hopeless love.

"One morn I missed him on the customed hill,
   Along the heath and near his favorite tree;   110

---

5. Cf. "the storied urn or animated bust" dedicated inside the church to "the proud" (line 41).

3. What attitude does "Elegy" take toward Aunt Irene? toward Uncle Robert? toward the mother? toward the father? How can you tell about the attitudes toward each? What individual words or factual details help to suggest the attitudes? Is "Elegy" an appropriate title for the poem? Why?

4. In Blake's poem "The Tyger," why is the "Tyger" described as "burning bright"? What is implied by such a strong visual image? What different attitudes does the poem imply toward the tiger? Are the attitudes contradictory? How do you feel about the tiger by the end of the poem?

WRITING SUGGESTIONS

1. Paraphrase—that is, put into different words line by line and stanza by stanza—Behn's "On Her Loving Two Equally." Summarize the poem's basic statement in one sentence. How accurately do your paraphrase and summary represent the tone of the poem?

2. Compare the tone of voice used in reading "Leaving the Motel" aloud to that in "Reunion." Pick out three or four key words from each poem that seem to help control the tone. Then, concentrating on the words you have isolated, write a short essay, of no more than 600 words, in which you compare the tones of the two poems.

2 SPEAKER

P oems are personal. The thoughts and feelings they express belong to a
specific person, and however general or universal their sentiments
seem to be, poems come to us as the expression of an individual
human voice. That voice is often the voice of the poet. But not always. Poets
sometimes create a "character" just as writers of fiction or drama do—people
who speak for them only indirectly. A character may, in fact, be very different
from the poet, just as a character in a play or story is different from the author,
and that person, the **speaker** of the poem, may express ideas or feelings very different from the poet's own. In the following poem, *two* individual voices in fact
speak, and it is clear that, rather than himself speaking directly to us, the poet,
Thomas Hardy, has chosen to create two speakers, both female, each of whom
has a distinctive voice, personality, and character.

THOMAS HARDY

The Ruined Maid

"O 'Melia,[1] my dear, this does everything crown!
Who could have supposed I should meet you in Town?
And whence such fair garments, such prosperi-ty?"—
"O didn't you know I'd been ruined?" said she.

—"You left us in tatters, without shoes or socks,   5
Tired of digging potatoes, and spudding up docks;[2]
And now you've gay bracelets and bright feathers three!"—
"Yes: that's how we dress when we're ruined," said she.

—"At home in the barton[3] you said 'thee' and 'thou,'
And 'thik oon,' and 'theäs oon,' and 't'other'; but now   10
Your talking quite fits 'ee for high compa-ny!"—
"Some polish is gained with one's ruin," said she.

—"Your hands were like paws then, your face blue and bleak
But now I'm bewitched by your delicate cheek,
And your little gloves fit as on any la-dy!"—   15
"We never do work when we're ruined," said she.

---

1. Short for Amelia.   2. Spading up weeds.   3. Farmyard.

—"You used to call home-life a hag-ridden dream,
And you'd sigh, and you'd sock;[4] but at present you seem
To know not of megrims[5] or melancho-ly!"—
"True. One's pretty lively when ruined," said she.

20

—"I wish I had feathers, a fine sweeping gown,
And a delicate face, and could strut about Town!"—
"My dear—a raw country girl, such as you be,
Cannot quite expect that. You ain't ruined," said she.

1866

The first voice, that of a young woman who has remained back on the farm, is designated typographically (that is, by the way the poem is printed): there are dashes at the beginning and end of each of her speeches. She speaks the first part of each stanza, usually the first three lines. The second young woman, a companion and co-worker on the farm in years gone by, regularly gets the last line in each stanza (and in the last stanza, two lines), so it is easy to tell who is talking at every point. Also, the two speakers are just as clearly distinguished by what they say, how they say it, and what sort of person each proves to be. The nameless stay-at-home shows little knowledge of the world, and everything surprises her: seeing her former companion at all, but especially seeing her well clothed, cheerful, and polished; and as the poem develops she shows increasing envy of her more worldly friend. She is the "raw country girl" (line 23) that the other speaker says she is, and she still speaks the country dialect ("fits 'ee," line 11, for example) that she notices her friend has lost (lines 9–11). The "ruined" young woman ('Melia), on the other hand, says little except to keep repeating the refrain about having been ruined, but even the slight variations she plays on that theme suggest her sophistication and amusement at her farm friend, although she still uses a rural "ain't" at the end. We are not told the full story of their lives (was the ruined young woman thrown out? did she run away from home or work?), but we know enough (that they've been separated for some time, that the stay-at-home did not know where the other had gone) to allow the dialogue to articulate the contrast between them. The style of speech of each speaker then does the rest.

It is equally obvious that there is a speaker (or, in this case, actually a singer) in stanzas 2 through 9 of this poem:

4. Deliver angry blows.　　5. Migraine headaches.

X. J. KENNEDY

In a Prominent Bar in Secaucus One Day

To the tune of "The Old Orange Flute" or the tune of
"Sweet Betsy from Pike"

In a prominent bar in Secaucus[6] one day
Rose a lady in skunk with a topheavy sway,
Raised a knobby red finger—all turned from their beer—
While with eyes bright as snowcrust she sang high and clear:

"Now who of you'd think from an eyeload of me   5
That I once was a lady as proud as could be?
Oh I'd never sit down by a tumbledown drunk
If it wasn't, my dears, for the high cost of junk.

"All the gents used to swear that the white of my calf
Beat the down of a swan by a length and a half.   10
In the kerchief of linen I caught to my nose
Ah, there never fell snot, but a little gold rose.

"I had seven gold teeth and a toothpick of gold.
My Virginia cheroot was a leaf of it rolled
And I'd light it each time with a thousand in cash—   15
Why the bums used to fight if I flicked them an ash.

"Once the toast of the Biltmore,[7] the belle of the Taft,
I would drink bottle beer at the Drake, never draft,
And dine at the Astor on Salisbury steak
With a clean tablecloth for each bite I did take.   20

"In a car like the Roxy[8] I'd roll to the track,
A steel-guitar trio, a bar in the back,
And the wheels made no noise, they turned over so fast,
Still it took you ten minutes to see me go past.

"When the horses bowed down to me that I might choose,   25
I bet on them all, for I hated to lose.
Now I'm saddled each night for my butter and eggs
And the broken threads race down the backs of my legs.

"Let you hold in mind, girls, that your beauty must pass
Like a lovely white clover that rusts with its grass.   30
Keep your bottoms off barstools and marry you young
Or be left—an old barrel with many a bung.

6. A small town on the Hackensack River in New Jersey, a few miles west of Manhattan.   7. Like the Taft, Drake, and Astor, a once-fashionable New York hotel.   8. A luxurious old New York theater and movie house, the site of many "world premieres" in the heyday of Hollywood.

"For when time takes you out for a spin in his car
You'll be hard-pressed to stop him from going too far
35   And be left by the roadside, for all your good deeds,
Two toadstools for tits and a face full of weeds."

All the house raised a cheer, but the man at the bar
Made a phonecall and up pulled a red patrol car
And she blew us a kiss as they copped her away
40   From that prominent bar in Secaucus, N.J.   1961

  Again, we learn about the character primarily through her own words,
although we don't have to believe everything she tells us about her past. From
her introduction in the first stanza we get some general notion of her appearance and condition, but it is she who tells us that she is a junkie (line 8), a
prostitute (line 27), and that her face and figure are pretty well shot (lines 32,
36). That information could make her a sad case, and the poem might lament
her state or allow her to lament it, but instead the poem presents her in a light
and friendly way. She is anxious to give advice and sound moral (line 31, for
example), but she's also enormously cheerful about herself, and her spirit
repeatedly bursts through her song. Her performance gives her a lot of pleasure
as she exaggerates outrageously about her former luxury and prominence, and
even her departure in a patrol car she chooses to treat as a grand exit, throwing
a kiss to her audience. The comedy is bittersweet, perhaps, but she is allowed
to present herself, through her own words and attitudes, as a likable character—someone who has survived life's disappointments and retained her dignity
and her sense of theatricality. The glorious fiction of her life, narrated with
energy and polish in the manner of a practiced and accomplished liar, betrays
some rather naive notions of good taste and luxurious living (lines 18–26). But
this "lady in skunk" has a picturesque and engaging style, a refreshing sense of
humor about herself, and a flair for drama. Like the cheap fur she wears, her
experiences in what she considers high life satisfy her sense of style and celebration. The self-portrait accumulates, almost completely through how she talks
about herself, and the poet develops our attitude toward her by allowing her to
recount her story herself, in her own words—or rather in words chosen for her
by the author.

  The following poem uses the idea of speaker in a very different way and for
quite different tonal purposes.

ADRIENNE RICH

Letters in the Family

I: Catalonia, 1936

Dear Parents:
             I'm the daughter
you didn't bless when she left,
an unmarried woman wearing a khaki knapsack
with a poor mark in Spanish.
                          I'm writing now
from a plaster-dusted desk in a town   5
pocked street by street with hand grenades,
some of them, dear ones, thrown by me.
This is a school: the children are at war.
You don't need honors in schoolroom Spanish here
to be of use and my right arm   10
's as strong as anyone's. I sometimes think
all languages are spoken here,
even mine, which you got zero in.
Don't worry. Don't try to write. I'm happy,
if you could know it.
                    Rochelle.   15

II: Yugoslavia, 1944[9]

Dear Chana,
          where are you now?
Am sending this pocket-to-pocket
(though we both know pockets we'd hate to lie in).
They showed me that poem you gave Reuven,
about the match: 20
Chana, you know, I never was
for martyrdom. I thought we'd try our best,
ragtag mission that we were,
then clear out if the signals looked too bad.
Something in you drives things ahead for me   25
but if I can I mean to stay alive.
We're none of us giants, you know,
just small, frail, inexperienced romantic people.

---

9. "See *Hannah Senesh: Her Life and Diary* (New York: Schocken, 1973). Born in Budapest, 1921, Hannah Senesh became a Zionist and emigrated to Palestine at the age of eighteen; her mother and brother remained in Europe. In 1943, she joined an expedition of Jews who trained under the British to parachute behind Nazi lines in Europe and connect with the partisan underground, to rescue Jews in Hungary, Romania, and Czechoslovakia. She was arrested by the Nazis, imprisoned, tortured, and executed in November 1944. Like the other letter-writers, 'Esther' is an imagined person.
  See also Ruth Whitman's long poem, *The Testing of Hannah Senesh* (Detroit: Wayne State University Press, 1986)." (Rich's note)

But there are things we learn.
You know the sudden suck of empty space
between the jump and the ripcord pull?
I hate it. I hate it so,
I've hated you for your dropping
ecstatically in free-fall, in the training,
your look, dragged on the ground, of knowing
precisely why you were there.
My mother's
still in Palestine. And yours
still there in Hungary. Well, there we are.
When this is over—
I'm
your earthbound friend to the end, still yours—
Esther.

III: Southern Africa, 1986

Dear children:
We've been walking nights
a long time over rough terrain,
sometimes through marshes. Days we hide
under what bushes we can find.
Our stars steer us. I write
on my knee by a river with a weary hand,
and the weariness will come through
this letter that should tell you
nothing but love. I can't say where we are,
what weeds are in bloom, what birds cry at dawn.
The less you know the safer.
But not to know how you are going on—
Matile's earache, Emma's lessons, those tell-tale
eyes and tongues, so quick—are you remembering
to be brave and wise and strong?
At the end of this hard road
we'll sit all together at one meal
and I'll tell you everything: the names
of our comrades, how the letters
were routed to you, why I left.
And I'll stop and say, "Now you,
grown so big, how was it for you, those times?
Look, I know you in detail, every inch of each
sweet body, haven't I washed and dried you
a thousand times?"
And we'll eat and tell our stories
together. That is my reason.
Ma.

1989

As in "The Ruined Maid," this poem uses different voices, and here they are clearly distinguished as different "historical" characters—Rochelle, Esther, and "Ma," women from three separate places and times who in letter form tell their own stories. In each case, the individual story is part of some larger historical moment, and although all three characters are (as the author's footnote points out) fictional, the three stories together present a kind of history of female heroism in difficult cultural moments.

Read the poem aloud and notice how different in tone the three voices sound; each woman has distinctive expressions and syntax of her own. All are in part defined by their relationships to families left behind, but all are defined even more fully by their own idealistic determination to resist the larger social and political forces in the cultures where they are at the time they write their letters. Telling stories, the pleasure identified by the third speaker as the ultimate purpose of her actions (lines 56–62), is important to all three speakers as a way of defining themselves in relation to their families; to the poem, the telling of separate stories by the different speakers becomes the collective means to exemplify the power of women in history in action.

Some speakers in poems are not, however, nearly so heroic or attractive, and some poems create a speaker who makes us dislike him or her, also because of what the poet makes him or her say, as the following poem does. Here the speaker, as the title implies, is a monk, but he shows himself to be most unmonklike: mean, self-righteous, and despicable.

ROBERT BROWNING

Soliloquy of the Spanish Cloister[1]

> Gr-r-r—there go, my heart's abhorrence!
>   Water your damned flower-pots, do!
> If hate killed men, Brother Lawrence,
>   God's blood, would not mine kill you!
> What? your myrtle-bush wants trimming?   5
>   Oh, that rose has prior claims—
> Needs its leaden vase filled brimming?
>   Hell dry you up with its flames!
>
> At the meal we sit together:
>   *Salve tibi!*[2] I must hear   10
> Wish talk of the kind of weather,
>   Sort of season, time of year:

---

1. Monastery.   2. "Hail to thee" (Latin). Italics usually indicate the words of Brother Lawrence.

Not a plenteous cork-crop: scarcely
    Dare we hope oak-galls,[3] I doubt:
What's the Latin name for "parsley"?
    What's the Greek name for Swine's Snout?

Whew! We'll have our platter burnished,
    Laid with care on our own shelf!
With a fire-new spoon we're furnished,
    And a goblet for ourself,
Rinsed like something sacrificial
    Ere 'tis fit to touch our chaps[4]—
Marked with L. for our initial!
    (He-he! There his lily snaps!)

Saint, forsooth! While brown Dolores
    —Squats outside the Convent bank
With Sanchicha, telling stories,
    Steeping tresses in the tank,
Blue-black, lustrous, thick like horsehairs,
    —Can't I see his dead eye glow,
Bright as 'twere a Barbary corsair's?[5]
    (That is, if he'd let it show!)

When he finishes refection,[6]
    Knife and fork he never lays
Cross-wise, to my recollection,
    As do I, in Jesu's praise.
I the Trinity illustrate,
    Drinking watered orange-pulp—
In three sips the Arian[7] frustrate;
    —While he drains his at one gulp.

Oh, those melons? If he's able
    We're to have a feast! so nice!
One goes to the Abbot's table,
    All of us get each a slice.
How go on your flowers? None double?
    Not one fruit-sort can you spy?
Strange!—And I, too, at such trouble,
    —Keep them close-nipped on the sly!

There's a great text in Galatians,
    Once you trip on it, entails
Twenty-nine distinct damnations,[8]
    One sure, if another fails:
If I trip him just a-dying,
    Sure of heaven as sure can be,

3. Abnormal growth on oak trees, used for tanning.   4. Jaws.   5. African pirate's.   6. A meal.   7. A heretical sect that denied the Trinity.   8. Galatians 5:15–23 provides a long list of possible offenses, but they do not add up to 29.

Spin him round and send him flying   55
    Off to hell, a Manichee?[9]
Or, my scrofulous French novel
    On gray paper with blunt type!
Simply glance at it, you grovel
    Hand and foot in Belial's gripe:[1]   60
If I double down its pages
    At the woeful sixteenth print,
When he gathers his greengages,
    Ope a sieve and slip it in't?

Or, there's Satan!—one might venture   65
    ledge one's soul to him, yet leave
Such a flaw in the indenture
    –As he'd miss till, past retrieve,
Blasted lay that rose-acacia
    We're so proud of! *Hy, Zy, Hine* . . .[2]   70
'St, there's Vespers! *Plena gratiâ*
    Ave, Virgo.[3] Gr-r-r—you swine!

                                            1842

Not many poems begin with a growl, and this harsh sound turns out to be
fair warning that we are about to get to know a real beast, even though he is in
the clothing of a religious man. In line 1, he has already shown himself to hold
a most uncharitable attitude toward his fellow monk, Brother Lawrence, and
by line 4 he has uttered two profanities and admitted his intense feelings of
hatred and vengefulness. His ranting and roaring is full of exclamation points
(four in the first stanza!), and he reveals his own personality and character
when he imagines curses and unflattering nicknames for Brother Lawrence or
plots malicious jokes on him. By the end, we have accumulated no knowledge
of Brother Lawrence that makes him seem a fit target for such rage (except that
he is pious, dutiful, and pleasant—perhaps enough to make this sort of speaker
despise him), but we have discovered the speaker to be lecherous (stanza 4),
full of false piety (stanza 5), malicious in trivial matters (stanza 6), ready to use
his theological learning to sponsor damnation rather than salvation (stanza 7),
a closet reader and viewer of pornography within the monastery (stanza 8)—
even willing to risk his own soul in order to torment Brother Lawrence (last
stanza).

    The speaker is made to characterize himself; the details accrue and accu-
mulate into a fairly full portrait, and here we do not have even an opening and

9. A heretic. According to the Manichean heresy, the world was divided into the forces of good and
evil, equally powerful.   1. In the clutches of Satan.   2. Possibly the beginning of an incantation or curse.   3. The opening words of the *Ave Maria*, here reversed: "Full of grace, Hail,
Virgin" (Latin).

closing "objective" description (as in "In a Prominent Bar") or another speaker (as in "The Ruined Maid") to give us perspective. Except for the moments when the speaker mimics or parodies Brother Lawrence (usually in italic type), we have only the speaker's own words and thoughts. But that is enough; the poet has controlled them so carefully that we clearly know what he thinks of the speaker he has created—that he is a mean-spirited, vengeful hypocrite, a thoroughly disreputable and unlikable character. The whole poem has been about him and his attitudes; the point of the poem has been to characterize the speaker and develop in us a dislike of him and what he stands for—total hypocrisy.

In reading a poem like this aloud, we would want our voice to suggest all the unlikable features of a hypocrite. We would also need to suggest, through the tone of voice we used, the author's contemptuous mocking of the rage and hypocrisy, and we would want, like an actor, to create strong disapproval in the hearer. The poem's words (the ones the author has given to the speaker) clearly imply those attitudes, and we would want our voice to express them. Usually there is much more to a poem than the identification and characterization of the speaker, but in many cases it is necessary to identify the speaker and determine his or her character before we can appreciate what else goes on in the poem. And sometimes, as here, in looking for the speaker of the poem, we come near to the center of the poem itself.

Sometimes the effect of a poem depends on our recognizing the temporal position of the speaker as well as her or his identity. The following poem, for example, quickly makes plain that a childhood experience is at the center of the action and that the speaker is female:

TESS GALLAGHER

Sudden Journey

Maybe I'm seven in the open field—
the straw-grass so high
only the top of my head makes a curve
of brown in the yellow. Rain then.
First a little. A few drops on my
wrist, the right wrist. More rain.
My shoulders, my chin. Until I'm looking up
to let my eyes take the bliss.
I open my face. Let the teeth show. I
pull my shirt down past the collar-bones.
I'm still a boy under my breast spots.

I can drink anywhere. The rain. My
skin shattering. Up suddenly, needing
to gulp, turning with my tongue, my arms out
running, running in the hard, cold plenitude   15
of all those who reach earth by falling.   1984

The sense of adventure and wonder here has a lot to do with the childlike
syntax and words at the beginning of the poem. Sentences are short, observations direct and simple. The rain becomes exciting and blissful and totally
absorbing as the child's actions and reactions take over the poem in lines 2–13.
But not all of the poem takes place in a child's mind in spite of the precise and
impressive re-creation of childish responses and feelings. The opening line
makes clear that we are sliding into a supposition of the past; "maybe I'm
seven" makes clear that we, as conspiring adults, are pretending ourselves into
earlier time. And at the end the word "plenitude"—crucial to interpreting the
poem's full effect and meaning—makes clear that we are finding an adult perspective on the incident. Elsewhere, too, the adult world gives the incident
meaning. In line 12, for example, the joke about being able to drink anywhere
depends on an adult sense of what being a boy might mean. The "journey" of
the poem's title is not only the little girl's running in the rain but also the adult
movement into a past re-created and newly understood.

The speaker in the following poem positions herself very differently, but we
do not get a very full sense of her until the poem is well along. As you read, try
to imitate the tone of voice you think this kind of person would use. Exactly
when do you begin to feel that you know what she is like?

DOROTHY PARKER

A Certain Lady

Oh, I can smile for you, and tilt my head,
    And drink your rushing words with eager lips,
And paint my mouth for you a fragrant red,
    And trace your brows with tutored finger-tips.
When you rehearse your list of loves to me,   5
    Oh, I can laugh and marvel, rapturous-eyed.
And you laugh back, nor can you ever see
    The thousand little deaths my heart has died.
And you believe, so well I know my part,
    That I am gay as morning, light as snow,   10
And all the straining things within my heart
    You'll never know.

Oh, I can laugh and listen, when we meet,
   And you bring tales of fresh adventurings—
Of ladies delicately indiscreet,
   Of lingering hands, and gently whispered things.
And you are pleased with me, and strive anew
   To sing me sagas of your late delights.
Thus do you want me—marveling, gay, and true—
   Nor do you see my staring eyes of nights.
And when, in search of novelty, you stray,
   Oh, I can kiss you blithely as you go . . .
And what goes on, my love, while you're away,
   You'll never know.   1937

To whom does the speaker seem to be talking? What sort of person is he? How do you feel about him? Which habits and attitudes of his do you like least? How soon can you tell that the speaker is not altogether happy about his conversation and conduct? In what tone of voice would you read the first 22 lines aloud? What attitude would you try to express toward the person spoken to? What tone would you use for the last two lines? How would you describe the speaker's personality? What aspects of her behavior are most crucial to the poem's effect?

It is easy to assume that the speaker in a poem is an extension of the poet. Is the speaker in this poem Dorothy Parker? Maybe. A lot of Parker's poems present a similar world-weary posture and a kind of cynicism about romantic love (look, for example, at "Comment" on p. 687). But the poem is hardly an example of self-revelation, a giving away of personal secrets. If it were, it would be silly, not to say risky, to address her lover in a way that gives damaging facts about a pose she has been so careful to set up.

In poems such as "The Ruined Maid," "In a Prominent Bar," and "Soliloquy of the Spanish Cloister," we are in no danger of mistaking the speaker for the poet, once we have recognized that poets may create speakers who participate in specific situations much as in fiction or drama. When there is a pointed discrepancy between the speaker and what we know of the poet— when the speaker is a woman, for example, and the poet is a man—we know we have a created speaker to contend with and that the point (or at least *one* point) in the poem is to observe the characterization carefully. In "A Certain Lady" we may be less sure, and in other poems the discrepancy between speaker and poet may be even more uncertain. What are we to make, for example, of the speaker in "Woodchucks" in the previous chapter? Is that speaker the real Maxine Kumin? At best (without knowing something quite specific about the author) we can only say "maybe" to that question. What we can be sure of is the sort of person the speaker is portrayed to be—someone (man? or woman?) surprised to discover feelings and attitudes that contradict values apparently held confidently. And that is exactly what we need to know for the poem to have its effect.

A similar kind of self-mocking of the speaker is present in the following poem, but here the mockery is put to less revelatory, more comic ends.

A. R. AMMONS

Needs

I want something suited to my special needs
I want chrome hubcaps, pin-on attachments
and year round use year after year
I want a workhorse with smooth uniform cut,
    dozer blade and snow blade & deluxe steering   5
    wheel
I want something to mow, throw snow, tow
    and sow with
I want precision reel blades
I want a console styled dashboard   10
I want an easy spintype recoil starter
I want combination bevel and spur gears, 14
    gauge stamped steel housing and
    washable foam element air cleaner
I want a pivoting front axle and extrawide   15
    turf tires
I want an inch of foam rubber inside a vinyl
    covering
and especially if it's not too much, if I
can deserve it, even if I can't pay for it   20
I want to mow while riding.   1970

The poet here may be teasing himself about his desire for comfort and ease—and showing how readily advertisements and catalog descriptions manipulate us. But the speaker doesn't have to be the author for the teasing to work. In fact, the effect is to tease those attitudes no matter who holds them by teasing a speaker who illustrates the attitudes. It doesn't matter to the poem whether the speaker is the poet himself or some totally invented character. If the speaker is a version of the poet himself—perhaps a *side* of his personality that he is exploring—the portrait is still fictional in an important sense. The poem presents not a whole human being (*no* poem could do that) but only a version of him—a mood perhaps, an aspect, an attitude, a part of that person. The poet presents someone with an obsession, in this case a small and not very damaging one, and allows him to spout phrases as if he were reciting from an ad or a sales catalog. The "portrait" is made more comic by a clear sense the poem projects that what we have is only a part of the person, an interest grown too intense, gone askew, gotten out of proportion, something that happens to most of us from time to time. All we know about the speaker is that he has a one-track mind, that he is obsessed by his own luxurious comfort. He may not even be a "he": there is nothing in the poem that makes us certain that the speaker is male. It is customary to think of the speaker in a poem written by a man as "he" and in a poem written by a woman as "she" (as in Maxine Kumin's "Woodchucks") unless the poem presents contrary evidence, but it is merely a convenience, a habit, nothing more.

Even when poets present themselves as if they were speaking directly to us in their own voices, their poems present only a partial portrait, something considerably less than the full personality and character of the poet. Even when there is not an obviously created character—someone with distinct characteristics that are different from those of the poet—strategies of characterization are used to present the person speaking in one way and not another. Even in a poem like the following one, which contains identifiable autobiographical details, it is still a good idea to talk of the speaker instead of the poet, although here it is probable that the poet is writing about a personal, actual experience.

WILLIAM WORDSWORTH

She Dwelt among the Untrodden Ways

> She dwelt among the untrodden ways
>   Beside the springs of Dove,[4]
> A Maid whom there were none to praise
>   And very few to love:
>
> A violet by a mossy stone
>   Half hidden from the eye!
> —Fair as a star, when only one
>   Is shining in the sky.
>
> She lived unknown, and few could know
>   When Lucy ceased to be;
> But she is in her grave, and, oh,
>   The difference to me!

5

10

1800

It is hard to say whether this poem is more about Lucy or about how the speaker feels about her death. Her simple life, far removed from fame and

4. A small stream in the Lake District in northern England, near where Wordsworth lived in Dove Cottage at Grasmere.

known only to a few, is said nevertheless to have been beautiful. We know little about her beyond her name and where she lived, in a beautiful but then-isolated section of northern England. We don't know if she was young or old, only that the speaker thinks of her as "fair" and compares her to a "violet by a mossy stone." What we do know is that the speaker is deeply pained by her death, so deeply that he is almost inarticulate with grief, lapsing into simple exclamation ("oh," line 11) and unable to articulate the "difference" that her death makes.

Did Lucy actually live? Was she a friend of the poet? We don't know; the poem doesn't tell us, and even biographers of Wordsworth are unsure. What we do know is that Wordsworth was able to represent grief over the death very powerfully. Whether the speaker is the historical Wordsworth or not, that speaker is a major focus of the poem, and it is his feelings that the poem isolates and expresses. We need to recognize some characteristics of the speaker and be sensitive to his feelings for the poem to work.

The following poem similarly seems to draw upon an actual occurrence and present a speaker who is the poet herself.

SHARON OLDS

The Lifting

Suddenly my father lifted up his nightie, I
turned my head away but he cried out
Shar!, my nickname, so I turned and looked.
He was sitting in the high cranked-up hospital bed with the
gown up, around his neck,   5
to show me the weight he had lost. I looked
where his solid ruddy stomach had been
and I saw the skin fallen into loose
soft hairy rippled folds
lying in a pool of folds   10
down at the base of his abdomen,
the gaunt torso of a big man
who will die soon. Right away
I saw how much his hips are like mine,
the long, white angles, and then   15
how much his pelvis is shaped like my daughter's,
a chambered whelk-shell hollowed out,
I saw the folds of skin like something
poured, a thick batter, I saw
his rueful smile, the cast-up eyes as he   20
shows me his old body, he knows

25

30

I will be interested, he knows I will find him
appealing. If anyone had told me I would sit
by him and he would pull up his nightie and I would look
at him, his naked body, the thick
bud of his glans, his penis in all that
dark hair, look at him
in affection and uneasy wonder
I would not have believed it. But now I can still
see the tiny snowflakes, white and
night-blue, on the cotton of the gown as it
rises the way we were promised at death it would rise,
the veils would fall from our eyes, we would know everything.

1990

Other poems by Olds written at about the same time also recount moments in the approaching death of a father—compare, for example, "The Glass" on p. 662—and the similar situations may suggest that the poet was herself struggling with such an event. But even if we were to read enough about the poet's life to be sure that the poem was based on an actual event, we would still have to be careful about assuming that the speaker was, plainly and simply, the poet herself. It may well be that the "I" in this poem is very close to the historical Sharon Olds in 1990, but we are still well advised as readers to think of the speaker in the poem as the woman characterized specifically in the text and not necessarily as altogether identical to the poet.

The poems we have looked at in this chapter—and the group that follows at the end of the chapter—all suggest the value of beginning the reading of any poem with a simple question: Who is speaking and what do we know about him or her? Putting together the evidence that the poem presents in answer to this question can often take us a long way into the poem. For some poems, this question won't help a great deal because the speaking voice is too indistinct or the character behind the poem too scantily presented, but in many cases asking this question will lead you toward the central experience the poem offers.

▼   ▼   ▼

HENRY REED

Lessons of the War

JUDGING DISTANCES

Not only how far away, but the way that you say it
Is very important. Perhaps you may never get
The knack of judging a distance, but at least you know
How to report on a landscape: the central sector,
The right of arc and that, which we had last Tuesday,   5
    And at least you know

That maps are of time, not place, so far as the army
Happens to be concerned—the reason being,
Is one which need not delay us. Again, you know
There are three kinds of tree, three only, the fir and the poplar,   10
And those which have bushy tops to; and lastly
    That things only seem to be things.

A barn is not called a barn, to put it more plainly,
Or a field in the distance, where sheep may be safely grazing.
You must never be over-sure. You must say, when reporting: 15
At five o'clock in the central sector is a dozen
Of what appear to be animals; whatever you do,
    Don't call the bleeders *sheep*.

I am sure that's quite clear; and suppose, for the sake of example,
The one at the end, asleep, endeavors to tell us   20
What he sees over there to the west, and how far away,
After first having come to attention. There to the west,
On the fields of summer the sun and the shadows bestow
    Vestments of purple and gold.

The still white dwellings are like a mirage in the heat,   25
And under the swaying elms a man and a woman
Lie gently together. Which is, perhaps, only to say
That there is a row of houses to the left of arc,
And that under some poplars a pair of what appear to be humans
    Appear to be loving.   30

Well that, for an answer, is what we might rightly call
Moderately satisfactory only, the reason being,
Is that two things have been omitted, and those are important.
The human beings, now: in what direction are they,
And how far away, would you say? And do not forget   35
    There may be dead ground in between.

There may be dead ground in between; and I may not have got
The knack of judging a distance; I will only venture

A guess that perhaps between me and the apparent lovers,
(Who, incidentally, appear by now to have finished,)
At seven o'clock from the houses, is roughly a distance
    Of about one year and a half.

40

1946

AUDRE LORDE

Hanging Fire

I am fourteen
and my skin has betrayed me
the boy I cannot live without
still sucks his thumb
in secret
how come my knees are
always so ashy
what if I die
before morning
and momma's in the bedroom
with the door closed.

I have to learn how to dance
in time for the next party
my room is too small for me
suppose I die before graduation
they will sing sad melodies
but finally
tell the truth about me
There is nothing I want to do
and too much
that has to be done
and momma's in the bedroom
with the door closed.

Nobody even stops to think
about my side of it
I should have been on Math Team
my marks were better than his
why do I have to be
the one
wearing braces
I have nothing to wear tomorrow
will I live long enough
to grow up
and momma's in the bedroom
with the door closed.

1978

JUDITH ORTIZ COFER

The Changeling

As a young girl
vying for my father's attention,
I invented a game that made him look up
from his reading and shake his head
as if both baffled and amused.   5

In my brother's closet, I'd change
into his dungarees—the rough material
molding me into boy shape; hide
my long hair under an army helmet
he'd been given by Father, and emerge   10
transformed into the legendary Ché[5]
of grown-up talk.

Strutting around the room,
I'd tell of life in the mountains,
of carnage and rivers of blood,   15
and of manly feasts with rum and music
to celebrate victories *para la libertad*.[6]
He would listen with a smile
to my tales of battles and brotherhood
until Mother called us to dinner.   20

She was not amused
by my transformations, sternly forbidding me
from sitting down with them as a man.
She'd order me back to the dark cubicle
that smelled of adventure, to shed   25
my costume, to braid my hair furiously
with blind hands, and to return invisible,
as myself,
to the real world of her kitchen.   1993

JOHN BETJEMAN

In Westminster Abbey[7]

Let me take this other glove off
As the *vox humana*[8] swells,

5. Ché Guevara (1928–1967), martyred companion of Fidel Castro.   6. "For freedom" (Spanish).   7. Gothic church in London in which English monarchs are crowned and famous Englishmen are buried (see lines 5, 39–40).   8. Organ tones that resemble the human voice.

GWENDOLYN BROOKS

We Real Cool

THE POOL PLAYERS,
SEVEN AT THE GOLDEN SHOVEL.

We real cool. We
Left school. We

Lurk late. We
Strike straight. We

5   Sing sin. We
Thin gin. We

Jazz June. We
Die soon.   1950

SIR THOMAS WYATT

They Flee from Me

They flee from me, that sometime did me seek,
With naked foot stalking in my chamber.
I have seen them, gentle, tame, and meek,
That now are wild, and do not remember
5   That sometime they put themselves in danger
To take bread at my hand; and now they range,
Busily seeking with a continual change.

Thankéd be Fortune it hath been otherwise,
Twenty times better; but once in special,
10   In thin array, after a pleasant guise,
When her loose gown from her shoulders did fall,
And she me caught in her arms long and small.[4]
And therewith all sweetly did me kiss
And softly said, "Dear heart, how like you this?"

15   It was no dream, I lay broad waking.
But all is turned, thorough[5] my gentleness,
Into a strange fashion of forsaking;
And I have leave to go, of her goodness,
And she also to use newfangleness.[6]
20   But since that I so kindely[7] am servéd,
I fain[8] would know what she hath deservéd.   1557

4. Slender.   5. Through.   6. Fondness for novelty.   7. In a way natural to women.
8. Eagerly.

ADRIENNE RICH

[My mouth hovers across your breasts][9]

3.

My mouth hovers across your breasts
in the short grey winter afternoon
in this bed   we are delicate
and tough   so hot with joy we amaze ourselves
tough   and delicate   we play rings   5
around each other   our daytime candle burns
with its peculiar light   and if the snow
begins to fall outside   filling the branches
and if the night falls   without announcement
these are the pleasures of winter   10
sudden, wild and delicate   your fingers
exact   my tongue exact at the same moment
stopping to laugh at a joke
my love   hot on your scent   on the cusp of winter

1983–85   1986

STEVIE SMITH

I Remember

It was my bridal night I remember,
An old man of seventy-three
I lay with my young bride in my arms,
A girl with t.b.
It was wartime, and overhead   5
The Germans were making a particularly heavy raid on Hampstead.
What rendered the confusion worse, perversely
Our bombers had chosen that moment to set out for Germany.
Harry, do they ever collide?
I do not think it has ever happened,   10
Oh my bride, my bride.

1957

9. This poem is taken from Rich's series "Tracking Poems."

SEAMUS HEANEY

The Outlaw

Kelly's kept an unlicensed bull, well away
From the road: you risked fine but had to pay

The normal fee if cows were serviced there.
Once I dragged a nervous Friesian on a tether

5   Down a lane of alder, shaggy with catkin,
Down to the shed the bull was kept in.

I gave Old Kelly the clammy silver, though why
I could not guess. He grunted a curt 'Go by

Get up on that gate.' And from my lofty station
10   I watched the business-like conception.

The door, unbolted, whacked back against the wall.
The illegal sire fumbled from his stall

Unhurried as an old steam engine shunting,
He circled, snored and nosed. No hectic panting,

15   Just the unfussy ease of a good tradesman;
Then an awkward, unexpected jump, and

His knobbed forelegs straddling her flank,
He slammed life home, impassive as a tank,

Dropping off like a tipped-up load of sand.
20   'She'll do,' said Kelly and tapped his ash-plant

Across her hindquarters. 'If not, bring her back.'
I walked ahead of her, the rope now slack

While Kelly whooped and prodded his outlaw
Who, in his own time, resumed the dark, the straw.   1969

MARGARET ATWOOD

Death of a Young Son by Drowning

He, who navigated with success
the dangerous river of his own birth
once more set forth

on a voyage of discovery
into the land I floated on   5
but could not touch to claim.

His feet slid on the bank,
the currents took him;
he swirled with ice and trees in the swollen water

and plunged into distant regions,   10
his head a bathysphere;
through his eyes' thin glass bubbles

he looked out, reckless adventurer
on a landscape stranger than Uranus
we have all been to and some remember.   15

There was an accident; the air locked,
he was hung in the river like a heart.
They retrieved the swamped body,

cairn of my plans and future charts,
with poles and hooks   20
from among the nudging logs.

It was spring, the sun kept shining, the new grass
leapt to solidity;
my hands glistened with details.

After the long trip I was tired of waves.   25
My foot hit rock. The dreamed sails
collapsed, ragged.

        I planted him in his country
        like a flag.   1970

WALT WHITMAN

[I celebrate myself, and sing myself]

I celebrate myself, and sing myself,
And what I assume you shall assume,
For every atom belonging to me as good belongs to you.

I loafe and invite my soul,
I lean and loafe at my ease observing a spear of summer grass.   5

My tongue, every atom of my blood, form'd from this soil, this air,
Born here of parents born here from parents the same, and their parents the
    same,
I, now thirty-seven years old in perfect health begin,
Hoping to cease not till death.

10 Creeds and schools in abeyance,
Retiring back a while sufficed at what they are, but never forgotten,
I harbor for good or bad, I permit to speak at every hazard,
Nature without check with original energy.   1855, 1881

▼ ▼ ▼

SPEAKER A Glossary

speaker: the person, not necessarily the author, who is the voice of the poem

---

QUESTIONS

1. In "Lessons of the War: Judging Distances," what indicators are there that different voices speak within the poem? Where, exactly, do the changes of speaker take place? How would you characterize each speaker? What words or phrases are especially effective in establishing the different speakers' characters and values?

2. What, precisely, do we know about the speaker in "Hanging Fire"? How much self-confidence does she have? How can you tell? How does she feel about herself?

3. List all the facts we know about the speaker of "In Westminster Abbey." Which facts are especially important in our view of her? Explain the significance of the poem's setting.

4. Characterize the speaker in "The Outlaw." What in particular fascinates him about the breeding operation? What, exactly, does he see? How do the two participants respond to the central event? How do the observers respond? Why does the poem describe the path to Kelly's so fully? Why does the "nervous Friesian" have to be dragged? Why is the money paid to Kelly described as "clammy silver" (line 7)? Why does the speaker decide to employ an "unlicensed bull"? What or whom does the title of the poem refer to?

5. What kind of journey does the mother make in "Death of a Young Son by Drowning"? How are the son's and mother's journeys related? Explain the final image in lines 28–29.

WRITING SUGGESTIONS

1. In your college library, do some basic research on Westminster Abbey—its location and appearance, its history, its symbolic status in England. Look up some brief summary (an encyclopedia entry will do) of the effects of World War II on London. Then write a two-page essay on the importance of setting to the tone of "In Westminster Abbey."

2. The speakers in "Needs" and "The Outlaw" both reveal themselves to have desires and needs that they are not themselves fully conscious of. Analyze carefully just what elements in the poem make clear to us the "secret" aspects of their characters. Compare the character of the speaker (and the strategies used to characterize her) in Maxine Kumin's "Woodchucks" (p. 684). Choose either "Needs" or "The Outlaw" to compare in detail with "Woodchucks," and write a short (600–700 word) essay in which you characterize the speakers in the two poems, making clear what kind of attitude each poem develops toward its speaker.

3. Analyze carefully the way "Mirror" is narrated. Evaluate the strategy of using a nonhuman speaker through which to present the words of the poem. Write a brief, two-paragraph account of the poem in which you explain the advantages and disadvantages of its choice of speaker.

4. Make a list of all the "facts" we learn about the speaker in "Twenty-year Marriage." What, exactly, is the setting of the poem? How much do we know about the husband? How much do we learn about the marriage? What is the speaker's attitude toward tonight? toward the marriage? toward the past? Once you are clear about exactly what is going on in the poem, write an answer, as if written by the husband.

3 SITUATION AND SETTING

Questions about speaker ("Who?" questions) in a poem almost always lead to questions of "Where?" "When?" and "Why?" Identifying the speaker usually is, in fact, part of a larger process of defining the entire imagined **situation** in a poem: What is happening? Where is it happening? Who is the speaker speaking to? Who else is present? Why is this event occurring? In order to understand the dialogue in "The Ruined Maid," for example, we need to recognize that the friends are meeting after an extended period of separation, and that they meet in a town setting rather than the rural area in which they grew up together. We infer (from the opening lines) that the meeting is accidental, and that no other friends are present for the conversation. The poem's whole "story" depends on their situation: after leading separate lives for some time they have some catching up to do. We don't know what specific town is involved, or what year, season, or time of day because those details are not important to the poem's effect. But crucial to the poem are the where and when questions that define the situation and relationship of the two speakers, and the answer to the why question—that the meeting is by chance—is important too. In another poem we looked at in the previous chapter, "A Certain Lady," the specific moment and place are not important, but we do need to notice that the "lady" is talking to (or having an imaginary conversation with) her lover and that they are talking about a relationship of some duration.

Sometimes a *specific* time and place (**setting**) may be important. The "lady in skunk" sings her life story "in a prominent bar in Secaucus," a smelly and unfashionable town in New Jersey, but on no particular occasion ("one day"). In "Soliloquy of the Spanish Cloister," the setting (a monastery) adds to the irony because of the gross inappropriateness of such sentiments and attitudes in a supposedly holy place, and the setting of "In Westminster Abbey" similarly helps us to judge the speaker's ideas, attitudes, and self-conception.

The title of the following poem suggests that place may be important, and it is, although you may be surprised to discover exactly what exists at this address and what uses the speaker makes of it.

JAMES DICKEY

Cherrylog Road

Off Highway 106
At Cherrylog Road I entered
The '34 Ford without wheels,
Smothered in kudzu,[1]
With a seat pulled out to run   5
Corn whiskey down from the hills,

And then from the other side
Crept into an Essex
With a rumble seat of red leather
And then out again, aboard   10
A blue Chevrolet, releasing
The rust from its other color,

Reared up on three building blocks.
None had the same body heat;
I changed with them inward, toward   15
The weedy heart of the junkyard,
For I knew that Doris Holbrook
Would escape from her father at noon

And would come from the farm
To seek parts owned by the sun   20
Among the abandoned chassis,
Sitting in each in turn
As I did, leaning forward
As in a wild stock-car race

In the parking lot of the dead.   25
Time after time, I climbed in
And out the other side, like
An envoy or movie star
Met at the station by crickets.
A radiator cap raised its head,   30

Become a real toad or a kingsnake
As I neared the hub of the yard,
Passing through many states,
Many lives, to reach
Some grandmother's long Pierce-Arrow   35
Sending platters of blindness forth

---

1. A rapidly growing vine, introduced from Japan to combat erosion but now covering whole fields
and groves of trees, especially in the deep South.

From its nickel hubcaps
And spilling its tender upholstery
On sleepy roaches,
40   The glass panel in between
Lady and colored driver
Not all the way broken out,

The back-seat phone
Still on its hook.
45   I got in as though to exclaim,
"Let us go to the orphan asylum,
John; I have some old toys
For children who say their prayers."

I popped with sweat as I thought
50   I heard Doris Holbrook scrape
Like a mouse in the southern-state sun
That was eating the paint in blisters
From a hundred car tops and hoods.
She was tapping like code,

55   Loosening the screws,
Carrying off headlights,
Sparkplugs, bumpers,
Cracked mirrors and gear-knobs,
Getting ready, already,
60   To go back with something to show

Other than her lips' new trembling
I would hold to me soon, soon,
Where I sat in the ripped back seat
Talking over the interphone,
65   Praying for Doris Holbrook
To come from her father's farm

And to get back there
With no trace of me on her face
To be seen by her red-haired father
70   Who would change, in the squalling barn,
Her back's pale skin with a strop,
Then lay for me

In a bootlegger's roasting car
With a string-triggered 12-gauge shotgun
75   To blast the breath from the air.
Not cut by the jagged windshields,
Through the acres of wrecks she came
With a wrench in her hand,

Through dust where the blacksnake dies
80   Of boredom, and the beetle knows

The compost has no more life.
Someone outside would have seen
The oldest car's door inexplicably
Close from within:

I held her and held her and held her,   85
Convoyed at terrific speed
By the stalled, dreaming traffic around us,
So the blacksnake, stiff
With inaction, curved back
Into life, and hunted the mouse   90

With deadly overexcitement,
The beetles reclaimed their field
As we clung, glued together,
With the hooks of the seat springs
Working through to catch us red-handed   95
Amidst the gray breathless batting

That burst from the seat at our backs.
We left by separate doors
Into the changed, other bodies
Of cars, she down Cherrylog Road   100
And I to my motorcycle
Parked like the soul of the junkyard

Restored, a bicycle fleshed
With power, and tore off
Up Highway 106, continually   105
Drunk on the wind in my mouth,
Wringing the handlebar for speed,
Wild to be wreckage forever.   1964

The *exact* location of the junkyard is not important (there is no Highway
106 near the real Cherrylog Road in North Georgia), but we do need to know
that the setting is rural, that the time is summer and that the summer is hot,
and that moonshine whiskey is native to the area. Following the story is no
problem once we have sorted out these few facts, and we are prepared to meet
the cast of characters: Doris Holbrook, her red-haired father, and the speaker.
About each we learn just enough to appreciate the sense of vitality, adventure,
and power that constitute the major effects of the poem.

The situation of lovemaking in another setting than the junkyard would not
produce the same effects, and the exotic sense of a forbidden meeting in this
unlikely place helps to re-create the speaker's sense of the episode. For him, it
is memorable (notice all the tiny details he remembers), powerful (notice his
reaction when he gets back on his motorcycle), dreamlike (notice the sense of

time standing still, especially in lines 85–89), and important (notice how the speaker perceives his environment as changed by their lovemaking, lines 88–91 and 98–100). The wealth of details about setting also helps us to raise other, related questions. Why does the speaker fantasize about being shot by the father (lines 72–75)? Why, in a poem so full of details, do we find out so little about what Doris Holbrook looks like? What gives us the sense that this incident is a composite of episodes, an event that was repeated many times? What gives us the impression that the events occurred long ago? What makes the speaker feel so powerful at the end? What does he mean when he talks of himself as being "wild to be wreckage forever"? All of the poem's attention to the speaker's reactions, reflections, and memories is intricately tied up with the particulars of setting. Making love in a junkyard is crucial to the speaker's sense of both power and wreckage, and to him Doris is merely a matter of excitement, adventure, and pale skin, appreciated because she makes the world seem different and because she is willing to take risks and to suffer for meeting him like this. The more we probe the poem with questions about situation, the more likely we are to catch the poem's full effect.

The plot of "Cherrylog Road" is fairly easy to sort out, but its effect is more complex than the simple story suggests. The next poem we will look at is, at first glance, much more difficult to follow. Part of the difficulty is that the poem is from an earlier age and its language and syntax may seem a bit unfamiliar, and part is because the action in the poem is so closely connected to what is being said. But its opening lines—addressed to someone who is resisting the speaker's suggestions—disclose the situation, and gradually we can figure out the scene: a man is trying to convince a woman that they should make love. When a flea happens by, the speaker uses it for an unlikely example; it becomes part of his argument. And once we recognize the situation, we can readily follow (and be amused by) the speaker's witty and intricate argument.

JOHN DONNE

The Flea

Mark but this flea, and mark in this[2]
How little that which thou deny'st me is;
It sucked me first, and now sucks thee,
And in this flea our two bloods mingled be;

2. Medieval preachers and rhetoricians asked their hearers to "mark" (look at) an object that illustrated a moral or philosophical lesson they wished to emphasize.

Thou know'st that this cannot be said   5
A sin, nor shame, nor loss of maidenhead.
    Yet this enjoys before it woo,
    And pampered³ swells with one blood made of two,
    And this, alas, is more than we would do.⁴

Oh stay, three lives in one flea spare,   10
Where we almost, yea more than, married are.
This flea is you and I, and this
Our marriage bed, and marriage temple is;
Though parents grudge, and you, we're met
And cloistered in these living walls of jet.   15
    Though use⁵ make you apt to kill me,
    Let not to that, self-murder added be,
    And sacrilege, three sins in killing three.

Cruel and sudden, hast thou since
Purpled thy nail in blood of innocence?   20
Wherein could this flea guilty be,
Except in that drop which it sucked from thee?
Yet thou triumph'st, and say'st that thou
Find'st not thyself, nor me, the weaker now;
    'Tis true; then learn how false, fears be;   25
    Just so much honor, when thou yield'st to me,
    Will waste, as this flea's death took life from thee.   1633

The scene in "The Flea" develops almost as it would in the theater. Action
occurs even as the poem is being written. Between stanzas 1 and 2, the woman
makes a move to kill the flea (as stanza 2 opens, the speaker is trying to stop
her), and between stanzas 2 and 3 she has squashed the flea with her fingernail. Once we make sense of what the speaker says, the action is just as clear
from the words as if we had stage directions in the margin. All of the speaker's
verbal cleverness and all of his specious arguments follow from the situation,
and in this poem (as in "Soliloquy of the Spanish Cloister" or "In Westminster
Abbey") we watch as if we were observing a scene in a play. The speaker is, in
effect, giving a dramatic monologue for our benefit.

Neither time nor place is important to "The Flea," except that the speaker
and his friend must be assumed to be in the same place and to have the leisure
for some playfulness. The situation could occur anywhere a man, a woman,
and a flea could be together: indoors, outdoors, morning, evening, city, country, in cottage or palace, on a boat or in a bedroom. We do know, from the

---

3. Fed luxuriously.   4. According to contemporary medical theory, conception involved the literal mingling of the lovers' blood.   5. Habit.

date of publication of the poem (1633), that the poet was writing about people of almost four centuries ago, but the conduct he describes might equally happen in later ages. Only the habits of language (and perhaps the speaker's religious attitudes) date the poem; the situation could just as easily be set in any age or place.

The two poems that follow have simpler plots, but in each case the heart of the poem is in the basic situation:

RITA DOVE

Daystar

She wanted a little room for thinking:
but she saw diapers steaming on the line,
a doll slumped behind the door.

So she lugged a chair behind the garage
5   to sit out the children's naps.

Sometimes there were things to watch —
the pinched armor of a vanished cricket,
a floating maple leaf. Other days
she stared until she was assured
10 when she closed her eyes
she'd see only her own vivid blood.

She had an hour, at best, before Liza appeared
pouting from the top of the stairs.
And just *what* was mother doing
15 out back with the field mice? Why,

building a palace. Later
that night when Thomas rolled over and
lurched into her, she would open her eyes
and think of the place that was hers
20 for an hour — where
she was nothing,
pure nothing, in the middle of the day.   1986

LINDA PASTAN

To a Daughter Leaving Home

When I taught you
at eight to ride
a bicycle, loping along
beside you
as you wobbled away   5
on two round wheels,
my own mouth rounding
in surprise when you pulled
ahead down the curved
path of the park,   10
I kept waiting
for the thud
of your crash as I
sprinted to catch up,
while you grew   15
smaller, more breakable
with distance,
pumping, pumping
for your life, screaming
with laughter,   20
the hair flapping
behind you like a
handkerchief waving
goodbye.   1988

Both these poems involve motherhood, but they take entirely different
stances about it and have very different tones. The mother in "Daystar" is overwhelmed by the demands of young children and needs a room of her own. All
she can manage, however, is a brief hour in a chair behind the garage. The situation is virtually the whole story here. Nothing really happens except that
daily events (washing diapers, picking up toys, looking at crickets and leaves,
explaining the world to children, having sex) crowd her brief private hour and
make it precious. Being "nothing" (lines 21 and 22) takes on great value in
these circumstances, and the poem makes much of the setting: an isolated
chair behind the garage. Setting in poems often means something much more
specific about a particular culture or social history, but here time and place are
given value by the circumstances of the situation for one frazzled mother.

The particulars of time and place in "To a Daughter Leaving Home" are
even less specific, but the incident the poem describes happened a long time

ago, and it is important to notice that its vividness in the poem is a function of memory. The mother is the speaker here, and we are told very little about her, at least directly. But she is thinking back nostalgically to a moment long ago when her daughter made an earlier (but briefer) departure from home, and the poem implies the occasion for her doing so. The daughter now is old enough to "leave" home in a full sense; the poem does not tell us why or what the present circumstances are, but the title tells us the situation. We may infer quite a bit about the speaker here—her affection for the daughter, the kind of mother she has been, her anxiety at the new departure that seems to reflect the earlier wobbly ride into the distance—but as in "Daystar" the poem is all situation. There are almost no details of present action, and we have no specific information about place or time for either the remembered event or the present one.

Some poems, however, depend heavily on historical specifics and a knowledge of actual places and events. The following poem, for example, depends not only on knowing some facts about a particular event but on the parallels between that event and circumstances surrounding the poet and his immediate readers.

JOHN MILTON

On the Late Massacre in Piedmont

Avenge, O Lord, thy slaughtered saints, whose bones
Lie scattered on the Alpine mountains cold;
Even them who kept thy truth so pure of old
When all our fathers worshiped stocks and stones,
Forget not: in thy book record their groans
Who were thy sheep and in their ancient fold
Slain by the bloody Piemontese that rolled
Mother with infant down the rocks. Their moans
The vales redoubled to the hills, and they
To heaven. Their martyred blood and ashes sow
O'er all th' Italian fields, where still doth sway
The triple tyrant:[6] that from these may grow
A hundredfold, who having learnt thy way
Early may fly the Babylonian woe.[7]

1673

6. The Pope's tiara featured three crowns.   7. In Milton's day, Protestants often likened the Roman Church to Babylonian decadence, called the church "the whore of Babylon," and read Revelation 17 and 18 as an allegory of its coming destruction.

The "slaughtered saints" were members of the Waldensians—a heretical sect that had long been settled in southern France and northern Italy (the Piedmont). Though a minority, the Waldensians were allowed freedom of worship until 1655, when their protection under the law was taken away and locals attacked them, killing large numbers. This poem, then, is not a private meditation, but rather a public statement about a well-known "news" event. The reader, to fully understand the poem and respond to it meaningfully, must therefore be acquainted with its historical context, including the massacre itself and the significance it had for Milton and his English audience.

Milton wrote the poem shortly after the Piedmont massacre of 1655 became known in England, and implicit in its "meaning" is a parallel Milton's readers would have felt between the events in the Piedmont and current English politics. Milton signals the analogy early on by calling the dead Piedmontese "saints," the term then regularly used by English Protestants of the Puritan stamp to describe themselves, and to thereby assert their belief that every individual Christian—not just those few "special" religious heroes singled out in the Catholic tradition—lived a heroic life. By identifying the Waldensians with the English Puritans—their beliefs were in some ways quite similar, and both were minorities in a larger political and cultural context—Milton was warning his fellow Puritans that, if the Stuart monarchy were reestablished, what had just happened to the Waldensians could happen to them as well. Following the Restoration in 1660, tight restrictions were in fact placed on the Puritan "sects" under the new monarchy. In lines 12 and 14, the poem alludes to dangers of religious rule by dominant groups by invoking standard images of Catholic power and persecution; the heir to the English throne (who succeeded to the throne as Charles II in 1660) was spending his exile in Catholic Europe and was, because of his sympathetic treatment of Catholic associates and friends, thought perhaps to be himself a Catholic. Chauvinistic Englishmen, who promoted rivalries with Catholic powers like France, considered him a traitor.

Many poems, like this one, make use of historical occurrences and situations to create a widely evocative set of angers, sympathies, and conclusions. Sometimes a poet's intention in recording a particular moment or event is to commemorate it or comment upon it. A poem written about a specific occasion is usually called an **occasional poem**, and such a poem is **referential**; that is, it *refers* to a certain historical time or event. Often it is hard to place ourselves fully enough in another time or place to imagine sympathetically what a particular historical moment would have been like, and even the best poetic efforts do not necessarily transport us there. For such poems we need, at the least, specific historical information—plus a willingness on our part as readers to be transported, by a name, a date, or a dramatic situation.

Time or place may, of course, be used much less specifically and still be important to a poem; frequently a poem's setting draws upon common notions of a particular time or place. Setting a poem in a garden, for example, or writing about apples almost inevitably reminds us of the Garden of Eden because it is part of the Western heritage of belief or knowledge. Even people who don't read at all or who lack Judeo-Christian religious commitments are likely to know about Eden, and a poet writing in our culture can count on that. An **allusion** is a reference to something outside the poem that carries a history of meaning and strong emotional associations. (There's a longer account of allusion in Chapter 11.) For example, gardens may carry suggestions of innocence and order, or temptation and the Fall, or both, depending on how the poem handles the allusion. Well-known places from history or myth may be popularly associated with particular ideas or values or ways of life.

The place involved in a poem is its **spatial setting,** and the time is its **temporal setting.** The temporal setting may involve a specific date or an era, a season of the year or a time of day. We tend, for example, to think of spring as a time of discovery and growth, and poems set in spring are likely to make use of that association; morning usually suggests discovery as well—beginnings, vitality, the world fresh and new—even to those of us who in reality take our waking slow. Temporal or spatial setting is often used to influence our expectation of theme and tone, although the poet may then go on to surprise us by making something very different of our expectation. Setting is often an important factor in creating the mood in poems just as in stories, plays, or films. Often the details of setting have a lot to do with the way we ultimately respond to the poem's subject or theme, as in this poem:

SYLVIA PLATH

Point Shirley

From Water-Tower Hill to the brick prison
The shingle booms, bickering under
The sea's collapse.
Snowcakes break and welter. This year
5 The gritted wave leaps
The seawall and drops onto a bier

Of quahog chips,[8]
Leaving a salty mash of ice to whiten

In my grandmother's sand yard. She is dead,
Whose laundry snapped and froze here, who   10
Kept house against
What the sluttish, rutted sea could do.
Squall waves once danced
Ship timbers in through the cellar window;
A thresh-tailed, lanced   15
Shark littered in the geranium bed—

Such collusion of mulish elements
She wore her broom straws to the nub.
Twenty years out
Of her hand; the house still hugs in each drab   20
Stucco socket
The purple egg-stones: from Great Head's knob
To the filled-in Gut
The sea in its cold gizzard ground those rounds.

Nobody wintering now behind   25
The planked-up windows where she set
Her wheat loaves
And apple cakes to cool. What is it
Survives, grieves
So, over this battered, obstinate spit   30
Of gravel? The waves'
Spewed relics clicker masses in the wind,

Gray waves the stub-necked eiders ride.
A labor of love, and that labor lost.
Steadily the sea   35
Eats at Point Shirley. She died blessed,
And I come by
Bones, bones only, pawed and tossed,
A dog-faced sea.
The sun sinks under Boston, bloody red.   40

I would get from these dry-papped stones
The milk your love instilled in them.
The black ducks dive.
And though your graciousness might stream,
And I contrive,   45
Grandmother, stones are nothing of home
To that spumiest dove.
Against both bar and tower the black sea runs.   1960

8. Chips from quahog clam shells, common on the New England coast.

One does not have to know the New England coast by personal experience to find it vividly re-created in Plath's poem. A reader who knows that coast or another like it may have an advantage in being able to respond more quickly to the poem's precision of description, but the poem does not depend on the reader's having such knowledge. The precise location of Point Shirley, near Boston, is not especially important, but visualization of the setting is. Crucial to the poem's tone and mood is the sense of the sea as aggressor, a force powerful enough to change the contours of the coast and invade the privacy of yards and homes. The energy, relentlessness, and impersonality of the sea met their match, though only temporarily, in the speaker's grandmother, who "[k]ept house against / What the sluttish, rutted sea could do" (lines 11–12). The grandmother *belonged* in this setting, and it seemed hers, but twenty years of her absence (since her death) now begin to show. Still, the marks of her obstinacy and love are there, although ultimately doomed by the sea's more enduring power.

Details—and how they are amassed—are important here rather than historic particulars of time and place. The grays and whites and drab colors of the sea and its leavings provide both a visual sense of the scene and the mood for the poem. The stubbornness that the speaker admired in the grandmother comes to seem a part of that tenacious grayness. Nothing happens rapidly here; things wear down. Even the "bloody red" (line 40) of the sun's setting—an ominous sign that adds a vivid fright to the dullness rather than brightening it—makes promises that seem slow and long-term. The toughness of the boarded-up house is a monument to the grandmother's loving care and becomes a way for the speaker to touch her human spirit, but the poem's final emphasis is on the relentless black sea, which continues to run against the landmarks and fortresses that had been identified with the setting in the very first line.

Questions about situation and setting begin as simple questions of identification but often become more complex when we sort out all the implications. Often it takes only a moment to determine a poem's situation, but it may take much longer to discover all of the things that time and place imply, for their meanings may depend upon visual details, or upon actual historical occurrences, or upon habitual ways of thinking about certain times and places—or all three at once. As you read the following poem, notice how the setting—another shore—prepares us for the speaker's moods and ideas, and then watch how the movement of his mind is affected by what he sees.

MATTHEW ARNOLD

Dover Beach[9]

The sea is calm tonight.
The tide is full, the moon lies fair
Upon the straits; on the French coast the light
Gleams and is gone; the cliffs of England stand,
Glimmering and vast, out in the tranquil bay.   5
Come to the window, sweet is the night-air!
Only, from the long line of spray
Where the sea meets the moon-blanched land,
Listen! you hear the grating roar
Of pebbles which the waves draw back, and fling, 10
At their return, up the high strand,
Begin, and cease, and then again begin,
With tremulous cadence slow, and bring
The eternal note of sadness in.

Sophocles long ago   15
Heard it on the Aegean, and it brought
Into his mind the turbid ebb and flow
Of human misery;[1] we
Find also in the sound a thought,
Hearing it by this distant northern sea. 20

The Sea of Faith
Was once, too, at the full, and round earth's shore
Lay like the folds of a bright girdle furled.
But now I only hear
Its melancholy, long, withdrawing roar, 25
Retreating, to the breath
Of the night-wind, down the vast edges drear
And naked shingles[2] of the world.

Ah, love, let us be true
To one another! for the world, which seems 30
To lie before us like a land of dreams,
So various, so beautiful, so new,
Hath really neither joy, nor love, nor light,
Nor certitude, nor peace, nor help for pain;
And we are here as on a darkling plain 35
Swept with confused alarms of struggle and flight,
Where ignorant armies clash by night.

ca. 1851

---

9. At the narrowest point on the English Channel. The lights on the French coast (lines 3–4) would
be about 20 miles away. 1. In *Antigone*, lines 583–91, the chorus compares the fate of the house
of Oedipus to the waves of the sea. 2. Pebble-strewn beaches.

Exactly what is the dramatic situation in "Dover Beach"? How soon are you aware that someone is being spoken to? How much are we told about the person spoken to? How would you describe the speaker's mood? What does the speaker's mood have to do with time and place? Do any details of present place and time help to account for his tendency to talk repeatedly of the past and the future? How important is it to the poem's total effect that the beach here involves an international border? What particulars of the Dover Beach seem especially important to the poem's themes? to its emotional effects?

Sometimes time and place may carry even greater resonance in a poem because pieces of history are recovered or rehearsed. In the following poem, for example, the whole history of Manifest Destiny ultimately is invoked in a situation that at first only seems to involve a quiet walk in a California small town. Here the "clear night in Live Oak" (line 1) quickly allows us to see large episodes in American and Mexican history.

ADRIENNE RICH

Walking down the Road

On a clear night in Live Oak you can see
the stars glittering low as from the deck
of a frigate.
In Live Oak without pavements you can walk
5   the fronts of old homesteads, past tattered palms,
original rosebushes, thick walnut trees
ghosts of the liveoak groves
the whitemen cleared. On a night like this
the old California thickens and bends
10 the Baja streams out like lava-melt
we are no longer the United States
we're a lost piece of Mexico
maybe dreaming the destruction
of the Indians, reading the headlines,
15 how the gringos marched into Mexico City
forcing California into the hand
of Manifest Destiny, law following greed.
And the pale lies trapped in the flickering boxes
here in Live Oak tonight, they too follow.
20 One thing follows on another, that is time:
Carmel in its death-infested prettiness,
thousands of skeletons stacked in the *campo santo:*[3]

3. Sacred field, cemetery (Spanish).

the spring fouled by the pickaxe:
the flag dragged on to the moon:
the crystal goblet smashed: grains of the universe   25
flashing their angry tears, here in Live Oak.   1989

Not all poems have an identifiable situation or setting, just as not all poems
have a speaker who is entirely distinct from the author. Poems that simply present a series of thoughts and feelings directly, in a contemplative, meditative,
or reflective way, may not set up any kind of action, plot, or situation at all, preferring to speak directly without the intermediary of a dramatic device. But
most poems depend crucially upon a sense of place, a sense of time, and an
understanding of human interaction in scenes that resemble the strategies of
drama or film. And questions about these matters will often lead you to define
not only the "facts" but also the feelings central to a poem's design upon us.

▼   ▼   ▼

ROBERT BROWNING

My Last Duchess

FERRARA[4]

That's my last Duchess painted on the wall,
Looking as if she were alive. I call
That piece a wonder, now: Frà Pandolf's hands[5]
Worked busily a day, and there she stands.
Will't please you sit and look at her? I said   5
"Frà Pandolf" by design, for never read
Strangers like you that pictured countenance,
The depth and passion of its earnest glance,
But to myself they turned (since none puts by
The curtain I have drawn for you, but I)   10
And seemed as they would ask me, if they durst,
How such a glance came there; so, not the first
Are you to turn and ask thus. Sir, 'twas not
Her husband's presence only, called that spot
Of joy into the Duchess' cheek: perhaps   15

---

4. Alfonso II, Duke of Ferrara in Italy in the mid-16th century, is the presumed speaker of the poem,
which is loosely based on historical events. The duke's first wife—whom he had married when she
was 14—died under suspicious circumstances at 17, and he then negotiated through an agent (to
whom the poem is spoken) for the hand of the niece of the Count of Tyrol in Austria.   **5.** Frà
Pandolf is, like Claus (line 56), fictitious.

Frà Pandolf chanced to say "Her mantle laps
Over my lady's wrist too much," or "Paint
Must never hope to reproduce the faint
Half-flush that dies along her throat": such stuff
20 Was courtesy, she thought, and cause enough
For calling up that spot of joy. She had
A heart—how shall I say?—too soon made glad,
Too easily impressed; she liked whate'er
She looked on, and her looks went everywhere.
25 Sir, 'twas all one! My favor at her breast,
The dropping of the daylight in the West,
The bough of cherries some officious fool
Broke in the orchard for her, the white mule
She rode with round the terrace—all and each
30 Would draw from her alike the approving speech,
Or blush, at least. She thanked men,—good! but thanked
Somehow—I know not how—as if she ranked
My gift of a nine-hundred-years-old name
With anybody's gift. Who'd stoop to blame
35 This sort of trifling? Even had you skill
In speech—which I have not—to make your will
Quite clear to such an one, and say, "Just this
Or that in you disgusts me; here you miss,
Or there exceed the mark"—and if she let
40 Herself be lessoned so, nor plainly set
Her wits to yours, forsooth, and made excuse,
—E'en then would be some stooping; and I choose
Never to stoop. Oh sir, she smiled, no doubt,
Whene'er I passed her; but who passed without
45 Much the same smile? This grew; I gave commands;
Then all smiles stopped together. There she stands
As if alive. Will 't please you rise? We'll meet
The company below, then. I repeat,
The Count your master's known munificence
50 Is ample warrant that no just pretense
Of mine for dowry will be disallowed;
Though his fair daughter's self, as I avowed
At starting, is my object. Nay, we'll go
Together down, sir. Notice Neptune, though,
55 Taming a sea-horse, thought a rarity,
Which Claus of Innsbruck cast in bronze for me!   1842

LOUISE GLÜCK

Labor Day

Requiring something lovely on his arm
Took me to Stamford, Connecticut, a quasi-farm,
His family's; later picking up the mammoth
Girlfriend of Charlie, meanwhile trying to pawn me off
On some third guy also up for the weekend.   5
But Saturday we still were paired; spent
it sprawled across that sprawling acreage
Until the grass grew limp
With damp. Like me. Johnston-baby, I can still see
The pelted clover, burrs' prickle fur and gorged   10
Pastures spewing infinite tiny bells. You pimp.   1969

RICHARD SNYDER

A Mongoloid Child Handling Shells on the Beach

She turns them over in her slow hands,
as did the sea sending them to her;
broken bits from the mazarine maze,
they are the calmest things on this sand.
The unbroken children splash and shout,   5
rough as surf, gay as their nesting towels.
But she plays soberly with the sea's
small change and hums back to it its slow vowels.   1971

ELIZABETH ALEXANDER

Boston Year

My first week in Cambridge a car full of white boys
tried to run me off the road, and spit through the window,
open to ask directions. I was always asking directions
and always driving: to an Armenian market
in Watertown to buy figs and string cheese, apricots,   5
dark spices and olives from barrels, tubes of paste
with unreadable Arabic labels. I ate
stuffed grape leaves and watched my lips swell in the mirror.
The floors of my apartment would never come clean.

10
Whenever I saw other colored people
in bookshops, or museums, or cafeterias, I'd gasp,
smile shyly, but they'd disappear before I spoke.
What would I have said to them? Come with me? Take
me home? Are you my mother? No. I sat alone

15
in countless Chinese restaurants eating almond
cookies, sipping tea with spoons and spoons of sugar.
Popcorn and coffee was dinner. When I fainted
from migraine in the grocery store, a Portuguese
man above me mouthed: "No breakfast." He gave me

20
orange juice and chocolate bars. The color red
sprang into relief singing Wagner's *Walküre*.[6]
Entire tribes gyrated and drummed in my head.
I learned the samba from a Brazilian man
so tiny, so festooned with glitter I was certain

25
that he slept inside a filigreed, Fabergé egg.
No one at the door: no salesmen, Mormons, meter
readers, exterminators, no Harriet Tubman,
no one. Red notes sounding in a grey trolley town.   1990

DOROTHY LIVESAY

Green Rain

I remember long veils of green rain
Feathered like the shawl of my grandmother—
Green from the half-green of the spring trees
Waving in the valley.

5
I remember the road
Like the one which leads to my grandmother's house,
A warm house, with green carpets,
Geraniums, a trilling canary
And shining horse-hair chairs;

10
And the silence, full of the rain's falling
Was like my grandmother's parlor
Alive with herself and her voice, rising and falling—
Rain and wind intermingled.

I remember on that day

15
I was thinking only of my love
And of my love's house.
But now I remember the day
As I remember my grandmother.
I remember the rain as the feathery fringe of her shawl.   p. 1929

6. One of four operas in *Der Ring des Nibelungen* (*The Ring of the Nibelung*) by German composer
Richard Wagner (1813–1883).

EMILY BRONTË

The Night-Wind

In summer's mellow midnight,
A cloudless moon shone through
Our open parlor window
And rosetrees wet with dew.

I sat in silent musing,   5
The soft wind waved my hair:
It told me Heaven was glorious,
And sleeping Earth was fair.

I needed not its breathing
To bring such thoughts to me,   10
But still it whispered lowly,
"How dark the woods will be!

"The thick leaves in my murmur
Are rustling like a dream,
And all their myriad voices   15
Instinct[7] with spirit seem."

I said, "Go, gentle singer,
Thy wooing voice is kind,
But do not think its music
Has power to reach my mind.   20

"Play with the scented flower,
The young tree's supple bough,
And leave my human feelings
In their own course to flow."

The wanderer would not leave me;   25
Its kiss grew warmer still—
"O come," it sighed so sweetly,
"I'll win thee 'gainst thy will.

"Have we not been from childhood friends?
Have I not loved thee long?   30
As long as thou hast loved the night
Whose silence wakes my song.

"And when thy heart is laid at rest
Beneath the church-yard stone
I shall have time enough to mourn   35
And thou to be alone."

September 11, 1840   1850

7. Infused.

APRIL BERNARD

Praise Psalm of the City-Dweller

for C. B.

Lift your heads, all you peoples, to the wet heat rising in the airshaft,
to the pigeon feathers scattered on the sills, to the grey
triangle of sky that drifts like a soft, wet shawl

For this is the day of the heat, when yellow sedans herd like goats,
5   when the smell of the body contains its own joyful death

See how the young men of the city weep and fall upon one another's
shoulders, see how they turn their shining faces away from us who stand
encumbered by the changing sky

There was a place made, a clearing in the wilderness of bricks,
10   where they gathered to sing—the microphone warbled,
the hot smell of tar and hope fanned in wings of smoke

Shout singing in your praises, all you peoples, for there will be more
days like this, when the mouths of all the dogs fall open, pink
and quivering, and the cats lie down like lambs and close their eyes

15   While the hot grey heat rises like tissue from the skin, accumulating
in clouds of tears, there will be more days

Break the stick across your knee, O my brother, begin again
in the heat of further days   1993

ARCHIBALD LAMPMAN

In November

The hills and leafless forests slowly yield
        To the thick-driving snow. A little while
        And night shall darken down. In shouting file
The woodmen's carts go by me homeward-wheeled,
5   Past the thin fading stubbles, half concealed,
        Now golden-gray, sowed softly through with snow,
        Where the last ploughman follows still his row,
Turning black furrows through the whitening field.
Far off the village lamps begin to gleam,
10   Fast drives the snow, and no man comes this way;
        The hills grow wintry white, and bleak winds moan
        About the naked uplands. I alone
Am neither sad, nor shelterless, nor gray,
Wrapped round with thought, content to watch and dream.   1888

SUSAN MUSGRAVE

I Am Not a Conspiracy
Everything Is Not Paranoid
The Drug Enforcement Administration Is
Not Everywhere

Paul comes from Toronto on Sunday
to photograph me here in my
new image. We drive to a cornfield
where I stand looking uncomfortable.
The corn-god has an Irish accent—   5
I can hear him whispering, "Whiskey!"

And the cows. They, too, are in the
corn, entranced like figures in effigy.
Last summer in Mexico I saw purses at the
market made from unborn calfskin—   10
I've been wondering where they came from
ever since, the soft skins I ran my hands
down over, that made me feel like shuddering.

I was wrong. The corn-god is whispering
"Cocaine!" He is not Irish, after all,   15
but D.E.A. wanting to do business. He
demands to know the names of all my friends,
wants me to tell him who's dealing.

I confess I'm growing restless as the
camera goes on clicking, standing naked in the   20
high-heel shoes I bought last summer in Mexico.
"We want names," say the cows, who suddenly
look malevolent. They are tearing the ears
off the innocent corn. They call it an
investigation.   25

Paul calls to them, "Come here, cows!"
though I don't even want them in the picture.
What Paul sees is something different from
me; my skin feels like shuddering when those
cows run their eyes down over me.   30

"But didn't you smuggle this poem into Canada?"
asks the cow with the mirrored sunglasses.
"As far as we can tell, this is not a
Canadian poem. Didn't you write it
in Mexico?"   1985   35

WILLIAM SHAKESPEARE

[Full many a glorious morning have I seen]

Full many a glorious morning have I seen
Flatter the mountain-tops with sovereign eye,
Kissing with golden face the meadows green,
Gilding pale streams with heavenly alchymy;
Anon permit the basest clouds to ride
With ugly rack[8] on his celestial face,
And from the forlorn world his visage hide,
Stealing unseen to west with this disgrace:
Even so my sun one early morn did shine,
With all-triumphant splendor on my brow;
But, out! alack! he was but one hour mine,
The region cloud hath mask'd him from me now.
    Yet him for this my love no whit disdaineth;
    Suns of the world may stain when heaven's sun staineth.   1609

5

10

JOHN DONNE

The Good-Morrow

I wonder, by my troth, what thou and I
    Did, till we loved? were we not weaned till then?
But sucked on country pleasures, childishly?
    Or snorted we in the Seven Sleepers' den?[9]
'Twas so; but[1] this, all pleasures fancies be.
If ever any beauty I did see,
Which I desired, and got,[2] twas but a dream of thee.

And now good-morrow to our waking souls,
    Which watch not one another out of fear;
For love, all love of other sights controls,
    And makes one little room an everywhere.
Let sea-discoverers to new worlds have gone,
Let maps to other,[3] worlds on worlds have shown,
Let us possess one world, each hath one, and is one.

My face in thine eye, thine in mine appears,[4]
    And true plain hearts do in the faces rest;

5

10

15

8. Moss.   9. According to tradition, seven Christian youths escaped Roman persecution by sleep-ing in a cave for 187 years. *Snorted:* snored.   1. Except for.   2. Sexually possessed. *Beauty:* Beautiful woman.   3. Other people.   4. I.e., each is reflected in the other's eyes.

Where can we find two better hemispheres,
   Without sharp north, without declining west?
Whatever dies was not mixed equally,[5]
If our two loves be one, or, thou and I
Love so alike that none do slacken, none can die.   1633   20

MARILYN CHIN

Aubade

The candle that would not burn
will never share its glory.

Waking is this easy:
Sunday; Haunauma Bay,[6] your birthday,
and we—too comfortable to notice
the sea forging inward,

that before the picture window   5
our special pine, dwarfed and hunched
through decades of seastorm and salty air,
has uprooted to die in the rain.

And in our sleep, the years have proceeded toward the horizon
like a school of uninteresting driftwood   10
or tortoises plodding disconsolately
to find what lurks at the edge.

What lurks there might be disaster:
the charred aftermath of Rome and Cathay, or
more deceptive, a sea of new aquatic flora   15
bathed in eternal dawn light.

But today as clouds give way to sunshine,
we wake as tourists of yet another decade.
Our tongues stale with last night's lovemaking,
our eyes bleared with tomorrow's dreams.   20

For now, let each candle gutter, as they do
and celebrate earth's mundane surprises:
family, lovers, friends,
clams in the mudflat for the taking.   1987

---

5. Perfectly mixed elements, according to scholastic philosophy, were stable and immortal.   6. On Oahu, east of Honolulu.

JONATHAN SWIFT

A Description of the Morning

Now hardly here and there a hackney-coach[7]
Appearing, showed the ruddy morn's approach.
Now Betty[8] from her master's bed had flown,
And softly stole to discompose her own.
5 The slip shod 'prentice from his master's door
Had pared the dirt, and sprinkled round the floor.
Now Moll had whirled her mop with dext'rous airs,
Prepared to scrub the entry and the stairs.
The youth with broomy stumps began to trace
10 The kennel-edge[9] where wheels had worn the place.
The small-coal man[1] was heard with cadence deep,
Till drowned in shriller notes of chimney-sweep:
Duns[2] at his lordship's gate began to meet;
And brick-dust Moll had screamed through half the street.[3]
15 The turnkey now his flock returning sees,
Duly let out a-nights to steal for fees.[4]
The watchful bailiffs take their silent stands,[5]
And schoolboys lag with satchels in their hands.   p. 1709

SYLVIA PLATH

Morning Song

Love set you going like a fat gold watch.
The midwife slapped your footsoles, and your bald cry
Took its place among the elements.

Our voices echo, magnifying your arrival. New statue.
5 In a drafty museum, your nakedness
Shadows our safety. We stand round blankly as walls.

I'm no more your mother
Than the cloud that distils a mirror to reflect its own slow
Effacement at the wind's hand.

10 All night your moth-breath
Flickers among the flat pink roses. I wake to listen:

---

7. Hired coach. *Hardly:* Scarcely; i.e., they are just beginning to appear.   8. A stock name for a servant girl. Moll (lines 7, 14) is a frequent lower-class nickname.   9. Edge of the gutter that ran down the middle of the street. *Trace:* "To find old Nails." (Swift's note)   1. A seller of coal and charcoal.   2. Bill collectors.   3. Selling powdered brick that was used to clean knives.
4. Jailers collected fees from prisoners for their keep and often let them out at night so they could steal to pay expenses.   5. Looking for those on their "wanted" lists.

A far sea moves in my ear.

One cry, and I stumble from bed, cow-heavy and floral
In my Victorian nightgown.
Your mouth opens clean as a cat's. The window square   15
Whitens and swallows its dull stars. And now you try
Your handful of notes;
The clear vowels rise like balloons.   1961

▼ ▼ ▼

SITUATION AND SETTING A Glossary

allusion: a reference to a text or myth, outside the poem itself, that carries
  its own history of meaning
occasional poem: a poem written about or for a specific occasion, public
  or private
referential: making use of a specific historical moment or event
setting: the time and place of the poem's action
situation: the context of the poem's action, what is happening when the
  poem begins
spatial setting: the place of a poem
temporal setting: the time of a poem

QUESTIONS

1. What facts do we actually have about the speaker of "My Last Duchess"?
On what basis do we form our evaluation of him? How does the setting contribute to the characterization? At what point in reading the poem do you become aware of the precise situation?

2. How much do we know about the child in "A Mongoloid Child Handling Shells on the Beach"? What do each of the following words contribute to the portrait of her: "slow" (lines 1, 8), "unbroken" (line 5), "soberly" (line 7), "hums" (line 8)? How does the boisterousness of the other children help to characterize the main character? What does the seaside setting contribute to the poem? What is the poem's tone?

3. What is the plot of "Labor Day"? How long ago did the central events occur? How can you tell? In what ways has the speaker's attitudes toward the events changed?

4. What do we come to know about the speaker in "Boston Year"? about the other residents of Boston? What kinds of attitudes toward her tastes does the speaker encounter? toward her color? What kind of year was it, all things considered? How is Boston itself characterized? What details in the poem justify the final images of red and gray?

WRITING SUGGESTIONS

1. Choose one of the poems you've read in this chapter and try to connect it to an experience in your own life that has helped you to appreciate the poem. Write a page or two explaining how the poem speaks to your particular situation.

2. What, exactly, happens in "The Good-Morrow"? How does the speaker feel about his lover? about the night of love? about himself? What is the evidence for his feelings about each of these things? What does the dawn have to do with the speaker's state of mind? with the tone of the poem? Write a brief two-page paper about the significance of the time setting.

3. Consult at least three handbooks of literary terms, and compare their definitions of *aubade* and *aube*. Consider the poems at the end of this chapter by Shakespeare, Donne, Chin, Swift, and Plath. Choose *one* of these poems and analyze how closely it relates to the tradition of morning poems described in the handbooks. Write a short essay (no more than two pages long) in which you explain how the poem achieves its effects by employing and modifying or rejecting the standard expectations of how mornings are to be described in poetry.

4. Consult a handbook of classical literature, and find out how Roman poets represented sunrises mythologically. (Hint: look up Phoebus, then— guided by the handbook or a reference librarian—look at several poems in which Phoebus or his fiery car is described in detail.) Consider carefully the opening lines of Swift's "A Description of the Morning." Write a short account (no more than three paragraphs) of how Swift's first two lines work: in what ways do they use and modify the standard mythological expectations? What do you make of the comparison of modern ordinary life to mythic patterns? What kind of evaluation of modern life (or of mythology) seems to be implied?

STUDENT WRITING

Below is an excerpt from one student's first response to Linda Pastan's "To a Daughter Leaving Home." The student's assignment was similar to Writing Suggestion number 1. Note how she asks Pastan questions about meaning as a way of articulating her own response to and questions about the poem.

A Letter to an Author

Kimberly Smith

Dear Linda,

I read your poem "To a Daughter Leaving Home" and it really grabbed my attention. I felt as if I were in your head knowing exactly how you felt when you wrote it. It was a feeling that a father, mother or even a child could understand. I also understand that you were born in New York, as I was. After reading the poem and finding out that we were born in the same place, I felt a connection to you. I came to Tucson from New Jersey and it was a very big culture shock. Knowing you are from the east gave me an easy feeling, a feeling of home.

I can remember back when I learned how to ride a bike. My father gave me the incentive that if I could ride to him without falling, then he would take me out for a lobster dinner. So, I did. I was ten and I got on that bike and peddled away until I could catch my balance and my Dad could let me go. I know now that learning to ride my bike meant more than my father watching me ride down the road. It was a symbol of freedom and growing up. It was time for my parents to let go a little more. I saw that same feeling in your poem also. Is that what you meant? Did you intend the bike image to portray a feeling of growing up and moving along in life?

It seemed to me that you wrote the poem to represent stages of a child's life. The first stage is from the beginning to the line "on two round wheels" (line 6). This stage, I believe, is when a baby is learning to walk and he or she wobbles around until getting the hang of it. The second stage is until the line "sprinted to catch up" (line 14). These are the elementary years and maybe junior high, when the child is trying to be on her own and do things for herself. I can remember this stage very well. I thought that I was at an age where I did not need my parents' help anymore. I used to say, "Mom, I am eleven years old and I am old enough to stay alone. I don't need a baby-sitter." The next stage, which I believe is one of the biggest changes in a child's life, ends at the line "with laughter" (line 20). This stage, to me, is very clearly marked high school. The idea about growing more distant I related to very well. That is because I definitely grew up a lot and learned a lot during high school. I got a car and finally felt like an individual, with her own mind. I was able to make my own decisions which was very important to me.

The language you have chosen is very simple, just like the stages of a child's life. Your sentences are short and to the point. I believe that you arranged the poem in the way you did to show a balance. The arrangement of the poem on paper is straight, just like a bike ride and just as parents want their child's life to be. I believe that you chose your words very carefully. For example, "thud" (line 12) has a deep and powerful meaning. It coincides with the last word of the poem, "goodbye" (line 24). Thud is a very final word as if you fell and you heard a big thud. "Goodbye" (line 24) has that same meaning here. You get a feeling of the end instead of just a new beginning. That is what I felt when I read those words. Did you intend to show that same connection between the words "thud" (line 12) and "goodbye" (line 24) that I saw?

There is one impression that I am getting from you in your poem that I do not agree with. I am not sure if you are intending this, but I got the feeling that you have the idea that as children go farther away that they become more fragile. That may be true in some cases, but if children are brought up in an environment that they are held in a glass box all of their life, then, in that case, it is definitely about time that they moved out on their own. Everyone is going to make mistakes but they only mean something if you can fix them yourself. I always tell my father that I appreciate his advice but sometimes I need to figure things out on my own and that making mistakes is all about growing up.

I learned a lot from your poem. I hope you enjoy my comments and feelings.

Yours truly,

Kimberly Smith

4 LANGUAGE

Fiction and drama depend upon language just as poetry does, but in a poem almost everything comes down to the particular meanings and implications of individual words. In stories and plays, we are likely to keep our attention primarily on character and plot—what is happening in front of us or in the action as we imagine it in our minds—and although words are crucial to how we imagine the characters and how we respond to what happens to them, we are not as likely to pause over any one word as we may need to in a poem. Because poems often are short and use only a few words, a lot depends on every single one. Poetry sometimes feels like prose that is distilled: only the most essential words are there. Just barely enough is said to communicate in the most basic way, using the most elemental signs of meaning and feeling—and each chosen for exactly the right shade of meaning. But elemental does not necessarily mean simple, and these signs may be very rich in their meanings and complex in their effects.

Precision and Ambiguity

Let's look first at two poems that create some of their major effects by emphasizing a single key word.

RICHARD ARMOUR

Hiding Place

A speaker at a meeting of the New York State Frozen Food Locker Association declared that the best hiding place in event of an atomic explosion is a frozen-food locker, where "radiation will not penetrate."[1]

—NEWS ITEM

Move over, ham
And quartered cow,

1. Before home freezers became popular, many Americans rented lockers in specially equipped commercial buildings.

759

My Geiger says
The time is now.

Yes, now I lay me
Down to sleep,
And if I die,
At least I'll keep.

1954

YVOR WINTERS

At the San Francisco Airport

to my daughter, 1954

This is the terminal: the light
Gives perfect vision, false and hard;
The metal glitters, deep and bright.
Great planes are waiting in the yard—
They are already in the night.

And you are here beside me, small,
Contained and fragile, and intent
On things that I but half recall—
Yet going whither you are bent.
I am the past, and that is all.

But you and I in part are one:
The frightened brain, the nervous will,
The knowledge of what must be done,
The passion to acquire the skill
To face that which you dare not shun.

The rain of matter upon sense
Destroys me momently. The score:
There comes what will come. The expense
Is what one thought, and something more—
One's being and intelligence.

This is the terminal, the break.
Beyond this point, on lines of air,
You take the way that you must take;
And I remain in light and stare—
In light, and nothing else, awake.

1954

In "Hiding Place," almost all the poem's comedy depends on the final
word, "keep." In the child's prayer that the poem echoes, to "pray the Lord my

soul to keep" does not exactly involve cold storage (though it implies, theologically, a distinct lack of afterlife heat), and so the poem depends upon an outrageous double meaning. The key word is chosen because it can mean more than one thing; in this case, the importance of the word involves its **ambiguity** (an ability to mean more than one thing) rather than its **precision** (exactness).

In the second poem, the several possible meanings of a single word are probed more soberly and thoughtfully. What does it *mean* to be in a place called a "terminal"? the poem asks. As the parting of father and daughter is explored, carefully, the place of parting and the means of transportation begin to take on meanings larger than their simple referential ones. The poem is full of contrasts—young and old, light and dark, past and present, security and adventure. The father ("I am the past," line 10) remains in the light, among known objects and experience familiar to his many years; the daughter is about to depart into the night, the unknown, the uncertain future. But they both share a sense of the necessity of the parting, of the need for the daughter to mature, gain knowledge, acquire experience. Is she going off to school? to college? to her first job? We don't know, but her plane ride clearly means a new departure and a clean break with childhood, dependency, the past.

So much depends upon the word "terminal." It refers to the airport building, of course, but it also implies a boundary, an extremity, an end, something that is limited, a place where a connection is broken. Important as well is the unambiguous meaning of certain words, i.e., what these other words **denote.** The final stanza is articulated flatly, as if the speaker has recovered completely from the momentary confusion of stanza 4, when "being and intelligence" are lost in the emotion of the parting itself. The words "break," "point," "way," and "remain" are almost completely unemotional and colorless; they do not make value judgments or offer personal views, but rather define and describe. The sharp articulation of the last stanza stresses the **denotations** of the words employed. It is as if the speaker is trying to disengage himself from the emotion of the situation and just give the facts.

Words, however, are more than hard blocks of meaning on whose sense everyone agrees. They also have a more personal side, and they carry emotional force and shades of suggestion. The words we use indicate not only what we mean but how we feel about it, and we choose words that we hope will engage others emotionally and persuasively, in conversation and daily usage as well as in poems. A person who holds office is, quite literally (and unemotionally), an "officeholder," a word that clearly denotes what he or she does. But if we want to convince someone that an officeholder is wise, trustworthy, and deserving of political support we may call that person a "political leader" or perhaps a "statesman"; whereas if we want to promote distrust or contempt of officeholders we might call them "politicians" or "bureaucrats" or "political hacks." These latter words have clear **connotations**—suggestions of emotional coloration that imply our attitude and invite a similar one on the part of our hearers. What words **connote** can be just as important to a poem as what they denote, although some poems depend primarily on denotation and some more on connotation.

"At the San Francisco Airport" seems to depend primarily on denotation; the speaker tries to *specify* the meanings and implications of the parting with his daughter, and his tendency to split categories neatly for the two of them at first contributes to the sense of clarity and certainty which the speaker wants to project. He is the past (line 10) and what remains (line 24); he has age and experience, his life is the known quantity, he stands in the light. She, on the other hand, is committed to the adventure of going into the night; she seems small, fragile, and her identity exists in the uncertain future. Yet the connotations of some words carry strong emotional force as well as clear definition: that the daughter seems "small" and "fragile" to the speaker suggests his fear for her, something quite different from her sense of adventure. The neat, clean categories keep breaking down, and the speaker's feelings keep showing through. In stanza 1, the speaker tells us that the light in the terminal gives "perfect vision" but he also notices, indirectly, its artificial quality: it is "false" and "hard," suggesting the limits of the rationalism he tries to maintain. That artificial light shines over most of the poem and honors the speaker's effort, but the whole poem represents his struggle, and in stanza 4 the signals of disturbance are very strong as, despite an insistence on a vocabulary of calculation, his rational facade collapses completely. If we have observed his verbal strategies carefully, we should not be surprised to find him at the end just *staring* in the artificial light, merely awake, although the poem has shown him to be unconsciously awake to much more than he will candidly admit.

"At the San Francisco Airport" is an unusually intricate and complicated poem, and it offers us, if we are willing to examine very precisely its carefully crafted fabric, an unusually rich insight into how complex it is to be human and to have human feelings and foibles when we think we must be rational machines. But connotations can work more simply. The following epitaph, for example, even though it describes the mixed feelings one person has about another, depends heavily on the common connotations of fairly common words.

WALTER DE LA MARE

Slim Cunning Hands

Slim cunning hands at rest, and cozening eyes—
Under this stone one loved too wildly lies;
How false she was, no granite could declare;
Nor all earth's flowers, how fair.   1950

What the speaker in "Slim Cunning Hands" remembers about the dead woman—her hands, her eyes—tells part of the story; her physical presence was clearly important to him, and the poem's other nouns—stone, granite, flowers—all remind us of her death and its finality. All these words denote objects having to do with rituals that memorialize a departed life. Granite and stone connote finality as well, and flowers connote fragility and suggest the shortness of life (which is why they have become the symbolic language of funerals). The way the speaker talks about the woman expresses, in just a few words, the complexity of his love for her. She was loved, he says, too "wildly"—by him perhaps, and apparently by others. The excitement she offered is suggested by the word, and also the lack of control. The words "cunning" and "cozening" help us interpret both her wildness and falsity; they suggest her calculation, cleverness, and untrustworthiness as well as her skill, persuasiveness, and ability to please. And the word "fair," a simple yet very inclusive word, suggests how totally attractive the speaker finds her: her beauty is just as incapable of being expressed by flowers as her fickleness is of being expressed in something as permanent as stone. Simple words here tell us perhaps all we need to know of a long story—or at least the speaker's version of it.

Words like "fair" and "cozening" are clearly loaded; they imply more emotionally than they literally mean. They have strong, clear connotations and tell us what to think, what evaluation to make, and they suggest the basis for the evaluation. Both words in the title of the following poem turn out to be key ones in its meaning and effect:

PAT MORA

Gentle Communion

Even the long-dead are willing to move.
Without a word, she came with me from the desert.

Mornings she wanders through my rooms
making beds, folding socks.

5   Since she can't hear me anymore,
Mamande[2] ignores the questions I never knew
to ask, about her younger days, her red
hair, the time she fell and broke her nose
in the snow. I will never know.

10   When I try to make her laugh,
to disprove her sad album face, she leaves
the room, resists me as she resisted
grinning for cameras, make-up, English.

While I write, she sits and prays,
15   feet apart, legs never crossed,
the blue housecoat buttoned high
as her hair dries white, girlish
around her head and shoulders.

She closes her eyes, bows her head,
20   and like a child presses her hands together,
her patient flesh steeple, the skin
worn, like the pages of her prayer book.

Sometimes I sit in her wide-armed
chair as I once sat in her lap.
25   Alone, we played a quiet I Spy.
She peeled grapes I still taste.

She removes the thin skin, places
the luminous coolness on my tongue.
I know not to bite or chew. I wait
30   for the thick melt,
our private green honey.   1991

Neither of the words in the title appears in the text itself, but both resonate throughout the poem. "Communion" is the more powerful of the words; here, it comes to imply the close ritualized relationship between the speaker and "Mamande." Mamande has long been dead but now returns, recalling to the speaker a host of memories and providing a sense of history and family identity. To the speaker, the reunion has a powerful value, reminding her of rituals, habits, and beliefs that "place" her and affirm her heritage. The past is strong in the speaker's mind and in the poem. Many details are recalled from album photographs—the blue housecoat (line 16), the sad face (line 11), the white hair that was once red (lines 7–8 and 17), the posture at prayer (lines 19–22),

2. A child's conflation of *mama grande* (Spanish for "grandmother").

the big chair (lines 23–24), the plain old-fashioned style (line 13)—and the speaker's childhood memories fade into them as she recalls a specific intimate moment.

The full effect of the word "communion"—which describes an intimate moment of union and a ritual—comes only in the final lines when the speaker remembers the secret of the grapes and recalls their sensuous feel and taste. The moment brings together the experience of different generations and cultures and represents a sacred sharing: the Spanish grandmother had resisted English, modernity, and show (line 13), and the speaker is a poet, writing (and publishing) in English, but the two have a common "private" (line 31) moment ritually shared and forever memorable. At the end, too, the full sense of "gentle" becomes evident—a word that sums up the softness, quietness, and understatedness of the experience, the personal qualities of "Mamande," and the unpretentious but dignified social level of the family heritage. Throughout the text, other words—ordinary, simple, and precise—are chosen with equal care to suggest the sense of personal dignity, revealed identity, and verbal power that the speaker comes to accept as her own. Look especially at the words "move" (line 1), "steeple" (line 21), and "luminous" (line 28).

In the two poems that follow we can readily see why the specific words are chosen because, although both poems express a male preference for the same sort of feminine appearance, the grounds of appeal are vastly different.

BEN JONSON

Still to Be Neat[3]

Still[4] to be neat, still to be dressed,
As you were going to a feast;
Still to be powdered, still perfumed;
Lady, it is to be presumed,
Though art's hid causes are not found,   5
All is not sweet, all is not sound.

Give me a look, give me a face
That makes simplicity a grace;
Robes loosely flowing, hair as free;
Such sweet neglect more taketh me   10
Than all th' adulteries of art.
They strike mine eyes, but not my heart.   1609

---

3. A song from Jonson's play *The Silent Woman* (1609–10).   4. Continually.

ROBERT HERRICK

Delight in Disorder

A sweet disorder in the dress
Kindles in clothes a wantonness.
A lawn[5] about the shoulders thrown
Into a fine distraction;
5   An erring lace, which here and there
Enthralls the crimson stomacher,[6]
A cuff neglectful, and thereby
Ribbands[7] to flow confusedly;
A winning wave, deserving note,
10 In the tempestuous petticoat;
A careless shoestring, in whose tie
I see a wild civility;
Do more bewitch me than when art
Is too precise[8] in every part.   1648

The poem "Still to Be Neat" begins by describing a woman who looks too neat and orderly; she seems too perfect to be believed, the speaker says, and he has to assume that there is a reason for such overly fastidious grooming, that she is covering up something. He worries that something is wrong underneath—that not all is "sweet" and "sound." "Sweet" could mean several things; its meaning becomes clearer when it is repeated in the next stanza in a more specific context. "Sound" begins to suggest the speaker's moral earnestness: it is a strong word, implying a suspicion that something is deeply wrong.

When "sweet" is repeated in line 10, it has taken on specific attributes from what the speaker has said about things he likes in a less calculated physical appearance. Now it appears to mean easy, attractive, unpremeditated. And when the speaker springs "adulteries" on us in the next line as a description of the woman's cosmeticizing, it is clear what he fears—that the appearance of the too neat, too made-up woman covers serious flaws, that she is trying to appear as someone she is not. "Adulteries" suggests the addition of something foreign, something unlike her own nature, and it is a strong, disapproving word. The "soundness" he had worried about involves her integrity; his objection is certainly moral, probably sexual. He wants a woman to be simple and chaste; he wants women to be just what they seem to be.

The speaker in "Delight in Disorder" wants his women easy and simple

5. Scarf of fine linen.   6. Ornamental covering for the breasts.   7. Ribbons.   8. In the 16th and 17th centuries Puritans were often called Precisians because of their fastidiousness.

too, but for different reasons. He finds disorder "sweet" (line 1), and seems almost to be answering the first speaker, providing a different rationale for art-less appearance. His grounds of preference are clear early: his support of "wantonness" (line 2) is close to the opposite in its moral suppositions of the first speaker's disapproval of "adulteries." This speaker wants a careless look because he thinks it's sexy, and many of the words he chooses suggest sensual-ity and availability: "distraction" (line 4), "erring" (line 5), "tempestuous" (line 10), "wild" (line 12). The speakers in the two poems read informality of dress very differently and have very different expectations of the person who dresses in a particular way. We find out quite a lot about each speaker. Their common subject allows us to see clearly how different they are, and how what one sees is in the eye of the beholder, how values and assumptions are built into the words one chooses even for description. Jonson has created a speaker who wants an informally clad woman who has a natural grace and ease of manner because she is confident of herself, dependable, and chaste. Herrick has cre-ated a speaker who finds informality of dress fetching and sexy and indicative of sensuality and availability.

Words are the starting point for all poetry, and almost every word is likely to be significant, either denotatively, connotatively, or both. Poets who know their craft pick each word with care to express exactly what needs to be expressed and to suggest every emotional shade that the poem is calculated to evoke in us. Often individual words qualify and amplify one another—suggestions clar-ify other suggestions, and meanings grow upon meanings—and thus the way the words are put together can be important too. Notice, for example, that in "Slim Cunning Hands" the final emphasis is on how *fair* in appearance the woman was; the speaker's last word describes the quality he can't forget in spite of her lack of a different kind of fairness and his distrust of her, the quality that, even though it doesn't justify everything else, mitigates all the disappointment and hurt.

That word does not stand all by itself, however, any more than any other word in a poem can be considered all alone. Every word exists within larger units of meaning—sentences, patterns of comparisons and contrasts, the whole poem—and where the word is and how it is used are often important. The final word or words may be especially emphatic (as in "Slim Cunning Hands"), and words that are repeated take on a special intensity, as "terminal" does in "At the San Francisco Airport" or as "chartered" and "cry" do in "London" (p. 875). Certain words often stand out, because they are used in an unusual way (like "chartered" in "London" or "adulteries" in "Still to Be Neat") or because they are given an artificial prominence—through unusual sentence structure, for example, or because the title calls special attention to them.

Sometimes word choice in poems is less dramatic and less obviously "significant" but equally important. Simple appropriateness is often, in fact, what makes the words in a poem work, and when words do not call special attention to themselves they are sometimes the most effective. Precision of denotation may be just as impressive and productive of specific effects as the resonance or ambiguous suggestiveness of connotation. Often poems achieve their power by a combination of verbal effects, setting off elaborate figures of speech (which we will discuss shortly) or other complicated strategies with simple words chosen to mark exact actions, moments, or states of mind. Notice, for example, how carefully the following poem produces its complex description of emotional patterns by delineating precise stages (which are then elaborated) of feeling.

EMILY DICKINSON

[After great pain, a formal feeling comes—]

> After great pain, a formal feeling comes—
> The Nerves sit ceremonious, like Tombs—
> The stiff Heart questions was it He, that bore,
> And Yesterday, or Centuries before?
>
> 5   The Feet, mechanical, go round—
> Of Ground, or Air, or Ought—
> A Wooden way
> Regardless grown,
> A Quartz contentment, like a stone—
>
> 10   This is the Hour of Lead—
> Remembered, if outlived,
> As Freezing Persons recollect the Snow—
> ca. 1862   First—Chill—then Stupor—then the letting go—

In the following poem, notice how the title calls upon us to wonder, from the beginning, how playful and how patterned the boy's bedtime romp with his father is. As you read it, try to be conscious of the emotional effects created by the choice of words that seem to be key ones. Which words establish the bond between the two males?

THEODORE ROETHKE

My Papa's Waltz

The whiskey on your breath
Could make a small boy dizzy;
But I hung on like death:
Such waltzing was not easy.

We romped until the pans   5
Slid from the kitchen shelf;
My mother's countenance
Could not unfrown itself.

The hand that held my wrist
Was battered on one knuckle;   10
At every step you missed
My right ear scraped a buckle.

You beat time on my head
With a palm caked hard by dirt,
Then waltzed me off to bed   15
Still clinging to your shirt.   1948

Exactly what is the situation in "My Papa's Waltz"? What are the economic
circumstances in the family? How can you tell? What indications are there of
the family's social class? of the father's line of work? How would you characterize the speaker? How does the poem indicate his pleasure in the bedtime ritual? Which words suggest the boy's excitement? Which suggest his anxiety?
How can you tell how the speaker feels about his father? What clues are there
about what the mother is like? How can you tell that the experience is remembered at some years' distance? What clues are there in the word choice that an
adult is remembering a childhood experience? In what sense is the poem a tribute to memories of the father? How would you describe the poem's tone?

The subtlety and force of word choice is sometimes very much affected by
word order, the way the sentences are put together. Sometimes poems are
driven to unusual word order because of the demands of rhyme and meter, but
ordinarily poets use word order very much as prose writers do, to create a particular emphasis. When an unusual word order is used, you can be pretty sure
that something there merits special attention. Notice the odd constructions in
the second and third stanzas of "My Papa's Waltz"—the way the speaker talks
about the abrasion of buckle on ear in line 12, for example. He does not say
that the buckle scraped his ear, but rather puts it the other way round—a big

difference in the kind of effect created, for it avoids placing blame and refuses to specify any unpleasant effect. Had he said that the buckle scraped his ear—the normal way of putting it—we would have to worry about the fragile ear. The **syntax** (sentence structure) of the poem channels our feeling and helps to control what we think of the "waltz."

The most curious part of the poem is the second stanza, for it is there that the silent mother appears, and the syntax there is peculiar in two places. In lines 5–6, the connection between the romping and the pans falling is stated oddly: "We romped *until* the pans / Slid from the kitchen shelf." The speaker does not say that they knocked down the pans or imply that there was awkward-ness, but he does suggest energetic activity and duration. He implies intensity, almost design—as though the romping would not be complete until the pans fell. And the sentence about the mother—odd but effective—makes her posi-tion clear. She is a silent bystander in this male ritual, and her frown seems molded on her face. It is not as if she is frightened or angry but as if she too is performing a ritual, holding a frown on her face as if it is part of her role in the ritual, as well as perhaps a facet of her stern character. The syntax implies that she *has to* maintain the frown, and the falling of the pans almost seems to be for her benefit. She disapproves, but she is still their audience.

Word order is not always as complicated or crucial as it is in "My Papa's Waltz," but poets often manipulate the ordinary prose order of a sentence to make a specific point or create a specific emphasis or effect. In the passage below from *Paradise Lost*, for example, notice how the syntax first sets a formal tone for the passage, then calls attention to the complexities of theology that it expresses, and (in lines 44ff.) imitates, by holding back key elements of the grammar, the Fall that is being described.

Sometimes poems create, as well, a powerful sense of the way minds and emotions work by varying normal syntactical order in special ways. Listen, for example, in the following poem to the speaker's sudden loss of vocal control in the midst of what seems to be a calm analysis of her feelings about sexual behavior.

SHARON OLDS

Sex Without Love

How do they do it, the ones who make love
without love? Beautiful as dancers,
gliding over each other like ice-skaters

over the ice, fingers hooked
inside each other's bodies, faces
red as steak, wine, wet as the   5
children at birth whose mothers are going to
give them away. How do they come to the
come to the   come to the   God   come to the
still waters, and not love   10
the one who came there with them, light
rising slowly as steam off their joined
skin? These are the true religious,
the purists, the pros, the ones who will not
accept a false Messiah, love the   15
priest instead of the God. They do not
mistake the lover for their own pleasure,
they are like great runners: they know they are alone
with the road surface, the cold, the wind,
the fit of their shoes, their over-all cardio-   20
vascular health—just factors, like the partner
in the bed, and not the truth, which is the
single body alone in the universe
against its own best time.   1984

    The poem starts calmly enough, with a simple rhetorical question implying
that the speaker just cannot understand sex without love. The second through
fourth lines compare such sexual activity with some distant aesthetic, with two
carefully delineated examples, and the speaker—although plainly disapproving—seems coolly, almost chillingly, in control of the analysis and evaluation.
But by the end of the fourth line, something begins to seem odd: "hooked"
seems too ugly and extreme a way to characterize the lovers' fingers, however
much the speaker may disapprove, and by line 6, the syntax seems to break
down. How does "wine" fit the syntax of the line? Is it parallel with "steak,"
another example of redness? or is it somehow related to the last part of the sentence, parallel with "faces"? But neither of these possibilities quite works. At
best, the punctuation is faulty; at worst the speaker's mind is working too fast
for the language it can generate, scrambling its images. We can't yet be quite
sure what is going on, but by the ninth line the lack of control is manifest with
the compulsive repeating (three times) of "come to the" and the interjected
"God."

    Such verbal behavior—here concretized by the way the poem orders its
words—invites us to reevaluate the speaker's moralism relative to her emotional involvement with the issues and with her representation of sexuality
itself. The speaker's values, as well as those who have sex without love, become
a subject for evaluation.

Words are the basic building materials of poetry. They are of many kinds and are used in many different ways and in different—sometimes surprising— combinations. Words are seldom simple, even when we know their meanings and recognize their syntax as conventional and transparent. The careful examination of them individually and collectively is a crucial part of the process of reading poems, and learning exactly what kinds of questions to ask about the words that poems use and how poems use them is one of the most basic—and rewarding—skills a reader of poetry can develop.

Here is a group of poems illustrating varieties of word usages and word orders. The discussion of language continues later in this chapter with an explanation of figures of speech.

▼   ▼   ▼

GERARD MANLEY HOPKINS

Pied Beauty[9]

Glory be to God for dappled things—
  For skies of couple-color as a brinded[1] cow;
    For rose-moles all in stipple[2] upon trout that swim;
Fresh-firecoal chestnut-falls;[3] finches' wings;
5   Landscape plotted and pieced—fold, fallow, and plow;
    And all trades, their gear and tackle and trim.
All things counter, original, spare, strange;
  Whatever is fickle, freckled (who knows how?)
    With swift, slow; sweet, sour; adazzle, dim;
10 He fathers-forth whose beauty is past change:
            Praise him.   1877

WILLIAM CARLOS WILLIAMS

The Red Wheelbarrow

so much depends
upon

a red wheel
barrow

9. Particolored beauty: having patches or sections of more than one color.   1. Streaked or spotted.   2. Rose-colored dots or flecks.   3. Fallen chestnuts as red as burning coals.

glazed with rain   5
water

beside the white
chickens.   1923

E. E. CUMMINGS

[in Just-][4]

in Just-
spring   when the world is mud-
luscious the little
lame balloonman

whistles   far   and wee   5

and eddieandbill come
running from marbles and
piracies and it's
spring

when the world is puddle-wonderful   10

the queer
old balloonman whistles
far   and   wee
and bettyandisbel come dancing

from hop-scotch and jump-rope and   15
it's
spring
and
    the
        goat-footed   20

balloonMan   whistles
far
and
wee[5]   1923

---

4. *Chansons innocentes* I.   **5.** Pan, whose Greek name means "everything," is traditionally represented with a syrinx (or the pipes of Pan). The upper half of his body is human, the lower half goat, and as the father of Silenus he is associated with the spring rites of Dionysus.

RICARDO PAU-LLOSA

Foreign Language

Every object is a room
you walk words into.
Take an apple, its windows peeling.
In your hands the apple's
5   door opens a crack
and the words barge through
like salesmen confident of a kill.
The gerund opens the mail,
the verb's hands rumble through
10   the refrigerator, an adverb
caresses the daughter's knee,
the noun, its feet on the sofa,
says everything is as it should be.
Teeth tear through the walls of the apple
15   like a plane crashing in the suburbs.
The mouth is full of a wet white word
you can't pronounce, a pronoun
reading the newspaper in the living room.
When you bit, you never knew what hit you.

1992

SUSAN MUSGRAVE

Hidden Meaning

Imagine hailing a taxi
and the driver is a poet.
You could say, "Tell me a poem
and take me to Costa Rica."
5   As you drive away.

Imagine getting into a taxi
where the driver is a *real* poet.
You could quote Robert Penn Warren
without feeling ridiculous: "Driver,
10   do you truly, truly know what flesh is?"

Imagine getting into a taxi
and it's snowy Saskatchewan
and the poet has not made a dollar.
The snow goes on falling
15   and now you're both stuck in it; poetry

gets you nowhere faster than anything.

Imagine breaking into a taxi
and finding two poets frozen together.
You'd look at one another as if the world
had meaning for the first time, hidden   20
meaning, and wouldn't it be a kind
of terrible occasion.   1991

EMILY DICKINSON

[I dwell in Possibility—]

I dwell in Possibility—
A fairer House than Prose—
More numerous of Windows—
Superior—for Doors—

Of Chambers as the Cedars—   5
Impregnable of Eye—
And for an Everlasting Roof
The Gambrels[6] of the Sky—

Of Visitors—the fairest—
For Occupation—This—   10
The spreading wide my narrow Hands
ca. 1862   To gather Paradise—

JOHN MILTON

from Paradise Lost[7]

I

Of man's first disobedience, and the fruit[8]
Of that forbidden tree whose mortal taste
Brought death into the world, and all our woe,
With loss of Eden, till one greater Man
Restore us, and regain the blissful seat,   5

6. Roofs with double slopes.   7. The opening lines of Books I and II and a short passage from
Book III. The first passage states the poem's subject, and the second describes Satan's beginning
address to the council of fallen angels meeting to discuss strategy; in the third, God is looking down
from Heaven at his new human creation and watching Satan approach the Earth.   8. The apple,
but also the consequences.

Sing, Heav'nly Muse,[9] that, on the secret top
Of Oreb, or of Sinai, didst inspire
That shepherd who first taught the chosen seed
In the beginning how the Heav'ns and Earth
Rose out of Chaos: or, if Sion hill
Delight thee more, and Siloa's brook that flowed
Fast[1] by the oracle of God, I thence
Invoke thy aid to my adventurous song,
That with no middle flight intends to soar
Above th' Aonian mount,[2] while it pursues
Things unattempted yet in prose or rhyme.
And chiefly thou, O Spirit,[3] that dost prefer
Before all temples th' upright heart and pure,
Instruct me, for thou know'st; thou from the first
Wast present, and, with mighty wings outspread,
Dovelike sat'st brooding on the vast abyss,
And mad'st it pregnant: what in me is dark
Illumine; what is low, raise and support;
That, to the height of this great argument,[4]
I may assert Eternal Providence,
And justify the ways of God to men.
    Say first (for Heav'n hides nothing from thy view,
Nor the deep tract of Hell), say first what cause
Moved our grand parents, in that happy state,
Favored of Heav'n so highly, to fall off
From their Creator, and transgress his will
For one restraint, lords of the world besides?[5]
Who first seduced them to that foul revolt?
Th' infernal serpent; he it was, whose guile,
Stirred up with envy and revenge, deceived
The mother of mankind, what time[6] his pride
Had cast him out from Heav'n, with all his host
Of rebel angels, by whose aid, aspiring
To set himself in glory above his peers,
He trusted to have equaled the Most High,

10

15

20

25

30

35

40

---

9. Addressing one of the muses and asking for aid is a convention for the opening lines of an epic;
Milton complicates the standard procedure here by describing sources and circumstances of Judeo-
Christian revelation rather than specifically invoking one of the nine classical muses. Sinai is the
spur of Mount Oreb, where Moses ("That shepherd," line 8, who was traditionally regarded as
author of the first five books of the Bible) received the Law; Sion hill and Siloa (lines 10–11), near
Jerusalem, correspond to the traditional mountain (Helicon) and springs of classical tradition. Later,
in Book VII, Milton calls upon Urania, the muse of astronomy, but he does not mention by name
the muse of epic poetry, Calliope.   1. Close.   2. Mt. Helicon, home of the classical muses.
3. The divine voice that inspired the Hebrew prophets. Genesis 1:2 says that "the Spirit of God
moved upon the face of the waters" as part of the process of Creation; Milton follows tradition in
making the inspirational and communicative function of God present in Creation itself. The passage echoes and merges many biblical references to Creation and divine revelation.   4. Subject.   5. In all other respects. For: because of.   6. When.

If he opposed; and with ambitious aim
Against the throne and monarchy of God,
Raised impious war in Heav'n and battle proud,
With vain attempt. Him the Almighty Power
Hurled headlong flaming from th' ethereal sky,   45
With hideous ruin and combustion down
To bottomless perdition, there to dwell
In adamantine chains and penal fire,
Who durst defy th' Omnipotent to arms.[7]

*   *   *

II

High on a throne of royal state, which far
Outshone the wealth of Ormus and of Ind,[8]
Or where the gorgeous East with richest hand
Show'rs on her kings barbaric pearl and gold,
Satan exalted sat, by merit raised   5
To that bad eminence; and, from despair
Thus high uplifted beyond hope, aspires
Beyond thus high, insatiate to pursue
Vain war with Heav'n, and by success[9] untaught,
His proud imaginations thus displayed: 10
    "Powers and Dominions, Deities of Heav'n,
For since no deep within her gulf can hold
Immortal vigor, though oppressed and fall'n,
I give not Heav'n for lost. From this descent
Celestial virtues rising will appear   15
More glorious and more dread than from no fall,
And trust themselves to fear no second fate.
Me though just right and the fixed laws of Heav'n
Did first create your leader, next, free choice,
With what besides, in council or in fight,   20
Hath been achieved of merit, yet this loss,
Thus far at least recovered, hath much more
Established in a safe unenvied throne
Yielded with full consent. The happier state
In Heav'n, which follows dignity, might draw   25
Envy from each inferior; but who here
Will envy whom the highest place exposes
Foremost to stand against the Thunderer's aim
Your bulwark, and condemns to greatest share
Of endless pain? Where there is then no good   30
For which to strive, no strife can grow up there
From faction; for none sure will claim in hell

---

7. After invoking the muse and giving a brief summary of the poem's subject, an epic regularly
begins *in medias res* (in the midst of things).   8. India. *Ormus:* Hormuz, an island in the Persian
Gulf, famous for pearls.   9. Outcome, either good or bad.

Precédence, none, whose portion is so small
Of present pain, that with ambitious mind
35   Will covet more. With this advantage then
To union, and firm faith, and firm accord,
More than can be in Heav'n, we now return
To claim our just inheritance of old,
Surer to prosper than prosperity
40   Could have assured us; and by what best way,
Whether of open war or covert guile,
We now debate; who can advise, may speak."

        *   *   *

III

        *   *   *

56   Now had th' Almighty Father from above,
From the pure empyrean where he sits
High throned above all height, bent down his eye,
His own works and their works at once to view:
60   About him all the sanctities of Heav'n[1]
Stood thick as stars, and from his sight received
Beatitude past utterance; on his right
The radiant image of his glory sat,
His only Son. On earth he first beheld
65   Our two first parents, yet the only two
Of mankind, in the happy garden placed,
Reaping immortal fruits of joy and love,
Uninterrupted joy, unrivaled love,
In blissful solitude. He then surveyed
70   Hell and the gulf between, and Satan there
Coasting the wall of Heav'n on this side Night
In the dun air sublime,[2] and ready now
To stoop[3] with wearied wings and willing feet
On the bare outside of this world, that seemed
75   Firm land embosomed without firmament,
Uncertain which, in ocean or in air.   1667

Metaphor and Simile

   The language of poetry is almost always visual and pictorial. Rather than depending primarily on abstract ideas and elaborate reasoning, poems depend mainly upon concrete and specific words that create images in our minds.

1. The hierarchies of angels.   2. Aloft in the twilight atmosphere.   3. Swoop down, like a bird of prey.

Poems thus help us to see things fresh and new, or to feel them suggestively through our other physical senses, such as hearing or touch. But, most often, poetry uses the sense of sight in that it helps us form, in our minds, visual impressions, images that communicate more directly than concepts. We "see" yellow leaves on a branch, a father and son waltzing precariously, or two lovers sitting together on the bank of a stream, so that our response begins from a vivid impression of exactly what is happening. Some people think that those media and arts that challenge the imagination of a hearer or reader—radio drama, for example, or poetry—allow us to respond more fully than those (such as television or theater) that actually show things more fully to our physical senses. Certainly they leave more to our imagination, to our mind's eye.

But being visual does not just mean describing, telling us facts, indicating shapes, colors, and specific details and giving us precise discriminations through exacting verbs, nouns, adverbs, and adjectives. Often the vividness of the picture in our minds depends upon comparisons. What we are trying to imagine is pictured in terms of something else familiar to us, and we are asked to think of one thing as if it were something else. Many such comparisons, or **figures of speech,** in which something is pictured or figured forth in terms of something already familiar to us, are taken for granted in daily life. Things we can't see or that aren't familiar to us are imaged as things we already know; for example, God is said to be like a father, Italy is said to be shaped like a boot, life is compared to a forest, a journey, or a sea. Poems use **figurative language** much of the time. A poem may insist that death is like a sunset or sex like an earthquake or that the way to imagine how it feels to be spiritually secure is to think of the way a shepherd takes care of his sheep. The pictorialness of our imagination may *clarify* things for us—scenes, states of mind, ideas—but at the same time it stimulates us to think of how those pictures make us *feel*. Pictures, even when they are mental pictures or imagined visions, may be both denotative and connotative, just as individual words are: they may clarify and make precise, and they may channel our feelings.

In the poem that follows, the poet helps us to visualize the old age and approaching death of the speaker by making comparisons with familiar things—the coming of winter, the approach of sunset, and the dying embers of a fire.

WILLIAM SHAKESPEARE

[That time of year thou mayst in me behold]

That time of year thou mayst in me behold
When yellow leaves, or none, or few, do hang
Upon those boughs which shake against the cold,
Bare ruined choirs, where late the sweet birds sang.
In me thou see'st the twilight of such day
As after sunset fadeth in the west;
Which by and by[1] black night doth take away,
Death's second self,[2] that seals up all in rest.
In me thou see'st the glowing of such fire,
That on the ashes of his youth doth lie,
As the deathbed whereon it must expire,
Consumed with that which it was nourished by.
This thou perceiv'st, which makes thy love more strong,
To love that well which thou must leave ere long.   1609

The first four lines of "That time of year" evoke images of the late autumn;
but notice that the poet does not have the speaker say directly that his physical
condition and age make him resemble autumn. He draws the comparison without stating that it is a comparison: you can see, he says, my own state in the
coming of winter, when the leaves are almost all off the trees. The speaker portrays himself *indirectly* by talking about the passing of the year. The poem uses
metaphor; that is, one thing is pictured *as if* it were something else. "That
time of year" goes on to another metaphor in lines 5–8 and still another in
lines 9–12, and each of the metaphors contributes to our understanding of the
speaker's sense of his old age and approaching death. More important, however, is the way the metaphors give us feelings, an emotional sense of the speaker's age and of his own attitude toward aging. Through the metaphors we
come to understand, appreciate, and to some extent share the increasing sense
of anxiety and urgency that the poem expresses. Our emotional sense of the
poem is largely influenced by the way each metaphor is developed and by the
way each metaphor leads, with its own kind of internal logic, to another.

The images of late autumn in the first four lines all suggest loneliness, loss,
and nostalgia for earlier times. As in the rest of the poem, our eyes are imagined to be the main vehicle for noticing the speaker's age and condition; the

---

1. Shortly.   2. Sleep.

phrase "thou mayst in me behold" (line 1) introduces what we are asked to see, and in both lines 5 and 9 we are similarly told "In me thou see'st. . . ." The picture of the trees shedding their leaves suggests that autumn is nearly over, and we can imagine trees either with yellow leaves, or without leaves, or with just a trace of foliage remaining—the latter perhaps most feelingly suggesting the bleakness and loneliness that characterize the change of seasons, the ending of the life cycle. But other senses are invoked too. The boughs shaking against the cold represent an appeal to our tactile sense, and the next line appeals to our sense of hearing, although only as a reminder that the birds no longer sing. (Notice how exact the visual representation is of the bare, or nearly bare, limbs, even as the cold and the lack of birds are noted; birds lined up like a choir on risers would have made a striking visual image on the barren limbs one above the other, but now there is only the *reminder* of what used to be. The present is quiet, bleak, trembly, and lonely.)

The next four lines are slightly different in tone, and the color changes. From a black-and-white landscape with a few yellow leaves, we come upon a rich and almost warm reminder of a faded sunset. But a somber note does enter the poem in these lines through another figure of speech, **personification,** which involves treating an abstraction, such as death or justice or beauty, as if it were a person. The poem is talking about the coming of night and of sleep, and Sleep is personified and identified as the "second self" of Death (that is, as a kind of "double" for death). The main emphasis is on how night and sleep close in on our sense of twilight, and only secondarily does a reminder of death enter the poem. But it does enter.

The third metaphor—that of the dying embers of a fire—begins in line 9 and continues to color and warm the bleak cold that the poem began with, but it also sharpens the reminder of death. The three main metaphors in the poem work in a way to make our sense of old age and approaching death more familiar, but also more immediate: moving from barren trees, to fading twilight, to dying embers suggests a sensuous increase of color and warmth, but also an increasing urgency. The first metaphor involves a whole season, or at least a segment of one, a matter of days or possibly weeks; the second involves the passing of a single day, reducing the time scale to a matter of minutes, and the third draws our attention to that split second when a glowing ember fades into a gray ash. The final part of the fire metaphor introduces the most explicit sense of death so far, as the metaphor of embers shifts into a direct reminder of death. Embers which had been a metaphor of the speaker's aging body now themselves become, metaphorically, a deathbed; the vitality that nourishes youth is used up just as a log in a fire is. The urgency of the reminder of coming death has now peaked. It is friendlier but now seems immediate and inevitable, a natural part of the life process, and the final two lines then make an explicit plea to make good and intense use of the remaining moments of human relationship.

"That time of year" represents an unusually intricate use of images to organize a poem and focus its emotional impact. Not all poems are so skillfully made, and not all depend on such a full and varied use of metaphor. But most poems use metaphors for at least part of their effect, and often a poem is based on a single metaphor that is fully developed as the major way of making the poem's statement and impact, as in the following poem about the role of a mother and wife.

LINDA PASTAN

Marks

My husband gives me an A
for last night's supper,
an incomplete for my ironing,
a B plus in bed.
My son says I am average,
an average mother, but if
I put my mind to it
I could improve.
My daughter believes
in Pass / Fail and tells me
I pass. Wait 'til they learn
I'm dropping out.   1978

The speaker in "Marks" is obviously not thrilled with the idea of continually being judged, and the metaphor of marks (or grades) as a way of talking about her performance of roles in the family suggests her irritation. The list of the roles implies the many things expected of her, and the three different systems of marking (letter grades, categories to be checked off on a chart, and pass / fail) detail the difficulties of multiple standards. The poem retains the language of schooldays all the way to the end ("learn," line 11; "dropping out," line 12), and the major effect of the poem depends on the irony of the speaker's surrendering to the metaphor the family has thrust upon her; if she is to be judged as if she were a student, she retains the right to leave the system. Ironically, she joins the system (adopts the metaphor for herself) in order to defeat it.

The following poem depends from the beginning—even from its title—on a single metaphor and the values associated with it.

DAVID WAGONER

My Father's Garden

On his way to the open hearth where white-hot steel
Boiled against furnace walls in wait for his lance
To pierce the fireclay and set loose demons
And dragons in molten tons, blazing
Down to the huge satanic caldrons,   5
Each day he would pass the scrapyard, his kind of garden.

In rusty rockeries of stoves and brake drums,
In grottoes of sewing machines and refrigerators,
He would pick flowers for us: small gears and cogwheels
With teeth like petals, with holes for anthers,   10
Long stalks of lead to be poured into toy soldiers,
Ball bearings as big as grapes to knock them down.

He was called a melter. He tried to keep his brain
From melting in those tyger-mouthed mills
Where the same steel reappeared over and over   15
To be reborn in the fire as something better
Or worse: cannons or cars, needles or girders,
Flagpoles, swords, or plowshares.

But it melted. His classical learning ran
Down and away from him, not burning bright.   20
His fingers culled a few cold scraps of Latin
And Greek, *magna sine laude*,[3] for crosswords
And brought home lumps of tin and sewer grills
As if they were his ripe prize vegetables.   1987

The poem is a tribute to the speaker's father and the things he understands and values in his ordinary, workingman's life. The father is a "melter" (line 13) in the steel mills (lines 14–15), and what he values are the things made from what he helps to produce. His avocation has developed from his vocation: he collects metal objects from the scrapyard and brings them home just as some other men would pick flowers for their families. The scrapyard is, says the

3. Without great distinction; a reversal of the usual *magna cum laude*.

speaker, "his kind of garden" (line 6). The life led by the father has been a hard one, but he shows love for his children in the only way he knows how— by bringing home things that mean something to him and that can be made into toys his children will come to value. Describing these scraps as the products of his garden—"As if they were his ripe prize vegetables" (line 24)—has the effect of making them seem home-grown, carefully tended, nurtured by the father into a useful beauty. Instead of crude and ugly pieces of scrap, they become—through the metaphor of the poem—examples of value and beauty corresponding to the warm feelings the speaker has for a father who did what he could with what he knew and what he had.

Poets often are self-conscious and explicit about the ways they use language metaphorically, and sometimes (as in the following poem) they celebrate the richness of language that makes their art possible:

ROBERT FRANCIS

Hogwash

The tongue that mothered such a metaphor
Only the purest purist could despair of.

Nobody ever called swill sweet but isn't
Hogwash a daisy in a field of daisies?

5   What beside sports and flowers could you find
To praise better than the American language?

Bruised by American foreign policy
What shall I soothe me, what defend me with

But a handful of clean unmistakable words—
10   Daisies, daisies, in a field of daisies?   1965

The poet here claims little for his own invention and not much for the art of poetry, insisting that the American language itself is responsible for miraculous conceptions. The poet plays cheerfully here with what words offer—the pun on "purest" and "purist" (line 2), for example, and the taunting (but misleading) similarity of the beginnings of "swill" and "sweet" (line 3)—but insists that poems and poets only articulate things already realized in common speech, where metaphors are "mothered" (line 1). "Hogwash," although never explicitly glossed or discussed in the poem, is the primary example: What *does* "hogwash" mean? How do hogs wash themselves and in what? to what purpose and effect? How did the term get invented as a metaphor, and what are its visual implications? And what is it doing as an example of beauty in a poem about "clean unmistakable words" (line 9)? But then the poem plays even more fully with "daisy" (lines 4 and 10) as metaphor and idiomatic expression. A "daisy" is a great success, a breakthrough, a beaut, a perfect example, and the word "hogwash" is such a daisy, an instance of such a success: a "daisy in a field of daisies," a success of successes, a wonder in a language full of wonders.

Not everything American, according to this poem, is as praiseworthy as its language, and the word "hogwash" ultimately has its context established in the poem's fourth stanza when the speaker finally tells us why the word is so sooth-ing and so pertinent. Poets, the poem says, need words and metaphors that are not always images of beauty because the world is full of things that are not alto-gether beautiful, and metaphors of ugliness can be "daisies" too.

Not all poets feel as positive as Robert Francis claims to be here about the raw materials they have to work with in language. Ultimately, of course, the modesty of the poet's claims about his own inventiveness becomes as comic as the metaphor of "hogwash" itself and the poem's characterization of foreign policy, for it is the poem that makes this particular use of the metaphor, no matter where or when it was invented: the wit belongs to the poem, not the lan-guage. Poets make use of whatever idioms, expressions, inherited metaphors, and traditions of language come their way, and they turn them to their own uses, sometimes quite surprisingly.

The difficulty of conveying what some experiences are like and how we feel about them sometimes leads poets to startling comparisons and figures of speech that may at first seem far-fetched but that, in one way or another, do in fact suggest the quality of the experience or the feelings associated with it. Sometimes they use a series of metaphors, as if no single act of visualization will serve but several together may suggest the full complexity of the experi-ence or cumulatively define the feeling precisely. Metaphors open up virtually endless possibilities of comparison, giving words a chance to be more than words, offering our mind's eye a challenge to keep up with the fertile and artic-ulate imagination of writers who make it their business to see things that ordi-nary people miss, noticing the most surprising likenesses and conveying feelings more powerfully than politicians usually do.

Sometimes, in poetry as in prose, comparisons are made explicitly, as in the following poem.

ROBERT BURNS

A Red, Red Rose

O, my luve's like a red, red rose
That's newly sprung in June.
O, my luve is like the melodie
That's sweetly played in tune.

5   As fair art thou, my bonnie lass,
So deep in luve am I;
And I will luve thee still, my dear,
Till a' the seas gang[4] dry.

Till a' the seas gang dry, my dear,
10 And the rocks melt wi' the sun;
And I will luve thee still, my dear,
While the sands o' life shall run.

And fare thee weel, my only luve,
And fare thee weel a while!
15 And I will come again, my luve,
Though it were ten thousand mile.   1796

The first four lines make two explicit comparisons: the speaker says that his love is "like a rose" and "like a melodie." Such *explicit* comparison is called a **simile,** and usually (as here) the comparison involves the words "like" or "as." Similes work much as do metaphors, except that they usually are used more passingly, more incidentally; they make a quick comparison and usually do not elaborate, whereas metaphors often extend over a long section of a poem (in which case they are called **extended metaphors**) or even over the whole poem, as in "Marks" (in which case they are called **controlling metaphors**).

The two similes in "A Red, Red Rose" assume that we already have a favorable opinion of roses and of melodies. Here the poet does not develop the comparison or even remind us of attractive details about roses or tunes. He pays the quick compliment and moves on. Similes sometimes develop more elaborate comparisons than this and occasionally even control long sections of a poem (in which case they are called **analogies**), but usually a simile is briefer and relies more fully on something we already know. The speaker in "My Papa's Waltz" says that he hung on "like death"; he doesn't have to explain or elaborate the comparison: we know the anxiety he refers to.

Like metaphors, similes may imply both meaning and feeling; they may

4. Go.

both explain something and invoke feelings about it. All figurative language involves an attempt to clarify something *and* to help readers feel a certain way about it. Saying that one's love is like a rose implies a delicate and fragile beauty and invites our senses into play so that we can share sensuously a response to fragrant appeal and soft touch, just as the shivering boughs and dying embers in "That time of year" explain separation and loss at the same time that they allow us to share the cold sense of loneliness and the warmth of old friendship.

Once you are alerted to look for them you will find figures of speech in poem after poem; they are among the most common devices through which poets share their vision with us.

The following poem uses a variety of metaphors to describe sexual experiences.

ADRIENNE RICH

Two Songs

1

Sex, as they harshly call it,
I fell into this morning
at ten o'clock, a drizzling hour
of traffic and wet newspapers.
I thought of him who yesterday   5
clearly didn't
turn me to a hot field
ready for plowing,
and longing for that young man
piercéd me to the roots   10
bathing every vein, etc.[5]
All day he appears to me
touchingly desirable,
a prize one could wreck one's peace for.
I'd call it love if love   15
didn't take so many years
but lust too is a jewel
a sweet flower and what
pure happiness to know
all our high-toned questions   20
breed in a lively animal.

---

5. See the opening lines of the Prologue to Chaucer's *Canterbury Tales*.

2

That "old last act"!
And yet sometimes
all seems post coitum triste[6]
and I a mere bystander.
Somebody else is going off,
getting shot to the moon.
Or, a moon-race!
Split seconds after
my opposite number lands
I make it—
we lie fainting together
at a crater-edge
heavy as mercury in our moonsuits
till he speaks
in a different language
yet one I've picked up
through cultural exchanges . . .
we murmur the first moonwords:
Spasibo.[7] *Thanks. O.K.*

1964

    The first "song" begins straightforwardly as narration ("Sex . . . I fell into this morning / at ten o'clock"), but the vividness of sex and desire is communicated mostly by figure. The narrator describes her body as "a hot field / ready for plowing" (lines 7–8)—quite unlike her resistant body yesterday—and her longing is also described by metaphor, in this case an elaborate one borrowed from another poem. After so sensual and urgent a beginning, the song turns more thoughtful and philosophical, but even the intellectual sorting between love and lust comes to depend on figures: lust is a "jewel" (line 17) and a "flower" (line 18). After the opening pace and excitement those later metaphors seem calm and tame, moving the poem from the lust of its beginning to a contemplative reflection on the value and beauty of momentary physical pleasures.

    The second song depends on two closely related metaphors, and here the metaphors for sex are highly self-conscious and a little comic. The song begins on a plaintive note, considering the classic melancholic feeling after sex; the speaker pictures herself as isolated, left out, "a bystander" (line 25), while someone else is having sexual pleasure. This pleasure of others is described through two colloquial expressions (both metaphors) for sexual climax: "going off" (line 26) and "getting shot to the moon" (line 27). Suddenly the narrator pretends to

---

6. Sadness after sexual union.   7. Russian for "thanks."

take sex as space travel seriously and creates a metaphor of her own: sexual partners running a "moon-race" (line 28). The rest of the poem enacts the metaphor in the context of the space race between the United States and Russia in the early 1960s. The race, not exactly even but close enough, is described in detail, and the speaker tells her story in a self-conscious comic way. These are international relations, foreign affairs, and the lovers appropriately say their thank-yous separately in Russian and English, then communicate an international "O.K."

▼ ▼ ▼

RANDALL JARRELL

The Death of the Ball Turret Gunner[8]

From my mother's sleep I fell into the State,
And I hunched in its belly till my wet fur froze.
Six miles from earth, loosed from its dream of life,
I woke to black flak and the nightmare fighters.
When I died they washed me out of the turret with a hose.   1945   5

HART CRANE

Forgetfulness

Forgetfulness is like a song
That, freed from beat and measure, wanders.
Forgetfulness is like a bird whose wings are reconciled,
Outspread and motionless,—
A bird that coasts the wind unwearyingly.   5

Forgetfulness is rain at night,
Or an old house in a forest,—or a child.
Forgetfulness is white,—white as a blasted tree,
And it may stun the sybil into prophecy,
Or bury the Gods.   10

I can remember much forgetfulness.   p. 1918

8. "A ball turret was a plexiglass sphere set into the belly of a B-17 or B-24 and inhabited by two .50 caliber machine-guns and one man, a short, small man. When this gunner tracked with his machine-guns a fighter attacking his bomber from below, he revolved with the turret; hunched upside-down in his little sphere, he looked like the foetus in the womb. The fighters which attacked him were armed with cannon firing explosive shells. The hose was a steam hose." (Jarrell's note)

CAROLYN FORCHÉ

Taking Off My Clothes

I take off my shirt, I show you.
I shaved the hair out under my arms.
I roll up my pants, I scraped off the hair
on my legs with a knife, getting white.

5 My hair is the color of chopped maples
My eyes dark as beans cooked in the south.
(Coal fields in the moon on torn-up hills)

Skin polished as a Ming bowl
showing its blood cracks, its age, I have hundreds
10 of names for the snow, for this, all of them quiet.

In the night I come to you and it seems a shame.
to waste my deepest shudders on a wall of a man.

You recognize strangers,
think you lived through destruction.
15 You can't explain this night, my face, your memory.

You want to know what I know?
Your own hands are lying.

1976

AGHA SHAHID ALI

The Dacca Gauzes

 . . . for a whole year he sought
to accumulate the most exquisite
Dacca gauzes.
—OSCAR WILDE / *The Picture
of Dorian Gray*

Those transparent Dacca gauzes
known as woven air, running
water, evening dew:

a dead art now, dead over
5 a hundred years. "No one
now knows," my grandmother says,

"what it was to wear
or touch that cloth." She wore
it once, an heirloom sari from

her mother's dowry, proved
genuine when it was pulled, all
six yards, through a ring.   10

Years later when it tore,
many handkerchiefs embroidered
with gold-thread paisleys   15

were distributed among
the nieces and daughters-in-law.
Those too now lost.

In history we learned: the hands
of weavers were amputated,   20
the looms of Bengal silenced,

and the cotton shipped raw
by the British to England.
History of little use to her,

my grandmother just says   25
how the muslins of today
seem so coarse and that only

in autumn, should one wake up
at dawn to pray, can one
feel that same texture again.   30

One morning, she says, the air
was dew-starched: she pulled
it absently through her ring.   1987

JOHN DONNE

[Batter my heart, three-personed God . . .][9]

Batter my heart, three-personed God; for You
As yet but knock, breathe, shine, and seek to mend;
That I may rise and stand, o'erthrow me, and bend
Your force, to break, blow, burn, and make me new.
I, like an usurped town, to another due,   5
Labor to admit You, but Oh, to no end!
Reason, Your viceroy[1] in me, me should defend,
But is captived, and proves weak or untrue.
Yet dearly I love You, and would be loved fain,[2]

9. *Holy Sonnets,* 14.   1. One who rules as the representative of a higher power.   2. Gladly.

10 But am betrothed unto Your enemy:
Divorce me, untie or break that knot again,
Take me to You, imprison me, for I,
Except You enthrall me, never shall be free,
Nor ever chaste, except You ravish me.

1633

ANONYMOUS[3]

The Twenty-third Psalm

The Lord is my shepherd; I shall not want.
He maketh me to lie down in green pastures: he leadeth me beside
    the still waters.
He restoreth my soul: he leadeth me in the paths of righteousness
    for his name's sake.
Yea, though I walk through the valley of the shadow of death,
    I will fear no evil: for thou art with me;
    thy rod and thy staff they comfort me.
Thou preparest a table before me in the presence of mine enemies:
5   thou anointest my head with oil; my cup runneth over.
Surely goodness and mercy shall follow me all the days of my life:
    and I will dwell in the house of the Lord for ever.

Symbol

The word "symbol" is often used sloppily and sometimes pretentiously, but
properly used the term suggests one of the most basic things about poems—
their ability to get beyond what words signify and make larger claims about
meanings in the verbal world. All words go beyond themselves. They are not
simply a collection of sounds: they signify something beyond their sounds,
often things or actions or ideas. Words describe not only a verbal universe but
a world in which actions occur, acts have implications, and events mean.
Sometimes words not only signify something beyond themselves—a rock or a
tree or a cloud—but symbolize something as well—solidity or life or dreams.
Words can—when their implications are agreed on by tradition, convention, or
habit—stand for things beyond their most immediate meanings or significa-
tions and become symbols, and even simple words that have accumulated no

3. Traditionally attributed to King David. The English translation printed here is from the King
James Version.

special power from previous use may be given special significance in special circumstances—either in poetry or in life itself.

A **symbol** is, put simply, something that stands for something else. The everyday world is full of common examples; a flag, a logo, a trademark, or a skull and crossbones all suggest things beyond themselves, and everyone is likely to understand what their display is meant to indicate, whether or not the viewer shares a commitment to what the object represents. In common usage a prison is a symbol of confinement, constriction, and loss of freedom, and in specialized traditional usage a cross may symbolize oppression, cruelty, suffering, death, resurrection, triumph, or the intersection of two separate things, traditions, or ideas (as in crossroads and crosscurrents, for example). The specific symbolic significance is controlled by the context; a reader may often decide what it is by looking at contiguous details in the poem and by examining the poem's attitude toward a particular tradition or body of beliefs. A star means one kind of thing to a Jewish poet and something else to a Christian poet, still something else to a sailor or actor. In a very literal sense, words themselves are all symbols (they stand for an object, action, or quality, not just for letters or sounds), but symbols in poetry are said to be those words and groups of words that have a range of reference beyond their literal signification or denotation.

Poems sometimes create a symbol out of a thing, action, or event that has no previously agreed upon symbolic significance. In the following poem, for example, a random gesture is given symbolic significance.

SHARON OLDS

Leningrad Cemetery, Winter of 1941[1]

That winter, the dead could not be buried.
The ground was frozen, the gravediggers weak from hunger,
the coffin wood used for fuel. So they were covered with something
and taken on a child's sled to the cemetery
in the sub-zero air. They lay on the soil,   5
some of them wrapped in dark cloth
bound with rope like the tree's ball of roots
when it waits to be planted; others wound in sheets,
their pale, gauze, tapered shapes
stiff as cocoons that will split down the center   10
when the new life inside is prepared;
but most lay like corpses, their coverings
coming undone, naked calves

---

1. The 900-day siege of Leningrad during World War II began in September 1941.

15

> hard as corded wood spilling
> from under a cloak, a hand reaching out
> with no sign of peace, wanting to come back
> even to the bread made of glue and sawdust,
> even to the icy winter, and the siege.   p. 1979

All of the corpses—frozen, neglected, beginning to be in disarray—vividly stamp upon our minds a sense of the horrors of war, and the detailed picture of the random, uncounted clutter of bodies is likely to stick in our minds long after we have finished reading the poem. Several of the details are striking, and the poem's language heightens our sense of them. The corpses wound in sheets, for example, are described in "their pale, gauze, tapered shapes," and they are compared to cocoons that one day will split and emit new life; and the limbs that dangle loose when the coverings come undone are said to be "hard as corded wood spilling." But clearly the most memorable sight is the hand dangling from one corpse that is coming unwrapped, for the poet invests that hand with special significance, giving its gesture *meaning*. The hand is described as "reaching out . . . wanting to come back": it is as if the dead can still gesture even if they cannot speak, and the gesture seems to signify the desire of the dead to come back at any price. They would be glad to be alive, even under the grim conditions that attend the living in Leningrad during this grim war. Suddenly the grimness that we—living—have been witnessing pales by comparison with what the dead have lost simply by being dead. The hand has been made to *symbolize* the desire of the dead to return, to be alive, to be still among us, anywhere. The hand reaches out in the poem as a gesture that means; the poet has made it a symbol of desire.

The whole array of dead bodies in the poem might be said to be symbolic as well. As a group, they stand for the human waste that the war has produced, and their dramatic visual presence on the scene provides the poem with a dramatic visualization of how war and its requirements have no time for decency, not even the decency of burial. The bodies are a symbol in the sense that they stand for what the poem as a whole asserts.

The poem that follows also arises out of a historical moment, but this time the event is a personal one that the poet gives a significance by the interpretation he puts upon it.

JAMES DICKEY

The Leap

The only thing I have of Jane MacNaughton
Is one instant of a dancing-class dance.
She was the fastest runner in the seventh grade,
My scrapbook says, even when boys were beginning
To be as big as the girls,   5
But I do not have her running in my mind,
Though Frances Lane is there, Agnes Fraser,
Fat Betty Lou Black in the boys-against-girls
Relays we ran at recess: she must have run

Like the other girls, with her skirts tucked up   10
So they would be like bloomers,
But I cannot tell; that part of her is gone.
What I do have is when she came,
With the hem of her skirt where it should be
For a young lady, into the annual dance   15
Of the dancing class we all hated, and with a light
Grave leap, jumped up and touched the end
Of one of the paper-ring decorations

To see if she could reach it. She could,
And reached me now as well, hanging in my mind   20
From a brown chain of brittle paper, thin
And muscular, wide-mouthed, eager to prove
Whatever it proves when you leap
In a new dress, a new womanhood, among the boys
Whom you easily left in the dust   25
Of the passionless playground. If I said I saw
In the paper where Jane MacNaughton Hill,

Mother of four, leapt to her death from a window
Of a downtown hotel, and that her body crushed-in
The top of a parked taxi, and that I held   30
Without trembling a picture of her lying cradled
In that papery steel as though lying in the grass,
One shoe idly off, arms folded across her breast,
I would not believe myself. I would say
The convenient thing, that it was a bad dream   35
Of maturity, to see that eternal process

Most obsessively wrong with the world
Come out of her light, earth-spurning feet
Grown heavy: would say that in the dusty heels
Of the playground some boy who did not depend   40
On speed of foot, caught and betrayed her.

Jane, stay where you are in my first mind:
It was odd in that school, at that dance.
I and the other slow-footed yokels sat in corners
Cutting rings out of drawing paper

45

Before you leapt in your new dress
And touched the end of something I began,
Above the couples struggling on the floor,
New men and women clutching at each other
And prancing foolishly as bears: hold on
To that ring I made for you, Jane—
My feet are nailed to the ground
By dust I swallowed thirty years ago—
While I examine my hands.

50

                                                                                    1967

Memory is crucial to "The Leap." The fact that Jane MacNaughton's graceful leap in dancing class has stuck in the speaker's mind for all these years
means that this leap was important to him, meant something to him, stood for
something in his mind. For the speaker, the leap is an "instant" and the "only
thing" he has of Jane. Its grace and ease are what he remembers, and he struggles at several points to articulate its meaning (lines 15–26, 44–50), but even
without articulation or explanation it is there in his head as a visual memory, a
symbol for him of something beyond himself, something he cannot do, something he wanted to be. What that leap had stood for, or symbolized, was boldness, confidence, accomplishment, maturity, the ability to go beyond her
fellow students in dancing class—the transcending of childhood by someone
beginning to be a woman. Her feet now seem "earth-spurning" (line 38) in that
original leap, and they separate her from everyone else. Jane MacNaughton
was beyond the speaker's abilities and any attempt he could make to articulate
his hopes, but not beyond his dreams. And even before articulation, she symbolized that dream.

The leap to her death seems cruelly ironic in the context of her earlier
leap. In memory she is suspended in air, as if there were no gravity, no coming
back to earth, as if life could exist as dream. And so the photograph, re-created
in precise detail, is a cruel dashing of the speaker's dream—a detailed record
of the ending of a leap, a denial of the suspension in which his memory had
held her. His dream is grounded; her mortality is insistent. But what the
speaker wants to hang on to (line 42) is still that symbolic moment which,
although now confronted in more mature implications, will never be altogether replaced or surrendered.

The leap is ultimately symbolic in the *poem*, too, not just in the speaker's mind. In the poem (and for us as readers) the symbolism of the leap is double: the first leap is aspiration, and the second is frustration of high hopes; the two are complementary, one unable to be imagined without the other. The poem is horrifying in some ways, a dramatic reminder that human beings don't ultimately transcend their mortality, their limits, no matter how heroic or unencumbered by gravity they may seem to an observer. But it is not altogether sad and despairing either, partly because it notices and affirms the validity of the original leap and partly because another symbol is created and elaborated in the poem. That symbol is the paper chain.

The chain connects Jane to the speaker both literally and figuratively. It is, in part, *his* paper chain which she had leaped to touch in dancing class (lines 18–19), and he thinks of her first leap as "touch[ing] the end of something I began" (line 47). He and the other "slow-footed," earthbound "yokels" (line 44) were the makers of the chain, and thus they are connected to her original leap, just as a photograph glimpsed in the paper connects the speaker to her second leap. The paper in the chain is "brittle" (line 21), and its creators seem dull artisans compared to the artistic performer that Jane was. They are heavy and left in the dust (lines 25, 52–53), and she is "light" (line 16) and able to transcend them but even in transcendence touching their lives and what they are able to do. And so the paper chain becomes the poem's symbol of linkage, connecting lower accomplishment to higher possibility, the artisan to the artist, material substance to the act of imagination. And the speaker at the end examines the hands that made the chain because those hands certify his connection to her and the imaginative leap she had made for him. The chain thus symbolizes not only the lower capabilities of those who cannot leap like the budding Jane could, but (later) the connection with her leap as both transcendence and mortality. Like the leap itself, the chain has been elevated to special meaning, given symbolic significance, by the poet's treatment of it. A leap and a chain have no necessary significance in themselves to most of us—at least no significance that we have all agreed upon together—but they may be given significance in specific circumstances or a specific text.

But some objects and acts do have a significance built in because of past usage. Over the years some things have acquired an agreed-upon significance, an accepted value in our minds. They already stand for something before the poet cites them; they are **traditional symbols.** Their uses in poetry have to do with the fact that poets can count on a recognition of their traditional suggestions and meanings outside the poem, and the poem does not have to propose or argue a particular symbolic value. Birds, for example, traditionally symbolize flight, freedom from confinement, detachment from earthbound limits, the ability to soar beyond rationality and transcend mortal limits. Traditionally, birds have also been linked with imagination, especially poetic imagination, and poets often identify with them as pure and ideal singers of songs, as in Keats's "Ode to a Nightingale." One of the most traditional symbols is the rose. It may be a simple and fairly plentiful flower in its season, but it has been allowed to stand for particular qualities for so long that to name it raises predictable expectations. Its beauty, delicacy, fragility, shortness of life, and depth of color have made it a symbol of the transitoriness of beauty, and countless poets have counted on its accepted symbolism—sometimes to compliment a friend (as Burns does in "A Red, Red Rose") or sometimes to make a point about the nature of symbolism. The following poem draws on, in a quite traditional way, the traditional meanings.

JOHN CLARE

Love's Emblem

Go, rose, my Chloe's[2] bosom grace:
   How happy should I prove,
Could I supply that envied place
   With never-fading love.

5   Accept, dear maid, now summer glows,
   This pure, unsullied gem,
Love's emblem in a full-blown rose,
   Just broken from the stem.

Accept it as a favorite flower
10   For thy soft breast to wear;
'Twill blossom there its transient hour,
   A favorite of the fair.

Upon thy cheek its blossom glows,
   As from a mirror clear,
15   Making thyself a living rose,
   In blossom all the year.

It is a sweet and favorite flower
   To grace a maiden's brow,
Emblem of love without its power—
20   A sweeter rose art thou.

2. A standard "poetic" name for a woman in traditional love poetry.

The rose, like hues of insect wing,
   May perish in an hour;
'Tis but at best a fading thing,
   But thou'rt a living flower.

The roses steeped in morning dews
   Would every eye enthrall,
But woman, she alone subdues;
   Her beauty conquers all.

25

1873

The speaker in "Love's Emblem" sends the rose to Chloe to decorate her
bosom (lines 1, 10) and reflect the blush of her cheek and brow (lines 13, 18),
and he goes on to mention some of the standard meanings: the rose is pure
(line 6), transitory (line 11), fragrant, beautiful, and always appreciated (line
17). The poet need not elaborate or argue these things; he counts on the tradition, habits of mind built on familiarity and repetition. To say that the rose is
an emblem of love is to say that it traditionally symbolizes love, and the
speaker expects Chloe to accept his gift readily; she will understand it as a compliment, a pledge, and a bond. She will understand, too, that her admirer is
being conventional and complimentary in going on to call her (and women in
general) a rose (line 20), except that her qualities are said to be more lasting
than those of a momentary flower.

    Poems often use traditional symbols to invoke predictable responses—in
effect using shortcuts to meaning and power by repeating acts of signification
and symbolization sanctioned by time and habit. But often poets examine the
tradition even as they employ it, and sometimes they revise or reverse meanings built into the tradition. Some of the poems at the end of this chapter question the usual meanings of roses in poetry and evaluate as they go. Symbols do
not necessarily stay the same over time, and poets often turn even the most
traditional of symbols to their own original uses. Knowing the traditions of
poetry—reading a lot of poems and observing how they tend to use certain
words, metaphors, and symbols—can be very useful in reading new poems, but
traditions modify and individual poems do highly individual things. Knowing
the past never means being able to predict new texts with confidence. Symbolism makes things happen, but individual poets and texts determine what will
happen and how.

    Sometimes symbols—traditional or not—become so insistent in the world
of a poem that the larger referential world is left almost totally behind. In such
cases the symbol is everything, and the poem does not just *use* symbols but

becomes a **symbolic poem,** usually a highly individualized one dependent on an internal system introduced by the individual poet.

Here is an example of such a poem:

WILLIAM BLAKE

The Sick Rose[3]

> O rose, thou art sick.
> The invisible worm
> That flies in the night
> In the howling storm
>
> Has found out thy bed
> Of crimson joy,
> And his dark secret love
> Does thy life destroy.

5

1794

The poem does not seem to be about a rose, but about what the rose represents—not in this case something altogether understandable through the traditional meanings of rose.

We know that the rose is usually associated with beauty and love, often with sex; and here several key terms have sexual connotations: "bed," "worm," and "crimson joy." The violation of the rose by the worm is the poem's main concern; the violation seems to have involved secrecy, deceit, and "dark" motives, and the result is sickness rather than the joy of love. The poem is sad; it involves a sense of hurt and tragedy, nearly of despair. The poem cries out against the misuse of the rose, against its desecration, implying that instead of a healthy joy in sensuality and sexuality, in this case, there has been destruction and hurt because of misunderstanding and repression and lack of sensitivity.

But to say so much about this poem I have had to extrapolate from other poems by this poet, and have introduced information from outside the poem. Fully symbolic poems often require that, and thus they ask us to go beyond the formal procedures of reading that we have discussed so far. As presented in this poem, the rose is not part of the normal world that we ordinarily see, and it is symbolic in a special sense. The poet does not simply take an object from that everyday world and give it special significance, making it a symbol in the same sense that the leap is a symbol, or the corpse's hand. Here the rose seems to

---

3. In Renaissance emblem books, the scarab beetle, worm, and rose are closely associated: the beetle feeds on dung, and the smell of the rose is fatal to it.

belong to its own world, a world made entirely inside the poem or the poet's head. The rose is not referential or not primarily so. The whole poem is symbolic; it is not paraphrasable; it lives in its own world. But what is the rose here a symbol of? In general terms, we can say from what the poem tells us; but we may not be as confident as we can be in the more nearly everyday world of "The Leap" or "Leningrad Cemetery, Winter of 1941," poems that contain actions we recognize from the world of probabilities in which we live. In "The Sick Rose," it seems inappropriate to ask the standard questions: What rose? Where? Which worm? What are the particulars here? In the world of this poem worms can fly and may be invisible. We are altogether in a world of meanings that have been formulated according to a particular system of knowledge and code of belief. We will only feel comfortable and confident in that world if we read many poems written by the poet (in this case William Blake) within the same symbolic system.

Negotiation of meanings in symbolic poems can be very difficult indeed. The skill of reading symbolic poems is an advanced skill that depends on special knowledge of authors and of the special traditions they work from, but the symbols you will usually find in poems are referential, and these meanings are readily discoverable from the careful study of the poems themselves, as in poems like "The Leap" and "Love's Emblem."

▼   ▼   ▼

EDMUND WALLER

Song

Go, lovely rose!
Tell her that wastes her time and me
    That now she knows,
When I resemble[4] her to thee,
How sweet and fair she seems to be.   5

    Tell her that's young,
And shuns to have her graces spied,
    That hadst thou sprung
In deserts, where no men abide,
Thou must have uncommended died.   10

4. Compare.

Small is the worth
Of beauty from the light retired;
Bid her come forth,
Suffer herself to be desired,
15   And not blush so to be admired.

Then die! that she
The common fate of all things rare
May read in thee;
How small a part of time they share
20   That are so wondrous sweet and fair!   1645

JOHN GAY

[Virgins are like the fair Flower in its Lustre] (*from* The Beggar's Opera)

Virgins are like the fair Flower in its Lustre,
Which in the Garden enamels the Ground;
Near it the Bees in Play flutter and cluster,
And gaudy Butterflies frolick around.
5   But, when once pluck'd, 'tis no longer alluring,
To Covent-Garden[5] 'tis sent, (as yet sweet,)
There fades, and shrinks, and grows past all enduring,
Rots, stinks, and dies, and is trod under feet.   1728

EMILY DICKINSON

[Go not too near a House of Rose—]

Go not too near a House of Rose—
The depredation of a Breeze
Or inundation of a Dew
Alarms its walls away—

5   Nor try to tie the Butterfly,
Nor climb the Bars of Ecstasy,
In insecurity to lie
ca. 1878   Is Joy's insuring quality.

---

5. A fruit and vegetable market in London (but also a haven for prostitutes).

WILLIAM CARLOS WILLIAMS

Poem

The rose fades
and is renewed again
by its seed, naturally
but where

save in the poem   5
shall it go
to suffer no diminution
of its splendor   1962

ALFRED, LORD TENNYSON

Now Sleeps the Crimson Petal[6]

Now sleeps the crimson petal, now the white;
Nor waves the cypress in the palace walk;
Nor winks the gold fin in the porphyry font;[7]
The firefly wakens; waken thou with me.

Now droops the milk-white peacock like a ghost,   5
And like a ghost she glimmers on to me.

Now lies the Earth all Danaë[8] to the stars,
And all thy heart lies open unto me.

Now slides the silent meteor on, and leaves
A shining furrow, as thy thoughts in me.   10

Now folds the lily all her sweetness up,
And slips into the bosom of the lake;
So fold thyself, my dearest, thou, and slip
Into my bosom and be lost in me.   1847

DOROTHY PARKER

One Perfect Rose

A single flow'r he sent me, since we met.
All tenderly his messenger he chose;

6. A song from *The Princess.*   7. Stone fishbowl. *Porphyry:* a red stone containing fine white crystals.   8. A princess, confined in a tower, seduced by Zeus after he became a shower of gold in order to gain access to her.

Deep-hearted, pure, with scented dew still wet—
   One perfect rose.

5 I knew the language of the floweret;
   "My fragile leaves," it said, "his heart enclose."
Love long has taken for his amulet
   One perfect rose.

Why is it no one ever sent me yet
10   One perfect limousine, do you suppose?
Ah no, it's always just my luck to get
   One perfect rose.   1937

KATHA POLLITT

Two Fish

Those speckled trout we glimpsed in a pool last year
you'd take for an image of love: it too should be
graceful, elusive, tacit, moving surely
among half-lights of mingled dim and clear,
5 forced to no course, of no fixed residence,
its only end its own swift elegance.
What would you say
if you saw what I saw the other day:
that pool heat-choked and fevered where sick blue
10 bubbled green scum and blistered water lily?
A white like a rolled-back eye or fish's belly
I thought I saw far out—but doubtless you
prefer to think our trout had left together
to seek a place with less inclement weather.   1981

ROO BORSON

After a Death

Seeing that there's no other way,
I turn his absence into a chair.
I can sit in it,
gaze out through the window.
5 I can do what I do best
and then go out into the world.
And I can return then with my useless love,
to rest,
because the chair is there.   1989

GEORGE PEELE

A Farewell to Arms[9]

His golden locks time hath to silver turned;
    Oh, time too swift, oh, swiftness never ceasing!
His youth 'gainst time and age hath ever spurned,[1]
    But spurned in vain; youth waneth by increasing.
Beauty, strength, youth, are flowers but fading seen;   5
Duty, faith, love, are roots, and ever green.

His helmet now shall make a hive for bees,
    And lover's sonnets turned to holy psalms,
A man-at-arms must now serve on his knees,
    And feed on prayers, which are age his[2] alms;   10
But though from court to cottage he depart,
His saint is sure of his unspotted heart.

And when he saddest sits in homely cell,
    He'll teach his swains this carol for a song:
Blest be the hearts that wish my sovereign well,   15
    Cursed be the souls that think her any wrong!
Goddess, allow this aged man his right,
To be your beadsman[3] now, that was your knight.   1590

HOWARD NEMEROV

The Town Dump

"The art of our necessities is strange,
That can make vile things precious."[4]

A mile out in the marshes, under a sky
Which seems to be always going away
In a hurry, on that Venetian land threaded
With hidden canals, you will find the city
Which seconds ours (so cemeteries, too,   5
Reflect a town from hillsides out of town),
Where Being most Becomingly[5] ends up
Becoming some more. From cardboard tenements,
Windowed with cellophane, or simply tenting
In paper bags, the angry mackerel eyes   10

9. From *Polyhymnia*, a verse description of a 1590 jousting tournament on Queen Elizabeth's birthday. Sir Henry Lee, who had for years been the queen's champion in such contests, retired that year (at age 60) in favor of a younger man.   **1.** Kicked.   **2.** Age's (a common Elizabethan possessive form).   **3.** One who prays for the soul of another (OED).   **4.** *King Lear*, Act III, scene 2, 70–71.   **5.** "Being" and "Becoming" have been, since Heraclitus, the standard antinomies in Western philosophy, standing for (respectively) the eternal and that which changes.

Glare at you out of stove-in, sunken heads
Far from the sea; the lobster, also, lifts
An empty claw in his most minatory
Of gestures; oyster, crab, and mussel shells
15   Lie here in heaps, savage as money hurled
Away at the gate of hell. If you want results,
These are results.
                    Objects of value or virtue,
However, are also to be picked up here,
Though rarely, lying with bones and rotten meat,
20   Eggshells and mouldy bread, banana peels
No one will skid on, apple cores that caused
Neither the fall of man nor a theory
Of gravitation.[6] People do throw out
The family pearls by accident, sometimes,
25   Not often; I've known dealers in antiques
To prowl this place by night, with flashlights, on
The off-chance of somebody's having left
Derelict chairs which will turn out to be
By Hepplewhite,[7] a perfect set of six
30   Going to show, I guess, that in any sty
Someone's heaven may open and shower down
Riches responsive to the right dream; though
It is a small chance, certainly, that sends
The ghostly dealer, heavy with fly-netting
35   Over his head, across these hills in darkness,
Stumbling in cut-glass goblets, lacquered cups,
And other products of his dreamy midden[8]
Penciled with light and guarded by the flies.

For there are flies, of course. A dynamo
40   Composed, by thousands, of our ancient black
Retainers, hums here day and night, steady
As someone telling[9] beads, the hum becoming
A high whine at any disturbance; then,
Settled again, they shine under the sun
45   Like oil-drops, or are invisible as night,
By night,
                    All this continually smoulders,
Crackles, and smokes with mostly invisible fires
Which, working deep, rarely flash out and flare,
And never finish. Nothing finishes;
50   The flies, feeling the heat, keep on the move.

---

6. According to legend, Sir Isaac Newton's discovery of the principle of gravitation followed his being hit on the head by a falling apple.   7. A late 18th-century cabinet maker and furniture designer, famed for his simplification of neoclassic lines. No pieces known to have been actually made by Hepplewhite survive.   8. Refuse heap. (The term is usually used to describe those primitive refuse heaps that have been untouched for centuries and in which archeologists dig for shards and artifacts of older cultures.)   9. Counting.

Among the flies, the purefying fires,
The hunters by night, acquainted with the art
Of our necessities, and the new deposits
That each day wastes with treasure, you may say
There should be ratios. You may sum up   55
The results if you want results. But I will add
That wild birds, drawn to the carrion and flies,
Assemble in some numbers here, their wings
Shining with light, their flight enviably free,
Their music marvelous, though sad, and strange.   1958   60

▼ ▼ ▼

Language A Glossary

ambiguity: the ability to mean more than one thing
analogy: a comparison based on certain resemblances between things that
  are otherwise unlike
connotation: what is suggested by a word, apart from what it explicitly
  describes
connote: to suggest something in addition to explicit meaning
controlling metaphors: metaphors that dominate or organize an entire
  poem
denote: to mean or stand for
denotation: a direct and specific meaning (as distinct from implication)
extended metaphors: detailed and complex metaphors that extend over a
  long section of a poem
figurative language: language that uses figures of speech
figures of speech: comparisons in which something is pictured or figured
  forth in other, more familiar terms
metaphor: one thing pictured as if it were something else, suggesting a
  likeness or analogy between them
personification (or **prosopopeia**): treating an abstraction as if it were a
  person, endowing it with human-like qualities
precision: exactness, accuracy of language or description
simile: a direct, explicit comparison of one thing to another, and usually
  using the words "like" or "as" to draw the connection
symbol: something that stands for something else
symbolic poem: a poem in which the use of symbols is so pervasive and
  internally consistent that the larger referential world is distanced, if not
  forgotten
syntax: the formal arrangement of words in a sentence
traditional symbols: symbols that, through years of usage, have acquired
  an agreed-on significance, an accepted meaning
word order: the positioning of words in relation to one another

QUESTIONS

1. List all of the neologisms and other unusual words in "Pied Beauty." Find the most precise synonym you can for each. How can you tell exactly what these words contribute to the poem? Explain the effects of the repeated consonant sounds (alliteration) and repeated vowel sounds (assonance) in the poem. What are the advantages of making up original words to describe highly individualized effects? What are the disadvantages?

2. Compare "I dwell in Possibility—" with two other Dickinson poems, "A narrow Fellow in the Grass" (p. 833) and "After great pain, a formal feeling comes—." What patterns of word use do you see in the three poems? What kinds of vocabulary do they have in common? what patterns of syntax? what strategies of organization?

3. Read aloud the passage from *Paradise Lost*. Then ask a friend to read the passage aloud as well. As the friend reads, note which words—and which choices of word order—provide especially useful guides for reading aloud. Make a list of all the lines in which the "normal" word order would be different if the poem were not written in a metrical form designed for reading aloud. In each case in which the poem uses unusual word order, try to figure out exactly what effect is produced by the variation.

4. Characterize as fully as you can the speaker in "Batter my heart, three-personed God." Explain how the metaphor of invasion and resistance works in the poem. What effect does this central metaphor have on our conception of the speaker? Explain the terms "imprison" (line 12) and "enthrall" (line 13). Explain "chaste" and "ravish" (line 14). How do these two sets of terms relate to the poem's central metaphor?

5. List every term in "The Twenty-third Psalm" that relates to the central metaphor of sheepherding. Explain the metaphors of anointing and the over-full cup in line 5. (If you have trouble with this metaphor and do not understand the historical/cultural reference, ask a reference librarian to guide you to biblical commentaries that explain the practices referred to here.) What is the "house of the Lord" (line 6), and how does it relate to the basic metaphor of the psalm? (Again, if you are not sure of the historical/cultural reference, consult biblical commentaries or other historical sources on social and economic structures of the ancient Middle East.)

6. List all of the material objects and human activities in "A Farewell to Arms" that symbolize the active world of the knight. List all the objects and activities that symbolize the contemplative life of the beadsman. What,

according to the poem, are the relative values of the "golden" and "silver" (line 1) worlds?

7. Compare the symbolism of the fish and seafood in "The Town Dump" with that of the two trout in "Two Fish."

WRITING SUGGESTIONS

1. Read back through the poems you have read so far in the course, and pick out one in which a single word seems to you crucial to that poem's total effect. Write a short essay in which you work out carefully how the poem's meaning and tone depend upon that one word.

2. With the help of a reference librarian, find several pictures of B-17 bombers, and study carefully the design and appearance of the ball turret. Try to find a picture of the gunner at work in the turret, and note carefully his body position. Explain, in a paragraph, how the poem uses the visual details of the ball turret to create the fetal and birth metaphors in the poem.

3. Consider carefully the symbolism of the trout in "Two Fish." Exactly how do the fish become symbolic to the lovers? How do they become invested with meaning? What do this year's trout look like? Is the difference between last year's trout and this year's in the fish themselves or in their settings? What power does the weather have over the fish? What is the implied moral for the lovers? What does each lover believe about what the trout represent? What are the temperamental differences between the two lovers? What does the poem conclude about the "meaning" of the fish? Write an essay of about three pages in which you show how the poem opens and develops the question of what "symbols" mean.

4. With the help of a reference librarian, find at least half a dozen more poems that are about roses. Read them all carefully, and make a list of all the things that the rose seems to stand for in the poems. Write a paragraph about each poem showing how a specific symbolism for rose is established.

5 THE SOUNDS OF POETRY

A lot of what happens in a poem happens in your mind's eye, but some of it happens in your voice. Poems are full of sounds and silences as well as words and sentences that are meaningful. Besides choosing words for their meanings, poets sometimes choose words because they involve certain sounds, and poems use sound effects to create a mood or establish a tone, just as films do. Sometimes the sounds of words are crucial to what is happening in the text of the poem.

The following poem explores the sounds of a particular word, tries them on, and analyzes them in relation to the word itself.

HELEN CHASIN

The Word *Plum*

The word *plum* is delicious

pout and push, luxury of
self-love, and savoring murmur

full in the mouth and falling
like fruit

taut skin
pierced, bitten, provoked into
juice, and tart flesh

question
and reply, lip and tongue
of pleasure.   1968

The poem savors the sounds of the word as well as the taste and feel of the fruit itself. It is almost as if the poem is tasting the sounds and rolling them carefully on the tongue. The second and third lines even replicate the *p, l, uh,* and *m* sounds of the word while at the same time imitating the squishy sounds of eating the fruit. Words like "delicious" and "luxury" sound juicy, and other words imitate sounds of satisfaction and pleasure—"murmur," for example. Even the process of eating is in part re-created aurally. The tight, clipped sounds of "taut skin / pierced" suggest the way teeth sharply break the skin and slice quickly into the solid flesh of a plum, and as the tartness is described, the words ("provoked," "question") force the lips to pucker and the tongue and palate to meet and hold, as if the mouth were savoring a tart fruit. The poet is having fun here re-creating the various sense appeals of a plum, teasing the sounds and meanings out of available words. The words must mean something appropriate and describe something accurately first of all, of course, but when they can also imitate the sounds and feel of the process, they can do double duty. Not all poems manipulate sound as consciously or as fully as "The Word *Plum*," but many poems at least contain passages in which the sounds of life are reproduced by the human voice reading the poem. To get the full effect of this poem—and of many others—reading aloud is essential; that way, you can pay attention to the vocal rhythms and articulate the sounds as the poem calls for them to be reproduced by the human voice.

Almost always a poem's effect will be helped by reading it aloud, using your voice to pronounce the words so that the poem becomes a spoken communication. Historically, poetry began as an oral phenomenon, and often poems that seem very difficult when looked at silently come alive when they are turned into sound. Early bards chanted their verses, and the music of poetry—its cadences and rhythms—developed from this kind of performance. Often performances of primitive poetry (and sometimes in later ages) were accompanied by some kind of musical instrument. The rhythms of any poem become clearer when you say or hear them.

Poetry is, almost always, a vocal art, dependent on the human voice to become its full self (for some exceptions look at the shaped verse in Chapter 7). In a sense, it begins to exist as a real phenomenon when a reader reads and actualizes it. Poems don't really achieve their full meaning when they merely exist on a page; a poem on a page is more a score or set of stage directions for a poem than a poem itself. Sometimes, in fact, it is hard to experience the poem at all unless you hear it. A good poetry reading might easily convince you of the importance of a good voice sensitive to the poem's requirements, but you can also persuade yourself by reading poems aloud in the privacy of your own room. An audience is even better, however, because then there is someone to share the pleasure in the sounds themselves and consider what they imply. At its oral best, much poetry is communal.

MONA VAN DUYN

What the Motorcycle Said

Br-r-r-am-m-m, rackety-am-m, OM, *Am:*
All—r-r-room, r-r-ram, ala-bas-ter—
Am, the world's my oyster.

I hate plastic, wear it black and slick,
hate hardhats, wear one on my head,
that's what the motorcycle said.

Passed phonies in Fords, knocked down billboards, landed
on the other side of The Gap, and Whee,
bypassed history.

When I was born (The Past), baby knew best.
They shook when I bawled, took Freud's path,
threw away their wrath.

R-r-rackety-am-m. *Am.* War, rhyme,
soap, meat, marriage, the Phantom Jet
are shit, and like that.

Hate pompousness, punishment, patience, am into Love,
hate middle-class moneymakers, live on Dad,
that's what the motorcycle said.

Br-r-r-am-m-m. It's Nowsville, man. Passed Oldies, Uglies,
Straighties, Honkies. I'll never be
mean, tired or unsexy.

Passed cigarette suckers, souses, mother-fuckers,
losers, went back to Nature and found
how to get VD, stoned.

Passed a cow, too fast to hear her moo, "I rolled
our leaves of grass into one ball.
I am the grassy All."

Br-r-r-am-m-m, rackety-am-m, OM, *Am:*
All—gr-r-rin, oooohgah, gl-l-utton—
Am, the world's my smilebutton.   1973

Saying this poem as if you were a motorcycle with the power of speech
(sort of) is part of the poem's fun, and the rich, loud sounds of a motorcycle
revving up concentrate and intensify the effect and enrich the pleasure. It's a
shame not to hear a poem like this aloud; a lot of it is missed if you don't try to
imitate the sounds or to pick up the motor's rhythms in the poem. A perfor-

mance here is clearly worth it: a human being as motorcycle, motorcycle as human being.

And it's a good poem, too. It does something interesting, important, and maybe a bit subversive. The speaking motorcycle seems to take on the values of some of its riders, the noisy and obtrusive ones that readers are most likely to associate with motorcycles. The riders made fun of here are themselves sort of mindless and mechanical; they are the sort who have cult feelings about their group, who travel in packs, and who live no life beyond their machines. The speaking motorcycle, like such riders, grooves on power and speed, lives for the moment, and has little respect for people, the past, institutions, or for anything beyond its own small world. It is self-centered, modish, ignorant, and inarticulate; but it is proud as well, mighty proud, and feels important in its own sounds. That's what the motorcycle says.

The following poem uses sound effects efficiently, too.

KENNETH FEARING

Dirge

1-2-3 was the number he played but today the number came 3-2-1;
Bought his Carbide at 30, and it went to 29; had the favorite at Bowie[1] but the
    track was slow—

O executive type, would you like to drive a floating-power, knee-action, silk-
    upholstered six? Wed a Hollywood star? Shoot the course in 58? Draw to the
    ace, king, jack?
O fellow with a will who won't take no, watch out for three cigarettes on the
    same, single match; O democratic voter born in August under Mars, beware
    of liquidated rails—

Denouement to denouement, he took a personal pride in the certain, certain
    way he lived his own, private life,
But nevertheless, they shut off his gas; nevertheless, the bank foreclosed; never-
    theless, the landlord called; nevertheless, the radio broke,

And twelve o'clock arrived just once too often,
Just the same he wore one gray tweed suit, bought one straw hat, drank one
    straight Scotch, walked one short step, took one long look, drew one deep
    breath,
Just one too many,

5

1. A racetrack in Maryland. *Carbide:* the Union Carbide Corporation.

10 And wow he died as wow he lived,
Going whop to the office and blooie home to sleep and biff got married and
    bam had children and oof got fired,
Zowie did he live and zowie did he die,
With who the hell are you at the corner of his casket, and where the hell're we
    going on the right-hand silver knob, and who the hell cares walking second
    from the end with an American Beauty[2] wreath from why the hell not,
Very much missed by the circulation staff of the New York Evening Post; deeply,
    deeply mourned by the B.M.T.[3]
Wham, Mr. Roosevelt; pow, Sears Roebuck; awk, big dipper; bop, summer rain;
15   Bong, Mr., bong, Mr., bong, Mr., bong.

1935

As the title implies, "Dirge" is a kind of musical lament, in this case for a
certain sort of businessman who took a lot of chances and saw his investments
and life go down the drain in the depression of the early 1930s. Reading this
poem aloud is a big help partly because it contains expressive cartoon words
that echo the action, words like "oof" and "blooie" (which primarily carry their
meaning in their sounds, for they have practically no literal or referential meaning). Reading aloud also helps us notice that the poem employs rhythms much
as a song would and that it frequently shifts its pace and mood. Notice how
carefully the first two lines are balanced, and then how quickly the rhythm
shifts as the "executive type" begins to be addressed directly in line 3. (Line 2 is
long and dribbles over in the narrow pages of a book like this; a lot of the lines
here are especially long, and the irregularity of the line lengths is one aspect of
the special sound effects the poem creates.) In the direct address, the poem
first picks up a series of advertising features, which it recites in rapid-fire order
rather like the advertising phrases in "Needs" (p. 713). In stanza 3 here, the
rhythm shifts again, but the poem gives us helpful clues about how to read.
Line 5 sounds like prose and is long, drawn out, and rather dull (rather like its
subject), but line 6 sets up a regular (and monotonous) rhythm with its
repeated "nevertheless," which punctuates the rhythm like a drumbeat: "But
nevertheless, *tuh-tuh-tuh-tuh-tuh*; nevertheless, *tuh-tuh-tuh-tuh*; nevertheless,
tuh-tuh-tuh-tuh; nevertheless *tuh-tuh-tuh-tuh-tuh*." In the next stanza, the repetitive phrasing comes again, this time guided by the word "one" in cooperation
with other words of one syllable: "wore *one* gray tweed suit, bought *one* straw
hat, *tuh* one *tuh-tuh, tuh* one *tuh-tuh, tuh* one *tuh-tuh, tuh* one *tuh-tuh*." And
then a new rhythm and a new technique in stanza 5 as the language of comic

2. A variety of rose.   3. A New York City subway line.

books is imitated to describe in violent, exaggerated terms the routine of his life. You have to say words like "whop" and "zowie" aloud and in the rhythm of the whole sentence to get the full effect of how boring his life is, no matter how he tries to jazz it up with exciting words. And so it goes—repeated words, shifting rhythms, emphasis on routine and averageness—until the final bell ("Bong . . . bong . . . bong . . . bong") tolls rhythmically for the dead man in the final clanging line.

Sometimes sounds in poems just provide special effects, rather like a musical score behind a film, setting mood and getting us into an appropriate frame of mind. But often sound and meaning go hand in hand, and the poet finds words that in their sounds echo the action. A word that captures or approximates the sound of what it describes, such as "splash" or "squish" or "murmur" is called an **onomatopoeic** word, and the device itself is called **onomatopoeia.** And similar things can be done poetically with pacing and rhythm, sounds and pauses. The punctuation, the length of vowels, and the combination of consonant sounds help to control the way we read so that we imitate what is being described. The poems at the end of this discussion (pp. 821–835) suggest several ways that such imitations of pace and pause may occur: by echoing the lapping of waves on a shore, for example ("Like as the waves"), or reproducing the rhythms of a musical style ("Queen of the Blues" or "Dear John, Dear Coltrane").

Here is a classic passage in which a skillful poet talks about the virtues of making the sound echo the sense—and shows at the same time how to do it:

ALEXANDER POPE

Sound and Sense[4]

But most by numbers[5] judge a poet's song,   337
And smooth or rough, with them, is right or wrong;
In the bright muse though thousand charms conspire,[6]
Her voice is all these tuneful fools admire,   340
Who haunt Parnassus[7] but to please their ear,
Not mend their minds; as some to church repair,
Not for the doctrine, but the music there.
These, equal syllables[8] alone require,

4. From *An Essay on Criticism,* Pope's poem on the art of poetry and the problems of literary criticism. The passage excerpted here follows a discussion of several common weaknesses of critics; failure to regard an author's intention, for example, or overemphasis on clever metaphors and ornate style.   5. Meter, rhythm, sound.   6. Unite.   7. A mountain in Greece, traditionally associated with the muses and considered the seat of poetry and music.   8. Regular accents.

345 Though oft the ear the open vowels tire,
While expletives[9] their feeble aid do join,
And ten low words oft creep in one dull line,
While they ring round the same unvaried chimes,
With sure returns of still expected rhymes.
350 Where'er you find "the cooling western breeze,"
In the next line, it "whispers through the trees";
If crystal streams "with pleasing murmurs creep,"
The reader's threatened (not in vain) with "sleep."
Then, at the last and only couplet fraught
355 With some unmeaning thing they call a thought,
A needless Alexandrine[1] ends the song,
That, like a wounded snake, drags its slow length along.
Leave such to tune their own dull rhymes, and know
What's roundly smooth, or languishingly slow;
360 And praise the easy vigor of a line,
Where Denham's strength and Waller's[2] sweetness join.
True ease in writing comes from art, not chance,
As those move easiest who have learned to dance.
'Tis not enough no harshness gives offense,
365 The sound must seem an echo to the sense:
Soft is the strain when Zephyr[3] gently blows,
And the smooth stream in smoother numbers flows;
But when loud surges lash the sounding shore,
The hoarse, rough verse should like the torrent roar.
370 When Ajax[4] strives, some rock's vast weight to throw,
The line too labors, and the words move slow;
Not so, when swift Camilla[5] scours the plain,
Flies o'er th' unbending corn, and skims along the main.
Hear how Timotheus'[6] varied lays surprise,
375 And bid alternate passions fall and rise!
While, at each change, the son of Libyan Jove[7]
Now burns with glory, and then melts with love;
Now his fierce eyes with sparkling fury glow,
Now sighs steal out, and tears begin to flow:
380 Persians and Greeks like turns of nature[8] found,
And the world's victor stood subdued by sound!
The pow'r of music all our hearts allow,
And what Timotheus was, is DRYDEN now.   1711

9. Filler words, such as "do."   1. A six-foot line, sometimes used in pen-tameter poems to vary
the pace mechanically. Line 357 is an alexandrine.   2. Sir John Denham and Edmund Waller,
17th-century poets credited with perfecting the heroic couplet.   3. The west wind.   4. A
Greek hero of the Trojan War, noted for his strength.   5. A woman warrior in *The Aeneid*.
6. The court-musician of Alexander the Great, celebrated in a famous poem by Dryden (see line
383) for the power of his music over Alexander's emotions.   7. In Greek tradition, the chief god
of any people was often given the name Zeus (Jove), and the chief god of Libya (the Greek name
for all of Africa) was called Zeus Ammon. Alexander visited his oracle and was proclaimed son of
the god.   8. Similar alternations of emotion.

A lot of things are going on here simultaneously. The poem uses a number of echoic or onomatopoeic words, and pleasant and unpleasant consonant sounds are used in some lines to underline a particular point or add some mood music. When the poet talks about a particular weakness in poetry, he illustrates it at the same time—by using open vowels (line 345), expletives (line 346), monosyllabic words (line 347), predictable rhymes (lines 350–53), or long, slow lines (line 357). And the good qualities of poetry he talks about and illustrates as well (line 360, for example). But the main effects of the passage come from an interaction of several strategies at once. The effects are fairly simple and easy to spot, but their causes involve a lot of poetic ingenuity. In line 340, for example, a careful cacophonous effect is achieved by the repetition of the o͞o vowel sound and the repetition of the *l* consonant sound together with the interruption (twice) of the rough *f* sound in the middle; no one wants to be caught admiring that music when the poet gets through with us, but the careful harmony of the preceding sounds has set us up beautifully. And the pace of lines 347, 357, and 359 is carefully controlled by clashing consonant sounds as well as by the use of long vowels. Line 347 moves incredibly slowly and seems much longer than it is because almost all the one-syllable words end in a consonant that refuses to blend with the beginning of the next word, making the words hard to say without distinct, awkward pauses between them. In lines 357 and 359, long vowels such as those in "wounded," "snake," "slow," "along," "roundly," and "smooth" help to slow down the pace, and the trick of juxtaposing awkward, unpronounceable consonants is again employed. The commas also provide nearly a full stop in the midst of these lines to slow us down still more. Similarly, the harsh lashing of the shore in lines 368–69 is partly accomplished by onomatopoeia, partly by a shift in the pattern of stress, which creates irregular waves in line 368, and partly by the dominance of rough consonants in line 369. (In Pope's time, the English *r* was still trilled gruffly so that it could be made to sound extremely rrrough and harrrsh.) Almost every line in this passage demonstrates how to make sound echo sense.

As "Sound and Sense" and "Dirge" suggest, sound is most effectively manipulated in poetry when the rhythm of the voice is carefully controlled so that not only are the proper sounds heard, but they are heard at precisely the right moment. Pace and rhythm are nearly as important to a good poem as they are to a good piece of music. The human voice naturally develops certain rhythms in speech; some syllables and some words receive more stress than others, and a careful poet controls the flow of stresses so that, in many poems, a certain basic rhythm develops almost like a quiet percussion instrument in the background. Not all poems are metered, and not all metered poems follow a single dominant rhythm, but many poems are written in one pervasive pattern, and it is useful to look for patterns of stress.

Here is a poem that names and illustrates many of the meters. If you hear someone reading it aloud and chart the unstressed (˘) and stressed (‾) syllables you should have a chart similar to that done by the poet himself in the text.

SAMUEL TAYLOR COLERIDGE

Metrical Feet

LESSON FOR A BOY

Trŏchĕe trīps frŏm lōng tŏ shŏrt;[9]
From long to long in solemn sort
Slōw Spōndēe stālks; strŏng fōot! yet ill able
Ĕvĕr tŏ cōme ŭp wĭth Dāctўl trĭsýllăblĕ.
5   Ĭāmbĭcs mārch frŏm shŏrt tŏ lōng—
With ă lēap ănd ă bōund thĕ swĭft Ānăpĕsts thrōng;
One syllable long, with one short at each side,
Ămphĭbrăchўs hāstes wĭth ă stātelў stride—
First ănd lāst bēĭng lōng, mĭddlĕ shŏrt, Ămphĭmācer
10   Strīkes hĭs thŭndērĭng hōofs lĭke ă prōud hĭgh-brĕd Rācer.
If Derwent[1] be innocent, steady, and wise,
And delight in the things of earth, water, and skies;
Tender warmth at his heart, with these meters to show it,
With sound sense in his brains, may make Derwent a poet—
15   May crown him with fame, and must win him the love
Of his father on earth and his Father above.
            My dear, dear child!
Could you stand upon Skiddaw,[2] you would not from its whole ridge
See a man who so loves you as your fond S. T. COLERIDGE.

1806

The following poem exemplifies **dactylic** rhythm (‾˘˘, or a stressed syllable followed by two unstressed ones).

---

9. The long and short marks over syllables are Coleridge's.   1. Written originally for Coleridge's son Hartley, the poem was later adapted for his younger son, Derwent.   2. A mountain in the lake country of northern England (where Coleridge lived in his early years), near the town of Derwent.

WENDY COPE

Emily Dickinson

Higgledy-piggledy
Emily Dickinson
Liked to use dashes
Instead of full stops.

Nowadays, faced with such   5
Idiosyncrasy,
Critics and editors
Send for the cops.   1986

Limericks rely on **anapestic** meter (˘˘¯, or two unstressed syllables followed by a stressed one), although usually the first two syllables are in iambic meter (see below).

ANONYMOUS

[A staid schizophrenic named Struther]

A staid schizophrenic named Struther,
When told of the death of his brother,
    Said: "Yes, I am sad;
    It makes me feel bad,
But then, I still have each other."   5

The following poem is composed in the more common **trochaic** meter (¯˘, a stressed syllable followed by an unstressed one).

SIR JOHN SUCKLING

Song

Why so pale and wan, fond Lover?
    Prithee why so pale?

Will, when looking well can't move her,
   Looking ill prevail?
   Prithee why so pale?

Why so dull and mute, young Sinner?
   Prithee why so mute?
Will, when speaking well can't win her,
   Saying nothing do 't?
   Prithee why so mute?

Quit, quit, for shame, this will not move,
   This cannot take her;
If of her self she will not love,
   Nothing can make her,
   The Devil take her.
                                    1646

The basic meter in the following poem, as in "Sound and Sense," is the most common one in English, **iambic** (˘¯, an unstressed syllable followed by a stressed one).

JOHN DRYDEN

To the Memory of Mr. Oldham[3]

Farewell, too little, and too lately known,
Whom I began to think and call my own;
For sure our souls were near allied, and thine
Cast in the same poetic mold with mine.
One common note on either lyre did strike,
And knaves and fools we both abhorred alike.
To the same goal did both our studies drive;
The last set out the soonest did arrive.
Thus Nisus fell upon the slippery place,
While his young friend performed and won the race.[4]
O early ripe! to thy abundant store
What could advancing age have added more?
It might (what nature never gives the young)
Have taught the numbers[5] of thy native tongue.
But satire needs not those, and wit will shine
Through the harsh cadence of a rugged line.[6]
A noble error, and but seldom made,

3. John Oldham (1653–1683), who like Dryden (see lines 3–6) wrote satiric poetry.   4. In Vergil's *Aeneid* (Book V), Nisus (who is leading the race) falls and then trips the second runner so that his friend Euryalus can win.   5. Rhythms.   6. In Dryden's time, *r*'s were pronounced with a harsh, trilling sound.

When poets are by too much force betrayed.
Thy generous fruits, though gathered ere their prime,
Still showed a quickness; and maturing time   20
But mellows what we write to the dull sweets of rhyme.
Once more, hail and farewell; farewell, thou young,
But ah too short, Marcellus[7] of our tongue;
Thy brows with ivy, and with laurels bound;
But fate and gloomy night encompass thee around.   1684   25

Once you have figured out the basic rhythm of a poem, you can often find
some interesting things by looking carefully at the departures from the pattern.
Departures from the basic iambic meter of "To the Memory of Mr. Oldham,"
for example, suggest some of the imaginative things that poets can do within
the apparently very restrictive requirements of traditional meter. Try marking
the stressed and unstressed syllables in "To the Memory of Mr. Oldham" and
then look carefully at each place that varies from the basic iambic pattern.
Which of these variations call special attention to a particular sound or
action being talked about in the poem? Which ones specifically mimic or
echo the sense? Which variations seem to exist primarily for emphasis? Which
ones seem primarily intended to mark structural breaks in the poem?

▼ ▼ ▼

GWENDOLYN BROOKS

Queen of the Blues

Mame was singing
At the Midnight Club.
And the place was red
With blues.
She could shake her body   5
Across the floor.
For what did she have
To lose?

She put her mama
Under the ground   10
Two years ago.

7. The nephew of the Roman emperor Augustus; he died at 20, and Vergil celebrated him in *The
Aeneid*, Book VI.

(Was it three?)
She covered that grave
With roses and tears.
15   (A handsome thing
To see.)

She didn't have any
Legal pa
To glare at her,
20   To shame
Her off the floor
Of the Midnight Club.
Poor Mame.

She didn't have any
25   Big brother
To shout
"No sister of mine ! . . ."
She didn't have any
Small brother
30   To think she was everything
Fine.

She didn't have any
Baby girl
With velvet
35   Pop-open eyes.
She didn't have any
Sonny boy
To tell sweet
Sonny boy lies.

40   "Show me a man
What will love me
Till I die.
Now show me a man
What will love me
45   Till I die.
Can't find no such a man
No matter how hard
You try.
Go 'long, baby.
50   Ain't a true man left
In Chi.

"I loved my daddy.
But what did my daddy
Do?
55   I loved my daddy.

But what did my daddy
Do?
Found him a brown-skin chicken
What's gonna be
Black and blue.   60

"I was good to my daddy.
Gave him all my dough.
I say, I was good to my daddy.
I gave him all of my dough.
Scrubbed hard in them white folks'   65
Kitchens
Till my knees was rusty
And so'."

The M.C. hollered,
"Queen of the blues   70
Folks, this is strictly
The queen of the blues!"
She snapped her fingers.
She rolled her hips.
What did she have   75
To lose?

But a thought ran through her
Like a fire.
"Men don't tip their
Hats to me.   80
They pinch my arms
And they slap my thighs.
But when has a man
Tipped his hat to me?"

Queen of the blues!   85
Queen of the blues!
Strictly, strictly,
The queen of the blues!

Men are low down
Dirty and mean.   90
Why don't they tip
Their hats to a queen?   1945

MICHAEL HARPER

Dear John, Dear Coltrane

a love supreme, a love supreme[8]
a love supreme, a love supreme

Sex fingers toes
in the marketplace
near your father's church
in Hamlet, North Carolina—[9]
witness to this love
in this calm fallow
of these minds,
there is no substitute for pain:
genitals gone or going,
seed burned out,
you tuck the roots in the earth,
turn back, and move
by river through the swamps,
singing: *a love supreme, a love supreme;*
what does it all mean?
Loss, so great each black
woman expects your failure
in mute change, the seed gone.
You plod up into the electric city—
your song now crystal and
the blues. You pick up the horn
with some will and blow
into the freezing night:
a love supreme, a love supreme—

Dawn comes and you cook
up the thick sin 'tween
impotence and death, fuel
the tenor sax cannibal
heart, genitals and sweat
that makes you clean—
a love supreme, a love supreme—

Why you so black?
cause I am
why you so funky?
cause I am

8. Coltrane wrote "A Love Supreme" in response to a spiritual experience in 1957, which led to his quitting heroin and alcohol. The record was released in 1965.   9. Coltrane's birthplace. His family shared a house with Coltrane's grandfather, who was the minister of St. Stephen's AME Zion Church there.

why you so black
cause I am
why you so sweet?
cause I am
why you so black?   40
cause I am
a love supreme, a love supreme:

So sick
you couldn't play *Naima*,[1]
so flat we ached   45
for song you'd concealed
with your own blood,
your diseased liver gave
out its purity,
the inflated heart   50
pumps out, the tenor kiss,
tenor love:
a love supreme, a love supreme—
a love supreme, a love supreme—   1970

WILLIAM SHAKESPEARE

[Like as the waves make towards the pebbled shore]

Like as the waves make towards the pebbled shore,
So do our minutes hasten to their end,
Each changing place with that which goes before,
In sequent toil all forwards do contend.[2]
Nativity, once in the main[3] of light,   5
Crawls to maturity, wherewith being crowned,
Crooked[4] eclipses 'gainst his glory fight,
And Time that gave doth now his gift confound.[5]
Time doth transfix[6] the flourish set on youth
And delves the parallels[7] in beauty's brow,   10
Feeds on the rarities of nature's truth,
And nothing stands but for his scythe to mow.
And yet to times in hope[8] my verse shall stand,
Praising thy worth, despite his cruel hand.   1609

---

1. A song Coltrane wrote for and named after his wife, recorded in 1959.   2. Struggle. *Sequent:*
successive.   3. High seas. *Nativity:* newborn life.   4. Perverse.   5. Bring to nothing.
6. Pierce.   7. Lines, wrinkles.   8. In the future.

ALFRED, LORD TENNYSON

Break, Break, Break

Break, break, break,
　　On thy cold gray stones, O Sea!
And I would that my tongue could utter
　　The thoughts that arise in me.

5　　O, well for the fisherman's boy,
　　That he shouts with his sister at play!
O, well for the sailor lad,
　　That he sings in his boat on the bay!

And the stately ships go on
10　　To their haven under the hill;
But O for the touch of a vanished hand,
　　And the sound of a voice that is still!

Break, break, break,
　　At the foot of thy crags, O Sea!
15　　But the tender grace of a day that is dead
　　Will never come back to me.

ca. 1834

THOMAS NASHE

A Litany in Time of Plague

Adieu, farewell, earth's bliss;
This world uncertain is;
Fond[9] are life's lustful joys;
Death proves them all but toys;[1]
5　　None from his darts can fly;
I am sick, I must die.
　　Lord, have mercy on us!

Rich men, trust not in wealth,
Gold cannot buy you health;
10　　Physic himself must fade.
All things to end are made,
The plague full swift goes by;
I am sick, I must die.
　　Lord, have mercy on us!

9. Foolish.　　1. Trifles.

Beauty is but a flower   15
Which wrinkles will devour;
Brightness falls from the air;
Queens have died young and fair;
Dust hath closed Helen's eye.
I am sick, I must die.   20
    Lord, have mercy on us!

Strength stoops unto the grave,
Worms feed on Hector brave;
Swords may not fight with fate,
Earth still holds ope her gate.   25
"Come, come!" the bells do cry.
I am sick, I must die.
    Lord, have mercy on us.

Wit with his wantonness
Tasteth death's bitterness;   30
Hell's executioner
Hath no ears for to hear
What vain art can reply.
I am sick, I must die.
    Lord, have mercy on us.   35

Haste, therefore, each degree,
To welcome destiny;
Heaven is our heritage,
Earth but a player's stage;
Mount we unto the sky.   40
I am sick, I must die.
    Lord, have mercy on us.   1600

STEVIE SMITH

Our Bog is Dood

Our Bog is dood, our Bog is dood,
They lisped in accents mild,
But when I asked them to explain
They grew a little wild.
How do you know your Bog is dood   5
My darling little child?

We know because we wish it so
That is enough, they cried,
And straight within each infant eye
Stood up the flame of pride,   10

And if you do not think it so
You shall be crucified.

Then tell me, darling little ones,
What's dood, suppose Bog is?
Just what we think, the answer came,
Just what we think it is.
They bowed their heads. Our Bog is ours
And we are wholly his.

But when they raised them up again
They had forgotten me
Each one upon each other glared
In pride and misery
For what was dood, and what their Bog
They never could agree.

Oh sweet it was to leave them then,
And sweeter not to see,
And sweetest of all to walk alone
Beside the encroaching sea,
The sea that soon should drown them all,
That never yet drowned me.

1950

EDGAR ALLAN POE

The Raven

Once upon a midnight dreary, while I pondered, weak and weary,
Over many a quaint and curious volume of forgotten lore,
While I nodded, nearly napping, suddenly there came a tapping,
As of some one gently rapping, rapping at my chamber door.
" 'Tis some visitor," I muttered, "tapping at my chamber door—
   Only this, and nothing more."

Ah, distinctly I remember it was in the bleak December,
And each separate dying ember wrought its ghost upon the floor.
Eagerly I wished the morrow;—vainly I had sought to borrow
From my books surcease of sorrow—sorrow for the lost Lenore—
For the rare and radiant maiden whom the angels name Lenore—
   Nameless here for evermore.

And the silken sad uncertain rustling of each purple curtain
Thrilled me—filled me with fantastic terrors never felt before;
So that now, to still the beating of my heart, I stood repeating
" 'Tis some visitor entreating entrance at my chamber door;—
Some late visitor entreating entrance at my chamber door;—
   This it is, and nothing more."

Presently my soul grew stronger; hesitating then no longer,
"Sir," said I, "or Madam, truly your forgiveness I implore;   20
But the fact is I was napping, and so gently you came rapping,
And so faintly you came tapping, tapping at my chamber door,
That I scarce was sure I heard you"—here I opened wide the door;—
          Darkness there, and nothing more.

Deep into that darkness peering, long I stood there wondering, fearing,   25
Doubting, dreaming dreams no mortal ever dared to dream before;
But the silence was unbroken, and the darkness gave no token,
And the only word there spoken was the whispered word, "Lenore!"
This I whispered, and an echo murmured back the word, "Lenore!"—
          Merely this, and nothing more.   30

Back into the chamber turning, all my soul within me burning,
Soon I heard again a tapping somewhat louder than before.
"Surely," said I, "surely that is something at my window lattice;
Let me see, then, what thereat is, and this mystery explore—
Let my heart be still a moment and this mystery explore;—   35
          'Tis the wind and nothing more!"

Open here I flung the shutter, when, with many a flirt and flutter,
In there stepped a stately raven of the saintly days of yore;
Not the least obeisance made he; not an instant stopped or stayed he;
But, with mien of lord or lady, perched above my chamber door—   40
Perched upon a bust of Pallas[2] just above my chamber door—
          Perched, and sat, and nothing more.

Then this ebony bird beguiling my sad fancy into smiling,
By the grave and stern decorum of the countenance it wore,
"Though thy crest be shorn and shaven, thou," I said, "art sure no craven,   45
Ghastly grim and ancient raven wandering from the Nightly shore—
Tell me what thy lordly name is on the Night's Plutonian shore!"
          Quoth the raven, "Nevermore."

Much I marvelled this ungainly fowl to hear discourse so plainly,
Though its answer little meaning—little relevancy bore,   50
For we cannot help agreeing that no living human being
Ever yet was blessed with seeing bird above his chamber door—
Bird or beast upon the sculptured bust above his chamber door,
          With such name as "Nevermore."

But the raven, sitting lonely on the placid bust, spoke only   55
That one word, as if his soul in that one word he did outpour.
Nothing farther then he uttered—not a feather then he fluttered—
Till I scarcely more than muttered "Other friends have flown before—
On the morrow *he* will leave me, as my hopes have flown before."
          Then the bird said "Nevermore."   60

---

2. Athena, the Greek goddess of wisdom.

Startled at the stillness broken by reply so aptly spoken,
"Doubtless," said I, "what it utters is its only stock and store
Caught from some unhappy master whom unmerciful Disaster
Followed fast and followed faster till his songs one burden bore —
65   Till the dirges of his Hope that melancholy burden bore
          Of 'Never — nevermore.' "

But the raven still beguiling all my sad soul into smiling,
Straight I wheeled a cushioned seat in front of bird and bust and door;
Then, upon the velvet sinking, I betook myself to linking
70   Fancy unto fancy, thinking what this ominous bird of yore —
What this grim, ungainly, ghastly, gaunt, and ominous bird of yore
          Meant in croaking "Nevermore."

This I sat engaged in guessing, but no syllable expressing
To the fowl whose fiery eyes now burned into my bosom's core;
75   This and more I sat divining, with my head at ease reclining
On the cushion's velvet lining that the lamplight gloated o'er,
But whose velvet violet lining with the lamplight gloating o'er,
          She shall press, ah, nevermore!

Then, methought, the air grew denser, perfumed from an unseen censer
80   Swung by angels whose faint foot-falls tinkled on the tufted floor.
"Wretch," I cried, "thy God hath lent thee — by these angels he hath sent thee
Respite — respite and nepenthe[3] from thy memories of Lenore!
Quaff, oh quaff this kind nepenthe and forget this lost Lenore!"
          Quoth the raven, "Nevermore."

85   "Prophet!" said I, "thing of evil! — prophet still, if bird or devil! —
Whether Tempter sent, or whether tempest tossed thee here ashore,
Desolate, yet all undaunted, on this desert land enchanted —
On this home by Horror haunted — tell me truly, I implore —
Is there — *is* there balm in Gilead?[4] — tell me — tell me, I implore!"
90   Quoth the raven, "Nevermore."

"Prophet!" said I, "thing of evil — prophet still, if bird or devil!
by that Heaven that bends above us — by that God we both adore —
Tell this soul with sorrow laden if, within the distant Aidenn,
It shall clasp a sainted maiden whom the angels name Lenore —
95   Clasp a rare and radiant maiden whom the angels name Lenore."
          Quoth the raven, "Nevermore."

"Be that word our sign of parting, bird or fiend!" I shrieked upstarting —
"Get thee back into the tempest and the Night's Plutonian shore!
Leave no black plume as a token of that lie thy soul hath spoken!
100   Leave my loneliness unbroken! — quit the bust above my door!
Take thy beak from out my heart, and take thy form from off my door!"
          Quoth the raven, "Nevermore."

---

3. A drug reputed by the Greeks to cause forgetfulness or sorrow.   4. Cf. Jeremiah 8:22.

And the raven, never flitting, still is sitting, still is sitting
On the pallid bust of Pallas just above my chamber door;
And his eyes have all the seeming of a demon's that is dreaming,   105
And the lamp-light o'er him streaming throws his shadow on the floor;
And my soul from out that shadow that lies floating on the floor
        Shall be lifted—nevermore!   1844

GERARD MANLEY HOPKINS

Spring and Fall:

to a young child

Márgarét áre you gríeving
Over Goldengrove unleaving?
Leáves, like the things of man, you
With your fresh thoughts care for, can you?
Áh! ás the heart grows older   5
It will come to such sights colder
By and by, nor spare a sigh
Though worlds of wanwood leafmeal[5] lie;
And yet you wíll weep and know why.
Now no matter, child, the name: 10
Sórrow's spríngs áre the same.
Nor mouth had, no nor mind, expressed
What heart heard of, ghost[6] guessed:
It ís the blight man was born for,
1880   It is Margaret you mourn for.   15

JUDITH WRIGHT

"Dove-Love"

The dove purrs—over and over the dove
purrs its declaration. The wind's tone
changes from tree to tree, the creek on stone
alters its sob and fall, but still the dove
goes insistently on, telling its love   5
    "I could eat you."

And in captivity, they say, doves do.
Gentle, methodical, starting with the feet
(the ham-pink succulent toes

---

5. Broken up, leaf by leaf (analogous to "piecemeal"). *Wanwood*: pale, gloomy woods.   6. Soul.

10   on their thin stems of rose),
baring feather by feather the wincing meat:
     "I could eat you."

That neat suburban head, that suit of grey,
watchful conventional eye and manicured claw—
15   these also rhyme with us. The doves play
on one repetitive note that plucks the raw
helpless nerve, their soft "I do. I do.
     I could eat you."

                                                            1962

MARGE PIERCY

To Have Without Holding

Learning to love differently is hard,
love with the hands wide open, love
with the doors banging on their hinges,
the cupboard unlocked, the wind
5   roaring and whimpering in the rooms
rustling the sheets and snapping the blinds
that thwack like rubber bands
in an open palm.

It hurts to love wide open
10   stretching the muscles that feel
as if they are made of wet plaster,
then of blunt knives, then
of sharp knives.

It hurts to thwart the reflexes
15   of grab, of clutch; to love and let
go again and again. It pesters to remember
the lover who is not in the bed,
to hold back what is owed to the work
that gutters like a candle in a cave
20   without air, to love consciously,
conscientiously, concretely, constructively.

I can't do it, you say it's killing
me, but you thrive, you glow
on the street like a neon raspberry,
25   You float and sail, a helium balloon
bright bachelor's button blue and bobbing
on the cold and hot winds of our breath,
as we make and unmake in passionate
diastole and systole the rhythm
30   of our unbound bonding, to have

and not to hold, to love
with minimized malice, hunger
and anger moment by moment balanced.   1980

IRVING LAYTON

The Way the World Ends

Before me on the dancestand
A god's vomit or damned by his decrees
The excited twitching couples shook and
Wriggled like giant parentheses.

A pallid Canadienne   5
Raised a finger and wetted her lip,
and echoing the nickelodeon
'Chip,' she breathed drowsily, 'Chip, chip.'

Aroused, her slavish partner
Smiled, showed his dentures through sodapop gas,   10
And 'chip' he said right back to her
And 'chip, chip' she said and shook her ass.

Denture to denture, 'Pas mal'[7]
They whispered and were glad, jerked to and fro:
Their distorted bodies like bits of steel   15
Controlled by that throbbing dynamo.

They stomped, flung out their arms, groaned;
And in a flash I saw the cosmos end
And last of all the black night cover this:
'Chip, chip' and a shake of the ass.   1956   20

EMILY DICKINSON

[A narrow Fellow in the Grass]

A narrow Fellow in the Grass
Occasionally rides—
You may have met Him—did you not
His notice sudden is—

The Grass divides as with a Comb—   5
A spotted shaft is seen—
And then it closes at your feet
And opens further on—

7. Not bad (French).

He likes a Boggy Acre
A Floor too cool for Corn —
Yet when a Boy, and Barefoot —
I more than once at Noon

Have passed, I thought, a Whip lash
Unbraiding in the Sun
When stooping to secure it
It wrinkled, and was gone —

Several of Nature's People
I know, and they know me —
I feel for them a transport
Of cordiality —

But never met this Fellow
Attended, or alone
Without a tighter breathing
And Zero at the Bone —

1866

ROBERT HERRICK

To the Virgins, to Make Much of Time

Gather ye rosebuds while ye may,
    Old time is still a-flying;
And this same flower that smiles today
    Tomorrow will be dying.

The glorious lamp of heaven, the sun,
    The higher he's a-getting,
The sooner will his race be run,
    And nearer he's to setting.

That age is best which is the first,
    When youth and blood are warmer;
But being spent, the worse, and worst
    Times still succeed the former.

Then be not coy, but use your time,
    And, while ye may, go marry;
For, having lost but once your prime,
    You may forever tarry.

1648

JEAN TOOMER

Reapers

Black reapers with the sound of steel on stones
Are sharpening scythes. I see them place the hones[8]
In their hip-pockets as a thing that's done,
And start their silent swinging, one by one.
Black horses drive a mower through the weeds   5
And there, a field rat, startled, squealing bleeds.
His belly close to ground. I see the blade,
Blood-stained, continue cutting weeds and shade.   1923

▼ ▼ ▼

THE SOUNDS OF POETRY A Glossary

anapestic: two unstressed syllables followed by a stressed one
dactylic: a stressed syllable followed by two unstressed ones
iambic: an unstressed syllable followed by a stressed one
onamatopoeia: a word capturing or approximating the sound of what it
   describes
trochaic: a stressed syllable followed by an unstressed one

QUESTIONS

1. Read "Persimmons" (p. 671) and Galway Kinnell's "Blackberry Eating"
(p. 1071), and compare their sound effects with those in "The Word *Plum.*"
How visual an image does each poem create? To what purposes does Li-Young
Lee put the visual qualities of the persimmon? Which other of the five senses
are evoked in each poem? to what specific purpose?

2. Read the following poems aloud: "Break, Break, Break," "A Litany in
Time of Plague," and "The Raven." As you read each, try to be especially conscious of the way punctuation and spacing guide your pauses and of the pace
you develop as you become accustomed to the prevailing rhythms of the
poem.

8. Instruments for sharpening blades.

3. Scan—that is, mark all of the stressed syllables and chart their pattern—"Like as the waves make towards the pebbled shore." What variations do you find on the basic iambic pentameter pattern? What functions do the variations perform in each case?

4. Read "To the Virgins, to Make Much of Time" aloud. Then have someone else read it aloud to you. Compare the *pace* of the readings. Compare the stress on particular words and syllables. To what extent does the basic metrical pattern in the poem come to control the voice? Do you notice more similarities in the two readings as you and the other reader progress through the poem? why?

WRITING SUGGESTIONS

1. Read "Sound and Sense" over carefully twice—once silently and once aloud—and then mark the stressed and unstressed syllables. Draw up a chart indicating, line by line, exactly what the patterns of stress are, and then single out all the lines that have major variations from the basic iambic pentameter pattern. Pick out half a dozen lines with variations that seem to you worthy of comment, and write a paragraph on each in which you show how the metrical pattern contributes to the specific effects achieved in that line. (You will probably notice that in most of the lines other strategies also contribute to the sound effects, but confine your discussion to the achievement through metrical pattern.)

2. Try your hand at writing limericks in imitation of "A staid schizophrenic named Struther" (study the rhythmic patterns and line lengths carefully, and imitate them exactly in your poem). Begin your limerick with "There once was a ——— named ———" (use a name for which you think you can find a comic rhyme).

3. Scan line by line Suckling's "Song." In an essay of no more than 500 words, show in detail how the varied metrical pattern in the final stanza abruptly changes the tone of the poem and reverses the poem's direction.

4. Read "Anglosaxon Street" (p. 893) aloud. Then go through the poem line by line and pick out half a dozen words and patterns of sound that seem to you especially effective in creating vocal effects. Analyze carefully the effects created by each of these words or word groups, and try to account for exactly how the passage works. Then, using these examples as the primary (though not necessarily the exclusive) basis, write a three-page paper on the uses of sound in the poem.

6 INTERNAL STRUCTURE

"Proper words in proper places": that is the way one great writer of English prose (Jonathan Swift) described good writing. Finding appropriate words is not the easiest of tasks for a poet, and already we have looked at some of the implications for readers of the verbal choices a poet makes. But a poet's decision about where to put those words—how to arrange them for maximum effect—is also difficult, for individual words, metaphors, and symbols not only exist as part of a phrase or sentence or rhythmic pattern but also as part of the larger whole of the poem itself. How are the words to be ordered and the poem organized? What will come first and what last? What will be its "plot"? How will it be conceived as a whole? How is some sort of structure to be created? What principle or idea of organization will inform the poem? How are words, sentences, images, ideas, and feelings to be put together into something that holds together, seems complete, and will have a certain effect upon us as readers?

Looking at these questions from the point of view of the poet (What shall I plan? Where shall I begin?) can help the reader notice the effect of structural decisions. Every poem is different from every other one, and independent, individual decisions must therefore be made about how to organize. But there are also patterns of organization that poems fall into, sometimes because of the subject matter, sometimes because of the effect intended, sometimes for other reasons. Often poets consciously decide on a particular organizational strategy; sometimes they may reach instinctively for one or happen into a structure that suits the needs of the moment, one onto which a creator can hang the words and sentences one by one and group by group.

When there is a story to be told, the organization of a poem may be fairly simple. Here, for example, is a poem that tells a fairly simple story, largely in chronological fashion (first . . . , and then . . .):

EDWIN ARLINGTON ROBINSON

Mr. Flood's Party

Old Eben Flood, climbing alone one night
Over the hill between the town below
And the forsaken upland hermitage

That held as much as he should ever know
On earth again of home, paused warily.
The road was his and not a native near;
And Eben, having leisure, said aloud,
For no man else in Tilbury Town to hear:

"Well, Mr. Flood, we have the harvest moon
Again, and we may not have many more;
The bird is on the wing, the poet says,[1]
And you and I have said it here before.
Drink to the bird." He raised up to the light
The jug that he had gone so far to fill,
And answered huskily: "Well, Mr. Flood,
Since you propose it, I believe I will."

Alone, as if enduring to the end
A valiant armor of scarred hopes outworn
He stood there in the middle of the road
Like Roland's ghost winding a silent horn.[2]
Below him, in the town among the trees,
Where friends of other days had honored him,
A phantom salutation of the dead
Rang thinly till old Eben's eyes were dim

Then, as a mother lays her sleeping child
Down tenderly, fearing it may awake
He set the jug down slowly at his feet
With trembling care, knowing that most things break;
And only when assured that on firm earth
It stood, as the uncertain lives of men
Assuredly did not, he paced away,
And with his hand extended paused again:

"Well, Mr. Flood, we have not met like this
In a long time; and many a change has come
To both of us, I fear, since last it was
We had a drop together. Welcome home!"
Convivially returning with himself,
Again he raised the jug up to the light;
And with an acquiescent quaver said:
"Well, Mr. Flood, if you insist, I might.

"Only a very little, Mr. Flood—
For auld lang syne. No more, sir; that will do."
So, for the time, apparently it did,
And Eben evidently thought so too;
For soon amid the silver loneliness

---

1. Edward Fitzgerald, in "The Rubáiyat of Omar Khayyám" (more or less a translation of an Arab original), so describes the "Bird of Time." 2. In French legend Roland's powerful ivory horn was used to warn his allies of impending attack.

Of night he lifted up his voice and sang,
Secure, with only two moons listening,
Until the whole harmonious landscape rang—
"For auld lang syne." The weary throat gave out,
The last word wavered, and the song was done.   50
He raised again the jug regretfully
And shook his head, and was again alone.
There was not much that was ahead of him,
And there was nothing in the town below—
Where strangers would have shut the many doors   55
That many friends had opened long ago.   1921

The fairly simple **narrative structure** here is based on the gradual
unfolding of the story. Old Eben is introduced and "placed" in relation to the
town and his home, and then the "plot" unfolds: he sits down in the road,
reviews his life, reflects on the present, and has a drink. Several drinks, in fact,
as he thinks about passing time and growing old; and he sings and considers
going "home." Not much happens really: what we get is a vignette of Mr.
Flood between two places and two times, but there *is* action, and the poem's
movement—its organization and structure—depends on it: Mr. Flood in
motion, in stasis, and then, again, contemplating motion. Here is story, and
chronological movement, such as it is. You could say that a narrative of sort
takes place (rather like that in "Cherrylog Road" [p. 729]), though sparely.
The poem's organization—its structural principle—involves the passing of
time, action moving forward, a larger story being revealed by the few moments
depicted here.

"Mr. Flood's Party" presents about as much story as a short poem ever does,
but as with most poems the emphasis is not really on the developing action—
which all seems fairly predictable once we "get" who Eben is, how old he is,
and what "position" he occupies in the communal memory of Tilbury Town
and vice versa. Rather, the movement forward in time dictates the shape of the
poem, determines the way it presents its images, ideas, themes. There's an
easy-to-follow chronology here, and nearly everything takes place within it: you
could say that a story is told—with a beginning, middle, and end—and that
time structures how the revelation of facts takes place.

But even here, in one of the most simple of narrative structures, there are
complications to be noted. One complication is in the use of time itself, for
"old" time and "present" time seem posed against each other as a structural
principle too, one in tension with the chronological movement: Eben's past, as
contrasted with his present and limited future, focuses the poem's attention,

and in some ways the contrast between what was and what is seems even more important than the brief movement through present time that gets the most obvious attention in the poem. Then, too, "character"—Eben's character and that of the townspeople of later generations—gets a lot of the poem's attention, even as the chronology moves forward. More than one structural principle is at work here. We may identify the main movement of the poem as chronological and its principal structure as narrative, but to be fair and full in our discussion we have to note several other competing organizational forces at work, principles of comparison and contrast, for example, and of descriptive elaboration.

Most poems work with this kind of complexity, and identifying a single structure behind any poem involves a sense of what kind of organizational principle makes it work—while at the same time recognizing that other principles repeatedly, perhaps continually, compete for our attention. A poem's *structure* involves its conceptual framework—what principle best explains its organization and movement—and it is often useful to identify one particular structure that gives the poem its shape. But it is well to recognize from the start that most poems follow paradigmatic models loosely. As with other "elements" of a poem, finding an appropriate label to describe the structure of a particular poem can help in analyzing the poem's other aspects, but there is nothing magic in the label itself.

Purely narrative poems are often very long, much longer than can be included in a book like this, and often there are many features that are not, strictly speaking, closely connected to the narrative or linked to a strict chronology. Very often a poem moves on from a narrative of an event to some sort of commentary or reflection upon it, as in "Auto Wreck" (p. 853). Reflection can be included along the way or may be implicit in the way the story is narrated, as in "Woodchucks" (p. 684), where our major attention is more on the narrator and her responses than on the events in the story as such.

Just as poems sometimes take on a structure rather like that of a story, they sometimes borrow the structures of plays. The following poem has a **dramatic structure**; it consists of a series of scenes, each of which is presented vividly and in detail:

HOWARD NEMEROV

The Goose Fish

On the long shore, lit by the moon
To show them properly alone,

Two lovers suddenly embraced
So that their shadows were as one.
The ordinary night was graced
For them by the swift tide of blood   5
That silently they took at flood.
And for a little time they prized
        Themselves emparadised.

Then, as if shaken by stage-fright   10
Beneath the hard moon's bony light,
They stood together on the sand
Embarrassed in each other's sight
But still conspiring hand in hand,
Until they saw, there underfoot,   15
As though the world had found them out,
The goose fish turning up, though dead,
        His hugely grinning head.

There in the china light he lay,
Most ancient and corrupt and gray.   20
They hesitated at his smile,
Wondering what it seemed to say
To lovers who a little while
Before had thought to understand,
By violence upon the sand,   25
The only way that could be known
        To make a world their own.

It was a wide and moony grin
Together peaceful and obscene;
They knew not what he would express,   30
So finished a comedian
He might mean failure or success,
But took it for an emblem of
Their sudden, new and guilty love
To be observed by, when they kissed,   35
        That rigid optimist.

So he became their patriarch,
Dreadfully mild in the half-dark.
His throat that the sand seemed to choke,
His picket teeth, these left their mark   40
But never did explain the joke
That so amused him, lying there
While the moon went down to disappear
Along the still and tilted track
        That bears the zodiac.   1955   45

The first stanza sets the scene—a sandy shore in moonlight—and presents, in fact, the major action of the poem. The rest of the poem dramatizes the lovers' reactions: their initial embarrassment and feelings of guilt (stanza 2), their attempt to interpret the goose fish's smile (stanza 3), their decision to make him, whatever his meaning, the "emblem" of their love (stanza 4), and their acceptance of the fish's ambiguity and of their own relationship (stanza 5). The five stanzas do not exactly present five different scenes, but they do present separate dramatic moments, even if only a few minutes apart. Almost like a play of five very short acts, the poem traces the drama of the lovers' discovery of themselves, of their coming to terms with the meaning of their action. As in many plays, the central event (their love-making) is not the central focus of the drama, although the drama is based upon that event and could not take place without it. Here, that event is depicted only briefly but very vividly through figurative language: "they took at flood" the "swift tide of blood," and the immediate effect is to make them briefly feel "emparadised." But the poem concentrates on their later reactions, not on the act of love itself.

Their sudden discovery of the fish is a rude shock and injects a grotesque, almost macabre note into the poem. From a vision of paradise, the poem seems for a moment to turn toward a gothic horror story when the lovers discover that they have, after all, been seen—and by such a ghoulish spectator. The last three stanzas gradually re-create the intruder in their minds, as they are forced to admit that their act of love does not exist in isolation as they had at first hoped, and they begin to see it as part of a continuum, as part of their relationship to the larger world, even (at the end) putting it into the context of the rotating world and its seasons as the moon disappears into its zodiac. In retrospect, we can see that even at the moment of passion they were in touch with larger processes controlled by the presiding mood (the "swift tide of blood"), but neither the lovers nor we had understood their act as such then, and the poem is about their gradual recognition of their "place" in time and space.

Stages of feeling and knowing rather than specific visual scenes are responsible for the poem's progress, and its dramatic structure depends upon internal perceptions and internal states of mind rather than dialogue and events. Visualization and images help to organize the poem too. Notice in particular how the two most striking visual features of the poem—the fish and the moon—are presented stanza by stanza. In stanza 1, the fish is not yet noticed, and the moon exists plain; it is only mentioned, not described, and its light serves as a stage spotlight to assure not center-stage attention, but rather total privacy: it is a kind of lookout for the lovers. The stage imagery, barely suggested by the light in stanza 1, is articulated in stanza 2, and there the moon is said to be "hard" and its light "bony'"; its features have characteristics that seem more appropriate to the fish, which has now become visible. In stanza 3, the moon's light has come to seem fragile ("china") as it is said to expose the fish directly; the role of the moon as lookout and protector seems abandoned, or at least endangered. No moon appears in stanza 4, but the fish's grin is described as "wide and moony," almost as if the two onlookers, one earthly and dead, the other heavenly and eternal, had become merged in the poem, as they nearly had been by the imagery in stanza 2. And by stanza 5, the fish has become a friend—by now he is a comedian, optimist, emblem, and a patriarch of their love—and his new position in collaboration with the lovers is presided over by the moon going about its eternal business. The moon has provided the stage light for the poem and the means by which not only the fish but the meaning of the lovers' act has been discovered. The moon has also helped to organize the poem, partly as a dramatic accessory, partly as imagery.

The following poem is also dramatic, but it seems to represent a composite of several similar experiences (compare Blake's "London" [p. 875] and Dickey's "Cherrylog Road" [p. 729]) rather than a single event—a fairly common pattern in dramatic poems:

PHILIP LARKIN

Church Going

Once I am sure there's nothing going on
I step inside, letting the door thud shut.
Another church: matting, seats, and stone,
And little books; sprawlings of flowers, cut
For Sunday, brownish now; some brass and stuff   5
Up at the holy end; the small neat organ;
And a tense, musty, unignorable silence,
Brewed God knows how long. Hatless, I take off
My cycle-clips in awkward reverence,

Move forward, run my hand around the font.   10
From where I stand, the roof looks almost new—
Cleaned, or restored? Someone would know: I don't.
Mounting the lectern, I peruse a few
Hectoring large-scale verses, and pronounce
"Here endeth" much more loudly than I'd meant.   15
The echoes snigger briefly. Back at the door
I sign the book, donate an Irish sixpence,
Reflect the place was not worth stopping for.

Yet stop I did: in fact I often do,
And always end much at a loss like this,
Wondering what to look for; wondering, too,
When churches fall completely out of use
What we shall turn them into, if we shall keep
A few cathedrals chronically on show,
Their parchment, plate and pyx in locked cases,
And let the rest rent-free to rain and sheep.
Shall we avoid them as unlucky places?

Or, after dark, will dubious women come
To make their children touch a particular stone;
Pick simples[3] for a cancer; or on some
Advised night see walking a dead one?
Power of some sort or other will go on
In games, in riddles, seemingly at random;
But superstition, like belief, must die,
And what remains when disbelief has gone?
Grass, weedy pavement, brambles, buttress, sky,

A shape less recognizable each week,
A purpose more obscure. I wonder who
Will be the last, the very last, to seek
This place for what it was; one of the crew
That tap and jot and know what rood-lofts[4] were?
Some ruin-bibber,[5] randy for antique,
Or Christmas-addict, counting on a whiff
Of gown-and-bands and organ-pipes and myrrh?
Or will he be my representative,

Bored, uninformed, knowing the ghostly silt
Dispersed, yet tending to this cross of ground
Through suburb scrub because it held unspilt
So long and equably what since is found
Only in separation—marriage, and birth,
And death, and thoughts of these—for whom was built
This special shell? For, though I've no idea
What this accoutered frowsty barn is worth,
It pleases me to stand in silence here;

A serious house on serious earth it is,
In whose blent air all our compulsions meet,
Are recognized, and robed as destinies.
And that much never can be obsolete,
Since someone will forever be surprising
A hunger in himself to be more serious,

---

3. Medicinal herbs.   4. Galleries atop the screens (on which crosses are mounted) that divide
the naves or main bodies of churches from the choirs or chancels.   5. Literally, ruin-drinker:
someone extremely attracted to antiquarian objects.

And gravitating with it to this ground,
Which, he once heard, was proper to grow wise in,
If only that so many dead lie round.   1955

Ultimately, the poem's emphasis is upon what it means to visit churches, what sort of phenomenon church buildings represent, and what is to be made of the fact that "church going" (in the usual sense of the word) has declined so much. The poem uses a *different* sort of church going (visitation by tourists) to consider larger philosophical questions about the relationship of religion to culture and history. The poem is, finally, a rather philosophical one about the directions of English culture, and through an enumeration of religious objects and rituals it reviews the history of how we got to our present historical circumstance. It tells a kind of story first, through one lengthy dramatized scene, in order to comment later on what the place and the experience may mean, and the larger conclusion derives from the particulars of what the speaker does and touches. The action is really over by the end of stanza 2, and that action, we are told, stands for many such visits to similar churches; after that, all is reflection and discussion, five stanzas' worth.

"Church Going" is a curious poem in many ways. It goes to a lot of trouble to characterize its speaker, who seems a rather odd choice as a commentator on the state of religion. His informal attire (he takes off his cycle-clips at the end of stanza 1) and his not exactly worshipful behavior do not at first make us expect him to be a serious philosopher about what all this means. He is not disrespectful or sacrilegious, and before the end of stanza 1 he has tried to describe the "awkward reverence" he feels, but his overly somber imitation of part of the service stamps him as playful, a little satirical, and as a tourist here, not someone who regularly drops in for prayer or meditation in the usual sense. And yet those early details do give him credentials, in a way; he clearly knows the names of religious objects and has some of the history of churches in his grasp. Clearly he does this sort of church going often ("Yet stop I did; in fact I often do," line 19) because he wonders seriously what it all means — now — in comparison to what it meant to religious worshipers in times past. Ultimately, he takes the church itself seriously and its cultural meaning and function just as seriously (lines 55ff.), and understands the importance of the church in the history of his culture. In this poem, the drama is, relatively speaking, brief, but it gives a context for the more digressive and rambling free-floating reflections that grow out of the dramatic experience.

Sometimes poems are organized by contrasts, setting one thing up conveniently against another that is quite different. Look, for example, at the two worlds in the following poem, and notice how carefully the contrasts between the two worlds are developed.

PAT MORA

Sonrisas

I live in a doorway
between two rooms, I hear
quiet clicks, cups of black
coffee, *click, click* like facts
5   budgets, tenure, curriculum,
from careful women in crisp beige
suits, quick beige smiles
that seldom sneak into their eyes.

I peek
10   in the other room señoras
in faded dresses stir sweet
milk coffee, laughter whirls
with steam from fresh *tamales*
      sh, sh, mucho ruido,[6]
15   they scold one another,
press their lips, trap smiles
in their dark, Mexican eyes.   1986

Here different words, habits, and values characterize the different worlds of the two sets of characters, and the poem is largely organized on the basis of the contrasts between them. The meaning of the poem (the difference between the two worlds) is very nearly the same as the structure itself.

Poems often have **discursive structures** too; that is, they are sometimes organized like a treatise, an argument, or an essay. "First," they say, "and second . . . and third. . . ." This sort of 1-2-3 structure takes a variety of forms depending on what one is enumerating or arguing. Here, for example, is a poem that is about three people who have died. The poem honors all three, but makes clear and sharp distinctions between them. As you read the poem, try to articulate just what sort of person each of the three is represented to be.

6. A lot of noise.

JAMES WRIGHT

Arrangements with Earth for Three Dead Friends

Sweet earth, he ran and changed his shoes to go
Outside with other children through the fields.
He panted up the hills and swung from trees
Wild as a beast but for the human laughter
That tumbled like a cider down his cheeks.   5
Sweet earth, the summer has been gone for weeks,
And weary fish already sleeping under water
Below the banks where early acorns freeze.
Receive his flesh and keep it cured of colds.
Button his coat and scarf his throat from snow.   10

And now, bright earth, this other is out of place
In what, awake, we speak about as tombs.
He sang in houses when the birds were still
And friends of his were huddled round till dawn
After the many nights to hear him sing.   15
Bright earth, his friends remember how he sang
Voices of night away when wind was one.
Lonely the neighborhood beneath your hill
Where he is waved away through silent rooms.
Listen for music, earth, and human ways.   20

Dark earth, there is another gone away,
But she was not inclined to beg of you
Relief from water falling or the storm.
She was aware of scavengers in holes
Of stone, she knew the loosened stones that fell   25
Indifferently as pebbles plunging down a well
And broke for the sake of nothing human souls.
Earth, hide your face from her where dark is warm.
She does not beg for anything, who knew
The change of tone, the human hope gone gray.   1957   30

Why, in stanza 1, is the earth represented as a parent? What does
addressing the earth here as "sweet" seem to mean? How does the address to
earth as "bright" fit the dead person described in stanza 2? In what different
senses is the person described in stanza 3 "dark"? Why is the earth asked to
give attention secretly to this person? Exactly what kind of person was she?
How does the poem make you feel about her? Is there any cumulative point in
describing three such different people in the same poem? What is accom-

plished by having the poem's three stanzas addressed to various aspects of earth? Similar discursive structures help to organize poems such as Shelley's "Ode to the West Wind" (p. 856), where the wind is shown driving a leaf in Part I, a cloud in Part II, a wave in Part III, and then, after a summary and statement of the speaker's ambitious hope in Part IV, is asked to make the speaker a lyre in Part V.

Poems may borrow their organizational strategies from many places, imitating chronological, visual, or discursive shapes in reality or in other works of art. Sometimes poems strive to be almost purely descriptive of someone or something (using **descriptive structures**), in which case organizational decisions have to be made much as a painter or photographer would make them, deciding first how the whole scene should look, then putting the parts into proper place for the whole. But there are differences demanded by the poetic medium: a poem has to present the details sequentially, not all at once as an actual picture more or less can, so the poet must decide where the description starts (at the left? center? top?) and what sort of movement to use (linear across the scene? clockwise?). But if having words instead of paint or film has some disadvantages, it also has particular assets: figurative language can be a part of description, or an adjunct to it. A poet can insert a comparison at any point without necessarily disturbing the unity of what he or she describes.

Some poems use **imitative structures,** mirroring as exactly as possible the structure of something that already exists as an object and can be seen — another poem perhaps, as in Koch's "Variations on a Theme by William Carlos Williams" (p. 993). Or a poem may use **reflective** (or **meditative**) **structures,** pondering a subject, theme, or event, and letting the mind play with it, skipping (sometimes illogically but still usefully) from one sound to another, or to related thoughts or objects as the mind receives them.

Here is a poem that involves several different organizational principles but ultimately takes its structure from an important emotional shift in the speaker's attitude as her mind reviews, ponders, and rethinks events of long ago.

SHARON OLDS

The Victims

When Mother divorced you, we were glad. She took it and
took it, in silence, all those years and then
kicked you out, suddenly, and her
kids loved it. Then you were fired, and we

grinned inside, the way people grinned when   5
Nixon's helicopter lifted off the South
Lawn for the last time.[7] We were tickled
to think of your office taken away,
your secretaries taken away,
your lunches with three double bourbons,   10
your pencils, your reams of paper. Would they take your
suits back, too, those dark
carcasses hung in your closet, and the black
noses of your shoes with their large pores?
She had taught us to take it, to hate you and take it   15
until we pricked with her for your
annihilation, Father. Now I
pass the bums in doorways, the white
slugs of their bodies gleaming through slits in their
suits of compressed silt, the stained   20
flippers of their hands, the underwater
fire of their eyes, ships gone down with the
lanterns lit, and I wonder who took it and
took it from them in silence until they had
given it all away and had nothing   25
left but this.   1984

"The Victims" divides basically into two parts. In the first two-thirds of the
poem (from line 1 to the middle of line 17), the speaker evokes her father (the
"you" of lines 1, 3, etc.), who had been guilty of terrible habits and behavior
when the speaker was young and was kicked out suddenly and divorced by the
speaker's mother (lines 1–3). He was then fired from his job (line 4) and lost
his whole way of life (lines 8–12), and the speaker (taught by the mother, lines
15–17) recalls celebrating every defeat and every loss ("we pricked with her for
your annihilation," lines 16–17). The mother is regarded as a victim ("she took
it and took it, in silence, all those years" [lines 1–2]), and the speaker forms an
indivisible unit with her and the other children ("her kids," lines 3–4). They
are the "we" of the first part of the poem. They were "glad" (line 1) at the
divorce; they "loved it" (line 4) when the mother kicked out the father; they
"grinned" (line 5) when the father was fired; they were "tickled" (line 7) when
he lost his job, his secretaries, and his daily life. Only at the end of the first section does the speaker (now older but remembering what it was like to be a
child) recognize that the mother was responsible for the easy, childish vision of
the father's guilt ("she had taught us to take it, to hate you and take it" [line

7. When Richard Nixon resigned the U.S. presidency on August 8, 1974, his exit from the White
House (by helicopter from the lawn) was televised live.

15]); nevertheless, all sympathy in this part of the poem is with the mother and her children, while all of the imagery is entirely unfavorable to the father. The family reacted to the father's misfortunes the way observers responded to the retreat in disgrace of Richard Nixon from the U.S. presidency. The father seems to have led a luxurious and insensitive life, with lots of support in his office (lines 8–11), fancy clothes (lines 12–14), and decadent lunches (line 10); his artificial identity seemed haunting and daunting (lines 11–14) to the speaker as child.

But in line 17, the poem shifts focus and shifts gears. The "you" in the poem is now, suddenly, "Father." A bit of sympathy begins to surface for "bums in doorways" (line 18), who begin to seem like victims too; their bodies are "slugs" (line 19), their suits are made of residual waste pressed into regimented usefulness (lines 19–20), and their hands are constricted into mechanical "flippers" (line 21). Their eyes contain fire (line 22), but it is as if they retain only a spark of life in their submerged and dying state. The speaker has not forgotten the cruelty and insensitivity remembered in the first part of the poem, but the blame seems to have shifted somewhat and the father is not the only villain, nor are the mother and children the only victims. Look carefully at how the existence of street people recalls earlier details about the father, how sympathy for his plight is elicited from us, and how the definition of victim shifts.

Imagery, words, attitudes, and narrative are different in the two parts of the poem, and the second half carefully qualifies the first, as if to illustrate the more mature and considered attitudes of the speaker in her older years—a qualification of the easy imitation of the earlier years when the mother's views were thoroughly dominant and seemed sensible and adequate. Change has governed the poem's structure here; differences in age, attitude, and tone are supported by entirely different sets of terms, attitudes, and versions of causality.

The paradigms (or models) for organizing poems are, finally, not all that different from those of prose. It may be easier to organize something short rather than something long, but the question of intensity becomes comparatively more important in shorter works. Basically, the problem of how to organize one's material is, for the writer, first of all a matter of deciding what kind of thing one wants to create, of having its purposes and effects clearly in mind. That means that every poem will differ somewhat from every other, but it also means that patterns of purpose—narrative, dramatic, discursive, descriptive, imitative, or reflective—may help writers organize and formulate their ideas. A consciousness of purpose and effect can help the reader see *how* a poem proceeds toward its goal. Seeing how a poem is organized is, in turn, often a good way of seeing where it is going and what its real concerns and purposes may be. Often a poem's organization helps to make clear the particular effects that the poet wishes to generate. In a good poem, means and end are closely related, and a reader who is a good observer of one will be able to discover the other.

▼ ▼ ▼

ANONYMOUS

Sir Patrick Spens

The king sits in Dumferling toune,[8]
    Drinking the blude-reid[9] wine:
"O whar will I get guid sailor,
    To sail this ship of mine?"

Up and spake an eldern knicht,   5
    Sat at the king's richt knee:
"Sir Patrick Spens is the best sailor
    That sails upon the sea."

The king has written a braid[1] letter
    And signed it wi' his hand,   10
And sent it to Sir Patrick Spens,
    Was walking on the sand.

The first line that Sir Patrick read,
    A loud lauch[2] lauched he;
The next line that Sir Patrick read,   15
    The tear blinded his ee.[3]

"O wha is this has done this deed,
    This il deed done to me,
To send me out this time o' the year,
    To sail upon the sea?   20

"Make haste, make haste, my merry men all,
    Our guid ship sails the morn."
"O say na sae,[4] my master dear,
    For I fear a deadly storm.

"Late, late yestre'en I saw the new moon   25
    Wi' the auld moon in her arm,
And I fear, I fear, my dear mastér,
    That we will come to harm."

8. Town.   9. Blood-red.   1. Broad: explicit.   2. Laugh.   3. Eye.   4. Not so.

O our Scots nobles were richt laith[5]
    To weet their cork-heeled shoon,[6]
But lang owre a'[7] the play were played
    Their hats they swam aboon.[8]

O lang, lang, may their ladies sit,
    Wi' their fans into their hand,
Or ere they see Sir Patrick Spens
    Come sailing to the land.

O lang, lang, may the ladies stand
    Wi' their gold kems[9] in their hair,
Waiting for their ain[1] dear lords,
    For they'll see them na mair.

Half o'er, half o'er to Aberdour
    It's fifty fadom deep,
And there lies guid Sir Patrick Spens
    Wi' the Scots lords at his feet.   Probably 13th cent.

T. S. ELIOT

Journey of the Magi[2]

"A cold coming we had of it,
Just the worst time of the year
For a journey, and such a long journey:
The ways deep and the weather sharp,
The very dead of winter."[3]
And the camels galled, sore-footed, refractory,
Lying down in the melting snow.
There were times we regretted
The summer palaces on slopes, the terraces,
And the silken girls bringing sherbet.
Then the camel men cursing and grumbling
And running away, and wanting their liquor and women,
And the night-fires going out, and the lack of shelters,
And the cities hostile and the towns unfriendly
And the villages dirty and charging high prices:
A hard time we had of it.
At the end we preferred to travel all night,
Sleeping in snatches,
With the voices singing in our ears, saying
That this was all folly.

5. Right loath: very reluctant.   6. To wet their cork-heeled shoes. Cork was expensive, and therefore such shoes were a mark of wealth and status.   7. Before all.   8. Their hats swam above them.   9. Combs.   1. Own.   2. The wise men who followed the star of Bethlehem. See Matthew 2:1–12.   3. An adaptation of a passage from a 1622 sermon by Lancelot Andrewes.

Then at dawn we came down to a temperate valley,
Wet, below the snow line, smelling of vegetation;
With a running stream and a water-mill beating the darkness,
And three trees on the low sky,[4]
And an old white horse galloped away in the meadow.   25
Then we came to a tavern with vine-leaves over the lintel,
Six hands at an open door dicing for pieces of silver,
And feet kicking the empty wine-skins.
But there was no information, and so we continued
And arrived at evening, not a moment too soon   30
Finding the place; it was (you may say) satisfactory.

All this was a long time ago, I remember,
And I would do it again, but set down
This set down
This: were we led all that way for   35
Birth or Death? There was a Birth, certainly,
We had evidence and no doubt. I had seen birth and death,
But had thought they were different; this Birth was
Hard and bitter agony for us, like Death, our death.
We returned to our places, these Kingdoms,[5]   40
But no longer at ease here, in the old dispensation,
With an alien people clutching their gods.
I should be glad of another death.   1927

KARL SHAPIRO

Auto Wreck

Its quick soft silver bell beating, beating,
And down the dark one ruby flare
Pulsing out red light like an artery,
The ambulance at top speed floating down
Past beacons and illuminated clocks   5
Wings in a heavy curve, dips down,
And brakes speed, entering the crowd.
The doors leap open, emptying light;
Stretchers are laid out, the mangled lifted
And stowed into the little hospital.   10
Then the bell, breaking the hush, tolls once,

---

4. Suggestive of the three crosses of the Crucifixion (Luke 23:32–33). The Magi see several objects that suggest later events in Christ's life: pieces of silver (see Matthew 26:14–16), the dicing (see Matthew 27:35), the white horse (see Revelation 6:2 and 19:11–16), and the empty wine-skins (see Matthew 9:14–17, possibly relevant also to lines 41–42).   **5.** The Bible only identifies the wise men as "from the East," and subsequent tradition has made them kings. In Persia, magi were members of an ancient priestly caste.

And the ambulance with its terrible cargo
Rocking, slightly rocking, moves away,
As the doors, an afterthought, are closed.

15 We are deranged, walking among the cops
Who sweep glass and are large and composed.
One is still making notes under the light.
One with a bucket douches ponds of blood
Into the street and gutter.
20 One hangs lanterns on the wrecks that cling,
Empty husks of locusts, to iron poles.

Our throats were tight as tourniquets,
Our feet were bound with splints, but now,
Like convalescents intimate and gauche,
25 We speak through sickly smiles and warn
With the stubborn saw of common sense,
The grim joke and the banal resolution.
The traffic moves around with care,
But we remain, touching a wound
30 That opens to our richest horror.
Already old, the question Who shall die?
Becomes unspoken Who is innocent?

For death in war is done by hands;
Suicide has cause and stillbirth, logic;
35 And cancer, simple as a flower, blooms.
But this invites the occult mind,
Cancels our physics with a sneer,
And spatters all we knew of denouement
Across the expedient and wicked stones.   1942

ROO BORSON

Save Us From

Save us from night,
from bleak open highways
without end, and the fluorescent
oases of gas stations,
5 from the gunning of immortal
engines past midnight,
when time has no meaning,
from all-night cafés,
their ghoulish slices of pie,
10 and the orange ruffle on the
apron of the waitress,

the matching plastic chairs,
from orange and brown and
all unearthly colors,
banish them back to the test tube,   15
save us from them,
from those bathrooms with a
moonscape of skin in the mirror,
from fatigue, its merciless brightness,
when each cell of the body stands on end,   20
and the sensation of teeth,
and the mind's eternal sentry,
and the unmapped city
with its cold bed.
Save us from insomnia,   25
its treadmill,
its school bells and factory bells,
from living-rooms like the tomb,
their plaid chesterfields
and galaxies of dust,   30
from chairs without arms,
from any matched set of furniture,
from floor-length drapes which
close out the world,
from padded bras and rented suits,   35
from any object in which horror is concealed.
Save us from waking after nightmares,
save us from nightmares,
from other worlds,
from the mute, immobile contours   40
of dressers and shoes,
from another measureless day, save us.   1989

WILLIAM CARLOS WILLIAMS

The Dance

In Brueghel's great picture, The Kermess,[6]
the dancers go round, they go round and
around, the squeal and the blare and the
tweedle of bagpipes, a bugle and fiddles
tipping their bellies (round as the thick-   5
sided glasses whose wash they impound)
their hips and their bellies off balance
to turn them. Kicking and rolling about

6. A drawing by Pieter Brueghel the elder (1525?–1569).

10　the Fair Grounds, swinging their butts, those
shanks must be sound to bear up under such
rollicking measures, prance as they dance
in Brueghel's great picture, The Kermess.　　　　　　1944

PERCY BYSSHE SHELLEY

Ode to the West Wind

I

O wild West Wind, thou breath of Autumn's being,
Thou, from whose unseen presence the leaves dead
Are driven, like ghosts from an enchanter fleeing,

Yellow, and black, and pale, and hectic red,
5　Pestilence-stricken multitudes: O thou,
Who chariotest to their dark wintry bed

The wingéd seeds, where they lie cold and low,
Each like a corpse within its grave, until
Thine azure sister of the Spring shall blow

10　Her clarion[7] o'er the dreaming earth, and fill
(Driving sweet buds like flocks to feed in air)
With living hues and odors plain and hill:

Wild Spirit, which art moving everywhere;
Destroyer and preserver; hear, oh, hear!

II

15　Thou on whose stream, mid the steep sky's commotion,
Loose clouds like earth's decaying leaves are shed,
Shook from the tangled boughs of Heaven and Ocean,

Angels[8] of rain and lightning: there are spread
On the blue surface of thine aéry surge,
20　Like the bright hair uplifted from the head

Of some fierce Maenad,[9] even from the dim verge
Of the horizon to the zenith's height,
The locks of the approaching storm. Thou dirge

Of the dying year, to which this closing night
25　Will be the dome of a vast sepulcher,
Vaulted with all thy congregated might

---

7. Trumpet-call.　　8. Messengers.　　9. A frenzied female votary of Dionysus, the Greek god of
vegetation and fertility who was supposed to die in the fall and rise again each spring.

Of vapors, from whose solid atmosphere
Black rain, and fire, and hail will burst: oh, hear!

III

Thou who didst waken from his summer dreams
The blue Mediterranean, where he lay,   30
Lulled by the coil of his crystálline streams,

Beside a pumice isle in Baiae's bay,[1]
And saw in sleep old palaces and towers
Quivering within the wave's intenser day,

All overgrown with azure moss and flowers   35
So sweet, the sense faints picturing them! Thou
For whose path the Atlantic's level powers

Cleave themselves into chasms, while far below
The sea-blooms and the oozy woods which wear
The sapless foliage of the ocean, know   40

Thy voice, and suddenly grow gray with fear,
And tremble and despoil themselves:[2] oh, hear!

IV

If I were a dead leaf thou mightest bear;
If I were a swift cloud to fly with thee;
A wave to pant beneath thy power, and share   45

The impulse of thy strength, only less free
Than thou, O uncontrollable! If even
I were as in my boyhood, and could be

The comrade of thy wanderings over Heaven,
As then, when to outstrip thy skyey speed   50
Scarce seemed a vision; I would ne'er have striven

As thus with thee in prayer in my sore need.
Oh, lift me as a wave, a leaf, a cloud!
I fall upon the thorns of life! I bleed!

A heavy weight of hours has chained and bowed   55
One too like thee: tameless, and swift, and proud.

V

Make me thy lyre, even as the forest is:
What if my leaves are falling like its own!
The tumult of thy mighty harmonies

---

1. Where Roman emperors had erected villas, west of Naples.   2. "The vegatation at the bottom
of the sea . . . sympathizers with that of the land in the change of seasons." (Shelley's note)

60 Will take from both a deep, autumnal tone,
Sweet though in sadness. Be thou, Spirit fierce,
My spirit! Be thou me, impetuous one!

Drive my dead thoughts over the universe
Like withered leaves to quicken a new birth!
65 And, by the incantation of this verse,

Scatter, as from an unextinguished hearth
Ashes and sparks, my words among mankind!
Be through my lips to unawakened earth

The trumpet of a prophecy! O Wind,
70 If Winter comes, can Spring be far behind?   1820

MARGARET ATWOOD

Siren Song

This is the one song everyone
would like to learn: the song
that is irresistible:

the song that forces men
5 to leap overboard in squadrons
even though they see the beached skulls

the song nobody knows
because anyone who has heard it
is dead, and the others can't remember.

10 Shall I tell you the secret
and if I do, will you get me
out of this bird suit?

I don't enjoy it here
squatting on this island
15 looking picturesque and mythical

with these two feathery maniacs,
I don't enjoy singing
this trio, fatal and valuable.

I will tell the secret to you,
20 to you, only to you.
Come closer. This song

is a cry for help: Help me!
Only you, only you can,
you are unique

at last. Alas   25
it is a boring song
but it works every time.   1974

LOUISE BOGAN

Cartography

As you lay in sleep
I saw the chart
Of artery and vein
Running from your heart,

Plain as the strength   5
Marked upon the leaf
Along the length,
Mortal and brief,

Of your gaunt hand.
I saw it clear: 10
The wiry brand
Of the life we bear

Mapped like the great
Rivers that rise
Beyond our fate   15
And distant from our eyes.   1941

▼   ▼   ▼

INTERNAL STRUCTURE A Glossary

descriptive structure: determined by the requirements of describing
   someone or something
discursive structure: organized in the form of a treatise, argument, or essay
dramatic structure: consisting of a series of scenes, each of which is presented vividly and in detail
imitative structure: mirroring as exactly as possible the structure of something that already exists as an object and can be seen
narrative structure: based on a straightforward chronological framework
reflective/meditative structure: pondering a subject, theme, or event, and
   letting the mind play with it, skipping from one sound to another, or to
   related thoughts or objects as the mind receives them

QUESTIONS

1. How many different "scenes" can you identify in "Sir Patrick Spens"? Where does each scene begin and end? How are the transitions made from scene to scene? How is the "fading" effect between scenes accomplished?

2. Why does the last line of "The Dance" repeat the first line? How do the line breaks early in the poem help to control the poem's rhythm and pace? What differences do you notice in the choice of words early in the poem and then later? How is the poem organized?

3. What words and patterns are repeated in the different stanzas of "Ode to the West Wind"? What differences are there from stanza to stanza? What "progress" does the poem make? In what sense is the poem "revolutionary" or "cyclical"? What contribution to the structure of the poem do the sound patterns make? How do the rhymes and repeated stanza patterns contribute to the tone of the poem? to its meaning?

4. Look back over the poems you have read earlier in the course, and pick out one of them that seems to you particularly effective in the way it is put together. Read it over several times and consider carefully how it is organized, i.e., what principles of structure it uses. What does the choice of speaker, situation, and setting have to do with its structure? What other artistic decisions seem to you crucial in creating the poem's structure?

WRITING SUGGESTIONS

1. After doing the reading and analysis suggested in question 4 above, write a detailed essay in which you consider fully the structural principles at work in the poem. The length of your essay will depend on the length of the poem you choose—but also on the complexity of its structure.

2. Look back at "Cherrylog Road" (p. 729) and reread it carefully. Then look for another poem in which memory of a much earlier event plays an important structural function. Compare the poems in detail, noting how (in each case) memory influences the way the event is reconstructed. What details of the event are in each case omitted in the retelling? What parts are lengthened or dwelt upon? What, in each case, is the point of having the event recalled later rather than from an immediate recollection?

Write a three- or four-page essay comparing the structuring function of memory in the two poems, noting in each case exactly how the structural principles at work in the poem help to create the poem's final tone.

STUDENT WRITING

Below is one student's response to the first Writing Suggestion. The student focuses primarily on the phrases in "The Victims" that involve "taking" as he describes the structure of the poem.

Structure and Language in "The Victims"
by Sharon Olds

In Sharon Olds' poem "The Victims" we hear a son or daughter, already grown, speaking to a father whom he/she lost as a result of divorce. It reads like part accusation and part confession. As the poem progresses attitudes such as bitterness and spite toward the father soften, and at the end the reader is left with the same ambivalent feelings as the speaker herself[1] feels.

The poem is divided into two parts, from line 1 to line 17 and from there to the end. The first portion is in many ways a narration, the story line. The speaker relives the experience. Both the language ("her kids loved it," "we grinned inside," "We were tickled") and symbolism (the comparison of suits to carcasses and shoe tips to noses) used here suggest that this is a child's perspective on the situation. This portion is also spoken in the past tense. In the second portion we hear a more reflective and contemplative adult. It is spoken in the present tense ("Now I . . ." [line 17]), and combines both the speaker's bitterness (which dominates the first portion) as well as her pity and sense of guilt towards her father.

The two portions are framed by similar phrases: "She took it and took it, in silence . . ." (line 1), "She had taught us to take it, to hate you and take it . . ." (line 15), "I wonder who took it and took it from them in silence . . ." (lines 23—24). In the final lines of the poem these words take on a deep meaning and enable the reader to read the poem in a completely different manner.

When we first read the words "took it and took it in silence" we assume the mother took some sort of abuse in silence. She taught her children to take the abuse in silence and to hate their father. The final repetition of that phrase: "I wonder who took it and took it from them in silence until they had given it all away and had nothing left but this" (lines 23—26), reminds us of the meaning of the word "take." "Taking it" can mean taking abuse, but it can also mean taking in the ordinary sense as in taking money or a gift or love. One is active and one is passive. If we adopt the active form, the poem is still meaningful, only this time it is the father who is the victim. He is the one who gave all he had. The mother took and took (money, love, attention) and taught her children to take and to hate. One hint to support this interpretation might be the first line of the poem, which suggests that the mother was something more than a passive victim ("When mother divorced you . . . ," ". . . kicked you out . . ."). Again the ambiguity of the phrase strengthens the sense of ambivalence which a child must feel when her parents divorce. It is never clear who "the Victims" are in the poem, perhaps all of them.

Silence is another strong theme in the poem. Note the following examples: "took it, in silence" (line 2), "we grinned inside . . ." (line 5), "I wonder . . ." (line 23), "took it from them in silence . . ." (line 24). The strongest example of the silence, the lack of communication, and the alienation comes in the last section and the metaphor of the bums in doorways. The speaker compares her father to the drunken bums she sees and describes them in such a way that the image of fish or sunken ships becomes vivid ("white slugs of their bodies," "slits in their suits of compressed silt," "stained flippers," "underwater fire of their eyes"). The father is in some other, "underwater" world where sounds from the outside are inaudible. The only sound we hear in this poem is the speaker's voice. Silence and alienation predominated in her childhood, and now as an adult she is still unable to reach her father.

While on the surface this poem seems to be one
of anger and accusation, a closer reading
indicates a deeper, more complex view of human
experience. Things are seldom as clearly defined
and one-sided as they appear to a child.

1. It is not apparent whether the speaker is male or female. I chose to
refer to her as a female simply because the poet is a female. It seems that
the experience and feelings related are not exclusive to one sex or the
other.

7 EXTERNAL FORM

M ost poems of more than a few lines are divided into **stanzas,** groups of lines divided from other groups by white space on the page. Putting some space between groupings of lines has the effect of sectioning the poem, giving its physical appearance a series of divisions that often mark breaks in thought, changes of scenery or imagery, or other shifts in structure or direction. In "The Flea" (p. 732), for example, the stanza divisions mark distinctive stages in the action; between the first and second stanzas, the speaker stops his companion from killing the flea, and between the second and third stanzas, the companion follows through on her intention and kills the flea. In "The Goose Fish" (p. 840), the stanzas mark stages in the self-perception of the lovers; each of the stanzas is a more or less distinct scene, and the scenes unfold almost like a series of slides. Not all stanzas are quite so neatly patterned as are the ones in these two poems, but any formal division of a poem into stanzas is important to consider—what appear to be gaps or silences may be structural indicators.

Historically, stanzas have most often been organized by patterns of rhyme, and thus stanza divisions have been a visual indicator of patterns in sound. In most traditional stanza forms, the pattern of rhyme is repeated in stanza after stanza throughout the poem, until voice and ear become familiar with the pattern and come to expect it and, in a sense, to depend on it. The accumulation of pattern allows us to "hear" variations as well, just as we do in music. The rhyme thus becomes an organizational device in the poem—a formal, external determiner of organization, as distinguished from the internal, structural determiners we considered in Chapter 6—and ordinarily the metrical patterns stay constant from stanza to stanza. In Shelley's "Ode to the West Wind," for example, the first and third lines in each stanza rhyme, and the middle line then rhymes with the first and third lines of the next stanza. (In indicating rhyme, a different letter of the alphabet is conventionally used to represent each sound; in the following example, if we begin with "being" as *a* and "dead" as *b*, then "fleeing" is also *a*, and "red" and "bed" are *b*.)

O wild West Wind, thou breath of Autumn's being,	*a*
Thou, from whose unseen presence the leaves dead	*b*
Are driven, like ghosts from an enchanter fleeing,	*a*
Yellow, and black, and pale, and hectic red,	*b*
Pestilence-stricken multitudes: O thou,	*c*

Who chariotest to their dark wintry bed	*b*
The wingéd seeds, where they lie cold and low,	*c*
Each like a corpse within its grave, until	*d*
Thine azure sister of the Spring shall blow	*c*

In this stanza form, known as **terza rima,** the stanzas are linked to each other by a common sound: one rhyme sound from each stanza is picked up in the next stanza, and so on to the end of the poem or one section of the poem. This stanza form was used by the great Italian poet Dante in *The Divine Comedy*, written in the early 1300s. Terza rima is not all that common in English because it is a rhyme-rich stanza form—that is, it requires many rhymes—and English is, relatively speaking, a rhyme-poor language (not as rich in rhyme possibilities as such languages as Italian or French). One reason for this is that English derives from so many different language families that it has fewer similar word endings than languages that have remained more "pure," i.e., more dependent for vocabulary on the roots and patterns found in a single language family.

Contemporary poets seldom use rhyme, finding it neither necessary nor appealing, but until the twentieth century the music of rhyme was central to both the sound and the formal conception of most poems. Because poetry was originally an oral art (and its texts not always written down) various kinds of **memory devices** (sometimes called **mnemonic devices**) were built into poems to help reciters remember them. Rhyme was one such device, and most people still find it easier to memorize poetry that rhymes. The simple pleasure of hearing familiar sounds repeated may also help to account for the traditional popularity of rhyme, and perhaps plain habit (for both poets and hearers) had a lot to do with why rhyme flourished for so many centuries as a standard expectation. No doubt, too, rhyme helped to give poetry a special quality that distinguished it from prose, a significant advantage in ages that worried about decorum and propriety and were anxious to preserve a strong sense of poetic tradition. Some ages have been very concerned that poetry should not in any way be mistaken for prose or made to serve prosaic functions, and the literary critics and theorists in those ages made extraordinary efforts to emphasize the distinctions between poetry, which was thought to be artistically superior, and prose, which was thought to be primarily utilitarian. A pride in elitism and a fear that an expanded reading public could ultimately dilute the possibilities of traditional art forms have been powerful cultural forces in Western civilization, and if such forces were not themselves responsible for creating rhyme in poetry, they at least helped to preserve a sense of its necessity.

But there are at least two other reasons for rhyme. One is complex and hard to state justly without long explanations. It involves traditional ideas about the symmetrical relationship of different aspects of the world and the function of poetry to reflect the universe as human learning understood it. Most poets in earlier centuries assumed that rhyme was proper to verse, perhaps even essential. They would have felt themselves eccentric to compose poems any other way. Some poets did experiment—very successfully—with **blank verse** (that is, verse that did not rhyme but that nevertheless had strict metrical requirements), but the cultural pressure for rhyme was almost constant. Why? As noted above, custom or habit may account for part of the assumption that rhyme was necessary, but probably not all of it. Rather, the poets' sense that poetry was an imitation of larger relationships in the universe made it seem natural to use rhyme to represent or re-create a sense of harmony, correspondence, symmetry, and order. The sounds of poetry were thus reminders of the harmonious cosmos, of the music of the spheres that animated the planets, the processes of nature, the interrelationship of all created things and beings. Probably poets never said to themselves, "I shall now tunefully emulate the harmony of God's carefully ordered universe," but the tendency to use rhyme and other repetitions or re-echoings of sound (such as **alliteration** or **assonance**) nevertheless stemmed ultimately from basic assumptions about how the universe worked. In a modern world increasingly perceived as fragmented, rambling, and unrelated, there is of course less of a tendency to testify to a sense of harmony and symmetry. It would be too easy and too mechanical to think that rhyme in a poem specifically means that the poet has a firm sense of cosmic order, and that an unrhymed poem testifies to chaos, but cultural assumptions do affect the expectations of both poets and readers, and cultural tendencies create a kind of pressure upon the individual creator. If you take a survey course (or a series of related "period" courses in English or American literature), you will readily notice the diminishing sense of the need for—or relevance of—rhyme.

One other reason for using rhyme is that it provides a kind of discipline for the poet, a way of harnessing poetic talents and keeping a rein on the imagination, so that the results are ordered, controlled, put into some kind of meaningful and recognizable form. Robert Frost used to be fond of saying that writing poems without rhyme was like playing tennis without a net. Writing good poetry does require a lot of discipline, and Frost speaks for many (perhaps most) traditional poets in suggesting that rhyme can be a major source of that discipline. But it is not the only possible source, and more recent poets have usually felt they would rather play by new rules or invent their own as they go along; they have therefore sought their sources of discipline elsewhere, preferring the more spare tones that unrhymed poetry provides. It is not that contemporary poets cannot think of rhyme words or that they do not care about the sounds of their poetry; rather, recent poets have consciously decided not to work with rhyme and to use instead other aural devices and other strategies for organizing stanzas, just as they have chosen to work with experimental and variable rhythms instead of writing primarily in the traditional English meters. Some few modern poets, though, have protested the abandonment of rhyme and have continued to write rhymed verse successfully in a more or less traditional way.

The amount and density of rhyme vary widely in stanza and verse forms, from elaborate and intricate patterns of rhyme to more casual or spare sound repetitions. The **Spenserian stanza,** for example, is even more rhyme rich than terza rima, using only three rhyme sounds in nine rhymed lines, as in Keats's *The Eve of St. Agnes*:

Her falt'ring hand upon the balustrade,	*a*
Old Angela was feeling for the stair,	*b*
When Madeline, St. Agnes' charméd maid,	*a*
Rose, like a missioned spirit, unaware:	*b*
With silver taper's light, and pious care,	*b*
She turned, and down the agéd gossip led	*c*
To a safe level matting. Now prepare,	*b*
Young Porphyro, for gazing on that bed;	*c*
She comes, she comes again, like ring dove frayed and fled	*c*

On the other hand, the **ballad stanza** has only one set of rhymes in four lines; lines 1 and 3 in each stanza do not rhyme at all (from "Sir Patrick Spens"):

The king sits in Dumferling toune,	*a*
Drinking the blude-reid wine:	*b*
"O whar will I get guid sailor,	*c*
To sail this ship of mine?"	*b*

Most stanzas have a metrical pattern as well as a rhyme scheme. Terza rima, for example, involves iambic meter (unstressed and stressed syllables alternating regularly) and each line has five beats (pentameter). Most of the Spenserian stanza (the first eight lines) is also in iambic pentameter, but the ninth line in each stanza has one extra foot (it is iambic hexameter). The ballad stanza, also iambic, as are most English stanza and verse forms, alternates three-beat and four-beat lines; lines 1 and 3 are unrhymed iambic tetrameter, and lines 2 and 4 are rhymed iambic trimeter.

Stanza Forms

Many stanza forms are represented in this book. Some have names because they have been used over and over by different poets. Others were invented for a particular use in a particular poem and may never be repeated again. Most traditional stanzas are based on rhyme schemes, but some use other kinds of predictable sound patterns; early English poetry, for example, used alliteration to construct a balance between the first and second half of each line (see Earle Birney's "Anglosaxon Street" [p. 893] for a modern imitation of this principle). Sometimes, especially when a strong community of poets interacts with each other, highly elaborate *verse forms* have been developed that set up stanzas as part of a scheme for the whole poem. The poets of medieval Provence were especially inventive, subtle, and elaborate in their construction of complex verse forms, some of which have been copied by poets ever since. The **sestina,** for example, depends on the measured repetition of words in particular places; see, for example, "Sestina" (p. 883), and try to decipher the pattern. (There are also double and even triple sestinas, tough tests of a poet's ingenuity.) And the **villanelle,** another Provençal form, depends on the patterned repetition of whole lines (see Dylan Thomas's "Do Not Go Gentle into That Good Night" [p. 881]). Different cultures and different languages develop their own patterns and measures — not all poetries are parallel to English poetry — and they vary from age to age as well as nation to nation.

You can probably deduce the principles involved in each of the following stanza or verse forms by looking carefully at a poem that uses it; if you have trouble, look at the definitions in the glossary on p. 894.

heroic couplet	"Sound and Sense"	p. 815
tetrameter couplet	"To His Coy Mistress"	p. 974
limerick	"A staid schizophrenic named Struther"	p. 819
free verse	"Dirge"	p. 813
blank verse	from *Paradise Lost*	p. 775

What are stanza forms good for? What use is it to recognize them? Why do poets bother? Matters discussed in this chapter so far have suggested two reasons: 1. Breaks between stanzas provide convenient pauses for reader and writer, something roughly equivalent to paragraphs in prose. The eye thus picks up the places where some kind of pause or break occurs. 2. Poets sometimes use stanza forms, as they do rhyme itself, as a discipline: writing in a certain kind of stanza form imposes a shape on their act of imagination. But visual spaces and unexpected print divisions also mean that poems sometimes *look* unusual and require special visual attention, attention that does not always follow the logic of sound patterns or syntax. At the end of this chapter (just after a detailed consideration of one kind of verse form—the sonnet—you will find poems that employ special configurations and shapes to establish their meanings and effects.

The Sonnet

The **sonnet** is one of the most persistent verse forms. From its origins in the Middle Ages as a prominent form in Italian and French poetry, it dominated English poetry in the late sixteenth and early seventeenth centuries and then was revived several times from the early nineteenth century onward. A sonnet, except for some early experiments with length, is always fourteen lines long and is usually written in iambic pentameter. It is usually printed as if it were a *single* stanza, although in reality it has several formal divisions that represent its rhyme schemes and formal breaks. As a popular and traditional verse form in English for more than four centuries, the sonnet has been surprisingly resilient even in ages that largely reject rhyme. It continues to attract a variety of poets, including (curiously) radical and even revolutionary poets who find its firm structure very useful. Its uses, although quite varied, can be illustrated fairly precisely. As a verse form, the sonnet is contained, compact, demanding; whatever it does, it must do concisely and quickly. To be effective, it must take advantage of the possibilities inherent in its shortness and its relative rigidity. It is best suited to intensity of feeling and concentration of expression. Not too surprisingly, one subject it frequently discusses is confinement itself.

WILLIAM WORDSWORTH

Nuns Fret Not

Nuns fret not at their convent's narrow room;
And hermits are contented with their cells;
And students with their pensive citadels;
Maids at the wheel, the weaver at his loom,
Sit blithe and happy; bees that soar for bloom,
High as the highest Peak of Furness-fells,[1]
Will murmur by the hour in foxglove bells:[2]

5

1. Mountains in England's Lake District, where Wordsworth lived.   2. Flowers from which digitalis (a heart medicine) began to be made in 1799.

In truth the prison, unto which we doom
Ourselves, no prison is: and hence for me,
In sundry moods, 'twas pastime to be bound   10
Within the sonnet's scanty plot of ground;
Pleased if some souls (for such there needs must be)
Who have felt the weight of too much liberty,
Should find brief solace there, as I have found.   1807

Most sonnets are structured according to one of two principles of division. On one principle, the sonnet divides into three units of four lines each and a final unit of two lines, and sometimes the line spacing reflects this division. On the other, the fundamental break is between the first eight lines (called an octave) and the last six (called a sestet). The 4-4-4-2 sonnet is usually called the **English** or **Shakespearean sonnet,** and ordinarily its rhyme scheme reflects the structure: the scheme of *abab cdcd efef gg* is the classic one, but many variations from that pattern still reflect the basic 4-4-4-2 division. The 8-6 sonnet is usually called the **Italian** or **Petrarchan sonnet** (the Italian poet Petrarch was an early master of this structure), and its "typical" rhyme scheme is *abbaabba cdecde,* although it too produces many variations that still reflect the basic division into two parts.

The two kinds of sonnet structures are useful for two different sorts of argument. The 4-4-4-2 structure works very well for constructing a poem that wants to make a three-step argument (with a quick summary at the end), or for setting up brief, cumulative images. "That time of year thou mayst in me behold" (p. 780), for example, uses the 4-4-4-2 structure to mark the progressive steps toward death and the parting of friends by using three distinct images, then summarizing. "Let me not to the marriage of true minds" (p. 669) works very similarly, following the kind of organization that in Chapter 6 was referred to as the 1-2-3 structure—and doing it compactly and economically.

Here, on the other hand, is a poem that uses the 8-6 pattern:

HENRY CONSTABLE

[My lady's presence makes the roses red]

My lady's presence makes the roses red,
Because to see her lips they blush for shame.
The lily's leaves, for envy, pale became,
And her white hands in them this envy bred.

5 The marigold the leaves abroad doth spread,
Because the sun's and her power is the same.
The violet of purple colour came,
Dyed in the blood she made my heart to shed.
In brief: all flowers from her their virtue take;
10 From her sweet breath their sweet smells do proceed;
The living heat which her eyebeams doth make
Warmeth the ground and quickeneth the seed.
The rain, wherewith she watereth the flowers,
Falls from mine eyes, which she dissolves in showers. 1594

The first eight lines argue that the lady's presence is responsible for the color of all of nature's flowers, and the final six lines summarize and extend that argument to smells and heat—and finally to the rain that the lady draws from the speaker's eyes. That kind of two-part structure, in which the octave states a proposition or generalization and the sestet provides a particularization or application of it, has a variety of uses. The final lines may, for example, reverse the first eight and achieve a paradox or irony in the poem, or the poem may nearly balance two comparable arguments. Basically, the 8-6 structure lends itself to poems with two points to make, or to those that wish to make one point and then illustrate it.

Sometimes the neat and precise structure I have described is altered— either slightly, as in "Nuns Fret Not" above (where the 8-6 structure is more of an 8½-5½ structure), or more radically as particular needs or effects may demand. And the two basic structures certainly do not define all the structural possibilities within a fourteen-line poem, even if they do suggest the most traditional ways of taking advantage of the sonnet's compact and well-kept container.

The sonnets in this chapter by Sidney, Shakespeare, and Constable survive from a golden age of English sonnet writing in the late sixteenth century, an age that set the pattern for expectations in the English tradition of form, subject matter, and tone. The sonnet came to England from Italy via France, and imitations of Petrarch's famous sonnet sequence to Laura became the rage. Thousands upon thousands of sonnets were written in those years, often in sequences of a hundred or more sonnets each; the sequences explored the many moods of love and usually had a light thread of narrative that purported to recount a love affair between the male poet and a female lover who was almost always golden-haired, beautiful, disdainful, and inaccessible. Her beauty was described in a series of exaggerated comparisons: her eyes were like the sun ("When Nature made her chief work, Stella's eyes"), her teeth like

pearls, her cheeks like roses, her skin like ivory, and so on, but the adherence
to these conventions was always playful, and it became a game of wit to play
variations upon expectations ("My lady's presence makes the roses red" and
"My mistress' eyes are nothing like the sun"). Sometimes the female lover was
disdainful, unavailable, or rejecting, and sometimes male friendship or homosexual love rivaled the usual male / female relationship. Almost always teasing
and witty, these poems were not necessarily as true to life as they pretended,
but they provided historically an expectation of what sonnets were to be.

Many modern sonnets continue to be about love or private life, and many
continue to use a personal, apparently open and sincere tone. But poets often
find the sonnet's compact form and rigid demands equally useful for many varieties of subject, theme, and tone. Besides love, sonnets often treat other subjects: politics, philosophy, discovery of a new world. And tones vary widely too,
from the anger and remorse of "Th' expense of spirit in a waste of shame"
(p. 1063) and righteous outrage of "On the Late Massacre in Piedmont"
(p. 736) to the tender awe of "How Do I Love Thee?" (p. 652). Many poets
seem to take the kind of comfort Wordsworth describes in the careful limits of
the form, finding in its two basic variations (the English sonnet such as "My
mistress' eyes" [p. 879] and the Italian sonnet such as "On First Looking into
Chapman's Homer" [p. 923]) a sufficiency of convenient ways to organize their
materials into coherent structures.

▼   ▼   ▼

JOHN KEATS

On the Sonnet

If by dull rhymes our English must be chained,
And like Andromeda,[3] the sonnet sweet
Fettered, in spite of painéd loveliness,
Let us find, if we must be constrained,
Sandals more interwoven and complete   5
To fit the naked foot of Poesy:[4]
Let us inspect the lyre, and weigh the stress
Of every chord,[5] and see what may be gained

---

3. Who, according to Greek myth, was chained to a rock so that she would be devoured by a sea
monster. She was rescued by Perseus, who married her. When she died she was placed among the
stars.   **4.** In a letter that contained this sonnet, Keats expressed impatience with the traditional
Petrarchan and Shakespearean sonnet forms: "I have been endeavoring to discover a better sonnet
stanza than we have."   **5.** Lyre-string.

10   By ear industrious, and attention meet;
        Misers of sound and syllable, no less
        Than Midas[6] of his coinage, let us be
        Jealous of dead leaves in the bay-wreath crown;[7]
1819   So, if we may not let the Muse be free,
        She will be bound with garlands of her own.

WILLIAM WORDSWORTH

The world is too much with us

        The world is too much with us; late and soon,
        Getting and spending, we lay waste our powers:
        Little we see in Nature that is ours;
        We have given our hearts away, a sordid boon![8]
5   This Sea that bares her bosom to the moon;
        The winds that will be howling at all hours,
        And are up-gathered now like sleeping flowers;
        For this, for every thing, we are out of tune;
        It moves us not.—Great God! I'd rather be
10   A Pagan suckled in a creed outworn;
        So might I, standing on this pleasant lea,
        Have glimpses that would make me less forlorn;
        Have sight of Proteus rising from the sea;
1802–04   Or hear old Triton[9] blow his wreathed horn.   1807

▼ ▼ ▼

HELEN CHASIN

Joy Sonnet in a Random Universe

        Sometimes I'm happy: la la la la la la la
        la la la la la la la la la la la la la la la la la
        la la la la. Tum tum ti tum. La la la la la la
        la la la la la la la la la la la la la la la la la la.
5   Hey nonny nonny. La la la la la la la la la
        la la la la la la la la la la la. Vo do di o do.
        Poo poo pi doo. La la la la la la la la la la
        la la la la la la la la la la la la la la la la la la
        la la. Whack a doo. La la la la la la la. Sh-

6. The legendary king of Phrygia who asked, and got, the power to turn all he touched to gold.
7. The bay tree was sacred to Apollo, god of poetry, and bay wreaths came to symbolize true poetic achievement. The withering of the bay tree is sometimes considered an omen of death. *Jealous:* suspiciously watchful.   8. Gift.   9. A sea deity, usually represented as blowing on a conch shell. *Proteus:* an old man of the sea who (in *The Odyssey*) could assume a variety of shapes.

boom, sh-boom. La la la la la la la la la la   10
la la la la la la la la la la la la la la la la la la la
la la. Dum di dum. La la la la la la la la la
la la la la la la la la la. Tra la la. Tra la la
la la la la la la la la la la. Yeah yeah yeah.   1968

PERCY BYSSHE SHELLEY

Ozymandias[1]

I met a traveler from an antique land
Who said: Two vast and trunkless legs of stone
Stand in the desert. . . . Near them, on the sand,
Half sunk, a shattered visage lies, whose frown,
And wrinkled lip, and sneer of cold command,   5
Tell that its sculptor well those passions read
Which yet survive, stamped on these lifeless things,
The hand that mocked them, and the heart that fed:
And on the pedestal these words appear:
"My name is Ozymandias, King of Kings: 10
Look on my works, ye Mighty, and despair!"
Nothing beside remains. Round the decay
Of that colossal wreck, boundless and bare
The lone and level sands stretch far away.   1818

WILLIAM WORDSWORTH

London, 1802

Milton! thou should'st be living at this hour:
England hath need of thee: she is a fen
Of stagnant waters: altar, sword, and pen,
Fireside, the heroic wealth of hall and bower,
Have forfeited their ancient English dower   5
Of inward happiness. We are selfish men;
Oh! raise us up, return to us again;
And give us manners, virtue, freedom, power.
Thy soul was like a star, and dwelt apart:
Thou hadst a voice whose sound was like the sea: 10
Pure as the naked heavens, majestic, free,

---

1. The Greek name for Rameses II, 13th-century B.C. pharaoh of Egypt. According to a first-century B.C. Greek historian, Diodorus Siculus, the largest statue in Egypt was inscribed: "I am Ozymandias, king of kings; if anyone wishes to know what I am and where I lie, let him surpass me in some of my exploits."

So didst thou travel on life's common way,
In cheerful godliness; and yet thy heart
1802   The lowliest duties on herself did lay.

HELENE JOHNSON

Sonnet to a Negro in Harlem

You are disdainful and magnificent—
Your perfect body and your pompous gait,
Your dark eyes flashing solemnly with hate,
Small wonder that you are incompetent
5   To imitate those whom you so despise—
Your shoulders towering high above the throng,
Your head thrown back in rich, barbaric song,
Palm trees and mangoes stretched before your eyes.
Let others toil and sweat for labor's sake
10   And wring from grasping hands their meed of gold.
Why urge ahead your supercilious feet?
Scorn will efface each footprint that you make.
I love your laughter arrogant and bold.
You are too splendid for this city street.   p. 1927

CLAUDE McKAY

The Harlem Dancer

Applauding youths laughed with young prostitutes
And watched her perfect, half-clothed body sway;
Her voice was like the sound of blended flutes
Blown by black players upon a picnic day.
5   She sang and danced on gracefully and calm,
The light gauze hanging loose about her form;
To me she seemed a proudly-swaying palm
Grown lovelier for passing through a storm.
Upon her swarthy neck black shiny curls
10   Luxuriant fell; and tossing coins in praise,
The wine-flushed, bold-eyed boys, and even the girls,
Devoured her shape with eager, passionate gaze;
But looking at her falsely-smiling face,
I knew her self was not in that strange place.   1922

JOHN MILTON

[When I consider how my light is spent]

When I consider how my light is spent,
   Ere half my days, in this dark world and wide,
   And that one talent which is death to hide[2]
   Lodged with me useless, though my soul more bent
To serve therewith my Maker, and present   5
   My true account, lest he returning chide;
   "Doth God exact day-labor, light denied?"
   I fondly ask; but Patience to prevent[3]
That murmur, soon replies, "God doth not need
   Either man's work or his own gifts; who best   10
   Bear his mild yoke, they serve him best. His state
Is kingly. Thousands at his bidding speed
   And post o'er land and ocean without rest:
1652?   They also serve who only stand and wait."   1673

ARCHIBALD LAMPMAN

Winter Evening

To-night the very horses springing by
Toss gold from whitened nostrils. In a dream
The streets that narrow to the westward gleam
Like rows of golden palaces; and high
From all the crowded chimneys tower and die   5
A thousand aureoles. Down in the west
The brimming plains beneath the sunset rest,
One burning sea of gold. Soon, soon shall fly
The glorious vision, and the hours shall feel
A mightier master; soon from height to height,   10
With silence and the sharp unpitying stars,
Stern creeping frosts, and winds that touch like steel,
Out of the depth beyond the eastern bars,
Glittering and still shall come the awful night.   1899

---

2. In the parable of the talents (Matthew 25), the servants who earned interest on their master's money (his talents) while he was away were called "good and faithful"; the one who hid the money and simply returned it was condemned and sent away. Usury, a deadly sin under Catholicism, was regarded by Puritans as a metaphor for attaining salvation.   3. Forestall. *Fondly*: foolishly.

SIR CHARLES G. D. ROBERTS

The Potato Harvest

A high bare field, brown from the plough, and borne
  Aslant from sunset; amber wastes of sky
  Washing the ridge; a clamor of crows that fly
In from the wide flats where the spent tides mourn
To yon their rocking roosts in pines wind-torn;
  A line of grey snake-fence that zigzags by
  A pond and cattle; from the homestead nigh
The long deep summonings of the supper horn.

Black on the ridge, against that lonely flush,
  A cart, and stoop-necked oxen; ranged beside
    Some barrels; and the day-worn harvest-folk,
Here emptying their baskets, jar the hush
  With hollow thunders. Down the dusk hillside
    Lumbers the wain; and day fades out like smoke.   1886

GWENDOLYN BROOKS

First Fight. Then Fiddle.

First fight. Then fiddle. Ply the slipping string
With feathery sorcery; muzzle the note
With hurting love; the music that they wrote
Bewitch, bewilder. Qualify to sing
Threadwise. Devise no salt, no hempen thing
For the dear instrument to bear. Devote
The bow to silks and honey. Be remote
A while from malice and from murdering.
But first to arms, to armor. Carry hate
In front of you and harmony behind.
Be deaf to music and to beauty blind.
Win war. Rise bloody, maybe not too late
For having first to civilize a space
Wherein to play your violin with grace.   1949

CLAUDE McKAY

The White House

Your door is shut against my tightened face,
And I am sharp as steel with discontent;

But I possess the courage and the grace
To bear my anger proudly and unbent.
The pavement slabs burn loose beneath my feet, 5
And passion rends my vitals as I pass,
A chafing savage, down the decent street,
Where boldly shines your shuttered door of glass.
Oh, I must search for wisdom every hour,
Deep in my wrathful bosom sore and raw, 10
And find in it the superhuman power
To hold me to the letter of your law!
Oh, I must keep my heart inviolate
Against the poison of your deadly hate. 1937

SIR PHILIP SIDNEY

[When Nature made her chief work, Stella's eyes]⁴

When Nature made her chief work, Stella's eyes,
In color black⁵ why wrapped she beams so bright?
Would she in beamy black, like painter wise,
Frame daintiest luster mixed of shades and light?
Or did she else that sober hue devise, 5
In object best to knit and strength our sight,
Lest if no veil those brave gleams did disguise,
They sunlike should more dazzle than delight?
Or would she her miraculous power show,
That, whereas black seems Beauty's contrary, 10
She even in black doth make all beauties flow?
Both so and thus: she, minding⁶ Love should be
Placed ever there, gave him this mourning weed
1582 To honor all their deaths who for her bleed.

WILLIAM SHAKESPEARE

[My mistress' eyes are nothing like the sun]

My mistress' eyes are nothing like the sun;
Coral is far more red than her lips' red;

4. From Sidney's sonnet sequence *Astrophel and Stella*, usually credited with having started the vogue of sonnet sequences in Elizabethan England. 5. Black was frequently used in the Renaissance to mean absence of light, and ugly or foul (see line 10). 6. Remembering that.

If snow be white, why then her breasts are dun;[7]
If hairs be wires, black wires grow on her head.
I have seen roses damasked[8] red and white,
But no such roses see I in her cheeks;
And in some perfumes is there more delight
Than in the breath that from my mistress reeks.
I love to hear her speak, yet well I know
That music hath a far more pleasing sound;
I grant I never saw a goddess go;[9]
My mistress, when she walks, treads on the ground.
And yet, by heaven, I think my love as rare
As any she belied with false compare.

1609

DIANE ACKERMAN

Sweep Me Through Your Many-Chambered Heart

Sweep me through your many-chambered heart
if you like, or leave me here, flushed
amid the sap-ooze and blossom: one more dish
in the banquet called April, or think me hard-
won all your days full of women. Weeks
later, till I felt your arms around
me like a shackle, heard all the sundown
wizardries the fired body speaks.
Tell me why, if it was no more than this,
the unmuddled tumble, the renegade kiss,
today, rapt in a still life and unaware,
my paintbrush dropped like an amber hawk;
thinking I'd heard your footfall on the stair,
I listened, heartwise, for the knock.

1978

EDNA ST. VINCENT MILLAY

[What lips my lips have kissed, and where, and why]

What lips my lips have kissed, and where, and why,
I have forgotten, and what arms have lain
Under my head till morning; but the rain
Is full of ghosts tonight, that tap and sigh

---

7. Mouse-colored.   8. Variegated.   9. Walk.

Upon the glass and listen for reply, 5
And in my heart there stirs a quiet pain
For unremembered lads that not again
Will turn to me at midnight with a cry.
Thus in the winter stands the lonely tree,
Nor knows what birds have vanished one by one, 10
Yet knows its boughs more silent than before:
I cannot say what loves have come and gone;
I only know that summer sang in me
A little while, that in me sings no more. 1923

Examples of Stanza Forms

DYLAN THOMAS

Do Not Go Gentle into That Good Night[1]

Do not go gentle into that good night,
Old age should burn and rave at close of day;
Rage, rage against the dying of the light.

Though wise men at their end know dark is right,
Because their words had forked no lightning they 5
Do not go gentle into that good night.

Good men, the last wave by, crying how bright
Their frail deeds might have danced in a green bay,
Rage, rage against the dying of the light.

Wild men who caught and sang the sun in flight, 10
And learn, too late, they grieved it on its way,
Do not go gentle into that good night.

Grave men, near death, who see with blinding sight
Blind eyes could blaze like meteors and be gay,
Rage, rage against the dying of the light. 15

And you, my father, there on the sad height,
Curse, bless, me now with your fierce tears, I pray.
Do not go gentle into that good night.
Rage, rage against the dying of the light. 1952

1. Written during the final illness of the poet's father.

MARIANNE MOORE

Poetry

I, too, dislike it: there are things that are important beyond all this fiddle.
    Reading it, however, with a perfect contempt for it, one discovers in
    it after all, a place for the genuine.
        Hands that can grasp, eyes
5   that can dilate, hair that can rise
           if it must, these things are important not because a

high-sounding interpretation can be put upon them but because they are
    useful. When they become so derivative as to become unintelligible,
    the same thing may be said for all of us, that we
10   do not admire what
        we cannot understand: the bat
           holding on upside down or in quest of something to

eat, elephants pushing, a wild horse taking a roll, a tireless wolf under
    a tree, the immovable critic twitching his skin like a horse that feels a flea, the ba
15   ball fan, the statistician —
        nor is it valid
           to discriminate against "business documents and

school-books"[2]; all these phenomena are important. One must make a distinction
    however: when dragged into prominence by half poets, the result is not poetry,
20   nor till the poets among us can be
        "literalists of
        the imagination"[3] — above
           insolence and triviality and can present

for inspection, "imaginary gardens with real toads in them," shall we have
25   it. In the meantime, if you demand on the one hand,
    the raw material of poetry in
        all its rawness and
        that which is on the other hand
           genuine, you are interested in poetry.   1921

2. "*Diary of Tolstoy*, p. 84: 'Where the boundary between prose and poetry lies, I shall never be able to understand. The question is raised in manuals of style, yet the answer to it lies beyond me. Poetry is verse: prose is not verse. Or else poetry is everything with the exception of business documents and school books.' " (Moore's note)   3. " 'Literalists of the imagination.' Yeats, *Ideas of Good and Evil* (A. H. Bullen, 1903), p. 182. 'The limitation of his view was from the very intensity of his vision; he was a too literal realist of imagination, as others are of nature; and because he believed that the figures seen by the mind's eye, when exalted by inspiration, were 'eternal existences," symbols of divine essences, he hated every grace of style that might obscure their lineaments.' " (Moore's note)

ELIZABETH BISHOP

Sestina

September rain falls on the house.
In the failing light, the old grandmother
sits in the kitchen with the child
beside the Little Marvel Stove,
reading the jokes from the almanac,   5
laughing and talking to hide her tears.

She thinks that her equinoctial tears
and the rain that beats on the roof of the house
were both foretold by the almanac,
but only known to a grandmother.   10
The iron kettle sings on the stove.
She cuts some bread and says to the child,

It's time for tea now; but the child
is watching the teakettle's small hard tears
dance like mad on the hot black stove,   15
the way the rain must dance on the house.
Tidying up, the old grandmother
hangs up the clever almanac

on its string. Birdlike, the almanac
hovers half open above the child,   20
hovers above the old grandmother
and her teacup full of dark brown tears.
She shivers and says she thinks the house
feels chilly, and puts more wood in the stove.

It was to be, says the Marvel Stove.   25
I know what I know, says the almanac.
With crayons the child draws a rigid house
and a winding pathway. Then the child
puts in a man with buttons like tears
and shows it proudly to the grandmother.   30

But secretly, while the grandmother
busies herself about the stove,
the little moons fall down like tears
from between the pages of the almanac
into the flower bed the child   35
has carefully placed in the front of the house.

Time to plant tears, says the almanac.
The grandmother sings to the marvellous stove
and the child draws another inscrutable house.   1965

ISHMAEL REED

beware :   do not read this poem

tonite   ,   thriller was
abt an ol woman   , so vain she
surrounded herself w /
    many mirrors

5   it got so bad that finally she
locked herself indoors & her
whole life became the
    mirrors

one day the villagers broke
10   into her house   ,   but she was too
swift for them   .   she disappeared
    into a mirror

each tenant who bought the house
after that   ,   lost a loved one to
15   the ol woman in the mirror :
    first a little girl
    then a young woman
    then the young woman / s husband

the hunger of this poem is legendary
20   it has taken in many victims
back off from this poem
it has drawn in yr feet
back off from this poem
it has drawn in yr legs

25   back off from this poem
it is a greedy mirror
you are into this poem   .   from
    the waist down
nobody can hear you can they   ?
30   this poem has had you up to here
    belch
this poem aint got no manners
you cant call out frm this poem
relax now & go w / this poem
35   move & roll on to this poem
do not resist this poem
this poem has yr eyes
this poem has his head
this poem has his arms
40   this poem has his fingers

this poem has his fingertips
this poem is the reader & the
reader this poem

statistic : the us bureau of missing persons reports
              that in 1968 over 100,000 people disappeared   45
              leaving no solid clues
                     nor trace   only
       a space   in the lives of their friends   1970

ARCHIBALD MacLEISH

Ars Poetica[4]

A poem should be palpable and mute
As a globed fruit,

Dumb
As old medallions to the thumb,

Silent as the sleeve-worn stone   5
Of casement ledges where the moss has grown—

A poem should be wordless
As the flight of birds.

A poem should be motionless in time
As the moon climbs.   10

Leaving, as the moon releases
Twig by twig the night-entangled trees,

Leaving, as the moon behind the winter leaves,
Memory by memory the mind—

A poem should be motionless in time   15
As the moon climbs.

A poem should be equal to:
Not true.

For all the history of grief
An empty doorway and a maple leaf.   20

For love
The leaning grasses and two lights above the sea—

A poem should not mean
But be.   1926

---

4. "The Art of Poetry," title of a poetical treatise by the Roman poet Horace (65–8 B.C.).

The Way a Poem Looks

Stanza breaks and other kinds of print spaces are important, primarily to guide the voice and mind to a clearer sense of sound and meaning. But there are exceptions. A few poems are written to be seen rather than heard, and their appearance on the page is crucial to their effect. The poem "l(a," for example, tries to visualize typographically what the poet asks you to see in your mind's eye. Occasionally, too, poems are composed in a specific shape so that the poem looks like a physical object. The poems that follow in this chapter—some old, some new—illustrate ways in which visual effects may be created. Even though poetry has traditionally been thought of as oral—words to be said, sung, or performed rather than looked at—the idea that poems can also be related to painting and the visual arts is an old one. Theodoric in ancient Greece is credited with inventing **technopaegnia**—that is, the construction of poems with visual appeal. Once, the shaping of words to resemble an object was thought to have mystical power, but more recent attempts at **concrete poetry** or **shaped verse** are usually playful exercises (such as Robert Holland-er's "You Too? Me Too—Why Not? Soda Pop" [p. 978], which is shaped like a Coke bottle) that attempt to supplement (or replace) verbal meanings with devices from painting and sculpture.

Reading a poem like "Easter Wings" aloud wouldn't make much sense. Our eyes are everything for a poem like that. A more frequent poetic device involves asking the eyes to become a guide for the voice. The following poem depends upon recognition of some standard typographical symbols and knowl-edge of their names. We have to say those names to read the poem.

FRANKLIN P. ADAMS

Composed in the Composing Room

At stated .ic times
I love to sit and—off rhymes
Till ,tose at last I fall
Exclaiming "I don't ∧ all."

Though I'm an * objection   5
By running this in this here §
This ☞ of the Fleeting Hour,
This lofty -ician Tower—

A ¶er's hope dispels
All fear of deadly ‖.   10
You think these [ ] are a pipe?
Well, not on your †eotype.   1914

We create the right term here when we verbalize, putting the visual signs together with the words or letters printed in the poem, for example making the word "periodic" out of ".ic" or "high Phoenician" out of "-ician." Like "Easter Wings," "Composed in the Composing Room" uses typography in an extreme way; here the eyes (and mind) are drawn into a punlike game that offers more puzzle-solving pleasure than emotional effect. More often poets give us—by the visual placement of sounds—a guide to reading, inviting us to regulate the pace of our reading, notice pauses or silences, pay attention both to the syntax of the poem and to the rhetoric of the voice, thus providing us a kind of musical score for reading.

E. E. CUMMINGS

[Buffalo Bill 's][1]

Buffalo Bill 's
        defunct
                who used to
                        ride a watersmooth-silver
                                                    stallion
        and break onetwothreefourfive pigeonsjustlikethat   5
                                                    Jesus

he was a handsome man
                        and what i want to know is
        how do you like your blueeyed boy   10
Mister Death   1923

1. Portraits XXI.

The unusual spacing of words here, with some run together and others widely separated, provides a guide to reading, regulating both speed and sense, so that the poem can capture aloud some of the excitement and wonder of a boy's enthusiasm for a theatrical act as spectacular as that of Buffalo Bill. A good reader-aloud, with only this typographical guidance, can capture some of the wide-eyed boy's responses, remembered now in retrospect long after Buffalo Bill himself is dead.

In prose, syntax and punctuation are the main guides to the voice of a reader, providing indicators of emphasis, pace, and speed; in poetry as well they are more conventional and more common guides than extreme forms of typography, such as in "Buffalo Bill 's." Reading a poem sensitively is in some ways a lot like reading a piece of prose sensitively: one has to pay close attention to the way the sentences are put together and how they are punctuated. A good reader makes use of appropriate pauses as well as thundering emphasis; silence as well as sound is part of any poem, and reading punctuation is as important as knowing how to say the words.

Beyond punctuation, the placement and spacing of lines on the page may be helpful to a reader even when that placement is not as radical as it is in "Buffalo Bill 's." The fact that poetry looks different from prose is not an accident; decisions to make lines one length instead of another have as much to do with vocal breaks and phrasing as with functions of syntax or meaning. In a good poem, there are few accidents, not even in the way the poem meets the eye, for as readers our eyes are the most direct route to our voices; they are our scanner and director, our prompter and guide.

The eye also may help the ear in poetry in another way—guiding us to notice repeated sounds by repeated visual patterns in letters. The most common rhymes in poems occur at the ends of lines, and the arrangement of lines (the typography of the poem) often calls attention to the pattern of sounds because of the similar appearance of line-ending words, as in sonnets and other traditional verse forms and sometimes in radically unconventional patterns. Not all words that rhyme have similar spellings, of course, but similarities of word appearance seem to imply a relationship of sound too, and many poems hint at their stanza patterns and verse forms by their spatial arrangement and repeated patterns at ends of lines. The following poem takes advantage of such expectations and plays with them by forcing a letter into arbitrary line relationships, forcing words ("stew," line 2) in order to create rhymes, setting up rhyme patterns and then breaking them (lines 9–11), using false or near rhymes (lines 10–11), and creating long lines with multisyllabic rhymes that seem silly (the final two lines).

STEVIE SMITH

The Jungle Husband

Dearest Evelyn, I often think of you
Out with the guns in the jungle stew
Yesterday I hittapotamus
I put the measurements down for you but they got lost in the fuss
It's not a good thing to drink out here 5
You know, I've practically given it up dear.
Tomorrow I am going alone a long way
Into the jungle. It is all grey
But green on top
Only sometimes when a tree has fallen 10
The sun comes down plop, it is quite appalling.
You never want to go in a jungle pool
In the hot sun, it would be the act of a fool
Because it's always full of anacondas, Evelyn, not looking ill-fed
I'll say. So no more now, from your loving husband, Wilfred.   1957   15

Visual devices are often entertainments to amuse, puzzle, or tease readers of poetry whose chief expectations are about sound, but sometimes poets achieve surprising (and lasting) original effects by manipulations of print space. Stanzas—visual breaks in poems that indicate some kind of unit of meaning or measurement—ultimately are more than visual devices, for they point to structural questions and ultimately frame and formalize the content of poems. But they involve—as do the similar visual patterns of words that rhyme—part of the "score" of poems, and suggest one more way that sight becomes a guide to sound in many poems.

▼   ▼   ▼

GEORGE HERBERT

Easter Wings

Lord, who createdst man in wealth and store,[2]
Though foolishly he lost the same,
Decaying more and more,
Till he became
Most poor:
With thee
O let me rise
As larks,[3] harmoniously,
And sing this day thy victories:
Then shall the fall further the flight in me.

My tender age in sorrow did begin;
And still with sicknesses and shame
Thou didst so punish sin,
That I became
Most thin.
With thee
Let me combine,
And feel this day thy victory;
For, if I imp[4] my wing on thine,
Affliction shall advance the flight in me.

1633

ROBERT HERRICK

The Pillar of Fame

Fame's pillar here, at last, we set,
Out-during *Marble*, *Brass*, or *Jet*,[5]
Charmed and enchanted so,
As to withstand the blow
Of   overthrow:
Nor shall the seas,
Or   OUTRAGES
Of storms o'erbear
What we up-rear;
Tho Kingdoms fall,
This   pillar   never   shall
Decline   or   waste   at   all;
But stand for ever by his own
Firm and well fixed foundation.

1648

2. In plenty.   3. Which herald the morning.   4. Engraft. In falconry, to engraft feathers in a damaged wing, so as to restore the powers of flight (OED).   5. Black lignite or black marble. *Out-during:* outlasting.

BARBARA HOWES

Mirror Image: Port-au-Prince

> *Au petit*
> *Salon de Coiffeur,*
> Monique's / hands fork
> like lightning, like a baton
> rise / to lead her client's hair   5
> in *repassage:* she irons out the kinks.
> Madame's brown cheek / is dusted over with a
> paler shade / of costly powder. Nails and lips are red.
>
> Her matching lips and nails incarnadined, / in the
> next booth Madam consults her face / imprisoned   10
> in the glass. Her lovely tan / is almost
> gone. Oh, watch Yvonne's astute /
> conductor fingers set the
> permanent, / *In little*
> *Drawing-room of*   15
> *Hairdresser!*   1954

E. E. CUMMINGS

[l(a]

l(a

le

af

fa

ll   5

s)

one

l

iness   1958

NORA DAUENHAUER

Tlingit Concrete Poem

```
                                t ' a  n
                              a              i
                              a   k
            x ' a a x ' x ' a a x ' x ' a a x ' x ' a a x ' x ' a a x
             a a x ' x ' a a x ' x ' a a x ' x ' a a x ' x ' a a x ' x
            ' x ' a a x ' x ' a a x ' x ' a a x ' x ' a a x ' x ' a a x ' x ' a
          x ' x ' a a x ' x ' a a x ' x ' a a x ' x ' a a x ' x ' a a x ' x ' a a x
        a a x ' x ' a a x ' x ' a a x ' x ' a a x ' x ' a a x ' x ' a a x ' x ' a a x '
       ' a a x ' x ' a a x ' x ' a a x ' x ' a a x ' x ' a a x ' x ' a a x ' x ' a a x ' x
      x ' a a x ' x ' a a x ' x ' a a x ' x ' a a x ' x ' a a x ' x ' a a x ' x ' a a x ' x '
     ' x ' a a x ' x ' a a x ' x ' a a x ' x ' a a x ' x ' a a x ' x ' a a x ' x ' a a x ' x '
     ' x ' a a x ' x ' a a x ' x ' a a x ' x ' a a x ' x ' a a x ' x ' a a x ' x ' a a x ' x ' a
     ' x ' a a x ' x ' a a x ' x ' a a x ' x ' a a x ' x ' a a x ' x ' a a x ' x ' a a x ' x ' a
    x ' x ' a a x ' x ' a a x ' x ' a a x ' x ' a a x ' x ' a a x ' x ' a a x ' x ' a a x ' x ' a
    x ' x ' a a x ' x ' a a x ' x ' a a x ' x ' a a x ' x ' a a x ' x ' a a x ' x ' a a x ' x ' a
    x ' x ' a a x ' x ' a a x ' x ' a a x ' x ' a a x ' x ' a a x ' x ' a a x ' x ' a a x ' x ' a
    x ' x ' a a x ' x ' a a x ' x ' a a x ' x ' a a x ' x ' a a x ' x ' a a x ' x ' a a x ' x ' a
     ' x ' a a x ' x ' a a x ' x ' a a x ' x ' a a x ' x ' a a x ' x ' a a x ' x ' a a x ' x ' a
     ' x ' a a x ' x ' a a x ' x ' a a x ' x ' a a x ' x ' a a x ' x ' a a x ' x ' a a x ' x '
     ' x ' a a x ' x ' a a x ' x ' a a x ' x ' a a x ' x ' a a x ' x ' a a x ' x ' a a x ' x '
      x ' a a x ' x ' a a x ' x ' a a x ' x ' a a x ' x ' a a x ' x ' a a x ' x ' a a x ' x '
       ' a a x ' x ' a a x ' x ' a a x ' x ' a a x ' x ' a a x ' x ' a a x ' x ' a a x ' x
       ' a a x ' x ' a a x ' x ' a a x ' x ' a a x ' x ' a a x ' x ' a a x ' x ' a a x '
        a a x ' x ' a a x ' x ' a a x ' x ' a a x ' x ' a a x ' tl ' u k w x ' a a x ' x ' a a x '
         a x ' x ' a a x ' x ' a a x ' x ' a a x ' x ' a a x ' x ' a a x ' x ' a a x ' x ' a a x
          x ' x ' a a x ' x ' a a x ' x ' a a x ' x ' a a x ' x ' a a x ' x ' a a x ' x ' a a
           ' x ' a a x ' x ' a a x ' x ' a a x ' x ' a a x ' x ' a a x ' x ' a a x ' x ' a
            ' a a x ' x ' a a x ' x ' a a x ' x ' a a x ' x ' a a x ' x ' a a x ' x
             a x ' x ' a a x ' x ' a a x ' x ' a a x ' x ' a a x ' x ' a a x
              ' x ' a a x ' x ' a a x ' x ' a a x ' x ' a a x ' x ' a
               ' a a x ' x ' a a x ' x ' a a x ' x ' a a x ' x '
                ' x ' a a x ' x ' a a x ' x ' a a
                 ' x ' a a
```

akat'ani = stem
x'aax' = apple
tl'ukwx = worm

1984

JOHN HOLLANDER

A State of Nature

Some broken
Iroquois adze
prounded southward
and resembled this
outlined once But now   5
boundaries foul-lines
and even sea-coasts are
naturally involved with
mappers and followers of
borders So that we who grew   10
up here might think <u>That steak is
shaped too much like New York to be real</u> And like
the shattered flinty implement whose ghost lives
inside our sense of what this rough chunk should
by right of history recall the language spoken by   15
its shapers now inhabits only streams and lakes and
hills The natural names are only a chattering and mean
only the land they label How shall we live in a forest of
such murmurs with
no ideas but in   20
forms a state
whose name
passes
for
a city   25
1969

EARLE BIRNEY

Anglosaxon Street

Dawn drizzle ended   dampness steams from
blotching brick and   blank plasterwaste
Faded housepatterns   hoary and finicky
unfold stuttering   stick like a phonograph

Here is a ghetto   gotten for goyim   5
O with care denuded   of nigger and kike
No coonsmell rankles   reeks only cellarrot
Ottar[6] of carexhaust   catcorpse and cookinggrease
Imperial hearts   heave in this haven
Cracks across windows   are welded with slogans   10
There'll Always Be An England   enhances geraniums
and V's for Victory   vanquish the housefly

6. Roselike fragrance.

Ho! with climbing sun   march the bleached beldames
festooned with shopping bags   farded[7] flatarched
15   bigthewed Saxonwives   stepping over buttrivers
waddling back wienerladen   to suckle smallfry

Hoy! with sunslope   shrieking over hydrants
flood from learninghall   the lean fingerlings
Nordic nobblecheeked[8]   not all clean of nose
20   leaping Commandowise   into leprous lanes

What! after whistleblow!   spewed from wheelboat
after daylight doughtiness   dire handplay
in sewertrench or sandpit   come Saxonthegns
Junebrown Jutekings[9]   jawslack for meat

25   Sit after supper   on smeared doorsteps
not humbly swearing   hatedeeds on Huns
profiteers politicians   pacifists Jews

Then by twobit magic   to muse in movie
unlock picturehoard   or lope to alehall
30   soaking bleakly   in beer skittleless

Home again to hotbox   and humid husbandhood
in slumbertrough adding   sleepily to Anglekin
Alongside in lanenooks   carling and leman[1]
caterwaul and clip[2]   careless of Saxonry
35   with moonglow and haste   and a higher heartbeat

Slumbers now slumtrack   unstinks cooling
waiting brief for milkmaid   mornstar and worldrise

Toronto 1942, revised 1966

▼ ▼ ▼

EXTERNAL FORM A Glossary

alliteration: the repetition of sounds in nearby words; alliteration usually
involves the initial consonant sounds of words (and sometimes internal
consonants in stressed syllables)

assonance: the repetition of vowel sounds in a line or series of lines; assonance often affects pace (by unbalancing short and long vowel patterns)
and the way words included in the pattern tend to seem underscored

---

7. Rouged.   8. Pimpled.   9. Refers to the Jutes, the German tribe that invaded England in
the fifth century and spearheaded the Anglo-Saxon conquest. *Saxonthegns:* Freemen who provided
military services for the Saxon lords.   1. Lover. *Carling:* old woman.   2. Embrace.

ballad stanza: a four-line stanza, the second and fourth lines of which are iambic trimeter and rhyme with each other; the first and third lines, in iambic tetrameter, do not rhyme

blank verse: unrhymed iambic pentameter

concrete poetry/shaped verse: an attempt to supplement (or replace) verbal meaning with visual devices from painting and sculpture

English or **Shakespearian sonnet:** three four-line stanzas and a couplet (two lines), rhymed *abab cdcd efef gg*

free verse: poetry that avoids regularized meter and has no significant recurrent stress rhythms, although it may use other repetitive patterns — of words, phrases, or structures

heroic couplet: a pair of rhymed lines of iambic pentameter

Italian or **Petrarchan sonnet:** an octave (eight lines) and a sestet (six lines); typically rhymed *abbaabba cdecde*, although it has many variations that still reflect the basic division into two parts

limerick: two lines of rhymed trimeter, two lines of rhymed dimeter, and an additional line of trimeter, the last word of which is the same as, or rhymes with, the last word of the first line

memory devices / mnemonic devices: forms, such as rhyme, built into poems to help reciters remember them

sestina: six six-line stanzas and a final three-line stanza, all unrhymed; but the final word in each line of the first stanza then becomes the final word in other stanzas (though in a different specific pattern); the final stanza uses these words again in a specified way, one in each half line

sonnet: a form, usually only a single stanza, that offers several related possibilities for its rhyme scheme, but is always fourteen lines long and usually written in iambic pentameter

Spenserian stanza: eight lines of iambic pentameter and a ninth line of iambic hexameter, called an alexandrine, rhymed *ababbcbcc*

stanzas: groups of lines with a specific cogency of their own and usually set off from one another by a space

syllabic verse: a form in which the poet establishes a precise number of syllables to a line and repeats them in subsequent stanzas

technopaegnia: the construction of poems with visual appeal

terza rima: the three-line stanza in which Dante wrote *The Divine Comedy*; each iambic pentameter stanza *(aba)* interlocks with the next through rhyme *(bcb, cdc, ded,* etc.)

tetrameter couplet: a pair of rhymed, four-beat lines

villanelle: contains five three-line stanzas and a final four-line stanza; only two rhyme sounds are permitted in the entire poem, and the first and third lines of the first stanza are repeated, alternately, as the third line of subsequent stanzas until the last

QUESTIONS

1. Chart the rhyme scheme of Keats's "On the Sonnet," and then, after a careful reading of the poem aloud, mark the major structural breaks in the poem. At what points do the structural breaks and the breaks in rhyme pattern coincide? At what points do they conflict? Can you account for the variations in terms of the poem's meaning?

2. Describe the structure of "Ozymandias." In what sense is it an Italian sonnet? Why do some of the rhythm sounds in the first eight lines contrast with rhymes in the last six?

3. What justification is there for calling "Joy Sonnet in a Random Universe" a sonnet?

4. What conventions of description is "My mistress' eyes are nothing like the sun" working against? How can you tell? Describe the tone of the poem. What strategies, beyond the basic one of inverting conventions, help to create the poem's special tone?

5. Characterize the "you" in "Sonnet to a Negro in Harlem." Describe the speaker's tone toward him. Describe the function of setting in the poem.

6. What principles seem to determine the form of "Anglosaxon Street"? How do sound patterns in the poem relate to its form?

WRITING SUGGESTIONS

1. Consider the structure of "The White House" and the poem's themes of confinement and exclusion. In what specific ways does the poem use the tight restrictions of the sonnet form? Write an essay of about two pages on the way content and form interact in the poem.

2. Compare "The Harlem Dancer" (also by Claude McKay) with "The White House," considering the very different uses the sonnet form accommodates. Write a parallel essay to that above in which you show how "The Harlem Dancer" uses the sonnet form to further its themes and tones.

3. Consider carefully the structure and sequencing in "First Fight. Then Fiddle." Notice how various uses of sound in the poem (rhyme, onomatapoeia, and alliteration, for example) help to enforce its themes and tones. In an essay of about 600 words, show the relationship between "sound and sense" in the poem.

8 THE WHOLE TEXT

n the previous seven chapters, we have been thinking about one thing at a time—symbolism, meter, stanza form, and so on—and each poem has been read and discussed primarily in terms of a single problem. Learning to deal with one problem at a time is good educational practice and in the long run will make you a more careful and more effective reader of poems. Still, the elements of poems do not work individually but in combination, and in considering even the simplest elements (speaker, for example, or setting) we have noticed how categories overlap—how, for example, the question of setting in "Cherrylog Road" quickly merges into questions about the speaker, his state of mind, his personality, his distance from the central events in the poem. Thinking about a single issue never fully does justice to an individual poem; no poem depends for all its effects on just one device or one element of craft. Poems are complex wholes that demand varieties of attention, and ultimately *all* the questions you have been learning to ask need to be applied to any poem you read. Reading any poem fully and well involves all the questions about craft, form, and tradition that you can think to ask. Not all questions are equally relevant to all poems, of course, but moving systematically through your whole list of questions will ultimately enable you to get beyond the fragmentation of particular issues and approach the whole poem. It is now time to think about how the various elements of poems work together to create the effects of the whole poem.

Here is a short poem in which several of the issues we have considered come up almost simultaneously:

ELIZABETH JENNINGS

Delay

The radiance of that star that leans on me
Was shining years ago. The light that now
Glitters up there my eye may never see
And so the time lag teases me with how

Love that loves now may not reach me until   5
Its first desire is spent. The star's impulse
Must wait for eyes to claim it beautiful
And love arrived may find us somewhere else.   1953

In most poems, several issues come up more or less at once, and the analytic practice of separating issues is a convenience rather than an assertion of priority or order. In "Delay," a lot of the basic questions (about speaker, situation, and setting, for example) seem to be put on hold in the beginning, but if we proceed systematically the poem begins to open itself to us. The first line identifies the "I" (or rather, in this case, "me") of the poem as an observer of the bright star that is the main object in the poem and the principal source of its imagery, its "plot," and its analogical argument. But we learn little detail about the speaker. She surfaces again in lines 4 and 5 and with someone else ("us") in line 8, but she is always in the objective case—acted on rather than acting. All that is certain about her is that she has some knowledge of the time it takes light from the stars to reach her and that she contemplates deeply and at length about the meaning and effect of such time lags. We are given even less detail about setting and situation; somewhere the speaker is watching a bright star and meditating on the fact that she is seeing it long, long after its actual light was sent forth. Her location is not specified, and the time, though probably night, could be any night (we do know that the speaker lives in the age of modern astronomy, i.e., that the speed of light and the distance of the stars from Earth are understood); the only other explicit clues we have about situation involves the "us" of the final line and the fact that the speaker's concern with time seems oddly personal, something that matters to her emotional life—not merely a matter of stellar knowledge.

The poem's language helps us understand much more about the speaker and her situation, as does the poem's structure and stanza form. The most crucial word in the first stanza is probably the verb "leans" (line 1); certainly it is the most unusual and surprising word. Because a star cannot literally *lean* on its observer, the word seems to suggest the speaker's perception of her relationship to the star. Perhaps she feels that the star impinges on her, that she is somehow *subject* to its influence, though not in the popular, astrological sense. Here the star influences the speaker because she understands something about the way the universe works and can apply her knowledge of light and light years in an analogical way to her own life: it "leans" because it tells her something about how observers are affected by their relationships to what they observe. And it is worth noticing how fully the speaker thinks of herself as object rather than actor. Here, as throughout the poem, she is acted upon; things happen *to* her—the star leans on her, the time lag teases her (line 4), love may not reach her (line 5), and she (along with someone else) is the object sought in the final line.

Other crucial words also help clarify the speaker and her situation. The words "radiance" (line 1) and "[g]litters" (line 3) are fairly standard ones to describe stars, but here their standard meanings are carefully qualified by their position in time. The radiance is from years ago and seems to be unavailable to the speaker, who now sees only glitter, something far less warm and resonant. And the word "impulse" in line 6 invokes technical knowledge about light. Here a star is not impulsive or quickly spent but must "wait" for its reception in the eye of the beholder where it becomes "beautiful"; in physics, an impulse combines force and duration. Hence, the receiver of light—the beholder, the acted upon—becomes important, and we begin to see why the speaker always appears as object: she is the receiver and interpreter, and the light is not complete—its duration not established—until she receives and interprets it. The star does, after all, *lean* on (depend on) her in some objective sense as well as the subjective one in which she first seems to report it.

The stanza form suggests that the poem may have stages and that its meaning may emerge in two parts, a suggestion that is in fact confirmed by the poem's form and structure. The first stanza is entirely about stars and stargazing, but the second stanza establishes the analogy with love that becomes the poem's central metaphor. Now, too, more becomes clear about the speaker and her situation. Her concern is about delay, "time lag" (line 4), and the fact that "Love that loves now may not reach me until / Its first desire is spent" (lines 5–6), a strong indication that her initial observation of the star is driven by feeling and her emotional context. Her attempt to put the remoteness of feeling into a perspective that will enable understanding and patience becomes the "plot" of the poem, and her final calm recognition about "us"—that "love arrived may find us somewhere else"—is, if not comforting, nevertheless a recognition that patience is important and that some things do last. Even the sounds of the poem—in this case the way rhyme is used—help support the meaning of the poem and the tone it achieves. The rhymes in the first part of the poem reflect perfectly the stable sense of ancient stars, while in the second stanza the sounds involve near-rhyme: there is harmony here, but in human life and emotion nothing is quite perfect.

Here is another short poem that deserves similar detailed attention to its several elements:

ANONYMOUS

Western Wind

Western wind, when wilt thou blow,
  The small rain down can rain?
Christ, if my love were in my arms
  And I in my bed again!   15th century

Perhaps the most obvious thing here is the poem's structure: its first two
lines seem to have little to do with the last two. How are we to account for
these two distinct and apparently unrelated directions, the calm concern with
natural processes in the first part and the emotional outburst about loneliness
and lovelessness in the second? The best route to the whole poem is still to
begin with the most simple of questions—who? when? where? what is happening?—and proceed to more difficult and complex ones.

As in "Delay," the speaker here offers little explicit autobiography. In the
first two lines, there is no personal information. The question these lines ask
could be delivered quite impersonally; they could be part of a philosophical
meditation. The abbreviated syntax at the end of line 1 (the question of causality is not fully stated, and we have to supply the "so that" implied at the end of
the line) may suggest strong feeling and emotional upset, but it tells us nothing
intimate and offers little information except that the time is spring (that's when
the western wind blows). No place is indicated, no year, no particulars of situation. But the next two lines, while remaining inexplicit about exact details,
make the speaker's situation clear enough: his love is no longer in his arms,
and he wishes she were. (We don't really know genders here, and my guess is
based on typical practice in the fifteenth century.)

The poem's language is a study in contrast, and it guides us to see the two-
part structure clearly. The question asked of the wind in the first two lines
involves straightforward, steady language, but the third line bursts with agony
and personal despair. The power of the first word of the third line—especially
in an age of belief—suggests a speaker ready to state his loss in the strongest
possible terms, and the parallel statements of loss in lines 3 and 4 suggest not
only the speaker's physical relationship to his love but also his displacement
from home: he is deprived of both place and love, human contact and contact
with his past. His longing for a world ordered according to his past experience
is structured to parallel his longing for the spring wind that brings the world
back to life. The two parts of the poem both express a desire for return—to life,

to order, to causal relationships within the world. Setting has in fact become a central theme in the poem, and what the poem expresses tonally involves a powerful desire for stability and belonging—an effect that grows out of our sense of the speaker's situation and character. Speaker, setting, language, and structure here intertwine to create the intense focus of the poem.

Here is another short poem in which the several elements noticeably interrelate:

ROBERT HERRICK

Upon Julia's Clothes

Whenas in silks my Julia goes
Then, then, methinks, how sweetly flows
That liquefaction of her clothes.

Next, when I cast mine eyes, and see
That brave[1] vibration, each way free,   5
O, how that glittering taketh me!   1648

The poem is unabashed in its admiration of the way Julia looks, and nearly everything in its six short lines contributes to its celebratory tone. Perhaps the most striking thing about the poem involves its unusual, highly suggestive use of words. "[G]oes" at the end of line 1 may be the first word to call special attention to itself, though we will return in a minute to the very first word of the poem. "Walks" or "moves" would seem to be more obvious choices; "goes" is more neutral and less specific and in most circumstances would seem an inferior choice, but here the point seems to be to describe Julia in a kind of seamless and unspecified motion and from a specific angle, because the poem is anxious to record the effect of Julia's movement on the speaker (already a second element becomes crucial) rather than the specifics of Julia herself. Another word that seems especially important is "liquefaction" (line 3), also an unusual and suggestive word about motion. Again it implies no specific kind of motion, just smoothness and seamlessness, and it is applied not to Julia but to her clothes—the kind of indirection that doesn't really fool anybody. Other words that might repay a close look include "vibration" in line 5 (the speaker is finally willing to be a little more direct), "brave" and "free" (also in line 5), and "glittering" and "taketh" in line 6.

1. Handsome, showy.

Had we begun conventionally by thinking about speaker, situation, and setting, we would have quickly noticed the precise way that the speaker chose to clothe Julia: "in silks," which move almost as one with her body. And we would have noticed that the speaker positions himself almost as voyeur (standing for us as observers, of course, but also for himself as the central figure in the poem). Not much detail about situation or setting is given (and the speaker is characterized only as a viewer and appreciator), but one thing about the scene is crucial. It takes us back to the first word of the poem, "whenas." The slightly quaint quality of the word may at first obscure, to a modern reader, just what it tells us about the situation, that it is a *kind* of scene rather than a single event. "Whenas" is very close to "whenever"; the speaker's claim seems to be that he responds this way *whenever* Julia dons her silks—apparently fairly often, at least in his memory or imagination.

Most of the speaker's language is sensual and rather provocative (he is anxious to share his responses with others so that *everyone* will know just how "taking" Julia is), but there is one rather elaborate (though somewhat disguised) metaphor that suggests his awareness of his own calculation and its consequences. In the beginning of the second stanza he describes how he "cast" his eyes: it is a metaphor from fishing, a frequent one in love poetry about luring, chasing, and catching. Julia is the object. The metaphor continues two lines later, but the angler is himself caught: he is taken by the "glittering" lure. This turning of the tables, drawing as it does on a traditional, common image that is then modified to help characterize the speaker, gives a little depth to the show: whatever the slither and glitter, there is not just showing off and sensuality but a catch in this angling.

Many other elements in the poem are worth comment, especially because they quickly relate to each other. Consider the way the poet uses sounds, first of all in picking words like "liquefaction" that are themselves virtually onomatopoeic, but then also using rhyme very cleverly. There are only two rhyme sounds in the poem, one in the first stanza, the other in the second. The long *ee* of the second becomes almost exclamatory, and the three words of the first seem to become linked in a kind of separate grammar of their own, as if "goes," "flows," and "clothes" were all part of a single action—pretty much what the poem claims on a thematic level. A lot is going on in this short and simple poem, and although a reader can get at it step by step by thinking about element after element, the interlocking of the elements is finally what is most impressive. It's easy to see that the plot here reenacts the familiar stances of woman as object and man as gazer, but we need to be flexible enough in our analysis and reading to consider not only all the analytical categories, but also the ways in which they work together.

Going back to poems read earlier in the course—with the methods and approaches you have learned since then—can be a useful exercise in seeing how different elements of poems interrelate. Look, for example, at the stanza divisions in "Cherrylog Road" and consider how the neatly spaced, apparently discrete units work against the sometimes frantic pacing of the poem. Or consider the character of the speaker, or the fundamental metaphor of "wreckage" that sponsors the poem, relative to the idea of speaker. Go back and read "Woodchucks" while thinking about structural questions, or consider how the effaced speaker works in "Aunt Jennifer's Tigers"; or think about metaphor in "The Vacuum."

Here are seven new poems to analyze. As you read them, think about the elements discussed in the first seven chapters—but rather than thinking about a single element at a time, try to consider relationships, how the different elements combine to make you respond not to a single device but to a complex set of strategies and effects.

▼ ▼ ▼

W. H. AUDEN

Musée des Beaux Arts[2]

About suffering they were never wrong,
The Old Masters: how well they understood
Its human position; how it takes place
While someone else is eating or opening a window or just walking dully along;
How, when the aged are reverently, passionately waiting   5
For the miraculous birth, there always must be
Children who did not specially want it to happen, skating
On a pond at the edge of the wood:
They never forgot
That even the dreadful martyrdom must run its course   10
Anyhow in a corner, some untidy spot
Where the dogs go on with their doggy life and the torturer's horse
Scratches its innocent behind on a tree.

2. The Museum of the Fine Arts, in Brussels.

In Brueghel's *Icarus*,[3] for instance: how everything turns away
Quite leisurely from the disaster; the plowman may
Have heard the splash, the forsaken cry,
But for him it was not an important failure; the sun shone
As it had to on the white legs disappearing into the green
Water; and the expensive delicate ship that must have seen
Something amazing, a boy falling out of the sky,
Had somewhere to get to and sailed calmly on.

1938

GEORGE HERBERT

The Collar

I struck the board[4] and cried, "No more;
                I will abroad!
What? shall I ever sigh and pine?
My lines[5] and life are free, free as the road,
        Loose as the wind, as large as store.[6]
                Shall I be still in suit?[7]
Have I no harvest but a thorn
To let me blood, and not restore
What I have lost with cordial[8] fruit?
                Sure there was wine
Before my sighs did dry it; there was corn
        Before my tears did drown it.
        Is the year only lost to me?
        Have I no bays[9] to crown it,
No flowers, no garlands gay? All blasted?
                All wasted?
Not so, my heart; but there is fruit,
                And thou hast hands.
Recover all thy sigh-blown age
On double pleasures: leave thy cold dispute
Of what is fit, and not. Forsake thy cage,
                Thy rope of sands,[1]

---

3. *Landscape with the Fall of Icarus*, by Pieter Brueghel the elder (1525?–1569), located in the Brussels Museum. According to Greek myth, Daedalus and his son Icarus escaped from imprisonment by using homemade wings of wax; but Icarus flew too near the sun, the wax melted, and he fell into the sea and drowned. In the Brueghel painting the central figure is a peasant plowing, and several other figures are more immediately noticeable than Icarus who, disappearing into the sea, is easy to miss in the lower right-hand corner. Equally ignored by the figures is a dead body in the woods. 4. Table. 5. Lot. 6. A storehouse; i.e., in abundance. 7. In service to another. 8. Reviving, restorative. 9. Wreaths of triumph. 1. Moral restrictions.

Which petty thoughts have made, and made to thee
  Good cable, to enforce and draw,
      And be thy law,
While thou didst wink[2] and wouldst not see.
      Away! take heed;
      I will abroad.   25
Call in thy death's-head[3] there; tie up thy fears.
      He that forbears   30
  To suit and serve his need,
      Deserves his load."
But as I raved and grew more fierce and wild
      At every word,
Methought I heard one calling, *Child!*   35
  And I replied, *My Lord.*   1633

ANNE SEXTON

With Mercy for the Greedy

for my friend, Ruth, who urges me to make an appointment
for The Sacrament of Confession

Concerning your letter in which you ask
me to call a priest and in which you ask
me to wear The Cross that you enclose;
your own cross,
your dog bitten cross,   5
no larger than a thumb,
small and wooden, no thorns, this rose.

I pray to its shadow,
that gray place
where it lies on your letter . . . deep, deep.   10
I detest my sins and I try to believe
in The Cross. I touch its tender hips, its dark jawed face,
its solid neck, its brown sleep.

True. There is
a beautiful Jesus.   15
He is frozen to his bones like a chunk of beef.
How desperately he wanted to pull his arms in!
How desperately I touch his vertical and horizontal axes!
But I can't. Need is not quite belief.

2. I.e., close your eyes to the weaknesses of such restrictions.   3. *Memento mori,* a skull intended
to remind people of their mortality.

20 All morning long
I have worn
your cross, hung with package string around my throat.
It tapped me lightly as a child's heart might,
tapping second hand, softly waiting to be born.
25 Ruth, I cherish the letter you wrote.

My friend, my friend, I was born
doing reference work in sin, and born
confessing it. This is what poems are:
with mercy
30 for the greedy;
they are the tongue's wrangle,
the world's pottage, the rat's star.   p. 1961

EMILY DICKINSON

[My Life had stood—a Loaded Gun—]

My Life had stood—a Loaded Gun—
In Corners—till a Day
The Owner passed—identified—
And carried Me away—

5 And now We roam in Sovereign Woods—
And now We hunt the Doe—
And every time I speak for Him—
The Mountains straight reply—

And do I smile, such cordial light
10 Upon the Valley glow—
It is as a Vesuvian face
Had let its pleasure through—

And when at Night—Our good Day done—
I guard My Master's Head—
15 'Tis better than the Eider-Duck's
Deep Pillow—to have shared—

To foe of His—I'm deadly foe—
None stir the second time—
On whom I lay a Yellow Eye—
20 Or an emphatic Thumb—

Though I than He—may longer live
He longer must—than I—
For I have but the power to kill,
ca. 1863   Without—the power to die—

ROBERT FROST

Design

I found a dimpled spider, fat and white,
On a white heal-all,[4] holding up a moth
Like a white piece of rigid satin cloth —
Assorted characters of death and blight
Mixed ready to begin the morning right,   5
Like the ingredients of a witches' broth —
A snow-drop spider, a flower like a froth,
And dead wings carried like a paper kite.

What had that flower to do with being white,
The wayside blue and innocent heal-all?   10
What brought the kindred spider to that height,
Then steered the white moth thither in the night?
What but design of darkness to appall? —
If design govern in a thing so small.   1936

ADRIENNE RICH

Living in Sin

She had thought the studio would keep itself;
no dust upon the furniture of love.
Half heresy, to wish the taps less vocal,
the panes relieved of grime. A plate of pears,
a piano with a Persian shawl, a cat   5
stalking the picturesque amusing mouse
had risen at his urging.
Not that at five each separate stair would writhe
under the milkman's tramp; that morning light
so coldly would delineate the scraps   10
of last night's cheese and three sepulchral bottles;
that on the kitchen shelf among the saucers
a pair of beetle-eyes would fix her own —
envoy from some village in the moldings . . .
Meanwhile, he, with a yawn,   15
sounded a dozen notes upon the keyboard,
declared it out of tune, shrugged at the mirror,
rubbed at his beard, went out for cigarettes;
while she, jeered by the minor demons,
pulled back the sheets and made the bed and found 20

4. A plant, also called the "all-heal" and "self-heal," with tightly clustered violet-blue flowers.

a towel to dust the table-top,
and let the coffee-pot boil over on the stove.
By evening she was back in love again,
though not so wholly but throughout the night
25   she woke sometimes to feel the daylight coming
like a relentless milkman up the stairs.   1955

ANONYMOUS

[My love in her attire doth show her wit]

My love in her attire doth show her wit,
    It doth so well become her;
For every season she hath dressings fit,
    For winter, spring, and summer.
5   No beauty she doth miss
    When all her robes are on;
But beauty's self she is
    When all her robes are gone.   1602

▼ ▼ ▼

QUESTIONS

1. Consider the setting of "Musée des Beaux Arts" both in the sense of the painting and of its location in the museum. In what different ways do the two settings become important? How does the use of setting relate to the way the speaker is conceived? Define the role played by all of the other characters in the poem, including the people on the ship. Whose attitudes (or perhaps words) are being echoed or parodied in line 20? Describe the poem's structure.

2. Consider the elements of speaker and situation simultaneously when you analyze "The Collar."

3. Consider the interrelation of the elements of speaker, words and word order, and stanza form in "My Life had stood—a Loaded Gun—."

4. Consider the interrelationships among speaker, structure, stanza form, and tone in "Design."

5. Compare Herrick's "Upon Julia's Clothes" with the anonymous "My love in her attire." In what ways does sound affect feeling in each? In what way does sound affect meaning? tone?

WRITING SUGGESTIONS

1. Find a reproduction of the Brueghel painting on which Auden's poem is based. "Read" the painting carefully, and notice which details Auden mentions and which he does not. What aspect(s) of the painting does he choose to emphasize? What does he ignore? Write a three-page essay in which you show exactly how Auden *uses* the Brueghel painting in his poem.

2. Consider "Design" as a sonnet. What features of the sonnet seem especially important to the effects Frost achieves here? Consider the structure, rhyme scheme, and imagery of the poem. Now look at another Frost poem, "Range-Finding" (p. 1096), and ask the same questions about this poem. Which poem seems to you to use the sonnet form more effectively? why?

Write a four- to five-page essay, comparing the two poems and evaluating their use of the sonnet form.

STUDENT WRITING

Below is a whole-text analysis of Maxine Kumin's "Woodchucks" (p. 684). In it, the student addresses the setting, language, tone, structure, rhythm, and, finally, the meaning of the poem.

Tragedy in Five Stanzas: "Woodchucks"

Meaghan E. Parker

Maxine Kumin's poem, "Woodchucks," is not, as the title might suggest, about cute, furry woodchucks, but instead describes how the speaker changes as she tries to kill them, revealing aspects of human attitudes towards killing. The speaker undergoes an internal conflict as she realizes her capacity for murder during her battle with the woodchucks. She is caught up in the age-old struggle of humans against nature, except that this time, it takes place in the modern, technological world. This battle is presented in five dramatic scenes, marked by six-line stanzas; the poem's structure echoes the format of a classical tragedy in five acts. The poem is subtly organized, each stanza rhyming *abcacb,* and more or less employing a pentameter line, mixing iambs with anapests. Although the rhyme and meter remain mostly constant over the course of this highly structured poem, the tone and pacing change with each stanza, as the speaker's attitudes transform during the struggle with the woodchucks. The poet indicates the development of the speaker's internal conflict by employing word choice to change the tone from slightly humorous and relaxed to indignant martial righteousness and finally to a harsh and primitive hunter's voice, and utilizing pacing and meter to build the action to its climax.

The poem is set in small-town North America, where the speaker grows marigolds, broccoli, carrots, roses and chard in her garden. Although the speaker buys the gas bomb from the "Feed and Grain Exchange," she is not a farmer, since she has only a "vegetable patch" (lines 2 and 11). Therefore, her killing of the woodchucks is not an occupational or economic necessity; the woodchucks were merely a nuisance, and the

speaker is sort of dabbling in killing. The first
line states that the "gassing . . . didn't turn
out right," not that it didn't work, emphasizing
with this understatement the dilettantish air of
the speaker's activities (line 1). The first
stanza employs a playful humor: the gas is called
a "knockout bomb," like some comic-book weapon,
and the speaker makes a pun on the word
"airtight" (lines 2—4). The store "featured" the
bomb, as if it were displayed and advertised as a
consumer desirable, not as a agent of death (line
3). Line 3 utilizes anapestic feet to add to the
humorous tone, and most of the lines of stanza 1
are composed of long clauses, creating an even,
calm pacing. The speaker and her compatriots
("we") had a made a "case against them,"
suggesting that the decision to kill the
woodchucks was a calm, rational, legal event, yet
the woodchucks evade the law by escaping "out of
range" underground (lines 4—6). The escalation of
the battle is indicated by the military term
"range" and the woodchucks' refusal to play by
the rules (line 6).

The second stanza is less light-hearted; even
though the irrepressible woodchucks "turned up
again" "up to scratch," they are now unmistakably
opponents to the "we," who attacked them with
"cyanide" (lines 7—9). The weapon seems more
sinister now; not just gas from a "merciful"
"knockout bomb," but murderous cyanide. The last

three lines are a litany of the woodchuck's crimes against nature, each one described as increasing in savagery and wanton destruction. First, they merely "brought down the marigolds," but in a "matter of course," thoughtless way, then they "took over" the vegetables, as if they were marauding bandits conquering the speaker's territory (lines 10—11). The speaker is horrified at the "nipping" and "beheading" of the vegetables; the use of the execution-style word "beheading" to create indignation at the death of a plant is ironic, probably consciously on the part of the speaker, since she had tried to execute the woodchuck (line 12). The litany of crimes is reeled off in quick anapestic feet, subtly hinting at the irony of the speaker's anger at the woodchucks and the ridiculousness of the escalating battle.

The action picks up pace in stanza 3, the center of the poem and the point at which the speaker makes her transformation from silent killer to murderous hunter. She indignantly implies that the woodchucks would steal "the food from our mouths": a cliché that is supposed to indicate what heartless criminals the woodchucks are, even though the poem does not indicate that the speaker is a subsistence farmer who would starve without the vegetables (line 13). Even so, she enjoys the feel of the gun, "righteously thrilling" to have the weapon of her justified

revenge in her hands (line 13). The ".22" and the
"bullets' neat noses" feel right and good, and
while the woodchucks are depersonalized into the
enemy, the bullets gain "noses" (line 14). The
killer is "righteous," "fallen from grace" and
"puffed with Darwinian pieties"; these heavy-
handed, Bible-thumping words echo religious and
political leaders' sermons against evil enemies.
The pace of the first four lines of this stanza is
heavy and martial, booming with polysyllabic
words and stirring phrases. The meter is the most
irregular in this stanza, with the two stressed
syllables and similar sounds of *"lapsed"* and
"pacifist" pounding the contrast home between the
speaker's current manifestation as righteous
killer and her former beliefs (line 15). Lines 15
and 16 begin with a stress, on "I" and "puffed";
the majority of the other lines in the poem begin
with an unstressed syllable, so this pair of
exceptions stands out, at the exact center of the
poem, and present the turning point of her
attitudes towards killing. Now "fallen from
grace," she is "puffed" like a self-righteous
windbag, and exchanges her pacifism for the maxim
of survival of the fittest (lines 15–16). Line 17
begins the switch in tone from martial
sloganeering to impersonal, hunting slang, as the
speaker "drew a bead" on a woodchuck and kills
him. His death is contrasted with the
perennialness of the "everbearing roses," for

whose sake he dies; this phrase indicates an
undercurrent of regret at the killing of the
woodchuck (line 18).

The fourth stanza speeds up, using short,
harsh clashing words in short simple clauses,
instead of the sermonizing phrases of the last
stanza. The speaker says she "dropped the
mother": "drop" is a crude, impersonal, and
unfeeling word for "shot dead," and indicates the
speaker's new callous attitude towards the
killing of the woodchucks (line 19). Similarly,
the description of the woodchuck "flipflopp[ing] in
the air" is gratuitous and violent, and the
stress on "flip," since the first syllable of the
line should be unstressed, emphasizes the visual
image of the helpless, blown-away woodchuck (line
20). The speaker immediately moves on: "another
baby next" is killed without comment (line 22).
In the same line, she counts down "O one-two-
three" for the three woodchucks she's killed, and
the three strong stresses lead into the climax of
the poem, where she announces what she's become:
"murderer" and "hawkeye killer" (lines 23—24).
The killer comes "on stage forthwith," as the
speaker appears fully transformed by her killing,
her capability for murderous action arising from
her nature to triumph over her professed pacifism.
The stage metaphor reinforces the five-act tragic
structure that the poem mirrors and line 24
brings the poem to its climax in the fourth
stanza.

Throughout the poem, the poet uses the directions down and up to contrast life and death. The woodchucks "turn up" alive (line 7), "up to scratch" (line 9) from their "sub-sub-basement," but then they "brought down the marigolds" (line 10), so they "died down in the . . . roses" (line 18), "flipflopped and fell" after being "dropped" (lines 19—20). The speaker, on the other hand, was "up to scratch" (line 9) but "[fell] from grace" (line 15), so the "murderer inside [her] rose up hard," as her former pacifist self died down and was reborn as a killer (line 23). In the final stanza, the speaker, now living as this new self, describes her continuing struggle with the woodchuck and the tolls this battle is taking on her, as she remains "cocked and ready day after day after day" and her obsession with hunting this elusive prey keeps her awake at night, dreaming of shooting (lines 26—28). The pacing slows, as the action falls from the climax, and an unenumerated amount of time elapses, but still there is not resolution and thus no victory; the speaker realizes she has lost already to the woodchucks; the tragedy is that they have already stolen her former innocence of murder and killing and now she will never have peace. The final two lines echo the beginning of the poem: "gassing" from line 1 and "gassed" from line 30 are each stressed syllables beginning a line, thus neatly bookending the poem. The speaker suggests that if the woodchucks had died from the gas, she would not have directly confronted the woodchucks and their deaths and thus undergone this tragic change into an obsessive hunter. However, this statement contains a telling historical allusion which suggests that the gassing wouldn't have been an easy moral way out either: the speaker wishes they had died "gassed underground the quiet Nazi way" (line 30). The speaker wished the deaths had been quiet, efficient, clean, non-confrontational and unwitnessed by her, so she could deny any complicity to her conscience. However, this indicates an important contradiction: gassing is still murder, as the Nazis made abundantly clear, no matter how "merciful." The poet draws a parallel between what we consider the "mercy killing" of animals and the "murder" of human beings, and thus the poem describes how delusions of righteousness cause people to wield unnecessary power over others, and how this damages and changes their sense of self as they realize and accept the human capability for acts of murder.

Exploring
Contexts

9 THE AUTHOR'S WORK AS CONTEXT: JOHN KEATS

P oems are not all written in the same style, as if they were produced by a
corporation or put together in a committee. Even though all poets
share the same medium (language) and usually have some common
notions of their craft, they put the unique resources of their individual minds
and consciousnesses into what they create. A poet may rely on tradition extensively and use devices that others have developed without surrendering his or
her own individuality, just as the integrity and uniqueness of an individual are
not compromised by characteristics the individual may share with others—
political affiliations, religious beliefs, tastes in clothes and music. Sometimes
this uniqueness is hard to define—what exactly is it that defines the singular
personality of an individual?—but it is always there, and we recognize and
depend upon it in our relationships with other people. And so with poets: most
don't make a conscious effort to put an individual stamp on their work; they
don't have to. The stamp is there, just in the way they choose subjects, words,
configurations. Every individual's consciousness uniquely marks what it
records, imagines, and decides to print. The poems of John Keats, for example,
are among the most distinctive in the English language. In this chapter, we
will (after considering what makes the poems of any poet distinctive) look at
the features of his poems that stamp them specifically as his own, and in the

next chapter (on the poems of Adrienne Rich), we will look at how development and change occur *within* the continuity of a poet's consciousness.

Experienced readers can often identify a poem as the distinctive work of an individual poet even though they may never have seen the poem before, much as experienced listeners can identify a particular composer, singer, or group after hearing only a few phrases of a piece of new music. Such an ability depends upon a lot of reading of that author, or a lot of listening to music, but any reasonably sensitive reader can learn to do it with great accuracy. Developing this ability, however, is not really an end in itself; rather, it is a by-product of learning to notice the particular, distinctive qualities in the workmanship of any poet. Once you've read several poems by the same poet, you will usually begin to notice some features that the poems all have in common, and gradually you may come to think of those features as characteristic. The poem that follows was written by Howard Nemerov, whose work you have read in some earlier chapters. Before you read it, you may want to look back at his poems printed earlier in this book and remind yourself of what those poems were like, or to compare other of his poems later in the book. (The index will help you find them all.)

HOWARD NEMEROV

A Way of Life

It's been going on a long time.
For instance, these two guys, not saying much, who slog
Through sun and sand, fleeing the scene of their crime,
Till one turns, without a word, and smacks
His buddy flat with the flat of an axe,
Which cuts down on the dialogue
Some, but is viewed rather as normal than sad
By me, as I wait for the next ad.

It seems to me it's been quite a while
Since the last vision of blonde loveliness
Vanished, her shampoo and shower and general style
Replaced by this lean young lunk-
head parading along with a gun in his back to confess
How yestereve, being drunk
And in a state of existential despair,
He beat up his grandma and pawned her invalid chair.

But here at last is a pale beauty
Smoking a filter beside a mountain stream,

Brief interlude, before the conflict of love and duty
Gets moving again, as sheriff and posse expound,   20
Between jail and saloon, the American Dream
Where Justice, after considerable horsing around,
Turns out to be Mercy; when the villain is knocked off,
A kindly uncle offers syrup for my cough.

And now these clean-cut athletic types   25
In global hats are having a nervous debate
As they stand between their individual rocket ships
Which have landed, appropriately, on some rocks
Somewhere in Space, in an atmosphere of hate
Where one tells the other to pull up his socks   30
And get going, he doesn't say where; they fade,
And an angel food cake flutters in the void.

I used to leave now and again;
No more. A lot of violence in American life
These days, mobsters and cops all over the scene.   35
But there's a lot of love, too, mixed with the strife,
And kitchen-kindness, like a bedtime story
With rich food and a more kissable depilatory.
Still, I keep my weapons handy, sitting here
Smoking and shaving and drinking the dry beer.   1967   40

What does this poem have in common with Nemerov's other poems? The
concern with contemporary life, the tendency to concentrate on modern conveniences and luxuries, and the interest in isolating and defining aspects of the
distinctively modern sensibility are all characteristic of Nemerov, as is the tendency to create a short drama, with a speaker who is not altogether admirable.
Several of Nemerov's other poems also share an attitude that seems deeply
imbedded in this poem, a kind of antiromanticism that emerges when someone tries to sound or feel *too* proud or cheerful and is shown, by events in the
poem, to be part of a grimmer reality instead. The concentration upon one or
more physical objects is also characteristic, and often (as in "The Vacuum")
the main object is a mechanical one that symbolizes modernity and our modern dependency on things rather than our concern with human relationships.
Americanness is emphasized here too, as if the poem were concerned to help
us define our culture and its habits and values. The mood of loneliness is also
typical of Nemerov, and so is the poem's witty conversational style. The verbal
wit here—although not as prominent as the puns and double-entendres of
"Boom!" (p. 976)—is characteristically informal. Often it seems to derive
from the language of commercials and street speech, and the undercutting of

this language by the poet—having a paranoid and simple-minded speaker talk about a gangster in "a state of existential despair"—is similar to the strategy of "Boom!" or "The Vacuum." The regular stanzas, rhymed but not in a traditional or regular way and with a number of near-rhymes, are also typical (look, for example, at "The Goose Fish," p. 840). Nemerov's thematic interests and ideas, his verbal style, and his cast of mind are all plainly visible in "A Way of Life."

Noticing common features does not mean that every poem by a particular author will be predictable and contain all these features. Most poets like to experiment with new subjects, tones, forms, and various kinds of poetic strategies and devices. But a characteristic way of thinking—the distinct stamp imposed by a unique consciousness—is likely to be visible anyway. The work of any writer will have certain *tendencies* that are identifiable, although not all of them will show up in any one poem.

Of what practical use is it to notice the distinctive voice and mind of a particular poet? One use (not the most important one for the casual reader, but one that nonetheless gives pleasure) is the pleasant surprise that occurs when you recognize something familiar. Reading a new poem by a familiar poet is a bit like meeting an old friend whose face or conversation reminds you of experiences you have had together. Poetic friendships can be treasures just as personal friendships are, even though they are necessarily more distant and somewhat more abstract. Just as novelty—meeting something or someone altogether new to you—is one kind of pleasure, so revisiting or recalling the familiar is another, its equal and opposite. Just *knowing* and *recognizing* often feel good—in and of themselves.

There are other reasons as well to look at the various works of a single writer. Just as you learn from watching other people—seeing how they react and respond to people and events, observing how they cope with various situations—you also learn from watching poets at work, seeing how they learn and develop, how they change their minds, how they discover the reach and limits of their imaginations and talents, how they find their distinctive voices and come to terms with their own identities. Watching someone at work over a period of years (as you can Adrienne Rich in the next chapter) is a little like watching an autobiography unfold, except that the individual poems continue to exist separately and for themselves at the same time they provide a record of a distinctive but gradually changing and evolving consciousness.

A third reason to study in some detail the work of an individual is a very practical one: the more you know about the poet, the better a reader you are likely to be of any individual poem by that poet. It is not so much that the external facts of a writer's life find their way into whatever he or she writes—be it poem, essay, letter, or autobiography—but that a reader gets used to habits and manners, and learns what to expect. Coming to a new poem by a poet you already know is not completely a new experience. You adjust faster, know what to look for, have some specific expectations (although they may be unconscious and unarticulated) of what the poem will be like. The more poems you read by any author, the better a reader you are likely to be of any one poem.

Before you read the following poem by John Donne, look at the poems by him that appear elsewhere in this book (check the index of authors). What features in these poems seem most striking and distinctive to you as you review them as a group?

JOHN DONNE

The Sun Rising

Busy old fool, unruly sun,
    Why dost thou thus,
Through windows, and through curtains, call on us?
Must to thy motions lovers' seasons run?
      Saucy pedantic wretch, go chide   5
      Late schoolboys, and sour prentices,[1]
Go tell court-huntsmen that the king will ride,
Call country ants[2] to harvest offices;
Love, all alike, no season knows, nor clime,
Nor hours, days, months, which are the rags of time.   10

      Thy beams, so reverend and strong
    Why shouldst thou think?
I could eclipse and cloud them with a wink,
But that I would not lose her sight so long:
      If her eyes have not blinded thine,   15
      Look, and tomorrow late, tell me
Whether both the Indias[3] of spice and mine
Be where thou left'st them, or lie here with me.
Ask for those kings whom thou saw'st yesterday,
And thou shalt hear, all here in one bed lay.   20

      She is all states, and all princes I,
    Nothing else is.

1. Apprentices.   2. Farmworkers.   3. The East and West Indies, commercial sources of spices and gold.

Princes do but play us; compared to this,
All honor's mimic, all wealth alchemy.[4]

25

Thou, sun, art half as happy as we,
In that the world's contracted thus;
Thine age asks[5] ease, and since thy duties be
To warm the world, that's done in warming us.
Shine here to us, and thou art every where;

30

This bed thy center[6] is, these walls thy sphere.   1633

Is "The Sun Rising" somewhat easier to read than the first Donne poem
you read this term? What kind of expectations did you have of the poem, knowing it was by the same author as other poems you had read? How conscious
were you of those expectations? Did they enable you to ask more intelligent
questions of the poem as you read it? How conscious were you, as you read, of
the subject matter of other Donne poems? of their themes? tone? style? form?
sound effects? of other poetic devices? Did you consciously expect a speaker
and a dramatic situation? How quickly did you decide what the situation was?
How quickly did you identify the setting? Did you find that you had certain
expectations of the speaker once you had sensed the poem's subject and situation? In retrospect, how similar to other Donne poems does this one seem? In
what specific ways? In what ways were your responses to this poem conditioned
by what you already knew from other Donne poems?

The skills involved here are progressive: they don't come all at once like a
flash of lightning. Rather, they develop over time, as do most of the more
sophisticated contextual reading skills we will be considering in the later chapters of this book, and they develop in conjunction with skills you have already
worked on in earlier chapters. Don't worry if you still have difficulty with a
new Donne poem. You are in good company: Donne isn't easy. But the more
you read, the better you will get. Reading ten or a dozen poems by a single
author is better than reading three or four, not only because your generalizations and the expectations they create will be more reliable but also because
you will feel increasingly comfortable. Spending some hours in the library reading several new poems by a poet you like and admire can be a very satisfying
experience; work with any author long enough, and you will begin to feel positively at home. But even then, a good poet will still surprise you in every new
poem, at least to some extent. Being reliable and distinctive is not the same as
being predictable.

The poems that follow—all written by John Keats—vary quite a bit in sub-

4. Imposture, like the "scientific" procedures for turning base metals into gold. *Mimic:* hypocritical.
5. Requires.   6. Of orbit.

ject matter, tone, choice of verse form, and length. But they also have a coherence that derives from their having been conceived by the same imagination—
the experiences of one young man in the early nineteenth century inform
them all. As you read them over, you will note what they have in common,
how they repeatedly suggest the pervasive sensuous and sensual quality of his
work, his fascination with medieval times and gothic states of mind, his
attraction both to nature and to highly ornate artifices, his distinctive patterns
of phrasing and use of poetic devices, and the recurrent contrasts in his work
between an external world of "objective" reality and internal states of "subjective" consciousness. Prose selections from a preface and from several of Keats's
personal letters underscore some of his most persistent poetic and personal concerns. The poems are arranged chronologically, and a chronology of his life
suggests the potential relevance of biographical information.

▼   ▼   ▼

JOHN KEATS

On First Looking into Chapman's Homer[7]

Much have I traveled in the realms of gold,
And many goodly states and kingdoms seen;
Round many western islands have I been
Which bards in fealty[8] to Apollo hold.
Oft of one wide expanse had I been told   5
That deep-browed Homer ruled as his demesne;
Yet did I never breathe its pure serene[9]
Till I heard Chapman speak out loud and bold:
Then felt I like some watcher of the skies
When a new planet swims into his ken;[1]   10
Or like stout Cortez[2] when with eagle eyes
He stared at the Pacific—and all his men
Looked at each other with a wild surmise—
Silent, upon a peak in Darien.   1816

---

7. George Chapman's were among the most famous Renaissance translations; his *Iliad* was completed in 1611, *The Odyssey* in 1616. Keats wrote the sonnet after being led to Chapman by his former
teacher and reading *The Iliad* all night long.   8. Literally, the loyalty owed by a vassal to his
feudal lord. Apollo was the Greek god of poetry and music.   9. Atmosphere.   1. Range of
vision.   2. Actually, Balboa; he first viewed the Pacific from Darien, in Panama.

On the Grasshopper and the Cricket

The poetry of earth is never dead:
When all the birds are faint with the hot sun,
And hide in cooling trees, a voice will run
From hedge to hedge about the new-mown mead;
That is the grasshopper's—he takes the lead
In summer luxury—he has never done
With his delights; for when tired out with fun
He rests at ease beneath some pleasant weed.
The poetry of earth is ceasing never:
On a lone winter evening, when the frost
Has wrought a silence, from the stove there shrills
The cricket's song, in warmth increasing ever,
And seems to one in drowsiness half lost,
The grasshopper's among some grassy hills.

December 30, 1816

On Seeing the Elgin Marbles[3]

My spirit is too weak—mortality
Weighs heavily on me like unwilling sleep,
And each imagined pinnacle and steep
Of godlike hardship tells me I must die
Like a sick eagle looking at the sky.
Yet 'tis a gentle luxury to weep
That I have not the cloudy winds to keep
Fresh for the opening of the morning's eye.
Such dim-conceived glories of the brain
Bring round the heart an indescribable feud;
So do these wonders a most dizzy pain,
That mingles Grecian grandeur with the rude
Wasting of old Time—with a billowy main—
A sun—a shadow of a magnitude.

1817

---

3. Figures and friezes from the Athenian Parthenon. They were purchased from the Turks (who controlled Athens) by Lord Elgin, brought to England in 1806, and then sold to the British Museum, where Keats saw them.

from Endymion (Book I)[4]

A thing of beauty is a joy for ever:
Its loveliness increases; it will never
Pass into nothingness; but still will keep
A bower quiet for us, and a sleep
Full of sweet dreams, and health, and quiet breathing.   5
Therefore, on every morrow, are we wreathing
A flowery band to bind us to the earth,
Spite of despondence, of the inhuman dearth
Of noble natures, of the gloomy days,
Of all the unhealthy and o'er-darkened ways   10
Made for our searching: yes, in spite of all,
Some shape of beauty moves away the pall
From our dark spirits. Such the sun, the moon,
Trees old, and young sprouting a shady boon
For simple sheep; and such are daffodils   15
With the green world they live in; and clear rills
That for themselves a cooling covert make
'Gainst the hot season; the mid forest brake,[5]
Rich with a sprinkling of fair musk-rose blooms:
And such too is the grandeur of the dooms[6]   20
We have imagined for the mighty dead;
All lovely tales that we have heard or read:
An endless fountain of immortal drink,
Pouring unto us from the heaven's brink.
    Nor do we merely feel these essences   25
For one short hour; no, even as the trees
That whisper round a temple become soon
Dear as the temple's self, so does the moon,
The passion poesy, glories infinite,
Haunt us till they become a cheering light   30
Unto our souls, and bound to us so fast,
That, whether there be shine, or gloom o'ercast,
1817   They always must be with us, or we die.

When I Have Fears

When I have fears that I may cease to be
Before my pen has gleaned my teeming brain,
Before high-piléd books, in charact'ry,
Hold like rich garners the full-ripened grain;

4. Keats's long poem about the myth of a mortal (Endymion) loved by the goddess of the moon.
5. Thicket.   6. Judgments.

5   When I behold, upon the night's starred face,
Huge cloudy symbols of a high romance,
And think that I may never live to trace
Their shadows, with the magic hand of chance;
And when I feel, fair creature of an hour!
10   That I shall never look upon thee more,
Never have relish in the faery power
Of unreflecting love!—then on the shore
Of the wide world I stand alone, and think
1818   Till Love and Fame to nothingness do sink.

To Sleep

O soft embalmer of the still midnight,
Shutting, with careful fingers and benign,
Our gloom-pleased eyes, embowered from the light,
Enshaded in forgetfulness divine;
5   O soothest[7] Sleep! if so it please thee, close,
In midst of this thine hymn, my willing eyes,
Or wait the amen, ere thy poppy[8] throws
Around my bed its lulling charities;
Then save me, or the passéd day will shine
10   Upon my pillow, breeding many woes;
Save me from curious conscience, that still lords[9]
Its strength for darkness, burrowing like a mole;
Turn the key deftly in the oiléd wards,[1]
And seal the hushéd casket of my soul.

April 1819

Ode to a Nightingale

I

My heart aches, and a drowsy numbness pains
   My sense, as though of hemlock I had drunk,
Or emptied some dull opiate to the drains
   One minute past, and Lethe-wards[2] had sunk:
5   'Tis not through envy of thy happy lot,
   But being too happy in thine happiness,

---

7. Softest.   8. Because opium derives from it, the poppy was associated with sleep.   9. Marshals. *Curious:* scrupulous.   1. Ridges in a lock that distinguish proper from improper keys.
2. Toward the river of forgetfulness (Lethe) in Hades.

That thou, light-wingéd Dryad[3] of the trees,
    In some melodious plot
Of beechen green, and shadows numberless,
    Singest of summer in full-throated ease.   10

II

O, for a draught of vintage! that hath been
    Cooled a long age in the deep-delvéd earth,
Tasting of Flora[4] and the country green,
    Dance, and Provençal song,[5] and sunburnt mirth!
O for a beaker full of the warm South,   15
    Full of the true, the blushful Hippocrene,[6]
        With beaded bubbles winking at the brim,
            And purple-stainéd mouth;
    That I might drink, and leave the world unseen,
    And with thee fade away into the forest dim: 20

III

Fade far away, dissolve, and quite forget
    What thou among the leaves hast never known,
The weariness, the fever, and the fret
    Here, where men sit and hear each other groan;
Where palsy shakes a few, sad, last gray hairs,   25
    Where youth grows pale, and specter-thin, and dies;
        Where but to think is to be full of sorrow
            And leaden-eyed despairs,
    Where Beauty cannot keep her lustrous eyes,
    Or new Love pine at them beyond tomorrow.   30

IV

Away! away! for I will fly to thee,
    Not charioted by Bacchus and his pards,[7]
But on the viewless[8] wings of Poesy,
    Though the dull brain perplexes and retards:
Already with thee! tender is the night,   35
    And haply the Queen-Moon is on her throne,
        Clustered around by all her starry Fays;[9]
            But here there is no light,
Save what from heaven is with the breezes blown
    Through verdurous glooms and winding mossy ways.   40

---

3. Wood nymph.   4. Roman goddess of flowers.   5. The medieval troubadors of Provence were famous for their love songs.   6. The fountain of the Muses on Mt. Helicon, whose waters bring poetic inspiration.   7. The Roman god of wine was sometimes portrayed in a chariot drawn by leopards.   8. Invisible.   9. Fairies.

V

I cannot see what flowers are at my feet,
    Nor what soft incense hangs upon the boughs,
But, in embalméd[1] darkness, guess each sweet
    Wherewith the seasonable month endows
45   The grass, the thicket, and the fruit-tree wild;
        White hawthorn, and the pastoral eglantine;[2]
        Fast fading violets covered up in leaves;
          And mid-May's eldest child,
    The coming musk-rose, full of dewy wine,
50   The murmurous haunt of flies on summer eves.

VI

Darkling[3] I listen; and, for many a time
    I have been half in love with easeful Death,
Called him soft names in many a muséd rhyme,
    To take into the air my quiet breath;
55 Now more than ever seems it rich to die,
    To cease upon the midnight with no pain,
        While thou art pouring forth thy soul abroad
          In such an ecstasy!
    Still wouldst thou sing, and I have ears in vain—
60   To thy high requiem become a sod.

VII

Thou wast not born for death, immortal Bird!
    No hungry generations tread thee down;
The voice I hear this passing night was heard
    In ancient days by emperor and clown:
65 Perhaps the selfsame song that found a path
    Through the sad heart of Ruth,[4] when, sick for home,
        She stood in tears amid the alien corn;
          The same that ofttimes hath
    Charmed magic casements, opening on the foam
70   Of perilous seas, in faery lands forlorn.

VIII

Forlorn! the very word is like a bell
    To toll me back from thee to my sole self!

---

1. Fragrant, aromatic.   2. Sweetbriar or honeysuckle.   3. In the dark.   4. A virtuous Moabite widow who, according to the Old Testament Book of Ruth, left her own country to accompany her mother-in-law Naomi back to Naomi's native land. She supported herself as a gleaner.

Adieu! the fancy cannot cheat so well
    As she is famed to do, deceiving elf.
Adieu! adieu! thy plaintive anthem fades   75
    Past the near meadows, over the still stream,
        Up the hillside; and now 'tis buried deep
            In the next valley-glades:
Was it a vision, or a waking dream?
    Fled is that music:—Do I wake or sleep?   80

May 1819

Ode on a Grecian Urn

I

Thou still unravished bride of quietness,
    Thou foster-child of silence and slow time,
Sylvan[5] historian, who canst thus express
    A flowery tale more sweetly than our rhyme:
What leaf-fringed legend haunts about thy shape   5
    Of deities or mortals, or of both,
        In Tempe or the dales of Arcady?[6]
What men or gods are these? What maidens loath?
    What mad pursuit? What struggle to escape?
        What pipes and timbrels? What wild ecstasy?   10

II

Heard melodies are sweet, but those unheard
    Are sweeter; therefore, ye soft pipes, play on;
Not to the sensual[7] ear, but, more endeared,
    Pipe to the spirit ditties of no tone:
Fair youth, beneath the trees, thou canst not leave   15
    Thy song, nor ever can those trees be bare;
        Bold Lover, never, never canst thou kiss,
Though winning near the goal—yet, do not grieve
    She cannot fade, though thou hast not thy bliss,
        For ever wilt thou love, and she be fair!   20

---

5. Rustic. The urn depicts a woodland scene.   6. Arcadia. Tempe is a beautiful valley near Mt. Olympus in Greece, and the valley ("dales") of Arcadia a picturesque section of the Peloponnesus; both came to be associated with the pastoral ideal.   7. Of the senses, as distinguished from the "ear" of the spirit or imagination.

III

Ah, happy, happy boughs! that cannot shed
　　Your leaves, nor ever bid the Spring adieu;
And, happy melodist, unweariéd,
　　For ever piping songs for ever new;
More happy love! more happy, happy love!
　　For ever warm and still to be enjoyed,
　　　　For ever panting, and for ever young;
All breathing human passion far above,
　　That leaves a heart high-sorrowful and cloyed,
　　　　A burning forehead, and a parching tongue.

IV

Who are these coming to the sacrifice?
　　To what green altar, O mysterious priest,
Lead'st thou that heifer lowing at the skies,
　　And all her silken flanks with garlands dressed?
What little town by river or sea shore,
　　Or mountain-built with peaceful citadel,
　　　　Is emptied of this folk, this pious morn?
And, little town, thy streets for evermore
　　Will silent be; and not a soul to tell
　　　　Why thou art desolate, can e'er return.

V

O Attic shape! Fair attitude! with brede[8]
　　Of marble men and maidens overwrought,[9]
With forest branches and the trodden weed;
　　Thou, silent form, dost tease us out of thought
As doth eternity: Cold Pastoral!
　　When old age shall this generation waste,
　　　　Thou shalt remain, in midst of other woe
Than ours, a friend to man, to whom thou say'st,
　　Beauty is truth, truth beauty[1]—that is all
　　　　Ye know on earth, and all ye need to know.

May 1819

---

8. Woven pattern. *Attic:* Attica was the district of ancient Greece surrounding Athens.　　**9.** Ornamented all over.　　**1.** In some texts of the poem "Beauty is truth, truth beauty" is in quotation marks and in some texts it is not, leading to critical disagreements about whether the last line and a half are also inscribed on the urn or spoken by the poet.

Ode on Melancholy

I

No, no, go not to Lethe,[2] neither twist
  Wolfsbane, tight-rooted, for its poisonous wine;[3]
Nor suffer thy pale forehead to be kissed
  By nightshade, ruby grape of Proserpine;
Make not your rosary of yew-berries,[4]   5
  Nor let the beetle, nor the death-moth be
    Your mournful Psyche,[5] nor the downy owl
A partner in your sorrow's mysteries;
  For shade to shade will come too drowsily,
    And drown the wakeful anguish of the soul.   10

II

But when the melancholy fit shall fall
  Sudden from heaven like a weeping cloud,
That fosters the droop-headed flowers all,
  And hides the green hill in an April shroud;
Then glut thy sorrow on a morning rose,   15
  Or on the rainbow of the salt sand-wave,
    Or on the wealth of globéd peonies;
Or if thy mistress some rich anger shows,
  Emprison her soft hand, and let her rave,
    And feed deep, deep upon her peerless eyes.   20

III

She[6] dwells with Beauty—Beauty that must die;
  And Joy, whose hand is ever at his lips
Bidding adieu; and aching Pleasure nigh,
  Turning to poison while the bee-mouth sips:
Ay, in the very temple of Delight   25
  Veiled Melancholy has her sov'reign shrine,
    Though seen of none save him whose strenuous tongue
Can burst Joy's grape against his palate fine;[7]
  His soul shall taste the sadness of her might,
    And be among her cloudy trophies hung.[8]   30

May 1819

2. The river of forgetfulness in Hades.   3. Like nightshade (line 4), wolfsbane is a poisonous plant. *Proserpine*: queen of Hades.   4. Which often grow in cemeteries and which are traditionally associated with death.   5. *Psyche* means both "soul" and "breath," and sometimes it was anciently represented by a moth leaving the mouth at death. Owls and beetles were also traditionally associated with darkness and death.   6. The goddess Melancholy, whose chief place of worship ("shrine") is described in lines 25–26.   7. Sensitive, discriminating.   8. The ancient Greeks and Romans hung trophies in their gods' temples.

To Autumn

I

Season of mists and mellow fruitfulness,
  Close bosom-friend of the maturing sun;
Conspiring with him how to load and bless
  With fruit the vines that round the thatch-eves run;
To bend with apples the mossed cottage-trees,
  And fill all fruit with ripeness to the core;
    To swell the gourd, and plump the hazel shells
With a sweet kernel; to set budding more,
  And still more, later flowers for the bees,
    Until they think warm days will never cease,
      For Summer has o'er-brimmed their clammy cells.

II

Who hath not seen thee oft amid thy store?
  Sometimes whoever seeks abroad may find
Thee sitting careless on a granary floor,
  Thy hair soft-lifted by the winnowing wind;[9]
Or on a half-reaped furrow sound asleep,
  Drowsed with the fume of poppies, while thy hook[1]
    Spares the next swath and all its twinéd flowers:
And sometimes like a gleaner thou dost keep
  Steady thy laden head across a brook;
  Or by a cider-press, with patient look,
    Thou watchest the last oozings hours by hours.

III

Where are the songs of Spring? Ay, where are they?
  Think not of them, thou hast thy music too—
While barréd clouds bloom the soft-dying day,
  And touch the stubble-plains with rosy hue;
Then in a wailful choir the small gnats mourn
  Among the river sallows,[2] borne aloft
    Or sinking as the light wind lives or dies;
And full-grown lambs loud bleat from hilly bourn;[3]
  Hedge-crickets sing; and now with treble soft
  The red-breast whistles from a garden-croft;[4]
    And gathering swallows twitter in the skies.

September 19, 1819

---

9. Which sifts the grain from the chaff.   1. Scythe or sickle.   2. Willows.   3. Domain.
4. An enclosed garden near a house.

from Letter to Benjamin Bailey, November 22, 1817[5]

* * * I am certain of nothing but of the holiness of the Heart's affections and the truth of Imagination—What the imagination seizes as Beauty must be truth—whether it existed before or not—for I have the same Idea of all our Passions as of Love they are all in their sublime, creative of essential Beauty * * The Imagination may be compared to Adam's dream[6]—he awoke and found it truth. I am the more zealous in this affair, because I have never yet been able to perceive how any thing can be known for truth by consequitive reasoning—and yet it must be—Can it be that even the greatest Philosopher ever ~~when~~ arrived at his goal without putting aside numerous objections—However it may be, O for a Life of Sensations rather than of Thoughts! It is "a Vision in the form of Youth" a Shadow of reality to come—and this consideration has further conv[i]nced me for it has come as auxiliary to another favorite Speculation of mine, that we shall enjoy ourselves here after by having what we called happiness on Earth repeated in a finer tone and so repeated—And yet such a fate can only befall those who delight in sensation rather than hunger as you do after Truth—Adam's dream will do here and seems to be a conviction that Imagination and its empyreal reflection is the same as human Life and its spiritual repetition. But as I was saying—the simple imaginative Mind may have its rewards in the repeti[ti]on of its own silent Working coming continually on the spirit with a fine suddenness—to compare great things with small—have you never by being surprised with an old Melody—in a delicious place—by a delicious voice, fe[l]t over again your very speculations and surmises at the time it first operated on your soul—do you not remember forming to yourself the singer's face more beautiful that [*for* than] it was possible and yet with the elevation of the Moment you did not think so—even then you were mounted on the Wings of Imagination so high—that the Prototype must be here after—that delicious face you will see—What a time! I am continually running away from the subject—sure this cannot be exactly the case with a complex Mind—one that is imaginative and at the same time careful of its fruits—who would exist partly on sensation partly on thought—to whom it is necessary that years should bring the philosophic Mind—such an one I consider your's and therefore it is necessary to your eternal Happiness that you not only ~~have~~ drink this old Wine of Heaven which I shall call the redigestion of our most ethereal Musings on Earth; but also increase in knowledge and know all things. * * *

---

5. Keats's private letters, often carelessly written, are reprinted uncorrected.   6. In *Paradise Lost*, VIII, 460–90.

from Letter to George and Thomas Keats, December 21, 1817

* * * I spent Friday evening with Wells[7] & went the next morning to see *Death on the Pale horse.*[8] It is a wonderful picture, when West's age is considered; But there is nothing to be intense upon; no women one feels mad to kiss, no face swelling into reality. the excellence of every Art is its intensity, capable of making all disagreeables evaporate, from their being in close relationship with Beauty & Truth—Examine King Lear & you will find this examplified throughout; but in this picture we have unpleasantness without any momentous depth of speculation excited, in which to bury its repulsiveness—The picture is larger than Christ rejected—I dined with Haydon the sunday after you left, & had a very pleasant day, I dined too (for I have been out too much lately) with Horace Smith & met his two Brothers with Hill & Kingston & one Du Bois,[9] they only served to convince me, how superior humour is to wit in respect to enjoyment—These men say things which make one start, without making one feel, they are all alike; their manners are alike; they all know fashionables; they have a mannerism in their very eating & drinking, in their mere handling a Decanter—They talked of Kean[1] & his low company—Would I were with that company instead of yours said I to myself! I know such like acquaintance will never do for me & yet I am going to Reynolds, on wednesday—Brown & Dilke walked with me & back from the Christmas pantomime. I had not a dispute but a disquisition with Dilke, on various subjects; several things dovetailed in my mind, & at once it struck me, what quality went to form a Man of Achievement especially in Literature & which Shakespeare posessed so enormously—I mean *Negative Capability*, that is when man is capable of being in uncertainties, Mysteries, doubts, without any irritable reaching after fact & reason—Coleridge, for instance, would let go by a fine isolated verisimilitude caught from the Penetralium of mystery, from being incapable of remaining content with half knowledge. This pursued through Volumes would perhaps take us no further than this, that with a great poet the sense of Beauty overcomes every other consideration, or rather obliterates all consideration.

Letter to John Hamilton Reynolds, February 19, 1818

I have an idea that a Man might pass a very pleasant life in this manner—let him on any certain day read a certain Page of full Poesy or distilled Prose and let him wander with it, and muse upon it, and reflect from it, and bring home

7. Charles Wells (1800–1879), an author.   8. By Benjamin West (1738–1820), American painter and president of the Royal Academy; *Christ Rejected* (mentioned below) is also by West.
9. Thomas Hill (1760–1840), a book collector, and Edward duBois (1774–1850), a journalist.
1. Edmund Kean (1789–1833), a famous Shakespearean actor.

to it, and prophesy upon it, and dream upon it—untill it becomes stale—but when will it do so? Never—When Man has arrived at a certain ripeness in intellect any one grand and spiritual passage serves him as a starting post towards all "the two-and-thirty Pallaces"[2] How happy is such a "voyage of conception," what delicious diligent Indolence! A doze upon a Sofa does not hinder it, and a nap upon Clover engenders ethereal finger-pointings—the prattle of a child gives it wings, and the converse of middle age a strength to beat them—a strain of musick conducts to "an odd angle of the Isle",[3] and when the leaves whisper it puts a girdle round the earth",[4] Nor will this sparing touch of noble Books be any irreverance to their Writers—for perhaps the honors paid by Man to Man are trifles in comparison to the Benefit done by great Works to the "Spirit and pulse of good" by their mere passive existence. Memory should not be called knowledge—Many have original minds who do not think it—they are led away by Custom—Now it appears to me that almost any Man may like the Spider spin from his own inwards his own airy Citadel—the points of leaves and twigs on which the Spider begins her work are few and she fills the Air with a beautiful circuiting: man should be content with as few points to tip with the fine Webb of his Soul and weave a tapestry empyrean—full of Symbols for his spiritual eye, of softness for his spiritual touch, of space for his wandering of distinctness for his Luxury—But the Minds of Mortals are so different and bent on such diverse Journeys that it may at first appear impossible for any common taste and fellowship to exist ~~bettween~~ between two or three under these suppositions—It is however quite the contrary—Minds would leave each other in contrary directions, traverse each other in Numberless points, and all [for at] last greet each other at the Journeys end—An old Man and a child would talk together and the old Man be led on his Path, and the child left thinking—Man should not dispute or assert but whisper results to his neighbor, and thus by every germ of Spirit sucking the Sap from mould ethereal every human might become great, and Humanity instead of being a wide heath of Furse[5] and Briars with here and there a remote Oak or Pine, would become a grand democracy of Forest Trees. It has been an old Comparison for our urging on—the Bee hive—however it seems to me that we should rather be the flower than the Bee—for it is a false notion that more is gained by receiving than giving—no, the receiver and the giver are equal in their benefits—The f[l]ower I doubt not receives a fair guerdon from the Bee—its leaves blush deeper in the next spring—and who shall say between Man and Woman which is the most delighted? Now it is more noble to sit like Jove that [for than] to fly like Mercury—let us not therefore go hurrying about and collecting honey bee like, buzzing here and there impatiently from a knowledge of what is to be arrived at; but let us open our leaves like a flower and be passive and receptive—budding patiently under the eye of Apollo and taking hints from every noble insect that favors us with a visit—sap will be given us for Meat and dew for drink—I was led into these thoughts, my dear Reynolds, by the beauty of the morning operating on a sense of Idleness—

---

2. "Places of delight" in Buddhism.   3. *The Tempest*, Act I, scene 2, 223.   4. The phrase is from *A Midsummer Night's Dream*, Act II, scene 1, 175.   5. *The Tempest*, Act II, scene 1, 68–69.

I have not read any Books—the Morning said I was right—I had no Idea but of the Morning, and the Thrush said I was right—seeming to say—

> O thou whose face hath felt the Winter's wind,
> Whose eye has seen the snow-clouds hung in mist,
> And the black elm tops 'mong the freezing stars,
> To thee the spring will be a harvest-time.
> O thou, whose only book has been the light
> Of supreme darkness which thou feddest on
> Night after night when Phœbus was away,
> To thee the spring shall be a triple morn.
> O fret not after knowledge—I have none,
> And yet my song comes native with the warmth.
> O fret not after knowledge—I have none,
> And yet the Evening listens. He who saddens
> At thought of idleness cannot be idle,
> And he's awake who thinks himself asleep.

Now I am sensible all this is a mere sophistication, however it may neighbor to any truths, to excuse my own indolence—so I will not deceive myself that Man should be equal with jove—but think himself very well off as a sort of scullion-Mercury, or even a humble Bee—It is not [*for* no] matter whether I am right or wrong either one way or another, if there is sufficient to lift a little time from your Shoulders.

from Letter to John Taylor, February 27, 1818

* * * It is a sorry thing for me that any one should have to overcome Prejudices in reading my Verses—that affects me more than any hyper-criticism on any particular Passage. In *Endymion* I have most likely but moved into the Go-cart from the leading strings. In Poetry I have a few Axioms, and you will see how far I am from their Centre. 1st I think Poetry should surprise by a fine excess and not by Singularity—it should strike the Reader as a wording of his own highest thoughts, and appear almost a Remembrance—2nd Its touches of Beauty should never be half way therby making the reader breathless instead of content: the rise, the progress, the setting of imagery should like the Sun come natural natural too him—shine over him and set soberly although in magnificence leaving him in the Luxury of twilight—but it is easier to think what Poetry should be than to write it—and this leads me on to another axiom. That if Poetry comes not as naturally as the Leaves to a tree it had better not come at all. However it may be with me I cannot help looking into new countries with "O for a Muse of fire to ascend!"[6]—If Endymion serves me as a Pioneer perhaps I ought to be content. I have great reason to be content, for thank God I can read and perhaps

6. *Henry V*, Prologue, 1.

understand Shakspeare to his depths, and I have I am sure many friends, who, if I fail, will attribute any change in my Life and Temper to Humbleness rather than to Pride—to a cowering under the Wings of great Poets rather than to a Bitterness that I am not appreciated. I am anxious to get Endymion printed that I may forget it and proceed. * * *

from the Preface to *Endymion,* dated April 10, 1818

The imagination of a boy is healthy, and the mature imagination of a man is healthy; but there is a space of life between, in which the soul is in a ferment, the character undecided, the way of life uncertain, the ambition thick-sighted: thence proceeds mawkishness, and all the thousand bitters which those men I speak of must necessarily taste in going over the following pages.

I hope I have not in too late a day touched the beautiful mythology of Greece, and dulled its brightness: for I wish to try once more, before I bid it farewell.

CHRONOLOGY

1795 John Keats born October 31 at Finsbury, just north of London, the eldest child of Thomas and Frances Jennings Keats. Thomas Keats was head ostler at a livery stable.

1797–1803 Birth of three younger brothers and sisters: George in 1797, Thomas in 1799, Frances Mary (Fanny) in 1803.

1803 With George, begins school in Enfield.

1804 Father killed by a fall from his horse, April 15. On June 27 his mother remarries, and the children go to live with their maternal grandparents at Enfield. The grandfather dies a year later, and the children move with their grandmother to Lower Edmonton.

1809 Begins a literary friendship with Charles Cowden Clarke, the son of the headmaster at the Enfield school, and develops a strong interest in reading.

1810 Mother dies of tuberculosis, after a long illness.

1811 Leaves school to become apprenticed to an apothecary-surgeon in Edmonton; completes a prose translation of the *Aeneid,* begun at school.

1814 Earliest known attempts at writing verse. In December his grandmother dies, and the family home is broken up.

1815 In October moves to next stage of his medical training at Guy's Hospital, south of the Thames in London.

1816 On May 5 his first published poem, "O Solitude," appears in Leigh Hunt's *Examiner.* In October writes "On First Looking into Chapman's Homer," published in December. Meets Hunt, Benjamin Haydon, John Hamilton Reynolds, and Shelley. By the spring of 1817, gives up the idea of medical practice.

1817   In March, moves with brothers to Hampstead, sees the Elgin Marbles with Haydon, and publishes his first collection of *Poems*. Composes *Endymion* between April and November. Reads Milton, Shakespeare, and Coleridge and rereads Wordsworth during the year.

1818   *Endymion* published in April, unfavorably reviewed in September, defended by Reynolds in October. During the summer goes on walking tour of the lake country and Scotland, but returns to London in mid-August with a sore throat and severe chills. His brother Tom also seriously ill by late summer, dying on December 1. In September, Keats first meets Fanny Brawne (eighteen years old), with whom he arrives at an "understanding" by Christmas.

1819   Writes *The Eve of St. Agnes* in January, revises it in September. Fanny Brawne and her mother move into the other half of the double house in which Keats lives in April. During April and May writes "La Belle Dame sans Merci" and all the major odes except "To Autumn," written in September. Rental arrangements force separation from Fanny Brawne during the summer (Keats on Isle of Wight from June to August), and in the fall he tries to break his dependence on her, but they become engaged by Christmas. Earlier in December suffers a recurrence of his sore throat.

1820   In February has a severe hemorrhage and in June an attack of blood-spitting. In July his doctor orders him to Italy for the winter; he sails in September and finally arrives in Rome on November 15. In July a volume of poems published, *Lamia, Isabella, The Eve of St. Agnes and Other Poems.* Fanny Brawne nurses him through the late summer.

1821   Dies at 11 P.M., February 23. Buried in the English Cemetery at Rome.

▼   ▼   ▼

QUESTIONS

1. Once you have read at least half a dozen poems by Keats, make a list of the ideas that you have found in more than one poem. Make a list as well of any distinctive stylistic features you have noticed. What kinds of experiences or events does he tend to write about? Do you notice any pattern in his use of speaker? Does he have favorite words that he uses in a particular way? What about metaphors? What are his habits in putting poems together? (You might want to look ahead to some examples of his revisions in Chapter 13.) In which poems do you feel as if you want to know more about the author and his experiences before you can interpret them confidently?

2. What stanza forms does Keats seem especially fond of? How do you explain his fondness for repeated rhymes? What kinds of tonal effects are produced by the rhyme-rich sound patterns of the poem? What effect on meaning does the emphasis on rhyme have?

3. What kinds of images dominate Keats's poems? What kinds of settings?

Do Keats's poems tend to have a distinctive, describable speaker? What tones are characteristic of Keats?

WRITING SUGGESTION

Pick out *one* poem that seems to you "typical" in that it uses many of the strategies found in other poems by Keats and displays themes that seem central to his work. Write a detailed paper (of eight to ten pages) in which you analyze the poem you have chosen, showing how it is typical of Keats's work.

10 THE AUTHOR'S WORK IN CONTEXT: ADRIENNE RICH

The poet featured in this chapter, Adrienne Rich, has had a long and very distinguished career. By many readers and critics, she is regarded as the best poet writing today. And a careful reader of her work will find similarities of interest, strategy, and taste from her earliest poems—published shortly after World War II, in 1951—to her newest ones. There is a distinctive mind and orientation at work in all her poems; one can speak about characteristic features in Rich's poetry just as surely as one does about characteristic features in the work of Donne, Keats, or Nemerov. Throughout her career of more than forty years so far, Rich has, for example, steadfastly remained interested in social and political issues and has often concentrated on themes relating to women's consciousness and the societal roles of women. Furthermore, her poems have always been conceived with a powerful sense of functional structure and cast into lyric modes that reflect sensitively their respective moods and tones. And the voice has always been firm and clear, setting out images vividly and taking a stand in matters of conscience. But over the years the voice has changed quite a lot too, and Rich's views on a number of issues have modified and developed. Many of the changes in Rich's ideas and attitudes reflect changing concerns among American (and especially women) intellectuals in the second half of the twentieth century, and her poems represent both changed social conditions and sharply altered social, political, and philosophical attitudes. But they also reflect altered personal circumstances and changes in lifestyle and expressions of sexual preference. Rich married in her early twenties and had three children by the time she was thirty; many of her early poems are about heterosexual love, and some of them are quite explicitly about sex (see, for example, "Two Songs," p. 787). More recently she has been involved in a long-term lesbian relationship and has written, again quite explicitly, about sex between women (see, for example, "My mouth hovers," p. 723). In her poems one can trace not only the contours of her changing personal and political life and commitments, but (even more important for the study of poetry generally) one can see as well how changes *within* the poet and *in her social and cultural context* alter the themes and

directions of her work and even change the formal nature of what she tries
to do.

In addition to the poems gathered in this chapter, there are seven other
poems by Adrienne Rich printed elsewhere in the book. If you have been proceeding linearly through the book, you have already read most of these poems
and may have noticed both the cogency of mind they show and the variations
in theme and attitude as Rich has developed and changed during her life and
career. One way to study Rich as an "author in context" is to read carefully
what she has to say about herself and her poems: she is unusually straightforward, explicit, and articulate, and to read her describing her own development
is to be guided carefully through her changing ideas about what is important
both to the individual subjective consciousness and to societal attitudes and
changing roles. Gathered at the end of this chapter are a series of excerpts
from Rich's writing about herself and about poetry more generally, and you
can use these self-conscious reflections as a kind of commentary on the poems
included here and elsewhere in the book.

Here is a chronological list of all the poems and prose commentary
included elsewhere in this book; you can deal with the issues of an author in
context in one of three ways: 1) read the commentary, then the poems; 2) read
the poems, then the commentary; or 3) read the poems and commentary inter-
mixed, in chronological order. Each selection is dated, usually (as throughout
this volume) by publication date below the poem on the right, but sometimes
(when Rich herself has been insistent about it) by the date of composition
listed below the poem on the left.

Aunt Jennifer's Tigers	(1951)	p. 685
Living in Sin	(1955)	p. 907
Two Songs	(1964)	p. 787
[My mouth hovers across your breasts]	(1986)	p. 723
Letters in the Family	(1989)	p. 705
Walking down the Road	(1989)	p. 742
Delta	(1989)	p. 1039

An even better way to study Adrienne Rich (or any poet) is to go to the
library and read all (or as much as you can find) of her writing, and consider
in detail how the various texts interact. Most poets, even John Keats, who lived
only to age twenty-five, change a lot during their careers, and many of the
changes correspond to larger social and cultural changes in their own time and
nation. The best way to think about the contexts of a poet's life and career is to
read as much as possible of their own work along with that of relevant contemporaries. Watching a poet develop within various traditions and contexts can

lead to a far more balanced assessment of a particular career and also to a more exact assessment of what poetry is about in a particular time, era, or culture.

Studying Rich's career in context suggests a number of larger literary, cultural, and historical issues— the kinds of issues that will be explored more fully in the next two chapters. You may well want to think about Adrienne Rich again after you have read the poems in the other chapters—especially the poems in the *Ideas and Consciousness* section of Chapter 12.

▼ ▼ ▼

ADRIENNE RICH

At a Bach Concert

Coming by evening through the wintry city
We said that art is out of love with life.
Here we approach a love that is not pity.

This antique discipline, tenderly severe,
Renews belief in love yet masters feeling,
Asking of us a grace in what we bear.

Form is the ultimate gift that love can offer—
The vital union of necessity
With all that we desire, all that we suffer.

A too-compassionate art is half an art.
Only such proud restraining purity
Restores the else-betrayed, too-human heart.   1951

Storm Warnings

The glass has been falling all the afternoon,
And knowing better than the instrument
What winds are walking overhead, what zone
Of gray unrest is moving across the land,
I leave the book upon a pillowed chair
And walk from window to closed window, watching
Boughs strain against the sky

And think again, as often when the air
Moves inward toward a silent core of waiting,
How with a single purpose time has traveled

By secret currents of the undiscerned
Into this polar realm. Weather abroad
And weather in the heart alike come on
Regardless of prediction.

Between foreseeing and averting change   15
Lies all the mastery of elements
Which clocks and weatherglasses cannot alter.
Time in the hand is not control of time,
Nor shattered fragments of an instrument
A proof against the wind; the wind will rise,   20
We can only close the shutters.

I draw the curtains as the sky goes black
And set a match to candles sheathed in glass
Against the keyhole draught, the insistent whine
Of weather through the unsealed aperture.   25
This is our sole defense against the season;
These are the things that we have learned to do
Who live in troubled regions.   1951

Snapshots of a Daughter-in-Law

1

You, once a belle in Shreveport,
with henna-colored hair, skin like a peachbud,
still have your dresses copied from that time,
and play a Chopin prelude
called by Cortot: *"Delicious recollections*   5
float like perfume through the memory."

Your mind now, mouldering like wedding-cake,
heavy with useless experience, rich
with suspicion, rumor, fantasy,
crumbling to pieces under the knife-edge   10
of mere fact. In the prime of your life.

Nervy, glowering, your daughter
wipes the teaspoons, grows another way.

2

Banging the coffee-pot into the sink
she hears the angels chiding, and looks out   15
past the raked gardens to the sloppy sky.
Only a week since They said: *Have no patience.*

The next time it was: *Be insatiable.*
Then: *Save yourself; others you cannot save.*[1]
10   Sometimes she's let the tapstream scald her arm,
a match burn to her thumbnail,

or held her hand above the kettle's snout
right in the woolly steam. They are probably angels,
since nothing hurts her any more, except
25   each morning's grit blowing into her eyes.

3

A thinking woman sleeps with monsters.
The beak that grips her, she becomes. And Nature,
that sprung-lidded, still commodious
steamer-trunk of *tempora* and *mores*[2]
30   gets stuffed with it all: the mildewed orange-flowers,
the female pills, the terrible breasts
of Boadicea[3] beneath flat foxes' heads and orchids.

Two handsome women, gripped in argument,
each proud, acute, subtle, I hear scream
35   across the cut glass and majolica
like Furies[4] cornered from their prey:
The argument *ad feminam*,[5] all the old knives
that have rusted in my back, I drive in yours,
ma semblable, ma soeur![6]

4

40   Knowing themselves too well in one another:
their gifts no pure fruition, but a thorn,
the prick filed sharp against a hint of scorn . . .
Reading while waiting
for the iron to heat,
45   writing, *My Life had stood—a Loaded Gun—*[7]
in that Amherst pantry while the jellies boil and scum,

---

1. According to Matthew 27:42, the chief priests, scribes, and elders mocked the crucified Jesus by saying, "He saved others; himself he cannot save."   2. Times and customs.   3. Queen of the ancient Britons. When her husband died, the Romans seized the territory he ruled and scourged Boadicea; she then led a heroic but ultimately unsuccessful revolt.   4. In Roman mythology, the three sisters were the avenging spirits of retributive justice.   5. "To the woman" (Latin). The *argumentum ad hominem* (literally, argument to the man) is (in logic) an argument aimed at a person's individual prejudices or special interests.   6. "My mirror-image [or "double"], my sister." Baudelaire, in the prefatory poem to *Les Fleurs du Mal*, addresses (and attacks) his "hypocrite reader" as "mon semblable, mon frère" ("my double, my brother").   7. " 'My Life had stood—a Loaded Gun—' [Poem No. 754], Emily Dickinson, *Complete Poems*, ed. T. H. Johnson, 1960, p. 369." (Rich's note)

or, more often,
iron-eyed and beaked and purposed as a bird,
dusting everything on the whatnot every day of life.

5

Dulce ridens, dulce loquens,[8]   50
she shaves her legs until they gleam
like petrified mammoth-tusk.

6

When to her lute Corinna sings[9]
neither words nor music are her own;
only the long hair dipping   55
over her cheek, only the song
of silk against her knees
and these
adjusted in reflections of an eye.

Poised, trembling and unsatisfied, before   60
an unlocked door, that cage of cages,
tell us, you bird, you tragical machine—
is this *fertilisante douleur?*[1] Pinned down
by love, for you the only natural action,
are you edged more keen   65
to prise the secrets of the vault? has Nature shown
her household books to you, daughter-in-law,
that her sons never saw?

7

"To have in this uncertain world some stay
which cannot be undermined, is   70
of the utmost consequence."[2]
                    Thus wrote
a woman, partly brave and partly good,
who fought with what she partly understood.
Few men about her would or could do more,
hence she was labeled harpy, shrew and whore.   75

---

8. "Sweet [or "winsome"] laughter, sweet chatter." The phrase (slightly modified here) concludes
Horace's *Ode,* 1, 22, describing the appeal of a mistress.   9. The opening line of a famous Elizabethan lyric (by Thomas Campion) in which Corinna's music is said to control totally the poet's
happiness or despair.   1. "Enriching pain" (French).   2. "'. . . is of the utmost consequence,'
from Mary Wollstonecraft, *Thoughts on the Education of Daughters,* London, 1787." (Rich's note)

8

"You all die at fifteen," said Diderot,[3]
and turn part legend, part convention.
Still, eyes inaccurately dream
behind closed windows blankening with steam.
80   Deliciously, all that we might have been,
all that we were—fire, tears,
wit, taste, martyred ambition—
stirs like the memory of refused adultery
the drained and flagging bosom of our middle years.

9

85   *Not that it is done well, but*
that it is done at all?[4] Yes, think
of the odds! or shrug them off forever.
This luxury of the precocious child,
Time's precious chronic invalid,—
90   would we, darlings, resign it if we could?
Our blight has been our sinecure:
mere talent was enough for us—
glitter in fragments and rough drafts.

Sigh no more, ladies.
                                Time is male
95   and in his cups drinks to the fair.
Bemused by gallantry, we hear
our mediocrities over-praised,
indolence read as abnegation,
slattern thought styled intuition,
100 every lapse forgiven, our crime
only to cast too bold a shadow
or smash the mould straight off.

For that, solitary confinement,
tear gas, attrition shelling.
Few applicants for that honor.

---

3. " 'Vous mourez toutes a quinze ans,' from the *Lettres à Sophie Volland*, quoted by Simone de Beauvoir in *Le Deuxième Sexe*, vol. II, pp. 123–4." (Rich's note) Editor of the *Encyclopédie* (the central document of the French Enlightenment), Diderot became disillusioned with the traditional education of women and undertook an experimental education for his own daughter.   **4.** Samuel Johnson's comment on women preachers: "Sir, a woman's preaching is like a dog's walking on his hinder legs. It is not done well, but you are surprised to find it done at all." (Boswell's *Life of Johnson*, ed. L. F. Powell and G. B. Hill, Oxford: Clarendon, 1934–64, I, 463)

10

Well,
she's long about her coming, who must be
more merciless to herself than history.[5]
Her mind full to the wind, I see her plunge
breasted and glancing through the currents,
taking the light upon her
at least as beautiful as any boy
or helicopter,
                poised, still coming,
her fine blades making the air wince

but her cargo
no promise then:
delivered
palpable
ours.

105

110

115

1958–60

In *When We Dead Awaken*, Rich describes her consciousness during the time she was writing this poem:

Over two years I wrote a 10-part poem called "Snapshots of a Daughter-in-Law," in a longer, looser mode than I've ever trusted myself with before. It was an extraordinary relief to write that poem. It strikes me now as too literary, too dependent on allusion; I hadn't found the courage yet to do without authorities, or even to use the pronoun "I"—the woman in the poem is always "she." One section of it, #2, concerns a woman who thinks she is going mad; she is haunted by voices telling her to resist and rebel, voices which she can hear but not obey.

Orion

Far back when I went zig-zagging
through tamarack pastures
you were my genius, you
my cast-iron Viking, my helmed
lion-heart king in prison.
Years later now you're young

5

5. "Cf. *Le Deuxième Sexe*, vol. II, p. 574: '. . . . elle arrive du fond des ages, de Thèbes, de Minos, de Chichen Itza; et elle est aussi le totem planté au coeur de la brousse africaine; c'est un helicoptère et c'est un oiseau; et voilà la plus grande merveille: sous ses cheveux peints le bruissement des feuillages devient une pensée et des paroles s'échappent de ses seins.' " (Rich's note)

my fierce half-brother, staring
down from that simplified west
your breast open, your belt dragged down
10 by an oldfashioned thing, a sword
the last bravado you won't give over
though it weighs you down as you stride

and the stars in it are dim
and maybe have stopped burning.
15 But you burn, and I know it;
as I throw back my head to take you in
an old transfusion happens again:
divine astronomy is nothing to it.

Indoors I bruise and blunder,
20 break faith, leave ill enough
alone, a dead child born in the dark.
Night cracks up over the chimney,
pieces of time, frozen geodes
come showering down in the grate.

25 A man reaches behind my eyes
and finds them empty
a woman's head turns away
from my head in the mirror
children are dying my death
30 and eating crumbs of my life.

Pity is not your forte.
Calmly you ache up there
pinned aloft in your crow's nest,
my speechless pirate!
35 You take it all for granted
and when I look you back

it's with a starlike eye
shooting its cold and egotistical spear
where it can do least damage.
40 Breathe deep! No hurt, no pardon
out here in the cold with you
you with your back to the wall.   1965

In *When We Dead Awaken*, Rich describes "Orion" as

a poem of reconstruction with a part of myself I had felt I was losing—the active
principle, the energetic imagination, the "half-brother" whom I projected, as I had
for many years, into the constellation Orion. It's no accident that the words "cold
and egotistical" appear in this poem, and are applied to myself. The choice still
seemed to be between "love"—womanly, maternal love, altruistic love—a love

defined and ruled by the weight of an entire culture—and egotism—a force directed by men into creation, achievement, ambition, often at the expense of others, but justifiably so. For weren't they men, and wasn't that their destiny as womanly love was ours? I know now that the alternatives are false ones—that the word "love" is itself in need of re-vision.

Leaflets

1

The big star, and that other
lonely on black glass
overgrown with frozen
lesions, endless night
the Coal Sack gaping   5
black veins of ice on the pane
spelling a word:
     Insomnia
not manic but ordinary
to start out of sleep
turning off and on   10
this seasick neon
vision, this
division

the head clears of sweet smoke
and poison gas   15

life without caution
the only worth living
love for a man
love for a woman
love for the facts   20
protectless

that self-defense be not
the arm's first motion

memory not only
cards of identity   25

that I can live half a year
as I have never lived up to this time—[6]

6. Quoted from a letter by Anton Chekhov to I. L. Scheglov, March 22, 1890, explaining his forth-coming visit to Saghalien, an island penal colony. Chekhov (1860–1904), the Russian playwright and short story writer, had contracted tuberculosis at age 23 (see line 28).

Chekhov coughing up blood almost daily
the steamer edging in toward the penal colony
30   chained men dozing on deck
five forest fires lighting the island

lifelong that glare, waiting.

2

Your face
        stretched like a mask
                begins to tear
as you speak of Che Guevara[7]
35   Bolivia, Nanterre
I'm too young to be your mother
you're too young to be my brother

your tears are not political
they are real water, burning
40   as the tears of Telemachus
burned

Over Spanish Harlem the moon
swells up, a fire balloon
fire gnawing the edge
of this crushed-up newspaper

45   now
the bodies come whirling
coal-black, ash-white
out of torn windows
and the death columns blacken
50   whispering
Who'd choose this life?

We're fighting for a slash of recognition,
a piercing to the pierced heart.
Tell me what you are going through—[8]

55   but the attention flickers
               and will flicker
a matchflame in poison air
a thread, a hair of light
                sum of all answer
60   to the *Know that I exist!* of all existing things.

---

7. Latin American revolutionary theorist and an early leader in the Castro regime in Cuba. Guevara was killed in the abortive Bolivian revolution in 1967. *Nanterre:* one site of the 1968 French student uprising.   8. "Simone Weil: 'The love of a fellow-creature in all its fullness consists simply in the ability to say to him: "What are you going through" ' — *Waiting For God.*" (Rich's note)

3

If, says the Dahomeyan devil,[9]
someone has courage to enter the fire
the young man will be restored to life.

If, the girl whispers,
I do not go into the fire   65
I will not be able to live with my soul.

(Her face calm and dark as amber
under the dyed butterfly turban
her back scarified in ostrich-skin patterns.)

4

Crusaders' wind glinting   70
off linked scales of sea
ripping the ghostflags
galloping at the fortress
Acre, bloodcaked, lionhearted
raw vomit curdling in the sun   75
gray walkers walking
straying with a curbed intentness
in and out the inclosures
the gallows, the photographs
of dead Jewish terrorists, aged 15   80
their fading faces wide-eyed
and out in the crusading sunlight
gray strayers still straying
dusty paths
the mad who live in the dried-up moat   85
of the War Museum

what are we coming to
what wants these things of us
who wants them

5

The strain of being born   90
       over and over has torn your smile into pieces
Often I have seen it broken
       and then re-membered
and wondered how a beauty
       so anarch, so ungelded   95
will be cared for in this world.

9. Legba the trickster.

I want to hand you this
leaflet streaming with rain or tears
    but the words coming clear
something you might find crushed into your hand
    after passing a barricade
and stuff in your raincoat pocket.
    I want this to reach you
who told me once that poetry is nothing sacred
    —no more sacred that is
than other things in your life—
    to answer yes, if life is uncorrupted
no better poetry is wanted.

    I want this to be yours
in the sense that if you find and read it
    it will be there in you already
and the leaflet then merely something
    to leave behind, a little leaf
in the drawer of a sublet room.
    What else does it come down to
but handing on scraps of paper
    little figurines or phials
no stronger than the dry clay they are baked in
    yet more than dry clay or paper
because the imagination crouches in them.
    If we needed fire to remind us
that all true images
    were scooped out of the mud
where our bodies curse and flounder
    then perhaps that fire is coming
to sponge away the scribes and time-servers
    and much that you would have loved will be lost as well
before you could handle it and know it
    just as we almost miss each other
in the ill cloud of mistrust, who might have touched
    hands quickly, shared food or given blood
for each other. I am thinking how we can use what we have
    to invent what we need.

Winter–Spring 1968

Planetarium

*(Thinking of Caroline Herschel, 1750–1848,
astronomer, sister of William; and others)*

A woman in the shape of a monster
a monster in the shape of a woman
the skies are full of them

a woman   "in the snow
among the Clocks and instruments   5
or measuring the ground with poles"

in her 98 years to discover
8 comets

she whom the moon ruled
like us   10
levitating into the night sky
riding the polished lenses

Galaxies of women, there
doing penance for impetuousness
ribs chilled   15
in those spaces   of the mind

An eye,
       "virile, precise and absolutely certain"
       from the mad webs of Uranisborg
                     encountering the NOVA   20

every impulse of light exploding
from the core
as life flies out of us

       Tycho[1] whispering at last
       "Let me not seem to have lived in vain"   25

What we see, we see
and seeing is changing

the light that shrivels a mountain
and leaves a man alive

Heartbeat of the pulsar   30
heart sweating through my body

1. Tycho Brahe (1546–1601), Danish astronomer whose cosmology tried to fuse the Ptolemaic and Copernican systems. He discovered and described (*De Nova Stella*, 1573) a new star in what had previously been considered a fixed star-system. Uranisborg (line 19) was Tycho's famous and elaborate palace-laboratory-observatory.

The radio impulse
pouring in from Taurus
      I am bombarded yet   I stand

35   I have been standing all my life in the
direct path of a battery of signals
the most accurately transmitted most
untranslatable language in the universe
I am a galactic cloud so deep   so invo-

40   luted that a light wave could take 15
years to travel through me   And has
taken   I am an instrument in the shape
of a woman trying to translate pulsations
into images   for the relief of the body

45   and the reconstruction of the mind.

1968

Rich describes this poem, in *When We Dead Awaken*, as a "companion poem to 'Orion,'" above:

at last the woman in the poem and the woman writing the poem become the same person. . . . It was written after a visit to a real planetarium, where I read an account of the work of Caroline Herschel, the astronomer, who worked with her brother William, but whose name remained obscure, as his did not.

Dialogue

She sits with one hand poised against her head, the
other turning an old ring to the light
for hours our talk has beaten
like rain against the screens

5   a sense of August and heat-lightning
I get up, go to make tea, come back
we look at each other
then she says (and this is what I live through
over and over)—she says: *I do not know*

10   *if sex is an illusion*

I do not know
who I was when I did those things
or who I said I was
or whether I willed to feel

15   *what I had read about*
or who in fact was there with me

or whether I knew, even then
that there was doubt about these things

1972

Diving into the Wreck

First having read the book of myths,
and loaded the camera,
and checked the edge of the knife-blade,
I put on
the body-armor of black rubber   5
the absurd flippers
the grave and awkward mask.
I am having to do this
not like Cousteau with his
assiduous team   10
aboard the sun-flooded schooner
but here alone.

There is a ladder.
The ladder is always there
hanging innocently   15
close to the side of the schooner.
We know what it is for,
we who have used it.
Otherwise
it's a piece of maritime floss   20
some sundry equipment.

I go down.
Rung after rung and still
the oxygen immerses me
the blue light   25
the clear atoms
of our human air.
I go down.
My flippers cripple me,
I crawl like an insect down the ladder   30
and there is no one
to tell me when the ocean
will begin.

First the air is blue and then
it is bluer and then green and then   35
black I am blacking out and yet
my mask is powerful
it pumps my blood with power
the sea is another story

40   the sea is not a question of power
    I have to learn alone
    to turn my body without force
    in the deep element.

    And now: it is easy to forget
45   what I came for
    among so many who have always
    lived here
    swaying their crenellated fans
    between the reefs
50   and besides
    you breathe differently down here.

    I came to explore the wreck.
    The words are purposes.
    The words are maps.
55   I came to see the damage that was done
    and the treasures that prevail.
    I stroke the beam of my lamp
    slowly along the flank
    of something more permanent
60   than fish or weed

    the thing I came for:
    the wreck and not the story of the wreck
    the thing itself and not the myth
    the drowned face always staring
65   toward the sun
    the evidence of damage
    worn by salt and sway into this threadbare beauty
    the ribs of the disaster
    curving their assertion
70   among the tentative haunters.

    This is the place.
    And I am here, the mermaid whose dark hair
    streams black, the merman in his armored body
    We circle silently
75   about the wreck
    we dive into the hold.
    I am she: I am he
    whose drowned face sleeps with open eyes
    whose breasts still bear the stress
80   whose silver, copper, vermeil cargo lies
    obscurely inside barrels
    half-wedged and left to rot
    we are the half-destroyed instruments
    that once held to a course

the water-eaten log   85
the fouled compass

We are, I am, you are
by cowardice or courage
the one who find our way
back to this scene   90
carrying a knife, a camera
a book of myths
in which
our names do not appear.

1972

Power

Living   in the earth-deposits   of our history

Today a backhoe divulged   out of a crumbling flank of earth
one bottle   amber   perfect   a hundred-year-old
cure for fever   or melancholy   a tonic
for living on this earth   in the winters of this climate   5

Today I was reading about Marie Curie:
she must have known she suffered   from radiation sickness
her body bombarded for years   by the element
she had purified
It seems she denied to the end   10
the source of the cataracts on her eyes
the cracked and suppurating skin   of her finger-ends
till she could no longer hold   a test-tube or a pencil

She died   a famous woman   denying
her wounds   15
denying
her wounds   came   from the same source as her power

1974   1978

Origins and History of Consciousness

I

Night-life. Letters, journals, bourbon
sloshed in the glass. Poems crucified on the wall,
dissected, their bird-wings severed

like trophies. No one lives in this room
5 without living through some kind of crisis.

No one lives in this room
without confronting the whiteness of the wall
behind the poems, planks of books,
photographs of dead heroines.
10 Without contemplating last and late
the true nature of poetry. The drive
to connect. The dream of a common language.

Thinking of lovers, their blind faith, their
experienced crucifixions,
15 my envy is not simple. I have dreamed of going to bed
as walking into clear water ringed by a snowy wood
white as cold sheets, thinking, *I'll freeze in there.*
My bare feet are numbed already by the snow
but the water
20 is mild, I sink and float
like a warm amphibious animal
that has broken the net, has run
through fields of snow leaving no print;
this water washes off the scent—
25 *You are clear now*
of the hunter, the trapper
the wardens of the mind—

yet the warm animal dreams on
of another animal
30 swimming under the snow-flecked surface of the pool,
and wakes, and sleeps again.

No one sleeps in this room without
the dream of a common language.

II

It was simple to meet you, simple to take your eyes
35 into mine, saying: these are eyes I have known
from the first. . . . It was simple to touch you
against the hacked background, the grain of what we
had been, the choices, years. . . . It was even simple
to take each other's lives in our hands, as bodies.
40 What is not simple: to wake from drowning
from where the ocean beat inside us like an afterbirth
into this common, acute particularity
these two selves who walked half a lifetime untouching—
to wake to something deceptively simple: a glass
45 sweated with dew, a ring of the telephone, a scream

of someone beaten up far down in the street
causing each of us to listen to her own inward scream

knowing the mind of the mugger and the mugged
as any woman must who stands to survive this city,
this century, this life . . .   50

each of us having loved the flesh in its clenched or loosened beauty
better than trees or music (yet loving those too
as if they were flesh—and they are—but the flesh
of beings unfathomed as yet in our roughly literal life).

III

It's simple to wake from sleep with a stranger,   55
dress, go out, drink coffee,
enter a life again. It isn't simple
to wake from sleep into the neighborhood
of one neither strange nor familiar
whom we have chosen to trust. Trusting, untrusting,   60
we lowered ourselves into this, let ourselves
downward hand over hand as on a rope that quivered
over the unsearched. . . . We did this. Conceived
of each other, conceived each other in a darkness
which I remember as drenched in light.   65
                            I want to call this, life.

But I can't call it life until we start to move
beyond this secret circle of fire
where our bodies are giant shadows flung on a wall
where the night becomes our inner darkness, and sleeps   70
like a dumb beast, head on her paws, in the corner.

1972–74   1978

For the Record

The clouds and the stars didn't wage this war
the brooks gave no information
if the mountain spewed stones of fire into the river
it was not taking sides
the raindrop faintly swaying under the leaf   5
had no political opinions

and if here or there a house
filled with backed-up raw sewage
or poisoned those who lived there
with slow fumes, over years   10

the houses were not at war
nor did the tinned-up buildings

intend to refuse shelter
to homeless old women and roaming children
15   they had no policy to keep them roaming
or dying, no, the cities were not the problem
the bridges were non-partisan
the freeways burned, but not with hatred

Even the miles of barbed-wire
20   stretched around crouching temporary huts
designed to keep the unwanted
at a safe distance, out of sight
even the boards that had to absorb
year upon year, so many human sounds

25   so many depths of vomit, tears
slow-soaking blood
had not offered themselves for this
The trees didn't volunteer to be cut into boards
nor the thorns for tearing flesh
30   Look around at all of it

and ask whose signature
is stamped on the orders, traced
in the corner of the building plans
Ask where the illiterate, big-bellied
35   women were, the drunks and crazies,
the ones you fear most of all: ask where you were.   1983

from Talking with Adrienne Rich[2]

* * * I think of myself as using poetry as a chief means of self-exploration—one of several means, of which maybe another would be dreams, really thinking about, paying attention to dreams, but the poem, like the dream, does this through images and it is in the images of my poems that I feel I am finding out more about my own experience, my sense of things. But I don't think of myself as having a position or a self-description which I'm then going to present in the poem.

When I started writing poetry I was tremendously conscious of, and very much in need of, a formal structure that could be obtained from outside, into which I could pour whatever I had, whatever I thought I had to express. But I think that was a part of a whole thing that I see, now as a teacher, very much

2. A transcript of a conversation recorded March 9, 1971, and printed in the *Ohio Review*, Fall 1971.

with young writers, of using language more as a kind of façade than as either self-revelation or as a probe into one's own consciousness. I think I would attribute a lot of the change in my poetry simply to the fact of growing older, undergoing certain kinds of experiences, realizing that formal metrics were not going to suffice me in dealing with those experiences, realizing that experience itself is much more fragmentary, much more sort of battering, much ruder than these structures would allow, and it had to find its own form.

I have a very strong sense about the existence of poetry in daily life and poetry being part of the world as it is, and that the attempt to reduce poetry to what is indited on a page just limits you terribly. . . . The poem is the poetry of things lodged in the innate shape of the experience. My saying "The moment of change is the only poem" is the kind of extreme statement you feel the need to make at certain times if only to force someone to say, "But I always thought a poem is something written on a piece of paper," you know, and to say: "But look, how did those words get on that piece of paper." There had to be a mind; there had to be an experience; the mind had to go through certain shocks, certain stresses, certain strains, and if you're going to carry the poem back to its real beginnings it's that moment of change. I feel that we are always writing.

When I was in my twenties * * * I was going through a very sort of female thing—of trying to distinguish between the ego that is capable of writing poems, and then this other kind of being that you're asked to be if you're a woman, who is, in a sense, denying that ego. I had great feelings of split about that for many years actually, and there are a lot of poems I couldn't write even, because I didn't want to confess to having that much aggression, that much ego, that much sense of myself. I had always thought of my first book as being a book of very well-tooled poems of a sort of very bright student, which I was at that time, but poems in which the unconscious things never got to the surface. But there's a poem in that book about a woman who sews a tapestry and the tapestry has figures of tigers on it. But the woman is represented as being completely—her hand is burdened by the weight of the wedding band, and she's meek, and she's fearful, and the only way in which she can express any other side of her nature is in embroidering these tigers. Well, I thought of that as almost a formal exercise, but when I go back and look at that poem I really think it's saying something about what I was going through. And now that's lessened a great deal for all sorts of reasons—that split.

from An Interview with Adrienne Rich[3]

I would have said ten or fifteen years ago that I would not even want to identify myself as a woman poet. That term *has* been used pejoratively; I just don't think

3. By David Kalstone, in the *Saturday Review*, April 22, 1972.

it can be at this point. You know, for a woman the act of creation is prototypically to produce children, while the act of creating with language—I'm not saying that women writers haven't been accepted; certainly, more have been accepted than women lawyers or doctors. Still, a woman writer feels, she is going against the grain—or there has been this sense until very recently (if there isn't still). Okay, it's all right to be a young thing and write verse. But a friend of mine was telling me about meeting a noted poet at a cocktail party. She'd sent him a manuscript for a contest he was judging. She went up to him and asked him about it, and he looked at her and said, "Young girls *are* poems; they shouldn't write them." This attitude toward women poets manifests itself so strongly that you are made to feel you are becoming the thing you are not.

If a man is writing, he's gone through all the nonsense and said "Okay, I am a poet and I'm still a man. They don't cancel each other out or, if they do, then I'll opt to be a poet." He's not writing for a hostile sex, a breed of critics who by virtue of their sex are going to look at his language and pass judgment on it. That does happen to a woman. I don't know why the woman poet has been slower than the woman novelist in taking risks though I'm very grateful that this is no longer so. I feel that I dare to think further than I would have dared to think ten years ago—and *that* certainly is going to affect my writing. And I now dare to entertain thoughts and speculations that then would have seemed unthinkable.

Many of the male writers whom I very much admire—Galway Kinnell, James Wright, W. S. Merwin—are writing poetry of such great desolation. They come from different backgrounds, write in different ways, and yet all seem to write out of a sense of doom, as if we were fated to carry on these terribly flawed relationships. I think it's expressive of a feeling that "we, the masters, have created a world that's impossible to live in and that probably may not be livable in, in a very literal sense. What we thought, what we'd been given to think is our privilege, our right, and our sexual prerogative has led to this, to our doom." I guess a lot of women—if not a lot of women poets—are feeling that there has to be some other way, that human life is messed-up but that it doesn't have to be *this* desolate.

Today, much poetry by women is charged with anger and uses voices of rage and anger that I don't think were ever used in poetry before. In poets like Sylvia Plath and Diane Wakoski, say, those voices are so convincing that it is impossible to describe them by using those favorite adjectives of phallic criticism—shrill and hysterical. Well, Sylvia Plath is dead. I always maintained from the first time I read her last poems that her suicide was not necessary, that she could have gone on and written poems that would have given us even more insight into the states of anger and willfulness, even of self-destructiveness, that women experience. She didn't need literally to destroy herself in order to reflect and express those things. Diane Wakoski is a young woman. She's changing a lot and will continue to change. What I admire in her, besides her energy and dynamism and quite a beautiful gift for snatching the image that she wants out of the air, is her honesty. No woman has written before about her face and said she hated it, that it had served her ill, that she wished she could throw acid in it. That's very shocking. But I think all women, even the most beautiful women, at times have felt that in a kind of self-hatred. Because the *face* is supposed to be the *woman.*

A lot of poetry is becoming more oral. Certainly, it's true of women and black poets. Reading black poetry on the printed page gives no sense of the poem, if you're going to look at that poetry the way you look at poems by Richard Wilbur. Yet you can hear these poets read and realize it's the oldest kind of poetry.

I think the energy of language comes somewhat from the pressure and need and unbearableness of what's being done to you. It's not the same energy you find in the blues. The blues are a grief language, a lost language, and a cry of pain, usually in a woman's voice, which is interesting. For a long time you sing the blues, and then you begin to say, "I'm tired of singing the blues. I want something else." And that's what you're hearing now. There seems to be a connection between an oppressed condition and having access to certain kinds of energy, vitality, and subjectivity. For women as well as blacks. Though I don't feel there is a necessary cause-and-effect relationship; what seems to happen is that being on top, being in a powerful position leads to a divorce between one's unruly, chaotic, revolutionary sensitivity and one's reason, sense of order and of maintaining a hold. And, therefore, you have at the bottom of the pile, so to speak, a kind of churning energy that gets lost up there among the administrators.

I don't know how or whether poetry changes anything. But neither do I know how or whether bombing or even community organizing changes anything when we are pitted against a massive patriarchal system armed with supertechnology. I believe in subjectivity—that a lot of male Left leaders have turned into Omnipotent Administrators, because their "masculinity" forced them to deny their subjectivity. I believe in dreams and visions and "the madness of art." And at moments I can conceive of a women's movement that will show the way to humanizing technology and fusing dreams and skills and visions and reason to begin the healing of the human race. But I don't want women to take over the world and run it the way men have, or to take on—yet again!—the burden of carrying the subjectivity of the race. Women are a vanguard now, and I believe will increasingly become so, because we have—Western women, Third World women, all women—known and felt the pain of the human condition most consistently. But in the end it can't be women alone.

from When We Dead Awaken: Writing as Re-Vision[4]

Most, if not all, human lives are full of fantasy—passive daydreaming which need not be acted on. But to write poetry or fiction, or even to think well, is not to fantasize, or to put fantasies on paper. For a poem to coalesce, for a character or an action to take shape, there has to be an imaginative transformation of reality which is in no way passive. And a certain freedom of the mind is needed—freedom to press on, to enter the currents of your thought like a glider pilot, knowing that your motion can be sustained, that the buoyancy of your attention will not be suddenly snatched away. Moreover, if the imagination is to transcend and transform experience it has to question, to challenge, to conceive of alternatives, perhaps to the very life you are living at that moment. You have to be free to play around with the notion that day might be night, love might be hate, nothing can be too sacred for the imagination to turn into its opposite or to call experimentally by another name. For writing is re-naming. Now, to be maternally with small children all day in the old way, to be with a man in the old way of marriage, requires a holding-back, a putting-aside of that imaginative activity, and demands instead a kind of conservatism. I want to make it clear that I am *not* saying that in order to write well, or think well, it is necessary to become unavailable to others, or to become a devouring ego. This has been the myth of the masculine artist and thinker; and I do not accept it. But to be a female human being trying to fulfill traditional female functions in a traditional way *is* in direct conflict with the subversive function of the imagination. The word traditional is important here. There must be ways, and we will be finding out more and more about them, in which the energy of creation and the energy of relation can be united. But in those earlier years I always felt the conflict as a failure of love in myself. I had thought I was choosing a full life: the life available to most men, in which sexuality, work, and parenthood could coexist. But I felt, at twenty-nine, guilt toward the people closest to me, and guilty toward my own being.

I wanted, then, more than anything, the one thing of which there was never enough: time to think, time to write. The fifties and early sixties were years of rapid revelations: the sit-ins and marches in the South, the Bay of Pigs, the early antiwar movement, raised large questions—questions for which the masculine world of the academy around me seemed to have expert and fluent answers. But I needed to think for myself—about pacifism and dissent and violence, about poetry and society, and about my own relationship to all these things. For about ten years I was reading in fierce snatches, scribbling in notebooks, writing poetry in fragments; I was looking desperately for clues, because if there were no clues then I thought I might be insane. I wrote in a notebook about this time:

4. First published in *College English* in 1972; this version slightly revised, is included in *On Lies, Secrets, and Silence: Selected Prose: 1966–1978* (1979).

Paralyzed by the sense that there exists a mesh of relationships—e.g., between my anger at the children, my sensual life, pacifism, sex (I mean sex in its broadest significance, not merely sexual desire)—an interconnectedness which, if I could see it, make it valid, would give me back myself, make it possible to function lucidly and passionately. Yet I grope in and out among these dark webs.

I think I began at this point to feel that politics was not something "out there" but something "in here" and of the essence of my condition.

In the late fifties I was able to write, for the first time, directly about experiencing myself as a woman. The poem was jotted in fragments during children's naps, brief hours in a library, or at 3 A.M. after rising with a wakeful child. I despaired of doing any continuous work at this time. Yet I began to feel that my fragments and scraps had a common consciousness and a common theme, one which I would have been very unwilling to put on paper at an earlier time because I had been taught that poetry should be "universal," which meant, of course, nonfemale. Until then I had tried very much *not* to identify myself as a female poet.

How Does a Poet Put Bread on the Table?[5]

But how does a poet put bread on the table? Rarely, if ever, by poetry alone. Of the four lesbian poets at the Nuyorican Poets Café about whose lives I know something, one directs an underfunded community arts project, two are untenured college teachers, one an assistant dean of students at a state university. Of other poets I know, most teach, often part time, without security but year round; two are on disability; one does clerical work; one cleans houses; one is a paid organizer; one has a paid editing job. Whatever odd money comes in erratically from readings and workshops, grants, permissions fees, royalties, prizes can be very odd money indeed, never to be counted on and almost always small: checks have to be chased down, grants become fewer and more competitive in a worsening political and economic climate. Most poets who teach at universities are untenured, without pension plans or group health insurance, or are employed at public and community colleges with heavy teaching loads and low salaries. Many give unpaid readings and workshops as part of their political "tithe."

Inherited wealth accounts for the careers of some poets: to inherit wealth is to inherit time. Most of the poets I know, hearing of a sum of money, translate it not into possessions, but into time—that precious immaterial necessity of our lives. It's true that a poem can be attempted in brief interstitial moments, pulled out of the pocket and worked on while waiting for a bus or riding a train or while children nap or while waiting for a new batch of clerical work or blood samples to come in. But only certain kinds of poems are amenable to these

5. From *What Is Found There: Notebooks on Poetry and Politics* (1993).

conditions. Sometimes the very knowledge of coming interruption dampens the flicker. And there is a difference between the ordinary "free" moments stolen from exhausting family strains, from alienating labor, from thought chained by material anxiety, and those other moments that sometimes arrive in a life being lived at its height though under extreme tension; perhaps we are waiting to initiate some act we believe will catalyze change but whose outcome is uncertain; perhaps we are facing personal or communal crisis in which everything unimportant seems to fall away and we are left with our naked lives, the brevity of life itself, and words. At such times we may experience a speeding-up of our imaginative powers, images and voices rush together in a kind of inevitability, what was externally fragmented is internally recognized, and the hand can barely keep pace.

But such moments presuppose other times: when we could simply stare into the wood grain of a door, or the trace of bubbles in a glass of water as long as we wanted to, *almost* secure in the knowledge that there would be no interruption—times of slowness, or purposelessness.

Often such time feels like a luxury, guiltily seized when it can be had, fearfully taken because it does not seem like work, this abeyance, but like "wasting time" in a society where personal importance—even job security—can hinge on acting busy, where the phrase "keeping busy" is a common idiom, where there is, for activists, so much to be done.

Most, if not all, of the names we know in North American poetry are the names of people who have had some access to freedom in time—that privilege of some which is actually a necessity for all. The struggle to limit the working day is a sacred struggle for the worker's freedom in time. To feel herself or himself, for a few hours or a weekend, as a free being with choices—to plant vegetables and later sit on the porch with a cold beer, to write poetry or build a fence or fish or play cards, to walk without a purpose, to make love in the day-time. To sleep late. Ordinary human pleasures, the self's re-creation. Yet every working generation has to reclaim that freedom in time, and many are brutally thwarted in the effort. Capitalism is based on the abridgment of that freedom.

Poets in the United States have either had some kind of private means, or help from people with private means, have held full-time, consuming jobs, or have chosen to work in low-paying, part-time sectors of the economy, saving their creative energies for poetry, keeping their material wants simple. Interstitial living, where the art itself is not expected to bring in much money, where the artist may move from a clerical job to part-time, temporary teaching to subsistence living on the land to waitressing or doing construction or translating, typesetting, or ghostwriting. In the 1990s this kind of interstitial living is more difficult, risky, and wearing than it has ever been, and this is a loss to all the arts—as much as the shrinkage of arts funding, the censorship-by-clique, the censorship by the Right, the censorship by distribution.

A Communal Poetry[6]

One day in New York in the late 1980s, I had lunch with a poet I'd known for more than twenty years. Many of his poems were—are—embedded in my life. We had read together at the antiwar events of the Vietnam years. Then, for a long time, we hardly met. As a friend, he had seemed to me withheld, defended in a certain way I defined as masculine and with which I was becoming in general impatient; yet often, in their painful beauty, his poems told another story. On this day, he was as I had remembered him: distant, stiff, shy perhaps. The conversation stumbled along as we talked about our experiences with teaching poetry, which seemed a safe ground. I made some remark about how long it was since last we'd talked. Suddenly, his whole manner changed: *You disappeared! You simply disappeared.* I realized he meant not so much from his life as from a landscape of poetry to which he though we both belonged and were in some sense loyal.

If anything, those intervening years had made me feel more apparent, more visible—to myself and to others—as a poet. The powerful magnet of the women's liberation movement—and the women's poetry movement it released—had drawn me to coffeehouses where women were reading new kinds of poems; to emerging "journals of liberation" that published women's poems, often in a context of political articles and the beginnings of feminist criticism; to bookstores selling chapbooks and pamphlets from the new women's presses; to a woman poet's workshops with women in prison; to meetings with other women poets in Chinese restaurants, coffee shops, apartments, where we talked not only of poetry, but of the conditions that make it possible or impossible. It had never occurred to me that I was disappearing—rather, that I was, along with other women poets, beginning to appear. In fact, we were taking part in an immense shift in human consciousness.

My old friend had, I believe, not much awareness of any of this. It was, for him, so off-to-the-edge, so out-of-the-way; perhaps so dangerous, it seemed I had sunk, or dived, into a black hole. Only later, in a less constrained and happier meeting, were we able to speak of the different ways we had perceived that time.

He thought there had been a known, defined poetic landscape and that as poetic contemporaries we simply shared it. But whatever poetic "generation" I belonged to, in the 1950s I was a mother, under thirty, raising three small children. Notwithstanding the prize and the fellowship to Europe that my first book of poems had won me, there was little or no "appearance" I then felt able to claim as a poet, against that other profound and as yet unworded reality.

6. From *What Is Found There: Notebooks on Poetry and Politics* (1993).

CHRONOLOGY

1929   Born in Baltimore, Maryland, May 16. Began writing poetry as a child under the encouragement and supervision of her father, Dr. Arnold Rich, from whose "very Victorian, pre-Raphaelite" library, Rich later recalled, she read Tennyson, Keats, Arnold, Blake, Rossetti, Swinburne, Carlyle, and Pater.

1951   A.B., Radcliffe College. Phi Beta Kappa. *A Change of World* chosen by W. H. Auden for the Young Poets Award and published.

1952–53   Guggenheim Fellowship; travel in Europe and England. Marriage to Alfred H. Conrad, an economist who taught at Harvard. Residence in Cambridge, Massachusetts, 1953–66.

1955   Birth of David Conrad. Publication of *The Diamond Cutters and Other Poems,* which won the Ridgely Torrence Memorial Award of the Poetry Society of America.

1957   Birth of Paul Conrad.

1959   Birth of Jacob Conrad.

1960   National Institute of Arts and Letters Award for poetry. Phi Beta Kappa poet at William and Mary College.

1961–62   Guggenheim Fellowship; residence with family in the Netherlands.

1962   Bollingen Foundation grant for translation of Dutch poetry.

1962–63   Amy Lowell Travelling Fellowship.

1963   *Snapshots of a Daughter-in-Law* published. Bess Hokin Prize of *Poetry* magazine.

1965   Phi Beta Kappa poet at Swarthmore College.

1966   *Necessities of Life* published, nominated for the National Book Award. Phi Beta Kappa poet at Harvard College. Move to New York City, where Alfred Conrad taught at City College of New York. Residence there from 1966 on. Increasingly active politically in protests against the Indochina war.

1966–68   Lecturer at Swarthmore College.

1967–69   Adjunct Professor of Writing in the Graduate School of the Arts, Columbia University.

1967   *Selected Poems* published in Britain. Litt.D., Wheaton College.

1968   Eunice Tietjens Memorial Prize of *Poetry* magazine. Began teaching in the SEEK and Open Admissions Programs at City College of New York.

1969   *Leaflets* published.

1970   Death of Alfred Conrad.

1971   *The Will to Change* published. Shelley Memorial Award of the Poetry Society of America. Increasingly identifies with the women's movement as a radical feminist.

1972–73   Fanny Hurst Visiting Professor of Creative Literature at Brandeis University.

1973   *Diving into the Wreck* published.

1973–74   Ingram Merrill Foundation research grant; began work on a book on the history and myths of motherhood.

1974   National Book Award for *Diving into the Wreck.* Rich rejected the award as an individual, but accepted it, in a statement written with Audre Lorde and Alice Walker, two other nominees, in the name of all women:

> We . . . together accept this award in the name of all the women whose voices have gone and still go unheard in a patriarchal world, and in the name of those who, like us, have been tolerated as token women in this

culture, often at great cost and in great pain. . . . We symbolically join here in refusing the terms of patriarchal competition and declaring that we will share this prize among us, to be used as best we can for women. . . . We dedicate this occasion to the struggle for self-determination of all women, of every color, identification or derived class . . . the women who will not understand yet; the silent women whose voices have been denied us, the articulate women who have given us strength to do our work.

Professor of English, City College of New York.

1975   *Poems: Selected and New* published.

1976   Professor of English at Douglass College. *Of Woman Born: Motherhood as Experience and Institution* published. *Twenty-one Love Poems* published.

1978   *The Dream of a Common Language: Poems 1974–1977* published.

1979   *On Lies, Secrets, and Silence: Selected Prose 1966–1978* published. Leaves Douglass College and New York City; moves to Montague, Massachusetts; edits, with Michelle Cliff, the lesbian-feminist journal, *Sinister Wisdom.*

1981   *A Wild Patience Has Taken Me This Far: Poems 1978–1981* published.

1984   *The Fact of a Doorframe: Poems Selected and New 1950–1984* published. Moves to Santa Cruz, California.

1986   *Blood, Bread, and Poetry: Selected Prose 1979–1985* published. Professor of English at Stanford University.

1989   *Time's Power: Poems 1985–1988* published.

1990   Member of the Department of Literature of the American Academy and Institute of Arts and Letters.

1991   *An Atlas of the Difficult World* published.

1992   Wins *Los Angeles Times* Book Prize for *An Atlas of the Difficult World*, the Lenore Marshall/*Nation* Prize for Poetry, and Nicholas Roerich Museum Poet's Prize; is co-winner of the Frost Silver Medal for distinguished lifetime achievement.

1993   *What Is Found There: Notebooks on Poetry and Politics* published.

1994   Awarded MacArthur fellowship.

▼ ▼ ▼

QUESTION

What significant differences do you notice among the poems by Adrienne Rich that appear throughout this volume? Can you tell quickly an early Rich poem from a later one? What are the differences in subject matter? in style? in situation? in strategies of argument? Try to read all the Rich poems in the book at one sitting, working in poems to be found elsewhere in the text in their appropriate chronological place. Characterize, as fully as you can, the voice of the poems written in the 1950s; in the '60s; '70s; '80s. In what ways does the voice seem to change? What similarities do you see in her work from beginning to end?

WRITING SUGGESTIONS

1. In what sense is "At a Bach Concert" typical of Rich's early poetry? Compare "Storm Warnings" and "Aunt Jennifer's Tigers" in terms of the comments Rich makes about her early work in the passage quoted from *When We Dead Awaken: Writing as Re-Vision* (p. 964). What "typical" features do the poems share? Write a detailed analysis (about 1,500 words) of "At a Bach Concert" showing how it is (or is not) typical of Rich's early work.

2. Carefully considering plot, characterization, and structure, write an essay in which you detail the ways "Diving into the Wreck" is and is not typical of Rich's recent work. (Alternate version: Are there other poems that strike you as more typical of later Rich? If so, choose one and show how it is characteristic of Rich's later ideas and strategies.)

▼   ▼   ▼

11 LITERARY TRADITION AS CONTEXT

The more poetry you read, the better a reader of poetry you are likely to be. This is not just because your skills will improve and develop, but also because you will come to know more about the poetic tradition and can thus understand more fully how poets draw upon each other. Poets are conscious of other poets, and often they refer to each other's work or use it as a starting point for their own, in ways that may not be immediately obvious to an outsider. Poetry can be treated as a form of argument: poets agree or disagree over basic matters. Sometimes a quiet (or even noisy) competitiveness is at the bottom of their concern with what other poems have done or can do; at other times, playfulness and a sense of humor about poetic possibilities take over, and the competitiveness dwindles to fun and poetic games. And often poets want to tap the rich mine of artistic expression in order to share in the bounty of our heritage. In any case, a poet's consciousness of what others have done leads to a sense of tradition that is often hard to articulate but nevertheless is very important to the effects of poetry—and this sense of tradition is something of a problem for a relatively new reader of poetry. How can I possibly read this poem intelligently, we are likely to ask sometimes in exasperation, until I've read all the other poems ever written? It's a real problem. Poets don't actually expect that all of their readers have Ph.D.'s in literature, but sometimes it *seems* as if they do. For some poets—Milton, T. S. Eliot, and Richard Wilbur are examples—it does help if one has read practically everything imaginable.

Why are poets so dependent on each other? What is the point of their relentless consciousness of what has already been done by others? Why do they repeatedly answer, allude to, and echo other poems? Why is a sense of tradition so important to them?

A sense of common task, a kind of communality of purpose, accounts for some traditional poetic practice, and the competitive desire of individual poets to achieve a place in the English and American poetic tradition accounts for more. Many poets are anxious to be counted among those who achieve, through their writing, a place in history; and a way of establishing that place is to define for oneself the relationship between one's own work and that of others whose place is already secure. There is, for many poets, a sense of a serious and abiding cultural tradition that they wish to share and pass on; but also important is a shared sense of playfulness, a kind of poetic gamesmanship. Making words dance on the page or in our heads provides in itself a satisfaction and delight for many writers—pride in craft that is like the pride of a painter or potter or tennis player. Often poets set themselves a particular task to see what they can do. One way of doing that is to introduce a standard traditional **motif** (a recurrent device, formula, or situation that deliberately connects a poem with common patterns of existing thought), and then to play variations on it much as a musician might do. Another way is to provide an alternative answer to a question that has repeatedly been asked and answered in a traditional way. Poetic playfulness by no means excludes serious intention—the poems in this chapter often make important statements about their subject, however humorous they may be in their method. Some teasing of the tradition and of other poets is pure fun, a kind of kidding among good friends; some is rather more harsh and represents an attempt to see the world very differently—to define and articulate a very different set of attitudes and values.

The English poetic tradition is a rich and varied heritage, and individual poets draw upon it in countless ways. You have probably noticed, in the poems you have read so far, a number of allusions, glances at the tradition or at individual expressions of it. The more poems you read, the more you will notice and the more you will yourself become a comfortable member of the audience poets write for. Poets do expect a lot from readers—not always but often enough to make a new reader feel nervous and sometimes inadequate. The other side of that discomfort comes when you begin to notice things that other readers don't. The groups of poems in this chapter illustrate some of the ways that the tradition energizes individual poets and suggest some of the things poets like to do with their heritage.

Echo and Allusion

The poems in this group illustrate the familiar poetic strategy of echoing or alluding to other texts as a way of importing meaning into a particular poem, similar to the strategy of "sampling" words in rap music. An **echo** may simply recall a word, phrase, or sound in another text as a way of associating what is going on in *this* poem with something in another, familiar text. The familiarity itself may sometimes be the point: writers often like to associate what they do with what has already been thought or expressed, especially if they can sound like a text that is already much admired. Echoes of Shakespeare (or other much admired writers) often have the function of implying that this new text shares concerns (and therefore insight or quality?) with something that has gone before. An **allusion** more insistently connects a particular word, phrase, or section of a poem with some similar formulation in a previous text; it *invokes* a previous text as a kind of gloss on this one; that is, it asks the reader to interpret this text in the light of some previous one, depending explicitly on the reader's recognition of the previous text and asking for interpretation based on the implied similarity.

Strategies of echo and allusion can be very complicated, for the question of just how much of one text can carry over—or be forcibly brought over—into another one cannot be answered categorically.

Often poets quote—or echo with variations—a passage from another text in order to suggest some thematic, ideological, tonal, or other link. Sometimes the purpose is simply to invoke an idea or attitude from another text, another place, or another culture. Thus, in Adrienne Rich's "Two Songs" (p. 787) Chaucer's familiar formulation of the rites of spring (with its description of all things coming to life, their vital juices flowing, as they follow the natural progress of the seasons) is introduced into the text to suggest the way the sap rises and bodies merge in ordinary lusty human beings. The speaker's attraction to a lover is thus put into a larger human perspective, and her sense of herself as a subject and object of lust comes to seem ordinary, part of the natural course of events.

The second poem in *Echo and Allusion* belongs, uncomfortably, in the *carpe diem* ("seize the day") tradition; but unlike ordinary *carpe diem* poems it is moralistic. It undercuts the speaker by having him allude to familiar biblical passages that imply a condemnation of live-for-today attitudes and ideas. By echoing Satan's tempting addresses to Eve in Genesis, the speaker in "Come, My Celia" condemns himself in the eyes of readers and becomes a seducer-tempter instead of a libertine-hero. The other poems here variously recall individual lines, passages, poems, ideas, or traditions in order to establish a particular stance or develop a position or attitude. The meaning of each poem derives primarily from a sorting through of the allusion.

Poems do not necessarily need earlier texts to exist or have meaning, but prior texts may set up what happens in a particular poem or govern how it is to be construed. Allusion is the strategy of using one text to comment on—and influence the interpretation of—another. It is one of the most popular, familiar, and frequent strategies that poets use.

ANDREW MARVELL

To His Coy Mistress

Had we but world enough, and time,
This coyness,[1] lady, were no crime.
We would sit down, and think which way
To walk, and pass our long love's day.
Thou by the Indian Ganges' side
Shouldst rubies[2] find: I by the tide
Of Humber[3] would complain. I would
Love you ten years before the Flood,
And you should if you please refuse
Till the conversion of the Jews.[4]
My vegetable love[5] should grow
Vaster than empires, and more slow;
An hundred years should go to praise
Thine eyes, and on thy forehead gaze;
Two hundred to adore each breast,
But thirty thousand to the rest.
An age at least to every part,
And the last age should show your heart.
For, lady, you deserve this state;[6]
Nor would I love at lower rate.
    But at my back I always hear
Time's wingéd chariot hurrying near;
And yonder all before us lie
Deserts of vast eternity.
Thy beauty shall no more be found,
Nor, in thy marble vault, shall sound
My echoing song; then worms shall try
That long preserved virginity,
And your quaint honor turn to dust,
And into ashes all my lust:
The grave's a fine and private place,
But none, I think, do there embrace.
    Now therefore, while the youthful hue
Sits on thy skin like morning dew,[7]
And while thy willing soul transpires[8]
At every pore with instant fires,
Now let us sport us while we may,

5

10

15

20

25

30

35

---

1. Hesitancy, modesty (not necessarily suggesting calculation).   2. Talismans that are supposed
to preserve virginity.   3. A small river that flows through Marvell's home town of Hull. *Complain:*
write love complaints, conventional songs lamenting the cruelty of love.   4. Which, according
to popular Christian belief, will occur just before the end of the world.   5. Which is capable
only of passive growth, not of consciousness. The "vegetable soul" is lower than the other two
divisions of the soul, "animal" and "rational."   6. Dignity.   7. The text reads "glew." "Lew"
(warmth) has also been suggested as an emendation.   8. Breathes forth.

And now, like am'rous birds of prey,
Rather at once our time devour
Than languish in his slow-chapped[9] pow'r.   40
Let us roll all our strength and all
Our sweetness up into one ball,
And tear our pleasures with rough strife
Thorough[1] the iron gates of life.
Thus, though we cannot make our sun   45
Stand still,[2] yet we will make him run.[3]   1681

BEN JONSON

Come, My Celia[4]

Come, my Celia, let us prove,[5]
While we can, the sports of love;
Time will not be ours forever:
He at length our good will sever.
Spend not, then, his gifts in vain;   5
Suns that set may rise again,
But if once we lose this light,
'Tis with us perpetual night.
Why should we defer our joys?
Fame and rumor are but toys.   10
Cannot we delude the eyes
Of a few poor household spies?
Or his easier ears beguile,
Thus removéd by our wile?
'Tis no sin love's fruits to steal,   15
But the sweet thefts to reveal;
To be taken, to be seen,
These have crimes accounted been.   1606

MARIANNE MOORE

Love in America?

Whatever it is, it's a passion—
a benign dementia that should be
engulfing America, fed in a way
the opposite of the way

9. Slow-jawed. Chronos (Time), ruler of the world in early Greek myth, devoured all of his children except Zeus, who was hidden. Later, Zeus seized power (see line 46 and note).   1. Through.
2. To lengthen his night of love with Alcmene, Zeus made the sun stand still.   3. Each sex act was believed to shorten life by one day.   4. A song from *Volpone*, sung by the play's villain and would-be seducer. Part of the poem paraphrases *Catullus*, V.   5. Try.

5

in which the Minotaur[6] was fed.
It's a Midas[7] of tenderness;
    from the heart;
nothing else. From one with ability
to bear being misunderstood—

10

    take the blame, with "nobility
    that is action,"[8] identifying itself with
    pioneer unperfunctoriness

without brazenness[9] or
bigness of overgrown
undergrown shallowness.

15

Whatever it is, let it be without
affectation.

Yes, yes, yes, *yes.*   1967

HOWARD NEMEROV

Boom!

SEES BOOM IN RELIGION, TOO

Atlantic City, June 23, 1957 (AP).—President Eisenhower's pastor
said tonight that Americans are living in a period of "unprecedented religious activity" caused partially by paid vacations, the
eight-hour day and modern conveniences.
    "These fruits of material progress," said the Rev. Edward L. R.
Elson of the National Presbyterian Church, Washington, "have
provided the leisure, the energy, and the means for a level of
human and spiritual values never before reached."

Here at the Vespasian-Carlton,[1] it's just one
religious activity after another; the sky
is constantly being crossed by cruciform
airplanes, in which nobody disbelieves
for a second and the tide, the tide

5

of spiritual progress and prosperity
miraculously keeps rising, to a level
never before attained. The churches are full,
the beaches are full, and the filling-stations

---

6. "The Minotaur demanded a virgin to devour once a year." (Moore's note)   7. "Midas, who
had the golden touch, was inconvenienced when eating or picking things up." (Moore's note)   8. "Unamuno said that what we need as a cure for unruly youth is 'nobility that is action.'"
(Moore's note)   9. "*without brazenness or bigness* ... Winston Churchill: 'Modesty becomes a
man.'" (Moore's note)   1. Vespasian was emperor of Rome 70–79, shortly after the reign of
Nero. In French, *vespasienne* means public toilet.

are full, God's great ocean is full   10
of paid vacationers praying an eight-hour day
to the human and spiritual values, the fruits,
the leisure, the energy, and the means, Lord,
the means for the level, the unprecedented level,
and the modern conveniences, which also are full.   15
Never before, O Lord, have the prayers and praises
from belfry and phonebooth, from ballpark and barbecue
the sacrifices, so endlessly ascended.

It was not thus when Job in Palestine
sat in the dust and cried, cried bitterly;[2]   20
when Damien kissed the lepers on their wounds
it was not thus;[3] it was not thus
when Francis worked a fourteen-hour day
strictly for the birds;[4] when Dante took
a week's vacation without pay and it rained   25
part of the time,[5] O Lord, it was not thus.

But now the gears mesh and the tires burn
and the ice chatters in the shaker and the priest
in the pulpit and Thy Name, O Lord,
is kept before the public, while the fruits   30
ripen and religion booms and the level rises
and every modern convenience runneth over,
that it may never be with us as it hath been
with Athens and Karnak and Nagasaki,[6]
nor Thy sun for one instant refrain from shining   35
on the rainbow Buick by the breezeway
or the Chris Craft with the uplift life raft;
that we may continue to be the just folks we are,
plain people with ordinary superliners and
disposable diaperliners, people of the stop'n'shop   40
'n'pray as you go, of hotel, motel, boatel,
the humble pilgrims of no deposit no return
and please adjust thy clothing, who will give to Thee,
if Thee will keep us going, our annual
Miss Universe, for Thy Name's Sake, Amen.   1960   45

---

2. According to the Book of Job, he was afflicted with the loss of prosperity, children, and health as a test of his faith. His name means, in Hebrew, "he cries"; see especially Job 2:7–13.   3. "Father Damien" (Joseph Damien de Veuster, 1840–1889), a Roman Catholic missionary from Belgium, was known for his work among lepers in Hawaii; he ultimately contracted leprosy himself and died there.   4. St. Francis of Assisi, 13th-century founder of the Franciscan order, was noted for his love of all living things, and one of the most famous stories about him tells of his preaching to the birds. *Strictly for the birds*: a mid-20th-century expression for worthless or unfashionable activity. 5. Dante's journey through Hell, Purgatory, and Paradise (in *The Divine Comedy*) takes a week, beginning on Good Friday, 1300. It rains in the third chasm of Hell.   6. Athens, the cultural center of ancient Greek civilization; Karnak, a village on the Nile, built on the site of ancient Thebes; Nagasaki, a large Japanese port city, virtually destroyed by a U.S. atomic bomb in 1945.

ROBERT HOLLANDER

You Too? Me Too—Why Not?
Soda Pop

```
                 I am
                 look
                 ing at
              the Co
              caCola
              bottle
              which is
              green wi
              th ridges
              just–like
          c       c       c
          o       o       o
          l       l       l
          u       u       u
          m       m       m
          n       n       n
          s       s       s
```

and on itself it says

COCA-COLA
reg.u.s.pat.off.

exactly like an art pop
statue of that kind of
bottle but not so green
that the juice inside
gives other than the co-
lor it has when I pour
it out in a clear glass
glass on this table top
(It's making me thirsty
all this winking and
beading of Hippocrene
please let me pause
drinking the fluid in)
ah! it is enticing how each
color is the same
brown in green bottle
brown in uplifted glass
making each utensil on
the table laid a brown
fork in a brown shade
making me long to watch
them harvesting the crop
which makes the deep-aged
rich brown wine of America
that is to say which makes
soda   pop   p. 1968

WILLIAM BLAKE

The Lamb

Little Lamb, who made thee?
Dost thou know who made thee?
Gave thee life, and bid thee feed
By the stream and o'er the mead;
Gave thee clothing of delight,   5
Softest clothing woolly bright;
Gave thee such a tender voice,
Making all the vales rejoice?
Little Lamb, who made thee?
Dost thou know who made thee?   10

Little Lamb, I'll tell thee!
Little Lamb, I'll tell thee:
He is calléd by thy name,
For he calls himself a Lamb,
He is meek and he is mild;   15
He became a little child.
I a child and thou a lamb,
We are calléd by his name.
Little Lamb, God bless thee!
Little Lamb, God bless thee!   1789   20

WILLIAM SHAKESPEARE

[Not marble, nor the gilded monuments]

Not marble, nor the gilded monuments
Of princes, shall outlive this powerful rhyme;
But you shall shine more bright in these conténts
Than unswept stone, besmeared with sluttish time.
When wasteful war shall statues overturn,   5
And broils root out the work of masonry,
Nor Mars his sword nor war's quick fire shall burn
The living record of your memory.
'Gainst death and all-oblivious enmity
Shall you pace forth; your praise shall still find room   10
Even in the eyes of all posterity
That wear this world out to the ending doom.[7]
So, till the judgment that yourself arise,
You live in this, and dwell in lovers' eyes.   1609

7. Judgment Day.

Poetic "Kinds"

There are all sorts of poems. By now you have experienced poems on a variety of subjects and with all kinds of tones—short poems, long poems, poems that rhyme and poems that don't. And there are, of course, many other sorts of poems that we haven't looked at. Some poems, for example, are thousands of lines long and differ rather substantially from the poems that can be included in a book like this.

Poems may be classified in a variety of ways, by subject, topic, or theme; by their length, appearance, and formal features; by the way they are organized; by the level of language they use; by the poet's intention and what kinds of effects the poem tries to generate.

Classification may be, of course, simply an intellectual exercise. Recognizing a poem that is, for example, an elegy (like *Lycidas* [p. 1110]), a parody, or a satire, may be very much like the satisfaction involved in recognizing a scarlet tanager, a weeping willow, a French phrase, or a 1967 Ford Thunderbird. Just *knowing* what others don't know gives us a sense of importance, accomplishment, and power. But there are also *uses* for classification: we can experience a poem more fully if we understand early on exactly what kind of poem we are dealing with. A fuller response is possible because the poet has consciously chosen to play by certain defined rules, and the **conventions** he or she employs indicate certain standard ways of saying things to achieve certain expected effects. The **tradition** that is involved in a particular poetic kind is thus employed by the poet in order to produce predictable standard responses.

A poem that calls itself an "elegy," for example, gives us fair warning of what to expect: its label tells that it will be a serious poem memorializing the death of someone, and we may reasonably expect that its tone will be sad or angry about the death, reflective about the meaning and direction of the dead person's life, and perhaps ruminative about the implications of the death itself. For example, much of the humor and fun in the following poem is premised on the assumption that readers will recognize the kind of poem they are reading.

CHRISTOPHER MARLOWE

The Passionate Shepherd to His Love

Come live with me and be my love,
And we will all the pleasures prove[1]
That valleys, groves, hills, and fields,
Woods, or steepy mountain yields.

And we will sit upon the rocks,   5
Seeing the shepherds feed their flocks,
By shallow rivers to whose falls
Melodious birds sing madrigals.

And I will make thee beds of roses
And a thousand fragrant posies,   10
A cap of flowers, and a kirtle[2]
Embroidered all with leaves of myrtle;

A gown made of the finest wool
Which from our pretty lambs we pull;
Fair lined slippers for the cold,   15
With buckles of the purest gold;

A belt of straw and ivy buds,
With coral clasps and amber studs:
And if these pleasures may thee move,
Come live with me, and be my love.   20

The shepherd swains[3] shall dance and sing
For thy delight each May morning:
If these delights thy mind may move,
Then live with me and be my love.   1600

A beginning reader of poetry might easily protest that a plea such as this
one is unrealistic and fanciful and thus feel unsure of the poem's tone. What
could such a reader think of a speaker who constructs his argument in such a
dreamlike way? But the traditions behind the poem and the conventions of the
poetic kind make its intention and effects quite clear. "The Passionate Shepherd" is a pastoral poem, a poetic kind that concerns itself with the simple life
of country folk and describes that life in stylized, idealized terms. The people
in a pastoral poem are usually (as here) shepherds, although they may be fishermen or other rustics who lead an outdoor life and are involved in tending to
basic human needs in a simplified society; the world of the poem is one of sim-

---

1. Try.   2. Gown.   3. Youths.

plicity, beauty, music, and love. The world always seems timeless in pastoral; people are eternally young, and the season is always spring, usually May. Nature seems endlessly green and the future entirely golden. Difficulty, frustration, disappointment, and obligation do not belong in this world at all; it is blissfully free of problems. Shepherds sing instead of tending sheep, and they make love and play music instead of having to watch out for wolves in the night. If only the shepherd boy and shepherd girl can agree with each other to make love joyously and passionately, they will live happily ever after. The language of pastoral is informal and fairly simple, although always a bit more sophisticated than that of real shepherds with real problems and real sheep.

Unrealistic? Of course. No real shepherd gets to spend even a single whole day like that, and certainly the world of simple country folk includes ferocities of nature, human falsehood and knavery, disease, bad weather, old age, moments that are not all green and gold. And probably no poet ever thought that shepherds really live that way, but it is an attractive fantasy, and poets who write pastoral simply choose one formulaic way to isolate a series of idealized moments. Fantasies can be personal and private, of course, but there is also a certain pleasure in shared public fantasies, and one central moment is that moment in a love relationship when two people are contemplating the joys of ecstatic love. The vision here is self-consciously constructed by poets in order to present a certain tone, attitude, and wholeness; it is a world that is self-existent, self-contained, and self-referential.

Pastoral poems are not written by shepherds. No doubt shepherds have fantasies too, but theirs probably involve ways of life far removed from sheepfolds and nights outdoors. Pastoral poems are usually written, as here, by city poets who are consciously indulging their "isn't it pretty to think so" thoughts. Pastoral poems involve an urban fantasy of rural bliss. It can be lovely to contemplate a world in which the birds sing only for our delight and other shepherds take care of the sheep, a world in which there is no work that does not turn into magic and in which the lambs bring themselves to us so that we can transform their wool instantly into a beautiful gown. It is also fun to "answer" such a vision. The next subsection of this chapter contains three poems that directly "answer" Marlowe's poem and thus offer a kind of critique of the pastoral vision. But in a sense none is necessary; the pastoral poet builds an awareness of artificiality into the whole idea of the poem. It is conceived in full consciousness that its fantasy avoids implication, and in filtering that implication carefully out of the poem, poets implicitly provide their own criticism of the fantasy world. Satire is, in a sense, the other side of the pastoral world—a city poet who fantasizes about being a shepherd usually knows all about dirt and grime and human failure and urban corruption—and satire and pastoral are often seen as complementary poetic kinds.

Several other poetic kinds are exemplified in this book; and each has its own characteristics and conventions that have become established by tradition, repetition, and habit.

epic	from *Paradise Lost*	p. 775
pastoral	"The Passionate Shepherd to His	
	Love"	p. 981
elegy	*Lycidas*	p. 1110
lyric	"The Lamb"	p. 979
ballad	"Sir Patrick Spens"	p. 851
protest poem	"Hard Rock Returns . . ."	p. 681
aubade	"The Sun Rising"	p. 921
confessional poem	"Skunk Hour"	p. 1106
meditation	"Love Calls Us . . ."	p. 1047
dramatic monologue	"My Last Duchess"	p. 743
soliloquy	"Soliloquy of the Spanish Cloister"	p. 707

You will find definitions and brief descriptions of these poetic kinds in the glossary. Each of these established kinds is worthy of detailed discussion and study, and your teacher may want to examine in depth how the conventions of several different kinds work. Here, we have chosen to examine in depth one particular poetic kind, the **epigram,** by including quite a few poems that typify it.

The poems that follow are all epigrams, and together they add up almost to a definition of that poetic kind. Like most poetic kinds, the epigram has a history that shaped its form and content. Originally, an epigram was an inscription upon some object such as a monument, triumphal arch, tombstone, or gate; hence brevity and conciseness were absolutely necessary. But over a period of time, the term "epigram" came to mean a short poem that tried to attract concentrated attention in the same way that an inscription attracts the eyes of passersby.

As the poems here suggest, epigrams have been popular over a long period of time. The modern tradition of epigrams has two more or less separate ancient sources, one in Greece, one in Rome. In classical Greece, epigrams were composed over a period of two thousand years; the earliest surviving ones date from the eighth century B.C. Apparently there were several anthologies of epigrams in early times, and fragments of these anthologies were later preserved, especially in large collections like the so-called *Greek Anthology,* which dates from the tenth century A.D. Largely short inscriptions, these epigrams also included some love poems (including many on homosexual love), comments on life and morality, riddles, etc. The father of the Roman tradition is generally agreed to be Martial (Marcus Valerius Martialis, A.D. 40?–104?), whose epigrams are witty and satirical. Modern epigrams have more frequently followed Martial's lead, but occasionally the distinctive influence of the older Greek tradition can be seen in the sadder poignancy of such poems as "Parting in Wartime."

Knowing what to do with a poem often is aided by knowing what it is, or what it means to be. Many modern poems are not consciously conceived in terms of a traditional kind, and not all older poems are either, but a knowledge of kind can often provide one more way of deciding what to look for in a poem, helping one to find the right questions to ask.

▼ ▼ ▼

SAMUEL TAYLOR COLERIDGE

What Is an Epigram?

What is an epigram? a dwarfish whole,
Its body brevity, and wit its soul.   p. 1802

BEN JONSON

Epitaph on Elizabeth, L. H.

Wouldst thou hear what man can say
In a little? Reader, stay.
Underneath this stone doth lie
As much beauty as could die;
5 Which in life did harbor give
To more virtue than doth live.
If at all she had a fault,
Leave it buried in this vault.
One name was Elizabeth;
10 Th' other, let it sleep with death:
Fitter, where it died, to tell,
Than that it lived at all. Farewell.   1616

MARTIAL

[You've told me, Maro, whilst you live][4]

You've told me, Maro, whilst you live
You'd not a single penny give,
But that whene'er you chanced to die,
You'd leave a handsome legacy;
You must be mad beyond redress,   5
If my next wish you cannot guess.

ca. 100

MARTIAL

[Fair, rich, and young? How rare is her perfection][5]

Fair, rich, and young? How rare is her perfection,
Were it not mingled with one foul infection?
I mean, so proud a heart, so cursed a tongue,
As makes her seem, nor fair, nor rich, nor young.

ca. 80–85

JOHN GAY

My Own Epitaph

Life is a jest; and all things show it.
I thought so once; but now I know it.   1720

RICHARD CRASHAW

An Epitaph upon a Young Married Couple, Dead and Buried Together

To these, whom death again did wed,
This grave's their second marriage-bed.
For though the hand of fate could force
'Twixt soul and body a divorce,
It could not sunder man and wife   5
'Cause they both livéd but one life.

---

4. Translated from the Latin by F. Lewis.   5. Translated from the Latin by Sir John Harington.

Peace, good reader. Do not weep.
Peace, the lovers are asleep.
They, sweet turtles,[6] folded lie
10 In the last knot love could tie.
And though they lie as they were dead,
Their pillow stone, their sheets of lead,
(Pillow hard, and sheets not warm)
Love made the bed; they'll take no harm;
15 Let them sleep, let them sleep on.
Till this stormy night be gone,
Till th' eternal morrow dawn;
Then the curtains will be drawn
And they wake into a light,
20 Whose day shall never die in night.   1646

X. J. KENNEDY

Epitaph for a Postal Clerk

Here lies wrapped up tight in sod
Henry Harkins c/o God.
On the day of Resurrection
May be opened for inspection.   1961

COUNTEE CULLEN

For a Lady I Know

She even thinks that up in heaven
Her class lies late and snores,
While poor black cherubs rise at seven
To do celestial chores.   1925

J. V. CUNNINGHAM

History of Ideas

God is love. Then by inversion
Love is God, and sex conversion.   1947

6. Turtledoves.

WENDY COPE

Another Christmas Poem

Bloody Christmas, here again.
Let us raise a loving cup:
Peace on earth, goodwill to men,
And make them do the washing-up.   1986

WALTER SAVAGE LANDOR

The Georges[7]

George the First was always reckoned
Vile, but viler George the Second;
And what mortal ever heard
Any good of George the Third?
When from earth the Fourth descended   5
(God be praised!) the Georges ended.   p. 1855

PETER PINDAR

Epigram

Midas, they say, possessed the art of old
Of turning whatsoe'er he touched to gold;
This modern statesmen can reverse with ease—
ca. 1780   Touch *them* with gold, *they'll turn to what you please.*

HOWARD NEMEROV

Epigram: Political Reflexion

loquitur the sparrow in the zoo[8]

No bars are set too close, no mesh too fine
To keep me from the eagle and the lion,
Whom keepers feed that I may freely dine.
This goes to show that if you have the wit
To be small, common, cute, and live on shit,   5
Though the cage fret kings, you may make free with it.   1958

7. British kings who ruled successively from 1714 to 1830.   8. I.e., the sparrow is the speaker.

EDNA ST. VINCENT MILLAY

First Fig

My candle burns at both ends;
  It will not last the night;
But ah, my foes, and oh, my friends—
  It gives a lovely light!   1920

Second Fig

Safe upon the solid rock the ugly houses stand:
Come and see my shining palace built upon the sand!   1920

FRANCES CORNFORD

Parting in Wartime

How long ago Hector[9] took off his plume,
Not wanting that his little son should cry,
Then kissed his sad Andromache good-bye—
And now we three in Euston[1] waiting-room.   1948

Imitating and Answering

Poems often respond directly—sometimes point by point or even line by line or word by word—to another poem. Often the point is teasing or comic, but often too there is a real issue behind the idea of such a facetious answer, a serious criticism perhaps of the poem's point or the tradition it represents, or sometimes an attempt to provide a different way of looking at the issue. Sometimes poems follow their models rather slavishly in order to emphasize their likeness; sometimes key words or details are substituted so that readers will easily notice the differences in tone or attitude.

Often these poems seem rather self-conscious—as if the poets who write

9. The noblest chieftain in ancient Troy and husband to Andromache.   1. A London railway station.

them are aware of the tradition they share and are each trying to do something a little bit different. However "sincere" these poems may be, their sense of play is equally important. The first three poems playfully pick on Christopher Marlowe's "The Passionate Shepherd to His Love" (p. 981). In effect, all of them provide "answers" to that poem. It is as if "his love" were telling the shepherd what is the matter with his argument, and the poets are answering Marlowe, too. These poets know full well what Marlowe was doing in the fantasy of his original poem, and they clearly have a lot of fun telling him how people in various circumstances might feel about his fantasy. There is in the end a lot of joy in their "realistic" deflation of his magic, and not much hostility. The poems by Koch, Skirrow, Hecht, and Cope poke gentle fun at other famous works, offering a summary or another version of what might have happened in each (see, respectively, "This Is Just to Say" [p. 1138], "Ode on a Grecian Urn" [p. 929], "Dover Beach" [p. 741], and "Not marble, nor the gilded monuments" [p. 979]).

A *parody* is a poem that imitates another poem closely but changes details for a comic or critical effect. Strictly speaking, only two of the poems that follow (those by Koch and Cope) are parodies—that is, they pretend to write in the style of the original poem but comically exaggerate that style and change the content. The others make fun of an original in less direct phraseological ways, but they share a similar objective of answering an original, even though they use very different styles to alter, totally, the poetic intention of that original. "Ode on a Grecian Urn Summarized" teases Keats as well as the whole notion of poetic summaries; the effects of the summary are not very much like those of the Keats poem. "The Dover Bitch," on the other hand, is as its subtitle suggests much more than just a different perspective on the situation presented in "Dover Beach"; it uses the tradition to criticize art and life.

All these poems offer a revised version of what reality may be like (as does one of the poems in the next subsection, "Penelope," by telling a familiar literary story from a different—in this case the woman's—point of view). Poems like these may have a serious purpose, but their method is comic and usually light. And fun is not always easy to explain intellectually or to demonstrate.

SIR WALTER RALEGH

The Nymph's Reply to the Shepherd

If all the world and love were young,
And truth in every shepherd's tongue,

These pretty pleasures might me move
To live with thee and be thy love.

5   Time drives the flocks from field to fold,
When rivers rage, and rocks grow cold,
And Philomel[1] becometh dumb;
The rest complain of cares to come.

The flowers do fade, and wanton fields
10   To wayward winter reckoning yields:
A honey tongue, a heart of gall,
Is fancy's spring, but sorrow's fall.

Thy gowns, thy shoes, thy beds of roses,
Thy cap, thy kirtle, and thy posies
15   Soon break, soon wither, soon forgotten;
In folly ripe, in reason rotten.

Thy belt of straw and ivy buds,
Thy coral clasps and amber studs,
All these in me no means can move
20   To come to thee and be thy love.

But could youth last, and love still breed,
Had joys no date,[2] nor age no need,
Then these delights my mind might move
To live with thee and be thy love.   1600

WILLIAM CARLOS WILLIAMS

Raleigh Was Right

We cannot go to the country
for the country will bring us no peace
What can the small violets tell us
that grow on furry stems in
5   the long grass among lance shaped leaves?

Though you praise us
and call to mind the poets
who sung of our loveliness
it was long ago!
10   long ago! when country people
would plow and sow with
flowering minds and pockets at ease—
if ever this were true.

1. The nightingale.   2. End.

Not now. Love itself a flower
with roots in a parched ground.   15
Empty pockets make empty heads.
Cure it if you can but
do not believe that we can live
today in the country
for the country will bring us no peace.   1941   20

E. E. CUMMINGS

[(ponder,darling,these busted statues]

(ponder,darling,these busted statues
of yon motheaten forum be aware
notice what hath remained
—the stone cringes
clinging to the stone,how obsolete   5

lips utter their extant smile. . . .
remark

a few deleted of texture
or meaning monuments and dolls

resist Them Greediest Paws of careful   10
time all of which is extremely
unimportant)whereas Life

matters if or

when the your- and my-
idle vertical worthless   15
self unite in a peculiarly
momentary

partnership(to instigate
constructive
                    Horizontal   20
business. . . . even so,let us make haste
—consider well this ruined aqueduct

lady,
which used to lead something into somewhere)   1926

PETER DE VRIES

To His Importunate Mistress

ANDREW MARVELL UPDATED

Had we but world enough, and time,
My coyness, lady, were a crime,
But at my back I always hear
Time's wingèd chariot, striking fear
The hour is nigh when creditors
Will prove to be my predators.
As wages of our picaresque,
Bag lunches bolted at my desk
Must stand as fealty to you
For each expensive rendezvous.
Obeisance at your marble feet
Deserves the best-appointed suite,
And would have, lacked I not the pelf
To pleasure also thus myself;
But aptly sumptuous amorous scenes
Rule out the rake of modest means.

Since mistress presupposes wife,
It means a doubly costly life;
For fools by second passion fired
A second income is required,
The earning which consumes the hours
They'd hoped to spend in rented bowers.
To hostelries the worst of fates
That weekly raise their daily rates!
I gather, lady, from your scoffing
A bloke more solvent in the offing.
So revels thus to rivals go
For want of monetary flow.
How vexing that inconstant cash
The constant suitor must abash,
Who with excuses vainly pled
Must rue the undishevelled bed,
And that for paltry reasons given
His conscience may remain unriven.

p. 1986

KENNETH KOCH

Variations on a Theme by William Carlos Williams

1

I chopped down the house that you had been saving to live in next
    summer.
I am sorry, but it was morning, and I had nothing to do
and its wooden beams were so inviting.

2

We laughed at the hollyhocks together
and then I sprayed them with lye.   5
Forgive me. I simply do not know what I am doing.

3

I gave away the money that you had been saving to live on for the
    next ten years.
The man who asked for it was shabby
and the firm March wind on the porch was so juicy and cold.

4

Last evening we went dancing and I broke your leg.   10
Forgive me. I was clumsy, and
I wanted you here in the wards, where I am the doctor!   1962

DESMOND SKIRROW

Ode on a Grecian Urn Summarized

Gods chase
Round vase.
What say?
What play?
Don't know.   5
Nice, though.   p. 1960

ANTHONY HECHT

The Dover Bitch

A CRITICISM OF LIFE

for Andrews Wanning

So there stood Matthew Arnold and this girl
With the cliffs of England crumbling away behind them,
And he said to her, "Try to be true to me,
And I'll do the same for you, for things are bad
5 All over, etc., etc."
Well now, I knew this girl. It's true she had read
Sophocles in a fairly good translation
And caught that bitter allusion to the sea,[3]
But all the time he was talking she had in mind
10 The notion of what his whiskers would feel like
On the back of her neck. She told me later on
That after a while she got to looking out
At the lights across the channel, and really felt sad,
Thinking of all the wine and enormous beds
15 And blandishments in French and the perfumes.
And then she got really angry. To have been brought
All the way down from London, and then be addressed
As a sort of mournful cosmic last resort
Is really tough on a girl, and she was pretty.
20 Anyway, she watched him pace the room
And finger his watch-chain and seem to sweat a bit,
And then she said one or two unprintable things.
But you mustn't judge her by that. What I mean to say is,
She's really all right. I still see her once in a while
25 And she always treats me right. We have a drink
And I give her a good time, and perhaps it's a year
Before I see her again, but there she is,
Running to fat, but dependable as they come.
And sometimes I bring her a bottle of *Nuit d'Amour.*   1968

WENDY COPE

[Not only marble, but the plastic toys]

Not only marble, but the plastic toys
From cornflake packets will outlive this rhyme:

3. In Sophocles' *Antigone*, lines 583–91. See "Dover Beach," lines 9–18.

I can't immortalize you, love—our joys
Will lie unnoticed in the vault of time.
When Mrs Thatcher has been cast in bronze 5
And her administration is a page
In some O-level text-book,[4] when the dons
Have analysed the story of our age,
When travel firms sell tours of outer space
And aeroplanes take off without a sound 10
And Tulse Hill has become a trendy place
And Upper Norwood's on the underground[5]
Your beauty and my name will be forgotten—
My love is true, but all my verse is rotten. 1986

Mythology and Myth

The poems in this group draw on a tradition that is larger than just
"literary." Mythologies involve whole systems of belief, usually cultural in
scope, and the familiar literary formulations of these mythologies are just the
surface articulations of a larger view of why the world works the way it does.

Every culture develops stories to explain itself. These stories, about who we
are and why we are the way we are, constitute what are often called **myths.**
Calling something a myth does not mean that it is false. In fact, it means
nearly the opposite, for cultures that subscribe to various myths, or that have
ever subscribed to particular myths about culture or history, become infused
with and defined by those views. Myth, in the sense in which it is used here,
involves explanations of life that are more or less universally shared within a
particular culture; it is a frame of reference that people within the culture
understand and share. A sharing of this frame of reference does not mean that
all people within a culture are carbon copies of each other or that popular
stereotypes represent reality accurately, nor does it mean that every individual
in the culture *knows* the perceived history and can articulate its events, ideas,
and values. But it does mean that a shared history and a shared set of symbols
lie behind any particular culture and that the culture is to some extent aware
of its distinctiveness from other cultures.

A **culture** may be of many sizes and shapes. Often we think of a nation as a
culture (and so speak of American culture, American history, the myth of
America, the American dream, the American frame of reference), and it is

---

4. A text designed to prepare secondary school students for the first hurdle in entrance exams for
British universities. *Dons*: academics.   5. London subway.

equally useful to make smaller and larger divisions—as long as there is some commonality of history and some cohesiveness of purpose within the group. One can speak of southern culture, for example, or of urban culture, or of the drug culture, or of the various popular music cultures, or of a culture associated with a particular political belief, economic class, or social group. Most of us belong, willingly or not, to a number of such cultures at one time, and to some extent our identity and destiny are linked with the distinctive features of those cultures and with the ways each culture perceives its identity, values, and history. Some of these cultures we choose to join; some are thrust upon us by birth and circumstances. It is these larger and more persistent forms of culture—not those chosen by an individual—that are illustrated in this chapter.

Poets, aware of their heritage, often like to probe its history and beliefs and plumb its depths, just as they like to articulate and play variations on the poetic tradition they feel a part of. For poetry written in the English language over the last four hundred years or so, both the Judeo-Christian frame of reference and the classical frame of reference (drawing on the civilizations of ancient Greece and Rome) have been quite important. Western culture, a broad culture that includes many nations and many religious and social groups, is largely defined within these two frames of reference—or it has been until quite recently. As religious belief in the west has eroded over the past two or three centuries, and as classical civilization has been less emphasized and less studied, poets have felt increasingly less comfortable in assuming that their audiences share a knowledge of their systems, but they have often continued to use them to isolate and articulate human traits that have cultural continuity and importance. More recently, poets have drawn on other cultural myths—Native American, African, and Asian, for example—to expand our sense of common heritage and give new meaning to the "American" and "Western" experience. The poems that follow draw on details from different myths and do so in a variety of different ways and tones.

JOHN HOLLANDER

Adam's Task

> And Adam gave names to all cattle, and to the fowl of the air, and
> to every beast of the field . . .
>
> —Gen. 2:20

Thou, paw-paw-paw; thou, glurd; thou, spotted
Glurd; thou, whitestap, lurching through

The high-grown brush; thou, pliant-footed,
  Implex; thou, awagabu.

Every burrower, each flier   5
  Came for the name he had to give:
Gay, first work, ever to be prior,
  Not yet sunk to primitive.

Thou, verdle; thou, McFleery's pomma;
  Thou; thou; thou—three types of grawl;   10
Thou, flisket; thou, kabasch; thou, comma-
  Eared mashawk; thou, all; thou, all.

Were, in a fire of becoming,
  Laboring to be burned away,
Then work, half-measuring, half-humming,   15
  Would be as serious as play.

Thou, pambler; thou, rivarn; thou, greater
  Wherret, and thou, lesser one;
Thou, sproal; thou, zant; thou, lily-eater.
  Naming's over. Day is done.   1971   20

SUSAN DONNELLY

Eve Names the Animals

To me, *lion* was sun on a wing
over the garden. *Dove,*
a burrowing, blind creature.

I swear that man
never knew animals. Words   5
he lined up according to size,

while elephants slipped flat-eyed
through water

and trout
hurtled from the underbrush, tusked   10
and ready for battle.

The name he gave me stuck
me to him. He did it to comfort me,
for not being first.

Mornings, while he slept,   15
I got away. Pickerel
hopped on the branches above me.
Only spider accompanied me,

nosing everywhere,
running up to lick my hand.

20

Poor finch. I suppose I was
woe to him—
the way he'd come looking for me,
not wanting either of us

25
to be ever alone

But to myself I was
palomino
    raven
        fox . . .

I strung words

30
by their stems and wore them
as garlands on my long walks.

The next day
I'd find them withered.

35
I liked change.

1985

CHRISTINA ROSSETTI

Eve

"While I sit at the door,
Sick to gaze within,
Mine eye weepeth sore
For sorrow and sin:

5
As a tree my sin stands
To darken all lands;
Death is the fruit it bore.

"How have Eden bowers grown
Without Adam to bend them!

10
How have Eden flowers blown,
Squandering their sweet breath,
Without me to tend them!
The Tree of Life was ours,
Tree twelvefold-fruited,[1]

15
Most lofty tree that flowers,
Most deeply rooted:
I chose the Tree of Death.[2]

1. The tree of life is so described in Revelation 22:2, 14, but the account there is of the New Jerusalem, not of Eden.   2. The Genesis account distinguishes between the tree of life and the tree of the knowledge of good and evil; the latter is forbidden, and eating of it brings labor, sickness, and death into the world. See Genesis 2:9, 3:1–24.

"Hadst thou but said me nay,
   Adam, my brother,
I might have pined away—
   I, but none other: 20
God might have let thee stay
   Safe in our garden,
By putting me away
   Beyond all pardon.   25

"I, Eve, sad mother
   Of all who must live,
I, not another,
   Plucked bitterest fruit to give
My friend, husband, lover.   30
O wanton eyes run over!
Who but I should grieve?—
   Cain hath slain his brother:[3]
Of all who must die mother,
   Miserable Eve!"   35

Thus she sat weeping,
   Thus Eve our mother,
Where one lay sleeping
   Slain by his brother.
Greatest and least   40
   Each piteous beast
To hear her voice
   Forgot his joys
And set aside his feast.

The mouse paused in his walk   45
   And dropped his wheaten stalk:
Grave cattle wagged their heads
   In rumination;
The eagle gave a cry
   From his cloud station: 50
Larks on thyme beds
   Forbore to mount or sing;
Bees dropped upon the wing;
   The raven perched on high
Forgot his ration;   55
   The conies[4] in their rock,
A feeble nation,
   Quaked sympathetical;
The mocking-bird left off to mock;
   Huge camels knelt as if   60
In deprecation;

3. Abel (see Genesis 4:1–15).   4. A common term for rabbits, but here probably the small pachyderms mentioned in Proverbs 30:26.

The kind hart's tears were falling;
Chattered the wistful stork;
Dove-voices with a dying fall
Cooed desolation
65 Answering grief by grief.

Only the serpent in the dust,
Wriggling and crawling,
Grinned an evil grin, and thrust
70 1865 His tongue out with its fork.

ALFRED, LORD TENNYSON

Ulysses[5]

It little profits that an idle king,
By this still hearth, among these barren crags,
Matched with an agéd wife,[6] I mete and dole
Unequal laws unto a savage race,
5 That hoard, and sleep, and feed, and know not me.

I cannot rest from travel; I will drink
Life to the lees.[7] All times I have enjoyed
Greatly, have suffered greatly, both with those
That loved me, and alone; on shore, and when
10 Through scudding drifts the rainy Hyades[8]
Vexed the dim sea. I am become a name;
For always roaming with a hungry heart
Much have I seen and known—cities of men
And manners, climates, councils, governments,
15 Myself not least, but honored of them all—
And drunk delight of battle with my peers,
Far on the ringing plains of windy Troy.
I am a part of all that I have met;
Yet all experience is an arch wherethrough
20 Gleams that untraveled world, whose margin fades
For ever and for ever when I move.
How dull it is to pause, to make an end,
To rust unburnished, not to shine in use!
As though to breathe were life. Life piled on life
25 Were all too little, and of one to me
Little remains; but every hour is saved
From that eternal silence, something more,

5. After the end of the Trojan War, Ulysses (or Odysseus), king of Ithaca and one of the Greek heroes of the war, returned to his island home (line 34). Homer's account of the situation is in *The Odyssey*, Book XI, but Dante's account of Ulysses in *The Inferno*, XXVI, is the more immediate background of the poem. 6. Penelope. 7. All the way down to the bottom of the cup.
8. A group of stars that were supposed to predict rain when they rose at the same time as the sun.

A bringer of new things; and vile it were
For some three suns to store and hoard myself,
And this gray spirit yearning in desire   30
To follow knowledge like a sinking star,
Beyond the utmost bound of human thought.

   This is my son, mine own Telemachus,
To whom I leave the scepter and the isle—
Well-loved of me, discerning to fulfill   35
This labor by slow prudence to make mild
A rugged people, and through soft degrees
Subdue them to the useful and the good.
Most blameless is he, centered in the sphere
Of common duties, decent not to fail   40
In offices of tenderness, and pay
Meet adoration to my household gods,
When I am gone. He works his work, I mine.

   There lies the port; the vessel puffs her sail:
There gloom the dark, broad seas. My mariners,   45
Souls that have toiled, and wrought, and thought with me—
That ever with a frolic welcome took
The thunder and the sunshine, and opposed
Free hearts, free foreheads—you and I are old;
Old age hath yet his honor and his toil.   50
Death closes all; but something ere the end,
Some work of noble note, may yet be done,
Not unbecoming men that strove with Gods.
The lights begin to twinkle from the rocks;
The long day wanes; the slow moon climbs; the deep 55
Moans round with many voices. Come, my friends.
'Tis not too late to seek a newer world.
Push off, and sitting well in order smite
The sounding furrows; for my purpose holds
To sail beyond the sunset, and the baths   60
Of all the western stars, until I die.
It may be that the gulfs will wash us down;[9]
It may be we shall touch the Happy Isles,[1]
And see the great Achilles, whom we knew.
Though much is taken, much abides; and though   65
We are not now that strength which in old days
Moved earth and heaven, that which we are, we are:
One equal temper of heroic hearts,
Made weak by time and fate, but strong in will
To strive, to seek, to find, and not to yield.   70

1833

9. Beyond the Gulf of Gibraltar was supposed to be a chasm that led to Hades.   1. Elysium, the Islands of the Blessed, where heroes like Achilles (line 64) abide after death.

JAMES HARRISON

Penelope[2]

for Ken

Oh, I have no illusions as to what
he's been up to all these years—a sea
nymph here, a minor goddess there, and a free
for all with the odd monster to give the plot
the necessary epic tone. Not   5
that I'm saying he goes out of his way to be
led astray. It happens quite naturally,
I'm sure. But it happens.
                        So, since suitors squat
on my doorstep, why so squeamish? In the first
place because it's the property they're out   10
to get, with me as an afterthought perhaps.
Then they're so callow. But mostly, having nursed
forebearance for twenty years, I'm not about
to have him forgiving me my only lapse.   1983

MIRIAM WADDINGTON

Ulysses Embroidered

You've come
at last from
all your journeying
to the old blind woman
in the tower,   5
Ulysses.

After all adventurings
through seas and
mountains through
giant battles,   10
storms and death,
from pinnacles
to valleys;

Past sirens
naked on rocks   15

---

2. "*Penelope*—wife of Ulysses, stuck at home the ten years he spent fighting Troy, and the further ten it took him to find his way back to Ithaca." (Harrison's note)

between Charybdis
and Scylla, from
dragons' teeth,
from sleep in
stables choking   20
on red flowers
walking through weeds
and through shipwreck.

And now you are
climbing the stairs,   25
taking shape,
a figure in shining
thread rising from
a golden shield:
a medallion   30
emblazoned in
tapestry you grew
from the blind hands
of Penelope.

Her tapestry   35
saw everything,
her stitches
embroidered the
painful colors
of her breath the   40
long sighing touch
of her hands.

She made many
journeys.   1992

EDNA ST. VINCENT MILLAY

An Ancient Gesture

I thought, as I wiped my eyes on the corner of my apron:
Penelope did this too.
And more than once: you can't keep weaving all day
And undoing it all through the night;
Your arms get tired, and the back of your neck gets tight   5
And along towards morning, when you think it will never be light,
And your husband has been gone, and you don't know where, for years,
Suddenly you burst into tears;
There is simply nothing else to do.
And I thought, as I wiped my eyes on the corner of my apron: 10

This is an ancient gesture, authentic, antique,
In the very best tradition, classic, Greek;
Ulysses did this too.
But only as a gesture,—a gesture which implied
To the assembled throng that he was much too moved to speak.
He learned it from Penelope . . .
Penelope, who really cried.

1954

LANGSTON HUGHES

The Negro Speaks of Rivers

I've known rivers:
I've known rivers ancient as the world and older than the flow of human blood
   in human veins.

My soul has grown deep like the rivers.

I bathed in the Euphrates when dawns were young.
I built my hut near the Congo and it lulled me to sleep.
I looked upon the Nile and raised the pyramids above it.
I heard the singing of the Mississippi when Abe Lincoln went down to New
   Orleans, and I've seen its muddy bosom turn all golden in the sunset.

I've known rivers:
Ancient, dusky rivers.

My soul has grown deep like the rivers.

1926

JUNE JORDAN

Something Like a Sonnet for Phillis Miracle Wheatley

Girl from the realm of birds florid and fleet
flying full feather in far or near weather
Who fell to a dollar lust coffled like meat
Captured by avarice and hate spit together
Trembling asthmatic alone on the slave block
built by a savagery travelling by carriage
viewed like a species of flaw in the livestock
A child without safety of mother or marriage

Chosen by whimsy but born to surprise
They taught you to read but you learned how to write
Begging the universe into your eyes:

They dressed you in light but you dreamed with the night.
From Africa singing of justice and grace,
Your early verse sweetens the fame of our Race.   1989

MAYA ANGELOU

Africa

Thus she had lain
sugar cane sweet
deserts her hair
golden her feet
mountains her breasts   5
two Niles her tears
Thus she has lain
Black through the years.

Over the white seas
rime white and cold   10
brigands ungentled
icicle bold
took her young daughters
sold her strong sons
churched her with Jesus   15
bled her with guns.
Thus she has lain.

Now she is rising
remember her pain
remember the losses   20
her screams loud and vain
remember her riches
her history slain
now she is striding
although she had lain.   1975   25

DEREK WALCOTT

A Far Cry from Africa

A wind is ruffling the tawny pelt
Of Africa. Kikuyu,[3] quick as flies,

---

3. An East African tribe whose members, as Mau Mau fighters, conducted an eight-year terrorist campaign against British colonial settlers in Kenya.

Batten upon the bloodstreams of the veldt.[4]
Corpses are scattered through a paradise.
5 Only the worm, colonel of carrion, cries:
"Waste no compassion on these separate dead!"
Statistics justify and scholars seize
The salients of colonial policy.
What is that to the white child hacked in bed?
10 To savages, expendable as Jews?

Threshed out by beaters,[5] the long rushes break
In a white dust of ibises whose cries
Have wheeled since civilization's dawn
From the parched river or beast-teeming plain.
15 The violence of beast on beast is read
As natural law, but upright man
Seeks his divinity by inflicting pain.
Delirious as these worried beasts, his wars
Dance to the tightened carcass of a drum,
20 While he calls courage still that native dread
Of the white peace contracted by the dead.

Again brutish necessity wipes its hands
Upon the napkin of a dirty cause, again
A waste of our compassion, as with Spain,[6]
25 The gorilla wrestles with the superman.
I who am poisoned with the blood of both,
Where shall I turn, divided to the vein?
I who have cursed
The drunken officer of British rule, how choose
30 Between this Africa and the English tongue I love?
Betray them both, or give back what they give?
How can I face such slaughter and be cool?
How can I turn from africa and live?   1962

ISHMAEL REED

I Am a Cowboy in the Boat of Ra

The devil must be forced to reveal any such physical evil (potions,
charms, fetishes, etc.) still outside the body and these must be
burned.
—*Rituale Romanum*, published 1947, endorsed by the coat of
arms and introduction letter from Francis Cardinal Spellman

---

4. Open country, neither cultivated nor forest (Afrikaans).   5. In big-game hunting, natives are
hired to beat the brush, driving birds—such as ibises—and animals into the open.   6. The Spanish Civil War (1936–39), in which the Loyalists were supported by liberals in the West and militarily
by Soviet Communists, and the rebels by Nazi Germany and Fascist Italy.

I am a cowboy in the boat of Ra,[7]
sidewinders in the saloons of fools
bit my forehead like O
the untrustworthiness of Egyptologists
Who do not know their trips. Who was that   5
dog-faced man?[8] they asked, the day I rode
from town.

School marms with halitosis cannot see
the Nefertiti[9] fake chipped on the run by slick
germans, the hawk behind Sonny Rollins' head or   10
the ritual beard of his axe,[1] a longhorn winding
its bells thru the Field of Reeds.

I am a cowboy in the boat of Ra. I bedded
down with Isis,[2] Lady of the Boogaloo, dove
down deep in her horny, stuck up her Wells-Far-ago   15
in daring midday get away. "Start grabbing the
blue," i said from top of my double crown.

I am a cowboy in the boat of Ra. Ezzard Charles[3]
of the Chisholm Trail. Took up the bass but they
blew off my thumb. Alchemist in ringmanship but a   20
sucker for the right cross.

I am a cowboy in the boat of Ra. Vamoosed from
the temple i bide my time. The price on the wanted
poster was a-going down, outlaw alias copped my stance
and moody greenhorns were making me dance; while my mouth's   25
shooting iron got its chambers jammed.

I am a cowboy in the boat of Ra. Boning-up in
the ol West i bide my time. You should see
me pick off these tin cans whippersnappers. I
write the motown long plays for the comeback of   30
Osiris.[4] Make them up when stars stare at sleeping
steer out here near the campfire. Women arrive
on the backs of goats and throw themselves on
my Bowie.[5]

I am a cowboy in the boat of Ra. Lord of the lash,   35
the Loup Garou[6] Kid. Half breed son of Pisces and

---

7. Chief of the ancient Egyptian gods, creator and protector of humans and vanquisher of Evil.
8. The Egyptian god of the dead, Anubis was usually depicted as a man with the head of a dog or
jackal.   9. Fourteenth-century B.C. Egyptian queen; elsewhere Reed says that German scholars
are responsible for the notion that her dynasty was white.   1. Saxophone. *Sonny Rollins:* jazz
great of the late 1950s and early 1960s.   2. Principal goddess of ancient Egypt.   3. World
heavyweight boxing champion, 1949–51.   4. Husband of Isis and constant foe of his brother Set
(line 48). Tricked by Set, he died violently but later rose from the dead.   5. Large hunting knife.
6. French for werewolf; in voodoo, a priest who has run amok or gone mad.

Aquarius. I hold the souls of men in my pot. I do
the dirty boogie with scorpions. I make the bulls
keep still and was the first swinger to grape the taste.

40 I am a cowboy in his boat. Pope Joan[7] of the
Ptah Ra. C / mere a minute willya doll?
Be a good girl and
Bring me my Buffalo horn of black powder
Bring me my headdress of black feathers
45 Bring me my bones of Ju-Ju snake
Go get my eyelids of red paint.
Hand me my shadow
I'm going into town after Set

I am a cowboy in the boat of Ra
50 look out Set   here i come Set
to get Set   to sunset Set
to unseat Set   to Set down Set
              usurper of the Royal couch
              imposter RAdio of Moses' bush[8]
55   party pooper O hater of dance
              vampire outlaw of the milky way   1969

JUDITH ORTIZ COFER

How to Get a Baby

To receive the *waiwaia* (spirit children) in the water seems to be
the most usual way of becoming pregnant. . . . They come along
on large tree trunks, and they may be attached to seascum and
dead leaves floating on the surface.
      —BRONISLAW MALINOWSKI,
      Baloma: The Spirits of the Dead in the Trobriand Islands

Go to the sea
the morning after a rainstorm,
preferably
fresh from your man's arms—
5 the *waiwaia* are drawn
to love smell.
They are tiny luminous fish

7. Mythical female pope, supposed to have succeeded to the papacy in 855. *Ptah Ra*: chief god of
Memphis, capital of ancient Egypt.   8. Which, according to Exodus 3:2, burned but was not
consumed and from which Moses heard the voice of God telling him to lead the Israelites out of
Egypt.

and blind. You must call
the soul of your child
in the name of your ancestors: 10
Come to me, little fish, come
to Tamala, Tudava, come to me.
Sit in shallow water
up to your waist until the tide
pulls away from you   15
like an exhausted lover.
You will by then
be carrying new life.
Make love that night,
and every night,   20
to let the little one
who chooses you know
she is one with your joy.   1993

ALBERTO ALVARO RÍOS

Advice to a First Cousin

The way the world works is like this:
for the bite of scorpions, she says,
my grandmother to my first cousin,
because I might die and someone must know,
go to the animal jar   5
the one with the soup of green herbs
mixed with the scorpions I have been putting in
still alive. Take one out
put it on the bite. It has had time to think
there with the others—put the lid back tight—   10
and knows that a biting is not the way to win
a finger or a young girl's foot.
It will take back into itself the hurting
the redness and the itching and its marks.

But the world works like this, too: 15
look out for the next scorpion you see,
she says, and makes a big face to scare me
thereby instructing my cousin, look out!
for one of the scorpion's many
illegitimate and unhappy sons.   20
It will be smarter, more of the devil.
It will have lived longer than these dead ones.
It will know from them something more
about the world, in the way mothers know
when something happens to a child, or how   25
I knew from your sadness you had been bitten.

It will learn something stronger than biting.
Look out most for that scorpion, she says,
making a big face to scare me again and it works
30 I go—crying—she lets me go—they laugh,
the way you must look out for men
who have not yet bruised you.   1985

DUNCAN CAMPBELL SCOTT

The Onondaga[9] Madonna

She stands full-throated and with careless pose,
This woman of a weird and waning race,
The tragic savage lurking in her face,
Where all her pagan passion burns and glows;
5 Her blood is mingled with her ancient foes,
And thrills with war and wildness in her veins;
Her rebel lips are dabbled with the stains
Of feuds and forays and her father's woes.
And closer in the shawl about her breast,
10 The latest promise of her nation's doom,
Paler than she her baby clings and lies,
The primal warrior gleaming from his eyes;
He sulks, and burdened with his infant gloom,
He draws his heavy brows and will not rest.   1898

CATHY SONG

A Mehinaku Girl in Seclusion

When the pequi fruit blossomed,
I went into seclusion.
A red flower
dropped out of my body
5 and stained the red dirt of the earth
one color. With one color
I became married to the earth.
I went to live by myself
in the hut at the end of the village.

There no one must see me.
10 For three years,
no one must touch me.

9. One of the five groups of Native Americans forming what became known as the League of Five Nations, or the Iroquois Confederacy, the Onondaga originated in upper New York State; many moved to Canada after the American Revolution and now form part of the Six Nations Reserve near Brantford, Ontario.

The men carve the spirit birds
and dream of me
becoming beautiful in the dark.   15
They say my skin
will be as delicate as the light
that touches the spider's web.
The women walk to the river
and bathe and time passes.   20

One woman, the old one,
brings me news of the harvest,
the names of the children who are born.
The children are taught
to make babies out of mud,   25
babies in the shape of gourds.
The children cry when the rains come.

When the rain comes I slip out
and circle the dirt plaza.
I pause as if to drink at each door.   30
At each door,
the sound of the sleeping.
I return before the first
hint of light,
return to hear   35
the click of my spinning.

I will learn to become
mistress of the hammocks.
The man who will be my husband
shall be proud.   40
When I walk beside him
to bathe in the river,
I will say with my body,
He is mine.
The manioc bread he eats   45
becomes the children I will bear.
His hammocks are not tattered.
Ask him. Yes, ask him.
I am learning to say this
with my body.   1988   50

LOUISE ERDRICH

Jacklight

The same Chippewa word is used both for flirting and hunting
game, while another Chippewa word connotes both using force
in intercourse and also killing a bear with one's bare hands.

—DUNNING 1959

We have come to the edge of the woods,
out of brown grass where we slept, unseen,
out of knotted twigs, out of leaves creaked shut,
out of hiding.

5   At first the light wavered, glancing over us.
Then it clenched to a fist of light that pointed,
searched out, divided us.
Each took the beams like direct blows the heart answers.
Each of us moved forward alone.

10 We have come to the edge of the woods,
drawn out of ourselves by this night sun,
this battery of polarized acids,
that outshines the moon.

We smell them behind it
15 but they are faceless, invisible,
We smell the raw steel of their gun barrels,
mink oil on leather, their tongues of sour barley.
We smell their mother buried chin-deep in wet dirt.

We smell their fathers with scoured knuckles,
20 teeth cracked from hot marrow.
We smell their sisters of crushed dogwood, bruised apples,
of fractured cups and concussions of burnt hooks.

We smell their breath steaming lightly behind the jacklight.
We smell the itch underneath the caked guts on their clothes.
25 We smell their minds like silver hammers
cocked back, held in readiness
for the first of us to step into the open.

We have come to the edge of the woods,
out of brown grass where we slept, unseen,
30 out of leaves creaked shut, out of our hiding.
We have come here too long.

It is their turn now,
their turn to follow us. Listen,
they put down their equipment.
35 It is useless in the tall brush.
And now they take the first steps, not knowing
how deep the woods are and lightless.
How deep the woods are.   1984

▼   ▼   ▼

LITERARY TRADITION AS CONTEXT A Glossary

aubade: a morning song in which the coming of dawn is either celebrated or denounced as a nuisance

ballad: a narrative poem that is, or originally was, meant to be sung; characterized by repetition and often by a repeated refrain (recurrent phrase or series of phrases), ballads were originally a folk creation, transmitted orally from person to person and age to age

confessional poem: a relatively new (or recently defined) kind in which the speaker describes a confused, chaotic state of mind, which becomes a metaphor for the larger world

conventions: standard ways of saying things in verse, employed to achieve certain expected effects

dramatic monologue: a monologue set in a specific situation and spoken to someone

echo: a reference that recalls a word, phrase, or sound in another text

elegy: in classical times, any poem on any subject written in "elegiac" meter, but since the Renaissance usually a formal lament for the death of a particular person

epic: a poem that celebrates, in a continuous narrative, the achievements of mighty heroes and heroines, usually in founding a nation or developing a culture, and uses elevated language and a grand, high style

epigram: originally any poem carved in stone (on tombstones, buildings, gates, etc.), but in modern usage a very short, usually witty verse with a quick turn at the end

lyric: originally designated poems meant to be sung to the accompaniment of a lyre; now a short poem in which the speaker expresses intense personal emotion rather than describing a narrative or dramatic situation

meditation: a contemplation of some physical object as a way of reflecting upon some larger truth, often (but not necessarily) a spiritual one

motif: a recurrent device, formula, or situation that deliberately connects a poem with common patterns of existing thought

myth: stories that are more or less universally shared within a culture to explain its history, traditions

pastoral: a poem (also called an eclogue, a bucolic, or an idyll) that describes the simple life of country folk, usually shepherds who live a timeless, painless (and sheepless) life in a world that is full of beauty, music, and love, and that remains forever green

protest poem: an attack, sometimes indirect, on institutions or social injustices

soliloquy: a monologue in which the character is alone and speaking only to him- or herself

tradition: an inherited, established, or customary practice

QUESTIONS

1. How, specifically, is the speaker undercut in Jonson's "Come, My Celia"? Explain how the strategy of allusion works in this poem.

2. Are Moore's notes to "Love in America" adequate to explain the allusions in her poem? What other information do you wish to have? After you have unearthed that information in your college library, show in detail how each separate allusion in the poem works. How would you paraphrase the poem? Why is there a question mark in the poem's title?

3. List all the metaphors you can find in "An Epitaph upon a Young Married Couple, Dead and Buried Together." How closely are the metaphors related to each other? Which metaphors seem especially appropriate to an epitaph? to the epigram as a poetic kind?

4. Which epitaph in the chapter seems to you the most likely actually to end up on a tombstone? Why? What features would prevent most of the "epitaphs" here from actually being used? Which epitaph here seems to you the wittiest? In what, exactly, does the wit consist? Do you like the epigrams better or worse that have a "sting" at the end? Why?

5. Read through a number of the very short poems in this book and pick out one of no more than eight lines that does not seem to you to qualify as an epigram. What features of the poem make that label inappropriate? On the basis of what you know about poetic kinds, can you assign a label to it?

6. Read the Cummings poem "(ponder,darling,these busted statues" closely in relation to "To His Coy Mistress." In what specific ways does it echo Marvell's poem? Which images are specifically derived from Marvell? In what specific ways does the Cummings poem undercut the argument of the Marvell poem? In what ways does it undercut its own argument? to what purpose?

7. Indicate the specific ways in which Ralegh's poem "replies" to Marlowe's. In what points does Williams agree with Ralegh? What, exactly, is "unfair" about Skirrow's summary of Keats? How do you think Keats would justify himself against Skirrow's summary?

8. What attitudes toward Adam and Eve are displayed in the Donnelly, Hollander, and Rossetti poems? Which poems develop the strongest negative attitudes toward their "heroes" or "heroines"? How does Harrison's version of the Ulysses story differ from Tennyson's? How do Waddington's and Millay's versions differ? What values are associated with Africa in the Hughes, Angelou, and Reed poems? What is the "cowboy" doing in Reed's poem?

WRITING SUGGESTIONS

1. In what specific ways is "To His Coy Mistress" anchored to its historical or cultural context? Can you tell that it is written by a 17th-century poet? How? What historical or cultural "allusions" anchor the poem to its specific moment in time? to its philosophical or thematic contexts? In what specific ways does the de Vries poem establish itself as contemporary? Write a short (500–700 word) essay in which you show how de Vries undercuts the assumptions of Marvell. (Alternative: write a short essay in which you show how Cummings undercuts the assumptions of Marvell.)

2. Choose randomly any six of the epigrams in this chapter, and try to decide on the basis of them what a good definition of the epigram might be. Write down your definition, mentioning any features of epigram that seem to you crucial to the kind. Then choose a seventh poem from the chapter, one that seems to you entirely typical of the epigram kind, and write a brief, three-paragraph analysis of it, showing exactly how it uses features mentioned in your definition.

3. Using one of the poems in this chapter as your model, try your hand at writing an epigram (of no more than four lines) of your own. When you have completed your poem, write a brief paragraph about it, describing how you have used features characteristic of the poetic kind.

4. Using a poetry index (available in the reference section of your college library), find half a dozen poems that use the term "elegy" in their titles, and compare their tones and strategies. Try to decide what features and expectations seem to be central to the poetic kind. Then look back at "On My First Son" (p. 659), often said to be a typical elegy, and write a brief (two-page) analysis of the poem in which you show how it uses and transforms the expectations associated with the elegy as a poetic kind.

5. In an essay of about three pages, show how the primary effects of "I Am a Cowboy in the Boat of Ra" relate to its use of cultural myths. (Alternative: apply this same question to Rossetti's "Eve," Tennyson's "Ulysses," or Song's "A Mehinaku Girl in Seclusion.")

12 HISTORY AND CULTURE AS CONTEXT

T
he more you know, the better a reader of poetry you are likely to be. And that goes for general knowledge as well as knowledge of other poetry and literary traditions. Poems often draw upon a larger fund of human knowledge about all sorts of things, asking us to bring to bear on a poem facts and values we have taken on from earlier reading or from our experiences in the world more generally. The first section of this book—the introductory chapter on *Reading, Responding, and Writing* and the first eight chapters—suggests how practice makes interpretation easier and better: the more you read and the more close analysis you do, the better interpreter you are likely to become. But in this "contextual" section we are concerned with information you need to read richly and fully—information about authors, about events that influenced them or became the inspiration or basis for their writing, and about literary traditions that provide a context for their work. Poets always write in a specific time, under particular circumstances, and with some awareness of the world around them, whether or not they specifically refer to it in a particular poem. In this chapter, our concern is with the specifically historical and cultural—events, movements, ideas that directly influence poets or that poets in some way represent in the poems they write.

Very little that you know will ultimately go to waste in your reading of poetry. The best potential reader of poetry is someone who has already developed reading skills to perfection, read everything, thought deeply about all kinds of things, and who is wise beyond belief—wise enough to know exactly how to apply what she or he knows accurately to a given text. But that is the ideal reader we all strive to be, not the one any of us actually is. Although no poet really expects any reader to be all those things, good readers try. And sometimes poets seem to write as if they expect such skills and knowledge. Poems can be just as demanding—or at least requestful—of readers about historical information as about the intricacies of language and form. Poems not only *refer to* people, places, and events—things that exist in time—but they also *are* themselves products of given moments, participating in both the potentialities and the limitations of the times in which they were created.

Things that happen every day frequently find their way into poetry in an easy and yet often forceful manner. Making love in a junkyard, as in "Cherrylog Road," is one kind of example; a reader doesn't need to know what particular junkyard was involved—or imaginatively involved—in order to understand the poem, but a reader does need to know what an auto junkyard was like in the mid-twentieth century, with more or less whole car bodies being scattered in various states of disarray over a large plot of ground. But what if, over the next generation or two, junkyards completely disappear as other ways are found to dispose of old cars? Already a lot of old cars are crushed into small metal blocks, especially in large cities. But what if the metal is all melted down, or the junk is orbited into space? If that should happen, readers then will have never seen a junkyard, and they will need a footnote to explain what such junkyards were like. The history of junkyards will not be lost—there will be pictures, films, records, and someone will write definitive books about the forms and functions of junkyards, probably even including the fact that lovers occasionally visited them—but the public memory of junkyards will soon disappear. No social customs, nothing that is made, no institutions or sites last forever.

Readers may still be able to experience "Cherrylog Road" when junkyards disappear, but they will need some help, and they may think its particulars a little quaint, much as we regard literature that involves horses and buggies—or even making love in the back seat of a parked car—as quaint now. Institutions change, habits change, times change, places and settings change—all kinds of particulars change, even when people's wants, needs, and foibles pretty much go on in the same way. Footnotes never provide a precise or adequate substitute for the ease and pleasure that come from already knowing, but they can help us understand and pave the way for feeling and experience. A kind of imaginative historical sympathy can be simulated and in fact created, for poems from earlier times that refer to specific contemporary details (and that have now become to us, in our own time, *historical* details) often describe human nature and human experiences very much as we still know and experience them. Today's poem may need tomorrow's footnote, but the poem need not be tomorrow's puzzle or only a curiosity or fossil.

The following poem, not many years old, already requires some explanation, not only because the factual details of its occasion may not be known to every reader, but also because the whole spirit of the poem may be difficult to appreciate unless one knows its circumstances.

RAYMOND R. PATTERSON

You Are the Brave

You are the brave who do not break
In the grip of the mob when the blow comes straight
To the shattered bone; when the sockets shriek;
When your arms lie twisted under your back.

5   Good men holding their courage slack
In their frightened pockets see how weak
The work that is done; and feel the weight
Of your blood on the ground for their spirits' sake;

And build their anger, stone on stone;
10   1962   Each silently, but not alone.

I can remember teaching this poem in class during the Vietnam War and
finding that a lot of students were hostile to it because they assumed it to be a
poem in praise of patriotism and war. More recently it has seemed to some
readers to be about Lebanon, or Bosnia, or a variety of other sites of painful violence. Sometimes the difficulty about factual information is that one doesn't
know that one *needs* specific information. In a poem like "You Are the Brave,"
it is fairly easy to assume (incorrectly, but understandably) that the conflict
involved is a war and that the speaker addresses, and honors, a group of soldiers. Actually, there are clues in the poem that this conflict is, if as bitter as
war, one in which mob violence (line 2) and enforced restraint (line 4) are
involved. The date of the poem is a clue too—1962, when the American civil
rights struggle was at its height. Once that "fact" is noticed, the whole historical context of the poem, if not its *immediate* occasion in terms of one specific
civil rights march in one place on one day, becomes clear. In fact, since the
poem doesn't mention a particular time and place, we may assume that it is
not about the particulars of one specific incident, but instead gathers the kind
of details that characterized many moments of the early 1960s. The poem's
details (generalized details about mob resentments and brutalities in a situation
of passive resistance), its metaphors in the second and third stanzas, and its dignified tone of praise for "the brave" all make sense readily when the right information is available. The poem does not mention specific time and place
because its concern is not confined to one event, but its location in time is
important to finding what it refers to. Poems may be referential to one single
event or moment, or to some larger situation that may span weeks, months, or
even years. The amount of particularity in the poem will tell you.

How do you know what you need to know? The easiest clue is your own puzzlement. When it seems that something is happening in a poem that you don't recognize—and yet the poem makes no apparent effort to clarify it—you have a clue that readers at the time the poem was written must have recognized something that is not now such common knowledge. Once you know you don't know, it only takes a little work to find out: most college libraries contain far more information than you will ever need, and the trick is to search efficiently. Your ability to find the information will depend upon how well you know the written reference materials and computer searches available to you. Practice helps. Knowledge accumulates. Most poems printed in textbooks like this one will be annotated for you with basic facts, but often you may need additional information to interpret the poem's full meaning and resonance. An editor, trying to satisfy the needs of a variety of readers, may not always decide to write the footnote you in particular may need, so there could be digging to do in the library for any poem you read, certainly for those you come upon in magazines and books of poetry without footnotes. Few poets like to footnote their own work (they'd rather let you struggle a little to appreciate them), and besides, many things that now need footnotes didn't when they were written, as in "You Are the Brave."

The two poems that follow both require from the reader some specific "referential" information, but they differ considerably in their emphasis on the particularities of time and place. The first poem, "Channel Firing," reflects and refers to a moment just before the outbreak of World War I when British naval forces were preparing for combat by taking gunnery practice in the English Channel. The second, "Sonnet: The Ladies' Home Journal," reflects a longer cultural moment in which attitudes and assumptions, rather than some specific event, are crucial to understanding the poem.

THOMAS HARDY

Channel Firing

That night your great guns, unawares,
Shook all our coffins as we lay,
And broke the chancel window squares,[1]
We thought it was the Judgment-day

And sat upright. While drearisome   5
Arose the howl of wakened hounds:

1. The windows near the altar in a church.

The mouse let fall the altar-crumb,[2]
The worms drew back into the mounds,

The glebe cow[3] drooled. Till God called, "No;
10   It's gunnery practice out at sea
Just as before you went below;
The world is as it used to be:

"All nations striving strong to make
Red war yet redder. Mad as hatters
15   They do no more for Christés sake
Than you who are helpless in such matters.

"That this is not the judgment-hour
For some of them's a blessed thing,
For if it were they'd have to scour
20   Hell's floor for so much threatening . . .

"Ha, ha. It will be warmer when
I blow the trumpet (if indeed
I ever do; for you are men,
And rest eternal sorely need)."

25   So down we lay again. "I wonder,
Will the world ever saner be,"
Said one, "than when He sent us under
In our indifferent century!"

And many a skeleton shook his head.
30   "Instead of preaching forty year,"
My neighbor Parson Thirdly said,
"I wish I had stuck to pipes and beer."

Again the guns disturbed the hour,
Roaring their readiness to avenge.
35   As far inland as Stourton Tower,
April 1914   And Camelot, and starlit Stonehenge.[4]

---

2. Breadcrumbs from the Blessed Sacrament.   3. Parish cow pastured on the meadow next to the churchyard.   4. Stourton Tower, built in the 18th century to commemorate King Alfred's ninth-century victory over the Danes, in Stourhead Park, Wiltshire. Camelot is the legendary site of King Arthur's court, said to have been in Cornwall or Somerset. Stonehenge, a circular formation of upright stones dating from about 1800 B.C., is on Salisbury Plain, Wiltshire; it is thought to have been a ceremonial site for political and religious occasions or an early scientific experiment in astronomy.

SANDRA GILBERT

Sonnet: The Ladies' Home Journal

The brilliant stills of food, the cozy
glossy, bygone life—mashed potatoes
posing as whipped cream, a neat mom
conjuring shapes from chaos, trimming the flame—
how we ached for all that,   5
that dance of love in the living room,
those paneled walls, that kitchen golden
as the inside of a seed: how we leaned
on those shiny columns of advice,
stroking the *thank yous*, the firm thighs, the wise   10
closets full of soap.

> But even then
we knew it was the lies we loved, the lies
we wore like Dior coats,[5] the clean-cut airtight
lies that laid out our lives in black and white.   1984

"Channel Firing" is not ultimately *about* World War I, for its emphasis is
finally on how human behavior stays the same from age to age, but it begins
from a particular historical vantage point. It would be difficult to make much
sense of the poem if the reader were not to recognize the importance of that
specific reference, and the poem's situation (with a waking corpse as the main
speaker) is difficult enough to sort out even with the clue of the careful dating
at the end (the date here is actually a part of the poem, recorded on the manuscript by the author and always printed as part of the text). The firing of the
guns has awakened the dead who are buried near the channel, and in their
puzzlement they assume it is Judgment Day, time for them to arise, until God
enters and tells them what is happening. Much of the poem's effect depends
on character portrayal—a God who laughs and sounds cynical, a parson who
regrets his selfless life and wishes he had indulged himself more—as well as
the sense that nothing ever changes. But particularity of time and place are crucial to this sense of changelessness; even so important a contemporary moment
as the beginning of a world war—a moment viewed by most people at the time
as unique and world-changing—fades into a timeless parade of moments that
stretches over centuries of history. The geographical particulars cited at the

5. Designer coats by Christian Dior.

end—as the sound of the guns moves inland to be heard in place after place—make the same point. Great moments in history are all encompassed in the sound of the guns and its message about human behavior. Times, places, and events, however important they seem, all become part of some larger pattern that denies individuality or uniqueness.

The particulars in "Sonnet: The Ladies' Home Journal" work rather differently—to remind us not of a specific time that readers need to identify but to characterize a way of seeing and thinking. The referentiality here is more cultural than historical; it is based more on ideas and attitudes characteristic of a particular period than on a specific moment or location. The pictures in the magazine stand for a whole way of thinking about women that was characteristic of the time when the *Ladies' Home Journal* flourished as a popular magazine. The poem implicitly contrasts the "lies" (line 12) of the magazine with the truth of the present—that women's lives and values are not to be seen as some fantasized sense of beautiful food, motherhood, social rituals, and commercial products. Two vastly different cultural attitudes—that of the poem's present, with its skeptical view of traditional women's roles, and that of a past that equated the superficiality of glossy photographs with gender identity—are at the heart of the poem. It is about cultural attitudes and their effects on actual human beings. Readers need to know what the *Ladies' Home Journal* was like in order to understand the poem; we do not need to know the date or contents of a specific issue, only that this popular magazine reflected the attitudes and values of a whole age and culture. The referentiality of this poem involves information about ideas and consciousness more than time and event.

To get at appropriate factual, cultural, and historical information, it is important to learn to ask three kinds of questions. One kind is obvious: it is the "Do I understand the reference to . . . ?" kind. When events, places, or people unfamiliar to you come up, you will need to find out what or who they are. The second kind of question is more difficult: How do you know, in a poem like "You Are the Brave," that you need to know more? When there are no specific references to look up, no people or events to identify, how do you know that there is a specific context? To get at this sort of question, you have to trust two people: the poet, and yourself. Learning to trust yourself, your own responses, is the more difficult—you can just decide to trust the poet. Usually, good poets know what they are doing. If they do, they will not want to puzzle you more than necessary, so that you can safely assume that something that is not self-explanatory will merit close attention and possibly some digging in the library. (Poets do make mistakes and miscalculations about their readers, but in an introductory way it is usually safe to assume they know what they are doing and why they are doing it.) References that are not in themselves clear (such as "the grip of the mob" or the "arms . . . twisted under your back" in "You Are the Brave") provide a strong clue that you need more information. And that is why you need to trust yourself: when something doesn't click, when the information given you does not seem enough, you need to trust your puzzlement and try to find the missing facts that will allow the poem to make sense. But how? Often the date of the poem is a help, as in "You Are the Brave." Sometimes the title gives a clue or a point of departure. Sometimes you can discover, by reading about the author, some of the things he or she was interested in or concerned about. There is no single all-purpose way to discover what to look for, but that kind of research—looking for clues, adding up the evidence—can be interesting in itself and very rewarding when it is successful.

The third question is why? For every factual reference, one needs to ask why. Why does the poem refer to this particular person instead of some other? What function does the reference serve?

Beyond the level of simply understanding that a particular poem is about an event or place or movement is the matter of developing a full sense of historical context, a sense of the larger significance and resonance of the historical occurrence or attitude referred to. Often a poem expects you to bring with you some sense of that significance; just as often it works to continue your education, telling you more, wanting you to understand and appreciate on the level of feeling some further things about this occurrence.

What we need to bring to our reading varies from poem to poem. For example, "Dulce et Decorum Est" (below), needs our knowledge that poison gas was used in World War I; the green tint through which the speaker sees the world in lines 13–14 comes from green glass in the goggles of the gas mask he has just put on. But some broader matters are important as well. Harder to specify but probably even more important is the climate of opinion that surrounded the war. To idealists, it was "the war to end all wars," and many participants—as well as politicians and propagandists—considered it a sacred mission, regarding the threat of Germany's expansionist policy as dangerous to Western civilization. No doubt you will read the poem more intelligently— and with more feeling—the more you know about World War I, and the same is true of poems about any historical occurrence or that refer to things that happen or situations that exist in a temporal or spatial context. But it is also true that your sense of these events will grow as a result of reading sensitively and thoughtfully the poems themselves. Facts are no substitute for skills. Once you have read individually the poems in this section, try taking a breather; and then at one sitting read them all again. Reading poetry can be a form of gaining knowledge as well as an aesthetic experience. One doesn't go to poetry to

seek information as such, but poems often give us more than we came for. The
ways to wisdom are paved with facts, and although poetry is not primarily a
data-conscious art, it often requires us to be aware, sometimes in detail, of its
referents in the real world.

Times, Places, and Events

IRVING LAYTON

From Colony to Nation

A dull people,
but the rivers of this country
are wide and beautiful

A dull people
5   enamoured of childish games,
but food is easily come by
and plentiful

Some with a priest's voice
in their cage of ribs: but
10   on high mountain-tops and in thunderstorms
the chirping is not heard

Deferring to beadle and censor;
not ashamed for this,
but given over to horseplay,
15   the making of money

A dull people, without charm or
ideas,
settling into the clean empty look
of a Mountie or dairy farmer
20   as into a legacy

One can ignore them
(the silences, the vast distances help)
and suppose them at the bottom
of one of the meaner lakes,
25   their bones not even picked for souvenirs.

                                          1956

CLAUDE McKAY

America

Although she feeds me bread of bitterness,
And sinks into my throat her tiger's tooth,
Stealing my breath of life, I will confess
I love this cultured hell that tests my youth!
Her vigor flows like tides into my blood,   5
Giving me strength erect against her hate.
Her bigness sweeps my being like a flood.
Yet as a rebel fronts a king in state,
I stand within her walls with not a shred
Of terror, malice, not a word of jeer.   10
Darkly I gaze into the days ahead,
And see her might and granite wonders there,
Beneath the touch of Time's unerring hand,
Like priceless treasures sinking in the sand.   1922

LANGSTON HUGHES

Harlem (A Dream Deferred)

What happens to a dream deferred?

Does it dry up
like a raisin in the sun?
Or fester like a sore—
And then run?   5
Does it stink like rotten meat?
Or crust and sugar over—
like a syrupy sweet?

Maybe it just sags
like a heavy load.   10

Or does it explode?   1951

ROBERT HAYDEN

Frederick Douglass[1]

When it is finally ours, this freedom, this liberty, this beautiful
and terrible thing, needful to man as air,
usable as earth; when it belongs at last to all,
when it is truly instinct, brain matter, diastole, systole,
5   reflex action; when it is finally won; when it is more
than the gaudy mumbo jumbo of politicians:
this man, this Douglass, this former slave, this Negro
beaten to his knees, exiled, visioning a world
where none is lonely, none hunted, alien,
10   this man, superb in love and logic, this man
shall be remembered. Oh, not with statues' rhetoric,
not with legends and poems and wreaths of bronze alone,
but with the lives grown out of his life, the lives
fleshing his dream of the beautiful, needful thing.   1966

THOMAS HARDY

The Convergence of the Twain

LINES ON THE LOSS OF THE "TITANIC"[2]

I

In a solitude of the sea
Deep from human vanity,
And the Pride of Life that planned her, stilly couches she.

II

Steel chambers, late the pyres
5   Of her salamandrine[3] fires,
Cold currents thrid,[4] and turn to rhythmic tidal lyres.

III

Over the mirrors meant
To glass the opulent
The sea-worm crawls—grotesque, slimed, dumb, indifferent.

1. Frederick Douglass (1817–1895), escaped slave. Douglass was involved in the Underground Railroad, and became the publisher of the famous abolitionist newspaper the *North Star*, in Rochester,
N.Y.   2. On the night of April 14, 1912, the *Titanic*, the largest ship afloat and on her maiden
voyage to New York from Southampton, collided with an iceberg in the North Atlantic and sank in
less than three hours; 1,500 of 2,206 passengers were lost.   3. Bright red; the salamander was
supposed to be able to live in fire.   4. Thread.

IV

Jewels in joy designed
To ravish the sensuous mind
Lie lightless, all their sparkles bleared and black and blind.   10

V

Dim moon-eyed fishes near
Gaze at the gilded gear
And query: "What does this vaingloriousness down here?" . . .   15

VI

Well: while was fashioning
This creature of cleaving wing,
The Immanent Will that stirs and urges everything

VII

Prepared a sinister mate
For her—so gaily great—   20
A Shape of Ice, for the time far and dissociate.

VIII

And as the smart ship grew
In stature, grace, and hue,
In shadowy silent distance grew the Iceberg too.

IX

Alien they seemed to be: 25
No mortal eye could see
The intimate welding of their later history,

X

Or sign that they were bent
By paths coincident
On being anon twin halves of one august event,   30

XI

Till the Spinner of the Years
Said "Now!" And each one hears,
And consummation comes, and jars two hemispheres.   1914

WILFRED OWEN

Dulce et Decorum Est[5]

Bent double, like old beggars under sacks,
Knock-kneed, coughing like hags, we cursed through sludge,
Till on the haunting flares we turned our backs
And towards our distant rest began to trudge.
Men marched asleep. Many had lost their boots
But limped on, blood-shod. All went lame; all blind;
Drunk with fatigue; deaf even to the hoots
Of disappointed shells that dropped behind.

Gas! Gas! Quick, boys!—An ecstasy of fumbling,
Fitting the clumsy helmets just in time;
But someone still was yelling out and stumbling
And floundering like a man in fire or lime.—
Dim, through the misty panes and thick green light
As under a green sea, I saw him drowning.

In all my dreams, before my helpless sight,
He plunges at me, guttering, choking, drowning.

If in some smothering dreams you too could pace
Behind the wagon that we flung him in,
And watch the white eyes writhing in his face,
His hanging face, like a devil's sick of sin;
If you could hear, at every jolt, the blood
Come gargling from the froth-corrupted lungs,
Obscene as cancer, bitter as the cud
Of vile, incurable sores on innocent tongues,—
My friend, you would not tell with such high zest
To children ardent for some desperate glory,
The old Lie: Dulce et decorum est
Pro patria mori.

1917

RICHARD EBERHART

The Fury of Aerial Bombardment

You would think the fury of aerial bombardment
Would rouse God to relent; the infinite spaces

5. Part of a phrase from Horace, quoted in full in the last lines: "It is sweet and proper to die for one's country."

Are still silent. He looks on shock-pried faces.
History, even, does not know what is meant.

You would feel that after so many centuries   5
God would give man to repent; yet he can kill
As Cain could, but with multitudinous will,
No farther advanced than in his ancient furies.

Was man made stupid to see his own stupidity?
Is God by definition indifferent, beyond us all?   10
Is the eternal truth man's fighting soul
Wherein the Beast ravens in its own avidity?

Of Van Wettering I speak, and Averill,
Names on a list, whose faces I do not recall
But they are gone to early death, who late in school   15
Distinguished the belt feed lever from the belt holding pawl.[6]   1947

ROBERT BRINGHURST

For the Bones of Josef Mengele, Disinterred June 1985

Master of Auschwitz, angel of death,
murderer, deep in Brazil they are breaking
your bones—or somebody's bones: my
bones, your bones, his bones, whose
bones does not matter. Deep in Brazil they are breaking   5
bones like loaves of old bread. The angel
of death is not drowning but eating.

Speak! they are saying. *Speak! speak!*
If you don't speak we will open and read you!
Something you too might have said in your time.   10
Are these bones guilty? they say. And the bones
are already talking. The bones, with guns
to their heads, are already saying, *Yes!*
Yes! It is true, we are guilty!

Butcher, baker, lampshade and candlestick   15
maker: yes, it is true. But the bones? The bones,
earth, metals, teeth, the body?
These are not guilty. The minds of the dead
are not to be found in the bones of the dead.
The minds of the dead are not anywhere to be found,   20
outside the minds of the living.   1986

6. Machine-gun parts.

MARY JO SALTER

Welcome to Hiroshima

is what you first see, stepping off the train:
a billboard brought to you in living English
by Toshiba Electric. While a channel
silent in the TV of the brain

5   projects those flickering re-runs of a cloud
that brims its risen columnful like beer
and, spilling over, hangs its foamy head,
you feel a thirst for history: what year

it started to be safe to breathe the air,
10   and when to drink the blood and scum afloat
on the Ohta River. But no, the water's clear,
they pour it for your morning cup of tea

in one of the countless sunny coffee shops
whose plastic dioramas advertise
15   mutations of cuisine behind the glass:
a pancake sandwich; a pizza someone tops

with a maraschino cherry. Passing by
the Peace Park's floral hypocenter (where
how bravely, or with what mistaken cheer,
20   humanity erased its own erasure),

you enter the memorial museum
and through more glass are served, as on a dish
of blistered grass, three mannequins. Like gloves
a mother clips to coatsleeves, strings of flesh

25   hang from their fingertips; or as if tied
to recall a duty for us, *Reverence*
the dead whose mourners too shall soon be dead,
but all commemoration's swallowed up

in questions of bad taste, how re-created
30   horror mocks the grim original,
and thinking at last *They should have left it all*
you stop. This is the wristwatch of a child.

Jammed on the moment's impact, resolute
to communicate some message, although mute,
35   it gestures with its hands at eight-fifteen
and eight-fifteen and eight-fifteen again

while tables of statistics on the wall
update the news by calling on a roll

of tape, death gummed on death, and in the case
adjacent, an exhibit under glass   40

is glass itself: a shard the bomb slammed in
a woman's arm at eight-fifteen, but some
three decades on—as if to make it plain
hope's only as renewable as pain,

and as if all the unsung   45
debasements of the past may one day come
rising to the surface once again—
worked its filthy way out like a tongue.   1984

WILLIAM STAFFORD

At the Bomb Testing Site

At noon in the desert a panting lizard
waited for history, its elbows tense,
watching the curve of a particular road
as if something might happen.

It was looking at something farther off   5
than people could see, an important scene
acted in stone for little selves
at the flute end of consequences.

There was just a continent without much on it
under a sky that never cared less.   10
Ready for a change, the elbows waited.
The hands gripped hard on the desert.   1966

DUDLEY RANDALL

Ballad of Birmingham

*(On the bombing of a church in
Birmingham, Alabama, 1963)*

"Mother dear, may I go downtown
Instead of out to play,
And march the streets of Birmingham
In a Freedom March today?"

"No, baby, no, you may not go,   5
For the dogs are fierce and wild,

And clubs and hoses, guns and jails
Aren't good for a little child."

"But, mother, I won't be alone.
Other children will go with me,
And march the streets of Birmingham
To make our country free."

"No, baby, no, you may not go,
For I fear those guns will fire.
But you may go to church instead
And sing in the children's choir."

She has combed and brushed her night-dark hair,
And bathed rose petal sweet,
And drawn white gloves on her small brown hands,
And white shoes on her feet.

The mother smiled to know her child
Was in the sacred place,
But that smile was the last smile
To come upon her face.

For when she heard the explosion,
Her eyes grew wet and wild.
She raced through the streets of Birmingham
Calling for her child.

She clawed through bits of glass and brick,
Then lifted out a shoe.
"Oh, here's the shoe my baby wore,
But, baby, where are you?"

1969

AI

Riot Act, April 29, 1992

I'm going out and get something.
I don't know what.
I don't care.
Whatever's out there, I'm going to get it.
Look in those shop windows at boxes
and boxes of Reeboks and Nikes
to make me fly through the air
like Michael Jordan
like Magic.
While I'm up there, I see Spike Lee.
Looks like he's flying too
straight through the glass
that separates me

from the virtual reality
I watch everyday on TV.   15
I know the difference between
what it is and what it isn't.
Just because I can't touch it
doesn't mean it isn't real.
All I have to do is smash the screen,   20
reach in and take what I want.
Break out of prison.
South Central homey's newly risen
from the night of living dead,
but this time he lives,   25
he gets to give the zombies
a taste of their own medicine.
Open wide and let me in,
or else I'll set your world on fire,
but you pretend that you don't hear.   30
You haven't heard the word is coming down
like the hammer of the gun
of this black son, locked out of the big house,
while massa looks out the window and sees only smoke.
Massa doesn't see anything else,   35
not because he can't,
but because he won't.
He'd rather hear me talking about mo' money,
mo' honeys and gold chains
and see me carrying my favorite things   40
from looted stores
than admit that underneath my Raiders' cap,
the aftermath is staring back
unblinking through the camera's lens,
courtesy of CNN,   45
my arms loaded with boxes of shoes
that I will sell at the swap meet
to make a few cents on the declining dollar.
And if I destroy myself
and my neighborhood   50
"ain't nobody's business, if I do,"
but the police are knocking hard
at my door
and before I can open it,
they break it down   55
and drag me in the yard.
They take me in to be processed and charged,
to await trial,
while Americans forget
the day the wealth finally trickled down   60
to the rest of us.
                                                                    1993

Ideas and Consciousness

ANNA LAETITIA BARBAULD

Washing-Day

The Muses are turned gossips; they have lost
The buskined step, and clear high-sounding phrase,
Language of gods. Come then, domestic Muse,
In slipshod measure loosely prattling on
5   Of farm or orchard, pleasant curds and cream,
Or drowning flies, or shoe lost in the mire
By little whimpering boy, with rueful face;
Come, Muse, and sing the dreaded Washing-Day.
Ye who beneath the yoke of wedlock bend,
10   With bowèd soul, full well ye ken the day
Which week, smooth sliding after week, brings on
Too soon;—for to that day nor peace belongs
Nor comfort;—ere the first grey streak of dawn,
The red-armed washers come and chase respose.
15   Nor pleasant smile, nor quaint device of mirth,
E'er visited that day: the very cat,
From the wet kitchen scared, and reeking hearth,
Visits the parlor,—an unwonted guest.
The silent breakfast-meal is soon dispatched;
20   Uninterrupted, save by anxious looks
Cast at the lowering sky, if sky should lower.
From that last evil, O preserve us, heavens!
For should the skies pour down, adieu to all
Remains of quiet: then expect to hear
25   Of sad disasters—dirt and gravel stains
Hard to efface, and loaded lines at once
Snapped short—and linen-horse by dog thrown down,
And all the petty miseries of life.
Saints have been calm while stretched upon the rack,
30   And Guatimozin smiled on burning coals;
But never yet did housewife notable
Greet with a smile a rainy washing-day.
—But grant the welkin fair, require not thou
Who call'st thyself perchance the master there,
35   Or study swept, or nicely dusted coat,
Or usual 'tendance;—ask not, indiscreet,
Thy stockings mended, though the yawning rents
Gape wide as Erebus; nor hope to find
Some snug recess impervious: shouldst thou try

The 'customed garden walks, thine eye shall rue   40
The budding fragrance of thy tender shrubs,
Myrtle or rose, all crushed beneath the weight
Of coarse-checked apron—with impatient hand
Twitched off when showers impend: or crossing lines
Shall mar thy musings, as the wet cold sheet   45
Flaps in thy face abrupt. Woe to the friend
Whose evil stars have urged him forth to claim
On such a day the hospitable rites!
Looks, blank at best, and stinted courtesy,
Shall he receive. Vainly he feeds his hopes   50
With dinner of roast chicken, savoury pie,
Or tart or pudding:—pudding he nor tart
That day shall eat; nor, though the husband try,
Mending what can't be helped, to kindle mirth
From cheer deficient, shall his consort's brow   55
Clear up propitious:—the unlucky guest
In silence dines, and early slinks away.
I well remember, when a child, the awe
This day struck into me; for then the maids,
I scarce knew why, looked cross, and drove me from them: 60
Nor soft caress could I obtain, nor hope
Usual indulgencies; jelly or creams,
Relic of costly suppers, and set by
For me their petted one; or buttered toast,
When butter was forbid; or thrilling tale   65
Of ghost, or witch, or murder—so I went
And sheltered me beside the parlour fire:
There my dear grandmother, eldest of forms,
Tended the little ones, and watched from harm,
Anxiously fond, though oft her spectacles   70
With elfin cunning hid, and oft the pins
Drawn from her ravelled stocking, might have soured
One less indulgent.—
At intervals my mother's voice was heard,
Urging dispatch: briskly the work went on,   75
All hands employed to wash, to rinse, to wring,
To fold, and starch, and clap, and iron, and plait.
Then would I sit down, and ponder much
Why washings were. Sometimes through hollow bowl
Of pipe amused we blew, and sent aloft   80
The floating bubbles; little dreaming then
To see, Montgolfier, thy silken ball
Ride buoyant through the clouds—so near approach
The sports of children and the toils of men.
Earth, air, and sky, and ocean, hath its bubbles,   85
And verse is one of them—this most of all.   1797

MARGE PIERCY

What's That Smell in the Kitchen?

All over America women are burning dinners.
It's lambchops in Peoria; it's haddock
in Providence; it's steak in Chicago;
tofu delight in Big Sur; red
5 rice and beans in Dallas.
All over America women are burning
food they're supposed to bring with calico
smile on platters glittering like wax.
Anger sputters in her brainpan, confined
10 but spewing out missiles of hot fat.
Carbonized despair presses like a clinker
from a barbecue against the back of her eyes.
If she wants to grill anything, it's
her husband spitted over a slow fire.
15 If she wants to serve him anything
it's a dead rat with a bomb in its belly
ticking like the heart of an insomniac.
Her life is cooked and digested,
nothing but leftovers in Tupperware.
20 Look, she says, once I was roast duck
on your platter with parsley but now I am Spam.
Burning dinner is not incompetence but war.   1983

ELIZABETH[1]

When I Was Fair and Young

When I was fair and young, and favor graced me,
    Of many was I sought, their mistress for to be;
But I did scorn them all, and answered them therefore,
    "Go, go, go, seek some otherwhere,
5   Importune me no more!"

How many weeping eyes I made to pine with woe,
    How many sighing hearts, I have no skill to show;
Yet I the prouder grew, and answered them therefore,
    "Go, go, go, seek some otherwhere,
10   Importune me no more!"

Then spake fair Venus' son, that proud victorious boy,[2]
    And said: "Fine dame, since that you be so coy,

---

1. The attribution of this poem to Queen Elizabeth I of England (1533–1603) is likely but not certain.
2. Cupid.

I will so pluck your plumes that you shall say no more,
 'Go, go, go, seek some otherwhere,
  Importune me no more!' "   15

When he had spake these words, such change grew in my breast
 That neither night nor day since that, I could take any rest.
Then lo! I did repent that I had said before,
 "Go, go, go, seek some otherwhere,
ca. 1585? Importune me no more!"   20

KATHERINE PHILIPS

L'amitié: To Mrs. M. Awbrey

Soul of my soul, my Joy, my crown, my friend!
A name which all the rest doth comprehend;
How happy are we now, whose souls are grown,
By an incomparable mixture, One:
Whose well acquainted minds are now as near   5
As Love, or vows, or secrets can endear.
I have no thought but what's to thee reveal'd,
Nor thou desire that is from me conceal'd.
Thy heart locks up my secrets richly set,
And my breast is thy private cabinet.   10
Thou shedst no tear but what my moisture lent,
And if I sigh, it is thy breath is spent.
United thus, what horror can appear
Worthy our sorrow, anger, or our fear?
Let the dull world alone to talk and fight,   15
And with their vast ambitions nature fright;
Let them despise so innocent a flame,
While Envy, Pride, and Faction play their game:
But we by Love sublim'd so high shall rise,
To pity Kings, and Conquerors despise,   20
Since we that sacred union have engrossed,
Which they and all the sullen world have lost. 1667

EDNA ST. VINCENT MILLAY

[Women have loved before as I love now]

Women have loved before as I love now;
At least, in lively chronicles of the past—
Of Irish waters by a Cornish prow
Or Trojan waters by a Spartan mast

5   Much to their cost invaded—here and there,
Hunting the amorous line, skimming the rest,
I find some woman bearing as I bear
Love like a burning city in the breast.
I think however that of all alive
10   I only in such utter, ancient way
Do suffer love; in me alone survive
The unregenerate passions of a day
When treacherous queens, with death upon the tread,
Heedless and wilful, took their knights to bed.   1931

LIZ ROSENBERG

Married Love

The trees are uncurling their first
green messages: Spring, and some man
lets his arm brush my arm in a darkened
theatre. Faint-headed, I fight the throb.
5   Later I dream
the gas attendant puts a cool hand
on my breast, asking a question.
Slowly I rise through the surface of the dream,
brushing his hand and my own heat away.

10   Young, I burned to marry. Married,
the smolder goes on underground,
clutching at weeds, writhing everywhere.
I'm trying to talk to a friend on burning
issues, flaming from the feet up,
15   drinking in his breath, touching his wrist.
I want to grab the pretty woman
on the street, seize the falcon
by its neck, beat my way into whistling steam.

I turn to you in the dark, oh husband,
20   watching your lit breath circle the pillow.
Then you turn to me, throwing first one limb
and then another over me, in the easy brotherly
lust of marriage. I cling to you
as if I were a burning ship and you
25   could save me, as if I won't go sliding down
beneath you soon; as if our lives are made of rise
and fall, and we could ride this out forever,
with longing's thunder rolling heavy in our arms.   1986

ADRIENNE RICH

Delta

If you have taken this rubble for my past
raking through it for fragments you could sell
know that I long ago moved on
deeper into the heart of the matter
If you think you can grasp me, think again: 5
my story flows in more than one direction
a delta springing from the riverbed
with its five fingers spread   1989

JUDITH ORTIZ COFER

Unspoken

When I hug you tight at bedtime
you wince in pain for the tender
swelling of new breasts.
Nothing is said, both of us aware
of the covenant of silence   5
we must maintain through the rending
apart that is adolescence.
        But it won't always
be confusion and hurting, the body
will find itself through this pain;   10
remember Michelangelo, who believed
that in marble, form already exists,
the artist's hands simply pulling it out
into the world.
        I want to tell you about men: 15
the pleasure of a lover's hands on skin
you think may rip at elbows and knees
stretching over a frame like clothes
you've almost outgrown; of the moment
when a woman first feels   20
a baby's mouth at her breast, opening her
like the hand of God in Genesis, the moment
when all that led to this seems right.
        Instead I say, *sweet dreams*,
for the secrets hidden under the blanket   25
like a forbidden book

I'm not supposed to know you've read.   1993

SHARON OLDS

The Elder Sister

When I look at my elder sister now
I think how she had to go first, down through the
birth canal, to force her way
head-first through the tiny channel,
5   the pressure of Mother's muscles on her brain,
the tight walls scraping her skin.
Her face is still narrow from it, the long
hollow cheeks of a Crusader on a tomb,
and her inky eyes have the look of someone who has
10   been in prison a long time and
knows they can send her back. I look at her
body and think how her breasts were the first to
rise, slowly, like swans on a pond.
By the time mine came along, they were just
15   two more birds in the flock, and when the hair
rose on the white mound of her flesh, like
threads of water out of the ground, it was the
first time, but when mine came
they knew about it. I used to think
20   only in terms of her harshness, sitting and
pissing on me in bed, but now I
see I had her before me always
like a shield. I look at her wrinkles, her clenched
jaws, her frown-lines—I see they are
25   the dents on my shield, the blows that did not reach me.
She protected me, not as a mother
protects a child, with love, but as a
hostage protects the one who makes her
escape as I made my escape, with my sister's
30   body held in front of me.   1984

ERICA JONG

Penis Envy

I envy men who can yearn
with infinite emptiness
toward the body of a woman,

hoping that the yearning
5   will make a child,
that the emptiness itself
will fertilize the darkness.

Women have no illusions about this,
being at once
houses, tunnels,   10
cups & cupbearers,
knowing emptiness as a temporary state
between two fullnesses,
& seeing no romance in it.

If I were a man   15
doomed to that infinite emptiness,
& having no choice in the matter,
I would, like the rest, no doubt,
find a woman
& christen her moonbelly,   20
madonna, gold-haired goddess
& make her the tent of my longing,
the silk parachute of my lust,
the blue-eyed icon of my sacred sexual itch,
the mother of my hunger.   25

But since I am a woman,
I must not only inspire the poem
but also type it,
not only conceive the child
but also bear it,   30
not only bear the child
but also bathe it,
not only bathe the child
but also feed it,
not only feed the child   35
but also carry it
everywhere, everywhere . . .

while men write poems
on the mysteries of motherhood.

I envy men who can yearn   40
with infinite emptiness.   1975

DOROTHY PARKER

Indian Summer

In youth, it was a way I had
    To do my best to please,
And change, with every passing lad,
    To suit his theories.

But now I know the things I know,
And do the things I do;
And if you do not like me so,
To hell, my love, with you!

1937

KAY SMITH

Annunciation

for Kathy

In all the old paintings
The Virgin is reading—
No one knows what,
When she is disturbed
By an angel with a higher mission,
Beyond books.

She looks up reluctantly,
Still marking the place with her finger.
The angel is impressive,
With red shoes and just
A hint of wing and shine everywhere.
Listening to the measured message
The Virgin bows her head,
Her eyes aslant
Between the angel and the book.

At the Uffizi[3]
We stood
Before a particularly beautiful angel
And a hesitant Sienese Virgin,
We two sometimes women.
Believing we could ignore
All messages,
Unobliged to wings or words,
We laughed in the vibrant space
Between the two,
Somewhere in the angled focus
Of the Virgin's eye.

Now, in the harder times,
I do not laugh so often;

---

3. The richest art gallery in Italy, located in Florence. Its collection includes a painting of the Annunciation by the 14th-century Sienese painter Simone Martini.

Still the cheap postcard in my room   30
Glints with the angel's robe.
I look with envy
At the angel and the book,
Wishing I had chosen
One or the other,   35
Anything but the space between.   1986

PAULETTE JILES

Paper Matches

My aunts washed dishes while the uncles
squirted each other on the lawn with
garden hoses. Why are we in here,
I said, and they are out there.
That's the way it is,   5
said Aunt Hetty, the shrivelled-up one.
I have the rages that small animals have,
being small, being animal.
Written on me was a message,
"At Your Service" like a book of   10
paper matches. One by one we were
taken out and struck.
We come bearing supper.
our heads on fire.   1973

▼ ▼ ▼

QUESTIONS

1. What additional information would you like to have about the events
referred to in "Frederick Douglass" and "Ballad of Birmingham"? What details
in these poems seem to require additional information about the events on
which each is based? What details about the life and writings of Frederick
Douglass, and about his character, would help your reading of "Frederick
Douglass"? What do you make of the mention of "dogs," "clubs," and "hoses"
in "Ballad of Birmingham"? What did "Freedom March" mean in 1969? Given
the poem's structure and its portrayal of children's voices and attitudes, what
difference might it make to your reading of the poem if you had factual information about the actual casualties of the bombing? If you were editing this

poem, what other footnotes would you provide? Reread "Sir Patrick Spens" (p. 851). In what ways does Randall's poem allude to it? why?

2. What details about the physical suffering from poison gas are specifically suggested in "Dulce et Decorum Est"? what details about the physical effects of atomic explosions in "Welcome to Hiroshima"? How accurate are these representations? Using the reference resources in your college library, look up news accounts of gassings in World War I and the atomic bombing of Hiroshima, and compare the journalistic details with those given in the poems. How careful does each poet seem to have been in representing historical events? What evidence do you find of distortion or "poetic license"? Which details are specifically chosen for powerful rhetorical effects in each poem?

3. Compare the images of fire and burning in "What's That Smell in the Kitchen?," "Married Love," and "Paper Matches." How are the images used differently in each poem? What common thread of meaning informs the images in these poems? On what kind of cultural assumptions about women and their roles do these images seem to be based? In what ways are these images like other images of passion in other poems you have read? In what ways are the images like other images of destruction?

4. What is the relationship between burning "to marry" (line 10), "burning issues" (lines 13–14), and the "burning ship" (line 24) in "Married Love"? What, exactly, is the dramatic situation in the poem? In what specific ways does the speaker's attitude change in the course of the poem? How do you interpret the poem's "as ifs" in final stanza? What is the poem's ultimate attitude toward "married love"?

5. Which poems in the *Ideas and Consciousness* group are especially concerned to suggest the importance of physical space? In what ways do they portray its absence? In what ways do they represent the male sense of a woman's "place"? How does the image of "rubble" in "Delta" (line 1) relate to the images of place, material evidence, and destruction in other poems? Why does the speaker of "Delta" describe herself and her past as ungraspable (line 5)? In what sense has she "moved on" (line 3) beyond the "rubble"? Explain the ironies in the phrase "the heart of the matter" (line 4). Explain the poem's title.

6. What images of passivity, deferentiality, and compliance can you find about women in the poems in this group? How is each image treated in the individual poem? In what ways do images of assertion and resistance compete with these images?

WRITING SUGGESTIONS

1. Using reference materials available in your college's library, construct a short but detailed narrative (of about 500–700 words) of the Birmingham bombing. Then "read" the poem in the context of the full story, showing how the poem uses specific details of the incident to create its effects.

2. Compare the speaker of Millay's "Women have loved before as I love now" with Jong's "Penis Envy." In an essay of about 800 words, show how each speaker characterizes herself through attitudes toward other people.

13 THE PROCESS OF
CREATION

Poems do not write themselves. Even if the idea for a poem comes in a flash (as it sometimes does), poets often struggle to get the final effect just right. For some poems that means draft after draft, and sometimes poets write more than one version of a poem and allow them to compete as rival authorized texts, or later revise the poem and alter it in some crucial way. Often a study of the manuscript or of the several drafts suggests the various kinds of decisions a poet may make as a poem moves toward its final form. In this chapter you will find examples of several poems as they take shape—or take different forms—in the poet's mind.

The first example involves early drafts of the first stanza of Richard Wilbur's "Love Calls Us to the Things of This World," which in its finished form is printed right after the drafts. Wilbur is one of the most careful craftsmen writing today, and in the early drafts of the first stanza we can see him moving toward the brilliant and surprising effects he achieves in the "final" version, that is, the version the poet decided to publish. Someone is just awaking, and through a window sees laundry on a clothesline blowing in the breeze. But he is not quite awake and not quite sure what he sees: his body and soul, the poet says playfully in lines 26 and 27, are not yet quite reunited, and he seems for a moment still suspended in a world of spirit and dream; the blowing clothes look like disembodied angels. Ultimately, the poem captures that sense of suspension between worlds, the uncertainty of where one is and what is happening in that first half-conscious moment when normal physical laws don't seem to apply. It is a delicate moment to catch, and in the six successive drafts printed below we can see the poet moving toward the more precise effect of the completed poem.

In the first three drafts the speaker seems to speak about himself—not quite right because that device makes him too conscious, and part of the basic effect of the poem involves a lack of consciousness and control. By the fourth draft "My eyes came open" has become "The eyes open," and the effect of being a little lost and unsure of identity is becoming clearer. Another major change in the early drafts is that the sound of the laundry pulley changes from "squeak" to "shriek" to "cry": the first two words capture the shrill sound of a moving pulley faithfully, but "cry" makes it seem personal and human, and now it is as if the pulleys were in fact calling the speaker from sleep. The image changes too: in the first draft the world of sleep is a brothel, but those connotations are eliminated in later drafts, and instead by the sixth draft the "spirit" has become "soul" and is bodiless. Every new draft changes the conception just a little, and in the drafts printed here we can see effects gradually getting clearer in the poet's mind and falling into place. Notice how rhyme appears in draft and then disappears again, notice how the poet tries out and rejects words that don't have quite the right connotation: "wallow" (draft c), "frothing" (draft d), "rout" (draft f). In a detailed set of drafts like this one, we can see the poet weighing different visual and verbal possibilities, choosing every single word with care.

The other poems and passages similarly give us a chance to compare the effects of more than one version of a poem or passage. In several cases, a poem is "finished" in more than one version, and the poets invite us to choose among the competing versions instead of choosing one themselves. In each selection a few crucial words create significant differences in the text.

▼ ▼ ▼

1. Early drafts of the first stanza of "Love Calls Us to the Things of This World," reprinted by permission of the author:

    (a) My eyes came open to the squeak of pulleys
        My spirit, shocked from the brothel of itself

    (b) My eyes came open to the shriek of pulleys,
        And the soul, spirited from its proper wallow,
        Hung in the air as bodiless and hollow

    (c) My eyes came open to the pulleys' cry.
        The soul, spirited from its proper wallow,
        Hung in the air as bodiless and hollow
        As light that frothed upon the wall opposing;
        But what most caught my eyes at their unclosing
        Was two gray ropes that yanked across the sky.
        One after one into the window frame
        . . . the hosts of laundry came

    (d)   The eyes open to a cry of pulleys,
        And the soul, so suddenly spirited from sleep,
        As morning sunlight frothing on the floor,
            While just outside the window
        The air is solid with a dance of angels.

(e)   The eyes open to a cry of pulleys,
And spirited from sleep, the astounded soul
Hangs for a moment bodiless and simple
As dawn light in the moment of its breaking:
        Outside the open window
        The air is crowded with a

(f)   The eyes open to a cry of pulleys,
And spirited from sleep, the astounded soul
Hangs for a moment bodiless and simple
As false dawn
        Outside the open window,
        Their air is leaping with a rout of angels.
        Some are in bedsheets, some are in dresses,
        it does not seem to matter

Final Version, 1956

The eyes open to a cry of pulleys,
And spirited from sleep, the astounded soul
Hangs for a moment bodiless and simple
As false dawn.
                    Outside the open window
The morning air is all awash with angels.

Some are in bed-sheets, some are in blouses,
Some are in smocks: but truly there they are.
Now they are rising together in calm swells
Of halcyon[1] feeling, filling whatever they wear
With the deep joy of their impersonal breathing;
    Now they are flying in place,[2] conveying
The terrible speed of their omnipresence, moving
And staying like white water; and now of a sudden
They swoon down into so rapt a quiet
That nobody seems to be there.
                            The soul shrinks

From all that it is about to remember,
From the punctual rape of every blesséd day,
And cries,
            "Oh, let there be nothing on earth but laundry,
Nothing but rosy hands in the rising steam
And clear dances done in the sight of heaven."

Yet, as the sun acknowledges
With a warm look the world's hunks and colors,

1. Serene.   2. Like planes in a formation.

The soul descends once more in bitter love
To accept the waking body, saying now
In a changed voice as the man yawns and rises,

    "Bring them down from their ruddy gallows;
Let there be clean linen for the backs of thieves;   30
Let lovers go fresh and sweet to be undone,
And the heaviest nuns walk in a pure floating
Of dark habits,
          keeping their difficult balance."

2. Two versions of Keats's "Bright star! would I were stedfast as thou art!"

Original Version, 1819

Bright star! would I were stedfast as thou art!
Not in lone splendor hung amid the night;
Not watching, with eternal lids apart,
Like Nature's devout sleepless Eremite,
The morning waters at their priestlike task   5
Of pure ablution round earth's human shores;
Or, gazing on the new soft fallen mask
Of snow upon the mountains and moors:—
No;—yet still stedfast, still unchangeable.
Cheek-pillow'd on my Love's white ripening breast,   10
To touch, for ever, its warm sink and swell,
Awake, for ever, in a sweet unrest;
To hear, to feel her tender taken breath,
Half-passionless, and so swoon on to death.

Revised Version, 1820

Bright star! would I were steadfast as thou art—
  Not in lone splendor hung aloft the night
And watching, with eternal lids apart,
  Like nature's patient, sleepless Eremite,
The moving waters at their priestlike task   5
  Of pure ablution round earth's human shores,
Or gazing on the new soft fallen mask
  Of snow upon the mountains and the moors—
No—yet still steadfast, still unchangeable,
  Pillowed upon my fair love's ripening breast,   10
To feel for ever its soft fall and swell,
  Awake for ever in a sweet unrest,
Still, still to hear her tender-taken breath,
And so live ever—or else swoon to death.

3. Two published versions of Keats's "La Belle Dame sans Merci: A Ballad."

Original Version, 1819

I

O what can ail thee, knight-at-arms,
    Alone and palely loitering?
The sedge has withered from the lake,
    And no birds sing.

II

O what can ail thee, knight-at-arms,
    So haggard and so woe-begone?
The squirrel's granary is full,
    And the harvest's done.

III

I see a lily on thy brow,
    With anguish moist and fever dew,
And on thy cheeks a fading rose
    Fast withereth too.

IV

I met a lady in the meads[3]
    Full beautiful—a faery's child,
Her hair was long her foot was light,
    And her eyes were wild.

V

I made a garland for her head,
    And bracelets too, and fragrant zone,[4]
She looked at me as she did love,
    And made sweet moan.

VI

I set her on my pacing steed,
    And nothing else saw all day long,
For sidelong would she bend, and sing
    A faery's song.

VII

She found me roots of relish sweet
    And honey wild, and manna dew,
And sure in language strange she said,
    "I love thee true."

3. Meadows.   4. Girdle.

VIII

She took me to her elfin grot,
   And there she wept, and sighed full sore,   30
And there I shut her wild wild eyes
    With kisses four.

IX

And there she lulléd me asleep,
   And there I dreamed—Ah! woe betide!
The latest[5] dream I ever dreamed   35
    On the cold hill side.

Revised Version, 1820

I

Ah, what can ail thee, wretched wight,
   Alone and palely loitering;
The sedge is withered from the lake,
    And no birds sing.

II

Ah, what can ail thee, wretched wight,   5
   So haggard and so woe-begone?
The squirrel's granary is full,
    And the harvest's done.

III

I see a lily on thy brow,
   With anguish moist and fever dew;   10
And on thy cheek a fading rose
    Fast withereth too.

IV

I met a lady in the meads
   Full beautiful, a fairy's child;
Her hair was long, her foot was light,   15
    And her eyes were wild.

V

I set her on my pacing steed,
   And nothing else saw all day long;
For sideways would she lean, and sing
    A fairy's song.   20

5. Last.

VI

I made a garland for her head,
   And bracelets too, and fragrant zone:
She looked at me as she did love,
   And made sweet moan.

VII

25   She found me roots of relish sweet,
   And honey wild, and manna dew;
And sure in language strange she said,
   "I love thee true."

VIII

She took me to her elfin grot,
30   And there she gazed and sighéd deep,
And there I shut her wild sad eyes—
   So kissed to sleep.

IX

And there we slumbered on the moss,
   And there I dreamed, ah woe betide,
35   The latest dream I ever dreamed
   On the cold hill side.

X

I saw pale kings and princes too,
   Pale warriors, death-pale were they all;
They cried—"La Belle Dame sans Merci
40   Hath thee in thrall!"

XI

I saw their starved lips in the gloam,
   With horrid warning gapéd wide,
And I awoke and found me here,
   On the cold hill's side.

XII

45   And this is why I sojourn here,
   Alone and palely loitering,
Though the sedge has withered from the lake,
   And no birds sing.

4. Three versions of Alexander Pope's "Ode on Solitude."

1709 Manuscript Version

Happy the man, who free from care,
The business and the noise of towns,
Contented breathes his native air,
   In his own grounds.

Whose herds with milk, whose fields with bread,   5
Whose flocks supply him with attire,
Whose trees in summer yield him shade,
    In winter fire.

Blest! who can unconcern'dly find
His years slide silently away,   10
In health of body, peace of mind,
    Quiet by day,

Repose at night; study and ease
Together mix'd; sweet recreation,
And innocence, which most does please,   15
    With meditation.

Thus let me live, unseen, unknown;
Thus unlamented let me die;
Steal from the world, and not a stone
    Tell where I lie.   20

First Printed Version, 1717

How happy he, who free from care,
The rage of courts, and noise of towns;
Contented breathes his native air,
    In his own grounds.
Whose herds with milk, whose fields with bread,   5
Whose flocks supply him with attire.
Whose trees in summer yield him shade,
    In winter fire.
Blest! who can unconcern'dly find
Hours, days, and years slide swift away,   10
In health of body, peace of mind,
    Quiet by day,
Sound sleep by night; study and ease
Together mix'd; sweet recreation,
And innocence, which most does please,   15
    With meditation.
Thus let me live, unheard, unknown;
Thus unlamented let me die;
Steal from the world, and not a stone
    Tell where I lie.   20

Final Version, 1736

Happy the man, whose wish and care
A few paternal acres bound,
Content to breathe his native air,
    In his own ground.

5   Whose herds with milk, whose fields with bread,
    Whose flocks supply him with attire,
    Whose trees in summer yield him shade,
        In winter fire.

    Blest! who can unconcern'dly find
10   Hours, days, and years slide soft away,
    In health of body, peace of mind,
        Quiet by day,

    Sound sleep by night; study and ease
    Together mix'd; sweet recreation,
15   And innocence, which most does please,
        With meditation.

    Thus let me live, unseen, unknown;
    Thus unlamented let me die;
    Steal from the world, and not a stone
20   Tell where I lie.

5. This famous folk ballad was sung and recited in many variations; here are two written versions. Neither version can be dated precisely.

    "O where ha' you been, Lord Randal, my son?
    And where ha' you been, my handsome young man?"
    "I ha' been at the greenwood; mother, mak my bed soon,
    For I'm wearied wi' huntin', and fain wad[6] lie down."

5   "And wha met ye there, Lord Randal, my son?
    And wha met you there, my handsome young man?"
    "O I met wi' my true-love; mother, mak my bed soon,
    For I'm wearied wi' huntin', and fain wad lie down."

    "And what did she give you, Lord Randal, my son?
10   And what did she give you, my handsome young man?"
    "Eels fried in a pan; mother, mak my bed soon,
    For I'm wearied wi' huntin', and fain wad lie down."

    "And wha gat your leavin's, Lord Randal, my son?
    And wha gat your leavin's, my handsome young man?"
15   "My hawks and my hounds; mother, mak my bed soon,
    For I'm wearied wi' huntin', and fain wad lie down."

    "And what becam of them, Lord Randal, my son?
    And what becam of them, my handsome young man?"
    "They stretched their legs out and died; mother, mak my bed soon,
20   For I'm wearied wi' huntin', and fain wad lie down."

    "O I fear you are poisoned, Lord Randal, my son!
    I fear you are poisoned, my handsome young man!"

6. Would like to.

"O yes, I am poisoned; mother, mak my bed soon,
For I'm sick at the heart, and I fain wad lie down."

"What d'ye leave to your mother, Lord Randal, my son?   25
What d'ye leave to your mother, my handsome young man?"
"Four and twenty milk kye;[7] mother, mak my bed soon,
For I'm sick at the heart, and I fain wad lie down."

"What d'ye leave to your sister, Lord Randal, my son?
What d'ye leave to your sister, my handsome young man?"   30
"My gold and my silver; mother, mak my bed soon,
For I'm sick at the heart, and I fain wad lie down."

"What d'ye leave to your brother, Lord Randal, my son?
What d'ye leave to your brother, my handsome young man?"
"My houses and my lands; mother, mak my bed soon,   35
For I'm sick at the heart, and I fain wad lie down."

"What d'ye leave to your true-love, Lord Randal, my son?
What d'ye leave to your true-love, my handsome young man?"
"I leave her hell and fire; mother, mak my bed soon,
For I'm sick at the heart, and I fain wad lie down."   40

Shorter Version

"O where hae ye been, Lord Randal, my son?
O where hae ye been, my handsome young man?"
"I hae been to the wild wood; mother, make my bed soon,
For I'm weary wi' hunting, and fain wald lie down."

"Where gat ye your dinner, Lord Randal, my son?   5
Where gat ye your dinner, my handsome young man?"
"I dined wi' my true-love; mother, make my bed soon,
For I'm weary wi' hunting, and fain wald lie down."

"What gat ye to your dinner, Lord Randal, my son?
What gat ye to your dinner, my handsome young man?"   10
"I gat eels boiled in broo; mother, make my bed soon,
For I'm weary wi' hunting, and fain wald lie down."

"What became of your bloodhounds, Lord Randal, my son?
What became of your bloodhounds, my handsome young man?"
"O they swelled and they died; mother, make my bed soon,   15
For I'm weary wi' hunting, and fain wald lie down."

"O I fear ye are poisoned, Lord Randal, my son!
O I fear ye are poisoned, my handsome young man!"
"O yes! I am poisoned; mother, make my bed soon,
For I'm sick at the heart, and I fain wald lie down."   20

7. Cows.

6. "Poetry," by Marianne Moore, appears on page 882 in a version that was originally published in 1921. Here are two later versions.

The 1925 Version

> I too, dislike it:
> there are things that are important beyond all this fiddle.
> The bat, upside down; the elephant pushing,
> the tireless wolf under a tree,
> 5   the base-ball fan, the statistician —
> "business documents and schoolbooks" —
> these phenomena are pleasing,
> but when they have been fashioned
> into that which is unknowable,
> 10   we are not entertained.
> It may be said of all of us
> that we do not admire what we cannot understand;
> enigmas are not poetry.

The version Moore chose to print in her *Complete Poems* in 1967:

> I, too, dislike it.
>   Reading it, however, with a perfect contempt for it, one discovers in
> it after all, a place for the genuine.

7. Two versions of Emily Dickinson's "Safe in their Alabaster Chambers–":

1859 Version

> Safe in their Alabaster Chambers —
> Untouched by Morning
> And untouched by Noon —
> Sleep the meek members of the Resurrection —
> 5   Rafter of satin,
> And Roof of stone.
>
> Light laughs the breeze
> In her Castle above them —
> Babbles the Bee in a stolid Ear,
> 10   Pipe the Sweet Birds in ignorant cadence —
> Ah, what sagacity perished here!

1861 Version

> Safe in their Alabaster Chambers —
> Untouched by Morning —
> And untouched by Noon —
> Lie the meek members of the Resurrection —
> 5   Rafter of Satin — and Roof of Stone!

Grand go the Years—in the Crescent—above them—
Worlds scoop their Arcs—
And Firmaments—row—
Diadems—drop—and Doges—surrender—
Soundless as dots—on a Disc of Snow—   10

8. Drafts of "The Tyger" by William Blake. The final version, published in 1790, can be found on page 698.

First Draft[8]

The Tyger

1   Tyger Tyger burning bright
     In the forests of the night
     What immortal hand or eye
     ~~Dare~~ Could frame thy fearful symmetry

              Burnt in
2   ~~In what~~ distant deeps or skies
     ~~The cruel~~ ~~Burnt the~~ fire of thine eyes
     On what wings dare he aspire
     What the hand dare sieze the fire

3   And what shoulder & what art
     Could twist the sinews of thy heart
     And when thy heart began to beat
     What dread hand & what dread feet

     ~~Could fetch it from the furnace deep~~
     ~~And in thy horrid ribs dare steep~~
     ~~In the well of sanguine woe~~
     ~~In what clay & what mould~~
     ~~Were thy eyes of fury rolld~~

     ~~Where~~   where
4   ~~What~~ the hammer ~~what~~ the chain
     In what furnace was thy brain
                                   dread grasp
     What the anvil what ~~the arm~~ ~~arm~~ ~~grasp~~ ~~clasp~~
     Dare ~~Could~~ its deadly terrors ~~clasp~~ ~~grasp~~ clasp

6   Tyger Tyger burning bright
     In the forests of the night
     What immortal hand & eye
              frame
     Dare ~~form~~ thy fearful symmetry

8. These drafts have been taken from a notebook used by William Blake, called the Rossetti MS because it was once owned by Dante Gabriel Rossetti, the Victorian poet and painter; David V. Erdman's edition of *The Notebook of William Blake* (1973) contains a photographic facsimile. The stanza numbers were written by Blake in the manuscript.

Trial Stanzas

> Burnt in distant deeps or skies
> The cruel fire of thine eye,
> Could heart descend or wings aspire
> What the hand dare sieze the fire
>
>   dare he ~~smile laugh~~
> 5 3 And ~~did he laugh~~ his work to see
>   ankle
>   ~~What the~~ shoulder ~~what the knee~~
>   Dare
> 4   ~~Did~~ he who made the lamb make thee
> 1   When the stars threw down their spears
> 2   And waterd heaven with their tears

Second Full Draft

> Tyger Tyger burning bright
> In the forests of the night
> What Immortal hand & eye
> Dare frame thy fearful symmetry
>
> And what shoulder & what art
> Could twist the sinews of thy heart
> And when thy heart began to beat
> What dread hand & what dread feet
>
> When the stars threw down their spears
> And waterd heaven with their tears
> Did he smile his work to see
> Did he who made the lamb make thee
>
> Tyger Tyger burning bright
> In the forests of the night
> What immortal hand & eye
> Dare frame thy fearful symmetry

Evaluating Poetry

How do you know a good poem when you see one? This is not an easy question to answer—partly because deciding about the *value* of poems is a complex, difficult, and often lengthy process, and partly because there is no single and absolute criterion that will measure texts and neatly divide the good from the not so good. People who long for a nice, infallible sorter—some test that will automatically pick out the best poems and distinguish variations of quality much as a litmus test separates acids from bases—often are frustrated at what they perceive to be the "relativity" of judgment in evaluating poems. But because an issue is complex does not mean it is impossible, and even if there is no easy and absolute standard to be discovered, there are nevertheless distinctions to be made. Some poems are better—that is, more consistently effective with talented and experienced readers—than others. Even if we cannot sensibly rate poems on a 1 to 10 scale or agree on the excellence of a single poem, it is possible to set out some criteria that are helpful to readers who may not yet have developed confidence in their own judgments. It isn't necessary, of course, to spend all of our time asking about quality and being judgmental about poetry. But because life isn't long enough to read everything, it is often useful to separate those poems that are likely to be worth your time from those that aren't. Besides, the process of sorting—in which you begin to articulate your own judgments and poetic values—can be a very useful strategy in making yourself a better reader and a more informed, better-educated, and wiser person. Evaluating poems can be, among other things, a way to learn more about yourself, for what you like in poetry has a lot to say about where your own values really lie.

"I like it." That simple, unreflective statement about a poem is often a way to begin the articulation of standards—as long as your next move is to ask yourself why. Answers to *why* questions are often, at first, quite simple, even for experienced and sophisticated readers. "I like the way it sounds" or "I like its rhythm and pace" might be good, if partial, reasons for liking a poem. The popularity of nursery rhymes and simple childish ditties, or even the haunting, predictable, and repeated sounds and phrases of a poem like "The Raven" owe a lot (if not necessarily everything) to the use of sound. Another frequent answer might be: "because it is TRUE" or "because I agree with what it says." All of us are apt to like sentiments or ideas that resemble our own more than those that challenge or disturb us, though bad formulations of some idea we treasure, like bad behavior in someone we love, can sometimes be more embarrassing than comforting. But the longer we struggle with our reasons for liking a poem, the more complex and revealing our answers are likely to be: "I like the *way* it expresses something I had thought but had never quite been able to articulate." "I like the way its sounds and rhythms imitate the sounds of what is being described." "I like the way it presents conflicting emotions, balancing negative and positive feelings that seem to exist at the same time in about equal intensity." "I like its precision in describing just how something like that affects a person." Such statements as "I like . . ." begin to quietly cross the border into the area of "I admire," and to include a second clause, beginning with "because," that offers complex reasons for that admiration.

What kinds of reasons might we expect different readers to agree on? *Groups* of readers might well agree on certain ideas—questions of politics or economics or religion, for example—but not readers across the board. More likely to generate consensus are technical criteria, questions of craft. How precise are the word choices at crucial moments in the poem? How rich, suggestive, and resonant are the words that open up the poem to larger statements and claims? How appropriate are the metaphors and other figures of speech? How original and imaginative? How carefully is the poem's situation set up? How clearly? How full and appropriate is the characterization of the speaker? How well-matched are the speaker, situation, and setting with the poem's sentiments and ideas? How consistent is the poem's tone? How appropriate to its themes? How carefully worked out is the poem's structure? How appropriate to the desired effects are the line breaks, the stanza breaks, and the pattern of rhythms and sounds?

One way of seeing how good a poem is in its various aspects is to look at what it is not—to consider the choices *not* made by the poet. Often it is possible to consider what a poem would be like if a different artistic choice had been made, as a way of seeing the importance of the choice actually made. What if, for example, Sylvia Plath had described a black *crow* in rainy weather instead of a rook? What if William Carlos Williams had described a *white* wheelbarrow? Sometimes we have the benefit, if we have a working manuscript or an autobiographical account of composition, of actually watching the process of selection. Look again, for example, at the several drafts of the first stanza of "Love Calls Us to the Things of This World":

(a) My eyes came open to the squeak of pulleys
My spirit, shocked from the brothel of itself

(b) My eyes came open to the shriek of pulleys,
And the soul, spirited from its proper wallow,
Hung in the air as bodiless and hollow

(c) My eyes came open to the pulleys' cry.
The soul, spirited from its proper wallow,
Hung, in the air as bodiless and hollow
As light that frothed upon the wall opposing;
But what most caught my eyes at their unclosing
Was two gray ropes that yanked across the sky.
One after one into the window frame
. . . the hosts of laundry came

(d)   The eyes open to a cry of pulleys,
And the soul, so suddenly spirited from sleep,
As morning sunlight frothing on the floor,
        While just outside the window
The air is solid with a dance of angels.

(e)   The eyes open to a cry of pulleys,
And spirited from sleep, the astounded soul
Hangs for a moment bodiless and simple
As dawn light in the moment of its breaking:
        Outside the open window
The air is crowded with a

(f)   The eyes open to a cry of pulleys,
And spirited from sleep, the astounded soul
Hangs for a moment bodiless and simple
As false dawn
        Outside the open window,
Their air is leaping with a rout of angels.
        Some are in bedsheets, some are in dresses,
        it does not seem to matter.

Notice how much more appropriate to the total poem is the choice of "cry" over "shriek" or "squeak" to describe the sound of pulleys or how much more effective than the metaphor of a spirit's "brothel" is the image of the soul hanging "bodiless." Notice the things Wilbur excised from the early drafts as well as the things he added when the poem became more clear and more of a piece in his mind. Read some of the other revised versions of poems or passages printed in Chapter 13. Do you think all the revisions improve on the originals? in what specific way? What are your criteria for deciding? Do any of the revisions seem pointless to you—or (worse) make the poem less than it was?

Let's look again at one of the first poems we discussed, Adrienne Rich's "Aunt Jennifer's Tigers" (p. 685). Some of the power of this poem comes from the poet's clear and sympathetic engagement with Aunt Jennifer's situation, but the effects are carefully generated through a series of specific technical choices. Rich herself may or may not have made all these choices consciously; her later comments on the poem suggest that her creative instincts, as well as her then-repressed sense of gender, may have governed some decisions more fully than her own deliberate calculations. But however conscious, the choices of speaker, situation, metaphor, and connotative words work brilliantly together to create a strong feminist statement, almost a manifesto on the subject of mastery and compliance.

In a sense there is no speaker in this poem, no specified personality—only a faceless niece who observes the central character—but the effacing of this speaker in the light of the vivid Jennifer amounts to a brilliant artistic decision. Jennifer, powerless to articulate and possibly even to understand her own plight, nevertheless is allowed almost to speak for herself, primarily through her hands. The seeming refusal of the narrator to do more than simply describe Jennifer's hands and their product gives Jennifer the crucial central role; she is the center of attention throughout, and the poem emphasizes only what one sees, with little apparent "editorial" comment (though the speaker does make three evaluative statements, saying that Jennifer was "mastered" by her ordeals [line 10], and noting that her hands are "terrified" [line 9] and that the wedding band "sits heavily" [line 9] on one of them). The tigers are ultimately more eloquent than the speaker seems to be: they "prance" (lines 1 and 12) and "pace" (line 4), and they are "proud" (line 12) and unafraid of men (lines 3 and 12), embodying the guarded message Jennifer sends to the world even though she herself is "mastered" and "ringed" (line 10). The brightly conceived colors in the tapestry, the expressive description of Jennifer's fingers and hands (note especially the excitement implied in "fluttering" [line 5]), and the action of the panel itself combine with the characterization of Jennifer to present a strong statement of generational repression—and boldness. The image of knitting as art, suggestive of the way the classical Fates determine the future and the nature of things, also hints at what is involved in Rich's art. The quality of the poem lies in the care, precision, and imaginativeness of Rich's craftsmanship. In later years, Rich has become clearer and more vocal about her values, but the direction and intensity of her vision are already apparent in this excellent poem taken from her first book, published more then forty years ago.

Here is another celebrated poem that similarly accomplishes a great deal in a short space:

WILLIAM SHAKESPEARE

[Th' expense of spirit in a waste of shame]

Th' expense[1] of spirit in a waste[2] of shame
Is lust in action; and, till action, lust
Is perjured, murderous, bloody, full of blame,
Savage, extreme, rude, cruel, not to trust;
Enjoyed no sooner but despiséd straight: 5
Past reason hunted; and no sooner had,
Past reason hated, as a swallowed bait,
On purpose laid to make the taker mad:
Mad in pursuit, and in possession so;
Had, having, and in quest to have, extreme;   10
A bliss in proof;[3] and proved, a very woe;
Before, a joy proposed; behind, a dream.
All this the world well knows; yet none knows well
To shun the heaven that leads men to this hell.   1609

Here the speaker *is* fully characterized, and the economical skill with which the characterization is achieved is one of the most striking aspects of the poem. The poem sets up its situation carefully and, at first, not altogether clearly. But the delay in clarity is functional: we do not know for a while just what disturbs the speaker so much, except that it has to do with "lust in action" (line 2). What we do know quickly is how powerful his feeling is. The two explosive *p*'s in the first half of the first line get the poem off to a fast and powerful start, and by the fourth line the speaker has listed nine separate unpleasant human characteristics driven by lust. He virtually spits them out. Here is one angry speaker, and it swiftly becomes clear that he is speaking from (undescribed) personal experience.

But the poem is not only angry and negative about lust. It also admits that there are definite, and powerful, pleasures in lust: it is "enjoyed" (line 5) at the time ("a bliss in proof," line 11), and anticipated with pleasure ("a joy proposed," line 12). Such inconsistencies (or at least complexities) in the speaker's

1. Expending.   2. Using up; also, desert.   3. In the act.

opinion are characteristic of the poem. Everything about his views, and according to him about lust itself, is "extreme" (line 10). There are no easy conclusions about lust in the first twelve lines of the poem, just a confusing movement back and forth between positives and negatives. The powerful condemnation of lust in the beginning—detailed in terms of how it makes people feel about themselves and how it affects their actions—quickly shifts into admissions of pleasure and joy, but then shifts back again. No opinion sticks for long. The only consistent thing about the speaker's feelings is his certainty of lust's power—to drive individuals to behavior that they may love or hate. Only at the end is there any kind of reasoned conclusion, and the "moral" is hardly comforting: everybody knows what I've been saying, the speaker says, and yet nobody knows how to avoid lust and its consequences because its pleasures are so sensational, both in prospect and in actual experience ("the heaven that leads men to this hell").

The vacillation of the speaker's opinions and moods is not the only confusing thing about the poem's organization. His account of lust repeatedly skips around in time. Are we talking here about lust at the time it is being satisfied ("lust in action")? Or are we talking about desire and anticipation? Or are we talking about what happens afterward? The answer is all three, and the discussion is hardly systematic. The first line and a half describe the present, and the meter of the first line even imitates the rhythms and force of male ejaculation: note how the basic iambic pentameter strategy of the poem does not regularize until near the end of the second line. But soon we are talking about what happens before lust in action ("till action," line 2), and by line 5, after. Lines 6 and 7 contrast before and after, and line 9 compares before and during. Line 10 describes all three positions in time ("Had, having, and in quest to have"). Line 11 compares during and after, line 12 before and after. The poem, or rather the speaker, does not seem able to decide exactly what he wants to talk about and what he thinks of his subject.

All this shifting around in focus and in feelings could easily be regarded as a serious flaw. Don't we expect a short poem, and especially a sonnet, to be very carefully organized and carefully focused toward a single end? Shouldn't the poet make up his mind about what he thinks and what the poem is about? It would be easy to construct an argument, on the basis of consistency or clarity of purpose, that this is not a very good poem, that perhaps the greatest poet in the English language was not, here, at the top of his form. But doing so would ignore the power of the poem's effects and underrate another principle of consistency—that of character. If we regard the poem as representative of a mind wrestling with the complex feelings brought about by lust—someone out of control because of lust, conscious enough to see his plight but unable to do anything about it—we can see a higher consistency here that helps explain the poem's powerful effect on many readers. Here is an account of a human mind grappling with a universal human experience, the subject of many much longer works of literature. Lust is beautiful but terrifying, certainly to be avoided but impossible to avoid. Shakespeare has managed, in the unlikely space of fourteen lines and in a form in which we expect tight organization and intense focus, to portray succinctly the human recognition of confusion and powerlessness in the face of a passion larger than our ability to control it.

Here is a parody of Shakespeare's poem:

WENDY COPE

[The expense of spirits is a crying shame]

The expense of spirits is a crying shame,
So is the cost of wine. What bard[4] today
Can live like old Khayyám?[5] It's not the same—
A loaf and Thou and Tesco's Beaujolais.
I had this bird[6] called Sharon, fond of gin—   5
Could knock back six or seven. At the price
I paid a high wage for each hour of sin
And that was why I only had her twice.
Then there was Tracy, who drank rum and Coke,
So beautiful I didn't mind at first   10
But love grows colder. Now some other bloke
Is subsidizing Tracy and her thirst.
I need a woman, honest and sincere,
Who'll come across on half a pint of beer.   1986

Gone here are, among other things, the agony and the complexity. In one sense, this poem makes fun of both the emotion and the tortured uncertainty in the Shakespeare original: here the speaker is clear, and simple, in what he wants, and there is no negotiation or kidding oneself about the urgency and value of sex. Cope creates a very different kind of poem, one that stands on its own in depicting sexual and economic values, but that also retains a close

---

4. Poet.   **5.** In Edward Fitzgerald's poem *The Rubáiyat of Omar Khayyám* (more or less a translation of an Arab original), the poet longs for "a loaf of bread, a jug of wine, and Thou." *Tesco's:* a British supermarket that sells a cheap house-brand of Beaujolais.   **6.** British slang for female sex object.

dependence, quite beyond the verbal phrasing, on the Shakespeare original. Had there not been the anxiety, anger, desire, and hesitation in the original poem, this poem could not have existed: the original makes the parody possible in more than just the sense of being a point to take off from or a model to react against.

But just as Shakespeare's poem is a basis for Cope's, the Cope poem becomes a criticism and interpretation of Shakespeare's. Not only does Cope tease Shakespeare about excessive agonizing and debilitating uncertainty; she also, through her own simplifications of situation and theme, calls strong attention to the complexities in the psychology of Shakespeare's speaker and to the elaborate structure of Shakespeare's sonnet—grossly and comically simplified in the Cope speaker, who just wants to get somebody into bed no matter what. There are no afterthoughts in Cope, no hesitations; there is no self-consciousness or awareness of larger consequences or feelings. Cope's poem leads us, as sensitive parodies very often do, to notice details in the original—details that may actually help us with analysis.

Is the Cope poem in itself a good one? Certainly it's clever in its use of verbal patterns that exist in the original, in getting a lot of mileage out of the different meanings of "expense" and "spirit," and in turning the direction of the whole poem in a way that responds dramatically to (or answers) the original. But ultimately a full evaluation of Cope's parody would consider not just its witty changing of expectations, clever word play, and tonal manipulation, but also its commentary on the Shakespeare original—and the insights it offers about why poems are created and what they can do.

Here is another poem that is something of a challenge to evaluate:

JOHN DONNE

Song

> Go, and catch a falling star,
>   Get with child a mandrake root,[7]
> Tell me, where all past years are,
>   Or who cleft the devil's foot,
> Teach me to hear mermaids singing
> Or to keep off envy's stinging,
>   And find
>   What wind
> Serves to advance an honest mind.

5

7. The forked mandrake root is said to look vaguely human.

If thou beest born to strange sights,[8]　　　　　　10
　　Things invisible to see,
Ride ten thousand days and nights,
　　Till age snow white hairs on thee;
Thou, when thou return'st, wilt tell me
All strange wonders that befell thee,　　　　　　15
　　　　And swear
　　　　No where
Lives a woman true, and fair.

If thou find'st one, let me know:
　　Such a pilgrimage were sweet.　　　　　　　20
Yet do not, I would not go,
　　Though at next door we might meet:
Though she were true when you met her,
And last till you write your letter,
　　　　Yet she　　　　　　　　　　　　25
　　　　Will be
False, ere I come, to two, or three.　　　1633

One immediate problem to confront here is the irregular, jerky rhythm. In
a poem called "Song," we are likely to expect music, harmony, something
pleasant and (within limits) predictable in its rhythm and movement. But this
"song" is nothing like that. At first its message sounds lyrical and romantic: to
go and catch a falling star is, if impossible, a romantic thing to propose, a motif
that often comes up (and has for centuries) in love poems and popular songs;
and lines 3 and 5 propose similar traditional romantic activities that evoke wonder and pleasure in contemplation. But the activities suggested in the alternate
lines (2, 4, and 6) contrast sharply; they are just as bold in their unromantic or
antiromantic sentiments. Making a mandrake root pregnant does not sound
like an especially pleasant male activity, however much such a root may look
like a female body, and knowledge of the devil's cleft foot or envy's stinging are
not usually the stuff of romantic poems or songs. Besides, the strange interrup-
tions of easy rhythm (indicated by commas) in otherwise pleasant lines like 1
and 3 suggest that something less than lyrical is going on there too.

By the time we get to the last stanza, what is going on is a lot clearer. We
have here a portrait of an angry and disillusioned man who is obsessed with
the infidelity of women. He is talking to another man, apparently someone
who has far more positive, perhaps even romantic, notions of women, and the
poem is a kind of argument, except that the disillusioned speaker does all the
talking. He pretends to take into account some traditional romantic rhetoric

8. I.e., if you have supernatural powers.

but turns it all on its head, intermixing the traditional impossible quests of lovers with a quest of his own—to find a "woman true, and fair" (line 18). But he knows cynically—he would probably say from experience, though he offers no evidence of his experience and no account of why he feels the way he does—that all these quests are impossible. This is one bitter man, and the song he sings has nothing to do with love or romance.

If we were to evaluate this "song" on the basis of harmonic and romantic expectations, looking for evenness of rhythms, pleasant sounds, and an attractive series of images consonant with romantic attitudes, we would certainly find it wanting. But again (as with the Shakespeare poem above) a larger question of appropriateness begs to be applied. Is the musical, imagistic, and organizational strategy consonant with the poem's total focus and force? Do the sounds and tone of the poem "work" in terms of the speaker portrayed here and the kind of artistic project this poem represents? The displeasure we feel in the speaker's words, images, feelings, and attitudes ultimately needs to be directed toward the speaker; the poet has done a good job of portraying a character whose bitterness, however generated, is unpleasant and off-putting. The poem "works" on its own terms. We may or may not like to hear attitudes like this expressed in a poem; we may or may not approve of using a pretended "song" to mouth such sentiments. But whether or not we "like" the poem in terms of what it says, we can evaluate, through close analysis of its several different elements (much as we have been doing analytically in earlier chapters), how *well* it does what it does. There are, of course, still larger questions of whether what it tries to do is worth doing, and readers of different philosophical or political persuasions may differ widely in their opinions and evaluations of that matter.

Different people do admire different things, and when we talk about criteria for evaluating poetry, we are talking about, at best, elements that a fairly large number of people have, over a long period of time, agreed on as important. There may be substantial agreement about political or social values in a particular group, and a consensus may exist among, say, misogynists or feminists about the value of such a poem as Donne's "Song." But more general agreements that bridge social and ideological divisions are more likely to involve the kinds of matters that have come up for analysis in earlier chapters, matters involving how well a poem *works*, how well it uses the resources it has within its conceptual limits. For some readers, ideology is everything, and there is no such thing as quality beyond political views or moral conclusions. But for others, different, more pluralistic evaluations can be made about accomplishment and quality.

Consistency. Appropriateness. Coherence. Effectiveness. Such terms are likely to be key ones for most readers in making their evaluations—as they have been in this discussion. But individual critics or readers will often have their own emphases, their own axes to grind. For some critics in past generations, "organic unity" was the key to all evaluation, whether a poem achieved, like something grown in nature, a wholeness of conception and effect. For others, the key term may be "tension" or "ambiguity" or "complexity" or "simplicity" or "authenticity" or "cultural truth" or "representation" or "psychological accuracy." With experience, you will develop your own set of criteria that may or may not involve a single ruling concept or term. But wherever (and whenever) you come out, you will learn something about yourself and your values in the process of articulating exactly what you like and admire—and why.

▼   ▼   ▼

IRVING LAYTON

Street Funeral

Tired of chewing
the flesh
of other animals;
Tired of subreption and conceit;
of the child's   5
bewildered conscience
fretting the sly man;
Tired of holding down
a job; of giving insults,
taking insults;   10
Of excited fornication,
failing heart valves,
septic kidneys . . .

This frosty morning,
the coffin wood bursting   15
into brilliant flowers,
Is he glad
that after all the lecheries,
betrayals, subserviency,
After all the lusts,   20
false starts, evasions
he can begin

the unobstructed change
into clean grass
Done forever
with the insult
of birth,
the long adultery
with illusion?   1956

25

REGINA BARRECA

Nighttime Fires

When I was five in Louisville
we drove to see nighttime fires. Piled seven of us,
all pajamas and running noses, into the Olds,
drove fast toward smoke. It was after my father
lost his job, so not getting up in the morning
gave him time: awake past midnight, he read old newspapers
with no news, tried crosswords until he split the pencil
between his teeth, mad. When he heard
the wolf whine of the siren, he woke my mother,
and she pushed and shoved
us all into waking. Once aroused we longed for burnt wood
and a smell of flames high into the pines. My old man liked
driving to rich neighborhoods best, swearing in a good mood
as he followed fire engines that snaked like dragons
and split the silent streets. It was festival, carnival.

If there were a Cadillac or any car
in a curved driveway, my father smiled a smile
from a secret, brittle heart.
His face lit up in the heat given off by destruction
like something was being made, or was being set right.
I bent my head back to see where sparks
ate up the sky. My father who never held us
would take my hand and point to falling cinders that
covered the ground like snow, or, excited, show us
the swollen collapse of a staircase. My mother
watched my father, not the house. She was happy
only when we were ready to go, when it was finally over
and nothing else could burn.
Driving home, she would sleep in the front seat
as we huddled behind. I could see his quiet face in the
rearview mirror, eyes like hallways filled with smoke.   1986

5

10

15

20

25

30

GEOFFREY HILL

In Memory of Jane Fraser

When snow like sheep lay in the fold
And winds went begging at each door
And the far hills were blue with cold
And a cold shroud lay on the moor

She kept the siege. And every day   5
We watched her brooding over death
Like a strong bird above its prey.
The room filled with the kettle's breath.

Damp curtains glued against the pane
Sealed time away. Her body froze   10
As if to freeze us all and chain
Creation to a stunned repose.

She died before the world could stir.
In March the ice unloosed the brook
And water ruffled the sun's hair.   15
Dead cones upon the altar shook.   1959

GALWAY KINNELL

Blackberry Eating

I love to go out in late September
among the fat, overripe, icy, black blackberries
to eat blackberries for breakfast,
the stalks very prickly, a penalty
they earn for knowing the black art   5
of blackberry-making; and as I stand among them
lifting the stalks to my mouth, the ripest berries
fall almost unbidden to my tongue,
as words sometimes do, certain peculiar words
like *strengths* or *squinched*,   10
many-lettered, one-syllabled lumps,
which I squeeze, squinch open, and splurge well
in the silent, startled, icy, black language
of blackberry-eating in late September.   1980

EMILY DICKINSON

[The Brain—is wider than the Sky—]

The Brain—is wider than the Sky—
For—put them side by side—
The one the other will contain
With ease—and You—beside—

The Brain is deeper than the sea—
For—hold them—Blue to Blue—
The one the other will absorb—
As Sponges—Buckets—do—

The Brain is just the weight of God—
For—Heft them—Pound for Pound—
And they will differ—if they do—
As Syllable from Sound—

ca. 1862

▼ ▼ ▼

QUESTIONS

1. What seems to you the most important single factor in whether you like or dislike a poem? Read back over the poems in the course that you have liked most; what do they have in common?

2. How adaptable do you think you are in adjusting to a poem's emphases? Which poems have you liked though you didn't especially like the conclusions they came to?

3. How important to you is the *precision* of words in a poem? Do you tend to like poems better if they are definite and explicit in what they say? if they are ambiguous, uncertain, or complex?

4. Which chapters in the first section of this textbook (up through Chapter 8) have you found most useful? most surprising? Which did you enjoy most? From which did you learn the most about yourself and your tastes and values?

5. What do you value most in poetry generally? Do you read poems that are not assigned? Do you read poems outside this textbook or outside the course? If so, what kinds of poems do you tend to seek out?

6. How important to you is the *tone* of a poem? Do you tend to like funny poems more than serious ones? tragic situations more than comic ones? unusual treatments of standard or predictable subjects and themes?

7. Which poem in this chapter did you most enjoy reading? Which one did

you like best after reading the commentary about it? Are there any poems you have read this term that you have violently disliked? What about them particularly irritated you?

8. Are certain subjects or themes always appealing to you? always unappealing? What variable seems to you most important in determining whether you will like or dislike a poem?

WRITING SUGGESTIONS

1. Choose one poem that you especially admire and one that you do not. Write a two- or three-page essay about each in which you try to show what specific accomplishments (or lack of them) lead you to your evaluative conclusions. Treat each poem in detail, and suggest fully not only how but *why* things "work"—or don't work. Try to construct your argument as "objectively" as possible, so that you are not simply pitting your personal judgment against someone else's. (Alternative: find two poems that are very much alike in subject matter, theme, or situation, but that seem to you to succeed to different degrees. Write one *comparative* essay in which you account for the difference in quality by showing in detail the difference between what works and what does not.)

2. Discuss with classmates a variety of poems you have read this term, and choose one poem about which a number of you disagree. Discuss among yourselves the different perspectives you have on the poem, and try to sort out in the discussion exactly what issues are at stake. Take notes on the discussion, trying to be clear about how your position differs from that of other students. Once you believe that you have the issues sorted out and can be clear about your own position, write a two- or three-page personal letter to your instructor in which you outline a position contrary to your own and then answer it point by point. Be sure to make clear in your letter the *grounds* for your evaluative position, positive or negative—that is, the principles or values on which you base your evaluation. (Hint: in the conversation with classmates, try to steer the discussion to a clear disagreement on no more than two or three points, and in your letter focus carefully on these points. State the arguments of your classmates as effectively and forcefully as you can so that your own argument will be as probing and sophisticated as you can make it.)

3. Choose a poem you have read this term that you admire but really don't like very much. In thinking over the poem again, try to account for the conflict

between your feelings and judgment: what questions of content or form, social or political assumption, personal style, or manner of argument in the poem seem to make it less attractive to you? In a personal letter to a friend who is not in the class and who thus has not heard the class discussions of the issues, describe your dilemma, being careful to first outline why you think the poem is admirable. Say frankly what your personal reservations about the poem are, and at the end use the discussion of the poem to talk about your own values, in poetry and in general.

Reading More Poetry

W. H. AUDEN

In Memory of W. B. Yeats

(d. January, 1939)

I

He disappeared in the dead of winter:
The brooks were frozen, the airports almost deserted,
And snow disfigured the public statues;
The mercury sank in the mouth of the dying day.
What instruments we have agree   5
The day of his death was a dark cold day.

Far from his illness
The wolves ran on through the evergreen forests,
The peasant river was untempted by the fashionable quays;
By mourning tongues   10
The death of the poet was kept from his poems.

But for him it was his last afternoon as himself,
An afternoon of nurses and rumors;
The provinces of his body revolted,
The squares of his mind were empty,   15
Silence invaded the suburbs,
The current of his feeling failed; he became his admirers.

Now he is scattered among a hundred cities
And wholly given over to unfamiliar affections,
To find his happiness in another kind of wood   20
And be punished under a foreign code of conscience.
The words of a dead man
Are modified in the guts of the living.

But in the importance and noise of tomorrow
25 When the brokers are roaring like beasts on the floor of the Bourse,[1]
And the poor have the sufferings to which they are fairly accustomed,
And each in the cell of himself is almost convinced of his freedom,
A few thousand will think of this day
As one thinks of a day when one did something slightly unusual.
30 What instruments we have agree
The day of his death was a dark cold day.

II

You were silly like us; your gift survived it all:
The parish of rich women, physical decay,
Yourself. Mad Ireland hurt you into poetry.
35 Now Ireland has her madness and her weather still,
For poetry makes nothing happen: it survives
In the valley of its making where executives
Would never want to tamper, flows on south
From ranches of isolation and the busy griefs,
40 Raw towns that we believe and die in; it survives,
A way of happening, a mouth.

III

Earth, receive an honored guest:
William Yeats is laid to rest.
Let the Irish vessel lie
45 Emptied of its poetry.

In the nightmare of the dark
All the dogs of Europe bark,
And the living nations wait,
Each sequestered in its hate;

50 Intellectual disgrace
Stares from every human face,
And the seas of pity lie
Locked and frozen in each eye.

Follow, poet, follow right
55 To the bottom of the night,
With your unconstraining voice
Still persuade us to rejoice;

With the farming of a verse
Make a vineyard of the curse,
60 Sing of human unsuccess
In a rapture of distress;

1. The Paris stock exchange.

In the deserts of the heart
Let the healing fountain start,
In the prison of his days
1939   Teach the free man how to praise.   65

ELIZABETH BISHOP

The Armadillo

for Robert Lowell

This is the time of year
when almost every night
the frail, illegal fire balloons appear.
Climbing the mountain height,

rising toward a saint   5
still honored in these parts,
the paper chambers flush and fill with light
that comes and goes, like hearts.

Once up against the sky it's hard
to tell them from the stars—   10
planets, that is—the tinted ones:
Venus going down, or Mars,

or the pale green one. With a wind,
they flare and falter, wobble and toss;
but if it's still they steer between   15
the kite sticks of the Southern Cross,

receding, dwindling, solemnly
and steadily forsaking us,
or, in the downdraft from a peak,
suddenly turning dangerous.   20

Last night another big one fell.
It splattered like an egg of fire
against the cliff behind the house.
The flame ran down. We saw the pair

of owls who nest there flying up   25
and up, their whirling black-and-white
stained bright pink underneath, until
they shrieked up out of sight.

The ancient owls' nest must have burned.
Hastily, all alone,   30

a glistening armadillo left the scene,
rose-flecked, head down, tail down,

and then a baby rabbit jumped out,
short-eared, to our surprise.
35　So soft!—a handful of intangible ash
with fixed, ignited eyes.

Too pretty, dreamlike mimicry!
O falling fire and piercing cry
and panic, and a weak mailed fist
40　*clenched ignorant against the sky!*　　　　　　1965

SAMUEL TAYLOR COLERIDGE

Kubla Khan: or, a Vision in a Dream[2]

In Xanadu did Kubla Khan
　A stately pleasure-dome decree:
Where Alph, the sacred river, ran
Through caverns measureless to man
5　　Down to a sunless sea.
So twice five miles of fertile ground
With walls and towers were girdled round:
And here were gardens bright with sinuous rills
Where blossomed many an incense-bearing tree;
10　And here were forests ancient as the hills,
Enfolding sunny spots of greenery.
But oh! that deep romantic chasm which slanted
Down the green hill athwart a cedarn cover![3]
A savage place! as holy and enchanted
15　As e'er beneath a waning moon was haunted
By woman wailing for her demon-lover![4]
And from this chasm, with ceaseless turmoil seething,
As if this earth in fast thick pants were breathing,
A mighty fountain momently was forced,
20　Amid whose swift half-intermitted burst
Huge fragments vaulted like rebounding hail,
Or chaffy grain beneath the thresher's flail:
And 'mid these dancing rocks at once and ever
It flung up momently the sacred river.
25　Five miles meandering with a mazy motion

2. Coleridge said he wrote this fragment immediately after waking from an opium dream and that after he was interrupted by a caller he was unable to finish the poem. 　3. From side to side of a cover of cedar trees. 　4. In a famous and often imitated German ballad, the lady Lenore is carried off on horseback by the specter of her lover and married to him at his grave.

Through wood and dale the sacred river ran,
Then reached the caverns measureless to man,
And sank in tumult to a lifeless ocean:
And 'mid this tumult Kubla heard from far
Ancestral voices prophesying war!   30

    The shadow of the dome of pleasure
    Floated midway on the waves;
    Where was heard the mingled measure
    From the fountain and the caves.
It was a miracle of rare device,   35
A sunny pleasure-dome with caves of ice!
    A damsel with a dulcimer
    In a vision once I saw:
    It was an Abyssinian maid,
    And on her dulcimer she played,   40
    Singing of Mount Abora.
    Could I revive within me
    Her symphony and song,
    To such a deep delight 'twould win me,
That with music loud and long,   45
I would build that dome in air,
That sunny dome! those caves of ice!
And all who heard should see them there,
And all should cry, Beware! Beware!
His flashing eyes, his floating hair!   50
Weave a circle round him thrice,
And close your eyes with holy dread,
For he on honey-dew hath fed,
And drunk the milk of Paradise.   1798

HART CRANE

To Emily Dickinson

You who desired so much—in vain to ask—
Yet fed your hunger like an endless task,
Dared dignify the labor, bless the quest—
Achieved that stillness ultimately best,

Being, of all, least sought for: Emily, hear!   5
O sweet, dead Silencer, most suddenly clear
When singing that Eternity possessed
And plundered momently in every breast;

—Truly no flower yet withers in your hand.
The harvest you descried and understand   10

Needs more than wit to gather, love to bind.
Some reconcilement of remotest mind—

Leaves Ormus rubyless, and Ophir⁵ chill.
Else tears heap all within one clay-cold hill.   1933

Exile

(after the Chinese)

My hands have not touched pleasure since your hands,—
No,—nor my lips freed laughter since 'farewell',
And with the day, distance again expands
Voiceless between us, as an uncoiled shell.

5   Yet love endures, though starving and alone.
A dove's wings cling about my heart each night
With surging gentleness, and the blue stone
Set in the tryst-ring has but worn more bright.   p. 1918

Episode of Hands

The unexpected interest made him flush.
Suddenly he seemed to forget the pain,—
Consented,—and held out
One finger from the others.

5   The gash was bleeding, and a shaft of sun
That glittered in and out among the wheels,
Fell lightly, warmly, down into the wound.

And as the fingers of the factory owner's son,
That knew a grip for books and tennis
10   As well as one for iron and leather,—
As his taut, spare fingers wound the gauze
Around the thick bed of the wound,
His own hands seemed to him
Like wings of butterflies
15   Flickering in sunlight over summer fields.

The knots and notches,—many in the wide
Deep hand that lay in his,—seemed beautiful.

---

5. An ancient country from which Solomon secured gold and precious stones. *Ormus:* Presumably Ormuz, an ancient city on the Persian Gulf.

They were like the marks of wild ponies' play,—
Bunches of new green breaking a hard turf.

And factory sounds and factory thoughts   20
Were banished from him by that larger, quieter hand
That lay in his with the sun upon it.
And as the bandage knot was tightened
1920   The two men smiled into each other's eyes.

E. E. CUMMINGS

[anyone lived in a pretty how town]

anyone lived in a pretty how town
(with up so floating many bells down)
spring summer autumn winter
he sang his didn't he danced his did.

Women and men(both little and small)   5
cared for anyone not at all
they sowed their isn't they reaped their same
sun moon stars rain

children guessed(but only a few
and down they forgot as up they grew   10
autumn winter spring summer)
that noone loved him more by more

when by now and tree by leaf
she laughed his joy she cried his grief
bird by snow and stir by still   15
anyone's any was all to her

someones married their everyones
laughed their cryings and did their dance
(sleep wake hope and then)they
said their nevers they slept their dream   20

stars rain sun moon
(and only the snow can begin to explain
how children are apt to forget to remember
with up so floating many bells down)

one day anyone died i guess   25
(and noone stooped to kiss his face)
busy folk buried them side by side
little by little and was by was

all by all and deep by deep
and more by more they dream their sleep   30

noone and anyone earth by april
wish by spirit and if by yes.

Women and men(both dong and ding)
summer autumn winter spring
35 reaped their sowing and went their came
sun moon stars rain   1940

WARING CUNEY

No Images

She does not know
Her beauty,
She thinks her brown body
Has no glory.

5   If she could dance
Naked,
Under palm trees
And see her image in the river
She would know.

10 But there are no palm trees
On the street,
And dish water gives back no images.   p. 1926

H. D. (HILDA DOOLITTLE)

Sea Rose

Rose, harsh rose,
marred and with stint of petals,
meagre flower, thin,
sparse of leaf,

5   more precious
than a wet rose
single on a stem—
you are caught in the drift.

Stunted, with small leaf,
10 you are flung on the sand,
you are lifted
in the crisp sand
that drives in the wind.

Can the spice-rose
drip such acrid fragrance
hardened in a leaf?   1916   15

Garden

I

You are clear
O rose, cut in rock,
hard as the descent of hail.

I could scrape the color
from the petals   5
like spilt dye from a rock.

If I could break you
I could break a tree.
If I could stir
I could break a tree—   10
I could break you.

II

O wind, rend open the heat,
cut apart the heat,
rend it to tatters.

Fruit cannot drop   15
through this thick air—
fruit cannot fall into heat
that presses up and blunts
the points of pears
and rounds the grapes.   20

Cut the heat—
plough through it,
turning it on either side
of your path.   1916

EMILY DICKINSON

[Because I could not stop for Death—]

Because I could not stop for Death—
He kindly stopped for me—
The Carriage held but just Ourselves—
And Immortality.

5   We slowly drove—He knew no haste
And I had put away
My labor and my leisure too,
For His Civility—

We passed the School, where Children strove
10   At Recess—in the Ring—
We passed the Fields of Gazing Grain—
We passed the Setting Sun—

Or rather—He passed Us—
The Dews drew quivering and chill—
15   For only Gossamer,[6] my Gown—
My Tippet—only Tulle[7]—

We paused before a House that seemed
A Swelling of the Ground—
The Roof was scarcely visible—
20   The Cornice—in the Ground—

Since then—'tis Centuries—and yet
Feels shorter than the Day
I first surmised the Horses' Heads
ca. 1863   Were toward Eternity—

[I reckon—when I count at all—]

I reckon—when I count at all—
First—Poets—Then the Sun—
Then Summer—Then the Heaven of God—
And then—the List is done—

5   But, looking back—the First so seems
To Comprehend the Whole—
The Others look a needless Show—
So I write—Poets—All—

---

6. A soft sheer fabric.   7. A fine net fabric. *Tippet:* scarf.

Their Summer—lasts a Solid Year—
They can afford a Sun   10
The East—would deem extravagant—
And if the Further Heaven—

Be Beautiful as they prepare
For Those who worship Them—
It is too difficult a Grace—   15
ca. 1862   To justify the Dream—

[My life closed twice before its close—]

My life closed twice before its close—
It yet remains to see
If Immortality unveil
A third event to me

So huge, so hopeless to conceive   5
As these that twice befell.
Parting is all we know of heaven,
And all we need of hell.   1896

[We do not play on Graves—]

We do not play on Graves—
Because there isn't Room—
Besides—it isn't even—it slants
And People come—

And put a Flower on it—   5
And hang their faces so—
We're fearing that their Hearts will drop—
And crush our pretty play—

And so we move as far
As Enemies—away—   10
Just looking round to see how far
ca. 1862   It is—Occasionally—

[Wild Nights—Wild Nights!]

Wild Nights—Wild Nights!
Were I with thee

Wild Nights should be
Our luxury!

Futile—the Winds—
To a Heart in port—
Done with the Compass—
Done with the Chart!

Rowing in Eden—
Ah, the Sea!
Might I but moor—Tonight—
In Thee!

ca. 1861

[She dealt her pretty words like Blades—]

She dealt her pretty words like Blades—
How glittering they shone—
And every One unbared a Nerve
Or wantoned with a Bone—

She never deemed—she hurt—
That—is not Steel's Affair—
A vulgar grimace in the Flesh—
How ill the Creatures bear—

To Ache is human—not polite—
The Film upon the eye
Mortality's old Custom—
Just locking up—to Die.

1862

[The Wind begun to knead the Grass—]

The Wind begun to knead the Grass—
As Women do a Dough—
He flung a Hand full at the Plain—
A Hand full at the Sky—
The Leaves unhooked themselves from Trees—
And started all abroad—
The Dust did scoop itself like Hands—
And throw away the Road—
The Wagons quickened on the Street—
The Thunders gossiped low—

The Lightning showed a Yellow Head—
And then a livid Toe—
The Birds put up the Bars to Nests—
The Cattle flung to Barns—
Then came one drop of Giant Rain—   15
And then, as if the Hands
That held the Dams—had parted hold—
The Waters Wrecked the Sky—
But overlooked my Father's House—
1864   Just Quartering a Tree—   20

JOHN DONNE

The Canonization

For God's sake hold your tongue and let me love!
    Or chide my palsy or my gout,
My five gray hairs or ruined fortune flout;
With wealth your state, your mind with arts improve,
    Take you a course, get you a place,   5
    Observe his Honor or his Grace,
Or the king's real or his stampéd face[8]
    Contemplate; what you will, approve,
        So you will let me love.

Alas, alas, who's injured by my love?   10
    What merchant's ships have my sighs drowned?
Who says my tears have overflowed his ground?
When did my colds a forward spring remove?
    When did the heats which my veins fill
    Add one man to the plaguy bill?[9]   15
Soldiers find wars, and lawyers find out still
    Litigious men which quarrels move,
        Though she and I do love.

Call us what you will, we are made such by love.
    Call her one, me another fly,   20
We're tapers[1] too, and at our own cost die;
And we in us find th' eagle and the dove.[2]
    The phoenix riddle[3] hath more wit[4]

8. On coins.   9. List of plague victims.   1. Which consume themselves. To "die" is Renaissance slang for consummating the sexual act, which was popularly believed to shorten life by one day. *Fly*: a traditional symbol of transitory life.   2. Traditional symbols of strength and purity. 3. According to tradition, only one phoenix existed at a time, dying in a funeral pyre of its own making and being reborn from its own ashes. The bird's existence was thus a riddle akin to a religious mystery (line 27), and a symbol sometimes fused with Christian representations of immortality.   4. Meaning.

By us; we two, being one, are it.
So to one neutral thing both sexes fit,
    We die and rise the same, and prove
        Mysterious by this love.

We can die by it, if not live by love;
    And if unfit for tombs and hearse
Our legend be, it will be fit for verse;[5]
And if no piece of chronicle we prove,
    We'll build in sonnets[6] pretty rooms
    (As well a well-wrought urn becomes[7]
The greatest ashes, as half-acre tombs),
    And by these hymns all shall approve
        Us canonized for love.

And thus invoke us: "You whom reverent love
    Made one another's hermitage,
You to whom love was peace, that now is rage,
Who did the whole world's soul extract, and drove[8]
    Into the glasses of your eyes
    (So made such mirrors and such spies
That they did all to you epitomize)
    Countries, towns, courts; beg from above
        A pattern of your love!"

1633

[Death, be not proud, though some have callèd thee]

Death be not proud, though some have callèd thee
Mighty and dreadful, for thou art not so;
For those whom thou think'st thou dost overthrow
Die not, poor Death, nor yet canst thou kill me.
From rest and sleep, which but thy pictures[9] be,
Much pleasure; then from thee much more must flow,
And soonest[1] our best men with thee do go,
Rest of their bones, and soul's delivery.[2]
Thou art slave to Fate, Chance, kings, and desperate men,
And dost with Poison, War, and Sickness dwell;
And poppy or charms can make us sleep as well,
And better than thy stroke; why swell'st[3] thou then?
One short sleep past, we wake eternally
And death shall be no more; Death, thou shalt die.

1633

---

5. I.e., if we don't turn out to be an authenticated piece of historical narrative.   6. Love poems.
In Italian, *stanza* means room.   7. Befits.   8. Compressed.   9. Likenesses.   1. Most
willingly.   2. Deliverance.   3. Puff with pride.

A Valediction: Forbidding Mourning

As virtuous men pass mildly away,
   And whisper to their souls to go,
Whilst some of their sad friends do say,
   "The breath goes now," and some say, "No,"

So let us melt, and make no noise,   5
   No tear-floods, nor sigh-tempests move;
'Twere profanation of our joys
   To tell the laity our love.

Moving of the earth[4] brings harms and fears,
   Men reckon what it did and meant;   10
But trepidation of the spheres,[5]
   Though greater far, is innocent.

Dull sublunary[6] lovers' love
   (Whose soul is sense) cannot admit
Absence, because it doth remove   15
   Those things which elemented[7] it.

But we, by a love so much refined
   That our selves know not what it is,
Inter-assured of the mind,
   Care less, eyes, lips, and hands to miss.   20

Our two souls therefore, which are one,
   Though I must go, endure not yet
A breach, but an expansion,
   Like gold to airy thinness beat.

If they be two, they are two so   25
   As stiff twin compasses are two:
Thy soul, the fixed foot, makes no show
   To move, but doth, if the other do;

And though it in the center sit,
   Yet when the other far doth roam,   30
It leans, and hearkens after it,
   And grows erect, as that comes home.

Such wilt thou be to me, who must,
   Like the other foot, obliquely run;
Thy firmness makes my circle[8] just,   35
   And makes me end where I begun.

1611?

4. Earthquakes.   5. The Renaissance hypothesis that the celestial spheres trembled and thus caused unexpected variations in their orbits. Such movements are "innocent" because earthlings do not observe or fret about them.   6. Below the moon: i.e., changeable. According to the traditional cosmology that Donne invokes here, the moon was considered the dividing line between the immutable celestial world and the earthly mortal one.   7. Comprised.   8. A traditional symbol of perfection.

RITA DOVE

Parsley[9]

1. THE CANE FIELDS

There is a parrot imitating spring
in the palace, its feathers parsley green.
Out of the swamp the cane appears

to haunt us, and we cut it down. El General
5   searches for a word; he is all the world
there is. Like a parrot imitating spring,

we lie down screaming as rain punches through
and we come up green. We cannot speak an R—
out of the swamp, the cane appears

10   and then the mountain we call in whispers *Katalina*.[1]
The children gnaw their teeth to arrowheads.
There is a parrot imitating spring.

El General has found his word: *perejil*.
Who says it, lives. He laughs, teeth shining
15   out of the swamp. The cane appears

in our dreams, lashed by wind and streaming.
And we lie down. For every drop of blood
there is a parrot imitating spring.
Out of the swamp the cane appears.

2. THE PALACE

20   The word the general's chosen is parsley.
It is fall, when thoughts turn
to love and death; the general thinks
of his mother, how she died in the fall
and he planted her walking cane at the grave
25   and it flowered, each spring stolidly forming
four-star blossoms. The general

pulls on his boots, he stomps to
her room in the palace, the one without
curtains, the one with a parrot
30   in a brass ring. As he paces he wonders
Who can I kill today. And for a moment

9. "On October 2, 1957, Rafael Trujillo (1891–1961), dictator of the Dominican Republic, ordered 20,000 blacks killed because they could not pronounce the letter 'r' in *perejil*, the Spanish word for parsley." (Dove's note)   1. I.e., "Katarina."

the little knot of screams
is still. The parrot, who has traveled

all the way from Australia in an ivory
cage, is, coy as a widow, practising   35
spring. Ever since the morning
his mother collapsed in the kitchen
while baking skull-shaped candies
for the Day of the Dead,[2] the general
has hated sweets. He orders pastries   40
brought up for the bird; they arrive

dusted with sugar on a bed of lace.
The knot in his throat starts to twitch;
he sees his boots the first day in battle
splashed with mud and urine   45
as a soldier falls at his feet amazed—
how stupid he looked—at the sound
of artillery. *I never thought it would sing*
the soldier said, and died. Now

the general sees the fields of sugar   50
cane, lashed by rain and streaming.
He sees his mother's smile, the teeth
gnawed to arrowheads. He hears
the Haitians sing without R's
as they swing the great machetes: 55
Katalina, they sing, *Katalina*,

mi madle, mi amol en muelte.[3] God knows
his mother was no stupid woman; she
could roll an R like a queen. Even
a parrot can roll an R! In the bare room   60
the bright feathers arch in a parody
of greenery, as the last pale crumbs
disappear under the blackened tongue. Someone

calls out his name in a voice
so like his mother's, a startled tear   65
splashes the tip of his right boot.
My mother, my love in death.
The general remembers the tiny green sprigs
men of his village wore in their capes
to honor the birth of a son. He will   70
order many, this time, to be killed

for a single, beautiful word.   1983

2. All Souls' Day, November 1.   3. Line 67 translates this phrase.

JOHN DRYDEN

[Why should a foolish marriage vow][4]

Why should a foolish marriage vow,
    Which long ago was made,
Oblige us to each other now
    When passion is decayed?
5   We loved, and we loved, as long as we could,
    Till our love was loved out in us both;
But our marriage is dead when the pleasure is fled:
    'Twas pleasure first made it an oath.

If I have pleasures for a friend,
10   And farther love in store,
What wrong has he whose joys did end,
    And who could give no more?
'Tis a madness that he should be jealous of me,
    Or that I should bar him of another:
15 For all we can gain is to give ourselves pain,
    When neither can hinder the other.

1671

PAUL LAWRENCE DUNBAR

We Wear the Mask

We wear the mask that grins and lies,
It hides our cheeks and shades our eyes,—
This debt we pay to human guile;
With torn and bleeding hearts we smile,
5 And mouth with myriad subtleties.

Why should the world be over-wise,
In counting all our tears and sighs?
Nay, let them only see us, while
    We wear the mask.

10 We smile, but, O great Christ, our cries
To thee from tortured souls arise.
We sing, but oh the clay is vile
Beneath our feet, and long the mile;
But let the world dream otherwise,
15   We wear the mask!

1896

4. A song from Dryden's play, *Marriage à la Mode*.

T. S. ELIOT

The Love Song of J. Alfred Prufrock

S'io credesse che mia risposta fosse
A persona che mai tornasse al mondo,
Questa fiamma staria senza piu scosse.
Ma perciocche giammai di questo fondo
Non torno vivo alcun, s'i'odo il vero,
Senza tema d'infamia ti rispondo.[5]

Let us go then, you and I,
When the evening is spread out against the sky
Like a patient etherized upon a table;
Let us go, through certain half-deserted streets,
The muttering retreats   5
Of restless nights in one-night cheap hotels
And sawdust restaurants with oyster-shells:
Streets that follow like a tedious argument
Of insidious intent
To lead you to an overwhelming question . . .   10
Oh, do not ask, "What is it?"
Let us go and make our visit.

In the room the women come and go
Talking of Michelangelo.

The yellow fog that rubs its back upon the window-panes,   15
The yellow smoke that rubs its muzzle on the window-panes
Licked its tongue into the corners of the evening,
Lingered upon the pools that stand in drains,
Let fall upon its back the soot that falls from chimneys,
Slipped by the terrace, made a sudden leap,   20
And seeing that it was a soft October night,
Curled once about the house, and fell asleep.

And indeed there will be time[6]
For the yellow smoke that slides along the street,

5. Dante's *Inferno*, XXVII, 61–66. In the Eighth Chasm, Dante and Vergil meet Count Guido de Montefeltrano, one of the False Counselors. The spirits there are in the form of flames, and Guido speaks from the trembling tip of the flame, responding to Dante's request that he tell his life story: "If I thought that my answer were to someone who would ever go back to Earth, this flame would be still, without any more movement. But because no one has ever gone back alive from this chasm (if what I hear is true) I answer you without fear of infamy."   6. See Ecclesiastes 3:1 ff.: "To everything there is a season, and a time to every purpose under the heaven: A time to be born, and a time to die; a time to plant, and a time to pluck up that which is planted; A time to kill, and a time to heal. . . ." Also see Marvell's "To His Coy Mistress": "Had we but world enough and time. . . ."

25 Rubbing its back upon the window-panes;
There will be time, there will be time
To prepare a face to meet the faces that you meet;
There will be time to murder and create,
And time for all the works and days[7] of hands
30 That lift and drop a question on your plate;
Time for you and time for me,
And time yet for a hundred indecisions,
And for a hundred visions and revisions,
Before the taking of a toast and tea.

35 In the room the women come and go
Talking of Michelangelo.

And indeed there will be time
To wonder, "Do I dare?" and, "Do I dare?"
Time to turn back and descend the stair,
40 With a bald spot in the middle of my hair—
(They will say: "How his hair is growing thin!")
My morning coat, my collar mounting firmly to the chin,
My necktie rich and modest, but asserted by a simple pin—
(They will say: "But how his arms and legs are thin!")
45 Do I dare
Disturb the universe?
In a minute there is time
For decisions and revisions which a minute will reverse.

For I have known them all already, known them all:—
50 Have known the evenings, mornings, afternoons,
I have measured out my life with coffee spoons;
I know the voices dying with a dying fall
Beneath the music from a farther room.
So how should I presume?

55 And I have known the eyes already, known them all—
The eyes that fix you in a formulated phrase,
And when I am formulated, sprawling on a pin,
When I am pinned and wriggling on the wall,
Then how should I begin
60 To spit out all the butt-ends of my days and ways?
And how should I presume?

And I have known the arms already, known them all—
Arms that are braceleted and white and bare
(But in the lamplight, downed with light brown hair!)
65 Is it perfume from a dress
That makes me so digress?

7. Hesiod's ancient Greek didactic poem *Works and Days* prescribed in practical detail how to conduct one's life.

Arms that lie along a table, or wrap about a shawl.
　　And should I then presume?
　　And how should I begin?

Shall I say, I have gone at dusk through narrow streets　　　　　70
And watched the smoke that rises from the pipes
Of lonely men in shirt-sleeves, leaning out of windows? . . .

　　I should have been a pair of ragged claws
Scuttling across the floors of silent seas.
　　　　　. . . . .
And the afternoon, the evening, sleeps so peacefully!　　　　　75
Smoothed by long fingers,
Asleep . . . tired . . . or it malingers,
Stretched on the floor, here beside you and me.
Should I, after tea and cakes and ices,
Have the strength to force the moment to its crisis?　　　　　80
But though I have wept and fasted, wept and prayed,
Though I have seen my head (grown slightly bald) brought in upon a platter,[8]
I am no prophet—and here's no great matter;
I have seen the moment of my greatness flicker,
And I have seen the eternal Footman hold my coat, and snicker,　　　　　85
And in short, I was afraid.

　　And would it have been worth it, after all,
After the cups, the marmalade, the tea,
Among the porcelain, among some talk of you and me,
Would it have been worth while,　　　　　90
To have bitten off the matter with a smile,
To have squeezed the universe into a ball[9]
To roll it toward some overwhelming question,
To say: "I am Lazarus,[1] come from the dead,
Come back to tell you all, I shall tell you all"—　　　　　95
If one, settling a pillow by her head,
　　Should say: "That is not what I meant at all.
　　That is not it, at all."

　　And would it have been worth it, after all,
Would it have been worth while,　　　　　100
After the sunsets and the dooryards and the sprinkled streets,
After the novels, after the teacups, after the skirts that trail along the floor—
And this, and so much more?—
It is impossible to say just what I mean!

8. See Matthew 14:1–12 and Mark 6:17–29: John the Baptist was decapitated, upon Salome's request and at Herod's command, and his head delivered on a platter. 　　9. See Marvell's "To His Coy Mistress," lines 41–42: "Let us roll all our strength and all / our sweetness up into one ball. . . . 　　1. One Lazarus was raised from the dead by Jesus (see John 1:1 to 2:2), and another (in the parable of the rich man Dives) is discussed in terms of returning from the dead to warn the living (Luke 16:19–31).

105 But as if a magic lantern[2] threw the nerves in patterns on a screen:
Would it have been worth while
If one, settling a pillow or throwing off a shawl,
And turning toward the window, should say:
    "That is not it at all,
110   That is not what I meant, at all."

No! I am not Prince Hamlet, nor was meant to be;
Am an attendant lord,[3] one that will do
To swell a progress,[4] start a scene or two,
Advise the prince; no doubt, an easy tool,
115 Deferential, glad to be of use,
Politic, cautious, and meticulous;
Full of high sentence, but a bit obtuse;
At times, indeed, almost ridiculous—
Almost, at times, the Fool.

120   I grow old . . . I grow old . . .
I shall wear the bottoms of my trousers rolled.

    Shall I part my hair behind? Do I dare to eat a peach?
I shall wear white flannel trousers, and walk upon the beach.
I have heard the mermaids singing, each to each.

125   I do not think that they will sing to me.

    I have seen them riding seaward on the waves
Combing the white hair of the waves blown back
When the wind blows the water white and black.

    We have lingered in the chambers of the sea
130 By sea-girls wreathed with seaweed red and brown
Till human voices wake us, and we drown.   1917

ROBERT FROST

Range-Finding

The battle rent a cobweb diamond-strung
And cut a flower beside a groundbird's nest
Before it stained a single human breast.
The stricken flower bent double and so hung.
5 And still the bird revisited her young.
A butterfly its fall had dispossessed,
A moment sought in air his flower of rest,
Then lightly stooped to it and fluttering clung.

---

2. A nonelectric projector used as early as the 17th century.   3. Like Polonius in *Hamlet,* who is full of maxims ("high sentence," line 117).   4. Procession of state.

On the bare upland pasture there had spread
O'ernight 'twixt mullein[5] stalks a wheel of thread   10
And straining cables wet with silver dew.
A sudden passing bullet shook it dry.
The indwelling spider ran to greet the fly,
But finding nothing, sullenly withdrew.   1916

The Road Not Taken

Two roads diverged in a yellow wood,
And sorry I could not travel both
And be one traveler, long I stood
And looked down one as far as I could
To where it bent in the undergrowth;   5

Then took the other, as just as fair,
And having perhaps the better claim,
Because it was grassy and wanted wear;
Though as for that the passing there
Had worn them really about the same,   10

And both that morning equally lay
In leaves no step had trodden black.
Oh, I kept the first for another day!
Yet knowing how way leads on to way,
I doubted if I should ever come back.   15

I shall be telling this with a sigh
Somewhere ages and ages hence:
Two roads diverged in a wood, and I—
I took the one less traveled by,
And that has made all the difference.   1916   20

Stopping by Woods on a Snowy Evening

Whose woods these are I think I know.
His house is in the village, though;
He will not see me stopping here
To watch his woods fill up with snow.

My little horse must think it queer   5
To stop without a farmhouse near

5. Weed.

Between the woods and frozen lake
The darkest evening of the year.

He gives his harness bells a shake
To ask if there is some mistake.
The only other sound's the sweep
Of easy wind and downy flake.

The woods are lovely, dark, and deep,
But I have promises to keep,
And miles to go before I sleep,
And miles to go before I sleep.

1923

THOMAS HARDY

The Darkling Thrush

I leant upon a coppice gate
    When Frost was specter gray,
And Winter's dregs made desolate
    The weakening eye of day.
The tangled bine-stems scored the sky
    Like strings of broken lyres,
And all mankind that haunted nigh
    Had sought their household fires.

The land's sharp features seemed to be
    The Century's corpse outleant,
His crypt the cloudy canopy,
    The wind his death-lament.
The ancient pulse of germ and birth
    Was shrunken hard and dry,
And every spirit upon earth
    Seemed fervorless as I.

At once a voice arose among
    The bleak twigs overhead
In a full-hearted evensong
    Of joy illimited;
An aged thrush, frail, gaunt, and small,
    In blast-beruffled plume,
Had chosen thus to fling his soul
    Upon the growing gloom.

So little cause for carolings
    Of such ecstatic sound
Was written on terrestrial things

Afar or nigh around,
That I could think there trembled through
His happy good-night air
Some blessed Hope, whereof he knew
And I was unaware.

30

December 31, 1900

During Wind and Rain

They sing their dearest songs—
He, she, all of them—yea,
Treble and tenor and bass,
    And one to play;
    With the candles mooning each face. . . .
        Ah, no; the years O!
How the sick leaves reel down in throngs!

5

They clear the creeping moss—
Elders and juniors—aye,
Making the pathway neat
    And the garden gay;
And they build a shady seat. . . .
    Ah, no; the years, the years;
See, the white stormbirds wing across!

10

They are blithely breakfasting all—
Men and maidens—yea,
Under the summer tree,
    With a glimpse of the bay,
While pet fowl come to the knee. . . .
    Ah, no; the years O!
And the rotten rose is ripped from the wall.

15

20

They change to a high new house,
He, she, all of them—aye,
Clocks and carpets, and chairs
    On the lawn all day,
And brightest things that are theirs. . . .
    Ah, no; the years, the years;
Down their carved names the rain drop ploughs.

25

1917

GERARD MANLEY HOPKINS

God's Grandeur

The world is charged with the grandeur of God.
   It will flame out, like shining from shook foil;[6]
   It gathers to a greatness, like the ooze of oil
Crushed. Why do men then now not reck his rod?[7]
Generations have trod, have trod, have trod;
   And all is seared with trade; bleared, smeared with toil;
   And wears man's smudge and shares man's smell: the soil
Is bare now, nor can foot feel, being shod.

And for all this, nature is never spent;
   There lives the dearest freshness deep down things;
And though the last lights off the black West went
   Oh, morning, at the brown brink eastward, springs—
Because the Holy Ghost over the bent
   World broods with warm breast and with ah! bright wings.

1918

The Windhover[8]

to Christ our Lord

I caught this morning morning's minion,[9] king-
   dom of daylight's dauphin,[1] dapple-dawn-drawn Falcon, in his riding
   Of the rolling level underneath him steady air, and striding
High there, how he rung upon the rein of a wimpling[2] wing
In his ecstasy! then off, off forth on swing,
   As a skate's heel sweeps smooth on a bow-bend: the hurl and gliding
   Rebuffed the big wind. My heart in hiding
Stirred for a bird,—the achieve of, the mastery of the thing!

Brute beauty and valor and act, oh, air, pride, plume, here
   Buckle![3] AND the fire that breaks from thee then, a billion
Times told lovelier, more dangerous, O my chevalier![4]

6. "I mean foil in its sense of leaf or tinsel.... Shaken goldfoil gives off broad glares like sheet lightning and also, and this is true of nothing else, owing to its zig-zag dints and creasings and network of small many cornered facets, a sort of fork lightning too." *Letters of Gerard Manley Hopkins to Robert Bridges*, ed. C. C. Abbott, 1955, p. 169.   7. Heed his authority.   8. A small hawk, the kestrel, which habitually hovers in the air, headed into the wind.   9. Favorite, beloved.   1. Heir to regal splendor.   2. Rippling.   3. Several meanings may apply: to join closely, to prepare for battle, to grapple with, to collapse.   4. Horseman, knight.

No wonder of it: sheér plód makes plow down sillion[5]
Shine, and blue-bleak embers, ah my dear,
Fall, gall themselves, and gash gold-vermilion.

1877

LANGSTON HUGHES

Theme for English B

The instructor said,

> Go home and write
> a page tonight.
> And let that page come out of you—
> Then, it will be true.   5

I wonder if it's that simple?
I am twenty-two, colored, born in Winston-Salem.
I went to school there, then Durham,[6] then here
to this college[7] on the hill above Harlem.
I am the only colored student in my class.   10
The steps from the hill lead down into Harlem,
through a park, then I cross St. Nicholas,[8]
Eighth Avenue, Seventh, and I come to the Y,
the Harlem Branch Y, where I take the elevator
up to my room, sit down, and write this page: 15

It's not easy to know what is true for you or me
at twenty-two, my age. But I guess I'm what
I feel and see and hear, Harlem, I hear you:
hear you, hear me—we two—you, me, talk on this page.
(I hear New York, too.) Me—who?   20

Well, I like to eat, sleep, drink, and be in love.
I like to work, read, learn, and understand life.
I like a pipe for a Christmas present,
or records—Bessie,[9] bop, or Bach.
I guess being colored doesn't make me *not* like   25
the same things other folks like who are other races.
So will my page be colored that I write?

Being me, it will not be white.
But it will be
a part of you, instructor.   30

5. The narrow strip of land between furrows in an open field divided for separate cultivation.
6. Winston-Salem and Durham are cities in North Carolina.   7. Columbia University.
8. An avenue east of Columbia University.   9. Bessie Smith (1898?–1937), famous blues singer.

You are white—
yet a part of me, as I am a part of you.
That's American.
Sometimes perhaps you don't want to be a part of me.
35   Nor do I often want to be a part of you.
But we are, that's true!
As I learn from you,
I guess you learn from me—
although you're older—and white—
40   and somewhat more free.

This is my page for English B.   1959

BEN JONSON

To Penshurst[1]

Thou art not, Penshurst, built to envious show,
Of touch[2] or marble; nor canst boast a row
Of polished pillars, or a roof of gold;
Thou hast no lantern[3] whereof tales are told,
5   Or stair, or courts; but stand'st an ancient pile,
And, these grudged at,[4] art reverenced the while.
Thou joy'st in better marks, of soil, of air,
Of wood, of water; therein thou art fair.
Thou hast thy walks for health, as well as sport;
10   Thy mount, to which the dryads do resort,
Where Pan and Bacchus[5] their high feasts have made
Beneath the broad beech and the chestnut shade,
That taller tree, which of a nut was set
At his great birth[6] where all the Muses met.
15   There in the writhéd bark are cut the names
Of many a sylvan, taken with his flames;[7]
And thence the ruddy satyrs oft provoke
The lighter fauns to reach thy Lady's Oak.[8]
Thy copse too, named of Gamage,[9] thou hast there,
20   That never fails to serve thee seasoned deer

1. The country seat (in Kent) of the Sidney family, owned by Sir Robert, brother of the poet, Sir Philip. Jonson's celebration of the estate is one of the earliest "house" poems and a prominent example of topographical or didactic-descriptive poetry.   2. Touchstone: basanite, a smooth dark stone similar to black marble.   3. A glassed or open tower or dome atop the roof.   4. I.e., although these (more pretentious structures) are envied. The while: anyway.   5. Ancient gods of nature and wine, both associated with spectacular feasting and celebration.   6. Sir Philip Sidney's, on November 30, 1554; the tree stood for nearly 150 years.   7. Inspired by Sidney's love poetry.   8. Where, according to legend, a former lady of the house (Lady Leicester) began labor pains. Satyrs: half-men, half-goats who participated in the rites of Bacchus.   9. The maiden name of the owner's wife. Copse: thicket.

When thou wouldst feast, or exercise, thy friends.
The lower land, that to the river bends,
Thy sheep, thy bullocks, kine, and calves do feed;
The middle grounds thy mares and horses breed.
Each bank doth yield thee conies;[1] and the tops,   25
Fertile of wood, Ashore and Sidney's copse,
To crown thy open table, doth provide
The purpled pheasant with the speckled side;
The painted partridge lies in every field,
And for thy mess is willing to be killed.   30
And if the high-swollen Medway[2] fail thy dish,
Thou hast thy ponds that pay thee tribute fish,
Fat agéd carps that run into thy net,
And pikes, now weary their own kind to eat,
As loath the second draught[3] or cast to stay,   35
Officiously[4] at first themselves betray;
Bright eels that emulate them, and leap on land
Before the fisher, or into his hand.
Then hath thy orchard fruit, thy garden flowers,
Fresh as the air, and new as are the hours.   40
The early cherry, with the later plum,
Fig, grape, and quince, each in his time doth come:
The blushing apricot and woolly peach
Hang on thy walls, that every child may reach.
And though thy walls be of the country stone,   45
They're reared with no man's ruin, no man's groan;
There's none that dwell about them wish them down,
But all come in, the farmer and the clown,[5]
And no one empty-handed, to salute
Thy lord and lady, though they have no suit.[6]   50
Some bring a capon, some a rural cake,
Some nuts, some apples; some that think they make
The better cheeses bring 'em, or else send
By their ripe daughters, whom they would commend
This way to husbands, and whose baskets bear   55
An emblem of themselves in plum or pear.
But what can this (more than express their love)
Add to thy free[7] provisions, far above
The need of such? whose liberal board doth flow
With all that hospitality doth know;   60
Where comes no guest but is allowed to eat,
Without his fear, and of thy lord's own meat;
Where the same beer and bread, and selfsame wine,
That is his lordship's shall be also mine.

1. Rabbits.   2. A river bordering the estate.   3. Of a net. *Stay*: await.   4. Obligingly.   5. Rustic, peasant.   6. Request for favors.   7. Generous.

65 　And I not fain[8] to sit (as some this day
　　At great men's tables), and yet dine away.[9]
　　Here no man tells[1] my cups; nor, standing by,
　　A waiter doth my gluttony envý,
　　But gives me what I call, and lets me eat;
70 　He knows below he shall find plenty of meat.
　　Thy tables hoard not up for the next day;
　　Nor, when I take my lodging, need I pray
　　For fire, or lights, or livery;[2] all is there,
　　As if thou then wert mine, or I reigned here:
75 　There's nothing I can wish, for which I stay.
　　That found King James when hunting late this way
　　With his brave son, the prince,[3] they saw thy fires
　　Shine bright on every hearth, as the desires
　　Of thy Penates had been set on flame
80 　To entertain them; or the country came
　　With all their zeal to warm their welcome here.
　　What (great I will not say, but) sudden cheer
　　Didst thou then make 'em! and what praise was heaped
　　On thy good lady then! who therein reaped
85 　The just reward of her high housewifery;[4]
　　To have her linen, plate, and all things nigh,
　　When she was far; and not a room but dressed
　　As if it had expected such a guest!
　　These, Penshurst, are thy praise, and yet not all.
90 　Thy lady's noble, fruitful, chaste withal.
　　His children thy great lord may call his own,
　　A fortune in this age but rarely known.
　　They are, and have been, taught religion; thence
　　Their gentler spirits have sucked innocence.
95 　Each morn and even they are taught to pray,
　　With the whole household, and may, every day,
　　Read in their virtuous parents' noble parts
　　The mysteries of manners, arms, and arts.
　　Now, Penshurst, they that will proportion[5] thee
100 　With other edifices, when they see
　　Those proud, ambitious heaps, and nothing else,
　　May say, their lords have built, but thy lord dwells.　　　1616

---

8. Obliged.　　9. Possibly, "elsewhere," because they do not get enough to eat; or "away" in the sense of far from the party of honor.　　1. Counts.　　2. Provisions (or, possibly, servants).
3. Prince Henry, who died in 1612.　　4. Domestic economy.　　5. Compare.

A. M. KLEIN

Heirloom

My father bequeathed me no wide estates;
No keys and ledgers were my heritage;
Only some holy books with *yahrzeit*[6] dates
Writ mournfully upon a blank front page—

Books of the Baal Shem Tov,[7] and of his wonders;   5
Pamphlets upon the devil and his crew;
Prayers against road demons, witches, thunders;
And sundry other tomes for a good Jew.

Beautiful: though no pictures on them, save
The scorpion crawling on a printed track;   10
The Virgin floating on a scriptural wave,
Square letters twinkling in the Zodiac.

The snuff left on this page, now brown and old,
The tallow stains of midnight liturgy—
These are my coat of arms, and these unfold   15
My noble lineage, my proud ancestry!

And my tears, too, have stained this heirloomed ground,
When reading in these treatises some weird
Miracle, I turned a leaf and found
A white hair fallen from my father's beard.   1940   20

RICHARD LOVELACE

To Amarantha, that She Would Dishevel Her Hair

Amarantha sweet and fair,
Ah, braid no more that shining hair!
As my curious hand or eye
Hovering round thee, let it fly.

Let it fly as unconfined   5
As its calm ravisher, the wind,
Who hath left his darling, th' East,
To wanton o'er that spicy nest.

---

6. Anniversary of the death of a parent or near relative.   7. A title given to someone who possesses
the secret knowledge of Jewish holy men and who therefore could work miracles.

Every tress must be confessed
But neatly tangled at the best,
   Like a clue[8] of golden thread,
Most excellently raveléd.

Do not then wind up that light
In ribands, and o'ercloud in night;
   Like the sun in's early ray,
But shake your head and scatter day.

See, 'tis broke! Within this grove,
The bower and the walks of love,
   Weary lie we down and rest
And fan each other's panting breast.

Here we'll strip and cool our fire
In cream below, in milk-baths higher;
   And when all wells are drawn dry,
I'll drink a tear out of thine eye.

Which our very joys shall leave,
That sorrows thus we can deceive;
   Or our very sorrows weep,
That joys so ripe so little keep.   1649

ROBERT LOWELL

Skunk Hour

for Elizabeth Bishop

Nautilus Island's hermit
heiress still lives through winter in her Spartan cottage;
her sheep still graze above the sea.
Her son's a bishop. Her farmer
is first selectman[9] in our village,
she's in her dotage.

Thirsting for
the hierarchic privacy
of Queen Victoria's century,
she buys up all
the eyesores facing her shore,
and lets them fall.

8. Ball.   9. An elected New England town official.

The season's ill—
we've lost our summer millionaire,
who seemed to leap from an L. L. Bean[1]
catalogue. His nine-knot yawl
was auctioned off to lobstermen.
A red fox stain covers Blue Hill. 15

And now our fairy
decorator brightens his shop for fall,
his fishnet's filled with orange cork,
orange, his cobbler's bench and awl,
there is no money in his work,
he'd rather marry. 20

One dark night,
my Tudor Ford climbed the hill's skull,
I watched for love-cars. Lights turned down,
they lay together, hull to hull,
where the graveyard shelves on the town. . . .
My mind's not right. 25 30

A car radio bleats,
"Love, O careless Love. . . ."[2] I hear
my ill-spirit sob in each blood cell,
as if my hand were at its throat. . . .
I myself am hell;
nobody's here— 35

only skunks, that search
in the moonlight for a bite to eat.
They march on their soles up Main Street:
white stripes, moonstruck eyes' red fire
under the chalk-dry and spar spire
of the Trinitarian Church. 40

I stand on top
of our back steps and breathe the rich air—
a mother skunk with her column of kittens swills the garbage pail.
She jabs her wedge head in a cup
of sour cream, drops her ostrich tail,
and will not scare. 45

1959

1. Famous old Maine sporting goods firm. 2. A popular song.

ANDREW MARVELL

The Garden

How vainly men themselves amaze[3]
To win the palm, the oak, or bays,[4]
And their incessant labors see
Crowned from some single herb, or tree,
Whose short and narrow-vergèd[5] shade
Does prudently their toils upbraid;
While all flowers and all trees do close[6]
To weave the garlands of repose!

Fair Quiet, have I found thee here,
And Innocence, thy sister dear?
Mistaken long, I sought you then
In busy companies of men.
Your sacred plants,[7] if here below,
Only among the plants will grow;
Society is all but rude[8]
To[9] this delicious solitude.

No white nor red was ever seen
So am'rous as this lovely green.
Fond lovers, cruel as their flame,
Cut in these trees their mistress' name:
Little, alas, they know, or heed
How far these beauties hers exceed!
Fair trees, wheresoe'er your barks I wound,
No name shall but your own be found.

When we have run our passion's heat,
Love hither makes his best retreat.
The gods, that mortal beauty chase,
Still in a tree did end their race:
Apollo hunted Daphne so,
Only that she might laurel grow;
And Pan did after Syrinx speed,
Not as a nymph, but for a reed.[1]

What wondrous life is this I lead!
Ripe apples drop about my head;
The luscious clusters of the vine

3. Become frenzied.   4. Awards for athletic, civic, and literary achievements.   5. Narrowly cropped.   6. Unite.   7. Cuttings.   8. Barbarous.   9. Compared to.   1. In Ovid's *Metamorphoses*, Daphne, pursued by Apollo, is turned into a laurel, and Syrinx, pursued by Pan, into a reed that Pan makes into a flute.

Upon my mouth do crush their wine;
The nectarine and curious[2] peach
Into my hands themselves do reach;
Stumbling on melons, as I pass,
Insnared with flowers, I fall on grass.   40

    Meanwhile the mind, from pleasure less,
Withdraws into its happiness;[3]
The mind, that ocean where each kind
Does straight its own resemblance find;[4]
Yet it creates, transcending these,   45
Far other worlds and other seas,
Annihilating[5] all that's made
To a green thought in a green shade.

    Here at the fountain's sliding foot,
Or at some fruit tree's mossy root,   50
Casting the body's vest[6] aside,
My soul into the boughs does glide:
There, like a bird, it sits and sings,
Then whets[7] and combs its silver wings,
And, till prepared for longer flight,   55
Waves in its plumes the various[8] light.

    Such was that happy garden-state,
While man there walked without a mate:
After a place so pure, and sweet,
What other help could yet be meet![9]   60
But 'twas beyond a mortal's share
To wander solitary there:
Two paradises 'twere in one
To live in paradise alone.

    How well the skillful gardener drew   65
Of flowers and herbs this dial[1] new,
Where, from above, the milder sun
Does through a fragrant zodiac run;
And as it works, th' industrious bee
Computes its time as well as we!   70
How could such sweet and wholesome hours
Be reckoned but with herbs and flowers?   1681

2. Exquisite. 3. I.e., the mind withdraws from lesser sense pleasure into contemplation.
4. All land creatures were supposed to have corresponding sea-creatures. 5. Reducing to nothing by comparison. 6. Vestment, clothing; the flesh is being considered as simply clothing for
the soul. 7. Preens. 8. Many-colored. 9. Appropriate. 1. A garden planted in the
shape of a sundial, complete with zodiac.

JOHN MILTON

Lycidas[2]

In this monody the author bewails a learned friend, unfortunately
drowned in his passage from Chester on the Irish Seas, 1637.[3] And
by occasion foretells the ruin of our corrupted clergy then in their
height.

Yet once more, O ye laurels, and once more
Ye myrtles brown, with ivy never sere,[4]
I come to pluck your berries harsh and crude,[5]
And with forced fingers rude,
5   Shatter your leaves before the mellowing year.
Bitter constraint, and sad occasion dear,[6]
Compels me to disturb your season due:
For Lycidas is dead, dead ere his prime,
Young Lycidas, and hath not left his peer.
10   Who would not sing for Lycidas? He knew
Himself to sing, and build the lofty rhyme.
He must not float upon his wat'ry bier
Unwept, and welter[7] to the parching wind,
Without the meed[8] of some melodious tear.
15   Begin then, sisters of the sacred well,[9]
That from beneath the seat of Jove doth spring,
Begin, and somewhat loudly sweep the string.
Hence with denial vain and coy excuse;
So may some gentle muse[1]
20   With lucky words favor my destined urn,
And as he passes turn,
And bid fair peace be to my sable shroud.
For we were nursed upon the self-same hill,
Fed the same flock, by fountain, shade, and rill.
25   Together both, ere the high lawns[2] appeared
Under the opening eyelids of the morn,
We drove afield, and both together heard
What time the gray-fly winds[3] her sultry horn,
Batt'ning[4] our flocks with the fresh dews of night,
30   Oft till the star that rose, at ev'ning, bright,

2. The name of a shepherd in Vergil's *Eclogue*, III. Milton's elegy works from the convention of
treating the dead man as if he were a shepherd and also transforms other details to a pastoral setting
and situation.   3. Edward King, a student with Milton at Cambridge, and at the time of his death
a young clergyman. *Monody:* a song sung by a single voice.   4. Withered. The laurel, myrtle,
and ivy were all materials used to construct traditional evergreen garlands signifying poetic accomplishment. *Brown:* dusky, dark.   5. Unripe.   6. Dire.   7. Tumble about.   8. Tribute.
9. The muses, who lived on Mt. Helicon. At the foot of the mountain were two fountains, or wells,
where the muses danced around Jove's altar.   1. Poet.   2. Grasslands: pastures.   3. Blows;
i.e., the insect hum of midday.   4. Fattening.

Towards Heav'n's descent had sloped his westering wheel.
Meanwhile the rural ditties were not mute,
Tempered to the oaten flute;[5]
Rough satyrs danced, and fauns with clov'n heel,
From the glad sound would not be absent long,   35
And old Damaetas[6] loved to hear our song.
 But O the heavy change, now thou art gone,
Now thou art gone, and never must return!
Thee, shepherd, thee the woods and desert caves,
With wild thyme and the gadding[7] vine o'ergrown,   40
And all their echoes mourn.
The willows and the hazel copses[8] green
Shall now no more be seen,
Fanning their joyous leaves to thy soft lays.
As killing as the canker[9] to the rose,   45
Or taint-worm to the weanling herds that graze,
Or frost to flowers, that their gay wardrobe wear,
When first the white-thorn blows:[1]
Such, Lycidas, thy loss to shepherd's ear.
 Where were ye, nymphs,[2] when the remorseless deep   50
Closed o'er the head of your loved Lycidas?
For neither were ye playing on the steep,
Where your old Bards, the famous Druids, lie,
Nor on the shaggy top of Mona high,
Nor yet where Deva spreads her wizard stream:[3]   55
Ay me, I fondly[4] dream!
Had ye been there—for what could that have done?
What could the Muse[5] herself that Orpheus bore,
The Muse herself, for her enchanting[6] son
Whom universal nature did lament,   60
When by the rout that made the hideous roar,
His gory visage down the stream was sent,
Down the swift Hebrus to the Lesbian shore?
 Alas! What boots[7] it with uncessant care
To tend the homely slighted shepherd's trade,   65
And strictly meditate the thankless Muse?
Were it not better done, as others use[8]
To sport with Amaryllis in the shade,

5. Shepherds' pipes. 6. A traditional pastoral name, possibly referring here to a Cambridge tutor.
7. Wandering. 8. Thickets. 9. Cankerworm. 1. Blossoms. 2. Nature deities.
3. The River Dee, reputed to have prophetic powers. *Mona:* the Isle of Anglesey. The steep (line
52) may be a burial ground, in northern Wales, for Druids, ancient priests and magicians; all three
locations are near the place where King drowned. 4. Foolishly. 5. Calliope, the muse of
epic poetry, whose son Orpheus was torn limb from limb by frenzied orgiasts. His head, thrown into
the Hebrus (lines 62–63), floated into the sea and finally to Lesbos, where it was buried. 6. Orpheus was reputed to be able to charm even inanimate things with his music; he once persuaded
Pluto to release his dead wife, Eurydice, from the infernal regions. 7. Profits. 8. Customarily do. Amaryllis (line 68) and Neaera (line 69) are stock names of women celebrated in pastoral
love poetry.

Or with the tangles of Neaera's hair?
70 Fame is the spur that the clear spirit doth raise
(That last infirmity of noble mind)
To scorn delights, and live laborious days;
But the fair guerdon⁹ when we hope to find,
And think to burst out into sudden blaze,
75 Comes the blind Fury¹ with th' abhorréd shears,
And slits the thin-spun life. "But not the praise,"
Phoebus² replied, and touched my trembling ears:
"Fame is no plant that grows on mortal soil,
Nor in the glistering foil³
80 Set off to th' world, nor in broad rumor lies,
But lives and spreads aloft by those pure eyes
And perfect witness of all-judging Jove;
As he pronounces lastly on each deed,
Of so much fame in Heav'n expect thy meed."
85 O fountain Arethuse,⁴ and thou honored flood,
Smooth-sliding Mincius, crowned with vocal reeds,
That strain I heard was of a higher mood.
But now my oat⁵ proceeds,
And listens to the herald of the sea,⁶
90 That came in Neptune's plea.
He asked the waves and asked the felon-winds,
What hard mishap hath doomed this gentle swain,⁷
And questioned every gust of rugged wings
That blows from off each beakéd promontory.
95 They knew not of his story,
And sage Hippotades⁸ their answer brings:
That not a blast was from his dungeon strayed;
The air was calm, and on the level brine,
Sleek Panopë⁹ with all her sisters played.
100 It was that fatal and perfidious bark
Built in th' eclipse, and rigged with curses dark,
That sunk so low that sacred head of thine,
Next Camus,¹ reverend sire, went footing slow,
His mantle hairy, and his bonnet sedge,
105 Inwrought with figures dim, and on the edge

9. Reward.   1. Atropos, the Fate who cuts the threads of human life after they are spun and measured by her two sisters.   2. Apollo, god of poetic inspiration. In Roman tradition, touching the ears of one's hearers meant asking them to remember what they heard.   3. Flashy setting, used to make inferior gems glitter.   4. A Sicilian fountain, associated with the pastoral poetry of Theocritus. The River Mincius (line 86) is associated with Vergil's pastorals.   5. Oaten pipe: pastoral song.   6. Triton, who maintains the innocence of Neptune, the Roman god of the sea, in the death of Lycidas.   7. Youth, shepherd, poet.   8. Aeolus, god of the winds and son of Hippotas.   9. According to Vergil, the greatest of the Nereids (sea nymphs).   1. God of the River Cam, which flows through Cambridge.

Like to that sanguine flower inscribed with woe.[2]
"Ah! who hath reft," quoth he, "my dearest pledge?"
Last came, and last did go,
The pilot of the Galilean Lake;[3]
Two massy keys he bore of metals twain   110
(The golden opes, the iron shuts amain).
He shook his mitered locks, and stern bespake:
"How well could I have spared for thee, young swain,
Enow[4] of such as for their bellies' sake
Creep and intrude, and climb into the fold![5]   115
Of other care they little reck'ning make,
Than how to scramble at the shearers' feast,
And shove away the worthy bidden guest.
Blind mouths! that scarce themselves know how to hold
A sheep-hook,[6] or have learned aught else the least   120
That to the faithful herdman's art belongs!
What recks it[7] them? What need they? They are sped,[8]
And when they list,[9] their lean and flashy songs
Grate on their scrannel[1] pipes of wretched straw.
The hungry sheep look up and are not fed,   125
But swoln with wind, and the rank mist they draw,
Rot inwardly, and foul contagion spread,
Besides what the grim wolf with privy paw[2]
Daily devours apace, and nothing said;
But that two-handed engine[3] at the door   130
Stands ready to smite once, and smite no more."
        Return, Alpheus,[4] the dread voice is past,
That shrunk thy streams; return, Sicilian Muse,
And call the vales, and bid them hither cast
Their bells and flowrets of a thousand hues.   135
Ye valleys low, where the mild whispers use,[5]
Of shades and wanton winds and gushing brooks,
On whose fresh lap the swart star[6] sparely looks,

---

2. The hyacinth, which was supposed to bear marks that meant "alas" because the flower was created by Phoebus from the blood of a youth he had killed accidentally.   3. St. Peter, a fisherman before he became a disciple. According to Matthew 16:19, Christ promised him "the keys of the kingdom of heaven"; he was traditionally regarded as the first head of the Church, hence the bishop's miter in line 112.   4. The old plural of "enough."   5. According to John 10:1, "He that entereth not by the door into the sheepfold, but climbeth up some other way . . . is a thief and a robber."   6. A bishop's staff was shaped like a sheephook to suggest his role as "pastor" (shepherd) of the flock of saints.   7. Does it matter to.   8. Have attained their purpose—but also, destroyed.   9. Desire.   1. Feeble.   2. The Roman Catholic Church.   3. Not identified. Guesses include the two-handed sword of the archangel Michael, the two houses of Parliament, and St. Peter's keys.   4. A river god who, according to Ovid, fell in love with Arethusa. She fled in the form of an underground stream and became a fountain in Sicily, but Alpheus dived under the sea and at last his waters mingled with hers. See above, line 85. *Sicilian Muse:* the muse of Theocritus.   5. Frequent.   6. Sirius, the Dog Star, which supposedly withers plants in late summer.

Throw hither all your quaint enameled eyes,
140 That on the green turf suck the honeyed showers,
And purple all the ground with vernal flowers.
Bring the rathe[7] primrose that forsaken dies,
The tufted crow-toe, and pale jessamine,
The white pink, and the pansy freaked[8] with jet,
145 The glowing violet,
The musk-rose, and the well-attired woodbine,
With cowslips wan that hang the pensive head,
And every flower that sad embroidery wears.
Bid amaranthus[9] all his beauty shed,
150 And daffodillies fill their cups with tears,
To strew the laureate hearse[1] where Lycid lies.
For so to interpose a little ease,
Let our frail thoughts dally with false surmise.
Ay me! Whilst thee the shores and sounding seas
155 Wash far away, where'er thy bones are hurled,
Whether beyond the stormy Hebrides,[2]
Where thou perhaps under the whelming tide
Visit'st the bottom of the monstrous world;[3]
Or whether thou to our moist vows denied,
160 Sleep'st by the fable of Bellerus old,[4]
Where the great vision of the guarded mount
Look toward Namancos and Bayona's hold;
Look homeward, Angel, now, and melt with ruth.[5]
And, O ye dolphins,[6] waft the hapless youth.
165 Weep no more, woeful shepherds, weep no more,
For Lycidas your sorrow is not dead,
Sunk though he be beneath the wat'ry floor,
So sinks the day-star[7] in the ocean bed,
And yet anon repairs his drooping head,
170 And tricks[8] his beams, and with new-spangled ore
Flames in the forehead of the morning sky:
So Lycidas sunk low, but mounted high,
Through the dear might of him that walked the waves,[9]
Where, other groves and other streams along,
175 With nectar pure his oozy locks he laves,
And hears the unexpressive nuptial song,[1]
In the blest kingdoms meek of joy and love.

7. Early.　8. Flecked.　9. A legendary flower that cannot fade.　1. Bier.　2. Islands off Scotland, the northern edge of the sea where King drowned.　3. World where monsters live.　4. A legendary giant, supposedly buried at Land's End in Cornwall. At the tip of Land's End is St. Michael's Mount (line 161), from which the archangel is pictured looking south across the Atlantic toward Spanish (Catholic) strongholds (Namancos and Bayona, line 162).　5. Pity. 6. According to Roman legend, dolphins brought the body of a drowned youth, Melicertes, to land, where a temple was erected to him as the protector of sailors.　7. The sun. 8. Dresses.　9. Christ. See Matthew 14:25–26.　1. Sung at the "marriage of the Lamb," according to Revelation 19, *unexpressive:* inexpressible.

There entertain him all the saints above,
In solemn troops and sweet societies
That sing, and singing in their glory move,   180
And wipe the tears forever from his eyes.
Now, Lycidas, the shepherds weep no more;
Henceforth thou art the genius[2] of the shore,
In thy large recompense, and shalt be good
To all that wander in that perilous flood.   185
   Thus sang the uncouth swain[3] to th' oaks and rills,
While the still morn went out with sandals gray;
He touched the tender stops of various quills,[4]
With eager thought warbling his Doric[5] lay.
And now the sun had stretched out all the hills,   190
And now was dropped into the western bay.
At last he rose, and twitched his mantle blue:
Tomorrow to fresh woods, and pastures new.   1637

MICHAEL ONDAATJE

King Kong Meets Wallace Stevens

Take two photographs—
Wallace Stevens and King Kong
(Is it significant that I eat bananas as I write this?)

Stevens is portly, benign, a white brush cut
striped tie. Businessman but   5
for the dark thick hands, the naked brain
the thought in him.

Kong is staggering
lost in New York streets again
a spawn of annoyed cars at his toes.   10
The mind is nowhere.
Fingers are plastic, electric under the skin.
He's at the call of Metro-Goldwyn-Mayer.

Meanwhile W. S. in his suit
is thinking chaos is thinking fences.   15
In his head—the seeds of fresh pain
his exorcising,
the bellow of locked blood.

The hands drain from his jacket,
pose in the murderer's shadow.   1979   20

---

2. Protecting deity.   3. Unlettered shepherd: i.e., Milton.   4. Reeds in the shepherd's pipes.
5. The Greek dialect of Theocritus, Bion, and Moschus, the first writers of pastoral.

SYLVIA PLATH

Black Rook in Rainy Weather

On the stiff twig up there
Hunches a wet black rook
Arranging and rearranging its feathers in the rain.
I do not expect a miracle
5   Or an accident

To set the sight on fire
In my eye, nor seek
Any more in the desultory weather some design,
But let spotted leaves fall as they fall,
10   Without ceremony, or portent

Although, I admit, I desire,
Occasionally, some backtalk
From the mute sky, I can't honestly complain:
A certain minor light may still
15   Leap incandescent

Out of kitchen table or chair
As if a celestial burning took
Possession of the most obtuse objects now and then—
Thus hallowing an interval
20   Otherwise inconsequent

By bestowing largesse, honor,
One might say love. At any rate, I now walk
Wary (for it could happen
Even in this dull, ruinous landscape); skeptical,
25   Yet politic; ignorant

Of whatever angel may choose to flare
Suddenly at my elbow. I only know that a rook
Ordering its black feathers can so shine
As to seize my senses, haul
30   My eyelids up, and grant

A brief respite from fear
Of total neutrality. With luck,
Trekking stubborn through this season
Of fatigue, I shall
35   Patch together a content

Of sorts. Miracles occur,
If you care to call those spasmodic
Tricks of radiance miracles. The wait's begun again,
The long wait for the angel,
40   For that rare, random descent.[6]   1960

6. According to Acts 2, the Holy Ghost at Pentecost descended like a tongue of fire upon Jesus' disciples.

Lady Lazarus

I have done it again.
One year in every ten
I manage it—

A sort of walking miracle, my skin
Bright as a Nazi lampshade,   5
My right foot

A paperweight,
My face a featureless, fine
Jew linen.

Peel off the napkin   10
O my enemy.
Do I terrify?—

The nose, the eye pits, the full set of teeth?
The sour breath
Will vanish in a day.   15

Soon, soon the flesh
The grave cave ate will be
At home on me

And I a smiling woman.
I am only thirty.   20
And like the cat I have nine times to die.

This is Number Three.
What a trash
To annihilate each decade.

What a million filaments.   25
The peanut-crunching crowd
Shoves in to see

Them unwrap me hand and foot—
The big strip tease.
Gentlemen, ladies   30

These are my hands
My knees.
I may be skin and bone,

Nevertheless, I am the same, identical woman.
The first time it happened I was ten.   35
It was an accident.

The second time I meant
To last it out and not come back at all.
I rocked shut

40   As a seashell.
    They had to call and call
    And pick the worms off me like sticky pearls.

    Dying
    Is an art, like everything else.
45   I do it exceptionally well.

    I do it so it feels like hell.
    I do it so it feels real.
    I guess you could say I've a call.

    It's easy enough to do it in a cell.
50   It's easy enough to do it and stay put.
    It's the theatrical

    Comeback in broad day
    To the same place, the same face, the same brute
    Amused shout:

55   "A miracle!"
    That knocks me out.
    There is a charge

    For the eyeing of my scars, there is a charge
    For the hearing of my heart—
60   It really goes.

    And there is a charge, a very large charge
    For a word or a touch
    Or a bit of blood

    Or a piece of my hair or my clothes.
65   So, so Herr Doktor.
    So, Herr Enemy.

    I am your opus,
    I am your valuable,
    The pure gold baby

70   That melts to a shriek.
    I turn and burn.
    Do not think I underestimate your great concern

    Ash, ash—
    You poke and stir.
75   Flesh, bone, there is nothing there—

    A cake of soap,
    A wedding ring,
    A gold filling.

    Herr God, Herr Lucifer
80   Beware
    Beware.

Out of the ash
I rise with my red hair
And I eat men like air.   1965

EZRA POUND

The Garden

En robe de parade.
—SAMAIN[7]

Like a skein of loose silk blown against a wall
She walks by the railing of a path in Kensington Gardens,[8]
And she is dying piece-meal
        of a sort of emotional anæmia.

And round about there is a rabble   5
Of the filthy, sturdy, unkillable infants of the very poor.
They shall inherit the earth.

In her is the end of breeding.
Her boredom is exquisite and excessive.
She would like some one to speak to her,   10
And is almost afraid that I
        will commit that indiscretion.   1916

In a Station of the Metro[9]

The apparition of these faces in the crowd;
Petals on a wet, black bough.   p. 1913

JOHN CROWE RANSOM

Bells for John Whiteside's Daughter

There was such speed in her little body,
And such lightness in her footfall,

---

7. Albert Samain, late 19th-century French poet. The phrase is from the first line of the prefatory poem in his first book of poems, *Au Jardin de l'Infante:* "Mon âme est une infante en robe de parade" ("My soul is an Infanta in ceremonial dress"). An "Infanta" is a daughter of the Spanish royal family, which, long inbred, had for many years been afflicted with a rare blood disease, hemophilia.   8. A fashionable park near the center of London.   9. The Paris subway.

It is no wonder her brown study[1]
Astonishes us all.

5   Her wars were bruited in our high window.
We looked among orchard trees and beyond
Where she took arms against her shadow,
Or harried unto the pond

The lazy geese, like a snow cloud
10   Dripping their snow on the green grass,
Tricking and stopping, sleepy and proud,
Who cried in goose, Alas,

For the tireless heart within the little
Lady with rod that made them rise
15   From their noon apple-dreams and scuttle
Goose-fashion under the skies!

But now go the bells, and we are ready,
In one house we are sternly stopped
To say we are vexed at her brown study,
20   Lying so primly propped.   1924

THEODORE ROETHKE

The Dream

1

I met her as a blossom on a stem
Before she ever breathed, and in that dream
The mind remembers from a deeper sleep:
Eye learned from eye, cold lip from sensual lip.
5   My dream divided on a point of fire;
Light hardened on the water where we were;
A bird sang low; the moonlight sifted in;
The water rippled, and she rippled on.

2

She came toward me in the flowing air,
10   A shape of change, encircled by its fire.
I watched her there, between me and the moon;
The bushes and the stones danced on and on;
I touched her shadow when the light delayed;
I turned my face away, and yet she stayed.

1. Stillness, as if in meditation or deep thought.

A bird sang from the center of a tree;   15
She loved the wind because the wind loved me.

3

Love is not love until love's vulnerable.
She slowed to sigh, in that long interval.
A small bird flew in circles where we stood;
The deer came down, out of the dappled wood.   20
All who remember, doubt. Who calls that strange?
I tossed a stone, and listened to its plunge.
She knew the grammar of least motion, she
Lent me one virtue, and I live thereby.

4

She held her body steady in the wind;   25
Our shadows met, and slowly swung around;
She turned the field into a glittering sea;
I played in flame and water like a boy
And I swayed out beyond the white seafoam;
Like a wet log, I sang within a flame.   30
In that last while, eternity's confine,
I came to love, I came into my own.   1958

I Knew a Woman

I knew a woman, lovely in her bones,
When small birds sighed, she would sigh back at them;
Ah, when she moved, she moved more ways than one:
The shapes a bright container can contain!
Of her choice virtues only gods should speak;   5
Or English poets who grew up on Greek
(I'd have them sing in chorus, cheek to cheek).

How well her wishes went! She stroked my chin,
She taught me Turn, and Counter-turn, and Stand;[2]
She taught me Touch, that undulant white skin;   10
I nibbled meekly from her proffered hand;
She was the sickle; I, poor I, the rake,
Coming behind her for her pretty sake
(But what prodigious mowing we did make).

Love likes a gander, and adores a goose: 15
Her full lips pursed, the errant note to seize;

2. Literary terms for the parts of a Pindaric ode.

She played it quick, she played it light and loose;
My eyes, they dazzled at her flowing knees;
Her several parts could keep a pure repose,
20 Or one hip quiver with a mobile nose
(She moved in circles, and those circles moved).

Let seed be grass, and grass turn into hay:
I'm martyr to a motion not my own;
What's freedom for? To know eternity.
25 I swear she cast a shadow white as stone.
But who would count eternity in days?
These old bones live to learn her wanton ways:
(I measure time by how a body sways).   1958

The Waking

I wake to sleep, and take my waking slow.
I feel my fate in what I cannot fear.
I learn by going where I have to go.

We think by feeling. What is there to know?
5 I hear my being dance from ear to ear.
I wake to sleep, and take my waking slow.

Of those so close beside me, which are you?
God bless the Ground! I shall walk softly there,
And learn by going where I have to go.

10 Light takes the Tree; but who can tell us how?
The lowly worm climbs up a winding stair;
I wake to sleep, and take my waking slow.

Great Nature has another thing to do
To you and me; so take the lively air,
15 And, lovely, learn by going where to go.

This shaking keeps me steady. I should know.
What falls away is always. And is near.
I wake to sleep, and take my waking slow.
I learn by going where I have to go.   1953

MURIEL RUKEYSER

Reading Time : 1 Minute 26 Seconds

The fear of poetry is the
fear : mystery and fury of a midnight street

of windows whose low voluptuous voice
issues, and after that there is no peace.

That round waiting moment in the   5
theatre : curtain rises, dies into the ceiling
and here is played the scene with the mother
bandaging a revealed son's head.   The bandage is torn off.
Curtain goes down.   And here is the moment of proof.

That climax when the brain acknowledges the world,   10
all values extended into the blood awake.
Moment of proof.   And as they say Brancusi did,
building his bird to extend through soaring air,
as Kafka planned stories that draw to eternity
through time extended.   And the climax strikes.   15

Love touches so, that months after the look of
blue stare of love, the footbeat on the heart
is translated into the pure cry of birds
following air-cries, or poems, the new scene.
Moment of proof.   That strikes long after act.   20

They fear it.   They turn away, hand up palm out
fending off moment of proof, the straight look, poem.
The prolonged wound-consciousness after the bullet's shot.
The prolonged love after the look is dead,
the yellow joy after the song of the sun.   1939   25

Myth

Long afterward, Oedipus, old and blinded, walked the
roads.   He smelled a familiar smell.   It was
the Sphinx.   Oedipus said, "I want to ask one question.
Why didn't I recognize my mother?"   "You gave the
wrong answer," said the Sphinx.   "But that was what   5
made everything possible," said Oedipus.   "No," she said.
"When I asked, What walks on four legs in the morning,
two at noon, and three in the evening, you answered,
Man.   You didn't say anything about woman."
"When you say Man," said Oedipus, "you include women   10
too. Everyone knows that."   She said, "That's what
you think."   1973

WILLIAM SHAKESPEARE

[Hark, hark! the lark at heaven's gate sings][3]

Hark, hark! the lark at heaven's gate sings,
And Phoebus'[4] gins arise,
His steeds to water at those springs
On chaliced[5] flowers that lies;
5   And winking Mary-buds[6] begin
To ope their golden eyes:
With every thing that pretty is,
My lady sweet, arise!
Arise, arise!

ca. 1610

[Two loves I have of comfort and despair]

Two loves I have of comfort and despair,
Which like two spirits do suggest[7] me still:
The better angel is a man right fair,
The worser spirit a woman, color'd ill.[8]
5   To win me soon to hell, my female evil
Tempteth my better angel from my side,
And would corrupt my saint to be a devil,
Wooing his purity with her foul pride.
And whether that my angel be turn'd fiend
10   Suspect I may, but not directly tell
But being both from me,[9] both to each friend,
I guess one angel in another's hell:
Yet this shall I ne'er know, but live in doubt,
Till my bad angel fire[1] my good one out.

1609

Spring[2]

When daisies pied and violets blue
And ladysmocks all silver-white

---

3. From *Cymbeline*, Act II, scene 3.   4. Apollo, the sun god.   5. Cup-shaped.   6. Buds of
marigolds.   7. Tempt. *Still*: constantly.   8. Badly.   9. Away from me. *Both to each friend*:
friends to each other.   1. Drive out with fire ("fire" was Elizabethan slang for venereal disease).
2. Like "Winter" (below), a song from *Love's Labors Lost*, Act V, scene 2.

And cuckoobuds of yellow hue
  Do paint the meadows with delight,
The cuckoo then, on every tree,   5
Mocks married men;[3] for thus sings he,
          Cuckoo;
Cuckoo, cuckoo: Oh word of fear,
Unpleasing to a married ear!

When shepherds pipe on oaten straws,   10
  And merry larks are plowmen's clocks,
When turtles tread,[4] and rooks, and daws,
  And maidens bleach their summer smocks,
The cuckoo then, on every tree,
Mocks married men; for thus sings he,   15
          Cuckoo;
Cuckoo, cuckoo: Oh word of fear,
ca. 1595   Unpleasing to a married ear!

Winter

When icicles hang by the wall
  And Dick the shepherd blows[5] his nail,
And Tom bears logs into the hall,
  And milk comes frozen home in pail.
When blood is nipped and ways be foul,   5
Then nightly sings the staring owl,
          Tu-who;
Tu-whit, tu-who: a merry note,
While greasy Joan doth keel[6] the pot.

When all aloud the wind doth blow,   10
  And coughing drowns the parson's saw,[7]
And birds sit brooding in the snow,
  And Marian's nose looks red and raw,
When roasted crabs[8] hiss in the bowl,
Then nightly sings the staring owl,   15
          Tu-who;
Tu-whit, tu-who: a merry note
ca. 1595   While greasy Joan doth keel the pot.

---

3. By the resemblance of its call to the word "cuckold."   **4.** Copulate. *Turtles:* turtle-doves.   **5.** Breathes on for warmth. *Nail:* fingernail; i.e., hands.   **6.** Cool: stir to keep it from boiling over.   **7.** Maxim, proverb.   **8.** Crabapples.

WALLACE STEVENS

Anecdote of the Jar

I placed a jar in Tennessee,
And round it was, upon a hill.
It made the slovenly wilderness
Surround that hill.

5 The wilderness rose up to it,
And sprawled around, no longer wild.
The jar was round upon the ground
And tall and of a port in air.

It took dominion everywhere.
10 The jar was gray and bare.
It did not give of bird or bush,
Like nothing else in Tennessee.

1923

The Emperor of Ice-Cream

Call the roller of big cigars,
The muscular one, and bid him whip
In kitchen cups concupiscent curds.[9]
Let the wenches dawdle in such dress
5 As they are used to wear, and let the boys
Bring flowers in last month's newspapers.
Let be be finale of seem.[1]
The only emperor is the emperor of ice-cream.

Take from the dresser of deal,
10 Lacking the three glass knobs, that sheet
On which she embroidered fantails[2] once
And spread it so as to cover her face.
If her horny feet protrude, they come
To show how cold she is, and dumb.
15 Let the lamp affix its beam.
The only emperor is the emperor of ice-cream.

1923

9. "The words 'concupiscent curds' have no genealogy; they are merely expressive: at least, I hope they are expressive. They express the concupiscence of life, but, by contrast with the things in relation in the poem, they express or accentuate life's destitution, and it is this that gives them something more than a cheap lustre." Wallace Stevens, *Letters* (New York: Knopf, 1966), p. 500.   1. ". . . the true sense of Let be be the finale of seem is let being become the conclusion of denouement of appearing to be: in short, ice cream is an absolute good. The poem is obviously not about ice cream, but about being as distinguished from seeming to be." Stevens, *Letters*, p. 341. 2. Fantail pigeons.

Sunday Morning

I

Complacencies of the peignoir, and late
Coffee and oranges in a sunny chair,
And the green freedom of a cockatoo
Upon a rug mingle to dissipate
The holy hush of ancient sacrifice.   5
She dreams a little, and she feels the dark
Encroachment of that old catastrophe,[3]
As a calm darkens among water-lights.
The pungent oranges and bright, green wings
Seem things in some procession of the dead,   10
Winding across wide water, without sound,
The day is like wide water, without sound,
Stilled for the passing of her dreaming feet
Over the seas, to silent Palestine,
Dominion of the blood and sepulchre.   15

II

Why should she give her bounty to the dead?
What is divinity if it can come
Only in silent shadows and in dreams?
Shall she not find in comforts of the sun,
In pungent fruit and bright, green wings, or else   20
In any balm or beauty of the earth,
Things to be cherished like the thought of heaven.
Divinity must live within herself:
Passions of rain, or moods in falling snow;
Grievings in loneliness, or unsubdued   25
Elations when the forest blooms; gusty
Emotions on wet roads on autumn nights;
All pleasures and all pains, remembering
The bough of summer and the winter branch.
These are the measures destined for her soul.   30

III

Jove in the clouds has his inhuman birth.
No mother suckled him, no sweet land gave
Large-mannered motions to his mythy mind,
He moved among us, as a muttering king,
Magnificent, would move among his hinds,[4]   35
Until our blood, commingling, virginal,

---

3. The Crucifixion.   4. Lowliest rural subjects.

With heaven, brought such requital to desire
The very hinds discerned it, in a star.[5]
Shall our blood fail? Or shall it come to be
The blood of paradise? And shall the earth
Seem all of paradise that we shall know?
The sky will be much friendlier then than now,
A part of labor and a part of pain,
And next in glory to enduring love,
Not this dividing and indifferent blue.

IV

She says, "I am content when wakened birds,
Before they fly, test the reality
Of misty fields, by their sweet questionings;
But when the birds are gone, and their warm fields
Return no more, where, then, is paradise?"
There is not any haunt of prophecy,
Nor any old chimera of the grave,
Neither the golden underground, nor isle
Melodious, where spirits gat[6] them home,
Nor visionary south, nor cloudy palm
Remote on heaven's hill, that has endured
As April's green endures, or will endure
Like her remembrance of awakened birds,
Or her desire for June and evening, tipped
By the consummation of the swallow's wings.

V

She says, "But in contentment I still feel
The need of some imperishable bliss."
Death is the mother of beauty; hence from her,
Alone, shall come fulfillment to our dreams
And our desires. Although she strews the leaves
Of sure obliteration on our paths,
The path sick sorrow took, the many paths
Where triumph rang its brassy phrase, or love
Whispered a little out of tenderness,
She makes the willow shiver in the sun
For maidens who were wont to sit and gaze
Upon the grass, relinquished to their feet.
She causes boys to pile new plums and pears
On disregarded plate.[7] The maidens taste
And stray impassioned in the littering leaves.

5. The star of Bethlehem. 6. Got. 7. "Plate is used in the sense of so-called family plate. Disregarded refers to the disuse into which things fall that have been possessed for a long time. I mean, therefore, that death releases and renews. What the old have come to disregard, the young inherit and make use of." Stevens, *Letters*, pp. 183–84.

VI

Is there no change of death in paradise?
Does ripe fruit never fall? Or do the boughs
Hang always heavy in that perfect sky,
Unchanging, yet so like our perishing earth,
With rivers like our own that seek for seas   80
They never find, the same receding shores
That never touch with inarticulate pang?
Why set the pear upon those river-banks
Or spice the shores with odors of the plum?
Alas, that they should wear our colors there,   85
The silken weavings of our afternoons,
And pick the strings of our insipid lutes!
Death is the mother of beauty, mystical,
Within whose burning bosom we devise
Our earthly mothers awaiting, sleeplessly.   90

VII

Supple and turbulent, a ring of men
Shall chant in orgy[8] on a summer morn
Their boisterous devotion to the sun,
Not as a god, but as a god might be,
Naked among them, like a savage source.   95
Their chant shall be a chant of paradise,
Out of their blood, returning to the sky;
And in their chant shall enter, voice by voice,
The windy lake wherein their lord delights,
The trees, like serafin,[9] and echoing hills,   100
That choir among themselves long afterward.
They shall know well the heavenly fellowship
Of men that perish and of summer morn.
And whence they came and whither they shall go
The dew upon their feet shall manifest.   105

VIII

She hears, upon that water without sound,
A voice that cries, "The tomb in Palestine
Is not the porch of spirits lingering.
It is the grave of Jesus, where he lay."
We live in an old chaos of the sun,   110
Or old dependency of day and night,
Or island solitude, unsponsored, free,
Of that wide water, inescapable.
Deer walk upon our mountains, and the quail

8. Ceremonial revelry.   9. Seraphim, the highest of the nine orders of angels.

115   Whistle about us their spontaneous cries;
    Sweet berries ripen in the wilderness;
    And, in the isolation of the sky,
    At evening, casual flocks of pigeons make
    Ambiguous undulations as they sink,
120   1915   Downward to darkness, on extended wings.

ALFRED, LORD TENNYSON

Tears, Idle Tears[1]

    Tears, idle tears, I know not what they mean,
    Tears from the depth of some divine despair
    Rise in the heart, and gather to the eyes,
    In looking on the happy autumn-fields,
5   And thinking of the days that are no more.

    Fresh as the first beam glittering on a sail,
    That brings our friends up from the underworld,
    Sad as the last which reddens over one
    That sinks with all we love below the verge;
10   So sad, so fresh, the days that are no more.

    Ah, sad and strange as in dark summer dawns
    The earliest pipe of half-awakened birds
    To dying ears, when unto dying eyes
    The casement slowly grows a glimmering square;
15   So sad, so strange, the days that are no more.

    Dear as remembered kisses after death,
    And sweet as those by hopeless fancy feigned
    On lips that are for others; deep as love,
    Deep as first love, and wild with all regret;
20   1847   O Death in Life, the days that are no more!

DYLAN THOMAS

Fern Hill

    Now as I was young and easy under the apple boughs
    About the lilting house and happy as the grass was green,
        The night above the dingle starry,
          Time let me hail and climb
5   Golden in the heydays of his eyes,

1. A song from *The Princess*, a long narrative poem about what the mid-19th century called the "new woman."

And honored among wagons I was prince of the apple towns
And once below a time I lordly had the trees and leaves
    Trail with daisies and barley
    Down the rivers of the windfall light.

And as I was green and carefree, famous among the barns   10
About the happy yard and singing as the farm was home,
    In the sun that is young once only,
        Time let me play and be
    Golden in the mercy of his means,
And green and golden I was huntsman and herdsman, the calves   15
Sang to my horn, the foxes on the hills barked clear and cold,
        And the sabbath rang slowly
    In the pebbles of the holy streams.

All the sun long it was running, it was lovely, the hay
Fields high as the house, the tunes from the chimneys, it was air   20
    And playing, lovely and watery
        And fire green as grass.
    And nightly under the simple stars
As I rode to sleep the owls were bearing the farm away,
All the moon long I heard, blessed among stables, the nightjars[2]   25
    Flying with the ricks,[3] and the horses
        Flashing into the dark.

And then to awake, and the farm, like a wanderer white
With the dew, come back, the cock on his shoulder: it was all
    Shining, it was Adam and maiden,   30
        The sky gathered again
    And the sun grew round that very day.
So it must have been after the birth of the simple light
In the first, spinning place, the spellbound horses walking warm
    Out of the whinnying green stable   35
        On to the fields of praise.

And honored among foxes and pheasants by the gay house
Under the new made clouds and happy as the heart was long,
    In the sun born over and over,
        I ran my heedless ways,   40
    My wishes raced through the house-high hay
And nothing I cared, at my sky-blue trades, that time allows
In all his tuneful turning so few and such morning songs
    Before the children green and golden
    Follow him out of grace,   45

Nothing I cared, in the lamb white days, that time would take me
Up to the swallow-thronged loft by the shadow of my hand,
    In the moon that is always rising,

2. Birds.   3. Haystacks.

₅₀

Nor that riding to sleep
I should hear him fly with the high fields
And wake to the farm forever fled from the childless land.
Oh as I was young and easy in the mercy of his means,
Time held me green and dying
Though I sang in my chains like the sea.

In My Craft or Sullen Art

In my craft or sullen art
Exercised in the still night
When only the moon rages
And the lovers lie abed
₅
With all their griefs in their arms,
I labor by singing light
Not for ambition or bread
Or the strut and trade of charms
On the ivory stages
₁₀
But for the common wages
Of their most secret heart.

Not for the proud man apart
From the raging moon I write
On these spindrift[4] pages
₁₅
Nor for the towering dead
With their nightingales and psalms
But for the lovers, their arms
Round the griefs of the ages,
Who pay no praise or wages
₂₀
Nor heed my craft or art.

JEAN TOOMER

Song of the Son[5]

Pour O pour that parting soul in song,
O pour it in the sawdust glow of night,
Into the velvet pine-smoke air tonight,
And let the valley carry it along.
₅
And let the valley carry it along.

O land and soil, red soil and sweet-gum tree,
So scant of grass, so profligate of pines,

---

4. Literally, wind-driven sea spray.   5. From the novel *Cane*.

Now just before an epoch's sun declines
Thy son, in time, I have returned to thee,
Thy son, I have in time returned to thee.   10

In time, for though the sun is setting on
A song-lit race of slaves, it has not set;
Though late, O soil, it is not too late yet
To catch thy plaintive soul, leaving, soon gone,
Leaving, to catch thy plaintive soul soon gone.   15

O Negro slaves, dark purple ripened plums,
Squeezed, and bursting in the pine-wood air,
Passing, before they strip the old tree bare
One plum was saved for me, one seed becomes

An everlasting song, a singing tree,   20
Caroling softly souls of slavery,
What they were, and what they are to me,
Caroling softly souls of slavery.   1923

DIANE WAKOSKI

A Poet Recognizing the Echo
of the Voice

I. ISOLATION OF BEAUTIFUL WOMEN

"How were you able to get ten of the world's
most beautiful women to marry you?"
"I just asked them. You know, men all over
the world dream about Lana Turner, desire
her, want to be with her. But very very
few ever ask her to marry them."
                    —paraphrase of an interview with
                    ARTIE SHAW

We are burning
in our heads
at night,
bonfires of our own bodies.
Persia reduces our heads   5
to star sapphires and lapis lazuli.[6]
Silver threads itself
into the lines of our throats
and glitters every time we speak.

6. Blue gems.

10 Old alchemical riddles[7]
are solved in the dreams of men
who marry other women and think of us.
Anyone who sees us
will hold our small hands,
15 like mirrors in which they see themselves,
and try to initial our arms
with desperation.
Everyone wants to come close to
the cinnamon of our ears.
20 Every man wants to explore our bodies
and fill up our minds.
Riding their motorcycles along collapsing grey highways,
they sequester their ambivalent hunting clothes
between our legs,
25 reminding themselves of their value
by quoting mining stock prices, and ours.
But men do not marry us,
do not ask us to share their lives,
do not survive the bonfires
30 hot enough to melt steel.
To alchemize rubies.

We live the loneliness
that men run after,
and we,
35 the precious rocks of the earth
are made harder,
more fiery
more beautiful,
more complex,
40 by all the pressing,
the burying,
the plundering;

even your desertions,
your betrayals,
45 your failure to understand and love us,
your unwillingness to face the world
as staunchly as we do;
these things
which ravage us,
50 cannot destroy our lives,
though they often take our bodies.
We are the earth.
We wake up

7. Problems. Alchemy was devoted to finding an elixir that would turn baser metals to gold (line 31).

finding ourselves
glinting in the dark
after thousands of years   55
of pressing.

II. Movement to Establish My Identity

I know what wages beauty gives,
How hard a life her servant lives . . . .
—"To A Young Beauty," w. b. yeats

A woman wakes up
finds herself
glinting in the dark;   60
the earth holds her
as a precious rock
in a mine

her breath is a jumble
of sediments,   65
of mixed strata,
of the valuable,
beautiful,
of bulk.

All men are miners;   70
willing to work hard
and cover themselves with pit dirt;
to dig out;
to weigh;
to possess.   75

Mine is a place.
Mine is a designation.
A man says, "it is mine,"
but he hacks,
chops apart the mine   80
to discover,
to plunder,
what's in it / Plunder,
that is the word.
Plunder.   85

A woman wakes up
finds herself
scarred
but still glinting
in the dark.   90

III. Beauty

> only God, my dear,
> Could love you for yourself alone
> And not your yellow hair.
> —"For Anne Gregory," W. B. YEATS

and if I cut off my long hair,
if I stopped speaking,
if I stopped dreaming for other people about parts of the car,
stopped handing them tall creamy flowered silks
95 and loosing the magnificent hawks to fly in their direction,
stopped exciting them with the possibilities
of a thousand crystals under the fingernail
to look at while writing a letter,
if I stopped crying for the salvation of the tea ceremony,
100 stopped rushing in excitedly with a spikey bird-of-paradise,[8]
and never let them see how accurate my pistol shooting is,
who would I be?

Where is the real me
I want them all to love?

105 We are all the textures we wear.

We frighten men with our steel;
we fascinate them with our silk;
we seduce them with our cinnamon;
we rule them with our sensuous voices;
110 we confuse them with our submissions.
Is there anywhere
a man
who
will not punish us
115 for our beauty?

He is the one
we all search for,
chanting names for exotic oceans of the moon.

He is the one
120 we all anticipate,
pretending these small pedestrians
jaywalking into our lives
are he.
He is the one
125 we all anticipate;
beauty looks for its match,

8. A bright, spectacular plant.

confuses the issue
with a mystery that does not exist:
the rock
that cannot burn.   130

We are burning
in our heads at night
the incense of our histories, finding
you have used our skulls
for ashtrays.   1970   135

WALT WHITMAN

Facing West from California's Shores

Facing west, from California's shores,
Inquiring, tireless, seeking what is yet unfound,
I, a child, very old, over waves, towards the house of maternity,[9] the land of
    migrations, look afar,
Look off the shores of my Western sea, the circle almost circled:
For starting westward from Hindustan, from the vales of Kashmere,   5
From Asia, from the north, from the God, the sage, and the hero,
From the south, from the flowery peninsulas and the spice islands,
Long having wandered since, round the earth having wandered,
Now I face home again, very pleased and joyous;
(But where is what I started for, so long ago?   10
And why is it yet unfound?)   1860

I Hear America Singing

I hear America singing, the varied carols I hear,
Those of mechanics, each one singing his as it should be blithe and strong,
The carpenter singing his as he measures his plank or beam,
The mason singing his as he makes ready for work, or leaves off work,
The boatman singing what belongs to him in his boat, the deckhand singing on
    the steamboat deck,   5
The shoemaker singing as he sits on his bench, the hatter singing as he stands,
The wood-cutter's song, the ploughboy's on his way in the morning, or at noon
    intermission or at sundown,

9. Asia, as the supposed birthplace of the human race.

The delicious singing of the mother, or of the young wife at work, or of the girl
    sewing or washing,
Each singing what belongs to him or her and to none else,
The day what belongs to the day—at night the party of young fellows, robust,
    friendly,
Singing with open mouths their strong melodious songs.   1860

A Noiseless Patient Spider

A noiseless patient spider,
I marked where on a little promontory it stood isolated,
Marked how to explore the vacant vast surrounding,
It launched forth filament, filament, filament, out of itself,
Ever unreeling them, ever tirelessly speeding them.

And you O my soul where you stand,
Surrounded, detached, in measureless oceans of space,
Ceaselessly musing, venturing, throwing, seeking the spheres to connect them,
Till the bridge you will need be formed, till the ductile anchor hold,
Till the gossamer thread you fling catch somewhere, O my soul.   1881

WILLIAM CARLOS WILLIAMS

This Is Just to Say

I have eaten
the plums
that were in
the icebox

and which
you were probably
saving
for breakfast

Forgive me
they were delicious
so sweet
and so cold   1934

WILLIAM WORDSWORTH

Lines Composed a Few Miles above Tintern Abbey on Revisiting the Banks of the Wye During a Tour, July 13, 1798[1]

Five years have passed; five summers, with the length
Of five long winters! and again I hear
These waters, rolling from their mountain-springs
With a soft inland murmur. Once again
Do I behold these steep and lofty cliffs,   5
That on a wild secluded scene impress
Thoughts of more deep seclusion; and connect
The landscape with the quiet of the sky.
The day is come when I again repose
Here, under this dark sycamore, and view   10
These plots of cottage-ground, these orchard tufts,
Which at this season, with their unripe fruits,
Are clad in one green hue, and lose themselves
'Mid groves and copses.[2] Once again I see
These hedge-rows, hardly hedge-rows, little lines   15
Of sportive wood run wild: these pastoral farms,
Green to the very door; and wreaths of smoke
Sent up, in silence, from among the trees!
With some uncertain notice, as might seem
Of vagrant dwellers in the houseless woods,   20
Or of some hermit's cave, where by his fire
The hermit sits alone.
              These beauteous forms,
Through a long absence, have not been to me
As is a landscape to a blind man's eye;
But oft, in lonely rooms, and 'mid the din   25
Of towns and cities, I have owed to them,
In hours of weariness, sensations sweet,
Felt in the blood, and felt along the heart;
And passing even into my purer mind,
With tranquil restoration—feelings too   30
Of unremembered pleasure: such, perhaps,
As have no slight or trivial influence
On that best portion of a good man's life,
His little, nameless, unremembered acts
Of kindness and of love. Nor less, I trust,   35

1. Wordsworth had first visited the Wye valley and the ruins of the medieval abbey there in 1793, while on a solitary walking tour. He was 23 then, 28 when he wrote this poem.   2. Thickets.

To them I may have owed another gift,
Of aspect more sublime; that blesséd mood,
In which the burthen[3] of the mystery,
In which the heavy and the weary weight
40   Of all this unintelligible world,
Is lightened—that serene and blesséd mood,
In which the affections gently lead us on—
Until, the breath of this corporeal frame
And even the motion of our human blood
45   Almost suspended, we are laid asleep
In body, and become a living soul;
While with an eye made quiet by the power
Of harmony, and the deep power of joy,
We see into the life of things.
                        If this
50   Be but a vain belief, yet, oh! how oft—
In darkness and amid the many shapes
Of joyless daylight; when the fretful stir
Unprofitable, and the fever of the world,
Have hung upon the beatings of my heart—
55   How oft, in spirit, have I turned to thee,
O sylvan Wye! thou wanderer through the woods,
How often has my spirit turned to thee!

    And now, with gleams of half-extinguished thought,
With many recognitions dim and faint,
60   And somewhat of a sad perplexity,
The picture of the mind revives again;
While here I stand, not only with the sense
Of present pleasure, but with pleasing thoughts
That in this moment there is life and food
65   For future years. And so I dare to hope,
Though changed, no doubt, from what I was when first
I came among these hills; when like a roe
I bounded o'er the mountains, by the sides
Of the deep rivers, and the lonely streams,
70   Wherever nature led: more like a man
Flying from something that he dreads than one
Who sought the thing he loved. For nature then
(The coarser[4] pleasures of my boyish days,
And their glad animal movements all gone by)
75   To me was all in all—I cannot paint
What then I was. The sounding cataract
Haunted me like a passion; the tall rock,
The mountain, and the deep and gloomy wood,
Their colors and their forms, were then to me
80   An appetite; a feeling and a love,

3. Burden.   4. Physical.

That had no need of a remoter charm.
By thought supplied, nor any interest
Unborrowed from the eye. That time is past,
And all its aching joys are now no more,
And all its dizzy raptures. Not for this   85
Faint I,[5] nor mourn nor murmur; other gifts
Have followed; for such loss, I would believe,
Abundant recompense. For I have learned
To look on nature, not as in the hour
Of thoughtless youth; but hearing oftentimes   90
The still, sad music of humanity,
Nor harsh nor grating, though of ample power
To chasten and subdue. And I have felt
A presence that disturbs me with the joy
Of elevated thoughts, a sense sublime   95
Of something far more deeply interfused,
Whose dwelling is the light of setting suns,
And the round ocean and the living air,
And the blue sky, and in the mind of man:
A motion and a spirit, that impels   100
All thinking things, all objects of all thought,
And rolls through all things. Therefore am I still
A lover of the meadows and the woods
And mountains; and of all that we behold
From this green earth; of all the mighty world   105
Of eye, and ear—both what they half create,
And what perceive; well pleased to recognize
In nature and the language of the sense
The anchor of my purest thoughts, the nurse,
The guide, the guardian of my heart, and soul   110
Of all my moral being.   Nor perchance,
If I were not thus taught, should I the more
Suffer my genial spirits[6] to decay:
For thou art with me here upon the banks
Of this fair river; thou my dearest Friend,[7]   115
My dear, dear Friend; and in thy voice I catch
The language of my former heart, and read
My former pleasures in the shooting lights
Of thy wild eyes. Oh! yet a little while
May I behold in thee what I was once,   120
My dear, dear Sister! and this prayer I make,
Knowing that Nature never did betray
The heart that loved her; 'tis her privilege,
Through all the years of this our life, to lead
From joy to joy: for she can so inform   125

5. Am I discouraged.   6. Natural disposition; i.e., the spirits that are part of his individual genius.   7. His sister Dorothy.

The mind that is within us, so impress
With quietness and beauty, and so feed
With lofty thoughts, that neither evil tongues,
Rash judgments, nor the sneers of selfish men,
130 Nor greetings where no kindness is, nor all
The dreary intercourse of daily life,
Shall e'er prevail against us, or disturb
Our cheerful faith that all which we behold
Is full of blessings. Therefore let the moon
135 Shine on thee in thy solitary walk;
And let the misty mountain-winds be free
To blow against thee: and, in after years,
When these wild ecstasies shall be matured
Into a sober pleasure; when thy mind
140 Shall be a mansion for all lovely forms,
Thy memory be as a dwelling-place
For all sweet sounds and harmonies; oh! then,
If solitude, or fear, or pain, or grief,
Should be thy portion, with what healing thoughts
145 Of tender joy wilt thou remember me,
And these my exhortations! No, perchance—
If I should be where I no more can hear
Thy voice, nor catch from thy wild eyes these gleams
Of past existence—wilt thou then forget
150 That on the banks of this delightful stream
We stood together; and that I, so long
A worshiper of Nature, hither came
Unwearied in that service; rather say
With warmer love—oh! with far deeper zeal
155 Of holier love. Nor wilt thou then forget,
That after many wanderings, many years
Of absence, these steep woods and lofty cliffs,
And this green pastoral landscape, were to me
More dear, both for themselves and for thy sake!   1798

W. B. YEATS

Easter 1916[8]

I have met them at close of day
Coming with vivid faces
From counter or desk among gray

8. On Easter Monday 1916, an Irish Republic was proclaimed by nationalist leaders, who launched an unsuccessful revolt against the British government. After a week of street fighting, the Easter Rebellion was put down. A number of prominent nationalists were executed, including the four leaders mentioned in lines 75–76, all of whom Yeats knew personally.

Eighteenth-century houses.
I have passed with a nod of the head   5
Or polite meaningless words,
Or have lingered awhile and said
Polite meaningless words,
And thought before I had done
Of a mocking tale or a gibe   10
To please a companion
Around the fire at the club,
Being certain that they and I
But lived where motley is worn:
All changed, changed utterly: 15
A terrible beauty is born.

That woman's[9] days were spent
In ignorant good-will,
Her nights in argument
Until her voice grew shrill.   20
What voice more sweet than hers
When, young and beautiful,
She rode to harriers?
This man[1] had kept a school
And rode our wingéd horse;[2]   25
This other[3] his helper and friend
Was coming into his force;
He might have won fame in the end,
So sensitive his nature seemed,
So daring and sweet his thought.   30
This other man[4] I had dreamed
A drunken, vainglorious lout.
He had done most bitter wrong
To some who are near my heart,
Yet I number him in the song;   35
He, too, has resigned his part
In the casual comedy;
He, too, has been changed in his turn,
Transformed utterly:
A terrible beauty is born.   40

9. Countess Constance Georgina Markiewicz, a beautiful and well-born young woman from County Sligo who became a vigorous and bitter nationalist. At first condemned to death, she later had her sentence commuted to life imprisonment, and she gained amnesty in 1917.   1. Patrick Pearse, who led the assault on the Dublin Post Office, from which the proclamation of a republic was issued. A schoolmaster by profession, he had vigorously supported the restoration of the Gaelic language in Ireland and was an active political writer and poet.   2. Pegasus, a traditional symbol of poetic inspiration.   3. Thomas MacDonagh, also a writer and teacher.   4. Major John MacBride, who had married Yeats's beloved Maud Gonne in 1903 but separated from her two years later.

Hearts with one purpose alone
Through summer and winter seem
Enchanted to a stone
To trouble the living stream.
45 The horse that comes from the road,
The rider, the birds that range
From cloud to tumbling cloud,
Minute by minute they change;
A shadow of cloud on the stream
50 Changes minute by minute;
A horse-hoof slides on the brim,
And a horse plashes within it;
The long-legged moor-hens dive,
And hens to moor-cocks call;
55 Minute by minute they live:
The stone's in the midst of all.

Too long a sacrifice
Can make a stone of the heart.
O when may it suffice?
60 That is Heaven's part, our part
To murmur name upon name,
As a mother names her child
When sleep at last has come
On limbs that had run wild.
65 What is it but nightfall?
No, no, not night but death;
Was it needless death after all?
For England may keep faith[5]
For all that is done and said.
70 We know their dream; enough
To know they dreamed and are dead;
And what if excess of love
Bewildered them till they died?
I write it out in a verse—
75 MacDonagh and MacBride
And Connolly[6] and Pearse
Now and in time to be,
Wherever green is worn,
Are changed, changed utterly;
80 1916 A terrible beauty is born.

---

5. Before the uprising the English had promised eventual home rule to Ireland.   6. James Connolly, the leader of the Easter uprising.

The Second Coming[7]

Turning and turning in the widening gyre[8]
The falcon cannot hear the falconer;
Things fall apart; the center cannot hold;
Mere anarchy is loosed upon the world,
The blood-dimmed tide is loosed, and everywhere   5
The ceremony of innocence is drowned;
The best lack all conviction, while the worst
Are full of passionate intensity.
Surely some revelation is at hand;
Surely the Second Coming is at hand.   10
The Second Coming! Hardly are those words out
When a vast image out of *Spiritus Mundi*[9]
Troubles my sight: somewhere in sands of the desert
A shape with lion body and the head of a man,
A gaze blank and pitiless as the sun,   15
Is moving its slow thighs, while all about it
Reel shadows of the indignant desert birds.[1]
The darkness drops again; but now I know
That twenty centuries of stony sleep
Were vexed to nightmare by a rocking cradle,   20
And what rough beast, its hour come round at last,
Slouches towards Bethlehem to be born?   p. 1920

Leda and the Swan[2]

A sudden blow: the great wings beating still
Above the staggering girl, her thighs caressed

7. The Second Coming of Christ, according to Matthew 24:29–44, will come after a time of "tribulation." Disillusioned by Ireland's continued civil strife, Yeats saw his time as the end of another historical cycle. In *A Vision* (1937) Yeats describes his view of history as dependent on cycles of about 2,000 years: the birth of Christ had ended the cycle of Greco-Roman civilization, and now the Christian cycle seemed near an end, to be followed by an antithetical cycle, ominous in its portents.   8. Literally, the widening spiral of a falcon's flight. "Gyre" is Yeats's term for a cycle of history, which he diagramed in terms of a series of interpenetrating cones.   9. Or *Anima Mundi*, the spirit or soul of the world. Yeats considered this universal consciousness or memory a fund from which poets drew their images and symbols.   1. Yeats later wrote of the "brazen winged beast . . . described in my poem *The Second Coming*" as "associated with laughing, ecstatic destruction." "Our civilization was about to reverse itself, or some new civilization about to be born from all that our age had rejected . . . ; because we had worshiped a single god it would worship many."
2. According to Greek myth, Zeus took the form of a swan to seduce Leda, who became the mother of Helen of Troy and also of Clytemnestra, Agamemnon's wife and murderer. Helen's abduction from her husband. Menelaus, brother of Agamemnon, began the Trojan War (line 10). Yeats described the visit of Zeus to Leda as an annunciation like that to Mary (see Luke 1:26–38): "I imagine the annunciation that founded Greece as made to Leda. . . ." (*A Vision*).

By the dark webs, her nape caught in his bill,
He holds her helpless breast upon his breast.

5 How can those terrified vague fingers push
The feathered glory from her loosening thighs?
And how can body, laid in that white rush,
But feel the strange heart beating where it lies?

10 A shudder in the loins engenders there
The broken wall, the burning roof and tower
And Agamemnon dead.
                              Being so caught up,
So mastered by the brute blood of the air,
Did she put on his knowledge with his power
1923 Before the indifferent beak could let her drop?

Sailing to Byzantium[3]

I

That[4] is no country for old men. The young
In one another's arms, birds in the trees
—Those dying generations—at their song,
The salmon-falls, the mackerel-crowded seas
5 Fish, flesh, or fowl, commend all summer long
Whatever is begotten, born, and dies.
Caught in that sensual music all neglect
Monuments of unaging intellect.

II

An aged man is but a paltry thing,
10 A tattered coat upon a stick, unless
Soul clap its hands and sing, and louder sing
For every tatter in its mortal dress,
Nor is there singing school but studying
Monuments of its own magnificence;
15 And therefore I have sailed the seas and come
To the holy city of Byzantium.

3. The ancient name of Istanbul, the capital and holy city of Eastern Christendom from the late fourth century until 1453. It was famous for its stylized and formal mosaics, its symbolic, nonnaturalistic art, and its highly developed intellectual life. Yeats repeatedly uses it to symbolize a world of artifice and timelessness, free from the decay and death of the natural and sensual world.   4. Ireland, as an instance of the natural, temporal world.

III

O sages standing in God's holy fire
As in the gold mosaic of a wall,
Come from the holy fire, perne in a gyre,[5]
And be the singing-masters of my soul.   20
Consume my heart away; sick with desire
And fastened to a dying animal
It knows not what it is; and gather me
Into the artifice of eternity.

IV

Once out of nature I shall never take   25
My bodily form from any natural thing,
But such a form as Grecian goldsmiths make
Of hammered gold and gold enameling
To keep a drowsy Emperor awake;[6]
Or set upon a golden bough[7] to sing   30
To lords and ladies of Byzantium
Of what is past, or passing, or to come.   1927

Among School Children

I

I walk through the long schoolroom questioning;
A kind old nun in a white hood replies;
The children learn to cipher and to sing,
To study reading-books and history,
To cut and sew, be neat in everything   5
In the best modern way—the children's eyes
In momentary wonder stare upon
A sixty-year-old smiling public man.[8]

5. I.e., whirl in a coiling motion, so that his soul may merge with its motion as the timeless world invades the cycles of history and nature. "Perne" is Yeats's coinage (from the noun "pirn"): to spin around in the kind of spiral pattern that thread makes as it comes off a bobbin or spool.   6. "I have read somewhere that in the Emperor's palace at Byzantium was a tree made of gold and silver, and artificial birds that sang." (Yeats's note)   7. In Book VI of *The Aeneid*, the sybil tells Aeneas that he must pluck a golden bough from a nearby tree in order to descend to Hades. There is only one such branch there, and when it is plucked an identical one takes its place.   8. At 60 (in 1925) Yeats had been a senator of the Irish Free State.

II

I dream of a Ledaean body,[9] bent
Above a sinking fire, a tale that she
Told of a harsh reproof, or trivial event
That changed some childish day to tragedy—
Told, and it seemed that our two natures blent
Into a sphere from youthful sympathy,
Or else, to alter Plato's parable,
Into the yolk and white of the one shell.[1]

III

And thinking of that fit of grief or rage
I look upon one child or t'other there
And wonder if she stood so at that age—
For even daughters of the swan can share
Something of every paddler's heritage—
And had that color upon cheek or hair,
And thereupon my heart is driven wild:
She stands before me as a living child.

IV

Her present image floats into the mind—
Did Quattrocento finger[2] fashion it
Hollow of cheek as though it drank the wind
And took a mess of shadows for its meat?
And I though never of Ledaean kind
Had pretty plumage once—enough of that,
Better to smile on all that smile, and show
There is a comfortable kind of old scarecrow.

V

What youthful mother, a shape upon her lap
Honey of generation[3] had betrayed,

9. Like that of Helen of Troy, daughter of Leda. The memory dream is of Maud Gonne (see also lines 29–30), with whom Yeats had long been hopelessly in love.   1. In Plato's *Symposium,* the origin of human love is explained by parable: Human beings were once spheres, but Zeus was fearful of their power and cut them in half; now each half longs to be reunited with its missing half. Helen and Pollux were hatched from one of two eggs born to Leda after her union with Zeus in the form of a swan; the other contained Castor and Clytemnestra. According to Yeats in *A Vision,* "from one of [Leda's] eggs came Love and from the other War."   2. The hand of a 15th-century artist. Yeats especially admired Botticelli, and in *A Vision* praises his "deliberate strangeness everywhere [that] gives one an emotion of mystery which is new to painting."   3. Porphyry, a third-century Greek scholar and neoplatonic philosopher, says "honey of generation" means the "pleasure arising from copulation" that draws souls "downward" to generation.

And that must sleep, shriek, struggle to escape   35
As recollection or the drug decide,
Would think her son, did she but see that shape
With sixty or more winters on its head,
A compensation for the pang of his birth,
Or the uncertainty of his setting forth?   40

VI

Plato thought nature but a spume that plays
Upon a ghostly paradigm of things;[4]
Solider Aristotle played the taws
Upon the bottom of a king of kings;[5]
World-famous golden-thighed Pythagoras[6]   45
Fingered upon a fiddle-stick or strings
What a star sang and careless Muses heard:
Old clothes upon old sticks to scare a bird.

VII

Both nuns and mothers worship images,
But those the candles light are not as those   50
That animate a mother's reveries
But keep a marble or a bronze repose.
And yet they too break hearts—O Presences
That passion, piety or affection knows,
And that all heavenly glory symbolize—   55
O self-born mockers of man's enterprise;

VIII

Labor is blossoming or dancing where
The body is not bruised to pleasure soul,
Nor beauty born out of its own despair,
Nor blear-eyed wisdom out of midnight oil.   60
O chestnut-tree, great-rooted blossomer,
Are you the leaf, the blossom or the bole?
O body swayed to music, O brightening glance,
How can we know the dancer from the dance?   1927

---

4. Plato considered the world of nature an imperfect and illusory copy of the ideal world.   5. Aristotle, the teacher of Alexander the Great, disciplined him with a strap ("taw," line 43). His philosophy, insisting on the interdependence of form and matter, took the world of nature far more seriously than did Plato's.   6. Pythagoras (580?–500? B.C.), the Greek mathematician and philosopher, was highly revered, and one legend describes his godlike golden thighs.

Byzantium

The unpurged images of day recede;
The Emperor's drunken soldiery are abed;
Night resonance recedes, night-walkers' song
After great cathedral gong;
5   A starlit or a moonlit dome[7] disdains
All that man is,
All mere complexities,
The fury and the mire of human veins.

Before me floats an image, man or shade,
10 Shade more than man, more image than a shade;
For Hades' bobbin bound in mummy-cloth
May unwind the winding path;
A mouth that has no moisture and no breath
Breathless mouths may summon;
15 I hail the superhuman;
I call it death-in-life and life-in-death.

Miracle, bird or golden handiwork,
More miracle than bird or handiwork,
Planted on the star-lit golden bough
20 Can like the cocks of Hades crow,[8]
Or, by the moon embittered, scorn aloud
In glory of changeless metal
Common bird or petal
And all complexities of mire or blood.

25 At midnight on the Emperor's pavement flit
Flames that no faggot feeds, nor steel has lit,
Nor storm disturbs, flames begotten of flame,
Where blood-begotten spirits come
And all complexities of fury leave,
30 Dying into a dance,
An agony of trance,
An agony of flame that cannot singe a sleeve.

Astraddle on the dolphin's mire and blood,[9]
Spirit after spirit! The smithies break the flood,
35 The golden smithies of the Emperor!
Marbles of the dancing floor

---

7. According to Yeats's philosophy, the full moon ("moonlit") represents the mind "completely absorbed in being."   8. As the bird of dawn, the cock has from antiquity been a symbol of rebirth and resurrection.   9. In ancient art, dolphins symbolize the soul moving from one state to another, and sometimes they provide a vehicle for the dead. Palaemon, for example, in Greek tradition is often mounted on a dolphin.

Break bitter furies of complexity,
Those images that yet
Fresh images beget,
That dolphin-torn, that gong-tormented sea.   1932   40

DRAMA

DRAMA

▽   ▽   ▽

Drama: Reading, Responding, Writing

Plays are generally written to be performed—by actors, on a stage, for an audience. Playwrights create plays in full consciousness of the possibilities that go beyond words and texts and extend to physical actions, stage devices, and other bits of theatricality that can be used to create special effects and modify responses. Consequently, responding to a stage production of a play involves physical senses as well as the imagination. Furthermore, your responses are not wholly a private matter. Responding to a theatrical production is, in part, communal: you respond not just as an individual but as part of an audience sharing the moment.

To attend a play—to see and hear it as part of an audience—represents a different kind of experience from the usually solitary act of reading. Plays are performed before live audiences of real people who respond directly and immediately to them, unlike texts that may lie silent and undisturbed in a book for days or even years at a time. When plays are acted out on a stage you see actions and hear words spoken; real live human beings, standing for imaginary characters, deliver lines and perform actions that you listen to and watch. Furthermore, you sit with others who are also watching and responding to the play. You and the other members of the audience have, at a single instant, a common experience that you have deliberately sought: you have assembled for the explicit purpose of seeing a play.

But you are not directly experiencing the author's text. It has been mediated by the director and actors who have brought it to the stage and to your eyes and ears. These mediators are interpreters of the play, and they perform for viewers part of the act of imagination that readers must perform for themselves. In poems and stories, only the written text stands between author and reader, but in plays all of the people involved in a particular production—the director, producer, actors, even stage designers—help to interpret the author's text for a specific audience. Consciously or not, every director puts an interpretation on every scene by the way he or she stages the action; timing, casting, set design, physical interaction, and the phrasing and tone of every speech affect how the play will come across. Every syllable uttered by every actor in some sense affects the outcome; tone of voice and the slightest body gesture are, for an actor, equivalent to the choices of words and sentence rhythm for a writer.

Every performance is a unique expression of a collaborative effort. Actors must remember hundreds of lines and perform movements on stage at certain times; the stagehands must change sets and install props between scenes; light and sound effects must occur on certain visual and aural cues. In any of these areas a single change or error—a new inflection at the end of a line or a misplaced prop—guarantees that a given performance will be unique. Nor are any two audiences the same, and the character of an audience inevitably affects the performance. A warm, responsive audience will bring out the best in the performers, as any actor will tell you, while a crowd's cold indifference often results in a tepid or stiff production. For these reasons, no staged realization of a play can ever duplicate another.

Just as no two single performances are ever identical, no two interpretations are ever exactly the same. It is common to speak of Olivier's Hamlet (meaning the performance of the title role by Sir Laurence Olivier), of Dame Maggie Smith's or Glenda Jackson's Hedda Gabler, or Zeffirelli's *Romeo and Juliet* (meaning the film directed by Franco Zeffirelli), because in each case the hand of the actor or director leads to a distinctive interpretation of the play. In the written text Hamlet may be regarded as indecisive, melancholy, conniving, mad, vindictive, ambitious, or some combination of these things; individual performances emphasize one attribute or another, always at some expense to other characteristics and interpretations. No play can be all things to an audience in any one performance or run. And no two members of the audience will respond to all of these signals in exactly the same way.

It is this limitation of the performed play, its multiple variables but necessary restriction of the several possible meanings of the work to one interpretation, that led the nineteenth-century writer Charles Lamb to come home from the theater vowing never to see another play of Shakespeare's on the stage. He found that no matter how good the performance, the enacted play restricted his imagination and robbed the play of some of the richness he found in reading it—and imagining it—for himself.

It is not necessary to renounce the theater or deprive ourselves of the thrilling experience of a brilliantly directed and performed interpretation of a play, but it is useful to reassert the quite different claims of reading drama as *literature*, as something written, the letters of the alphabet forming words on the page. Reading drama (we are somewhat arbitrarily here using the term "drama" to mean the written and read play, as opposed to the performed one) is not a poor substitute for seeing a play; it is simply a different kind of experience, literary rather than theatrical.

In some ways reading a play is no different from reading a story or novel. In both cases we anticipate what is to happen next and what it all means. In reading both narrative and drama we imagine the characters, setting, action; and in reading both we respond to the symbolic suggestiveness of images and we project configurations of thematic significance. The chief difference between narrative and drama on the page is the absence, in drama, of a mediator, someone standing between the reader and the work and helping us relate to the characters, actions, and meanings. It is for this reason that reading drama is for many a greater strain on the imagination: the reader is his or her own mediator, narrator, interpreter.

Reading drama is not only a compelling literary experience in itself, but even the strain it puts upon our imagination is rewarding. For not only are we freer to incorporate the play into our own being, but in becoming our own mediator we see how our imagination or our response to story-telling language really works. It is customary to assume that we "cast characters" in our minds, paint in the scenic backdrops, place the furniture and props, and choreograph the action. While we no doubt do some of this, it seems that most of our imaginations are not so well stocked, and that we do not fully recreate what the playwright had in her or his mind's eye. We can ask ourselves whom we might cast as Hamlet or Hedda Gabler, but most of us do not have a full and fixed visual image of a character: we have a shape here, a profile there, adding a feature, mannerism, or gesture as we read on, mainly on the basis of suggestions in the text, though sometimes according to memories of theatrical performances or movies seen previously.

In reading drama where dialogue is more or less all we have, we reconstruct character and personality from what the character says; we do this by relating our own experiences to what we are reading, responding in terms of expectations based on what we have felt in comparable situations. We've known someone who said things like this, or remember another play or story that suggests such attitudes and statements. So what we imagine as we read depends greatly upon our repertoire of experiences of life and literature. A character, even at the end of a play, is less a solid reconstruction than a series of frames like those that make up a moving picture, each a little different. When we have seen an actress playing Blanche DuBois in A *Streetcar Named Desire* and see her as we read the play, we are no longer reading that play but watching it in our minds, more or less remembering a play we once saw.

To say this is not necessarily to agree with Charles Lamb—an actress can show us something in a part we might not have seen for ourselves. If we would go to the theater more often we would have a spectrum of performances to lend depth to our reading. But to read a play we have never seen is not to watch in the mind's eye a single, well-defined figure incorporating a character throughout the one, three, or five acts. We *watch* plays, but we *read* drama. Though we must take every opportunity to see a play performed to enrich our own reading of it, and though we should take advantage of our silent reading to include all the alternatives we can, each time we read a play we do our own interpreting, make our own choices and omissions. Reading, we perform all the parts, and we may want to ask ourselves how we would act this or that role, read this or that line; what kind of person we should try to imagine ourselves being; what, if we were that person, our motivations might be, and so on. But most important, perhaps, we want to be aware of what choices are available and what making one choice or another means.

As with fiction and poetry, writing about drama usually sharpens your responses and focuses your reading. When you write about drama, you are—in a very real sense—performing the role that directors and actors take on in a stage performance: you are giving your "reading" of the text, interpreting it to guide other readers' responses. But you are also, as when you write about a story or a poem, molding your own response, by forcing yourself to be clear about just what your response is. The virtue of writing about drama, as in writing about any text, lies mainly in your having to be precise and articulate about how the text affects you. Normally, you consider what a play says to you and how the theatrical or imagined action is to be interpreted before you actually begin to write about it, but the act of writing will give shape to your initial impressions and lead to further reflection and insight. Your reading of texts in drama (and in fiction and poetry) is considerably enhanced by your writing about them, just as the process of responding itself is often clarified by your putting into words what has happened to you as a result of confronting the text.

Just as writing about a play after you have read it may help you to formulate or clarify your response, jotting down your thoughts before you've finished it may help you to clarify your expectations. If when someone is speaking you always finish his or her sentence, you are not being a good listener, but, if when reading you always project forward, to what may happen next, or what a certain character will finally be revealed to be like, or what a play will show or suggest, you are being a good reader. As with fiction and poetry, expectation or anticipation should always be part of your response. One way to capture this kind of response is to stop your reading at some reasonable point—the end of a scene or an act, or when you are puzzled or where the action seems to pause briefly—and write out how you think the action will proceed, how the play will end, what its characters will ultimately seem like to you, and what the play will seem to say or show.

There is still another form of written response, one in which you imitate, parody, or write a sequel to the original. Read Tom Stoppard's *Rosencrantz and Guildenstern Are Dead* as a response to *Hamlet,* for example. Such responses also, even in the case of parody, make you read more carefully, attend to form and content more carefully, articulate your responses more fully. (And they can also be fun.)

Plays often reflect the drama of everyday life, but (like other forms of literature and art) they concentrate life and hold it up to examination. Many scenes in plays could be slices of actual conversations, and sometimes playwrights make a special effort to have their dialogue take on the informality—or even the sloppiness and banality—of ordinary talk. Sometimes, too, the actions portrayed are everyday actions—drinking a cup of coffee, watching a bus go by, working out the subtleties of a relationship with a friend. Not all plays are about grand machinations of state or great loves or noble deeds (although some are), and not all artistic shapings of actuality into drama are formalized into traditional structures (although many are). Plays may be short, have only two or three characters, portray the routine matters of everyday life, and present conflicts that are personal or even trivial as well as moments of national or cosmic significance. They may as likely ask us to respond to ordinary and everyday emotions as to public or national issues. Sometimes it takes greater artistic control to make a very simple scene compelling than it does to portray grander actions that are more laden with deep conflict and greater in import. Here, for example, is a very brief contemporary piece of drama. Its author, Harold Pinter, does not call it a play but only a "sketch," a short piece suitable for staging and containing key elements of dramatic art.

HAROLD PINTER

The Black and White

The FIRST OLD WOMAN *is sitting at a milk bar table. Small. A* SECOND OLD WOMAN *approaches. Tall. She is carrying two bowls of soup, which are covered by two plates, on each of which is a slice of bread. She puts the bowls down on the table carefully.*

SECOND: You see that one come up and speak to me at the counter? [*She takes the bread plates off the bowls, takes two spoons from her pocket, and places the bowls, plates, and spoons.*]

FIRST: You got the bread, then?

SECOND: I didn't know how I was going to carry it. In the end I put the plates on top of the soup.

FIRST: I like a bit of bread with my soup. [*They begin the soup. Pause.*]

SECOND: Did you see that one come up and speak to me at the counter?

FIRST: Who?

SECOND: Comes up to me, he says, hullo, he says, what's the time by your clock? Bloody liberty. I was just standing there getting your soup.

FIRST: It's tomato soup.

SECOND: What's the time by your clock? he says.

FIRST: I bet you answered him back.

SECOND: I told him all right. Go on, I said, why don't you get back into your scraghole, I said, clear off out of it before I call a copper. [*Pause.*]

FIRST: I not long got here.

SECOND: Did you get the all-night bus?

FIRST: I got the all-night bus straight here.

SECOND: Where from?

FIRST: Marble Arch.

SECOND: Which one?

FIRST: The two-nine-four, that takes me all the way to Fleet Street.

SECOND: So does the two-nine-one. [*Pause.*] I see you talking to two strangers as I come in. You want to stop talking to strangers, old piece of boot like you, you mind who you talk to.

FIRST: I wasn't talking to any strangers. [*Pause. The* FIRST OLD WOMAN *follows the progress of a bus through the window.*] That's another all-night bus gone down. [*Pause.*] Going up the other way. Fulham way. [*Pause.*] That was a two-nine-seven. [*Pause.*] I've never been up that way. [*Pause.*] I've been down to Liverpool Street.

SECOND: That's up the other way.

FIRST: I don't fancy going down there, down Fulham way, and all up there.

SECOND: Uh-uh.

FIRST: I've never fancied that direction much. [*Pause.*]

SECOND: How's your bread? [*Pause.*]

FIRST: Eh?

SECOND: Your bread.

FIRST: All right. How's yours? [*Pause.*]

SECOND: They don't charge for the bread if you have soup.

FIRST: They do if you have tea.

SECOND: If you have tea they do. [*Pause.*] You talk to strangers they'll take you in. Mind my word. Coppers'll take you in.

FIRST: I don't talk to strangers.

SECOND: They took me away in the wagon once.

FIRST: They didn't keep you though.

SECOND: They didn't keep me, but that was only because they took a fancy to me. They took a fancy to me when they got me in the wagon.

FIRST: Do you think they'd take a fancy to me?

SECOND: I wouldn't bank on it.

[*The* FIRST OLD WOMAN *gazes out of the window.*]

FIRST: You can see what goes on from this top table. [*Pause.*] It's better than going down to that place on the embankment, anyway.

SECOND: Yes, there's not too much noise.

FIRST: There's always a bit of noise.

SECOND: Yes, there's always a bit of life. [*Pause.*]

FIRST: They'll be closing down soon to give it a scrub-round.

SECOND: There's a wind out. [*Pause.*]

FIRST: I wouldn't mind staying.

SECOND: They won't let you.

FIRST: I know. [*Pause.*] Still, they only close hour and half, don't they? [*Pause.*] It's not long. [*Pause.*] You can go along, then come back.

SECOND: I'm going. I'm not coming back.

FIRST: When it's light I come back. Have my tea.

SECOND: I'm going. I'm going up to the Garden.

FIRST: I'm not going down there. [*Pause.*] I'm going up to Waterloo Bridge.

SECOND: You'll just about see the last two-nine-six come up over the river.

FIRST: I'll just catch a look of it. Time I get up there. [*Pause.*] It don't look like an all-night bus in daylight, do it?

1959

All the elements of drama are here in rather elementary form: there is a bit of story, mostly implied, about the lives of two women; action on a modest scale, with the emphasis on timing and relatively insignificant movements and props to underscore the women's dependence on the everyday; characterization sufficient to give a quite clear idea of what the two women's lives are like; dialogue enough to suggest the characters' thoughts and feelings and to show how their lives intersect. Even a small element of conflict is present, just enough to make the scene interesting and lively and to highlight the quiet desperation of the women's lives.

What is such a sketch about? Why is it interesting? What makes it worth seeing, worth reading, worth studying, worth thinking about and responding to? What makes it "drama"?

It's easy enough to say what it's "about"—the essentially eventless lives of two elderly, lonely women who create a simple kind of sociality between each other and in relation to their rather mechanized, anonymous, modern environment. The order of their lives is built on the predictable schedules of London's night buses and the odd opening and closing hours of an almost-all-night eatery. It reflects human routines in which not much—not even sleep—happens and in which little connection to other people exists. The women therefore create an artificial community with other riders and other patrons who are in fact unknown to them except by rituals, habits, and eccentricities.

And with each other they develop some elemental sense of human relationship—a sort of parody of a conventional domestic relationship. One might say (although it sounds almost too pretentious and formal to describe this piece) that the sketch is about loneliness and a quest for meaning. But the point is less to prove or assert something profound or thematic than to present, poignantly, a sense of what life—or a brief slice of life—is like for two isolated people who feel rather passed by. We read its details readily in terms of simple daily encounters we've had ourselves, and respond to its relative lack of action because we know from experience what to expect in moments like these.

The question of what makes the sketch interesting, memorable, and dramatic is more complicated. Once in a while we may witness, in life, a scene or vignette that seems to offer a poignant sense of some aspect of human life. When we come upon such a moment, it is sort of art by accident, and in a way that is what Pinter manages to recreate here. We could walk in on a scene like this, and the sketch goes out of its way to give that impression. The set is simple, the props are few and common, there is nothing especially complicated about the setting or the way the action is set up. A production of the sketch is not likely to seem much like a production, and one can imagine the actors making it seem as little like a play—as untheatrical—as possible. They probably would not even seem to be actors. This is about as close to a segment of life as one can get, certainly far less portentous than a scene in *Oedipus the King* or *Hamlet*, far less organized and contrived than the carefully orchestrated confrontations in television soap operas.

Yet the scene is very powerful. The action is efficient, there are no irrelevancies, except in the sense that the whole sketch depends on the conventional perceptions of two rather marginal lives. The two main characters quickly reveal themselves. The setting gives them an opportunity to present, quickly and compactly, their situation and to imply their feelings. The action—almost nonaction—reflects the story of their lives and the theme of the sketch. And the setting and props—in their simplicity and spareness—not only set the stage for the dialogue but also reflect accurately the whole world of the women's lives. All things work together quickly and efficiently to create an impression, a vivid visual sense of the way some people (probably people most members of the audience wouldn't know much about) actually live, and a brief sense of both how those people feel about their lives and how we do.

Some readers will respond to this play personally and profoundly. They will find it symbolic, an epiphany, a sudden insight into and encapsulation of the very nature of modern or modern urban life, not just for the old ladies, but for us all. Indeed, it is possible that even other readers, those who do not respond in such terms, would agree that the tone, the feeling you get, the emotional response to this brief play is "depressing" and yet that somehow, despite its banality and lack of overt symbols and preaching about "life," it also gives the impression of having a meaning beyond itself.

Trifles, though a short one-act play, is five times as long as Pinter's sketch, and has five characters (not counting the Wrights, about whom, though they never appear, we learn a good deal) to Pinter's two. It has a more conventional plot and a more conventionally presented "point" or theme than *The Black and White*, though both contain the same dramatic elements. For example, the setting and characters of *Trifles* appear as realistic as those of Pinter's sketch, but this play seems to belong to a conventional genre—the detective story—and its plot and exposition (the sheriff asking Hale to tell the county attorney, and thus the audience, what he found in the Wright farmhouse the day before) seem contrived, theatrical, and conventional. It would not be difficult to believe that Pinter stumbled across the scene that makes up *The Black and White* or that we ourselves might do so tomorrow; it would be very difficult to believe that we could accidentally encounter the scene and events of *Trifles*.

SUSAN GLASPELL

Trifles

CHARACTERS

SHERIFF	MRS. PETERS, *Sheriff's wife*
COUNTY ATTORNEY	MRS. HALE
HALE	

SCENE: *The kitchen in the now abandoned farmhouse of* JOHN WRIGHT, *a gloomy kitchen, and left without having been put in order—unwashed pans under the sink, a loaf of bread outside the bread-box, a dish-towel on the table—other signs of incompleted work. At the rear the outer door opens and the* SHERIFF *comes in followed by the* COUNTY ATTORNEY *and* HALE. *The* SHERIFF *and* HALE *are men in middle life, the* COUNTY ATTORNEY *is a young man; all are much bundled up and go at once to the stove. They are followed by the two women—the* SHERIFF's *wife first; she is a slight wiry woman, a thin nervous face.* MRS. HALE *is larger and would ordinarily be called more comfortable looking, but she is disturbed now and looks fearfully about as she enters. The women have come in slowly, and stand close together near the door.*

COUNTY ATTORNEY: [*Rubbing his hands.*] This feels good. Come up to the fire, ladies.

MRS. PETERS: [*After taking a step forward.*] I'm not—cold.

SHERIFF: [*Unbuttoning his overcoat and stepping away from the stove as if to mark the beginning of official business.*] Now, Mr. Hale, before we move things about, you explain to Mr. Henderson just what you saw when you came here yesterday morning.

COUNTY ATTORNEY: By the way, has anything been moved? Are things just as you left them yesterday?

SHERIFF: [*Looking about.*] It's just the same. When it dropped below zero last night I thought I'd better send Frank out this morning to make a fire for us— no use getting pneumonia with a big case on, but I told him not to touch anything except the stove—and you know Frank.

COUNTY ATTORNEY: Somebody should have been left here yesterday.

SHERIFF: Oh—yesterday. When I had to send Frank to Morris Center for that man who went crazy—I want you to know I had my hands full yesterday. I knew you could get back from Omaha by today and as long as I went over everything here myself—

COUNTY ATTORNEY: Well, Mr. Hale, tell just what happened when you came here yesterday morning.

HALE: Harry and I had started to town with a load of potatoes. We came along the road from my place and as I got here I said, "I'm going to see if I can't get John Wright to go in with me on a party telephone." I spoke to Wright about it once before and he put me off, saying folks talked too much anyway, and all he asked was peace and quiet—I guess you know about how much he talked himself; but I thought maybe if I went to the house and talked about it before his wife, though I said to Harry that I didn't know as what his wife wanted made much difference to John—

COUNTY ATTORNEY: Let's talk about that later, Mr. Hale. I do want to talk about that, but tell now just what happened when you got to the house.

HALE: I didn't hear or see anything; I knocked at the door, and still it was all quiet inside. I knew they must be up, it was past eight o'clock. So I knocked again, and I thought I heard somebody say, "Come in." I wasn't sure, I'm not sure yet, but I opened the door—this door [*Indicating the door by which the two women are still standing.*] and there in that rocker—[*Pointing to it.*] sat Mrs. Wright.

[*They all look at the rocker.*]

COUNTY ATTORNEY: What—was she doing?

HALE: She was rockin' back and forth. She had her apron in her hand and was kind of—pleating it.

COUNTY ATTORNEY: And how did she—look?

HALE: Well, she looked queer.

COUNTY ATTORNEY: How do you mean—queer?

HALE: Well, as if she didn't know what she was going to do next. And kind of done up.

COUNTY ATTORNEY: How did she seem to feel about your coming?

HALE: Why, I don't think she minded—one way or other. She didn't pay much attention. I said, "How do, Mrs. Wright, it's cold, ain't it?" And she said, "Is it?"—and went on kind of pleating at her apron. Well, I was surprised; she didn't ask me to come up to the stove, or to set down, but just sat there, not even looking at me, so I said, "I want to see John." And then she—laughed. I guess you would call it a laugh. I thought of Harry and the team outside, so I said a little sharp: "Can't I see John?" "No," she says, kind o' dull like. "Ain't he home?" says I. "Yes," says she, "he's home." "Then why can't I see him?" I asked her, out of patience. " 'Cause he's dead," says she. "*Dead?*" says I. She just nodded her head, not getting a bit excited, but rockin' back and forth. "Why—where is he?" says I, not knowing what to say. She just pointed upstairs—like that. [*Himself pointing to the room above.*] I got up, with the idea of going up there. I walked from there to here—then I says, "Why, what did he die of?" "He died of a rope round his neck," says she, and just went on pleatin' at her apron. Well, I went out and called Harry. I thought I might—need help. We went upstairs and there he was lyin'—

COUNTY ATTORNEY: I think I'd rather have you go into that upstairs, where you can point it all out. Just go on now with the rest of the story.

HALE: Well, my first thought was to get that rope off. It looked . . . [*Stops, his face twitches.*] . . . but Harry, he went up to him, and he said, "No, he's dead all right, and we'd better not touch anything." So we went back down stairs. She was still sitting that same way. "Has anybody been notified?" I asked. "No," says she unconcerned. "Who did this, Mrs. Wright?" said Harry. He said it business-like—and she stopped pleatin' of her apron. "I don't know," she says. "You don't *know?*" says Harry. "No," says she. "Weren't you sleepin' in the bed with him?" says Harry. "Yes," says she, "but I was on the inside." "Somebody slipped a rope round his neck and strangled him and you didn't wake up?" says Harry. "I didn't wake up," she said after him. We must 'a looked as if we didn't see how that could be, for after a minute she said, "I sleep sound." Harry was going to ask her more questions but I said maybe we ought to let her tell her story first to the coroner, or the sheriff, so Harry went fast as he could to Rivers' place, where there's a telephone.

COUNTY ATTORNEY: And what did Mrs. Wright do when she knew that you had gone for the coroner?

HALE: She moved from that chair to this one over here [*Pointing to a small chair in the corner.*] and just sat there with her hands held together and looking down. I got a feeling that I ought to make some conversation, so I said I had come in to see if John wanted to put in a telephone, and at that she started to laugh, and then she stopped and looked at me—scared. [*The* COUNTY ATTORNEY, *who has had his notebook out, makes a note.*] I dunno, maybe it wasn't scared. I wouldn't like to say it was. Soon Harry got back, and then Dr. Lloyd came, and you, Mr. Peters, and so I guess that's all I know that you don't.

COUNTY ATTORNEY: [*Looking around.*] I guess we'll go upstairs first—and then out to the barn and around there. [*To the* SHERIFF.] You're convinced that there was nothing important here—nothing that would point to any motive?

SHERIFF: Nothing here but kitchen things.

[*The* COUNTY ATTORNEY, *after again looking around the kitchen, opens the door of a cupboard closet. He gets up on a chair and looks on a shelf. Pulls his hand away, sticky.*]

COUNTY ATTORNEY: Here's a nice mess.

[*The women draw nearer.*]

MRS. PETERS: [*To the other woman.*] Oh, her fruit; it did freeze. [*To the* LAWYER.] She worried about that when it turned so cold. She said the fire'd go out and her jars would break.

SHERIFF: Well, can you beat the women! Held for murder and worryin' about her preserves.

COUNTY ATTORNEY: I guess before we're through she may have something more serious than preserves to worry about.

HALE: Well, women are used to worrying over trifles.

[*The two women move a little closer together.*]

COUNTY ATTORNEY: [*With the gallantry of a young politician.*] And yet, for all their worries, what would we do without the ladies? [*The women do not unbend. He goes to the sink, takes a dipperful of water from the pail and pouring it into a basin, washes his hands. Starts to wipe them on the roller-towel, turns it for a cleaner place.*] Dirty towels! [*Kicks his foot against the pans under the sink.*] Not much of a housekeeper, would you say, ladies?

MRS. HALE: [*Stiffly.*] There's a great deal of work to be done on a farm.

COUNTY ATTORNEY: To be sure. And yet [*With a little bow to her.*] I know there are some Dickson county farmhouses which do not have such roller towels. [*He gives it a pull to expose its length again.*]

MRS. HALE: Those towels get dirty awful quick. Men's hands aren't always as clean as they might be.

COUNTY ATTORNEY: Ah, loyal to your sex, I see. But you and Mrs. Wright were neighbors. I suppose you were friends, too.

MRS. HALE: [*Shaking her head.*] I've not seen much of her of late years. I've not been in this house—it's more than a year.

COUNTY ATTORNEY: And why was that? You didn't like her?

MRS. HALE: I liked her all well enough. Farmers' wives have their hands full, Mr. Henderson. And then—

COUNTY ATTORNEY: Yes—?

MRS. HALE: [*Looking about.*] It never seemed a very cheerful place.

COUNTY ATTORNEY: No—it's not cheerful. I shouldn't say she had the homemaking instinct.

MRS. HALE: Well, I don't know as Wright had, either.

COUNTY ATTORNEY: You mean that they didn't get on very well?

MRS. HALE: No, I don't mean anything. But I don't think a place'd be any cheerfuller for John Wright's being in it.

COUNTY ATTORNEY: I'd like to talk more of that a little later. I want to get the lay of things upstairs now. [*He goes to the left, where three steps lead to a stair door.*]

SHERIFF: I suppose anything Mrs. Peters does'll be all right. She was to take in some clothes for her, you know, and a few little things. We left in such a hurry yesterday.

COUNTY ATTORNEY: Yes, but I would like to see what you take, Mrs. Peters, and keep an eye out for anything that might be of use to us.

MRS. PETERS: Yes, Mr. Henderson. [*The women listen to the men's steps on the stairs, then look about the kitchen.*]

MRS. HALE: I'd hate to have men coming into my kitchen, snooping around and criticizing. [*She arranges the pans under sink which the* LAWYER *had shoved out of place.*]

MRS. PETERS: Of course it's no more than their duty.

MRS. HALE: Duty's all right, but I guess that deputy sheriff that came out to make the fire might have got a little of this on. [*Gives the roller towel a pull.*] Wish I'd thought of that sooner. Seems mean to talk about her for not having things slicked up when she had to come away in such a hurry.

MRS. PETERS: [*Who has gone to a small table in the left rear corner of the room, and lifted one end of a towel that covers a pan.*] She had bread set. [*Stands still.*]

MRS. HALE: [*Eyes fixed on a loaf of bread beside the bread box, which is on a low shelf at the other side of the room. Moves slowly toward it.*] She was going to put this in there. [*Picks up loaf, then abruptly drops it. In a manner of returning to familiar things.*] It's a shame about her fruit. I wonder if it's all gone. [*Gets up on the chair and looks.*] I think there's some here that's all right, Mrs. Peters. Yes—here; [*Holding it toward the window.*] this is cherries, too. [*Looking again.*] I declare I believe that's the only one. [*Gets down, bottle in her hand. Goes to the sink and wipes it off on the outside.*] She'll feel awful bad after all her hard work in the hot weather. I remember the afternoon I put up my cherries last summer. [*She puts the bottle on the big kitchen table, center of the room. With a sigh, is about to sit down in the rocking-chair. Before she is seated realizes what chair it is; with a slow look at it, steps back. The chair, which she has touched, rocks back and forth.*]

MRS. PETERS: Well, I must get those things from the front room closet. [*She goes to the door at the right, but after looking into the other room, steps back.*] You coming with me, Mrs. Hale? You could help me carry them. [*They go in the other room; reappear,* MRS. PETERS *carrying a dress and skirt,* MRS. HALE *following with a pair of shoes.*] My, it's cold in there. [*She puts the clothes on the big table, and hurries to the stove.*]

MRS. HALE: [*Examining the skirt.*] Wright was close. I think maybe that's why she kept so much to herself. She didn't even belong to the Ladies Aid. I suppose she felt she couldn't do her part, and then you don't enjoy things when you feel shabby. She used to wear pretty clothes and be lively, when she was Minnie Foster, one of the town girls singing in the choir. But that— oh, that was thirty years ago. This all you was to take in?

MRS. PETERS: She said she wanted an apron. Funny thing to want, for there isn't much to get you dirty in jail, goodness knows. But I suppose just to make her feel more natural. She said they was in the top drawer in this cupboard. Yes, here. And then her little shawl that always hung behind the door. [*Opens stair door and looks.*] Yes, here it is. [*Quickly shuts door leading upstairs.*]

MRS. HALE: [*Abruptly moving toward her.*] Mrs. Peters?

MRS. PETERS: Yes, Mrs. Hale?

MRS. HALE: Do you think she did it?

MRS. PETERS: [*In a frightened voice.*] Oh, I don't know.

MRS. HALE: Well, I don't think she did. Asking for an apron and her little shawl. Worrying about her fruit.

MRS. PETERS: [*Starts to speak, glances up, where footsteps are heard in the room above. In a low voice.*] Mr. Peters says it looks bad for her. Mr. Henderson is awful sarcastic in a speech and he'll make fun of her sayin' she didn't wake up.

MRS. HALE: Well, I guess John Wright didn't wake when they was slipping that rope under his neck.

MRS. PETERS: No, it's strange. It must have been done awful crafty and still. They say it was such a—funny way to kill a man, rigging it all up like that.

MRS. HALE: That's just what Mr. Hale said. There was a gun in the house. He says that's what he can't understand.

MRS. PETERS: Mr. Henderson said coming out that what was needed for the case was a motive; something to show anger, or—sudden feeling.

MRS. HALE: [*Who is standing by the table.*] Well, I don't see any signs of anger around here. [*She puts her hand on the dish towel which lies on the table, stands looking down at table, one half of which is clean, the other half messy.*] It's wiped to here. [*Makes a move as if to finish work, then turns and looks at loaf of bread outside the bread box. Drops towel. In that voice of coming back to familiar things.*] Wonder how they are finding things upstairs. I hope she had it a little more red-up[1] up there. You know, it seems kind of *sneaking.* Locking her up in town and then coming out here and trying to get her own house to turn against her!

MRS. PETERS: But Mrs. Hale, the law is the law.

MRS. HALE: I s'pose 'tis. [*Unbuttoning her coat.*] Better loosen up your things, Mrs. Peters. You won't feel them when you go out.

[MRS. PETERS *takes off her fur tippet, goes to hang it on hook at back of room, stands looking at the under part of the small corner table.*]

MRS. PETERS: She was piecing a quilt. [*She brings the large sewing basket and they look at the bright pieces.*]

MRS. HALE: It's log cabin pattern. Pretty, isn't it? I wonder if she was goin' to quilt it or just knot it?

[*Footsteps have been heard coming down the stairs. The* SHERIFF *enters followed by* HALE *and the* COUNTY ATTORNEY.]

SHERIFF: They wonder if she was going to quilt it or just knot it!

[*The men laugh, the women look abashed.*]

COUNTY ATTORNEY: [*Rubbing his hands over the stove.*] Frank's fire didn't do much up there, did it? Well, let's go out to the barn and get that cleared up.

[*The men go outside.*]

MRS. HALE: [*Resentfully.*] I don't know as there's anything so strange, our takin' up our time with little things while we're waiting for them to get the evidence. [*She sits down at the big table smoothing out a block with decision.*] I don't see as it's anything to laugh about.

MRS. PETERS: [*Apologetically.*] Of course they've got awful important things on their minds. [*Pulls up a chair and joins* MRS. HALE *at the table.*]

MRS. HALE: [*Examining another block.*] Mrs. Peters, look at this one. Here, this is the one she was working on, and look at the sewing! All the rest of it has been so nice and even. And look at this! It's all over the place! Why, it looks as if she didn't know what she was about! [*After she has said this they look at each other, then start to glance back at the door. After an instant* MRS. HALE *has pulled at a knot and ripped the sewing.*]

MRS. PETERS: Oh, what are you doing, Mrs. Hale?

MRS. HALE: [*Mildly.*] Just pulling out a stitch or two that's not sewed very good. [*Threading the needle.*] Bad sewing always made me fidgety.

MRS. PETERS: [*Nervously.*] I don't think we ought to touch things.

MRS. HALE: I'll just finish up this end. [*Suddenly stopping and leaning forward.*] Mrs. Peters?

MRS. PETERS: Yes, Mrs. Hale?

MRS. HALE: What do you suppose she was so nervous about?

1. Tidied up.

MRS. PETERS: Oh—I don't know. I don't know as she was nervous. I sometimes sew awful queer when I'm just tired. [MRS. HALE *starts to say something, looks at* MRS. PETERS, *then goes on sewing.*] Well I must get these things wrapped up. They may be through sooner than we think. [*Putting apron and other things together.*] I wonder where I can find a piece of paper, and string.

MRS. HALE: In that cupboard, maybe.

MRS. PETERS: [*Looking in cupboard.*] Why, here's a bird-cage. [*Holds it up.*] Did she have a bird, Mrs. Hale?

MRS. HALE: Why, I don't know whether she did or not—I've not been here for so long. There was a man around last year selling canaries cheap, but I don't know as she took one; maybe she did. She used to sing real pretty herself.

MRS. PETERS: [*Glancing around.*] Seems funny to think of a bird here. But she must have had one, or why would she have a cage? I wonder what happened to it.

MRS. HALE: I s'pose maybe the cat got it.

MRS. PETERS: No, she didn't have a cat. She's got that feeling some people have about cats—being afraid of them. My cat got in her room and she was real upset and asked me to take it out.

MRS. HALE: My sister Bessie was like that. Queer, ain't it?

MRS. PETERS: [*Examining the cage.*] Why, look at this door. It's broke. One hinge is pulled apart.

MRS. HALE: [*Looking too.*] Looks as if someone must have been rough with it.

MRS. PETERS: Why, yes. [*She brings the cage forward and puts it on the table.*]

MRS. HALE: I wish if they're going to find any evidence they'd be about it. I don't like this place.

MRS. PETERS: But I'm awful glad you came with me, Mrs. Hale. It would be lonesome for me sitting here alone.

MRS. HALE: It would, wouldn't it? [*Dropping her sewing.*] But I tell you what I do wish, Mrs. Peters. I wish I had come over sometimes when *she* was here. I—[*Looking around the room.*]—wish I had.

MRS. PETERS: But of course you were awful busy, Mrs. Hale—your house and your children.

MRS. HALE: I could've come. I stayed away because it weren't cheerful—and that's why I ought to have come. I—I've never liked this place. Maybe because it's down in a hollow and you don't see the road. I dunno what it is, but it's a lonesome place and always was. I wish I had come over to see Minnie Foster sometimes. I can see now—[*Shakes her head.*]

MRS. PETERS: Well, you mustn't reproach yourself, Mrs. Hale. Somehow we just don't see how it is with other folks until—something comes up.

MRS. HALE: Not having children makes less work—but it makes a quiet house, and Wright out to work all day, and no company when he did come in. Did you know John Wright, Mrs. Peters?

MRS. PETERS: Not to know him; I've seen him in town. They say he was a good man.

MRS. HALE: Yes—good; he didn't drink, and kept his word as well as most, I guess, and paid his debts. But he was a hard man, Mrs. Peters. Just to pass the time of day with him—[*Shivers.*] Like a raw wind that gets to the bone.

[*Pauses, her eye falling on the cage.*] I should think she would 'a wanted a bird. But what do you suppose went with it?

MRS. PETERS: I don't know, unless it got sick and died. [*She reaches over and swings the broken door, swings it again, both women watch it.*]

MRS. HALE: You weren't raised round here, were you? [MRS. PETERS *shakes her head.*] You didn't know—her?

MRS. PETERS: Not till they brought her yesterday.

MRS. HALE: She—come to think of it, she was kind of like a bird herself—real sweet and pretty, but kind of timid and—fluttery. How—she—did—change. [*Silence; then as if struck by a happy thought and relieved to get back to everyday things.*] Tell you what, Mrs. Peters, why don't you take the quilt in with you? It might take up her mind.

MRS. PETERS: Why, I think that's a real nice idea, Mrs. Hale. There couldn't possibly be any objection to it, could there? Now, just what would I take? I wonder if her patches are in here—and her things. [*They look in the sewing basket.*]

MRS. HALE: Here's some red. I expect this has got sewing things in it. [*Brings out a fancy box.*] What a pretty box. Looks like something somebody would give you. Maybe her scissors are in here. [*Opens box. Suddenly puts her hand to her nose.*] Why— [MRS. PETERS *bends nearer, then turns her face away.*] There's something wrapped up in this piece of silk.

MRS. PETERS: Why, this isn't her scissors.

MRS. HALE: [*Lifting the silk.*] Oh, Mrs. Peters—it's—

[MRS. PETERS *bends closer.*]

MRS. PETERS: It's the bird.

MRS. HALE: [*Jumping up.*] But, Mrs. Peters—look at it! Its neck! Look at its neck! It's all—other side *to.*

MRS. PETERS: Somebody—wrung—its—neck.

[*Their eyes meet. A look of growing comprehension, of horror. Steps are heard outside.* MRS. HALE *slips box under quilt pieces, and sinks into her chair. Enter* SHERIFF *and* COUNTY ATTORNEY. MRS. PETERS *rises.*]

COUNTY ATTORNEY: [*As one turning from serious things to little pleasantries.*] Well ladies, have you decided whether she was going to quilt it or knot it?

MRS. PETERS: We think she was going to—knot it.

COUNTY ATTORNEY: Well, that's interesting, I'm sure. [*Seeing the bird-cage.*] Has the bird flown?

MRS. HALE: [*Putting more quilt pieces over the box.*] We think the—cat got it.

COUNTY ATTORNEY: [*Preoccupied.*] Is there a cat?

[MRS. HALE *glances in a quick covert way at* MRS. PETERS.]

MRS. PETERS: Well, not *now.* They're superstitious, you know. They leave.

COUNTY ATTORNEY: [*To* SHERIFF PETERS, *continuing an interrupted conversation.*] No sign at all of anyone having come from the outside. Their own rope. Now let's go up again and go over it piece by piece. [*They start upstairs.*] It would have to have been someone who knew just the—

[MRS. PETERS *sits down. The two women sit there not looking at one another, but as if peering into something and at the same time holding back. When they talk now it is in the manner of feeling their way over strange ground, as if afraid of what they are saying, but as if they cannot help saying it.*]

MRS. HALE: She liked the bird. She was going to bury it in that pretty box.

MRS. PETERS: [*In a whisper.*] When I was a girl—my kitten—there was a boy took a hatchet, and before my eyes—and before I could get there—[*Covers her face an instant.*] If they hadn't held me back I would have—[*Catches herself, looks upstairs where steps are heard, falters weakly.*]—hurt him.

MRS. HALE: [*With a slow look around her.*] I wonder how it would seem never to have had any children around. [*Pause.*] No, Wright wouldn't like the bird—a thing that sang. She used to sing. He killed that, too.

MRS. PETERS: [*Moving uneasily.*] We don't know who killed the bird.

MRS. HALE: I knew John Wright.

MRS. PETERS: It was an awful thing was done in this house that night, Mrs. Hale. Killing a man while he slept, slipping a rope around his neck that choked the life out of him.

MRS. HALE: His neck. Choked the life out of him. [*Her hand goes out and rests on the bird-cage.*]

MRS. PETERS: [*With rising voice.*] We don't know who killed him. We don't know.

MRS. HALE: [*Her own feeling not interrupted.*] If there's been years and years of nothing, then a bird to sing to you, it would be awful—still, after the bird was still.

MRS. PETERS: [*Something within her speaking.*] I know what stillness is. When we homesteaded in Dakota, and my first baby died—after he was two years old, and me with no other then—

MRS. HALE: [*Moving.*] How soon do you suppose they'll be through, looking for the evidence?

MRS. PETERS: I know what stillness is. [*Pulling herself back.*] The law has got to punish crime, Mrs. Hale.

MRS. HALE: [*Not as if answering that.*] I wish you'd seen Minnie Foster when she wore a white dress with blue ribbons and stood up there in the choir and sang. [*A look around the room.*] Oh, I *wish* I'd come over here once in a while! That was a crime! That was a crime! Who's going to punish that?

MRS. PETERS: [*Looking upstairs.*] We mustn't—take on.

MRS. HALE: I might have known she needed help! I know how things can be—for women. I tell you, it's queer, Mrs. Peters. We live close together and we live far apart. We all go through the same things—it's all just a different kind of the same thing. [*Brushes her eyes, noticing the bottle of fruit, reaches out for it.*] If I was you, I wouldn't tell her her fruit was gone. Tell her it *ain't*. Tell her it's all right. Take this in to prove it to her. She—she may never know whether it was broke or not.

MRS. PETERS: [*Takes the bottle, looks about for something to wrap it in; takes petticoat from the clothes brought from the other room, very nervously begins winding this around the bottle. In a false voice.*] My, it's a good thing the men couldn't hear us. Wouldn't they just laugh! Getting all stirred up over a little thing like a—dead canary. As if that could have anything to do with—with— wouldn't they *laugh!*

[*The men are heard coming down stairs.*]

MRS. HALE: [*Under her breath.*] Maybe they would—maybe they wouldn't.
COUNTY ATTORNEY: No, Peters, it's all perfectly clear except a reason for doing it. But you know juries when it comes to women. If there was some definite thing. Something to show—something to make a story about—a thing that would connect up with this strange way of doing it—

[*The women's eyes meet for an instant. Enter* HALE *from outer door.*]

HALE: Well, I've got the team around. Pretty cold out there.
COUNTY ATTORNEY: I'm going to stay here a while by myself. [*To the* SHERIFF.] You can send Frank out for me, can't you? I want to go over everything. I'm not satisfied that we can't do better.
SHERIFF: Do you want to see what Mrs. Peters is going to take in?

[*The* LAWYER *goes to the table, picks up the apron, laughs.*]

COUNTY ATTORNEY: Oh, I guess they're not very dangerous things the ladies have picked out. [*Moves a few things about, disturbing the quilt pieces which cover the box. Steps back.*] No, Mrs. Peters doesn't need supervising. For that matter, a sheriff's wife is married to the law. Ever think of it that way, Mrs. Peters?
MRS. PETERS: Not—just that way.
SHERIFF: [*Chuckling.*] Married to the law. [*Moves toward the other room.*] I just want you to come in here a minute, George. We ought to take a look at these windows.
COUNTY ATTORNEY: [*Scoffingly.*] Oh, windows!
SHERIFF: We'll be right out, Mr. Hale.

[HALE *goes outside. The* SHERIFF *follows the* COUNTY ATTORNEY *into the other room. Then* MRS. HALE *rises, hands tight together, looking intensely at* MRS. PETERS, *whose eyes make a slow turn, finally meeting* MRS. HALE's. *A moment* MRS. HALE *holds her, then her own eyes point the way to where the box is concealed. Suddenly* MRS. PETERS *throws back quilt pieces and tries to put the box in the bag she is wearing. It is too big. She opens box, starts to take bird out, cannot touch it, goes to pieces, stands there helpless. Sound of a knob turning in the other room.* MRS. HALE *snatches the box and puts it in the pocket of her big coat. Enter* COUNTY ATTORNEY *and* SHERIFF.]

COUNTY ATTORNEY: [*Facetiously.*] Well, Henry, at least we found out that she was not going to quilt it. She was going to—what is it you call it, ladies?
MRS. HALE: [*Her hand against her pocket.*] We call it—knot it, Mr. Henderson.

CURTAIN

1920

Our responses to *Trifles* are not so uncertain or difficult to define as our responses to *The Black and White* were; *Trifles* is clearly a play and not a sketch or a slice of life. Hale's story first generates curiosity rather than expectation: Mrs. Wright's conduct at first seems strange—at least to the point where she says her husband is dead, and "died of a rope round his neck"—and then seems suspicious: could she actually have slept so soundly that she was unaware that someone had put a rope around his neck and pulled him upright, killing him? Though there is still some curiosity to know what actually happened and some anticipation about the discovery of the murderer or perhaps how the men will discover that Mrs. Wright is the murderer, our attention is distracted and our response diverted by another facet of the action: Hale's sexist remark, "Well, women are used to worrying over trifles," and later the men's scoffing laughter at the women's conjecture as to whether Mrs. Wright was going to hand-quilt or knot the quilt she was making. There may well be some difference in response based on the reader's gender. Women might pick up the sexism earlier, in the county attorney's refusal to listen when Hale suggests that Mrs. Wright's desires may not have been very important to Wright, or the sheriff's dismissive remark that there is "Nothing here but kitchen things." How offensive are these remarks? To what extent do you feel they justify the women's suppression of evidence (which the men might not have thought "real" evidence in any case)? Where do your sympathies lie? Do you want Mrs. Wright to get away with it? Does it seem justifiable homicide? Does the play strongly suggest an answer to these questions? Does the answer make you like or dislike the play? How important is our acceptance or rejection of the social theme to our emotional response to the play?

▼   ▼   ▼

QUESTIONS

1. How, besides size, would you differentiate the two old women in *The Black and White*? Which woman seems dominant? more "worldly"? What evidence can you use to support your answer? How would you describe the tone of the sketch? What feelings in you does it generate? What are the three topics of conversation between the two women? Which seems to interest them most? Can you imagine any reason why? If so, what does it suggest about the lives being depicted?

2. All three of the men in *Trifles* seem sexist; indicate at least one bit of dialogue by each that would support this judgment. What do you learn of the

character and attitudes of John Wright, the murdered man? How does the situation in the Wright household reflect on the relations between Peters, Hale, and their wives? Describe the differences between Mrs. Peters and Mrs. Hale; how does Mrs. Wright resemble and differ from them? What is the effect of the last line of the play?

WRITING SUGGESTIONS

1. With a map of London and perhaps a London Transport bus guide, locate the milk bar and the other places mentioned in *The Black and White* — Waterloo Bridge, Fulham, [Covent] Garden, etc. How much of greater London is involved? What can you learn about the area encompassed? How does that relate to the definition of the lives of the women and the tone of the sketch? How do the directions the women travel differentiate them?

2. (a) Write a sketch of a scene that you have witnessed or experienced or can discover that seems to have a mood and a meaning, not necessarily similar to Pinter's in tone or outlook but only in its suggestion of encapsulating a way of life, OR,

    (b) write a parody of the Pinter sketch.

3. (a) Write a brief sketch of the trial of Mrs. Wright, OR

    (b) write a brief of your case for or against, OR,

    (c) write a brief parody of the "feminism" of *Trifles*, OR,

    (d) describe an incident in which male chauvinism (sexism) caused a blunder or oversight.

4. Argue that Caryl Zook's (the student paper that follows) reading of the details of the play is too insistently feminist, that Henderson, for example, is not being dominant, but polite in inviting (not ordering) the "ladies" to come up to the fire; that the sheriff's remark that there's "Nothing here but kitchen things" is not dismissive of women but just a direct response to the question of what he saw in the kitchen, etc. (OR, counter such a counterargument.)

STUDENT WRITING

In the paper that follows, Caryl Zook examines each twist in the action of *Trifles* in terms of the behavior demonstrated by the men and the women. Her style and tone are informal, but her feelings about the play are strong, and she convincingly uses details to support her reading.

<u>Trifles</u>

Caryl Zook

<u>Trifles</u>: The title is at once descriptive and ironic. The males in the play are, in varying degrees, patronizing to the women and self-important in all they do. While the men are assuming that all women's concerns are trifles, the women are solving the case through their understanding of the importance of the little things. It is therefore easy for them to hide the evidence necessary to solve the case from the men.

The county attorney, Mr. Henderson, asserts his dominance from the first lines of the play when he almost orders them to "Come up to the fire, ladies." Mrs. Peters, the more timid of the two women in the scenes and trained to obey, starts to comply, then answers, "I'm not--cold."

Sheriff Peters says, "Nothing here but kitchen things" (p. 1166), implying that these are "women's" things, things of no significance. The county attorney checks a high shelf and pulls his hand away, sticky. "Here's a nice mess," he says, attaching no significance to this "trifle." Mrs. Peters realizes that almost all of Mrs. Wright's preserves had frozen and broken, as Mrs. Wright had anticipated and feared. She tells her husband, but he says, "Well, can you beat the women!" (interesting choice of words). "Held for murder and worryin' about her preserves." Hale adds, "Well, women are used to worrying over trifles." Like food, like the long hours of labor this woman must have invested to preserve a winter's worth of food for the family. Trifles. Furthermore, it was out of the sheriff's neglect to keep a fire at the house that the jars froze and broke.

The men got a good laugh at the women, who discovered that Mrs. Wright was piecing a quilt, when the sheriff says, "They wonder if she was going to quilt it or just knot it!" (p. 1169), as if this was obviously a ridiculously trivial issue. It was a little pleasantry, a diversion for the county attorney to use as small talk, "Well, ladies, have you decided whether she was going to quilt it or knot it?" Mrs. Peters says, "We think she was going to--knot it." Was she reluctant to talk about Minnie Wright's knot-tying abilities? "Well, that's interesting, I'm sure," said the county attorney. He, of course, was concerned about more pressing matters, such as how to prove who tied the knot in the rope around the neck of John Wright (p. 1171).

Ironically, while the men were parading around
being important and humorous at the expense of
"the ladies," the ladies were solving the crime.
Mrs. Hale realizes that it may have been the
deputy who got the towel dirty. Mrs. Peters
discovers a canary with a broken neck. They
conclude that Mr. Wright killed it and this was
the motive for the crime. They decide that
justice will be best served, however, by removing
this evidence in a show of solidarity with
another mistreated, over-worked, under-
appreciated female. Perhaps the attitude of the
males on the scene, whose belittling definition of
"women's work" as trifles, was another motivation
for the protective actions the women took on
behalf of a victimized sister. Anything the women
did was unimportant by comparison to what the men
do. The long, hot hours spent canning and the
months spent quilting a cover, rather than
knotting it, are trifles also. Even if the men
knew that Minnie Foster had loved to sing and
that she bought a canary to bring some small joy
into her childless life and that John Wright
killed the songbird precisely because it made her
happy, would they have seen it as a motive for
murder? Or would they have dismissed it as
"trifles"?

Glaspell has woven a tightly bound plot. The
major elements of the mystery are interconnected.

John Wright died, according to Mrs. Wright, ". . . of a rope around his neck." The women figured out that Mrs. Wright had bought a canary to sing, like she used to sing, and Mr. Wright had strangled it to death. She was, they determined, going to knot the quilt. Perhaps she could knot a rope when she wanted to. But let's not tell the men.

Understanding the Text

1 CHARACTERIZATION

People—their activities, habits, eccentricities, and personalities—are ultimately the center of almost all the stories that literature tells. Just as literature is written for human eyes and has no meaningful existence as text unless people read and respond, literature has people at the center of attention within the text, even when animals or gods are the ostensible subject, for the attention is always on human behavior and human characteristics.

Someone who appears in a work is called a **character,** the same word we use to refer to those qualities of mind, spirit, and behavior that make one individual different from every other. The identity of terms is not mere coincidence, for the creation of an imaginary character by author and reader is almost always based on some conception of human character and of individual differences.

Plays have a special engagement with character because of the visual and concrete manner in which they portray people on the stage, and written drama must create its world only through stage directions and dialogue. Stories or poems may comment on a character or editorialize rather directly, but plays have to *reveal* character—that is, let characters dramatize the kind of people they are by their own words and actions. Other characters may, of course, express opinions about a particular character, and our feelings as readers or members of the audience may be influenced by such rumor and innuendo, but all characters who appear on the stage or on the drama's page ultimately have to be credible in their own terms.

It it thus the first task of a play to introduce the people with whom we are to be concerned and to establish the central facts of their characters. The first page of text of most plays contains a complete list of the persons whose lives are to be presented dramatically, the **dramatis personae.** Many play programs offer this list, the names of the actors playing the parts, and sometimes even a brief description of each of the characters and of the relationships among them. Some plays, older ones especially, have someone appear on stage and recite a prologue that explains directly what the audience needs to know about the plot and characters. Still, whatever textual aids may be provided for curious readers or introductory matter for the audience, the play on page or stage has to present characters as if from scratch.

Getting Out, for example, uses some conventional strategies of telling us about Arlene's character, providing exposition—that is, what we need to know before the main action of the play gets underway—about both character and plot. In the opening lines of Act I, the warden's voice tells us her last name, describes her crimes, summarizes her time in prison, and offers a legal view of her prospects. A little later, we see for ourselves how others respond to Arlene, and we hear Arlene's repeated insistence on how she differs from the younger Arlie: "Arlie girl landed herself in prison. Arlene is out, O. K.?"

Whether Arlene in *Getting Out* is a "different person" from Arlie, or what the relationship is between her (and anyone's) past and present selves, seems to be what the play is about: can we really change? how much is our present—and future—determined by who we were in the past? what future do we project for Arlie / Arlene in the time after the end of the play? How do these questions affect our understanding of the title? Does it simply refer to getting out of prison?

In a live production, two different actors portray Arlie and Arlene, the same character at two different times in her life. A reader can manufacture his or her own resemblances of body type, gesture, and cues, but must also decide how much weight to give Arlene's fears and needs and how much to believe in her change. The staging of her character is very complicated because the plot involves repeated "flashbacks" to her teenage years. The main action occurs when Arlene is getting out of prison and trying to reestablish her life, but repeatedly we see glimpses of her as an adolescent ("Arlie"), before she has been to prison. The author provides a helpful introductory note explaining the differences between Arlene ("late twenties") and Arlie ("Arlene as a teenager"): "Arlie is the violent kid Arlene was until her last stretch in prison. In a sense, she is Arlene's memory of herself, called up by her fears, needs and even simple word cues. There should be hints in both physical type and gesture that

Arlie and Arlene are the same person seen at different times in her life." The stage directions suggest casting considerations as well as hints about behavior and body language for each actor. Because Arlie and Arlene are often onstage at the same time, their "reflection" of each other is crucial to the effect. In this case, a single "character" has two different manifestations, both portrayed on stage and often simultaneously. The portrayal of Arlie shows us where Arlene has come from and how she came to be the Arlene we see on another part of the stage. The device of representing the character's past alongside her present provides a context for our understanding her responses to the main action of the play—Arlene's adjustment to "ordinary" life after prison. Much of what we know about the main character thus derives from what we know of her earlier life, which is portrayed through her own earlier words, actions, and appearance. On the stage, director and actor may suggest to what degree she is determined by her past or to what degree she has changed. From the page, the reader must be director and actors and decide such issues, or allow an ambiguity—the two possible answers to such questions to remain hovering in the air above the text of the play.

Often, it is minor (or even inconsequential) characters who provide the initial information, sometimes hardly appearing again after performing their expository function. The main character seldom appears until he or she has been fully prepared for. In *Hedda Gabler*, for example, the title character does not appear until more than two hundred lines have been spoken. Her entrance is anticipated and announced, as if with a flourish of trumpets.

Our first, indirect impressions of her are rather positive. We hear what a beauty she is, how sought-after she was, and how prominent her family is. She has just returned from her honeymoon, and it is from her new husband and his Aunt Juliana that we hear about Hedda and learn how lucky they feel that she has—rather inexplicably—chosen to marry the unprepossessing Tesman. There are cautionary hints that Hedda is less than perfect, however. Tesman says she insisted on having all her baggage with her on the journey, which suggests self-indulgence or at least a certain amount of eccentricity that is hard to reconcile with her image as a cool and classy beauty. Aunt Juliana is a bit shocked by Hedda's having removed the chintz covers from the furniture and the pretension of using the drawing-room as a parlor. When Hedda enters, she is a bit snappy with both her husband and his aunt. It is quite possible, however, that the reader or audience shares Hedda's low opinion of her new groom and his family; we may be on her side and wonder how she came to be married to a rather unattractive, thick-skulled, bloodless oaf like Tesman. Her self-centeredness and cruelty are only very gradually revealed (and perhaps we, who have been on her side against the "inferior" Tesman, come to recognize that we too have been guilty of snobbishness, confusing class and worth).

The titles of such plays as *Hamlet*, *Hedda Gabler*, *Antigone*, and *Oedipus the King* imply that the play will center on a single character, and in most cases the expectations created by titles are fulfilled in the play itself: the main character (or **protagonist**) is not only at the center of the action but is also the chief object of the playwright's (and the reader's or audience's) concern. Defining the character of the protagonist (sometimes by comparison with a competitor, or **antagonist**) often becomes the consuming interest of the play, and the action seems designed to illustrate, or clarify, or develop that character, or sometimes to make him or her a complex, unfathomable, mysterious being. Even titles that do not use proper names can indicate focus on a single character or character type—*Death of a Salesman*, for example, which suggests that the emphasis is on a type rather than an individual. Occasionally, of course, a title may be a mere convenience (in which case it means nothing about the play's focus), or it may set up misleading or ambiguous expectations to arouse or divert our attention. Does the title *Getting Out* refer to Arlene or Arlie? Which of them is getting out? of where?

Not all plays focus on characters, though all involve characters and characterization. The reader, without the image of a living actor in view, must imaginatively create or recreate that image. Or, to be more precise, the reader must build, project, revise, compound, and complicate the image of the characters throughout the reading of the play.

In *Getting Out*, for example, the reader has to decide what the relationship is between the angry, out-of-control Arlie and the more thoughtful, subdued, and determined Arlene, and keep in mind how the past affects the present to imagine how Arlene is likely to be in the future. Those attending a performance of the play are guided by visual and aural clues provided by the juxtaposing of the two actors and the scenes of past and present, but the text of the play—the dialogue, stage directions, and responses of other characters—provides the primary basis of interpreting both Arlie and Arlene. A reader simply has to imagine what the actors, directors, and stage managers would provide in a staged performance. A good performance can suggest things the reader may have missed; many good performances may reveal a richness the single reader might overlook. But a good reading may also be richer than any one performance. Making sense of the main character is an interpretive act that draws most immediately on what the text or performance tell us. As readers we draw on things we already know or assume—what we infer from language, action, and reaction and what we already believe about human psychology and how a person's past affects present and future behavior. As viewers we are guided by and interact with what the director, actors, and stage managers assume, believe, or know. A play like *Getting Out* tries to reopen in our minds questions about past and present, about youthful predilections and the effects of subsequent events on later choices, but it has to work through language with assumptions we already make.

Not all the characters in a play are the heroes or heroines or villains, protagonists or antagonists. If we are to imagine the play vividly and make sense of the action, structure, and themes of the work, we must pay attention to the supporting or minor characters as well as to the leading figures. Characters are so categorized according to their functions within the play. But characters can also be categorized by what they require of those who are to act the part. There are demanding and challenging roles, juicy parts and dull or routine ones, roles for stars, character-actors, comedians, and novices. Characters can also be categorized by their cultural identities (Jewish mothers, Roumanian raven-haired beauties, pious frauds, social climbers). These sometimes verge on (or are subsumed by) **stereotypes:** characters based on conscious or unconscious cultural assumptions that sex, age, ethnic or national identification, occupation, marital status, and so on are predictably accompanied by certain character traits, actions, even values. Stereotypes, especially disparaging ones, can be a weakness in a play if they involve important characters who do not develop or become individualized, or whose motives are inadequately explored. However, no matter how individualized characters ultimately turn out to be, they often begin as some identifiable "type" of person that the audience will recognize and have certain expectations about.

Overturning or modifying these expectations of character is a method often employed to surprise a reader or audience, and to make a character a deeper, more interesting study. Hedda Gabler, as we have seen, is at first a Great Beauty. She is also rich, spoiled, ambitious, used to having her own way. Less and less attractive as she reveals herself more and more, yet pitiable because she is beginning to age and panic, and more and more helpless in a trap only in part of her own making, she begins as a quite predictable stereotype but becomes more and more complex, as does our response to her.

Tesman similarly begins as a type, almost as a comic type—the other-worldly and somewhat absent-minded professor who does not really understand veiled allusions to pregnancy, who has little sense of money, who is affectionate without suspicion, who is generally unsophisticated about the ways of the world and very trusting of human nature. Although he is always more simple and straightforward than Hedda, and his annoying mannerisms (his habit of ending most of his sentences with "what," for example) continue to categorize him, as the play develops he, too, becomes complicated, no longer simply a simple stereotype. His part, too, though not so challenging as that of Hedda, demands interpretation, nuance, and subtlety from an actor and understanding from the reader.

No matter how magnificent a performance may be, the actors must make choices—how to read a line, what body language to use, what gestures, if any, or stage "business" to bring to bear. Of course this means choosing how *not* to perform a scene as well, though some other way may be equally true to the text and equally or similarly effective. A performance is an interpretation, a "reading" of the play one way rather than another—or any other.

How would you play Hedda Gabler? What are the possibilities reading the play reveals? You might play her as an aristocratic beauty trapped into a dull marriage in the ugly, tacky world of the bourgeoisie, driven by boredom, frustration, and abhorrence to acts of cruelty; or as a thoroughly spoiled brat, used to primacy and getting her own way, who lashes out at the weak and innocent and uses everyone to satisfy her need and greed; or as . . . . Is her reverence for her dead father touching? admirable? unhealthy? To what degree is she more sinned against than sinning? Ibsen, in starkly realistic, hands-off fashion, does not mediate. Not one in the play seems to speak for him—or us. There may be clues in the context Ibsen sketches in, her social background and family upbringing, but the play does not seem to offer them either as "explanations" or justification of her nature and acts.

Suppose you wanted to show that she was some subtle mixture of both lady and brat. How would you read the lines early in the play where she seems more sympathetic in order to suggest the brat beneath? And how would you read the later lines when her cruelty emerges to suggest the pitiable lady beneath her selfishness and greed? How would you play off the emotions and sympathies of the "audience" yet play fair? For example, in a rather early episode Hedda mistakes Aunt Juliana's new hat for an old one that must belong to the maid. Still enthralled by her, we as readers or audience may have our own sense of social superiority tickled by her obvious superiority to the bumbling Tesmans. Later in the play, when Hedda's spoiled, unstable, cruel character has been more and more clearly revealed, we learn that this "mistake" was deliberate, that Hedda was deliberately trying to put down Tesman's doting, flighty, but well-meaning and vulnerable aunt. How do we reveal her cruelty for what it is, while still suggesting the lovely and suffering woman beneath? Do we simply play the early part for sympathy and the later portions of the play as a bitter exposé? That would have its own merit, engaging the reader/audience/ourselves in the romantic self-deception and then showing Hedda and ourselves up for what we are. But should we—and if so, how could we—suggest hypocrisy and selfishness from the beginning? No actress can completely embody all the suggestions and possibilities of the character as we imagine her in our reading, yet many great actresses have played the role, and when we have seen three or four portrayals, our image of the possibilities will surely be further enriched. No wonder actresses clamor for this role just as actors do for the part of Hamlet.

Every production of a play (and, in a sense, every performance) is an interpretation. Not just the "adaptations," setting a Greek or Elizabethan play in modern times and performing in modern dress, but even a production and performance that seeks to get at the "heart" or "essence" of the play is a "reading," a diagnosis or analysis of just what is vital and essential in the play. Interpretation does not necessarily mean getting the author's "intention," however. John Malkovich, in the 1983–84 production of *Death of a Salesman,* did not project Biff Loman as an outgoing, successful, hail-fellow-well-met jock, though that is what Arthur Miller intended and how he wanted the part played. Malkovich saw Biff as only pretending, playing the part of the jock. Big-time athletes, he insisted, don't glad-hand people; they wait for people to come to them. The actor did not change the author's words, but by body language, stage business, and carriage suggested his own view of the nature of the character.

Once the playwright sets down the words in the many-faceted language of the multiple communities of readers and audience, readers, directors, and actors are free to read those words as they will, within the limits of the language, the culture, and reason. The effect of Malkovich's interpretation and performance was revolutionary and convincing. Reading the play now, perhaps we will see Biff as more complex, more ambiguous — not the jock, for sure, but not a pretender for sure either.

Characterization on the stage involves four more or less separate processes. The first involves the **conception** of the character in the playwright's mind, at the moment when the play begins to be an idea, when the playwright first begins to construct — or even dream about — a plot, structure, or theme that will ultimately be an element of the drama. Characters may develop or change radically in the process of conception, and nothing in the process is really complete or final until the other three processes are also complete. The second process involves **presentation** of the character by the playwright through the words and actions specified in the text. The artistic decision about how much to present and when to present it (structural decisions, really) can have an important effect not only on how the audience responds to a character but also on what sort of character ultimately is realized in the play. The full effect of the characterization developed by the playwright is possible only when the play is fleshed out on the stage with a live actor playing the part and adding the final personal touches to the role, whether these are subtle shadings or bold new interpretations, with body gestures, facial expressions, and tones of voice. In **casting** a play—that is, in deciding what actors are to play the parts—a director takes a major step in determining how a character might seem to the audience, for the choice of actor determines not only the physical appearance, quality of voice, and degree of presence that a character will present on the stage, but also more subtle and more significant details of presentation. The **acting** itself is the last of the four steps in characterization. The embodying of a character onstage in a fully realized production is the ultimate creative act in an art that goes beyond words and stage directions and is ultimately an exercise in a complex form of impersonation. In this step one person becomes for a brief while someone different, first conceived in one form in the imagination of the playwright, developed in modified form in words by that playwright, partially interpreted by the director, and then embodied by the actor as someone other than him- or herself, but within his or her individual resources, experiences, abilities.

In a play performed on the stage we in the audience have a role, but a somewhat reduced role: actors tell us that no two performances are exactly alike, in part due to the nature of the audience. However, the actors and director have made choices and limited our freedom to interpret. Though as readers we may be the poorer for lacking the inspired insights of a great director and great actors, we are the richer for not being subjected to someone else's choices, for not having to settle on one interpretation, for the opportunity to hold complex, even contradictory, possibilities in mind, to "change character" as the words shift, while retaining all the possibilities we have gone through.

▼ ▼ ▼

MARSHA NORMAN

Getting Out

CHARACTERS

ARLENE, *a thin, drawn woman in her late twenties who has just served an eight-year prison term for murder*

ARLIE, *Arlene at various times earlier in her life*

BENNIE, *an Alabama prison guard in his fifties*

MOTHER, *Arlene's mother*

SCHOOL PRINCIPAL, *female*

RONNIE, *a teenager in a juvenile institution*

CARL, *Arlene's former pimp and partner in various crimes, in his late twenties*

GUARD [EVANS]
GUARD [CALDWELL]
DOCTOR, *a psychiatrist in a juvenile institution*

WARDEN, *superintendent of Pine Ridge Correctional Institute for Women*
RUBY, *Arlene's upstairs neighbor, a cook in a diner, also an ex-con, in her late thirties*

PLAYWRIGHT'S NOTES

ARLIE is *the violent kid* ARLENE *was until her last stretch in prison.* ARLIE *may walk through the apartment quite freely, but no one there will acknowledge her presence. Most of her scenes take place in the prison areas.*

ARLIE, *in a sense, is* ARLENE's *memory of herself, called up by fears, needs and even simple word cues. The memory haunts, attacks and warns. But mainly, the memory will not go away.*

ARLIE's *life should be as vivid as* ARLENE's *if not as continuous. There must be hints in both physical type and gesture that* ARLIE *and* ARLENE *are the same person, though seen at different times in her life. They both speak with a country twang, but* ARLENE *is suspicious and guarded, withdrawal is always a possibility.* ARLIE *is unpredictable and incorrigible. The change seen in* ARLIE *during the second act represents a movement toward the adult* ARLENE, *but the transition should never be complete. Only in the final scene are they enjoyably aware of each other.*

The life in the prison "surround" needs to convince without distracting. The guards do not belong to any specific institution, but rather to all the places where ARLENE *has done time.*

PROLOGUE

Beginning five minutes before the houselights come down, the following announcements are broadcast over the loudspeaker. A woman's voice is preferred, a droning tone is essential.

LOUDSPEAKER VOICE: Kitchen workers, all kitchen workers report immediately to the kitchen. Kitchen workers to the kitchen. The library will not be open today. Those scheduled for book checkout should remain in morning work assignments. Kitchen workers to the kitchen. No library hours today. Library hours resume tomorrow as usual. All kitchen workers to the kitchen.

Frances Mills, you have a visitor at the front gate. All residents and staff, all residents and staff . . . . Do not, repeat, do not, walk on the front lawn today or use the picnic tables on the front lawn during your break after lunch or dinner.

Your attention please. The exercise class for Dorm A residents has been cancelled. Mrs. Fischer should be back at work in another month. She thanks you for your cards and wants all her girls to know she had an eight-pound baby girl.

Doris Creech, see Mrs. Adams at the library before lunch. Frances Mills, you have a visitor at the front gate. The Women's Associates' picnic for the beauty school class has been postponed until Friday. As picnic lunches have already been prepared, any beauty school member who so wishes, may pick up a picnic lunch and eat it at her assigned lunch table during the regular lunch period.

Frances Mills, you have a visitor at the front gate. Doris Creech to see Mrs. Adams at the library before lunch. I'm sorry, that's Frankie Hill, you have a visitor at the front gate. Repeat, Frankie Hill, not Frances Mills, you have a visitor at the front gate.

ACT I

The play is set in a dingy one-room apartment in a rundown section of downtown Louisville, Kentucky. There is a twin bed and one chair. There is a sink, an apartment-size combination stove and refrigerator, and a counter with cabinets above. Dirty curtains conceal the bars on the outside of the single window. There is one closet and a door to the bathroom. The door to the apartment opens into a hall.

A catwalk stretches above the apartment and a prison cell, stage right, connects to it by stairways. An area downstage and another stage left complete the enclosure of the apartment by playing areas for the past. The apartment must seem imprisoned.

Following the prologue, lights fade to black and the warden's voice is heard on tape.

WARDEN'S VOICE: The Alabama State Parole Board hereby grants parole to Holsclaw, Arlene, subject having served eight years at Pine Ridge Correctional Institute for the second-degree murder of a cab driver in conjunction with a filling station robbery involving attempted kidnapping of attendant. Crime occurred during escape from Lakewood State Prison where subject Holsclaw was serving three years for forgery and prostitution. Extensive juvenile records from the state of Kentucky appended hereto.

[*As the warden continues, light comes up on* ARLENE, *walking around the cell, waiting to be picked up for the ride home.* ARLIE *is visible, but just barely, down center.*]

WARDEN'S VOICE: Subject now considered completely rehabilitated is returned to Kentucky under interstate parole agreement in consideration of family residence and appropriate support personnel in the area. Subject will remain under the supervision of Kentucky parole officers for a period of five years. Prospects for successful integration into community rated good. Psychological evaluation, institutional history and health records attached in Appendix C, this document.

BENNIE'S VOICE: Arlie!

[ARLENE *leaves the cell as light comes up on* ARLIE, *seated down center. She tells this story rather simply. She enjoys it, but its horror is not lost on her. She may be doing some semiabsorbing activity such as painting her toenails.*]

ARLIE: So, there was this little kid, see, this creepy little fucker next door. Had glasses an somethin' wrong with his foot. I don't know, seven, maybe. Anyhow, ever time his daddy went fishin', he'd bring this kid back some frogs. They built this little fence around 'em in the backyard like they was pets or somethin'. An we'd try to go over an see 'em but he'd start screamin' to his mother to come out an git rid of us. Real snotty like. So we got sick of him bein' such a goody-goody an one night me an June snuck over there an put all his dumb ol' frogs in this sack. You never heared such a fuss. [*Makes croaking sounds.*] Slimy bastards, frogs. We was plannin' to let 'em go all over the place, but when they started jumpin' an all, we just figured they was askin' for it. So, we taken 'em out front to the porch an we throwed 'em, one at a time, into the street. [*Laughs.*] Some of 'em hit cars goin' by but most of 'em jus' got squashed, you know, runned over? It was great, seein' how far we could throw 'em, over back of our backs an under our legs an God, it was really fun watchin' 'em fly through the air then *splat* [*Claps hands.*] all over somebody's car window or somethin'. Then the next day, we was waitin' and this little kid comes out in his backyard lookin' for his stupid frogs and he don't see any an he gets so crazy, cryin' and everything. So me an June goes over an tells him we seen this big mess out in the street, an he goes out an sees all them frogs' legs and bodies an shit all over the everwhere, an, man, it was so funny. We 'bout killed ourselves laughin'. Then his mother come out and she wouldn't let him go out an pick up all the pieces, so he jus' had to stand there watchin' all the cars go by smush his little babies right into the street. I's gonna run out an git him a frog's head, but June yellin' at me "Arlie, git over here fore some car slips on them frog guts an crashes into you." [*Pause.*] I never had so much fun in one day in my whole life.

[ARLIE *remains seated as* ARLENE *enters the apartment. It is late evening. Two sets of footsteps are heard coming up the stairs.* ARLENE *opens the door and walks into the room. She stands still, surveying the littered apartment.* BENNIE *is heard dragging a heavy trunk up the stairs.* BENNIE *is wearing his guard uniform. He is a heavy man, but obviously used to physical work.*]

BENNIE: [*From outside.*] Arlie?

ARLENE: Arlene.

BENNIE: Arlene? [*Bringing the trunk just inside the door.*]

ARLENE: Leave it. I'll git it later.

BENNIE: Oh, now, let me bring it in for you. You ain't as strong as you was.

ARLENE: I ain't as mean as I was. I'm strong as ever. You go on now. [*Beginning to walk around the room.*]

ARLIE: [*Irritated, as though someone is calling her.*] Lay off! [*Gets up and walks past* BENNIE.]

BENNIE: [*Scoots the trunk into the room a little further.*] Go on where, Arlie?

ARLENE: I don't know where. How'd I know where you'd be goin'?

BENNIE: I can't go till I know you're gonna do all right.

ARLENE: Look, I'm gonna do all right. I done all right before Pine Ridge, an I done all right at Pine Ridge. An I'm gonna do all right here.

BENNIE: But you don't know nobody. I mean, nobody nice.

ARLENE: Lay off.

BENNIE: Nobody to take care of you.

ARLENE: [*Picking up old newspapers and other trash from the floor.*] I kin take
care of myself. I been doin' it long enough.

BENNIE: Sure you have, an you landed yourself in prison doin' it. Arlie girl.

ARLENE: [*Wheels around.*] Arlie girl landed herself in prison. Arlene is out, okay?

BENNIE: Hey, now, I know we said we wasn't gonna say nuthin' about that, but
I been lookin' after you for a long time. I been watchin' you eat your dinner
for eight years now. I got used to it, you know?

ARLENE: Well, you kin jus' git unused to it.

BENNIE: Then why'd you ask me to drive you all the way up here?

ARLENE: I didn't, now. That was all your big idea.

BENNIE: And what were you gonna do? Ride the bus, pick up some soldier, git
yourself in another mess of trouble?

[ARLIE *struts back into the apartment, speaking as if to a soldier in a bar.*]

ARLIE: Okay, who's gonna buy me a beer?

ARLENE: You oughta go by Fort Knox on your way home.

ARLIE: Fuckin' soldiers, don't care where they get theirself drunk.

ARLENE: You'd like it.

ARLIE: Well, Arlie girl, take your pick.

ARLENE: They got tanks right out on the grass to look at.

ARLIE: [*Now appears to lean on a bar rail.*] You git that haircut today, honey?

BENNIE: I just didn't want you givin' your twenty dollars the warden gave you to
the first pusher you come across.

[ARLIE *laughs.*]

ARLENE: That's what you think I been waitin' for?

[A GUARD *appears and motions for* ARLIE *to follow him.*]

ARLIE: Yeah! I heard ya.

[*The* GUARD *takes* ARLIE *to the cell and slams the door.*]

BENNIE: But God almighty, I hate to think what you'd done to the first ol' bugger
tried to make you in that bus station. You got grit, Arlie girl. I gotta credit
you for that.

ARLIE: [*From the cell, as she dumps a plate of food on the floor.*] Officer!

BENNIE: The screamin' you'd do. Wake the dead.

ARLENE: Uh-huh.

BENNIE: [*Proudly.*] An there ain't nobody can beat you for throwin' plates.

ARLIE: Are you gonna clean up this shit or do I have to sit here and look at it till
I vomit?

[A GUARD *comes in to clean it up.*]

BENNIE: Listen, ever prison in Alabama's usin' plastic forks now on account of
what you done.

ARLENE: You can quit talkin' just anytime now.

ARLIE: Some life you got, fatso. Bringin' me my dinner then wipin' it off the
walls. [*Laughs.*]

BENNIE: Some of them officers was pretty leery of you. Even the chaplain.

ARLENE: No he wasn't either.

BENNIE: Not me, though. You was just wild, that's all.

ARLENE: Animals is wild, not people. That's what he said.

ARLIE: [*Mocking.*] Good behavior, good behavior. Shit.

BENNIE: Now what could that four-eyes chaplain know about wild? [ARLENE *looks up sharply.*] Okay. Not wild, then . . .

ARLIE: I kin git outta here anytime I want. [*Leaves the cell.*]

BENNIE: But you got grit, Arlie.

ARLENE: I have said for you to call me Arlene.

BENNIE: Okay okay.

ARLENE: Huh?

BENNIE: Don't git riled. You want me to call you Arlene, then Arlene it is. Yes ma'am. Now, [*Slapping the trunk.*] where do you want this? [*No response.*] Arlene, I said, where do you want this trunk?

ARLENE: I don't care. [BENNIE *starts to put it at the foot of the bed.*] No! [*Then calmer.*] I seen it there too long. [BENNIE *is irritated.*] Maybe over here. [*Points to a spot near the window.*] I could put a cloth on it and sit an look out the . . . [*She pulls the curtains apart, sees the bars on the window.*] What's these bars doin' here?

BENNIE: [*Stops moving the trunk.*] I think they're to keep out burglars, you know. [*Sits on the trunk.*]

ARLENE: Yeah, I know.

[ARLIE *appears on the catwalk, as if stopped during a break-in.*]

ARLIE: We ain't breakin' in, cop, we're just admirin' this beautiful window.

ARLENE: I don't want them there. Pull them out.

BENNIE: You can't go tearin' up the place, Arlene. Landlord wouldn't like it.

ARLIE: [*To the unseen policeman.*] Maybe I got a brick in my hand and maybe I don't.

BENNIE: Not one bit.

ARLIE: An I'm standin' on this garbage can because I like to, all right?

ARLENE: [*Walking back toward* BENNIE.] I ain't gonna let no landlord tell me what to do.

BENNIE: The landlord owns the building. You gotta do what he says or he'll throw you out right on your pretty little behind. [*Gives her a familiar pat.*]

ARLENE: [*Slaps his hand away.*] You watch your mouth. I won't have no dirty talk.

ARLIE: Just shut the fuck up, cop! Go bust a wino or somethin'. [*Returns to the cell.*]

ARLENE: [*Points down right.*] Here, put the trunk over here.

BENNIE: [*Carrying the trunk over to the spot she has picked.*] What you got in here, anyhow? Rocks? Rocks from the rock pile?

ARLENE: That ain't funny.

BENNIE: Oh sweetie, I didn't mean nuthin' by that.

ARLENE: And I ain't your sweetie.

BENNIE: We really did have us a rock pile, you know, at the old men's prison, yes we did. And those boys, time they did nine or ten years carryin' rocks around, they was pret-ty mean, I'm here to tell you. And strong? God.

ARLENE: Well, what did you expect? [*Beginning to unpack the trunk.*]

BENNIE: You're tellin' me. It was dumb, I kept tellin' the warden that. They coulda killed us all, easy, anytime, that outfit. Except, we did have the guns.

ARLENE: Uh-huh.

BENNIE: One old bastard sailed a throwin' rock at me one day, woulda took my eye out if I hadn't turned around just then. Still got the scar, see? [*Reaches up to the back of his head.*]

ARLENE: You shoot him?

BENNIE: Nope. Somebody else did. I forget who. Hey! [*Walking over to the window.*] These bars won't be so bad. Maybe you could get you some plants so's you don't even see them. Yeah, plants'd do it up just fine. Just fine.

ARLENE: [*Pulls a cheaply framed picture of Jesus out of the trunk.*] Chaplain give me this.

BENNIE: He got it for free, I bet.

ARLENE: Now, look here. That chaplain was good to me, so you can shut up about him.

BENNIE: [*Backing down.*] Fine. Fine.

ARLENE: Here. [*Handing him the picture.*] You might as well be useful fore you go.

BENNIE: Where you want it?

ARLENE: Don't matter.

BENNIE: Course it matters. Wouldn't want me puttin' it inside the closet, would you? You gotta make decisions now, Arlene. Gotta decide things.

ARLENE: I don't care.

BENNIE: [*Insisting.*] Arlene.

ARLENE: [*Pointing to a prominent position on the apartment wall, center.*] There.

BENNIE: Yeah. Good place. See it first thing when you get up.

[ARLENE *lights a cigarette, as* ARLIE *retrieves a hidden lighter from the toilet in the cell.*]

ARLIE: There's ways . . . gettin' outta bars . . . [*Lights a fire in the cell, catching her blouse on fire too.*]

BENNIE: [*As* ARLIE *is lighting the fire.*] This ol' nail's pretty loose. I'll find something better to hang it with . . . somewhere or other . . .

[ARLIE *screams and the* DOCTOR *runs toward her, getting the attention of a* GUARD *who has been goofing off on the catwalk.*]

ARLIE: Let me outta here! There's a fuckin' fire in here!

[*The* DOCTOR *arrives at the cell, pats his pockets as if looking for the keys.*]

ARLIE: Officer!

DOCTOR: Guard!

[GUARD *begins his run to the cell.*]

ARLIE: It's burnin' me!

DOCTOR: Hurry!

GUARD (EVANS): I'm comin'! I'm comin'!

DOCTOR: What the hell were you—

GUARD (EVANS): [Fumbling for the right key.] Come on, come on.

DOCTOR: [Urgent.] For Chrissake!

[The GUARD gets the door open, they rush in. The DOCTOR, wrestling ARLIE to the ground, opens his bag.]

DOCTOR: Lay still, dammit.

[ARLIE collapses. The DOCTOR gives an injection.]

DOCTOR: [Grabbing his hand.] Ow!

GUARD (EVANS): [Lifting ARLIE up to the bed.] Get bit, Doc?

DOCTOR: You going to let her burn this place down before you start payin' attention up there?

GUARD (EVANS): [Walks to the toilet, feels under the rim.] Uh-huh.

BENNIE: There, that what you had in mind?

ARLENE: Yeah, thanks.

GUARD (EVANS): She musta had them matches hid right here.

BENNIE: [Staring at the picture he's hung.] How you think he kept his beard trimmed all nice?

ARLENE: [Preoccupied with unloading the trunk.] Who?

BENNIE: [Pointing to the picture.] Jesus.

DOCTOR: I'll have to report you for this, Evans.

ARLENE: I don't know.

DOCTOR: That injection should hold her. I'll check back later. [Leaves.]

GUARD (EVANS): [Walking over to the bed.] Report me, my ass. We got cells don't have potties, Holsclaw. [Begins to search her and the bed, handling her very roughly.] So where is it now? Got it up your pookie, I bet. Oh, that'd be good. Doc comin' back an me with my fingers up your . . . roll over . . . don't weigh hardly nuthin', do you, dollie?

BENNIE: Never seen him without a moustache either.

ARLENE: Huh?

BENNIE: The picture.

GUARD (EVANS): Aw now . . . . [Finding the lighter under the mattress.] That wasn't hard at all. Don't you know 'bout hide an seek, Arlie, girl? Gonna hide somethin', hide it where it's fun to find it. [Standing up, going to the door.] Crazy fuckin' someday-we-ain't-gonna-come-save-you bitch!

[GUARD slams cell door and leaves.]

BENNIE: Well, Arlie girl, that ol' trunk's 'bout as empty as my belly.

ARLENE: You have been talkin' 'bout your belly ever since we left this mornin'.

BENNIE: You hungry? Them hotdogs we had give out around Nashville.

ARLENE: No. Not really.

BENNIE: You gotta eat, Arlene.

ARLENE: Says who?

BENNIE: [*Laughs.*] How 'bout I pick us up some chicken, give you time to clean yourself up. We'll have a nice little dinner, just the two of us.

ARLENE: I git sick if I eat this late. Besides, I'm tired.

BENNIE: You'll feel better soon's you git somethin' on your stomach. Like I always said, "Can't plow less'n you feed the mule."

ARLENE: I ain't never heard you say that.

BENNIE: There's lots you don't know about me, Arlene. You been seein' me ever day, but you ain't been payin' attention. You'll get to like me now we're out.

ARLENE: You . . . was always out.

BENNIE: Yes sir, I'm gonna like bein' retired. I kin tell already. An I can take care of you, like I been, only now—

ARLENE: You tol' me you was jus' takin' a vacation.

BENNIE: I was gonna tell you.

ARLENE: You had some time off an nothin' to do . . .

BENNIE: Figured you knew already.

ARLENE: You said you ain't never seen Kentucky like you always wanted to. Now you tell me you done quit at the prison?

BENNIE: They wouldn't let me drive you up here if I was still on the payroll, you know. Rules, against the rules. Coulda got me in big trouble doin' that.

ARLENE: You ain't goin' back to Pine Ridge?

BENNIE: Nope.

ARLENE: An you drove me all the way up here plannin' to stay here?

BENNIE: I was thinkin' on it.

ARLENE: Well what are you gonna do?

BENNIE: [*Not positive, just a possibility.*] Hardware.

ARLENE: Sell guns?

BENNIE: [*Laughs.*] Nails. Always wanted to. Some little store with bins and barrels full of nails and screws. Count 'em out. Put 'em in little sacks.

ARLENE: I don't need nobody hangin' around remindin' me where I been.

BENNIE: We had us a good time drivin' up here, didn't we? You throwin' that tomato outta the car . . . hit that no litterin' sign square in the middle. [*Grabs her arm as if to feel the muscle.*] Good arm you got.

ARLENE: [*Pulling away sharply.*] Don't you go grabbin' me.

BENNIE: Listen, you take off them clothes and have yourself a nice hot bath. [*Heading for the bathroom.*] See, I'll start the water. And me, I'll go get us some chicken. [*Coming out of the bathroom.*] You like slaw or potato salad?

ARLENE: Don't matter.

BENNIE: [*Asking her to decide.*] Arlene . . .

ARLENE: Slaw.

BENNIE: One big bucket of slaw comin' right up. An extra rolls. You have a nice bath, now, you hear? I'll take my time so's you don't have to hurry fixin' yourself up.

ARLENE: I ain't gonna do no fixin'.

BENNIE: [*A knowing smile.*] I know how you gals are when you get in the tub. You got any bubbles?

ARLENE: What?

BENNIE: Bubbles. You know, stuff to make bubbles with. Bubble bath.

ARLENE: I thought you was goin'.

BENNIE: Right. Right. Goin' right now.

[BENNIE *leaves, locking the door behind him. He has left his hat on the bed.* ARLENE *checks the stove and refrigerator.*]

GUARD (CALDWELL): [*Opening the cell door, carrying a plastic dinner carton.*] Got your grub, girlie.

ARLIE: Get out!

GUARD (CALDWELL): Can't. Doc says you gotta take the sun today.

ARLIE: You take it! I ain't hungry.

[*The* GUARD *and* ARLIE *begin to walk to the downstage table area.*]

GUARD (CALDWELL): You gotta eat, Arlie.

ARLIE: Says who?

GUARD (CALDWELL): Says me. Says the warden. Says the Department of Corrections. Brung you two rolls.

ARLIE: And you know what you can do with your—

GUARD (CALDWELL): Stuff 'em in your bra, why don't you?

ARLIE: Ain't you got somebody to go beat up somewhere?

GUARD (CALDWELL): Gotta see you get fattened up.

ARLIE: What do you care?

[ARLENE *goes into the bathroom.*]

GUARD (CALDWELL): Oh, we care all right. [*Setting the food down on the table.*] Got us a two-way mirror in the shower room. [*She looks up, hostile.*] And you don't know which one it is, do you? [*He forces her onto the seat.*] Yes ma'am. Eat. [*Pointing to the food.*] We sure do care if you go gittin' too skinny. [*Walks away but continues to watch her.*] Yes ma'am. We care a hog-lickin' lot.

ARLIE: [*Throws the whole carton at him.*] Sons-a-bitches!

[MOTHER'S *knock is heard on the apartment door.*]

MOTHER'S VOICE: Arlie? Arlie girl you in there?

[ARLENE *walks out of the bathroom. She stands still, looking at the door.* ARLIE *hears the knock at the same time and slips into the apartment and over to the bed, putting the pillow between her legs and holding the yellow teddy bear* ARLENE *has unpacked. The knocking gets louder.*]

MOTHER'S VOICE: Arlie?

ARLIE: [*Pulling herself up weakly on one elbow, speaking with the voice of a very young child.*] Mama? Mama?

[ARLENE *walks slowly toward the door.*]

MOTHER'S VOICE: [*Now pulling the doorknob from the outside, angry that the door is locked.*] Arlie? I know you're in there.

ARLIE: I can't git up, Mama. [*Hands between her legs.*] My legs is hurt.

MOTHER'S VOICE: What's takin' you so long?

ARLENE: [*Smoothing out her dress.*] Yeah, I'm comin'. [*Puts* BENNIE's *hat out of sight under the bed.*] Hold on.

MOTHER'S VOICE: I brung you some stuff but I ain't gonna stand here all night.

[ARLENE *opens the door and stands back.* MOTHER *looks strong but badly worn. She is wearing her cab driver's uniform and is carrying a plastic laundry basket stuffed with cleaning fluids, towels, bug spray, etc.*]

ARLENE: I didn't know if you'd come.

MOTHER: Ain't I always?

ARLENE: How are you?

[ARLENE *moves as if to hug her.* MOTHER *stands still,* ARLENE *backs off.*]

MOTHER: 'Bout the same. [*Walking into the room.*]

ARLENE: I'm glad to see you.

MOTHER: [*Not looking at* ARLENE.] You look tired.

ARLENE: It was a long drive.

MOTHER: [*Putting the laundry basket on the trunk.*] Didn't fatten you up none, I see. [*Walks around the room, looking the place over.*] You always was too skinny. [ARLENE *straightens her clothes again.*] Shoulda beat you like your daddy said. Make you eat.

ARLIE: Nobody done this to me, Mama. [*Protesting, in pain.*] No! No!

MOTHER: He weren't a mean man, though, your daddy.

ARLIE: Was . . . [*Quickly.*] my bike. My bike hurt me. The seat bumped me.

MOTHER: You remember that black chewing gum he got you when you was sick?

ARLENE: I remember he beat up on you.

MOTHER: Yeah, [*Proudly.*] and he was real sorry a coupla times. [*Looking in the closet.*] Filthy dirty. Hey! [*Slamming the closet door.* ARLENE *jumps at the noise.*] I brung you all kinda stuff. Just like Candy not leavin' you nuthin'. [*Walking back to the basket.*] Some kids I got.

ARLIE: [*Curling up into a ball.*] No, Mama, don't touch it. It'll git well. It git well before.

ARLENE: Where is Candy?

MOTHER: You got her place so what do you care? I got her outta my house so whatta I care? This'll be a good place for you.

ARLENE: [*Going to the window.*] Wish there was a yard, here.

MOTHER: [*Beginning to empty the basket.*] Nice things, see? Bet you ain't had no colored towels where you been.

ARLENE: No.

MOTHER: [*Putting some things away in cabinets.*] No place like home. Got that up on the kitchen wall now.

ARLIE: I don't want no tea, Mama.

ARLENE: Yeah?

MOTHER: [*Repeating* ARLENE's *answers.*] No . . . yeah? . . . You forgit how to talk? I ain't gonna be here all that long. Least you can talk to me while I'm here.

ARLENE: You ever git that swing you wanted?

MOTHER: Dish towels, an see here? June sent along this teapot. You drink tea, Arlie?

ARLENE: No.

MOTHER: June's havin' another baby. Don't know when to quit, that girl. Course, I ain't one to talk. [*Starting to pick up trash on the floor.*]

ARLENE: Have you seen Joey?

ARLIE: I'm tellin' you the truth.

MOTHER: An Ray . . .

ARLIE: [*Pleading.*] Daddy didn't do nuthin' to me.

MOTHER: Ray ain't had a day of luck in his life.

ARLIE: Ask him. He saw me fall on my bike.

MOTHER: Least bein' locked up now, he'll keep off June till the baby gits here.

ARLENE: Have you seen Joey?

MOTHER: Your daddy ain't doin' too good right now. Man's been dyin' for ten years, to hear him tell it. You'd think he'd git tired of it an jus' go ahead . . . pass on.

ARLENE: [*Wanting an answer.*] Mother . . .

MOTHER: Yeah, I seen 'im. 'Bout two years ago. Got your stringy hair.

ARLENE: You got a picture?

MOTHER: You was right to give him up. Foster homes is good for some kids.

ARLIE: Where's my Joey-bear? Yellow Joey-bear? Mama?

ARLENE: How'd you see him?

MOTHER: I was down at Detention Center pickin' up Pete. [*Beginning her serious cleaning now.*]

ARLENE: [*Less than interested.*] How is he?

MOTHER: I could be workin' at the Detention Center I been there so much. All I gotta do's have somethin' big goin' on an I git a call to come after one of you. Can't jus' have kids, no, gotta be pickin' 'em up all over town.

ARLENE: You was just tellin' me—

MOTHER: Pete is taller, that's all.

ARLENE: You was just tellin' me how you saw Joey.

MOTHER: I'm comin' back in the cab an I seen him waitin' for the bus.

ARLENE: What'd he say?

MOTHER: Oh, I didn't stop. [ARLENE *looks up quickly, hurt and angry.*] If the kid don't even know you, Arlie, he sure ain't gonna know who I am.

ARLENE: How come he couldn't stay at Shirley's?

MOTHER: 'Cause Shirley never was crazy about washin' more diapers. She's the only smart kid I got. Anyway, social worker only put him there till she could find him a foster home.

ARLENE: But I coulda seen him.

MOTHER: Thatta been trouble, him bein' in the family. Kid wouldn't have known who to listen to, Shirley or you.

ARLENE: But I'm his mother.

MOTHER: See, now you don't have to be worryin' about him. No kids, no worryin'.

ARLENE: He just had his birthday, you know.

ARLIE: Don't let Daddy come in here, Mama. Just you an me. Mama?

ARLENE: When I git workin', I'll git a nice rug for this place. He could come live here with me.

MOTHER: Fat chance.

ARLENE: I done my time.

MOTHER: You never really got attached to him anyway.

ARLENE: How do you know that?

MOTHER: Now don't you go gettin' het up. I'm telling you . . .

ARLENE: But . . .

MOTHER: Kids need rules to go by an he'll get 'em over there.

ARLIE: [Screaming.] No Daddy! I didn't tell her nuthin'. I didn't! I didn't! [Gets up from the bed, terrified.]

MOTHER: Here, help me with these sheets. [Hands ARLENE the sheets from the laundry basket.] Even got you a spread. Kinda goes with them curtains. [ARLENE is silent.] You ain't thanked me, Arlie girl.

ARLENE: [Going to the other side of the bed.] They don't call me Arlie no more. It's Arlene now.

[ARLENE and MOTHER make up the bed. ARLIE jumps up, looks around and goes over to MOTHER's purse. She looks through it hurriedly and pulls out the wallet. She takes some money and runs down left, where she is caught by a SCHOOL PRINCIPAL.]

PRINCIPAL: Arlie? You're in an awfully big hurry for such a little girl. [Brushes at ARLIE's hair.] That is you under all that hair, isn't it? [ARLIE resists this gesture.] Now, you can watch where you're going.

ARLIE: Gotta git home.

PRINCIPAL: But school isn't over for another three hours. And there's peanut butter and chili today.

ARLIE: Ain't hungry. [Struggling free.]

[The PRINCIPAL now sees ARLIE's hands clenched behind her back.]

PRINCIPAL: What do we have in our hands, Arlie?

ARLIE: Nuthin'.

PRINCIPAL: Let me see your hands, Arlie. Open up your hands.

[ARLIE brings her hands around in front, opening them, showing crumpled dollars.]

ARLIE: It's my money. I earned it.

PRINCIPAL: [Taking the money.] And how did we earn this money?

ARLIE: Doin' things.

PRINCIPAL: What kind of things?

ARLIE: For my daddy.

PRINCIPAL: Well, we'll see about that. You'll have to come with me.

[ARLIE *resists as the* PRINCIPAL *pulls her.*]

ARLIE: No.

PRINCIPAL: Your mother was right after all. She said put you in a special school. [*Quickly.*] No, what she said was put you away somewhere and I said, no, she's too young, well I was wrong. I have four hundred other children to take care of here and what have I been doing? Breaking up your fights, talking to your truant officer and washing your writing off the bathroom wall. Well, I've had enough. You've made your choice. You *want* out of regular school and you're going to *get* out of regular school.

ARLIE: [*Becoming more violent.*] You can't make me go nowhere, bitch!

PRINCIPAL: [*Backing off in cold anger.*] I'm not making you go. You've earned it. You've worked hard for this, well, they're used to your type over there. They'll know exactly what to do with you. [*She stalks off, leaving* ARLIE *alone.*]

MOTHER: [*Smoothing out the spread.*] Spread ain't new, but it don't look so bad. Think we got it right after we got you. No, I remember now. I was pregnant with you an been real sick the whole time.

[ARLENE *lights a cigarette,* MOTHER *takes one,* ARLENE *retrieves the pack quickly.*]

MOTHER: Your daddy brung me home this big bowl of chili an some jelly dough-nuts. Some fare from the airport give him a big tip. Anyway, I'd been eatin' peanut brittle all day, only thing that tasted any good. Then in he come with this chili an no sooner'n I got in bed I thrown up all over everwhere. Lucky I didn't throw you up, Arlie girl. Anyhow, that's how come us to get a new spread. This one here. [*Sits on the bed.*]

ARLENE: You drivin' the cab any?

MOTHER: Any? Your daddy ain't drove it at all a long time now. Six years, seven maybe.

ARLENE: You meet anybody nice?

MOTHER: Not anymore. Mostly drivin' old ladies to get their shoes. Guess it got around the nursin' homes I was reliable. [*Sounds funny to her.*] You remember that time I took you drivin' with me that night after you been in a fight an that soldier bought us a beer? Shitty place, hole in the wall?

ARLENE: You made me wait in the car.

MOTHER: [*Standing up.*] Think I'd take a child of mine into a dump like that?

ARLENE: You went in.

MOTHER: Weren't no harm in it. [*Walking over for the bug spray.*] I didn't always look so bad, you know.

ARLENE: You was pretty.

MOTHER: [*Beginning to spray the floor.*] You could look better'n you do. Do somethin' with your hair. I always thought if you'd looked better you wouldn't have got in so much trouble.

ARLENE: [*Pleased and curious.*] Joey got my hair?

MOTHER: And skinny.

ARLENE: I took some beauty school at Pine Ridge.

MOTHER: Yeah, a beautician?

ARLENE: I don't guess so.

MOTHER: Said you was gonna work.

ARLENE: They got a law here. Ex-cons can't get no license.

MOTHER: Shoulda stayed in Alabama, then. Worked there.

ARLENE: They got a law there, too.

MOTHER: Then why'd they give you the trainin'?

ARLENE: I don't know.

MOTHER: Maybe they thought it'd straighten you out.

ARLENE: Yeah.

MOTHER: But you are gonna work, right?

ARLENE: Yeah. Cookin' maybe. Somethin' that pays good.

MOTHER: You? Cook? [*Laughs.*]

ARLENE: I could learn it.

MOTHER: Your daddy ain't never forgive you for that bologna sandwich. [ARLENE *laughs a little, finally enjoying a memory.*] Oh, I wish I'd seen you spreadin' that Colgate on that bread. He'd have smelled that toothpaste if he hadn't been so sloshed. Little snotty-nosed kid tryin' to kill her daddy with a bologna sandwich. An him bein' so pleased when you brung it to him . . . [*Laughing.*]

ARLENE: He beat me good.

MOTHER: Well, now, Arlie, you gotta admit you had it comin' to you. [*Wiping tears from laughing.*]

ARLENE: I guess.

MOTHER: You got a broom?

ARLENE: No.

MOTHER: Well, I got one in the cab I brung just in case. I can't leave it here, but I'll sweep up fore I go. [*Walking toward the door.*] You jus' rest till I git back. Won't find no work lookin' the way you do.

[MOTHER *leaves.* ARLENE *finds some lipstick and a mirror in her purse, makes an attempt to look better while* MOTHER *is gone.*]

ARLIE: [*Jumps up, as if talking to another kid.*] She is not skinny!

ARLENE: [*Looking at herself in the mirror.*] I guess I could . . .

ARLIE: And she don't have to git them stinky permanents. Her hair just comes outta her head curly.

ARLENE: Some lipstick.

ARLIE: [*Serious.*] She drives the cab to buy us stuff, 'cause we don't take no charity from nobody, 'cause we got money 'cause she earned it.

ARLENE: [*Closing the mirror, dejected, afraid* MOTHER *might be right.*] But you're too skinny and you got stringy hair. [*Sitting on the floor.*]

ARLIE: [*More angry.*] She drives at night 'cause people needs rides at night. People goin' to see their friends that are sick, or people's cars broken down an they gotta get to work at the . . . nobody calls my mama a whore!

MOTHER: [*Coming back in with the broom.*] If I'd known you were gonna sweep up with your butt, I wouldn't have got this broom. Get up! [*Sweeps at* ARLENE *to get her to move.*]

ARLIE: You're gonna take that back or I'm gonna rip out all your ugly hair and stuff it down your ugly throat.

ARLENE: [*Tugging at her own hair.*] You still cut hair?

MOTHER: [*Noticing some spot on the floor.*] Gonna take a razor blade to get out this paint.

ARLENE: Nail polish.

ARLIE: Wanna know what I know about your mama? She's dyin'. Somethin's eatin' up her insides piece by piece, only she don't want you to know it.

MOTHER: [*Continuing to sweep.*] So, you're callin' yourself Arlene, now?

ARLENE: Yes.

MOTHER: Don't want your girlie name no more?

ARLENE: Somethin' like that.

MOTHER: They call you Arlene in prison?

ARLENE: Not at first when I was bein' hateful. Just my number then.

MOTHER: You always been hateful.

ARLENE: There was this chaplain, he called me Arlene from the first day he come to talk to me. Here, let me help you. [*She reaches for the broom.*]

MOTHER: I'll do it.

ARLENE: You kin rest.

MOTHER: Since when? [ARLENE *backs off.*] I ain't hateful, how come I got so many hateful kids? [*Sweeping harder now.*] Poor dumb-as-hell Pat, stealin' them wigs, Candy screwin' since day one, Pete cuttin' up ol' Mac down at the grocery, June sellin' dope like it was Girl Scout cookies, and you . . . thank God I can't remember it all.

ARLENE: [*A very serious request.*] Maybe I could come out on Sunday for . . . you still make that pot roast?

MOTHER: [*Now sweeping over by the picture of Jesus.*] That your picture?

ARLENE: That chaplain give it to me.

MOTHER: The one give you your "new name."

ARLENE: Yes.

MOTHER: It's crooked. [*Doesn't straighten it.*]

ARLENE: I liked those potatoes with no skins. An that ketchup squirter we had, jus' like in a real restaurant.

MOTHER: People that run them institutions now, they jus' don't know how to teach kids right. Let 'em run around an get in more trouble. They should get you up at the crack of dawn an set you to scrubbin' the floor. That's what kids need. Trainin'. Hard work.

ARLENE: [*A clear request.*] I'll probably git my Sundays off.

MOTHER: Sunday . . . is my day to clean house now.

[ARLENE *gets the message, finally walks over to straighten the picture.* MOTHER *now feels a little bad about this rejection, stops sweeping for a moment.*]

MOTHER: I woulda wrote you but I didn't have nuthin' to say. An no money to send, so what's the use?

ARLENE: I made out.

MOTHER: They pay you for workin'?

ARLENE: 'Bout three dollars a month.

MOTHER: How'd you make it on three dollars a month? [*Answers her own question.*] You do some favors?

ARLENE: [*Sitting down in the chair under the picture, a somewhat smug look.*] You jus' can't make it by yourself.

MOTHER: [*Pauses, suspicious, then contemptuous.*] You play, Arlie?

ARLENE: You don't know nuthin' about that.

MOTHER: I hear things. Girls callin' each other "mommy" an bringin' things back from the canteen for their "husbands." Makes me sick. You got family, Arlie, what you want with that playin'? Don't want nobody like that in my house.

ARLENE: You don't know what you're talkin' about.

MOTHER: I still got two kids at home. Don't want no bad example. [*Not finishing the sweeping. Has all the dirt in one place, but doesn't get it up off the floor yet.*]

ARLENE: I could tell them some things.

MOTHER: [*Vicious.*] Like about that cab driver.

ARLENE: Look, that was a long time ago. I wanna work, now, make somethin' of myself. I learned to knit. People'll buy nice sweaters. Make some extra money.

MOTHER: We sure could use it.

ARLENE: An then if I have money, maybe they'd let me take Joey to the fair, buy him hotdogs an talk to him. Make sure he ain't foolin' around.

MOTHER: What makes you think he'd listen to you? Alice, across the street? Her sister took care her kids while she was at Lexington. You think they pay any attention to her now? Ashamed, that's what. One of 'em told me his mother done died. Gone to see a friend and died there.

ARLENE: Be different with me and Joey.

MOTHER: He don't even know who you are, Arlie.

ARLENE: [*Wearily.*] Arlene.

MOTHER: You forgot already what you was like as a kid. At Waverly, tellin' them lies about that campin' trip we took, sayin' your daddy made you watch while he an me . . . you know. I'd have killed you then if them social workers hadn't been watchin'.

ARLENE: Yeah.

MOTHER: Didn't want them thinkin' I weren't fit. Well, what do they know?

Each time you'd get out of one of them places, you'd be actin' worse than ever. Go right back to that junkie, pimp, Carl, sellin' the stuff he steals, savin' his ass from the police. He follow you home this time, too?

ARLENE: He's got four more years at Bricktown.

MOTHER: Glad to hear it. Here . . . [*Handing her a bucket.*] Water.

[ARLENE *fills up the bucket and* MOTHER *washes several dirty spots on the walls, floor and furniture.* ARLENE *knows better than to try to help. The doctor walks downstage to find* ARLIE *for their counseling session.*]

DOCTOR: So you refuse to go to camp?

ARLIE: Now why'd I want to go to your fuckin' camp? Camp's for babies. You can go shit in the woods if you want to, but I ain't goin'.

DOCTOR: Oh, you're goin'.

ARLIE: Wanna bet?

MOTHER: Arlie, I'm waitin'. [*For the water.*]

ARLIE: 'Sides, I'm waitin'.

DOCTOR: Waiting for what?

ARLIE: For Carl to come git me.

DOCTOR: And who is Carl?

ARLIE: Jus' some guy. We're goin' to Alabama.

DOCTOR: You don't go till we say you can go.

ARLIE: Carl's got a car.

DOCTOR: Does he have a driver's license to go with it?

ARLIE: [*Enraged, impatient.*] I'm goin' now.

[ARLIE *stalks away, then backs up toward the* DOCTOR *again. He has information she wants.*]

DOCTOR: Hey!

ARLENE: June picked out a name for the baby?

MOTHER: Clara . . . or Clarence. Got it from this fancy shampoo she bought.

ARLIE: I don't feel good. I'm pregnant, you know.

DOCTOR: The test was negative.

ARLIE: Well, I should know, shouldn't I?

DOCTOR: No. You want to be pregnant, is that it?

ARLIE: I wouldn't mind. Kids need somebody to bring 'em up right.

DOCTOR: Raising children is a big responsibility, you know.

ARLIE: Yeah, I know it. I ain't dumb. Everybody always thinks I'm so dumb.

DOCTOR: You could learn if you wanted to. That's what the teachers are here for.

ARLIE: Shit.

DOCTOR: Or so they say.

ARLIE: All they teach us is about geography. Why'd I need to know about Africa. Jungles and shit.

DOCTOR: They want you to know about other parts of the world.

ARLIE: Well, I ain't goin' there so whatta I care?

DOCTOR: What's this about Cindy?

ARLIE: [*Hostile.*] She told Mr. Dawson some lies about me.

DOCTOR: I bet.

ARLIE: She said I fuck my daddy for money.

DOCTOR: And what did you do when she said that?

ARLIE: What do you think I did? I beat the shit out of her.

DOCTOR: And that's a good way to work out your problem?

ARLIE: [*Proudly.*] She ain't done it since.

DOCTOR: She's been in traction, since.

ARLIE: So, whatta I care? She say it again, I'll do it again. Bitch!

ARLENE: [*Looking down at the dirt* MOTHER *is gathering on the floor.*] I ain't got a can. Just leave it.

MOTHER: And have you sweep it under the bed after I go? [*Wraps the dirt in a piece of newspaper and puts it in her laundry basket.*]

DOCTOR: [*Looking at his clipboard.*] You're on unit cleanup this week.

ARLIE: I done it last week!

DOCTOR: Then you should remember what to do. The session is over. [*Getting up, walking away.*] And stand up straight! And take off that hat!

[DOCTOR *and* ARLIE *go offstage as* MOTHER *finds* BENNIE's *hat.*]

MOTHER: This your hat?

ARLENE: No.

MOTHER: Guess Candy left it here.

ARLENE: Candy didn't leave nuthin'.

MOTHER: Then whose is it? [ARLENE *doesn't answer.*] Do you know whose hat this is? [ARLENE *knows she made a mistake.*] I'm askin' you a question and I want an answer. [ARLENE *turns her back.*] Whose hat is this? You tell me right now, whose hat is this?

ARLENE: It's Bennie's.

MOTHER: And who's Bennie?

ARLENE: Guy drove me home from Pine Ridge. A guard.

MOTHER: [*Upset.*] I knew it. You been screwin' a goddamn guard. [*Throws the hat on the bed.*]

ARLENE: He jus' drove me up here, that's all.

MOTHER: Sure.

ARLENE: I git sick on the bus.

MOTHER: You expect me to believe that?

ARLENE: I'm tellin' you, he jus'—

MOTHER: No man alive gonna drive a girl five hundred miles for nuthin'.

ARLENE: He ain't never seen Kentucky.

MOTHER: It ain't Kentucky he wants to see.

ARLENE: He ain't gettin' nuthin' from me.

MOTHER: That's what you think.

ARLENE: He done some nice things for me at Pine Ridge. Gum, funny stories.

MOTHER: He'd be tellin' stories all right, tellin' his buddies where to find you.

ARLENE: He's gettin' us some dinner right now.

MOTHER: And how're you gonna pay him? Huh? Tell me that.

ARLENE: I ain't like that no more.

MOTHER: Oh you ain't. I'm your mother. I know what you'll do.

ARLENE: I tell you I ain't.

MOTHER: I knew it. Well, when you got another bastard in you, don't come cryin' to me, 'cause I done told you.

ARLENE: Don't worry.

MOTHER: An I'm gettin' myself outta here fore your boyfriend comes back.

ARLENE: [*Increasing anger.*] He ain't my boyfriend.

MOTHER: I been a lotta things, but I ain't dumb, Arlene. ["*Arlene*" *is mocking.*]

ARLENE: I didn't say you was. [*Beginning to know how this is going to turn out.*]

MOTHER: Oh no? You lied to me!

ARLENE: How?

MOTHER: You took my spread without even sayin' thank you. You're hintin' at comin' to my house for pot roast just like nuthin' ever happened, an all the time you're hidin' a goddamn guard under your bed. [*Furious.*] Uh-huh.

ARLENE: [*Quietly.*] Mama?

MOTHER: [*Cold, fierce.*] What?

ARLENE: What kind of meat makes a pot roast?

MOTHER: A roast makes a pot roast. Buy a roast. Shoulder, chuck . . .

ARLENE: Are you comin' back?

MOTHER: You ain't got no need for me.

ARLENE: I gotta ask you to come see me?

MOTHER: I come tonight, didn't I, an nobody asked me?

ARLENE: Just forget it.

MOTHER: [*Getting her things together.*] An if I hadn't told them about this apartment, you wouldn't be out at all, how 'bout that!

ARLENE: Forget it!

MOTHER: Don't you go talkin' to me that way. You remember who I am. I'm the one took you back after all you done all them years. I brung you that teapot. I scrubbed your place. You remember that when you talk to me.

ARLENE: Sure.

MOTHER: Uh-huh. [*Now goes to the bed, rips off the spread and stuffs it in her basket.*] I knowed I shouldn't have come. You ain't changed a bit.

ARLENE: Same hateful brat, right?

MOTHER: [*Arms full, heading for the door.*] Same hateful brat. Right.

ARLENE: [*Rushing toward her.*] Mama . . .

MOTHER: Don't you touch me.

[MOTHER *leaves.* ARLENE *stares out the door, stunned and hurt. Finally, she slams the door and turns back into the room.*]

ARLENE: No! Don't you touch Mama, Arlie.

[RONNIE, *a fellow juvenile offender, runs across the catwalk, waving a necklace and being chased by* ARLIE.]

RONNIE: Arlie got a boyfriend, Arlie got a boyfriend. [*Throws the necklace downstage.*] Whoo!

ARLIE: [*Chasing him.*] Ronnie, you ugly mother, I'll smash your fuckin' —

ARLENE: [*Getting more angry.*] You might steal all —

RONNIE: [*Running down the stairs.*] Arlie got a boyfriend . . .

ARLIE: Gimme that necklace or I'll —

ARLENE: — or eat all Mama's precious pot roast.

RONNIE: [*As they wrestle downstage.*] You'll tell the doctor on me? And get your private room back? [*Laughing.*]

ARLENE: [*Cold and hostile.*] No, don't touch Mama, Arlie. 'Cause you might slit Mama's throat. [*Goes into the bathroom.*]

ARLIE: You wanna swallow all them dirty teeth?

RONNIE: Tell me who give it to you.

ARLIE: No, you tell me where it's at.

[RONNIE *breaks away, pushing* ARLIE *in the opposite direction, and runs for the necklace.*]

RONNIE: It's right here. [*Drops it down his pants.*] Come an git it.

ARLIE: Oh now, that was really ignorant, you stupid pig.

RONNIE: [*Backing away, daring her.*] Jus' reach right in. First come, first served.

ARLIE: Now, how you gonna pee after I throw your weenie over the fence?

RONNIE: You ain't gonna do that, girl. You gonna fall in love.

[ARLIE *turns vicious, pins* RONNIE *down, attacking. This is no longer play. He screams. The* DOCTOR *appears on the catwalk.*]

DOCTOR: Arlie! [*Heads down the stairs to stop this.*]

CARL'S VOICE: [*From outside the apartment door.*] Arlie!

DOCTOR: Arlie!

ARLIE: Stupid, ugly —

RONNIE: Help!

[ARLIE *runs away and hides down left.*]

DOCTOR: That's three more weeks of isolation, Arlie. [*Bending down to* RONNIE.] You all right? Can you walk?

RONNIE: [*Looking back to* ARLIE *as he gets up in great pain.*] She was tryin' to kill me.

DOCTOR: Yeah. Easy now. You should've known, Ronnie.

ARLIE: [*Yelling at* RONNIE.] You'll get yours, crybaby.

CARL'S VOICE: Arlie . . .

ARLIE: Yeah, I'm comin'!

CARL'S VOICE: Bad-lookin' dude says move your ass an open up this here door, girl.

[ARLENE *does not come out of the bathroom.* CARL *twists the door knob violently, then kicks in the door and walks in.* CARL *is thin and cheaply dressed.* CARL's *walk and manner are imitative of black pimps, but he can't quite carry it off.*]

CARL: Where you at, mama?

ARLENE: Carl?

CARL: Who else? You 'spectin' Leroy Brown?

ARLENE: I'm takin' a bath!

CARL: [*Walking toward the bathroom.*] I like my ladies clean. Matter of professional pride.

ARLENE: Don't come in here.

CARL: [*Mocking her tone.*] Don't come in here. I seen it all before, girl.

ARLENE: I'm gittin' out. Sit down or somethin'.

CARL: [*Talking loud enough for her to hear him through the door.*] Ain't got the time. [*Opens her purse, then searches the trunk.*] Jus' come by to tell you it's tomorrow. We be takin' our feet to the New York street. [*As though she will be pleased.*] No more fuckin' around with these jiveass southern turkeys. We're goin' to the big city, baby. Get you some red shades and some red shorts an' the johns be linin' up fore we hit town. Four tricks a night. How's that sound? No use wearin' out that cute ass you got. Way I hear it, only way to git busted up there's be stupid, an I ain't lived this long bein' stupid.

ARLENE: [*Coming out of the bathroom wearing a towel.*] That's exactly how you lived your whole life—bein' stupid.

CARL: Arlie . . . [*Moving in on her.*] be sweet, sugar.

ARLENE: Still got your curls.

CARL: [*Trying to hug her.*] You're looking okay yourself.

ARLENE: Oh, Carl. [*Noticing the damage to the door, breaking away from any closeness he might try to force.*]

CARL: [*Amused.*] Bent up your door, some.

ARLENE: How come you're out?

CARL: Sweetheart, you done broke out once, been nabbed and sent to Pine Ridge and got yourself paroled since I been in. I got a right to a little free time too, ain't that right?

ARLENE: You escape?

CARL: Am I standin' here or am I standin' here? They been fuckin' with you, I can tell.

ARLENE: They gonna catch you.

CARL: [*Going to the window.*] Not where we're going. Not a chance.

ARLENE: Where you goin' they won't git you?

CARL: Remember that green hat you picked out for me down in Birmingham? Well, I ain't ever wore it yet, but I kin wear it in New York 'cause New York's where you wear whatever you feel like. One guy tol' me he saw this dude wearin' a whole ring of feathers roun' his leg, right here [*Grabs his leg above the knee.*] an he weren't in no circus nor no Indian neither.

ARLENE: I ain't seen you since Birmingham. How come you think I wanna see you now?

[ARLIE *appears suddenly, confronts* CARL.]

ARLIE: [*Pointing as if there is a trick waiting.*] Carl, I ain't goin' with that dude, he's weird.

CARL: 'Cause we gotta go collect the johns' money, that's "how come."

ARLIE: I don't need you pimpin' for me.

ARLENE: [*Very strong.*] I'm gonna work.

CARL: Work?

ARLENE: Yeah.

CARL: What's this "work"?

ARLIE: You always sendin' me to them ol' droolers . . .

CARL: You kin do two things, girl —

ARLIE: They slobberin' all over me . . .

CARL: Breakin' out an hookin'.

ARLIE: They tyin' me to the bed!

ARLENE: I mean real work.

ARLIE: [*Now screaming, gets further away from him.*] I could git killed working for you. Some sicko, some crazy drunk . . .

[ARLIE *goes offstage. A* GUARD *puts her in the cell sometime before* BENNIE's *entrance.*]

CARL: You forget, we seen it all on TV in the day room, you bustin' outta Lakewood like that. Fakin' that palsy fit, then beatin' that guard half to death with his own key ring. Whoo-ee! Then that spree you went on . . . stoppin' at that fillin' station for some cash, then kidnappin' the old dude pumpin' the gas.

ARLENE: Yeah.

CARL: Then that cab driver comes outta the bathroom an tries to mess with you and you shoots him with his own piece. [*Fires an imaginary pistol.*] That there's nice work, mama. [*Going over to her, putting his arms around her.*]

ARLENE: That gun . . . it went off, Carl.

CARL: [*Getting more determined with his affection.*] That's what guns do, doll. They go off.

BENNIE'S VOICE: [*From outside.*] Arlene? Arlene?

CARL: Arlene? [*Jumping up.*] Well, la-de-da.

[BENNIE *opens the door, carrying the chicken dinners. He is confused, seeing* ARLENE *wearing a towel and talking to* CARL.]

ARLENE: Bennie, this here's Carl.

CARL: You're interruptin', Jack. Me an Arlie got business.

BENNIE: She's callin' herself Arlene.

CARL: I call my ladies what I feel like, chicken man, an you call yourself "gone."

BENNIE: I don't take orders from you.

CARL: Well, you been takin' orders from somebody, or did you git that outfit at the army surplus store?

ARLENE: Bennie brung me home from Pine Ridge.

CARL: [*Walking toward him.*] Oh, it's a guard now, is it? That chicken break out or what? [*Grabs the chicken.*]

BENNIE: I don't know what you're doin' here, but —

CARL: What you gonna do about it, huh? Lock me up in the toilet? You an who else, Batman?

BENNIE: [*Taking the chicken back, walking calmly to the counter.*] Watch your mouth, punk.

CARL: [*Kicks a chair toward* BENNIE.] Punk!

ARLENE: [*Trying to stop this.*] I'm hungry.

BENNIE: You heard her, she's hungry.

CARL: [*Vicious.*] Shut up! [*Mocking.*] Ossifer.

BENNIE: Arlene, tell this guy if he knows what's good for him . . .

CARL: [*Walking to the counter where* BENNIE *has left the chicken.*] Why don't you write me a parkin' ticket? [*Shoves the chicken on the floor.*] Don't fuck with me, dad. It ain't healthy.

[BENNIE *pauses. A real standoff. Finally,* BENNIE *bends down and picks up the chicken.*]

BENNIE: You ain't worth dirtyin' my hands.

[CARL *walks by him, laughing.*]

CARL: Hey, Arlie. I got some dude to see. [*For* BENNIE's *benefit as he struts to the door.*] What I need with another beat-up guard? All that blood, jus' ugly up my threads. [*Very sarcastic.*] Bye y'all.

ARLENE: Bye, Carl.

[CARL *turns back quickly at the door, stopping* BENNIE, *who was following him.*]

CARL: You really oughta shine them shoes, man. [*Vindictive laugh, slams the door in* BENNIE's *face.*]

BENNIE: [*Relieved, trying to change the atmosphere.*] Well, how 'bout if we eat? You'll catch your death dressed like that.

ARLENE: Turn around then.

[ARLENE *gets a shabby housecoat from the closet. She puts it on over her towel, buttons it up, then pulls the towel out from under it. This has the look of a prison ritual.*]

BENNIE: [*As she is dressing.*] Your parole officer's gonna tell you to keep away from guys like that . . . for your own good, you know. Those types, just like the suckers on my tomatoes back home. Take everything right outta you. Gotta pull 'em off, Arlie, uh, Arlene.

ARLENE: Now, I'm decent now.

BENNIE: You hear what I said?

ARLENE: [*Going to the bathroom for her hairbrush.*] I told him that. That's exactly what I did tell him.

BENNIE: Who was that anyhow? [*Sits down on the bed, opens up the chicken.*]

ARLENE: [*From the bathroom.*] Long time ago, me an Carl took a trip together.

BENNIE: When you was a kid, you mean?

ARLENE: I was at this place for kids.

BENNIE: And Carl was there?

ARLENE: No, he picked me up an we went to Alabama. There was this wreck an all. I ended up at Lakewood for forgery. It was him that done it. Got me pregnant too.

BENNIE: That was Joey's father?

ARLENE: Yeah, but he don't know that. [*Sits down.*]

BENNIE: Just as well. Guy like that, don't know what they'd do.

ARLENE: Mother was here while ago. Says she's seen Joey. [*Taking a napkin from* BENNIE.]

BENNIE: Wish I had a kid. Life ain't, well, complete, without no kids to play ball with an take fishin'. Dorrie, though, she had them backaches an that neuralgia, day I married her to the day she died. Good woman though. No drinkin', no card playin', real sweet voice . . . what was that song she used to sing? . . . Oh, yeah . . .

ARLENE: She says Joey's a real good-lookin' kid.

BENNIE: Well, his mom ain't bad.

ARLENE: At Lakewood, they tried to git me to have an abortion.

BENNIE: They was just thinkin' of you, Arlene.

ARLENE: [*Matter-of-fact, no self-pity.*] I told 'em I'd kill myself if they done that. I would have too.

BENNIE: But they took him away after he was born.

ARLENE: Yeah. [BENNIE *waits, knowing she is about to say more.*] An I guess I went crazy after that. Thought if I could jus' git out an find him . . .

BENNIE: I don't remember any of that on the TV.

ARLENE: No.

BENNIE: Just remember you smilin' at the cameras, yellin' how you tol' that cab driver not to touch you.

ARLENE: I never seen his cab. [*Forces herself to eat.*]

ARLIE: [*In the cell, holding a pillow and singing.*] Rock-a-bye baby, in the tree top, when the wind blows, the cradle will . . . [*Not remembering.*] cradle will . . . [*Now talking.*] What you gonna be when you grow up, pretty boy baby? You gonna be a doctor? You gonna give people medicine an take out they . . . no, don't be no doctor . . . be . . . be a preacher . . . sayin' Our Father who is in heaven . . . heaven, that's where people go when they dies, when doctors can't save 'em or somebody kills 'em fore they even git a chance to . . . no, don't be no preacher neither . . . be . . . go to school an learn good [*Tone begins to change.*] so you kin . . . make everybody else feel so stupid all the time. Best thing you to be is stay a baby 'cause nobody beats up on babies or puts them . . . [*Much more quiet.*] that ain't true, baby. People is mean to babies, so you stay right here with me so nobody kin git you an make you cry an they lay one finger on you [*Hostile.*] an I'll beat the screamin' shit right out of 'em. They even blow on you an I'll kill 'em.

[BENNIE *and* ARLENE *have finished their dinner.* BENNIE *puts one carton of slaw in the refrigerator, then picks up all the paper, making a garbage bag out of one of the sacks.*]

BENNIE: Ain't got a can, I guess. Jus' use this ol' sack for now.

ARLENE: I ain't never emptyin' another garbage can.

BENNIE: Yeah, I reckon you know how by now. [*Yawns.*] You 'bout ready for bed?

ARLENE: [*Stands up.*] I s'pose.

BENNIE: [*Stretches.*] Little tired myself.

ARLENE: [*Dusting the crumbs off the bed.*] Thanks for the chicken.

BENNIE: You're right welcome. You look beat. How 'bout I rub your back. [*Grabs her shoulders.*]

ARLENE: [*Pulling away.*] No. [*Walking to the sink.*] You go on now.

BENNIE: Oh come on. [*Wiping his hands on his pants.*] I ain't all that tired.

ARLENE: *I'm* tired.

BENNIE: Well, see then, a back rub is just what the doctor ordered.

ARLENE: No. I don't . . . [*Pulling away.*]

[BENNIE *grabs her shoulders and turns her around, sits her down hard on the trunk, starts rubbing her back and neck.*]

BENNIE: Muscles git real tightlike, right in here.

ARLENE: You hurtin' me.

BENNIE: Has to hurt a little or it won't do no good.

ARLENE: [*Jumps, he has hurt her.*] Oh, stop it! [*She slips away from him and out into the room. She is frightened.*]

BENNIE: [*Smiling, coming after her, toward the bed.*] Be lot nicer if you was layin' down. Wouldn't hurt as much.

ARLENE: Now, I ain't gonna start yellin'. I'm jus' tellin' you to go.

BENNIE: [*Straightens up as though he's going to cooperate.*] Okay then. I'll jus' git my hat.

[*He reaches for the hat, then turns quickly, grabs her and throws her down on the bed. He starts rubbing again.*]

BENNIE: Now, you just relax. Don't you go bein' scared of me.

ARLENE: You ain't gettin' nuthin' from me.

BENNIE: I don't want nuthin', honey. Jus' tryin' to help you sleep.

ARLENE: [*Struggling.*] Don't you call me honey.

[BENNIE *stops rubbing, but keeps one hand on her back. He rubs her hair with his free hand.*]

BENNIE: See? Don't that feel better?

ARLENE: Let me up.

BENNIE: Why, I ain't holdin' you down.

ARLENE: Then let me up.

BENNIE: [*Takes hands off.*] Okay. Git up.

[ARLENE *turns over slowly, begins to lift herself up on her elbows.* BENNIE *puts one hand on her leg.*]

ARLENE: Move your hand. [*She gets up, moves across the room.*]

BENNIE: I'd be happy to stay here with you tonight. Make sure you'll be all right. You ain't spent a night by yourself for a long time.

ARLENE: I remember how.

BENNIE: Well how you gonna git up? You got a alarm?

ARLENE: It ain't all that hard.

BENNIE: [*Puts one hand in his pocket, leers a little.*] Oh yeah it is. [*Walks toward her again.*] Gimme a kiss. Then I'll go.

ARLENE: [*Edging along the counter, seeing she's trapped.*] You stay away from me.

[BENNIE *reaches for her, clamping her hands behind her, pressing up against her.*]

BENNIE: Now what's it going to hurt you to give me a little ol' kiss?

ARLENE: [*Struggling.*] Git out! I said git out!

BENNIE: You don't want me to go. You're jus' beginning to git interested. Your ol' girlie temper's flarin' up. I like that in a woman.

ARLENE: Yeah, you'd love it if I'd swat you one. [*Getting away from him.*]

BENNIE: I been hit by you before. I kin take anything you got.

ARLENE: I could mess you up good.

BENNIE: Now, Arlie, You ain't had a man in a long time. And the ones you had been no-count.

ARLENE: Git out!

[*She slaps him. He returns the slap.*]

BENNIE: [*Moving in.*] Ain't natural goin' without it too long. Young thing like you. Git all shriveled up.

ARLENE: All right, you sunuvabitch, you asked for it!

[*She goes into a violent rage, hitting and kicking him.* BENNIE *overpowers her capably, prison-guard style.*]

BENNIE: [*Amused.*] Little outta practice, ain't you?

ARLENE: [*Screaming.*] I'll kill you, you creep!

[*The struggle continues,* BENNIE *pinning her arms under his legs as he kneels over her on the bed.* ARLENE *is terrified and in pain.*]

BENNIE: You will? You kill ol' Bennie . . . kill ol' Bennie like you done that cab driver?

[*A cruel reminder he employs to stun and mock her.* ARLENE *looks as though she has been hit.* BENNIE, *still fired up, unzips his pants.*]

ARLENE: [*Passive, cold and bitter.*] This how you got your Dorrie, rapin'?

BENNIE: [*Unbuttoning his shirt.*] That what you think this is, rape?

ARLENE: I oughta know.

BENNIE: Uh-huh.

ARLENE: First they unzip their pants.

[BENNIE *pulls his shirttail out.*]

ARLENE: Sometimes they take off their shirt.

BENNIE: They do huh?

ARLENE: But mostly, they just pull it out and stick it in.

BENNIE *stops, finally hearing what she has been saying. He straightens up, obviously shocked. He puts his arms back in his shirt.*]

BENNIE: Don't you call me no rapist. [*Pause, then insistent.*] No, I ain't no rapist, Arlie. [*Gets up, begins to tuck his shirt back in and zip up his pants.*]

ARLENE: And I ain't Arlie.

[ARLENE *remains on the bed as he continues dressing.*]

BENNIE: No I guess you ain't.

ARLENE: [*Quietly and painfully.*] Arlie coulda killed you.

END OF ACT I

PROLOGUE

These announcements are heard during the last five minutes of the intermission.

LOUDSPEAKER VOICE: Garden workers will, repeat, will, report for work this afternoon. Bring a hat and raincoat and wear boots. All raincoats will be checked at the front gate at the end of work period and returned to you after supper.

Your attention please. A checkerboard was not returned to the recreation area after dinner last night. Anyone with information regarding the black and red checkerboard missing from the recreation area will please contact Mrs. Duvall after lunch. No checkerboards or checkers will be distributed until this board is returned.

Betty Rickey and Mary Alice Wolf report to the laundry. Doris Creech and Arlie Holsclaw report immediately to the superintendent's office. The movie this evening will be *Dirty Harry* starring Clint Eastwood. Doris Creech and Arlie Holsclaw report to the superintendent's office immediately.

The bus from St. Mary's this Sunday will arrive at 1:00 P.M. as usual. Those residents expecting visitors on that bus will gather on the front steps promptly at 1:20 and proceed with the duty officer to the visiting area after it has been confirmed that you have a visitor on the bus.

Attention all residents. Attention all residents. [*Pause.*] Mrs. Helen Carson has taught needlework classes here at Pine Ridge for thirty years. She will be retiring at the end of this month and moving to Florida where her husband has bought a trailer park. The resident council and the superintendent's staff has decided on a suitable retirement present. We want every resident to participate in this project—which is—a quilt, made from scraps of material collected from the residents and sewn together by residents and staff alike. The procedure will be as follows. A quilting room has been set up in an empty storage area just off the infirmary. Scraps of fabric will be collected as officers do evening count. Those residents who would enjoy cutting up old uniforms and bedding no longer in use should sign up for this detail with your dorm officer. If you would like to sign your name or send Mrs. Carson some special message on your square of fabric, the officers will of have tubes of embroidery paint for that purpose. The backing for the quilt has been donated by the Women's Associates as well as the refreshments for the retirement party to be held after lunch on the thirtieth. Thank you very much for your attention and participation in this worthwhile tribute to someone we are all fond of here. You may resume work at this time. Doris Creech and Arlie Holsclaw report to the superintendent's office immediately.

ACT II

Lights fade. When they come up, it is the next morning. ARLENE *is asleep on the bed.* ARLIE *is locked in a maximum-security cell. We do not see the officer to whom she speaks.*

ARLIE: No, I don't have to shut up, neither. You already got me in seg-re-ga-tion, what else you gonna do? I got all day to sleep, while everybody else is out bustin' ass in the laundry. [*Laughs.*] Hey! I know . . . you ain't gotta go do no dorm count, I'll just tell you an you jus' sit. Huh? You 'preciate that? Ease them corns you been moanin' about . . . yeah . . . okay. Write this down. [*Pride, mixed with alternating contempt and amusement.*] Startin' down by the john on the back side, we got Mary Alice. Sleeps with her pillow stuffed in her mouth. Says her mom says it'd keep her from grindin' down her teeth or somethin'. She be suckin' that pillow like she gettin' paid for it. [*Laughs.*] Next, it's Betty the Frog. Got her legs all opened out like some fuckin' . . . [*Makes croaking noises.*] Then it's Doris eatin' pork rinds. Thinks somebody gonna grab 'em outta her mouth if she eats 'em during the day. Doris ain't dumb. She fat, but she ain't dumb. Hey! You notice how many girls is fat here? Then it be Rhonda, snoring', Marvene, wheezin', and Suzanne, coughin'. Then Clara an Ellie be still whisperin'. Family shit, who's gettin' outta line, which girls is gittin' a new work 'signment, an who kin git extra desserts an for how much. Them's the two really run this place. My bed right next to Ellie, for sure it's got some of her shit hid in it by now. Crackers or some crap gonna leak out all over my sheets. Last time I found a fuckin' grilled cheese in my pillow. Even had two of them little warty pickles. Christ! Okay. Linda and Lucille. They be real quite, but they ain't sleppin'. Prayin', that's them. Linda be sayin' them Hell Marys till you kin just about scream. An Lucille, she tol' me once she didn't believe in no God, jus' some stupid spirits whooshin' aroun' everwhere makin' people do stuff. Weird. Now, I'm goin' back down the other side there's . . . [*Screams.*] I'd like to see you try it! I been listenin' at you for the last three hours. Your husband's gettin' laid off an your lettuce is gettin' eat by rabbits. Crap City. *You* shut up! Whadda

I care if I wake everybody up? I want the nurse . . . I'm gettin' sick in here . . . an there's bugs in here!

[*The light comes up in the apartment. Faint morning traffic sounds are heard.* ARLENE *does not wake up. The* WARDEN *walks across the catwalk. A* GUARD *catches up with him near* ARLIE's *cell.* BENNIE *is stationed at the far end of the walk.*]

LOUDSPEAKER VOICE: Dorm A may now eat lunch.

GUARD (EVANS): Warden, I thought 456 . . . [*Nodding in* ARLIE's *direction.*] was leavin' here.

WARDEN: Is there some problem?

GUARD (EVANS): Oh, we can take care of her all right. We're just tired of takin' her shit, if you'll pardon the expression.

ARLIE: You ain't seen nuthin' yet, you mother.

WARDEN: Washington will decide on her transfer. Till then, you do your job.

GUARD (EVANS): She don't belong her. Rest of—

LOUDSPEAKER VOICE: Betty Rickey and Mary Alice Wolf report to the laundry.

GUARD (EVANS): Most of these girls are mostly nice people, go along with things. She needs a cage.

ARLIE: [*Vicious.*] I need a knife.

WARDEN: [*Very curt.*] Had it occurred to you that we could send the rest of them home and just keep her? [*Walks away.*]

LOUDSPEAKER VOICE: Dorm A may now eat lunch. A Dorm to lunch.

GUARD (EVANS): [*Turning around, muttering to himself.*] Oh, that's a swell idea. Let everybody out except bitches like Holsclaw. [*She makes an obscene gesture at him, he turns back toward the catwalk.*] Smartass warden, thinks he's runnin' a hotel.

BENNIE: Give you some trouble, did she?

GUARD (EVANS): I can wait.

BENNIE: For what?

GUARD (EVANS): For the day she tries gettin' out an I'm here by myself. I'll show that screechin' slut a thing or two.

BENNIE: That ain't the way, Evans.

GUARD (EVANS): The hell it ain't. Beat the livin'—

BENNIE: Outta a little thing like her? Gotta do her like all the rest. You got your shorts washed by givin' Betty Rickey Milky Ways. You git your chairs fixed givin' Frankie Hill extra time in the shower with Lucille Smith. An you git ol' Arlie girl to behave herself with a stick of gum. Gotta have her brand, though.

GUARD (EVANS): You screwin' that wildcat?

BENNIE: [*Starts walk to* ARLIE's *cell.*] Watch. [ARLIE *is silent as he approaches, but is watching intently.*] Now, [*To nobody in particular.*] where was that piece of Juicy Fruit I had in this pocket. Gotta be here somewhere. [*Takes a piece of gum out of his pocket and drops it within* ARLIE's *reach.*] Well, [*Feigning disappointment.*] I guess I already chewed it. [ARLIE *reaches for the gum and gets it.*] Oh, [*Looking down at her now.*] how's it goin', kid?

ARLIE: Okay.

[ARLIE *says nothing more, but unwraps the gum and chews it.* BENNIE *leaves the cell area, motioning to the other* GUARD *as if to say, "See, that's how it's done." A loud siren goes by in the street below the apartment.* ARLENE *bolts up out of bed, then turns back to it quickly, making it up in a frenzied, ritual manner. As she tucks the spread up under the pillow, the siren stops and so does she. For the first time, now, she realizes where she is and the inappropriateness of the habit she has just played out. A jackhammer noise gets louder. She walks over to the window and looks out. There is a wolf-whistle from a worker below. She shuts the window in a fury. She looks around the room as if trying to remember what she is doing there. She looks at her watch, now aware that it is late and that she has slept in her clothes.*]

ARLENE: People don't sleep in their clothes, Arlene. An people git up fore noon.

[ARLENE *makes a still-disoriented attempt to pull herself together—changing shoes, combing her hair, washing her face—as prison life continues on the catwalk. The* WARDEN *walks toward* ARLIE, *stopping some distance from her but talking directly to her, as he checks files or papers.*]

WARDEN: Good afternoon, Arlie.
ARLIE: Fuck you. [WARDEN *walks away.*] Wait! I wanna talk to you.
WARDEN: I'm listening.
ARLIE: When am I gittin' outta here?
WARDEN: That's up to you.
ARLIE: The hell it is.
WARDEN: When you can show that you can be with the other girls, you can get out.
ARLIE: How'm I supposed to prove that bein' in here?
WARDEN: And then you can have mail again and visitors.
ARLIE: You're just fuckin' with me. You ain't ever gonna let me out. I been in this ad-just-ment room four months, I think.
WARDEN: Arlie, you see the other girls in the dorm walking around, free to do whatever they want? If we felt the way you seem to think we do, everyone would be in lockup. When you get out of segregation, you can go to the records office and have your time explained to you.
ARLIE: It won't make no sense.
WARDEN: They'll go through it all very slowly . . . when you're eligible for parole, how many days of good time you have, how many industrial days you've earned, what constitutes meritorious good time . . . and how many days you're set back for your write-ups and all your time in segregation.
ARLIE: I don't even remember what I done to git this lockup.
WARDEN: Well, I do. And if you ever do it again, or anything like it again, you'll be right back in lockup where you will stay until you forget *how* to do it.
ARLIE: What was it?
WARDEN: You just remember what I said.
ARLENE: Now then . . . [*Sounds as if she has something in mind to do. Looks as though she doesn't.*]
ARLIE: What was it?

WARDEN: Oh, and Arlie, the prison chaplain will be coming by to visit you today.
ARLIE: I don't want to see no chaplain!
WARDEN: Did I ask you if you wanted to see the chaplain? No, I did not. I said, the chaplain will be coming by to visit you today. [*To an unseen guard.*] Mrs. Roberts, why hasn't this light bulb been replaced?
ARLIE: [*Screaming.*] Get out of my hall!

[*The* WARDEN *walks away.* ARLENE *walks to the refrigerator and opens it. She picks out the carton of slaw* BENNIE *put there last night. She walks away from the door, then turns around, remembering to close it. She looks at the slaw, as a* GUARD *comes up to* ARLIE'*s cell with a plate.*]

ARLENE: I ain't never eatin' no more scrambled eggs.
GUARD (CALDWELL): Chow time, cutie pie.
ARLIE: These eggs ain't scrambled, they's throwed up! And I want a fork!

[ARLENE *realizes she has no fork, then fishes one out of the garbage sack from last night. She returns to the bed, takes a bite of slaw and gets her wallet out of her purse. She lays the bills out on the bed one at a time.*]

ARLENE: That's for coffee . . . and that's for milk and bread . . . an that's cookies . . . an cheese and crackers . . . and shampoo an soap . . . and bacon an livercheese. No, pickle loaf . . . an ketchup and some onions . . . an peanut butter an jelly . . . and shoe polish. Well, ain't no need gettin' everything all at once. Coffee, milk, ketchup, cookies, cheese, onions, jelly. Coffee, milk . . . oh, shampoo . . .
[*There is a banging on the door.*]

RUBY'S VOICE: [*Yelling.*] Candy, I gotta have my five dollars back.
ARLENE: [*Quickly stuffing her money back in her wallet.*] Candy ain't here!
RUBY'S VOICE: It's Ruby, upstairs. She's got five dollars I loaned her . . . Arlie? That Arlie? Candy told me her sister be . . . .
[ARLENE *opens the door hesitantly.*]

RUBY: It is Arlie, right?
ARLENE: It's Arlene. [*Does not extend her hand.*]
RUBY: See, I got these shoes in layaway . . .[*Puts her hand back in her pocket.*] she said you been . . . you just got . . . you seen my money?
ARLENE: No
RUBY: I don't get 'em out today they go back on the shelf.
ARLENE: [*Doesn't understand.*] They sell your shoes?
RUBY: Yeah. Welcome back.
ARLENE: Thank you.
RUBY: She coulda put it in my mailbox.

[RUBY *starts to leave.* ARLENE *is closing the door when* RUBY *turns around.*]

RUBY: Uh . . . listen . . . if you need a phone, I got one most of the time.
ARLENE: I do have to make this call.

RUBY: Ain't got a book though . . . well, I got one but it's holdin' up my bed. [*Laughs.*]

ARLENE: I got the number.

RUBY: Well, then . . .

ARLENE: Would you . . . wanna come in?

RUBY: You sure I'm not interruptin' anything?

ARLENE: I'm s'posed to call my parole officer.

RUBY: Good girl. Most of them can't talk but you call 'em anyway. [ARLENE *does not laugh.*] Candy go back to that creep?

ARLENE: I guess.

RUBY: I's afraid of that. [*Looking around.*] Maybe an envelope with my name on it? Really cleaned out the place, didn't she?

ARLENE: Yeah. Took everything.

[*They laugh a little.*]

RUBY: Didn't have much. Didn't do nuthin' here 'cept . . . sleep.

ARLENE: Least the rent's paid till the end of the month. I'll be workin' by then.

RUBY: You ain't seen Candy in a while.

ARLENE: No. Think she was in the seventh grade when—

RUBY: She's growed up now, you know.

ARLENE: Yeah. I was thinkin' she might come by.

RUBY: Honey, she won't be comin' by. He keeps all his . . . [*Starting over.*] his place is pretty far from here. But . . . [*Stops, trying to decide what to say.*]

ARLENE: But what?

RUBY: But she had a lot of friends, you know. *They* might be comin' by.

ARLENE: Men, you mean.

RUBY: Yeah. [*Quietly, waiting for* ARLENE'S *reaction.*]

ARLENE: [*Realizing the truth.*] Mother said he was her boyfriend.

RUBY: I shouldn't have said nuthin'. I jus' didn't want you to be surprised if some john showed up, his tongue hangin' out an all. [*Sits down on the bed.*]

ARLENE: It's okay. I shoulda known anyway. [*Now suddenly angry.*] No, it ain't okay. Guys got their dirty fingernails all over her. Some pimp's out buyin' green pants while she . . . Goddamn her.

RUBY: Hey now, that ain't your problem. [*Moves toward her,* ARLENE *backs away.*]

ARLIE: [*Pointing.*] You stick your hand in here again Doris an I'll bit it off.

RUBY: She'll figure it out soon enough.

ARLIE: [*Pointing to another person.*] An you, you ain't my mama, so you can cut the mama crap.

ARLENE: I wasn't gonna cuss no more.

RUBY: Nuthin' in the parole rules says you can't get pissed. My first day outta Gilbertsville I done the damn craziest . . . [ARLENE *looks around, surprised to hear she has done time.*] Oh yeah, a long time ago, but . . . hell, I heaved a whole gallon of milk right out the window my first day.

ARLENE: [*Somewhat cheered.*] It hit anybody?

RUBY: It bounced! Made me fell a helluva lot better. I said, "Ruby, if a gallon of milk can bounce back, so kin you."

ARLENE: That's really what you thought?

RUBY: Well, not exactly. I had to keep sayin' it for 'bout a year fore I finally believed it. I's moppin' this lady's floor once an she come in an heard me sayin' "gallon a milk, gallon a milk," fired me. She did. Thought I was too crazy to mop her floors.

[RUBY *laughs, but is still bitter.* ARLENE *wasn't listening.* RUBY *wants to change the subject now.*]

RUBY: Hey! You have a good trip? Candy said you was in Arkansas.

ARLENE: Alabama. It was okay. This guard, well he used to be a guard, he just quit. He ain't never seen Kentucky, so he drove me. [*Watching for* RUBY'S *response.*]

RUBY: Pine Ridge?

ARLENE: Yeah.

RUBY: It's coed now, ain't it?

ARLENE: Yeah. That's dumb, you know. They put you with men so's they can git you if you're seen with 'em.

RUBY: S'posed to be more natural, I guess.

ARLENE: I guess.

RUBY: Well, I say it sucks. Still a prison. No matter how many pictures they stick up on the walls or how many dirty movies they show, you still gotta be counted five times a day. [*Now beginning to worry about* ARLENE'S *silence.*] You don't seem like Candy said.

ARLENE: She tell you I was a killer?

RUBY: More like the meanest bitch that ever walked. I seen lots worse than you.

ARLENE: I been lots worse.

RUBY: Got to you, didn't it?

[ARLENE *doesn't respond, but* RUBY *knows she's right.*]

RUBY: Well, you jus' gotta git over it. Bein' out, you gotta—

ARLENE: Don't you start in on me.

RUBY: [*Realizing her tone.*] Right, sorry.

ARLENE: It's okay.

RUBY: Ex-cons is the worst. I'm sorry.

ARLENE: It's okay.

RUBY: Done that about a year ago. New waitress we had. Gave my little goin'-straight speech, "No booze, no men, no buyin' on credit," shit like that, she quit that very night. Stole my fuckin' raincoat on her way out. Some speech, huh? [*Laughs, no longer resenting this theft.*]

ARLENE: You a waitress?

RUBY: I am the Queen of Grease. Make the finest french fries you ever did see.

ARLENE: You make a lot of money?

RUBY: I sure know how to. But I ain't about to go back inside for doin' it. Cookin' out's better'n eatin' in, I say.

ARLENE: You think up all these things you say?

RUBY: Know what I hate? Makin' salads—cuttin' up all that stuff 'n floppin' it in a bowl. Some day . . . some day . . . I'm gonna hear "tossed salad" an I'm gonna do jus' that. Toss out a tomato, toss out a head a lettuce, toss out a big ol' carrot. [*Miming the throwing and enjoying herself immensely.*]

ARLENE: [*Laughing.*] Be funny seein' all that stuff flyin' outta the kitchen.

RUBY: Hey Arlene! [*Gives her a friendly pat.*] You had your lunch yet?

ARLENE: [*Pulling away immediately.*] I ain't hungry.

RUBY: [*Carefully.*] I got raisin toast.

ARLENE: No. [*Goes over to the sink, twists knobs as if to stop a leak.*]

ARLIE: Whaddaya mean, what did she do to me? You got eyes or is they broke? You only seein' what you feel like seein'. I git ready to protect myself from a bunch of weirdos an then you look.

ARLENE: Sink's stopped up. [*Begins to work on it.*]

ARLIE: You ain't seein' when they's leavin' packs of cigarettes on my bed an then thinking I owe 'em or somethin'.

RUBY: Stopped up, huh? [*Squashing a bug on the floor.*]

ARLIE: You ain't lookin' when them kitchen workers lets up their mommies in line nights they know they only baked half enough brownies.

RUBY: Let me try.

ARLIE: You ain't seein' all the letters comin' in an goin' out with visitors. I'll tell you somethin'. One of them workmen buries dope for Betty Rickey in little plastic bottles under them sticker bushes at the water tower. You see that? No, you only seein' me. Well, you don't see shit.

RUBY: [*A quiet attempt.*] Gotta git you some Drano if you're gonna stay here.

ARLIE: I'll tell you what she done. Doris brung me some rollers from the beauty-school class. Three fuckin' pink rollers. Them plastic ones with the little holes. I didn't ask her. She jus' done it.

RUBY: Let me give her a try.

ARLENE: I can fix my own sink.

ARLIE: I's stupid. I's thinkin' maybe she were different from all them others. Then that night everbody disappears from the john and she's wantin' to brush my hair. Sure, brush my hair. How'd I know she was gonna crack her head open on the sink. I jus' barely even touched her.

RUBY: [*Walking to the bed now, digging through her purse.*] Want a Chiclet?

ARLIE: You ain't asked what she was gonna do to me. Huh? When you gonna ask that? You don't give a shit about that 'cause Doris such a good girl.

ARLENE: [*Giving up.*] Don't work.

RUBY: We got a dishwasher quittin' this week if you're interested.

ARLENE: I need somethin' that pays good.

RUBY: You type?

ARLENE: No.

RUBY: Do any clerk work?

ARLENE: No.

RUBY: Any keypunch?

ARLENE: No.

RUBY: Well, then I hate to tell you, but all us old-timers already got all the good cookin' and cleanin' jobs. [*Smashes another bug, goes to the cabinet to look for the bug spray.*] She even took the can of Raid! Just as well, empty anyway. [ARLENE *doesn't respond.*] She hit the bugs with it. [*Still no response.*] Now, there's that phone call you was talkin' about.

ARLENE: Yeah.

RUBY: [*Walking toward the door.*] An I'll git you that number for the dishwashin' job, just in case. [ARLENE *backs off.*] How 'bout cards? You play any cards? Course you do. I get sick of beatin' myself all the time at solitaire. Damn borin' bein' so good at it.

ARLENE: [*Goes for her purse.*] Maybe I'll jus' walk to the corner an make my call from there.

RUBY: It's always broke.

ARLENE: What?

RUBY: The phone . . . at the corner. Only it ain't at the corner. It's inside the A & P.

ARLENE: Maybe it'll be fixed.

RUBY: Look, I ain't gonna force you to play cards with me. It's time for my programs anyway.

ARLENE: I gotta git some pickle loaf an . . . things.

RUBY: Suit yourself. I'll be there if you change your mind.

ARLENE: I have some things I gotta do here first.

RUBY: [*Trying to leave on a friendly basis.*] Look, I'll charge you a dime if it'll make you feel better.

ARLENE: [*Takes her seriously.*] Okay.

RUBY: [*Laughs, then realizes* ARLENE *is serious.*] Mine's the one with the little picture of Johnny Cash on the door.

[RUBY *leaves. Singing to the tune of "I'll Toe the Line,"* BENNIE *walks across the catwalk carrying a tray with cups and a pitcher of water.* ARLENE *walks toward the closet. She is delaying going to the store, but is determined to go. She checks little things in the room, remembers to get a scarf, changes shoes, checks her wallet. Finally, as she is walking out, she stops and looks at the picture of Jesus, then moves closer, having noticed a dirty spot. She goes back into the bathroom for a tissue, wets it in her mouth, then dabs at the offending spot. She puts the tissue in her purse, then leaves the room when noted.*]

BENNIE: I keep my pants up with a piece of twine. I keep my eyes wide open all the time. Da da da da-da da da da da da. If you'll be mine, please pull the twine.

ARLIE: You can't sing for shit.

BENNIE: [*Starts down the stairs toward* ARLIE'*s cell.*] You know what elephants got between their toes?

ARLIE: I don't care.

BENNIE: Slow natives. [*Laughs.*]

ARLIE: That ain't funny.

GUARD (EVANS): [*As* BENNIE *opens* ARLIE'*s door.*] Hey, Davis.

BENNIE: Conversation is rehabilitatin', Evans. Want some water?

ARLIE: Okay.

BENNIE: How about some Kool-Aid to go in it? [*Gives her a glass of water.*]

ARLIE: When does the chaplain come?

BENNIE: Want some gum?

ARLIE: Is it today?

BENNIE: Kool-Aid's gone up, you know. Fifteen cents and tax. You get out, you'll learn all about that.

ARLIE: Does the chaplain come today?

BENNIE: [*Going back up the catwalk.*] Income tax, sales tax, property tax, gas and electric, water, rent—

ARLIE: Hey!

BENNIE: Yeah, he's comin', so don't mess up.

ARLIE: I ain't.

BENNIE: What's he tell you anyway, get you so starry-eyed?

ARLIE: He jus' talks to me.

BENNIE: I talk to you.

ARLIE: Where's Frankie Hill?

BENNIE: Gone.

ARLIE: Out?

BENNIE: Pretty soon.

ARLIE: When.

BENNIE: Miss her don't you? Ain't got nobody to bullshit with. Stories you gals tell . . . whoo-ee!

ARLIE: Get to cut that grass now, Frankie, honey.

BENNIE: Huh?

ARLIE: Stupidest thing she said. [*Gently.*] Said first thing she was gonna do when she got out—

[ARLENE *leaves the apartment.*]

BENNIE: Get laid.

ARLIE: Shut up. First thing was gonna be going to the garage. Said it always smelled like car grease an turpur . . . somethin'.

BENNIE: Turpentine.

ARLIE: Yeah, an gasoline, wet. An she'll bend down an squirt oil in the lawn-mower, red can with a long pointy spout. Then cut the grass in the backyard, up an back, up an back. They got this grass catcher on it. Says she likes scoopin' up that cut grass an spreadin' it out under the trees. Says it makes her real hungry for some lunch. [*A quiet curiosity about all this.*]

BENNIE: I got a power mower, myself.

ARLIE: They done somethin' to her. Took out her nerves or somethin'. She . . .

BENNIE: She jus' got better, that's all.

ARLIE: Hah. Know what else? They give her a fork to eat with last week. A fork. A fuckin' fork. Now how long's it been since I had a fork to eat with?

BENNIE: [*Getting ready to leave the cell.*] Wish I could help you with that, honey.

ARLIE: [*Loud.*] Don't call me honey.

BENNIE: [*Locks the door behind him.*] That's my girl.

ARLIE: I ain't your girl.

BENNIE: [*On his way back up the stairs.*] Screechin' wildcat.

ARLIE: [*Very quiet.*] What time is it?

[ARLENE *walks back into the apartment. She is out of breath and has some trouble getting the door open. She is carrying a big sack of groceries. As she sets the bag on the counter, it breaks open, spilling cans and packages all over the floor. She just stands and looks at the mess. She takes off her scarf and sets down her purse, still looking at the spilled groceries. Finally, she bends down and picks up the package of pickle loaf. She starts to put it on the counter, then turns suddenly and throws it at the door. She stares at it as it falls.*]

ARLENE: Bounce? [*In disgust.*] Shit.

[ARLENE *sinks to the floor. She tears open the package of pickle loaf and eats a piece of it. She is still angry, but is completely unable to do anything about her anger.*]

ARLIE: Who's out there? Is anybody out there? [*Reading.*] Depart from evil and do good. [*Yelling.*] Now, you pay attention out there 'cause this is right out of the Lord's mouth. [*Reading.*] And dwell, that means live, dwell for-ever-more. [*Speaking.*] That's like for longer than I've been in here or longer than . . . this Bible the chaplain give me's got my name right in the front of it. Hey! Somebody's s'posed to be out there watchin' me. Wanna hear some more? [*Reading.*] For the Lord for . . . [*The word is forsaketh.*] I can't read in here, you turn on my light, you hear me? Or let me out and I'll go read it in the TV room. Please let me out. I won't scream or nuthin'. I'll just go right to sleep, okay? Somebody! I'll go right to sleep. Okay? You won't even know I'm there. Hey! Goddammit, somebody let me out of here, I can't stand it in here anymore. Somebody! [*Her spirit finally broken.*]

ARLENE: [*She draws her knees up, wraps her arms around them and rests her head on her arms.*] Jus' gotta git a job an make some money an everything will be all right. You hear me, Arlene? You git yourself up an go find a job. [*Continues to sit.*] An you kin start by cleanin' up this mess you made 'cause food don't belong on the floor.

[ARLENE *still doesn't get up.* CARL *appears in the doorway of the apartment. When he sees* ARLENE *on the floor, he goes into a fit of vicious, sadistic laughter.*]

CARL: What's happenin', mama? You havin' lunch with the bugs?

ARLENE: [*Quietly.*] Fuck off.

CARL: [*Threatening.*] What'd you say?

ARLENE: [*Reconsidering.*] Go away.

CARL: You watch your mouth or I'll close it up for you.

[ARLENE *stands up now.* CARL *goes to the window and looks out, as if checking for someone.*]

ARLENE: They after you, ain't they?

[CARL *sniffs, scratches at his arm. He finds a plastic bag near the bed, stuffed with brightly colored knitted things. He pulls out baby sweaters, booties and caps.*]

CARL: What the fuck is this?

ARLENE: You leave them be.

CARL: You got a baby hid here somewhere? I found its little shoes. [*Laughs, dangling them in front of him.*]

ARLENE: [*Chasing him.*] Them's mine.

CARL: Aw sugar, I ain't botherin' nuthin'. Just lookin'. [*Pulls more out of the sack, dropping one or two booties on the floor, kicking them away.*]

ARLENE: [*Picking up what he's dropped.*] I ain't tellin' you again. Give me them.

CARL: [*Turns around quickly, walking away with a few of the sweaters.*] How much these go for?

ARLENE: I don't know yet.

CARL: I'll jus' take care of 'em for you—a few coin for the trip. You *are* gonna have to pay your share, you know.

ARLENE: You give me them. I ain't goin' with you. [*She walks toward him.*]

CARL: You ain't?

[*Mocking,* ARLENE *walks up close to him now, taking the bag in her hands. He knocks her away and onto the bed.*]

CARL: Straighten up, girlie. [*Now kneels over her.*] You done forgot how to behave yourself. [*Moves as if to threaten her, but kisses her on the forehead, then moves out into the room.*]

ARLENE: [*Sitting up.*] I worked hard on them things. They's nice, too, for babies and little kids.

CARL: I bet you fooled them officers good, doin' this shit. [*Throws the bag in the sink.*]

ARLENE: I weren't—

CARL: I kin see that scene. They sayin' . . . [*Puts on a high southern voice.*] "I'd jus' love one a them nice yella sweaters."

ARLENE: They liked them.

CARL: Those turkeys, sure they did. Where else you gonna git your free sweaters an free washin' an free step-right-up-git-your-convict-special-shoe-shine. No, don't give me no money, officer. I's jus' doin' this 'cause I likes you.

ARLENE: They give 'em for Christmas presents.

CARL: [*Checks the window again, then peers into the grocery sack.*] What you got sweet, mama? [*Pulls out a box of cookies and begins to eat them.*]

ARLIE: I'm sweepin', Doris, 'cause it's like a pigpen in here. So you might like it, but I don't, so if you got some mops, I'll take one of them too.

ARLENE: You caught another habit, didn't you?

CARL: You turned into a narc or what?

ARLENE: You scratchin' an sniffin' like crazy.

CARL: I see a man eatin' cookies an that's what you see too.

ARLENE: An you was laughin' at me sittin' on the floor! You got cops lookin' for you an you ain't scored yet this morning. You better get yourself back to prison where you can git all you need.

CARL: Since when Carl couldn't find it if he really wanted it?

ARLENE: An I bought them cookies for me.

CARL: An I wouldn't come no closer if I's you.

ARLENE: [*Stops, then walks to the door.*] Then take the cookies an git out.

CARL: [*Imitating* BENNIE.] Oh, please, Miss Arlene, come go with Carl to the big city. We'll jus' have us the best time.

ARLENE: I'm gonna stay here an git a job an save up money so's I kin git Joey. [*Opening the door.*] Now, I ain't s'posed to see no ex-cons.

CARL: [*Big laugh.*] You don't know nobody else. Huh, Arlie? Who you know ain't a con-vict?

ARLENE: I'll meet 'em.

CARL: And what if they don't wanna meet you? You ain't exactly a nice girl, you know. An you gotta be jivin' about that job shit. [*Throws the sack of cookies on the floor.*]

ARLENE: [*Retrieving the cookies.*] I kin work.

CARL: Doin' what?

ARLENE: I don't know. Cookin', cleanin', somethin' that pays good.

CARL: You got your choice, honey. You can do cookin' an cleanin' *or* you can do somethin' that pays good. You ain't gonna git rich working on your knees. You come with me an you'll have money. You stay here, you won't have shit.

ARLENE: Ruby works an she does okay.

CARL: You got any Kool-Aid? [*Looking in the cabinets, moving* ARLENE *out of his way.*] Ruby who?

ARLENE: Upstairs. She cooks. Works nights an has all day to do jus' what she wants.

CARL: And what, exactly, do she do? See flicks take rides in cabs to pick up see-through shoes?

ARLENE: She watches TV, plays cards, you know.

CARL: Yeah, I know. Sounds just like the day room in the fuckin' joint.

ARLENE: She likes it.

CARL: [*Exasperated.*] All right. Say you stay here an *finally* find yourself some job. [*Grabs the picture of Jesus off the wall.*] This your boyfriend?

ARLENE: The chaplain give it to me.

CARL: Say it's dishwashin', okay? [ARLENE *doesn't answer.*] Okay?

ARLENE: Okay. [*Takes the picture, hangs it back up.*]

CARL: An you git maybe seventy-five a week. Seventy-five for standin' over a sink full of greasy gray water, fishin' out blobs of bread an lettuce. People puttin' pieces of chewed-up meat in their napkins and you gotta pick it out. Eight hours a day, six days a week, to make seventy-five lousy pictures of Big Daddy George. Now, how long it'll take you to make seventy-five workin' for me?

ARLENE: A night.

[*She sits on the bed,* CARL *pacing in front of her.*]

CARL: Less than a night. Two hours maybe. Now, it's the same fuckin' seventy-five bills. You can either work all week for it or make it in two hours. You work two hours a night for me an how much you got in a week? [ARLENE *looks puzzled by the multiplication required. He sits down beside her, even more disgusted.*] Two seventy-five's is a hundred and fifty. Three hundred-and-fifties is four hundred and fifty. You stay here you git seventy-five a week. You come with me an you git four hundred and fifty a week. Now, four hundred and fifty, Arlie, is *more* than seventy-five. You stay here you gotta work eight hours a day and your hands git wrinkled and your feet swell up. [*Suddenly distracted.*] There was this guy at Bricktown had webby toes like a duck. [*Back now.*] You come home with me you work two hours a night an you kin sleep all mornin' an spend the day buyin' eyelashes and tryin' out perfume. Come home, have some guy openin' the door for you sayin', "Good evenin', Miss Holsclaw, nice night now ain't it?" [*Puts his arm around her.*]

ARLENE: It's Joey I'm thinkin' about.

CARL: If you was a kid, would you want your mom to git so dragged out washin' dishes she don't have no time for you an no money to spend on you? You come with me, you kin send him big orange bears an Sting-Ray bikes with his name wrote on the fenders. He'll like that. Holsclaw. [*Amused.*] Kinda sounds like coleslaw, don't it? Joey be tellin' all his friends 'bout his mom livin' up in New York City an bein' so rich an sendin' him stuff all the time.

ARLENE: I want to be with him.

CARL: [*Now stretches out on the bed, his head in her lap.*] So, fly him up to see you. Take him on that boat they got goes roun' the island. Take him up to the Empire State Building, let him play King Kong. [*Rubs her hair, unstudied tenderness.*] He be talkin' 'bout that trip his whole life.

ARLENE: [*Smoothing his hair.*] I don't want to go back to prison, Carl.

CARL: [*Jumps up, moves toward the refrigerator.*] There any chocolate milk? [*Distracted again.*] You know they got this motel down in Mexico named after me? Carlsbad Cabins. [*Proudly.*] Who said anything about goin' back to prison? [*Slams the refrigerator door, really hostile.*] What do you think I'm gonna be doin'? Keepin' you out, that's what!

ARLENE: [*Stands up.*] Like last time? Like you gettin' drunk? Like you lookin' for kid junkies to beat up?

CARL: God, ain't it hot in this dump. You gonna come or not? You wanna wash dishes, I could give a shit. [*Yelling.*] But you comin' with me, you say it right now, lady! [*Grabs her by the arm.*] Huh?

[*There is a knock on the door.*]

RUBY'S VOICE: Arlene?

CARL: [*Yelling.*] She ain't here!

RUBY'S VOICE: [*Alarmed.*] Arlene! You all right?

ARLENE: That's Ruby I was tellin' you about.

CARL: [*Catches* ARLENE'*s arm again, very rough.*] We ain't through!

RUBY: [*Opening the door.*] Hey! [*Seeing the rough treatment.*] Goin' to the store. [*Very firm.*] Thought maybe you forgot somethin'.

CARL: [*Turns* ARLENE *loose.*] You this cook I been hearin' about?

RUBY: I cook. So what?

CARL: Buys you nice shoes, don't it, cookin'? Why don't you hock your watch an have somethin' done to your hair? If you got a watch.

RUBY: Why don't you drop by the coffee shop. I'll spit in your eggs.

CARL: They let you bring home the half-eat chili dogs?

RUBY: You . . . you got half-eat chili dogs for brains. [*To* ARLENE.] I'll stop by later. [*Contemptuous look for* CARL.]

ARLENE: No. Stay.

[CARL *gets the message. He goes over to the sink to get a drink of water out of the faucet, then looks down at his watch.*]

CARL: Piece a shit. [*Thumps it with his finger.*] Shoulda took the dude's hat, Jack. Guy preachin' about the end of the world ain't gonna own a watch that works.

ARLENE: [*Walks over to the sink, bends over* CARL.] You don't need me. I'm gittin' too old for it, anyway.

CARL: I don't discuss my business with strangers in the room. [*Heads for the door.*]

ARLENE: When you leavin'?

CARL: Six. You wanna come, meet me at this bar. [*Gives her a brightly colored matchbook.*] I'm havin' my wheels delivered.

ARLENE: You stealin' a car?

CARL: Take a cab. [*Gives her a dollar.*] You don't come . . . well, I already laid it out for you. I ain't never lied to you, have I girl?

ARLENE: No.

CARL: Then you be there. That's all the words I got. [*Makes an unconscious move toward her.*] I don't beg nobody. [*Backs off.*] Be there.

[*He turns abruptly and leaves.* ARLENE *watches him go, folding up the money in the matchbook. The door remains open.*]

ARLIE: [*Reading, or trying to, from a small Testament.*] For the Lord forsaketh not his saints, but the seed of the wicked shall be cut off.

[RUBY *walks over to the counter, starts to pick up some of the groceries lying on the floor, then stops.*]

RUBY: I 'magine you'll want to be puttin' these up yourself. [ARLENE *continues to stare out the door.*] He do this?

ARLENE: No.

RUBY: Can't trust these sacks. I seen bag boys punchin' holes in 'em at the store.

ARLENE: Can't trust anybody. [*Finally turning around.*]

RUBY: Well, you don't want to trust him, that's for sure.

ARLENE: We spent a lot of time together, me an Carl.

RUBY: He live here?

ARLENE: No, he jus' broke outta Bricktown near where I was. I got word there sayin' he'd meet me. I didn't believe it then, but he don't lie, Carl don't.

RUBY: You thinkin' of goin' with him?

ARLENE: They'll catch him. I told him but he don't listen.

RUBY: Funny ain't it, the number a men come without ears.

ARLENE: How much that dishwashin' job pay?

RUBY: I don't know. Maybe seventy-five.

ARLENE: That's what he said.

RUBY: He tell you you was gonna wear out your hands and knees grubbin' for nuthin', git old an be broke an never have a nice dress to wear? [*Sitting down.*]

ARLENE: Yeah.

RUBY: He tell you nobody's gonna wanna be with you 'cause you done time?

ARLENE: Yeah.

RUBY: He tell you your kid gonna be ashamed of you an nobody's gonna believe you if you tell 'em you changed?

ARLENE: Yeah.

RUBY: Then he was right. [*Pauses.*] But when you make your two nickels, you can keep both of 'em.

ARLENE: [*Shattered by these words.*] Well, I can't do that.

RUBY: Can't do what?

ARLENE: Live like that. Be like bein' dead.

RUBY: You kin always call in sick . . . stay home, send out for pizza an watch your Johnny Carson on TV . . . or git a bus way out Preston Street an go bowlin'.

ARLENE: [*Anger building.*] What am I gonna do? I can't git no work that will pay good 'cause I can't do nuthin'. It'll be years fore I have a nice rug for this place. I'll never even have some ol' Ford to drive around, I'll never take Joey to no fair. I won't be invited home for pot roast and I'll have to wear this fuckin' dress for the rest of my life. What kind of life is that?

RUBY: It's outside.

ARLENE: Outside? Honey I'll either be *inside* this apartment or *inside* some kitchen sweatin' over the sink. Outside's where you get to do what you want, not where you gotta do some shit job jus' so's you can eat worse than you did in prison. That ain't why I quit bein' so hateful, so I could come back and rot in some slum.

RUBY: [*Word "slum" hits hard.*] Well, you can wash dishes to pay the rent on your "slum," or you can spread your legs for any shit that's got the ten dollars.

ARLENE: [*Not hostile.*] I don't need you agitatin' me.

RUBY: An I don't live in no slum.

ARLENE: [*Sensing* RUBY's *hurt.*] Well, I'm sorry . . . it's just . . . I thought . . . [*Increasingly upset.*]

RUBY: [*Finishing her sentence.*] . . . it was gonna be different. Well, it ain't. And the sooner you believe it, the better off you'll be.

[*A* GUARD *enters* ARLIE's *cell.*]

ARLIE: Where's the chaplain? I got somethin' to tell him.

ARLENE: They said I's . . .

GUARD (CALDWELL): He ain't comin'.

ARLENE: . . . he tol' me if . . . I thought once Arlie . . .

ARLIE: It's Tuesday. He comes to see me on Tuesday.

GUARD (CALDWELL): Chaplain's been transferred, dollie. Gone. Bye-bye. You know.

ARLENE: He said the meek, meek, them that's quiet and good . . . the meek . . . as soon as Arlie . . .

RUBY: What, Arlene? Who said what?

ARLIE: He's not comin' back?

ARLENE: At Pine Ridge there was . . .

ARLIE: He woulda told me if he couldn't come back.

ARLENE: I was . . .

GUARD (CALDWELL): He left this for you.

ARLENE: I was . . .

GUARD (CALDWELL): Picture of Jesus, looks like.

ARLENE: . . . this chaplain . . .

RUBY: [Trying to call her back from this hysteria.] Arlene . . .

ARLIE: [Hysterical.] I need to talk to him.

ARLENE: This chaplain . . .

ARLIE: You tell him to come back and see me.

ARLENE: I was in lockup . . .

ARLIE: [A final, anguished plea.] I want the chaplain!

ARLENE: I don't know . . . years . . .

RUBY: And . . .

ARLENE: This chaplain said I had . . . said Arlie was my hateful self and she was hurtin' me and God would find some way to take her away . . . and it was God's will so I could be the meek . . . the meek, them that's quiet and good an git whatever they want . . . I forgit that word . . . they git the earth.

RUBY: Inherit.

ARLENE: Yeah. And that's why I done it.

RUBY: Done what?

ARLENE: What I done. 'Cause the chaplain he said . . . I'd sit up nights waitin' for him to come talk to me.

RUBY: Arlene, what did you do? What are you talkin' about?

ARLENE: They tol' me . . . after I's out an it was all over . . . they said after the chaplain got transferred . . . I didn't know why he didn't come no more till after . . . they said it was three whole nights at first, me screamin' to God to come git Arlie an kill her. They give me this medicine an thought I's better . . . then that night it happened, the officer was in the dorm doin' count . . . an they didn't hear nuthin' but they come back out where I was an I'm standin' there tellin' 'em to come see, real quiet I'm tellin' 'em, but there's all this blood all over my shirt an I got this fork I'm holdin' real tight in my hand . . . [Clenches one hand now, the other hand fumbling with the front of her dress as if she's going to show RUBY.] this fork, they said Doris stole it from

the kitchen an give it to me so I'd kill myself and shut up botherin' her . . .
an there's all these holes all over me where I been stabbin' myself an I'm
sayin' Arlie is dead for what she done to me, Arlie is dead an it's God's will
. . . I didn't scream it, I was jus' sayin' it over and over . . . Arlie is dead, Arlie
is dead . . . they couldn't git that fork outta my hand till . . . I woke up in the
infirmary and they said I almost died. They said they's glad I didn't. [*Smiling.*] They said did I feel better now an they was real nice, bringing me
chocolate puddin' . . .

RUBY: I'm sorry, Arlene.

[RUBY *reaches out for her, but* ARLENE *pulls away sharply.*]

ARLENE: I'd be eatin' or jus' lookin' at the ceiling an git a tear in my eye, but it'd
jus' dry up, you know, it didn't run out or nuthin'. An then pretty soon, I's
well, an officers was sayin' they's seein' such a change in me an givin' me
yarn to knit sweaters an how'd I like to have a new skirt to wear an sometimes
lettin' me chew gum. They said things ain't never been as clean as when I's
doin' the housekeepin' at the dorm. [*So proud.*] An then I got in the honor
cottage an nobody was foolin' with me no more or nuthin'. An I didn't git
mad like before or nuthin'. I jus' done my work an knit . . . an I don't think
about it, what happened, 'cept . . . [*Now losing control.*] people here keep
callin' me Arlie an . . . [*Has trouble saying "Arlie"*] I didn't mean to do it,
what I done . . .

RUBY: Oh, honey . . .

ARLENE: I did . . . [*This is very difficult.*] I mean, Arlie was a pretty mean kid, but
I did . . . [*Very quickly.*] I didn't know what I . . .

[ARLENE *breaks down completely, screaming, crying, falling over into* RUBY's
lap.]

ARLENE: [*Grieving for this lost self.*] Arlie!

[RUBY *rubs her back, her hair, waiting for the calm she knows will come.*]

RUBY: [*Finally, but very quietly.*] You can still . . . [*Stops to think of how to say
it.*] . . . you can still love people that's gone.

[RUBY *continues to hold her tenderly, rocking as with a baby. A terrible crash
is heard on the steps outside the apartment.*]

BENNIE'S VOICE: Well, chicken-pluckin', hog-kickin' shit!
RUBY: Don't you move now, it's just somebody out in the hall.
ARLENE: That's —
RUBY: It's okay Arlene. Everything's gonna be just fine. Nice and quiet now.
ARLENE: That's Bennie that guard I told you about.
RUBY: I'll get it. You stay still now. [*She walks to the door and looks out into the
hall, hands on hips.*] Why you dumpin' them flowers on the stairs like
that? Won't git no sun at all! [*Turns back to* ARLENE.] Arlene, there's a man
plantin' a garden out in the hall. You think we should call the police or get
him a waterin' can?

[BENNIE *appears in the doorway, carrying a box of dead-looking plants.*]

BENNIE: I didn't try to fall, you know.

RUBY: [*Blocking the door.*] Well, when you git ready to *try*, I wanna watch!

ARLENE: I thought you's gone.

RUBY: [*To* BENNIE.] You got a visitin' pass?

BENNIE: [*Coming into the room.*] Arlie . . . [*Quickly.*] Arlene. I brung you some plants. You know, plants for your window. Like we talked about, so's you don't see them bars.

RUBY: [*Picking up one of the plants.*] They sure is scraggly-lookin' things. Next time, git plastic.

BENNIE: I'm sorry I dropped 'em, Arlene. We kin get 'em back together an they'll do real good. [*Setting them down on the trunk.*] These ones don't take the sun. I asked just to make sure. Arlene?

RUBY: You up for seein' this petunia killer?

ARLENE: It's okay. Bennie, this is Ruby, upstairs.

BENNIE: [*Bringing one flower over to show* ARLENE, *stuffing it back into its pot.*] See? It ain't dead.

RUBY: Poor little plant. It comes from a broken home.

BENNIE: [*Walks over to the window, getting the box and holding it up.*] That's gonna look real pretty. Cheerful-like.

RUBY: Arlene ain't gettin' the picture yet. [*Walking to the window and holding her plant up too, posing.*] Now.

[ARLENE *looks, but is not amused.*]

BENNIE: [*Putting the plants back down.*] I jus' thought, after what I done last night . . . I jus' wanted to do somethin' nice.

ARLENE: [*Calmer now.*] They is nice. Thanks.

RUBY: Arlene says you're a guard.

BENNIE: I was. I quit. Retired.

ARLENE: Bennie's goin' back to Alabama.

BENNIE: Well, I ain't leavin' right away. There's this guy at the motel says the bass is hittin' pretty good right now. Thought I might fish some first.

ARLENE: Then he's goin' back.

BENNIE: [*To* RUBY *as he washes his hands.*] I'm real fond of this little girl. I ain't goin' till I'm sure she's gonna do okay. Thought I might help some.

RUBY: Arlene's had about all the help she can stand.

BENNIE: I got a car, Arlene. An money. An . . . [*Reaching into his pocket.*] I brung you some gum.

ARLENE: That's real nice, too. An I 'preciate what you done, bringin' me here an all, but . . .

BENNIE: Well, look. Least you can take my number at the motel an give me a ring if you need somethin'. [*Holds out a piece of paper.*] Here, I wrote it down for you. [ARLENE *takes the paper.*] Oh, an somethin' else, these towel things . . . [*Reaching into his pocket, pulling out a package of towelettes.*] they was in the chicken last night. I thought I might be needin' 'em, but they give us new towels every day at that motel.

ARLENE: Okay then. I got your number.

BENNIE: [*Backing up toward the door.*] Right. Right. Any ol' thing, now. Jus' any ol' thing. You even run outta gum an you call.

RUBY: Careful goin' down.

ARLENE: Bye Bennie.

BENNIE: Right. The number now. Don't lose it. You know, in case you need somethin'.

ARLENE: No.

[BENNIE *leaves,* ARLENE *gets up and picks up the matchbook* CARL *gave her and holds it with* BENNIE's *piece of paper.* RUBY *watches a moment, sees* ARLENE *trying to make this decision, knows that what she says now is very important.*]

RUBY: We had this waitress put her phone number in matchbooks, give 'em to guys left her nice tips. Anyway, one night this little ol' guy calls her and comes over and says he works at this museum an he don't have any money but he's got this hat belonged to Queen Victoria. An she felt real sorry for him so she screwed him for this little ol' lacy hat. Then she takes the hat back the next day to the museum thinkin' she'll git a reward or somethin' an you know what they done? [*Pause.*] Give her a free membership. Tellin' her thanks so much an we're so grateful an wouldn't she like to see this mummy they got downstairs . . . an all the time jus' stallin' . . . waiting 'cause they called the police.

ARLENE: You do any time for that?

RUBY: [*Admitting the story was about her.*] County jail.

ARLENE: [*Quietly, looking at the matchbook.*] County jail. [*She tears up the matchbook and drops it in the sack of trash.*] You got any Old Maids?

RUBY: Huh?

ARLENE: You know.

RUBY: [*Surprised and pleased.*] Cards?

ARLENE: [*Laughs a little.*] It's the only one I know.

RUBY: Old Maid, huh? [*Not her favorite game.*]

ARLENE: I gotta put my food up first.

RUBY: 'Bout an hour?

ARLENE: I'll come up.

RUBY: Great. [*Stops by the plants on her way to the door, smiles.*] These plants is real ugly.

[RUBY *exits.* ARLENE *watches her, then turns back to the groceries still on the floor. Slowly, but with great determination, she picks up the items one at a time and puts them away in the cabinet above the counter.* ARLIE *appears on the catwalk. There is one light on each of them.*]

ARLIE: Hey! You 'member that time we was playin' policeman an June locked me up in Mama's closet an then took off swimmin'? An I stood around with them dresses itchin' my ears an crashin' into that door tryin' to git outta there? It was dark in there. So, finally, [*Very proud.*] I went around an peed in all Mama's shoes. But then she come home an tried to git in the closet only June taken the key so she said, "Who's in there?" an I said, "It's me!" and she said, "What you doin' in there?" an I started gigglin' an she started pullin' on the door an yellin', "Arlie, what you doin' in there?" [*Big laugh.*]

[ARLENE *has begun to smile during the story. Now they speak together, both standing as Mama did, one hand on her hip.*]

ARLIE AND ARLENE: Arlie, what you doin' in there?

ARLENE: [*Still smiling and remembering, stage dark except for one light on her face.*] Aw shoot.

[*Light dims on* ARLENE's *fond smile as* ARLIE *laughs once more.*]

END OF PLAY

1977

HENRIK IBSEN

Hedda Gabler[1]

CHARACTERS

GEORGE TESMAN, *research graduate in cultural history*

HEDDA, *his wife*

MISS JULIANA TESMAN, *his aunt*

MRS. ELVSTED

JUDGE BRACK

EILERT LOEVBORG

BERTHA, *a maid*

The action takes place in TESMAN's *villa in the fashionable quarter of town.*

ACT I

SCENE: A *large drawing room, handsomely and tastefully furnished; decorated in dark colors. In the rear wall is a broad open doorway, with curtains drawn back to either side. It leads to a smaller room, decorated in the same style as the drawing room. In the right-hand wall of the drawing room, a folding door leads out to the hall. The opposite wall, on the left, contains french windows, also with curtains drawn back on either side. Through the glass we can see part of a verandah, and trees in autumn colors. Downstage stands an oval table, covered by a cloth and surrounded by chairs. Downstage right, against the wall, is a broad stove tiled with dark porcelain; in front of it stand a high-backed armchair, a cushioned footrest, and two footstools. Upstage right, in an alcove, is a corner sofa, with a small, round table. Downstage left, a little away from the wall, is another sofa. Upstage of the french windows, a piano. On either side of the open doorway in the rear wall stand what-nots holding ornaments of terra cotta and majolica. Against the rear wall of the smaller room can be seen a sofa, a table, and a couple*

1. Translated by Michael Meyer.

of chairs. Above this sofa hangs the portrait of a handsome old man in general's uniform. Above the table a lamp hangs from the ceiling, with a shade of opalescent, milky glass. All round the drawing room bunches of flowers stand in vases and glasses. More bunches lie on the tables. The floors of both rooms are covered with thick carpets. Morning light. The sun shines in through the french windows.

MISS JULIANA TESMAN, *wearing a hat and carrying a parasol, enters from the hall, followed by* BERTHA, *who is carrying a bunch of flowers wrapped in paper.* MISS TESMAN *is about sixty-five, of pleasant and kindly appearance. She is neatly but simply dressed in grey outdoor clothes.* BERTHA, *the maid, is rather simple and rustic-looking. She is getting on in years.*

MISS TESMAN: [*Stops just inside the door, listens, and says in a hushed voice.*] No, bless my soul! They're not up yet.

BERTHA: [*Also in hushed tones.*] What did I tell you, miss? The boat didn't get in till midnight. And when they did turn up—Jesus, miss, you should have seen all the things Madam made me unpack before she'd go to bed!

MISS TESMAN: Ah, well. Let them have a good lie in. But let's have some nice fresh air waiting for them when they do come down. [*Goes to the french windows and throws them wide open.*]

BERTHA: [*Bewildered at the table, the bunch of flowers in her hand.*] I'm blessed if there's a square inch left to put anything. I'll have to let it lie here, miss. [*Puts it on the piano.*]

MISS TESMAN: Well, Bertha dear, so now you have a new mistress. Heaven knows it nearly broke my heart to have to part with you.

BERTHA: [*Snivels.*] What about me, Miss Juju? How do you suppose I felt? After all the happy years I've spent with you and Miss Rena?

MISS TESMAN: We must accept it bravely, Bertha. It was the only way. George needs you to take care of him. He could never manage without you. You've looked after him ever since he was a tiny boy.

BERTHA: Oh, but Miss Juju, I can't help thinking about Miss Rena, lying there all helpless, poor dear. And that new girl! She'll never learn the proper way to handle an invalid.

MISS TESMAN: Oh, I'll manage to train her. I'll do most of the work myself, you know. You needn't worry about my poor sister, Bertha dear.

BERTHA: But Miss Juju, there's another thing. I'm frightened Madam may not find me suitable.

MISS TESMAN: Oh, nonsense, Bertha. There may be one or two little things to begin with——

BERTHA: She's a real lady. Wants everything just so.

MISS TESMAN: But of course she does! General Gabler's daughter! Think of what she was accustomed to when the General was alive. You remember how we used to see her out riding with her father? In that long black skirt? With the feather in her hat?

BERTHA: Oh, yes, miss. As if I could forget! But, Lord! I never dreamed I'd live to see a match between her and Master Georgie.

MISS TESMAN: Neither did I. By the way, Bertha, from now on you must stop calling him Master Georgie. You must say: Dr. Tesman.

BERTHA: Yes, Madam said something about that too. Last night—the moment they'd set foot inside the door. Is it true, then, miss?

MISS TESMAN: Indeed it is. Just imagine, Bertha, some foreigners have made him a doctor.[2] It happened while they were away. I had no idea till he told me when they got off the boat.

BERTHA: Well, I suppose there's no limit to what he won't become. He's that clever. I never thought he'd go in for hospital work, though.

MISS TESMAN: No, he's not that kind of doctor. [Nods impressively.] In any case, you may soon have to address him by an even grander title.

BERTHA: You don't say! What might that be, miss?

MISS TESMAN: [Smiles.] Ah! If you only knew! [Moved.] Dear God, if only poor dear Joachim could rise out of his grave and see what his little son has grown into! [Looks round.] But Bertha, why have you done this? Taken the chintz covers off all the furniture!

BERTHA: Madam said I was to. Can't stand chintz covers on chairs, she said.

MISS TESMAN: But surely they're not going to use this room as a parlor?

BERTHA: So I gathered, miss. From what Madam said. He didn't say anything. The Doctor.

[GEORGE TESMAN comes into the rear room, from the right, humming, with an open, empty traveling bag in his hand. He is about thirty-three, of medium height and youthful appearance, rather plump, with an open, round, contented face, and fair hair and beard. He wears spectacles, and is dressed in comfortable, indoor clothes.]

MISS TESMAN: Good morning! Good morning, George!

TESMAN: [In open doorway.] Auntie Juju! Dear Auntie Juju! [Comes forward and shakes her hand.] You've come all the way out here! And so early! What?

MISS TESMAN: Well, I had to make sure you'd settled in comfortably.

TESMAN: But you can't have had a proper night's sleep.

MISS TESMAN: Oh, never mind that.

TESMAN: We were so sorry we couldn't give you a lift. But you saw how it was— Hedda had so much luggage—and she insisted on having it all with her.

MISS TESMAN: Yes, I've never seen so much luggage.

BERTHA: [To TESMAN.] Shall I go and ask Madam if there's anything I can lend her a hand with?

TESMAN: Er—thank you, Bertha; no, you needn't bother. She says if she wants you for anything she'll ring.

BERTHA: [Over to right.] Oh. Very good.

TESMAN: Oh, Bertha—take this bag, will you?

BERTHA: [Takes it.] I'll put it in the attic. [Goes out into the hall.]

TESMAN: Just fancy, Auntie Juju, I filled that whole bag with notes for my book. You know, it's really incredible what I've managed to find rooting through

2. Awarded him a doctoral degree.

those archives. By Jove! Wonderful old things no one even knew existed——

MISS TESMAN: I'm sure you didn't waste a single moment of your honeymoon, George dear.

TESMAN: No, I think I can truthfully claim that. But, Auntie Juju, do take your hat off. Here. Let me untie it for you. What?

MISS TESMAN: [As he does so.] Oh dear, oh dear! It's just as if you were still living at home with us.

TESMAN: [Turns the hat in his hand and looks at it.] I say! What a splendid new hat!

MISS TESMAN: I bought it for Hedda's sake.

TESMAN: For Hedda's sake? What?

MISS TESMAN: So that Hedda needn't be ashamed of me, in case we ever go for a walk together.

TESMAN: [Pats her cheek.] You still think of everything, don't you, Auntie Juju? [Puts the hat down on a chair by the table.] Come on, let's sit down here on the sofa. And have a little chat while we wait for Hedda.

[They sit. She puts her parasol in the corner of the sofa.]

MISS TESMAN: [Clasps both his hands and looks at him.] Oh, George, it's so wonderful to have you back, and be able to see you with my own eyes again! Poor dear Joachim's own son!

TESMAN: What about me! It's wonderful for me to see you again, Auntie Juju. You've been a mother to me. And a father, too.

MISS TESMAN: You'll always keep a soft spot in your heart for your old aunties, won't you, George dear?

TESMAN: I suppose Auntie Rena's no better? What?

MISS TESMAN: Alas, no. I'm afraid she'll never get better, poor dear. She's lying there just as she has for all these years. Please God I may be allowed to keep her for a little longer. If I lost her I don't know what I'd do. Especially now I haven't you to look after.

TESMAN: [Pats her on the back.] There, there, there!

MISS TESMAN: [With a sudden change of mood.] Oh but George, fancy you being a married man! And to think it's you who've won Hedda Gabler! The beautiful Hedda Gabler! Fancy! She was always so surrounded by admirers.

TESMAN: [Hums a little and smiles contentedly.] Yes, I suppose there are quite a few people in this town who wouldn't mind being in my shoes. What?

MISS TESMAN: And what a honeymoon! Five months! Nearly six.

TESMAN: Well, I've done a lot of work, you know. All those archives to go through. And I've had to read lots of books.

MISS TESMAN: Yes, dear, of course. [Lowers her voice confidentially.] But tell me, George—haven't you any—any extra little piece of news to give me?

TESMAN: You mean, arising out of the honeymoon?

MISS TESMAN: Yes.

TESMAN: No, I don't think there's anything I didn't tell you in my letters. My doctorate, of course—but I told you about that last night, didn't I?

MISS TESMAN: Yes, yes, I didn't mean that kind of thing. I was just wondering—
are you—are you expecting——?

TESMAN: Expecting what?

MISS TESMAN: Oh, come on George, I'm your old aunt!

TESMAN: Well actually—yes, I am expecting something.

MISS TESMAN: I knew it!

TESMAN: You'll be happy to hear that before very long I expect to become a
professor.

MISS TESMAN: Professor?

TESMAN: I think I may say that the matter has been decided. But, Auntie Juju,
you know about this.

MISS TESMAN: [*Gives a little laugh.*] Yes, of course. I'd forgotten. [*Changes her
tone.*] But we were talking about your honeymoon. It must have cost a dreadful amount of money, George?

TESMAN: Oh well, you know, that big research grant I got helped a good deal.

MISS TESMAN: But how on earth did you manage to make it do for two?

TESMAN: Well, to tell the truth it was a bit tricky. What?

MISS TESMAN: Especially when one's traveling with a lady. A little bird tells me
that makes things very much more expensive.

TESMAN: Well, yes, of course it does make things a little more expensive. But
Hedda has to do things in style, Auntie Juju. I mean, she has to. Anything
less grand wouldn't have suited her.

MISS TESMAN: No, no, I suppose not. A honeymoon abroad seems to be the
vogue nowadays. But tell me, have you had time to look round the
house?

TESMAN: You bet. I've been up since the crack of dawn.

MISS TESMAN: Well, what do you think of it?

TESMAN: Splendid. Absolutely splendid. I'm only wondering what we're going to
do with those two empty rooms between that little one and Hedda's bedroom.

MISS TESMAN: [*Laughs slyly.*] Ah, George dear, I'm sure you'll manage to find
some use for them—in time.

TESMAN: Yes, of course, Auntie Juju, how stupid of me. You're thinking of my
books. What?

MISS TESMAN: Yes, yes, dear boy. I was thinking of your books.

TESMAN: You know, I'm so happy for Hedda's sake that we've managed to get
this house. Before we became engaged she often used to say this was the
only house in town she felt she could really bear to live in. It used to belong
to Mrs. Falk—you know, the Prime Minister's widow.

MISS TESMAN: Fancy that! And what a stroke of luck it happened to come into
the market. Just as you'd left on your honeymoon.

TESMAN: Yes, Auntie Juju, we've certainly had all the luck with us. What?

MISS TESMAN: But, George dear, the expense! It's going to make a dreadful hole
in your pocket, all this.

TESMAN: [*A little downcast.*] Yes, I—I suppose it will, won't it?

MISS TESMAN: Oh, George, really!

TESMAN: How much do you think it'll cost? Roughly, I mean? What?

MISS TESMAN: I can't possibly say till I see the bills.

TESMAN: Well, luckily Judge Brack's managed to get it on very favorable terms. He wrote and told Hedda so.

MISS TESMAN: Don't you worry, George dear. Anyway I've stood security for all the furniture and carpets.

TESMAN: Security? But dear, sweet Auntie Juju, how could you possibly stand security?

MISS TESMAN: I've arranged a mortgage on our annuity.

TESMAN: [*Jumps up.*] What? On your annuity? And—Auntie Rena's?

MISS TESMAN: Yes. Well, I couldn't think of any other way.

TESMAN: [*Stands in front of her.*] Auntie Juju, have you gone completely out of your mind? That annuity's all you and Auntie Rena have.

MISS TESMAN: All right, there's no need to get so excited about it. It's a pure formality, you know. Judge Brack told me so. He was so kind as to arrange it all for me. A pure formality; those were his very words.

TESMAN: I dare say. All the same——

MISS TESMAN: Anyway, you'll have a salary of your own now. And, good heavens, even if we did have to fork out a little—tighten our belts for a week or two— why, we'd be happy to do so for your sake.

TESMAN: Oh, Auntie Juju! Will you never stop sacrificing yourself for me?

MISS TESMAN: [*Gets up and puts her hands on his shoulders.*] What else have I to live for but to smooth your road a little, my dear boy? You've never had any mother or father to turn to. And now at last we've achieved our goal. I won't deny we've had our little difficulties now and then. But now, thank the good Lord, George dear, all your worries are past.

TESMAN: Yes, it's wonderful really how everything's gone just right for me.

MISS TESMAN: Yes! And the enemies who tried to bar your way have been struck down. They have been made to bite the dust. The man who was your most dangerous rival has had the mightiest fall. And now he's lying there in the pit he dug for himself, poor misguided creature.

TESMAN: Have you heard any news of Eilert? Since I went away?

MISS TESMAN: Only that he's said to have published a new book.

TESMAN: What! Eilert Loevborg? You mean—just recently? What?

MISS TESMAN: So they say. I don't imagine it can be of any value, do you? When your new book comes out, that'll be another story. What's it going to be about?

TESMAN: The domestic industries of Brabant[3] in the Middle Ages.

MISS TESMAN: Oh, George! The things you know about!

TESMAN: Mind you, it may be some time before I actually get down to writing it. I've made these very extensive notes, and I've got to file and index them first.

MISS TESMAN: Ah, yes! Making notes; filing and indexing; you've always been wonderful at that. Poor dear Joachim was just the same.

3. Prosperous duchy (1190–1477), now divided between Belgium and the Netherlands.

TESMAN: I'm looking forward so much to getting down to that. Especially now I've a home of my own to work in.

MISS TESMAN: And above all, now that you have the girl you set your heart on, George dear.

TESMAN: [*Embraces her.*] Oh, yes, Auntie Juju, yes! Hedda's the loveliest thing of all! [*Looks towards the doorway.*] I think I hear her coming. What?

[HEDDA *enters the rear room from the left, and comes into the drawing room. She is a woman of twenty-nine. Distinguished, aristocratic face and figure. Her complexion is pale and opalescent. Her eyes are steel-grey, with an expression of cold, calm serenity. Her hair is of a handsome auburn color, but is not especially abundant. She is dressed in an elegant, somewhat loose-fitting morning gown.*]

MISS TESMAN: [*Goes to greet her.*] Good morning, Hedda dear! Good morning!

HEDDA: [*Holds out her hand.*] Good morning, dear Miss Tesman. What an early hour to call. So kind of you.

MISS TESMAN. [*Seems somewhat embarrassed.*] And has the young bride slept well in her new home?

HEDDA: Oh—thank you, yes. Passably well.

TESMAN: [*Laughs.*] Passably. I say, Hedda, that's good! When I jumped out of bed, you were sleeping like a top.

HEDDA: Yes. Fortunately. One has to accustom oneself to anything new, Miss Tesman. It takes time. [*Looks left.*] Oh, that maid's left the french windows open. This room's flooded with sun.

MISS TESMAN. [*Goes towards the windows.*] Oh—let me close them.

HEDDA: No, no, don't do that. Tesman dear, draw the curtains. This light's blinding me.

TESMAN: [*At the windows.*] Yes, yes, dear. There, Hedda, now you've got shade and fresh air.

HEDDA: This room needs fresh air. All these flowers—But my dear Miss Tesman, won't you take a seat?

MISS TESMAN: No, really not, thank you. I just wanted to make sure you have everything you need. I must see about getting back home. My poor dear sister will be waiting for me.

TESMAN: Be sure to give her my love, won't you? Tell her I'll run over and see her later today.

MISS TESMAN: Oh yes, I'll tell her that. Oh, George—— [*Fumbles in the pocket of her skirt.*] I almost forgot. I've brought something for you.

TESMAN. What's that, Auntie Juju? What?

MISS TESMAN: [*Pulls out a flat package wrapped in newspaper and gives it to him.*] Open and see, dear boy.

TESMAN: [*Opens the package.*] Good heavens! Auntie Juju, you've kept them! Hedda, this is really very touching. What?

HEDDA: [*By the what-nots, on the right.*] What is it, Tesman?

TESMAN: My old shoes! My slippers, Hedda!

HEDDA: Oh, them. I remember you kept talking about them on our honeymoon.

TESMAN: Yes, I missed them dreadfully. [*Goes over to her.*] Here, Hedda, take a look.

HEDDA: [*Goes away towards the stove.*] Thanks, I won't bother.

TESMAN: [*Follows her.*] Fancy, Hedda, Auntie Rena's embroidered them for me. Despite her being so ill. Oh, you can't imagine what memories they have for me.

HEDDA: [*By the table.*] Not for me.

MISS TESMAN: No, Hedda's right there, George.

TESMAN: Yes, but I thought since she's one of the family now——

HEDDA: [*Interrupts.*] Tesman, we really can't go on keeping this maid.

MISS TESMAN: Not keep Bertha?

TESMAN: What makes you say that, dear? What?

HEDDA: [*Points.*] Look at that! She's left her old hat lying on the chair.

TESMAN: [*Appalled, drops his slippers on the floor.*] But, Hedda——!

HEDDA: Suppose someone came in and saw it?

TESMAN: But Hedda—that's Auntie Juju's hat.

HEDDA: Oh?

MISS TESMAN: [*Picks up the hat.*] Indeed it's mine. And it doesn't happen to be old, Hedda dear.

HEDDA: I didn't look at it very closely, Miss Tesman.

MISS TESMAN: [*Tying on the hat.*] As a matter of fact, it's the first time I've worn it. As the good Lord is my witness.

TESMAN: It's very pretty, too. Really smart.

MISS TESMAN: Oh, I'm afraid it's nothing much really. [*Looks round.*] My parasol? Ah, here it is. [*Takes it.*] This is mine, too. [*Murmurs.*] Not Bertha's.

TESMAN: A new hat and a new parasol! I say, Hedda, fancy that!

HEDDA: Very pretty and charming.

TESMAN: Yes, isn't it? What? But Auntie Juju, take a good look at Hedda before you go. Isn't she pretty and charming?

MISS TESMAN: Dear boy, there's nothing new in that. Hedda's been a beauty ever since the day she was born. [*Nods and goes right.*]

TESMAN: [*Follows her.*] Yes, but have you noticed how strong and healthy she's looking? And how she's filled out since we went away?

MISS TESMAN: [*Stops and turns.*] Filled out?

HEDDA: [*Walks across the room.*] Oh, can't we forget it?

TESMAN: Yes, Auntie Juju—you can't see it so clearly with that dress on. But I've good reason to know——

HEDDA: [*By the french windows, impatiently.*] You haven't good reason to know anything.

TESMAN: It must have been the mountain air up there in the Tyrol——

HEDDA: [*Curtly, interrupts him.*] I'm exactly the same as when I went away.

TESMAN: You keep on saying so. But you're not. I'm right, aren't I, Auntie Juju?

MISS TESMAN: [*Has folded her hands and is gazing at her.*] She's beautiful—beautiful. Hedda is beautiful. [*Goes over to* HEDDA, *takes her head between her hands, draws it down and kisses her hair.*] God bless and keep you, Hedda Tesman. For George's sake.

HEDDA: [*Frees herself politely.*] Oh—let me go, please.

MISS TESMAN: [*Quietly, emotionally.*] I shall come see you both every day.

TESMAN: Yes, Auntie Juju, please do. What?

MISS TESMAN: Good-bye! Good-bye!

[*She goes out into the hall.* TESMAN *follows her. The door remains open.* TES- MAN *is heard sending his love to* AUNT RENA *and thanking* MISS TESMAN *for his slippers. Meanwhile* HEDDA *walks up and down the room raising her arms and clenching her fists as though in desperation. Then she throws aside the curtains from the french windows and stands there, looking out. A few moments later,* TESMAN *returns and closes the door behind him.*]

TESMAN: [*Picks up his slippers from the floor.*] What are you looking at, Hedda?

HEDDA: [*Calm and controlled again.*] Only the leaves. They're so golden. And withered.

TESMAN: [*Wraps up the slippers and lays them on the table.*] Well, we're in September now.

HEDDA: [*Restless again.*] Yes. We're already into September.

TESMAN: Auntie Juju was behaving rather oddly, I thought, didn't you? Almost as though she was in church or something. I wonder what came over her. Any idea?

HEDDA: I hardly know her. Does she often act like that?

TESMAN: Not to the extent she did today.

HEDDA: [*Goes away from the french windows.*] Do you think she was hurt by what I said about the hat?

TESMAN: Oh, I don't think so. A little at first, perhaps——

HEDDA: But what a thing to do, throw her hat down in someone's drawing room. People don't do such things.

TESMAN: I'm sure Auntie Juju doesn't do it very often.

HEDDA: Oh well, I'll make it up with her.

TESMAN: Oh Hedda, would you?

HEDDA: When you see them this afternoon invite her to come out here this evening.

TESMAN: You bet I will! I say, there's another thing which would please her enormously.

HEDDA: Oh?

TESMAN: If you could bring yourself to call her Auntie Juju. For my sake, Hedda? What?

HEDDA: Oh no, really Tesman, you mustn't ask me to do that. I've told you so once before. I'll try to call her Aunt Juliana. That's as far as I'll go.

TESMAN: [*After a moment.*] I say, Hedda, is anything wrong? What?

HEDDA: I'm just looking at my old piano. It doesn't really go with all this.

TESMAN: As soon as I start getting my salary we'll see about changing it.

HEDDA: No, no, don't let's change it. I don't want to part with it. We can move it into that little room and get another one to put in here.

TESMAN: [*A little downcast.*] Yes, we—might do that.

HEDDA: [*Picks up the bunch of flowers from the piano.*] These flowers weren't here when we arrived last night.

TESMAN: I expect Auntie Juju brought them.

HEDDA: Here's a card. [*Takes it out and reads.*] "Will come back later today." Guess who it's from?

TESMAN: No idea. Who? What?

HEDDA: It says: "Mrs. Elvsted."

TESMAN: No, really? Mrs. Elvsted! She used to be Miss Rysing, didn't she?

HEDDA: Yes. She was the one with that irritating hair she was always showing off. I hear she used to be an old flame of yours.

TESMAN: [*Laughs.*] That didn't last long. Anyway, that was before I got to know you, Hedda. By Jove, fancy her being in town!

HEDDA: Strange she should call. I only knew her at school.

TESMAN: Yes, I haven't seen her for—oh, heaven knows how long. I don't know how she manages to stick it out up there in the north. What?

HEDDA: [*Thinks for a moment, then says suddenly.*] Tell me, Tesman, doesn't he live somewhere up in those parts? You know—Eilert Loevborg?

TESMAN: Yes, that's right. So he does. [BERTHA *enters from the hall.*]

BERTHA. She's here again, madam. The lady who came and left the flowers. [*Points.*] The ones you're holding.

HEDDA: Oh, is she? Well, show her in.

[BERTHA *opens the door for* MRS. ELVSTED *and goes out.* MRS. ELVSTED *is a delicately built woman with gentle, attractive features. Her eyes are light blue, large, and somewhat prominent, with a frightened, questioning expression. Her hair is extremely fair, almost flaxen, and is exceptionally wavy and abundant. She is two or three years younger than* HEDDA. *She is wearing a dark visiting dress, in good taste but not quite in the latest fashion.*]

HEDDA: [*Goes cordially to greet her.*] Dear Mrs. Elvsted, good morning. How delightful to see you again after all this time.

MRS. ELVSTED: [*Nervously, trying to control herself.*] Yes, it's many years since we met.

TESMAN: And since *we* met. What?

HEDDA: Thank you for your lovely flowers.

MRS. ELVSTED: Oh, please—I wanted to come yesterday afternoon. But they told me you were away——

TESMAN: You've only just arrived in town, then? What?

MRS. ELVSTED: I got here yesterday, around midday. Oh, I became almost desperate when I heard you weren't here.

HEDDA: Desperate? Why?

TESMAN: My dear Mrs. Rysing—Elvsted——

HEDDA: There's nothing wrong, I hope?

MRS. ELVSTED: Yes, there is. And I don't know anyone else here whom I can turn to.

HEDDA: [*Puts the flowers down on the table.*] Come and sit with me on the sofa——

MRS. ELVSTED: Oh, I feel too restless to sit down.

HEDDA: You must. Come along, now. [*She pulls* MRS. ELVSTED *down on to the sofa and sits beside her.*]

TESMAN: Well? Tell us, Mrs.—er——

HEDDA: Has something happened at home?

MRS. ELVSTED: Yes—that is, yes and no. Oh, I do hope you won't misunderstand me——

HEDDA: Then you'd better tell us the whole story, Mrs. Elvsted.

TESMAN: That's why you've come. What?

MRS. ELVSTED: Yes—yes, it is. Well, then—in case you don't already know—Eilert Loevborg is in town.

HEDDA: Loevborg here?

TESMAN: Eilert back in town? By Jove, Hedda, did you hear that?

HEDDA: Yes, of course I heard.

MRS. ELVSTED: He's been here a week. A whole week! In this city. Alone. With all those dreadful people——

HEDDA: But my dear Mrs. Elvsted, what concern is he of yours?

MRS. ELVSTED: [Gives her a frightened look and says quickly.] He's been tutoring the children.

HEDDA: Your children?

MRS. ELVSTED: My husband's. I have none.

HEDDA: Oh, you mean your stepchildren.

MRS. ELVSTED: Yes.

TESMAN: [Gropingly.] But was he sufficiently—I don't know how to put it—sufficiently regular in his habits to be suited to such a post? What?

MRS. ELVSTED: For the past two to three years he has been living irreproachably.

TESMAN: You don't say! By Jove, Hedda, hear that?

HEDDA: I hear.

MRS. ELVSTED: Quite irreproachably, I assure you. In every respect. All the same—in this big city—with money in his pockets—I'm so dreadfully frightened something may happen to him.

TESMAN: But why didn't he stay up there with you and your husband?

MRS. ELVSTED: Once his book had come out, he became restless.

TESMAN: Oh, yes—Auntie Juju said he's brought out a new book.

MRS. ELVSTED: Yes, a big new book about the history of civilization. A kind of general survey. It came out a fortnight ago. Everyone's been buying it and reading it—it's created a tremendous stir——

TESMAN: Has it really? It must be something he's dug up, then.

MRS. ELVSTED: You mean from the old days?

TESMAN: Yes.

MRS. ELVSTED: No, he's written it all since he came to live with us.

TESMAN: Well, that's splendid news, Hedda. Fancy that!

MRS. ELVSTED: Oh, yes! If only he can go on like this!

HEDDA: Have you met him since you came here?

MRS. ELVSTED: No, not yet, I had such dreadful difficulty finding his address. But this morning I managed to track him down at last.

HEDDA: [Looks searchingly at her.] I must say I find it a little strange that your husband—hm——

MRS. ELVSTED: [*Starts nervously.*] My husband! What do you mean?

HEDDA: That he should send you all the way here on an errand of this kind. I'm surprised he didn't come himself to keep an eye on his friend.

MRS. ELVSTED: Oh, no, no—my husband hasn't the time. Besides, I—er—wanted to do some shopping here.

HEDDA: [*With a slight smile.*] Ah. Well, that's different.

MRS. ELVSTED: [*Gets up quickly, restlessly.*] Please, Mr. Tesman, I beg you—be kind to Eilert Loevborg if he comes here. I'm sure he will. I mean, you used to be such good friends in the old days. And you're both studying the same subject, as far as I can understand. You're in the same field, aren't you?

TESMAN: Well, we used to be, anyway.

MRS. ELVSTED: Yes—so I beg you earnestly, do please, please, keep an eye on him. Oh, Mr. Tesman, do promise me you will.

TESMAN: I shall be only too happy to do so, Mrs. Rysing.

HEDDA: Elvsted.

TESMAN: I'll do everything for Eilert that lies in my power. You can rely on that.

MRS. ELVSTED: Oh, how good and kind you are! [*Presses his hands.*] Thank you, thank you, thank you. [*Frightened.*] My husband's so fond of him, you see.

HEDDA: [*Gets up.*] You'd better send him a note, Tesman. He may not come to you of his own accord.

TESMAN: Yes, that'd probably be the best plan, Hedda. What?

HEDDA: The sooner the better. Why not do it now?

MRS. ELVSTED: [*Pleadingly.*] Oh yes, if only you would!

TESMAN: I'll do it this very moment. Do you have his address, Mrs.—er—Elvsted?

MRS. ELVSTED: Yes. [*Takes a small piece of paper from her pocket and gives it to him.*]

TESMAN: Good, good. Right, well I'll go inside and——[*Looks round.*] Where are my slippers? Oh yes, here. [*Picks up the package and is about to go.*]

HEDDA: Try to sound friendly. Make it a nice long letter.

TESMAN: Right, I will.

MRS. ELVSTED: Please don't say anything about my having seen you.

TESMAN: Good heavens no, of course not. What? [*Goes out through the rear room to the right.*]

HEDDA: [*Goes over to* MRS. ELVSTED, *smiles, and says softly.*] Well! Now we've killed two birds with one stone.

MRS. ELVSTED: What do you mean?

HEDDA: Didn't you realize I wanted to get him out of the room?

MRS. ELVSTED: So that he could write the letter?

HEDDA: And so that I could talk to you alone.

MRS. ELVSTED: [*Confused.*] About this?

HEDDA: Yes, about this.

MRS. ELVSTED: [*In alarm.*] But there's nothing more to tell, Mrs. Tesman. Really there isn't.

HEDDA: Oh, yes there is. There's a lot more. I can see that. Come along, let's sit down and have a little chat.

[*She pushes* MRS. ELVSTED *down into the armchair by the stove and seats herself on one of the footstools.*]

MRS. ELVSTED: [*Looks anxiously at her watch.*] Really, Mrs. Tesman, I think I ought to be going now.

HEDDA: There's no hurry. Well? How are things at home?

MRS. ELVSTED: I'd rather not speak about that.

HEDDA: But my dear, you can tell me. Good heavens, we were at school together.

MRS. ELVSTED: Yes, but you were a year senior to me. Oh, I used to be terribly frightened of you in those days.

HEDDA: Frightened of me?

MRS. ELVSTED: Yes, terribly frightened. Whenever you met me on the staircase you used to pull my hair.

HEDDA: No, did I?

MRS. ELVSTED: Yes. And once you said you'd burn it all off.

HEDDA: Oh, that was only in fun.

MRS. ELVSTED: Yes, but I was so silly in those days. And then afterwards—I mean, we've drifted so far apart. Our backgrounds were so different.

HEDDA: Well, now we must try to drift together again. Now listen. When we were at school we used to call each other by our Christian names—

MRS. ELVSTED: No, I'm sure you're mistaken.

HEDDA: I'm sure I'm not. I remember it quite clearly. Let's tell each other our secrets, as we used to in the old days. [*Moves closer on her footstool.*] There, now. [*Kisses her on the cheek.*] You must call me Hedda.

MRS. ELVSTED: [*Squeezes her hands and pats them.*] Oh, you're so kind. I'm not used to people being so nice to me.

HEDDA: Now, now, now. And I shall call you Tora, the way I used to.

MRS. ELVSTED: My name is Thea.

HEDDA: Yes, of course. Of course. I meant Thea. [*Looks at her sympathetically.*] So you're not used to kindness, Thea? In your own home?

MRS. ELVSTED: Oh, if only I had a home! But I haven't. I've never had one.

HEDDA: [*Looks at her for a moment.*] I thought that was it.

MRS. ELVSTED: [*Stares blankly and helplessly.*] Yes—yes—yes.

HEDDA: I can't remember exactly now, but didn't you first go to Mr. Elvsted as a housekeeper?

MRS. ELVSTED: Governess, actually. But his wife—at the time, I mean—she was an invalid, and had to spend most of her time in bed. So I had to look after the house too.

HEDDA: But in the end, you became mistress of the house.

MRS. ELVSTED: [*Sadly.*] Yes, I did.

HEDDA: Let me see. Roughly how long ago was that?

MRS. ELVSTED: When I got married, you mean?

HEDDA: Yes.

MRS. ELVSTED: About five years.

HEDDA: Yes; it must be about that.

MRS. ELVSTED: Oh, those five years! Especially that last two or three. Oh, Mrs. Tesman, if you only knew——

HEDDA: [Slaps her hand gently.] Mrs. Tesman? Oh, Thea!

MRS. ELVSTED: I'm sorry, I'll try to remember. Yes—if you had any idea——

HEDDA: [Casually.] Eilert Loevborg's been up here too, for about three years, hasn't he?

MRS. ELVSTED: [Looks at her uncertainly.] Eilert Loevborg? Yes, he has.

HEDDA: Did you know him before? When you were here?

MRS. ELVSTED: No, not really. That is—I knew him by name, of course.

HEDDA: But up there, he used to visit you?

MRS. ELVSTED: Yes, he used to come and see us every day. To give the children lessons. I found I couldn't do that as well as manage the house.

HEDDA: I'm sure you couldn't. And your husband——? I suppose being a magistrate he has to be away from home a good deal?

MRS. ELVSTED: Yes. You see, Mrs. —— you see, Hedda, he has to cover the whole district.

HEDDA: [Leans against the arm of MRS. ELVSTED's chair.] Poor, pretty little Thea! Now you must tell me the whole story. From beginning to end.

MRS. ELVSTED: Well—what do you want to know?

HEDDA: What kind of a man is your husband, Thea? I mean, as a person. Is he kind to you?

MRS. ELVSTED: [Evasively.] I'm sure he does his best to be.

HEDDA: I only wonder if he isn't too old for you. There's more than twenty years between you, isn't there?

MRS. ELVSTED: [Irritably.] Yes, there's that too. Oh, there are so many things. We're different in every way. We've nothing in common. Nothing whatever.

HEDDA: But he loves you, surely? In his own way?

MRS. ELVSTED: Oh, I don't know. I think he just finds me useful. And then I don't cost much to keep. I'm cheap.

HEDDA: Now you're being stupid.

MRS. ELVSTED: [Shakes her head.] It can't be any different. With him. He doesn't love anyone except himself. And perhaps the children—a little.

HEDDA: He must be fond of Eilert Loevborg, Thea.

MRS. ELVSTED: [Looks at her.] Eilert Loevborg? What makes you think that?

HEDDA: Well, if he sends you all the way down here to look for him——[Smiles almost imperceptibly.] Besides, you said so yourself to Tesman.

MRS. ELVSTED: [With a nervous twitch.] Did I? Oh yes, I suppose I did. [Impulsively, but keeping her voice low.] Well, I might as well tell you the whole story. It's bound to come out sooner or later.

HEDDA: But my dear Thea——?

MRS. ELVSTED: My husband had no idea I was coming here.

HEDDA: What? Your husband didn't know?

MRS. ELVSTED: No, of course not. As a matter of fact, he wasn't even there. He was away at the assizes. Oh, I couldn't stand it any longer, Hedda! I just couldn't. I'd be so dreadfully lonely up there now.

HEDDA: Go on.

MRS. ELVSTED: So I packed a few things. Secretly. And went.

HEDDA: Without telling anyone?

MRS. ELVSTED: Yes. I caught the train and came straight here.

HEDDA: But my dear Thea! How brave of you!

MRS. ELVSTED: [Gets up and walks across the room.] Well, what else could I do?

HEDDA: But what do you suppose your husband will say when you get back?

MRS. ELVSTED: [By the table, looks at her.] Back there? To him?

HEDDA: Yes. Surely——?

MRS. ELVSTED: I shall never go back to him.

HEDDA: [Gets up and goes closer.] You mean you've left your home for good?

MRS. ELVSTED: Yes. I didn't see what else I could do.

HEDDA: But to do it so openly!

MRS. ELVSTED: Oh, it's no use trying to keep a thing like that secret.

HEDDA: But what do you suppose people will say?

MRS. ELVSTED: They can say what they like. [Sits sadly, wearily on the sofa.] I had to do it.

HEDDA: [After a short silence.] What do you intend to do now? How are you going to live?

MRS. ELVSTED: I don't know. I only know that I must live wherever Eilert Loevborg is. If I am to go on living.

HEDDA: [Moves a chair from the table, sits on it near MRS. ELVSTED and strokes her hands.] Tell me, Thea, how did this—friendship between you and Eilert Loevborg begin?

MRS. ELVSTED: Oh, it came about gradually. I developed a kind of—power over him.

HEDDA: Oh?

MRS. ELVSTED: He gave up his old habits. Not because I asked him to. I'd never have dared to do that. I suppose he just noticed I didn't like that kind of thing. So he gave it up.

HEDDA: [Hides a smile.] So you've made a new man of him. Clever little Thea!

MRS. ELVSTED: Yes—anyway, he says I have. And he's made a —sort of—real person of me. Taught me to think—and to understand all kinds of things.

HEDDA: Did he give you lessons too?

MRS. ELVSTED: Not exactly lessons. But he talked to me. About—oh, you've no idea—so many things! And then he let me work with him. Oh, it was wonderful. I was so happy to be allowed to help him.

HEDDA: Did he allow you to help him!

MRS. ELVSTED: Yes. Whenever he wrote anything we always—did it together.

HEDDA: Like good pals?

MRS. ELVSTED: [Eagerly.] Pals! Yes—why, Hedda, that's exactly the word he used! Oh, I ought to feel so happy. But I can't. I don't know if it will last.

HEDDA: You don't seem very sure of him.

MRS. ELVSTED: [Sadly.] Something stands between Eilert Loevborg and me. The shadow of another woman.

HEDDA: Who can that be?

MRS. ELVSTED: I don't know. Someone he used to be friendly with in—in the old days. Someone he's never been able to forget.

HEDDA: What has he told you about her?

MRS. ELVSTED: Oh, he only mentioned her once, casually.

HEDDA: Well! What did he say?

MRS. ELVSTED: He said when he left her she tried to shoot him with a pistol.

HEDDA: [*Cold, controlled.*] What nonsense. People don't do such things. The kind of people we know.

MRS. ELVSTED: No, I think it must have been that red-haired singer he used to—

HEDDA: Ah yes, very probably.

MRS. ELVSTED: I remember they used to say she always carried a loaded pistol.

HEDDA: Well then, it must be her.

MRS. ELVSTED: But Hedda, I hear she's come back, and is living here. Oh, I'm so desperate——!

HEDDA: [*Glances toward the rear room.*] Ssh! Tesman's coming. [*Gets up and whispers.*] Thea, we mustn't breathe a word about this to anyone.

MRS. ELVSTED: [*Jumps up.*] Oh, no, no! Please don't!

[GEORGE TESMAN *appears from the right in the rear room with a letter in his hand, and comes into the drawing room.*]

TESMAN: Well, here's my little epistle all signed and sealed.

HEDDA: Good. I think Mrs. Elvsted wants to go now. Wait a moment—I'll see you as far as the garden gate.

TESMAN: Er—Hedda, do you think Bertha could deal with this?

HEDDA: [*Takes the letter.*] I'll give her instructions.

[BERTHA *enters from the hall.*]

BERTHA: Judge Brack is here and asks if he may pay his respects to Madam and the Doctor.

HEDDA: Yes, ask him to be so good as to come in. And—wait a moment—drop this letter in the post box.

BERTHA: [*Takes the letter.*] Very good, madam.

[*She opens the door for* JUDGE BRACK, *and goes out.* JUDGE BRACK *is forty-five; rather short, but well-built, and elastic in his movements. He has a roundish face with an aristocratic profile. His hair, cut short, is still almost black, and is carefully barbered. Eyes lively and humorous. Thick eyebrows. His moustache is also thick, and is trimmed square at the ends. He is wearing outdoor clothes which are elegant but a little too youthful for him. He has a monocle in one eye; now and then he lets it drop.*]

BRACK: [*Hat in hand, bows.*] May one presume to call so early?

HEDDA: One may presume.

TESMAN: [*Shakes his hand.*] You're welcome here any time. Judge Brack—Mrs. Rysing.

[HEDDA *sighs.*]

BRACK: [*Bows.*] Ah—charmed——

HEDDA: [*Looks at him and laughs.*] What fun to be able to see you by daylight for once, Judge.

BRACK: Do I look—different?

HEDDA: Yes. A little younger, I think.

BRACK: Obliged.

TESMAN: Well, what do you think of Hedda? What? Doesn't she look well? Hasn't she filled out——?

HEDDA: Oh, do stop it. You ought to be thanking Judge Brack for all the inconvenience he's put himself to——

BRACK: Nonsense, it was a pleasure——

HEDDA: You're a loyal friend. But my other friend is pining to get away. Au revoir, Judge. I won't be a minute.

[*Mutual salutations.* MRS. ELVSTED *and* HEDDA *go out through the hall.*]

BRACK: Well, is your wife satisfied with everything?

TESMAN: Yes, we can't thank you enough. That is—we may have to shift one or two things around, she tells me. And we're short of one or two little items we'll have to purchase.

BRACK: Oh? Really?

TESMAN: But you musn't worry your head about that. Hedda says she'll get what's needed. I say, why don't we sit down? What?

BRACK: Thanks, just for a moment. [*Sits at the table.*] There's something I'd like to talk to you about, my dear Tesman.

TESMAN: Oh? Ah yes, of course. [*Sits.*] After the feast comes the reckoning. What?

BRACK: Oh, never mind about the financial side—there's no hurry about that. Though I could wish we'd arranged things a little less palatially.

TESMAN: Good heavens, that'd never have done. Think of Hedda, my dear chap. You know her. I couldn't possibly ask her to live like a suburban housewife.

BRACK: No, no—that's just the problem.

TESMAN: Anyway, it can't be long now before my nomination[4] comes through.

BRACK: Well, you know, these things often take time.

TESMAN: Have you heard any more news? What?

BRACK: Nothing definite. [*Changing the subject.*] Oh, by the way, I have one piece of news for you.

TESMAN: What?

BRACK: Your old friend Eilert Loevborg is back in town.

TESMAN: I know that already.

BRACK: Oh? How did you hear that?

TESMAN: She told me. That lady who went out with Hedda.

BRACK: I see. What was her name? I didn't catch it.

TESMAN: Mrs. Elvsted.

---

4. To a professorship at the university.

BRACK: Oh, the magistrate's wife. Yes, Loevborg's been living up near them, hasn't he?

TESMAN: I'm delighted to hear he's become a decent human being again.

BRACK: Yes, so they say.

TESMAN: I gather he's published a new book, too. What?

BRACK: Indeed he has.

TESMAN: I hear it's created rather a stir.

BRACK: Quite an unusual stir.

TESMAN: I say, isn't that splendid news! He's such a gifted chap—and I was afraid he'd gone to the dogs for good.

BRACK: Most people thought he had.

TESMAN: But I can't think what he'll do now. How on earth will he manage to make ends meet? What?

[As he speaks his last words, HEDDA enters from the hall.]

HEDDA: [To BRACK, laughs slightly scornfully.] Tesman is always worrying about making ends meet.

TESMAN: We were talking about poor Eilert Loevborg, Hedda dear.

HEDDA: [Gives him a quick look.] Oh, were you? [Sits in the armchair by the stove and asks casually.] Is he in trouble?

TESMAN: Well, he must have run through his inheritance long ago by now. And he can't write a new book every year. What? So I'm wondering what's going to become of him.

BRACK: I may be able to enlighten you there.

TESMAN: Oh?

BRACK: You mustn't forget he has relatives who wield a good deal of influence.

TESMAN: Relatives? Oh, they've quite washed their hands of him, I'm afraid.

BRACK: They used to regard him as the hope of the family.

TESMAN: Used to, yes. But he's put an end to that.

HEDDA: Who knows? [With a little smile.] I hear the Elvsteds have made a new man of him.

BRACK: And then this book he's just published——

TESMAN: Well, let's hope they find something for him. I've just written him a note. Oh, by the way, Hedda, I asked him to come over and see us this evening.

BRACK: But my dear chap, you're coming to me this evening. My bachelor party. You promised me last night when I met you at the boat.

HEDDA: Had you forgotten, Tesman?

TESMAN: Good heavens, yes, I'd quite forgotten.

BRACK: Anyway, you can be quite sure he won't turn up here.

TESMAN: Why do you think that? What?

BRACK: [A little unwillingly, gets up and rests his hands on the back of his chair.] My dear Tesman—and you, too, Mrs. Tesman—there's something I feel you ought to know.

TESMAN: Concerning Eilert?

BRACK: Concerning him and you.

TESMAN: Well, my dear Judge, tell us, please!

BRACK: You must be prepared for your nomination not to come through quite as quickly as you hope and expect.

TESMAN: [*Jumps up uneasily.*] Is anything wrong? What?

BRACK: There's a possibility that the appointment may be decided by competition——

TESMAN: Competition! By Jove, Hedda, fancy that!

HEDDA: [*Leans further back in her chair.*] Ah! How interesting!

TESMAN: But who else——? I say, you don't mean——?

BRACK: Exactly. By competition with Eilert Loevborg.

TESMAN: [*Clasps his hands in alarm.*] No, no, but this is inconceivable! It's absolutely impossible! What?

BRACK: Hm. We may find it'll happen, all the same.

TESMAN: No, but—Judge Brack, they couldn't be so inconsiderate toward me! [*Waves his arms.*] I mean, by Jove, I—I'm a married man! It was on the strength of this that Hedda and I *got* married! We ran up some pretty hefty debts. And borrowed money from Auntie Juju! I mean, good heavens, they practically promised me the appointment. What?

BRACK: Well, well, I'm sure you'll get it. But you'll have to go through a competition.

HEDDA: [*Motionless in her armchair.*] How exciting, Tesman. It'll be a kind of duel, by Jove.

TESMAN: My dear Hedda, how can you take it so lightly?

HEDDA: [*As before.*] I'm not. I can't wait to see who's going to win.

BRACK: In any case, Mrs. Tesman, it's best you should know how things stand. I mean before you commit yourself to these little items I hear you're threatening to purchase.

HEDDA: I can't allow this to alter my plans.

BRACK: Indeed? Well, that's your business. Good-bye. [*To* TESMAN.] I'll come and collect you on the way home from my afternoon walk.

TESMAN: Oh, yes, yes. I'm sorry, I'm all upside down just now.

HEDDA: [*Lying in her chair, holds out her hand.*] Good-bye, Judge. See you this afternoon.

BRACK: Thank you. Good-bye, good-bye.

TESMAN: [*Sees him to the door.*] Good-bye, my dear Judge. You will excuse me, won't you?

[JUDGE BRACK *goes out through the hall.*]

TESMAN: [*Pacing up and down.*] Oh, Hedda! One oughtn't to go plunging off on wild adventures. What?

HEDDA: [*Looks at him and smiles.*] Like you're doing?

TESMAN: Yes. I mean, there's no denying it, it was a pretty big adventure to go off and get married and set up house merely on expectation.

HEDDA: Perhaps you're right.

TESMAN: Well, anyway, we have our home, Hedda. By Jove, yes. The home we dreamed of. And set our hearts on. What?

HEDDA: [*Gets up slowly, wearily.*] You agreed that we should enter society. And keep open house. That was the bargain.

TESMAN: Yes. Good heavens, I was looking forward to it all so much. To seeing you play hostess to a select circle! By Jove! What? Ah, well, for the time being we shall have to make do with each other's company, Hedda. Perhaps have Auntie Juju in now and then. Oh dear, this wasn't all what you had in mind——

HEDDA: I won't be able to have a liveried footman. For a start.

TESMAN: Oh no, we couldn't possibly afford a footman.

HEDDA: And that thoroughbred horse you promised me——

TESMAN: [*Fearfully.*] Thoroughbred horse!

HEDDA: I mustn't even think of that now.

TESMAN: Heaven forbid!

HEDDA: [*Walks across the room.*] Ah, well. I still have one thing left to amuse myself with.

TESMAN: [*Joyfully.*] Thank goodness for that. What's that, Hedda? What?

HEDDA: [*In the open doorway, looks at him with concealed scorn.*] My pistols, George darling.

TESMAN: [*Alarmed.*] Pistols!

HEDDA: [*Her eyes cold.*] General Gabler's pistols. [*She goes into the rear room and disappears.*]

TESMAN: [*Runs to the doorway and calls after her.*] For heaven's sake, Hedda dear, don't touch those things. They're dangerous. Hedda—please—for my sake! What?

ACT II

SCENE: *The same as in Act I except that the piano has been removed and an elegant little writing table, with a bookcase, stands in its place. By the sofa on the left a smaller table has been placed. Most of the flowers have been removed.* MRS. ELVSTED's *bouquet stands on the larger table, downstage. It is afternoon.*

HEDDA, *dressed to receive callers, is alone in the room. She is standing by the open french windows, loading a revolver. The pair to it is lying in an open pistol case on the writing table.*

HEDDA: [*Looks down into the garden and calls.*] Good afternoon, Judge.

BRACK: [*In the distance, below.*] Afternoon, Mrs. Tesman.

HEDDA: [*Raises the pistol and takes aim.*] I'm going to shoot you, Judge Brack.

BRACK: [*Shouts from below.*] No no, no! Don't aim that thing at me!

HEDDA: This'll teach you to enter houses by the back door. [*Fires.*]

BRACK: [*Below.*] Have you gone completely out of your mind?

HEDDA: Oh dear! Did I hit you?

BRACK: [*Still outside.*] Stop playing these silly tricks.

HEDDA: All right, Judge. Come along in.

[JUDGE BRACK, *dressed for a bachelor party, enters through the french windows. He has a light overcoat on his arm.*]

BRACK: For God's sake! Haven't you stopped fooling around with those things yet? What are you trying to hit?

HEDDA: Oh, I was just shooting at the sky.

BRACK: [*Takes the pistol gently from her hand.*] By your leave, ma'am. [*Looks at it.*] Ah, yes—I know this old friend well. [*Looks around.*] Where's the case? Oh, yes. [*Puts the pistol in the case and closes it.*] That's enough of that little game for today.

HEDDA: Well, what on earth *am* I to do?

BRACK: You haven't had any visitors?

HEDDA: [*Closes the french windows.*] Not one. I suppose the best people are all still in the country.

BRACK: Your husband isn't home yet?

HEDDA: [*Locks the pistol case away in a drawer of the writing table.*] No. The moment he'd finished eating he ran off to his aunties. He wasn't expecting you so early.

BRACK: Ah, why didn't I think of that? How stupid of me.

HEDDA: [*Turns her head and looks at him.*] Why stupid?

BRACK: I'd have come a little sooner.

HEDDA: [*Walks across the room.*] There'd have been no one to receive you. I've been in my room since lunch, dressing.

BRACK: You haven't a tiny crack in the door through which we might have negotiated?

HEDDA: You forgot to arrange one.

BRACK: Another stupidity.

HEDDA: Well, we'll have to sit down here. And wait. Tesman won't be back for some time.

BRACK: Sad. Well, I'll be patient.

[HEDDA *sits on the corner of the sofa.* BRACK *puts his coat over the back of the nearest chair and seats himself, keeping his hat in his hand. Short pause. They look at each other.*]

HEDDA: Well?

BRACK: [*In the same tone of voice.*] Well?

HEDDA: I asked first.

BRACK: [*Leans forward slightly.*] Yes, well, now we can enjoy a nice, cosy little chat—Mrs. Hedda.

HEDDA: [*Leans further back in her chair.*] It seems such ages since we had a talk. I don't count last night or this morning.

BRACK: You mean: *à deux?*

HEDDA: Mm—yes. That's roughly what I meant.

BRACK: I've been longing so much for you to come home.

HEDDA: So have I.

BRACK: You? Really, Mrs. Hedda? And I thought you were having such a wonderful honeymoon.

HEDDA: Oh, yes. Wonderful!

BRACK: But your husband wrote such ecstatic letters.

HEDDA: He! Oh, yes! He thinks life has nothing better to offer than rooting around in libraries and copying old pieces of parchment, or whatever it is he does.

BRACK: [*A little maliciously.*] Well, that *is* his life. Most of it, anyway.

HEDDA: Yes, I know. Well, it's all right for him. But for me! Oh no, my dear Judge. I've been bored to death.

BRACK: [*Sympathetically.*] Do you mean that? Seriously?

HEDDA: Yes. Can you imagine? Six whole months without ever meeting a single person who was one of us, and to whom I could talk about the kind of things we talk about.

BRACK: Yes, I can understand. I'd miss that, too.

HEDDA: That wasn't the worst, though.

BRACK: What was?

HEDDA: Having to spend every minute of one's life with—with the same person.

BRACK: [*Nods.*] Yes. What a thought! Morning; noon; and——

HEDDA: [*Coldly.*] As I said: every minute of one's life.

BRACK: I stand corrected. But dear Tesman is such a clever fellow, I should have thought one ought to be able——

HEDDA: Tesman is only interested in one thing, my dear Judge. His special subject.

BRACK: True.

HEDDA: And people who are only interested in one thing don't make the most amusing company. Not for long, anyway.

BRACK: Not even when they happen to be the person one loves?

HEDDA: Oh, don't use that sickly, stupid word.

BRACK: [*Starts.*] But, Mrs. Hedda——!

HEDDA: [*Half laughing, half annoyed.*] You just try it, Judge. Listening to the history of civilization morning, noon and——

BRACK: [*Corrects her.*] Every minute of one's life.

HEDDA: All right. Oh, and those domestic industries of Brabant in the Middle Ages! That really is beyond the limit.

BRACK: [*Looks at her searchingly.*] But, tell me—if you feel like this why on earth did you—? Ha——

HEDDA: Why on earth did I marry George Tesman?

BRACK: If you like to put it that way.

HEDDA: Do you think it so very strange?

BRACK: Yes—and no, Mrs. Hedda.

HEDDA: I'd danced myself tired, Judge. I felt my time was up——[*Gives a slight shudder.*] No, I mustn't say that. Or even think it.

BRACK: You've no rational cause to think it.

HEDDA: Oh—cause, cause——[*Looks searchingly at him.*] After all, George Tesman—well, I mean, he's a very respectable man.

BRACK: Very respectable, sound as a rock. No denying that.

HEDDA: And there's nothing exactly ridiculous about him. Is there?

BRACK: Ridiculous? No-no, I wouldn't say that.

HEDDA: Mm. He's very clever at collecting material and all that, isn't he? I mean, he may go quite far in time.

BRACK: [Looks at her a little uncertainly.] I thought you believed, like everyone else, that he would become a very prominent man.

HEDDA: [Looks tired.] Yes, I did. And when he came and begged me on his bended knees to be allowed to love and to cherish me, I didn't see why I shouldn't let him.

BRACK: No, well—if one looks at it like that——

HEDDA: It was more than my other admirers were prepared to do, Judge dear.

BRACK: [Laughs.] Well, I can't answer for the others. As far as I myself am concerned, you know I've always had a considerable respect for the institution of marriage. As an institution.

HEDDA: [Lightly.] Oh, I've never entertained any hopes of you.

BRACK: All I want is to have a circle of friends whom I can trust, whom I can help with advice or—or by any other means, and into whose houses I may come and go as a—trusted friend.

HEDDA: Of the husband?

BRACK: [Bows.] Preferably, to be frank, of the wife. And of the husband too, of course. Yes, you know, this kind of—triangle is a delightful arrangement for all parties concerned.

HEDDA: Yes, I often longed for a third person while I was away. Oh, those hours we spent alone in railway compartments——

BRACK: Fortunately your honeymoon is now over.

HEDDA: [Shakes her head.] There's a long way still to go. I've only reached a stop on the line.

BRACK: Why not jump out and stretch your legs a little, Mrs. Hedda?

HEDDA: I'm not the jumping sort.

BRACK: Aren't you?

HEDDA: No. There's always someone around who——

BRACK: [Laughs.] Who looks at one's legs?

HEDDA: Yes. Exactly.

BRACK: Well, but surely——

HEDDA: [With a gesture of rejection.] I don't like it. I'd rather stay where I am. Sitting in the compartment. À deux.

BRACK: But suppose a third person were to step into the compartment?

HEDDA: That would be different.

BRACK: A trusted friend—someone who understood——

HEDDA: And was lively and amusing——

BRACK: And interested in—more subjects than one——

HEDDA: [Sighs audibly.] Yes, that'd be a relief.

BRACK: [Hears the front door open and shut.] The triangle is completed.

HEDDA: [Half under breath.] And the train goes on.

[GEORGE TESMAN, *in grey walking dress with a soft felt hat, enters from the hall. He has a number of paper-covered books under his arm and in his pockets.*]

TESMAN: [*Goes over to the table by the corner sofa.*] Phew! It's too hot to be lugging all this around. [*Puts the books down.*] I'm positively sweating, Hedda. Why, hullo, hullo! You here already, Judge? What? Bertha didn't tell me.

BRACK: [*Gets up.*] I came in through the garden.

HEDDA: What are all those books you've got there?

TESMAN: [*Stands glancing through them.*] Oh, some new publications dealing with my special subject. I had to buy them.

HEDDA. Your special subject?

BRACK: His special subject, Mrs. Tesman.

[BRACK *and* HEDDA *exchange a smile.*]

HEDDA: Haven't you collected enough material on your special subject?

TESMAN: My dear Hedda, one can never have too much. One must keep abreast of what other people are writing.

HEDDA: Yes. Of course.

TESMAN: [*Rooting among the books.*] Look—I bought a copy of Eilert Loevborg's new book, too. [*Holds it out to her.*] Perhaps you'd like to have a look at it, Hedda? What?

HEDDA. No, thank you. Er—yes, perhaps I will, later.

TESMAN: I glanced through it on my way home.

BRACK: What's your opinion—as a specialist on the subject?

TESMAN: I'm amazed how sound and balanced it is. He never used to write like that. [*Gathers his books together.*] Well, I must get down to these at once. I can hardly wait to cut the pages.[5] Oh, I've got to change, too. [*To* BRACK.] We don't have to be off just yet, do we? What?

BRACK: Heavens, no. We've plenty of time yet.

TESMAN: Good, I needn't hurry, then. [*Goes with his books, but stops and turns in the doorway.*] Oh, by the way, Hedda, Auntie Juju won't be coming to see you this evening.

HEDDA: Won't she? Oh—the hat, I suppose.

TESMAN: Good heavens, no. How could you think such a thing of Auntie Juju? Fancy——! No, Auntie Rena's very ill.

HEDDA: She always is.

TESMAN: Yes, but today she's been taken really bad.

HEDDA: Oh, then it's quite understandable that the other one should want to stay with her. Well, I shall have to swallow my disappointment.

TESMAN: You can't imagine how happy Auntie Juju was in spite of everything. At your looking so well after the honeymoon!

---

5. Books used to be sold with the pages folded but uncut as they came from the printing press; the owner had to cut the pages in order to read the book.

HEDDA: [*Half beneath her breath, as she rises.*] Oh, these everlasting aunts!

TESMAN: What?

HEDDA: [*Goes over to the french windows.*] Nothing.

TESMAN: Oh. All right. [*Goes into the rear room and out of sight.*]

BRACK: What was that about the hat?

HEDDA: Oh, something that happened with Miss Tesman this morning. She'd put her hat down on a chair. [*Looks at him and smiles.*] And I pretended to think it was the servant's.

BRACK: [*Shakes his head.*] But my dear Mrs. Hedda, how could you do such a thing? To that poor old lady?

HEDDA: [*Nervously, walking across the room.*] Sometimes a mood like that hits me. And I can't stop myself. [*Throws herself down in the armchair by the stove.*] Oh, I don't know how to explain it.

BRACK: [*Behind her chair.*] You're not really happy. That's the answer.

HEDDA: [*Stares ahead of her.*] Why on earth should I be happy? Can you give me a reason?

BRACK: Yes. For one thing you've got the home you always wanted.

HEDDA: [*Looks at him.*] You really believe that story?

BRACK: You mean it isn't true?

HEDDA: Oh, yes, it's partly true.

BRACK: Well?

HEDDA: It's true I got Tesman to see me home from parties last summer——

BRACK: It was a pity my home lay in another direction.

HEDDA: Yes. Your interests lay in another direction, too.

BRACK: [*Laughs.*] That's naughty of you, Mrs. Hedda. But to return to you and Tesman——

HEDDA: Well, we walked past this house one evening. And poor Tesman was fidgeting in his boots trying to find something to talk about. I felt sorry for the great scholar——

BRACK: [*Smiles incredulously.*] Did you? Hm.

HEDDA: Yes, honestly I did. Well, to help him out of his misery, I happened to say quite frivolously how much I'd love to live in this house.

BRACK: Was that all?

HEDDA: That evening, yes.

BRACK: But—afterwards?

HEDDA: Yes. My little frivolity had its consequences, my dear Judge.

BRACK: Our little frivolities do. Much too often, unfortunately.

HEDDA: Thank you. Well, it was our mutual admiration for the late Prime Minister's house that brought George Tesman and me together on common ground. So we got engaged, and we got married, and we went on our honeymoon, and—Ah well, Judge, I've—made my bed and I must lie in it, I was about to say.

BRACK: How utterly fantastic! And you didn't really care in the least about the house?

HEDDA: God knows I didn't.

BRACK: Yes, but now that we've furnished it so beautifully for you?

HEDDA: Ugh—all the rooms smell of lavender and dried roses. But perhaps Auntie Juju brought that in.

BRACK: [Laughs.] More likely the Prime Minister's widow, rest her soul.

HEDDA: Yes, it's got the odor of death about it. It reminds me of the flowers one has worn at a ball—the morning after. [Clasps her hands behind her neck, leans back in the chair and looks up at him.] Oh, my dear Judge, you've no idea how hideously bored I'm going to be out here.

BRACK: Couldn't you find some kind of occupation, Mrs. Hedda? Like your husband?

HEDDA: Occupation? That'd interest me?

BRACK: Well—preferably.

HEDDA: God knows what. I've often thought——[Breaks off.] No, that wouldn't work either.

BRACK: Who knows? Tell me about it.

HEDDA: I was thinking—if I could persuade Tesman to go into politics, for example.

BRACK: [Laughs.] Tesman! No, honestly, I don't think he's quite cut out to be a politician.

HEDDA: Perhaps not. But if I could persuade him to have a go at it?

BRACK: What satisfaction would that give you? If he turned out to be no good? Why do you want to make him do that?

HEDDA: Because I'm bored. [After a moment.] You feel there's absolutely no possibility of Tesman becoming Prime Minister, then?

BRACK: Well, you know, Mrs. Hedda, for one thing he'd have to be pretty well off before he could become that.

HEDDA: [Gets up impatiently.] There you are! [Walks across the room.] It's this wretched poverty that makes life so hateful. And ludicrous. Well, it is!

BRACK: I don't think that's the real cause.

HEDDA: What is, then?

BRACK: Nothing really exciting has ever happened to you.

HEDDA: Nothing serious, you mean?

BRACK: Call it that if you like. But now perhaps it may.

HEDDA: [Tosses her head.] Oh, you're thinking of this competition for that wretched professorship? That's Tesman's affair. I'm not going to waste my time worrying about that.

BRACK: Very well, let's forget about that then. But suppose you were to find yourself faced with what people call—to use the conventional phrase—the most solemn of human responsibilities? [Smiles.] A new responsibility, little Mrs. Hedda.

HEDDA: [Angrily.] Be quiet! Nothing like that's going to happen.

BRACK: [Warily.] We'll talk about it again in a year's time. If not earlier.

HEDDA: [Curtly.] I've no leanings in that direction, Judge. I don't want any— responsibilities.

BRACK: But surely you must feel some inclination to make use of that—natural talent which every woman—

HEDDA: [*Over by the french windows.*] Oh, be quiet, I say! I often think there's only one thing for which I have any natural talent.

BRACK: [*Goes closer.*] And what is that, if I may be so bold as to ask?

HEDDA: [*Stands looking out.*] For boring myself to death. Now you know. [*Turns, looks toward the rear room and laughs.*] Talking of boring, here comes the Professor.

BRACK: [*Quietly, warningly.*] Now, now, now, Mrs. Hedda!

[GEORGE TESMAN, *in evening dress, with gloves and hat in his hand, enters through the rear room from the right.*]

TESMAN: Hedda, hasn't any message come from Eilert? What?

HEDDA: No.

TESMAN: Ah, then we'll have him here presently. You wait and see.

BRACK: You really think he'll come?

TESMAN: Yes, I'm almost sure he will. What you were saying about him this morning is just gossip.

BRACK: Oh?

TESMAN: Yes. Auntie Juju said she didn't believe he'd ever dare to stand in my way again. Fancy that!

BRACK: Then everything in the garden's lovely.

TESMAN: [*Puts his hat, with his gloves in it, on a chair, right.*] Yes, but you really must let me wait for him as long as possible.

BRACK: We've plenty of time. No one'll be turning up at my place before seven or half past.

TESMAN: Ah, then we can keep Hedda company a little longer. And see if he turns up. What?

HEDDA: [*Picks up BRACK's coat and hat and carries them over to the corner sofa.*] And if the worst comes to the worst, Mr. Loevborg can sit here and talk to me.

BRACK: [*Offering to take his things from her.*] No, please. What do you mean by "if the worst comes to the worst"?

HEDDA: If he doesn't want to go with you and Tesman.

TESMAN: [*Looks doubtfully at her.*] I say, Hedda, do you think it'll be all right for him to stay here with you? What? Remember Auntie Juju isn't coming.

HEDDA: Yes, but Mrs. Elvsted is. The three of us can have a cup of tea together.

TESMAN: Ah, that'll be all right then.

BRACK: [*Smiles.*] It's probably the safest solution as far as he's concerned.

HEDDA: Why?

BRACK: My dear Mrs. Tesman, you always say of my little bachelor parties that they should be attended only by men of the strongest principles.

HEDDA: But Mr. Loevborg is a man of principle now. You know what they say about a reformed sinner——

[BERTHA *enters from the hall.*]

BERTHA: Madam, there's a gentleman here who wants to see you——

HEDDA: Ask him to come in.

TESMAN: [*Quietly.*] I'm sure it's him. By Jove. Fancy that!

[EILERT LOEVBORG *enters from the hall. He is slim and lean, of the same age as* TESMAN, *but looks older and somewhat haggard. His hair and beard are of a blackish-brown; his face is long and pale, but with a couple of reddish patches on his cheekbones. He is dressed in an elegant and fairly new black suit, and carries black gloves and a top hat in his hand. He stops just inside the door and bows abruptly. He seems somewhat embarrassed.*]

TESMAN: [*Goes over and shakes his hand.*] My dear Eilert! How grand to see you again after all these years!

EILERT LOEVBORG: [*Speaks softly.*] It was good of you to write, George. [*Goes nearer to* HEDDA.] May I shake hands with you, too, Mrs. Tesman?

HEDDA: [*Accepts his hand.*] Delighted to see you, Mr. Loevborg. [*With a gesture.*] I don't know if you two gentlemen——

LOEVBORG: [*Bows slightly.*] Judge Brack, I believe.

BRACK: [*Also with a slight bow.*] Correct. We—met some years ago——

TESMAN: [*Puts his hands on* LOEVBORG's *shoulders.*] Now you're to treat this house just as though it were your own home, Eilert. Isn't that right, Hedda? I hear you've decided to settle here again? What?

LOEVBORG: Yes, I have.

TESMAN: Quite understandable. Oh, by the bye—I've just bought your new book. Though to tell the truth I haven't found time to read it yet.

LOEVBORG: You needn't bother.

TESMAN: Oh? Why?

LOEVBORG: There's nothing much in it.

TESMAN: By Jove, fancy hearing that from you!

BRACK: But everyone's praising it.

LOEVBORG: That was exactly what I wanted to happen. So I only wrote what I knew everyone would agree with.

BRACK: Very sensible.

TESMAN: Yes, but my dear Eilert——

LOEVBORG: I want to try to re-establish myself. To begin again—from the beginning.

TESMAN: [*A little embarrassed.*] Yes, I—er—suppose you do. What?

LOEVBORG: [*Smiles, puts down his hat and takes a package wrapped in paper from his coat pocket.*] But when this gets published—George Tesman—read it. This is my real book. The one in which I have spoken with my own voice.

TESMAN: Oh, really? What's it about?

LOEVBORG: It's the sequel.

TESMAN: Sequel? To what?

LOEVBORG: To the other book.

TESMAN: The one that's just come out?

LOEVBORG: Yes.

TESMAN: But my dear Eilert, that covers the subject right up to the present day.

LOEVBORG: It does. But this is about the future.

TESMAN: The future! But, I say, we don't know anything about that.

LOEVBORG: No. But there are one or two things that need to be said about it. [*Opens the package.*] Here, have a look.

TESMAN: Surely that's not your handwriting?

LOEVBORG: I dictated it. [*Turns the pages.*] It's in two parts. The first deals with the forces that will shape our civilization. [*Turns further on towards the end.*] And the second indicates the direction in which that civilization may develop.

TESMAN: Amazing! I'd never think of writing about anything like that.

HEDDA: [*By the french windows, drumming on the pane.*] No. You wouldn't.

LOEVBORG: [*Puts the pages back into their cover and lays the package on the table.*] I brought it because I thought I might possibly read you a few pages this evening.

TESMAN: I say, what a kind idea! Oh, but this evening——? [*Glances at* BRACK.] I'm not quite sure whether——

LOEVBORG: Well, some other time, then. There's no hurry.

BRACK: The truth is, Mr. Loevborg, I'm giving a little dinner this evening. In Tesman's honor, you know.

LOEVBORG: [*Looks round for his hat.*] Oh—then I mustn't——

BRACK: No, wait a minute. Won't you do me the honor of joining us?

LOEVBORG: [*Curtly, with decision.*] No I can't. Thank you so much.

BRACK: Oh, nonsense. Do—please. There'll only be a few of us. And I can promise you we shall have some good sport, as Mrs. Hed—as Mrs. Tesman puts it.

LOEVBORG: I've no doubt. Nevertheless——

BRACK: You could bring your manuscript along and read it to Tesman at my place. I could lend you a room.

TESMAN: By Jove, Eilert, that's an idea. What?

HEDDA: [*Interposes.*] But Tesman, Mr. Loevborg doesn't want to go. I'm sure Mr. Loevborg would much rather sit here and have supper with me.

LOEVBORG: [*Looks at her.*] With you, Mrs. Tesman?

HEDDA: And Mrs. Elvsted.

LOEVBORG: Oh. [*Casually.*] I ran into her this afternoon.

HEDDA: Did you? Well, she's coming here this evening. So you really must stay, Mr. Loevborg. Otherwise she'll have no one to see her home.

LOEVBORG: That's true. Well—thank you, Mrs. Tesman, I'll stay then.

HEDDA: I'll just tell the servant.

[*She goes to the door which leads into the hall, and rings.* BERTHA *enters.* HEDDA *talks softly to her and points towards the rear room.* BERTHA *nods and goes out.*]

TESMAN: [*To* LOEVBORG, *as* HEDDA *does this.*] I say, Eilert. This new subject of yours—the—er—future—is that the one you're going to lecture about?

LOEVBORG: Yes.

TESMAN: They told me down at the bookshop that you're going to hold a series of lectures here during the autumn.

LOEVBORG: Yes, I am, I—hope you don't mind, Tesman.

TESMAN: Good heavens, no! But——?

LOEVBORG: I can quite understand it might queer your pitch a little.

TESMAN: [*Dejectedly*.] Oh well, I can't expect you to put them off for my sake.

LOEVBORG: I'll wait till your appointment's been announced.

TESMAN: You'll wait! But—but—aren't you going to compete with me for the post? What?

LOEVBORG: No. I only want to defeat you in the eyes of the world.

TESMAN: Good heavens! Then Auntie Juju was right after all! Oh, I knew it, I knew it! Hear that, Hedda? Fancy! Eilert *doesn't* want to stand in our way.

HEDDA: [*Curtly*.] Our? Leave me out of it, please.

[*She goes towards the rear room, where* BERTHA *is setting a tray with decanters and glasses on the table.* HEDDA *nods approval, and comes back into the drawing room.* BERTHA *goes out.*]

TESMAN: [*While this is happening*.] Judge Brack, what do you think about all this? What?

BRACK: Oh, I think honor and victory can be very splendid things——

TESMAN: Of course they can. Still——

HEDDA: [*Looks at* TESMAN *with a cold smile*.] You look as if you'd been hit by a thunderbolt.

TESMAN: Yes, I feel rather like it.

BRACK: There was a black cloud looming up, Mrs. Tesman. But it seems to have passed over.

HEDDA: [*Points toward the rear room*.] Well, gentlemen, won't you go in and take a glass of cold punch?

BRACK: [*Glances at his watch*.] A stirrup cup? Yes, why not?

TESMAN: An admirable suggestion, Hedda. Admirable! Oh, I feel so relieved!

HEDDA: Won't you have one, too, Mr. Loevborg?

LOEVBORG: No, thank you. I'd rather not.

BRACK: Great heavens, man, cold punch isn't poison. Take my word for it.

LOEVBORG: Not for everyone, perhaps.

HEDDA: I'll keep Mr. Loevborg company while you drink.

TESMAN: Yes, Hedda dear, would you?

[*He and* BRACK *go into the rear room, sit down, drink punch, smoke cigarettes and talk cheerfully during the following scene.* EILERT LOEVBORG *remains standing by the stove.* HEDDA *goes to the writing table.*]

HEDDA: [*Raising her voice slightly*.] I've some photographs I'd like to show you, if you'd care to see them. Tesman and I visited the Tyrol[6] on our way home.

[*She comes back with an album, places it on the table by the sofa and sits in the upstage corner of the sofa.* EILERT LOEVBORG *comes toward her, stops and looks at her. Then he takes a chair and sits down on her left, with his back toward the rear room.*]

6. Region in the Alps, now primarily in Austria, near the Italian border.

HEDDA: [*Opens the album.*] You see these mountains, Mr. Loevborg? That's the Ortler group. Tesman has written the name underneath. You see: "The Ortler Group near Meran."

LOEVBORG: [*Has not taken his eyes from her; says softly, slowly.*] Hedda—Gabler!

HEDDA: [*Gives him a quick glance.*] Ssh!

LOEVBORG: [*Repeats softly.*] Hedda Gabler!

HEDDA: [*Looks at the album.*] Yes, that used to be my name. When we first knew each other.

LOEVBORG: And from now on—for the rest of my life—I must teach myself never to say: Hedda Gabler.

HEDDA: [*Still turning the pages.*] Yes, you must. You'd better start getting into practice. The sooner the better.

LOEVBORG: [*Bitterly.*] Hedda Gabler married? And to George Tesman?

HEDDA: Yes. Well—that's life.

LOEVBORG: Oh, Hedda, Hedda! How could you throw yourself away like that?

HEDDA: [*Looks sharply at him.*] Stop it.

LOEVBORG: What do you mean?

[TESMAN *comes in and goes toward the sofa.*]

HEDDA: [*Hears him coming and says casually.*] And this, Mr. Loevborg, is the view from the Ampezzo valley. Look at those mountains. [*Glances affectionately up at* TESMAN.] What did you say those curious mountains were called, dear?

TESMAN: Let me have a look. Oh, those are the Dolomites.

HEDDA: Of course. Those are the Dolomites, Mr. Loevborg.

TESMAN: Hedda, I just wanted to ask you, can't we bring some punch in here? A glass for you, anyway. What?

HEDDA: Thank you, yes. And a biscuit or two, perhaps.

TESMAN: You wouldn't like a cigarette?

HEDDA: No.

TESMAN: Right.

[*He goes into the rear room and over to the right.* BRACK *is sitting there, glancing occasionally at* HEDDA *and* LOEVBORG.]

LOEVBORG: [*Softly, as before.*] Answer me, Hedda. How could you do it?

HEDDA: [*Apparently absorbed in the album.*] If you go on calling me Hedda I won't talk to you any more.

LOEVBORG: Mayn't I even when we're alone?

HEDDA: No. You can think it. But you mustn't say it.

LOEVBORG: Oh, I see. Because you love George Tesman.

HEDDA: [*Glances at him and smiles.*] Love? Don't be funny.

LOEVBORG: You don't love him?

HEDDA: I don't intend to be unfaithful to him. That's not what I want.

LOEVBORG: Hedda—just tell me one thing——

HEDDA: Ssh!

[TESMAN *enters from the rear room, carrying a tray.*]

TESMAN: Here we are! Here come the goodies! [*Puts the tray down on the table.*]

HEDDA: Why didn't you ask the servant to bring it in?

TESMAN: [*Fills the glasses.*] I like waiting on you, Hedda.

HEDDA: But you've filled both glasses. Mr. Loevborg doesn't want to drink.

TESMAN: Yes, but Mrs. Elvsted'll be here soon.

HEDDA: Oh yes, that's true. Mrs. Elvsted——

TESMAN: Had you forgotten her? What?

HEDDA: We're so absorbed with these photographs. [*Shows him one.*] You remember this little village?

TESMAN: Oh, that one down by the Brenner Pass. We spent a night there——

HEDDA: Yes, and met all those amusing people.

TESMAN: Oh yes, it was there, wasn't it? By Jove, if only we could have had you with us, Eilert! Ah, well. [*Goes back into the other room and sits down with* BRACK.]

LOEVBORG: Tell me one thing, Hedda.

HEDDA: Yes?

LOEVBORG: Didn't you love me either? Not—just a little?

HEDDA: Well now, I wonder? No, I think we were just good pals—Really good pals who could tell each other anything. [*Smiles.*] You certainly poured your heart out to me.

LOEVBORG: You begged me to.

HEDDA: Looking back on it, there was something beautiful and fascinating—and brave—about the way we told each other everything. That secret friendship no one else knew about.

LOEVBORG: Yes, Hedda, yes! Do you remember? How I used to come up to your father's house in the afternoon—and the General sat by the window and read his newspapers—with his back toward us——

HEDDA: And we sat on the sofa in the corner——

LOEVBORG: Always reading the same illustrated magazine——

HEDDA: We hadn't any photograph album.

LOEVBORG: Yes, Hedda. I regarded you as a kind of confessor. Told you things about myself which no one else knew about—then. Those days and nights of drinking and— Oh, Hedda, what power did you have to make me confess such things?

HEDDA: Power? You think I had some power over you?

LOEVBORG: Yes—I don't know how else to explain it. And all those—oblique questions you asked me——

HEDDA: You knew what they meant.

LOEVBORG: But that you could sit there and ask me such questions! So unashamedly——

HEDDA: I thought you said they were oblique.

LOEVBORG: Yes, but you asked them so unashamedly. That you could question me about—about that kind of thing!

HEDDA: You answered willingly enough.

LOEVBORG: Yes—that's what I can't understand—looking back on it. But tell me, Hedda—what you felt for me—wasn't that—love? When you asked me those questions and made me confess my sins to you, wasn't it because you wanted to wash me clean?

HEDDA: No, not exactly.

LOEVBORG: Why did you do it, then?

HEDDA: Do you find it so incredible that a young girl, given the chance to do so without anyone knowing, should want to be allowed a glimpse into a forbidden world of whose existence she is supposed to be ignorant?

LOEVBORG: So that was it?

HEDDA: One reason. One reason—I think.

LOEVBORG: You didn't love me, then. You just wanted—knowledge. But if that was so, why did you break it off?

HEDDA: That was your fault.

LOEVBORG: It was you who put an end to it.

HEDDA: Yes, when I realized that our friendship was threatening to develop into something—something else. Shame on you, Eilert Loevborg! How could you abuse the trust of your dearest friend?

LOEVBORG: [Clenches his fists.] Oh, why didn't you do it? Why didn't you shoot me dead? As you threatened to?

HEDDA: I was afraid. Of the scandal.

LOEVBORG: Yes, Hedda. You're a coward at heart.

HEDDA: A dreadful coward. [Changes her tone.] Luckily for you. Well, now you've found consolation with the Elvsteds.

LOEVBORG: I know what Thea's been telling you.

HEDDA: I dare say you told her about us.

LOEVBORG: Not a word. She's too silly to understand that kind of thing.

HEDDA: Silly?

LOEVBORG: She's silly about that kind of thing.

HEDDA: And I am a coward. [Leans closer to him, without looking him in the eyes, and says quietly.] But let me tell you something. Something you don't know.

LOEVBORG: [Tensely.] Yes?

HEDDA: My failure to shoot you wasn't my worst act of cowardice that evening.

LOEVBORG: [Looks at her for a moment, realizes her meaning and whispers passionately.] Oh, Hedda! Hedda Gabler! Now I see what was behind those questions. Yes! It wasn't knowledge you wanted! It was life!

HEDDA: [Flashes a look at him and says quietly.] Take care! Don't you delude yourself!

[It has begun to grow dark. BERTHA, from outside, opens the door leading into the hall.]

HEDDA: [Closes the album with a snap and cries, smiling.] Ah, at last! Come in, Thea dear!

[MRS. ELVSTED *enters from the hall, in evening dress. The door is closed behind her.*]

HEDDA: [*On the sofa, stretches out her arms toward her.*] Thea darling, I thought you were never coming!

[MRS. ELVSTED *makes a slight bow to the gentlemen in the rear room as she passes the open doorway, and they to her. Then she goes to the table and holds out her hand to* HEDDA. EILERT LOEVBORG *has risen from his chair. He and* MRS. ELVSTED *nod silently to each other.*]

MRS. ELVSTED: Perhaps I ought to go in and say a few words to your husband?
HEDDA: Oh, there's no need. They're happy by themselves. They'll be going soon.
MRS. ELVSTED: Going?
HEDDA. Yes, they're off on a spree this evening.
MRS. ELVSTED: [*Quickly, to* LOEVBORG.] You're not going with them?
LOEVBORG: No.
HEDDA: Mr. Loevborg is staying here with us.
MRS. ELVSTED: [*Takes a chair and is about to sit down beside him.*] Oh, how nice it is to be here!
HEDDA: No, Thea darling, not there. Come over here and sit beside me. I want to be in the middle.
MRS. ELVSTED: Yes, just as you wish.

[*She goes right the table and sits on the sofa, on* HEDDA's *right.* LOEVBORG *sits down again in his chair.*]

LOEVBORG: [*After a short pause, to* HEDDA.] Isn't she lovely to look at?
HEDDA: [*Strokes her hair gently.*] Only to look at?
LOEVBORG: Yes. We're just good pals. We trust each other implicitly. We can talk to each other quite unashamedly.
HEDDA: No need to be oblique?
MRS. ELVSTED: [*Nestles close to* HEDDA *and says quietly.*] Oh, Hedda, I'm so happy. Imagine—he says I've inspired him!
HEDDA: [*Looks at her with a smile.*] Dear Thea! Does he really?
LOEVBORG: She has the courage of her convictions, Mrs. Tesman.
MRS. ELVSTED: I? Courage?
LOEVBORG: Absolute courage. Where friendship is concerned.
HEDDA: Yes. Courage. Yes. If only one had that——
LOEVBORG: Yes?
HEDDA. One might be able to live. In spite of everything. [*Changes her tone suddenly.*] Well, Thea darling, now you're going to drink a nice glass of cold punch.
MRS. ELVSTED: No, thank you. I never drink anything like that.
HEDDA: Oh. You, Mr. Loevborg?
LOEVBORG: Thank you, I don't either.

MRS. ELVSTED: No, he doesn't, either.

HEDDA: [*Looks into his eyes.*] But if I want you to?

LOEVBORG: That doesn't make any difference.

HEDDA: [*Laughs.*] Have I no power over you at all? Poor me!

LOEVBORG: Not where this is concerned.

HEDDA: Seriously, I think you should. For your own sake.

MRS. ELVSTED: Hedda!

LOEVBORG: Why?

HEDDA: Or perhaps I should say for other people's sake.

LOEVBORG: What do you mean?

HEDDA: People might think you didn't feel absolutely and unashamedly sure of yourself. In your heart of hearts.

MRS. ELVSTED: [*Quietly.*] Oh, Hedda, no!

LOEVBORG: People can think what they like. For the present.

MRS. ELVSTED: [*Happily.*] Yes, that's true.

HEDDA: I saw it so clearly in Judge Brack a few minutes ago.

LOEVBORG: Oh. What did you see?

HEDDA: He smiled so scornfully when he saw you were afraid to go in there and drink with them.

LOEVBORG: Afraid! I wanted to stay here and talk to you.

MRS. ELVSTED: That was only natural, Hedda.

HEDDA: But the Judge wasn't to know that. I saw him wink at Tesman when you showed you didn't dare to join their wretched little party.

LOEVBORG: Didn't dare! Are you saying I didn't dare?

HEDDA: I'm not saying so. But that was what Judge Brack thought.

LOEVBORG: Well, let him.

HEDDA: You're not going, then?

LOEVBORG: I'm staying here with you and Thea.

MRS. ELVSTED: Yes, Hedda, of course he is.

HEDDA: [*Smiles, and nods approvingly to* LOEVBORG.] Firm as a rock! A man of principle! That's how a man should be! [*Turns to* MRS. ELVSTED *and strokes her cheek.*] Didn't I tell you so this morning when you came here in such a panic——

LOEVBORG: [*Starts.*] Panic?

MRS. ELVSTED: [*Frightened.*] Hedda! But—Hedda!

HEDDA: Well, now you can see for yourself. There's no earthly need for you to get scared to death just because——[*Stops.*] Well! Let's all three cheer up and enjoy ourselves.

LOEVBORG: Mrs. Tesman, would you mind explaining to me what this is all about?

MRS. ELVSTED: Oh, my God, my God, Hedda, what are you saying? What are you doing?

HEDDA: Keep calm. That horrid Judge has his eye on you.

LOEVBORG: Scared to death, were you? For my sake?

MRS. ELVSTED: [*Quietly, trembling.*] Oh, Hedda! You've made me so unhappy!

LOEVBORG: [*Looks coldly at her for a moment. His face is distorted.*] So that was how much you trusted me.

MRS. ELVSTED: Eilert dear, please listen to me——

LOEVBORG: [*Takes one of the glasses of punch, raises it and says quietly, hoarsely.*] Skoal, Thea! [*Empties the glass, puts it down and picks up one of the others.*]

MRS. ELVSTED: [*Quietly.*] Hedda, Hedda! Why did you want this to happen?

HEDDA: I—want it? Are you mad?

LOEVBORG: Skoal to you too, Mrs. Tesman. Thanks for telling me the truth. Here's to the truth! [*Empties his glass and refills it.*]

HEDDA: [*Puts her hand on his arm.*] Steady. That's enough for now. Don't forget the party.

MRS. ELVSTED: No, no, no!

HEDDA: Ssh! They're looking at you.

LOEVBORG: [*Puts down his glass.*] Thea, tell me the truth——

MRS. ELVSTED: Yes!

LOEVBORG: Did your husband know you were following me?

MRS. ELVSTED: Oh, Hedda!

LOEVBORG: Did you and he have an agreement that you should come here and keep an eye on me? Perhaps he gave you the idea? After all, he's a magistrate. I suppose he needed me back in his office. Or did he miss my companionship at the card table?

MRS. ELVSTED: [*Quietly, sobbing.*] Eilert, Eilert!

LOEVBORG: [*Seizes a glass and is about to fill it.*] Let's drink to him, too.

HEDDA: No more now. Remember you're going to read your book to Tesman.

LOEVBORG: [*Calm again, puts down his glass.*] That was silly of me, Thea. To take it like that, I mean. Don't be angry with me, my dear. You'll see—yes, and they'll see, too—that though I fell, I—I have raised myself up again. With your help, Thea.

MRS. ELVSTED: [*Happily.*] Oh, thank God!

[BRACK *has meanwhile glanced at his watch. He and* TESMAN *get up and come into the drawing room.*]

BRACK: [*Takes his hat and overcoat.*] Well, Mrs. Tesman. It's time for us to go.

HEDDA: Yes, I suppose it must be.

LOEVBORG: [*Gets up.*] Time for me too, Judge.

MRS. ELVSTED: [*Quietly, pleadingly.*] Eilert, please don't!

HEDDA: [*Pinches her arm.*] They can hear you.

MRS. ELVSTED: [*Gives a little cry.*] Oh!

LOEVBORG: [*To* BRACK.] You were kind enough to ask me to join you.

BRACK: Are you coming?

LOEVBORG: If I may.

BRACK: Delighted.

LOEVBORG: [*Puts the paper package in his pocket and says to* TESMAN.] I'd like to show you one or two things before I send it off to the printer.

TESMAN: I say, that'll be fun. Fancy——! Oh, but Hedda, how'll Mrs. Elvsted get home? What?

HEDDA: Oh, we'll manage somehow.

LOEVBORG: [*Glances over toward the ladies.*] Mrs. Elvsted? I shall come back and collect her, naturally. [*Goes closer.*] About ten o'clock, Mrs. Tesman? Will that suit you?

HEDDA: Yes. That'll suit me admirably.

TESMAN: Good, that's settled. But you mustn't expect me back so early, Hedda.

HEDDA: Stay as long as you c—as long as you like, dear.

MRS. ELVSTED: [*Trying to hide her anxiety.*] Well then, Mr. Loevborg, I'll wait here till you come.

LOEVBORG: [*His hat in his hand.*] Pray do, Mrs. Elvsted.

BRACK: Well, gentlemen, now the party begins. I trust that, in the words of a certain fair lady, we shall enjoy good sport.

HEDDA: What a pity the fair lady can't be there, invisible.

BRACK: Why invisible?

HEDDA: So as to be able to hear some of your uncensored witticisms, your honor.

BRACK: [*Laughs.*] Oh, I shouldn't advise the fair lady to do that.

TESMAN: [*Laughs too.*] I say, Hedda, that's good. By Jove! Fancy that!

BRACK: Well, good night, ladies, good night!

LOEVBORG: [*Bows farewell.*] About ten o'clock, then.

[BRACK, LOEVBORG *and* TESMAN *go out through the hall. As they do so* BERTHA *enters from the rear room with a lighted lamp. She puts it on the drawing-room table, then goes out the way she came.*]

MRS. ELVSTED: [*Has got up and is walking uneasily to and fro.*] Oh Hedda, Hedda! How is all this going to end?

HEDDA: At ten o'clock, then. He'll be here. I can see him. With a crown of vine-leaves in his hair. Burning and unashamed!

MRS. ELVSTED: Oh, I do hope so!

HEDDA: Can't you see? Then he'll be himself again! He'll be a free man for the rest of his days!

MRS. ELVSTED: Please God you're right.

HEDDA: That's how he'll come! [*Gets up and goes closer.*] You can doubt him as much as you like. I believe in him! Now we'll see which of us——

MRS. ELVSTED: You're after something, Hedda.

HEDDA: Yes, I am. For once in my life I want to have the power to shape a man's destiny.

MRS. ELVSTED: Haven't you that power already?

HEDDA: No, I haven't. I've never had it.

MRS. ELVSTED: What about your husband?

HEDDA: Him! Oh, if you could only understand how poor I am. And you're allowed to be so rich, so rich! [*Clasps her passionately.*] I think I'll burn your hair off after all!

MRS. ELVSTED: Let me go! Let me go! You frighten me, Hedda!

BERTHA: [*In the open doorway.*] I've laid tea in the dining room, madam.

HEDDA: Good, we're coming.

MRS. ELVSTED: No, no, no! I'd rather go home alone! Now—at once!

HEDDA: Rubbish! First you're going to have some tea, you little idiot. And then—at ten o'clock—Eilert Loevborg will come. With a crown of vine-leaves in his hair![7] [*She drags* MRS. ELVSTED *almost forcibly toward the open doorway.*]

ACT III

SCENE: *The same. The curtains are drawn across the open doorway, and also across the french windows. The lamp, half turned down, with a shade over it, is burning on the table. In the stove, the door of which is open, a fire has been burning, but it is now almost out.*

MRS. ELVSTED, *wrapped in a large shawl and with her feet resting on a footstool, is sitting near the stove, huddled in the armchair.* HEDDA *is lying asleep on this sofa, fully dressed, with a blanket over her.*

MRS. ELVSTED: [*After a pause, suddenly sits up in her chair and listens tensely. Then she sinks wearily back again and sighs.*] Not back yet! Oh, God! Oh, God! Not back yet!

[BERTHA *tiptoes cautiously in from the hall. She has a letter in her hand.*]

MRS. ELVSTED: [*Turns and whispers.*] What is it? Has someone come?
BERTHA: [*Quietly.*] Yes, a servant's just called with this letter.
MRS. ELVSTED: [*Quickly, holding out her hand.*] A letter! Give it to me!
BERTHA: But it's for the Doctor, madam.
MRS. ELVSTED: Oh. I see.
BERTHA: Miss Tesman's maid brought it. I'll leave it here on the table.
MRS. ELVSTED: Yes, do.
BERTHA: [*Puts down the letter.*] I'd better put the lamp out. It's starting to smoke.
MRS. ELVSTED: Yes, put it out. It'll soon be daylight.
BERTHA: [*Puts out the lamp.*] It's daylight already, madam.
MRS. ELVSTED: Yes. Broad day. And not home yet.
BERTHA: Oh dear, I was afraid this would happen.
MRS. ELVSTED: Were you?
BERTHA: Yes. When I heard that a certain gentleman had returned to town, and saw him go off with them. I've heard all about him.
MRS. ELVSTED: Don't talk so loud. You'll wake your mistress.
BERTHA: [*Looks at the sofa and sighs.*] Yes. Let her go on sleeping, poor dear. Shall I put some more wood on the fire?
MRS. ELVSTED: Thank you, don't bother on my account.
BERTHA: Very good. [*Goes quietly out through the hall.*]
HEDDA: [*Wakes as the door closes and looks up.*] What's that?
MRS. ELVSTED: It was only the maid.
HEDDA: [*Looks round.*] What am I doing here? Oh, now I remember. [*Sits up on the sofa, stretches herself and rubs her eyes.*] What time is it, Thea?
MRS. ELVSTED: It's gone seven.

7. Worshippers of Dionysus, Greek god of wine, wore garlands of vine leaves as a sign of divine intoxication.

HEDDA: When did Tesman get back?

MRS. ELVSTED: He's not back yet.

HEDDA: Not home yet?

MRS. ELVSTED: [Gets up.] No one's come.

HEDDA: And we sat up waiting for them till four o'clock.

MRS. ELVSTED: God! How I waited for him!

HEDDA: [Yawns and says with her hand in front of her mouth.] Oh, dear. We might have saved ourselves the trouble.

MRS. ELVSTED: Did you manage to sleep?

HEDDA: Oh, yes. Quite well, I think. Didn't you get any?

MRS. ELVSTED: Not a wink. I couldn't, Hedda. I just couldn't.

HEDDA: [Gets up and comes over to her.] Now, now, now. There's nothing to worry about. I know what's happened.

MRS. ELVSTED: What? Please tell me.

HEDDA: Well, obviously the party went on very late——

MRS. ELVSTED: Oh dear, I suppose it must have. But——

HEDDA: And Tesman didn't want to come home and wake us all up in the middle of the night. [Laughs.] Probably wasn't too keen to show his face either, after a spree like that.

MRS. ELVSTED: But where could he have gone?

HEDDA: I should think he's probably slept at his aunts'. They keep his old room for him.

MRS. ELVSTED: No, he can't be with them. A letter came for him just now from Miss Tesman. It's over there.

HEDDA: Oh? [Looks at the envelope.] Yes, it's Auntie Juju's handwriting. Well, he must still be at Judge Brack's, then. And Eilert Loevborg is sitting there, reading to him. With a crown of vine-leaves in his hair.

MRS. ELVSTED: Hedda, you're only saying that. You don't believe it.

HEDDA: Thea, you really are a little fool.

MRS. ELVSTED: Perhaps I am.

HEDDA: You look tired to death.

MRS. ELVSTED: Yes. I am tired to death.

HEDDA: Go to my room and lie down for a little. Do as I say, now; don't argue.

MRS. ELVSTED: No, no. I couldn't possibly sleep.

HEDDA: Of course you can.

MRS. ELVSTED: But your husband'll be home soon. And I must know at once——

HEDDA: I'll tell you when he comes.

MRS. ELVSTED: Promise me, Hedda?

HEDDA: Yes, don't worry. Go and get some sleep.

MRS. ELVSTED: Thank you. All right, I'll try.

[She goes out through the rear room. HEDDA goes to the french windows and draws the curtains. Broad daylight floods into the room. She goes to the writing table, takes a small hand mirror from it and arranges her hair. Then she goes to the door leading into the hall and presses the bell. After a few moments, BERTHA enters.]

BERTHA: Did you want anything, madam?

HEDDA: Yes, put some more wood on the fire. I'm freezing.

BERTHA: Bless you, I'll soon have this room warmed up. [*She rakes the embers together and puts a fresh piece of wood on them. Suddenly she stops and listens.*] There's someone at the front door, madam.

HEDDA: Well, go and open it. I'll see to the fire.

BERTHA: It'll burn up in a moment.

[*She goes out through the hall.* HEDDA *kneels on the footstool and puts more wood in the stove. After a few seconds,* GEORGE TESMAN *enters from the hall. He looks tired, and rather worried. He tiptoes toward the open doorway and is about to slip through the curtains.*]

HEDDA: [*At the stove, without looking up.*] Good morning.

TESMAN: [*Turns.*] Hedda! [*Comes nearer.*] Good heavens, are you up already? What?

HEDDA: Yes, I got up very early this morning.

TESMAN: I was sure you'd still be sleeping. Fancy that!

HEDDA: Don't talk so loud. Mrs. Elvsted's asleep in my room.

TESMAN: Mrs. Elvsted? Has she stayed the night here?

HEDDA: Yes. No one came to escort her home.

TESMAN: Oh. No, I suppose not.

HEDDA: [*Closes the door of the stove and gets up.*] Well. Was it fun?

TESMAN: Have you been anxious about me? What?

HEDDA: Not in the least. I asked if you'd had fun.

TESMAN: Oh yes, rather! Well, I thought, for once in a while—The first part was the best; when Eilert read his book to me. We arrived over an hour too early—what about that, eh? By Jove! Brack had a lot of things to see to, so Eilert read to me.

HEDDA: [*Sits at the right-hand side of the table.*] Well? Tell me about it.

TESMAN: [*Sits on a footstool by the stove.*] Honestly, Hedda, you've no idea what a book that's going to be. It's really one of the most remarkable things that's ever been written. By Jove!

HEDDA: Oh, never mind about the book——

TESMAN: I'm going to make a confession to you, Hedda. When he'd finished reading a sort of beastly feeling came over me.

HEDDA: Beastly feeling?

TESMAN: I found myself envying Eilert for being able to write like that. Imagine that, Hedda!

HEDDA: Yes. I can imagine.

TESMAN: What a tragedy that with all those gifts he should be so incorrigible.

HEDDA: You mean he's less afraid of life than most men?

TESMAN: Good heavens, no. He just doesn't know the meaning of the word moderation.

HEDDA: What happened afterwards?

TESMAN: Well, looking back on it I suppose you might almost call it an orgy, Hedda.

HEDDA: Had he vine-leaves in his hair?

TESMAN: Vine-leaves? No, I didn't see any of them. He made a long, rambling oration in honor of the woman who'd inspired him to write this book. Yes, those were the words he used.

HEDDA: Did he name her?

TESMAN: No. But I suppose it must be Mrs. Elvsted. You wait and see!

HEDDA: Where did you leave him?

TESMAN: On the way home. We left in a bunch—the last of us, that is—and Brack came with us to get a little fresh air. Well, then, you see, we agreed we ought to see Eilert home. He'd had a drop too much.

HEDDA: You don't say?

TESMAN: But now comes the funny part, Hedda. Or I should really say the tragic part. Oh, I'm almost ashamed to tell you. For Eilert's sake, I mean——

HEDDA: Why, what happened?

TESMAN: Well, you see, as we were walking toward town I happened to drop behind for a minute. Only for a minute—er—you understand——

HEDDA: Yes, yes——?

TESMAN: Well then, when I ran on to catch them up, what do you think I found by the roadside. What?

HEDDA: How on earth should I know?

TESMAN: You mustn't tell anyone, Hedda. What? Promise me that—for Eilert's sake. [*Takes a package wrapped in paper from his coat pocket.*] Just fancy! I found this.

HEDDA: Isn't this the one he brought here yesterday?

TESMAN: Yes! The whole of that precious, irreplaceable manuscript! And he went and lost it! Didn't even notice! What about that? By Jove! Tragic.

HEDDA: But why didn't you give it back to him?

TESMAN: I didn't dare to, in the state he was in.

HEDDA: Didn't you tell any of the others?

TESMAN: Good heavens, no. I didn't want to do that. For Eilert's sake, you understand.

HEDDA: Then no one else knows you have his manuscript?

TESMAN: No. And no one must be allowed to know.

HEDDA: Didn't it come up in the conversation later?

TESMAN: I didn't get a chance to talk to him any more. As soon as we got into the outskirts of town, he and one or two of the others gave us the slip. Disappeared, by Jove!

HEDDA: Oh? I suppose they took him home.

TESMAN: Yes, I imagine that was the idea. Brack left us, too.

HEDDA: And what have you been up to since then?

TESMAN: Well, I and one or two of the others—awfully jolly chaps, they were—went back to where one of them lived, and had a cup of morning coffee. Morning-after coffee—what? Ah, well. I'll just lie down for a bit and give Eilert time to sleep it off, poor chap, then I'll run over and give this back to him.

HEDDA: [*Holds out her hand for the package.*] No, don't do that. Not just yet. Let me read it first.

TESMAN: Oh no, really, Hedda dear, honestly, I daren't do that.

HEDDA: Daren't?

TESMAN: No—imagine how desperate he'll be when he wakes up and finds his manuscript's missing. He hasn't any copy, you see. He told me so himself.

HEDDA: Can't a thing like that be rewritten?

TESMAN: Oh no, not possibly, I shouldn't think. I mean, the inspiration, you know——

HEDDA: Oh, yes. I'd forgotten that. [*Casually.*] By the way, there's a letter for you.

TESMAN: Is there? Fancy that!

HEDDA: [*Holds it out to him.*] It came early this morning.

TESMAN: I say, it's from Auntie Juju! What on earth can it be? [*Puts the package on the other footstool, opens the letter, reads it and jumps up.*] Oh, Hedda! She says poor Auntie Rena's dying.

HEDDA: Well, we've been expecting that.

TESMAN: She says if I want to see her I must go quickly. I'll run over at once.

HEDDA: [*Hides a smile.*] Run?

TESMAN: Hedda dear, I suppose you wouldn't like to come with me? What about that, eh?

HEDDA: [*Gets up and says wearily and with repulsion.*] No, no, don't ask me to do anything like that. I can't bear illness or death. I loathe anything ugly.

TESMAN: Yes, yes. Of course. [*In a dither.*] My hat? My overcoat? Oh yes, in the hall. I do hope I won't get there too late, Hedda? What?

HEDDA: You'll be all right if you run.

[BERTHA *enters from the hall.*]

BERTHA: Judge Brack's outside and wants to know if he can come in.

TESMAN: At this hour? No, I can't possibly receive him now.

HEDDA: I can. [*To* BERTHA.] Ask his honor to come in.

[BERTHA *goes.*]

HEDDA: [*Whispers quickly.*] The manuscript, Tesman. [*She snatches it from the footstool.*]

TESMAN: Yes, give it to me.

HEDDA: No, I'll look after it for now.

[*She goes over to the writing table and puts it in the bookcase.* TESMAN *stands dithering, unable to get his gloves on.* JUDGE BRACK *enters from the hall.*]

HEDDA: [*Nods to him*] Well, you're an early bird.

BRACK: Yes, aren't I? [*To* TESMAN.] Are you up and about, too?

TESMAN: Yes, I've got to go and see my aunts. Poor Auntie Rena's dying.

BRACK: Oh dear, is she? Then you mustn't let me detain you. At so tragic a——

TESMAN: Yes, I really must run. Good-bye! Good-bye! [*Runs out through the hall.*]

HEDDA: [*Goes nearer.*] You seem to have had excellent sport last night—Judge.

BRACK: Indeed yes, Mrs. Hedda. I haven't even had time to take my clothes off.

HEDDA: *You* haven't either?

BRACK: As you see. What's Tesman told you about last night's escapades?

HEDDA: Oh, only some boring story about having gone and drunk coffee somewhere.

BRACK: Yes, I've heard about that coffee party. Eilert Loevborg wasn't with them, I gather?

HEDDA: No, they took him home first.

BRACK: Did Tesman go with him?

HEDDA: No, one or two of the others, he said.

BRACK: [*Smiles.*] George Tesman is a credulous man, Mrs. Hedda.

HEDDA: God knows. But—has something happened?

BRACK: Well, yes, I'm afraid it has.

HEDDA: I see. Sit down and tell me. [*She sits on the left of the table,* BRACK *at the long side of it, near her.*] Well?

BRACK: I had a special reason for keeping track of my guests last night. Or perhaps I should say some of my guests.

HEDDA: Including Eilert Loevborg?

BRACK: I must confess—yes.

HEDDA: You're beginning to make me curious.

BRACK: Do you know where he and some of my other guests spent the latter half of last night, Mrs. Hedda?

HEDDA: Tell me. If it won't shock me.

BRACK: Oh, I don't think it'll shock you. They found themselves participating in an exceedingly animated *soirée.*

HEDDA: Of a sporting character?

BRACK: Of a highly sporting character.

HEDDA: Tell me more.

BRACK: Loevborg had received an invitation in advance—as had the others. I knew all about that. But he had refused. As you know, he's become a new man.

HEDDA: Up at the Elvsteds', yes. But he went?

BRACK: Well, you see, Mrs. Hedda, last night at my house, unhappily, the spirit moved him.

HEDDA: Yes, I hear he became inspired.

BRACK: Somewhat violently inspired. And as a result, I suppose, his thoughts strayed. We men, alas, don't always stick to our principles as firmly as we should.

HEDDA: I'm sure you're an exception, Judge Brack. But go on about Loevborg.

BRACK: Well, to cut a long story short, he ended up in the establishment of a certain Mademoiselle Danielle.

HEDDA: Mademoiselle Danielle?

BRACK: She was holding the *soirée*. For a selected circle of friends and admirers.

HEDDA: Has she got red hair?

BRACK: She has.

HEDDA: A singer of some kind?

BRACK: Yes—among other accomplishments. She's also a celebrated huntress—
of men, Mrs. Hedda. I'm sure you've heard about her. Eilert Loevborg used
to be one of her most ardent patrons. In his salad days.

HEDDA: And how did all this end?

BRACK: Not entirely amicably, from all accounts. Mademoiselle Danielle began
by receiving him with the utmost tenderness and ended by resorting to her
fists.

HEDDA: Against Loevborg?

BRACK: Yes. He accused her, or her friends, of having robbed him. He claimed
his pocketbook had been stolen. Among other things. In short, he seems to
have made a bloodthirsty scene.

HEDDA: And what did this lead to?

BRACK: It led to a general free-for-all, in which both sexes participated. Fortunately, in the end the police arrived.

HEDDA: The police too?

BRACK: Yes. I'm afraid it may turn out to be rather an expensive joke for Master
Eilert. Crazy fool!

HEDDA: Oh?

BRACK: Apparently he put up a very violent resistance. Hit one of the constables
on the ear and tore his uniform. He had to accompany them to the police
station.

HEDDA: Where did you learn all this?

BRACK: From the police.

HEDDA: [*To herself.*] So that's what happened. He didn't have a crown of vine-
leaves in his hair.

BRACK: Vine-leaves, Mrs. Hedda?

HEDDA: [*In her normal voice again.*] But, tell me, Judge, why do you take such a
close interest in Eilert Loevborg?

BRACK: For one thing it'll hardly be a matter of complete indifference to me if
it's revealed in court that he came there straight from my house.

HEDDA: Will it come to court?

BRACK: Of course. Well, I don't regard that as particularly serious. Still, I thought
it my duty, as a friend of the family, to give you and your husband a full
account of his nocturnal adventures.

HEDDA: Why?

BRACK: Because I've a shrewd suspicion that he's hoping to use you as a kind of
screen.

HEDDA: What makes you think that?

BRACK: Oh, for heaven's sake, Mrs. Hedda, we're not blind. You wait and see.
This Mrs. Elvsted won't be going back to her husband just yet.

HEDDA: Well, if there were anything between those two there are plenty of other
places where they could meet.

BRACK: Not in anyone's home. From now on every respectable house will once again be closed to Eilert Loevborg.

HEDDA: And mine should be too, you mean?

BRACK: Yes. I confess I should find it more than irksome if this gentleman were to be granted unrestricted access to this house. If he were superfluously to intrude into——

HEDDA: The triangle?

BRACK: Precisely. For me it would be like losing a home.

HEDDA: [Looks at him and smiles.] I see. You want to be the cock of the walk.

BRACK: [Nods slowly and lowers his voice.] Yes, that is my aim. And I shall fight for it with—every weapon at my disposal.

HEDDA: [As her smile fades.] You're a dangerous man, aren't you? When you really want something.

BRACK: You think so?

HEDDA: Yes. I'm beginning to think so. I'm deeply thankful you haven't any kind of hold over me.

BRACK: [Laughs equivocally.] Well, well, Mrs. Hedda—perhaps you're right. If I had, who knows what I might not think up?

HEDDA: Come, Judge Brack. That sounds almost like a threat.

BRACK: [Gets up.] Heaven forbid! In the creation of a triangle—and its continuance—the question of compulsion should never arise.

HEDDA: Exactly what I was thinking.

BRACK: Well, I've said what I came to say. I must be getting back. Good-bye, Mrs. Hedda. [Goes toward the french windows.]

HEDDA: [Gets up.] Are you going out through the garden?

BRACK: Yes, it's shorter.

HEDDA: Yes. And it's the back door, isn't it?

BRACK: I've nothing against back doors. They can be quite intriguing—sometimes.

HEDDA: When people fire pistols out of them, for example?

BRACK: [In the doorway, laughs.] Oh, people don't shoot tame cocks.

HEDDA: [Laughs too.] I suppose not. When they've only got one.

[They nod good-bye, laughing. He goes. She closes the french windows behind him, and stands for a moment, looking out pensively. Then she walks across the room and glances through the curtains in the open doorway. Goes to the writing table, takes LOEVBORG's package from the bookcase and is about to leaf through the pages when BERTHA is heard remonstrating loudly in the hall. HEDDA turns and listens. She hastily puts the package back in the drawer, locks it and puts the key on the inkstand. EILERT LOEVBORG, with his overcoat on and his hat in his hand, throws the door open. He looks somewhat confused and excited.]

LOEVBORG: [Shouts as he enters.] I must come in, I tell you! Let me pass! [He closes the door, turns, sees HEDDA, controls himself immediately and bows.]

HEDDA: [At the writing table.] Well, Mr. Loevborg, this is rather a late hour to be collecting Thea.

LOEVBORG: And an early hour to call on you. Please forgive me.

HEDDA: How do you know she's still here?

LOEVBORG: They told me at her lodgings that she has been out all night.

HEDDA: [*Goes to the table.*] Did you notice anything about their behavior when they told you?

LOEVBORG: [*Looks at her, puzzled.*] Notice anything?

HEDDA: Did they sound as if they thought it—strange?

LOEVBORG: [*Suddenly understands.*] Oh, I see what you mean. I'm dragging her down with me. No, as a matter of fact I didn't notice anything. I suppose Tesman isn't up yet?

HEDDA: No, I don't think so.

LOEVBORG: When did he get home?

HEDDA: Very late.

LOEVBORG: Did he tell you anything?

HEDDA: Yes. I gather you had a merry party at Judge Brack's last night.

LOEVBORG: He didn't tell you anything else?

HEDDA. I don't think so. I was so terribly sleepy——

[MRS. ELVSTED *comes through the curtains in the open doorway.*]

MRS. ELVSTED: [*Runs toward him.*] Oh, Eilert! At last!

LOEVBORG: Yes—at last. And too late.

MRS. ELVSTED: What is too late?

LOEVBORG: Everything—now. I'm finished, Thea.

MRS. ELVSTED: Oh, no, no! Don't say that!

LOEVBORG: You'll say it yourself, when you've heard what I——

MRS. ELVSTED: I don't want to hear anything!

HEDDA: Perhaps you'd rather speak to her alone? I'd better go.

LOEVBORG: No, stay.

MRS. ELVSTED: But I don't want to hear anything, I tell you!

LOEVBORG: It's not about last night.

MRS. ELVSTED: Then what——?

LOEVBORG: I want to tell you that from now on we must stop seeing each other.

MRS. ELVSTED: Stop seeing each other!

HEDDA: [*Involuntarily.*] I knew it!

LOEVBORG: I have no further use for you, Thea.

MRS. ELVSTED: You can stand there and say that! No further use for me! Surely I can go on helping you? We'll go on working together, won't we?

LOEVBORG: I don't intend to do any more work from now on.

MRS. ELVSTED: [*Desperately.*] Then what use have I for my life?

LOEVBORG: You must try to live as if you had never known me.

MRS. ELVSTED: But I can't!

LOEVBORG: Try to, Thea. Go back home——

MRS. ELVSTED: Never! I want to be wherever you are! I won't let myself be driven away like this! I want to stay here—and be with you when the book comes out.

HEDDA: [*Whispers.*] Ah, yes! The book!

LOEVBORG: [*Looks at her.*] Our book; Thea's and mine. It belongs to both of us.

MRS. ELVSTED: Oh, yes! I feel that, too! And I've a right to be with you when it comes into the world. I want to see people respect and honor you again. And the joy! The joy! I want to share it with you!

LOEVBORG: Thea—our book will never come into the world.

HEDDA: Ah!

MRS. ELVSTED: Not——?

LOEVBORG: It cannot. Ever.

MRS. ELVSTED: Eilert—what have you done with the manuscript? Where is it?

LOEVBORG: Oh Thea, please don't ask me that!

MRS. ELVSTED: Yes, yes—I must know. I've a right to know. Now!

LOEVBORG: The manuscript. I've torn it up.

MRS. ELVSTED: [*Screams.*] No, no!

HEDDA: [*Involuntarily.*] But that's not——!

LOEVBORG: [*Looks at her.*] Not true, you think?

HEDDA: [*Controls herself.*] Why—yes, of course it is, if you say so. It just sounded so incredible——

LOEVBORG: It's true, nevertheless.

MRS. ELVSTED: Oh, my God, my God, Hedda—he's destroyed his own book!

LOEVBORG: I have destroyed my life. Why not my life's work, too?

MRS. ELVSTED: And you—did this last night?

LOEVBORG: Yes, Thea. I tore it into a thousand pieces. And scattered them out across the fjord. It's good, clean, salt water. Let it carry them away; let them drift in the current and the wind. And in a little while, they will sink. Deeper and deeper. As I shall, Thea.

MRS. ELVSTED: Do you know, Eilert—this book—all my life I shall feel as though you'd killed a little child?

LOEVBORG: You're right. It is like killing a child.

MRS. ELVSTED: But how could you? It was my child, too!

HEDDA. [*Almost inaudibly.*] Oh—the child——!

MRS. ELVSTED: [*Breathes heavily.*] It's all over, then. Well—I'll go now, Hedda.

HEDDA: You're not leaving town?

MRS. ELVSTED: I don't know what I'm going to do. I can't see anything except—darkness. [*She goes out through the hall.*]

HEDDA: [*Waits a moment.*] Aren't you going to escort her home, Mr. Loevborg?

LOEVBORG: I? Through the streets? Do you want me to let people see her with me?

HEDDA: Of course I don't know what else may have happened last night. But is it so utterly beyond redress?

LOEVBORG: It isn't just last night. It'll go on happening. I know it. But the curse of it is, I don't want to live that kind of life. I don't want to start all that again. She's broken my courage. I can't spit in the eyes of the world any longer.

HEDDA: [*As though to herself.*] That pretty little fool's been trying to shape a man's destiny. [*Looks at him.*] But how could you be so heartless toward her?

LOEVBORG: Don't call me heartless!

HEDDA: To go and destroy the one thing that's made her life worth living? You don't call that heartless?

LOEVBORG: Do you want to know the truth, Hedda?

HEDDA: The truth?

LOEVBORG: Promise me first—give me your word—that you'll never let Thea know about this.

HEDDA: I give you my word.

LOEVBORG: Good. Well; what I told her just now was a lie.

HEDDA: About the manuscript?

LOEVBORG: Yes. I didn't tear it up. Or throw it in the fjord.

HEDDA: You didn't? But where is it, then?

LOEVBORG: I destroyed it, all the same. I destroyed it, Hedda!

HEDDA: I don't understand.

LOEVBORG: Thea said that what I had done was like killing a child.

HEDDA: Yes. That's what she said.

LOEVBORG: But to kill a child isn't the worst thing a father can do to it.

HEDDA: What could be worse than that?

LOEVBORG: Hedda—suppose a man came home one morning, after a night of debauchery, and said to the mother of his child: "Look here. I've been wandering round all night. I've been to—such-and-such a place and such-and-such a place. And I had our child with me. I took him to—these places. And I've lost him. Just—lost him. God knows where he is or whose hands he's fallen into."

HEDDA: I see. But when all's said and done, this was only a book——

LOEVBORG: Thea's heart and soul were in that book. It was her whole life.

HEDDA: Yes. I understand.

LOEVBORG: Well, then you must also understand that she and I cannot possibly ever see each other again.

HEDDA: Where will you go?

LOEVBORG: Nowhere. I just want to put an end to it all. As soon as possible.

HEDDA: [Takes a step toward him.] Eilert Loevborg, listen to me. Do it—beautifully!

LOEVBORG: Beautifully? [Smiles.] With a crown of vine-leaves in my hair? The way you used to dream of me—in the old days?

HEDDA: No. I don't believe in that crown any longer. But—do it beautifully, all the same. Just this once. Good-bye. You must go now. And don't come back.

LOEVBORG: Adieu, madam. Give my love to George Tesman. [Turns to go.]

HEDDA: Wait. I want to give you a souvenir to take with you.

[She goes over to the writing table, opens the drawer and the pistol-case, and comes back to LOEVBORG with one of the pistols.]

LOEVBORG: [Looks at her.] This? Is this the souvenir?

HEDDA: [Nods slowly.] You recognize it? You looked down its barrel once.

LOEVBORG: You should have used it then.

HEDDA: Here! Use it now!

LOEVBORG: [*Puts the pistol in his breast pocket.*] Thank you.
HEDDA: Do it beautifully, Eilert Loevborg. Only promise me that!
LOEVBORG: Good-bye, Hedda Gabler.

[*He goes out through the hall.* HEDDA *stands by the door for a moment, listening. Then she goes over to the writing table, takes out the package containing the manuscript, glances inside it, pulls some of the pages half out and looks at them. Then she takes it to the armchair by the stove and sits down with the package in her lap. After a moment, she opens the door of the stove; then she opens the packet.*]

HEDDA: [*Throws one of the pages into the stove and whispers to herself.*] I'm burning your child, Thea! You with your beautiful wavy hair! [*She throws a few more pages into the stove.*] The child Eilert Loevborg gave you. [*Throws the rest of the manuscript in.*] I'm burning it! I'm burning your child!

ACT IV

SCENE: *The same. It is evening. The drawing room is in darkness. The small room is illuminated by the hanging lamp over the table. The curtains are drawn across the french windows.* HEDDA, *dressed in black, is walking up and down in the darkened room. Then she goes into the small room and crosses to the left. A few chords are heard from the piano. She comes back into the drawing room.*

BERTHA *comes through the small room from the right with a lighted lamp, which she places on the table in front of the corner sofa in the drawing room. Her eyes are red with crying, and she has black ribbons on her cap. She goes quietly out, right.* HEDDA *goes over to the french windows, draws the curtains slightly to one side and looks out into the darkness.*

A few moments later, MISS TESMAN *enters from the hall. She is dressed in mourning, with a black hat and veil.* HEDDA *goes to meet her and holds out her hand.*

MISS TESMAN: Well, Hedda, here I am in the weeds of sorrow. My poor sister has ended her struggles at last.
HEDDA: I've already heard. Tesman sent me a card.
MISS TESMAN: Yes, he promised me he would. But I thought, no, I must go and break the news of death to Hedda myself—here, in the house of life.
HEDDA: It's very kind of you.
MISS TESMAN: Ah, Rena shouldn't have chosen a time like this to pass away. This is no moment for Hedda's house to be a place of mourning.
HEDDA: [*Changing the subject.*] She died peacefully, Miss Tesman?
MISS TESMAN: Oh, it was quite beautiful! The end came so calmly. And she was so happy at being able to see George once again. And say good-bye to him. Hasn't he come home yet?
HEDDA: No. He wrote that I mustn't expect him too soon. But please sit down.
MISS TESMAN: No, thank you, Hedda dear—bless you. I'd like to. But I've so little

time. I must dress her and lay her out as well as I can. She shall go to her grave looking really beautiful.

HEDDA: Can't I help with anything?

MISS TESMAN: Why, you mustn't think of such a thing! Hedda Tesman mustn't let her hands be soiled by contact with death. Or her thoughts. Not at this time.

HEDDA: One can't always control one's thoughts.

MISS TESMAN: [Continues.] Ah, well, that's life. Now we must start to sew poor Rena's shroud. There'll be sewing to be done in this house too before long, I shouldn't wonder. But not for a shroud, praise God.

[GEORGE TESMAN enters from the hall.]

HEDDA: You've come at last! Thank heavens!

TESMAN: Are you here, Auntie Juju? With Hedda? Fancy that!

MISS TESMAN: I was just on the point of leaving, dear boy. Well, have you done everything you promised me?

TESMAN: No, I'm afraid I forgot half of it. I'll have to run over again tomorrow. My head's in a complete whirl today. I can't collect my thoughts.

MISS TESMAN: But George dear, you mustn't take it like this.

TESMAN: Oh? Well—er—how should I?

MISS TESMAN: You must be happy in your grief. Happy for what's happened. As I am.

TESMAN: Oh, yes, yes. You're thinking of Aunt Rena.

HEDDA: It'll be lonely for you now, Miss Tesman.

MISS TESMAN: For the first few days, yes. But it won't last long, I hope. Poor dear Rena's little room isn't going to stay empty.

TESMAN: Oh? Whom are you going to move in there? What?

MISS TESMAN: Oh, there's always some poor invalid who needs care and attention.

HEDDA: Do you really want another cross like that to bear?

MISS TESMAN: Cross! God forgive you, child. It's been no cross for me.

HEDDA: But now—if a complete stranger comes to live with you——?

MISS TESMAN: Oh, one soon makes friends with invalids. And I need so much to have someone to live for. Like you, my dear. Well, I expect there'll soon be work in this house too for an old aunt, praise God!

HEDDA: Oh—please!

TESMAN: By Jove, yes! What a splendid time the three of us could have together if——

HEDDA: If?

TESMAN: [Uneasily.] Oh, never mind. It'll all work out. Let's hope so—what?

MISS TESMAN: Yes, yes. Well, I'm sure you two would like to be alone. [Smiles.] Perhaps Hedda may have something to tell you, George. Good-bye. I must go home to Rena. [Turns to the door.] Dear God, how strange! Now Rena is with me and with poor dear Joachim.

TESMAN: Fancy that. Yes, Auntie Juju! What?

[MISS TESMAN *goes out through the hall.*]

HEDDA: [*Follows* TESMAN *coldly and searchingly with her eyes.*] I really believe this death distresses you more than it does her.

TESMAN: Oh, it isn't just Auntie Rena. It's Eilert I'm so worried about.

HEDDA: [*Quickly.*] Is there any news of him?

TESMAN: I ran over to see him this afternoon. I wanted to tell him his manuscript was in safe hands.

HEDDA: Oh? You didn't find him?

TESMAN: No. He wasn't at home. But later I met Mrs. Elvsted and she told me he'd been here early this morning.

HEDDA: Yes, just after you'd left.

TESMAN: It seems he said he'd torn the manuscript up. What?

HEDDA: Yes, he claimed to have done so.

TESMAN: You told him we had it, of course?

HEDDA: No. [*Quickly.*] Did you tell Mrs. Elvsted?

TESMAN: No, I didn't like to. But you ought to have told him. Think if he should go home and do something desperate! Give me the manuscript, Hedda. I'll run over to him with it right away. Where did you put it?

HEDDA: [*Cold and motionless, leaning against the armchair.*] I haven't got it any longer.

TESMAN: Haven't got it? What on earth do you mean?

HEDDA: I've burned it.

TESMAN: [*Starts, terrified.*] Burned it! Burned Eilert's manuscript!

HEDDA: Don't shout. The servant will hear you.

TESMAN: Burned it! But in heaven's name——! Oh, no, no, no! This is impossible!

HEDDA: Well, it's true.

TESMAN: But Hedda, do you realize what you've done? That's appropriating lost property! It's against the law! By Jove! You ask Judge Brack and see if I'm not right.

HEDDA: You'd be well advised not to talk about it to Judge Brack or anyone else.

TESMAN: But how could you go and do such a dreadful thing? What on earth put the idea into your head? What came over you? Answer me! What?

HEDDA: [*Represses an almost imperceptible smile.*] I did it for your sake, George.

TESMAN: For my sake?

HEDDA: When you came home this morning and described how he'd read his book to you——

TESMAN: Yes, yes?

HEDDA: You admitted you were jealous of him.

TESMAN: But, good heavens, I didn't mean it literally!

HEDDA: No matter. I couldn't bear the thought that anyone else should push you into the background.

TESMAN: [*Torn between doubt and joy.*] Hedda—is this true? But—but—but I never realized you loved me like that! Fancy——

HEDDA: Well, I suppose you'd better know. I'm going to have—— [*Breaks off and says violently.*] No, no—you'd better ask your Auntie Juju. She'll tell you.

TESMAN: Hedda! I think I understand what you mean. [*Clasps his hands.*] Good heavens, can it really be true! What?

HEDDA: Don't shout. The servant will hear you.

TESMAN: [*Laughing with joy.*] The servant! I say, that's good! The servant! Why, that's Bertha! I'll run out and tell her at once!

HEDDA: [*Clenches her hands in despair.*] Oh, it's destroying me, all this—it's destroying me!

TESMAN: I say, Hedda, what's up? What?

HEDDA: [*Cold, controlled.*] Oh, it's all so—absurd—George.

TESMAN: Absurd? That I'm so happy? But surely——? Ah, well—perhaps I won't say anything to Bertha.

HEDDA: No, do. She might as well know too.

TESMAN: No, no, I won't tell her yet. But Auntie Juju—I must let her know! And you—you called me George! For the first time! Fancy that! Oh, it'll make Auntie Juju so happy, all this! So very happy!

HEDDA: Will she be happy when she hears I've burned Eilert Loevborg's manuscript—for your sake?

TESMAN: No, I'd forgotten about that. Of course no one must be allowed to know about the manuscript. But that you're burning with love for me, Hedda, I must certainly let Auntie Juju know that. I say, I wonder if young wives often feel like that toward their husbands? What?

HEDDA: You might ask Auntie Juju about that too.

TESMAN: I will, as soon as I get the chance. [*Looks uneasy and thoughtful again.*] But I say, you know, that manuscript. Dreadful business. Poor Eilert!

[MRS. ELVSTED, *dressed as on her first visit, with hat and overcoat, enters from the hall.*]

MRS. ELVSTED: [*Greets them hastily and tremulously.*] Oh, Hedda dear, do please forgive me for coming here again.

HEDDA: Why, Thea, what's happened?

TESMAN: Is it anything to do with Eilert Loevborg? What?

MRS. ELVSTED: Yes—I'm so dreadfully afraid he may have met with an accident.

HEDDA: [*Grips her arm.*] You think so?

TESMAN: But, good heavens, Mrs. Elvsted, what makes you think that?

MRS. ELVSTED: I heard them talking about him at the boarding-house, as I went in. Oh, there are the most terrible rumors being spread about him in town today.

TESMAN: Fancy. Yes, I heard about them too. But I can testify that he went straight home to bed. Fancy that!

HEDDA: Well—what did they say in the boarding-house?

MRS. ELVSTED: Oh, I couldn't find out anything. Either they didn't know, or else—— They stopped talking when they saw me. And I didn't dare to ask.

TESMAN: [*Fidgets uneasily.*] We must hope—we must hope you misheard them, Mrs. Elvsted.

MRS. ELVSTED: No, no, I'm sure it was he they were talking about. I heard them say something about a hospital——

TESMAN: Hospital!

HEDDA: Oh no, surely that's impossible!

MRS. ELVSTED: Oh, I became so afraid. So I went up to his rooms and asked to see him.

HEDDA: Do you think that was wise, Thea?

MRS. ELVSTED: Well, what else could I do? I couldn't bear the uncertainty any longer.

TESMAN: But you didn't manage to find him either? What?

MRS. ELVSTED: No. And they had no idea where he was. They said he hadn't been home since yesterday afternoon.

TESMAN: Since yesterday? Fancy that!

MRS. ELVSTED: I'm sure he must have met with an accident.

TESMAN: Hedda, I wonder if I ought to go into town and make one or two enquiries?

HEDDA: No, no, don't you get mixed up in this.

[JUDGE BRACK *enters from the hall, hat in hand.* BERTHA, *who has opened the door for him, closes it. He looks serious and greets them silently.*]

TESMAN: Hullo, my dear Judge. Fancy seeing you!

BRACK: I had to come and talk to you.

TESMAN: I can see Auntie Juju's told you the news.

BRACK: Yes, I've heard about that too.

TESMAN: Tragic, isn't it?

BRACK: Well, my dear chap, that depends how you look at it.

TESMAN: [*Looks uncertainly at him.*] Has something else happened?

BRACK: Yes.

HEDDA: Another tragedy?

BRACK: That also depends on how you look at it, Mrs. Tesman.

MRS. ELVSTED: Oh, it's something to do with Eilert Loevborg!

BRACK: [*Looks at her for a moment.*] How did you guess? Perhaps you've heard already——?

MRS. ELVSTED: [*Confused.*] No, no, not at all—I——

TESMAN: For heaven's sake, tell us!

BRACK: [*Shrugs his shoulders.*] Well, I'm afraid they've taken him to the hospital. He's dying.

MRS. ELVSTED: [*Screams.*] Oh God, God!

TESMAN: The hospital! Dying!

HEDDA: [*Involuntarily.*] So quickly!

MRS. ELVSTED: [*Weeping.*] Oh, Hedda! And we parted enemies!

HEDDA: [*Whispers.*] Thea—Thea!

MRS. ELVSTED: [*Ignoring her.*] I must see him! I must see him before he dies!

BRACK: It's no use, Mrs. Elvsted. No one's allowed to see him now.

MRS. ELVSTED: But what's happened to him? You must tell me!

TESMAN: He hasn't tried to do anything to himself? What?

HEDDA: Yes, he has. I'm sure of it.

TESMAN: Hedda, how can you——?

BRACK: [*Who has not taken his eyes from her.*] I'm afraid you've guessed correctly, Mrs. Tesman.

MRS. ELVSTED: How dreadful!

TESMAN: Attempted suicide! Fancy that!

HEDDA: Shot himself!

BRACK: Right again, Mrs. Tesman.

MRS. ELVSTED: [*Tries to compose herself.*] When did this happen, Judge Brack?

BRACK: This afternoon. Between three and four.

TESMAN: But, good heavens—where? What?

BRACK: [*A little hesitantly.*] Where? Why, my dear chap, in his rooms of course.

MRS. ELVSTED: No, that's impossible. I was there soon after six.

BRACK: Well, it must have been somewhere else, then. I don't know exactly. I only know that they found him. He'd shot himself—through the breast.

MRS. ELVSTED: Oh, how horrible! That he should end like that!

HEDDA: [*To* BRACK.] Through the breast, you said?

BRACK: That is what I said.

HEDDA: Not through the head?

BRACK: Through the breast, Mrs. Tesman.

HEDDA: The breast. Yes; yes. That's good, too.

BRACK: Why, Mrs. Tesman?

HEDDA: Oh—no, I didn't mean anything.

TESMAN: And the wound's dangerous you say? What?

BRACK: Mortal. He's probably already dead.

MRS. ELVSTED: Yes, yes—I feel it! It's all over. All over. Oh Hedda——!

TESMAN: But, tell me, how did you manage to learn all this?

BRACK: [*Curtly.*] From the police. I spoke to one of them.

HEDDA: [*Loudly, clearly.*] At last! Oh, thank God!

TESMAN: [*Appalled.*] For God's sake, Hedda, what are you saying?

HEDDA: I am saying there's beauty in what he has done.

BRACK: Mm—Mrs. Tesman——

TESMAN: Beauty! Oh, but I say!

MRS. ELVSTED: Hedda, how can you talk of beauty in connection with a thing like this?

HEDDA: Eilert Loevborg has settled his account with life. He's had the courage to do what—what he had to do.

MRS. ELVSTED: No, that's not why it happened. He did it because he was mad.

TESMAN: He did it because he was desperate.

HEDDA: You're wrong! I know!

MRS. ELVSTED: He must have been mad. The same as when he tore up the manuscript.

BRACK: [*Starts.*] Manuscript? Did he tear it up?

MRS. ELVSTED: Yes. Last night.

TESMAN: [*Whispers.*] Oh, Hedda, we shall never be able to escape from this.

BRACK: Hm. Strange.

TESMAN: [*Wanders round the room.*] To think of Eilert dying like that. And not leaving behind him the thing that would have made his name endure.

MRS. ELVSTED: If only it could be pieced together again!

TESMAN: Yes, fancy! If only it could! I'd give anything——

MRS. ELVSTED: Perhaps it can, Mr. Tesman.

TESMAN: What do you mean?

MRS. ELVSTED: [*Searches in the pocket of her dress.*] Look! I kept the notes he dictated it from.

HEDDA: [*Takes a step nearer.*] Ah!

TESMAN: You kept them, Mrs. Elvsted! What?

MRS. ELVSTED: Yes, here they are. I brought them with me when I left home. They've been in my pocket ever since.

TESMAN: Let me have a look.

MRS. ELVSTED: [*Hands him a wad of small sheets of paper.*] They're in a terrible muddle. All mixed up.

TESMAN: I say, just fancy if we can sort them out! Perhaps if we work on them together——?

MRS. ELVSTED: Oh, yes! Let's try, anyway!

TESMAN: We'll manage it. We must! I shall dedicate my life to this.

HEDDA: *You*, George? Your life?

TESMAN: Yes—well, all the time I can spare. My book'll have to wait. Hedda, you do understand? What? I owe it to Eilert's memory.

HEDDA: Perhaps.

TESMAN: Well, my dear Mrs. Elvsted, you and I'll have to pool our brains. No use crying over spilt milk, what? We must try to approach this matter calmly.

MRS. ELVSTED: Yes, yes, Mr. Tesman. I'll do my best.

TESMAN: Well, come over here and let's start looking at these notes right away. Where shall we sit? Here? No, the other room. You'll excuse us, won't you, Judge? Come along with me, Mrs. Elvsted.

MRS. ELVSTED: Oh, God! If only we can manage to do it!

[TESMAN *and* MRS. ELVSTED *go into the rear room. He takes off his hat and overcoat. They sit at the table beneath the hanging lamp and absorb themselves in the notes.* HEDDA *walks across to the stove and sits in the armchair. After a moment,* BRACK *goes over to her.*]

HEDDA: [*Half aloud.*] Oh, Judge! This act of Eilert Loevborg's—doesn't it give one a sense of release!

BRACK: Release, Mrs. Hedda? Well, it's a release for him, of course——

HEDDA: Oh, I don't mean him—I mean me! The release of knowing that someone can do something really brave! Something beautiful!

BRACK: [*Smiles.*] Hm—my dear Mrs. Hedda——

HEDDA: Oh, I know what you're going to say. You're a bourgeois at heart too, just like—ah, well!

BRACK: [*Looks at her.*] Eilert Loevborg has meant more to you than you're willing to admit to yourself. Or am I wrong?

HEDDA: I'm not answering questions like that from you. I only know that Eilert Loevborg has had the courage to live according to his own principles. And now, at last, he's done something big! Something beautiful! To have the courage and the will to rise from the feast of life so early!

BRACK: It distresses me deeply, Mrs. Hedda, but I'm afraid I must rob you of that charming illusion.

HEDDA: Illusion?

BRACK: You wouldn't have been allowed to keep it for long, anyway.

HEDDA: What do you mean?

BRACK: He didn't shoot himself on purpose.

HEDDA: Not on purpose?

BRACK: No. It didn't happen quite the way I told you.

HEDDA: Have you been hiding something? What is it?

BRACK: In order to spare poor Mrs. Elvsted's feelings, I permitted myself one or two small—equivocations.

HEDDA: What?

BRACK: To begin with, he is already dead.

HEDDA: He died at the hospital?

BRACK: Yes. Without regaining consciousness.

HEDDA: What else haven't you told us?

BRACK: The incident didn't take place at his lodgings.

HEDDA: Well, that's utterly unimportant.

BRACK: Not utterly. The fact is, you see, that Eilert Loevborg was found shot in Mademoiselle Danielle's boudoir.

HEDDA: [Almost jumps up, but instead sinks back in her chair.] That's impossible. He can't have been there today.

BRACK: He was there this afternoon. He went to ask for something he claimed they'd taken from him. Talked some crazy nonsense about a child which had got lost——

HEDDA: Oh! So that was the reason!

BRACK: I thought at first he might have been referring to his manuscript. But I hear he destroyed that himself. So he must have meant his pocketbook—I suppose.

HEDDA: Yes, I suppose so. So they found him there?

BRACK: Yes; there. With a discharged pistol in his breast pocket. The shot had wounded him mortally.

HEDDA: Yes. In the breast.

BRACK: No. In the—hm—stomach. The—lower part——

HEDDA: [Looks at him with an expression of repulsion.] That too! Oh, why does everything I touch become mean and ludicrous? It's like a curse!

BRACK: There's something else, Mrs. Hedda. It's rather disagreeable, too.

HEDDA: What?

BRACK: The pistol he had on him——

HEDDA: Yes? What about it?

BRACK: He must have stolen it.

HEDDA: [Jumps up.] Stolen it! That isn't true! He didn't!

BRACK: It's the only explanation. He must have stolen it. Ssh!

[TESMAN and MRS. ELVSTED have got up from the table in the rear room and come into the drawing room.]

TESMAN. [*His hands full of papers.*] Hedda, I can't see properly under that lamp. Think!

HEDDA: I am thinking.

TESMAN: Do you think we could possibly use your writing table for a little? What?

HEDDA: Yes, of course. [*Quickly.*] No, wait! Let me tidy it up first.

TESMAN: Oh, don't you trouble about that. There's plenty of room.

HEDDA: No, no, let me tidy it up first, I say. I'll take this in and put them on the piano. Here.

[*She pulls an object, covered with sheets of music, out from under the bookcase, puts some more sheets on top and carries it all into the rear room and away to the left.* TESMAN *puts his papers on the writing table and moves the lamp over from the corner table. He and* MRS. ELVSTED *sit down and begin working again.* HEDDA *comes back.*]

HEDDA: [*Behind* MRS. ELVSTED's *chair, ruffles her hair gently.*] Well, my pretty Thea! And how is work progressing on Eilert Loevborg's memorial?

MRS. ELVSTED: [*Looks up at her, dejectedly.*] Oh, it's going to be terribly difficult to get these into any order.

TESMAN: We've got to do it. We must! After all, putting other people's papers into order is rather my specialty, what?

[HEDDA *goes over to the stove and sits on one of the footstools.* BRACK *stands over her, leaning against the armchair.*]

HEDDA: [*Whispers.*] What was that you were saying about the pistol?

BRACK: [*Softly.*] I said he must have stolen it.

HEDDA: Why do you think that?

BRACK: Because any other explanation is unthinkable, Mrs. Hedda, or ought to be.

HEDDA: I see.

BRACK: [*Looks at her for a moment.*] Eilert Loevborg was here this morning. Wasn't he?

HEDDA: Yes.

BRACK: Were you alone with him?

HEDDA: For a few moments.

BRACK: You didn't leave the room while he was here?

HEDDA: No.

BRACK: Think again. Are you sure you didn't go out for a moment?

HEDDA: Oh—yes, I might have gone into the hall. Just for a few seconds.

BRACK: And where was your pistol-case during this time?

HEDDA: I'd locked it in that——

BRACK: Er—Mrs. Hedda?

HEDDA: It was lying over there on my writing table.

BRACK: Have you looked to see if both the pistols are still there?

HEDDA: No.

BRACK: You needn't bother. I saw the pistol Loevborg had when they found him. I recognized it at once. From yesterday. And other occasions.

HEDDA: Have you got it?

BRACK: No. The police have it.

HEDDA: What will the police do with this pistol?

BRACK: Try to trace the owner.

HEDDA: Do you think they'll succeed?

BRACK: [Leans down and whispers.] No, Hedda Gabler. Not as long as I hold my tongue.

HEDDA: [Looks nervously at him.] And if you don't?

BRACK: [Shrugs his shoulders.] You could always say he'd stolen it.

HEDDA: I'd rather die!

BRACK: [Smiles.] People say that. They never do it.

HEDDA: [Not replying.] And suppose the pistol wasn't stolen? And they trace the owner? What then?

BRACK: There'll be a scandal, Hedda.

HEDDA: A scandal!

BRACK: Yes, a scandal. The thing you're so frightened of. You'll have to appear in court. Together with Mademoiselle Danielle. She'll have to explain how it all happened. Was it an accident, or was it—homicide? Was he about to take the pistol from his pocket to threaten her? And did it go off? Or did she snatch the pistol from his hand, shoot him and then put it back in his pocket? She might quite easily have done it. She's a resourceful lady, is Mademoiselle Danielle.

HEDDA: But I had nothing to do with this repulsive business.

BRACK: No. But you'll have to answer one question. Why did you give Eilert Loevborg this pistol? And what conclusions will people draw when it is proved you did give it to him?

HEDDA: [Bows her head.] That's true. I hadn't thought of that.

BRACK: Well, luckily there's no danger as long as I hold my tongue.

HEDDA: [Looks up at him.] In other words, I'm in your power, Judge. From now on, you've got your hold over me.

BRACK: [Whispers, more slowly.] Hedda, my dearest—believe me—I will not abuse my position.

HEDDA: Nevertheless, I'm in your power. Dependent on your will, and your demands. Not free. Still not free! [Rises passionately.] No. I couldn't bear that. No.

BRACK: [Looks half-derisively at her.] Most people resign themselves to the inevitable, sooner or later.

HEDDA: [Returns his gaze.] Possibly they do. [She goes across to the writing table.]

HEDDA: [Represses an involuntary smile and says in TESMAN's voice.] Well, George. Think you'll be able to manage? What?

TESMAN: Heaven knows, dear. This is going to take months and months.

HEDDA: [In the same tone as before.] Fancy that, by Jove! [Runs her hands gently through MRS. ELVSTED's hair.] Doesn't it feel strange, Thea? Here you are working away with Tesman just the way you used to work with Eilert Loevborg.

MRS. ELVSTED: Oh—if only I can inspire your husband too!

HEDDA: Oh, it'll come. In time.

TESMAN: Yes—do you know, Hedda, I really think I'm beginning to feel a bit—well—that way. But you go back and talk to Judge Brack.

HEDDA: Can't I be of use to you two in any way?

TESMAN: No, none at all. [*Turns his head.*] You'll have to keep Hedda company from now on, Judge, and see she doesn't get bored. If you don't mind.

BRACK: [*Glances at* HEDDA.] It'll be a pleasure.

HEDDA: Thank you. But I'm tired this evening. I think I'll lie down on the sofa in there for a little while.

TESMAN: Yes, dear—do. What?

[HEDDA *goes into the rear room and draws the curtain behind her. Short pause. Suddenly she begins to play a frenzied dance melody on the piano.*]

MRS. ELVSTED: [*Starts up from her chair.*] Oh, what's that?

TESMAN: [*Runs to the doorway.*] Hedda dear, please! Don't play dance music tonight! Think of Auntie Rena. And Eilert.

HEDDA: [*Puts her head out through the curtains.*] And Auntie Juju. And all the rest of them. From now on I'll be quiet. [*Closes the curtains behind her.*]

TESMAN: [*At the writing table.*] It distresses her to watch us doing this. I say, Mrs. Elvsted, I've an idea. Why don't you move in with Auntie Juju? I'll run over each evening, and we can sit and work there. What?

MRS. ELVSTED: Yes, that might be the best plan.

HEDDA: [*From the rear room.*] I can hear what you're saying, Tesman. But how shall I spend the evenings out here?

TESMAN: [*Looking through his papers.*] Oh, I'm sure Judge Brack'll be kind enough to come over and keep you company. You won't mind my not being here, Judge?

BRACK: [*In the armchair, calls gaily.*] I'll be delighted, Mrs. Tesman. I'll be here every evening. We'll have great fun together, you and I.

HEDDA: [*Loud and clear.*] Yes, that'll suit you, won't it, Judge? The only cock on the dunghill——!

[*A shot is heard from the rear room.* TESMAN, MRS. ELVSTED *and* JUDGE BRACK *start from their chairs.*]

TESMAN: Oh, she's playing with those pistols again.

[*He pulls the curtains aside and runs in.* MRS. ELVSTED *follow him.* HEDDA *is lying dead on the sofa. Confusion and shouting.* BERTHA *enters in alarm from the right.*]

TESMAN: [*Screams to* BRACK.] She's shot herself! Shot herself in the head! By Jove! Fancy that!

BRACK: [*Half paralyzed in the armchair.*] But, good God! People don't do such things!

1890

▼   ▼   ▼

CHARACTERIZATION A Glossary

acting: the last of the four steps in characterization in a performed play, for in the actual production the actor makes something distinctive of her or his talents in relation to the author's original conception and to the author's presentation

antagonist: the opponent of the protagonist or main character; the villain

casting: the third step in the creation of a character on the stage; deciding what actors are to play the parts

character: someone who acts, appears, or is referred to in a work

conception: the first step in the creation of a dramatic character, whether for written text or performed play; the original idea, when the playwright first begins to construct—or even dream about—a plot, or the characters, structure, or theme that will be an element of the play

dramatis personae: a list of the persons either in the play program or at the top of the first page of the written play whose lives are to be presented dramatically

hero/heroine: the leading male/female character, usually larger than life. See **protagonist.**

presentation: the second step in the creation of a character for the written text and the performed play; the representation of the character by the playwright in the words and actions specified in the text

protagonist: the main character of a play

stereotype: characters based on conscious or unconscious cultural assumptions that sex, age, ethnic or national identification, occupation, marital status, and so on are predictably accompanied by certain character traits, actions, even values

QUESTIONS

Getting Out

1. In what ways does Arlene differ from Arlie? What evidence does the play present that Arlene has changed over the years? Why is Arlene so insistent on not being called Arlie? Has she truly changed?

2. What is Bennie like? What are his motives in driving Arlene to her new home? How do you know? What devices are used to characterize Bennie? In what ways is Bennie like the guards in the Arlie scenes? In what ways is he different?

3. How is Ruby characterized? Carl? What strategies does the play use to influence your evaluation of each of these characters?

4. If you were staging *Getting Out*, how would you emphasize visually the connection between Arlie and Arlene? What vocal echoes would you try to create? How would you direct the actors who play Arlie and Arlene in their body language?

Hedda Gabler

1. How much do you learn of Hedda's life, of Tesman, of the situation, in the brief conversation between Miss Tesman and Bertha that opens the play? What indications are there of differences in class (or "life-style") between the Tesmans and Gablers in that conversation?

2. In what way did Tesman not "waste time" on his honeymoon? What does this suggest about him? his marriage? the future? What other details in the first five or six pages reinforce your understanding of his character, his professional accomplishments, and your expectations of what will happen later in the play? How is Tesman distinguished from the stereotypical absent-minded professor?

3. What is the important element in Hedda's attire when she first enters?

4. What expectations are aroused by the first part of the scene in Act I in which Mrs. Elvsted pays a call (before Tesman leaves the room)? What does Hedda get out of Mrs. Elvsted after Tesman leaves? How does she do it? Why? What new expectations are aroused by the Hedda–Thea conversation? Hedda is amazed by Mrs. Elvsted's open break with social conformity in deserting her husband; what are Hedda's attitudes toward society and the appearance that she makes in that society?

5. Why is Hedda so intrigued by the "competition" between George Tes-

man and Loevborg? Why does Judge Brack find the competition suited to his purposes?

6. How does the first act end? What is the effect of that ending? What does it fill in about the past and what expectations does it arouse about what is to happen later?

7. What are Loevborg's strengths? weaknesses? How are they related?

8. Why is George so shocked at the subject of Loevborg's new book? How are their approaches to their professions and to life different?

9. When Hedda suggests to George that Loevborg is "less afraid of life than most men," George responds, "Good heavens, no. He just doesn't know the meaning of the word moderation." Whose assessment is more accurate?

10. Does Mrs. Elvsted's inspiration of George and her plans to move in with Miss Tesman complete a new triangle excluding Hedda? What does Hedda's imitation of George in the last scene ("Fancy that, by Jove!") indicate regarding this turn of events?

WRITING SUGGESTIONS

1. Note the similarities in the stage directions describing the sets (and, indeed, in the rooms themselves) in *Hedda Gabler* and *The Little Foxes* (in the next chapter). Beginning with setting, write a comparative analysis of the two plays as examples of realism.

2. Write on the relation of social class to character and events in *Hedda Gabler*, in the course of your essay suggesting what segments of society Hedda, George, Loevborg, and Judge Brack represent.

3. Write on the themes of courage and cowardice in *Hedda Gabler*. You will probably want to treat the scenes between Hedda and Loevborg, and between Hedda, Mrs. Elvsted, and Loevborg in Act II, and, of course, Hedda's suicide.

4. Write two character sketches, one of Arlie at age ten and another of Arlene at age thirty-five. Then, imagine a dialogue between the two and write a transcript of their conversation.

5. Write an autobiography for Carl. Invent incidents in his past that help to explain his present character. Try to imitate as exactly as you can the language he uses in the play.

6. Write a review of an imaginary performance of *Getting Out*. Be sure to indicate in some detail how the past and present are staged in this particular performance, and evaluate how effective the staging is in interpreting the character of Arlie / Arlene.

2 STRUCTURE

An important part of any storyteller's task, whether the story is to be narrative or dramatic, is the invention, selection, and arrangement of the action. What will happen—including the introduction of characters, the unfolding of events, the development of theme, and the resolution of situational problems—cannot properly be called a full-scale **plot** until some principles of order and organization are introduced and questions of character, story line, and theme are somehow brought together.

Plot in plays usually involves a conflict, and dramatic structure centrally concerns the presentation—quite literally the embodiment or fleshing out—of that conflict. A conflict whose outcome is never in doubt may have other kinds of interest, but it is not truly dramatic. In a dramatic conflict each of the opposing forces—whether one character versus another, one group of characters versus another group, the values of an individual versus those of a group or society or nature, or one idea or ideology versus another one—at one point or another seems to have a chance to triumph.

In *Hamlet*, for example, our interest in the struggle between Hamlet and Claudius depends on their being evenly matched. Claudius has possession of the throne and the queen, but Hamlet's relation to the late king and his popularity with the people offset his opponent's strengths. Early in the play Claudius has the upper hand, but, realizing that he has underestimated Hamlet, he overreacts. Until he stops the play-within-the-play, the king seems firmly in command; in the end, however, Claudius does not triumph.

The king's outburst in *Hamlet* exemplifies the kind of event around which dramatic structure is built. The typical structure of a dramatic plot involves five distinct stages in the progression of the conflict. The first of these, the **exposition**, presents the situation as it exists at the opening of the play, introducing the characters and defining the relationships among them. Most of the exposition in *Trifles* is given early in the play by Hale's account of what he had found at the farmhouse, but somewhat more is provided a little later by Mrs. Hale's hint that all was not well with the Wrights and, even further, her comments about how different (and happier) Mrs. Wright was before her marriage. In the second stage of dramatic progression, the **rising action**, events complicate the original situation and generate conflicts among characters or values. These events often begin before the exposition is complete, furthering the story even as we learn about the situation and the characters involved. The rising action flows in a single direction, until, at a crucial moment, something happens to change its direction, such as a sudden revelation. In *Trifles* the rising action is the gradual piling up of "trifling" clues—frozen preserves, dirty towels, bread setting—until the women find the dead canary. This discovery is the third stage of dramatic progression, the **climax** or **turning point.** The fourth stage is the **falling action,** the unwinding or unknotting of the complication, which often occurs much more quickly than the rising action. The final stage of dramatic progression is its **conclusion,** sometimes called the **catastrophe** (from a Greek word meaning "to overturn"). The central conflict is resolved, a stable situation is reestablished, and the drama is done.

Dramatic progression is not structured exactly the same way in every play, but the basic pattern in most plays is quite similar. In *Hamlet,* the exposition—the situation at the beginning of the play—is mostly set forth in the first act. What do we need to know to understand the major conflicts in the play? We must know about the death of the old king, the accession of Claudius rather than young Hamlet, the marriage of Claudius and Gertrude, Hamlet's return from Wittenberg, and the threat of invasion from Fortinbras. We also need to know something about the nature of the characters involved in the situation. Shakespeare uses two major devices to present this information: the recent return of Horatio from Wittenberg (and his need to be brought up to date) and Claudius's speech at the beginning of Act I, scene 2. In these and other ways we learn where things stand. But even as this background is being revealed, things start to happen. The rising action begins, introducing new elements that complicate the story: the appearance of the ghost, Claudius's refusal to allow Hamlet to return to Wittenberg, Hamlet's growing involvement with Ophelia, the return of Rosencrantz and Guildenstern, and so forth. These and other complications affect the action without changing its basic direction. They also set up or prepare us for events later in the play: for example, Laertes' departure for Paris sets up his return in Act IV. The climax, or turning point, occurs when the king loses control of himself at the play-within-the-play. From then on it is Hamlet who more or less controls the situation. During the falling action the various strands of the plot begin to work themselves out. What happens to Ophelia? What is the result of Rosencrantz and Guildenstern's return? When such questions have been settled, we move to the conclusion of the play, the reestablishment of a new stable situation. The conclusion takes place in the final scene, where order is finally restored by the promise of Fortinbras as king.

Similarly, in *The Little Foxes* the opening scenes establish the characters and outline the various kinds of emotional and thematic conflict. There is regional conflict between the values of the South, as represented by the Hubbard and Giddens families, and the North, as represented by the Chicago interests of William Marshall. There is class conflict between the old landed South of Birdie and the new commercialization represented by Oscar and Ben—the paternalistic values represented by Lionnet versus those of stores and factories. There are racial conflicts, generational conflicts, conflicts among siblings and between husbands and wives. And most immediately and powerfully, there are struggles of will among strong individuals, most notably involving Regina and her several antagonists—both her brothers, her daughter, her husband.

But even before all the givens of character and situation are clear to us, the tension (rising action) begins to develop over details of the family's deal with Mr. Marshall, a deal that is designed to ease some of the major ideological conflicts (North and South, land and commerce) but that heightens other conflicts instead (between generations, siblings, marriage partners, and other individuals). The climax comes near the end of Act II, when Ben and Oscar decide to steal the bonds and leave Regina out of the deal. The falling action sorts out the implications for the several characters and families and leads to the final struggle between Regina and Horace and the related struggles between Regina and Zan and Regina and her brothers, and the conclusion involves baring the loneliness and fears of Regina and a recognition on all sides that their continued existence depends on silence and lies.

Even a sketch like *The Black and White* or a short play like *Trifles* contains all five stages of dramatic progression, although some are in abbreviated or truncated form. In *The Black and White*, for example, the exposition is barely completed when the play ends. The action is minimal and so is the conflict. What little disagreement there is between the two characters—the rising action—quickly climaxes through their discussion of how to handle strangers as their joint worry about uselessness and pointlessness surfaces, and together they face the fact that neither has anyplace to go when the milk bar closes (the falling action). The brief conclusion shows them planning how to cope individually with the alien world (by mentioning familiar sights and going to familiar places) as the night ends and dawn comes on. This is not high drama with fireworks and physical conflict, but even in its shortened and subdued form a basic dramatic structure shapes the single scene.

There are other structural devices by which a play can be organized and made meaningful and effective. Thematic concerns, for example, often hold together varieties of characters and winding plots. In *The Little Foxes*, the concern to define southern culture and values brings together the various kinds of conflict—between races, classes, generations, families, individuals, and ways of life. Careful and intricate plot calculations, in which difficult situations keep in tension the precise strengths and weaknesses of crucial characters, also structure plays in subtle but analyzable ways. In *The Little Foxes*, the negotiable bonds in Leo's possession make possible not only the theft of Regina's share in the family investment but also set up the final isolation of Regina from both her husband and daughter. Making Leo an assistant at the bank, creating him as a weak, immature, opportunistic, and gossipy character, and having his private knowledge of the bonds in the safe deposit box surface at precisely the right moment allow developments in the plot to conflict with aspects of Regina's character—her greed and ambition, her romanticism, her lack of human loyalty and inability to love—in ways that make event after event seem nearly inevitable.

Another structural device involves **dramatic irony**, the fulfillment of a plan, action, or expectation in a surprising way, often the opposite of what the characters intend. One example occurs in *Trifles* when the women keep noticing all the everyday things—"trifles"—in the house while the official investigators—the men—keep looking for large and unusual things. Finding "nothing . . . but kitchen things," and thinking they have no clues at all, the men condescend to the women's concerns: "Women are used to worrying about trifles." Their observation is ironic, but the irony is on them. Here the play's title sets up the dramatic irony of moment after moment and observation after observation, for two wholly different ways of observing and reasoning are explored from beginning to end, and the action continually comments on the dominant male assumptions.

Another example involves the way, at the end of *The Little Foxes*, Regina's clever manipulativeness first seems to be rewarded and then is thwarted. Her insistence that Horace return home from Baltimore so that she can persuade him to join in the family's get-rich-quick scheme becomes a nightmare for her when he proves to have become, during his absence, both stronger and smarter, and when Horace reveals the terms of his will she recognizes that her own "will"—to be rich and have a new life in Chicago—is going to be defeated. There are more turns of dramatic irony, as well. When Horace's sudden attack again gives Regina control over his medicine, his life, and his ability to make his will, she again seems not only to have triumphed over her husband but over her brothers as well—only to find again that her shrewdest and most cruel plans fail to get her what she wants.

Besides structures like dramatic irony or thematic coherence that pull parts of a play together, and the five structural stages that shape dramatic action, most plays also have formal divisions, such as acts and scenes. In the Greek theater scenes were separated by choral odes (see, for example, *Oedipus the King*). In many French plays, a new scene begins with any significant entrance or exit. Many "classic" plays, like *Hamlet,* have five acts (because the poet Horace suggested that number), but modern plays tend to have two or three acts. Formal divisions are the result of the content of the individual play—where sharp breaks can be emotionally effective by creating suspense or giving readers a relief from tension—or the conventions of the period: the expectation in the modern theater, for example, that audiences will have one or two intermissions in a public performance. Divisions may vary from the one-act, one-scene play—such as *The Black and White*—to such long multiact plays as Eugene O'Neill's *Mourning Becomes Electra.*

The ways that interest is sustained, that the rise and fall of emotion are controlled, and that character and plot are revealed depend heavily on length and the mode of presentation conceived for the drama. Closet dramas written primarily for private reading are likely to have a different pace than musicals or farces that depend heavily on physical movement or pratfalls, and soap operas or serials broken into many episodes are likely to use all kinds of subplots and subconflicts to create smaller structural units within some larger shape. Dramas that are written as performance texts but read as literary texts retain in their printed state features that may have been dictated by conventions, circumstances, or accidents of performance.

Dramatic progression, dramatic irony, and even the formal divisions of a play are present to the reader as well as the viewer of the performance of a play, but of course in performance a play takes definite form on a stage or acting area rather than in the less defined theater of the reader's mind. The design and significance of the acting area vary in different times and places, and knowing something about stage history often helps readers to appreciate how features of the text came to be and how the action might be imagined. In the Greek theater, the audience was seated on a raised semicircle of seats (**amphitheater**) halfway around a circular area (**orchestra**) used primarily for dancing by the chorus. At the back of the orchestra was the **skene** or stage house, representing the palace or temple before which the action took place. Shakespeare's stage, in contrast, basically involved a rectangular area built inside one end of a generally round enclosure, so that the audience was on three sides of the principal acting area. There were additional acting areas on either side of this stage, as well as a recessed area at the back of the stage, which could represent Gertrude's chamber in *Hamlet,* for example, and an upper acting area, which could serve as Juliet's balcony, for example.

Modern stages are of three basic types. The **proscenium** stage evolved during the nineteenth century and is still the most common. The proscenium or proscenium arch is an architectural element that separates the auditorium from the stage and makes the action seem more real because the audience views it through an invisible fourth wall. The proscenium stage lends itself to the use of a curtain, which can be lowered and raised—or closed and parted— between acts or scenes. Sometimes a part of the acting area is on the auditorium side of the proscenium. This area is called an **apron** or forestage. The second type of modern stage is the **thrust stage,** in which the audience is seated around three sides of the major acting area. All of the action may take place on this projecting area, or some may occur in the extended area of the fourth side. In an **arena stage,** the third type, the audience is seated all the way around the acting area, and players make their entrances and exits through the auditorium.

Naturally playwrights must often take into account the sort of stage their play will be performed on. An arena stage, for example, imposes severe limitations on the sets that may be used, in order that viewing not be obstructed from any side. Sometimes an author or director may find ways to overcome certain limitations of a given type of stage, as Marsha Norman did by using flashbacks in *Getting Out.* Nevertheless, when writing she knew the problems she confronted given the particular nature of the stage she was writing for.

The conventions of dramatic writing and stage production have of course changed considerably since the advent of theater. These conventions involve, for example the way playwrights convey the notion of place. The audience knows that the stage is a stage, but they accept it as a public square or a room in a castle or an empty road. In *Trifles* we accept the stage as a kitchen in a midwest farmhouse. There must be one door leading to the outside of the house, another leading to the upstairs, and a third leading to another room. There must be at least a sink, a cupboard, a stove, a small table and a large kitchen table, and a rocking chair. The play is written for a proscenium stage. If the play is to work, the designer must make the audience aware of the objects, doors, chairs, and so on required by the action. Many medieval plays were, by contrast, written to be performed on small wagons that could be moved from town to town, and although the action could spill into the street or the audience, no elaborate stage settings or entrances or exits could be physically represented: much more of the "place" had to be left to the audience's imagination, as in radio plays or plays written primarily for readers.

The convention of place also involves how place is changed. In a modern play like *The Little Foxes,* such a change involves lowering a curtain or darkening the stage while different sets and props are arranged. In Greek drama, generally there was no change of place and the action was set up to involve only one place. When, in *Oedipus the King*, the presence of Tiresias is required, escorts are sent to bring him. (Films, on the other hand, can change location quickly without demanding any spatial imagination on the part of viewers, and can create a sense of place that is more dreamy, or symbolic, or suggestive than what many plays are capable of, since there are no props or sets to change or physical stage to be limited by.)

In Shakespeare's theater the conventions of place are quite different: the acting area does not represent a specific place, but assumes a temporary identity according to the characters who inhabit it, their costumes, and their speeches. At the opening of *Hamlet* we know we are at a sentry station because a man dressed as a soldier challenges two others. By line 15, we know that we are in Denmark because the actors profess to be "liegemen to the Dane." At the end of the scene the actors leave the stage and in a sense take the sentry station with them. Shortly a group of people dressed in court costumes and a man and a woman wearing crowns appear. A theater audience must surmise, from costumes and dialogue, that the acting area has now become a "chamber of state"; as readers of the text, we could also infer the change of place from the identity of the characters and their words, but our text provides more information than a performance can, identifying the changed place in a stage direction. Often, in fact, readers of plays have more—and more accurate—guidance than viewers of plays, for they have the clues beyond dialogue from which actors and directors make decisions about tone or staging.

Readers of plays usually have the convenience of stage directions to indicate exactly where they are, but readers have greater demands placed on them as well, for they are allowed to keep open matters of interpretation that viewers of a play will have had decided by the director. Readers, for example, can put to work their own strategies of textual interpretation to decide how "real" the ghost is, and they can juggle more than one possibility at a time, while a viewer of a performance will have "seen" either an apparent illusion or a realistic presence. The mists can only cover so much in a production, but for a reader the mist can linger much longer, until an entire coherent interpretation of events merges. Thus, in one sense, a reader's text of a play is richer and more uncertain, more open to individual interpretation, than a production mediated by a director and acting company.

Conventions have also changed in the treatment of time, with respect to both stage production and the way a text is written. Renaissance commentators on classical drama argued that in order to insure maximum dramatic impact the action of a play should represent a very short time—sometimes as short as the actual performance (two or three hours), and certainly no longer than a single day. It is this concentration or **unity of time** that impels a dramatist to select the moment when a stable situation should change and to fill in the necessary prior details by exposition or even by some more elaborate device, such as the enacted dreams and memories in *Death of a Salesman*. The action from the beginning to the end of the play thus can represent a rather long time span, even years, a very short period of actual time. You might look back over the plays you have read so far and note how much time elapses from beginning to end and what devices, if any, concentrate the represented time and thus heighten the impact of the action.

Even within the classical drama with its restricted time span, there are conventions to mark the passing of represented time when it is supposed to pass at a greater rate than that of viewing or reading time. The choral odes in *Oedipus the King* are an example of one convention for representing the passage of time. The elapsed time between scenes may be that necessary to send for the shepherd from Mount Cithaeron and allow for his return or the much shorter time needed for Oedipus to enter his palace, discover Jocasta's suicide, blind himself, and return.

The time covered by the ode is shorter or longer as necessary, without real reference to the length of the ode. In Elizabethan drama the break between scenes covers whatever time is necessary without a formal device like the choral odes. Sometimes the time is short, like the break between Hamlet's departure to see his mother at the end of Act III, scene 2, and the entrance of the king with Rosencrantz and Guildenstern at the beginning of the next scene; at other times the elapsed time between might be as long as that between scenes 4 and 5 of Act IV, during which the news of Polonius's death reaches Paris and Laertes returns to Denmark and there rallies his friends. In *Hamlet* we cannot tell exactly what the time span is, but in a time of relatively primitive transportation Laertes goes to Paris, remains there for a time, and returns to Denmark; Fortinbras goes from Norway to Poland, fights a war, and returns to Denmark; and news of the deaths of Rosencrantz and Guildenstern, who leave for England between scenes 3 and 4 of Act IV, is brought back. The point is not that Shakespeare was sloppy about time; he worked, as did other playwrights of his era, within conventions that audiences and readers understood, and modern readers of his text have to adjust to these assumptions or they will spend a lot of energy worrying about "inconsistencies" or "inaccuracies" that are readily explained by historical habits of performance, reading, and interpretation.

In reading fiction we recognize that what is going on in represented time is often supposed to be taking much longer than it takes us to read the words describing it. The time that is supposed to pass within one sentence can vary greatly from that which passes in another. In reading fiction, we are used to making such adjustments. In plays, however, modern readers or audiences might expect the passage of time to be more clearly marked—by stage directions, or scene or act endings. Not so, necessarily, in Shakespeare. The first scene of *Hamlet*, for example, opens just on the stroke of midnight, yet in fewer than forty lines—with no obvious warning to the reader that so much time has passed—we learn it is one o'clock. And a hundred lines later the cock crows, and soon Horatio says that it is dawn. In reading this scene, we have little difficulty in adjusting represented time to reading time, but if we enact plays within our imagination while we read them we need to be aware of this "undramatic" handling of time. In performance, some sort of stage business must suggest the passing of represented time: those watching for the ghost may sit still for what seems to an audience a long time—a couple of minutes—or get up and stretch and walk about the stage, or lie down, toss and turn, perhaps sleep.

Drama is both a literary and performed art, and a play exists separately on page and stage. In reading plays, we use our imagination much as we do in stories to portray to ourselves the way the action is unfolding, but there is a difference. When we read stories we have a mediator, a narrator to guide us. When we read plays, we know that in another manifestation they are staged, produced, performed, and that another set of consciousnesses would mediate if we were viewing the plays in performance. As readers, we take all the roles ourselves and do not portion them out to actors; we set our own stage in our own minds. We become, in effect, our own producers, directors, and actors, but with the reader's latitude to keep multiple possibilities in mind. We become not just viewers of a staged production created by an intermediary, but imagining readers of a play—staging and restaging it in the mind's eye, mediated by our producer-selves.

▼ ▼ ▼

WILLIAM SHAKESPEARE

Hamlet

CHARACTERS

CLAUDIUS, *King of Denmark*
HAMLET, *son of the former and nephew
    to the present King*
POLONIUS, *Lord Chamberlain*
HORATIO, *friend of Hamlet*
LAERTES, *son of Polonius*
VOLTEMAND
CORNELIUS
ROSENCRANTZ
GUILDENSTERN ⎬ *courtiers*
OSRIC
A GENTLEMAN
A PRIEST

MARCELLUS ⎱
BERNARDO ⎰ *officers*
FRANCISCO, *a soldier*
REYNALDO, *servant to Polonius*
PLAYERS
TWO CLOWNS, *gravediggers*
FORTINBRAS, *Prince of Norway*
A NORWEGIAN CAPTAIN
ENGLISH AMBASSADORS
GERTRUDE, *Queen of Denmark, and
    mother of Hamlet*
OPHELIA, *daughter of Polonius*
GHOST OF HAMLET'S FATHER

LORDS, LADIES, OFFICERS, SOLDIERS, SAILORS, MESSENGERS, AND ATTENDANTS

SCENE: *The action takes place in or near the royal castle of Denmark at
Elsinore.*

ACT I

SCENE 1

A guard station atop the castle. Enter BERNARDO *and* FRANCISCO, *two sentinels.*

BERNARDO: Who's there?
FRANCISCO: Nay, answer me. Stand and unfold yourself.
BERNARDO: Long live the king!
FRANCISCO: Bernardo?
5 BERNARDO: He.
FRANCISCO: You come most carefully upon your hour.
BERNARDO: 'Tis now struck twelve. Get thee to bed, Francisco.
FRANCISCO: For this relief much thanks. 'Tis bitter cold,
    And I am sick at heart.
BERNARDO: Have you had quiet guard?
10 FRANCISCO: Not a mouse stirring.
BERNARDO: Well, good night.
    If you do meet Horatio and Marcellus,
    The rivals[1] of my watch, bid them make haste.

[*Enter* HORATIO *and* MARCELLUS.]

---

1. Companions.

FRANCISCO: I think I hear them. Stand, ho! Who is there?
HORATIO: Friends to this ground.
MARCELLUS: And liegemen to the Dane.[2]   15
FRANCISCO: Give you good night.
MARCELLUS: O, farewell, honest soldier!
    Who hath relieved you?
FRANCISCO: Bernardo hath my place.
    Give you good night.   [*Exit* FRANCISCO.]
MARCELLUS: Holla, Bernardo!
BERNARDO: Say—
    What, is Horatio there?
HORATIO: A piece of him.
BERNARDO: Welcome, Horatio. Welcome, good Marcellus.   20
HORATIO: What, has this thing appeared again tonight?
BERNARDO: I have seen nothing.
MARCELLUS: Horatio says 'tis but our fantasy,
    And will not let belief take hold of him
    Touching this dreaded sight twice seen of us.   25
    Therefore I have entreated him along
    With us to watch the minutes of this night,
    That if again this apparition come,
    He may approve[3] our eyes and speak to it.
HORATIO: Tush, tush, 'twill not appear.
BERNARDO: Sit down awhile,   30
    And let us once again assail your ears,
    That are so fortified against our story,
    What we have two nights seen.
HORATIO: Well, sit we down.
    And let us hear Bernardo speak of this.
BERNARDO: Last night of all,   35
    When yond same star that's westward from the pole[4]
    Had made his course t' illume that part of heaven
    Where now it burns, Marcellus and myself,
    The bell then beating one—

[*Enter* GHOST.]

MARCELLUS: Peace, break thee off. Look where it comes again.   40
BERNARDO: In the same figure like the king that's dead.
MARCELLUS: Thou art a scholar; speak to it, Horatio.
BERNARDO: Looks 'a[5] not like the king? Mark it, Horatio.
HORATIO: Most like. It harrows me with fear and wonder.
BERNARDO: It would be spoke to.

2. The "Dane" is the King of Denmark, who is also called "Denmark," as in line 48 of this scene.
In line 61 the same figure is used for the King of Norway.   3. Confirm the testimony of.   4. Pole-
star.   5. He.

45 MARCELLUS: Speak to it, Horatio.
HORATIO: What art thou that usurp'st this time of night
    Together with that fair and warlike form
    In which the majesty of buried Denmark
    Did sometimes march? By heaven I charge thee, speak.
MARCELLUS: It is offended.
50 BERNARDO: See, it stalks away.
HORATIO: Stay. Speak, speak. I charge thee, speak.   [*Exit* GHOST.]
MARCELLUS: 'Tis gone and will not answer.
BERNARDO: How now, Horatio! You tremble and look pale.
    Is not this something more than fantasy?
55   What think you on't?
HORATIO: Before my God, I might not this believe
    Without the sensible[6] and true avouch
    Of mine own eyes.
MARCELLUS: Is it not like the king?
HORATIO: As thou art to thyself.
60   Such was the very armor he had on
    When he the ambitious Norway combated.
    So frowned he once when, in an angry parle,[7]
    He smote the sledded Polacks on the ice.
    'Tis strange.
MARCELLUS: Thus twice before, and jump[8] at this dead hour,
65   With martial stalk hath he gone by our watch.
HORATIO: In what particular thought to work I know not,
    But in the gross and scope of mine opinion,
    This bodes some strange eruption to our state.
MARCELLUS: Good now, sit down, and tell me he that knows,
70   Why this same strict and most observant watch
    So nightly toils the subject[9] of the land,
    And why such daily cast of brazen cannon
    And foreign mart for implements of war;
    Why such impress of shipwrights, whose sore task
75   Does not divide the Sunday from the week.
    What might be toward that this sweaty haste
    Doth make the night joint-laborer with the day?
    Who is't that can inform me?
HORATIO: That can I.
    At last, the whisper goes so. Our last king,
80   Whose image even but now appeared to us,
    Was as you know by Fortinbras of Norway,
    Thereto pricked on by a most emulate pride,
    Dared to the combat; in which our valiant Hamlet
    (For so this side of our known world esteemed him)

6. Of the senses.   7. Parley.   8. Precisely.   9. People.

Did slay this Fortinbras; who by a sealed compact   85
Well ratified by law and heraldry,
Did forfeit, with his life, all those his lands
Which he stood seized of,[1] to the conqueror;
Against the which a moiety competent[2]
Was gagéd[3] by our king; which had returned   90
To the inheritance of Fortinbras,
Had he been vanquisher; as, by the same covenant
And carriage of the article designed,
His fell to Hamlet. Now, sir, young Fortinbras,
Of unimprovéd mettle hot and full,   95
Hath in the skirts of Norway here and there
Sharked up a list of lawless resolutes
For food and diet to some enterprise
That hath a stomach in't; which is no other,
As it doth well appear unto our state,   100
But to recover of us by strong hand
And terms compulsatory, those foresaid lands
So by his father lost; and this, I take it,
Is the main motive of our preparations,
The source of this our watch, and the chief head   105
Of this post-haste and romage[4] in the land.
BERNARDO: I think it be no other but e'en so.
  Well may it sort[5] that this portentous figure
  Comes arméd through our watch so like the king
  That was and is the question of these wars.   110
HORATIO: A mote[6] it is to trouble the mind's eye.
  In the most high and palmy state of Rome,
  A little ere the mightiest Julius fell,
  The graves stood tenantless, and the sheeted dead
  Did squeak and gibber in the Roman streets;   115
  As stars with trains of fire, and dews of blood,
  Disasters in the sun; and the moist star,
  Upon whose influence Neptune's empire stands,[7]
  Was sick almost to doomsday with eclipse.
  And even the like precurse[8] of feared events,   120
  As harbingers preceding still the fates
  And prologue to the omen coming on,
  Have heaven and earth together demonstrated
  Unto our climatures[9] and countrymen.

  [Enter GHOST.]

---

1. Possessed.   2. Portion of similar value.   3. Pledged.   4. Stir.   5. Chance.
6. Speck of dust.   7. Neptune was the Roman sea god; the "moist star" is the moon.   8. Precursor.   9. Regions.

125   But soft, behold, lo where it comes again!
    I'll cross it[1] though it blast me.—Stay, illusion.

    [*It spreads (its) arms.*]

    If thou hast any sound or use of voice,
    Speak to me.
    If there be any good thing to be done,
130   That may to thee do ease, and grace to me,
    Speak to me.
    If thou art privy to thy country's fate,
    Which happily foreknowing may avoid,
    O, speak!
135   Or if thou hast uphoarded in thy life
    Extorted treasure in the womb of earth,
    For which, they say, you spirits oft walk in death,

    [*The cock crows.*]

    Speak of it. Stay, and speak. Stop it, Marcellus.
MARCELLUS: Shall I strike at it with my partisan[2]?
HORATIO: Do, if it will not stand.
BERNARDO: 'Tis here.
140 HORATIO: 'Tis here.
MARCELLUS: 'Tis gone.   [*Exit* GHOST.]
    We do it wrong, being so majestical,
    To offer it the show of violence;
    For it is as the air, invulnerable,
145   And our vain blows malicious mockery.
BERNARDO: It was about to speak when the cock crew.
HORATIO: And then it started like a guilty thing
    Upon a fearful summons. I have heard
    The cock, that is the trumpet to the morn,
150   Doth with his lofty and shrill-sounding throat
    Awake the god of day, and at his warning,
    Whether in sea or fire, in earth or air,
    Th' extravagant and erring[3] spirit hies
    To his confine; and of the truth herein
155   This present object made probation.[4]
MARCELLUS: It faded on the crowing of the cock.
    Some say that ever 'gainst that season comes
    Wherein our Savior's birth is celebrated,
    This bird of dawning singeth all night long,
160   And then, they say, no spirit dare stir abroad,

---

1. Horatio means either that he will move across the ghost's path in order to stop him or that he will make the sign of the cross to gain power over him. The stage direction that follows is somewhat ambiguous. "It" seems to refer to the ghost, but the movement would be appropriate to Horatio.
2. Halberd.   3. Wandering out of bounds.   4. Proof.

The nights are wholesome, then no planets strike,
No fairy takes,[5] nor witch hath power to charm,
So hallowed and so gracious is that time.
HORATIO: So have I heard and do in part believe it.
But look, the morn in russet mantle clad   165
Walks o'er the dew of yon high eastward hill.
Break we our watch up, and by my advice
Let us impart what we have seen tonight
Unto young Hamlet, for upon my life
This spirit, dumb to us, will speak to him.   170
Do you consent we shall acquaint him with it,
As needful in our loves, fitting our duty?
MARCELLUS: Let's do't, I pray, and I this morning know
Where we shall find him most convenient.   *[Exeunt.]*

SCENE 2

A *chamber of state. Enter* KING CLAUDIUS, QUEEN GERTRUDE, HAMLET,
POLONIUS, LAERTES, OPHELIA, VOLTEMAND, CORNELIUS *and other members of the
court.*

KING: Though yet of Hamlet our dear brother's death
  The memory be green, and that it us befitted
  To bear our hearts in grief, and our whole kingdom
  To be contracted in one brow of woe,
  Yet so far hath discretion fought with nature   5
  That we with wisest sorrow think on him,
  Together with remembrance of ourselves.
  Therefore our sometime sister, now our queen,
  Th' imperial jointress[6] to this warlike state,
  Have we, as 'twere with a defeated joy,   10
  With an auspicious and a dropping eye,
  With mirth in funeral, and with dirge in marriage,
  In equal scale weighing delight and dole,
  Taken to wife; nor have we herein barred
  Your better wisdoms, which have freely gone   15
  With this affair along. For all, our thanks.
  Now follows that you know young Fortinbras,
  Holding a weak supposal of our worth,
  Or thinking by our late dear brother's death
  Our state to be disjoint and out of frame,   20
  Colleaguéd with this dream of his advantage,
  He hath not failed to pester us with message
  Importing the surrender of those lands

---

5. Enchants.   6. A "jointress" is a widow who holds a *jointure* or life interest in the estate of her
deceased husband.

Lost by his father, with all bands of law,
25 To our most valiant brother. So much for him.
Now for ourself, and for this time of meeting,
Thus much the business is: we have here writ
To Norway, uncle of young Fortinbras—
Who, impotent and bedrid, scarcely hears
30 Of this his nephew's purpose—to suppress
His further gait[7] herein, in that the levies,
The lists, and full proportions are all made
Out of his subject; and we here dispatch
You, good Cornelius, and you, Voltemand,
35 For bearers of this greeting to old Norway,
Giving to you no further personal power
To business with the king, more than the scope
Of these dilated[8] articles allow.
Farewell, and let your haste commend your duty.

CORNELIUS: ⎫
40 VOLTEMAND: ⎬ In that, and all things will we show our duty.

KING: We doubt it nothing, heartily farewell.

                                 [*Exeunt* VOLTEMAND *and* CORNELIUS.]

And now, Laertes, what's the news with you?
You told us of some suit. What is't, Laertes?
You cannot speak of reason to the Dane
45 And lose your voice. What wouldst thou beg, Laertes,
That shall not be my offer, not thy asking?
The head is not more native to the heart,
The hand more instrumental[9] to the mouth,
Than is the throne of Denmark to thy father.
What wouldst thou have, Laertes?

50 LAERTES: My dread lord,
Your leave and favor to return to France,
From whence, though willingly, I came to Denmark
To show my duty in your coronation,
Yet now I must confess, that duty done,
55 My thoughts and wishes bend again toward France,
And bow them to your gracious leave and pardon.

KING: Have you your father's leave? What says Polonius?

POLONIUS: He hath, my lord, wrung from me my slow leave
By laborsome petition, and at last
60 Upon his will I sealed my hard consent.
I do beseech you give him leave to go.

KING: Take thy fair hour, Laertes. Time be thine,
And thy best graces spend it at thy will.

7. Progress.   8. Fully expressed.   9. Serviceable.

But now, my cousin[1] Hamlet, and my son—
HAMLET: [*Aside.*] A little more than kin, and less than kind.   65
KING: How is it that the clouds still hang on you?
HAMLET: Not so, my lord. I am too much in the sun.
QUEEN: Good Hamlet, cast thy nighted color off,
    And let thine eye look like a friend on Denmark.
    Do not for ever with thy vailéd lids[2]   70
    Seek for thy noble father in the dust.
    Thou know'st 'tis common—all that lives must die,
    Passing through nature to eternity.
HAMLET: Ay, madam, it is common.
QUEEN: If it be,
    Why seems it so particular with thee?   75
HAMLET: Seems, madam? Nay, it is. I know not "seems."
    'Tis not alone my inky cloak, good mother,
    Nor customary suits of solemn black,
    Nor windy suspiration of forced breath,
    No, nor the fruitful river in the eye,   80
    Nor the dejected havior[3] of the visage,
    Together with all forms, moods, shapes of grief,
    That can denote me truly. These indeed seem,
    For they are actions that a man might play,
    But I have that within which passes show—   85
    These but the trappings and the suits of woe.
KING: 'Tis sweet and commendable in your nature, Hamlet,
    To give these mourning duties to your father,
    But you must know your father lost a father,
    That father lost, lost his, and the survivor bound   90
    In filial obligation for some term
    To do obsequious[4] sorrow. But to persever
    In obstinate condolement is a course
    Of impious stubbornness. 'Tis unmanly grief.
    It shows a will most incorrect to[5] heaven,   95
    A heart unfortified, a mind impatient,
    An understanding simple and unschooled.
    For what we know must be, and is as common
    As any the most vulgar thing to sense,
    Why should we in our peevish opposition   100
    Take it to heart? Fie, 'tis a fault to heaven,
    A fault against the dead, a fault to nature,
    To reason most absurd, whose common theme
    Is death of fathers, and who still hath cried,
    From the first corse[6] till he that died today,   105
    "This must be so." We pray you throw to earth

1. "Cousin" is used here as a general term of kinship.   2. Lowered eyes.   3. Appearance.
4. Suited for funeral obsequies.   5. Uncorrected toward.   6. Corpse.

This unprevailing woe, and think of us
As of a father, for let the world take note
You are the most immediate[7] to our throne,
110   And with no less nobility of love
Than that which dearest father bears his son
Do I impart toward you. For your intent
In going back to school in Wittenberg,
It is most retrograde[8] to our desire,
115   And we beseech you, bend you to remain
Here in the cheer and comfort of our eye,
Our chiefest courtier, cousin, and our son.
QUEEN: Let not thy mother lose her prayers, Hamlet.
I pray thee stay with us, go not to Wittenberg.
120   HAMLET: I shall in all my best obey you, madam.
KING: Why, 'tis a loving and a fair reply.
Be as ourself in Denmark. Madam, come.
This gentle and unforced accord of Hamlet
Sits smiling to my heart, in grace whereof,
125   No jocund health that Denmark drinks today
But the great cannon to the clouds shall tell,
And the king's rouse the heaven shall bruit[9] again,
Respeaking earthly thunder. Come away.

[*Flourish. Exeunt all but* HAMLET.]

HAMLET: O, that this too too solid flesh would melt,
130   Thaw, and resolve itself into a dew,
Or that the Everlasting had not fixed
His canon[1] 'gainst self-slaughter. O God, God,
How weary, stale, flat, and unprofitable
Seem to me all the uses of this world!
135   Fie on't, ah, fie, 'tis an unweeded garden
That grows to seed. Things rank and gross in nature
Possess it merely.[2] That it should come to this,
But two months dead, nay, not so much, not two.
So excellent a king, that was to this
140   Hyperion to a satyr,[3] so loving to my mother,
That he might not beteem[4] the winds of heaven
Visit her face too roughly. Heaven and earth,
Must I remember? Why, she would hang on him
As if increase of appetite had grown
145   By what it fed on, and yet, within a month—
Let me not think on't. Frailty, thy name is woman—
A little month, or ere those shoes were old

7. Next in line.   8. Contrary.   9. Echo. *Rouse:* carousal.   1. Law.   2. Entirely.   3. Hyperion, a Greek god, stands here for beauty in contrast to the monstrous satyr, a lecherous creature, half man and half goat.   4. Permit.

With which she followed my poor father's body
Like Niobe,[5] all tears, why she, even she—
O God, a beast that wants discourse of reason   150
Would have mourned longer—married with my uncle,
My father's brother, but no more like my father
Than I to Hercules.[6] Within a month,
Ere yet the salt of most unrighteous tears
Had left the flushing in her gallèd eyes,   155
She married. O, most wicked speed, to post
With such dexterity to incestuous sheets!
It is not, nor it cannot come to good.
But break my heart, for I must hold my tongue.

[*Enter* HORATIO, MARCELLUS, *and* BERNARDO.]

HORATIO: Hail to your lordship!
HAMLET: I am glad to see you well.   160
    Horatio—or I do forget myself.
HORATIO: The same, my lord, and your poor servant ever.
HAMLET: Sir, my good friend, I'll change[7] that name with you.
    And what make you from Wittenberg, Horatio?
    Marcellus?   165
MARCELLUS: My good lord!
HAMLET: I am very glad to see you. [*To* BERNARDO.] Good even, sir.—
    But what, in faith, make you from Wittenberg?
HORATIO: A truant disposition, good my lord.
HAMLET: I would not hear your enemy say so,   170
    Nor shall you do my ear that violence
    To make it truster of your own report
    Against yourself. I know you are no truant.
    But what is your affair in Elsinore?
    We'll teach you to drink deep ere you depart.   175
HORATIO: My lord, I came to see your father's funeral.
HAMLET: I prithee do not mock me, fellow-student,
    I think it was to see my mother's wedding.
HORATIO: Indeed, my lord, it followed hard upon.
HAMLET: Thrift, thrift, Horatio. The funeral-baked meats   180
    Did coldly furnish forth the marriage tables.
    Would I had met my dearest[8] foe in heaven
    Or ever I had seen that day, Horatio!
    My father—methinks I see my father.
HORATIO: Where, my lord?
HAMLET: In my mind's eye, Horatio.   185

5. In Greek mythology Niobe was turned to stone after a tremendous fit of weeping over the death of her 14 children, a misfortune brought about by her boasting over her fertility.   6. The demigod Hercules was noted for his strength and the series of spectacular labors that it allowed him to accomplish.   7. Exchange.   8. Bitterest.

HORATIO: I saw him once, 'a was a goodly king.
HAMLET: 'A was a man, take him for all in all,
    I shall not look upon his like again.
HORATIO: My lord, I think I saw him yesternight.
190   HAMLET: Saw who?
HORATIO: My lord, the king your father.
HAMLET: The king my father?
HORATIO: Season your admiration[9] for a while
    With an attent ear till I may deliver[1]
    Upon the witness of these gentlemen
    This marvel to you.
195   HAMLET: For God's love, let me hear!
HORATIO: Two nights together had these gentlemen,
    Marcellus and Bernardo, on their watch
    In the dead waste and middle of the night
    Been thus encountered. A figure like your father,
200   Armed at point exactly, cap-a-pe,[2]
    Appears before them, and with solemn march
    Goes slow and stately by them. Thrice he walked
    By their oppressed and fear-surprisèd eyes
    Within his truncheon's[3] length, whilst they, distilled
205   Almost to jelly with the act of fear,
    Stand dumb and speak not to him. This to me
    In dreadful secrecy impart they did,
    And I with them the third night kept the watch,
    Where, as they had delivered, both in time,
210   Form of the thing, each word made true and good,
    The apparition comes. I knew your father.
    These hands are not more like.
HAMLET: But where was this?
MARCELLUS: My lord, upon the platform where we watch.
HAMLET: Did you not speak to it?
HORATIO: My lord, I did,
215   But answer made it none. Yet once methought
    It lifted up it head and did address
    Itself to motion, like as it would speak;
    But even then the morning cock crew loud,
    And at the sound it shrunk in haste away
    And vanished from our sight.
220   HAMLET: 'Tis very strange.
HORATIO: As I do live, my honored lord, 'tis true,
    And we did think it writ down in our duty
    To let you know of it.

---

9. Moderate your wonder.   1. Relate. *Attent:* attentive.   2. From head to toe. *Exactly:* completely.   3. Baton of office.

HAMLET: Indeed, sirs, but
   This troubles me. Hold you the watch tonight?
ALL: We do, my lord.
HAMLET: Armed, say you?
ALL: Armed, my lord.   225
HAMLET: From top to toe?
ALL: My lord, from head to foot.
HAMLET: Then saw you not his face.
HORATIO: O yes, my lord, he wore his beaver[4] up.
HAMLET: What, looked he frowningly?
HORATIO: A countenance more in sorrow than in anger.   230
HAMLET: Pale or red?
HORATIO: Nay, very pale.
HAMLET: And fixed his eyes upon you?
HORATIO: Most constantly.
HAMLET: I would I had been there.
HORATIO: It would have much amazed you.
HAMLET: Very like.
   Stayed it long?   235
HORATIO: While one with moderate haste might tell a hundred.
BOTH: Longer, longer.
HORATIO: Not when I saw't.
HAMLET: His beard was grizzled, no?
HORATIO: It was as I have seen it in his life,
   A sable silvered.
HAMLET: I will watch tonight.   240
   Perchance 'twill walk again.
HORATIO: I warr'nt it will.
HAMLET: If it assume my noble father's person,
   I'll speak to it though hell itself should gape[5]
   And bid me hold my peace. I pray you all,
   If you have hitherto concealed this sight,   245
   Let it be tenable[6] in your silence still,
   And whatsomever else shall hap tonight,
   Give it an understanding but no tongue.
   I will requite your loves. So fare you well.
   Upon the platform 'twixt eleven and twelve   250
   I'll visit you.
ALL: Our duty to your honor.
HAMLET: Your loves, as mine to you. Farewell.   [*Exeunt all but* HAMLET.]
   My father's spirit in arms? All is not well.
   I doubt[7] some foul play. Would the night were come!
   Till then sit still, my soul. Foul deeds will rise,   255
   Though all the earth o'erwhelm them, to men's eyes.   [*Exit.*]

---

4. Movable face protector.   5. Open (its mouth) wide.   6. Held.   7. Suspect.

SCENE 3

The dwelling of POLONIUS. *Enter* LAERTES *and* OPHELIA.

LAERTES: My necessaries are embarked. Farewell.
And, sister, as the winds give benefit
And convoy is assistant,[8] do not sleep,
But let me hear from you.

OPHELIA: Do you doubt that?

5 LAERTES: For Hamlet, and the trifling of his favor,
Hold it a fashion and a toy in blood,
A violet in the youth of primy[9] nature,
Forward, not permanent, sweet, not lasting,
The perfume and suppliance of a minute,
No more.

OPHELIA: No more but so?

10 LAERTES: Think it no more.
For nature crescent[1] does not grow alone
In thews and bulk, but as this temple[2] waxes
The inward service of the mind and soul
Grows wide withal. Perhaps he loves you now,
15 And now no soil nor cautel[3] doth besmirch
The virtue of his will, but you must fear,
His greatness weighted,[4] his will is not his own,
For he himself is subject to his birth.
He may not, as unvalued persons do,
20 Carve for himself, for on his choice depends
The safety and health of this whole state,
And therefore must his choice be circumscribed
Unto the voice[5] and yielding of that body
Whereof he is the head. Then if he says he loves you,
25 It fits your wisdom so far to believe it
As he in his particular act and place
May give his saying deed, which is no further
Than the main voice of Denmark goes withal.
Then weigh what loss your honor may sustain
30 If with too credent ear you list[6] his songs,
Or lose your heart, or your chaste treasure open
To his unmastered importunity.
Fear it, Ophelia, fear it, my dear sister,
And keep you in the rear of your affection,
35 Out of the shot and danger of desire.
The chariest[7] maid is prodigal enough

8. Means of transport is available.   9. Of the spring.   1. Growing.   2. Body.   3. Deceit.
4. Rank considered.   5. Assent.   6. Too credulous an ear you listen to.   7. Most circumspect.

If she unmask her beauty to the moon.
Virtue itself scapes not calumnious strokes.
The canker[8] galls the infants of the spring
Too oft before their buttons[9] be disclosed,   40
And in the morn and liquid dew of youth
Contagious blastments[1] are most imminent.
Be wary then; best safety lies in fear.
Youth to itself rebels, though none else near.
OPHELIA: I shall the effect of this good lesson keep   45
  As watchman to my heart. But, good my brother,
  Do not as some ungracious pastors do,
  Show me the steep and thorny way to heaven,
  Whiles like a puffed and reckless libertine
  Himself the primrose path of dalliance treads   50
  And recks not his own rede.[2]
LAERTES: O, fear me not.

[*Enter* POLONIUS.]

I stay too long. But here my father comes.
A double blessing is a double grace;
Occasion smiles upon a second leave.
POLONIUS: Yet here, Laertes? Aboard, aboard, for shame!   55
  The wind sits in the shoulder of your sail,
  And you are stayed for. There—my blessing with thee,
  And these few precepts in thy memory
  Look thou character.[3] Give thy thoughts no tongue,
  Nor any unproportioned thought his act.   60
  Be thou familiar, but by no means vulgar.
  Those friends thou hast, and their adoption tried,
  Grapple them unto thy soul with hoops of steel;
  But do not dull[4] thy palm with entertainment
  Of each new-hatched, unfledged comrade. Beware   65
  Of entrance to a quarrel, but being in,
  Bear't that th' opposéd[5] may beware of thee.
  Give every man thy ear, but few thy voice[6];
  Take each man's censure, but reserve thy judgment.
  Costly thy habit as thy purse can buy,   70
  But not expressed in fancy; rich not gaudy,
  For the apparel oft proclaims the man,
  And they in France of the best rank and station
  Are of a most select and generous chief[7] in that.
  Neither a borrower nor a lender be,   75
  For loan oft loses both itself and friend,

8. Rose caterpillar.   9. Buds.   1. Blights.   2. Heeds not his own advice.   3. Write.
4. Make callous.   5. Conduct it so that the opponent.   6. Approval.   7. Eminence.

And borrowing dulls th' edge of husbandry.
This above all, to thine own self be true,
And it must follow as the night the day
80   Thou canst not then be false to any man.
Farewell. My blessing season this in thee!
LAERTES: Most humbly do I take my leave, my lord.
POLONIUS: The time invites you. Go, your servants tend.[8]
LAERTES: Farewell, Ophelia, and remember well
What I have said to you.
85   OPHELIA: 'Tis in my memory locked,
And you yourself shall keep the key of it.
LAERTES: Farewell.   [*Exit.*]
POLONIUS: What is 't, Ophelia, he hath said to you?
OPHELIA: So please you, something touching the Lord Hamlet.
90   POLONIUS: Marry, well bethought.
'Tis told me he hath very oft of late
Given private time to you, and you yourself
Have of your audience been most free and bounteous.
If it be so—as so 'tis put on me,
95   And that in way of caution—I must tell you,
You do not understand yourself so clearly
As it behooves my daughter and your honor.
What is between you? Give me up the truth.
OPHELIA: He hath, my lord, of late made many tenders
100   Of his affection to me.
POLONIUS: Affection? Pooh! You speak like a green girl,
Unsifted in such perilous circumstance.
Do you believe his tenders, as you call them?
OPHELIA: I do not know, my lord, what I should think.
105   POLONIUS: Marry, I will teach you. Think yourself a baby
That you have ta'en these tenders for true pay
Which are not sterling. Tender yourself more dearly,
Or (not to crack the wind of the poor phrase,
Running it thus) you'll tender me a fool.
110   OPHELIA: My lord, he hath importuned me with love
In honorable fashion.
POLONIUS: Ay, fashion you may call it. Go to, go to.
OPHELIA: And hath given countenance[9] to his speech, my lord,
With almost all the holy vows of heaven.
115   POLONIUS: Ay, springes[1] to catch woodcocks. I do know,
When the blood burns, how prodigal the soul
Lends the tongue vows. These blazes, daughter,
Giving more light than heat, extinct in both
Even in their promise, as it is a-making,

8. Await.   9. Confirmation.   1. Snares.

You must not take for fire. From this time   120
Be something scanter of your maiden presence.
Set your entreatments[2] at a higher rate
Than a command to parle. For Lord Hamlet,
Believe so much in him that he is young,
And with a larger tether may he walk   125
Than may be given you. In few, Ophelia,
Do not believe his vows, for they are brokers,[3]
Not of that dye which their investments[4] show,
But mere implorators[5] of unholy suits,
Breathing like sanctified and pious bawds,   130
The better to beguile. This is for all:
I would not, in plain terms, from this time forth
Have you so slander any moment leisure
As to give words or talk with the Lord Hamlet.
Look to't, I charge you. Come your ways.   135
OPHELIA: I shall obey, my lord.   [*Exeunt.*]

SCENE 4

The guard station. Enter HAMLET, HORATIO *and* MARCELLUS.

HAMLET: The air bites shrewdly[6]; it is very cold.
HORATIO: It is a nipping and an eager[7] air.
HAMLET: What hour now?
HORATIO: I think it lacks of twelve.
MARCELLUS: No, it is struck.
HORATIO: Indeed? I heard it not. It then draws near the season   5
  Wherein the spirit held his wont to walk.

[*A flourish of trumpets, and two pieces go off.*]

  What does this mean, my lord?
HAMLET: The king doth wake tonight and takes his rouse.
  Keeps wassail, and the swagg'ring up-spring[8] reels,
  And as he drains his draughts of Rhenish down,   10
  The kettledrum and trumpet thus bray out
  The triumph of his pledge.
HORATIO: Is it a custom?
HAMLET: Ay, marry, is't,
  But to my mind, though I am native here
  And to the manner born, it is a custom   15
  More honored in the breach than the observance.
  This heavy headed revel east and west
  Makes us traduced and taxed of other nations.

2. Negotiations before a surrender.   3. Panderers.   4. Garments.   5. Solicitors.   6. Sharply.   7. Keen.   8. A German dance.

They clepe[9] us drunkards, and with swinish phrase
20 Soil our addition,[1] and indeed it takes
From our achievements, though performed at height,
The pith and marrow of our attribute.[2]
So oft it chances in particular men,
25 That for some vicious mole of nature in them,
As in their birth, wherein they are not guilty
(Since nature cannot choose his origin),
By the o'ergrowth of some complexion,
Oft breaking down the pales[3] and forts of reason,
Or by some habit that too much o'er-leavens
30 The form of plausive[4] manners—that these men,
Carrying, I say, the stamp of one defect,
Being nature's livery or fortune's star,
His virtues else, be they as pure as grace,
As infinite as man may undergo,
35 Shall in the general censure take corruption
From that particular fault. The dram of evil
Doth all the noble substance often doubt[5]
To his own scandal.

[*Enter* GHOST.]

HORATIO: Look, my lord, it comes.
HAMLET: Angels and ministers of grace defend us!
40 Be thou a spirit of health or goblin damned,
Bring with thee airs from heaven or blasts from hell,
Be thy intents wicked or charitable,
Thou com'st in such a questionable[6] shape
That I will speak to thee. I'll call thee Hamlet,
45 King, father, royal Dane. O, answer me!
Let me not burst in ignorance, but tell
Why thy canonized[7] bones, hearsèd in death,
Have burst their cerements[8]; why the sepulchre
Wherein we saw thee quietly interred
50 Hath oped his ponderous and marble jaws
To cast thee up again. What may this mean
That thou, dead corse, again in complete steel[9]
Revisits thus the glimpses of the moon,
Making night hideous, and we fools of nature
55 So horridly to shake our disposition
With thoughts beyond the reaches of our souls?
Say, why is this? wherefore? What should we do?

9. Call.   1. Reputation.   2. Honor.   3. Barriers.   4. Pleasing.   5. Put out.
6. Prompting question.   7. Buried in accordance with church canons.   8. Gravecloths.
9. Armor.

[GHOST *beckons.*]

HORATIO: It beckons you to go away with it,
   As if it some impartment[1] did desire
   To you alone.
MARCELLUS: Look with what courteous action   60
   It waves you to a more removéd[2] ground.
   But do not go with it.
HORATIO: No, by no means.
HAMLET: It will not speak; then I will follow it.
HORATIO: Do not, my lord.
HAMLET: Why, what should be the fear?
   I do not set my life at a pin's fee,[3]   65
   And for my soul, what can it do to that,
   Being a thing immortal as itself?
   It waves me forth again. I'll follow it
HORATIO: What if it tempt you toward the flood, my lord,
   Or to the deathful summit of the cliff   70
   That beetles[4] o'er his base into the sea,
   And there assume some other horrible form,
   Which might deprive your sovereignty of reason[5]
   And draw you into madness? Think of it.
   The very place puts toys of desperation,[6]   75
   Without more motive, into every brain
   That looks so many fathoms to the sea
   And hears it roar beneath.
HAMLET: It waves me still.
   Go on. I'll follow thee.
MARCELLUS: You shall not go, my lord.
HAMLET: Hold off your hands.
HORATIO: Be ruled, You shall not go.   80
HAMLET: My fate cries out
   And makes each petty artere in this body
   As hardy as the Nemean lion's nerve.[7]
   Still am I called. Unhand me, gentlemen.
   By heaven, I'll make a ghost of him that lets[8] me.   85
   I say, away! Go on. I'll follow thee.   [*Exeunt* GHOST *and* HAMLET.]
HORATIO: He waxes desperate with imagination.
MARCELLUS: Let's follow. 'Tis not fit thus to obey him.
HORATIO: Have after. To what issue will this come?
MARCELLUS: Something is rotten in the state of Denmark.   90

---

1. Communication.   2. Beckons you to a more distant.   3. Price.   4. Juts out.   5. Rational power. *Deprive:* take away.   6. Desperate fancies.   7. The Nemean lion was a mythological monster slain by Hercules as one of his twelve labors.   8. Hinders.

HORATIO: Heaven will direct it.
MARCELLUS: Nay, let's follow him.   [*Exeunt.*]

SCENE 5

Near the guard station. Enter GHOST *and* HAMLET.

HAMLET: Whither wilt thou lead me? Speak. I'll go no further.
GHOST: Mark me.
HAMLET: I will.
GHOST: My hour is almost come,
    When I to sulph'rous and tormenting flames
    Must render up myself.
HAMLET: Alas, poor ghost!
5   GHOST: Pity me not, but lend thy serious hearing
    To what I shall unfold.
HAMLET: Speak. I am bound to hear.
GHOST: So art thou to revenge, when thou shalt hear.
HAMLET: What?
GHOST: I am thy father's spirit,
10   Doomed for a certain term to walk the night,
    And for the day confined to fast in fires,
    Till the foul crimes done in my days of nature[9]
    Are burnt and purged away. But that I am forbid
    To tell the secrets of my prison house,
15   I could a tale unfold whose lightest word
    Would harrow up thy soul, freeze thy young blood,
    Make thy two eyes like stars start from their spheres,
    Thy knotted and combinéd[1] locks to part,
    And each particular hair to stand an end,
20   Like quills upon the fretful porpentine.[2]
    But this eternal blazon[3] must not be
    To ears of flesh and blood. List, list, O, list!
    If thou didst every thy dear father love—
HAMLET: O God!
25   GHOST: Revenge his foul and most unnatural murder.
HAMLET: Murder!
GHOST: Murder most foul, as in the best it is,
    But this most foul, strange, and unnatural.
HAMLET: Haste me to know't, that I, with wings as swift
30   As meditation or the thoughts of love,
    May sweep to my revenge.
GHOST: I find thee apt.
    And duller shouldst thou be than the fat weed

---

9. I.e., while I was alive.   1. Tangled.   2. Porcupine.   3. Description of eternity.

That rots itself in ease on Lethe[4] wharf, —
Wouldst thou not stir in this. Now, Hamlet, hear.
'Tis given out that, sleeping in my orchard,   35
A serpent stung me. So the whole ear of Denmark
Is by a forgéd process[5] of my death
Rankly abused. But know, thou noble youth,
The serpent that did sting thy father's life
Now wears his crown.

HAMLET: O my prophetic soul!   40
My uncle!

GHOST: Ay, that incestuous, that adulterate beast,
With witchcraft of his wits, with traitorous gifts—
O wicked wit and gifts that have the power
So to seduce!—won to his shameful lust   45
The will of my most seeming virtuous queen.
O Hamlet, what a falling off was there,
From me, whose love was of that dignity
That it went hand in hand even with the vow
I made to her in marriage, and to decline[6]   50
Upon a wretch whose natural gifts were poor
To those of mine!
But virtue, as it never will be moved,
Though lewdness court it in a shape of heaven,
So lust, though to a radiant angel linked,   55
Will sate itself in a celestial bed
And prey on garbage.
But soft, methinks I scent the morning air.
Brief let me be. Sleeping within my orchard,
My custom always of the afternoon,   60
Upon my secure hour thy uncle stole,
With juice of cursed hebona[7] in a vial,
And in the porches of my ears did pour
The leperous distilment, whose effect
Holds such an enmity with blood of man   65
That swift as quicksilver it courses through
The natural gates and alleys of the body,
And with a sudden vigor it doth posset[8]
And curd, like eager[9] droppings into milk,
The thin and wholesome blood. So did it mine,   70
And a most instant tetter barked about[1]
Most lazar-like[2] with vile and loathsome crust
All my smooth body.

---

4. The Lethe was one of the rivers of the classical underworld. Its specific importance was that its waters when drunk induced forgetfulness. The "fat weed" is the asphodel that grew there. 5. False report. 6. Sink. 7. A poison. 8. Coagulate. 9. Acid. *Curd:* curdle. 1. Covered like bark. *Tetter:* a skin disease. 2. Leper-like.

Thus was I sleeping by a brother's hand
75   Of life, of crown, of queen at once dispatched,
Cut off even in the blossoms of my sin,
Unhouseled, disappointed, unaneled,[3]
No reck'ning made, but sent to my account
With all my imperfections on my head.
80   O, horrible! O, horrible! most horrible!
If thou hast nature in thee, bear it not.
Let not the royal bed of Denmark be
A couch of luxury[4] and damnéd incest.
But howsomever thou pursues this act,
85   Taint not thy mind, nor let thy soul contrive
Against thy mother aught. Leave her to heaven,
And to those thorns that in her bosom lodge
To prick and sting her. Fare thee well at once.
The glowworm shows the matin[5] to be near,
90   And gins to pale his uneffectual fire.
Adieu, adieu, adieu. Remember me.   [*Exit.*]
HAMLET: O all you host of heaven! O earth! What else?
And shall I couple hell? O, fie! Hold, hold, my heart,
And you, my sinews, grow not instant old,
95   But bear me stiffly up. Remember thee?
Ay, thou poor ghost, whiles memory holds a seat
In this distracted globe.[6] Remember thee?
Yea, from the table[7] of my memory
I'll wipe away all trivial fond[8] records,
100   All saws of books, all forms, all pressures past
That youth and observation copied there,
And thy commandment all alone shall live
Within the book and volume of my brain,
Unmixed with baser matter. Yes, by heaven!
105   O most pernicious woman!
O villain, villain, smiling, damnéd villian!
My tables—meet it is I set it down
That one may smile, and smile, and be a villain.
At least I am sure it may be so in Denmark.
110   So, uncle, there you are. Now to my word:[9]
It is "Adieu, adieu. Remember me."
I have sworn't.

[*Enter* HORATIO *and* MARCELLUS.]

HORATIO: My lord, my lord!

---

3. The ghost means that he died without the customary rites of the church, that is, without receiving the Sacrament, without confession, and without Extreme Unction.   **4.** Lust.   **5.** Morning.
6. Skull.   **7.** Writing tablet.   **8.** Foolish.   **9.** For my motto.

MARCELLUS: Lord Hamlet!

HORATIO: Heavens secure him!

HAMLET: So be it!

MARCELLUS: Illo, ho, ho, my lord! 115

HAMLET: Hillo, ho, ho, boy![1] Come, bird, come.

MARCELLUS: How is't, my noble lord?

HORATIO: What news, my lord?

HAMLET: O, wonderful!

HORATIO: Good my lord, tell it.

HAMLET: No, you will reveal it.

HORATIO: Not I, my lord, by heaven.

MARCELLUS: Nor I, my lord.

HAMLET: How say you then, would heart of man once think it? 120
But you'll be secret?

BOTH: Ay, by heaven, my lord.

HAMLET: There's never a villain dwelling in all Denmark
But he's an arrant knave.

HORATIO: There needs no ghost, my lord, come from the grave 125
To tell us this.

HAMLET: Why, right, you are in the right,
And so without more circumstance at all
I hold it fit that we shake hands and part,
You, as your business and desire shall point you,
For every man hath business and desire 130
Such as it is, and for my own poor part,
I will go pray.

HORATIO: These are but wild and whirling words, my lord.

HAMLET: I am sorry they offend you, heartily;
Yes, faith, heartily.

HORATIO: There's no offence, my lord. 135

HAMLET: Yes, by Saint Patrick, but there is, Horatio,
And much offence too. Touching this vision here,
It is an honest ghost, that let me tell you.
For your desire to know what is between us,
O'ermaster't as you may. And now, good friends, 140
As you are friends, scholars, and soldiers,
Give me one poor request.

HORATIO: What is't, my lord? We will.

HAMLET: Never make known what you have seen tonight.

BOTH: My lord, we will not.

HAMLET: Nay, but swear't.

HORATIO: In faith, 145
My lord, not I.

MARCELLUS: Nor I, my lord, in faith.

1. A falconer's cry.

HAMLET: Upon my sword.
MARCELLUS: We have sworn, my lord, already.
HAMLET: Indeed, upon my sword, indeed.

[GHOST *cries under the stage.*]

GHOST: Swear.
HAMLET: Ha, ha, boy, say'st thou so? Art thou there, truepenny[2]?
150   Come on. You hear this fellow in the cellarage.[3]
            Consent to swear.
HORATIO: Propose the oath, my lord.
HAMLET: Never to speak of this that you have seen,
            Swear by my sword.
GHOST: [*Beneath.*] Swear.
155   HAMLET: Hic et ubique?[4] Then we'll shift our ground.
            Come hither, gentlemen,
            And lay your hands again upon my sword.
            Swear by my sword
            Never to speak of this that you have heard.
160   GHOST: [*Beneath.*] Swear by his sword.
HAMLET: Well said, old mole! Canst work i' th' earth so fast?
            A worthy pioneer[5]! Once more remove, good friends.
HORATIO: O day and night, but this is wondrous strange!
HAMLET: And therefore as a stranger give it welcome.
165   There are more things in heaven and earth, Horatio,
            Than are dreamt of in your philosophy.
            But come.
            Here as before, never, so help you mercy,
            How strange or odd some'er I bear myself
170   (As I perchance hereafter shall think meet
            To put an antic[6] disposition on),
            That you, at such times, seeing me, never shall,
            With arms encumbered[7] thus, or this head-shake,
            Or by pronouncing of some doubtful phrase,
175   As "Well, well, we know," or "We could, and if we would"
            Or "If we list to speak," or "There be, and if they might"
            Or such ambiguous giving out, to note
            That you know aught of me—this do swear,
            So grace and mercy at your most needed help you.
180   GHOST: [*Beneath.*] Swear.   [*They swear.*]
HAMLET: Rest, rest, perturbéd spirit! So, gentlemen,
            With all my love I do commend me to you,
            And what so poor a man as Hamlet is
            May do t'express his love and friending[8] to you,

---

2. Old fellow.   3. Below.   4. "Here and everywhere?"   5. Soldier who digs trenches.
6. Mad.   7. Folded.   8. Friendship.

God willing, shall not lack. Let us go in together,   185
And still your fingers on your lips, I pray.
The time is out of joint. O cursèd spite
That ever I was born to set it right!
Nay, come, let's go together.   [*Exeunt.*]

ACT II

Scene 1

The dwelling of POLONIUS. *Enter* POLONIUS *and* REYNALDO.

POLONIUS: Give him this money and these notes, Reynaldo.
REYNALDO: I will, my lord.
POLONIUS: You shall do marvellous wisely, good Reynaldo,
  Before you visit him, to make inquire[9]
  Of his behavior.
REYNALDO: My lord, I did intend it.   5
POLONIUS: Marry, well said, very well said. Look you, sir.
  Enquire me first what Danskers[1] are in Paris,
  And how, and who, what means, and where they keep,[2]
  What company, at what expense; and finding
  By this encompassment[3] and drift of question   10
  That they do know my son, come you more nearer
  Than your particular demands[4] will touch it.
  Take you as 'twere some distant knowledge of him,
  As thus, "I know his father and his friends,
  And in part him." Do you mark this, Reynaldo?   15
REYNALDO: Ay, very well, my lord.
POLONIUS: "And in part him, but," you may say, "not well,
  But if't be he I mean, he's very wild,
  Addicted so and so." And there put on him
  What forgeries you please; marry, none so rank[5]   20
  As may dishonor him. Take heed of that.
  But, sir, such wanton, wild, and usual slips
  As are companions noted and most known
  To youth and liberty.
REYNALDO: As gaming, my lord.
POLONIUS: Ay, or drinking, fencing, swearing, quarrelling,   25
  Drabbing[6]—you may go so far.
REYNALDO: My lord, that would dishonor him.
POLONIUS: Faith, no, as you may season it in the charge.[7]
  You must not put another scandal on him,
  That he is open to incontinency.[8]   30

9. Inquiry.   1. Danes.   2. Live.   3. Indirect means.   4. Direct questions.   5. Foul.
Forgeries: lies.   6. Whoring.   7. Soften the accusation.   8. Sexual excess.

That's not my meaning. But breathe his faults so quaintly[9]
That they may seem the taints of liberty,[1]
The flash and outbreak of a fiery mind,
A savageness in unreclaiméd[2] blood,
Of general assault.[3]

35 REYNALDO: But, my good lord—
POLONIUS: Wherefore should you do this?
REYNALDO: Ay, my lord,
I would know that.
POLONIUS: Marry, sir, here's my drift,
And I believe it is a fetch of warrant.[4]
You laying these slight sullies on my son,
40 As 'twere a thing a little soiled i' th' working,
Mark you,
Your party in converse,[5] him you would sound,
Having ever seen in the prenominate[6] crimes
The youth you breathe[7] of guilty, be assured
45 He closes with you in this consequence,
"Good sir," or so, or "friend," or "gentleman,"
According to the phrase or the addition
Of man and country.
REYNALDO: Very good, my lord.
POLONIUS: And then, sir, does 'a this—'a does—What was I about to say?
50 By the mass, I was about to say something.
Where did I leave?
REYNALDO: At "closes in the consequence."
POLONIUS: At "closes in the consequence"—ay, marry,
He closes thus: "I know the gentleman.
55 I saw him yesterday, or th' other day,
Or then, or then, with such, or such, and as you say,
There was 'a gaming, there o'ertook in's rouse,
There falling out at tennis," or perchance
"I saw him enter such a house of sale,"
60 Videlicet,[8] a brothel, or so forth.
See you, now—
Your bait of falsehood takes this carp of truth,
And thus do we of wisdom and of reach,[9]
With windlasses and with assays of bias,[1]
65 By indirections find directions out;
So by my former lecture and advice
Shall you my son. You have me, have you not?
REYNALDO: My lord, I have.

9. With delicacy.   1. Faults of freedom.   2. Untamed.   3. Touching everyone.
4. Permissible trick.   5. Conversation.   6. Already named.   7. Speak.   8. Namely.
9. Ability.   1. Indirect tests.

POLONIUS: God b'wi' ye; fare ye well.
REYNALDO: Good my lord.
POLONIUS: Observe his inclination in yourself. 70
REYNALDO: I shall, my lord.
POLONIUS: And let him ply[2] his music.
REYNALDO: Well, my lord.
POLONIUS: Farewell. [*Exit* REYNALDO.]

[*Enter* OPHELIA.]

How now, Ophelia, what's the matter?
OPHELIA: O my lord, my lord, I have been so affrighted!
POLONIUS: With what, i' th' name of God? 75
OPHELIA: My lord, as I was sewing in my closet,[3]
Lord Hamlet with his doublet all unbraced,[4]
No hat upon his head, his stockings fouled,
Ungartered and down-gyvéd[5] to his ankle,
Pale as his shirt, his knees knocking each other, 80
And with a look so piteous in purport
As if he had been looséd out of hell
To speak of horrors—he comes before me.
POLONIUS: Mad for thy love?
OPHELIA: My lord, I do not know,
But truly I do fear it.
POLONIUS: What said he? 85
OPHELIA: He took me by the wrist, and held me hard,
Then goes he to the length of all his arm,
And with his other hand thus o'er his brow,
He falls to such perusal of my face
As 'a would draw it. Long stayed he so. 90
At last, a little shaking of mine arm,
And thrice his head thus waving up and down,
He raised a sigh so piteous and profound
As it did seem to shatter all his bulk,[6]
And end his being. That done, he lets me go, 95
And with his head over his shoulder turned
He seemed to find his way without his eyes,
For out adoors he went without their helps,
And to the last bended[7] their light on me.
POLONIUS: Come, go with me. I will go seek the king. 100
This is the very ecstasy of love,
Whose violent property fordoes[8] itself,
And leads the will to desperate undertakings
As oft as any passion under heaven

---

2. Practice.   3. Chamber.   4. Unlaced. *Doublet:* jacket.   5. Fallen down like fetters.
6. Body.   7. Directed.   8. Destroys. *Property:* character.

105　That does afflict our natures. I am sorry.
　　　What, have you given him any hard words of late?
　　OPHELIA: No, my good lord, but as you did command
　　　I did repel[9] his letters, and denied
　　　His access to me.
　　POLONIUS:　　　　That hath made him mad.
110　I am sorry that with better heed and judgment
　　　I had not quoted[1] him. I feared he did but trifle,
　　　And meant to wrack[2] thee; but beshrew my jealousy.
　　　By heaven, it is as proper to our age
　　　To cast beyond ourselves in our opinions
115　As it is common for the younger sort
　　　To lack discretion. Come, go we to the king.
　　　This must be known, which being kept close, might move
　　　More grief to hide than hate to utter love.
　　　Come.　　　　　　　　　　　　　　　　　[*Exeunt.*]

SCENE 2

A *public room. Enter* KING, QUEEN, ROSENCRANTZ *and* GUILDENSTERN.

　　KING: Welcome, dear Rosencrantz and Guildenstern.
　　　Moreover that[3] we much did long to see you,
　　　The need we have to use you did provoke
　　　Our hasty sending. Something have you heard
5　Of Hamlet's transformation—so call it,
　　　Sith[4] nor th' exterior nor the inward man
　　　Resembles that it was. What it should be,
　　　More than his father's death, that thus hath put him
　　　So much from th' understanding of himself,
10　I cannot deem of. I entreat you both
　　　That, being of so young days[5] brought up with him,
　　　And sith so neighbored[6] to his youth and havior,
　　　That you vouchsafe your rest here in our court
　　　Some little time, so by your companies
15　To draw him on to pleasures, and to gather
　　　So much as from occasion you may glean,
　　　Whether aught to us unknown afflicts him thus,
　　　That opened lies within our remedy.
　　QUEEN: Good gentlemen, he hath much talked of you,
20　And sure I am two men there are not living
　　　To whom he more adheres. If it will please you
　　　To show us so much gentry[7] and good will
　　　As to expend your time with us awhile

9. Refuse.　　1. Observed.　　2. Harm.　　3. In addition to the fact that.　　4. Since.
5. From childhood.　　6. Closely allied.　　7. Courtesy.

For the supply and profit of our hope,
Your visitation shall receive such thanks   25
As fits a king's remembrance.
ROSENCRANTZ: Both your majesties
  Might, by the sovereign power you have of us,
  Put your dread pleasures more into command
  Than to entreaty.
GUILDENSTERN: But we both obey,
  And here give up ourselves in the full bent[8]   30
  To lay our service freely at your feet,
  To be commanded.
KING: Thanks, Rosencrantz and gentle Guildenstern.
QUEEN: Thanks, Guildenstern and gentle Rosencrantz.
  And I beseech you instantly to visit   35
  My too much changed son. Go, some of you,
  And bring these gentlemen where Hamlet is.
GUILDENSTERN: Heavens make our presence and our practices
  Pleasant and helpful to him!
QUEEN: Ay, amen!
                    [*Exeunt* ROSENCRANTZ *and* GUILDENSTERN.]

  [*Enter* POLONIUS.]

POLONIUS: Th' ambassadors from Norway, my good lord,   40
  Are joyfully returned.
KING: Thou still[9] hast been the father of good news.
POLONIUS: Have I, my lord? I assure you, my good liege,
  I hold my duty as I hold my soul,
  Both to my God and to my gracious king;   45
  And I do think—or else this brain of mine
  Hunts not the trial of policy[1] so sure
  As it hath used to do—that I have found
  The very cause of Hamlet's lunacy.
KING: O, speak of that, that do I long to hear.   50
POLONIUS: Give first admittance to th' ambassadors.
  My news shall be the fruit[2] to that great feast.
KING: Thyself do grace to them, and bring them in.   [*Exit* POLONIUS.]
  He tells me, my dear Gertrude, he hath found
  The head and source of all your son's distemper.   55
QUEEN: I doubt it is no other but the main,
  His father's death and our o'erhasty marriage.
KING: Well, we shall sift[3] him.

  [*Enter Ambassadors* (VOLTEMAND *and* CORNELIUS) *with* POLONIUS.]

                    Welcome, my good friends,
  Say, Voltemand, what from our brother Norway?

8. Completely.   9. Ever.   1. Statecraft.   2. Dessert.   3. Examine.

60 VOLTEMAND: Most fair return of greetings and desires.
Upon our first,[4] he sent out to suppress
His nephew's levies, which to him appeared
To be a preparation 'gainst the Polack,
But better looked into, he truly found
65 It was against your highness, whereat grieved,
That so his sickness, age, and impotence
Was falsely borne in hand, sends out arrests[5]
On Fortinbras, which he in brief obeys,
Receives rebuke from Norway, and in fine,
70 Makes vow before his uncle never more
To give th' assay[6] of arms against your majesty.
Whereon old Norway, overcome with joy,
Gives him threescore thousand crowns in annual fee,
And his commission to employ those soldiers,
75 So levied as before, against the Polack,
With an entreaty, herein further shown,   [*Gives* CLAUDIUS *a paper.*]
That it might please you to give quiet pass[7]
Through your dominions for this enterprise,
On such regards of safety and allowance
As therein are set down.
80 KING: It likes[8] us well,
And at our more considered time[9] we'll read,
Answer, and think upon this business.
Meantime we thank you for your well-took[1] labor.
Go to your rest; at night we'll feast together.
Most welcome home!   [*Exeunt* AMBASSADORS.]
85 POLONIUS: This business is well ended.
My liege and madam, to expostulate[2]
What majesty should be, what duty is,
Why day is day, night night, and time is time,
Were nothing but to waste night, day, and time.
90 Therefore, since brevity is the soul of wit,
And tediousness the limbs and outward flourishes,[3]
I will be brief. Your noble son is mad.
Mad call I it, for to define true madness,
What is't but to be nothing else but mad?
But let that go.
95 QUEEN: More matter with less art.
POLONIUS: Madam, I swear I use no art at all.
That he is mad, 'tis true: 'tis true 'tis pity,
And pity 'tis 'tis true. A foolish figure,
But farewell it, for I will use no art.
100 Mad let us grant him, then, and now remains

4. I.e., first appearance.   5. Orders to stop. *Falsely borne in hand:* deceived.   6. Trial.
7. Safe conduct.   8. Pleases.   9. Time for more consideration.   1. Successful.   2. Discuss.   3. Adornments.

That we find out the cause of this effect,
Or rather say the cause of this defect,
For this effect defective comes by cause.
Thus it remains, and the remainder thus.
Perpend.[4]   105
I have a daughter—have while she is mine—
Who in her duty and obedience, mark,
Hath given me this. Now gather, and surmise.
    "To the celestial, and my soul's idol, the most beautified
Ophelia."—That's an ill phrase, a vile phrase, "beautified" is a   110
vile phrase. But you shall hear. Thus:
    "In her excellent white bosom, these, etc."
QUEEN: Came this from Hamlet to her?
POLONIUS: Good madam, stay awhile. I will be faithful.

                "Doubt thou the stars are fire,   115
                    Doubt that the sun doth move;
                    Doubt truth to be a liar;
                    But never doubt I love.

    O dear Ophelia, I am ill at these numbers.[5] I have not art to reck-
on my groans, but that I love thee best, O most best, believe it.   120
Adieu.
            Thine evermore, most dear lady, whilst this machine[6] is to him,
            Hamlet."
This in obedience hath my daughter shown me,
And more above, hath his solicitings,   125
As they fell out by time, by means, and place,
All given to mine ear.
KING: But how hath she
Received his love?
POLONIUS: What do you think of me?
KING: As of a man faithful and honorable.
POLONIUS: I would fain prove so. But what might you think,   130
When I had seen this hot love on the wing.
(As I perceived it, I must tell you that,
Before my daughter told me), what might you,
Or my dear majesty your queen here, think,
If I had played the desk or table-book,   135
Or given my heart a winking, mute and dumb,
Or looked upon this love with idle sight,[7]
What might you think? No, I went round[8] to work,
And my young mistress thus I did bespeak:

---

4. Consider.   5. Verses.   6. Body.   7. Polonius means that he would have been at fault if,
having seen Hamlet's attention to Ophelia, he had winked at it or not paid attention, an "idle sight,"
and if he had remained silent and kept the information to himself, as if it were written in a "desk"
or "table-book."   8. Directly.

140   "Lord Hamlet is a prince out of thy star.[9]
        This must not be." And then I prescripts[1] gave her,
        That she should lock herself from his resort,
        Admit no messengers, receive no tokens.
        Which done, she took[2] the fruits of my advice;
145   And he repelled, a short tale to make,
        Fell into a sadness, then into a fast,
        Thence to a watch, thence into a weakness,
        Thence to a lightness, and by this declension,
        Into the madness wherein now he raves,
        And all we mourn for.
150 KING: Do you think 'tis this?
        QUEEN: It may be, very like.
        POLONIUS: Hath there been such a time—I would fain know that—
        That I have positively said "Tis so,"
        When it proved otherwise?
        KING: Not that I know.
        POLONIUS: [*Pointing to his head and shoulder.*] Take this from this, if this be
155   otherwise.
        If circumstances lead me, I will find
        Where truth is hid, though it were hid indeed
        Within the centre.[3]
        KING: How may we try it further?
        POLONIUS: You know sometimes he walks four hours together
        Here in the lobby.
160 QUEEN: So he does, indeed.
        POLONIUS: At such a time I'll loose[4] my daughter to him.
        Be you and I behind an arras[5] then.
        Mark the encounter. If he love her not,
        And be not from his reason fall'n thereon,
165   Let me be no assistant for a state,
        But keep a farm and carters.
        KING: We will try it.

        [*Enter* HAMLET *reading a book.*]

        QUEEN: But look where sadly the poor wretch comes reading.
        POLONIUS: Away, I do beseech you both away,
        I'll board[6] him presently.   [*Exeunt* KING *and* QUEEN.]
                  O, give me leave.
170   How does my good Lord Hamlet?
        HAMLET: Well, God-a-mercy.
        POLONIUS: Do you know me, my lord?
        HAMLET: Excellent well, you are a fishmonger.
        POLONIUS: Not I, my lord.

9. Beyond your sphere.   1. Orders.   2. Followed.   3. Of the earth.   4. Let loose.
5. Tapestry.   6. Accost.

HAMLET: Then I would you were so honest a man.   175
POLONIUS: Honest, my lord?
HAMLET: Ay, sir, to be honest as this world goes, is to be one man picked out of
    ten thousand.
POLONIUS: That's very true, my lord.
HAMLET: For if the sun breed maggots in a dead dog, being a god kissing   180
    carrion[7]—Have you a daughter?
POLONIUS: I have, my lord.
HAMLET: Let her not walk i' th' sun. Conception is a blessing, but as your daugh-
    ter may conceive—friend, look to't.
POLONIUS: How say you by that? [Aside.] Still harping on my daughter. Yet he   185
    knew me not at first. 'A said I was a fishmonger. 'A is far gone. And truly in
    my youth I suffered much extremity for love. Very near this. I'll speak to him
    again.—What do you read, my lord?
HAMLET: Words, words, words.
POLONIUS: What is the matter, my lord?   190
HAMLET: Between who?
POLONIUS: I mean the matter that you read, my lord.
HAMLET: Slanders, sir; for the satirical rogue says here that old men have grey
    beards, that their faces are wrinkled, their eyes purging thick amber and
    plum-tree gum, and that they have a plentiful lack of wit, together with most   195
    weak hams[8]—all which, sir, though I have it thus set down, for yourself, sir,
    shall grow old as I am, if like a crab you could go backward.
POLONIUS: [Aside.] Though this be madness, yet there is method in't.—Will you
    walk out of the air, my lord?
HAMLET: Into my grave?   200
POLONIUS: [Aside.] Indeed, that's out of the air. How pregnant sometime his
    replies are! a happiness that often madness hits on, which reason and sanity
    could not so prosperously be delivered of. I will leave him, and suddenly
    contrive the means of meeting between him and my daughter.—My lord. I
    will take my leave of you.   205
HAMLET: You cannot take from me anything that I will more willingly part
    withal—except my life, except my life, except my life.

    [Enter GUILDENSTERN and ROSENCRANTZ.]

POLONIUS: Fare you well, my lord.
HAMLET: These tedious old fools!
POLONIUS: You go to seek the Lord Hamlet. There he is.   210
ROSENCRANTZ: [To POLONIUS.] God save you, sir!   [Exit POLONIUS.]
GUILDENSTERN: My honored lord!
ROSENCRANTZ: My most dear lord!
HAMLET: My excellent good friends! How dost thou, Guildenstern?
    Ah, Rosencrantz! Good lads, how do you both?   215
ROSENCRANTZ: As the indifferent[9] children of the earth.

---

7. A reference to the belief of the period that maggots were produced spontaneously by the action
of sunshine on carrion.   8. Limbs.   9. Ordinary.

GUILDENSTERN: Happy in that we are not over-happy;
    On Fortune's cap we are not the very button.[1]
HAMLET: Nor the soles of her shoe?
220 ROSENCRANTZ: Neither, my lord.
HAMLET: Then you live about her waist, or in the middle of her favors.
GUILDENSTERN: Faith, her privates we.
HAMLET: In the secret parts of Fortune? O, most true, she is a strumpet.[2] What
    news?
225 ROSENCRANTZ: None, my lord, but that the world's grown honest.
HAMLET: Then is doomsday near. But your news is not true. Let me question
    more in particular. What have you, my good friends, deserved at the hands
    of Fortune, that she sends you to prison hither?
GUILDENSTERN: Prison, my lord?
230 HAMLET: Denmark's a prison.
ROSENCRANTZ: Then is the world one.
HAMLET: A goodly one, in which there are many confines, wards[3] and dungeons.
    Denmark being one o' th' worst.
ROSENCRANTZ: We think not so, my lord.
235 HAMLET: Why then 'tis none to you; for there is nothing either good or bad, but
    thinking makes it so. To me it is a prison.
ROSENCRANTZ: Why then your ambition makes it one. 'Tis too narrow for your
    mind.
HAMLET: O God, I could be bounded in a nutshell and count myself a king of
240 infinite space, where it not that I have bad dreams.
GUILDENSTERN: Which dreams indeed are ambition; for the very substance of
    the ambitious is merely the shadow of a dream.
HAMLET: A dream itself is but a shadow.
ROSENCRANTZ: Truly, and I hold ambition of so airy and light a quality that it is
245 but a shadow's shadow.
HAMLET: Then are our beggars bodies, and our monarchs and outstretched
    heroes the beggars' shadows. Shall we to th' court? for, by my fay,[4] I cannot
    reason.
BOTH: We'll wait upon you.
250 HAMLET: No such matter. I will not sort[5] you with the rest of my servants; for to
    speak to you like an honest man, I am most dreadfully attended. But in the
    beaten way of friendship, what make you at Elsinore?
ROSENCRANTZ: To visit you, my lord; no other occasion.
HAMLET: Beggar that I am, I am even poor in thanks, but I thank you; and sure,
255 dear friends, my thanks are too dear a halfpenny.[6] Were you not sent for? Is
    it your own inclining? Is it a free visitation? Come, come, deal justly with
    me. Come, come, nay speak.
GUILDENSTERN: What should we say, my lord?

1. I.e., on top.   2. Prostitute. Hamlet is indulging in characteristic ribaldry. Guildenstern means
that they are "privates" = ordinary citizens, but Hamlet takes him to mean "privates" = sexual
organs and "middle of her favors" = waist = sexual organs.   3. Cells.   4. Faith.   5. Include.   6. Not worth a halfpenny.

HAMLET: Why anything but to th' purpose. You were sent for, and there is a kind
of confession in your looks, which your modesties have not craft enough to
color. I know the good king and queen have sent for you.

ROSENCRANTZ: To what end, my lord?

HAMLET: That you must teach me. But let me conjure you by the rights of our
fellowship, by the consonancy of our youth, by the obligation of our ever-
preserved love, and by what more dear a better proposer can charge you
withal, be even and direct[7] with me whether you were sent for or no.

ROSENCRANTZ: [Aside to GUILDENSTERN.] What say you?

HAMLET: [Aside.] Nay, then, I have an eye of you.—If you love me, hold not off.

GUILDENSTERN: My lord, we were sent for.

HAMLET: I will tell you why; so shall my anticipation prevent your discovery,[8]
and your secrecy to the king and queen moult no feather. I have of late—
but wherefore I know not—lost all my mirth, forgone all custom of exercises;
and indeed it goes so heavily with my disposition, that this goodly frame the
earth seems to me a sterile promontory, this most excellent canopy the air,
look you, this brave o'er-hanging firmament, this majestical roof fretted[9]
with golden fire, why it appeareth nothing to me but a foul and pestilent
congregation of vapors. What a piece of work is a man, how noble in reason,
how infinite in faculties, in form and moving, how express[1] and admirable
in action, how like an angel in apprehension, how like a god: the beauty of
the world, the paragon of animals. And yet to me, what is this quintessence
of dust? Man delights not me, nor woman neither, though by your smiling
you seem to say so.

ROSENCRANTZ: My lord, there was no such stuff in my thoughts.

HAMLET: Why did ye laugh, then, when I said "Man delights not me"?

ROSENCRANTZ: To think, my lord, if you delight not in man, what lenten entertainment the players shall receive from you. We coted[2] them on the way,
and hither are they coming to offer you service.

HAMLET: He that plays the king shall be welcome—his majesty shall have tribute
on me; the adventurous knight shall use his foil and target; the lover shall
not sigh gratis; the humorous[3] man shall end his part in peace; the clown
shall make those laugh whose lungs are tickle o' th' sere;[4] and the lady shall
say her mind freely, or the blank verse shall halt for't. What players are they?

ROSENCRANTZ: Even those you were wont to take such delight in, the tragedians
of the city.

HAMLET: How chances it they travel? Their residence, both in reputation and
profit, was better both ways.

ROSENCRANTZ: I think their inhibition comes by the means of the late innovation.

HAMLET: Do they hold the same estimation they did when I was in the city? Are
they so followed?

ROSENCRANTZ: No, indeed, are they not.

HAMLET: How comes it? Do they grow rusty?

7. Straightforward.   8. Disclosure.   9. Ornamented with fretwork.   1. Well built.
2. Passed. *Lenten:* scanty.   3. Eccentric. *Foil and target:* sword and shield.   4. Easily set off.

ROSENCRANTZ: Nay, their endeavor keeps in the wonted pace; but there is, sir, an eyrie of children, little eyases,[5] that cry out on the top of question,[6] and are most tyrannically clapped for't. These are now the fashion, and so be-
305 rattle the common stages (so they call them) that many wearing rapiers are afraid of goose quills[7] and dare scarce come thither.[8]

HAMLET: What, are they children? Who maintains 'em? How are they escoted[9]? Will they pursue the quality no longer than they can sing? Will they not say afterwards, if they should grow themselves to common players (as it is most
310 like, if their means are no better), their writers do them wrong to make them exclaim against their own succession[1]?

ROSENCRANTZ: Faith, there has been much to do on both sides; and the nation holds it no sin to tarre[2] them to controversy. There was for a while no money bid for argument,[3] unless the poet and the player went to cuffs[4] in the ques-
315 tion.

HAMLET: Is't possible?

GUILDENSTERN: O, there has been much throwing about of brains.

HAMLET: Do the boys carry it away?

ROSENCRANTZ: Ay, that they do, my lord. Hercules and his load too.[5]

320 HAMLET: It is not very strange, for my uncle is King of Denmark, and those that would make mouths[6] at him while my father lived give twenty, forty, fifty, a hundred ducats apiece for his picture in little.[7] 'Sblood, there is something in this more than natural, if philosophy could find it out.

[A flourish.]

GUILDENSTERN: There are the players.

325 HAMLET: Gentlemen, you are welcome to Elsinore. Your hands. Come then, th' appurtenance of welcome is fashion and ceremony. Let me comply with you in this garb, lest my extent[8] to the players, which I tell you must show fairly outwards should more appear like entertainment[9] than yours. You are wel- come. But my uncle-father and aunt-mother are deceived.

330 GUILDENSTERN: In what, my dear lord?

HAMLET: I am but mad north-north-west; when the wind is southerly I know a hawk from a handsaw.[1]

[Enter POLONIUS.]

POLONIUS: Well be with you, gentlemen.

---

5. Little hawks.   6. With a loud, high delivery.   7. Pens of satirical writers.   8. The passage refers to the emergence at the time of the play of theatrical companies made up of children from London choir schools. Their performances became fashionable and hurt the business of the estab- lished companies. Hamlet says that if they continue to act, "pursue the quality," when they are grown, they will find that they have been damaging their own future careers.   9. Supported. 1. Future careers.   2. Urge.   3. Paid for a play plot.   4. Blows.   5. During one of his labors Hercules assumed for a time the burden of the Titan Atlas, who supported the heavens on his shoulder. Also a reference to the effect on business at Shakespeare's theater, the Globe. 6. Sneer.   7. Miniature.   8. Fashion. *Comply with*: welcome.   9. Cordiality.   1. A "hawk" is a plasterer's tool; Hamlet may also be using "handsaw" = hernshaw = heron.

HAMLET: Hark you, Guildenstern—and you too—at each ear a hearer.
   That great baby you see there is not yet out of his swaddling clouts.[2]   335
ROSENCRANTZ: Happily he is the second time come to them, for they say an old
   man is twice a child.
HAMLET: I will prophesy he comes to tell me of the players. Mark it.
   —You say right, sir, a Monday morning, 'twas then indeed.
POLONIUS: My lord, I have news to tell you.   340
HAMLET: My lord, I have news to tell you.
   When Roscius was an actor in Rome—[3]
POLONIUS: The actors are come hither, my lord.
HAMLET: Buzz, buzz.
POLONIUS: Upon my honor—   345
HAMLET: Then came each actor on his ass—
POLONIUS: The best actors in the world, either for tragedy, comedy, history, pas-
   toral, pastoral-comical, historical-pastoral, tragical-historical, tragical-comi-
   cal-historical-pastoral, scene individable, or poem unlimited. Seneca cannot
   be too heavy nor Plautus too light. For the law of writ and the liberty, these   350
   are the only men.[4]
HAMLET: O Jephtha, judge of Israel, what a treasure hadst thou![5]
POLONIUS: What a treasure had he, my lord?
HAMLET: Why—

   "One fair daughter, and no more,   355
   The which he loved passing well."

POLONIUS: [Aside.] Still on my daughter.
HAMLET: Am I not i' th' right, old Jephtha?
POLONIUS: If you call me Jephtha, my lord, I have a daughter that I love passing
   well.   360
HAMLET: Nay, that follows not.
POLONIUS: What follows then, my lord?
HAMLET: Why—

   "As by lot, God wot"

and then, you know,   365

   "It came to pass, as most like it was."

The first row of the pious chanson[6] will show you more, for look
where my abridgement[7] comes.

---

2. Wrappings for an infant.   3. Roscius was the most famous actor of classical Rome.   4. Seneca and Plautus were Roman writers of tragedy and comedy, respectively. The "law of writ" refers
to plays written according to such rules as the three unities; the "liberty" to those written otherwise.
5. To insure victory, Jephtha promised to sacrifice the first creature to meet him on his return.
Unfortunately, his only daughter outstripped his dog and was the victim of his vow. The biblical
story is told in Judges 11.   6. Song. Row: stanza.   7. That which cuts short by interrupting.

[*Enter the* PLAYERS.]

370 You are welcome, masters; welcome, all.—I am glad to see thee well.—
Welcome, good friends.—O, old friend! Why thy face is valanced[8] since I
saw thee last. Com'st thou to beard me in Denmark?—What, my young lady
and mistress? By'r lady, your ladyship is nearer to heaven than when I saw
you last by the altitude of a chopine.[9] Pray God your voice, like a piece of
uncurrent gold, be not cracked within the ring.—Masters, you are all wel-
375 come. We'll e'en to't like French falconers, fly at anything we see. We'll
have a speech straight. Come give us a taste of your quality,[1] come a passionate speech.

FIRST PLAYER: What speech, my good lord?

HAMLET: I heard thee speak me a speech once, but it was never acted, or if it
380 was, not above once, for the play, I remember, pleased not the million; 'twas
caviary to the general.[2] But it was—as I received it, and others whose judgments in such matters cried in the top of[3] mine—an excellent play, well
digested[4] in the scenes, set down with as much modesty as cunning. I remember one said there were no sallets[5] in the lines to make the matter savory, nor
385 no matter in the phrase that might indict the author of affectation, but called
it an honest method, as wholesome as sweet, and by very much more handsome than fine. One speech in't I chiefly loved. 'Twas Æneas' tale to Dido,
and thereabout of it especially where he speaks of Priam's slaughter.[6] If it live
in your memory, begin at this line—let me see, let me see:

390   "The rugged Pyrrhus, like th' Hyrcanian beast"[7]—

'tis not so; it begins with Pyrrhus—

      "The rugged Pyrrhus, he whose sable arms,
      black as his purpose, did the night resemble
      When he lay couchéd in th' ominous horse,[8]
395   Hath now this dread and black complexion smeared
      With heraldry more dismal; head to foot
      Now is he total gules, horridly tricked[9]
      With blood of fathers, mothers, daughters, sons,
      Baked and impasted with the parching[1] streets,

---

8. Fringed (with a beard).   9. A reference to the contemporary theatrical practice of using boys
to play women's parts. The company's "lady" has grown in height by the size of a woman's thick-
soled shoe, "chopine," since Hamlet saw him last. The next sentence refers to the possibility, suggested by his growth, that the young actor's voice may soon begin to change.   1. Trade.
2. Masses. *Caviary*: caviar.   3. Were weightier than.   4. Arranged.   5. Spicy passages.
6. Aeneas, fleeing with his band from fallen Troy (Ilium), arrives in Carthage, where he tells Dido,
the queen of Carthage, of the fall of Troy. Here he is describing the death of Priam, the aged king
of Troy, at the hands of Pyrrhus, the son of the slain Achilles.   7. Tiger.   8. I.e., the Trojan
horse.   9. Adorned. *Total gules*: completely red.   1. Burning. *Impasted*: crusted.

That lend a tyrannous and a damnéd light 400
To their lord's murder. Roasted in wrath and fire,
And thus o'er-sizéd with coagulate[2] gore,
With eyes like carbuncles, the hellish Pyrrhus
Old grandsire Priam seeks."

So proceed you. 405
POLONIUS: Fore God, my lord, well spoken, with good accent and good
discretion.
FIRST PLAYER: "Anon he finds him[3]
Striking too short at Greeks. His antique[4] sword,
Rebellious[5] to his arm, lies where it falls, 410
Repugnant to command. Unequal matched,
Pyrrhus at Priam drives, in rage strikes wide.
But with the whiff and wind of his fell sword
Th' unnervéd father falls. Then senseless[6] Ilium,
Seeming to feel this blow, with flaming top 415
Stoops[7] to his base, and with a hideous crash
Takes prisoner Pyrrhus' ear. For, lo! his sword,
Which was declining[8] on the milky head
Of reverend Priam, seemed i' th' air to stick.
So as a painted tyrant Pyrrhus stood, 420
And like a neutral to his will and matter,[9]
Did nothing.
But as we often see, against some storm,
A silence in the heavens, the rack[1] stand still,
The bold winds speechless, and the orb below 425
As hush as death, anon the dreadful thunder
Doth rend the region; so, after Pyrrhus' pause,
A rouséd vengeance sets him new awork,[2]
And never did the Cyclops' hammers fall
On Mars's armor, forged for proof eterne,[3] 430
With less remorse than Pyrrhus' bleeding sword
Now falls on Priam.
Out, out, thou strumpet, Fortune! All you gods,
In general synod take away her power,
Break all the spokes and fellies[4] from her wheel, 435
And bowl the round nave[5] down the hill of heaven
As low as to the fiends."

---

2. Clotted. *O'er-sized:* glued over.   3. I.e., Pyrrhus finds Priam.   4. Which he used when
young.   5. Refractory.   6. Without feeling.   7. Falls.   8. About to fall.   9. Between
his will and the fulfillment of it.   1. Clouds.   2. To work.   3. Mars, as befits a Roman war
god, had armor made for him by the blacksmith god Vulcan and his assistants, the Cyclops. It was
suitably impenetrable, of "proof eterne."   4. Parts of the rim.   5. Hub. *Bowl:* roll.

POLONIUS: This is too long.

HAMLET: It shall to the barber's with your beard. — Prithee say on. He's for a jig,[6]
or a tale of bawdry, or he sleeps. Say on; come to Hecuba.[7]

FIRST PLAYER: "But who, ah woe! had seen the mobled[8] queen—"

HAMLET: "The mobled queen"?

POLONIUS: That's good. "Mobled queen" is good.

FIRST PLAYER: "Run barefoot up and down, threat'ning the flames
  With bisson rheum, a clout[9] upon that head
  Where late the diadem stood, and for a robe,
  About her lank and all o'er-teeméd loins,
  A blanket, in the alarm of fear caught up—
  Who this had seen, with tongue in venom steeped,
  'Gainst Fortune's state[1] would treason have pronounced.
  But if the gods themselves did see her then,
  When she saw Pyrrhus make malicious sport
  In mincing[2] with his sword her husband's limbs,
  The instant burst of clamor that she made,
  Unless things mortal move them not at all,
  Would have made milch[3] the burning eyes of heaven,
  And passion in the gods."

POLONIUS: Look whe'r[4] he has not turned his color, and has tears in's eyes.
Prithee no more.

HAMLET: 'Tis well. I'll have thee speak out the rest of this soon. — Good my
lord, will you see the players well bestowed[5]? Do you hear, let them be well
used, for they are the abstract[6] and brief chronicles of the time; after your
death you were better have a bad epitaph than their ill report while you live.

POLONIUS: My lord, I will use them according to their desert.

HAMLET: God's bodkin, man, much better. Use every man after his desert, and
who shall 'scape whipping? Use them after your own honor and dignity. The
less they deserve, the more merit is in your bounty. Take them in.

POLONIUS: Come, sirs.

HAMLET: Follow him, friends. We'll hear a play tomorrow. [Aside to FIRST PLAYER.]
Dost thou hear me, old friend, can you play "The Murder of Gonzago"?

FIRST PLAYER: Ay, my lord.

HAMLET: We'll ha't tomorrow night. You could for a need study a speech of
some dozen or sixteen lines which I would set down and insert in't, could
you not?

FIRST PLAYER: Ay, my lord.

HAMLET: Very well. Follow that lord, and look you mock him not.

[Exeunt POLONIUS and PLAYERS.]

---

6. A comic act.   7. Hecuba was the wife of Priam and queen of Troy. Her "loins" are described
below as "o'erteemed" because of her unusual fertility. The number of her children varies in different accounts, but 20 is a safe minimum.   8. Muffled (in a hood).   9. Cloth. *Bisson
rheum*: blinding tears.   1. Government.   2. Cutting up.   3. Tearful (*lit.* milk-giving).
4. Whether.   5. Provided for.   6. Summary.

My good friends, I'll leave you till night. You are welcome to Elsinore.
ROSENCRANTZ: Good my lord.

[*Exeunt* ROSENCRANTZ *and* GUILDENSTERN.]

HAMLET: Ay, so God b'wi'ye. Now I am alone.
    O, what a rogue and peasant slave am I!   480
    Is it not monstrous that this player here,
    But in a fiction, in a dream of passion,
    Could force his soul so to his own conceit[7]
    That from her working all his visage wanned[8];
    Tears in his eyes, distraction in his aspect[9]   485
    A broken voice, and his whole function suiting
    With forms to his conceit? And all for nothing,
    For Hecuba!
    What's Hecuba to him or he to Hecuba,
    That he should weep for her? What would he do   490
    Had he the motive and the cue for passion
    That I have? He would drown the stage with tears,
    And cleave the general ear with horrid speech,
    Make mad the guilty, and appal the free,
    Confound the ignorant, and amaze indeed   495
    The very faculties of eyes and ears.
    Yet I,
    A dull and muddy-mettled rascal, peak[1]
    Like John-a-dreams, unpregnant[2] of my cause,
    And can say nothing; no, not for a king   500
    Upon whose property and most dear life
    A damned defeat was made. Am I a coward?
    Who calls me villain, breaks my pate across,
    Plucks off my beard and blows it in my face,
    Tweaks me by the nose, gives me the lie i' th' throat   505
    As deep as to the lungs? Who does me this?
    Ha, 'swounds, I should take it; for it cannot be
    But I am pigeon-livered and lack gall[3]
    To make oppression bitter, or ere this
    I should 'a fatted all the region kites[4]   510
    With this slave's offal. Bloody, bawdy villain!
    Remorseless, treacherous, lecherous, kindless[5] villain!
    Why, what an ass am I! This is most brave,
    That I, the son of a dear father murdered,
    Prompted to my revenge by heaven and hell,   515
    Must like a whore unpack[6] my heart with words,
    And fall a-cursing like a very drab,

---

7. Imagination.   8. Grew pale.   9. Face.   1. Mope. *Muddy-mettled:* dull-spirited.
2. Not quickened by. *John-a-dreams:* a man dreaming.   3. Bitterness.   4. Birds of prey of the area.   5. Unnatural.   6. Relieve.

A scullion[7]! Fie upon't! foh!
About, my brains. Hum—I have heard
520   That guilty creatures sitting at a play,
Have by the very cunning of the scene
Been struck so to the soul that presently
They have proclaimed[8] their malefactions;
For murder, though it have no tongue, will speak
525   With most miraculous organ. I'll have these players
Play something like the murder of my father
Before mine uncle. I'll observe his looks.
I'll tent him to the quick. If 'a do blench,[9]
I know my course. The spirit that I have seen
530   May be a devil, and the devil hath power
T' assume a pleasing shape, yea, and perhaps
Out of my weakness and my melancholy,
As he is very potent with such spirits,
Abuses me to damn me. I'll have grounds
535   More relative[1] than this. The play's the thing
Wherein I'll catch the conscience of the king.   [*Exit.*]

ACT III

Scene 1

A room in the castle. Enter KING, QUEEN, POLONIUS, OPHELIA, ROSENCRANTZ *and* GUILDENSTERN.

KING: And can you by no drift of conference[2]
   Get from him why he puts on this confusion,
   Grating so harshly all his days of quiet
   With turbulent[3] and dangerous lunacy?
5 ROSENCRANTZ: He does confess he feels himself distracted,
   But from what cause 'a will by no means speak.
GUILDENSTERN: Nor do we find him forward to be sounded,[4]
   But with a crafty madness keeps aloof
   When we would bring him on to some confession
   Of his true state.
10 QUEEN: Did he receive you well?
ROSENCRANTZ: Most like a gentleman.
GUILDENSTERN: But with much forcing of his disposition.[5]
ROSENCRANTZ: Niggard of question,[6] but of our demands
   Most free in his reply.

---

7. In some versions of the play, the word "stallion," a slang term for a prostitute, appears in place of "scullion."   8. Admitted.   9. Turn pale. *Tent:* try.   1. Conclusive.   2. Line of conversation.   3. Disturbing.   4. Questioned. *Forward:* eager.   5. Conversation.   6. To our questions.

QUEEN: Did you assay[7] him
   To any pastime?   15
ROSENCRANTZ: Madam, it so fell out that certain players
   We o'er-raught[8] on the way. Of these we told him,
   And there did seem in him a kind of joy
   To hear of it. They are here about the court,
   And as I think, they have already order   20
   This night to play before him.
POLONIUS: 'Tis most true,
   And he beseeched me to entreat your majesties
   To hear and see the matter.[9]
KING: With all my heart, and it doth much content me
   To hear him so inclined.   25
   Good gentlemen, give him a further edge,
   And drive his purpose[1] into these delights.
ROSENCRANTZ: We shall, my lord.   [*Exeunt* ROSENCRANTZ *and* GUILDENSTERN.]
KING: Sweet Gertrude, leave us too,
   For we have closely sent for Hamlet hither,
   That he, as 'twere by accident, may here   30
   Affront[2] Ophelia.
   Her father and myself (lawful espials[3])
   Will so bestow ourselves that, seeing unseen,
   We may of their encounter frankly judge,
   And gather by him, as he is behaved,   35
   If't be th' affiction of his love or no
   That thus he suffers for.
QUEEN: I shall obey you.—
   And for your part, Ophelia, I do wish
   That your good beauties be the happy cause
   Of Hamlet's wildness. So shall I hope your virtues   40
   Will bring him to his wonted[4] way again,
   To both your honors.
OPHELIA: Madam, I wish it may.   [*Exit* QUEEN.]
POLONIUS: Ophelia, walk you here.—Gracious,[5] so please you,
   We will bestow ourselves.—[*To* OPHELIA.] Read on this book,
   That show of such an exercise may color[6]   45
   Your loneliness.—We are oft to blame in this,
   'Tis too much proved, that with devotion's visage
   And pious action we do sugar o'er
   The devil himself.
KING: [*Aside.*]   O, 'tis too true.
   How smart a lash that speech doth give my conscience!   50
   The harlot's cheek, beautied with plast'ring[7] art,

---

7. Tempt.   8. Passed.   9. Performance.   1. Sharpen his intention.   2. Confront.
3. Justified spies.   4. Usual.   5. Majesty.   6. Explain. *Exercise:* act of devotion.
7. Thickly painted.

Is not more ugly to the thing that helps it
Than is my deed to my most painted word.
O heavy burden!

55 POLONIUS: I hear him coming. Let's withdraw, my lord.

[*Exeunt* KING *and* POLONIUS.]

[*Enter* HAMLET.]

HAMLET: To be, or not to be, that is the question:
Whether 'tis nobler in the mind to suffer
The slings and arrows of outrageous fortune,
Or to take arms against a sea of troubles,
60 And by opposing end them. To die, to sleep—
No more; and by a sleep to say we end
The heartache, and the thousand natural shocks
That flesh is heir to. 'Tis a consummation
Devoutly to be wished—to die, to sleep—
65 To sleep, perchance to dream, ay there's the rub;
For in that sleep of death what dreams may come
When we have shuffled off this mortal coil[8]
Must give us pause—there's the respect[9]
That makes calamity of so long life.
70 For who would bear the whips and scorns of time,
Th' oppressor's wrong, the proud man's contumely,[1]
The pangs of despised love, the law's delay,
The insolence of office, and the spurns[2]
That patient merit of th' unworthy takes,
75 When he himself might his quietus[3] make
With a bare bodkin? Who would fardels[4] bear,
To grunt and sweat under a weary life,
But that the dread of something after death,
The undiscovered country, from whose bourn[5]
80 No traveller returns, puzzles the will,
And makes us rather bear those ills we have
Than fly to others that we know not of?
Thus conscience does make cowards of us all;
And thus the native[6] hue of resolution
85 Is sicklied o'er with the pale cast of thought,
And enterprises of great pitch and moment[7]
With this regard their currents turn awry
And lose the name of action.—Soft you now,
The fair Ophelia.—Nymph, in thy orisons[8]
Be all my sins remembered.

---

8. Turmoil.   9. Consideration.   1. Insulting behavior.   2. Rejections.   3. Settlement.
4. Burdens. *Bodkin:* dagger.   5. Boundary.   6. Natural.   7. Importance. *Pitch:* height.
8. Prayers.

OPHELIA: Good my lord,   90
   How does your honor for this many a day?
HAMLET: I humbly thank you, well, well, well.
OPHELIA: My lord, I have remembrances of yours
   That I have longed long to re-deliver.
   I pray you now receive them.
HAMLET: No, not I,   95
   I never gave you aught.
OPHELIA: My honored lord, you know right well you did,
   And with them words of so sweet breath composed
   As made the things more rich. Their perfume lost,
   Take these again, for to the noble mind   100
   Rich gifts wax[9] poor when givers prove unkind.
   There, my lord.
HAMLET: Ha, ha! are you honest[1]?
OPHELIA: My lord?
HAMLET: Are you fair?   105
OPHELIA: What means your lordship?
HAMLET: That if you be honest and fair, your honesty should admit no discourse
   to your beauty.
OPHELIA: Could beauty, my lord, have better commerce[2] than with honesty?
HAMLET: Ay, truly, for the power of beauty will sooner transform honesty from   110
   what it is to a bawd than the force of honesty can translate beauty into his
   likeness. This was sometimes a paradox, but now the time gives it proof. I
   did love you once.
OPHELIA: Indeed, my lord, you made me believe so.
HAMLET: You should not have believed me, for virtue cannot so inoculate[3] our   115
   old stock but we shall relish of it. I loved you not.
OPHELIA: I was the more deceived.
HAMLET: Get thee to a nunnery.[4] Why wouldst thou be a breeder of sinners? I
   am myself indifferent[5] honest, but yet I could accuse me of such things that
   it were better my mother had not borne me: I am very proud, revengeful,   120
   ambitious, with more offences at my beck[6] than I have thoughts to put them
   in, imagination to give them shape, or time to act them in. What should
   such fellows as I do crawling between earth and heaven? We are arrant[7]
   knaves all; believe none of us. Go thy ways to a nunnery. Where's your
   father?   125
OPHELIA: At home, my lord.
HAMLET: Let the doors be shut upon him, that he may play the fool nowhere
   but in's own house. Farewell.
OPHELIA: O, help him, you sweet heavens!
HAMLET: If thou dost marry, I'll give thee this plague for thy dowry: be thou as   130

9. Become.   1. Chaste.   2. Intercourse.   3. Change by grafting.   4. With typical ribaldry Hamlet uses "nunnery" in two senses, the second as a slang term for brothel.   5. Moderately.   6. Command.   7. Thorough.

chaste as ice, as pure as snow, thou shalt not escape calumny. Get thee to a
nunnery, farewell. Or if thou wilt needs marry, marry a fool, for wise men
know well enough what monsters[8] you make of them. To a nunnery, go, and
quickly too. Farewell.

135   OPHELIA: Heavenly powers, restore him!

  HAMLET: I have heard of your paintings well enough. God hath given you one
face, and you make yourselves another. You jig, you amble, and you lisp;[9]
you nickname God's creatures, and make your wantonness your ignorance.[1]
Go to, I'll no more on't, it hath made me mad. I say we will have no more
140   marriage. Those that are married already, all but one, shall live. The rest
shall keep as they are. To a nunnery, go.   [*Exit.*]

  OPHELIA: O, what a noble mind is here o'erthrown!
The courtier's, soldier's, scholar's, eye, tongue, sword,
Th' expectancy and rose[2] of the fair state,
145   The glass of fashion and the mould[3] of form,
Th' observed of all observers, quite quite down!
And I of ladies most deject and wretched,
That sucked the honey of his music[4] vows,
Now see that noble and most sovereign reason
150   Like sweet bells jangled, out of time and harsh;
That unmatched form and feature of blown[5] youth
Blasted with ecstasy. O, woe is me
T' have seen what I have seen, see what I see!

  [*Enter* KING *and* POLONIUS.]

  KING: Love! His affections do not that way tend,
155   Nor what he spake, though it lacked form a little,
Was not like madness. There's something in his soul
O'er which his melancholy sits on brood,[6]
And I do doubt the hatch and the disclose[7]
Will be some danger; which to prevent,
160   I have in quick determination
Thus set it down: he shall with speed to England
For the demand of our neglected tribute.
Haply the seas and countries different,
With variable objects, shall expel
165   This something-settled matter in his heart
Whereon his brains still beating puts him thus
From fashion of himself. What think you on't?

  POLONIUS: It shall do well. But yet do I believe
The origin and commencement of his grief
170   Sprung from neglected love.—How now, Ophelia?

8. Horned because cuckolded.   9. Walk and talk affectedly.   1. Hamlet means that women
call things by pet names and then blame the affectation on ignorance.   2. Ornament. *Expectancy:* hope.   3. Model. *Glass:* mirror.   4. Musical.   5. Full-blown.   6. I.e., like a hen.
7. Result. *Doubt:* fear.

You need not tell us what Lord Hamlet said,
We heard it all.—My lord, do as you please,
But if you hold it fit, after the play
Let his queen-mother all alone entreat him
To show his grief. Let her be round[8] with him,   175
And I'll be placed, so please you, in the ear[9]
Of all their conference. If she find him not,[1]
To England send him; or confine him where
Your wisdom best shall think.
KING: It shall be so.
Madness in great ones must not unwatched go.   [*Exeunt.*]   180

SCENE 2

A public room in the castle. Enter HAMLET *and three of the* PLAYERS.

HAMLET: Speak the speech, I pray you, as I pronounced it to you, trippingly on
the tongue; but if you mouth it as many of our players do, I had as lief the
town-crier spoke my lines. Nor do not saw the air too much with your hand
thus, but use all gently, for in the very torrent, tempest, and as I may say,
whirlwind of your passion, you must acquire and beget a temperance that   5
may give it smoothness. O, it offends me to the soul to hear a robustious
periwig-pated[2] fellow tear a passion to tatters, to very rags, to split the ears of
the groundlings, who for the most part are capable of[3] nothing but inexplicable dumb shows and noise. I would have such a fellow whipped for o'erdoing
Termagant. It out-herods Herod.[4] Pray you avoid it.   10
FIRST PLAYER: I warrant your honor.
HAMLET: Be not too tame neither, but let your own discretion be your tutor. Suit
the action to the word, the word to the action, with this special observance,
that you o'erstep not the modesty of nature; for anything so o'erdone is from[5]
the purpose of playing, whose end both at the first, and now, was and is, to   15
hold as 'twere the mirror up to nature, to show virtue her own feature, scorn
her own image, and the very age and body of the time his form and pressure.[6]
Now this overdone, or come tardy off, though it makes the unskilful[7] laugh,
cannot but make the judicious grieve, the censure[8] of the which one must
in your allowance o'erweigh a whole theatre of others. O, there be players   20
that I have seen play—and heard others praise, and that highly—not to speak
it profanely, that neither having th' accent of Christians, nor the gait of
Christian, pagan, nor man, have so strutted and bellowed that I have thought
some of nature's journeymen[9] had made men, and not made them well, they
imitated humanity so abominably.   25

8. Direct.   9. Hearing.   1. Does not discover his problem.   2. Bewigged. *Robustious:*
noisy.   3. I.e., capable of understanding. *Groundlings:* the spectators who paid least.   4. Termagant, a "Saracen" deity, and the biblical Herod were stock characters in popular drama noted for
the excesses of sound and fury used by their interpreters.   5. Contrary to.   6. Shape.   7. Ignorant.   8. Judgment.   9. Inferior craftsmen.

FIRST PLAYER: I hope we have reformed that indifferently[1] with us.

HAMLET: O, reform it altogether. And let those that play your clowns speak no more than is set down for them, for there be of them that will themselves laugh, to set on some quantity of barren[2] spectators to laugh too, though in the meantime some necessary question of the play be then to be considered. That's villainous, and shows a most pitiful ambition in the fool that uses it. Go, make you ready.   *[Exeunt* PLAYERS.*]*

30

[Enter POLONIUS, GUILDENSTERN, *and* ROSENCRANTZ.*]*

How now, my lord? Will the king hear this piece of work?

POLONIUS: And the queen too, and that presently.

HAMLET: Bid the players make haste.   *[Exit* POLONIUS.*]*

35

Will you two help to hasten them?

ROSENCRANTZ: Ay, my lord.   *[Exeunt they two.]*

HAMLET: What, ho, Horatio!

[Enter HORATIO.*]*

HORATIO: Here, sweet lord, at your service.

40

HAMLET: Horatio, thou art e'en as just a man
   As e'er my conversation coped[3] withal.

HORATIO: O my dear lord!

HAMLET: Nay, do not think I flatter,
   For what advancement may I hope from thee,
   That no revenue hast but thy good spirits

45

   To feed and clothe thee? Why should the poor be flattered?
   No, let the candied tongue lick absurd pomp,
   And crook the pregnant[4] hinges of the knee
   Where thrift[5] may follow fawning. Dost thou hear?
   Since my dear soul was mistress of her choice

50

   And could of men distinguish her election,
   S'hath sealed thee for herself, for thou hast been
   As one in suff'ring all that suffers nothing,
   A man that Fortune's buffets and rewards
   Hast ta'en with equal thanks; and blest are those

55

   Whose blood and judgment are so well commingled
   That they are not a pipe[6] for Fortune's finger
   To sound what stop[7] she please. Give me that man
   That is not passion's slave, and I will wear him
   In my heart's core, ay, in my heart of heart,

60

   As I do thee. Something too much of this.
   There is a play tonight before the king.
   One scene of it comes near the circumstance
   Which I have told thee of my father's death.

---

1. Somewhat.   2. Dull-witted.   3. Encountered.   4. Quick to bend.   5. Profit.
6. Musical instrument.   7. Note. *Sound:* play.

I prithee, when thou seest that act afoot,
Even with the very comment[8] of thy soul 65
Observe my uncle. If his occulted[9] guilt
Do not itself unkennel[1] in one speech,
It is a damnéd ghost that we have seen,
And my imaginations are as foul
As Vulcan's stithy. Give him heedful note,[2] 70
For I mine eyes will rivet to his face,
And after we will both our judgments join
In censure of his seeming.[3]
HORATIO: Well, my lord.
If 'a steal aught the whilst this play in playing,
And 'scape detecting, I will pay[4] the theft. 75

[*Enter Trumpets and Kettledrums*, KING, QUEEN, POLONIUS, OPHELIA, ROSEN-
CRANTZ, GUILDENSTERN, *and other* LORDS *attendant.*]

HAMLET: They are coming to the play. I must be idle.
Get you a place.
KING: How fares our cousin Hamlet?
HAMLET: Excellent, i' faith, of the chameleon's dish.[5] I eat the air, promise-
crammed. You cannot feed capons so. 80
KING: I have nothing with this answer, Hamlet. These words are not mine.
HAMLET: No, nor mine now. [*To* POLONIUS.] My lord, you played once i' th'
university, you say?
POLONIUS: That did I, my lord, and was accounted a good actor.
HAMLET: What did you enact? 85
POLONIUS: I did enact Julius Cæsar. I was killed i' th' Capitol; Brutus killed
me.[6]
HAMLET: It was a brute part of him to kill so capital a calf there. Be the players
ready?
ROSENCRANTZ: Ay, my lord, they stay upon your patience.[7] 90
QUEEN: Come hither, my dear Hamlet, sit by me.
HAMLET: No, good mother, here's metal more attractive.
POLONIUS: [*To the* KING.] O, ho! do you mark that?
HAMLET: Lady, shall I lie in your lap?

[*Lying down at* OPHELIA'*s feet.*]

OPHELIA: No, my lord. 95
HAMLET: I mean, my head upon your lap?
OPHELIA: Ay, my lord.
HAMLET: Do you think I meant country matters[8]?

8. Keenest observation.   9. Hidden.   1. Break loose.   2. Careful attention. *Stithy:* smithy.
3. Manner.   4. Repay.   5. A reference to a popular belief that the chameleon subsisted on a
diet of air. Hamlet has deliberately misunderstood the king's question.   6. The assassination of
Julius Caesar by Brutus and others is the subject of another play by Shakespeare.   7. Leisure.
Stay: wait.   8. Presumably, rustic misbehavior, but here and elsewhere in this exchange Hamlet
treats Ophelia to some ribald double meanings.

OPHELIA: I think nothing, my lord.

100 HAMLET: That's a fair thought to lie between maids' legs.

OPHELIA: What is, my lord?

HAMLET: Nothing.

OPHELIA: You are merry, my lord.

HAMLET: Who, I?

105 OPHELIA: Ay, my lord.

HAMLET: O God, your only jig-maker[9]! What should a man do but be merry? For look you how cheerfully my mother looks, and my father died within's two hours.

OPHELIA: Nay, 'tis twice two months, my lord.

110 HAMLET: So long? Nay then, let the devil wear black, for I'll have a suit of sables. O heavens! die two months ago, and not forgotten yet? Then there's hope a great man's memory may outlive his life half a year, but by'r lady 'a must build churches then, or else shall 'a suffer not thinking on, with the hobby-horse, whose epitaph is "For O, for O, the hobby-horse is forgot!"[1]

The trumpets sound. Dumb Show follows. Enter a KING *and a* QUEEN *very lovingly; the* QUEEN *embracing him and he her. She kneels, and makes show of protestation unto him. He takes her up, and declines[2] his head upon her neck. He lies him down upon a bank of flowers; she, seeing him asleep, leaves him. Anon come in another man, takes off his crown, kisses it, pours poison in the sleeper's ears, and leaves him. The* QUEEN *returns, finds the* KING *dead, makes passionate action. The* POISONER *with some three or four come in again, seem to condole with her. The dead body is carried away. The* POISONER *woos the* QUEEN *with gifts; she seems harsh awhile, but in the end accepts love.*

[*Exeunt.*]

115 OPHELIA: What means this, my lord?

HAMLET: Marry, this is miching mallecho[3]; it means mischief.

OPHELIA: Belike this show imports the argument[4] of the play.

[*Enter* PROLOGUE.]

HAMLET: We shall know by this fellow. The players cannot keep counsel; they'll tell all.

120 OPHELIA: Will 'a tell us what this show meant?

HAMLET: Ay, or any show that you will show him. Be not you ashamed to show, he'll not shame to tell you what it means.

OPHELIA: You are naught, you are naught. I'll mark[5] the play.

PROLOGUE: *For us, and for our tragedy,*

125   *Here stooping to your clemency,*

      We beg your hearing patiently. [*Exit.*]

HAMLET: Is this a prologue, or the posy[6] of a ring?

---

9. Writer of comic scenes. **1.** In traditional games and dances one of the characters was a man respresented as riding a horse. The horse was made of something like cardboard and was worn about the "rider's" waist. **2.** Lays. **3.** Sneaking crime. **4.** Plot. *Imports:* explains. **5.** Attend to. *Naught:* obscene. **6.** Motto engraved inside.

OPHELIA: 'Tis brief, my lord.

HAMLET: As woman's love.

[*Enter the* PLAYER KING *and* QUEEN.]

PLAYER KING: *Full thirty times hath Phœbus' cart gone round*   130
Neptune's salt wash and Tellus' orbéd ground,
And thirty dozen moons with borrowed sheen[7]
About the world have times twelve thirties been,
Since love our hearts and Hymen did our hands
Unite comutual in most sacred bands.[8]   135

PLAYER QUEEN: *So many journeys may the sun and moon*
Make us again count o'er ere love be done!
But woe is me, you are so sick of late,
So far from cheer and from your former state,
That I distrust[9] *you. Yet though I distrust,*   140
Discomfort you, my lord, it nothing must.
For women's fear and love hold quantity,[1]
In neither aught, or in extremity.[2]
Now what my love is proof hath made you know,
And as my love is sized,[3] *my fear is so.*   145
Where love is great, the littlest doubts are fear;
Where little fears grow great, great love grows there.

PLAYER KING: *Faith, I must leave thee, love, and shortly too;*
My operant powers their functions leave[4] *to do.*
And thou shalt live in this fair world behind,   150
Honored, beloved, and haply one as kind
For husband shalt thou —

PLAYER QUEEN: *O, confound the rest!*
Such love must needs be treason in my breast.
In second husband let me be accurst!
None wed the second but who killed the first.[5]   155

HAMLET: That's wormwood.

PLAYER QUEEN: *The instances*[6] *that second marriage move*
Are base respects[7] *of thrift, but none of love.*
A second time I kill my husband dead,
When second husband kisses me in bed.   160

PLAYER KING: *I do believe you think what now you speak,*
But what we do determine oft we break.
Purpose is but the slave to memory,
Of violent birth, but poor validity;

---

7. Light.   8. The speech contains several references to Greek mythology. Phoebus was the sun
god, and his chariot or "cart" the sun. The "salt wash" of Neptune is the ocean; Tellus was an earth
goddess, and her "orbed ground" is the Earth, or globe. Hymen was the god of marriage. *Comutual:*
mutually.   9. Fear for.   1. Agree in weight.   2. Without regard to too much or too little.   3. In size.   4. Cease. *Operant powers:* active forces.   5. Though there is some ambiguity, she seems to mean that the only kind of woman who would remarry is one who has killed or
would kill her first husband.   6. Causes.   7. Concerns.

165   *Which now, like fruit unripe, sticks on the tree,*
       But fall unshaken when they mellow be.
       Most necessary 'tis that we forget
       To pay ourselves what to ourselves is debt.
       What to ourselves in passion we propose,
170   *The passion ending, doth the purpose lose.*
       The violence of either grief or joy
       Their own enactures[8] with themselves destroy.
       Where joy most revels, grief doth most lament;
       Grief joys, joy grieves, on slender accident.
175   *This world is not for aye,[9] nor 'tis not strange*
       That even our loves should with our fortunes change;
       For 'tis a question left us yet to prove,
       Whether love lead fortune, or else fortune love.
       The great man down, you mark his favorite flies;
180   *The poor advanced makes friends of enemies;*
       And hitherto doth love on fortune tend,
       For who not needs shall never lack a friend,
       And who in want a hollow[1] friend doth try,
       Directly seasons him[2] his enemy.
185   *But orderly to end where I begun,*
       Our wills and fates do so contrary run
       That our devices[3] still are overthrown;
       Our thoughts are ours, their ends none of our own.
       So think thou wilt no second husband wed,
190   *But die thy thoughts when thy first lord is dead.*
PLAYER QUEEN: *Nor earth to me give food, nor heaven light,*
       Sport and repose lock from me day and night,
       To desperation turn my trust and hope,
       An anchor's cheer[4] in prison be my scope,
195   *Each opposite that blanks[5] the face of joy*
       Meet what I would have well, and it destroy,
       Both here and hence[6] pursue me lasting strife,
       If once a widow, ever I be wife!
HAMLET: If she should break it now!
200 PLAYER KING: *'Tis deeply sworn. Sweet, leave me here awhile.*
       My spirits grow dull, and fain I would beguile
       The tedious day with sleep.   *[Sleeps.]*
PLAYER QUEEN: *Sleep rock thy brain,*
       And never come mischance between us twain!   *[Exit.]*
HAMLET: Madam, how like you this play?
205 QUEEN: The lady doth protest too much, methinks.
HAMLET: O, but she'll keep her word.
KING: Have you heard the argument? Is there no offence in't?

---

8. Actions.   9. Eternal.   1. False.   2. Ripens him into.   3. Plans.   4. Anchorite's
food.   5. Blanches.   6. In the next world.

HAMLET: No, no, they do but jest, poison in jest; no offence i' th' world.

KING: What do you call the play?

HAMLET: "The Mouse-trap." Marry, how? Tropically.[7] This play is the image of   210
a murder done in Vienna. Gonzago is the duke's name; his wife, Baptista.
You shall see anon. 'Tis a knavish piece of work, but what of that? Your
majesty, and we that have free souls, it touches us not. Let the galled jade
wince, our withers are unwrung.[8]

[Enter LUCIANUS.]

This is one Lucianus, nephew to the king.   215

OPHELIA: You are as good as a chorus, my lord.

HAMLET: I could interpret between you and your love, if I could see the puppets
dallying.

OPHELIA: You are keen, my lord, you are keen.

HAMLET: It would cost you a groaning to take off mine edge.   220

OPHELIA: Still better, and worse.

HAMLET: So you mistake your husbands.—Begin, murderer. Leave thy damn-
able faces and begin. Come, the croaking raven doth bellow for revenge.

LUCIANUS: *Thoughts black, hands apt, drugs fit, and time agreeing,*
Confederate season,[9] else no creature seeing,   225
Thou mixture rank, of midnight weeds collected,
With Hecate's ban thrice blasted, thrice infected,[1]
Thy natural magic[2] and dire property
On wholesome life usurps immediately.   [*Pours the poison in his ears.*]

HAMLET: 'A poisons him i' th' garden for his estate. His name's Gonzago. The   230
story is extant, and written in very choice Italian. You shall see anon how
the murderer gets the love of Gonzago's wife.

OPHELIA: The king rises.

HAMLET: What, frighted with false fire?

QUEEN: How fares my lord?   235

POLONIUS: Give o'er the play.

KING: Give me some light. Away!

POLONIUS: Lights, lights, lights!   [*Exeunt all but* HAMLET *and* HORATIO.]

HAMLET:

Why, let the strucken deer go weep,
The hart ungallèd[3] play.
For some must watch while some must sleep;   240
Thus runs the world away.

Would not this, sir, and a forest of feathers[4]—if the rest of my fortunes turn
Turk with me—with two Provincial roses on my razed shoes, get me a fellowship in a cry of players?[5]   245

7. Figuratively.   8. A "galled jade" is a horse, particularly one of poor quality, with a sore back.
The "withers" are the ridge between a horse's shoulders; "unwrung withers" are not chafed by the
harness.   9. A helpful time for the crime.   1. Hecate was a classical goddess of witchcraft.
2. Native power.   3. Uninjured.   4. Plumes.   5. Hamlet asks Horatio if "this" recitation,
accompanied with a player's costume, including plumes and rosettes on shoes that have been

HORATIO: Half a share.

HAMLET: A whole one, I.

> For thou dost know, O Damon dear,[6]
> This realm dismantled was
> Of Jove himself, and now reigns here
> A very, very—peacock.

250

HORATIO: You might have rhymed.

HAMLET: O good Horatio, I'll take the ghost's word for a thousand pound. Didst perceive?

255

HORATIO: Very well, my lord.

HAMLET: Upon the talk of the poisoning.

HORATIO: I did very well note[7] him.

HAMLET: Ah, ha! Come, some music. Come, the recorders.[8]

> For if the king like not the comedy.
> Why then, belike he likes it not, perdy.[9]

260

Come, some music.

[*Enter* ROSENCRANTZ *and* GUILDENSTERN.]

GUILDENSTERN: Good my lord, vouchsafe me a word with you.

HAMLET: Sir, a whole history.

GUILDENSTERN: The king, sir—

265

HAMLET: Ay, sir, what of him?

GUILDENSTERN: Is in his retirement marvellous distempered.[1]

HAMLET: With drink, sir?

GUILDENSTERN: No, my lord, with choler.[2]

HAMLET: Your wisdom should show itself more richer to signify this to the doc-

270

tor, for for me to put him to his purgation[3] would perhaps plunge him into more choler.

GUILDENSTERN: Good my lord, put your discourse into some frame,[4] and start not so wildly from my affair.

HAMLET: I am tame, sir. Pronounce.

275

GUILDENSTERN: The queen your mother, in most great affliction of spirit, hath sent me to you.

HAMLET: You are welcome.

GUILDENSTERN: Nay, good my lord, this courtesy is not of the right breed. If it shall please you to make me a wholesome[5] answer, I will do your mother's

---

slashed for decorative effect, might not entitle him to become a shareholder in a theatrical company in the event that Fortune goes against him, "turn Turk." *Cry:* company.   6. Damon was a common name for a young man or a shepherd in lyric, especially pastoral poetry. Jove was the chief god of the Romans. Readers may supply for themselves the rhyme referred to by Horatio.   7. Observe. 8. Wooden, end-blown flutes.   9. *Par Dieu* (by God).   1. Vexed. *Retirement:* place to which he has retired.   2. Bile.   3. Treatment with a laxative.   4. Order. *Discourse:* speech. 5. Reasonable.

commandment. If not, your pardon and my return[6] shall be the end of my
business.

HAMLET: Sir, I cannot.

ROSENCRANTZ: What, my lord?

HAMLET: Make you a wholesome answer; my wit's diseased. But, sir, such answer
as I can make, you shall command, or rather, as you say, my mother. Therefore no more, but to the matter. My mother, you say—

ROSENCRANTZ: Then thus she says: your behavior hath struck her into amazement and admiration.[7]

HAMLET: O wonderful son, that can so stonish a mother! But is there no sequel
at the heels of his mother's admiration? Impart.[8]

ROSENCRANTZ: She desires to speak with you in her closet[9] ere you go to bed.

HAMLET: We shall obey, were she ten times our mother. Have you any further
trade[1] with us?

ROSENCRANTZ: My lord, you once did love me.

HAMLET: And do still, by these pickers and stealers.[2]

ROSENCRANTZ: Good my lord, what is your cause of distemper? You do surely
bar the door upon your own liberty, if you deny your griefs to your friend.

HAMLET: Sir, I lack advancement.

ROSENCRANTZ: How can that be, when you have the voice of the king himself
for your succession in Denmark?

HAMLET: Ay, sir, but "while the grass grows"—the proverb[3] is something musty.

[*Enter the* PLAYERS *with recorders.*]

O, the recorders! Let me see one. To withdraw with you[4]—why do you go
about to recover the wind of me, as if you would drive me into a toil?[5]

GUILDENSTERN: O my lord, if my duty be too bold, my love is too unmannerly.

HAMLET: I do not well understand that. Will you play upon this pipe[6]?

GUILDENSTERN: My lord, I cannot.

HAMLET: I pray you.

GUILDENSTERN: Believe me, I cannot.

HAMLET: I do beseech you.

GUILDENSTERN: I know no touch of it,[7] my lord.

HAMLET: It is as easy as lying. Govern these ventages[8] with your fingers and
thumb, give it breath with your mouth, and it will discourse most eloquent
music. Look you, these are the stops.[9]

GUILDENSTERN: But these cannot I command to any utt'rance of harmony. I
have not the skill.

HAMLET: Why, look you now, how unworthy a thing you make of me! You
would play upon me, you would seem to know my stops, you would pluck
out the heart of my mystery, you would sound[1] me from my lowest note to

---

6. I.e., to the queen.   7. Wonder.   8. Tell me.   9. Bedroom.   1. Business.
2. Hands.   3. The proverb ends "the horse starves."   4. Let me step aside.   5. The figure
is from hunting. Hamlet asks why Guildenstern is attempting to get windward of him, as if he would
drive him into a net.   6. Recorder.   7. Have no ability.   8. Holes. *Govern:* cover and uncover.   9. Wind-holes.   1. Play.

the top of my compass[2]; and there is much music, excellent voice, in this little organ, yet cannot you make it speak. 'Sblood, do you think I am easier to be played on than a pipe? Call me what instrument you will, though you can fret[3] me, you cannot play upon me.

[*Enter* POLONIUS.]

God bless you, sir!

POLONIUS: My lord, the queen would speak with you, and presently.[4]

HAMLET: Do you see yonder cloud that's almost in shape of a camel?

POLONIUS: By th' mass, and 'tis like a camel indeed.

HAMLET: Methinks it is like a weasel.

POLONIUS: It is backed like a weasel.

HAMLET: Or like a whale.

POLONIUS: Very like a whale.

HAMLET: Then I will come to my mother by and by. [*Aside.*] They fool me to the top of my bent.[5]—I will come by and by.

POLONIUS: I will say so. [*Exit.*]

HAMLET: "By and by" is easily said. Leave me, friends. [*Exeunt all but* HAMLET.]
  'Tis now the very witching time of night,
  When churchyards yawn, and hell itself breathes out
  Contagion to this world. Now could I drink hot blood,
  And do such bitter business as the day
  Would quake to look on. Soft, now to my mother.
  O heart, lose not thy nature; let not ever
  The soul of Nero[6] enter this firm bosom.
  Let me be cruel, not unnatural;
  I will speak daggers to her, but use none.
  My tongue and soul in this be hypocrites—
  How in my words somever she be shent,[7]
  To give them seals[8] never, my soul, consent! [*Exit.*]

SCENE 3

A room in the castle. Enter KING, ROSENCRANTZ *and* GUILDENSTERN.

KING: I like him not,[9] nor stands it safe with us
  To let his madness range.[1] Therefore prepare you.
  I your commission will forthwith dispatch,
  And he to England shall along with you.
  The terms of our estate[2] may not endure
  Hazard so near's as doth hourly grow
  Out of his brows.

---

2. Range.   3. "Fret" is used in a double sense, to annoy and to play a guitar or similar instrument using the "frets" or small bars on the neck.   4. At once.   5. Treat me as an utter fool. 6. The Roman emperor Nero, known for his excesses, was believed to have been responsible for the death of his mother.   7. Shamed.   8. Fulfillment in action.   9. Distrust him.   1. Roam freely.   2. Condition of the state.

GUILDENSTERN: We will ourselves provide,[3]
　　Most holy and religious fear it is
　　To keep those many many bodies safe
　　That live and feed upon your majesty.
ROSENCRANTZ: The single and peculiar[4] life is bound   10
　　With all the strength and armor of the mind
　　To keep itself from noyance,[5] but much more
　　That spirit upon whose weal[6] depends and rests
　　The lives of many. The cess[7] of majesty
　　Dies not alone, but like a gulf[8] doth draw   15
　　What's near it with it. It is a massy[9] wheel
　　Fixed on the summit of the highest mount,
　　To whose huge spokes ten thousand lesser things
　　Are mortised and adjoined,[1] which when it falls,   20
　　Each small annexment, petty consequence,
　　Attends[2] the boist'rous ruin. Never alone
　　Did the king sigh, but with a general groan.
KING: Arm you, I pray you, to this speedy voyage,
　　For we will fetters put about this fear,   25
　　Which now goes too free-footed.
ROSENCRANTZ: We will haste us.

　　　　　　　　　　[*Exeunt* ROSENCRANTZ *and* GUILDENSTERN.]

[*Enter* POLONIUS.]

POLONIUS: My lord, he's going to his mother's closet.
　　Behind the arras I'll convey[3] myself
　　To hear the process. I'll warrant she'll tax him home,[4]
　　And as you said, and wisely was it said,   30
　　'Tis meet that some more audience than a mother,
　　Since nature makes them partial, should o'erhear
　　The speech, of vantage.[5] Fare you well, my liege.
　　I'll call upon you ere you go to bed,
　　And tell you what I know.
KING: Thanks, dear my lord.   [*Exit* POLONIUS.]   35
　　O, my offence is rank, it smells to heaven;
　　It hath the primal eldest curse[6] upon't,
　　A brother's murder. Pray can I not,
　　Though inclination be as sharp as will.
　　My stronger guilt defeats my strong intent,   40
　　And like a man to double business[7] bound,
　　I stand in pause where I shall first begin,
　　And both neglect. What if this cursèd hand

3. Equip (for the journey).   4. Individual.   5. Harm.   6. Welfare.   7. Cessation.
8. Whirlpool.   9. Massive.   1. Attached.   2. Joins in.   3. Station.   4. Sharply. *Process:* proceedings.   5. From a position of vantage.   6. I.e., of Cain.   7. Two mutually opposed interests.

Were thicker than itself with brothers' blood,
45   Is there not rain enough in the sweet heavens
To wash it white as snow? Whereto serves mercy
But to confront the visage of offence?
And what's in prayer but this twofold force,
To be forestallèd[8] ere we come to fall,
50   Or pardoned being down[9]? Then I'll look up.
My fault is past. But, O, what form of prayer
Can serve my turn? "Forgive me my foul murder"?
That cannot be, since I am still possessed
Of those effects[1] for which I did the murder—
55   My crown, mine own ambition, and my queen.
May one be pardoned and retain th' offence[2]?
In the corrupted currents of this world
Offence's gilded[3] hand may shove by justice,
And oft 'tis seen the wicked prize itself
60   Buys out the law. But 'tis not so above.
There is no shuffling; there the action[4] lies
In his true nature, and we ourselves compelled,
Even to the teeth and forehead of[5] our faults,
To give in evidence. What then? What rests[6]?
65   Try what repentance can. What can it not?
Yet what can it when one can not repent?
O wretched state? O bosom black as death!
O limèd[7] soul, that struggling to be free
Art more engaged! Help, angels! Make assay.
70   Bow, stubborn knees, and heart with strings of steel,
Be soft as sinews of the new-born babe.
All may be well.   [*He kneels.*]

[*Enter* HAMLET.]

HAMLET: Now might I do it pat,[8] now 'a is a-praying,
And now I'll do't—and so 'a goes to heaven,
75   And so am I revenged. That would be scanned.[9]
A villain kills my father, and for that,
I, his sole son, do this same villain send
To heaven.
Why, this is hire and salary, not revenge.
80   'A took my father grossly, full of bread,[1]
With all his crimes broad blown, as flush[2] as May;
And how his audit stands who knows save heaven?
But in our circumstance and course of thought

8. Prevented (from sin).   9. Having sinned.   1. Gains.   2. I.e., benefits of the offence.
3. Bearing gold as a bribe.   4. Case at law.   5. Face-to-face with.   6. Remains.
7. Caught as with birdlime.   8. Easily.   9. Deserves consideration.   1. In a state of sin and
without fasting.   2. Vigorous. *Broad blown:* full-blown.

'Tis heavy with him; and am I then revenged
To take him in the purging of his soul, 85
When he is fit and seasoned³ for his passage?
No.
Up, sword, and know thou a more horrid hent.⁴
When he is drunk, asleep, or in his rage,
Or in th' incestuous pleasure of his bed, 90
At game a-swearing, or about some act
That has no relish⁵ of salvation in't—
Then trip him, that his heels may kick at heaven,
And that his soul may be as damned and black
As hell, whereto it goes. My mother stays. 95
This physic⁶ but prolongs thy sickly days. [*Exit.*]
KING: [*Rising.*] My words fly up, my thoughts remain below.
Words without thoughts never to heaven go. [*Exit.*]

SCENE 4

The Queen's chamber. Enter QUEEN *and* POLONIUS.

POLONIUS: 'A will come straight. Look you lay home to⁷ him.
Tell him his pranks have been too broad⁸ to bear with,
And that your grace hath screen'd⁹ and stood between
Much heat and him. I'll silence me even here.
Pray you be round.
QUEEN: I'll warrant you. Fear¹ me not. 5
Withdraw, I hear him coming.

[POLONIUS *goes behind the arras. Enter* HAMLET.]

HAMLET: Now, mother, what's the matter?
QUEEN: Hamlet, thou hast thy father much offended.
HAMLET: Mother, you have my father much offended.
HAMLET: Come, come, you answer with an idle tongue. 10
HAMLET: Go, go, you question with a wicked tongue.
QUEEN: Why, how now, Hamlet?
HAMLET: What's the matter now?
QUEEN: Have you forgot me?
HAMLET: No, by the rood,² not so.
You are the queen, your husband's brother's wife,
And would it were not so, you are my mother. 15
QUEEN: Nay, then I'll set those to you that can speak.
HAMLET: Come, come, and sit you down. You shall not budge.
You go not till I set you up a glass³

---

3. Ready.   4. Opportunity.   5. Flavor.   6. Medicine.   7. Be sharp with.   8. Outrageous.   9. Acted as a fire screen.   1. Doubt.   2. Cross.   3. Mirror.

Where you may see the inmost part of you.

20 QUEEN: What wilt thou do? Thou wilt not murder me?
Help, ho!

POLONIUS: [*Behind.*] What, ho! help!

HAMLET: [*Draws.*] How now, a rat?
Dead for a ducat, dead!

[*Kills* POLONIUS *with a pass through the arras.*]

25 POLONIUS: [*Behind.*] O, I am slain!

QUEEN: O me, what hast thou done?

HAMLET: Nay, I know not.
Is it the king?

QUEEN: O, what a rash and bloody deed is this!

HAMLET: A bloody deed!—almost as bad, good mother,

30 As kill a king and marry with his brother.

QUEEN: As kill a king?

HAMLET: Ay, lady, it was my word.   [*Parting the arras.*]
Thou wretched, rash, intruding fool, farewell!
I took thee for thy better. Take thy fortune.
Thou find'st to be too busy[4] is some danger.—

35 Leave wringing of your hands. Peace, sit you down
And let me wring your heart, for so I shall
If it be made of penetrable stuff,
If damnéd custom have not brazed it[5] so
That it be proof and bulwark against sense.[6]

40 QUEEN: What have I done that thou dar'st wag thy tongue
In noise so rude against me?

HAMLET: Such an act
That blurs the grace and blush of modesty,
Calls virtue hypocrite, takes off the rose
From the fair forehead of an innocent love.

45 And sets a blister[7] there, makes marriage-vows
As false as dicers' oaths. O, such a deed
As from the body of contraction[8] plucks
The very soul, and sweet religion makes
A rhapsody of words. Heaven's face does glow

50 And this solidity and compound mass[9]
With heated visage, as against the doom[1]—
Is though-sick at the act.

QUEEN: Ay me, what act
That roars so loud and thunders in the index[2]?

HAMLET: Look here upon this picture[3] and on this,

55 The counterfeit presentment of two brothers.

4. Officious.   5. Plated it with brass   6. Feeling. *Proof*: armor.   7. Brand.   8. The marriage contract.   9. Meaningless mass (Earth).   1. Judgment Day.   2. Table of contents.
3. Portrait.

See what a grace was seated on this brow:
Hyperion's curls, the front[4] of Jove himself,
An eye like Mars, to threaten and command,
A station like the herald Mercury[5]
New lighted[6] on a heaven-kissing hill—   60
A combination and a form indeed
Where every god did seem to set his seal,[7]
To give the world assurance of a man.
This was your husband. Look you now what follows.
Here is your husband, like a mildewed ear   65
Blasting his wholesome brother. Have you eyes?
Could you on this fair mountain leave to feed,
And batten[8] on this moor? Ha! have you eyes?
You cannot call it love, for at your age
The heyday in the blood is tame, it's humble,   70
And waits upon the judgment, and what judgment
Would step from this to this? Sense sure you have
Else could you not have motion, but sure that sense
Is apoplexed[9] for madness would not err,
Nor sense to ecstasy was ne'er so thralled   75
But it reserved some quantity[1] of choice
To serve in such a difference. What devil was't
That thus hath cozened you at hoodman-blind[2]?
Eyes without feeling, feeling without sight,
Ears without hands or eyes, smelling sans[3] all,   80
Or but a sickly part of one true sense
Could not so mope.[4] O shame! where is thy blush?
Rebellious hell,
If thou canst mutine[5] in a matron's bones,
To flaming youth let virtue be as wax   85
And melt in her own fire. Proclaim no shame
When the compulsive ardor gives the charge,[6]
Since frost itself as actively doth burn,
And reason panders[7] will.

QUEEN: O Hamlet, speak no more!
Thou turn'st my eyes into my very soul;   90
And there I see such black and grainéd[8] spots
As will not leave their tinct.[9]

HAMLET: Nay, but to live
In the rank sweat of an enseaméd[1] bed,
Stewed in curruption, honeying and making love

---

4. Forehead.   5. In Roman mythology, Mercury served as the messenger of the gods. *Station:*
bearing.   6. Newly alighted.   7. Mark of approval.   8. Feed greedily.   9. Paralyzed.
1. Power.   2. Blindman's buff. *Cozened:* cheated.   3. Without.   4. Be stupid.   5. Commit mutiny.   6. Attacks.   7. Pimps for.   8. Ingrained.   9. Lose their color.   1. Greasy.

Over the nasty sty—

QUEEN: O, speak to me no more!

These words like daggers enter in my ears;

No more, sweet Hamlet.

HAMLET: A murderer and a villain,

A slave that is not twentieth part the tithe[2]

Of your precedent lord, a vice of kings,[3]

A cutpurse[4] of the empire and the rule,

That from a shelf the precious diadem stole

And put it in his pocket—

QUEEN: No more.

[*Enter* GHOST.]

HAMLET: A king of shreds and patches—

Save me and hover o'er me with your wings,

You heavenly guards! What would your gracious figure?

QUEEN: Alas, he's mad.

HAMLET: Do you not come your tardy[5] son to chide,

That lapsed in time and passion lets go by

Th' important acting of your dread command?

O, say!

GHOST: Do not forget. This visitation

Is but to whet thy almost blunted purpose.

But look, amazement on thy mother sits.

O, step between her and her fighting soul!

Conceit[6] in weakest bodies strongest works.

Speak to her, Hamlet.

HAMLET: How is it with you, lady?

QUEEN: Alas, how is't with you,

That you do bend[7] your eye on vacancy,

And with th' incorporal air do hold discourse?

Forth at your eyes your spirits wildly peep,

And as the sleeping soldiers in th' alarm,

Your bedded hairs like life in excrements[8]

Start up and stand an end. O gentle son,

Upon the heat and flame of thy distemper

Sprinkle cool patience. Whereon do you look?

HAMLET: On him, on him! Look you how pale he glares.

His form and cause conjoined,[9] preaching to stones,

Would make them capable.[1]—Do not look upon me,

Lest with piteous action you convert

My stern effects.[2] Then what I have to do

2. One-tenth.   3. The "Vice," a common figure in the popular drama, was a clown or buffoon.
Precedent lord: first husband.   4. Pickpocket.   5. Slow to act.   6. Imagination.   7. Turn.
8. Nails and hair.   9. Working together.   1. Of responding.   2. Deeds.

Will want true color—tears perchance for blood.

QUEEN: To whom do you speak this?

HAMLET: Do you see nothing there?

QUEEN: Nothing at all, yet all that is I see.   135

HAMLET: Nor did you nothing hear?

QUEEN: No, nothing but ourselves.

HAMLET: Why, look you there. Look how it steals away.
   My father, in his habit[3] as he lived!
   Look where he goes even now out at the portal.   *[Exit* GHOST.]   140

QUEEN: This is the very coinage[4] of your brain.
   Ths bodiless creation ecstasy[5]
   Is very cunning[6] in.

HAMLET: My pulse as yours doth temperately keep time,
   And makes as healthful music. It is not madness   145
   That I have uttered. Bring me to the test,
   And I the matter will re-word, which madness
   Would gambol[7] from. Mother, for love of grace,
   Lay not that flattering unction[8] to your soul,
   That not your trespass but my madness speaks.   150
   It will but skin and film the ulcerous place
   Whiles rank corruption, mining[9] all within,
   Infects unseen. Confess yourself to heaven,
   Repent what's past, avoid what is to come.
   And do not spread the compost on the weeds,   155
   To make them ranker. Forgive me this my virtue,
   For in the fatness of these pursy[1] times
   Virtue itself of vice must pardon beg,
   Yea, curb[2] and woo for leave to do him good.

QUEEN: O Hamlet, thou hast cleft my heart in twain.   160

HAMLET: O, throw away the worser part of it,
   And live the purer with the other half.
   Good night—but go not to my uncle's bed.
   Assume a virtue, if you have it not.
   That monster custom[3] who all sense doth eat   165
   Of habits evil, is angel yet in this,
   That to the use of actions fair and good
   He likewise gives a frock or livery
   That aptly[4] is put on. Refrain tonight,
   And that shall lend a kind of easiness   170
   To the next abstinence; the next more easy;
   For use almost can change the stamp of nature,
   And either curb the devil, or throw him out
   With wondrous potency. Once more, good night,

---

3. Costume.   **4.** Invention.   **5.** Madness.   **6.** Skilled.   **7.** Shy away.   **8.** Ointment.
9. Undermining.   **1.** Bloated.   **2.** Bow.   **3.** Habit.   **4.** Easily.

175 And when you are desirous to be blest,
I'll blessing beg of you. For this same lord
I do repent; but heaven hath pleased it so,
To punish me with this, and this with me,
That I must be their scourge and minister.
180 I will bestow[5] him and will answer well
The death I gave him. So, again, good night.
I must be cruel only to be kind.
Thus bad begins and worse remains behind.
One word more, good lady.
QUEEN: What shall I do?
185 HAMLET: Not this, by no means, that I bid you do:
Let the bloat[6] king tempt you again to bed,
Pinch wanton[7] on your cheek, call you his mouse,
And let him, for a pair of reechy[8] kisses,
Or paddling in your neck with his damned fingers,
190 Make you to ravel[9] all this matter out,
That I essentially am not in madness,
But mad in craft. 'Twere good you let him know,
For who that's but a queen, fair, sober, wise,
Would from a paddock, from a bat, a gib,[1]
195 Such dear concernings hide? Who would so do?
No, in despite of sense and secrecy,
Unpeg the basket on the house's top,
Let the birds fly, and like the famous ape,
To try conclusions, in the basket creep
200 And break your own neck down.[2]
QUEEN: Be thou assured, if words be made of breath
And breath of life, I have no life to breathe
What thou hast said to me.
HAMLET: I must to England; you know that?
QUEEN: Alack,
205 I had forgot. 'Tis so concluded on.
HAMLET: There's letters sealed, and my two school-fellows,
Whom I will trust as I will adders fanged,
They bear the mandate; they must sweep[3] my way
And marshal me to knavery. Let it work,
210 For 'tis the sport to have the enginer
Hoist with his own petar; and 't shall go hard
But I will delve[4] one yard below their mines
And blow them at the moon. O, 'tis most sweet

---

5. Dispose of.   6. Bloated.   7. Lewdly.   8. Foul.   9. Reveal.   1. Tomcat. *Paddock*:
toad.   2. Apparently a reference to a now-lost fable in which an ape, finding a basket containing
a cage of birds on a housetop, opens the cage. The birds fly away. The ape, thinking that if he were
in the basket he too could fly, enters, jumps out, and breaks his neck.   3. Prepare. *Mandate*:
command.   4. Dig.

When in one line two crafts directly meet.[5]
This man shall set me packing.   215
I'll lug the guts into the neighbor room.
Mother, good night. Indeed, this counsellor
Is now most still, most secret, and most grave,
Who was in life a foolish prating knave.
Come sir, to draw toward an end with you.   220
Good night, mother.

        [*Exit the* QUEEN. *Then exit* HAMLET *tugging* POLONIUS.]

ACT IV

SCENE 1

A room in the castle. Enter KING, QUEEN, ROSENCRANTZ *and* GUILDENSTERN.

KING: There's matter in these sighs, these profound heaves,
  You must translate[6]; 'tis fit we understand them.
  Where is your son?
QUEEN: Bestow this place on us a little while.

        [*Exeunt* ROSENCRANTZ *and* GUILDENSTERN.]

  Ah, mine own lord, what have I seen tonight!   5
KING: What, Gertrude? How does Hamlet?
QUEEN: Mad as the sea and wind when both contend
  Which is the mightier. In his lawless fit,
  Behind the arras hearing something stir,
  Whips out his rapier, cries "A rat, a rat!"   10
  And in this brainish apprehension[7] kills
  The unseen good old man.
KING: O heavy deed!
  It had been so with us had we been there.
  His liberty is full of threats to all—
  To your yourself, to us, to every one.   15
  Alas, how shall this bloody deed be answered?
  It will be laid to us, whose providence[8]
  Should have kept short, restrained, and out of haunt,[9]
  This mad young man. But so much was our love,
  We would not understand what was most fit;   20
  But, like the owner of a foul disease,
  To keep it from divulging, let it feed
  Even on the pith of life. Where is he gone?

5. The "enginer," or engineer, is a military man who is here described as being blown up by a bomb
of his own construction, "hoist with his own petar." The military figure continues in the succeeding
lines where Hamlet describes himself as digging a countermine or tunnel beneath the one Claudius
is digging to defeat Hamlet. In line 214 the two tunnels unexpectedly meet.   6. Explain.   7. Insane notion.   8. Prudence.   9. Away from court.

QUEEN: To draw apart the body he hath killed,
25   O'er whom his very madness, like some ore
     Among a mineral of metals base,
     Shows itself pure: 'a weeps for what is done.
KING: O Gertrude, come away!
     The sun no sooner shall the mountains touch
30   But we will ship him hence, and this vile deed
     We must with all our majesty and skill
     Both countenance and excuse. Ho, Guildenstern!

[*Enter* ROSENCRANTZ *and* GUILDENSTERN.]

     Friends both, go join you with some further aid.
     Hamlet in madness hath Polonius slain,
35   And from his mother's closet hath he dragged him.
     Go seek him out; speak fair, and bring the body
     Into the chapel. I pray you haste in this.
                         [*Exeunt* ROSENCRANTZ *and* GUILDENSTERN.]
     Come, Gertrude, we'll call up our wisest friends
     And let them know both what we mean to do
40   And what's untimely done;
     Whose whisper o'er the world's diameter,
     As level as the cannon to his blank,[1]
     Transports his poisoned shot—may miss our name,
     And hit the woundless air. O, come away!
45   My soul is full of discord and dismay.   [*Exeunt.*]

SCENE 2

A passageway. Enter HAMLET.

HAMLET: Safely stowed.—But soft, what noise? Who calls on Hamlet?
     O, here they come.

[*Enter* ROSENCRANTZ, GUILDENSTERN, *and* OTHERS.]

ROSENCRANTZ: What have you done, my lord, with the dead body?
HAMLET: Compounded it with dust, whereto 'tis kin.
5 ROSENCRANTZ: Tell us where 'tis, that we may take it thence
     And bear it to the chapel.
HAMLET: Do not believe it.
ROSENCRANTZ: Believe what?
HAMLET: That I can keep your counsel and not mine own. Besides, to be de-
10   manded of a sponge—what replication[2] should be made by the son of a king?
ROSENCRANTZ: Take you me for a sponge, my lord?
HAMLET: Ay, sir, that soaks up the king's countenance,[3] his rewards, his author-

1. Mark. *Level:* direct.   2. Answer. *Demanded of:* questioned by.   3. Favor.

ities. But such officers do the king best service in the end. He keeps them
like an apple in the corner of his jaw, first mouthed to be last swallowed.
When he needs what you have gleaned, it is but squeezing you and, sponge, 15
you shall be dry again.

ROSENCRANTZ: I understand you not, my lord.

HAMLET: I am glad of it. A knavish speech sleeps in a foolish ear.

ROSENCRANTZ: My lord, you must tell us where the body is, and go with us to
the king. 20

HAMLET: The body is with the king, but the king is not with the body.
The king is a thing—

GUILDENSTERN: A thing, my lord!

HAMLET: Of nothing. Bring me to him. Hide fox, and all after.[4]   [*Exeunt.*]

SCENE 3

A room in the castle. Enter KING.

KING: I have sent to seek him, and to find the body.
How dangerous is it that this man goes loose!
Yet must not we put the strong law on him.
He's loved of the distracted[5] multitude,
Who like not in their judgment but their eyes, 5
And where 'tis so, th' offender's scourge[6] is weighed,
But never the offence. To bear all smooth and even,
This sudden sending him away must seem
Deliberate pause.[7] Diseases desperate grown
By desperate appliance are relieved, 10
Or not at all.

[*Enter* ROSENCRANTZ, GUILDENSTERN, *and all the rest.*]

How now! what hath befall'n?

ROSENCRANTZ: Where the dead body is bestowed, my lord,
We cannot get from him.

KING: But where is he?

ROSENCRANTZ: Without, my lord; guarded, to know[8] your pleasure.

KING: Bring him before us.

ROSENCRANTZ: Ho! bring in the lord. 15

[*They enter with* HAMLET.]

KING: Now, Hamlet, where's Polonius?

HAMLET: At supper.

KING: At supper? Where?

HAMLET: Not where he eats, but where 'a is eaten. A certain convocation of
politic[9] worms are e'en at him. Your worm is your only emperor for diet. 20

4. Apparently a reference to a children's game like hide-and-seek.   5. Confused.   6. Punishment.   7. I.e., not an impulse.   8. Await.   9. Statesmanlike. *Convocation:* gathering.

We fat all creatures else to fat us, and we fat ourselves for maggots. Your fat king and your lean beggar is but variable service—two dishes, but to one table. That's the end.

KING: Alas, alas!

25 HAMLET: A man may fish with the worm that hath eat of a king, and eat of the fish that hath fed of that worm.

KING: What dost thou mean by this?

HAMLET: Nothing but to show you how a king may go a progress through the guts of a beggar.

30 KING: Where is Polonius?

HAMLET: In heaven. Send thither to see. If your messenger find him not there, seek him i' th' other place yourself. But if, indeed, you find him not within this month, you shall nose[1] him as you go up the stairs into the lobby.

KING: [To ATTENDANTS.] Go seek him there.

35 HAMLET: 'A will stay till you come.   [Exeunt ATTENDANTS.]

KING: Hamlet, this deed, for thine especial safety—
  Which we do tender, as we dearly[2] grieve
  For that which thou hast done—must send thee hence
  With fiery quickness. Therefore prepare thyself.

40 The bark is ready, and the wind at help,
  Th' associates tend, and everything is bent
  For England.

HAMLET: For England?

KING: Ay, Hamlet.

HAMLET: Good.

KING: So it is, if thou knew'st our purposes.

HAMLET: I see a cherub that sees them. But come, for England!

45   Farewell, dear mother.

KING: Thy loving father, Hamlet.

HAMLET: My mother. Father and mother is man and wife, man and wife is one flesh. So, my mother. Come, for England.   [Exit.]

KING: Follow him at foot[3]; tempt him with speed aboard.

50   Delay it not; I'll have him hence tonight.
  Away! for everything is sealed and done
  That else leans on th' affair. Pray you make haste. [Exeunt all but the KING.]
  And, England, if my love thou hold'st at aught—
  As my great power thereof may give thee sense,[4]

55   Since yet thy cicatrice[5] looks raw and red
  After the Danish sword, and thy free awe
  Pays homage to us—thou mayst not coldly set[6]
  Our sovereign process,[7] which imports at full
  By letters congruing[8] to that effect

60   The present death of Hamlet. Do it, England,

---

1. Smell.   2. Deeply. *Tender:* consider.   3. Closely.   4. Of its value.   5. Wound scar.
6. Set aside.   7. Mandate.   8. Agreeing.

For like the hectic[9] in my blood he rages,
And thou must cure me. Till I know 'tis done,
Howe'er my haps, my joys were ne'er begun.   [*Exit.*]

SCENE 4

Near Elsinore. Enter FORTINBRAS *with his army.*

FORTINBRAS: Go, captain, from me greet the Danish king.
Tell him that by his license Fortinbras
Craves the conveyance[1] of a promised march
Over his kingdom. You know the rendezvous.
If that his majesty would aught with us,   5
We shall express our duty in his eye,[2]
And let him know so.
CAPTAIN: I will do't, my lord.
FORTINBRAS: Go softly on.   [*Exeunt all but the* CAPTAIN.]

[*Enter* HAMLET, ROSENCRANTZ, GUILDENSTERN, *and* OTHERS.]

HAMLET: Good sir, whose powers are these?
CAPTAIN: They are of Norway, sir.   10
HAMLET: How purposed, sir, I pray you?
CAPTAIN: Against some part of Poland.
HAMLET: Who commands them, sir?
CAPTAIN: The nephew to old Norway, Fortinbras.
HAMLET: Goes it against the main[3] of Poland, sir,   15
Or for some frontier?
CAPTAIN: Truly to speak, and with no addition,[4]
We go to gain a little patch of ground
That hath in it no profit but the name.
To pay five ducats,[5] five, I would not farm it;   20
Nor will it yield to Norway or the Pole
A ranker rate should it be sold in fee.[6]
HAMLET: Why, then the Polack never will defend it.
CAPTAIN: Yes, it is already garrisoned.
HAMLET: Two thousand souls and twenty thousand ducats   25
Will not debate the question of this straw.
This is th' imposthume[7] of much wealth and peace,
That inward breaks, and shows no cause without
Why the man dies. I humbly thank you, sir.
CAPTAIN: God b'wi'ye, sir.   [*Exit.*]
ROSENCRANTZ: Will't please you go, my lord?   30
HAMLET: I'll be with you straight. Go a little before.   [*Exeunt all but* HAMLET.]
How all occasions do inform against me,

9. Chronic fever.   1. Escort.   2. Presence.   3. Central part.   4. Exaggeration.
5. I.e., in rent.   6. Outright. *Ranker:* higher.   7. Abscess.

And spur my dull revenge! What is a man,
If his chief good and market[8] of his time
35 Be but to sleep and feed? A beast, no more.
Sure he that made us with such large discourse,[9]
Looking before and after, gave us not
That capability and godlike reason
To fust[1] in us unused. Now, whether it be
40 Bestial oblivion, or some craven scruple
Of thinking too precisely on th' event[2]—
A thought which, quartered, hath but one part wisdom
And ever three parts coward—I do not know
Why yet I live to say "This thing's to do,"
45 Sith[3] I have cause, and will, and strength, and means,
To do't. Examples gross as earth exhort me.
Witness this army of such mass and charge,[4]
Led by a delicate and tender prince,
Whose spirit, with divine ambition puffed,
50 Makes mouths at[5] the invisible event,
Exposing what is mortal and unsure
To all that fortune, death, and danger dare,
Even for an eggshell. Rightly to be great
Is not to stir without great argument,
55 But greatly to find quarrel in a straw
When honor's at the stake. How stand I then,
That have a father killed, a mother stained,
Excitements of my reason and my blood,
And let all sleep, while to my shame I see
60 The imminent death of twenty thousand men
That for a fantasy and trick of fame
Go to their graves like beds, fight for a plot
Whereon the numbers cannot try the cause,
Which is not tomb enough and continent
65 To hide the slain?[6] O, from this time forth,
My thoughts be bloody, or be nothing worth!   [*Exit.*]

SCENE 5

A room in the castle. Enter QUEEN, HORATIO *and a* GENTLEMAN.

QUEEN: I will not speak with her.
GENTLEMAN: She is importunate, indeed distract.
    Her mood will needs to be pitied.

---

8. Occupation.   9. Ample reasoning power.   1. Grow musty.   2. Outcome.   3. Since.
4. Expense.   5. Scorns.   6. The plot of ground involved is so small that it cannot contain the
number of men involved in fighting or furnish burial space for the number of those who will die.

QUEEN: What would she have?
GENTLEMAN: She speaks much of her father, says she hears
    There's tricks i' th' world, and hems, and beats her heart,   5
    Spurns enviously at straws,[7] speaks things in doubt
    That carry but half sense. Her speech is nothing,
    Yet the unshaped use of it doth move
    The hearers to collection[8]; they yawn at it,
    And botch the words up fit to their own thoughts,   10
    Which, as her winks and nods and gestures yield them,
    Indeed would make one think there might be thought,
    Though nothing sure, yet much unhappily.
HORATIO: 'Twere good she were spoken with, for she may strew
    Dangerous conjectures in ill-breeding minds.   15
QUEEN: Let her come in.   [*Exit* GENTLEMAN.]
    [*Aside.*] To my sick soul, as sin's true nature is,
    Each toy seems prologue to some great amiss.[9]
    So full of artless jealousy is guilt,
    It spills itself in fearing to be spilt.   20

    [*Enter* OPHELIA *distracted.*]

OPHELIA: Where is the beauteous majesty of Denmark?
QUEEN: How now, Ophelia!

                [OPHELIA *sings.*]

        How should I your true love know
                From another one?
        By his cockle hat and staff,[1]   25
        And his sandal shoon.[2]

QUEEN: Alas, sweet lady, what imports this song?
OPHELIA: Say you? Nay, pray you mark.

                [*Sings.*]

        He is dead and gone, lady,
                He is dead and gone;   30
        At his head a grass-green turf,
                At his heels a stone.

    O, ho!
QUEEN: Nay, but Ophelia—
OPHELIA: Pray you mark.

                [*Sings.*]

        White his shroud as the mountain snow—

7. Takes offense at trifles.   8. An attempt to order.   9. Catastrophe. *Toy*: trifle.   1. A "cockle
hat," one decorated with a shell, indicated that the wearer had made a pilgrimage to the shrine of
St. James at Compostela in Spain. The staff also marked the carrier as a pilgrim.   2. Shoes.

[*Enter* KING.]

35   QUEEN: Alas, look here, my lord.

[OPHELIA:]

> Larded all with sweet flowers;
> Which bewept to the grave did not go
> With true-love showers.

KING: How do you, pretty lady?

40   OPHELIA: Well, God dild[3] you! They say the owl was a baker's daughter. Lord, we know what we are, but know not what we may be. God be at your table!

KING: Conceit[4] upon her father.

OPHELIA: Pray let's have no words of this, but when they ask you what it means, say you this:

[*Sings.*]

45
> Tomorrow is Saint Valentine's day,
>   All in the morning betime,
> And I a maid at your window,
>   To be your Valentine.

> Then up he rose, and donn'd his clo'es,
50
>   And dupped[5] the chamber-door,
> Let in the maid, that out a maid
>   Never departed more.

KING: Pretty Ophelia!

OPHELIA: Indeed, without an oath, I'll make an end on't.

[*Sings.*]

55
> By Gis[6] and by Saint Charity,
>   Alack, and fie for shame!
> Young men will do't, if they come to't;
>   By Cock,[7] they are to blame.

> Quoth she "before you tumbled me,
60
>   You promised me to wed."

He answers:

> "So would I'a done, by yonder sun,
>   An thou hadst not come to my bed."

KING: How long hath she been thus?

65   OPHELIA: I hope all will be well. We must be patient, but I cannot choose but weep to think they would lay him i' th' cold ground. My brother shall know of it, and so I thank you for your good counsel. Come, my coach! Good

---

3. Yield.   4. Thought.   5. Opened.   6. Jesus.   7. God.

night, ladies, good night. Sweet ladies, good night, good night.   [*Exit.*]
KING: Follow her close; give her good watch, I pray you.

[*Exeunt* HORATIO *and* GENTLEMAN.]

O, this is the poison of deep grief; it springs   70
All from her father's death, and now behold!
O Gertrude, Gertrude!
When sorrows come, they come not single spies,
But in battalions: first, her father slain;
Next, your son gone, and he most violent author   75
Of his own just remove; the people muddied,[8]
Thick and unwholesome in their thoughts and whispers
For good Polonius' death; and we have done but greenly[9]
In hugger-mugger[1] to inter him; poor Ophelia
Divided from herself and her fair judgment,   80
Without the which we are pictures, or mere beasts;
Last, and as much containing as all these,
Her brother is in secret come from France,
Feeds on his wonder, keeps himself in clouds,
And wants not buzzers to infect his ear   85
With pestilent speeches of his father's death,
Wherein necessity, of matter beggared,[2]
Will nothing stick our person to arraign[3]
In ear and ear.[4] O my dear Gertrude, this,
Like to a murd'ring piece,[5] in many places   90
Gives me superfluous death. Attend,

[*A noise within. Enter a* MESSENGER.]

Where are my Switzers[6]? Let them guard the door.
What is the matter?
MESSENGER: Save yourself, my lord.
The ocean, overpeering of his list,[7]
Eats not the flats with more impiteous[8] haste   95
Then young Laertes, in a riotous head,[9]
O'erbears your officers. The rabble call him lord,
And as the world were now but to begin,
Antiquity forgot, custom not known,
The ratifiers and props of every word,   100
They cry "Choose we, Laertes shall be king."
Caps, hands, and tongues, applaud it to the clouds,
"Laertes shall be king, Laertes king."
QUEEN: How cheerfully on the false trail they cry![1]

8. Disturbed.   9. Without judgment.   1. Haste.   2. Short on facts.   3. Accuse. *Stick:*
hesitate.   4. From both sides.   5. A weapon designed to scatter its shot.   6. Swiss guards.
7. Towering above its limits.   8. Pitiless.   9. With an armed band.   1. As if following
the scent.

[*A noise within.*]

105   O, this is counter,[2] you false Danish dogs!
KING: The doors are broke.

[*Enter* LAERTES, *with* OTHERS.]

LAERTES: Where is this king?—Sirs, stand you all without.
ALL: No, let's come in.
LAERTES: I pray you give me leave.
ALL: We will, we will.   [*Exeunt his followers.*]
110   LAERTES: I thank you. Keep[3] the door.—O thou vile king,
       Give me my father!
QUEEN: Calmly, good Laertes.
LAERTES: That drop of blood that's calm proclaims me bastard,
       Cries cuckold to my father, brands the harlot
       Even here between the chaste unsmirchéd brow
       Of my true mother.
115   KING: What is the cause, Laertes,
       That thy rebellion looks so giant-like?
       Let him go, Gertrude. Do not fear[4] our person.
       There's such divinity doth hedge a king
       That treason can but peep to[5] what it would,
120   Acts little of his will. Tell me, Laertes.
       Why thou art thus incensed. Let him go, Gertrude.
       Speak, man.
LAERTES: Where is my father?
KING: Dead.
QUEEN: But not by him.
KING: Let him demand[6] his fill.
LAERTES: How came he dead? I'll not be juggled with.
125   To hell allegiance, vows to the blackest devil,
       Conscience and grace to the profoundest pit!
       I dare damnation. To this point I stand,
       That both the worlds I give to negligence,[7]
       Let come what comes, only I'll be revenged
130   Most throughly for my father.
KING: Who shall stay you?
LAERTES: My will, not all the world's.
       And for my means, I'll husband[8] them so well
       They shall go far with little.
KING: Good Laertes,
       If you desire to know the certainty
135   Of your dear father, is't writ in your revenge

2. Backward.   3. Guard.   4. Fear for.   5. Look at over or through a barrier.   6. Question.   7. Disregard. *Both the worlds:* i.e., this and the next.   8. Manage.

That, swoopstake,[9] you will draw both friend and foe,
    Winner and loser?
LAERTES: None but his enemies.
KING: Will you know them, then?
LAERTES: To his good friends thus wide I'll ope my arms,
    And like the kind life-rend'ring pelican,[1]   140
    Repast them with my blood.
KING: Why, now you speak
    Like a good child and a true gentleman.
    That I am guiltless of your father's death,
    And am most sensibly in grief for it,
    It shall as level[2] to your judgment 'pear   145
    As day does to your eye.

[A *noise within*: "Let her come in."]

LAERTES: How now? What noise is that?

[*Enter* OPHELIA.]

O, heat dry up my brains! tears seven times salt
    Burn out the sense and virtue[3] of mine eye!
    By heaven, thy madness shall be paid with weight   150
    Till our scale turn the beam. O rose of May,
    Dear maid, kind sister, sweet Ophelia!
    O heavens! is't possible a young maid's wits
    Should be as mortal as an old man's life?
    Nature is fine[4] in love, and where 'tis fine   155
    It sends some precious instances of itself
    After the thing it loves.[5]

[OPHELIA *sings*.]
            They bore him barefac'd on the bier;
                Hey non nonny, nonny, hey nonny;
            And in his grave rain'd many a tear—   160

    Fare you well, my dove!
LAERTES: Hadst thou thy wits, and didst persuade revenge,
    It could not move thus.
OPHELIA: You must sing "A-down, a-down, and you call him a-down-a." O,
    how the wheel becomes it! It is the false steward, that stole his master's   165
    daughter.[6]

9. Sweeping the board.   1. The pelican was believed to feed her young with her own blood.
2. Plain.   3. Function. *Sense*: feeling.   4. Refined.   5. Laertes means that Ophelia, because of her love for her father, gave up her sanity as a token of grief at his death.   6. The "wheel"
refers to the "burden" or refrain of a song, in this case "A-down, a-down, and you call him a-down-
a." The ballad to which she refers was about a false steward. Others have suggested that the "wheel"
is the Wheel of Fortune, a spinning wheel to whose rhythm such a song might have been sung or a
kind of dance movement performed by Ophelia as she sings.

LAERTES: This nothing's more than matter.

OPHELIA: There's a rosemary, that's for remembrance. Pray you, love, remember. And there is pansies, that's for thoughts.

170 LAERTES: A document[7] in madness, thoughts and remembrance fitted.

OPHELIA: There's fennel for you, and columbines. There's rue for you, and here's some for me. We may call it herb of grace a Sundays. O, you must wear your rue with a difference. There's a daisy. I would give you some violets, but they withered all when my father died. They say 'a made a good end.

[*Sings.*]

175   For bonny sweet Robin is all my joy.

LAERTES: Thought and affliction, passion, hell itself,
    She turns to favor[8] and to prettiness.

[OPHELIA *sings.*]

        And will 'a not come again?
        And will 'a not come again?
180   No, no, he is dead,
            Go to thy death-bed,
        He never will come again.

        His beard was as white as snow,
        All flaxen was his poll[9];
185   He is gone, he is gone,
            And we cast away moan:
        God-a-mercy on his soul!

    And of all Christian souls, I pray God. God b'wi'you.   [*Exit.*]

LAERTES: Do you see this, O God?

190 KING: Laertes, I must commune with your grief,
    Or you deny me right. Go but apart,
    Make choice of whom your wisest friends you will,
    And they shall hear and judge 'twixt you and me.
    If by direct or by collateral[1] hand
195   They find us touched,[2] we will our kingdom give,
    Our crown, our life, and all that we call ours,
    To you in satisfaction; but if not,
    Be you content to lend your patience to us,
    And we shall jointly labor with your soul
    To give it due content.

200 LAERTES: Let this be so.
    His means of death, his obscure funeral—
    No trophy, sword, nor hatchment,[3] o'er his bones,
    No noble rite nor formal ostentation[4]—

---

7. Lesson.   8. Beauty.   9. Head.   1. Indirect.   2. By guilt.   3. Coat of arms.
4. Pomp.

Cry to be heard, as 'twere from heaven to earth,
That I must call't in question.

KING: So you shall;   205
And where th' offence is, let the great axe fall.
I pray you go with me.   [*Exeunt.*]

Scene 6

Another room in the castle. Enter HORATIO *and a* GENTLEMAN.

HORATIO: What are they that would speak with me?
GENTLEMAN: Sea-faring men, sir. They say they have letters for you.
HORATIO: Let them come in.   [*Exit* GENTLEMAN.]
   I do not know from what part of the world
   I should be greeted, if not from Lord Hamlet.   5

[*Enter* SAILORS.]

SAILOR: God bless you, sir.
HORATIO: Let him bless thee too.
SAILOR: 'A shall, sir, an't please him. There's a letter for you, sir—it came from
   th' ambassador that was bound for England—if your name be Horatio, as I
   am let to know[5] it is.   10
HORATIO: [*Reads.*] "Horatio, when thou shalt have overlooked[6] this, give these
   fellows some means[7] to the king. They have letters for him. Ere we were two
   days old at sea, a pirate of very warlike appointment[8] gave us chase. Finding
   ourselves too slow of sail, we put on a compelled valor, and in the grapple I
   boarded them. On the instant they got clear of our ship, so I alone became   15
   their prisoner. They have dealt with me like thieves of mercy, but they knew
   what they did; I am to do a good turn for them. Let the king have the letters
   I have sent, and repair thou to me with as much speed as thou wouldest fly
   death. I have words to speak in thine ear will make thee dumb; yet are they
   much too light for the bore of the matter.[9] These good fellows will bring thee   20
   where I am. Rosencrantz and Guildenstern hold their course for England. Of
   them I have much to tell thee. Farewell.
                                    He that thou knowest thine, Hamlet."
   Come, I will give you way[1] for these your letters,
   And do't the speedier that you may direct me   25
   To him from whom you brought them.   [*Exeunt.*]

5. Informed.   6. Read through.   7. Access.   8. Equipment.   9. A figure from gunnery,
referring to shot that is too small for the size of the weapons to be fired.   1. Means of delivery.

SCENE 7

Another room in the castle. Enter KING *and* LAERTES.

KING: Now must your conscience my acquittance seal,[2]
 And you must put me in your heart for friend,
 Sith you have heard, and with a knowing ear,
 That he which hath your noble father slain
5 Pursued my life.
LAERTES: It well appears. But tell me
 Why you proceeded not against these feats,
 So criminal and so capital in nature,
 As by your safety, greatness, wisdom, all things else,
 You mainly were stirred up.
KING: O, for two special reasons,
10 Which may to you, perhaps, seem much unsinewed,[3]
 But yet to me th' are strong. The queen his mother
 Lives almost by his looks, and for myself—
 My virtue or my plague, be it either which—
 She is so conjunctive[4] to my life and soul
15 That, as the star moves not but in his sphere,[5]
 I could not but by her. The other motive,
 Why to a public count[6] I might not go,
 Is the great love the general gender[7] bear him,
 Who, dipping all his faults in their affection,
20 Work like the spring that turneth wood to stone,[8]
 Convert his gyves[9] to graces; so that my arrows,
 Too slightly timbered[1] for so loud a wind,
 Would have reverted to my bow again,
 But not where I have aimed them.
25 LAERTES: And so have I a noble father lost,
 A sister driven into desp'rate terms,
 Whose worth, if praises may go back again,
 Stood challenger on mount of all the age
 For her perfections. But my revenge will come.
30 KING: Break not your sleeps for that. You must not think
 That we are made of stuff so flat and dull
 That we can let our beard be shook with danger,
 And think it pastime. You shortly shall hear more.
 I loved you father, and we love our self,
35 And that, I hope, will teach you to imagine—

2. Grant me innocent.   3. Weak.   4. Closely joined.   5. A reference to the Ptolemaic cosmology in which planets and stars were believed to revolve in crystalline spheres concentrically
about the Earth.   6. Reckoning.   7. Common people.   8. Certain English springs contain
so much lime that a lime covering will be deposited on a log placed in one of them for a length of
time.   9. Fetters.   1. Shafted.

[*Enter a* MESSENGER *with letters.*]

MESSENGER: These to your majesty; this to the queen.
KING: From Hamlet! Who brought them?
MESSENGER: Sailors, my lord, they say. I saw them not.
    They were given me by Claudio; he received them
    Of him that brought them.
KING: Laertes, you shall hear them. —   40
    Leave us.   [*Exit* MESSENGER.]
    [*Reads.*] "High and mighty, you shall know I am set naked on your king-
    dom. Tomorrow shall I beg leave to see your kingly eyes; when I shall, first
    asking your pardon thereunto, recount the occasion of my sudden and more
    strange return.   45
                Hamlet."
    What should this mean? Are all the rest come back?
    Or is it some abuse,[2] and no such thing?
LAERTES: Know you the hand?
KING: 'Tis Hamlet's character.[3] "Naked"!
    And in a postscript here, he says "alone."   50
    Can you devise[4] me?
LAERTES: I am lost in it, my lord. But let him come.
    It warms the very sickness in my heart
    That I shall live and tell him to his teeth   55
    "Thus didest thou."
KING: If it be so, Laertes —
    As how should it be so, how otherwise? —
    Will you be ruled by me?
LAERTES: Ay, my lord,
    So you will not o'errule me to a peace.
KING: To thine own peace. If he be now returned,   60
    As checking at[5] his voyage, and that he means
    No more to undertake it, I will work him
    To an exploit now ripe in my device,
    Under the which he shall not choose but fall;
    And for his death no wind of blame shall breathe   65
    But even his mother shall uncharge[6] the practice
    And call it accident.
LAERTES: My lord, I will be ruled;
    The rather if you could devise it so
    That I might be the organ.[7]
KING: It falls right.
    You have been talked of since your travel much,   70
    And that in Hamlet's hearing, for a quality

---

2. Trick.   3. Handwriting.   4. Explain it to.   5. Turning aside from.   6. Not accuse.
7. Instrument.

Wherein they say you shine. Your sum of parts
Did not together pluck such envy from him
As did that one, and that, in my regard,
Of the unworthiest siege.[8]

75   LAERTES: What part is that, my lord?
KING: A very riband in the cap of youth,
Yet needful too, for youth no less becomes
The light and careless livery that it wears
Than settled age his sables and his weeds,[9]

80   Importing health and graveness. Two months since
Here was a gentleman of Normandy.
I have seen myself, and served against, the French,
And they can[1] well on horseback, but this gallant
Had witchcraft in't. He grew unto his seat,

85   And to such wondrous doing brought his horse,
As had he been incorpsed and demi-natured
With the brave beast. So far he topped my thought
That I, in forgery[2] of shapes and tricks,
Come short of what he did.[3]

LAERTES: A Norman was't?
90   KING: A Norman.
LAERTES: Upon my life, Lamord.
KING: The very same.
LAERTES: I know him well. He is the brooch indeed
And gem of all the nation.
KING: He made confession[4] of you,

95   And gave you such a masterly report
For art and exercise in your defence,[5]
And for your rapier most especial,
That he cried out 'twould be a sight indeed
If one could match you. The scrimers[6] of their nation

100   He swore had neither motion, guard, nor eye,
If you opposed them. Sir, this report of his
Did Hamlet so envenom with his envy
That he could nothing do but wish and beg
Your sudden coming o'er, to play with you.
Now out of this—

105   LAERTES: What out of this, my lord?
KING: Laertes, was your father dear to you?

---

8. Rank.   9. Dignified clothing.   1. Perform.   2. Imagination.   3. The gentleman referred to was so skilled in horsemanship that he seemed to share one body with the horse, "incorpsed." The king further extends the compliment by saying that he appeared like the mythical centaur, a creature who was man from the waist up and horse from the waist down, therefore "deminatured."   4. Gave a report.   5. Skill in fencing.   6. Fencers.

Or are you like the painting of a sorrow,
A face without a heart?
LAERTES: Why ask you this?
KING: Not that I think you did not love your father,
But that I know love is begun by time,   110
And that I see in passages of proof,[7]
Time qualifies the spark and fire of it.
There lives within the very flame of love
A kind of wick or snuff that will abate it,
And nothing is at a like goodness still,   115
For goodness, growing to a plurisy,[8]
Dies in his own too much.[9] That we would do,
We should do when we would; for this "would" changes,
And hath abatements and delays as many
As there are tongues, are hands, are accidents,   120
And then this "should" is like a spendthrift's sigh
That hurts by easing. But to the quick of th' ulcer—
Hamlet comes back; what would you undertake
To show yourself in deed your father's son
More than in words?
LAERTES: To cut his throat i' th' church.   125
KING: No place indeed should murder sanctuarize[1];
Revenge should have no bounds. But, good Laertes,
Will you do this? Keep close within your chamber.
Hamlet returned shall know you are come home.
We'll put on those shall praise your excellence,   130
And set a double varnish[2] on the fame
The Frenchman gave you, bring you in fine[3] together,
And wager on your heads. He, being remiss,[4]
Most generous, and free from all contriving,
Will not peruse[5] the foils, so that with ease,   135
Or with a little shuffling, you may choose
A sword unbated,[6] and in a pass of practice
Requite him for your father.
LAERTES: I will do't,
And for that purpose I'll anoint my sword.
I bought an unction of a mountebank   140
So mortal that but dip a knife in it,
Where it draws blood no cataplasm[7] so rare,
Collected from all simples[8] that have virtue
Under the moon, can save the thing from death
That is but scratched withal. I'll touch my point   145

---

7. Tests of experience.   8. Fullness.   9. Excess.   1. Provide sanctuary for murder.
2. Gloss.   3. In short.   4. Careless.   5. Examine.   6. Not blunted.   7. Poultice.
8. Herbs.

1386 ▾ William Shakespeare

> With this contagion, that if I gall[9] him slightly,
> It may be death.

KING: Let's further think of this,
> Weigh what convenience both of time and means
> May fit us to our shape. If this should fail,
150 And that our drift look[1] through our bad performance,
> 'Twere better not assayed. Therefore this project
> Should have a back or second that might hold
> If this did blast in proof.[2] Soft, let me see.
> We'll make a solemn wager on your cunnings—
155 I ha't.
> When in your motion you are hot and dry—
> As make your bouts more violent to that end—
> And that he calls for drink, I'll have preferred him
> A chalice for the nonce, whereon but sipping,
160 If he by chance escape your venomed stuck,[3]
> Our purpose may hold there.—But stay, what noise?

[*Enter* QUEEN.]

QUEEN: One woe doth tread upon another's heel,
> So fast they follow. Your sister's drowned, Laertes.
LAERTES: Drowned? O, where?
165 QUEEN: There is a willow grows aslant the brook
> That shows his hoar leaves in the glassy stream.
> Therewith fantastic garlands did she make
> Of crowflowers, nettles, daisies, and long purples
> That liberal shepherds give a grosser[4] name,
170 But our cold[5] maids do dead men's fingers call them.
> There on the pendent boughs her coronet weeds
> Clamb'ring to hang, an envious[6] sliver broke,
> When down her weedy trophies and herself
> Fell in the weeping brook. Her clothes spread wide,
175 And mermaid-like awhile they bore her up,
> Which time she chanted snatches of old tunes,
> As one incapable[7] of her own distress,
> Or like a creature native and indued[8]
> Unto that element. but long it could not be
180 Till that her garments, heavy with their drink,
> Pulled the poor wretch from her melodious lay
> To muddy death.
LAERTES: Alas, then she is drowned?
QUEEN: Drowned, drowned.
LAERTES: Too much of water hast thou, poor Ophelia,

---

9. Scratch.   1. Intent become obvious.   2. Fail when tried.   3. Thrust.   4. Coarser.
Liberal: vulgar.   5. Chaste.   6. Malicious.   7. Unaware.   8. Habituated.

And therefore I forbid my tears; but yet 185
It is our trick; nature her custom holds,
   Let shame say what it will. When these are gone,
The woman will be out. Adieu, my lord.
I have a speech o' fire that fain would blaze
But that this folly drowns it.   *[Exit.]*

KING: Let's follow, Gertrude. 190
   How much I had to do to calm his rage!
   Now fear I this will give it start again;
   Therefore let's follow.   *[Exeunt.]*

ACT V

SCENE 1

A churchyard. Enter two CLOWNS.[9]

CLOWN: Is she to be buried in Christian burial when she wilfully seeks her own
   salvation?
OTHER: I tell thee she is. Therefore make her grave straight. The crowner hath
   sat on her,[1] and finds it Christian burial.
CLOWN: How can that be, unless she drowned herself in her own defence? 5
OTHER: Why, 'tis found so.
CLOWN: It must be "se offendendo"[2]; it cannot be else. For here lies the point:
   if I drown myself wittingly, it argues an act, and an act hath three branches—
   it is to act, to do, to perform; argal,[3] she drowned herself wittingly.
OTHER: Nay, but hear you, Goodman Delver. 10
CLOWN: Give me leave. Here lies the water; good. Here stands the man; good.
   If the man go to this water and drown himself, it is, will he, nill he, he
   goes—mark you that. But if the water come to him and drown him, he
   drowns not himself. Argal, he that is not guilty of his own death shortens not
   his own life. 15
OTHER: But is this law?
CLOWN: Ay, marry, is't; crowner's quest[4] law.
OTHER: Will you ha' the truth on't? If this had not been a gentle woman, she
   should have been buried out o' Christian burial.
CLOWN: Why, there thou say'st. And the more pity that great folk should have 20
   count'nance[5] in this world to drown or hang themselves more than their
   even-Christen.[6] Come, my spade. There is no ancient gentlemen but
   gard'ners, ditchers, and grave-makers. They hold up Adam's profession.
OTHER: Was he a gentleman?
CLOWN: 'A was the first that ever bore arms. 25
OTHER: Why, he had none.

9. Rustics.   1. Held an inquest. *Crowner:* coroner.   2. An error for *se defendendo,* in self-
defense.   3. Therefore.   4. Inquest.   5. Approval.   6. Fellow Christians.

CLOWN: What, art a heathen? How dost thou understand the Scripture? The
Scripture says Adam digged. Could he dig without arms? I'll put another
question to thee. If thou answerest me not to the purpose, confess thyself—

30 OTHER: Go to.

CLOWN: What is he that builds stronger than either the mason, the shipwright,
or the carpenter?

OTHER: The gallows-maker, for that frame outlives a thousand tenants.

CLOWN: I like thy wit well, in good faith. The gallows does well. But how does
35   it well? It does well to those that do ill. Now thou dost ill to say the gallows is
built stronger than the church. Argal, the gallows may do well to thee. To't
again,[7] come.

OTHER: Who builds stronger than a mason, a shipwright, or a carpenter?

CLOWN: Ay tell me that, and unyoke.[8]

40 OTHER: Marry, now I can tell.

CLOWN: To't.

OTHER: Mass, I cannot tell.

CLOWN: Cudgel thy brains no more about it, for your dull ass will not mend his
pace with beating. And when you are asked this question next, say "a grave
45   maker." The houses he makes lasts till doomsday. Go, get thee in, and fetch
me a stoup[9] of liquor.   [Exit OTHER CLOWN.]

[Enter HAMLET and HORATIO as CLOWN digs and sings.]

    In youth, when I did love, did love,
      Methought it was very sweet,
    To contract the time for-a my behove,[1]
50   O, methought there-a was nothing-a meet.[2]

HAMLET: Has this fellow no feeling of his business, that 'a sings in grave-making?

HORATIO: Custom hath made it in him a property of easiness.

HAMLET: 'Tis e'en so. The hand of little employment hath the daintier sense.

[CLOWN sings.]

    But age, with his stealing steps,
      Hath clawed me in his clutch,
55   And hath shipped me into the land,
      As if I had never been such.

[Throws up a skull.]

HAMLET: That skull had a tongue in it, and could sing once. How the knave
jowls[3] it to the ground, as if 'twere Cain's jawbone, that did the first murder!
60   This might be the pate of a politician, which this ass now o'erreaches[4]; one
that would circumvent God, might it not?

7. Guess again.   8. Finish the matter.   9. Mug.   1. Advantage. *Contract:* shorten.
2. The gravedigger's song is a free version of "The aged lover renounceth love" by Thomas, Lord
Vaux, published in *Tottel's Miscellany,* 1557.   3. Hurls.   4. Gets the better of.

HORATIO: It might, my lord.

HAMLET: Or of a courtier, which could say, "Good morrow, sweet lord! How does thou, sweet lord?" This might be my Lord Such-a-one, that praised my Lord Such-a-one's horse, when 'a meant to beg it, might it not? 65

HORATIO: Ay, my lord.

HAMLET: Why, e'en so, and now my Lady Worm's, chapless,[5] and knock'd abut the mazzard[6] with a sexton's spade. Here's fine revolution,[7] an we had the trick to see't. Did these bones cost no more the breeding but to play at loggets with them[8]? Mine ache to think on't. 70

[CLOWN sings.]

A pick-axe and a spade, a spade,
    For and a shrouding sheet:
O, a pit of clay for to be made
    For such a guest is meet.

[Throws up another skull.]

HAMLET: There's another. Why may not that be the skull of a lawyer? Where be 75
his quiddities now, his quillets, his cases, his tenures, and his tricks? Why
does he suffer this mad knave now to knock him about the sconce[9] with a
dirty shovel, and will not tell him of his action of battery? Hum! This fellow
might be in's time a great buyer of land, with his statutes, his recognizances,
his fines, his double vouchers, his recoveries. Is this the fine[1] of his fines, 80
and the recovery of his recoveries, to have his fine pate full of fine dirt? Will
his vouchers vouch him no more of his purchases, and double ones too, than
the length and breadth of a pair of indentures[2]? The very conveyances of his
lands will scarcely lie in this box, and must th' inheritor himself have no
more, ha?[3] 85

HORATIO: Not a jot more, my lord.

HAMLET: Is not parchment made of sheepskins?

HORATIO: Ay, my lord, and of calves' skins too.

HAMLET: They are sheep and calves which seek out assurance in that. I will
speak to this fellow. Whose grave's this, sirrah? 90

CLOWN: Mine, sir.

[Sings.]

O, a pit of clay for to be made—

HAMLET: I think it be thine indeed, for thou liest in't.

CLOWN: You lie out on't, sir, and therefore 'tis not yours. For my part, I do not
lie in't, yet it is mine. 95

HAMLET: Thou dost lie in't, to be in't and say it is thine. 'Tis for the dead, not
for the quick[4]; therefore thou liest.

---

5. Lacking a lower jaw. 6. Head. 7. Skill. 8. "Loggets" were small pieces of wood
thrown as part of a game. 9. Head. 1. End. 2. Contracts. 3. In this speech Hamlet
reels off a list of legal terms relating to property transactions. 4. Living.

CLOWN: 'Tis a quick lie, sir; 'twill away again from me to you.

HAMLET: What man dost thou dig it for?

100 CLOWN: For no man, sir.

HAMLET: What woman, then?

CLOWN: For none neither.

HAMLET: Who is to be buried in't?

CLOWN: One that was a woman, sir; but, rest her soul, she's dead.

105 HAMLET: How absolute the knave is! We must speak by the card,[5] or equivocation will undo us. By the Lord, Horatio, this three years I have took note of it, the age is grown so picked[6] that the toe of the peasant comes so near the heel of the courtier, he galls his kibe.[7] How long hast thou been a grave-maker?

CLOWN: Of all the days i' th' year, I came to't that day that our last King Hamlet

110 overcame Fortinbras.

HAMLET: How long is that since?

CLOWN: Cannot you tell that? Every fool can tell that. It was that very day that young Hamlet was born—he that is mad, and sent into England.

HAMLET: Ay, marry, why was he sent into England?

115 CLOWN: Why, because 'a was mad. 'A shall recover his wits there; or, if 'a do not, 'tis no great matter there.

HAMLET: Why?

CLOWN: 'Twill not be seen in him there. There the men are as mad as he.

HAMLET: How came he mad?

120 CLOWN: Very strangely, they say.

HAMLET: How strangely?

CLOWN: Faith, e'en with losing his wits.

HAMLET: Upon what ground?

CLOWN: Why, here in Denmark. I have been sexton here, man and boy, thirty

125 years.

HAMLET: How long will a man lie i' th' earth ere he rot?

CLOWN: Faith, if 'a be not rotten before 'a die—as we have many pocky[8] corses now-a-days that will scarce hold the laying in—'a will last you some eight

130 year or nine year. A tanner will last you nine year.

HAMLET: Why he more than another?

CLOWN: Why, sir, his hide is so tanned with his trade that 'a will keep out water a great while; and your water is a sore decayer of your whoreson dead body. Here's a skull now hath lien[9] you i' th' earth three and twenty years.

HAMLET: Whose was it?

135 CLOWN: A whoreson mad fellow's it was. Whose do you think it was?

HAMLET: Nay, I know not.

CLOWN: A pestilence on him for a mad rogue! 'A poured a flagon of Rhenish on my head once. This same skull, sir, was, sir, Yorick's skull, the king's jester.

HAMLET: [Takes the skull.] This?

140 CLOWN: E'en that.

5. Exactly. *Absolute:* precise.   6. Refined.   7. Rubs a blister on his heel.   8. Corrupted by syphilis   9. Lain. *Whoreson:* bastard (not literally).

HAMLET: Alas, poor Yorick! I knew him, Horatio—a fellow of infinite jest, of most excellent fancy. He hath bore me on his back a thousand times, and now how abhorred in my imagination it is! My gorge[1] rises at it. Here hung those lips that I have kissed I know not how oft. Where be your gibes now, your gambols, your songs, your flashes of merriment that were wont to set the table on a roar? Not one now to mock your own grinning? Quite chap-fall'n[2]? Now get you to my lady's chamber, and tell her, let her paint an inch thick, to this favor[3] she must come. Make her laugh at that. Prithee, Horatio, tell me one thing. 145

HORATIO: What's that, my lord? 150

HAMLET: Dost thou think Alexander looked o' this fashion i' th' earth?

HORATIO: E'en so.

HAMLET: And smelt so? Pah! *[Throws down the skull.]*

HORATIO: E'en so, my lord.

HAMLET: To what base uses we may return, Horatio! Why may not imagination trace the noble dust of Alexander till 'a find it stopping a bung-hole? 155

HORATIO: 'Twere to consider too curiously[4] to consider so.

HAMLET: No, faith, not a jot, but to follow him thither with modesty[5] enough, and likelihood to lead it. Alexander died, Alexander was buried, Alexander returneth to dust; the dust is earth; of earth we make loam; and why of that loam whereto he was converted might they not stop a beerbarrel? 160

> Imperious Cæsar, dead and turned to clay,
> Might stop a hole to keep the wind away.
> O, that that earth which kept the world in awe
> Should patch a wall t'expel the winter's flaw[6]! 165

But soft, but soft awhile! Here comes the king,
The queen, the courtiers.

[Enter KING, QUEEN, LAERTES, and the Corse with a PRIEST and LORDS attendant.]

       Who is this they follow?
And with such maiméd[7] rites? This doth betoken
The corse they follow did with desperate hand
Fordo it own life. 'Twas of some estate.[8] 170
Couch[9] we awhile and mark.   *[Retires with HORATIO.]*

LAERTES: What ceremony else[1]?

HAMLET: That is Laertes, a very noble youth. Mark.

LAERTES: What ceremony else?

PRIEST: Here obsequies have been as far enlarged[2] 175
As we have warranty. Her death was doubtful,
And but that great command o'ersways the order,[3]

---

1. Throat.   2. Lacking a lower jaw.   3. Appearance.   4. Precisely.   5. Moderation.
6. Gusty wind.   7. Cut short.   8. Rank. *Fordo:* destroy.   9. Conceal ourselves.   1. More.
2. Extended.   3. Usual rules.

She should in ground unsanctified been lodged
Till the last trumpet. For charitable prayers,
180 Shards, flints, and pebbles, should be thrown on her.
Yet here she is allowed her virgin crants,[4]
Her maiden strewments,[5] and the bringing home
Of bell and burial.
LAERTES: Must there no more be done?
PRIEST: No more be done.
185 We should profane the service of the dead
To sing a requiem and such rest to her
As to peace-parted souls.
LAERTES: Lay her i' th' earth,
And from her fair and unpolluted flesh
May violets spring! I tell thee, churlish priest,
190 A minist'ring angel shall my sister be
When thou liest howling.[6]
HAMLET: What, the fair Ophelia!
QUEEN: Sweets to the sweet. Farewell! [Scatters flowers.]
I hoped thou shouldst have been my Hamlet's wife.
I thought thy bride-bed to have decked, sweet maid,
And not have strewed thy grave.
195 LAERTES: O, treble woe
Fall ten times treble on that curséd head
Whose wicked deed thy most ingenious sense[7]
Deprived thee of! Hold off the earth awhile,
Till I have caught her once more in mine arms. [Leaps into the grave.]
200 Now pile your dust upon the quick and dead,
Till of this flat a mountain you have made
T' o'er-top old Pelion or the skyish head
Of blue Olympus.[8]
HAMLET: [Coming forward.] What is he whose grief
205 Bears such an emphasis, whose phrase of sorrow
Conjures[9] the wand'ring stars, and makes them stand
Like wonder-wounded hearers? This is I,
Hamlet the Dane.

[HAMLET leaps into the grave and they grapple.]

LAERTES: The devil take thy soul!
HAMLET: Thou pray'st not well.

---

4. Wreaths. 5. Flowers strewn on the grave. 6. In Hell. 7. Lively mind. 8. The ri-
valry between Laertes and Hamlet in this scene extends even to their rhetoric. Pelion and Olympus,
mentioned here by Laertes, and Ossa, mentioned below by Hamlet, are Greek mountains noted in
mythology for their height. Olympus was the reputed home of the gods, and the other two were
piled one on top of the other by the Giants in an attempt to reach the top of Olympus and overthrow
the gods. 9. Casts a spell on.

I prithee take thy fingers from my throat,   210
For though I am not splenitive[1] and rash,
Yet have I in me something dangerous,
Which let thy wisdom fear. Hold off thy hand.
KING: Pluck them asunder.
QUEEN: Hamlet! Hamlet!   215
ALL: Gentlemen!
HORATIO: Good my lord, be quiet.

[*The* ATTENDANTS *part them, and they come out of the grave.*]

HAMLET: Why, I will fight with him upon this theme
   Until my eyelids will no longer wag.[2]
QUEEN: O my son, what theme?   220
HAMLET: I loved Ophelia. Forty thousand brothers
   Could not with all their quantity of love
   Make up my sum. What wilt thou do for her?
KING: O, he is mad, Laertes.
QUEEN: For love of God, forbear[3] him.   225
HAMLET: 'Swounds, show me what th'owt do.
   Woo't[4] weep, woo't fight, woo't fast, woo't tear thyself,
   Woo't drink up eisel,[5] eat a crocodile?
   I'll do't. Dost come here to whine?
   To outface[6] me with leaping in her grave?   230
   Be buried quick with her, and so will I.
   And if thou prate of mountains, let them throw
   Millions of acres on us, till our ground,
   Singeing his pate against the burning zone,[7]
   Make Ossa like a wart! Nay, an thou'lt mouth,   235
   I'll rant as well as thou.
QUEEN: This is mere madness;
   And thus awhile the fit will work on him.
   Anon, as patient as the female dove
   When that her golden couplets[8] are disclosed,
   His silence will sit drooping.
HAMLET: Hear you, sir.   240
   What is the reason that you use me thus?
   I loved you ever. But it is no matter.
   Let Hercules himself do what he may,
   The cat will mew, and dog will have his day.
KING: I pray thee, good Horatio, wait upon[9] him.   245

[*Exeunt* HAMLET *and* HORATIO.]

---

1. Hot-tempered.   2. Move.   3. Bear with.   4. Will you.   5. Vinegar.   6. Get the
best of.   7. Sky in the torrid zone.   8. Pair of eggs.   9. Attend.

[*To* LAERTES.] Strengthen your patience in our last night's speech.
We'll put the matter to the present push.[1]—
Good Gertrude, set some watch over your son.—
This grave shall have a living monument.
250　　An hour of quiet shortly shall we see;
Till then in patience our proceeding be.　　　　　[*Exeunt.*]

SCENE 2

A hall or public room. Enter HAMLET *and* HORATIO.

HAMLET: So much for this, sir; now shall you see the other.
　　You do remember all the circumstance?
HORATIO: Remember it, my lord!
HAMLET: Sir, in my heart there was a kind of fighting
5　　That would not let me sleep. Methought I lay
　　Worse than the mutines in the bilboes.[2] Rashly,
　　And praised be rashness for it—let us know,
　　Our indiscretion sometime serves us well,
　　When our deep plots do pall; and that should learn[3] us
10　　There's a divinity that shapes our ends,
　　Rough-hew them how we will—
HORATIO:　　　　　　　　　　That is most certain.
HAMLET: Up from my cabin,
　　My sea-gown scarfed[4] about me, in the dark
　　Groped I to find out them, had my desire,
15　　Fingered their packet, and in fine[5] withdrew
　　To mine own room again, making so bold,
　　My fears forgetting manners, to unseal
　　Their grand commission; where I found, Horatio—
　　Ah, royal knavery!—an exact[6] command,
20　　Larded[7] with many several sorts of reasons,
　　Importing Denmark's health, and England's too,
　　With, ho! such bugs and goblins in my life,[8]
　　That on the supervise,[9] no leisure bated,
　　No, not to stay the grinding of the axe,
　　My head should be struck off.
25　HORATIO:　　　　　　　　　　Is't possible?
HAMLET: Here's the commission; read it at more leisure.
　　But wilt thou hear now how I did proceed?
HORATIO: I beseech you.
HAMLET: Being thus benetted[1] round with villainies,

---

1. Immediate trial.　　　2. Stocks. *Mutines:* mutineers.　　　3. Teach.　　　4. Wrapped.
5. Quickly. *Fingered:* stole.　　6. Precisely stated.　　7. Garnished.　　8. Such dangers if I remained alive.　　9. As soon as the commission was read.　　1. Caught in a net.

Or I could make a prologue to my brains,   30
They had begun the play. I sat me down,
Devised a new commission, wrote it fair.[2]
I once did hold it, as our statists[3] do,
A baseness to write fair, and labored much
How to forget that learning; but sir, now   35
It did me yeoman's service. Wilt thou know
Th' effect[4] of what I wrote?
HORATIO: Ay, good my lord.
HAMLET: An earnest conjuration from the king,
As England was his faithful tributary,[5]
As love between them like the palm might flourish,   40
As peace should still her wheaten garland wear
And stand a comma 'tween their amities[6]
And many such like as's of great charge,[7]
That on the view and knowing of these contents,
Without debatement[8] further more or less,   45
He should those bearers put to sudden death,
Not shriving-time allowed.[9]
HORATIO: How was this sealed?
HAMLET: Why, even in that was heaven ordinant,[1]
I had my father's signet in my purse,
Which was the model of that Danish seal,   50
Folded the writ up in the form of th' other,
Subscribed it, gave't th' impression,[2] placed it safely,
The changeling[3] never known. Now, the next day
Was our sea-fight, and what to this was sequent[4]
Thou knowest already.   55
HORATIO: So Guildenstern and Rosencrantz go to't.
HAMLET: Why, man, they did make love to this employment.
They are not near my conscience; their defeat[5]
Does by their own insinuation grow.
'Tis dangerous when the baser nature comes   60
Between the pass and fell[6] incensèd points
Of mighty opposites.
HORATIO: Why, what a king is this!
HAMLET: Does it not, think thee, stand me now upon—
He that hath killed my king and whored my mother,
Popped in between th' election and my hopes,   65
Thrown out his angle[7] for my proper life,
And with such coz'nage[8]—is't not perfect conscience
To quit[9] him with this arm? And is't not be be damned

2. Legibly. *Devised:* made.   3. Politicians.   4. Contents.   5. Vassal.   6. Link friendships.   7. Import.   8. Consideration.   9. Without time for confession.   1. Operative.
2. Of the seal.   3. Alteration.   4. Followed.   5. Death. *Are not near:* do not touch.
6. Cruel. *Pass:* thrust.   7. Fishhook.   8. Trickery.   9. Repay.

To let this canker of our nature come
70   In further evil?
HORATIO: It must be shortly known to him from England
  What is the issue[1] of the business there.
HAMLET: It will be short[2]; the interim is mine.
  And a man's life's no more than to say "one."
75   But I am very sorry, good Horatio,
  That to Laertes I forgot myself;
  For by the image of my cause I see
  The portraiture of his. I'll court his favors.
  But sure the bravery[3] of his grief did put me
  Into a tow'ring passion.
80 HORATIO: Peace; who comes here?

  [*Enter* OSRIC.]

OSRIC: Your lordship is right welcome back to Denmark.
HAMLET: I humbly thank you, sir. [*Aside to* HORATIO.] Dost know this water-fly?
HORATIO: [*Aside to* HAMLET.] No, my good lord.
HAMLET: [*Aside to* HORATIO.] Thy state is the more gracious, for 'tis a vice to
85   know him. He hath much land, and fertile. Let a beast be lord of beasts, and
  his crib shall stand at the king's mess. 'Tis a chough,[4] but as I say, spacious
  in the possession of dirt.
OSRIC: Sweet lord, if your lordship were at leisure, I should impart a thing to
  you from his majesty.
90 HAMLET: I will receive it, sir, with all diligence of spirit. Put your bonnet to his
  right use. 'Tis for the head.
OSRIC: I thank your lordship, it is very hot.
HAMLET: No, believe me, 'tis very cold; the wind is northerly.
OSRIC: It is indifferent[5] cold, my lord, indeed.
95 HAMLET: But yet methinks it is very sultry and hot for my complexion.[6]
OSRIC: Exceedingly, my lord; it is very sultry, as 'twere—I cannot tell how. My
  lord, his majesty bade me signify to you that 'a has laid a great wager on your
  head. Sir, this is the matter—
HAMLET: I beseech you, remember.   [*Moves him to put on his hat.*]
100 OSRIC: Nay, good my lord; for my ease, in good faith. Sir, here is newly come to
  court Laertes; believe me, an absolute[7] gentleman, full of most excellent
  differences,[8] of very soft society and great showing.[9] Indeed, to speak feelingly of him, he is the card or calendar of gentry, for you shall find in him
  the continent[1] of what part a gentleman would see.
105 HAMLET: Sir, his definement[2] suffers no perdition in you, though I know to
  divide him inventorially would dozy[3] th' arithmetic of memory, and yet but
  yaw[4] neither in respect of his quick sail. But in the verity of extolment, I take

1. Outcome.   2. Soon.   3. Exaggerated display.   4. Jackdaw.   5. Moderately.
6. Temperament.   7. Perfect.   8. Qualities.   9. Good manners.   1. Sum total. *Calendar:* measure.   2. Description.   3. Daze. *Divide him inventorially*: examine bit by bit.
4. Steer wildly.

him to be a soul of great article,[5] and his infusion[6] of such dearth and rareness as, to make true diction of him, his semblage[7] is his mirror, and who else would trace him, his umbrage,[8] nothing more. 110

OSRIC: Your lordship speaks most infallibly of him.

HAMLET: The concernancy,[9] sir? Why do we wrap the gentleman in our more rawer breath[1]?

OSRIC: Sir?

HORATIO: Is't not possible to understand in another tongue? You will to't, sir, 115 really.

HAMLET: What imports the nomination[2] of this gentleman?

OSRIC: Of Laertes?

HORATIO: [Aside.] His purse is empty already. All's golden words are spent.

HAMLET: Of him, sir. 120

OSRIC: I know you are not ignorant—

HAMLET: I would you did, sir; yet, in faith, if you did, it would not much approve me. Well, sir.

OSRIC: You are not ignorant of what excellence Laertes is—

HAMLET: I dare not confess that, lest I should compare[3] with him in excellence; 125 but to know a man well were to know himself.

OSRIC: I mean, sir, for his weapon; but in the imputation[4] laid on him by them, in his meed he's unfellowed.[5]

HAMLET: What's his weapon?

OSRIC: Rapier and dagger. 130

HAMLET: That's two of his weapons—but well.

OSRIC: The king, sir, hath wagered with him six Barbary horses, against the which he has impawned,[6] as I take it, six French rapiers and poniards, with their assigns,[7] as girdle, hangers, and so. Three of the carriages, in faith, are very dear to fancy,[8] very responsive to the hilts, most delicate carriages, and 135 of very liberal conceit.[9]

HAMLET: What call you the carriages?

HORATIO: [Aside to HAMLET.] I knew you must be edified by the margent[1] ere you had done.

OSRIC: The carriages, sir, are the hangers. 140

HAMLET: The phrase would be more germane to the matter if we could carry a cannon by our sides. I would it might be hangers till then. But on! Six Barbary horses against six French swords, their assigns, and three liberal conceited carriages; that's the French bet against the Danish. Why is this all impawned, as you call it? 145

OSRIC: The king, sir, hath laid, sir, that in a dozen passes between yourself and him he shall not exceed you three hits; he hath laid on twelve for nine, and it

---

5. Scope.   6. Nature.   7. Rival. *Diction:* telling.   8. Shadow. *Trace:* keep pace with.
9. Meaning.   1. Cruder words.   2. Naming.   3. I.e., compare myself.   4. Reputation.
5. Unequaled in his excellence.   6. Staked.   7. Appurtenances.   8. Finely designed.
9. Elegant design. *Delicate:* well adjusted.   1. Marginal gloss.

would come to immediate trial if your lordship would vouchsafe the answer.

HAMLET: How if I answer no?

150 OSRIC: I mean, my lord, the opposition of your person in trial.

HAMLET: Sir, I will walk here in the hall. If it please his majesty, it is the breathing time[2] of day with me. Let the foils be brought, the gentleman willing, and the king hold his purpose; I will win for him an I can. If not, I will gain nothing but my shame and the odd hits.

155 OSRIC: Shall I deliver you so?

HAMLET: To this effect, sir, after what flourish your nature will.

OSRIC: I commend my duty to your lordship.

HAMLET: Yours, yours. [*Exit* OSRIC.] He does well to commend it himself; there are no tongues else for's turn.

160 HORATIO: This lapwing runs away with the shell on his head.[3]

HAMLET: 'A did comply, sir, with his dug[4] before 'a sucked it. Thus has he, and many more of the same bevy that I know the drossy age dotes on, only got the tune of the time; and out of an habit of encounter, a king of yesty[5] collection which carries them through and through the most fanned and

165 winnowed opinions; and do but blow them to their trial, the bubbles are out.

[*Enter a* LORD.]

LORD: My lord, his majesty commended him to you by young Osric, who brings back to him that you attend[6] him in the hall. He sends to know if your pleasure hold to play with Laertes, or that you will take longer time.

HAMLET: I am constant to my purposes; they follow the king's pleasure. If his
170 fitness speaks, mine is ready; now or whensoever, provided I be so able as now.

LORD: The king and queen and all are coming down.

HAMLET: In happy time.

LORD: The queen desires you to use some gentle entertainment[7] to Laertes
175 before you fall to play.

HAMLET: She well instructs me. [*Exit* LORD.]

HORATIO: You will lose this wager, my lord.

HAMLET: I do not think so. Since he went into France I have been in continual practice. I shall win at the odds. But thou wouldst not think how ill[8] all's
180 here about my heart. But it's no matter.

HORATIO: Nay, good my lord—

HAMLET: It is but foolery, but it is such a kind of gaingiving[9] as would perhaps trouble a woman.

HORATIO: If your mind dislike anything, obey it. I will forestall their repair[1]
185 hither, and say you are not fit.

---

2. Time for exercise.   3. The lapwing was thought to be so precocious that it could run immediately after being hatched, even, as here, with bits of the shell still on its head.   4. Mother's breast. *Comply:* deal formally.   5. Yeasty.   6. Await.   7. Cordiality.   8. Uneasy.   9. Misgiving.   1. Coming.

HAMLET: Not a whit, we defy augury. There is special providence in the fall of a
sparrow. If it be now, 'tis not to come; if it be not to come, it will be now; if
it be not now, yet it will come. The readiness is all. Since no man of aught
he leaves knows, what is't to leave betimes? Let be.

[A *table prepared. Enter* TRUMPETS, DRUMS, *and* OFFICERS *with cushions*;
KING, QUEEN, OSRIC *and* ATTENDANTS *with foils, daggers, and* LAERTES.]

KING: Come, Hamlet, come and take this hand from me.   190

[*The* KING *puts* LAERTES' *hand into* HAMLET'*s*.]

HAMLET: Give me your pardon, sir. I have done you wrong,
But pardon 't as you are a gentleman.
This presence[2] knows, and you must needs have heard,
How I am punished with a sore distraction.
What I have done   195
That might your nature, honor, and exception,[3]
Roughly awake, I here proclaim was madness.
Was 't Hamlet wronged Laertes? Never Hamlet.
If Hamlet from himself be ta'en away,
And when he's not himself does wrong Laertes,   200
Then Hamlet does it not, Hamlet denies it.
Who does it then? His madness. If't be so,
Hamlet is of the faction that is wronged;
His madness is poor Hamlet's enemy.
Sir, in this audience,   205
Let my disclaiming from[4] a purposed evil
Free[5] me so far in your most generous thoughts
That I have shot my arrow o'er the house
And hurt my brother.
LAERTES: I am satisfied in nature,
Whose motive in this case should stir me most   210
To my revenge. But in my terms of honor
I stand aloof, and will no reconcilement
Till by some elder masters of known honor
I have a voice[6] and precedent of peace
To keep my name ungored.[7] But till that time   215
I do receive your offered love like love,
And will not wrong it.
HAMLET: I embrace it freely,
And will this brother's wager frankly[8] play.
Give us the foils.
LAERTES: Come, one for me.
HAMLET: I'll be your foil, Laertes. In mine ignorance   220

2. Company.   3. Resentment.   4. Denying of.   5. Absolve.   6. Authority.   7. Un-
shamed.   8. Without rancor.

Your skill shall, like a star i' th' darkest night,
Stick fiery off[9] indeed.

LAERTES: You mock me, sir.

HAMLET: No, by this hand.

KING: Give them the foils, young Osric. Cousin Hamlet,
You know the wager?

225   HAMLET: Very well, my lord;
Your Grace has laid the odds o' th' weaker side.

KING: I do not fear it, I have seen you both;
But since he is bettered[1] we have therefore odds.

LAERTES: This is too heavy; let me see another.

230   HAMLET: This likes me well. These foils have all a[2] length?

[*They prepare to play.*]

OSRIC: Ay, my good lord.

KING: Set me the stoups of wine upon that table.
If Hamlet give the first or second hit,
Or quit in answer of[3] the third exchange,

235   Let all the battlements their ordnance fire.
The king shall drink to Hamlet's better breath,
And in the cup an union[4] shall he throw,
Richer than that which four successive kings
In Denmark's crown have worn. Give me the cups,

240   And let the kettle[5] to the trumpet speak,
The trumpet to the cannoneer without,
The cannons to the heavens, the heaven to earth,
"Now the king drinks to Hamlet." Come, begin—

[*Trumpets the while.*]

And you, the judges, bear a wary eye.

HAMLET: Come on, sir.

LAERTES: Come, my lord.

[*They play.*]

HAMLET: One.

LAERTES: No.

245   HAMLET: Judgment?

OSRIC: A hit, a very palpable hit.

[*Drums, trumpets, and shot. Flourish; a piece goes off.*]

LAERTES: Well, again.

KING: Stay, give me drink. Hamlet, this pearl is thine.
Here's to thy health. Give him the cup.

---

9. Shine brightly.   1. Reported better.   2. The same. *Likes:* suits.   3. Repay.   4. Pearl.
5. Kettledrum.

HAMLET: I'll play this bout first; set it by awhile.   250
   Come.

[*They play.*]

   Another hit; what say you?
LAERTES: I do confess't.
KING: Our son shall win.
QUEEN: He's fat,[6] and scant of breath.
   Here, Hamlet, take my napkin, rub thy brows.   255
   The queen carouses to thy fortune, Hamlet.
HAMLET: Good madam!
KING: Gertrude, do not drink.
QUEEN: I will, my lord; I pray you pardon me.
KING: [*Aside.*] It is the poisoned cup; it is too late.   260
HAMLET: I dare not drink yet, madam; by and by.
QUEEN: Come, let me wipe thy face.
LAERTES: My lord, I'll hit him now.
KING: I do not think't.
LAERTES: [*Aside.*] And yet it is almost against my conscience.
HAMLET: Come, for the third, Laertes. You do but dally.   265
   I pray you pass[7] with your best violence;
   I am afeard you make a wanton of me.[8]
LAERTES: Say you so? Come on.

[*They play.*]

OSRIC: Nothing, neither way.
LAERTES: Have at you now!   270

[LAERTES *wounds* HAMLET: *then, in scuffling, they change rapiers, and* HAM-
LET *wounds* LAERTES.]

KING: Part them. They are incensed.
HAMLET: Nay, come again.

[*The* QUEEN *falls.*]

OSRIC: Look to the queen there, ho!
HORATIO: They bleed on both sides. How is it, my lord?
OSRIC: How is't, Laertes?   275
LAERTES: Why, as a woodcock to mine own springe,[9] Osric.
   I am justly killed with mine own treachery.
HAMLET: How does the queen?
KING: She swoons to see them bleed.
QUEEN: No, no, the drink, the drink! O my dear Hamlet!
   The drink, the drink! I am poisoned.   [*Dies.*]   280

6. Out of shape.   7. Attack.   8. Trifle with me.   9. Snare.

HAMLET: O, villainy! Ho! let the door be locked.
    Treachery! seek it out.
LAERTES: It is here, Hamlet. Hamlet, thou art slain;
    No med'cine in the world can do thee good.
285   In thee there is not half an hour's life.
    The treacherous instrument is in thy hand,
    Unbated[1] and envenomed. The foul practice
    Hath turned itself on me. Lo, here I lie,
    Never to rise again. Thy mother's poisoned.
290   I can no more. The king, the king's to blame.
HAMLET: The point envenomed too?
    Then, venom, to thy work.   [Hurts the KING.]
ALL: Treason! treason!
KING: O, yet defend me, friends. I am but hurt.[2]
295 HAMLET: Here, thou incestuous, murd'rous, damnéd Dane,
    Drink off this potion. Is thy union here?
    Follow my mother.

    [The KING dies.]

LAERTES: He is justly served.
    It is a poison tempered[3] by himself.
    Exchange forgiveness with me, noble Hamlet.
300   Mine and my father's death come not upon thee,
    Nor thine on me!   [Dies.]
HAMLET: Heaven make thee free of[4] it! I follow thee.
    I am dead, Horatio. Wretched queen, adieu!
    You that look pale and tremble at this chance,[5]
305   That are but mutes or audience to this act,
    Had I but time, as this fell sergeant Death
    Is strict in his arrest,[6] O, I could tell you—
    But let it be. Horatio, I am dead:
    Thou livest; report me and my cause aright
    To the unsatisfied.[7]
310 HORATIO: Never believe it.
    I am more an antique Roman than a Dane.
    Here's yet some liquor left.
HAMLET: As th'art a man,
    Give me the cup. Let go. By heaven, I'll ha't.
    O God, Horatio, what a wounded name,
315   Things standing thus unknown, shall live behind me!
    If thou didst ever hold me in thy heart,
    Absent thee from felicity awhile,

---

1. Unblunted.   2. Wounded.   3. Mixed.   4. Forgive.   5. Circumstance.   6. Summons to court.   7. Uninformed.

And in this harsh world draw thy breath in pain,
To tell my story.

[*A march afar off.*]

                    What warlike noise is this?

OSRIC: Young Fortinbras, with conquest come from Poland,   320
    To th' ambassadors of England gives
    This warlike volley.[8]

HAMLET: O, I die, Horatio!
    The potent poison quite o'er-crows[9] my spirit.
    I cannot live to hear the news from England,
    But I do prophesy th' election lights   325
    On Fortinbras. He has my dying voice.[1]
    So tell him, with th' occurrents,[2] more and less,
    Which have solicited[3]—the rest is silence.   [*Dies.*]

HORATIO: Now cracks a noble heart. Good night, sweet prince,
    And flights of angels sing thee to thy rest!   330

[*March within.*]

Why does the drum come hither?

[*Enter* FORTINBRAS, *with the* AMBASSADORS *and with drum, colors, and* ATTEN-
DANTS.]

FORTINBRAS: Where is this sight?

HORATIO: What is it you would see?
    If aught of woe or wonder, cease your search.

FORTINBRAS: This quarry cries on havoc.[4] O proud death,
    What feast is toward[5] in thine eternal cell   335
    That thou so many princes at a shot
    So bloodily hast struck?

AMBASSADORS: The sight is dismal;
    And our affairs from England come too late.
    The ears are senseless[6] that should give us hearing
    To tell him his commandment is fulfilled,   340
    That Rosencrantz and Guildenstern are dead.
    Where should we have our thanks?

HORATIO: Not from his mouth,
    Had it th' ability of life to thank you.
    He never gave commandment for their death.
    But since, so jump[7] upon this bloody question,   345

8. The staging presents some difficulties here. Unless Osric is clairvoyant, he must have left the
stage at some point and returned. One possibility is that he might have left to carry out Hamlet's
order to lock the door (line 281) and returned when the sound of the distant march is heard.   9. Overcomes.   1. Support.   2. Circumstances.   3. Brought about this scene.   4. The game
killed in the hunt proclaims a slaughter.   5. In preparation.   6. Without sense of hearing.   7. Exactly.

You from the Polack wars, and you from England,
Are here arrived, give orders that these bodies
High on a stage be placed to the view,
And let me speak to th' yet unknowing world

350   How these things came about. So shall you hear
Of carnal, bloody, and unnatural acts;
Of accidental judgments, casual[8] slaughters;
Of deaths put on by cunning and forced cause;
And, in this upshot,[9] purposes mistook

355   Fall'n on th' inventors' heads. All this can I
Truly deliver.

FORTINBRAS: Let us haste to hear it,
And call the noblest to the audience.[1]
For me, with sorrow I embrace my fortune.
I have some rights of memory[2] in this kingdom,

360   Which now to claim my vantage[3] doth invite me.

HORATIO: Of that I shall have also cause to speak,
And from his mouth whose voice will draw on more.
But let this same be presently performed,
Even while men's minds are wild, lest more mischance
On plots and errors happen.

365   FORTINBRAS: Let four captains
Bear Hamlet like a soldier to the stage,
For he was likely, had he been put on,[4]
To have proved most royal; and for his passage
The soldier's music and the rite of war

370   Speak loudly for him.
Take up the bodies. Such a sight as this
Becomes the field, but here shows much amiss.
Go, bid the soldiers shoot.

                    [*Exeunt marching. A peal of ordnance shot off.*]

ca. 1600

---

8. Brought about by apparent accident.   9. Result.   1. Hearing.   2. Succession.   3. Position.   4. Elected king.

LILLIAN HELLMAN

The Little Foxes

Take us the foxes, the little foxes,
—that spoil the vines:
for our vines have tender grapes.[1]

CHARACTERS

ADDIE

CAL

OSCAR HUBBARD

BIRDIE HUBBARD, *his wife*

LEO HUBBARD, *Oscar and Birdie's son*

HORACE GIDDENS

REGINA GIDDENS, *Horace's wife*

ALEXANDRA GIDDENS, *Horace and Regina's daughter*

BENJAMIN HUBBARD

WILLIAM MARSHALL

The scene of the play is the living room of the GIDDENS *house, in a small town in the South.*

Act I: The Spring of 1900, evening.

Act II: A week later, early morning.

Act III: Two weeks later, late afternoon.

There has been no attempt to write Southern dialect. It is to be understood that the accents are Southern.

ACT I

SCENE: *The living room of the* GIDDENS *house, in a small town in the deep South, the Spring of 1900. Upstage is a staircase leading to the second story. Upstage, right, are double doors to the dining room. When these doors are open we see a section of the dining room and the furniture. Upstage, left, is an entrance hall with a coat-rack and umbrella stand. There are large lace-curtained windows on the left wall. The room is lit by a center gas chandelier and painted china oil lamps on the tables. Against the wall is a large piano. Downstage, right, are a high couch, a large table, several chairs. Against the left back wall are a table and several chairs. Near the window there are a smaller couch and tables. The room is good-looking, the furniture expensive; but it reflects no particular taste. Everything is of the best and that is all.*

AT RISE: ADDIE, *a tall, nice-looking Negro woman of about fifty-five, is closing the windows. From behind the closed dining-room doors there is the sound of voices. After a second,* CAL, *a middle-aged Negro, comes in from the entrance hall carrying a tray with glasses and a bottle of port.* ADDIE *crosses, takes the tray from him, puts it on table, begins to arrange it.*

ADDIE: [*Pointing to the bottle.*] You gone stark out of your head?

CAL: No, smart lady, I ain't. Miss Regina told me to get out that bottle. [*Points*

1. Song of Solomon 2:15.

to bottle.] That very bottle for the mighty honored guest. When Miss Regina changes orders like that you can bet your dime she got her reason.

ADDIE: [*Points to dining room.*] Go on. You'll be needed.

CAL: Miss Zan she had two helpings frozen fruit cream and she tell that honored guest, she tell him that you make the best frozen fruit cream in all the South.

ADDIE: [*Smiles, pleased.*] Did she? Well, see that Belle saves a little for her. She like it right before she go to bed. Save a few little cakes, too, she like—

[*The dining-room doors are opened and quickly closed again by* BIRDIE HUBBARD. BIRDIE *is a woman of about forty, with a pretty, well-bred, faded face. Her movements are usually nervous and timid, but now, as she comes running into the room, she is gay and excited.* CAL *turns to* BIRDIE.]

BIRDIE: Oh, Cal. [*Closes door.*] I want you to get one of the kitchen boys to run home for me. He's to look in my desk drawer and—[*To* ADDIE.] My, Addie. What a good supper! Just as good as good can be.

ADDIE: You look pretty this evening, Miss Birdie, and young.

BIRDIE: [*Laughing.*] Me, young? [*Turns back to* CAL.] Maybe you better find Simon and tell him to do it himself. He's too look in my desk, the left drawer, and bring my music album right away. Mr. Marshall is very anxious to see it because of his father and the opera in Chicago. [*To* ADDIE.] Mr. Marshall is such a polite man with his manners and very educated and cultured and I've told him all about how my mama and papa used to go to Europe for the music—[*Laughs. To* ADDIE.] Imagine going all the way to Europe just to listen to music. Wouldn't that be nice, Addie? Just to sit there and listen and—[*Turns and steps to* CAL.] Left drawer, Cal. Tell him that twice because he forgets. And tell him not to let any of the things drop out of the album and to bring it right in here when he comes back.

[*The dining-room doors are opened and quickly closed by* OSCAR HUBBARD. *He is a man in his late forties.*]

CAL: Yes'm. But Simon he won't get it right. But I'll tell him.

BIRDIE: Left drawer, Cal, and tell him to bring the blue book and—

OSCAR: [*Sharply.*] Birdie.

BIRDIE: [*Turning nervously.*] Oh, Oscar. I was just sending Simon for my music album.

OSCAR: [*To* CAL.] Never mind about the album. Miss Birdie has changed her mind.

BIRDIE: But, really, Oscar. Really I promised Mr. Marshall. I—

[CAL *looks at them, exits.*]

OSCAR: Why do you leave the dinner table and go running about like a child?

BIRDIE: [*Trying to be gay.*] But, Oscar, Mr. Marshall said most specially he *wanted* to see my album. I told him about the time Mama met Wagner,[2] and Mrs. Wagner gave her the signed program and the big picture. Mr. Marshall wants to see that. Very, very much. We had such a nice talk and—

2. Richard Wagner (1813–1883), German composer.

OSCAR: [*Taking a step to her.*] You have been chattering to him like a magpie. You haven't let him be for a second. I can't think he came South to be bored with you.

BIRDIE: [*Quickly, hurt.*] He wasn't bored. I don't believe he was bored. He's a very educated, cultured gentleman. [*Her voice rises.*] I just don't believe it. You always talk like that when I'm having a nice time.

OSCAR: [*Turning to her, sharply.*] You have had too much wine. Get yourself in hand now.

BIRDIE: [*Drawing back, about to cry, shrilly.*] What am I doing? I am not doing anything. What am I doing?

OSCAR: [*Taking a step to her, tensely.*] I said get yourself in hand. Stop acting like a fool.

BIRDIE: [*Turns to him, quietly.*] I don't believe he was bored. I just don't believe it. Some people like music and like to talk about it. That's all I was doing.

[LEO HUBBARD *comes hurrying through the dining-room door. He is a young man of twenty, with a weak kind of good looks.*]

LEO: Mama! Papa! They are coming in now.

OSCAR: [*Softly.*] Sit down, Birdie. Sit down now.

[BIRDIE *sits down, bows her head as if to hide her face. The dining-room doors are opened by* CAL. *We see people beginning to rise from the table.* REGINA GIDDENS *comes in with* WILLIAM MARSHALL. REGINA *is a handsome woman of forty.* MARSHALL *is forty-five, pleasant-looking, self-possessed. Behind them comes* ALEXANDRIA GIDDENS, *a very pretty, rather delicate-looking girl of seventeen. She is followed by* BENJAMIN HUBBARD, *fifty-five, with a large jovial face and the light graceful movements that one often finds in large men.*]

REGINA: Mr. Marshall, I think you're trying to console me. Chicago may be the noisiest, dirtiest city in the world but I should still prefer it to the sound of our horses and the smell of our azaleas. I should like crowds of people, and theatres, and lovely women—*Very* lovely women, Mr. Marshall?

MARSHALL: [*Crossing to sofa.*] In Chicago? Oh, I suppose so. But I can tell you this: I've never dined there with three *such* lovely ladies.

[ADDIE *begins to pass the port.*]

BEN: Our Southern women are well favored.

LEO: [*Laughs.*] But one must go to Mobile for the ladies, sir. Very elegant worldly ladies, too.

BEN: [*Looks at him very deliberately.*] Worldly, eh? *Worldly*, did you say?

OSCAR: [*Hastily, to* LEO.] Your Uncle Ben means that worldliness is not a mark of beauty in any woman.

LEO: [*Quickly.*] Of course, Uncle Ben. I didn't mean—

MARSHALL: Your port is excellent, Mrs. Giddens.

REGINA: Thank you, Mr. Marshall. We had been saving that bottle, hoping we could open it just for you.

ALEXANDRA: [*As* ADDIE *comes to her with the tray.*] Oh. May I *really*, Addie?

ADDIE: Better ask Mama.

ALEXANDRA: May I, Mama?

REGINA: [*Nods, smiles.*] In Mr. Marshall's honor.

ALEXANDRA: [*Smiles.*] Mr. Marshall, this will be the first taste of port I've ever had.

[ADDIE *serves* LEO.]

MARSHALL: No one ever had their first taste of a better port. [*He lifts his glass in a toast; she lifts hers; they both drink.*] Well, I suppose it is all true, Mrs. Giddens.

REGINA: What is true?

MARSHALL: That you Southerners occupy a unique position in America. You live better than the rest of us, you eat better, you drink better. I wonder you find time, or want to find time, to do business.

BEN: A great many Southerners don't.

MARSHALL: Do all of you live here together?

REGINA: Here with me? [*Laughs.*] Oh, no. My brother Ben lives next door. My brother Oscar and his family live in the next square.

BEN: But we are a very close family. We've always *wanted* it that way.

MARSHALL: That is very pleasant. Keeping your family together to share each other's lives. My family moves around too much. My children seem never to come home. Away at school in the winter; in the summer, Europe with their mother—

REGINA: [*Eagerly.*] Oh, yes. Even down here we read about Mrs. Marshall in the society pages.

MARSHALL: I dare say. She moves about a great deal. And all of you are part of the same business? Hubbard Sons?

BEN: [*Motions to* OSCAR.] Oscar and me. [*Motions to* REGINA.] My sister's good husband is a banker.

MARSHALL: [*Looks at* REGINA, *surprised.*] Oh.

REGINA: I am so sorry that my husband isn't here to meet you. He's been very ill. He is at Johns Hopkins.[3] But he will be home soon. We think he is getting better now.

LEO: I work for Uncle Horace. [REGINA *looks at him.*] I mean I work for Uncle Horace at his bank. I keep an eye on things while he's away.

REGINA: [*Smiles.*] Really, Leo?

BEN: [*Looks at* LEO, *then to* MARSHALL.] Modesty in the young is as excellent as it is rare. [*Looks at* LEO *again.*]

OSCAR: [*To* LEO.] Your uncle means that a young man should speak more modestly.

LEO: [*Hastily, taking a step to* BEN.] Oh, I didn't mean, sir—

MARSHALL: Oh, Mrs. Hubbard. Where's that Wagner autograph you promised to let me see? My train will be leaving soon and—

BIRDIE: The autograph? Oh. Well. Really, Mr. Marshall, I didn't mean to chatter

---

3. A well-respected hospital in Baltimore.

so about it. Really I—[*Nervously, looking at* OSCAR.] You must excuse me. I didn't get it because, well, because I had—I—I had a little headache and—

OSCAR: My wife is a miserable victim of headaches.

REGINA: [*Quickly.*] Mr. Marshall said at supper that he would like you to play for him, Alexandra.

ALEXANDRA: [*Who has been looking at* BIRDIE.] It's not I who play well, sir. It's my aunt. She plays just wonderfully. She's my teacher. [*Rises. Eagerly.*] May we play a duet? May we, Mama?

BIRDIE: [*Taking* ALEXANDRA's *hand.*] Thank you, dear. But I have my headache now. I—

OSCAR: [*Sharply.*] Don't be stubborn, Birdie. Mr. Marshall wants you to play.

MARSHALL: Indeed I do. If your headache isn't—

BIRDIE: [*Hesitates, then gets up, pleased.*] But I'd like to, sir. Very much. [*She and* ALEXANDRA *go to the piano.*]

MARSHALL: It's very remarkable how you Southern aristocrats have kept together. Kept together and kept what belonged to you.

BEN: You misunderstand, sir. Southern aristocrats have *not* kept together and have *not* kept what belonged to them.

MARSHALL: [*Laughs, indicates room.*] You don't call this keeping what belongs to you?

BEN: But we are not aristocrats. [*Points to* BIRDIE *at the piano.*] Our brother's wife is the only one of us who belongs to the Southern aristocracy.

[BIRDIE *looks towards* BEN.]

MARSHALL: [*Smiles.*] My information is that you people have been here, and solidly here, for a long time.

OSCAR: And so we have. Since our great-grandfather.

BEN: [*Smiles.*] Who was *not* an aristocrat, like Birdie's.

MARSHALL: [*A little sharply.*] You make great distinctions.

BEN: Oh, they have been made for us. And maybe they are important distinctions. [*Leans forward, intimately.*] Now you take Birdie's family. When my great-grandfather came here they were the highest-tone plantation owners in this state.

LEO: [*Steps to* MARSHALL. *Proudly.*] My mother's grandfather was *governor* of the state before the war.

OSCAR: They owned the plantation, Lionnet. You may have heard of it, sir?

MARSHALL: [*Laughs.*] No, I've never heard of anything but brick houses on a lake, and cotton mills.

BEN: Lionnet in its day was the best cotton land in the South. It still brings us in a fair crop. [*Sits back.*] Ah, they were great days for those people—even when I can remember. They had the best of everything. [BIRDIE *turns to them.*] Cloth from Paris, trips to Europe, horses you can't raise any more, niggers to lift their fingers—

BIRDIE: [*Suddenly.*] We were good to our people. Everybody knew that. We were better to them than—

[MARSHALL *looks up at* BIRDIE.]

REGINA: Why, Birdie. You aren't playing.

BEN: But when the war comes these fine gentlemen ride off and leave the cotton, *and* the women, to rot.

BIRDIE: My father was killed in the war. He was a fine soldier, Mr. Marshall. A fine man.

REGINA: Oh, certainly, Birdie. A famous soldier.

BEN: [*To* BIRDIE.] But that isn't the tale I am telling Mr. Marshall. [*To* MAR-SHALL.] Well, sir, the war ends. [BIRDIE *goes back to piano.*] Lionnet is almost ruined, and the sons finish ruining it. And there were thousands like them. Why? [*Leans forward.*] Because the Southern aristocrat can adapt himself to nothing. Too high-tone to try.

MARSHALL: Sometimes it is difficult to learn new ways.

[BIRDIE *and* ALEXANDRA *begin to play.* MARSHALL *leans forward, listening.*]

BEN: Perhaps, perhaps. [*He sees that* MARSHALL *is listening to the music. Irritated, he turns to* BIRDIE *and* ALEXANDRA *at the piano, then back to* MARSHALL.] You're right, Mr. Marshall. It is difficult to learn new ways. But maybe that's why it's profitable. *Our* grandfather and *our* father learned the new ways and learned how to make them pay. They work. [*Smiles nastily.*] *They* are in trade. Hubbard Sons, Merchandise. Others, Birdie's family, for example, look down on them. [*Settles back in chair.*] To make a long story short, Lionnet now belongs to *us.* [BIRDIE *stops playing.*] Twenty years ago we took over their land, their cotton, and their daughter.

[BIRDIE *rises and stands stiffly by the piano.* MARSHALL, *who has been watching her, rises.*]

MARSHALL: May I bring you a glass of port, Mrs. Hubbard?

BIRDIE: [*Softly.*] No, thank you, sir. You are most polite.

REGINA: [*Sharply, to* BEN.] You are boring Mr. Marshall with these ancient family tales.

BEN: I hope not. I hope not. I am trying to make an important point—[*Bows to* MARSHALL.] for our future business partner.

OSCAR: [*To* MARSHALL.] My brother always says that it's folks like us who have struggled and fought to bring to our land some of the posperity of your land.

BEN: Some people call that patriotism.

REGINA: [*Laughs gaily.*] I hope you don't find my brothers too obvious, Mr. Marshall. I'm afraid they mean that this is the time for the ladies to leave the gentlemen to talk business.

MARSHALL: [*Hastily.*] Not at all. We settled everything this afternoon. [MARSHALL *looks at his watch.*] I have only a few minutes before I must leave for the train. [*Smiles at her.*] And I insist they be spent with you.

REGINA: *And* with another glass of port.

MARSHALL: Thank you.

BEN: [*To* REGINA.] My sister is right. [*To* MARSHALL.] I am a plain man and I am trying to say a plain thing. A man ain't only in business for what he can get out of it. It's got to give him something here. [*Puts hand to his breast.*] That's every bit as true for the nigger picking cotton for a silver quarter, as it is for you and me. [REGINA *gives* MARSHALL *a glass of port.*] If it don't give him something here, then he don't pick the cotton right. Money isn't all. Not by three shots.

MARSHALL: Really? Well, I always thought it was a great deal.

REGINA: And so did I, Mr. Marshall.

MARSHALL: [*Leans forward. Pleasantly, but with meaning.*] Now you don't have to convince me that you are the right people for the deal. I wouldn't be here if you hadn't convinced me six months ago. You want the mill here, and I want it here. It isn't my business to find out *why* you want it.

BEN: To bring the machine to the cotton, and not the cotton to the machine.

MARSHALL: [*Amused.*] You have a turn for neat phrases, Hubbard. Well, however grand your reasons are, mine are simple: I want to make money and I believe I'll make it on you. [*As* BEN *starts to speak, he smiles.*] Mind you, I have no objections to more high-minded reasons. They are mighty valuable in business. It's fine to have partners who so closely follow the teachings of Christ. [*Gets up.*] And now I must leave for my train.

REGINA: I'm sorry you won't stay over with us, Mr. Marshall, but you'll come again. Any time you like.

BEN: [*Motions to* LEO, *indicating the bottle.*] Fill them up, boy, fill them up. [LEO *moves around filling the glasses as* BEN *speaks.*] Down here, sir, we have a strange custom. We drink the *last* drink for a toast. That's to prove that the Southerner is always still on his feet for the last drink. [*Picks up his glass.*] It was Henry Frick, your Mr. Henry Frick,[4] who said, "Railroads are the Rembrandts of investments." Well, *I* say, "Southern cotton mills *will be* the Rembrandts of investment." So I give you the firm of Hubbard Sons and Marshall, Cotton Mills, and to it a long and prosperous life.

[*They all pick up their glasses.* MARSHALL *looks at them, amused. Then he, too, lifts his glass, smiles.*]

OSCAR: The children will drive you to the depot. Leo! Alexandra! You will drive Mr. Marshall down.

LEO: [*Eagerly, looks at* BEN *who nods.*] Yes, sir. [*To* MARSHALL.] Not often Uncle Ben lets *me* drive the horses. And a beautiful pair they are. [*Starts for hall.*] Come on, Zan.

ALEXANDRA: May I drive tonight, Uncle Ben, please? I'd like to and—

BEN: [*Shakes his head, laughs.*] In your evening clothes? Oh, no, my dear.

ALEXANDRA: But Leo always—[*Stops, exits quickly.*]

REGINA: I don't like to say good-bye to you, Mr. Marshall.

MARSHALL: Then we won't say good-bye. You have promised that you would come and let me show you Chicago. Do I have to make you promise again?

---

4. (1849–1919), American industrialist; "your" because he was a Northerner. *Rembrandts*: valuable paintings by the great Dutch artist (1606–1669), here representing the highest quality.

REGINA: [*Looks at him as he presses her hand.*] I promise again.

MARSHALL: [*Touches her hand again, then moves to* BIRDIE.] Good-bye, Mrs. Hubbard.

BIRDIE: [*Shyly, with sweetness and dignity.*] Good-bye, sir.

MARSHALL: [*As he passes* REGINA.] Remember.

REGINA: I will.

OSCAR: We'll see you to the carriage.

[MARSHALL *exits, followed by* BEN *and* OSCAR. *For a second* REGINA *and* BIRDIE *stand looking after them. Then* REGINA *throws up her arms, laughs happily.*]

REGINA: And there, Birdie, goes the man who has opened the door to our future.

BIRDIE: [*Surprised to the unaccustomed friendliness.*] What?

REGINA: [*Turning to her.*] Our future. Yours and mine, Ben's and Oscar's, the children—[*Looks at* BIRDIE's *puzzled face, laughs.*] Our future! [*Gaily.*] You were charming at supper, Birdie. Mr. Marshall certainly thought so.

BIRDIE: [*Pleased.*] Why, Regina! Do you think he did?

REGINA: Can't you tell when you're being admired?

BIRDIE: Oscar said I bored Mr. Marshall. [*Then quietly.*] But he admired *you.* He told me so.

REGINA: What did he say?

BIRDIE: He said to me, "I hope your sister-in-law will come to Chicago. Chicago will be at her feet." He said the ladies would bow to your manners and the gentlemen to your looks.

REGINA: Did he? He seems a lonely man. Imagine being lonely with all that money. I don't think he likes his wife.

BIRDIE: Not like his wife? What a thing to say.

REGINA: She's away a great deal. He said that several times. And once he made fun of her being so social and high-tone. But that fits in all right. [*Sits back, arms on back of sofa, stretches.*] Her being social, I mean. She can introduce me. It won't take long with an introduction from her.

BIRDIE: [*Bewildered.*] Introduce you? In Chicago? You mean you really might go? Oh, Regina, you can't leave here. What about Horace?

REGINA: Don't look so scared about everything, Birdie. I'm going to live in Chicago. I've always wanted to. And now there'll be plenty of money to go with.

BIRDIE: But Horace won't be able to move around. You know what the doctor wrote.

REGINA: There'll be millions, Birdie, millions. You know what I've always said when people told me we were rich? I said I think you should either be a nigger or a millionaire. In between, like us, what for? [*Laughs. Looks at* BIRDIE.] But I'm not going away tomorrow, Birdie. There's plenty of time to worry about Horace when he comes home. If he ever decides to come home.

BIRDIE: Will we be going to Chicago? I mean, Oscar and Leo and me?

REGINA: You? I shouldn't think so. [*Laughs.*] Well, we must remember tonight. It's a very important night and we mustn't forget it. We shall plan all the things we'd like to have and then we'll really have them. Make a wish, Birdie, any wish. It's bound to come true now.

[BEN *and* OSCAR *enter.*]

BIRDIE: [*Laughs.*] Well. Well, I don't know. Maybe. [REGINA *turns to look at* BEN.] Well, I guess I'd know right off what I wanted.

[OSCAR *stands by the upper window, waves to the departing carriage.*]

REGINA [*Looks up at* BEN, *smiles. He smiles back at her.*] Well, you did it.

BEN: Looks like it might be we did.

REGINA: [*Springs up, laughs.*] Looks like it! Don't pretend. You're like a cat who's been licking the cream. [*Crosses to wine bottle.*] Now we must all have a drink to celebrate.

OSCAR: The children, Alexandra and Leo, make a very handsome couple, Regina. Marshall remarked himself what fine young folks they were. How well they looked together!

REGINA: [*Sharply.*] Yes. You said that before, Oscar.

BEN: Yes, sir. It's beginning to look as if the deal's all set. I may not be a subtle man—but—[*Turns to them. After a second.*] Now somebody ask me how I know the deal is set.

OSCAR: What do you mean, Ben?

BEN: You remember I told him that down here we drink the *last* drink for a toast?

OSCAR: [*Thoughtfully.*] Yes. I never heard that before.

BEN: Nobody's ever heard it before. God forgives those who invent what they need. I already had his signature. But we've all done business with men whose word over a glass is better than a bond. Anyway it don't hurt to have both.

OSCAR: [*Turns to* REGINA.] You understand what Ben means?

REGINA: [*Smiles.*] Yes, Oscar. I understand. I understood immediately.

BEN: [*Looks at her admiringly.*] Did you, Regina? Well, when he lifted his glass to drink, I closed my eyes and saw the bricks going into place.

REGINA: And *I* saw a lot more than that.

BEN: Slowly, slowly. As yet we have only our hopes.

REGINA: Birdie and I have just been planning what we want. I know what I want. What will you want, Ben?

BEN: Caution. Don't count the chickens. [*Leans back, laughs.*] Well, God would allow us a little daydreaming. Good for the soul when you've worked hard enough to deserve it. [*Pauses.*] I think I'll have a stable. For a long time I've had my good eyes on Carter's in Savannah. A rich man's pleasure, the sport of kings, why not the sport of Hubbards? Why not?

REGINA: [*Smiles.*] Why not? What will you have, Oscar?

OSCAR: I don't know. [*Thoughtfully.*] The pleasure of seeing the bricks grow will be enough for me.

BEN: Oh, of course. Our *greatest* pleasure will be to see the bricks grow. But we are all entitled to a little side indulgence.

OSCAR: Yes, I suppose so. Well, then, I think we might take a few trips here and there, eh, Birdie?

BIRDIE: [*Surprised at being consulted.*] Yes, Oscar. I'd like that.

OSCAR: We might even make a regular trip to Jekyll Island.[5] I've heard the Cornelly place is for sale. We might think about buying it. Make a nice change. Do you good, Birdie, a change of climate. Fine shooting on Jekyll, the best.

BIRDIE: I'd like—

OSCAR: [*Indulgently.*] What would you like?

BIRDIE: Two things. Two things I'd like most.

REGINA: Two! I should like a thousand. You are modest, Birdie.

BIRDIE: [*Warmly, delighted with the unexpected interest.*] I should like to have Lionnet back. I know you own it now, but I'd like to see it fixed up again, the way Mama and Papa had it. Every year it used to get a nice coat of paint—Papa was very particular about the paint—and the lawn was so smooth all the way down to the river, with the trims of zinnias and red-feather plush. And the figs and blue little plums and the scuppernongs— [*Smiles. Turns to* REGINA.] The organ is still there and it wouldn't cost much to fix. We could have parties for Zan, the way Mama used to have for me.

BEN: That's a pretty picture, Birdie. Might be a most pleasant way to live. [*Dismissing* BIRDIE.] What do you want, Regina?

BIRDIE: [*Very happily, not noticing that they are no longer listening to her.*] I could have a cutting garden. Just where Mama's used to be. Oh, I do think we could be happier there. Papa used to say that *nobody* had ever lost their temper at Lionnet, and *nobody* ever would. Papa would never let anybody be nasty-spoken or mean. No, sir. He just didn't like it.

BEN: What do you want, Regina?

REGINA: I'm going to Chicago. And when I'm settled there and know the right people and the right things to buy—because I certainly don't now—I shall go to Paris and buy them. [*Laughs.*] I'm going to leave you and Oscar to count the bricks.

BIRDIE: Oscar. Please let me have Lionnet back.

OSCAR: [*To* REGINA.] You are serious about moving to Chicago?

BEN: She is going to see the great world and leave us in the little one. Well, we'll come and visit you and meet all the great and be proud to think you are our sister.

REGINA: [*Gaily.*] Certainly. And you won't even have to learn to be subtle, Ben. Stay as you are. You will be rich and the rich don't have to be subtle.

OSCAR: But what about Alexandra? She's seventeen. Old enough to be thinking about marrying.

BIRDIE: And, Oscar, I have one more wish. Just one more wish.

OSCAR: [*Turns.*] What is it, Birdie? What are you saying?

BIRDIE: I want you to stop shooting. I mean, so much. I don't like to see animals and birds killed just for the killing. You only throw them away—

BEN: [*To* REGINA.] It'll take a great deal of money to live as you're planning, Regina.

REGINA: Certainly. But there'll be plenty of money. You have estimated the profits very high.

---

5. In Georgia, on the Atlantic coast.

BEN: I have—

BIRDIE: [OSCAR *is looking at her furiously.*] And you never let anybody else shoot, and the niggers need it so much to keep from starving. It's wicked to shoot food just because you like to shoot, when poor people need it so—

BEN: [*Laughs.*] I have estimated the profits very high—for myself.

REGINA: What did you say?

BIRDIE: I've always wanted to speak about it, Oscar.

OSCAR: [*Slowly, carefully.*] What are you chattering about?

BIRDIE: [*Nervously.*] I was talking about Lionnet and—and about your shooting—

OSCAR: You are exciting yourself.

REGINA: [*To* BEN.] I didn't hear you. There was so much talking.

OSCAR: [*To* BIRDIE.] You have been acting very childish, very excited, all evening.

BIRDIE: Regina asked me what I'd like.

REGINA: What did you say, Ben?

BIRDIE: Now that we'll be so rich everybody was saying what they would like, so I said what I would like, too.

BEN: I said—[*He is interrupted by* OSCAR.]

OSCAR: [*To* BIRDIE.] Very well, We've all heard you. That's enough now.

BEN: I am waiting. [*They stop.*] I am waiting for you to finish. You and Birdie. Four conversations are three too many. [BIRDIE *slowly sits down.* BEN *smiles, to* REGINA.] I said that I had, and I do, estimate the profits very high—for myself, and Oscar, of course.

REGINA: [*Slowly.*] And what does that mean?

[BEN *shrugs, looks towards* OSCAR.]

OSCAR: [*Looks at* BEN, *clears throat.*] Well, Regina, it's like this. For forty-nine per cent Marshall will put up four hundred thousand dollars. For forty-one per cent—[*Smiles archly.*] a controlling interest, mind you, we will put up two hundred and twenty-five thousand dollars besides offering him certain benefits that our [*Looks at* BEN.] local position allows us to manage. Ben means that two hundred and twenty-five thousand dollars is a lot of money.

REGINA: I know the terms and I know it's a lot of money.

BEN: [*Nodding.*] It is.

OSCAR: Ben means that we are ready with our two-thirds of the money. Your third, Horace's I mean, doesn't seem to be ready. [*Raises his hand as* REGINA *starts to speak.*] Ben has written to Horace, I have written, and you have written. He answers. But he never mentions this business. Yet we have explained it to him in great detail, and told him the urgency. Still he never mentions it. Ben has been very patient, Regina. Naturally, you are our sister and we want you to benefit from anything we do.

REGINA: And in addition to your concern for me, you do not want control to go out of the family. [*To* BEN.] That right, Ben?

BEN: That's cynical. [*Smiles.*] Cynicism is an unpleasant way of saying the truth.

OSCAR: No need to be cynical. We'd have no trouble raising the third share, the share that you want to take.

REGINA: I am sure you could get the third share, the share you were saving for me. But that would give you a strange partner. And strange partners sometimes want a great deal. [*Smiles unpleasantly.*] But perhaps it would be wise for you to find him.

OSCAR: Now, now. Nobody says we *want* to do that. We would like to have you in and you would like to come in.

REGINA: Yes. I certainly would.

BEN: [*Laughs, puts up his hand.*] But we haven't heard from Horace.

REGINA: I've given my word that Horace will put up the money. That should be enough.

BEN: Oh, it was enough. I took your word. But I've got to have more than your word now. The contracts will be signed this week, and Marshall will want to see our money soon after. Regina, Horace has been in Baltimore for five months. I know that you've written him to come home, and that he hasn't come.

OSCAR: It's beginning to look as if he doesn't want to come home.

REGINA: Of course he wants to come home. You can't move around with heart trouble at any moment you choose. You know what doctors are like once they get their hands on a case like this—

OSCAR: They can't very well keep him from answering letters, can they? [REGINA *turns to* BEN.] They couldn't keep him from arranging for the money if he wanted to—

REGINA: Has it occurred to you that Horace is also a good business man?

BEN: Certainly. He is a shrewd trader. Always has been. The bank is proof of that.

REGINA: Then, possibly, he may be keeping silent because he doesn't think he is getting enough for his money. [*Looks at* OSCAR.] Seventy-five thousand he has to put up. That's a lot of money, too.

OSCAR: Nonsense. He knows a good thing when he hears it. He knows that we can make *twice* the profit on cotton goods manufactured *here* than can be made in the North.

BEN: That isn't what Regina means. [*Smiles.*] May I interpret you, Regina? [*To* OSCAR.] Regina is saying that Horace wants *more* than a third of our share.

OSCAR: But he's only putting up a third of the money. You put up a third and you get a third. What else *could* he expect?

REGINA: Well, *I* don't know. I don't know about these things. It would seem that if you put up a third you should only get a third. But then again, there's no law about it, is there? I should think that if you knew your money was very badly needed, well, you just might say, I want more, I want a bigger share. You boys have done that. I've heard you say so.

BEN: [*After a pause, laughs.*] So you believe he has deliberately held out? For a larger share? [*Leaning forward.*] Well, I *don't* believe it. But I *do* believe that's what *you* want. Am I right, Regina?

REGINA: Oh, I shouldn't like to be too definite. But I *could* say that I wouldn't like to persuade Horace unless he did get a larger share. I must look after his interests. It seems only natural—

OSCAR: And where would the larger share come from?

REGINA: I don't know. That's not my business. [*Giggles.*] But perhaps it could come off your share, Oscar.

[REGINA *and* BEN *laugh.*]

OSCAR: [*Rises and wheels furiously on both of them as they laugh.*] What kind of talk is this?

BEN: I haven't said a thing.

OSCAR: [*To* REGINA.] *You* are talking very big tonight.

REGINA: [*Stops laughing.*] Am I? Well, you should know me well enough to know that I wouldn't be asking for things I didn't think I could get.

OSCAR: Listen. I don't believe you can even get Horace to come home, much less get money from him or talk quite so big about what you want.

REGINA: Oh, I can get him home.

OSCAR: Then why haven't you?

REGINA: I thought I should fight his battles for him, before he came home. Horace is a very sick man. And even if *you* don't care how sick he is, I do.

BEN: Stop this foolish squabbling. How can you get him home?

REGINA: I will send Alexandra to Baltimore. She will ask him to come home. She will say that she *wants* him to come home, and that *I* want him to come home.

BIRDIE: [*Suddenly.*] Well, of course she wants him here, but he's sick and maybe he's happy where he is.

REGINA: [*Ignores* BIRDIE, *to* BEN.] You agree that he will come home if she asks him to, if she says that I miss him and want him—

BEN: [*Looks at her, smiles.*] I admire you, Regina. And I agree. That's settled now and—[*Starts to rise.*]

REGINA: [*Quickly.*] But before she brings him home, I want to know what he's going to get.

BEN: What do you want?

REGINA: Twice what you offered.

BEN: Well, you won't get it.

OSCAR: [*To* REGINA.] I think you've gone crazy.

REGINA: I don't want to fight, Ben—

BEN: I don't either. You won't get it. There isn't any chance of that. [*Roguishly.*] You're holding us up, and that's not pretty, Regina, not pretty. [*Holds up his hand as he sees she is about to speak.*] But we need you, and I don't want to fight. Here's what I'll do: I'll give Horace forty percent, instead of the thirty-three and a third he really should get. I'll do that, provided he is home and his money is up within two weeks. How's that?

REGINA: All right.

OSCAR: I've asked before: where is this extra share coming from?

BEN: [*Pleasantly.*] From you. From your share.

OSCAR: [*Furiously.*] From me, is it? That's just fine and dandy. That's my reward. For thirty-five years I've worked my hands to the bone for you. For thirty-five years I've done all the things you didn't want to do. And this is what I—

BEN: [*Turns slowly to look at* OSCAR. OSCAR *breaks off.*] My, my. I am being attacked tonight on all sides. First by my sister, then by my brother. And I ain't a man who likes being attacked. I can't believe that God wants the strong to parade their strength, but I don't mind doing it if it's got to be done. [*Leans back in his chair.*] You ought to take these things better, Oscar. I've made you money in the past. I'm going to make you more money now. You'll be a very rich man. What's the difference to any of us if a little more goes here, a little less goes there—it's all in the family. And it will stay in the family. I'll never marry. [ADDIE *enters, begins to gather the glasses from the table.* OSCAR *turns to* BEN.] So my money will go to Alexandra and Leo. They may even marry some day and—

[ADDIE *looks at* BEN.]

BIRDIE: [*Rising.*] Marry—Zan and Leo—

OSCAR: [*Carefully.*] That would make a great difference in my feelings. If they married.

BEN: Yes, that's what I mean. Of course it would make a difference.

OSCAR: [*Carefully.*] Is that what *you* mean, Regina?

REGINA: Oh, it's too far away. We'll talk about it in a few years.

OSCAR: I want to talk about it now.

BEN: [*Nods.*] Naturally.

REGINA: There's a lot of things to consider. They are first cousins, and—

OSCAR: That isn't unusual. Our grandmother and grandfather were first cousins.

REGINA: [*Giggles.*] And look at us.

[BEN *giggles.*]

OSCAR: [*Angrily.*] You're both being very gay with my money.

BEN: [*Sighs.*] These quarrels. I dislike them so. [*Leans forward to* REGINA.] A marriage might be a very wise arrangement, for several reasons. And then, Oscar has given up something for you. You should try to manage something for him.

REGINA: I haven't said I was opposed to it. But Leo is a wild boy. There were those times when he took a little money from the bank and—

OSCAR: That's all past history—

REGINA: Oh, I know. And I know all young men are wild. I'm only mentioning it to show you that there are considerations—

BEN: [*Irritated because she does not understand that he is trying to keep* OSCAR *quiet.*] All right, so there are. But please assure Oscar that you will think about it very seriously.

REGINA: [*Smiles, nods.*] Very well. I assure Oscar that I will think about it seriously.

OSCAR: [*Sharply.*] That is not an answer.

REGINA: [*Rises.*] My, you're in a bad humor and you shall put me in one. I have said all that I am willing to say now. After all, Horace has to give his consent too.

OSCAR: Horace will do what you tell him to.

REGINA: Yes, I think he will.

OSCAR: And I have your word that you will try to—

REGINA: [*Patiently.*] Yes, Oscar. You have my word that I will think about it. Now do leave me alone.

[*There is the sound of the front door being closed.*]

BIRDIE: I—Alexandra is only seventeen. She—

REGINA: [*Calling.*] Alexandra? Are you back?

ALEXANDRA: Yes, Mama.

LEO: [*Comes into the room.*] Mr. Marshall got off safe and sound. Weren't those fine clothes he had? You can always spot clothes made in a good place. Looks like maybe they were done in England. Lots of men in the North send all the way to England for their stuff.

BEN: [*To* LEO.] Were you careful driving the horses?

LEO: Oh, yes, sir. I was.

[ALEXANDRA *has come in on* BEN's *question, hears the answer, looks angrily at* LEO.]

ALEXANDRA: It's a lovely night. You should have come, Aunt Birdie.

REGINA: Were you gracious to Mr. Marshall?

ALEXANDRA: I think so, Mama. I liked him.

REGINA: Good. And now I have great news for you. You are going to Baltimore in the morning to bring your father home.

ALEXANDRA: [*Gasps, then delighted.*] Me? Papa said I should come? That must mean—[*Turns to* ADDIE.] Addie, he must be well. Think of it, he'll be back home again. We'll bring him home.

REGINA: You are going alone, Alexandra.

ADDIE: [ALEXANDRA *has turned in surprise.*] Going alone? Going by herself? A child that age! Mr. Horace ain't going to like Zan traipsing up there by herself.

REGINA: [*Sharply.*] Go upstairs and lay out Alexandra's things.

ADDIE: He'd expect me to be along—

REGINA: I'll be up in a few minutes to tell you what to pack. [ADDIE *slowly begins to climb the steps. To* ALEXANDRA.] I should think you'd like going alone. At your age it certainly would have delighted me. You're a strange girl, Alexandra. Addie has babied you so much.

ALEXANDRA: I only thought it would be more fun if Addie and I went together.

BIRDIE: [*Timidly.*] Maybe I could go with her, Regina. I'd really like to.

REGINA: She is going alone. She is getting old enough to take some responsibilities.

OSCAR: She'd better learn now. She's almost old enough to get married. [*Jovially, to* LEO, *slapping him on shoulder.*] Eh, son?

LEO: Huh?

OSCAR: [*Annoyed with* LEO *for not understanding.*] Old enough to get married, you're thinking, eh?

LEO: Oh, yes, sir. [*Feebly.*] Lots of girls get married at Zan's age. Look at Mary Prester and Johanna and—

REGINA: Well, she's not getting married tomorrow. But she is going to Baltimore tomorrow, so let's talk about that. [*To* ALEXANDRA.] You'll be glad to have Papa home again.

ALEXANDRA: I wanted to go before, Mama. You remember that. But you said *you* couldn't go, and that *I* couldn't go alone.

REGINA: I've changed my mind. [*Too casually.*] You're to tell Papa how much you missed him, and that he must come home now—for your sake. Tell him that you *need* him home.

ALEXANDRA: Need him home? I don't understand.

REGINA: There is nothing for you to understand. You are simply to say what I have told you.

BIRDIE: [*Rises.*] He may be too sick. She couldn't do that—

ALEXANDRA: Yes. He may be too sick to travel. I couldn't make him think he had to come home for me, if he is too sick to—

REGINA: [*Looks at her, sharply, challengingly.*] You *couldn't* do what I tell you to do, Alexandra?

ALEXANDRA: [*Quietly.*] No. I couldn't. If I thought it would hurt him.

REGINA: [*After a second's silence, smiles pleasantly.*] But you are doing this for Papa's own good. [*Takes* ALEXANDRA's *hand.*] You must let me be the judge of his condition. It's the best possible cure for him to come home and be taken care of here. He mustn't stay there any longer and listen to those alarmist doctors. You are doing this entirely for his sake. Tell your papa that I want him to come home, that I miss him very much.

ALEXANDRA: [*Slowly.*] Yes, Mama.

REGINA: [*To the others. Rises.*] I must go and start getting Alexandra ready now. Why don't you all go home?

BEN: [*Rises.*] I'll attend to the railroad ticket. One of the boys will bring it over. Good night, everybody. Have a nice trip, Alexandra. The food on the train is very good. The celery is so crisp. Have a good time and act like a little lady. [*Exits.*]

REGINA: Good night, Ben. Good night, Oscar—[*Playfully.*] Don't be so glum, Oscar. It makes you look as if you had chronic indigestion.

BIRDIE: Good night, Regina.

REGINA: Good night, Birdie. [*Exits upstairs.*]

OSCAR: [*Starts for hall.*] Come along.

LEO: [*To* ALEXANDRA.] Imagine your not wanting to go! What a little fool you are. Wish it were me. What I could do in a place like Baltimore!

ALEXANDRA: [*Angrily, looking away from him.*] Mind your business. I can guess the kind of things *you* could do.

LEO: [*Laughs.*] Oh, no, you couldn't. [*He exits.*]

REGINA: [*Calling from the top of the stairs.*] Come on, Alexandra.

BIRDIE: [*Quickly, softly.*] Zan.

ALEXANDRA: I don't understand about my going, Aunt Birdie. [*Shrugs.*] But anyway, Papa will be home again. [*Pats* BIRDIE's *arm.*] Don't worry about me. I can take care of myself. Really I can.

BIRDIE: [*Shakes her head, softly.*] That's not what I'm worried about. Zan—

ALEXANDRA: [*Comes close to her.*] What's the matter?

BIRDIE: It's about Leo—

ALEXANDRA: [*Whispering.*] He beat the horses. That's why we were late getting back. We had to wait until they cooled off. He always beats the horses as if—

BIRDIE: [*Whispering frantically, holding* ALEXANDRA's *hands.*] He's my son. My own son. But you are more to me—more to me than my own child. I love you more than anybody else—

ALEXANDRA: Don't worry about the horses. I'm sorry I told you.

BIRDIE: [*Her voice rising.*] I am not worrying about the horses. I am worrying about *you.* You are *not* going to marry Leo. I am not going to let them do that to you—

ALEXANDRA: Marry? To Leo? [*Laughs.*] I wouldn't marry, Aunt Birdie. I've never even thought about it—

BIRDIE: But they have thought about it. [*Wildly.*] Zan, I couldn't stand to think about such a thing. You and—

[OSCAR *has come into the doorway on* ALEXANDRA's *speech. He is standing quietly, listening.*]

ALEXANDRA: [*Laughs.*] But I'm not going to marry. And I'm certainly not going to marry Leo.

BIRDIE: Don't you understand? They'll make you. They'll make you—

ALEXANDRA: [*Takes* BIRDIE's *hands, quietly, firmly.*] That's foolish, Aunt Birdie. I'm grown now. Nobody can make me do anything.

BIRDIE: I just couldn't stand—

OSCAR: [*Sharply.*] Birdie. [BIRDIE *looks up, draws quickly away from* ALEXANDRA. *She stands rigid, frightened. Quietly.*] Birdie, get your hat and coat.

ADDIE: [*Calls from upstairs.*] Come on, baby. Your mama's waiting for you, and she ain't nobody to keep waiting.

ALEXANDRA: All right. [*Then softly, embracing* BIRDIE.] Good night, Aunt Birdie. [*As she passes* OSCAR.] Good night, Uncle Oscar. [BIRDIE *begins to move slowly towards the door as* ALEXANDRA *climbs the stairs.* ALEXANDRA *is almost out of view when* BIRDIE *reaches* OSCAR *in the doorway. As* BIRDIE *quietly attempts to pass him, he slaps her hard, across the face.* BIRDIE *cries out, puts her hand to her face. On the cry,* ALEXANDRA *turns, begins to run down the stairs.*] Aunt Birdie! What happened? What happened? I—

BIRDIE: [*Softly, without turning.*] Nothing, darling. Nothing happened. [*Quickly, as if anxious to keep* ALEXANDRA *from coming close.*] Now go to bed. [OSCAR *exits.*] Nothing happened. [*Turns to* ALEXANDRA *who is holding her hand.*] I only—I only twisted my ankle. [*She goes out.* ALEXANDRA *stands on the stairs looking after her as if she were puzzled and frightened.*]

CURTAIN

ACT II

SCENE: *Same as Act I. A week later, morning.*

AT RISE: *The light comes from the open shutter of the right window; the other shutters are tightly closed.* ADDIE *is standing at the window, looking out. Near the dining-room doors are brooms, mops, rags, etc. After a second,* OSCAR *comes into the entrance hall, looks in the room, shivers, decides not to take his hat and coat off, comes into the room. At the sound of the door,* ADDIE *turns to see who has come in.*

ADDIE: [*Without interest.*] Oh, it's you, Mr. Oscar.

OSCAR: What is this? It's not night. What's the matter here? [*Shivers.*] Fine thing at this time of the morning. Blinds all closed. [ADDIE *begins to open shutters.*] Where's Miss Regina? It's cold in here.

ADDIE: Miss Regina ain't down yet.

OSCAR: She had any word?

ADDIE: [*Wearily.*] No, sir.

OSCAR: Wouldn't you think a girl that age could get on a train at one place and have sense enough to get off at another?

ADDIE: Something must have happened. If Zan say she was coming last night, she's coming last night. Unless something happened. Sure fire disgrace to let a baby like that go all that way alone to bring home a sick man without—

OSCAR: You do a lot of judging around here, Addie, eh? Judging of your white folks, I mean.

ADDIE: [*Looks at him, sighs.*] I'm tired. I been up all night watching for them.

REGINA: [*Speaking from the upstairs hall.*] Who's downstairs, Addie? [*She appears in a dressing gown, peers down from the landing.* ADDIE *picks up broom, dustpan and brush and exits.*] Oh, it's you, Oscar. What are you doing here so early? I haven't been down yet. I'm not finished dressing.

OSCAR: [*Speaking up to her.*] You had any word from them?

REGINA: No.

OSCAR: Then something certainly has happened. People don't just say they are arriving on Thursday night, and they haven't come by Friday morning.

REGINA: Oh, nothing has happened. Alexandra just hasn't got sense enough to send a message.

OSCAR: If nothing's happened, then why aren't they here?

REGINA: You asked me that ten times last night. My, you do fret so, Oscar. Anything might have happened. They may have missed connections in Atlanta, the train may have been delayed—oh, a hundred things could have kept them.

OSCAR: Where's Ben?

REGINA: [*As she disappears upstairs.*] Where should he be? At home, probably. Really, Oscar, I don't tuck him in his bed and I don't take him out of it. Have some coffee and don't worry so much.

OSCAR: Have some coffee? There isn't any coffee. [*Looks at his watch, shakes his head. After a second* CAL *enters with a large silver tray, coffee urn, small cups, newspaper.*] Oh, there you are. Is everything in this fancy house always late?

CAL: [*Looks at him surprised.*] You ain't out shooting this morning, Mr. Oscar?

OSCAR: First day I missed since I had my head cold. First day I missed in eight years.

CAL: Yes, sir. I bet you. Simon he say you had a mighty good day yesterday morning. That's what Simon say. [*Brings* OSCAR *coffee and newspaper.*]

OSCAR: Pretty good, pretty good.

CAL: [*Laughs slyly.*] Bet you got enough bobwhite and squirrel to give every nigger in town a Jesus-party. Most of 'em ain't had no meat since the cotton picking was over. Bet they'd give anything for a little piece of that meat—

OSCAR: [*Turns his head to look at* CAL.] Cal, if I catch a nigger in this town going shooting, you know what's going to happen.

[LEO *enters.*]

CAL: [*Hastily.*] Yes, sir, Mr. Oscar. I didn't say nothing about nothing. It was Simon who told me and— Morning, Mr. Leo. You gentlemen having your breakfast with us here?

LEO: The boys in the bank don't know a thing. They haven't had any message.

[CAL *waits for an answer, gets none, shrugs, moves to door, exits.*]

OSCAR: [*Peers at* LEO.] What you doing here, son?

LEO: You told me to find out if the boys at the bank had any message from Uncle Horace or Zan—

OSCAR: I told you if they had a message to bring it here. I told you that if they didn't have a message to stay at the bank and do your work.

LEO: Oh, I guess I misunderstood.

OSCAR: You didn't misunderstand. You just were looking for any excuse to take an hour off. [LEO *pours a cup of coffee.*] You got to stop that kind of thing. You got to start settling down. You going to be a married man one of these days.

LEO: Yes, sir.

OSCAR: You also got to stop with that woman in Mobile. [*As* LEO *is about to speak.*] You're young and I haven't got no objections to outside women. That is, I haven't got no objections so long as they don't interfere with serious things. Outside women are all right in their place, but *now* isn't their place. You got to realize that.

LEO: [*Nods.*] Yes, sir. I'll tell her. She'll act all right about it.

OSCAR: Also, you got to start working harder at the bank. You got to convince your Uncle Horace you going to make a fit husband for Alexandra.

LEO: What do you think has happened to them? Supposed to be here last night—[*Laughs.*] Bet you Uncle Ben's mighty worried. Seventy-five thousand dollars worried.

OSCAR: [*Smiles happily.*] Ought to be worried. Damn well ought to be. First he don't answer the letters, then he don't come home— [*Giggles.*]

LEO: What will happen if Uncle Horace don't come home or don't—

OSCAR: Or don't put up the money? Oh, we'll get it from outside. Easy enough.

LEO: [*Surprised.*] But *you* don't want outsiders.

OSCAR: What do I care who gets my share? I been shaved already. Serve Ben right if he had to give away some of his.

LEO: Damn shame what they did to you.

OSCAR: [*Looking up the stairs.*] Don't talk so loud. Don't you worry. When I die, you'll have as much as the rest. You might have yours *and* Alexandra's. I'm not so easily licked.

LEO: I wasn't thinking of myself, Papa—

OSCAR: Well, you should be, you should be. It's every man's duty to think of himself.

LEO: You think Uncle Horace don't want to go in on this?

OSCAR: [*Giggles.*] That's my hunch. He hasn't showed any signs of loving it yet.

LEO: [*Laughs.*] But he hasn't listened to Aunt Regina yet, either. Oh, he'll go along. It's too good a thing. Why wouldn't he want to? He's got plenty and plenty to invest with. He don't even have to sell anything. Eighty-eight thousand worth of Union Pacific bonds sitting right in his safe deposit box. All he's got to do is open the box.

OSCAR: [*After a pause. Looks at his watch.*] Mighty late breakfast in this fancy house. Yes, he's had those bonds for fifteen years. Bought them when they were low and just locked them up.

LEO: Yeah. Just has to open the box and take them out. That's all. Easy as easy can be. [*Laughs.*] The things in that box! There's all those bonds, looking mighty fine. [OSCAR *slowly puts down his newspaper and turns to* LEO.] Then right next to them is a baby shoe of Zan's and a cheap old cameo on a string, and, *and*—nobody'd believe this—a piece of an old violin. Not even a whole violin. Just a piece of an old thing, a piece of a violin.

OSCAR: [*Very softly, as if he were trying to control his voice.*] A piece of a violin! What do you think of that!

LEO: Yes, sirree. A lot of other crazy things, too. A poem, I guess it is, signed with his mother's name, and two old schoolbooks with notes and—[LEO *catches* OSCAR's *look. His voice trails off. He turns his head away.*]

OSCAR: [*Very softly.*] How do you know what's in the box, son?

LEO: [*Stops, draws back, frightened, realizing what he has said.*] Oh, well. Well, er. Well, one of the boys, sir. It was one of the boys at the bank. He took old Manders' keys. It was Joe Horns. He just up and took Manders' keys and, and—well, took the box out. [*Quickly.*] Then they all asked me if I wanted to see, too. So I looked a little, I guess, but then I made them close up the box quick and I told them never—

OSCAR: [*Looks at him.*] Joe Horns, you say? He opened it?

LEO: Yes, sir, yes, he did. My word of honor. [*Very nervously looking away.*] I suppose that don't excuse *me* for looking—[*Looking at* OSCAR.] but I did make him close it up and put the keys back in Manders' drawer—

OSCAR: [*Leans forward, very softly.*] Tell me the truth, Leo. I am not going to be angry with you. Did you open the box yourself?

LEO: No, sir, I didn't. I told you I didn't. No, I—

OSCAR: [*Irritated, patient.*] I am *not* going to be angry with you. [*Watching* LEO *carefully.*] Sometimes a young fellow deserves credit for looking round him to see what's going on. Sometimes that's a good sign in a fellow your age. [OSCAR *rises.*] Many great men have made their fortune with their eyes. Did you open the box?

LEO: [*Very puzzled.*] No. I—

OSCAR: [*Moves to* LEO.] Did you open the box? It may have been—well, it may have been a good thing if you had.

LEO: [*After a long pause.*] I opened it.

OSCAR: [*Quickly.*] Is that the truth? [LEO *nods.*] Does anybody else know that you opened it? Come, Leo, don't be afraid of speaking the truth to me.

LEO: No. Nobody knew. Nobody was in the bank when I did it. But—

OSCAR: Did your Uncle Horace ever know you opened it?

LEO: [*Shakes his head.*] He only looks in it once every six months when he cuts the coupons,[6] and sometimes Manders even does that for him. Uncle Horace don't even have the keys. Manders keeps them for him. Imagine not looking at all that. You can bet if I had the bonds, I'd watch 'em like—

OSCAR: If you had them. [LEO *watches him.*] If you had them. Then you could have a share in the mill, you and me. A fine, big share, too. [*Pauses, shrugs.*] Well, a man can't be shot for wanting to see his son get on in the world, can he, boy?

LEO: [*Looks up, begins to understand.*] No, he can't. Natural enough. [*Laughs.*] But I haven't got the bonds and Uncle Horace has. And now he can just sit back and wait to be a millionaire.

OSCAR: [*Innocently.*] You think your Uncle Horace likes you well enough to lend you the bonds if he decides not to use them himself?

LEO: Papa, it must be that you haven't had your breakfast! [*Laughs loudly.*] Lend me the bonds! My God—

OSCAR: [*Disappointed.*] No, I suppose not. Just a fancy of mine. A loan for three months, maybe four, easy enough for us to pay it back then. Anyway, this is only April—[*Slowly counting the months on his fingers.*] and if he doesn't look at them until Fall, he wouldn't even miss them out of the box.

LEO: That's it. He wouldn't even miss them. Ah, well—

OSCAR: No, sir. Wouldn't even miss them. How could he miss them if he never looks at them? [*Sighs as* LEO *stares at him.*] Well, here we are sitting around waiting for him to come home and invest his money in something he hasn't lifted his hand to get. But I can't help thinking he's acting strange. You laugh when I say he could lend you the bonds if he's not going to use them himself. But would it hurt him?

LEO: [*Slowly looking at* OSCAR.] No. No, it wouldn't.

OSCAR: People ought to help other people. But that's not always the way it happens. [BEN *enters, hangs his coat and hat in hall. Very carefully.*] And so sometimes you got to think of yourself. [*As* LEO *stares at him,* BEN *appears in the doorway.*] Morning, Ben.

---

6. In order to receive his interest payments.

BEN: [*Coming in, carrying his newspaper.*] Fine sunny morning. Any news from the runaways?

REGINA: [*On the staircase.*] There's no news or you would have heard it. Quite a convention so early in the morning, aren't you all? [*Goes to coffee urn.*]

OSCAR: You rising mighty late these days. Is that the way they do things in Chicago society?

BEN: [*Looking at his paper.*] Old Carter died up in Senateville. Eighty-one is a good time for us all, eh? What do you think has really happened to Horace, Regina?

REGINA: Nothing.

BEN: [*Too casually.*] You don't think maybe he never started from Baltimore and never intends to start?

REGINA: [*Irritated.*] Of course they've started. Didn't I have a letter from Alexandra? What is so strange about people arriving late? He has that cousin in Savannah he's so fond of. He may have stopped to see him. They'll be along today some time, very flattered that you and Oscar are so worried about them.

BEN: I'm a natural worrier. Especially when I am getting ready to close a business deal and one of my partners remains silent *and* invisible.

REGINA: [*Laughs.*] Oh, is that it? I thought you were worried about Horace's health.

OSCAR: Oh, that too. Who could help but worry? I'm worried. This is the first day I haven't shot since my head cold.

REGINA: [*Starts towards dining room.*] Then you haven't had your breakfast. Come along.

[OSCAR *and* LEO *follow her.*]

BEN: Regina. [*She turns at dining-room door.*] That cousin of Horace's has been dead for years and, in any case, the train does not go through Savannah.

REGINA: [*Laughs, continues into dining room, seats herself.*] Did he die? You're always remembering about people dying. [BEN *rises.*] Now I intend to eat my breakfast in peace, and read my newspaper.

BEN: [*Goes towards dining room as he talks.*] This is second breakfast for me. My first was bad. Celia ain't the cook she used to be. Too old to have taste any more. If she hadn't belonged to Mama, I'd send her off to the country.

[OSCAR *and* LEO *start to eat.* BEN *seats himself.*]

LEO: Uncle Horace will have some tales to tell, I bet. Baltimore is a lively town.

REGINA: [*To* CAL.] The grits isn't hot enough. Take it back.

CAL: Oh, yes'm. [*Calling into kitchen as he exits.*] Grits didn't hold the heat. Grits didn't hold the heat.

LEO: When I was at school three of the boys and myself took a train once and went over to Baltimore. It was so big we thought we were in Europe. I was just a kid then—

REGINA: I find it very pleasant [ADDIE *enters.*] to have breakfast alone. I hate chattering before I've had something hot. [CAL *closes the dining-room doors.*] Do be still, Leo.

[ADDIE *comes into the room, begins gathering up the cups, carries them to the large tray. Outside there are the sounds of voices. Quickly* ADDIE *runs into the hall. A few seconds later she appears again in the doorway, her arm around the shoulders of* HORACE GIDDENS, *supporting him.* HORACE *is a tall man of about forty-five. He has been good looking, but now his face is tired and ill. He walks stiffly, as if it were an enormous effort, and carefully, as if he were unsure of his balance.* ADDIE *takes off his overcoat and hangs it on the hall tree. She then helps him to a chair.*]

HORACE: How are you, Addie? How have you been?

ADDIE: I'm all right, Mr. Horace. I've just been worried about you.

[ALEXANDRA *enters. She is flushed and excited, her hat awry, her face dirty. Her arms are full of packages, but she comes quickly to* ADDIE.]

ALEXANDRA: Now don't tell me how worried you were. We couldn't help it and there was no way to send a message.

ADDIE: [*Begins to take packages from* ALEXANDRA.] Yes, sir, I was mighty worried.

ALEXANDRA: We had to stop in Mobile over night. Papa— [*Looks at him.*] Papa didn't feel well. The trip was too much for him, and I made him stop and rest— [*As* ADDIE *takes the last package.*] No, don't take that. That's father's medicine. I'll hold it. It mustn't break. Now, about the stuff outside. Papa must have his wheel chair. I'll get that and the valises—

ADDIE: [*Very happy, holding* ALEXANDRA's *arms.*] Since when you got to carry your own valises? Since when I ain't old enough to hold a bottle of medicine? [HORACE *coughs.*] You feel all right, Mr. Horace?

HORACE: [*Nods.*] Glad to be sitting down.

ALEXANDRA: [*Opening package of medicine.*] He doesn't feel all right. [ADDIE *looks at her, then at* HORACE.] He just says that. The trip was very hard on him, and now he must go right to bed.

ADDIE: [*Looking at him carefully.*] Them fancy doctors, they give you help?

HORACE: They did their best.

ALEXANDRA: [*Has become conscious of the voices in the dining room.*] I bet Mama was worried. I better tell her we're here now. [*She starts for door.*]

HORACE: Zan. [*She stops.*] Not for a minute, dear.

ALEXANDRA: Oh, Papa, you feel bad again. I knew you did. Do you want your medicine?

HORACE: No, I don't feel that way. I'm just tired, darling. Let me rest a little.

ALEXANDRA: Yes, but Mama will be mad if I don't tell her we're here.

ADDIE: They're all in there eating breakfast.

ALEXANDRA: Oh, are they all here? Why do they *always* have to be here? I was hoping Papa wouldn't have to see anybody, that it would be nice for him and quiet.

ADDIE: Then let your papa rest for a minute.

HORACE: Addie, I bet your coffee's as good as ever. They don't have such good coffee up North. [*Looks at the urn.*] Is it as good, Addie? [ADDIE *starts for coffee urn.*]

ALEXANDRA: No. Dr. Reeves said not much coffee. Just now and then. I'm the nurse now, Addie.

ADDIE: You'd be a better one if you didn't look so dirty. Now go and take a bath, Miss Grown-up. Change your linens, get out a fresh dress and give your hair a good brushing—go on—

ALEXANDRA: Will you be all right, Papa?

ADDIE: Go on.

ALEXANDRA: [*On stairs, talks as she goes up.*] The pills Papa must take once every four hours. And the bottle only when—only if he feels very bad. Now don't move until I come back and don't talk much and remember about his medicine, Addie—

ADDIE: Ring for Belle and have her help you and then I'll make you a fresh breakfast.

ALEXANDRA: [*As she disappears.*] How's Aunt Birdie? Is she here?

ADDIE: It ain't right for you to have coffee? It will hurt you?

HORACE: [*Slowly.*] Nothing can make much difference now. Get me a cup, Addie. [*She looks at him, crosses to urn, pours a cup.*] Funny. They can't make coffee up North. [ADDIE *brings him a cup.*] They don't like red pepper, either. [*He takes the cup and gulps it greedily.*] God, that's good. You remember how I used to drink it? Ten, twelve cups a day. So strong it had to stain the cup. [*Then slowly.*] Addie, before I see anybody else, I want to know why Zan came to fetch me home. She's tried to tell me, but she doesn't seem to know herself.

ADDIE: [*Turns away.*] I don't know. All I know is big things are going on. Everybody going to be high-tone rich. Big rich. You too. All because smoke's going to start out of a building that ain't even up yet.

HORACE: I've heard about it.

ADDIE: And, er— [*Hesitates—steps to him.*] And—well, Zan, she going to marry Mr. Leo in a little while.

HORACE: [*Looks at her, then very slowly.*] What are you talking about?

ADDIE: That's right. That's the talk. God help us.

HORACE: [*Angrily.*] What's the talk?

ADDIE: I'm telling you. There's going to be a wedding— [*Angrily turns away.*] Over my dead body there is.

HORACE: [*After a second, quietly.*] Go and tell them I'm home.

ADDIE: [*Hesitates.*] Now you ain't to get excited. You're to be in your bed—

HORACE: Go on, Addie. Go and say I'm back. [ADDIE *opens dining-room doors. He rises with difficulty, stands stiff, as if he were in pain, facing the dining room.*]

ADDIE: Miss Regina. They're home. They got here—

REGINA: Horace! [REGINA *quickly rises, runs into the room. Warmly.*] Horace! You've finally arrived. [*As she kisses him, the others come forward, all talking together.*]

BEN: [*In doorway, carrying a napkin.*] Well, sir, you had us all mighty worried.

[*He steps forward. They shake hands.* ADDIE *exits.*]

OSCAR: You're a sight for sore eyes.

HORACE: Hello, Ben.

[LEO *enters, eating a biscuit.*]

OSCAR: And what is that costume you have on?

BIRDIE: [*Looking at* HORACE.] Now that you're home, you'll feel better. Plenty of good rest and we'll take such fine care of you. [*Stops.*] But where is Zan? I missed her so much.

OSCAR: I asked you what is that strange costume you're parading around in?

BIRDIE: [*Nervously, backing towards stairs.*] Me? Oh! It's my wrapper. I was so excited about Horace I just rushed out of the house—

OSCAR: Did you come across the square dressed that way? My dear Birdie, I—

HORACE: [*To* REGINA, *wearily.*] Yes, it's just like old times.

REGINA: [*Quickly to* OSCAR.] Now, no fights. This is a holiday.

BIRDIE: [*Runs quickly up the stairs.*] Zan! Zannie!

OSCAR: Birdie! [*She stops.*]

BIRDIE: Oh. Tell Zan I'll be back in a little while. [*Whispers.*] Sorry, Oscar. [*Exits.*]

REGINA: [*To* OSCAR *and* BEN.] Why don't you go finish your breakfast and let Horace rest for a minute?

BEN: [*Crossing to dining room with* OSCAR.] Never leave a meal unfinished. There are too many poor people who need the food. Mighty glad to see you home, Horace. Fine to have you back. Fine to have you back.

OSCAR: [*To* LEO *as* BEN *closes dining-room doors.*] Your mother has gone crazy. Running around the streets like a woman—

[*The moment* REGINA *and* HORACE *are alone, they become awkward and self-conscious.*]

REGINA: [*Laughs awkwardly.*] Well. Here we are. It's been a long time. [HORACE *smiles.*] Five months. You know, Horace, I wanted to come and be with you in the hospital, but I didn't know where my duty was. Here, or with you. But you know how much I *wanted* to come.

HORACE: That's kind of you, Regina. There was no need to come.

REGINA: Oh, but there was. Five months lying there all by yourself, no kinfolks, no friends. Don't try to tell me you didn't have a bad time of it.

HORACE: I didn't have a bad time. [*As she shakes her head, he becomes insistent.*] No, I didn't, Regina. Oh, at first when I—when I heard the news about myself—but after I got used to that, I liked it there.

REGINA: You *liked* it? [*Coldly.*] Isn't that strange. You liked it so well you didn't want to come home?

HORACE: That's not the way to put it. [*Then, kindly, as he sees her turn her head away.*] But there I was and I got kind of used to it, kind of to like lying there and thinking. [*Smiles.*] I never had much time to think before. And time's become valuable to me.

REGINA: It sounds almost like a holiday.

HORACE: [*Laughs.*] It was, sort of. The first holiday I've had since I was a little kid.

REGINA: And here I was thinking you were in pain and—

HORACE: [*Quietly.*] I was in pain.

REGINA: And instead you were having a holiday! A holiday of thinking. Couldn't you have done that here?

HORACE: I wanted to do it before I came here. I was thinking about us.

REGINA: About us? About you and me? Thinking about you and me after all these years. [*Unpleasantly.*] You shall tell me everything you thought—some day.

HORACE: [*There is silence for a minute.*] Regina. [*She turns to him.*] Why did you send Zan to Baltimore?

REGINA: Why? Because I wanted you home. You can't make anything suspicious out of that, can you?

HORACE: I didn't mean to make anything suspicious about it. [*Hesitantly, taking her hand.*] Zan said you wanted me to come home. I was so pleased at that and touched, it made me feel good.

REGINA: [*Taking away her hand, turns.*] Touched that I should want you home?

HORACE: [*Sighs.*] I'm saying all the wrong things as usual. Let's try to get along better. There isn't so much more time. Regina, what's all this crazy talk I've been hearing about Zan and Leo? Zan and Leo marrying?

REGINA: [*Turning to him, sharply.*] Who gossips so much around here?

HORACE: [*Shocked.*] Regina!

REGINA: [*Annoyed, anxious to quiet him.*] It's some foolishness that Oscar thought up. I'll explain later. I have no intention of allowing any such arrangement. It was simply a way of keeping Oscar quiet in all this business I've been writing you about—

HORACE: [*Carefully.*] What has Zan to do with any business of Oscar's? Whatever it is, you had better put it out of Oscar's head immediately. You know what I think of Leo.

REGINA: But there's no need to talk about it now.

HORACE: There is no need to talk about it ever. Not as long as I live. [HORACE *stops, slowly turns to look at her.*] As long as I live. I've been in a hospital for five months. Yet since I've been here you have not once asked me about—about my health. [*Then gently.*] Well, I suppose they've written you. I can't live very long.

REGINA: [*Coldly.*] I've never understood why people have to talk about this kind of thing.

HORACE: [*There is a silence. Then he looks up at her, his face cold.*] You misunderstand. I don't intend to gossip about my sickness. I thought it was only fair to tell you. I was not asking for your sympathy.

REGINA: [*Sharply, turns to him.*] What do the doctors think caused your bad heart?

HORACE: What do you mean?

REGINA: They didn't think it possible, did they, that your fancy women may have—

HORACE: [*Smiles unpleasantly.*] Caused my heart to be bad? I don't think that's the best scientific theory. You don't catch heart trouble in bed.

REGINA: [*Angrily.*] I didn't think you did. I only thought you might catch a bad conscience—in bed, as you say.

HORACE: I didn't tell them about my bad conscience. Or about my fancy women. Nor did I tell them that my wife has not wanted me in bed with her for— [*Sharply.*] How long is it, Regina? [REGINA *turns to him.*] Ten years? Did you bring me home for this, to make me feel guilty again? That means you want something. But you'll not make me feel guilty any more. My "thinking" has made a difference.

REGINA: I see that it has. [*She looks towards dining-room door. Then comes to him, her manner warm and friendly.*] It's foolish for us to fight this way. I didn't mean to be unpleasant. I was stupid.

HORACE: [*Wearily.*] God knows I didn't either. I came home wanting so much not to fight, and then all of a sudden there we were. I got hurt and—

REGINA: [*Hastily.*] It's all my fault. I didn't ask about—about your illness because I didn't want to remind you of it. Anyway I never believe doctors when they talk about—[*Brightly.*] when they talk like that.

HORACE: [*Not looking at her.*] Well, we'll try our best with each other. [*He rises.*]

REGINA: [*Quickly.*] I'll try. Honestly, I will. Horace, Horace, I know you're tired but, but—couldn't you stay down here a few minutes longer? I want Ben to tell you something.

HORACE: Tomorrow.

REGINA: I'd like to now. It's very important to me. It's very important to all of us. [*Gaily, as she moves toward dining room.*] Important to your beloved daughter. She'll be a very great heiress—

HORACE: Will she? That's nice.

REGINA: [*Opens doors.*] Ben, are you finished breakfast?

HORACE: Is this the mill business I've had so many letters about?

REGINA: [*To* BEN.] Horace would like to talk to you now.

HORACE: Horace would not like to talk to you now. I am very tired, Regina—

REGINA: [*Comes to him.*] Please. You've said we'll try our best with each other. I'll try. Really, I will. Please do this for me now. You will see what I've done while you've been away. How I watched your interests. [*Laughs gaily.*] And I've done very well too. But things can't be delayed any longer. Everything must be settled this week— [HORACE *sits down.* BEN *enters.* OSCAR *has stayed in the dining room, his head turned to watch them.* LEO *is pretending to read the newspaper.*] Now you must tell Horace all about it. Only be quick because he is very tired and must go to bed. [HORACE *is looking up at her. His face hardens as she speaks.*] But I think your news will be better for him than all the medicine in the world.

BEN: [*Looking at* HORACE.] It could wait. Horace may not feel like talking today.

REGINA: What an old faker you are! You know it can't wait. You know it must be finished this week. You've been just as anxious for Horace to get here as I've been.

BEN: [*Very jovial.*] I suppose I have been. And why not? Horace has done Hubbard Sons many a good turn. Why shouldn't I be anxious to help him now?

REGINA: [*Laughs.*] Help him! Help him when you need him, that's what you mean.

BEN: What a woman you married, Horace. [*Laughs awkwardly when* HORACE *does not answer.*] Well, then I'll make it quick. You know what I've been telling you for years. How I've always said that every one of us little Southern business men had great things—[*Extends his arms.*]—right beyond our finger tips. It's been my dream: my dream to make those fingers grow longer. I'm a lucky man, Horace, a lucky man. To dream and to live to get what you've dreamed of. That's *my* idea of a lucky man. [*Looks at his fingers as his arm drops slowly.*] For thirty years I've cried bring the cotton mills to the cotton. [HORACE *opens medicine bottle.*] Well, finally I got up nerve to go to Marshall Company in Chicago.

HORACE: I know all this. [*He takes the medicine.* REGINA *rises, steps to him.*]

BEN: Can I get you something?

HORACE: Some water, please.

REGINA: [*Turns quickly.*] Oh, I'm sorry. Let me. [*Brings him a glass of water. He drinks as they wait in silence.*] You feel all right now?

HORACE: Yes. You wrote me. I know all that.

[OSCAR *enters from dining room.*]

REGINA: [*Triumphantly.*] But you don't know that in the last few days Ben has agreed to give us—you, I mean—a much larger share.

HORACE: Really? That's very generous of him.

BEN: [*Laughs.*] It wasn't so generous of me. It was smart of Regina.

REGINA: [*As if she were signaling* HORACE.] I explained to Ben that perhaps you hadn't answered his letters because you didn't think he was offering you enough, and that the time was getting short and you could guess how much he needed you—

HORACE: [*Smiles at her, nods.*] And I could guess that he wants to keep control in the family?

REGINA: [*To* BEN, *triumphantly.*] Exactly. [*To* HORACE.] So I did a little bargaining for you and convinced my brothers they weren't the only Hubbards who had a business sense.

HORACE: Did you have to convince them of that? How little people know about each other! [*Laughs.*] But you'll know better about Regina next time, eh, Ben? [BEN, REGINA, HORACE *laugh together.* OSCAR's *face is angry.*] Now let's see. We're getting a bigger share. [*Looking at* OSCAR.] Who's getting less?

BEN: Oscar.

HORACE: Well, Oscar, you've grown very unselfish. What's happened to you?

[LEO *enters from dining room.*]

BEN: [*Quickly, before* OSCAR *can answer.*] Oscar doesn't mind. Not worth fighting about now, eh, Oscar?

OSCAR: [*Angrily.*] I'll get mine in the end. You can be sure of that. I've got my son's future to think about.

HORACE: [*Sharply.*] Leo? Oh, I see. [*Puts his head back, laughs.* REGINA *looks at him nervously.*] I am beginning to see. Everybody will get theirs.

BEN: I knew you'd see it. Seventy-five thousand, and that seventy-five thousand will make you a million.

OSCAR: And how you feel? Tip-top, I bet, because that's the way you're looking.

HORACE: [*Coldly, irritated with* OSCAR'S *lie.*] Hello, Oscar. Hello, Leo, how are you?

LEO: [*Shaking hands.*] I'm fine, sir. But a lot better now that you're back.

REGINA: Now sit down. What did happen to you and where's Alexandra? I am so excited about seeing you that I almost forgot about her.

HORACE: I didn't feel good, a little weak, I guess, and we stopped over night to rest. Zan's upstairs washing off the train dirt.

REGINA: Oh, I am so sorry the trip was hard on you. I didn't think that—

HORACE: Well, it's just as if I had never been away. All of you here—

BEN: Waiting to welcome you home.

[BIRDIE *bursts in. She is wearing a flannel kimono and her face is flushed and excited.*]

BIRDIE: [*Runs to him, kisses him.*] Horace!

HORACE: [*Warmly pressing her arm.*] I was just wondering where you were, Birdie.

BIRDIE: [*Excited.*] Oh, I would have been here. I didn't know you were back until Simon said he saw the buggy. [*She draws back to look at him. Her face sobers.*] Oh, you don't look well, Horace. No, you don't.

REGINA: [*Laughs.*] Birdie, what a thing to say—

HORACE: [*Looking at* OSCAR.] Oscar thinks I look very well.

OSCAR: [*Annoyed. Turns on* LEO.] Don't stand there holding that biscuit in your hand.

LEO: Oh, well. I'll just finish my breakfast, Uncle Horace, and then I'll give you all the news about the bank— [*He exits into the dining room.*]

REGINA: [*Steps to table, leaning forward.*] It will, Horace, it will.

HORACE: I believe you. [*After a second.*] Now I can understand Oscar's self-sacrifice, but what did you have to promise Marshall Company besides the money you're putting up?

BEN: They wouldn't take promises. They wanted guarantees.

HORACE: Of what?

BEN: [*Nods.*] Water power. Free and plenty of it.

HORACE: You got them that, of course.

BEN: Cheap. You'd think the Governor of a great state would make his price a little higher. From pride, you know. [HORACE *smiles.* BEN *smiles.*] Cheap wages. "What do you mean by cheap wages?" I say to Marshall. "Less than Massachusetts," he says to me, "and that averages eight a week." "Eight a week! By God," I tell him, "I'd work for eight a week myself." Why, there ain't a mountain white or a town nigger but wouldn't give his right arm for three silver dollars every week, eh, Horace?

HORACE: Sure. And they'll take less than that when you get around to playing them off against each other. You can save a little money that way, Ben.

[*Angrily.*] And make them hate each other just a little more than they do now.

REGINA: What's all this about?

BEN: [*Laughs.*] There'll be no trouble from anybody, white or black. Marshall said that to me. "What about strikes? That's all we've had in Massachusetts for the last three years." I say to him, "What's a strike? I never heard of one. Come South, Marshall. We got good folks and we don't stand for any fancy fooling."

HORACE: You're right. [*Slowly.*] Well, it looks like you made a good deal for yourselves, and for Marshall, too. [*To* BEN.] Your father used to say he made the thousands and you boys would make the millions. I think he was right. [*Rises.*]

REGINA: [*They are all looking at* HORACE. *She laughs nervously.*] Millions for *us*, too.

HORACE: Us? You and me? I don't think so. We've got enough money, Regina. We'll just sit by and watch the boys grow rich. [*They watch* HORACE *tensely as he begins to move towards the staircase. He passes* LEO, *looks at him for a second.*] How's everything at the bank, Leo?

LEO: Fine, sir. Everything is fine.

HORACE: How are all the ladies in Mobile? [HORACE *turns to* REGINA, *sharply.*] Whatever made you think I'd let Zan marry—

REGINA: Do you mean that you are turning this down? Is it possible that's what you mean?

BEN: No, that's not what he means. Turning down a fortune. Horace is tired. He'd rather talk about it tomorrow—

REGINA: We can't keep putting it off this way. Oscar must be in Chicago by the end of the week with the money and contracts.

OSCAR: [*Giggles, pleased.*] Yes, sir. Got to be there end of the week. No sense going without the money.

REGINA: [*Tensely.*] I've waited long enough for your answer. I'm not going to wait any longer.

HORACE: [*Very deliberately.*] I'm very tired now, Regina.

BEN: [*Hastily.*] Now, Horace probably has his reasons. Things he'd like explained. Tomorrow will do. I can—

REGINA: [*Turns to* BEN, *sharply.*] I want to know his reasons now! [*Turns back to* HORACE.]

HORACE: [*As he climbs the steps.*] I don't know them all myself. Let's leave it at that.

REGINA: We shall not leave it at that! We have waited for you here like children. Waited for you to come home.

HORACE: So that you could invest my money. So this is why you wanted me home? Well, I had hoped— [*Quietly.*] If you are disappointed, Regina, I'm sorry. But I must do what I think best. We'll talk about it another day.

REGINA: We'll talk about it now. Just you and me.

HORACE: [*Looks down at her. His voice is tense.*] Please, Regina. It's been a hard trip. I don't feel well. Please leave me alone now.

REGINA: [*Quietly.*] I want to talk to you, Horace. I'm coming up. [*He looks at her for a minute, then moves on again out of sight. She begins to climb the stairs.*]

BEN: [*Softly.* REGINA *turns to him as he speaks.*] Sometimes it is better to wait for the sun to rise again. [*She does not answer.*] And sometimes, as our mother used to tell you, [REGINA *starts up stairs.*] it's unwise for a good-looking woman to frown. [BEN *rises, moves towards stairs.*] Softness and a smile do more to the heart of men —

[*She disappears.* BEN *stands looking up the stairs. There is a long silence. Then, suddenly,* OSCAR *giggles.*]

OSCAR: Let us hope she'll change his mind. Let us hope.

[*After a second* BEN *crosses to table, picks up his newspaper.* OSCAR *looks at* BEN. *The silence makes* LEO *uncomfortable.*]

LEO: The paper says twenty-seven cases of yellow fever in New Orleans. Guess the flood-waters caused it. [*Nobody pays attention.*] Thought they were building the levees high enough. Like the niggers always say: a man born of woman can't build nothing high enough for the Mississippi. [*Gets no answer. Gives an embarrassed laugh.*]

[*Upstairs there is the sound of voices. The voices are not loud, but* BEN, OSCAR, LEO *become conscious of them.* LEO *crosses to landing, looks up, listens.*]

OSCAR: [*Pointing up.*] Now just suppose she doesn't change his mind? Just suppose he keeps on refusing?

BEN: [*Without conviction.*] He's tired. It was a mistake to talk to him today. He's a sick man, but he isn't a crazy one.

OSCAR: [*Giggles.*] But just suppose he is crazy. What then?

BEN: [*Puts down his paper, peers at* OSCAR.] Then we'll go outside for the money. There's plenty who would give it.

OSCAR: And plenty who will want a lot for what they give. The ones who are rich enough to give will be smart enough to want. That means we'd be working for them, don't it, Ben?

BEN: You don't have to tell me the things I told you six months ago.

OSCAR: Oh, you're right not to worry. She'll change his mind. She always has. [*There is a silence. Suddenly* REGINA's *voice becomes louder and sharper. All of them begin to listen now. Slowly* BEN *rises, goes to listen by the staircase.* OSCAR, *watching him, smiles. As they listen* REGINA's *voice becomes very loud.* HORACE's *voice is no longer heard.*] Maybe. But I don't believe it. I never did believe he was going in with us.

BEN: [*Turning on him.*] What the hell do you expect me to do?

OSCAR: [*Mildly.*] Nothing. You done your almighty best. Nobody could blame you if the whole thing just dripped away right through our fingers. You can't do a thing. But there may be something I could do for us. [OSCAR *rises.*] Or, I might better say, Leo could do for us. [BEN *stops, turns, looks at* OSCAR. LEO *is staring at* OSCAR.] Ain't that true, son? Ain't it true you might be able to help your own kinfolks?

LEO: [*Nervously taking a step to him.*] Papa, I—

BEN: [*Slowly.*] How would he help us, Oscar?

OSCAR: Leo's got a friend. Leo's friend owns eighty-eight thousand dollars in Union Pacific bonds. [BEN *turns to look at* LEO.] Leo's friend don't look at the bonds much—not for five or six months at a time.

BEN: [*After a pause.*] Union Pacific. Uh, huh. Let me understand. Leo's friend would—would lend him these bonds and he—

OSCAR: [*Nods.*] Would be kind enough to lend them to us.

BEN: Leo.

LEO: [*Excited, comes to him.*] Yes, sir?

BEN: When would your friend be wanting the bonds back?

LEO: [*Very nervous.*] I don't know. I—well, I—

OSCAR: [*Sharply. Steps to him.*] You told me he won't look at them until Fall—

LEO: Oh, that's right. But I—not till Fall. Uncle Horace never—

BEN: [*Sharply.*] Be still.

OSCAR: [*Smiles at* LEO.] Your uncle doesn't wish to know your friend's name.

LEO: [*Starts to laugh.*] That's a good one. Not know his name—

OSCAR: Shut up, Leo! [LEO *turns away slowly, moves to table.* BEN *turns to* OSCAR.] He won't look at them again until September. That gives us five months. Leo will return the bonds in three months. And we'll have no trouble raising the money once the mills are going up. Will Marshall accept bonds?

[BEN *stops to listen to sudden sharp voices from above. The voices are now very angry and very loud.*]

BEN: [*Smiling.*] Why not? Why not? [*Laughs.*] Good. We are lucky. We'll take the loan from Leo's friend—I think he will make a safer partner than our sister. [*Nods towards stairs. Turns to* LEO.] How soon can you get them?

LEO: Today. Right now. They're in the safe-deposit box and—

BEN: [*Sharply.*] I don't want to know where they are.

OSCAR: [*Laughs.*] We will keep it secret from you. [*Pats* BEN's *arm.*]

BEN: [*Smiles.*] Good. Draw a check for our part. You can take the night train for Chicago. Well, Oscar [*holds out his hand*], good luck to us.

OSCAR: Leo will be taken care of?

LEO: I'm entitled to Uncle Horace's share. I'd enjoy being a partner—

BEN: [*Turns to stare at him.*] You would? You can go to hell, you little—[*Starts towards* LEO.]

OSCAR: [*Nervously.*] Now, now. He didn't mean that. I only want to be sure he'll get something out of all this.

BEN: Of course. We'll take care of him. We won't have any trouble about that. I'll see you at the store.

OSCAR: [*Nods.*] That's settled then. Come on, son. [*Starts for door.*]

LEO: [*Puts out his hand.*] I didn't mean just that. I was only going to say what a great day this was for me and—

[BEN *ignores his hand.*]

BEN: Go on.

[LEO *looks at him, turns, follows* OSCAR *out.* BEN *stands where he is, thinking. Again the voices upstairs can be heard.* REGINA'*s voice is high and furious.* BEN *looks up, smiles, winces at the noise.*]

ALEXANDRA: [*Upstairs.*] Mama—Mama—don't . . . [*The noise of running footsteps is heard and* ALEXANDRA *comes running down the steps, speaking as she comes.*] Uncle Ben! Uncle Ben! Please go up. Please make Mama stop. Uncle Ben, he's sick, he's so sick. How can Mama talk to him like that— please, make her stop. She'll—

BEN: Alexandra, you have a tender heart.

ALEXANDRA: [*Crying.*] Go on up, Uncle Ben, please—

[*Suddenly the voices stop. A second later there is the sound of a door being slammed.*]

BEN: Now you see. Everything is over. Don't worry. [*He starts for the door.*] Alexandra, I want you to tell your mother how sorry I am that I had to leave. And don't worry so, my dear. Married folk frequently raise their voices, unfortunately. [*He starts to put on his hat and coat as* REGINA *appears on the stairs.*]

ALEXANDRA: [*Furiously.*] How can you treat Papa like this? He's sick. He's very sick. Don't you know that? I won't let you.

REGINA: Mind your business, Alexandra. [*To* BEN. *Her voice is cold and calm.*] How much longer can you wait for the money?

BEN: [*Putting on his coat.*] He has refused? My, that's too bad.

REGINA: He will change his mind. I'll find a way to make him. What's the longest you can wait now?

BEN: I could wait until next week. But I can't wait until next week. [*He giggles, pleased at the joke.*] I could but I can't. Could and can't. Well, I must go now. I'm very late—

REGINA: [*Coming downstairs towards him.*] You're not going. I want to talk to you.

BEN: I was about to give Alexandra a message for you. I wanted to tell you that Oscar is going to Chicago tonight, so we can't be here for our usual Friday supper.

REGINA: [*Tensely.*] Oscar is going to Chi— [*Softly.*] What do you mean?

BEN: Just that. Everything is settled. He's going on to deliver to Marshall—

REGINA: [*Taking a step to him.*] I demand to know what— You are lying. You are trying to scare me. *You haven't got the money.* How could you have it? You can't have— [BEN *laughs.*] You will wait until I—

[HORACE *comes into view on the landing.*]

BEN: You are getting out of hand. Since when do I take orders from you?

REGINA: Wait, you—[BEN *stops.*] How *can* he go to Chicago? Did a ghost arrive with the money? [BEN *starts for the hall.*] I don't believe you. Come back here. [REGINA *starts after him.*] Come back here, you— [*The door slams. She stops in the doorway, staring, her fists clenched. After a pause she turns slowly.*]

HORACE: [*Very quietly.*] It's a great day when you and Ben cross swords. I've been waiting for it for years.

ALEXANDRA: Papa, Papa, please go back! You will—

HORACE: And so they don't need you, and so you will not have your millions, after all.

REGINA: [*Turns slowly.*] You hate to see anybody live now, don't you? You hate to think that I'm going to be alive and have what I want.

HORACE: I should have known you'd think that was the reason.

REGINA: Because you're going to die and you know you're going to die.

ALEXANDRA: [*Shrilly.*] Mama! Don't— Don't listen, Papa. Just don't listen. Go away—

HORACE: Not to keep you from getting what you want. Not even partly that. [*Holding to the rail.*] I'm sick of you, sick of this house, sick of my life here. I'm sick of your brothers and their dirty tricks to make a dime. There must be better ways of getting rich than cheating niggers on a pound of bacon. Why should I give you the money? [*Very angrily.*] To pound the bones of this town to make dividends for you to spend? You wreck the town, you and your brothers, *you* wreck the town and live on it. Not me. Maybe it's easy for the dying to be honest. But it's not my fault I'm dying. [ADDIE *enters, stands at door quietly.*] I'll do no more harm now. I've done enough. I'll die my own way. And I'll do it without making the world any worse. I leave that to you.

REGINA: [*Looks up at him slowly, calmly.*] I hope you die. I hope you die soon. [*Smiles.*] I'll be waiting for you to die.

ALEXANDRA: [*Shrieking.*] Papa! Don't—Don't listen—Don't—

ADDIE: Come here, Zan. Come out of this room.

[ALEXANDRA *runs quickly to* ADDIE, *who holds her.* HORACE *turns slowly and starts upstairs.*]

CURTAIN

ACT III

SCENE: *Same as Act I. Two weeks later. It is late afternoon and it is raining.*

AT RISE: HORACE *is sitting near the window in a wheel chair. On the table next to him is a safe-deposit box, and a small bottle of medicine.* BIRDIE *and* ALEXANDRA *are playing the piano. On a chair is a large sewing basket.*

BIRDIE: [*Counting for* ALEXANDRA.] One and two and three and four. One and two and three and four. [*Nods—turns to* HORACE.] We once played together, Horace. Remember?

HORACE: [*Has been looking out of the window.*] What, Birdie?

BIRDIE: We played together. You and me.

ALEXANDRA: *Papa* used to play?

BIRDIE: Indeed he did. [ADDIE *appears at the door in a large kitchen apron. She is wiping her hands on a towel.*] He played the fiddle and very well, too.

ALEXANDRA: [*Turns to smile at* HORACE.] I never knew—

ADDIE: Where's your mama?

ALEXANDRA: Gone to Miss Safronia's to fit her dresses.

[ADDIE *nods, starts to exit.*]

HORACE: Addie.

ADDIE: Yes, Mr. Horace.

HORACE: [*Speaks as if he had made a sudden decision.*] Tell Cal to get on his things. I want him to go an errand.

[ADDIE *nods, exits.* HORACE *moves nervously in his chair, looks out of the window.*]

ALEXANDRA: [*Who has been watching him.*] It's too bad it's been raining all day, Papa. But you can go out in the yard tomorrow. Don't be restless.

HORACE: I'm not restless, darling.

BIRDIE: I remember so well the time we played together, your papa and me. It was the first time Oscar brought me here to supper. I had never seen all the Hubbards together before, and you know what a ninny I am and how shy. [*Turns to look at* HORACE.] You said you could play the fiddle and you'd be much obliged if I'd play with you. *I* was obliged to *you*, all right, all right. [*Laughs when he does not answer her.*] Horace, you haven't heard a word I've said.

HORACE: Birdie, when did Oscar get back from Chicago?

BIRDIE: Yesterday. Hasn't he been here yet?

ALEXANDRA: [*Stops playing.*] No. Neither has Uncle Ben since—since that day.

BIRDIE: Oh, I didn't know it was *that* bad. Oscar never tells me anything—

HORACE: [*Smiles, nods.*] The Hubbards have had their great quarrel. I knew it would come some day. [*Laughs.*] It came.

ALEXANDRA: It came. It certainly came all right.

BIRDIE: [*Amazed.*] But Oscar was in such a good humor when he got home, I didn't—

HORACE: Yes, I can understand that.

[ADDIE *enters carrying a large tray with glasses, a carafe of elderberry wine and a plate of cookies, which she puts on the table.*]

ALEXANDRA: Addie! A party! What for?

ADDIE: Nothing for. I had the fresh butter, so I made the cakes, and a little elderberry does the stomach good in the rain.

BIRDIE: Isn't this nice! A party just for us. Let's play party music, Zan. [ALEXANDRA *begins to play a gay piece.*]

ADDIE: [*To* HORACE, *wheeling his chair to center.*] Come over here, Mr. Horace, and don't be thinking so much. A glass of elderberry will do more good.

[ALEXANDRA *reaches for a cake.* BIRDIE *pours herself a glass of wine.*]

ALEXANDRA: Good cakes, Addie. It's nice here. Just us. Be nice if it could always be this way.

BIRDIE: [*Nods happily.*] Quiet and restful.

ADDIE: Well, it won't be that way long. Little while now, even sitting here, you'll hear the red bricks going into place. The next day the smoke'll be pushing out the chimneys and by church time that Sunday every human born of woman will be living on chicken. That's how Mr. Ben's been telling the story.

HORACE: [*Looks at her.*] They believe it that way?

ADDIE: Believe it? They use to believing what Mr. Ben orders. There ain't been so much talk around here since Sherman's army didn't come near.[7]

HORACE: [*Softly.*] They are fools.

ADDIE: [*Nods, sits down with the sewing basket.*] You ain't born in the South unless you're a fool.

BIRDIE: [*Has drunk another glass of wine.*] But we didn't play together after that night. Oscar said he didn't like me to play on the piano. [*Turns to* ALEXANDRA.] You know what he said that night?

ALEXANDRA: Who?

BIRDIE: Oscar. He said that music made him nervous. He said he just sat and waited for the next note. [ALEXANDRA *laughs.*] He wasn't poking fun. He meant it. Ah, well—[*She finishes her glass, shakes her head.* HORACE *looks at her, smiles.*] Your papa don't like to admit it, but he's been mighty kind to me all these years. [*Running the back of her hand along his sleeve.*] Often he'd step in when somebody said something and once—[*She stops, turns away, her face still.*] Once he stopped Oscar from—[*She stops, turns. Quickly.*] I'm sorry I said that. Why, here I am so happy and yet I think about bad things. [*Laughs nervously.*] That's not right, now, is it?

[*She pours a drink.* CAL *appears in the door. He has on an old coat and is carrying a torn umbrella.*]

ALEXANDRA: Have a cake, Cal.

CAL: [*Comes in, takes a cake.*] Yes'm. You want me, Mr. Horace?

HORACE: What time is it, Cal?

CAL: 'Bout ten minutes before it's five.

HORACE: All right. Now you walk yourself down to the bank.

CAL: It'll be closed. Nobody'll be there but Mr. Manders, Mr. Joe Horns, Mr. Leo—

HORACE: Go in the back way. They'll be at the table, going over the day's business. [*Points to the deposit box.*] See that box?

CAL: [*Nods.*] Yes, sir.

7. Union general William Tecumseh Sherman (1820–1891) fought vigorously in the deep South in the Civil War, most notably in his famous and destructive march from Atlanta to Savannah, November–December 1864.

HORACE: You tell Mr. Manders that Mr. Horace says he's much obliged to him for bringing the box, it arrived all right.

CAL: [*Bewildered.*] He know you got the box. He bring it himself Wednesday. I opened the door to him and he say, "Hello, Cal, coming on to summer weather."

HORACE: You say just what I tell you. Understand?

[BIRDIE *pours another drink, stands at table.*]

CAL: No, sir. I ain't going to say I understand. I'm going down and tell a man he give you something he already know he give you, and you say "understand."

HORACE: Now, Cal.

CAL: Yes, sir. I just going to say you obliged for the box coming all right. I ain't going to understand it, but I'm going to say it.

HORACE: And tell him I want him to come over here after supper, and to bring Mr. Sol Fowler with him.

CAL: [*Nods.*] He's to come after supper and bring Mr. Sol Fowler, your attorney-*at*-law, with him.

HORACE: [*Smiles.*] That's right. Just walk right in the back room and say your piece. [*Slowly.*] In front of everybody.

CAL: Yes, sir. [*Mumbles to himself as he exits.*]

ALEXANDRA: [*Who has been watching* HORACE.] Is anything the matter, Papa?

HORACE: Oh, no. Nothing.

ADDIE: Miss Birdie, that elderberry going to give you a headache spell.

BIRDIE: [*Beginning to be drunk. Gaily.*] Oh, I don't think so. I don't think it will.

ALEXANDRA: [*As* HORACE *puts his hand to this throat.*] Do you want your medicine, Papa?

HORACE: No, no. I'm all right, darling.

BIRDIE: Mama used to give me elderberry wine when I was a little girl. For hiccoughs. [*Laughs.*] You know, I don't think people get hiccoughs any more. Isn't that funny? [BIRDIE *laughs.* HORACE *and* ALEXANDRA *laugh.*] I used to get hiccoughs just when I shouldn't have.

ADDIE: [*Nods.*] And nobody gets growing pains no more. That is funny. Just as if there was some style in what you get. One year an ailment's stylish and the next year it ain't.

BIRDIE: [*Turns.*] I remember. It was my first big party, at Lionnet I mean, and I was so excited, and there I was with hiccoughs and Mama laughing. [*Softly. Looking at carafe.*] Mama always laughed. [*Picks up carafe.*] A big party, a lovely dress from Mr. Worth[8] in Paris, France, and hiccoughs. [*Pours drink.*] My brother pounding me on the back and Mama with the elderberry bottle, laughing at me. Everybody was on their way to come, and I was such a ninny, hiccoughing away. [*Drinks.*] You know, that was the first day I ever saw Oscar Hubbard. The Ballongs were selling their horses and he was going there to buy. He passed and lifted his hat—we could see him from the window—and my brother, to tease Mama, said maybe we should have invited

8. Charles Frederick Worth (1825–1895), founder of the influential fashion house Maison Worth.

the Hubbards to the party. He said Mama didn't like them because they kept a store, and he said that was old-fashioned of her. [*Her face lights up.*] And then, and *then*, I saw Mama angry for the first time in my life. She said that wasn't the reason. She said she was old-fashioned, but not that way. She said she was old-fashioned enough not to like people who killed animals they couldn't use, and who made their money charging awful interest to poor, ignorant niggers and cheating them on what they bought. She was very angry, Mama was. I had never seen her face like that. And then suddenly she laughed and said, "Look, I've frightened Birdie out of the hiccoughs." [*Her head drops. Then softly.*] And so she had. They were all gone. [*Moves to sofa, sits.*]

ADDIE: Yeah, they got mighty well off cheating niggers. Well, there are people who eat the earth and eat all the people on it like in the Bible with the locusts.[9] Then there are people who stand around and watch them eat it. [*Softly.*] Sometimes I think it ain't right to stand and watch them do it.

BIRDIE: [*Thoughtfully.*] Like I say, if we could only go back to Lionnet. Everybody'd be better there. They'd be good and kind. I like people to be kind. [*Pours drink.*] Don't you, Horace; don't you like people to be kind?

HORACE: Yes, Birdie.

BIRDIE: [*Very drunk now.*] Yes, that was the first day I ever saw Oscar. Who would have thought— [*Quickly.*] You all want to know something? Well, I don't like Leo. My very own son, and I don't like him. [*Laughs, gaily.*] My, I guess I even like Oscar more.

ALEXANDRA: Why did you marry Uncle Oscar?

ADDIE: [*Sharply.*] That's no question for you to be asking.

HORACE: [*Sharply.*] Why not? She's heard enough around here to ask anything.

ALEXANDRA: Aunt Birdie, why did you marry Uncle Oscar?

BIRDIE: I don't know. I thought I liked him. He was kind to me and I thought it was because he liked me too. But that wasn't the reason— [*Wheels on* ALEXANDRA.] Ask why *he* married *me*. I can tell you that: He's told it to me often enough.

ADDIE: [*Leaning forward.*] Miss Birdie, don't—

BIRDIE: [*Speaking very rapidly, tensely.*] My family was good and the cotton on Lionnet's fields was better. Ben Hubbard wanted the cotton and [*Rises.*] Oscar Hubbard married it for him. He was kind to me, then. He used to smile at me. He hasn't smiled at me since. Everybody knew that's what he married me for. [ADDIE *rises.*] Everybody but me. Stupid, stupid me.

ALEXANDRA: [*To* HORACE, *holding his hand, softly.*] I see. [*Hesitates.*] Papa, I mean—when you feel better couldn't we go away? I mean, by ourselves. Couldn't we find a way to go—

HORACE: Yes, I know what you mean. We'll try to find a way. I promise you, darling.

ADDIE: [*Moves to* BIRDIE.] Rest a bit, Miss Birdie. You get talking like this you'll get a headache and—

9. Exodus 10:12–16.

BIRDIE: [*Sharply, turning to her.*] I've never had a headache in my life. [*Begins to cry hysterically.*] You know it as well as I do. [*Turns to* ALEXANDRA.] I never had a headache, Zan. That's a lie they tell for me. I drink. All by myself, in my own room, by myself, I drink. Then, when they want to hide it, they say, "Birdie's got a headache again" —

ALEXANDRA: [*Comes to her quickly.*] Aunt Birdie.

BIRDIE: [*Turning away.*] Even you won't like me now. You won't like me any more.

ALEXANDRA: I love you. I'll always love you.

BIRDIE: [*Furiously.*] Well, don't Don't love me. Because in twenty years you'll just be like me. They'll do all the same things to you. [*Begins to laugh hysterically.*] You know what? In twenty-two years I haven't had a whole day of happiness. Oh, a little, like today with you all. But never a single, whole day. I say to myself, if only I had one more *whole* day, then — [*The laugh stops.*] And that's the way you'll be. And you'll trail after them, just like me, hoping they won't be so mean that day or say something to make you feel so bad — only you'll be worse off because you haven't got my Mama to remember — [*Turns away, her head drops. She stands quietly, swaying a little, holding onto the sofa.* ALEXANDRA *leans down, puts her cheek on* BIRDIE's *arm.*]

ALEXANDRA: [*To* BIRDIE.] I guess we were all trying to make a happy day. You know, we sit around and try to pretend nothing's happened. We try to pretend we are not here. We make believe we are just by ourselves, some place else, and it doesn't seem to work. [*Kisses* BIRDIE's *hand.*] Come now, Aunt Birdie, I'll walk you home. You and me. [*She takes* BIRDIE's *arm. They move slowly out.*]

BIRDIE: [*Softly as they exit.*] You and me.

ADDIE: [*After a minute.*] Well. First time I ever heard Miss Birdie say a word. [HORACE *looks at her.*] Maybe it's good for her. I'm just sorry Zan had to hear it. [HORACE *moves his head as if he were uncomfortable.*] You feel bad, don't you? [*He shrugs.*]

HORACE: So you didn't want Zan to hear? It would be nice to let her stay innocent, like Birdie at her age. Let her listen now. Let her see everything. How else is she going to know that she's got to get away? I'm trying to show her that. I'm trying, but I've only got a little time left. She can even hate me when I'm dead, if she'll only learn to hate and fear this.

ADDIE: Mr. Horace —

HORACE: Pretty soon there'll be nobody to help her but you.

ADDIE: [*Crossing to him.*] What can I do?

HORACE: Take her away.

ADDIE: How can I do that? Do you think they'd let me just go away with her?

HORACE: I'll fix it so they can't stop you when you're ready to go. You'll go, Addie?

ADDIE: [*After a second, softly.*] Yes, sir. I promise.

[*He touches her arm, nods.*]

HORACE: [*Quietly.*] I'm going to have Sol Fowler make me a new will. They'll make trouble, but you make Zan stand firm and Fowler'll do the rest. Addie,

I'd like to leave you something for yourself. I always wanted to.

ADDIE: [*Laughs.*] Don't you do that, Mr. Horace. A nigger woman in a white man's will! I'd never get it nohow.

HORACE: I know. But upstairs in the armoire drawer there's seventeen hundred dollar bills. It's money left from my trip. It's in an envelope with your name. It's for you.

ADDIE: Seventeen hundred dollar bills! My God, Mr. Horace, I won't know how to count up that high. [*Shyly.*] It's mighty kind and good of you. I don't know what to say for thanks—

CAL: [*Appears in doorway.*] I'm back. [*No answer.*] I'm back.

ADDIE: So we see.

HORACE: Well?

CAL: Nothing. I just went down and spoke my piece. Just like you told me. I say, "Mr. Horace he thank you mightily for the safe box arriving in good shape and he say you come right after supper to his house and bring Mr. Attorney-at-law Sol Fowler with you." Then I wipe my hands on my coat. Every time I ever told a lie in my whole life, I wipe my hands right after. Can't help doing it. Well, while I'm wiping my hands, Mr. Leo jump up and say to me, "What box? What you talking about?"

HORACE: [*Smiles.*] Did he?

CAL: And Mr. Leo say he got to leave a little early cause he got something to do. And then Mr. Manders say Mr. Leo should sit right down and finish up his work and stop acting like somebody made him Mr. President. So he sit down. Now, just like I told you, Mr. Manders was mighty surprised with the message because he knows right well he brought the box—[*Points to box, sighs.*] But he took it all right. Some men take everything easy and some do not.

HORACE: [*Puts his head back, laughs.*] Mr. Leo was telling the truth; he *has* got something to do. I hope Manders don't keep him too long. [*Outside there is the sound of voices.* CAL *exits.* ADDIE *crosses quickly to* HORACE, *puts basket on table, begins to wheel his chair towards the stairs. Sharply.*] No. Leave me where I am.

ADDIE: But that's Miss Regina coming back.

HORACE: [*Nods, looking at door.*] Go away, Addie.

ADDIE: [*Hesitates.*] Mr. Horace. Don't talk no more today. You don't feel well and it won't do no good—

HORACE: [*As he hears footsteps in the hall.*] Go on.

[*She looks at him for a second, then picks up her sewing from table and exits as* REGINA *comes in from hall.* HORACE's *chair is now so placed that he is in front of the table with the medicine.* REGINA *stands in the hall, shakes umbrella, stands it in the corner, takes off her cloak and throws it over the banister. She stares at* HORACE.]

REGINA: [*As she takes off her gloves.*] We had agreed that you were to stay in your part of this house and I in mine. This room is *my* part of the house. Please don't come down here again.

HORACE: I won't.

REGINA: [*Crosses towards bell-cord.*] I'll get Cal to take you upstairs.

HORACE: [*Smiles.*] Before you do I want to tell you that after all, we have invested our money in Hubbard Sons and Marshall, Cotton Manufacturers.

REGINA: [*Stops, turns, stares at him.*] What are you talking about? You haven't seen Ben— When did you change your mind?

HORACE: I didn't change my mind. *I* didn't invest the money. [*Smiles.*] It was invested for me.

REGINA: [*Angrily.*] What—?

HORACE: I had eighty-eight thousand dollars' worth of Union Pacific bonds in that safe-deposit box. They are not there now. Go and look. [*As she stares at him, he points to the box.*] Go and look, Regina. [*She crosses quickly to the box, opens it.*] Those bonds are as negotiable as money.

REGINA: [*Turns back to him.*] What kind of joke are you playing now? Is this for my benefit?

HORACE: I don't look in that box very often, but three days ago, on Wednesday it was, because I had made a decision—

REGINA: I want to know what you are talking about.

HORACE: [*Sharply.*] Don't interrupt me again. Because I had made a decision, I sent for the box. The bonds were gone. Eighty-eight thousand dollars gone. [*He smiles at her.*]

REGINA: [*After a moment's silence, quietly.*] Do you think I'm crazy enough to believe what you're saying?

HORACE: [*Shrugs.*] Believe anything you like.

REGINA: [*Stares at him, slowly.*] Where did they go to?

HORACE: They are in Chicago. With Mr. Marshall, I should guess.

REGINA: What did they do? Walk to Chicago? Have you really gone crazy?

HORACE: Leo took the bonds.

REGINA: [*Turns sharply then speaks softly, without conviction.*] I don't believe it.

HORACE: [*Leans forward.*] I wasn't there but I can guess what happened. This fine gentleman, to whom you were willing to marry your daughter, took the keys and opened the box. You remember that the day of the fight Oscar went to Chicago? Well, he went with my bonds that his son Leo had stolen for him. [*Pleasantly.*] And for Ben, of course, too.

REGINA: [*Slowly, nods.*] When did you find out the bonds were gone?

HORACE: Wednesday night.

REGINA: I thought that's what you said. Why have you waited three days to do anything? [*Suddenly laughs.*] This *will* make a fine story.

HORACE: [*Nods.*] Couldn't it?

REGINA: [*Still laughing.*] A fine story to hold over their heads. How could they be such fools? [*Turns to him.*]

HORACE: But I'm not going to hold it over their heads.

REGINA: [*The laugh stops.*] What?

HORACE: [*Turns his chair to face her.*] I'm going to let them keep the bonds—as a loan from you. An eighty-eight-thousand-dollar loan; they should be grateful to you. They will be, I think.

REGINA: [*Slowly, smiles.*] I see. You are punishing me. But I won't let you punish me. If you won't do anything, I will. Now. [*She starts for door.*]

HORACE: You won't do anything. Because you can't. [REGINA *stops.*] It won't do you any good to make trouble because I shall simply say that I lent them the bonds.

REGINA: [*Slowly.*] You would do that?

HORACE: Yes. For once in your life I am tying your hands. There is nothing for you to do.

[*There is silence. Then she sits down.*]

REGINA: I see. You are going to lend them the bonds and let them keep all the profit they make on them, and there is nothing I can do about it. Is that right?

HORACE: Yes.

REGINA: [*Softly.*] Why did you say that I was making this gift?

HORACE: I was coming to that. I am going to make a new will, Regina, leaving you eighty-eight thousand dollars in Union Pacific bonds. The rest will go to Zan. It's true that your brothers have borrowed your share for a little while. After my death I advise you to talk to Ben and Oscar. They won't admit anything and Ben, I think, will be smart enough to see that he's safe. Because I knew about the theft and said nothing. Nor will I say anything as long as I live. Is that clear to you?

REGINA: [*Nods, softly, without looking at him.*] You will not say anything as long as you live.

HORACE: That's right. And by that time they will probably have replaced your bonds, and then they'll belong to you and nobody but us will ever know what happened. [*Stops, smiles.*] They'll be around any minute to see what I am going to do. I took good care to see that word reached Leo. They'll be mighty relieved to know I'm going to do nothing and Ben will think it all a capital joke on you. And that will be the end of that. There's nothing you can do to them, nothing you can do to me.

REGINA: You hate me very much.

HORACE: No.

REGINA: Oh, I think you do. [*Puts her head back, sighs.*] Well, we haven't been very good together. Anyway, I don't hate you either. I have only contempt for you. I've always had.

HORACE: From the very first?

REGINA: I think so.

HORACE: I was in love with *you*. But why did *you* marry *me*?

REGINA: I was lonely when I was young.

HORACE: *You* were lonely?

REGINA: Not the way people usually mean. Lonely for all the things I wasn't going to get. Everybody in this house was so busy and there was so little place for what I wanted. I wanted the world. Then, and then— [*Smiles.*] Papa died and left the money to Ben and Oscar.

HORACE: And you married me?

REGINA: Yes, I thought—But I was wrong. You were a small-town clerk then. You haven't changed.

HORACE: [*Nods, smiles.*] And that wasn't what you wanted.

REGINA: No. No, it wasn't what I wanted. [*Pauses, leans back, pleasantly.*] It took me a little while to find out I had made a mistake. As for you—I don't know. It was almost as if I couldn't stand the kind of man you were— [*Smiles, softly.*] I used to lie there at night, praying you wouldn't come near—

HORACE: Really? It was as bad as that?

REGINA: [*Nods.*] Remember when I went to Doctor Sloan and I told you he said there was something the matter with me and that you shouldn't touch me any more?

HORACE: I remember.

REGINA: But you believed it. I couldn't understand that. I couldn't understand that anybody could be such a soft fool. That was when I began to despise you.

HORACE: [*Puts his hand to his throat, looks at the bottle of medicine on table.*] Why didn't you leave me?

REGINA: I told you I married you for something. It turned out it was only for this. [*Carefully.*] This wasn't what I wanted, but it was something. I never thought about it much but if I had [HORACE *puts his hand to his throat.*] I'd have known that you would die before I would. But I couldn't have known that you would get heart trouble so early and so bad. I'm lucky, Horace. I've always been lucky. [HORACE *turns slowly to the medicine.*] I'll be lucky again.

[HORACE *looks at her. The he puts his hand to his throat. Because he cannot reach the bottle he moves the chair closer. He reaches for the medicine, takes out the cork, picks up the spoon. The bottle slips and smashes on the table. He draws in his breath, gasps.*]

HORACE: Please. Tell Addie— The other bottle is upstairs. [REGINA *has not moved. She does not move now. He stares at her. Then, suddenly as if he understood, he raises his voice. It is a panic-stricken whisper, too small to be heard outside the room.*] Addie! Addie! Come—

[*Stops as he hears the softness of his voice. He makes a sudden, furious spring from the chair to the stairs, taking the first few steps as if he were a desperate runner. On the fourth step he slips, gasps, grasps the rail, makes a great effort to reach the landing. When he reaches the landing, he is on his knees. His knees give way, he falls on the landing, out of view.* REGINA *has not turned during his climb up the stairs. Now she waits a second. Then she goes below the landing, speaks up.*]

REGINA: Horace. Horace. [*When there is no answer, she turns, calls.*] Addie! Cal! Come in here. [*She starts up the steps.* ADDIE *and* CAL *appear. Both run towards the stairs.*] He's had an attack. Come up here. [*They run up the steps quickly.*]

CAL: My God. Mr. Horace—

[*They cannot be seen now.*]

REGINA: [*Her voice comes from the head of the stairs.*] Be still, Cal. Bring him in here.

[*Before the footsteps and the voices have completely died away,* ALEXANDRA *appears in the hall door, in her raincloak and hood. She comes into the room, begins to unfasten the cloak, suddenly looks around, sees the empty wheel chair, begins to move swiftly as if to look in the dining room. At the same moment* ADDIE *runs down the stairs.* ALEXANDRA *turns and stares up at* ADDIE.]

ALEXANDRA: Addie! What?

ADDIE: [*Takes* ALEXANDRA *by the shoulders.*] I'm going for the doctor. Go upstairs.

[ALEXANDRA *looks at her, then quickly breaks away and runs up the steps.* ADDIE *exits. The stage is empty for a minute. Then the front door bell begins to ring. When there is no answer, it rings again. A second later* LEO *appears in the hall, talking as he comes in.*]

LEO: [*Very nervous.*] Hello. [*Irritably.*] Never saw any use ringing a bell when a door was open. If you are going to ring a bell, then somebody should answer it. [*Gets in the room, looks around, puzzled, listens, hears no sound.*] Aunt Regina. [*He moves around restlessly.*] Addie. [*Waits.*] Where the hell— [*Crosses to the bell cord, rings it impatiently, waits, gets no answer, calls.*] Cal! Cal!

[CAL *appears on the stair landing.*]

CAL: [*His voice is soft, shaken.*] Mr. Leo. Miss Regina says you stop that screaming noise.

LEO: [*Angrily.*] Where is everybody?

CAL: Mr. Horace he got an attack. He's bad. Miss Regina says you stop that noise.

LEO: Uncle Horace—What—What happened? [CAL *starts down the stairs, shakes his head, begins to move swiftly off.* LEO *looks around wildly.*] But when— You seen Mr. Oscar or Mr. Ben? [CAL *shakes his head. Moves on.* LEO *grabs him by the arm.*] Answer me, will you?

CAL: No, I ain't seen 'em. I ain't got time to answer you. I got to get things. [CAL *runs off.*]

LEO: But what's the matter with him? When did this happen—[*Calling after* CAL.] You'd think Papa'd be some place where you could find him. I been chasing him all afternoon.

[OSCAR *and* BEN *come into the room, talking excitedly.*]

OSCAR: I hope it's not a bad attack.

BEN: It's the first one he's had since he came home.

LEO: Papa, I've been looking all over town for you and Uncle Ben—

BEN: Where is he?

OSCAR: Addie said it was sudden.

BEN: [*To* LEO.] Where is he? When did it happen?

LEO: Upstairs. Will you listen to me, please? I been looking for you for—
OSCAR: [*To* BEN.] You think we should go up?

[BEN, *looking up the steps, shakes his head.*]

BEN: I don't know. I don't know.
OSCAR: [*Shakes his head.*] But he was all right—
LEO: [*Yelling.*] *Will you listen to me?*
OSCAR: [*Sharply.*] What is the matter with you?
LEO: I been trying to tell you. I been trying to find you for an hour—
OSCAR: Tell me what?
LEO: Uncle Horace knows about the bonds. He knows about them. He's had the box since Wednesday—
BEN: [*Sharply.*] Stop shouting! What the hell are you talking about?
LEO: [*Furiously.*] I'm telling you he knows about the bonds. Ain't that clear enough—
OSCAR: [*Grabbing* LEO's *arm.*] You God-damn fool! Stop screaming!
BEN: Now what happened? Talk quietly.
LEO: You heard me. Uncle Horace knows about the bonds. He's known since Wednesday.
BEN: [*After a second.*] How do you known that?
LEO: Because Cal comes down to Manders and says the box came O.K. and—
OSCAR: [*Trembling.*] That might not mean a thing—
LEO: [*Angrily.*] No? It might not, huh? Then he says Manders should come here tonight and bring Sol Fowler with him. I guess that don't mean a thing either.
OSCAR: [*To* BEN.] Ben— What— Do you think he's seen the—
BEN: [*Motions to the box.*] There's the box. [*Both* OSCAR *and* LEO *turn sharply.* LEO *makes a leap to the box.*] You ass. Put it down. What are you going to do with it, eat it?
LEO: I'm going to— [*Starts.*]
BEN: [*Furiously.*] Put it down. Don't touch it again. Now sit down and shut up for a minute.
OSCAR: Since Wednesday. [*To* LEO.] You said he had it since Wednesday. Why didn't he say something— [*To* BEN.] I don't understand—
LEO: [*Taking a step.*] I can put it back. I can put it back before anybody knows.
BEN: [*Who is standing at the table, softly.*] He's had it since Wednesday. Yet he hasn't said a word to us.
OSCAR: Why? Why?
LEO: What's the difference why? He was getting ready to say plenty. He was going to say it to Fowler tonight—
OSCAR: [*Angrily.*] Be still. [*Turns to* BEN, *looks at him, waits.*]
BEN: [*After a minute.*] I don't believe that.
LEO: [*Wildly.*] You don't believe it? What do I care what *you* believe? I do the dirty work and then—
BEN: [*Turning his head sharply to* LEO.] I'm remembering that. I'm remembering that, Leo.
OSCAR: What do you mean?

LEO: You—

BEN: [To OSCAR.] If you don't shut that little fool up, I'll show you what I mean. For some reason he knows, but he don't say a word.

OSCAR: Maybe he didn't know that *we*—

BEN: [Quickly.] That Leo— He's no fool. Does Manders know the bonds are missing?

LEO: How could I tell? I was half crazy. I don't think so. Because Manders seemed kind of puzzled and—

OSCAR: But we got to find out—[He breaks off as CAL comes into the room carrying a kettle of hot water.]

BEN: How is he, Cal?

CAL: I don't know, Mr. Ben. He was bad. [Going towards stairs.]

OSCAR: But when did it happen?

CAL: [Shrugs.] He wasn't feeling bad early. [ADDIE comes in quickly from the hall.] Then there he is next thing on the landing, fallen over, his eyes tight—

ADDIE: [To CAL.] Dr. Sloan's over at the Ballongs. Hitch the buggy and go get him. [She takes the kettle and cloths from him, pushes him, runs up the stair.] Go on.

[She disappears. CAL exits.]

BEN: Never seen Sloan anywhere when you need him.

OSCAR: [Softly.] Sounds bad.

LEO: He would have told *her* about it. Aunt Regina. He would have told his own wife—

BEN: [Turning to LEO.] Yes, he might have told her. But they weren't on such pretty terms and maybe he didn't. Maybe he didn't. [Goes quickly to LEO.] Now, listen to me. If she doesn't know, it may work out all right. If she does know, you're to say he lent you the bonds.

LEO: Lent them to me! Who's going to believe that?

BEN: Nobody.

OSCAR: [To LEO.] Don't you understand? It can't do no harm to say it—

LEO: Why should I say he lent them to me? Why not to you? [Carefully.] Why not to Uncle Ben?

BEN: [Smiles.] Just because he didn't lend them to me. Remember that.

LEO: But all he has to do is say he didn't lend them to me—

BEN: [Furiously.] But for some reason, he doesn't seem to be talking, does he?

[There are footsteps above. They all stand looking at the stairs. REGINA begins to come slowly down.]

BEN: What happened?

REGINA: He's had a bad attack.

OSCAR: Too bad. I'm so sorry we weren't here when—when Horace needed us.

BEN: When *you* needed us.

REGINA: [Looks at him.] Yes.

BEN: How is he? Can we—can we go up?

REGINA: [Shakes her head.] He's not conscious.

OSCAR: [*Pacing around.*] It's that—it's that bad? Wouldn't you think Sloan could be found quickly, just once, just once?

REGINA: I don't think there is much for him to do.

BEN: Oh, don't talk like that. He's come through attacks before. He will now.

[REGINA *sits down. After a second she speaks softly.*]

REGINA: Well. We haven't seen each other since the day of our fight.

BEN: [*Tenderly.*] That was nothing. Why, you and Oscar and I used to fight when we were kids.

OSCAR: [*Hurriedly.*] Don't you think we should go up? Is there anything we can do for Horace—

BEN: You don't feel well. Ah—

REGINA: [*Without looking at them.*] No, I don't. [*Slight pause.*] Horace told me about the bonds this afternoon.

[*There is an immediate shocked silence.*]

LEO: The bonds. What do you mean? What bonds? What—

BEN: [*Looks at him furiously. Then to REGINA.*] The Union Pacific bonds? Horace's Union Pacific bonds?

REGINA: Yes.

OSCAR: [*Steps to her, very nervously.*] Well. Well what—what about them? What—what could he say?

REGINA: He said that Leo had stolen the bonds and given them to you.

OSCAR: [*Aghast, very loudly.*] That's ridiculous, Regina, absolutely—

LEO: I don't know what you're talking about. What would I— Why—

REGINA: [*Wearily to BEN.*] Isn't it enough that he stole them from me? Do I have to listen to this in the bargain?

OSCAR: You are talking—

LEO: I didn't steal anything. I don't know why—

REGINA: [*To BEN.*] Would you ask them to stop that, please?

[*There is silence for a minute.* BEN *glowers at* OSCAR *and* LEO.]

BEN: Aren't we starting at the wrong end, Regina? What did Horace tell you?

REGINA: [*Smiles at him.*] He told me that Leo had stolen the bonds.

LEO: I didn't steal—

REGINA: Please. Let me finish. Then he told me that he was going to pretend that he had lent them to you [LEO *turns sharply to* REGINA, *then looks at* OSCAR, *then looks back at* REGINA.] as a present from me—to my brothers. He said there was nothing I could do about it. He said the rest of his money would go to Alexandra. That is all.

[*There is a silence.* OSCAR *coughs,* LEO *smiles slyly.*]

LEO: [*Taking a step to her.*] I told you he had lent them—I could have told you—

REGINA: [*Ignores him, smiles sadly at* BEN.] So I'm very badly off, you see. [*Carefully.*] But Horace said there was nothing I could do about it as long as he was alive to say he had lent you the bonds.

BEN: You shouldn't feel that way. It can all be explained, all be adjusted. It isn't as bad—

REGINA: So you, at least, are willing to admit that the bonds were stolen?

[OSCAR *laughs nervously.*]

BEN: I admit no such thing. It's possible that Horace made up that part of the story to tease you—[*Looks at her.*] Or perhaps to punish you. Punish you.

REGINA: [*Sadly.*] It's not a pleasant story. I feel bad, Ben, naturally. I hadn't thought—

BEN: Now you shall have the bonds safely back. That was the understanding, wasn't it, Oscar?

OSCAR: Yes.

REGINA: I'm glad to know that. [*Smiles.*] Ah, I had greater hopes—

BEN: Don't talk that way. That's foolish. [*Looks at his watch.*] I think we ought to drive out for Sloan ourselves. If we can't find him we'll go over to Senateville for Doctor Morris. And don't think I'm dismissing this other business. I'm not. We'll have it all out on a more appropriate day.

REGINA: [*Looks up, quietly.*] I don't think you had better go yet. I think you had better stay and sit down.

BEN: We'll be back with Sloan.

REGINA: Cal has gone for him. I don't want you to go.

BEN: Now don't worry and—

REGINA: You will come back in this room and sit down. I have something more to say.

BEN: [*Turns, comes towards her.*] Since when do I take orders from you?

REGINA: [*Smiles.*] You don't—yet. [*Sharply.*] Come back, Oscar. You too, Leo.

OSCAR: [*Sure of himself, laughs.*] My dear Regina—

BEN: [*Softly, pats her hand.*] Horace has already clipped your wings and very wittily. Do I have to clip them, too? [*Smiles at her.*] You'd get farther with a smile, Regina. I'm a soft man for a woman's smile.

REGINA: I'm smiling, Ben. I'm smiling because you are quite safe while Horace lives. But I don't think Horace will live. And if he doesn't live I shall want seventy-five per cent in exchange for the bonds.

BEN: [*Steps back, whistles, laughs.*] Greedy! What a greedy girl you are! You want so much of everything.

REGINA: Yes. And if I don't get what I want I am going to put all three of you in jail.

OSCAR: [*Furiously.*] You're mighty crazy. Having just admitted—

BEN: And on what evidence would you put Oscar and Leo in jail?

REGINA: [*Laughs, gaily.*] Oscar, listen to him. He's getting ready to swear that it was you and Leo! What do you say to that? [OSCAR *turns furiously towards* BEN.] Oh, don't be angry, Oscar. I'm going to see that he goes in with you.

BEN: Try anything you like, Regina. [*Sharply.*] And now we can stop all this and say good-bye to you. [ALEXANDRA *comes slowly down the steps.*] It's his money and he's obviously willing to let us borrow it. [*More pleasantly.*] Learn to make threats when you can carry them through. For how many years have I told you a good-looking woman gets more by being soft and appealing? Mama used to tell you that. [*Looks at his watch.*] Where the hell is Sloan? [*To* OSCAR.] Take the buggy and—

[*As* BEN *turns to* OSCAR, *he sees* ALEXANDRA. *She walks stiffly. She goes slowly to the lower window, her head bent. They all turn to look at her.*]

OSCAR: [*After a second, moving toward her.*] What? Alexandra—

[*She does not answer. After a second,* ADDIE *comes slowly down the stairs, moving as if she were very tired. At the foot of steps, she looks at* ALEXANDRA, *then turns and slowly crosses to door and exits.* REGINA *rises.* BEN *looks nervously at* ALEXANDRA, *at* REGINA.]

OSCAR: [*As* ADDIE *passes him, irritably to* ALEXANDRA.] Well, what is— [*Turns into room—sees* ADDIE *at foot of steps.*] —what's? [BEN *puts up a hand, shakes his head.*] My God, I didn't know—who *could* have known—I didn't know he was that sick. Well, well—I—

[REGINA *stands quietly, her back to them.*]

BEN: [*Softly, sincerely.*] Seems like yesterday when he first came here.
OSCAR: [*Sincerely, nervously.*] Yes, that's true. [*Turns to* BEN.] The whole town loved him and respected him.
ALEXANDRA: [*Turns.*] Did you love him, Uncle Oscar?
OSCAR: Certainly, I— What a strange thing to ask! I—
ALEXANDRA: Did you love him, Uncle Ben?
BEN: [*Simply.*] He had—
ALEXANDRA: [*Suddenly starts to laugh very loudly.*] And you, Mama, did you love him, too?
REGINA: I know what you feel, Alexandra, but please try to control yourself.
ALEXANDRA: [*Still laughing.*] I'm trying, Mama. I'm trying very hard.
BEN: Grief makes some people laugh and some people cry. It's better to cry, Alexandra.
ALEXANDRA: [*The laugh has stopped. Tensely moves toward* REGINA.] What was Papa doing on the staircase?

[BEN *turns to look at* ALEXANDRA.]

REGINA: Please go and lie down, my dear. We all need time to get over shocks like this. [ALEXANDRA *does not move.* REGINA's *voice becomes softer, more insistent.*] Please go, Alexandra.
ALEXANDRA: No, Mama. I'll wait. I've got to talk to you.
REGINA: Later. Go and rest now.
ALEXANDRA: [*Quietly.*] I'll wait, Mama. I've plenty of time.
REGINA: [*Hesitates, stares, makes a half shrug, turns back to* BEN.] As I was saying. Tomorrow morning I am going up to Judge Simmes. I shall tell him about Leo.
BEN: [*Motioning toward* ALEXANDRA.] Not in front of the child, Regina. I—

REGINA: [*Turns to him. Sharply.*] I didn't ask her to stay. Tomorrow morning I go to Judge Simmes—

OSCAR: And what proof? What proof of all this—

REGINA: [*Turns sharply.*] None. I won't need any. The bonds are missing and they are with Marshall. That will be enough. If it isn't, I'll add what's necessary.

BEN: I'm sure of that.

REGINA: [*Turns to BEN.*] You can be quite sure.

OSCAR: We'll deny—

REGINA: Deny your heads off. You couldn't find a jury that wouldn't weep for a woman whose brothers steal from her. And you couldn't find twelve men in this state you haven't cheated and hate you for it.

OSCAR: What kind of talk is this? You couldn't do anything like that! We're your own brothers. [*Points upstairs.*] How can you talk that way when upstairs not five minutes ago—

REGINA: [*Slowly.*] There are people who can never go back, who must finish what they start. I am one of those people, Oscar. [*After a slight pause.*] Where was I? [*Smiles at BEN.*] Well, they'll convict you. But I won't care much if they don't. [*Leans forward, pleasantly.*] Because by that time you'll be ruined. I shall also tell my story to Mr. Marshall, who likes me, I think, and who will not want to be involved in your scandal. A respectable firm like Marshall and Company. The deal would be off in an hour. [*Turns to them angrily.*] And you know it. Now I don't want to hear any more from any of you. *You'll do no more bargaining in this house.* I'll take my seventy-five per cent and we'll forget the story forever. That's one way of doing it, and the way I prefer. You know me well enough to know that I don't mind taking the other way.

BEN: [*After a second, slowly.*] None of us have ever known you well enough, Regina.

REGINA: You're getting old, Ben. Your tricks aren't as smart as they used to be. [*There is no answer. She waits, then smiles.*] All right. I take it that's settled and I get what I asked for.

OSCAR: [*Furiously to BEN.*] Are you going to let her do this—

BEN: [*Turns to look at him, slowly.*] You have a suggestion?

REGINA: [*Puts her arms above her head, stretches, laughs.*] No, he hasn't. All right. Now, Leo, I have forgotten that you ever saw the bonds. [*Archly, to BEN and OSCAR.*] And as long as you boys both behave yourselves, I've forgotten that we ever talked about them. You can draw up the necessary papers tomorrow.

[BEN *laughs,* LEO *stares at him, starts for door. Exits.* OSCAR *moves towards door angrily.* REGINA *looks at* BEN, *nods, laughs with him. For a second,* OSCAR *stands in the door, looking back at them. Then he exits.*]

REGINA: You're a good loser, Ben. I like that.

BEN: [*He picks up his coat, then turns to her.*] Well, I say to myself, what's the good? You and I aren't like Oscar. We're not sour people. I think that comes from a good digestion. Then, too, one loses today and wins tomorrow. I say to myself, years of planning and I get what I want. Then I don't get it. But I'm not discouraged. The century's turning, the world is open. Open for people like you and me. Ready for us, waiting for us. After all this is just the beginning. There are hundreds of Hubbards sitting in rooms like this throughout the country. All their names aren't Hubbard, but they are all Hubbards and they will own this country some day. We'll get along.

REGINA: [Smiles.] I think so.

BEN: Then, too, I say to myself, things may change. [Looks at ALEXANDRA.] I agree with Alexandra. What is a man in a wheel chair doing on a staircase? I ask myself that.

REGINA: [Looks up at him.] And what do you answer?

BEN: I have no answer. But maybe some day I will. Maybe never, but maybe some day. [Smiles. Pats her arm.] When I do, I'll let you know. [Goes towards hall.]

REGINA: When you do, write me. I will be in Chicago. [Gaily.] Ah, Ben, if Papa had only left me his money.

BEN: I'll see you tomorrow.

REGINA: Oh, yes. Certainly. You'll be sort of working for me now.

BEN: [As he passes ALEXANDRA, smiles.] Alexandra, you're turning out to be a right interesting girl. [Looks at REGINA.] Well, good night all. [He exits.]

REGINA: [Sits quietly for a second, stretches, turns to look at ALEXANDRA.] What do you want to talk to me about, Alexandra?

ALEXANDRA: [Slowly.] I've changed my mind. I don't want to talk. There's nothing to talk about now.

REGINA: You're acting very strange. Not like yourself. You've had a bad shock today. I know that. And you loved Papa, but you must have expected this to come some day. You know how sick he was.

ALEXANDRA: I knew. We all knew.

REGINA: It will be good for you to get away from here. Good for me, too. Time heals most wounds, Alexandra. You're young, you shall have all the things I wanted. I'll make the world for you the way I wanted it to be for me. [Uncomfortably.] Don't sit there staring. You've been around Birdie so much you're getting just like her.

ALEXANDRA: [Nods.] Funny. That's what Aunt Birdie said today.

REGINA: [Nods.] Be good for you to get away from all this.

[ADDIE enters.]

ADDIE: Cal is back, Miss Regina. He says Dr. Sloan will be coming in a few minutes.

REGINA: We'll go in a few weeks. A few weeks! That means two or three Saturdays, two or three Sundays. [Sighs.] Well, I'm very tired. I shall go to bed. I don't want any supper. Put the lights out and lock up. [ADDIE moves to the piano lamp, turns it out.] You go to your room, Alexandra. Addie will bring you something hot. You look very tired. [Rises. To ADDIE.] Call me when Dr.

Sloan gets here. I don't want to see anybody else. I don't want any condolence calls tonight. The whole town will be over.

ALEXANDRA: Mama, I'm not coming with you. I'm not going to Chicago.

REGINA: [*Turns to her.*] You're very upset, Alexandra.

ALEXANDRA: [*Quietly.*] I mean what I say. With all my heart.

REGINA: We'll talk about it tomorrow. The morning will make a difference.

ALEXANDRA: It won't make any difference. And there isn't anything to talk about. I am going away from you. Because I want to. Because I know Papa would want me to.

REGINA: [*Puzzled, careful, polite.*] You *know* your papa wanted you to go away from me?

ALEXANDRA: Yes.

REGINA: [*Softly.*] And if I say no?

ALEXANDRA: [*Looks at her.*] Say it, Mama, say it. And see what happens.

REGINA: [*Softly, after a pause.*] And if I make you stay?

ALEXANDRA: That would be foolish. It wouldn't work in the end.

REGINA: You're very serious about it, aren't you? [*Crosses to stairs.*] Well, you'll change your mind in a few days.

ALEXANDRA: You only change your mind when you want to. And I won't want to.

REGINA: [*Going up the steps.*] Alexandra, I've come to the end of my rope. Somewhere there has to be what I want, too. Life goes too fast. Do what you want; think what you want; go where you want. I'd like to keep you with me, but I won't make you stay. Too many people used to make me do too many things. No, I won't make you stay.

ALEXANDRA: You couldn't, Mama, because I want to leave here. As I've never wanted anything in my life before. Because now I understand what Papa was trying to tell me. [*Pause.*] All in one day: Addie said there were people who ate the earth and other people who stood around and watched them do it. And just now Uncle Ben said the same thing. Really, he said the same thing. [*Tensely.*] Well, tell him for me, Mama, I'm not going to stand around and watch you do it. Tell him I'll be fighting as hard as he'll be fighting [*Rises.*] some place where people don't just stand around and watch.

REGINA: Well, you have spirit, after all. I used to think you were all sugar water. We don't have to be bad friends. I don't want us to be bad friends, Alexandra. [*Starts, stops, turns to* ALEXANDRA.] Would you like to come and talk to me, Alexandra? Would you—would you like to sleep in my room tonight?

ALEXANDRA: [*Takes a step towards her.*] Are you afraid, Mama?

[REGINA *does not answer. She moves slowly out of sight.* ADDIE *comes to* ALEXANDRA, *presses her arm.*]

CURTAIN

1939

▼   ▼   ▼

STRUCTURE A Glossary

amphitheater: the raised semicircle of seats on which the audience sat in ancient Greek theater

apron: a forestage, an area of the stage in proscenium theater that extends outward from the curtain, toward the audience

arena stage: a stage in which the action takes place in the midst of the audience, that is, with the audience seated all around the stage action. Also called theater-in-a-circle or theater-in-the-round

catastrophe: the conclusion, the fifth part of dramatic progression

climax: the turning point between rising and falling action, the third part of dramatic progression

conclusion: the final part of dramatic progression, the catastrophe

conflict: the central tension in drama. Conflict may be between individuals or groups, between an individual and some particular group, between ideas or values, or various combinations of the above

dramatic irony: the fulfillment of a plan, action, or expectation in a surprising way, often the opposite of what the characters intended

exposition: the situation of events and the givens of character at the beginning of a play; the first part of dramatic progression

falling action: the unwinding of the plot toward a conclusion, the fourth part of dramatic progression

orchestra: the circular area in ancient Greek theater, which was used primarily for dancing by the chorus

plot: the entire conception of action and character in a play, including its structure

proscenium: the kind of stage in which the action takes place in a designated area isolated from the audience. A proscenium arch, often with a pull or drop curtain, normally divides the stage cleanly from the audience, and the illusion created is of an audience seeing through one wall of a room or from one side of an outdoor scene

rising action: the tangling of the plot, the setting up of conflict; the second part of dramatic progression

skene: in ancient Greek theater, the stage house representing the palace or temple in front of which the action takes place

thrust stage: a stage surrounded on three sides by the audience

turning point: the climax, the third part of dramatic progression: the point at which rising action ends and falling action begins

unity of time: the critical doctrine that the represented action in a play should not exceed the performance time on the stage. Literally understood, unity of time would mean that a play that takes two hours to perform represents fictional time of two hours, but in practice even the most rigid proponents of unity of time allow a play to represent fictional time up to a day

QUESTIONS

Hamlet

1. Read over the first act of the play carefully, and make a list of all the exposition we are given here—relationships between characters, events that have taken place before the play begins, conflicts of various kinds and issues at stake. What *else* happens in Act I? What kinds of emotions are aroused? With what issues do we become concerned? Whose problems do we care about? In what specific ways is the action moved forward?

2. Review carefully all the action in Act III, scene 2. Summarize exactly what happens in the scene, and specify exactly what we learn. Do we learn the same thing that Hamlet does? What structural functions does the scene perform? If you were producing the play, how would you have Claudius act at the end of the scene when he calls for more light? What facial expressions would you give him? What hand gestures?

3. How are Rosencrantz and Guildenstern characterized in the play? In what ways are they alike? In what ways different? What suggestions do you find in the text as to why their fate is paired so closely? What other "pairs" of characters are in the play? Which characters are specifically compared to each other in terms of temperament or habit? What does the device of pairing have to do with the play's structure?

4. What different strategies are used to characterize Laertes? Describe his relationship to his sister; to his father; to Hamlet. Describe his "role" in the plot. If he were to be eliminated from the play, what specific things that seem to you crucial to the play's structure and effects would be missing? Can you conceive of another character or group of characters who could be introduced into the play to perform those structural functions? Make a list of all the things that such a character or group would have to be or do.

5. Study the character of Polonius carefully and review all of his lines and actions. What other characters is he paired with, by relationship or parallel function? How do those pairings help us to evaluate Polonius and draw conclusions about him? What structural role does he perform in the play?

The Little Foxes

1. How much of Act I seems to you to be exposition? Exactly what are we told and by whom? At what point in Act I do you begin to have a sense of what individual characters are like and how they are related to each other? Where does the rising action begin?

2. Exactly what part of Act II constitutes the play's turning point? Where does the falling action begin? In what does the play's final stability consist?

3. What different pasts haunt the different characters in the play? In what specific ways do memories of the past, or nostalgia for it, affect the motivations of individual characters? How much of the plot is driven by a sense of the past? Which characters are motivated by the future? In what ways are economic status and social class related to a sense of the past?

4. In what specific ways is the setting of the play important? Does it make any difference that the action occurs in the spring? In what ways are the material objects mentioned in the stage directions important to characterization? to the play's themes?

5. Who is the most important character in the play? On what basis did you decide: centrality to the plot? attractiveness? psychological complexity? obsession to manipulate others? power?

6. What does the play's title mean?

WRITING SUGGESTIONS

Hamlet

1. Paraphrase, as exactly as you can, Hamlet's "To be or not to be" soliloquy. Summarize it in no more than two sentences. In your summary, what distortions are you particularly concerned about? In what ways did you find it difficult to communicate tone in your paraphrase?

2. Pretend that you have been given the job of reading the play in order to prepare actors for their performance in it. Choose five characters from the play, and write (as if for the actor about to play the part) a full description of each of them (about 300 words each). Describe physical appearance, voice, gestures, personality, temperament, conflicts, character flaws, everything you think the actor needs to know to play the part according to your interpretation of the play.

3. In an essay of about four pages, analyze the characterization of Ophelia and assess her structural function in the play.

The Little Foxes

1. Write a brief character sketch of Leo, outlining his most obvious characteristics. Then read back through the play carefully and notice at what points his various stereotypical characteristics reveal themselves. How important to

the play are other people's opinions of Leo? When do you become aware that you have formed a strong opinion about him? Exactly what function does he perform in the plot? Which of his distinctive characteristics are crucial to the plot? In an essay of about three pages, analyze Leo's role in the plot and show exactly how the structure of the play depends on the gradual revelation of his character.

2. Write a short (600-word) essay describing Birdie's role in the plot.

3. "Chicago" has a specific symbolic value for several of the play's characters, a symbolism that does not necessarily correspond to the "real" Chicago Mr. Marshall is from. Which characters develop a particular "image" of Chicago—either from the past or because of what it might hold in the future? Make a list of the qualities Chicago represents to individual characters. Note especially what kinds of notions Regina has about Chicago. In an essay about Regina's character (an essay of about 1,000 words), show the importance of "Chicago" to her consciousness, and note how other people's visions of the city help to clarify Regina's character and values.

STUDENT WRITING

The Play's the Thing:
Deception in <u>Hamlet</u>

Jeanette Sperhac

Early in Act I we are introduced to the young
Prince Hamlet who, distraught over his father's
death, is defending the utter sincerity of his
grief. Alongside the wily banter of the court and
the murky circumstances of his mother's marriage,
Hamlet's distress is astonishingly genuine and
true. But Hamlet's honesty does not appear to
last; his hopelessness leads him to don an "antic
disposition" and reciprocate the deceit of those
around him. He is driven to feign madness, to toy
with the sensibilities of courtiers, friends, and
even his mother, and to plot the exposure of the
king's monstrous crime; these acts seem to be
breaches of his honesty, yet all actually uphold
a higher end, avenging King Hamlet's murder.
Hamlet's seeming descent from sincerity to
deceit, and the nested plots and false
appearances that ensnare him, can be traced to
his first speech, that of an "honest" man.

Hamlet's opening speech resounds with his
ideals. "I know not 'seems,'" he claims
(I.2.76), seeking to dispel his mother's
misgivings about his mourning. Not merely

claiming sincerity, Hamlet is making a statement
fundamental to his character; all that he knows,
all that he recognizes, is <u>what</u> <u>is</u>. Appearances
are transitory and fleeting; in his distracted
state, Hamlet knows and acknowledges only that
his father is dead, that his mother's remarriage
is suspect, that his grief <u>is</u> <u>warranted</u>. When
Hamlet learns later that his father's ghost
desires revenge, that fact becomes Hamlet's
warrant to do whatever he must to frame Claudius.
Further insight into Hamlet's character can be
ascertained from "I have that within which
passeth show" (I.2.85), which, on the surface,
articulates the all-encompassing nature of his
grief. Once again, there are strong
undercurrents; Hamlet knows that he is able to
project a false appearance, to act a part that
still "passes show" and seems true. Hamlet's first
speech makes evident two seemingly contradictory
qualities, his conviction and honesty opposite
his ability to lie and deceive.

It can hardly be surprising that Hamlet
plunges into the rampant currents of deception,
feigning madness and playing parts for those
around him. The "actions that a man might play"
to which Hamlet alluded in his opening speech
(I.2.84) begin to unfold. Of Polonius he makes a
"tedious old fool" (II.2.209) by bantering
endlessly with the man until he is certain that
the prince is mad with unrequited love; Hamlet is
harsher with Polonius's daughter, berating

Ophelia and mocking his own fond letters to her:
"I did love you once . . . [but] you should not
have believed me . . . I loved you not"
(III.1.113—17). Hamlet is torn upon the subject
of his mother; though he is tempted to reproach
her, though she is playing along with Claudius,
his father's ghost has warned him to leave her
alone. With his mother, as throughout, Hamlet's
justification for his actions and his play-acting
lies in the genuine motive that lies
paradoxically behind his antic disposition. The
ghost of King Hamlet has given irrevocable
orders; Hamlet, in his distress, is compelled to
obey them, and is drawn deeper into his playing.

Most fundamental of all Hamlet's play-acting
is that which involves Claudius, for revenge upon
Claudius is Hamlet's true objective. Directly
connected to the king is Hamlet's playing and
counterplaying with Rosencrantz and Guildenstern,
who, at Claudius's request, assume the guises of
concerned friends. The perceptive prince cuts
instantly through what "seems"; he knows that
they are informers. His uncanny sense for what
"is" identifies their true intent. In the course
of their three-way playing, Hamlet taunts
Rosencrantz and Guildenstern with his knowledge,
continually mocks them, and even forces them to
admit to their doings. "Though you can fret me,
you cannot play upon me," Hamlet laughs
(III.2.320—21); though Rosencrantz and
Guildenstern are hired to spy on him, though it

is purportedly their game, Hamlet is the one in
control; it is he who plays upon them.

Of the final and most shattering instances of
"playing," the framing of Claudius belongs
completely to Hamlet; the exposure of the king's
monstrous crime is Hamlet's great scheme. The
prince's interest in the traveling players is
misinterpreted by Claudius as a healthy
diversion; the king never suspects that the crux
of Hamlet's revenge lies in the players' art.
Claudius's forced admission of the king's murder
happens bizarrely, paradoxically, not
acknowledged under confrontation, but whimpered
in the dark in the response to posed figures on a
stage. Hamlet has surpassed his own play-acting
and the guile and tact of the court; he turns the
false projection of an actor into a vehicle of
justice. In his finest moment, Hamlet harnesses
the actor's art to accuse Claudius; it is as if
the prince is gone so far into playing that he
must use puppets for his true intent.

The final scene could be viewed as Claudius's
reply to the "Mousetrap." Challenged to an
apparently harmless fencing match, Hamlet is
doomed to lose his life, either to the tainted
foil of Laertes, his "sporting" opponent, or to
the poisoned goblet held by Claudius. The prince
is hopelessly trapped; no guise can transport him
now, no perception foresee the consequences of
the scene. Deception heaped upon deception has
caught up with Hamlet at last, and upstaged by

Claudius's guile, the prince drags Denmark down
with him.

Central to <u>Hamlet</u> are currents of deception:
apparent truths, apparent sentiments, apparent
relationships and the submerged realities which
they misrepresent. Though the prince's opening
speech shows a veneer of sincerity, it
foreshadows the trickery that Hamlet is capable
of, the playing and seeming that he will
undertake to serve an ironically pure end. To
obey his murdered father, a loyal son plays at
deception, aiming to achieve justice; labyrinths
of deceit produce a kind of final truth, once
appearances are shed and the actual emerges.
These entangled plots and jumbled motives within
<u>Hamlet</u> are all evident from the prince's opening
speech.

3 THE WHOLE TEXT

Though it is possible to represent the elements of fiction or poetry in an introduction to literature by devoting a chapter to each element and giving full-length texts as examples, it is not so for drama. In considering drama, we have in this volume represented only the elements of characterization and structure in their own chapters, each containing two plays. In this chapter we will look at such other elements as **setting, tone,** and **theme** for the first time and look again at character and plot. But while all of these elements will be glanced at separately, it will become clear that they are not really so distinct: that character is shown in action, that action or plot relates to setting, that setting relates to tone, and that theme involves all elements at once. For if we analyze the separate parts of a text in order to understand them, we must then put them back together to fully comprehend the text itself. It is for this reason that we examine them all in one chapter entitled "The Whole Text."

Before reading *Pygmalion* and analyzing its elements and how they interrelate, for a few moments let us look back at *Trifles.* The **setting** in Glaspell's play is the kitchen of a midwestern farmhouse in which a murder has occurred. Having the action unfold in the kitchen, traditionally considered the woman's part of the house, relates to the play's **theme** or central idea—that men and women have different views of reality, that women viewing "trifles," like details in a kitchen, can discover truths as well or better than men who believe themselves to be concerned only with more important matters. The plot—the finding of the "trifling" bits of evidence that implicate Mrs. Wright in the murder of her husband and the suggestions of John Wright's abusive behavior that lead the women to band together in her defense and to suppress evidence that the men would think trifling—depends on the setting and embodies the theme. The characters of Mrs. Peters, the sheriff's wife, and Mrs. Hale are interrelated with plot and theme. Mrs. Hale is the more observant of the women and less subordinate to her husband and a man's way of looking at things, while Mrs. Peters is more conventional, less willing to defy male authority. In convincing her, Mrs. Hale and the evidence convince most viewers that Mrs. Wright had good reason to murder her husband.

As you read *Pygmalion*, keep in mind the individual elements, and how sometimes a given action, sentence, or word may be related to several elements at once. Notice the structure (exposition, rising action, and so on), the characters and their characterization, the setting, the tone, and the theme, but be aware too of how impossible it is at times to separate plot from character, character from theme, or any one element from another or from all the others.

▼   ▼   ▼

BERNARD SHAW

Pygmalion

A ROMANCE IN FIVE ACTS

CHARACTERS

CLARA EYNSFORD HILL	HENRY HIGGINS
MRS. EYNSFORD HILL	A SARCASTIC BYSTANDER
A BYSTANDER	MRS. PEARCE
FREDDY EYNSFORD HILL	ALFRED DOOLITTLE
ELIZA DOOLITTLE	MRS. HIGGINS
COLONEL PICKERING	PARLORMAID

Period: The present.

ACT I: *The Portico of St. Paul's, Covent Garden.* 11:15 P.M.

ACT II: PROFESSOR HIGGINS's *phonetic laboratory, Wimpole Street. Next day.* 11 A.M.

ACT III: *The drawing room in* MRS. HIGGINS's *flat on Chelsea Embankment. Several months later. At-home day.*

ACT IV: *The same as Act II. Several months later. Midnight.*

ACT V: *The same as Act III. The following morning.*

NOTE: *In the dialogue an e upside down indicates the indefinite vowel, sometimes called obscure or neutral, for which, though it is one of the commonest sounds in English speech, our wretched alphabet has no letter.*

ACT I

London at 11:15 P.M. *Torrents of heavy summer rain. Cab whistles blowing frantically in all directions.* PEDESTRIANS *running for shelter into the portico of St. Paul's church (not Wren's cathedral but Inigo Jones's church in Covent Garden vegetable market), among them a* LADY *and her* DAUGHTER *in evening dress. All are peering out gloomily at the rain, except one* MAN *with his back turned to the rest, wholly preoccupied with a notebook in which he is writing.*

The church clock strikes the first quarter.

THE DAUGHTER: [*In the space between the central pillars, close to the one on her left.*] I'm getting chilled to the bone. What can Freddy be doing all this time? He's been gone twenty minutes.

THE MOTHER: [*On her* DAUGHTER's *right.*] Not so long. But he ought to have got us a cab by this.

A BYSTANDER: [*On the* LADY's *right.*] He wont[1] get no cab not until half-past eleven, missus, when they come back after dropping their theatre fares.

THE MOTHER: But we must have a cab. We cant stand here until half-past eleven. It's too bad.

THE BYSTANDER: Well, it aint my fault, missus.

THE DAUGHTER: If Freddy had a bit of gumption, he would have got one at the theatre door.

THE MOTHER: What could he have done, poor boy?

THE DAUGHTER: Other people got cabs. Why couldnt he?

[FREDDY *rushes in out of the rain from the Southampton Street side, and comes between them closing a dripping umbrella. He is a young man of twenty, in evening dress, very wet round the ankles.*]

THE DAUGHTER: Well, havnt you got a cab?

FREDDY: Theres not one to be had for love or money.

THE MOTHER: Oh, Freddy, there must be one. You cant have tried.

THE DAUGHTER: It's too tiresome. Do you expect us to go and get one ourselves?

FREDDY: I tell you theyre all engaged. The rain was so sudden: nobody was prepared; and everybody had to take a cab. Ive been to Charing Cross one way and nearly to Ludgate Circus the other; and they were all engaged.

THE MOTHER: Did you try Trafalgar Square?

FREDDY: There wasnt one at Trafalgar Square.

THE DAUGHTER: Did you try?

FREDDY: I tried as far as Charing Cross Station. Did you expect me to walk to Hammersmith?[2]

THE DAUGHTER: You havnt tried at all.

THE MOTHER: You really are very helpless, Freddy. Go again; and dont come back until you have found a cab.

FREDDY: I shall simply get soaked for nothing.

THE DAUGHTER: And what about us? Are we to stay here all night in this draught, with next to nothing on? You selfish pig—

FREDDY: Oh, very well: I'll go, I'll go. [*He opens his umbrella and dashes off Strandwards, but comes into collision with a* FLOWER GIRL *who is hurrying in for shelter, knocking her basket out of her hands. A blinding flash of lightning, followed instantly by a rattling peal of thunder, orchestrates the incident.*]

THE FLOWER GIRL: Nah then, Freddy: look wh' y' gowin, deah.

FREDDY: Sorry. [*He rushes off.*]

THE FLOWER GIRL: [*Picking up her scattered flowers and replacing them in the basket.*] Theres menners f' yer! Tə-oo banches o voylets trod into the mad. [*She sits down on the plinth of the column, sorting her flowers, on the* LADY's *right. She is not at all a romantic figure. She is perhaps eighteen, perhaps*

---

1. Shaw insisted on eliminating apostrophes from most contractions—wont, cant, didnt, etc.
2. Freddie has walked about two blocks in either direction to reach Charing Cross Station and Ludgate Circus. Trafalgar Square is another block beyond Charing Cross Station, and Hammersmith is about ten miles beyond that.

twenty, hardly older. She wears a little sailor hat of black straw that has long been exposed to the dust and soot of London and has seldom if ever been brushed. Her hair needs washing rather badly: its mousy color can hardly be natural. She wears a shoddy black coat that reaches nearly to her knees and is shaped to her waist. She has a brown skirt with a coarse apron. Her boots are much the worse for wear. She is no doubt as clean as she can afford to be; but compared to the ladies she is very dirty. Her features are no worse than theirs; but their condition leaves something to be desired; and she needs the services of a dentist.]

THE MOTHER: How do you know that my son's name is Freddy, pray?

THE FLOWER GIRL: Ow, eez yə-ooa san, is e? Wal, fewd dan y' də-ooty bawmz a mather should, eed now bettern to spawl a pore gel's flahrzn than ran awy athaht pyin. Will ye-oo py me fthem? [*Here, with apologies, this desperate attempt to represent her dialect without a phonetic alphabet must be abandoned as unintelligible outside London.*]

THE DAUGHTER: Do nothing of the sort, mother. The idea!

THE MOTHER: Please allow me, Clara. Have you any pennies?

THE DAUGHTER: No. Ive nothing smaller than sixpence.

THE FLOWER GIRL: [*Hopefully.*] I can give you change for a tanner,[3] kind lady.

THE MOTHER: [*To* CLARA.] Give it to me. [CLARA *parts reluctantly.*] Now. [*To the* GIRL.] This is for your flowers.

THE FLOWER GIRL: Thank you kindly, lady.

THE DAUGHTER: Make her give you the change. These things are only a penny a bunch.

THE MOTHER: Do hold your tongue, Clara. [*To the* GIRL.] You can keep the change.

THE FLOWER GIRL: Oh, thank you, lady.

THE MOTHER: Now tell me how you know that young gentleman's name.

THE FLOWER GIRL: I didnt.

THE MOTHER: I heard you call him by it. Dont try to deceive me.

THE FLOWER GIRL: [*Protesting.*] Who's trying to deceive you? I called him Freddy or Charlie same as you might yourself if you was talking to a stranger and wished to be pleasant.

THE DAUGHTER: Sixpence thrown away! Really, mamma, you might have spared Freddy that. [*She retreats in disgust behind the pillar.*]

[*An elderly* GENTLEMAN *of the amiable military type rushes into the shelter, and closes a dripping umbrella. He is in the same plight as* FREDDY, *very wet about the ankles. He is in evening dress, with a light overcoat. He takes the place left vacant by the* DAUGHTER.]

THE GENTLEMAN: Phew!

THE MOTHER: [*To the* GENTLEMAN.] Oh sir, is there any sign of its stopping?

THE GENTLEMAN: I'm afraid not. It started worse than ever about two minutes ago. [*He goes to the plinth beside the* FLOWER GIRL; *puts up his foot on it; and stoops to turn down his trouser ends.*]

---

3. Slang for sixpence (six pennies), loosely equivalent to a half-dollar in 1990s U.S. currency.

THE MOTHER: Oh dear! [*She retires sadly and joins her* DAUGHTER.]

THE FLOWER GIRL: [*Taking advantage of the military* GENTLEMAN's *proximity to establish friendly relations with him.*] If it's worse, it's a sign it's nearly over. So cheer up, Captain; and buy a flower off a poor girl.

THE GENTLEMAN: I'm sorry. I havnt any change.

THE FLOWER GIRL: I can give you change, Captain.

THE GENTLEMAN: For a sovereign[4]? Ive nothing less.

THE FLOWER GIRL: Garn! Oh do buy a flower off me, Captain. I can change half-a-crown.[5] Take this for tuppence.[6]

THE GENTLEMAN: Now dont be troublesome: theres a good girl. [*Trying his pockets.*] I really havnt any change—Stop: heres three hapence,[7] if thats any use to you. [*He retreats to the other pillar.*]

THE FLOWER GIRL: [*Disappointed, but thinking three halfpence better than nothing.*] Thank you, sir.

THE BYSTANDER: [*To the* GIRL.] You be careful: give him a flower for it. Theres a bloke here behind taking down every blessed word youre saying. [*All turn to the* MAN *who is taking notes.*]

THE FLOWER GIRL: [*Springing up terrified.*] I aint done nothing wrong by speaking to the gentleman. Ive a right to sell flowers if I keep off the kerb. [*Hysterically.*] I'm a respectable girl: so help me, I never spoke to him except to ask him to buy a flower off me.

[*General hubbub, mostly sympathetic to the* FLOWER GIRL, *but deprecating her excessive sensibility. Cries of* Dont start hollerin. Who's hurting you? Nobody's going to touch you. Whats the good of fussing? Steady on. Easy easy, etc., *come from the elderly staid spectators, who pat her comfortingly. Less patient ones bid her shut her head, or ask her roughly what is wrong with her. A remoter group, not knowing what the matter is, crowd in and increase the noise with question and answer:* Whats the row? What-she do? Where is he? A tec[8] taking her down. What! him? Yes: him over there: Took money off the gentleman, etc.]

THE FLOWER GIRL: [*Breaking through them to the* GENTLEMAN, *crying wildly.*] Oh, sir, dont let him charge me. You dunno what it means to me. Theyll take away my character and drive me on the streets for speaking to gentlemen. They—

THE NOTE TAKER: [*Coming forward on her right, the rest crowding after him.*] There! there! there! there! who's hurting you, you silly girl? What do you take me for?

THE BYSTANDER: It's aw rawt: e's a genleman: look at his bɔ-oots [*Explaining to the* NOTE TAKER.] She thought you was a copper's nark, sir.

THE NOTE TAKER: [*With quick interest.*] Whats a copper's nark?

---

4. Gold coin worth a pound (20 shillings), loosely equivalent to 20 dollars in 1990s U.S. currency.
5. Two and one-half shillings, loosely equivalent to two and a half dollars in 1990s currency.   6. Two pennies.   7. Half a penny.   8. Detective.

THE BYSTANDER: [*Inapt at definition.*] It's a—well, it's a copper's nark, as you might say. What else would you call it? A sort of informer.

THE FLOWER GIRL: [*Still hysterical.*] I take my Bible oath I never said a word—

THE NOTE TAKER: [*Overbearing but good-humored.*] Oh, shut up, shut up. Do I look like a policeman?

THE FLOWER GIRL: [*Far from reassured.*] Then what did you take down my words for? How do I know whether you took me down right? You just shew me what youve wrote about me. [*The NOTE TAKER opens his book and holds it steadily under her nose, though the pressure of the mob trying to read it over his shoulders would upset a weaker man.*] Whats that? That aint proper writing. I cant read that.

THE NOTE TAKER: I can. [*Reads, reproducing her pronunciation exactly.*] "Cheer ap, Keptin; n' baw ya flahr orf a pore gel."

THE FLOWER GIRL: [*Much distressed.*] It's because I called him Captain. I meant no harm. [*To the GENTLEMAN.*] Oh, sir, dont let him lay a charge agen me for a word like that. You—

THE GENTLEMAN: Charge! I make no charge. [*To the NOTE TAKER.*] Really, sir, if you are a detective, you need not begin protecting me against molestation by young women until I ask you. Anybody could see that the girl meant no harm.

THE BYSTANDERS GENERALLY: [*Demonstrating against police espionage.*] Course they could. What business is it of yours? You mind your own affairs. He wants promotion, he does. Taking down people's words! Girl never said a word to him. What harm if she did? Nice thing a girl cant shelter from the rain without being insulted, etc., etc., etc. [*She is conducted by the more sympathetic demonstrators back to her plinth, where she resumes her seat and struggles with her emotion.*]

THE BYSTANDER: He aint a tec. He's a blooming busybody: thats what he is. I tell you, look at his bɜ-oots.

THE NOTE TAKER: [*Turning on him genially.*] And how are all your people down at Selsey?

THE BYSTANDER: [*Suspiciously.*] Who told you my people come from Selsey?

THE NOTE TAKER: Never you mind. They did. [*To the GIRL.*] How do you come to be up so far east? You were born in Lisson Grove.

THE FLOWER GIRL: [*Appalled.*] Oh, what harm is there in my leaving Lisson Grove? It wasnt fit for a pig to live in; and I had to pay four-and-six a week. [*In tears.*] Oh, boo—hoo—oo—

THE NOTE TAKER: Live where you like; but stop that noise.

THE GENTLEMAN: [*To the GIRL.*] Come, come! he cant touch you: you have a right to live where you please.

A SARCASTIC BYSTANDER: [*Thrusting himself between the NOTE TAKER and the GENTLEMAN.*] Park Lane, for instance. I'd like to go into the Housing Question with you, I would.

THE FLOWER GIRL: [*Subsiding into a brooding melancholy over her basket, and talking very low-spiritedly to herself.*] I'm a good girl, I am.

THE SARCASTIC BYSTANDER: [*Not attending to her.*] Do you know where *I* come from?

THE NOTE TAKER: [*Promptly.*] Hoxton. [*Titterings. Popular interest in the* NOTE TAKER's *performance increases.*]

THE SARCASTIC ONE: [*Amazed.*] Well, who said I didnt? Bly me! you know everything, you do.

THE FLOWER GIRL: [*Still nursing her sense of injury.*] Aint no call to meddle with me, he aint.

THE BYSTANDER: [*To her.*] Of course he aint. Dont you stand it from him. [*To the* NOTE TAKER.] See here: what call have you to know about people what never offered to meddle with you?

THE FLOWER GIRL: Let him say what he likes. I dont want to have no truck with him.

THE BYSTANDER: You take us for dirt under your feet, dont you? Catch you taking liberties with a gentleman!

THE SARCASTIC BYSTANDER: Yes: tell him where he come from if you want to go fortune-telling.

THE NOTE TAKER: Cheltenham, Harrow, Cambridge, and India.

THE GENTLEMAN: Quite right. [*Great laughter. Reaction in the* NOTE TAKER's *favor. Exclamations of* He knows all about it. Told him proper. Hear him tell the toff[9] where he come from? *etc.*] May I ask, sir, do you do this for your living at a music hall?

THE NOTE TAKER: I've thought of that. Perhaps I shall some day.

[*The rain has stopped; and the persons on the outside of the crowd begin to drop off.*]

THE FLOWER GIRL: [*Resenting the reaction.*] He's no gentleman, he aint, to interfere with a poor girl.

THE DAUGHTER: [*Out of patience, pushing her way rudely to the front and displacing the* GENTLEMAN, *who politely retires to the other side of the pillar.*] What on earth is Freddy doing? I shall get pneumownia if I stay in this draught any longer.

THE NOTE TAKER: [*To himself, hastily making a note of her pronunciation of "monia."*] Earlscourt.

THE DAUGHTER: [*Violently.*] Will you please keep your impertinent remarks to yourself.

THE NOTE TAKER: Did I say that out loud? I didnt mean to. I beg your pardon. Your mother's Epsom, unmistakeably.

THE MOTHER: [*Advancing between her* DAUGHTER *and the* NOTE TAKER.] How very curious! I was brought up in Largelady Park, near Epsom.

THE NOTE TAKER: [*Uproariously amused.*] Ha! ha! What a devil of a name! Excuse me. [*To the* DAUGHTER.] You want a cab, do you?

THE DAUGHTER: Dont dare speak to me.

THE MOTHER: Oh please, please, Clara. [*Her* DAUGHTER *repudiates her with an*

---

9. Slang for "gentleman," slightly derogatory.

angry shrug and retires haughtily.] We should be so grateful to you, sir, if you found us a cab. [*The* NOTE TAKER *produces a whistle.*] Oh, thank you. [*She joins her* DAUGHTER.]

[*The* NOTE TAKER *blows a piercing blast.*]

THE SARCASTIC BYSTANDER: There! I knowed he was a plainclothes copper.

THE BYSTANDER: That aint a police whistle: thats a sporting whistle.

THE FLOWER GIRL: [*Still preoccupied with her wounded feelings.*] He's no right to take away my character. My character is the same to me as any lady's.

THE NOTE TAKER: I dont know whether youve noticed it; but the rain stopped about two minutes ago.

THE BYSTANDER: So it has. Why didnt you say so before? and us losing our time listening to your silliness! [*He walks off towards the Strand.*]

THE SARCASTIC BYSTANDER: I can tell where you come from. You come from Anwell. Go back there.

THE NOTE TAKER: [*Helpfully.*] Hanwell.[1]

THE SARCASTIC BYSTANDER: [*Affecting great distinction of speech.*] Thenk you, teacher. Haw haw! So long [*He touches his hat with mock respect and strolls off.*]

THE FLOWER GIRL: Frightening people like that! How would he like it himself?

THE MOTHER: It's quite fine now, Clara. We can walk to a motor bus. Come. [*She gathers her skirts above her ankles and hurries off towards the Strand.*]

THE DAUGHTER: But the cab—[*Her* MOTHER *is out of hearing.*] Oh, how tiresome! [*She follows angrily.*]

[*All the rest have gone except the* NOTE TAKER, *the* GENTLEMAN, *and the* FLOWER GIRL, *who sits arranging her basket, and still pitying herself in murmurs.*]

THE FLOWER GIRL: Poor girl! Hard enough for her to live without being worried and chivied.[2]

THE GENTLEMAN: [*Returning to his former place on the* NOTE TAKER's *left.*] How do you do it, if I may ask?

THE NOTE TAKER: Simply phonetics. The science of speech. Thats my profession: also my hobby. Happy is the man who can make a living by his hobby! You can spot an Irishman or a Yorkshireman by his brogue. *I* can place any man within six miles. I can place him within two miles in London. Sometimes within two streets.

THE FLOWER GIRL: Ought to be ashamed of himself, unmanly coward!

THE GENTLEMAN: But is there a living in that?

THE NOTE TAKER: Oh yes. Quite a fat one. This is an age of upstarts. Men begin in Kentish Town with £80 a year, and end in Park Lane with a hundred thousand. They want to drop Kentish Town; but they give themselves away every time they open their mouths. Now I can teach them—

THE FLOWER GIRL: Let him mind his own business and leave a poor girl—

1. Parish in Middlesex County, eight miles west of London.   2. Worried and hounded.

THE NOTE TAKER: [*Explosively.*] Woman: cease this detestable boohooing instantly; or else seek the shelter of some other place of worship.

THE FLOWER GIRL: [*With feeble defiance.*] Ive a right to be here if I like, same as you.

THE NOTE TAKER: A woman who utters such depressing and disgusting sounds has no right to be anywhere—no right to live. Remember that you are a human being with a soul and the divine gift of articulate speech: that your native language is the language of Shakespear and Milton and The Bible; and dont sit there crooning like a bilious pigeon.

THE FLOWER GIRL: [*Quite overwhelmed, looking up at him in mingled wonder and deprecation without daring to raise her head.*] Ah-ah-ah-ow-ow-ow-oo!

THE NOTE TAKER: [*Whipping out his book.*] Heavens! what a sound! [*He writes; then holds out the book and reads, reproducing her vowels exactly.*] Ah-ah-ah-ow-ow-ow-oo!

THE FLOWER GIRL: [*Tickled by the performance, and laughing in spite of herself.*] Garn!

THE NOTE TAKER: You see this creature with her kerbstone English: the English that will keep her in the gutter to the end of her days. Well, sir, in three months I could pass that girl off as a duchess at an ambassador's garden party. I could even get her a place as lady's maid or shop assistant, which requires better English.

THE FLOWER GIRL: Whats that you say?

THE NOTE TAKER: Yes, you squashed cabbage leaf, you disgrace to the noble architecture of these columns, you incarnate insult to the English language: I could pass you off as the Queen of Sheba. [*To the* GENTLEMAN.] Can you believe that?

THE GENTLEMAN: Of course I can. I am myself a student of Indian dialects; and—

THE NOTE TAKER: [*Eagerly.*] Are you? Do you know Colonel Pickering, the author of Spoken Sanscrit?

THE GENTLEMAN: I am Colonel Pickering. Who are you?

THE NOTE TAKER: Henry Higgins, author of Higgins's Universal Alphabet.

PICKERING: [*With enthusiasm.*] I came from India to meet you.

HIGGINS: I was going to India to meet you.

PICKERING: Where do you live?

HIGGINS: 27A Wimpole Street. Come and see me tomorrow.

PICKERING: I'm at the Carlton. Come with me now and lets have a jaw over some supper.

HIGGINS: Right you are.

THE FLOWER GIRL: [*To* PICKERING, *as he passes her.*] Buy a flower, kind gentleman. I'm short for my lodging.

PICKERING: I really havnt any change. I'm sorry. [*He goes away.*]

HIGGINS: [*Shocked at the* GIRL's *mendacity.*] Liar. You said you could change half-a-crown.

THE FLOWER GIRL: [*Rising in desperation.*] You ought to be stuffed with nails, you ought. [*Flinging the basket at his feet.*] Take the whole blooming basket for sixpence.

[*The church clock strikes the second quarter.*]

HIGGINS: [*Hearing in it the voice of God, rebuking him for his Pharisaic want of charity to the poor* GIRL.] A reminder. [*He raises his hat solemnly; then throws a handful of money into the basket and follows* PICKERING.]

THE FLOWER GIRL: [*Picking up a half-crown.*] Ah-ow-ooh! [*Picking up a couple of florins.*[3]] Aaah-ow-ooh! [*Picking up several coins.*] Aaaaaah-ow-ooh! [*Picking up a half-sovereign.*[4]] Aaaaaaaaaaaah-ow-ooh!!!

FREDDY: [*Springing out of a taxicab.*] Got one at last. Hallo! [*To the* GIRL.] Where are the two ladies that were here?

THE FLOWER GIRL: They walked to the bus when the rain stopped.

FREDDY: And left me with a cab on my hands! Damnation!

THE FLOWER GIRL: [*With grandeur.*] Never mind, young man. I'm going home in a taxi. [*She sails off to the cab. The driver puts his hand behind him and holds the door firmly shut against her. Quite understanding his mistrust, she shews him her handful of money.*] A taxi fare aint no object to me, Charlie. [*He grins and opens the door.*] Here. What about the basket?

THE TAXIMAN: Give it here. Tuppence extra.

LIZA: No: I dont want nobody to see it. [*She crushes it into the cab and gets in, continuing the conversation through the window.*] Goodbye, Freddy.

FREDDY: [*Dazedly raising his hat.*] Goodbye.

TAXIMAN: Where to?

LIZA: Bucknam Pellis [Buckingham Palace].

TAXIMAN: What d'ye mean—Bucknam Pellis?

LIZA: Dont you know where it is? In the Green Park, where the King lives. Goodbye, Freddy. Dont let me keep you standing there. Goodbye.

FREDDY: Goodbye. [*He goes.*].

TAXIMAN: Here? Whats this about Bucknam Pellis? What business have you at Bucknam Pellis?

LIZA: Of course I havnt none. But I wasnt going to let him know that. You drive me home.

TAXIMAN: And wheres home?

LIZA: Angel Court, Drury Lane, next Meiklejohn's oil shop.

TAXIMAN: That sounds more like it, Judy. [*He drives off.*]

* * *

Let us follow the taxi to the entrance to Angel Court, a narrow little archway between two shops, one of them Meiklejohn's oil shop. When it stops there, Eliza gets out, dragging her basket with her.

LIZA: How much?

TAXIMAN: [*Indicating the taximeter.*] Cant you read? A shilling.

LIZA: A shilling for two minutes!!

TAXIMAN: Two minutes or ten: it's all the same.

---

3. Two shillings, loosely equivalent to two dollars in 1990s U.S. currency.   4. Ten shillings (half-pound), loosely equivalent to ten dollars in 1990s U.S. currency.

LIZA: Well, I dont call it right.

TAXIMAN: Ever been in a taxi before?

LIZA: [*With dignity.*] Hundreds and thousands of times, young man.

TAXIMAN: [*Laughing at her.*] Good for you, Judy. Keep the shilling, darling, with best love from all at home. Good luck! [*He drives off.*]

LIZA: [*Humiliated.*] Impidence!

[*She picks up the basket and trudges up the alley with it to her lodging: a small room with very old wall paper hanging loose in the damp places. A broken pane in the window is mended with paper. A portrait of a popular actor and a fashion plate of ladies' dresses, all wildly beyond poor* ELIZA'S *means, both torn from newspapers, are pinned up on the wall. A birdcage hangs in the window; but its tenant died long ago: it remains as a memorial only.*

These are the only visible luxuries: the rest is the irreducible minimum of poverty's needs: a wretched bed heaped with all sorts of coverings that have any warmth in them, a draped packing case with a basin and jug on it and a little looking glass over it, a chair and table, the refuse of some suburban kitchen, and an American alarum clock on the shelf above the unused fire-place: the whole lighted with a gas lamp with a penny in the slot meter. Rent: four shillings a week.]

Here ELIZA, *chronically weary, but too excited to go to bed, sits, counting her new riches and dreaming and planning what to do with them, until the gas goes out, when she enjoys for the first time the sensation of being able to put in another penny without grudging it. This prodigal mood does not extinguish her gnawing sense of the need for economy sufficiently to prevent her from calculating that she can dream and plan in bed more cheaply and warmly than sitting up without a fire. So she takes off her shawl and skirt and adds them to the miscellaneous bedclothes. Then she kicks off her shoes and gets into bed without any further change.*

ACT II

Next day at 11 A.M. HIGGINS'S *laboratory in Wimpole Street. It is a room on the first floor, looking on the street, and was meant for the drawing room. The double doors are in the middle of the back wall; and persons entering find in the corner to their right two tall file cabinets at right angles to one another against the walls. In this corner stands a flat writing-table, on which are a phonograph, a laryngoscope, a row of tiny organ pipes with a bellows, a set of lamp chimneys for singing flames with burners attached to a gas plug in the wall by an indiarubber tube, several tuning-forks of different sizes, a life-size image of half a human head, shewing in section the vocal organs, and a box containing a supply of wax cylinders for the phonograph.*

Further down the room, on the same side, is a fireplace, with a comfortable leather-covered easy-chair at the side of the hearth nearest the door, and a coal-scuttle. There is a clock on the mantel-piece. Between the fireplace and the phonograph table is a stand for newspapers.

On the other side of the central door, to the left of the visitor, is a cabinet of shallow drawers. On it is a telephone and the telephone directory. The corner beyond, and most of the side wall, is occupied by a grand piano, with the keyboard at the end furthest from the door, and a bench for the player extending the full length of the keyboard. On the piano is a dessert dish heaped with fruit and sweets, mostly chocolates.

The middle of the room is clear. Besides the easy-chair, the piano bench, and two chairs at the phonograph table, there is one stray chair. It stands near the fireplace. On the walls, engravings: mostly Piranesis[5] and mezzotint portraits. No paintings.

PICKERING *is seated at the table, putting down some cards and a tuning-fork which he has been using.* HIGGINS *is standing up near him, closing two or three file drawers which are hanging out. He appears in the morning light as a robust, vital, appetizing sort of man of forty or thereabouts, dressed in a professional-looking black frock-coat with a white linen collar and black silk tie. He is of the energetic, scientific type, heartily, even violently interested in everything that can be studied as a scientific subject, and careless about himself and other people, including their feelings. He is, in fact, but for his years and size, rather like a very impetuous baby "taking notice" eagerly and loudly, and requiring almost as much watching to keep him out of unintended mischief. His manner varies from genial bullying when he is in a good humor to stormy petulance when anything goes wrong; but he is so entirely frank and void of malice that he remains likeable even in his least reasonable moments.*

HIGGINS: [*As he shuts the last drawer.*] Well, I think thats the whole show.

PICKERING: It's really amazing. I havnt taken half of it in, you know.

HIGGINS: Would you like to go over any of it again?

PICKERING: [*Rising and coming to the fireplace, where he plants himself with his back to the fire.*] No, thank you: not now. I'm quite done up for this morning.

HIGGINS: [*Following him, and standing beside him on his left.*] Tired of listening to sounds?

PICKERING: Yes. It's a fearful strain. I rather fancied myself because I can pronounce twenty-four distinct vowel sounds; but your hundred and thirty beat me. I cant hear a bit of difference between most of them.

HIGGINS: [*Chuckling, and going over to the piano to eat sweets.*] Oh, that comes with practice. You hear no difference at first; but you keep on listening, and presently you find theyre all as different as A from B. [MRS. PEARCE *looks in: she is* HIGGINS's *housekeeper*]. Whats the matter?

MRS. PEARCE: [*Hesitating, evidently perplexed.*] A young woman asks to see you, sir.

HIGGINS: A young woman! What does she want?

MRS. PEARCE: Well, sir, she says youll be glad to see her when you know what she's come about. She's quite a common girl, sir. Very common indeed. I should have sent her away, only I thought perhaps you wanted her to talk

5. Giovanni Battista Piranesi (1720–1778), a Neoclassical master in the art of etching, whose prints of Roman architecture helped stimulate the 18th-century enthusiasm for the Classical style.

into your machines. I hope Ive not done wrong; but really you see such queer people sometimes—youll excuse me, I'm sure, sir—

HIGGINS: Oh, thats all right, Mrs. Pearce. Has she an interesting accent?

MRS. PEARCE: Oh, something dreadful, sir, really. I dont know how you can take an interest in it.

HIGGINS: [*To* PICKERING.] Lets have her up. Shew her up, Mrs. Pearce [*He rushes across to his working table and picks out a cylinder to use on the phonograph.*]

MRS. PEARCE: [*Only half resigned to it.*] Very well, sir. It's for you to say. [*She goes downstairs.*]

HIGGINS: This is rather a bit of luck. I'll shew you how I make records. We'll set her talking; and I'll take it down first in Bell's Visible Speech; then in broad Romic[6]; and then we'll get her on the phonograph so that you can turn her on as often as you like with the written transcript before you.

MRS. PEARCE: [*Returning.*] This is the young woman, sir.

[*The* FLOWER GIRL *enters in state. She has a hat with three ostrich feathers, orange, sky-blue, and red. She has a nearly clean apron, and the shoddy coat has been tidied a little. The pathos of this deplorable figure, with its innocent vanity and consequential air, touches* PICKERING, *who has already straightened himself in the presence of* MRS. PEARCE. *But as to* HIGGINS, *the only distinction he makes between men and women is that when he is neither bullying nor exclaiming to the heavens against some feather-weight cross, he coaxes women as a child coaxes its nurse when it wants to get anything out of her.*]

HIGGINS: [*Brusquely, recognizing her with unconcealed disappointment, and at once, babylike, making an intolerable grievance of it.*] Why, this is the girl I jotted down last night. She's no use: Ive got all the records I want of the Lisson Grove lingo; and I'm not going to waste another cylinder on it. [*To the* GIRL.] Be off with you: I dont want you.

THE FLOWER GIRL: Dont you be so saucy. You aint heard what I come for yet. [*To* MRS. PEARCE, *who is waiting at the door for further instructions.*] Did you tell him I come in a taxi?

MRS. PEARCE: Nonsense, girl! what do you think a gentleman like Mr. Higgins cares what you came in?

THE FLOWER GIRL: Oh, we are proud! He aint above giving lessons, not him: I heard him say so. Well, I aint come here to ask for any compliment; and if my money's not good enough I can go elsewhere.

HIGGINS: Good enough for what?

THE FLOWER GIRL: Good enough for yə-oo. Now you know, dont you? I'm come to have lessons, I am. And to pay for em te-oo: make no mistake.

HIGGINS: [*Stupent.*[7]] Well!!! [*Recovering his breath with a gasp.*] What do you expect me to say to you?

---

6. A system of phonetic transcription devised by Dr. Henry Sweet.   7. In a state of stupor or amazement.

THE FLOWER GIRL: Well, if you was a gentleman, you might ask me to sit down, I think. Dont I tell you I'm bringing you business?

HIGGINS: Pickering: shall we ask this baggage to sit down, or shall we throw her out of the window?

THE FLOWER GIRL: [*Running away in terror to the piano, where she turns at bay.*] Ah-ah-oh-ow-ow-ow-oo! [*Wounded and whimpering.*] I wont be called a baggage when Ive offered to pay like any lady.

[*Motionless, the* TWO MEN *stare at her from the other side of the room, amazed.*]

PICKERING: [*Gently.*] But what is it you want?

THE FLOWER GIRL: I want to be a lady in a flower shop stead of sellin at the corner of Tottenham Court Road. But they wont take me unless I can talk more genteel. He said he could teach me. Well, here I am ready to pay him—not asking any favor—and he treats me zif I was dirt.

MRS. PEARCE: How can you be such a foolish ignorant girl as to think you could afford to pay Mr. Higgins?

THE FLOWER GIRL: Why shouldnt I? I know what lessons cost as well as you do; and I'm ready to pay.

HIGGINS: How much?

THE FLOWER GIRL: [*Coming back to him, triumphant.*] Now youre talking! I thought youd come off it when you saw a chance of getting back a bit of what you chucked at me last night. [*Confidentially.*] Youd had a drop in, hadnt you?

HIGGINS: [*Peremptorily.*] Sit down.

THE FLOWER GIRL: Oh, if youre going to make a compliment of it—

HIGGINS: [*Thundering at her.*] Sit down.

MRS. PEARCE: [*Severely.*] Sit down, girl. Do as youre told.

THE FLOWER GIRL: Ah-ah-ah-ow-ow-oo! [*She stands, half rebellious, half bewildered.*]

PICKERING: [*Very courteous.*] Wont you sit down? [*He places the stray chair near the hearthrug between himself and* HIGGINS.].

LIZA: [*Coyly.*] Dont mind if I do. [*She sits down.* PICKERING *returns to the hearthrug.*]

HIGGINS: Whats your name?

THE FLOWER GIRL: Liza Doolittle.

HIGGINS: [*Declaiming gravely.*]

    Eliza, Elizabeth, Betsy and Bess,

    They went to the woods to get a bird's nes':

PICKERING: They found a nest with four eggs in it:

HIGGINS: They took one apiece, and left three in it.

[*They laugh heartily at their own fun.*]

LIZA: Oh, dont be silly.

MRS. PEARCE: [*Placing herself behind* ELIZA's *chair.*] You mustnt speak to the gentleman like that.

LIZA: Well, why wont he speak sensible to me?

HIGGINS: Come back to business. How much do you propose to pay me for the lessons?

LIZA: Oh, I know whats right. A lady friend of mine gets French lessons for eighteenpence an hour from a real French gentleman. Well, you wouldnt have the face to ask me the same for teaching me my own language as you would for French; so I wont give more than a shilling. Take it or leave it.

HIGGINS: [*Walking up and down the room, rattling his keys and his cash in his pockets.*] You know, Pickering, if you consider a shilling, not as a simple shilling, but as a percentage of this girl's income, it works out as fully equivalent to sixty or seventy guineas from a millionaire.

PICKERING: How so?

HIGGINS: Figure it out. A millionaire has about £150 a day. She earns about half-a-crown.

LIZA: [*Haughtily.*] Who told you I only—

HIGGINS: [*Continuing.*] She offers me two-fifths of her day's income for a lesson. Two-fifths of a millionaire's income for a day would be somewhere about £60. It's handsome. By George, it's enormous! it's the biggest offer I ever had.

LIZA: [*Rising, terrified.*] Sixty pounds! What are you talking about? I never offered you sixty pounds. Where would I get—

HIGGINS: Hold your tongue.

LIZA: [*Weeping.*] But I aint got sixty pounds. Oh—

MRS. PEARCE: Dont cry, you silly girl. Sit down. Nobody is going to touch your money.

HIGGINS: Somebody is going to touch you,with a broomstick, if you dont stop snivelling. Sit down.

LIZA: [*Obeying slowly.*] Ah-ah-ah-ow-oo-o! One would think you was my father.

HIGGINS: If I decide to teach you, I'll be worse than two fathers to you. Here! [*He offers her his silk handkerchief.*]

LIZA: Whats this for?

HIGGINS: To wipe your eyes. To wipe any part of your face that feels moist. Remember: thats your handkerchief; and thats your sleeve. Dont mistake the one for the other if you wish to become a lady in a shop.

[LIZA, *utterly bewildered, stares helplessly at him.*]

MRS. PEARCE: It's no use talking to her like that, Mr. Higgins: she doesnt understand you. Besides, youre quite wrong: she doesnt do it that way at all. [*She takes the handkerchief.*]

LIZA: [*Snatching it*] Here! You give me that handkerchief. He gev it to me, not to you.

PICKERING: [*Laughing*] He did. I think it must be regarded as her property, Mrs. Pearce.

MRS. PEARCE: [*Resigning herself.*] Serve you right, Mr. Higgins.

PICKERING: Higgins: I'm interested. What about the ambassador's garden party? I'll say youre the greatest teacher alive if you make that good. I'll bet you all the expenses of the experiment you cant do it. And I'll pay for the lessons.

LIZA: Oh, you are real good. Thank you, Captain.

HIGGINS: [*Tempted, looking at her.*] It's almost irresistible. She's so deliciously low—so horribly dirty—

LIZA: [*Protesting extremely.*] Ah-ah-ah-ah-ow-ow-oo-oo!!! I aint dirty: I washed my face and hands afore I come, I did.

PICKERING: Youre certainly not going to turn her head with flattery, Higgins.

MRS. PEARCE: [*Uneasy.*] Oh, dont say that, sir: theres more ways than one of turning a girl's head; and nobody can do it better than Mr. Higgins, though he may not always mean it. I do hope, sir, you wont encourage him to do anything foolish.

HIGGINS: [*Becoming excited as the idea grows on him.*] What is life but a series of inspired follies? The difficulty is to find them to do. Never lose a chance: it doesnt come every day. I shall make a duchess of this draggletailed guttersnipe.

LIZA: [*Strongly deprecating this view of her.*] Ah-ah-ah-ow-ow-oo!

HIGGINS: [*Carried away.*] Yes: in six months—in three if she has a good ear and a quick tongue—I'll take her anywhere and pass her off as anything. We'll start today: now! this moment! Take her away and clean her, Mrs. Pearce. Monkey Brand, if it wont come off any other way. Is there a good fire in the kitchen?

MRS. PEARCE: [*Protesting.*] Yes; but—

HIGGINS: [*Storming on.*] Take all her clothes off and burn them. Ring up Whiteley or somebody for new ones. Wrap her up in brown paper til they come.

LIZA: Youre no gentleman, youre not, to talk of such things. I'm a good girl, I am; and I know what the like of you are, I do.

HIGGINS: We want none of your Lisson Grove prudery here, young woman. Youve got to learn to behave like a duchess. Take her away, Mrs. Pearce. If she gives you any trouble, wallop her.

LIZA: [*Springing up and running between* PICKERING *and* MRS. PEARCE *for protection.*] No! I'll call the police, I will.

MRS. PEARCE: But Ive no place to put her.

HIGGINS: Put her in the dustbin.

LIZA: Ah-ah-ah-ow-ow-oo!

PICKERING: Oh come, Higgins! be reasonable.

MRS. PEARCE: [*Resolutely.*] You must be reasonable, Mr. Higgins: really you must. You cant walk over everybody like this.

[HIGGINS, *thus scolded, subsides. The hurricane is succeeded by a zephyr of amiable surprise.*]

HIGGINS: [*With professional exquisiteness of modulation.*] I walk over everybody! My dear Mrs. Pearce, my dear Pickering, I never had the slightest intention of walking over anyone. All I propose is that we should be kind to this poor girl. We must help her to prepare and fit herself for her new station in life. If I did not express myself clearly it was because I did not wish to hurt her delicacy, or yours.

[LIZA, *reassured, steals back to her chair.*]

MRS. PEARCE: [*To* PICKERING.] Well, did you ever hear anything like that, sir?

PICKERING: [*Laughing heartily.*] Never, Mrs. Pearce: never.

HIGGINS: [*Patiently.*] Whats the matter?

MRS. PEARCE: Well, the matter is, sir, that you cant take a girl up like that as if you were picking up a pebble on the beach.

HIGGINS: Why not?

MRS. PEARCE: Why not! But you dont know anything about her. What about her parents? She may be married.

LIZA: Garn!

HIGGINS: There! As the girl very properly says, Garn! Married indeed! Dont you know that a woman of that class looks a worn out drudge of fifty a year after she's married?

LIZA: Whood marry me?

HIGGINS: [*Suddenly resorting to the most thrillingly beautiful low tones in his best elocutionary style.*] By George, Eliza, the streets will be strewn with the bodies of men shooting themselves for your sake before Ive done with you.

MRS. PEARCE: Nonsense, sir. You mustnt talk like that to her.

LIZA: [*Rising and squaring herself determinedly.*] I'm going away. He's off his chump, he is. I dont want no balmies teaching me.

HIGGINS: [*Wounded in his tenderest point by her insensibility to his elocution.*] Oh, indeed! I'm mad, am I? Very well, Mrs. Pearce: you neednt order the new clothes for her. Throw her out.

LIZA: [*Whimpering.*] Nah-ow. You got no right to touch me.

MRS. PEARCE: You see now what comes of being saucy. [*Indicating the door.*] This way, please.

LIZA: [*Almost in tears.*] I didnt want no clothes. I wouldnt have taken them. [*She throws away the handkerchief.*] I can buy my own clothes.

HIGGINS: [*Deftly retrieving the handkerchief and intercepting her on her reluctant way to the door.*] Youre an ungrateful wicked girl. This is my return for offering to take you out of the gutter and dress you beautifully and make a lady of you.

MRS. PEARCE: Stop, Mr. Higgins. I wont allow it. It's you that are wicked. Go home to your parents, girl; and tell them to take better care of you.

LIZA: I aint got no parents. They told me I was big enough to earn my own living and turned me out.

MRS. PEARCE: Wheres your mother?

LIZA: I aint got no mother. Her that turned me out was my sixth stepmother. But I done without them. And I'm a good girl, I am.

HIGGINS: Very well, then, what on earth is all this fuss about? The girl doesnt belong to anybody—is no use of anybody but me. [*He goes to* MRS. PEARCE *and begins coaxing.*] You can adopt her, Mrs. Pearce: I'm sure a daughter would be a great amusement to you. Now dont make any more fuss. Take her downstairs; and—

MRS. PEARCE: But whats to become of her? Is she to be paid anything? Do be sensible, sir.

HIGGINS: Oh, pay her whatever is necessary: put it down in the housekeeping book. [*Impatiently.*] What on earth will she want with money? She'll have her food and her clothes. She'll only drink if you give her money.

LIZA: [*Turning on him.*] Oh you are a brute. It's a lie: nobody ever saw the sign of liquor on me. [*To* PICKERING.] Oh, sir: youre a gentleman: dont let him speak to me like that.

PICKERING: [*In good-humored remonstrance.*] Does it occur to you, Higgins, that the girl has some feelings?

HIGGINS: [*Looking critically at her.*] Oh no, I dont think so. Not any feelings that we need bother about. [*Cheerily.*] Have you, Eliza?

LIZA: I got my feelings same as anyone else.

HIGGINS: [*To* PICKERING, *reflectively.*] You see the difficulty?

PICKERING: Eh? What difficulty?

HIGGINS: To get her to talk grammar. The mere pronunciation is easy enough.

LIZA: I dont want to talk grammar. I want to talk like a lady in a flower-shop.

MRS. PEARCE: Will you please keep to the point, Mr. Higgins. I want to know on what terms the girl is to be here. Is she to have any wages? And what is to become of her when youve finished your teaching? You must look ahead a little.

HIGGINS: [*Impatiently.*] Whats to become of her if I leave her in the gutter? Tell me that, Mrs. Pearce.

MRS. PEARCE: Thats her own business, not yours, Mr. Higgins.

HIGGINS: Well, when Ive done with her, we can throw her back into the gutter; and then it will be her own business again; so thats all right.

LIZA: Oh, youve no feeling heart in you: you dont care for nothing but yourself. [*She rises and takes the floor resolutely.*] Here! Ive had enough of this. I'm going. [*Making for the door.*] You ought to be ashamed of yourself, you ought.

HIGGINS: [*Snatching a chocolate cream from the piano, his eyes suddenly beginning to twinkle with mischief.*] Have some chocolates, Eliza.

LIZA: [*Halting, tempted.*] How do I know what might be in them? Ive heard of girls being drugged by the like of you.

[HIGGINS *whips out his penknife; cuts a chocolate in two; puts one half into his mouth and bolts it; and offers her the other half.*]

HIGGINS: Pledge of good faith, Eliza. I eat one half: you eat the other. [LIZA *opens her mouth to retort: he pops the half chocolate into it.*] You shall have boxes of them, barrels of them, every day. You shall live on them. Eh?

LIZA: [*Who has disposed of the chocolate after being nearly choked by it.*] I wouldnt have ate it, only I'm too ladylike to take it out of my mouth.

HIGGINS: Listen, Eliza. I think you said you came in a taxi.

LIZA: Well, what if I did? Ive as good a right to take a taxi as anyone else.

HIGGINS: You have, Eliza; and in future you shall have as many taxis as you want. You shall go up and down and round the town in a taxi every day. Think of that, Eliza.

MRS. PEARCE: Mr. Higgins: youre tempting the girl. It's not right. She should think of the future.

HIGGINS: At her age! Nonsense! Time enough to think of the future when you havnt any future to think of. No, Eliza: do as this lady does: think of other people's futures; but never think of your own. Think of chocolates, and taxis, and gold, and diamonds.

LIZA: No: I dont want no gold and no diamonds. I'm a good girl, I am. [*She sits down again, with an attempt at dignity.*]

HIGGINS: You shall remain so, Eliza, under the care of Mrs. Pearce. And you shall marry an officer in the Guards, with a beautiful moustache: the son of a marquis, who will disinherit him for marrying you, but will relent when he sees your beauty and goodness—

PICKERING: Excuse me, Higgins; but I really must interfere. Mrs. Pearce is quite right. If this girl is to put herself in your hands for six months for an experiment in teaching, she must understand thoroughly what she's doing.

HIGGINS: How can she? She's incapable of understanding anything. Besides, do any of us understand what we are doing? If we did, would we ever do it?

PICKERING: Very clever, Higgins; but not to the present point. [*To* ELIZA.] Miss Doolittle—

LIZA: [*Overwhelmed.*] Ah-ah-ow-oo!

HIGGINS: There! Thats all youll get out of Eliza. Ah-ah-ow-oo! No use explaining. As a military man you ought to know that. Give her her orders: thats enough for her. Eliza: you are to live here for the next six months, learning how to speak beautifully, like a lady in a florist's shop. If youre good and do whatever youre told, you shall sleep in a proper bedroom, and have lots to eat, and money to buy chocolates and take rides in taxis. If youre naughty and idle you will sleep in the back kitchen among the black beetles, and be walloped by Mrs. Pearce with a broomstick. At the end of six months you shall go to Buckingham Palace in a carriage, beautifully dressed. If the King finds out youre not a lady, you will be taken by the police to the Tower of London, where your head will be cut off as a warning to other presumptuous flower girls. If you are not found out, you shall have a present of seven-and-sixpence to start life with as a lady in a shop. If you refuse this offer you will be a most ungrateful wicked girl; and the angels will weep for you. [*To* PICKERING.] Now are you satisfied, Pickering? [*To* MRS. PEARCE.] Can I put it more plainly and fairly, Mrs. Pearce?

MRS. PEARCE: [*Patiently.*] I think youd better let me speak to the girl properly in private. I dont know that I can take charge of her or consent to the arrangement at all. Of course I know you dont mean her any harm; but when you get what you call interested in people's accents, you never think or care what may happen to them or you. Come with me, Eliza.

HIGGINS: Thats all right. Thank you, Mrs. Pearce. Bundle her off to the bathroom.

LIZA: [*Rising reluctantly and suspiciously.*] Youre a great bully, you are. I wont stay here if I dont like. I wont let nobody wallop me. I never asked to go to Bucknam Palace, I didnt. I was never in trouble with the police, not me. I'm a good girl—

MRS. PEARCE: Dont answer back, girl. You dont understand the gentleman.

Come with me. [*She leads the way to the door, and holds it open for* ELIZA.]

LIZA: [*As she goes out.*] Well, what I say is right. I wont go near the King, not if I'm going to have my head cut off. If I'd known what I was letting myself in for, I wouldnt have come here. I always been a good girl; and I never offered to say a word to him; and I dont owe him nothing; and I dont care; and I wont be put upon; and I have my feelings the same as anyone else—

[MRS. PEARCE *shuts the door; and* ELIZA's *plaints are no longer audible.*]

* * *

ELIZA *is taken upstairs to the third floor greatly to her surprise; for she expected to be taken down to the scullery. There* MRS. PEARCE *opens a door and takes her into a spare bedroom.*

MRS. PEARCE: I will have to put you here. This will be your bedroom.

LIZA: O-h, I couldnt sleep here, missus. It's too good for the likes of me. I should be afraid to touch anything. I aint a duchess yet, you know.

MRS. PEARCE: You have got to make yourself as clean as the room: then you wont be afraid of it. And you must call me Mrs. Pearce, not missus. [*She throws open the door of the dressingroom, now modernized as a bathroom.*]

LIZA: Gawd! whats this? Is this where you wash clothes? Funny sort of copper I call it.

MRS. PEARCE: It is not a copper. This is where we wash ourselves, Eliza, and where I am going to wash you.

LIZA: You expect me to get into that and wet myself all over! Not me. I should catch my death. I knew a woman did it every Saturday night; and she died of it.

MRS. PEARCE: Mr. Higgins has the gentlemen's bathroom downstairs; and he has a bath every morning, in cold water.

LIZA: Ugh! He's made of iron, that man.

MRS. PEARCE: If you are to sit with him and the Colonel and be taught you will have to do the same. They wont like the smell of you if you dont. But you can have the water as hot as you like. There are two taps: hot and cold.

LIZA: [*Weeping.*] I couldnt. I dursnt. It's not natural: it would kill me. Ive never had a bath in my life: not what youd call a proper one.

MRS. PEARCE: Well, dont you want to be clean and sweet and decent, like a lady? You know you can't be a nice girl inside if youre a dirty slut outside.

LIZA: Boohoo!!!!

MRS. PEARCE: Now stop crying and go back into your room and take off all your clothes. Then wrap yourself in this [*Taking down a gown from its peg and handing it to her.*] and come back to me. I will get the bath ready.

LIZA: [*All tears.*] I cant. I wont. I'm not used to it. Ive never took off all my clothes before. It's not right: it's not decent.

MRS. PEARCE: Nonsense, child. Dont you take off all your clothes every night when you go to bed?

LIZA: [*Amazed.*] No. Why should I? I should catch my death. Of course I take off my skirt.

MRS. PEARCE: Do you mean that you sleep in the underclothes you wear in the daytime?

LIZA: What else have I to sleep in?

MRS. PEARCE: You will never do that again as long as you live here. I will get you a proper nightdress.

LIZA: Do you mean change into cold things and lie awake shivering half the night? You want to kill me, you do.

MRS. PEARCE: I want to change you from a frowzy slut to a clean respectable girl fit to sit with the gentlemen in the study. Are you going to trust me and do what I tell you or be thrown out and sent back to your flower basket?

LIZA: But you dont know what the cold is to me. You dont know how I dread it.

MRS. PEARCE: Your bed wont be cold here: I will put a hot water bottle in it. [Pushing her into the bedroom.] Off with you and undress.

LIZA: Oh, if only I'd a known what a dreadful thing it is to be clean I'd never have come. I didnt know when I was well off. I—[MRS. PEARCE pushes her through the door, but leaves it partly open lest her prisoner should take to flight.]

[MRS. PEARCE puts on a pair of white rubber sleeves, and fills the bath, mixing hot and cold, and testing the result with the bath thermometer. She perfumes it with a handful of bath salts and adds a palmful of mustard. She then takes a formidable looking long handled scrubbing brush and soaps it profusely with a ball of scented soap.

ELIZA comes back with nothing on but the bath gown huddled tightly round her, a piteous spectacle of abject terror.]

MRS. PEARCE: Now come along. Take that thing off.

LIZA: Oh I couldnt, Mrs. Pearce: I reely couldnt. I never done such a thing.

MRS. PEARCE: Nonsense. Here: step in and tell me whether it's hot enough for you.

LIZA: Ah-oo! Ah-oo! It's too hot.

MRS. PEARCE: [Deftly snatching the gown away and throwing ELIZA down on her back.] It wont hurt you. [She sets to work with the scrubbing brush.]

[ELIZA's screams are heartrending.]

* * *

Meanwhile the COLONEL has been having it out with HIGGINS about ELIZA. PICKERING has come from the hearth to the chair and seated himself astride of it with his arms on the back to cross-examine him.

PICKERING: Excuse the straight question, Higgins. Are you a man of good character where women are concerned?

HIGGINS: [Moodily.] Have you ever met a man of good character where women are concerned?

PICKERING: Yes: very frequently.

HIGGINS: [Dogmatically, lifting himself on his hands to the level of the piano, and sitting on it with a bounce.] Well, I havnt. I find that the moment I let a woman make friends with me, she becomes jealous, exacting, suspicious, and a damned nuisance. I find that the moment I let myself make friends with a woman, I become selfish and tyrannical. Women upset everything. When you let them into your life, you find that the woman is driving at one thing and youre driving at another.

PICKERING: At what, for example?

HIGGINS: [Coming off the piano restlessly.] Oh, Lord knows! I suppose the woman wants to live her own life; and the man wants to live his; and each tries to drag the other on to the wrong tack. One wants to go north and the other south; and the result is that both have to go east, though they both hate the east wind. [He sits down on the bench at the keyboard.] So here I am, a confirmed old bachelor, and likely to remain so.

PICKERING: [Rising and standing over him gravely.] Come, Higgins! You know what I mean. If I'm to be in this business I shall feel responsible for that girl. I hope it's understood that no advantage is to be taken of her position.

HIGGINS: What! That thing! Sacred, I assure you. [Rising to explain.] You see, she'll be a pupil; and teaching would be impossible unless pupils were sacred. Ive taught scores of American millionairesses how to speak English: the best looking women in the world. I'm seasoned. They might as well be blocks of wood. I might as well be a block of wood. It's—

[MRS. PEARCE opens the door. She has ELIZA's hat in her hand. PICKERING retires to the easy-chair at the hearth and sits down.]

HIGGINS: [Eagerly.] Well, Mrs. Pearce: is it all right?

MRS. PEARCE: [At the door.] I just wish to trouble you with a word, if I may, Mr. Higgins.

HIGGINS: Yes, certainly. Come in. [She comes forward.] Dont burn that, Mrs. Pearce. I'll keep it as a curiosity. [He takes the hat.]

MRS. PEARCE: Handle it carefully, sir, please. I had to promise her not to burn it; but I had better put it in the oven for a while.

HIGGINS: [Putting it down hastily on the piano.] Oh! thank you. Well, what have you to say to me?

PICKERING: Am I in the way?

MRS. PEARCE: Not at all, sir. Mr. Higgins: will you please be very particular what you say before the girl?

HIGGINS: [Sternly.] Of course. I'm always particular about what I say. Why do you say this to me?

MRS. PEARCE: [Unmoved.] No, sir: youre not at all particular when youve mislaid anything or when you get a little impatient. Now it doesnt matter before me: I'm used to it. But you really must not swear before the girl.

HIGGINS: [Indignantly.] I swear! [Most emphatically.] I never swear. I detest the habit. What the devil do you mean?

MRS. PEARCE: [Stolidly.] Thats what I mean, sir. You swear a great deal too much. I dont mind your damning and blasting, and what the devil and where the devil and who the devil—

HIGGINS: Mrs. Pearce: this language from your lips! Really!

MRS. PEARCE: [*Not to be put off.*]—but there is a certain word I must ask you not to use. The girl used it herself when she began to enjoy the bath. It begins with the same letter as bath. She knows no better: she learnt it at her mother's knee. But she must not hear it from your lips.

HIGGINS: [*Loftily.*] I cannot charge myself with having ever uttered it, Mrs. Pearce. [*She looks at him steadfastly. He adds, hiding an uneasy conscience with a judicial air.*] Except perhaps in a moment of extreme and justifiable excitement.

MRS. PEARCE: Only this morning, sir, you applied it to your boots, to the butter, and to the brown bread.

HIGGINS: Oh, that! Mere alliteration, Mrs. Pearce, natural to a poet.

MRS. PEARCE: Well, sir, whatever you choose to call it, I beg you not to let the girl hear you repeat it.

HIGGINS: Oh, very well, very well. Is that all?

MRS. PEARCE: No, sir. We shall have to be very particular with this girl as to personal cleanliness.

HIGGINS: Certainly. Quite right. Most important.

MRS. PEARCE: I mean not to be slovenly about her dress or untidy in leaving things about.

HIGGINS: [*Going to her solemnly.*] Just so. I intended to call your attention to that. [*He passes on to* PICKERING, *who is enjoying the conversation immensely.*] It is these little things that matter, Pickering. Take care of the pence and the pounds will take care of themselves is as true of personal habits as of money. [*He comes to anchor on the hearthrug, with the air of a man in an unassailable position.*]

MRS. PEARCE: Yes, sir. Then might I ask you not to come down to breakfast in your dressing-gown, or at any rate not to use it as a napkin to the extent you do, sir. And if you would be so good as not to eat everything off the same plate, and to remember not to put the porridge saucepan out of your hand on the clean tablecloth, it would be a better example to the girl. You know you nearly choked yourself with a fishbone in the jam only last week.

HIGGINS: [*Routed from the hearthrug and drifting back to the piano.*] I may do these things sometimes in absence of mind; but surely I dont do them habitually. [*Angrily.*] By the way: my dressing-gown smells most damnably of benzine.

MRS. PEARCE: No doubt it does, Mr. Higgins. But if you will wipe your fingers—

HIGGINS: [*Yelling.*] Oh very well, very well: I'll wipe them in my hair in future.

MRS. PEARCE: I hope youre not offended, Mr. Higgins.

HIGGINS: [*Shocked at finding himself thought capable of an unamiable sentiment.*] Not at all, not at all. Youre quite right, Mrs. Pearce: I shall be particularly careful before the girl. Is that all?

MRS. PEARCE: No, sir. Might she use some of those Japanese dresses you brought from abroad? I really cant put her back into her old things.

HIGGINS: Certainly. Anything you like. Is that all?

MRS. PEARCE: Thank you, sir. Thats all. [*She goes out.*]

HIGGINS: You know, Pickering, that woman has the most extraordinary ideas about me. Here I am, a shy, diffident sort of man. Ive never been able to feel really grown-up and tremendous, like other chaps. And yet she's firmly persuaded that I'm an arbitrary overbearing bossing kind of person. I cant account for it.

[MRS. PEARCE *returns.*]

MRS. PEARCE: If you please, sir, the trouble's beginning already. Theres a dustman downstairs, Alfred Doolittle, wants to see you. He says you have his daughter here.

PICKERING: [*Rising.*] Phew! I say!

HIGGINS: [*Promptly.*] Send the blackguard up.

MRS. PEARCE: Oh, very well, sir. [*She goes out.*]

PICKERING: He may not be a blackguard, Higgins.

HIGGINS: Nonsense. Of course he's a blackguard.

PICKERING: Whether he is or not, I'm afraid we shall have some trouble with him.

HIGGINS: [*Confidently.*] Oh no: I think not. If theres any trouble he shall have it with me, not I with him. And we are sure to get something interesting out of him.

PICKERING: About the girl?

HIGGINS: No. I mean his dialect.

PICKERING: Oh!

MRS. PEARCE: [*At the door.*] Doolittle, sir. [*She admits* DOOLITTLE *and retires.*]

[ALFRED DOOLITTLE *is an elderly but vigorous dustman, clad in the costume of his profession, including a hat with a back brim covering his neck and shoulders. He has well marked and rather interesting features, and seems equally free from fear and conscience. He has a remarkably expressive voice, the result of a habit of giving vent to his feelings without reserve. His present pose is that of wounded honor and stern resolution.*]

DOOLITTLE: [*At the door, uncertain which of the two gentlemen is his man.*] Professor Iggins?

HIGGINS: Here. Good morning. Sit down.

DOOLITTLE: Morning, Governor. [*He sits down magisterially.*] I come about a very serious matter, Governor.

HIGGINS: [*To* PICKERING.] Brought up in Hounslow. Mother Welsh, I should think. [DOOLITTLE *opens his mouth, amazed.* HIGGINS *continues.*] What do you want, Doolittle?

DOOLITTLE: [*Menacingly.*] I want my daughter: thats what I want. See?

HIGGINS: Of course you do. Youre her father, arnt you? You dont suppose anyone else wants her, do you? I'm glad to see you have some spark of family feeling left. She's upstairs. Take her away at once.

DOOLITTLE: [*Rising, fearfully taken aback.*] What!

HIGGINS: Take her away. Do you suppose I'm going to keep your daughter for you?

DOOLITTLE: [*Remonstrating.*] Now, now, look here, Governor. Is this reasonable? Is it fairity to take advantage of a man like this? The girl belongs to me. You got her. Where do I come in? [*He sits down again.*]

HIGGINS: Your daughter had the audacity to come to my house and ask me to teach her how to speak properly so that she could get a place in a flower-shop. This gentleman and my housekeeper have been here all the time. [*Bullying him.*] How dare you come here and attempt to blackmail me? You sent her here on purpose.

DOOLITTLE: [*Protesting.*] No, Governor.

HIGGINS: You must have. How else could you possibly know that she is here?

DOOLITTLE: Dont take a man up like that, Governor.

HIGGINS: The police shall take you up. This is a plant—a plot to extort money by threats. I shall telephone for the police. [*He goes resolutely to the telephone and opens the directory.*]

DOOLITTLE: Have I asked you for a brass farthing? I leave it to the gentleman here: have I said a word about money?

HIGGINS: [*Throwing the book aside and marching down on* DOOLITTLE *with a poser.*] What else did you come for?

DOOLITTLE: [*Sweetly.*] Well, what would a man come for? Be human, Governor.

HIGGINS: [*Disarmed.*] Alfred: did you put her up to it?

DOOLITTLE: So help me, Governor, I never did. I take my Bible oath I aint seen the girl these two months past.

HIGGINS: Then how did you know she was here?

DOOLITTLE: [*"Most musical, most melancholy."*] I'll tell you, Governor, if youll only let me get a word in. I'm willing to tell you. I'm wanting to tell you. I'm waiting to tell you.

HIGGINS: Pickering: this chap has a certain natural gift of rhetoric. Observe the rhythm of his native woodnotes wild. "I'm willing to tell you: I'm wanting to tell you: I'm waiting to tell you." Sentimental rhetoric! thats the Welsh strain in him. It also accounts for his mendacity and dishonesty.

PICKERING: Oh, please, Higgins: I'm west country[8] myself. [*To* DOOLITTLE.] How did you know the girl was here if you didnt send her?

DOOLITTLE: It was like this, Governor. The girl took a boy in the taxi to give him a jaunt. Son of her landlady, he is. He hung about on the chance of her giving him another ride home. Well, she sent him back for her luggage when she heard you was willing for her to stop here. I met the boy at the corner of Long Acre and Endell Street.

HIGGINS: Public house. Yes?

DOOLITTLE: The poor man's club, Governor: why shouldnt I?

PICKERING: Do let him tell his story, Higgins.

DOOLITTLE: He told me what was up. And I ask you, what was my feelings and my duty as a father? I says to the boy, "You bring me the luggage," I says—

PICKERING: Why didnt you go for it yourself?

DOOLITTLE: Landlady wouldnt have trusted me with it, Governor. She's that kind of woman: you know. I had to give the boy a penny afore he trusted me

---

8. Wales is in west Britain.

with it, the little swine. I brought it to her just to oblige you like, and make myself agreeable. Thats all.

HIGGINS: How much luggage?

DOOLITTLE: Musical instrument, Governor. A few pictures, a trifle of jewelry, and a bird-cage. She said she didnt want no clothes. What was I to think from that, Governor? I ask you as a parent what was I to think?

HIGGINS: So you came to rescue her from worse than death, eh?

DOOLITTLE: [Appreciatively: relieved at being so well understood.] Just so, Governor. Thats right.

PICKERING: But why did you bring her luggage if you intended to take her away?

DOOLITTLE: Have I said a word about taking her away? Have I now?

HIGGINS: [Determinedly.] Youre going to take her away, double quick. [He crosses to the hearth and rings the bell.]

DOOLITTLE: [Rising.] No, Governor. Dont say that. I'm not the man to stand in my girl's light. Heres a career opening for her, as you might say; and —

[MRS. PEARCE opens the door and awaits orders.]

HIGGINS: Mrs. Pearce: this is Eliza's father. He has come to take her away. Give her to him. [He goes back to the piano, with an air of washing his hands of the whole affair.]

DOOLITTLE: No. This is a misunderstanding. Listen here —

MRS. PEARCE: He cant take her away, Mr. Higgins: how can he? You told me to burn her clothes.

DOOLITTLE: Thats right. I cant carry the girl through the streets like a blooming monkey, can I? I put it to you.

HIGGINS: You have put it to me that you want your daughter. Take your daughter. If she has no clothes go out and buy her some.

DOOLITTLE: [Desperate.] Wheres the clothes she come in? Did I burn them or did your missus here?

MRS. PEARCE: I am the housekeeper, if you please. I have sent for some clothes for your girl. When they come you can take her away. You can wait in the kitchen. This way, please.

[DOOLITTLE, much troubled, accompanies her to the door; then hesitates; finally turns confidentially to HIGGINS.]

DOOLITTLE: Listen here, Governor. You and me is men of the world aint we?

HIGGINS: Oh! Men of the world, are we? Youd better go, Mrs. Pearce.

MRS. PEARCE: I think so, indeed, sir. [She goes, with dignity.]

PICKERING: The floor is yours, Mr. Doolittle.

DOOLITTLE: [To PICKERING] I thank you, Governor. [To HIGGINS, who takes refuge on the piano bench, a little overwhelmed by the proximity of his visitor; for DOOLITTLE has a professional flavour of dust about him.] Well, the truth is, Ive taken a sort of fancy to you, Governor; and if you want the girl, I'm not so set on having her back home again but what I might be open to an arrangement. Regarded in the light of a young woman, she's a fine handsome girl. As a daughter she's not worth her keep; and so I tell you straight.

All I ask is my rights as a father; and youre the last man alive to expect me to let her go for nothing; for I can see youre one of the straight sort, Governor. Well, whats a five-pound note to you? and whats Eliza to me? [*He turns to his chair and sits down judicially.*]

PICKERING: I think you ought to know, Doolittle, that Mr. Higgins's intentions are entirely honorable.

DOOLITTLE: Course they are, Governor. If I thought they wasn't, I'd ask fifty.

HIGGINS: [*Revolted.*] Do you mean to say that you would sell your daughter for £50?

DOOLITTLE: Not in a general way I wouldnt; but to oblige a gentleman like you I'd do a good deal, I do assure you.

PICKERING: Have you no morals, man?

DOOLITTLE: [*Unabashed.*] Cant afford them, Governor. Neither could you if you was as poor as me. Not that I mean any harm, you know. But if Liza is going to have a bit out of this, why not me too?

HIGGINS: [*Troubled.*] I dont know what to do, Pickering. There can be no question that as a matter of morals it's a positive crime to give this chap a farthing. And yet I feel a sort of rough justice in his claim.

DOOLITTLE: Thats it, Governor. Thats all I say. A father's heart, as it were.

PICKERING: Well, I know the feeling; but really it seems hardly right—

DOOLITTLE: Dont say that, Governor. Dont look at it that way. What am I, Governors both? I ask you, what am I? I'm one of the undeserving poor: thats what I am. Think of what that means to a man. It means that he's up agen middle class morality all the time. If theres anything going, and I put in for a bit of it, it's always the same story: "Youre undeserving; so you cant have it." But my needs is as great as the most deserving widow's that ever got money out of six different charities in one week for the death of the same husband. I dont need less than a deserving man: I need more. I dont eat less hearty than him; and I drink a lot more. I want a bit of amusement, cause I'm a thinking man. I want cheerfulness and a song and a band when I feel low. Well, they charge me just the same for everything as they charge the deserving. What is middle class morality? Just an excuse for never giving me anything. Therefore, I ask you, as two gentlemen, not to play that game on me. I'm playing straight with you. I aint pretending to be deserving. I'm undeserving; and I mean to go on being undeserving. I like it; and thats the truth. Will you take advantage of a man's nature to do him out of the price of his own daughter what he's brought up and fed and clothed by the sweat of his brow until she's growed big enough to be interesting to you two gentlemen? Is five pounds unreasonable? I put it to you; and I leave it to you.

HIGGINS: [*Rising, and going over to* PICKERING.] Pickering: if we were to take this man in hand for three months, he could choose between a seat in the Cabinet and a popular pulpit in Wales.

PICKERING: What do you say to that, Doolittle?

DOOLITTLE: Not me, Governor, thank you kindly. Ive heard all the preachers and all the prime ministers—for I'm a thinking man and game for politics or religion or social reform same as all the other amusements—and I tell you it's a dog's life any way you look at it. Undeserving poverty is my line. Taking one station in society with another, it's—it's—well, it's the only one that has any ginger in it, to my taste.

HIGGINS: I suppose we must give him a fiver.

PICKERING: He'll make a bad use of it, I'm afraid.

DOOLITTLE: Not me, Governor, so help me I wont. Dont you be afraid that I'll save it and spare it and live idle on it. There wont be a penny of it left by Monday: I'll have to go to work same as if I'd never had it. It wont pauperize me, you bet. Just one good spree for myself and the missus, giving pleasure to ourselves and employment to others, and satisfaction to you to think it's not been throwed away. You couldnt spend it better.

HIGGINS: [*Taking out his pocket book and coming between* DOOLITTLE *and the piano.*] This is irresistible. Lets give him ten. [*He offers two notes to the* DUSTMAN.]

DOOLITTLE: No, Governor. She wouldnt have the heart to spend ten; and perhaps I shouldnt neither. Ten pounds is a lot of money: it makes a man feel prudent like; and then goodbye to happiness. You give me what I ask you, Governor: not a penny more, and not a penny less.

PICKERING: Why dont you marry that missus of yours? I rather draw the line at encouraging that sort of immorality.

DOOLITTLE: Tell her so, Governor: tell her so. I'm willing. It's me that suffers by it. Ive no hold on her. I got to be agreeable to her. I got to give her presents. I got to buy her clothes something sinful. I'm a slave to that woman, Governor, just because I'm not her lawful husband. And she knows it too. Catch her marrying me! Take my advice, Governor: marry Eliza while she's young and dont know no better. If you dont youll be sorry for it after. If you do, she'll be sorry for it after; but better her than you, because youre a man, and she's only a woman and dont know how to be happy anyhow.

HIGGINS: Pickering: if we listen to this man another minute, we shall have no convictions left. [*To* DOOLITTLE.] Five pounds I think you said.

DOOLITTLE: Thank you kindly, Governor.

HIGGINS: Youre sure you wont take ten?

DOOLITTLE: Not now. Another time, Governor.

HIGGINS: [*Handing him a five-pound note.*] Here you are.

DOOLITTLE: Thank you, Governor. Good morning. [*He hurries to the door, anxious to get away with his booty. When he opens it he is confronted with a dainty and exquisitely clean young* JAPANESE LADY *in a simple blue cotton kimono printed cunningly with small white jasmine blossoms.* MRS. PEARCE *is with her. He gets out of her way deferentially and apologizes.*] Beg pardon, miss.

THE JAPANESE LADY: Garn! Dont you know your own daughter?

DOOLITTLE:		Bly me! it's Eliza!
HIGGINS:	*exclaiming*	Whats that? This!
PICKERING:	*simultaneously*	By Jove!

LIZA: Don't I look silly?

HIGGINS: Silly?

MRS. PEARCE: [*At the door.*] Now, Mr. Higgins, please dont say anything to make the girl conceited about herself.

HIGGINS: [*Conscientiously.*] Oh! Quite right, Mrs. Pearce. [*To* ELIZA.] Yes: damned silly.

MRS. PEARCE: Please, sir.

HIGGINS: [*Correcting himself.*] I mean extremely silly.

LIZA: I should look all right with my hat on. [*She takes up her hat; puts it on; and walks across the room to the fireplace with a fashionable air.*]

HIGGINS: A new fashion, by George! And it ought to look horrible!

DOOLITTLE: [*With fatherly pride.*] Well, I never thought she'd clean up as good looking as that, Governor. She's a credit to me, aint she?

LIZA: I tell you, it's easy to clean up here. Hot and cold water on tap, just as much as you like, there is. Woolly towels, there is; and a towel horse[9] so hot, it burns your fingers. Soft brushes to scrub yourself, and a wooden bowl of soap smelling like primroses. Now I know why ladies is so clean. Washing's a treat for them. Wish they could see what it is for the like of me!

HIGGINS: I'm glad the bathroom met with your approval.

LIZA: It didnt: not all of it; and I dont care who hears me say it. Mrs. Pearce knows.

HIGGINS: What was wrong, Mrs. Pearce?

MRS. PEARCE: [*Blandly.*] Oh, nothing, sir. It doesnt matter.

LIZA: I had a good mind to break it. I didnt know which way to look. But I hung a towel over it, I did.

HIGGINS: Over what?

MRS. PEARCE: Over the looking-glass, sir.

HIGGINS: Doolittle: you have brought your daughter up too strictly.

DOOLITTLE: Me! I never brought her up at all, except to give her a lick of a strap now and again. Dont put it on me, Governor. She aint accustomed to it, you see: thats all. But she'll soon pick up your free-and-easy ways.

LIZA: I'm a good girl, I am; and I wont pick up no free-and-easy ways.

HIGGINS: Eliza: if you say again that youre a good girl, your father shall take you home.

LIZA: Not him. You dont know my father. All he come here for was to touch you for some money to get drunk on.

DOOLITTLE: Well, what else would I want money for? To put into the plate in church, I suppose. [*She puts out her tongue at him. He is so incensed by this that* PICKERING *presently finds it necessary to step between them.*] Dont you give me none of your lip; and dont let me hear you giving this gentleman any of it neither, or youll hear from me about it. See?

HIGGINS: Have you any further advice to give her before you go, Doolittle? Your blessing, for instance.

DOOLITTLE: No, Governor: I aint such a mug as to put up my children to all I know myself. Hard enough to hold them in without that. If you want Eliza's mind improved, Governor, you do it yourself with a strap. So long, gentlemen. [*He turns to go.*]

9. Towel rack of pipes through which hot water runs, heating towels.

HIGGINS: [*Impressively.*] Stop. Youll come regularly to see your daughter. It's your duty, you know. My brother is a clergyman; and he could help you in your talks with her.

DOOLITTLE: [*Evasively.*] Certainly, I'll come, Governor. Not just this week, because I have a job at a distance. But later on you may depend on me. Afternoon, gentlemen. Afternoon, maam. [*He touches his hat to* MRS. PEARCE, *who disdains the salutation and goes out. He winks at* HIGGINS, *thinking him probably a fellow sufferer from* MRS. PEARCE's *difficult disposition, and follows her.*]

LIZA: Dont you believe the old liar. He'd as soon you set a bulldog on him as a clergyman. You wont see him again in a hurry.

HIGGINS: I dont want to, Eliza. Do you?

LIZA: Not me. I dont want never to see him again, I dont. He's a disgrace to me, he is, collecting dust, instead of working at his trade.

PICKERING: What is his trade, Eliza?

LIZA: Talking money out of other people's pockets into his own. His proper trade's a navvy; and he works at it sometimes too—for exercise—and earns good money at it. Aint you going to call me Miss Doolittle any more?

PICKERING: I beg your pardon, Miss Doolittle. It was a slip of the tongue.

LIZA: Oh, I dont mind; only it sounded so genteel. I should just like to take a taxi to the corner of Tottenham Court Road and get out there and tell it to wait for me, just to put the girls in their place a bit. I wouldnt speak to them, you know.

PICKERING: Better wait til we get you something really fashionable.

HIGGINS: Besides, you shouldnt cut your old friends now that you have risen in the world. Thats what we call snobbery.

LIZA: You dont call the like of them my friends now, I should hope. Theyve took it out of me often enough with their ridicule when they had the chance; and now I mean to get a bit of my own back. But if I'm to have fashionable clothes, I'll wait. I should like to have some. Mrs. Pearce says youre going to give me some to wear in bed at night different to what I wear in the day-time; but it do seem a waste of money when you could get something to shew. Besides, I never could fancy changing into cold things on a winter night.

MRS. PEARCE: [*Coming back.*] Now, Eliza. The new things have come for you to try on.

LIZA: Ah-ow-oo-ooh! [*She rushes out.*]

MRS. PEARCE: [*Following her.*] Oh, don't rush about like that, girl. [*She shuts the door behind her.*]

HIGGINS: Pickering: we have taken on a stiff job.

PICKERING: [*With conviction.*] Higgins: we have.

*   *   *

There seems to be some curiosity as to what HIGGINS's *lessons to* ELIZA *were like. Well, here is a sample: the first one.*

Picture ELIZA, *in her new clothes, and feeling her inside put out of step by a lunch, dinner, and breakfast of a kind to which it is unaccustomed, seated with*

HIGGINS *and the* COLONEL *in the study, feeling like a hospital out-patient at a first encounter with the doctors.*

HIGGINS, *constitutionally unable to sit still, discomposes her still more by striding restlessly about. But for the reassuring presence and quietude of her friend the* COLONEL *she would run for her life, even back to Drury Lane.*

HIGGINS: Say your alphabet.

LIZA: I know my alphabet. Do you think I know nothing? I dont need to be taught like a child.

HIGGINS: [*Thundering.*] Say your alphabet.

PICKERING: Say it, Miss Doolittle. You will understand presently. Do what he tells you; and let him teach you in his own way.

LIZA: Oh well, if you put it like that—Ahyee, bəyee, cəyee, dəyee—

HIGGINS: [*With the roar of a wounded lion.*] Stop. Listen to this, Pickering. This is what we pay for as elementary education. This unfortunate animal has been locked up for nine years in school at our expense to teach her to speak and read the language of Shakespear and Milton. And the result is Ahyee, Bə-yee, Cə-yee, Də-yee. [*To* ELIZA.] Say A, B, C, D.

LIZA: [*Almost in tears.*] But I'm sayin it. Ahyee, Bəyee, Cə-yee—

HIGGINS: Stop. Say a cup of tea.

LIZA: A cappətə-ee.

HIGGINS: Put your tongue forward until it squeezes against the top of your lower teeth. Now say cup.

LIZA: C-c-c—I cant. C-Cup.

PICKERING: Good. Splendid, Miss Doolittle.

HIGGINS: By Jupiter, she's done it at the first shot. Pickering: We shall make a duchess of her. [*To* ELIZA.] Now do you think you could possibly say tea? Not tə-yee, mind: if you ever say bə-yee cə-yee də-yee again you shall be dragged round the room three times by the hair of your head. [*Fortissimo.*] T, T, T, T.

LIZA: [*Weeping.*] I cant hear no difference cep that it sounds more genteel-like when you say it.

HIGGINS: Well, if you can hear that difference, what the devil are you crying for? Pickering: give her a chocolate.

PICKERING: No, no. Never mind crying a little, Miss Doolittle: you are doing very well; and the lessons wont hurt. I promise you I wont let him drag you round the room by your hair.

HIGGINS: Be off with you to Mrs. Pearce and tell her about it. Think about it. Try to do it by yourself: and keep your tongue well forward in your mouth instead of trying to roll it up and swallow it. Another lesson at half-past four this afternoon. Away with you.

[ELIZA, *still sobbing, rushes from the room.*]

And that is the sort of ordeal poor ELIZA *has to go through for months before we meet her again on her first appearance in London society of the professional class.*

ACT III

It is MRS. HIGGINS's *at-home day. Nobody has yet arrived. Her drawing room, in a flat on Chelsea Embankment, has three windows looking on the river; and the ceiling is not so lofty as it would be in an older house of the same pretension. The windows are open, giving access to a balcony with flowers in pots. If you stand with your face to the windows, you have the fireplace on your left and the door in the right-hand wall close to the corner nearest the windows.*

MRS. HIGGINS *was brought up on Morris and Burne Jones[1]; and her room, which is very unlike her son's room in Wimpole Street, is not crowded with furniture and little tables and nicknacks. In the middle of the room there is a big ottoman; and this, with the carpet, the Morris wall-papers, and the Morris chintz window curtains and brocade covers of the ottoman and its cushions, supply all the ornament, and are much too handsome to be hidden by odds and ends of useless things. A few good oil-paintings from the exhibitions in the Grosvenor Gallery thirty years ago (the Burne Jones, not the Whistler[2] side of them) are on the walls. The only landscape is a Cecil Lawson on the scale of a Rubens.[3] There is a portrait of* MRS. HIGGINS *as she was when she defied fashion in her youth in one of the beautiful Rossettian[4] costumes which, when caricatured by people who did not understand, led to the absurdities of popular estheticism in the eighteen-seventies.*

In the corner diagonally opposite the door MRS. HIGGINS, *now over sixty and long past taking the trouble to dress out of the fashion, sits writing at an elegantly simple writing-table with a bell button within reach of her hand. There is a Chippendale chair further back in the room between her and the window nearest her side. At the other side of the room, further forward, is an Elizabethan chair roughly carved in the taste of Inigo Jones.[5] On the same side a piano in a decorated case. The corner between the fireplace and the window is occupied by a divan cushioned in Morris chintz.*

It is between four and five in the afternoon.

The door is opened violently; and HIGGINS *enters with his hat on.*

MRS. HIGGINS: [*Dismayed.*] Henry! [*Scolding him.*] What are you doing here today? It is my at-home day: you promised not to come. [*As he bends to kiss her, she takes his hat off, and presents it to him.*]

HIGGINS: Oh bother! [*He throws the hat down on the table.*]

MRS. HIGGINS: Go home at once.

---

1. William Morris (1834–1896), poet, painter, designer, and leader in the 19th-century decorative arts; Edward Burne-Jones (1833–1898), late Pre-Raphaelite painter and associate of Morris's spartan aesthetic movement.   2. James A. McNeill Whistler (1834–1903), American painter whose early work was associated with the Realism of Courbet et al., and thus antithetical to the Pre-Raphaelite influences associated with Burne-Jones.   3. Cecil Lawson (1851–1882), English landscape painter. Peter Paul Rubens (1577–1640), a Flemish painter of the Baroque style, known for tremendously dynamic, violent, and powerful works.   4. After Dante Gabriel Rossetti, (1828–1882), a Pre-Raphaelite painter whose subject matter was exotically beautiful women from medieval literature and romantic legend.   5. Inigo Jones (1573–1652), architect to James I and Charles I, responsible for England's move toward Italian Renaissance architectural principles in the early 17th century.

HIGGINS: [*Kissing her.*] I know, mother. I came on purpose.

MRS. HIGGINS: But you mustnt. I'm serious, Henry. You offend all my friends: they stop coming whenever they meet you.

HIGGINS: Nonsense! I know I have no small talk; but people dont mind. [*He sits on the settee.*]

MRS. HIGGINS: Oh! dont they? Small talk indeed! What about your large talk? Really, dear, you mustnt stay.

HIGGINS: I must. Ive a job for you. A phonetic job.

MRS. HIGGINS: No use, dear. I'm sorry; but I cant get round your vowels; and though I like to get pretty postcards in your patent shorthand, I always have to read the copies in ordinary writing you so thoughtfully send me.

HIGGINS: Well, this isnt a phonetic job.

MRS. HIGGINS: You said it was.

HIGGINS: Not your part of it. Ive picked up a girl.

MRS. HIGGINS: Does that mean that some girl has picked you up?

HIGGINS: Not at all. I dont mean a love affair.

MRS. HIGGINS: What a pity!

HIGGINS: Why?

MRS. HIGGINS: Well, you never fall in love with anyone under forty-five. When will you discover that there are some rather nice-looking young women about?

HIGGINS: Oh, I cant be bothered with young women. My idea of a lovable woman is somebody as like you as possible. I shall never get into the way of seriously liking young women: some habits lie too deep to be changed. [*Rising abruptly and walking about, jingling his money and his keys in his trouser pockets.*] Besides, theyre all idiots.

MRS. HIGGINS: Do you know what you would do if you really loved me, Henry?

HIGGINS: Oh bother! What? Marry, I suppose.

MRS. HIGGINS: No. Stop fidgeting and take your hands out of your pockets. [*With a gesture of despair, he obeys and sits down again.*] Thats a good boy. Now tell me about the girl.

HIGGINS: She's coming to see you.

MRS. HIGGINS: I dont remember asking her.

HIGGINS: You didnt. *I* asked her. If youd known her you wouldnt have asked her.

MRS. HIGGINS: Indeed! Why?

HIGGINS: Well, it's like this. She's a common flower girl. I picked her off the kerbstone.

MRS. HIGGINS: And invited her to my at-home!

HIGGINS: [*Rising and coming to her to coax her.*] Oh, thatll be all right. Ive taught her to speak properly; and she has strict orders as to her behavior. She's to keep to two subjects: the weather and everybody's health—Fine day and How do you do, you know—and not to let herself go on things in general. That will be safe.

MRS. HIGGINS: Safe! To talk about our health! about our insides! perhaps about our outsides! How could you be so silly, Henry?

HIGGINS: [*Impatiently.*] Well, she must talk about something. [*He controls himself and sits down again.*] Oh, she'll be all right: dont you fuss. Pickering is in it with me. Ive a sort of bet on that I'll pass her off as a duchess in six months. I started on her some months ago; and she's getting on like a house on fire. I shall win my bet. She has a quick ear; and she's been easier to teach than my middle-class pupils because she's had to learn a complete new language. She talks English almost as you talk French.

MRS. HIGGINS: Thats satisfactory, at all events.

HIGGINS: Well, it is and it isnt.

MRS. HIGGINS: What does that mean?

HIGGINS: You see, Ive got her pronunciation all right; but you have to consider not only how a girl pronounces, but what she pronounces; and that's where—

[*They are interrupted by the* PARLORMAID, *announcing guests.*]

THE PARLORMAID: Mrs. and Miss Eynsford Hill. [*She withdraws.*]

HIGGINS: Oh Lord! [*He rises; snatches his hat from the table; and makes for the door; but before he reaches it his mother introduces him.*]

[MRS. *and* MISS EYNSFORD HILL *are the mother and daughter who sheltered from the rain in Covent Garden. The mother is well bred, quiet, and has the habitual anxiety of straitened means. The daughter has acquired a gay air of being very much at home in society: the bravado of genteel poverty.*]

MRS. EYNSFORD HILL: [*To* MRS. HIGGINS.] How do you do? [*They shake hands.*]

MISS EYNSFORD HILL: How d'you do? [*She shakes.*]

MRS. HIGGINS: [*Introducing.*] My son Henry.

MRS. EYNSFORD HILL: Your celebrated son! I have so longed to meet you, Professor Higgins.

HIGGINS: [*Glumly, making no movement in her direction.*] Delighted. [*He backs against the piano and bows brusquely.*]

MISS EYNSFORD HILL: [*Going to him with confident familiarity.*] How do you do?

HIGGINS: [*Staring at her.*] Ive seen you before somewhere. I havnt the ghost of a notion where; but Ive heard your voice. [*Drearily.*] It doesnt matter. Youd better sit down.

MRS. HIGGINS: I'm sorry to say that my celebrated son has no manners. You mustnt mind him.

MISS EYNSFORD HILL: [*Gaily.*] I dont. [*She sits in the Elizabethan chair.*]

MRS. EYNSFORD HILL: [*A little bewildered.*] Not at all. [*She sits on the ottoman between her* DAUGHTER *and* MRS. HIGGINS, *who has turned her chair away from the writing-table.*]

HIGGINS: Oh, have I been rude? I didnt mean to be.

[*He goes to the central window, through which, with his back to the company, he contemplates the river and the flowers in Battersea Park on the opposite bank as if they were a frozen desert.*
The PARLORMAID *returns, ushering in* PICKERING.]

THE PARLORMAID: Colonel Pickering. [*She withdraws.*]

PICKERING: How do you do, Mrs. Higgins?

MRS. HIGGINS: So glad youve come. Do you know Mrs. Eynsford Hill—Miss

Eynsford Hill? [*Exchange of bows. The* COLONEL *brings the Chippendale chair a little forward between* MRS. HILL *and* MRS. HIGGINS, *and sits down.*]

PICKERING: Has Henry told you what weve come for?

HIGGINS: [*Over his shoulder.*] We were interrupted: damn it!

MRS. HIGGINS: Oh Henry, Henry, really!

MRS. EYNSFORD HILL: [*Half rising.*] Are we in the way?

MRS. HIGGINS: [*Rising and making her sit down again.*] No, no. You couldnt have come more fortunately: we want you to meet a friend of ours.

HIGGINS: [*Turning hopefully.*] Yes, by George! We want two or three people. Youll do as well as anybody else.

[*The* PARLORMAID *returns, ushering* FREDDY.]

THE PARLORMAID: Mr. Eynsford Hill.

HIGGINS: [*Almost audibly, past endurance.*] God of Heaven! another of them.

FREDDY: [*Shaking hands with* MRS. HIGGINS.] Ahdedo?

MRS. HIGGINS: Very good of you to come. [*Introducing.*] Colonel Pickering.

FREDDY: [*Bowing.*] Ahdedo?

MRS. HIGGINS: I dont think you know my son, Professor Higgins.

FREDDY: [*Going to* HIGGINS.] Ahdedo?

HIGGINS: [*Looking at him much as if he were a pickpocket.*] I'll take my oath Ive met you before somewhere. Where was it?

FREDDY: I dont think so.

HIGGINS: [*Resignedly.*] It dont matter, anyhow. Sit down.

[*He shakes* FREDDY's *hand, and almost slings him on to the ottoman with his face to the windows; then comes round to the other side of it.*]

HIGGINS: Well, here we are, anyhow! [*He sits down on the ottoman next to* FREDDY.] And now what the devil are we going to talk about until Eliza comes?

MRS. HIGGINS: Henry: you are the life and soul of the Royal Society's soirées; but really youre rather trying on more commonplace occasions.

HIGGINS: Am I? Very sorry. [*Beaming suddenly.*] I suppose I am, you know. [*Uproariously.*] Ha, ha!

MISS EYNSFORD HILL: [*Who considers* HIGGINS *quite eligible matrimonially.*] I sympathize. *I* havnt any small talk. If people would only be frank and say what they really think!

HIGGINS: [*Relapsing into gloom.*] Lord forbid!

MRS. EYNSFORD HILL: [*Taking up her daughter's cue.*] But why?

HIGGINS: What they think they ought to think is bad enough, Lord knows; but what they really think would break up the whole show. Do you suppose it would be really agreeable if I were to come out now with what *I* really think?

MISS EYNSFORD HILL: [*Gaily.*] Is it so very cynical?

HIGGINS: Cynical! Who the dickens said it was cynical? I mean it wouldnt be decent.

MRS. EYNSFORD HILL: [*Seriously.*] Oh! I'm sure you dont mean that, Mr. Higgins.

HIGGINS: You see, we're all savages, more or less. We're supposed to be civilized and cultured—to know all about poetry and philosophy and art and science, and so on; but how many of us know even the meanings of these names? [*To* MISS HILL.] What do you know of poetry? [*To* MRS. HILL.] What do you know of science? [*Indicating* FREDDY.] What does he know of art or science or anything else? What the devil do you imagine I know of philosophy?

MRS. HIGGINS: [*Warningly.*] Or of manners, Henry?

THE PARLORMAID: [*Opening the door.*] Miss Doolittle. [*She withdraws.*]

HIGGINS: [*Rising hastily and running to* MRS. HIGGINS.] Here she is, mother. [*He stands on tiptoe and makes signs over his mother's head to* ELIZA *to indicate to her which lady is her hostess.*]

[ELIZA, *who is exquisitely dressed, produces an impression of such remarkable distinction and beauty as she enters that they all rise, quite fluttered. Guided by* HIGGINS's *signals, she comes to* MRS. HIGGINS *with studied grace.*]

LIZA: [*Speaking with pedantic correctness of pronunciation and great beauty of tone.*] How do you do, Mrs. Higgins? [*She gasps slightly in making sure of the H in Higgins, but is quite successful.*] Mr. Higgins told me I might come.

MRS. HIGGINS: [*Cordially.*] Quite right: I'm very glad indeed to see you.

PICKERING: How do you do, Miss Doolittle?

LIZA: [*Shaking hands with him.*] Colonel Pickering, is it not?

MRS. EYNSFORD HILL: I feel sure we have met before, Miss Doolittle. I remember your eyes.

LIZA: How do you do? [*She sits down on the ottoman gracefully in the place just left vacant by* HIGGINS.]

MRS. EYNSFORD HILL: [*Introducing.*] My daughter Clara.

LIZA: How do you do?

CLARA: [*Impulsively.*] How do you do? [*She sits down on the ottoman beside* ELIZA, *devouring her with her eyes.*]

FREDDY: [*Coming to their side of the ottoman.*] Ive certainly had the pleasure.

MRS. EYNSFORD HILL: [*Introducing.*] My son Freddy.

LIZA: How do you do?

[FREDDY *bows and sits down in the Elizabethan chair, infatuated.*]

HIGGINS: [*Suddenly.*] By George, yes: it all comes back to me! [*They stare at him.*] Covent Garden! [*Lamentably.*] What a damned thing!

MRS. HIGGINS: Henry, please! [*He is about to sit on the edge of the table.*] Dont sit on my writing-table: youll break it.

HIGGINS: [*Sulkily.*] Sorry.

[*He goes to the divan, stumbling into the fender and over the fire-irons on his way; extricating himself with muttered imprecations; and finishing his disastrous journey by throwing himself so impatiently on the divan that he almost breaks it.* MRS. HIGGINS *looks at him, but controls herself and says nothing. A long and painful pause ensues.*]

MRS. HIGGINS: [*At last, conversationally.*] Will it rain, do you think?

LIZA: The shallow depression in the west of these islands is likely to move slowly in an easterly direction. There are no indications of any great change in the barometrical situation.

FREDDY: Ha! ha! how awfully funny!

LIZA: What is wrong with that, young man? I bet I got it right.

FREDDY: Killing!

MRS. EYNSFORD HILL: I'm sure I hope it wont turn cold. Theres so much influenza about. It runs right through our whole family regularly every spring.

LIZA: [Darkly.] My aunt died of influenza: so they said.

MRS. EYNSFORD HILL: [Clicks her tongue sympathetically.]!!!!

LIZA: [In the same tragic tone.] But it's my belief they done the old woman in.

MRS. HIGGINS: [Puzzled.] Done her in?

LIZA: Y-e-e-e-es, Lord love you! Why should she die of influenza? She come through diptheria right enough the year before. I saw her with my own eyes. Fairly blue with it, she was. They all thought she was dead; but my father he kept ladling gin down her throat til she came to so sudden that she bit the bowl off the spoon.

MRS. EYNSFORD HILL: [Startled.] Dear me!

LIZA: [Piling up the indictment.] What call would a woman with that strength in her have to die of influenza? What become of her new straw hat that should have come to me? Somebody pinched it; and what I say is, them as pinched it done her in.

MRS. EYNSFORD HILL: What does doing her in mean?

HIGGINS: [Hastily.] Oh, thats the new small talk. To do a person in means to kill them.

MRS. EYNSFORD HILL: [To ELIZA, horrified.] You surely dont believe that your aunt was killed?

LIZA: Do I not! Them she lived with would have killed her for a hat-pin, let alone a hat.

MRS. EYNSFORD HILL: But it cant have been right for your father to pour spirits down her throat like that. It might have killed her.

LIZA: Not her. Gin was mother's milk to her. Besides, he'd poured so much down his own throat that he knew the good of it.

MRS. EYNSFORD HILL: Do you mean that he drank?

LIZA: Drank! My word! Something chronic.

MRS. EYNSFORD HILL: How dreadful for you!

LIZA: Not a bit. It never did him no harm what I could see. But then he did not keep it up regular. [Cheerfully.] On the burst, as you might say, from time to time. And always more agreeable when he had a drop in. When he was out of work, my mother used to give him fourpence and tell him to go out and not come back until he'd drunk himself cheerful and loving-like. Theres lots of women has to make their husbands drunk to make them fit to live with. [Now quite at her ease.] You see, it's like this. If a man has a bit of a conscience, it always takes him when he's sober; and then it makes him low-spirited. A drop of booze just takes that off and makes him happy. [To FREDDY, who is in convulsions of suppressed laughter.] Here! what are you sniggering at?

FREDDY: The new small talk. You do it so awfully well.

LIZA: If I was doing it proper, what was you laughing at? [*To* HIGGINS.] Have I said anything I oughtnt?

MRS. HIGGINS: [*Interposing.*] Not at all, Miss Doolittle.

LIZA: Well, thats a mercy, anyhow. [*Expansively.*] What I always say is—

HIGGINS: [*Rising and looking at his watch.*] Ahem!

LIZA: [*Looking round at him; taking the hint; and rising.*] Well: I must go. [*They all rise.* FREDDY *goes to the door.*] So pleased to have met you. Goodbye. [*She shakes hands with* MRS. HIGGINS.]

MRS. HIGGINS: Goodbye.

LIZA: Goodbye, Colonel Pickering.

PICKERING: Goodbye, Miss Doolittle. [*They shake hands.*]

LIZA: [*Nodding to the others.*] Goodbye, all.

FREDDY: [*Opening the door for her.*] Are you walking across the Park, Miss Doolittle? If so—

LIZA: [*With perfectly elegant diction.*] Walk! Not bloody likely. [*Sensation.*] I am going in a taxi. [*She goes out.*]

[PICKERING *gasps and sits down.* FREDDY *goes out on the balcony to catch another glimpse of* ELIZA.]

MRS. EYNSFORD HILL: [*Suffering from shock.*] Well, I really cant get used to the new ways.

CLARA: [*Throwing herself discontentedly into the Elizabethan chair.*] Oh, it's all right, mamma, quite right. People will think we never go anywhere or see anybody if you are so old-fashioned.

MRS. EYNSFORD HILL: I daresay I am very old-fashioned; but I do hope you wont begin using that expression, Clara. I have got accustomed to hear you talking about men as rotters, and calling everything filthy and beastly; though I do think it horrible and unladylike. But this last is really too much. Dont you think so, Colonel Pickering?

PICKERING: Dont ask me. Ive been away in India for several years; and manners have changed so much that I sometimes dont know whether I'm at a respectable dinner-table or in a ship's forecastle.

CLARA: It's all a matter of habit. Theres no right or wrong in it. Nobody means anything by it. And it's so quaint, and gives such a smart emphasis to things that are not in themselves very witty. I find the new small talk delightful and quite innocent.

MRS. EYNSFORD HILL: [*Rising.*] Well, after that, I think it's time for us to go.

[PICKERING *and* HIGGINS *rise.*]

CLARA: [*Rising.*] Oh yes: we have three at-homes to go to still. Goodbye, Mrs. Higgins. Goodbye, Colonel Pickering. Goodbye, Professor Higgins.

HIGGINS: [*Coming grimly at her from the divan, and accompanying her to the door.*] Goodbye. Be sure you try on that small talk at the three at-homes. Dont be nervous about it. Pitch it in strong.

CLARA: [*All smiles.*] I will. Goodbye. Such nonsense, all this early Victorian prudery!

HIGGINS: [*Tempting her.*] Such damned nonsense!

CLARA: Such bloody nonsense!

MRS. EYNSFORD HILL: [*Convulsively.*] Clara!

CLARA: Ha! ha! [*She goes out radiant, conscious of being thoroughly up to date, and is heard descending the stairs in a stream of silvery laughter.*]

FREDDY: [*To the heavens at large.*] Well, I ask you— [*He gives it up, and comes to* MRS. HIGGINS.] Goodbye.

MRS. HIGGINS: [*Shaking hands.*] Goodbye. Would you like to meet Miss Doolittle again?

FREDDY: [*Eagerly.*] Yes, I should, most awfully.

MRS. HIGGINS: Well, you know my days.

FREDDY: Yes. Thanks awfully. Goodbye. [*He goes out.*]

MRS. EYNSFORD HILL: Goodbye, Mr. Higgins.

HIGGINS: Goodbye. Goodbye.

MRS. EYNSFORD HILL: [*To* PICKERING.] It's no use. I shall never be able to bring myself to use that word.

PICKERING: Dont. It's not compulsory, you know. Youll get on quite well without it.

MRS. EYNSFORD HILL: Only, Clara is so down on me if I am not positively reeking with the latest slang. Goodbye.

PICKERING: Goodbye. [*They shake hands.*]

MRS. EYNSFORD HILL: [*To* MRS. HIGGINS.] You mustnt mind Clara. [PICKERING, *catching from her lowered tone that this is not meant for him to hear, discreetly joins* HIGGINS *at the window.*] We're so poor! and she gets so few parties, poor child! She doesnt quite know. [MRS. HIGGINS, *seeing that her eyes are moist, takes her hand sympathetically and goes with her to the door.*] But the boy is nice. Dont you think so?

MRS. HIGGINS: Oh, quite nice. I shall always be delighted to see him.

MRS. EYNSFORD HILL: Thank you, dear. Goodbye. [*She goes out.*]

HIGGINS: [*Eagerly.*] Well? Is Eliza presentable? [*He swoops on his mother and drags her to the ottoman, where she sits down in* ELIZA's *place with her son on her left.*]

[PICKERING *returns to his chair on her right.*]

MRS. HIGGINS: You silly boy, of course she's not presentable. She's a triumph of your art and of her dressmaker's; but if you suppose for a moment that she doesnt give herself away in every sentence she utters, you must be perfectly cracked about her.

PICKERING: But dont you think something might be done? I mean something to eliminate the sanguinary element from her conversation.

MRS. HIGGINS: Not as long as she is in Henry's hands.

HIGGINS: [*Aggrieved.*] Do you mean that my language is improper?

MRS. HIGGINS: No, dearest: it would be quite proper—say on a canal barge; but it would not be proper for her at a garden party.

HIGGINS: [*Deeply injured.*] Well I must say—

PICKERING: [*Interrupting him.*] Come, Higgins: you must learn to know yourself. I havnt heard such language as yours since we used to review the volunteers in Hyde Park twenty years ago.

HIGGINS: [*Sulkily.*] Oh, well, if you say so, I suppose I dont always talk like a bishop.

MRS. HIGGINS: [*Quieting* HENRY *with a touch.*] Colonel Pickering: will you tell me what is the exact state of things in Wimpole Street?

PICKERING: [*Cheerfully: as if this completely changed the subject.*] Well, I have come to live there with Henry. We work together at my Indian Dialects; and we think it more convenient—

MRS. HIGGINS: Quite so. I know all about that: it's an excellent arrangement. But where does this girl live?

HIGGINS: With us, of course. Where should she live?

MRS. HIGGINS: But on what terms? Is she a servant? If not, what is she?

PICKERING: [*Slowly.*] I think I know what you mean, Mrs. Higgins.

HIGGINS: Well, dash me if *I* do! Ive had to work at the girl every day for months to get her to her present pitch. Besides, she's useful. She knows where my things are, and remembers my appointments and so forth.

MRS. HIGGINS: How does your housekeeper get on with her?

HIGGINS: Mrs. Pearce? Oh, she's jolly glad to get so much taken off her hands; for before Eliza came, she used to have to find things and remind me of my appointments. But she's got some silly bee in her bonnet about Eliza. She keeps saying "You dont think, sir": doesnt she, Pick?

PICKERING: Yes: thats the formula. "You dont think, sir." Thats the end of every conversation about Eliza.

HIGGINS: As if I ever stop thinking about the girl and her confounded vowels and consonants. I'm worn out, thinking about her, and watching her lips and her teeth and her tongue, not to mention her soul, which is the quaintest of the lot.

MRS. HIGGINS: You certainly are a pretty pair of babies, playing with your live doll.

HIGGINS: Playing! The hardest job I ever tackled: make no mistake about that, mother. But you have no idea how frightfully interesting it is to take a human being and change her into a quite different human being by creating a new speech for her. It's filling up the deepest gulf that separates class from class and soul from soul.

PICKERING: [*Drawing his chair closer to* MRS. HIGGINS *and bending over to her eagerly.*] Yes: it's enormously interesting. I assure you, Mrs. Higgins, we take Eliza very seriously. Every week—every day almost—there is some new change. [*Closer again.*] We keep records of every stage—dozens of gramophone disks and photographs—

HIGGINS: [*Assailing her at the other ear.*] Yes, by George: it's the most absorbing experiment I ever tackled. She regularly fills our lives up: doesnt she, Pick?

PICKERING: We're always talking Eliza.

HIGGINS: Teaching Eliza.

PICKERING: Dressing Eliza.
MRS. HIGGINS: What!
HIGGINS: Inventing new Elizas.

HIGGINS: [*Speaking together.*] You now, she has the most extraordinary quickness of ear:
PICKERING: I assure you, my dear Mrs. Higgins, that girl

HIGGINS: just like a parrot. Ive tried her with every
PICKERING: is a genius. She can play the piano quite beautifully.

HIGGINS: possible sort of sound that a human being can make
PICKERING: We have taken her to classical concerts and to music

HIGGINS: Continental dialects, African dialects, Hottentot
PICKERING: halls; and it's all the same to her: she plays everything

HIGGINS: [*Speaking together.*] clicks, things it took me years to get hold of; and
PICKERING: she hears right off when she comes home, whether it's

HIGGINS: she picks them up like a shot, right away, as if she had
PICKERING: Beethoven and Brahms or Lehar and Lionel Monckton;[6]

HIGGINS: been at it all her life.
PICKERING: though six months ago, she'd never as much as touched a piano—

MRS. HIGGINS: [*Putting her fingers in her ears, as they are by this time shouting one another down with an intolerable noise.*] Sh-sh-sh—sh! [*They stop.*]
PICKERING: I beg your pardon. [*He draws his chair back apologetically.*]
HIGGINS: Sorry. When Pickering starts shouting nobody can get a word in edgeways.
MRS. HIGGINS: Be quiet, Henry. Colonel Pickering: dont you realize that when Eliza walked into Wimpole Street, something walked in with her?
PICKERING: Her father did. But Henry soon got rid of him.
MRS. HIGGINS: It would have been more to the point if her mother had. But as her mother didnt something else did.
PICKERING: But what?
MRS. HIGGINS: [*Unconsciously dating herself by the word.*] A problem.
PICKERING: Oh, I see. The problem of how to pass her off as a lady.
HIGGINS: I'll solve that problem. Ive half solved it already.
MRS. HIGGINS: No, you two infinitely stupid male creatures: the problem of what is to be done with her afterwards.

6. German composers Ludwig van Beethoven (1770–1827) and Johannes Brahms (1833–1897); Hungarian operetta composer Franz Lehar (1870–1948) and English operetta composer Lionel Monckton (1862–1924).

HIGGINS: I dont see anything in that. She can go her own way, with all the advantages I have given her.

MRS. HIGGINS: The advantages of that poor woman who was here just now! The manners and habits that disqualify a fine lady from earning her own living without giving her a fine lady's income! Is that what you mean?

PICKERING: [*Indulgently, being rather bored.*] Oh, that will be all right, Mrs. Higgins. [*He rises to go.*]

HIGGINS: [*Rising also.*] We'll find her some light employment.

PICKERING: She's happy enough. Dont you worry about her. Goodbye. [*He shakes hands as if he were consoling a frightened child, and makes for the door.*]

HIGGINS: Anyhow, theres no good bothering now. The thing's done. Goodbye, mother. [*He kisses her, and follows* PICKERING.]

PICKERING: [*Turning for a final consolation.*] There are plenty of openings. We'll do whats right. Goodbye.

HIGGINS: [*To* PICKERING *as they go out together.*] Lets take her to the Shakespear exhibition at Earls Court.

PICKERING: Yes: lets. Her remarks will be delicious.

HIGGINS: She'll mimic all the people for us when we get home.

PICKERING: Ripping. [*Both are heard laughing as they go downstairs.*]

MRS. HIGGINS: [*Rises with an impatient bounce, and returns to her work at the writing-table. She sweeps a litter of disarranged papers out of her way; snatches a sheet of paper from her stationery case; and tries resolutely to write. At the third line she gives it up; flings down her pen; grips the table angrily and exclaims.*] Oh, men! men!! men!!!

✻   ✻   ✻

Clearly ELIZA *will not pass as a duchess yet; and* HIGGINS's *bet remains unwon. But the six months are not yet exhausted; and just in time* ELIZA *does actually pass as a princess. For a glimpse of how she did it imagine an Embassy in London one summer evening after dark. The hall door has an awning and a carpet across the sidewalk to the kerb, because a grand reception is in progress. A small crowd is lined up to see the guests arrive.*

A Rolls-Royce car drives up. PICKERING *in evening dress, with medals and orders, alights, and hands out* ELIZA, *in opera cloak, evening dress, diamonds, fan, flowers and all accessories.* HIGGINS *follows. The car drives off; and the three go up the steps and into the house, the door opening for them as they approach.*

Inside the house they find themselves in a spacious hall from which the grand staircase rises. On the left are the arrangements for the gentlemen's cloaks. The male guests are depositing their hats and wraps there.

On the right is a door leading to the ladies' cloakroom. Ladies are going in cloaked and coming out in splendor. PICKERING *whispers to* ELIZA *and points out the ladies' room. She goes into it.* HIGGINS *and* PICKERING *take off their overcoats and take tickets for them from the attendant.*

One of the guests, occupied in the same way, has his back turned. Having taken his ticket, he turns round and reveals himself as an important looking YOUNG

MAN *with an astonishingly hairy face. He has an enormous moustache, flowing out into luxuriant whiskers. Waves of hair cluster on his brow. His hair is cropped closely at the back, and glows with oil. Otherwise he is very smart. He wears several worthless orders. He is evidently a foreigner, guessable as a whiskered Pandour from Hungary; but in spite of the ferocity of his moustache he is amiable and genially voluble.*

Recognizing HIGGINS, *he flings his arms wide apart and approaches him enthusiastically.*

WHISKERS: Maestro, maestro. [*He embraces* HIGGINS *and kisses him on both cheeks.*] You remember me?

HIGGINS: No I dont. Who the devil are you?

WHISKERS: I am your pupil: your first pupil, your best and greatest pupil. I am little Nepommuck, the marvellous boy. I have made your name famous throughout Europe. You teach me phonetic. You cannot forget ME.

HIGGINS: Why dont you shave?

NEPOMMUCK: I have not your imposing appearance, your chin, your brow. Nobody notice me when I shave. Now I am famous: they call me Hairy Faced Dick.

HIGGINS: And what are you doing here among all these swells?

NEPOMMUCK: I am interpreter. I speak 32 languages. I am indispensable at these international parties. You are great cockney specialist: you place a man anywhere in London the moment he open his mouth. I place any man in Europe.

[*A* FOOTMAN *hurries down the grand staircase and comes to* NEPOMMUCK.]

FOOTMAN: You are wanted upstairs. Her Excellency cannot understand the Greek gentleman.

NEPOMMUCK: Thank you, yes, immediately.

[*The* FOOTMAN *goes and is lost in the crowd.*]

NEPOMMUCK: [*To* HIGGINS.] This Greek diplomatist pretends he cannot speak nor understand English. He cannot deceive me. He is the son of a Clerkenwell watchmaker. He speaks English so villainously that he dare not utter a word of it without betraying his origin. I help him to pretend; but I make him pay through the nose. I make them all pay. Ha Ha! [*He hurries upstairs.*]

PICKERING: Is this fellow really an expert? Can he find out Eliza and blackmail her?

HIGGINS: We shall see. If he finds her out I lose my bet.

[ELIZA *comes from the cloakroom and joins them.*]

PICKERING: Well, Eliza, now for it. Are you ready?

LIZA: Are you nervous, Colonel?

PICKERING: Frightfully. I feel exactly as I felt before my first battle. It's the first time that frightens.

LIZA: It is not the first time for me, Colonel. I have done this fifty times—
hundreds of times—in my little piggery in Angel Court in my day-dreams. I
am in a dream now. Promise me not to let Professor Higgins wake me; for if
he does I shall forget everything and talk as I used to in Drury Lane.

PICKERING: Not a word, Higgins. [*To* ELIZA.] Now, ready?

LIZA: Ready.

PICKERING: Go.

[*They mount the stairs,* HIGGINS *last.* PICKERING *whispers to the* FOOTMAN *on the first landing.*]

FIRST LANDING FOOTMAN: Miss Doolittle, Colonel Pickering, Professor Higgins.

SECOND LANDING FOOTMAN: Miss Doolittle, Colonel Pickering, Professor Higgins.

[*At the top of the staircase the* AMBASSADOR *and his* WIFE, *with* NEPOMMUCK *at her elbow, are receiving.*]

HOSTESS: [*Taking* ELIZA's *hand.*] How d'ye do?

HOST: [*Same play.*] How d'ye do? How d'ye do, Pickering?

LIZA: [*With a beautiful gravity that awes her* HOSTESS.] How do you do? [*She passes on to the drawingroom.*]

HOSTESS: Is that your adopted daughter, Colonel Pickering? She will make a
sensation.

PICKERING: Most kind of you to invite her for me. [*He passes on.*]

HOSTESS: [*To* NEPOMMUCK.] Find out all about her.

NEPOMMUCK: [*Bowing.*] Excellency—[*He goes into the crowd.*]

HOST: How d'ye do, Higgins? You have a rival here tonight. He introduced himself as your pupil. Is he any good?

HIGGINS: He can learn a language in a fortnight—knows dozens of them. A sure
mark of a fool. As a phonetician, no good whatever.

HOSTESS: How d'ye do, Professor?

HIGGINS: How do you do? Fearful bore for you this sort of thing. Forgive my
part in it. [*He passes on.*]

[*In the drawingroom and its suite of salons the reception is in full swing.* ELIZA
*passes through. She is so intent on her ordeal that she walks like a somnambu-
list in a desert instead of a débutante in a fashionable crowd. They stop talking
to look at her, admiring her dress, her jewels, and her strangely attractive self.
Some of the younger ones at the back stand on their chairs to see.*

The HOST *and* HOSTESS *come in from the staircase and mingle with their
guests.* HIGGINS, *gloomy and contemptuous of the whole business, comes into
the group where they are chatting.*]

HOSTESS: Ah, here is Professor Higgins: he will tell us. Tell us all about the
wonderful young lady, Professor.

HIGGINS: [*Almost morosely.*] What wonderful young lady?

HOSTESS: You know very well. They tell me there has been nothing like her in London since people stood on their chairs to look at Mrs. Langtry.[7]

[NEPOMMUCK *joins the group, full of news.*]

HOSTESS: Ah, here you are at last, Nepommuck. Have you found out all about the Doolittle lady?

NEPOMMUCK: I have found out all about her. She is a fraud.

HOSTESS: A fraud! Oh no.

NEPOMMUCK: YES, yes. She cannot deceive me. Her name cannot be Doolittle.

HIGGINS: Why?

NEPOMMUCK: Because Doolittle is an English name. And she is not English.

HOSTESS: Oh, nonsense! She speaks English perfectly.

NEPOMMUCK: Too perfectly. Can you shew me any English woman who speaks English as it should be spoken? Only foreigners who have been taught to speak it speak it well.

HOSTESS: Certainly she terrified me by the way she said How d'ye do. I had a schoolmistress who talked like that; and I was mortally afraid of her. But if she is not English what is she?

NEPOMMUCK: Hungarian.

ALL THE REST: Hungarian!

NEPOMMUCK: Hungarian. And of royal blood. I am Hungarian. My blood is royal.

HIGGINS: Did you speak to her in Hungarian?

NEPOMMUCK: I did. She was very clever. She said "Please speak to me in English: I do not understand French." French! She pretends not to know the difference between Hungarian and French. Impossible: she knows both.

HIGGINS: And the blood royal? How did you find that out?

NEPOMMUCK: Instinct, maestro, instinct. Only the Magyar races can produce that air of the divine right, those resolute eyes. She is a princess.

HOST: What do you say, Professor?

HIGGINS: I say an ordinary London girl out of the gutter and taught to speak by an expert. I place her in Drury Lane.

NEPOMMUCK: Ha ha ha! Oh, maestro, maestro, you are mad on the subject of cockney dialects. The London gutter is the whole world for you.

HIGGINS: [*To the* HOSTESS.] What does your Excellency say?

HOSTESS: Oh, of course I agree with Nepommuck. She must be a princess at least.

HOST: Not necessarily legitimate, of course. Morganatic perhaps. But that is undoubtedly her class.

HIGGINS: I stick to my opinion.

HOSTESS: Oh, you are incorrigible.

[*The group breaks up, leaving* HIGGINS *isolated.* PICKERING *joins him.*]

PICKERING: Where is Eliza? We must keep an eye on her.

7. English actress Lillie Langtry (1852–1929), a renowned beauty.

[ELIZA *joins them.*]

LIZA: I dont think I can bear much more. The people all stare so at me. An old lady has just told me that I speak exactly like Queen Victoria. I am sorry if I have lost your bet. I have done my best; but nothing can make me the same as these people.

PICKERING: You have not lost it, my dear. You have won it ten times over.

HIGGINS: Let us get out of this. I have had enough of chattering to these fools.

PICKERING: Eliza is tired; and I am hungry. Let us clear out and have supper somewhere.

ACT IV

The Wimpole Street laboratory. Midnight. Nobody in the room. The clock on the mantelpiece strikes twelve. The fire is not alight: it is a summer night.

Presently HIGGINS *and* PICKERING *are heard on the stairs.*

HIGGINS: [*Calling down to* PICKERING.] I say, Pick: lock up, will you? I shant be going out again.

PICKERING: Right. Can Mrs. Pearce go to bed? We dont want anything more, do we?

HIGGINS: Lord, no!

[ELIZA *opens the door and is seen on the lighted landing in all the finery in which she has just won* HIGGINS's *bet for him. She comes to the hearth, and switches on the electric lights there. She is tired: her pallor contrasts strongly with her dark eyes and hair; and her expression is almost tragic. She takes off her cloak; puts her fan and gloves on the piano; and sits down on the bench, brooding and silent.* HIGGINS, *in evening dress, with overcoat and hat, comes in, carrying a smoking jacket which he has picked up downstairs. He takes off the hat and overcoat; throws them carelessly on the newspaper stand; disposes of his coat in the same way; puts on the smoking jacket; and throws himself wearily into the easy-chair at the hearth.* PICKERING, *similarly attired, comes in. He also takes off his hat and overcoat, and is about to throw them on* HIGGINS's *when he hesitates.*]

PICKERING: I say: Mrs. Pearce will row if we leave these things lying about in the drawing room.

HIGGINS: Oh, chuck them over the bannisters into the hall. She'll find them there in the morning and put them away all right. She'll think we were drunk.

PICKERING: We are, slightly. Are there any letters?

HIGGINS: I didnt look. [PICKERING *takes the overcoats and hats and goes downstairs.* HIGGINS *begins half singing half yawning an air from* La Fanciulla del Golden West.[8] *Suddenly he stops and exclaims.*] I wonder where the devil my slippers are!

8. *The Girl of the Golden West* (1910), a three-act opera by Puccini.

[ELIZA *looks at him darkly; then rises suddenly and leaves the room.*
HIGGINS *yawns again, and resumes his song.*
PICKERING *returns, with the contents of the letter-box in his hand.*]

PICKERING: Only circulars, and this coroneted billet-doux for you. [*He throws the circulars into the fender, and posts himself on the hearthrug, with his back to the grate.*]
HIGGINS: [*Glancing at the billet-doux.*] Money-lender. [*He throws the letter after the circulars.*]

[ELIZA *returns with a pair of large down-at-heel slippers. She places them on the carpet before* HIGGINS, *and sits as before without a word.*]

HIGGINS: [*Yawning again.*] Oh Lord! What an evening! What a crew! What a silly tomfoolery! [*He raises his shoe to unlace it, and catches sight of the slippers. He stops unlacing and looks at them as if they had appeared there of their own accord.*] Oh! theyre there, are they?
PICKERING: [*Stretching himself.*] Well, I feel a bit tired. It's been a long day. The garden party, a dinner party, and the reception! Rather too much of a good thing. But youve won your bet, Higgins. Eliza did the trick, and something to spare, eh?
HIGGINS: [*Fervently.*] Thank God it's over!

[ELIZA *flinches violently; but they take no notice of her; and she recovers herself and sits stonily as before.*]

PICKERING: Were you nervous at the garden party? I was. Eliza didnt seem a bit nervous.
HIGGINS: Oh, she wasnt nervous. I knew she'd be all right. No: it's the strain of putting the job through all these months that has told on me. It was interesting enough at first, while we were at the phonetics; but after that I got deadly sick of it. If I hadnt backed myself to do it I should have chucked the whole thing up two months ago. It was a silly notion: the whole thing has been a bore.
PICKERING: Oh come! the garden party was frightfully exciting. My heart began beating like anything.
HIGGINS: Yes, for the first three minutes. But when I saw we were going to win hands down, I felt like a bear in a cage, hanging about doing nothing. The dinner was worse: sitting gorging there for over an hour, with nobody but a damned fool of a fashionable woman to talk to! I tell you, Pickering, never again for me. No more artificial duchesses. The whole thing has been simple purgatory.
PICKERING: Youve never been broken in properly to the social routine. [*Strolling over to the piano.*] I rather enjoy dipping into it occasionally myself: it makes me feel young again. Anyhow, it was a great success: an immense success. I was quite frightened once or twice because Eliza was doing it so well. You see, lots of the real people cant do it at all: theyre such fools that they think style comes by nature to people in their position; and so they never learn.

Theres always something professional about doing a thing superlatively well.

HIGGINS: Yes: thats what drives me mad: the silly people dont know their own silly business. [*Rising.*] However, it's over and done with; and now I can go to bed at last without dreading tomorrow.

[ELIZA's *beauty becomes murderous.*]

PICKERING: I think I shall turn in too. Still, it's been a great occasion: a triumph for you. Goodnight. [*He goes*].

HIGGINS: [*Following him.*] Goodnight. [*Over his shoulder, at the door.*] Put out the lights, Eliza; and tell Mrs. Pearce not to make coffee for me in the morning: I'll take tea. [*He goes out.*]

[ELIZA *tries to control herself and feel indifferent as she rises and walks across to the hearth to switch off the lights. By the time she gets there she is on the point of screaming. She sits down in* HIGGINS's *chair and holds on hard to the arms. Finally she gives way and flings herself furiously on the floor, raging.*]

HIGGINS: [*In despairing wrath outside.*] What the devil have I done with my slippers? [*He appears at the door.*]

LIZA: [*Snatching up the slippers, and hurling them at him one after the other with all her force.*] There are your slippers. And there. Take your slippers; and may you never have a day's luck with them!

HIGGINS: [*Astounded.*] What on earth—! [*He comes to her.*] Whats the matter? Get up. [*He pulls her up.*] Anything wrong?

LIZA: [*Breathless.*] Nothing wrong—with you. Ive won your bet for you, havent I? Thats enough for you. *I* dont matter, I suppose.

HIGGINS: You won my bet! You! Presumptuous insect! *I* won it. What did you throw those slippers at me for?

LIZA: Because I wanted to smash your face. I'd like to kill you, you selfish brute. Why didnt you leave me where you picked me out of—in the gutter? You thank God it's all over, and that now you can throw me back again there, do you? [*She crisps her fingers frantically.*]

HIGGINS: [*Looking at her in cool wonder.*] The creature is nervous, after all.

LIZA: [*Gives a suffocated scream of fury, and instinctively darts her nails at his face.*]!!

HIGGINS: [*Catching her wrists.*] Ah! would you? Claws in, you cat. How dare you shew your temper to me? Sit down and be quiet. [*He throws her roughly into the easy-chair.*]

LIZA: [*Crushed by superior strength and weight.*] Whats to become of me? Whats to become of me?

HIGGINS: How the devil do I know whats to become of you? What does it matter what becomes of you?

LIZA: You dont care. I know you dont care. You wouldnt care if I was dead. I'm nothing to you—not so much as them slippers.

HIGGINS: [*Thundering.*] Those slippers.

LIZA: [*With bitter submission.*] Those slippers. I didnt think it made any difference now.

[*A pause.* ELIZA *hopeless and crushed.* HIGGINS *a little uneasy.*]

HIGGINS: [*In his loftiest manner.*] Why have you begun going on like this? May I ask whether you complain of your treatment here?

LIZA: No.

HIGGINS: Has anybody behaved badly to you? Colonel Pickering? Mrs. Pearce? Any of the servants?

LIZA: No.

HIGGINS: I presume you dont pretend that *I* have treated you badly?

LIZA: No.

HIGGINS: I am glad to hear it. [*He moderates his tone.*] Perhaps youre tired after the strain of the day. Will you have a glass of champagne? [*He moves towards the door.*]

LIZA: No. [*Recollecting her manners.*] Thank you.

HIGGINS: [*Good-humored again.*] This has been coming on you for some days. I suppose it was natural for you to be anxious about the garden party. But thats all over now. [*He pats her kindly on the shoulder. She writhes.*] Theres nothing more to worry about.

LIZA: No. Nothing more for you to worry about. [*She suddenly rises and gets away from him by going to the piano bench, where she sits and hides her face.*] Oh God! I wish I was dead.

HIGGINS: [*Staring after her in sincere surprise.*] Why? In heaven's name, why? [*Reasonably, going to her.*] Listen to me, Eliza. All this irritation is purely subjective.

LIZA: I dont understand. I'm too ignorant.

HIGGINS: It's only imagination. Low spirits and nothing else. Nobody's hurting you. Nothing's wrong. You go to bed like a good girl and sleep it off. Have a little cry and say your prayers: that will make you comfortable.

LIZA: I heard your prayers. "Thank God it's all over!"

HIGGINS: [*Impatiently.*] Well, dont you thank God it's all over? Now you are free and can do what you like.

LIZA: [*Pulling herself together in desperation.*] What am I fit for? What have you left me fit for? Where am I to go? What am I to do? Whats to become of me?

HIGGINS: [*Enlightened, but not at all impressed.*] Oh, thats whats worrying you, is it? [*He thrusts his hands into his pockets, and walks about in his usual manner, rattling the contents of his pockets, as if condescending to a trivial subject out of pure kindness.*] I shouldnt bother about it if I were you. I should imagine you wont have much difficulty in settling yourself somewhere or other, though I hadnt quite realized that you were going away. [*She looks quickly at him: he does not look at her, but examines the dessert stand on the piano and decides that he will eat an apple.*] You might marry, you know. [*He bites a large piece out of the apple and munches it noisily.*] You see, Eliza, all men are not confirmed old bachelors like me and the Colonel. Most men are the marrying sort (poor devils!); and youre not bad-looking: it's quite a pleasure to look at you sometimes—not now, of course, because youre crying and looking as ugly as the very devil; but when youre all right and quite yourself, youre what I should call attractive. That is, to the people in the marrying line, you understand. You go to bed and have a good nice rest; and then get up and look at yourself in the glass; and you wont feel so cheap.

[ELIZA *again looks at him, speechless, and does not stir.*
    The look is quite lost on him: he eats his apple with a dreamy expression of happiness, as it is quite a good one.]

HIGGINS: [*A genial afterthought occurring to him.*] I daresay my mother could find some chap or other who would do very well.

LIZA: We were above that at the corner of Tottenham Court Road.

HIGGINS: [*Waking up.*] What do you mean?

LIZA: I sold flowers. I didnt sell myself. Now youve made a lady of me I'm not fit to sell anything else. I wish youd left me where you found me.

HIGGINS: [*Slinging the core of the apple decisively into the grate.*] Tosh, Eliza. Dont you insult human relations by dragging all this cant about buying and selling into it. You neednt marry the fellow if you dont like him.

LIZA: What else am I to do?

HIGGINS: Oh, lots of things. What about your old idea of a florist's shop? Pickering could set you up in one: he has lots of money. [*Chuckling.*] He'll have to pay for all those togs you have been wearing today; and that, with the hire of the jewellery, will make a big hole in two hundred pounds. Why, six months ago you would have thought it the millennium to have a flower shop of your own. Come! youll be all right. I must clear off to bed: I'm devilish sleepy. By the way, I came down for something: I forget what it was.

LIZA: Your slippers.

HIGGINS: Oh yes, of course. You shied them at me. [*He picks them up, and is going out when she rises and speaks to him.*]

LIZA: Before you go, sir—

HIGGINS: [*Dropping the slippers in his surprise at her calling him Sir.*] Eh?

LIZA: Do my clothes belong to me or to Colonel Pickering?

HIGGINS: [*Coming back into the room as if her question were the very climax of unreason.*] What the devil use would they be to Pickering?

LIZA: He might want them for the next girl you pick up to experiment on.

HIGGINS: [*Shocked and hurt.*] Is that the way you feel towards us?

LIZA: I dont want to hear anything more about that. All I want to know is whether anything belongs to me. My own clothes were burnt.

HIGGINS: But what does it matter? Why need you start bothering about that in the middle of the night?

LIZA: I want to know what I may take away with me. I dont want to be accused of stealing.

HIGGINS: [*Now deeply wounded.*] Stealing! You shouldnt have said that, Eliza. That shews a want of feeling.

LIZA: I'm sorry. I'm only a common ignorant girl; and in my station I have to be careful. There cant be any feelings between the like of you and the like of me. Please will you tell me what belongs to me and what doesnt?

HIGGINS: [*Very sulky.*] You may take the whole damned houseful if you like. Except the jewels. Theyre hired. Will that satisfy you? [*He turns on his heel and is about to go in extreme dudgeon.*]

LIZA: [*Drinking in his emotion like nectar, and nagging him to provoke a further supply.*] Stop, please. [*She takes off her jewels.*] Will you take these to your room and keep them safe? I dont want to run the risk of their being missing.

HIGGINS: [*Furious.*] Hand them over. [*She puts them into his hands.*] If these belonged to me instead of to the jeweller, I'd ram them down your ungrateful throat. [*He perfunctorily thrusts them into his pockets, unconsciously decorating himself with the protruding ends of the chains.*]

LIZA: [*Taking a ring off.*] This ring isnt the jeweller's: it's the one you bought me in Brighton. I dont want it now. [HIGGINS *dashes the ring violently into the fireplace, and turns on her so threateningly that she crouches over the piano with her hands over her face, and exclaims.*] Dont you hit me.

HIGGINS: Hit you! You infamous creature, how dare you accuse me of such a thing? It is you who have hit me. You have wounded me to the heart.

LIZA: [*Thrilling with hidden joy.*] I'm glad. Ive got a little of my own back, anyhow.

HIGGINS: [*With dignity, in his finest professional style.*] You have caused me to lose my temper: a thing that has hardly ever happened to me before. I prefer to say nothing more tonight. I am going to bed.

LIZA: [*Pertly.*] Youd better leave a note for Mrs. Pearce about the coffee; for she wont be told by me.

HIGGINS: [*Formally.*] Damn Mrs. Pearce; and damn the coffee; and damn you; and [*Wildly.*] damn my own folly in having lavished my hard-earned knowledge and the treasure of my regard and intimacy on a heartless guttersnipe. [*He goes out with impressive decorum, and spoils it by slamming the door savagely.*]

[ELIZA *goes down on her knees on the hearthrug to look for the ring. When she finds it she considers for a moment what to do with it. Finally she flings it down on the dessert stand and goes upstairs in a tearing rage.*]

*   *   *

The furniture of ELIZA's room has been increased by a big wardrobe and a sumptuous dressing-table. She comes in and switches on the electric light. She goes to the wardrobe; opens it; and pulls out a walking dress, a hat, and a pair of shoes, which she throws on the bed. She takes off her evening dress and shoes; then takes a padded hanger from the wardrobe; adjusts it carefully in the evening dress; and hangs it in the wardrobe, which she shuts with a slam. She puts on her walking shoes, her walking dress, and hat. She takes her wrist watch from the dressing-table and fastens it on. She pulls on her gloves; takes her vanity bag; and looks into it to see that her purse is there before hanging it on her wrist. She makes for the door. Every movement expresses her furious resolution.

She takes a last look at herself in the glass.

She suddenly puts out her tongue at herself; then leaves the room, switching off the electric light at the door.

Meanwhile, in the street outside, FREDDY EYNSFORD HILL, *lovelorn, is gazing up at the second floor, in which one of the windows is still lighted.*

The light goes out.

FREDDY: Goodnight, darling, darling, darling.

[ELIZA *comes out, giving the door a considerable bang behind her.*]

LIZA: Whatever are you doing here?

FREDDY: Nothing. I spend most of my nights here. It's the only place where I'm happy. Dont laugh at me, Miss Doolittle.

LIZA: Dont you call me Miss Doolittle, do you hear? Liza's good enough for me. [*She breaks down and grabs him by the shoulders.*] Freddy: you dont think I'm a heartless guttersnipe, do you?

FREDDY: Oh no, no, darling: how can you imagine such a thing? You are the loveliest, dearest—

[*He loses all self-control and smothers her with kisses. She, hungry for comfort, responds. They stand there in one another's arms.*

An elderly police CONSTABLE *arrives.*]

CONSTABLE: [*Scandalized.*] Now then! Now then!! Now then!!!

[*They release one another hastily.*]

FREDDY: Sorry, constable. Weve only just become engaged.

[*They run away.*]

The CONSTABLE *shakes his head, reflecting on his own courtship and on the vanity of human hopes. He moves off in the opposite direction with slow professional steps.*

The flight of the lovers takes them to Cavendish Square. There they halt to consider their next move.

LIZA: [*Out of breath.*] He didnt half give me a fright, that copper. But you answered him proper.

FREDDY: I hope I havent taken you out of your way. Where were you going?

LIZA: To the river.

FREDDY: What for?

LIZA: To make a hole in it.

FREDDY [*Horrified.*] Eliza, darling. What do you mean? What's the matter?

LIZA: Never mind. It doesnt matter now. There's nobody in the world now but you and me, is there?

FREDDY: Not a soul.

[*They indulge in another embrace, and are again surprised by a much younger* CONSTABLE.]

SECOND CONSTABLE. Now then, you two! Whats this? Where do you think you are? Move along here, double quick.

FREDDY: As you say, sir, double quick.

They run away again, and are in Hanover Square before they stop for another conference.

FREDDY: I had no idea the police were so devilishly prudish.

LIZA: It's their business to hunt girls off the streets.

FREDDY: We must go somewhere. We cant wander about the streets all night.

LIZA: Cant we? I think it'd be lovely to wander about for ever.

FREDDY: Oh, darling.

[*They embrace again, oblivious of the arrival of a crawling taxi. It stops.*]

TAXIMAN: Can I drive you and the lady anywhere, sir?

[*They start asunder.*]

LIZA: Oh, Freddy, a taxi. The very thing.

FREDDY: But, damn it, Ive no money.

LIZA: I have plenty. The Colonel thinks you should never go out without ten pounds in your pocket. Listen. We'll drive about all night; and in the morning I'll call on old Mrs. Higgins and ask her what I ought to do. I'll tell you all about it in the cab. And the police wont touch us there.

FREDDY: Righto! Ripping. [*To the* TAXIMAN.] Wimbledon Common. [*They drive off.*]

ACT V

MRS. HIGGINS's *drawing room. She is at her writing-table as before. The* PARLORMAID *comes in.*

THE PARLORMAID: [*At the door.*] Mr. Henry, maam, is downstairs with Colonel Pickering.

MRS. HIGGINS: Well, shew them up.

THE PARLORMAID: Theyre using the telephone, maam. Telephoning to the police, I think.

MRS. HIGGINS: What!

THE PARLORMAID: [*Coming further in and lowering her voice.*] Mr. Henry is in a state, maam. I thought I'd better tell you.

MRS. HIGGINS: If you had told me that Mr. Henry was not in a state it would have been more surprising. Tell them to come up when theyve finished with the police. I suppose he's lost something.

THE PARLORMAID: Yes, maam [*Going.*]

MRS. HIGGINS: Go upstairs and tell Miss Doolittle that Mr. Henry and the Colonel are here. Ask her not to come down til I send for her.

THE PARLORMAID: Yes, maam.

[HIGGINS *bursts in. He is, as the* PARLORMAID *has said, in a state.*]

HIGGINS: Look here, mother: heres a confounded thing!

MRS. HIGGINS: Yes, dear. Good morning. [*He checks his impatience and kisses her, whilst the* PARLORMAID *goes out.*] What is it?

HIGGINS: Eliza's bolted.

MRS. HIGGINS: [*Calmly continuing her writing.*] You must have frightened her.

HIGGINS: Frightened her! nonsense! She was left last night, as usual, to turn out the lights and all that; and instead of going to bed she changed her clothes and went right off: her bed wasnt slept in. She came in a cab for her things before seven this morning; and that fool Mrs. Pearce let her have them without telling me a word about it. What am I to do?

MRS. HIGGINS: Do without, I'm afraid, Henry. The girl has a perfect right to leave if she chooses.

HIGGINS: [*Wandering distractedly across the room.*] But I cant find anything. I dont know what appointments Ive got. I'm—

[PICKERING *comes in.* MRS. HIGGINS *puts down her pen and turns away from the writing-table.*]

PICKERING: [*Shaking hands.*] Good morning, Mrs. Higgins. Has Henry told you? [*He sits down on the ottoman.*]

HIGGINS: What does that ass of an inspector say? Have you offered a reward?

MRS. HIGGINS: [*Rising in indignant amazement.*] You dont mean to say you have set the police after Eliza.

HIGGINS: Of course. What are the police for? What else could we do? [*He sits in the Elizabethan chair.*]

PICKERING: The inspector made a lot of difficulties. I really think he suspected us of some improper purpose.

MRS. HIGGINS: Well, of course he did. What right have you to go to the police and give the girl's name as if she were a thief, or a lost umbrella, or something? Really! [*She sits down again, deeply vexed.*]

HIGGINS: But we want to find her.

PICKERING: We cant let her go like this, you know, Mrs. Higgins. What were we to do?

MRS. HIGGINS: You have no more sense, either of you, than two children. Why—

[*The* PARLORMAID *comes in and breaks off the conversation.*]

THE PARLORMAID: Mr. Henry: a gentleman wants to see you very particular. He's been sent on from Wimpole Street.

HIGGINS: Oh, bother! I cant see anyone now. Who is it?

THE PARLORMAID: A Mr. Doolittle, sir.

PICKERING: Doolittle! Do you mean the dustman?

THE PARLORMAID: Dustman! Oh no, sir: a gentleman.

HIGGINS: [*Springing up excitedly.*] By George, Pick, it's some relative of hers that she's gone to. Somebody we know nothing about. [*To the* PARLORMAID.] Send him up, quick.

THE PARLORMAID: Yes, sir. [*She goes.*]

HIGGINS: [*Eagerly, going to his mother.*] Genteel relatives! now we shall hear something. [*He sits down in the Chippendale chair.*]

MRS. HIGGINS: Do you know any of her people?

PICKERING: Only her father: the fellow we told you about.

THE PARLORMAID: [*Announcing.*] Mr. Doolittle. [*She withdraws.*].

[DOOLITTLE *enters. He is resplendently dressed as for a fashionable wedding, and might, in fact, be the bridegroom. A flower in his buttonhole, a dazzling silk hat, and patent leather shoes complete the effect. He is too concerned with the business he has come on to notice* MRS. HIGGINS. *He walks straight to* HIGGINS, *and accosts him with vehement reproach.*]

DOOLITTLE: [*Indicating his own person.*] See here! Do you see this? You done this.

HIGGINS: Done what, man?

DOOLITTLE: This, I tell you. Look at it. Look at this hat. Look at this coat.

PICKERING: Has Eliza been buying you clothes?

DOOLITTLE: Eliza! not she. Why would she buy me clothes?

MRS. HIGGINS: Good morning, Mr. Doolittle. Wont you sit down?

DOOLITTLE: [*Taken aback as he becomes conscious that he has forgotten his hostess.*] Asking your pardon, maam. [*He approaches her and shakes her proffered hand.*] Thank you. [*He sits down on the ottoman, on* PICKERING's *right.*] I am that full of what has happened to me that I cant think of anything else.

HIGGINS: What the dickens has happened to you?

DOOLITTLE: I shouldnt mind if it had only happened to me: anything might happen to anybody and nobody to blame but Providence, as you might say. But this is something that you done to me: yes, you, Enry Iggins.

HIGGINS: Have you found Eliza?

DOOLITTLE: Have you lost her?

HIGGINS: Yes.

DOOLITTLE: You have all the luck, you have. I aint found her; but she'll find me quick enough now after what you done to me.

MRS. HIGGINS: But what has my son done to you, Mr. Doolittle?

DOOLITTLE: Done to me! Ruined me. Destroyed my happiness. Tied me up and delivered me into the hands of middle class morality.

HIGGINS: [*Rising intolerantly and standing over* DOOLITTLE.] Youre raving. Youre drunk. Youre mad. I gave you five pounds. After that I had two conversations with you, at half-a-crown an hour. Ive never seen you since.

DOOLITTLE: Oh! Drunk am I? Mad am I? Tell me this. Did you or did you not write a letter to an old blighter in America that was giving five millions to found Moral Reform Societies all over the world, and that wanted you to invent a universal language for him?

HIGGINS: What! Ezra D. Wannafeller! He's dead. [*He sits down again carelessly.*]

DOOLITTLE: Yes: he's dead; and I'm done for. Now did you or did you not write a letter to him to say that the most original moralist at present in England, to the best of your knowledge, was Alfred Doolittle, a common dustman?

HIGGINS: Oh, after your first visit I remember making some silly joke of the kind.

DOOLITTLE: Ah! you may well call it a silly joke. It put the lid on me right enough. Just give him the chance he wanted to shew that Americans is not like us: that they reckonize and respect merit in every class of life, however humble. Them words is in his blooming will, in which, Henry Higgins, thanks to your silly joking, he leaves me a share in his Predigested Cheese Trust worth three thousand a year on condition that I lecture for his Wanna-feller Moral Reform World League as often as they ask me up to six times a year.

HIGGINS: The devil he does! Whew! [*Brightening suddenly.*] What a lark!

PICKERING: A safe thing for you, Doolittle. They wont ask you twice.

DOOLITTLE: It aint the lecturing I mind. I'll lecture them blue in the face, I will, and not turn a hair. It's making a gentleman of me that I object to. Who asked him to make a gentleman of me? I was happy. I was free. I touched pretty nigh everybody for money when I wanted it, same as I touched you, Enry Iggins. Now I am worrited; tied neck and heels; and everybody touches me for money. It's a fine thing for you, says my solicitor. Is it? says I. You mean it's a good thing for you, I says. When I was a poor man and had a solicitor once when they found a pram in the dust cart, he got me off, and got shut of me and got me shut of him as quick as he could. Same with the doctors: used to shove me out of the hospital before I could hardly stand on my legs, and nothing to pay. Now they finds out that I'm not a healthy man and cant live unless they looks after me twice a day. In the house I'm not let do a hand's turn for myself: somebody else must do it and touch me for it. A year ago I hadnt a relative in the world except two or three that wouldnt speak to me. Now Ive fifty, and not a decent week's wages among the lot of them. I have to live for others and not for myself: thats middle class morality. You talk of losing Eliza. Dont you be anxious: I bet she's on my doorstep by this: she that could support herself easy by selling flowers if I wasnt respect-able. And the next one to touch me will be you, Enry Iggins. I'll have to learn to speak middle class language from you, instead of speaking proper English. Thats where youll come in; and I daresay thats what you done it for.

MRS. HIGGINS: But, my dear Mr. Doolittle, you need not suffer all this if you are really in earnest. Nobody can force you to accept this bequest. You can repudiate it. Isnt that so, Colonel Pickering?

PICKERING: I believe so.

DOOLITTLE: [*Softening his manner in deference to her sex.*] Thats the tragedy of it, maam. It's easy to say chuck it; but I havnt the nerve. Which of us has? We're all intimidated. Intimidated, maam: thats what we are. What is there for me if I chuck it but the workhouse in my old age? I have to dye my hair already to keep my job as a dustman. If I was one of the deserving poor, and had put by a bit, I could chuck it; but then why should I, acause the deserv-ing poor might as well be millionaires for all the happiness they ever has. They dont know what happiness is. But I, as one of the undeserving poor, have nothing between me and the pauper's uniform but this here blasted three thousand a year that shoves me into the middle class. (Excuse the expression, maam; youd use it yourself if you had my provocation.) Theyve got you every way you turn: it's a choice between the Skilly of the workhouse and the Char Bydis[9] of the middle class; and I havnt the nerve for the workhouse. Intimidated: thats what I am. Broke. Bought up. Happier men than me will call for my dust, and touch me for their tip; and I'll look on helpless, and envy them. And thats what your son has brought me to. [*He is overcome by emotion.*]

MRS. HIGGINS: Well, I'm very glad youre not going to do anything foolish, Mr. Doolittle. For this solves the problem of Eliza's future. You can provide for her now.

DOOLITTLE: [*With melancholy resignation.*] Yes, maam: I'm expected to provide for everyone now, out of three thousand a year.

HIGGINS: [*Jumping up.*] Nonsense! he cant provide for her. He shant provide for her. She doesnt belong to him. I paid him five pounds for her. Doolittle: either youre an honest man or a rogue.

DOOLITTLE: [*Tolerantly.*] A little of both, Henry, like the rest of us: a little of both.

HIGGINS: Well, you took that money for the girl; and you have no right to take her as well.

MRS. HIGGINS: Henry: dont be absurd. If you want to know where Eliza is, she is upstairs.

HIGGINS: [*Amazed.*] Upstairs!!! Then I shall jolly soon fetch her downstairs. [*He makes resolutely for the door.*]

MRS. HIGGINS: [*Rising and following him.*] Be quiet, Henry. Sit down.

HIGGINS: I—

MRS. HIGGINS: Sit down, dear; and listen to me.

HIGGINS: Oh very well, very well, very well. [*He throws himself ungraciously on the ottoman, with his face towards the windows.*] But I think you might have told us this half an hour ago.

MRS. HIGGINS: Eliza came to me this morning. She told me of the brutal way you two treated her.

HIGGINS: [*Bounding up again.*] What!

PICKERING: [*Rising also.*] My dear Mrs. Higgins, she's been telling you stories. We didnt treat her brutally. We hardly said a word to her; and we parted on particularly good terms. [*Turning on* HIGGINS.] Higgins: did you bully her after I went to bed?

HIGGINS: Just the other way about. She threw my slippers in my face. She behaved in the most outrageous way. I never gave her the slightest provocation. The slippers came bang into my face the moment I entered the room— before I had uttered a word. And used perfectly awful language.

PICKERING: [*Astonished.*] But why? What did we do to her?

MRS. HIGGINS: I think I know pretty well what you did. The girl is naturally rather affectionate, I think. Isnt she, Mr. Doolittle?

---

9. Mistake for Scylla and Charybdis. Scylla is an Italian rock and Charybdis is a nearby whirlpool. Used allusively, it refers to the danger of avoiding one peril only to encounter its opposite.

DOOLITTLE: Very tender-hearted, maam. Takes after me.

MRS. HIGGINS: Just so. She had become attached to you both. She worked very hard for you, Henry. I dont think you quite realize what anything in the nature of brain work means to a girl of her class. Well, it seems that when the great day of trial came, and she did this wonderful thing for you without making a single mistake, you two sat there and never said a word to her, but talked together of how glad you were that it was all over and how you had been bored with the whole thing. And then you were surprised because she threw your slippers at you! *I* should have thrown the fire-irons at you.

HIGGINS: We said nothing except that we were tired and wanted to go to bed. Did we, Pick?

PICKERING: [*Shrugging his shoulders.*] That was all.

MRS. HIGGINS: [*Ironically.*] Quite sure?

PICKERING: Absolutely. Really, that was all.

MRS. HIGGINS: You didnt thank her, or pet her, or admire her, or tell her how splendid she'd been.

HIGGINS: [*Impatiently.*] But she knew all about that. We didnt make speeches to her, if thats what you mean.

PICKERING: [*Conscience stricken.*] Perhaps we were a little inconsiderate. Is she very angry?

MRS. HIGGINS: [*Returning to her place at the writing-table.*] Well, I'm afraid she wont go back to Wimpole Street, especially now that Mr. Doolittle is able to keep up the position you have thrust on her; but she says she is quite willing to meet you on friendly terms and to let bygones be bygones.

HIGGINS: [*Furious.*] Is she, by George? Ho!

MRS. HIGGINS: If you promise to behave yourself, Henry, I'll ask her to come down. If not, go home; for you have taken up quite enough of my time.

HIGGINS: Oh, all right. Very well. Pick: you behave yourself. Let us put on our best Sunday manners for this creature that we picked out of the mud. [*He flings himself sulkily into the Elizabethan chair.*]

DOOLITTLE: [*Remonstrating.*] Now, now, Enry Iggins! Have some consideration for my feelings as a middle class man.

MRS. HIGGINS: Remember your promise, Henry. [*She presses the bell-button on the writing-table.*] Mr. Doolittle: will you be so good as to step out on the balcony for a moment. I dont want Eliza to have the shock of your news until she has made it up with these two gentlemen. Would you mind?

DOOLITTLE: As you wish, lady. Anything to help Henry to keep her off my hands. [*He disappears through the window.*]

[*The* PARLORMAID *answers the bell.* PICKERING *sits down in* DOOLITTLE'*s place.*]

MRS. HIGGINS: Ask Miss Doolittle to come down, please.

THE PARLORMAID: Yes, maam. [*She goes out.*]

MRS. HIGGINS: Now, Henry: be good.

HIGGINS: I am behaving myself perfectly.

PICKERING: He is doing his best, Mrs. Higgins.

[*A pause.* HIGGINS *throws back his head; stretches out his legs; and begins to whistle.*]

MRS. HIGGINS: Henry, dearest, you dont look at all nice in that attitude.

HIGGINS: [*Pulling himself together.*] I was not trying to look nice, mother.

MRS. HIGGINS: It doesnt matter, dear. I only wanted to make you speak.

HIGGINS: Why?

MRS. HIGGINS: Because you cant speak and whistle at the same time.

[HIGGINS *groans. Another very trying pause.*]

HIGGINS: [*Springing up, out of patience.*] Where the devil is that girl? Are we to wait here all day?

[ELIZA *enters, sunny, self-possessed, and giving a staggeringly convincing exhibition of ease of manner. She carries a little work-basket, and is very much at home.* PICKERING *is too much taken aback to rise.*]

LIZA: How do you do, Professor Higgins? Are you quite well?

HIGGINS: [*Choking.*] Am I—[*He can say no more.*]

LIZA: But of course you are: you are never ill. So glad to see you again, Colonel Pickering. [*He rises hastily; and they shake hands.*] Quite chilly this morning, isnt it? [*She sits down on his left. He sits beside her.*]

HIGGINS: Dont you dare try this game on me. I taught it to you; and it doesnt take me in. Get up and come home; and dont be a fool.

[ELIZA *takes a piece of needlework from her basket, and begins to stitch at it, without taking the least notice of this outburst.*]

MRS. HIGGINS: Very nicely put, indeed, Henry. No woman could resist such an invitation.

HIGGINS: You let her alone, mother. Let her speak for herself. You will jolly soon see whether she has an idea that I havnt put into her head or a word that I havnt put into her mouth. I tell you I have created this thing out of the squashed cabbage leaves of Covent Garden; and now she pretends to play the fine lady with me.

MRS. HIGGINS: [*Placidly.*] Yes, dear; but youll sit down, wont you?

[HIGGINS *sits down again, savagely.*]

LIZA: [*To* PICKERING, *taking no apparent notice of* HIGGINS, *and working away deftly.*] Will you drop me altogether now that the experiment is over, Colonel Pickering?

PICKERING: Oh dont. You mustnt think of it as an experiment. It shocks me, somehow.

LIZA: Oh, I'm only a squashed cabbage leaf—

PICKERING: [*Impulsively.*] No.

LIZA: [*Continuing quietly.*]—but I owe so much to you that I should be very unhappy if you forgot me.

PICKERING: It's very kind of you to say so, Miss Doolittle.

LIZA: It's not because you paid for my dresses. I know you are generous to everybody with money. But it was from you that I learnt really nice manners; and that is what makes one a lady, isnt it? You see it was so very difficult for me with the example of Professor Higgins always before me. I was brought up to be just like him, unable to control myself, and using bad language on the slightest provocation. And I should never have known that ladies and gentlemen didnt behave like that if you hadnt been there.

HIGGINS: Well!!

PICKERING: Oh, thats only his way, you know. He doesnt mean it.

LIZA: Oh, I didnt mean it either, when I was a flower girl. It was only my way. But you see I did it; and thats what makes the difference after all.

PICKERING: No doubt. Still, he taught you to speak; and I couldnt have done that, you know.

LIZA: [*Trivially.*] Of course: that is his profession.

HIGGINS: Damnation!

LIZA: [*Continuing.*] It was just like learning to dance in the fashionable way: there was nothing more than that in it. But do you know what began my real education?

PICKERING: What?

LIZA: [*Stopping her work for a moment.*] Your calling me Miss Doolittle that day when I first came to Wimpole Street. That was the beginning of self-respect for me. [*She resumes her stitching.*] And there were a hundred little things you never noticed, because they came naturally to you. Things about standing up and taking off your hat and opening doors—

PICKERING: Oh, that was nothing.

LIZA: Yes: things that shewed you thought and felt about me as if I were something better than a scullery-maid; though of course I know you would have been just the same to a scullery-maid if she had been let into the drawing room. You never took off your boots in the dining room when I was there.

PICKERING: You mustnt mind that. Higgins takes off his boots all over the place.

LIZA: I know. I am not blaming him. It is his way, isnt it? But it made such a difference to me that you didnt do it. You see, really and truly, apart from the things anyone can pick up (the dressing and the proper way of speaking, and so on), the difference between a lady and a flower girl is not how she behaves, but how she's treated. I shall always be a flower girl to Professor Higgins, because he always treats me as a flower girl, and always will; but I know I can be a lady to you, because you always treat me as a lady, and always will.

MRS. HIGGINS: Please dont grind your teeth, Henry.

PICKERING: Well, this is really very nice of you, Miss Doolittle.

LIZA: I should like you to call me Eliza, now, if you would.

PICKERING: Thank you. Eliza, of course.

LIZA: And I should like Professor Higgins to call me Miss Doolittle.

HIGGINS: I'll see you damned first.

MRS. HIGGINS: Henry! Henry!

PICKERING: [*Laughing.*] Why dont you slang back at him? Dont stand it. It would do him a lot of good.

LIZA: I cant. I could have done it once; but now I cant go back to it. You told me, you know, that when a child is brought to a foreign country, it picks up the language in a few weeks, and forgets its own. Well, I am a child in your country. I have forgotten my own language, and can speak nothing but yours. Thats the real break-off with the corner of Tottenham Court Road. Leaving Wimpole Street finishes it.

PICKERING: [*Much alarmed.*] Oh! but youre coming back to Wimpole Street, arnt you? Youll forgive Higgins?

HIGGINS: [*Rising.*] Forgive! Will she, by George! Let her go. Let her find out how she can get on without us. She will relapse into the gutter in three weeks without me at her elbow.

[DOOLITTLE *appears at the centre window. With a look of dignified reproach at* HIGGINS, *he comes slowly and silently to his daughter, who, with her back to the window, is unconscious of his approach.*]

PICKERING: He's incorrigible, Eliza. You wont relapse, will you?

LIZA: No: not now. Never again. I have learnt my lesson. I dont believe I could utter one of the old sounds if I tried. [DOOLITTLE *touches her on her left shoulder. She drops her work, losing her self-possession utterly at the spectacle of her father's splendor.*] A-a-a-a-a-ah-ow-ooh!

HIGGINS: [*With a crow of triumph.*] Aha! Just so. A-a-a-a-ahowooh! A-a-a-a-ah-ow-ooh! A-a-a-ahowooh! Victory! Victory! [*He throws himself on the divan, folding his arms, and spraddling arrogantly.*]

DOOLITTLE: Can you blame the girl? Dont look at me like that, Eliza. It aint my fault. Ive come into some money.

LIZA: You must have touched a millionaire this time, dad.

DOOLITTLE: I have. But I'm dressed something special today. I'm going to St. George's, Hanover Square. Your stepmother is going to marry me.

LIZA: [*Angrily.*] Youre going to let yourself down to marry that low common woman!

PICKERING: [*Quietly.*] He ought to, Eliza. [*To* DOOLITTLE.] Why has she changed her mind?

DOOLITTLE: [*Sadly.*] Intimidated, Governor. Intimidated. Middle class morality claims its victim. Wont you put on your hat, Liza, and come and see me turned off?

LIZA: If the Colonel says I must, I—I'll [*Almost sobbing.*] I'll demean myself. And get insulted for my pains, like enough.

DOOLITTLE: Dont be afraid: she never comes to words with anyone now, poor woman! respectability has broke all the spirit out of her.

PICKERING: [*Squeezing* ELIZA's *elbow gently.*] Be kind to them, Eliza. Make the best of it.

LIZA: [*Forcing a little smile for him through her vexation.*] Oh well, just to shew theres no ill feeling. I'll be back in a moment. [*She goes out.*]

DOOLITTLE: [*Sitting down beside* PICKERING.] I feel uncommon nervous about the ceremony, Colonel. I wish youd come and see me through it.

PICKERING: But youve been through it before, man. You were married to Eliza's mother.

DOOLITTLE: Who told you that, Colonel?

PICKERING: Well, nobody told me. But I concluded—naturally—

DOOLITTLE: No: that aint the natural way, Colonel: it's only the middle class way. My way was always the undeserving way. But dont say nothing to Eliza. She dont know: I always had a delicacy about telling her.

PICKERING: Quite right. We'll leave it so, if you dont mind.

DOOLITTLE: And youll come to the church, Colonel, and put me through straight?

PICKERING: With pleasure. As far as a bachelor can.

MRS. HIGGINS: May I come, Mr. Doolittle? I should be very sorry to miss your wedding.

DOOLITTLE: I should indeed be honored by your condescension, maam; and my poor old woman would take it as a tremenjous compliment. She's been very low, thinking of the happy days that are no more.

MRS. HIGGINS: [*Rising.*] I'll order the carriage and get ready. [*The men rise, except* HIGGINS.] I shant be more than fifteen minutes. [*As she goes to the door* ELIZA *comes in, hatted and buttoning her gloves.*] I'm going to the church to see your father married, Eliza. You had better come in the brougham with me. Colonel Pickering can go on with the bridegroom.

[MRS. HIGGINS *goes out.* ELIZA *comes to the middle of the room between the centre window and the ottoman.* PICKERING *joins her.*]

DOOLITTLE: Bridegroom! What a word! It makes a man realize his position, somehow. [*He takes up his hat and goes towards the door.*]

PICKERING: Before I go, Eliza, do forgive Higgins and come back to us.

LIZA: I dont think dad would allow me. Would you, dad?

DOOLITTLE: [*Sad but magnanimous.*] They played you off very cunning, Eliza, them two sportsmen. It if had been only one of them, you could have nailed him. But you see, there was two; and one of them chaperoned the other, as you might say. [*To* PICKERING.] It was artful of you, Colonel; but I bear no malice: I should have done the same myself. I been the victim of one woman after another all my life; and I dont grudge you two getting the better of Eliza. I shant interfere. It's time for us to go, Colonel. So long, Henry. See you in St. George's, Eliza. [*He goes out.*]

PICKERING: [*Coaxing.*] Do stay with us, Eliza. [*He follows* DOOLITTLE.]

[ELIZA *goes out on the balcony to avoid being alone with* HIGGINS. *He rises and joins her there. She immediately comes back into the room and makes for the door; but he goes along the balcony quickly and gets his back to the door before she reaches it.*]

HIGGINS: Well, Eliza, youve had a bit of your own back, as you call it. Have you had enough? and are you going to be reasonable? Or do you want any more?

LIZA: You want me back only to pick up your slippers and put up with your tempers and fetch and carry for you.

HIGGINS: I havnt said I wanted you back at all.

LIZA: Oh, indeed. Then what are we talking about?

HIGGINS: About you, not about me. If you come back I shall treat you just as I have always treated you. I cant change my nature; and I dont intend to change my manners. My manners are exactly the same as Colonel Pickering's.

LIZA: Thats not true. He treats a flower girl as if she was a duchess.

HIGGINS: And I treat a duchess as if she was a flower girl.

LIZA: I see. [*She turns away composedly, and sits on the ottoman, facing the window.*] The same to everybody.

HIGGINS: Just so.

LIZA: Like father.

HIGGINS: [*Grinning, a little taken down.*] Without accepting the comparison at all points, Eliza, it's quite true that your father is not a snob, and that he will be quite at home in any station of life to which his eccentric destiny may call him. [*Seriously.*] The great secret, Eliza, is not having bad manners or good manners or any other particular sort of manners, but having the same manner for all human souls: in short, behaving as if you were in Heaven, where there are no third-class carriages, and one soul is as good as another.

LIZA: Amen. You are a born preacher.

HIGGINS: [*Irritated.*] The question is not whether I treat you rudely, but whether you ever heard me treat anyone else better.

LIZA: [*With sudden sincerity.*] I dont care how you treat me. I dont mind your swearing at me. I shouldnt mind a black eye: Ive had one before this. But [*Standing up and facing him.*] I wont be passed over.

HIGGINS: Then get out of my way; for I wont stop for you. You talk about me as if I were a motor bus.

LIZA: So you are a motor bus: all bounce and go, and no consideration for anyone. But I can do without you: dont think I cant.

HIGGINS: I know you can. I told you you could.

LIZA: [*Wounded, getting away from him to the other side of the ottoman with her face to the hearth.*] I know you did, you brute. You wanted to get rid of me.

HIGGINS: Liar.

LIZA: Thank you. [*She sits down with dignity.*]

HIGGINS: You never asked yourself, I suppose, whether I could do without you.

LIZA: [*Earnestly.*] Dont you try to get round me. Youll have to do without me.

HIGGINS: [*Arrogant.*] I can do without anybody. I have my own soul: my own spark of divine fire. But [*With sudden humility.*] I shall miss you, Eliza. [*He sits down near her on the ottoman.*] I have learnt something from your idiotic notions: I confess that humbly and gratefully. And I have grown accustomed to your voice and appearance. I like them, rather.

LIZA: Well, you have both of them on your gramophone and in your book of photographs. When you feel lonely without me, you can turn the machine on. It's got no feelings to hurt.

HIGGINS: I cant turn your soul on. Leave me those feelings; and you can take away the voice and the face. They are not you.

LIZA: Oh, you are a devil. You can twist the heart in a girl as easy as some could twist her arms to hurt her. Mrs. Pearce warned me. Time and again she has wanted to leave you; and you always got round her at the last minute. And you dont care a bit for her. And you dont care a bit for me.

HIGGINS: I care for life, for humanity; and you are a part of it that has come my way and been built into my house. What more can you or anyone ask?

LIZA: I wont care for anybody that doesnt care for me.

HIGGINS: Commercial principles, Eliza. Like [*Reproducing her Covent Garden pronunciation with professional exactness.*] s'yollin voylets [selling violets], isnt it?

LIZA: Dont sneer at me. It's mean to sneer at me.

HIGGINS: I have never sneered in my life. Sneering doesnt become either the human face or the human soul. I am expressing my righteous contempt for Commercialism. I dont and wont trade in affection. You call me a brute because you couldnt buy a claim on me by fetching my slippers and finding my spectacles. You were a fool: I think a woman fetching a man's slippers is a disgusting sight: did I ever fetch your slippers? I think a good deal more of you for throwing them in my face. No use slaving for me and then saying you want to be cared for: who cares for a slave? If you come back, come back for the sake of good fellowship; for youll get nothing else. Youve had a thousand times as much out of me as I have out of you; and if you dare to set up your little dog's tricks of fetching and carrying slippers against my creation of a Duchess Eliza, I'll slam the door in your silly face.

LIZA: What did you do it for if you didnt care for me?

HIGGINS: [*Heartily.*] Why, because it was my job.

LIZA: You never thought of the trouble it would make for me.

HIGGINS: Would the world ever have been made if its maker had been afraid of making trouble? Making life means making trouble. Theres only one way of escaping trouble; and thats killing things. Cowards, you notice, are always shrieking to have troublesome people killed.

LIZA: I'm no preacher: I dont notice things like that. I notice that you dont notice me.

HIGGINS: [*Jumping up and walking about intolerantly.*] Eliza: youre an idiot. I waste the treasures of my Miltonic mind by spreading them before you. Once for all, understand that I go my way and do my work without caring twopence what happens to either of us. I am not intimidated, like your father and your stepmother. So you can come back or go to the devil: which you please.

LIZA: What am I to come back for?

HIGGINS: [*Bouncing up on his knees on the ottoman and leaning over it to her.*] For the fun of it. Thats why I took you on.

LIZA: [*With averted face.*] And you may throw me out tomorrow if I dont do everything you want me to?

HIGGINS: Yes; and you may walk out tomorrow if I dont do everything you want me to.

LIZA: And live with my stepmother?

HIGGINS: Yes, or sell flowers.

LIZA: Oh! if I only could go back to my flower basket! I should be independent of both you and father and all the world! Why did you take my independence from me? Why did I give it up? I'm a slave now, for all my fine clothes.

HIGGINS: Not a bit. I'll adopt you as my daughter and settle money on you if you like. Or would you rather marry Pickering?

LIZA: [Looking fiercely round at him.] I wouldnt marry you if you asked me; and youre nearer my age than what he is.

HIGGINS: [Gently.] Than he is: not "than what he is."

LIZA: [Losing her temper and rising.] I'll talk as I like. Youre not my teacher now.

HIGGINS: [Reflectively.] I dont suppose Pickering would, though. He's as confirmed an old bachelor as I am.

LIZA: Thats not what I want; and dont you think it. Ive always had chaps enough wanting me that way. Freddy Hill writes to me twice and three times a day, sheets and sheets.

HIGGINS: [Disagreeably surprised.] Damn his impudence! [He recoils and finds himself sitting on his heels.]

LIZA: He has a right to if he likes, poor lad. And he does love me.

HIGGINS: [Getting off the ottoman.] You have no right to encourage him.

LIZA: Every girl has a right to be loved.

HIGGINS: What! By fools like that?

LIZA: Freddy's not a fool. And if he's weak and poor and wants me, may be he'd make me happier than my betters that bully me and dont want me.

HIGGINS: Can he make anything of you? Thats the point.

LIZA: Perhaps I could make something of him. But I never thought of us making anything of one another; and you never think of anything else. I only want to be natural.

HIGGINS: In short, you want me to be as infatuated about you as Freddy? Is that it?

LIZA: No I dont. Thats not the sort of feeling I want from you. And dont you be too sure of yourself or of me. I could have been a bad girl if I'd liked. Ive seen more of some things than you, for all your learning. Girls like me can drag gentlemen down to make love to them easy enough. And they wish each other dead the next minute.

HIGGINS: Of course they do. Then what in thunder are we quarrelling about?

LIZA: [Much troubled.] I want a little kindness. I know I'm a common ignorant girl, and you a book-learned gentleman; but I'm not dirt under your feet. What I done [Correcting herself.] what I did was not for the dresses and the taxis: I did it because we were pleasant together and I come—came—to care for you; not to want you to make love to me, and not forgetting the difference between us, but more friendly like.

HIGGINS: Well, of course. Thats just how I feel. And how Pickering feels. Eliza: youre a fool.

LIZA: Thats not a proper answer to give me. [She sinks on the chair at the writing-table in tears.]

HIGGINS: It's all youll get until you stop being a common idiot. If youre going to be a lady, youll have to give up feeling neglected if the men you know dont spend half their time snivelling over you and the other half giving you black eyes. If you cant stand the coldness of my sort of life, and the strain of it, go back to the gutter. Work til youre more a brute than a human being; and then cuddle and squabble and drink til you fall asleep. Oh, it's a fine life, the life of the gutter. It's real: it's warm: it's violent: you can feel it through the thickest skin: you can taste it and smell it without any training or any work. Not like Science and Literature and Classical Music and Philosophy and Art. You find me cold, unfeeling, selfish, dont you? Very well: be off with you to the sort of people you like. Marry some sentimental hog or other with lots of money, and a thick pair of lips to kiss you with and a thick pair of boots to kick you with. If you cant appreciate what youve got, youd better get what you can appreciate.

LIZA: [*Desperate.*] Oh, you are a cruel tyrant. I cant talk to you: you turn everything against me: I'm always in the wrong. But you know very well all the time that youre nothing but a bully. You know I cant go back to the gutter, as you call it, and that I have no real friends in the world but you and the Colonel. You know well I couldnt bear to live with a low common man after you two; and it's wicked and cruel of you to insult me by pretending I could. You think I must go back to Wimpole Street because I have nowhere else to go but father's. But dont you be too sure that you have me under your feet to be trampled on and talked down. I'll marry Freddy, I will, as soon as I'm able to support him.

HIGGINS: [*Thunderstruck.*] Freddy!!! that young fool! That poor devil who couldnt get a job as an errand boy even if he had the guts to try for it! Woman: do you not understand that I have made you a consort for a king?

LIZA: Freddy loves me: that makes him king enough for me. I dont want him to work: he wasnt brought up to it as I was. I'll go and be a teacher.

HIGGINS: Whatll you teach, in heaven's name?

LIZA: What you taught me. I'll teach phonetics.

HIGGINS: Ha! ha! ha!

LIZA: I'll offer myself as an assistant to that hairy-faced Hungarian.

HIGGINS: [*Rising in a fury.*] What! That impostor! that humbug! that toadying ignoramus! Teach him my methods! my discoveries! You take one step in his direction and I'll wring your neck. [*He lays hands on her.*] Do you hear?

LIZA: [*Defiantly non-resistant.*] Wring away. What do I care? I knew youd strike me some day. [*He lets her go, stamping with rage at having forgotten himself, and recoils so hastily that he stumbles back into his seat on the ottoman.*] Aha! Now I know how to deal with you. What a fool I was not to think of it before! You cant take away the knowledge you gave me. You said I had a finer ear than you. And I can be civil and kind to people, which is more than you can. Aha! [*Purposely dropping her aitches to annoy him.*] Thats done you, Enry Iggins, it az. Now I dont care that [*Snapping her fingers.*] for your bullying and your big talk. I'll advertize it in the papers that your duchess is only a flower girl that you taught, and that she'll teach anybody to be a duchess just the same in six months for a thousand guineas. Oh, when I think of myself crawling under your feet and being trampled on and called names, when all the time I had only to lift up my finger to be as good as you. I could just kick myself.

HIGGINS: [*Wondering at her.*] You damned impudent slut, you! But it's better than snivelling; better than fetching slippers and finding spectacles, isnt it? [*Rising.*] By George, Eliza, I said I'd make a woman of you; and I have. I like you like this.

LIZA: Yes: you turn round and make up to me now that I'm not afraid of you, and can do without you.

HIGGINS: Of course I do, you little fool. Five minutes ago you were like a millstone round my neck. Now youre a tower of strength: a consort battleship. You and I and Pickering will be three old bachelors together instead of only two men and a silly girl.

[MRS. HIGGINS *returns, dressed for the wedding.* ELIZA *instantly becomes cool and elegant.*]

MRS. HIGGINS: The carriage is waiting, Eliza. Are you ready?

LIZA: Quite. Is the Professor coming?

MRS. HIGGINS: Certainly not. He cant behave himself in church. He makes remarks out loud all the time on the clergyman's pronunciation.

LIZA: Then I shall not see you again, Professor. Goodbye. [*She goes to the door.*]

MRS. HIGGINS: [*Coming to* HIGGINS.] Goodbye, dear.

HIGGINS: Goodbye, mother. [*He is about to kiss her, when he recollects something.*] Oh, by the way, Eliza, order a ham and a Stilton cheese, will you? And buy me a pair of reindeer gloves, number eights, and a tie to match that new suit of mine. You can choose the color. [*His cheerful, careless, vigorous voice shews that he is incorrigible.*]

LIZA: [*Disdainfully.*] Number eights are too small for you if you want them lined with lamb's wool. You have three new ties that you have forgotten in the drawer of your washstand. Colonel Pickering prefers double Gloucester to Stilton; and you dont notice the difference. I telephoned Mrs. Pearce this morning not to forget the ham. What you are to do without me I cannot imagine. [*She sweeps out.*]

MRS. HIGGINS: I'm afraid youve spoilt that girl, Henry. I should be uneasy about you and her if she were less fond of Colonel Pickering.

HIGGINS: Pickering! Nonsense: she's going to marry Freddy. Ha ha! Freddy! Freddy!! Ha ha ha ha ha!!!!! [*He roars with laughter as the play ends*].

CURTAIN

The rest of the story need not be shewn in action, and indeed, would hardly need telling if our imaginations were not so enfeebled by their lazy dependence on the ready-mades and reach-me-downs of the ragshop in which Romance keeps its stock of "happy endings" to misfit all stories. Now, the history of Eliza

Doolittle, though called a romance because the transfiguration it records seems exceedingly improbable, is common enough. Such transfigurations have been achieved by hundreds of resolutely ambitious young women since Nell Gwynne set them the example by playing queens and fascinating kings in the theatre in which she began by selling oranges. Nevertheless, people in all directions have assumed, for no other reason than that she became the heroine of a romance, that she must have married the hero of it. This is unbearable, not only because her little·drama, if acted on such a thoughtless assumption, must be spoiled, but because the true sequel is patent to anyone with a sense of human nature in general, and of feminine instinct in particular.

Eliza, in telling Higgins she would not marry him if he asked her, was not coquetting: she was announcing a well-considered decision. When a bachelor interests, and dominates, and teaches, and becomes important to a spinster, as Higgins with Eliza, she always, if she has character enough to be capable of it, considers very seriously indeed whether she will play for becoming that bachelor's wife, especially if he is so little interested in marriage that a determined and devoted woman might capture him if she set herself resolutely to do it. Her decision will depend a good deal on whether she is really free to choose; and that, again, will depend on her age and income. If she is at the end of her youth, and has no security for her livelihood, she will marry him because she must marry anybody who will provide for her. But at Eliza's age a good-looking girl does not feel that pressure: she feels free to pick and choose. She is therefore guided by her instinct in the matter. Eliza's instinct tells her not to marry Higgins. It does not tell her to give him up. It is not in the slightest doubt as to his remaining one of the strongest personal interests in her life. It would be very sorely strained if there was another woman likely to supplant her with him. But as she feels sure of him on that last point, she has no doubt at all as to her course, and would not have any, even if the difference of twenty years in age, which seems so great to youth, did not exist between them.

As our own instincts are not appealed to by her conclusion, let us see whether we cannot discover some reason in it. When Higgins excused his indifference to young women on the ground that they had an irresistible rival in his mother, he gave the clue to his inveterate old-bachelordom. The case is uncommon only to the extent that remarkable mothers are uncommon. If an imaginative boy has a sufficiently rich mother who has intelligence, personal grace, dignity of character without harshness, and a cultivated sense of the best art of her time to enable her to make her house beautiful, she sets a standard for him against which very few women can struggle, besides effecting for him a disengagement of his affections, his sense of beauty, and his idealism from his

specifically sexual impulses. This makes him a standing puzzle to the huge
number of uncultivated people who have been brought up in tasteless homes by
commonplace or disagreeable parents, and to whom, consequently, literature,
painting, sculpture, music, and affectionate personal relations come as modes
of sex if they come at all. The word passion means nothing else to them; and
that Higgins could have a passion for phonetics and idealize his mother instead
of Eliza, would seem to them absurd and unnatural. Nevertheless, when we
look round and see that hardly anyone is too ugly or disagreeable to find a wife
or a husband if he or she wants one, whilst many old maids and bachelors are
above the average in quality and culture, we cannot help suspecting that the
disentanglement of sex from the associations with which it is so commonly confused, a disentanglement which persons of genius achieve by sheer intellectual
analysis, is sometimes produced or aided by parental fascination.

Now, though Eliza was incapable of thus explaining to herself Higgins's formidable powers of resistance to the charm that prostrated Freddy at the first
glance, she was instinctively aware that she could never obtain a complete grip
of him, or come between him and his mother (the first necessity of the married
woman). To put it shortly, she knew that for some mysterious reason he had not
the makings of a married man in him, according to her conception of a husband
as one to whom she would be his nearest and fondest and warmest interest.
Even had there been no mother-rival, she would still have refused to accept an
interest in herself that was secondary to philosophic interests. Had Mrs. Higgins
died, there would still have been Milton and the Universal Alphabet. Landor's
remark that to those who have the greatest power of loving, love is a secondary
affair, would not have recommended Landor to Eliza. Put that along with her
resentment of Higgins's domineering superiority, and her mistrust of his coaxing
cleverness in getting round her and evading her wrath when he had gone too
far with his impetuous bullying, and you will see that Eliza's instinct had good
grounds for warning her not to marry her Pygmalion.

And now, whom did Eliza marry? For if Higgins was a predestinate old bachelor, she was most certainly not a predestinate old maid. Well, that can be told
very shortly to those who have not guessed it from the indications she has herself
given them.

Almost immediately after Eliza is stung into proclaiming her considered
determination not to marry Higgins, she mentions the fact that young Mr. Frederick Eynsford Hill is pouring out his love for her daily through the post. Now
Freddy is young, practically twenty years younger than Higgins: he is a gentleman (or, as Eliza would qualify him, a toff), and speaks like one. He is nicely
dressed, is treated by the Colonel as an equal, loves her unaffectedly, and is not

her master, nor ever likely to dominate her in spite of his advantage of social standing. Eliza has no use for the foolish romantic tradition that all women love to be mastered, if not actually bullied and beaten. "When you go to women" says Nietzsche[1] "take your whip with you." Sensible despots have never confined that precaution to women: they have taken their whips with them when they have dealt with men, and been slavishly idealized by the men over whom they have flourished the whip much more than by women. No doubt there are slavish women as well as slavish men; and women, like men, admire those that are stronger than themselves. But to admire a strong person and to live under that strong person's thumb are two different things. The weak may not be admired and hero-worshipped; but they are by no means disliked or shunned; and they never seem to have the least difficulty in marrying people who are too good for them. They may fail in emergencies; but life is not one long emergency: it is mostly a string of situations for which no exceptional strength is needed, and with which even rather weak people can cope if they have a stronger partner to help them out. Accordingly, it is a truth everywhere in evidence that strong people, masculine or feminine, not only do not marry stronger people, but do not shew any preference for them in selecting their friends. When a lion meets another with a louder roar "the first lion thinks the last a bore." The man or woman who feels strong enough for two, seeks for every other quality in a partner than strength.

The converse is also true. Weak people want to marry strong people who do not frighten them too much; and this often leads them to make the mistake we describe metaphorically as "biting off more than they can chew." They want too much for too little; and when the bargain is unreasonable beyond all bearing, the union becomes impossible: it ends in the weaker party being either discarded or borne as a cross, which is worse. People who are not only weak, but silly or obtuse as well, are often in these difficulties.

This being the state of human affairs, what is Eliza fairly sure to do when she is placed between Freddy and Higgins? Will she look forward to a lifetime of fetching Higgins's slippers or to a lifetime of Freddy fetching hers? There can be no doubt about the answer. Unless Freddy is biologically repulsive to her, and Higgins biologically attractive to a degree that overwhelms all her other instincts, she will, if she marries either of them, marry Freddy.

And that is just what Eliza did.

Complications ensued; but they were economic, not romantic. Freddy had no money and no occupation. His mother's jointure, a last relic of the opulence of Largelady Park, had enabled her to struggle along in Earlscourt with an air of

1. German philosopher Friedrich Nietzsche (1844–1900).

gentility, but not to procure any serious secondary education for her children, much less give the boy a profession. A clerkship at thirty shillings a week was beneath Freddy's dignity, and extremely distasteful to him besides. His prospects consisted of a hope that if he kept up appearances somebody would do something for him. The something appeared vaguely to his imagination as a private secretaryship or a sinecure of some sort. To his mother it perhaps appeared as a marriage to some lady of means who could not resist her boy's niceness. Fancy her feelings when he married a flower girl who had become disclassed under extraordinary circumstances which were now notorious!

It is true that Eliza's situation did not seem wholly ineligible. Her father, though formerly a dustman, and now fantastically disclassed, had become extremely popular in the smartest society by a social talent which triumphed over every prejudice and every disadvantage. Rejected by the middle class, which he loathed, he had shot up at once into the highest circles by his wit, his dustmanship (which he carried like a banner), and his Nietzschean transcendence of good and evil. At intimate ducal dinners he sat on the right hand of the Duchess; and in country houses he smoked in the pantry and was made much of by the butler when he was not feeding in the dining room and being consulted by cabinet ministers. But he found it almost as hard to do all this on four thousand a year as Mrs. Eynsford Hill to live in Earlscourt on an income so pitiably smaller that I have not the heart to disclose its exact figure. He absolutely refused to add the last straw to his burden by contributing to Eliza's support.

Thus Freddy and Eliza, now Mr. and Mrs. Eynsford Hill, would have spent a penniless honeymoon but for a wedding present of £500 from the Colonel to Eliza. It lasted a long time because Freddy did not know how to spend money, never having had any to spend, and Eliza, socially trained by a pair of old bachelors, wore her clothes as long as they held together and looked pretty, without the least regard to their being many months out of fashion. Still, £500 will not last two young people for ever; and they both knew, and Eliza felt as well, that they must shift for themselves in the end. She could quarter herself on Wimpole Street because it had come to be her home; but she was quite aware that she ought not to quarter Freddy there, and that it would not be good for his character if she did.

Not that the Wimpole Street bachelors objected. When she consulted them, Higgins declined to be bothered about her housing problem when that solution was so simple. Eliza's desire to have Freddy in the house with her seemed of no more importance than if she had wanted an extra piece of bedroom furniture. Pleas as to Freddy's character, and the moral obligation on him to earn his own living, were lost on Higgins. He denied that Freddy had any character, and declared that if he tried to do any useful work some competent person would have the trouble of undoing it: a procedure involving a net loss to the community, and great unhappiness to Freddy himself, who was obviously intended by Nature for such light work as amusing Eliza, which, Higgins declared, was a much more useful and honorable occupation than working in the city. When Eliza referred again to her project of teaching phonetics, Higgins abated not a jot of his violent opposition to it. He said she was not within ten years of being qualified to meddle with his pet subject; and as it was evident that the Colonel agreed with him, she felt she could not go against them in this grave matter, and that she had no right, without Higgins's consent, to exploit the knowledge he had given her; for his knowledge seemed to her as much his private property as his watch: Eliza was no communist. Besides, she was superstitiously devoted to them both, more entirely and frankly after her marriage than before it.

It was the Colonel who finally solved the problem, which had cost him much perplexed cogitation. He one day asked Eliza, rather shyly, whether she had quite given up her notion of keeping a flower shop. She replied that she had thought of it, but had put it out of her head, because the Colonel had said, that day at Mrs. Higgins's, that it would never do. The Colonel confessed that when he said that, he had not quite recovered from the dazzling impression of the day before. They broke the matter to Higgins that evening. The sole comment vouchsafed by him very nearly led to a serious quarrel with Eliza. It was to the effect that she would have in Freddy an ideal errand boy.

Freddy himself was next sounded on the subject. He said he had been thinking of a shop himself; though it had presented itself to his pennilessness as a small place in which Eliza should sell tobacco at one counter whilst he sold newspapers at the opposite one. But he agreed that it would be extraordinarily jolly to go early every morning with Eliza to Covent Garden and buy flowers on the scene of their first meeting: a sentiment which earned him many kisses from his wife. He added that he had always been afraid to propose anything of the sort, because Clara would make an awful row about a step that must damage her matrimonial chances, and his mother could not be expected to like it after clinging for so many years to that step of the social ladder on which retail trade is impossible.

This difficulty was removed by an event highly unexpected by Freddy's mother. Clara, in the course of her incursions into those artistic circles which were the highest within her reach, discovered that her conversational qualifications were expected to include a grounding in the novels of Mr. H. G. Wells.[2]

2. H. G. Wells (1866–1946), English novelist, scientific visionary, and social prophet.

She borrowed them in various directions so energetically that she swallowed them all within two months. The result was a conversion of a kind quite common today. A modern Acts of the Apostles[3] would fill fifty whole Bibles if anyone were capable of writing it.

Poor Clara, who appeared to Higgins and his mother as a disagreeable and ridiculous person, and to her own mother as in some inexplicable way a social failure, had never seen herself in either light; for, though to some extent ridiculed and mimicked in West Kensington like everybody else there, she was accepted as a rational and normal—or shall we say inevitable?—sort of human being. At worst they called her The Pusher; but to them no more than to herself had it ever occurred that she was pushing the air, and pushing it in a wrong direction. Still, she was not happy. She was growing desperate. Her one asset, the fact that her mother was what the Epsom greengrocer called a carriage lady, had no exchange value, apparently. It had prevented her from getting educated, because the only education she could have afforded was education with the Earlscourt greengrocer's daughter. It had led her to seek the society of her mother's class; and that class simply would not have her, because she was much poorer than the greengrocer, and, far from being able to afford a maid, could not afford even a housemaid, and had to scrape along at home with an illiberally treated general servant. Under such circumstances nothing could give her an air of being a genuine product of Largelady Park. And yet its tradition made her regard a marriage with anyone within her reach as an unbearable humiliation. Commercial people and professional people in a small way were odious to her. She ran after painters and novelists; but she did not charm them; and her bold attempts to pick up and practise artistic and literary talk irritated them. She was, in short, an utter failure, an ignorant, incompetent, pretentious, unwelcome, penniless, useless little snob; and though she did not admit these disqualifications (for nobody ever faces unpleasant truths of this kind until the possibility of a way out dawns on them) she felt their effects too keenly to be satisfied with her position.

Clara had a startling eyeopener when, on being suddenly wakened to enthusiasm by a girl of her own age who dazzled her and produced in her a gushing desire to take her for a model, and gain her friendship, she discovered that this exquisite apparition had graduated from the gutter in a few months time. It shook her so violently, that when Mr. H. G. Wells lifted her on the point of his puissant pen, and placed her at the angle of view from which the life she was leading and the society to which she clung appeared in its true relation to real human needs and worthy social structure, he effected a conversion and a convic-

3. Fifth book of the New Testament.

tion of sin comparable to the most sensational feats of General Booth or Gypsy Smith.[4] Clara's snobbery went bang. Life suddenly began to move with her. Without knowing how or why, she began to make friends and enemies. Some of the acquaintances to whom she had been a tedious or indifferent or ridiculous affliction, dropped her: others became cordial. To her amazement she found that some "quite nice" people were saturated with Wells, and that this accessibility to ideas was the secret of their niceness. People she had thought deeply religious, and had tried to conciliate on that tack with disastrous results, suddenly took an interest in her, and revealed a hostility to conventional religion which she had never conceived possible except among the most desperate characters. They made her read Galsworthy[5]; and Galsworthy exposed the vanity of Largelady Park and finished her. It exasperated her to think that the dungeon in which she had languished for so many unhappy years had been unlocked all the time, and that the impulses she had so carefully struggled with and stifled for the sake of keeping well with society, were precisely those by which alone she could have come into any sort of sincere human contact. In the radiance of these discoveries, and the tumult of their reaction, she made a fool of herself as freely and conspicuously as when she so rashly adopted Eliza's expletive in Mrs. Higgins's drawing room; for the new-born Wellsian had to find her bearings almost as ridiculously as a baby; but nobody hates a baby for its ineptitudes, or thinks the worse of it for trying to eat the matches; and Clara lost no friends by her follies. They laughed at her to her face this time; and she had to defend herself and fight it out as best she could.

When Freddy paid a visit to Earlscourt (which he never did when he could possibly help it) to make the desolating announcement that he and his Eliza were thinking of blackening the Largelady scutcheon by opening a shop, he found the little household already convulsed by a prior announcement from Clara that she also was going to work in an old furniture shop in Dover Street, which had been started by a fellow Wellsian. This appointment Clara owed, after all, to her old social accomplishment of Push. She had made up her mind that, cost what it might, she would see Mr. Wells in the flesh; and she had achieved her end at a garden party. She had better luck than so rash an enterprise deserved. Mr. Wells came up to her expectations. Age had not withered him, nor could custom stale his infinite variety in half an hour.[6] His pleasant neatness and compactness, his small hands and feet, his teeming ready brain, his unaffected accessibility, and a certain fine apprehensiveness which stamped

4. General William Booth (1829–1912), founder and leader of the Salvation Army, and Gypsy Rodney Smith (1860–1947), English evangelist with the National Free Church Council and an associate of General Booth's.　　**5.** English playwright and novelist John Galsworthy (1867–1933).　　**6.** From Shakespeare's *Antony and Cleopatra*, II.2.243: "Age cannot wither her, nor custom stale / her infinite variety."

him as susceptible from his topmost hair to his tipmost toe, proved irresistible. Clara talked of nothing else for weeks and weeks afterwards. And as she happened to talk to the lady of the furniture shop, and that lady also desired above all things to know Mr. Wells and sell pretty things to him, she offered Clara a job on the chance of achieving that end through her.

And so it came about that Eliza's luck held, and the expected opposition to the flower shop melted away. The shop is in the arcade of a railway station not very far from the Victoria and Albert Museum; and if you live in that neighborhood you may go there any day and buy a buttonhole from Eliza.

Now here is a last opportunity for romance. Would you not like to be assured that the shop was an immense success, thanks to Eliza's charms and her early business experience in Covent Garden? Alas! the truth is the truth: the shop did not pay for a long time, simply because Eliza and her Freddy did not know how to keep it. True, Eliza had not to begin at the very beginning: she knew the names and prices of the cheaper flowers; and her elation was unbounded when she found that Freddy, like all youths educated at cheap, pretentious, and thoroughly inefficient schools, knew a little Latin. It was very little, but enough to make him appear to her a Porson or Bentley,[7] and to put him at his ease with botanical nomenclature. Unfortunately he knew nothing else; and Eliza, though she could count money up to eighteen shillings or so, and had acquired a certain familiarity with the language of Milton from her struggles to qualify herself for winning Higgins's bet, could not write out a bill without utterly disgracing the establishment. Freddy's power of stating in Latin that Balbus built a wall and that Gaul was divided into three parts[8] did not carry with it the slightest knowledge of accounts or business: Colonel Pickering had to explain to him what a cheque book and a bank account meant. And the pair were by no means easily teachable. Freddy backed up Eliza in her obstinate refusal to believe that they could save money by engaging a bookkeeper with some knowledge of the business. How, they argued, could you possibly save money by going to extra expense when you already could not make both ends meet? But the Colonel, after making the ends meet over and over again, at last gently insisted; and Eliza, humbled to the dust by having to beg from him so often, and stung by the uproarious derision of Higgins, to whom the notion of Freddy succeeding at anything was a joke that never palled, grasped the fact that business, like phonetics, has to be learned.

On the piteous spectacle of the pair spending their evenings in shorthand

---

7. Classical scholars Richard Porson (1759–1808) and Richard Bentley (1662–1742).   8. Freddie's ability to say such things in Latin reflects his fragmented and partial "schoolboy's" understanding of Roman history.

schools and polytechnic classes, learning bookkeeping and typewriting with incipient junior clerks, male and female, from the elementary schools, let me not dwell. There were even classes at the London School of Economics, and a humble personal appeal to the director of that institution to recommend a course bearing on the flower business. He, being a humorist, explained to them the method of the celebrated Dickensian essay on Chinese Metaphysics by the gentleman who read an article on China and an article on Metaphysics and combined the information. He suggested that they should combine the London School with Kew Gardens. Eliza, to whom the procedure of the Dickensian gentleman seemed perfectly correct (as in fact it was) and not in the least funny (which was only her ignorance), took the advice with entire gravity. But the effort that cost her the deepest humiliation was a request to Higgins, whose pet artistic fancy, next to Milton's verse, was caligraphy, and who himself wrote a most beautiful Italian hand, that he would teach her to write. He declared that she was congenitally incapable of forming a single letter worthy of the least of Milton's words; but she persisted; and again he suddenly threw himself into the task of teaching her with a combination of stormy intensity, concentrated patience, and occasional bursts of interesting disquisition on the beauty and nobility, the august mission and destiny, of human handwriting. Eliza ended by acquiring an extremely uncommercial script which was a positive extension of her personal beauty, and spending three times as much on stationery as anyone else because certain qualities and shapes of paper became indispensable to her. She could not even address an envelope in the usual way because it made the margins all wrong.

Their commercial schooldays were a period of disgrace and despair for the young couple. They seemed to be learning nothing about flower shops. At last they gave it up as hopeless, and shook the dust of the shorthand schools, and the polytechnics, and the London School of Economics from their feet for ever. Besides, the business was in some mysterious way beginning to take care of itself. They had somehow forgotten their objections to employing other people. They came to the conclusion that their own way was the best, and that they had really a remarkable talent for business. The Colonel, who had been compelled for some years to keep a sufficient sum on current account at his bankers to make up their deficits, found that the provision was unnecessary: the young people were prospering. It is true that there was not quite fair play between them and their competitors in trade. Their week-ends in the country cost them nothing, and saved them the price of their Sunday dinners; for the motor car was the Colonel's; and he and Higgins paid the hotel bills. Mr. F. Hill, florist and green-grocer (they soon discovered that there was money in asparagus; and asparagus led to other vegetables), had an air which stamped the business as classy; and in private life he was still Frederick Eynsford Hill, Esquire. Not that there was any swank about him: nobody but Eliza knew that he had been christened Frederick Challoner. Eliza herself swanked like anything.

That is all. That is how it has turned out. It is astonishing how much Eliza still manages to meddle in the housekeeping at Wimpole Street in spite of the shop and her own family. And it is notable that though she never nags her husband, and frankly loves the Colonel as if she were his favorite daughter, she has never got out of the habit of nagging Higgins that was established on the fatal night when she won his bet for him. She snaps his head off on the faintest provocation, or on none. He no longer dares to tease her by assuming an abysmal inferiority of Freddy's mind to his own. He storms and bullies and derides; but she stands up to him so ruthlessly that the Colonel has to ask her from time to time to be kinder to Higgins; and it is the only request of his that brings a mulish expression into her face. Nothing but some emergency or calamity great enough to break down all likes and dislikes, and throw them both back on their common humanity—and may they be spared any such trial!—will ever alter this. She knows that Higgins does not need her, just as her father did not need her. The very scrupulousness with which he told her that day that he had become used to having her there, and dependent on her for all sorts of little services, and that he should miss her if she went away (it would never have occurred to Freddy or the Colonel to say anything of the sort) deepens her inner certainty that she is "no more to him than them slippers"; yet she has a sense, too, that his indifference is deeper than the infatuation of commoner souls. She is immensely interested in him. She has even secret mischievous moments in which she wishes she could get him alone, on a desert island, away from all ties and with nobody else in the world to consider, and just drag him off his pedestal and see him making love like any common man. We all have private imaginations of that sort. But when it comes to business, to the life that she really leads as distinguished from the life of dreams and fancies, she likes Freddy and she likes the Colonel; and she does not like Higgins and Mr. Doolittle. Galatea never does quite like Pygmalion: his relation to her is too godlike to be altogether agreeable.

1914, revised 1941

In staging a play, "sets" are more important than "setting," so let us first look at the "sets." The staging of the original version of *Pygmalion* was relatively simple. Each of the five acts had only one scene and there were in all only three sets: the portico of St. Paul's Church in the first act, Higgins's laboratory in his Wimpole Street residence in Acts II and IV, and his mother's drawing room in her home on Chelsea Embankment in Acts III and V. Consequently there were no sudden stage shifts, and, except for the rain in the first scene, not much in the way of special effects. To keep matters simple, we will stick to that early version, ignoring the "movie" material added after the successful 1941 film version of the play—passages that are marked in your text by asterisks.

The setting of *Pygmalion* is more or less contemporary (that is, early twentieth-century) London, chiefly in the upper-class districts of Regents Park (Higgins's laboratory on Wimpole Street) and Chelsea Embankment. The setting in the first act, however, is on the portico of St. Paul's in central London, near the produce market—Covent Garden—the theaters, and the East End, where the "lower" class—the cockneys—lived, and where accidental encounters of the upper and lower classes were possible. On the night of the first act, the rain drives the Eynsford Hills and Pickering into the company of the flower girl, Eliza Doolittle, and assorted, chiefly working-class bystanders and keeps them together for a time. A well-dressed note taker is also there, not accidentally, and his mysterious activities arouse the suspicions of the bystanders, who fear he is a policeman or spy. This initial setting and the action of the characters dramatize the issue of class and class conflict, one of the themes of the play. The note taker—we soon learn his name is Henry Higgins—is obsessed with phonetics and can identify a person's neighborhood (and thus class) from that person's speech. He is further characterized as arrogant, unconventional, ironic, and even insulting in his brusqueness: "dont sit there crooning like a bilious pigeon," he tells the flower girl at one point; and later, "A woman who utters such depressing and disgusting sounds has no right . . . . to live." But there also seems to be an almost idealistic and humane contempt for class distinction beneath his sometimes cruel candor. He seems to believe that it is only differences in speech that distinguish the classes: he tells her to remember she has "a soul and the divine gift of articulate speech," and he swears he can so train her speech as to pass her off as a duchess. (It is not that he believes the educated upper classes speak better English; he contemptuously says that being a lady's maid or shop assistant requires better English than being a duchess.) His character and his speech set the ironic tone, his character and his project will soon generate the plot, and are all immediately related to the theme of class and its artificiality.

The **tone** of the play at the end of the first act is somewhat like that of Higgins. It is witty, iconoclastic, unsentimental, satiric, and even caustic. At this early stage, most readers or viewers will feel an almost guilty complicity with Higgins's arrogant and unconventional attitudes toward the phoniness of individuals as well as that of "society." While the class theme set out in the first act denies the superiority of the upper class, the play does not indulge in lauding the virtues of the poor or of being poor: Eliza's extravagance, when she takes a cab and tells the driver that "a taxi fare ain't no object to me," comically and a little shockingly reinforces the unconventional tone of the first act. Like Freddy's own mother and sister, most readers and viewers are somewhat contemptuous and condescending toward "poor Freddy" Eynsford Hill, who, though clearly a "gentleman," is characterized not as superior, but more as an amiable klutz, a foolish and naive young man, especially in contrast to Higgins's shocking sophistication and originality and even to Eliza's breezy "realism." As the first act ends, after great effort Freddy has come up at last with a cab—now that one is no longer necessary—and characterization, tone, and theme are blended once again. And since it seems unlikely that he and his family have been introduced only to disappear, and that the contrast between him and Higgins is without significance, expectations are aroused that Freddy will have some sort of role in the plot, and, perhaps, in defining the theme.

The first act serves chiefly as exposition. The plot begins to "rise" in Act II, when Eliza comes to Higgins to take lessons in being a lady and he makes a bet with Pickering that he can pass her off as a duchess within six months. Eliza's comic insistence at this point that she will pay for her lessons further characterizes her, gets the plot going, and reinforces both the play's ironic tone and the theme of human qualities transcending class. Similarly, the stage directions near the beginning of the act indicating that Higgins makes no distinction between men and women further develop his character while reinforcing our ambivalence toward him; we generally agree that treating men and women equally is "good," but failing to notice women as women is "bad." This character trait contributes to the play's ironic tone and arouses the expectation that, in the ordinary course of events, and the ordinary course of plots, Higgins will learn to appreciate the differences between men and women. The introduction of Alfred Doolittle hilariously exaggerates the ironic amorality and unconventionality of the scene, though we are a little shocked by his bland and imperturbable willingness to "sell" his daughter, for he cannot "afford" middle-class morality. This is comic, but, like Higgins's unconventionality and apparent cruelty, it is also disturbing.

The climax of the plot comes when Eliza is accepted by the Eynsford Hills (and, in the revised, movie version, with her being accepted at the embassy party) and Higgins wins his bet. The falling action centers on a question raised earlier by Mrs. Higgins but kept in the background while Eliza becomes a lady: now that she has been taken out of her life of poverty and given a taste of cleanliness and luxury and a new accent, what will become of her? Higgins's casual, unsentimental attitude is no longer entirely comic. At this point the movie-makers of *Pygmalion* and the musical-makers of *My Fair Lady*, and, no doubt, most readers, insist on a romantic ending. Bernard Shaw's narrative post-script insists otherwise. Indeed, the logic of the play, the character of Higgins, the unsentimental tone, the unconventionality of theme, reality, and the nature of British society in the early twentieth century all point to frustrating romantic expectations. However, we do not have to believe Shaw the story-teller—D. H. Lawrence tells us to trust the tale and not the teller—but we do have to trust the play, and at this point we begin to interpret the text. The tale or play, however, does not in or by itself answer all questions, solve all prob-lems of meaning, or yield a single, definitive interpretation. Though interpreta-tion rests on the details of the text, it is also conditioned by social, historical, and literary contexts and by the reader's own experiences, premises, and val-ues. Interpretation will, most likely, never be absolutely definitive, or certain.

▼   ▼   ▼

QUESTIONS

1. What is the attitude of the lower class to the upper and middle classes as shown in the first act? How does Shaw characterize the three classes and the relationship between them? Which class comes off best?

2. What is your first impression of Freddy? What do his mother and sister think of him? Support your answer with examples from the play.

3. What is your first impression of Eliza? Can you understand the first lines she speaks? There is a stage direction announcing that Shaw will no longer rep-resent her speech phonetically, and he does not. How would this be handled on the stage? Would her early and later speech be different?

4. Higgins defies conventional class distinctions. Is this because he believes all human beings equally good? equally bad? Higgins seems uninhibitedly out-spoken, but when, in Act III, Clara (Miss Eynsford Hill) suggests that people should be frank and say what they really think, Higgins says, "Lord forbid!" because "we're all savages, more or less." How does that relate to the theme of equality and the falseness of class distinctions? What evidence is there in the

play that we are "savages"? What does being "savage" mean?

5. What do the engravings in Higgins's home and lab and the absence of paintings (Act II) suggest about his character? Both Leslie Howard in the movie *Pygmalion* and Rex Harrison in *My Fair Lady* are rather slightly built, and for some viewers this goes along with Higgins's vinegary, sarcastic manner, but the text says Higgins is "robust." Does the casting suggest a stereotype or convention? How would Anthony Hopkins or Mel Gibson as Higgins affect your understanding of his character? the play?

6. What is Higgins's view of himself? Does it contrast with what we have read or seen of him from the outside? Is this merely comic or does it suggest that all our views of ourselves are equally false? Knowing this view of himself, would you play Higgins a little differently than you would not knowing this?

7. In what way are Higgins's and Alfred Doolittle's attitudes and behavior similar? Why will Doolittle take five pounds for his daughter but not ten? What use does he promise to put the money to? Why will the woman he lives with not marry him? How does this relate to the reversal of conventional expectations?

8. What is the "new small talk" (Act III)? the "sanguinary element" in that "small talk"? In what way is the "small talk" like the fairy tale of the Emperor's new clothes? Though this scene seems comically exaggerated, what elements of "truth" or "reality" are in it? What does it suggest about society and its "rules"?

9. How is Act IV the climax or turning point? How does it initiate and present the falling action? What is the tone of this act? How does it differ from that of much of the rest of the play? To what extent is your opinion of Higgins changed? At this point, or early in Act V, review Pickering's role and his character. Does his character suggest qualities that are almost inevitably associated with his class? If so, does this mean that Eliza, whom Pickering admires and protects and who understands and values him, has, indeed, been transformed into a "lady"? How, then, is class defined by the characters of Pickering and the transformed Eliza?

WRITING SUGGESTIONS

1. Shaw's postscript tells us that Eliza marries Freddy, not Higgins. Write an argumentative essay that takes one of the two following positions; use concrete evidence and take into account your "opponent's" possible counterarguments:

(a) If we are to trust the tale and not the teller, as D. H. Lawrence advises us to do, argue, *using evidence from the text,* that Shaw is wrong, that what he says is not in the play but only his interpretation of the play, and that from the play we can show that Liza really does marry Higgins, as both the movie and the later musical, *My Fair Lady,* "show."

(b) But Bernard Shaw knows best: argue that the whole tone of the play is ironic and undermines conventional expectation, that Eliza marries Higgins is the expected comic resolution and therefore *not* the one that is consistent with the play. Using passages showing the reversals of ordinary expectations, the upsetting of conventions and middle-class morality, and adopting some of Shaw's argument in his afterword, try to prove your point.

2. Is Higgins a sexist? Analyze the attitude toward gender in *Pygmalion.* If Higgins were to marry Eliza how would this reinforce or change what the play seems to be saying about gender?

3. From the beginning of the play to the very end there are reversals of conventions and thus of conventional expectations. List as many of these as you can find. Write an essay that either

(a) forms from these a consistent view of society and morality; or,

(b) discriminates between those that justifiably "question authority" or social conventions and those that are themselves questionable—sexist, inhumane, snobbish in their own way, etc.

4. Look up the classical story of Pygmalion and read one or two versions other than Shaw's. Show how the means Pygmalion uses to create a woman (art, the gods, phonetics, etc.) and the relationship of Pygmalion to his creation embody different themes and derive from and embody different attitudes (toward art and science, men and women, etc.).

5. What does each of the scenes from the movie—scenes that were not in the first version of the play—add to the plot, characterization, theme, tone, setting? Which of these would be easy to stage? difficult? impossible? Which of those that were possible, would you include in your "production" of the play? Why?

Exploring
Contexts

4 THE AUTHOR'S WORK AS CONTEXT: ANTON CHEKHOV

Making comparisons is an inevitable activity of the mind, and as we read drama we can enlarge our understanding of a work by making comparisons—between this play and our own experience, between this play and other plays of the season, between this play and others by the same dramatist. No doubt you have already been making such comparisons as you've been reading the plays in this book.

Take *Hamlet* as an example: if you have read other tragedies or histories by Shakespeare, you may already be aware that the question of royal succession was of paramount importance to Shakespeare and his audience and may thus understand the emphasis laid upon it in this play. Moreover, whatever Shakespeare plays you have read or will go on to read, comparisons will show you how Shakespeare continually made his verse line more fluid and dramatic. Thus every new Shakespeare play you encounter will increase your knowledge of Shakespeare's "world." A writer's world involves not only his or her individual mind and personal consciousness, but also the larger cultural and historical world in which he or she lives. Understanding Shakespearean plays becomes easier as we read more of them not only because we come to understand better what Shakespeare was interested in, how his mind worked, and what kinds of characters, plots, and dramatic situations he liked to create, but also because we begin to know more about the details of life in the England in which he lived four centuries ago. This chapter focuses on the work of Anton Chekhov, a playwright who lived three hundred years after Shakespeare but still a full century before the present time; in a culture unfamiliar to most contemporary American readers: Czarist Russia.

Chekhov was in many ways a "product" of the late nineteenth-century Russia in which he grew up, but he was of course also an individual with a life and history of his own. Born in 1860 in southern Russia, he was the son of a poor grocer. His ancestors had been serfs. His father—pious, rigid, and something of a bully—was deeply committed to Anton's education, and sent him to the classical *gimnaziya* (grammar school) in his home town. Eventually the elder Chekhov went bankrupt, and moved his family six hundred miles north to Moscow, except Anton, who stayed behind to complete his schooling. When he finished three years later (in 1879), Anton joined his family and enrolled as a medical student at Moscow University. He received his medical degree in 1884. By that time he had begun to show symptoms of tuberculosis, which would take his life at the age of forty-four.

Even as a young child, Chekhov is said to have shown a flair for the theatrical—he loved mimicry, practical jokes, and play acting—and in grammar school he acted in several plays and wrote a number of his own, though he systematically destroyed them. But early in his university years—in an effort to help relieve his family's poverty—he began to write short stories and comic sketches, which he published in a variety of magazines. He also began to write a regular gossip column for a popular magazine. Before he was thirty, he had published dozens of stories and established a certain popular reputation, but not until 1888—when he published "The Steppe" in a major literary journal—did he begin to write the "serious" stories on which his international reputation as a writer of short stories is now based. In fact, Chekhov's early reputation was as a story writer; his major plays were written much later, during the last eight years of his life (1896–1904). But as early as 1880 (at the age of twenty), he began work on a long and strange play, *Platonov*, which was neither performed during his lifetime nor discovered until many years after his death. In its uncut form it takes almost seven hours to perform. Although the play's loudly proclaimed emotional rampages, rampant on-stage violence, and complicated plot line make it quite unlike Chekhov's more famous plays, in which very little "action" happens on stage, one can still see in *Platonov* many characteristic Chekhovian concerns. As his principal English translator, Ronald Hingley, has pointed out, *Platonov* "has much to say to those who wish to examine the roots of his art." About 1888—just as he was reaching maturity as a short story writer—Chekhov began experimenting with short theatrical farces, almost as if he continued to need an outlet for his often outrageous comic sense as his narrative prose became more serious and more fully controlled. Most of these pieces (like *The Bear*, which is included here) are what Chekhov himself called "vaudevilles"—wildly exuberant sketches heavily dependent on stereotypical characters and situations. Sometimes they seem unfinished and a bit out of control, but they are very funny in themselves and they help us to see more clearly the absurdity and humor in Chekhov's important later plays, which some producers, readers, and critics tend to regard in too solemn a way. Chekhov's social criticism is always telling and often biting, but he always has a powerful sense of irony about human behavior that grows out of the social and cultural particulars of late nineteenth- and early twentieth-century Russia.

Chekhov's early writing is not now much remembered, but the three dozen or so stories written after 1888 and four of his later plays—*The Seagull, Uncle Vanya, The Three Sisters,* and *The Cherry Orchard*—are internationally regarded as masterpieces and remain in the repertory in many cities and countries throughout the world. As with any author, the ideal way to appreciate Chekhov would be to read all of his stories and plays in succession. Their common themes, strategies, and cultural analyses would shine through clearly and richly, each work contributing to your understanding of the next. Your insights into Chekhov's most mature work would consequently be much deeper than if you were to begin with or read only that material. But given the limitations of this book, we provide here three examples to introduce you to Chekhov's work: the first a brief "vaudeville" written when Chekhov was about twenty-eight years old, then a stage monologue, and finally his final major play, produced only weeks before his death.

One way to begin the study of an author in the context of his or her work is to consider what you know or can easily find out about the author's life, and then read the text with some of the issues suggested there in mind. Chekhov, for example, lived in a time of social transition in Russia. Power of the old propertied classes was shifting noticeably into the hands of a rising entrepreneurial class; his own family's difficult and troubled economic history suggests some of the social transitions characteristic of Russia in the last decades of Czarist rule. Many of the challenges that Chekhov faced—the uncertain economic climate that brought his father's bankruptcy, the scrambling, hackwork writing that enabled Chekhov to scrape out a living early on, the climate-aggravated illness that dominated most of his life—are closely related to larger national issues and situations and often find their way, at least obliquely, into his plays. But the larger, more powerful sense of deep cultural change and of shifting power among social classes is everywhere in Chekhov. Much of the

anxiety and social unease is understandable in generational terms; it is not surprising that older generations deplored the loss of family closeness, identity
with the land, and traditional community they associated with their way of life,
nor is it surprising that members of the younger generation found traditional
loyalties boring, stifling, and inferior to city life and the greater mobility among
social classes and groups of people it offered. Chekhov himself, torn from his
ancestral home by economic and career needs, understood very well what it
was like to lose familiarity and security, but what is most surprising is the tonal
complexity he maintains in the face of deep personal and cultural change. He
seems to understand both what it was like to lose a familiar way of life and to
achieve new distinction or wealth. And he maintains a firm sense of the absurd
among human beings in all classes.

In *The Cherry Orchard*, for example, representatives of all classes and
groups come in for comic, often even satiric treatment: Lyuba Ranevsky, for
example, is ridiculous both in her inability to face economic reality (she keeps
hoping that money will mysteriously appear out of the past) and in her romantic attachments to the past and her exploitive lover in Paris (though the play is
also powerfully respectful of the real human loss that the cherry orchard represents). Lopakhin, too, is a caricature of his class and type; he is nouveau riche,
acquisitive, and a bit gleeful about the fall of his social betters. Others in the
play—the eternal student, the governess, the romantic and maritally ambitious
daughters, and even the aged manservant Firs (pathetic and poignant though
he is)—all come in for richly comic treatment, as well, resulting from their
inevitable encounters with economic and cultural change, shifting values, and
exigencies of situation that result in changed human circumstances.

Social and cultural issues get central attention in *The Cherry Orchard*,
although they by no means overshadow Chekhov's interest in the depiction of
individual characters. In a sense, the conflicts here—between generations,
between past and present values, between haves and have-nots, and between
different sets and kinds of social standards—are "universal,"—they recur in a
variety of places and times—but the specific representations of conflict have to
do with the particulars of Chekhov's having grown up in Russia in the late
nineteenth century. You don't have to know about Chekhov's life or the details
of Russian social change to understand the several complicated issues in the
play, but knowing such details helps considerably in seeing exactly what the
conflicts are about and why the sympathies with different characters are so
complicated. For Chekhov and his contemporaries, these issues were not
abstract; they were materials that could be worked out in imaginative fictions.

Another way to consider the authorial context is to read an author's texts comparatively. If you do not have time to read a writer's entire canon to see how one work illuminates all the others (and readers usually don't unless they are producing or acting in a play or doing a detailed scholarly study), you can learn a lot by comparing two works and noticing what themes, concerns, and strategies are shared. It is not only ideas and feelings that authors tend to carry over from one text to another, but dramatic devices and rhetorical strategies as well.

The Bear is a short, early play, and although it does not have the polish or complexity of Chekhov's later, more sophisticated efforts, it suggests many of the qualities Chekhov has come to be prized for. In many ways it is a very simple piece, depicting only a brief moment, an elemental conflict, and a quite predictable character revelation. But even so, one can see many of the elements that have come to be acclaimed in Chekhov's mature drama. The main characters—Mrs. Popov, Smirnov, and even the servant Luke—all have distinctive personalities that they display quite fully in so short a play, and all are somewhat more complicated than they themselves think. Much of the comedy here involves Mrs. Popov's view of herself as a faithful, loyal, and steadfast widow who finds that she has feelings she doesn't begin to understand. But Smirnov and Luke similarly find themselves beyond their depth to understand both emotion and situation; the central conflict here involves a tension between devotion to the past and a present that seems far less valuable and resonant but that also carries a powerful, vital appeal of its own. The central sources of tension are far less complex and interesting here than in The Cherry Orchard, but the same situations, plots, and schemes are present, the characters are similar, and even the themes and tones are recognizable. The Bear does not predict the later success of mature plays such as The Cherry Orchard, but it does readily show a distinctive mind at work on a persistent and characteristic set of issues. The older Chekhov may see the issues of land, family, loyalty, and ownership as more serious and lasting, but even in a brief, almost trivial play like The Bear one can see the young writer grappling with major cultural problems involving the rise of a new moneyed class with different social assumptions and ethical values and the decay of an older, more ordered world of social and personal expectation. One can also see here a deep interest in the analysis of feelings and an inclination to expose the difference in the way people believe they feel and what they demonstrate through their actions, something that comes out in more full and complex ways with several characters in The Cherry Orchard. And one can even see in these two plays a continuity of tone that derives from a consistent sense of human absurdity and inability to deal realistically with change and circumstance. The Cherry Orchard is not hilariously funny in its portrayal of the deterioration of older social values—its attitude is more ambivalent than words like "humor" or "satire" would suggest—but one can see in such a play not only irony and gentle teasing of classic attitudes but a certain lightness of touch and a recognition that even serious or tragic themes have their absurdity and their humorous aspects.

▼   ▼   ▼

ANTON CHEKHOV

The Bear[1]

A FARCE IN ONE ACT

Dedicated to N. N. Solovtsov

CHARACTERS

MRS. HELEN POPOV, *a young widow*   LUKE, *Mrs. Popov's old manservant*
with dimpled cheeks, a landowner

GREGORY SMIRNOV, *a landowner in*
early middle age

The action takes place in the drawing-room of MRS. POPOV's *country house.*

SCENE 1

MRS. POPOV, *in deep mourning, with her eyes fixed on a snapshot, and* LUKE.

LUKE: This won't do, madam, you're just making your life a misery. Cook's out with the maid picking fruit, every living creature's happy and even our cat knows how to enjoy herself—she's parading round the yard trying to pick up a bird or two. But here you are cooped up inside all day like you was in a convent cell—you never have a good time. Yes, it's true. Nigh on twelve months it is since you last set foot outdoors.

MRS. POPOV: And I'm never going out again, why should I? My life's finished. He lies in his grave, I've buried myself inside these four walls—we're both dead.

LUKE: There you go again! I don't like to hear such talk, I don't. Your husband died and that was that—God's will be done and may he rest in peace. You've shed a few tears and that'll do, it's time to call it a day—you can't spend your whole life a-moaning and a-groaning. The same thing happened to me once, when my old woman died, but what did I do? I grieved a bit, shed a tear or two for a month or so and that's all she's getting. Catch me wearing sackcloth

1. Translated by Ronald Hingley

and ashes for the rest of my days, it'd be more than the old girl was worth! [*Sighs.*] You've neglected all the neighbours—won't go and see them or have them in the house. We never get out and about, lurking here like dirty great spiders, saving your presence. The mice have been at my livery too. And it's not for any lack of nice people either—the county's full of 'em, see. There's the regiment stationed at Ryblovo and them officers are a fair treat, a proper sight for sore eyes they are. They have a dance in camp of a Friday and the brass band plays most days. This ain't right, missus. You're young, and pretty as a picture with that peaches-and-cream look, so make the most of it. Them looks won't last for ever, you know. If you wait another ten years to come out of your shell and lead them officers a dance, you'll find it's too late.

MRS. POPOV: [*Decisively.*] Never talk to me like that again, please. When Nicholas died my life lost all meaning, as you know. You may think I'm alive, but I'm not really. I swore to wear this mourning and shun society till my dying day, do you hear? Let his departed spirit see how I love him! Yes, I realize you know what went on—that he was often mean to me, cruel and, er, unfaithful even, but I'll be true to the grave and show him how much I can love. And he'll find me in the next world just as I was before he died.

LUKE: Don't talk like that—walk round the garden instead. Or else have Toby or Giant harnessed and go and see the neighbours.

MRS. POPOV: Oh dear! [*Weeps.*]

LUKE: Missus! Madam! What's the matter? For heaven's sake!

MRS. POPOV: He was so fond of Toby—always drove him when he went over to the Korchagins' place and the Vlasovs'. He drove so well too! And he looked so graceful when he pulled hard on the reins, remember? Oh Toby, Toby! See he gets an extra bag of oats today.

LUKE: Very good, madam.

[*A loud ring.*]

MRS. POPOV: [*Shudders.*] Who is it? Tell them I'm not at home.

LUKE: Very well, madam. [*Goes out.*]

SCENE 2

MRS. POPOV, *alone.*

MRS. POPOV: [*Looking at the snapshot.*] Now you shall see how I can love and forgive, Nicholas. My love will only fade when I fade away myself, when this poor heart stops beating. [*Laughs, through tears.*] Well, aren't you ashamed of yourself? I'm your good, faithful little wifie, I've locked myself up and I'll be faithful to the grave, while you—aren't you ashamed, you naughty boy? You deceived me and you used to make scenes and leave me alone for weeks on end.

SCENE 3

MRS. POPOV *and* LUKE.

LUKE: [*Comes in, agitatedly.*] Someone's asking for you, madam. Wants to see you——

MRS. POPOV: Then I hope you told them I haven't received visitors since the day my husband died.

LUKE: I did, but he wouldn't listen—his business is very urgent, he says.

MRS. POPOV: *I am not at home!*

LUKE: So I told him, but he just swears and barges straight in, drat him. He's waiting in the dining-room.

MRS. POPOV: [*Irritatedly.*] All right, ask him in here then. Aren't people rude?

[LUKE *goes out.*]

MRS. POPOV: Oh, aren't they all a bore? What do they want with me, why must they disturb my peace? [*Sighs.*] Yes, I see I really shall have to get me to a nunnery. [*Reflects.*] I'll take the veil, that's it.

SCENE 4

MRS. POPOV, LUKE *and* SMIRNOV.

SMIRNOV: [*Coming in, to* LUKE.] You're a fool, my talkative friend. An ass. [*Seeing* MRS. POPOV, *with dignity.*] May I introduce myself, madam? Gregory Smirnov, landed gentleman and lieutenant of artillery retired. I'm obliged to trouble you on most urgent business.

MRS. POPOV: [*Not holding out her hand.*] What do you require?

SMIRNOV: I had the honour to know your late husband. He died owing me twelve hundred roubles—I have his two IOUs. Now I've some interest due to the land-bank tomorrow, madam, so may I trouble you to let me have the money today?

MRS. POPOV: Twelve hundred roubles—. How did my husband come to owe you that?

SMIRNOV: He used to buy his oats from me.

MRS. POPOV: [*Sighing, to* LUKE.] Oh yes—Luke, don't forget to see Toby has his extra bag of oats. [LUKE *goes out. To* SMIRNOV.] Of course I'll pay if Nicholas owed you something, but I've nothing on me today, sorry. My manager will be back from town the day after tomorrow and I'll get him to pay you whatever it is then, but for the time being I can't oblige. Besides, it's precisely seven months today since my husband died and I am in no fit state to discuss money.

SMIRNOV: Well, I'll be in a fit state to go bust with a capital B if I can't pay that interest tomorrow. They'll have the bailiffs in on me.

MRS. POPOV: You'll get your money the day after tomorrow.

SMIRNOV: I don't want it the day after tomorrow, I want it now.

MRS. POPOV: I can't pay you now, sorry.

SMIRNOV: And I can't wait till the day after tomorrow.

MRS. POPOV: Can I help it if I've no money today?

SMIRNOV: So you can't pay then?

MRS. POPOV: Exactly.

SMIRNOV: I see. And that's your last word, is it?

MRS. POPOV: It is.

SMIRNOV: Your last word? You really mean it?

MRS. POPOV: I do.

SMIRNOV: [Sarcastic.] Then I'm greatly obliged to you, I'll put it in my diary! [Shrugs.] And people expect me to be cool and collected! I met the local excise man on my way here just now. "My dear Smirnov," says he, "why are you always losing your temper?" But how can I help it, I ask you? I'm in desperate need of money! Yesterday morning I left home at crack of dawn. I call on everyone who owes me money, but not a soul forks out. I'm dog-tired. I spend the night in some God-awful place—by the vodka barrel in a Jewish pot-house. Then I fetch up here, fifty miles from home, hoping to see the colour of my money, only to be fobbed off with this "no fit state" stuff! How *can* I keep my temper?

MRS. POPOV: I thought I'd made myself clear. You can have your money when my manager gets back from town.

SMIRNOV: It's not your manager I'm after, it's you. What the blazes, pardon my language, do I want with your manager?

MRS. POPOV: I'm sorry, my dear man, but I'm not accustomed to these peculiar expressions and to this tone. I have closed my ears. [Hurries out.]

SCENE 5

SMIRNOV, *alone.*

SMIRNOV: Well, what price that! "In no fit state!" Her husband died seven months ago, if you please! Now have I got my interest to pay or not? I want a straight answer—yes or no? All right, your husband's dead, you're in no fit state and so on and so forth, and your blasted manager's hopped it. But what am I supposed to do? Fly away from my creditors by balloon, I take it! Or go and bash the old brain-box against a brick wall? I call on Gruzdev—not at home. Yaroshevich is in hiding. I have a real old slanging-match with Kurit-syn and almost chuck him out of the window. Mazutov has the belly-ache, and this creature's "in no fit state." Not one of the swine will pay. This is what comes of being too nice to them and behaving like some snivelling no-hoper or old woman. It doesn't pay to wear kid gloves with this lot! All right, just you wait—I'll give you something to remember me by! You don't make a monkey out of me, blast you! I'm staying here—going to stick around till she coughs up. Pah! I feel well and truly riled today. I'm shaking like a leaf, I'm so furious—choking I am. Phew, my God, I really think I'm going to pass out! [Shouts.] Hey, you there!

SCENE 6

SMIRNOV *and* LUKE.

LUKE: [*Comes in.*] What is it?
SMIRNOV: Bring me some kvass or water, will you?

[LUKE *goes out.*]

SMIRNOV: What a mentality, though! You need money so bad you could shoot
yourself, but she won't pay, being "in no fit state to discuss money," if you
please! There's female logic for you and no mistake! That's why I don't like
talking to women. Never have. Talk to a woman—why, I'd rather sit on top
of a powder magazine! Pah! It makes my flesh creep, I'm so fed up with her,
her and that great trailing dress! Poetic creatures they call 'em! Why, the
very sight of one gives me cramp in both legs, I get so aggravated.

SCENE 7

SMIRNOV *and* LUKE.

LUKE: [*Comes in and serves some water.*] Madam's unwell and won't see anyone.
SMIRNOV: You clear out!

[LUKE *goes out.*]

SMIRNOV: "Unwell and won't see anyone." All right then, don't! I'm staying put,
chum, and I don't budge one inch till you unbelt. Be ill for a week and I'll
stay a week, make it a year and a year I'll stay. I'll have my rights, lady! As for
your black dress and dimples, you don't catch me that way—we know all
about those dimples! [*Shouts through the window.*] Unhitch, Simon, we're
here for some time—I'm staying put. Tell the stable people to give my horses
oats. And you've got that animal tangled in the reins again, you great oaf!
[*Imitates him.*] "I don't care." I'll give you don't care! [*Moves away from the
window.*] How ghastly—it's unbearably hot, no one will pay up, I had a bad
night, and now here's this female with her long black dress and her states.
I've got a headache. How about a glass of vodka? That might be an idea.
[*Shouts.*] Hey, you there!
LUKE: [*Comes in.*] What is it?
SMIRNOV: Bring me a glass of vodka.

[LUKE *goes out.*]

SMIRNOV: Phew! [*Sits down and looks himself over.*] A fine specimen I am, I must
say—dust all over me, my boots dirty, unwashed, hair unbrushed, straw on
my waistcoat. I bet the little woman took me for a burglar. [*Yawns.*] It's not
exactly polite to turn up in a drawing-room in this rig! Well, anyway, I'm not
a guest here, I'm collecting money. And there's no such thing as correct wear
for the well-dressed creditor.
LUKE: [*Comes in and gives him the vodka.*] This is a liberty, sir.

SMIRNOV: [*Angrily.*] What!

LUKE: I, er, it's all right, I just——

SMIRNOV: Who do you think you're talking to? You hold your tongue!

LUKE: [*Aside.*] Now we'll never get rid of him, botheration take it! It's an ill wind brought him along.

[LUKE *goes out.*]

SMIRNOV: Oh, I'm so furious! I could pulverize the whole world, I'm in such a rage. I feel quite ill. [*Shouts.*] Hey, you there!

SCENE 8

MRS. POPOV *and* SMIRNOV.

MRS. POPOV: [*Comes in, with downcast eyes.*] Sir, in my solitude I have grown unaccustomed to the sound of human speech, and I can't stand shouting. I must urgently request you not to disturb my peace.

SMIRNOV: Pay up and I'll go.

MRS. POPOV: As I've already stated quite plainly, I've no ready cash. Wait till the day after tomorrow.

SMIRNOV: I've also had the honour of stating quite plainly that I need the money today, not the day after tomorrow. If you won't pay up now, I'll have to put my head in a gas-oven tomorrow.

MRS. POPOV: Can I help it if I've no cash in hand? This is all rather odd.

SMIRNOV: So you won't pay up now, eh?

MRS. POPOV: I can't.

SMIRNOV: In that case I'm not budging, I'll stick around here till I do get my money. [*Sits down.*] You'll pay the day after tomorrow, you say? Very well, then I'll sit here like this till the day after tomorrow. I'll just stay put exactly as I am. [*Jumps up.*] I ask you—have I got that interest to pay tomorrow or haven't I? Think I'm trying to be funny, do you?

MRS. POPOV: Kindly don't raise your voice at me, sir—we're not in the stables.

SMIRNOV: I'm not discussing stables, I'm asking whether my interest falls due tomorrow. Yes or no?

MRS. POPOV: You don't know how to treat a lady.

SMIRNOV: Oh yes I do.

MRS. POPOV: Oh no you don't. You're a rude, ill-bred person. Nice men don't talk to ladies like that.

SMIRNOV: Now, this *is* a surprise! How do you want me to talk then? In French, I suppose? [*In an angry, simpering voice.*] Madame, *je voo pree*. You won't pay me—how perfectly delightful. Oh, *pardong*, I'm sure—sorry you were troubled! Now isn't the weather divine today? And that black dress looks too, too charming! [*Bows and scrapes.*]

MRS. POPOV: That's silly. And not very clever.

SMIRNOV: [*Mimics her.*] "Silly, not very clever." I don't know how to treat a lady, don't I? Madam, I've seen more women in my time than you have house-sparrows. I've fought three duels over women. There have been twenty-one women in my life. Twelve times it was me broke it off, the other nine got in first. Oh yes! Time was I made an ass of myself, slobbered, mooned around, bowed and scraped and practically crawled on my belly. I loved, I suffered, I sighed at the moon, I languished, I melted, I grew cold. I loved passionately, madly, in every conceivable fashion, damn me, burbling nineteen to the dozen about women's emancipation and wasting half my substance on the tender passion. But now—no thank you very much! I can't be fooled any more, I've had enough. Black eyes, passionate looks, crimson lips, dimpled cheeks, moonlight, "Whispers, passion's bated breathing"—I don't give a tinker's cuss for the lot now, lady. Present company excepted, all women, large or small, are simpering, mincing, gossipy creatures. They're great haters. They're eyebrow-deep in lies. They're futile, they're trivial, they're cruel, they're outrageously illogical. And as for having anything upstairs [*Taps his forehead.*]—I'm sorry to be so blunt, but the very birds in the trees can run rings round your average blue-stocking. Take any one of these poetical creations. Oh, she's all froth and fluff, she is, she's half divine, she sends you into a million raptures. But you take a peep inside her mind, and what do you see? A common or garden crocodile! [*Clutches the back of a chair, which cracks and breaks.*] And yet this crocodile somehow thinks its great life-work, privilege and monopoly is the tender passion—that's what really gets me! But damn and blast it, and crucify me upside down on that wall if I'm wrong—does a woman know how to love any living creature apart from lapdogs? Her love gets no further than snivelling and slobbering. The man suffers and makes sacrifices, while she just twitches the train of her dress and tries to get him squirming under her thumb, that's what her love adds up to! You must know what women are like, seeing you've the rotten luck to be one. Tell me frankly, did you ever see a sincere, faithful, true woman? You know you didn't. Only the old and ugly ones are true and faithful. You'll never find a constant woman, not in a month of Sundays you won't, not once in a blue moon!

MRS. POPOV: Well, I like that! Then who is true and faithful in love to your way of thinking? Not men by any chance?

SMIRNOV: Yes, madam. Men.

MRS. POPOV: Men! [*Gives a bitter laugh.*] Men true and faithful in love! That's rich, I must say. [*Vehemently.*] What right have you to talk like that? Men true and faithful! If it comes to that, the best man I've ever known was my late husband, I may say. I loved him passionately, with all my heart as only an intelligent young woman can. I gave him my youth, my happiness, my life, my possessions. I lived only for him. I worshipped him as an idol. And— what do you think? This best of men was shamelessly deceiving me all along the line! After his death I found a drawer in his desk full of love letters, and when he was alive—oh, what a frightful memory!—he used to leave me on my own for weeks on end, he carried on with other girls before my very eyes, he was unfaithful to me, he spent my money like water, and he joked about my feelings for him. But I loved him all the same, and I've been faithful to him. What's more, I'm still faithful and true now that he's dead. I've buried myself alive inside these four walls and I shall go round in these widow's weeds till my dying day.

SMIRNOV: [*With a contemptuous laugh.*] Widow's weeds! Who do you take me for? As if I didn't know why you wear this fancy dress and bury yourself indoors! Why, it sticks out a mile! Mysterious and romantic, isn't it? Some army cadet or hack poet may pass by your garden, look up at your windows and think: "There dwells Tamara, the mysterious princess, the one who buried herself alive from love of her husband." Who do you think you're fooling?

MRS. POPOV: [*Flaring up.*] What! You dare to take that line with me!

SMIRNOV: Buries herself alive—but doesn't forget to powder her nose!

MRS. POPOV: You dare adopt that tone!

SMIRNOV: Don't you raise your voice to me, madam, I'm not one of your servants. Let me call a spade a spade. Not being a woman, I'm used to saying what I think. So stop shouting, pray.

MRS. POPOV: It's you who are shouting, not me. Leave me alone, would you mind?

SMIRNOV: Pay up, and I'll go.

MRS. POPOV: You'll get nothing out of me.

SMIRNOV: Oh yes I shall.

MRS. POPOV: Just to be awkward, you won't get one single copeck. And you can leave me alone.

SMIRNOV: Not having the pleasure of being your husband or fiancé, I'll trouble you not to make a scene. [*Sits down.*] I don't like it.

MRS. POPOV: [*Choking with rage.*] Do I see you sitting down?

SMIRNOV: You most certainly do.

MRS. POPOV: Would you mind leaving?

SMIRNOV: Give me my money. [*Aside.*] Oh, I'm in such a rage! Furious I am!

MRS. POPOV: I've no desire to bandy words with cads, sir. Kindly clear off! [*Pause.*] Well, are you going or aren't you?

SMIRNOV: No.

MRS. POPOV: No?

SMIRNOV: No!

MRS. POPOV: Very well then! [*Rings.*]

SCENE 9

The above and LUKE.

MRS. POPOV: Show this gentleman out, Luke.

LUKE: [*Goes up to* SMIRNOV.] Be so good as to leave, sir, when you're told, sir. No point in——

SMIRNOV: [*Jumping up.*] You hold your tongue! Who do you think you're talking to? I'll carve you up in little pieces.

LUKE: [*Clutching at his heart.*] Heavens and saints above us! [*Falls into an armchair.*] Oh, I feel something terrible—fair took my breath away, it did.

MRS. POPOV: But where's Dasha? Dasha! [*Shouts.*] Dasha! Pelageya! Dasha! [*Rings.*]

LUKE: Oh, they've all gone fruit-picking. There's no one in the house. I feel faint. Fetch water.

MRS. POPOV: Be so good as to clear out!

SMIRNOV: Couldn't you be a bit more polite?

MRS. POPOV: [*Clenching her fists and stamping.*] You uncouth oaf! You have the manners of a bear! Think you own the place? Monster!

SMIRNOV: What! You say that again!

MRS. POPOV: I called you an ill-mannered oaf, a monster!

SMIRNOV: [*Advancing on her.*] Look here, what right have you to insult me?

MRS. POPOV: All right, I'm insulting you. So what? Think I'm afraid of you?

SMIRNOV: Just because you look all romantic, you can get away with anything— is that your idea? This is duelling talk!

LUKE: Heavens and saints above us! Water!

SMIRNOV: Pistols at dawn!

MRS. POPOV: Just because you have big fists and the lungs of an ox you needn't think I'm scared, see? Think you own the place, don't you!

SMIRNOV: We'll shoot it out! No one calls me names and gets away with it, weaker sex or no weaker sex.

MRS. POPOV: [*Trying to shout him down.*] You coarse lout!

SMIRNOV: Why should it only be us men who answer for our insults? It's high time we dropped that silly idea. If women want equality, let them damn well have equality! I challenge you, madam!

MRS. POPOV: Want to shoot it out, eh? Very well.

SMIRNOV: This very instant!

MRS. POPOV: Most certainly! My husband left some pistols, I'll fetch them instantly. [*Moves hurriedly off and comes back.*] I'll enjoy putting a bullet through that thick skull, damn your infernal cheek! [*Goes out.*]

SMIRNOV: I'll pot her like a sitting bird. I'm not one of your sentimental young puppies. She'll get no chivalry from me!

LUKE: Kind sir! [*Kneels.*] Grant me a favour, pity an old man and leave this place. First you frighten us out of our wits, now you want to fight a duel.

SMIRNOV: [*Not listening.*] A duel! There's true women's emancipation for you! That evens up the sexes with a vengeance! I'll knock her off as a matter of principle. But what a woman! [*Mimics her.*] "Damn your infernal cheek! I'll put a bullet through that thick skull." Not bad, eh? Flushed all over, flashing eyes, accepts my challenge! You know, I've never seen such a woman in my life.

LUKE: Go away, sir, and I'll say prayers for you till the day I die.

SMIRNOV: There's a regular woman for you, something I do appreciate! A proper woman—not some namby-pamby, wishy-washy female, but a really red-hot bit of stuff, a regular pistol-packing little spitfire. A pity to kill her, really.

LUKE: [*Weeps.*] Kind sir—do leave. Please!

SMIRNOV: I definitely like her. Definitely! Never mind her dimples, I like her. I wouldn't mind letting her off what she owes me, actually. And I don't feel angry any more. Wonderful woman!

SCENE 10

The above and MRS. POPOV.

MRS. POPOV: [*Comes in with the pistols.*] Here are the pistols. But before we start would you mind showing me how to fire them? I've never had a pistol in my hands before.

LUKE: Lord help us! Mercy on us! I'll go and find the gardener and coachman. What have we done to deserve this? [*Goes out.*]

SMIRNOV: [*Examining the pistols.*] Now, there are several types of pistol. There are Mortimer's special duelling pistols with percussion caps. Now, yours here are Smith and Wessons, triple action with extractor, centre-fired. They're fine weapons, worth a cool ninety roubles the pair. Now, you hold a revolver like this. [*Aside.*] What eyes, what eyes! She's hot stuff all right!

MRS. POPOV: Like this?

SMIRNOV: Yes, that's right. Then you raise the hammer and take aim like this. Hold your head back a bit, stretch your arm out properly. Right. And then with this finger you press this little gadget and that's it. But the great thing is—don't get excited and do take your time about aiming. Try and see your hand doesn't shake.

MRS. POPOV: All right. We can't very well shoot indoors, let's go in the garden.

SMIRNOV: Very well. But I warn you, I'm firing in the air.

MRS. POPOV: Oh, this is the limit! Why?

SMIRNOV: Because, because—. That's my business.

MRS. POPOV: Got cold feet, eh? I see. Now don't shilly-shally, sir. Kindly follow me. I shan't rest till I've put a bullet through your brains, damn you. Got the wind up, have you?

SMIRNOV: Yes.

MRS. POPOV: That's a lie. Why won't you fight?

SMIRNOV: Because, er, because you, er, I like you.

MRS. POPOV: [*With a vicious laugh.*] He likes me! He dares to say he likes me! [*Points to the door.*] I won't detain you.

SMIRNOV: [*Puts down the revolver without speaking, picks up his peaked cap and moves off; near the door he stops and for about half a minute the two look at each other without speaking; then he speaks, going up to her hesitantly.*] Listen. Are you still angry? I'm absolutely furious myself, but you must see— how can I put it? The fact is that, er, it's this way, actually—. [*Shouts.*] Anyway, can I help it if I like you? [*Clutches the back of a chair, which cracks and breaks.*] Damn fragile stuff, furniture! I like you! Do you understand? I, er, I'm almost in love.

MRS. POPOV: Keep away from me, I loathe you.

SMIRNOV: God, what a woman! Never saw the like of it in all my born days. I'm sunk! Without trace! Trapped like a mouse!

MRS. POPOV: Get back or I shoot.

SMIRNOV: Shoot away. I'd die happily with those marvellous eyes looking at me, that's what you can't see—die by that dear little velvet hand. Oh, I'm crazy!

Think it over and make your mind up now, because once I leave this place we shan't see each other again. So make your mind up. I'm a gentleman and a man of honour, I've ten thousand a year, I can put a bullet through a coin in mid air and I keep a good stable. Be my wife.

MRS. POPOV: [*Indignantly brandishes the revolver.*] A duel! We'll shoot it out!

SMIRNOV: I'm out of my mind! Nothing makes any sense. [*Shouts.*] Hey, you there—water!

MRS. POPOV: [*Shouts.*] We'll shoot it out!

SMIRNOV: I've lost my head, fallen for her like some damfool boy! [*Clutches her hand. She shrieks with pain.*] I love you! [*Kneels.*] I love you as I never loved any of my twenty-one other women—twelve times it was me broke it off, the other nine got in first. But I never loved anyone as much as you. I've gone all sloppy, soft and sentimental. Kneeling like an imbecile, offering my hand! Disgraceful! Scandalous! I haven't been in love for five years, I swore not to, and here I am crashing head over heels, hook, line and sinker! I offer you my hand. Take it or leave it. [*Gets up and hurries to the door.*]

MRS. POPOV: Just a moment.

SMIRNOV: [*Stops.*] What is it?

MRS. POPOV: Oh, never mind, just go away. But wait. No, go, go away. I hate you. Or no—don't go away. Oh, if you knew how furious I am! [*Throws the revolver on the table.*] My fingers are numb from holding this beastly thing. [*Tears a handkerchief in her anger.*] Why are you hanging about? Clear out!

SMIRNOV: Good-bye.

MRS. POPOV: Yes, yes, go away! [*Shouts.*] Where are you going? Stop. Oh, go away then. I'm so furious! Don't you come near me, I tell you.

SMIRNOV: [*Going up to her.*] I'm so fed up with myself! Falling in love like a schoolboy! Kneeling down! It's enough to give you the willies! [*Rudely.*] I love you! Oh, it's just what the doctor ordered, this is! There's my interest due in tomorrow, haymaking's upon us—and *you* have to come along! [*Takes her by the waist.*] I'll never forgive myself.

MRS. POPOV: Go away! You take your hands off me! I, er, hate you! We'll sh-shoot it out!

[*A prolonged kiss.*]

SCENE 11

The above, LUKE *with an axe, the gardener with a rake, the coachman with a pitchfork and some workmen with sundry sticks and staves.*

LUKE: [*Seeing the couple kissing.*] Mercy on us! [*Pause.*]

MRS. POPOV: [*Lowering her eyes.*] Luke, tell them in the stables—Toby gets no oats today.

CURTAIN

1888

ANTON CHEKHOV

On the Injurious Effects of Tobacco[1]

A MONOLOGUE FOR THE STAGE IN ONE ACT

DRAMATIS PERSONA

IVAN IVANOVICH NYUKHIN, *the husband of his wife, who maintains a music school and a boarding school for girls*

The scene is the platform stage of a provincial club.

NYUKHIN: [*Has long burnsides without mustache; dressed in an old, shabby frock coat; enters majestically, bows, and adjusts his waistcoat.*] Dear ladies and, in one way or another, dear gentlemen. [*Combing his burnsides.*] It was proposed to my wife, that I—for the purpose of charity—give a popular lecture of some sort or other. Well, hmm? If it's to be a lecture, then let it be a lecture—it doesn't matter to me anyway. I am not a professor, of course, and I am a stranger to university degrees, but nonetheless, all the same, here am I, for already thirty years without stopping, and it's even possible to say, for the sake of injury to my own health and so on, I've been working on questions of a strictly scientific character, which I turn over in my mind and sometimes even write, can you imagine it, scientific articles; that is, not quite scientific, but which are, excuse the expression, not unlike scientific, as it were. By the way, the other day an enormous article was written by me under the title, "On the Injurious Effects of Certain Insects." My daughters liked it very much, especially the part on bedbugs. I just read it through and tore it up. It doesn't matter, you know, whatever you may write, because you can't do without Persian powder.[2] Bedbugs are even in our piano . . . For the subject of my lecture today I have chosen, so to speak, the injurious effects which come about in humankind by the consumption of tobacco. I myself smoke, but my wife ordered me to lecture today on the injurious effects of tobacco, and, consequently, what else can you say but do it. If it's to be about tobacco, then let it be about tobacco—it doesn't matter to me anyway, and as for you, dear gentlemen, I propose that you treat my present lecture with proper respect, otherwise I can't be held responsible for the way it turns out. Be there anyone here who is intimidated by the dry, scientific lecture, or who just doesn't like it, then that person need not listen and should leave at once. [*Adjusts his waistcoat.*] I especially ask the attention of the gentlemen present here who are doctors, who may draw from my lecture a good deal of

---

1. This monologue was originally published in Chekhov's *Collected Works* (*Sobranie sočinenij*), XIV, in 1903 and is the last version written by him, supposedly in September 1902. This translation is by Eugene K. Bristow, from *O vrede tabaka*, as published in *Collected Works*, IX, 602–06.
2. An insecticide to ward off bugs.

useful information, since tobacco, apart from its injurious activities, is also utilized in medicine. Thus, for example, if a fly is placed in a snuffbox, then it will expire, in all likelihood, from nervous disorder. Tobacco is, for the most part, a plant . . . When I lecture, I usually wink my right eye, but don't pay any attention to it; it comes from nervous excitement.[3] I am a very nervous person, generally speaking, but my eye began to wink in the year eighteen hundred and eighty-nine, on the thirteenth of September, the very same day that my wife gave birth, in one way or another, to her fourth daughter, Varvara. All my daughters were born on the thirteenth. Or rather [*Having glanced at his watch.*], in view of the shortage of time, we dare not wander away from the subject of the lecture. It should be pointed out to you, my wife maintains a music school and a private boarding school; that is, not quite a boarding school, but which is not unlike something of that sort. Confidentially speaking, my wife likes to complain about the lack of money, but she's socked away a little something, some forty or fifty thousand, and I don't have a kopek to my soul, not even part of one—well, what's the use of talking about it! In the boarding school, I am the head of the housekeeping department. I buy provisions, check up on the servants, write down the expenses, bind and stitch notebooks, exterminate bedbugs, walk my wife's little dog, catch mice . . . Yesterday evening my duty lay in issuing to the cook butter and flour, because pancakes were intended. Well, sir, to put it in one word, today, when the pancakes had already been fried, my wife came to the cook and said that three pupils would not be eating pancakes, because they had swollen glands. In this way it turned out that we had fried several superfluous pancakes. What were we supposed to do with them? At first, my wife ordered them to be carried to the cellar, but then she thought; she thought and said: "Eat these pancakes yourself, you sloppy dummy." When she's out of sorts, that's what she calls me: sloppy dummy, or asp, or Satan. What kind of Satan am I, anyway? She is always out of sorts. And I didn't eat them, but I stuffed them down without chewing, because I am always hungry. Yesterday, for example, she didn't give me anything for dinner. "You sloppy dummy," she said, "What's the use of feeding you . . ." Still, however [*Looks at his watch.*], we've forgotten ourselves and have wandered somewhat away from our subject. Shall we continue. Though, of course, you'd be much more inclined now to listen to a love song, or some sort of symphony or other, or an aria . . . [*Sings and conducts.*] "In the thick of battle we do not bat an eye . . ." I can't really remember where that's from . . . By the way, I forgot to tell you that in the music school belonging to my wife, in addition to running the housekeeping department, my duties also include the teaching of mathematics, physics, chemistry, geography, history, solfeggio, literature, and so on. For dancing, singing, and drawing, my wife charges a special fee, though I'm also the one who teaches dancing and singing. Our music school is located in Five Dog Lane, number thirteen. That's why, in all likelihood, my life is so unfortunate, since the number of the house we live in is thirteen. And my daughters were born on the thirteenth, and in our

---

3. *Èto ot volnenija*; literally, "it's from agitation."

house we have thirteen windows . . . Well, what's the use of talking about it! As to negotiations, it's possible to find my wife at home anytime, and the prospectus of the school, if you like, is sold by the porter at the door at thirty kopeks a copy. [*Takes several brochures out of his pocket.*] And here am I, if you like, able to share. Only thirty kopeks a copy! Who'd like one? [*Pause.*] No one wants a copy? Well, what about twenty kopeks! [*Pause.*] Isn't that the limit. Yes, house number thirteen! Nothing comes through for me, I'm putting on years, becoming stupid . . . Here am I giving a lecture, I look like I'm cheerful, but inside myself I'd like to cry out in full voice or fly away somewhere or other to the end of the world. And there's no one at all to complain to, I even want to start crying . . . You will say: your daughters . . . What daughters? I talk to them, but they only laugh . . . My wife has seven daughters . . . No, I'm sorry, it seems there are six . . . [*Quickly.*] Seven! The oldest of them, Anna, is twenty-seven; the youngest, seventeen. Dear gentlemen! [*Looks around.*] I'm not happy, I've turned into a fool, a nonentity; but, in reality, you see before you the happiest of fathers. In reality, that's as it should be, and I dare not say otherwise. If only you knew! I've lived with my wife thirty-three years, and I can say those were the best years of my life, oh, by no means the best, but in general, that is. They've flown by, to put it in one word, like one twinkling, happy moment. As a matter of fact, damn them all, damn them to hell. [*Looks around.*] Or rather she, of course, still hasn't arrived, she isn't here, and it's possible to say whatever I like . . . I get terribly frightened . . . frightened when she looks at me. Well, like I was saying: my daughters have taken so long in getting married, because, in all likelihood, they are shy and because men never see them. My wife doesn't want to give parties, she never invites anyone to dinners, she is as tightfisted as they come, a bilious and pugnacious lady, and that's why no one ever stops by our place, but . . . I can let you in on a secret . . . [*Walks closer to the footlights.*] It's possible to see the daughters of my wife on high holidays at the home of their aunt, Natalya Semyonovna, the very same person who suffers from rheumatism and goes around in that yellow dress with black dots, just as if cockroaches were splattered all over her. Refreshments are handed out there, too. And when my wife isn't around there, then it's possible for this . . . [*Smacks himself on the neck.*] It should be pointed out to you, I get drunk on one glass, and from this comes such a good feeling in my soul, and at the same time, such sorrow that I can't possibly express; for some reason, memories of my youth come back, and for some reason, the longing to run away, oh, if you only knew, how much the longing! [*Carried away.*] To run away, to throw everything down, and to run without once looking back . . . Where to? It doesn't matter where . . . if only to run away from this rotten, vulgar, cheap life, which has turned me into an old, pitiful fool, an old, pitiful idiot, to run away from this stupid, petty, malicious, malicious, malicious money-grubber, from my wife, who tortured me for thirty-three years, to run away from music, from the kitchen, from the wife's money, from all this nonsense, pettiness and vulgarity . . . and to stop somewhere far, far away in the field and to stand there like a tree, a post, a garden scarecrow, under the wide sky, and the whole night through, watch how the silent, bright moon is hanging

over you, and to forget, to forget[4] . . . Oh, how I long to remember nothing!
. . How much I long to tear off this obscene old frock coat I wore thirty years
ago at my wedding . . . [*Tears off his frock coat.*], in which I constantly give
lectures for the purposes of charity . . . That's for you! [*Stamps on the frock
coat.*] That's for you! I am old, poor, dilapidated, like this very same waistcoat
with its shabby, used-up old back . . . [*Shows the back.*] I don't need anything!
I'm superior to this, more clean and pure. Once upon a time I was young,
intelligent, I studied at the university, I had dreams, I took for granted I was
a human being . . . Now I don't need anything! Nothing except peace . . .
except peace! [*Having glanced to the side, quickly puts on the frock coat.*]
However, my wife is standing in the wings . . . She has arrived and is waiting
for me there . . . [*Looks at his watch.*] Time has already passed . . . If she
asks, then, please, I beg you, tell her that the lecture was . . . that the sloppy
dummy, that is, I, conducted himself with dignity. [*Looks to the side, clears
his throat.*] She is looking here . . . [*Having raised his voice.*] Proceeding
from this proposition, that tobacco contains a horrible poison, of which I
have only just spoken, under no circumstances is it proper to smoke, and I
permit myself, in one way or another, to hope that this my lecture, "On the
Injurious Effects of Tobacco," will be of service. I have said everything. *Dixi
et animam levavi!*[5] [*Bows and majestically leaves.*]

1902

ANTON CHEKHOV

The Cherry Orchard[1]

A COMEDY IN FOUR ACTS

CHARACTERS

MRS. LYUBA RANEVSKY, *an estate-owner*

ANYA, *her daughter, aged* 17

VARYA, *her adopted daughter, aged* 24

LEONID GAYEV, *Mrs. Ranevsky's brother*

YERMOLAY LOPAKHIN, *a businessman*

PETER TROFIMOV, *a student*

BORIS SIMEONOV-PISHCHIK, *an estate-owner*

CHARLOTTE, *a governess*

SIMON YEPIKHODOV, *a clerk*

DUNYASHA, *a maid*

FIRS, *a manservant, aged* 87

YASHA, *a young manservant*

A PASSER-BY

A STATIONMASTER

A POST OFFICE CLERK

GUESTS *and* SERVANTS

The action takes place on MRS. RANEVSKY's *estate*

4. This last version, although hilarious and ridiculous in parts, is shaped in great measure by Chekhov's introduction of *nastroenie*, or mood; by his heightening of Nyukhin's unconscious hatred for his wife; and by his coupling of both *nastroenie* and hatred with the absurd and farcical action of taking off his coat and stamping on it. By shedding and attempting to destroy his coat, Nyukhin acts out the dream (false) of casting aside his role of henpecked husband and of taking on an entirely new life style.   **5.** "I have spoken and alleviated my soul!"   **1.** Translated by Ronald Hingley.

ACT I

A room which is still known as "the nursery." One of the doors leads to ANYA's *room. Dawn is breaking and the sun will soon be up. It is May. The cherry trees are in bloom, but it is cold and frosty in the orchard. The windows of the room are shut.*

Enter DUNYASHA *carrying a candle, and* LOPAKHIN *with a book in his hand.*

LOPAKHIN: The train's arrived, thank God. What time is it?

DUNYASHA: Nearly two o'clock. [*Blows out the candle.*] It's already light.

LOPAKHIN: How late was the train then? A couple of hours at least. [*Yawns and stretches himself.*] And a prize idiot I am, making an ass of myself like this. I come out here specially so I can go and meet them at the station, then suddenly fall asleep and wake up too late. Dropped off in the chair. What a nuisance. You might have woken me.

DUNYASHA: I thought you'd gone. [*Listens.*] It sounds as if they're coming.

LOPAKHIN: [*Listening.*] No, they're not. There's the luggage to be got out and all that. [*Pause.*] Mrs. Ranevsky's been living abroad for five years and I've no idea what she's like now. She was always such a nice woman, unaffected and easy to get on with. I remember when I was a lad of fifteen and my father— he's not alive now, but he kept the village shop in those days—punched me in the face and made my nose bleed. We'd come round here for something or other and he had a bit of drink inside him. Mrs. Ranevsky—I can see her now—was still quite a slip of a girl. She brought me over to the wash-stand here in this very room, the nursery as it was. "Don't cry, little peasant," she said. "You'll soon be right as rain." [*Pause.*] Little peasant. It's true my father was a peasant, but here am I in my white waistcoat and brown boots, barging in like a bull in a china shop. The only thing is, I am rich. I have plenty of money, but when you really get down to it I'm just another country bumpkin. [*Turns the pages of his book.*] I was reading this book and couldn't make sense of it. Fell asleep over it. [*Pause.*]

DUNYASHA: The dogs have been awake all night, they can tell the family are coming.

LOPAKHIN: What's up with you, Dunyasha?

DUNYASHA: My hands are shaking. I think I'm going to faint.

LOPAKHIN: You're too sensitive altogether, my girl. You dress like a lady and do your hair like one too. We can't have that. Remember your place.

[YEPIKHODOV *comes in carrying a bunch of flowers. He wears a jacket and brightly polished high boots which make a loud squeak. Once inside the room he drops the flowers.*]

YEPIKHODOV: [*Picking up the flowers.*] The gardener sent these, says they're to go in the dining-room. [*Hands the flowers to* DUNYASHA.]

LOPAKHIN: And you might bring me some kvass.

DUNYASHA: Yes sir. [*Goes out.*]

YEPIKHODOV: There are three degrees of frost this morning and the cherry trees are in full bloom. I can't say I think much of our climate. [*Sighs.*] That I can't. It isn't exactly co-operative, our climate isn't. Then if you'll permit a further observation, Mr. Lopakhin, I bought these boots the day before yesterday and, as I make so bold to assure you, they squeak like something out of this world. What could I put on them?

LOPAKHIN: Leave me alone. I'm tired of you.

YEPIKHODOV: Every day something awful happens to me. Not that I complain, I'm used to it. Even raise a smile.

[DUNYASHA *comes in and hands* LOPAKHIN *the kvass.*]

YEPIKHODOV: I'll be off. [*Bumps into a chair and knocks it over.*] You see. [*With an air of triumph.*] There you are, if you'll pardon my language, that's just the kind of thing I mean, actually. Quite remarkable really. [*Goes out.*]

DUNYASHA: The fact is Yepikhodov has proposed to me, Mr. Lopakhin.

LOPAKHIN: Oh yes.

DUNYASHA: I really don't know what to do. He's the quiet type, only sometimes he gets talking and you can't make head or tail of what he says. It sounds ever so nice and romantic, but it just doesn't make sense. I do sort of like him, and he's crazy about me. He's a most unfortunate man, every day something goes wrong. That's why he gets teased here. They call him "Simple Simon."

LOPAKHIN: [*Pricking up his ears.*] I think I hear them coming.

DUNYASHA: They're coming! Oh, whatever's the matter with me? I've gone all shivery.

LOPAKHIN: Yes, they really are coming. Let's go and meet them. I wonder if she'll know me, we haven't seen each other for five years.

DUNYASHA: [*Agitated.*] I'm going to faint. Oh dear, I'm going to faint.

[*Two carriages are heard driving up to the house.* LOPAKHIN *and* DUNYASHA *hurry out. The stage is empty. Noises begin to be heard from the adjoining rooms.* FIRS, *who has been to meet* MRS. RANEVSKY *at the station, hurries across the stage leaning on a stick. He wears an old-fashioned servant's livery and a top hat. He mutters something to himself, but not a word can be understood. The noises off stage become louder. A voice is heard:* "Let's go through here." *Enter, on their way through the room,* MRS. RANEVSKY, ANYA, *and* CHARLOTTE, *with a small dog on a lead, all dressed in travelling clothes,* VARYA, *wearing an overcoat and a scarf over her head,* GAYEV, SIMEONOV-PISHCHIK, LOPAKHIN, DUNYASHA *carrying a bundle and an umbrella, and other servants with luggage.*]

ANYA: Let's go through here. You remember this room, don't you, Mother?

MRS. RANEVSKY: [*Happily, through tears.*] The nursery!

VARYA: How cold it is, my hands are quite numb. [*To* MRS. RANEVSKY.] Your rooms are just as they were, Mother, the white one and the mauve one.

MRS. RANEVSKY: The nursery! My lovely, heavenly room! I slept in here when I was a little girl. [*Weeps.*] And now I feel like a little girl again. [*Kisses her brother and* VARYA, *and then her brother again.*] Varya hasn't changed a bit, she still looks like a nun. And I recognized Dunyasha. [*Kisses* DUNYASHA.]

GAYEV: The train was two hours late. Pretty good, eh? What price that for efficiency?

CHARLOTTE: [*To* PISHCHIK.] My dog eats nuts too.

PISHCHIK: [*With surprise.*] Extraordinary thing.

[*All go out except* ANYA *and* DUNYASHA.]

DUNYASHA: We've been longing for you to get here. [*Helps* ANYA *off with her overcoat and hat.*]

ANYA: I've travelled four nights without sleep, and now I'm frozen.

DUNYASHA: You left before Easter in the snow and frost. What a difference now. Darling Anya! [*Laughs and kisses her.*] I've been longing to see you again, my precious angel. I must tell you at once, I can't keep it to myself a minute longer——

ANYA: [*Listlessly.*] Whatever is it this time?

DUNYASHA: Yepikhodov—you know, the clerk—proposed to me just after Easter.

ANYA: Can't you talk about something else? [*Tidying her hair.*] I've lost all my hair-pins. [*She is very tired and is actually swaying on her feet.*]

DUNYASHA: I really don't know what to think. He loves me so much, he really does.

ANYA: [*Fondly, looking through the door into her room.*] My own room, my own windows, just as if I'd never been away. I'm home again! I'll get up tomorrow and run straight out into the orchard. Oh, if I could only go to sleep. I didn't sleep at all on the way back, I was so worried.

DUNYASHA: Mr. Trofimov arrived the day before yesterday.

ANYA: [*Joyfully.*] Peter!

DUNYASHA: He's sleeping in the bath-house, in fact he's living there. Afraid of being in the way, he says. [*With a glance at her pocketwatch.*] Someone ought to wake him up, but your sister said not to. 'Don't you wake him,' she said.

[VARYA *comes in. She has a bunch of keys on her belt.*]

VARYA: Dunyasha, go and get some coffee quickly. Mother wants some.

DUNYASHA: I'll see to it at once. [*Goes out.*]

VARYA: Well, thank heavens you're back. You're home again. [*Affectionately.*] My lovely, darling Anya's home again.

ANYA: I've had a terrible time.

VARYA: So I can imagine.

ANYA: I left just before Easter and it was cold then. On the way there Charlotte kept talking and doing those awful tricks of hers. Why you ever landed me with Charlotte——

VARYA: But you couldn't have gone on your own, darling. A girl of seventeen!

ANYA: It was cold and snowing when we got to Paris. My French is atrocious. I find Mother living on the fourth floor somewhere and when I get there she has visitors, French people—some ladies and an old priest with a little book. The place is full of smoke and awfully uncomfortable. Suddenly I felt sorry for Mother, so sorry, I took her head in my arms and held her and just couldn't let go. Afterwards Mother was terribly sweet to me and kept crying.

VARYA: [*Through tears.*] Don't, Anya, I can't bear it.

ANYA: She'd already sold her villa near Menton and had nothing left, nothing at all. I hadn't any money either, there was hardly enough for the journey. And Mother simply won't understand. If we have a meal in a station restaurant she asks for all the most expensive things and tips the waiters a rouble each. And Charlotte's no better. Then Yasha has to have his share as well, it was simply awful. Mother has this servant Yasha, you know, we've brought him with us—

VARYA: Yes, I've seen him. Isn't he foul?

ANYA: Well, how is everything? Have you paid the interest?

VARYA: What a hope.

ANYA: My God, how dreadful.

VARYA: This estate is up for sale in August.

ANYA: Oh my God!

LOPAKHIN: [*Peeping round the door and mooing like a cow.*] Moo-oo-oo. [*Disappears.*]

VARYA: [*Through tears.*] Oh, I could give him such a—. [*Shakes her fist.*]

ANYA: [*Quietly embracing* VARYA.] Has he proposed, Varya? [VARYA *shakes her head.*] But he does love you. Why can't you get it all settled? What are you both waiting for?

VARYA: I don't think anything will come of it. He's so busy he can't be bothered with me, he doesn't even notice me. Wretched man, I'm fed up with the sight of him. Everyone's talking about our wedding and congratulating us, when there's nothing in it at all actually and the whole thing's so vague. [*In a different tone of voice.*] You've got a brooch that looks like a bee or something.

ANYA: [*Sadly.*] Yes, Mother bought it. [*Goes to her room, now talking away happily like a child.*] Do you know, in Paris I went up in a balloon.

VARYA: My lovely, darling Anya's home again.

[DUNYASHA *has returned with the coffee-pot and is making coffee.*]

VARYA: [*Standing near the door.*] You know, darling, while I'm doing my jobs round the house I spend the whole day dreaming. I imagine marrying you off to a rich man. That would set my mind at rest and I'd go off to a convent, then on to Kiev and Moscow, wandering from one holy place to another. I'd just wander on and on. What bliss!

ANYA: The birds are singing in the orchard. What time is it?

VARYA: It must be nearly three. Time you were asleep, dear. [*Going into* ANYA's *room.*] What bliss!

[*Enter* YASHA *with a rug and a travelling bag.*]

YASHA: [*Crossing the stage and speaking in a refined manner.*] Is one permitted to pass this way?

DUNYASHA: I wouldn't have known you, Yasha. You've changed so much since you've been abroad.

YASHA: H'm! And who might you be?

DUNYASHA: When you left here I was no bigger than this. [*Shows her height from the floor.*] I'm Dunyasha, Theodore Kozoyedov's daughter. You won't remember me.

YASHA: H'm! Tasty little morsel. [*Looks round, then embraces her. She gives a squeak and drops a saucer.* YASHA *hurries out.*]

VARYA: [*In the doorway, speaking angrily.*] What is it now?

DUNYASHA: [*Through tears.*] I've broken a saucer.

VARYA: That's supposed to be lucky.

ANYA: [*Coming out of her room.*] Someone ought to let Mother know that Peter's here.

VARYA: I told them not to wake him up.

ANYA: [*Thoughtfully.*] It's six years since Father died. And a month after that our brother Grisha was drowned in the river. He was a lovely little boy, only seven years old. It was too much for Mother, she went away, just dropped everything and went. [*Shudders.*] How well I understand her, if only she knew. [*Pause.*] Peter Trofimov was Grisha's tutor, he might bring back memories.

[FIRS *comes in wearing a jacket and a white waistcoat.*]

FIRS: [*Goes to the coffee-pot, anxiously.*] The mistress is going to have her coffee here. [*Puts on white gloves.*] Is it made? [*To* DUNYASHA, *sternly.*] You there! What about the cream?

DUNYASHA: Oh, goodness me. [*Goes out quickly.*]

FIRS: [*Fussing around the coffee-pot.*] The girl's a nincompoop. [*Muttering to himself.*] They've come from Paris. There was a time when the old master used to go to Paris, went by carriage. [*Laughs.*]

VARYA: What is it, Firs?

FIRS: Beg pardon, Miss Varya? [*Happily.*] The mistress is home. Home at last. Now I can die happy. [*Weeps with joy.*]

[*Enter* MRS. RANEVSKY, GAYEV *and* SIMEONOV-PISHCHIK, *the last wearing a sleeveless coat of fine cloth and wide trousers tucked inside his boots. As he comes in,* GAYEV *moves his arms and body as if making billiard shots.*]

MRS. RANEVSKY: How does it go now? Let me remember. "Pot the red in the corner. Double into the middle."

GAYEV: Screw shot into the corner. At one time, dear sister, we both used to sleep in this room. And now I'm fifty-one, unlikely as it may sound.

LOPAKHIN: Yes, time marches on.

GAYEV: What's that?

LOPAKHIN: Time. It marches on, I was saying.

GAYEV: This place smells of cheap scent.

ANYA: I'm going to bed. Good night, Mother. [*Kisses her mother.*]

MRS. RANEVSKY: My own beautiful little baby. [*Kisses* ANYA's *hands.*] Are you glad to be home? I still can't get used to it.

ANYA: Good night, Uncle.

GAYEV: [*Kissing her face and hands.*] God bless you. You look so like your mother. [*To his sister.*] You were just like her at that age, Lyuba.

[ANYA *shakes hands with* LOPAKHIN *and* PISHCHIK, *goes out and shuts the door behind her.*]

MRS. RANEVSKY: She's completely worn out.

PISHCHIK: Yes, it must have been a long journey.

VARYA: [*To* LOPAKHIN *and* PISHCHIK.] Well, gentlemen? It's nearly three o'clock. Time you were on your way.

MRS. RANEVSKY: [*Laughing.*] Varya, you haven't changed a bit. [*Draws* VARYA *towards her and kisses her.*] I'll just drink this coffee, then we'll all go. [FIRS *puts a hassock under her feet.*] Thank you, my dear. I've got used to coffee, I drink it day and night. Thank you, dear old friend. [*Kisses* FIRS.]

VARYA: I'll go and see if they've brought all the luggage. [*Goes out.*]

MRS. RANEVSKY: Is it really me sitting here? [*Laughs.*] I feel like dancing and waving my arms about. [*Covers her face with her hands.*] But perhaps I'm only dreaming. God knows, I love my country, I love it dearly. I couldn't see anything from the train, I was crying so much. [*Through tears.*] But I must drink my coffee. Thank you, Firs. Thank you, dear old friend. I'm so glad you're still alive.

FIRS: The day before yesterday.

GAYEV: He's a bit deaf.

LOPAKHIN: I have to leave for Kharkov soon, about half past four. What a nuisance. I'd like to have seen a bit more of you and had a talk. You're just as wonderful as ever.

PISHCHIK: [*Breathes heavily.*] Even prettier. In that Parisian outfit. Well and truly bowled me over, and no mistake.

LOPAKHIN: This brother of yours calls me a lout of a peasant out for what I can get, but that doesn't bother me a bit. Let him talk. You just believe in me as you used to, that's all I ask, and look at me in the old way, with those wonderful, irresistible eyes. Merciful heavens! My father was a serf, belonged to your father and your grandfather before him. But you—you've done so much for me in the past that I've forgotten all that and love you as a brother. Or even more.

MRS. RANEVSKY: I can't sit still, I really can't. [*Jumps up and walks about in great excitement.*] I'll die of happiness. Laugh at me if you want, I'm silly. My own dear little book-case. [*Kisses the book-case.*] My own little table——

GAYEV: Nanny died while you were abroad.

MRS. RANEVSKY: [*Sitting down and drinking her coffee.*] Yes, God rest her soul. Someone wrote to me about it.

GAYEV: Anastasy has died too. Petrushka—remember the chap with the squint?—left me for another job, he's with the chief of police in town now. [*Takes a packet of sweets from his pocket and sucks one.*]

PISHCHIK: My daughter Dashenka sends her regards.

LOPAKHIN: I feel I want to tell you something nice and cheerful. [*With a glance at his watch.*] I'm just leaving and there isn't time to say much. Anyway, I'll be brief. As you know, the cherry orchard's being sold to pay your debts and the auction's on the twenty-second of August. But you needn't worry, dear friend, you can sleep in peace because there's a way out. Here's my plan. Please listen carefully. Your estate's only twelve miles or so from town and the new railway isn't far away. If you divide the cherry orchard and the land along the river into building plots and lease them out for summer cottages you'll have a yearly income of at least twenty-five thousand roubles.

GAYEV: Oh really, what rubbish.

MRS. RANEVSKY: I don't quite follow you, Yermolay.

LOPAKHIN: You'll get at least ten roubles an acre from your tenants every year. And if you advertise right away I bet you anything you won't have a scrap of land left by autumn, it'll all be snapped up. In fact I congratulate you. You're saved. The situation's magnificent and there's a good depth of river. But of course you will have to do a spot of tidying and clearing up. For instance, you'll have to pull down all the old buildings, let's say, and this house—it's no more use anyway, is it?—and cut down the old cherry orchard——

MRS. RANEVSKY: Cut it down? My dear man, forgive me, you don't know what you're talking about. If there's one interesting, in fact quite remarkable, thing in the whole county it's our cherry orchard.

LOPAKHIN: The only remarkable thing about that orchard is its size. It only gives a crop every other year and then no one knows what to do with the cherries. Nobody wants to buy them.

GAYEV: This orchard is even mentioned in the Encyclopaedia.

LOPAKHIN: [*With a glance at his watch.*] If we don't make a plan and get something decided, that orchard—and the whole estate with it—is going to be auctioned on the twenty-second of August, you can make up your minds to that. There's no other way out, you can take it from me. And that's flat.

FIRS: In the old days, forty or fifty years ago, the cherries used to be dried, preserved and bottled. They used to make jam out of them, and time was——

GAYEV: Be quiet please, Firs.

FIRS: Time was when dried cherries used to be sent to Moscow and Kharkov by the wagon-load. They fetched a lot of money. Soft and juicy those dried cherries were, sweet and tasty. People had the knack of it in those days.

MRS. RANEVSKY: But where's the recipe now?

FIRS: Forgotten. No one remembers it.

PISHCHIK: [*To* MRS. RANEVSKY.] How are things in Paris, eh? Eat any frogs?

MRS. RANEVSKY: I ate crocodiles.

PISHCHIK: Extraordinary thing.

LOPAKHIN: Until lately everyone in the countryside was a gentleman or a peasant, but now there are these holiday visitors as well. All our towns, even the smallest, are surrounded by summer cottages nowadays. And it looks as though in twenty years or so there are going to be fantastic numbers of these holiday-makers. So far your holiday-maker only has his tea on the balcony, but he may very well start growing things on his bit of land and then this cherry orchard will become a happy, rich, prosperous place.

GAYEV: [*Indignantly.*] That's all rubbish.

[*Enter* VARYA *and* YASHA.]

VARYA: Two telegrams came for you, Mother. [*Picks out a key and unlocks the old-fashioned book-case with a jingling noise.*] Here you are.

MRS. RANEVSKY: They're from Paris. [*Tears them up without reading them.*] I've finished with Paris.

GAYEV: Lyuba, do you know how old this book-case is? Last week I pulled out the bottom drawer and saw some figures burnt on it. This book-case was made exactly a hundred years ago. Not bad, eh? We might celebrate its centenary. It's an inanimate object, but all the same it is a book-case, you can't get away from that.

PISHCHIK: [*In amazement.*] A hundred years. Extraordinary thing.

GAYEV: Yes, this really is quite something. [*Feeling round the book-case.*] Dear and most honoured book-case. In you I salute an existence devoted for over a hundred years to the glorious ideals of virtue and justice. In the course of the century your silent summons to creative work has never faltered, upholding [*Through tears.*] in several generations of our line confidence and faith in a better future and fostering in us the ideals of virtue and social consciousness. [*Pause.*]

LOPAKHIN: Yes.

MRS. RANEVSKY: Dear Leonid, you haven't changed a bit.

GAYEV: [*Somewhat embarrassed.*] In off on the right into the corner. Screw shot into the middle.

LOPAKHIN: [*After a glance at his watch.*] Well, time for me to go.

YASHA: [*Handing some medicine to* MRS. RANEVSKY.] Would you care to take your pills now?

PISHCHIK: Don't ever take medicine, dear lady, it doesn't do any good. Or harm, if it comes to that. Here, give it to me, dearest lady. [*Takes the pills, pours them out on the palm of his hand, blows on them, puts them in his mouth and washes them down with kvass.*] There you are.

MRS. RANEVSKY: [*Terrified.*] You must be crazy!

PISHCHIK: I've taken the lot.

LOPAKHIN: You greedy pig. [*Everyone laughs.*]

FIRS: The gentleman was here at Easter. Ate over a gallon of pickled gherkins. [*Mutters.*]

MRS. RANEVSKY: What's he saying?

VARYA: He's been muttering like this for three years now. We've got used to it.

YASHA: It's a case of *anno domini*.

[CHARLOTTE *crosses the stage wearing a white dress. She is very thin and tightly laced and has a lorgnette attached to her belt.*]

LOPAKHIN: I'm sorry, Miss Charlotte, I haven't had a chance to say hallo. [*Tries to kiss her hand.*]

CHARLOTTE: [*Withdrawing her hand.*] If I let you kiss my hand it'll be my elbow next, then my shoulder——

LOPAKHIN: This is my unlucky day. [*Everyone laughs.*] Do us a trick, Charlotte.

MRS. RANEVSKY: Yes, do us a trick, Charlotte.

CHARLOTTE: Not now. I want to go to bed. [*Goes out.*]

LOPAKHIN: We'll meet again in three weeks. [*Kisses* MRS. RANEVSKY's *hand.*] Good-bye for now. I must go. [*To* GAYEV.] Fare you well [*Kisses* PISHCHIK.] for I must leave you. [*Shakes hands with* VARYA, *then with* FIRS *and* YASHA.] I don't really feel like going. [*To* MRS. RANEVSKY.] Think it over about those cottages, let me know if you decide to go ahead and I'll get you a loan of fifty thousand or so. Give it some serious thought.

VARYA: [*Angrily.*] Oh, do for heaven's sake go.

LOPAKHIN: All right, I'm going. [*Goes.*]

GAYEV: Ill-bred lout. Oh, I beg your pardon, Varya's going to marry him. He's Varya's "young man."

VARYA: Don't overdo it, Uncle.

MRS. RANEVSKY: But I should be only too pleased, Varya. He's such a nice man.

PISHCHIK: A most worthy fellow. Got to hand it to him. My daughter Dashenka says so too. She says all sorts of things actually. [*Gives a snore, but wakes up again straight away.*] By the way, dear lady, can you lend me two hundred and forty roubles? I've interest to pay on a mortgage tomorrow.

VARYA: [*Terrified.*] We haven't got it. Really.

MRS. RANEVSKY: Honestly, I've no money at all.

PISHCHIK: It'll turn up. [*Laughs.*] Never say die. The times I've thought, "This is the end of me, I'm finished." And then, lo and behold, they run a railway line over my land or something and I get some money. And sooner or later something will turn up this time, you'll see. Dashenka will win two hundred thousand. She has a ticket in the lottery.

MRS. RANEVSKY: I've finished my coffee. Now for some rest.

FIRS: [*Reprovingly, brushing* GAYEV's *clothes.*] You've got the wrong trousers on again. What am I to do with you?

VARYA: [*In a low voice.*] Anya's asleep. [*Quietly opens a window.*] The sun's up now and it's not cold. Look, Mother, what marvellous trees! And the air is glorious. The starlings are singing.

GAYEV: [*Opening another window.*] The orchard is white all over. Lyuba, you haven't forgotten that long avenue, have you? It runs on and on, straight as an arrow. And it gleams on moonlit nights, remember? You can't have forgotten?

MRS. RANEVSKY: [*Looking through the window at the orchard.*] Oh, my childhood, my innocent childhood! This is the nursery where I slept and I used to look out at the orchard from here. When I woke up every morning happiness awoke with me, and the orchard was just the same in those days. Nothing's changed. [*Laughs happily.*] White! All white! Oh, my orchard! After the damp, dismal autumn and the cold winter here you are, young again and full of happiness. The angels in heaven have not forsaken you. If I could only shake off the heavy burden that weighs me down, if only I could forget my past.

GAYEV: Yes, and now the orchard's to be sold to pay our debts, unlikely as it may sound.

MRS. RANEVSKY: Look! Mother's walking in the orchard. In a white dress. [*Laughs happily.*] It's Mother.

GAYEV: Where?

VARYA: Really, Mother, what things you say!

MRS. RANEVSKY: There's no one there, I just imagined it. On the right at the turning to the summer-house there's a little white tree which has leant over, it looks like a woman.

[*Enter* TROFIMOV. *He is dressed in a shabby student's uniform and wears spectacles.*]

MRS. RANEVSKY: What a superb orchard! The great banks of white blossom, the blue sky——

TROFIMOV: Mrs. Ranevsky! [*She looks round at him.*] I'll just pay my respects and go away at once. [*Kisses her hand with great feeling.*] I was told to wait till later in the morning, but I was too impatient.

[MRS. RANEVSKY *looks at him in bewilderment.*]

VARYA: [*Through tears.*] This is Peter Trofimov.

TROFIMOV: I'm Peter Trofimov. I was Grisha's tutor. Can I have changed so much?

[MRS. RANEVSKY *embraces him and weeps quietly.*]

GAYEV: [*Embarrassed.*] There, Lyuba, don't cry.

VARYA: [*Weeping.*] I did tell you to wait till later, Peter.

MRS. RANEVSKY: Grisha, my—my little boy. Grisha, my son——

VARYA: It can't be helped, Mother, it was God's will.

TROFIMOV: [*Gently, through tears.*] Don't cry. Please don't.

MRS. RANEVSKY: [*Weeping quietly.*] I lost my little boy—drowned. Why? Why did it happen, my dear? [*In a quieter voice.*] Anya's asleep in there and here I am raising my voice and making all this noise. Well, Peter? Why have you grown so ugly? And why do you look so old?

TROFIMOV: A woman in the train called me "that seedy-looking gent."

MRS. RANEVSKY: You were only a boy in those days, just a nice little undergraduate. But now you're losing your hair and wear these spectacles. You can't still be a student, surely? [*Moves towards the door.*]

TROFIMOV: I'll obviously be a student for the rest of time.

MRS. RANEVSKY: [*Kisses her brother and then* VARYA.] Well, go to bed then. You look older too, Leonid.

PISHCHIK: [*Follows her.*] So we're off to bed now. Oh dear, my gout. I'd better stay the night here. And to-morrow morning, Lyuba my sweetheart, that little matter of two hundred and forty roubles.

GAYEV: Can't he think about anything else?

PISHCHIK: Two hundred and forty roubles to pay the interest on my mortgage.

MRS. RANEVSKY: But I've no money, my dear man.

PISHCHIK: I'll pay you back, dearest lady. A trifling sum.

MRS. RANEVSKY: All right then, Leonid will let you have it. Leonid, give him the money.

GAYEV: What, me give it him? Not likely!

MRS. RANEVSKY: Let him have it, what else can we do? He needs it, he'll pay us back.

[MRS. RANEVSKY, TROFIMOV, PISHCHIK *and* FIRS *go out.* GAYEV, VARYA, *and* YASHA *remain behind.*]

GAYEV: My sister hasn't lost her habit of throwing money about. [*To* YASHA.] Out of the way, my man, you smell like a farmyard.

YASHA: [*With an ironical grin.*] You haven't changed a bit, Mr. Gayev sir.

GAYEV: What's that? [*To* VARYA.] What did he say?

VARYA: [*To* YASHA.] Your mother's come from the village. She's been waiting in the servants' quarters since yesterday and wants to see you.

YASHA: Why can't she leave me alone?

VARYA: You—you ought to be ashamed of yourself!

YASHA: What's the big idea? Couldn't she have come tomorrow? [*Goes out.*]

VARYA: Mother's just the same as ever, hasn't changed a bit. She'd give everything away if we let her.

GAYEV: Yes. [*Pause.*] When a lot of different remedies are suggested for a disease, that means it can't be cured. I've been thinking and racking my brains. I have plenty of remedies, any amount of them, and that means I haven't really got one. It would be a good thing if somebody left us some money. It would be a good thing to marry Anya to a very rich man. And it would be a good thing to go to Yaroslavl and try our luck with our aunt the Countess. Aunty is rich, you know, very much so.

VARYA: [*Crying.*] May God help us.

GAYEV: Stop that crying. Aunty's rich enough, but she doesn't like us. To start with, my sister married a lawyer, a social inferior——.

[ANYA *appears in the doorway.*]

GAYEV: She married beneath her, and the way she's behaved—well, she hasn't exactly been a model of propriety, has she? She's a good, kind, splendid person and I love her very much, but make what allowances you like, she's still a loose woman and you can't get away from it. It shows in every movement she makes.

VARYA: [*In a whisper.*] Anya's in the doorway.

GAYEV: What's that? [*Pause.*] Curious thing, there's something in my right eye. Can't see properly. And on Thursday when I was at the County Court——

[ANYA *comes in.*]

VARYA: Why aren't you asleep, Anya?

ANYA: I can't. I just can't get to sleep.

GAYEV: My dear child. [*Kisses* ANYA's *face and hands.*] My little child. [*Through tears.*] You're not my niece, you're an angel, you're everything in the world to me. Do, do believe me.

ANYA: I do believe you, Uncle. Everyone loves and respects you. But, Uncle dear, you should keep quiet, just keep quiet. What were you saying just now about my mother, about your own sister? What made you say it?

GAYEV: Yes, yes. [*Takes her hand and covers his face with it.*] You're quite right, it was dreadful of me. Oh God! God, help me! And that speech I made to the book-case just now. How silly of me. And it was only when I'd finished that I saw how silly it was.

VARYA: It's true, Uncle dear, you oughtn't to talk. Just don't talk, that's all.

ANYA: If you stop talking you'll feel easier in your own mind.

GAYEV: I am silent. [*Kisses* ANYA's *and* VARYA's *hands.*] I am silent. There is something rather important, though. I was at the County Court last Thursday and—well, a lot of us got talking about this and that and about several other things as well. It seems we might manage to borrow some money and pay the interest to the bank.

VARYA: May God help us.

GAYEV: I'm going back there on Tuesday and I'll talk to them again. [*To* VARYA.] Stop that crying. [*To* ANYA.] Your mother's going to speak to Lopakhin and I'm sure he won't let her down. And when you've had a rest you can go and see your great-aunt the Countess at Yaroslavl. This way we'll be tackling the thing from three different directions at once and we simply can't fail. We shall pay that interest, I'm sure of it. [*Puts a sweet in his mouth.*] I give you my word of honour, I swear by anything you like, this estate isn't going to be sold. [*Elatedly.*] As I hope to be happy, I swear it. Here's my hand and you can call me a good-for-nothing scoundrel if I let it come to an auction. I won't, on that I'll stake my life.

ANYA: [*Has reverted to a calmer mood and is happy.*] What a good person you are, Uncle, you're so sensible. [*Embraces him.*] I feel calm now. Calm and happy.

[*Enter* FIRS.]

FIRS: [*Reproachfully.*] Mr. Leonid, sir, you're past praying for. When are you going to bed?

GAYEV: At once, at once. You can go, Firs. It's all right, I'll undress myself. Well, children, bed-time. The details will keep till morning and you go to bed now. [*Kisses* ANYA *and* VARYA.] I'm a man of the eighties. No one has a good word to say for those days, but still I've suffered quite a bit for my convictions, I can tell you. Do you wonder the peasants like me so much? You have to know your peasant of course. You have to know how to——

ANYA: Uncle, you're off again.

VARYA: Uncle dear, do be quiet.

FIRS: [*Angrily.*] Mr. Leonid, sir!

GAYEV: I'm coming, I'm coming. Go to bed. Off two cushions into the middle. Pot the white. [*Goes off with* FIRS *tottering after him.*]

ANYA: I'm not worried now. I don't feel like going to Yaroslavl and I don't like my great-aunt, but I do feel less worried. Thanks to Uncle. [*Sits down.*]

VARYA: We must get to bed. I'm just going. Oh, something unpleasant happened here while you were away. As you know, there's no one living in the old servants' quarters except some of our old folk—Yefim, Polya, Yevstigney, oh yes, and Karp. They began letting odd tramps and people spend the night there. I kept quiet about it. But then I heard of a story they'd spread that I'd said they must be fed on nothing but dried peas. Out of meanness if you please. It was all Yevstigney's doing. All right, I thought. If that's the way things are, then you just wait. I sent for the man. [*Yawns.*] He came. "What's all this?" I said. "You stupid so-and-so." [*Looks at* ANYA]. Anya, dear! [*Pause.*] She's asleep. [*Takes* ANYA *by the arm.*] Come to bed, dear. Come on. [*Leads her by the arm.*] My little darling's gone to sleep. Come on. [*They move off.*]

[A *shepherd's pipe is heard playing from far away on the other side of the orchard.* TROFIMOV *crosses the stage, catches sight of* VARYA *and* ANYA *and stops.*]

VARYA: Sh! She's asleep—asleep. Come on, my dear.

ANYA: [*Quietly, half asleep.*] I'm so tired. I keep hearing bells. Uncle—dear—Mother and Uncle——

VARYA: Come on, dear, come on. [*They go into* ANYA's *room.*]

TROFIMOV: [*Deeply moved.*] Light of my being! My springtime!

CURTAIN

ACT II

In the open country. A small, tumble-down old chapel long ago abandoned. Near it a well, some large stones which look like old tombstones and an old bench. A road can be seen leading to GAYEV's *estate. Dark poplar trees loom on one side and beyond them the cherry orchard begins. There is a row of telegraph poles in the distance and far, far away on the horizon are the dim outlines of a big town, visible only in very fine, clear weather. It will soon be sunset.* CHARLOTTE, YASHA *and* DUNYASHA *are sitting on the bench.* YEPIKHODOV *stands near them playing a guitar, while the others sit lost in thought.* CHARLOTTE *wears a man's old peaked cap. She has taken a shot-gun from her shoulder and is adjusting the buckle on the strap.*

CHARLOTTE: [*Meditatively.*] I haven't any proper identity papers. I don't know how old I am and I always think of myself as a young girl. When I was little, Father and Mother used to go on tour round all the fairs giving performances, and very good ones too. I used to do the dive of death and lots of other tricks. When Father and Mother died a German lady adopted me and began educating me. Well, I grew up and became a governess. But where I come from and who I am I've no idea. Who my parents were I don't know either, very likely they weren't even married. [*Takes a cucumber out of her pocket and starts eating it.*] I don't know anything. [*Pause.*] I'm longing for someone to talk to, but there isn't anyone. I'm alone in the world.

YEPIKHODOV: [*Playing the guitar and singing.*]

"I'm tired of the world and its bustle,
I'm tired of my friends and my foes."

How nice it is to play a mandolin.

DUNYASHA: That isn't a mandolin, it's a guitar. [*Looks at herself in a hand-mirror, and powders her face.*]

YEPIKHODOV: To a man crazed with love it's a mandolin. [*Sings softly.*]

"If only my heart were delighted
By the warmth of an ardour requited."

[YASHA *joins in.*]

CHARLOTTE: The awful way these people sing—ugh! Like a lot of hyenas.

DUNYASHA: [*To* YASHA.] You're ever so lucky to have been abroad, though.

YASHA: Yes, of course. My sentiments precisely. [*Yawns, then lights a cigar.*]

YEPIKHODOV: It stands to reason. Abroad everything's pretty comprehensive like. Has been for ages.

YASHA: Oh, definitely.

YEPIKHODOV: I'm a cultured sort of person and read all kinds of remarkable books, but I just can't get a line on what it is I'm really after. Shall I go on living or shall I shoot myself, I mean? But anyway, I always carry a revolver. Here it is. [*Shows them his revolver.*]

CHARLOTTE: Well, that's that. I'm off. [*Slings the gun over her shoulder.*] Yepikhodov, you're a very clever man and a most alarming one. Women must be quite crazy about you. Brrr! [*Moves off.*] These clever men are all so stupid, I've no one to talk to. I'm lonely, oh so lonely. I'm on my own in the world, and—and who I am and what I'm for is a mystery. [*Goes out slowly.*]

YEPIKHODOV: Actually, other considerations apart, there's something I really must explain about myself at this juncture, which is that fate treats me most unkindly, like a storm buffeting a small boat. If I'm mistaken—which I allow is possible—why is it, to take a case in point, that I wake up this morning and there, sitting on my chest, is a spider of gigantic proportions? This size. [*Uses both hands to show the size.*] Or I pick up a glass of kvass to have a drink and lo and behold there's something highly improper inside it like a black-beetle. [*Pause.*] Have you ever read Buckle's *History of Civilization?* [*Pause.*] Might I trouble you for the favour of a few words, Miss Dunyasha?

DUNYASHA: All right, carry on.

YEPIKHODOV: I should prefer it to be in private. [*Sighs.*]

DUNYASHA: [*Embarrassed.*] Very well then, only first go and get me my cape. You'll find it in the cupboard or somewhere. It's rather damp out here.

YEPIKHODOV: Oh certainly, I'm sure. At your service. Now I know what to do with my revolver. [*Takes the guitar and goes out strumming it.*]

YASHA: Simple Simon! The man's a fool, between you and me. [*Yawns.*]

DUNYASHA: Heavens, I hope he doesn't go and shoot himself. [*Pause.*] I've grown so nervous and I feel worried all the time. The master and mistress took me in when I was a little girl and now I've lost touch with the way ordinary people live. Look at my hands, as white as white could be, just like a lady's.

Yes, I've become all soft and refined and ladylike and easily frightened. I'm scared of everything. If you deceive me, Yasha, I can't think what it'll do to my nerves.

YASHA: [*Kissing her.*] Tasty little morsel. A girl should know her place, mind. There's nothing I dislike so much as loose behaviour in a girl.

DUNYASHA: I'm so much in love with you. You're so educated, you can talk about anything. [*Pause.*]

YASHA: [*Yawning.*] That's true enough. To my way of thinking, if a girl's in love with anybody that proves she's immoral. [*Pause.*] How nice to smoke a cigar out of doors. [*Pricks up his ears.*] There's somebody coming. It's the missis and the others.

[DUNYASHA *embraces him impulsively.*]

YASHA: Go back to the house as if you'd been down to the river for a bathe. Take that path, or else you'll meet them and they'll think we've been walking out together. I can't have that.

DUNYASHA: [*Coughing quietly.*] Your cigar's given me an awful headache. [*Goes off.*]

[YASHA *remains behind, sitting near the chapel. Enter* MRS. RANEVSKY, GAYEV *and* LOPAKHIN.]

LOPAKHIN: You must make up your minds once and for all, time's running out. And anyway it's a perfectly simple matter. Are you prepared to lease your land for summer cottages or aren't you? You can answer it in one word—yes or no. Just one single word.

MRS. RANEVSKY: Who's smoking disgusting cigars round here? [*Sits down.*]

GAYEV: How handy it is now they've built the railway. [*Sits down.*] We've been into town for lunch. Pot the red in the middle. I must go indoors now and have a game.

MRS. RANEVSKY: There's no hurry.

LOPAKHIN: One single word. [*Imploringly.*] Do give me an answer.

GAYEV: [*Yawning.*] What's that?

MRS. RANEVSKY: [*Looking in her purse.*] Yesterday I had lots of money, but I've hardly any left today. My poor Varya tries to save by feeding us all on milk soup and the old servants in the kitchen get nothing but peas to eat, while I go round simply squandering money, I can't think why. [*Drops her purse, scattering some gold coins.*] There, now I've dropped it all. [*Is annoyed.*]

YASHA: Allow me to pick it up, madam. [*Picks up the coins.*]

MRS. RANEVSKY: Please do, Yasha. Oh, whatever made me go out to lunch? That beastly restaurant of yours with its music and tablecloths smelling of soap. Does one have to drink so much, Leonid? Or eat so much? Or talk so much? You talked much too much again in the restaurant today, all most unsuitable stuff about the seventies and the decadent movement. And just think who you were speaking to. Fancy talking about the decadents to the waiters.

LOPAKHIN: Quite so.

GAYEV: [*Making a gesture of dismissal with his hands.*] I'm a hopeless case, obvi-

ously. [*To* YASHA, *irritably.*] Why is it I always see you hanging about everywhere?

YASHA: [*Laughing.*] I just can't help laughing when I hear your voice.

GAYEV: [*To his sister.*] Either he goes or I do.

MRS. RANEVSKY: You may leave, Yasha. Off with you.

YASHA: [*Returning the purse to* MRS. RANEVSKY.] I'll go at once. [*Hardly able to
contain his laughter.*] This very instant. [*Goes out.*]

LOPAKHIN: Do you know who's thinking of buying your property? A rich man
called Deriganov. They say he's coming to the auction himself.

MRS. RANEVSKY: Oh? Where did you hear that?

LOPAKHIN: It's what they're saying in town.

GAYEV: Our aunt in Yaroslavl has promised to send money, but when she'll send
it and how much it'll be, nobody knows.

LOPAKHIN: How much is she sending? A hundred thousand roubles? Two hundred thousand?

MRS. RANEVSKY: Oh, about ten or fifteen thousand, and we're lucky to get that
much.

LOPAKHIN: With due respect, I've never met anyone as scatterbrained as you two,
or as odd and unbusinesslike either. I tell you in plain language that your
place is up for sale and you can't even seem to take it in.

MRS. RANEVSKY: But what are we to do about it? You tell us that.

LOPAKHIN: I *do* tell you. I tell you every day. Every day I say the same thing over
and over again. The cherry orchard and the rest of the land must be leased
out for summer cottages. You must act at once, without delay, the auction's
almost on top of us. Do get that into your heads. Once you definitely decide
on those cottages you can raise any amount of money and you'll be all right.

MRS. RANEVSKY: Cottages, summer visitors. Forgive me, but all that's so frightfully vulgar.

GAYEV: I entirely agree.

LOPAKHIN: I'm going to burst into tears or scream or faint. This is too much. I've
had about all I can stand! [*To* GAYEV.] You're an old woman.

GAYEV: What's that?

LOPAKHIN: I say you're an old woman. [*Makes to leave.*]

MRS. RANEVSKY: [*Terrified.*] No, don't go away, my dear man. Stay with us, I
implore you. Perhaps we'll think of something.

LOPAKHIN: "Think"? This isn't a question of thinking.

MRS. RANEVSKY: Don't go away, I beg you. Besides, it's more amusing with you
around. [*Pause.*] I keep expecting something awful to happen, as if the house
was going to collapse around our ears.

GAYEV: [*Deep in thought.*] Off the cushion into the corner. Across into the middle——

MRS. RANEVSKY: I suppose we've committed so many sins——

LOPAKHIN: Oh? What sins have you committed?

GAYEV: [*Putting a sweet in his mouth.*] People say I've wasted my substance on
boiled sweets. [*Laughs.*]

MRS. RANEVSKY: Oh, my sins. Look at the mad way I've always wasted money, spent it like water, and I married a man who could do nothing but run up debts. My husband died of champagne, he drank like a fish, and then I had the bad luck to fall in love with someone else and have an affair with him. And just then came my first punishment, and what a cruel blow that was! In the river here—. My little boy was drowned and I went abroad, went right away, never meaning to return or see the river again. I shut my eyes and ran away, not knowing what I was doing, and *he* followed me. It was a cruel, brutal thing to do. I bought a villa near Menton because he fell ill there and for three years I had no rest, nursing him day and night. He utterly wore me out. All my feelings seemed to have dried up inside me. Then last year, when the villa had to be sold to pay my debts, I left for Paris where he robbed me, deserted me and took up with another woman. I tried to poison myself. It was all so stupid and humiliating. Then I suddenly longed to be back in Russia, back in my own country with my little girl. [*Dries her eyes.*] Lord, Lord, be merciful, forgive me my sins. Don't punish me any more. [*Takes a telegram from her pocket.*] This came from Paris today. He asks my forgiveness and begs me to go back. [*Tears up the telegram.*] Isn't that music I hear? [*Listens.*]

GAYEV: That's our famous Jewish band. You remember, the four fiddles, flute and double-bass?

MRS. RANEVSKY: Are they still about then? We must get them round here some time and have a party.

LOPAKHIN: [*Listening.*] I don't hear anything. [*Sings quietly.*]

> "For a spot of cash your Prussian
> Will frenchify a Russian."

[*Laughs.*] I saw a rather good play at the theatre last night, something really funny.

MRS. RANEVSKY: I don't suppose it was a bit funny. You people shouldn't go and see plays, you should try watching your own performance instead. What drab lives you all lead and what a lot of rubbish you talk!

LOPAKHIN: Quite right. To be honest, the life we lead is preposterous. [*Pause.*] My father was a peasant, an idiot who understood nothing, taught me nothing and just beat me when he was drunk, with a stick too. As a matter of fact I'm just as big a numskull and idiot myself. I never learned anything and my handwriting's awful. A pig could write about as well as I do, I'm ashamed to let anyone see it.

MRS. RANEVSKY: You ought to get married, my friend.

LOPAKHIN: Yes, that's true enough.

MRS. RANEVSKY: Why not marry Varya? She's a very nice girl.

LOPAKHIN: True.

MRS. RANEVSKY: She's a nice simple creature. She works all day long, and the great thing is she loves you. And you've been fond of her for some time too.

LOPAKHIN: All right, I've nothing against it. She is a very nice girl. [*Pause.*]

GAYEV: I've been offered a job in a bank. At six thousand roubles a year. Had you heard?

MRS. RANEVSKY: What, you in a bank! You stay where you are.

[FIRS *comes in with an overcoat.*]

FIRS: [*To* GAYEV.] Please put this on, Mr. Leonid sir. It's damp out here.

GAYEV: [*Putting on the overcoat.*] You are a bore, my dear fellow.

FIRS: We can't have this. Goes off in the morning without so much as a word. [*Inspects him.*]

MRS. RANEVSKY: How you have aged, Firs!

FIRS: Beg pardon, madam?

LOPAKHIN: Your mistress says you look a lot older.

FIRS: Well, I've been alive a long time. They were arranging my wedding before your Dad was so much as thought of. [*Laughs.*] And when the serfs were freed I was already head valet. But I wouldn't have any of their freedom, I stayed on with the master and mistress. [*Pause.*] As I recall, everyone was very pleased, but what they were so pleased about they'd no idea themselves.

LOPAKHIN: Oh, it was a good life all right. At least there were plenty of floggings.

FIRS: [*Not hearing him.*] Yes, those were the days. The serfs had their masters and the masters had their serfs, but now everything's at sixes and sevens and you can't make head or tail of it.

GAYEV: Keep quiet a minute, Firs. I have to go to town tomorrow. I've been promised an introduction to a general who might let us have a loan.

LOPAKHIN: It won't come off and you won't pay the interest either, of that you may be sure.

MRS. RANEVSKY: He's only talking nonsense. There is no such general.

[*Enter* TROFIMOV, ANYA *and* VARYA.]

GAYEV: Ah, here come the children.

ANYA: Look, there's Mother.

MRS. RANEVSKY: [*Affectionately.*] Come, come to me. My darling girls. [*Embracing* ANYA *and* VARYA.] If you only knew how much I love you both. Sit beside me, that's right. [*All sit down.*]

LOPAKHIN: Our eternal student never strays far from the young ladies.

TROFIMOV: Mind your own business.

LOPAKHIN: He's nearly fifty and he's still a student.

TROFIMOV: Oh, stop making these idiotic jokes.

LOPAKHIN: But why so angry, my dear fellow?

TROFIMOV: Can't you leave me alone?

LOPAKHIN: [*Laughing.*] Just let me ask you one question. What's your opinion of me?

TROFIMOV: My opinion of you is simply this, Lopakhin. You're a rich man. You'll soon be a millionaire. Now, as part of the process whereby one form of matter is converted into another, nature needs beasts of prey which devour everything in their path. You fulfil that need. [*Everyone laughs.*]

VARYA: Oh Peter, couldn't you tell us something about the planets instead?

MRS. RANEVSKY: No, let's go on with what we were talking about yesterday.

TROFIMOV: What was that?

GAYEV: Pride.

TROFIMOV: We talked a lot yesterday, but we didn't get anywhere. A proud man in your sense of the word has something mystical about him. You may be right in a way. But if we look at the thing quite simply and don't try to be too clever, then what room is there for pride and what's the sense of it anyway, if in fact man is a pretty poor physiological specimen and if the great majority of the human race is crude, stupid and profoundly miserable? It's time we stopped admiring ourselves. The only thing to do is to work.

GAYEV: We shall all die anyway.

TROFIMOV: Why be so sure of that? And what does it mean anyway, "to die"? Perhaps man has a hundred senses and perhaps when he dies he loses only the five we know, while the other ninety-five live on.

MRS. RANEVSKY: How clever you are, Peter.

LOPAKHIN: [Ironically.] Oh, brilliant!

TROFIMOV: Mankind marches on, going from strength to strength. All that now eludes us will one day be well within our grasp, but, as I say, we must work and we must do all we can for those who are trying to find the truth. Here in Russia very few people do work at present. The kind of Russian intellectuals I know, far and away the greater part of them anyway, aren't looking for anything. They don't do anything. They still don't know the meaning of hard work. They call themselves an intelligentsia, but they speak to their servants as inferiors and treat the peasants like animals. They don't study properly, they never read anything serious, in fact they don't do anything at all. Science is something they just talk about and they know precious little about art. Oh, they're all very earnest. They all go round looking extremely solemn. They talk of nothing but weighty issues and they discuss abstract problems, while all the time everyone knows the workers are abominably fed and sleep without proper bedding, thirty or forty to a room—with bed-bugs everywhere, to say nothing of the stench, the damp, the moral degradation. And clearly all our fine talk is just meant to pull wool over our own eyes and other people's too. Tell me, where are those children's crèches that there's all this talk about? Where are the libraries? They're just things people write novels about, we haven't actually got any of them. What we have got is dirt, vulgarity and squalor. I loathe all these earnest faces. They scare me, and so do earnest conversations. Why can't we keep quiet for a change?

LOPAKHIN: I'm always up by five o'clock, you know. I work from morning till night, and then—well, I'm always handling money, my own and other people's, and I can see what sort of men and women I have around me. You only have to start a job of work to realize how few decent, honest folk there are about. When I can't sleep I sometimes think—the Lord gave us these huge forests, these boundless plains, these vast horizons, and we who live among them ought to be real giants.

MRS. RANEVSKY: You're calling for giants. They're all very well in fairy-tales, but elsewhere they might be rather alarming.

[YEPIKHODOV crosses the back of the stage playing his guitar.]

MRS. RANEVSKY: [*Pensively.*] There goes Yepikhodov.

ANYA: [*Pensively.*] There goes Yepikhodov.

GAYEV: The sun has set, my friends.

TROFIMOV: Yes.

GAYEV: [*In a quiet voice, as if giving a recitation.*] Nature, glorious Nature, glowing with everlasting radiance, so beautiful, so cold—you, whom men call
mother, in whom the living and the dead are joined together, you who give
life and take it away——

VARYA: [*Imploring him.*] Uncle dear!

ANYA: Uncle, you're off again.

TROFIMOV: You'd far better pot the red in the middle.

GAYEV: I am silent. Silent.

> [*Everyone sits deep in thought. It is very quiet. All that can be heard is* FIRS's
> *low muttering. Suddenly a distant sound is heard. It seems to come from the
> sky and is the sound of a breaking string. It dies away sadly.*]

MRS. RANEVSKY: What was that?

LOPAKHIN: I don't know. A cable must have broken somewhere away in the
mines. But it must be a long, long way off.

GAYEV: Or perhaps it was a bird, a heron or something.

TROFIMOV: Or an owl.

MRS. RANEVSKY: [*Shudders.*] There was something disagreeable about it. [*Pause.*]

FIRS: The same thing happened before the troubles, the owl hooting and the
samovar humming all the time.

GAYEV: What "troubles" were those?

FIRS: When the serfs were given their freedom. [*Pause.*]

MRS. RANEVSKY: Come, let's go in, everyone. It's getting late. [*To* ANYA.] You've
tears in your eyes. What is it, child? [*Embraces her.*]

ANYA: It's nothing, Mother. I'm all right.

TROFIMOV: There's somebody coming.

> [*The* PASSER-BY *appears. He wears a shabby, white peaked cap and an over-
> coat. He is slightly drunk.*]

PASSER-BY: Excuse me asking, but am I right for the station this way?

GAYEV: Yes. Follow that road.

PASSER-BY: I'm uncommonly obliged to you. [*With a cough.*] Splendid weather,
this. [*Declaiming.*] "Brother, my suffering brother!" "Come out to the Volga,
you whose groans— ." [*To* VARYA.] Miss, could you spare a few copecks for a
starving Russian?

> [VARYA *takes fright and shrieks.*]

LOPAKHIN: [*Angrily.*] Even where you come from there's such a thing as being
polite.

MRS. RANEVSKY: [*Flustered.*] Here, have this. [*Looks in her purse.*] I've no silver.
Never mind, here's some gold.

PASSER-BY: I'm uncommonly obliged to you. [*Goes off.*]

[*Everyone laughs.*]

VARYA: [*Frightened.*] I'm going. I'm going away from here. Oh Mother, we've no food in the house for the servants and you gave him all that money.

MRS. RANEVSKY: What's to be done with me? I'm so silly. I'll give you all I have when we get home. Yermolay, lend me some more money.

LOPAKHIN: At your service.

MRS. RANEVSKY: Come on, everybody, it's time to go in. Varya, we've just fixed you up with a husband. Congratulations.

VARYA: [*Through tears.*] Don't make jokes about it, Mother.

LOPAKHIN: Amelia, get thee to a nunnery.

GAYEV: My hands are shaking. It's a long time since I had a game of billiards.

LOPAKHIN: Amelia, nymph, in thy orisons, be all my sins remembered.

MRS. RANEVSKY: Come on, all of you. It's nearly supper time.

VARYA: That man scared me. I still feel quite shaken.

LOPAKHIN: May I remind you all that the cherry orchard's going to be sold on the twenty-second of August? You must think about it. Give it some thought.

[*All go off except* TROFIMOV *and* ANYA.]

ANYA: [*Laughing.*] We should be grateful to that man for frightening Varya. Now we're alone.

TROFIMOV: Varya's afraid we might fall in love, so she follows us about for days on end. With her narrow outlook she can't understand that we're above love. To rid ourselves of the pettiness and the illusions which stop us being free and happy, that's the whole meaning and purpose of our lives. Forward then! We are marching triumphantly on towards that bright star shining there far away. On, on! No falling back, my friends.

ANYA: [*Clapping her hands.*] What splendid things you say! [*Pause.*] Isn't it heavenly here today?

TROFIMOV: Yes, it's wonderful weather.

ANYA: What have you done to me, Peter? Why is it I'm not so fond of the cherry orchard as I used to be? I loved it so dearly. I used to think there was no better place on earth than our orchard.

TROFIMOV: All Russia is our orchard. The earth is so wide, so beautiful, so full of wonderful places. [*Pause.*] Just think, Anya. Your grandfather, your great-grandfather and all your ancestors owned serfs, they owned human souls. Don't you see that from every cherry-tree in the orchard, from every leaf and every trunk, men and women are gazing at you? Don't you hear their voices? Owning living souls, that's what has changed you all so completely, those who went before and those alive today, so that your mother, you yourself, your uncle—you don't realize that you're actually living on credit. You're living on other people, the very people you won't even let inside your own front door. We're at least a couple of hundred years behind the times. So far we haven't got anywhere at all and we've no real sense of the past. We just talk in airy generalizations, complain of boredom or drink vodka. But if we're to start living in the present isn't it abundantly clear that we've first got to redeem our past and make a clean break with it? And we can only redeem it by suffering and getting down to some real work for a change. You must understand that, Anya.

ANYA: The house we live in hasn't really been ours for a long time and I mean to leave it, I promise you.

TROFIMOV: If you have the keys of the place throw them in the well and go away. Be free, free as the wind.

ANYA: [Carried away.] How beautifully you put it.

TROFIMOV: Believe me, Anya. Trust me. I'm not yet thirty. I'm young and I'm still a student, but I've had my share of hardship. In winter time I'm always half-starved, ill, worried, desperately poor. And I've been landed in some pretty queer places. I've seen a thing or two in my time, I can tell you. Yet always, every moment of the day and night, I've been haunted by mysterious visions of the future. Happiness is coming, Anya, I feel it. I already see it—

ANYA: [Pensively.] The moon is rising.

[YEPIKHODOV is heard playing his guitar, the same sad tune as before. The moon rises. Somewhere near the poplars VARYA is looking for ANYA and calling, "Anya, where are you?"]

TROFIMOV: Yes, the moon is rising. [Pause.] Here it is! Happiness is here. Here it comes, nearer, ever nearer. Already I hear its footsteps. And if we never see it, if we never know it, what does that matter? Others will see it.

VARYA: [Off stage.] Anya! Where are you?

TROFIMOV: Varya's at it again. [Angrily.] She really is infuriating.

ANYA: Oh well, let's go down to the river. It's lovely there.

TROFIMOV: Come on then. [They move off.]

VARYA: [Off stage.] Anya! Anya!

CURTAIN

ACT III

The drawing-room. Beyond it, through an archway, the ballroom. The chandelier is lit. The Jewish band mentioned in Act II is heard playing in the entrance-hall. It is evening. In the ballroom they are dancing a grand rond. SIMEONOV-PISHCHIK's voice is heard: "Promenade à une paire!" They come into the drawing-room, the first two dancers being PISHCHIK and CHARLOTTE. TROFIMOV and MRS. RANEVSKY form the second pair, ANYA and the POST OFFICE CLERK the third, VARYA and the STATIONMASTER the fourth and so on. VARYA is quietly weeping and dries her eyes as she dances. The last couple consists of DUNYASHA and a partner. They cross the drawing-room. PISHCHIK shouts, "Grand rond, balancez!" and "Les cavaliers à genoux et remerciez vos dames!"

FIRS, wearing a tail-coat, brings in soda-water on a tray. PISHCHIK and TROFIMOV come into the drawing-room.

PISHCHIK: I've got high blood pressure, I've twice had a stroke and it's hard work dancing. Still, as the saying goes, those who run with the pack must wag their tails, even if they can't raise a bark. I'm as strong as a horse, though. My old father—he liked his little joke, God bless him—sometimes spoke about the family pedigree and he reckoned that the ancient line of the Simeonov-Pishchiks comes from a horse, the one Caligula made a senator. [*Sits down.*] Trouble is though, I've no money. A hungry dog thinks only of his supper. [*Snores, but wakes up again at once.*] I'm just the same, can't think of anything but money.

TROFIMOV: You know, you really are built rather like a horse.

PISHCHIK: Well, and why not? The horse is a fine animal. You can sell a horse.

[*From an adjoining room comes the sound of people playing billiards.* VARYA *appears in the ballroom beneath the archway.*]

TROFIMOV: [*Teasing her.*] Mrs. Lopakhin! Mrs. Lopakhin!

VARYA: [*Angrily.*] Seedy-looking gent!

TROFIMOV: Yes, I am a seedy-looking gent and I'm proud of it.

VARYA: [*Brooding unhappily.*] We've gone and hired this band, but how are we to pay them?

[*Goes out.*]

TROFIMOV: [*To* PISHCHIK.] Think of all the energy you've wasted in your time looking for money to pay interest on your loans. If you'd used it on something else you might have turned the world upside down by now.

PISHCHIK: Nietzsche, the philosopher—tremendous fellow, very famous, colossally clever chap—says in his works that there's nothing wrong with forging bank-notes.

TROFIMOV: Have you read Nietzsche then?

PISHCHIK: Well, Dashenka told me about it actually. And the way I'm fixed now, forging a few bank-notes is about my only way out. I have to pay three hundred and ten roubles the day after tomorrow. So far I've got a hundred and thirty. [*Feels his pockets in alarm.*] My money's gone! I've lost my money! [*Through tears.*] Where is it? [*Happily.*] Oh, here it is in the lining. That gave me quite a turn.

[MRS. RANEVSKY *and* CHARLOTTE *come in.*]

MRS. RANEVSKY: [*Hums a Caucasian dance tune, the* Lezginka.] Why is Leonid so long? What can he be doing in town? [*To* DUNYASHA.] Dunyasha, ask the band if they'd care for some tea.

TROFIMOV: Most likely the auction didn't even take place.

MRS. RANEVSKY: What a time to have the band here and what a time to give a party! Oh well, never mind. [*Sits down and hums quietly.*]

CHARLOTTE: [*Handing* PISHCHIK *a pack of cards.*] Here's a pack of cards. Think of a card.

PISHCHIK: All right.

CHARLOTTE: Now shuffle the pack. That's fine. Now give them to me, my dearest Mr. Pishchik. *Ein, zwei, drei!* And now look in your coat pocket. Is it there?

PISHCHIK: [*Taking a card out of his coat pocket.*] The eight of spades, you're quite right. [*In amazement.*] Extraordinary thing.

CHARLOTTE: [*Holding the pack of cards on the palm of her hand, to* TROFIMOV.] Tell me quick, what's the top card?

TROFIMOV: Well, say the queen of spades.

CHARLOTTE: And here she is! [*To* PISHCHIK.] Right. What's the top card now?

PISHCHIK: The ace of hearts.

CHARLOTTE: Correct. [*Claps her hand on the pack of cards, which disappears.*] What fine weather we've had today. [*She is answered by a mysterious female voice which seems to come from under the floor:* "Oh yes, magnificent weather, madam."] Oh you're so nice, quite charming in fact. [*The voice:* "I likes you very much too, madam."]

STATIONMASTER: [*Clapping his hands.*] Hurrah for our lady ventriloquist!

PISHCHIK: [*Astonished.*] Extraordinary thing. Miss Charlotte, you're utterly bewitching, I've quite fallen in love with you.

CHARLOTTE: In love? [*Shrugging her shoulders.*] As if you were capable of love. *Guter Mensch, aber schlechter Musikant.*

TROFIMOV: [*Claps* PISHCHIK *on the shoulder.*] Good for the old horse.

CHARLOTTE: Your attention, please. Another trick. [*Takes a rug from a chair.*] Here's a very fine rug, I'd like to sell it. [*Shakes it.*] Doesn't anyone want to buy?

PISHCHIK: [*Astonished.*] Extraordinary thing.

CHARLOTTE: *Ein, zwei, drei!* [*Quickly snatches up the rug, which she had allowed to fall down, to reveal* ANYA *standing behind it.* ANYA *curtsies, runs to her mother and embraces her, then runs back into the ballroom amid general enthusiasm.*]

MRS. RANEVSKY: [*Claps.*] Well done, well done!

CHARLOTTE: Now for another. *Ein, zwei, drei!* [*Raises the rug. Behind it stands* VARYA, *who bows.*]

PISHCHIK: [*Astonished.*] Extraordinary thing.

CHARLOTTE: The performance is over. [*Throws the rug at* PISHCHIK, *curtsies and runs off into the ballroom.*]

PISHCHIK: [*Hurries after her.*] What a naughty girl! Not bad, eh? Not bad at all. [*Goes out.*]

MRS. RANEVSKY: And still no sign of Leonid. I can't think what he's been up to in town all this time. The thing must be over by now. Either the estate's sold or the auction didn't take place, so why keep us in suspense all this time?

VARYA: [*Trying to console her.*] Uncle's bought it, he must have.

TROFIMOV: [*With a sneer.*] Oh, of course.

VARYA: Our great-aunt sent him the authority to buy it in her name and transfer the mortgage to her. She's doing it for Anya's sake. Uncle will buy it, God willing, I'm sure of that.

MRS. RANEVSKY: Your great-aunt in Yaroslavl sent fifteen thousand to buy the estate in her name—she doesn't trust us—but that much wouldn't even pay the interest. [*Covers her face with her hands.*] My fate, my whole future is being decided today.

TROFIMOV: [*Teasing* VARYA.] Mrs. Lopakhin!

VARYA: [*Angrily.*] Hark at the eternal student. He's already been sent down from the university twice.

MRS. RANEVSKY: Why are you so cross, Varya? If he teases you about Lopakhin, what of it? If you want to marry Lopakhin, do—he's a nice, attractive man. And if you don't want to, don't. Nobody's forcing you, darling.

VARYA: I'm perfectly serious about this, Mother, I must tell you quite plainly. He is a nice man and I do like him.

MRS. RANEVSKY: Well, marry him then. What are you waiting for? That's what I can't see.

VARYA: I can't very well propose to him myself, can I? Everyone's been talking to me about him for the last two years. Everyone goes on and on about it, but he either says nothing or just makes jokes. And I see his point. He's making money, he has his business to look after and he hasn't time for me. If I had just a bit of money myself—even a hundred roubles would do—I'd drop everything and go right away. I'd go to a convent.

TROFIMOV: What bliss!

VARYA: [*To* TROFIMOV.] Our student must show how witty he is, mustn't he? [*In a gentle voice, tearfully.*] Oh, you have grown ugly, Peter, and you do look old. [*She has stopped crying and speaks to* MRS. RANEVSKY.] But I can't stand having nothing to do, Mother, I must be doing something every minute of the day.

[*Enter* YASHA.]

YASHA: [*Hardly able to restrain his laughter.*] Yepikhodov's broken a billiard cue. [*Goes out.*]

VARYA: What is Yepikhodov doing here? And who said he could play billiards? I can't make these people out. [*Goes out.*]

MRS. RANEVSKY: Don't tease her, Peter. Don't you see she's unhappy enough already?

TROFIMOV: She's a great deal too officious. Why can't she mind her own business? She's been pestering me and Anya all summer, afraid we might have a love affair. What's it got to do with her? Not that I ever gave her cause to think such a thing, anyway, I'm beyond such trivialities. We are above love.

MRS. RANEVSKY: While I'm supposed to be beneath it, I imagine. [*Greatly agitated.*] Why isn't Leonid back? If only I knew whether the estate's been sold or not. I feel that such an awful thing just couldn't happen, so I don't know what to think, I'm at my wits' end. I'm liable to scream or do something silly. Help me, Peter. Oh, say something, do, for heaven's sake speak.

TROFIMOV: What does it matter whether the estate's been sold today or not? All that's over and done with. There's no turning back, that avenue is closed. Don't worry, my dear. But don't try and fool yourself either. For once in your life you must face the truth.

MRS. RANEVSKY: What truth? You can see what's true or untrue, but I seem to have lost my sight, I see nothing. You solve the most serious problems so confidently, but tell me, dear boy, isn't that because you're young—not old enough for any of your problems to have caused you real suffering? You face the future so bravely, but then you can't imagine anything terrible happening, can you? And isn't that because you're still too young to see what life's really like? You're bolder, more honest, more profound than we are, but try and put yourself in our place, do show a little generosity and spare my feelings. You see, I was born here, my father and mother lived here, and my grandfather too. I love this house. Without the cherry orchard life has no meaning for me and if it really must be sold then you'd better sell me with it. [*Embraces* TROFIMOV *and kisses him on the forehead.*] My little boy was drowned here, you know. [*Weeps.*] Don't be too hard on me, my good kind friend.

TROFIMOV: As you know, I feel for you with all my heart.

MRS. RANEVSKY: Well, that isn't the way to say it, it really isn't. [*Takes out her handkerchief. A telegram falls to the floor.*] I'm so depressed today, you just can't imagine. I hate all this noise. Every sound sends a shiver right through me. I'm trembling all over, but I can't go to my room, the silence frightens me when I'm on my own. Don't think too badly of me, Peter. I love you as my own son. I'd gladly let Anya marry you, I honestly would, only you really must study, dear boy, you must take your degree. You never do anything, you just drift about from place to place, that's what's so peculiar. Well, it is, isn't it? And you should do something about that beard, make it grow somehow. [*Laughs.*] You do look funny.

TROFIMOV: [*Picks up the telegram.*] I don't pretend to be particularly good-looking.

MRS. RANEVSKY: That telegram's from Paris. I get one every day. One came yesterday and there's another today. That crazy creature is ill and in trouble again. He asks my forgiveness, begs me to come to him, and I really ought to go over to Paris and be near him for a bit. You look very disapproving, Peter, but what else can I do, my dear boy, what else can I do? He's ill, he's lonely and unhappy, and who'll look after him there? Who'll stop him making a fool of himself and give him his medicine at the right time? And then, why make a secret of it, why not say so? I love him, that's obvious. I love him, I love him. He's a millstone round my neck and he's dragging me down with him, but I love my millstone and I can't live without it. [*Presses* TROFIMOV's *hand.*] Don't think badly of me, Peter, and don't say anything, don't talk.

TROFIMOV: [*Through tears.*] Excuse me being so blunt, for heaven's sake, but he did rob you.

MRS. RANEVSKY: No, no, no, you mustn't say that. [*Puts her hands over her ears.*]

TROFIMOV: Why, the man's a swine and you're the only one who doesn't know it. He's a little swine, a nobody——

MRS. RANEVSKY: [*Angry, but restraining herself.*] You're twenty-six or twenty-seven, but you're still a schoolboy.

TROFIMOV: What if I am?

MRS. RANEVSKY: You should be more of a man. At your age you should understand people in love. And you should be in love yourself, you should fall in love. [*Angrily.*] Yes, I mean it. And you're not all that pure and innocent either, you're just a prig, a ridiculous freak, a kind of monster——

TROFIMOV: [*Horrified.*] She can't know what she's saying!

MRS. RANEVSKY: "I am above love!" You're not above love, you're just what our friend Firs calls a nincompoop. Fancy being your age and not having a mistress!

TROFIMOV: [*Horrified.*] This is outrageous. She can't know what she's saying! [*Goes quickly into the ballroom clutching his head.*] It's outrageous. I can't stand it, I'm going. [*Goes out, but immediately comes back.*] All is over between us. [*Goes out into the hall.*]

MRS. RANEVSKY: [*Shouting after him.*] Peter, wait a minute. Don't be silly, I was only joking. Peter!

[*There is a sound of rapid footsteps on the staircase in the hall and then of someone suddenly falling downstairs with a crash.* ANYA *and* VARYA *scream, but this is at once followed by laughter.*]

MRS. RANEVSKY: What's going on out there?

[ANYA *runs in.*]

ANYA: [*Laughing.*] Peter fell downstairs. [*Runs out.*]

MRS. RANEVSKY: What a funny boy Peter is.

[*The* STATIONMASTER *stands in the middle of the ballroom and begins to declaim* The Sinful Woman *by Aleksey Tolstoy. The others listen, but he has only recited a few lines when the sound of a waltz comes from the hall and the recitation is broken off. Everyone dances.* TROFIMOV, ANYA, VARYA, *and* MRS. RANEVSKY *pass through from the hall.*]

MRS. RANEVSKY: Now, Peter. There now, my dear good boy. Please forgive me. Let's dance. [*Dances with* PETER.]

[ANYA *and* VARYA *dance together.* FIRS *comes in and stands his walking-stick near the side door.* YASHA *has also gone in from the drawing-room and is watching the dancing.*]

YASHA: How goes it, old boy?

FIRS: I don't feel so good. We used to have generals, barons and admirals at our dances in the old days, but now we send for the post office clerk and the stationmaster and even they aren't all that keen to come. I feel so frail somehow. The old master, Mr. Leonid's grandfather, used to dose us all with powdered sealing-wax no matter what was wrong with us. I've been taking sealing-wax every day for the last twenty years or more. Maybe that's what's kept me alive.

YASHA: Granddad, you make me tired. [*Yawns.*] It's time you were dead.

FIRS: Get away with you. Nincompoop! [*Mutters.*]

[TROFIMOV *and* MRS. RANEVSKY *dance in the ballroom, then in the drawing-room.*]

MRS. RANEVSKY: Thank you. I think I'll sit down a bit. [*Sits down.*] I'm tired.

[*Enter* ANYA.]

ANYA: [*Excitedly.*] There was someone in the kitchen just now saying the cherry orchard's been sold today.

MRS. RANEVSKY: Sold? Who to?

ANYA: He didn't say. He's gone away now. [*She and* TROFIMOV *dance off into the ballroom.*]

YASHA: It was only some old man's gossip. Nobody from here.

FIRS: And Mr. Leonid hasn't come yet, he's still not back. He's only got his light overcoat on and he'll catch cold, like as not. These young people never stop to think.

MRS. RANEVSKY: Oh, I shall die. Yasha, go and find out who bought it.

YASHA: But he's been gone some time, that old fellow. [*Laughs.*]

MRS. RANEVSKY: [*Somewhat annoyed.*] Well, what's so funny? What are you so pleased about?

YASHA: Yepikhodov really is a scream. The man's so futile. Simple Simon!

MRS. RANEVSKY: Firs, if the estate's sold where will you go?

FIRS: I'll go wherever you tell me.

MRS. RANEVSKY: Why do you look like that? Aren't you well? You ought to be in bed, you know.

FIRS: Oh yes. [*With amusement.*] I go off to bed and then who'll do the serving and look after everything? There's only me to run the whole house.

YASHA: [*To* MRS. RANEVSKY.] Mrs. Ranevsky, may I ask you something, please? If you go back to Paris, do me a favour and take me with you. I can't stay here, that's out of the question. [*Looks round, in an undertone.*] It goes without saying, you can see for yourself, this is an uncivilized country and no one has any morals. Besides it's boring, the food they give you in the kitchen is something awful and on top of that there's old Firs wandering round mumbling and speaking out of turn. Do take me with you. Please.

[*Enter* PISHCHIK.]

PISHCHIK: May I have the pleasure of a little waltz, you ravishing creature? [MRS. RANEVSKY *goes with him.*] But I'll have a hundred and eighty roubles off you, my bewitching friend. That I will. [*Dances.*] Just a hundred and eighty roubles, that's all. [*They go into the ballroom.*]

YASHA: [*Singing softly.*] "Couldst thou but sense the trembling of my heart——"

[*In the ballroom a woman in a grey top hat and check trousers is seen jumping and waving her arms about. Shouts are heard:* "Well done, Charlotte!"]

DUNYASHA: [*Stops to powder her face.*] Miss Anya told me to join in the dancing. There are lots of gentlemen and only a few ladies. But I get giddy when I dance and it makes my heart beat so. I say, Mr. Firs, the man from the post office has just told me something that gave me quite a turn.

[*The music becomes quieter.*]

FIRS: What was that?

DUNYASHA: "You're like a flower," he said.

YASHA: [*Yawning.*] Shockin' ignorance. [*Goes out.*]

DUNYASHA: Like a flower. I'm such a sensitive girl and I like it ever so when people say such nice things.

FIRS: You'll end up in a real old mess.

[*Enter* YEPIKHODOV.]

YEPIKHODOV: You don't seem to want to see me, Miss Dunyasha, I might be an insect or something. [*Sighs.*] Oh, what a life!

DUNYASHA: What do you want?

YEPIKHODOV: Undoubtedly you may be right. [*Sighs.*] But of course, if one looks at things from a certain angle, as I venture to assert if you'll excuse my frankness, you've finally reduced me to a state of mind. I know what I'm up against. Every day something goes wrong, but I got used to that long ago, so I just smile at my fate. You gave me your promise, and though I——

DUNYASHA: Please! Can't we talk about it some other time? And you leave me alone now. I'm in a sort of dream. [*Plays with her fan.*]

YEPIKHODOV: Every day something goes wrong, but, as I make so bold to assert, I just smile. Even raise a laugh.

[VARYA *comes in from the ballroom.*]

VARYA: Are you still here, Simon? Really, you don't listen to anything you're told. [*To* DUNYASHA.] Be off with you, Dunyasha. [*To* YEPIKHODOV.] First you play billiards and break a cue, and now you wander round the drawing-room as if you were a guest.

YEPIKHODOV: You've no right to tell me off, permit me to inform you.

VARYA: I'm not telling you off, I'm just telling you. All you do is drift about from one place to another, you never do a stroke of work. Goodness knows why we keep a clerk at all.

YEPIKHODOV: [*Offended.*] Whether I work or drift about and whether I eat or play billiards, these are questions for older and wiser heads than yours.

VARYA: How dare you talk to me like that! [*Flaring up.*] How dare you! So I don't know what I'm talking about, don't I? Then get out of here! This instant!

YEPIKHODOV: [*Cowed.*] I must ask you to express yourself in a more refined manner.

VARYA: [*Losing her temper.*] Get out of here this instant! Out you go! [*He moves towards the door, and she follows him.*] Simple Simon! You clear out of here! Out of my sight! [YEPIKHODOV *goes out. His voice is heard from behind the door:* "I shall lodge a complaint."] Oh, so you're coming back, are you? [*Picks up the stick which* FIRS *left near the door.*] Come on then. All right—. Come on, I'll teach you. Ah, so you are coming, are you? Then take that. [*Lashes out just as* LOPAKHIN *comes in.*]

LOPAKHIN: Thank you very much.

VARYA: [*Angrily and derisively.*] I'm extremely sorry.

LOPAKHIN: Not at all. Thank you for such a warm welcome.

VARYA: Oh, don't mention it. [*Moves away, then looks round and asks gently.*] I didn't hurt you, did I?

LOPAKHIN: No, it's all right. I'm going to have a whacking great bruise, though.

[*Voices in the ballroom: "Lopakhin's arrived! Yermolay! Mr. Lopakhin!"*]

PISHCHIK: As large as life and twice as natural. [*Embraces* LOPAKHIN.] There's a slight whiff of brandy about you, dear old boy. We're having a pretty good time here too.

[MRS. RANEVSKY *comes in.*]

MRS. RANEVSKY: Is it you, Yermolay? Why have you been so long? Where's Leonid?

LOPAKHIN: We came together. He'll be along in a moment.

MRS. RANEVSKY: [*Agitated.*] Well? Did the auction take place? For heaven's sake speak!

LOPAKHIN: [*Embarrassed and fearing to betray his delight.*] The auction was over by four o'clock. We missed our train and had to wait till half past nine. [*Gives a heavy sigh.*] Oh dear, I feel a bit dizzy. [*Enter* GAYEV. *He carries some packages in his right hand and wipes away his tears with his left.*]

MRS. RANEVSKY: What happened, Leonid? Leonid, please! [*Impatiently, in tears.*] Hurry up! Tell me, for God's sake!

GAYEV: [*Not answering her and making a gesture of resignation with his hand. To* FIRS, *weeping.*] Here, take this, some anchovies and Black Sea herrings. I haven't eaten all day. I've had a frightful time. [*The door into the billiard room is open. The click of billiard balls is heard and* YASHA's *voice: "Seven and eighteen!"* GAYEV's *expression changes and he stops crying.*] I'm terribly tired. Come and help me change, Firs. [*Goes off through the ballroom to his own room followed by* FIRS.]

PISHCHIK: What happened at the sale? For heaven's sake tell us!

MRS. RANEVSKY: Was the cherry orchard sold?

LOPAKHIN: It was.

MRS. RANEVSKY: Who bought it?

LOPAKHIN: I did. [*Pause.*]

[MRS. RANEVSKY *is overwhelmed and would have fallen if she had not been standing near an armchair and a table.* VARYA *takes the keys from her belt, throws them on the floor in the middle of the drawing-room and goes out.*]

LOPAKHIN: I bought it. Just a moment, everybody, if you don't mind. I feel a bit muddled, I can't talk. [*Laughs.*] When we got to the auction Deriganov was already there. Gayev only had fifteen thousand, and straight off Deriganov bid thirty on top of the arrears on the mortgage. I saw how things were going, so I weighed in myself and bid forty. He bid forty-five. I went up to fifty-five. He kept raising his bid five thousand, you see, and I was going up in tens. Anyway, it finished in the end. I bid ninety thousand roubles plus the arrears. And I got it. And now the cherry orchard is mine. Mine! [*Gives a loud laugh.*] Great God in heaven, the cherry orchard's mine! Tell me I'm drunk or crazy, say it's all a dream. [*Stamps his feet.*] Don't laugh at me. If my father and grandfather could only rise from their graves and see what happened, see how their Yermolay—Yermolay who was always being beaten, who could hardly write his name and ran round barefoot in winter—how this same Yermolay bought this estate, the most beautiful place in the world. I've bought the estate where my father and grandfather were slaves, where they weren't even allowed inside the kitchen. I must be dreaming, I must be imagining it all. It can't be true. This is all a figment of your imagination wrapped in the mists of obscurity. [*Picks up the keys, smiling fondly.*] She threw away the keys to show she's not in charge here now. [*Jingles the keys.*] Oh well, never mind. [*The band is heard tuning up.*] Hey, you in the band, give us a tune, I want to hear you. Come here, all of you, and you just watch Yermolay Lopakhin get his axe into that cherry orchard, watch the trees come crashing down. We'll fill the place with cottages. Our grandchildren and our great-grandchildren will see a few changes round here. Music, boys!

[*The band plays.* MRS. RANEVSKY *has sunk into a chair and is weeping bitterly.*]

LOPAKHIN: [*Reproachfully.*] But why, oh why, didn't you listen to me before? My poor dear friend, you can't put the clock back now. [*With tears.*] Oh, if all this could be over quickly, if our miserable, mixed-up lives could somehow hurry up and change.
PISHCHIK: [*Taking him by the arm, in an undertone.*] She's crying. Come into the other room and leave her alone. Come on. [*Takes him by the arm and leads him into the ballroom.*]
LOPAKHIN: Hey, what's up? You in the band, let's have you playing properly. Let's have everything the way *I* want it. [*Ironically.*] Here comes the new squire, the owner of the cherry orchard! [*Accidentally jogs a small table, nearly knocking over the candelabra.*] I can pay for everything. [*Goes out with* PISHCHIK.]

[*There is no one left in the ballroom or drawing-room except* MRS. RANEVSKY, *who sits hunched up, weeping bitterly. The band plays quietly.* ANYA *and* TROFIMOV *come in quickly.* ANYA *goes up to her mother and kneels down in front of her.* TROFIMOV *stays by the entrance to the ballroom.*]

ANYA: Mother! Mother, are you crying? My lovely, kind, good mother. My precious, I love you. God bless you. The cherry orchard's sold, it's gone. That's true, quite true, but don't cry, Mother, you still have your life to live. You're still here with your kind and innocent heart. Come with me, dear, come away. We shall plant a new orchard, more glorious than this one. And when you see it everything will make sense to you. Your heart will be filled with happiness—deep happiness and peace, descending from above like the sun at evening time. And then you'll smile again, Mother. Come, my dear, come with me.

CURTAIN

ACT IV

The scene is the same as in Act I. There are no window-curtains or pictures. Only a few pieces of furniture are left and have been stacked in one corner as if for sale. There is a feeling of emptiness. Suitcases, travelling bags and so on have been piled up near the outside door and at the back of the stage. The voices of VARYA *and* ANYA *can be heard through the door, left, which is open.* LOPAKHIN *stands waiting.* YASHA *is holding a tray with glasses of champagne on it.* YEPIKHO-DOV *is roping up a box in the hall. There is a murmur off stage at the rear, the voices of peasants who have come to say good-bye.* GAYEV's *voice is heard:* "Thank you, my good fellows, thank you very much."

YASHA: Some village people have come to say good-bye. If you ask my opinion, sir, the lower orders mean well, but they haven't got much sense.

[*The murmur of voices dies away.* MRS. RANEVSKY *and* GAYEV *come in through the hall. She is not crying, but she is pale, her face is working and she cannot speak.*]

GAYEV: You gave them your purse, Lyuba. You shouldn't do such things, you really shouldn't.

MRS. RANEVSKY: I couldn't help it, just couldn't help it.

[*Both go out.*]

LOPAKHIN: [*Calling through the door after them.*] Come along, please, come on. Let's have a little glass together before we go. I didn't think of bringing any from town and I could only get one bottle at the station. Come on. [*Pause.*] What's the matter? None of you want any? [*Come back from the door.*] I wouldn't have bought it if I'd known. All right then, I won't have any either. [YASHA *carefully places the tray on a chair.*] You have some, Yasha, anyway.

YASHA: Here's to those that are leaving. And good luck to them that aren't. [*Drinks.*] This champagne isn't the genuine article, you can take it from me.

LOPAKHIN: And at eight roubles a bottle. [*Pause.*] It's damn cold in here.

YASHA: The stoves haven't been lit today. Never mind, we're going away. [*Laughs.*]

LOPAKHIN: What's the joke?

YASHA: I feel so pleased.

LOPAKHIN: It's October now, but it might be summer, it's so fine and sunny. Good building weather. [*Glances at his watch and calls through the door.*] I say, don't forget the train leaves in forty-seven minutes. So we must start for the station twenty minutes from now. Better get a move on.

[TROFIMOV *comes in from outside. He wears an overcoat.*]

TROFIMOV: I think it's time we were off. The carriages are at the door. Damn it, where are my galoshes? They've disappeared. [*Through the door.*] Anya, I've lost my galoshes. I can't find them anywhere.

LOPAKHIN: I've got to go to Kharkov. We're all taking the same train. I'm spending the winter in Kharkov—I've been kicking my heels round here quite
long enough and I'm fed up with doing nothing. I can't stand not working—
look, I don't know what to do with my arms. See the absurd way they flop
about as if they belonged to someone else.

TROFIMOV: We'll soon be gone and then you can get back to your useful labours
again.

LOPAKHIN: Come on, have a drink.

TROFIMOV: Not for me, thank you.

LOPAKHIN: So you're off to Moscow, are you?

TROFIMOV: Yes, I'm seeing them as far as town and going on to Moscow
tomorrow.

LOPAKHIN: I see. Ah well, I daresay the professors haven't started lecturing yet,
they'll be waiting for you to turn up.

TROFIMOV: Oh, mind your own business.

LOPAKHIN: How many years is it you've been at the university?

TROFIMOV: Can't you say something new for a change? That joke's played out.
[Looks for his galoshes.] Look here, you and I may never meet again, so let
me give you a word of advice before we say good-bye. Stop waving your arms
about. Cure yourself of that stupid habit. What's more, all this stuff about
building cottages and working out that the owners will end up as smallhold-
ers—that's just as stupid as waving your arms about. Anyway, never mind, I
still like you. You have sensitive fingers like an artist's and you're a fine,
sensitive person too, deep down inside you.

LOPAKHIN: [Embracing him.] Good-bye, Peter. Thanks for everything. Let me
give you some money for the journey, you may need it.

TROFIMOV: I don't. Why should I?

LOPAKHIN: Because you haven't any.

TROFIMOV: Yes I have, thank you very much. I got some for a translation, it's
here in my pocket. [Anxiously.] But I still can't find my galoshes.

VARYA: [From another room.] Oh, take the beastly things. [Throws a pair of
galoshes on to the stage.]

TROFIMOV: Why are you so angry, Varya? I say, these aren't my galoshes.

LOPAKHIN: I put nearly three thousand acres down to poppy in the spring and
made a clear forty thousand roubles. And when my poppies were in flower,
that was a sight to see. What I'm trying to say is, I've made forty thousand
and I'd like to lend it you because I can afford to. So why turn it down? I'm
a peasant, I put it to you straight.

TROFIMOV: Your father was a peasant and mine worked in a chemist's shop, all
of which proves precisely nothing. [LOPAKHIN takes out his wallet.] Oh, put
it away, for heaven's sake. If you offered me two hundred thousand I still
wouldn't take it. I'm a free man. And all the things that mean such a lot to
you all, whether you're rich or poor—why, they have no more power over
me than a bit of thistledown floating on the breeze. I can get on without
you, I can pass you by. I'm strong and proud. Mankind is marching towards

a higher truth, towards the greatest possible happiness on earth, and I'm in the vanguard.

LOPAKHIN: Will you get there?

TROFIMOV: I shall. [*Pause.*] I'll either get there or show others the way.

[*There is the sound of an axe striking a tree in the distance.*]

LOPAKHIN: Well, good-bye, my dear fellow. It's time to go. You and I look down our noses at each other, but life goes on without bothering about us. When I work for a long time at a stretch I feel a bit calmer, and I too seem to know why I exist. But there are lots of people in Russia, old boy, and why some of them exist is anyone's guess. Oh well, never mind, that's not what makes the world go round. I hear Gayev's taken a job at the bank at six thousand a year. He'll never stick it out, though, he's too lazy.

ANYA: [*In the doorway.*] Mother says would you mind waiting till she's gone before cutting down the orchard.

TROFIMOV: Yes, you really might have shown more tact, I must say. [*Goes out through the hall.*]

LOPAKHIN: Right, I'll see to it. Those people are the limit. [*Goes out after him.*]

ANYA: Has Firs been taken to hospital yet?

YASHA: I told them to this morning. They must have taken him, I reckon.

ANYA: [*To* YEPIKHODOV, *who is passing through the ballroom.*] Simon, please find out if Firs has been taken to hospital.

YASHA: [*Offended.*] I told Yegor this morning. Why keep on and on about it?

YEPIKHODOV: The aged Firs, or so I have finally concluded, is beyond repair. It's time he was gathered to his fathers. As for me, I can only envy him. [*Has placed a suitcase on a hat box and squashed it.*] Oh look, that had to happen. I knew it. [*Goes out.*]

YASHA: [*With a sneer.*] Simple Simon.

VARYA: [*From behind the door.*] Has Firs been taken to hospital?

ANYA: Yes.

VARYA: Then why didn't they take the letter to the doctor?

ANYA: Well, we'll have to send it on after him. [*Goes out.*]

VARYA: [*From the next room.*] Where's Yasha? Tell him his mother's come to say good-bye.

YASHA: [*With an impatient gesture.*] Oh, this is too much.

[*All this time* DUNYASHA *has been busy with the luggage. Now that* YASHA *is alone she goes up to him.*]

DUNYASHA: You might at least look at me, Yasha. You're going away, deserting me. [*Weeps and throws her arms round his neck.*]

YASHA: Why all the tears? [*Drinks champagne.*] I'll be back in Paris in a week. Tomorrow we catch the express and then you won't see us for smoke. I can hardly believe it somehow. *Veev la France!* It doesn't suit me here, this isn't the life for me and that's that. I've seen enough ignorance to last me a lifetime. [*Drinks champagne.*] So why the tears? You be a good girl and then you won't have anything to cry about.

DUNYASHA: [*Powders her face, looking in a hand-mirror.*] Write to me from Paris. You know, I did love you Yasha, I loved you so much. Oh Yasha, I'm such a soft-hearted girl.

YASHA: Somebody's coming. [*Attends to the suitcases, humming quietly.*]

[MRS. RANEVSKY, GAYEV, ANYA *and* CHARLOTTE *come in.*]

GAYEV: We ought to be going, there's not much time left. [*Looks at* YASHA.] Someone round here smells of herring.

MRS. RANEVSKY: We'd better be getting into the carriages in about ten minutes. [*Looks round the room.*] Good-bye, house. Good-bye, dear old place. Winter will pass, spring will come again and then you won't be here any more, you'll be pulled down. These walls have seen a few sights in their time. [*Kisses her daughter with great feeling.*] My treasure, you look radiant, your eyes are sparkling like diamonds. Are you very pleased? You are, aren't you?

ANYA: Oh yes, I am. This is the start of a new life, Mother.

GAYEV: [*Happily.*] It's quite true, everything's all right now. Before the cherry orchard was sold we were all worried and upset, but when things were settled once and for all and we'd burnt our boats, we all calmed down and actually cheered up a bit. I'm working at a bank now, I'm a financier. Pot the red in the middle. And you can say what you like, Lyuba, you're looking a lot better, no doubt about it.

MRS. RANEVSKY: Yes. I'm not so much on edge, that's true. [*Someone helps her on with her hat and coat.*] And I'm sleeping better. Take my things out, Yasha, it's time. [*To* ANYA.] We'll soon be seeing each other again, child. I'm going to Paris and I'll live on the money your great-aunt sent from Yaroslavl to buy the estate—good old Aunty! Not that it'll last very long.

ANYA: You'll come back soon, Mother. You will, won't you? I'm going to study and pass my school exams and then I'll work and help you. We'll read together, won't we, Mother—all sorts of books? [*Kisses her mother's hands.*] We'll read during the autumn evenings. We'll read lots of books and a wonderful new world will open up before us. [*Dreamily.*] Do come back, Mother.

MRS. RANEVSKY: I will, my precious. [*Embraces her daughter.*]

[LOPAKHIN *comes in.* CHARLOTTE *quietly hums a tune.*]

GAYEV: Charlotte's happy, she's singing.

CHARLOTTE: [*Picking up a bundle which looks like a swaddled baby.*] Rock-a-bye, baby. [*A baby's cry is heard.*] Hush, my darling, my dear little boy. [*The cry is heard again.*] You poor little thing! [*Throws the bundle down.*] And please will you find me another job? I can't go on like this.

LOPAKHIN: We'll find you something, Charlotte, don't worry.

GAYEV: Everyone's deserting us. Varya's going, suddenly no one wants us any more.

CHARLOTTE: I haven't anywhere to live in town. I shall have to go away. [*Sings quietly.*] Anyway, I don't care.

[PISHCHIK *comes in.*]

LOPAKHIN: Oh, look who's come! Wonders will never cease.

PISHCHIK: [*Out of breath.*] Phew, I say, let me get my breath back. I'm all in. My good friends—. Give me some water.

GAYEV: Wants to borrow money, I'll be bound. I'll keep out of harm's way, thank you very much. [*Goes out.*]

PISHCHIK: Haven't been here for ages, dearest lady. [*To* LOPAKHIN.] You here too? Glad to see you. Tremendously clever fellow you are. Here. Take this. [*Gives* LOPAKHIN *money.*] Four hundred roubles. That leaves eight hundred and forty I owe you.

LOPAKHIN: [*Amazed, shrugging his shoulders.*] I must be seeing things. Where can you have got it?

PISHCHIK: Just a moment, I'm so hot. Most extraordinary occurrence. Some Englishmen came along and found a kind of white clay on my land. [*To* MRS. RANEVSKY.] And there's four hundred for you, you ravishing creature. [*Hands over the money.*] You'll get the rest later. [*Drinks some water.*] A young fellow on the train was just saying that some great philosopher advises everyone to go and jump off a roof. "Just you jump," he tells them, "and you'll find that solves your problem." [*With astonishment.*] Extraordinary things. More water, please.

LOPAKHIN: But what Englishmen?

PISHCHIK: I've leased them this land with the clay on it for twenty-four years. But now you must excuse me, I can't stay. Must be running along. Going to see Znoykov. And Kardamonov. Owe them all money. [*Drinks.*] And the very best of luck to you. I'll look in on Thursday.

MRS. RANEVSKY: We're just leaving for town and I'm going abroad tomorrow.

PISHCHIK: What! [*Deeply concerned.*] Why go to town? Oh, I see, the furniture and luggage. Well, never mind. [*Through tears.*] It doesn't matter. Colossally clever fellows, these English. Never mind. All the best to you. God bless you. It doesn't matter. Everything in this world comes to an end. [*Kisses* MRS. RANEVSKY's *hand.*] If you should ever hear that my end has come, just remember—remember the old horse, and say, "There once lived such-and-such a person, a certain Simeonov-Pishchik, may his bones rest in peace." Remarkable weather we're having. Yes. [*Goes out in great distress, but at once returns and speaks from the doorway.*] Dashenka sends her regards. [*Goes out.*]

MRS. RANEVSKY: Well, now we can go. I'm leaving with two worries. One is old Firs, who's ill. [*With a glance at her watch.*] We still have about five minutes.

ANYA: Firs has been taken to hospital, Mother. Yasha sent him off this morning.

MRS. RANEVSKY: My other worry's Varya. She's used to getting up early and working, and now she has nothing to do she's like a fish out of water. She's grown thin and pale and she's always crying, poor thing. [*Pause.*] As you know very well, Yermolay, I had hoped—to see her married to you, and it did look as if that was how things were shaping. [*Whispers to* ANYA, *who nods to* CHAR-LOTTE. *They both go out.*] She loves you, you're fond of her, and I haven't the faintest idea why you seem to avoid each other. It makes no sense to me.

LOPAKHIN: It makes no sense to me either, to be quite honest. It's a curious business, isn't it? If it's not too late I don't mind going ahead even now. Let's get it over and done with. I don't feel I'll ever propose to her without you here.

MRS. RANEVSKY: That's a very good idea. Why, it won't take more than a minute. I'll call her at once.

LOPAKHIN: There's even champagne laid on. [*Looks at the glasses.*] They're empty, someone must have drunk it. [YASHA *coughs.*] That's what I call really knocking it back.

MRS. RANEVSKY: [*Excitedly.*] I'm so glad. We'll go out. Yasha, *allez!* I'll call her. [*Through the door.*] Varya, leave what you're doing and come here a moment. Come on! [*Goes out with* YASHA.]

LOPAKHIN: [*With a glance at his watch.*] Yes. [*Pause.*]

[*Suppressed laughter and whispering are heard from behind the door. After some time* VARYA *comes in.*]

VARYA: [*Spends a long time examining the luggage.*] That's funny, I can't find it anywhere.

LOPAKHIN: What are you looking for?

VARYA: I packed it myself and I still can't remember. [*Pause.*]

LOPAKHIN: Where are you going now, Varya?

VARYA: Me? To the Ragulins'. I've arranged to look after their place, a sort of housekeeper's job.

LOPAKHIN: That's in Yashnevo, isn't it? It must be fifty odd miles from here. [*Pause.*] So life has ended in this house.

VARYA: [*Examining the luggage.*] Oh, where can it be? Or could I have put it in the trunk? Yes, life has gone out of this house. And it will never come back.

LOPAKHIN: Well, I'm just off to Kharkov. By the next train. I have plenty to do there. And I'm leaving Yepikhodov in charge here, I've taken him on.

VARYA: Oh, have you?

LOPAKHIN: This time last year we already had snow, remember? But now it's calm and sunny. It's a bit cold though. Three degrees of frost, I should say.

VARYA: I haven't looked. [*Pause.*] Besides, our thermometer's broken. [*Pause.*]

[*A voice at the outer door:* "Mr. Lopakhin!"]

LOPAKHIN: [*As if he had long been expecting this summons.*] I'm just coming. [*Goes out quickly.*]

[VARYA *sits on the floor with her head on a bundle of clothes, quietly sobbing. The door opens and* MRS. RANEVSKY *comes in cautiously.*]

MRS. RANEVSKY: Well? [*Pause.*] We'd better go.

VARYA: [*Has stopped crying and wiped her eyes.*] Yes, Mother, it's time. I can get to the Ragulins' today so long as I don't miss my train.

MRS. RANEVSKY: [*Calling through the door.*] Put your things on, Anya.

[ANYA *comes in followed by* GAYEV *and* CHARLOTTE. GAYEV *wears a warm overcoat with a hood. Servants and coachmen come in.* YEPIKHODOV *attends to the luggage.*]

MRS. RANEVSKY: Now we really can be on our way.

ANYA: [*Joyfully.*] On our way!

GAYEV: My friends, my dear good friends! As I leave this house for the last time, how can I be silent? How can I refrain from expressing as I leave the feelings that overwhelm my entire being?

ANYA: [*Beseechingly.*] Uncle.

VARYA: Uncle dear, please don't.

GAYEV: [*Despondently.*] Double the red into the middle. I am silent.

[TROFIMOV *comes in followed by* LOPAKHIN.]

TROFIMOV: Well everybody, it's time to go.

LOPAKHIN: My coat please, Yepikhodov.

MRS. RANEVSKY: I'll just stay another minute. I feel as though I'd never really looked at the walls or ceilings of this house before and now I can hardly take my eyes off them, I love them so dearly.

GAYEV: I remember when I was six years old sitting in this window on Trinity Sunday and watching Father go off to church.

MRS. RANEVSKY: Have they taken all the luggage out?

LOPAKHIN: It looks like it. [*Putting on his coat, to* YEPIKHODOV.] Make sure everything's all right, Yepikhodov, will you?

YEPIKHODOV: [*Speaking in a hoarse voice.*] Don't worry, Mr. Lopakhin!

LOPAKHIN: What's wrong with your voice?

YEPIKHODOV: I've just had some water, I must have swallowed something.

YASHA: [*Contemptuously.*] Shockin' ignorance.

MRS. RANEVSKY: When we've gone there will be no one left here. No one at all.

LOPAKHIN: Not till spring.

VARYA: [*Pulls an umbrella out of a bundle in such a way that it looks as if she meant to hit someone with it.* LOPAKHIN *pretends to be frightened.*] Oh, don't be silly, I didn't do it on purpose.

TROFIMOV: Come on, everyone, let's get into the carriages. It's time. The train will be in soon.

VARYA: There your galoshes are, Peter, just by that suitcase. [*Tearfully.*] And what dirty old things they are.

TROFIMOV: [*Putting on his galoshes.*] Come on, everyone.

GAYEV: [*Greatly distressed, afraid of bursting into tears.*] The train. The station. In off into the middle, double the white into the corner.

MRS. RANEVSKY: Come on then.

LOPAKHIN: Is everyone here? Nobody left behind? [*Locks the side door on the left.*] There are some things stored in there, so I'd better keep it locked. Come on.

ANYA: Good-bye, house. Good-bye, old life.

TROFIMOV: And welcome, new life. [*Goes out with* ANYA.]

[VARYA *looks round the room and goes out slowly.* YASHA *and* CHARLOTTE, *with her dog, follow.*]

LOPAKHIN: Till the spring then. Come along, everyone. Till we meet again. [*Goes out.*]

[MRS. RANEVSKY *and* GAYEV *are left alone. They seem to have been waiting for this moment and fling their arms round each other, sobbing quietly, restraining themselves, afraid of being heard.*]

GAYEV: [*In despair.*] My sister, my dear sister——

MRS. RANEVSKY: Oh, my dear, sweet, beautiful orchard. My life, my youth, my happiness, good-bye. Good-bye.

ANYA: [*Off stage, happily and appealingly.*] Mother!

TROFIMOV: [*Off stage, happily and excitedly.*] Hallo there!

MRS. RANEVSKY: One last look at the walls and the windows. Our dear mother loved to walk about this room.

GAYEV: Oh Lyuba, my dear sister——

ANYA: [*Off stage.*] Mother!

TROFIMOV: [*Off stage.*] Hallo there!

MRS. RANEVSKY: We're coming. [*They go out.*]

[*The stage is empty. The sound of all the doors being locked, then of carriages leaving. It grows quiet. In the silence a dull thud is heard, the noise of an axe striking a tree. It sounds lonely and sad. Footsteps are heard.* FIRS *appears from the door, right. He is dressed as always in jacket and white waistcoat, and wears slippers. He is ill.*]

FIRS: [*Goes up to the door and touches the handle.*] Locked. They've gone. [*Sits on the sofa.*] They forgot me. Never mind, I'll sit here a bit. And Mr. Leonid hasn't put his fur coat on, I'll be bound, he'll have gone off in his light one. [*Gives a worried sigh.*] I should have seen to it, these young folk have no sense. [*Mutters something which cannot be understood.*] Life's slipped by just as if I'd never lived at all. [*Lies down.*] I'll lie down a bit. You've got no strength left, got nothing left, nothing at all. You're just a—nincompoop. [*Lies motionless.*]

[*A distant sound is heard. It seems to come from the sky and is the sound of a breaking string. It dies away sadly. Silence follows, broken only by the thud of an axe striking a tree far away in the orchard.*]

CURTAIN

1903–1904

ANTON CHEKHOV

Passages from Letters[1]

To D. V. Grigorovich,[2] March 28, 1886

. . . If I do have a gift that should be respected, I confess before your pure heart that up to now I haven't respected it. I felt that I had it, but got used to considering it insignificant. There are plenty of purely external reasons to make an individual unfair, extremely suspicious, and distrustful of himself, and I reflect now that there have been plenty of such reasons in my case. All my friends and relatives were always condescending toward my writing and constantly advised me in a friendly way not to give up real work for scribbling. I have hundreds of friends in Moscow, a score of whom write, and I cannot recall a single one who read my work or considered me an artist. There is a so-called "literary circle" in Moscow: talents and mediocrities of all shapes and sizes gather once a week in a restaurant and exercise their tongues. If I were to go there and read them a mere snippet of your letter, they would laugh in my face. During the five years I have been roaming around editorial offices I managed to succumb to the general view of my literary insignificance, quickly got used to looking at my work condescendingly, and—kept plugging away! That's the first reason. The second is that I am a doctor and am up to my ears in medical work, so that the proverb about chasing two hares has cost me more sleep than anyone else.

I write all this merely to justify myself to you in the smallest way for my deep sin. Up to now I have treated my literary work extremely lightly, carelessly, haphazardly. I do not remember working more than a day on *any single* story of mine, and I wrote *The Huntsman*, which you liked, when I went swimming! I wrote my stories as reporters write their news about fires: mechanically, half-consciously, without worrying about either the reader or themselves. I wrote and constantly tried not to waste images and scenes which I valued on these stories, and I tried to save them and carefully hide them, God only knows why.

Suvorin's[3] very friendly and, so far as I can see, sincere letter, was the first thing to impel me to look at my work critically. I began to get ready to write something significant, but I still had no faith in my own literary significance. Then suddenly, completely unexpectedly, your letter came. Forgive the comparison, but it acted on me like an order "to leave town within twenty-four hours!" that is, I suddenly felt an absolute necessity to hurry, to get out of the place I was stuck in as quickly as possible. . . .

1. Translated by Ralph E. Matlaw. 2. D. V. Grigorovich (1822–1899), an important writer in the 1840s and the later part of the century, had written to Chekhov on March 25, 1886, praising his outstanding talent and urging him to write more seriously. 3. A. S. Suvorin (1833–1911), influential publisher of the conservative paper *New Times*, became Chekhov's closest friend.

I will liberate myself from deadlines, but not at once. There is no possibility of getting out of the rut into which I have fallen. I don't mind starving as I have already done, but there are others involved too. I give my leisure to writing, two or three hours a day and a little bit of the night, that is, time that is suitable only for trifling work. This summer, when I will have more leisure and will have to earn less, I will undertake something serious. . . .

To A. N. Pleshcheev,[4] October 4, 1888

. . . Write to me after you've read my *Name-Day Party*. You won't like it, but I am not afraid of you or Anna Mikhailovna.[5] I am afraid of those who will look for tendenciousness between the lines and who are determined to see me either as a liberal or a conservative. I am neither a liberal nor a conservative, neither a gradualist nor a monk nor an indifferentist. I would like to be nothing more than a free artist, and I regret that God did not give me the gift to be one. I hate falseness and coercion in all their forms and consistorial secretaries are just as repellent to me as Notovich and Gradovsky.[6] Pharisaism, stupidity, and arbitrariness reign not merely in merchants' houses and police stations: I see them in science, in literature, among the young. That is why I have no particular passion for either policemen or butchers or scientists or writers or the young. I consider brand-names and labels a prejudice. My holy of holies is the human body, health, intelligence, talent, inspiration, love, and absolute freedom, freedom from force and falseness in whatever form they express themselves. That's the platform I'd subscribe to if I were a great artist. . . .

To A. N. Pleshcheev, October 9, 1888

. . . Is there really no "ideology" apparent in my last story [*The Name-Day Party*] either? Once you remarked to me that the element of protest is missing from my work, that there is neither sympathy nor antipathy in them. But don't I protest against falsehood from the beginning of the story to its end? Isn't that ideology? No? Well then, that means that I don't know how to bite, or that I am a flea. . . .

To A. S. Suvorin, October 27, 1888

. . . I sometimes preach heresy, but I have never yet gone so far as to deny a place in art to topical questions altogether. In conversations with the writing fraternity I always insist that the artist's function is not to solve narrowly specialized questions. It is bad for the artist to undertake something he doesn't understand. We have specialists for specialized questions; it is their function to discuss the peasant commune, the fate of capitalism, the evil of drink, shoes, women's diseases. The artist, however, must treat only what he understands; his sphere is as limited as that of any other specialist's, I repeat that and always insist on it.

---

4. I. L. Shcheglov-Leontiev (1825–1893), poet and editor of the *Northern Herald*, in which Chekhov published. **5.** A. M. Efreinova, publisher of the *Northern Herald*. **6.** Two supposedly unscrupulous left-wing journalists.

Only somebody who has never written or had anything to do with images could say that there are no questions in his realm, that there is nothing but answers. The artist observes, chooses, guesses, compounds—these actions in themselves already presuppose a question at the origin; if the artist did not pose a question to himself at the beginning then there was nothing to guess or to choose. To be as brief as possible, I'll end with psychiatry: if you deny questions and intentions in creative work you must acknowledge that the artist creates unintentionally, without purpose, under the influence of a temporary aberration; therefore, if an author were to brag to me that he wrote a tale purely by inspiration, without previously having pondered his intentions, I would call him insane.

You are right in demanding that an artist approach his work consciously, but you are confusing two concepts: *the solution of a problem and the correct formulation of a problem*. Only the second is required of the artist. Not a single problem is resolved in *Anna Karenina* or *Onegin*, but they satisfy you completely only because all the problems in them are formulated correctly. The judge is required to formulate the questions correctly, but the decision is left to the jurors, each according to his own taste. . . .

▼   ▼   ▼

QUESTIONS

1. Sometimes the title of *The Bear* is translated as *The Brute*. Which title seems to you to describe best the action of the play? Why?

2. In what different ways does the dialogue indicate that Mrs. Popov is not entirely honest about her feelings?

3. Describe in detail the character of Luke. How is his character revealed? In what ways is he like Firs in *The Cherry Orchard?* Do any other characters in *The Bear* remind you of characters in *The Cherry Orchard?* In what specific ways?

4. Why is there so little "action" in *The Cherry Orchard?* Describe the full "plot" of the play. How much of the action takes place offstage?

5. Explain how the billiard talk helps to characterize Gayev. Which other characters deploy language in peculiar ways that help to characterize them?

6. How do you respond to Trofimov? What are his likable characteristics? What is his function in the plot?

7. How do you respond to Charlotte? Why? What kind of social class does she seem to belong to?

8. If you were staging the play, what kind of furniture would you use in the opening scene to help characterize Lyubov Ranevsky?

9. If you were directing the play, how sympathetic would you try to make Firs? How would you do it?

WRITING SUGGESTIONS

1. Read another full-length play by Chekhov. Choose one character from that play who is similar to a character in either *The Bear* or *The Cherry Orchard*, and write a four- or five-page paper comparing how Chekhov *introduces* the two characters.

2. Read a full-length biography of Chekhov. In what specific ways does knowledge of Chekhov's life help you to interpret *The Cherry Orchard*?

3. Read at least three short stories that Chekhov wrote after 1888, and compare the kinds of themes in them to *The Cherry Orchard*. Choose one of the stories, and in a four-page paper discuss the different ways in which Chekhov explores the themes in the story and in the play.

5 LITERARY CONTEXT: TRAGEDY AND COMEDY

C lassifying literary texts serves a variety of purposes for historians and literary critics who may need to "place" a literary work in history, suggest its relationship to other texts, or make a value judgment about its literary quality or cultural value. But classification is not just an activity for "professionals," and a knowledge of literary categories and definitions is not useful only for those who enjoy sorting and labeling. Classification can also be important to students and ordinary readers, for a knowledge of categories and what they stand for can aid in the interpretation and enjoyment of individual texts. Just as the generic divisions of poetry, fiction, and drama tell you something about what to expect when you pick up a text, so particular kinds of dramas—tragedies, for example, or comedies—provide certain expectations of what will go on and how. Knowing something about the nature of tragedy can make you a better, more attentive reader of *Oedipus the King*, and understanding the nature of literary categories can help you to a more satisfying relationship with literary texts more generally.

Authors sometimes label their texts specifically to help readers know what to expect, thereby entering into a kind of contract of expectation with readers. Fiction writers who call their books "romances," for example, are telling their readers to expect stories that are romantic, idealistic, improbable, full of fantasy, and characterized by love and emotional fulfillment. Playwrights too have historically labeled their texts to lure or warn readers. **Pastoral plays** promise to be about shepherds living in an idealized world reminiscent of the idealistic values of some primitive golden age. **Farces** promise broad humor and wild antics, perhaps slapstick or pratfalls or other physical humor or perhaps easy puns and verbal highjinks, but certainly something entertaining, not too taxing, and not too serious. **Satires** promise critical commentary on some person or situation or event, often political or involving some specific cultural or social situation of contemporary relevance. Not all pastoral plays, farces, and satires do exactly what they promise, but if they label themselves as such, they set up readers to expect a certain kind of text—a text that will treat predictable subject matter and behave in predictable fashion. Often these labels imply a certain kind of structure, a certain kind of language, and a value structure. A title such as *The Tragedy of Hamlet, Prince of Denmark* gives us an idea, from the moment we read it, of what to expect—not just a plot, ending, and tone of a particular kind but an imagined world that operates according to habits and laws.

Not all plays (or texts of any other kind) are given labels by their authors, but many unlabeled texts are nevertheless conceived along lines that have to do with previous practice and traditional classifications, and many texts are therefore classified by critics or by their earliest viewers and readers as belonging to traditional groups. We might, for example, describe a film as a whodunit or a spaghetti Western, or we might call a TV program a sitcom or a soap, and have a reasonable expectation that others would know, at least roughly speaking, what kind of thing we had been watching.

Tragedy and **comedy** are two of the oldest and most enduring dramatic forms, and many contemporary plays continued to be called, by their authors or by critics, by these names. Many people believe that tragedy and comedy still provide convenient ways to organize and present experience because they testify to, and reflect, basic ways of viewing human history. You can sometimes get into a pretty lively argument about whether a particular play should properly be called a tragedy; when *Death of a Salesman* first appeared, all kinds of critics, students, theatergoers, and readers argued with its author and with each other about whether the play was truly tragic. Many individuals often have very different opinions about the propriety of certain labels for particular texts, and often somewhat different notions of everything that such labels imply; nevertheless most people admit the necessity of labels, and believe that some general agreement about definition is possible, despite quibbling over details.

The broad parameters of comedy and tragedy have been established since the time of Aristotle, who first tried to define tragedy by describing contemporary examples in the fourth century B.C. The most fundamental aspects of Aristotelian definition may be summarized as depending upon three categories of assumption—the order of values implicit in the play, the nature of character in the play, and the nature of the conclusion.

In a tragedy like *Oedipus the King*, values are universal and beyond the control of humankind. Right and wrong are determined not by any agreement between individuals, but by the will of the gods, or some other preterhuman force. When the oracle tells Oedipus that his fate is to kill his father and marry his mother, Oedipus is revolted by the prospect. In human terms he is certainly right to try to avoid such a fate—but in terms of the value system that rules the play, his attempt to circumvent the will of the gods is what destroys him.

In a comedy like *The Importance of Being Earnest*, on the other hand, values are social and determined by the general opinion of society. In moral terms there is no reason why Jack and Gwendolen should not marry and get about the business of establishing a family. They are healthy, unmarried people; the only problems about their intention to marry are social ones. Gwendolen's children cannot achieve their "proper" place in society unless her husband is a suitable choice, a man of good family, some social position, and adequate means to provide an appropriate education for them. Implicit in this consideration is the fact that comedy tends to endorse the values of society, sometimes at the expense of individual needs or values. Lady Bracknell may be amusing, but she is also right, because she understands how her society works, what is acceptable and what is not.

A second characteristic feature of these dramatic categories is their treatment of character. Tragedy, for example, tends to focus on a single individual, a person of high rank who confronts the universe and his fate as an individual, a hero. He is ultimately doomed to defeat because, although a good and noble person, the tragic figure has a flaw of character or a limitation of knowledge— some mark of humanity—that offsets all his goodness. Oedipus wishes to know and to control his own destiny, but he learns too much and is destroyed. Had Oedipus been the son of a shepherd rather than of a king, perhaps the gods would not have taken such an unfortunate interest in his fate.

Comic figures are quite different. Since comedies are concerned with society and social roles, comic characters are often defined in those terms. In *The Importance of Being Earnest* both Jack and Algernon are, for plot purposes, unmarried young men who are not eminently eligible husbands-to-be, Jack because of his uncertain parentage and Algernon because of his lack of money. They have individual traits—Algernon eats too much and enjoys pretense, Jack is more straightforward, or wishes to be—but what distinguishes them is not so important as what they have in common according to societal standards. Many comic characters go even further and become stereotypes. Lady Bracknell, for example, is a middle-aged, meddling matron, ideally placed by age and position to exert tremendous social influence. However ridiculous Lady Bracknell appears, she understands her society and its rules thoroughly. Other stereotypes in the same play are Miss Prism, the desperate spinster, and Dr. Chasuble, the slightly dim clergyman.

A third defining feature of tragedy and comedy can be found in their endings. In most tragedies, the hero is enlightened; he or she comes to understand the meaning of his or her deeds and to accept an appropriate punishment. At the end of *Oedipus the King* the blind hero sees and understands. He accepts his ostracism, and when he leaves Thebes he is a chastened but wiser man. Many tragic heroes die, as Hamlet does, but it is not death that ends the tragedy, it is understanding. Hamlet understands what has happened and in his last moments tries to restore order to the kingdom, asking for himself only that people may know the truth about what he has done. In comedy, on the other hand, the resolution occurs when one or more characters take a proper social role. This is most frequently defined in terms of the marriage of an eligible young woman and an equally eligible young man. The society of *Earnest* believes that young men like Jack and Algernon and young women like Gwendolen and Cecily should marry and get about the business of having children and raising them to provide for the continuation of the society. Even the marriage of Miss Prism and Dr. Chasuble serves social purposes. The society of the play prefers married clergymen to celibates and has no really useful function for a middle-aged spinster.

The two plays that follow represent tragedy and comedy in something close to pure form, and in each the assumptions as well as the features of their genre are manifest. Many good plays are examples far less clear, and over the years many plays have consciously mixed the conventions and assumptions of these two lasting kinds. Many other categories have been used over the centuries to describe the shape and assumptions of groups of dramatic texts. Modern and postmodern plays most often mix genres in a conscious way, and they tend to emphasize their desire to reflect and depict ordinary reality as their authors perceive it to be (that is, they aim to be *mimetic*) rather than following some predetermined shape or set of assumptions about some universal tone and standard kind of ending.

▼ ▼ ▼

SOPHOCLES

Oedipus the King[1]

CHARACTERS

OEDIPUS, *King of Thebes*
JOCASTA, *His Wife*
CREON, *His Brother-in-Law*
TEIRESIAS, *an Old Blind Prophet*
A PRIEST

FIRST MESSENGER
SECOND MESSENGER
A HERDSMAN
A CHORUS *of Old Men of Thebes*

SCENE: *In front of the palace of* OEDIPUS *at Thebes. To the right of the stage near the altar stands the* PRIEST *with a crowd of children.* OEDIPUS *emerges from the central door.*

1. Translated by David Grene.

OEDIPUS: Children, young sons and daughters of old Cadmus,[2]
    why do you sit here with your suppliant crowns?
    The town is heavy with a mingled burden
    of sounds and smells, of groans and hymns and incense;
    I did not think it fit that I should hear   5
    of this from messengers but came myself,—
    I Oedipus whom all men call the Great.

[*He turns to the* PRIEST.]

    You're old and they are young; come, speak for them.
    What do you fear or want, that you sit here
    suppliant? Indeed I'm willing to give all   10
    that you may need; I would be very hard
    should I not pity suppliants like these.
PRIEST: O ruler of my country, Oedipus,
    you see our company around the altar;
    you see our ages; some of us, like these,   15
    who cannot yet fly far, and some of us
    heavy with age; these children are the chosen
    among the young, and I the priest of Zeus.
    Within the market place sit others crowned
    with suppliant garlands, at the double shrine   20
    of Pallas[3] and the temple where Ismenus
    gives oracles by fire. King, you yourself
    have seen our city reeling like a wreck
    already; it can scarcely lift its prow
    out of the depths, out of the bloody surf.   25
    A blight is on the fruitful plants of the earth,
    A blight is on the cattle in the fields,
    a blight is on our women that no children
    are born to them; a God that carries fire,
    a deadly pestilence, is on our town,   30
    strikes us and spares not, and the house of Cadmus
    is emptied of its people while black Death
    grows rich in groaning and in lamentation.
    We have not come as suppliants to this altar
    because we thought of you as of a God,   35
    but rather judging you the first of men
    in all the chances of this life and when
    we mortals have to do with more than man.
    You came and by your coming saved our city,
    freed us from tribute which we paid of old   40
    to the Sphinx, cruel singer. This you did
    in virtue of no knowledge we could give you,

---

2. The founder of Thebes.   3. Athena, the goddess of wisdom.

in virtue of no teaching; it was God
that aided you, men say, and you are held
45 with God's assistance to have saved our lives.
Now Oedipus, Greatest in all men's eyes,
here falling at your feet we all entreat you,
find us some strength for rescue.
Perhaps you'll hear a wise word from some God,
50 perhaps you will learn something from a man
(for I have seen that for the skilled of practice
the outcome of their counsels live the most).
Noblest of men, go, and raise up our city,
go,—and give heed. For now this land of ours
55 calls you its savior since you saved it once.
So, let us never speak about your reign
as of a time when first our feet were set
secure on high, but later fell to ruin.
Raise up our city, save it and raise it up.
60 Once you have brought us luck with happy omen;
be no less now in fortune.
If you will rule this land, as now you rule it,
better to rule it full of men than empty.
For neither tower nor ship is anything
65 when empty, and none live in it together.
OEDIPUS: I pity you, children. You have come full of longing,
but I have known the story before you told it
only too well. I know you are all sick,
yet there is not one of you, sick though you are,
70 that is as sick as I myself.
Your several sorrows each have single scope
and touch but one of you. My spirit groans
for city and myself and you at once.
You have not roused me like a man from sleep;
75 know that I have given many tears to this,
gone many ways wandering in thought,
but as I thought I found only one remedy
and that I took. I sent Menoeceus' son
Creon, Jocasta's brother, to Apollo,
80 to his Pythian temple,
that he might learn there by what act or word
I could save this city. As I count the days,
it vexes me what ails him; he is gone
far longer than he needed for the journey.
85 But when he comes, then, may I prove a villain,
if I shall not do all the God commands.
PRIEST: Thanks for your gracious words. Your servants here
signal that Creon is this moment coming.

OEDIPUS: His face is bright. O holy Lord Apollo,
   grant that his news too may be bright for us   90
   and bring us safety.
PRIEST: It is happy news,
   I think, for else his head would not be crowned
   with sprigs of fruitful laurel.
OEDIPUS: We will know soon,
   he's within hail. Lord Creon, my good brother,   95
   what is the word you bring us from the God?

[CREON *enters.*]

CREON: A good word,—for things hard to bear themselves
   if in the final issue all is well
   I count complete good fortune.
OEDIPUS: What do you mean?
   What you have said so far   100
   leaves me uncertain whether to trust or fear.
CREON: If you will hear my news before these others
   I am ready to speak, or else to go within.
OEDIPUS: Speak it to all;
   the grief I bear, I bear it more for these   105
   than for my own heart.
CREON: I will tell you, then,
   what I heard from the God.
   King Phoebus[4] in plain words commanded us
   to drive out a pollution from our land,
   pollution grown ingrained within the land;   110
   drive it out, said the God, not cherish it,
   till it's past cure.
OEDIPUS: What is the rite
   of purification? How shall it be done?
CREON: By banishing a man, or expiation
   of blood by blood, since it is murder guilt   115
   which holds our city in this destroying storm.
OEDIPUS: Who is this man whose fate the God pronounces?
CREON: My Lord, before you piloted the state
   we had a king called Laius.
OEDIPUS: I know of him by hearsay. I have not seen him.   120
CREON: The God commanded clearly: let some one
   punish with force this dead man's murderers.
OEDIPUS: Where are they in the world? Where would a trace
   of this old crime be found? It would be hard
   to guess where.
CREON: The clue is in this land;   125

---

4. Apollo, the god of truth.

that which is sought is found;
the unheeded thing escapes:
so said the God.

OEDIPUS: Was it at home,
or in the country that death came upon him,
130   or in another country travelling?

CREON: He went, he said himself, upon an embassy,
but never returned when he set out from home.

OEDIPUS: Was there no messenger, no fellow traveller
who knew what happened? Such a one might tell
135   something of use.

CREON: They were all killed save one. He fled in terror
and he could tell us nothing in clear terms
of what he knew, nothing, but one thing only.

OEDIPUS: What was it?
140   If we could even find a slim beginning
in which to hope, we might discover much.

CREON: This man said that the robbers they encountered
were many and the hands that did the murder
were many; it was no man's single power.

145 OEDIPUS: How could a robber dare a deed like this
were he not helped with money from the city,
money and treachery?

CREON: That indeed was thought.
But Laius was dead and in our trouble
there was none to help.

150 OEDIPUS: What trouble was so great to hinder you
inquiring out the murder of your king?

CREON: The riddling Sphinx induced us to neglect
mysterious crimes and rather seek solution
of troubles at our feet.

155 OEDIPUS: I will bring this to light again. King Phoebus
fittingly took this care about the dead,
and you too fittingly.
And justly you will see in me an ally,
a champion of my country and the God.
160   For when I drive pollution from the land
I will not serve a distant friend's advantage,
but act in my own interest. Whoever
he was that killed the king may readily
wish to dispatch me with his murderous hand;
165   so helping the dead king I help myself.

Come, children, take your suppliant boughs and go;
up from the altars now. Call the assembly

and let it meet upon the understanding
that I'll do everything. God will decide
whether we prosper or remain in sorrow.

PRIEST: Rise, children—it was this we came to seek,
which of himself the king now offers us.
May Phoebus who gave us the oracle
come to our rescue and stay the plague.

[*Exeunt all but the* CHORUS.]

CHORUS: [*Strophe.*] What is the sweet spoken word of God from the shrine of
    Pythorich in gold
that has come to glorious Thebes?
I am stretched on the rack of doubt, and terror and trembling hold
my heart, O Delian Healer, and I worship full of fears
for what doom you will bring to pass, new or renewed in the revolving years.
Speak to me, immortal voice,
child of golden Hope.

[*Antistrophe.*]

First I call on you, Athene, deathless daughter of Zeus,
and Artemis, Earth Upholder,
who sits in the midst of the market place in the throne which men call
    Fame,
and Phoebus, the Far Shooter, three averters of Fate,
come to us now, if ever before, when ruin rushed upon the state,
you drove destruction's flame away
out of our land.

[*Strophe.*]

Our sorrows defy number;
all the ship's timbers are rotten;
taking of thought is no spear for the driving away of the plague.
There are no growing children in this famous land;
there are no women bearing the pangs of childbirth.
You may see them one with another, like birds swift on the wing,
quicker than fire unmastered,
speeding away to the coast of the Western God.

[*Antistrophe.*]

In the unnumbered deaths
of its people the city dies;
those children that are born lie dead on the naked earth
unpitied, spreading contagion of death; and grey haired mothers and wives
everywhere stand at the altar's edge, suppliant, moaning;

170

175

180

185

190

195

200

the hymn to the healing God rings out but with it the wailing voices are
  blended.
From these our sufferings grant us, O golden Daughter of Zeus,
glad-faced deliverance.

[*Strophe.*]

205 There is no clash of brazen shields but our fight is with the War God,
a War God ringed with the cries of men, a savage God who burns us;
grant that he turn in racing course backwards out of our country's bounds
to the great palace of Amphitrite[5] or where the waves of the Thracian sea
deny the stranger safe anchorage.
210 Whatsoever escapes the night
at last the light of day revisits;
so smite the War God, Father Zeus,
beneath your thunderbolt,
for you are the Lord of the lightning, the lightning that carries fire.

[*Antistrophe.*]

215 And your unconquered arrow shafts, winged by the golden corded bow,
Lycean King, I beg to be at our side for help;
and the gleaming torches of Artemis with which she scours the Lycean hills,
and I call on the God with the turban of gold, who gave his name to this
  country of ours,
the Bacchic God with the wind flushed face,
220 Evian One, who travel
with the Maenad[6] company,
combat the God that burns us
with your torch of pine;
for the God that is our enemy is a God unhonoured among the Gods.

[OEDIPUS *returns.*]

225 OEDIPUS: For what you ask me—if you will hear my words,
and hearing welcome them and fight the plague,
you will find strength and lightening of your load
Hark to me; what I say to you, I say
as one that is a stranger to the story
230 as stranger to the deed. For I would not
be far upon the track if I alone
were tracing it without a clue. But now,
since after all was finished, I became
a citizen among you, citizens—
235 now I proclaim to all the men of Thebes:
who so among you knows the murderer

5. The Atlantic Ocean.   6. Female worshipers of Bacchus.

by whose hand Laius, son of Labdacus,
died—I command him to tell everything
to me,—yes, though he fears himself to take the blame
on his own head; for bitter punishment   240
he shall have none, but leave this land unharmed.
Or if he knows the murderer, another,
a foreigner, still let him speak the truth.
For I will pay him and be grateful, too.
But if you shall keep silence, if perhaps   245
some one of you, to shield a guilty friend,
or for his own sake shall reject my words—
hear what I shall do then:
I forbid that man, whoever he be, my land,
my land where I hold sovereignty and throne;   250
and I forbid any to welcome him
or cry him greeting or make him a sharer
in sacrifice or offering to the Gods,
or give him water for his hands to wash.
I command all to drive him from their homes,   255
since he is our pollution, as the oracle
of Pytho's God proclaimed him now to me.
So I stand forth a champion of the God
and of the man who died.
Upon the murderer I invoke this curse—   260
whether he is one man and all unknown,
or one of many—may he wear out his life
in misery to miserable doom!
If with my knowledge he lives at my hearth
I pray that I myself may feel my curse.   265
On you I lay my charge to fulfill all this
for me, for the God, and for this land of ours
destroyed and blighted, by the God forsaken.

Even were this no matter of God's ordinance
it would not fit you so to leave it lie,   270
unpurified, since a good man is dead
and one that was a king. Search it out.
Since I am now the holder of his office,
and have his bed and wife that once was his,
and had his line not been unfortunate   275
we would have common children—(fortune leaped
upon his head)—because of all these things,
I fight in his defence as for my father,
and I shall try all means to take the murderer
of Laius the son of Labdacus   280

the son of Polydorus and before him
of Cadmus and before him of Agenor.
Those who do not obey me, may the Gods
grant no crops springing from the ground they plough

285   nor children to their women! May a fate
like this, or one still worse than this consume them!
For you whom these words please, the other Thebans,
may Justice as your ally and all the Gods
live with you, blessing you now and for ever!

290 CHORUS: As you have held me to my oath, I speak:
I neither killed the king nor can declare
the killer; but since Phoebus set the quest
it is his part to tell who the man is.
OEDIPUS: Right; but to put compulsion on the Gods

295   against their will—no man can do that.
CHORUS: May I then say what I think second best?
OEDIPUS: If there's a third best, too, spare not to tell it.
CHORUS: I know that what the Lord Teiresias
sees, is most often what the Lord Apollo

300   sees. If you should inquire of this from him
you might find out most clearly.
OEDIPUS: Even in this my actions have not been sluggard.
On Creon's word I have sent two messengers
and why the prophet is not here already
I have been wondering.

305 CHORUS: His skill apart
there is besides only an old faint story.
OEDIPUS: What is it?
I look at every story.
CHORUS: It was said
that he was killed by certain wayfarers.

310 OEDIPUS: I heard that, too, but no one saw the killer.
CHORUS: Yet if he has a share of fear at all,
his courage will not stand firm, hearing your curse.
OEDIPUS: The man who in the doing did not shrink
will fear no word.
CHORUS: Here comes his prosecutor:

315   led by your men the godly prophet comes
in whom alone of mankind truth is native.

[*Enter* TEIRESIAS, *led by a* LITTLE BOY.]

OEDIPUS: Teiresias, you are versed in everything,
things teachable and things not to be spoken,
things of the heaven and earth-creeping things.

320   You have no eyes but in your mind you know

with what a plague our city is afflicted.
My lord, in you alone we find a champion,
in you alone one that can rescue us.
Perhaps you have not heard the messengers,
but Phoebus sent in answer to our sending   325
an oracle declaring that our freedom
from this disease would only come when we
should learn the names of those who killed King Laius,
and kill them or expel from our country.
Do not begrudge us oracles from birds,   330
or any other way of prophecy
within your skill; save yourself and the city,
save me; redeem the debt of our pollution
that lies on us because of this dead man.
We are in your hands; pains are most nobly taken   335
to help another when you have means and power.
TEIRESIAS: Alas, how terrible is wisdom when
it brings no profit to the man that's wise!
This I knew well, but had forgotten it,
else I would not have come here.
OEDIPUS: What is this?   340
How sad you are now you have come!
TEIRESIAS: Let me
go home. It will be easiest for us both
to bear our several destinies to the end
if you will follow my advice.
OEDIPUS: You'd rob us
of this your gift of prophecy? You talk   345
as one who had no care for law nor love
for Thebes who reared you.
TEIRESIAS: Yes, but I see that even your own words
miss the mark; therefore I must fear for mine.
OEDIPUS: For God's sake if you know of anything,   350
do not turn from us; all of us kneel to you,
all of us here, your suppliants.
TEIRESIAS: All of you here know nothing. I will not
bring to the light of day my troubles, mine—
rather than call them yours.
OEDIPUS: What do you mean?   355
You know of something but refuse to speak.
Would you betray us and destroy the city?
TEIRESIAS: I will not bring this pain upon us both,
neither on you nor on myself. Why is it
you question me and waste your labour? I   360
will tell you nothing.

OEDIPUS: You would provoke a stone! Tell us, you villain,
    tell us, and do not stand there quietly
    unmoved and balking at the issue.
365 TEIRESIAS: You blame my temper but you do not see
    your own that lives within you; it is me
    you chide.
OEDIPUS: Who would not feel his temper rise
    at words like these with which you shame our city?
370 TEIRESIAS: Of themselves things will come, although I hide them
    and breathe no word of them.
OEDIPUS: Since they will come
    tell them to me.
TEIRESIAS: I will say nothing further.
    Against this answer let your temper rage
    as wildly as you will.
OEDIPUS: Indeed I am
375   so angry I shall not hold back a jot
    of what I think. For I would have you know
    I think you were complotter of the deed
    and doer of the deed save in so far
    as for the actual killing. Had you had eyes
380   I would have said alone you murdered him.
TEIRESIAS: Yes? Then I warn you faithfully to keep
    the letter of your proclamation and
    from this day forth to speak no word of greeting
    to these nor me; you are the land's pollution.
385 OEDIPUS: How shamelessly you started up this taunt!
    How do you think you will escape?
TEIRESIAS: I have.
    I have escaped; the truth is what I cherish
    and that's my strength.
OEDIPUS: And who has taught you truth?
    Not your profession surely!
TEIRESIAS: You have taught me,
390   for you have made me speak against my will.
OEDIPUS: Speak what? Tell me again that I may learn it better.
TEIRESIAS: Did you not understand before or would you
    provoke me into speaking?
OEDIPUS: I did not grasp it,
    not so to call it known. Say it again.
395 TEIRESIAS: I say you are the murderer of the king
    whose murderer you seek.
OEDIPUS: Not twice you shall
    say calumnies like this and stay unpunished.
TEIRESIAS: Shall I say more to tempt your anger more?

OEDIPUS: As much as you desire; it will be said
    in vain.
TEIRESIAS: I say that with those you love best   400
    you live in foulest shame unconsciously
    and do not see where you are in calamity.
OEDIPUS: Do you imagine you can always talk
    like this, and live to laugh at it hereafter?
TEIRESIAS: Yes, if the truth has anything of strength.   405
OEDIPUS: It has, but not for you; it has no strength
    for you because you are blind in mind and ears
    as well as in your eyes.
TEIRESIAS: You are a poor wretch
    to taunt me with the very insults which
    every one soon will heap upon yourself.   410
OEDIPUS: Your life is one long night so that you cannot
    hurt me or any other who sees the light.
TEIRESIAS: It is not fate that I should be your ruin,
    Apollo is enough; it is his care
    to work this out.
OEDIPUS: Was this your own design   415
    or Creon's?
TEIRESIAS: Creon is no hurt to you,
    but you are to yourself.
OEDIPUS: Wealth, sovereignty and skill outmatching skill
    for the contrivance of an envied life!
    Great store of jealousy fill your treasury chests,   420
    if my friend Creon, friend from the first and loyal,
    thus secretly attacks me, secretly
    desires to drive me out and secretly
    suborns this juggling, trick devising quack,
    this wily beggar who has only eyes   425
    for his own gains, but blindness in his skill.
    For, tell me, where have you seen clear, Teiresias,
    with your prophetic eyes? When the dark singer,
    the sphinx, was in your country, did you speak
    word of deliverance to its citizens?   430
    And yet the riddle's answer was not the province
    of a chance comer. It was a prophet's task
    and plainly you had no such gift of prophecy
    from birds nor otherwise from any God
    to glean a word of knowledge. But I came,   435
    Oedipus, who knew nothing, and I stopped her.
    I solved the riddle by my wit alone.
    Mine was no knowledge got from birds. And now
    you would expel me,

440   because you think that you will find a place
    by Creon's throne. I think you will be sorry,
    both you and your accomplice, for your plot
    to drive me out. And did I not regard you
    as an old man, some suffering would have taught you
445   that what was in your heart was treason.
  CHORUS: We look at this man's words and yours, my king,
    and we find both have spoken them in anger.
    We need no angry words but only thought
    how we may best hit the God's meaning for us.
450   TEIRESIAS: If you are king, at least I have the right
    no less to speak in my defence against you.
    Of that much I am master. I am no slave
    of yours, but Loxias', and so I shall not
    enroll myself with Creon for my patron.
455   Since you have taunted me with being blind,
    here is my word for you.
    You have your eyes but see not where you are
    in sin, nor where you live, nor whom you live with.
    Do you know who your parents are? Unknowing
460   you are an enemy to kith and kin
    in death, beneath the earth, and in this life.
    A deadly footed, double striking curse,
    from father and mother both, shall drive you forth
    out of this land, with darkness on your eyes,
465   that now have such straight vision. Shall there be
    a place will not be harbour to your cries,
    a corner of Cithaeron[7] will not ring
    in echo to your cries, soon, soon,—
    when you shall learn the secret of your marriage,
470   which steered you to a haven in this house,—
    haven no haven, after lucky voyage?
    And of the multitude of other evils
    establishing a grim equality
    between you and your children, you know nothing.
475   So, muddy with contempt my words and Creon's!
    Misery shall grind no man as it will you.
  OEDIPUS: Is it endurable that I should hear
    such words from him? Go and a curse go with you
    Quick, home with you! Out of my house at once!!
480   TEIRESIAS: I would not have come either had you not called me.
  OEDIPUS: I did not know then you would talk like a fool—

7. The mountain where Oedipus was abandoned as a child.

or it would have been long before I called you.
TEIRESIAS: I am a fool then, as it seems to you—
but to the parents who have bred you, wise.
OEDIPUS: What parents? Stop! Who are they of all the world?   485
TEIRESIAS: This day will show your birth and will destroy you.
OEDIPUS: How needlessly your riddles darken everything.
TEIRESIAS: But it's in riddle answering you are strongest.
OEDIPUS: Yes. Taunt me where you will find me great.
TEIRESIAS: It is this very luck that has destroyed you.   490
OEDIPUS: I do not care, if it has saved this city.
TEIRESIAS: Well, I will go. Come, boy, lead me away.
OEDIPUS: Yes, lead him off. So long as you are here,
you'll be a stumbling block and a vexation;
once gone, you will not trouble me again.
TEIRESIAS: I have said   495
what I came here to say not fearing your
countenance: there is no way you can hurt me.
I tell you, king, this man, this murderer
(whom you have long declared you are in search of,
indicting him in threatening proclamation   500
as murderer of Laius)—he is here.
In name he is a stranger among citizens
but soon he will be shown to be a citizen
true native Theban, and he'll have no joy
of the discovery: blindness for sight   505
and beggary for riches his exchange,
he shall go journeying to a foreign country
tapping his way before him with a stick.
He shall be proved father and brother both
to his own children in his house; to her   510
that gave him birth, a son and husband both;
a fellow sower in his father's bed
with that same father that he murdered.
Go within, reckon that out, and if you find me
mistaken, say I have no skill in prophecy.   515
[*Exeunt separately* TEIRESIAS *and* OEDIPUS.]
CHORUS: [*Strophe.*] Who is the man proclaimed
by Delphi's prophetic rock
as the bloody handed murderer,
the doer of deeds that none dare name?
   Now is the time for him to run   520
with a stronger foot
than Pegasus[8]

8. Winged horse.

for the child of Zeus leaps in arms upon him
with fire and the lightning bolt,
525   and terribly close on his heels
are the Fates[9] that never miss.

[*Antistrophe.*]

Lately from snowy Parnassus[1]
clearly the voice flashed forth,
bidding each Theban track him down,
530   the unknown murderer.
In the savage forests he lurks and in
the caverns like
the mountain bull.
He is sad and lonely, and lonely his feet
535   that carry him far from the navel of earth;
but its prophecies, ever living,
flutter around his head.

[*Strophe.*]

The augur has spread confusion,
terrible confusion;
540   I do not approve what was said
nor can I deny it.
I do not know what to say;
I am in a flutter of foreboding;
I never heard in the present
545   nor past of a quarrel between
the sons of Labdacus and Polybus,[2]
that I might bring as proof
in attacking the popular fame
of Oedipus, seeking
550   to take vengeance for undiscovered
death in the line of Labdacus.

[*Antistrophe.*]

Truly Zeus and Apollo are wise
and in human things all knowing;
but amongst men there is no
555   distinct judgment, between the prophet
and me—which of us is right.
One man may pass another in wisdom
but I would never agree

9. Spirits called upon to avenge crimes.   1. Mountain sacred to Apollo.   2. King who adopted
Oedipus.

with those that find fault with the king
till I should see the word   560
proved right beyond doubt. For once
in visible form the Sphinx
came on him and all of us
saw his wisdom and in that test
he saved the city. So he will not be condemned by my mind.   565

[*Enter* CREON.]

CREON: Citizens, I have come because I heard
deadly words spread about me, that the king
accuses me. I cannot take that from him.
If he believes that in these present troubles
he has been wronged by me in word or deed   570
I do not want to live on with the burden
of such a scandal on me. The report
injures me doubly and most vitally—
for I'll be called a traitor to my city
and traitor also to my friends and you.   575
CHORUS: Perhaps it was a sudden gust of anger
that forced that insult from him, and no judgment.
CREON: But did he say that it was in compliance
with schemes of mine that the seer told him lies?
CHORUS: Yes, he said that, but why, I do not know.   580
CREON: Were his eyes straight in his head? Was his mind right
when he accused me in this fashion?
CHORUS: I do not know; I have no eyes to see
what princes do. Here comes the king himself.

[*Enter* OEDIPUS.]

OEDIPUS: You, sir, how is it you come here? Have you so much   585
brazen-faced daring that you venture in
my house although you are proved manifestly
the murderer of that man, and though you tried,
openly, highway robbery of my crown?
For God's sake, tell me what you saw in me,   590
what cowardice or what stupidity,
that made you lay a plot like this against me?
Did you imagine I should not observe
the crafty scheme that stole upon me or
seeing it, take no means to counter it?   595
Was it not stupid of you to make the attempt,
to try to hunt down royal power without
the people at your back or friends? For only

600 with the people at your back or money can
the hunt end in the capture of a crown.
CREON: Do you know what you're doing? Will you listen
to words to answer yours, and then pass judgment?
OEDIPUS: You're quick to speak, but I am slow to grasp you,
for I have found you dangerous,—and my foe.
605 CREON: First of all hear what I shall say to that.
OEDIPUS: At least don't tell me that you are not guilty.
CREON: If you think obstinacy without wisdom
a valuable possession, you are wrong.
OEDIPUS: And you are wrong if you believe that one,
610 a criminal, will not be punished only
because he is my kinsman.
CREON: This is but just—
but tell me, then, of what offense I'm guilty?
OEDIPUS: Did you or did you not urge me to send
to this prophetic mumbler?
CREON: I did indeed,
615 and I shall stand by what I told you.
OEDIPUS: How long ago is it since Laius . . .
CREON: What about Laius? I don't understand.
OEDIPUS: Vanished—died—was murdered?
CREON: It is long,
a long, long time to reckon.
OEDIPUS: Was this prophet
in the profession then?
620 CREON: He was, and honoured
as highly as he is today.
OEDIPUS: At that time did he say a word about me?
CREON: Never, at least when I was near him.
OEDIPUS: You never made a search for the dead man?
625 CREON: We searched, indeed, but never learned of anything.
OEDIPUS: Why did our wise old friend not say this then?
CREON: I don't know; and when I know nothing, I
usually hold my tongue.
OEDIPUS: You know this much,
and can declare this much if you are loyal.
630 CREON: What is it? If I know, I'll not deny it.
OEDIPUS: That he would not have said that I killed Laius
had he not met you first.
CREON: You know yourself
whether he said this, but I demand that I
should hear as much from you as you from me.
635 OEDIPUS: Then hear,—I'll not be proved a murderer.
CREON: Well, then. You're married to my sister.

OEDIPUS: Yes,
   that I am not disposed to deny.
CREON: You rule
   this country giving her an equal share
   in the government?
OEDIPUS: Yes, everything she wants
   she has from me.
CREON: And I, as thirdsman to you,   640
   am rated as the equal of you two?
OEDIPUS: Yes, and it's there you've proved yourself false friend.
CREON: Not if you will reflect on it as I do.
   Consider, first, if you think any one
   would choose to rule and fear rather than rule   645
   and sleep untroubled by a fear if power
   were equal in both cases. I, at least,
   I was not born with such a frantic yearning
   to be a king—but to do what kings do.
   And so it is with every one who has learned   650
   wisdom and self-control. As it stands now,
   the prizes are all mine—and without fear.
   But if I were the king myself, I must
   do much that went against the grain.
   How should despotic rule seem sweeter to me   655
   than painless power and an assured authority?
   I am not so besotted yet that I
   want other honours than those that come with profit.
   Now every man's my pleasure; every man greets me;
   now those who are your suitors fawn on me,—   660
   success for them depends upon my favour.
   Why should I let all this go to win that?
   My mind would not be traitor if it's wise;
   I am no treason lover, of my nature,
   nor would I ever dare to join a plot.   665
   Prove what I say. Go to the oracle
   at Pytho and inquire about the answers,
   if they are as I told you. For the rest,
   if you discover I laid any plot
   together with the seer, kill me, I say,   670
   not only by your vote but by my own.
   But do not charge me on obscure opinion
   without some proof to back it. It's not just
   lightly to count your knaves as honest men,
   nor honest men as knaves. To throw away   675
   an honest friend is, as it were, to throw
   your life away, which a man loves the best.

In time you will know all with certainty;
time is the only test of honest men,
680 one day is space enough to know a rogue.
CHORUS: His words are wise, king, if one fears to fall.
Those who are quick of temper are not safe.
OEDIPUS: When he that plots against me secretly
moves quickly, I must quickly counterplot.
685 If I wait taking no decisive measure
his business will be done, and mine be spoiled.
CREON: What do you want to do then? Banish me?
OEDIPUS: No, certainly; kill you, not banish you.[3]
CREON: I do not think that you've your wits about you.
OEDIPUS: For my own interests, yes.
690 CREON: But for mine, too,
you should think equally.
OEDIPUS: You are a rogue.
CREON: Suppose you do not understand?
OEDIPUS: But yet
I must be ruler.
CREON: Not if you rule badly.
OEDIPUS: O, city, city!
CREON: I too have some share
695 in the city; it is not yours alone.
CHORUS: Stop, my lords! Here—and in the nick of time
I see Jocasta coming from the house;
with her help lay the quarrel that now stirs you.

[*Enter* JOCASTA.]

JOCASTA: For shame! Why have you raised this foolish squabbling
700 brawl? Are you not ashamed to air your private
griefs when the country's sick? Go in, you, Oedipus,
and you, too, Creon, into the house. Don't magnify
your nothing troubles.
CREON: Sister, Oedipus,
your husband, thinks he has the right to do
705 terrible wrongs—he has but to choose between
two terrors: banishing or killing me.
OEDIPUS: He's right, Jocasta; for I find him plotting
with knavish tricks against my person.
CREON: That God may never bless me! May I die
710 accursed, if I have been guilty of
one tittle of the charge you bring against me!

3. *Translator's note:* Two lines omitted here owing to the confusion in the dialogue consequent on the loss of a third line. The lines as they stand in Jebb's edition (1902) are: OED.: That you may show what manner of thing is envy. / CREON: You speak as one that will not yield or trust. / [OED. *lost line.*]

JOCASTA: I beg you, Oedipus, trust him in this,
    spare him for the sake of this his oath to God,
    for my sake, and the sake of those who stand here.
CHORUS: Be gracious, be merciful,   715
    we beg of you.
OEDIPUS: In what would you have me yield?
CHORUS: He has been no silly child in the past.
    He is strong in his oath now.
    Spare him.   720
OEDIPUS: Do you know what you ask?
CHORUS: Yes.
OEDIPUS: Tell me then.
CHORUS: He has been your friend before all men's eyes; do not cast him
    away dishonoured on an obscure conjecture.   725
OEDIPUS: I would have you know that this request of yours
    really requests my death or banishment.
CHORUS: May the Sun God, king of Gods, forbid! May I die without God's
    blessing, without friends' help, if I had any such thought. But my
    spirit is broken by my unhappiness for my wasting country; and   730
    this would but add troubles amongst ourselves to the other
    troubles.
OEDIPUS: Well, let him go then—if I must die ten times for it,
    or be sent out dishonoured into exile.
    It is your lips that prayed for him I pitied,   735
    not his; wherever he is, I shall hate him.
CREON: I see you sulk in yielding and you're dangerous
    when you are out of temper; natures like yours
    are justly heaviest for themselves to bear.
OEDIPUS: Leave me alone! Take yourself off, I tell you.   740
CREON: I'll go, you have not known me, but they have,
    and they have known my innocence.

    [*Exit.*]

CHORUS: Won't you take him inside, lady?
JOCASTA: Yes, when I've found out what was the matter.
CHORUS: There was some misconceived suspicion of a story, and on the other   745
    side the sting of injustice.
JOCASTA: So, on both sides?
CHORUS: Yes.
JOCASTA: What was the story?
CHORUS: I think it best, in the interests of the country, to leave it where it   750
    ended.
OEDIPUS: You see where you have ended, straight of judgment
    although you are, by softening my anger.
CHORUS: Sir, I have said before and I say again—be sure that I would have been
    proved a madman, bankrupt in sane council, if I should put you away, you   755

who steered the country I love safely when she was crazed with troubles.
God grant that now, too, you may prove a fortunate guide for us.

JOCASTA: Tell me, my lord, I beg of you, what was it
that roused your anger so?

OEDIPUS: Yes, I will tell you.
760   I honour you more than I honour them.
         It was Creon and the plots he laid against me.

JOCASTA: Tell me—if you can clearly tell the quarrel—

OEDIPUS: Creon says
         that I'm the murderer of Laius.

JOCASTA: Of his own knowledge or on information?

765 OEDIPUS: He sent this rascal prophet to me, since
         he keeps his own mouth clean of any guilt.

JOCASTA: Do not concern yourself about this matter;
         listen to me and learn that human beings
         have no part in the craft of prophecy.
770   Of that I'll show you a short proof.
         There was an oracle once that came to Laius,—
         I will not say that it was Phoebus' own,
         but it was from his servants—and it told him
         that it was fate that he should die a victim
775   at the hands of his own son, a son to be born
         of Laius and me. But, see now, he,
         the king, was killed by foreign highway robbers
         at a place where three roads meet—so goes the story;
         and for the son—before three days were out
780   after his birth King Laius pierced his ankles
         and by the hands of others cast him forth
         upon a pathless hillside. So Apollo
         failed to fulfill his oracle to the son,
         that he should kill his father, and to Laius
785   also proved false in that the thing he feared,
         death at his son's hands, never came to pass.
         So clear in this case were the oracles,
         so clear and false. Give them no heed, I say;
         what God discovers need of, easily
         he shows to us himself.

790 OEDIPUS: O dear Jocasta,
         as I hear this from you, there comes upon me
         a wandering of the soul—I could run mad.

JOCASTA: What trouble is it, that you turn again
         and speak like this?

OEDIPUS: I thought I heard you say
795   that Laius was killed at a crossroads.

JOCASTA: Yes, that was how the story went and still
         that word goes round.

OEDIPUS: Where is this place, Jocasta,
    where he was murdered?
JOCASTA: Phocis is the country
    and the road splits there, one of two roads from Delphi,
    another comes from Daulia.
OEDIPUS: How long ago is this?   800
JOCASTA: The news came to the city just before
    you became king and all men's eyes looked to you.
    What is it, Oedipus, that's in your mind?
OEDIPUS: What have you designed, O Zeus, to do with me?
JOCASTA: What is the thought that troubles your heart?   805
OEDIPUS: Don't ask me yet—tell me of Laius—
    How did he look? How old or young was he?
JOCASTA: He was a tall man and his hair was grizzled
    already—nearly white—and in his form
    not unlike you.
OEDIPUS: O God, I think I have   810
    called curses on myself in ignorance.
JOCASTA: What do you mean? I am terrified
    when I look at you.
OEDIPUS: I have a deadly fear
    that the old seer had eyes. You'll show me more
    if you can tell me one more thing.
JOCASTA: I will.   815
    I'm frightened,—but if I can understand,
    I'll tell you all you ask.
OEDIPUS: How was his company?
    Had he few with him when he went this journey,
    or many servants, as would suit a prince?
JOCASTA: In all there were but five, and among them   820
    a herald; and one carriage for the king.
OEDIPUS: It's plain—it's plain—who was it told you this?
JOCASTA: The only servant that escaped safe home.
OEDIPUS: Is he at home now?
JOCASTA: No, when he came home again
    and saw you king and Laius was dead,   825
    he came to me and touched my hand and begged
    that I should send him to the fields to be
    my shepherd and so he might see the city
    as far off as he might. So I
    sent him away. He was an honest man,   830
    as slaves go, and was worthy of far more
    than what he asked of me.
OEDIPUS: O, how I wish that he could come back quickly!
JOCASTA: He can. Why is your heart so set on this?
OEDIPUS: O dear Jocasta, I am full of fears   835

that I have spoken far too much; and therefore
I wish to see this shepherd.

JOCASTA: He will come;
but, Oedipus, I think I'm worthy too
to know what it is that disquiets you.

840   OEDIPUS: It shall not be kept from you, since my mind
has gone so far with its forebodings. Whom
should I confide in rather than you, who is there
of more importance to me who have passed
through such a fortune?

845   Polybus was my father, king of Corinth,
and Merope, the Dorian, my mother.
I was held greatest of the citizens
in Corinth till a curious chance befell me
as I shall tell you—curious, indeed,

850   but hardly worth the store I set upon it.
There was a dinner and at it a man,
a drunken man, accused me in his drink
of being bastard. I was furious
but held my temper under for that day.

855   Next day I went and taxed my parents with it;
they took the insult very ill from him,
the drunken fellow who had uttered it.
So I was comforted for their part, but
still this thing rankled always, for the story

860   crept about widely. And I went at last
to Pytho, though my parents did not know.
But Phoebus sent me home again unhonoured
in what I came to learn, but he foretold
other and desperate horrors to befall me,

865   that I was fated to lie with my mother,
and show to daylight an accursed breed
which men would not endure, and I was doomed
to be murderer of the father that begot me.
When I heard this I fled, and in the days

870   that followed I would measure from the stars
the whereabouts of Corinth—yes, I fled
to somewhere where I should not see fulfilled
the infamies told in that dreadful oracle.
And as I journeyed I came to the place

875   where, as you say, this king met with his death.
Jocasta, I will tell you the whole truth.
When I was near the branching of the crossroads,
going on foot, I was encountered by
a herald and a carriage with a man in it,

880   just as you tell me. He that led the way

and the old man himself wanted to thrust me
out of the road by force. I became angry
and struck the coachman who was pushing me.
When the old man saw this he watched his moment,
and as I passed he struck me from his carriage,   885
full on the head with his two pointed goad.
But he was paid in full and presently
my stick had struck him backwards from the car
and he rolled out of it. And then I killed them
all. If it happened there was any tie   890
of kinship twixt this man and Laius,
who is then now more miserable than I,
what man on earth so hated by the Gods,
since neither citizen nor foreigner
may welcome me at home or even greet me,   895
but drive me out of doors? And it is I,
I and no other have so cursed myself.
And I pollute the bed of him I killed
by the hands that killed him. Was I not born evil?
Am I not utterly unclean? I had to fly   900
and in my banishment not even see
my kindred nor set foot in my own country,
or otherwise my fate was to be yoked
in marriage with my mother and kill my father,
Polybus who begot me and had reared me.   905
Would not one rightly judge and say that on me
these things were sent by some malignant God?
O no, no, no—O holy majesty
of God on high, may I not see that day!
May I be gone out of men's sight before   910
I see the deadly taint of this disaster
come upon me.

CHORUS: Sir, we too fear these things. But until you see this man face to face
and hear his story, hope.

OEDIPUS: Yes, I have just this much of hope—to wait until the herdsman comes.   915

JOCASTA: And when he comes, what do you want with him?

OEDIPUS: I'll tell you; if I find that his story is the same as yours, I at least will be
clear of this guilt.

JOCASTA: Why what so particularly did you learn from my story?

OEDIPUS: You said that he spoke of highway *robbers* who killed Laius. Now if he   920
uses the same number, it was not I who killed him. One man cannot be the
same as many. But if he speaks of a man travelling alone, then clearly the
burden of the guilt inclines towards me.

JOCASTA: Be sure, at least, that this was how he told the story. He cannot unsay
it now, for every one in the city heard it—not I alone. But, Oedipus, even if   925
he diverges from what he said then, he shall never prove that the murder of

Laius squares rightly with the prophecy—for Loxias declared that the king
should be killed by his own son. And that poor creature did not kill him
surely,— for he died himself first. So as far as prophecy goes, henceforward
930   I shall not look to the right hand or the left.
OEDIPUS: Right. But yet, send some one for the peasant to bring him here; do
       not neglect it.
JOCASTA: I will send quickly. Now let me go indoors. I will do nothing except
       what pleases you.

[*Exeunt.*]

935   CHORUS: [*Strophe.*] May destiny ever find me
       pious in word and deed
       prescribed by the laws that live on high:
       laws begotten in the clear air of heaven,
       whose only father is Olympus;
940   no mortal nature brought them to birth,
       no forgetfulness shall lull them to sleep;
       for God is great in them and grows not old.

       [*Antistrophe.*]

       Insolence breeds the tyrant, insolence
       if it is glutted with a surfeit, unseasonable, unprofitable,
945   climbs to the roof-top and plunges
       sheer down to the ruin that must be,
       and there its feet are no service.
       But I pray that the God may never
       abolish the eager ambition that profits the state.
950   For I shall never cease to hold the God as our protector.

       [*Strophe.*]

       If a man walks with haughtiness
       of hand or word and gives no heed
       to Justice and the shrines of Gods
       despises—may an evil doom
955   smite him for his ill-starred pride of heart!—
       if he reaps gains without justice
       and will not hold from impiety
       and his fingers itch for untouchable things.
       When such things are done, what man shall contrive
960   to shield his soul from the shafts of the God?
       When such deeds are held in honour,
       why should I honour the Gods in the dance?

       [*Antistrophe.*]

       No longer to the holy place,
       to the navel of earth I'll go

to worship, nor to Abae 965
nor to Olympia,
unless the oracles are proved to fit,
for all men's hands to point at.
O Zeus, if you are rightly called
the sovereign lord, all-mastering, 970
let this not escape you nor your ever-living power!
The oracles concerning Laius
are old and dim and men regard them not.
Apollo is nowhere clear in honour; God's service perishes.

[*Enter* JOCASTA, *carrying garlands.*]

JOCASTA: Princes of the land, I have had the thought to go 975
to the Gods' temples, bringing in my hand
garlands and gifts of incense, as you see.
For Oedipus excites himself too much
at every sort of trouble, not conjecturing,
like a man of sense, what will be from what was, 980
but he is always at the speaker's mercy,
when he speaks terrors. I can do no good
by my advice, and so I came as suppliant
to you, Lycaean Apollo, who are nearest.
These are the symbols of my prayer and this 985
my prayer: grant us escape free of the curse.
Now when we look to him we are all afraid;
he's pilot of our ship and he is frightened.

[*Enter* MESSENGER.]

MESSENGER: Might I learn from you, sirs, where is the house of Oedipus? Or
best of all, if you know, where is the king himself? 990
CHORUS: This is his house and he is within doors. This lady is his wife and
mother of his children.
MESSENGER: God bless you, lady, and God bless your household! God bless
Oedipus' noble wife!
JOCASTA: God bless you, sir, for your kind greeting! What do you want of us that 995
you have come here? What have you to tell us?
MESSENGER: Good news, lady. Good for your house and for your husband.
JOCASTA: What is your news? Who sent you to us?
MESSENGER: I come from Corinth and the news I bring will give you pleasure.
Perhaps a little pain too. 1000
JOCASTA: What is this news of double meaning?
MESSENGER: The people of the Isthmus will choose Oedipus to be their king.
That is the rumour there.
JOCASTA: But isn't their king still old Polybus?
MESSENGER: No. He is in his grave. Death has got him. 1005
JOCASTA: Is that the truth? Is Oedipus' father dead?

MESSENGER: May I die myself if it be otherwise!

JOCASTA: [*To a* SERVANT.] Be quick and run to the King with the news! O oracles of the Gods, where are you now? It was from this man Oedipus fled, lest he should be his murderer! And now he is dead, in the course of nature, and
1010   not killed by Oedipus.

[*Enter* OEDIPUS.]

OEDIPUS: Dearest Jocasta, why have you sent for me?

JOCASTA: Listen to this man and when you hear reflect what is the outcome of the holy oracles of the Gods.

1015   OEDIPUS: Who is he? What is his message for me?

JOCASTA: He is from Corinth and he tells us that your father Polybus is dead and gone.

OEDIPUS: What's this you say, sir? Tell me yourself.

MESSENGER: Since this is the first matter you want clearly told: Polybus has
1020   gone down to death. You may be sure of it.

OEDIPUS: By treachery or sickness?

MESSENGER: A small thing will put old bodies asleep.

OEDIPUS: So he died of sickness, it seems,—poor old man!

MESSENGER: Yes, and of age—the long years he had measured.

1025   OEDIPUS: Ha! Ha! O dear Jocasta, why should one
            look to the Pythian hearth[4]? Why should one look
            to the birds screaming overhead? They prophesied
            that I should kill my father! But he's dead,
            and hidden deep in earth, and I stand here
1030   who never laid a hand on spear against him,—
            unless perhaps he died of longing for me,
            and thus I am his murderer. But they,
            the oracles, as they stand—he's taken them
            away with him, they're dead as he himself is,
            and worthless.

1035   JOCASTA: That I told you before now.

OEDIPUS: You did, but I was misled by my fear.

JOCASTA: Then lay no more of them to heart, not one

OEDIPUS: But surely I must fear my mother's bed?

JOCASTA: Why should man fear since chance is all in all
1040   for him, and he can clearly foreknow nothing?
            Best to live lightly, as one can, unthinkingly.
            As to your mother's marriage bed,—don't fear it.
            Before this, in dreams too, as well as oracles,
            many a man has lain with his own mother.
1045   But he to whom such things are nothing bears
            his life most easily.

OEDIPUS: All that you say would be said perfectly

4. Delphi.

if she were dead; but since she lives I must
still fear, although you talk so well, Jocasta.
JOCASTA: Still in your father's death there's light of comfort? 1050
OEDIPUS: Great light of comfort; but I fear the living.
MESSENGER: Who is the woman that makes you afraid?
OEDIPUS: Merope, old man, Polybus' wife.
MESSENGER: What about her frightens the queen and you?
OEDIPUS: A terrible oracle, stranger, from the Gods. 1055
MESSENGER: Can it be told? Or does the sacred law
     forbid another to have knowledge of it?
OEDIPUS: O no! Once on a time Loxias said
     that I should lie with my own mother and
     take on my hands the blood of my own father. 1060
     And so for these long years I've lived away
     from Corinth; it has been to my great happiness;
     but yet it's sweet to see the face of parents.
MESSENGER: This was the fear which drove you out of Corinth?
OEDIPUS: Old man, I did not wish to kill my father. 1065
MESSENGER: Why should I not free you from this fear, sir,
     since I have come to you in all goodwill?
OEDIPUS: You would not find me thankless if you did.
MESSENGER: Why, it was just for this I brought the news, —
     to earn your thanks when you had come safe home. 1070
OEDIPUS: No, I will never come near my parents.
MESSENGER: Son,
     it's very plain you don't know what you're doing.
OEDIPUS: What do you mean, old man? For God's sake, tell me.
MESSENGER: If your homecoming is checked by fears like these.
OEDIPUS: Yes, I'm afraid that Phoebus may prove right. 1075
MESSENGER: The murder and the incest?
OEDIPUS: Yes, old man;
     that is my constant terror.
MESSENGER: Do you know
     that all your fears are empty?
OEDIPUS: How is that,
     if they are father and mother and I their son?
MESSENGER: Because Polybus was no kin to you in blood. 1080
OEDIPUS: What, was not Polybus my father?
MESSENGER: No more than I but just so much.
OEDIPUS: How can
     my father be my father as much as one
     that's nothing to me?
MESSENGER: Neither he nor I
     begat you.
OEDIPUS: Why then did he call me son? 1085
MESSENGER: A gift he took you from these hands of mine.

OEDIPUS: Did he love so much what he took from another's hand?

MESSENGER: His childlessness before persuaded him.

OEDIPUS: Was I a child you bought or found when I
 was given to him?

1090 MESSENGER: On Cithaeron's slopes
 in the twisting thickets you were found.

OEDIPUS: And why
 were you a traveller in those parts?

MESSENGER: I was
 in charge of mountain flocks.

OEDIPUS: You were a shepherd?
 A hireling vagrant?

1095 MESSENGER: Yes, but at least at that time
 the man that saved your life, son.

OEDIPUS: What ailed me when you took me in your arms?

MESSENGER: In that your ankles should be witnesses.

OEDIPUS: Why do you speak of that old pain?

MESSENGER: I loosed you;
 the tendons of your feet were pierced and fettered, —

1100 OEDIPUS: My swaddling clothes brought me a rare disgrace.

MESSENGER: So that from this you're called your present name.

OEDIPUS: Was this my father's doing or my mother's?
 For God's sake, tell me.

MESSENGER: I don't know, but he
 who gave you to me has more knowledge than I.

1105 OEDIPUS: You yourself did not find me then? You took me
 from someone else?

MESSENGER: Yes, from another shepherd.

OEDIPUS: Who was he? Do you know him well enough
 to tell?

MESSENGER: He was called Laius' man.

OEDIPUS: You mean the king who reigned here in the old days?

MESSENGER: Yes, he was that man's shepherd.

1110 OEDIPUS: Is he alive
 still, so that I could see him?

MESSENGER: You who live here
 would know that best.

OEDIPUS: Do any of you here
 know of this shepherd whom he speaks about
 in town or in the fields? Tell me. It's time

1115 that this was found out once for all.

CHORUS: I think he is none other than the peasant
 whom you have sought to see already; but
 Jocasta here can tell us best of that.

OEDIPUS: Jocasta, do you know about this man

1120 whom we have sent for? Is he the man he mentions?

JOCASTA: Why ask of whom he spoke? Don't give it heed;
nor try to keep in mind what has been said.
It will be wasted labour.

OEDIPUS: With such clues
I could not fail to bring my birth to light.

JOCASTA: I beg you—do not hunt this out—I beg you,
if you have any care for your own life.
What I am suffering is enough.

OEDIPUS: Keep up
your heart, Jocasta. Though I'm proved a slave,
thrice slave, and though my mother is thrice slave,
you'll not be shown to be of lowly lineage.

JOCASTA: O be persuaded by me, I entreat you;
do not do this.

OEDIPUS: I will not be persuaded to let be
the chance of finding out the whole thing clearly.

JOCASTA: It is because I wish you well that I
give you this counsel—and it's the best counsel.

OEDIPUS: Then the best counsel vexes me, and has
for some while since.

JOCASTA: O Oedipus, God help you!
God keep you from the knowledge of who you are!

OEDIPUS: Here, some one, go and fetch the shepherd for me;
and let her find her joy in her rich family!

JOCASTA: O Oedipus, unhappy Oedipus!
that is all I can call you, and the last thing
that I shall ever call you.

[*Exit.*]

CHORUS: Why has the queen gone, Oedipus, in wild
grief rushing from us? I am afraid that trouble
will break out of this silence.

OEDIPUS: Break out what will! I at least shall be
willing to see my ancestry, though humble.
Perhaps she is ashamed of my low birth,
for she has all a woman's high-flown pride.
But I account myself a child of Fortune,
beneficent Fortune, and I shall not be
dishonoured. She's the mother from whom I spring;
the months, my brothers, marked me, now as small,
and now again as mighty. Such is my breeding,
and I shall never prove so false to it,
as not to find the secret of my birth.

CHORUS: [*Strophe.*] If I am a prophet and wise of heart
you shall not fail, Cithaeron,
by the limitless sky, you shall not!—

1125

1130

1135

1140

1145

1150

1155

1160

to know at tomorrow's full moon
that Oedipus honours you,
as native to him and mother and nurse at once;

1165   and that you are honoured in dancing by us, as finding favour in sight of our
king.
Apollo, to whom we cry, find these things pleasing!

[*Antistrophe.*]

Who was it bore you, child? One of
the long-lived nymphs who lay with Pan[5] —
1170   the father who treads the hills?
Or was she a bride of Loxias, your mother? The grassy slopes
are all of them dear to him. Or perhaps Cyllene's king[6]
or the Bacchants' God[7] that lives on the tops
of the hills received you a gift from some
1175   one of the Helicon Nymphs,[8] with whom he mostly plays?

[*Enter an* OLD MAN, *led by* OEDIPUS' *servants.*]

OEDIPUS: If some one like myself who never met him
may make a guess, — I think this is the herdsman,
whom we were seeking. His old age is consonant
with the other. And besides, the men who bring him
1180   I recognize as my own servants. You
perhaps may better me in knowledge since
you've seen the man before.

CHORUS: You can be sure
I recognize him. For if Laius
had ever an honest shepherd, this was he.

1185   OEDIPUS: You, sir, from Corinth, I must ask you first,
is this the man you spoke of?

MESSENGER: This is he
before your eyes.

OEDIPUS: Old man, look here at me
and tell me what I ask you. Were you ever
a servant of King Laius?

HERDSMAN: I was, —
1190   no slave he bought but reared in his own house.

OEDIPUS: What did you do as work? How did you live?

HERDSMAN: Most of my life was spent among the flocks.

OEDIPUS: In what part of the country did you live?

HERDSMAN: Cithaeron and the places near to it.

1195   OEDIPUS: And somewhere there perhaps you knew this man?

---

5. God of nature; half-man, half-goat.   6. Mountain reputed to be the birthplace of Hermes, the
messenger of the gods.   7. Dionysus, the god of wine.   8. The Muses; nine sister goddesses
who presided over poetry, music, and the arts.

HERDSMAN: What was his occupation? Who?
OEDIPUS: This man here
    have you had any dealings with him?
HERDSMAN: No—
    not such that I can quickly call to mind.
MESSENGER: That is no wonder, master. But I'll make him remember what he
    does not know. For I know, that he well knows the country of Cithaeron,   1200
    how he with two flocks, I with one kept company for three years—each year
    half a year—from spring till autumn time and then when winter came I
    drove my flocks to our fold home again and he to Laius' steadings. Well—
    am I right or not in what I said we did?
HERDSMAN: You're right—although it's a long time ago.   1205
MESSENGER: Do you remember giving me a child
    to bring up as my foster child?
HERDSMAN: What's this?
    Why do you ask this question?
MESSENGER: Look old man,
    here he is—here's the man who was that child!
HERDSMAN: Death take you! Won't you hold your tongue?
OEDIPUS: No, no,   1210
    do not find fault with him, old man. Your words
    are more at fault than his.
HERDSMAN: O best of masters,
    how do I give offense?
OEDIPUS: When you refuse
    to speak about the child of whom he asks you.
HERDSMAN: He speaks out of his ignorance, without meaning.   1215
OEDIPUS: If you'll not talk to gratify me, you
    will talk with pain to urge you.
HERDSMAN: O please, sir,
    don't hurt an old man, sir.
OEDIPUS: [To the SERVANTS.] Here, one of you,
    twist his hands behind him.
HERDSMAN: Why, God help me, why?
    What do you want to know?
OEDIPUS: You gave a child   1220
    to him,—the child he asked you of?
HERDSMAN: I did.
    I wish I'd died the day I did.
OEDIPUS: You will
    unless you tell me truly.
HERDSMAN: And I'll die
    far worse if I should tell you.
OEDIPUS: This fellow
    is bent on more delays, as it would seem.   1225
HERDSMAN: O no, no! I have told you that I gave it.

OEDIPUS: Where did you get this child from? Was it your own or did you get it
    from another?

HERDSMAN: Not
    my own at all; I had it from some one.

1230   OEDIPUS: One of these citizens? or from what house?

HERDSMAN: O master, please—I beg you, master, please
    don't ask me more.

OEDIPUS: You're a dead man if I
    ask you again.

HERDSMAN: It was one of the children
    of Laius.

OEDIPUS: A slave? Or born in wedlock?

1235   HERDSMAN: O God, I am on the brink of frightful speech.

OEDIPUS: And I of frightful hearing. But I must hear.

HERDSMAN: The child was called his child; but she within,
    your wife would tell you best how all this was.

OEDIPUS: *She* gave it to you?

HERDSMAN: Yes, she did, my lord.

OEDIPUS: To do what with it?

1240   HERDSMAN: Make away with it.

OEDIPUS: She was so hard—its mother?

HERDSMAN: Aye, through fear
    of evil oracles.

OEDIPUS: Which?

HERDSMAN: They said that he
    should kill his parents.

OEDIPUS: How was it that you
    gave it away to this old man?

HERDSMAN: O master,

1245   I pitied it, and thought that I could send it
    off to another country and this man
    was from another country. But he saved it
    for the most terrible troubles. If you are
    the man he says you are, you're bred to misery.

1250   OEDIPUS: O, O, O, they will all come,
    all come out clearly! Light of the sun, let me
    look upon you no more after today!
    I who first saw the light bred of a match
    accursed, and accursed in my living

1255   with them I lived with, cursed in my killing.

[*Exeunt all but the* CHORUS.]

CHORUS: [*Strophe.*] O generations of men, how I
    count you as equal with those who live
    not at all!
    What man, what man on earth wins more

of happiness than a seeming
and after that turning away?
Oedipus, you are my pattern of this,
Oedipus, you and your fate!
Luckless Oedipus, whom of all men
I envy not at all.

[*Antistrophe.*]

In as much as he shot his bolt
beyond the others and won the prize
of happiness complete—
O Zeus—and killed and reduced to nought
the hooked taloned maid of the riddling speech,
standing a tower against death for my land:
hence he was called my king and hence
was honoured the highest of all
honours; and hence he ruled
in the great city of Thebes.

[*Strophe.*]

But now whose tale is more miserable?
Who is there lives with a savager fate?
Whose troubles so reverse his life as his?

O Oedipus, the famous prince
for whom a great haven
the same both as father and son
sufficed for generation,
how, O how, have the furrows ploughed
by your father endured to bear you, poor wretch,
and hold their peace so long?

[*Antistrophe.*]

Time who sees all has found you out
against your will; judges your marriage accursed,
begetter and begot at one in it.

O child of Laius,
would I had never seen you.
I weep for you and cry
a dirge of lamentation.

To speak directly, I drew my breath
from you at the first and so now I lull
my mouth to sleep with your name.

[*Enter a* SECOND MESSENGER.]

SECOND MESSENGER: O Princes always honoured by our country,
what deeds you'll hear of and what horrors see,

1260

1265

1270

1275

1280

1285

1290

1295

what grief you'll feel, if you as true born Thebans
care for the house of Labdacus's sons.

1300 Phasis nor Ister cannot purge this house,
I think, with all their streams, such things
it hides, such evils shortly will bring forth
into the light, whether they will or not;
and troubles hurt the most
1305 when they prove self-inflicted.

CHORUS: What we had known before did not fall short
of bitter groaning's worth; what's more to tell?

SECOND MESSENGER: Shortest to hear and tell—our glorious queen
Jocasta's dead.

CHORUS: Unhappy woman! How?

1310 SECOND MESSENGER: By her own hand. The worst of what was done
you cannot know. You did not see the sight.
Yet in so far as I remember it
you'll hear the end of our unlucky queen.
When she came raging into the house she went
1315 straight to her marriage bed, tearing her hair
with both her hands, and crying upon Laius
long dead—Do you remember, Laius,
that night long past which bred a child for us
to send you to your death and leave
1320 a mother making children with her son?
And then she groaned and cursed the bed in which
she brought forth husband by her husband, children
by her own child, an infamous double bond.
How after that she died I do not know,—
1325 for Oedipus distracted us from seeing.
He burst upon us shouting and we looked
to him as he paced frantically around,
begging us always: Give me a sword, I say,
to find this wife no wife, this mother's womb,
1330 this field of double sowing whence I sprang
and where I sowed my children! As he raved
some god showed him the way—none of us there.
Bellowing terribly and led by some
invisible guide he rushed on the two doors,—
1335 wrenching the hollow bolts out of their sockets,
he charged inside. There, there, we saw his wife
hanging, the twisted rope around her neck.
When he saw her, he cried out fearfully
and cut the dangling noose. Then, as she lay,
1340 poor woman, on the ground, what happened after,
was terrible to see. He tore the brooches—
the gold chased brooches fastening her robe—

away from her and lifting them up high
dashed them on his own eyeballs, shrieking out
such things as: they will never see the crime   1345
I have committed or had done upon me!
Dark eyes, now in the days to come look on
forbidden faces, do not recognize
those whom you long for—with such imprecations
he struck his eyes again and yet again   1350
with the brooches. And the bleeding eyeballs gushed
and stained his beard—no sluggish oozing drops
but a black rain and bloody hail poured down.

So it has broken—and not on one head
but troubles mixed for husband and for wife.   1355
The fortune of the days gone by was true
good fortune—but today groans and destruction
and death and shame—of all ills can be named
not one is missing.
CHORUS: Is he now in any ease from pain?
SECOND MESSENGER: He shouts   1360
for some one to unbar the doors and show him
to all the men of Thebes, his father's killer,
his mother's—no I cannot say the word,
it is unholy—for he'll cast himself,
out of the land, he says, and not remain   1365
to bring a curse upon his house, the curse
he called upon it in his proclamation. But
he wants for strength, aye, and some one to guide him;
his sickness is too great to bear. You, too,
will be shown that. The bolts are opening.   1370
Soon you will see a sight to waken pity
even in the horror of it.

[*Enter the blinded* OEDIPUS.]

CHORUS: This is a terrible sight for men to see!
I never found a worse!
Poor wretch, what madness came upon you!   1375
What evil spirit leaped upon your life
to your ill-luck—a leap beyond man's strength!
Indeed I pity you, but I cannot
look at you, though there's much I want to ask
and much to learn and much to see.   1380
I shudder at the sight of you.
OEDIPUS: O, O,
where am I going? Where is my voice
borne on the wind to and fro?
Spirit, how far have you sprung?   1385

CHORUS: To a terrible place whereof men's ears
    may not hear, nor their eyes behold it.
OEDIPUS: Darkness!
    Horror of darkness enfolding, resistless, unspeakable visitant sped by an ill
1390   wind in haste!
    madness and stabbing pain and memory
    of evil deeds I have done!
CHORUS: In such misfortunes it's no wonder
    if double weighs the burden of your grief.
1395 OEDIPUS: My friend,
    you are the only one steadfast, the only one that attends on me;
    you still stay nursing the blind man.
    Your care is not unnoticed. I can know
    your voice, although this darkness is my world.
1400 CHORUS: Doer of dreadful deeds, how did you dare
    so far to do despite to your own eyes?
    what spirit urged you to it?
OEDIPUS: It was Apollo, friends, Apollo,
    that brought this bitter bitterness, my sorrows to completion.
1405   But the hand that struck me
    was none but my own.
    Why should I see
    whose vision showed me nothing sweet to see?
CHORUS: These things are as you say.
1410 OEDIPUS: What can I see to love?
    What greeting can touch my ears with joy?
    Take me away, and haste—to a place out of the way!
    Take me away, my friends, the greatly miserable,
    the most accursed, whom God too hates
1415   above all men on earth!
CHORUS: Unhappy in your mind and your misfortune,
    would I had never known you!
OEDIPUS: Curse on the man who took
    the cruel bonds from off my legs, as I lay in the field.
1420   He stole me from death and saved me,
    no kindly service.
    Had I died then
    I would not be so burdensome to friends.
CHORUS: I, too, could have wished it had been so.
1425 OEDIPUS: Then I would not have come
    to kill my father and marry my mother infamously.
    Now I am godless and child of impurity,
    begetter in the same seed that created my wretched self.
    If there is any ill worse than ill,
1430   that is the lot of Oedipus.

CHORUS: I cannot say your remedy was good;
    you would be better dead than blind and living.
OEDIPUS: What I have done here was best done—don't tell me
    otherwise, do not give me further counsel.
    I do not know with what eyes I could look   1435
    upon my father when I die and go
    under the earth, nor yet my wretched mother—
    those two to whom I have done things deserving
    worse punishment than hanging. Would the sight
    of children, bred as mine are, gladden me?   1440
    No, not these eyes, never. And my city,
    its towers and sacred places of the Gods,
    of these I robbed my miserable self
    when I commanded all to drive *him* out,
    the criminal since proved by God impure   1445
    and of the race of Laius.
    To this guilt I bore witness against myself—
    with what eyes shall I look upon my people?
    No. If there were a means to choke the fountain
    of hearing I would not have stayed my hand   1450
    from locking up my miserable carcase,
    seeing and hearing nothing; it is sweet
    to keep our thoughts out of the range of hurt.

    Cithaeron, why did you receive me? why
    having received me did you not kill me straight?   1455
    And so I had not shown to men my birth.

    O Polybus and Corinth and the house,
    the old house that I used to call my father's—
    what fairness you were nurse to, and what foulness
    festered beneath! Now I am found to be   1460
    a sinner and a son of sinners. Crossroads,
    and hidden glade, oak and the narrow way
    at the crossroads, that drank my father's blood
    offered you by my hands, do you remember
    still what I did as you looked on, and what   1465
    I did when I came here? O marriage, marriage!
    you bred me and again when you had bred
    bred children of your child and showed to men
    brides, wives and mothers and the foulest deeds
    that can be in this world of ours.   1470

    Come—it's unfit to say what is unfit
    to do.—I beg of you in God's name hide me
    somewhere outside your country, yes, or kill me,

or throw me into the sea, to be forever
1475   out of your sight. Approach and deign to touch me
for all my wretchedness, and do not fear.
No man but I can bear my evil doom.
CHORUS: Here Creon comes in fit time to perform
or give advice in what you ask of us.
1480   Creon is left sole ruler in your stead.
OEDIPUS: Creon! Creon! What shall I say to him?
How can I justly hope that he will trust me?
In what is past I have been proved towards him
an utter liar.

[*Enter* CREON.]

CREON: Oedipus, I've come
1485   not so that I might laugh at you nor taunt you
with evil of the past. But if you still
are without shame before the face of men
reverence at least the flame that gives all life,
our Lord the Sun, and do not show unveiled
1490   to him pollution such that neither land
nor holy rain nor light of day can welcome.

[*To a* SERVANT.]

Be quick and take him in. It is most decent
that only kin should see and hear the troubles
of kin.
OEDIPUS: I beg you, since you've torn me from
1495   my dreadful expectations and have come
in a most noble spirit to a man
that has used you vilely—do a thing for me.
I shall speak for your own good, not for my own.
CREON: What do you need that you would ask of me?
1500 OEDIPUS: Drive me from here with all the speed you can
to where I may not hear a human voice.
CREON: Be sure, I would have done this had not I
wished first of all to learn from the God the course
of action I should follow.
OEDIPUS: But his word
1505   has been quite clear to let the parricide,
the sinner, die.
CREON: Yes, that indeed was said.
But in the present need we had best discover
what we should do.
OEDIPUS: And will you ask about
a man so wretched?

CREON: Now even you will trust
the God.
OEDIPUS: So. I command you—and will beseech you—   1510
to her that lies inside that house give burial
as you would have it; she is yours and rightly
you will perform the rites for her. For me—
never let this my father's city have me
living a dweller in it. Leave me live   1515
in the mountains where Cithaeron is, that's called
my mountain, which my mother and my father
while they were living would have made my tomb.
So I may die by their decree who sought
indeed to kill me. Yet I know this much: 1520
no sickness and no other thing will kill me.
I would not have been saved from death if not
for some strange evil fate. Well, let my fate
go where it will.
Creon, you need not care
about my sons; they're men and so wherever   1525
they are, they will not lack a livelihood.
But my two girls—so sad and pitiful—
whose table never stood apart from mine,
and everything I touched they always shared—
O Creon, have a thought for them! And most   1530
I wish that you might suffer me to touch them
and sorrow with them.

[*Enter* ANTIGONE *and* ISMENE, OEDIPUS' *two daughters.*]

O my lord! O true noble Creon! Can I
really be touching them, as when I saw?
What shall I say?   1535
Yes, I can hear them sobbing—my two darlings!
and Creon has had pity and has sent me
what I loved most?
Am I right?
CREON: You're right: it was I gave you this   1540
because I knew from old days how you loved them
as I see now.
OEDIPUS: God bless you for it, Creon,
and may God guard you better on your road
than he did me!
O children,
where are you? Come here, come to my hands,   1545
a brother's hands which turned your father's eyes,
those bright eyes you knew once, to what you see,

a father seeing nothing, knowing nothing,
begetting you from his own source of life.
1550   I weep for you—I cannot see your faces—
I weep when I think of the bitterness
there will be in your lives, how you must live
before the world. At what assemblages
of citizens will you make one? to what
1555   gay company will you go and not come home
in tears instead of sharing in the holiday?
And when you're ripe for marriage, who will he be,
the man who'll risk to take such infamy
as shall cling to my children, to bring hurt
1560   on them and those that marry with them? What
curse is not there? "Your father killed his father
and sowed the seed where he had sprung himself
and begot you out of the womb that held him."
These insults you will hear. Then who will marry you?
1565   No one, my children; clearly you are doomed
to waste away in barrenness unmarried.
Son of Menoeceus, since you are all the father
left these two girls, and we, their parents, both
are dead to them—do not allow them wander
1570   like beggars, poor and husbandless.
They are of your own blood.
And do not make them equal with myself
in wretchedness; for you can see them now
so young, so utterly alone, save for you only.
1575   Touch my hand, noble Creon, and say yes.
If you were older, children, and were wiser,
there's much advice I'd give you. But as it is,
let this be what you pray: give me a life
wherever there is opportunity
1580   to live, and better life than was my father's.
CREON: Your tears have had enough of scope; now go within the house.
OEDIPUS: I must obey, though bitter of heart.
CREON: In season, all is good.
OEDIPUS: Do you know on what conditions I obey?
CREON: You tell me them,
and I shall know them when I hear.
1585   OEDIPUS: That you shall send me out
to live away from Thebes.
CREON: That gift you must ask of the God.
OEDIPUS: But I'm now hated by the Gods.
CREON: So quickly you'll obtain your prayer.
OEDIPUS: You consent then?
CREON: What I do not mean, I do not use to say.

OEDIPUS: Now lead me away from here.
CREON: Let go the children, then, and come.
OEDIPUS: Do not take them from me.
CREON: Do not seek to be master in everything,   1590
  for the things you mastered did not follow you throughout your life.

[*As* CREON *and* OEDIPUS *go out.*]

CHORUS: You that live in my ancestral Thebes, behold this Oedipus,—
  him who knew the famous riddles and was a man most masterful;
  not a citizen who did not look with envy on his lot—
  see him now and see the breakers of misfortune swallow him!   1595
  Look upon that last day always. Count no mortal happy till
  he has passed the final limit of his life secure from pain.

THE END

ca. 429 B.C.E.

OSCAR WILDE

The Importance of Being Earnest

CHARACTERS

ALGERNON MONCRIEFF	MISS PRISM
LANE	CECILY CARDEW
ERNEST WORTHING	CANON CHASUBLE
LADY AUGUSTA BRACKNELL	MERRIMAN
GWENDOLEN FAIRFAX	

ACT I

SCENE: *Morning room in* ALGERNON's *flat in Half-Moon Street.*[1]
The room is luxuriously and artistically furnished. The sound of a piano is heard in the adjoining room.

[LANE *is arranging afternoon tea on the table, and after the music has ceased,* ALGERNON *enters.*]

ALGERNON: Did you hear what I was playing, Lane?
LANE: I didn't think it polite to listen, sir.
ALGERNON: I'm sorry for that, for your sake. I don't play accurately—anyone can
  play accurately—but I play with wonderful expression. As far as the piano is
  concerned, sentiment is my forte. I keep science for Life.

1. Half-Moon Street runs north from Piccadilly near Hyde Park. Like many of the addresses in the
play, it is in Mayfair, a very fashionable section of London.

LANE: Yes, sir.

ALGERNON: And, speaking of the science of Life, have you got the cucumber sandwiches cut for Lady Bracknell?

LANE: Yes, sir. [*Hands them on a salver.*]

ALGERNON: [*Inspects them, takes two, and sits down on the sofa.*] Oh! . . . . by the way, Lane, I see from your book that on Thursday night, when Lord Shoreham and Mr. Worthing were dining with me, eight bottles of champagne are entered as having been consumed.

LANE: Yes, sir; eight bottles and a pint.

ALGERNON: Why is it that at a bachelor's establishment the servants invariably drink the champagne? I ask merely for information.

LANE: I attribute it to the superior quality of the wine, sir. I have often observed that in married households the champagne is rarely of a first-rate brand.

ALGERNON: Good heavens! Is marriage so demoralizing as that?

LANE: I believe it *is* a very pleasant state, sir. I have had very little experience of it myself up to the present. I have only been married once. That was in consequence of a misunderstanding between myself and a young person.

ALGERNON: [*Languidly.*] I don't know that I am much interested in your family life, Lane.

LANE: No, sir; it is not a very interesting subject. I never think of it myself.

ALGERNON: Very natural, I am sure. That will do, Lane, thank you.

LANE: Thank you, sir. [LANE *goes out.*]

ALGERNON: Lane's views on marriage seem somewhat lax. Really, if the lower orders don't set us a good example, what on earth is the use of them? They seem, as a class, to have absolutely no sense of moral responsibility.

[*Enter* LANE.]

LANE: Mr. Ernest Worthing.

[*Enter* JACK. LANE *goes out.*]

ALGERNON: How are you, my dear Ernest? What brings you up to town?

JACK: Oh, pleasure, pleasure! What else should bring one anywhere? Eating as usual, I see, Algy!

ALGERNON: [*Stiffly.*] I believe it is customary in good society to take some slight refreshment at five o'clock. Where have you been since last Thursday?

JACK: [*Sitting down on the sofa.*] In the country.

ALGERNON: What on earth do you do there?

JACK: [*Pulling off his gloves.*] When one is in town one amuses oneself. When one is in the country one amuses other people. It is excessively boring.

ALGERNON: And who are the people you amuse?

JACK: [*Airily.*] Oh, neighbors, neighbors.

ALGERNON: Got nice neighbors in your part of Shropshire?

JACK: Perfectly horrid! Never speak to one of them.

ALGERNON: How immensely you must amuse them! [*Goes over and takes sandwich.*] By the way, Shropshire is your county, is it not?

JACK: Eh? Shropshire? Yes, of course.[2] Hallo! Why all these cups? Why cucumber sandwiches? Why such reckless extravagance in one so young? Who is coming to tea?

ALGERNON: Oh! merely Aunt Augusta and Gwendolen.

JACK: How perfectly delightful!

ALGERNON: Yes, that is all very well; but I am afraid Aunt Augusta won't quite approve of your being here.

JACK: May I ask why?

ALGERNON: My dear fellow, the way you flirt with Gwendolen is perfectly disgraceful. It is almost as bad as the way Gwendolen flirts with you.

JACK: I am in love with Gwendolen. I have come up to town expressly to propose to her.

ALGERNON: I thought you had come up for pleasure? . . . I call that business.

JACK: How utterly unromantic you are!

ALGERNON: I really don't see anything romantic in proposing. It is very romantic to be in love. But there is nothing romantic about a definite proposal. Why, one may be accepted. One usually is, I believe. Then the excitement is all over. The very essence of romance is uncertainty. If ever I get married, I'll certainly try to forget the fact.

JACK: I have no doubt about that, dear Algy. The divorce court was specially invented for people whose memories are so curiously constituted.

ALGERNON: Oh! there is no use speculating on that subject. Divorces are made in heaven — [JACK *puts out his hand to take a sandwich.* ALGERNON *at once interferes.*] Please don't touch the cucumber sandwiches. They are ordered specially for Aunt Augusta. [*Takes one and eats it.*]

JACK: Well, you have been eating them all the time.

ALGERNON: That is quite a different matter. She is my aunt. [*Takes plate from below.*] Have some bread and butter. The bread and butter is for Gwendolen. Gwendolen is devoted to bread and butter.

JACK: [*Advancing to table and helping himself.*] And very good bread and butter it is too.

ALGERNON: Well, my dear fellow, you need not eat as if you were going to eat it all. You behave as if you were married to her already. You are not married to her already, and I don't think you ever will be.

JACK: Why on earth do you say that?

ALGERNON: Well, in the first place, girls never marry the men they flirt with. Girls don't think it right.

JACK: Oh, that is nonsense!

ALGERNON: It isn't. It is a great truth. It accounts for the extraordinary number of bachelors that one sees all over the place. In the second place, I don't give my consent.

JACK: Your consent!

---

2. As we learn later, Jack's country place is in Hertfordshire, to the north of London. He is attempting to deceive Algernon by giving a false location to the west, on the Welsh border.

ALGERNON: My dear fellow, Gwendolen is my first cousin. And before I allow you to marry her, you will have to clear up the whole question of Cecily. [*Rings bell.*]

JACK: Cecily! What on earth do you mean? What do you mean, Algy, by Cecily? I don't know anyone of the name of Cecily.

[*Enter* LANE.]

ALGERNON: Bring me that cigarette case Mr. Worthing left in the smoking-room the last time he dined here.

LANE: Yes, sir. [LANE *goes out.*]

JACK: Do you mean to say you have had my cigarette case all this time? I wish to goodness you had let me know. I have been writing frantic letters to Scotland Yard about it. I was very nearly offering a large reward.

ALGERNON: Well, I wish you would offer one. I happen to be more than usually hard up.

JACK: There is no good offering a large reward now that the thing is found.

[*Enter* LANE *with the cigarette case on a salver.* ALGERNON *takes it at once.* LANE *goes out.*]

ALGERNON: I think that is rather mean of you, Ernest, I must say. [*Opens case and examines it.*] However, it makes no matter, for, now that I look at the inscription inside, I find that the thing isn't yours after all.

JACK: Of course it's mine. [*Moving to him.*] You have seen me with it a hundred times, and you have no right whatsoever to read what is written inside. It is a very ungentlemanly thing to read a private cigarette case.

ALGERNON: Oh! it is absurd to have a hard-and-fast rule about what one should read and what one shouldn't. More than half of modern culture depends on what one shouldn't read.

JACK: I am quite aware of the fact, and I don't propose to discuss modern culture. It isn't the sort of thing one should talk of in private. I simply want my cigarette case back.

ALGERNON: Yes; but this isn't your cigarette case. This cigarette case is a present from someone of the name of Cecily, and you said you didn't know anyone of that name.

JACK: Well, if you want to know, Cecily happens to be my aunt.

ALGERNON: Your aunt!

JACK: Yes. Charming old lady she is, too. Lives at Tunbridge Wells.³ Just give it back to me, Algy.

ALGERNON: [*Retreating to back of sofa.*] But why does she call herself Cecily if she is your aunt and lives at Tunbridge Wells? [*Reading.*] "From little Cecily with her fondest love."

JACK: [*Moving to sofa and kneeling upon it.*] My dear fellow, what on earth is there in that? Some aunts are tall, some aunts are not tall. That is a matter that surely an aunt may be allowed to decide for herself. You seem to think

---

3. Tunbridge Wells is a resort town in Kent, to the southeast of London.

that every aunt should be exactly like your aunt! That is absurd! For heaven's sake give me back my cigarette case. [*Follows* ALGY *round the room.*]

ALGERNON: Yes. But why does your aunt call you her uncle? "From little Cecily, with her fondest love to her dear Uncle Jack." There is no objection, I admit, to an aunt being a small aunt, but why an aunt, no matter what her size may be, should call her own nephew her uncle, I can't quite make out. Besides, your name isn't Jack at all; it is Ernest.

JACK: It isn't Ernest; it's Jack.

ALGERNON: You have always told me it was Ernest. I have introduced you to everyone as Ernest. You answer to the name of Ernest. You look as if your name was Ernest. You are the most earnest looking person I ever saw in my life. It is perfectly absurd your saying that your name isn't Ernest. It's on your cards. Here is one of them. [*Taking it from case.*] "Mr. Ernest Worthing, B. 4, The Albany."[4] I'll keep this as a proof that your name is Ernest if ever you attempt to deny it to me, or to Gwendolen, or to anyone else. [*Puts the card in his pocket.*]

JACK: Well, my name is Ernest in town and Jack in the country, and the cigarette case was given to me in the country.

ALGERNON: Yes, but that does not account for the fact that your small Aunt Cecily, who lives at Tunbridge Wells, calls you her dear uncle. Come, old boy, you had much better have the thing out at once.

JACK: My dear Algy, you talk exactly as if you were a dentist. It is very vulgar to talk like a dentist when one isn't a dentist. It produces a false impression.

ALGERNON: Well, that is exactly what dentists always do. Now, go on! Tell me the whole thing. I may mention that I have always suspected you of being a confirmed and secret Bunburyist; and I am quite sure of it now.

JACK: Bunburyist? What on earth do you mean by a Bunburyist?

ALGERNON: I'll reveal to you the meaning of that incomparable expression as soon as you are kind enough to inform me why you are Ernest in town and Jack in the country.

JACK: Well, produce my cigarette case first.

ALGERNON: Here it is. [*Hands cigarette case.*] Now produce your explanation, and pray make it improbable. [*Sits on sofa.*]

JACK: My dear fellow, there is nothing improbable about my explanation at all. In fact it's perfectly ordinary. Old Mr. Thomas Cardew, who adopted me when I was a little boy, made me in his will guardian to his granddaughter, Miss Cecily Cardew. Cecily, who addresses me as her uncle from motives of respect that you could not possibly appreciate, lives at my place in the country under the charge of her admirable governess, Miss Prism.

ALGERNON: Where is that place in the country, by the way?

JACK: That is nothing to you, dear boy. You are not going to be invited. . . . I may tell you candidly that the place is not in Shropshire.

ALGERNON: I suspected that, my dear fellow! I have Bunburyed all over Shrop-

---

4. An apartment building for single gentlemen on Piccadilly, to the east of Algernon's flat.

shire on two separate occasions. Now, go on. Why are you Ernest in town and Jack in the country?

JACK: My dear Algy, I don't know whether you will be able to understand my real motives. You are hardly serious enough. When one is placed in the position of guardian, one has to adopt a very high moral tone on all subjects. It's one's duty to do so. And as a high moral tone can hardly be said to conduce very much to either one's health or one's happiness, in order to get up to town I have always pretended to have a younger brother of the name of Ernest, who lives in the Albany, and gets into the most dreadful scrapes. That, my dear Algy, is the whole truth pure and simple.

ALGERNON: The truth is rarely pure and never simple. Modern life would be very tedious if it were either, and modern literature a complete impossibility!

JACK: That wouldn't be at all a bad thing.

ALGERNON: Literary criticism is not your forte, my dear fellow. Don't try it. You should leave that to people who haven't been at a university. They do it so well in the daily papers. What you really are is a Bunburyist. I was quite right in saying you were a Bunburyist. You are one of the most advanced Bunburyists I know.

JACK: What on earth do you mean?

ALGERNON: You have invented a very useful young brother called Ernest, in order that you may be able to come up to town as often as you like. I have invented an invaluable permanent invalid called Bunbury, in order that I may be able to go down into the country whenever I choose. Bunbury is perfectly invaluable. If it wasn't for Bunbury's extraordinary bad health, for instance, I wouldn't be able to dine with you at Willis's[5] tonight, for I have been really engaged to Aunt Augusta for more than a week.

JACK: I haven't asked you to dine with me anywhere tonight.

ALGERNON: I know. You are absurdly careless about sending out invitations. It is very foolish of you. Nothing annoys people so much as not receiving invitations.

JACK: You had much better dine with your Aunt Augusta.

ALGERNON: I haven't the smallest intention of doing anything of the kind. To begin with, I dined there on Monday, and once a week is quite enough to dine with one's own relations. In the second place, whenever I do dine there I am always treated as a member of the family, and sent down with either no woman at all, or two. In the third place, I know perfectly well whom she will place me next to, tonight. She will place me next Mary Farquhar, who always flirts with her own husband across the dinner table. That is not very pleasant. Indeed, it is not even decent . . . and that sort of thing is enormously on the increase. The amount of women in London who flirt with their own husbands is perfectly scandalous. It looks so bad. It is simply washing one's clean linen in public. Besides, now that I know you to be a confirmed Bun-

---

5. A well-known establishment for dining on King Street, off St. James's Street and quite near Picadilly.

buryist, I naturally want to talk to you about Bunburying. I want to tell you the rules.

JACK: I'm not a Bunburyist at all. If Gwendolen accepts me, I am going to kill my brother, indeed I think I'll kill him in any case. Cecily is a little too much interested in him. It is rather a bore. So I am going to get rid of Ernest. And I strongly advise you to do the same with Mr. . . . with your invalid friend who has the absurd name.

ALGERNON: Nothing will induce me to part with Bunbury, and if you ever get married, which seems to me extremely problematic, you will be very glad to know Bunbury. A man who marries without knowing Bunbury has a very tedious time of it.

JACK: That is nonsense. If I marry a charming girl like Gwendolen, and she is the only girl I ever saw in my life that I would marry, I certainly won't want to know Bunbury.

ALGERNON: Then your wife will. You don't seem to realize, that in married life three is company and two is none.

JACK: [*Sententiously.*] That, my dear young friend, is the theory that the corrupt French drama has been propounding for the last fifty years.[6]

ALGERNON: Yes; and that the happy English home has proved in half the time.

JACK: For heaven's sake, don't try to be cynical. It's perfectly easy to be cynical.

ALGERNON: My dear fellow, it isn't easy to be anything nowadays. There's such a lot of beastly competition about. [*The sound of an electric bell is heard.*] Ah! that must be Aunt Augusta. Only relatives, or creditors, ever ring in that Wagnerian manner.[7] Now, if I get her out of the way for ten minutes, so that you can have an opportunity for proposing to Gwendolen, may I dine with you tonight at Willis's?

JACK: I suppose so, if you want to.

ALGERNON: Yes, but you must be serious about it. I hate people who are not serious about meals. It is so shallow of them.

[*Enter* LANE.]

LANE: Lady Bracknell and Miss Fairfax.

[ALGERNON *goes forward to meet them. Enter* LADY BRACKNELL *and* GWEN-DOLEN.]

LADY BRACKNELL: Good afternoon, dear Algernon, I hope you are behaving very well.

ALGERNON: I'm feeling very well, Aunt Augusta.

LADY BRACKNELL: That's not quite the same thing. In fact the two things rarely go together. [*Sees* JACK *and bows to him with icy coldness.*]

ALGERNON: [*To* GWENDOLEN.] Dear me, you are smart!

GWENDOLEN: I am always smart! Aren't I, Mr. Worthing?

6. Beginning in the middle of the 19th century, French drama produced plays dealing with subjects such as adultery, prostitution, and illegitimacy. The heavily censored English theater either avoided such subjects or dealt with them more circumspectly.   7. Many earlier listeners to the music of Richard Wagner found it extremely loud and, consequently, peremptory in demanding attention.

JACK: You're quite perfect, Miss Fairfax.

GWENDOLEN: Oh! I hope I am not that. It would leave no room for developments, and I intend to develop in many directions. [GWENDOLEN *and* JACK *sit down together in the corner.*]

LADY BRACKNELL: I'm sorry if we are a little late, Algernon, but I was obliged to call on dear Lady Harbury. I hadn't been there since her poor husband's death. I never saw a woman so altered; she looks quite twenty years younger. And now I'll have a cup of tea, and one of those nice cucumber sandwiches you promised me.

ALGERNON: Certainly, Aunt Augusta. [*Goes over to teatable.*]

LADY BRACKNELL: Won't you come and sit here, Gwendolen?

GWENDOLEN: Thanks, mamma, I'm quite comfortable where I am.

ALGERNON: [*Picking up empty plate in horror.*] Good heavens! Lane! Why are there no cucumber sandwiches? I ordered them specially.

LANE: [*Gravely.*] There were no cucumbers in the market this morning, sir. I went down twice.

ALGERNON: No cucumbers!

LANE: No, sir. Not even for ready money.

ALGERNON: That will do, Lane, thank you.

LANE: Thank you, sir.

ALGERNON: I am greatly distressed, Aunt Augusta, about there being no cucumbers, not even for ready money.

LADY BRACKNELL: It really makes no matter, Algernon. I had some crumpets with Lady Harbury, who seems to me to be living entirely for pleasure now.

ALGERNON: I hear her hair has turned quite gold from grief.

LADY BRACKNELL: It certainly has changed its color. From what cause I, of course, cannot say. [ALGERNON *crosses and hands tea.*] Thank you. I've quite a treat for you tonight, Algernon. I am going to send you down with Mary Farquhar. She is such a nice woman, and so attentive to her husband. It's delightful to watch them.

ALGERNON: I am afraid, Aunt Augusta, I shall have to give up the pleasure of dining with you tonight after all.

LADY BRACKNELL: [*Frowning.*] I hope not, Algernon. It would put my table completely out. Your uncle would have to dine upstairs. Fortunately he is accustomed to that.

ALGERNON: It is a great bore, and, I need hardly say, a terrible disappointment to me, but the fact is I have just had a telegram to say that my poor friend Bunbury is very ill again. [*Exchanges glances with* JACK.] They seem to think I should be with him.

LADY BRACKNELL: It is very strange. This Mr. Bunbury seems to suffer from curiously bad health.

ALGERNON: Yes; poor Bunbury is a dreadful invalid.

LADY BRACKNELL: Well, I must say, Algernon, that I think it is high time that Mr. Bunbury made up his mind whether he was going to live or to die. This shilly-shallying with the question is absurd. Nor do I in any way approve of the modern sympathy with invalids. I consider it morbid. Illness of any kind is hardly a thing to be encouraged in others. Health is the primary duty of life. I am always telling that to your poor uncle, but he never seems to take much notice . . . as far as any improvement in his ailments goes. I should be obliged if you would ask Mr. Bunbury, from me, to be kind enough not to have a relapse on Saturday, for I rely on you to arrange my music for me. It is my last reception, and one wants something that will encourage conversation, particularly at the end of the season when everyone has practically said whatever they had to say, which, in most cases, was probably not much.

ALGERNON: I'll speak to Bunbury, Aunt Augusta, if he is still conscious, and I think I can promise you he'll be all right by Saturday. Of course the music is a great difficulty. You see, if one plays good music, people don't listen, and if one plays bad music, people don't talk. But I'll run over the program I've drawn out, if you will kindly come into the next room for a moment.

LADY BRACKNELL: Thank you, Algernon. It is very thoughtful of you. [*Rising, and following* ALGERNON.] I'm sure the program will be delightful, after a few expurgations. French songs I cannot possibly allow. People always seem to think that they are improper, and either look shocked, which is vulgar, or laugh, which is worse. But German sounds a thoroughly respectable language, and indeed, I believe is so. Gwendolen, you will accompany me.

GWENDOLEN: Certainly, mamma.

[LADY BRACKNELL *and* ALGERNON *go into the music room*, GWENDOLEN *remains behind.*]

JACK: Charming day it has been, Miss Fairfax.

GWENDOLEN: Pray don't talk to me about the weather, Mr. Worthing. Whenever people talk to me about the weather, I always feel quite certain that they mean something else. And that makes me so nervous.

JACK: I do mean something else.

GWENDOLWN: I thought so. In fact, I am never wrong.

JACK: And I would like to be allowed to take advantage of Lady Bracknell's temporary absence . . .

GWENDOLEN. I would certainly advise you to do so. Mamma has a way of coming back suddenly into a room that I have often had to speak to her about.

JACK: [*Nervously.*] Miss Fairfax, ever since I met you I have admired you more than any girl . . . I have ever met since . . . I met you.

GWENDOLEN: Yes, I am quite aware of the fact. And I often wish that in public, at any rate, you had been more demonstrative. For me you have always had an irresistible fascination. Even before I met you I was far from indifferent to you. [JACK *looks at her in amazement.*] We live, as I hope you know, Mr. Worthing, in an age of ideals. The fact is constantly mentioned in the more expensive monthly magazines, and has reached the provincial pulpits, I am told: and my ideal has always been to love someone of the name of Ernest. There is something in that name that inspires absolute confidence. The moment Algernon first mentioned to me that he had a friend called Ernest, I knew I was destined to love you.

JACK: You really love me, Gwendolen?

GWENDOLEN: Passionately!

JACK: Darling! You don't know how happy you've made me.

GWENDOLEN: My own Ernest!

JACK: But you don't really mean to say that you couldn't love me if my name wasn't Ernest?

GWENDOLEN: But your name is Ernest.

JACK: Yes, I know it is. But supposing it was something else? Do you mean to say you couldn't love me then?

GWENDOLEN: [Glibly.] Ah! that is clearly a metaphysical speculation, and like most metaphysical speculations has very little reference at all to the actual facts of real life, as we know them.

JACK: Personally, darling, to speak quite candidly, I don't much care about the name of Ernest . . . I don't think the name suits me at all.

GWENDOLEN: It suits you perfectly. It is a divine name. It has a music of its own. It produces vibrations.

JACK: Well, really, Gwendolen, I must say that I think there are lots of other much nicer names. I think Jack, for instance, a charming name.

GWENDOLEN: Jack? . . . No, there is very little music in the name Jack, if any at all, indeed. It does not thrill. It produces absolutely no vibrations. . . . I have known several Jacks, and they all, without exception, were more than usually plain. Besides, Jack is a notorious domesticity for John! And I pity any woman who is married to a man called John. She would probably never be allowed to know the entrancing pleasure of a single moment's solitude. The only really safe name is Ernest.

JACK: Gwendolen, I must get christened at once—I mean we must get married at once. There is no time to be lost.

GWENDOLWN: Married, Mr. Worthing?

JACK: [Astounded.] Well . . . surely. You know that I love you, and you led me to believe, Miss Fairfax, that you were not absolutely indifferent to me.

GWENDOLEN: I adore you. But you haven't proposed to me yet. Nothing has been said at all about marriage. The subject has not even been touched on.

JACK: Well . . . may I propose to you now?

GWENDOLEN: I think it would be an admirable opportunity. And to spare you any possible disappointment, Mr. Worthing, I think it only fair to tell you quite frankly beforehand that I am fully determined to accept you.

JACK: Gwendolen!

GWENDOLEN: Yes, Mr. Worthing, what have you got to say to me?

JACK: You know what I have got to say to you.

GWENDOLEN: Yes, but you don't say it.

JACK: Gwendolen, will you marry me? [Goes on his knees.]

GWENDOLEN: Of course I will, darling. How long you have been about it! I am afraid you have had very little experience in how to propose.

JACK: My own one, I have never loved anyone in the world but you.

GWENDOLEN: Yes, but men often propose for practice. I know my brother Gerald does. All my girlfriends tell me so. What wonderfully blue eyes you have,

Ernest! They are quite, quite blue. I hope you will always look at me just like that, especially when there are other people present.

[*Enter* LADY BRACKNELL.]

LADY BRACKNELL: Mr. Worthing! Rise, sir, from this semi-recumbent posture. It is most indecorous.

GWENDOLEN: Mamma! [*He tries to rise; she restrains him.*] I must beg you to retire. This is no place for you. Besides, Mr. Worthing has not quite finished yet.

LADY BRACKNELL: Finished what, may I ask?

GWENDOLEN: I am engaged to Mr. Worthing, mamma.

[*They rise together.*]

LADY BRACKNELL: Pardon me, you are not engaged to anyone. When you do become engaged to someone, I, or you father, should his health permit him, will inform you of the fact. An engagement should come on a young girl as a surprise, pleasant or unpleasant, as the case may be. It is hardly a matter that she could be allowed to arrange for herself. . . . And now I have a few questions to put to you, Mr. Worthing. While I am making these inquiries, you, Gwendolen, will wait for me below in the carriage.

GWENDOLEN: [*Reproachfully.*] Mamma!

LADY BRACKNELL: In the carriage, Gwendolen! [GWENDOLEN *goes to the door. She and* JACK *blow kisses to each other behind* LADY BRACKNELL's *back.* LADY BRACKNELL *looks vaguely about as if she could not understand what the noise was. Finally turns round.*] Gwendolen, the carriage!

GWENDOLEN: Yes, mamma. [*Goes out, looking back at* JACK.]

LADY BRACKNELL: [*Sitting down.*] You can take a seat, Mr. Worthing.

[*Looks in her pocket for notebook and pencil.*]

JACK: Thank you, Lady Bracknell, I prefer standing.

LADY BRACKNELL: [*Pencil and notebook in hand.*] I feel bound to tell you that you are not down on my list of eligible young men, although I have the same list as the dear Duchess of Bolton has. We work together, in fact. However, I am quite ready to enter your name, should your answers be what a really affectionate mother requires. Do you smoke?

JACK: Well, yes, I must admit I smoke.

LADY BRACKNELL: I am glad to hear it. A man should always have an occupation of some kind. There are far too many idle men in London as it is. How old are you?

JACK: Twenty-nine.

LADY BRACKNELL: A very good age to be married at. I have always been of opinion that a man who desires to get married should know either everything or nothing. Which do you know?

JACK: [*After some hesitation.*] I know nothing, Lady Bracknell.

LADY BRACKNELL: I am pleased to hear it. I do not approve of anything that tampers with natural ignorance. Ignorance is like a delicate exotic fruit; touch it and the bloom is gone. The whole theory of modern education is radically unsound. Fortunately in England, at any rate, education produces no effect whatsoever. If it did, it would prove a serious danger to the upper classes, and probably lead to acts of violence in Grosvenor Square.[8] What is your income?

JACK: Between seven and eight thousand a year.[9]

LADY BRACKNELL: [*Makes a note in her book.*] In land, or in investments?

JACK: In investments, chiefly.

LADY BRACKNELL: That is satisfactory. What between the duties expected of one during one's lifetime, and the duties exacted from one after one's death, land has ceased to be either a profit or a pleasure. It gives one position, and prevents one from keeping it up. That's all that can be said about land.

JACK: I have a country house with some land, of course, attached to it, about fifteen hundred acres, I believe; but I don't depend on that for my real income. In fact, as far as I can make out, the poachers are the only people who make anything out of it.

LADY BRACKNELL: A country house! How many bedrooms? Well, that point can be cleared up afterwards. You have a town house, I hope? A girl with a simple, unspoiled nature, like Gwendolen, could hardly be expected to reside in the country.

JACK: Well, I own a house in Belgrave Square,[1] but it is let by the year to Lady Bloxham. Of course, I can get it back whenever I like, at six months' notice.

LADY BRACKNELL: Lady Bloxham? I don't know her.

JACK: Oh, she goes about very little. She is a lady considerably advanced in years.

LADY BRACKNELL: Ah, nowadays that is no guarantee of respectability of character. What number in Belgrave Square?

JACK: 149.

LADY BRACKNELL: [*Shaking her head.*] The unfashionable side. I thought there was something. However, that could easily be altered.

JACK: Do you mean the fashion, or the side?

LADY BRACKNELL: [*Sternly.*] Both, if necessary, I presume. What are your politics?

JACK: Well, I am afraid I really have none. I am a Liberal Unionist.

LADY BRACKNELL: Oh, they count as Tories.[2] They dine with us. Or come in the evening, at any rate. Now to minor matters. Are your parents living?

JACK: I have lost both my parents.

LADY BRACKNELL: Both? To lose one parent may be regarded as a misfortune — to lose *both* seems like carelessness. Who was your father? He was evidently a man of some wealth. Was he born in what the Radical papers call the purple of commerce, or did he rise from the ranks of aristocracy?

JACK: I am afraid I really don't know. The fact is, Lady Bracknell, I said I had

8. A fashionable location in Mayfair.　　9. A considerable income for the time.　　1. Belgrave Square is near the southeast corner of Hyde Park in Belgravia, another fashionable section of London.　　2. Members of the Conservative Party. Opposed to home rule for Ireland, they joined forces with the Liberal Unionists, who had split from the Liberal Party over the issue.

lost my parents. It would be nearer the truth to say that my parents seem to have lost me. . . . I don't actually know who I am by birth. I was . . . well, I was found.

LADY BRACKNELL: Found!

JACK: The late Mr. Thomas Cardew, an old gentleman of a very charitable and kindly disposition, found me, and gave me the name of Worthing, because he happened to have a first-class ticket for Worthing in his pocket at the time. Worthing is a place in Sussex. It is a seaside resort.

LADY BRACKNELL: Where did the charitable gentleman who had a first-class ticket for this seaside resort find you?

JACK: [Gravely.] In a handbag.

LADY BRACKNELL: A handbag?

JACK: [Very seriously.] Yes, Lady Bracknell. I was in a handbag—a somewhat large, black leather handbag, with handles to it—an ordinary handbag, in fact.

LADY BRACKNELL: In what locality did this Mr. James, or Thomas, Cardew come across this ordinary handbag?

JACK: In the cloak room at Victoria Station.[3] It was given to him in mistake for his own.

LADY BRACKNELL: The cloak room at Victoria Station?

JACK: Yes. The Brighton line.

LADY BRACKNELL: The line is immaterial. Mr. Worthing, I confess I feel somewhat bewildered by what you have just told me. To be born, or at any rate, bred in a handbag, whether it had handles or not, seems to me to display a contempt for the ordinary decencies of family life that reminds one of the worst excesses of the French Revolution. And I presume you know what that unfortunate movement led to? As for the particular locality in which the handbag was found, a cloak room at a railway station might serve to conceal a social indiscretion—has probably, indeed, been used for that purpose before now—but it could hardly be regarded as an assured basis for a recognized position in good society.

JACK: May I ask you then what you would advise me to do? I need hardly say I would do anything in the world to ensure Gwendolen's happiness.

LADY BRACKNELL: I would strongly advise you, Mr. Worthing, to try and acquire some relations as soon as possible, and to make a definite effort to produce at any rate one parent, of either sex, before the season is quite over.

JACK: Well, I don't see how I could possibly manage to do that. I can produce the handbag at any moment, it is in my dressing room at home. I really think that should satisfy you, Lady Bracknell.

LADY BRACKNELL: Me, sir! What has it to do with me? You can hardly imagine that I and Lord Bracknell would dream of allowing our only daughter—a girl brought up with the utmost care—to marry into a cloak room, and form an alliance with a parcel? Good morning, Mr. Worthing!

[LADY BRACKNELL sweeps out in majestic indignation.]

3. Major railroad terminus in London.

JACK: Good morning! [ALGERNON, *from the other room, strikes up the Wedding March.* JACK *looks perfectly furious, and goes to the door.*] For goodness' sake don't play that ghastly tune, Algy! How idiotic you are!

[*The music stops, and* ALGERNON *enters cheerily.*]

ALGERNON: Didn't it go off all right, old boy? You don't mean to say Gwendolen refused you? I know it is a way she has. She is always refusing people. I think it is most ill-natured of her.

JACK: Oh, Gwendolen is as right as a trivet.[4] As far as she is concerned, we are engaged. Her mother is perfectly unbearable. Never met such a Gorgon[5] . . . I don't really know what a Gorgon is like, but I am quite sure that Lady Bracknell is one. In any case, she is a monster, without being a myth, which is rather unfair . . . I beg your pardon, Algy, I suppose I shouldn't talk about your own aunt in that way before you.

ALGERNON: My dear boy, I love hearing my relations abused. It is the only thing that makes me put up with them at all. Relations are simply a tedious pack of people who haven't got the remotest knowledge of how to live, nor the smallest instinct about when to die.

JACK: Oh, that is nonsense!

ALGERNON: It isn't!

JACK: Well, I won't argue about the matter. You always want to argue about things.

ALGERNON: That is exactly what things were originally made for.

JACK: Upon my word, if I thought that, I'd shoot myself . . . [*A pause.*] You don't think there is any chance of Gwendolen becoming like her mother in about a hundred and fifty years, do you, Algy?

ALGERNON: All women become like their mothers. That is their tragedy. No man does. That's his.

JACK: Is that clever?

ALGERNON: It is perfectly phrased! and quite as true as any observation in civilized life should be.

JACK: I am sick to death of cleverness. Everybody is clever nowadays. You can't go anywhere without meeting clever people. The thing has become an absolute public nuisance. I wish to goodness we had a few fools left.

ALGERNON: We have.

JACK: I should extremely like to meet them. What do they talk about?

ALGERNON: The fools? Oh! about the clever people, of course.

JACK: What fools!

ALGERNON: By the way, did you tell Gwendolen the truth about your being Ernest in town, and Jack in the country?

JACK: [*In a very patronizing manner.*] My dear fellow, the truth isn't quite the sort of thing one tells to a nice sweet refined girl. What extraordinary ideas you have about the way to behave to a woman!

---

4. A proverbial expression, referring to the solidity of a tripod on its three legs.   5. A mythological creature of horrible aspect, the Gorgon had snakes in place of hair. According to myth, those who looked on a Gorgon were turned to stone by the experience.

ALGERNON: The only way to behave to a woman is to make love to her, if she is pretty, and to someone else if she is plain.

JACK: Oh, that is nonsense.

ALGERNON: What about your brother? What about the profligate Ernest?

JACK: Oh, before the end of the week I shall have got rid of him. I'll say he died in Paris of apoplexy. Lots of people die of apoplexy, quite suddenly, don't they?

ALGERNON: Yes, but it's hereditary, my dear fellow. It's a sort of thing that runs in families. You had much better say a severe chill.

JACK: You are sure a severe chill isn't hereditary, or anything of that kind?

ALGERNON: Of course it isn't!

JACK: Very well, then. My poor brother Ernest is carried off suddenly in Paris, by a severe chill. That gets rid of him.

ALGERNON: But I thought you said that . . . Miss Cardew was a little too much interested in your poor brother Ernest? Won't she feel his loss a good deal?

JACK: Oh, that is all right. Cecily is not a silly romantic girl, I am glad to say. She has got a capital appetite, goes on long walks, and pays no attention at all to her lessons.

ALGERNON: I would rather like to see Cecily.

JACK: I will take very good care you never do. She is excessively pretty, and she is only just eighteen.

ALGERNON: Have you told Gwendolen yet that you have an excessively pretty ward who is only just eighteen?

JACK: Oh! one doesn't blurt these things out to people. Cecily and Gwendolen are perfectly certain to be extremely great friends. I'll bet you anything you like that half an hour after they have met, they will be calling each other sister.

ALGERNON: Women only do that when they have called each other a lot of other things first. Now, my dear boy, if we want to get a good table at Willis's, we really must go and dress. Do you know it is nearly seven?

JACK: [*Irritably.*] Oh! it always is nearly seven.

ALGERNON: Well, I'm hungry.

JACK: I never knew you when you weren't. . . .

ALGERNON: What shall we do after dinner? Go to the theater?

JACK: Oh no! I loathe listening.

ALGERNON: Well, let us go to the club?

JACK: Oh, no! I hate talking.

ALGERNON: Well, we might trot around to the Empire[6] at ten?

JACK: Oh no! I can't bear looking at things. It is so silly.

ALGERNON: Well, what shall we do?

JACK: Nothing!

ALGERNON: It is awfully hard work doing nothing. However, I don't mind hard work where there is no definite object of any kind.

6. The Empire Theatre of Varieties, a music hall on Leicester Square.

[*Enter* LANE.]

LANE: Miss Fairfax.

[*Enter* GWENDOLEN. LANE *goes out.*]

ALGERNON: Gwendolen, upon my word!

GWENDOLEN: Algy, kindly turn your back. I have something very particular to say to Mr. Worthing.

ALGERNON: Really, Gwendolen, I don't think I can allow this at all.

GWENDOLEN: Algy, you always adopt a strictly immoral attitude towards life. You are not quite old enough to do that.

[ALGERNON *retires to the fireplace.*]

JACK: My own darling!

GWENDOLEN: Ernest, we may never be married. From the expression on mamma's face I fear we never shall. Few parents nowadays pay any regard to what their children say to them. The old-fashioned respect for the young is fast dying out. Whatever influence I ever had over mamma, I lost at the age of three. But although she may prevent us from becoming man and wife, and I may marry someone else, and marry often, nothing that she can possibly do can alter my eternal devotion to you.

JACK: Dear Gwendolen!

GWENDOLEN: The story of your romantic origin, as related to me by mamma, with unpleasing comments, has naturally stirred the deeper fibers of my nature. Your Christian name has an irresistible fascination. The simplicity of your character makes you exquisitely incomprehensible to me. Your town address at the Albany I have. What is your address in the country?

JACK: The Manor House, Woolton, Hertfordshire.

[ALGERNON, *who has been carefully listening, smiles to himself, and writes the address on his shirt-cuff. Then picks up the Railway Guide.*]

GWENDOLEN: There is a good postal service, I suppose? It may be necessary to do something desperate. That of course will require serious consideration. I will communicate with you daily.

JACK: My own one!

GWENDOLEN: How long do you remain in town?

JACK: Till Monday.

GWENDOLEN: Good! Algy, you may turn round now.

ALGERNON: Thanks, I've turned round already.

GWENDOLEN: You may also ring the bell.

JACK: You will let me see you to your carriage, my own darling?

GWENDOLEN: Certainly.

JACK: [*To* LANE, *who now enters.*] I will see Miss Fairfax out.

LANE: Yes, sir.

[JACK *and* GWENDOLEN *go off.* LANE *presents several letters on a salver to* ALGERNON. *It is to be surmised that they are bills, as* ALGERNON, *after looking at the envelopes, tears them up.*]

ALGERNON: A glass of sherry, Lane.

LANE: Yes, sir.

ALGERNON: Tomorrow, Lane, I'm going Bunburying.

LANE: Yes, sir.

ALGERNON: I shall probably not be back till Monday. You can put up my dress clothes, my smoking jacket, and all the Bunbury suits . . .

LANE: Yes, sir. [*Handing sherry.*]

ALGERNON: I hope tomorrow will be a fine day, Lane.

LANE: It never is, sir.

ALGERNON: Lane, you're a perfect pessimist.

LANE: I do my best to give satisfaction, sir.

[*Enter* JACK. LANE *goes off.*]

JACK: There's a sensible, intellectual girl! the only girl I ever cared for in my life. [ALGERNON *is laughing immoderately.*] What on earth are you so amused at?

ALGERNON: Oh, I'm a little anxious about poor Bunbury, that is all.

JACK: If you don't take care, your friend Bunbury will get you into a serious scrape some day.

ALGERNON: I love scrapes. They are the only things that are never serious.

JACK: Oh, that's nonsense, Algy. You never talk anything but nonsense.

ALGERNON: Nobody ever does.

[JACK *looks indignantly at him, and leaves the room.* ALGERNON *lights a cigarette, reads his shirt-cuff, and smiles.*]

ACT-DROP

ACT II

SCENE: *Garden at the Manor House. A flight of gray stone steps leads up to the house. The garden, an old-fashioned one, full of roses. Time of year, July. Basket chairs, and a table covered with books, are set under a large yew tree.*

[MISS PRISM *discovered seated at the table.* CECILY *is at the back watering flowers.*]

MISS PRISM: [*Calling.*] Cecily, Cecily! Surely such a utilitarian occupation as the watering of flowers is rather Moulton's duty than yours? Especially at a moment when intellectual pleasures await you. Your German grammar is on the table. Pray open it at page fifteen. We will repeat yesterday's lesson.

CECILY: [*Coming over very slowly.*] But I don't like German. It isn't at all a becoming language. I know perfectly well that I look quite plain after my German lesson.

MISS PRISM: Child, you know how anxious your guardian is that you should improve yourself in every way. He laid particular stress on your German, as he was leaving for town yesterday. Indeed, he always lays stress on your German when he is leaving for town.

CECILY: Dear Uncle Jack is so very serious! Sometime he is so serious that I
    think he cannot be quite well.

MISS PRISM: [*Drawing herself up.*] Your guardian enjoys the best of health, and
    his gravity of demeanor is especially to be commended in one so compara-
    tively young as he is. I know no one who has a higher sense of duty and
    responsibility.

CECILY: I suppose that is why he often looks a little bored when we three are
    together.

MISS PRISM: Cecily! I am surprised at you. Mr. Worthing has many troubles in
    his life. Idle merriment and triviality would be out of place in his conversa-
    tion. You must remember his constant anxiety about that unfortunate young
    man his brother.

CECILY: I wish Uncle Jack would allow that unfortunate young man, his brother,
    to come down here sometimes. We might have a good influence over him,
    Miss Prism. I am sure you certainly would. You know German, and geology,
    and things of that kind influence a man very much. [CECILY *begins to write*
    in her diary.]

MISS PRISM: [*Shaking her head.*] I do not think that even I could produce any
    effect on a character that according to his own brother's admission is irre-
    trievably weak and vacillating. Indeed I am not sure that I would desire to
    reclaim him. I am not in favor of this modern mania for turning bad people
    into good people at a moment's notice. As a man sows so let him reap. You
    must put away your diary, Cecily. I really don't see why you should keep a
    diary at all.

CECILY: I keep a diary in order to enter the wonderful secrets of my life. If I
    didn't write them down I should probably forget all about them.

MISS PRISM: Memory, my dear Cecily, is the diary that we all carry about with
    us.

CECILY: Yes, but it usually chronicles the things that have never happened, and
    couldn't possibly have happened. I believe that memory is responsible for
    nearly all the three-volume novels that Mudie sends us.[7]

MISS PRISM: Do not speak slightingly of the three-volume novel, Cecily. I wrote
    one myself in earlier days.

CECILY: Did you really, Miss Prism? How wonderfully clever you are! I hope it
    did not end happily? I don't like novels that end happily. They depress me
    so much.

MISS PRISM: The good ended happily, and the bad unhappily. That is what fic-
    tion means.

CECILY: I suppose so. But it seems very unfair. And was your novel ever pub-
    lished?

MISS PRISM: Alas! no. The manuscript unfortunately was abandoned. I use the

---

7. From the 1860s to the 1890s most novels were published in three volumes. Because of the resultant price, most readers could not afford to buy copies and obtained them by subscription from
lending libraries, of which Mudie's in London was by far the largest.

word in the sense of lost or mislaid. To your work, child, these speculations are profitless.

CECILY: [*Smiling.*] But I see dear Dr. Chasuble coming up through the garden.

MISS PRISM: [*Rising and advancing.*] Dr. Chasuble! This is indeed a pleasure.

[*Enter* CANON CHASUBLE.]

CHASUBLE: And how are we this morning? Miss Prism, you are, I trust, well?

CECILY: Miss Prism has just been complaining of a slight headache. I think it would do her so much good to have a short stroll with you in the park, Dr. Chasuble.

MISS PRISM: Cecily, I have not mentioned anything about a headache.

CECILY: No, dear Miss Prism, I know that, but I felt instinctively that you had a headache. Indeed I was thinking about that, and not about my German lesson, when the Rector came in.

CHASUBLE: I hope, Cecily, you are not inattentive.

CECILY: Oh, I am afraid I am.

CHASUBLE: That is strange. Were I fortunate enough to be Miss Prism's pupil, I would hang upon her lips. [MISS PRISM *glares.*] I spoke metaphorically.—My metaphor was drawn from bees. Ahem! Mr. Worthing, I suppose, has not returned from town yet?

MISS PRISM: We do not expect him till Monday afternoon.

CHASUBLE: Ah yes, he usually likes to spend his Sunday in London. He is not one of those whose sole aim is enjoyment, as, by all accounts, that unfortunate young man his brother seems to be. But I must not disturb Egeria[8] and her pupil any longer.

MISS PRISM: Egeria? My name is Laetitia, Doctor.

CHASUBLE: [*Bowing.*] A classical allusion merely, drawn from the Pagan authors. I shall see you both no doubt at Evensong[9]?

MISS PRISM: I think, dear Doctor, I will have a stroll with you. I find I have a headache after all, and a walk might do it good.

CHASUBLE: With pleasure, Miss Prism, with pleasure. We might go as far as the schools and back.

MISS PRISM: That would be delightful. Cecily, you will read your Political Economy[1] in my absence. The chapter on the Fall of the Rupee you may omit. It is somewhat too sensational. Even these metallic problems have their melodramatic side. [*Goes down the garden with* CANON CHASUBLE.]

CECILY: [*Picks up books and throws them back on table.*] Horrid Political Economy! Horrid Geography! Horrid, horrid German!

[*Enter* MERRIMAN *with a card on a salver.*]

MERRIMAN: Mr. Ernest Worthing has just driven over from the station. He has brought his luggage with him.

---

8. A nymph in classical mythology, famous as the wise counselor of Numa Pompilius, the second of the legendary kings of Rome.   9. Evening church services.   1. I.e., book about economics.

CECILY: [*Takes the card and reads it.*] "Mr. Ernest Worthing, B. 4, The Albany, W." Uncle Jack's brother! Did you tell him Mr. Worthing was in town?

MERRIMAN: Yes, Miss. He seemed very much disappointed. I mentioned that you and Miss Prism were in the garden. He said he was anxious to speak to you privately for a moment.

CECILY. Ask Mr. Ernest Worthing to come here. I suppose you had better talk to the housekeeper about a room for him.

MERRIMAN: Yes, Miss. [MERRIMAN *goes off.*]

CECILY: I have never met any really wicked person before. I feel rather frightened. I am so afraid he will look just like everyone else. [*Enter* ALGERNON, *very gay and debonair.*] He does!

ALGERNON: [*Raising his hat.*] You are my little cousin Cecily, I'm sure.

CECILY: You are under some strange mistake. I am not little. In fact, I believe I am more than usually tall for my age. [ALGERNON *is rather taken aback.*] But I am your cousin Cecily. You, I see from your card, are Uncle Jack's brother, my cousin Ernest, my wicked cousin Ernest.

ALGERNON: Oh! I am not really wicked at all, cousin Cecily. You mustn't think that I am wicked.

CECILY: If you are not, then you have certainly been deceiving us all in a very inexcusable manner. I hope you have not been leading a double life, pretending to be wicked and being really good all the time. That would be hypocrisy.

ALGERNON: [*Looks at her in amazement.*] Oh! Of course I have been rather reckless.

CECILY: I am glad to hear it.

ALGERNON: In fact, now you mention the subject, I have been very bad in my own small way.

CECILY: I don't think you should be so proud of that, though I am sure it must have been very pleasant.

ALGERNON: It is much pleasanter being here with you.

CECILY: I can't understand how you are here at all. Uncle Jack won't be back till Monday afternoon.

ALGERNON: That is a great disappointment. I am obliged to go up by the first train on Monday morning. I have a business appointment that I am anxious . . . to miss.

CECILY: Couldn't you miss it anywhere but in London?

ALGERNON: No: the appointment is in London.

CECILY: Well, I know, of course, how important it is not to keep a business engagement, if one wants to retain any sense of the beauty of life, but still I think you had better wait till Uncle Jack arrives. I know he wants to speak to you about your emigrating.

ALGERNON: About my what?

CECILY: Your emigrating. He has gone up to buy your outfit.

ALGERNON: I certainly wouldn't let Jack buy my outfit. He has no taste in neckties at all.

CECILY: I don't think you will require neckties. Uncle Jack is sending you to Australia.

ALGERNON: Australia? I'd sooner die.

CECILY: Well, he said at dinner on Wednesday night, that you would have to choose between this world, the next world, and Australia.

ALGERNON: Oh, well! The accounts I have received of Australia and the next world are not particularly encouraging. This world is good enough for me, cousin Cecily.

CECILY: Yes, but are you good enough for it?

ALGERNON: I'm afraid I'm not that. That is why I want you to reform me. You might make that your mission, if you don't mind, cousin Cecily.

CECILY: I'm afraid I've no time, this afternoon.

ALGERNON: Well, would you mind my reforming myself this afternoon?

CECILY: It is rather Quixotic of you. But I think you should try.

ALGERNON: I will. I feel better already.

CECILY: You are looking a little worse.

ALGERNON: That is because I am hungry.

CECILY: How thoughtless of me. I should have remembered that when one is going to lead an entirely new life, one requires regular and wholesome meals. Won't you come in?

ALGERNON: Thank you. Might I have a buttonhole[2] first? I never have any appetite unless I have a buttonhole first.

CECILY: A Maréchal Niel? [Picks up scissors.]

ALGERNON: No, I'd sooner have a pink rose.

CECILY: Why? [Cuts a flower.]

ALGERNON: Because you are like a pink rose, cousin Cecily.

CECILY: I don't think it can be right for you to talk to me like that. Miss Prism never says such things to me.

ALGERNON: Then Miss Prism is a shortsighted old lady. [CECILY puts the rose in his buttonhole.] You are the prettiest girl I ever saw.

CECILY: Miss Prism says that all good looks are a snare.

ALGERNON: They are a snare that every sensible man would like to be caught in.

CECILY: Oh! I don't think I would care to catch a sensible man. I shouldn't know what to talk to him about.

[They pass into the house. MISS PRISM and DR. CHASUBLE return.]

MISS PRISM: You are too much alone, dear Dr. Chasuble. You should get married. A misanthrope I can understand—a womanthrope, never!

CHASUBLE: [With a scholar's shudder.] Believe me, I do not deserve so neologistic a phrase. The precept as well as the practice of the Primitive Church was distinctly against matrimony.

MISS PRISM: [Sententiously.] That is obviously the reason why the Primitive

---

2. A "buttonhole" is a flower to be worn on the lapel of a man's coat, in this case the Maréchal Niel, a popular yellow rose of the period.

Church has not lasted up to the present day. And you do not seem to realize, dear Doctor, that by persistently remaining single, a man converts himself into a permanent public temptation. Men should be more careful; this very celibacy leads weaker vessels astray.

CHASUBLE: But is a man not equally attractive when married?

MISS PRISM: No married man is ever attractive except to his wife.

CHASUBLE: And often, I've been told, not even to her.

MISS PRISM: That depends on the intellectual sympathies of the woman. Maturity can always be depended on. Ripeness can be trusted. Young women are green. [DR. CHASUBLE *starts.*] I spoke horticulturally. My metaphor was drawn from fruits. But where is Cecily?

CHASUBLE: Perhaps she followed us to the schools.

[*Enter* JACK *slowly from the back of the garden. He is dressed in the deepest mourning, with crape hat-band and black gloves.*]

MISS PRISM: Mr. Worthing!

CHASUBLE: Mr. Worthing?

MISS PRISM: This is indeed a surprise. We did not look for you till Monday afternoon.

JACK: [*Shakes* MISS PRISM's *hand in a tragic manner.*] I have returned sooner than I expected. Dr. Chasuble, I hope you are well?

CHASUBLE: Dear Mr. Worthing, I trust this garb of woe does not betoken some terrible calamity?

JACK: My brother.

MISS PRISM: More shameful debts and extravagance?

CHASUBLE: Still leading his life of pleasure?

JACK: [*Shaking his head.*] Dead!

CHASUBLE: Your brother Ernest dead?

JACK: Quite dead.

MISS PRISM: What a lesson for him! I trust he will profit by it.

CHASUBLE: Mr. Worthing, I offer you my sincere condolence. You have at least the consolation of knowing that you were always the most generous and forgiving of brothers.

JACK: Poor Ernest! He had many faults, but it is a sad, sad blow.

CHASUBLE: Very sad indeed. Were you with him at the end?

JACK: No. He died abroad; in Paris, in fact. I had a telegram last night from the manager of the Grand Hotel.

CHASUBLE: Was the cause of death mentioned?

JACK: A severe chill, it seems.

MISS PRISM: As a man sows, so shall he reap.

CHASUBLE: [*Raising his hand.*] Charity, dear Miss Prism, charity! None of us are perfect. I myself am peculiarly susceptible to drafts. Will the interment take place here?

JACK: No. He seemed to have expressed a desire to be buried in Paris.

CHASUBLE: In Paris! [*Shakes his head.*] I fear that hardly points to any very serious state of mind at the last. You would no doubt wish me to make some slight allusion to this tragic domestic affliction next Sunday. [JACK *presses his hand convulsively.*] My sermon on the meaning of the manna in the wilderness can be adapted to almost any occasion, joyful, or, as in the present case, distressing. [*All sigh.*] I have preached it at harvest celebrations, christenings, confirmations, on days of humiliation and festal days. The last time I delivered it was in the Cathedral, as a charity sermon on behalf of the Society for the Prevention of Discontent among the Upper Orders. The Bishop, who was present, was much struck by some of the analogies I drew.

JACK: Ah! That reminds me, you mentioned christenings, I think, Dr. Chasuble? I suppose you know how to christen all right? [DR. CHASUBLE *looks astounded.*] I mean, of course, you are continually christening, aren't you?

MISS PRISM: It is, I regret to say, one of the Rector's most constant duties in this parish. I have often spoken to the poorer classes on the subject. But they don't seem to know what thrift is.

CHASUBLE: But is there any particular infant in whom you are interested, Mr. Worthing? Your brother was, I believe, unmarried, was he not?

JACK: Oh yes.

MISS PRISM: [*Bitterly.*] People who live entirely for pleasure usually are.

JACK: But it is not for any child, dear Doctor. I am very fond of children. No! the fact is, I would like to be christened myself, this afternoon, if you have nothing better to do.

CHASUBLE: But surely, Mr. Worthing, you have been christened already?

JACK: I don't remember anything about it.

CHASUBLE: But have you any grave doubts on the subject?

JACK: I certainly intend to have. Of course I don't know if the thing would bother you in any way, or if you think I am a little too old now.

CHASUBLE: Not at all. The sprinkling, and, indeed, the immersion of adults is a perfectly canonical practice.

JACK: Immersion!

CHASUBLE: You need have no apprehensions. Sprinkling is all that is necessary, or indeed I think advisable. Our weather is so changeable. At what hour would you wish the ceremony performed?

JACK: Oh, I might trot round about five if that would suit you.

CHASUBLE: Perfectly, perfectly! In fact I have two similar ceremonies to perform at that time. A case of twins that occurred recently in one of the outlying cottages on your own estate. Poor Jenkins the carter, a most hard-working man.

JACK: Oh! I don't see much fun in being christened along with other babies. It would be childish. Would half-past five do?

CHASUBLE: Admirably! Admirably! [*Takes out watch.*] And now, dear Mr. Worthing, I will not intrude any longer into a house of sorrow. I would merely beg you not to be too much bowed down by grief. What seem to us bitter trials are often blessings in disguise.

MISS PRISM: This seems to me a blessing of an extremely obvious kind.

[*Enter* CECILY *from the house.*]

CECILY: Uncle Jack! Oh, I am pleased to see you back. But what horrid clothes you have got on! Do go and change them.

MISS PRISM: Cecily!

CHASUBLE: My child! my child!

[CECILY *goes towards* JACK; *he kisses her brow in a melancholy manner.*]

CECILY: What is the matter, Uncle Jack? Do look happy! You look as if you had toothache, and I have got such a surprise for you. Who do you think is in the dining room? Your brother!

JACK: Who?

CECILY: Your brother Ernest. He arrived about half an hour ago.

JACK: What nonsense! I haven't got a brother!

CECILY: Oh, don't say that. However badly he may have behaved to you in the past he is still your brother. You couldn't be so heartless as to disown him. I'll tell him to come out. And you will shake hands with him, won't you, Uncle Jack? [*Runs back into the house.*]

CHASUBLE: These are very joyful tidings.

MISS PRISM: After we had all been resigned to his loss, his sudden return seems to me peculiarly distressing.

JACK: My brother is in the dining room? I don't know what it all means. I think it is perfectly absurd. [*Enter* ALGERNON *and* CECILY *hand in hand. They come slowly up to* JACK.] Good heavens! [*Motions* ALGERNON *away.*]

ALGERNON: Brother John, I have come down from town to tell you that I am very sorry for all the trouble I have given you, and that I intend to lead a better life in the future. [JACK *glares at him and does not take his hand.*]

CECILY: Uncle Jack, you are not going to refuse your own brother's hand?

JACK: Nothing will induce me to take his hand. I think his coming down here disgraceful. He knows perfectly well why.

CECILY: Uncle Jack, do be nice. There is some good in everyone. Ernest has just been telling me about his poor invalid friend Mr. Bunbury whom he goes to visit so often. And surely there must be much good in one who is kind to an invalid, and leaves the pleasures of London to sit by a bed of pain.

JACK: Oh! he has been talking about Bunbury, has he?

CECILY: Yes, he has told me all about poor Mr. Bunbury, and his terrible state of health.

JACK: Bunbury! Well, I won't have him talk to you about Bunbury or about anything else. It is enough to drive one perfectly frantic.

ALGERNON: Of course I admit that the faults were all on my side. But I must say that I think that Brother John's coldness to me is peculiarly painful. I expected a more enthusiastic welcome, especially considering it is the first time I have come here.

CECILY: Uncle Jack, if you don't shake hands with Ernest, I will never forgive you.

JACK: Never forgive me?

CECILY: Never, never, never!

JACK: Well, this is the last time I shall ever do it. [*Shakes hands with* ALGERNON *and glares.*]

CHASUBLE: It's pleasant, is it not, to see so perfect a reconciliation? I think we might leave the two brothers together.

MISS PRISM: Cecily, you will come with us.

CECILY: Certainly, Miss Prism. My little task of reconciliation is over.

CHASUBLE: You have done a beautiful action today, dear child.

MISS PRISM: We must not be premature in our judgments.

CECILY: I feel very happy.

[*They all go off.*]

JACK: You young scoundrel, Algy, you must get out of this place as soon as possible. I don't allow any Bunburying here.

[*Enter* MERRIMAN.]

MERRIMAN: I have put Mr. Ernest's things in the room next to yours, sir. I suppose that is all right?

JACK: What?

MERRIMAN: Mr. Ernest's luggage, sir. I have unpacked it and put it in the room next to your own.

JACK: His luggage?

MERRIMAN: Yes, sir. Three portmanteaus, a dressing case, two hat-boxes, and a large luncheon basket.

ALGERNON: I am afraid I can't stay more than a week this time.

JACK: Merriman, order the dogcart[3] at once. Mr. Ernest has been suddenly called back to town.

MERRIMAN: Yes, sir. [*Goes back into the house.*]

ALGERNON: What a fearful liar you are, Jack. I have not been called back to town at all.

JACK: Yes, you have.

ALGERNON: I haven't heard anyone call me.

JACK: Your duty as a gentleman calls you back.

ALGERNON: My duty as a gentleman has never interfered with my pleasures in the smallest degree.

JACK: I can quite understand that.

ALGERNON: Well, Cecily is a darling.

JACK: You are not to talk of Miss Cardew like that. I don't like it.

ALGERNON: Well, I don't like your clothes. You look perfectly ridiculous in them. Why on earth don't you go up and change? It is perfectly childish to be in deep mourning for a man who is actually staying for a whole week with you in your house as a guest. I call it grotesque.

JACK: You are certainly not staying with me for a whole week as a guest or anything else. You have got to leave . . . by the four-five train.

3. A light, two-wheeled carriage, usually drawn by one horse; it has two transverse seats positioned back to back.

ALGERNON: I certainly won't leave you so long as you are in mourning. It would be most unfriendly. If I were in mourning you would stay with me, I suppose. I should think it very unkind if you didn't.

JACK: Well, will you go if I change my clothes?

ALGERNON: Yes, if you are not too long. I never saw anybody take so long to dress, and with such little result.

JACK: Well, at any rate, that is better than being always overdressed as you are.

ALGERNON: If I am occasionally a little overdressed, I make up for it by being always immensely overeducated.

JACK: Your vanity is ridiculous, your conduct an outrage, and your presence in my garden utterly absurd. However, you have got to catch the four-five, and I hope you will have a pleasant journey back to town. This Bunburying, as you call it, has not been a great success for you. [Goes into the house.]

ALGERNON: I think it has been a great success. I'm in love with Cecily, and that is everything. [Enter CECILY at the back of the garden. She picks up the can and begins to water the flowers.] But I must see her before I go, and make arrangements for another Bunbury. Ah, there she is.

CECILY: Oh, I merely came back to water the roses. I thought you were with Uncle Jack.

ALGERNON: He's gone to order the dogcart for me.

CECILY: Oh, is he going to take you for a nice drive?

ALGERNON: He's going to send me away.

CECILY: Then have we got to part?

ALGERNON: I am afraid so. It's very painful parting.

CECILY: It is always painful to part from people whom one has known for a very brief space of time. The absence of old friends one can endure with equanimity. But even a momentary separation from anyone to whom one has just been introduced is almost unbearable.

ALGERNON: Thank you.

[Enter MERRIMAN.]

MERRIMAN: The dogcart is at the door, sir. [ALGERNON looks appealingly at CECILY.]

CECILY: It can wait, Merriman . . . for . . . five minutes.

MERRIMAN: Yes, Miss. [Exit MERRIMAN.]

ALGERNON: I hope, Cecily, I shall not offend you if I state quite frankly and openly that you seem to me to be in every way the visible personification of absolute perfection.

CECILY: I think your frankness does you great credit, Ernest. If you will allow me I will copy your remarks into my diary. [Goes over to table and begins writing in diary.]

ALGERNON: Do you really keep a diary? I'd give anything to look at it. May I?

CECILY: Oh no. [Puts her hand over it.] You see, it is simply a very young girl's record of her own thoughts and impressions, and consequently meant for publication. When it appears in volume form I hope you will order a copy. But pray, Ernest, don't stop. I delight in taking down from dictation. I have reached "absolute perfection." You can go on. I am quite ready for more.

ALGERNON: [*Somewhat taken aback.*] Ahem! Ahem!

CECILY: Oh, don't cough, Ernest. When one is dictating one should speak fluently and not cough. Besides, I don't know how to spell a cough. [*Writes as ALGERNON speaks.*]

ALGERNON: [*Speaking very rapidly.*] Cecily, ever since I first looked upon your wonderful and incomparable beauty, I have dared to love you wildly, passionately, devotedly, hopelessly.

CECILY: I don't think that you should tell me that you love me wildly, passionately, devotedly, hopelessly. Hopelessly doesn't seem to make much sense, does it?

ALGERNON: Cecily!

[*Enter MERRIMAN.*]

MERRIMAN: The dogcart is waiting, sir.

ALGERNON: Tell it to come round next week, at the same hour.

MERRIMAN: [*Looks at CECILY, who makes no sign.*] Yes, sir. [*MERRIMAN retires.*]

CECILY: Uncle Jack would be very much annoyed if he knew you were staying on till next week, at the same hour.

ALGERNON: Oh, I don't care about Jack. I don't care for anybody in the whole world but you. I love you, Cecily. You will marry me, won't you?

CECILY: You silly boy! Of course. Why, we have been engaged for the last three months.

ALGERNON: For the last three months?

CECILY: Yes, it will be exactly three months on Thursday.

ALGERNON: But how did we become engaged?

CECILY: Well, ever since dear Uncle Jack first confessed to us that he had a younger brother who was very wicked and bad, you of course have formed the chief topic of conversation between myself and Miss Prism. And of course a man who is much talked about is always very attractive. One feels there must be something in him after all. I daresay it was foolish of me, but I fell in love with you, Ernest.

ALGERNON: Darling! And when was the engagement actually settled?

CECILY: On the 14th of February last. Worn out by your entire ignorance of my existence, I determined to end the matter one way or the other, and after a long struggle with myself I accepted you under this dear old tree here. The next day I bought this little ring in your name, and this is the little bangle with the true lovers' knot I promised you always to wear.

ALGERNON: Did I give you this? It's very pretty, isn't it?

CECILY: Yes, you've wonderfully good taste, Ernest. It's the excuse I've always given for your leading such a bad life. And this is the box in which I keep all your dear letters. [*Kneels at table, opens box, and produces letters tied up with blue ribbon.*]

ALGERNON: My letters! But my own sweet Cecily, I have never written you any letters.

CECILY: You need hardly remind me of that, Ernest. I remember only too well that I was forced to write your letters for you. I always wrote three times a week, and sometimes oftener.

ALGERNON: Oh, do let me read them, Cecily?

CECILY: Oh, I couldn't possibly. They would make you far too conceited. [*Replaces box.*] The three you wrote me after I had broken off the engagement are so beautiful, and so badly spelled, that even now I can hardly read them without crying a little.

ALGERNON: But was our engagement ever broken off?

CECILY: Of course it was. On the 22nd of last March. You can see the entry if you like. [*Shows diary.*] "Today I broke off my engagement with Ernest. I feel it is better to do so. The weather still continues charming."

ALGERNON: But why on earth did you break if off? What had I done? I had done nothing at all. Cecily, I am very much hurt indeed to hear you broke it off. Particularly when the weather was so charming.

CECILY: It would hardly have been a really serious engagement if it hadn't been broken off at least once. But I forgave you before the week was out.

ALGERNON: [*Crossing to her, and kneeling.*] What a perfect angel you are, Cecily.

CECILY: You dear romantic boy. [*He kisses her, she puts her fingers through his hair.*] I hope your hair curls naturally, does it?

ALGERNON: Yes, darling, with a little help from others.

CECILY: I am so glad.

ALGERNON: You'll never break off our engagement again, Cecily?

CECILY: I don't think I could break it off now that I have actually met you. Besides, of course, there is the question of your name.

ALGERNON: Yes, of course. [*Nervously.*]

CECILY: You must not laugh at me, darling, but it had always been a girlish dream of mine to love someone whose name was Ernest. [ALGERNON *rises,* CECILY *also.*] There is something in that name that seems to inspire absolute confidence. I pity any poor married woman whose husband is not called Ernest.

ALGERNON: But, my dear child, do you mean to say you could not love me if I had some other name?

CECILY: But what name?

ALGERNON: Oh, any name you like—Algernon—for instance . . . .

CECILY: But I don't like the name of Algernon.

ALGERNON: Well, my own dear, sweet, loving little darling, I really can't see why you should object to the name of Algernon. It is not at all a bad name. In fact, it is rather an aristocratic name. Half of the chaps who get into the Bankruptcy Court are called Algernon. But seriously, Cecily . . . [*Moving to her.*] . . . if my name was Algy, couldn't you love me?

CECILY: [*Rising.*] I might respect you, Ernest, I might admire your character, but I fear that I should not be able to give you my undivided attention.

ALGERNON: Ahem! Cecily! [*Picking up hat.*] Your Rector here is, I suppose, thoroughly experienced in the practice of all the rites and ceremonials of the Church?

CECILY: Oh, yes. Dr. Chasuble is a most learned man. He has never written a single book, so you can imagine how much he knows.

ALGERNON: I must see him at once on a most important christening—I mean on most important business.

CECILY: Oh!

ALGERNON: I shan't be away more than half an hour.

CECILY: Considering that we have been engaged since February the 14th, and that I only met you today for the first time, I think it is rather hard that you should leave me for so long a period as half an hour. Couldn't you make it twenty minutes?

ALGERNON: I'll be back in no time. [*Kisses her and rushes down the garden.*]

CECILY: What an impetuous boy he is! I like his hair so much. I must enter his proposal in my diary.

[*Enter* MERRIMAN.]

MERRIMAN: A Miss Fairfax has just called to see Mr. Worthing. On very important business, Miss Fairfax states.

CECILY: Isn't Mr. Worthing in his library?

MERRIMAN: Mr. Worthing went over in the direction of the rectory some time ago.

CECILY: Pray ask the lady to come out here; Mr. Worthing is sure to be back soon. And you can bring tea.

MERRIMAN: Yes, Miss. [*Goes out.*]

CECILY: Miss Fairfax! I suppose one of the many good elderly women who are associated with Uncle Jack in some of his philanthropic work in London. I don't quite like women who are interested in philanthropic work. I think it is so forward of them.

[*Enter* MERRIMAN.]

MERRIMAN: Miss Fairfax.

[*Enter* GWENDOLEN. *Exit* MERRIMAN.]

CECILY: [*Advancing to meet her.*] Pray let me introduce myself to you. My name is Cecily Cardew.

GWENDOLEN: Cecily Cardew? [*Moving to her and shaking hands.*] What a very sweet name! Something tells me that we are going to be great friends. I like you already more than I can say. My first impressions of people are never wrong.

CECILY: How nice of you to like me so much after we have known each other such a comparatively short time. Pray sit down.

GWENDOLEN: [*Still standing up.*] I may call you Cecily, may I not?

CECILY: With pleasure!

GWENDOLEN: And you will always call me Gwendolen, won't you?

CECILY: If you wish.

GWENDOLEN: Then that is all quite settled, is it not?

CECILY: I hope so. [*A pause. They both sit down together.*]

GWENDOLEN: Perhaps this might be a favorable opportunity for my mentioning who I am. My father is Lord Bracknell. You have never heard of papa, I suppose?

CECILY: I don't think so.

GWENDOLEN: Outside the family circle, papa, I am glad to say, is entirely unknown. I think that is quite as it should be. The home seems to me to be the proper sphere for the man. And certainly once a man begins to neglect his domestic duties he becomes painfully effeminate, does he not? And I don't like that. It makes men so very attractive. Cecily, mamma, whose views on education are remarkably strict, has brought me up to be extremely short-sighted; it is part of her system; so do you mind my looking at you through my glasses?

CECILY: Oh! not at all, Gwendolen. I am very fond of being looked at.

GWENDOLEN: [*After examining* CECILY *carefully through a lorgnette.*] You are here on a short visit, I suppose.

CECILY: Oh no! I live here.

GWENDOLEN: [*Severely.*] Really? Your mother, no doubt, or some female relative of advanced years, resides here also?

CECILY: Oh no! I have no mother, nor, in fact, any relations.

GWENDOLEN: Indeed?

CECILY: My dear guardian, with the assistance of Miss Prism, has the arduous task of looking after me.

GWENDOLEN: Your guardian?

CECILY: Yes, I am Mr. Worthing's ward.

GWENDOLEN: Oh! It is strange he never mentioned to me that he had a ward. How secretive of him! He grows more interesting hourly. I am not sure, however, that the news inspires me with feelings of unmixed delight. [*Rising and going to her.*] I am very fond of you, Cecily; I have liked you ever since I met you! But I am bound to state that now that I know that you are Mr. Worthing's ward, I cannot help expressing a wish you were—well just a little older than you seem to be—and not quite so very alluring in appearance. In fact, if I may speak candidly—

CECILY: Pray do! I think that whenever one has anything unpleasant to say, one should always be quite candid.

GWENDOLEN: Well, to speak with perfect candor, Cecily, I wish that you were fully forty-two, and more than usually plain for your age. Ernest has a strong upright nature. He is the very soul of truth and honor. Disloyalty would be as impossible to him as deception. But even men of the noblest possible moral character are extremely susceptible to the influence of the physical charms of others. Modern, no less than ancient history, supplies us with many most painful examples of what I refer to. If it were not so, indeed, history would be quite unreadable.

CECILY: I beg your pardon, Gwendolen, did you say Ernest?

GWENDOLEN: Yes.

CECILY: Oh, but it is not Mr. Ernest Worthing who is my guardian. It is his brother—his elder brother.

GWENDOLEN: [*Sitting down again.*] Ernest never mentioned to me that he had a brother.

CECILY: I am sorry to say they have not been on good terms for a long time.

GWENDOLEN: Ah! that accounts for it. And now that I think of it I have never heard any man mention his brother. The subject seems distasteful to most men. Cecily, you have lifted a load from my mind. I was growing almost anxious. It would have been terrible if any cloud had come across a friendship like ours, would it not? Of course you are quite, quite sure that it is not Mr. Ernest Worthing who is your guardian?

CECILY: Quite sure. [*A pause.*] In fact, I am going to be his.

GWENDOLEN: [*Inquiringly.*] I beg your pardon?

CECILY: [*Rather shy and confidingly.*] Dearest Gwendolen, there is no reason why I should make a secret of it to you. Our little county newspaper is sure to chronicle the fact next week. Mr. Ernest Worthing and I are engaged to be married.

GWENDOLEN: [*Quite politely, rising.*] My darling Cecily, I think there must be some slight error. Mr. Ernest Worthing is engaged to me. The announcement will appear in the *Morning Post* on Saturday at the latest.

CECILY: [*Very politely, rising.*] I am afraid you must be under some misconception. Ernest proposed to me exactly ten minutes ago. [*Shows diary.*]

GWENDOLEN: [*Examines diary through her lorgnette carefully.*] It is certainly very curious, for he asked me to be his wife yesterday afternoon at 5:30. If you would care to verify the incident, pray do so. [*Produces diary of her own.*] I never travel without my diary. One should always have something sensational to read in the train. I am so sorry, dear Cecily, if it is any disappointment to you, but I am afraid *I* have the prior claim.

CECILY: It would distress me more than I can tell you, dear Gwendolen, if it caused you any mental or physical anguish, but I feel bound to point out that since Ernest proposed to you he clearly has changed his mind.

GWENDOLEN: [*Meditatively.*] If the poor fellow has been entrapped into any foolish promise I shall consider it my duty to rescue him at once, and with a firm hand.

CECILY: [*Thoughtfully and sadly.*] Whatever unfortunate entanglement my dear boy may have got into, I will never reproach him with it after we are married.

GWENDOLEN: Do you allude to me, Miss Cardew, as an entanglement? You are presumptuous. On an occasion of this kind it becomes more than a moral duty to speak one's mind. It becomes a pleasure.

CECILY: Do you suggest, Miss Fairfax, that I entrapped Ernest into an engagement? How dare you? This is no time for wearing the shallow mask of manners. When I see a spade I call it a spade.

GWENDOLEN: [*Satirically.*] I am glad to say that I have never seen a spade. It is obvious that our social spheres have been widely different.

[*Enter* MERRIMAN, *followed by the footman. He carries a salver, tablecloth, and plate stand.* CECILY *is about to retort. The presence of the servants exercises a restraining influence, under which both girls chafe.*]

MERRIMAN: Shall I lay tea here as usual, Miss?

CECILY: [*Sternly, in a calm voice.*] Yes, as usual.

[MERRIMAN *begins to clear table and lay cloth. A long pause.* CECILY *and* GWENDOLEN *glare at each other.*]

GWENDOLEN: Are there many interesting walks in the vicinity, Miss Cardew?

CECILY: Oh! yes! a great many. From the top of one of the hills quite close one can see five counties.

GWENDOLEN: Five counties! I don't think I should like that. I hate crowds.

CECILY: [*Sweetly.*] I suppose that is why you live in town?

[GWENDOLEN *bites her lip, and beats her foot nervously with her parasol.*]

GWENDOLEN: [*Looking round.*] Quite a well-kept garden this is, Miss Cardew.

CECILY: So glad you like it, Miss Fairfax.

GWENDOLEN: I had no idea there were any flowers in the country.

CECILY: Oh, flowers are as common here, Miss Fairfax, as people are in London.

GWENDOLEN: Personally I cannot understand how anybody manages to exist in the country, if anybody who is anybody does. The country always bores me to death.

CECILY: Ah! This is what the newspapers call agricultural depression, is it not? I believe the aristocracy are suffering very much from it just at present. It is almost an epidemic amongst them, I have been told. May I offer you some tea, Miss Fairfax?

GWENDOLEN: [*With elaborate politeness.*] Thank you. [*Aside.*] Detestable girl! But I require tea!

CECILY: [*Sweetly.*] Sugar?

GWENDOLEN: [*Superciliously.*] No, thank you. Sugar is not fashionable any more.

[CECILY *looks angrily at her, takes up the tongs and puts four lumps of sugar into the cup.*]

CECILY: [*Severely.*] Cake or bread and butter?

GWENDOLEN: [*In a bored manner.*] Bread and butter, please. Cake is rarely seen at the best houses nowadays.

CECILY: [*Cuts a very large slice of cake, and puts it on the tray.*] Hand that to Miss Fairfax.

[MERRIMAN *does so, and goes out with footman.* GWENDOLEN *drinks the tea and makes a grimace. Puts down cup at once, reaches out her hand to the bread and butter, looks at it, and finds it is cake. Rises in indignation.*]

GWENDOLEN: You have filled my tea with lumps of sugar, and though I asked most distinctly for bread and butter, you have given me cake. I am known for the gentleness of my disposition, and the extraordinary sweetness of my nature, but I warn you, Miss Cardew, you may go too far.

CECILY: [*Rising.*] To save my poor, innocent, trusting boy from the machinations of any other girl there are no lengths to which I would not go.

GWENDOLEN: From the moment I saw you I distrusted you. I felt that you were false and deceitful. I am never deceived in such matters. My first impressions of people are invariably right.

CECILY: It seems to me, Miss Fairfax, that I am trespassing on your valuable time. No doubt you have many other calls of a similar character to make in the neighborhood.

[*Enter* JACK.]

GWENDOLEN: [*Catching sight of him.*] Ernest! My own Ernest!

JACK: Gwendolen! Darling! [*Offers to kiss her.*]

GWENDOLEN: [*Drawing back.*] A moment! May I ask if you are engaged to be married to this young lady? [*Points to* CECILY.]

JACK: [*Laughing.*] To dear little Cecily! Of course not! What could have put such an idea into your pretty little head?

GWENDOLEN: Thank you. You may! [*Offers her cheek.*]

CECILY: [*Very sweetly.*] I knew there must be some misunderstanding, Miss Fairfax. The gentleman whose arm is at present round your waist is my dear guardian, Mr. John Worthing.

GWENDOLEN: I beg your pardon?

CECILY: This is Uncle Jack.

GWENDOLEN: [*Receding.*] Jack! Oh!

[*Enter* ALGERNON.]

CECILY: Here is Ernest.

ALGERNON: [*Goes straight over to* CECILY *without noticing anyone else.*] My own love! [*Offers to kiss her.*]

CECILY: [*Drawing back.*] A moment, Ernest! May I ask you—are you engaged to be married to this young lady?

ALGERNON: [*Looking round.*] To what young lady? Good heavens! Gwendolen!

CECILY: Yes! to good heavens, Gwendolen, I mean to Gwendolen.

ALGERNON: [*Laughing.*] Of course not! What could have put such an idea into your pretty little head?

CECILY: Thank you. [*Presenting her cheek to be kissed.*] You may. [ALGERNON *kisses her.*]

GWENDOLEN: I felt there was some slight error, Miss Cardew. The gentleman who is now embracing you is my cousin, Mr. Algernon Moncrieff.

CECILY: [*Breaking away from* ALGERNON.] Algernon Moncrieff! Oh! [*The two girls move towards each other and put their arms round each other's waists as if for protection.*] Are you called Algernon?

ALGERNON: I cannot deny it.

CECILY: Oh!

GWENDOLEN: Is your name really John?

JACK: [*Standing rather proudly.*] I could deny it if I liked, I could deny anything if I liked. But my name certainly is John. It has been John for years.

CECILY: [*To* GWENDOLEN.] A gross deception has been practiced on both of us.
GWENDOLEN: My poor wounded Cecily!
CECILY: My sweet wronged Gwendolen!
GWENDOLEN: [*Slowly and seriously.*] You will call me sister, will you not?

[*They embrace.* JACK *and* ALGERNON *groan and walk up and down.*]

CECILY: [*Rather brightly.*] There is just one question I would like to be allowed
to ask my guardian.
GWENDOLEN: An admirable idea! Mr. Worthing, there is just one question I
would like to be permitted to put to you. Where is your brother Ernest? We
are both engaged to be married to your brother Ernest, so it is a matter of
some importance to us to know where your brother Ernest is at present.
JACK: [*Slowly and hesitatingly.*] Gwendolen—Cecily—it is very painful for me
to be forced to speak the truth. It is the first time in my life that I have ever
been reduced to such a painful position, and I am really quite inexperienced
in doing anything of the kind. However I will tell you quite frankly that I
have no brother Ernest. I have no brother at all. I never had a brother in my
life, and I certainly have not the smallest intention of ever having one in the
future.
CECILY: [*Surprised.*] No brother at all?
JACK: [*Cheerily.*] None!
GWENDOLEN: [*Severely.*] Had you never a brother of any kind?
JACK: [*Pleasantly.*] Never. Not even of any kind.
GWENDOLEN: I am afraid it is quite clear, Cecily, that neither of us is engaged
to be married to anyone.
CECILY: It is not a very pleasant position for a young girl suddenly to find herself
in. Is it?
GWENDOLEN: Let us go into the house. They will hardly venture to come after
us there.
CECILY: No, men are so cowardly, aren't they?

[*They retire into the house with scornful looks.*]

JACK: This ghastly state of things is what you call Bunburying, I suppose?
ALGERNON: Yes, and a perfectly wonderful Bunbury it is. The most wonderful
Bunbury I have ever had in my life.
JACK: Well, you've no right whatsoever to Bunbury here.
ALGERNON: That is absurd. One has a right to Bunbury anywhere one chooses.
Every serious Bunburyist knows that.
JACK: Serious Bunburyist! Good heavens!
ALGERNON: Well, one must be serious about something, if one wants to have
any amusement in life. I happen to be serious about Bunburying. What on
earth you are serious about I haven't got the remotest idea. About everything,
I should fancy. You have such an absolutely trivial nature.
JACK: Well, the only small satisfaction I have in the whole of this wretched
business is that your friend Bunbury is quite exploded. You won't be able to

run down to the country quite so often as you used to do, dear Algy. And a very good thing too.

ALGERNON: Your brother is a little off-color, isn't he, dear Jack? You won't be able to disappear to London quite so frequently as your wicked custom was. And not a bad thing either.

JACK: As for your conduct towards Miss Cardew, I must say that your taking in a sweet, simple, innocent girl like that is quite inexcusable. To say nothing of the fact that she is my ward.

ALGERNON: I can see no possible defense at all for your deceiving a brilliant, clever, thoroughly experienced young lady like Miss Fairfax. To say nothing of the fact that she is my cousin.

JACK: I wanted to be engaged to Gwendolen, that is all. I love her.

ALGERNON: Well, I simply wanted to be engaged to Cecily. I adore her.

JACK: There is certainly no chance of your marrying Miss Cardew.

ALGERNON: I don't think there is much likelihood, Jack, of you and Miss Fairfax being united.

JACK: Well, that is no business of yours.

ALGERNON: If it was my business, I wouldn't talk about it. [*Begins to eat muffins.*] It is very vulgar to talk about one's business. Only people like stockbrokers do that, and then merely at dinner parties.

JACK: How can you sit there, calmly eating muffins when we are in this horrible trouble, I can't make out. You seem to me to be perfectly heartless.

ALGERNON: Well, I can't eat muffins in an agitated manner. The butter would probably get on my cuffs. One should always eat muffins quite calmly. It is the only way to eat them.

JACK: I say it's perfectly heartless your eating muffins at all, under the circumstances.

ALGERNON: When I am in trouble, eating is the only thing that consoles me. Indeed, when I am in really great trouble, as anyone who knows me intimately will tell you, I refuse everything except food and drink. At the present moment I am eating muffins because I am unhappy. Besides, I am particularly fond of muffins. [*Rising.*]

JACK: [*Rising.*] Well, that is no reason why you should eat them all in that greedy way. [*Takes muffins from* ALGERNON.]

ALGERNON: [*Offering tea cake.*] I wish you would have tea cake instead. I don't like tea cake.

JACK: Good heavens! I suppose a man may eat his own muffins in his own garden.

ALGERNON: But you have just said it was perfectly heartless to eat muffins.

JACK: I said it was perfectly heartless of you, under the circumstances. That is a very different thing.

ALGERNON: That may be. But the muffins are the same. [*He seizes the muffin dish from* JACK.]

JACK: Algy, I wish to goodness you would go.

ALGERNON: You can't possibly ask me to go without having some dinner. It's absurd. I never go without my dinner. No one ever does, except vegetarians and people like that. Besides I have just made arrangements with Dr. Chasuble to be christened at a quarter to six under the name of Ernest.

JACK: My dear fellow, the sooner you give up that nonsense the better. I made arrangements this morning with Dr. Chasuble to be christened myself at 5:30, and I naturally will take the name of Ernest. Gwendolen would wish it. We can't both be christened Ernest. It's absurd. Besides, I have a perfect right to be christened if I like. There is no evidence at all that I ever have been christened by anybody. I should think it extremely probable I never was, and so does Dr. Chasuble. It is entirely different in your case. You have been christened already.

ALGERNON: Yes, but I have not been christened for years.

JACK: Yes, but you have been christened. That is the important thing.

ALGERNON: Quite so. So I know my constitution can stand it. If you are not quite sure about your ever having been christened, I must say I think it rather dangerous your venturing on it now. It might make you very unwell. You can hardly have forgotten that someone very closely connected with you was very nearly carried off this week in Paris by a severe chill.

JACK: Yes, but you said yourself that a severe chill was not hereditary.

ALGERNON: It usen't to be, I know—but I daresay it is now. Science is always making wonderful improvements in things.

JACK: [*Picking up the muffin dish.*] Oh, that is nonsense; you are always talking nonsense.

ALGERNON: Jack, you are at the muffins again! I wish you wouldn't. There are only two left. [*Takes them.*] I told you I was particularly fond of muffins.

JACK: But I hate tea cake.

ALGERNON: Why on earth then do you allow tea cake to be served up for your guests? What ideas you have of hospitality!

JACK: Algernon! I have already told you to go. I don't want you here. Why don't you go!

ALGERNON: I haven't quite finished my tea yet! and there is still one muffin left.

[*JACK groans, and sinks into a chair.* ALGERNON *still continues eating.*]

ACT-DROP

ACT III

SCENE: *Morning room at the Manor House.*

[GWENDOLEN *and* CECILY *are at the window, looking out into the garden.*]

GWENDOLEN: The fact that they did not follow us at once into the house, as anyone else would have done, seems to me to show that they have some sense of shame left.

CECILY: They have been eating muffins. That looks like repentance.

GWENDOLEN: [*After a pause.*] They don't seem to notice us at all. Couldn't you cough?

CECILY: But I haven't got a cough.

GWENDOLEN: They're looking at us. What effrontery!

CECILY: They're approaching. That's very forward of them.

GWENDOLEN: Let us preserve a dignified silence.

CECILY: Certainly. It's the only thing to do now.

[*Enter* JACK *followed by* ALGERNON. *They whistle some dreadful popular air from a British Opera.*]

GWENDOLEN: This dignified silence seems to produce an unpleasant effect.

CECILY: A most distasteful one.

GWENDOLEN: But we will not be the first to speak.

CECILY: Certainly not.

GWENDOLEN: Mr. Worthing, I have something very particular to ask you. Much depends on your reply.

CECILY: Gwendolen, your common sense is invaluable. Mr. Moncrieff, kindly answer me the following question. Why did you pretend to be my guardian's brother?

ALGERNON: In order that I might have an opportunity of meeting you.

CECILY: [*To* GWENDOLEN.] That certainly seems a satisfactory explanation, does it not?

GWENDOLEN: Yes, dear, if you can believe him.

CECILY: I don't. But that does not affect the wonderful beauty of his answer.

GWENDOLEN: True. In matters of grave importance, style, not sincerity is the vital thing. Mr. Worthing, what explanation can you offer to me for pretending to have a brother? Was it in order that you might have an opportunity of coming up to town to see me as often as possible?

JACK: Can you doubt it, Miss Fairfax?

GWENDOLEN: I have the gravest doubts upon the subject. But I intend to crush them. This is not the moment for German skepticism.[4] [*Moving to* CECILY.] Their explanations appear to be quite satisfactory, especially Mr. Worthing's. That seems to me to have the stamp of truth upon it.

CECILY: I am more than content with what Mr. Moncrieff said. His voice alone inspires one with absolute credulity.

GWENDOLEN: Then you think we should forgive them?

CECILY: Yes. I mean no.

GWENDOLEN: True! I had forgotten. There are principles at stake that one cannot surrender. Which of us should tell them? The task is not a pleasant one.

CECILY: Could we not both speak at the same time?

GWENDOLEN: An excellent idea! I nearly always speak at the same time as other people. Will you take the time from me?

CECILY: Certainly [GWENDOLEN *beats time with uplifted finger.*]

GWENDOLEN AND CECILY: [*Speaking together.*] Your Christian names are still an insuperable barrier. That is all!

---

4. A reference to such philosophical movements as the Materialism of Ludwig Feuerbach (1804–1872) and such theological movements as the "Higher Criticism," which subjected the Bible to the same kind of study as that accorded other books.

JACK AND ALGERNON: [*Speaking together.*] Our Christian names! Is that all? But we are going to be christened this afternoon.

GWENDOLEN: [*To* JACK.] For my sake you are prepared to do this terrible thing?

JACK: I am.

CECILY: [*To* ALGERNON.] To please me you are ready to face this fearful ordeal?

ALGERNON: I am!

GWENDOLEN: How absurd to talk of the equality of the sexes! Where questions of self-sacrifice are concerned, men are infinitely beyond us.

JACK: We are. [*Clasps hands with* ALGERNON.]

CECILY: They have moments of physical courage of which we women know absolutely nothing.

GWENDOLEN: [*To* JACK.] Darling!

ALGERNON: [*To* CECILY.] Darling. [*They fall into each other's arms.*]

[*Enter* MERRIMAN. *When he enters he coughs loudly, seeing the situation.*]

MERRIMAN: Ahem! Ahem! Lady Bracknell!

JACK: Good heavens!

[*Enter* LADY BRACKNELL. *The couples separate in alarm. Exit* MERRIMAN.]

LADY BRACKNELL: Gwendolen! What does this mean?

GWENDOLEN: Merely that I am engaged to be married to Mr. Worthing, mamma.

LADY BRACKNELL: Come here. Sit down. Sit down immediately. Hesitation of any kind is a sign of mental decay in the young, of physical weakness in the old. [*Turns to* JACK.] Apprised, sir, of my daughter's sudden flight by her trusty maid, whose confidence I purchased by means of a small coin, I followed her at once by a luggage train. Her unhappy father is, I am glad to say, under the impression that she is attending a more than usually lengthy lecture by the University Extension Scheme on the Influence of a permanent income on Thought. I do not propose to undeceive him. Indeed I have never unde-ceived him on any question. I would consider it wrong. But of course, you will clearly understand that all communication between yourself and my daughter must cease immediately from this moment. On this point, as indeed on all points, I am firm.

JACK: I am engaged to be married to Gwendolen, Lady Bracknell!

LADY BRACKNELL: You are nothing of the kind, sir. And now, as regards Algernon! . . . Algernon!

ALGERNON: Yes, Aunt Augusta.

LADY BRACKNELL: May I ask if it is in this house that your invalid friend Mr. Bunbury resides?

ALGERNON: [*Stammering.*] Oh! No! Bunbury doesn't live here. Bunbury is some-where else at present. In fact, Bunbury is dead.

LADY BRACKNELL: Dead! When did Mr. Bunbury die? His death must have been extremely sudden.

ALGERNON: [*Airily.*] Oh! I killed Bunbury this afternoon. I mean poor Bunbury died this afternoon.

LADY BRACKNELL: What did he die of?

ALGERNON: Bunbury? Oh, he was quite exploded.

LADY BRACKNELL: Exploded! Was he the victim of a revolutionary outrage? I was not aware that Mr. Bunbury was interested in social legislation. If so, he is well punished for his morbidity.

ALGERNON: My dear Aunt Augusta, I mean he was found out! The doctors found out that Bunbury could not live, that is what I mean—so Bunbury died.

LADY BRACKNELL: He seems to have had great confidence in the opinion of his physicians. I am glad, however, that he made up his mind at the last to some definite course of action, and acted under proper medical advice. And now that we have finally got rid of this Mr. Bunbury, may I ask, Mr. Worthing, who is that young person whose hand my nephew Algernon is now holding in what seems to me a peculiarly unnecessary manner?

JACK: That lady is Miss Cecily Cardew, my ward.

[LADY BRACKNELL *bows coldly to* CECILY.]

ALGERNON: I am engaged to be married to Cecily, Aunt Augusta.

LADY BRACKNELL: I beg your pardon?

CECILY: Mr. Moncrieff and I are engaged to be married, Lady Bracknell.

LADY BRACKNELL: [*With a shiver, crossing to the sofa and sitting down.*] I do not know whether there is anything peculiarly exciting in the air of this particular part of Hertfordshire, but the number of engagements that go on seems to me considerably above the proper average that statistics have laid down for our guidance. I think some preliminary inquiry on my part would not be out of place. Mr. Worthing, is Miss Cardew at all connected with any of the larger railway stations in London? I merely desire information. Until yesterday I had no idea that there were any families or persons whose origin was a terminus.

[JACK *looks perfectly furious, but restrains himself.*]

JACK: [*In a clear, cold voice.*] Miss Cardew is the granddaughter of the late Mr. Thomas Cardew of 149, Belgrave Square, S.W.; Gervase Park, Dorking, Surrey; and the Sporran, Fifeshire, N.B.[5]

LADY BRACKNELL: That sounds not unsatisfactory. Three addresses always inspire confidence, even in tradesmen. But what proof have I of their authenticity?

JACK: I have carefully preserved the Court Guides of the period. They are open to your inspection, Lady Bracknell.

LADY BRACKNELL: [*Grimly.*] I have known strange errors in that publication.

JACK: Miss Cardew's family solicitors are Messrs. Markby, Markby, and Markby.

LADY BRACKNELL: Markby, Markby, and Markby? A firm of the very highest position in their profession. Indeed I am told that one of the Mr. Markbys is occasionally to be seen at dinner parties. So far I am satisfied.

JACK: [*Very irritably.*] How extremely kind of you, Lady Bracknell! I have also in

5. In addition to his London residence in Belgrave Square (already referred to in Act 1), Mr. Cardew maintained establishments in the south of England (Dorking, Surrey) and in Scotland (Fifeshire; N.B., North Britain).

my possession, you will be pleased to hear, certificates of Miss Cardew's birth, baptism, whooping cough, registration, vaccination, confirmation, and the measles; both the German and the English variety.

LADY BRACKNELL: Ah! A life crowded with incident, I see; though perhaps somewhat too exciting for a young girl. I am not myself in favor of premature experiences. [*Rises, looks at her watch.*] Gwendolen! the time approaches for our departure. We have not a moment to lose. As a matter of form, Mr. Worthing, I had better ask you if Miss Cardew has any little fortune?

JACK: Oh! about a hundred and thirty thousand pounds in the Funds.[6] That is all. Good-bye, Lady Bracknell. So pleased to have seen you.

LADY BRACKNELL: [*Sitting down again.*] A moment, Mr. Worthing. A hundred and thirty thousand pounds! And in the Funds! Miss Cardew seems to me a most attractive young lady, now that I look at her. Few girls of the present day have any really solid qualities, any of the qualities that last, and improve with time. We live, I regret to say, in an age of surfaces. [*To* CECILY.] Come over here, dear. [CECILY *goes across.*] Pretty child! your dress is sadly simple, and your hair seems almost as Nature might have left it. But we can soon alter all that. A thoroughly experienced French maid produces a really marvelous result in a very brief space of time. I remember recommending one to young Lady Lancing, and after three months her own husband did not know her.

JACK: [*Aside.*] And after six months nobody knew her.

LADY BRACKNELL: [*Glares at* JACK *for a few moments. Then bends, with a practiced smile, to* CECILY.] Kindly turn round, sweet child. [CECILY *turns completely round.*] No, the side view is what I want. [CECILY *presents her profile.*] Yes, quite as I expected. There are distinct social possibilities in your profile. The two weak points in our age are its want of principle and its want of profile. The chin a little higher, dear. Style largely depends on the way the chin is worn. They are worn very high, just at present. Algernon!

ALGERNON: Yes, Aunt Augusta!

LADY BRACKNELL: There are distinct social possibilities in Miss Cardew's profile.

ALGERNON: Cecily is the sweetest, dearest, prettiest girl in the whole world. And I don't care twopence about social possibilities.

LADY BRACKNELL: Never speak disrespectfully of Society, Algernon. Only people who can't get into it do that. [*To* CECILY.] Dear child, of course you know that Algernon has nothing but his debts to depend upon. But I do not approve of mercenary marriages. When I married Lord Bracknell I had no fortune of any kind. But I never dreamed for a moment of allowing that to stand in my way. Well, I suppose I must give my consent.

ALGERNON: Thank you, Aunt Augusta.

LADY BRACKNELL: Cecily, you may kiss me!

CECILY: [*Kisses her.*] Thank you, Lady Bracknell.

LADY BRACKNELL: You may also address me as Aunt Augusta for the future.

CECILY: Thank you, Aunt Augusta.

6. Stock of the British National Debt.

LADY BRACKNELL: The marriage, I think, had better take place quite soon.

ALGERNON: Thank you, Aunt Augusta.

CECILY: Thank you, Aunt Augusta.

LADY BRACKNELL: To speak frankly, I am not in favor of long engagements. They give people the opportunity of finding out each other's character before marriage, which I think is never advisable.

JACK: I beg your pardon for interrupting you, Lady Bracknell, but this engagement is quite out of the question. I am Miss Cardew's guardian, and she cannot marry without my consent until she comes of age. That consent I absolutely decline to give.

LADY BRACKNELL: Upon what grounds may I ask? Algernon is an extremely, I may almost say an ostentatiously, eligible young man. He has nothing, but he looks everything. What more can one desire?

JACK: It pains me very much to have to speak frankly to you, Lady Bracknell, about your nephew, but the fact is that I do not approve at all of his moral character. I suspect him of being untruthful.

[ALGERNON *and* CECILY *look at him in indignant amazement.*]

LADY BRACKNELL: Untruthful! My nephew Algernon? Impossible! He is an Oxonian.[7]

JACK: I fear there can be no possible doubt about the matter. This afternoon, during my temporary absence in London on an important question of romance, he obtained admission to my house by means of the false pretense of being my brother. Under an assumed name he drank, I've just been informed by the butler, an entire pint bottle of my Perrier-Jouet, Brut, '89[8]; a wine I was specially reserving for myself. Continuing his disgraceful deception, he succeeded in the course of the afternoon in alienating the affections of my only ward. He subsequently stayed to tea, and devoured every single muffin. And what makes his conduct all the more heartless is, that he was perfectly well aware from the first that I have no brother, that I never had a brother, and that I don't intend to have a brother, not even of any kind. I distinctly told him so myself yesterday afternoon.

LADY BRACKNELL: Ahem! Mr. Worthing, after careful consideration I have decided entirely to overlook my nephew's conduct to you.

JACK: That is very generous of you, Lady Bracknell. My own decision, however, is unalterable. I decline to give my consent.

LADY BRACKNELL: [*To* CECILY.] Come here, sweet child. [CECILY *goes over.*] How old are you, dear?

CECILY: Well, I am really only eighteen, but I always admit to twenty when I go to evening parties.

LADY BRACKNELL: You are perfectly right in making some slight alteration. Indeed, no woman should ever be quite accurate about her age. It looks so calculating. . . . [*In a meditative manner.*] Eighteen, but admitting to twenty at evening parties. Well, it will not be very long before you are of age and

---

7. A graduate of Oxford University.   8. A very fine champagne.

free from the restraints of tutelage. So I don't think your guardian's consent is, after all, a matter of any importance.

JACK: Pray excuse me, Lady Bracknell, for interrupting you again, but it is only fair to tell you that according to the terms of her grandfather's will Miss Cardew does not come legally of age till she is thirty-five.

LADY BRACKNELL: That does not seem to me to be a grave objection. Thirty-five is a very attractive age. London society is full of women of the very highest birth who have, of their own free choice, remained thirty-five for years. Lady Dumbleton is an instance in point. To my own knowledge she has been thirty-five ever since she arrived at the age of forty, which was many years ago now. I see no reason why our dear Cecily should not be even still more attractive at the age you mention than she is at present. There will be a large accumulation of property.

CECILY: Algy, could you wait for me till I was thirty-five?

ALGERNON: Of course I could, Cecily. You know I could.

CECILY: Yes, I felt it instinctively, but I couldn't wait all that time. I hate waiting even five minutes for anybody. It always makes me rather cross. I am not punctual myself, I know, but I do like punctuality in others, and waiting, even to be married, is quite out of the question.

ALGERNON: Then what is to be done, Cecily?

CECILY: I don't know, Mr. Moncrieff.

LADY BRACKNELL: My dear Mr. Worthing, as Miss Cardew states positively that she cannot wait till she is thirty-five—a remark which I am bound to say seems to me to show a somewhat impatient nature—I would beg of you to reconsider your decision.

JACK: But my dear Lady Bracknell, the matter is entirely in your own hands. The moment you consent to my marriage with Gwendolen, I will most gladly allow your nephew to form an alliance with my ward.

LADY BRACKNELL: [*Rising and drawing herself up.*] You must be quite aware that what you propose is out of the question.

JACK: Then a passionate celibacy is all that any of us can look forward to.

LADY BRACKNELL: This is not the destiny I propose for Gwendolen. Algernon, of course, can choose for himself. [*Pulls out her watch.*] Come, dear; [GWENDOLEN *rises.*] we have already missed five, if not six, trains. To miss any more might expose us to comment on the platform.

[*Enter* CANON CHASUBLE.]

CHASUBLE: Everything is quite ready for the christenings.

LADY BRACKNELL: The christenings, sir! Is not that somewhat premature!

CHASUBLE: [*Looking rather puzzled, and pointing to* JACK *and* ALGERNON.] Both these gentlemen have expressed a desire for immediate baptism.

LADY BRACKNELL: At their age? The idea is grotesque and irreligious! Algernon, I forbid you to be baptized. I will not hear of such excesses. Lord Bracknell would be highly displeased if he learned that that was the way in which you wasted your time and money.

CHASUBLE: Am I to understand then that there are to be no christenings at all this afternoon?

JACK: I don't think that, as things are now, it would be of much practical value to either of us, Dr. Chasuble.

CHASUBLE: I am grieved to hear such sentiments from you, Mr. Worthing. They savor of the heretical views of the Anabaptists,[9] views that I have completely refuted in four of my unpublished sermons. However, as your present mood seems to be one peculiarly secular, I will return to the church at once. Indeed, I have just been informed by the pew-opener[1] that for the last hour and a half Miss Prism has been waiting for me in the vestry.

LADY BRACKNELL: [*Starting*.] Miss Prism! Did I hear you mention a Miss Prism?

CHASUBLE: Yes, Lady Bracknell. I am on my way to join her.

LADY BRACKNELL: Pray allow me to detain you for a moment. This matter may prove to be one of vital importance to Lord Bracknell and myself. Is this Miss Prism a female of repellent aspect, remotely connected with education?

CHASUBLE: [*Somewhat indignantly*.] She is the most cultivated of ladies, and the very picture of respectability.

LADY BRACKNELL: It is obviously the same person. May I ask what position she holds in your household?

CHASUBLE: [*Severely*.] I am a celibate, madam.

JACK: [*Interposing*.] Miss Prism, Lady Bracknell, has been for the last three years Miss Cardew's esteemed governess and valued companion.

LADY BRACKNELL: In spite of what I hear of her, I must see her at once. Let her be sent for.

CHASUBLE: [*Looking off*.] She approaches; she is nigh.

[*Enter* MISS PRISM *hurriedly*.]

MISS PRISM: I was told you expected me in the vestry, dear Canon. I have been waiting for you there for an hour and three quarters. [*Catches sight of* LADY BRACKNELL, *who has fixed her with a stony glare*. MISS PRISM *grows pale and quails. She looks anxiously round as if desirous to escape*.]

LADY BRACKNELL: [*In a severe, judicial voice*.] Prism! [MISS PRISM *bows her head in shame*.] Come here, Prism! [MISS PRISM *approaches in a humble manner*.] Prism! Where is that baby? [*General consternation*. THE CANON *starts back in horror*. ALGERNON *and* JACK *pretend to be anxious to shield* CECILY *and* GWENDOLEN *from hearing the details of a terrible public scandal*.] Twenty-eight years ago, Prism, you left Lord Bracknell's house, Number 104, Upper Grosvenor Street, in charge of a perambulator that contained a baby, of the male sex. You never returned. A few weeks later, through the elaborate inves-

9. A 16th-century religious group, most nearly like contemporary Mennonites. Dr. Chasuble, however, is probably using the term loosely to apply to a group more like contemporary Baptists.   1. An usher. Since most pews were completely enclosed, his duties would have included opening the gate that provided entrance for the worshipers. In addition, since most pews were rented for the use of specific persons, he would have been responsible for seeing that worshipers were seated in the correct pews.

tigations of the Metropolitan police, the perambulator was discovered at midnight, standing by itself in a remote corner of Bayswater.[2] It contained the manuscript of a three-volume novel of more than usually revolting sentimentality. [MISS PRISM *starts in involuntary indignation.*] But the baby was not there! [*Everyone looks at* MISS PRISM.] Prism! Where is that baby? [*A pause.*]

MISS PRISM: Lady Bracknell, I admit with shame that I do not know. I only wish I did. The plain facts of the case are these. On the morning of the day you mention, a day that is forever branded on my memory, I prepared as usual to take the baby out in its perambulator. I had also with me a somewhat old, but capacious handbag, in which I had intended to place the manuscript of a work of fiction that I had written during my few unoccupied hours. In a moment of mental abstraction, for which I never can forgive myself, I deposited the manuscript in the bassinette, and placed the baby in the handbag.

JACK: [*Who has been listening attentively.*] But where did you deposit the handbag?

MISS PRISM: Do not ask me, Mr. Worthing.

JACK: Miss Prism, this is a matter of no small importance to me. I insist on knowing where you deposited the handbag that contained that infant.

MISS PRISM: I left it in the cloak room of one of the larger railway stations in London.

JACK: What railway station?

MISS PRISM: [*Quite crushed.*] Victoria. The Brighton line. [*Sinks into a chair.*]

JACK: I must retire to my room for a moment. Gwendolen, wait here for me.

GWENDOLEN: If you are not too long, I will wait here for you all my life.

[*Exit* JACK *in great excitement.*]

CHASUBLE: What do you think this means, Lady Bracknell?

LADY BRACKNELL: I dare not even suspect, Dr. Chasuble. I need hardly tell you that in families of high position strange coincidences are not supposed to occur. They are hardly considered the thing.

[*Noises heard overhead as if someone was throwing trunks about. Everyone looks up.*]

CECILY: Uncle Jack seems strangely agitated.

CHASUBLE: Your guardian has a very emotional nature.

LADY BRACKNELL: This noise is extremely unpleasant. It sounds as if he was having an argument. I dislike arguments of any kind. They are always vulgar, and often convincing.

CHASUBLE: [*Looking up.*] It has stopped now. [*The noise is redoubled.*]

LADY BRACKNELL: I wish he would arrive at some conclusion.

GWENDOLEN: This suspense is terrible. I hope it will last.

[*Enter* JACK *with a handbag of black leather in his hand.*]

---

2. A fashionable residential section to the north of Hyde Park and Kensington Gardens.

JACK: [*Rushing over to* MISS PRISM.] Is this the handbag, Miss Prism? Examine it carefully before you speak. The happiness of more than one life depends on your answer.

MISS PRISM: [*Calmly.*] It seems to be mine. Yes, here is the injury it received through the upsetting of a Gower Street omnibus in younger and happier days. Here is the stain on the lining caused by the explosion of a temperance beverage, an incident that occurred at Leamington. And here, on the lock, are my initials. I had forgotten that in an extravagant mood I had had them placed there. The bag is undoubtedly mine. I am delighted to have it so unexpectedly restored to me. It has been a great inconvenience being without it all these years.

JACK: [*In a pathetic voice.*] Miss Prism, more is restored to you than this handbag. I was the baby you placed in it.

MISS PRISM: [*Amazed.*] You!

JACK: [*Embracing her.*] Yes . . . mother!

MISS PRISM: [*Recoiling in indignant astonishment.*] Mr. Worthing! I am unmarried!

JACK: Unmarried! I do not deny that is a serious blow. But after all, who has the right to cast a stone against one who has suffered? Cannot repentance wipe out an act of folly? Why should there be one law for men, and another for women? Mother, I forgive you. [*Tries to embrace her again.*]

MISS PRISM: [*Still more indignant.*] Mr. Worthing, there is some error. [*Pointing to* LADY BRACKNELL.] There is the lady who can tell you who you really are.

JACK: [*After a pause.*] Lady Bracknell, I hate to seem inquisitive, but would you kindly inform me who I am?

LADY BRACKNELL: I am afraid that the news I have to give you will not altogether please you. You are the son of my poor sister, Mrs. Moncrieff, and consequently Algernon's elder brother.

JACK: Algy's elder brother! Then I have a brother after all. I knew I had a brother! I always said I had a brother! Cecily—how could you have ever doubted that I had a brother? [*Seizes hold of* ALGERNON.] Dr. Chasuble, my unfortunate brother. Miss Prism, my unfortunate brother. Gwendolen, my unfortunate brother. Algy, you young scoundrel, you will have to treat me with more respect in the future. You have never behaved to me like a brother in all your life.

ALGERNON: Well, not till today, old boy, I admit. I did my best, however, though I was out of practice. [*Shakes hands.*]

GWENDOLEN: [*To* JACK.] My own! But what own are you? What is your Christian name, now that you have become someone else?

JACK: Good heavens! . . . I had quite forgotten that point. Your decision on the subject of my name is irrevocable, I suppose?

GWENDOLEN: I never change, except in my affections.

CECILY: What a noble nature you have, Gwendolen!

JACK: Then the question had better be cleared up at once. Aunt Augusta, a moment. At the time when Miss Prism left me in the handbag, had I been christened already?

LADY BRACKNELL: Every luxury that money could buy, including christening, had been lavished on you by your fond and doting parents.

JACK: Then I was christened! That is settled. Now, what name was I given? Let me know the worst.

LADY BRACKNELL: Being the eldest son you were naturally christened after your father.

JACK: [*Irritably.*] Yes, but what was my father's Christian name?

LADY BRACKNELL: [*Meditatively.*] I cannot at the present moment recall what the General's Christian name was. But I have no doubt he had one. He was eccentric, I admit. But only in later years. And that was the result of the Indian climate, and marriage, and indigestion, and other things of that kind.

JACK: Algy! Can't you recollect what our father's Christian name was?

ALGERNON: My dear boy, we were never even on speaking terms. He died before I was a year old.

JACK: His name would appear in the Army Lists of the period, I suppose, Aunt Augusta?

LADY BRACKNELL: The General was essentially a man of peace, except in his domestic life. But I have no doubt his name would appear in any military directory.

JACK: The Army Lists of the last forty years are here. These delightful records should have been my constant study. [*Rushes to bookcase and tears the books out.*] M. Generals . . . Mallam, Maxbohm, Magley, what ghastly names they have—Markby, Migsby, Mobbs, Moncrieff! Lieutenant 1840, Captain, Lieutenant Colonel, Colonel, General 1869, Christian names, Ernest John. [*Puts book very quietly down and speaks quite calmly.*] I always told you, Gwendolen, my name was Ernest, didn't I? Well it is Ernest after all. I mean it naturally is Ernest.

LADY BRACKNELL: Yes, I remember now that the General was called Ernest. I knew I had some particular reason for disliking the name.

GWENDOLEN: Ernest! My own Ernest! I felt from the first that you could have no other name!

JACK: Gwendolen, it is a terrible thing for a man to find out suddenly that all his life he has been speaking nothing but the truth. Can you forgive me?

GWENDOLEN: I can. For I feel that you are sure to change.

JACK: My own one!

CHASUBLE: [*To* MISS PRISM.] Laetitia! [*Embraces her.*]

MISS PRISM: [*Enthusiastically.*] Frederick! At last!

ALGERNON: Cecily! [*Embraces her.*] At last!

JACK: Gwendolen! [*Embraces her.*] At last!

LADY BRACKNELL: My nephew, you seem to be displaying signs of triviality.

JACK: On the contrary, Aunt Augusta, I've now realized for the first time in my life the vital Importance of Being Earnest.

CURTAIN

1899

▼ ▼ ▼

QUESTIONS

Oedipus the King

1. Summarize the story before the play opens. What actually happens in the play itself? What period of time is covered? How important is setting to this play? In what specific ways?

2. How, exactly, does the chorus function in this play? What is the significance of the chorus being made up of Theban citizens? Which opinions of the chorus are most important to the effects of the play?

3. Characterize Tiresias. How much does the play itself actually tell us about Tiresias? What function does he perform in the plot? in the play's structure?

4. In what specific ways is the plot of *Oedipus the King* tragic?

The Importance of Being Earnest

1. What initial obstacles are there to a comic resolution of the romantic plot? How are they resolved? Trace the structure of the resolution, and show where the various structural parts of the play (exposition, rising action, climax, falling action, and conclusion) occur in the text.

2. Characterize Lady Bracknell. Trace the different ways that the character and her role are made clear. What is her structural role in the play?

3. What characters in the play seem to you simple stereotypes? Exactly how are attitudes toward these characters developed? Which characters rise "above" or go "beyond" stereotypes? What kinds of qualities separate stereotypes from the more complex characters? Which names are especially significant in suggesting the nature of character? Which names are noncharacterizing or neutral?

4. Wilde is often praised for his wit and the skill with which he develops conversational repartee. Choose three speeches that seem to you especially witty, and explain in detail exactly how they work, in what their wit consists. What patterns of verbal wit do you notice in the play? How dependent is the tone on language? What human values does the play seem to support? What has the preoccupation of the play with language to do with these values?

WRITING SUGGESTIONS

Oedipus the King

1. In an essay of about three pages, compare Oedipus at the beginning of the play with Oedipus at the end. Explain the differences in terms of tragic form.

2. Try to recount the events of the play from the point of view of Jocasta. In what sense is the play a tragedy for her? Write a persuasive essay in which you argue that the play is Jocasta's story.

3. What are the more significant and distinctive elements in the character of Oedipus? In what sense is he responsible for his fate? In what sense is he a victim? How heroic is he? Write an essay appraising Oedipus's character and assessing his responsibility for the things that befall him.

The Importance of Being Earnest

1. Recount in as few words as possible the plot of the play. Then retell the story structurally as a "typical" comic plot. On the basis of this retelling, write a short (two-page) essay in which you show how Wilde structures his play along classical comic lines.

2. Choose one character in the play who seems to you not as fully developed as he or she might be. Construct a new scene for the play in which this character is allowed, through dialogue and action, to reveal him or herself more fully.

3. Defend the use of comic stereotypes in the play in an essay that suggests how the various stereotypical characters help to create the basic comic plot.

6 CULTURE AS CONTEXT: SOCIAL AND HISTORICAL SETTING

Time conditions all texts, but a sense of time is particularly important for readers of drama. Events in drama often seem more immediate than in poems or stories, and the demands of time seem more pressing. Immediacy is an important feature of drama, and not only in performance. Reading drama involves a strong sense of presentness as well, for all the action takes place in the present tense regardless of what time period is being represented. Nothing in drama is narrated or recounted: action is all in words and gestures happening right now. And all the action takes place rather fast; novels often take many hours to read, but most plays can easily be read in the time it would take to perform them on stage, two or three hours, even when the action they represent covers several years in time.

But whatever the illusion of presentness, plays often deal with extensive and complicated dislocations in time, and readers of drama are often asked to make sophisticated moves that involve an adjustment to more than the illusion of immediacy. Even though action seems to be taking place as we read, the plot may be set far in the past, and we are often asked as readers to bring to bear specific historical information on the times being represented. Sensitive reading of a play may depend on making some fairly complicated distinctions between different time frames.

Three different levels of time operate in most plays. First, play texts represent some particular time—the temporal setting—in which the action takes place. We can call this **plot time.** Second, texts reflect the time when the author was writing, and the conditions and assumptions of that time find their way into the conception and style of the text. This feature of textual time we may call **authorial time.** Third, readers read a text in a particular time frame of their own, and sometimes conditions and assumptions then are very different from those that obtain in either the text's present or the author's present. We may call this time **reader time.**

These three levels of time often interact importantly in the way we interpret a text. When, for example, we read—as American readers in the 1990s—a play written by Shakespeare in the early seventeenth century about the Danish court of many centuries earlier, we have three time schemes operating at once. We are reading about a time (and place) centuries remote from us, and the text in which these events are represented reflects values, writing conditions, habits of language, and dramatic conventions of a second time—centuries later than the action but still almost four centuries earlier than the time in which we read. Values in these three times are not going to be identical, and how we interpret the actions and thoughts of Hamlet in part depends not only on our own assumptions about what he ought to do or might do, but on what we know about the expectations of human events in two earlier ages. Suspending these three "settings" in our minds as we read—and consciously making comparisons when we perceive conflicts of values—is an important part of interpretation and response. We perceive at one and the same time three different Hamlets—ours (the reader's), Shakespeare's (the text's), and the "historical" Hamlet known to his contemporaries in medieval Denmark. In this particular case, the play does not ask us to know anything very specific about the historical Hamlet; we do not need to know, for example, the history of ancient Elsinore. All we really need to know is that the Danish monarchy passes within families but not necessarily to the eldest son.

Many plays explicitly invoke a particular era as the time of action, and often they specify (in stage directions or interjected comments) information about the era that is relevant to the interpretation of specific episodes. But sometimes we have to supply historical or cultural facts from outside the text, and often we have to adjust our expectations because the "world" of the play— its "present" time in some past age in some specific place—is very different from our own world. People may share some characteristics across ages and cultures, but behavior and motivation are often conditioned by cultural habits and situations, and often we are asked to think carefully about the particulars of a time and place very different from our own. Identifying the setting of a play— in both time and place—and considering carefully its historical situation are often crucial to understanding what happens and why.

The 1957 setting of *Fences*, for example, is very important to the interpretation of Troy Maxson's resistance to his son's participation in sports. Troy is fifty-three at the time the play begins; he had himself been a talented athlete and had played in the Negro League against players like Satchel Paige who had gone on to become well-known stars after major-league baseball finally admitted black players in 1947. Troy often reminisces about his youthful athletic exploits (hitting homers off Paige, for example), and he is clearly proud of his accomplishments, but his athletic success has brought him nothing in later life except memories. He had been well past his peak when blacks were first allowed in the major leagues (and thus when significant salaries and public fame became available to black players). He doesn't say so but it is clear that, at forty-three, he never got the chance that the younger Jackie Robinson did.

In 1946, just after the end of World War II, Robinson became the first black to be signed in what was then called "organized baseball"—that is, the elaborate system of major and minor professional leagues for white players. The Negro League, in which the quality of play was thought by many to be as high as in the majors, was not part of "organized baseball," and salaries there were very much lower, and most of white America knew nothing of the players. After a year in the minors (at Montreal, which was then the top farm team of the Brooklyn Dodgers), Robinson—at age twenty-eight—was promoted to the "parent" Dodgers. Robinson was a war veteran, a college graduate, and incredibly talented. He immediately became a star, thus opening careers for scores of young black athletes. Robinson went on to bat over .300 for six consecutive years in the late 1940s and early 1950s, and he compiled a lifetime average of .311, even though he was over thirty years old for most of his major-league career. He retired at the end of the 1956 season, just a year before the action of *Fences* begins.

Troy's slighting references to Robinson and other black players younger than himself who had major-league careers reflect his frustration and bitterness at having been left out of the reform, and he still finds it impossible to believe that sports can be the road to success for blacks, even though by 1957 a great many professional black athletes had achieved national fame and commanded large salaries. By 1981, when the play was written, sports had come to be considered one of the most direct routes from the ghetto to public success, and Troy's combination of self-pity and blindness to his son's opportunities makes him a figure both pathetic and repressive. His refusal to encourage his son's potential to advance beyond the status of Troy's own generation becomes one of the play's "fences"—one of the text's reminders that some barriers are sustained by human failings, in this case within the black culture as well as within the white systems. Troy's attitudes about the relationship between athletic prowess and later success in life would be a good bit more understandable in 1957 than 1981. The irony of Troy's insistence that his son quit football to work at the A & P and that he refuse athletic scholarship opportunities depends heavily on the advances made by black athletes between 1957 and 1981. Readers or viewers in 1981—or in the 1990s—are likely to regard this aspect of Troy's fathering more critically than many people would have in 1957; the text does not ask us to like Troy for his attitudes, only to understand what his world looked like, to him, at a time when history had not yet followed the course that we take for granted.

The specter of World War II is also important to the play. Gabriel is a casualty of the war and receives a small pension as a result of the disabling head wound that has altered his mind. Like Troy, he is a victim of white society and public policy, and he bears his wound publicly (though he is himself unaware of his condition) as a reminder of the sacrifice he has made. Unlike Troy, he bears no bitterness; he simply does not understand what has happened to him, and he sees his inheritance beyond racial terms. He is able to imagine himself as Heaven's trumpeter, right there with St. Peter, largely because he does not understand the fences that govern expectations. (Lyons, by contrast, is painfully aware of the limits imposed on him by his color, his background, and his education, and the most he can imagine for his musicianship is a marginal living.)

In 1957, the present of the play, World War II was still a vivid memory, and daily life was still conditioned by its aftermath. The relative plenty and peace that seemed impressive when compared to the scarcities and dangers of the war were frequently celebrated, and if we remember the complacent and self-satisfied attitudes generally attributed now to the 1950s, we will understand better the weekly struggle Troy faces. He has a menial job and little chance for promotion, though he is affected enough by the general optimism about success and fairness that he protests the discrimination that divides black and white expectations on his job. And then he is unable to take advantage of the opportunity when fairness unexpectedly triumphs, because he has never learned to drive and doesn't understand the "rules" about "qualification."

The war shadows the action of the play well beyond the specific wound to Gabriel; 1957 takes us back in time to a world related to our own but quite different in both the events of daily life and the expectations created by them. But the play invites us to make connections between that world and ours, causal connections. We are conscious of looking back to an earlier time because the text emphasizes the distance.

Authorial time here is 1981, a quarter century later. The play's events are self-consciously distanced in time; the twenty-four intervening years provide some perspective. In 1981, World War II seemed distant, well over, and any portrayal of postwar optimism was far removed from the moment—the Iranian hostage crisis, runaway inflation, a new administration elected under the banner of returning to old-fashioned values, a tough stance on national defense and the shadow of the debacle in Vietnam, the public display of patriotism and a chauvinistic championing of American frontier values, a retreat from affirmative action and a reliance on competitive, appetitive instincts. *Fences* recalls a world that in 1981 was a generation old; when Troy describes the habits he has fallen into and is made to seem the reason that some problems have been passed along to a new generation, he seems to represent old attitudes and old solutions that are up against the values of a rising generation that will be in some ways different, in some ways more like, the values blackness embodied in 1981.

The author of *Fences*, August Wilson, has continued to write plays about the past of black families, self-consciously going back to different decades in different plays to suggest not only different stages in growing black consciousness but the kinds of attitudes and responses to crises that obtained within black families set apart from, but always circumscribed by, the larger white world of America. Wilson's interest is very much in suggesting what present-day life is like, especially for black people, and his play of 1990, *The Piano Lesson*, is self-consciously a play of the 1990s even though its action takes place a generation before *Fences* and involves the history of an old material object, a piano, that has been passed down through several generations. For Wilson (and for most playwrights who set their plays in earlier times), the past leads to the present and helps the present learn how it got here. It not only represents events (World War II, or the integration of major-league baseball) that helped to cause change; it also represents attitudes and individual acts of behavior that led to new conditions and an evolved set of issues and problems. The kind of fencing that this play is about suggests both the power of family and generational influence (a theme that is universal) and the kinds of particulars associated with one family's story conditioned by specific patterns of social and cultural history. *Fences* is about America in the 1950s in much the same way that *Death of a Salesman* is about the American 1940s—the values, the consciousness, the habits, the immediate outcomes—except that *Fences* emphatically distances itself in time and makes the audience conscious of the difference as a way of articulating the power of a past on the present, whereas *Death of a Salesman*—written in 1949 about present events—is itself implicated in those values and assumptions.

Recreating a sense of a historical past is, we have been noticing, important to the act of reading when a text is set in an earlier time. But we have also been noticing difference—the implied contrast between the world represented in a play (plot time) and the world at the time the play is written (authorial time). But we are not reading *Fences* in 1981 or *Death of a Salesman* in 1949. Often the perspective from which we read, especially when we are reading relatively recent plays, is quite similar to that in authorial time, for often it is simply pastness that is at stake, but in older plays—*Oedipus the King*, for example, or *Hamlet*—we are often conscious of being far removed from the text's assumptions and values. We do not share the sense of urgency about Greek history and myth, and we are, as late-twentieth-century American readers, not so anxious about how power and control are passed along in monarchies (though there are plenty of other urgencies that translate readily—anxieties about whether our actions are somehow predetermined, for example, or about what we should do with our knowledge of evil). And sometimes, too, even more recent plays are already distanced from us by events that have intervened between authorial time and reader time.

Readers of the 1990s are not all that far removed in years from the time in which Wilson wrote *Fences*, but some things have changed that well may influence how we respond. Some readers of this book will hardly be able to remember what life was like for themselves in 1981, let alone what the world was doing in larger terms. In the 1990s, we are much more removed from World War II, the shifts in Eastern Europe and in China having made us think in quite different international terms. The self-conscious removal from the 1950s that we described as having been built into the play is even more striking to readers now. Reader time has begun to be quite distinct from authorial time, and we may have to reach back further to retrieve the relevant facts about baseball, or the war, or daily life in Pittsburgh to understand the issues in the play. And we also read with a somewhat different perspective. In 1981 the integration of baseball seemed a powerful symbol of progress and disappearing distinctions between black and white opportunity. In the 1990s the symbol has become more mixed. Statistical studies have emphasized the difference between the opportunities available to blacks and to whites as "fringe" players, the lack of blacks in managerial and management positions in baseball has drawn a lot of attention, and the exploitation of football players, especially black players, by colleges has gotten a lot of press. We therefore read Troy's skepticism about the sports opportunities for his son rather differently than we would have in 1981; Troy sounds like some of the spokespeople for black capitalism in the Reagan administration. Generally speaking, the longer the time between the writing of a text and the reading of it, the more differences of attitude and assumption will have appeared. Often readers must adjust their sights somewhat to understand the perspective that went into the positioning of the action that the act of writing represents, as well as adjusting to the historical present of the play.

Plays that represent a specific historical event—the Lizzie Borden case in *Blood Relations*, for example—make the act of reading at once easier and more difficult. The easy part is that we are alerted to the fact that we have to know something about that historical moment. We may well have heard the familiar rhyme:

> Lizzie Borden took an ax
> And gave her mother forty whacks;
> When she saw what she had done
> She gave her father forty-one!

And we may well know that the murder of Lizzie's parents (actually it was her father and stepmother) occurred in 1892 and that Lizzie was ultimately acquitted. We might even have heard something, rumors at least, of Lizzie's character and behavior and be aware of her reputation for oddness. If we don't know these things we can readily find them out, and texts that consciously represent public historical events usually count on this knowledge. But there are more subtle aspects of historical consciousness that do not come from going to the library to research an event, and Pollock's play is very much about these subtleties.

What was life like in Fall River, Massachusetts, in the late nineteenth century? What was it like to be a spinster in such a time and such a community? What kinds of expectations of behavior and value were imposed then on a woman like Lizzie? How free were individuals in this "Victorian" age to behave eccentrically, and what sorts of conclusions were drawn about "odd" behavior? Such information is not readily found in encyclopedia articles about an event or even in "factual" books on the subject. Often, as in *Blood Relations*, the text will reconstruct ordinary life so as to make us aware of the subtle particularities of the historical moment, but we have to be open to that re-creation and not assume we have mastered the "history" when we disinter "facts" about the event. It is often easy to mislead ourselves, in any text that renders a historical event, into thinking that factual research prepares us with the "right" knowledge. The "right" knowledge may in fact be far more complex, and it is important to allow the text to lead us to the "right" history rather than imposing the standard public version of history. Writers are often attracted to historical events and historical moments because they want to reinterpret history or to examine some kind of motivation or behavior within a definable cultural context. Fact and legend interact in *Blood Relations* with a highly subjective interpretation of history, culture, and the psychological analysis of human behavior, and readers of the 1990s may want to know just as much about authorial time here as about historical time—just as much about the playwright of 1981 and her Canadian context as about the Lizzie Borden of a century earlier and her New England context.

▼ ▼ ▼

SHARON POLLOCK

Blood Relations

CHARACTERS

MISS LIZZIE, *who will play* BRIDGET, *the Irish maid*

THE ACTRESS, *who will play* LIZZIE BORDEN

HARRY, *Mrs. Borden's brother*

EMMA, *Lizzie's older sister*

ANDREW [MR. BORDEN], *Lizzie's father*

ABIGAIL [MRS. BORDEN], *Lizzie's step-mother*

DR. PATRICK, *the Irish doctor, sometimes* THE DEFENSE

SETTING

The time proper is late Sunday afternoon and evening, late fall, in Fall River,[1] 1902; the year of the "dream thesis," if one might call it that, is 1892.

The playing areas include (a) within the BORDEN *house: the dining room from which there is an exit to the kitchen; the parlour; a flight of stairs leading to the second floor; and (b) in the* BORDEN *yard: the walk outside the house; the area in which the birds are kept.*

PRODUCTION NOTE: *Action must be free-flowing. There can be no division of the script into scenes by blackout, movement of furniture, or sets. There may be freezes of some characters while other scenes are being played. There is no necessity to "get people off" and "on" again for, with the exception of* THE ACTRESS *and* MISS LIZZIE *(and* EMMA *in the final scene), all characters are imaginary, and all action in reality would be taking place between* MISS LIZZIE *and* THE ACTRESS *in the dining room and parlour of her home.*

THE DEFENSE *may actually be seen, may be a shadow, or a figure behind a scrim.*

While MISS LIZZIE *exits and enters with her* BRIDGET *business, she is a presence, often observing unobtrusively when as* BRIDGET *she takes no part in the action.*

ACT I

Lights up on the figure of A WOMAN *standing centre stage. It is a somewhat formal pose. A pause. She speaks.*

[THE ACTRESS:]

"Since what I am about to say must be but that
Which contradicts my accusation, and
The testimony on my part no other
But what comes from myself, it shall scare boot[2] me

---

1. Town in southeastern Massachusetts.   2. Profit.

To say 'Not Guilty.'
But, if Powers Divine
Behold our human action as they do,
I doubt not than but innocence shall make
False accusation blush and tyranny
Tremble at . . . at . . ."

[*She wriggles the fingers of an outstretched hand searching for the word.*]

"Aaaat" . . . Bollocks!!³

[*She raises her script, takes a bite of chocolate.*]

"Tremble at Patience," patience patience! . . .

[MISS LIZZIE *enters from the kitchen with tea service.* THE ACTRESS's *attention drifts to* MISS LIZZIE. THE ACTRESS *watches* MISS LIZZIE *sit in the parlour and proceed to pour two cups of tea.* THE ACTRESS *sucks her teeth a bit to clear the chocolate as she speaks.*]

THE ACTRESS: Which . . . is proper, Lizzie?

MISS LIZZIE: Proper?

THE ACTRESS: To pour first the cream, and add the tea—or first tea and add cream. One is proper. Is the way you do the proper way, the way it's done in circles where it counts?

MISS LIZZIE: Sugar?

THE ACTRESS: Well, is it?

MISS LIZZIE: I don't know, sugar?

THE ACTRESS: Mmmn. [MISS LIZZIE *adds sugar.*] I suppose if we had Mrs. Beeton's *Book of Etiquette*, we could look it up.

MISS LIZZIE: I do have it, shall I get it?

THE ACTRESS: No. . . . You could ask your sister, she might know.

MISS LIZZIE: Do you want this tea or not?

THE ACTRESS: I hate tea.

MISS LIZZIE: You drink it every Sunday.

THE ACTRESS: I drink it because you like to serve it.

MISS LIZZIE: Pppu.

THE ACTRESS: It's true. You've no idea how I suffer from this toast and tea ritual. I really do. The tea upsets my stomach and the toast makes me fat because I eat so much of it.

MISS LIZZIE: Practice some restraint then.

THE ACTRESS: Mmmmm. . . . Why don't we ask your sister which is proper?

MISS LIZZIE: You ask her.

THE ACTRESS: How can I? She doesn't speak to me. I don't think she even sees me. She gives no indication of it. [*She looks up the stairs.*] What do you suppose she does up there every Sunday afternoon?

MISS LIZZIE: She sulks.

3. Balls!!

THE ACTRESS: And reads the Bible I suppose, and Mrs. Beeton's *Book of Etiquette*. Oh Lizzie. . . . What a long day. The absolutely longest day. . . . When does that come anyway, the longest day?

MISS LIZZIE: June.

THE ACTRESS: Ah yes, June. [*She looks at* MISS LIZZIE.] June?

MISS LIZZIE: June.

THE ACTRESS: Mmmmmm. . . .

MISS LIZZIE: I know what you're thinking.

THE ACTRESS: Of course you do. . . . I'm thinking . . . shall I pour the sherry—or will you.

MISS LIZZIE: No.

THE ACTRESS: I'm thinking . . . June . . . in Fall River.

MISS LIZZIE: No.

THE ACTRESS: August in Fall River? [*She smiles. Pause.*]

MISS LIZZIE: We could have met in Boston.

THE ACTRESS: I prefer it here.

MISS LIZZIE: You don't find it . . . a trifle boring?

THE ACTRESS: Au contraire. [MISS LIZZIE *gives a small laugh at the affectation.*] What?

MISS LIZZIE: I find it a trifle boring . . . I know what you're doing. You're soaking up the ambience.

THE ACTRESS: Nonsense, Lizzie. I come to see you.

MISS LIZZIE: Why?

THE ACTRESS: Because . . . of us. [*Pause.*]

MISS LIZZIE: You were a late arrival last night. Later than usual.

THE ACTRESS: Don't be silly.

MISS LIZZIE: I wonder why.

THE ACTRESS: The show was late, late starting, late coming down.

MISS LIZZIE: And?

THE ACTRESS: And—then we all went out for drinks.

MISS LIZZIE: We?

THE ACTRESS: The other members of the cast.

MISS LIZZIE: Oh yes.

THE ACTRESS: And then I caught a cab . . . all the way from Boston. . . . Do you know what it cost?

MISS LIZZIE: I should. I paid the bill, remember?

THE ACTRESS: [*Laughs.*] Of course. What a jumble all my thoughts are. There're too many words running round inside my head today. It's terrible.

MISS LIZZIE: It sounds it.

[*Pause.*]

THE ACTRESS: . . . You know . . . you do this thing . . . you stare at me . . . You look directly at my eyes. I think . . . you think . . . that if I'm lying . . . it will come up, like lemons on a slot machine. [*She makes a gesture at her eyes.*] Tick. Tick . . . [*Pause.*] In the alley, behind the theater the other day, there were some kids. You know what they were doing?

MISS LIZZIE: How could I?

THE ACTRESS: They were playing skip rope, and you know what they were singing?

[*She sings, and claps her hands arhythmically to:*]

"Lizzie Borden took an ax
Gave her mother forty whacks,
When the job was nicely done,
She gave her father forty-one."

MISS LIZZIE: Did you stop them?

THE ACTRESS: No.

MISS LIZZIE: Did you tell them I was acquitted?

THE ACTRESS: No.

MISS LIZZIE: What did you do?

THE ACTRESS: I shut the window.

MISS LIZZIE: A noble gesture on my behalf.

THE ACTRESS: We were doing lines—the noise they make is dreadful. Sometimes they play ball, ka-thunk, ka-thunk, ka-thunk against the wall. Once I saw them with a cat and—

MISS LIZZIE: And you didn't stop them?

THE ACTRESS: That time I stopped them. [THE ACTRESS *crosses to table where there is a gramophone. She prepares to play a record. She stops.*] Should I?

MISS LIZZIE: Why not?

THE ACTRESS: Your sister, the noise upsets her.

MISS LIZZIE: And she upsets me. On numerous occasions.

THE ACTRESS: You're incorrigible, Lizzie. [THE ACTRESS *holds out her arms to* MISS LIZZIE. *They dance the latest "in" dance, a Scott Joplin composition. It requires some concentration, but they chat while dancing rather formally in contrast to the music.*] . . . Do you think your jawline's heavy?

MISS LIZZIE: Why do you ask?

THE ACTRESS: They said you had jowls.

MISS LIZZIE: Did they.

THE ACTRESS: The reports of the day said you were definitely jowly.

MISS LIZZIE: That was ten years ago.

THE ACTRESS: Imagine. You were only thirty-four.

MISS LIZZIE: Yes.

THE ACTRESS: It happened here, this house.

MISS LIZZIE: You're leading.

THE ACTRESS: I know.

MISS LIZZIE: . . . I don't think I'm jowly. Then or now. Do you?

THE ACTRESS: Lizzie? Lizzie.

MISS LIZZIE: What?

THE ACTRESS: . . . did you?

MISS LIZZIE: Did I what?

[*Pause.*]

THE ACTRESS: You never tell *me* anything. [*She turns off the music.*]

MISS LIZZIE: I tell you everything.

THE ACTRESS: No you don't!

MISS LIZZIE: Oh yes, I tell you the most personal things about myself, my thoughts, my dreams, my—

THE ACTRESS: But never that one thing. . . . [*She lights a cigarette.*]

MISS LIZZIE: And don't smoke those—they stink. [THE ACTRESS *ignores her, inhales, exhales a volume of smoke in* MISS LIZZIE'S *direction.*] Do you suppose . . . people buy you drinks . . . or cast you even . . . because you have a "liaison" with Lizzie Borden? Do you suppose they do that?

THE ACTRESS: They cast me because I'm good at what I do.

MISS LIZZIE: They never pry? They never ask? What's she really like? Is she really jowly? Did she? Didn't she?

THE ACTRESS: What could I tell them? You never tell me anything.

MISS LIZZIE: I tell you everything.

THE ACTRESS: But that! [*Pause.*] You think everybody talks about you—they don't.

MISS LIZZIE: Here they do.

THE ACTRESS: You think they talk about you.

MISS LIZZIE: But never to me.

THE ACTRESS: Well . . . you give them lots to talk about.

MISS LIZZIE: You know you're right, your mind is a jumble.

THE ACTRESS: I told you so.

[*Pause.*]

MISS LIZZIE: You remind me of my sister.

THE ACTRESS: Oh God, in what way?

MISS LIZZIE: Day in, day out, ten years now, sometimes at breakfast as she rolls little crumbs of bread in little balls, sometimes at noon, or late at night . . . "Did you, Lizzie?" "Lizzie, did you?"

THE ACTRESS: Ten years, day in, day out?

MISS LIZZIE: Oh yes. She sits there where Papa used to sit and I sit there, where I have always sat. She looks at me and at her plate, then at me, and at her plate, then at me and then she says "Did you Lizzie?" "Lizzie, did you?"

THE ACTRESS: [*A nasal imitation of* EMMA'S *voice.*] "Did-you-Lizzie—Lizzie-did-you." [*Laughs.*]

MISS LIZZIE: Did I what?

THE ACTRESS: [*Continues her imitation of* EMMA.] "You know."

MISS LIZZIE: Well, what do you think?

THE ACTRESS: "Oh, I believe you didn't, in fact I know you didn't, what a thought! After all, you were acquitted."

MISS LIZZIE: Yes, I was.

THE ACTRESS: "But sometimes when I'm on the street . . . or shopping . . . or at the church even, I catch somebody's eye, they look away . . . and I think to myself "Did-you-Lizzie—Lizzie-did-you."

MISS LIZZIE: [*Laughs.*] Ah, poor Emma.

THE ACTRESS: [*Dropping her* EMMA *imitation.*] Well, did you?

MISS LIZZIE: Is it important?

THE ACTRESS: Yes.

MISS LIZZIE: Why?

THE ACTRESS: I have . . . a compulsion to know the truth.

MISS LIZZIE: The truth?

THE ACTRESS: Yes.

MISS LIZZIE: . . . Sometimes I think you look like me, and you're not jowly.

THE ACTRESS: No.

MISS LIZZIE: You look like me, or how I think I look, or how I ought to look . . . sometimes you think like me . . . do you feel that?

THE ACTRESS: Sometimes.

MISS LIZZIE: [*Triumphant.*] You shouldn't have to ask then. You should know. "Did I, didn't I." You tell me.

THE ACTRESS: I'll tell you what I think . . . I think . . . that you're aware there is a certain fascination in the ambiguity. . . . You always paint the background but leave the rest to my imagination. Did Lizzie Borden take an ax? . . . If you didn't I should be disappointed . . . and if you did I should be horrified.

MISS LIZZIE: And which is worse?

THE ACTRESS: To have murdered one's parents, or to be a pretentious small-town spinster? I don't know.

MISS LIZZIE: Why're you so cruel to me?

THE ACTRESS: I'm teasing, Lizzie. I'm only teasing. Come on, paint the background again.

MISS LIZZIE: Why?

THE ACTRESS: Perhaps you'll give something away.

MISS LIZZIE: Which you'll dine out on.

THE ACTRESS: Of course. [*Laughs.*] Come on, Lizzie. Come on.

MISS LIZZIE: A game.

THE ACTRESS: What?

MISS LIZZIE: A game? . . . And you'll play me.

THE ACTRESS: Oh—

MISS LIZZIE: It's your stock in trade, my love.

THE ACTRESS: All right. . . . A game!

MISS LIZZIE: Let me think . . . Bridget . . . Brrridget. We had a maid then. And her name was Bridget. Oh, she was a great one for stories, stood like this, very straight back, and her hair . . . and there she was in the courtroom in her new dress on the stand. "Do you swear to tell the truth, the whole truth, and nothing but the truth, so help you God?" [*Imitates Irish accent.*] "I do sir," she said.

"Would you give the court your name."

"Bridget O'Sullivan, sir."

[*Very faint echo of the voice of* THE DEFENSE *under* MISS LIZZIE's *next line.*]

"And occupation."

"I'm like what you'd call a maid, sir. I do a bit of everything, cleanin' and cookin'."

[*The actual voice of* THE DEFENSE *is heard alone; he may also be seen.*]

THE DEFENSE: You've been in Fall River how long?

MISS LIZZIE: [*Who continues as* BRIDGET, *while* THE ACTRESS (*who will play* LIZZIE) *observes.*] Well now, about five years sir, ever since I came over. I worked up on the hill for a while but it didn't—well, you could say, suit me, too lah-de-dah—so I—

THE DEFENSE: Your employer in June of 1892 was?

BRIDGET: Yes sir. Mr. Borden, sir. Well, more rightly, Mrs. Borden for she was the one who—

THE DEFENSE: Your impression of the household?

BRIDGET: Well . . . the man of the house, Mr. Borden, was a bit of a . . . tightwad, and Mrs. B. could nag you into the grave, still she helped with the dishes and things which not everyone does when they hire a maid. [HARRY *appears on the stairs; approaches* BRIDGET *stealthily. She is unaware of him.*] Then there was the daughters, Miss Emma and Lizzie, and that day, Mr. Wingate, Mrs. B's brother who'd stayed for the night and was—[*He grabs her ass with both hands. She screams.*] Get off with you!

HARRY: Come on, Bridget, give me a kiss!

BRIDGET: I'll give you a good poke in the nose if you don't keep your hands to yourself.

HARRY: Ohhh-hh-hh Bridget!

BRIDGET: Get away you old sod!

HARRY: Haven't you missed me?

BRIDGET: I have not! I was pinched black and blue last time—and I'll be sufferin' the same before I see the end of you this time.

HARRY: [*Tilts his ass at her.*] You want to see my end?

BRIDGET: You're a dirty old man.

HARRY: If Mr. Borden hears that, you'll be out on the street. [*Grabs her.*] Where's my kiss!

BRIDGET: [*Dumps glass of water on his head.*] There! [HARRY *splutters.*] Would you like another? You silly thing you—and leave me towels alone!

HARRY: You've soaked my shirt.

BRIDGET: Shut up and pour yourself a cup of coffee.

HARRY: You got no sense of fun, Bridget.

BRIDGET: Well now, if you tried actin' like the gentleman farmer you're supposed to be, Mr. Wingate—

HARRY: I'm tellin' you you can't take a joke.

BRIDGET: If Mr. Borden sees you jokin', it's not his maid he'll be throwin' out on the street, but his brother-in-law, and that's the truth.

HARRY: What's between you and me's between you and me, eh?

BRIDGET: There ain't nothin' between you and me.

HARRY: . . . Finest cup of coffee in Fall River.

BRIDGET: There's no gettin' on the good side of me now, it's too late for that.

HARRY: . . . Bridget? . . . You know what tickles my fancy?

BRIDGET: No and I don't want to hear.

HARRY: It's your Irish temper.

BRIDGET: It is, is it? . . . Can I ask you something?

HARRY: Ooohhh—anything.

BRIDGET: [*Innocently.*] Does Miss Lizzie know you're here? . . . I say does Miss Lizzie—

HARRY: Why do you bring her up.

BRIDGET: She don't then, eh? [*Teasing.*] It's a surprise visit?

HARRY: No surprise to her father.

BRIDGET: Oh?

HARRY: We got business.

BRIDGET: I'd of thought the last bit of business was enough.

HARRY: It's not for— [*you to say.*]

BRIDGET: You don't learn a thing, from me or Lizzie, do you?

HARRY: Listen here—

BRIDGET: You mean you've forgotten how mad she was when you got her father to sign the rent from the mill house over to your sister? Oh my.

HARRY: She's his wife, isn't she?

BRIDGET: [*Lightly.*] Second wife.

HARRY: She's still got her rights.

BRIDGET: Who am I to say who's got a right? But I can tell you this—Miss Lizzie don't see it that way.

HARRY: It don't matter how Miss Lizzie sees it.

BRIDGET: Oh it matters enough—she had you thrown out last time, didn't she? By jasus that was a laugh!

HARRY: You mind your tongue.

BRIDGET: And after you left, you know what happened?

HARRY: Get away.

BRIDGET: She and sister Emma got her father's rent money from the other mill house to make it all even-steven—and now, here you are back again? What kind of business you up to this time? [*Whispers in his ear.*] Mind Lizzie doesn't catch you.

HARRY: Get away!

BRIDGET: [*Laughs.*] Ohhhh—would you like some more coffee, sir? It's the finest coffee in all Fall River! [*She pours it.*] Thank you sir. You're welcome, sir. [*She exits to the kitchen.*]

HARRY: There'll be no trouble this time! Do you hear me!

BRIDGET: [*Off.*] Yes sir.

HARRY: There'll be no trouble. [*Sees a basket of crusts.*] What the hell's this? I said is this for breakfast!

BRIDGET: [*Entering.*] Is what for—oh no—Mr. Borden's not economizin' to that degree yet, it's the crusts for Miss Lizzie's birds.

HARRY: What birds?

BRIDGET: Some kind of pet pigeons she's raisin' out in the shed. Miss Lizzie loves her pigeons.

HARRY: Miss Lizzie loves kittens and cats and horses and dogs. What Miss Lizzie doesn't love is people.

BRIDGET: *Some* people. [*She looks past* HARRY *to* THE ACTRESS / LIZZIE. HARRY *turns to follow* BRIDGET'*s gaze.* BRIDGET *speaks, encouraging an invitation for* THE ACTRESS *to join her.*] Good mornin' Lizzie.

THE ACTRESS: [*She is a trifle tentative in the role of* LIZZIE.] Is the coffee on?

BRIDGET: Yes ma'am.

LIZZIE: I'll have some then.

BRIDGET: Yes ma'am.

[*She makes no move to get it, but watches as* LIZZIE *stares at* HARRY.]

HARRY: Well . . . I think . . . maybe I'll . . . just split a bit of that kindling out back.

[*He exits.* LIZZIE *turns to* BRIDGET.]

LIZZIE: Silly ass.

BRIDGET: Oh Lizzie.

[*She laughs. She enjoys* THE ACTRESS / LIZZIE'*s comments as she guides her into her role by "painting the background."*]

LIZZIE: Well, he is. He's a silly ass.

BRIDGET: Can you remember him last time with your Papa? Oh, I can still hear him. "Now Andrew, I've spent my life raisin' horses and I'm gonna tell you somethin'—a *woman* is just like a *horse!* You keep her on a tight rein, or she'll take the bit in her teeth and next thing you know, road, destination, and purpose is all behind you, and you'll be damn lucky if she don't pitch you right in a sewer ditch!"

LIZZIE: Stupid bugger.

BRIDGET: Oh Lizzie, what language! What would your father say if he heard you?

LIZZIE: Well . . . I've never used a word I didn't hear from him first.

BRIDGET: Do you think he'd be congratulatin' you?

LIZZIE: Possibly. [BRIDGET *gives a subtle shake of her head.*] Not.

BRIDGET: Possibly not is right. . . . And what if *Mrs.* B. should hear you?

LIZZIE: I hope and pray that she does. . . . Do you know what I think, Bridget? I think there's nothing wrong with Mrs. B. . . . that losing eighty pounds and tripling her intellect wouldn't cure.

BRIDGET: [*Loving it.*] You ought to be ashamed.

LIZZIE: It's the truth, isn't it?

BRIDGET: Still, what a way to talk of your mother.

LIZZIE: Step-mother.

BRIDGET: Still you don't mean it, do you?

LIZZIE: Don't I? [*Louder.*] She's a *silly ass* too!

BRIDGET: Shhhh.

LIZZIE: It's all right, she's deaf as a picket fence when she wants to be. . . . What's he here for?

BRIDGET: Never said.

LIZZIE: He's come to worm more money out of Papa I bet.

BRIDGET: Lizzie.

LIZZIE: What.

BRIDGET: Your sister, Lizzie.

[BRIDGET *indicates* EMMA, LIZZIE *turns to see her on the stairs.*]

EMMA: You want to be quiet, Lizzie, a body can't sleep for the racket upstairs.

LIZZIE: Oh?

EMMA: You've been makin' too much noise.

LIZZIE: It must have been Bridget, she dropped a pot, didn't you, Bridget.

EMMA: A number of pots from the sound of it.

BRIDGET: I'm all thumbs this mornin', ma'am.

EMMA: You know it didn't sound like pots.

LIZZIE: Oh.

EMMA: Sounded more like voices.

LIZZIE: Oh?

EMMA: Sounded like your voice, Lizzie.

LIZZIE: Maybe you dreamt it.

EMMA: I wish I had, for someone was using words no lady would use.

LIZZIE: When Bridget dropped the pot, she did say "pshaw!" didn't you, Bridget.

BRIDGET: Pshaw! That's what I said.

EMMA: That's not what I heard.

[BRIDGET *will withdraw.*]

LIZZIE: Pshaw?

EMMA: If mother heard you, you know what she's say.

LIZZIE: She's not my mother or yours.

EMMA: Well she married our father twenty-seven years ago, if that doesn't make her our mother—

LIZZIE: It doesn't.

EMMA: Don't talk like that.

LIZZIE: I'll talk as I like.

EMMA: We're not going to fight, Lizzie. We're going to be quiet and have our breakfast!

LIZZIE: Is that what we're going to do?

EMMA: Yes.

LIZZIE: Oh.

EMMA: At least—that's what I'm going to do.

LIZZIE: Bridget, Emma wants her breakfast!

EMMA: I could have yelled myself.

LIZZIE: You could, but you never do.

[BRIDGET *serves* EMMA, EMMA *is reluctant to argue in front of* BRIDGET.]

EMMA: Thank you, Bridget.

LIZZIE: Did you know Harry Wingate's back for a visit? . . . He must have snuck in late last night so I wouldn't hear him. Did you? [EMMA *shakes her head.* LIZZIE *studies her.*] Did you know he was coming?

EMMA: No.

LIZZIE: No?

EMMA: But I do know he wouldn't be here unless Papa asked him.

LIZZIE: That's not the point. You know what happened last time he was here. Papa was signing property over to her.

EMMA: Oh Lizzie.

LIZZIE: Oh Lizzie nothing. It's bad enough Papa's worth thousands of dollars, and here we are, stuck in this tiny bit of a house on Second Street, when we should be up on the hill—and that's her doing. Or hers and Harry's.

EMMA: Shush.

LIZZIE: I won't shush. They cater to Papa's worst instincts.

EMMA: They'll hear you.

LIZZIE: I don't care if they do. It's true, isn't it? Papa tends to be miserly, he probably has the first penny he ever earned—or more likely *she* has it.

EMMA: You talk rubbish.

LIZZIE: Papa *can* be very warm-hearted and generous *but he needs encouragement.*

EMMA: If Papa didn't save his money, Papa wouldn't have any money.

LIZZIE: And neither will we if he keeps signing things over to her.

EMMA: I'm not going to listen.

LIZZIE: Well try thinking.

EMMA: Stop it.

LIZZIE: [*Not a threat, a simple statement of fact.*] Someday Papa will die—

EMMA: Don't say that.

LIZZIE: Some day Papa will die. And I don't intend to spend the rest of my life licking Harry Wingate's boots, or toadying to his sister.

MRS. BORDEN: [*From the stairs.*] What's that?

LIZZIE: Nothing.

MRS. BORDEN: [*Making her way downstairs.*] Eh?

LIZZIE: I said, nothing!

BRIDGET: [*Holds out basket of crusts.* LIZZIE *looks at it.*] For your birds, Miss Lizzie.

LIZZIE: [*She takes the basket.*] You want to know what I think? I think she's a fat cow and I hate her. [*She exits.*]

EMMA: Morning, Mother.

MRS. BORDEN: Morning Emma.

EMMA: . . . Did you have a good sleep.

[BRIDGET *will serve breakfast.*]

MRS. BORDEN: So so. . . . It's the heat you know. It never cools off proper at night. It's too hot for a good sleep.

EMMA: . . . Is Papa up?

MRS. BORDEN: He'll be down in a minute . . . sooo. . . . What's wrong with Lizzie this morning?

EMMA: Nothing.

MRS. BORDEN: . . . Has Harry come down?

EMMA: I'm not sure.

MRS. BORDEN: Bridget. Has Harry come down?

BRIDGET: Yes ma'am.

MRS. BORDEN: And?

BRIDGET: And he's gone out back for a bit.

MRS. BORDEN: Lizzie see him?

BRIDGET: Yes ma'am. [*Beats it back to the kitchen.*]

[EMMA *concentrates on her plate.*]

MRS. BORDEN: . . . You should have said so. . . . She have words with him?

EMMA: Lizzie has more manners than that.

MRS. BORDEN: She's incapable of disciplining herself like a lady and we all know it.

EMMA: Well she doesn't make a habit of picking fights with people.

MRS. BORDEN: That's just it. She does.

EMMA: Well—she may—

MRS. BORDEN: And you can't deny that.

EMMA: [*Louder.*] Well this morning she may have been a bit upset because no one told her he was coming and when she came down he was here. But that's all there was to it.

MRS. BORDEN: If your father wants my brother in for a stay, he's to ask Lizzie's permission I suppose.

EMMA: No.

MRS. BORDEN: You know, Emma—

EMMA: She didn't argue with him or anything like that.

MRS. BORDEN: You spoiled her. You may have had the best of intentions, but you spoiled her.

[MISS LIZZIE / BRIDGET *is speaking to* ACTRESS / LIZZIE.]

MISS LIZZIE / BRIDGET: I was thirty-four years old, and I still daydreamed. . . . I did . . . I daydreamed . . . I dreamt that my name was Lisbeth . . . and I lived up on the hill in a corner house . . . and my hair wasn't red. I hate red hair. When I was little, everyone teased me. . . . When I was little, we never stayed in this house for the summer, we'd go to the farm. . . . I remember . . . my knees were always covered with scabs, god knows how I got them, but you know what I'd do? I'd sit in the field, and haul up my skirts, and my petticoat and my bloomers and roll down my stockings and I'd *pick* the scabs on my knees! And Emma would catch me! You know what she'd say? "Nice little girls don't have scabs on their knees!"

[*They laugh.*]

ACTRESS / LIZZIE: Poor Emma.

MISS LIZZIE / BRIDGET: I dreamt . . . someday I'm going to live . . . in a corner house on the hill. . . . I'll have parties, grand parties. I'll be . . . witty, not biting, but witty. Everyone will be witty. Everyone who is *anyone* will want to come to my parties . . . and if . . . I can't . . . live in a corner house on the hill . . . I'll live on the farm, all by myself on the farm! There was a barn there, with barn cats and barn kittens and two horses and barn swallows that lived in the eaves. . . . The birds I kept here were pigeons, not swallows. . . . They were grey, a dull grey . . . but . . . when the sun struck their feathers, I'd see blue, a steel blue with a sheen, and when they'd move in the sun they were bright blue and maroon and over it all, an odd sparkle as if you'd . . . grated a new silver dollar and the gratings caught in their feathers. . . . Most of the time they were dull . . . and stupid perhaps . . . but they weren't really. They were . . . hiding I think. . . . They knew me. . . . They liked me. . . . The truth . . . is . . .

ACTRESS / LIZZIE: The truth is . . . thirty-four is too old to daydream. . . .

MRS. BORDEN: The truth is she's spoilt rotten. [MR. BORDEN *will come downstairs and take his place at the table.* MRS. BORDEN *continues for his benefit.* MR. BORDEN *ignores her. He has learned the fine art of tuning her out. He is not intimidated or hen-pecked.*] And we're paying the piper for that. In most of the places I've been the people who pay the piper call the tune. Of course I haven't had the advantage of a trip to Europe with a bunch of lady friends like our Lizzie had three years ago, all expenses paid by her father.

EMMA: Morning Papa.

MR. BORDEN: Mornin'.

MRS. BORDEN: I haven't had the benefit of that experience. . . . Did you know Lizzie's seen Harry?

MR. BORDEN: Has she.

MRS. BORDEN: You should have met him down town. You should never have asked him to stay over.

MR. BORDEN: Why not?

MRS. BORDEN: You know as well as I do why not. I don't want a repeat of last time. She didn't speak civil for months.

MR. BORDEN: There's no reason for Harry to pay for a room when we've got a spare one. . . . Where's Lizzie?

EMMA: Out back feeding the birds.

MR. BORDEN: She's always out at those birds.

EMMA: Yes Papa.

MR. BORDEN: And tell her to get a new lock for the shed. There's been someone in it again.

EMMA: All right.

MR. BORDEN: It's those little hellions from next door. We had no trouble with them playin' in that shed before, they always played in their own yard before.

EMMA: . . . Papa?

MR. BORDEN: It's those damn birds, that's what brings them into the yard.

EMMA: . . . About Harry . . .

MR. BORDEN: What about Harry?

EMMA: Well . . . I was just wondering why . . . [he's here.]

MR. BORDEN: You never mind Harry—did you speak to Lizzie about Johnny MacLeod?

EMMA: I ah—

MR. BORDEN: Eh?

EMMA: I said I tried to—

MR. BORDEN: What do you mean, you tried to.

EMMA: Well, I was working my way round to it but—

MR. BORDEN: What's so difficult about telling Lizzie Johnny MacLeod wants to call?

EMMA: Then why don't you tell her? I'm always the one that has to go running to Lizzie telling her this and telling her that, and taking the abuse for it!

MRS. BORDEN: We all know why that is, she can wrap her father round her little finger, always has, always could. If everything else fails, she throws a tantrum and her father buys her off, trip to Europe, rent to the mill house, it's all the same.

EMMA: Papa, what's Harry here for?

MR. BORDEN: None of your business.

MRS. BORDEN: And don't you go runnin' to Lizzie stirring things up.

EMMA: You know I've never done that!

MR. BORDEN: What she means—

EMMA: [With anger but little fatigue.] I'm tired, do you hear? Tired!

[She gets up from the table and leaves for upstairs.]

MR. BORDEN: Emma!

EMMA: You ask Harry here, you know there'll be trouble, and when I try to find out what's going on, so once again good old Emma can stand between you and Lizzie, all you've got to say is "none of your business!" Well then, it's your business, you look after it, because I'm not! [She exits.]

MRS. BORDEN: . . . She's right.

MR. BORDEN: That's enough. I've had enough. I don't want to hear from you too.

MRS. BORDEN: I'm only saying she's right. You have to talk straight and plain to Lizzie and tell her things she don't want to hear.

MR. BORDEN: About the farm?

MRS. BORDEN: About Johnny MacLeod! Keep your mouth shut about the farm and she won't know the difference.

MR. BORDEN: All right.

MRS. BORDEN: Speak to her about Johnny MacLeod.

MR. BORDEN: All right!

MRS. BORDEN: You know what they're sayin' in town. About her and that doctor.

[MISS LIZZIE / BRIDGET is speaking to THE ACTRESS / LIZZIE.]

MISS LIZZIE / BRIDGET: They're saying if you live on Second Street and you need a housecall, and you don't mind the Irish, call Dr. Patrick. Dr. Patrick is very prompt with his Second Street house calls.

ACTRESS / LIZZIE: Do they really say that?

MISS LIZZIE / BRIDGET: No they don't. I'm telling a lie. But he is very prompt with a Second Street call, do you know why that is?

ACTRESS / LIZZIE: Why?

MISS LIZZIE / BRIDGET: Well—he's hoping to see someone who lives on Second Street—someone who's yanking up her skirt and showing her ankle—so she can take a decent-sized step—and forgetting everything she was ever taught in Miss Cornelia's School for Girls, and talking to the Irish as if she never heard of the Pope! Oh yes, he's very prompt getting to Second Street . . . getting away is something else. . . .

DR. PATRICK: Good morning, Miss Borden!

LIZZIE: I haven't decided . . . if it is . . . or it isn't. . . .

DR. PATRICK: No, you've got it all wrong. The proper phrase is "good morning, Dr. Patrick," and then you smile, discreetly of course, and lower the eyes just a titch, twirl the parasol—

LIZZIE: The parasol?

DR. PATRICK: The parasol, but not too fast; and then you murmur in a voice that was ever sweet and low, "And how are you doin' this morning, Dr. Patrick?" Your education's been sadly neglected, Miss Borden.

LIZZIE: You're forgetting something. You're married—and Irish besides—I'm supposed to ignore you.

DR. PATRICK: No.

LIZZIE: Yes. Don't you realize Papa and Emma have fits everytime we engage in "illicit conversation." They're having fits right now.

DR. PATRICK: Well, does Mrs. Borden approve?

LIZZIE: Ahhh. She's the real reason I keep stopping and talking. Mrs. Borden is easily shocked. I'm hoping she dies from the shock.

DR. PATRICK: [Laughs.] Why don't you . . . run away from home, Lizzie?

LIZZIE: Why don't you "run away" with me?

DR. PATRICK: Where'll we go?

LIZZIE: Boston.

DR. PATRICK: Boston?

LIZZIE: For a start.

DR. PATRICK: And when will we go?

LIZZIE: Tonight.

DR. PATRICK: But you don't really mean it, you're havin' me on.

LIZZIE: I do mean it.

DR. PATRICK: How can you joke—and look so serious?

LIZZIE: It's a gift.

DR. PATRICK: [Laughs.] Oh Lizzie—

LIZZIE: Look!

DR. PATRICK: What is it?

LIZZIE: It's those little beggars next door. Hey! Hey get away! Get away there!

. . . They break into the shed to get at my birds and Papa gets angry.

DR. PATRICK: It's a natural thing.

LIZZIE: Well Papa doesn't like it.

DR. PATRICK: They just want to look at them.

LIZZIE: Papa says what's his is his own—you need a formal invitation to get into our yard. . . . [*Pause.*] How's your wife?

DR. PATRICK: My wife.

LIZZIE: Shouldn't I ask that? I thought nice polite ladies always inquired after the wives of their friends or acquaintances or . . . whatever.

[HARRY *observes them.*]

DR. PATRICK: You've met my wife, my wife is always the same.

LIZZIE: How boring for you.

DR. PATRICK: Uh-huh.

LIZZIE: And for her—

DR. PATRICK: Yes indeed.

LIZZIE: And for me.

DR. PATRICK: Do you know what they say, Lizzie? They say if you live on Second Street, and you need a house call, and you don't mind the Irish, call Dr. Patrick. Dr. Patrick is very prompt with his Second Street house calls.

LIZZIE: I'll tell you what I've heard them say—Second Street is a nice place to visit, but you wouldn't want to live there. I certainly don't.

HARRY: Lizzie.

LIZZIE: Well, look who's here. Have you had the pleasure of meeting my uncle, Mr. Wingate.

DR. PATRICK: No Miss Borden, that pleasure has never been mine.

LIZZIE: That's exactly how I feel.

DR. PATRICK: Mr. Wingate, sir.

HARRY: Dr. . . . Patrick is it?

DR. PATRICK: Yes it is, sir.

HARRY: Who's sick? [In other words, "*What the hell are you doing here?*"]

LIZZIE: No one. He just dropped by for a visit; you see Dr. Patrick and I are very old, very dear friends, isn't that so?

[HARRY *stares at* DR. PATRICK.]

DR. PATRICK: Well . . . [LIZZIE *jabs him in the ribs.*] Ouch! . . . It's her sense of humor, sir . . . a rare trait in a woman. . . .

HARRY: You best get in, Lizzie, it's gettin' on for lunch.

LIZZIE: Don't be silly, we just had breakfast.

HARRY: You best get in!

LIZZIE: . . . Would you give me your arm, Dr. Patrick?

[*She moves away with* DR. PATRICK, *ignoring* HARRY.]

DR. PATRICK: Now see what you've done?

LIZZIE: What?

DR. PATRICK: You've broken two of my ribs and ruined my reputation all in one blow.

LIZZIE: It's impossible to ruin an Irishman's reputation.

DR. PATRICK: [*Smiles.*] . . . I'll be seeing you, Lizzie . . .

MISS LIZZIE / BRIDGET: They're sayin' it's time you were married.

LIZZIE: What time is that?

MISS LIZZIE / BRIDGET: You need a place of your own.

LIZZIE: How would getting married get me that?

MISS LIZZIE / BRIDGET: Though I don't know what man would put up with your moods!

LIZZIE: What about me putting up with his!

MISS LIZZIE / BRIDGET: Oh Lizzie!

LIZZIE: What's the matter, don't men have moods?

HARRY: I'm tellin' you, as God is my witness, she's out in the walk talkin' to that Irish doctor, and he's fallin' all over her.

MRS. BORDEN: What's the matter with you. For her own sake you should speak to her.

MR. BORDEN: I will.

HARRY: The talk around town can't be doin' you any good.

MRS. BORDEN: Harry's right.

HARRY: Yes sir.

MRS. BORDEN: He's tellin' you what you should know.

HARRY: If a man can't manage his own daughter, how the hell can he manage a business—that's what people say, and it don't matter a damn whether there's any sense in it or not.

MR. BORDEN: I know that.

MRS. BORDEN: Knowin' is one thing, doin' something about it is another. What're you goin' to do about it?

MR. BORDEN: God damn it! I said I was goin' to speak to her and I am!

MRS. BORDEN: Well speak good and plain this time!

MR. BORDEN: Jesus Christ woman!

MRS. BORDEN: Your "speakin' to Lizzie" is a ritual around here.

MR. BORDEN: Abbie—

MRS. BORDEN: She talks, you listen, and nothin' changes!

MR. BORDEN: That's enough!

MRS. BORDEN: Emma isn't the only one that's fed to the teeth!

MR. BORDEN: Shut up!

MRS. BORDEN: You're gettin' old, Andrew! You're gettin' old! [*She exits.*]

[*An air of embarrassment from* MR. BORDEN *at having words in front of* HARRY. MR. BORDEN *fumbles with his pipe.*]

HARRY: [*Offers his pouch of tobacco.*] Here . . . have some of mine.

MR. BORDEN: Don't mind if I do. . . . Nice mix.

HARRY: It is.

MR. BORDEN: . . . I used to think . . . by my seventies . . . I'd be bouncin' a grandson on my knee. . . .

HARRY: Not too late for that.

MR. BORDEN: Nope . . . never had any boys . . . and girls . . . don't seem to have the same sense of family. . . . You know it's all well and good to talk about speakin' plain to Lizzie, but the truth of the matter is, if Lizzie puts her mind to a thing, she does it, and if she don't, she don't.

HARRY: It's up to you to see she does.

MR. BORDEN: It's like Abigail says, knowin' is one thing, doin' is another. . . . You're lucky you never brought any children into the world, Harry, you don't have to deal with them.

HARRY: Now that's no way to be talkin'.

MR. BORDEN: There's Emma . . . Emma's a good girl . . . when Abbie and I get on, there'll always be Emma. . . . Well! You're not sittin' here to listen to me and my girls, are you, you didn't come here for that. Business, eh Harry?

[HARRY *whips out a sheet of figures.*]

MISS LIZZIE / BRIDGET: I can remember distinctly . . . that moment I was undressing for bed, and I looked at my knees—and there were no scabs! At last! I thought I'm the nice little girl Emma wants me to be! . . . But it wasn't that at all. I was just growing up. I didn't fall down so often. . . . [*She smiles.*] Do you suppose . . . do you suppose there's a formula, a magic formula for being "a woman"? Do you suppose every girl baby receives it at birth, it's the last thing that happens just before birth, the magic formula is stamped indelibly on the brain—Ka Thud!! [*Her mood of amusement changes.*] . . . and . . . through some terrible oversight . . . perhaps the death of my mother . . . I didn't get that Ka Thud!! I was born . . . defective. . . . [*She looks at* THE ACTRESS.]

LIZZIE: [*Low.*] No.

MISS LIZZIE / BRIDGET: Not defective?

LIZZIE: Just . . . born.

THE DEFENSE: Gentlemen of the Jury! I ask you to look at the defendant, Miss Lizzie Borden. I ask you to recall the nature of the crime of which she is accused. I ask you—do you believe Miss Lizzie Borden, the youngest daughter of a scion of our community, a recipient of the fullest amenities our society can bestow upon its most fortunate members, do you believe Miss Lizzie Borden capable of wielding the murder weapon—thirty-two blows, gentlemen, thirty-two blows—fracturing Abigail Borden's skull, leaving her bloody and broken body in an upstairs bedroom, then, Miss Borden, with no hint of frenzy, hysteria, or trace of blood upon her person, engages in casual conversation with the maid, Bridget O'Sullivan, while awaiting her father's return home, upon which, after sending Bridget to her attic room, Miss Borden deals thirteen blows to the head of her father, and minutes later—in a state utterly comparable with that of a loving daughter upon discovery of murder most foul—Miss Borden calls for aid! Is this the aid we give her? Accusation of the most heinous and infamous of crimes? Do you believe Miss Lizzie Borden capable of these acts? I can tell you I do not!! I can tell you these acts of violence are acts of madness!! Gentlemen! If this gentlewoman is capable of such an act—I say to you—look to your daughters—if this gentlewoman is capable of such an act, which of us can lie abed at night, hear a step upon the stairs, a rustle in the hall, a creak outside the door. . . . Which of you can plump your pillow, nudge your wife, close your eyes, and sleep? Gentlemen, Lizzie Borden is not mad. Gentlemen, Lizzie Borden is not guilty.

MR. BORDEN: Lizzie?

LIZZIE: Papa . . . have you and Harry got business?

HARRY: 'lo Lizzie. I'll ah . . . finish up later.

[*He exits with the figures.* LIZZIE *watches him go.*].

MR. BORDEN: Lizzie?

LIZZIE: What?

MR. BORDEN: Could you sit down a minute?

LIZZIE: If it's about Dr. Patrick again, I—

MR. BORDEN: It isn't.

LIZZIE: Good.

MR. BORDEN: But we could start there.

LIZZIE: Oh Papa.

MR. BORDEN: Sit down Lizzie.

LIZZIE: But I've heard it all before, another chat for a wayward girl.

MR. BORDEN: [*Gently.*] Bite your tongue, Lizzie.

[*She smiles at him, there is affection between them. She has the qualities he would like in a son but deplores in a daughter.*]

MR. BORDEN: Now . . . first off . . . I want you to know that I . . . understand about you and the doctor.

LIZZIE: What do you understand?

MR. BORDEN: I understand . . . that it's a natural thing.

LIZZIE: What is?

MR. BORDEN: I'm saying there's nothing unnatural about an attraction between a man and a woman. That's a natural thing.

LIZZIE: I find Dr. Patrick . . . amusing and entertaining . . . if that's what you mean . . . is that what you mean?

MR. BORDEN: This attraction . . . points something up—you're a woman of thirty-four years—

LIZZIE: I know that.

MR. BORDEN: Just listen to me, Lizzie. . . . I'm choosing my words, and I want you to listen. Now . . . in most circumstances . . . a woman of your age would be married, eh? have children, be running her own house, that's the natural thing, eh? [*Pause.*] Eh, Lizzie?

LIZZIE: I don't know.

MR. BORDEN: Of course you know.

LIZZIE: You're saying I'm unnatural . . . am I supposed to agree, is that what you want?

MR. BORDEN: No, I'm not saying that! I'm saying the opposite to that! . . . I'm saying the feelings you have towards Dr. Patrick—

LIZZIE: What feelings?

MR. BORDEN: What's . . . what's happening here, I can understand, but what you have to understand is that he's a married man, and there's nothing for you there.

LIZZIE: If he weren't married, Papa, I wouldn't be bothered talking to him! . . . It's just a game, Papa, it's a game.

MR. BORDEN: A game.

LIZZIE: You have no idea how boring it is looking eligible, interested, and alluring, when I feel none of the three. So I play games. And it's a blessed relief to talk to a married man.

MR. BORDEN: What're his feelings for you?

LIZZIE: I don't know, I don't care. Can I go now?

MR. BORDEN: I'm not finished yet! . . . You know Mr. MacLeod, Johnny MacLeod?

LIZZIE: I know his three little monsters.

MR. BORDEN: He's trying to raise three boys with no mother!

LIZZIE: That's not my problem! I'm going.

MR. BORDEN: Lizzie!

LIZZIE: What!

MR. BORDEN: Mr. MacLeod's asked to come over next Tuesday.

LIZZIE: I'll be out that night.

MR. BORDEN: No you won't!

LIZZIE: Yes I will! . . . Whose idea was this?

MR. BORDEN: No one's.

LIZZIE: That's a lie. She wants to get rid of me.

MR. BORDEN: I want what's best for you!

LIZZIE: No you don't! 'Cause you don't care what I want!

MR. BORDEN: You don't know what you want!

LIZZIE: But I know what you want! You want me living my life by the Farmer's Almanac; having everyone over for Christmas dinner, waiting up for my husband; and *serving at socials!*

MR. BORDEN: It's good enough for your mother!

LIZZIE: She is *not* my *mother!*

MR. BORDEN: . . . John MacLeod is looking for a wife.

LIZZIE: No, god damn it, he isn't!

MR. BORDEN: Lizzie!

LIZZIE: He's looking for a housekeeper and it isn't going to be me!

MR. BORDEN: You've a filthy mouth!

LIZZIE: Is that why you hate me?

MR. BORDEN: You don't make sense.

LIZZIE: Why is it when I pretend things I don't feel, that's when you like me?

MR. BORDEN: You talk foolish.

LIZZIE: I'm supposed to be a mirror. I'm supposed to reflect what you want to see, but everyone wants something different. If no one looks in the mirror, I'm not even there, I don't exist!

MR. BORDEN: Lizzie, you talk foolish!

LIZZIE: No, I don't, that isn't true.

MR. BORDEN: About Mr. MacLeod—

LIZZIE: You can't make me get married!

MR. BORDEN: Lizzie, do you want to spend the rest of your life in this house?

LIZZIE: No . . . No . . . I want out of it, but I won't get married to do it.

MRS. BORDEN: [*On her way through to the kitchen.*] You've never been asked.

LIZZIE: Oh listen to her! I must be some sort of failure, then, eh? You had no son and a daughter that failed? What does that make you, Papa?!

MR. BORDEN: I want you to think about Johnny MacLeod!

LIZZIE: To hell with him!!! [MR. BORDEN *appears defeated. After a moment,* LIZZIE *goes to him, she holds his hand, strokes his hair.*] Papa? . . . Papa, I love you, I try to be what you want, really I do try, I try . . . but . . . I don't want to get married. I wouldn't be a good mother, I—

MR. BORDEN: How do you know—

LIZZIE: I know it! . . . I want out of all this . . . I hate this house, I hate . . . I want out. Try to understand how I feel. . . . Why can't I do something? . . . Eh? I mean . . . I could . . . I could go into your office. . . . I could . . . learn how to keep books?

MR. BORDEN: Lizzie.

LIZZIE: Why can't I do something like that?

MR. BORDEN: For god's sake, talk sensible.

LIZZIE: All right then! Why can't we move up on the hill to a house where we aren't in each other's laps!

MRS. BORDEN: [*Returning from kitchen.*] Why don't you move out!

LIZZIE: Give me the money and I'll go!

MRS. BORDEN: Money.

LIZZIE: And give me enough that I won't ever have to come back!

MRS. BORDEN: She always gets round to money!

LIZZIE: You drive me to it!

MRS. BORDEN: She's crazy!

LIZZIE: You drive me to it!

MRS. BORDEN: She should be locked up!

LIZZIE: [*Begins to smash the plates in the dining-room.*] There!! There!!

MR. BORDEN: Lizzie!

MRS. BORDEN: Stop her!

LIZZIE: There!

[MR. BORDEN *attempts to restrain her.*]

MRS. BORDEN: For god's sake, Andrew!

LIZZIE: Lock me up! Lock me up!

MR. BORDEN: Stop it! Lizzie!

[*She collapses against him, crying.*]

LIZZIE: Oh, Papa, I can't stand it.

MR. BORDEN: There, there, come on now, it's all right, listen to me, Lizzie, it's all right.

MRS. BORDEN: You may as well get down on your knees.

LIZZIE: Look at her. She's jealous of me. She can't stand it whenever you're nice to me.

MR. BORDEN: There now.

MRS. BORDEN: Ask her about Dr. Patrick.

MR. BORDEN: I'll handle this my way.

LIZZIE: He's an entertaining person, there're very few around!

MRS. BORDEN: Fall River ain't Paris and ain't that a shame for our Lizzie!

LIZZIE: One trip three years ago and you're still harping on it; it's true, Papa, an elephant never forgets!

MR. BORDEN: Show some respect!

LIZZIE: She's a fat cow and I hate her!

[MR. BORDEN *slaps* LIZZIE. *There is a pause as he regains control of himself.*]

MR. BORDEN: Now . . . now . . . you'll see Mr. MacLeod Tuesday night.

LIZZIE: No.

MR. BORDEN: God damn it!! I said you'll see Johnny MacLeod Tuesday night!!

LIZZIE: No.

MR. BORDEN: Get the hell upstairs to your room!

LIZZIE: No.

MR. BORDEN: I'm telling you to go upstairs to your room!!

LIZZIE: I'll go when I'm ready.

MR. BORDEN: I said, Go!

[He grabs her arm to move her forcibly, she hits his arm away.]

LIZZIE: No! . . . There's something you don't understand, Papa. You can't make me do one thing that I don't want to do. I'm going to keep on doing just what I want just when I want—like always!

MR. BORDEN: [Shoves her to the floor to gain a clear exit from the room. He stops on the stairs, looks back to her on the floor.] . . . I'm . . . [He continues off.]

MRS. BORDEN: [Without animosity.] You know, Lizzie, your father keeps you. You know you got nothing but what he gives you. And that's a fact of life. You got to come to deal with facts. I did.

LIZZIE: And married Papa.

MRS. BORDEN: And married your father. You never made it easy for me. I took on a man with two little ones, and Emma was your mother.

LIZZIE: You got stuck so I should too, is that it?

MRS. BORDEN: What?

LIZZIE: The reason I should marry Johnny MacLeod.

MRS. BORDEN: I just know, this time, in the end, you'll do what your Papa says, you'll see.

LIZZIE: No, I won't. I have a right. A right that frees me from all that.

MRS. BORDEN: No, Lizzie, you got no rights.

LIZZIE: I've a legal right to one-third because I am his flesh and blood.

MRS. BORDEN: What you don't understand is your father's not dead yet, your father's got many good years ahead of him, and when his time comes, well, we'll see what his will says then. . . . Your father's no fool, Lizzie. . . . Only a fool would leave money to you. [*She exits.*]

[*After a moment,* BRIDGET *enters from the kitchen.*]

BRIDGET: Ah Lizzie . . . you outdid yourself that time. [*She is comforting* LIZZIE.] . . . Yes you did . . . an elephant never forgets!

LIZZIE: Oh Bridget.

BRIDGET: Come on now.

LIZZIE: I can't help it.

BRIDGET: Sure you can . . . sure you can . . . stop your cryin' and come and sit down . . . you want me to tell you a story?

LIZZIE: No.

BRIDGET: Sure, a story. I'll tell you a story. Come on now . . . now . . . before I worked here I worked up on the hill and the lady of the house . . . are you listenin'? Well, she swore by her cook, finest cook in creation, yes, always bowin' and scrapin' and smilin' and givin' up her day off if company arrived. Oh the lady of the house she loved that cook—and I'll tell you her name! It was Mary! Now listen! Do you know what Mary was doin'? [LIZZIE *shakes her head.*] Before eatin' the master'd serve drinks in the parlour—and out in the kitchen, Mary'd be spittin' in the soup!

LIZZIE: What?

BRIDGET: She'd spit in the soup! And she'd smile when they served it!

LIZZIE: No.

BRIDGET: Yes. I've seen her cut up hair for an omelette.

LIZZIE: You're lying.

BRIDGET: Cross me heart. . . . They thought it was pepper!

LIZZIE: Oh, Bridget!

BRIDGET: These two eyes have seen her season up mutton stew when it's off and gone bad.

LIZZIE: Gone bad?

BRIDGET: Oh and they et it, every bit, and the next day they was hit with . . . *stomach flu!* so cook called it. By jasus, Lizzie, I daren't tell you what she served up in their food, for fear you'd be sick!!

LIZZIE: That's funny. . . . [*A fact—*LIZZIE *does not appear amused.*]

BRIDGET: [*Starts to clear up the dishes.*] Yes, well, I'm tellin' you I kept on the good side of cook.

[LIZZIE *watches her for a moment.*]

LIZZIE: . . . Do you . . . like me?

BRIDGET: Sure I do. . . . You should try bein' more like cook, Lizzie. Smile and get round them. You can do it.

LIZZIE: It's not . . . *fair* that I have to.

BRIDGET: There ain't nothin' fair in this world.

LIZZIE: Well then . . . well then, I don't want to!

BRIDGET: You dream, Lizzie . . . you dream dreams . . . Work. Be sensible. What could you do?

LIZZIE: I could

MISS LIZZIE / BRIDGET: No.

LIZZIE: I could

MISS LIZZIE / BRIDGET: No.

LIZZIE: I could

MISS LIZZIE / BRIDGET: No!

LIZZIE: I . . . dream.

MISS LIZZIE / BRIDGET: You dream . . . of a carousel . . . you see a carousel . . . you see lights that go on and go off . . . you see yourself on a carousel horse, a red-painted horse with its head in the air, and green staring eyes, and a white flowing mane, it looks wild! . . . It goes up and comes down, and the carousel whirls round with music and lights, on and off . . . and you watch . . . watch yourself on the horse. You're wearing a mask, a white mask like the mane of the horse, it looks like your face except that it's rigid and white . . . and it changes! With each flick of the lights, the expression, it changes, but always so rigid and hard, like the flesh of the horse that is red that you ride. You ride with no hands! No hands on this petrified horse, its head flung in the air, its wide staring eyes like those of a doe run down by the dogs! . . . And each time you go round, your hands rise a fraction nearer the mask . . . and the music and the carousel and the horse . . . they all three slow down, and they stop. . . . You can reach out and touch . . . you . . . you on the horse . . . with your hands so at the eyes. . . . You look into the eyes! [A *sound from* LIZZIE, *she is horrified and frightened. She covers her eyes.*] There are none! None! Just black holes in a white mask. . . . [*Pause.*] Only a dream. . . . The eyes of your birds . . . are round . . . and bright . . . a light shines from inside . . . they . . . can see into your heart . . . they're pretty . . . they love you. . . .

MR. BORDEN: I want this settled, Harry, I want it settled while Lizzie's out back.

[MISS LIZZIE / BRIDGET *draws* LIZZIE's *attention to the* MR. BORDEN / HARRY *scene.* LIZZIE *listens, will move closer.*]

HARRY: You know I'm for that.

MR. BORDEN: I want it all done but the signin' of the papers tomorrow, that's if I decide to—

HARRY: You can't lose, Andrew. The farm's just lyin' fallow.

MR. BORDEN: Well, let's see what you got.

HARRY: [*Gets out his papers.*] Look at this . . . I'll run horse auctions and a buggy rental—now I'll pay no rent for the house or pasturage but you get twenty percent, eh? That figure there—

MR. BORDEN: Mmmn.

HARRY: From my horse auctions last year, it'll go up on the farm and you'll get twenty percent off the top. . . . My buggy rental won't do so well . . . that's that figure there, approximate . . . but it all adds up, eh? Adds up for you.

MR. BORDEN: It's a good deal, Harry, but . . .

HARRY: Now I know why you're worried—but the farm will still be in the family, 'cause aren't I family? and whenever you or the girls want to come over for a visit, why I'll send a buggy from the rental, no need for you to have the expense of a horse, eh?

MR. BORDEN: It looks good on paper.

HARRY: There's . . . ah . . . something else, it's a bit awkward but I got to mention it; I'll be severin' a lot of my present connections, and what I figure I've a right to, is some kind of guarantee. . . .

MR. BORDEN: You mean a renewable lease for the farm?

HARRY: Well—what I'm wondering is . . . No offense, but you're an older man, Andrew . . . now if something should happen to you, where would the farm stand in regards to your will? That's what I'm wondering.

MR. BORDEN: I've not made a will.

HARRY: You know best—but I wouldn't want to be in a position where Lizzie would be havin' anything to do with that farm. The less she knows now the better, but she's bound to find out—I don't feel I'm steppin' out of line by bringin' this up.

[LIZZIE *is within earshot. She is staring at* HARRY *and* MR. BORDEN. *They do not see her.*]

MR. BORDEN: No.

HARRY: If you mind you come right out and say so.

MR. BORDEN: That's all right.

HARRY: Now . . . if you . . . put the farm—in Abbie's name, what do you think?

MR. BORDEN: I don't know, Harry.

HARRY: I don't want to push.

MR. BORDEN: . . . I should make a will . . . I want the girls looked after, it don't seem like they'll marry . . . and Abbie, she's younger than me, I know Emma will see to her, still . . . money-wise I got to consider these things . . . it makes a difference no men in the family.

HARRY: You know you can count on me for whatever.

MR. BORDEN: If . . . *If* I changed title to the farm, Abbie'd have to come down to the bank, I wouldn't want Lizzie to know.

HARRY: You can send a note for her when you get to the bank; she can say it's a note from a friend, and come down and meet you. Simple as that.

MR. BORDEN: I'll give it some thought.

HARRY: You see, Abbie owns the farm, it's no difference to you, but it gives me protection.

MR. BORDEN: Who's there?

HARRY: It's Lizzie.

MR. BORDEN: What do you want? . . . Did you lock the shed? . . . Is the shed locked! [LIZZIE *makes a slow motion which* MR. BORDEN *takes for assent.*] Well you make sure it stays locked! I don't want anymore of those god damned. . . . I . . . ah . . . I think we about covered everything, Harry, we'll . . . ah . . . we'll let it go till tomorrow.

HARRY: Good enough . . . well . . . I'll just finish choppin' that kindlin', give a shout when it's lunchtime. [*He exits.*]

[LIZZIE *and* MR. BORDEN *stare at each other for a moment.*]

LIZZIE: [*Very low.*] What are you doing with the farm? [MR. BORDEN *slowly picks up the papers, places them in his pocket.*] Papa! . . . Papa. I want you to show me what you put in your pocket.

MR. BORDEN: It's none of your business.

LIZZIE: The farm is my business.

MR. BORDEN: It's nothing.

LIZZIE: Show me!

MR. BORDEN: I said it's nothing!

[LIZZIE *makes a quick move towards her father to seize the paper from his pocket. Even more quickly and smartly he slaps her face. It is all very quick and clean. A pause as they stand frozen.*]

HARRY: [*Off.*] Andrew, there's a bunch of kids broken into the shed!

MR. BORDEN: Jesus Christ.

LIZZIE: [*Whispers.*] What about the farm.

MR. BORDEN: You! You and those god damn birds! I've told you! I've told you time and again!

LIZZIE: What about the farm!

MR. BORDEN: Jesus Christ . . . You never listen! Never!

HARRY: [*Enters carrying the hand hatchet.*] Andrew!!

MR. BORDEN: [*Grabs the hand hatchet from* HARRY, *turns to* LIZZIE.] There'll be no more of your god damn birds in this yard!!

LIZZIE: No! [MR. BORDEN *raises the hatchet and smashes it into the table as* LIZZIE *screams.*] No Papa!! Nooo!!

[*The hatchet is embedded in the table.* MR. BORDEN *and* HARRY *assume a soft freeze as* ACTRESS / LIZZIE *whirls to see* MISS LIZZIE / BRIDGET *observing the scene.*]

LIZZIE: Nooo!

MISS LIZZIE: I loved them.

BLACKOUT

ACT II

Lights come up on THE ACTRESS / LIZZIE *sitting at the dining room table. She is very still, her hands clasped in her lap.* MISS LIZZIE / BRIDGET *is near her. She too is very still. A pause.*

ACTRESS / LIZZIE: [*Very low.*] Talk to me.

MISS LIZZIE / BRIDGET: I remember . . .

ACTRESS / LIZZIE: [*Very low.*] No.

MISS LIZZIE / BRIDGET: On the farm, Papa's farm, Harry's farm, when I was little and thought it was my farm and I loved it, we had some puppies, the farm dog had puppies, brown soft little puppies with brown ey . . . [*She does not complete the word "eyes."*] And one of the puppies got sick. I didn't know it was sick, it seemed like the others, but the mother, she knew. It would lie at the back of the box, she would lie in front of it while she nursed all the others. They ignored it, that puppy didn't exist for the others. . . . I think inside it was different, and the mother thought the difference she sensed was a sickness . . . and after a while . . . anyone could tell it was sick. It had nothing to eat! . . . And papa took it and drowned it. That's what you do on a farm with things that are different.

ACTRESS / LIZZIE: Am I different?

MISS LIZZIE / BRIDGET: You kill them.

[ACTRESS / LIZZIE *looks at* MISS LIZZIE / BRIDGET. MISS LIZZIE / BRIDGET *looks towards the top of the stairs.* BRIDGET *gets up and exits to the kitchen.* EMMA *appears at the top of the stairs. She is dressed for travel and carries a small suitcase and her gloves. She stares down at* LIZZIE *still sitting at the table. After several moments* LIZZIE *becomes aware of that gaze and turns to look at* EMMA. EMMA *then descends the stairs. She puts down her suitcase. She is not overjoyed at seeing* LIZZIE, *having hoped to get away before* LIZZIE *arose, nevertheless she begins with an excess of enthusiasm to cover the implications of her departure.*]

EMMA: Well! You're up early . . . Bridget down? . . . did you put the coffee on? [*She puts her gloves on the table.*] My goodness, Lizzie, cat got your tongue?

[*She exits to the kitchen.* LIZZIE *picks up the gloves.* EMMA *returns.*]

EMMA: Bridget's down, she's in the kitchen. . . . Well . . . looks like a real scorcher today, doesn't it? . . .

LIZZIE: What's the bag for?

EMMA: I . . . decided I might go for a little trip, a day or two, get away from the heat. . . . The girls've rented a place out beach way and I thought . . . with the weather and all . . .

LIZZIE: How can you do that?

EMMA: Do what? . . . Anyway I thought I might stay with them a few days. . . . Why don't you come with me?

LIZZIE: No.

EMMA: Just for a few days, come with me.

LIZZIE: No.

EMMA: You know you like the water.

LIZZIE: I said no!

EMMA: Oh, Lizzie.

[*Pause.*]

LIZZIE: I don't see how you can leave me like this.

EMMA: I asked you to come with me.

LIZZIE: You know I can't do that.

EMMA: Why not?

LIZZIE: Someone has to *do* something, you just run away from things.

[*Pause.*]

EMMA: . . . Lizzie . . . I'm sorry about the—[*birds.*]

LIZZIE: No!

EMMA: Papa was angry.

LIZZIE: I don't want to talk about it.

EMMA: He's sorry now.

LIZZIE: Nobody *listens* to me, can't you hear me? I said *don't* talk about it. I don't want to talk about it. Stop talking about it!!

[BRIDGET *enters with the coffee.*]

EMMA: Thank you, Bridget. [BRIDGET *withdraws.*] Well! . . . I certainly can use this this morning. . . . Your coffee's there.

LIZZIE: I don't want it.

EMMA: You're going to ruin those gloves.

LIZZIE: I don't care.

EMMA: Since they're not yours.

[LIZZIE *bangs the gloves down on the table. A pause. Then* EMMA *picks them up and smooths them out.*]

LIZZIE: Why are you leaving me?

EMMA: I feel like a visit with the girls. Is there something wrong with that?

LIZZIE: How can you go now?

EMMA: I don't know what you're getting at.

LIZZIE: I heard them. I heard them talking yesterday. Do you know what they're saying?

EMMA: How could I

LIZZIE: "How could I?" What do you mean "How could I?" Did you know?

EMMA: No, Lizzie, I did not.

LIZZIE: *Did-not-what.*

EMMA: Know.

LIZZIE: But you know now. How do you know now?

EMMA: I've put two and two together and I'm going over to the girls for a visit!

LIZZIE: Please Emma!

EMMA: It's too hot.

LIZZIE: I need you, don't go.

EMMA: I've been talking about this trip.

LIZZIE: That's a lie.

EMMA: They're expecting me.

LIZZIE: You're lying to me!

EMMA: I'm going to the girls' place. You can come if you want, you can stay if you want. I planned this trip and I'm taking it!

LIZZIE: Stop lying!

EMMA: If I want to tell a little white lie to avoid an altercation in this house, I'll do so. Other people have been doing it for years!

LIZZIE: You don't understand, you don't understand anything.

EMMA: Oh, I understand enough.

LIZZIE: You don't! Let me explain it to you. You listen carefully, you listen. . . . Harry's getting the farm, can you understand that? Harry is here and he's moving on the farm and he's going to be there, on the farm, living on the farm. *Our farm.* Do you understand that? . . . Do you understand that!

EMMA: Yes.

LIZZIE: Harry's going to be on the farm. That's the first thing. . . . No . . . no it isn't. . . . The first thing . . . was the mill house, that was the first thing! And *now* the farm. You see there's a pattern, Emma, you can see that, can't you?

EMMA: I don't—

LIZZIE: You can see it! The mill house, then the farm, and the next thing is the papers for the farm—do you know what he's doing, Papa's doing? He's signing the farm over to her. It will never be ours, we will never have it, not ever. It's ours by rights, don't you feel that?

EMMA: The farm—has always meant a great deal to me, yes.

LIZZIE: Then what are you doing about it! You can't leave me now . . . but that's not all. Papa's going to make a will, and you can see the pattern, can't you, and if the pattern keeps on, what do you suppose his will will say. What do you suppose, answer me!

EMMA: I don't know.

LIZZIE: Say it!

EMMA: He'll see we're looked after.

LIZZIE: I don't want to be looked after! What's the matter with you? Do you really want to spend the rest of your life with that cow, listening to her drone on and on for years! That's just what they think you'll do. Papa'll leave you a monthly allowance, just like he'll leave me, just enough to keep us all living together. We'll be worth millions on paper, and be stuck in this house and by and by Papa will die and Harry will move in and you will wait on that cow while she gets fatter and fatter and I—will—sit in my room.

EMMA: Lizzie.

LIZZIE: We have to do something, you can see that. We have to do something!

EMMA: There nothing we can do.

LIZZIE: Don't say that.

EMMA: All right, then, what can we do?

LIZZIE: I . . . I . . . don't know. But we have to do something, you have to help me, you can't go away and leave me alone, you can't do that.

EMMA: Then—

LIZZIE: You know what I thought? I thought you could talk to him, really talk to him, make him understand that we're people. *Individual people,* and we have to live separate lives, and his will should make it possible for us to do that. And the farm can't go to Harry.

EMMA: You know it's no use.

LIZZIE: I can't talk to him anymore. Everytime I talk to him I make everything worse. I hate him, no. No I don't. I hate her. [EMMA *looks at her broach watch.*] Don't look at the time.

EMMA: I'll miss my connections.

LIZZIE: No!

EMMA: [*Puts on her gloves.*] Lizzie. There's certain things we have to face. One of them is, we can't change a thing.

LIZZIE: I won't let you go!

EMMA: I'll be back on the week-end.

LIZZIE: He killed my birds! He took the ax and he killed them! Emma, I ran out and held them in my hands, I felt their hearts throbbing and pumping and the blood gushed out of their necks, it was all over my hands, don't you care about that?

EMMA: I . . . I . . . have a train to catch.

LIZZIE: He didn't care how much he hurt me and you don't care either. Nobody cares.

EMMA: I . . . have to go now.

LIZZIE: That's right. Go away. I don't even like you, Emma. Go away! [EMMA *leaves,* LIZZIE *runs after her calling.*] I'm sorry for all the things I told you! Things I really felt! You pretended to me, and I don't like you!! Go away!! [LIZZIE *runs to the window and looks out after* EMMA's *departing figure. After a moment she slowly turns back into the room.* MISS LIZZIE / BRIDGET *is there.*] I want to die . . . I want to die, but something inside won't let me . . . inside something says *no.* [*She shuts her eyes.*] I can do anything.

DEFENSE: Miss Borden. [*Both* LIZZIES *turn.*] Could you describe the sequence of events upon your father's arrival home?

LIZZIE: [*With no animation.*] Papa came in . . . we exchanged a few words . . . Bridget and I spoke of the yard goods sale down town, whether she would buy some. She went up to her room . . .

DEFENSE: And then?

LIZZIE: I went out back . . . through the yard . . . I picked up several pears from the ground beneath the trees . . . I went into the shed . . . I stood looking out the window and ate the pears . . .

DEFENSE: How many?

LIZZIE: Four.

DEFENSE: It wasn't warm, stifling in the shed?

LIZZIE: No, it was cool.

DEFENSE: What were you doing, apart from eating the pears?

LIZZIE: I suppose I was thinking. I just stood there, looking out the window, thinking, and eating the pears I'd picked up.

DEFENSE: You're fond of pears?

LIZZIE: Otherwise, I wouldn't eat them.

DEFENSE: Go on.

LIZZIE: I returned to the house. I found—Papa. I called for Bridget.

[MRS. BORDEN *descends the stairs.* LIZZIE *and* BRIDGET *turn to look at her.* MRS. BORDEN *is only aware of* LIZZIE's *stare. Pause.*]

MRS. BORDEN: . . . What're you staring at? I said what're you staring at?

LIZZIE: [*Continuing to stare at* MRS. BORDEN.] Bridget.

BRIDGET: Yes ma'am.

[*Pause.*]

MRS. BORDEN: Just coffee and a biscuit this morning, Bridget, it's too hot for a decent breakfast.

BRIDGET: Yes ma'am.

[*She exits for the biscuit and coffee.* LIZZIE *continues to stare at* MRS. BORDEN.]

MRS. BORDEN: . . . Tell Bridget I'll have it in the parlour.

[LIZZIE *is making an effort to be pleasant, to be "good."* MRS. BORDEN *is more aware of this as unusual behavior from* LIZZIE *than were she to be rude, biting, or threatening.* LIZZIE, *at the same time, feels caught in a dimension other than the one in which the people around her are operating. For* LIZZIE, *a bell-jar effect. Simple acts seem filled with significance.* LIZZIE *is trying to fulfill other people's expectations of "normal."*]

LIZZIE: It's not me, is it?

MRS. BORDEN: What?

LIZZIE: You're not moving into the parlor because of me, are you?

MRS. BORDEN: What?

LIZZIE: I'd hate to think I'd driven you out of your own dining-room.

MRS. BORDEN: No.

LIZZIE: Oh good, because I'd hate to think that was so.

MRS. BORDEN: It's cooler in the parlor.

LIZZIE: You know, you're right.

MRS. BORDEN: Eh?

LIZZIE: It is cooler. . . . [BRIDGET *enters with the coffee and biscuit.*] I will, Bridget. [*She takes the coffee and biscuit, gives it to* MRS. BORDEN. LIZZIE *watches her eat and drink.* MRS. BORDEN *eats the biscuit delicately.* LIZZIE's *attention is caught by it.*] Do you like that biscuit?

MRS. BORDEN: It could be lighter.

LIZZIE: You're right. [MR. BORDEN *enters, makes his way into the kitchen,* LIZZIE *watches him pass.*] You know, Papa doesn't look well, Papa doesn't look well at all. Papa looks sick.

MRS. BORDEN: He had a bad night.

LIZZIE: Oh?

MRS. BORDEN: Too hot.

LIZZIE: But it's cooler in here, isn't it . . . [*Not trusting her own evaluation of the degree of heat.*] Isn't it?

MRS. BORDEN: Yes, yes, it's cooler in here.

[MR. BORDEN *enters with his coffee.* LIZZIE *goes to him.*]

LIZZIE: Papa? You should go in the parlor. It's much cooler in there, really it is.

[*He goes into the parlor.* LIZZIE *remains in the dining-room She sits at the table, folds her hands in her lap.* MR. BORDEN *begins to read the paper.*]

MRS. BORDEN: . . . I think I'll have Bridget do the windows today . . . they need doing . . . get them out of the way first thing. . . . Anything in the paper, Andrew?

MR. BORDEN: [*As he continues to read.*] Nope.

MRS. BORDEN: There never is . . . I don't know why we buy it.

MR. BORDEN: [*Reading.*] Yup.

MRS. BORDEN: You going out this morning?

MR. BORDEN: Business.

MRS. BORDEN: . . . Harry must be having a bit of a sleep-in.

MR. BORDEN: Yup.

MRS. BORDEN: He's always up by—[HARRY *starts down the stairs.*] Well, speak of the devil—coffee and biscuits?

HARRY: Sounds good to me.

[MRS. BORDEN *starts off to get it.* LIZZIE *looks at her, catching her eye.* MRS. BORDEN *stops abruptly.*]

LIZZIE: [*Her voice seems too loud.*] Emma's gone over to visit at the girls' place. [MR. BORDEN *lowers his paper to look at her.* HARRY *looks at her. Suddenly aware of the loudness of her voice, she continues softly, too softly.*] . . . Till the week-end.

MR. BORDEN: She didn't say she was going, when'd she decide that?

[LIZZIE *looks down at her hands, doesn't answer. A pause. Then* MRS. BORDEN *continues out to the kitchen.*]

HARRY: Will you be ah . . . going down today?

MR. BORDEN: This mornin'. I got . . . business at the bank.

[*A look between them. They are very aware of* LIZZIE's *presence in the dining-room.*]

HARRY: This mornin' eh? Well now . . . that works out just fine for me. I can . . . I got a bill to settle in town myself. [LIZZIE *turns her head to look at them.*] I'll be on my way after that.

MR. BORDEN: Abbie'll be disappointed you're not stayin' for lunch.

HARRY: 'Nother time.

MR. BORDEN: [*Aware of* LIZZIE's *gaze.*] I . . . I don't know where she is with that coffee. I'll—

HARRY: Never you mind, you sit right there, I'll get it.

[*He exits.* LIZZIE *and* MR. BORDEN *look at each other. The bell-jar effect is lessened.*]

LIZZIE: [*Softly.*] Good mornin' Papa.

MR. BORDEN: Mornin' Lizzie.

LIZZIE: Did you have a good sleep?

MR. BORDEN: Not bad.

LIZZIE: Papa?

MR. BORDEN: Yes Lizzie.

LIZZIE: You're a very strong-minded person, Papa, do you think I'm like you?

MR. BORDEN: In some ways . . . perhaps.

LIZZIE: I must be like someone.

MR. BORDEN: You resemble your mother.

LIZZIE: I look like my mother?

MR. BORDEN: A bit like your mother.

LIZZIE: But my mother's dead.

MR. BORDEN: Lizzie—

LIZZIE: I remember you told me she died because she was sick . . . I was born and she died . . . Did you love her?

MR. BORDEN: I married her.

LIZZIE: Can't you say if you loved her.

MR. BORDEN: Of course I did, Lizzie.

LIZZIE: Did you hate me for killing her?

MR. BORDEN: You don't think of it that way, it was just something that happened.

LIZZIE: Perhaps she just got tired and died. She didn't want to go on, and the chance came up and she took it. I could understand that. . . . Perhaps she was like a bird, she could see all the blue sky and she wanted to fly away but she couldn't. She was caught, Papa, she was caught in a horrible snare, and she saw a way out and she took it. . . . Perhaps it was a very brave thing to do, Papa, perhaps it was the only way, and she hated to leave because she loved us so much, but she couldn't breathe all caught in the snare. . . . [*Long pause.*] Some people have very small wrists, have you noticed. Mine aren't . . . [*There is a murmur from the kitchen, then muted laughter.* MR. BORDEN *looks towards it.*] Papa! . . . I'm a very strong person.

MRS. BORDEN: [*Off, laughing.*] You're tellin' tales out of school, Harry!

HARRY: [*Off.*] God's truth. You should have seen the buggy when they brought it back.

MRS. BORDEN: [*Off.*] You've got to tell Andrew. [*Pokes her head in.*] Andrew, come on out here, Harry's got a story. [*Off.*] Now you'll have to start at the beginning again, oh my goodness.

[MR. BORDEN *starts for the kitchen. He stops, and looks back at* LIZZIE.]

LIZZIE: Is there anything you want to tell me, Papa?

MRS. BORDEN: [*Off.*] Andrew!

LIZZIE: [*Softly, an echo.*] Andrew.

MR. BORDEN: What is it, Lizzie?

LIZZIE: If I promised to be a good girl forever and ever, would anything change?

MR. BORDEN: I don't know what you're talkin' about.

LIZZIE: I would be lying . . . Papa! . . . Don't do any business today. Don't go out. Stay home.

MR. BORDEN: What for?

LIZZIE: Everyone's leaving. Going away. Everyone's left.

MRS. BORDEN: [*Off.*] Andrew!

LIZZIE: [*Softly, an echo.*] Andrew.

MR. BORDEN: What is it?

LIZZIE: I'm calling you. [MR. BORDEN *looks at her for a moment, then leaves for the kitchen.* DR. PATRICK *is heard whistling very softly.* LIZZIE *listens.*] Listen . . . can you hear it . . . can you?

MISS LIZZIE / BRIDGET: I can hear it. . . . It's stopped.

[DR. PATRICK *can't be seen. Only his voice is heard.*]

DR. PATRICK: [*Very low.*] Lizzie?

LIZZIE: [*Realization.*] I could hear it before—[*you.*] [*Pause.*] It sounded so sad I wanted to cry.

MISS LIZZIE / BRIDGET: You mustn't cry.

LIZZIE: I mustn't cry.

DR. PATRICK: I bet you know this one. [*He whistles an Irish jig.*]

LIZZIE: I know that! [*She begins to dance.*]

[DR. PATRICK *enters. He claps in time to the dance.* LIZZIE *finishes the jig.* DR. PATRICK *applauds.*]

DR. PATRICK: Bravo! Bravo!!

LIZZIE: You didn't know I could do that, did you?

DR. PATRICK: You're a woman of many talents, Miss Borden.

LIZZIE: You're not making fun of me?

DR. PATRICK: I would never do that.

LIZZIE: I can do anything I want.

DR. PATRICK: I'm sure you can.

LIZZIE: If I wanted to die—I could even do that, couldn't I.

DR. PATRICK: Well now, I don't think so.

LIZZIE: Yes, I could!

DR. PATRICK: Lizzie—

LIZZIE: You wouldn't know—you can't see into my heart.

DR. PATRICK: I think I can.

LIZZIE: Well you can't!

DR. PATRICK: . . . It's only a game.

LIZZIE: I never play games.

DR. PATRICK: Sure you do.

LIZZIE: I hate games.

DR. PATRICK: You're playin' one now.

LIZZIE: You don't even know me!

DR. PATRICK: Come on Lizzie, we don't want to fight. I know what we'll do . . . we'll start over. . . . Shut your eyes, Lizzie. [*She does so.*] Good mornin' Miss Borden. . . . Good mornin' Miss Borden. . . .

LIZZIE: . . . I haven't decided. . . . [*She slowly opens her eyes.*] . . . if it is or it isn't.

DR. PATRICK: Much better . . . and now . . . would you take my arm, Miss Borden? How about a wee promenade?

LIZZIE: There's nowhere to go.

DR. PATRICK: That isn't so. . . . What about Boston? . . . Do you think it's too far for a stroll? . . . I know what we'll do, we'll walk 'round to the side and you'll show me your birds. [*They walk.*] . . . I waited last night but you never showed up . . . there I was, travellin' bag and all, and you never appeared . . . I know what went wrong! We forgot to agree on an hour! Next time, Lizzie, you must set the hour. . . . Is this where they're kept? [LIZZIE *nods, she opens the cage and looks in it.*] It's empty. [*He laughs.*] And you say you never play games?

LIZZIE: They're gone.

DR. PATRICK: You've been havin' me on again, yes you have.

LIZZIE: They've run away.

DR. PATRICK: Did they really exist?

LIZZIE: I had blood on my hands.

DR. PATRICK: What do you say?

LIZZIE: You can't see it now, I washed it off, see?

DR. PATRICK: [*Takes her hands.*] Ah Lizzie. . . .

LIZZIE: Would you . . . help someone die?

DR. PATRICK: Why do you ask that?

LIZZIE: Some people are better off dead. I might be better off dead.

DR. PATRICK: You're a precious and unique person, Lizzie, and you shouldn't think things like that.

LIZZIE: Precious and unique?

DR. PATRICK: All life is precious and unique.

LIZZIE: I am precious and unique? . . . I *am* precious and unique. You said that.

DR. PATRICK: Oh, I believe it.

LIZZIE: And I am. I know it. People mix things up on you, you have to be careful. I am a person of worth.

DR. PATRICK: Sure you are.

LIZZIE: Not like that fat cow in there.

DR. PATRICK: Her life too is—

LIZZIE: No!

DR. PATRICK: Liz—

LIZZIE: Do you know her?

DR. PATRICK: That doesn't matter.

LIZZIE: Yes it does, it does matter.

DR. PATRICK: You can't be—

LIZZIE: You're a doctor, isn't that right?

DR. PATRICK: Right enough there.

LIZZIE: So, tell me, tell me, if a dreadful accident occurred . . . and two people were dying . . . but you could only save one. . . . Which would you save?

DR. PATRICK: You can't ask questions like that.

LIZZIE: Yes I can, come on, it's a game. How does a doctor determine? If one were old and the other were young—would you save the younger one first?

DR. PATRICK: Lizzie.

LIZZIE: You said you liked games! If one were a bad person and the other was good, was trying to be good, would you save the one who was good and let the bad person die?

DR. PATRICK: I don't know.

LIZZIE: Listen! If you could go back in time . . . what would you do if you met a person who was evil and wicked?

DR. PATRICK: Who?

LIZZIE: I don't know, Attila the Hun!

DR. PATRICK: [Laughs.] Oh my.

LIZZIE: Listen, if you met Attila the Hun, and you were in a position to kill him, would you do it?

DR. PATRICK: I don't know.

LIZZIE: Think of the suffering he caused, the unhappiness.

DR. PATRICK: Yes, but I'm a doctor, not an assassin.

LIZZIE: I think you're a coward.

[Pause.]

DR. PATRICK: What I do is try to save lives . . .

LIZZIE: But you put poison out for the slugs in your garden.

DR. PATRICK: You got something mixed up.

LIZZIE: I've never been clearer. Everything's clear. I've lived all of my life for this one moment of absolute charity! If war were declared, would you serve?

DR. PATRICK: I would fight in a war.

LIZZIE: You wouldn't fight, you would kill—you'd take a gun and shoot people, people who'd done nothing to you, people who were trying to be good, you'd kill them! And you say you wouldn't kill Attila the Hun, or that that stupid cow's life is precious—*My life is precious!!*

DR. PATRICK: To you.

LIZZIE: Yes to me, are you stupid!?

DR. PATRICK: And hers is to her.

LIZZIE: I don't care about her! [Pause.] I'm glad you're not my doctor, you can't make decisions, can you? You are a coward. [DR. PATRICK starts off.] You're afraid of your wife . . . you can *only* play games. . . . If I really wanted to go to Boston, you wouldn't come with me because you're a coward! *I'm not a coward!!* [LIZZIE turns to watch MRS. BORDEN sit with needle work. After a moment MRS. BORDEN looks at LIZZIE, aware of her scrutiny.] . . . Where's Papa?

MRS. BORDEN: Out.

LIZZIE: And Mr. Wingate?

MRS. BORDEN: He's out too.

LIZZIE: So what are you going to do . . . Mrs. Borden?

MRS. BORDEN: I'm going to finish this up.

LIZZIE: You do that. . . . [Pause.] Where's Bridget?

MRS. BORDEN: Out back washing windows. . . . You got clean clothes to go upstairs, they're in the kitchen.

[*Pause.*]

LIZZIE: Did you know Papa killed my birds with the ax? He chopped off their heads. [MRS. BORDEN *is uneasy.*] . . . It's all right. At first I felt bad, but I feel better now. I feel much better now. . . . I am a woman of decision, Mrs. Borden. When I decide to do things, I do them, yes, I do. [*Smiles.*] How many times has Papa said—when Lizzie puts her mind to a thing, she does it—and I do. . . . It's always me who puts the slug poison out because they eat all the flowers and you don't like that, do you? They're bad things, they must die. You see, not all life is precious, is it? [MRS. BORDEN *after a moment makes an attempt casually to gather together her things, to go upstairs. She does not want to be in the room with* LIZZIE.] Where're you going?

MRS. BORDEN: Upstairs. . . . [*An excuse.*] The spare room needs changing.

[*A knock at the back door. . . . A second knock.*]

LIZZIE: Someone's at the door. . . . [*A third knock.*] I'll get it. [*She exits to the kitchen.* MRS. BORDEN *waits.* LIZZIE *returns. She's a bit out of breath. She carries a pile of clean clothes which she puts on the table. She looks at* MRS. BORDEN.] Did you want something?

MRS. BORDEN: Who was it?—the door?

LIZZIE: Oh yes. I forgot. I had to step out back for a moment and—it's a note. A message for you.

MRS. BORDEN: Oh.

LIZZIE: Shall I open it?

MRS. BORDEN: That's all right. [*She holds out her hand.*]

LIZZIE: Looks like Papa's handwriting. . . . [*She passes over the note.*] Aren't you going to open it?

MRS. BORDEN: I'll read it upstairs.

LIZZIE: Mrs. Borden! . . . Would you mind . . . putting my clothes in my room? [*She gets some clothes from the table,* MRS. BORDEN *takes them, something she would never normally do. Before she can move away,* LIZZIE *grabs her arm.*] Just a minute . . . I would like you to look into my eyes. What's the matter? Nothing's wrong. It's an experiment. . . . Look right into them. Tell me . . . what do you see . . . can you see anything?

MRS. BORDEN: . . . Myself.

LIZZIE: Yes. When a person dies, retained on her eye is the image of the last thing she saw. Isn't that interesting?

[*Pause.* MRS. BORDEN *slowly starts upstairs.* LIZZIE *picks up remaining clothes on table. The hand hatchet is concealed beneath them. She follows* MRS. BORDEN *up the stairs.*]

LIZZIE: Do you know something? If I were to kill someone, I would come up behind them very slowly and quietly. They would never even hear me, they would never turn around. [MRS. BORDEN *stops on the stairs. She turns around to look at* LIZZIE, *who is behind her.*] They would be too frightened to turn around even if they heard me. They would be so afraid they'd see what they feared. [MRS. BORDEN *makes a move which might be an effort to go past* LIZZIE *back down the stairs.* LIZZIE *stops her.*] Careful. Don't fall. [MRS. BORDEN *turns and slowly continues up the stairs with* LIZZIE *behind her.*] And then, I would strike them down. With them not turning around, they would retain no image of me on their eye. It would be better that way.

[LIZZIE *and* MRS. BORDEN *disappear at the top of the stairs. The stage is empty for a moment.* BRIDGET *enters. She carries the pail for washing the windows. She sets the pail down, wipes her forehead. She stands for a moment looking towards the stairs as if she might have heard a sound. She picks up the pail and exits to the kitchen.* LIZZIE *appears on the stairs. She is carrying the pile of clothes she carried upstairs. The hand hatchet is concealed under the clothes.* LIZZIE *descends the stairs, she seems calm, self-possessed. She places the clothes on the table. She pauses, then she slowly turns to look at* MRS. BORDEN's *chair at the table. After a moment she moves to it, pauses a moment, then sits down in it. She sits there at ease, relaxed, thinking.* BRIDGET *enters from the kitchen, she sees* LIZZIE, *she stops, she takes in* LIZZIE *sitting in* MRS. BORDEN's *chair.* BRIDGET *glances towards the stairs, back to* LIZZIE. LIZZIE *looks, for the first time, at* BRIDGET.]

LIZZIE: We must hurry before Papa gets home.

BRIDGET: Lizzie?

LIZZIE: I have it all figured out, but you have to help me, Bridget, you have to help me.

BRIDGET: What have you done?

LIZZIE: He would never leave me the farm, not with her on his back, but now [*She gets up from the chair.*] I will have the farm, and I will have the money, yes, to do what I please! And you too Bridget, I'll give you some of my money but you've got to help me. [*She moves towards* BRIDGET, who backs away a step.] Don't be afraid, it's me, it's Lizzie, you like me!

BRIDGET: What have you done? [*Pause. She moves towards the stairs.*]

LIZZIE: Don't go up there!

BRIDGET: You killed her!

LIZZIE: Someone broke in and they killed her.

BRIDGET: They'll know!

LIZZIE: Not if you help me.

BRIDGET: I can't, Miss Lizzie, I can't!

LIZZIE: [*Grabs* BRIDGET's *arm.*] Do you want them to hang me? Is that what you want? Oh Bridget, look! Look! [*She falls to her knees.*] I'm begging for my life, I'm begging. Deny me, and they will kill me. Help me, Bridget, please help me.

BRIDGET: But . . . what . . . could we do?

LIZZIE: [*Up off her knees.*] Oh I have it all figured out. I'll go down town as quick as I can and you leave the doors open and go back outside and work on the windows.

BRIDGET: I've finished them, Lizzie.

LIZZIE: Then do them again! Remember last year when the burglar broke in? Today someone broke in and she caught them.

BRIDGET: They'll never believe us.

LIZZIE: Have coffee with Lucy next door, stay with her till Papa gets home and he'll find her, and then each of us swears she was fine when we left, she was all right when we left!—it's going to work, Bridget, I know it!

BRIDGET: Your papa will guess.

LIZZIE: [*Getting ready to leave for downtown.*] If he found me here he might guess, but he won't.

BRIDGET: Your papa will know!

LIZZIE: Papa loves me, if he has another story to believe, he'll believe it. He'd want to believe it, he'd have to believe it.

BRIDGET: Your papa will know.

LIZZIE: Why aren't you happy? I'm happy. We both should be happy! [LIZZIE *embraces* BRIDGET. LIZZIE *steps back a pace.*] Now—how do I look? [MR. BORDEN *enters.* BRIDGET *sees him.* LIZZIE *slowly turns to see what* BRIDGET *is looking at.*] Papa?

MR. BORDEN: What is it? Where's Mrs. Borden?

BRIDGET: I . . . don't know . . . sir . . . I . . . just came in, sir.

MR. BORDEN: Did she leave the house?

BRIDGET: Well, sir . . .

LIZZIE: She went out. Someone delivered a message and she left. [LIZZIE *takes off her hat and looks at her father.*] . . . You're home early, Papa.

MR. BORDEN: I wanted to see Abbie. She's gone out, has she? Which way did she go? [LIZZIE *shrugs, he continues, more thinking aloud.*] Well . . . I . . . I . . . best wait for her here. I don't want to miss her again.

LIZZIE: Help Papa off with his coat, Bridget. . . . I hear there's a sale of dress goods on downtown. Why don't you go buy yourself a yard?

BRIDGET: Oh . . . I don't know, ma'am.

LIZZIE: You don't want any?

BRIDGET: I don't know.

LIZZIE: Then . . . why don't you go upstairs and lie down. Have a rest before lunch.

BRIDGET: I don't think I should.

LIZZIE: Nonsense.

BRIDGET: Lizzie, I—

LIZZIE: You go up and lie down. I'll look after things here. [LIZZIE *smiles at* BRIDGET. BRIDGET *starts up the stairs, suddenly stops. She looks back at* LIZ-ZIE.] It's all right go on . . . it's all right. [BRIDGET *continues up the stairs. For the last bit of interchange,* MR. BORDEN *has lowered the paper he's reading.* LIZZIE *looks at him.*] Hello papa. You look so tired. . . . I make you unhappy. . . . I don't like to make you unhappy. I love you.

MR. BORDEN: [*Smiles and takes her hand.*] I'm just getting old, Lizzie.

LIZZIE: You've got on my ring. Do you remember when I gave you that? . . . When I left Miss Cornelia's—it was in a little blue velvet box, you hid it behind your back, and you said, "Guess which hand, Lizzie!" And I guessed. And you gave it to me and you said, "It's real gold, Lizzie, it's for you because you are very precious to me." Do you remember, Papa? [MR. BORDEN *nods.*] And I took it out of the little blue velvet box, and I took your hand, and I put my ring on your finger and I said "thank you, Papa, I love you." . . . You've never taken it off . . . see how it bites into the flesh of your finger. [*She presses his hand to her face.*] I forgive you, Papa, I forgive you for killing my birds. . . . You look so tired, why don't you lie down and rest, put your feet up, I'll undo your shoes for you. [*She kneels and undoes his shoes.*]

MR. BORDEN: You're a good girl.

LIZZIE: I could never stand to have you hate me, Papa. Never. I would do anything rather than have you hate me.

MR. BORDEN: I don't hate you, Lizzie.

LIZZIE: I would not want you to find out anything that would make you hate me. Because I love you.

MR. BORDEN: And I love you, Lizzie, you'll always be precious to me.

LIZZIE: [*Looks at him, and then smiles.*] Was I—when I had scabs on my knees?

MR. BORDEN: [*Laughs.*] Oh yes. Even then.

LIZZIE: [*Laughs.*] Oh Papa! . . . Kiss me! [*He kisses her on the forehead.*] Thank you, Papa.

MR. BORDEN: Why're you crying?

LIZZIE: Because I'm so happy. Now . . . put your feet up and get to sleep . . . that's right . . . shut your eyes . . . go to sleep . . . go to sleep . . .

[*She starts to hum, continues humming as* MR. BORDEN *falls asleep.* MISS LIZZIE / BRIDGET *appears on the stairs unobstrusively.* LIZZIE *still humming, moves to the table, slips her hand under the clothes, withdraws the hatchet. She approaches her father with the hatchet behind her back. She stops humming. A pause, then she slowly raises the hatchet very high to strike him. Just as the hatchet is about to start its descent, there is a black out. Children's voices are heard singing:*

> "Lizzie Borden took an ax,
> Gave her mother forty whacks,
> When the job was nicely done,
> She gave her father forty-one!
> Forty-one!
> Forty-one!"

The singing increases in volume and in distortion as it nears the end of the verse till the last words are very loud but discernible, just. Silence. Then the sound of slow measured heavy breathing which is growing into a wordless sound of hysteria. Light returns to the stage, dim light from late in the day. THE ACTRESS *stands with the hatchet raised in the same position in which we saw her before the blackout, but the couch is empty. Her eyes are shut. The sound comes from her.* MISS LIZZIE *is at the foot of the stairs. She moves to* THE ACTRESS, *reaches up to take the hatchet from her. When* MISS LIZZIE's *hand touches* THE ACTRESS's, THE ACTRESS *releases the hatchet and whirls around to face* MISS LIZZIE, *who is left holding the hatchet.* THE ACTRESS *backs away from* MISS LIZZIE. *There is a flickering of light at the top of the stairs.*]

EMMA: [*From upstairs.*] Lizzie! Lizzie! You're making too much noise! [EMMA *descends the stairs carrying an oil lamp.* THE ACTRESS *backs away from* LIZZIE, *turns and runs into the kitchen.* MISS LIZZIE *turns to see* EMMA. *The hand hatchet is behind* MISS LIZZIE's *back concealed from* EMMA. EMMA *pauses for a moment.*] Where is she?

MISS LIZZIE: Who?

[*A pause, then* EMMA *moves to the window and glances out.*]

EMMA: It's raining.
MISS LIZZIE: I know.
EMMA: [*Puts the lamp down, sits, lowers her voice.*] Lizzie.
MISS LIZZIE: Yes?
EMMA: I want to speak to you, Lizzie.
MISS LIZZIE: Yes Emma.
EMMA: That . . . actress who's come up from Boston.
MISS LIZZIE: What about her?
EMMA: People talk.
MISS LIZZIE: You needn't listen.
EMMA: In your position you should do nothing to *inspire talk*.
MISS LIZZIE: People need so little in the way of inspiration. And Miss Cornelia's classes didn't cover "Etiquette for Acquitted Persons."
EMMA: Common sense should tell you what you ought or ought not do.
MISS LIZZIE: Common sense is repugnant to me. I prefer uncommon sense.
EMMA: I forbid her in this house, Lizzie!

[*Pause.*]

MISS LIZZIE: Do you?
EMMA: [*Backing down, softly.*] It's . . . disgraceful.
MISS LIZZIE: I see. [*She turns away from* EMMA *a few steps.*]
EMMA: I simply cannot—
MISS LIZZIE: You could always leave.
EMMA: Leave?
MISS LIZZIE: Move. Away. Why don't you?
EMMA: I—
MISS LIZZIE: You could never, could you?
EMMA: If I only—
MISS LIZZIE: Knew.
EMMA: Lizzie, did you?
MISS LIZZIE: Oh Emma, do you intend asking me that question from now till death us do part?
EMMA: It's just—
MISS LIZZIE: For if you do, I may well take something sharp to you.

EMMA: Why do you joke like that!

MISS LIZZIE: [*Turning back to* EMMA *who sees the hatchet for the first time.* EMMA'*s reaction is not any verbal or untoward movement. She freezes as* MISS LIZZIE *advances on her.*] Did you never stop and think that if I did, then you were guilty too?

EMMA: What?

[THE ACTRESS *will enter unobtrusively on the periphery. We are virtually unaware of her entrance until she speaks and moves forward.*]

MISS LIZZIE: It was you who brought me up, like a mother to me. Almost like a mother. Did you ever stop and think that I was like a puppet, your puppet. My head your hand, yes, your hand working my mouth, me saying all the things you felt like saying, me doing all the things you felt like doing, me spewing forth, me hitting out, and you, you—!

THE ACTRESS: [*Quietly.*] Lizzie.

[MISS LIZZIE *is immediately in control of herself.*]

EMMA: [*Whispers.*] I wasn't even here that day.

MISS LIZZIE: I can swear to that.

EMMA: Do you want to drive me mad?

MISS LIZZIE: Oh yes.

EMMA: You didn't . . . did you?

MISS LIZZIE: Poor . . . Emma.

THE ACTRESS: Lizzie. [*She takes the hatchet from* MISS LIZZIE.] Lizzie, you did.

MISS LIZZIE: I didn't. [THE ACTRESS *looks to the hatchet—then to the audience.*] You did.

BLACKOUT

1981

AUGUST WILSON

Fences[1]

CHARACTERS

TROY MAXSON
JIM BONO, *Troy's friend*
ROSE, *Troy's wife*
LYONS, *Troy's oldest son by
    previous marriage*

GABRIEL, *Troy's brother*
CORY, *Troy and Rose's son*
RAYNELL, *Troy's daughter*

SETTING

The setting is the yard which fronts the only entrance to the MAXSON *household, an ancient two-story brick house set back off a small alley in a big-city*

1. The text is from the third printing of the *New American Library* edition of the play (1986).

neighborhood. The entrance to the house is gained by two or three steps leading to a wooden porch badly in need of paint.

A relatively recent addition to the house and running its full width, the porch lacks congruence. It is a sturdy porch with a flat roof. One or two chairs of dubious value sit at one end where the kitchen window opens onto the porch. An old-fashioned icebox stands silent guard at the opposite end.

The yard is a small dirt yard, partially fenced, except for the last scene, with a wooden sawhorse, a pile of lumber, and other fence-building equipment set off to the side. Opposite is a tree from which hangs a ball made of rags. A baseball bat leans against the tree. Two oil drums serve as garbage receptacles and sit near the house at right to complete the setting.

THE PLAY

Near the turn of the century, the destitute of Europe sprang on the city with tenacious claws and an honest and solid dream. The city devoured them. They swelled its belly until it burst into a thousand furnaces and sewing machines, a thousand butcher shops and bakers' ovens, a thousand churches and hospitals and funeral parlors and money-lenders. The city grew. It nourished itself and offered each man a partnership limited only by his talent, his guile, and his willingness and capacity for hard work. For the immigrants of Europe, a dream dared and won true.

The descendants of African slaves were offered no such welcome or participation. They came from places called the Carolinas and the Virginias, Georgia, Alabama, Mississippi, and Tennessee. They came strong, eager, searching. The city rejected them and they fled and settled along the riverbanks and under bridges in shallow, ramshackle houses made of sticks and tar-paper. They collected rags and wood. They sold the use of their muscles and their bodies. They cleaned houses and washed clothes, they shined shoes, and in quiet desperation and vengeful pride, they stole, and lived in pursuit of their own dream. That they could breathe free, finally, and stand to meet life with the force of dignity and whatever eloquence the heart could call upon.

By 1957, the hard-won victories of the European immigrants had solidified the industrial might of America. War had been confronted and won with new energies that used loyalty and patriotism as its fuel. Life was rich, full, and flourishing. The Milwaukee Braves won the World Series, and the hot winds of change that would make the sixties a turbulent, racing, dangerous, and provocative decade had not yet begun to blow full.

ACT I

SCENE 1

It is 1957. TROY *and* BONO *enter the yard, engaged in conversation.* TROY *is fifty-three years old, a large man with thick, heavy hands; it is this largeness that he strives to fill out and make an accommodation with. Together with his black-*

ness, his largeness informs his sensibilities and the choices he has made in his life.

Of the two men, BONO *is obviously the follower. His commitment to their friendship of thirty-odd years is rooted in his admiration of* TROY's *honesty, capacity for hard work, and his strength, which* BONO *seeks to emulate.*

It is Friday night, payday, and the one night of the week the two men engage in a ritual of talk and drink. TROY *is usually the most talkative and at times he can be crude and almost vulgar, though he is capable of rising to profound heights of expression. The men carry lunch buckets and wear or carry burlap aprons and are dressed in clothes suitable to their jobs as garbage collectors.*

BONO: Troy, you ought to stop that lying!

TROY: I ain't lying! The nigger had a watermelon this big. [*He indicates with his hands.*] Talking about . . . "What watermelon, Mr. Rand?" I liked to fell out! "What watermelon, Mr. Rand?" . . . And it sitting there big as life.

BONO: What did Mr. Rand say?

TROY: Ain't said nothing. Figure if the nigger too dumb to know he carrying a watermelon, he wasn't gonna get much sense out of him. Trying to hide that great big old watermelon under his coat. Afraid to let the white man see him carry it home.

BONO: I'm like you . . . I ain't got no time for them kind of people.

TROY: Now what he look like getting mad cause he see the man from the union talking to Mr. Rand?

BONO: He come to me talking about . . . "Maxson gonna get us fired." I told him to get away from me with that. He walked away from me calling you a troublemaker. What Mr. Rand say?

TROY: Ain't said nothing. He told me to go down the Commissioner's office next Friday. They called me down there to see them.

BONO: Well, as long as you got your complaint filed, they can't fire you. That's what one of them white fellows tell me.

TROY: I ain't worried about them firing me. They gonna fire me cause I asked a question? That's all I did. I went to Mr. Rand and asked him, "Why? Why you got the white mens driving and the colored lifting?" Told him, "what's the matter, don't I count? You think only white fellows got sense enough to drive a truck. That ain't no paper job! Hell, anybody can drive a truck. How come you got all whites driving and the colored lifting?" He told me "take it to the union." Well, hell, that's what I done! Now they wanna come up with this pack of lies.

BONO: I told Brownie if the man come and ask him any questions . . . just tell the truth! It ain't nothing but something they done trumped up on you cause you filed a complaint on them.

TROY: Brownie don't understand nothing. All I want them to do is change the job description. Give everybody a chance to drive the truck. Brownie can't see that. He ain't got that much sense.

BONO: How you figure he be making out with that gal be up at Taylors' all the time . . . that Alberta gal?

TROY: Same as you and me. Getting just as much as we is. Which is to say nothing.

BONO: It is, huh? I figure you doing a little better than me . . . and I ain't saying what I'm doing.

TROY: Aw, nigger, look here . . . I know you. If you had got anywhere near that gal, twenty minutes later you be looking to tell somebody. And the first one you gonna tell . . . that you gonna want to brag to . . . is gonna be me.

BONO: I ain't saying that. I see where you be eyeing her.

TROY: I eye all the women. I don't miss nothing. Don't never let nobody tell you Troy Maxson don't eye the women.

BONO: You been doing more than eyeing her. You done bought her a drink or two.

TROY: Hell yeah, I bought her a drink! What that mean? I bought you one, too. What that mean cause I buy her a drink? I'm just being polite.

BONO: It's alright to buy her one drink. That's what you call being polite. But when you wanna be buying two or three . . . that's what you call eyeing her.

TROY: Look here, as long as you known me . . . you ever known me to chase after women?

BONO: Hell yeah! Long as I done known you. You forgetting I knew you when.

TROY: Naw, I'm talking about since I been married to Rose?

BONO: Oh, not since you been married to Rose. Now, that's the truth, there. I can say that.

TROY: Alright then! Case closed.

BONO: I see you be walking up around Alberta's house. You supposed to be at Taylors' and you be walking around there.

TROY: What you watching where I'm walking for? I ain't watching after you.

BONO: I seen you walking around there more than once.

TROY: Hell, you liable to see me walking anywhere! That don't mean nothing cause you see me walking around there.

BONO: Where she come from anyway? She just kinda showed up one day.

TROY: Tallahassee. You can look at her and tell she one of them Florida gals. They got some big healthy women down there. Grow them right up out the ground. Got a little bit of Indian in her. Most of them niggers down in Florida got some Indian in them.

BONO: I don't know about that Indian part. But she damn sure big and healthy. Woman wear some big stockings. Got them great big old legs and hips as wide as the Mississippi River.

TROY: Legs don't mean nothing. You don't do nothing but push them out of the way. But them hips cushion the ride!

BONO: Troy, you ain't got no sense.

TROY: It's the truth! Like you riding on Goodyears!

[ROSE *enters from the house. She is ten years younger than* TROY, *her devotion to him stems from her recognition of the possibilities of her life without him: a succession of abusive men and their babies, a life of partying and running the streets, the Church, or aloneness with its attendant pain and frustration. She recognizes* TROY'S *spirit as a fine and illuminating one and she either ignores or forgives his faults, only some of which she recognizes. Though she doesn't drink, her presence is an integral part of the Friday night rituals. She alternates between the porch and the kitchen, where supper preparations are under way.*]

ROSE: What you all out here getting into?

TROY: What you worried about what we getting into for? This is men talk, woman.

ROSE: What I care what you all talking about? Bono, you gonna stay for supper?

BONO: No, I thank you, Rose. But Lucille say she cooking up a pot of pigfeet.

TROY: Pigfeet! Hell, I'm going home with you! Might even stay the night if you got some pigfeet. You got something in there to top them pigfeet, Rose?

ROSE: I'm cooking up some chicken. I got some chicken and collard greens.

TROY: Well, go on back in the house and let me and Bono finish what we was talking about. This is men talk. I got some talk for you later. You know what kind of talk I mean. You go on and powder it up.

ROSE: Troy Maxson, don't you start that now!

TROY: [*Puts his arm around her.*] Aw, woman . . . come here. Look here, Bono . . . when I met this woman . . . I got out that place, say, "Hitch up my pony, saddle up my mare . . . there's a woman out there for me somewhere. I looked here. Looked there. Saw Rose and latched on to her." I latched on to her and told her—I'm gonna tell you the truth—I told her, "Baby, I don't wanna marry, I just wanna be your man." Rose told me . . . tell him what you told me, Rose.

ROSE: I told him if he wasn't the marrying kind, then move out the way so the marrying kind could find me.

TROY: That's what she told me. "Nigger, you in my way. You blocking the view! Move out the way so I can find me a husband." I thought it over two or three days. Come back—

ROSE: Ain't no two or three days nothing. You was back the same night.

TROY: Come back, told her . . . "Okay, baby . . . but I'm gonna buy me a banty rooster and put him out there in the backyard . . . and when he see a stranger come, he'll flap his wings and crow . . ." Look here, Bono, I could watch the front door by myself . . . it was that back door I was worried about.

ROSE: Troy, you ought not talk like that. Troy ain't doing nothing but telling a lie.

TROY: Only thing is . . . when we first got married . . . forget the rooster . . . we ain't had no yard!

BONO: I hear you tell it. Me and Lucille was staying down there on Logan Street. Had two rooms with the outhouse in the back. I ain't mind the outhouse none. But when that goddamn wind blow through there in the winter . . . that's what I'm talking about! To this day I wonder why in the hell I ever stayed down there for six long years. But see, I didn't know I could do no better. I thought only white folks had inside toilets and things.

ROSE: There's a lot of people don't know they can do no better than they doing now. That's just something you got to learn. A lot of folks still shop at Bella's.

TROY: Ain't nothing wrong with shopping at Bella's. She got fresh food.

ROSE: I ain't said nothing about if she got fresh food. I'm talking about what she charge. She charge ten cents more than the A&P.

TROY: The A&P ain't never done nothing for me. I spends my money where I'm treated right. I go down to Bella, say, "I need a loaf of bread, I'll pay you on Friday." She give it to me. What sense that make when I got money to go and spend it somewhere else and ignore the person who done right by me? That ain't in the Bible.

ROSE: We ain't talking about what's in the Bible. What sense it make to shop there when she overcharge?

TROY: You shop where you want to. I'll do my shopping where the people been good to me.

ROSE: Well, I don't think it's right for her to overcharge. That's all I was saying.

BONO: Look here . . . I got to get on. Lucille going be raising all kind of hell.

TROY: Where you going, nigger? We ain't finished this pint. Come here, finish this pint.

BONO: Well, hell, I am . . . if you ever turn the bottle loose.

TROY: [*Hands him the bottle.*] The only thing I say about the A&P is I'm glad Cory got that job down there. Help him take care of his school clothes and things. Gabe done moved out and things getting tight around here. He got that job. . . . He can start to look out for himself.

ROSE: Cory done went and got recruited by a college football team.

TROY: I told that boy about that football stuff. The white man ain't gonna let him get nowhere with that football. I told him when he first come to me with it. Now you come telling me he done went and got more tied up in it. He ought to go and get recruited in how to fix cars or something where he can make a living.

ROSE: He ain't talking about making no living playing football. It's just something the boys in school do. They gonna send a recruiter by to talk to you. He'll tell you he ain't talking about making no living playing football. It's a honor to be recruited.

TROY: It ain't gonna get him nowhere. Bono'll tell you that.

BONO: If he be like you in the sports . . . he's gonna be alright. Ain't but two men ever played baseball as good as you. That's Babe Ruth and Josh Gibson. Them's the only two men ever hit more home runs than you.

TROY: What it ever get me? Ain't got a pot to piss in or a window to throw it out of.

ROSE: Times have changed since you was playing baseball, Troy. That was before the war. Times have changed a lot since then.

TROY: How in hell they done changed?

ROSE: They got lots of colored boys playing ball now. Baseball and football.

BONO: You right about that, Rose. Times have changed, Troy. You just come along too early.

TROY: There ought not never have been no time called too early! Now you take that fellow . . . what's that fellow they had playing right field for the Yankees back then? You know who I'm talking about, Bono. Used to play right field for the Yankees?

ROSE: Selkirk?

TROY: Selkirk! That's it! Man batting .269, understand? .269. What kind of sense that make? I was hitting .432 with thirty-seven home runs! Man batting .269 and playing right field for the Yankees! I saw Josh Gibson's daughter yesterday. She walking around with raggedy shoes on her feet. Now I bet you Selkirk's daughter ain't walking around with raggedy shoes on her feet. I bet you that!

ROSE: They got a lot of colored baseball players now. Jackie Robinson was the first. Folks had to wait for Jackie Robinson.

TROY: I done seen a hundred niggers play baseball better than Jackie Robinson. Hell, I know some teams Jackie Robinson couldn't even make! What you talking about Jackie Robinson. Jackie Robinson wasn't nobody. I'm talking about if you could play ball then they ought to have let you play. Don't care what color you were. Come telling me I come along too early. If you could play . . . then they ought to have let you play. [TROY *takes a long drink from the bottle.*]

ROSE: You gonna drink yourself to death. You don't need to be drinking like that.

TROY: Death ain't nothing. I done seen him. Done wrassled with him. You can't tell me nothing about death. Death ain't nothing but a fastball on the outside corner. And you know what I'll do to that! Lookee here, Bono . . . am I lying? You get one of them fastballs, about waist high, over the outside corner of the plate where you can get the meat of the bat on it . . . and good god! You can kiss it goodbye. Now, am I lying?

BONO: Naw, you telling the truth there. I seen you do it.

TROY: If I'm lying . . . that 450 feet worth of lying! [*Pause.*] That's all death is to me. A fastball on the outside corner.

ROSE: I don't know why you want to get on talking about death.

TROY: Ain't nothing wrong with talking about death. That's part of life. Everybody gonna die. You gonna die, I'm gonna die. Bono's gonna die. Hell, we all gonna die.

ROSE: But you ain't got to talk about it. I don't like to talk about it.

TROY: You the one brought it up. Me and Bono was talking about baseball . . . you tell me I'm gonna drink myself to death. Ain't that right, Bono? You know I don't drink this but one night out of the week. That's Friday night. I'm gonna drink just enough to where I can handle it. Then I cuts it loose. I leave it alone. So don't you worry about me drinking myself to death. 'Cause I ain't worried about Death. I done seen him. I done wrestled with him. Look here, Bono . . . I looked up one day and Death was marching straight at me. Like Soldiers on Parade! The Army of Death marching straight at me. The middle of July, 1941. It got real cold just like it be winter. It seem like Death himself reached out and touched me on the shoulder. He touch me just like I touch you. I got cold as ice and Death standing there grinning at me.

ROSE: Troy, why don't you hush that talk.

TROY: I say . . . "What you want, Mr. Death? You be wanting me? You done brought your army to be getting me?" I looked him dead in the eye. I wasn't fearing nothing. I was ready to tangle. Just like I'm ready to tangle now. The Bible say be ever vigilant. That's why I don't get but so drunk. I got to keep watch.

ROSE: Troy was right down there in Mercy Hospital. You remember he had pneumonia? Laying there with a fever talking plumb out of his head.

TROY: Death standing there staring at me . . . carrying that sickle in his hand. Finally he say, "You want bound over for another year?" See, just like that . . . "You want bound over for another year?" I told him, "Bound over hell! Let's settle this now!" It seem like he kinda fell back when I said that, and all the cold went out of me. I reached down and grabbed that sickle and threw it just as far as I could throw it . . . and me and him commenced to wrestling. We wrestled for three days and three nights. I can't say where I found the strength from. Every time it seemed like he was gonna get the best of me, I'd reach way down deep inside myself and find the strength to do him one better.

ROSE: Every time Troy tell that story he find different ways to tell it. Different things to make up about it.

TROY: I ain't making up nothing. I'm telling you the facts of what happened. I wrestled with Death for three days and three nights and I'm standing here to tell you about it. [Pause.] Alright. At the end of the third night we done weakened each other to where we can't hardly move. Death stood up, throwed on his robe . . . had him a white robe with a hood on it. He throwed on that robe and went off to look for his sickle. Say, "I'll be back." Just like that. "I'll be back." I told him, say, "Yeah, but . . . you gonna have to find me!" I wasn't no fool. I wasn't going looking for him. Death ain't nothing to play with. And I know he's gonna get me. I know I got to join his army . . . his camp followers. But as long as I keep my strength and see him coming . . . as long as I keep up my vigilance . . . he's gonna have to fight to get me. I ain't going easy.

BONO: Well, look here, since you got to keep up your vigilance . . . let me have the bottle.

TROY: Aw hell, I shouldn't have told you that part. I should have left out that part.

ROSE: Troy be talking that stuff and half the time don't even know what he be talking about.

TROY: Bono know me better than that.

BONO: That's right. I know you. I know you got some Uncle Remus[2] in your blood. You got more stories than the devil got sinners.

TROY: Aw hell, I done seen him too! Done talked with the devil.

ROSE: Troy, don't nobody wanna be hearing all that stuff.

2. Old slave and folk philosopher whose proverbs and stories were recorded by Joel Chandler Harris (1848–1908).

[LYONS *enters the yard from the street. Thirty-four years old,* TROY's *son by a previous marriage, he sports a neatly trimmed goatee, sport coat, white shirt, tieless and buttoned at the collar. Though he fancies himself a musician, he is more caught up in the rituals and "idea" of being a musician than in the actual practice of the music. He has come to borrow money from* TROY, *and while he knows he will be successful, he is uncertain as to what extent his lifestyle will be held up to scrutiny and ridicule.*]

LYONS: Hey, Pop.

TROY: What you come "Hey, Popping" me for?

LYONS: How you doing, Rose? [*He kisses her.*] Mr. Bono, how you doing?

BONO: Hey, Lyons . . . how you been?

TROY: He must have been doing alright. I ain't seen him around here last week.

ROSE: Troy, leave your boy alone. He come by to see you and you wanna start all that nonsense.

TROY: I ain't bothering Lyons. [*Offers him the bottle.*] Here . . . get you a drink. We got an understanding. I know why he come by to see me and he know I know.

LYONS: Come on, Pop . . . I just stopped by to say hi . . . see how you was doing.

TROY: You ain't stopped by yesterday.

ROSE: You gonna stay for supper, Lyons? I got some chicken cooking in the oven.

LYONS: No, Rose . . . thanks. I was just in the neighborhood and thought I'd stop by for a minute.

TROY: You was in the neighborhood alright, nigger. You telling the truth there. You was in the neighborhood cause it's my payday.

LYONS: Well, hell, since you mentioned it . . . let me have ten dollars.

TROY: I'll be damned! I'll die and go to hell and play blackjack with the devil before I give you ten dollars.

BONO: That's what I wanna know about . . . that devil you done seen.

LYONS: What . . . Pop done seen the devil? You too much, Pops.

TROY: Yeah, I done seen him. Talked to him too!

ROSE: You ain't seen no devil. I done told you that man ain't had nothing to do with the devil. Anything you can't understand, you want to call it the devil.

TROY: Look here, Bono . . . I went down to see Hertzberger about some furniture. Got three rooms for two-ninety-eight. That what it say on the radio. "Three rooms . . . two-ninety-eight." Even made up a little song about it. Go down there . . . man tell me I can't get no credit. I'm working every day and can't get no credit. What to do? I got an empty house with some raggedy furniture in it. Cory ain't got no bed. He's sleeping on a pile of rags on the floor. Working every day and can't get no credit. Come back here—Rose'll tell you—madder than hell. Sit down . . . try to figure what I'm gonna do. Come a knock on the door. Ain't been living here but three days. Who know I'm here? Open the door . . . devil standing there bigger than life. White fellow . . . got on good clothes and everything. Standing there with a clipboard in his hand. I ain't had to say nothing. First words come out of his mouth was . . . "I understand you need some furniture and can't get no credit." I liked to fell over. He say "I'll give you all the credit you want, but you got to pay the interest on it." I told him, "Give me three rooms worth and charge whatever you want." Next day a truck pulled up here and two men unloaded them three rooms. Man what drove the truck give me a book. Say send ten dollars, first of every month to the address in the book and everything will be alright. Say if I miss a payment the devil was coming back and it'll be hell to pay. That was fifteen years ago. To this day . . . the first of the month I send my ten dollars, Rose'll tell you.

ROSE: Troy lying.

TROY: I ain't never seen that man since. Now you tell me who else that could have been but the devil? I ain't sold my soul or nothing like that, you understand. Naw, I wouldn't have truck with the devil about nothing like that. I got my furniture and pays my ten dollars the first of the month just like clockwork.

BONO: How long you say you been paying this ten dollars a month?

TROY: Fifteen years!

BONO: Hell, ain't you finished paying for it yet? How much the man done charged you.

TROY: Aw hell, I done paid for it. I done paid for it ten times over! The fact is I'm scared to stop paying it.

ROSE: Troy lying. We got that furniture from Mr. Glickman. He ain't paying no ten dollars a month to nobody.

TROY: Aw hell, woman. Bono know I ain't that big a fool.

LYONS: I was just getting ready to say . . . I know where there's a bridge for sale.

TROY: Look here, I'll tell you this . . . it don't matter to me if he was the devil. It don't matter if the devil give credit. Somebody has got to give it.

ROSE: It ought to matter. You going around talking about having truck with the devil . . . God's the one you gonna have to answer to. He's the one gonna be at the Judgment.

LYONS: Yeah, well, look here, Pop . . . let me have that ten dollars. I'll give it back to you. Bonnie got a job working at the hospital.

TROY: What I tell you, Bono? The only time I see this nigger is when he wants something. That's the only time I see him.

LYONS: Come on, Pop, Mr. Bono don't want to hear all that. Let me have the ten dollars. I told you Bonnie working.

TROY: What that mean to me? "Bonnie working." I don't care if she working. Go ask her for the ten dollars if she working. Talking about "Bonnie working." Why ain't you working?

LYONS: Aw, Pop, you know I can't find no decent job. Where am I gonna get a job at? You know I can't get no job.

TROY: I told you I know some people down there. I can get you on the rubbish if you want to work. I told you that the last time you came by here asking me for something.

LYONS: Naw, Pop . . . thanks. That ain't for me. I don't wanna be carrying nobody's rubbish. I don't wanna be punching nobody's time clock.

TROY: What's the matter, you too good to carry people's rubbish? Where you think that ten dollars you talking about come from? I'm just supposed to haul people's rubbish and give my money to you cause you too lazy to work. You too lazy to work and wanna know why you ain't got what I got.

ROSE: What hospital Bonnie working at? Mercy?

LYONS: She's down at Passavant working in the laundry.

TROY: I ain't got nothing as it is. I give you that ten dollars and I got to eat beans the rest of the week. Naw . . . you ain't getting no ten dollars here.

LYONS: You ain't got to be eating no beans. I don't know why you wanna say that.

TROY: I ain't got no extra money. Gabe done moved over to Miss Pearl's paying her the rent and things done got tight around here. I can't afford to be giving you every payday.

LYONS: I ain't asked you to give me nothing. I asked you to loan me ten dollars. I know you got ten dollars.

TROY: Yeah, I got it. You know why I got it? Cause I don't throw my money away out there in the streets. You living the fast life . . . wanna be a musician . . . running around in them clubs and things . . . then, you learn to take care of yourself. You ain't gonna find me going and asking nobody for nothing. I done spent too many years without.

LYONS: You and me is two different people, Pop.

TROY: I done learned my mistake and learned to do what's right by it. You still trying to get something for nothing. Life don't owe you nothing. You owe it to yourself. Ask Bono. He'll tell you I'm right.

LYONS: You got your way of dealing with the world . . . I got mine. The only thing that matters to me is the music.

TROY: Yeah, I can see that! It don't matter how you gonna eat . . . where your next dollar is coming from. You telling the truth there.

LYONS: I know I got to eat. But I got to live too. I need something that gonna help me to get out of the bed in the morning. Make me feel like I belong in the world. I don't bother nobody. I just stay with my music cause that's the only way I can find to live in the world. Otherwise there ain't no telling what I might do. Now I don't come criticizing you and how you live. I just come by to ask you for ten dollars. I don't wanna hear all that about how I live.

TROY: Boy, your mama did a hell of a job raising you.

LYONS: You can't change me, Pop. I'm thirty-four years old. If you wanted to change me, you should have been there when I was growing up. I come by to see you . . . ask for ten dollars and you want to talk about how I was raised. You don't know nothing about how I was raised.

ROSE: Let the boy have ten dollars, Troy.

TROY: [To LYONS.] What the hell you looking at me for? I ain't got no ten dollars. You know what I do with my money. [To ROSE.] Give him ten dollars if you want him to have it.

ROSE: I will. Just as soon as you turn it loose.

TROY: [Handing ROSE the money.] There it is. Seventy-six dollars and forty-two cents. You see this, Bono? Now, I ain't gonna get but six of that back.

ROSE: You ought to stop telling that lie. Here, Lyons. [*She hands him the money.*]

LYONS: Thanks, Rose. Look . . . I got to run . . . I'll see you later.

TROY: Wait a minute. You gonna say, "thanks, Rose" and ain't gonna look to see where she got that ten dollars from? See how they do me, Bono?

LYONS: I know she got it from you, Pop. Thanks. I'll give it back to you.

TROY: There he go telling another lie. Time I see that ten dollars . . . he'll be owing me thirty more.

LYONS: See you, Mr. Bono.

BONO: Take care, Lyons!

LYONS: Thanks, Pop. I'll see you again. [LYONS *exits the yard.*]

TROY: I don't know why he don't go and get him a decent job and take care of that woman he got.

BONO: He'll be alright, Troy. The boy is still young.

TROY: The *boy* is thirty-four years old.

ROSE: Let's not get off into all that.

BONO: Look here . . . I got to be going. I got to be getting on. Lucille gonna be waiting.

TROY: [*Puts his arm around* ROSE.] See this woman, Bono? I love this woman. I love this woman so much it hurts. I love her so much . . . I done run out of ways of loving her. So I got to go back to basics. Don't you come by my house Monday morning talking about time to go to work . . . 'cause I'm still gonna be stroking!

ROSE: Troy! Stop it now!

BONO: I ain't paying him no mind, Rose. That ain't nothing but gin-talk. Go on, Troy. I'll see you Monday.

TROY: Don't you come by my house, nigger! I done told you what I'm gonna be doing.

[*The lights go down to black.*]

SCENE 2

The lights come up on ROSE *hanging up clothes. She hums and sings softly to herself. It is the following morning.*

ROSE: [*Singing.*]

        Jesus, be a fence all around me every day
        Jesus, I want you to protect me as I travel on my way.
        Jesus, be a fence all around me every day.

[TROY *enters from the house.*]

ROSE: [*Continues singing.*]

        Jesus, I want you to protect me
        As I travel on my way.

[*To* TROY.]

'Morning. You ready for breakfast? I can fix it soon as I finish hanging up these clothes?

TROY: I got the coffee on. That'll be alright. I'll just drink some of that this morning.

ROSE: That 651 hit yesterday. That's the second time this month. Miss Pearl hit for a dollar . . . seem like those that need the least always get lucky. Poor folks can't get nothing.

TROY: Them numbers don't know nobody. I don't know why you fool with them. You and Lyons both.

ROSE: It's something to do.

TROY: You ain't doing nothing but throwing your money away.

ROSE: Troy, you know I don't play foolishly. I just play a nickel here and a nickel there.

TROY: That's two nickels you done thrown away.

ROSE: Now I hit sometimes . . . that makes up for it. It always comes in handy when I do hit. I don't hear you complaining then.

TROY: I ain't complaining now. I just say it's foolish. Trying to guess out of six hundred ways which way the number gonna come. If I had all the money niggers, these Negroes, throw away on numbers for one week—just one week—I'd be a rich man.

ROSE: Well, you wishing and calling it foolish ain't gonna stop folks from playing numbers. That's one thing for sure. Besides . . . some good things come from playing numbers. Look where Pope done bought him that restaurant off of numbers.

TROY: I can't stand niggers like that. Man ain't had two dimes to rub together. He walking around with his shoes all run over bumming money for cigarettes. Alright. Got lucky there and hit the numbers . . .

ROSE: Troy, I know all about it.

TROY: Had good sense, I'll say that for him. He ain't throwed his money away. I seen niggers hit the numbers and go through two thousand dollars in four days. Man brought him that restaurant down there . . . fixed it up real nice . . . and then didn't want nobody to come in it! A Negro go in there and can't get no kind of service. I seen a white fellow come in there and order a bowl of stew. Pope picked all the meat out the pot for him. Man ain't had nothing but a bowl of meat! Negro come behind him and ain't got nothing but the potatoes and carrots. Talking about what numbers do for people, you picked a wrong example. Ain't done nothing but make a worser fool out of him than he was before.

ROSE: Troy, you ought to stop worrying about what happened at work yesterday.

TROY: I ain't worried. Just told me to be down there at the Commissioner's office on Friday. Everybody think they gonna fire me. I ain't worried about them firing me. You ain't got to worry about that. [*Pause.*] Where's Cory? Cory in the house? [*Calls.*] Cory?

ROSE: He gone out.

TROY: Out, huh? He gone out 'cause he know I want him to help me with this fence. I know how he is. That boy scared of work.

[GABRIEL *enters. He comes halfway down the alley and, hearing* TROY's *voice, stops.*]

TROY: [*Continues.*] He ain't done a lick of work in his life.

ROSE: He had to go to football practice. Coach wanted them to get in a little extra practice before the season start.

TROY: I got his practice . . . running out of here before he get his chores done.

ROSE: Troy, what is wrong with you this morning? Don't nothing set right with you. Go on back in there and go to bed . . . get up on the other side.

TROY: Why something got to be wrong with me? I ain't said nothing wrong with me.

ROSE: You got something to say about everything. First it's the numbers . . . then it's the way the man runs his restaurant . . . then you done got on Cory. What's it gonna be next? Take a look up there and see if the weather suits you . . . or is it gonna be how you gonna put up the fence with the clothes hanging in the yard.

TROY: You hit the nail on the head then.

ROSE: I know you like I know the back of my hand. Go on in there and get you some coffee . . . see if that straighten you up. 'Cause you ain't right this morning.

[TROY *starts into the house and sees* GABRIEL. GABRIEL *starts singing.* TROY's *brother, he is seven years younger than* TROY. *Injured in World War II, he has a metal plate in his head. He carries an old trumpet tied around his waist and believes with every fiber of his being that he is the Archangel Gabriel. He carries a chipped basket with an assortment of discarded fruits and vegetables he has picked up in the strip district and which he attempts to sell.*]

GABRIEL: [*Singing.*]

> Yes ma'am, I got plums
> You ask me how I sell them
> Oh ten cents apiece
> Three for a quarter
> Come and buy now
> 'Cause I'm here today
> And tomorrow I'll be gone

[GABRIEL *enters.*]

GABRIEL: Hey, Rose!

ROSE: How you doing, Gabe?

GABRIEL: There's Troy . . . Hey, Troy!

TROY: Hey, Gabe. [*Exit into kitchen.*]

ROSE: [*To* GABRIEL.] What you got there?

GABRIEL: You know what I got, Rose. I got fruits and vegetables.

ROSE: [*Looking in basket.*] Where's all these plums you talking about?

GABRIEL: I ain't got no plums today, Rose. I was just singing that. Have some tomorrow. Put me in a big order for plums. Have enough plums tomorrow for St. Peter and everybody. [TROY *re-enters from kitchen, crosses to steps. To* ROSE.] Troy's mad at me.

TROY: I ain't mad at you. What I got to be mad at you about? You ain't done nothing to me.

GABRIEL: I just moved over to Miss Pearl's to keep out from in your way. I ain't mean no harm by it.

TROY: Who said anything about that? I ain't said anything about that.

GABRIEL: You ain't mad at me, is you?

TROY: Naw . . . I ain't mad at you, Gabe. If I was mad at you I'd tell you about it.

GABRIEL: Got me two rooms. In the basement. Got my own door too. Wanna see my key? [*He holds up a key.*] That's my own key! Ain't nobody else got a key like that. That's my key! My two rooms!

TROY: Well, that's good, Gabe. You got your own key . . . that's good.

ROSE: You hungry, Gabe? I was just fixing to cook Troy his breakfast.

GABRIEL: I'll take some biscuits. You got some biscuits? Did you know when I was in heaven . . . every morning me and St. Peter would sit down by the gate and eat some big fat biscuits? Oh, yeah! We had us a good time. We'd sit there and eat us them biscuits and then St. Peter would go off to sleep and tell me to wake him up when it's time to open the gates for the judgment.

ROSE: Well, come on . . . I'll make up a batch of biscuits. [ROSE *exits into the house.*]

GABRIEL: Troy . . . St. Peter got your name in the book. I seen it. It say . . . Troy Maxson. I say . . . I know him! He got the same name like what I got. That's my brother!

TROY: How many times you gonna tell me that, Gabe?

GABRIEL: Ain't got my name in the book. Don't have to have my name. I done died and went to heaven. He got your name though. One morning St. Peter was looking at his book . . . marking it up for the judgment . . . and he let me see your name. Got it in there under M. Got Rose's name . . . I ain't seen it like I seen yours . . . but I know it's in there. He got a great big book. Got everybody's name what was ever been born. That's what he told me. But I seen your name. Seen it with my own eyes.

TROY: Go on in the house there. Rose going to fix you something to eat.

GABRIEL: Oh, I ain't hungry. I done had breakfast with Aunt Jemimah. She come by and cooked me up a whole mess of flapjacks. Remember how we used to eat them flapjacks?

TROY: Go on in the house and get you something to eat now.

GABRIEL: I got to go sell my plums. I done sold some tomatoes. Got me two quarters. Wanna see? [*He shows* TROY *his quarters.*] I'm gonna save them and buy me a new horn so St. Peter can hear me when it's time to open the gates. [GABRIEL *stops suddenly. Listens.*] Hear that? That's the hellhounds. I got to chase them out of here. Go on get out of here! Get out!

[GABRIEL *exits singing.*]

> Better get ready for the judgment
> Better get ready for the judgment
> My lord is coming down

[ROSE *enters from the house.*]

TROY: He gone off somewhere.
GABRIEL: [*Offstage.*]

> Better get ready for the judgment
> Better get ready for the judgment morning
> Better get ready for the judgment
> My God is coming down

ROSE: He ain't eating right. Miss Pearl say she can't get him to eat nothing.
TROY: What you want me to do about it, Rose? I done did everything I can for the man. I can't make him get well. Man got half his head blown away . . . what you expect?
ROSE: Seem like something ought to be done to help him.
TROY: Man don't bother nobody. He just mixed up from that metal plate he got in his head. Ain't no sense for him to go back into the hospital.
ROSE: Least he be eating right. They can help him take care of himself.
TROY: Don't nobody wanna be locked up, Rose. What you wanna lock him up for? Man go over there and fight the war . . . messin' around with them Japs, get half his head blown off . . . and they give him a lousy three thousand dollars. And I had to swoop down on that.
ROSE: Is you fixing to go into that again?
TROY: That's the only way I got a roof over my head . . . cause of that metal plate.
ROSE: Ain't no sense you blaming yourself for nothing. Gabe wasn't in no condition to manage that money. You done what was right by him. Can't nobody say you ain't done what was right by him. Look how long you took care of him . . . till he wanted to have his own place and moved over there with Miss Pearl.
TROY: That ain't what I'm saying, woman! I'm just stating the facts. If my brother didn't have that metal plate in his head . . . I wouldn't have a pot to piss in or a window to throw it out of. And I'm fifty-three years old. Now see if you can understand that! [TROY *gets up from the porch and starts to exit the yard.*]
ROSE: Where you going off to? You been running out of here every Saturday for weeks. I thought you was gonna work on this fence?
TROY: I'm gonna walk down to Taylors'. Listen to the ball game. I'll be back in a bit. I'll work on it when I get back.

[*He exits the yard. The lights go to black.*]

SCENE 3

The lights come up on the yard. It is four hours later. ROSE *is taking down the clothes from the line.* CORY *enters carrying his football equipment.*

ROSE: Your daddy liked to had a fit with you running out of here this morning without doing your chores.

CORY: I told you I had to go to practice.

ROSE: He say you were supposed to help him with this fence.

CORY: He been saying that the last four or five Saturdays, and then he don't never do nothing, but go down to Taylors'. Did you tell him about the recruiter?

ROSE: Yeah, I told him.

CORY: What he say?

ROSE: He ain't said nothing too much. You get in there and get started on your chores before he gets back. Go on and scrub down them steps before he gets back here hollering and carrying on.

CORY: I'm hungry. What you got to eat, Mama?

ROSE: Go on and get started on your chores. I got some meat loaf in there. Go on and make you a sandwich . . . and don't leave no mess in there. [CORY *exits into the house.* ROSE *continues to take down the clothes.* TROY *enters the yard and sneaks up and grabs her from behind.*] Troy! Go on, now. You liked to scared me to death. What was the score of the game? Lucille had me on the phone and I couldn't keep up with it.

TROY: What I care about the game? Come here, woman. [*He tries to kiss her.*]

ROSE: I thought you went down Taylors' to listen to the game. Go on, Troy! You supposed to be putting up this fence.

TROY: [*Attempting to kiss her again.*] I'll put it up when I finish with what is at hand.

ROSE: Go on, Troy. I ain't studying you.

TROY: [*Chasing after her.*] I'm studying you . . . fixing to do my homework!

ROSE: Troy, you better leave me alone.

TROY: Where's Cory? That boy brought his butt home yet?

ROSE: He's in the house doing his chores.

TROY: [*Calling.*] Cory! Get your butt out here, boy! [ROSE *exits into the house with the laundry.* TROY *goes over to the pile of wood, picks up a board, and starts sawing.* CORY *enters from the house.*] You just now coming in here from leaving this morning?

CORY: Yeah, I had to go to football practice.

TROY: Yeah, what?

CORY: Yessir.

TROY: I ain't but two seconds off you noway. The garbage sitting in there overflowing . . . you ain't done none of your chores . . . and you come in here talking about, "Yeah."

CORY: I was just getting ready to do my chores now, Pop . . .

TROY: Your first chore is to help me with this fence on Saturday. Everything else come after that. Now get that saw and cut them boards.

[CORY *takes the saw and begins cutting the boards.* TROY *continues working. There is a long pause.*]

CORY: Hey, Pop . . . why don't you buy a TV?

TROY: What I want with a TV? What I want one of them for?

CORY: Everybody got one. Earl, Ba Bra . . . Jesse!

TROY: I ain't asked you who had one. I say what I want with one?

CORY: So you can watch it. They got lots of things on TV. Baseball games and everything. We could watch the World Series.

TROY: Yeah . . . and how much this TV cost?

CORY: I don't know. They got them on sale for around two hundred dollars.

TROY: Two hundred dollars, huh?

CORY: That ain't that much, Pop.

TROY: Naw, it's just two hundred dollars. See that roof you got over your head at night? Let me tell you something about that roof. It's been over ten years since that roof was last tarred. See now . . . the snow come this winter and sit up there on that roof like it is . . . and it's gonna seep inside. It's just gonna be a little bit . . . ain't gonna hardly notice it. Then the next thing you know, it's gonna be leaking all over the house. Then the wood rot from all that water and you gonna need a whole new roof. Now, how much you think it cost to get that roof tarred?

CORY: I don't know.

TROY: Two hundred and sixty-four dollars . . . cash money. While you thinking about a TV, I got to be thinking about the roof . . . and whatever else go wrong around here. Now if you had two hundred dollars, what would you do . . . fix the roof or buy a TV?

CORY: I'd buy a TV. Then when the roof started to leak . . . when it needed fixing . . . I'd fix it.

TROY: Where you gonna get the money from? You done spent it for a TV. You gonna sit up and watch the water run all over your brand new TV.

CORY: Aw, Pop. You got money. I know you do.

TROY: Where I got it at, huh?

CORY: You got it in the bank.

TROY: You wanna see my bankbook? You wanna see that seventy-three dollars and twenty-two cents I got sitting up in there.

CORY: You ain't got to pay for it all at one time. You can put a down payment on it and carry it on home with you.

TROY: Not me. I ain't gonna owe nobody nothing if I can help it. Miss a payment and they come and snatch it right out your house. Then what you got? Now, soon as I get two hundred dollars clear, then I'll buy a TV. Right now, as soon as I get two hundred and sixty-four dollars, I'm gonna have this roof tarred.

CORY: Aw . . . Pop!

TROY: You go on and get you two hundred dollars and buy one if ya want it. I got better things to do with my money.

CORY: I can't get no two hundred dollars. I ain't never seen two hundred dollars.

TROY: I'll tell you what . . . you get you a hundred dollars and I'll put the other hundred with it.

CORY: Alright, I'm gonna show you.

TROY: You gonna show me how you can cut them boards right now.

[CORY *begins to cut the boards. There is a long pause.*]

CORY: The Pirates won today. That makes five in a row.

TROY: I ain't thinking about the Pirates. Got an all-white team. Got that boy . . . that Puerto Rican boy . . . Clemente. Don't even half-play him. That boy could be something if they give him a chance. Play him one day and sit him on the bench the next.

CORY: He gets a lot of chances to play.

TROY: I'm talking about playing regular. Playing every day so you can get your timing. That's what I'm talking about.

CORY: They got some white guys on the team that don't play every day. You can't play everybody at the same time.

TROY: If they got a white fellow sitting on the bench . . . you can bet your last dollar he can't play! The colored guy got to be twice as good before he get on the team. That's why I don't want you to get all tied up in them sports. Man on the team and what it get him? They got colored on the team and don't use them. Same as not having them. All them teams the same.

CORY: The Braves got Hank Aaron and Wes Covington. Hank Aaron hit two home runs today. That makes forty-three.

TROY: Hank Aaron ain't nobody. That's what you supposed to do. That's how you supposed to play the game. Ain't nothing to it. It's just a matter of timing . . . getting the right follow-through. Hell, I can hit forty-three home runs right now!

CORY: Not off no major-league pitching, you couldn't.

TROY: We had better pitching in the Negro leagues. I hit seven home runs off of Satchel Paige. You can't get no better than that!

CORY: Sandy Koufax. He's leading the league in strikeouts.

TROY: I ain't thinking of no Sandy Koufax.

CORY: You got Warren Spahn and Lew Burdette. I bet you couldn't hit no home runs off of Warren Spahn.

TROY: I'm through with it now. You go on and cut them boards. [*Pause.*] Your mama tells me you got recruited by a college football team? Is that right?

CORY: Yeah. Coach Zellman say the recruiter gonna be coming by to talk to you. Get you to sign the permission papers.

TROY: I thought you supposed to be working down there at the A&P. Ain't you suppose to be working down there after school?

CORY: Mr. Stawicki say he gonna hold my job for me until after the football season. Say starting next week I can work weekends.

TROY: I thought we had an understanding about this football stuff? You suppose to keep up with your chores and hold that job down at the A&P. Ain't been around here all day on a Saturday. Ain't none of your chores done . . . and now you telling me you done quit your job.

CORY: I'm gonna be working weekends.

TROY: You damn right you are! And ain't no need for nobody coming around here to talk to me about signing nothing.

CORY: Hey, Pop . . . you can't do that. He's coming all the way from North Carolina.

TROY: I don't care where he coming from. The white man ain't gonna let you get nowhere with that football noway. You go on and get your book-learning so you can work yourself up in that A&P or learn how to fix cars or build houses or something, get you a trade. That way you can have something can't nobody take away from you. You go on and learn how to put your hands to some good use. Besides hauling people's garbage.

CORY: I get good grades, Pop. That's why the recruiter wants to talk with you. You got to keep up your grades to get recruited. This way I'll be going to college. I'll get a chance . . .

TROY: First, you gonna get your butt down there to the A&P and get your job back.

CORY: Mr. Stawicki done already hired somebody else 'cause I told him I was playing football.

TROY: You a bigger fool than I thought . . . to let somebody take away your job so you can play some football. Where you gonna get your money to take out your girlfriend and whatnot? What kind of foolishness is that to let somebody take away your job?

CORY: I'm still gonna be working weekends.

TROY: Naw . . . naw. You getting your butt out of here and finding you another job.

CORY: Come on, Pop! I got to practice. I can't work after school and play football too. The team needs me. That's what Coach Zellman say . . .

TROY: I don't care what nobody else say. I'm the boss . . . you understand? I'm the boss around here. I do the only saying what counts.

CORY: Come on, Pop!

TROY: I asked you . . . Did you understand?

CORY: Yeah . . .

TROY: What!

CORY: Yessir.

TROY: You go down there to that A&P and see if you can get your job back. If you can't do both . . . then you quit the football team. You've got to take the crookeds with the straights.

CORY: Yessir. [*Pause.*] Can I ask you a question?

TROY: What the hell you wanna ask me? Mr. Stawicki the one you got the questions for.

CORY: How come you ain't never liked me?

TROY: Liked you? Who the hell say I got to like you? What law is there say I got to like you? Wanna stand up in my face and ask a damn fool-ass question like that. Talking about liking somebody. Come here, boy, when I talk to you. [CORY *comes over to where* TROY *is working. He stands slouched over and* TROY *shoves him on his shoulder.*] Straighten up, goddammit! I asked you a question . . . what law is there say I got to like you?

CORY: None.

TROY: Well, alright then! Don't you eat every day? [*Pause.*] Answer me when I talk to you! Don't you eat every day?

CORY: Yeah.

TROY: Nigger, as long as you in my house, you put that sir on the end of it when you talk to me!

CORY: Yes . . . sir.

TROY: You eat every day.

CORY: Yessir!

TROY: Got a roof over your head.

CORY: Yessir!

TROY: Got clothes on your back.

CORY: Yessir.

TROY: Why you think that is?

CORY: Cause of you.

TROY: Aw, hell I know it's 'cause of me . . . but why do you think that is?

CORY: [*Hesitant.*] Cause you like me.

TROY: Like you? I go out of here every morning . . . bust my butt . . . putting up with them crackers every day . . . cause I like you? You about the biggest fool I ever saw. [*Pause.*] It's my job. It's my responsibility! You understand that? A man got to take care of his family. You live in my house . . . sleep you behind on my bedclothes . . . fill you belly up with my food . . . cause you my son. You my flesh and blood. Not 'cause I like you! 'Cause it's my duty to take care of you. I owe a responsibility to you! Let's get this straight right here . . . before it go along any further . . . I ain't got to like you. Mr. Rand don't give me my money come payday cause he likes me. He gives me cause he owe me. I done give you everything I had to give you. I gave you your life! Me and your mama worked that out between us. And liking your black ass wasn't part of the bargain. Don't you try and go through life worrying about if somebody like you or not. You best be making sure they doing right by you. You understand what I'm saying, boy?

CORY: Yessir.

TROY: Then get the hell out of my face, and get on down to that A&P.

[ROSE *has been standing behind the screen door for much of the scene. She enters as* CORY *exits.*]

ROSE: Why don't you let the boy go ahead and play football, Troy? Ain't no harm in that. He's just trying to be like you with the sports.

TROY: I don't want him to be like me! I want him to move as far away from my life as he can get. You the only decent thing that ever happened to me. I wish him that. But I don't wish him a thing else from my life. I decided seventeen years ago that boy wasn't getting involved in no sports. Not after what they did to me in the sports.

ROSE: Troy, why don't you admit you was too old to play in the major leagues? For once . . . why don't you admit that?

TROY: What do you mean too old? Don't come telling me I was too old. I just wasn't the right color. Hell, I'm fifty-three years old and I can do better than Selkirk's .269 right now!

ROSE: How's was you gonna play ball when you were over forty? Sometimes I can't get no sense out of you.

TROY: I got good sense, woman. I got sense enough not to let my boy get hurt over playing no sports. You been mothering that boy too much. Worried about if people like him.

ROSE: Everything that boy do . . . he do for you. He wants you to say "Good job, son." That's all.

TROY: Rose, I ain't got time for that. He's alive. He's healthy. He's got to make his own way. I made mine. Ain't nobody gonna hold his hand when he get out there in that world.

ROSE: Times have changed from when you was young, Troy. People change. The world's changing around you and you can't even see it.

TROY: [Slow, methodical.] Woman . . . I do the best I can do. I come in here every Friday. I carry a sack of potatoes and a bucket of lard. You all line up at the door with your hands out. I give you the lint from my pockets. I give you my sweat and my blood. I ain't got no tears. I done spent them. We go upstairs in that room at night . . . and I fall down on you and try to blast a hole into forever. I get up Monday morning . . . find my lunch on the table. I go out. Make my way. Find my strength to carry me through to the next Friday. [Pause.] That's all I got, Rose. That's all I got to give. I can't give nothing else.

[TROY exits into the house. The lights go down to black.]

SCENE 4

It is Friday. Two weeks later. CORY starts out of the house with his football equipment. The phone rings.

CORY: [Calling.] I got it! [He answers the phone and stands in the screen door talking.] Hello? Hey, Jesse. Naw . . . I was just getting ready to leave now.

ROSE: [Calling.] Cory!

CORY: I told you, man, them spikes is all tore up. You can use them if you want, but they ain't no good. Earl got some spikes.

ROSE: [Calling.] Cory!

CORY: [Calling to ROSE.] Mam? I'm talking to Jesse. [Into phone.] When she say that? [Pause.] Aw, you lying, man. I'm gonna tell her you said that.

ROSE: [Calling.] Cory, don't you go nowhere!

CORY: I got to go to the game, Ma! [Into the phone.] Yeah, hey, look, I'll talk to you later. Yeah, I'll meet you over Earl's house. Later. Bye, Ma!

[CORY exits the house and starts out the yard.]

ROSE: Cory, where you going off to? You got that stuff all pulled out and thrown all over your room.

CORY: [In the yard.] I was looking for my spikes. Jesse wanted to borrow my spikes.

ROSE: Get up there and get that cleaned up before your daddy gets back in here.

CORY: I got to go to the game! I'll clean it up *when I get back.* [CORY *exits.*]

ROSE: That's all he need to do is see that room all messed up.

[ROSE *exits into the house.* TROY *and* BONO *enter the yard.* TROY *is dressed in clothes other than his work clothes.*]

BONO: He told him the same thing he told you. Take it to the union.

TROY: Brownie ain't got that much sense. Man wasn't thinking about nothing. He wait until I confront them on it . . . then he wanna come crying seniority. [*Calls.*] Hey, Rose!

BONO: I wish I could have seen Mr. Rand's face when he told you.

TROY: He couldn't get it out of his mouth! Liked to bit his tongue! When they called me down there to the Commissioner's office . . . he thought they was gonna fire me. Like everybody else.

BONO: I didn't think they was gonna fire you. I thought they was gonna put you on the warning paper.

TROY: Hey, Rose! [*To* BONO.] Yeah, Mr. Rand like to bit his tongue. [TROY *breaks the seal on the bottle, takes a drink, and hands it to* BONO.]

BONO: I see you ran right down to Taylors' and told that Alberta gal.

TROY: [*Calling.*] Hey Rose! [*To* BONO.] I told everybody. Hey Rose! I went down there to cash my check.

ROSE: [*Entering from the house.*] Hush all that hollering, man! I know you out here. What they say down there at the Commissioner's office?

TROY: You supposed to come when I call you, woman. Bono'll tell you that. [*To* BONO.] Don't Lucille come when you call her?

ROSE: Man, hush your mouth. I ain't no dog . . . talk about "come when you call me."

TROY: [*Puts his arm around* ROSE.] You hear this, Bono? I had me an old dog used to get uppity like that. You say, "C'mere, Blue!" . . . and he just lay there and look at you. End up getting a stick and chasing him away trying to make him come.

ROSE: I ain't studying you and your dog. I remember you used to sing that old song.

TROY: [*He sings.*] Hear it ring! Hear it ring! I had a dog his name was Blue.

ROSE: Don't nobody wanna hear you sing that old song.

TROY: [*Sings.*] You know Blue was mighty true.

ROSE: Used to have Cory running around here singing that song.

BONO: Hell, I remember that song myself.

TROY: [*Singing.*]

You know Blue was a good old dog.
Blue treed a possum in a hollow log.

That was my daddy's song. My daddy made up that song.

ROSE: I don't care who made it up. Don't nobody wanna hear you sing it.

TROY: [*Makes a song like calling a dog.*] Come here, woman.

ROSE: You come in here carrying on, I reckon they ain't fired you. What they say down there at the Commissioner's office?

TROY: Look here, Rose . . . Mr. Rand called me into his office today when I got back from talking to them people down there . . . it come from up top . . . he called me in and told me they was making me a driver.

ROSE: Troy, you kidding!

TROY: No I ain't. Ask Bono.

ROSE: Well, that's great, Troy. Now you don't have to hassle them people no more.

[LYONS *enters from the street.*]

TROY: Aw hell, I wasn't looking to see you today. I thought you was in jail. Got it all over the front page of the *Courier* about them raiding Sefus' place . . . where you be hanging out with all them thugs.

LYONS: Hey, Pop . . . that ain't got nothing to do with me. I don't go down there gambling. I go down there to sit in with the band. I ain't got nothing to do with the gambling part. They got some good music down there.

TROY: They got some rogues . . . is what they got.

LYONS: How you been, Mr. Bono? Hi, Rose.

BONO: I see where you playing down at the Crawford Grill tonight.

ROSE: How come you ain't brought Bonnie like I told you. You should have brought Bonnie with you, she ain't been over in a month of Sundays.

LYONS: I was just in the neighborhood . . . thought I'd stop by.

TROY: Here he come . . .

BONO: Your daddy got a promotion on the rubbish. He's gonna be the first colored driver. Ain't got to do nothing but sit up there and read the paper like them white fellows.

LYONS: Hey, Pop . . . if you knew how to read you'd be alright.

BONO: Naw . . . naw . . . you mean if the nigger knew how to *drive* he'd be all right. Been fighting with them people about driving and ain't even got a license. Mr. Rand know you ain't got no driver's license?

TROY: Driving ain't nothing. All you do is point the truck where you want it to go. Driving ain't nothing.

BONO: Do Mr. Rand know you ain't got no driver's license? That's what I'm talking about. I ain't asked if driving was easy. I asked if Mr. Rand know you ain't got no driver's license.

TROY: He ain't got to know. The man ain't got to know my business. Time he find out, I have two or three driver's licenses.

LYONS: [*Going into his pocket.*] Say, look here, Pop . . .

TROY: I knew it was coming. Didn't I tell you, Bono? I know what kind of "Look here, Pop" that was. The nigger fixing to ask me for some money. It's Friday night. It's my payday. All them rogues down there on the avenue . . . the ones that ain't in jail . . . and Lyons is hopping in his shoes to get down there with them.

LYONS: See, Pop . . . if you give somebody else a chance to talk sometime, you'd see that I was fixing to pay you back your ten dollars like I told you. Here . . . I told you I'd pay you when Bonnie got paid.

TROY: Naw . . . you go ahead and keep that ten dollars. Put it in the bank. The next time you feel like you wanna come by here and ask me for something . . . you go on down there and get that.

LYONS: Here's your ten dollars, Pop. I told you I don't want you to give me nothing. I just wanted to borrow ten dollars.

TROY: Naw . . . go on and keep that for the next time you want to ask me.

LYONS: Come on, Pop . . . here go your ten dollars.

ROSE: Why don't you go on and let the boy pay you back, Troy?

LYONS: Here you go, Rose. If you don't take it I'm gonna have to hear about it for the next six months. [He hands her the money.]

ROSE: You can hand yours over here too, Troy.

TROY: You see this, Bono. You see how they do me.

BONO: Yeah, Lucille do me the same way.

[GABRIEL is heard singing offstage. He enters.]

GABRIEL: Better get ready for the Judgment! Better get ready for . . . Hey! . . . Hey! . . . There's Troy's boy!

LYONS: How you doing, Uncle Gabe?

GABRIEL: Lyons . . . the King of the Jungle! Rose . . . hey, Rose. Got a flower for you. [He takes a rose from his pocket.] Picked it myself. That's the same rose like you is!

ROSE: That's right nice of you, Gabe.

LYONS: What you been doing, Uncle Gabe?

GABRIEL: Oh, I been chasing hellhounds and waiting on the time to tell St. Peter to open the gates.

LYONS: You been chasing hellhounds, huh? Well . . . you doing the right thing, Uncle Gabe. Somebody got to chase them.

GABRIEL: Oh, yeah . . . I know it. The devil's strong. The devil ain't no pushover. Hellhounds snipping at everybody's heels. But I got my trumpet waiting on the judgment time.

LYONS: Waiting on the Battle of Armageddon, huh?

GABRIEL: Ain't gonna be too much of a battle when God get to waving that Judgment sword. But the peoples gonna have a hell of a time trying to get into heaven if them gates ain't open.

LYONS: [Putting his arm around GABRIEL.] You hear this, Pop. Uncle Gabe, you alright!

GABRIEL: [Laughing with LYONS.] Lyons! King of the Jungle.

ROSE: You gonna stay for supper, Gabe. Want me to fix you a plate?

GABRIEL: I'll take a sandwich, Rose. Don't want no plate. Just wanna eat with my hands. I'll take a sandwich.

ROSE: How about you, Lyons? You staying? Got some short ribs cooking.

LYONS: Naw, I won't eat nothing till after we finished playing. [Pause.] You ought to come down and listen to me play, Pop.

TROY: I don't like that Chinese music. All that noise.

ROSE: Go on in the house and wash up, Gabe . . . I'll fix you a sandwich.

GABRIEL: [*To* LYONS, *as he exits.*] Troy's mad at me.

LYONS: What you mad at Uncle Gabe for, Pop.

ROSE: He thinks Troy's mad at him cause he moved over to Miss Pearl's.

TROY: I ain't mad at the man. He can live where he want to live at.

LYONS: What he move over there for? Miss Pearl don't like nobody.

ROSE: She don't mind him none. She treats him real nice. She just don't allow all that singing.

TROY: She don't mind that rent he be paying . . . that's what she don't mind.

ROSE: Troy, I ain't going through that with you no more. He's over there cause he want to have his own place. He can come and go as he please.

TROY: Hell, he could come and go as he please here. I wasn't stopping him. I ain't put no rules on him.

ROSE: It ain't the same thing, Troy. And you know it. [GABRIEL *comes to the door.*] Now, that's the last I wanna hear about that. I don't wanna hear nothing else about Gabe and Miss Pearl. And next week . . .

GABRIEL: I'm ready for my sandwich, Rose.

ROSE: And next week . . . when that recruiter come from that school . . . I want you to sign that paper and go on and let Cory play football. Then that'll be the last I have to hear about that.

TROY: [*To* ROSE *as she exits into the house.*] I ain't thinking about Cory nothing.

LYONS: What . . . Cory got recruited? What school he going to?

TROY: That boy walking around here smelling his piss . . . thinking he's grown. Thinking he's gonna do what he want, irrespective of what I say. Look here, Bono . . . I left the Commissioner's office and went down to the A&P . . . that boy ain't working down there. He lying to me. Telling me he got his job back . . . telling me he working weekends . . . telling me he working after school . . . Mr. Stawicki tell me he ain't working down there at all!

LYONS: Cory just growing up. He's just busting at the seams trying to fill out your shoes.

TROY: I don't care what he's doing. When he get to the point where he wanna disobey me . . . then it's time for him to move on. Bono'll tell you that. I bet he ain't never disobeyed his daddy without paying the consequences.

BONO: I ain't never had a chance. My daddy came on through . . . but I ain't never knew him to see him . . . or what he had on his mind or where he went. Just moving on through. Searching out the New Land. That's what the old folks used to call it. See a fellow moving around from place to place . . . woman to woman . . . called it searching out the New Land. I can't say if he ever found it. I come along, didn't want no kids. Didn't know if I was gonna be in one place long enough to fix on them right as their daddy. I figured I was going searching too. As it turned out I been hooked up with Lucille near about as long as your daddy been with Rose. Going on sixteen years.

TROY: Sometimes I wish I hadn't known my daddy. My daddy ain't cared nothing about no kids. A kid to him wasn't nothing. All he wanted was for you to learn how to walk so he could start you to working. When it come time for eating . . . he ate first. If there was anything left over, that's what you got. Man would sit down and eat two chickens and give you the wing.

LYONS: You ought to stop that, Pop. Everybody feed their kids. No matter how hard times is . . . everybody care about their kids. Make sure they have something to eat.

TROY: The only thing my daddy cared about was getting them bales of cotton in to Mr. Lubin. That's the only thing that mattered to him. Sometimes I used to wonder why he was living. Wonder why the devil hadn't come and got him. "Get them bales of cotton in to Mr. Lubin" and find out he owe him money . . .

LYONS: He should have just went on and left when he saw he couldn't get nowhere. That's what I would have done.

TROY: How he gonna leave with eleven kids? And where he gonna go? He ain't knew how to do nothing but farm. No, he was trapped and I think he knew it. But I'll say this for him . . . he felt a responsibility toward us. Maybe he ain't treated us the way I felt he should have . . . but without that responsibility he could have walked off and left us . . . made his own way.

BONO: A lot of them did. Back in those days what you talking about . . . they walk out their front door and just take on down one road or another and keep on walking.

LYONS: There you go! That's what I'm talking about.

BONO: Just keep on walking till you come to something else. Ain't you never heard of nobody having the walking blues? Well, that's what you call it when you just take off like that.

TROY: My daddy ain't had them walking blues! What you talking about? He stayed right there with his family. But he was just as evil as he could be. My mama couldn't stand him. Couldn't stand that evilness. She run off when I was about eight. She sneaked off one night after he had gone to sleep. Told me she was coming back for me. I ain't never seen her no more. All his women run off and left him. He wasn't good for nobody. When my turn come to head out, I was fourteen and got to sniffing around Joe Canewell's daughter. Had us an old mule we called Greyboy. My daddy sent me out to do some plowing and I tied up Greyboy and went to fooling around with Joe Canewell's daughter. We done found us a nice little spot, got real cozy with each other. She about thirteen and we done figured we was grown anyway . . . so we down there enjoying ourselves . . . ain't thinking about nothing. We didn't know Greyboy had got loose and wandered back to the house and my daddy was looking for me. We down there by the creek enjoying ourselves when my daddy come up on us. Surprised us. He had them leather straps off the mule and commenced to whupping me like there was no tomorrow. I jumped up, mad and embarrassed. I was scared of my daddy. When he commenced to whupping on me . . . quite naturally I run to get out of the way. [Pause.] Now I thought he was mad cause I ain't done my work. But I see where he was chasing me off so he could have the gal for himself. When I see what the matter of it was, I lost all fear of my daddy.

Right there is where I become a man . . . at fourteen years of age. [*Pause.*]
Now it was my turn to run him off. I picked up them same reins that he had
used on me. I picked up them reins and commenced to whupping on him.
The gal jumped up and run off . . . and when my daddy turned to face me,
I could see why the devil had never come to get him . . . cause he was the
devil himself. I don't know what happened. When I woke up, I was laying
right there by the creek, and Blue . . . this old dog we had . . . was licking
my face. I thought I was blind. I couldn't see nothing. Both my eyes were
swollen shut. I layed there and cried. I didn't know what I was gonna do.
The only thing I knew was the time had come for me to leave my daddy's
house. And right there the world suddenly got big. And it was a long time
before I could cut it down to where I could handle it. Part of that cutting
down was when I got to the place where I could feel him kicking in my
blood and knew that the only thing that separated us was the matter of a few
years.

[GABRIEL *enters from the house with a sandwich.*]

LYONS: What you got there, Uncle Gabe?
GABRIEL: Got me a ham sandwich. Rose gave me a ham sandwich.
TROY: I don't know what happened to him. I done lost touch with everybody
except Gabriel. But I hope he's dead. I hope he found some peace.
LYONS: That's a heavy story, Pop. I didn't know you left home when you was
fourteen.
TROY: And didn't know nothing. The only part of the world I knew was the forty-
two acres of Mr. Lubin's land. That's all I knew about life.
LYONS: Fourteen's kinda young to be out on your own. [*Phone rings.*] I don't
even think I was ready to be out on my own at fourteen. I don't know what
I would have done.
TROY: I got up from the creek and walked on down to Mobile. I was through
with farming. Figured I could do better in the city. So I walked the two
hundred miles to Mobile.
LYONS: Wait a minute . . . you ain't walked no two hundred miles, Pop. Ain't
nobody gonna walk no two hundred miles. You talking about some walking
there.
BONO: That's the only way you got anywhere back in them days.
LYONS: Shhh. Damn if I wouldn't have hitched a ride with somebody!
TROY: Who you gonna hitch it with? They ain't had no cars and things like they
got now. We talking about 1918.
ROSE: [*Entering.*] What you all out here getting into?
TROY: [*To* ROSE.] I'm telling Lyons how good he got it. He don't know nothing
about this I'm talking.
ROSE: Lyons, that was Bonnie on the phone. She say you supposed to pick her
up.
LYONS: Yeah, okay, Rose.
TROY: I walked on down to Mobile and hitched up with some of them fellows

that was heading this way. Got up here and found out . . . not only couldn't you get a job . . . you couldn't find no place to live. I thought I was in freedom. Shhh. Colored folks living down there on the riverbanks in whatever kind of shelter they could find for themselves. Right down there under the Brady Street Bridge. Living in shacks made of sticks and tarpaper. Messed around there and went from bad to worse. Started stealing. First it was food. Then I figured, hell, if I steal money I can buy me some food. Buy me some shoes too! One thing led to another. Met your mama. I was young and anxious to be a man. Met your mama and had you. What I do that for? Now I got to worry about feeding you and her. Got to steal three times as much. Went out one day looking for somebody to rob . . . that's what I was, a robber. I'll tell you the truth. I'm ashamed of it today. But it's the truth. Went to rob this fellow . . . pulled out my knife . . . and he pulled out a gun. Shot me in the chest. It felt just like somebody had taken a hot branding iron and laid it on me. When he shot me I jumped at him with my knife. They tell me I killed him and they put me in the penitentiary and locked me up for fifteen years. That's where I met Bono. That's where I learned how to play baseball. Got out that place and your mama had taken you and went on to make life without me. Fifteen years was a long time for her to wait. But that fifteen years cured me of that robbing stuff. Rose'll tell you. She asked me when I met her if I had gotten all that foolishness out of my system. And I told her, "Baby, it's you and baseball all what count with me." You hear me, Bono? I meant it too. She say, "Which one comes first?" I told her, "Baby, there ain't no doubt it's baseball . . . but you stick and get old with me and we'll both outlive this baseball." Am I right, Rose? And it's true.

ROSE: Man, hush your mouth. You ain't said no such thing. Talking about, "Baby, you know you'll always be number one with me." That's what you was talking.

TROY: You hear that, Bono? That's why I love her.

BONO: Rose'll keep you straight. You get off the track, she'll straighten you up.

ROSE: Lyons, you better get on up and get Bonnie. She waiting on you.

LYONS: [Gets up to go.] Hey, Pop, why don't you come down to the Grill and hear me play?

TROY: I ain't going down there. I'm too old to be sitting around in them clubs.

BONO: You got to be good to play down at the Grill.

LYONS: Come on, Pop . . .

TROY: I got to get up in the morning.

LYONS: You ain't got to stay long.

TROY: Naw, I'm gonna get my supper and go on to bed.

LYONS: Well, I got to go. I'll see you again.

TROY: Don't you come around my house on my payday!

ROSE: Pick up the phone and let somebody know you coming. And bring Bonnie with you. You know I'm always glad to see her.

LYONS: Yeah, I'll do that, Rose. You take care now. See you, Pop. See you, Mr. Bono. See you, Uncle Gabe.

GABRIEL: Lyons! King of the Jungle!

[LYONS *exits.*]

TROY: Is supper ready, woman? Me and you got some business to take care of. I'm gonna tear it up too!

ROSE: Troy, I done told you now!

TROY: [*Puts his arm around* BONO.] Aw hell, woman . . . this is Bono. Bono like family. I done known this nigger since . . . how long I done know you?

BONO: It's been a long time.

TROY: I done known this nigger since Skippy was a pup. Me and him done been through some times.

BONO: You sure right about that.

TROY: Hell, I done know him longer than I known you. And we still standing shoulder to shoulder. Hey, look here, Bono . . . a man can't ask for no more than that. [*Drinks to him.*] I love you, nigger.

BONO: Hell, I love you too . . . but I got to get home see my woman. You got yours in hand. I got to go get mine.

[BONO *starts to exit as* CORY *enters the yard, dressed in his football uniform. He gives* TROY *a hard, uncompromising look.*]

CORY: What you do that for, Pop? [*He throws his helmet down in the direction of* TROY.]

ROSE: What's the matter? Cory . . . what's the matter?

CORY: Papa done went up to the school and told Coach Zellman I can't play football no more. Wouldn't even let me play the game. Told him to tell the recruiter not to come.

ROSE: Troy . . .

TROY: What you Troying me for. Yeah, I did it. And the boy know why I did it.

CORY: Why you wanna do that to me? That was the one chance I had.

ROSE: Ain't nothing wrong with Cory playing football, Troy.

TROY: The boy lied to me. I told the nigger if he wanna play football . . . to keep up his chores and hold down that job at the A&P. That was the conditions. Stopped down there to see Mr. Stawicki . . .

CORY: I can't work after school during the football season, Pop! I tried to tell you that Mr. Stawicki's holding my job for me. You don't never want to listen to nobody. And then you wanna go and do this to me!

TROY: I ain't done nothing to you. You done it to yourself.

CORY: Just cause you didn't have a chance! You just scared I'm gonna be better than you, that's all.

TROY: Come here.

ROSE: Troy . . .

[CORY *reluctantly crosses over to* TROY.]

TROY: Alright! See. You done made a mistake.

CORY: I didn't even do nothing!

TROY: I'm gonna tell you what your mistake was. See . . . you swung at the ball and didn't hit it. That's strike one. See, you in the batter's box now. You swung and you missed. That's strike one. Don't you strike out!

[*Lights fade to black.*]

ACT II

Scene 1

The following morning. CORY *is at the tree hitting the ball with the bat. He tries to mimic* TROY, *but his swing is awkward, less sure.* ROSE *enters from the house.*

ROSE: Cory, I want you to help me with this cupboard.

CORY: I ain't quitting the team. I don't care what Poppa say.

ROSE: I'll talk to him when he gets back. He had to go see about your Uncle Gabe. The police done arrested him. Say he was disturbing the peace. He'll be back directly. Come on in here and help me clean out the top of this cupboard. [CORY *exits into the house.* ROSE *sees* TROY *and* BONO *coming down the alley.*] Troy . . . what they say down there?

TROY: Ain't said nothing. I give them fifty dollars and they let him go. I'll talk to you about it. Where's Cory?

ROSE: He's in there helping me clean out these cupboards.

TROY: Tell him to get his butt out here.

[TROY *and* BONO *go over to the pile of wood.* BONO *picks up the saw and begins sawing.*]

TROY: [*To* BONO.] All they want is the money. That makes six or seven times I done went down there and got him. See me coming they stick out their hands.

BONO: Yeah, I know what you mean. That's all they care about . . . that money. They don't care about what's right. [*Pause.*] Nigger, why you got to go and get some hard wood? You ain't doing nothing but building a little old fence. Get you some soft pine wood. That's all you need.

TROY: I know what I'm doing. This is outside wood. You put pine wood inside the house. Pine wood is inside wood. This here is outside wood. Now you tell me where the fence is gonna be?

BONO: You don't need this wood. You can put it up with pine wood and it'll stand as long as you gonna be here looking at it.

TROY: How you know how long I'm gonna be here, nigger? Hell, I might just live forever. Live longer than old man Horsely.

BONO: That's what Magee used to say.

TROY: Magee's a damn fool. Now you tell me who you ever heard of gonna pull their own teeth with a pair of rusty pliers?

BONO: The old folks . . . my granddaddy used to pull his teeth with pliers. They ain't had no dentists for the colored folks back then.

TROY: Get clean pliers! You understand? Clean pliers! Sterilize them! Besides we ain't living back then. All Magee had to do was walk over to Doc Goldblums.

BONO: I see where you and that Tallahassee gal . . . that Alberta . . . I see where you all done got tight.

TROY: What you mean "got tight"?

BONO: I see where you be laughing and joking with her all the time.

TROY: I laughs and jokes with all of them, Bono. You know me.

BONO: That ain't the kind of laughing and joking I'm talking about.

[CORY *enters from the house.*]

CORY: How you doing, Mr. Bono?

TROY: Cory? Get that saw from Bono and cut some wood. He talking about the wood's too hard to cut. Stand back there, Jim, and let that young boy show you how it's done.

BONO: He's sure welcome to it. [CORY *takes the saw and begins to cut the wood.*] Whew-e-e! Look at that. Big old strong boy. Look like Joe Louis.[3] Hell, must be getting old the way I'm watching that boy whip through that wood.

CORY: I don't see why Mama want a fence around the yard noways.

TROY: Damn if I know either. What the hell she keeping out with it? She ain't got nothing nobody want.

BONO: Some people build fences to keep people out . . . and other people build fences to keep people in. Rose wants to hold on to you all. She loves you.

TROY: Hell, nigger, I don't need nobody to tell me my wife loves me, Cory . . . go on in the house and see if you can find that other saw.

CORY: Where's it at?

TROY: I said find it! Look for it till you find it! [CORY *exits into the house.*] What's that supposed to mean? Wanna keep us in?

BONO: Troy . . . I done known you seem like damn near my whole life. You and Rose both. I done know both of you all for a long time. I remember when you met Rose. When you was hitting them baseball out the park. A lot of them old gals was after you then. You had the pick of the litter. When you picked Rose, I was happy for you. That was the first time I knew you had any sense. I said . . . My man Troy knows what he's doing . . . I'm gonna follow this nigger . . . he might take me somewhere. I been following you too. I done learned a whole heap of things about life watching you. I done learned how to tell where the shit lies. How to tell it from the alfalfa. You done learned me a lot of things. You showed me how to not make the same mistakes . . . to take life as it comes along and keep putting one foot in front of the other. [*Pause.*] Rose a good woman, Troy.

TROY: Hell, nigger, I know she a good woman. I been married to her for eighteen years. What you got on your mind, Bono?

BONO: I just say she a good woman. Just like I say anything. I ain't got to have nothing on my mind.

---

3. Louis (1914–1981), boxing's world heavyweight champion from 1937 to 1949, achieved a level of fame and popularity previously unheard of for an African-American in the United States.

TROY: You just gonna say she a good woman and leave it hanging out there like that? Why you telling me she a good woman?

BONO: She loves you, Troy. Rose loves you.

TROY: You saying I don't measure up. That's what you trying to say. I don't measure up cause I'm seeing this other gal. I know what you trying to say.

BONO: I know what Rose means to you, Troy. I'm just trying to say I don't want to see you mess up.

TROY: Yeah, I appreciate that, Bono. If you was messing around on Lucille I'd be telling you the same thing.

BONO: Well, that's all I got to say. I just say that because I love you both.

TROY: Hell, you know me . . . I wasn't out there looking for nothing. You can't find a better woman than Rose. I know that. But seems like this woman just stuck onto me where I can't shake her loose. I done wrestled with it, tried to throw her off me . . . but she just stuck on tighter. Now she's stuck on for good.

BONO: You's in control . . . that's what you tell me all the time. You responsible for what you do.

TROY: I ain't ducking the responsibility of it. As long as it sets right in my heart . . . then I'm okay. Cause that's all I listen to. It'll tell me right from wrong every time. And I ain't talking about doing Rose no bad turn. I love Rose. She done carried me a long ways and I love and respect her for that.

BONO: I know you do. That's why I don't want to see you hurt her. But what you gonna do when she find out? What you got then? If you try and juggle both of them . . . sooner or later you gonna drop one of them. That's common sense.

TROY: Yeah, I hear what you saying, Bono. I been trying to figure a way to work it out.

BONO: Work it out right, Troy. I don't want to be getting all up between you and Rose's business . . . but work it so it come out right.

TROY: Aw hell, I get all up between you and Lucille's business. When you gonna get that woman that refrigerator she been wanting? Don't tell me you ain't got no money now. I know who your banker is. Mellon don't need that money bad as Lucille want that refrigerator. I'll tell you that.

BONO: Tell you what I'll do . . . when you finish building this fence for Rose . . . I'll buy Lucille that refrigerator.

TROY: You done stuck your foot in your mouth now! [TROY *grabs up a board and begins to saw.* BONO *starts to walk out the yard.*] Hey, nigger . . . where you going?

BONO: I'm going home. I know you don't expect me to help you now. I'm protecting my money. I wanna see you put that fence up by yourself. That's what I want to see. You'll be here another six months without me.

TROY: Nigger, you ain't right.

BONO: When it comes to my money . . . I'm right as fireworks on the Fourth of July.

TROY: Alright, we gonna see now. You better get out your bankbook.

[BONO *exits, and* TROY *continues to work.* ROSE *enters from the house.*]

ROSE: What they say down there? What's happening with Gabe?

TROY: I went down there and got him out. Cost me fifty dollars. Say he was disturbing the peace. Judge set up a hearing for him in three weeks. Say to show cause why he shouldn't be recommitted.

ROSE: What was he doing that cause them to arrest him?

TROY: Some kids was teasing him and he run them off home. Say he was howling and carrying on. Some folks seen him and called the police. That's all it was.

ROSE: Well, what's you say? What'd you tell the judge?

TROY: Told him I'd look after him. It didn't make no sense to recommit the man. He stuck out his big greasy palm and told me to give him fifty dollars and take him on home.

ROSE: Where's he at now? Where'd he go off to?

TROY: He's gone on about his business. He don't need nobody to hold his hand.

ROSE: Well, I don't know. Seem like that would be the best place for him if they did put him into the hospital. I know what you're gonna say. But that's what I think would be best.

TROY: The man done had his life ruined fighting for what? And they wanna take and lock him up. Let him be free. He don't bother nobody.

ROSE: Well, everybody got their own way of looking at it I guess. Come on and get your lunch. I got a bowl of lima beans and some cornbread in the oven. Come on get something to eat. Ain't no sense you fretting over Gabe. [ROSE *turns to go into the house.*]

TROY: Rose . . . got something to tell you.

ROSE: Well, come on . . . wait till I get this food on the table.

TROY: Rose! [*She stops and turns around.*] I don't know how to say this. [*Pause.*] I can't explain it none. It just sort of grows on you till it gets out of hand. It starts out like a little bush . . . and the next thing you know it's a whole forest.

ROSE: Troy . . . what are you talking about?

TROY: I'm talking, woman, let me talk. I'm trying to find a way to tell you . . . I'm gonna be a daddy. I'm gonna be somebody's daddy.

ROSE: Troy . . you're not telling me this? You're gonna be . . . what?

TROY: Rose . . . now . . . see . . .

ROSE: You telling me you gonna be somebody's daddy? You telling your *wife* this?

[GABRIEL *enters from the street. He carries a rose in his hand.*]

GABRIEL: Hey, Troy! Hey, Rose!

ROSE: I have to wait eighteen years to hear something like this.

GABRIEL: Hey, Rose . . . I got a flower for you. [*He hands it to her.*] That's a rose. Same rose like you is.

ROSE: Thanks, Gabe.

GABRIEL: Troy, you ain't mad at me is you? Them bad mens come and put me away. You ain't mad at me is you?

TROY: Naw, Gabe, I ain't mad at you.

ROSE: Eighteen years and you wanna come with this.

GABRIEL: [*Takes a quarter out of his pocket.*] See what I got? Got a brand new quarter.

TROY: Rose . . . it's just . . .

ROSE: Ain't nothing you can say, Troy. Ain't no way of explaining that.

GABRIEL: Fellow that give me this quarter had a whole mess of them. I'm gonna keep this quarter till it stop shining.

ROSE: Gabe, go on in the house there. I got some watermelon in the frigidaire. Go on and get you a piece.

GABRIEL: Say, Rose . . . you know I was chasing hellhounds and them bad mens come and get me and take me away. Troy helped me. He come down there and told them they better let me go before he beat them up. Yeah, he did!

ROSE: You go on and get you a piece of watermelon, Gabe. Them bad mens is gone now.

GABRIEL: Okay, Rose . . . gonna get me some watermelon. The kind with the stripes on it. [GABRIEL *exits into the house.*]

ROSE: Why, Troy? Why? After all these years to come dragging this in to me now. It don't make no sense at your age. I could have expected this ten or fifteen years ago, but not now.

TROY: Age ain't got nothing to do with it, Rose.

ROSE: I done tried to be everything a wife should be. Everything a wife could be. Been married eighteen years and I got to live to see the day you tell me you been seeing another woman and done fathered a child by her. And you know I ain't never wanted no half nothing in my family. My whole family is half. Everybody got different fathers and mothers . . . my two sisters and my brother. Can't hardly tell who's who. Can't never sit down and talk about Papa and Mama. It's your papa and your mama and my papa and my mama . . .

TROY: Rose . . . stop it now.

ROSE: I ain't never wanted that for none of my children. And now you wanna drag your behind in here and tell me something like this.

TROY: You ought to know. It's time for you to know.

ROSE: Well, I don't want to know, goddamn it!

TROY: I can't just make it go away. It's done now. I can't wish the circumstance of the thing away.

ROSE: And you don't want to either. Maybe you want to wish me and my boy away. Maybe that's what you want? Well, you can't wish us away. I've got eighteen years of my life invested in you. You ought to have stayed upstairs in my bed where you belong.

TROY: Rose . . . now listen to me . . . we can get a handle on this thing. We can talk this out . . . come to an understanding.

ROSE: All of a sudden it's "we." Where was "we" at when you was down there rolling around with some godforsaken woman? "We" should have come to an understanding before you started making a damn fool of yourself. You're a day late and a dollar short when it comes to an understanding with me.

TROY: It's just . . . She gives me a different idea . . . a different understanding about myself. I can step out of this house and get away from the pressures and problems . . . be a different man. I ain't got to wonder how I'm gonna pay the bills or get the roof fixed. I can just be a part of myself that I ain't never been.

ROSE: What I want to know . . . is do you plan to continue seeing her? That's all you can say to me.

TROY: I can sit up in her house and laugh. Do you understand what I'm saying. I can laugh out loud . . . and it feels good. It reaches all the way down to the bottom of my shoes. [*Pause.*] Rose, I can't give that up.

ROSE: Maybe you ought to go on and stay down there with her . . . if she a better woman than me.

TROY: It ain't about nobody being a better woman or nothing. Rose, you ain't the blame. A man couldn't ask for no woman to be a better wife than you've been. I'm responsible for it. I done locked myself into a pattern trying to take care of you all that I forgot about myself.

ROSE: What the hell was I there for? That was my job, not somebody else's.

TROY: Rose, I done tried all my life to live decent . . . to live a clean . . . hard . . . useful life. I tried to be a good husband to you. In every way I knew how. Maybe I come into the world backwards, I don't know. But . . . you born with two strikes on you before you come to the plate. You got to guard it closely . . . always looking for the curve-ball on the inside corner. You can't afford to let none get past you. You can't afford a call strike. If you going down . . . you going down swinging. Everything lined up against you. What you gonna do. I fooled them, Rose. I bunted. When I found you and Cory and a halfway decent job . . . I was safe. Couldn't nothing touch me. I wasn't gonna strike out no more. I wasn't going back to the penitentiary. I wasn't gonna lay in the streets with a bottle of wine. I was safe. I had me a family. A job. I wasn't gonna get that last strike. I was on first looking for one of them boys to knock me in. To get me home.

ROSE: You should have stayed in my bed, Troy.

TROY: Then, when I saw that gal . . . she firmed up my backbone. And I got to thinking that if I tried . . . I just might be able to steal second. Do you understand after eighteen years I wanted to steal second.

ROSE: You should have held me tight. You should have grabbed me and held on.

TROY: I stood on first base for eighteen years and I thought . . . well, goddamn it . . . go on for it!

ROSE: We're not talking about baseball! We're talking about you going off to lay in bed with another woman . . . and then bring it home to me. That's what we're talking about. We ain't talking about no baseball.

TROY: Rose, you're not listening to me. I'm trying the best I can to explain it to you. It's not easy for me to admit that I been standing in the same place for eighteen years.

ROSE: I been standing with you! I been right here with you, Troy. I got a life too. I gave eighteen years of my life to stand in the same spot with you. Don't you think I ever wanted other things? Don't you think I had dreams and hopes? What about my life? What about me? Don't you think it ever crossed my mind to want to know other men? That I wanted to lay up somewhere and forget about my responsibilities? That I wanted someone to make me laugh so I could feel good? You not the only one who's got wants and needs. But I held on to you, Troy. I took all my feelings, my wants and needs, my dreams . . . and I buried them inside you. I planted a seed and watched and prayed over it. I planted myself inside you and waited to bloom. And it didn't take me no eighteen years to find out the soil was hard and rocky and it wasn't never gonna bloom. But I held on to you, Troy. I held you tighter. You was my husband. I owed you everything I had. Every part of me I could find to give you. And upstairs in that room . . . with the darkness falling in on me . . . I gave everything I had to try and erase the doubt that you wasn't the finest man in the world. And wherever you was going . . . I wanted to be there with you. Cause you was my husband. Cause that's the only way I was gonna survive as your wife. You always talking about what you give . . . and what you don't have to give. But you take too. You take . . . and don't even know nobody's giving!

[ROSE *turns to exit into the house;* TROY *grabs her arm.*]

TROY: You say I take and don't give!
ROSE: Troy! You're hurting me!
TROY: You say I take and don't give!
ROSE: Troy . . . you're hurting my arm! Let go!
TROY: I done give you everything I got. Don't you tell that lie on me.
ROSE: Troy!
TROY: Don't you tell that lie on me!

[CORY *enters from the house.*]

CORY: Mama!
ROSE: Troy, you're hurting me.
TROY: Don't you tell me about no taking and giving.

[CORY *comes up behind* TROY *and grabs him.* TROY, *surprised, is thrown off balance just as* CORY *throws a glancing blow that catches him on the chest and knocks him down.* TROY *is stunned, as is* CORY.]

ROSE: Troy. Troy. No! [TROY *gets to his feet and starts at* CORY.] Troy . . . no. Please! Troy!

[ROSE *pulls on* TROY *to hold him back.* TROY *stops himself.*]

TROY: [*To* CORY.] Alright. That's strike two. You stay away from around me, boy. Don't you strike out. You living with a full count.[4] Don't you strike out.

[TROY *exits out the yard as the lights go down.*]

4. In baseball, a count of three balls and two strikes.

SCENE 2

It is six months later, early afternoon. TROY *enters from the house and starts to exit the yard.* ROSE *enters from the house.*

ROSE: Troy, I want to talk to you.

TROY: All of a sudden, after all this time, you want to talk to me, huh? You ain't wanted to talk to me for months. You ain't wanted to talk to me last night. You ain't wanted no part of me then. What you wanna talk to me about now?

ROSE: Tomorrow's Friday.

TROY: I know what day tomorrow is. You think I don't know tomorrow's Friday? My whole life I ain't done nothing but look to see Friday coming and you got to tell me it's Friday.

ROSE: I want to know if you're coming home.

TROY: I always come home, Rose. You know that. There ain't never been a night I ain't come home.

ROSE: That ain't what I mean . . . and you know it. I want to know if you're coming straight home after work.

TROY: I figure I'd cash my check . . . hang out at Taylors' with the boys . . . maybe play a game of checkers . . .

ROSE: Troy, I can't live like this. I won't live like this. You livin' on borrowed time with me. It's been going on six months now you ain't been coming home.

TROY: I be here every night. Every night of the year. That's 365 days.

ROSE: I want you to come home tomorrow after work.

TROY: Rose . . . I don't mess up my pay. You know that now. I take my pay and I give it to you. I don't have no money but what you give me back. I just want to have a little time to myself . . . a little time to enjoy life.

ROSE: What about me? When's my time to enjoy life?

TROY: I don't know what to tell you, Rose. I'm doing the best I can.

ROSE: You ain't been home from work but time enough to change your clothes and run out . . . and you wanna call that the best you can do?

TROY: I'm going over to the hospital to see Alberta. She went into the hospital this afternoon. Look like she might have the baby early. I won't be gone long.

ROSE: Well, you ought to know. They went over to Miss Pearl's and got Gabe today. She said you told them to go ahead and lock him up.

TROY: I ain't said no such thing. Whoever told you that telling a lie. Pearl ain't doing nothing but telling a big fat lie.

ROSE: She ain't had to tell me. I read it on the papers.

TROY: I ain't told them nothing of the kind.

ROSE: I saw it right there on the papers.

TROY: What it say, huh?

ROSE: It said you told them to take him.

TROY: Then they screwed that up, just the way they screw up everything. I ain't worried about what they got on the paper.

ROSE: Say the government send part of his check to the hospital and the other part to you.

TROY: I ain't got nothing to do with that if that's the way it works. I ain't made up the rules about how it work.

ROSE: You did Gabe just like you did Cory. You wouldn't sign the paper for Cory . . . but you signed for Gabe. You signed that paper.

[*The telephone is heard ringing inside the house.*]

TROY: I told you I ain't signed nothing, woman! The only thing I signed was the release form. Hell, I can't read, I don't know what they had on the paper! I ain't signed nothing about sending Gabe away.

ROSE: I said send him to the hospital . . . you said let him be free . . . now you done went down there and signed him to the hospital for half his money. You went back on yourself, Troy. You gonna have to answer for that.

TROY: See now . . . you been over there talking to Miss Pearl. She done got mad cause she ain't getting Gabe's rent money. That's all it is. She's liable to say anything.

ROSE: Troy, I seen where you signed the paper.

TROY: You ain't seen nothing I signed. What she doing got papers on my brother anyway? Miss Pearl telling a big fat lie. And I'm gonna tell her about it too! You ain't seen nothing I signed. Say . . . you ain't seen nothing I signed.

[ROSE *exits into the house to answer the telephone. Presently she returns.*]

ROSE: Troy . . . that was the hospital. Alberta had the baby.

TROY: What she have? What is it?

ROSE: It's a girl.

TROY: I better get on down to the hospital to see her.

ROSE: Troy . . .

TROY: Rose . . . I got to go see her now. That's only right . . . what's the matter . . . the baby's alright, ain't it?

ROSE: Alberta died having the baby.

TROY: Died . . . you say she's dead? Alberta's dead?

ROSE: They said they done all they could. They couldn't do nothing for her.

TROY: The baby? How's the baby?

ROSE: They say it's healthy. I wonder who's gonna bury her.

TROY: She had family, Rose. She wasn't living in the world by herself.

ROSE: I know she wasn't living in the world by herself.

TROY: Next thing you gonna want to know if she had any insurance.

ROSE: Troy, you ain't got to talk like that.

TROY: That's the first thing that jumped out your mouth. "Who's gonna bury her?" Like I'm fixing to take on that task for myself.

ROSE: I am your wife. Don't push me away.

TROY: I ain't pushing nobody away. Just give me some space. That's all. Just give me some room to breathe.

[ROSE *exits into the house.* TROY *walks about the yard.*]

TROY: [*With a quiet rage that threatens to consume him.*] Alright . . . Mr. Death. See now . . . I'm gonna tell you what I'm gonna do. I'm gonna take and build me a fence around this yard. See? I'm gonna build me a fence around what belongs to me. And then I want you to stay on the other side. See? You stay over there until you're ready for me. Then you come on. Bring your army. Bring your sickle. Bring your wrestling clothes. I ain't gonna fall down on my vigilance this time. You ain't gonna sneak up on me no more. When you ready for me . . . when the top of your list say Troy Maxson . . . that's when you come around here. You come up and knock on the front door. Ain't nobody else got nothing to do with this. This is between you and me. Man to man. You stay on the other side of that fence until you ready for me. Then you come up and knock on the front door. Anytime you want. I'll be ready for you.

[*The lights go down to black.*]

SCENE 3

The lights come up on the porch. It is late evening three days later. ROSE *sits listening to the ball game waiting for* TROY. *The final out of the game is made and* ROSE *switches off the radio.* TROY *enters the yard carrying an infant wrapped in blankets. He stands back from the house and calls.*

[ROSE *enters and stands on the porch. There is a long, awkward silence, the weight of which grows heavier with each passing second.*]

TROY: Rose . . . I'm standing here with my daughter in my arms. She ain't but a wee bittie little old thing. She don't know nothing about grownups' business. She innocent . . . and she ain't got no mama.

ROSE: What you telling me for, Troy? [*She turns and exits into the house.*]

TROY: Well . . . I guess we'll just sit out here on the porch. [*He sits down on the porch. There is an awkward indelicateness about the way he handles the baby. His largeness engulfs and seems to swallow it. He speaks loud enough for* ROSE *to hear.*] A man's got to do what's right for him. I ain't sorry for nothing I done. It felt right in my heart. [*To the baby.*] What you smiling at? Your daddy's a big man. Got these great big old hands. But sometimes he's scared. And right now your daddy's scared cause we sitting out here and ain't got no home. Oh, I been homeless before. I ain't had no little baby with me. But I been homeless. You just be out on the road by your lonesome and you see one of them trains coming and you just kinda go like this . . .

[*He sings as a lullaby.*]

> Please, Mr. Engineer let a man ride the line
> Please, Mr. Engineer let a man ride the line
> I ain't got no ticket please let me ride the blinds

[ROSE *enters from the house.* TROY *hearing her steps behind him, stands and faces her.*]

TROY: She's my daughter, Rose. My own flesh and blood. I can't deny her no
more than I can deny them boys. [*Pause.*] You and them boys is my family.
You and them and this child is all I got in the world. So I guess what I'm
saying is . . . I'd appreciate it if you'd help me take care of her.

ROSE: Okay, Troy . . . you're right. I'll take care of your baby for you . . . cause
. . . like you say . . . she's innocent . . . and you can't visit the sins of the father
upon the child. A motherless child has got a hard time. [*She takes the baby
from him.*] From right now . . . this child got a mother. But you a womanless
man.

[ROSE *turns and exits into the house with the baby. Lights go down to black.*]

Scene 4

It is two months later. LYONS *enters from the street. He knocks on the door and*
calls.

LYONS: Hey, Rose! [*Pause.*] Rose!

ROSE: [*From inside the house.*] Stop that yelling. You gonna wake up Raynell. I
just got her to sleep.

LYONS: I just stopped by to pay Papa this twenty dollars I owe him. Where's Papa
at?

ROSE: He should be here in a minute. I'm getting ready to go down to the
church. Sit down and wait on him.

LYONS: I got to go pick up Bonnie over her mother's house.

ROSE: Well, sit it down there on the table. He'll get it.

LYONS: [*Enters the house and sets the money on the table.*] Tell Papa I said
thanks. I'll see you again.

ROSE: Alright, Lyons. We'll see you.

[LYONS *starts to exit as* CORY *enters.*]

CORY: Hey, Lyons.

LYONS: What's happening, Cory. Say man, I'm sorry I missed your graduation.
You know I had a gig and couldn't get away. Otherwise, I would have been
there. So what you doing?

CORY: I'm trying to find a job.

LYONS: Yeah, I know how that go, man. It's rough out here. Jobs are scarce.

CORY: Yeah, I know.

LYONS: Look here, I got to run. Talk to Papa . . . he know some people. He'll be
able to help get you a job. Talk to him . . . see what he say.

CORY: Yeah . . . alright, Lyons.

LYONS: You take care. I'll talk to you soon. We'll find some time to talk.

[LYONS *exits the yard.* CORY *wanders over to the tree, picks up the bat and
assumes a batting stance. He studies an imaginary pitcher and swings. Dissatisfied with the result, he tries again.* TROY *enters. They eye each other for a beat.*
CORY *puts the bat down and exits the yard.* TROY *starts into the house as* ROSE
exits with RAYNELL. *She is carrying a cake.*]

TROY: I'm coming in and everybody's going out.

ROSE: I'm taking this cake down to the church for the bakesale. Lyons was by to see you. He stopped by to pay you your twenty dollars. It's laying in there on the table.

TROY: [Going into his pocket.] Well . . . here go this money.

ROSE: Put it in there on the table, Troy. I'll get it.

TROY: What time you coming back?

ROSE: Ain't no use in you studying me. It don't matter what time I come back.

TROY: I just asked you a question, woman. What's the matter . . . can't I ask you a question?

ROSE: Troy, I don't want to go into it. Your dinner's in there on the stove. All you got to do is heat it up. And don't you be eating the rest of them cakes in there. I'm coming back for them. We having a bakesale at the church tomorrow.

[ROSE exits the yard. TROY sits down on the steps, takes a pint bottle from his pocket, opens it, and drinks. He begins to sing.]

TROY: [Singing.]

> Hear it ring! Hear it ring!
> Had an old dog his name was Blue
> You know Blue was mighty true
> You know Blue as a good old dog
> Blue trees a possum in a hollow log
> You know from that he was a good old dog

[BONO enters the yard.]

BONO: Hey, Troy.

TROY: Hey, what's happening, Bono?

BONO: I just thought I'd stop by to see you.

TROY: What you stop by and see me for? You ain't stopped by in a month of Sundays. Hell, I must owe you money or something.

BONO: Since you got your promotion I can't keep up with you. Used to see you everyday. Now I don't even know what route you working.

TROY: They keep switching me around. Got me out in Greentree now . . . hauling white folks' garbage.

BONO: Greentree, huh? You lucky, at least you ain't got to be lifting them barrels. Damn if they ain't getting heavier. I'm gonna put in my two years and call it quits.

TROY: I'm thinking about retiring myself. How's Lucille?

BONO: You got it easy. You can *drive* for another five years.

TROY: It ain't the same, Bono. It ain't like working the back of the truck. Ain't got nobody to talk to . . . feel like you working by yourself. Naw, I'm thinking about retiring. How's Lucille?

BONO: She alright. Her arthritis get to acting up on her sometime. Saw Rose on my way in. She going down to the church, huh?

TROY: Yeah, she took up going down there. All them preachers looking for some-body to fatten their pockets. [*Pause.*] Got some gin here.

BONO: Naw, thanks. I just stopped by to say hello.

TROY: Hell, nigger . . . you can take a drink. I ain't never known you to say no to a drink. You ain't got to work tomorrow.

BONO: I just stopped by. I'm fixing to go over to Skinner's. We got us a domino game going over his house every Friday.

TROY: Nigger, you can't play no dominoes. I used to whup you four games out of five.

BONO: Well, that learned me. I'm getting better.

TROY: Yeah? Well, that's alright.

BONO: Look here . . . I got to be getting on. Stop by sometime, huh?

TROY: Yeah, I'll do that, Bono. Lucille told Rose you bought her a new refriger-ator.

BONO: Yeah, Rose told Lucille you had finally built your fence . . . so I figured we'd call it even.

TROY: I knew you would.

BONO: Yeah . . . okay. I'll be talking to you.

TROY: Yeah, take care, Bono. Good to see you. I'm gonna stop over.

BONO: Yeah. Okay, Troy.

[BONO *exits.* TROY *drinks from the bottle.*]

TROY: [*Singing.*]

> Old Blue died and I dig his grave
> Let him down with a golden chain
> Every night when I hear old Blue bark
> I know Blue treed a possum in Noah's Ark.
> Hear it ring! Hear it ring!

[CORY *enters the yard. They eye each other for a beat.* TROY *is sitting in the middle of the steps.* CORY *walks over.*]

CORY: I got to get by.

TROY: Say what? What's you say?

CORY: You in my way. I got to get by.

TROY: You got to get by where? This is my house. Bought and paid for. In full. Took me fifteen years. And if you wanna go in my house and I'm sitting on the steps . . . you say excuse me. Like your mama taught you.

CORY: Come on, Pop . . . I got to get by.

[CORY *starts to maneuver his way past* TROY. TROY *grabs his leg and shoves him back.*]

TROY: You just gonna walk over top of me?

CORY: I live here too!

TROY: [*Advancing toward him.*] You just gonna walk over top of me in my own house?

CORY: I ain't scared of you.

TROY: I ain't asked if you was scared of me. I asked you if you was fixing to walk over top of me in my own house? That's the question. You ain't gonna say excuse me? You just gonna walk over top of me?

CORY: If you wanna put it like that.

TROY: How else am I gonna put it?

CORY: I was walking by you to go into the house cause you sitting on the steps drunk, singing to yourself. You can put it like that.

TROY: Without saying excuse me?? [CORY *doesn't respond.*] I asked you a question. Without saying excuse me??

CORY: I ain't got to say excuse me to you. You don't count around here no more.

TROY: Oh, I see . . . I don't count around here no more. You ain't got to say excuse me to your daddy. All of a sudden you done got so grown that your daddy don't count around here no more . . . Around here in his own house and yard that he done paid for with the sweat of his brow. You done got so grown to where you gonna take over. You gonna take over my house. Is that right? You gonna wear my pants. You gonna go in there and stretch out on my bed. You ain't got to say excuse me cause I don't count around here no more. Is that right?

CORY: That's right. You always talking this dumb stuff. Now, why don't you just get out my way.

TROY: I guess you got someplace to sleep and something to put in your belly. You got that, huh? You got that? That's what you need. You got that, huh?

CORY: You don't know what I got. You ain't got to worry about what I got.

TROY: You right! You one hundred percent right! I done spent the last seventeen years worrying about what you got. Now it's your turn, see? I'll tell you what you do. You grown . . . we done established that. You a man. Now, let's see you act like one. Turn your behind around and walk out this yard. And when you get out there in the alley . . . you can forget about this house. See? Cause this is my house. You go on and be a man and get your own house. You can forget about this. 'Cause this is mine. You go on and get yours cause I'm through with doing for you.

CORY: You talking about what you did for me . . . what'd you ever give me?

TROY: Them feet and bones! That pumping heart nigger! I give you more than anybody else is ever gonna give you.

CORY: You ain't never gave me nothing! You ain't never done nothing but hold me back. Afraid I was gonna be better than you. All you ever did was try and make me scared of you. I used to tremble every time you called my name. Every time I heard your footsteps in the house. Wondering all the time . . . what's Papa gonna say if I do this? . . . What's he gonna say if I do that? . . . what's Papa gonna say if I turn on the radio? And Mama, too . . . she tries . . . but she's scared of you.

TROY: You leave your mama out of this. She ain't got nothing to do with this.

CORY: I don't know how she stand you . . . after what you did to her.

TROY: I told you to leave your mama out of this! [*He advances toward* CORY.]

CORY: What you gonna do . . . give me a whupping? You can't whup me no more. You're too old. You just an old man.

TROY: [*Shoves him on his shoulder.*] Nigger! That's what you are. You just another nigger on the street to me!

CORY: You crazy! You know that?

TROY: Go on now! You got the devil in you. Get on away from me!

CORY: You just a crazy old man . . . talking about I got the devil in me.

TROY: Yeah, I'm crazy! If you don't get on the other side of that yard . . . I'm gonna show you how crazy I am! Go on . . . get the hell out of my yard.

CORY: It ain't your yard. You took Uncle Gabe's money he got from the army to buy this house and then you put him out.

TROY: [TROY *advances on* CORY.] Get your black ass out of my yard!

[TROY's *advance backs* CORY *up against the tree.* CORY *grabs up the bat.*]

CORY: I ain't going nowhere! Come on . . . put me out! I ain't scared of you.

TROY: That's my bat!

CORY: Come on!

TROY: Put my bat down!

CORY: Come on, put me out. [CORY *swings at* TROY, *who backs across the yard.*] What's the matter? You so bad . . . put me out!

[TROY *advances toward* CORY.]

CORY: [*Backing up.*] Come on! Come on!

TROY: You're gonna have to use it! You wanna draw that bat back on me . . . you're gonna have to use it.

CORY: Come on! . . . Come on!

[CORY *swings the bat at* TROY *a second time. He misses.* TROY *continues to advance toward him.*]

TROY: You're gonna have to kill me! You wanna draw that bat back on me. You're gonna have to kill me.

[CORY, *backed up against the tree, can go no farther.* TROY *taunts him. He sticks out his head and offers him a target.*]

TROY: Come on! Come on!

[CORY *is unable to swing the bat.* TROY *grabs it.*]

TROY: Then I'll show you.

[CORY *and* TROY *struggle over the bat. The struggle is fierce and fully engaged.* TROY *ultimately is the stronger, and takes the bat from* CORY *and stands over him ready to swing. He stops himself.*]

TROY: Go on and get away from around my house.

[CORY, *stung by his defeat, picks himself up, walks slowly out of the yard and up the alley.*]

CORY: Tell Mama I'll be back for my things.

TROY: They'll be on the other side of that fence.

[CORY *exits.*]

TROY: I can't taste nothing. Helluljah! I can't taste nothing no more. [TROY *assumes a batting posture and begins to taunt Death, the fastball on the outside corner.*] Come on! It's between you and me now! Come on! Anytime you want! Come on! I be ready for you . . . but I ain't gonna be easy.

[*The lights go down on the scene.*]

SCENE 5

The time is 1965. The lights come up in the yard. It is the morning of TROY's *funeral. A funeral plaque with a light hangs beside the door. There is a small garden plot off to the side. There is noise and activity in the house as* ROSE, LYONS *and* BONO *have gathered. The door opens and* RAYNELL, *seven years old, enters dressed in a flannel nightgown. She crosses to the garden and pokes around with a stick.* ROSE *calls from the house.*

ROSE: Raynell!

RAYNELL: Mam?

ROSE: What you doing out there?

RAYNELL: Nothing.

[ROSE *comes to the door.*]

ROSE: Girl, get in here and get dressed. What you doing?

RAYNELL: Seeing if my garden growed.

ROSE: I told you it ain't gonna grow overnight. You got to wait.

RAYNELL: It don't look like it never gonna grow. Dag!

ROSE: I told you a watched pot never boils. Get in here and get dressed.

RAYNELL: This ain't even no pot, Mama.

ROSE: You just have to give it a chance. It'll grow. Now you come on and do what I told you. We got to be getting ready. This ain't no morning to be playing around. You hear me?

RAYNELL: Yes, mam.

[ROSE *exits into the house.* RAYNELL *continues to poke at her garden with a stick.* CORY *enters. He is dressed in a Marine corporal's uniform, and carries a duffel bag. His posture is that of a military man, and his speech has a clipped sternness.*]

CORY: [*To* RAYNELL.] Hi. [*Pause.*] I bet your name is Raynell.

RAYNELL: Uh huh.

CORY: Is your mama home?

[RAYNELL *runs up on the porch and calls through the screendoor.*]

RAYNELL: Mama . . . there's some man out here. Mama?

[ROSE *comes to the door.*]

ROSE: Cory? Lord have mercy! Look here, you all! [ROSE *and* CORY *embrace in a tearful reunion as* BONO *and* LYONS *enter from the house dressed in funeral clothes.*]

BONO: Aw, looka here . . .

ROSE: Done got all grown up!

CORY: Don't cry, Mama. What you crying about?

ROSE: I'm just so glad you made it.

CORY: Hey Lyons. How you doing, Mr. Bono.

[LYON *goes to embrace* CORY.]

LYONS: Look at you, man. Look at you. Don't he look good, Rose. Got them Corporal stripes.

ROSE: What took you so long.

CORY: You know how the Marines are, Mama. They got to get all their paperwork straight before they let you do anything.

ROSE: Well, I'm sure glad you made it. They let Lyons come. Your Uncle Gabe's still in the hospital. They don't know if they gonna let him out or not. I just talked to them a little while ago.

LYONS: A Corporal in the United States Marines.

BONO: Your daddy knew you had it in you. He used to tell me all the time.

LYONS: Don't he look good, Mr. Bono?

BONO: Yeah, he remind me of Troy when I first met him. [*Pause.*] Say, Rose, Lucille's down at the church with the choir. I'm gonna go down and get the pallbearers lined up. I'll be back to get you all.

ROSE: Thanks, Jim.

CORY: See you, Mr. Bono.

LYONS: [*With his arm around* RAYNELL.] Cory . . . look at Raynell. Ain't she precious? She gonna break a whole lot of hearts.

ROSE: Raynell, come and say hello to your brother. This is your brother, Cory. You remember Cory.

RAYNELL: No, Mam.

CORY: She don't remember me, Mama.

ROSE: Well, we talk about you. She heard us talk about you. [*To* RAYNELL.] This is your brother, Cory. Come on and say hello.

RAYNELL: Hi.

CORY: Hi. So you're Raynell. Mama told me a lot about you.

ROSE: You all come on into the house and let me fix you some breakfast. Keep up your strength.

CORY: I ain't hungry, Mama.

LYONS: You can fix me something, Rose. I'll be in there in a minute.

ROSE: Cory, you sure you don't want nothing. I know they ain't feeding you right.

CORY: No, Mama . . . thanks. I don't feel like eating. I'll get something later.

ROSE: Raynell . . . get on upstairs and get that dress on like I told you.

[ROSE *and* RAYNELL *exit into the house.*]

LYONS: So . . . I hear you thinking about getting married.

CORY: Yeah, I done found the right one, Lyons. It's about time.

LYONS: Me and Bonnie been split up about four years now. About the time Papa retired. I guess she just got tired of all them changes I was putting her through. [*Pause.*] I always knew you was gonna make something out yourself. Your head was always in the right direction. So . . . you gonna stay in . . . make it a career. . . put in your twenty years?

CORY: I don't know. I got six already, I think that's enough.

LYONS: Stick with Uncle Sam and retire early. Ain't nothing out here. I guess Rose told you what happened with me. They got me down the workhouse. I thought I was being slick cashing other people's checks.

CORY: How much time you doing?

LYONS: They give me three years. I got that beat now. I ain't got but nine more months. It ain't so bad. You learn to deal with it like anything else. You got to take the crookeds with the straights. That's what Papa used to say. He used to say that when he struck out. I seen him strike out three times in a row . . . and the next time up he hit the ball over the grandstand. Right out there in Homestead Field. He wasn't satisfied hitting in the seats . . . he want to hit it over everything! After the game he had two hundred people standing around waiting to shake his hand. You got to take the crookeds with the straights. Yeah, Papa was something else.

CORY: You still playing?

LYONS: Cory . . . you know I'm gonna do that. There's some fellows down there we got us a band . . . we gonna try and stay together when we get out . . . but yeah, I'm still playing. It still helps me to get out of bed in the morning. As long as it do that I'm gonna be right there playing and trying to make some sense out of it.

ROSE: [*Calling.*] Lyons, I got these eggs in the pan.

LYONS: Let me go on and get these eggs, man. Get ready to go bury Papa. [*Pause.*] How you doing? You doing alright?

[CORY *nods.* LYONS *touches him on the shoulder and they share a moment of silent grief.* LYONS *exits into the house.* CORY *wanders about the yard.* RAYNELL *enters.*]

RAYNELL: Hi.

CORY: Hi.

RAYNELL: Did you used to sleep in my room?

CORY: Yeah . . . that used to be my room.

RAYNELL: That's what Papa call it. "Cory's room." It got your football in the closet.

[ROSE *comes to the door.*]

ROSE: Raynell, get in there and get them good shoes on.

RAYNELL: Mama, can't I wear these. Them other one hurt my feet.

ROSE: Well, they just gonna have to hurt your feet for a while. You ain't said they hurt your feet when you went down to the store and got them.

RAYNELL: They didn't hurt then. My feet done got bigger.

ROSE: Don't you give me no backtalk now. You get in there and get them shoes on. [RAYNELL *exits into the house.*] Ain't too much changed. He still got that piece of rag tied to that tree. He was out here swinging that bat. I was just ready to go back in the house. He swung that bat and then he just fell over. Seem like he swung it and stood there with this grin on his face . . . and then he just fell over. They carried him on down to the hospital, but I knew there wasn't no need . . . why don't you come on in the house?

CORY: Mama . . . I got something to tell you. I don't know how to tell you this . . . but I've got to tell you . . . I'm not going to Papa's funeral.

ROSE: Boy, hush your mouth. That's your daddy you talking about. I don't want hear that kind of talk this morning. I done raised you to come to this? You standing there all healthy and grown talking about you ain't going to your daddy's funeral?

CORY: Mama . . . listen . . .

ROSE: I don't want to hear it, Cory. You just get that thought out of your head.

CORY: I can't drag Papa with me everywhere I go. I've got to say no to him. One time in my life I've got to say no.

ROSE: Don't nobody have to listen to nothing like that. I know you and your daddy ain't seen eye to eye, but I ain't got to listen to that kind of talk this morning. Whatever was between you and your daddy . . . the time has come to put it aside. Just take it and set it over there on the shelf and forget about it. Disrespecting your daddy ain't gonna make you a man, Cory. You got to find a way to come to that on your own. Not going to your daddy's funeral ain't gonna make you a man.

CORY: The whole time I was growing up . . . living in his house . . . Papa was like a shadow that followed you everywhere. It weighed on you and sunk into your flesh. It would wrap around you and lay there until you couldn't tell which one was you anymore. That shadow digging in your flesh. Trying to crawl in. Trying to live through you. Everywhere I looked, Troy Maxson was staring back at me . . . hiding under the bed . . . in the closet. I'm just saying I've got to find a way to get rid of that shadow, Mama.

ROSE: You just like him. You got him in you good.

CORY: Don't tell me that, Mama.

ROSE: You Troy Maxson all over again.

CORY: I don't want to be Troy Maxson. I want to be me.

ROSE: You can't be nobody but who you are, Cory. That shadow wasn't nothing but you growing into yourself. You either got to grow into it or cut it down to fit you. But that's all you got to make life with. That's all you got to measure yourself against that world out there. Your daddy wanted you to be everything he wasn't . . . and at the same time he tried to make you into everything he was. I don't know if he was right or wrong . . . but I do know he meant to do more good than he meant to do harm. He wasn't always right. Sometimes when he touched he bruised. And sometimes when he took me in his arms he cut. When I first met your daddy I thought . . . Here is a man I can lay down with and make a baby. That's the first thing I thought when I seen him. I was thirty years old and had done seen my share of men. But when he walked up to me and said, "I can dance a waltz that'll make you dizzy," I thought, Rose Lee, here is a man that you can open yourself up to and be filled to bursting. Here is a man that can fill all them empty spaces you been tipping around the edges of. One of them empty spaces was being somebody's mother. I married your daddy and settled down to cooking his supper and keeping clean sheets on the bed. When your daddy walked through the house he was so big he filled it up. That was my first mistake. Not to make him leave some room for me. For my part in the matter. But at that time I wanted that. I wanted a house that I could sing in. And that's what your daddy gave me. I didn't know to keep up his strength I had to give up little pieces of mine. I did that. I took on his life as mine and mixed up the pieces so that you couldn't hardly tell which was which anymore. It was my choice. It was my life and I didn't have to live it like that. But that's what life offered me in the way of being a woman, and I took it. I grabbed hold of it with both hands. By the time Raynell came into the house, me and your daddy had done lost touch with one another. I didn't want to make my blessing off of nobody's misfortune . . . but I took on to Raynell like she was all them babies I had wanted and never had. [*The phone rings.*] Like I'd been blessed to relive a part of my life. And if the Lord see fit to keep up my strength . . . I'm gonna do her just like your daddy did you . . . I'm gonna give her the best of what's in me.

RAYNELL: [*Entering, still with her old shoes.*] Mama . . . Reverend Tollivier on the phone.

[ROSE *exits into the house.*]

RAYNELL: Hi.
CORY: Hi.
RAYNELL: You in the Army or the Marines?
CORY: Marines.
RAYNELL: Papa said it was the Army. Did you know Blue?
CORY: Blue? Who's Blue?
RAYNELL: Papa's dog what he sing about all the time.

CORY: [*Singing.*]

Hear it ring! hear it ring!
I had a dog his name was Blue
You know Blue was mighty true
You know Blue was a good old dog
Blue treed a possum in a hollow log
You know from that he was a good old dog.
Hear it ring! Hear it ring!

[RAYNELL *joins in singing.*]

[CORY *and* RAYNELL]

Blue treed a possum out on a limb
Blue looked at me and I looked at him
Grabbed that possum and put him in a sack
Blue stayed there till I came back
Old Blue's feets was big and round
Never allowed a possum to touch the ground.

Old Blue died and I dug his grave
I dug his grave with a silver spade
Let him down with a golden chain
And every night I call his name
Go on Blue, you good dog you
Go on Blue, you good dog you

[RAYNELL]

Blue laid down and died like a man
Blue laid down and died . . .

[BOTH]

Blue laid down and died like a man
Now he's treeing possums in the Promised Land
I'm gonna tell you this to let you know
Blue's gone where the good dogs go
When I hear old Blue bark
When I heard old Blue bark
Blue treed a possum in Noah's Ark
Blue treed a possum in Noah's Ark.

[ROSE *comes to the screen door.*]

ROSE: Cory, we gonna be ready to go in a minute.
CORY: [*To* RAYNELL.] You go on in the house and change them shoes like Mama
told you so we can go to papa's funeral.
RAYNELL: Okay, I'll be right back.

[RAYNELL *exits into the house.* CORY *gets up and crosses over to the tree.* ROSE
stands in the screen door watching him. GABRIEL *enters from the alley.*]

GABRIEL: [*Calling.*] Hey, Rose!
ROSE: Gabe?
GABRIEL: I'm here, Rose. Hey Rose, I'm here!

[ROSE *enters from the house.*]

ROSE: Lord . . . Look here, Lyons!
LYONS: See, I told you, Rose . . . I told you they'd let him come.
CORY: How you doing, Uncle Gabe?

LYONS: How you doing, Uncle Gabe?

GABRIEL: Hey, Rose. It's time. It's time to tell St. Peter to open the gates. Troy, you ready? You ready, Troy. I'm gonna tell St. Peter to open the gates. You get ready now.

[GABRIEL, *with great fanfare, braces himself to blow. The trumpet is without a mouthpiece. He puts the end of it into his mouth and blows with great force, like a man who has been waiting some twenty-odd years for this single moment. No sound comes out of the trumpet. He braces himself and blows again with the same result. A third time he blows. There is a weight of impossible description that falls away and leaves him bare and exposed to a frightful realization. It is a trauma that a sane and normal mind would be unable to withstand. He begins to dance. A slow, strange dance, eerie and life-giving. A dance of atavistic signature and ritual.* LYONS *attempts to embrace him.* GABRIEL *pushes* LYONS *away. He begins to howl in what is an attempt at song, or perhaps a song turning back into itself in an attempt at speech. He finishes his dance and the gates of heaven stand open as wide as God's closet.*]

GABRIEL: That's the way that go!

BLACKOUT

1986

▼   ▼   ▼

QUESTIONS

Blood Relations

1. What does the stage direction mean in asserting, at the beginning, that ". . . with the exception of THE ACTRESS and MISS LIZZIE (and EMMA in the final scene), all characters are imaginary . . ."?

2. Explain the relationship between the time frames of 1892 and 1902. In what ways does the play show its consciousness of having been written almost 90 years after the deaths took place? What effects in the play depend on the reader's (or audience's) distance from the historical events?

3. Given the uncertainties of time and identity in *Blood Relations*, it is not always easy to know exactly what the "facts" are. How do you get your bearings in the play? How do you *know* what really happened? What authority do you trust here?

Fences

1. How many meanings does the title take on in the course of the play? If you were staging the play, what strategies of staging and lighting would you use

to highlight the visual suggestions of the title? How finished or permanent would you make the fence seem? What other aspects of setting help to set up the major themes of the play?

2. Which characters in the play seem to you the most sympathetic? What devices of characterization make their distinctive individualities clear? What strategies are used to make them sympathetic? How sympathetic is Troy?

3. Examine carefully the play's attitudes toward the male characters as a group and toward the female characters. Does the play take a stand on gendered behaviors? Does more blame seem to be placed on one gender or the other?

4. In what specific ways do the values and habits of the white world impinge on the characters? What attitude does the play take toward white behavior and white institutions?

WRITING SUGGESTIONS

Blood Relations

1. With the help of a reference librarian, discover as many facts as you can about the actual episode involving Lizzie Borden, her trial, and daily life in the town in which Lizzie lived. Which events in the play are based on accepted historical "facts"? What things in the play seem invented purposely to distort or contradict "historical facts"? For what purpose?

2. How does the play reveal the character of Lizzie Borden—her values, desires, motivations? Write an essay on the characterization of Lizzie in *Blood Relations* in which you show what is revealed when and make clear what aspects of her life and character are left ambiguous.

Fences

1. Like the other plays of August Wilson, *Fences* seems to be very much about conflicts and continuities between generations. Write a four- or five-page essay on the theme of generations in *Fences*, showing the various manifestations of generational influence that the play features. How powerful, according to the play, is tradition from generation to generation? How powerful is generational rebellion?

2. In the reference department of your college library, look up Satchel Paige, and find out as much as you can about his career in the Negro League before he moved to "organized baseball." How long did he pitch in the

majors? How old was he on his last appearance in the majors? Look up the roster for the world-champion Milwaukee Braves in 1957, and check the records of black players on that team. What additional ironies does Troy's attitude bear in the light of that particular baseball year?

3. According to this play, how do people free themselves from the power of the past? Write a three- or four-page interpretive essay in which you show how the play resolves the question of the tyranny of the past.

4. According to the play, who is responsible for the kinds of difficulties faced by Troy and his family? Write an interpretive essay in which you show how the play investigates themes of responsibility and causality.

Evaluating Drama

H ow can you tell if a play is good? Why are some plays said to be
"great"? On what grounds are plays like *Hamlet* or *Oedipus the King*
agreed to be so important that they are performed, season after season, in place after place, for hundreds or thousands of years? Why do actors try
to build reputations on playing classic parts—like Ophelia or Hamlet, Hedda
Gabler or Willy Loman—rather than staking their careers on new plays or less
famous roles? Who decides that a particular play is that important? Why do
people continue to buy and read some plays over and over while others die on
the shelf or never get printed at all? Is there a qualitative difference between
"great" and "good," or between "good" and "satisfactory," or are such distinctions subjective, arbitrary, or accidental? What criteria are useful in trying to
assess the literary or dramatic quality of a play? What other kinds of values—
political, cultural, social, moral, or ideological—are relevant in judging plays?

These questions are important ones, but the answers are not always easy.
Even intelligent, knowledgeable, and well-meaning people do not always agree
about matters of pleasure, importance, or quality. Besides, judgments vary from
age to age and culture to culture, and plays judged highly in one time and
place do not necessarily hold their reputations later and elsewhere. Some plays
are better when read and some better when performed. Some are effective in
some ways, ineffective in others. It is not easy to develop a logical, consistent,
and useful set of criteria that will automatically sort plays into the great, the
good, the indifferent, and the bad, and it is not clear that such a system would
be a good idea even if it were workable. Systems that try to be "timeless"
quickly discover that times do change and that both cultural and historical considerations do influence "objective" judgments in ways that cannot always be
understood, let alone predicted.

Still, quality is not an irrelevant consideration, and if judgments are sometimes difficult and frustrating, they are also inevitable. We all judge all the
time, and the question is whether we try to judge on some reasonable basis

that we can communicate to others or whether we settle for gut feelings and first impressions. Evaluating is not, of course, something that only critics or experts do. We all do it all the time, often from the moment a curtain goes up or we read the opening words of a text. Timing can, in fact, be a major issue, for sometimes we are tempted to evaluate too fast, before we have appropriate grounds for deciding. We may be confident in our likes and dislikes and feel that we are entitled to make a judgment right away, but haste can be a problem if we go on inadequate or inaccurate information. We might, for example, decide from the moment that Willy Loman makes his first speech in *Death of a Salesman* that we just don't like him. We might decide quickly that he is too pathetic, self-pitying, whiny, inconsistent, and confused for our taste. And that could turn out to be a good judgment. But some crucial questions need to be confronted before a final judgment is made. Is his first appearance misleading, and will we like him better later if we stay tuned? Are his unattractive qualities part of the point? Are his weaknesses a crucial part of the plot, a way of suggesting complexity of character, or developing the play's structural conflicts, or setting up its themes? Seeing the implications of the way we respond to Willy and relating them to the total play add up to an evaluation, but the initial feelings might not, in themselves, represent the total evaluation.

Still, most evaluation does begin with feelings, and first impressions are not to be ignored. At the very least, our feelings and impressions—even when they are not fully thought through or rationalized—are guides to responses. And, finally, our own feelings are all—or nearly all—we have, at least to begin with. But feelings and impressions may be modified by clear thinking about various issues, and feelings can sometimes be educated to become more sensitive. Besides, whether it is feelings or thoughts that lead us to like or admire (or despise or distrust) a particular work, sorting out the reasons is a useful part of learning to read effectively and resonantly.

Before we cast our first impressions in cement we need to finish reading the play and think back on its parts—character, structure, theme—to see how they relate, to see the play as a whole. Discovering a play's wholeness—its fundamental direction and thrust—is not of course an easy matter. In fact, it is impossible to do all at once. But you have been learning, in this course, how to think carefully about wholeness by looking systematically at parts, and in fact you can readily apply the kinds of issues brought up chapter by chapter in this book to get at some sense of the whole, as Chapter 3 attempts to do. Ask yourself about the play's themes; the way it conceives character and how it defines, reveals, and values individual characters; the kinds of conflicts that are developed and resolved; the responses the play achieves. How well are the parts or elements put together? Your considered evaluation—the one you are willing to stand behind, at least for the moment—involves first of all close reading and a careful analysis of the relationship of parts to the whole.

Let's go back to the issue of first impressions and the character of Willy Loman in *Death of a Salesman*. Willy is plainly the central figure in the play. The title suggests that it is his death—and the kind of life that leads to it—that the play is about. Willy's inability to cope with his problems, from the very first moment of the play when he returns home from a disastrous sales trip, is the focus of almost all the action. We learn quickly that his mental and emotional health is in jeopardy, that he is failing as a salesman, that he likes to think that he is successful and very well liked but that he is increasingly aware that his notions of himself do not match well with reality. His image of himself as a father and husband is similarly fraught with contradiction: his "boys"—now grown men—have no jobs, no directions for their lives, no prospects of success, and no clear values. What they really believe in is pleasure to be achieved without personal effort or developed skills, and their disappointment promises to become as disastrous as Willy's. And Willy's marriage, haunted by trivial on-the-road episodes that sound like dramatizations of conventional jokes about traveling salesmen, is characterized by pain and disillusionment too. Willy, for all his bluff and hot air, is a disappointment to himself in all parts of his life, and the text leads us to be judgmental about a number of aspects of Willy's behavior—his bad fathering, his self-delusion, his philandering, his nostalgia for the past that repeatedly keeps him from facing problems in the present. It is his character that seems central to the play's focus and effect—do we despise him or pity him for his flaws?—and the themes of dream and disillusion play themselves out in relation to his career and his life.

Structurally, the play reveals Willy's character through a combination of present incident and flashbacks to the past. We actually "see" much of Willy's failure, and "watch" the various dramatic ironies that underscore the loss of the dream—for example, the flashback to the woman in Hartford to whom Willy gives nylon stockings (rare and expensive in the years just after World War II), framed by two scenes in which Linda is mending old hosiery. And the repeated juxtaposition of scenes involving Willy's dreams and ambitions with those involving his compromises and failures dramatizes over and over both his fallings short and the reasons behind them.

The theme of responsibility or blame seems closely related to questions of character that the play highlights from the first scene onward, so that, in one sense, the play seems to be, like *Hedda Gabler*, primarily an examination of character. But the play also articulates some larger questions of responsibility, asking whether Willy is fully responsible for himself and implying (also as in *Hedda Gabler*) that societal values may have in part made Willy who he is. "Nobody dast blame this man," Charley insists after his death. Is he just being sentimental at such a moment? Is he unwilling to accept Willy's flaws for what they are? Is he as a character unable to understand the implications of individual behavior, or is his understanding superior to that of others (including us as readers) who find Willy culpable for his own misery? Are people like Uncle Ben—more consistent, more focused in their goals, more ruthless—to be preferred to the impressionable and trusting Willy, who seems to believe what he has been told about how life works, about dreams of success, about the values that are appreciated in American society? What are we ultimately to make of unquestioned conventional values and the way society tells us that ordinary people should live? How does what we believe about individual responsibility and social forces influence our judgment of the play? How do the questions raised by the play influence our beliefs?

Questions about how to read Charley's eulogy come close to the center of the play's meaning, and we will return in a moment to the implications of such questions for an evaluation of the total play. But first let's review the issues of evaluation growing out of the analysis of character that we have been discussing. We might expect a character to be consistent, but Willy is not. (There are several striking passages early on that you might cite as evidence—when, for example, Willy accuses Biff of being "a lazy bum" and only two lines later says, "There's one thing about Biff—he's not lazy"; or when, a little later in Act I, he calls Chevrolet "the greatest car ever built" and a few moments later rails against "that goddam Chevrolet, they ought to prohibit the manufacture of the car!") Yet Willy is convincing, for, if we think about it, most people we know are *not* consistent. In that respect, Willy is more realistic than mere consistency would make him. In the case of Willy, then, if we do not leap too immediately to a first impression, we evaluate not the consistency of character, but the consistency of characterization—how fully and how well does the play portray Willy's inconsistency? And we might wish to ask quite a variety of questions about Willy's characterization. How clear is the presentation of inconsistency? How well does what Willy says establish his character? Are they things someone like him might really say and not just words put in his mouth to illustrate a point? What other facets of Willy's character are related to his inconsistency, and are they all fully integrated into some total portrait of a person who then seems both whole (a fully portrayed or "three-dimensional" character) and representative (someone we recognize as like actual human beings we have seen or know about)? Does the sequence of events in the presentation of character make sense? Do the scenes illustrate the character and persuade us that Willy is actually like that? Do they succeed in developing a certain attitude—hatred, sympathy, contempt—toward him? Do we care about his existence and have an interest in his fate? Are we clearer, for reading the play, about what makes human beings act the way they do?

Evaluative questions almost tumble over one another once you begin to raise them in a particular category. You could ask similar questions about other characters in the play—about consistency and effectiveness, about meaning, about relationship to other characters, to the play's total effect and theme—and you could ask related questions about structure and the way the play works out, and presents, the plot and stage action in order to render theme and idea into feeling and effect. How carefully is Willy's character differentiated from that of other characters? And you could raise questions of functionality about minor characters and small incidents: What does Uncle Ben do for the play? How does the character of Bernard work to clarify other characters and further the play's theme? Why is the woman from Boston introduced into the play?

Careful evaluation always takes us back to the text to look for evidence and to an examination of our own values and beliefs. It is important to accumulate that evidence to answer individual questions you might raise and to examine the evidence thoughtfully. One important reason for such care is that it helps us mediate between rational considerations and emotional ones. Both are important, for plays are neither logical syllogisms nor structures of pure feeling, and we respond to them not as robots or pure bundles of passion, but as human beings who both feel and think. Let us return to Charley's eulogy for Willy to see if we can sort out what the issues are in how we read—and evaluate—his statement of nonblame.

Death of a Salesman has now held the stage for more than forty years, and both audiences and readers have come to regard it as a "classic" American play. Hundreds of thousands of people seem to have been moved by it, moved enough to pay money to see or read it and to advise others to do so as well. What do they see in it? We cannot know the answer for every single viewer or reader. We can, however, get some idea by listening to what issues they repeatedly argue about. One that has surfaced most frequently has to do with Charley's evaluation of Willy. Do we agree with him? Should we? Does Arthur Miller agree? Does the text of the play offer a clear answer, or is the indeterminacy of the text crucial to the play's continued popularity and success?

Again, the issue of evaluation comes down to questions of consistency and inconsistency, though this time of a different kind. Is the statement that Willy cannot be blamed for his fate consistent with the play's portrayal of him and its presentation of questions of cause and effect? We have looked enough at the characterization here to say with certainty that Willy is presented as having made important mistakes: he has not always been a good role model for his sons, he has been an unfaithful husband, he deludes himself about his likability and his ambition, he vacillates in what he thinks about important issues, he sometimes seems to hold strong traditional values (about the wrongness of stealing, for example) and sometimes he seems to wink at violations of these values. But how fully is he responsible? How much of his attitude derives from a shared sense of how life works, of what is rewarded in an economy of salesmanship and being well liked, of what American culture is about? To discuss the issue intelligently, we have to consider not only the question of why Charley lets Willy off the hook but whether the whole play does. Is the play about personal responsibility or about societal influence? How well and how clearly does the play makes its point? Does the play divide the responsibility between individual and society? How effective is it in making us face questions of value and questions of responsibility? Answering such questions takes us back once again deep into the language of the play and forces us to examine not only what Willy says but how he says it, how often he seems to be echoing some master language of the culture. And relevant too are the languages of other characters in the play—Linda, Biff, Hap, Bernard, Uncle Ben, Howard. Do they all speak the language of value? Are they all subject to some larger system of determined values to which they can only respond with some limited individuality? How does the question of individuality and characterization relate to Charley's assertion about blame and to the larger cause-effect themes of the play?

Evaluation may be closely related to interpretation: if you believe the play says that society is to blame but you yourself believe this is a dodge of personal responsibility, of morality, you may not like the play. If you agree about what the play says and agree *with* what it says you may like the play. There is even another possibility. You may believe in either society's or the individual's responsibility but recognize that there are those who believe otherwise, that the issue is complex, that the best presentation of the issue is such that it can be read either way.

Even though evaluation may ultimately depend on highly subjective judgments and good readers may reasonably differ from each other, questions of evaluation are very close to analytical questions, and determining meaning and effect takes you very quickly to questions of value. And vice versa. Often asking questions about how good a play is will get you closer to questions of what it is about and of what you value than you may at first be aware. Questions of value are not, finally, of a different order from other questions that help us read more carefully and enjoyably, and evaluation is not only an understandable outcome of reading texts but an integral part of the process of reading itself.

Samuel Johnson, the most respected arbiter of taste in England in the late eighteenth century, said that "nothing can please many and please long but just representations of general nature." Johnson was trying to explain why Shakespeare had continued to charm readers and playgoers for a century and a half, and what he says is both a common-sense argument about actual responses to texts (based on consensus and durability) and a proposition about what literature has to say about reality. Good literature, says Johnson, accurately reflects patterns that exist across culture and time; to last, literature must have something important ("just") to say about what does not change from time to time or place to place ("general nature"). Plays last, says Johnson, when they accurately portray what human nature is like, the way things are, the universals that transcend the interests of individuals and local times and places.

Not everyone in Johnson's own time agreed that such a universal standard could be found, and in the enlarged and varied world of cultural relativity of the late twentieth century, fewer still believe that any universals exist. Still, his point is an interesting one even for relativists. We still want to believe that literature can teach us something, that it has a vision of reality from which we can learn, and even if we do not expect universal plots and characters that assure us that life and times are ever the same, we continue to expect representations of reality that we can recognize as related to our own. The accuracy of that representation (its "just"-ness, in Johnson's terms) is likely to remain important; we want our playwrights to know the world and be able to represent it faithfully, and we are apt to want the representation to be enough like our own world for it to seem in some sense applicable. We are interested in people in other times and other cultures primarily because their experiences, even in other circumstances, have some potential analogy to us. We want a playwright's sense of reality—of what the world is like, and how people will behave—to be similar enough to our own that our own world will seem clearer after reading about the one represented in the play.

A play like A Midsummer Night's Dream may not at first seem to be of a kind that can be evaluated according to Johnson's test, for the characters, the plot, and the language of the play all are fairly strange by "normal," "realistic" standards. Johnson himself, in fact, wrote some fairly critical things about the play, objecting especially to the way Shakespeare combines the fairy mythology of one historical period with the court world of an entirely different age, though he did finally approve—and enjoy—the "wild, Fantastical. . . ." Certainly, there is plenty in the play to like—the hijinks of Puck, the romantic plot at court with its solvable complications, the lunkish physical comedy of the mechanic players, the verbal wit in line after line, the memorable (and by now famous and familiar) lines about the "course of true love" that plainly state the play's theme, the careful and lively presentation of a wide variety of characters, the ingenious plotting, the engaging resolution of human conflicts. It is easy to find good, solid textual evidence that would enable us to analyze, and praise, the conception and presentation of characters, the effective and appropriate uses of language to delineate characters and further plot and theme, and the careful interlocking of the several plots and the three entirely different sets of characters. But what about the question of whether the play represents some recognizable reality that we can relate to in a sympathetic way? What are we to think of a world that presents royal lovers alongside simple laborers trying to mount a theatrical production and that then mixes in a magical group of fairies? Is this a mix from which we are likely to garner useful knowledge about what life is like?

Whether a text accurately represents human life, behavior, and conversation as we know it is often very important to readers. We want to think about the probable, if not necessarily the real, and often we want to feel that we are learning about the way the world works, what people are like, what kinds of stories other people are involved in. We do not necessarily expect to find ourselves in other people's stories, but we expect to find recognizable people. They do not have to be "universal" in the way that Johnson seems to imply— we have to believe that all times, places, and people are pretty much alike to regard literature as representational—but they need to represent people we can understand in predicaments we can sympathize with.

But how can we "understand" or "sympathize with" a cast of characters comprising a duke and a queen impatient to marry each other, a set of clumsy would-be actors who are really a carpenter, a weaver, a bellows-mender, a tinker, a joiner, and a tailor, and—of another order altogether—fairies with their own king and queen? If it is a little hard to relate to the first pair of characters because of their high position, the middle group (at least as Shakespeare presents them) seems as difficult because their position is too low: even in our most awkward and most unself-possessed moments we are not likely to "identify" with figures like these. As for the third group, watching fairies at work and play around their court seems an unlikely way to find human "representation."

In this play, however, representation comes to mean something else: the play openly operates as fantasy, and the three different worlds that seem impossible to conceive on the same stage all ultimately become so tangled up with each other—and in such creative and entertaining ways—that we have the illusion of complicated conflicts and relationships being worked out across whole orders of being. To ask whether we have ever seen anyone in the real world who resembles Puck would be to ask, for this play, the wrong question. A key to seeing what is going on in this play is flexibility in applying standards and terms—even so basic a standard and term as representation. Ultimately, many readers feel that they *are* represented by the characters in A *Midsummer Night's Dream*, not because they resemble some one character in the play but because the play gives us insights into human aspiration and the pleasures and perils of romantic love in a social class or order of beings. Not all discovery in literature is solemn and high-minded; some is odd and unpredictable and full of belly laughs.

Questions about evaluation are ultimately questions about what values we share and with whom. Some readers will find it easier to appreciate—and like—a world like that of A *Midsummer Night's Dream* than will others. Sometimes, values shared throughout a whole culture or an entire age determine how a text will be received and evaluated; sometimes the sharing involves smaller, more local or more select groups—people of a particular political persuasion, or of a certain social class, or of a certain age or ethnic group, or those with common religious or philosophical beliefs. To some extent your values are determined by your community, but if you are strong enough you can choose your group by choosing your values, in your readings as in your social and political life.

Evaluations of some features of plays—of whether language is used precisely or effectively, for example, or whether characters are presented consistently and winningly—may sometimes seem almost value-free. Can't we decide such issues without regard to our social, economic, religious, or political biases and presuppositions? The answer seems to be that what we bring to a text, and where we bring it from, is likely to influence our judgment at every point. But the fact that our judgments are both highly subjective—subject to our individual biases and preferences—and influenced by the ideologies and cultural identities we participate in does not mean that evaluation is predetermined and beyond discussion or change. The more we read, the more conscious we are of how literary meaning and effect are conditioned by the text, the more aware we are of what we believe and why, of what we bring to a text. We are therefore more open to other influences. The better we can articulate our values and adduce evidence from the text, the more we will be able to learn, to grow, and to teach. For we may have to bring our values into discussion in class and papers to try to convince—and be convinced.

Agreeing about the quality of a play is not ultimately the point. You may never convince someone else that a particular play is as good (or bad) as you think it to be. And you may never be convinced by the arguments of someone else. But having discussions about quality has virtues of its own. The grounds of judgment are ultimately more important than the judgment of any single play, and argument helps clarify the grounds of judgment. Knowing your own grounds of judgment may make a play more enjoyable and meaningful to you; certainly it will make you more aware of who you are as a reader and as a person, and allow you to grow.

▼   ▼   ▼

ARTHUR MILLER

Death of a Salesman

CERTAIN PRIVATE CONVERSATIONS IN
TWO ACTS AND A REQUIEM

CHARACTERS

WILLY LOMAN	UNCLE BEN
LINDA	HOWARD WAGNER
BIFF	JENNY
HAPPY	STANLEY
BERNARD	MISS FORSYTHE
THE WOMAN	LETTA
CHARLEY	

The action takes place in WILLY LOMAN's *house and yard and in various places he visits in the New York and Boston of today.*

ACT I

A melody is heard, playing upon a flute. It is small and fine, telling of grass and trees and the horizon. The curtain rises.

Before us is the Salesman's house. We are aware of towering, angular shapes behind it, surrounding it on all sides. Only the blue light of the sky falls upon the house and forestage; the surrounding area shows an angry flow of orange. As more light appears, we see a solid vault of apartment houses around the small, fragile-seeming home. An air of the dream clings to the place, a dream rising out of reality. The kitchen at center seems actual enough, for there is a kitchen table with three chairs, and a refrigerator. But no other fixtures are seen. At the back of the kitchen there is a draped entrance, which leads to the living-room. To the right of the kitchen, on a level raised two feet, is a bedroom furnished only with a brass bedstead and a straight chair. On a shelf over the bed a silver athletic trophy stands. A window opens onto the apartment house at the side.

Behind the kitchen, on a level raised six and a half feet, is the boys' bedroom, at present barely visible. Two beds are dimly seen, and at the back of the room a dormer window. (This bedroom is above the unseen living-room.) At the left a stairway curves up to it from the kitchen.

The entire setting is wholly or, in some places, partially transparent. The roof-line of the house is one-dimensional; under and over it we see the apartment buildings. Before the house lies an apron, curving beyond the forestage into the orchestra. This forward area serves as the back yard as well as the locale of all WILLY's *imaginings and of his city scenes. Whenever the action is in the present the actors observe the imaginary wall-lines, entering the house only through its door at the left. But in the scenes of the past these boundaries are broken, and characters enter or leave a room by stepping "through" a wall onto the forestage.*

From the right, WILLY LOMAN, *the Salesman, enters, carrying two large sample cases. The flute plays on. He hears but is not aware of it. He is past sixty years of age, dressed quietly. Even as he crosses the stage to the doorway of the house, his exhaustion is apparent. He unlocks the door, comes into the kitchen, and thankfully lets his burden down, feeling the soreness of his palms. A word-sigh escapes his lips—it might be "Oh, boy, oh, boy." He closes the door, then carries his cases out into the living-room, through the draped kitchen doorway.*

LINDA, *his wife, has stirred in her bed at the right. She gets out and puts on a robe, listening. Most often jovial, she has developed an iron repression of her exceptions to* WILLY's *behavior—she more than loves him, she admires him, as though his mercurial nature, his temper, his massive dreams and little cruelties, served her only as sharp reminders of the turbulent longings within him, longings which she shares but lacks the temperament to utter and follow to their end.*

LINDA: [*Hearing* WILLY *outside the bedroom, calls with some trepidation.*] Willy!

WILLY: It's all right. I came back.

LINDA: Why? What happened? [*Slight pause.*] Did something happen, Willy?

WILLY: No, nothing happened.

LINDA: You didn't smash the car, did you?

WILLY: [*With casual irritation.*] I said nothing happened. Didn't you hear me?

LINDA: Don't you feel well?

WILLY: I'm tired to the death. [*The flute has faded away. He sits on the bed beside her, a little numb.*] I couldn't make it. I just couldn't make it, Linda.

LINDA: [*Very carefully, delicately.*] Where were you all day? You look terrible.

WILLY: I got as far as a little above Yonkers. I stopped for a cup of coffee. Maybe it was the coffee.

LINDA: What?

WILLY: [*After a pause.*] I suddenly couldn't drive any more. The car kept going off onto the shoulder, y'know?

LINDA: [*Helpfully.*] Oh. Maybe it was the steering again. I don't think Angelo knows the Studebaker.

WILLY: No, it's me, it's me. Suddenly I realize I'm goin' sixty miles an hour and

I don't remember the last five minutes. I'm—I can't seem to—keep my mind to it.

LINDA: Maybe it's your glasses. You never went for your new glasses.

WILLY: No, I see everything. I came back ten miles an hour. It took me nearly four hours from Yonkers.

LINDA: [Resigned.] Well, you'll just have to take a rest, Willy, you can't continue this way.

WILLY: I just got back from Florida.

LINDA: But you didn't rest your mind. Your mind is overactive, and the mind is what counts, dear.

WILLY: I'll start out in the morning. Maybe I'll feel better in the morning. [She is taking off his shoes.] These goddam arch supports are killing me.

LINDA: Take an aspirin. Should I get you an aspirin? It'll soothe you.

WILLY: [With wonder.] I was driving along, you understand? And I was fine. I was even observing the scenery. You can imagine, me looking at scenery, on the road every week of my life. But it's so beautiful up there, Linda, the trees are so thick, and the sun is warm. I opened the windshield and just let the warm air bathe over me. And then all of a sudden I'm goin' off the road! I'm tellin' ya, I absolutely forgot I was driving. If I'd've gone the other way over the white line I might've killed somebody. So I went on again—and five minutes later I'm dreamin' again, and I nearly—[He presses two fingers against his eyes.] I have such thoughts, I have such strange thoughts.

LINDA: Willy, dear. Talk to them again. There's no reason why you can't work in New York.

WILLY: They don't need me in New York. I'm the New England man. I'm vital in New England.

LINDA: But you're sixty years old. They can't expect you to keep traveling every week.

WILLY: I'll have to send a wire to Portland. I'm supposed to see Brown and Morrison tomorrow morning at ten o'clock to show the line. Goddammit, I could sell them! [He starts putting on his jacket.]

LINDA: [Taking the jacket from him.] Why don't you go down to the place tomorrow and tell Howard you've simply got to work in New York? You're too accommodating, dear.

WILLY: If old man Wagner was alive I'da been in charge of New York now! That man was a prince, he was a masterful man. But that boy of his, that Howard, he don't appreciate. When I went north the first time, the Wagner Company didn't know where New England was!

LINDA: Why don't you tell those things to Howard, dear?

WILLY: [Encouraged.] I will, I definitely will. Is there any cheese?

LINDA: I'll make you a sandwich.

WILLY: No, go to sleep. I'll take some milk. I'll be up right away. The boys in?

LINDA: They're sleeping. Happy took Biff on a date tonight.

WILLY: [Interested.] That so?

LINDA: It was so nice to see them shaving together, one behind the other, in the bathroom. And going out together. You notice? The whole house smells of shaving lotion.

WILLY: Figure it out. Work a lifetime to pay off a house. You finally own it, and there's nobody to live in it.

LINDA: Well, dear, life is a casting off. It's always that way.

WILLY: No, no, some people—some people accomplish something. Did Biff say anything after I went this morning?

LINDA: You shouldn't have criticized him, Willy, especially after he just got off the train. You mustn't lose your temper with him.

WILLY: When the hell did I lose my temper? I simply asked him if he was making any money. Is that a criticism?

LINDA: But, dear, how could he make any money?

WILLY: [Worried and angered.] There's such an undercurrent in him. He became a moody man. Did he apologize when I left this morning?

LINDA: He was crestfallen, Willy. You know how he admires you. I think if he finds himself, then you'll both be happier and not fight any more.

WILLY: How can he find himself on a farm? Is that a life? A farmhand? In the beginning, when he was young, I thought, well, a young man, it's good for him to tramp around, take a lot of different jobs. But it's more than ten years now and he has yet to make thirty-five dollars a week!

LINDA: He's finding himself, Willy.

WILLY: Not finding yourself at the age of thirty-four is a disgrace!

LINDA: Shh!

WILLY: The trouble is he's lazy, goddammit!

LINDA: Willy, please!

WILLY: Biff is a lazy bum!

LINDA: They're sleeping. Get something to eat. Go on down.

WILLY: Why did he come home? I would like to know what brought him home.

LINDA: I don't know. I think he's still lost, Willy. I think he's very lost.

WILLY: Biff Loman is lost. In the greatest country in the world a young man with such—personal attractiveness, gets lost. And such a hard worker. There's one thing about Biff—he's not lazy.

LINDA: Never.

WILLY: [With pity and resolve.] I'll see him in the morning; I'll have a nice talk with him. I'll get him a job selling. He could be big in no time. My God! Remember how they used to follow him around in high school? When he smiled at one of them their faces lit up. When he walked down the street . . . [He loses himself in reminiscences.]

LINDA: [Trying to bring him out of it.] Willy, dear, I got a new kind of American-type cheese today. It's whipped.

WILLY: Why do you get American when I like Swiss?

LINDA: I just thought you'd like a change—

WILLY: I don't want a change! I want Swiss cheese. Why am I always being contradicted?

LINDA: [With a covering laugh.] I thought it would be a surprise.

WILLY: Why don't you open a window in here, for God's sake?

LINDA: [*With infinite patience.*] They're all open, dear.

WILLY: The way they boxed us in here. Bricks and windows, windows and bricks.

LINDA: We should've bought the land next door.

WILLY: The street is lined with cars. There's not a breath of fresh air in the neighborhood. The grass don't grow any more, you can't raise a carrot in the back yard. They should've had a law against apartment houses. Remember those two beautiful elm trees out there? When I and Biff hung the swing between them?

LINDA: Yeah, like being a million miles from the city.

WILLY: They should've arrested the builder for cutting those down. They massacred the neighborhood. [*Lost.*] More and more I think of those days, Linda. This time of year it was lilac and wisteria. And then the peonies would come out, and the daffodils. What fragrance in this room!

LINDA: Well, after all, people had to move somewhere.

WILLY: No, there's more people now.

LINDA: I don't think there's more people. I think—

WILLY: There's more people! That's what ruining this country! Population is getting out of control. The competition is maddening! Smell the stink from that apartment house! And another one on the other side . . . How can they whip cheese?

[*On* WILLY's *last line,* BIFF *and* HAPPY *raise themselves up in their beds, listening.*]

LINDA: Go down, try it. And be quiet.

WILLY: [*Turning to* LINDA, *guiltily.*] You're not worried about me, are you, sweetheart?

BIFF: What's the matter?

HAPPY: Listen!

LINDA: You've got too much on the ball to worry about.

WILLY: You're my foundation and my support, Linda.

LINDA: Just try to relax, dear. You make mountains out of mole-hills.

WILLY: I won't fight with him any more. If he wants to go back to Texas, let him go.

LINDA: He'll find his way.

WILLY: Sure. Certain men just don't get started till later in life. Like Thomas Edison, I think. Or B. F. Goodrich. One of them was deaf. [*He starts for the bedroom doorway.*] I'll put my money on Biff.

LINDA: And Willy—if it's warm Sunday we'll drive in the country. And we'll open the windshield, and take lunch.

WILLY: No, the windshields don't open on the new cars.

LINDA: But you opened it today.

WILLY: Me? I didn't. [*He stops.*] Now isn't that peculiar! Isn't that a remarkable— [*He breaks off in amazement and fright as the flute is heard distantly.*]

LINDA: What, darling?

WILLY: That is the most remarkable thing.

LINDA: What, dear?

WILLY: I was thinking of the Chevvy. [*Slight pause.*] Nineteen twenty-eight . . . when I had that red Chevvy— [*Breaks off.*] That funny? I coulda sworn I was driving that Chevvy today.

LINDA: Well, that's nothing. Something must've reminded you.

WILLY: Remarkable. *Ts.* Remember those days? The way Biff used to simonize that car? The dealer refused to believe there was eighty thousand miles on it. [*He shakes his head.*] Heh! [*To* LINDA.] Close your eyes, I'll be right up. [*He walks out of the bedroom.*]

HAPPY: [*To* BIFF.] Jesus, maybe he smashed up the car again!

LINDA: [*Calling after* WILLY.] Be careful on the stairs, dear! The cheese is on the middle shelf! [*She turns, goes over to the bed, takes his jacket, and goes out of the bedroom.*]

[*Light has risen on the boys' room. Unseen,* WILLY *is heard talking to himself,* "Eighty thousand miles," *and a little laugh.* BIFF *gets out of bed, comes downstage a bit, and stands attentively.* BIFF *is two years older than his brother* HAPPY, *well built, but in these days bears a worn air and seems less self-assured. He has succeeded less, and his dreams are stronger and less acceptable than* HAPPY's. HAPPY *is tall, powerfully made. Sexuality is like a visible color on him, or a scent that many women have discovered. He, like his brother, is lost, but in a different way, for he has never allowed himself to turn his face toward defeat and is thus more confused and hard-skinned, although seemingly more content.*]

HAPPY: [*Getting out of bed.*] He's going to get his license taken away if he keeps that up. I'm getting nervous about him, y'know, Biff?

BIFF: His eyes are going.

HAPPY: No, I've driven with him. He sees all right. He just doesn't keep his mind on it. I drove into the city with him last week. He stops at a green light and then it turns red and he goes. [*He laughs.*]

BIFF: Maybe he's color-blind.

HAPPY: Pop? Why he's got the finest eye for color in the business. You know that.

BIFF: [*Sitting down on his bed.*] I'm going to sleep.

HAPPY: You're not still sour on Dad, are you Biff?

BIFF: He's all right, I guess.

WILLY: [*Underneath them, in the living-room.*] Yes, sir, eighty thousand miles— eighty-two thousand!

BIFF: You smoking?

HAPPY: [*Holding out a pack of cigarettes.*] Want one?

BIFF: [*Taking a cigarette.*] I can never sleep when I smell it.

WILLY: What a simonizing job, heh!

HAPPY: [*With deep sentiment.*] Funny, Biff, y'know? Us sleeping in here again? The old beds. [*He pats his bed affectionately.*] All the talk that went across those two beds, huh? Our whole lives.

BIFF: Yeah. Lotta dreams and plans.

HAPPY: [*With a deep and masculine laugh.*] About five hundred women would like to know what was said in this room.

[*They share a soft laugh.*]

BIFF: Remember that big Betsy something—what the hell was her name—over on Bushwick Avenue?

HAPPY: [*Combing his hair.*] With the collie dog!

BIFF: That's the one. I got you in there, remember?

HAPPY: Yeah, that was my first time—I think. Boy, there was a pig! [*They laugh, almost crudely.*] You taught me everything I know about women. Don't forget that.

BIFF: I bet you forgot how bashful you used to be. Especially with girls.

HAPPY: Oh, I still am, Biff.

BIFF: Oh, go on.

HAPPY: I just control it, that's all. I think I got less bashful and you got more so. What happened, Biff? Where's the old humor, the old confidence? [*He shakes* BIFF's *knee.* BIFF *gets up and moves restlessly about the room.*] What's the matter?

BIFF: Why does Dad mock me all the time?

HAPPY: He's not mocking you, he—

BIFF: Everything I say there's a twist of mockery on his face. I can't get near him.

HAPPY: He just wants you to make good, that's all. I wanted to talk to you about Dad for a long time, Biff. Something's—happening to him. He—talks to himself.

BIFF: I noticed that this morning. But he always mumbled.

HAPPY: But not so noticeable. It got so embarrassing I sent him to Florida. And you know something? Most of the time he's talking to you.

BIFF: What's he say about me?

HAPPY: I can't make it out.

BIFF: What's he say about me?

HAPPY: I think the fact that you're not settled, that you're still kind of up in the air. . . .

BIFF: There's one or two things depressing him, Happy.

HAPPY: What do you mean?

BIFF: Never mind. Just don't lay it all to me.

HAPPY: But I think if you just got started—I mean—is there any future for you out there?

BIFF: I tell ya, Hap, I don't know what the future is. I don't know—what I'm supposed to want.

HAPPY: What do you mean?

BIFF: Well, I spent six or seven years after high school trying to work myself up. Shipping clerk, salesman, business of one kind or another. And it's a measly manner of existence. To get on that subway on the hot mornings in summer. To devote your whole life to keeping stock, or making phone calls, or selling or buying. To suffer fifty weeks of the year for the sake of a two-week vacation, when all you really desire is to be outdoors, with your shirt off. And always to have to get ahead of the next fella. And still—that's how you build a future.

HAPPY: Well, you really enjoy it on a farm? Are you content out there?

BIFF: [*With rising agitation.*] Hap, I've had twenty or thirty different kinds of jobs since I left home before the war, and it always turns out the same. I just realized it lately. In Nebraska when I herded cattle, and the Dakotas, and Arizona, and now in Texas. It's why I came home now, I guess, because I realized it. This farm I work on, it's spring there now, see? And they've got about fifteen new colts. There's nothing more inspiring or—beautiful than the sight of a mare and a new colt. And it's cool there now, see? Texas is cool now, and it's spring. And whenever spring comes to where I am, I suddenly get the feeling, my God, I'm not gettin' anywhere! What the hell am I doing, playing around with horses, twenty-eight dollars a week! I'm thirty-four years old. I oughta be makin' my future. That's when I come running home. And now, I get there, and I don't know what to do with myself. [*After a pause.*] I've always made a point of not wasting my life, and everytime I come back here I know that all I've done is to waste my life.

HAPPY: You're a poet, you know that, Biff? You're a—you're an idealist!

BIFF: No, I'm mixed up very bad. Maybe I oughta get married. Maybe I oughta get stuck into something. Maybe that's my trouble. I'm like a boy. I'm not married. I'm not in business, I just—I'm like a boy. Are you content, Hap? You're a success, aren't you? Are you content?

HAPPY: Hell, no!

BIFF: Why? You're making money, aren't you?

HAPPY: [*Moving about with energy, expressiveness.*] All I can do now is wait for the merchandise manager to die. And suppose I get to be merchandise manager? He's a good friend of mine, and he just built a terrific estate on Long Island. And he lived there about two months and sold it, and now he's building another one. He can't enjoy it once it's finished. And I know that's just what I would do. I don't know what the hell I'm workin' for. Sometimes I sit in my apartment—all alone. And I think of the rent I'm paying. And it's crazy. But then, it's what I always wanted. My own apartment, a car, and plenty of women. And still, goddammit, I'm lonely.

BIFF: [*With enthusiasm.*] Listen, why don't you come out West with me?

HAPPY: You and I, heh?

BIFF: Sure, maybe we could buy a ranch. Raise cattle, use our muscles. Men built like we are should be working out in the open.

HAPPY: [*Avidly.*] The Loman Brothers, heh?

BIFF: [*With vast affection.*] Sure, we'd be known all over the counties!

HAPPY: [*Enthralled.*] That's what I dream about, Biff. Sometimes I want to just rip my clothes off in the middle of the store and outbox that goddam merchandise manager. I mean I can outbox, outrun, and outlift anybody in that store, and I have to take orders from those common, petty sons-of-bitches till I can't stand it any more.

BIFF: I'm tellin' you, kid, if you were with me I'd be happy out there.

HAPPY: [*Enthused.*] See, Biff, everybody around me is so false that I'm constantly lowering my ideals . . .

BIFF: Baby, together we'd stand up for one another, we'd have someone to trust.

HAPPY: If I were around you—

BIFF: Hap, the trouble is we weren't brought up to grub for money. I don't know how to do it.

HAPPY: Neither can I!

BIFF: Then let's go!

HAPPY: The only thing is—what can you make out there?

BIFF: But look at your friend. Builds an estate and then hasn't the peace of mind to live in it.

HAPPY: Yeah, but when he walks into the store the waves part in front of him. That's fifty-two thousand dollars a year coming through the revolving door, and I got more in my pinky finger than he's got in his head.

BIFF: Yeah, but you just said—

HAPPY: I gotta show some of those pompous, self-important executives over there that Hap Loman can make the grade. I want to walk into the store the way he walks in. Then I'll go with you, Biff. We'll be together yet, I swear. But take those two we had tonight. Now weren't they gorgeous creatures?

BIFF: Yeah, yeah, most gorgeous I've had in years.

HAPPY: I get that any time I want, Biff. Whenever I feel disgusted. The only trouble is, it gets like bowling or something. I just keep knockin' them over and it doesn't mean anything. You still run around a lot?

BIFF: Naa. I'd like to find a girl—steady, somebody with substance.

HAPPY: That's what I long for.

BIFF: Go on! You'd never come home.

HAPPY: I would! Somebody with character, with resistance! Like Mom, y'know? You're gonna call me a bastard when I tell you this. That girl Charlotte I was with tonight is engaged to be married in five weeks. [*He tries on his new hat.*]

BIFF: No kiddin'!

HAPPY: Sure, the guy's in line for the vice-presidency of the store. I don't know what gets into me, maybe I just have an overdeveloped sense of competition or something, but I went and ruined her, and furthermore I can't get rid of her. And he's the third executive I've done that to. Isn't that a crummy characteristic? And to top it all, I go to their weddings! [*Indignantly, but laughing.*] Like I'm not supposed to take bribes. Manufacturers offer me a hundred-dollar bill now and then to throw an order their way. You know how honest I am, but it's like this girl, see. I hate myself for it. Because I don't want the girl, and, still, I take it and—I love it!

BIFF: Let's go to sleep.

HAPPY: I guess we didn't settle anything, heh?

BIFF: I just got one idea that I'm going to try.

HAPPY: What's that?

BIFF: Remember Bill Oliver?

HAPPY: Sure, Oliver is very big now. You want to work for him again?

BIFF: No, but when I quit he said something to me. He put his arm on my shoulder, and he said, "Biff, if you ever need anything, come to me."

HAPPY: I remember that. That sounds good.

BIFF: I think I'll go to see him. If I could get ten thousand or even seven or eight thousand dollars I could buy a beautiful ranch.

HAPPY: I bet he'd back you. 'Cause he thought highly of you, Biff. I mean, they all do. You're well liked, Biff. That's why I say to come back here, and we both have the apartment. And I'm tellin' you, Biff, any babe you want . . .

BIFF: No, with a ranch I could do the work I like and still be something. I just wonder though. I wonder if Oliver still thinks I stole that carton of basketballs.

HAPPY: Oh, he probably forgot that long ago. It's almost ten years. You're too sensitive. Anyway, he didn't really fire you.

BIFF: Well, I think he was going to. I think that's why I quit. I was never sure whether he knew or not. I know he thought the world of me, though. I was the only one he'd let lock up the place.

WILLY: [*Below.*] You gonna wash the engine, Biff?

HAPPY: Shh! [BIFF *looks at* HAPPY, *who is gazing down, listening.* WILLY *is mumbling in the parlor.*] You hear that?

[*They listen.* WILLY *laughs warmly.*]

BIFF: [*Growing angry.*] Doesn't he know Mom can hear that?

WILLY: Don't get your sweater dirty, Biff!

[*A look of pain crosses* BIFF's *face.*]

HAPPY: Isn't that terrible? Don't leave again, will you? You'll find a job here. You gotta stick around. I don't know what to do about him, it's getting embarrassing.

WILLY: What a simonizing job!

BIFF: Mom's hearing that!

WILLY: No kiddin', Biff, you got a date? Wonderful!

HAPPY: Go on to sleep. But talk to him in the morning, will you?

BIFF: [*Reluctantly getting into bed.*] With her in the house. Brother!

HAPPY: [*Getting into bed.*] I wish you'd have a good talk with him.

[*The light on their room begins to fade.*]

BIFF: [*To himself in bed.*] That selfish, stupid . . .

HAPPY: Sh . . . Sleep, Biff.

[*Their light is out. Well before they have finished speaking,* WILLY's *form is dimly seen below in the darkened kitchen. He opens the refrigerator, searches in there, and takes out a bottle of milk. The apartment houses are fading out, and the entire house and surroundings become covered with leaves. Music insinuates itself as the leaves appear.*]

WILLY: Just wanna be careful with those girls, Biff, that's all. Don't make any promises. No promises of any kind. Because a girl, y'know, they always believe what you tell 'em, and you're very young, Biff, you're too young to be talking seriously to girls. [*Light rises on the kitchen.* WILLY, *talking, shuts the refrigerator door and comes downstage to the kitchen table. He pours milk into a glass. He is totally immersed in himself, smiling faintly.*] Too young entirely, Biff. You want to watch your schooling first. Then when you're all set, there'll be plenty of girls for a boy like you. [*He smiles broadly at a kitchen chair.*] That so? The girls pay for you? [*He laughs.*] Boy, you must really be makin' a hit. [WILLY *is gradually addressing—physically—a point offstage, speaking through the wall of the kitchen, and his voice has been rising in volume to that of a normal conversation.*] I been wondering why you polish the car so careful. Ha! Don't leave the hubcaps, boys. Get the chamois to the hubcaps. Happy, use newspaper on the windows, it's the easiest thing. Show him how to do it, Biff! You see, Happy? Pad it up, use it like a pad. That's it, that's it, good work. You're doin' all right, Hap. [*He pauses, then nods in approbation for a few seconds, then looks upward.*] Biff, first thing we gotta do when we get time is clip that big branch over the house. Afraid it's gonna fall in a storm and hit the roof. Tell you what. We get a rope and sling her around, and then we climb up there with a couple of saws and take her down. Soon as you finish the car, boys, I wanna see ya. I got a surprise for you, boys.

BIFF: [*Offstage.*] Whatta ya got, Dad?

WILLY: No, you finish first. Never leave a job till you're finished—remember that. [*Looking toward the "big trees."*] Biff, up in Albany I saw a beautiful hammock. I think I'll buy it next trip, and we'll hang it right between those two elms. Wouldn't that be something? Just swingin' there under those branches. Boy, that would be . . .

[YOUNG BIFF *and* YOUNG HAPPY *appear from the direction* WILLY *was addressing.* HAPPY *carries rags and a pail of water.* BIFF, *wearing a sweater with a block "S," carries a football.*]

BIFF: [*Pointing in the direction of the car offstage.*] How's that, Pop, professional?

WILLY: Terrific. Terrific job, boys. Good work, Biff.

HAPPY: Where's the surprise, Pop?

WILLY: In the back seat of the car.

HAPPY: Boy! [*He runs off.*]

BIFF: What is it, Dad? Tell me, what'd you buy?

WILLY: [*Laughing, cuffs him.*] Never mind, something I want you to have.

BIFF: [*Turns and starts off.*] What is it, Hap?

HAPPY: [*Offstage.*] It's a punching bag!

BIFF: Oh, Pop!

WILLY: It's got Gene Tunney's[1] signature on it!

[HAPPY *runs onstage with a punching bag.*]

BIFF: Gee, how'd you know we wanted a punching bag?

WILLY: Well, it's the finest thing for the timing.

---

1. Tunney (1897–1978) was world heavyweight boxing champion from 1926 to 1928 and retired undefeated.

HAPPY: [*Lies down on his back and pedals with his feet.*] I'm losing weight, you notice, Pop?

WILLY: [*To* HAPPY.] Jumping rope is good too.

BIFF: Did you see the new football I got?

WILLY: [*Examining the ball.*] Where'd you get a new ball?

BIFF: The coach told me to practice my passing.

WILLY: That so? And he gave you the ball, heh?

BIFF: Well, I borrowed it from the locker room. [*He laughs confidentially.*]

WILLY: [*Laughing with him at the theft.*] I want you to return that.

HAPPY: I told you he wouldn't like it!

BIFF: [*Angrily.*] Well, I'm bringing it back!

WILLY: [*Stopping the incipient argument, to* HAPPY.] Sure, he's gotta practice with a regulation ball, doesn't he? [*To* BIFF.] Coach'll probably congratulate you on your initiative!

BIFF: Oh, he keeps congratulating my initiative all the time, Pop.

WILLY: That's because he likes you. If somebody else took that ball there'd be an uproar. So what's the report, boys, what's the report?

BIFF: Where'd you go this time, Dad? Gee we were lonesome for you.

WILLY: [*Pleased, puts an arm around each boy and they come down to the apron.*] Lonesome, heh?

BIFF: Missed you every minute.

WILLY: Don't say? Tell you a secret, boys. Don't breathe it to a soul. Someday I'll have my own business, and I'll never have to leave home any more.

HAPPY: Like Uncle Charley, heh?

WILLY: Bigger than Uncle Charley! Because Charley is not—liked. He's liked, but he's not—well liked.

BIFF: Where'd you go this time, Dad?

WILLY: Well, I got on the road, and I went north to Providence. Met the Mayor.

BIFF: The Mayor of Providence!

WILLY: He was sitting in the hotel lobby.

BIFF: What'd he say?

WILLY: He said, "Morning!" And I said, "You got a fine city here, Mayor." And then he had coffee with me. And then I went to Waterbury. Waterbury is a fine city. Big clock city, the famous Waterbury clock. Sold a nice bill there. And then Boston—Boston is the cradle of the Revolution. A fine city. And a couple of other towns in Mass., and on to Portland and Bangor and straight home!

BIFF: Gee, I'd love to go with you sometime, Dad.

WILLY: Soon as summer comes.

HAPPY: Promise?

WILLY: You and Hap and I, and I'll show you all the towns. America is full of beautiful towns and fine, upstanding people. And they know me, boys, they know me up and down New England. The finest people. And when I bring you fellas up, there'll be open sesame for all of us, 'cause one thing, boys: I have friends. I can park my car in any street in New England, and the cops protect it like their own. This summer, heh?

BIFF and HAPPY: [*Together.*] Yeah! You bet!

WILLY: We'll take our bathing suits.

HAPPY: We'll carry your bags, Pop!

WILLY: Oh, won't that be something! Me comin' into the Boston stores with you boys carryin' my bags. What a sensation! [BIFF *is prancing around, practicing passing the ball.*] You nervous, Biff, about the game?

BIFF: Not if you're gonna be there.

WILLY: What do they say about you in school, now that they made you captain?

HAPPY: There's a crowd of girls behind him everytime the classes change.

BIFF: [*Taking* WILLY's *hand.*] This Saturday, Pop, this Saturday—just for you, I'm going to break through for a touchdown.

HAPPY: You're supposed to pass.

BIFF: I'm takin' one play for Pop. You watch me, Pop, and when I take off my helmet, that means I'm breakin' out. Then you watch me crash through that line!

WILLY: [*Kisses* BIFF.] Oh, wait'll I tell this in Boston!

[BERNARD *enters in knickers. He is younger than* BIFF, *earnest and loyal, a worried boy.*]

BERNARD: Biff, where are you? You're supposed to study with me today.

WILLY: Hey, looka Bernard. What're you lookin' so anemic about, Bernard?

BERNARD: He's gotta study, Uncle Willy. He's got Regents[2] next week.

HAPPY: [*Tauntingly, spinning* BERNARD *around.*] Let's box, Bernard!

BERNARD: Biff! [*He gets away from* HAPPY.] Listen, Biff, I heard Mr. Birnbaum say that if you don't start studyin' math he's gonna flunk you, and you won't graduate. I heard him!

WILLY: You better study with him, Biff. Go ahead now.

BERNARD: I heard him!

BIFF: Oh, Pop, you didn't see my sneakers! [*He holds up a foot for* WILLY *to look at.*]

WILLY: Hey, that's a beautiful job of printing!

BERNARD: [*Wiping his glasses.*] Just because he printed University of Virginia on his sneakers doesn't mean they've got to graduate him, Uncle Willy!

WILLY: [*Angrily.*] What're you talking about? With scholarships to three universities they're gonna flunk him?

BERNARD: But I heard Mr. Birnbaum say—

WILLY: Don't be a pest, Bernard! [*To his boys.*] What an anemic!

BERNARD: Okay, I'm waiting for you in my house, Biff.

[BERNARD *goes off. The* LOMANS *laugh.*]

WILLY: Bernard is not well liked, is he?

BIFF: He's liked, but he's not well liked.

HAPPY: That's right, Pop.

WILLY: That's just what I mean. Bernard can get the best marks in school, y'un-

---

2. A statewide examination administered to New York high school students.

derstand, but when he gets out in the business world, y'understand, you are going to be five times ahead of him. That's why I thank Almighty God you're both built like Adonises. Because the man who makes an appearance in the business world, the man who creates personal interest, is the man who gets ahead. Be liked and you will never want. You take me, for instance. I never have to wait in line to see a buyer. "Willy Loman is here!" That's all they have to know, and I go right through.

BIFF: Did you knock them dead, Pop?

WILLY: Knocked 'em cold in Providence, slaughtered 'em in Boston.

HAPPY: [On his back, pedaling again.] I'm losing weight, you notice, Pop?

[LINDA enters, as of old, a ribbon in her hair, carrying a basket of washing.]

LINDA: [With youthful energy.] Hello, dear!

WILLY: Sweetheart!

LINDA: How'd the Chevvy run?

WILLY: Chevrolet, Linda, is the greatest car ever built. [To the boys.] Since when do you let your mother carry wash up the stairs?

BIFF: Grab hold there, boy!

HAPPY: Where to, Mom?

LINDA: Hang them up on the line. And you better go down to your friends, Biff. The cellar is full of boys. They don't know what to do with themselves.

BIFF: Ah, when Pop comes home they can wait!

WILLY: [Laughs appreciatively.] You better go down and tell them what to do, Biff.

BIFF: I think I'll have them sweep out the furnace room.

WILLY: Good work, Biff.

BIFF: [Goes through wall-line of kitchen to doorway at back and calls down.] Fellas! Everybody sweep out the furnace room! I'll be right down!

VOICES: All right! Okay, Biff.

BIFF: George and Sam and Frank, come out back! We're hangin' up the wash! Come on, Hap, on the double!

[He and HAPPY carry out the basket.]

LINDA: The way they obey him!

WILLY: Well, that training, the training. I'm tellin' you, I was sellin' thousands and thousands, but I had to come home.

LINDA: Oh, the whole block'll be at that game. Did you sell anything?

WILLY: I did five hundred gross in Providence and seven hundred gross in Boston.

LINDA: No! Wait a minute, I've got a pencil. [She pulls pencil and paper out of her apron pocket.] That makes your commission . . . Two hundred—my God! Two hundred and twelve dollars!

WILLY: Well, I didn't figure it yet, but . . .

LINDA: How much did you do?

WILLY: Well, I—I did—about a hundred and eighty gross in Providence. Well, no—it came to—roughly two hundred gross on the whole trip.

LINDA: [*Without hesitation.*] Two hundred gross. That's . . . [*She figures.*]

WILLY: The trouble was that three of the stores were half closed for inventory in Boston. Otherwise I woulda broke records.

LINDA: Well, it makes seventy dollars and some pennies. That's very good.

WILLY: What do we owe?

LINDA: Well, on the first there's sixteen dollars on the refrigerator—

WILLY: Why sixteen?

LINDA: Well, the fan belt broke, so it was a dollar eighty.

WILLY: But it's brand new.

LINDA: Well, the man said that's the way it is. Till they work themselves in, y'know.

[*They move through the wall-line into the kitchen.*]

WILLY: I hope we didn't get stuck on that machine.

LINDA: They got the biggest ads of any of them!

WILLY: I know, it's a fine machine. What else?

LINDA: Well, there's nine-sixty for the washing machine. And for the vacuum cleaner there's three and a half due on the fifteenth. Then the roof, you got twenty-one dollars remaining.

WILLY: It don't leak, does it?

LINDA: No, they did a wonderful job. Then you owe Frank for the carburetor.

WILLY: I'm not going to pay that man! That goddam Chevrolet, they ought to prohibit the manufacture of that car!

LINDA: Well, you owe him three and a half. And odds and ends, comes to around a hundred and twenty dollars by the fifteenth.

WILLY: A hundred and twenty dollars! My God, if business don't pick up I don't know what I'm gonna do!

LINDA: Well, next week you'll do better.

WILLY: Oh, I'll knock 'em dead next week. I'll go to Hartford. I'm very well liked in Hartford. You know, the trouble is, Linda, people don't seem to take to me.

[*They move onto the forestage.*]

LINDA: Oh, don't be foolish.

WILLY: I know it when I walk in. They seem to laugh at me.

LINDA: Why? Why would they laugh at you? Don't talk that way, Willy.

[WILLY *moves to the edge of the stage.* LINDA *goes into the kitchen and starts to darn stockings.*]

WILLY: I don't know the reason for it, but they just pass me by. I'm not noticed.

LINDA: But you're doing wonderful, dear. You're making seventy to a hundred dollars a week.

WILLY: But I gotta be at it ten, twelve hours a day. Other men—I don't know— they do it easier. I don't know why—I can't stop myself—I talk too much. A man oughta come in with a few words. One thing about Charley. He's a man of few words, and they respect him.

LINDA: You don't talk too much, you're just lively.

WILLY: [Smiling.] Well, I figure, what the hell, life is short, a couple of jokes. [To himself.] I joke too much! [The smile goes.]

LINDA: Why? You're—

WILLY: I'm fat. I'm very—foolish to look at, Linda. I didn't tell you, but Christmas time I happened to be calling on F. H. Stewarts, and a salesman I know, as I was going in to see the buyer I heard him say something about—walrus. And I—I cracked him right across the face. I won't take that. I simply will not take that. But they do laugh at me. I know that.

LINDA: Darling . . .

WILLY: I gotta overcome it. I know I gotta overcome it. I'm not dressing to advantage, maybe.

LINDA: Willy, darling, you're the handsomest man in the world—

WILLY: Oh, no, Linda.

LINDA: To me you are. [Slight pause.] The handsomest. [From the darkness is heard the laughter of a woman. WILLY doesn't turn to it, but it continues through LINDA's lines.] And the boys, Willy. Few men are idolized by their children the way you are.

[Music is heard as behind a scrim, to the left of the house, THE WOMAN, dimly seen, is dressing.]

WILLY: [With great feeling.] You're the best there is, Linda, you're a pal, you know that? On the road—on the road I want to grab you sometimes and just kiss the life outa you. [The laughter is loud now, and he moves into a brightening area at the left, where THE WOMAN has come from behind the scrim and is standing, putting on her hat, looking into a "mirror" and laughing.] 'Cause I get so lonely—especially when business is bad and there's nobody to talk to. I get the feeling that I'll never sell anything again, that I won't make a living for you, or a business, a business for the boys. [He talks through THE WOMAN's subsiding laughter. THE WOMAN primps at the "mirror."] There's so much I want to make for—

THE WOMAN: Me? You didn't make me, Willy. I picked you.

WILLY: [Pleased.] You picked me?

THE WOMAN: [Who is quite proper-looking, WILLY's age.] I did. I've been sitting at that desk watching all the salesmen go by, day in, day out. But you've got such a sense of humor, and we do have such a good time together, don't we?

WILLY: Sure, sure. [He takes her in his arms.] Why do you have to go now?

THE WOMAN: It's two o'clock . . .

WILLY: No, come on in! [He pulls her.]

THE WOMAN: . . . my sisters'll be scandalized. When'll you be back?

WILLY: Oh, two weeks about. Will you come up again?

THE WOMAN: Sure thing. You do make me laugh. It's good for me. [She squeezes his arm, kisses him.] And I think you're a wonderful man.

WILLY: You picked me, heh?

THE WOMAN: Sure. Because you're so sweet. And such a kidder.

WILLY: Well, I'll see you next time I'm in Boston.

THE WOMAN: I'll put you right through to the buyers.

WILLY: [*Slapping her bottom.*] Right. Well, bottoms up!

THE WOMAN: [*Slaps him gently and laughs.*] You just kill me, Willy. [*He suddenly grabs her and kisses her roughly.*] You kill me. And thanks for the stockings. I love a lot of stockings. Well, good night.

WILLY: Good night. And keep your pores open!

THE WOMAN: Oh, Willy!

[THE WOMAN *bursts out laughing, and* LINDA'S *laughter blends in.* THE WOMAN *disappears into the dark. Now the area at the kitchen table brightens.* LINDA *is sitting where she was at the kitchen table, but now is mending a pair of her silk stockings.*]

LINDA: You are, Willy. The handsomest man. You've got no reason to feel that—

WILLY: [*Coming out of* THE WOMAN'S *dimming area and going over to* LINDA.] I'll make it all up to you, Linda. I'll—

LINDA: There's nothing to make up, dear. You're doing fine, better than—

WILLY: [*Noticing her mending.*] What's that?

LINDA: Just mending my stockings. They're so expensive—

WILLY: [*Angrily, taking them from her.*] I won't have you mending stockings in this house! Now throw them out!

[LINDA *puts the stockings in her pocket.*]

BERNARD: [*Entering on the run.*] Where is he? If he doesn't study!

WILLY: [*Moving to the forestage, with great agitation.*] You'll give him the answers!

BERNARD: I do, but I can't on a Regents! That's a state exam! They're liable to arrest me!

WILLY: Where is he? I'll whip him, I'll whip him!

LINDA: And he'd better give back that football, Willy, it's not nice.

WILLY: Biff! Where is he? Why is he taking everything?

LINDA: He's too rough with the girls, Willy. All the mothers are afraid of him!

WILLY: I'll whip him!

BERNARD: He's driving the car without a license!

[THE WOMAN'S *laugh is heard.*]

WILLY: Shut up!

LINDA: All the mothers—

WILLY: Shut up!

BERNARD: [*Backing quietly away and out.*] Mr. Birnbaum says he's stuck up.

WILLY: Get outa here!

BERNARD: If he doesn't buckle down he'll flunk math! [*He goes off.*]

LINDA: He's right, Willy, you've gotta—

WILLY: [*Exploding at her.*] There's nothing the matter with him! You want him to be a worm like Bernard? He's got spirit, personality . . . [*As he speaks,* LINDA, *almost in tears, exits into the living room.* WILLY *is alone in the kitchen, wilting and staring. The leaves are gone. It is night again, and the apartment houses look down from behind.*] Loaded with it. Loaded! What is he stealing? He's giving it back, isn't he? Why is he stealing? What did I tell him? I never in my life told him anything but decent things.

[HAPPY *in pajamas has come down the stairs;* WILLY *suddenly becomes aware of* HAPPY's *presence.*]

HAPPY: Let's go now, come on.
WILLY: [*Sitting down at the kitchen table.*] Huh! Why did she have to wax the floors herself? Everytime she waxes the floors she keels over. She knows that!
HAPPY: Shh! Take it easy. What brought you back tonight?
WILLY: I got an awful scare. Nearly hit a kid in Yonkers. God! Why didn't I go to Alaska with my brother Ben that time! Ben! That man was a genius, that man was success incarnate! What a mistake! He begged me to go.
HAPPY: Well, there's no use in—
WILLY: You guys! There was a man started with the clothes on his back and ended up with diamond mines!
HAPPY: Boy, someday I'd like to know how he did it.
WILLY: What's the mystery? The man knew what he wanted and went out and got it! Walked into a jungle, and comes out, the age of twenty-one, and he's rich! The world is an oyster, but you don't crack it open on a mattress!
HAPPY: Pop, I told you I'm gonna retire you for life.
WILLY: You'll retire me for life on seventy goddam dollars a week? And your women and your car and your apartment, and you'll retire me for life! Christ's sake, I couldn't get past Yonkers today! Where are you guys, where are you? The woods are burning! I can't drive a car!

[CHARLEY *has appeared in the doorway. He is a large man, slow of speech, laconic, immovable. In all he says, despite what he says, there is pity, and now, trepidation. He has a robe over pajamas, slippers on his feet. He enters the kitchen.*]

CHARLEY: Everything all right?
HAPPY: Yeah, Charley, everything's . . .
WILLY: What's the matter?
CHARLEY: I heard some noise. I thought something happened. Can't we do something about the walls? You sneeze in here, and in my house hats blow off.
HAPPY: Let's go to bed, Dad. Come on.

[CHARLEY *signals to* HAPPY *to go.*]

WILLY: You go ahead, I'm not tired at the moment.
HAPPY: [*To* WILLY.] Take it easy, huh? [*He exits.*]
WILLY: What're you doin' up?
CHARLEY: [*Sitting down at the kitchen table opposite* WILLY.] Couldn't sleep good. I had a heartburn.
WILLY: Well, you don't know how to eat.
CHARLEY: I eat with my mouth.

WILLY: No, you're ignorant. You gotta know about vitamins and things like that.

CHARLEY: Come on, let's shoot. Tire you out a little.

WILLY: [*Hesitantly.*] All right. You got cards?

CHARLEY: [*Taking a deck from his pocket.*] Yeah, I got them. Someplace. What is it with those vitamins?

WILLY: [*Dealing.*] They build up your bones. Chemistry.

CHARLEY: Yeah, but there's no bones in a heartburn.

WILLY: What are you talkin' about? Do you know the first thing about it?

CHARLEY: Don't get insulted.

WILLY: Don't talk about something you don't know anything about.

[*They are playing. Pause.*]

CHARLEY: What're you doin' home?

WILLY: A little trouble with the car.

CHARLEY: Oh. [*Pause.*] I'd like to take a trip to California.

WILLY: Don't say.

CHARLEY: You want a job?

WILLY: I got a job, I told you that. [*After a slight pause.*] What the hell are you offering me a job for?

CHARLEY: Don't get insulted.

WILLY: Don't insult me.

CHARLEY: I don't see no sense in it. You don't have to go on this way.

WILLY: I got a good job. [*Slight pause.*] What do you keep comin' in here for?

CHARLEY: You want me to go?

WILLY: [*After a pause, withering.*] I can't understand it. He's going back to Texas again. What the hell is that?

CHARLEY: Let him go.

WILLY: I got nothin' to give him, Charley, I'm clean, I'm clean.

CHARLEY: He won't starve. None a them starve. Forget about him.

WILLY: Then what have I got to remember?

CHARLEY: You take it too hard. To hell with it. When a deposit bottle is broken you don't get your nickel back.

WILLY: That's easy enough for you to say.

CHARLEY: That ain't easy for me to say.

WILLY: Did you see the ceiling I put up in the living-room?

CHARLEY: Yeah, that's a piece of work. To put up a ceiling is a mystery to me. How do you do it?

WILLY: What's the difference?

CHARLEY: Well, talk about it.

WILLY: You gonna put up a ceiling?

CHARLEY: How could I put up a ceiling?

WILLY: Then what the hell are you bothering me for?

CHARLEY: You're insulted again.

WILLY: A man who can't handle tools is not a man. You're disgusting.

CHARLEY: Don't call me disgusting, Willy.

[UNCLE BEN, *carrying a valise and an umbrella, enters the forestage from around the right corner of the house. He is a stolid man, in his sixties, with a mustache and an authoritative air. He is utterly certain of his destiny, and there is an aura of far places about him. He enters exactly as* WILLY *speaks.*]

WILLY: I'm getting awfully tired, Ben.

[BEN's *music is heard.* BEN *looks around at everything.*]

CHARLEY: Good, keep playing; you'll sleep better. Did you call me Ben?

[BEN *looks at his watch.*]

WILLY: That's funny. For a second there you reminded me of my brother Ben.

BEN: I only have a few minutes. [*He strolls, inspecting the place.* WILLY *and* CHARLEY *continue playing.*]

CHARLEY: You never heard from him again, heh? Since that time?

WILLY: Didn't Linda tell you? Couple of weeks ago we got a letter from his wife in Africa. He died.

CHARLEY: That so.

BEN: [*Chuckling.*] So this is Brooklyn, eh?

CHARLEY: Maybe you're in for some of his money.

WILLY: Naa, he had seven sons. There's just one opportunity I had with that man . . .

BEN: I must make a train, William. There are several properties I'm looking at in Alaska.

WILLY: Sure, sure! If I'd gone with him to Alaska that time, everything would've been totally different.

CHARLEY: Go on, you'da froze to death up there.

WILLY: What're you talking about?

BEN: Opportunity is tremendous in Alaska, William. Surprised you're not up there.

WILLY: Sure, tremendous.

CHARLEY: Heh?

WILLY: There was the only man I ever met who knew the answers.

CHARLEY: Who?

BEN: How are you all?

WILLY: [*Taking a pot, smiling.*] Fine, fine.

CHARLEY: Pretty sharp tonight.

BEN: Is Mother living with you?

WILLY: No, she died a long time ago.

CHARLEY: Who?

BEN: That's too bad. Fine specimen of a lady, Mother.

WILLY: [*To* CHARLEY.] Heh?

BEN: I'd hoped to see the old girl.

CHARLEY: Who died?

BEN: Heard anything from Father, have you?

WILLY: [*Unnerved.*] What do you mean, who died?

CHARLEY: [*Taking a pot.*] What're you talkin' about?

BEN: [*Looking at his watch.*] William, it's half-past eight!

WILLY: [*As though to dispel his confusion he angrily stops* CHARLEY's *hand.*] That's my build!

CHARLEY: I put the ace—

WILLY: If you don't know how to play the game I'm not gonna throw my money away on you!

CHARLEY: [*Rising.*] It was my ace, for God's sake!

WILLY: I'm through, I'm through!

BEN: When did Mother die?

WILLY: Long ago. Since the beginning you never knew how to play cards.

CHARLEY: [*Picks up the cards and goes to the door.*] All right! Next time I'll bring a deck with five aces.

WILLY: I don't play that kind of game!

CHARLEY: [*Turning to him.*] You ought to be ashamed of yourself!

WILLY: Yeah?

CHARLEY: Yeah! [*He goes out.*]

WILLY: [*Slamming the door after him.*] Ignoramus!

BEN: [*As* WILLY *comes toward him through the wall-line of the kitchen.*] So you're William.

WILLY: [*Shaking* BEN's *hand.*] Ben! I've been waiting for you so long! What's the answer? How did you do it?

BEN: Oh, there's a story in that.

[LINDA *enters the forestage, as of old, carrying the wash basket.*]

LINDA: Is this Ben?

BEN: [*Gallantly.*] How do you do, my dear.

LINDA: Where've you been all these years? Willy's always wondered why you—

WILLY: [*Pulling* BEN *away from her impatiently.*] Where is Dad? Didn't you follow him? How did you get started?

BEN: Well, I don't know how much you remember.

WILLY: Well, I was just a baby, of course, only three or four years old—

BEN: Three years and eleven months.

WILLY: What a memory, Ben!

BEN: I have many enterprises, William, and I have never kept books.

WILLY: I remember I was sitting under the wagon in—was it Nebraska?

BEN: It was South Dakota, and I gave you a bunch of wild flowers.

WILLY: I remember you walking away down some open road.

BEN: [*Laughing.*] I was going to find Father in Alaska.

WILLY: Where is he?

BEN: At that age I had a very faulty view of geography, William. I discovered after a few days that I was heading due south, so instead of Alaska, I ended up in Africa.

LINDA: Africa!

WILLY: The Gold Coast!

BEN: Principally diamond mines.

LINDA: Diamond mines!

BEN: Yes, my dear. But I've only a few minutes—

WILLY: No! Boys! Boys! [*Young* BIFF *and* HAPPY *appear.*] Listen to this. This is your Uncle Ben, a great man! Tell my boys, Ben!

BEN: Why, boys, when I was seventeen I walked into the jungle, and when I was twenty-one I walked out. [*He laughs.*] And by God I was rich.

WILLY: [*To the boys.*] You see what I been talking about? The greatest things can happen!

BEN: [*Glancing at his watch.*] I have an appointment in Ketchikan Tuesday week.

WILLY: No, Ben! Please tell about Dad. I want my boys to hear. I want them to know the kind of stock they spring from. All I remember is a man with a big beard, and I was in Mamma's lap, sitting around a fire, and some kind of high music.

BEN: His flute. He played the flute.

WILLY: Sure, the flute, that's right!

[*New music is heard, a high, rollicking tune.*]

BEN: Father was a very great and a very wild-hearted man. We would start in Boston, and he'd toss the whole family into the wagon, and then he'd drive the team right across the country; through Ohio, and Indiana, Michigan, Illinois, and all the Western states. And we'd stop in the towns and sell the flutes that he'd made on the way. Great inventor, Father. With one gadget he made more in a week than a man like you could make in a lifetime.

WILLY: That's just the way I'm bringing them up, Ben—rugged, well liked, all-around.

BEN: Yeah? [*To* BIFF.] Hit that, boy—hard as you can. [*He pounds his stomach.*]

BIFF: Oh, no, sir!

BEN: [*Taking boxing stance.*] Come on, get to me! [*He laughs.*]

WILLY: Go to it, Biff! Go ahead, show him!

BIFF: Okay! [*He cocks his fist and starts in.*]

LINDA: [*To* WILLY.] Why must he fight, dear?

BEN: [*Sparring with* BIFF.] Good boy! Good boy!

WILLY: How's that, Ben, heh?

HAPPY: Give him the left, Biff!

LINDA: Why are you fighting?

BEN: Good boy! [*Suddenly comes in, trips* BIFF, *and stands over him, the point of his umbrella poised over* BIFF's *eye.*]

LINDA: Look out, Biff!

BIFF: Gee!

BEN: [*Patting* BIFF's *knee.*] Never fight fair with a stranger, boy. You'll never get out of the jungle that way. [*Taking* LINDA's *hand and bowing.*] It was an honor and a pleasure to meet you, Linda.

LINDA: [*Withdrawing her hand coldly, frightened.*] Have a nice—trip.

BEN: [*To* WILLY.] And good luck with your—what do you do?

WILLY: Selling.

BEN: Yes. Well . . . [*He raises his hand in farewell to all.*]

WILLY: No, Ben, I don't want you to think . . . [*He takes* BEN's *arm to show him.*] It's Brooklyn, I know, but we hunt too.

BEN: Really, now.

WILLY: Oh, sure, there's snakes and rabbits and—that's why I moved out here. Why, Biff can fell any one of these trees in no time! Boys! Go right over to where they're building the apartment house and get some sand. We're gonna rebuild the entire front stoop right now! Watch this, Ben!

BIFF: Yes, sir! On the double, Hap!

HAPPY: [*As he and* BIFF *run off.*] I lost weight, Pop, you notice?

[CHARLEY *enters in knickers, even before the boys are gone.*]

CHARLEY: Listen, if they steal any more from that building the watchman'll put the cops on them!

LINDA: [*To* WILLY.] Don't let Biff . . .

[BEN *laughs lustily.*]

WILLY: You shoulda seen the lumber they brought home last week. At least a dozen six-by-tens worth all kinds a money.

CHARLEY: Listen, if that watchman—

WILLY: I gave them hell, understand. But I got a couple of fearless characters there.

CHARLEY: Willy, the jails are full of fearless characters.

BEN: [*Clapping* WILLY *on the back, with a laugh at* CHARLEY.] And the stock exchange, friend!

WILLY: [*Joining in* BEN's *laughter.*] Where are the rest of your pants?

CHARLEY: My wife bought them.

WILLY: Now all you need is a golf club and you can go upstairs and go to sleep. [*To* BEN.] Great athlete! Between him and his son Bernard they can't hammer a nail!

BERNARD: [*Rushing in.*] The watchman's chasing Biff!

WILLY: [*Angrily.*] Shut up! He's not stealing anything!

LINDA: [*Alarmed, hurrying off left.*] Where is he? Biff, dear! [*She exits.*]

WILLY: [*Moving toward the left, away from* BEN.] There's nothing wrong. What's the matter with you?

BEN: Nervy boy. Good!

WILLY: [*Laughing.*] Oh, nerves of iron, that Biff!

CHARLEY: Don't know what it is. My New England man comes back and he's bleedin', they murdered him up there.

WILLY: It's contacts, Charley, I got important contacts!

CHARLEY: [*Sarcastically.*] Glad to hear it, Willy. Come in later, we'll shoot a little casino. I'll take some of your Portland money. [*He laughs at* WILLY *and exits.*]

WILLY: [*Turning to* BEN.] Business is bad, it's murderous. But not for me, of course.

BEN: I'll stop by on my way back to Africa.

WILLY: [*Longingly.*] Can't you stay a few days? You're just what I need, Ben, because I—I have a fine position here, but I—well, Dad left when I was such a baby and I never had a chance to talk to him and I still feel—kind of temporary about myself.

BEN: I'll be late for my train.

[*They are at opposite ends of the stage.*]

WILLY: Ben, my boys—can't we talk? They'd go into the jaws of hell for me, see, but I—

BEN: William, you're being first-rate with your boys. Outstanding, manly chaps!

WILLY: [*Hanging on to his words.*] Oh, Ben, that's good to hear! Because sometimes I'm afraid that I'm not teaching them the right kind of— Ben, how should I teach them?

BEN: [*Giving great weight to each word, and with a certain vicious audacity.*] William, when I walked into the jungle, I was seventeen. When I walked out I was twenty-one. And, by God, I was rich! [*He goes off into darkness around the right corner of the house.*]

WILLY: . . . was rich! That's just the spirit I want to imbue them with! To walk into a jungle! I was right! I was right! I was right!

[BEN *is gone, but* WILLY *is still speaking to him as* LINDA, *in nightgown and robe, enters the kitchen, glances around for* WILLY, *then goes to the door of the house, looks out and sees him. Comes down to his left. He looks at her.*]

LINDA: Willy, dear? Willy?

WILLY: I was right!

LINDA: Did you have some cheese? [*He can't answer.*] It's very late, darling. Come to bed, heh?

WILLY: [*Looking straight up.*] Gotta break your neck to see a star in this yard.

LINDA: You coming in?

WILLY: Whatever happened to that diamond watch fob? Remember? When Ben came from Africa that time? Didn't he give me a watch fob with a diamond in it?

LINDA: You pawned it, dear. Twelve, thirteen years ago. For Biff's radio correspondence course.

WILLY: Gee, that was a beautiful thing. I'll take a walk.

LINDA: But you're in your slippers.

WILLY: [*Starting to go around the house at the left.*] I was right! I was! [*Half to* LINDA, *as he goes, shaking his head.*] What a man! There was a man worth talking to. I was right!

LINDA: [*Calling after* WILLY.] But in your slippers, Willy!

[WILLY *is almost gone when* BIFF, *in his pajamas, comes down the stairs and enters the kitchen.*]

BIFF: What is he doing out there?

LINDA: Sh!

BIFF: God Almighty, Mom, how long has he been doing this?

LINDA: Don't, he'll hear you.

BIFF: What the hell is the matter with him?

LINDA: It'll pass by morning.

BIFF: Shouldn't we do anything?

LINDA: Oh, my dear, you should do a lot of things, but there's nothing to do, so go to sleep.

[HAPPY *comes down the stairs and sits on the steps.*]

HAPPY: I never heard him so loud, Mom.

LINDA: Well, come around more often; you'll hear him. [*She sits down at the table and mends the lining of* WILLY's *jacket.*]

BIFF: Why didn't you ever write me about this, Mom?

LINDA: How would I write to you? For over three months you had no address.

BIFF: I was on the move. But you know I thought of you all the time. You know that, don't you, pal?

LINDA: I know, dear, I know. But he likes to have a letter. Just to know that there's still a possibility for better things.

BIFF: He's not like this all the time, is he?

LINDA: It's when you come home he's always the worst.

BIFF: When I come home?

LINDA: When you write you're coming, he's all smiles, and talks about the future, and—he's just wonderful. And then the closer you seem to come, the more shaky he gets, and then, by the time you get here, he's arguing, and he seems angry at you. I think it's just that maybe he can't bring himself to—to open up to you. Why are you so hateful to each other? Why is that?

BIFF: [*Evasively.*] I'm not hateful, Mom.

LINDA: But you no sooner come in the door than you're fighting!

BIFF: I don't know why. I mean to change. I'm tryin', Mom, you understand?

LINDA: Are you home to stay now?

BIFF: I don't know. I want to look around, see what's doin'.

LINDA: Biff, you can't look around all your life, can you?

BIFF: I just can't take hold, Mom. I can't take hold of some kind of a life.

LINDA: Biff, a man is not a bird, to come and go with the springtime.

BIFF: Your hair . . . [*He touches her hair.*] Your hair got so gray.

LINDA: Oh, it's been gray since you were in high school. I just stopped dyeing it, that's all.

BIFF: Dye it again, will ya? I don't want my pal looking old. [*He smiles.*]

LINDA: You're such a boy! You think you can go away for a year and . . . You've got to get it into your head now that one day you'll knock on this door and there'll be strange people here—

BIFF: What are you talking about? You're not even sixty, Mom.

LINDA: But what about your father?

BIFF: [*Lamely.*] Well, I meant him too.

HAPPY: He admires Pop.

LINDA: Biff, dear, if you don't have any feeling for him, then you can't have any feeling for me.

BIFF: Sure I can, Mom.

LINDA: No. You can't just come to see me, because I love him. [*With a threat, but only a threat, of tears.*] He's the dearest man in the world to me, and I won't have anyone making him feel unwanted and low and blue. You've got to make up your mind now, darling, there's no leeway any more. Either he's your father and you pay him that respect, or else you're not to come here. I know he's not easy to get along with—nobody knows that better than me— but . . .

WILLY: [*From the left, with a laugh.*] Hey, hey, Biffo!

BIFF: [*Starting to go out after* WILLY.] What the hell is the matter with him? [HAPPY *stops him.*]

LINDA: Don't—don't go near him!

BIFF: Stop making excuses for him! He always, always wiped the floor with you. Never had an ounce of respect for you.

HAPPY: He's always had respect for—

BIFF: What the hell do you know about it?

HAPPY: [*Surlily.*] Just don't call him crazy!

BIFF: He's got no character—Charley wouldn't do this. Not in his own house— spewing out that vomit from his mind.

HAPPY: Charley never had to cope with what he's got to.

BIFF: People are worse off than Willy Loman. Believe me, I've seen them!

LINDA: Then make Charley your father, Biff. You can't do that, can you? I don't say he's a great man. Willy Loman never made a lot of money. His name was never in the paper. He's not the finest character that ever lived. But he's a human being, and a terrible thing is happening to him. So attention must be paid. He's not to be allowed to fall into his grave like an old dog. Attention, attention must be finally paid to such a person. You called him crazy—

BIFF: I didn't mean—

LINDA: No, a lot of people think he's lost his—balance. But you don't have to be very smart to know what his trouble is. The man is exhausted.

HAPPY: Sure!

LINDA: A small man can be just as exhausted as a great man. He works for a company thirty-six years this March, opens up unheard-of territories to their trademark, and now in his old age they take his salary away.

HAPPY: [*Indignantly.*] I didn't know that, Mom.

LINDA: You never asked, my dear! Now that you get your spending money some-place else you don't trouble your mind with him.

HAPPY: But I gave you money last—

LINDA: Christmas time, fifty dollars! To fix the hot water it cost ninety-seven fifty! For five weeks he's been on straight commission, like a beginner, an unknown!

BIFF: Those ungrateful bastards!

LINDA: Are they any worse than his sons? When he brought them business, when he was young, they were glad to see him. But now his old friends, the old buyers that loved him so and always found some order to hand him in a pinch—they're all dead, retired. He used to be able to make six, seven calls a day in Boston. Now he takes his valises out of the car and puts them back and takes them out again and he's exhausted. Instead of walking he talks now. He drives seven hundred miles, and when he gets there no one knows him any more, no one welcomes him. And what goes through a man's mind, driving seven hundred miles home without having earned a cent? Why shouldn't he talk to himself? Why? When he has to go to Charley and borrow fifty dollars a week and pretend to me that it's his pay? How long can that go on? How long? You see what I'm sitting here and waiting for? And you tell me he has no character? The man who never worked a day but for your benefit? When does he get the medal for that? Is this his reward—to turn around at the age of sixty-three and find his sons, who he loved better than his life, one a philandering bum—

HAPPY: Mom!

LINDA: That's all you are, my baby! [*To* BIFF.] And you! What happened to the love you had for him? You were such pals! How you used to talk to him on the phone every night! How lonely he was till he could come home to you!

BIFF: All right, Mom. I'll live here in my room, and I'll get a job. I'll keep away from him, that's all.

LINDA: No, Biff. You can't stay here and fight all the time.

BIFF: He threw me out of this house, remember that.

LINDA: Why did he do that? I never knew why.

BIFF: Because I know he's a fake and he doesn't like anybody around who knows!

LINDA: Why a fake? In what way? What do you mean?

BIFF: Just don't lay it all at my feet. It's between me and him—that's all I have to say. I'll chip in from now on. He'll settle for half my pay check. He'll be all right. I'm going to bed. [*He starts for the stairs.*]

LINDA: He won't be all right.

BIFF: [*Turning on the stairs, furiously.*] I hate this city and I'll stay here. Now what do you want?

LINDA: He's dying, Biff.

[HAPPY *turns quickly to her, shocked.*]

BIFF: [*After a pause.*] Why is he dying?

LINDA: He's been trying to kill himself.

BIFF: [*With great horror.*] How?

LINDA: I live from day to day.

BIFF: What're you talking about?

LINDA: Remember I wrote you that he smashed up the car again? In February?

BIFF: Well?

LINDA: The insurance inspector came. He said that they have evidence. That all these accidents in the last year—weren't—weren't—accidents.

HAPPY: How can they tell that? That's a lie.

LINDA: It seems there's a woman . . . [*She takes a breath as. . . .*]

BIFF: [*Sharply but contained.*] What woman?
LINDA: [*Simultaneously.*] . . . and this woman . . .
LINDA: What?
BIFF: Nothing. Go ahead.
LINDA: What did you say?
BIFF: Nothing. I just said what woman?
HAPPY: What about her?
LINDA: Well, it seems she was walking down the road and saw his car. She says that he wasn't driving fast at all, and that he didn't skid. She says he came to that little bridge, and then deliberately smashed into the railing, and it was only the shallowness of the water that saved him.
BIFF: Oh, no, he probably just fell asleep again.
LINDA: I don't think he fell asleep.
BIFF: Why not?
LINDA: Last month . . . [*With great difficulty.*] Oh, boys, it's so hard to say a thing like this! He's just a big stupid man to you, but I tell you there's more good in him than in many other people. [*She chokes, wipes her eyes.*] I was looking for a fuse. The lights blew out, and I went down the cellar. And behind the fuse box—it happened to fall out—was a length of rubber pipe—just short.
HAPPY: No kidding?
LINDA: There's a little attachment on the end of it. I knew right away. And sure enough, on the bottom of the water heater there's a new little nipple on the gas pipe.
HAPPY: [*Angrily.*] That—jerk.
BIFF: Did you have it taken off?
LINDA: I'm—I'm ashamed to. How can I mention it to him? Every day I go down and take away that little rubber pipe. But, when he comes home, I put it back where it was. How can I insult him that way? I don't know what to do. I live from day to day, boys. I tell you, I know every thought in his mind. It sounds so old-fashioned and silly, but I tell you he put his whole life into you and you've turned your backs on him. [*She is bent over in the chair, weeping, her face in her hands.*] Biff, I swear to God! Biff, his life is in your hands!
HAPPY: [*To* BIFF.] How do you like that damned fool!
BIFF: [*Kissing her.*] All right, pal, all right. It's all settled now. I've been remiss. I know that, Mom. But now I'll stay, and I swear to you, I'll apply myself. [*Kneeling in front of her, in a fever of self-reproach.*] It's just—you see, Mom, I don't fit in business. Not that I won't try. I'll try, and I'll make good.
HAPPY: Sure you will. The trouble with you in business was you never tried to please people.
BIFF: I know, I—
HAPPY: Like when you worked for Harrison's. Bob Harrison said you were tops, and then you go and do some damn fool thing like whistling whole songs in the elevator like a comedian.
BIFF: [*Against* HAPPY.] So what? I like to whistle sometimes.
HAPPY: You don't raise a guy to a responsible job who whistles in the elevator!

LINDA: Well, don't argue about it now.

HAPPY: Like when you'd go off and swim in the middle of the day instead of taking the line around.

BIFF: [*His resentment rising.*] Well, don't you run off? You take off sometimes, don't you? On a nice summer day?

HAPPY: Yeah, but I cover myself!

LINDA: Boys!

HAPPY: If I'm going to take a fade the boss can call any number where I'm supposed to be and they'll swear to him that I just left. I'll tell you something that I hate to say, Biff, but in the business world some of them think you're crazy.

BIFF: [*Angered.*] Screw the business world!

HAPPY: All right, screw it! Great, but cover yourself!

LINDA: Hap, Hap!

BIFF: I don't care what they think! They've laughed at Dad for years, and you know why? Because we don't belong in this nuthouse of a city! We should be mixing cement on some open plain, or—or carpenters. A carpenter is allowed to whistle!

[WILLY *walks in from the entrance of the house, at left.*]

WILLY: Even your grandfather was better than a carpenter. [*Pause. They watch him.*] You never grew up. Bernard does not whistle in the elevator, I assure you.

BIFF: [*As though to laugh* WILLY *out of it.*] Yeah, but you do, Pop.

WILLY: I never in my life whistled in an elevator! And who in the business world thinks I'm crazy?

BIFF: I didn't mean it like that, Pop. Now don't make a whole thing out of it, will ya?

WILLY: Go back to the West! Be a carpenter, a cowboy, enjoy yourself!

LINDA: Willy, he was just saying—

WILLY: I heard what he said!

HAPPY: [*Trying to quiet* WILLY.] Hey, Pop, come on now . . .

WILLY: [*Continuing over* HAPPY's *line.*] They laugh at me, heh? Go to Filene's, go to the Hub, go to Slattery's Boston. Call out the name Willy Loman and see what happens! Big shot!

BIFF: All right, Pop.

WILLY: Big!

BIFF: All right!

WILLY: Why do you always insult me?

BIFF: I didn't say a word. [*To* LINDA.] Did I say a word?

LINDA: He didn't say anything, Willy.

WILLY: [*Going to the doorway of the living-room.*] All right, good night, good night.

LINDA: Willy, dear, he just decided . . .

WILLY: [*To* BIFF.] If you get tired hanging around tomorrow, paint the ceiling I put up in the living-room.

BIFF: I'm leaving early tomorrow.

HAPPY: He's going to see Bill Oliver, Pop.

WILLY: [*Interestedly.*] Oliver? For what?

BIFF: [*With reserve, but trying, trying.*] He always said he'd stake me. I'd like to go into business, so maybe I can take him up on it.

LINDA: Isn't that wonderful?

WILLY: Don't interrupt. What's wonderful about it? There's fifty men in the City of New York who'd stake him. [*To* BIFF.] Sporting goods?

BIFF: I guess so. I know something about it and—

WILLY: He knows something about it! You know sporting goods better than Spalding, for God's sake! How much is he giving you?

BIFF: I don't know, I didn't even see him yet, but—

WILLY: Then what're you talkin' about?

BIFF: [*Getting angry.*] Well, all I said was I'm gonna see him, that's all!

WILLY: [*Turning away.*] Ah, you're counting your chickens again.

BIFF: [*Starting left for the stairs.*] Oh, Jesus, I'm going to sleep!

WILLY: [*Calling after him.*] Don't curse in this house!

BIFF: [*Turning.*] Since when did you get so clean?

HAPPY: [*Trying to stop them.*] Wait a . . .

WILLY: Don't use that language to me! I won't have it!

HAPPY: [*Grabbing* BIFF, *shouts.*] Wait a minute! I got an idea. I got a feasible idea. Come here, Biff, let's talk this over now, let's talk some sense here. When I was down in Florida last time, I thought of a great idea to sell sporting goods. It just came back to me. You and I, Biff—we have a line, the Loman Line. We train a couple of weeks, and put on a couple of exhibitions, see?

WILLY: That's an idea!

HAPPY: Wait! We form two basketball teams, see? Two water-polo teams. We play each other. It's a million dollars' worth of publicity. Two brothers, see? The Loman Brothers. Displays in the Royal Palms—all the hotels. And banners over the ring and the basketball court: "Loman Brothers." Baby, we could sell sporting goods!

WILLY: That is a one-million-dollar idea!

LINDA: Marvelous!

BIFF: I'm in great shape as far as that's concerned.

HAPPY: And the beauty of it is, Biff, it wouldn't be like a business. We'd be out playin' ball again . . .

BIFF: [*Enthused.*] Yeah, that's . . .

WILLY: Million-dollar . . .

HAPPY: And you wouldn't get fed up with it, Biff. It'd be the family again. There'd be the old honor, and comradeship, and if you wanted to go off for a swim or somethin'—well, you'd do it! Without some smart cooky gettin' up ahead of you!

WILLY: Lick the world! You guys together could absolutely lick the civilized world.

BIFF: I'll see Oliver tomorrow. Hap, if we could work that out . . .

LINDA: Maybe things are beginning to—

WILLY: [*Wildly enthused, to* LINDA.] Stop interrupting! [*To* BIFF.] But don't wear sport jacket and slacks when you see Oliver.

BIFF: No, I'll—

WILLY: A business suit, and talk as little as possible, and don't crack any jokes.

BIFF: He did like me. Always liked me.

LINDA: He loved you!

WILLY: [*To* LINDA.] Will you stop! [*To* BIFF.] Walk in very serious. You are not applying for a boy's job. Money is to pass. Be quiet, fine, and serious. Everybody likes a kidder, but nobody lends him money.

HAPPY: I'll try to get some myself, Biff. I'm sure I can.

WILLY: I see great things for you kids, I think your troubles are over. But remember, start big and you'll end big. Ask for fifteen. How much you gonna ask for?

BIFF: Gee, I don't know—

WILLY: And don't say "Gee." "Gee" is a boy's word. A man walking in for fifteen thousand dollars does not say "Gee!"

BIFF: Ten, I think, would be top though.

WILLY: Don't be so modest. You always started too low. Walk in with a big laugh. Don't look worried. Start off with a couple of your good stories to lighten things up. It's not what you say, it's how you say it—because personality always wins the day.

LINDA: Oliver always thought the highest of him—

WILLY: Will you let me talk?

BIFF: Don't yell at her, Pop, will ya?

WILLY: [*Angrily.*] I was talking, wasn't I?

BIFF: I don't like you yelling at her all the time, and I'm tellin' you, that's all.

WILLY: What're you, takin' over this house?

LINDA: Willy—

WILLY: [*Turning on her.*] Don't take his side all the time, goddammit!

BIFF: [*Furiously.*] Stop yelling at her!

WILLY: [*Suddenly pulling on his cheek, beaten down, guilt ridden.*] Give my best to Bill Oliver—he may remember me. [*He exits through the living-room doorway.*]

LINDA: [*Her voice subdued.*] What'd you have to start that for? [BIFF *turns away.*] You see how sweet he was as soon as you talked hopefully? [*She goes over to* BIFF.] Come up and say good night to him. Don't let him go to bed that way.

HAPPY: Come on, Biff, let's buck him up.

LINDA: Please, dear. Just say good night. It takes so little to make him happy. Come. [*She goes through the living-room doorway, calling upstairs from within the living-room.*] Your pajamas are hanging in the bathroom, Willy!

HAPPY: [*Looking toward where* LINDA *went out.*] What a woman! They broke the mold when they made her. You know that, Biff?

BIFF: He's off salary. My God, working on commission!

HAPPY: Well, let's face it: he's no hot-shot selling man. Except that sometimes, you have to admit, he's a sweet personality.

BIFF: [*Deciding.*] Lend me ten bucks, will ya? I want to buy some new ties.

HAPPY: I'll take you to a place I know. Beautiful stuff. Wear one of my striped shirts tomorrow.

BIFF: She got gray. Mom got awful old. Gee, I'm gonna go in to Oliver tomorrow and knock him for a —

HAPPY: Come on up. Tell that to Dad. Let's give him a whirl. Come on.

BIFF: [*Steamed up.*] You know, with ten thousand bucks, boy!

HAPPY: [*As they go into the living-room.*] That's the talk, Biff, that's the first time I've heard the old confidence out of you! [*From within the living-room, fading off.*] You're gonna live with me, kid, and any babe you want just say the word . . .

[*The last lines are hardly heard. They are mounting the stairs to their parents' bedroom.*]

LINDA: [*Entering her bedroom and addressing* WILLY, *who is in the bathroom. She is straightening the bed for him.*] Can you do anything about the shower? It drips.

WILLY: [*From the bathroom.*] All of a sudden everything falls to pieces! Goddam plumbing, oughta be sued, those people. I hardly finished putting it in and the thing . . . [*His words rumble off.*]

LINDA: I'm just wondering if Oliver will remember him. You think he might?

WILLY: [*Coming out of the bathroom in his pajamas.*] Remember him? What's the matter with you, you crazy? If he'd've stayed with Oliver he'd be on top by now! Wait'll Oliver gets a look at him. You don't know the average caliber any more. The average young man today—[*He is getting into bed.*]—is got a caliber of zero. Greatest thing in the world for him was to bum around. [BIFF *and* HAPPY *enter the bedroom. Slight pause.* WILLY *stops short, looking at* BIFF.] Glad to hear it, boy.

HAPPY: He wanted to say good night to you, sport.

WILLY: [*To* BIFF.] Yeah. Knock him dead, boy. What'd you want to tell me?

BIFF: Just take it easy, Pop. Good night. [*He turns to go.*]

WILLY: [*Unable to resist.*] And if anything falls off the desk while you're talking to him—like a package or something—don't you pick it up. They have office boys for that.

LINDA: I'll make a big breakfast—

WILLY: Will you let me finish? [*To* BIFF.] Tell him you were in the business in the West. Not farm work.

BIFF: All right, Dad.

LINDA: I think everything—

WILLY: [*Going right through her speech.*] And don't undersell yourself. No less than fifteen thousand dollars.

BIFF: [*Unable to bear him.*] Okay. Good night, Mom. [*He starts moving.*]

WILLY: Because you got a greatness in you, Biff, remember that. You got all kinds of greatness . . . [*He lies back, exhausted.* BIFF *walks out.*]

LINDA: [*Calling after* BIFF.] Sleep well, darling!

HAPPY: I'm gonna get married, Mom. I wanted to tell you.

LINDA: Go to sleep, dear.

HAPPY: [*Going.*] I just wanted to tell you.

WILLY: Keep up the good work. [HAPPY *exits.*] God . . . remember that Ebbets Field[3] game? The championship of the city?

LINDA: Just rest. Should I sing to you?

WILLY: Yeah. Sing to me. [LINDA *hums a soft lullaby.*] When that team came out—he was the tallest, remember?

LINDA: Oh, yes. And in gold.

[BIFF *enters the darkened kitchen, takes a cigarette, and leaves the house. He comes downstage into a golden pool of light. He smokes, staring at the night.*]

WILLY: Like a young god. Hercules—something like that. And the sun, the sun all around him. Remember how he waved to me? Right up from the field, with the representatives of three colleges standing by? And the buyers I brought, and the cheers when he came out—Loman, Loman, Loman! God Almighty, he'll be great yet. A star like that, magnificent, can never really fade away!

[*The light on* WILLY *is fading. The gas heater begins to glow through the kitchen wall, near the stairs, a blue flame beneath red coils.*]

LINDA: [*Timidly.*] Willy dear, what has he got against you?

WILLY: I'm so tired. Don't talk any more.

[BIFF *slowly returns to the kitchen. He stops, stares toward the heater.*]

LINDA: Will you ask Howard to let you work in New York?

WILLY: First thing in the morning. Everything'll be all right.

[BIFF *reaches behind the heater and draws out a length of rubber tubing. He is horrified and turns his head toward* WILLY's *room, still dimly lit, from which the strains of* LINDA's *desperate but monotonous humming rise.*]

WILLY: [*Staring through the window into the moonlight.*] Gee, look at the moon moving between the buildings!

[BIFF *wraps the tubing around his hand and quickly goes up the stairs.*]

CURTAIN

ACT II

Music is heard, gay and bright. The curtain rises as the music fades away. WILLY, *in shirt sleeves, is sitting at the kitchen table, sipping coffee, his hat in his lap.* LINDA *is filling his cup when she can.*

WILLY: Wonderful coffee. Meal in itself.

LINDA: Can I make you some eggs?

3. Stadium where the Dodgers, Brooklyn's major league baseball team, played from 1913 to 1957.

WILLY: No. Take a breath.

LINDA: You look so rested, dear.

WILLY: I slept like a dead one. First time in months. Imagine, sleeping till ten on a Tuesday morning. Boys left nice and early, heh?

LINDA: They were out of here by eight o'clock.

WILLY: Good work!

LINDA: It was so thrilling to see them leaving together. I can't get over the shaving lotion in this house!

WILLY: [Smiling.] Mmm—

LINDA: Biff was very changed this morning. His whole attitude seemed to be hopeful. He couldn't wait to get downtown to see Oliver.

WILLY: He's heading for a change. There's no question, there simply are certain men that take longer to get—solidified. How did he dress?

LINDA: His blue suit. He's so handsome in that suit. He could be a—anything in that suit!

[WILLY gets up from the table. LINDA holds his jacket for him.]

WILLY: There's no question, no question at all. Gee, on the way home tonight I'd like to buy some seeds.

LINDA: [Laughing.] That'd be wonderful. But not enough sun gets back there. Nothing'll grow any more.

WILLY: You wait, kid, before it's all over we're gonna get a little place out in the country, and I'll raise some vegetables, a couple of chickens . . .

LINDA: You'll do it yet, dear.

[WILLY walks out of his jacket. LINDA follows him.]

WILLY: And they'll get married, and come for a weekend. I'd build a little guest house. 'Cause I got so many fine tools, all I'd need would be a little lumber and some peace of mind.

LINDA: [Joyfully.] I sewed the lining . . .

WILLY: I could build two guest houses, so they'd both come. Did he decide how much he's going to ask Oliver for?

LINDA: [Getting him into the jacket.] He didn't mention it, but I imagine ten or fifteen thousand. You going to talk to Howard today?

WILLY: Yeah. I'll put it to him straight and simple. He'll just have to take me off the road.

LINDA: And Willy, don't forget to ask for a little advance, because we've got the insurance premium. It's the grace period now.

WILLY: That's a hundred . . . ?

LINDA: A hundred and eight, sixty-eight. Because we're a little short again.

WILLY: Why are we short?

LINDA: Well, you had the motor job on the car . . .

WILLY: That goddam Studebaker!

LINDA: And you got one more payment on the refrigerator . . .

WILLY: But it just broke again!

LINDA: Well, it's old, dear.

WILLY: I told you we should've bought a well-advertised machine. Charley bought a General Electric and it's twenty years old and it's still good, that son-of-a-bitch.

LINDA: But, Willy—

WILLY: Whoever heard of a Hastings refrigerator? Once in my life I would like to own something outright before it's broken! I'm always in a race with the junkyard! I just finished paying for the car and it's on its last legs. The refrigerator consumes belts like a goddam maniac. They time those things. They time them so when you finally paid for them, they're used up.

LINDA: [Buttoning up his jacket as he unbuttons it.] All told, about two hundred dollars would carry us, dear. But that includes the last payment on the mortgage. After this payment, Willy, the house belongs to us.

WILLY: It's twenty-five years!

LINDA: Biff was nine years old when we bought it.

WILLY: Well, that's a great thing. To weather a twenty-five year mortgage is—

LINDA: It's an accomplishment.

WILLY: All the cement, the lumber, the reconstruction I put in this house! There ain't a crack to be found in it any more.

LINDA: Well, it served its purpose.

WILLY: What purpose? Some stranger'll come along, move in, and that's that. If only Biff would take this house, and raise a family . . . [He starts to go.] Goodby, I'm late.

LINDA: [Suddenly remembering.] Oh, I forgot! You're supposed to meet them for dinner.

WILLY: Me?

LINDA: At Frank's Chop House on Forty-eighth near Sixth Avenue.

WILLY: Is that so! How about you?

LINDA: No, just the three of you. They're gonna blow you to a big meal!

WILLY: Don't say! Who thought of that?

LINDA: Biff came to me this morning, Willy, and he said, "Tell Dad, we want to blow him to a big meal." Be there six o'clock. You and your two boys are going to have dinner.

WILLY: Gee whiz! That's really somethin'. I'm gonna knock Howard for a loop, kid. I'll get an advance, and I'll come home with a New York job. Goddammit, now I'm gonna do it!

LINDA: Oh, that's the spirit, Willy!

WILLY: I will never get behind a wheel the rest of my life!

LINDA: It's changing, Willy, I can feel it changing!

WILLY: Beyond a question. G'by, I'm late. [He starts to go again.]

LINDA: [Calling after him as she runs to the kitchen table for a handkerchief.] You got your glasses?

WILLY: [Feels for them, then comes back in.] Yeah, yeah, got my glasses.

LINDA: [Giving him the handkerchief.] And a handkerchief.

WILLY: Yeah, handkerchief.

LINDA: And your saccharine?

WILLY: Yeah, my saccharine.

LINDA: Be careful on the subway stairs.

[*She kisses him, and a silk stocking is seen hanging from her hand.* WILLY *notices it.*]

WILLY: Will you stop mending stockings? At least while I'm in the house. It gets me nervous. I can't tell you. Please.

[LINDA *hides the stocking in her hand as she follows* WILLY *across the forestage in front of the house.*]

LINDA: Remember, Frank's Chop House.

WILLY: [*Passing the apron.*] Maybe beets would grow out there.

LINDA: [*Laughing.*] But you tried so many times.

WILLY: Yeah. Well, don't work hard today. [*He disappears around the right corner of the house.*]

LINDA: Be careful! [*As* WILLY *vanishes,* LINDA *waves to him. Suddenly the phone rings. She runs across the stage and into the kitchen and lifts it.*] Hello? Oh, Biff! I'm so glad you called, I just . . . Yes, sure, I just told him. Yes, he'll be there for dinner at six o'clock, I didn't forget. Listen, I was just dying to tell you. You know that little rubber pipe I told you about? That he connected to the gas heater? I finally decided to go down the cellar this morning and take it away and destroy it. But it's gone! Imagine? He took it away himself, it isn't there! [*She listens.*] When? Oh, then you took it. Oh—nothing, it's just that I'd hoped he'd taken it away himself. Oh, I'm not worried, darling, because this morning he left in such high spirits, it was like the old days! I'm not afraid any more. Did Mr. Oliver see you? . . . Well, you wait there then. And make a nice impression on him, darling. Just don't perspire too much before you see him. And have a nice time with Dad. He may have big news too! . . . That's right, a New York job. And be sweet to him tonight, dear. Be loving to him. Because he's only a little boat looking for a harbor. [*She is trembling with sorrow and joy.*] Oh, that's wonderful, Biff, you'll save his life. Thanks, darling. Just put your arm around him when he comes into the restaurant. Give him a smile. That's the boy . . . Good-by, dear. . . . You got your comb? . . . That's fine. Good-by, Biff dear.

[*In the middle of her speech,* HOWARD WAGNER, *thirty-six, wheels on a small typewriter table on which is a wire-recording machine and proceeds to plug it in. This is on the left forestage. Light slowly fades on* LINDA *as it rises on* HOWARD. HOWARD *is intent on threading the machine and only glances over his shoulder as* WILLY *appears.*]

WILLY: Pst! Pst!

HOWARD: Hello, Willy, come in.

WILLY: Like to have a little talk with you, Howard.

HOWARD: Sorry to keep you waiting. I'll be with you in a minute.

WILLY: What's that, Howard?

HOWARD: Didn't you ever see one of these? Wire recorder.

WILLY: Oh. Can we talk a minute?

HOWARD: Records things. Just got delivery yesterday. Been driving me crazy, the most terrific machine I ever saw in my life. I was up all night with it.

WILLY: What do you do with it?

HOWARD: I bought it for dictation, but you can do anything with it. Listen to this. I had it home last night. Listen to what I picked up. The first one is my daughter. Get this. [*He flicks the switch and "Roll out the Barrel" is heard being whistled.*] Listen to that kid whistle.

WILLY: That is lifelike, isn't it?

HOWARD: Seven years old. Get that tone.

WILLY: Ts, ts. Like to ask a little favor if you . . .

[*The whistling breaks off, and the voice of* HOWARD's *daughter is heard.*]

HIS DAUGHTER: "Now you, Daddy."

HOWARD: She's crazy for me! [*Again the same song is whistled.*] That's me! Ha! [*He winks.*]

WILLY: You're very good!

[*The whistling breaks off again. The machine runs silent for a moment.*]

HOWARD: Sh! Get this now, this is my son.

HIS SON: "The capital of Alabama is Montgomery; the capital of Arizona is Phoenix; the capital of Arkansas is Little Rock; the capital of California is Sacramento . . ." [*And on, and on.*]

HOWARD: [*Holding up five fingers.*] Five years old, Willy!

WILLY: He'll make an announcer some day!

HIS SON: [*Continuing.*] "The capital. . ."

HOWARD: Get that—alphabetical order! [*The machine breaks off suddenly.*] Wait a minute. The maid kicked the plug out.

WILLY: It certainly is a—

HOWARD: Sh, for God's sake!

HIS SON: "It's nine o'clock, Bulova watch time. So I have to go to sleep."

WILLY: That really is—

HOWARD: Wait a minute! The next is my wife.

[*They wait.*]

HOWARD'S VOICE: "Go on, say something." [*Pause.*] "Well, you gonna talk?"

HIS WIFE: "I can't think of anything."

HOWARD'S VOICE: "Well, talk—it's turning."

HIS WIFE: [*Shyly, beaten.*] "Hello." [*Silence.*] "Oh, Howard, I can't talk into this . . ."

HOWARD: [*Snapping the machine off.*] That was my wife.

WILLY: That is a wonderful machine. Can we—

HOWARD: I tell you, Willy, I'm gonna take my camera, and my bandsaw, and all my hobbies, and out they go. This is the most fascinating relaxation I ever found.

WILLY: I think I'll get one myself.

HOWARD: Sure, they're only a hundred and a half. You can't do without it. Supposing you wanna hear Jack Benny,[4] see? But you can't be at home at that hour. So you tell the maid to turn the radio on when Jack Benny comes on, and this automatically goes on with the radio . . .

WILLY: And when you come home you . . .

HOWARD: You can come home twelve o'clock, one o'clock, any time you like, and you get yourself a Coke and sit yourself down, throw the switch, and there's Jack Benny's program in the middle of the night!

WILLY: I'm definitely going to get one. Because lots of time I'm on the road, and I think to myself, what I must be missing on the radio!

HOWARD: Don't you have a radio in the car?

WILLY: Well, yeah, but who ever thinks of turning it on?

HOWARD: Say, aren't you supposed to be in Boston?

WILLY: That's what I want to talk to you about, Howard. You got a minute? [*He draws a chair in from the wing.*]

HOWARD: What happened? What're you doing here?

WILLY: Well . . .

HOWARD: You didn't crack up again, did you?

WILLY: Oh, no. No . . .

HOWARD: Geez, you had me worried there for a minute. What's the trouble?

WILLY: Well, tell you the truth, Howard. I've come to the decision that I'd rather not travel any more.

HOWARD: Not travel! Well, what'll you do?

WILLY: Remember, Christmas time, when you had the party here? You said you'd try to think of some spot for me here in town.

HOWARD: With us?

WILLY: Well, sure.

HOWARD: Oh, yeah, yeah. I remember. Well, I couldn't think of anything for you, Willy.

WILLY: I tell ya, Howard. The kids are all grown up, y'know. I don't need much any more. If I could take home—well, sixty-five dollars a week, I could swing it.

HOWARD: Yeah, but Willy, see I—

WILLY: I tell ya why, Howard. Speaking frankly and between the two of us, y'know—I'm just a little tired.

HOWARD: Oh, I could understand that, Willy. But you're a road man, Willy, and we do a road business. We've only got a half-dozen salesmen on the floor here.

WILLY: God knows, Howard, I never asked a favor of any man. But I was with the firm when your father used to carry you in here in his arms.

HOWARD: I know that, Willy, but—

4. Jack Benny (1894–1974), a vaudeville, radio, television, and motion picture star, hosted America's most popular radio show from 1932 to 1955.

WILLY: Your father came to me the day you were born and asked me what I thought of the name of Howard, may he rest in peace.

HOWARD: I appreciate that, Willy, but there just is no spot here for you. If I had a spot I'd slam you right in, but I just don't have a single solitary spot.

[*He looks for his lighter.* WILLY *has picked it up and gives it to him. Pause.*]

WILLY: [*With increasing anger.*] Howard, all I need to set my table is fifty dollars a week.

HOWARD: But where am I going to put you, kid?

WILLY: Look, it isn't a question of whether I can sell merchandise, is it?

HOWARD: No, but it's a business, kid, and everybody's gotta pull his own weight.

WILLY: [*Desperately.*] Just let me tell you a story, Howard—

HOWARD: 'Cause you gotta admit, business is business.

WILLY: [*Angrily.*] Business is definitely business, but just listen for a minute. You don't understand this. When I was a boy—eighteen, nineteen—I was already on the road. And there was a question in my mind as to whether selling had a future for me. Because in those days I had a yearning to go to Alaska. See, there were three gold strikes in one month in Alaska, and I felt like going out. Just for the ride, you might say.

HOWARD: [*Barely interested.*] Don't say.

WILLY: Oh, yeah, my father lived many years in Alaska. He was an adventurous man. We've got quite a little streak of self-reliance in our family. I thought I'd go out with my older brother and try to locate him, and maybe settle in the North with the old man. And I was almost decided to go, when I met a salesman in the Parker House. His name was Dave Singleman. And he was eighty-four years old, and he'd drummed merchandise in thirty-one states. And old Dave, he'd go up to his room, y'understand, put on his green velvet slippers—I'll never forget—and pick up his phone and call the buyers, and without ever leaving his room, at the age of eighty-four, he made a living. And when I saw that, I realized that selling was the greatest career a man could want. 'Cause what could be more satisfying than to be able to go, at the age of eighty-four, into twenty or thirty different cities, and pick up his phone and be remembered and loved and helped by so many different people? Do you know? when he died—and by the way he died the death of a salesman, in his green velvet slippers in the smoker of the New York, New Haven and Hartford, going into Boston—when he died, hundreds of salesmen and buyers were at his funeral. Things were sad on a lotta trains for months after that. [*He stands up.* HOWARD *has not looked at him.*] In those days there was personality in it, Howard. There was respect, and comradeship, and gratitude in it. Today, it's all cut and dried, and there's no chance for bringing friendship to bear—or personality. You see what I mean? They don't know me any more.

HOWARD: [*Moving away, toward the right.*] That's just the thing, Willy.

WILLY: If I had forty dollars a week—that's all I'd need. Forty dollars, Howard.

HOWARD: Kid, I can't take blood from a stone, I—

WILLY: [*Desperation is on him now.*] Howard, the year Al Smith[5] was nominated, your father came to me and—

HOWARD: [*Starting to go off.*] I've got to see some people, kid.

WILLY: [*Stopping him.*] I'm talking about your father! There were promises made across this desk! You mustn't tell me you've got people to see—I put thirty-four years into this firm, Howard, and now I can't pay my insurance! You can't eat the orange and throw the peel away—a man is not a piece of fruit! [*After a pause.*] Now pay attention. Your father—in 1928 I had a big year. I averaged a hundred and seventy dollars a week in commissions.

HOWARD: [*Impatiently.*] Now, Willy, you never averaged—

WILLY: [*Banging his hand on the desk.*] I averaged a hundred and seventy dollars a week in the year of 1928! And your father came to me—or rather, I was in the office here—it was right over this desk—and he put his hand on my shoulder—

HOWARD: [*Getting up.*] You'll have to excuse me, Willy, I gotta see some people. Pull yourself together. [*Going out.*] I'll be back in a little while.

[*On* HOWARD's *exit, the light on his chair grows very bright and strange.*]

WILLY: Pull myself together! What the hell did I say to him? My God, I was yelling at him! How could I! [WILLY *breaks off, staring at the light, which occupies the chair, animating it. He approaches this chair, standing across the desk from it.*] Frank, Frank, don't you remember what you told me that time? How you put your hand on my shoulder, and Frank . . . [*He leans on the desk and as he speaks the dead man's name he accidentally switches on the recorder, and instantly.*]

HOWARD'S SON: ". . . of New York is Albany. The capital of Ohio is Cincinnati, the capital of Rhode Island is . . ." [*The recitation continues.*]

WILLY: [*Leaping away with fright, shouting.*] Ha! Howard! Howard! Howard!

HOWARD: [*Rushing in.*] What happened?

WILLY: [*Pointing at the machine, which continues nasally, childishly, with the capital cities.*] Shut it off! Shut it off!

HOWARD: [*Pulling the plug out.*] Look, Willy . . .

WILLY: [*Pressing his hands to his eyes.*] I gotta get myself some coffee. I'll get some coffee . . .

[WILLY *starts to walk out.* HOWARD *stops him.*]

HOWARD: [*Rolling up the cord.*] Willy, look . . .

WILLY: I'll go to Boston.

HOWARD: Willy, you can't go to Boston for us.

WILLY: Why can't I go?

HOWARD: I don't want you to represent us. I've been meaning to tell you for a long time now.

WILLY: Howard, are you firing me?

5. Alfred E. Smith (1873–1944) was the Democratic presidential nominee who lost to Herbert Hoover in 1928.

HOWARD: I think you need a good long rest, Willy.

WILLY: Howard—

HOWARD: And when you feel better, come back, and we'll see if we can work something out.

WILLY: But I gotta earn money, Howard. I'm in no position to—

HOWARD: Where are your sons? Why don't your sons give you a hand?

WILLY: They're working on a very big deal.

HOWARD: This is no time for false pride, Willy. You go to your sons and you tell them that you're tired. You've got two great boys, haven't you?

WILLY: Oh, no question, no question, but in the meantime . . .

HOWARD: Then that's that, heh?

WILLY: All right, I'll go to Boston tomorrow.

HOWARD: No, no.

WILLY: I can't throw myself on my sons. I'm not a cripple!

HOWARD: Look, kid, I'm busy, I'm busy this morning.

WILLY: [Grasping HOWARD's arm.] Howard, you've got to let me go to Boston!

HOWARD: [Hard, keeping himself under control.] I've got a line of people to see this morning. Sit down, take five minutes, and pull yourself together, and then go home, will ya? I need the office, Willy. [He starts to go, turns, remembering the recorder, starts to push off the table holding the recorder.] Oh, yeah. Whenever you can this week, stop by and drop off the samples. You'll feel better, Willy, and then come back and we'll talk. Pull yourself together, kid, there's people outside.

[HOWARD exits, pushing the table off left. WILLY stares into space, exhausted. Now the music is heard—BEN's music—first distantly, then closer, closer. As WILLY speaks, BEN enters from the right. He carries valise and umbrella.]

WILLY: Oh, Ben, how did you do it? What is the answer? Did you wind up the Alaska deal already?

BEN: Doesn't take much time if you know what you're doing. Just a short business trip. Boarding ship in an hour. Wanted to say good-by.

WILLY: Ben, I've got to talk to you.

BEN: [Glancing at his watch.] Haven't the time, William.

WILLY: [Crossing the apron to BEN.] Ben, nothing's working out. I don't know what to do.

BEN: Now, look here, William. I've bought timberland in Alaska and I need a man to look after things for me.

WILLY: God, timberland! Me and my boys in those grand outdoors!

BEN: You've a new continent at your doorstep, William. Get out of these cities, they're full of talk and time payments and courts of law. Screw on your fists and you can fight for a fortune up there.

WILLY: Yes, yes! Linda, Linda!

[LINDA enters as of old, with the wash.]

LINDA: Oh, you're back?

BEN: I haven't much time.

WILLY: No, wait! Linda, he's got a proposition for me in Alaska.

LINDA: But you've got—[*To* BEN.] He's got a beautiful job here.

WILLY: But in Alaska, kid, I could—

LINDA: You're doing well enough, Willy!

BEN: [*To* LINDA.] Enough for what, my dear?

LINDA: [*Frightened of* BEN *and angry at him.*] Don't say those things to him! Enough to be happy right here, right now. [*To* WILLY, *while* BEN *laughs.*] Why must everybody conquer the world? You're well liked, and the boys love you, and someday—[*To* BEN.]—why, old man Wagner told him just the other day that if he keeps it up he'll be a member of the firm, didn't he, Willy?

WILLY: Sure, sure. I am building something with this firm, Ben, and if a man is building something he must be on the right track, mustn't he?

BEN: What are you building? Lay your hand on it. Where is it?

WILLY: [*Hesitantly.*] That's true, Linda, there's nothing.

LINDA: Why? [*To* BEN.] There's a man eighty-four years old—

WILLY: That's right, Ben, that's right. When I look at that man I say, what is there to worry about?

BEN: Bah!

WILLY: It's true, Ben. All he has to do is go into any city, pick up the phone, and he's making his living and you know why?

BEN: [*Picking up his valise.*] I've got to go.

WILLY: [*Holding* BEN *back.*] Look at this boy! [BIFF, *in his high school sweater, enters carrying suitcase.* HAPPY *carries* BIFF's *shoulder guards, gold helmet, and football pants.*] Without a penny to his name, three great universities are begging for him, and from there the sky's the limit, because it's not what you do, Ben. It's who you know and the smile on your face! It's contacts, Ben, contacts! The whole wealth of Alaska passes over the lunch table at the Commodore Hotel, and that's the wonder, the wonder of this country, that a man can end with diamonds here on the basis of being liked! [*He turns to* BIFF.] And that's why when you get out on that field today it's important. Because thousands of people will be rooting for you and loving you. [*To* BEN, *who has again begun to leave.*] And Ben! when he walks into a business office his name will sound out like a bell and all the doors will open to him! I've seen it, Ben, I've seen it a thousand times! You can't feel it with your hand like timber, but it's there!

BEN: Good-by, William.

WILLY: Ben, am I right? Don't you think I'm right? I value your advice.

BEN: There's a new continent at your doorstep, William. You could walk out rich. Rich! [*He is gone.*]

WILLY: We'll do it here, Ben! You hear me? We're gonna do it here!

[*Young* BERNARD *rushes in. The gay music of the Boys is heard.*]

BERNARD: Oh, gee, I was afraid you left already!

WILLY: Why? What time is it?

BERNARD: It's half-past one!

WILLY: Well, come on, everybody! Ebbets Field next stop! Where's the pennants? [*He rushes through the wall-line of the kitchen and out into the living room.*]

LINDA: [*To* BIFF.] Did you pack fresh underwear?

BIFF: [*Who has been limbering up.*] I want to go!

BERNARD: Biff, I'm carrying your helmet, ain't I?

HAPPY: No, I'm carrying the helmet.

BERNARD: Oh, Biff, you promised me.

HAPPY: I'm carrying the helmet.

BERNARD: How am I going to get in the locker room?

LINDA: Let him carry the shoulder guards. [*She puts her coat and hat on in the kitchen.*]

BERNARD: Can I, Biff? 'Cause I told everybody I'm going to be in the locker room.

HAPPY: In Ebbets Field it's the clubhouse.

BERNARD: I meant the clubhouse, Biff!

HAPPY: Biff!

BIFF: [*Grandly, after a slight pause.*] Let him carry the shoulder guards.

HAPPY: [*As he gives* BERNARD *the shoulder guards.*] Stay close to us now.

[WILLY *rushes in with the pennants.*]

WILLY: [*Handing them out.*] Everybody wave when Biff comes out on the field. [HAPPY *and* BERNARD *run off.*] You set now, boy?

[*The music has died away.*]

BIFF: Ready to go, Pop. Every muscle is ready.

WILLY: [*At the edge of the apron.*] You realize what this means?

BIFF: That's right, Pop.

WILLY: [*Feeling* BIFF's *muscles.*] You're comin' home this afternoon captain of the All-Scholastic Championship Team of the City of New York.

BIFF: I got it, Pop. And remember, pal, when I take off my helmet, that touchdown is for you.

WILLY: Let's go! [*He is starting out, with his arm around* BIFF, *when* CHARLEY *enters, as of old, in knickers.*] I got no room for you, Charley.

CHARLEY: Room? For what?

WILLY: In the car.

CHARLEY: You goin' for a ride? I wanted to shoot some casino.

WILLY: [*Furiously.*] Casino! [*Incredulously.*] Don't you realize what today is?

LINDA: Oh, he knows, Willy. He's just kidding you.

WILLY: That's nothing to kid about!

CHARLEY: No, Linda, what's goin' on?

LINDA: He's playing in Ebbets Field.

CHARLEY: Baseball in this weather?

WILLY: Don't talk to him. Come on, come on! [*He is pushing them out.*]

CHARLEY: Wait a minute, didn't you hear the news?

WILLY: What?

CHARLEY: Don't you listen to the radio? Ebbets Field just blew up.

WILLY: You go to hell! [CHARLEY laughs. Pushing them out.] Come on, come on!
We're late.

CHARLEY: [As they go.] Knock a homer, Biff, knock a homer!

WILLY: [The last to leave, turning to CHARLEY.] I don't think that was funny,
Charley. This is the greatest day of my life.

CHARLEY: Willy, when are you going to grow up?

WILLY: Yeah, heh? When this game is over, Charley, you'll be laughing out of
the other side of your face. They'll be calling him another Red Grange.[6]
Twenty-five thousand a year.

CHARLEY: [Kidding.] Is that so?

WILLY: Yeah, that's so.

CHARLEY: Well, then, I'm sorry, Willy. But tell me something.

WILLY: What?

CHARLEY: Who is Red Grange?

WILLY: Put up your hands. Goddam you, put up your hands! [CHARLEY, chuckling, shakes his head and walks away, around the left corner of the stage.
WILLY follows him. The music rises to a mocking frenzy.] Who the hell do you
think you are, better than everybody else? You don't know everything, you
big, ignorant, stupid . . . Put up your hands!

[Light rises, on the right side of the forestage, on a small table in the reception
room of CHARLEY's office. Traffic sounds are heard. BERNARD, now mature, sits
whistling to himself. A pair of tennis rackets and an overnight bag are on the
floor beside him.]

WILLY: [Offstage.] What are you walking away for? Don't walk away! If you're
going to say something say it to my face! I know you laugh at me behind my
back. You'll laugh out of the other side of your goddam face after this game.
Touchdown! Touchdown! Eighty thousand people! Touchdown! Right
between the goal posts.

[BERNARD is a quiet, earnest, but self-assured young man. WILLY's voice is
coming from right upstage now. BERNARD lowers his feet off the table and
listens. JENNY, his father's secretary, enters.]

JENNY: [Distressed.] Say, Bernard, will you go out in the hall?

BERNARD: What is that noise? Who is it?

JENNY: Mr. Loman. He just got off the elevator.

BERNARD: [Getting up.] Who's he arguing with?

JENNY: Nobody. There's nobody with him. I can't deal with him any more, and
your father gets all upset everytime he comes. I've got a lot of typing to do,
and your father's waiting to sign it. Will you see him?

6. Harold Edward Grange, All-American halfback at the University of Illinois (1923–1925), who
played professionally for the Chicago Bears.

WILLY: [*Entering.*] Touchdown! Touch—[*He sees* JENNY.] Jenny, Jenny, good to see you. How're ya? Workin'? Or still honest?

JENNY: Fine. How've you been feeling?

WILLY: Not much any more, Jenny. Ha, ha! [*He is surprised to see the rackets.*]

BERNARD: Hello, Uncle Willy.

WILLY: [*Almost shocked.*] Bernard! Well, look who's here! [*He comes quickly, guiltily to* BERNARD *and warmly shakes his hand.*]

BERNARD: How are you? Good to see you.

WILLY: What are you doing here?

BERNARD: Oh, just stopped by to see Pop. Get off my feet till my train leaves. I'm going to Washington in a few minutes.

WILLY: Is he in?

BERNARD: Yes, he's in his office with the accountant. Sit down.

WILLY: [*Sitting down.*] What're you going to do in Washington?

BERNARD: Oh, just a case I've got there, Willy.

WILLY: That so? [*Indicating the rackets.*] You going to play tennis there?

BERNARD: I'm staying with a friend who's got a court.

WILLY: Don't say. His own tennis court. Must be fine people, I bet.

BERNARD: They are, very nice. Dad tells me Biff's in town.

WILLY: [*With a big smile.*] Yeah, Biff's in. Working on a very big deal, Bernard.

BERNARD: What's Biff doing?

WILLY: Well, he's been doing very big things in the West. But he decided to establish himself here. Very big. We're having dinner. Did I hear your wife had a boy?

BERNARD: That's right. Our second.

WILLY: Two boys! What do you know!

BERNARD: What kind of a deal has Biff got?

WILLY: Well, Bill Oliver—very big sporting-goods man—he wants Biff very badly. Called him in from the West. Long distance, carte blanche, special deliveries. Your friends have their own private tennis court?

BERNARD: You still with the old firm, Willy?

WILLY: [*After a pause.*] I'm—I'm overjoyed to see how you made the grade, Bernard, overjoyed. It's an encouraging thing to see a young man really— really— Looks very good for Biff—very—[*He breaks off, then.*] Bernard— [*He is so full of emotion, he breaks off again.*]

BERNARD: What is it, Willy?

WILLY: [*Small and alone.*] What—what's the secret?

BERNARD: What secret?

WILLY: How—how did you? Why didn't he ever catch on?

BERNARD: I wouldn't know that, Willy.

WILLY: [*Confidentially, desperately.*] You were his friend, his boyhood friend. There's something I don't understand about it. His life ended after that Ebbets Field game. From the age of seventeen nothing good ever happened to him.

BERNARD: He never trained himself for anything.

WILLY: But he did, he did. After high school he took so many correspondence courses. Radio mechanics; television; God knows what, and never made the slightest mark.

BERNARD: [*Taking off his glasses.*] Willy, do you want to talk candidly?

WILLY: [*Rising, faces* BERNARD.] I regard you as a very brilliant man, Bernard. I value your advice.

BERNARD: Oh, the hell with the advice, Willy. I couldn't advise you. There's just one thing I've always wanted to ask you. When he was supposed to graduate, and the math teacher flunked him—

WILLY: Oh, that son-of-a-bitch ruined his life.

BERNARD: Yeah, but, Willy, all he had to do was go to summer school and make up that subject.

WILLY: That's right, that's right.

BERNARD: Did you tell him not to go to summer school?

WILLY: Me? I begged him to go. I ordered him to go!

BERNARD: Then why wouldn't he go?

WILLY: Why? Why! Bernard, that question has been trailing me like a ghost for the last fifteen years. He flunked the subject, and laid down and died like a hammer hit him!

BERNARD: Take it easy, kid.

WILLY: Let me talk to you—I got nobody to talk to. Bernard, Bernard, was it my fault? Y'see? It keeps going around in my mind, maybe I did something to him. I got nothing to give him.

BERNARD: Don't take it so hard.

WILLY: Why did he lay down? What is the story there? You were his friend!

BERNARD: Willy, I remember, it was June, and our grades came out. And he'd flunked math.

WILLY: That son-of-a-bitch!

BERNARD: No, it wasn't right then. Biff just got very angry, I remember, and he was ready to enroll in summer school.

WILLY: [*Surprised.*] He was?

BERNARD: He wasn't beaten by it at all. But then, Willy, he disappeared from the block for almost a month. And I got the idea that he'd gone up to New England to see you. Did he have a talk with you then? [WILLY *stares in silence.*] Willy?

WILLY: [*With a strong edge of resentment in his voice.*] Yeah, he came to Boston. What about it?

BERNARD: Well, just that when he came back—I'll never forget this, it always mystifies me. Because I'd thought so well of Biff, even though he'd always taken advantage of me. I loved him, Willy, y'know? And he came back after that month and took his sneakers—remember those sneakers with "University of Virginia" printed on them? He was so proud of those, wore them every day. And he took them down in the cellar, and burned them up in the furnace. We had a fist fight. It lasted at least half an hour. Just the two of us, punching each other down the cellar, and crying right through it. I've often thought of how strange it was that I knew he'd given up his life. What happened in Boston, Willy? [WILLY *looks at him as at an intruder.*] I just bring it up because you asked me.

WILLY: [*Angrily.*] Nothing. What do you mean, "What happened?" What's that got to do with anything?

BERNARD: Well, don't get sore.

WILLY: What are you trying to do, blame it on me? If a boy lays down is that my fault?

BERNARD: Now, Willy, don't get—

WILLY: Well, don't—don't talk to me that way! What does that mean, "What happened?"

[CHARLEY *enters. He is in his vest, and he carries a bottle of bourbon.*]

CHARLEY: Hey, you're going to miss that train. [*He waves the bottle.*]

BERNARD: Yeah, I'm going. [*He takes the bottle.*] Thanks, Pop. [*He picks up his rackets and bag.*] Good-by, Willy, and don't worry about it. You know, "If at first you don't succeed . . ."

WILLY: Yes, I believe in that.

BERNARD: But sometimes, Willy, it's better for a man just to walk away.

WILLY: Walk away?

BERNARD: That's right.

WILLY: But if you can't walk away?

BERNARD: [*After a slight pause.*] I guess that's when it's tough. [*Extending his hand.*] Good-by, Willy.

WILLY: [*Shaking* BERNARD's *hand.*] Good-by, boy.

CHARLEY: [*An arm on* BERNARD's *shoulder.*] How do you like this kid? Gonna argue a case in front of the Supreme Court.

BERNARD: [*Protesting.*] Pop!

WILLY: [*Genuinely shocked, pained, and happy.*] No! The Supreme Court!

BERNARD: I gotta run. 'By, Dad!

CHARLEY: Knock 'em dead, Bernard!

[BERNARD *goes off.*]

WILLY: [*As* CHARLEY *takes out his wallet.*] The Supreme Court! And he didn't even mention it!

CHARLEY: [*Counting out money on the desk.*] He don't have to—he's gonna do it.

WILLY: And you never told him what to do, did you? You never took any interest in him.

CHARLEY: My salvation is that I never took any interest in anything. There's some money—fifty dollars. I got an accountant inside.

WILLY: Charley, look . . . [*With difficulty.*] I got my insurance to pay. If you can manage it—I need a hundred and ten dollars. [CHARLEY *doesn't reply for a moment; merely stops moving.*] I'd draw it from my bank but Linda would know, and I . . .

CHARLEY: Sit down, Willy.

WILLY: [*Moving toward the chair.*] I'm keeping an account of everything, remember. I'll pay every penny back. [*He sits.*]

CHARLEY: Now listen to me, Willy.

WILLY: I want you to know I appreciate . . .

CHARLEY: [*Sitting down on the table.*] Willy, what're you doin'? What the hell is goin' on in your head?

WILLY: Why? I'm simply . . .

CHARLEY: I offered you a job. You can make fifty dollars a week. And I won't send you on the road.

WILLY: I've got a job.

CHARLEY: Without pay? What kind of job is a job without pay? [*He rises.*] Now, look kid, enough is enough. I'm no genius but I know when I'm being insulted.

WILLY: Insulted!

CHARLEY: Why don't you want to work for me?

WILLY: What's the matter with you? I've got a job.

BERNARD: Then what're you walkin' in here every week for?

WILLY: [*Getting up.*] Well, if you don't want me to walk in here—

CHARLEY: I am offering you a job!

WILLY: I don't want your goddam job!

CHARLEY: When the hell are you going to grow up?

WILLY: [*Furiously.*] You big ignoramus, if you say that to me again I'll rap you one! I don't care how big you are! [*He's ready to fight. Pause.*]

CHARLEY: [*Kindly, going to him.*] How much do you need, Willy?

WILLY: Charley, I'm strapped, I'm strapped. I don't know what to do. I was just fired.

CHARLEY: Howard fired you?

WILLY: That snotnose. Imagine that? I named him. I named him Howard.

CHARLEY: Willy, when're you gonna realize that them things don't mean anything? You named him Howard, but you can't sell that. The only thing you got in this world is what you can sell. And the funny thing is that you're a salesman, and you don't know that.

WILLY: I've always tried to think otherwise, I guess. I always felt that if a man was impressive, and well liked, that nothing—

CHARLEY: Why must everybody like you? Who liked J. P. Morgan? Was he impressive? In a Turkish bath he'd look like a butcher. But with his pockets on he was very well liked. Now listen, Willy, I know you don't like me, and nobody can say I'm in love with you, but I'll give you a job because—just for the hell of it, put it that way. Now what do you say?

WILLY: I—I just can't work for you, Charley.

CHARLEY: What're you, jealous of me?

WILLY: I can't work for you, that's all, don't ask me why.

CHARLEY: [*Angered, takes out more bills.*] You been jealous of me all your life, you damned fool! Here, pay your insurance. [*He puts the money in* WILLY'S *hand.*]

WILLY: I'm keeping strict accounts.

CHARLEY: I've got some work to do. Take care of yourself. And pay your insurance.

WILLY: [*Moving to the right.*] Funny, y'know? After all the highways and the trains, and the appointments, and the years, you end up worth more dead than alive.

CHARLEY: Willy, nobody's worth nothin' dead. [*After a slight pause.*] Did you hear what I said? [WILLY *stands still, dreaming.*] Willy!

WILLY: Apologize to Bernard for me when you see him. I didn't mean to argue with him. He's a fine boy. They're all fine boys, and they'll end up big—all of them. Someday they'll all play tennis together. Wish me luck, Charley. He saw Bill Oliver today.

CHARLEY: Good luck.

WILLY: [*On the verge of tears.*] Charley, you're the only friend I got. Isn't that a remarkable thing? [*He goes out.*]

CHARLEY: Jesus!

[CHARLEY *stares after him a moment and follows. All light blacks out. Suddenly raucous music is heard, and a red glow rises behind the screen at right.* STANLEY, *a young waiter, appears, carrying a table, followed by* HAPPY, *who is carrying two chairs.*]

STANLEY: [*Putting the table down.*] That's all right, Mr. Loman, I can handle it myself. [*He turns and takes the chairs from* HAPPY *and places them at the table.*]

HAPPY: [*Glancing around.*] Oh, this is better.

STANLEY: Sure, in the front there you're in the middle of all kinds a noise. Whenever you got a party. Mr. Loman, you just tell me and I'll put you back here. Y'know, there's a lotta people they don't like it private, because when they go out they like to see a lotta action around them because they're sick and tired to stay in the house by theirself. But I know you, you ain't from Hackensack. You know what I mean?

HAPPY: [*Sitting down.*] So how's it coming, Stanley?

STANLEY: Ah, it's a dog life. I only wish during the war they'd a took me in the Army. I couda been dead by now.

HAPPY: My brother's back, Stanley.

STANLEY: Oh, he come back, heh? From the Far West.

HAPPY: Yeah, big cattle man, my brother, so treat him right. And my father's coming too.

STANLEY: Oh, your father too!

HAPPY: You got a couple of nice lobsters?

STANLEY: Hundred per cent, big.

HAPPY: I want them with the claws.

STANLEY: Don't worry, I don't give you no mice. [HAPPY *laughs.*] How about some wine? It'll put a head on the meal.

HAPPY: No. You remember, Stanley, that recipe I brought you from overseas? With the champagne in it?

STANLEY: Oh, yeah, sure. I still got it tacked up yet in the kitchen. But that'll have to cost a buck apiece anyways.

HAPPY: That's all right.

STANLEY: What'd you, hit a number or somethin'?

HAPPY: No, it's a little celebration. My brother is—I think he pulled off a big deal today. I think we're going into business together.

STANLEY: Great! That's the best for you. Because a family business, you know what I mean?—that's the best.

HAPPY: That's what I think.

STANLEY: 'Cause what's the difference? Somebody steals? It's in the family. Know what I mean? [*Sotto voce.*] Like this bartender here. The boss is goin' crazy what kinda leak he's got in the cash register. You put it in but it don't come out.

HAPPY: [*Raising his head.*] Sh!

STANLEY: What?

HAPPY: You notice I wasn't lookin' right or left, was I?

STANLEY: No.

HAPPY: And my eyes are closed.

STANLEY: So what's the—?

HAPPY: Strudel's comin'.

STANLEY: [*Catching on, looks around.*] Ah, no there's no—[*He breaks off as a furred, lavishly dressed* GIRL *enters and sits at the next table. Both follow her with their eyes.*] Geez, how'd ya know?

HAPPY: I got radar or something. [*Staring directly at her profile.*] Oooooooo . . . Stanley.

STANLEY: I think, that's for you, Mr. Loman.

HAPPY: Look at that mouth. Oh, God. And the binoculars.

STANLEY: Geez, you got a life, Mr. Loman.

HAPPY: Wait on her.

STANLEY: [*Going to the* GIRL'*s table.*] Would you like a menu, ma'am?

GIRL: I'm expecting someone, but I'd like a—

HAPPY: Why don't you bring her—excuse me, miss, do you mind? I sell champagne, and I'd like you to try my brand. Bring her a champagne, Stanley.

GIRL: That's awfully nice of you.

HAPPY: Don't mention it. It's all company money. [*He laughs.*]

GIRL: That's a charming product to be selling, isn't it?

HAPPY: Oh, gets to be like everything else. Selling is selling, y'know.

GIRL: I suppose.

HAPPY: You don't happen to sell, do you?

GIRL: No, I don't sell.

HAPPY: Would you object to a compliment from a stranger? You ought to be on a magazine cover.

GIRL: [*Looking at him a little archly.*] I have been.

[STANLEY *comes in with a glass of champagne.*]

HAPPY: What'd I say before, Stanley? You see? She's a cover girl.

STANLEY: Oh, I could see, I could see.

HAPPY: [*To the* GIRL.] What magazine?

GIRL: Oh, a lot of them. [*She takes the drink.*] Thank you.

HAPPY: You know what they say in France, don't you? "Champagne is the drink of the complexion"—Hya, Biff!

[BIFF *has entered and sits with* HAPPY.]

BIFF: Hello, kid. Sorry I'm late.

HAPPY: I just got here. Uh, Miss—?

GIRL: Forsythe.

HAPPY: Miss Forsythe, this is my brother.

BIFF: Is Dad here?

HAPPY: His name is Biff. You might've heard of him. Great football player.

GIRL: Really? What team?

HAPPY: Are you familiar with football?

GIRL: No, I'm afraid I'm not.

HAPPY: Biff is quarterback with the New York Giants.

GIRL: Well, that's nice, isn't it? [*She drinks.*]

HAPPY: Good health.

GIRL: I'm happy to meet you.

HAPPY: That's my name, Hap. It's really Harold, but at West Point they called me Happy.

GIRL: [*Now really impressed.*] Oh, I see. How do you do? [*She turns her profile.*]

BIFF: Isn't Dad coming?

HAPPY: You want her?

BIFF: Oh, I could never make that.

HAPPY: I remember the time that idea would never come into your head. Where's the old confidence, Biff?

BIFF: I just saw Oliver—

HAPPY: Wait a minute. I've got to see that old confidence again. Do you want her? She's on call.

BIFF: Oh, no. [*He turns to look at the* GIRL.]

HAPPY: I'm telling you. Watch this. [*Turning to see the* GIRL.] Honey? [*She turns to him.*] Are you busy?

GIRL: Well, I am . . . but I could make a phone call.

HAPPY: Do that, will you, honey? And see if you can get a friend. We'll be here for a while. Biff is one of the greatest football players in the country.

GIRL: [*Standing up.*] Well, I'm certainly happy to meet you.

HAPPY: Come back soon.

GIRL: I'll try.

HAPPY: Don't try, honey, try hard. [*The* GIRL *exits.* STANLEY *follows, shaking his head in bewildered admiration.*] Isn't that a shame now? A beautiful girl like that? That's why I can't get married. There's not a good woman in a thousand. New York is loaded with them, kid!

BIFF: Hap, look—

HAPPY: I told you she was on call!

BIFF: [*Strangely unnerved.*] Cut it out, will ya? I want to say something to you.

HAPPY: Did you see Oliver?

BIFF: I saw him all right. Now look, I want to tell Dad a couple of things and I want you to help me.

HAPPY: What? Is he going to back you?

BIFF: Are you crazy? You're out of your goddam head, you know that?

HAPPY: Why? What happened?

BIFF: [*Breathlessly.*] I did a terrible thing today, Hap. It's been the strangest day I ever went through. I'm all numb, I swear.

HAPPY: You mean he wouldn't see you?

BIFF: Well, I waited six hours for him, see? All day. Kept sending my name in. Even tried to date his secretary so she'd get me to him, but no soap.

HAPPY: Because you're not showin' the old confidence, Biff. He remembered you, didn't he?

BIFF: [*Stopping* HAPPY *with a gesture.*] Finally, about five o'clock, he comes out. Didn't remember who I was or anything. I felt like such an idiot, Hap.

HAPPY: Did you tell him my Florida idea?

BIFF: He walked away. I saw him for one minute. I got so mad I could've torn the walls down! How the hell did I ever get the idea I was a salesman there? I even believed myself that I'd been a salesman for him! And then he gave me one look and—I realized what a ridiculous lie my whole life has been! We've been talking in a dream for fifteen years. I was a shipping clerk.

HAPPY: What'd you do?

BIFF: [*With great tension and wonder.*] Well, he left, see. And the secretary went out. I was all alone in the waiting-room. I don't know what came over me, Hap. The next thing I know I'm in his office—paneled walls, everything. I can't explain it. I—Hap, I took his fountain pen.

HAPPY: Geez, did he catch you?

BIFF: I ran out. I ran down all eleven flights. I ran and ran and ran.

HAPPY: That was an awful dumb—what'd you do that for?

BIFF: [*Agonized.*] I don't know, I just—wanted to take something, I don't know. You gotta help me, Hap, I'm gonna tell Pop.

HAPPY: You crazy? What for?

BIFF: Hap, he's got to understand that I'm not the man somebody lends that kind of money to. He thinks I've been spiting him all these years and it's eating him up.

HAPPY: That's just it. You tell him something nice.

BIFF: I can't.

HAPPY: Say you got a lunch date with Oliver tomorrow.

BIFF: So what do I do tomorrow?

HAPPY: You leave the house tomorrow and come back at night and say Oliver is thinking it over. And he thinks it over for a couple of weeks, and gradually it fades away and nobody's the worse.

BIFF: But it'll go on forever!

HAPPY: Dad is never so happy as when he's looking forward to something! [WILLY *enters.*] Hello, scout!

WILLY: Gee, I haven't been here in years!

[STANLEY *has followed* WILLY *in and sets a chair for him.* STANLEY *starts off but* HAPPY *stops him.*]

HAPPY: Stanley!

[STANLEY *stands by, waiting for an order.*]

BIFF: [*Going to* WILLY *with guilt, as to an invalid.*] Sit down, Pop. You want a
  drink?
WILLY: Sure, I don't mind.
BIFF: Let's get a load on.
WILLY: You look worried.
BIFF: N-no. [*To* STANLEY.] Scotch all around. Make it doubles.
STANLEY: Doubles, right. [*He goes.*]
WILLY: You had a couple already, didn't you?
BIFF: Just a couple, yeah.
WILLY: Well, what happened, boy? [*Nodding affirmatively, with a smile.*] Every-
  thing go all right?
BIFF: [*Takes a breath, then reaches out and grasps* WILLY'*s hand.*] Pal . . . [*He is
  smiling bravely, and* WILLY *is smiling too.*] I had an experience today.
HAPPY: Terrific, Pop.
WILLY: That so? What happened?
BIFF: [*High, slightly alcoholic, above the earth.*] I'm going to tell you everything
  from first to last. It's been a strange day. [*Silence. He looks around, composes
  himself as best he can, but his breath keeps breaking the rhythm of his voice.*]
  I had to wait quite a while for him, and —
WILLY: Oliver?
BIFF: Yeah, Oliver. All day, as a matter of cold fact. And a lot of — instances —
  facts, Pop, facts about my life came back to me. Who was it, Pop? Who ever
  said I was a salesman with Oliver?
WILLY: Well, you were.
BIFF: No, Dad, I was shipping clerk.
WILLY: But you were practically —
BIFF: [*With determination.*] Dad, I don't know who said it first, but I was never
  a salesman for Bill Oliver.
WILLY: What're you talking about?
BIFF: Let's hold on to the facts tonight, Pop. We're not going to get anywhere
  bullin' around. I was a shipping clerk.
WILLY: [*Angrily.*] All right, now listen to me —
BIFF: Why don't you let me finish?
WILLY: I'm not interested in stories about the past or any crap of that kind
  because the woods are burning, boys, you understand? There's a big blaze
  going on all around. I was fired today.
BIFF: [*Shocked.*] How could you be?
WILLY: I was fired, and I'm looking for a little good news to tell your mother,
  because the woman has waited and the woman has suffered. The gist of it is
  that I haven't got a story left in my head, Biff. So don't give me a lecture
  about facts and aspects. I am not interested. Now what've you got to say to
  me? [STANLEY *enters with three drinks. They wait until he leaves.*] Did you
  see Oliver?
BIFF: Jesus, Dad!

WILLY: You mean you didn't go up there?

HAPPY: Sure he went up there.

BIFF: I did. I—saw him. How could they fire you?

WILLY: [On the edge of his chair.] What kind of a welcome did he give you?

BIFF: He won't even let you work on commission?

WILLY: I'm out. [Driving.] So tell me, he gave you a warm welcome?

HAPPY: Sure, Pop, sure!

BIFF: [Driven.] Well, it was kind of—

WILLY: I was wondering if he'd remember you. [To HAPPY.] Imagine, man doesn't see him for ten, twelve years and gives him that kind of a welcome!

HAPPY: Damn right!

BIFF: [Trying to return to the offensive.] Pop, look—

WILLY: You know why he remembered you, don't you? Because you impressed him in those days.

BIFF: Let's talk quietly and get this down to the facts, huh?

WILLY: [As though BIFF had been interrupting.] Well, what happened? It's great news, Biff. Did he take you into his office or'd you talk in the waiting-room?

BIFF: Well, he came in, see and—

WILLY: [With a big smile.] What'd he say? Betcha he threw his arm around you.

BIFF: Well, he kinda—

WILLY: He's a fine man. [To HAPPY.] Very hard man to see, y'know.

HAPPY: [Agreeing.] Oh, I know.

WILLY: [To BIFF.] Is that where you had the drinks?

BIFF: Yeah, he gave me a couple of—no, no!

HAPPY: [Cutting in.] He told him my Florida idea.

WILLY: Don't interrupt. [To BIFF.] How'd he react to the Florida idea?

BIFF: Dad, will you give me a minute to explain?

WILLY: I've been waiting for you to explain since I sat down here! What happened? He took you into his office and what?

BIFF: Well—I talked. And—he listened, see.

WILLY: Famous for the way he listens, y'know. What was his answer?

BIFF: His answer was—[He breaks off, suddenly angry.] Dad, you're not letting me tell you what I want to tell you!

WILLY: [Accusing, angered.] You didn't see him, did you?

BIFF: I did see him!

WILLY: What'd you insult him or something? You insulted him, didn't you?

BIFF: Listen, will you let me out of it, will you just let me out of it!

HAPPY: What the hell!

WILLY: Tell me what happened!

BIFF: [To HAPPY.] I can't talk to him!

[A single trumpet note jars the ear. The light of green leaves stains the house, which holds the air of night and a dream. YOUNG BERNARD enters and knocks on the door of the house.]

YOUNG BERNARD: [Frantically.] Mrs. Loman, Mrs. Loman!

HAPPY: Tell him what happened!

BIFF: [*To* HAPPY.] Shut up and leave me alone!

WILLY: No, no. You had to go and flunk math!

BIFF: What math? What're you talking about?

YOUNG BERNARD: Mrs. Loman, Mrs. Loman!

[LINDA *appears in the house, as of old.*]

WILLY: [*Wildly.*] Math, math, math!

BIFF: Take it easy, Pop!

YOUNG BERNARD: Mrs. Loman!

WILLY: [*Furiously.*] If you hadn't flunked you'd've been set by now!

BIFF: Now, look, I'm gonna tell you what happened, and you're going to listen to me.

YOUNG BERNARD: Mrs. Loman!

BIFF: I waited six hours—

HAPPY: What the hell are you saying?

BIFF: I kept sending in my name but he wouldn't see me. So finally he . . . [*He continues unheard as light fades low on the restaurant.*]

YOUNG BERNARD: Biff flunked math!

LINDA: No!

YOUNG BERNARD: Birnbaum flunked him! They won't graduate him!

LINDA: But they have to. He's gotta go to the university. Where is he? Biff! Biff!

YOUNG BERNARD: No, he left. He went to Grand Central.

LINDA: Grand— You mean he went to Boston!

YOUNG BERNARD: Is Uncle Willy in Boston?

LINDA: Oh, maybe Willy can talk to the teacher. Oh, the poor, poor boy!

[*Light on house area snaps out.*]

BIFF: [*At the table, now audible, holding up a gold fountain pen.*] . . . so I'm washed up with Oliver, you understand? Are you listening to me?

WILLY: [*At a loss.*] Yeah, sure. If you hadn't flunked—

BIFF: Flunked what? What're you talking about?

WILLY: Don't blame everything on me! I didn't flunk math—you did! What pen?

HAPPY: That was awful dumb, Biff, a pen like that is worth—

WILLY: [*Seeing the pen for the first time.*] You took Oliver's pen?

BIFF: [*Weakening.*] Dad, I just explained it to you.

WILLY: You stole Bill Oliver's fountain pen!

BIFF: I didn't exactly steal it! That's just what I've been explaining to you!

HAPPY: He had it in his hand and just then Oliver walked in, so he got nervous and stuck it in his pocket!

WILLY: My God, Biff!

BIFF: I never intended to do it, Dad!

OPERATOR'S VOICE: Standish Arms, good evening!

WILLY: [*Shouting.*] I'm not in my room!

BIFF: [*Frightened.*] Dad, what's the matter? [*He and* HAPPY *stand up.*]

OPERATOR: Ringing Mr. Loman for you!

BIFF: [*Horrified, gets down on one knee before* WILLY.] Dad, I'll make good, I'll make good. [WILLY *tries to get to his feet.* BIFF *holds him down.*] Sit down now.

WILLY: No, you're no good, you're no good for anything.

BIFF: I am, Dad, I'll find something else, you understand? Now don't worry about anything. [*He holds up* WILLY's *face.*] Talk to me, Dad.

OPERATOR: Mr. Loman does not answer. Shall I page him?

WILLY: [*Attempting to stand, as though to rush and silence the* OPERATOR.] No, no, no!

HAPPY: He'll strike something, Pop.

WILLY: No, no . . .

BIFF: [*Desperately, standing over* WILLY.] Pop, listen! Listen to me! I'm telling you something good. Oliver talked to his partner about the Florida idea. You listening? He—he talked to his partner, and he came to me . . . I'm going to be all right, you hear? Dad, listen to me, he said it was just a question of the amount!

WILLY: Then you . . . got it?

HAPPY: He's gonna be terrific, Pop!

WILLY: [*Trying to stand.*] Then you got it, haven't you? You got it! You got it!

BIFF: [*Agonized, holds* WILLY *down.*] No, no. Look, Pop. I'm supposed to have lunch with them tomorrow. I'm just telling you this so you'll know that I can still make an impression, Pop. And I'll make good somewhere, but I can't go tomorrow, see?

WILLY: Why not? You simply—

BIFF: But the pen, Pop!

WILLY: You give it to him and tell him it was an oversight!

HAPPY: Sure, have lunch tomorrow!

BIFF: I can't say that—

WILLY: You were doing a crossword puzzle and accidentally used his pen!

BIFF: Listen, kid, I took those balls years ago, now I walk in with his fountain pen? That clinches it, don't you see? I can't face him like that! I'll try elsewhere.

PAGE'S VOICE: Paging Mr. Loman!

WILLY: Don't you want to be anything?

BIFF: Pop, how can I go back?

WILLY: You don't want to be anything, is that what's behind it?

BIFF: [*Now angry at* WILLY *for not crediting his sympathy.*] Don't take it that way! You think it was easy walking into that office after what I'd done to him? A team of horses couldn't have dragged me back to Bill Oliver!

WILLY: Then why'd you go?

BIFF: Why did I go? Why did I go! Look at you! Look at what's become of you!

[*Off left,* THE WOMAN *laughs.*]

WILLY: Biff, you're going to go to that lunch tomorrow, or—

BIFF: I can't go. I've got an appointment!

HAPPY: Biff for . . . !

WILLY: Are you spiting me?

BIFF: Don't take it that way! Goddammit!

WILLY: [*Strikes* BIFF *and falters away from the table.*] You rotten little louse! Are you spiting me?

THE WOMAN: Someone's at the door, Willy!

BIFF: I'm no good, can't you see what I am?

HAPPY: [*Separating them.*] Hey, you're in a restaurant! Now cut it out, both of you? [*The* GIRLS *enter.*] Hello, girls, sit down.

[THE WOMAN *laughs, off left.*]

MISS FORSYTHE: I guess we might as well. This is Letta.

THE WOMAN: Willy, are you going to wake up?

BIFF: [*Ignoring* WILLY.] How're ya, miss, sit down. What do you drink?

MISS FORSYTHE: Letta might not be able to stay long.

LETTA: I gotta get up early tomorrow. I got jury duty. I'm so excited! Were you fellows ever on a jury?

BIFF: No, but I been in front of them! [*The* GIRLS *laugh.*] This is my father.

LETTA: Isn't he cute? Sit down with us, Pop.

HAPPY: Sit him down, Biff!

BIFF: [*Going to him.*] Come on, slugger, drink us under the table. To hell with it! Come on, sit down, pal.

[*On* BIFF's *last insistence,* WILLY *is about to sit.*]

THE WOMAN: [*Now urgently.*] Willy, are you going to answer the door!

[THE WOMAN's *call pulls* WILLY *back. He starts right, befuddled.*]

BIFF: Hey, where are you going?

WILLY: Open the door.

BIFF: The door?

WILLY: The washroom . . . the door . . . where's the door?

BIFF: [*Leading* WILLY *to the left.*] Just go straight down.

[WILLY *moves left.*]

THE WOMAN: Willy, Willy, are you going to get up, get up, get up, get up?

[WILLY *exits left.*]

LETTA: I think it's sweet you bring your daddy along.

MISS FORSYTHE: Oh, he isn't really your father!

BIFF: [*At left, turning to her resentfully.*] Miss Forsythe, you've just seen a prince walk by. A fine, troubled prince. A hardworking, unappreciated prince. A pal, you understand? A good companion. Always for his boys.

LETTA: That's so sweet.

HAPPY: Well, girls, what's the program? We're wasting time. Come on, Biff. Gather round. Where would you like to go?

BIFF: Why don't you do something for him?

HAPPY: Me!

BIFF: Don't you give a damn for him, Hap?

HAPPY: What're you talking about? I'm the one who—

BIFF: I sense it, you don't give a good goddam about him. [*He takes the rolled-up hose from his pocket and puts it on the table in front of* HAPPY.] Look what I found in the cellar, for Christ's sake. How can you bear to let it go on?

HAPPY: Me? Who goes away? Who runs off and—

BIFF: Yeah, but he doesn't mean anything to you. You could help him—I can't! Don't you understand what I'm talking about? He's going to kill himself, don't you know that?

HAPPY: Don't I know it! Me!

BIFF: Hap, help him! Jesus . . . help him . . . Help me, help me, I can't bear to look at his face! [*Ready to weep, he hurries out, up right.*]

HAPPY: [*Starting after him.*] Where are you going?

MISS FORSYTHE: What's he so mad about?

HAPPY: Come on, girls, we'll catch up with him.

MISS FORSYTHE: [*As* HAPPY *pushes her out.*] Say, I don't like that temper of his!

HAPPY: He's just a little overstrung, he'll be all right!

WILLY: [*Off left, as* THE WOMAN *laughs.*] Don't answer! Don't answer!

LETTA: Don't you want to tell your father—

HAPPY: No, that's not my father. He's just a guy. Come on, we'll catch Biff, and, honey, we're going to paint this town! Stanley, where's the check! Hey, Stanley!

[*They exit.* STANLEY *looks toward left.*]

STANLEY: [*Calling to* HAPPY *indignantly.*] Mr. Loman! Mr. Loman!

[STANLEY *picks up a chair and follows them off. Knocking is heard off left.* THE WOMAN *enters, laughing.* WILLY *follows her. She is in a black slip; he is buttoning his shirt. Raw, sensuous music accompanies their speech.*]

WILLY: Will you stop laughing? Will you stop?

THE WOMAN: Aren't you going to answer the door? He'll wake the whole hotel.

WILLY: I'm not expecting anybody.

THE WOMAN: Whyn't you have another drink, honey, and stop being so damn self-centered?

WILLY: I'm so lonely.

THE WOMAN: You know you ruined me, Willy? From now on, whenever you come to the office, I'll see that you go right through to the buyers. No waiting at my desk any more, Willy. You ruined me.

WILLY: That's nice of you to say that.

THE WOMAN: Gee, you are self-centered! Why so sad? You are the saddest, self-centerdest soul I ever did see-saw. [*She laughs. He kisses her.*] Come on inside, drummer boy. It's silly to be dressing in the middle of the night. [*As knocking is heard.*] Aren't you going to answer the door?

WILLY: They're knocking on the wrong door.

THE WOMAN: But I felt the knocking. And he heard us talking in here. Maybe the hotel's on fire!

WILLY: [*His terror rising.*] It's a mistake.

THE WOMAN: Then tell them to go away!

WILLY: There's nobody there.

THE WOMAN: It's getting on my nerves, Willy. There's somebody standing out there and it's getting on my nerves!

WILLY: [*Pushing her away from him.*] All right, stay in the bathroom here, and don't come out. I think there's a law in Massachusetts about it, so don't come out. It may be that new room clerk. He looked very mean. So don't come out. It's a mistake, there's no fire.

[*The knocking is heard again. He takes a few steps away from her, and she vanishes into the wing. The light follows him, and now he is facing* YOUNG BIFF, *who carries a suitcase.* BIFF *steps toward him. The music is gone.*]

BIFF: Why didn't you answer?

WILLY: Biff! What are you doing in Boston?

BIFF: Why didn't you answer? I've been knocking for five minutes, I called you on the phone—

WILLY: I just heard you. I was in the bathroom and had the door shut. Did anything happen home?

BIFF: Dad—I let you down.

WILLY: What do you mean?

BIFF: Dad . . .

WILLY: Biffo, what's this about? [*Putting his arm around* BIFF.] Come on, let's go downstairs and get you a malted.

BIFF: Dad, I flunked math.

WILLY: Not for the term?

BIFF: The term. I haven't got enough credits to graduate.

WILLY: You mean to say Bernard wouldn't give you the answers?

BIFF: He did, he tried, but I only got a sixty-one.

WILLY: And they wouldn't give you four points?

BIFF: Birnbaum refused absolutely. I begged him, Pop, but he won't give me those points. You gotta talk to him before they close the school. Because if he saw the kind of man you are, and you just talked to him in your way, I'm sure he'd come through for me. The class came right before practice, see, and I didn't go enough. Would you talk to him? He'd like you, Pop. You know the way you could talk.

WILLY: You're on. We'll drive right back.

BIFF: Oh, Dad, good work! I'm sure he'll change for you!

WILLY: Go downstairs and tell the clerk I'm checkin' out. Go right down.

BIFF: Yes, sir! See, the reason he hates me, Pop—one day he was late for class so I got up at the blackboard and imitated him. I crossed my eyes and talked with a lithp.

WILLY: [*Laughing.*] You did? The kids like it?

BIFF: They nearly died laughing!

WILLY: Yeah? What'd you do?

BIFF: The thquare root of thixthy twee is . . . [WILLY *bursts out laughing;* BIFF *joins him.*] And in the middle of it he walked in!

[WILLY *laughs and* THE WOMAN *joins in offstage.*]

WILLY: [*Without hesitation.*] Hurry downstairs and—

BIFF: Somebody in there?

WILLY: No, that was next door.

[THE WOMAN *laughs offstage.*]

BIFF: Somebody got in your bathroom!

WILLY: No, it's the next room, there's a party—

THE WOMAN: [*Enters laughing. She lisps this.*] Can I come in? There's something in the bathtub, Willy, and it's moving!

[WILLY *looks at* BIFF, *who is staring open-mouthed and horrified at* THE WOMAN.]

WILLY: Ah—you better go back to your room. They must be finished painting by now. They're painting her room so I let her take a shower here. Go back, go back . . . [*He pushes her.*]

THE WOMAN: [*Resisting.*] But I've got to get dressed, Willy, I can't—

WILLY: Get out of here! Go back, go back . . . [*Suddenly striving for the ordinary.*] This is Miss Francis, Biff, she's a buyer. They're painting her room. Go back, Miss Francis, go back . . .

THE WOMAN: But my clothes, I can't go out naked in the hall!

WILLY: [*Pushing her offstage.*] Get outa here! Go back, go back!

[BIFF *slowly sits down on his suitcase as the argument continues offstage.*]

THE WOMAN: Where's my stockings? You promised me stockings, Willy!

WILLY: I have no stockings here!

THE WOMAN: You had two boxes of size nine sheers for me, and I want them!

WILLY: Here, for God's sake, will you get outa here!

THE WOMAN: [*Enters holding a box of stockings.*] I just hope there's nobody in the hall. That's all I hope. [*To* BIFF.] Are you football or baseball?

BIFF: Football.

THE WOMAN: [*Angry, humiliated.*] That's me too. G'night. [*She snatches her clothes from* WILLY, *and walks out.*]

WILLY: [*After a pause.*] Well, better get going. I want to get to the school first thing in the morning. Get my suits out of the closet. I'll get my valise. [BIFF *doesn't move.*] What's the matter? [BIFF *remains motionless, tears falling.*] She's a buyer. Buys for J. H. Simmons. She lives down the hall—they're painting. You don't imagine—[*He breaks off. After a pause.*] Now listen, pal, she's just a buyer. She sees merchandise in her room and they have to keep it looking just so . . . [*Pause. Assuming command.*] All right, get my suits. [BIFF *doesn't move.*] Now stop crying and do as I say. I gave you an order. Biff, I gave you an order! Is that what you do when I give you an order? How dare you cry! [*Putting his arm around* BIFF.] Now look, Biff, when you grow up you'll understand about these things. You mustn't—you mustn't overemphasize a thing like this. I'll see Birnbaum first thing in the morning.

BIFF: Never mind.

WILLY: [*Getting down beside* BIFF.] Never mind! He's going to give you those points. I'll see to it.

BIFF: He wouldn't listen to you.

WILLY: He certainly will listen to me. You need those points for the U. of Virginia.

BIFF: I'm not going there.

WILLY: Heh? If I can't get him to change that mark you'll make it up in summer school. You've got all summer to—

BIFF: [*His weeping breaking from him.*] Dad . . .

WILLY: [*Infected by it.*] Oh, my boy . . .

BIFF: Dad . . .

WILLY: She's nothing to me, Biff. I was lonely, I was terribly lonely.

BIFF: You—you gave her Mama's stockings! [*His tears break through and he rises to go.*]

WILLY: [*Grabbing for* BIFF.] I gave you an order!

BIFF: Don't touch me, you—liar!

WILLY: Apologize for that!

BIFF: You fake! You phony little fake! You fake!

[*Overcome, he turns quickly and weeping fully goes out with his suitcase.* WILLY *is left on the floor on his knees.*]

WILLY: I gave you an order! Biff, come back here or I'll beat you! Come back here! I'll whip you! [STANLEY *comes quickly in from the right and stands in front of* WILLY. WILLY *shouts at* STANLEY.] I gave you an order . . .

STANLEY: Hey, let's pick it up, pick it up, Mr. Loman. [*He helps* WILLY *to his feet.*] Your boys left with the chippies. They said they'll see you home.

[*A* SECOND WAITER *watches some distance away.*]

WILLY: But we were supposed to have dinner together.

[*Music is heard,* WILLY's *theme.*]

STANLEY: Can you make it?

WILLY: I'll—sure, I can make it. [*Suddenly concerned about his clothes.*] Do I— I look all right?

STANLEY: Sure, you look all right. [*He flicks a speck off* WILLY's *lapel.*]

WILLY: Here—here's a dollar.

STANLEY: Oh, your son paid me. It's all right.

WILLY: [*Putting it in* STANLEY's *hand.*] No, take it. You're a good boy.

STANLEY: Oh, no, you don't have to . . .

WILLY: Here—here's some more, I don't need it any more. [*After a slight pause.*] Tell me—is there a seed store in the neighborhood?

STANLEY: Seeds? You mean like to plant?

[*As* WILLY *turns,* STANLEY *slips the money back into his jacket pocket.*]

WILLY: Yes. Carrots, peas . . .

STANLEY: Well, there's hardware stores on Sixth Avenue, but it may be too late now.

WILLY: [*Anxiously.*] Oh, I'd better hurry. I've got to get some seeds. [*He starts off to the right.*] I've got to get some seeds, right away. Nothing's planted. I don't have a thing in the ground.

[WILLY *hurries out as the light goes down.* STANLEY *moves over to the right after him, watches him off. The other* WAITER *has been staring at* WILLY.]

STANLEY: [*To the* WAITER.] Well, whatta you looking at?

[*The* WAITER *picks up the chairs and moves off right.* STANLEY *takes the table and follows him. The light fades on this area. There is a long pause, the sound of the flute coming over. The light gradually rises on the kitchen, which is empty.* HAPPY *appears at the door of the house, followed by* BIFF. HAPPY *is carrying a large bunch of long-stemmed roses. He enters the kitchen, looks around for* LINDA. *Not seeing her, he turns to* BIFF, *who is just outside the house door, and makes a gesture with his hands, indicating "Not here, I guess." He looks into the living-room and freezes. Inside,* LINDA, *unseen, is seated,* WILLY's *coat on her lap. She rises ominously and quietly and moves toward* HAPPY, *who backs up into the kitchen, afraid.*]

HAPPY: Hey, what're you doing up? [LINDA *says nothing but moves toward him implacably.*] Where's Pop? [*He keeps backing to the right, and now* LINDA *is in full view in the doorway to the living-room.*] Is he sleeping?

LINDA: Where were you?

HAPPY: [*Trying to laugh it off.*] We met two girls, Mom, very fine types. Here, we brought you some flowers. [*Offering them to her.*] Put them in your room, Ma. [*She knocks them to the floor at* BIFF's *feet. He has now come inside and closed the door behind him. She stares at* BIFF, *silent.*] Now what'd you do that for? Mom, I want you to have some flowers—

LINDA: [*Cutting* HAPPY *off, violently to* BIFF.] Don't you care whether he lives or dies?

HAPPY: [*Going to the stairs.*] Come upstairs, Biff.

BIFF: [*With a flare of disgust, to* HAPPY.] Go away from me! [*To* LINDA.] What do you mean, lives or dies? Nobody's dying around here, pal.

LINDA: Get out of my sight! Get out of here!

BIFF: I wanna see the boss.

LINDA: You're not going near him!

BIFF: Where is he? [*He moves into the living-room and* LINDA *follows.*]

LINDA: [*Shouting after* BIFF.] You invite him for dinner. He looks forward to it all day—[BIFF *appears in his parents' bedroom, looks around and exits.*]—and then you desert him there. There's no stranger you'd do that to!

HAPPY: Why? He had a swell time with us. Listen, when I— [LINDA *comes back into the kitchen.*]—desert him I hope I don't outlive the day!

LINDA: Get out of here!

HAPPY: Now look, Mom . . .

LINDA: Did you have to go to women tonight? You and your lousy rotten whores!

[BIFF *re-enters the kitchen.*]

HAPPY: Mom, all we did was follow Biff around trying to cheer him up! [*To* BIFF.] Boy, what a night you gave me!

LINDA: Get out of here, both of you, and don't come back! I don't want you tormenting him any more. Go on now, get your things together! [*To* BIFF.] You can sleep in his apartment. [*She starts to pick up the flowers and stops herself.*] Pick up this stuff, I'm not your maid any more. Pick it up, you bum, you! [HAPPY *turns his back to her in refusal.* BIFF *slowly moves over and gets down on his knees, picking up the flowers.*] You're a pair of animals! Not one, not another living soul would have had the cruelty to walk out on that man in a restaurant!

BIFF: [*Not looking at her.*] Is that what he said?

LINDA: He didn't have to say anything. He was so humiliated he nearly limped when he came in.

HAPPY: But, Mom, he had a great time with us—

BIFF: [*Cutting him off violently.*] Shut up!

[*Without another word,* HAPPY *goes upstairs.*]

LINDA: You! You didn't even go in to see if he was all right!

BIFF: [*Still on the floor in front of* LINDA, *the flowers in his hand; with self-loathing.*] No. Didn't. Didn't do a damned thing. How do you like that, heh? Left him babbling in a toilet.

LINDA: You louse. You . . .

BIFF: Now you hit it on the nose! [*He gets up, throws the flowers in the wastebasket.*] The scum of the earth, and you're looking at him!

LINDA: Get out of here!

BIFF: I gotta talk to the boss, Mom. Where is he?

LINDA: You're not going near him. Get out of this house!

BIFF: [*With absolute assurance, determination.*] No. We're gonna have an abrupt conversation, him and me.

LINDA: You're not talking to him! [*Hammering is heard from outside the house, off right.* BIFF *turns toward the noise. Suddenly pleading.*] Will you please leave him alone?

BIFF: What's he doing out there?

LINDA: He's planting the garden!

BIFF: [*Quietly.*] Now? Oh, my God!

[BIFF *moves outside,* LINDA *following. The light dies down on them and comes up on the center of the apron as* WILLY *walks into it. He is carrying a flashlight, a hoe, and a handful of seed packets. He raps the top of the hoe sharply to fix it firmly, and then moves to the left, measuring off the distance with his foot. He holds the flashlight to look at the seed packets, reading off the instructions. He is in the blue of night.*]

WILLY: Carrots . . . quarter-inch apart. Rows . . . one-foot rows. [*He measures it off.*] One foot. [*He puts down a package and measures off.*] Beets. [*He puts down another package and measures again.*] Lettuce. [*He reads the package, puts it down.*] One foot—[*He breaks off as* BEN *appears at the right and moves slowly down to him.*] What a proposition, ts, ts. Terrific, terrific. 'Cause she's suffered, Ben, the woman has suffered. You understand me? A man can't go out the way he came in, Ben, a man has got to add up to something. You can't, you can't—[BEN *moves toward him as though to interrupt.*] You gotta consider, now. Don't answer so quick. Remember, it's a guaranteed twenty-thousand-dollar proposition. Now look, Ben, I want you to go through the ins and outs of this thing with me. I've got nobody to talk to, Ben, and the woman has suffered, you hear me?

BEN: [*Standing still, considering.*] What's the proposition?

WILLY: It's twenty thousand dollars on the barrelhead. Guaranteed, gilt-edged, you understand?

BEN: You don't want to make a fool of yourself. They might not honor the policy.

WILLY: How can they dare refuse? Didn't I work like a coolie to meet every premium on the nose? And now they don't pay off! Impossible!

BEN: It's called a cowardly thing, William.

WILLY: Why? Does it take more guts to stand here the rest of my life ringing up a zero?

BEN: [*Yielding.*] That's a point, William. [*He moves, thinking, turns.*] And twenty thousand—that *is* something one can feel with the hand, it is there.

WILLY: [*Now assured, with rising power.*] Oh, Ben, that's the whole beauty of it! I see it like a diamond, shining in the dark, hard and rough, that I can pick up and touch in my hand. Not like—like an appointment! This would not be another damned-fool appointment, Ben, and it changes all the aspects. Because he thinks I'm nothing, see, and so he spites me. But the funeral—[*Straightening up.*] Ben, that funeral will be massive! They'll come from Maine, Massachusetts, Vermont, New Hampshire! All the old-timers with the strange license plates—that boy will be thunder-struck, Ben, because he never realized—I am known! Rhode Island, New York, New Jersey—I am known, Ben, and he'll see it with his eyes once and for all. He'll see what I am, Ben! He's in for a shock, that boy!

BEN: [*Coming down to the edge of the garden.*] He'll call you a coward.

WILLY: [*Suddenly fearful.*] No, that would be terrible.

BEN: Yes. And a damned fool.

WILLY: No, no, he mustn't, I won't have that! [*He is broken and desperate.*]

BEN: He'll hate you, William.

[*The gay music of the Boys is heard.*]

WILLY: Oh, Ben, how do we get back to all the great times? Used to be so full of light, and comradeship, the sleigh-riding in winter, and the ruddiness on his cheeks. And always some kind of good news coming up, always something nice coming up ahead. And never even let me carry the valises in the house, and simonizing, simonizing that little red car! Why, why can't I give him something and not have him hate me?

BEN: Let me think about it. [*He glances at his watch.*] I still have a little time. Remarkable proposition, but you've got to be sure you're not making a fool of yourself.

[BEN *drifts off upstage and goes out of sight.* BIFF *comes down from the left.*]

WILLY: [*Suddenly conscious of* BIFF, *turns and looks up at him, then begins picking up the packages of seeds in confusion.*] Where the hell is that seed? [*Indignantly.*] You can't see nothing out here! They boxed in the whole goddam neighborhood!

BIFF: There are people all around here. Don't you realize that?

WILLY: I'm busy. Don't bother me.

BIFF: [*Taking the hoe from* WILLY.] I'm saying good-by to you, Pop. [WILLY *looks at him, silent, unable to move.*] I'm not coming back any more.

WILLY: You're not going to see Oliver tomorrow?

BIFF: I've got no appointment, Dad.

WILLY: He put his arm around you, and you've got no appointment?

BIFF: Pop, get this now, will you? Everytime I've left it's been a fight that sent me out of here. Today I realized something about myself and I tried to explain it to you and I—I think I'm just not smart enough to make any sense out of it for you. To hell with whose fault it is or anything like that. [*He takes* WILLY's *arm.*] Let's just wrap it up, heh? Come on in, we'll tell Mom. [*He gently tries to pull* WILLY *to left.*]

WILLY: [*Frozen, immobile, with guilt in his voice.*] No, I don't want to see her.

BIFF: Come on! [*He pulls again, and* WILLY *tries to pull away.*]

WILLY: [*Highly nervous.*] No, no, I don't want to see her.

BIFF: [*Tries to look into* WILLY's *face, as if to find the answer there.*] Why don't you want to see her?

WILLY: [*More harshly now.*] Don't bother me, will you?

BIFF: What do you mean, you don't want to see her? You don't want them calling you yellow, do you? This isn't your fault; it's me, I'm a bum. Now come inside! [WILLY *strains to get away.*] Did you hear what I said to you?

[WILLY *pulls away and quickly goes by himself into the house.* BIFF *follows.*]

LINDA: [*To* WILLY.] Did you plant, dear?

BIFF: [*At the door, to* LINDA.] All right, we had it out. I'm going and I'm not writing any more.

LINDA: [*Going to* WILLY *in the kitchen.*] I think that's the best way, dear. 'Cause there's no use drawing it out, you'll just never get along.

[WILLY *doesn't respond.*]

BIFF: People ask where I am and what I'm doing, you don't know, and you don't care. That way it'll be off your mind and you can start brightening up again. All right? That clears it, doesn't it? [WILLY *is silent, and* BIFF *goes to him.*] You gonna wish me luck, scout? [*He extends his hand.*] What do you say?

LINDA: Shake his hand, Willy.

WILLY: [*Turning to her, seething with hurt.*] There's no necessity to mention the pen at all, y'know.

BIFF: [*Gently.*] I've got no appointment, Dad.

WILLY: [*Erupting fiercely.*] He put his arm around . . . ?

BIFF: Dad, you're never going to see what I am, so what's the use of arguing? If I strike oil I'll send you a check. Meantime forget I'm alive.

WILLY: [*To* LINDA.] Spite, see?

BIFF: Shake hands, Dad.

WILLY: Not my hand.

BIFF: I was hoping not to go this way.

WILLY: Well, this is the way you're going. Good-by. [BIFF *looks at him a moment, then turns sharply and goes to the stairs.* WILLY *stops him with.*] May you rot in hell if you leave this house!

BIFF: [*Turning.*] Exactly what is it that you want from me?

WILLY: I want you to know, on the train, in the mountains, in the valleys, wherever you go, that you cut down your life for spite!

BIFF: No, no.

WILLY: Spite, spite, is the word of your undoing! And when you're down and out, remember what did it. When you're rotting somewhere beside the railroad tracks, remember, and don't you dare blame it on me!

BIFF: I'm not blaming it on you!

WILLY: I won't take the rap for this, you hear?

[HAPPY *comes down the stairs and stands on the bottom step, watching.*]

BIFF: That's just what I'm telling you!

WILLY: [*Sinking into a chair at the table, with full accusation.*] You're trying to put a knife in me—don't think I don't know what you're doing!

BIFF: All right, phony! Then let's lay it on the line. [*He whips the rubber tube out of his pocket and puts it on the table.*]

HAPPY: You crazy—

LINDA: Biff!

[*She moves to grab the hose, but* BIFF *holds it down with his hand.*]

BIFF: Leave it there! Don't move it!

WILLY: [*Not looking at it.*] What is that?

BIFF: You know goddam well what that is.

WILLY: [*Caged, wanting to escape.*] I never saw that.

BIFF: You saw it. The mice didn't bring it into the cellar! What is this supposed to do, make a hero out of you? This supposed to make me sorry for you?

WILLY: Never heard of it.

BIFF: There'll be no pity for you, you hear it? No pity!

WILLY: [*To* LINDA.] You hear the spite!

BIFF: No, you're going to hear the truth—what you are and what I am!

LINDA: Stop it!

WILLY: Spite!

HAPPY: [*Coming down toward* BIFF.] You cut it now!

BIFF: [*To* HAPPY.] The man don't know who we are! The man is gonna know! [*To* WILLY.] We never told the truth for ten minutes in this house!

HAPPY: We always told the truth!

BIFF: [*Turning on him.*] You big blow, are you the assistant buyer? You're one of the two assistants to the assistant, aren't you?

HAPPY: Well, I'm practically—

BIFF: You're practically full of it! We all are! And I'm through with it. [*To* WILLY.] Now hear this, Willy, this is me.

WILLY: I know you!

BIFF: You know why I had no address for three months? I stole a suit in Kansas City and I was in jail. [*To* LINDA, *who is sobbing.*] Stop crying. I'm through with it.

[LINDA *turns away from them, her hands covering her face.*]

WILLY: I suppose that's my fault!

BIFF: I stole myself out of every good job since high school!

WILLY: And whose fault is that?

BIFF: And I never got anywhere because you blew me so full of hot air I could never stand taking orders from anybody! That's whose fault it is!

WILLY: I hear that!

LINDA: Don't, Biff!

BIFF: It's goddam time you heard that! I had to be boss big shot in two weeks, and I'm through with it!

WILLY: Then hang yourself! For spite, hang yourself!

BIFF: No! Nobody's hanging himself, Willy! I ran down eleven flights with a pen in my hand today. And suddenly I stopped, you hear me? And in the middle of that office building, do you hear this? I stopped in the middle of that building and I saw—the sky. I saw the things that I love in this world. The work and the food and time to sit and smoke. And I looked at the pen and said to myself, what the hell am I grabbing this for? Why am I trying to become what I don't want to be? What am I doing in an office, making a contemptuous, begging fool of myself, when all I want is out there, waiting for me the minute I say I know who I am! Why can't I say that, Willy? [*He tries to make* WILLY *face him, but* WILLY *pulls away and moves to the left.*]

WILLY: [*With hatred, threateningly.*] The door of your life is wide open!

BIFF: Pop! I'm a dime a dozen, and so are you!

WILLY: [*Turning on him now in an uncontrolled outburst.*] I am not a dime a dozen! I am Willy Loman, and you are Biff Loman!

[BIFF *starts for* WILLY, *but is blocked by* HAPPY. *In his fury,* BIFF *seems on the verge of attacking his father.*]

BIFF: I am not a leader of men, Willy, and neither are you. You were never anything but a hard-working drummer who landed in the ash can like all the rest of them! I'm one dollar an hour, Willy! I tried seven states and couldn't raise it. A buck an hour! Do you gather my meaning? I'm not bringing home any prizes any more, and you're going to stop waiting for me to bring them home!

WILLY: [*Directly to* BIFF.] You vengeful, spiteful mut!

[BIFF *breaks from* HAPPY. WILLY, *in fright, starts up the stairs.* BIFF *grabs him.*]

BIFF: [*At the peak of his fury.*] Pop, I'm nothing! I'm nothing, Pop. Can't you understand that? There's no spite in it any more. I'm just what I am, that's all.

[BIFF's *fury has spent itself, and he breaks down, sobbing, holding on to* WILLY, *who dumbly fumbles for* BIFF's *face.*]

WILLY: [*Astonished.*] What're you doing? What're you doing? [*To* LINDA.] Why is he crying?

BIFF: [*Crying, broken.*] Will you let me go, for Christ's sake? Will you take that phony dream and burn it before something happens? [*Struggling to contain himself, he pulls away and moves to the stairs.*] I'll go in the morning. Put him—put him to bed. [*Exhausted,* BIFF *moves up the stairs to his room.*]

WILLY: [*After a long pause, astonished, elevated.*] Isn't that—isn't that remarkable? Biff—he likes me!

LINDA: He loves you, Willy!

HAPPY: [*Deeply moved.*] Always did, Pop.

WILLY: Oh, Biff! [*Staring wildly.*] He cried! Cried to me. [*He is choking with his love, and now cries out his promise.*] That boy—that boy is going to be magnificent!

[BEN *appears in the light just outside the kitchen.*]

BEN: Yes, outstanding, with twenty thousand behind him.

LINDA: [*Sensing the racing of his mind, fearfully, carefully.*] Now come to bed, Willy. It's all settled now.

WILLY: [*Finding it difficult not to rush out of the house.*] Yes, we'll sleep. Come on. Go to sleep, Hap.

BEN: And it does take a great kind of man to crack the jungle.

[*In accents of dread,* BEN's *idyllic music starts up.*]

HAPPY: [*His arm around* LINDA.] I'm getting married, Pop, don't forget it. I'm changing everything. I'm gonna run that department before the year is up. You'll see, Mom. [*He kisses her.*]

BEN: The jungle is dark but full of diamonds, Willy.

[WILLY *turns, moves, listening to* BEN.]

LINDA: Be good. You're both good boys, just act that way, that's all.

HAPPY: 'Night, Pop. [*He goes upstairs.*]

LINDA: [*To* WILLY.] Come, dear.

BEN: [*With greater force.*] One must go in to fetch a diamond out.

WILLY: [*To* LINDA, *as he moves slowly along the edge of the kitchen, toward the door.*] I just want to get settled down, Linda. Let me sit alone for a little.

LINDA: [*Almost uttering her fear.*] I want you upstairs.

WILLY: [*Taking her in his arms.*] In a few minutes, Linda. I couldn't sleep right now. Go on, you look awful tired. [*He kisses her.*]

BEN: Not like an appointment at all. A diamond is rough and hard to the touch.

WILLY: Go on now. I'll be right up.

LINDA: I think this is the only way, Willy.

WILLY: Sure, it's the best thing.

BEN: Best thing!

WILLY: The only way. Everything is gonna be—go on, kid, get to bed. You look so tired.

LINDA: Come right up.

WILLY: Two minutes. [LINDA *goes into the living-room, then reappears in her bedroom.* WILLY *moves just outside the kitchen door.*] Loves me. [*Wonderingly.*] Always loved me. Isn't that a remarkable thing? Ben, he'll worship me for it!

BEN: [*With promise.*] It's dark there, but full of diamonds.

WILLY: Can you imagine that magnificence with twenty thousand dollars in his pocket?

LINDA: [*Calling from her room.*] Willy! Come up!

WILLY: [*Calling into the kitchen.*] Yes! Yes. Coming! It's very smart, you realize that, don't you, sweetheart? Even Ben sees it. I gotta go, baby. 'By! 'By! [*Going over to* BEN, *almost dancing.*] Imagine? When the mail comes he'll be ahead of Bernard again!

BEN: A perfect proposition all around.

WILLY: Did you see how he cried to me? Oh, if I could kiss him, Ben!

BEN: Time, William, time!

WILLY: Oh, Ben, I always knew one way or another we were gonna make it, Biff and I!

BEN: [*Looking at his watch.*] The boat. We'll be late. [*He moves slowly off into the darkness.*]

WILLY: [*Elegiacally, turning to the house.*] Now when you kick off, boy, I want a seventy-yard boot, and get right down the field under the ball, and when you hit, hit low and hit hard, because it's important, boy. [*He swings around and faces the audience.*] There's all kinds of important people in the stands, and the first thing you know . . . [*Suddenly realizing he is alone.*] Ben! Ben, where do I . . . ? [*He makes a sudden movement of search.*] Ben, how do I . . . ?

LINDA: [*Calling.*] Willy, you coming up?

WILLY: [*Uttering a gasp of fear, whirling about as if to quiet her.*] Sh! [*He turns around as if to find his way; sounds, faces, voices, seem to be swarming in upon him and he flicks at them, crying.*] Sh! Sh! [*Suddenly music, faint and high, stops him. It rises in intensity, almost to an unbearable scream. He goes up and down on his toes, and rushes off around the house.*] Shhh!

LINDA: Willy? [*There is no answer.* LINDA *waits.* BIFF *gets up off his bed. He is still in his clothes.* HAPPY *sits up.* BIFF *stands listening.*] [*With real fear.*] Willy, answer me! Willy! [*There is the sound of a car starting and moving away at full speed.*] No!

BIFF: [*Rushing down the stairs.*] Pop!

[*As the car speeds off, the music crashes down in a frenzy of sound, which becomes the soft pulsation of a single cello string.* BIFF *slowly returns to his bedroom. He and* HAPPY *gravely don their jackets.* LINDA *slowly walks out of her room. The music has developed into a dead march. The leaves of day are appearing over everything.* CHARLEY *and* BERNARD, *somberly dressed, appear and knock on the kitchen door.* BIFF *and* HAPPY *slowly descend the stairs to the kitchen as* CHARLEY *and* BERNARD *enter. All stop a moment when* LINDA, *in clothes of mourning, bearing a little bunch of roses, comes through the draped doorway into the kitchen. She goes to* CHARLEY *and takes his arm. Now all move toward the audience, through the wall-line of the kitchen. At the limit of the apron,* LINDA *lays down the flowers, kneels, and sits back on her heels. All stare down at the grave.*]

REQUIEM

CHARLEY: It's getting dark, Linda.

[LINDA *doesn't react. She stares at the grave.*]

BIFF: How about it, Mom? Better get some rest, heh? They'll be closing the gate soon.

[LINDA *makes no move. Pause.*]

HAPPY: [*Deeply angered.*] He had no right to do that. There was no necessity for it. We would've helped him.

CHARLEY [*Grunting.*] Hmmm.

BIFF: Come along, Mom.

LINDA: Why didn't anybody come?

CHARLEY: It was a very nice funeral.

LINDA: But where are all the people he knew? Maybe they blame him.

CHARLEY: Naa. It's a rough world, Linda. They wouldn't blame him.

LINDA: I can't understand it. At this time especially. First time in thirty-five years we were just about free and clear. He only needed a little salary. He was even finished with the dentist.

CHARLEY: No man only needs a little salary.

LINDA: I can't understand it.

BIFF: There were a lot of nice days. When he'd come home from a trip; or on Sundays, making the stoop; finishing the cellar; putting on the new porch; when he built the extra bathroom; and put up the garage. You know something, Charley, there's more of him in that front stoop than in all the sales he ever made.

CHARLEY: Yeah. He was a happy man with a batch of cement.

LINDA: He was so wonderful with his hands.

BIFF: He had the wrong dreams. All, all, wrong.

HAPPY: [*Almost ready to fight* BIFF.] Don't say that!

BIFF: He never knew who he was.

CHARLEY: [*Stopping* HAPPY'*s movement and reply. To* BIFF.] Nobody dast blame this man. You don't understand: Willy was a salesman. And for a salesman, there is no rock bottom to the life. He don't put a bolt to a nut, he don't tell you the law or give you medicine. He's a man way out there in the blue, riding on a smile and a shoeshine. And when they start not smiling back— that's an earthquake. And then you get yourself a couple of spots on your hat, and you're finished. Nobody dast blame this man. A salesman is got to dream, boy. It comes with the territory.

BIFF: Charley, the man didn't know who he was.

HAPPY: [*Infuriated.*] Don't say that!

BIFF: Why don't you come with me, Happy?

HAPPY: I'm not licked that easily. I'm staying right in this city, and I'm gonna beat this racket! [*He looks at* BIFF, *his chin set.*] The Loman Brothers!

BIFF: I know who I am, kid.

HAPPY: All right, boy. I'm gonna show you and everybody else that Willy Loman did not die in vain. He had a good dream. It's the only dream you can have— to come out number-one-man. He fought it out here, and this is where I'm gonna win it for him.

BIFF: [*With a hopeless glance at* HAPPY, *bends toward his mother.*] Let's go, Mom.

LINDA: I'll be with you in a minute. Go on, Charley. [*He hesitates.*] I want to, just for a minute. I never had a chance to say good-by. [CHARLEY *moves away, followed by* HAPPY. BIFF *remains a slight distance up and left of* LINDA. *She sits there, summoning herself. The flute begins, not far away, playing behind her speech.*] Forgive me, dear. I can't cry. I don't know what it is, but I can't cry. I don't understand it. Why did you ever do that? Help me, Willy, I can't cry. It seems to me that you're just on another trip. I keep expecting you. Willy, dear, I can't cry. Why did you do it? I search and search and I search, and I can't understand it, Willy. I made the last payment on the house today. Today, dear. And there'll be nobody home. [*A sob rises in her throat.*] We're free and clear. [*Sobbing more fully, released.*] We're free. [BIFF *comes slowly toward her.*] We're free . . . We're free . . .

[BIFF *lifts her to her feet and moves out up right with her in his arms.* LINDA *sobs quietly.* BERNARD *and* CHARLEY *come together and follow them, followed by* HAPPY. *Only the music of the flute is left on the darkening stage as over the house the hard towers of the apartment buildings rise into sharp focus.*]

CURTAIN

1949

WILLIAM SHAKESPEARE

A Midsummer Night's Dream[1]

CHARACTERS

THESEUS, *Duke of Athens*
EGEUS, *father to Hermia*
LYSANDER, } *in love with Hermia*
DEMETRIUS,
PHILOSTRATE, *Master of the Revels to Theseus*
QUINCE, *a carpenter*
SNUG, *a joiner*
BOTTOM, *a weaver*
FLUTE, *a bellows-maker*
SNOUT, *a tinker*
STARVELING, *a tailor*

HIPPOLYTA, *Queen of the Amazons, betrothed to Theseus*
HERMIA, *daughter to Egeus, in love with Lysander*
HELENA, *in love with Demetrius*
OBERON, *King of the Fairies*
TITANIA, *Queen of the Fairies*
PUCK, *or Robin Goodfellow*
PEASEBLOSSOM,
COBWEB,
MOTH, } *fairies*
MUSTARDSEED,

Other FAIRIES *attending their king and queen*
ATTENDANTS *on Theseus and Hippolyta*

SCENE: *Athens, and a wood near it.*

ACT I

SCENE 1[2]

Enter THESEUS, HIPPOLYTA, PHILOSTRATE, *with others.*

THESEUS: Now, fair Hippolyta, our nuptial hour
  Draws on apace. Four happy days bring in
  Another moon; but, O, methinks, how slow
  This old moon wanes! She lingers[3] my desires,
  Like to a step-dame or a dowager[4]
  Long withering out a young man's revenue.
HIPPOLYTA: Four days will quickly steep themselves in night,
  Four nights will quickly dream away the time;
  And then the moon, like to a silver bow
  New-bent in heaven, shall behold the night
  Of our solemnities.
THESEUS: Go, Philostrate,
  Stir up the Athenian youth to merriments,
  Awake the pert and nimble spirit of mirth,

5

10

1. Edited and annotated by David Bevington (except footnotes set in brackets). 2. Location: Athens. The palace of Theseus. 3. Lengthens, protracts. 4. Widow with a jointure or dower. *Step-dame:* stepmother.

Turn melancholy forth to funerals;
15 The pale companion is not for our pomp.[5]   [*Exit* PHILOSTRATE.]
Hippolyta, I woo'd thee with my sword,[6]
And won thy love doing thee injuries;
But I will wed thee in another key,
With pomp, with triumph,[7] and with reveling.

[*Enter* EGEUS *and his daughter* HERMIA, *and* LYSANDER, *and* DEMETRIUS.]

20 EGEUS: Happy be Theseus, our renowned Duke!
THESEUS: Thanks, good Egeus. What's the news with thee?
EGEUS: Full of vexation come I, with complaint
     Against my child, my daughter Hermia.
     Stand forth, Demetrius. My noble lord,
25   This man hath my consent to marry her.
     Stand forth, Lysander. And, my gracious Duke,
     This man hath bewitch'd the bosom of my child.
     Thou, thou, Lysander, thou hast given her rhymes
     And interchang'd love-tokens with my child.
30   Thou hast by moonlight at her window sung
     With feigning[8] voice verses of feigning love,
     And stol'n the impression of her fantasy[9]
     With bracelets of thy hair, rings, gauds, conceits,[1]
     Knacks,[2] trifles, nosegays, sweetmeats—messengers
35   Of strong prevailment in unhardened youth.
     With cunning hast thou filch'd my daughter's heart,
     Turn'd her obedience, which is due to me,
     To stubborn harshness. And, my gracious Duke,
     Be it so she will not here before your Grace
40   Consent to marry with Demetrius,
     I beg the ancient privilege of Athens:
     As she is mine, I may dispose of her,
     Which shall be either to this gentleman
     Or to her death, according to our law
45   Immediately[3] provided in that case.
THESEUS: What say you, Hermia? Be advis'd, fair maid.
     To you your father should be as a god—
     One that compos'd your beauties, yea, and one
     To whom you are but as a form in wax
50   By him imprinted and within his power
     To leave the figure or disfigure[4] it.
     Demetrius is a worthy gentleman.

---

5. Ceremonial magnificence. *Companion:* fellow.   6. I.e., in a military engagement against the
Amazons, when Hippolyta was taken captive.   7. Public festivity.   8. (1) Counterfeiting; (2)
faining, desirous.   9. Made her fall in love with you (imprinting your image on her imagination)
by stealthy and dishonest means.   1. Fanciful trifles. *Gauds:* playthings.   2. Knickknacks.
3. Expressly.   4. Obliterate. *Leave:* i.e., leave unaltered.

HERMIA: So is Lysander.
THESEUS: In himself he is;
   But in this kind, wanting your father's voice,[5]
   The other must be held the worthier.   55
HERMIA: I would my father look'd but with my eyes.
THESEUS: Rather your eyes must with his judgment look.
HERMIA: I do entreat your Grace to pardon me.
   I know not by what power I am made bold,
   Nor how it may concern[6] my modesty,   60
   In such a presence here to plead my thoughts;
   But I beseech your Grace that I may know
   The worst that may befall me in this case,
   If I refuse to wed Demetrius.
THESEUS: Either to die the death, or to abjure   65
   Forever the society of men.
   Therefore, fair Hermia, question your desires,
   Know of your youth, examine well your blood,[7]
   Whether, if you yield not to your father's choice,
   You can endure the livery[8] of a nun,   70
   For aye to be in shady cloister mew'd,[9]
   To live a barren sister all your life,
   Chanting faint hymns to the cold fruitless moon.
   Thrice blessed they that master so their blood
   To undergo such maiden pilgrimage;   75
   But earthlier happy[1] is the rose distill'd,
   Than that which withering on the virgin thorn
   Grows, lives, and dies in single blessedness.
HERMIA: So will I grow, so live, so die, my lord,
   Ere I will yield my virgin patent[2] up   80
   Unto his lordship, whose unwished yoke
   My soul consents not to give sovereignty.
THESEUS: Take time to pause; and, by the next new moon—
   The sealing-day betwixt my love and me,
   For everlasting bond of fellowship—   85
   Upon that day either prepare to die
   For disobedience to your father's will,
   Or[3] else to wed Demetrius, as he would,
   Or on Diana's altar to protest[4]
   For aye austerity and single life.   90
DEMETRIUS: Relent, sweet Hermia, and, Lysander, yield
   Thy crazed[5] title to my certain right.
LYSANDER: You have her father's love, Demetrius;

---

5. Approval. *Kind:* respect. *Wanting:* lacking.   6. Befit.   7. Passions.   8. Habit.
9. Shut in (said of a hawk, poultry, and so on). *Aye:* ever.   1. Happier as respects this world.
2. Privilege.   3. Either.   4. Vow.   5. Cracked, unsound.

Let me have Hermia's. Do you marry him.

95 EGEUS: Scornful Lysander! True, he hath my love,
And what is mine my love shall render him.
And she is mine, and all my right of her
I do estate unto[6] Demetrius.

LYSANDER: I am, my lord, as well deriv'd[7] as he,
100 As well possess'd[8]; my love is more than his;
My fortunes every way as fairly[9] rank'd,
If not with vantage,[1] as Demetrius';
And, which is more than all these boasts can be,
I am belov'd of beauteous Hermia.
105 Why should not I then prosecute my right?
Demetrius, I'll avouch it to his head,[2]
Made love to Nedar's daughter, Helena,
And won her soul; and she, sweet lady, dotes,
Devoutly dotes, dotes in idolatry,
110 Upon this spotted[3] and inconstant man.

THESEUS: I must confess that I have heard so much,
And with Demetrius thought to have spoke thereof;
But, being over-full of self-affairs,
My mind did lose it. But, Demetrius, come,
115 And come, Egeus, you shall go with me;
I have some private schooling for you both.
For you, fair Hermia, look you arm[4] yourself
To fit your fancies[5] to your father's will;
Or else the law of Athens yields you up—
120 Which by no means we may extenuate[6]—
To death, or to a vow of single life.
Come, my Hippolyta. What cheer, my love?
Demetrius and Egeus, go[7] along.
I must employ you in some business
125 Against[8] our nuptial, and confer with you
Of something nearly that[9] concerns yourselves.

EGEUS: With duty and desire we follow you.

[*Exeunt (all but* LYSANDER *and* HERMIA).]

LYSANDER: How now, my love, why is your cheek so pale?
How chance the roses there do fade so fast?

130 HERMIA: Belike[1] for want of rain, which I could well
Beteem[2] them from the tempest of my eyes.

LYSANDER: Ay me! For aught that I could ever read,
Could ever hear by tale or history,

---

6. Settle or bestow upon.   7. Descended; i.e., as well born.   8. Endowed with wealth.
9. Handsomely.   1. Superiority.   2. I.e., face.   3. I.e., morally stained.   4. Take care
you prepare.   5. Likings, thoughts of love.   6. Mitigate.   7. I.e., come.   8. In preparation for.   9. That closely.   1. Very likely.   2. Grant, afford.

The course of true love never did run smooth;
But either it was different in blood[3]—   135
HERMIA: O cross,[4] too high to be enthrall'd to low!
LYSANDER: Or else misgraffed[5] in respect of years—
HERMIA: O spite, too old to be engag'd to young!
LYSANDER: Or else it stood upon the choice of friends[6]—
HERMIA: O hell, to choose love by another's eyes!   140
LYSANDER: Or, if there were a sympathy in choice,
    War, death, or sickness did lay siege to it,
    Making it momentany[7] as a sound,
    Swift as a shadow, short as any dream,
    Brief as the lightning in the collied[8] night,   145
    That, in a spleen, unfolds[9] both heaven and earth,
    And ere a man hath power to say "Behold!"
    The jaws of darkness do devour it up.
    So quick bright things come to confusion.[1]
HERMIA: If then true lovers have been ever cross'd,[2]   150
    It stands as an edict in destiny.
    Then let us teach our trial patience,[3]
    Because it is a customary cross,
    As due to love as thoughts and dreams and sighs,
    Wishes and tears, poor fancy's[4] followers.   155
LYSANDER: A good persuasion. Therefore, hear me, Hermia.
    I have a widow aunt, a dowager
    Of great revenue, and she hath no child.
    From Athens is her house remote seven leagues;
    And she respects[5] me as her only son.   160
    There, gentle Hermia, may I marry thee,
    And to that place the sharp Athenian law
    Cannot pursue us. If thou lovest me, then,
    Steal forth thy father's house tomorrow night;
    And in the wood, a league without the town,   165
    Where I did meet thee once with Helena
    To do observance to a morn of May,[6]
    There will I stay for thee.
HERMIA: My good Lysander!
    I swear to thee, by Cupid's strongest bow,
    By his best arrow[7] with the golden head,   170
    By the simplicity of Venus' doves,[8]

---

3. Hereditary station.   4. Vexation.   5. Ill grafted, badly matched.   6. Relatives.   7. Lasting but a moment.   8. Blackened (as with coal-dust), darkened.   9. Discloses. *In a spleen:* in a
swift impulse, in a violent flash.   1. Ruin. *Quick:* quickly; or, perhaps, living, alive.   2. Always
thwarted.   3. I.e., teach ourselves patience in this trial.   4. Amorous passion's.   5. Regards.
6. Perform the ceremonies of May Day.   7. [Cupid's best goldpointed arrows were supposed to
induce love, his blunt leaden arrows aversion.]   8. I.e., those that drew Venus's chariot. *Simplicity:* innocence.

By that which knitteth souls and prospers loves,
And by that fire which burn'd the Carthage queen,
When the false Troyan[9] under sail was seen,
By all the vows that ever men have broke,
In number more than ever women spoke,
In that same place thou hast appointed me
Tomorrow truly will I meet with thee.

LYSANDER: Keep promise, love. Look, here comes Helena.

[*Enter* HELENA.]

HERMIA: God speed fair[1] Helena, whither away?
HELENA: Call you me fair? That fair again unsay.
Demetrius loves your fair. O happy fair![2]
Your eyes are lodestars, and your tongue's sweet air[3]
More tuneable[4] than lark to shepherd's ear
When wheat is green, when hawthorn buds appear.
Sickness is catching. O, were favor[5] so,
Yours would I catch, fair Hermia, ere I go;
My ear should catch your voice, my eye your eye,
My tongue should catch your tongue's sweet melody.
Were the world mine, Demetrius being bated,[6]
The rest I'd give to be to you translated.[7]
O, teach me how you look, and with what art
You sway the motion[8] of Demetrius' heart.

HERMIA: I frown upon him, yet he loves me still.
HELENA: O that your frowns would teach my smiles such skill!
HERMIA: I give him curses, yet he gives me love.
HELENA: O that my prayers could such affection move[9]!
HERMIA: The more I hate, the more he follows me.
HELENA: The more I love, the more he hateth me.
HERMIA: His folly, Helena, is no fault of mine.
HELENA: None, but your beauty. Would that fault were mine!
HERMIA: Take comfort. He no more shall see my face.
Lysander and myself will fly this place.
Before the time I did Lysander see,
Seem'd Athens as a paradise to me.
O, then, what graces in my love do dwell,
That he hath turn'd a heaven unto a hell!

LYSANDER: Helen, to you our minds we will unfold.
Tomorrow night, when Phoebe[1] doth behold
Her silver visage in the wat'ry glass,[2]

9. [Dido, queen of Carthage, immolated herself on a funeral pyre after having been deserted by the
Trojan hero Aeneas.]   1. Fair-complexioned (generally regarded by the Elizabethans as more
beautiful than dark complexion).   2. Lucky fair one! *Fair:* beauty (even though Hermia is dark-
complexioned).   3. Music. *Lodestars:* guiding stars.   4. Tuneful, melodious.   5. Appearance, looks.   6. Excepted.   7. Transformed.   8. Impulse.   9. Arouse. *Affection:* passion.
1. Diana, the moon.   2. Mirror.

Decking with liquid pearl the bladed grass,
A time that lovers' flights doth still[3] conceal,
Through Athens' gates have we devis'd to steal.

HERMIA: And in the wood, where often you and I
    Upon faint[4] primrose beds were wont to lie,   215
    Emptying our bosoms of their counsel[5] sweet,
    There my Lysander and myself shall meet;
    And thence from Athens turn away our eyes,
    To seek new friends and stranger companies.
    Farewell, sweet playfellow. Pray thou for us,   220
    And good luck grant thee thy Demetrius!
    Keep word, Lysander. We must starve our sight
    From lovers' food till morrow deep midnight.   [Exit.]

LYSANDER: I will, my Hermia.
                        Helena, adieu.
    As you on him, Demetrius dote on you!   [Exit.]   225

HELENA: How happy some o'er other some can be![6]
    Through Athens I am thought as fair as she.
    But what of that? Demetrius thinks not so;
    He will not know what all but he do know.
    And as he errs, doting on Hermia's eyes,   230
    So I, admiring[7] of his qualities.
    Things base and vile, holding no quantity,[8]
    Love can transpose to form and dignity.
    Love looks not with the eyes, but with the mind,
    And therefore is wing'd Cupid painted blind.   235
    Nor hath Love's mind of any judgment taste;[9]
    Wings, and no eyes, figure[1] unheedy haste.
    And therefore is Love said to be a child,
    Because in choice he is so oft beguil'd.
    As waggish boys in game[2] themselves forswear,   240
    So the boy Love is perjur'd everywhere.
    For ere Demetrius look'd on Hermia's eyne,[3]
    He hail'd down oaths that he was only mine;
    And when this hail some heat from Hermia felt,
    So he dissolv'd, and show'rs of oaths did melt.   245
    I will go tell him of fair Hermia's flight.
    Then to the wood will he tomorrow night
    Pursue her; and for this intelligence[4]
    If I have thanks, it is a dear expense.[5]
    But herein mean I to enrich my pain,   250
    To have his sight thither and back again.   [Exit.]

3. Always.   4. Pale.   5. Secret thought.   6. Can be in comparison to some others.
7. Wondering at.   8. I.e., unsubstantial, unshapely.   9. I.e., nor has Love, which dwells in the
fancy or imagination, any taste or least bit of judgment or reason.   1. Are a symbol of.
2. Sport, jest.   3. Eyes (old form of plural).   4. Information.   5. I.e., a trouble worth taking. *Dear:* costly.

SCENE 2[6]

Enter QUINCE *the Carpenter, and* SNUG *the Joiner, and* BOTTOM *the Weaver, and* FLUTE *the Bellows-mender, and* SNOUT *the Tinker, and* STARVELING *the Tailor.*

QUINCE: Is all our company here?

BOTTOM: You were best to call them generally,[7] man by man, according to the scrip.[8]

QUINCE: Here is the scroll of every man's name which is thought fit, through all Athens, to play in our interlude before the Duke and the Duchess on his wedding-day at night.

BOTTOM: First, good Peter Quince, say what the play treats on, then read the names of the actors, and so grow to[9] a point.

QUINCE: Marry,[1] our play is "The most lamentable comedy and most cruel death of Pyramus and Thisby."

BOTTOM: A very good piece of work, I assure you, and a merry. Now, good Peter Quince, call forth your actors by the scroll. Masters, spread yourselves.

QUINCE: Answer as I call you. Nick Bottom, the weaver.

BOTTOM: Ready. Name what part I am for, and proceed.

QUINCE: You, Nick Bottom, are set down for Pyramus.

BOTTOM: What is Pyramus? A lover, or a tyrant?

QUINCE: A lover, that kills himself most gallant for love.

BOTTOM: That will ask some tears in the true performing of it. If I do it, let the audience look to their eyes. I will move storms; I will condole[2] in some measure. To the rest—yet my chief humor[3] is for a tyrant. I could play Ercles rarely, or a part to tear a cat in, to make all split.[4]

> "The raging rocks
> And shivering shocks
> Shall break the locks
>   Of prison gates;
> And Phibbus' car[5]
> Shall shine from far
> And make and mar
>   The foolish Fates."

This was lofty! Now name the rest of the players. This is Ercles' vein, a tyrant's vein. A lover is more condoling.

QUINCE: Francis Flute, the bellows-mender.

FLUTE: Here, Peter Quince.

QUINCE: Flute, you must take Thisby on you.

FLUTE: What is Thisby? A wand'ring knight?

5
10
15
20
25
30
35

6. Location: Athens. Quince's house (?).   7. [Bottom's blunder for *individually.*]   8. Script, written list.   9. Come to.   1. [A mild oath, originally the name of the Virgin Mary.]   2. Lament, arouse pity.   3. Inclination, whim.   4. I.e., cause a stir, bring the house down. *Ercles:* Hercules (the tradition of ranting came from Seneca's *Hercules Furens*). *Tear a cat:* i.e., rant.   5. Phoebus's, the sun-god's, chariot.

QUINCE: It is the lady that Pyramus must love.

FLUTE: Nay, faith, let not me play a woman. I have a beard coming.

QUINCE: That's all one.[6] You shall play it in a mask, and you may speak as small[7] as you will.

BOTTOM: An[8] I may hide my face, let me play Thisby too. I'll speak in a monstrous little voice, "Thisne, Thisne!" "Ah, Pyramus, my lover dear! Thy Thisby dear, and lady dear!"   40

QUINCE: No, no; you must play Pyramus; and, Flute, you Thisby.

BOTTOM: Well, proceed.

QUINCE: Robin Starveling, the tailor.   45

STARVELING: Here, Peter Quince.

QUINCE: Robin Starveling, you must play Thisby's mother. Tom Snout, the tinker.

SNOUT: Here, Peter Quince.

QUINCE: You, Pyramus' father; myself, Thisby's father; Snug, the joiner, you, the lion's part; and I hope here is a play fitted.   50

SNUG: Have you the lion's part written? Pray you, if it be, give it me, for I am slow of study.

QUINCE: You may do it extempore, for it is nothing but roaring.

BOTTOM: Let me play the lion too. I will roar that I will do any man's heart good to hear me. I will roar that I will make the Duke say, "Let him roar again, let him roar again."   55

QUINCE: An you should do it too terribly, you would fright the Duchess and the ladies, that they would shriek; and that were enough to hang us all.

ALL: That would hang us, every mother's son.

BOTTOM: I grant you, friends, if you should fright the ladies out of their wits, they would have no more discretion but to hang us; but I will aggravate[9] my voice so that I will roar[1] you as gently as any sucking dove; I will roar you an 'twere any nightingale.   60

QUINCE: You can play no part but Pyramus; for Pyramus is a sweet-fac'd man, a proper[2] man as one shall see in a summer's day, a most lovely gentleman-like man. Therefore you must needs play Pyramus.   65

BOTTOM: Well, I will undertake it. What beard were I best to play it in?

QUINCE: Why, what you will.

BOTTOM: I will discharge it in either your[3] straw-color beard, your orange-tawny beard, your purple-in-grain beard, or your French-crown-color[4] beard, your perfect yellow.   70

QUINCE: Some of your French crowns[5] have no hair at all, and then you will play barefac'd. But, masters, here are your parts. [He distributes parts.] And I am to entreat you, request you, and desire you, to con[6] them by tomorrow night; and meet me in the palace wood, a mile without the town, by moon-   75

6. It makes no difference.   7. High-pitched.   8. If.   9. [Bottom's blunder for diminish.]
1. I.e., roar for you.   2. Handsome.   3. I.e., you know the kind I mean. Discharge: perform.
4. I.e., color of a French crown, a gold coin. Purple-in-grain: dyed a very deep red (from grain, the name applied to the dried insect used to make the dye).   5. Heads bald from syphilis, the "French disease."   6. Learn by heart.

light. There will we rehearse; for if we meet in the city, we shall be dogg'd
with company, and our devices[7] known. In the meantime I will draw a bill[8]
of properties, such as our play wants. I pray you, fail me not.

BOTTOM: We will meet, and there we may rehearse most obscenely[9] and coura-
geously. Take pains, be perfect[1]; adieu.

QUINCE: At the Duke's oak we meet.

BOTTOM: Enough. Hold, or cut bow-strings.[2]   [*Exeunt.*]

ACT II

SCENE 1[3]

Enter a FAIRY *at one door, and Robin Goodfellow* (PUCK) *at another.*

PUCK: How now, spirit! Whither wander you?

FAIRY: Over hill, over dale,
    Thorough bush, thorough[4] brier,
    Over park, over pale,[5]
    Thorough flood, thorough fire,
    I do wander every where,
    Swifter than the moon's sphere;
    And I serve the Fairy Queen,
    To dew her orbs[6] upon the green.
    The cowslips tall her pensioners[7] be.
    In their gold coats spots you see;
    Those be rubies, fairy favors,[8]
    In those freckles live their savors.[9]
I must go seek some dewdrops here
And hang a pearl in every cowslip's ear.
Farewell, thou lob[1] of spirits; I'll be gone.
Our Queen and all her elves come here anon.[2]

PUCK: The King doth keep his revels here tonight.
Take heed the Queen come not within his sight.
For Oberon is passing fell and wrath,[3]
Because that she as her attendant hath
A lovely boy, stolen from an Indian king;
She never had so sweet a changeling.[4]
And jealous Oberon would have the child
Knight of his train, to trace[5] the forests wild.
But she perforce[6] withholds the loved boy,

---

7. Plans.   8. List.   9. [An unintentionally funny blunder, whatever Bottom meant to say.]
1. I.e., letter-perfect in memorizing your parts.   2. [An archer's expression not definitely explained, but probably meaning here "keep your promises, or give up the play."]   3. Location: A
wood near Athens.   4. Through.   5. Enclosure.   6. Circles; i.e., fairy rings. 7. Retainers,
members of the royal bodyguard.   8. Love tokens.   9. Sweet smells. 1. Country bumpkin.
2. At once.   3. Wrathful. *Fell:* exceedingly angry.   4. Child exchanged for another by the
fairies.   5. Range through.   6. Forcibly.

Crowns him with flowers and makes him all her joy.
And now they never meet in grove or green,
By fountain[7] clear, or spangled starlight sheen,
But they do square,[8] that all their elves for fear   30
Creep into acorn-cups and hide them there.
FAIRY: Either I mistake your shape and making quite,
  Or else you are that shrewd and knavish sprite[9]
Call'd Robin Goodfellow. Are not you he
That frights the maidens of the villagery,   35
Skim milk, and sometimes labor in the quern,[1]
And bootless[2] make the breathless huswife churn,
And sometime make the drink to bear no barm,[3]
Mislead night-wanderers, laughing at their harm?
Those that Hobgoblin call you and sweet Puck,   40
You do their work, and they shall have good luck.
Are you not he?
PUCK: Thou speakest aright;
  I am that merry wanderer of the night.
I jest to Oberon and make him smile
When I a fat and bean-fed horse beguile,   45
Neighing in likeness of a filly foal;
And sometime lurk I in a gossip's[4] bowl,
In very likeness of a roasted crab,[5]
And when she drinks, against her lips I bob
And on her withered dewlap[6] pour the ale.   50
The wisest aunt, telling the saddest[7] tale,
Sometime for three-foot stool mistaketh me;
Then slip I from her bum, down topples she,
And "tailor"[8] cries, and falls into a cough;
And then the whole quire[9] hold their hips and laugh,   55
And waxen in their mirth and neeze[1] and swear
A merrier hour was never wasted there.
But, room, fairy! Here comes Oberon.
FAIRY: And here my mistress. Would that he were gone!

[*Enter* OBERON, *the King of Fairies, at one door, with his train; and* TITANIA,
the Queen, at another, with hers.]

OBERON: Ill met by moonlight, proud Titania.   60
TITANIA: What, jealous Oberon? Fairies, skip hence.
  I have forsworn his bed and company.
OBERON: Tarry, rash wanton.[2] Am not I thy lord?

---

7. Spring.   8. Quarrel.   9. Spirit. *Shrewd:* mischievous.   1. Handmill.   2. In vain.
3. Yeast, head on the ale.   4. Old woman's.   5. Crab apple.   6. Loose skin on neck.
7. Most serious. *Aunt:* old woman.   8. [Possibly because she ends up sitting crosslegged on the
floor, looking like a tailor.]   9. Company.   1. Sneeze. *Waxen:* increase. 2. Head-strong
creature.

TITANIA: Then I must be thy lady; but I know
65   When thou hast stolen away from fairy land,
        And in the shape of Corin[3] sat all day,
        Playing on pipes of corn[4] and versing love
        To amorous Phillida. Why art thou here,
        Come from the farthest steep[5] of India,
70   But that, forsooth, the bouncing Amazon,
        Your buskin'd[6] mistress and your warrior love,
        To Theseus must be wedded, and you come
        To give their bed joy and prosperity.
OBERON: How canst thou thus for shame, Titania,
75   Glance at my credit with Hippolyta,[7]
        Knowing I know thy love to Theseus?
        Didst not thou lead him through the glimmering night
        From Perigenia,[8] whom he ravished?
        And make him with fair Aegles[9] break his faith,
80   With Ariadne and Antiopa[1]?
TITANIA: These are the forgeries of jealousy;
        And never, since the middle summer's spring,[2]
        Met we on hill, in dale, forest, or mead,
        By paved fountain or by rushy[3] brook,
85   Or in the beached margent[4] of the sea,
        To dance our ringlets[5] to the whistling wind,
        But with thy brawls thou hast disturb'd our sport.
        Therefore the winds, piping to us in vain,
        As in revenge, have suck'd up from the sea
90   Contagious[6] fogs; which falling in the land
        Hath every pelting[7] river made so proud
        That they have overborne their continents.[8]
        The ox hath therefore stretch'd his yoke in vain,
        The ploughman lost his sweat, and the green corn[9]
95   Hath rotted ere his youth attain'd a beard;
        The fold[1] stands empty in the drowned field,
        And crows are fatted with the murrion[2] flock;

---

3. Corin and Phillida are conventional names of pastoral lovers.   4. [Here, oat stalks.]
5. Mountain range.   6. Wearing half-boots called buskins.   7. Make insinuations about
my favored relationship with Hippolyta.   8. I.e., Perigouna, one of Theseus's conquests. (This
and the following women are named in Thomas North's translation of Plutarch's *Life of Theseus*.)
9. I.e., Aegle, for whom Theseus deserted Ariadne according to some accounts.   1. Queen
of the Amazons and wife of Theseus; elsewhere identified with Hippolyta, but here thought of as a
separate woman. *Ariadne*: the daughter of Minos, king of Crete, who helped Theseus to escape the
labyrinth after killing the Minotaur; later she was abandoned by Theseus.   2. Beginning
of midsummer.   3. Bordered with rushes. *Paved*: with pebbled bottom.   4. Edge, border. *In*:
on.   5. Dances in a ring. (See *orbs* in II.1.9.)   6. Noxious.   7. Paltry; or, striking, moving
forcefully.   8. Banks that contain them.   9. Grain of any kind.   1. Pen for sheep or cattle.
2. Having died of the murrain, plague.

The nine men's morris[3] is fill'd up with mud,
And the quaint mazes in the wanton[4] green
For lack of tread are undistinguishable.   100
The human mortals want their winter[5] here;
No night is now with hymn or carol bless'd.
Therefore[6] the moon, the governess of floods,
Pale in her anger, washes all the air,
That rheumatic[7] diseases do abound.   105
And thorough this distemperature[8] we see
The seasons alter: hoary-headed frosts
Fall in the fresh lap of the crimson rose,
And on old Hiems'[9] thin and icy crown
An odorous chaplet of sweet summer buds   110
Is, as in mockery, set. The spring, the summer,
The childing[1] autumn, angry winter, change
Their wonted liveries, and the mazed[2] world,
By their increase,[3] now knows not which is which.
And this same progeny of evils comes   115
From our debate,[4] from our dissension;
We are their parents and original.[5]
OBERON: Do you amend it then; it lies in you.
Why should Titania cross her Oberon?
I do but beg a little changeling boy,   120
To be my henchman.[6]
TITANIA: Set your heart at rest.
The fairy land buys not the child of me.
His mother was a vot'ress of my order,
And, in the spiced Indian air, by night,
Full often hath she gossip'd by my side,   125
And sat with me on Neptune's yellow sands,
Marking th' embarked traders on the flood,[7]
When we have laugh'd to see the sails conceive
And grow big-bellied with the wanton[8] wind;
Which she, with pretty and with swimming gait,   130
Following—her womb then rich with my young squire—
Would imitate, and sail upon the land
To fetch me trifles, and return again,
As from a voyage, rich with merchandise.

3. I.e., portion of the village green marked out in a square for a game played with nine pebbles or
pegs.   4. Luxuriant. *Mazes*: i.e., intricate paths marked out on the village green to be followed
rapidly on foot as a kind of contest.   5. I.e., regular winter season; or, proper observances of
winter, such as the *hymn* or *carol* in the next line. *Want*: lack.   6. I.e., as a result of our quarrel.
7. Colds, flu, and other respiratory infections.   8. Disturbance in nature.   9. The winter
god's.   1. Fruitful, pregnant.   2. Bewildered. *Liveries*: usual apparel.   3. Their yield, what
they produce.   4. Quarrel.   5. Origin.   6. Attendant, page.   7. Flood tide. *Traders*:
trading vessels.   8. Sportive.

135 But she, being mortal, of that boy did die;
And for her sake do I rear up her boy,
And for her sake I will not part with him.

OBERON: How long within this wood intend you stay?

TITANIA: Perchance till after Theseus' wedding-day.

140 If you will patiently dance in our round[9]
And see our moonlight revels, go with us;
If not, shun me, and I will spare[1] your haunts.

OBERON: Give me that boy, and I will go with thee.

TITANIA: Not for thy fairy kingdom. Fairies, away!

145 We shall chide downright, if I longer stay.   [*Exeunt* TITANIA *with her train.*]

OBERON: Well, go thy way. Thou shalt not from[2] this grove
Till I torment thee for this injury.
My gentle Puck, come hither. Thou rememb'rest
Since[3] once I sat upon a promontory,

150 And heard a mermaid on a dolphin's back
Uttering such dulcet and harmonious breath[4]
That the rude sea grew civil at her song
And certain stars shot madly from their spheres,
To hear the sea-maid's music.

PUCK: I remember.

155 OBERON: That very time I saw, but thou couldst not,
Flying between the cold moon and the earth,
Cupid all[5] arm'd. A certain aim he took
At a fair vestal[6] throned by the west,
And loos'd his love-shaft smartly from his bow,

160 As[7] it should pierce a hundred thousand hearts;
But I might[8] see young Cupid's fiery shaft
Quench'd in the chaste beams of the wat'ry moon,
And the imperial vot'ress passed on,
In maiden meditation, fancy-free.[9]

165 Yet mark'd I where the bolt of Cupid fell:
It fell upon a little western flower,
Before milk-white, now purple with love's wound,
And maidens call it love-in-idleness.[1]
Fetch me that flow'r; the herb I showed thee once.

170 The juice of it on sleeping eyelids laid
Will make or man or[2] woman madly dote
Upon the next live creature that it sees.
Fetch me this herb, and be thou here again
Ere the leviathan[3] can swim a league.

---

9. Circular dance.   1. Shun.   2. Go from.   3. When.   4. Voice, song.   5. Fully.
6. Vestal virgin (contains a complimentary allusion to Queen Elizabeth as a votaress of Diana and probably refers to an actual entertainment in her honor at Elvetham in 1591).   7. As if.
8. Could.   9. Free of love's spell.   1. Pansy, heartsease.   2. Either . . . or.   3. Sea-monster, whale.

PUCK: I'll put a girdle round about the earth   175
  In forty[4] minutes.   [*Exit.*]
OBERON: Having once this juice,
  I'll watch Titania when she is asleep,
  And drop the liquor of it in her eyes.
  The next thing then she waking looks upon,
  Be it on lion, bear, or wolf, or bull,   180
  On meddling monkey, or on busy ape,
  She shall pursue it with the soul of love.
  And ere I take this charm from off her sight,
  As I can take it with another herb,
  I'll make her render up her page to me.   185
  But who comes here? I am invisible,
  And I will overhear their conference.

[*Enter* DEMETRIUS, HELENA *following him.*]

DEMETRIUS: I love thee not, therefore pursue me not.
  Where is Lysander and fair Hermia?
  The one I'll slay, the other slayeth me.   190
  Thou told'st me they were stol'n unto this wood;
  And here am I, and wode[5] within this wood,
  Because I cannot meet my Hermia.
  Hence, get thee gone, and follow me no more.
HELENA: You draw me, you hard-hearted adamant[6];   195
  But yet you draw not iron, for my heart
  Is true as steel. Leave[7] you your power to draw,
  And I shall have no power to follow you.
DEMETRIUS: Do I entice you? Do I speak you fair[8]?
  Or, rather, do I not in plainest truth   200
  Tell you I do not nor I cannot love you?
HELENA: And even for that do I love you the more.
  I am your spaniel; and, Demetrius,
  The more you beat me, I will fawn on you.
  Use me but as your spaniel, spurn me, strike me,   205
  Neglect me, lose me; only give me leave,
  Unworthy as I am, to follow you.
  What worser place can I beg in your love—
  And yet a place of high respect with me—
  Than to be used as you use your dog?   210
DEMETRIUS: Tempt not too much the hatred of my spirit,
  For I am sick when I do look on thee.
HELENA: And I am sick when I look not on you.

4. [Used indefinitely.]   5. Mad (pronounced *wood* and often spelled so).   6. Lodestone,
magnet (with pun on *hard-hearted,* since adamant was also thought to be the hardest of all stones
and was confused with the diamond).   7. Give up.   8. Courteously.

DEMETRIUS: You do impeach[9] your modesty too much
    To leave the city and commit yourself
    Into the hands of one that loves you not,
    To trust the opportunity of night
    And the ill counsel of a desert[1] place
    With the rich worth of your virginity.
HELENA: Your virtue is my privilege. For that[2]
    It is not night when I do see your face,
    Therefore I think I am not in the night;
    Nor doth this wood lack worlds of company,
    For you in my respect[3] are all the world.
    Then how can it be said I am alone,
    When all the world is here to look on me?
DEMETRIUS: I'll run from thee and hide me in the brakes,[4]
    And leave thee to the mercy of wild beasts.
HELENA: The wildest hath not such a heart as you.
    Run when you will, the story shall be chang'd:
    Apollo flies and Daphne holds the chase,[5]
    The dove pursues the griffin, the mild hind[6]
    Makes speed to catch the tiger—bootless[7] speed,
    When cowardice pursues and valor flies.
DEMETRIUS: I will not stay thy questions.[8] Let me go!
    Or if thou follow me, do not believe
    But I shall do thee mischief in the wood.
HELENA: Ay, in the temple, in the town, the field,
    You do me mischief. Fie, Demetrius!
    Your wrongs do set a scandal on my sex.
    We cannot fight for love, as men may do;
    We should be woo'd and were not made to woo.   [*Exit* DEMETRIUS.]
    I'll follow thee and make a heaven of hell,
    To die upon[9] the hand I love so well.   [*Exit.*]
OBERON: Fare thee well, nymph. Ere he do leave this grove,
    Thou shalt fly him and he shall seek thy love.

[*Enter* PUCK.]

    Hast thou the flower there? Welcome, wanderer.
PUCK: Ay, there it is.   [*Offers the flower.*]
OBERON: I pray thee, give it me.
    I know a bank where the wild thyme blows,[1]
    Where oxlips[2] and the nodding violet grows,

215
220
225
230
235
240
245
250

---

9. Call into question.   1. Deserted.   2. Because. *Virtue:* goodness or power to attract. *Privilege:* safeguard, warrant.   3. As far as I am concerned.   4. Thickets.   5. [In the ancient myth, Daphne fled from Apollo and was saved from rape by being transformed into a laurel tree; here it is the female who *holds the chase,* or pursues, instead of the male.]   6. Female deer. *Griffin:* a fabulous monster with the head of an eagle and the body of a lion.   7. Fruitless. 8. Talk or argument. *Stay:* wait for.   9. By.   1. Blooms.   2. Flowers resembling cowslip and primrose.

Quite over-canopied with luscious woodbine,[3]
With sweet musk-roses and with eglantine.[4]
There sleeps Titania sometime of the night,
Lull'd in these flowers with dances and delight;
And there the snake throws[5] her enamel'd skin,   255
Weed[6] wide enough to wrap a fairy in.
And with the juice of this I'll streak[7] her eyes,
And make her full of hateful fantasies.
Take thou some of it, and seek through this grove.   [*Gives some love-juice.*]
A sweet Athenian lady is in love   260
With a disdainful youth. Anoint his eyes,
But do it when the next thing he espies
May be the lady. Thou shalt know the man
By the Athenian garments he hath on.
Effect it with some care, that he may prove   265
More fond on[8] her than she upon her love;
And look thou meet me ere the first cock crow.
PUCK: Fear not, my lord, your servant shall do so.   [*Exeunt.*]

SCENE 2[9]

Enter TITANIA, *Queen of Fairies, with her train.*

TITANIA: Come, now a roundel[1] and a fairy song;
Then, for the third part of a minute, hence—
Some to kill cankers[2] in the musk-rose buds,
Some war with rere-mice[3] for their leathern wings,
To make my small elves coats, and some keep back   5
The clamorous owl, that nightly hoots and wonders
At our quaint[4] spirits. Sing me now asleep.
Then to your offices and let me rest.

[FAIRIES *sing.*]

[FIRST FAIRY:]

You spotted snakes with double[5] tongue,
  Thorny hedgehogs, be not seen;
Newts[6] and blindworms, do no wrong,   10
  Come not near our fairy queen.
[*Chorus.*] Philomel,[7] with melody
  Sing in our sweet lullaby;

---

3. Honeysuckle.   4. Sweetbriar, a kind of rose. *Musk-rose:* a kind of large, sweet-scented rose.
5. Sloughs off, sheds.   6. Garment.   7. Anoint, touch gently.   8. Doting on.   9. Location: The wood.   1. Dance in a ring.   2. Cankerworms.   3. Bats.   4. Dainty.
5. Forked.   6. Water lizards (considered poisonous, as were *blindworms*—small snakes with tiny eyes—and spiders).   7. The nightingale (Philomela, daughter of King Pandion, was transformed into a nightingale, according to Ovid's *Metamorphoses* VI, after she had been raped by her sister

15   Lulla, lulla, lullaby, lulla, lulla, lullaby.
        Never harm,
        Nor spell nor charm,
     Come our lovely lady nigh.
     So, good night, with lullaby.

             [FIRST FAIRY:]

20   Weaving spiders, come not here;
     Hence, you long-legg'd spinners, hence!
     Beetles black, approach not near;
        Worm nor snail, do no offense.
     [*Chorus.*] Philomel, with melody, etc.

            [SECOND FAIRY:]

25   Hence, away! Now all is well.
     One aloof stand sentinel.

                         [*Exeunt* FAIRIES. TITANIA *sleeps.*]

     [*Enter* OBERON *and squeezes the flower on* TITANIA's *eyelids.*]

OBERON: What thou seest when thou dost wake,
     Do it for thy true-love take;
     Love and languish for his sake.
30   Be it ounce,[8] or cat, or bear,
     Pard,[9] or boar with bristled hair,
     In thy eye that shall appear
     When thou wak'st, it is thy dear.
     Wake when some vile thing is near.   [*Exit.*]

     [*Enter* LYSANDER *and* HERMIA.]

35   LYSANDER: Fair love, you faint with wand'ring in the wood;
     And to speak troth,[1] I have forgot our way.
     We'll rest us, Hermia, if you think it good,
     And tarry for the comfort of the day.
HERMIA: Be 't so, Lysander. Find you out a bed,
40   For I upon this bank will rest my head.
LYSANDER: One turf shall serve as pillow for us both,
     One heart, one bed, two bosoms, and one troth.[2]
HERMIA: Nay, good Lysander; for my sake, my dear,
     Lie further off yet, do not lie so near.
45   LYSANDER: O, take the sense, sweet, of my innocence![3]
     Love takes the meaning in love's conference.[4]
     I mean, that my heart unto yours is knit

Procne's husband, Tereus).   **8.** Lynx.   **9.** Leopard.   **1.** Truth.   **2.** Faith, trothplight.
3. I.e., interpret my intention as innocent.   **4.** I.e., when lovers confer, love teaches each lover
to interpret the other's meaning lovingly.

So that but one heart we can make of it;
Two bosoms interchained with an oath—
So then two bosoms and a single troth.   50
Then by your side no bed-room me deny,
For lying so, Hermia, I do not lie.[5]

HERMIA: Lysander riddles very prettily.
Now much beshrew[6] my manners and my pride
If Hermia meant to say Lysander lied.   55
But, gentle friend, for love and courtesy
Lie further off, in human[7] modesty;
Such separation as may well be said
Becomes a virtuous bachelor and a maid,
So far be distant; and, good night, sweet friend.   60
Thy love ne'er alter till thy sweet life end!

LYSANDER: Amen, amen, to that fair prayer, say I,
And then end life when I end loyalty!
Here is my bed. Sleep give thee all his rest!

HERMIA: With half that wish the wisher's eyes be press'd![8]   65

[*They sleep, separated by a short distance. Enter* PUCK.]

PUCK: Through the forest have I gone,
      But Athenian found I none
      On whose eyes I might approve[9]
      This flower's force in stirring love.
      Night and silence.—Who is here?   70
      Weeds of Athens he doth wear.
      This is he, my master said,
      Despised the Athenian maid;
      And here the maiden, sleeping sound,
      On the dank and dirty ground.   75
      Pretty soul! She durst not lie
      Near this lack-love, this kill-courtesy.
      Churl, upon thy eyes I throw
      All the power this charm doth owe.[1]   [*Applies the love-juice.*]
      When thou wak'st, let love forbid   80
      Sleep his seat on thy eyelid.
      So awake when I am gone,
      For I must now to Oberon.   [*Exit.*]

[*Enter* DEMETRIUS *and* HELENA, *running.*]

HELENA: Stay, though thou kill me, sweet Demetrius.
DEMETRIUS: I charge thee, hence, and do not haunt me thus.   85

---

5. Tell a falsehood (with a pun on *lie*, recline).   6. Curse (but mildly meant).   7. Courteous.
8. I.e., may we share your wish, so that your eyes too are *press'd*, closed, in sleep.   9. Test.
1. Own.

HELENA: O, wilt thou darkling[2] leave me? Do not so.

DEMETRIUS: Stay, on thy peril![3] I alone will go. [*Exit.*]

HELENA: O, I am out of breath in this fond[4] chase!
    The more my prayer, the lesser is my grace.[5]
90   Happy is Hermia, wheresoe'er she lies,[6]
    For she hath blessed and attractive eyes.
    How came her eyes so bright? Not with salt tears;
    If so, my eyes are oft'ner wash'd than hers.
    No, no, I am as ugly as a bear;
95   For beasts that meet me run away for fear.
    Therefore no marvel though Demetrius
    Do, as a monster, fly my presence thus.
    What wicked and dissembling glass of mine
    Made me compare with Hermia's sphery eyne?[7]
100   But who is here? Lysander, on the ground?
    Dead, or asleep? I see no blood, no wound.
    Lysander, if you live, good sir, awake.

LYSANDER: [*Awaking.*] And run through fire I will for thy sweet sake.
    Transparent[8] Helena! Nature shows art,
105   That through thy bosom makes me see thy heart.
    Where is Demetrius? O, how fit a word
    Is that vile name to perish on my sword!

HELENA: Do not say so, Lysander, say not so.
    What though he love your Hermia? Lord, what though?
110   Yet Hermia still loves you. Then be content.

LYSANDER: Content with Hermia? No! I do repent
    The tedious minutes I with her have spent.
    Not Hermia but Helena I love.
    Who will not change a raven for a dove?
115   The will of man is by his reason sway'd,
    And reason says you are the worthier maid.
    Things growing are not ripe until their season;
    So I, being young, till now ripe not to reason.[9]
    And touching now the point of human skill,[1]
120   Reason becomes the marshal to my will
    And leads me to your eyes, where I o'erlook[2]
    Love's stories written in love's richest book.

HELENA: Wherefore was I to this keen mockery born?
    When at your hands did I deserve this scorn?
125   Is 't not enough, is 't not enough, young man,
    That I did never, no, nor never can,
    Deserve a sweet look from Demetrius' eye,

2. In the dark.   3. I.e., on pain of danger to you if you don't obey me and stay.   4. Doting.
5. The favor I obtain.   6. Dwells.   7. Eyes as bright as stars in their spheres.   8. (1) Radiant; (2) Able to be seen through.   9. Mature enough to be reasonable.   1. Judgment. *Touching*: reaching. *Point*: summit.   2. Read.

But you must flout my insufficiency?
Good troth, you do me wrong, good sooth,[3] you do,
In such disdainful manner me to woo.   130
But fare you well. Perforce I must confess
I thought you lord of more true gentleness.[4]
O, that a lady, of[5] one man refus'd,
Should of another therefore be abus'd[6]!   [*Exit.*]
LYSANDER: She sees not Hermia. Hermia, sleep thou there,   135
And never mayst thou come Lysander near!
For as a surfeit of the sweetest things
The deepest loathing to the stomach brings,
Or as the heresies that men do leave
Are hated most of those they did deceive,   140
So thou, my surfeit and my heresy,
Of all be hated, but the most of me!
And, all my powers, address your love and might
To honor Helen and to be her knight!   [*Exit.*]
HERMIA: [*Awaking.*] Help me, Lysander, help me! Do thy best   145
To pluck this crawling serpent from my breast!
Ay me, for pity! What a dream was here!
Lysander, look how I do quake with fear.
Methought a serpent eat[7] my heart away,
And you sat smiling at his cruel prey.[8]   150
Lysander! What, remov'd? Lysander! Lord!
What, out of hearing? Gone? No sound, no word?
Alack, where are you? Speak, an if you hear.
Speak, of all loves![9] I swoon almost with fear.
No? Then I well perceive you are not nigh.   155
Either death, or you, I'll find immediately.

[*Exit. Manet* TITANIA *lying asleep.*]

ACT III

SCENE 1[1]

Enter the Clowns (QUINCE, SNUG, BOTTOM, FLUTE, SNOUT, *and* STARVELING.)

BOTTOM: Are we all met?
QUINCE: Pat, pat; and here's a marvailes convenient place for our rehearsal. This
green plot shall be our stage, this hawthorn brake our tiring-house,[2] and we
will do it in action as we will do it before the Duke.
BOTTOM: Peter Quince?   5

3. I.e., indeed, truly.   4. Courtesy. *Lord of:* i.e., possessor of.   5. By.   6. Ill treated.
7. Ate (pronounced *et*).   8. Act of preying.   9. For all love's sake.   1. Location: Scene
continues.   2. Attiring area, hence backstage. *Brake:* thicket.

QUINCE: What sayest thou, bully[3] Bottom?

BOTTOM: There are things in this comedy of Pyramus and Thisby that will never please. First, Pyramus must draw a sword to kill himself, which the ladies cannot abide. How answer you that?

SNOUT: By 'r lakin, a parlous[4] fear.

STARVELING: I believe we must leave the killing out, when all is done.[5]

BOTTOM: Not a whit. I have a device to make all well. Write me[6] a prologue; and let the prologue seem to say, we will do no harm with our swords and that Pyramus is not kill'd indeed; and, for the more better assurance, tell them that I Pyramus am not Pyramus, but Bottom the weaver. This will put them out of fear.

QUINCE: Well, we will have such a prologue, and it shall be written in eight and six.[7]

BOTTOM: No, make it two more; let it be written in eight and eight.

SNOUT: Will not the ladies be afeard of the lion?

STARVELING: I fear it, I promise you.

BOTTOM: Masters, you ought to consider with yourselves, to bring in—God shield us!—a lion among ladies,[8] is a most dreadful thing. For there is not a more fearful[9] wild-fowl than your lion living; and we ought to look to 't.

SNOUT: Therefore another prologue must tell he is not a lion.

BOTTOM: Nay, you must name his name, and half his face must be seen through the lion's neck, and he himself must speak through, saying thus, or to the same defect[1]: "Ladies"—or "Fair ladies—I would wish you"—or "I would request you"—or "I would entreat you—not to fear, not to tremble; my life for yours.[2] If you think I come hither as a lion, it were pity of my life.[3] No, I am no such thing; I am a man as other men are." And there indeed let him name his name, and tell them plainly he is Snug the joiner.

QUINCE: Well, it shall be so. But there is two hard things: that is, to bring the moonlight into a chamber; for, you know, Pyramus and Thisby meet by moonlight.

SNOUT: Doth the moon shine that night we play our play?

BOTTOM: A calendar, a calendar! Look in the almanac. Find out moonshine, find out moonshine. [*They consult an almanac.*]

QUINCE: Yes, it doth shine that night.

BOTTOM: Why then may you leave a casement of the great chamber window, where we play, open, and the moon may shine in at the casement.

QUINCE: Ay; or else one must come in with a bush of thorns and a lantern, and

---

3. I.e., worthy, jolly, fine fellow.   4. Perilous. *By 'r lakin:* by our ladykin; i.e., the Virgin Mary.
5. I.e., when all is said and done.   6. I.e., write at my suggestion. (*Me* is the ethic dative.)
7. Alternate lines of eight and six syllables, a common ballad measure.   8. [A contemporary pamphlet tells how at the christening in 1594 of Prince Henry, eldest son of King James VI of Scotland, later James I of England, a "blackmoor" instead of a lion drew the triumphal chariot since the lion's presence might have "brought some fear to the nearest."]   9. Fear-inspiring.
1. [Bottom's blunder for *effect*.]   2. I.e., I pledge my life to make your lives safe.   3. My life would be endangered.

say he comes to disfigure,[4] or to present,[5] the person of Moonshine. Then
there is another thing: we must have a wall in the great chamber; for Pyramus and Thisby, says the story, did talk through the chink of a wall.   45

SNOUT: You can never bring in a wall. What say you, Bottom?

BOTTOM: Some man or other must present Wall. And let him have some plaster,
or some loam, or some roughcast[6] about him, to signify wall; and let him
hold his fingers thus, and through that cranny shall Pyramus and Thisby
whisper.   50

QUINCE: If that may be, then all is well. Come, sit down, every mother's son,
and rehearse your parts. Pyramus, you begin. When you have spoken your
speech, enter into that brake, and so every one according to his cue.

[*Enter Robin* (PUCK).]

PUCK: What hempen home-spuns have we swagg'ring here,
So near the cradle of the Fairy Queen?
What, a play toward[7]? I'll be an auditor;   55
An actor too perhaps, if I see cause.

QUINCE: Speak, Pyramus. Thisby, stand forth.

BOTTOM: "Thisby, the flowers of odious savors sweet,"—

QUINCE: Odors, odors.   60

BOTTOM: —"Odors savors sweet;
So hath thy breath, my dearest Thisby dear.
But hark, a voice! Stay thou but here awhile,
And by and by I will to thee appear."   [*Exit.*]

PUCK: A stranger Pyramus than e'er played here.[8]   [*Exit.*]   65

FLUTE: Must I speak now?

QUINCE: Ay, marry, must you; for you must understand he goes but to see a noise
that he heard, and is to come again.

FLUTE: "Most radiant Pyramus, most lily-white of hue,
Of color like the red rose on triumphant brier,   70
Most brisky juvenal and eke most lovely Jew,[9]
As true as truest horse that yet would never tire.
I'll meet thee, Pyramus, at Ninny's tomb."

QUINCE: "Ninus'[1] tomb," man. Why, you must not speak that yet. That you
answer to Pyramus. You speak all your part at once, cues and all. Pyramus   75
enter. Your cue is past; it is, "never tire."

FLUTE: O—"As true as truest horse, that yet would never tire."

---

4. [Quince's blunder for *prefigure.*] *Bush of thorns*: bundle of thornbush faggots (part of the accoutre-
ments of the man in the moon, according to the popular notions of the time, along with his lantern
and his dog).   **5.** Represent   **6.** A mixture of lime and gravel used to plaster the outside of
buildings.   **7.** About to take place.   **8.** I.e., in this theater (?).   **9.** [Probably an absurd
repetition of the first syllable of *juvenal.*] *Briskly juvenal*: brisk youth. *Eke*: also.   **1.** Mythical
founder of Nineveh (whose wife, Semiramis, was supposed to have built the walls of Babylon where
the story of Pyramis and Thisbe [Thisby] takes place).

[*Enter* PUCK, *and* BOTTOM *as Pyramus with the ass head.*][2]

BOTTOM: "If I were fair,[3] Thisby, I were only thine."

QUINCE: O monstrous! O strange! We are haunted. Pray, masters! Fly, masters!
80   Help!   [*Exeunt* QUINCE, SNUG, FLUTE, SNOUT, *and* STARVELING.]

PUCK: I'll follow you, I'll lead you about a round,[4]
     Through bog, through bush, through brake, through brier.
     Sometime a horse I'll be, sometime a hound,
     A hog, a headless bear, sometime a fire[5];
85   And neigh, and bark, and grunt, and roar, and burn,
     Like horse, hound, hog, bear, fire, at every turn.   [*Exit.*]

BOTTOM: Why do they run away? This is a knavery of them to make me afeard.

[*Enter* SNOUT.]

SNOUT: O Bottom, thou art chang'd! what do I see on thee?

BOTTOM: What do you see? You see an ass-head of your own, do you?
                                                 [*Exit* SNOUT.]

[*Enter* QUINCE.]

90 QUINCE: Bless thee, Bottom, bless thee! Thou art translated.[6]   [*Exit.*]

BOTTOM: I see their knavery. This is to make an ass of me, to fright me, if they
     could. But I will not stir from this place, do what they can. I will walk up
     and down here, and I will sing, that they shall hear I am not afraid.

                            [*Sings.*]

     The woosel cock[7] so black of hue,
95   With orange-tawny bill,
     The throstle[8] with his note so true,
         The wren with little quill[9] —

TITANIA: [*Awaking.*] What angel wakes me from my flow'ry bed?

                     [BOTTOM *sings.*]

     The finch, the sparrow, and the lark,
100   The plain-song[1] cuckoo grey,
     Whose note full many a man doth mark,
         And dares not answer nay —[2]

For, indeed, who would set his wit to so foolish a bird? Who would give a
bird the lie,[3] though he cry "cuckoo" never so?[4]

105 TITANIA: I pray thee, gentle mortal, sing again.

---

2. [This stage direction, taken from the Folio, presumably refers to a standard stage property.]
3. Handsome.   4. Roundabout.   5. Will-o'-the-wisp.   6. Transformed.   7. Male
ousel or ouzel, blackbird.   8. Song thrush.   9. [Literally, a reed pipe; hence, the bird's piping
song.]   1. Singing a melody without variations.   2. I.e., cannot deny that he is a cuckold.
3. Call the bird a liar.   4. Ever so much.

Mine ear is much enamored of thy note;
So is mine eye enthralled to thy shape;
And thy fair virtue's force[5] perforce doth move me
On the first view to say, to swear, I love thee.

BOTTOM: Methinks, mistress, you should have little reason for that. And yet, to   110
say the truth, reason and love keep little company together nowadays. The
more the pity that some honest neighbors will not make them friends. Nay,
I can gleek[6] upon occasion.

TITANIA: Thou art as wise as thou art beautiful.

BOTTOM: Not so, neither. But if I had wit enough to get out of this wood, I have   115
enough to serve mine own turn.[7]

TITANIA: Out of this wood do not desire to go.
Thou shalt remain here, whether thou wilt or no.
I am a spirit of no common rate.[8]
The summer still doth tend upon my state;[9]   120
And I do love thee. Therefore, go with me.
I'll give thee fairies to attend on thee,
And they shall fetch thee jewels from the deep,
And sing while thou on pressed flowers dost sleep.
And I will purge thy mortal grossness so   125
That thou shalt like an airy spirit go.
Peaseblossom, Cobweb, Moth,[1] and Mustardseed!

[*Enter four* FAIRIES (PEASEBLOSSOM, COBWEB, MOTH, *and* MUSTARDSEED).]

PEASEBLOSSOM: Ready.

COBWEB: And I.

MOTH: And I.

MUSTARDSEED: And I.

ALL: Where shall we go?

TITANIA: Be kind and courteous to this gentleman.   130
Hop in his walks and gambol in his eyes;
Feed him with apricocks and dewberries,
With purple grapes, green figs, and mulberries;
The honey-bags steal from the humble-bees,
And for the night-tapers crop their waxen thighs   135
And light them at the fiery glow-worm's eyes,
To have my love to bed and to arise;
And pluck the wings from painted butterflies
To fan the moonbeams from his sleeping eyes.
Nod to him, elves, and do him courtesies.   140

---

5. The power of your beauty.   6. Scoff, jest.   7. Answer my purpose.   8. Rank, value.
9. Waits upon me as a part of my royal retinue. *Still*: ever, always.   1. I.e., mote, speck. (The
two words *moth* and *mote* were pronounced alike.)

PEASEBLOSSOM: Hail, mortal!

COBWEB: Hail!

MOTH: Hail!

MUSTARDSEED: Hail!

145 BOTTOM: I cry your worships mercy, heartily. I beseech your worship's name.

COBWEB: Cobweb.

BOTTOM: I shall desire you of more acquaintance, good Master Cobweb. If I cut my finger, I shall make bold with you.[2] Your name, honest gentleman?

PEASEBLOSSOM: Peaseblossom.

150 BOTTOM: I pray you, commend me to Mistress Squash,[3] your mother, and to Master Peascod,[4] your father. Good Master Peaseblossom, I shall desire you of more acquaintance too. Your name, I beseech you, sir?

MUSTARDSEED: Mustardseed.

BOTTOM: Good Master Mustardseed, I know your patience well.[5] That

155 same cowardly, giant-like ox-beef hath devour'd many a gentleman of your house. I promise you your kindred hath made my eyes water ere now. I desire you of more acquaintance, good Master Mustardseed.

TITANIA: Come wait upon him; lead him to my bower.

160 The moon methinks looks with a wat'ry eye;
And when she weeps,[6] weeps every little flower,
Lamenting some enforced[7] chastity.
Tie up my lover's tongue, bring him silently.   [*Exeunt.*]

SCENE 2[8]

Enter OBERON, King of Fairies.

OBERON: I wonder if Titania be awak'd;
Then, what it was that next came in her eye,
Which she must dote on in extremity.

[*Enter Robin Goodfellow (PUCK).*]

Here comes my messenger. How now, mad spirit?

5 What night-rule now about this haunted[9] grove?

PUCK: My mistress with a monster is in love.
Near to her close[1] and consecrated bower,
While she was in her dull[2] and sleeping hour,
A crew of patches, rude mechanicals,[3]

---

2. [Cobwebs were used to stanch bleeding.]   3. Unripe pea pod.   4. Ripe pea pod.
5. What you have endured.   6. I.e., she causes dew.   7. Forced, violated; or, possibly, constrained (since Titania at this moment is hardly concerned about chastity).   8. Location: The wood.   9. Much frequented. *Night-rule:* diversion for the night.   1. Secret, private.
2. Drowsy.   3. Ignorant artisans. *Patches:* clowns, fools.

That work for bread upon Athenian stalls,   10
Were met together to rehearse a play
Intended for great Theseus' nuptial day.
The shallowest thick-skin of that barren sort,[4]
Who Pyramus presented,[5] in their sport
Forsook his scene[6] and ent'red in a brake.   15
When I did him at this advantage take,
An ass's nole[7] I fixed on his head.
Anon his Thisby must be answered,
And forth my mimic[8] comes. When they him spy,
As wild geese that the creeping fowler eye,   20
Or russet-pated choughs, many in sort,[9]
Rising and cawing at the gun's report,
Sever[1] themselves and madly sweep the sky,
So, at his sight, away his fellows fly;
And, at our stamp, here o'er and o'er one falls;   25
He murder cries and help from Athens calls.
Their sense thus weak, lost with their fears thus strong,
Made senseless things begin to do them wrong,
For briers and thorns at their apparel snatch;
Some, sleeves—some, hats; from yielders all things catch.   30
I led them on in this distracted fear
And left sweet Pyramus translated there,
When in that moment, so it came to pass,
Titania wak'd and straightway lov'd an ass.
OBERON: This falls out better than I could devise.   35
　　But hast thou yet latch'd[2] the Athenian's eyes
　　With the love-juice, as I did bid thee do?
PUCK: I took him sleeping—that is finish'd too—
　　And the Athenian woman by his side,
　　That, when he wak'd, of force[3] she must be ey'd.   40

[Enter DEMETRIUS and HERMIA.]

OBERON: Stand close. This is the same Athenian.
PUCK: This is the woman, but not this the man.　　　　　　　[They stand aside.]
DEMETRIUS: O, why rebuke you him that loves you so?
　　Lay breath so bitter on your bitter foe.
HERMIA: Now I but chide; but I should use thee worse,   45
　　For thou, I fear, hast given me cause to curse.
　　If thou hast slain Lysander in his sleep,
　　Being o'er shoes in blood, plunge in the deep,

---

4. Stupid company or crew.　　5. Acted.　　6. Playing area.　　7. Noddle, head.　　8. Burlesque actor.　　9. In a flock. *Russet-pated choughs*: gray-headed jackdaws.　　1. I.e., scatter.
2. Moistened, anointed.　　3. Perforce.

And kill me too.
50 The sun was not so true unto the day
As he to me. Would he have stolen away
From sleeping Hermia? I'll believe as soon
This whole[4] earth may be bor'd and that the moon
May through the center creep and so displease
55 Her brother's noontide with th' Antipodes.[5]
It cannot be but thou hast murd'red him;
So should a murderer look, so dead,[6] so grim.
DEMETRIUS: So should the murdered look, and so should I,
Pierc'd through the heart with your stern cruelty.
60 Yet you, the murderer, look as bright, as clear,
As yonder Venus in her glimmering sphere.
HERMIA: What's this to my Lysander? Where is he?
Ah, good Demetrius, wilt thou give him me?
DEMETRIUS: I had rather give his carcass to my hounds.
65 HERMIA: Out, dog! Out, cur! Thou driv'st me past the bounds
Of maiden's patience. Hast thou slain him, then?
Henceforth be never numb'red among men!
O, once tell true, tell true, even for my sake!
Durst thou have look'd upon him being awake,
70 And hast thou kill'd him sleeping? O brave touch![7]
Could not a worm,[8] an adder, do so much?
An adder did it; for with doubler tongue
Than thine, thou serpent, never adder stung.
DEMETRIUS: You spend your passion on a mispris'd mood.[9]
75 I am not guilty of Lysander's blood,
Nor is he dead, for aught that I can tell.
HERMIA: I pray thee, tell me then that he is well.
DEMETRIUS: An if I could, what should I get therefore?
HERMIA: A privilege never to see me more.
80 And from thy hated presence part I so.
See me no more, whether he be dead or no. [Exit.]
DEMETRIUS: There is no following her in this fierce vein.
Here therefore for a while I will remain.
So sorrow's heaviness doth heavier[1] grow
85 For debt that bankrupt[2] sleep doth sorrow owe;
Which now in some slight measure it will pay,
If for his tender here I make some stay.[3] [They lie down and sleep.]

4. Solid.   5. The people on the opposite side of the Earth. *Her brother's:* i.e., the sun's.
6. Deadly, or deathly pale.   7. Noble exploit (said ironically).   8. Serpent.   9. Anger based
on misconception. *Passion:* violent feelings.   1. (1) Harder to bear; (2) more drowsy.   2. [De-
metrius is saying that his sleepiness adds to the weariness caused by sorrow.]   3. I.e., to a small
extent I will be able to "pay back" and hence find some relief from sorrow, if I pause here a while
(*make some stay*) while sleep "tenders" or offers itself by way of paying the debt owed to sorrow.

OBERON: What hast thou done? Thou hast mistaken quite
    And laid the love-juice on some true-love's sight.
    Of thy misprision[4] must perforce ensue   90
    Some true love turn'd and not a false turn'd true.
PUCK: Then fate o'er-rules, that, one man holding troth,[5]
    A million fail, confounding[6] oath on oath.
OBERON: About the wood go swifter than the wind,
    And Helena of Athens look thou find.   95
    All fancy-sick she is and pale of cheer[7]
    With sighs of love, that cost the fresh blood[8] dear.
    By some illusion see thou bring her here.
    I'll charm his eyes against she do appear.[9]
PUCK: I go, I go; look how I go,   100
    Swifter than arrow from the Tartar's bow.[1]   *[Exit.]*
OBERON: Flower of this purple dye,
    Hit with Cupid's archery.
    Sink in apple of his eye.   *[Applies love-juice to* DEMETRIUS's *eyes.]*
    When his love he doth espy,   105
    Let her shine as gloriously
    As the Venus of the sky.
    When thou wak'st, if she be by,
    Beg of her for remedy.

    [Enter PUCK.*]*

PUCK: Captain of our fairy band,   110
    Helena is here at hand,
    And the youth, mistook by me,
    Pleading for a lover's fee.[2]
    Shall we their fond pageant[3] see?
    Lord, what fools these mortals be!   115
OBERON: Stand aside. The noise they make
    Will cause Demetrius to awake.
PUCK: Then will two at once woo one;
    That must needs be sport alone[4];
    And those things do best please me   120
    That befall prepost'rously.[5]   *[They stand aside.]*

    [Enter LYSANDER *and* HELENA.*]*

---

4. Mistake.   5. Faith.   6. I.e., invalidating one oath with another.   7. Face. *Fancysick:*
lovesick.   8. [An allusion to the physiological theory that each sigh costs the heart a drop of
blood.]   9. In anticipation of her coming.   1. [Tartars were famed for their skill with the
bow.]   2. Privilege, reward.   3. Foolish exhibition.   4. Unequaled.   5. Out of the natural order.

LYSANDER: Why should you think that I should woo in scorn?
    Scorn and derision never come in tears.
    Look when[6] I vow, I weep; and vows so born,
125   In their nativity all truth appears.[7]
    How can these things in me seem scorn to you,
    Bearing the badge[8] of faith, to prove them true?
HELENA: You do advance[9] your cunning more and more.
    When truth kills truth,[1] O devilish-holy fray!
130   These vows are Hermia's. Will you give her o'er?
    Weigh oath with oath, and you will nothing weigh.
    Your vows to her and me, put in two scales,
    Will even weigh, and both as light as tales.[2]
LYSANDER: I had no judgment when to her I swore.
135 HELENA: Nor none, in my mind, now you give her o'er.
LYSANDER: Demetrius loves her, and he loves not you.
DEMETRIUS: [*Awaking.*] O Helen, goddess, nymph, perfect, divine!
    To what, my love, shall I compare thine eyne?
    Crystal is muddy. O, how ripe in show[3]
140   Thy lips, those kissing cherries, tempting grow!
    That pure congealed white, high Taurus'[4] snow,
    Fann'd with the eastern wind, turns to a crow[5]
    When thou hold'st up thy hand. O, let me kiss
    This princess of pure white, this seal[6] of bliss!
145 HELENA: O spite! O hell! I see you all are bent
    To set against me for your merriment.
    If you were civil and knew courtesy,
    You would not do me thus much injury.
    Can you not hate me, as I know you do,
150   But you must join in souls to mock me too?
    If you were men, as men you are in show,
    You would not use a gentle lady so—
    To vow, and swear, and superpraise my parts,[7]
    When I am sure you hate me with your hearts.
155   You both are rivals, and love Hermia;
    And now both rivals, to mock Helena.
    A trim[8] exploit, a manly enterprise,
    To conjure tears up in a poor maid's eyes
    With your derision! None of noble sort

---

6. Whenever.   7. I.e., vows made by one who is weeping give evidence thereby of their sincerity.   8. Identifying device such as that worn on servants' livery.   9. Carry forward, display.
1. I.e., one of Lysander's vows must invalidate the other.   2. Lies.   3. Appearance.
4. A lofty mountain range in Asia Minor.   5. I.e., seems black by contrast.   6. Pledge.
7. Qualities. *Superpraise:* overpraise.   8. Pretty, fine (said ironically).

Would so offend a virgin and extort[9]   160
A poor soul's patience, all to make you sport.

LYSANDER: You are unkind, Demetrius. Be not so;
For you love Hermia; this you know I know.
And here, with all good will, with all my heart,
In Hermia's love I yield you up my part;   165
And yours of Helena to me bequeath,
Whom I do love and will do till my death.

HELENA: Never did mockers waste more idle breath.

DEMETRIUS: Lysander, keep thy Hermia; I will none.[1]
If e'er I lov'd her, all that love is gone.   170
My heart to her but as guest-wise sojourn'd,
And now to Helen is it home return'd,
There to remain.

LYSANDER: Helen, it is not so.

DEMETRIUS: Disparage not the faith thou dost not know,
Lest, to thy peril, thou aby[2] it dear.   175
Look, where thy love comes; yonder is thy dear.

[Enter HERMIA.]

HERMIA: Dark night, that from the eye his[3] function takes,
The ear more quick of apprehension makes;
Wherein it doth impair the seeing sense,
It pays the hearing double recompense.   180
Thou art not by mine eye, Lysander, found;
Mine ear, I thank it, brought me to thy sound.
But why unkindly didst thou leave me so?

LYSANDER: Why should he stay, whom love doth press to go?

HERMIA: What love could press Lysander from my side?   185

LYSANDER: Lysander's love, that would not let him bide,
Fair Helena, who more engilds the night
Than all yon fiery oes[4] and eyes of light.
Why seek'st thou me? Could not this make thee know,
The hate I bear thee made me leave thee so?   190

HERMIA: You speak not as you think. It cannot be.

HELENA: Lo, she is one of this confederacy!
Now I perceive they have conjoin'd all three
To fashion this false sport, in spite of me.[5]
Injurious Hermia, most ungrateful maid!   195
Have you conspir'd, have you with these contriv'd[6]
To bait[7] me with this foul derision?

---

9. Twist, torture.   1. I.e., wish none of her.   2. Pay for.   3. Its.   4. I.e., circles, orbs,
stars.   5. To vex me.   6. Plotted.   7. Torment, as one sets on dogs to bait a bear.

Is all the counsel[8] that we two have shar'd,
The sisters' vows, the hours that we have spent,
200   When we have chid the hasty-footed time
For parting us—O, is all forgot?
All school-days friendship, childhood innocence?
We, Hermia, like two artificial[9] gods,
Have with our needles created both one flower,
205   Both on one sampler, sitting on one cushion,
Both warbling of one song, both in one key,
As if our hands, our sides, voices, and minds
Had been incorporate. So we grew together,
Like to a double cherry, seeming parted,
210   But yet an union in partition;
Two lovely[1] berries molded on one stem;
So, with two seeming bodies, but one heart;
Two of the first, like coats in heraldry,
Due but to one and crowned with one crest.[2]
215   And will you rent[3] our ancient love asunder,
To join with men in scorning your poor friend?
It is not friendly, 'tis not maidenly.
Our sex, as well as I, may chide you for it,
Though I alone do feel the injury.
220   HERMIA: I am amazed at your passionate words.
I scorn you not. It seems that you scorn me.
HELENA: Have you not set Lysander, as in scorn,
To follow me and praise my eyes and face?
And made your other love, Demetrius,
225   Who even but now did spurn me with his foot,
To call me goddess, nymph, divine and rare,
Precious, celestial? Wherefore speaks he this
To her he hates? And wherefore doth Lysander
Deny your love, so rich within his soul,
230   And tender[4] me, forsooth, affection,
But by your setting on, by your consent?
What though I be not so in grace[5] as you,
So hung upon with love, so fortunate,
But miserable most, to love unlov'd?
235   This you should pity rather than despise.
HERMIA: I understand not what you mean by this.
HELENA: Ay, do! Persever, counterfeit sad[6] looks,
Make mouths upon[7] me when I turn my back,

---

8. Confidential talk.   9. Skilled in art or creation.   1. Loving.   2. I.e., we have two separate bodies, just as a coat of arms in heraldry can be represented twice on a shield but surmounted by a single crest.   3. Rend.   4. Offer.   5. Favor.   6. Grave, serious.   7. I.e., makes mows, faces, grimaces at.

Wink each at other, hold the sweet jest up.
This sport, well carried,[8] shall be chronicled.   240
If you have any pity, grace, or manners,
You would not make me such an argument.[9]
But fare ye well. 'Tis partly my own fault,
Which death, or absence, soon shall remedy.
LYSANDER: Stay, gentle Helena; hear my excuse,   245
   My love, my life, my soul, fair Helena!
HELENA: O excellent!
HERMIA: Sweet, do not scorn her so.
DEMETRIUS: If she cannot entreat,[1] I can compel.
LYSANDER: Thou canst compel no more than she entreat.
   Thy threats have no more strength than her weak prayers.   250
   Helen, I love thee, by my life, I do!
   I swear by that which I will lose for thee,
   To prove him false that says I love thee not.
DEMETRIUS: I say I love thee more than he can do.
LYSANDER: If thou say so, withdraw, and prove it too.   255
DEMETRIUS: Quick, come!
HERMIA: Lysander, whereto tends all this?
LYSANDER: Away, you Ethiope[2]!   [He tries to break away from HERMIA.]
DEMETRIUS: No, no; he'll
   Seem to break loose; take on as you would follow,
   But yet come not. You are a tame man, go!
LYSANDER: Hang off,[3] thou cat, thou burr! Vile thing, let loose,   260
   Or I will shake thee from me like a serpent!
HERMIA: Why are you grown so rude? What change is this,
   Sweet love?
LYSANDER: Thy love? Out, tawny Tartar, out!
   Out, loathed med'cine[4]! O hated potion, hence!
HERMIA: Do you not jest?
HELENA: Yes, sooth,[5] and so do you.   265
LYSANDER: Demetrius, I will keep my word with thee.
DEMETRIUS: I would I had your bond, for I perceive
   A weak bond[6] holds you. I'll not trust your word.
LYSANDER: What, should I hurt her, strike her, kill her dead?
   Although I hate her, I'll not harm her so.   270
HERMIA: What, can you do me greater harm than hate?
   Hate me? Wherefore? O me, what news,[7] my love?
   Am not I Hermia? Are not you Lysander?
   I am as fair now as I was erewhile.[8]

---

8. Managed.   9. Subject for a jest.   1. I.e., succeed by entreaty.   2. [Referring to
Hermia's relatively dark hair and complexion; see also *tawny Tartar* six lines later.]   3. Let go.
4. I.e., poison.   5. Truly.   6. I.e., Hermia's arm (with a pun on *bond*, oath, in the previous
line).   7. What is the matter.   8. Just now.

275   Since night you lov'd me; yet since night you left me.
    Why, then you left me—O, the gods forbid!—
    In earnest, shall I say?
LYSANDER: Ay, by my life!
    And never did desire to see thee more.
    Therefore be out of hope, of question, of doubt;
280   Be certain, nothing truer. 'Tis no jest
    That I do hate thee and love Helena.
HERMIA: O me! You juggler! You cankerblossom[9]!
    You thief of love! What, have you come by night
    And stol'n my love's heart from him?
HELENA: Fine, i' faith!
285   Have you no modesty, no maiden shame,
    No touch of bashfulness? What, will you tear
    Impatient answers from my gentle tongue?
    Fie, fie! You counterfeit, you puppet,[1] you!
HERMIA: Puppet? Why so? Ay, that way goes the game.
290   Now I perceive that she hath made compare
    Between our statures; she hath urg'd her height,
    And with her personage, her tall personage,
    Her height, forsooth, she hath prevail'd with him.
    And are you grown so high in his esteem,
295   Because I am so dwarfish and so low?
    How low am I, thou painted maypole? Speak!
    How low am I? I am not yet so low
    But that my nails can reach unto thine eyes.

                  [*She flails at* HELENA, *but is restrained.*]
HELENA: I pray you, though you mock me, gentlemen,
300   Let her not hurt me. I was never curst[2];
    I have no gift at all in shrewishness;
    I am a right[3] maid for my cowardice.
    Let her not strike me. You perhaps may think,
    Because she is something[4] lower than myself,
    That I can match her.
HERMIA: Lower! Hark, again!
305 HELENA: Good Hermia, do not be so bitter with me.
    I evermore did love you, Hermia,
    Did ever keep your counsels, never wrong'd you;
    Save that, in love unto Demetrius,
310   I told him of your stealth[5] unto this wood.
    He followed you; for love I followed him.
    But he hath chid me hence and threat'ned me

---

9. Worm that destroys the flower bud (?).   1. (1) Counterfeit; (2) dwarfish woman (in reference to Hermia's smaller stature).   2. Shrewish.   3. True.   4. Somewhat.   5. Stealing away.

To strike me, spurn me, nay, to kill me too.
And now, so[6] you will let me quiet go,
To Athens will I bear my folly back   315
And follow you no further. Let me go.
You see how simple and how fond[7] I am.

HERMIA: Why, get you gone, Who is 't that hinders you?
HELENA: A foolish heart, that I leave here behind.
HERMIA: What, with Lysander?
HELENA: With Demetrius.   320
LYSANDER: Be not afraid; she shall not harm thee, Helena.
DEMETRIUS: No, sir, she shall not, though you take her part.
HELENA: O, when she is angry, she is keen and shrewd[8]!
    She was a vixen when she went to school;
    And though she be but little, she is fierce.   325
HERMIA: "Little" again! Nothing but "low" and "little"!
    Why will you suffer her to flout me thus?
    Let me come to her.
LYSANDER: Get you gone, you dwarf!
    You minimus, of hind'ring knot-grass[9] made!
    You bead, you acorn!
DEMETRIUS: You are too officious   330
    In her behalf that scorns your services.
    Let her alone. Speak not of Helena;
    Take not her part. For, if thou dost intend[1]
    Never so little show of love to her,
    Thou shalt aby[2] it.
LYSANDER: Now she holds me not;   335
    Now follow, if thou dar'st, to try whose right,
    Of thine or mine, is most in Helena.   [Exit.]
DEMETRIUS: Follow? Nay, I'll go with thee, cheek by jowl.[3]
                              [Exit, following LYSANDER.]
HERMIA: You, mistress, all this coil is 'long of[4] you.
    Nay, go not back.[5]
HELENA: I will not trust you, I,   340
    Nor longer stay in your curst company.
    Your hands than mine are quicker for a fray;
    My legs are longer, though, to run away.   [Exit.]
HERMIA: I am amaz'd, and know not what to say.   [Exit.]
OBERON: This is thy negligence. Still thou mistak'st,   345
    Or else committ'st thy knaveries willfully.
PUCK: Believe me, king of shadows, I mistook.

6. If only.   7. Foolish.   8. Shrewish.   9. A weed, an infusion of which was thought to
stunt the growth. *Minimus*: diminutive creature.   1. Give sign of.   2. Pay for.   3. I.e., side
by side.   4. On account of. *Coil*: turmoil, dissension.   5. I.e., don't retreat (Hermia is again
proposing a fight).

Did not you tell me I should know the man
By the Athenian garments he had on?
350 And so far blameless proves my enterprise
That I have 'nointed an Athenian's eyes;
And so far am I glad it so did sort[6]
As this their jangling I esteem a sport.
OBERON: Thou see'st these lovers seek a place to fight.
355 Hie therefore, Robin, overcast the night;
The starry welkin[7] cover thou anon
With drooping fog as black as Acheron,[8]
And lead these testy rivals so astray
As[9] one come not within another's way.
360 Like to Lysander sometime frame thy tongue,
Then stir Demetrius up with bitter wrong[1];
And sometime rail thou like Demetrius.
And from each other look thou lead them thus,
Till o'er their brows death-counterfeiting sleep
365 With leaden legs and batty[2] wings doth creep.
Then crush this herb[3] into Lysander's eye, [*Gives herb.*]
Whose liquor hath this virtuous[4] property,
To take from thence all error with his[5] might
And make his eyeballs roll with wonted[6] sight.
370 When they next wake, all this derision[7]
Shall seem a dream and fruitless vision,
And back to Athens shall the lovers wend
With league whose date[8] till death shall never end.
Whiles I in this affair do thee employ,
375 I'll to my queen and beg her Indian boy;
And then I will her charmed eye release
From monster's view, and all things shall be peace.
PUCK: My fairy lord, this must be done with haste,
For night's swift dragons[9] cut the clouds full fast,
380 And yonder shines Aurora's harbinger,[1]
At whose approach, ghosts, wand'ring here and there,
Troop home to churchyards. Damned spirits all,
That in crossways and floods have burial,[2]
Already to their wormy beds are gone.
385 For fear lest day should look their shames upon,

---

6. Turn out.   7. Sky.   8. River of Hades (here representing Hades itself).   9. That.
1. Insults.   2. Batlike.   3. I.e., the antidote (mentioned in II.1.184) to love-in-idleness.
4. Efficacious.   5. Its.   6. Accustomed.   7. Laughable business.   8. Term of existence.
9. [Supposed by Shakespeare to be yoked to the car of the goddess of night.]   1. The morning
star, precursor of dawn.   2. [Those who had committed suicide were buried at crossways, with a
stake driven through them; those drowned, i.e., buried in floods or great waters, would be condemned to wander disconsolate for want of burial rites.]

They willfully themselves exile from light
And must for aye[3] consort with black-brow'd night.
OBERON: But we are spirits of another sort.
  I with the Morning's love[4] have oft made sport,
  And, like a forester,[5] the groves may tread   390
  Even till the eastern gate, all fiery-red,
  Opening on Neptune with fair blessed beams,
  Turns into yellow gold his salt green streams.
  But, notwithstanding, haste; make no delay.
  We may effect this business yet ere day.   [*Exit.*]   395
PUCK: Up and down, up and down,
    I will lead them up and down.
    I am fear'd in field and town.
    Goblin, lead them up and down.
  Here comes one.   400

  [*Enter* LYSANDER.]

LYSANDER: Where art thou, proud Demetrius? Speak thou now.
PUCK: [*Mimicking* DEMETRIUS.] Here, villain, drawn[6] and ready. Where art thou?
LYSANDER: I will be with thee straight.[7]
PUCK: Follow me, then,
  To plainer[8] ground.

  [LYSANDER *wanders about,*[9] *following the voice. Enter* DEMETRIUS.]

DEMETRIUS: Lysander! Speak again!
  Thou runaway, thou coward, art thou fled?   405
  Speak! In some bush? Where dost thou hide thy head?
PUCK: [*Mimicking* LYSANDER.] Thou coward, art thou bragging to the stars,
  Telling the bushes that thou look'st for wars,
  And wilt not come? Come, recreant[1]; come, thou child,
  I'll whip thee with a rod. He is defil'd   410
  That draws a sword on thee.
DEMETRIUS: Yea, art thou there?
PUCK: Follow my voice. We'll try[2] no manhood here.   [*Exeunt.*]

  [LYSANDER *returns.*]

LYSANDER: He goes before me and still dares me on.
  When I come where he calls, then he is gone.
  The villain is much lighter-heel'd than I.   415
  I followed fast, but faster he did fly,
  That fallen am I in dark uneven way,

---

3. Forever.   4. Cephalus, a beautiful youth beloved by Aurora; or perhaps the goddess of the
dawn herself.   5. Keeper of a royal forest.   6. With drawn sword.   7. Immediately.
8. Smoother.   9. [It is not clearly necessary that Lysander exit at this point; neither exit nor
reentrance is indicated in the early texts.]   1. Cowardly wretch.   2. Test.

And here will rest me. [*Lies down.*] Come, thou gentle day!
For if but once thou show me thy grey light,
420 I'll find Demetrius and revenge this spite.   [*Sleeps.*]

[*Enter Robin (*PUCK*) and* DEMETRIUS.]

PUCK: Ho, ho, ho! Coward, why com'st thou not?
DEMETRIUS: Abide me, if thou dar'st; for well I wot[3]
Thou runn'st before me, shifting every place,
And dar'st not stand nor look me in the face.
425 Where art thou now?
PUCK: Come hither. I am here.
DEMETRIUS: Nay, then, thou mock'st me. Thou shalt buy this dear,[4]
If ever I thy face by daylight see.
Now, go thy way. Faintness constraineth me
To measure out my length on this cold bed.
430 By day's approach look to be visited.   [*Lies down and sleeps.*]

[*Enter* HELENA.]

HELENA: O weary night, O long and tedious night,
Abate[5] thy hours! Shine, comforts, from the east,
That I may back to Athens by daylight,
From these that my poor company detest;
435 And sleep, that sometimes shuts up sorrow's eye,
Steal me awhile from mine own company.   [*Lies down and sleeps.*]
PUCK: Yet but three? Come one more;
Two of both kinds makes up four.
Here she comes, curst and sad.
440 Cupid is a knavish lad,
Thus to make poor females mad.

[*Enter* HERMIA.]

HERMIA: Never so weary, never so in woe,
Bedabbled with the dew and torn with briers,
I can no further crawl, no further go;
445 My legs can keep no pace with my desires.
Here will I rest me till the break of day.
Heavens shield Lysander, if they mean a fray!   [*Lies down and sleeps.*]
PUCK: On the ground
Sleep sound.
450 I'll apply
To your eye,
Gentle lover, remedy.   [*Squeezing the juice on* LYSANDER's *eyes.*]
When thou wak'st,

---

3. Know.   4. Pay dearly for this.   5. Lessen, shorten.

> Thou tak'st
> True delight   455
> In the sight
> Of thy former lady's eye;
> And the country proverb known,
> That every man should take his own,
> In your waking shall be shown: 460
> Jack shall have Jill;
> Nought shall go ill;
> The man shall have his mare again, and all
> shall be well.   [*Exit. Manent the four lovers.*]

ACT IV

SCENE 1[6]

Enter TITANIA, *Queen of Fairies, and* BOTTOM *the Clown, and* FAIRIES: *and*
OBERON, *the King, behind them.*

TITANIA: Come, sit thee down upon this flow'ry bed,
    While I thy amiable cheeks do coy,[7]
    And stick musk-roses in thy sleek smooth head,
    And kiss thy fair large ears, my gentle joy.

[*They recline.*]

BOTTOM: Where's Peaseblossom?   5
PEASEBLOSSOM: Ready.
BOTTOM: Scratch my head, Peaseblossom. Where's Mounsieur Cobweb?
COBWEB: Ready.
BOTTOM: Mounsieur Cobweb, good mounsieur, get you your weapons in your
    hand, and kill me a red-hipp'd humble-bee on the top of a thistle; and, good   10
    mounsieur, bring me the honey-bag. Do not fret yourself too much in the
    action, mounsieur; and, good mounsieur, have a care the honey-bag break
    not; I would be loath to have you overflown with a honey-bag, signior.
    Where's Mounsieur Mustardseed?
MUSTARDSEED: Ready.   15
BOTTOM: Give me your neaf,[8] Mounsieur Mustardseed. Pray you, leave your
    curtsy,[9] good mounsieur.
MUSTARDSEED: What's your will?
BOTTOM: Nothing, good mounsieur, but to help Cavalery Cobweb[1] to scratch. I
    must to the barber's, mounsieur; for methinks I am marvailes hairy about the   20
    face; and I am such a tender ass, if my hair do but tickle me, I must scratch.

---

6. Location: Scene continues. The four lovers are still asleep on stage.   7. Caress. *Amiable:*
lovely.   8. Fist.   9. I.e., put on your hat.   1. [Seemingly an error, since Cobweb has been
sent to bring honey while Peaseblossom has been asked to scratch. *Cavalery:* Form of address for a
gentleman.]

TITANIA: What, wilt thou hear some music, my sweet love?

BOTTOM: I have a reasonable good ear in music. Let's have the tongs and the bones.[2]

[*Music: tongs, rural music.*][3]

25 TITANIA: Or say, sweet love, what thou desirest to eat.

BOTTOM: Truly, a peck of provender. I could munch your good dry oats. Methinks I have a great desire to a bottle of hay. Good hay, sweet hay, hath no fellow.[4]

TITANIA: I have a venturous fairy that shall seek
The squirrel's hoard, and fetch thee new nuts.

30 BOTTOM: I had rather have a handful or two of dried peas. But, I pray you, let none of your people stir me. I have an exposition[5] of sleep come upon me.

TITANIA: Sleep thou, and I will wind thee in my arms.
Fairies, be gone, and be all ways[6] away.   [*Exeunt* FAIRIES.]
So doth the woodbine the sweet honeysuckle
35 Gently entwist; the female ivy so
Enrings the barky fingers of the elm.
Oh, how I love thee! How I dote on thee!   [*They sleep.*]

[*Enter Robin Goodfellow* (PUCK).]

OBERON: [*Advancing.*] Welcome, good Robin. See'st thou this sweet sight?
Her dotage now I do begin to pity.
40 For, meeting her of late behind the wood,
Seeking sweet favors[7] for this hateful fool,
I did upbraid her and fall out with her.
For she his hairy temples then had rounded
With coronet of fresh and fragrant flowers;
45 And that same dew, which sometime[8] on the buds
Was wont to swell like round and orient pearls,[9]
Stood now within the pretty flouriets'[1] eyes
Like tears that did their own disgrace bewail.
When I had at my pleasure taunted her,
50 And she in mild terms begg'd my patience,
I then did ask of her her changeling child;
Which straight she gave me, and her fairy sent
To bear him to my bower in fairy land.
And, now I have the boy, I will undo
55 This hateful imperfection of her eyes.
And, gentle Puck, take this transformed scalp
From off the head of this Athenian swain,
That, he awaking when the other[2] do,

---

2. Instruments for rustic music. (The tongs were played like a triangle, whereas the bones were held between the fingers and used as clappers.)   3. [This stage direction is added from the Folio.] 4. Equal. *Bottle:* bundle.   5. [Bottom's word for *disposition.*]   6. In all directions. 7. I.e., gifts of flowers.   8. Formerly.   9. I.e., the most beautiful of all pearls, those coming from the Orient.   1. Flowerets'.   2. Others.

May all to Athens back again repair,
And think no more of this night's accidents   60
But as the fierce vexation of a dream.
But first I will release the Fairy Queen.   [*Squeezes juice in her eyes.*]
    Be as thou wast wont to be;
    See as thou wast wont to see.
    Dian's bud³ o'er Cupid's flower   65
    Hath such force and blessed power.
Now, my Titania, wake you, my sweet queen.
TITANIA: [*Waking.*] My Oberon! What visions have I seen!
    Methought I was enamor'd of an ass.
OBERON: There lies your love.
TITANIA: How came these things to pass?   70
    O, how mine eyes do loathe his visage now!
OBERON: Silence awhile. Robin, take off this head.
    Titania, music call, and strike more dead
    Than common sleep of all these five⁴ the sense.
TITANIA: Music, ho! Music, such as charmeth sleep!   75

[*Music.*]

PUCK: [*Removing the ass's head.*] Now, when thou wak'st, with thine own fool's
    eyes peep.
OBERON: Sound, music! Come, my queen, take hands with me,
    And rock the ground whereon these sleepers be.

[*Dance.*]

    Now thou and I are new in amity,   80
    And will tomorrow midnight solemnly⁵
    Dance in Duke Theseus' house triumphantly
    And bless it to all fair prosperity.
    There shall the pairs of faithful lovers be
    Wedded, with Theseus, all in jollity.   85
PUCK: Fairy King, attend, and mark:
    I do hear the morning lark.
OBERON: Then, my queen, in silence sad,⁶
    Trip we after night's shade.
    We the globe can compass soon,   90
    Swifter than the wand'ring moon.
TITANIA: Come, my lord, and in our flight
    Tell me how it came this night
    That I sleeping here was found
    With these mortals on the ground.   [*Exeunt.*]   95

3. [Perhaps the flower of the *agnus castus* or chaste-tree, supposed to preserve chastity; or perhaps
referring simply to Oberon's herb by which he can undo the effects of "Cupid's flower," the love-in-
idleness of II.1.166 f.].   4. I.e., the four lovers and Bottom.   5. Ceremoniously.   6. Sober.

[*Wind horn within. Enter* THESEUS *and all his train;* HIPPOLYTA, EGEUS.]

THESEUS: Go, one of you, find out the forester,
    For now our observation[7] is perform'd;
    And since we have the vaward[8] of the day,
    My love shall hear the music of my hounds.
100   Uncouple in the western valley; let them go.
    Dispatch, I say, and find the forester.   [*Exit an Attendant.*]
    We will, fair queen, up to the mountain's top
    And mark the musical confusion
    Of hounds and echo in conjunction.
105 HIPPOLYTA: I was with Hercules and Cadmus[9] once,
    When in a wood of Crete they bay'd[1] the bear
    With hounds of Sparta.[2] Never did I hear
    Such gallant chiding; for, besides the groves,
    The skies, the fountains, every region near
110   Seem'd all one mutual cry. I never heard
    So musical a discord, such sweet thunder.
THESEUS: My hounds are bred out of the Spartan kind,
    So flew'd, so sanded[3]; and their heads are hung
    With ears that sweep away the morning dew;
115   Crook-knee'd, and dewlapp'd[4] like Thessalian bulls;
    Slow in pursuit, but match'd in mouth like bells,
    Each under each. A cry more tuneable[5]
    Was never holla'd to, nor cheer'd with horn,
    In Crete, in Sparta, nor in Thessaly.
120   Judge when you hear. [*Sees the sleepers.*] But, soft! What nymphs are these?
EGEUS: My lord, this' my daughter here asleep;
    And this, Lysander; this Demetrius is;
    This Helena, old Nedar's Helena.
    I wonder of their being here together.
125 THESEUS: No doubt they rose up early to observe
    The rite of May, and, hearing our intent,
    Came here in grace of our solemnity.[6]
    But speak, Egeus. Is not this the day
    That Hermia should give answer of her choice?
130 EGEUS: It is, my lord.
THESEUS: Go, bid the huntsmen wake them with their horns.
                          [*Exit an Attendant.*]

---

7. I.e., observance to a morn of May (I.1.167).   8. Vanguard, i.e., earliest part.   9. Mythical founder of Thebes. (This story about him is unknown.)   1. Brought to bay.   2. [A breed famous in antiquity for their hunting skill.]   3. Of sandy color. *So flew'd:* similarly having large hanging chaps or fleshy covering of the jaw.   4. Having pendulous folds of skin under the neck. 5. Well tuned, melodious. *Match'd . . . each:* i.e., harmoniously matched in their various cries like a set of bells, from treble down to bass. *Cry:* pack of hounds.   6. I.e., observance of these same rites of May.

[*Shout within. Wind horns. They all start up.*]

Good morrow, friends. Saint Valentine[7] is past.
Begin these wood-birds but to couple now?
LYSANDER: Pardon, my lord.   [*They kneel.*]
THESEUS: I pray you all, stand up.
    I know you two are rival enemies;   135
    How comes this gentle concord in the world,
    That hatred is so far from jealousy
    To sleep by hate and fear no enmity?
LYSANDER: My lord, I shall reply amazedly,
    Half sleep, half waking; but as yet, I swear,   140
    I cannot truly say how I came here.
    But, as I think—for truly would I speak,
    And now I do bethink me, so it is—
    I came with Hermia hither. Our intent
    Was to be gone from Athens, where[8] we might,   145
    Without[9] the peril of the Athenian law—
EGEUS: Enough, enough, my lord; you have enough.
    I beg the law, the law, upon his head.
    They would have stol'n away; they would, Demetrius,
    Thereby to have defeated you and me,   150
    You of your wife and me of my consent,
    Of my consent that she should be your wife.
DEMETRIUS: My lord, fair Helen told me of their stealth,
    Of this their purpose hither to this wood,
    And I in fury hither followed them,   155
    Fair Helena in fancy following me.
    But, my good lord, I wot not by what power—
    But by some power it is—my love to Hermia,
    Melted as the snow, seems to me now
    As the remembrance of an idle gaud[1]   160
    Which in my childhood I did dote upon;
    And all the faith, the virtue of my heart,
    The object and the pleasure of mine eye,
    Is only Helena. To her, my lord,
    Was I betroth'd ere I saw Hermia,   165
    But like a sickness did I loathe this food;
    But, as in health, come to my natural taste,
    Now I do wish it, love it, long for it,
    And will for evermore be true to it.

---

7. [Birds were supposed to choose their mates on St. Valentine's Day.]   8. Wherever; or, to
where.   9. Outside of, beyond.   1. Worthless trinket.

170 THESEUS: Fair lovers, you are fortunately met.
Of this discourse we more will hear anon.
Egeus, I will overbear your will;
For in the temple, by and by, with us
These couples shall eternally be knit.
175 And, for the morning now is something[2] worn,
Our purpos'd hunting shall be set aside.
Away with us to Athens. Three and three,
We'll hold a feast in great solemnity.
Come, Hippolyta.   [*Exeunt* THESEUS, HIPPOLYTA, EGEUS, *and train.*]
180 DEMETRIUS: These things seem small and undistinguishable,
Like far-off mountains turned into clouds.
HERMIA: Methinks I see these things with parted[3] eye,
When every thing seems double.
HELENA: So methinks;
And I have found Demetrius like a jewel,
Mine own, and not mine own.[4]
185 DEMETRIUS: Are you sure
That we are awake? It seems to me
That yet we sleep, we dream. Do not you think
The Duke was here, and bid us follow him?
HERMIA: Yea, and my father.
HELENA: And Hippolyta.
190 LYSANDER: And he did bid us follow to the temple.
DEMETRIUS: Why, then, we are awake. Let's follow him,
And by the way let us recount our dreams.   [*Exeunt.*]
BOTTOM: [*Awaking.*] When my cue comes, call me, and I will answer. My next
is, "Most fair Pyramus." Heigh-ho! Peter Quince! Flute, the bellows-mender!
195 Snout, the tinker! Starveling! God's my life, stol'n hence, and left me asleep!
I have had a most rare vision. I have had a dream, past the wit of man to say
what dream it was. Man is but an ass, if he go about[5] to expound this dream.
Methought I was—there is no man can tell what. Methought I was—and
methought I had—but man is but a patch'd fool, if he will offer[6]
200 to say what methought I had. The eye of man hath not heard, the ear of man
hath not seen, man's hand is not able to taste, his tongue to conceive, nor
his heart to report, what my dream was. I will get Peter Quince to write a
ballad of this dream. It shall be called "Bottom's Dream," because it hath no
bottom; and I will sing it in the latter end of a play, before the Duke.
205 Peradventure, to make it the more gracious, I shall sing it at her[7] death.
                                                                      [*Exit.*]

---

2. Somewhat. *For:* since.   3. Improperly focused.   4. I.e., like a jewel that one finds by
chance and therefore possesses but cannot certainly consider one's own property.   5. Attempt.
6. Venture. *Patch'd:* wearing motley, i.e., a dress of various colors.   7. Thisby's(?).

SCENE 2[8]

Enter QUINCE, FLUTE, SNOUT, *and* STARVELING.

QUINCE: Have you sent to Bottom's house? Is he come home yet?
STARVELING: He cannot be heard of. Out of doubt he is transported.[9]
FLUTE: If he come not, then the play is marr'd. It goes not forward, doth it?
QUINCE: It is not possible. You have not a man in all Athens able to discharge[1]
    Pyramus but he.   5
FLUTE: No, he hath simply the best wit of any handicraft man in Athens.
QUINCE: Yea, and the best person too; and he is a very paramour for a sweet
    voice.
FLUTE: You must say "paragon." A paramour is, God bless us, a thing of naught.

[*Enter* SNUG *the Joiner.*]

SNUG: Masters, the Duke is coming from the temple, and there is two or three   10
    lords and ladies more married. If our sport had gone forward, we had all
    been made men.
FLUTE: O sweet bully Bottom! Thus hath he lost sixpence a day[2] during his life;
    he could not have scap'd sixpence a day. An the Duke had not given him
    sixpence a day for playing Pyramus, I'll be hang'd. He would have deserv'd   15
    it. Sixpence a day in Pyramus, or nothing.

[*Enter* BOTTOM.]

BOTTOM: Where are these lads? Where are these hearts[3]?
QUINCE: Bottom! O most courageous day! O most happy hour!
BOTTOM: Masters, I am to discourse wonders.[4] But ask me not what; for if I tell
    you, I am no true Athenian. I will tell you everything, right as it fell out. 20
QUINCE: Let us hear, sweet Bottom.
BOTTOM: Not a word of[5] me. All that I will tell you is, that the Duke hath din'd.
    Get your apparel together, good strings to your beards, new ribands[6] to your
    pumps; meet presently[7] at the palace; every man look o'er his part; for the
    short and the long is, our play is preferr'd.[8] In any case, let Thisby have   25
    clean linen; and let not him that plays the lion pare his nails, for they shall
    hang out for the lion's claws. And, most dear actors, eat no onions nor garlic,
    for we are to utter sweet breath; and I do not doubt but to hear them say, it
    is a sweet comedy. No more words. Away! Go away!   [*Exeunt.*]

---

8. Location: Athens. Quince's house(?).   9. Carried off by fairies; or, possibly, transformed.
1. Perform.   2. I.e., as a royal pension.   3. Good fellows.   4. Have wonders to relate.
5. Out of.   6. Ribbons. *Strings:* (to attach the beards).   7. Immediately.   8. Selected for
consideration.

ACT V

SCENE 1[9]

Enter THESEUS, HIPPOLYTA, *and* PHILOSTRATE, *Lords, and Attendants.*

HIPPOLYTA: 'Tis strange, my Theseus, that[1] these lovers speak of.
THESEUS: More strange than true. I never may[2] believe
    These antic fables, nor these fairy toys.[3]
    Lovers and madmen have such seething brains,
5   Such shaping fantasies,[4] that apprehend
    More than cool reason ever comprehends.
    The lunatic, the lover, and the poet
    Are of imagination all compact.[5]
    One sees more devils than vast hell can hold;
10   That is the madman. The lover, all as frantic,
    Sees Helen's beauty in a brow of Egypt.[6]
    The poet's eye, in a fine frenzy rolling,
    Doth glance from heaven to earth, from earth to heaven;
    And as imagination bodies forth
15   The forms of things unknown, the poet's pen
    Turns them to shapes and gives to airy nothing
    A local habitation and a name.
    Such tricks hath strong imagination
    That, if it would but apprehend some joy,
20   It comprehends some bringer[7] of that joy;
    Or in the night, imagining some fear,[8]
    How easy is a bush suppos'd a bear!
HIPPOLYTA: But all the story of the night told over,
    And all their minds transfigur'd so together,
25   More witnesseth than fancy's images[9]
    And grows to something of great constancy[1];
    But, howsoever, strange and admirable.[2]

    [*Enter lovers:* LYSANDER, DEMETRIUS, HERMIA, *and* HELENA.]

THESEUS: Here come the lovers, full of joy and mirth.
    Joy, gentle friends! Joy and fresh days of love
    Accompany your hearts!
30 LYSANDER: More than to us
    Wait in your royal walks, your board, your bed!
THESEUS: Come now, what masques, what dances shall we have,

9. Location: Athens. The palace of Theseus.   1. That which.   2. Can.   3. Trifling stories about fairies. *Antic:* strange, grotesque (with additional punning sense of *antique,* ancient.). 4. Imaginations.   5. Formed, composed.   6. I.e., face of a gypsy. *Helen's:* i.e., of Helen of Troy, pattern of beauty.   7. I.e., source.   8. Object of fear.   9. Testifies to something more substantial than mere imaginings.   1. Certainty.   2. Source of wonder. *Howsoever:* in any case.

To wear away this long age of three hours
Between our after-supper and bed-time?
Where is our usual manager of mirth?   35
What revels are in hand? Is there no play,
To ease the anguish of a torturing hour?
Call Philostrate.
PHILOSTRATE: Here, mighty Theseus.
THESEUS: Say, what abridgement³ have you for this evening?
    What masque? What music? How shall we beguile   40
    The lazy time, if not with some delight?
PHILOSTRATE: There is a brief⁴ how many sports are ripe.
    Make choice of which your Highness will see first.   [*Giving a paper.*]
THESEUS: [*Reads.*] "The battle with the Centaurs,⁵ to be sung
    By an Athenian eunuch to the harp."   45
    We'll none of that. That have I told my love,
    In glory of my kinsman⁶ Hercules.
    [*Reads.*] "The riot of the tipsy Bacchanals,
    Tearing the Thracian singer in their rage."⁷
    That is an old device; and it was play'd   50
    When I from Thebes came last a conqueror.
    [*Reads.*] "The thrice three Muses mourning for the death
    Of Learning, late deceas'd in beggary."⁸
    That is some satire, keen and critical,
    Not sorting with⁹ a nuptial ceremony.   55
    [*Reads.*] "A tedious brief scene of young Pyramus
    And his love Thisby; very tragical mirth."
    Merry and tragical? Tedious and brief?
    That is, hot ice and wondrous strange¹ snow.
    How shall we find the concord of this discord?   60
PHILOSTRATE: A play there is, my lord, some ten words long,
    Which is as brief as I have known a play;
    But by ten words, my lord, it is too long,
    Which makes it tedious. For in all the play
    There is not one word apt, one player fitted.   65
    And tragical, my noble lord, it is,
    For Pyramus therein doth kill himself.
    Which, when I saw rehears'd, I must confess,

---

3. Pastime (to abridge or shorten the evening).   **4.** Short written statement, list.   **5.** [Probably refers to the battle of the Centaurs and the Lapithae, when the Centaurs attempted to carry off Hippodamia, bride of Theseus's friend Pirothous.]   **6.** [Plutarch's *Life of Theseus* states that Hercules and Theseus were near kinsmen. Theseus is referring to a version of the battle of the Centaurs in which Hercules was said to be present.]   **7.** [(This was the story of the death of Orpheus, as told in *Metamorphoses*, XI.]   **8.** [Possibly an allusion to Spenser's *Teares of the Muses*, 1591, though "satires" deploring the neglect of learning and the creative arts were commonplace.] **9.** Befitting.   **1.** [Seemingly an error for some adjective that would contrast with *snow*, just as *hot* contrasts with *ice*.]

Made mine eyes water; but more merry tears
70 The passion of loud laughter never shed.
THESEUS: What are they that do play it?
PHILOSTRATE: Hard-handed men that work in Athens here,
Which never labor'd in their minds till now,
And now have toil'd their unbreathed[2] memories
75 With this same play, against[3] your nuptial.
THESEUS: And we will hear it.
PHILOSTRATE: No, my noble lord,
It is not for you. I have heard it over,
And it is nothing, nothing in the world;
Unless you can find sport in their intents,
80 Extremely stretch'd and conn'd[4] with cruel pain,
To do you service.
THESEUS: I will hear that play;
For never anything can be amiss
When simpleness and duty tender it.
Go, bring them in; and take your places, ladies.

[PHILOSTRATE *goes to summon the players.*]

85 HIPPOLYTA: I love not to see wretchedness o'ercharg'd[5]
And duty in his service[6] perishing.
THESEUS: Why, gentle sweet, you shall see no such thing.
HIPPOLYTA: He says they can do nothing in this kind.[7]
THESEUS: The kinder we, to give them thanks for nothing.
90 Our sport shall be to take what they mistake;
And what poor duty cannot do, noble respect
Takes it in might, not merit.[8]
Where I have come, great clerks[9] have purposed
To greet me with premeditated welcomes;
95 Where I have seen them shiver and look pale,
Make periods in the midst of sentences,
Throttle their practic'd accent[1] in their fears,
And in conclusion dumbly have broke off,
Not paying me a welcome. Trust me, sweet,
100 Out of this silence yet I pick'd a welcome;
And in the modesty of fearful duty
I read as much as from the rattling tongue
Of saucy and audacious eloquence.
Love, therefore, and tongue-tied simplicity
105 In least speak most, to my capacity.[2]

2. Unexercised. *Toil'd:* taxed.   3. In preparation for.   4. Memorized. *Stretch'd:* strained.
5. Incompetence overburdened.   6. Its attempt to serve.   7. Kind of thing.   8. Values it
for the effort made rather than for the excellence achieved.   9. Learned men.   1. I.e.,
rehearsed speech; or, usual way of speaking.   2. In my judgment and understanding. *Least:* i.e.,
saying least.

[PHILOSTRATE *returns.*]

PHILOSTRATE: So please your Grace, the Prologue is address'd.[3]
THESEUS: Let him approach.

[*Flourish of trumpets. Enter the Prologue* (QUINCE).]

PROLOGUE: If we offend, it is with our good will.
 That you should think, we come not to offend,
 But with good will. To show our simple skill,   110
 That is the true beginning of our end.
 Consider, then, we come but in despite.
 We do not come, as minding[4] to content you,
 Our true intent is. All for your delight
 We are not here. That you should here repent you,   115
 The actors are at hand; and, by their show,
 You shall know all that you are like to know.
THESEUS: This fellow doth not stand upon points.[5]
LYSANDER: He hath rid his prologue like a rough[6] colt; he knows not the stop.[7]
 A good moral, my lord: it is not enough to speak, but to speak true.   120
HIPPOLYTA: Indeed he hath play'd on his prologue like a child on a recorder; a
 sound, but not in government.[8]
THESEUS: His speech was like a tangled chain, nothing[9] impair'd, but all disor-
 der'd. Who is next?

[*Enter* PYRAMUS *and* THISBY, *and* WALL, *and* MOONSHINE, *and* LION.]

PROLOGUE: Gentles, perchance you wonder at this show;   125
 But wonder on, till truth make all things plain.
 This man is Pyramus, if you would know;
 This beauteous lady Thisby is certain.
 This man, with lime and rough-cast, doth present
 Wall, that vile Wall which did these lovers sunder;   130
 And through Wall's chink, poor souls, they are content
 To whisper. At the which let no man wonder.
 This man, with lantern, dog, and bush of thorn,
 Presenteth Moonshine; for, if you will know,
 By moonshine did these lovers think no scorn[1]   135
 To meet at Ninus' tomb, there, there to woo.
 This grisly beast, which Lion hight[2] by name,
 The trusty Thisby, coming first by night,
 Did scare away, or rather did affright;
 And, as she fled, her mantle she did fall,[3]   140

3. Ready. *Prologue:* speaker of the prologue.   4. Intending   5. (1) Heed niceties or
small points; (2) pay attention to punctuation in his reading. (The humor of Quince's speech is in
the blunders of its punctuation.)   6. Unbroken.   7. (1) The stopping of a colt by reining it in;
(2) punctuation mark.   8. Control. *Recorder:* a wind instrument like a flute or flageolet.
9. Not at all.   1. Think it no disgraceful matter.   2. Is called.   3. Let fall.

Which Lion vile with bloody mouth did stain.
Anon comes Pyramus, sweet youth and tall,[4]
And finds his trusty Thisby's mantle slain;
Whereat, with blade, with bloody blameful blade,
145 He bravely broach'd[5] his boiling bloody breast.
And Thisby, tarrying in mulberry shade,
His dagger drew, and died. For all the rest,
Let Lion, Moonshine, Wall, and lovers twain
At large[6] discourse, while here they do remain.

[*Exeunt* LION, THISBY, *and* MOONSHINE.]

150 THESEUS: I wonder if the lion be to speak.
DEMETRIUS: No wonder, my lord. One lion may, when many asses do.
WALL: In this same interlude it doth befall
That I, one Snout by name, present a wall;
And such a wall, as I would have you think,
155 That had in it a crannied hole or chink,
Through which the lovers, Pyramus and Thisby,
Did whisper often very secretly.
This loam, this rough-cast, and this stone doth show
That I am that same wall; the truth is so.
160 And this the cranny is, right and sinister,[7]
Through which the fearful lovers are to whisper.
THESEUS: Would you desire lime and hair to speak better?
DEMETRIUS: It is the wittiest partition[8] that ever I heard discourse, my lord.

[PYRAMUS *comes forward.*]

THESEUS: Pyramus draws near the wall. Silence!
165 PYRAMUS: O grim-look'd[9] night! O night with hue so black!
O night, which ever art when day is not!
O night, O night! Alack, alack, alack,
I fear my Thisby's promise is forgot.
And thou, O wall, O sweet, O lovely wall,
170 That stand'st between her father's ground and mine,
Thou wall, O wall, O sweet and lovely wall,
Show me thy chink, to blink through with mine eyne!

[WALL *holds up his fingers.*]

Thanks, courteous Wall. Jove shield thee well for this!
But what see I? No Thisby do I see.
175 O wicked wall, through whom I see no bliss!
Curs'd be thy stones for thus deceiving me!
THESEUS: The wall, methinks, being sensible,[1] should curse again.

4. Courageous.   5. Stabbed.   6. In full, at length.   7. I.e., the right side of it and the left; or, running from right to left, horizontally.   8. (1) Wall; (2) section of a learned treatise or oration.   9. Grim-looking.   1. Capable of feeling.

PYRAMUS: No, in truth, sir, he should not. "Deceiving me" is Thisby's cue: she is to enter now, and I am to spy her through the wall. You shall see, it will fall pat as I told you. Yonder she comes.   180

[*Enter* THISBY.]

THISBY: O wall, full often hast thou heard my moans,
    For parting my fair Pyramus and me.
    My cherry lips have often kiss'd thy stones,
    Thy stones with lime and hair knit up in thee.
PYRAMUS: I see a voice. Now will I to the chink,   185
    To spy an[2] I can hear my Thisby's face.
    Thisby!
THISBY: My love! Thou art my love, I think.
PYRAMUS: Think what thou wilt, I am thy lover's grace;[3]
    And, like Limander, am I trusty still.   190
THISBY: And I like Helen,[4] till the Fates me kill.
PYRAMUS: Not Shafalus to Procrus[5] was so true.
THISBY: As Shafalus to Procrus, I to you.
PYRAMUS: O, kiss me through the hole of this vile wall!
THISBY: I kiss the wall's hole, not your lips at all.   195
PYRAMUS: Wilt thou at Ninny's tomb meet me straightway?
THISBY: 'Tide life, 'tide[6] death, I come without delay.

                               [*Exeunt* PYRAMUS *and* THISBY.]

WALL: Thus have I, Wall, my part discharged so;
    And, being done, thus Wall away doth go.   [*Exit.*]
THESEUS: Now is the mural down between the two neighbors.   200
DEMETRIUS: No remedy, my lord, when walls are so willful to hear without warning.[7]
HIPPOLYTA: This is the silliest stuff that ever I heard.
THESEUS: The best in this kind are but shadows[8]; and the worst are no worse, if imagination amend them.   205
HIPPOLYTA: It must be your imagination then, and not theirs.
THESEUS: If we imagine no worse of them than they of themselves, they may pass for excellent men. Here come two noble beasts in, a man and a lion.

[*Enter* LION *and* MOONSHINE.]

LION: You, ladies, you, whose gentle hearts do fear
    The smallest monstrous mouse that creeps on floor,   210
    May now perchance both quake and tremble here,
    When lion rough in widest rage doth roar.
    Then know that I, as Snug the joiner, am
    A lion fell,[9] nor else no lion's dam;

2. If.   3. I.e., gracious lover.   4. [Blunders for "Leander" (*Limander*) and "Hero."]   5. [Blunders for "Cephalus" (*Shafalus*) and "Procris," also famous lovers.]   6. Betide, come.   7. I.e., without warning the parents. *To hear*: as to hear.   8. Likenesses, representations. *In this kind*: of this sort.   9. Fierce lion (with a play on the idea of *lion skin*).

215　For, if I should as lion come in strife
　　Into this place, 'twere pity on my life.
THESEUS: A very gentle beast, and of a good conscience.
DEMETRIUS: The very best at a beast, my lord, that e'er I saw.
LYSANDER: This lion is a very fox for his valor.[1]
220　THESEUS: True; and a goose for his discretion.[2]
DEMETRIUS: Not so, my lord; for his valor cannot carry his discretion; and the
　　fox carries the goose.
THESEUS: His discretion, I am sure, cannot carry his valor; for the goose carries
　　not the fox. It is well. Leave it to his discretion, and let us listen to the moon.
225　MOON: This lanthorn[3] doth the horned moon present—
DEMETRIUS: He should have worn the horns on his head.[4]
THESEUS: He is no crescent, and his horns are invisible within the circumfer-
　　ence.
MOON: This lanthorn doth the horned moon present;
230　　Myself the man i' th' moon do seem to be.
THESEUS: This is the greatest error of all the rest. The man should be put into
　　the lanthorn. How is it else the man i' th' moon?
DEMETRIUS: He dares not come there for the[5] candle; for, you see, it is already
　　in snuff.[6]
235　HIPPOLYTA: I am aweary of this moon. Would he would change!
THESEUS: It appears, by his small light of discretion, that he is in the wane; but
　　yet, in courtesy, in all reason, we must stay the time.
LYSANDER: Proceed, Moon.
MOON: All that I have to say is to tell you that the lanthorn is the moon, I, the
240　　man in the moon, this thorn-bush my thorn-bush, and this dog my dog.
DEMETRIUS: Why, all these should be in the lanthorn; for all these are in the
　　moon. But silence! Here comes Thisby.

　　[Enter THISBY.]

THISBY: This is old Ninny's tomb. Where is my love?
LION: [Roaring.] Oh—　　　　　　　　　　　　　　　　　　[THISBY runs off.]
245　DEMETRIUS: Well roar'd, Lion.
THESEUS: Well run, Thisby.
HIPPOLYTA: Well shone, Moon. Truly, the moon shines with a good grace.

　　[The LION shakes THISBY's mantle, and exit.]

THESEUS: Well mous'd,[7] Lion.
DEMETRIUS: And then came Pyramus.
250　LYSANDER: And so the lion vanish'd.

---

1. I.e., his valor consists of craftiness and discretion.　　2. I.e., as discreet as a goose, that is, more
foolish than discreet.　　3. [This original spelling, lanthorn, may suggest a play on the horn of
which lanterns were made, and also on a cuckold's horns; but the spelling lanthorn is not used
consistently for comic effect in this play or elsewhere. At V.1.134, for example, the word is lantern
in the original.]　　4. [As a sign of cuckoldry.]　　5. Because of the.　　6. (1) Offended; (2) in
need of snuffing.　　7. Shaken.

[*Enter* PYRAMUS.]

PYRAMUS: Sweet Moon, I thank thee for thy sunny beams;
　　I thank thee, Moon, for shining now so bright;
　　For, by thy gracious, golden, glittering gleams,
　　I trust to take of truest Thisby sight.
　　　　But stay, O spite!   255
　　　　But mark, poor knight,
　　　What dreadful dole[8] is here!
　　　　Eyes, do you see?
　　　　How can it be?
　　　O dainty duck! O dear!   260
　　　　Thy mantle good,
　　　What, stain'd with blood!
　　　Approach, ye Furies fell[9]!
　　　　O Fates, come, come,
　　　　Cut thread and thrum[1];   265
　　Quail, crush, conclude, and quell[2]!

THESEUS: This passion, and the death of a dear friend, would go near to make a
man look sad.[3]

HIPPOLYTA: Beshrew my heart, but I pity the man.

PYRAMUS: O wherefore, Nature, didst thou lions frame?   270
　　Since lion vile hath here deflow'r'd my dear,
　　Which is—no, no—which was the fairest dame
　　That liv'd, that lov'd, that lik'd, that look'd with cheer.[4]
　　　　Come, tears, confound,
　　　　Out, sword, and wound   275
　　　The pap of Pyramus;
　　　Ay, that left pap,
　　　Where heart doth hop.   [*Stabs himself.*]
　　Thus die I, thus, thus, thus.
　　　　Now am I dead,   280
　　　　Now am I fled;
　　　My soul is in the sky.
　　　Tongue, lose thy light;
　　　Moon, take thy flight.   [*Exit* MOONSHINE.]
　　Now die, die, die, die, die.   [*Dies.*]   285

DEMETRIUS: No die, but an ace,[5] for him; for he is but one.[6]

LYSANDER: Less than an ace, man; for he is dead, he is nothing.

THESEUS: With the help of a surgeon he might yet recover, and yet prove an ass.[7]

---

8. Grievous event.　　9. Fierce.　　1. The warp in weaving and the loose end of the warp.
2. Kill, destroy. *Quail*: overpower.　　3. I.e., if one had other reason to grieve, one might be sad,
but not from this absurd portrayal of passion.　　4. Countenance.　　5. The side of the die featur-
ing the single pip, or spot. (The pun is on *die* as a singular of *dice*; Bottom's performance is not
worth a whole *die* but rather one single face of it, one small portion.)　　6. (1) An individual person;
(2) unique.　　7. [With a pun on *ace*.]

HIPPOLYTA: How chance Moonshine is gone before Thisby comes back and finds
her lover?

THESEUS: She will find him by starlight. Here she comes; and her passion ends
the play.

[*Enter* THISBY.]

HIPPOLYTA: Methinks she should not use a long one for such a Pyramus. I hope
she will be brief.

DEMETRIUS: A mote will turn the balance, which Pyramus, which[8] Thisby, is
the better: he for a man, God warr'nt us; she for a woman, God bless us.

LYSANDER: She hath spied him already with those sweet eyes.

DEMETRIUS: And thus she means, videlicet[9]:

THISBY: Asleep, my love?
    What, dead, my dove?
      O Pyramus, arise!
        Speak, speak. Quite dumb?
        Dead, dead? A tomb
    Must cover thy sweet eyes.
        These lily lips,
        This cherry nose,
    These yellow cowslip cheeks,
      Are gone, are gone!
      Lovers, make moan.
    His eyes were green as leeks.
      O Sisters Three,[1]
      Come, come to me,
    With hands as pale as milk;
      Lay them in gore,
      Since you have shore[2]
    With shears his thread of silk.
      Tongue, not a word.
      Come, trusty sword,
    Come, blade, my breast imbrue[3]!   [*Stabs herself.*]
      And farewell, friends.
      Thus Thisby ends.
    Adieu, adieu, adieu.   [*Dies.*]

THESEUS: Moonshine and Lion are left to bury the dead.

DEMETRIUS: Ay, and Wall too.

BOTTOM: [*Starting up.*] No, I assure you; the wall is down that parted their fathers.
Will it please you to see the epilogue, or to hear a Bergomask dance[4] between
two of our company?

THESEUS: No epilogue, I pray you; for your play needs no excuse. Never excuse;
for when the players are all dead, there need none to be blam'd. Marry, if

---

8. Whether . . . or.   9. To wit. *Means:* moans, laments.   1. The Fates.   2. Shorn.
3. Stain with blood.   4. A rustic dance named from Bergamo, a province in the state of Venice.

he that writ it had play'd Pyramus and hang'd himself in Thisby's garter, it 330
would have been a fine tragedy; and so it is, truly, and very notably dis-
charg'd. But, come, your Bergomask. Let your epilogue alone. [*A dance.*]
The iron tongue of midnight hath told[5] twelve.
Lovers, to bed; 'tis almost fairy time.
I fear we shall outsleep the coming morn 335
As much as we this night have overwatch'd.[6]
This palpable-gross[7] play hath well beguil'd
The heavy[8] gait of night. Sweet friends, to bed.
A fortnight hold we this solemnity,
In nightly revels and new jollity. [*Exeunt.*] 340

[*Enter* PUCK.]

PUCK: Now the hungry lion roars,
    And the wolf behowls the moon;
Whilst the heavy ploughman snores,
    All with weary task fordone.[9]
Now the wasted brands[1] do glow, 345
    Whilst the screech-owl, screeching loud,
Puts the wretch that lies in woe
    In remembrance of a shroud.
Now it is the time of night
    That the graves, all gaping wide, 350
Every one lets forth his sprite,[2]
    In the churchway paths to glide.
And we fairies, that do run
    By the triple Hecate's[3] team
From the presence of the sun, 355
    Following darkness like a dream,
Now are frolic.[4] Not a mouse
Shall disturb this hallowed house.
I am sent with broom before,
To sweep the dust behind[5] the door. 360

[*Enter* OBERON *and* TITANIA, *King and Queen of Fairies, with all their train.*]

OBERON: Through the house give glimmering light,
    By the dead and drowsy fire;
Every elf and fairy sprite
    Hop as light as bird from brier;
And this ditty, after me, 365
    Sing, and dance it trippingly.

---

5. Counted, struck ("tolled"). 6. Stayed up too late. 7. Palpably gross, obviously crude.
8. Drowsy, dull. 9. Exhausted. 1. Burned-out logs. 2. Every grave lets forth its ghost.
3. [Hecate ruled in three capacities: as Luna or Cynthia in Heaven, as Diana on Earth, and as
Proserpina in Hell.] 4. Merry. 5. From behind. (Robin Goodfellow was a household spirit
who helped good housemaids and punished lazy ones.)

TITANIA: First, rehearse your song by rote,
    To each word a warbling note.
    Hand in hand, with fairy grace,
370   Will we sing, and bless this place.

[*Song and dance.*]

OBERON: Now, until the break of day,
    Through this house each fairy stray.
    To the best bride-bed will we,
    Which by us shall blessed be;
375   And the issue there create[6]
    Ever shall be fortunate.
    So shall all the couples three
    Ever true in loving be;
    And the blots of Nature's hand
380   Shall not in their issue stand;
    Never mole, hare lip, nor scar,
    Nor mark prodigious,[7] such as are
    Despised in nativity,
    Shall upon their children be.
385   With this field-dew consecrate,[8]
    Every fairy take his gait,[9]
    And each several[1] chamber bless,
    Through this palace, with sweet peace;
    And the owner of it blest
390   Ever shall in safety rest.
    Trip away; make no stay;
    Meet me all by break of day.   [*Exeunt* OBERON, TITANIA, *and train.*]

PUCK: If we shadows have offended,
    Think but this, and all is mended,
395   That you have but slumb'red here[2]
    While these visions did appear.
    And this weak and idle theme,
    No more yielding but[3] a dream,
    Gentles, do not reprehend.
400   If you pardon, we will mend.
    And, as I am an honest Puck,
    If we have unearned luck
    Now to scape the serpent's tongue,[4]
    We will make amends ere long;
405   Else the Puck a liar call.

---

6. Created.   7. Monstrous, unnatural.   8. Consecrated.   9. Go his way.   1. Separate.
2. I.e., that it is a "midsummer night's dream."   3. Yielding no more than.   4. I.e., hissing.

So, good night unto you all.
Give me your hands,[5] if we be friends,
And Robin shall restore amends.   [*Exit.*]

ca. 1594–1595

5. Applaud.

▼ ▼ ▼

STUDENT WRITING

In the student paper that follows, Sherry Schnake examines how characterization, sets and setting, and plot all contribute to a thematic analysis of the destructive clash between the American Dream and everyday reality.

Dream of a Salesman

Sherry Schnake

Success is an integral part of the American dream. However, as Arthur Miller points out in <u>Death of a Salesman</u>, when that dream is not based in reality it can lead to destruction. This is demonstrated in the character of Willy Loman, a salesman consumed by illusion. "He had all the wrong dreams," said his son Biff at Willy's funeral. Biff was right: Willy's dreams ruined his life and the lives of everyone he loved.

As the play opens, Willy is introduced as a tired man and gains sympathy from the reader. However, questions begin to arise about his integrity the first time he slips into the past. In this scene, when he learns his son Biff has stolen a football, he praises him for his initiative. He also tells his boys that as long as a person is well liked, it doesn't matter if he does poorly in school. As the play progresses, Willy reveals through his words and actions that being well liked is the center of his life's philosophy. Because Willy cannot fulfill this philosophy, he lives in an illusion. In it, he is popular and successful, even though in reality he is a failure.

Although the action of the play occurs in a twenty-four hour period, much more of Willy's life is revealed through his memories of the past, which he is continually reliving. The staging of the play supports the theme and symbolizes Willy's life. The scenery is all transparent, just as Willy and his dreams are. In scenes of the past there are no boundaries, for it was a time when Willy knew no limits. The fact that Willy fluctuates so freely from the past to the present emphasizes his inability to distinguish illusion from reality. The flashbacks also allow the reader to see how Willy and his sons' lives were shaped by the past.

Near the beginning of the play, Willy suggests to Biff that he ask for a loan to start a business from his former employer Bill Oliver. Willy assures Biff he will get it because Oliver always liked Biff. However, when Biff is rejected by Oliver, he confronts Willy in the climax of the play. At this point Biff tries to make Willy see that the dream they had both been living by was phony. Biff knows now that being well liked is not the key to success and happiness. He tries to make his father realize that that outlook has gotten them nowhere by exclaiming "I'm a dime a dozen and so are you!"

However, the dream is too deeply engraved in Willy's mind. It is ironic that Biff's attempt to make his father rid himself of his false dream only convinces Willy that his dream was right. When Biff cries to Willy in frustration, all Willy can see is that Biff likes him.

Biff's discontent with Willy began many years earlier. Through Willy's memories we learn that when Biff failed math he went to Boston to ask Willy to convince his teacher to pass him. There Biff found Willy with another woman. At that moment, Biff's image of his father was shattered. Because the false values Willy planted in his son were shattered also, Biff became a lost soul and didn't fully understand himself until his later confrontation with Willy.

Biff isn't the only one whose life is ruined by Willy's dream. Biff's brother Happy is usually ignored by Willy and overshadowed by Biff. Nonetheless, Happy enthusiastically embraces Willy's goals and will not let go of them even when they have failed his father. In this sense, he is less fortunate than Biff because he is destined to repeat his father's life.

Willy's illusions also adversely affect his wife Linda. She was always supportive of him, yet he took out his frustrations on her in the form of angry words and disrespect. His desire to be well liked led him to betray her with an affair.

Willy's dreams are further challenged by his

neighbor Charley and his brother Ben. Charley is
the antithesis of Willy: he is unconcerned with
popularity, and yet is successful. Ben represents
something Willy could never attain: he grabbed
success in an almost physical way and never
looked back.

Willy dies still clinging to his illusion. In
fact, he kills himself so that Biff can use his
insurance money to succeed in life. His painfully
small funeral that concludes the play is a
pathetic reminder that his dreams, indeed, were
wrong.

Thus, Willy's life and death were devoted to
false goals. Because of his inability to see
reality, he left Linda alone, he left Biff
disillusioned, and, sadly, he left Happy to
follow in his footsteps, chasing the wrong dreams.

Reading More Drama

SOPHOCLES

Antigone[1]

CHARACTERS

ANTIGONE	HAEMON
ISMENE	TEIRESIAS
CHORUS OF THEBAN ELDERS	A MESSENGER
CREON	EURYDICE
A SENTRY	SECOND MESSENGER

The two sisters ANTIGONE *and* ISMENE *meet in front of the palace gates in Thebes.*

ANTIGONE: Ismene, my dear sister,
    whose father was my father, can you think of any
    of all the evils that stem from Oedipus
    that Zeus does not bring to pass for us, while we yet live?
5   No pain, no ruin, no shame, and no dishonor
    but I have seen it in our mischiefs,
    yours and mine.
    And now what is the proclamation that they tell of
    made lately by the commander, publicly,
10   to all the people? Do you know it? Have you heard it?
    Don't you notice when the evils due to enemies
    are headed towards those we love?
ISMENE: Not a word, Antigone, of those we love,
    either sweet or bitter, has come to me since the moment
15   when we lost our two brothers,
    on one day, by their hands dealing mutual death.

1. Translated by David Grene.

Since the Argive army fled in this past night,
I know of nothing further, nothing
of better fortune or of more destruction.

ANTIGONE: *I* knew it well; that is why I sent for you   20
to come outside the palace gates
to listen to me, privately.

ISMENE: What is it? Certainly your words
come of dark thoughts.

ANTIGONE: Yes, indeed; for those two brothers of ours, in burial   25
has not Creon honored the one, dishonored the other?
Eteocles, they say he has used justly
with lawful rites and hid him in the earth
to have his honor among the dead men there.
But the unhappy corpse of Polyneices   30
he has proclaimed to all the citizens,
they say, no man may hide
in a grave nor mourn in funeral,
but leave unwept, unburied, a dainty treasure
for the birds that see him, for their feast's delight.   35
That is what, they say, the worthy Creon
has proclaimed for you and me—for me, I tell you—
and he comes here to clarify to the unknowing
his proclamation; he takes it seriously;
for whoever breaks the edict death is prescribed,   40
and death by stoning publicly.
There you have it; soon you will show yourself
as noble both in your nature and your birth,
or yourself as base, although of noble parents.

ISMENE: If things are as you say, poor sister, how   45
can I better them? how loose or tie the knot?

ANTIGONE: Decide if you will share the work, the deed.

ISMENE: What kind of danger is there? How far have your thoughts gone?

ANTIGONE: Here is this hand. Will you help it to lift the dead man?

ISMENE: Would you bury him, when it is forbidden the city?   50

ANTIGONE: At least he is my brother—and yours, too,
though you deny him. *I* will not prove false to him.

ISMENE: You are so headstrong. Creon has forbidden it.

ANTIGONE: It is not for him to keep me from my own.

ISMENE: O God!   55
Consider, sister, how our father died,
hated and infamous; how he brought to light
his own offenses; how he himself struck out
the sight of his two eyes;
his own hand was their executioner.   60
Then, mother and wife, two names in one, did shame
violently on her life, with twisted cords.
Third, our two brothers, on a single day,

poor wretches, themselves worked out their mutual doom.
65 Each killed the other, hand against brother's hand.
Now there are only the two of us, left behind,
and see how miserable our end shall be
if in the teeth of law we shall transgress
against the sovereign's decree and power.
70 You ought to realize we are only women,
not meant in nature to fight against men,
and that we are ruled, by those who are stronger,
to obedience in this and even more painful matters.
I do indeed beg those beneath the earth
75 to give me their forgiveness,
since force constrains me,
that I shall yield in this to the authorities.
Extravagant action is not sensible.
ANTIGONE: I would not urge you now; nor if you wanted
80 to act would I be glad to have you with me.
Be as you choose to be; but for myself
I myself will bury him. It will be good
to die, so doing. I shall lie by his side,
loving him as he loved me; I shall be
85 a criminal—but a religious one.
The time in which I must please those that are dead
is longer than I must please those of this world.
For there I shall lie forever. You, if you like,
can cast dishonor on what the gods have honored.
90 ISMENE: I will not put dishonor on them, but
to act in defiance of the citizenry,
my nature does not give me means for that.
ANTIGONE: Let that be your excuse. But I will go
to heap the earth on the grave of my loved brother.
95 ISMENE: How I fear for you, my poor sister!
ANTIGONE: Do not fear for me. Make straight your own path to destiny.
ISMENE: At least do not speak of this act to anyone else;
bury him in secret; I will be silent, too.
ANTIGONE: Oh, oh, no! shout it out. I will hate you still worse
100 for silence—should you not proclaim it,
to everyone.
ISMENE: You have a warm heart for such chilly deeds.
ANTIGONE: I know I am pleasing those I should please most.
ISMENE: *If* you can do it. But you are in love
105 with the impossible.
ANTIGONE: No. When I can no more, then I will stop.
ISMENE: It is better not to hunt the impossible
at all.
ANTIGONE: If you will talk like this I will loathe you,

and you will be adjudged an enemy—
justly—by the dead's decision. Let me alone   110
and my folly with me, to endure this terror.
No suffering of mine will be enough
to make me die ignobly.

ISMENE: Well, if you will, go on.   115
    Know this; that though you are wrong to go, your friends
    are right to love you.

CHORUS: Sun's beam, fairest of all
    that ever till now shone
    on seven-gated Thebes;   120
    O golden eye of day, you shone
    coming over Dirce's stream[2];
    You drove in headlong rout
    the whiteshielded man from Argos,
    complete in arms;   125
    his bits rang sharper
    under your urging.

Polyneices brought him here
against our land, Polyneices,
roused by contentious quarrel;   130
like an eagle he flew into our country,
with many men-at-arms,
with many a helmet crowned with horsehair.

He stood above the halls, gaping with murderous lances,
encompassing the city's   135
seven-gated mouth.
But before his jaws would be sated
with our blood, before the fire,
pine fed, should capture our crown of towers,
he went hence—   140
such clamor of war stretched behind his back,
from his dragon foe, a thing he could not overcome.

For Zeus, who hates the most
the boasts of a great tongue,
saw them coming in a great tide,   145
insolent in the clang of golden armor.
The god struck him down with hurled fire,
as he strove to raise the victory cry,
now at the very winning post.

The earth rose to strike him as he fell swinging.   150
In his frantic onslaught, possessed, he breathed upon us

2. River near Thebes.

with blasting winds of hate.
Sometimes the great god of war was on one side,
and sometimes he struck a staggering blow on the other;
155   the god was a very wheel horse on the right trace.

At seven gates stood seven captains,
ranged equals against equals, and there left
their brazen suits of armor
to Zeus, the god of trophies.
160   Only those two wretches born of one father and mother
set their spears to win a victory on both sides;
they worked out their share in a common death.

Now Victory, whose name is great, has come
to Thebes of many chariots
165   with joy to answer her joy,
to bring forgetfulness of these wars;
let us go to all the shrines of the gods
and dance all night long.
Let Bacchus lead the dance,
170   shaking Thebes to trembling.

But here is the king of our land,
Creon, son of Menoeceus;
in our new contingencies with the gods,
he is our new ruler.
175   He comes to set in motion some design—
what design is it? Because he has proposed
the convocation of the elders.
He sent a public summons for our discussion.
CREON: Gentlemen: as for our city's fortune,
180   the gods have shaken her, when the great waves broke,
but the gods have brought her through again to safety.
For yourselves, I chose you out of all and summoned you
to come to me, partly because I knew you
as always loyal to the throne—at first,
185   when Laïus was king, and then again
when Oedipus saved our city and then again
when he died and you remained with steadfast truth
to their descendants,
until they met their double fate upon one day,
190   striking and stricken, defiled each by a brother's murder.
Now here I am, holding all authority
and the throne, in virtue of kinship with the dead.

It is impossible to know any man—
I mean his soul, intelligence, and judgment—

until he shows his skill in rule and law.   195
I think that a man supreme ruler of a whole city,
if he does not reach for the best counsel for her,
but through some fear, keeps his tongue under lock and key,
him I judge the worst of any;
I have always judged so; and anyone thinking   200
another man more a friend than his own country,
I rate him nowhere. For my part, God is my witness,
who sees all, always, I would not be silent
if I saw ruin, not safety, on the way
towards my fellow citizens. I would not count   205
any enemy of my country as a friend—
because of what I know, that she it is
which gives us our security. If she sails upright
and we sail on her, friends will be ours for the making.
In the light of rules like these, I will make her greater still.   210

In consonance with this, I here proclaim
to the citizens about Oedipus' sons.
For Eteocles, who died this city's champion,
showing his valor's supremacy everywhere,
he shall be buried in his grave with every rite   215
of sanctity given to heroes under earth.
However, his brother, Polyneices, a returned exile,
who sought to burn with fire from top to bottom
his native city, and the gods of his own people;
who sought to taste the blood he shared with us,   220
and lead the rest of us to slavery—
I here proclaim to the city that this man
shall no one honor with a grave and none shall mourn.
You shall leave him without burial; you shall watch him
chewed up by birds and dogs and violated.   225
Such is my mind in the matter; never by me
shall the wicked man have precedence in honor
over the just. But he that is loyal to the state
in death, in life alike, shall have my honor.
CHORUS: Son of Menoeceus, so it is your pleasure   230
    to deal with foe and friend of this our city.
    To use any legal means lies in your power,
    both about the dead and those of us who live.
CREON: I understand, then, you will do my bidding.
CHORUS: Please lay this burden on some younger man.   235
CREON: Oh, watchers of the corpse I have already.
CHORUS: What else, then, do your commands entail?
CREON: That you should not side with those who disagree.

CHORUS: There is none so foolish as to love his own death.
240 CREON: Yes, indeed those are the wages, but often greed
has with its hopes brought men to ruin.

[*The* SENTRY *whose speeches follow represents a remarkable experiment in
Greek tragedy in the direction of naturalism of speech. He speaks with marked
clumsiness, partly because he is excited and talks almost colloquially. But also
the royal presence makes him think apparently that he should be rather grand
in his show of respect. He uses odd bits of archaism or somewhat stale poetical
passages, particularly in catch phrases. He sounds something like lower-level
Shakespearean characters, e.g. Constable Elbow, with his uncertainty about
benefactor and malefactor.*]

SENTRY: My lord, I will never claim my shortness of breath
is due to hurrying, nor were there wings in my feet.
I stopped at many a lay-by in my thinking;
245 I circled myself till I met myself coming back.
My soul accosted me with different speeches.
"Poor fool, yourself, why are you going somewhere
when once you get there you will pay the piper?"
"Well, aren't you the daring fellow! stopping again?
250 and suppose Creon hears the news from someone else—
don't you realize that you will smart for that?"
I turned the whole matter over. I suppose I may say
"I made haste slowly" and the short road became long.
However, at last I came to a resolve:
255 I must go to you; even if what I say
is nothing, really, still I shall say it.
I come here, a man with a firm clutch on the hope
that nothing can betide him save what is fated.
CREON: What is it then that makes you so afraid?
260 SENTRY: No, I want first of all to tell you my side of it.
I didn't do the thing; I never saw who did it.
It would not be fair for me to get into trouble.
CREON: You hedge, and barricade the thing itself.
Clearly you have some ugly news for me.
265 SENTRY: Well, you know how disasters make a man
hesitate to be their messenger.
CREON: For God's sake, tell me and get out of here!
SENTRY: Yes, I *will* tell you. Someone just now
buried the corpse and vanished. He scattered on the skin
270 some thirsty dust; he did the ritual,
duly, to purge the body of desecration.
CREON: What! Now who on earth could have done that?
SENTRY: I do not know. For there was there no mark
of axe's stroke nor casting up of earth
275 of any mattock; the ground was hard and dry,

unbroken; there were no signs of wagon wheels.
The doer of the deed had left no trace.
But when the first sentry of the day pointed it out,
there was for all of us a disagreeable
wonder. For the body had disappeared; 280
not in a grave, of course; but there lay upon him
a little dust as of a hand avoiding
the curse of violating the dead body's sanctity.
There were no signs of any beast nor dog
that came there; he had clearly not been torn. 285
There was a tide of bad words at one another,
guard taunting guard, and it might well have ended
in blows, for there was no one there to stop it.
Each one of us was the criminal but no one
manifestly so; all denied knowledge of it. 290
We were ready to take hot bars in our hands
or walk through fire, and call on the gods with oaths
that we had neither done it nor were privy
to a plot with anyone, neither in planning
nor yet in execution. 295
At last when nothing came of all our searching,
there was one man who spoke, made every head
bow to the ground in fear. For we could not
either contradict him nor yet could we see how
if we did what he said we would come out all right. 300
His word was that we must lay information
about the matter to yourself; we could not cover it.
This view prevailed and the lot of the draw chose me,
unlucky me, to win that prize. So here
I am. I did not want to come, 305
and you don't want to have me. I know that.
For no one likes the messenger of bad news.
CHORUS: My lord: I wonder, could this be God's doing?
This is the thought that keeps on haunting me.
CREON: Stop, before your words fill even me with rage, 310
that you should be exposed as a fool, and you so old.
For what you say is surely insupportable
when you say the gods took forethought for this corpse.
Is it out of excess of honor for the man,
for the favors that he did them, they should cover him? 315
This man who came to burn their pillared temples,
their dedicated offerings—and this land
and laws he would have scattered to the winds?
Or do you see the gods as honoring
criminals? This is not so. But what I am doing 320
now, and other things before this, some men disliked,

within this very city, and muttered against me,
secretly shaking their heads; they would not bow
justly beneath the yoke to submit to me.
325 I am very sure that these men hired others
to do this thing. I tell you the worse currency
that ever grew among mankind is money. This
sacks cities, this drives people from their homes,
this teaches and corrupts the minds of the loyal
330 to acts of shame. This displays
all kinds of evil for the use of men,
instructs in the knowledge of every impious act.
Those that have done this deed have been paid to do it,
but in the end they will pay for what they have done.

335 It is as sure as I still reverence Zeus—
know this right well—and I speak under oath—
if you and your fellows do not find this man
who with his own hand did the burial
and bring him here before me face to face,
340 your death alone will not be enough for me.
You will hang alive till you open up this outrage.
That will teach you in the days to come from what
you may draw profit—safely—from your plundering.
It's not from anything and everything
345 you can grow rich. You will find out
that ill-gotten gains ruin more than they save.
SENTRY: Have I your leave to say something—or should I
just turn and go?
CREON: Don't you know your talk is painful enough already?
350 SENTRY: Is the ache in your ears or in your mind?
CREON: Why do you dissect the whereabouts of my pain?
SENTRY: Because it is he who did the deed who hurts
your mind. I only hurt your ears that listen.
CREON: I am sure you have been a chatterbox since you were born.
355 SENTRY: All the same, I did not do this thing.
CREON: You might have done this, too, if you sold your soul.
SENTRY: It's a bad thing if one judges and judges wrongly.
CREON: You may talk as wittily as you like of judgment.
Only, if you don't bring to light those men
360 who have done this, you will yet come to say
that your wretched gains have brought bad consequences.
SENTRY: [Aside.] It were best that he were found, but whether
the criminal is taken or he isn't—
for that chance will decide—one thing is certain,
365 you'll never see me coming here again.

I never hoped to escape, never thought I could.
But now I have come off safe, I thank God heartily.

CHORUS: Many are the wonders, none
   is more wonderful than what is man.
   This it is that crosses the sea   370
   with the south winds storming and the waves swelling,
   breaking around him in roaring surf.
   He it is again who wears away
   the Earth, oldest of gods, immortal, unwearied,
   as the ploughs wind across her from year to year   375
   when he works her with the breed that comes from horses.

   The tribe of the lighthearted birds he snares
   and takes prisoner the races of savage beasts
   and the brood of the fish of the sea,
   with the close-spun web of nets.   380
   A cunning fellow is man. His contrivances
   make him master of beasts of the field
   and those that move in the mountains.
   So he brings the horse with the shaggy neck
   to bend underneath the yoke;   385
   and also the untamed mountain bull;
   and speech and windswift thought
   and the tempers that go with city living
   he has taught himself, and how to avoid
   the sharp frost, when lodging is cold   390
   under the open sky
   and pelting strokes of the rain.
   He has a way against everything,
   and he faces nothing that is to come
   without contrivance.   395
   Only against death
   can he call on no means of escape;
   but escape from hopeless diseases
   he has found in the depths of his mind.
   With some sort of cunning, inventive   400
   beyond all expectation
   he reaches sometimes evil,
   and sometimes good.

   If he honors the laws of earth,
   and the justice of the gods he has confirmed by oath,   405
   high is his city; no city
   has he with whom dwells dishonor
   prompted by recklessness.
   He who is so, may he never

410   share my hearth!
                may he never think my thoughts!

                Is this a portent sent by God?
                I cannot tell.
                I know her. How can I say
415   that this is not Antigone?
                Unhappy girl, child of unhappy Oedipus,
                what is this?
                Surely it is not you they bring here
                as disobedient to the royal edict,
420   surely not you, taken in such folly.
SENTRY: She is the one who did the deed;
                we took her burying him. But where is Creon?
CHORUS: He is just coming from the house, when you most need him.
CREON: What is this? What has happened that I come
425   so opportunely?
SENTRY: My lord, there is nothing
                that a man should swear he would never do.
                Second thoughts make liars of the first resolution.
                I would have vowed it would be long enough
430   before I came again, lashed hence by your threats.
                But since the joy that comes past hope, and against all hope,
                is like no other pleasure in extent,
                I have come here, though I break my oath in coming.
                I bring this girl here who has been captured
435   giving the grace of burial to the dead man.
                This time no lot chose me; this was my jackpot,
                and no one else's. Now, my lord, take her
                and as you please judge her and test her; I
                am justly free and clear of all this trouble.
440 CREON: This girl—how did you take her and from where?
SENTRY: She was burying the man. Now you know all.
CREON: Do you know what you are saying? Do you mean it?
SENTRY: She is the one; I saw her burying
                the dead man you forbade the burial of.
445   Now, do I speak plainly and clearly enough?
CREON: How was she seen? How was she caught in the act?
SENTRY: This is how it was. When we came there,
                with those dreadful threats of yours upon us,
                we brushed off all the dust that lay upon
450   the dead man's body, heedfully
                leaving it moist and naked.
                We sat on the brow of the hill, to windward,
                that we might shun the smell of the corpse upon us.
                Each of us wakefully urged his fellow

with torrents of abuse, not to be careless   455
in this work of ours. So it went on,
until in the midst of the sky the sun's bright circle
stood still; the heat was burning. Suddenly
a squall lifted out of the earth a storm of dust,
a trouble in the sky. It filled the plain,   460
ruining all the foliage of the wood
that was around it. The great empty air
was filled with it. We closed our eyes, enduring
this plague sent by the gods. When at long last
we were quit of it, why, then we saw the girl.   465

She was crying out with the shrill cry
of an embittered bird
that sees its nest robbed of its nestlings
and the bed empty. So, too, when she saw
the body stripped of its cover, she burst out in groans,   470
calling terrible curses on those that had done that deed;
and with her hands immediately
brought thirsty dust to the body; from a shapely brazen
urn, held high over it, poured a triple stream
of funeral offerings; and crowned the corpse.   475
When we saw that, we rushed upon her and
caught our quarry then and there, not a bit disturbed.
We charged her with what she had done, then and the first time.
She did not deny a word of it—to my joy,
but to my pain as well. It is most pleasant   480
to have escaped oneself out of such troubles
but painful to bring into it those whom we love.
However, it is but natural for me
to count all this less than my own escape.
CREON: You there, that turn your eyes upon the ground,   485
   do you confess or deny what you have done?
ANTIGONE: Yes, I confess; I will not deny my deed.
CREON: [To the SENTRY.] You take yourself off where you like.
   You are free of a heavy charge.
   Now, Antigone, tell me shortly and to the point,   490
   did you know the proclamation against your action?
ANTIGONE: I knew it; of course I did. For it was public.
CREON: And did you dare to disobey that law?
ANTIGONE: Yes, it was not Zeus that made the proclamation;
   nor did Justice, which lives with those below, enact   495
   such laws as that, for mankind. I did not believe
   your proclamation had such power to enable
   one who will someday die to override
   God's ordinances, unwritten and secure.

500 *They* are not of today and yesterday;
they live forever; none knows when first they were.
These are the laws whose penalties I would not
incur from the gods, through fear of any man's temper.

I know that I will die—of course I do—
505 even if you had not doomed me by proclamation.
If I shall die before my time, I count that
a profit. How can such as I, that live
among such troubles, not find a profit in death?
So for such as me, to face such a fate as this
510 is pain that does not count. But if I dared to leave
the dead man, my mother's son, dead and unburied,
that would have been real pain. The other is not.
Now, if you think me a fool to act like this,
perhaps it is a fool that judges so.
515 CHORUS: The savage spirit of a savage father
shows itself in this girl. She does not know
how to yield to trouble.
CREON: I would have you know the most fanatic spirits
fall most of all. It is the toughest iron,
520 baked in the fire to hardness, you may see
most shattered, twisted, shivered to fragments.
I know hot horses are restrained
by a small curb. For he that is his neighbor's slave cannot
be high in spirit. This girl had learned her insolence
525 before this, when she broke the established laws.
But here is still another insolence
in that she boasts of it, laughs at what she did.
I swear I am no man and she the man
if she can win this and not pay for it.
530 No; though she were my sister's child or closer
in blood than all that my hearth god acknowledges
as mine, neither she nor her sister should escape
the utmost sentence—death. For indeed I accuse her,
the sister, equally of plotting the burial.
535 Summon her. I saw her inside, just now,
crazy, distraught. When people plot
mischief in the dark, it is the mind which first
is convicted of deceit. But surely I hate indeed
the one that is caught in evil and then makes
540 that evil look like good.
ANTIGONE: Do you want anything
beyond my taking and my execution?
CREON: Oh, nothing! Once I have that I have everything.
ANTIGONE: Why do you wait, then? Nothing that you say

pleases me; God forbid it ever should.   545
So my words, too, naturally offend you.
Yet how could I win a greater share of glory
than putting my own brother in his grave?
All that are here would surely say that's true,
if fear did not lock their tongues up. A prince's power   550
is blessed in many things, not least in this,
that he can say and do whatever he likes.
CREON: You are alone among the people of Thebes
to see things in that way.
ANTIGONE: No, these do, too,   555
but keep their mouths shut for the fear of you.
CREON: Are you not ashamed to think so differently
from them?
ANTIGONE: There is nothing shameful in honoring my brother.
CREON: Was not he that died on the other side your brother?   560
ANTIGONE: Yes, indeed, of my own blood from father and mother.
CREON: Why then do you show a grace that must be impious
in *his* sight?
ANTIGONE: *That* other dead man
would never bear you witness in what you say.   565
CREON: Yes he would, if you put him only on equality
with one that was a desecrator.
ANTIGONE: It was his brother, not his slave, that died.
CREON: He died destroying the country the other defended.
ANTIGONE: The god of death demands these rites for both.   570
CREON: But the good man does not seek an *equal* share only,
with the bad.
ANTIGONE: Who knows
if in that other world this is true piety?
CREON: My enemy is still my enemy, even in death.
ANTIGONE: My nature is to join in love, not hate.   575
CREON: Go then to the world below, yourself, if you
must love. Love *them*. When I am alive no woman shall rule.
CHORUS: Here before the gates comes Ismene
shedding tears for the love of a brother.
A cloud over her brow casts shame   580
on her flushed face, as the tears wet
her fair cheeks.
CREON: You there, who lurked in my house, viper-like—
secretly drawing its lifeblood; I never thought
that I was raising two sources of destruction,   585
two rebels against my throne. Come tell me now,
will you, too, say you bore a hand in the burial
or will you swear that you know nothing of it?
ISMENE: I did it, yes—if she will say I did it

590   I bear my share in it, bear the guilt, too.
      ANTIGONE: Justice will not allow you what you refused
      and I will have none of your partnership.
      ISMENE: But in your troubles I am not ashamed
      to sail with you the sea of suffering.
595   ANTIGONE: Where the act was death, the dead are witnesses.
      I do not love a friend who loves in words.
      ISMENE: Sister, do not dishonor me, denying me
      a common death with you, a common honoring
      of the dead man.
600   ANTIGONE: Don't die with me, nor make your own
      what you have never touched. I that die am enough.
      ISMENE: What life is there for me, once I have lost you?
      ANTIGONE: Ask Creon; all your care was on his behalf.
      ISMENE: Why do you hurt me, when you gain nothing by it?
605   ANTIGONE: I am hurt by my own mockery—if I mock you.
      ISMENE: Even now—what can I do to help you still?
      ANTIGONE: Save yourself; I do not grudge you your escape.
      ISMENE: I cannot bear it! Not even to share your death!
      ANTIGONE: Life was your choice, and death was mine.
610   ISMENE: You cannot say I accepted that choice in silence.
      ANTIGONE: You were right in the eyes of one party, I in the other.
      ISMENE: Well then, the fault is equally between us.
      ANTIGONE: Take heart; you are alive, but my life died
      long ago, to serve the dead.
615   CREON: Here are two girls; I think that one of them
      has suddenly lost her wits—the other was always so.
      ISMENE: Yes, for, my lord, the wits that they are born with
      do not stay firm for the unfortunate.
      They go astray.
      CREON: Certainly yours do,
620   when you share troubles with the troublemaker.
      ISMENE: What life can be mine alone without her?
      CREON: Do not
      speak of her. She isn't, anymore.
      ISMENE: Will you kill your son's wife to be?
      CREON: Yes, there are other fields for him to plough.
625   ISMENE: Not with the mutual love of him and her.
      CREON: I hate a bad wife for a son of mine.
      ANTIGONE: Dear Haemon, how your father dishonors you.
      CREON: There is too much of you—and of your marriage!
      CHORUS: Will you rob your son of this girl?
630   CREON: Death—it is death that will stop the marriage for me.
      CHORUS: Your decision it seems is taken: she shall die.
      CREON: Both you and I have decided it. No more delay.

[*He turns to the* SERVANTS.]

Bring her inside, you. From this time forth,
these must be women, and not free to roam.
For even the stout of heart shrink when they see   635
the approach of death close to their lives.
CHORUS: Lucky are those whose lives
   know no taste of sorrow.
  But for those whose house has been shaken by God
  there is never cessation of ruin;   640
  it steals on generation after generation
  within a breed. Even as the swell
  is driven over the dark deep
  by the fierce Thracian winds
  I see the ancient evils of Labdacus' house   645
  are heaped on the evils of the dead.
  No generation frees another, some god
  strikes them down; there is no deliverance.
  Here was the light of hope stretched
  over the last roots of Oedipus' house,   650
  and the bloody dust due to the gods below
  has mowed it down—that and the folly of speech
  and ruin's enchantment of the mind.

  Your power, O Zeus, what sin of man can limit?
  All-aging sleep does not overtake it,   655
  nor the unwearied months of the gods; and you,
  for whom time brings no age,
  you hold the glowing brightness of Olympus.

  For the future near and far,
  and the past, this law holds good: 660
  nothing very great
  comes to the life of mortal man
  without ruin to accompany it.
  For Hope, widely wandering, comes to many of mankind
  as a blessing,   665
  but to many as the deceiver,
  using light-minded lusts;
  she comes to him that knows nothing
  till he burns his foot in the glowing fire.
  With wisdom has someone declared   670
  a word of distinction:
  that evil seems good to one whose mind
  the god leads to ruin,
  and but for the briefest moment of time

675   is his life outside of calamity.
          Here is Haemon, youngest of your sons.
          Does he come grieving
          for the fate of his bride to be,
          in agony at being cheated of his marriage?

680 CREON: Soon we will know that better than the prophets.
          My son, can it be that you have not heard
          of my final decision on your betrothed?
          Can you have come here in your fury against your father?
          Or have I your love still, no matter what I do?

685 HAEMON: Father, I am yours; with your excellent judgment
          you lay the right before me, and I shall follow it.
          No marriage will ever be so valued by me
          as to override the goodness of your leadership.
      CREON: Yes, my son, this should always be

690   in your very heart, that everything else
          shall be second to your father's decision.
          It is for this that fathers pray to have
          obedient sons begotten in their halls,
          that they may requite with ill their father's enemy

695   and honor his friend no less than he would himself.
          If a man have sons that are no use to him,
          what can one say of him but that he has bred
          so many sorrows to himself, laughter to his enemies?
          Do not, my son, banish your good sense

700   through pleasure in a woman, since you know
          that the embrace grows cold
          when an evil woman shares your bed and home.
          What greater wound can there be than a false friend?
          No. Spit on her, throw her out like an enemy,

705   this girl, to marry someone in Death's house.
          I caught her openly in disobedience
          alone out of all this city and I shall not make
          myself a liar in the city's sight. No, I will kill her.
          So let her cry if she will on the Zeus of kinship;

710   for if I rear those of my race and breeding
          to be rebels, surely I will do so with those outside it.
          For he who is in his household a good man
          will be found a just man, too, in the city.
          But he that breaches the law or does it violence

715   or thinks to dictate to those who govern him
          shall never have my good word.
          The man the city sets up in authority
          must be obeyed in small things and in just
          but also in their opposites.

720   I am confident such a man of whom I speak

will be a good ruler, and willing to be well ruled.
He will stand on his country's side, faithful and just,
in the storm of battle. There is nothing worse
than disobedience to authority.
It destroys cities, it demolishes homes;   725
it breaks and routs one's allies. Of successful lives
the most of them are saved by discipline.
So we must stand on the side of what is orderly;
we cannot give victory to a woman.
If we must accept defeat, let it be from a man;   730
we must not let people say that a woman beat us.
CHORUS: We think, if we are not victims of Time the Thief,
that you speak intelligently of what you speak.
HAEMON: Father, the natural sense that the gods breed
in men is surely the best of their possessions.   735
I certainly could not declare you wrong—
may I never know how to do so!—Still there might
be something useful that some other than you might think.
It is natural for me to be watchful on your behalf
concerning what all men say or do or find to blame.   740
Your face is terrible to a simple citizen;
it frightens him from words you dislike to hear.
But what I can hear, in the dark, are things like these:
the city mourns for this girl; they think she is dying
most wrongly and most undeservedly   745
of all womenkind, for the most glorious acts.
Here is one who would not leave her brother unburied,
a brother who had fallen in bloody conflict,
to meet his end by greedy dogs or by
the bird that chanced that way. Surely what she merits   750
is golden honor, isn't it? That's the dark rumor
that spreads in secret. Nothing I own
I value more highly, father, than your success.
What greater distinction can a son have than the glory
of a successful father, and for a father   755
the distinction of successful children?
Do not bear this single habit of mind, to think
that what you say and nothing else is true
A man who thinks that he alone is right,
or what he says, or what he is himself,   760
unique, such men, when opened up, are seen
to be quite empty. For a man, though he be wise,
it is no shame to learn—learn many things,
and not maintain his views too rigidly.
You notice how by streams in wintertime   765
the trees that yield preserve their branches safely,

but those that fight the tempest perish utterly.
The man who keeps the sheet of his sail tight
and never slackens capsizes his boat
770   and makes the rest of his trip keel uppermost.
Yield something of your anger, give way a little.
If a much younger man, like me, may have
a judgment, I would say it were far better
to be one altogether wise by nature, but,
775   as things incline not to be so, then it is good
also to learn from those who advise well.
CHORUS: My lord, if he says anything to the point,
you should learn from him, and you, too, Haemon,
learn from your father. Both of you
780   have spoken well.
CREON: Should we that are my age learn wisdom
from young men such as he is?
HAEMON: Not learn injustice, certainly. If I am young,
do not look at my years but what I do.
CREON: Is what you do to have respect for rebels?
785   HAEMON: I
would not urge you to be scrupulous
towards the wicked.
CREON: Is *she* not tainted by the disease of wickedness?
HAEMON: The entire people of Thebes says no to that.
790   CREON: Should the city tell me how I am to rule them?
HAEMON: Do you see what a young man's words these are of yours?
CREON: Must I rule the land by someone else's judgment
rather than my own?
HAEMON: There is no city
possessed by one man only.
795   CREON: Is not the city thought to be the ruler's?
HAEMON: You would be a fine dictator of a desert.
CREON: It seems this boy is on the woman's side.
HAEMON: If you are a woman—my care is all for you.
CREON: You villain, to bandy words with your own father!
800   HAEMON: I see your acts as mistaken and unjust.
CREON: Am I mistaken, reverencing my own office?
HAEMON: There is no reverence in trampling on God's honor.
CREON: Your nature is vile, in yielding to a woman.
HAEMON: You will not find me yield to what is shameful.
805   CREON: At least, your argument is all for her.
HAEMON: Yes, and for you and me—and for the gods below.
CREON: You will never marry her while her life lasts.
HAEMON: Then she must die—and dying destroy another.
CREON: Has your daring gone so far, to threaten me?
810   HAEMON: What threat is it to speak against empty judgments?

CREON: Empty of sense yourself, you will regret
    your schooling of me in sense.
HAEMON: If you were not
    my father, I would say you are insane.
CREON: You woman's slave, do not try to wheedle me.
HAEMON: You want to talk but never to hear and listen.   815
CREON: Is that so? By the heavens above you will not—
    be sure of that—get off scot-free, insulting,
    abusing me.

    [*He speaks to the* SERVANTS.]

            You people bring out this creature,
    this hated creature, that she may die before
    his very eyes, right now, next her would-be husband.   820
HAEMON: Not at my side! Never think that! She will not
    die by my side. But you will never again
    set eyes upon my face. Go then and rage
    with such of your friends as are willing to endure it.
CHORUS: The man is gone, my lord, quick in his anger.   825
    A young man's mind is fierce when he is hurt.
CREON: Let him go, and do and think things superhuman.
    But these two girls he shall not save from death.
CHORUS: Both of them? Do you mean to kill them both?
CREON: No, not the one that didn't do anything.   830
    You are quite right there.
CHORUS: And by what form of death do you mean to kill her?
CREON: I will bring her where the path is loneliest,
    and hide her alive in a rocky cavern there.
    I'll give just enough of food as shall suffice   835
    for a bare expiation, that the city may avoid pollution.
    In that place she shall call on Hades, god of death,
    in her prayers. That god only she reveres.
    Perhaps she will win from him escape from death
    or at least in that last moment will recognize   840
    her honoring of the dead is labor lost.
CHORUS: Love undefeated in the fight,
        Love that makes havoc of possessions,
        Love who lives at night in a young girl's soft cheeks,
        Who travels over sea, or in huts in the countryside—   845
        there is no god able to escape you
        nor anyone of men, whose life is a day only,
        and whom you possess is mad.

        You wrench the minds of just men to injustice,
        to their disgrace; this conflict among kinsmen   850
        it is you who stirred to turmoil.

The winner is desire. She gleaming kindles
from the eyes of the girl good to bed.
Love shares the throne with the great powers that rule.
855   For the golden Aphrodite[3] holds her play there
and then no one can overcome her.

Here I too am borne out of the course of lawfulness
when I see these things, and I cannot control
the springs of my tears
860   when I see Antigone making her way
to her bed—but the bed
that is rest for everyone.

ANTIGONE: You see me, you people of my country,
as I set out on my last road of all,
865   looking for the last time on this light of this sun—
never again. I am alive but Hades who gives sleep to everyone
is leading me to the shores of Acheron,[4]
though I have known nothing of marriage songs
nor the chant that brings the bride to bed.
870   My husband is to be the Lord of Death.

CHORUS: Yes, you go to the place where the dead are hidden,
but you go with distinction and praise.
You have not been stricken by wasting sickness;
you have not earned the wages of the sword;
875   it was your own choice and alone among mankind
you will descend, alive,
to that world of death.

ANTIGONE: But indeed I have heard of the saddest of deaths—
of the Phrygian stranger,[5] daughter of Tantalus,
880   whom the rocky growth subdued, like clinging ivy.
The rains never leave her, the snow never fails,
as she wastes away. That is how men tell the story.
From streaming eyes her tears wet the crags;
most like to her the god brings me to rest.

885 CHORUS: Yes, but she was a god, and god born,
and you are mortal and mortal born.
Surely it is great renown
for a woman that dies, that in life and death
her lot is a lot shared with demigods.

890 ANTIGONE: You mock me. In the name of our fathers' gods
why do you not wait till I am gone to insult me?
Must you do it face to face?
My city! Rich citizens of my city!

---

3. Goddess of love and beauty.   4. River in Hades.   5. Niobe, whose children were slain because of her boastfulness and who was herself turned into a stone on Mount Siphylus. Her tears became the mountain's streams.

You springs of Dirce, you holy groves of Thebes,
famed for its chariots! I would still have you as my witnesses,   895
with what dry-eyed friends, under what laws
I make my way to my prison sealed like a tomb.
Pity me. Neither among the living nor the dead
do I have a home in common—
neither with the living nor the dead.   900
CHORUS: You went to the extreme of daring
and against the high throne of Justice
you fell, my daughter, grievously.
But perhaps it was for some ordeal of your father
that you are paying requital.   905
ANTIGONE: You have touched the most painful of my cares—
the pity for my father, ever reawakened,
and the fate of all of our race, the famous Labdacids;
the doomed self-destruction of my mother's bed
when she slept with her own son,   910
my father.
What parents I was born of, God help me!
To them I am going to share their home,
the curse on me, too, and unmarried.
Brother, it was a luckless marriage you made,   915
and dying killed my life.
CHORUS: There *is* a certain reverence for piety.
But for him in authority,
he cannot see that authority defied;
it is your own self-willed temper   920
that has destroyed you.
ANTIGONE: No tears for me, no friends, no marriage. Brokenhearted
I am led along the road ready before me.
I shall never again be suffered
to look on the holy eye of the day.   925
But my fate claims no tears—
no friend cries for me.
CREON: [*To the* SERVANTS.] Don't you know that weeping and wailing before
    death
would never stop if one is allowed to weep and wail?
Lead her away at once. Enfold her   930
in that rocky tomb of hers—as I told you to.
There leave her alone, solitary,
to die if she so wishes
or live a buried life in such a home;
we are guiltless in respect of her, this girl.   935
But living above, among the rest of us, this life
she shall certainly lose.
ANTIGONE: Tomb, bridal chamber, prison forever

dug in rock, it is to you I am going
to join my people, that great number that have died,
whom in their death Persephone[6] received.
I am the last of them and I go down
in the worst death of all—for I have not lived
the due term of my life. But when I come
to that other world my hope is strong
that my coming will be welcome to my father,
and dear to you, my mother, and dear to you,
my brother deeply loved. For when you died,
with my own hands I washed and dressed you all,
and poured the lustral offerings on your graves.
And now, Polyneices, it was for such care of your body
that I have earned these wages.
Yet those who think rightly will think I did right
in honoring you. Had I been a mother
of children, and my husband been dead and rotten,
I would not have taken this weary task upon me
against the will of the city. What law backs me
when I say this? I will tell you:
If my husband were dead, I might have had another,
and child from another man, if I lost the first.
But when father and mother both were hidden in death
no brother's life would bloom for me again.
That is the law under which I gave you precedence,
my dearest brother, and that is why Creon thinks me
wrong, even a criminal, and now takes me
by the hand and leads me away,
unbedded, without bridal, without share
in marriage and in nurturing of children;
as lonely as you see me; without friends;
with fate against me I go to the vault of death
while still alive. What law of God have I broken?
Why should I still look to the gods in my misery?
Whom should I summon as ally? For indeed
because of piety I was called impious.
If this proceeding is good in the gods' eyes
I shall know my sin, once I have suffered.
But if Creon and his people are the wrongdoers
let their suffering be no worse than the injustice
they are meting out to me.

CHORUS: It is the same blasts, the tempests of the soul,
possess her.

CREON: Then for this her guards,

---

6. Abducted by Pluto, god of the underworld.

who are so slow, will find themselves in trouble.

ANTIGONE: [*Cries out.*] Oh, that word has come
    very close to death.

CREON: I will not comfort you   985
    with hope that the sentence will not be accomplished.

ANTIGONE: O my father's city, in Theban land,
    O gods that sired my race,
    I am led away, I have no more stay.
    Look on me, princes of Thebes,   990
    the last remnant of the old royal line;
    see what I suffer and who makes me suffer
    because I gave reverence to what claims reverence.

CHORUS: Danae suffered, too, when, her beauty lost, she gave
    the light of heaven in exchange for brassbound walls,   995
    and in the tomb-like cell was she hidden and held;
    yet she was honored in her breeding, child,
    and she kept, as guardian, the seed of Zeus
    that came to her in a golden shower.[7]
    But there is some terrible power in destiny   1000
    and neither wealth nor war
    nor tower nor black ships, beaten by the sea,
    can give escape from it.

    The hot-tempered son of Dryas,[8] the Edonian king,
    in fury mocked Dionysus,   1005
    who then held him in restraint
    in a rocky dungeon.
    So the terrible force and flower of his madness
    drained away. He came to know the god
    whom in frenzy he had touched with his mocking tongue,   1010
    when he would have checked the inspired women
    and the fire of Dionysus,
    when he provoked the Muses[9] that love the lyre.
    By the black rocks, dividing the sea in two,
    are the shores of the Bosporus, Thracian Salmydessus.   1015
    There the god of war who lives near the city
    saw the terrible blinding wound
    dealt by his savage wife
    on Phineus' two sons.
    She blinded and tore with the points of her shuttle,   1020
    and her bloodied hands, those eyes
    that else would have looked on her vengefully.
    As they wasted away, they lamented

---

7. Danae was locked away because it was prophesized that her son would kill her father. Zeus came down and impregnated her and the child who resulted fulfilled the prophesy.   8. Stricken with madness by Dionysus.   9. Nine sister goddesses of poetry, music, and the arts.

their unhappy fate that they were doomed
1025   to be born of a mother cursed in her marriage.
She traced her descent from the seed
of the ancient Erechtheidae.
In far-distant caves she was raised
among her father's storms, that child of Boreas,
1030   quick as a horse, over the steep hills,
a daughter of the gods.[1]
But, my child, the long-lived Fates[2]
bore hard upon her, too.

[*Enter* TEIRESIAS, *the blind prophet, led by a* BOY.]

TEIRESIAS: My lords of Thebes, we have come here together,
1035   one pair of eyes serving us both. For the blind
such must be the way of going, by a guide's leading.
CREON: What is the news, my old Teiresias?
TEIRESIAS: I will tell you; and you, listen to the prophet.
CREON: Never in the past have I turned from your advice.
1040 TEIRESIAS: And so you have steered well the ship of state.
CREON: I have benefited and can testify to that.
TEIRESIAS: Then realize you are on the razor edge
of danger.
CREON: What can that be? I shudder to hear those words.
1045 TEIRESIAS: When you learn the signs recognized by my art
you will understand.
I sat at my ancient place of divination
for watching the birds, where every bird finds shelter;
and I heard an unwonted voice among them;
1050   they were horribly distressed, and screamed unmeaningly.
I knew they were tearing each other murderously;
the beating of their wings was a clear sign.
I was full of fear; at once on all the altars,
as they were fully kindled, I tasted the offerings,
1055   but the god of fire refused to burn from the sacrifice,
and from the thighbones a dark stream of moisture
oozed from the embers, smoked and sputtered.
The gall bladder burst and scattered to the air
and the streaming thighbones lay exposed
1060   from the fat wrapped round them—
so much I learned from this boy here,
the fading prophecies of a rite that failed.
This boy here is my guide, as I am others'.

---

1. King Phineus's second wife blinded the children of his first wife, whom Phineus had imprisoned in a cave.   2. Spirits called upon to avenge crimes.

This is the city's sickness—and your plans are the cause of it.
For our altars and our sacrificial hearths   1065
are filled with the carrion meat of birds and dogs,
torn from the flesh of Oedipus' poor son.
So the gods will not take our prayers or sacrifice
nor yet the flame from the thighbones, and no bird
cries shrill and clear, so glutted   1070
are they with fat of the blood of the killed man.
Reflect on these things, son. All men
can make mistakes; but, once mistaken,
a man is no longer stupid nor accursed
who, having fallen on ill, tries to cure that ill,   1075
not taking a fine undeviating stand.
It is obstinacy that convicts of folly.
Yield to the dead man; do not stab him—
now he is gone—what bravery is this,
to inflict another death upon the dead?   1080
I mean you well and speak well for your good.
It is never sweeter to learn from a good counselor
than when he counsels to your benefit.
CREON: Old man, you are all archers, and I am your mark.
I must be tried by your prophecies as well.   1085
By the breed of you I have been bought and sold
and made a merchandise, for ages now.
But I tell you: make your profit from silver-gold
from Sardis and the gold from India
if you will. But this dead man you shall not hide   1090
in a grave, not though the eagles of Zeus should bear
the carrion, snatching it to the throne of Zeus itself.
Even so, I shall not so tremble at the pollution
to let you bury him.
                No, I am certain
no human has the power to pollute the gods.   1095
They fall, you old Teiresias, those men,
—so very clever—in a bad fall whenever
they eloquently speak vile words for profit.
TEIRESIAS: I wonder if there's a man who dares consider—
CREON: What do you mean? What sort of generalization   1100
   is this talk of yours?
TEIRESIAS: How much the best of possessions is the ability
   to listen to wise advice?
CREON: As I should imagine that the worst
   injury must be native stupidity.   1105
TEIRESIAS: Now that is exactly where your mind is sick.
CREON: I do not like to answer a seer with insults.

TEIRESIAS: But you do, when you say my prophecies are lies.

CREON: Well,

1110   the whole breed of prophets certainly loves money.

TEIRESIAS: And the breed that comes from princes loves to take
    advantage—base advantage.

CREON: Do you realize
    you are speaking in such terms of your own prince?

TEIRESIAS: I know. But it is through me you have saved the city.

1115 CREON: You are a wise prophet, but what you love is wrong.

TEIRESIAS: You will force me to declare what should be hidden
    in my own heart.

CREON: Out with it—
    but only if your words are not for gain.

TEIRESIAS: They won't be for *your* gain—that I am sure of.

1120 CREON: But realize you will not make a merchandise
    of my decisions.

TEIRESIAS: And you must realize
    that you will not outlive many cycles more
    of this swift sun before you give in exchange
    one of your own loins bred, a corpse for a corpse,
1125   for you have thrust one that belongs above
    below the earth, and bitterly dishonored
    a living soul by lodging her in the grave;
    while one that belonged indeed to the underworld
    gods you have kept on this earth without due share
1130   of rites of burial, of due funeral offerings,
    a corpse unhallowed. With all of this you, Creon,
    have nothing to do, nor have the gods above.
    These acts of yours are violence, on your part.
    And in requital the avenging Spirits
1135   of Death itself and the gods' Furies shall
    after *your* deeds, lie in ambush for you, and
    in their hands you shall be taken cruelly.
    Now, look at this and tell me I was bribed
    to say it! The delay will not be long
1140   before the cries of mourning in your house,
    of men and women. All the cities will stir in hatred
    against you, because their sons in mangled shreds
    received their burial rites from dogs, from wild beasts
    or when some bird of the air brought a vile stink
1145   to each city that contained the hearths of the dead.
    These are the arrows that archer-like I launched—
    you vexed me so to anger—at your heart.
    You shall not escape their sting. You, boy,
    lead me away to my house, so he may discharge
1150   his anger on younger men; so may he come to know

to bear a quieter tongue in his head and a better
mind than that now he carries in him.

CHORUS: That was a terrible prophecy, my lord.
The man has gone. Since these hairs of mine grew white
from the black they once were, he has never spoken   1155
a word of a lie to our city.

CREON: I know, I know.
My mind is all bewildered. To yield is terrible.
But by opposition to destroy my very being
with a self-destructive curse must also be reckoned   1160
in what is terrible.

CHORUS: You need good counsel, son of Menoeceus,
and need to take it.

CREON: What must I do, then? Tell me; I shall agree.

CHORUS: The girl—go now and bring her up from her cave,   1165
and for the exposed dead man, give him his burial.

CREON: That is really your advice? You would have me yield.

CHORUS: And quickly as you may, my lord. Swift harms
sent by the gods cut off the paths of the foolish.

CREON: Oh, it is hard; I must give up what my heart   1170
would have me do. But it is ill to fight
against what must be.

CHORUS: Go now, and do this;
do not give the task to others.

CREON: I will go,   1175
just as I am. Come, servants, all of you;
take axes in your hands; away with you
to the place you see, there.
For my part, since my intention is so changed,
as I bound her myself, myself will free her.   1180
I am afraid it may be best, in the end
of life, to have kept the old accepted laws.

CHORUS: You of many names,[3] glory of the Cadmeian
bride, breed of loud thundering Zeus;
you who watch over famous Italy;   1185
you who rule where all are welcome in Eleusis;
in the sheltered plains of Deo—
O Bacchus that dwells in Thebes,
the mother city of Bacchanals,
by the flowing stream of Ismenus,   1190
in the ground sown by the fierce dragon's teeth.

You are he on whom the murky gleam of torches glares,
above the twin peaks of the crag
where come the Corycean nymphs

3. Refers to Dionysus.

1195   to worship you, the Bacchanals;
         and the stream of Castalia has seen you, too;
         and you are he that the ivy-clad
         slopes of Nisaean hills,
         and the green shore ivy-clustered,
1200   sent to watch over the roads of Thebes,
         where the immortal Evoe chant[4] rings out.

         It is Thebes which you honor most of all cities,
         you and your mother both,
         she who died by the blast of Zeus' thunderbolt.
1205   And now when the city, with all its folk,
         is gripped by a violent plague,
         come with healing foot, over the slopes of Parnassus,
         over the moaning strait.
         You lead the dance of the fire-breathing stars,
1210   you are master of the voices of the night.
         True-born child of Zeus, appear,
         my lord, with your Thyiad attendants,
         who in frenzy all night long
         dance in your house, Iacchus,
1215   dispenser of gifts.
MESSENGER: You who live by the house of Cadmus and Amphion,[5]
         hear me. There is no condition of man's life
         that stands secure. As such I would not
         praise it or blame. It is chance that sets upright;
1220   it is chance that brings down the lucky and the unlucky,
         each in his turn. For men, that belong to death,
         there is no prophet of established things.
         Once Creon was a man worthy of envy—
         of my envy, at least. For he saved this city
1225   of Thebes from her enemies, and attained
         the throne of the land, with all a king's power.
         He guided it right. His race bloomed
         with good children. But when a man forfeits joy
         I do not count his life as life, but only
1230   a life trapped in a corpse.
         Be rich within your house, yes greatly rich,
         if so you will, and live in a prince's style.
         If the gladness of these things is gone, I would not
         give the shadow of smoke for the rest,
1235   as against joy.
CHORUS: What is the sorrow of our princes
         of which you are the messenger?
MESSENGER: Death; and the living are guilty of their deaths.

4. Come forth, come forth!   5. A name for Thebes.

CHORUS: But who is the murderer? Who the murdered? Tell us.

MESSENGER: Haemon is dead; the hand that shed his blood   1240
    was his very own.

CHORUS: Truly his own hand? Or his father's?

MESSENGER: His own hand, in his anger
    against his father for a murder.

CHORUS: Prophet, how truly you have made good your word!   1245

MESSENGER: These things are so; you may debate the rest.
    Here I see Creon's wife Eurydice
    approaching. Unhappy woman!
    Does she come from the house as hearing about her son
    or has she come by chance?   1250

EURYDICE: I heard your words, all you men of Thebes, as I
    was going out to greet Pallas[6] with my prayers.
    I was just drawing back the bolts of the gate
    to open it when a cry struck through my ears
    telling of my household's ruin. I fell backward   1255
    in terror into the arms of my servants; I fainted.
    But tell me again, what is the story? I
    will hear it as one who is no stranger to sorrow.

MESSENGER: Dear mistress, I will tell you, for I was there,
    and I will leave out no word of the truth.   1260
    Why should I comfort you and then tomorrow
    be proved a liar? The truth is always best.

    I followed your husband, at his heels, to the end of the plain
    where Polyneices' body still lay unpitied,
    and torn by dogs. We prayed to Hecate, goddess   1265
    of the crossroads, and also to Pluto[7]
    that they might restrain their anger and turn kind.
    And him we washed with sacred lustral water
    and with fresh-cut boughs we burned what was left of him
    and raised a high mound of his native earth;   1270
    then we set out again for the hollowed rock,
    death's stone bridal chamber for the girl.
    Someone then heard a voice of bitter weeping
    while we were still far off, coming from that unblest room.
    The man came to tell our master Creon of it.   1275
    As the king drew nearer, there swarmed about him
    a cry of misery but no clear words.
    He groaned and in an anguished mourning voice
    cried "Oh, am I a true prophet? Is this the road
    that I must travel, saddest of all my wayfaring?   1280
    It is my son's voice that haunts my ear. Servants,
    get closer, quickly. Stand around the tomb

6. Athena, goddess of wisdom.   7. King of the underworld. *Hecate:* Goddess of witchcraft.

and look. There is a gap there where the stones
have been wrenched away; enter there, by the very mouth,
1285 and see whether I recognize the voice of Haemon
or if the gods deceive me." On the command
of our despairing master we went to look.
In the furthest part of the tomb we saw her, hanging
by her neck. She had tied a noose of muslin on it.
1290 Haemon's hands were about her waist embracing her,
while he cried for the loss of his bride gone to the dead,
and for all his father had done, and his own sad love.
When Creon saw him he gave a bitter cry,
went in and called to him with a groan: "Poor son!
1295 what have you done? What can you have meant?
What happened to destroy you? Come out, I pray you!"
The boy glared at him with savage eyes, and then
spat in his face, without a word of answer.
He drew his double-hilted sword. As his father
1300 ran to escape him, Haemon failed to strike him,
and the poor wretch in anger at himself
leaned on his sword and drove it halfway in,
into his ribs. Then he folded the girl to him,
in his arms, while he was conscious still,
1305 and gasping poured a sharp stream of bloody drops
on her white cheeks. There they lie,
the dead upon the dead. So he has won
the pitiful fulfillment of his marriage
within death's house. In this human world he has shown
1310 how the wrong choice in plans is for a man
his greatest evil.
CHORUS: What do you make of this? My lady is gone,
without a word of good or bad.
MESSENGER: I, too,
am lost in wonder. I am inclined to hope
1315 that hearing of her son's death she could not
open her sorrow to the city, but chose rather
within her house to lay upon her maids
the mourning for the household grief. Her judgment
is good; she will not make any false step.
1320 CHORUS: I do not know. To me this over-heavy silence
seems just as dangerous as much empty wailing.
MESSENGER: I will go in and learn if in her passionate
heart she keeps hidden some secret purpose.
You are right; there is sometimes danger in too much silence.
1325 CHORUS: Here comes our king himself. He bears in his hands
a memorial all too clear;
it is a ruin of none other's making,
purely his own if one dare to say that.

CREON: The mistakes of a blinded man
    are themselves rigid and laden with death.   1330
    You look at us the killer and the killed
    of the one blood. Oh, the awful blindness
    of those plans of mine. My son, you were so young,
    so young to die. You were freed from the bonds of life
    through no folly of your own—only through mine.   1335
CHORUS: I think you have learned justice—but too late.
CREON: Yes, I have learned it to my bitterness. At this moment
    God has sprung on my head with a vast weight
    and struck me down. He shook me in my savage ways;
    he has overturned my joy, has trampled it,   1340
    underfoot. The pains men suffer
    are pains indeed.
SECOND MESSENGER: My lord, you have troubles and a store besides;
    some are there in your hands, but there are others
    you will surely see when you come to your house.   1345
CREON: What trouble can there be beside these troubles?
SECOND MESSENGER: The queen is dead. She was indeed true mother
    of the dead son. She died, poor lady,
    by recent violence upon herself.
CREON: Haven of death, you can never have enough.   1350
    Why, why do you destroy me?
    You messenger, who have brought me bitter news,
    what is this tale you tell?
    It is a dead man that you kill again—
    what new message of yours is this, boy?   1355
    Is this new slaughter of a woman
    a doom to lie on the pile of the dead?
CHORUS: You can see. It is no longer
    hidden in a corner.

[*By some stage device, perhaps the so-called eccyclema, the inside of the palace
is shown, with the body of the dead* QUEEN.]

CREON: Here is yet another horror   1360
    for my unhappy eyes to see.
    What doom still waits for me?
    I have but now taken in my arms my son,
    and again I look upon another dead face.
    Poor mother and poor son!   1365
SECOND MESSENGER: She stood at the altar, and with keen whetted knife
    she suffered her darkening eyes to close.
    First she cried in agony recalling the noble fate of Megareus,[8]
    who died before all this,
    and then for the fate of this son; and in the end   1370

8. Another son of Creon.

she cursed you for the evil you had done
in killing her sons.

CREON: I am distracted with fear. Why does not someone
strike a two-edged sword right through me?

1375   I am dissolved in an agony of misery.

SECOND MESSENGER: You were indeed accused
by her that is dead
of Haemon's and of Megareus' death.

CREON: By what kind of violence did she find her end?

1380 SECOND MESSENGER: Her own hand struck her to the entrails
when she heard of her son's lamentable death.

CREON: These acts can never be made to fit another
to free me from the guilt. It was I that killed her.
Poor wretch that I am, I say it is true!

1385   Servants, lead me away, quickly, quickly.
I am no more a live man than one dead.

CHORUS: What you say is for the best—if there be a best
in evil such as this. For the shortest way
is best with troubles that lie at our feet.

1390 CREON: O, let it come, let it come,
that best of fates that waits on my last day.
Surely best fate of all. Let it come, let it come!
That I may never see one more day's light!

CHORUS: These things are for the future. We must deal

1395   with what impends. What in the future is to care for
rests with those whose duty it is
to care for them.

CREON: At least, all that I want
is in that prayer of mine.

1400 CHORUS: Pray for no more at all. For what is destined
for us, men mortal, there is no escape.

CREON: Lead me away, a vain silly man
who killed you, son, and you, too, lady.
I did not mean to, but I did.

1405   I do not know where to turn my eyes
to look to, for support.
Everything in my hands is crossed. A most unwelcome fate
has leaped upon me.

CHORUS: Wisdom is far the chief element in happiness

1410   and, secondly, no irreverence towards the gods.
But great words of haughty men exact
in retribution blows as great
and in old age teach wisdom.

THE END

ca. 441 B.C.E.

TENNESSEE WILLIAMS

A Streetcar Named Desire

And so it was I entered the broken world
To trace the visionary company of love, its voice
An instant in the wind (I know not whither hurled)
But not for long to hold each desperate choice.
 — "The Broken Tower" by HART CRANE[1]

CHARACTERS

BLANCHE	PABLO
STELLA	A NEGRO WOMAN
STANLEY	A DOCTOR
MITCH	A NURSE (MATRON)
EUNICE	A YOUNG COLLECTOR
STEVE	A MEXICAN WOMAN

SCENE 1

The exterior of a two-story corner building on a street in New Orleans which is named Elysian Fields and runs between the L & N tracks and the river.[2] The section is poor but, unlike corresponding sections in other American cities, it has a raffish charm. The houses are mostly white frame, weathered grey, with rickety outside stairs and galleries and quaintly ornamented gables. This building contains two flats, upstairs and down. Faded white stairs ascend to the entrances of both.

It is first dark of an evening early in May. The sky that shows around the dim white building is a peculiarly tender blue, almost a turquoise, which invests the scene with a kind of lyricism and gracefully attenuates the atmosphere of decay. You can almost feel the warm breath of the brown river beyond the river warehouses with their faint redolences of bananas and coffee. A corresponding air is evoked by the music of Negro entertainers at a barroom around the corner. In this part of New Orleans you are practically always just around the corner, or a few doors down the street, from a tinny piano being played with the infatuated fluency of brown fingers. This "Blue Piano" expresses the spirit of the life which goes on here.

Two women, one white and one colored, are taking the air on the steps of the building. The white woman is EUNICE, who occupies the upstairs flat; the NEGRO WOMAN, a neighbor, for New Orleans is a cosmopolitan city where there is a relatively warm and easy intermingling of races in the old part of town.

---

1. American poet (1899–1932).   2. Elysian Fields is in fact a New Orleans street at the northern tip of the French Quarter, between the Louisville & Nashville railroad tracks and the Mississippi River. In Greek mythology, the Elysian Fields are the abode of the blessed in the afterlife; in Paris, the Champs Elysées is a grand boulevard.

Above the music of the "Blue Piano" the voices of people on the street can be heard overlapping.

[*Two men come around the corner,* STANLEY KOWALSKI *and* MITCH. *They are about twenty-eight, or thirty years old, roughly dressed in blue denim work clothes.* STANLEY *carries his bowling jacket and a red-stained package from a butcher's. They stop at the foot of the steps.*]

STANLEY: [*Bellowing.*] Hey there! Stella, baby!

[STELLA *comes out on the first floor landing, a gentle young woman, about twenty-five, and of a background obviously quite different from her husband's.*]

STELLA: [*Mildly.*] Don't holler at me like that. Hi, Mitch.
STANLEY: Catch!
STELLA: What?
STANLEY: Meat!

[*He heaves the package at her. She cries out in protest but manages to catch it: then she laughs breathlessly. Her husband and his companion have already started back around the corner.*]

STELLA: [*Calling after him.*] Stanley! Where are you going?
STANLEY: Bowling!
STELLA: Can I come watch?
STANLEY: Come on. [*He goes out.*]
STELLA: Be over soon. [*To the* WHITE WOMAN.] Hello, Eunice. How are you?
EUNICE: I'm all right. Tell Steve to get him a poor boy's sandwich[3] 'cause nothing's left here.

[*They all laugh; the* NEGRO WOMAN *does not stop.* STELLA *goes out.*]

NEGRO WOMAN: What was that package he th'ew at 'er? [*She rises from steps, laughing louder.*]
EUNICE: You hush, now!
NEGRO WOMAN: Catch what!

[*She continues to laugh.* BLANCHE *comes around the corner, carrying a valise. She looks at a slip of paper, then at the building, then again at the slip and again at the building. Her expression is one of shocked disbelief. Her appearance is incongruous to this setting. She is daintily dressed in a white suit with a fluffy bodice, necklace and earrings of pearl, white gloves and hat, looking as if she were arriving at a summer tea or cocktail party in the garden district. She is about five years older than* STELLA. *Her delicate beauty must avoid a strong light. There is something about her uncertain manner, as well as her white clothes, that suggests a moth.*]

EUNICE: [*Finally.*] What's the matter, honey? Are you lost?
BLANCHE: [*With faintly hysterical humor.*] They told me to take a street-car

---

3. Usually called just "poor boy" or "po' boy." Similar to a hero or submarine sandwich.

named Desire, and then transfer to one called Cemeteries[4] and ride six blocks and get off at—Elysian Fields!

EUNICE: That's where you are now.

BLANCHE: At Elysian Fields?

EUNICE: This here is Elysian Fields.

BLANCHE: They mustn't have—understood—what number I wanted . . .

EUNICE: What number you lookin' for?

[BLANCHE *wearily refers to the slip of paper.*]

BLANCHE: Six thirty-two.

EUNICE: You don't have to look no further.

BLANCHE: [*Uncomprehendingly.*] I'm looking for my sister, Stella DuBois, I mean—Mrs. Stanley Kowalski.

EUNICE: That's the party.—You just did miss her, though.

BLANCHE: This—can this be—her home?

EUNICE: She's got the downstairs here and I got the up.

BLANCHE: Oh. She's—out?

EUNICE: You noticed that bowling alley around the corner?

BLANCHE: I'm—not sure I did.

EUNICE: Well, that's where she's at, watchin' her husband bowl. [*There is a pause.*] You want to leave your suitcase here an' go find her?

BLANCHE: No.

NEGRO WOMAN: I'll go tell her you come.

BLANCHE: Thanks.

NEGRO WOMAN: You welcome. [*She goes out.*]

EUNICE: She wasn't expecting you?

BLANCHE: No. No, not tonight.

EUNICE: Well, why don't you just go in and make yourself at home till they get back.

BLANCHE: How could I—do that?

EUNICE: We own this place so I can let you in.

[*She gets up and opens the downstairs door. A light goes on behind the blind, turning it light blue.* BLANCHE *slowly follows her into the downstairs flat. The surrounding areas dim out as the interior is lighted. Two rooms can be seen, not too clearly defined. The one first entered is primarily a kitchen but contains a folding bed to be used by* BLANCHE. *The room beyond this is a bedroom. Off this room is a narrow door to a bathroom.*]

EUNICE: [*Defensively, noticing* BLANCHE's *look.*] It's sort of messed up right now but when it's clean it's real sweet.

BLANCHE: Is it?

EUNICE: Uh-huh, I think so. So you're Stella's sister?

BLANCHE: Yes. [*Wanting to get rid of her.*] Thanks for letting me in.

4. Desire is a street in New Orleans, Cemeteries the end of a streetcar line that stopped at a cemetery.

EUNICE: *Por nada*, as the Mexicans say, *por nada!*[5] Stella spoke of you.

BLANCHE: Yes?

EUNICE: I think she said you taught school.

BLANCHE: Yes.

EUNICE: And you're from Mississippi, huh?

BLANCHE: Yes.

EUNICE: She showed me a picture of your home-place, the plantation.

BLANCHE: Belle Reve?[6]

EUNICE: A great big place with white columns.

BLANCHE: Yes . . .

EUNICE: A place like that must be awful hard to keep up.

BLANCHE: If you will excuse me, I'm just about to drop.

EUNICE: Sure, honey. Why don't you set down?

BLANCHE: What I meant was I'd like to be left alone.

EUNICE: [*Offended.*] Aw. I'll make myself scarce, in that case.

BLANCHE: I didn't meant to be rude, but—

EUNICE: I'll drop by the bowling alley an' hustle her up. [*She goes out the door.*]

[BLANCHE *sits in a chair very stiffly with her shoulders slightly hunched and her legs pressed close together and her hands tightly clutching her purse as if she were quite cold. After a while the blind look goes out of her eyes and she begins to look slowly around. A cat screeches. She catches her breath with a startled gesture. Suddenly she notices something in a half opened closet. She springs up and crosses to it, and removes a whiskey bottle. She pours a half tumbler of whiskey and tosses it down. She carefully replaces the bottle and washes out the tumbler at the sink. Then she resumes her seat in front of the table.*]

BLANCHE: [*Faintly to herself.*] I've got to keep hold of myself!

[STELLA *comes quickly around the corner of the building and runs to the door of the downstairs flat.*]

STELLA: [*Calling out joyfully.*] Blanche!

[*For a moment they stare at each other. Then* BLANCHE *springs up and runs to her with a wild cry.*]

BLANCHE: Stella, oh, Stella, Stella! Stella for Star! [*She begins to speak with feverish vivacity as if she feared for either of them to stop and think. They catch each other in a spasmodic embrace.*] Now, then, let me look at you. But don't you look at me, Stella, no, no, no, not till later, not till I've bathed and rested! And turn that over-light off! Turn that off! I won't be looked at in this merciless glare! [STELLA *laughs and complies.*] Come back here now! Oh, my baby! Stella! Stella for Star! [*She embraces her again.*] I thought you would never come back to this horrible place! What am I saying? I didn't

5. "It's nothing." 6. "Beautiful Dream."

mean to say that. I meant to be nice about it and say—Oh, what a convenient location and such—Ha-a-ha! Precious lamb! You haven't said a *word* to me.

STELLA: You haven't given me a chance to, honey! [*She laughs, but her glance at* BLANCHE *is a little anxious.*]

BLANCHE: Well, now you talk. Open your pretty mouth and talk while I look around for some liquor! I know you must have some liquor on the place! Where could it be, I wonder? Oh, I spy, I spy! [*She rushes to the closet and removes the bottle; she is shaking all over and panting for breath as she tries to laugh. The bottle nearly slips from her grasp.*]

STELLA: [*Noticing.*] Blanche, you sit down and let me pour the drinks. I don't know what we've got to mix with. Maybe a Coke in the icebox. Look'n see, honey, while I'm—

BLANCHE: No Coke, honey, not with my nerves tonight! Where—where—where is—?

STELLA: Stanley? Bowling! He loves it. They're having a—found some soda!—tournament . . .

BLANCHE: Just water, baby, to chase it! Now don't get worried, your sister hasn't turned into a drunkard, she's just all shaken up and hot and tired and dirty! You sit down, now, and explain this place to me! What are you doing in a place like this?

STELLA: Now, Blanche—

BLANCHE: Oh, I'm not going to be hypocritical, I'm going to be honestly critical about it! Never, never, never in my worst dreams could I picture—Only Poe! Only Mr. Edgar Allan Poe!—could do it justice! Out there I suppose is the ghoul-haunted woodland of Weir![7] [*She laughs.*]

STELLA: No, honey, those are the L & N tracks.

BLANCHE: No, now seriously, putting joking aside. Why didn't you tell me, why didn't you write me, honey, why didn't you let me know?

STELLA: [*Carefully, pouring herself a drink.*] Tell you what, Blanche?

BLANCHE: Why, that you had to live in these conditions!

STELLA: Aren't you being a little intense about it? It's not that bad at all! New Orleans isn't like other cities.

BLANCHE: This has got nothing to do with New Orleans. You might as well say—forgive me, blessed baby! [*She suddenly stops short.*] The subject is closed!

STELLA: [*A little drily.*] Thanks.

[*During the pause,* BLANCHE *stares at her. She smiles at* BLANCHE.]

BLANCHE: [*Looking down at her glass, which shakes in her hand.*] You're all I've got in the world, and you're not glad to see me!

STELLA: [*Sincerely.*] Why, Blanche, you know that's not true.

BLANCHE: No?—I'd forgotten how quiet you were.

STELLA: You never did give me a chance to say much, Blanche. So I just got in the habit of being quiet around you.

BLANCHE: [*Vaguely.*] A good habit to get into . . . [*Then, abruptly.*] You haven't

7. From the refrain of Poe's gothic ballad *Ulalume* (1847).

asked me how I happened to get away from the school before the spring term
ended.

STELLA: Well, I thought you'd volunteer that information—if you wanted to tell
me.

BLANCHE: You thought I'd been fired?

STELLA: No, I—thought you might have—resigned . . .

BLANCHE: I was so exhausted by all I'd been through my—nerves broke. [*Nervously tamping cigarette.*] I was on the verge of—lunacy, almost! So Mr.
Graves—Mr. Graves is the high school superintendent—he suggested I take
a leave of absence. I couldn't put all of those details into the wire . . . [*She
drinks quickly.*] Oh, this buzzes right through me and feels so *good!*

STELLA: Won't you have another?

BLANCHE: No, one's my limit.

STELLA: Sure?

BLANCHE: You haven't said a word about my appearance.

STELLA: You look just fine.

BLANCHE: God love you for a liar! Daylight never exposed so total a ruin! But
you—you've put on some weight, yes, you're just as plump as a little partridge! And it's so becoming to you!

STELLA: Now, Blanche—

BLANCHE: Yes, it is, it is or I wouldn't say it! You just have to watch around the
hips a little. Stand up.

STELLA: Not now.

BLANCHE: You hear me? I said stand up! [STELLA *complies reluctantly.*] You
messy child, you, you've spilt something on that pretty white lace collar!
About your hair—you ought to have it cut in a feather bob with your dainty
features. Stella, you have a maid, don't you?

STELLA: No. With only two rooms it's—

BLANCHE: What? *Two* rooms, did you say?

STELLA: This one and—[*She is embarrassed.*]

BLANCHE: The other one? [*She laughs sharply. There is an embarrassed silence.*]
I am going to take just one little tiny nip more, sort of to put the stopper on,
so to speak. . . . Then put the bottle away so I won't be tempted. [*She rises.*]
I want you to look at *my* figure! [*She turns around.*] You know I haven't put
on one ounce in ten years, Stella? I weigh what I weighed the summer you
left Belle Reve. The summer Dad died and you left us . . .

STELLA: [*A little wearily.*] It's just incredible, Blanche, how well you're looking.

BLANCHE: [*They both laugh uncomfortably.*] But, Stella, there's only two rooms,
I don't see where you're going to put me!

STELLA: We're going to put you in here.

BLANCHE: What kind of bed's this—one of those collapsible things? [*She sits on
it.*]

STELLA: Does it feel all right?

BLANCHE: [*Dubiously.*] Wonderful, honey. I don't like a bed that gives much.
But there's no door between the two rooms, and Stanley—will it be decent?

STELLA: Stanley is Polish, you know.

BLANCHE: Oh, yes. They're something like Irish, aren't they?

STELLA: Well—

BLANCHE: Only not so—highbrow? [*They both laugh again in the same way.*] I brought some nice clothes to meet all your lovely friends in.

STELLA: I'm afraid you won't think they are lovely.

BLANCHE: What are they like?

STELLA: They're Stanley's friends.

BLANCHE: Polacks?

STELLA: They're a mixed lot, Blanche.

BLANCHE: Heterogeneous—types?

STELLA: Oh, yes. Yes, types is right!

BLANCHE: Well—anyhow—I brought nice clothes and I'll wear them. I guess you're hoping I'll say I'll put up at a hotel, but I'm not going to put up at a hotel. I want to be *near* you, got to be *with* somebody, I *can't* be *alone!* Because—as you must have noticed—I'm—*not* very *well.* . . . [*Her voice drops and her look is frightened.*]

STELLA: You seem a little bit nervous or overwrought or something.

BLANCHE: Will Stanley like me, or will I be just a visiting in-law, Stella? I couldn't stand that.

STELLA: You'll get along fine together, if you'll just try not to—well—compare him with men that we went out with at home.

BLANCHE: Is he so—different?

STELLA: Yes. A different species.

BLANCHE: In what way; what's he like?

STELLA: Oh, you can't describe someone you're in love with! Here's a picture of him! [*She hands a photograph to* BLANCHE.]

BLANCHE: An officer?

STELLA: A Master Sergeant in the Engineers' Corps. Those are decorations!

BLANCHE: He had those on when you met him?

STELLA: I assure you I wasn't just blinded by all the brass.

BLANCHE: That's not what I—

STELLA: But of course there were things to adjust myself to later on.

BLANCHE: Such as his civilian background! [STELLA *laughs uncertainly.*] How did he take it when you said I was coming?

STELLA: Oh, Stanley doesn't know yet.

BLANCHE: [*Frightened.*] You—haven't told him?

STELLA: He's on the road a good deal.

BLANCHE: Oh. Travels?

STELLA: Yes.

BLANCHE: Good. I mean—isn't it?

STELLA: [*Half to herself.*] I can hardly stand it when he is away for a night . . .

BLANCHE: Why, Stella!

STELLA: When he's away for a week I nearly go wild!

BLANCHE: Gracious!

STELLA: And when he comes back I cry on his lap like a baby . . . [*She smiles to herself.*]

BLANCHE: I guess that is what is meant by being in love . . . [STELLA *looks up with a radiant smile.*] Stella—

STELLA: What?

BLANCHE: [*In an uneasy rush.*] I haven't asked you the things you probably thought I was going to ask. And so I'll expect you to be understanding about what I have to tell *you.*

STELLA: What, Blanche? [*Her face turns anxious.*]

BLANCHE: Well, Stella—you're going to reproach me, I know that you're bound to reproach me—but before you do—take into consideration—you left! I stayed and struggled! You came to New Orleans and looked out for yourself! I stayed at Belle Reve and tried to hold it together! I'm not meaning this in any reproachful way, but *all* the burden descended on *my* shoulders.

STELLA: The best I could do was make my own living, Blanche.

[BLANCHE *begins to shake again with intensity.*]

BLANCHE: I know, I know. But you are the one that abandoned Belle Reve, not I! I stayed and fought for it, bled for it, almost died for it!

STELLA: Stop this hysterical outburst and tell me what's happened? What do you mean fought and bled? What kind of—

BLANCHE: I knew you would, Stella. I knew you would take this attitude about it!

STELLA: About—what?—please!

BLANCHE: [*Slowly.*] The loss—the loss . . .

STELLA: Belle Reve? Lost, is it? No!

BLANCHE: Yes, Stella.

[*They stare at each other across the yellow-checked linoleum of the table.* BLANCHE *slowly nods her head and* STELLA *looks slowly down at her hands folded on the table. The music of the "Blue Piano" grows louder.* BLANCHE *touches her handkerchief to her forehead.*]

STELLA: But how did it go? What happened?

BLANCHE: [*Springing up.*] You're a fine one to ask me how it went!

STELLA: Blanche!

BLANCHE: You're a fine one to sit there *accusing me* of it!

STELLA: *Blanche!*

BLANCHE: I, I, I took the blows in my face and my body! All of those deaths! The long parade to the graveyard! Father, Mother! Margaret, that dreadful way! So big with it, it couldn't be put in a coffin! But had to be burned like rubbish! You just came home in time for the funerals, Stella. And funerals are pretty compared to deaths. Funerals are quiet, but deaths—not always. Sometimes their breathing is hoarse, and sometimes it rattles, and sometimes they even cry out to you, "Don't let me go!" Even the old, sometimes, say, "Don't let me go." As if you were able to stop them! But funerals are quiet, with pretty flowers. And, oh, what gorgeous boxes they pack them away in! Unless you were there at the bed when they cried out, "Hold me!" you'd never suspect there was the struggle for breath and bleeding. You didn't dream, but I saw! *Saw! Saw!* And now you sit there telling me with your eyes that I let the place go! How in hell do you think all that sickness and dying was paid for? Death is expensive, Miss Stella! And old Cousin Jessie's right after Margaret's, hers! Why, the Grim Reaper had put up his tent on our doorstep! . . . Stella. Belle Reve was his headquarters! Honey—that's how it slipped through my fingers! Which of them left us a fortune? Which of them left a cent of insurance even? Only poor Jessie—one hundred to pay for her coffin. That was all, Stella! And I with my pitiful salary at the school. Yes, accuse me! Sit there and stare at me, thinking I let the place go! *I* let the place go? Where were *you!* In bed with your—Polack!

STELLA: [*Springing.*] Blanche! You be still! That's enough! [*She starts out.*]

BLANCHE: Where are you going?

STELLA: I'm going into the bathroom to wash my face.

BLANCHE: Oh, Stella, Stella, you're crying!

STELLA: Does that surprise you?

BLANCHE: Forgive me—I didn't mean to—

[*The sound of men's voices is heard.* STELLA *goes into the bathroom, closing the door behind her. When the men appear, and* BLANCHE *realizes it must be* STANLEY *returning, she moves uncertainly from the bathroom door to the dressing table, looking apprehensively toward the front door.* STANLEY *enters, followed by* STEVE *and* MITCH. STANLEY *pauses near his door,* STEVE *by the foot of the spiral stair, and* MITCH *is slightly above and to the right of them, about to go out. As the men enter, we hear some of the following dialogue.*]

STANLEY: Is that how he got it?

STEVE: Sure that's how he got it. He hit the old weather-bird for 300 bucks on a six-number-ticket.

MITCH: Don't tell him those things; he'll believe it. [MITCH *starts out.*]

STANLEY: [*Restraining* MITCH.] Hey, Mitch—come back here.

[BLANCHE, *at the sound of voices, retires in the bedroom. She picks up* STANLEY's *photo from dressing table, looks at it, puts it down. When* STANLEY *enters the apartment, she darts and hides behind the screen at the head of bed.*]

STEVE: [*To* STANLEY *and* MITCH.] Hey, are we playin' poker tomorrow?

STANLEY: Sure—at Mitch's.

MITCH: [*Hearing this, returns quickly to the stair rail.*] No—not at my place. My mother's still sick!

STANLEY: Okay, at my place . . . [MITCH *starts out again.*] But you bring the beer!

[MITCH *pretends not to hear—calls out "Good night, all," and goes out, singing.* EUNICE's *voice is heard, above.*]

EUNICE: Break it up down there! I made the spaghetti dish and ate it myself.

STEVE: [*Going upstairs.*] I told you and phoned you we was playing. [*To the men.*] Jax[8] beer!

8. A local brand.

EUNICE: You never phoned me once.

STEVE: I told you at breakfast—and phoned you at lunch . . .

EUNICE: Well, never mind about that. You just get yourself home here once in a while.

STEVE: You want it in the papers?

[More laughter and shouts of parting come from the men. STANLEY throws the screen door of the kitchen open and comes in. He is of medium height, about five feet eight or nine, and strongly, compactly built. Animal joy in his being is implicit in all his movements and attitudes. Since earliest manhood the center of his life has been pleasure with women, the giving and taking of it, not with weak indulgence, dependently, but with the power and pride of a richly feathered male bird among hens. Branching out from this complete and satisfying center are all the auxiliary channels of his life, such as his heartiness with men, his appreciation of rough humor, his love of good drink and food and games, his car, his radio, everything that is his, that bears his emblem of the gaudy seed-bearer. He sizes women up at a glance, with sexual classifications, crude images flashing into his mind and determining the way he smiles at them.]

BLANCHE: [Drawing involuntarily back from his stare.] You must be Stanley. I'm Blanche.

STANLEY: Stella's sister?

BLANCHE: Yes.

STANLEY: H'lo. Where's the little woman?

BLANCHE: In the bathroom.

STANLEY: Oh. Didn't know you were coming in town.

BLANCHE: I—uh—

STANLEY: Where you from, Blanche?

BLANCHE: Why, I—live in Laurel.

[He has crossed to the closet and removed the whiskey bottle.]

STANLEY: In Laurel, huh? Oh, yeah. Yeah, in Laurel, that's right. Not in my territory. Liquor goes fast in hot weather. [He holds the bottle to the light to observe its depletion.] Have a shot?

BLANCHE: No, I—rarely touch it.

STANLEY: Some people rarely touch it, but it touches them often.

BLANCHE: [Faintly.] Ha-ha.

STANLEY: My clothes're stickin' to me. Do you mind if I make myself comfortable? [He starts to remove his shirt.]

BLANCHE: Please, please do.

STANLEY: Be comfortable is my motto.

BLANCHE: It's mine, too. It's hard to stay looking fresh. I haven't washed or even powdered my face and—here you are!

STANLEY: You know you can catch cold sitting around in damp things, especially when you been exercising hard like bowling is. You're a teacher, aren't you?

BLANCHE: Yes.

STANLEY: What do you teach, Blanche?

BLANCHE: English.

STANLEY: I never was a very good English student. How long you here for, Blanche?

BLANCHE: I—don't know yet.

STANLEY: You going to shack up here?

BLANCHE: I thought I would if it's not inconvenient for you all.

STANLEY: Good.

BLANCHE: Traveling wears me out.

STANLEY: Well, take it easy.

[*A cat screeches near the window.* BLANCHE *springs up.*]

BLANCHE: What's that?

STANLEY: Cats . . . Hey, Stella!

STELLA: [*Faintly, from the bathroom.*] Yes, Stanley.

STANLEY: Haven't fallen in, have you? [*He grins at* BLANCHE. *She tries unsuccessfully to smile back. There is a silence.*] I'm afraid I'll strike you as being the unrefined type. Stella's spoke of you a good deal. You were married once, weren't you?

[*The music of the polka rises up, faint in the distance.*]

BLANCHE: Yes. When I was quite young.

STANLEY: What happened?

BLANCHE: The boy—the boy died. [*She sinks back down.*] I'm afraid I'm—going to be sick! [*Her head falls on her arms.*]

SCENE 2

It is six o'clock the following evening. BLANCHE *is bathing.* STELLA *is completing her toilette.* BLANCHE's *dress, a flowered print, is laid out on* STELLA's *bed.*

STANLEY *enters the kitchen from outside, leaving the door open on the perpetual "Blue Piano" around the corner.*

STANLEY: What's all this monkey doings?

STELLA: Oh, Stan! [*She jumps up and kisses him, which he accepts with lordly composure.*] I'm taking Blanche to Galatoire's[9] for supper and then to a show, because it's your poker night.

STANLEY: How about my supper, huh? I'm not going to no Galatoire's for supper!

STELLA: I put you a cold plate on ice.

STANLEY: Well, isn't that just dandy!

STELLA: I'm going to try to keep Blanche out till the party breaks up because I don't know how she would take it. So we'll go to one of the little places in the Quarter afterward and you'd better give me some money.

STANLEY: Where is she?

STELLA: She's soaking in a hot tub to quiet her nerves. She's terribly upset.

9. A famous old restaurant on Bourbon Street in the French Quarter.

STANLEY: Over what?

STELLA: She's been through such an ordeal.

STANLEY: Yeah?

STELLA: Stan, we've—lost Belle Reve!

STANLEY: The place in the country?

STELLA: Yes.

STANLEY: How?

STELLA: [*Vaguely.*] Oh, it had to be—sacrificed or something. [*There is a pause while* STANLEY *considers.* STELLA *is changing into her dress.*] When she comes in be sure to say something nice about her appearance. And, oh! Don't mention the baby. I haven't said anything yet, I'm waiting until she gets in a quieter condition.

STANLEY: [*Ominously.*] So?

STELLA: And try to understand her and be nice to her, Stan.

BLANCHE: [*Singing in the bathroom.*] "From the land of the sky blue water, They brought a captive maid!"

STELLA: She wasn't expecting to find us in such a small place. You see I'd tried to gloss things over a little in my letters.

STANLEY: So?

STELLA: And admire her dress and tell her she's looking wonderful. That's important with Blanche. Her little weakness!

STANLEY: Yeah. I get the idea. Now let's skip back a little to where you said the country place was disposed of.

STELLA: Oh!—yes . . .

STANLEY: How about that? Let's have a few more details on that subjeck.

STELLA: It's best not to talk much about it until she's calmed down.

STANLEY: So that's the deal, huh? Sister Blanche cannot be annoyed with business details right now!

STELLA: You saw how she was last night.

STANLEY: Uh-hum, I saw how she was. Now let's have a gander at the bill of sale.

STELLA: I haven't seen any.

STANLEY: She didn't show you no papers, no deed of sale or nothing like that, huh?

STELLA: It seems like it wasn't sold.

STANLEY: Well, what in hell was it then, give away? To charity?

STELLA: Shhh! She'll hear you.

STANLEY: I don't care if she hears me. Let's see the papers!

STELLA: There weren't any papers, she didn't show any papers, I don't care about papers.

STANLEY: Have you ever heard of the Napoleonic code?[1]

STELLA: No, Stanley, I haven't heard of the Napoleonic code and if I have, I don't see what it—

1. This codification of French law (1802), made by Napoleon as emperor, is the basis for Louisiana's civil law.

STANLEY: Let me enlighten you on a point or two, baby.

STELLA: Yes?

STANLEY: In the state of Louisiana we have the Napoleonic code according to which what belongs to the wife belongs to the husband and vice versa. For instance if I had a piece of property, or you had a piece of property—

STELLA: My head is swimming!

STANLEY: All right. I'll wait till she gets through soaking in a hot tub and then I'll inquire if *she* is acquainted with the Napoleonic code. It looks to me like you have been swindled, baby, and when you're swindled under the Napoleonic code I'm swindled *too*. And I don't like to be *swindled*.

STELLA: There's plenty of time to ask her questions later but if you do now she'll go to pieces again. I don't undertand what happened to Belle Reve but you don't know how ridiculous you are being when you suggest that my sister or I or anyone of our family could have perpetrated a swindle on anyone else.

STANLEY: Then where's the money if the place was sold?

STELLA: Not sold—*lost, lost!* [*He stalks into bedroom, and she follows him.*] Stanley!

[*He pulls open the wardrobe trunk standing in middle of room and jerks out an armful of dresses.*]

STANLEY: Open your eyes to this stuff! You think she got them out of a teacher's pay?

STELLA: Hush!

STANLEY: Look at these feathers and furs that she come here to preen herself in! What's this here? A solid-gold dress, I believe! And this one! What is these here? Fox-pieces! [*He blows on them.*] Genuine fox fur-pieces, a half a mile long! Where are your fox-pieces, Stella? Bushy snowwhite ones, no less! Where are your white fox-pieces?

STELLA: Those are inexpensive summer furs that Blanche has had a long time.

STANLEY: I got an acquaintance who deals in this sort of merchandise. I'll have him in here to appraise it. I'm willing to bet you there's thousands of dollars invested in this stuff here!

STELLA: Don't be such an idiot, Stanley!

[*He hurls the furs to the day bed. Then he jerks open small drawer in the trunk and pulls up a fistful of costume jewelry.*]

STANLEY: And what have we here? The treasure chest of a pirate!

STELLA: Oh, Stanley!

STANLEY: Pearls! Ropes of them! What is this sister of yours, a deep-sea diver? Bracelets of solid gold, too! Where are your pearls and gold bracelets?

STELLA: Shhh! Be still, Stanley!

STANLEY: And diamonds! A crown for an empress!

STELLA: A rhinestone tiara she wore to a costume ball.

STANLEY: What's rhinestone?

STELLA: Next door to glass.

STANLEY: Are you kidding? I have an acquaintance that works in a jewelry store. I'll have him in here to make an appraisal of this. Here's your plantation, or what was left of it, here!

STELLA: You have no idea how stupid and horrid you're being! Now close that trunk before she comes out of the bathroom!

[*He kicks the trunk partly closed and sits on the kitchen table.*]

STANLEY: The Kowalskis and the DuBoises have different notions.

STELLA: [*Angrily.*] Indeed they have, thank heavens!—*I'm* going outside. [*She snatches up her white hat and gloves and crosses to the outside door.*] You come out with me while Blanche is getting dressed.

STANLEY: Since when do you give me orders?

STELLA: Are you going to stay here and insult her?

STANLEY: You're damn tootin' I'm going to stay here.

[STELLA *goes out to the porch.* BLANCHE *comes out of the bathroom in a red satin robe.*]

BLANCHE: [*Airily.*] Hello, Stanley! Here I am, all freshly bathed and scented, and feeling like a brand new human being!

[*He lights a cigarette.*]

STANLEY: That's good.

BLANCHE: [*Drawing the curtains at the windows.*] Excuse me while I slip on my pretty new dress!

STANLEY: Go right ahead, Blanche.

[*She closes the drapes between the rooms.*]

BLANCHE: I understand there's to be a little card party to which we ladies are cordially *not* invited!

STANLEY: [*Ominously.*] Yeah?

[BLANCHE *throws off her robe and slips into a flowered print dress.*]

BLANCHE: Where's Stella?

STANLEY: Out on the porch.

BLANCHE: I'm going to ask a favor of you in a moment.

STANLEY: What could that be, I wonder?

BLANCHE: Some buttons in back! You may enter! [*He crosses through drapes with a smoldering look.*] How do I look?

STANLEY: You look all right.

BLANCHE: Many thanks! Now the buttons!

STANLEY: I can't do nothing with them.

BLANCHE: You men with your big clumsy fingers. May I have a drag on your cig?

STANLEY: Have one for yourself.

BLANCHE: Why, thanks! . . . It looks like my trunk has exploded.

STANLEY: Me an' Stella were helping you unpack.

BLANCHE: Well, you certainly did a fast and thorough job of it!

STANLEY: It looks like you raided some stylish shops in Paris.

BLANCHE: Ha-ha! Yes—clothes are my passion!

STANLEY: What does it cost for a string of fur-pieces like that?

BLANCHE: Why, those were a tribute from an admirer of mine!

STANLEY: He must have had a lot of—admiration!

BLANCHE: Oh, in my youth I excited some admiration. But look at me now! [*She smiles at him radiantly.*] Would you think it possible that I was once considered to be—attractive?

STANLEY: Your looks are okay.

BLANCHE: I was fishing for a compliment, Stanley.

STANLEY: I don't go in for that stuff.

BLANCHE: What—stuff?

STANLEY: Compliments to women about their looks. I never met a woman that didn't know if she was good-looking or not without being told, and some of them give themselves credit for more than they've got. I once went out with a doll who said to me, "I am the glamorous type, I am the glamorous type!" I said, "So what?"

BLANCHE: And what did she say then?

STANLEY: She didn't say nothing. That shut her up like a clam.

BLANCHE: Did it end the romance?

STANLEY: It ended the conversation—that was all. Some men are took in by this Hollywood glamor stuff and some men are not.

BLANCHE: I'm sure you belong in the second category.

STANLEY: That's right.

BLANCHE: I cannot imagine any witch of a woman casting a spell over you.

STANLEY: That's—right.

BLANCHE: You're simple, straightforward and honest, a little bit on the primitive side I should think. To interest you a woman would have to—[*She pauses with an indefinite gesture.*]

STANLEY: [*Slowly.*] Lay . . . her cards on the table.

BLANCHE: [*Smiling.*] Well, I never cared for wishy-washy people. That was why, when you walked in here last night, I said to myself—"My sister has married a man!"—Of course that was all that I could tell about you.

STANLEY: [*Booming.*] Now let's cut the re-bop[2]!

BLANCHE: [*Pressing hands to her ears.*] Ouuuuu!

STELLA: [*Calling from the steps.*] Stanley! You come out here and let Blanche finish dressing!

BLANCHE: I'm through dressing, honey.

STELLA: Well, you come out, then.

STANLEY: Your sister and I are having a little talk.

BLANCHE: [*Lightly.*] Honey, do me a favor. Run to the drugstore and get me a lemon Coke with plenty of chipped ice in it!—Will you do that for me, sweetie?

2. Nonsense syllables (from "bop," a form of jazz).

STELLA: [*Uncertainly.*] Yes. [*She goes around the corner of the building.*]

BLANCHE: The poor little thing was out there listening to us, and I have an idea she doesn't understand you as well as I do. . . . All right; now, Mr. Kowalski, let us proceed without any more double-talk. I'm ready to answer all questions. I've nothing to hide. What is it?

STANLEY: There is such a thing in this state of Louisiana as the Napoleonic code, according to which whatever belongs to my wife is also mine—and vice versa.

BLANCHE: My, but you have an impressive judicial air!

[*She sprays herself with her atomizer; then playfully sprays him with it. He seizes the atomizer and slams it down on the dresser. She throws back her head and laughs.*]

STANLEY: If I didn't know that you was my wife's sister I'd get ideas about you!

BLANCHE: Such as what!

STANLEY: Don't play so dumb. You know what!

BLANCHE: [*She puts the atomizer on the table.*] All right. Cards on the table. That suits me. [*She turns to* STANLEY.] I know I fib a good deal. After all, a woman's charm is fifty per cent illusion, but when a thing is important I tell the truth, and this is the truth: I haven't cheated my sister or you or anyone else as long as I have lived.

STANLEY: Where's the papers? In the trunk?

BLANCHE: Everything that I own is in that trunk. [STANLEY *crosses to the trunk, shoves it roughly open and begins to open compartments.*] What in the name of heaven are you thinking of! What's in the back of that little boy's mind of yours? That I am absconding with something, attempting some kind of treachery on my sister?—Let me do that! It will be faster and simpler . . . [*She crosses to the trunk and takes out a box.*] I keep my papers mostly in this tin box. [*She opens it.*]

STANLEY: What's them underneath? [*He indicates another sheaf of paper.*]

BLANCHE: These are love-letters, yellowing with antiquity, all from one boy. [*He snatches them up. She speaks fiercely.*] Give those back to me!

STANLEY: I'll have a look at them first!

BLANCHE: The touch of your hands insults them!

STANLEY: Don't pull that stuff!

[*He rips off the ribbon and starts to examine them.* BLANCHE *snatches them from him, and they cascade to the floor.*]

BLANCHE: Now that you've touched them I'll burn them!

STANLEY: [*Staring, baffled.*] What in hell are they?

BLANCHE: [*On the floor gathering them up.*] Poems a dead boy wrote. I hurt him the way that you would like to hurt me, but you can't! I'm not young and vulnerable any more. But my young husband was and I—never mind about that! Just give them back to me!

STANLEY: What do you mean by saying you'll have to burn them?

BLANCHE: I'm sorry, I must have lost my head for a moment. Everyone has something he won't let others touch because of their—intimate nature . . . [*She now seems faint with exhaustion and she sits down with the strong box and puts on a pair of glasses and goes methodically through a large stack of papers.*] Ambler & Ambler. Hmmmmm. . . . Crabtree. . . . More Ambler & Ambler.

STANLEY: What is Ambler & Ambler?

BLANCHE: A firm that made loans on the place.

STANLEY: Then it *was* lost on a mortgage?

BLANCHE: [*Touching her forehead.*] That must've been what happened.

STANLEY: I don't want no ifs, ands or buts! What's all the rest of them papers?

[*She hands him the entire box. He carries it to the table and starts to examine the papers.*]

BLANCHE: [*Picking up a large envelope containing more papers.*] There are thousands of papers, stretching back over hundreds of years, affecting Belle Reve as, piece by piece, our improvident grandfathers and father and uncles and brothers exchanged the land for their epic fornications—to put it plainly! [*She removes her glasses with an exhausted laugh.*] The four-letter word deprived us of our plantation, till finally all that was left—and Stella can verify that!—was the house itself and about twenty acres of ground, including a graveyard, to which now all but Stella and I have retreated. [*She pours the contents of the envelope on the table.*] Here all of them are, all papers! I hereby endow you with them! Take them, peruse them—commit them to memory, even! I think it's wonderfully fitting that Belle Reve should finally be this bunch of old papers in your big, capable hands! . . . I wonder if Stella's come back with my lemon Coke . . . [*She leans back and closes her eyes.*]

STANLEY: I have a lawyer acquaintance who will study these out.

BLANCHE: Present them to him with a box of aspirin tablets.

STANLEY: [*Becoming somewhat sheepish.*] You see, under the Napoleonic code— a man has to take an interest in his wife's affairs—especially now that she's going to have a baby.

[BLANCHE *opens her eyes. The "Blue Piano" sounds louder.*]

BLANCHE: Stella? Stella going to have a baby? [*Dreamily.*] I didn't know she was going to have a baby! [*She gets up and crosses to the outside door.* STELLA *appears around the corner with a carton from the drugstore.* STANLEY *goes into the bedroom with the envelope and the box. The inner rooms fade to darkness and the outside wall of the house is visible.* BLANCHE *meets* STELLA *at the foot of the steps to the sidewalk.*] Stella, Stella for star! How lovely to have a baby! It's all right. Everything's all right.

STELLA: I'm sorry he did that to you.

BLANCHE: Oh, I guess he's just not the type that goes for jasmine perfume, but maybe he's what we need to mix with our blood now that we've lost Belle Reve. We thrashed it out. I feel a bit shaky, but I think I handled it nicely, I laughed and treated it all as a joke. [STEVE *and* PABLO *appear, carrying a case of beer.*] I called him a little boy and laughed and flirted. Yes, I was flirting with your husband! [*As the men approach.*] The guests are gathering for the poker party. [*The two men pass between them, and enter the house.*] Which way do we go now, Stella—this way?

STELLA: No, this way. [*She leads* BLANCHE *away.*]

BLANCHE: [*Laughing.*] The blind are leading the blind!

[*A tamale* VENDOR *is heard calling.*]

VENDOR'S VOICE: Red-hot!

SCENE 3. THE POKER NIGHT

There is a picture of Van Gogh's of a billiard-parlor at night.[3] *The kitchen now suggests that sort of lurid nocturnal brilliance, the raw colors of childhood's spectrum. Over the yellow linoleum of the kitchen table hangs an electric bulb with a vivid green glass shade. The poker players—* STANLEY, STEVE, MITCH *and* PABLO—*wear colored shirts, solid blues, a purple, a red-and-white check, a light green, and they are men at the peak of their physical manhood, as coarse and direct and powerful as the primary colors. There are vivid slices of watermelon on the table, whiskey bottles and glasses. The bedroom is relatively dim with only the light that spills between the portieres and through the wide window on the street.*

For a moment, there is absorbed silence as a hand is dealt.

STEVE: Anything wild this deal?

PABLO: One-eyed jacks are wild.

STEVE: Give me two cards.

PABLO: You, Mitch?

MITCH: I'm out.

PABLO: One.

MITCH: Anyone want a shot?

STANLEY: Yeah. Me.

PABLO: Why don't somebody go to the Chinaman's and bring back a load of chop suey?

STANLEY: When I'm losing you want to eat! Ante up! Openers? Openers! Get y'r ass off the table, Mitch. Nothing belongs on a poker table but cards, chips and whiskey. [*He lurches up and tosses some watermelon rinds to the floor.*]

MITCH: Kind of on your high horse, ain't you?

STANLEY: How many?

STEVE: Give me three.

STANLEY: One.

MITCH: I'm out again. I oughta go home pretty soon.

STANLEY: Shut up.

MITCH: I gotta sick mother. She don't go to sleep until I come in at night.

STANLEY: Then why don't you stay home with her?

3. *The Night Café,* by Vincent Van Gogh, Dutch post-impressionist painter (1853–1890). *The Poker Night* was Williams's first title for *A Streetcar Named Desire.*

MITCH: She says to go out, so I go, but I don't enjoy it. All the while I keep wondering how she is.

STANLEY: Aw, for the sake of Jesus, go home, then!

PABLO: What've you got?

STEVE: Spade flush.

MITCH: You all are married. But I'll be alone when she goes.—I'm going to the bathroom.

STANLEY: Hurry back and we'll fix you a sugar-tit.

MITCH: Aw, go rut. [*He crosses through the bedroom into the bathroom.*]

STEVE: [*Dealing a hand.*] Seven card stud. [*Telling his joke as he deals.*] This ole farmer is out in back of his house sittin' down th'owing corn to the chickens when all at once he hears a loud cackle and this young hen comes lickety split around the side of the house with the rooster right behind her and gaining on her fast.

STANLEY: [*Impatient with the story.*] Deal!

STEVE: But when the rooster catches sight of the farmer th'owing the corn he puts on the brakes and lets the hen get away and starts pecking corn. And the old farmer says, "Lord God, I hopes I never gits *that* hongry!"

[STEVE *and* PABLO *laugh. The sisters appear around the corner of the building.*]

STELLA: The game is still going on.

BLANCHE: How do I look?

STELLA: Lovely, Blanche.

BLANCHE: I feel so hot and frazzled. Wait till I powder before you open the door. Do I look done in?

STELLA: Why no. You are as fresh as a daisy.

BLANCHE: One that's been picked a few days.

[STELLA *opens the door and they enter.*]

STELLA: Well, well, well. I see you boys are still at it?

STANLEY: Where you been?

STELLA: Blanche and I took in a show. Blanche, this is Mr. Gonzales and Mr. Hubbell.

BLANCHE: Please don't get up.

STANLEY: Nobody's going to get up, so don't be worried.

STELLA: How much longer is this game going to continue?

STANLEY: Till we get ready to quit.

BLANCHE: Poker is so fascinating. Could I kibitz?

STANLEY: You could not. Why don't you women go up and sit with Eunice?

STELLA: Because it is nearly two-thirty. [BLANCHE *crosses into the bedroom and partially closes the portieres.*] Couldn't you call it quits after one more hand?

[*A chair scrapes.* STANLEY *gives a loud whack of his hand on her thigh.*]

STELLA: [*Sharply.*] That's not fun, Stanley. [*The men laugh.* STELLA *goes into the bedroom.*] It makes me so mad when he does that in front of people.

BLANCHE: I think I will bathe.

STELLA: Again?

BLANCHE: My nerves are in knots. Is the bathroom occupied?

STELLA: I don't know.

[BLANCHE *knocks.* MITCH *opens the door and comes out, still wiping his hands on a towel.*]

BLANCHE: Oh!—good evening.

MITCH: Hello. [*He stares at her.*]

STELLA: Blanche, this is Harold Mitchell. My sister, Blanche DuBois.

MITCH: [*With awkward courtesy.*] How do you do, Miss DuBois.

STELLA: How is your mother now, Mitch?

MITCH: About the same, thanks. She appreciated your sending over that custard.—Excuse me, please.

[*He crosses slowly back into the kitchen, glancing back at* BLANCHE *and coughing a little shyly. He realizes he still has the towel in his hands and with an embarrassed laugh hands it to* STELLA. BLANCHE *looks after him with a certain interest.*]

BLANCHE: That one seems—superior to the others.

STELLA: Yes, he is.

BLANCHE: I thought he had a sort of sensitive look.

STELLA: His mother is sick.

BLANCHE: Is he married?

STELLA: No.

BLANCHE: Is he a wolf?

STELLA: Why, Blanche! [BLANCHE *laughs.*] I don't think he would be.

BLANCHE: What does—what does he do? [*She is unbuttoning her blouse.*]

STELLA: He's on the precision bench in the spare parts department. At the plant Stanley travels for.

BLANCHE: Is that something much?

STELLA: No. Stanley's the only one of his crowd that's likely to get anywhere.

BLANCHE: What makes you think Stanley will?

STELLA: Look at him.

BLANCHE: I've looked at him.

STELLA: Then you should know.

BLANCHE: I'm sorry, but I haven't noticed the stamp of genius even on Stanley's forehead.

[*She takes off the blouse and stands in her pink silk brassiere and white skirt in the light through the portieres. The game has continued in undertones.*]

STELLA: It isn't on his forehead and it isn't genius.

BLANCHE: Oh. Well, what is it, and where? I would like to know.

STELLA: It's a drive that he has. You're standing in the light, Blanche!

BLANCHE: Oh, am I!

[*She moves out of the yellow streak of light.* STELLA *has removed her dress and put on a light blue satin kimona.*]

STELLA: [*With girlish laughter.*] You ought to see their wives.

BLANCHE: [*Laughingly.*] I can imagine. Big, beefy things, I suppose.

STELLA: You know that one upstairs? [*More laughter.*] One time [*Laughing.*] the plaster—[*Laughing.*] cracked—

STANLEY: You hens cut out that conversation in there!

STELLA: You can't hear us.

STANLEY: Well, you can hear me and I said to hush up!

STELLA: This is my house and I'll talk as much as I want to!

BLANCHE: Stella, don't start a row.

STELLA: He's half drunk!—I'll be out in a minute.

[*She goes into the bathroom.* BLANCHE *rises and crosses leisurely to a small white radio and turns it on.*]

STANLEY: Awright, Mitch, you in?

MITCH: What? Oh!—No, I'm out!

[BLANCHE *moves back into the streak of light. She raises her arms and stretches, as she moves indolently back to the chair. Rhumba music comes over the radio.* MITCH *rises at the table.*]

STANLEY: Who turned that on in there?

BLANCHE: I did. Do you mind?

STANLEY: Turn it off!

STEVE: Aw, let the girls have their music.

PABLO: Sure, that's good, leave it on!

STEVE: Sounds like Xavier Cugat[4]! [STANLEY *jumps up and, crossing to the radio, turns it off. He stops short at the sight of* BLANCHE *in the chair. She returns his look without flinching. Then he sits again at the poker table. Two of the men have started arguing hotly.*] I didn't hear you name it.

PABLO: Didn't I name it, Mitch?

MITCH: I wasn't listenin'.

PABLO: What were you doing, then?

STANLEY: He was looking through them drapes. [*He jumps up and jerks roughly at curtains to close them.*] Now deal the hand over again and let's play cards or quit. Some people get ants when they win.

[MITCH *rises as* STANLEY *returns to his seat.*]

STANLEY: [*Yelling.*] Sit down!

MITCH: I'm going to the "head." Deal me out.

PABLO: Sure he's got ants now. Seven five-dollar bills in his pants pocket folded up tight as spitballs.

STEVE: Tomorrow you'll see him at the cashier's window getting them changed into quarters.

4. Cuban band leader, well known for composing and playing rhumbas.

STANLEY: And when he goes home he'll deposit them one by one in a piggy bank his mother give him for Christmas. [*Dealing.*] This game is Spit in the Ocean.

[MITCH *laughs uncomfortably and continues through the portieres. He stops just inside.*]

BLANCHE: [*Softly.*] Hello! The Little Boys' Room is busy right now.

MITCH: We've—been drinking beer.

BLANCHE: I hate beer.

MITCH: It's—a hot weather drink.

BLANCHE: Oh, I don't think so; it always makes me warmer. Have you got any cigs? [*She has slipped on the dark red satin wrapper.*]

MITCH: Sure.

BLANCHE: What kind are they?

MITCH: Luckies.

BLANCHE: Oh, good. What a pretty case. Silver?

MITCH: Yes. Yes; read the inscription.

BLANCHE: Oh, is there an inscription? I can't make it out. [*He strikes a match and moves closer.*] Oh! [*Reading with feigned difficulty.*] "And if God choose, / I shall but love thee better—after—death!" Why, that's from my favorite sonnet by Mrs. Browning[5]!

MITCH: You know it?

BLANCHE: Certainly I do!

MITCH: There's a story connected with that inscription.

BLANCHE: It sounds like a romance.

MITCH: A pretty sad one.

BLANCHE: Oh?

MITCH: The girl's dead now.

BLANCHE: [*In a tone of deep sympathy.*] Oh!

MITCH: She knew she was dying when she give me this. A very strange girl, very sweet—very!

BLANCHE: She must have been fond of you. Sick people have such deep, sincere attachments.

MITCH: That's right, they certainly do.

BLANCHE: Sorrow makes for sincerity, I think.

MITCH: It sure brings it out in people.

BLANCHE: The little there is belongs to people who have experienced some sorrow.

MITCH: I believe you are right about that.

BLANCHE: I'm positive that I am. Show me a person who hasn't known any sorrow and I'll show you a shuperficial—Listen to me! My tongue is a little—thick! You boys are responsible for it. The show let out at eleven and we couldn't come home on account of the poker game so we had to go some-

5. Elizabeth Barrett Browning, 19th-century British poet, was most famous for her sequence of love poems, *Sonnets from the Portuguese.*

where and drink. I'm not accustomed to having more than one drink. Two
is the limit—and *three!* [*She laughs.*] Tonight I had three.

STANLEY: Mitch!

MITCH: Deal me out. I'm talking to Miss—

BLANCHE: DuBois.

MITCH: Miss DuBois?

BLANCHE: It's a French name. It means woods and Blanche means white, so the
two together mean white woods. Like an orchard in spring! You can remember it by that.

MITCH: You're French?

BLANCHE: We are French by extraction. Our first American ancestors were
French Huguenots.

MITCH: You are Stella's sister, are you not?

BLANCHE: Yes, Stella is my precious little sister. I call her little in spite of the
fact she's somewhat older than I. Just slightly. Less than a year. Will you do
something for me?

MITCH: Sure. What?

BLANCHE: I bought this adorable little colored paper lantern at a Chinese shop
on Bourbon. Put it over the light bulb! Will you, please?

MITCH: Be glad to.

BLANCHE: I can't stand a naked light bulb, any more than I can a rude remark
or a vulgar action.

MITCH: [*Adjusting the lantern.*] I guess we strike you as being a pretty rough
bunch.

BLANCHE: I'm very adaptable—to circumstances.

MITCH: Well, that's a good thing to be. You are visiting Stanley and Stella?

BLANCHE: Stella hasn't been so well lately, and I came down to help her for a
while. She's very run down.

MITCH: You're not—?

BLANCHE: Married? No, no. I'm an old maid schoolteacher!

MITCH: You may teach school but you're certainly not an old maid.

BLANCHE: Thank you, sir! I appreciate your gallantry!

MITCH: So you are in the teaching profession?

BLANCHE: Yes. Ah, yes . . .

MITCH: Grade school or high school or—

STANLEY: [*Bellowing.*] Mitch!

MITCH: Coming!

BLANCHE: Gracious, what lung-power! . . . I teach high school. In Laurel.

MITCH: What do you teach? What subject?

BLANCHE: Guess!

MITCH: I bet you teach art or music? [BLANCHE *laughs delicately.*] Of course I
could be wrong. You might teach arithmetic.

BLANCHE: Never arithmetic, sir; never arithmetic! [*With a laugh.*] I don't even
know my multiplication tables! No, I have the misfortune of being an
English instructor. I attempt to instill a bunch of bobby-soxers and drugstore
Romeos with reverence for Hawthorne and Whitman and Poe!

MITCH: I guess that some of them are more interested in other things.

BLANCHE: How very right you are! Their literary heritage is not what most of them treasure above all else! But they're sweet things! And in the spring, it's touching to notice them making their first discovery of love! As if nobody had ever known it before! [*The bathroom door opens and* STELLA *comes out.* BLANCHE *continues talking to* MITCH.] Oh! Have you finished? Wait—I'll turn on the radio.

[*She turns the knobs on the radio and it begins to play "Wien, Wien, nur du allein."*[6] BLANCHE *waltzes to the music with romantic gestures.* MITCH *is delighted and moves in awkward imitation like a dancing bear.* STANLEY *stalks fiercely through the portieres into the bedroom. He crosses to the small white radio and snatches it off the table. With a shouted oath, he tosses the instrument out the window.*]

STELLA: Drunk—drunk—animal thing, you! [*She rushes through to the poker table.*] All of you—please go home! If any of you have one spark of decency in you—

BLANCHE: [*Wildly.*] Stella, watch out, he's—

[STANLEY *charges after* STELLA.]

MEN: [*Feebly.*] Take it easy, Stanley. Easy, fellow.—Let's all—

STELLA: You lay your hands on me and I'll—

[*She backs out of sight. He advances and disappears. There is the sound of a blow.* STELLA *cries out.* BLANCHE *screams and runs into the kitchen. The men rush forward and there is grappling and cursing. Something is overturned with a crash.*]

BLANCHE: [*Shrilly.*] My sister is going to have a baby!

MITCH: This is terrible.

BLANCHE: Lunacy, absolute lunacy!

MITCH: Get him in here, men.

[STANLEY *is forced, pinioned by the two men, into the bedroom. He nearly throws them off. Then all at once he subsides and is limp in their grasp. They speak quietly and lovingly to him and he leans his face on one of their shoulders.*]

STELLA: [*In a high, unnatural voice, out of sight.*] I want to go away, I want to go away!

MITCH: Poker shouldn't be played in a house with women.

[BLANCHE *rushes into the bedroom.*]

BLANCHE: I want my sister's clothes! We'll go to that woman's upstairs!

MITCH: Where is the clothes?

BLANCHE: [*Opening the closet.*] I've got them! [*She rushes through to* STELLA.] Stella, Stella, precious! Dear, dear little sister, don't be afraid!

6. "Vienna, Vienna, you are my only," a waltz from an operetta by Franz Lehár (1870–1948).

[*With her arm around* STELLA, BLANCHE *guides her to the outside door and upstairs.*]

STANLEY: [*Dully.*] What's the matter; what's happened?
MITCH: You just blew your top, Stan.
PABLO: He's okay, now.
STEVE: Sure, my boy's okay!
MITCH: Put him on the bed and get a wet towel.
PABLO: I think coffee would do him a world of good, now.
STANLEY: [*Thickly.*] I want water.
MITCH: Put him under the shower!

[*The men talk quietly as they lead him to the bathroom.*]

STANLEY: Let the rut go of me, you sons of bitches!

[*Sounds of blows are heard. The water goes on full tilt.*]

STEVE: Let's get quick out of here!

[*They rush to the poker table and sweep up their winnings on their way out.*]

MITCH: [*Sadly but firmly.*] Poker should not be played in a house with women.

[*The door closes on them and the place is still. The Negro entertainers in the bar around the corner play "Paper Doll"[7] slow and blue. After a moment* STANLEY *comes out of the bathroom dripping water and still in his clinging wet polka dot drawers.*]

STANLEY: Stella! [*There is a pause.*] My baby doll's left me! [*He breaks into sobs. Then he goes to the phone and dials, still shuddering with sobs.*] Eunice? I want my baby! [*He waits a moment; then he hangs up and dials again.*] Eunice! I'll keep on ringin' until I talk with my *baby*! [*An indistinguishable shrill voice is heard. He hurls phone to floor. Dissonant brass and piano sounds as the rooms dim out to darkness and the outer walls appear in the night light. The "Blue Piano" plays for a brief interval. Finally,* STANLEY *stumbles half-dressed out to the porch and down the wooden steps to the pavement before the building. There he throws back his head like a baying hound and bellows his wife's name:* "STELLA! STELLA, *sweetheart!* STELLA!"] Stell-*lahhhhh*!
EUNICE: [*Calling down from the door of her upper apartment.*] Quit that howling out there an' go back to bed!
STANLEY: I want my baby down here. Stella, Stella!
EUNICE: She ain't comin' down so you quit! Or you'll git th' law on you!
STANLEY: Stella!
EUNICE: You can't beat on a woman an' then call 'er back! She won't come! And her goin' t' have a baby! . . . You stinker! You whelp of a Polack, you! I hope they do haul you in and turn the fire hose on you, same as the last time!
STANLEY: [*Humbly.*] Eunice, I want my girl to come down with me!

7. Popular song of the early 1940s.

EUNICE: Hah! [*She slams her door.*]

STANLEY: [*With heaven-splitting violence.*] STELL-LAHHHHH!

[*The low-tone clarinet moans. The door upstairs opens again.* STELLA *slips down the rickety stairs in her robe. Her eyes are glistening with tears and her hair loose about her throat and shoulders. They stare at each other. Then they come together with low, animal moans. He falls to his knees on the steps and presses his face to her belly, curving a little with maternity. Her eyes go blind with tenderness as she catches his head and raises him level with her. He snatches the screen door open and lifts her off her feet and bears her into the dark flat.* BLANCHE *comes out the upper landing in her robe and slips fearfully down the steps.*]

BLANCHE: Where is my little sister? Stella? Stella?

[*She stops before the dark entrance of her sister's flat. Then catches her breath as if struck. She rushes down to the walk before the house. She looks right and left as if for a sanctuary. The music fades away.* MITCH *appears from around the corner.*]

MITCH: Miss DuBois?

BLANCHE: Oh!

MITCH: All quiet on the Potomac now?

BLANCHE: She ran downstairs and went back in there with him.

MITCH: Sure she did.

BLANCHE: I'm terrified!

MITCH: Ho-ho! There's nothing to be scared of. They're crazy about each other.

BLANCHE: I'm not used to such—

MITCH: Naw, it's a shame this had to happen when you just got here. But don't take it serious.

BLANCHE: Violence! Is so—

MITCH: Set down on the steps and have a cigarette with me.

BLANCHE: I'm not properly dressed.

MITCH: That don't make no difference in the Quarter.

BLANCHE: Such a pretty silver case.

MITCH: I showed you the inscription, didn't I?

BLANCHE: Yes. [*During the pause, she looks up at the sky.*] There's so much—so much confusion in the world . . . [*He coughs diffidently.*] Thank you for being so kind! I need kindness now.

SCENE 4

It is early the following morning. There is a confusion of street cries like a choral chant.

STELLA is lying down in the bedroom. Her face is serene in the early morning sunlight. One hand rests on her belly, rounding slightly with new maternity. From the other dangles a book of colored comics. Her eyes and lips have that almost narcotized tranquility that is in the faces of Eastern idols.

The table is sloppy with remains of breakfast and the debris of the preceding night, and STANLEY's *gaudy pyjamas lie across the threshold of the bathroom. The outside door is slightly ajar on a sky of summer brilliance.*

BLANCHE *appears at this door. She has spent a sleepless night and her appearance entirely contrasts with* STELLA's. *She presses her knuckles nervously to her lips as she looks through the door, before entering.*

BLANCHE: Stella?

STELLA: [*Stirring lazily.*] Hmmh?

[BLANCHE *utters a moaning cry and runs into the bedroom, throwing herself down beside* STELLA *in a rush of hysterical tenderness.*]

BLANCHE: Baby, my baby sister!

STELLA: [*Drawing away from her.*] Blanche, what is the matter with you?

[BLANCHE *straightens up slowly and stands beside the bed looking down at her sister with knuckles pressed to her lips.*]

BLANCHE: He's left?

STELLA: Stan? Yes.

BLANCHE: Will he be back?

STELLA: He's gone to get the car greased. Why?

BLANCHE: Why! I've been half crazy, Stella! When I found out you'd been insane enough to come back in here after what happened—I started to rush in after you!

STELLA: I'm glad you didn't.

BLANCHE: What were you thinking of? [STELLA *makes an indefinite gesture.*] Answer me! What? What?

STELLA: Please, Blanche! Sit down and stop yelling.

BLANCHE: All right, Stella. I will repeat the question quietly now. How could you come back in this place last night? Why, you must have slept with him!

[STELLA *gets up in a calm and leisurely way.*]

STELLA: Blanche, I'd forgotten how excitable you are. You're making much too much fuss about this.

BLANCHE: Am I?

STELLA: Yes, you are, Blanche. I know how it must have seemed to you and I'm awful sorry it had to happen, but it wasn't anything as serious as you seem to take it. In the first place, when men are drinking and playing poker anything can happen. It's always a powder-keg. He didn't know what he was doing. . . . He was as good as a lamb when I came back and he's really very, very ashamed of himself.

BLANCHE: And that—that makes it all right?

STELLA: No, it isn't all right for anybody to make such a terrible row, but— people do sometimes. Stanley's always smashed things. Why, on our wedding night—soon as we came in here—he snatched off one of my slippers and rushed about the place smashing light bulbs with it.

BLANCHE: He did—*what?*

STELLA: He smashed all the lightbulbs with the heel of my slipper! [*She laughs.*]

BLANCHE: And you—you *let* him? Didn't *run*, didn't *scream?*

STELLA: I was—sort of—thrilled by it. [*She waits for a moment.*] Eunice and you had breakfast?

BLANCHE: Do you suppose I wanted any breakfast?

STELLA: There's some coffee left on the stove.

BLANCHE: You're so—matter-of-fact about it, Stella.

STELLA: What other can I be? He's taken the radio to get it fixed. It didn't land on the pavement so only one tube was smashed.

BLANCHE: And you are standing there smiling!

STELLA: What do you want me to do?

BLANCHE: Pull yourself together and face the facts.

STELLA: What are they, in your opinion?

BLANCHE: In my opinion? You're married to a madman!

STELLA: No!

BLANCHE: Yes, you are, your fix is worse than mine is! Only you're not being sensible about it. I'm going to *do* something. Get hold of myself and make myself a new life!

STELLA: Yes?

BLANCHE: But you've given in. And that isn't right, you're not old! You can get out.

STELLA: [*Slowly and emphatically.*] I'm not in anything I want to get out of.

BLANCHE: [*Incredulously.*] What—Stella?

STELLA: I said I am not in anything that I have a desire to get out of. Look at the mess in this room! And those empty bottles! They went through two cases last night! He promised this morning that he was going to quit having these poker parties, but you know how long such a promise is going to keep. Oh, well, it's his pleasure, like mine is movies and bridge. People have got to tolerate each other's habits, I guess.

BLANCHE: I don't understand you. [STELLA *turns toward her.*] I don't understand your indifference. Is this a Chinese philosophy you've—cultivated?

STELLA: Is what—what?

BLANCHE: This—shuffling about and mumbling—"One tube smashed—beer bottles—mess in the kitchen!"—as if nothing out of the ordinary has happened! [STELLA *laughs uncertainly and picking up the broom, twirls it in her hands.*] Are you deliberately shaking that thing in my face?

STELLA: No.

BLANCHE: Stop it. Let go of that broom. I won't have you cleaning up for him!

STELLA: Then who's going to do it? Are you?

BLANCHE: I? I!

STELLA: No, I didn't think so.

BLANCHE: Oh, let me think, if only my mind would function! We've got to get hold of some money, that's the way out!

STELLA: I guess that money is always nice to get hold of.

BLANCHE: Listen to me. I have an idea of some kind. [*Shakily she twists a ciga-*

rette into her holder.] Do you remember Shep Huntleigh? [STELLA *shakes her head.*] Of course you remember Shep Huntleigh. I went out with him at college and wore his pin for a while. Well—

STELLA: Well?

BLANCHE: I ran into him last winter. You know I went to Miami during the Christmas holidays?

STELLA: No.

BLANCHE: Well, I did. I took the trip as an investment, thinking I'd meet someone with a million dollars.

STELLA: Did you?

BLANCHE: Yes. I ran into Shep Huntleigh—I ran into him on Biscayne Boulevard, on Christmas Eve, about dusk . . . getting into his car—Cadillac convertible; must have been a block long!

STELLA: I should think it would have been—inconvenient in traffic!

BLANCHE: You've heard of oil wells?

STELLA: Yes—remotely.

BLANCHE: He has them, all over Texas. Texas is literally spouting gold in his pockets.

STELLA: My, my.

BLANCHE: Y'know how indifferent I am to money. I think of money in terms of what it does for you. But he could do it, he could certainly do it!

STELLA: Do what, Blanche?

BLANCHE: Why—set us up in a—shop!

STELLA: What kind of shop?

BLANCHE: Oh, a—shop of some kind! He could do it with half what his wife throws away at the races.

STELLA: He's married?

BLANCHE: Honey, would I be here if the man weren't married? [STELLA *laughs a little.* BLANCHE *suddenly springs up and crosses to phone. She speaks shrilly.*] How do I get Western Union?—Operator! Western Union!

STELLA: That's a dial phone, honey.

BLANCHE: I can't dial, I'm too—

STELLA: Just dial O.

BLANCHE: O?

STELLA: Yes, "O" for Operator!

[BLANCHE *considers a moment; then she puts the phone down.*]

BLANCHE: Give me a pencil. Where is a slip of paper? I've got to write it down first—the message, I mean . . . [*She goes to the dressing table, and grabs up a sheet of Kleenex and an eyebrow pencil for writing equipment.*] Let me see now . . . [*She bites the pencil.*] "Darling Shep. Sister and I in desperate situation."

STELLA: I beg your pardon!

BLANCHE: "Sister and I in desperate situation. Will explain details later. Would you be interested in—?" [*She bites the pencil again.*] "Would you be—inter-

ested—in . . ." [*She smashes the pencil on the table and springs up.*] You
never get anywhere with direct appeals!

STELLA: [*With a laugh.*] Don't be so ridiculous, darling!

BLANCHE: But I'll think of something, I've *got* to think of—something! Don't
laugh at me, Stella! Please, please don't—I—I want you to look at the contents of my purse! Here's what's in it! [*She snatches her purse open.*] Sixty-
five measly cents in coin of the realm!

STELLA: [*Crossing to bureau.*] Stanley doesn't give me a regular allowance, he
likes to pay bills himself, but—this morning he gave me ten dollars to smooth
things over. You take five of it, Blanche, and I'll keep the rest.

BLANCHE: Oh, no. No, Stella.

STELLA: [*Insisting.*] I know how it helps your morale just having a little pocket-
money on you.

BLANCHE: No, thank you—I'll take to the streets!

STELLA: Talk sense! How did you happen to get so low on funds?

BLANCHE: Money just goes—it goes places. [*She rubs her forehead.*] Sometime
today I've got to get hold of a Bromo[8]!

STELLA: I'll fix you one now.

BLANCHE: Not yet—I've got to keep thinking!

STELLA: I wish you'd just let things go, at least for a—while.

BLANCHE: Stella, I can't live with him! You can, he's your husband. But how
could I stay here with him, after last night, with just those curtains between
us?

STELLA: Blanche, you saw him at his worst last night.

BLANCHE: On the contrary, I saw him at his best! What such a man has to offer
is animal force and he gave a wonderful exhibition of that! But the only way
to live with such a man is to—go to bed with him! And that's your job—not
mine!

STELLA: After you've rested a little, you'll see it's going to work out. You don't
have to worry about anything while you're here. I mean—expenses . . .

BLANCHE: I have to plan for us both, to get us both—out!

STELLA: You take it for granted that I am in something that I want to get out of.

BLANCHE: I take it for granted that you still have sufficient memory of Belle Reve
to find this place and these poker players impossible to live with.

STELLA: Well, you're taking entirely too much for granted.

BLANCHE: I can't believe you're in earnest.

STELLA: No?

BLANCHE: I understand how it happened—a little. You saw him in uniform, an
officer, not here but—

STELLA: I'm not sure it would have made any difference where I saw him.

BLANCHE: Now don't say it was one of those mysterious electric things between
people! If you do I'll laugh in your face.

STELLA: I am not going to say anything more at all about it!

BLANCHE: All right, then, don't!

8. Short for "Bromo Seltzer," a headache remedy.

STELLA: But there are things that happen between a man and a woman in the dark—that sort of make everything else seem—unimportant. [*Pause.*]

BLANCHE: What you are talking about is brutal desire—just—Desire!—the name of that rattle-trap streetcar that bangs through the Quarter, up one old narrow street and down another . . .

STELLA: Haven't you ever ridden on that streetcar?

BLANCHE: It brought me here.—Where I'm not wanted and where I'm ashamed to be . . .

STELLA: Then don't you think your superior attitude is a bit out of place?

BLANCHE: I am not being or feeling at all superior, Stella. Believe me I'm not! It's just this. This is how I look at it. A man like that is someone to go out with—once—twice—three times when the devil is in you. But live with? Have a child by?

STELLA: I have told you I love him.

BLANCHE: Then I *tremble* for you! I just—*tremble* for you. . . .

STELLA: I can't help your trembling if you insist on trembling!

[*There is a pause.*]

BLANCHE: May I—speak—*plainly*?

STELLA: Yes, do. Go ahead. As plainly as you want to.

[*Outside, a train approaches. They are silent till the noise subsides. They are both in the bedroom. Under cover of the train's noise* STANLEY *enters from outside. He stands unseen by the women, holding some packages in his arms, and overhears their following conversation. He wears an undershirt and grease-stained seersucker pants.*]

BLANCHE: Well—if you'll forgive me—he's *common*!

STELLA: Why, yes, I suppose he is.

BLANCHE: Suppose! You can't have forgotten that much of our bringing up, Stella, that you just *suppose* that any part of a gentleman's in his nature! *Not one particle, no!* Oh, if he was just—*ordinary*! Just plain—but good and wholesome, but—*no*. There's something downright—*bestial*—about him! You're hating me saying this, aren't you?

STELLA: [*Coldly.*] Go on and say it all, Blanche.

BLANCHE: He acts like an animal, has an animal's habits! Eats like one, moves like one, talks like one! There's even something—sub-human—something not quite to the stage of humanity yet! Yes, something—ape-like about him, like one of those pictures I've seen in—anthropological studies! Thousands and thousands of years have passed him right by, and there he is—Stanley Kowalski—survivor of the Stone Age! Bearing the raw meat home from the kill in the jungle! And you—*you* here—*waiting* for him! Maybe he'll strike you or maybe grunt and kiss you! That is, if kisses have been discovered yet! Night falls and the other apes gather! There in the front of the cave, all grunting like him, and swilling and gnawing and hulking! His poker night! you call it—this party of apes! Somebody growls—some creature snatches at something—the fight is on! *God!* Maybe we are a long way from being made in God's image, but Stella—my sister—there has been *some* progress since then! Such things as art—as poetry and music—such kinds of new light have come into the world since then! In some kinds of people some tenderer feelings have had some little beginning! That we have got to make *grow!* And *cling* to, and hold as our flag! In this dark march toward whatever it is we're approaching. . . . *Don't—don't hang back with the brutes!*

[*Another train passes outside.* STANLEY *hesitates, licking his lips. Then suddenly he turns stealthily about and withdraws through front door. The women are still unaware of his presence. When the train has passed he calls through the closed front door.*]

STANLEY: Hey! Hey, Stella!
STELLA: [*Who has listened gravely to* BLANCHE.] Stanley!
BLANCHE: Stell, I—

[*But* STELLA *has gone to the front door.* STANLEY *enters casually with his packages.*]

STANLEY: Hiyuh, Stella. Blanche back?
STELLA: Yes, she's back.
STANLEY: Hiyuh, Blanche. [*He grins at her.*]
STELLA: You must've got under the car.
STANLEY: Them darn mechanics at Fritz's don't know their ass fr'm—*Hey!*

[STELLA *has embraced him with both arms, fiercely, and full in the view of* BLANCHE. *He laughs and clasps her head to him. Over her head he grins through the curtains at* BLANCHE. *As the lights fade away, with a lingering brightness on their embrace, the music of the "Blue Piano" and trumpet and drums is heard.*]

SCENE 5

BLANCHE *is seated in the bedroom fanning herself with a palm leaf as she reads over a just-completed letter. Suddenly she bursts into a peal of laughter.* STELLA *is dressing in the bedroom.*

STELLA: What are you laughing at, honey?
BLANCHE: Myself, myself, for being such a liar! I'm writing a letter to Shep. [*She picks up the letter.*] "Darling Shep. I am spending the summer on the wing, making flying visits here and there. And who knows, perhaps I shall take a sudden notion to *swoop* down on *Dallas!* How would you feel about that? Ha-ha! [*She laughs nervously and brightly, touching her throat as if actually talking to Shep.*] Forewarned is forearmed, as they say!"—How does that sound?
STELLA: Uh-huh . . .
BLANCHE: [*Going on nervously.*] "Most of my sister's friends go north in the summer but some have homes on the Gulf and there has been a continued round of entertainments, teas, cocktails, and luncheons—"

[*A disturbance is heard upstairs at the Hubbells' apartment.*]

STELLA: Eunice seems to be having some trouble with Steve. [EUNICE's *voice shouts in terrible wrath.*]

EUNICE: I heard about you and that blonde!

STEVE: That's a damn lie!

EUNICE: You ain't pulling the wool over my eyes! I wouldn't mind if you'd stay down at the Four Deuces, but you always going up.

STEVE: Who ever seen me up?

EUNICE: I seen you chasing her 'round the balcony—I'm gonna call the vice squad!

STEVE: Don't you throw that at me!

EUNICE: [*Shrieking.*] You hit me! I'm gonna call the police!

[*A clatter of aluminum striking a wall is heard, followed by a man's angry roar, shouts and overturned furniture. There is a crash; then a relative hush.*]

BLANCHE: [*Brightly.*] Did he *kill* her?

[EUNICE *appears on the steps in daemonic disorder.*]

STELLA: No! She's coming downstairs.

EUNICE: Call the police, I'm going to call the police! [*She rushes around the corner.*]

[*They laugh lightly.* STANLEY *comes around the corner in his green and scarlet silk bowling shirt. He trots up the steps and bangs into the kitchen.* BLANCHE *registers his entrance with nervous gestures.*]

STANLEY: What's a matter with Eun-uss?

STELLA: She and Steve had a row. Has she got the police?

STANLEY: Naw. She's gettin' a drink.

STELLA: That's much more practical!

[STEVE *comes down nursing a bruise on his forehead and looks in the door.*]

STEVE: She here?

STANLEY: Naw, naw. At the Four Deuces.

STEVE: That rutting hunk! [*He looks around the corner a bit timidly, then turns with affected boldness and runs after her.*]

BLANCHE: I must jot that down in my notebook. Ha-ha! I'm compiling a notebook of quaint little words and phrases I've picked up here.

STANLEY: You won't pick up nothing here you ain't heard before.

BLANCHE: Can I count on that?

STANLEY: You can count on it up to five hundred.

BLANCHE: That's a mighty high number. [*He jerks open the bureau drawer, slams it shut and throws shoes in a corner. At each noise* BLANCHE *winces slightly. Finally she speaks.*] What sign were you born under?

STANLEY: [*While he is dressing.*] Sign?

BLANCHE: Astrological sign. I bet you were born under Aries. Aries people are forceful and dynamic. They dote on noise! They love to bang things around! You must have had lots of banging around in the army and now that you're out, you make up for it by treating inanimate objects with such a fury!

[STELLA *has been going in and out of closet during this scene. Now she pops her head out of the closet.*]

STELLA: Stanley was born just five minutes after Christmas.

BLANCHE: Capricorn—the Goat!

STANLEY: What sign were *you* born under?

BLANCHE: Oh, my birthday's next month, the fifteenth of September; that's under Virgo.

STANLEY: What's Virgo?

BLANCHE: Virgo is the Virgin.

STANLEY: [*Contemptuously.*] Hah! [*He advances a little as he knots his tie.*] Say, do you happen to know somebody named Shaw?

[*Her face expresses a faint shock. She reaches for the cologne bottle and dampens her handkerchief as she answers carefully.*]

BLANCHE: Why, everybody knows somebody named Shaw!

STANLEY: Well, this somebody named Shaw is under the impression he met you in Laurel, but I figure he must have got you mixed up with some other party because this other party is someone he met at a hotel called the Flamingo.

[BLANCHE *laughs breathlessly as she touches the cologne-dampened handkerchief to her temples.*]

BLANCHE: I'm afraid he does have me mixed up with this "other party." The Hotel Flamingo is not the sort of establishment I would dare to be seen in!

STANLEY: You know of it?

BLANCHE: Yes, I've seen it and smelled it.

STANLEY: You must've got pretty close if you could smell it.

BLANCHE: The odor of cheap perfume is penetrating.

STANLEY: That stuff you use is expensive?

BLANCHE: Twenty-five dollars an ounce! I'm nearly out. That's just a hint if you want to remember my birthday! [*She speaks lightly but her voice has a note of fear.*]

STANLEY: Shaw must've got you mixed up. He goes in and out of Laurel all the time so he can check on it and clear up any mistake.

[*He turns away and crosses to the portieres.* BLANCHE *closes her eyes as if faint. Her hand trembles as she lifts the handkerchief again to her forehead.* STEVE *and* EUNICE *come around corner.* STEVE's *arm is around* EUNICE's *shoulder and she is sobbing luxuriously and he is cooing love-words. There is a murmur of thunder as they go slowly upstairs in a tight embrace.*]

STANLEY: [*To* STELLA.] I'll wait for you at the Four Deuces!

STELLA: Hey! Don't I rate one kiss?

STANLEY: Not in front of your sister.

[*He goes out.* BLANCHE *rises from her chair. She seems faint; looks about her with an expression of almost panic.*]

BLANCHE: Stella! What have you heard about me?

STELLA: Huh?

BLANCHE: What have people been telling you about me?

STELLA: Telling?

BLANCHE: You haven't heard any—unkind—gossip about me?

STELLA: Why, no, Blanche, of course not!

BLANCHE: Honey, there was—a good deal of talk in Laurel.

STELLA: About *you,* Blanche?

BLANCHE: I wasn't so good the last two years or so, after Belle Reve had started to slip through my fingers.

STELLA: All of us do things we—

BLANCHE: I never was hard or self-sufficient enough. When people are soft—soft people have got to shimmer and glow—they've got to put on soft colors, the colors of butterfly wings, and put a—paper lantern over the light. . . . It isn't enough to be soft *and attractive.* And I—I'm fading now! I don't know how much longer I can turn the trick. [*The afternoon has faded to dusk.* STELLA *goes into the bedroom and turns on the light under the paper lantern. She holds a bottled soft drink in her hand.*] Have you been listening to me?

STELLA: I don't listen to you when you are being morbid! [*She advances with the bottled Coke.*]

BLANCHE: [*With abrupt change to gaiety.*] Is that Coke for me?

STELLA: Not for anyone else!

BLANCHE: Why, you precious thing, you! Is it just Coke?

STELLA: [*Turning.*] You mean you want a shot in it!

BLANCHE: Well, honey, a shot never does a Coke any harm! Let me! You mustn't wait on me!

STELLA: I like to wait on you, Blanche. It makes it seem more like home. [*She goes into the kitchen, finds a glass and pours a shot of whiskey into it.*]

BLANCHE: I have to admit I love to be waited on . . . [*She rushes into the bedroom.* STELLA *goes to her with the glass.* BLANCHE *suddenly clutches* STELLA's *free hand with a moaning sound and presses the hand to her lips.* STELLA *is embarrassed by her show of emotion.* BLANCHE *speaks in a choked voice.*] You're—you're—so *good* to me! And I—

STELLA: Blanche.

BLANCHE: I know, I won't! You hate me to talk sentimental! But honey, *believe* I feel things more than I *tell* you! I *won't* stay long! I won't, I *promise* I—

STELLA: Blanche!

BLANCHE: [*Hysterically.*] I won't, I promise, I'll go! Go soon! I will *really!* I won't hang around until he—throws me out . . .

STELLA: Now will you stop talking foolish?

BLANCHE: Yes, honey. Watch how you pour—that fizzy stuff foams over!

[BLANCHE *laughs shrilly and grabs the glass, but her hand shakes so it almost slips from her grasp.* STELLA *pours the Coke into the glass. It foams over and spills.* BLANCHE *gives a piercing cry.*]

STELLA: [*Shocked by the cry.*] Heavens!

BLANCHE: Right on my pretty white skirt!

STELLA: Oh . . . Use my hanky. Blot gently.

BLANCHE: [*Slowly recovering.*] I know—gently—gently . . .

STELLA: Did it stain?

BLANCHE: Not a bit. Ha-ha! Isn't that lucky? [*She sits down shakily, taking a grateful drink. She holds the glass in both hands and continues to laugh a little.*]

STELLA: Why did you scream like that?

BLANCHE: I don't know why I screamed! [*Continuing nervously.*] Mitch—Mitch is coming at seven. I guess I am just feeling nervous about our relations. [*She begins to talk rapidly and breathlessly.*] He hasn't gotten a thing but a good-night kiss, that's all I have given him, Stella. I want his respect. And men don't want anything they get too easy. But on the other hand men lose interest quickly. Especially when the girl is over—thirty. They think a girl over thirty ought to—the vulgar term is—"put out." . . . And I—I'm not "putting out." Of course he—he doesn't know—I mean I haven't informed him—of my real age!

STELLA: Why are you sensitive about your age?

BLANCHE: Because of hard knocks my vanity's been given. What I mean is—he thinks I'm sort of—prim and proper, you know! [*She laughs out sharply.*] I want to *deceive* him enough to make him—want me . . .

STELLA: Blanche, do you want *him*?

BLANCHE: I want to *rest*! I want to breathe quietly again! Yes—I *want* Mitch . . . *very badly*! Just think! If it happens! I can leave here and not be anyone's problem . . .

[*STANLEY comes around the corner with a drink under his belt.*]

STANLEY: [*Bawling.*] Hey, Steve! Hey, Eunice! Hey, Stella!

[*There are joyous calls from above. Trumpet and drums are heard from around the corner.*]

STELLA: [*Kissing BLANCHE impulsively.*] It *will* happen!

BLANCHE: [*Doubtfully.*] It will?

STELLA: It *will*! [*She goes across into the kitchen, looking back at BLANCHE.*] It will, honey, *it will*. . . . But don't take another drink! [*Her voice catches as she goes out the door to meet her husband.*]

[*BLANCHE sinks faintly back in her chair with her drink. EUNICE shrieks with laughter and runs down the steps. STEVE bounds after her with goat-like screeches and chases her around corner. STANLEY and STELLA twine arms as they follow, laughing. Dusk settles deeper. The music from the Four Deuces is slow and blue.*]

BLANCHE: Ah, me, ah, me, ah, me . . . [*Her eyes fall shut and the palm leaf fan drops from her fingers. She slaps her hand on the chair arm a couple of times.*

There is a little glimmer of lightning about the building. A YOUNG MAN *comes along the street and rings the bell.*] Come in. [*The* YOUNG MAN *appears through the portieres. She regards him with interest.*] Well, well! What can I do for *you?*

YOUNG MAN: I'm collecting for *The Evening Star.*

BLANCHE: I didn't know that stars took up collections.

YOUNG MAN: It's the paper.

BLANCHE: I know, I was joking—feebly! Will you—have a drink?

YOUNG MAN: No, ma'am. No, thank you. I can't drink on the job.

BLANCHE: Oh, well, now, let's see. . . . No, I don't have a dime! I'm not the lady of the house. I'm her sister from Mississippi. I'm one of those poor relations you've heard about.

YOUNG MAN: That's all right. I'll drop by later. [*He starts to go out. She approaches a little.*]

BLANCHE: Hey! [*He turns back shyly. She puts a cigarette in a long holder.*] Could you give me a light? [*She crosses toward him. They meet at the door between the two rooms.*]

YOUNG MAN: Sure. [*He takes out a lighter.*] This doesn't always work.

BLANCHE: It's temperamental? [*It flares.*] Ah!—thank you. [*He starts away again.*] Hey! [*He turns again, still more uncertainly. She goes close to him.*] Uh—what time is it?

YOUNG MAN: Fifteen of seven, ma'am.

BLANCHE: So late? Don't you just love these long rainy afternoons in New Orleans when an hour isn't just an hour—but a little piece of eternity dropped into your hands—and who knows what to do with it? [*She touches his shoulders.*] You—uh—didn't get wet in the rain?

YOUNG MAN: No, ma'am. I stepped inside.

BLANCHE: In a drugstore? And had a soda?

YOUNG MAN: Uh-huh.

BLANCHE: Chocolate?

YOUNG MAN: No, ma'am. Cherry.

BLANCHE: [*Laughing.*] Cherry!

YOUNG MAN: A cherry soda.

BLANCHE: You make my mouth water. [*She touches his cheek lightly, and smiles. Then she goes to the trunk.*]

YOUNG MAN: Well, I'd better be going—

BLANCHE: [*Stopping him.*] Young man! [*He turns. She takes a large, gossamer scarf from the trunk and drapes it about her shoulders. In the ensuing pause, the "Blue Piano" is heard. It continues through the rest of this scene and the opening of the next. The* YOUNG MAN *clears his throat and looks yearningly at the door.*] Young man! Young, young, young man! Has anyone ever told you that you look like a young Prince out of the Arabian Nights? [*The* YOUNG MAN *laughs uncomfortably and stands like a bashful kid.* BLANCHE *speaks softly to him.*] Well, you do, honey lamb! Come here. I want to kiss you, just once, softly and sweetly on your mouth! [*Without waiting for him to accept, she crosses quickly to him and presses her lips to his.*] Now run along, now, quickly! It would be nice to keep you, but I've got to be good—and keep my hands off children.

[*He stares at her a moment. She opens the door for him and blows a kiss at him as he goes down the steps with a dazed look. She stands there a little dreamily after he has disappeared. Then* MITCH *appears around the corner with a bunch of roses.*]

BLANCHE: [*Gaily.*] Look who's coming! My Rosenkavalier[9]! Bow to me first . . . now present them! *Ahhhh—Merciiii!* [*She looks at him over them, coquettishly pressing them to her lips. He beams at her self-consciously.*]

SCENE 6

It is about two A.M. *on the same evening. The outer wall of the building is visible.* BLANCHE *and* MITCH *come in. The utter exhaustion which only a neurasthenic personality can know is evident in* BLANCHE'*s voice and manner.* MITCH *is stolid but depressed. They have probably been out to the amusement park on Lake Pontchartrain, for* MITCH *is bearing, upside down, a plaster statuette of Mae West, the sort of prize won at shooting galleries and carnival games of chance.*

BLANCHE: [*Stopping lifelessly at the steps.*] Well—[MITCH *laughs uneasily.*] Well . . .

MITCH: I guess it must be pretty late—and you're tired.

BLANCHE: Even the hot tamale man has deserted the street, and he hangs on till the end. [MITCH *laughs uneasily again.*] How will you get home?

MITCH: I'll walk over to Bourbon and catch an owl-car.

BLANCHE: [*Laughing grimly.*] Is that street-car named Desire still grinding along the tracks at this hour?

MITCH: [*Heavily.*] I'm afraid you haven't gotten much fun out of this evening, Blanche.

BLANCHE: I spoiled it for *you.*

MITCH: No, you didn't, but I felt all the time that I wasn't giving you much—entertainment.

BLANCHE: I simply couldn't rise to the occasion. That was all. I don't think I've ever tried so hard to be gay and made such a dismal mess of it. I get ten points for trying!—I *did* try.

MITCH: Why did you try if you didn't feel like it, Blanche?

BLANCHE: I was just obeying the law of nature.

MITCH: Which law is that?

BLANCHE: The one that says the lady must entertain the gentleman—or no dice! See if you can locate my door key in this purse. When I'm so tired my fingers are all thumbs!

MITCH: [*Rooting in her purse.*] This it?

BLANCHE: No, honey, that's the key to my trunk which I must soon be packing.

9. *Knight of the Rose,* title of a romantic opera (1911) by Richard Strauss (1864–1949). *Merci:* thank you (French).

MITCH: You mean you are leaving here soon?

BLANCHE: I've outstayed my welcome.

MITCH: This it?

[*The music fades away.*]

BLANCHE: Eureka! Honey, you open the door while I take a last look at the sky. [*She leans on the porch rail. He opens the door and stands awkwardly behind her.*] I'm looking for the Pleiades,[1] the Seven Sisters, but these girls are not out tonight. Oh, yes they are, there they are! God bless them! All in a bunch going home from their little bridge party. . . . Y' get the door open? Good boy! I guess you—want to go now . . .

[*He shuffles and coughs a little.*]

MITCH: Can I—uh—kiss you—good night?

BLANCHE: Why do you always ask me if you may?

MITCH: I don't know whether you want me to or not.

BLANCHE: Why should you be so doubtful?

MITCH: That night when we parked by the lake and I kissed you, you—

BLANCHE: Honey, it wasn't the kiss I objected to. I liked the kiss very much. It was the other little—familiarity—that I—felt obliged to—discourage. . . . I didn't resent it! Not a bit in the world! In fact, I was somewhat flattered that you—desired me! But, honey, you know as well as I do that a single girl, a girl alone in the world, has got to keep a firm hold on her emotions or she'll be lost!

MITCH: [*Solemnly.*] Lost?

BLANCHE: I guess you are used to girls that like to be lost. The kind that get lost immediately, on the first date!

MITCH: I like you to be exactly the way that you are, because in all my—experience—I have never known anyone like you. [BLANCHE *looks at him gravely; then she bursts into laughter and then claps a hand to her mouth.*] Are you laughing at me?

BLANCHE: No, honey. The lord and lady of the house have not yet returned, so come in. We'll have a nightcap. Let's leave the lights off. Shall we?

MITCH: You just—do what you want to.

[BLANCHE *precedes him into the kitchen. The outer wall of the building disappears and the interiors of the two rooms can be dimly seen.*]

BLANCHE: [*Remaining in the first room.*] The other room's more comfortable—go on in. This crashing around in the dark is my search for some liquor.

MITCH: You want a drink?

BLANCHE: I want *you* to have a drink! You have been so anxious and solemn all evening, and so have I; we have both been anxious and solemn and now for these few last remaining moments of our lives together—I want to create—*joie de vivre!* I'm lighting a candle.

1. The seven daughters of Atlas who were metamorphosed into stars.

MITCH: That's good.

BLANCHE: We are going to be very Bohemian. We are going to pretend that we are sitting in a little artists' cafe on the Left Bank in Paris! [*She lights a candle stub and puts it in a bottle.*] *Je suis la Dame aux Camellias! Vous êtes—Armand!*[2] Understand French?

MITCH: [*Heavily.*] Naw. Naw, I—

BLANCHE: *Voulez-vous couchez avec moi ce soir? Vous ne comprenez pas? Ah, quelle dommage!*[3]—I mean it's a damned good thing. . . . I've found some liquor! Just enough for two shots without any dividends, honey . . .

MITCH: [*Heavily.*] That's—good.

[*She enters the bedroom with the drinks and the candle.*]

BLANCHE: Sit down! Why don't you take off your coat and loosen your collar?

MITCH: I better leave it on.

BLANCHE: No. I want you to be comfortable.

MITCH: I am ashamed of the way I perspire. My shirt is sticking to me.

BLANCHE: Perspiration is healthy. If people didn't perspire they would die in five minutes. [*She takes his coat from him.*] This is a nice coat. What kind of material is it?

MITCH: They call that stuff alpaca.

BLANCHE: Oh. Alpaca.

MITCH: It's very light-weight alpaca.

BLANCHE: Oh. Light-weight alpaca.

MITCH: I don't like to wear a wash-coat even in summer because I sweat through it.

BLANCHE: Oh.

MITCH: And it don't look neat on me. A man with a heavy build has got to be careful of what he puts on him so he don't look too clumsy.

BLANCHE: You are not too heavy.

MITCH: You don't think I am?

BLANCHE: You are not the delicate type. You have a massive bone-structure and a very imposing physique.

MITCH: Thank you. Last Christmas I was given a membership to the New Orleans Athletic Club.

BLANCHE: Oh, good.

MITCH: It was the finest present I ever was given. I work out there with the weights and I swim and I keep myself fit. When I started there, I was getting soft in the belly but now my belly is hard. It is so hard now that a man can punch me in the belly and it don't hurt me. Punch me! Go on! See? [*She pokes lightly at him.*]

BLANCHE: Gracious. [*Her hand touches her chest.*]

MITCH: Guess how much I weigh, Blanche?

2. "I am the Lady of the Camellias! You are—Armand!" Both are characters in the popular romantic play *La Dame aux Camélias* (1852) by the French author Alexandre Dumas (1824–1895); she is a courtesan who gives up her true love, Armand.　　3. "Would you like to sleep with me this evening? You don't understand? Ah, what a pity!"

BLANCHE: Oh, I'd say in the vicinity of—one hundred and eighty?

MITCH: Guess again.

BLANCHE: Not that much?

MITCH: No. More.

BLANCHE: Well, you're a tall man and you can carry a good deal of weight without looking awkward.

MITCH: I weigh two hundred and seven pounds and I'm six feet one and one half inches tall in my bare feet—without shoes on. And that is what I weigh stripped.

BLANCHE: Oh, my goodness, me! It's awe-inspiring.

MITCH: [*Embarrassed.*] My weight is not a very interesting subject to talk about. [*He hesitates for a moment.*] What's yours?

BLANCHE: My weight?

MITCH: Yes.

BLANCHE: Guess!

MITCH: Let me lift you.

BLANCHE: Samson[4]! Go on, lift me. [*He comes behind her and puts his hands on her waist and raises her lightly off the ground.*] Well?

MITCH: You are light as a feather.

BLANCHE: Ha-ha! [*He lowers her but keeps his hands on her waist.* BLANCHE *speaks with an affectation of demureness.*] You may release me now.

MITCH: Huh?

BLANCHE: [*Gaily.*] I said unhand me, sir. [*He fumblingly embraces her. Her voice sounds gently reproving.*] Now, Mitch. Just because Stanley and Stella aren't at home is no reason why you shouldn't behave like a gentleman.

MITCH: Just give me a slap whenever I step out of bounds.

BLANCHE: That won't be necessary. You're a natural gentleman, one of the very few that are left in the world. I don't want you to think that I am severe and old maid school-teacherish or anything like that. It's just—well—

MITCH: Huh?

BLANCHE: I guess it is just that I have—old-fashioned ideals! [*She rolls her eyes, knowing he cannot see her face.* MITCH *goes to the front door. There is a considerable silence between them.* BLANCHE *sighs and* MITCH *coughs self-consciously.*]

MITCH: [*Finally.*] Where's Stanley and Stella tonight?

BLANCHE: They have gone out. With Mr. and Mrs. Hubbell upstairs.

MITCH: Where did they go?

BLANCHE: I think they were planning to go to a midnight prevue at Loew's State.

MITCH: We should all go out together some night.

BLANCHE: No. That wouldn't be a good plan.

MITCH: Why not?

BLANCHE: You are an old friend of Stanley's?

MITCH: We was together in the Two-forty-first.[5]

BLANCHE: I guess he talks to you frankly?

---

4. Legendary strong man, in the Old Testament.   5. Battalion of Engineers, in World War II.

MITCH: Sure.

BLANCHE: Has he talked to you about me?

MITCH: Oh—not very much.

BLANCHE: The way you say that, I suspect that he has.

MITCH: No, he hasn't said much.

BLANCHE: But what he *has* said. What would you say his attitude toward me was?

MITCH: Why do you want to ask that?

BLANCHE: Well—

MITCH: Don't you get along with him?

BLANCHE: What do you think?

MITCH: I don't think he understands you.

BLANCHE: That is putting it mildly. If it weren't for Stella about to have a baby, I wouldn't be able to endure things here.

MITCH: He isn't—nice to you?

BLANCHE: He is insufferably rude. Goes out of his way to offend me.

MITCH: In what way, Blanche?

BLANCHE: Why, in every conceivable way.

MITCH: I'm surprised to hear that.

BLANCHE: Are you?

MITCH: Well, I—don't see how anybody could be rude to you.

BLANCHE: It's really a pretty frightful situation. You see, there's no privacy here. There's just these portieres between the two rooms at night. He stalks through the rooms in his underwear at night. And I have to ask him to close the bathroom door. That sort of commonness isn't necessary. You probably wonder why I don't move out. Well, I'll tell you frankly. A teacher's salary is barely sufficient for her living expenses. I didn't save a penny last year and so I had to come here for the summer. That's why I have to put up with my sister's husband. And he has to put up with me, apparently so much against his wishes. . . . Surely he must have told you how much he hates he!

MITCH: I don't think he hates you.

BLANCHE: He hates me. Or why would he insult me? The first time I laid eyes on him I thought to myself, that man is my executioner! That man will destroy me, unless——

MITCH: Blanche—

BLANCHE: Yes, honey?

MITCH: Can I ask you a question?

BLANCHE: Yes. What?

MITCH: How old are you?

[*She makes a nervous gesture.*]

BLANCHE: Why do you want to know?

MITCH: I talked to my mother about you and she said, "How old is Blanche?" And I wasn't able to tell her. [*There is another pause.*]

BLANCHE: You talked to your mother about me?

MITCH: Yes.

BLANCHE: Why?

MITCH: I told my mother how nice you were, and I liked you.

BLANCHE: Were you sincere about that?

MITCH: You know I was.

BLANCHE: Why did your mother want to know my age?

MITCH: Mother is sick.

BLANCHE: I'm sorry to hear it. Badly?

MITCH: She won't live long. Maybe just a few months.

BLANCHE: Oh.

MITCH: She worries because I'm not settled.

BLANCHE: Oh.

MITCH: She wants me to be settled down before she—[*His voice is hoarse and he clears his throat twice, shuffling nervously around with his hands in and out of his pockets.*]

BLANCHE: You love her very much, don't you?

MITCH: Yes.

BLANCHE: I think you have a great capacity for devotion. You will be lonely when she passes on, won't you? [MITCH *clears his throat and nods.*] I understand what that is.

MITCH: To be lonely?

BLANCHE: I loved someone, too, and the person I loved I lost.

MITCH: Dead? [*She crosses to the window and sits on the sill, looking out. She pours herself another drink.*] A man?

BLANCHE: He was a boy, just a boy, when I was a very young girl. When I was sixteen, I made the discovery—love. All at once and much, much too completely. It was like you suddenly turned a blinding light on something that had always been half in shadow, that's how it struck the world for me. But I was unlucky. Deluded. There was something different about the boy, a nervousness, a softness and tenderness which wasn't like a man's, although he wasn't the least bit effeminate looking—still—that thing was there. . . . He came to me for help. I didn't know that. I didn't find out anything till after our marriage when we'd run away and come back and all I knew was I'd failed him in some mysterious way and wasn't able to give the help he needed but couldn't speak of! He was in the quicksands and clutching at me—but I wasn't holding him out, I was slipping in with him! I didn't know that. I didn't know anything except I loved him unendurably but without being able to help him or help myself. Then I found out. In the worst of all possible ways. By coming suddenly into a room that I thought was empty— which wasn't empty, but had two people in it . . . the boy I had married and an older man who had been his friend for years . . . [*A locomotive is heard approaching outside. She claps her hands to her ears and crouches over. The headlight of the locomotive glares into the room as it thunders past. As the noise recedes she straightens slowly and continues speaking.*] Afterward we pretended that nothing had been discovered. Yes, the three of us drove out

2046 ▼ Tennessee Williams

to Moon Lake Casino, very drunk and laughing all the way. [*Polka music sounds, in a minor key faint with distance.*] We danced the "Varsouviana[6]!" Suddenly in the middle of the dance the boy I had married broke away from me and ran out of the casino. A few moments later—a shot! [*The polka stops abruptly.* BLANCHE *rises stiffly. Then, the polka resumes in a major key.*] I ran out—all did!—all ran and gathered about the terrible thing at the edge of the lake! I couldn't get near for the crowding. Then somebody caught my arm. "Don't go any closer! Come back! You don't want to see!" See? See what! Then I heard voices say—Allan! Allan! The Grey boy! He'd stuck the revolver into his mouth, and fired—so that the back of his head had been— blown away! [*She sways and covers her face.*] It was because—on the dance floor—unable to stop myself—I'd suddenly said—"I saw! I know! You disgust me . . . ." And then the searchlight which had been turned on the world was turned off again and never for one moment since has there been any light that's stronger than this—kitchen—candle . . .

[MITCH *gets up awkwardly and moves toward her a little. The polka music increases.* MITCH *stands beside her.*]

MITCH: [*Drawing her slowly into his arms.*] You need somebody. And I need somebody, too. Could it be—you and me, Blanche?

[*She stares at him vacantly for a moment. Then with a soft cry huddles in his embrace. She makes a sobbing effort to speak but the words won't come. He kisses her forehead and her eyes and finally her lips. The polka tune fades out. Her breath is drawn and released in long, grateful sobs.*]

BLANCHE: Sometimes—there's God—so quickly!

SCENE 7

It is late afternoon in mid-September.
The portieres are open and a table is set for a birthday supper, with cake and flowers.
STELLA *is completing the decorations as* STANLEY *comes in.*

STANLEY: What's all this stuff for?
STELLA: Honey, it's Blanche's birthday.
STANLEY: She here?
STELLA: In the bathroom.
STANLEY: [*Mimicking.*] "Washing out some things"?
STELLA: I reckon so.
STANLEY: How long she been in there?
STELLA: All afternoon.
STANLEY: [*Mimicking.*] "Soaking in a hot tub"?
STELLA: Yes.
STANLEY: Temperature 100 on the nose, and she soaks herself in a hot tub.

6. Fast Polish dance, similar to the polka.

STELLA: She says it cools her off for the evening.

STANLEY: And you run out an' get her cokes, I suppose? And serve 'em to Her Majesty in the tub? [STELLA *shrugs*.] Set down here a minute.

STELLA: Stanley, I've got things to do.

STANLEY: Set down! I've got th' dope on your big sister, Stella.

STELLA: Stanley, stop picking on Blanche.

STANLEY: That girl calls *me* common!

STELLA: Lately you been doing all you can think of to rub her the wrong way, Stanley, and Blanche is sensitive and you've got to realize that Blanche and I grew up under very different circumstances than you did.

STANLEY: So I been told. And told and told and told! You know she's been feeding us a pack of lies here?

STELLA: No, I don't and—

STANLEY: Well, she has, however. But now the cat's out of the bag! I found out some things!

STELLA: What—things?

STANLEY: Things I already suspected. But now I got proof from the most reliable sources—which I have checked on!

[BLANCHE *is singing in the bathroom a saccharine popular ballad which is used contrapuntally with* STANLEY's *speech.*]

STELLA: [*To* STANLEY.] Lower your voice!

STANLEY: Some canary bird, huh!

STELLA: Now please tell me quietly what you think you've found out about my sister.

STANLEY: Lie Number One: All this squeamishness she puts on! You should just know the line she's been feeding to Mitch. He thought she had never been more than kissed by a fellow! But Sister Blanche is no lily! Ha-ha! Some lily she is!

STELLA: What have you heard and who from?

STANLEY: Our supply-man down at the plant has been going through Laurel for years and he knows all about her and everybody else in the town of Laurel knows all about her. She is as famous in Laurel as if she was the President of the United States, only she is not respected by any party! This supply-man stops at a hotel called the Flamingo.

BLANCHE: [*Singing blithely.*] "Say, it's only a paper moon, Sailing over a cardboard sea—But it wouldn't be make-believe If you believed in me!"[7]

STELLA: What about the—Flamingo?

STANLEY: She stayed there, too.

STELLA: My sister lived at Belle Reve.

STANLEY: This is after the home-place had slipped through her lily-white fingers! She moved to the Flamingo! A second-class hotel which has the advantage of not interfering in the private social life of the personalities there! The Flamingo is used to all kinds of goings-on. But even the management of the

---

7. From "It's Only a Paper Moon" (1933), a popular song by Harold Arlen.

Flamingo was impressed by Dame Blanche! In fact they was so impressed by Dame Blanche that they requested her to turn in her room key—for permanently! This happened a couple of weeks before she showed here.

BLANCHE: [*Singing.*] "It's a Barnum and Bailey world, Just as phony as it can be—But it wouldn't be make-believe If you believed in me!"

STELLA: What—contemptible—lies!

STANLEY: Sure, I can see how you would be upset by this. She pulled the wool over your eyes as much as Mitch's!

STELLA: It's pure invention! There's not a word of truth in it and if I were a man and this creature had dared to invent such things in my presence—

BLANCHE: [*Singing.*] "Without your love, it's a honky-tonk parade! Without your love, It's a melody played In a penny arcade . . ."

STANLEY: Honey, I told you I thoroughly checked on these stories! Now wait till I finish. The trouble with Dame Blanche was that she couldn't put on her act any more in Laurel! They got wised up after two or three dates with her and then they quit, and she goes on to another, the same old line, same old act, same old hooey! But the town was too small for this to go on forever! And as time went by she became a town character. Regarded as not just different but downright loco—nuts. [STELLA *draws back.*] And for the last year or two she has been washed up like poison. That's why she's here this summer, visiting royalty, putting on all this act—because she's practically told by the mayor to get out of town! Yes, did you know there was an army camp near Laurel and your sister's was one of the places called "Out-of-Bounds"?

BLANCHE: "It's only a paper moon, Just as phony as it can be—But it wouldn't be make-believe If you believed in me!"

STANLEY: Well, so much for her being such a refined and particular type of girl. Which brings us to Lie Number Two.

BLANCHE: I don't want to hear any more!

STANLEY: She's not going back to teach school! In fact I am willing to bet you that she never had no idea of returning to Laurel! She didn't resign temporarily from the high school because of her nerves! No, siree, Bob! She didn't. They kicked her out of that high school before the spring term ended—and I hate to tell you the reason that step was taken! A seventeen-year-old boy—she'd gotten mixed up with!

BLANCHE: "It's a Barnum and Bailey world, Just as phony as it can be—"

[*In the bathroom the water goes on loud; little breathless cries and peals of laughter are heard as if a child were frolicking in the tub.*]

STELLA: This is making me—sick!

STANLEY: The boy's dad learned about it and got in touch with the high school superintendent. Boy, oh, boy, I'd like to have been in that office when Dame Blanche was called on the carpet! I'd like to have seen her trying to squirm out of that one! But they had her on the hook good and proper that time and she knew that the jig was all up! They told her she better move on to some fresh territory. Yep, it was practickly a town ordinance passed against her!

[*The bathroom door is opened and* BLANCHE *thrusts her head out, holding a towel about her hair.*]

BLANCHE: Stella!

STELLA: [*Faintly.*] Yes, Blanche?

BLANCHE: Give me another bath-towel to dry my hair with. I've just washed it.

STELLA: Yes, Blanche. [*She crosses in a dazed way from the kitchen to the bathroom door with a towel.*]

BLANCHE: What's the matter, honey?

STELLA: Matter? Why?

BLANCHE: You have such a strange expression on your face!

STELLA: Oh—[*She tries to laugh.*] I guess I'm a little tired!

BLANCHE: Why don't you bathe, too, soon as I get out?

STANLEY: [*Calling from the kitchen.*] How soon is that going to be?

BLANCHE: Not so terribly long! Possess your soul in patience!

STANLEY: It's not my soul, it's my kidneys I'm worried about! [BLANCHE *slams the door.* STANLEY *laughs harshly.* STELLA *comes slowly back into the kitchen.*] Well, what do you think of it?

STELLA: I don't believe all of those stories and I think your supply-man was mean and rotten to tell them. It's possible that some of the things he said are partly true. There are things about my sister I don't approve of—things that caused sorrow at home. She was always—flighty!

STANLEY: Flighty!

STELLA: But when she was young, very young, she married a boy who wrote poetry. . . . He was extremely good-looking. I think Blanche didn't just love him but worshipped the ground he walked on! Adored him and thought him almost too fine to be human! But then she found out—

STANLEY: What?

STELLA: This beautiful and talented young man was a degenerate. Didn't your supply-man give you that information?

STANLEY: All we discussed was recent history. That must have been a pretty long time ago.

STELLA: Yes, it was—a pretty long time ago . . .

[STANLEY *comes up and takes her by the shoulders rather gently. She gently withdraws from him. Automatically she starts sticking little pink candles in the birthday cake.*]

STANLEY: How many candles you putting in that cake?

STELLA: I'll stop at twenty-five.

STANLEY: Is company expected?

STELLA: We asked Mitch to come over for cake and ice-cream.

[STANLEY *looks a little uncomfortable. He lights a cigarette from the one he has just finished.*]

STANLEY: I wouldn't be expecting Mitch over tonight.

[STELLA *pauses in her occupation with candles and looks slowly around at* STANLEY.]

STELLA: *Why?*

STANLEY: Mitch is a buddy of mine. We were in the same outfit together—Two-forty-first Engineers. We work in the same plant and now on the same bowling team. You think I could face him if—

STELLA: Stanley Kowalski, did you—did you repeat what that—?

STANLEY: You're goddam right I told him! I'd have that on my conscience the rest of my life if I knew all that stuff and let my best friend get caught!

STELLA: Is Mitch through with her?

STANLEY: Wouldn't you be if—?

STELLA: I said, *Is Mitch through with her?*

[BLANCHE's *voice is lifted again, serenely as a bell. She sings "But it wouldn't be make-believe If you believed in me."*]

STANLEY: No, I don't think he's necessarily through with her—just wised up!

STELLA: Stanley, she thought Mitch was—going to—going to marry her. I was hoping so, too.

STANLEY: Well, he's not going to marry her. Maybe he *was*, but he's not going to jump in a tank with a school of sharks—now! [*He rises.*] Blanche! Oh, Blanche! Can I please get in my bathroom? [*There is a pause.*]

BLANCHE: Yes, indeed, sir! Can you wait one second while I dry?

STANLEY: Having waited one hour I guess one second ought to pass in a hurry.

STELLA: And she hasn't got her job? Well, what will she do!

STANLEY: She's not stayin' here after Tuesday. You know that, don't you? Just to make sure I bought her ticket myself. A bus ticket.

STELLA: In the first place, Blanche wouldn't go on a bus.

STANLEY: She'll go on a bus and like it.

STELLA: No, she won't, no, she won't, Stanley!

STANLEY: *She'll go!* Period. P.S. She'll go *Tuesday!*

STELLA: [*Slowly.*] What'll—she—do? What on earth will she—*do!*

STANLEY: Her future is mapped out for her.

STELLA: What do you mean?

[BLANCHE *sings.*]

STANLEY: Hey, canary bird! Toots! Get *OUT* of the *BATHROOM!*

[*The bathroom door flies open and* BLANCHE *emerges with a gay peal of laughter, but as* STANLEY *crosses past her, a frightened look appears in her face, almost a look of panic. He doesn't look at her but slams the bathroom door shut as he goes in.*]

BLANCHE: [*Snatching up a hairbrush.*] Oh, I feel so good after my long, hot bath, I feel so good and cool and—rested!

STELLA: [*Sadly and doubtfully from the kitchen.*] Do you, Blanche?

BLANCHE: [*Snatching up a hairbrush.*] Yes, I do, so refreshed! [*She tinkles her highball glass.*] A hot bath and a long, cold drink always give me a brand new outlook on life! [*She looks through the portieres at* STELLA, *standing between them, and slowly stops brushing.*] Something has happened!—What is it?

STELLA: [*Turning away quickly.*] Why, nothing has happened, Blanche.

BLANCHE: You're lying! Something has! [*She stares fearfully at* STELLA, *who pretends to be busy at the table. The distant piano goes into a hectic breakdown.*]

SCENE 8

Three quarters of an hour later.

The view through the big windows is fading gradually into a still-golden dusk. A torch of sunlight blazes on the side of a big water-tank or oil-drum across the empty lot toward the business district which is now pierced by pinpoints of lighted windows or windows reflecting the sunset.

The three people are completing a dismal birthday supper. STANLEY *looks sullen.* STELLA *is embarrassed and sad.*

BLANCHE *has a tight, artificial smile on her drawn face. There is a fourth place at the table which is left vacant.*

BLANCHE: [*Suddenly.*] Stanley, tell us a joke, tell us a funny story to make us all laugh. I don't know what's the matter, we're all so solemn. Is it because I've been stood up by my beau? [STELLA *laughs feebly.*] It's the first time in my entire experience with men, and I've had a good deal of all sorts, that I've actually been stood up by anybody! Ha-ha! I don't know how to take it. . . . Tell us a funny little story, Stanley! Something to help us out.

STANLEY: I didn't think you liked my stories, Blanche.

BLANCHE: I like them when they're amusing but not indecent.

STANLEY: I don't know any refined enough for your taste.

BLANCHE: Then let me tell one.

STELLA: Yes, you tell one, Blanche. You used to know lots of good stories.

[*The music fades.*]

BLANCHE: Let me see, now. . . . I must run through my repertoire! Oh, yes—I love parrot stories! Do you all like parrot stories? Well, this one's about the old maid and the parrot. This old maid, she had a parrot that cursed a blue streak and knew more vulgar expressions than Mr. Kowalski!

STANLEY: Huh.

BLANCHE: And the only way to hush the parrot up was to put the cover back on its cage so it would think it was night and go back to sleep. Well, one morning the old maid had just uncovered the parrot for the day—when who should she see coming up the front walk but the preacher! Well, she rushed back to the parrot and slipped the cover back on the cage and then she let in the preacher. And the parrot was perfectly still, just as quiet as a mouse, but just as she was asking the preacher how much sugar he wanted in his coffee—the parrot broke the silence with a loud—[*She whistles.*]—and said—"God *damn*, but that was a short day!" [*She throws back her head and laughs.* STELLA *also makes an ineffectual effort to seem amused.* STANLEY *pays no attention to the story but reaches way over the table to spear his fork into the remaining chop which he eats with his fingers.*] Apparently Mr. Kowalski was not amused.

STELLA: Mr. Kowalski is too busy making a pig of himself to think of anything else!

STANLEY: That's right, baby.

STELLA: Your face and your fingers are disgustingly greasy. Go and wash up and then help me clear the table.

[*He hurls a plate to the floor.*]

STANLEY: That's how I'll clear the table! [*He seizes her arm.*] Don't ever talk that way to me! "Pig—Polack—disgusting—vulgar—greasy!"—them kind of words have been on your tongue and your sister's too much around here! What do you two think you are? A pair of queens? Remember what Huey Long[8] said—"Every Man is a King!" And I am the king around here, so don't forget it! [*He hurls a cup and saucer to the floor.*] My place is cleared! You want me to clear your places?

[STELLA *begins to cry weakly.* STANLEY *stalks out on the porch and lights a cigarette. The Negro entertainers around the corner are heard.*]

BLANCHE: What happened while I was bathing? What did he tell you, Stella?

STELLA: Nothing, nothing, nothing!

BLANCHE: I think he told you something about Mitch and me! You know why Mitch didn't come but you won't tell me! [STELLA *shakes her head helplessly.*] I'm going to call him!

STELLA: I wouldn't call him, Blanche.

BLANCHE: I am, I'm going to call him on the phone.

STELLA: [*Miserably.*] I wish you wouldn't.

BLANCHE: I intend to be given some explanation from someone!

[*She rushes to the phone in the bedroom.* STELLA *goes out on the porch and stares reproachfully at her husband. He grunts and turns away from her.*]

STELLA: I hope you're pleased with your doings. I never had so much trouble swallowing food in my life, looking at that girl's face and the empty chair! [*She cries quietly.*]

BLANCHE: [*At the phone.*] Hello. Mr. Mitchell, please. . . . Oh. . . . I would like to leave a number if I may. Magnolia 9047. And say it's important to call. . . . Yes, very important. . . . Thank you. [*She remains by the phone with a lost, frightened look.*]

[STANLEY *turns slowly back toward his wife and takes her clumsily in his arms.*]

STANLEY: Stell, it's gonna be all right after she goes and after you've had the baby. It's gonna be all right again between you and me the way that it was.

8. Demagogic Louisiana politcal leader, governor, and senator (1893–1935).

You remember the way that it was? Them nights we had together? God, honey, it's gonna be sweet when we can make noise in the night the way that we used to and get the colored lights going with nobody's sister behind the curtains to hear us! [*Their upstairs neighbors are heard in bellowing laughter at something.* STANLEY *chuckles.*] Steve an' Eunice . . .

STELLA: Come on back in. [*She returns to the kitchen and starts lighting the candles on the white cake.*] Blanche?

BLANCHE: Yes. [*She returns from the bedroom to the table in the kitchen.*] Oh, those pretty, pretty little candles! Oh, don't burn them, Stella.

STELLA: I certainly will.

[STANLEY *comes back in.*]

BLANCHE: You ought to save them for baby's birthdays. Oh, I hope candles are going to glow in his life and I hope that his eyes are going to be like candles, like two blue candles lighted in a white cake!

STANLEY: [*Sitting down.*] What poetry!

BLANCHE: [*She pauses reflectively for a moment.*] I shouldn't have called him.

STELLA: There's lots of things could have happened.

BLANCHE: There's no excuse for it, Stella. I don't have to put up with insults. I won't be taken for granted.

STANLEY: Goddamn, it's hot in here with the steam from the bathroom.

BLANCHE: I've said I was sorry three times. [*The piano fades out.*] I take hot baths for my nerves. Hydrotherapy, they call it. You healthy Polack, without a nerve in your body, of course you don't know what anxiety feels like!

STANLEY: I am not a Polack. People from Poland are Poles, not Polacks. But what I am is a one-hundred-per-cent American, born and raised in the greatest country on earth and proud as hell of it, so don't ever call me a Polack.

[*The phone rings.* BLANCHE *rises expectantly.*]

BLANCHE: Oh, that's for me, I'm sure.

STANLEY: *I'm* not sure. Keep your seat. [*He crosses leisurely to phone.*] H'lo. Aw, yeh, hello, Mac.

[*He leans against wall, staring insultingly in at* BLANCHE. *She sinks back in her chair with a frightened look.* STELLA *leans over and touches her shoulder.*]

BLANCHE: Oh, keep your hands off me, Stella. What is the matter with you? Why do you look at me with that pitying look?

STANLEY: [*Bawling.*] QUIET IN THERE!—We've got a noisy woman on the place.—Go on, Mac. At Riley's? No, I don't wanta bowl at Riley's. I had a little trouble with Riley last week. I'm the team captain, ain't I? All right, then, we're not gonna bowl at Riley's, we're gonna bowl at the West Side or the Gala! All right, Mac. See you! [*He hangs up and returns to the table.* BLANCHE *fiercely controls herself, drinking quickly from her tumbler of water. He doesn't look at her but reaches in a pocket. Then he speaks slowly and with false amiability.*] Sister Blanche, I've got a little birthday remembrance for you.

BLANCHE: Oh, have you, Stanley? I wasn't expecting any, I—I don't know why Stella wants to observe my birthday! I'd much rather forget it—when you—reach twenty-seven! Well—age is a subject that you'd prefer to—ignore!

STANLEY: Twenty-seven?

BLANCHE: [*Quickly.*] What is it? Is it for *me*?

[*He is holding a little envelope toward her.*]

STANLEY: Yes, I hope you like it!

BLANCHE: Why, why—Why, it's a—

STANLEY: Ticket! Back to Laurel! On the Greyhound! Tuesday! [*The "Varsouviana" music steals in softly and continues playing.* STELLA *rises abruptly and turns her back.* BLANCHE *tries to smile. Then she tries to laugh. Then she gives both up and springs from the table and runs into the next room. She clutches her throat and then runs into the bathroom. Coughing, gagging sounds are heard.*] Well!

STELLA: You didn't need to do that.

STANLEY: Don't forget all that I took off her.

STELLA: You needn't have been so cruel to someone alone as she is.

STANLEY: Delicate piece she is.

STELLA: She is. She was. You didn't know Blanche as a girl. Nobody, nobody, was tender and trusting as she was. But people like you abused her, and forced her to change. [*He crosses into the bedroom, ripping off his shirt, and changes into a brilliant silk bowling shirt. She follows him.*] Do you think you're going bowling now?

STANLEY: Sure.

STELLA: You're not going bowling. [*She catches hold of his shirt.*] Why did you do this to her?

STANLEY: I done nothing to no one. Let go of my shirt. You've torn it.

STELLA: I want to know why. Tell me why.

STANLEY: When we first met, me and you, you thought I was common. How right you was, baby. I was common as dirt. You showed me the snapshot of the place with the columns. I pulled you down off them columns and how you loved it, having them colored lights going! And wasn't we happy together, wasn't it all okay till she showed here? [STELLA *makes a slight movement. Her look goes suddenly inward as if some interior voice had called her name. She begins a slow, shuffling progress from the bedroom to the kitchen, leaning and resting on the back of the chair and then on the edge of a table with a blind look and listening expression.* STANLEY, *finishing with his shirt, is unaware of her reaction.*] And wasn't we happy together? Wasn't it all okay? Till she showed here. Hoity-Toity, describing me as an ape. [*He suddenly notices the change in* STELLA.] Hey, what is it, Stell? [*He crosses to her.*]

STELLA: [*Quietly.*] Take me to the hospital.

[*He is with her now, supporting her with his arm, murmuring indistinguishably as they go outside.*]

SCENE 9

A while later that evening. BLANCHE *is seated in a tense hunched position in a bedroom chair that she has recovered with diagonal green and white stripes. She has on her scarlet satin robe. On the table beside chair is a bottle of liquor and a glass. The rapid, feverish polka tune, the "Varsouviana," is heard. The music is in her mind; she is drinking to escape it and the sense of disaster closing in on her, and she seems to whisper the words of the song. An electric fan is turning back and forth across her.*

MITCH *comes around the corner in work clothes: blue denim shirt and pants. He is unshaven. He climbs the steps to the door and rings.* BLANCHE *is startled.*

BLANCHE: Who is it, please?
MITCH: [*Hoarsely.*] Me. Mitch.

[*The polka tune stops.*]

BLANCHE: Mitch!—Just a minute. [*She rushes about frantically, hiding the bottle in a closet, crouching at the mirror and dabbing her face with cologne and powder. She is so excited that her breath is audible as she dashes about. At last she rushes to the door in the kitchen and lets him in.*] Mitch!—Y'know, I really shouldn't let you in after the treatment I have received from you this evening! So utterly uncavalier! But hello, beautiful! [*She offers him her lips. He ignores it and pushes past her into the flat. She looks fearfully after him as he stalks into the bedroom.*] My, my, what a cold shoulder! And such uncouth apparel! Why, you haven't even shaved! The unforgivable insult to a lady! But I forgive you. I forgive you because it's such a relief to see you. You've stopped that polka tune that I had caught in my head. Have you ever had anything caught in your head? No, of course you haven't, you dumb angel-puss, you'd never get anything awful caught in your head!

[*He stares at her while she follows him while she talks. It is obvious that he has had a few drinks on the way over.*]

MITCH: Do we have to have that fan on?
BLANCHE: No!
MITCH: I don't like fans.
BLANCHE: Then let's turn it off, honey. I'm not partial to them! [*She presses the switch and the fan nods slowly off. She clears her throat uneasily as* MITCH *plumps himself down on the bed in the bedroom and lights a cigarette.*] I don't know what there is to drink. I—haven't investigated.
MITCH: I don't want Stan's liquor.
BLANCHE: It isn't Stan's. Everything here isn't Stan's. Some things on the premises are actually mine! How is your mother? Isn't your mother well?
MITCH: Why?
BLANCHE: Something's the matter tonight, but never mind. I won't cross-examine the witness. I'll just— [*She touches her forehead vaguely. The polka tune*

starts up again.]—pretend I don't notice anything different about you!
That—music again . . .

MITCH: What music?

BLANCHE: The "Varsouviana"! The polka tune they were playing when Allan—
Wait! [*A distant revolver shot is heard.* BLANCHE *seems relieved.*] There now,
the shot! It always stops after that. [*The polka music dies out again.*] Yes, now
it's stopped.

MITCH: Are you boxed out of your mind?

BLANCHE: I'll go and see what I can find in the way of— [*She crosses into the
closet, pretending to search for the bottle.*] Oh, by the way, excuse me for
not being dressed. But I'd practically given you up! Had you forgotten your
invitation to supper?

MITCH: I wasn't going to see you any more.

BLANCHE: Wait a minute. I can't hear what you're saying and you talk so little
that when you do say something, I don't want to miss a single syllable of it.
. . . What am I looking around here for? Oh, yes—liquor! We've had so
much excitement around here this evening that I *am* boxed out of my mind!
[*She pretends suddenly to find the bottle. He draws his foot up on the bed and
stares at her contemptuously.*] Here's something. Southern Comfort! What is
that, I wonder?

MITCH: If you don't know, it must belong to Stan.

BLANCHE: Take your foot off the bed. It has a light cover on it. Of course you
boys don't notice things like that. I've done so much with this place since
I've been here.

MITCH: I bet you have.

BLANCHE: You saw it before I came. Well, look at it now! This room is almost—
dainty! I want to keep it that way. I wonder if this stuff ought to be mixed
with something? Ummm, it's sweet! It's terribly, terribly sweet! Why, it's a
liqueur, I believe! Yes, that's what it *is*, a liqueur! [MITCH *grunts.*] I'm afraid
you won't like it, but try it, and maybe you will.

MITCH: I told you already I don't want none of his liquor and I mean it. You
ought to lay off his liquor. He says you been lapping it up all summer like a
wild-cat!

BLANCHE: What a fantastic statement! Fantastic of him to say it, fantastic of you
to repeat it! I won't descend to the level of such cheap accusations to answer
them, even!

MITCH: Huh.

BLANCHE: What's in your mind? I see something in your eyes!

MITCH: [*Getting up.*] It's dark in here.

BLANCHE: I like it dark. The dark is comforting to me.

MITCH: I don't think I ever seen you in the light. [BLANCHE *laughs breathlessly.*]
That's a fact!

BLANCHE: Is it?

MITCH: I've never seen you in the afternoon.

BLANCHE: Whose fault is that?

MITCH: You never want to go out in the afternoon.

BLANCHE: Why, Mitch, you're at the plant in the afternoon!

MITCH: Not Sunday afternoon. I've asked you to go out with me sometimes on Sundays but you always make an excuse. You never want to go out till after six and then it's always some place that's not lighted much.

BLANCHE: There is some obscure meaning in this but I fail to catch it.

MITCH: What it means is I've never had a real good look at you, Blanche. Let's turn the light on here.

BLANCHE: [Fearfully.] Light? Which light? What for?

MITCH: This one with the paper thing on it.

[He tears the paper lantern off the light bulb. She utters a frightened gasp.]

BLANCHE: What did you do that for?

MITCH: So I can take a look at you good and plain!

BLANCHE: Of course you don't really mean to be insulting!

MITCH: No, just realistic.

BLANCHE: I don't want realism. I want magic! [MITCH laughs.] Yes, yes, magic! I try to give that to people. I misrepresent things to them. I don't tell truth, I tell what ought to be truth. And if that is sinful, then let me be damned for it!—Don't turn the light on!

[MITCH crosses to the switch. He turns the light on and stares at her. She cries out and covers her face. He turns the lights off again.]

MITCH: [Slowly and bitterly.] I don't mind you being older than what I thought. But all the rest of it—Christ! That pitch about your ideals being so old-fashioned and all the malarkey that you've dished out all summer. Oh, I knew you weren't sixteen any more. But I was a fool enough to believe you was straight.

BLANCHE: Who told you I wasn't—"straight"? My loving brother-in-law. And you believed him.

MITCH: I called him a liar at first. And then I checked on the story. First I asked our supply-man who travels through Laurel. And then I talked directly over long-distance to this merchant.

BLANCHE: Who is this merchant?

MITCH: Kiefaber.

BLANCHE: The merchant Kiefaber of Laurel! I know the man. He whistled at me. I put him in his place. So now for revenge he makes up stories about me.

MITCH: Three people, Kiefaber, Stanley and Shaw, swore to them!

BLANCHE: Rub-a-dub-dub, three men in a tub! And such a filthy tub!

MITCH: Didn't you stay at a hotel called The Flamingo?

BLANCHE: Flamingo? No! Tarantula was the name of it! I stayed at a hotel called The Tarantula Arms!

MITCH: [Stupidly] Tarantula?

BLANCHE: Yes, a big spider! That's where I brought my victims. [She pours herself another drink.] Yes, I had many intimacies with strangers. After the death of Allan—intimacies with strangers was all I seemed able to fill my empty heart with. . . . I think it was panic, just panic, that drove me from one to another, hunting for some protection—here and there, in the most—unlikely places—even, at last, in a seventeen-year-old boy but—somebody wrote the superintendent about it—"This woman is morally unfit for her position!" [*She throws back her head with convulsive, sobbing laughter. Then she repeats the statement, gasps, and drinks.*] True? Yes, I suppose—unfit somehow— anyway. . . . So I came here. There was nowhere else I could go. I was played out. You know what played out is? My youth was suddenly gone up the water-spout, and—I met you. You said you needed somebody. Well, I needed somebody, too. I thanked God for you, because you seemed to be gentle—a cleft in the rock of the world that I could hide in! But I guess I was asking, hoping—too much! Kiefaber, Stanley and Shaw have tied an old tin can to the tail of the kite.

[*There is a pause.* MITCH *stares at her dumbly.*]

MITCH: You lied to me, Blanche.
BLANCHE: Don't say I lied to you.
MITCH: Lies, lies, inside and out, all lies.
BLANCHE: Never inside, I didn't lie in my heart . . .

[*A vendor comes around the corner. She is a blind* MEXICAN WOMAN *in a dark shawl, carrying bunches of those gaudy tin flowers that lower-class Mexicans display at funerals and other festive occasions. She is calling barely audibly. Her figure is only faintly visible outside the building.*]

MEXICAN WOMAN: *Flores. Flores, Flores para los muertos.*[9] *Flores. Flores.*
BLANCHE: What? Oh! Somebody outside . . . . [*She goes to the door, opens it and stares at the* MEXICAN WOMAN.]
MEXICAN WOMAN: [*She is at the door and offers* BLANCHE *some of her flowers.*] *Flores? Flores para los muertos?*
BLANCHE: [*Frightened.*] No, no! Not now! Not now! [*She darts back into the apartment, slamming the door.*]
MEXICAN WOMAN: [*She turns away and starts to move down the street.*] *Flores para los muertos.*

[*The polka tune fades in.*]

BLANCHE: [*As if to herself.*] Crumble and fade and—regrets—recriminations . . . "If you'd done this, it wouldn't've cost me that!"
MEXICAN WOMAN: *Corones*[1] *para los muertos. Corones* . . .
BLANCHE: Legacies! Huh. . . . And other things such as bloodstained pillow-slips—"Her linen needs changing"—"Yes, Mother. But couldn't we get a colored girl to do it?" No, we couldn't of course. Everything gone but the—
MEXICAN WOMAN: *Flores.*
BLANCHE: Death—I used to sit here and she used to sit over there and death was as close as you are. . . . We didn't dare even admit we had ever heard of it!

---

9. "Flowers for the dead."   1. "Wreaths."

MEXICAN WOMAN: *Flores para los muertos, flores—flores . . .*

BLANCHE: The opposite is desire. So do you wonder? How could you possibly wonder! Not far from Belle Reve, before we had lost Belle Reve, was a camp where they trained young soldiers. On Sunday nights they would go in town to get drunk—

MEXICAN WOMAN: [*Softly.*] *Corones . . .*

BLANCHE: —and on the way back they would stagger onto my lawn and call— "Blanche! Blanche!"—the deaf old lady remaining suspected nothing. But sometimes I slipped outside to answer their calls. . . . Later the paddy-wagon would gather them up like daisies . . . the long way home . . . [*The* MEXICAN WOMAN *turns slowly and drifts back off with her soft mournful cries.* BLANCHE *goes to the dresser and leans forward on it. After a moment,* MITCH *rises and follows her purposefully. The polka music fades away. He places his hands on her waist and tries to turn her about.*] What do you want?

MITCH: [*Fumbling to embrace her.*] What I been missing all summer.

BLANCHE: Then marry me, Mitch!

MITCH: I don't think I want to marry you any more.

BLANCHE: No?

MITCH: [*Dropping his hands from her waist.*] You're not clean enough to bring in the house with my mother.

BLANCHE: Go away, then. [*He stares at her.*] Get out of here quick before I start screaming fire! [*Her throat is tightening with hysteria.*] Get out of here quick before I start screaming fire. [*He still remains staring. She suddenly rushes to the big window with its pale blue square of the soft summer light and cries wildly.*] Fire! Fire! Fire!

[*With a startled gasp,* MITCH *turns and goes out the outer door, clatters awkwardly down the steps and around the corner of the building.* BLANCHE *staggers back from the window and falls to her knees. The distant piano is slow and blue.*]

SCENE 10

It is a few hours later that night.

BLANCHE *has been drinking fairly steadily since* MITCH *left. She has dragged her wardrobe trunk into the center of the bedroom. It hangs open with flowery dresses thrown across it. As the drinking and packing went on, a mood of hysterical exhilaration came into her and she has decked herself out in a somewhat soiled and crumpled white satin evening gown and a pair of scuffed silver slippers with brilliants set in their heels.*

Now she is placing the rhinestone tiara on her head before the mirror of the dressing-table and murmuring excitedly as if to a group of spectral admirers.

BLANCHE: How about taking a swim, a moonlight swim at the old rock-quarry? If anyone's sober enough to drive a car! Ha-ha! Best way in the world to stop your head buzzing! Only you've got to be careful to dive where the deep pool is—if you hit a rock you don't come up till tomorrow . . . [*Tremblingly she lifts the hand mirror for a closer inspection. She catches her breath and slams the mirror face down with such violence that the glass cracks. She moans a little and attempts to rise.* STANLEY *appears around the corner of the building. He still has on the vivid green silk bowling shirt. As he rounds the corner the honky-tonk music is heard. It continues softly throughout the scene. He enters the kitchen, slamming the door. As he peers in at* BLANCHE, *he gives a low whistle. He has had a few drinks on the way and has brought some quart beer bottles home with him.*] How is my sister?

STANLEY: She is doing okay.

BLANCHE: And how is the baby?

STANLEY: [*Grinning amiably.*] The baby won't come before morning so they told me to go home and get a little shut-eye.

BLANCHE: Does that mean we are to be alone in here?

STANLEY: Yep. Just me and you, Blanche. Unless you got somebody hid under the bed. What've you got on those fine feathers for?

BLANCHE: Oh, that's right. You left before my wire came.

STANLEY: You got a wire?

BLANCHE: I received a telegram from an old admirer of mine.

STANLEY: Anything good?

BLANCHE: I think so. An invitation.

STANLEY: What to? A fireman's ball?

BLANCHE: [*Throwing back her head.*] A cruise of the Caribbean on a yacht!

STANLEY: Well, well. What do you know?

BLANCHE: I have never been so surprised in my life.

STANLEY: I guess not.

BLANCHE: It came like a bolt from the blue!

STANLEY: Who did you say it was from?

BLANCHE: An old beau of mine.

STANLEY: The one that give you the white fox-pieces?

BLANCHE: Mr. Shep Huntleigh. I wore his ATO pin my last year at college. I hadn't seen him again until last Christmas. I ran in to him on Biscayne Boulevard. Then—just now—this wire—inviting me on a cruise of the Caribbean! The problem is clothes. I tore into my trunk to see what I have that's suitable for the tropics!

STANLEY: And come up with that—gorgeous—diamond—tiara?

BLANCHE: This old relic? Ha-ha! It's only rhinestones.

STANLEY: Gosh. I thought it was Tiffany diamonds. [*He unbuttons his shirt.*]

BLANCHE: Well, anyhow, I shall be entertained in style.

STANLEY: Uh-huh. It goes to show, you never know what is coming.

BLANCHE: Just when I thought my luck had begun to fail me—

STANLEY: Into the picture pops this Miami millionaire.

BLANCHE: This man is not from Miami. This man is from Dallas.

STANLEY: This man is from Dallas?

BLANCHE: Yes, this man is from Dallas where gold spouts out of the ground!

STANLEY: Well, just so he's from somewhere! [*He starts removing his shirt.*]

BLANCHE: Close the curtains before you undress any further.

STANLEY: [*Amiably.*] This is all I'm going to undress right now. [*He rips the sack off a quart beer bottle.*] Seen a bottle-opener? [*She moves slowly toward the dresser, where she stands with her hands knotted together.*] I used to have a cousin who could open a beer bottle with his teeth. [*Pounding the bottle cap on the corner of table.*] That was his only accomplishment, all he could do—he was just a human bottle-opener. And then one time, at a wedding party, he broke his front teeth off! After that he was so ashamed of himself he used t' sneak out of the house when company came . . . [*The bottle cap pops off and a geyser of foam shoots up.* STANLEY *laughs happily, holding up the bottle over his head.*] Ha-ha! Rain from heaven! [*He extends the bottle toward her.*] Shall we bury the hatchet and make it a loving-cup? Huh?

BLANCHE: No, thank you.

STANLEY: Well, it's a red-letter night for us both. You having an oil millionaire and me having a baby. [*He goes to the bureau in the bedroom and crouches to remove something from the bottom drawer.*]

BLANCHE: [*Drawing back.*] What are you doing in here?

STANLEY: Here's something I always break out on special occasions like this. The silk pyjamas I wore on my wedding night!

BLANCHE: Oh.

STANLEY: When the telephone rings and they say, "You've got a son!" I'll tear this off and wave it like a flag! [*He shakes out a brilliant pyjama coat.*] I guess we are both entitled to put on the dog. [*He goes back to the kitchen with the coat over his arm.*]

BLANCHE: When I think of how divine it is going to be to have such a thing as privacy once more—I could weep with joy!

STANLEY: This millionaire from Dallas is not going to interfere with your privacy any?

BLANCHE: It won't be the sort of thing you have in mind. This man is a gentleman and he respects me. [*Improvising feverishly.*] What he wants is my companionship. Having great wealth sometimes makes people lonely! A cultivated woman, a woman of intelligence and breeding, can enrich a man's life—immeasurably! I have those things to offer, and this doesn't take them away. Physical beauty is passing. A transitory possession. But beauty of the mind and richness of the spirit and tenderness of the heart—and I have all of those things—aren't taken away, but grow! Increase with the years! How strange that I should be called a destitute woman! When I have all of these treasures locked in my heart. [*A choked sob comes from her.*] I think of myself as a very, very rich woman! But I have been foolish—casting my pearls before swine!

STANLEY: Swine, huh?

BLANCHE: Yes, swine! Swine! And I'm thinking not only of you but of your friend, Mr. Mitchell. He came to see me tonight. He dared to come here in his work clothes! And to repeat slander to me, vicious stories that he had gotten from you! I gave him his walking papers . . .

STANLEY: You did, huh?

BLANCHE: But then he came back. He returned with a box of roses to beg my forgiveness! He implored my forgiveness. But some things are not forgivable. Deliberate cruelty is not forgivable. It is the one unforgivable thing in my opinion and it is the one thing of which I have never, ever been guilty. And so I told him, I said to him, "Thank you," but it was foolish of me to think that we could ever adapt ourselves to each other. Our ways of life are too different. Our attitudes and our backgrounds are incompatible. We have to be realistic about such things. So farewell, my friend! And let there be no hard feelings . . .

STANLEY: Was this before or after the telegram came from the Texas oil millionaire?

BLANCHE: What telegram? No! No, after! As a matter of fact, the wire came just as—

STANLEY: As a matter of fact there wasn't no wire at all!

BLANCHE: Oh, oh!

STANLEY: There isn't no millionaire! And Mitch didn't come back with roses 'cause I know where he is—

BLANCHE: Oh!

STANLEY: There isn't a goddam thing but imagination!

BLANCHE: Oh!

STANLEY: And lies and conceit and tricks!

BLANCHE: Oh!

STANLEY: And look at yourself! Take a look at yourself in that worn-out Mardi Gras outfit, rented for fifty cents from some ragpicker! And with the crazy crown on! What queen do you think you are?

BLANCHE: Oh—God . . .

STANLEY: I've been on to you from the start! Not once did you pull any wool over this boy's eyes! You come in here and sprinkle the place with powder and spray perfume and cover the light-bulb with a paper lantern, and lo and behold the place has turned into Egypt and you are the Queen of the Nile! Sitting on your throne and swilling down my liquor! I say—*Ha!—Ha!* Do you hear me? *Ha—ha—ha!* [*He walks into the bedroom.*]

BLANCHE: Don't come in here! [*Lurid reflections appear on the walls around* BLANCHE. *The shadows are of a grotesque and menacing form. She catches her breath, crosses to the phone and jiggles the hook.* STANLEY *goes into the bathroom and closes the door.*] Operator, operator! Give me long-distance, please. . . . I want to get in touch with Mr. Shep Huntleigh of Dallas. He's so well known he doesn't require any address. Just ask anybody who—Wait!!—No, I couldn't find it right now. . . . Please understand, I—No! No, wait! . . . One moment! Someone is—Nothing! Hold on, please! [*She sets the phone down and crosses warily into the kitchen. The night is filled with inhuman voices like cries in a jungle. The shadows and lurid reflections move sinuously as flames along the wall spaces. Through the back wall of the rooms, which have become transparent, can be seen the sidewalk. A* PROSTITUTE *has rolled a* DRUNKARD. *He pursues her along the walk, overtakes her and there is a struggle. A policeman's whistle breaks it up. The figures disappear. Some moments later the* NEGRO WOMAN *appears around the corner with a sequined bag which the* PROSTITUTE *had dropped on the walk. She is rooting excitedly through it.* BLANCHE *presses her knuckles to her lips and returns slowly to the phone. She speaks in a hoarse whisper.*] Operator! Operator! Never mind long-distance. Get Western Union. There isn't time to be—Western—Western Union! [*She waits anxiously.*] Western Union? Yes! I—want to—Take down this message! "In desperate, desperate circumstances! Help me! Caught in a trap. Caught in—" *Oh!*

[*The bathroom door is thrown open and* STANLEY *comes out in the brilliant silk pyjamas. He grins at her as he knots the tassled sash about his waist. She gasps and backs away from the phone. He stares at her for a count of ten. Then a clicking becomes audible from the telephone, steady and rasping.*]

STANLEY: You left th' phone off th' hook.

[*He crosses to it deliberately and sets it back on the hook. After he has replaced it, he stares at her again, his mouth slowly curving into a grin, as he weaves between* BLANCHE *and the outer door. The barely audible "Blue Piano" begins to drum up louder. The sound of it turns into the roar of an approaching locomotive.* BLANCHE *crouches, pressing her fists to her ears until it has gone by.*]

BLANCHE: [*Finally straightening.*] Let me—let me get by you!
STANLEY: Get by me? Sure. Go ahead. [*He moves back a pace in the doorway.*]
BLANCHE: You—you stand over there! [*She indicates a further position.*]
STANLEY: You got plenty of room to walk by me now.
BLANCHE: Not with you there! But I've got to get out somehow!
STANLEY: You think I'll interfere with you? Ha-ha! [*The "Blue Piano" goes softy. She turns confusedly and makes a faint gesture. The inhuman jungle voices rise up. He takes a step toward her, biting his tongue, which protrudes between his lips. Softly.*] Come to think of it—maybe you wouldn't be bad to—interfere with . . .

[BLANCHE *moves backward through the door into the bedroom.*]

BLANCHE: Stay back! Don't you come toward me another step or I'll—
STANLEY: What?
BLANCHE: Some awful thing will happen! It will!
STANLEY: What are you putting on now?

[*They are now both inside the bedroom.*]

BLANCHE: I warn you, don't, I'm in danger!

[*He takes another step. She smashes a bottle on the table and faces him, clutching the broken top.*]

STANLEY: What did you do that for?
BLANCHE: So I could twist the broken end in your face!
STANLEY: I bet you would do that!
BLANCHE: I would! I will if you—

STANLEY: Oh! So you want some roughhouse! All right, let's have some rough-house! [*He springs toward her, overturning the table. She cries out and strikes at him with the bottle top but he catches her wrist.*] Tiger—tiger! Drop the bottle-top! Drop it! We've had this date with each other from the beginning!

[*She moans. The bottle-top falls. She sinks to her knees: He picks up her inert figure and carries her to the bed. The hot trumpet and drums from the Four Deuces sound loudly.*]

SCENE 11

It is some weeks later. STELLA is packing BLANCHE's things. Sounds of water can be heard running in the bathroom.

The portieres are partly open on the poker players—STANLEY, STEVE, MITCH and PABLO—who sit around the table in the kitchen. The atmosphere of the kitchen is now the same raw, lurid one of the disastrous poker night.

The building is framed by the sky of turquoise. STELLA has been crying as she arranges the flowery dresses in the open trunk.

EUNICE comes down the steps from her flat above and enters the kitchen. There is an outburst from the poker table.

STANLEY: Drew to an inside straight and made it, by God.
PABLO: *Maldita sea tu suerto!*
STANLEY: Put it in English, greaseball.
PABLO: I am cursing your rutting luck.
STANLEY: [*Prodigiously elated.*] You know what luck is? Luck is believing you're lucky. Take at Salerno.[2] I believed I was lucky. I figured that 4 out of 5 would not come through but I would . . . and I did. I put that down as a rule. To hold front position in this rat-race you've got to believe you are lucky.
MITCH: You . . . you . . . you . . . Brag . . . brag . . . bull . . . bull.

[STELLA *goes into the bedroom and starts folding a dress.*]

STANLEY: What's the matter with him?
EUNICE: [*Walking past the table.*] I always did say that men are callous things with no feelings but this does beat anything. Making pigs of yourselves. [*She comes through the portieres into the bedroom.*]
STANLEY: What's the matter with her?
STELLA: How is my baby?
EUNICE: Sleeping like a little angel. Brought you some grapes. [*She puts them on a stool and lowers her voice.*] Blanche?
STELLA: Bathing.
EUNICE: How is she?
STELLA: She wouldn't eat anything but asked for a drink.
EUNICE: What did you tell her?

2. Important beachhead in the Allied invasion of Italy in World War II.

STELLA: I—just told her that—we'd made arrangements for her to rest in the country. She's got it mixed in her mind with Shep Huntleigh.

[BLANCHE *opens the bathroom door slightly.*]

BLANCHE: Stella.

STELLA: Yes.

BLANCHE: That cool yellow silk—the bouclé. See if it's crushed. If it's not too crushed I'll wear it and on the lapel that silver and turquoise pin in the shape of a seahorse. You will find them in the heart-shaped box I keep my accessories in. And Stella . . . Try and locate a bunch of artificial violets in that box, too, to pin with the seahorse on the lapel of the jacket.

[*She closes the door.* STELLA *turns to* EUNICE.]

STELLA: I don't know if I did the right thing.

EUNICE: What else could you do?

STELLA: I couldn't believe her story and go on living with Stanley.

EUNICE: Don't ever believe it. Life has got to go on. No matter what happens, you've got to keep on going.

[*The bathroom door opens a little.*]

BLANCHE: [*Looking out.*] Is the coast clear?

STELLA: Yes, Blanche. [*To* EUNICE.] Tell her how well she's looking.

BLANCHE: Please close the curtains before I come out.

STELLA: They're closed.

STANLEY: —How many for you?

PABLO: Two.

STEVE: Three.

[BLANCHE *appears in the amber light of the door. She has a tragic radiance in her red satin robe following the sculptural lines of her body. The "Varsouviana" rises audibly as* BLANCHE *enters the bedroom.*]

BLANCHE: [*With faintly hysterical vivacity.*] I have just washed my hair.

STELLA: Did you?

BLANCHE: I'm not sure I got the soap out.

EUNICE: Such fine hair!

BLANCHE: [*Accepting the compliment.*] It's a problem. Didn't I get a call?

STELLA: Who from, Blanche?

BLANCHE: Shep Huntleigh . . .

STELLA: Why, not yet, honey!

BLANCHE: How strange! I—

[*At the sound of* BLANCHE's *voice* MITCH's *arm supporting his cards has sagged and his gaze is dissolved into space.* STANLEY *slaps him on the shoulder.*]

STANLEY: Hey, Mitch, come to!

[*The sound of this new voice shocks* BLANCHE. *She makes a shocked gesture, forming his name with her lips.* STELLA *nods and looks quickly away.* BLANCHE *stands quite still for some moments—the silver-backed mirror in her hand and a look of sorrowful perplexity as though all human experience shows on her face.* BLANCHE *finally speaks but with sudden hysteria.*]

BLANCHE: What's going on here? [*She turns from* STELLA *to* EUNICE *and back to* STELLA. *Her rising voice penetrates the concentration of the game.* MITCH *ducks his head lower but* STANLEY *shoves back his chair as if about to rise.* STEVE *places a restraining hand on his arm. Continuing.*] What's happened here? I want an explanation of what's happened here.

STELLA: [*Agonizingly.*] Hush! Hush!

EUNICE: Hush! Hush! Honey.

STELLA: Please, Blanche.

BLANCHE: Why are you looking at me like that? Is something wrong with me?

EUNICE: You look wonderful, Blanche. Don't she look wonderful?

STELLA: Yes.

EUNICE: I understand you are going on a trip.

STELLA: Yes, Blanche *is.* She's going on a vacation.

EUNICE: I'm green with envy.

BLANCHE: Help me, help me get dressed!

STELLA: [*Handing her dress.*] Is this what you—

BLANCHE: Yes, it will do! I'm anxious to get out of here—this place is a trap!

EUNICE: What a pretty blue jacket.

STELLA: It's lilac colored.

BLANCHE: You're both mistaken. It's Della Robbia blue.[3] The blue of the robe in the old Madonna pictures. Are these grapes washed? [*She fingers the bunch of grapes which* EUNICE *had brought in.*]

EUNICE: Huh?

BLANCHE: Washed, I said. Are they washed?

EUNICE: They're from the French Market.

BLANCHE: That doesn't mean they've been washed. [*The cathedral bells chime.*] Those cathedral bells—they're the only clean thing in the Quarter. Well, I'm going now. I'm ready to go.

EUNICE: [*Whispering.*] She's going to walk out before they get here.

STELLA: Wait, Blanche.

BLANCHE: I don't want to pass in front of those men.

EUNICE: Then wait'll the game breaks up.

STELLA: Sit down and . . .

[BLANCHE *turns weakly, hesitantly about. She lets them push her into a chair.*]

BLANCHE: I can smell the sea air. The rest of my time I'm going to spend on the sea. And when I die, I'm going to die on the sea. You know what I shall die of? [*She plucks a grape.*] I shall die of eating an unwashed grape one day out on the ocean. I will die—with my hand in the hand of some nice-looking ship's doctor, a very young one with a small blond mustache and a big silver

---

3. A shade of light blue seen in terra cottas made by the Della Robbia family in the Italian Renaissance.

watch. "Poor lady," they'll say, "the quinine did her no good. That unwashed grape has transported her soul to heaven." [*The cathedral chimes are heard.*] And I'll be buried at sea sewn up in a clean white sack and dropped overboard—at noon—in the blaze of summer—and into an ocean as blue as [*Chimes again.*] my first lover's eyes!

[*A* DOCTOR *and a* MATRON *have appeared around the corner of the building and climbed the steps to the porch. The gravity of their profession is exaggerated—the unmistakable aura of the state institution with its cynical detachment. The* DOCTOR *rings the doorbell. The murmur of the game is interrupted.*]

EUNICE: [*Whispering to* STELLA.] That must be them.

[STELLA *presses her fists to her lips.*]

BLANCHE: [*Rising slowly.*] What is it?
EUNICE: [*Affectedly casual.*] Excuse me while I see who's at the door.
STELLA: Yes.

[EUNICE *goes into the kitchen.*]

BLANCHE: [*Tensely.*] I wonder if it's for me.

[*A whispered colloquy takes place at the door.*]

EUNICE: [*Returning, brightly.*] Someone is calling for Blanche.
BLANCHE: It is for me, then! [*She looks fearfully from one to the other and then to the portieres. The "Varsouviana" faintly plays.*] Is it the gentleman I was expecting from Dallas?
EUNICE: I think it is, Blanche.
BLANCHE: I'm not quite ready.
STELLA: Ask him to wait outside.
BLANCHE: I . . .

[EUNICE *goes back to the portieres. Drums sound very softly.*]

STELLA: Everything packed?
BLANCHE: My silver toilet articles are still out.
STELLA: Ah!
EUNICE: [*Returning.*] They're waiting in front of the house.
BLANCHE: They! Who's "they"?
EUNICE: There's a lady with him.
BLANCHE: I cannot imagine who this "lady" could be! How is she dressed?
EUNICE: Just—just a sort of a—plain-tailored outfit.
BLANCHE: Possibly she's—[*Her voice dies out nervously.*]
STELLA: Shall we go, Blanche?
BLANCHE: Must we go through that room?
STELLA: I will go with you.
BLANCHE: How do I look?
STELLA: Lovely.
EUNICE: [*Echoing.*] Lovely.

[BLANCHE *moves fearfully to the portieres.* EUNICE *draws them open for her.* BLANCHE *goes into the kitchen.*]

BLANCHE: [*To the men.*] Please don't get up. I'm only passing through.

[*She crosses quickly to outside door.* STELLA *and* EUNICE *follow. The poker players stand awkwardly at the table—all except* MITCH, *who remains seated, looking down at the table.* BLANCHE *steps out on a small porch at the side of the door. She stops short and catches her breath.*]

DOCTOR: How do you do?

BLANCHE: You are not the gentleman I was expecting. [*She suddenly gasps and starts back up the steps. She stops by* STELLA, *who stands just outside the door, and speaks in a frightening whisper.*] That man isn't Shep Huntleigh.

[*The "Varsouviana" is playing distantly.* STELLA *stares back at* BLANCHE. EUNICE *is holding* STELLA's *arm. There is a moment of silence—no sound but that of* STANLEY *steadily shuffling the cards.* BLANCHE *catches her breath again and slips back into the flat. She enters the flat with a peculiar smile, her eyes wide and brilliant. As soon as her sister goes past her,* STELLA *closes her eyes and clenches her hands.* EUNICE *throws her arms comfortingly about her. Then she starts up to her flat.* BLANCHE *stops just inside the door.* MITCH *keeps staring down at his hands on the table, but the other men look at her curiously. At last she starts around the table toward the bedroom. As she does,* STANLEY *suddenly pushes back his chair and rises as if to block her way. The* MATRON *follows her into the flat.*]

STANLEY: Did you forget something?

BLANCHE: [*Shrilly.*] Yes! Yes, I forgot something!

[*She rushes past him into the bedroom. Lurid reflections appear on the walls in odd, sinuous shapes. The "Varsouviana" is filtered into a weird distortion, accompanied by the cries and noises of the jungle.* BLANCHE *seizes the back of a chair as if to defend herself.*]

STANLEY: [*Sotto voce.*] Doc, you better go in.

DOCTOR: [*Sotto voce, motioning to the* MATRON.] Nurse, bring her out.

[*The* MATRON *advances on one side,* STANLEY *on the other. Divested of all the softer properties of womanhood, the* MATRON *is a peculiarly sinister figure in her severe dress. Her voice is bold and toneless as a firebell.*]

MATRON: Hello, Blanche.

[*The greeting is echoed and re-echoed by other mysterious voices behind the walls, as if reverberated through a canyon of rock.*]

STANLEY: She says that she forgot something.

[*The echo sounds in threatening whispers.*]

MATRON: That's all right.

STANLEY: What did you forget, Blanche?

BLANCHE: I—I—

MATRON: It don't matter. We can pick it up later.

STANLEY: Sure. We can send it along with the trunk.

BLANCHE: [*Retreating in panic.*] I don't know you—I don't know you. I want to be—left alone—please!

MATRON: Now, Blanche!

ECHOES: [*Rising and falling.*] Now, Blanche—now, Blanche—now, Blanche!

STANLEY: You left nothing here but spilt talcum and old empty perfume bottles—unless it's the paper lantern you want to take with you. You want the lantern?

[*He crosses to dressing table and seizes the paper lantern, tearing it off the light bulb, and extends it toward her. She cries out as if the lantern was herself. The* MATRON *steps boldly toward her. She screams and tries to break past the* MATRON. *All the men spring to their feet.* STELLA *runs out to the porch, with* EUNICE *following to comfort her, simultaneously with the confused voices of the men in the kitchen.* STELLA *rushes into* EUNICE's *embrace on the porch.*]

STELLA: Oh, my God, Eunice help me! Don't let them do that to her, don't let them hurt her! Oh, God, oh, please God, don't hurt her! What are they doing to her? What are they doing? [*She tries to break from* EUNICE's *arms.*]

EUNICE: No, honey, no, no, honey. Stay here. Don't go back in there. Stay with me and don't look.

STELLA: What have I done to my sister? Oh, God, what have I done to my sister?

EUNICE: You done the right thing, the only thing you could do. She couldn't stay here; there wasn't no other place for her to go.

[*While* STELLA *and* EUNICE *are speaking on the porch the voices of the men in the kitchen overlap them.* MITCH *has started toward the bedroom.* STANLEY *crosses to block him.* STANLEY *pushes him aside.* MITCH *lunges and strikes at* STANLEY. STANLEY *pushes* MITCH *back.* MITCH *collapses at the table, sobbing. During the preceding scenes, the* MATRON *catches hold of* BLANCHE's *arm and prevents her flight.* BLANCHE *turns wildly and scratches at the* MATRON. *The heavy woman pinions her arms.* BLANCHE *cries out hoarsely and slips to her knees.*]

MATRON: These fingernails have to be trimmed. [*The* DOCTOR *comes into the room and she looks at him.*] Jacket, Doctor?

DOCTOR: Not unless necessary. [*He takes off his hat and now he becomes personalized. The unhuman quality goes. His voice is gentle and reassuring as he crosses to* BLANCHE *and crouches in front of her. As he speaks her name, her terror subsides a little. The lurid reflections fade from the walls, the inhuman cries and noises die out and her own hoarse crying is calmed.*] Miss DuBois. [*She turns her face to him and stares at him with desperate pleading. He smiles; then he speaks to the* MATRON.] It won't be necessary.

BLANCHE: [*Faintly.*] Ask her to let go of me.

DOCTOR: [*To the* MATRON.] Let go.

[*The* MATRON *releases her.* BLANCHE *extends her hands toward the* DOCTOR. *He draws her up gently and supports her with his arm and leads her through the portieres.*]

BLANCHE: [*Holding tight to his arm.*] Whoever you are—I have always depended on the kindness of strangers.

[*The poker players stand back as* BLANCHE *and the* DOCTOR *cross the kitchen to the front door. She allows him to lead her as if she were blind. As they go out on the porch,* STELLA *cries out her sister's name from where she is crouched a few steps up on the stairs.*]

STELLA: Blanche! Blanche, Blanche!

[BLANCHE *walks on without turning, followed by the* DOCTOR *and the* MATRON. *They go around the corner of the building.* EUNICE *descends to* STELLA *and places the child in her arms. It is wrapped in a pale blue blanket.* STELLA *accepts the child, sobbingly.* EUNICE *continues downstairs and enters the kitchen where the men, except for* STANLEY, *are returning silently to their places about the table.* STANLEY *has gone out on the porch and stands at the foot of the steps looking at* STELLA.]

STANLEY: [*A bit uncertainly.*] Stella? [*She sobs with inhuman abandon. There is something luxurious in her complete surrender to crying now that her sister is gone. Voluptuously, soothingly.*] Now, honey. Now, love. Now, now, love. [*He kneels beside her and his fingers find the opening of her blouse.*] Now, now, love, Now, love. . . .

[*The luxurious sobbing, the sensual murmur fade away under the swelling music of the "Blue Piano" and the muted trumpet.*]

STEVE: This game is seven-card stud.

CURTAIN

1947

CARYL CHURCHILL

Top Girls

CHARACTERS

MARLENE	POPE JOAN
ISABELLA BIRD	LOUISE
JOYCE	PATIENT GRISELDA
MRS. KIDD	NELL
LADY NIJO	JEANINE
WIN	WAITRESS
DULL GRET	KIT
ANGIE	SHONA

Act I
   Scene 1: *Restaurant. Saturday night.*
   Scene 2: *"Top Girls" Employment Agency. Monday morning.*
   Scene 3: JOYCE's *back yard. Sunday afternoon.*
Act II
   Scene 1: *Employment agency. Monday morning.*
   Scene 2: JOYCE's *kitchen. Sunday evening, a year earlier.*

NOTE ON CHARACTERS

ISABELLA BIRD (1831–1904) *lived in Edinburgh, travelled extensively between the ages of 40 and 70.*

LADY NIJO (b.1258) *Japanese, was an Emperor's courtesan and later a Buddhist nun who travelled on foot through Japan.*

DULL GRET *is the subject of the Brueghel[1] painting,* Dulle Griet, *in which a woman in an apron and armour leads a crowd of women charging through hell and fighting the devils.*

POPE JOAN, *disguised as a man, is thought to have been pope between 854–856.*

PATIENT GRISELDA *is the obedient wife whose story is told by Chaucer in* The Clerk's Tale *of* The Canterbury Tales.

NOTE ON LAYOUT

A speech usually follows the one immediately before it BUT:

1) *when one character starts speaking before the other has finished, the point of interruption is marked* /.

e.g. ISABELLA: This is the Emperor of Japan? / I once met the Emperor of
              Morocco.
      NIJO: In fact he was the ex-Emperor.

2) *a character sometimes continues speaking right through another's speech:*

e.g. ISABELLA: When I was forty I thought my life was over. / Oh I was pitiful.
              I was
      NIJO: I didn't say I felt it for twenty years. Not every minute.
      ISABELLA: sent on a cruise for my health and I felt even worse. Pains in
              my bones, pins and needles . . . etc.

3) *sometimes a speech follows on from a speech earlier than the one immediately before it, and continuity is marked**.

e.g. GRISELDA: I'd seen him riding by, we all had. And he'd seen me in the
            fields with the sheep.*
      ISABELLA: I would have been well suited to minding sheep.
      NIJO: And Mr. Nugent riding by.
      ISABELLA: Of course not, Nijo, I mean a healthy life in the open air.

---

1. Flemish painter Pieter Brueghel (1525–1569).

JOAN: *He just rode up while you were minding the sheep and asked you to marry him?

where "in the fields with the sheep" is the cue to both "I would have been" and "He just rode up."

ACT I

SCENE 1

Restaurant. Table set for dinner with white tablecloth. Six places. MARLENE *and* WAITRESS.

MARLENE: Excellent, yes, table for six. One of them's going to be late but we won't wait. I'd like a bottle of Frascati straight away if you've got one really cold.

[ISABELLA BIRD *arrives.*]

Here we are. Isabella.

ISABELLA: Congratulations, my dear.

MARLENE: Well, it's a step. It makes for a party. I haven't time for a holiday. I'd like to go somewhere exotic like you but I can't get away. I don't know how you could bear to leave Hawaii. / I'd like to lie

ISABELLA: I did think of settling.

MARLENE: in the sun forever, except of course I can't bear sitting still.

ISABELLA: I sent for my sister Hennie to come and join me. I said, Hennie we'll live here forever and help the natives. You can buy two sirloins of beef for what a pound of chops costs in Edinburgh. And Hennie wrote back, the dear, that yes, she would come to Hawaii if I wished, but I said she had far better stay where she was. Hennie was suited to life in Tobermory.

MARLENE: Poor Hennie.

ISABELLA: Do you have a sister?

MARLENE: Yes in fact.

ISABELLA: Hennie was happy. She was good. I did miss its face, my own pet. But I couldn't stay in Scotland. I loathed the constant murk.

MARLENE: Ah! [*She sees* LADY NIJO *arrive.*]

NIJO: Marlene!

MARLENE: I think a drink while we wait for the others. I think a drink anyway. What a week.

NIJO: It was always the men who used to get so drunk. I'd be one of the maidens, passing the sake.[2]

ISABELLA: I've had sake. Small hot drink. Quite fortifying after a day in the wet.

NIJO: One night my father proposed three rounds of three cups, which was normal, and then the Emperor should have said three rounds of three cups, but he said three rounds of nine cups, so you can imagine. Then the Emperor

2. A Japanese rice wine, served hot

passed his sake cup to my father and said, "Let the wild goose come to me this spring."

MARLENE: Let the what?

NIJO: It's a literary allusion to a tenth-century epic, / His Majesty was very cultured.

ISABELLA: This is the Emperor of Japan? / I once met the Emperor of Morocco.

NIJO: In fact he was the ex-Emperor.

MARLENE: But he wasn't old? / Did you, Isabella?

NIJO: Twenty-nine.

ISABELLA: Oh it's a long story.

MARLENE: Twenty-nine's an excellent age.

NIJO: Well I was only fourteen and I knew he meant something but I didn't know what. He sent me an eight-layered gown and I sent it back. So when the time came I did nothing but cry. My thin gowns were badly ripped. But even that morning when he left / —he'd a green

MARLENE: Are you saying he raped you?

NIJO: robe with a scarlet lining and very heavily embroidered trousers, I already felt different about him. It made me uneasy. No, of course not, Marlene, I belonged to him, it was what I was brought up for from a baby. I soon found I was sad if he stayed away. It was depressing day after day not knowing when he would come. I never enjoyed taking other women to him.

[*The* WAITRESS *brings the wine.*]

ISABELLA: I certainly never saw my father drunk. He was a clergyman. / And I didn't get married till I was fifty.

NIJO: Oh, my father was a very religious man. Just before he died he said to me, "Serve His Majesty, be respectful, if you lose his favour enter holy orders."

MARLENE: But he meant stay in a convent, not go wandering round the country.

NIJO: Priests were often vagrants, so why not a nun? You think I shouldn't / I still did what my father wanted.

MARLENE: No no, I think you should. I think it was wonderful.

[DULL GRET *arrives.*]

ISABELLA: I tried to do what my father wanted.

MARLENE: Gret, good. Nijo. Gret. / I know Griselda's going to be late, but should we wait for Joan? / Let's get you a drink.

[MARLENE *pours a drink for* GRET *while the others talk.*]

ISABELLA: Gret! [*Continues to* NIJO.] I tried to do what my father wanted. I tried to be a clergyman's daughter. Needlework, music, charitable schemes. I had a tumour removed from my spine and spent a great deal of time on the sofa. I studied the metaphysical poets and hymnology. / I thought I enjoyed intellectual pursuits.

NIJO: Ah, you like poetry. I come of a line of eight generations of poets. Father had a poem / in the anthology.

ISABELLA: My father taught me Latin although I was a girl. / But really I was

MARLENE: They didn't have Latin at my school.

ISABELLA: more suited to manual work. Cooking, washing, mending, riding horses. / Better than reading books, eh Gret? A rough life in the open air.*

NIJO: Oh but I'm sure you're very clever. *I can't say I enjoyed my rough life. What I enjoyed most was being the Emperor's favourite / and wearing thin silk.

ISABELLA: Did you have any horses, Gret?

GRET: Pig.

[POPE JOAN *arrives.*]

MARLENE: Oh Joan, thank God, we can order. Do you know everyone? We were just talking about learning Latin and being clever girls. Joan was by way of an infant prodigy. Of course you were. What excited you when you were ten?

JOAN: Because angels are without matter they are not individuals. Every angel is a species.

MARLENE: There you are.

[*They laugh. They look at menus.*]

ISABELLA: Yes, I forgot all my Latin. But my father was the mainspring of my life and when he died I was so grieved. I'll have the chicken, please, / and the soup.

NIJO: Of course you were grieved. My father was saying his prayers and he dozed off in the sun. So I touched his knee to rouse him. "I wonder what will happen," he said, and then he was dead before he finished the sentence. / If he'd

MARLENE: What a shock.

NIJO: died saying his prayers he would have gone straight to heaven. Waldorf salad.

JOAN: Death is the return of all creatures to God.

NIJO: I shouldn't have woken him.

JOAN: Damnation only means ignorance of the truth. I was always attracted by the teachings of John the Scot, though he was inclined to confuse / God and the world.*

ISABELLA: Grief always overwhelmed me at the time.

MARLENE: *What I fancy is a rare / steak.

ISABELLA: I am of course a member of the Church of England.

MARLENE: Gret?

GRET: Potatoes.

MARLENE: I haven't been to church for years. / I like Christmas carols.

ISABELLA: Good works matter more than church attendance.

MARLENE: Make that two steaks and a lot of potatoes. Rare. But I don't do good works either.

JOAN: Canelloni, please, / and a salad.

ISABELLA: Well, I tried, but oh dear. Hennie did good works.

NIJO: The first half of my life was all sin and the second / all repentance.*

MARLENE: Oh what about starters?

GRET: Soup.

JOAN: *And which did you like best?

MARLENE: Were your travels just a penance? Avocado vinaigrette. Didn't you / enjoy yourself?

JOAN: Nothing to start with for me, thank you.

NIJO: Yes, but I was very unhappy. / It hurt to remember the past.

MARLENE: And the wine list.

NIJO: I think that was repentance.

MARLENE: Well I wonder.

NIJO: I might have just been homesick.

MARLENE: Or angry.

NIJO: Not angry, no, / why angry?

GRET: Can we have some more bread?

MARLENE: Don't you get angry? I get angry.

NIJO: But what about?

MARLENE: Yes let's have two of number 45.

ISABELLA: I tried to understand Buddhism when I was in Japan / but all

MARLENE: And some more bread, please.

ISABELLA: this birth and death succeeding each other through eternities just filled me with the most profound melancholy. I do like something more active.

NIJO: You couldn't say I was inactive. I walked every day for twenty years.

ISABELLA: I don't mean walking. / I mean in the head.

NIJO: I vowed to copy five Mahayana³ sutras. / Do you know how long they are?

MARLENE: I don't think religious beliefs are something we have in common. Activity yes.

NIJO: My head was active. / My head ached.

JOAN: It's no good being active in heresy.

ISABELLA: What heresy? She's calling the Church of England / a heresy.

JOAN: There are some very attractive / heresies.

NIJO: I had never heard of Christianity. Never / heard of it. Barbarians.

MARLENE: Well I'm not a Christian. / And I'm not a Buddhist.

ISABELLA: You have heard of it?

MARLENE: We don't all have to believe the same.

ISABELLA: I knew coming to dinner with a pope we should keep off religion.

JOAN: I always enjoy a theological argument. But I won't try to convert you, I'm not a missionary. Anyway I'm a heresy myself.

ISABELLA: There are some barbaric practices in the east.

NIJO: Barbaric?

ISABELLA: Among the lower classes.

---

3. Buddhist texts.

NIJO: I wouldn't know.

ISABELLA: Well theology always made my head ache.

MARLENE: Oh good, some food.

[WAITRESS *is bringing the first course.*]

NIJO: How else could I have left the court if I wasn't a nun? When father died I had only His Majesty. So when I fell out of favour I had nothing. Religion is a kind of nothing / and I dedicated what was left of me to nothing.

ISABELLA: That's what I mean about Buddhism. It doesn't brace.

MARLENE: Come on, Nijo, have some wine.

NIJO: Haven't you ever felt like that? You've all felt / like that.

ISABELLA: You thought your life was over but it wasn't.

MARLENE: Yes but only for a few hours. Not twenty years.

ISABELLA: When I was forty I thought my life was over. / Oh I was pitiful. I was sent

NIJO: I didn't say I felt it for twenty years. Not every minute.

ISABELLA: on a cruise for my health and I felt even worse. Pains in my bones, pins and needles in my hands, swelling behind the ears, and—oh, stupidity. I shook all over, indefinable terror. And Australia seemed to me a hideous country, the acacias stank like drains. / I

NIJO: You were homesick.

ISABELLA: had a photograph for Hennie but I told her I wouldn't send it, my hair had fallen out and my clothes were crooked, I looked completely insane and suicidal.

NIJO: So did I, exactly, dressed as a nun. I was wearing walking shoes for the first time.

ISABELLA: I longed to go home, / but home to what? Houses are so perfectly dismal.*

NIJO: I longed to go back ten years.

MARLENE: *I thought travelling cheered you both up.

ISABELLA: Oh it did / of course. It was on

NIJO: I'm not a cheerful person, Marlene. I just laugh a lot.

ISABELLA: the trip from Australia to the Sandwich Isles, I fell in love with the sea. There were rats in the cabin and ants in the food but suddenly it was like a new world. I woke up every morning happy, knowing there would be nothing to annoy me. No nervousness. No dressing.

NIJO: Don't you like getting dressed? I adored my clothes. / When I was chosen

MARLENE: You had prettier colours than Isabella.

NIJO: to give sake to His Majesty's brother, the Emperor Kameyana, on his formal visit, I wore raw silk pleated trousers and a seven-layered gown in shades of red, and two outer garments, / yellow lined with green

MARLENE: Yes, all that silk must have been very—

JOAN: I dressed as a boy when I left home.*

NIJO: and a light green jacket. Lady Betto had a five-layered gown in shades of green and purple.

ISABELLA: *You dressed as a boy?

MARLENE: Of course, / for safety.

JOAN: It was easy, I was only twelve. / Also women weren't allowed in the library. We wanted to study in Athens.

MARLENE: You ran away alone?

JOAN: No, not alone, I went with my friend. / He was sixteen but I thought I

NIJO: Ah, an elopement.

JOAN: knew more science than he did and almost as much philosophy.

ISABELLA: Well I always travelled as a lady and I repudiated strongly any suggestion in the press that I was other than feminine.

MARLENE: I don't wear trousers in the office. / I could but I don't.

ISABELLA: There was no great danger to a woman of my age and appearance.

MARLENE: And you got away with it, Joan?

JOAN: I did then.

MARLENE: And nobody noticed anything?

JOAN: They noticed I was a very clever boy. / And when I shared a bed with my

MARLENE: I couldn't have kept pretending for so long.

JOAN: friend, that was ordinary—two poor students in a lodging house. I think I forgot I was pretending.

[*By now they have their food.*]

ISABELLA: Rocky Mountain Jim, Mr. Nugent, showed me no disrespect. He found it interesting, I think, that I could make scones and also lasso cattle. Indeed he declared his love for me, which was most distressing.

NIJO: What did he say? / We always sent poems first.

MARLENE: What did you say?

ISABELLA: I urged him to give up whisky, / but he said it was too late.

MARLENE: Oh Isabella.

ISABELLA: He had lived alone in the mountains for many years.

MARLENE: But did you—?

ISABELLA: Mr. Nugent was a man that any woman might love but none could marry. I came back to England.

NIJO: Did you write him a poem when you left? / Snow on the mountains. My sleeves

MARLENE: Did you never see him again?

ISABELLA: No, never.

NIJO: are wet with tears. In England no tears, no snow.

ISABELLA: Well, I say never. One morning very early in Switzerland, it was a year later, I had a vision of him as I last saw him / in his trapper's clothes with his

NIJO: A ghost!

ISABELLA: hair round his face, and that was the day, / I learnt later, he died with a

NIJO: Ah!

ISABELLA: bullet in his brain. / He just bowed to me and vanished.

MARLENE: Oh Isabella.

NIJO: When your lover dies—One of my lovers died. / The priest Ariake.

JOAN: My friend died. Have we all got dead lovers?

MARLENE: Not me, sorry.

NIJO: [*To* ISABELLA.] I wasn't a nun, I was still at court, but he was a priest, and when he came to me he dedicated his whole life to hell. / He knew that when he died he would fall into one of the three lower realms. And he died, he did die.

JOAN: [*To* MARLENE.] I'd quarrelled with him over the teachings of John the Scot, who held that our ignorance of God is the same as his ignorance of himself. He only knows what he creates because he creates everything he knows but he himself is above being—do you follow?

MARLENE: No, but go on.

NIJO: I couldn't bear to think / in what shape would he be reborn.*

JOAN: St. Augustine maintained that the Neo-Platonic Ideas are indivisible

ISABELLA: *Buddhism is really most uncomfortable.

JOAN: from God, but I agreed with John that the created world is essences derived from Ideas which derived from God. As Denys the Areopagite said— the pseudo-Denys—first we give God a name, then deny it, / then reconcile the contradiction

NIJO: In what shape would he return?

JOAN: by looking beyond—

MARLENE: Sorry, what? Denys said what?

JOAN: Well we disagreed about it, we quarrelled. And next day he was ill, / I

NIJO: Misery in this life and worse in the next, all because of me.

JOAN: was so annoyed with him, all the time I was nursing him I kept going over the arguments in my mind. Matter is not a means of knowing the essence. The source of the species is the Idea. But then I realised he'd never understand my arguments again, and that night he died. John the Scot held that the individual disintegrates / and there is no personal immortality.

ISABELLA: I wouldn't have you think I was in love with Jim Nugent. It was yearning to save him that I felt.

MARLENE: [*To* JOAN.] So what did you do?

JOAN: First I decided to stay a man. I was used to it. And I wanted to devote my life to learning. Do you know why I went to Rome? Italian men didn't have beards.

ISABELLA: The loves of my life were Hennie, my own pet, and my dear husband the doctor, who nursed Hennie in her last illness. I knew it would be terrible when Hennie died but I didn't know how terrible. I felt half of myself had gone. How could I go on my travels without that sweet soul waiting at home for my letters? It was Doctor Bishop's devotion to her in her last illness that made me decide to marry him. He and Hennie had the same sweet character. I had not.

NIJO: I thought his majesty had sweet character because when he found out about Ariake he was so kind. But really it was because he no longer cared for me. One night he even sent me out to a man who had been pursuing me. He lay awake on the other side of the screens and listened.

ISABELLA: I did wish marriage had seemed more of a step. I tried very hard to cope with the ordinary drudgery of life. I was ill again with carbuncles on the spine and nervous prostration. I ordered a tricycle, that was my idea of adventure then. And John himself fell ill, with erysipelas[4] and anaemia. I began to love him with my whole heart but it was too late. He was a skeleton with transparent white hands. I wheeled him on various seafronts in a bath-chair. And he faded and left me. There was nothing in my life. The doctors said I had gout / and my heart was much affected.

NIJO: There was nothing in my life, nothing, without the Emperor's favour. The Empress had always been my enemy, Marlene, she said I had no right to wear three-layered gowns. / But I was the adopted daughter of my grandfather the Prime Minister. I had been publicly granted permission to wear thin silk.

JOAN: There was nothing in my life except my studies. I was obsessed with pursuit of the truth. I taught at the Greek School in Rome, which St. Augustine had made famous. I was poor, I worked hard, I spoke apparently brilliantly, I was still very young, suddenly I was quite famous, I was everyone's favourite. Huge crowds came to hear me. The day after they made me cardinal I fell ill and lay two weeks without speaking, full of terror and regret. / But then I got up determined to

MARLENE: Yes, success is very alarming.

JOAN: go on. I was seized again / with a desperate longing for the absolute.

ISABELLA: Yes, yes, to go on. I sat in Tobermory among Hennie's flowers and sewed a complete outfit in Jaeger flannel. / I was fifty-six years old.

NIJO: Out of favour but I didn't die. I left on foot, nobody saw me go. For the next twenty years I walked through Japan.

GRET: Walking is good.

JOAN: Pope Leo died and I was chosen. All right then. I would be Pope. I would know God. I would know everything.

ISABELLA: I determined to leave my grief behind and set off for Tibet.

MARLENE: Magnificent all of you. We need some more wine, please, two bottles I think, Griselda isn't here yet, and I want to drink a toast to you all.

ISABELLA: To yourself surely, / we're here to celebrate your success.

NIJO: Yes, Marlene.

JOAN: Yes, what is it exactly, Marlene?

MARLENE: Well it's not Pope but it is managing director.*

JOAN: And you find work for people.

MARLENE: Yes, an employment agency.

NIJO: *Over all the women you work with. And the men.

ISABELLA: And very well deserved too. I'm sure it's just the beginning of something extraordinary.

MARLENE: Well it's worth a party.

ISABELLA: To Marlene.*

MARLENE: And all of us.

4. Inflammation of the skin.

JOAN: *Marlene.
NIJO: Marlene.
GRET: Marlene.

[*They drink to her.*]

MARLENE: Well we've all come a long way. To our courage and the way we changed our lives and our extraordinary achievements.

[*They laugh and drink.*]

ISABELLA: Such adventures. We were crossing a mountain pass at seven thousand feet, the cook was all to pieces, the muleteers suffered fever and snow blindness. But even though my spine was agony I managed very well.
MARLENE: Wonderful.
NIJO: Once I was ill for four months lying alone at an inn. Nobody to offer a horse to Buddha. I had to live for myself, and I did live.
ISABELLA: Of course you did. It was far worse returning to Tobermory. I always felt dull when I was stationary. / That's why I could never stay anywhere.
NIJO: Yes, that's it exactly. New sights. / The shrine by the beach, the moon shining on the sea. The goddess had vowed to save all living things. / She would even save the fishes. I was full of hope.
JOAN: I had thought the Pope would know everything. I thought God would speak to me directly. But of course he knew I was a woman.*
MARLENE: But nobody else even suspected?
JOAN: In the end I did take a lover again. He was one of my chamberlains. There are such a lot of servants when you're a Pope. The food's very good. And I realised I did know the truth. Because whatever the Pope says, that's true.
NIJO: What was he like, the chamberlain?
JOAN: He could keep a secret.
MARLENE: So you did know everything.
JOAN: Yes, I enjoyed being Pope. I consecrated bishops and let people kiss my feet. I received the King of England when he came to submit to the church. Unfortunately there were earthquakes, and some village reported it had rained blood, and in France there was a plague of giant grasshoppers, but I don't think that can have been my fault, do you?*

[*Laughter.*]

The grasshoppers fell on the English Channel / and were washed up on shore
NIJO: I once went to sea. It was very lonely. / I realised it made very little difference
GRET: Ah, boat.
NIJO: where I went.
JOAN: and their bodies rotted and poisoned the air and everyone in those parts died.

[*Laughter.*]

ISABELLA: *Such superstition! I was nearly murdered in China by a howling mob. They thought the barbarians ate babies and put them under railway sleepers to make the tracks steady, and ground up their eyes to make the lenses of cameras. / So they were shouting,

MARLENE: And you had a camera!

ISABELLA: "Child-eater, child-eater." Some people tried to sell girl babies to Europeans for cameras or stew!

[Laughter.]

MARLENE: So apart from the grasshoppers it was a great success.

JOAN: Yes, if it hadn't been for the baby I expect I'd have lived to an old age like Theodora of Alexandria, who lived as a monk. She was accused by a girl / who fell in love with her of being the father of her child and rather than say she was a woman she—

NIJO: But tell us what happened to your baby. I had some babies.

MARLENE: Didn't you think of getting rid of it?

JOAN: Wouldn't that be a worse sin than having it? / But a Pope with a child was about as bad as possible.

MARLENE: I don't know, you're the Pope.

JOAN: But I wouldn't have known how to get rid of it.

MARLENE: Other Popes had children, surely.

JOAN: They didn't give birth to them.

NIJO: Well you were a woman.

JOAN: Exactly and I shouldn't have been a woman. Women, children and lunatics can't be Pope.

MARLENE: So the only thing to do / was get rid of it somehow.

NIJO: You had to have it adopted secretly.

JOAN: But I didn't know what was happening. I thought I was getting fatter, but then I was eating more and sitting about, the life of a Pope is quite luxurious. I don't think I'd spoken to a woman since I was twelve. The chamberlain was the one who realised.

MARLENE: And by then it was too late.

JOAN: Oh I didn't want to pay attention. It was easier to do nothing.

NIJO: But you had to plan for having it. You had to say you were ill and go away.

JOAN: That's what I should have done I suppose.

MARLENE: Did you want them to find out?

NIJO: I too was often in embarrassing situations, there's no need for a scandal. My first child was His Majesty's, which unfortunately died, but my second was Akebono's. I was seventeen. He was in love with me when I was thirteen, he was very upset when I had to go to the Emperor, it was very romantic, a lot of poems. Now His Majesty hadn't been near me for two months so he thought I was four months pregnant when I was really six, so when I reached the ninth month / I announced I was seriously ill,

JOAN: I never knew what month it was.

NIJO: and Akebono announced he had gone on a religious retreat. He held me round the waist and lifted me up as the baby was born. He cut the cord with a short sword, wrapped the baby in white and took it away. It was only a girl but I was sorry to lose it. Then I told the Emperor that the baby had miscarried because of my illness, and there you are. The danger was past.

JOAN: But Nijo, I wasn't used to having a woman's body.

ISABELLA: So what happened?

JOAN: I didn't know of course that it was near the time. It was Rogation Day,[5] there was always a procession. I was on the horse dressed in my robes and a cross was carried in front of me, and all the cardinals were following, and all the clergy of Rome, and a huge crowd of people. / We set off from St. Peter's to go

MARLENE: Total Pope.

JOAN: to St. John's. I had felt a slight pain earlier, I thought it was something I'd eaten, and then it came back, and came back more often. I thought when this is over I'll go to bed. There were still long gaps when I felt perfectly all right and I didn't want to attract attention to myself and spoil the ceremony. Then I suddenly realised what it must be. I had to last out till I could get home and hide. Then something changed, my breath started to catch, I couldn't plan things properly any more. We were in a little street that goes between St. Clement's and the Colosseum, and I just had to get off the horse and sit down for a minute. Great waves of pressure were going through my body, I heard sounds like a cow lowing, they came out of my mouth. Far away I heard people screaming, "The Pope is ill, the Pope is dying." And the baby just slid out onto the road.*

MARLENE: The cardinals / won't have known where to put themselves.

NIJO: Oh dear, Joan, what a thing to do! In the street!

ISABELLA: *How embarrassing.

GRET: In a field, yah.

[*They are laughing.*]

JOAN: One of the cardinals said, "The Antichrist!" and fell over in a faint.

[*They all laugh.*]

MARLENE: So what did they do? They weren't best pleased.

JOAN: They took me by the feet and dragged me out of town and stoned me to death.

[*They stop laughing.*]

MARLENE: Joan, how horrible.

JOAN: I don't really remember.

NIJO: And the child died too?

JOAN: Oh yes, I think so, yes.

[*Pause.*]

5. The Monday, Tuesday, or Wednesday preceding Ascension Day.

ISABELLA: I never had any children. I was very fond of horses.

NIJO: I saw my daughter once. She was three years old. She wore a plum-red / small-sleeved gown. Akebono's wife

ISABELLA: Birdie was my favourite. A little Indian bay mare I rode in the Rocky Mountains.

NIJO: had taken the child because her own died. Everyone thought I was just a visitor. She was being brought up carefully so she could be sent to the palace like I was.

ISABELLA: Legs of iron and always cheerful, and such a pretty face. If a stranger led her she reared up like a bronco.

NIJO: I never saw my third child after he was born, the son of Ariake the priest. Ariake held him on his lap the day he was born and talked to him as if he could understand, and cried. My fourth child was Ariake's too. Ariake died before he was born. I didn't want to see anyone, I stayed alone in the hills. It was a boy again, my third son. But oddly enough I felt nothing for him.

MARLENE: How many children did you have, Gret?

GRET: Ten.

ISABELLA: Whenever I came back to England I felt I had so much to atone for. Hennie and John were so good. I did no good in my life. I spent years in self-gratification. So I hurled myself into committees, I nursed the people of Tobermory in the epidemic of influenza, I lectured the Young Women's Christian Association on Thrift. I talked and talked / explaining how the East was corrupt and vicious and I went to Korea and China not for pleasure but specially to report on the missions. My travels must do good to someone beside myself. I wore myself out with good causes.

MARLENE: Oh God, why are we all so miserable?

JOAN: The procession never went down that street again.

MARLENE: They rerouted it specially?

JOAN: Yes they had to go all round to avoid it. And they introduced a pierced chair.

MARLENE: A pierced chair?

JOAN: Yes, a chair made out of solid marble with a hole in the seat / and it was

MARLENE: You're not serious.

JOAN: in the Chapel of the Saviour, and after he was elected the Pope had to sit in it.

MARLENE: And someone looked up his skirts? / Not really!

ISABELLA: What an extraordinary thing.

JOAN: Two of the clergy / made sure he was a man.

NIJO: On their hands and knees!

MARLENE: A pierced chair!

GRET: Balls!

NIJO: Why couldn't he just pull up his robe?

JOAN: He had to sit there and look dignified.

[*They are quite drunk. They get the giggles.* GRISELDA *arrives.*]

MARLENE: Griselda! / There you are. Do you want to eat?

GRISELDA: I'm sorry I'm so late. No, no, don't bother.

MARLENE: Of course it's no bother. / Have you eaten.

GRISELDA: No really, I'm not hungry.

MARLENE: Well have some pudding.

GRISELDA: I never eat pudding.

MARLENE: Griselda, I hope you're not anorexic. We're having pudding, I am, and getting nice and fat.

GRISELDA: Oh if everyone is. I don't mind.

MARLENE: Now who do you know. This is Joan who was Pope in the ninth century, and Isabella Bird, the Victorian traveller, and Lady Nijo from Japan, Emperor's concubine and Buddhist nun, thirteenth century, nearer your own time, and Gret who was painted by Brueghel. Griselda's in Boccaccio and Petrarch and Chaucer because of her extraordinary marriage. I'd like profiterolles because they're disgusting.

JOAN: Zabaglione, please.

ISABELLA: Apple pie / and cream.

NIJO: What's this?

MARLENE: Zabaglione, it's Italian, it's what Joan's having, / it's delicious.

NIJO: A Roman Catholic / dessert? Yes please.

MARLENE: Gret?

GRET: Cake.

GRISELDA: Just cheese and biscuits, thank you.

MARLENE: Yes, Griselda's life is like a fairy story, except it starts with marrying the prince.

GRISELDA: He's only a marquis, Marlene.

MARLENE: Well everyone for miles around is his liege and he's absolute lord of life and death and you were the poor but beautiful peasant girl and he whisked you off. / Near enough a prince.

NIJO: How old were you?

GRISELDA: Fifteen.

NIJO: I was brought up in court circles and it was still a shock. Had you ever seen him before?

GRISELDA: I'd seen him riding by, we all had. And he'd seen me in the fields with the sheep.*

ISABELLA: I would have been well suited to minding sheep.

NIJO: And Mr. Nugent riding by.

ISABELLA: Of course not, Nijo, I mean a healthy life in the open air.

JOAN: *He just rode up while you were minding the sheep and asked you to marry him?

GRISELDA: No, no, it was on the wedding day. I was waiting outside the door to see the procession. Everyone wanted him to get married so there'd be an heir to look after us when he died, / and at last he

MARLENE: I don't think Walter wanted to get married. It is Walter? Yes.

GRISELDA: announced a day for the wedding but nobody knew who the bride was, we thought it must be a foreign princess, we were longing to see her.

Then the carriage stopped outside our cottage and we couldn't see the bride anywhere. And he came and spoke to my father.

NIJO: And your father told you to serve the Prince.

GRISELDA: My father could hardly speak. The Marquis said it wasn't an order, I could say no, but if I said yes I must always obey him in everything.

MARLENE: That's when you should have suspected.

GRISELDA: But of course a wife must obey her husband. / And of course I must obey the Marquis.*

ISABELLA: I swore to obey dear John, of course, but it didn't seem to arise. Naturally I wouldn't have wanted to go abroad while I was married.

MARLENE: *Then why bother to mention it at all? He'd got a thing about it, that's why.

GRISELDA: I'd rather obey the Marquis than a boy from the village.

MARLENE: Yes, that's a point.

JOAN: I never obeyed anyone. They all obeyed me.

NIJO: And what did you wear? He didn't make you get married in your own clothes? That would be perverse.*

MARLENE: Oh, you wait.

GRISELDA: *He had ladies with him who undressed me and they had a white silk dress and jewels for my hair.

MARLENE: And at first he seemed perfectly normal?

GRISELDA: Marlene, you're always so critical of him. / Of course he was normal, he was very kind.

MARLENE: But Griselda, come on, he took your baby.

GRISELDA: Walter found it hard to believe I loved him. He couldn't believe I would always obey him. He had to prove it.

MARLENE: I don't think Walter likes women.

GRISELDA: I'm sure he loved me, Marlene, all the time.

MARLENE: He just had a funny way / of showing it.

GRISELDA: It was hard for him too.

JOAN: How do you mean he took away your baby?

NIJO: Was it a boy?

GRISELDA: No, the first one was a girl.

NIJO: Even so it's hard when they take it away. Did you see it at all?

GRISELDA: Oh yes, she was six weeks old.

NIJO: Much better to do it straight away.

ISABELLA: But why did your husband take the child?

GRISELDA: He said all the people hated me because I was just one of them. And now I had a child they were restless. So he had to get rid of the child to keep them quiet. But he said he wouldn't snatch her, I had to agree and obey and give her up. So when I was feeding her a man came in and took her away. I thought he was going to kill her even before he was out of the room.

MARLENE: But you let him take her? You didn't struggle?

GRISELDA: I asked him to give her back so I could kiss her. And I asked him to bury her where no animals could dig her up. / It was Walter's child to do what he

ISABELLA: Oh my dear.

GRISELDA: liked with.*

MARLENE: Walter was bonkers.

GRET: Bastard.

ISABELLA: But surely, murder.

GRISELDA: I had promised.

MARLENE: I can't stand this. I'm going for a pee.

[MARLENE *goes out.*]

NIJO: No, I understand. Of course you had to, he was your life. And were you in
favour after that?

GRISELDA: Oh yes, we were very happy together. We never spoke about what
had happened.

ISABELLA: I can see you were doing what you thought was your duty. But didn't
it make you ill?

GRISELDA: No, I was very well, thank you.

NIJO: And you had another child?

GRISELDA: Not for four years, but then I did, yes, a boy.

NIJO: Ah a boy. / So it all ended happily.

GRISELDA: Yes he was pleased. I kept my son till he was two years old. A peasant's
grandson. It made the people angry. Walter explained.

ISABELLA: But surely he wouldn't kill his children / just because—

GRISELDA: Oh it wasn't true. Walter would never give in to people. He wanted
to see if I loved him enough.

JOAN: He killed his children / to see if you loved him enough?

NIJO: Was it easier the second time or harder?

GRISELDA: It was always easy because I always knew I would do what he said.

ISABELLA: I hope you didn't have any more children.

GRISELDA: Oh no, no more. It was twelve years till he tested me again.

ISABELLA: So whatever did he do this time? / My poor John, I never loved him
enough, and he would never have dreamt . . .

GRISELDA: He sent me away. He said the people wanted him to marry someone
else who'd give him an heir and he'd got special permission from the Pope.
So I said I'd go home to my father. I came with nothing / so I went with
nothing. I took

NIJO: Better to leave if your master doesn't want you.

GRISELDA: off my clothes. He let me keep a slip so he wouldn't be shamed. And
I walked home barefoot. My father came out in tears. Everyone was crying
except me.

NIJO: At least your father wasn't dead. / I had nobody.

ISABELLA: Well it can be a relief to come home. I loved to see Hennie's sweet
face again.

GRISELDA: Oh yes, I was perfectly content. And quite soon he sent for me again.

JOAN: I don't think I would have gone.

GRISELDA: But he told me to come. I had to obey him. He wanted me to help
prepare his wedding. He was getting married to a young girl from France /

and nobody except me knew how to arrange things the way he liked them.

NIJO: It's always hard taking him another woman.

JOAN: I didn't live a woman's life. I don't understand it.

GRISELDA: The girl was sixteen and far more beautiful than me. I could see why he loved her. / She had her younger brother with her as a page.

[MARLENE *comes back.*]

MARLENE: Oh God, I can't bear it. I want some coffee. Six coffees. Six brandies. / Double brandies.

GRISELDA: They all went in to the feast I'd prepared. And he stayed behind and put his arms round me and kissed me. / I felt half asleep with the shock.

NIJO: Oh, like a dream.

MARLENE: And he said, "This is your daughter and your son."

GRISELDA: Yes.

JOAN: What?

NIJO: Oh. Oh I see. You got them back.

ISABELLA: I did think it was remarkably barbaric to kill them but you learn not to say anything. / So he had them brought up secretly I suppose.

MARLENE: Walter's a monster. Weren't you angry? What did you do?

GRISELDA: Well I fainted. Then I cried and kissed the children. / Everyone was making a fuss of me.

NIJO: But did you feel anything for them?

GRISELDA: What?

NIJO: Did you feel anything for the children?

GRISELDA: Of course, I loved them.

JOAN: So you forgave him and lived with him?

GRISELDA: He suffered so much all those years.

ISABELLA: Hennie had the same sweet nature.

NIJO: So they dressed you again?

GRISELDA: Cloth of gold.

JOAN: I can't forgive anything.

MARLENE: You really are exceptional, Griselda.

NIJO: Nobody gave me back my children.

[NIJO *cries. The* WAITRESS *brings coffees and brandies.*]

ISABELLA: I can never be like Hennie. I was always so busy in England, a kind of business I detested. The very presence of people exhausted my emotional reserves. I could not be like Hennie however I tried. I tried and was as ill as could be. The doctor suggested a steel net to support my head, the weight of my own head was too much for my diseased spine. It is dangerous to put oneself in depressing circumstances. Why should I do it?

JOAN: Don't cry.

NIJO: My father and the Emperor both died in the autumn. So much pain.

JOAN: Yes, but don't cry.

NIJO: They wouldn't let me into the palace when he was dying. I hid in the room with his coffin, then I couldn't find where I'd left my shoes, I ran after the funeral procession in bare feet, I couldn't keep up. When I got there it was over, a few wisps of smoke in the sky, that's all that was left of him. What I want to know is, if I'd still been at court, would I have been allowed to wear full mourning?

MARLENE: I'm sure you would.

NIJO: Why do you say that? You don't know anything about it. Would I have been allowed to wear full mourning?

ISABELLA: How can people live in this dim pale island and wear our hideous clothes? I cannot and will not live the life of a lady.

NIJO: I'll tell you something that made me angry. I was eighteen, at the Full Moon Ceremony. They make a special rice gruel and stir it with their sticks, and then they beat their women across the loins so they'll have sons and not daughters. / So

MARLENE: What a sod.

NIJO: the Emperor beat us all very hard as usual—that's not it, Marlene, that's normal, what made us angry, he told his attendants they could beat us too. Well they had a wonderful time. / So Lady

MARLENE: I'd like another brandy please. Better make it six.

NIJO: Genki and I made a plan, and the ladies all hid in his rooms, and Lady Mashimizu stood guard with a stick at the door, and when His Majesty came in Genki seized him and I beat him till he cried out and promised he would never order anyone to hit us again. Afterwards there was a terrible fuss. The nobles were horrified. "We wouldn't even dream of stepping on your Majesty's shadow." And I had hit him with a stick. Yes, I hit him with a stick.

JOAN: Suave, mari magno turbantibus[6] aequora ventis,
    e terra magnum alterius spectare laborem;
    non quia vexari quemquamst iucunda voluptas,
    sed quibus ipse malis careas quia cernere suave est.
    Suave etiam belli / certamina magna tueri

GRISELDA: I do think—I do wonder—it would have been nicer if Walter hadn't had to.

JOAN: per campos instructa tua sine parte pericli.
    Sed nil dulcius est, bene quam munita tenere

---

6. From the Latin poet and philosopher Titus Lucretius Carus (97–54 B.C.) On the Nature of Things (trans. Cyril Bailey): Sweet it is, when on the great sea the winds are buffeting the waters, to gaze from the land on another's great struggles; not because it is pleasure or joy that anyone should be distressed, but because it is sweet to perceive from what misfortune you yourself are free. Sweet is it too, to behold great contests of war in full array over the plains, when you have no part in the danger. But nothing is more gladdening than to dwell in the calm high places, firmly embattled on the heights by the teaching of the wise, whence you can look down on others, and see them wandering hither and thither, going astray as they seek the way of life, in strife matching their wits or rival claims of birth, struggling night and day by surpassing effort to rise up to the height of power and gain possession of the world. Ah! miserable minds of men, blind hearts! In what darkness of life, in what great dangers ye spend this little span of years! to think that ye should not see that nature cries aloud for nothing else but that pain may be kept far sundered from the body, and that, withdrawn from care and fear, she may enjoy in mind the sense of pleasure.

edita doctrina sapientum templa serena,
despicere unde queas alios passimque videre
errare atque viam / palantis quaerere vitae,
ISABELLA: Why should I? Why should I?
MARLENE: Of course not.
NIJO: I hit him with a stick.
JOAN: certare ingenio, contendere nobilitate,
noctes atque dies niti praestante labore
ad summas emergere opes rerumque potiri.
O miseras hominum mentis, o pectora caeca!
qualibus in tenebris vitae quantisque periclis
degitur hoc aevi quodcumquest! nonne videre
nil aliud sibi naturam latrare, nisi utqui
corpore seiunctus dolor absit, / mente fruatur
iucundo sensu cura semota metuque?
ergo corpoream ad naturam pauca videmus
esse opus omnino, quae dement cumque dolorem,
delicias quoque uti multas substernere possint.
gratius interdum neque natura ipsa requirit,
si non aurea sunt iuvenum simulacra per aedes
lampadas igniferas manibus retinentia dextris,
lumina nocturnis epulis ut suppeditentur,
nec domus argento fulget auroque renidet
nec citharae reboant laqueata aurataque templa

[JOAN *has gradually faded under* GRET's *speech.*]

GRET: We come into hell through a big mouth. Hell's black and red. It's like
the village where I come from. There's a river and a bridge and houses.
There's places on fire like when the soldiers come. There's a big devil sat on
a roof with a big hole in his arse and he's scooping stuff out of it with a big
ladle and it's falling down on us, and it's money, so a lot of the women stop
and get some. But most of us is fighting the devils. There's lots of little devils,
our size, and we get them down all right and give them a beating. There's
lots of funny creatures round your feet, you don't like to look, like rats and
lizards, and nasty things, a bum with a face, and fish with legs, and faces on
things that don't have faces on. But they don't hurt, you just keep going.
Well we'd had worse, you see, we'd had the Spanish. We'd all had family
killed. Men on wheels. Babies on swords. I'd had enough, I was mad, I
hate the bastards. I come out my front door that morning and shout till my
neighbours come out and I said, "Come on, we're going where the evil come
from and pay the bastards out." And they all come out just as they was from
baking or washing in their aprons, and we push down the street and the
ground opens up and we go through a big mouth into a street just like ours
but in hell. I've got a sword in my hand from somewhere and I fill a basket
with gold cups they drink out of down there. You just keep running on

and fighting, you didn't stop for nothing. Oh we give them devils such a beating.

JOAN: Something something something[7] something mortisque timores
tum vacuum pectus—damn.
Quod si ridicula—
something something on and on and on
and and something splendorem purpureai.

ISABELLA: I thought I would have a last jaunt up the west river in China. Why not? But the doctors were so very grave I just went to Morocco. The sea was so wild I had to be landed by ship's crane in a coal bucket. My horse was a terror to me / a

JOAN: nos in luce timemus
something
terrorem

ISABELLA: powerful black charger.

[NIJO *is crying.*
JOAN *gets up and is sick in a corner.*
MARLENE *is drinking* ISABELLA's *brandy.*]

So off I went to visit the Berber sheikhs in full blue trousers and great brass spurs. I was the only European woman ever to have seen the Emperor of Morocco. I was seventy years old. What lengths to go to for a last chance of joy. I knew my return of vigour was only temporary, but how marvellous while it lasted.

SCENE 2

Employment agency. MARLENE *and* JEANINE.

MARLENE: Right Jeanine, you are Jeanine aren't you? Let's have a look. O's[8] and A's. / No A's, all those O's you

JEANINE: Six O's.

MARLENE: probably could have got an A. / Speeds, not brilliant, not too bad.

JEANINE: I wanted to go to work.

MARLENE: Well, Jeanine, what's your present job like?

JEANINE: I'm a secretary.

---

7. Fragments from a passage that reads: The dread of death leaves your heart empty, but if we see that these thoughts are mere mirth and mockery, and in very truth the fears of men and the cares that dog them fear not the clash of arms nor the weapons of war, but pass boldly among kings and lords of the world, nor dread the glitter that comes from gold nor the bright sheen of the purple robe, can you doubt that all such power belongs to reason alone, above all when the whole of life is but a struggle in darkness? For even as children tremble and fear everything in blinding darkness, so we sometimes dread in the light things that are no whit more to be feared than what children shudder at in the dark.   8. O-level and A-level examinations in the British school system. O-level tests basic knowledge and A-level tests advanced knowledge.

MARLENE: Secretary or typist?

JEANINE: I did start as a typist but the last six months I've been a secretary.

MARLENE: To?

JEANINE: To three of them, really, they share me. There's Mr. Ashford, he's the office manager, and Mr. Philby / is sales, and—

MARLENE: Quite a small place?

JEANINE: A bit small.

MARLENE: Friendly?

JEANINE: Oh it's friendly enough.

MARLENE: Prospects?

JEANINE: I don't think so, that's the trouble. Miss Lewis is secretary to the managing director and she's been there forever, and Mrs. Bradford / is—

MARLENE: So you want a job with better prospects?

JEANINE: I want a change.

MARLENE: So you'll take anything comparable?

JEANINE: No, I do want prospects. I want more money.

MARLENE: You're getting—?

JEANINE: Hundred.

MARLENE: It's not bad you know. You're what? Twenty?

JEANINE: I'm saving to get married.

MARLENE: Does that mean you don't want a long-term job, Jeanine?

JEANINE: I might do.

MARLENE: Because where do the prospects come in? No kids for a bit?

JEANINE: Oh no, not kids, not yet.

MARLENE: So you won't tell them you're getting married?

JEANINE: Had I better not?

MARLENE: It would probably help.

JEANINE: I'm not wearing a ring. We thought we wouldn't spend on a ring.

MARLENE: Saves taking it off.

JEANINE: I wouldn't take it off.

MARLENE: There's no need to mention it when you go for an interview. / Now

JEANINE: But what if they ask?

MARLENE: Jeanine do you have a feel for any particular kind of company?

JEANINE: I thought advertising.

MARLENE: People often do think advertising. I have got a few vacancies but I think they're looking for something glossier.

JEANINE: You mean how I dress? / I can

MARLENE: I mean experience.

JEANINE: dress different. I dress like this on purpose for where I am now.

MARLENE: I have a marketing department here of a knitwear manufacturer. / Marketing is near enough

JEANINE: Knitwear?

MARLENE: advertising. Secretary to the marketing manager, he's thirty-five, married, I've sent him a girl before and she was happy, left to have a baby, you won't want to mention marriage there. He's very fair I think, good at his job, you won't have to nurse him along. Hundred and ten, so that's better than you're doing now.

JEANINE: I don't know.

MARLENE: I've a fairly small concern here, father and two sons, you'd have more say potentially, secretarial and reception duties, only a hundred but the job's going to grow with the concern and then you'll be in at the top with new girls coming in underneath you.

JEANINE: What is it they do?

MARLENE: Lampshades. / This would be my first choice for you.

JEANINE: Just lampshades?

MARLENE: There's plenty of different kinds of lampshade. So we'll send you there, shall we, and the knitwear second choice. Are you free to go for an interview any day they call you?

JEANINE: I'd like to travel.

MARLENE: We don't have any foreign clients. You'd have to go elsewhere.

JEANINE: Yes I know. I don't really . . . I just mean . . .

MARLENE: Does your fiancé want to travel?

JEANINE: I'd like a job where I was here in London and with him and everything but now and then—I expect it's silly. Are there jobs like that?

MARLENE: There's personal assistant to a top executive in a multinational. If that's the idea you need to be planning ahead. Is that where you want to be in ten years?

JEANINE: I might not be alive in ten years.

MARLENE: Yes but you will be. You'll have children.

JEANINE: I can't think about ten years.

MARLENE: You haven't got the speeds anyway. So I'll send you to these two shall I? You haven't been to any other agency? Just so we don't get crossed wires. Now Jeanine I want you to get one of these jobs, all right? If I send you that means I'm putting myself on the line for you. Your presentation's OK, you look fine, just be confident and go in there convinced that this is the best job for you and you're the best person for the job. If you don't believe it they won't believe it.

JEANINE: Do you believe it?

MARLENE: I think you could make me believe it if you put your mind to it.

JEANINE: Yes, all right.

Scene 3

JOYCE's *back yard. The house with back door is upstage. Downstage a shelter made of junk, made by children. Two girls,* ANGIE *and* KIT, *are in it, squashed together.* ANGIE *is 16,* KIT *is 12. They cannot be seen from the house.* JOYCE *calls from the house.*

JOYCE: Angie. Angie are you out there?

[*Silence. They keep still and wait. When nothing else happens they relax.*]

ANGIE: Wish she was dead.

KIT: Wanna watch *The Exterminator*[9]?

ANGIE: You're sitting on my leg.

KIT: There's nothing on telly. We can have an ice cream. Angie?

ANGIE: Shall I tell you something?

KIT: Do you wanna watch *The Exterminator*?

ANGIE: It's X,[1] innit.

KIT: I can get into Xs.

ANGIE: Shall I tell you something?

KIT: We'll go to something else. We'll go to Ipswich. What's on the Odeon?

ANGIE: She won't let me, will she.

KIT: Don't tell her.

ANGIE: I've no money.

KIT: I'll pay.

ANGIE: She'll moan though, won't she.

KIT: I'll ask her for you if you like.

ANGIE: I've no money, I don't want you to pay.

KIT: I'll ask her.

ANGIE: She don't like you.

KIT: I still got three pounds birthday money. Did she say she don't like me? I'll go by myself then.

ANGIE: Your mum don't let you. I got to take you.

KIT: She won't know.

ANGIE: You'd be scared who'd sit next to you.

KIT: No I wouldn't.
She does like me anyway.
Tell me then.

ANGIE: Tell you what?

KIT: It's you she doesn't like.

ANGIE: Well I don't like her so tough shit.

JOYCE: [*Off.*] Angie. Angie. Angie. I know you're out there. I'm not coming out after you. You come in here.

[*Silence. Nothing happens.*]

ANGIE: Last night when I was in bed. I been thinking yesterday could I make things move. You know, make things move by thinking about them without touching them. Last night I was in bed and suddenly a picture fell down off the wall.

KIT: What picture?

ANGIE: My gran, that picture. Not the poster. The photograph in the frame.

KIT: Had you done something to make it fall down?

ANGIE: I must have done.

---

9. 1980 U.S. vigilante film remarkable for its extreme violence.   1. Film rating, indicating it is unsuitable for children.

KIT: But were you thinking about it?

ANGIE: Not about it, but about something.

KIT: I don't think that's very good.

ANGIE: You know the kitten?

KIT: Which one?

ANGIE: There only is one. The dead one.

KIT: What about it?

ANGIE: I heard it last night.

KIT: Where?

ANGIE: Out here. In the dark. What if I left you here in the dark all night?

KIT: You couldn't. I'd go home.

ANGIE: You couldn't.

KIT: I'd / go home.

ANGIE: No you couldn't, not if I said.

KIT: I could.

ANGIE: Then you wouldn't see anything. You'd just be ignorant.

KIT: I can see in the daytime.

ANGIE: No you can't. You can't hear it in the daytime.

KIT: I don't want to hear it.

ANGIE: You're scared that's all.

KIT: I'm not scared of anything.

ANGIE: You're scared of blood.

KIT: It's not the same kitten anyway. You just heard an old cat, / you just heard some old cat.

ANGIE: You don't know what I heard. Or what I saw. You don't know nothing because you're a baby.

KIT: You're sitting on me.

ANGIE: Mind my hair / you silly cunt.

KIT: Stupid fucking cow, I hate you.

ANGIE: I don't care if you do.

KIT: You're horrible.

ANGIE: I'm going to kill my mother and you're going to watch.

KIT: I'm not playing.

ANGIE: You're scared of blood.

[KIT *puts her hand under dress, brings it out with blood on her finger.*]

KIT: There, see, I got my own blood, so.

[ANGIE *takes* KIT's *hand and licks her finger.*]

ANGIE: Now I'm a cannibal. I might turn into a vampire now.

KIT: That picture wasn't nailed up right.

ANGIE: You'll have to do that when I get mine.

KIT: I don't have to.

ANGIE: You're scared.

KIT: I'll do it, I might do it. I don't have to just because you say. I'll be sick on you.

ANGIE: I don't care if you are sick on me, I don't mind sick. I don't mind blood. If I don't get away from here I'm going to die.

KIT: I'm going home.

ANGIE: You can't go through the house. She'll see you.

KIT: I won't tell her.

ANGIE: Oh great, fine.

KIT: I'll say I was by myself. I'll tell her you're at my house and I'm going there to get you.

ANGIE: She knows I'm here, stupid.

KIT: Then why can't I go through the house?

ANGIE: Because I said not.

KIT: My mum don't like you anyway.

ANGIE: I don't want her to like me. She's a slag.[2]

KIT: She is not.

ANGIE: She does it with everyone.

KIT: She does not.

ANGIE: You don't even know what it is.

KIT: Yes I do.

ANGIE: Tell me then.

KIT: We get it all at school, cleverclogs. It's on television. You haven't done it.

ANGIE: How do you know?

KIT: Because I know you haven't.

ANGIE: You know wrong then because I have.

KIT: Who with?

ANGIE: I'm not telling you / who with.

KIT: You haven't anyway.

ANGIE: How do you know?

KIT: Who with?

ANGIE: I'm not telling you.

KIT: You said you told me everything.

ANGIE: I was lying wasn't I.

KIT: Who with? You can't tell me who with because / you never—

ANGIE: Sh.

[JOYCE *has come out of the house. She stops half way across the yard and listens. They listen.*]

JOYCE: You there Angie? Kit? You there Kitty? Want a cup of tea? I've got some chocolate biscuits. Come on now I'll put the kettle on. Want a choccy biccy, Angie?

[*They all listen and wait.*]

Fucking rotten little cunt. You can stay there and die. I'll lock the back door.

[*They all wait.*
JOYCE *goes back to the house.*

2. Worthless or insignificant person.

[ANGIE *and* KIT *sit in silence for a while.*]

KIT: When there's a war, where's the safest place?

ANGIE: Nowhere.

KIT: New Zealand is, my mum said. Your skin's burned right off. Shall we go to New Zealand?

ANGIE: I'm not staying here.

KIT: Shall we go to New Zealand?

ANGIE: You're not old enough.

KIT: You're not old enough.

ANGIE: I'm old enough to get married.

KIT: You don't want to get married.

ANGIE: No but I'm old enough.

KIT: I'd find out where they were going to drop it and stand right in the place.

ANGIE: You couldn't find out.

KIT: Better than walking round with your skin dragging on the ground. Eugh. / Would you like walking round with your skin dragging on the ground?

ANGIE: You couldn't find out, stupid, it's a secret.

KIT: Where are you going?

ANGIE: I'm not telling you.

KIT: Why?

ANGIE: It's a secret.

KIT: But you tell me all your secrets.

ANGIE: Not the true secrets.

KIT: Yes you do.

ANGIE: No I don't.

KIT: I want to go somewhere away from the war.

ANGIE: Just forget the war.

KIT: I can't.

ANGIE: You have to. It's so boring.

KIT: I'll remember it at night.

ANGIE: There's not going to be a war. No war. No war. Right? No war. Now shut up.

KIT: How do you know?

ANGIE: How do you know there is?

KIT: How do you know there isn't?

ANGIE: I'm going to do something else anyway.

KIT: What? Angie come on. Angie.

ANGIE: It's a secret.

KIT: It can't be worse than the kitten. And killing your mother. And the war.

ANGIE: Well I'm not telling you so you can die for all I care.

KIT: My mother says there's something wrong with you playing with someone my age. She says why haven't you got friends your own age. People your own age know there's something funny about you. She says you're a bad influence. She says she's going to speak to your mother.

[ANGIE *twists* KIT's *arm till she cries out.*]

ANGIE: Say you're a liar.

KIT: She said it not me.

ANGIE: Say you eat shit.

KIT: You can't make me.

[ANGIE *lets go.*]

ANGIE: I don't care anyway. I'm leaving.

KIT: Go on then.

ANGIE: You'll all wake up one morning and find I've gone.

KIT: Good.

ANGIE: I'm not telling you when.

KIT: Go on then.

ANGIE: I'm sorry I hurt you.

KIT: I'm tired.

ANGIE: Do you like me?

KIT: I don't know.

ANGIE: You do like me.

KIT: I'm going home.

ANGIE: No you're not.

KIT: I'm tired.

ANGIE: She'll see you.

KIT: She'll give me a chocolate biscuit.

ANGIE: Kitty.

KIT: Tell me where you're going.

ANGIE: Sit down.

KIT: Go on then.

ANGIE: Swear?

KIT: Swear.

ANGIE: I'm going to London. To see my aunt.

KIT: And what?

ANGIE: That's it.

KIT: I see my aunt all the time.

ANGIE: I don't see my aunt.

KIT: What's so special?

ANGIE: It is special. She's special.

KIT: Why?

ANGIE: She is.

KIT: Why?

ANGIE: She is.

KIT: Why?

ANGIE: My mother hates her.

KIT: Why?

ANGIE: Because she does.

KIT: Perhaps she's not very nice.

ANGIE: She is nice.

KIT: How do you know?

ANGIE: Because I know her.
KIT: You said you never see her.
ANGIE: I saw her last year. You saw her.
KIT: Did I?
ANGIE: Never mind.
KIT: I remember her. That aunt. What's so special?
ANGIE: She gets people jobs.
KIT: What's so special?
ANGIE: I think I'm my aunt's child. I think my mother's really my aunt.
KIT: Why?
ANGIE: Because I do, now shut up.
KIT: I've been to London.
ANGIE: Now give us a cuddle and shut up because I'm sick.
KIT: You're sitting on my arm.

[*Silence.*
JOYCE *comes out and comes up to them quietly.*]

JOYCE: Come on.
KIT: Oh hello.
JOYCE: Time you went home.
KIT: We want to go to the Odeon.
JOYCE: What time?
KIT: Don't know.
JOYCE: What's on?
KIT: Don't know.
JOYCE: Don't know much do you?
KIT: That all right then?
JOYCE: Angie's got to clean her room first.
ANGIE: No I don't.
JOYCE: Yes you do, it's a pigsty.
ANGIE: Well I'm not.
JOYCE: Then you're not going. I don't care.
ANGIE: Well I am going.
JOYCE: You've no money, have you.
ANGIE: Kit's paying anyway.
JOYCE: No she's not.
KIT: I'll help you with your room.
JOYCE: That's nice.
ANGIE: No you won't. You wait here.
KIT: Hurry then.
ANGIE: I'm not hurrying. You just wait.

[ANGIE *goes into the house. Silence.*]

JOYCE: I don't know.

[*Silence.*]

How's school then?

KIT: All right.

JOYCE: What are you now? Third year?

KIT: Second year.

JOYCE: Your mum says you're good at English.

[*Silence.*]

Maybe Angie should've stayed on.

KIT: She didn't like it.

JOYCE: I didn't like it. And look at me. If your face fits at school it's going to fit other places too. It wouldn't make no difference to Angie. She's not going to get a job when jobs are hard to get. I'd be sorry for anyone in charge of her. She'd better get married. I don't know who'd have her, mind. She's one of those girls might never leave home. What do you want to be when you grow up, Kit?

KIT: Physicist.

JOYCE: What?

KIT: Nuclear physicist.

JOYCE: Whatever for?

KIT: I could, I'm clever.

JOYCE: I know you're clever, pet.

[*Silence.*]

I'll make a cup of tea.

[*Silence.*]

Looks like it's going to rain.

[*Silence.*]

Don't you have friends your own age?

KIT: Yes.

JOYCE: Well then.

KIT: I'm old for my age.

JOYCE: And Angie's simple is she? She's not simple.

KIT: I love Angie.

JOYCE: She's clever in her own way.

KIT: You can't stop me.

JOYCE: I don't want to.

KIT: You can't, so.

JOYCE: Don't be cheeky, Kitty. She's always kind to little children.

KIT: She's coming so you better leave me alone.

[ANGIE *comes out. She has changed into an old best dress, slightly small for her.*]

JOYCE: What you put that on for? Have you done your room? You can't clean your room in that.

ANGIE: I looked in the cupboard and it was there.

JOYCE: Of course it was there, it's meant to be there. Is that why it was a surprise, finding something in the right place? I should think she's surprised, wouldn't you Kit, to find something in her room in the right place.

ANGIE: I decided to wear it.

JOYCE: Not today, why? To clean your room? You're not going to the pictures till you've done your room. You can put your dress on after if you like.

[ANGIE *squats down in the rubble of the shelter and picks up a brick.*]

Have you done your room? You're not getting out of it, you know.

KIT: Angie, let's go.

JOYCE: She's not going till she's done her room.

KIT: It's starting to rain.

JOYCE: Come on, come on then. Hurry and do your room, Angie, and then you can go to the cinema with Kit. Oh it's wet, come on. We'll look up the time in the paper. Does your mother know, Kit, it's going to be a late night for you, isn't it. Hurry up, Angie. You'll spoil your dress. You make me sick.

[JOYCE *and* KIT *run in.*
ANGIE *stays where she is. Sound of rain.*
KIT *comes out of the house and shouts.*]

KIT: Angie. Angie, come on, you'll get wet.

[KIT *comes back to* ANGIE.]

ANGIE: I put on this dress to kill my mother.

KIT: I suppose you thought you'd do it with a brick.

ANGIE: You can kill people with a brick.

KIT: Well you didn't, so.

ACT II

SCENE 1

Office of "Top Girls" Employment Agency. Central desk area and small interviewing area. Monday morning. WIN *and* NELL *have just arrived for work.*

NELL: Coffee coffee coffee coffee / coffee.

WIN: The roses were smashing. / Mermaid.

NELL: Ohhh.

WIN: Iceberg. He taught me all their names.

[NELL *has some coffee now.*]

NELL: Ah. Now then.

WIN: He has one of the finest rose gardens in West Sussex. He exhibits.

NELL: He what?

WIN: His wife was visiting her mother. It was like living together.

NELL: Crafty, you never said.

WIN: He rang on Saturday morning.

NELL: Lucky you were free.

WIN: That's what I told him.

NELL: Did you hell.

WIN: Have you ever seen a really beautiful rose garden?

NELL: I don't like flowers. / I like swimming pools.

WIN: Marilyn. Esther's Baby. They're all called after birds.

NELL: Our friend's late. Celebrating all weekend I bet you.

WIN: I'd call a rose Elvis. Or John Conteh.

NELL: Is Howard in yet?

WIN: If he is he'll be bleeping us with a problem.

NELL: Howard can just hang onto himself.

WIN: Howard's really cut up.

NELL: Howard thinks because he's a fella the job was his as of right. Our Marlene's got far more balls than Howard and that's that.

WIN: Poor little bugger.

NELL: He'll live.

WIN: He'll move on.

NELL: I wouldn't mind a change of air myself.

WIN: Serious?

NELL: I've never been a staying put lady. Pastures new.

WIN: So who's the pirate?

NELL: There's nothing definite.

WIN: Inquiries?

NELL: There's always inquiries. I'd think I'd got bad breath if there stopped being inquiries. Most of them can't afford me. Or you.

WIN: I'm all right for the time being. Unless I go to Australia.

NELL: There's not a lot of room upward.

WIN: Marlene's filled it up.

NELL: Good luck to her. Unless there's some prospects moneywise.

WIN: You can but ask.

NELL: Can always but ask.

WIN: So what have we got? I've got a Mr. Holden I saw last week.

NELL: Any use?

WIN: Pushy. Bit of a cowboy.

NELL: Goodlooker?

WIN: Good dresser.

NELL: High flyer?

WIN: That's his general idea certainly but I'm not sure he's got it up there.

NELL: Prestel wants six high flyers and I've only seen two and a half.

WIN: He's making a bomb on the road but he thinks it's time for an office. I sent him to IBM but he didn't get it.

NELL: Prestel's on the road.

WIN: He's not overbright.

NELL: Can he handle an office?

WIN: Provided his secretary can punctuate he should go far.

NELL: Bear Prestel in mind then, I might put my head round the door. I've got that poor little nerd I should never had said I could help. Tender heart me.

WIN: Tender like old boots. How old?

NELL: Yes well forty-five.

WIN: Say no more.

NELL: He knows his place, he's not after calling himself a manager, he's just a poor little bod wants a better commission and a bit of sunshine.

WIN: Don't we all.

NELL: He's just got to relocate. He's got a bungalow in Dymchurch.

WIN: And his wife says.

NELL: The lady wife wouldn't care to relocate. She's going through the change.

WIN: It's his funeral, don't waste your time.

NELL: I don't waste a lot.

WIN: Good weekend you?

NELL: You could say.

WIN: Which one?

NELL: One Friday, one Saturday.

WIN: Aye—aye.

NELL: Sunday night I watched telly.

WIN: Which of them do you like best really?

NELL: Sunday was best, I liked the Ovaltine.

WIN: Holden, Barker, Gardner, Duke.

NELL: I've a lady here thinks she can sell.

WIN: Taking her on?

NELL: She's had some jobs.

WIN: Services?

NELL: No, quite heavy stuff, electric.

WIN: Tough bird like us.

NELL: We could do with a few more here.

WIN: There's nothing going here.

NELL: No but I always want the tough ones when I see them. Hang onto them.

WIN: I think we're plenty.

NELL: Derek asked me to marry him again.

WIN: He doesn't know when he's beaten.

NELL: I told him I'm not going to play house, not even in Ascot.

WIN: Mind you, you could play house.

NELL: If I chose to play house I would play house ace.

WIN: You could marry him and go on working.

NELL: I could go on working and not marry him.

[MARLENE *arrives.*]

MARLENE: Morning ladies.

[WIN *and* NELL *cheer and whistle.*]

Mind my head.

NELL: Coffee coffee coffee.

WIN: We're tactfully not mentioning you're late.

MARLENE: Fucking tube.

WIN: We've heard that one.

NELL: We've used that one.

WIN: It's the top executive doesn't come in as early as the poor working girl.

MARLENE: Pass the sugar and shut your face, pet.

WIN: Well I'm delighted.

NELL: Howard's looking sick.

WIN: Howard is sick. He's got ulcers and heart. He told me.

NELL: He'll have to stop then won't he.

WIN: Stop what?

NELL: Smoking, drinking, shouting. Working.

WIN: Well, working.

NELL: We're just looking through the day.

MARLENE: I'm doing some of Pam's ladies. They've been piling up while she's away.

NELL: Half a dozen little girls and an arts graduate who can't type.

WIN: I spent the whole weekend at his place in Sussex.

NELL: She fancies his rose garden.

WIN: I had to lie down in the back of the car so the neighbours wouldn't see me go in.

NELL: You're kidding.

WIN: It was funny.

NELL: Fuck that for a joke.

WIN: It was funny.

MARLENE: Anyway they'd see you in the garden.

WIN: The garden has extremely high walls.

NELL: I think I'll tell the wife.

WIN: Like hell.

NELL: She might leave him and you could have the rose garden.

WIN: The minute it's not a secret I'm out on my ear.

NELL: Don't know why you bother.

WIN: Bit of fun.

NELL: I think it's time you went to Australia.

WIN: I think it's pushy Mr. Holden time.

NELL: If you've any really pretty bastards, Marlene, I want some for Prestel.

MARLENE: I might have one this afternoon. This morning it's all Pam's secretarial.

NELL: Not long now and you'll be upstairs watching over us all.

MARLENE: Do you feel bad about it?

NELL: I don't like coming second.

MARLENE: Who does?

WIN: We'd rather it was you than Howard. We're glad for you, aren't we Nell.

NELL: Oh yes. Aces.

INTERVIEW

WIN *and* LOUISE.

WIN: Now Louise, hello, I have your details here. You've been very loyal to the one job I see.

LOUISE: Yes I have.

WIN: Twenty-one years is a long time in one place.

LOUISE: I feel it is. I feel it's time to move on.

WIN: And you are what age now?

LOUISE: I'm in my early forties.

WIN: Exactly?

LOUISE: Forty-six.

WIN: It's not necessarily a handicap, well it is of course we have to face that, but it's not necessarily a disabling handicap, experience does count for something.

LOUISE: I hope so.

WIN: Now between ourselves is there any trouble, any reason why you're leaving that wouldn't appear on the form?

LOUISE: Nothing like that.

WIN: Like what?

LOUISE: Nothing at all.

WIN: No long term understandings come to a sudden end, making for an insupportable atmosphere?

LOUISE: I've always completely avoided anything like that at all.

WIN: No personality clashes with your immediate superiors or inferiors?

LOUISE: I've always taken care to get on very well with everyone.

WIN: I only ask because it can affect the reference and it also affects your motivation, I want to be quite clear why you're moving on. So I take it the job itself no longer satisfies you. Is it the money?

LOUISE: It's partly the money. It's not so much the money.

WIN: Nine thousand is very respectable. Have you dependants?

LOUISE: No, no dependants. My mother died.

WIN: So why are you making a change?

LOUISE: Other people make changes.

WIN: But why are you, now, after spending most of your life in the one place?

LOUISE: There you are, I've lived for that company, I've given my life really you could say because I haven't had a great deal of social life, I've worked in the evenings. I haven't had office entanglements for the very reason you just mentioned and if you are committed to your work you don't move in many other circles. I had management status from the age of twenty-seven and you'll appreciate what that means. I've built up a department. And there it is, it works extremely well, and I feel I'm stuck there. I've spent twenty years in middle management. I've seen young men who I trained go on, in my own company or elsewhere, to higher things. Nobody notices me, I don't expect it, I don't attract attention by making mistakes, everybody takes it for granted that my work is perfect. They will notice me when I go, they will be sorry I think to lose me, they will offer me more money of course, I will refuse. They will see when I've gone what I was doing for them.

WIN: If they offer you more money you won't stay?

LOUISE: No I won't.

WIN: Are you the only woman?

LOUISE: Apart from the girls of course, yes. There was one, she was my assistant, it was the only time I took on a young woman assistant, I always had my doubts. I don't care greatly for working with women, I think I pass as a man at work. But I did take on this young women, her qualifications were excellent, and she did well, she got a department of her own, and left the company for a competitor where she's now on the board and good luck to her. She has a different style, she's a new kind of attractive well-dressed—I don't mean I don't dress properly. But there is a kind of woman who is thirty now who grew up in a different climate. They are not so careful. They take themselves for granted. I have had to justify my existence every minute, and I have done so, I have proved—well.

WIN: Let's face it, vacancies are going to be ones that might be filled by a rather younger man. And there are companies that will value your experience enough to take that chance. There are also fields that are easier for a woman, there is a cosmetic company here where your experience might be relevant. It's eight and a half, I don't know if that appeals.

LOUISE: I've proved I can earn money. It's more important to get away. I feel it's now or never. I sometimes / think—

WIN: You shouldn't talk too much at an interview.

LOUISE: I don't. I don't normally talk about myself. I know very well how to handle myself in an office situation. I only talk to you because it seems to me this is different, it's your job to understand me, surely. You asked the questions.

WIN: I think I understand you sufficiently.

LOUISE: Well good, that's good.

WIN: Do you drink?

LOUISE: Certainly not. I'm not a teetotaller, I think that's very suspect, it's seen as being an alcoholic if you're teetotal. What do you mean? I don't drink. Why?

WIN: I drink.

LOUISE: I don't.

WIN: Good for you.

MAIN OFFICE

MARLENE *and* ANGIE. ANGIE *arrives*.

ANGIE: Hello.

MARLENE: Have you an appointment?

ANGIE: It's me. I've come.

MARLENE: What? It's not Angie?

ANGIE: It was hard to find this place. I got lost.

MARLENE: How did you get past the receptionist? The girl on the desk, didn't she try to stop you?

ANGIE: What desk?

MARLENE: Never mind.

ANGIE: I just walked in. I was looking for you.

MARLENE: Well you found me.

ANGIE: Yes.

MARLENE: So where's your mum? Are you up in town for the day?

ANGIE: Not really.

MARLENE: Sit down. Do you feel all right?

ANGIE: Yes thank you.

MARLENE: So where's Joyce?

ANGIE: She's at home.

MARLENE: Did you come up on a school trip then?

ANGIE: I've left school.

MARLENE: Did you come up with a friend?

ANGIE: No. There's just me.

MARLENE: You came up by yourself, that's fun. What have you been doing? Shopping? Tower of London?

ANGIE: No, I just come here. I come to you.

MARLENE: That's very nice of you to think of paying your aunty a visit. There's not many nieces make that the first port of call. Would you like a cup of tea?

ANGIE: No thank you.

MARLENE: Coffee, orange?

ANGIE: No thank you.

MARLENE: Do you feel all right?

ANGIE: Yes thank you.

MARLENE: Are you tired from the journey?

ANGIE: Yes, I'm tired from the journey.

MARLENE: You sit there for a bit then. How's Joyce?

ANGIE: She's all right.

MARLENE: Same as ever.

ANGIE: Oh yes.

MARLENE: Unfortunately you've picked a day when I'm rather busy, if there's a day when I'm not, or I'd take you out to lunch and we'd go to Madame Tussaud's.[3] We could go shopping. What time do you have to be back? Have you got a day return?

ANGIE: No.

MARLENE: So what train are you going back on?

ANGIE: I came on the bus.

MARLENE: So what bus are you going back on? Are you staying the night?

ANGIE: Yes.

---

3. Wax museum that serves as a tourist attraction for London visitors.

MARLENE: Who are you staying with? Do you want me to put you up for the night, is that it?

ANGIE: Yes please.

MARLENE: I haven't got a spare bed.

ANGIE: I can sleep on the floor.

MARLENE: You can sleep on the sofa.

ANGIE: Yes please.

MARLENE: I do think Joyce might have phoned me. It's like her.

ANGIE: This is where you work is it?

MARLENE: It's where I have been working the last few years but I'm going to move into another office.

ANGIE: It's lovely.

MARLENE: My new office is nicer than this. There's just the one big desk in it for me.

ANGIE: Can I see it?

MARLENE: Not now, no, there's someone else in it now. But he's leaving at the end of next week and I'm going to do his job.

ANGIE: Is that good?

MARLENE: Yes, it's very good.

ANGIE: Are you going to be in charge?

MARLENE: Yes I am.

ANGIE: I knew you would be.

MARLENE: How did you know?

ANGIE: I knew you'd be in charge of everything.

MARLENE: Not quite everything.

ANGIE: You will be.

MARLENE: Well we'll see.

ANGIE: Can I see it next week then?

MARLENE: Will you still be here next week?

ANGIE: Yes.

MARLENE: Don't you have to go home?

ANGIE: No.

MARLENE: Why not?

ANGIE: It's all right.

MARLENE: Is it all right?

ANGIE: Yes, don't worry about it.

MARLENE: Does Joyce know where you are?

ANGIE: Yes of course she does.

MARLENE: Well does she?

ANGIE: Don't worry about it.

MARLENE: How long are you planning to stay with me then?

ANGIE: You know when you came to see us last year?

MARLENE: Yes, that was nice wasn't it.

ANGIE: That was the best day of my whole life.

MARLENE: So how long are you planning to stay?

ANGIE: Don't you want me?

MARLENE: Yes yes, I just wondered.

ANGIE: I won't stay if you don't want me.

MARLENE: No, of course you can stay.

ANGIE: I'll sleep on the floor. I won't be any bother.

MARLENE: Don't get upset.

ANGIE: I'm not, I'm not. Don't worry about it.

[MRS. KIDD *comes in.*]

MRS. KIDD: Excuse me.

MARLENE: Yes.

MRS. KIDD: Excuse me.

MARLENE: Can I help you?

MRS. KIDD: Excuse me bursting in on you like this but I have to talk to you.

MARLENE: I am engaged at the moment. / If you could go to reception—

MRS. KIDD: I'm Rosemary Kidd, Howard's wife, you don't recognise me but we
    did meet, I remember you of course / but you wouldn't—

MARLENE: Yes of course, Mrs. Kidd, I'm sorry, we did meet. Howard's about
    somewhere I expect, have you looked in his office?

MRS. KIDD: Howard's not about, no. I'm afraid it's you I've come to see if I could
    have a minute or two.

MARLENE: I do have an appointment in five minutes.

MRS. KIDD: This won't take five minutes. I'm very sorry. It is a matter of some
    urgency.

MARLENE: Well of course. What can I do for you?

MRS. KIDD: I just wanted a chat, an informal chat. It's not something I can sim-
    ply—I'm sorry if I'm interrupting your work. I know office work isn't like
    housework / which is all interruptions.

MARLENE: No no, this is my niece. Angie. Mrs. Kidd.

MRS. KIDD: Very pleased to meet you.

ANGIE: Very well thank you.

MRS. KIDD: Howard's not in today.

MARLENE: Isn't he?

MRS. KIDD: He's feeling poorly.

MARLENE: I didn't know. I'm sorry to hear that.

MRS. KIDD: The fact is he's in a state of shock. About what's happened.

MARLENE: What has happened?

MRS. KIDD: You should know if anyone. I'm referring to you being appointed
    managing director instead of Howard. He hasn't been at all well all weekend.
    He hasn't slept for three nights. I haven't slept.

MARLENE: I'm sorry to hear that, Mrs. Kidd. Has he thought of taking sleeping
    pills?

MRS. KIDD: It's very hard when someone has worked all these years.

MARLENE: Business life is full of little setbacks. I'm sure Howard knows that.
    He'll bounce back in a day or two. We all bounce back.

MRS. KIDD: But I've been behind him all the way. If you could see him you'd know what I'm talking about. What's it going to do to him working for a woman? I think if it was a man he'd get over it as something normal.

MARLENE: I think he's going to have to get over it.

MRS. KIDD: It's me that bears the brunt. I'm not the one that's been promoted. He's not being dominated by me, I've been right behind him, I put him first every inch of the way. And now what do I get? You women this, you women that. It's not my fault. You're going to have to be very careful how you handle him. He's very hurt.

MARLENE: Naturally I'll be tactful and pleasant to him, you don't start pushing someone round. I'll consult him over any decisions affecting his department. But that's no different, Mrs. Kidd, from any of my other colleagues.

MRS. KIDD: I think it is different, because he's a man.

MARLENE: I'm not quite sure why you came to see me.

MRS. KIDD: I had to do something.

MARLENE: Well you've done it, you've seen me. I think that's probably all we've time for. I'm sorry he's been taking it out on you. He really is a shit, Howard.

MRS. KIDD: But he's got a family to support. He's got three children. It's only fair.

MARLENE: Are you suggesting I give up the job to him then?

MRS. KIDD: It had crossed my mind if you were unavailable after all for some reason, he would be the natural second choice I think, don't you. I'm not asking.

MARLENE: Good.

MRS. KIDD: You mustn't tell him I came. He's very proud.

MARLENE: If he doesn't like what's happening here he can go and work somewhere else.

MRS. KIDD: Is that a threat?

MARLENE: I'm sorry but I do have some work to do.

MRS. KIDD: It's not that easy, a man of Howard's age. He's been here longer than you have. You don't care. I thought he was going too far in what he said about you but he's right. You're one of these ballbreakers, that's what you are. You'll end up miserable / and lonely. You're not natural.

MARLENE: I'm sorry but I do have some work to do.

MRS. KIDD: I'll stand by him, I've got feelings.

MARLENE: Could you please piss off?

MRS. KIDD: I thought if I saw you at least I'd be doing something.

[MRS. KIDD goes.]

MARLENE: I've got to go and do some work now. Will you come back later?

ANGIE: I think you were wonderful.

MARLENE: I've got to go and do some work now.

ANGIE: You told her to piss off.

MARLENE: Will you come back later?

ANGIE: Can't I stay here?

MARLENE: Don't you want to go sightseeing?

ANGIE: I'd rather stay here.

MARLENE: You can stay here I suppose, if it's not boring.
ANGIE: It's where I most want to be in the world.
MARLENE: I'll see you later then.

> [MARLENE *goes.*
> ANGIE *sits there.*]

INTERVIEW

NELL *and* SHONA.

NELL: Is this right? You are Shona?
SHONA: Yeh.
NELL: It says here you're twenty-nine.
SHONA: Yeh.
NELL: Too many late nights, me. So you've been where you are for four years, Shona, you're earning six basic and three commission. So what's the problem?
SHONA: No problem.
NELL: Why do you want a change?
SHONA: Just a change.
NELL: Change of product, change of area?
SHONA: Both.
NELL: But you're happy on the road?
SHONA: I like driving.
NELL: You're not after management status?
SHONA: I would like management status.
NELL: You'd be interested in titular management status but not come off the road?
SHONA: I want to be on the road, yeh.
NELL: So how many calls have you been making a day?
SHONA: Six.
NELL: And what proportion of those are successful?
SHONA: Six.
NELL: That's hard to believe.
SHONA: Four.
NELL: You find it easy to get the initial interest do you?
SHONA: Oh yeh, I get plenty of initial interest.
NELL: And what about closing?
SHONA: I close, don't I?
NELL: Because that's what an employer is going to have doubts about with a lady as I needn't tell you, whether she's got the guts to push through to a closing situation. They think we're too nice. They think we listen to the buyer's doubts. They think we consider his needs and his feelings.
SHONA: I never consider people's feelings.
NELL: I was selling for six years, I can sell anything, I've sold in three continents, and I'm jolly as they come but I'm not very nice.

SHONA: I'm not very nice.

NELL: What sort of time do you have on the road with the other reps? Get on all right? Handle the chat?

SHONA: I get on. Keep myself to myself.

NELL: Fairly much of a loner are you?

SHONA: Sometimes.

NELL: So what field are you interested in?

SHONA: Computers.

NELL: That's a top field as you know and you'll be up against some very slick fellas there, there's some very pretty boys in computers, it's an American-style field.

SHONA: That's why I want to do it.

NELL: Video systems appeal? That's a high-flying situation.

SHONA: Video systems appeal OK.

NELL: Because Prestel have half a dozen vacancies I'm looking to fill at the moment. We're talking in the area of ten to fifteen thousand here and upwards.

SHONA: Sounds OK.

NELL: I've half a mind to go for it myself. But it's good money here if you've got the top clients. Could you fancy it do you think?

SHONA: Work here?

NELL: I'm not in a position to offer, there's nothing officially going just now, but we're always on the lookout. There's not that many of us. We could keep in touch.

SHONA: I like driving.

NELL: So the Prestel appeals?

SHONA: Yeh.

NELL: What about ties?

SHONA: No ties.

NELL: So relocation wouldn't be a problem.

SHONA: No problem.

NELL: So just fill me in a bit more could you about what you've been doing.

SHONA: What I've been doing. It's all down there.

NELL: The bare facts are down here but I've got to present you to an employer.

SHONA: I'm twenty-nine years old.

NELL: So it says here.

SHONA: We look young. Youngness runs in the family in our family.

NELL: So just describe your present job for me.

SHONA: My present job at present. I have a car. I have a Porsche. I go up the M1 a lot. Burn up the M1 a lot. Straight up the M1 in the fast lane to where the clients are, Staffordshire, Yorkshire, I do a lot in Yorkshire. I'm selling electric things. Like dishwashers, washing machines, stainless steel tub are a feature and the reliability of the programme. After sales service, we offer a very good after sales service, spare parts, plenty of spare parts. And fridges, I sell a lot of fridges specially in the summer. People want to buy fridges in the summer because of the heat melting the butter and you get fed up standing the milk in a basin of cold water with a cloth over, stands to reason people don't want to do that in this day and age. So I sell a lot of them. Big ones with big freezers. Big freezers. And I stay in hotels at night when I'm away from home. On my expense account. I stay in various hotels. They know me, the ones I go to. I check in, have a bath, have a shower. Then I go down to the bar, have a gin and tonic, have a chat. Then I go into the dining room and have dinner. I usually have fillet steak and mushrooms, I like mushrooms. I like smoked salmon very much. I like having a salad on the side. Green salad. I don't like tomatoes.

NELL: Christ what a waste of time.

SHONA: Beg your pardon?

NELL: Not a word of this is true is it. /

SHONA: How do you mean?

NELL: You just filled in the form with a pack of lies.

SHONA: Not exactly.

NELL: How old are you?

SHONA: Twenty-nine.

NELL: Nineteen?

SHONA: Twenty-one.

NELL: And what jobs have you done? Have you done any?

SHONA: I could though, I bet you.

MAIN OFFICE

ANGIE *sitting as before.* WIN *comes in.*

WIN: Who's sitting in my chair?

ANGIE: What? Sorry.

WIN: Who's been eating my porridge?

ANGIE: What?

WIN: It's all right, I saw Marlene. Angie isn't it? I'm Win. And I'm not going out for lunch because I'm knackered. I'm going to set me down here and have a yoghurt. Do you like yoghurt?

ANGIE: No.

WIN: That's good because I've only got one. Are you hungry?

ANGIE: No.

WIN: There's a cafe on the corner.

ANGIE: No thank you. Do you work here?

WIN: How did you guess?

ANGIE: Because you look as if you might work here and you're sitting at the desk. Have you always worked here?

WIN: No I was headhunted. That means I was working for another outfit like this and this lot came and offered me more money. I broke my contract, there was a hell of a stink. There's not many top ladies about. Your aunty's a smashing bird.

ANGIE: Yes I know.

MARLENE: Fan are you? Fan of your aunty's?

ANGIE: Do you think I could work here?

WIN: Not at the moment.

ANGIE: How do I start?

WIN: What can you do?

ANGIE: I don't know. Nothing.

WIN: Type?

ANGIE: Not very well. The letters jump up when I do capitals. I was going to do a CSE in commerce but I didn't.

WIN: What have you got?

ANGIE: What?

WIN: CSE's,[4] O's.

ANGIE: Nothing, none of that. Did you do all that?

WIN: Oh yes, all that, and a science degree funnily enough. I started out doing medical research but there's no money in it. I thought I'd go abroad. Did you know they sell Coca-Cola in Russia and Pepsi-cola in China? You don't have to be qualified as much as you might think. Men are awful bullshitters, they like to make out jobs are harder than they are. Any job I ever did I started doing it better than the rest of the crowd and they didn't like it. So I'd get unpopular and I'd have a drink to cheer myself up. I lived with a fella and supported him for four years, he couldn't get work. After that I went to California. I like the sunshine. Americans know how to live. This country's too slow. Then I went to Mexico, still in sales, but it's no country for a single lady. I came home, went bonkers for a bit, thought I was five different people, got over that all right, the psychiatrist said I was perfectly sane and highly intelligent. Got married in a moment of weakness and he's inside now, he's been inside four years, and I've not been to see him too much this last year. I like this better than sales, I'm not really that aggressive. I started thinking sales was a good job if you want to meet people, but you're meeting people that don't want to meet you. It's no good if you like being liked. Here your clients want to meet you because you're the one doing them some good. They hope.

[ANGIE *has fallen asleep.* NELL *comes in.*]

NELL: You're talking to yourself, sunshine.

WIN: So what's new.

NELL: Who is this?

WIN: Marlene's little niece.

NELL: What's she got, brother, sister? She never talks about her family.

WIN: I was telling her my life story.

NELL: Violins?

WIN: No, success story.

NELL: You've heard Howard's had a heart attack?

WIN: No, when?

4. Certificate of Secondary Education.

NELL: I heard just now. He hadn't come in, he was at home, he's gone to hospital. He's not dead. His wife was here, she rushed off in a cab.

WIN: Too much butter, too much smoke. We must send him some flowers.

[MARLENE *comes in.*]

You've heard about Howard?

MARLENE: Poor sod.

NELL: Lucky he didn't get the job if that's what his health's like.

MARLENE: Is she asleep?

WIN: She wants to work here.

MARLENE: Packer in Tesco more like.

WIN: She's a nice kid. Isn't she?

MARLENE: She's a bit thick. She's a bit funny.

WIN: She thinks you're wonderful.

MARLENE: She's not going to make it.

SCENE 2

A year earlier. Sunday evening. JOYCE's *kitchen.* JOYCE, ANGIE, MARLENE. MARLENE *is taking presents out of a bright carrier bag.* ANGIE *has already opened a box of chocolates.*

MARLENE: Just a few little things. / I've

JOYCE: There's no need.

MARLENE: no memory for birthdays have I, and Christmas seems to slip by. So I think I owe Angie a few presents.

JOYCE: What do you say?

ANGIE: Thank you very much. Thank you very much, Aunty Marlene.

[*She opens a present. It is the dress from Act I, new.*]

ANGIE: Oh look, mum, isn't it lovely.

MARLENE: I don't know if it's the right size. She's grown up since I saw her. / I

ANGIE: Isn't it lovely.

MARLENE: knew she was always tall for her age.

JOYCE: She's a big lump.

MARLENE: Hold it up, Angie, let's see.

ANGIE: I'll put it on, shall I?

MARLENE: Yes, try it on.

JOYCE: Go on to your room then, we don't want / a strip show thank you.

ANGIE: Of course I'm going to my room, what do you think. Look mum, here's something for you. Open it, go on. What is it? Can I open it for you?

JOYCE: Yes, you open it, pet.

ANGIE: Don't you want to open it yourself? / Go on.

JOYCE: I don't mind, you can do it.

ANGIE: It's something hard. It's—what is it? A bottle. Drink is it? No, it's what? Perfume, look. What a lot. Open it, look, let's smell it. Oh it's strong. It's lovely. Put it on me. How do you do it? Put it on me.

JOYCE: You're too young.

ANGIE: I can play wearing it like dressing up.

JOYCE: And you're too old for that. Here, give it here, I'll do it, you'll tip the whole bottle over yourself / and we'll have you smelling all summer.

ANGIE: Put it on you. Do I smell? Put it on aunty too. Put it on aunty too. Let's all smell.

MARLENE: I didn't know what you'd like.

JOYCE: There's no danger I'd have it already, / that's one thing.

ANGIE: Now we all smell the same.

MARLENE: It's a bit of nonsense.

JOYCE: It's very kind of you Marlene, you shouldn't.

ANGIE: Now I'll put on the dress and then we'll see.

[ANGIE *goes.*]

JOYCE: You've caught me on the hop with the place in the mess. / If you'd let me.

MARLENE: That doesn't matter.

JOYCE: know you was coming I'd have got something in to eat. We had our dinner dinnertime. We're just going to have a cup of tea. You could have an egg.

MARLENE: No, I'm not hungry. Tea's fine.

JOYCE: I don't expect you take sugar.

MARLENE: Why not?

JOYCE: You take care of yourself.

MARLENE: How do you mean you didn't know I was coming?

JOYCE: You could have written. I know we're not on the phone but we're not completely in the dark ages, / we do have a postman.

MARLENE: But you asked me to come.

JOYCE: How did I ask you to come?

MARLENE: Angie said when she phoned up.

JOYCE: Angie phoned up, did she.

MARLENE: Was it just Angie's idea?

JOYCE: What did she say?

MARLENE: She said you wanted me to come and see you. / It was a couple of

JOYCE: Ha.

MARLENE: weeks ago. How was I to know that's a ridiculous idea? My diary's always full a couple of weeks ahead so we fixed it for this weekend. I was meant to get here earlier but I was held up. She gave me messages from you.

JOYCE: Didn't you wonder why I didn't phone you myself?

MARLENE: She said you didn't like using the phone. You're shy on the phone and can't use it. I don't know what you're like, do I.

JOYCE: Are there people who can't use the phone?

MARLENE: I expect so.

JOYCE: I haven't met any.

MARLENE: Why should I think she was lying?

JOYCE: Because she's like what she's like.

MARLENE: How do I know / what she's like?

JOYCE: It's not my fault you don't know what she's like. You never come and see her.

MARLENE: Well I have now / and you don't seem over the moon.*

JOYCE: Good.

    *Well I'd have got a cake if she'd told me.

[*Pause.*]

MARLENE: I did wonder why you wanted to see me.

JOYCE: I didn't want to see you.

MARLENE: Yes, I know. Shall I go?

JOYCE: I don't mind seeing you.

MARLENE: Great, I feel really welcome.

JOYCE: You can come and see Angie any time you like, I'm not stopping you. / you

MARLENE: Ta ever so.

JOYCE: know where we are. You're the one went away, not me. I'm right here where I was. And will be a few years yet I shouldn't wonder.

MARLENE: All right. All right.

[JOYCE *gives* MARLENE *a cup of tea.*]

JOYCE: Tea.

MARLENE: Sugar?

[JOYCE *passes* MARLENE *the sugar.*]

    It's very quiet down here.

JOYCE: I expect you'd notice it.

MARLENE: The air smells different too.

JOYCE: That's the scent.

MARLENE: No, I mean walking down the lane.

JOYCE: What sort of air you get in London then?

[ANGIE *comes in, wearing the dress. It fits.*]

MARLENE: Oh, very pretty. / You do look pretty, Angie.

JOYCE: That fits all right.

MARLENE: Do you like the colour?

ANGIE: Beautiful. Beautiful.

JOYCE: You better take it off, / you'll get it dirty.

ANGIE: I want to wear it. I want to wear it.

MARLENE: It is for wearing after all. You can't just hang it up and look at it.

ANGIE: I love it.

JOYCE: Well if you must you must.

ANGIE: If someone asks me what's my favourite colour I'll tell them it's this. Thank you very much, Aunty Marlene.

MARLENE: You didn't tell your mum you asked me down.

ANGIE: I wanted it to be a surprise.

JOYCE: I'll give you a surprise / one of these days.

ANGIE: I thought you'd like to see her. She hasn't been here since I was nine. People do see their aunts.

MARLENE: Is it that long? Doesn't time fly.

ANGIE: I wanted to.

JOYCE: I'm not cross.

ANGIE: Are you glad?

JOYCE: I smell nicer anyhow, don't I?

[KIT *comes in without saying anything, as if she lived there.*]

MARLENE: I think it was a good idea, Angie, about time. We are sisters after all. It's a pity to let that go.

JOYCE: This is Kitty, / who lives up the road. This is Angie's Aunty Marlene.

KIT: What's that?

ANGIE: It's a present. Do you like it?

KIT: It's all right. / Are you coming out?*

MARLENE: Hello, Kitty.

ANGIE: *No.

KIT: What's that smell?

ANGIE: It's a present.

KIT: It's horrible. Come on.*

MARLENE: Have a chocolate.

ANGIE: *No, I'm busy.

KIT: Coming out later?

ANGIE: No.

KIT: [*To* MARLENE.] Hello.

[KIT *goes without a chocolate.*]

JOYCE: She's a little girl Angie sometimes plays with because she's the only child lives really close. She's like a little sister to her really. Angie's good with little children.

MARLENE: Do you want to work with children, Angie? / Be a teacher or a nursery nurse?

JOYCE: I don't think she's ever thought of it.

MARLENE: What do you want to do?

JOYCE: She hasn't an idea in her head what she wants to do. / lucky to get anything.

MARLENE: Angie?

JOYCE: She's not clever like you.

[*Pause.*]

MARLENE: I'm not clever, just pushy.

JOYCE: True enough.

[MARLENE *takes a bottle of whisky out of the bag.*]

I don't drink spirits.

ANGIE: You do at Christmas.

JOYCE: It's not Christmas, is it?

ANGIE: It's better than Christmas.

MARLENE: Glasses?

JOYCE: Just a small one then.

MARLENE: Do you want some, Angie?

ANGIE: I can't, can I?

JOYCE: Taste it if you want. You won't like it.

MARLENE: We got drunk together the night your grandfather died.

JOYCE: We did not get drunk.

MARLENE: I got drunk. You were just overcome with grief.

JOYCE: I still keep up the grave with flowers.

MARLENE: Do you really?

JOYCE: Why wouldn't I?

MARLENE: Have you seen mother?

JOYCE: Of course I've seen mother.

MARLENE: I mean lately.

JOYCE: Of course I've seen her lately, I go every Thursday.

MARLENE: [*To* ANGIE.] Do you remember your grandfather?

ANGIE: He got me out of the bath one night in a towel.

MARLENE: Did he? I don't think he ever gave me a bath. Did he give you a bath,
    Joyce? He probably got soft in his old age. Did you like him?

ANGIE: Yes of course.

MARLENE: Why?

ANGIE: What?

MARLENE: So what's the news? How's Mrs. Paisley? Still going crazily? / and
    Dorothy. What happened to Dorothy?*

ANGIE: Who's Mrs. Paisley?

JOYCE: She went to Canada.

MARLENE: Did she? What to do?

JOYCE: I don't know. She just went to Canada.

MARLENE: Well good for her.

ANGIE: Mr. Connolly killed his wife.

MARLENE: What, Connolly at Whitegates?

ANGIE: They found her body in the garden. / Under the cabbages.

MARLENE: He was always so proper.

JOYCE: Stuck up git, Connolly. Best lawyer money could buy but he couldn't
    get out of it. She was carrying on with Matthew.

MARLENE: How old's Matthew then?

JOYCE: Twenty-one. He's got a motorbike.

MARLENE: I think he's about six.

ANGIE: How can he be six? He's six years older than me. / If he was six I'd be
    nothing, I'd be just born this minute.

JOYCE: Your aunty knows that, she's just being silly. She means it's so long since she's been here she's forgotten about Matthew.

ANGIE: You were here for my birthday when I was nine. I had a pink cake. Kit was only five then, she was four, she hadn't started school yet. She could read already when she went to school. You remember my birthday? / You remember me?

MARLENE: Yes, I remember the cake.

ANGIE: You remember me?

MARLENE: Yes, I remember you.

ANGIE: And mum and dad was there, and Kit was.

MARLENE: Yes, how is your dad? Where is he tonight? Up the pub?

JOYCE: No, he's not here.

MARLENE: I can see he's not here.

JOYCE: He moved out.

MARLENE: What? When did he? / Just recently?*

ANGIE: Didn't you know that? You don't know much.

JOYCE: *No, it must be three years ago. Don't be rude, Angie.

ANGIE: I'm not, am I aunty? What else don't you know?

JOYCE: You was in America or somewhere. You sent a postcard.

ANGIE: I've got that in my room. It's the Grand Canyon. Do you want to see it? Shall I get it? I can get it for you.

MARLENE: Yes, all right.

[ANGIE goes.]

JOYCE: You could be married with twins for all I know. You must have affairs and break up and I don't need to know about any of that so I don't see what the fuss is about.

MARLENE: What fuss?

[ANGIE comes back with the postcard.]

ANGIE: "Driving across the states for a new job in L.A. It's a long way but the car goes very fast. It's very hot. Wish you were here. Love from Aunty Marlene."

JOYCE: Did you make a lot of money?

MARLENE: I spent a lot.

ANGIE: I want to go to America. Will you take me?

JOYCE: She's not going to America, she's been to America, stupid.

ANGIE: She might go again, stupid. It's not something you do once. People who go keep going all the time, back and forth on jets. They go on Concorde and Laker[5] and get jet lag. Will you take me?

MARLENE: I'm not planning a trip.

ANGIE: Will you let me know?

JOYCE: Angie, / you're getting silly.

ANGIE: I want to be American.

5. The Concorde is the fastest (and most expensive) commercial airplane for transcontinental flights, and Laker is a transcontinental airline.

JOYCE: It's time you were in bed.

ANGIE: No it's not. / I don't have to go to bed at all tonight.

JOYCE: School in the morning.

ANGIE: I'll wake up.

JOYCE: Come on now, you know how you get.

ANGIE: How do I get? / I don't get anyhow.*

JOYCE: Angie.* Are you staying the night?

MARLENE: Yes, if that's all right. / I'll see you in the morning.

ANGIE: You can have my bed. I'll sleep on the sofa.

JOYCE: You will not, you'll sleep in your bed. / Think I can't see through that? I

ANGIE: Mum.

JOYCE: can just see you going to sleep / with us talking.

ANGIE: I would, I would go to sleep, I'd love that.

JOYCE: I'm going to get cross, Angie.

ANGIE: I want to show her something.

JOYCE: Then bed.

ANGIE: It's a secret.

JOYCE: Then I expect it's in your room so off you go. Give us a shout when you're ready for bed and your aunty'll be up and see you.

ANGIE: Will you?

MARLENE: Yes of course.

[ANGIE *goes.*
Silence.]

It's cold tonight.

JOYCE: Will you be all right on the sofa? You can / have my bed.

MARLENE: The sofa's fine.

JOYCE: Yes the forecast said rain tonight but it's held off.

MARLENE: I was going to walk down to the estuary but I've left it a bit late. Is it just the same?

JOYCE: They cut down the hedges a few years back. Is that since you were here?

MARLENE: But it's not changed down the end, all the mud? And the reeds? We used to pick them up when they were bigger than us. Are there still lapwings?

JOYCE: You get strangers walking there on a Sunday. I expect they're looking at the mud and the lapwings, yes.

MARLENE: You could have left.

JOYCE: Who says I wanted to leave?

MARLENE: Stop getting at me then, you're really boring.

JOYCE: How could I have left?

MARLENE: Did you want to?

JOYCE: I said how, / how could I.

MARLENE: If you'd wanted to you'd have done it.

JOYCE: Christ.

MARLENE: Are we getting drunk?

JOYCE: Do you want something to eat?

MARLENE: No, I'm getting drunk.

JOYCE: Funny time to visit, Sunday evening.

MARLENE: I came this morning. I spent the day—

ANGIE: [*Off.*] Aunty! Aunty Marlene!

MARLENE: I'd better go.

JOYCE: Go on then.

MARLENE: All right.

ANGIE: [*Off.*] Aunty! Can you hear me? I'm ready.

> [MARLENE *goes.*
> JOYCE *sits.*
> MARLENE *comes back.*]

JOYCE: So what's the secret?

MARLENE: It's a secret.

JOYCE: I know what it is anyway.

MARLENE: I bet you don't. You always said that.

JOYCE: It's her exercise book.

MARLENE: Yes, but you don't know what's in it.

JOYCE: It's some game, some secret society she has with Kit.

MARLENE: You don't know the password. You don't know the code.

JOYCE: You're really in it, aren't you. Can you do the handshake?

MARLENE: She didn't mention a handshake.

JOYCE: I thought they'd have a special handshake. She spends hours writing that but she's useless at school. She copies things out of books about black magic, and politicians out of the paper. It's a bit childish.

MARLENE: I think it's a plot to take over the world.

JOYCE: She's been in the remedial class the last two years.

MARLENE: I came up this morning and spent the day in Ipswich. I went to see mother.

JOYCE: Did she recognise you?

MARLENE: Are you trying to be funny?

JOYCE: No, she does wander.

MARLENE: She wasn't wandering at all, she was very lucid thank you.

JOYCE: You were very lucky then.

MARLENE: Fucking awful life she's had.

JOYCE: Don't tell me.

MARLENE: Fucking waste.

JOYCE: Don't talk to me.

MARLENE: Why shouldn't I talk? Why shouldn't I talk to you? / Isn't she my mother too?

JOYCE: Look, you've left, you've gone away, / we can do without you.

MARLENE: I left home, so what, I left home. People do leave home / it is normal.

JOYCE: We understand that, we can do without you.

MARLENE: We weren't happy. Were you happy?

JOYCE: Don't come back.

MARLENE: So it's just your mother is it, your child, you never wanted me round, /

JOYCE: Here we go.

MARLENE: you were jealous of me because I was the little one and I was clever.

JOYCE: I'm not clever enough for all this psychology / if that's what it is.

MARLENE: Why can't I visit my own family / without all this?*

JOYCE: Aah.

    *Just don't go on about mum's life when you haven't been to see her for how many years. / I go and see her every

MARLENE: It's up to me.

JOYCE: week.

MARLENE: Then don't go and see her every week.

JOYCE: Somebody has to.

MARLENE: No they don't. / Why do they?

JOYCE: How would I feel if I didn't go.

MARLENE: A lot better.

JOYCE: I hope you feel better.

MARLENE: It's up to me.

JOYCE: You couldn't get out of here fast enough.

MARLENE: Of course I couldn't get out of here fast enough. What was I going to do? Marry a dairyman who'd come home pissed? / Don't you fucking this fucking

JOYCE: Christ.

MARLENE: that fucking bitch fucking tell me what to fucking do fucking.

JOYCE: I don't know how you could leave your own child.

MARLENE: You were quick enough to take her.

JOYCE: What does that mean?

MARLENE: You were quick enough to take her.

JOYCE: Or what? Have her put in a home? Have some stranger / take her would you rather?

MARLENE: You couldn't have one so you took mine.

JOYCE: I didn't know that then.

MARLENE: Like hell, / married three years.

JOYCE: I didn't know that. Plenty of people / take that long.

MARLENE: Well it turned out lucky for you, didn't it.

JOYCE: Turned out all right for you by the look of you. You'd be getting a few less thousand a year.

MARLENE: Not necessarily.

JOYCE: You'd be stuck here / like you said.

MARLENE: I could have taken her with me.

JOYCE: You didn't want to take her with you. It's no good coming back now, Marlene, / and saying—

MARLENE: I know a managing director who's got two children, she breast feeds in the board room, she pays a hundred pounds a week on domestic help alone and she can afford that because she's an extremely high-powered lady earning a great deal of money.

JOYCE: So what's that got to do with you at the age of seventeen?

MARLENE: Just because you were married and had somewhere to live—

JOYCE: You could have lived at home. /

MARLENE: Don't be stupid.

JOYCE: Or live with me and Frank. / You

MARLENE: You never suggested.

JOYCE: said you weren't keeping it. You shouldn't have had it / if you wasn't

MARLENE: Here we go.

JOYCE: going to keep it. You was the most stupid, / for someone so clever you was the most stupid, get yourself pregnant, not go to the doctor, not tell.

MARLENE: You wanted it, you said you were glad, I remember the day, you said I'm glad you never got rid of it, I'll look after it, you said that down by the river. So what are you saying, sunshine, you don't want her?

JOYCE: Course I'm not saying that.

MARLENE: Because I'll take her, / wake her up and pack now.

JOYCE: You wouldn't know how to begin to look after her.

MARLENE: Don't you want her?

JOYCE: Course I do, she's my child.

MARLENE: Then what are you going on about / why did I have her?

JOYCE: You said I got her off you / when you didn't—

MARLENE: I said you were lucky / the way it—

JOYCE: Have a child now if you want one. You're not old.

MARLENE: I might do.

JOYCE: Good.

[Pause.]

MARLENE: I've been on the pill so long / I'm probably sterile.

JOYCE: Listen when Angie was six months I did get pregnant and I lost it because I was so tired looking after your fucking baby / because she cried so much— yes I

MARLENE: You never told me.

JOYCE: did tell you— / and the doctor

MARLENE: Well I forgot.

JOYCE: said if I'd sat down all day with my feet up I'd've kept it / and that's the only chance I ever had because after that—

MARLENE: I've had two abortions, are you interested? Shall I tell you about them? Well I won't, it's boring, it wasn't a problem. I don't like messy talk about blood / and what a bad time we all had. I

JOYCE: If I hadn't had your baby. The doctor said.

MARLENE: don't want a baby. I don't want to talk about gynaecology.

JOYCE: Then stop trying to get Angie off of me.

MARLENE: I come down here after six years. All night you've been saying I don't come often enough. If I don't come for another six years she'll be twenty-one, will that be OK?

JOYCE: That'll be fine, yes, six years would suit me fine.

[Pause.]

MARLENE: I was afraid of this. I only came because I thought you wanted . . . I just want . . .

[MARLENE *cries.*]

JOYCE: Don't grizzle, Marlene, for God's sake.
  Marly? Come on, pet. Love you really.
  Fucking stop it, will you?
MARLENE: No, let me cry. I like it.

[*They laugh,* MARLENE *begins to stop crying.*]

  I knew I'd cry if I wasn't careful.
JOYCE: Everyone's always crying in this house. Nobody takes any notice.
MARLENE: You've been wonderful looking after Angie.
JOYCE: Don't get carried away.
MARLENE: I can't write letters but I do think of you.
JOYCE: You're getting drunk. I'm going to make some tea.
MARLENE: Love you.

[JOYCE *gets up to make tea.*]

JOYCE: I can see why you'd want to leave. It's a dump here.
MARLENE: So what's this about you and Frank?
JOYCE: He was always carrying on, wasn't he. And if I wanted to go out in the
  evening he'd go mad, even if it was nothing, a class, I was going to go to an
  evening class. So he had this girlfriend, only twenty-two poor cow, and I said
  go on, off you go, hoppit. I don't think he even likes her.
MARLENE: So what about money?
JOYCE: I've always said I don't want your money.
MARLENE: No, does he send you money?
JOYCE: I've got four different cleaning jobs. Adds up. There's not a lot round
  here.
MARLENE: Does Angie miss him?
JOYCE: She doesn't say.
MARLENE: Does she see him?
JOYCE: He was never that fond of her to be honest.
MARLENE: He tried to kiss me once. When you were engaged.
JOYCE: Did you fancy him?
MARLENE: No, he looked like a fish.
JOYCE: He was lovely then.
MARLENE: Ugh.
JOYCE: Well I fancied him. For about three years.
MARLENE: Have you got someone else?
JOYCE: There's not a lot round here. Mind you, the minute you're on your own,
  you'd be amazed how your friends' husbands drop by. I'd sooner do without.
MARLENE: I don't see why you couldn't take my money.
JOYCE: I do, so don't bother about it.
MARLENE: Only got to ask.
JOYCE: So what about you? Good job?
MARLENE: Good for a laugh. / Got back
JOYCE: Good for more than a laugh I should think.

MARLENE: from the US of A bit wiped out and slotted into this speedy employment agency and still there.

JOYCE: You can always find yourself work then.

MARLENE: That's right.

JOYCE: And men?

MARLENE: Oh there's always men.

JOYCE: No one special?

MARLENE: There's fellas who like to be seen with a high-flying lady. Shows they've got something really good in their pants. But they can't take the day to day. They're waiting for me to turn into the little woman. Or maybe I'm just horrible of course.

JOYCE: Who needs them.

MARLENE: Who needs them. Well I do. But I need adventures more. So on on into the sunset. I think the eighties are going to be stupendous.

JOYCE: Who for?

MARLENE: For me. / I think I'm going up up up.

JOYCE: Oh for you. Yes, I'm sure they will.

MARLENE: And for the country, come to that. Get the economy back on its feet and whoosh. She's a tough lady, Maggie.[6] I'd give her a job. / She just needs to hang

JOYCE: You voted for them, did you?

MARLENE: in there. This country needs to stop whining. / Monetarism is not

JOYCE: Drink your tea and shut up, pet.

MARLENE: stupid. It takes time, determination. No more slop. / And

JOYCE: Well I think they're filthy bastards.

MARLENE: who's got to drive it on? First woman prime minister. Terrifico. Aces. Right on. / You must admit. Certainly gets my vote:

JOYCE: What good's first woman if it's her? I suppose you'd have liked Hitler if he was a woman. Ms. Hitler. Got a lot done, Hitlerina. / Great adventures.

MARLENE: Bosses still walking on the workers' faces? Still dadda's little parrot? Haven't you learned to think for yourself? I believe in the individual. Look at me.

JOYCE: I am looking at you.

MARLENE: Come on, Joyce, we're not going to quarrel over politics.

JOYCE: We are though.

MARLENE: Forget I mentioned it. Not a word about the slimy unions will cross my lips.

[Pause.]

JOYCE: You say mother had a wasted life.

MARLENE: Yes I do. Married to that bastard.

JOYCE: What sort of life did he have? /

MARLENE: Violent life?

JOYCE: Working in the fields like an animal. / Why wouldn't he want a drink.

MARLENE: Come off it.

6. Margaret Thatcher (b. 1925), British Conservative politician and prime minister.

JOYCE: You want a drink. He couldn't afford whisky.

MARLENE: I don't want to talk about him.

JOYCE: You started, I was talking about here. She had a rotten life because she had nothing. She went hungry.

MARLENE: She was hungry because he drank the money. / He used to hit her.

JOYCE: It's not all down to him / Their

MARLENE: She didn't hit him.

JOYCE: lives were rubbish. They were treated like rubbish. He's dead and she'll die soon and what sort of life / did they have?

MARLENE: I saw him one night. I came down.

JOYCE: Do you think I didn't? / They

MARLENE: I still have dreams.

JOYCE: didn't get to America and drive across it in a fast car. / Bad nights, they had bad days.

MARLENE: America, America, you're jealous. / I had to get out, I knew when I

JOYCE: Jealous?

MARLENE: was thirteen, out of their house, out of them, never let that happen to me, / never let him, make my own way, out.

JOYCE: Jealous of what you've done, you're ashamed of me if I came to your office, your smart friends, wouldn't you, I'm ashamed of you, think of nothing but yourself, you've got on, nothing's changed for most people / has it.

MARLENE: I hate the working class /

JOYCE: Yes you do.

MARLENE: which is what you're going to go on about now, it doesn't exist any more, it means lazy and stupid. / I don't

JOYCE: Come on, now we're getting it.

MARLENE: like the way they talk. I don't like beer guts and football vomit and saucy tits / and brothers and sisters—

JOYCE: I spit when I see a Rolls Royce, scratch it with my ring / Mercedes it was.

MARLENE: Oh very mature—

JOYCE: I hate the cows I work for / and their dirty dishes with blanquette of fucking veau.

MARLENE: and I will not be pulled down to their level by a flying picket and I won't be sent to Siberia / or a loony bin just because

JOYCE: No, you'll be on a yacht, you'll be head of Coca-Cola and you wait, the eighties is going to be stupendous all right because we'll get you lot off our backs—

MARLENE: I'm original and I support Reagan even if he is a lousy movie star because the reds are swarming up his map and I want to be free in a free world—

JOYCE: What? / What?

MARLENE: I know what I mean / by that—not shut up here.

JOYCE: So don't be round here when it happens because if someone's kicking you I'll just laugh.

[Silence.]

MARLENE: I don't mean anything personal. I don't believe in class. Anyone can do anything if they've got what it takes.
JOYCE: And if they haven't?
MARLENE: If they're stupid or lazy or frightened, I'm not going to help them get a job, why should I?
JOYCE: What about Angie?
MARLENE: What about Angie?
JOYCE: She's stupid, lazy and frightened, so what about her?
MARLENE: You run her down too much. She'll be all right.
JOYCE: I don't expect so, no. I expect her children will say what a wasted life she had. If she has children. Because nothing's changed and it won't with them in.
MARLENE: Them, them. / Us and them?
JOYCE: And you're one of them.
MARLENE: And you're us, wonderful us, and Angie's us / and mum and dad's us.
JOYCE: Yes, that's right, and you're them.
MARLENE: Come on, Joyce, what a night. You've got what it takes.
JOYCE: I know I have.
MARLENE: I didn't really mean all that.
JOYCE: I did.
MARLENE: But we're friends anyway.
JOYCE: I don't think so, no.
MARLENE: Well it's lovely to be out in the country. I really must make the effort to come more often.
I want to go to sleep.
I want to go to sleep.

[JOYCE *gets blankets for the sofa.*]

JOYCE: Goodnight then. I hope you'll be warm enough.
MARLENE: Goodnight. Joyce—
JOYCE: No, pet. Sorry.

[JOYCE *goes.*
MARLENE *sits wrapped in a blanket and has another drink.*
ANGIE *comes in.*]

ANGIE: Mum?
MARLENE: Angie? What's the matter?
ANGIE: Mum?
MARLENE: No, she's gone to bed. It's Aunty Marlene.
ANGIE: Frightening.
MARLENE: Did you have a bad dream? What happened in it? Well you're awake now, aren't you pet.
ANGIE: Frightening.

THE END

1982

WRITING
ABOUT
LITERATURE

INTRODUCTION

▼ ▼ ▼

Writing about literature ought to be easier than writing about anything else. When you write about painting, for example, you have
to translate shapes and colors and textures into words. When you
write about music, you have to translate various aspects and combinations of
sounds into words. When you write about that complex, mysterious, fleeting
thing called "reality" or "life," you have an even more difficult task. Worst of
all, perhaps, is trying to put into words all that is going on at any given
moment inside your particular and unique self. So you ought to be relieved to
know that you are going to write about literature — that is, use words to write
about words.

But writing about literature will not be easy if you haven't learned to *read*
literature, for in order to write about anything you have to know that something rather well. Helping you to learn to read literature is what the earlier
chapters of this book is about; this chapter is about the writing. (But, as you
will see, you cannot fully separate the writing from the reading.)

Another thing keeps writing about literature from being easy: writing itself
is not easy. Writing well requires a variety of language skills — a good working
vocabulary, for example — and a sense of how to order your ideas, of how to
link one idea or statement to another, of what to put in and what to leave out.
Worse, writing is not a finite or definite skill or art; you never really "know how
to write," you just learn how to write a little better about a little more. These
very words you are reading have been written and revised several times, even
though your editors have had a good many years of practice.

REPRESENTING THE LITERARY TEXT

Copying

f writing about literature is using words about words, what words should you use? Since most writers work very hard to get each word exactly right and in exactly the right order, there are no better words to use in discussing what the literature is about than those of the literary work itself. Faced with writing about a story, then, you could just write the story over again, word for word:

> Once upon a time there was a Siamese cat who pretended to be a lion and spoke inappropriate Zebraic. . .

and so on until the end. **Copying** texts was useful in medieval monasteries, but in our electronic age, with printing, word processors, and Fax machines available to us, it would not seem to be very useful. Besides, if you try to copy a text, you will probably find that spelling or punctuation errors, reversed word order, and missing or added or just different words seem mysteriously to appear. Still, it's a good exercise for teaching yourself accuracy and attention to detail, and you will probably discover things about the text you are copying that you would be unlikely to notice otherwise. Early in a literature course, particularly, copying can be a useful step in learning how to read and write about fiction, poetry, or drama; later, being able to copy a passage accurately will help when you want to quote a passage to illustrate or prove a point you are making. But copying is not, in itself, writing *about* literature.

Reading aloud, a variation of copying, may be a more original and interpretive exercise than copying itself, since by tone, emphasis, and pace you are clarifying the text or indicating the way you understand the text. But it, too, is not *writing* about literature, and you will not long be satisfied with merely repeating someone else's words. You will have perceptions, responses, and ideas that you will want to express for yourself about what you are reading. And having something to say and wanting to say or write it is the first and most significant step in learning to write about literature.

Paraphrase

If you look away from the text for a while and then write the same material but in your own words, you are writing a **paraphrase**.

For example, let's try to paraphrase the first sentence of Jane Austen's *Pride and Prejudice*: "It is a truth universally acknowledged that a single man in possession of a good fortune, must be in want of a wife." We can start by making "It is a truth" a little less formal: *It's true that*, perhaps. Now "universally acknowledged": *everybody acknowledges*, or, a little more loosely, *everybody agrees*. Now we may choose to drop the whole first clause and begin, *Everybody agrees that* "a single man"—*a bachelor*—"in possession of a good fortune"—*rich*—"must be in want of a wife"—*wants a wife*. Or is it *needs a wife*? Okay, *Everybody agrees that a rich bachelor needs* (or *wants*) *a wife*. You can see that the process of paraphrase is something like that of translation. We are translating Austen's nineteenth-century formal English prose into twentieth-century informal American prose.

But what good is that? First of all, it enables us to test whether we really understand what we are reading. Second, certain elements of the text become clearer: we may see now that Austen's sentence is meant to be ironic or humorous, and we now understand the two possible meanings of "in want of." Third, we can check our paraphrase with those of others, our classmates' versions, for example, to compare our understanding of the passage with theirs. Finally, we have learned how dependent literature is upon words. A paraphrase, no matter how precise, can render only an approximate equivalent of the meaning of a text—how *good* Austen's sentence is, how *flat* our paraphrase.

Paraphrasing, like copying, is not in itself an entirely satisfactory way of writing about literature, but, like copying, it can be a useful tool when you write about literature in other ways. In trying to explain or clarify a literary text for someone, to illustrate a point you are making about that text, or to remind your readers of or to acquaint them with a text or passage, you will at times want to paraphrase. Unlike an exact copy, a paraphrase, being in your own words, adds something of yours to the text or passage—your emphasis, your perspective, your understanding.

Summary

Paraphrase follows faithfully the outlines of the text. But if you stand back far enough from the text so as not to see its specific words or smaller details and put down briefly in your own words what you believe the work is about, you will have a **summary**. How briefly? Well, you could summarize the one hundred eight lines of Poe's "The Raven" in about one hundred eighty words or so, like this, for example:

> The speaker of Poe's "The Raven" is sitting in his room late at night reading in order to forget the death of his beloved Lenore. There's a tap at the door; after some hesitation he opens it and calls Lenore's name, but there is only an echo. When he goes back into his room he hears the rapping again, this time at his window, and when he opens it a raven enters. He asks the raven its name, and it answers very clearly, "Nevermore." When the speaker says that the bird, like his friends, will leave, the raven again says, "Nevermore." As the speaker's thoughts run back to Lenore, he realizes the aptness of the raven's word: she shall sit there nevermore. But, he says, sooner or later he will forget her and the grief will lessen. "Nevermore," the raven says again, too aptly. Now the speaker wants the bird to leave, but "Nevermore," the raven says once again. At the end, the speaker knows he'll never escape the raven or its dark message.

Or you could summarize the story of *Hamlet* in a single sentence: "A young man, seeking to avenge the murder of his father by his uncle, kills his uncle, but he himself and others die in the process." Has *too* much been left out? What do you feel it essential to add? Let's try again: "In Denmark, many centuries ago, a young prince avenged the murder of his father, the king, by his uncle, who had usurped the throne, but the prince himself was killed as were others, and a well-led foreign army had no trouble successfully invading the decayed and troubled state." A classmate may have written this summary: "From the ghost of his murdered father a young prince learns that his uncle, who has married the prince's mother, much to the young man's shame and disgust, is the father's murderer, and he plots revenge, feigning madness, acting erratically—even to insulting the woman he loves—and, though gaining his revenge, causes the suicide of his beloved and the deaths of others and, finally, of himself."

The last two, though accurate enough, sound like two different plays, don't they? To summarize means to select and emphasize and so to interpret: that is, not to replicate the text in miniature, as a reduced photograph might replicate the original, but while reducing it to change the angle of vision and even the filter, to represent the essentials as the reader or summarizer sees them. When you write a summary you should try to be as objective as possible; nevertheless, your summary will reflect not only the literary text but also your own understanding and attitudes. There's nothing wrong with your fingerprints or "mindprints" appearing on the summary, so long as you recognize that in summarizing you are doing more than copying, paraphrasing, or merely reflecting the literary text. You might learn something about both literature and yourself by comparing your summaries of, say, three or four short poems, a couple of short stories, or a play with summaries of the same works by several of your classmates. As you read their summaries, try to understand how each viewed the text differently from you. You might then write a composite summary that would include all that any one reader felt important. You might try the same exercise again on different texts. Has the practice made you more careful? More inclusive? Is there a greater degree of uniformity or inclusiveness in your summaries?

A good summary can be a form of literary criticism. Though you will seldom be called upon merely to summarize a work, a good deal of writing about literature requires that at some point or other you do summarize—a whole work, a particular incident or aspect, a stanza, chapter, or scene. But beware: a mere summary, no matter how accurate, will seldom fulfill an assignment for a critical essay.

REPLYING TO THE TEXT

Imitation and Parody

While paraphrase is something like translation—a faithful following of the original text but in different words—and summary is the faithful, but inevitably interpretive, reduction of the text, there is another kind of writing about literature that faithfully follows the manner or matter or both of a literary text, but that does so for different ends. It's called **imitation.**

For many generations, students were taught to write by "writing from models"—imitating good writing. Many serious works are, in one way or another, imitations: *The Aeneid*, for example, may be said to be an imitation of *The Odyssey*, and, in a very different way, so might James Joyce's *Ulysses*. You too may be able to learn a good deal about writing—and reading—by trying your hand at an imitation.

To write an imitation, first analyze the original—that is, break it down into its characteristics or qualities—and decide just what you want to preserve in your version. Sometimes you can poke fun at a work by imitating it but at the same time exaggerating its style or prominent characteristics, or placing it in an inappropriate context; that kind of imitation, a kind that is still popular, is called a **parody.** The list of qualities and the model might be much the same for a serious imitation and for a parody, only in a parody you can exaggerate a little—or a lot.

To parody Poe's "The Raven," we may decide to stick closely to Poe's rhythms, his use of repetitive mood words or of several words that mean almost the same thing, and his frequent use of alliteration (words that begin with the same sound). We might want to exaggerate the characteristic stylistic devices as C. L. Edson does in his parody; it begins,

> Once upon a midnight dreary, eerie, scary,
> I was wary, I was weary, full of worry, thinking of my lost Lenore,
> Of my cheery, airy, faerie, fierie Dearie—(Nothing more).

We may choose another kind of parody, keeping the form as close as possible to the original but applying it to a ludicrously unsuitable subject, as Pope does in his mock epic "The Rape of the Lock," where he uses pretentious epic machinery in a poem about cutting off a lock of a woman's hair. In writing such a parody of "The Raven," we will keep the rhythm closer to Poe's and the subject matter less close. How about this?

> Once upon a midday murky, crunching on a Christmas turkey,
> And guzzling giant Jereboams of gin . . .

And maybe we could use the "Nevermore" refrain as if it were an antacid commercial.

You will have noticed that in order to write a good imitation or parody you must read and reread the original very carefully, examine it, and identify just those elements and qualities that make it a unique and recognizable text. Since you admire works you wish to imitate, such close study should be a pleasure. You may or may not greatly admire a work you wish to parody, but parody itself is fun to do and fun to read. In either case, you are having fun while gaining a deeper, more intimate knowledge of the nature and details of a work of literature. Moreover, such close attention to how a professional piece of writing is put together and how its parts function together along with your effort to reproduce the effects in your own imitation or parody are sure to help you understand the process of writing and so help you improve your own ability to write about literature knowledgeably.

Re-creation and Reply

Sometimes a story, poem, or play will seem so partial, biased, or unrealistic that it will stimulate a response that is neither an imitation or a parody but a retort. While Christopher Marlowe's "shepherd" in "The Passionate Shepherd to His Love" paints an idyllic scene of love in the country for his beloved and pleads, "Come live with me and be my love," Sir Walter Ralegh apparently feels obliged to reply in the name of the beloved "nymph": it won't always be spring, she says in "The Nymph's Reply to the Shepherd"; we won't always be young, and, besides, I can scarcely trust myself to someone who offers me such a phony view of reality.

Ralegh's nymph confronts the invitation and the words of Marlowe's shepherd directly and almost detail for detail. In fiction the reply is less likely to be so directly verbal a retort and is more likely to involve a shift in perspective. It may tell the same story as the original but from a different angle, not only giving a different view of the same events and people but also adding details that the original focus ignored or could not perceive. In *Jane Eyre*, for example, Bertha Mason Rochester is the hero's bestial, mad wife, whom he has locked away upstairs and whose existence, when it comes to light, prevents for a time our heroine, our Jane, from marrying her heart's desire; Bertha is, in effect, the villainess. In *Wide Sargasso Sea*, Jean Rhys not only gives Bertha's side of Charlotte Brontë's story but tells us more details about Bertha's earlier life: poor Bertha was more sinned against than sinning, it turns out.

We may respond to a work whose view seems partial or distorted by shifting the perspective in time as well as in space. Are Francis Weed's marital and other problems solved by his recognition, at the end of "The Country Husband," that life in the suburbs can be, in its own way, as adventurous as more romantic kinds of existence? What will happen to him next spring? On his fortieth birthday? As he lies dying? What will the speaker of "My Papa's Waltz" be thinking about as he plays or dances with *his* daughter?

You may have noticed that while retorts can often be witty, they are also serious. Usually they say not merely, "That's not how the story went," but "That's not what life is really like." Try to read literature initially with the aim of understanding it and taking it at its highest value (rather than reducing it and quibbling). Try to "hear" what it is saying; avoid imposing your own notions of reality prematurely upon a work. Open your mind to learning from the work and let it broaden your views. Finally, read it critically as well, asking, "Is this the way things *really* are?" or, more generously, "If I were standing over there, where the story (author, character) is, would things really look that way?"

Perhaps the most familiar kind of literary re-creation or reply is the **adaptation**, especially that of fiction into film. (Among the stories in this anthology that have been made into feature-length films are "The Most Dangerous Game," "An Occurrence at Owl Creek Bridge," "The Lady with the Dog," "Blow-Up" and "The Rocking-Horse Winner.") In adaptation, the rather contradictory demands of faithfulness to the original and appropriateness to the new medium can teach us a great deal about both the content and the medium of the original. It is unlikely you will have the opportunity in this course to make a film based on a story but you can still try your hand at adapting a work or piece of a work to a new medium. You might want to turn "The Cask of Amontillado" into verse (probably as a dramatic monologue) or write a short story called *Hamlet* or a one-act play called "Young Goodman Brown." It is quite likely that you will learn not only about the nature of the original work but also something of the nature of the medium in which you are trying to work.

EXPLAINING THE TEXT

Description

To give an account of the form of a work or passage rather than merely a brief version of its content or plot (and a plot summary, even of a poem, is usually what we mean by "summary") you may wish to write a **description.** We have given a summary of Poe's "The Raven" earlier, concentrating there, as summaries tend to do, on subject and plot. A description, on the other hand, may concentrate on the form of the stanzas, the lines, the rhyme scheme, perhaps like this:

Poe's "The Raven" is a poem of one hundred eight lines divided into eighteen six-line stanzas. If in describing the rhyme scheme you were to look just at the ends of the lines, you would notice only one or two unusual features: not only is there only one rhyme sound per stanza, lines 2, 4, 5, and 6 rhyming, but one rhyme sound is the same in all eighteen stanzas, so that there are seventy-two lines ending with the sound "ore"; in addition, the fourth and fifth lines of each stanza end with the identical word, and in six of the stanzas that word is "door" and in four others "Lenore." There is even more repetition: the last line of six of the first seven stanzas ends with the words "nothing more," and the last eleven stanzas end with the word "Nevermore." The rhyming lines—other than the last, which is very short—in each stanza are fifteen syllables long, the unrhymed lines sixteen. The longer lines give the effect of shorter ones, however, and add still further to the frequency of repeated sounds, for the first half of each opening line rhymes with the second half of the line, and so do the halves of line 3. There is still more: the first half of line 4 rhymes with the halves of line 3 (in the first stanza the rhymes are "dreary" /"weary" and "napping" / "tapping" /"rapping"). So at least nine words in each eight-line stanza are involved in the regular rhyme scheme, and in many stanzas there are added instances of rhyme or repetition. As if this were not enough, all the half-line rhymes are rich feminine rhymes, where both the accented and the following unaccented syllables rhyme—"dreāry̆" /"weāry̆."

This is a detailed and complicated description of a complex and unusual pattern of rhymes. Though there are many other elements of the poem we could describe—images and symbols, for example—the unusual and dominant element in this poem is clearly the intricate and insistent pattern of rhyme and repetition. Moreover, this paragraph shows how you can describe at length, in depth, and with considerable complexity certain aspects of a work without mentioning the content at all. You can describe a play in comparable terms—acts, scenes, settings, time lapses perhaps—and you might describe a novel in terms of chapters, books, summary narration, dramatized scenes. In addition to describing the narrative structure or focus and voice of a short story, you might also describe the diction (word choice), the sentence structure, the amount of description of the characters or landscape, and so on.

Analysis

Like copying, paraphrase, and summary, a description of a work or passage rarely stands alone as a piece of writing about literature. It is, instead, a tool, a means of supporting a point or opinion. Even the description we have given above borders on **analysis**. To analyze is to break something down into its parts to discover what they are, and, usually, how they function in and relate to the whole. The description of the rhyme scheme of "The Raven" tells you what that scheme or pattern is but says nothing about how it functions in the poem. If you were to add such an account to the description, then, you would have analyzed one aspect of the poem. In order to do so, however, you would first have to decide what, in a general way, the poem is about: what its *theme* is. If you defined the theme of "The Raven" as "inconsolable grief," you could then write an analytical paper suggesting how the rhyme scheme reinforces that theme. You might begin something like this:

> Obsessive Rhyme in "The Raven"
>
> We all know that gloomy poem with that gloomy bird, Edgar Allan Poe's "The Raven." The time is midnight, the room is dark, the bird is black, and the poem is full of words like "dreary," "sad," "mystery," and "ghastly." We all know too it has a rather sing-song rhythm and repeated rhymes, but we do not often stop to think how the rhymes contribute to the mood or meaning. Before we do so here, perhaps it would be a good idea to describe in detail just what that rhyme scheme is.

Then follow with the description of the rhyme scheme, and go on like this:

> Of course the most obvious way in which the rhyme scheme reinforces the theme of inconsolable loss is through the emphatic repetition of "Nevermore." Since this refrain comes at the very end of each of the last stanzas it is even more powerful in its effect.

What is not so obvious as the effect of repeating "Nevermore" is the purpose of the over-all abundance and richness of rhyme. Some might say it is not abundant and rich but excessive and cloying. These harsh critics cynically add that in a way the rhymes and repetitions are appropriate to this poem because the whole poem is excessive and cloying: grief over loss, even intense grief, does, human experience tells us, pass away. This criticism is just, however, only if we have accurately defined the theme of the poem as "inconsolable sorrow." The very insistence of the rhyme and repetition, however, suggests we may need to adjust slightly our definition of that theme. Perhaps the poem is not about "inconsolable sorrow" in so neutral a way; maybe it would be better to say it is about obsessive grief. Then the insistent, pounding rhyme and repetition make sense (just as the closed-in dark chamber does). Obsessive repetition of words and sounds thus helps to create the meaning of the poem almost as much as the words themselves do.

Interpretation

Principles and Procedures

If you have been reading carefully, you may have noticed what looks like a catch: to turn description into analysis, you must relate what you are describing to the theme, the overall effect, and meaning of the text. But how do you know what the theme is? If analysis relates the part to the whole, how can you know the "whole" before you have analyzed each part? But then, how can you analyze each part—relating it to the whole—if you don't know what that whole is?

Interpretation, or the expression of your understanding of a literary work and its meaning, involves an initial general impression that is then supported and, often, modified by analysis of the particulars. It involves looking at the whole, the part, the whole, the part, the whole, the part, in a series of approximations and adjustments. (Note, in particular, the need to keep your mind open for modifications or changes rather than forcing your analysis to confirm your first impressions.)

This procedure should in turn suggest something of the nature and even the form of the critical essay, or essay of interpretation. The essay should present the overall theme and support that generalization with close analyses of the major elements of the text (or, in some essays, an analysis of one significant element)—showing how one or more of such elements as rhyme or speaker, plot or setting reinforce, define, or modify the theme of the story. Often the conclusion of such an essay will be a fuller, more refined statement of the theme.

Both the definition of and the procedures for interpreting a work suggest that a literary text is unified, probably around a theme, a meaning, and an effect. In interpreting, you therefore keep asking of each element or detail, "How does it fit? How does it contribute to *the* theme or whole?" In most instances, especially when you are writing on shorter works, if you dig hard and deep enough, you will find a satisfactory interpretation or central theme. Even after you have done your best, however, you must hold your "reading" or interpretation as a hypothesis rather than a final truth. Your experience of reading criticism has probably already shown you that more than one reading of a literary work is possible and that no reading exhausts the meaning and totality of a work. Nonetheless, you will want to begin reading a literary text as if it were going to make a central statement and create a single effect, no matter how complex. Try as conscientiously as you can to make sense of the work, to analyze it, show how its elements work together. In analyzing elements, you kept your initial sense of the whole as hypothesis and did not try to force evidence to fit your first impression. Here, too, you will want to hold your interpretation as a hypothesis even in its final stages, even at the end. It is, you must be sure, the fullest and best "reading" of the text you are capable of at this time, with the evidence and knowledge you have at this moment; but only that. In other words, an interpretation is "only an opinion." But just as your political and other opinions are not lightly held but are what you really feel and believe based on all you know and have experienced and all you have thought and felt, so your opinion or interpretation of a literary work should be as responsible as you can make it. Your opinions are a measure of your knowledge, intelligence, and sensibility. They should not be lightly changed but neither should they be obstinately and inflexibly held.

Reading and Theme Making

Because you need a sense of the whole text before you can analyze it, analysis and interpretation would seem to be possible only after repeated readings. Though obvious, logical, and partially true, this may not be *entirely* true. In reading, we actually anticipate theme or meaning much as we anticipate what will happen next. Often this anticipation or expectation of theme or effect begins with our first opening a book—or even before, in reading the title. If you were to read *Hamlet* in an edition that gives its full title—*The Tragedy of Hamlet, Prince of Denmark*—even if you had never heard of the play or its author before—you would have some idea or hypothesis about who the protagonist is, where the action will more than likely be set, how the play will end, and even some of the feelings it will arouse.

Such anticipation of theme and effect, projecting and modifying understanding and response, continues as you read. When you read the first four
words of "The Zebra Storyteller"—"Once upon a time . . ."—the strange title is
to some extent explained and the kind of story you are about to read and its
relation to everyday reality have been established. The title and the first short
section of "The Most Dangerous Game" arouse expectations of the supernatural, the frightening, the adventurous, creating suspense: "What will happen
next?" we ask as we read the first few paragraphs. The brief conversation about
hunting, toward the end of that section, not only educates our expectations but
also generates a moral and thematic question: "Are there really two animal
classes—the hunters and the hunted—and does being lucky enough to be
among the hunters justify insensitivity toward the feelings of the hunted?"
While the question may recede from the foreground of our attention for a
while, it has nonetheless been raised. It is, in addition, reinforced by the break
on the page, which forces us to pause and, even if but momentarily, reflect. It
comes forward again when General Zaroff introduces the subject of hunting.
At these two points, at least, a thematic hypothesis based on hunters and
hunted begins forming, however faintly, in our minds. That is enough to give
us grounds—even as we read the story for the first time—for an analysis of elements and their relationship to our very tentatively formulated theme, and perhaps for beginning to modify or modulate our articulation of that theme. Many
details in the story indicate that there is a political coloring to the theme: Zaroff is a Cossack—a people noted for fierceness—and is, or was, a Czarist general; he keeps a giant Cossack servant who was an official flogger under the
Czar; he refers to the Revolution of 1917 in Russia as a "debacle"; he is clearly
a racist. We may want to alter "hunter" and "hunted" in our first version of the
anticipated theme to something broader—"strong" and "weak," perhaps, or
"privileged" and "underprivileged," or we may need fuller definitions of the
implications of the terms "hunter" and "hunted."

Just as we have more than one expectation of what may happen next as we
read a story, poem, or play, so we may have more than one expectation of what
it is going to be "about" in the more general sense: as we read along we have
expectations or hypotheses of meaning, and so we consciously or unconsciously try to fit together the pieces of elements of what we are reading into a
pattern of significance. By the end of our first reading we should have a fairly
well-defined sense of what the work is "about," what it means, even how some
of the elements have worked together to produce that meaning and effect.
Indeed, isn't this the way we read when we are not reading for a class or performance? Don't most people read most stories, poems, plays only once? And
don't we usually think we have understood what we have read? Shouldn't we

be able to read a very short story in class just once and immediately write an interpretive paper based on that first reading?

This is not to say that we cannot understand more about a work by repeated readings, or that there is some virtue or purity of response in the naive first reading that is lost in closer study. Our first "reading"—"reading" in the sense of both "casting our eye over" and "interpretation"—is almost certain to be modified or refined by rereading: if nothing else, we know from the beginning what will happen next—what the most dangerous game is, and that the blow-up refers to a photograph. The theme or meaning is likely to be modulated by later readings, the way the elements function in defining or embodying meaning is likely to be clearer; the effect of the second reading is certain to be different from that of the first. It may be instructive to reread several times the short work we interpreted in class after a single reading, write a new interpretive essay, and see how our understanding has been changed and enriched by subsequent readings.

Opinions, Right and Wrong

Just as each of our separate readings is different, so naturally one reader's fullest and "final" reading, interpretation, or opinion will differ somewhat from another's. Seldom will readers agree entirely with any full statement of the theme of a literary text. Nor is one of these interpretations entirely "right" and all the others necessarily "wrong." For no thematic summary, no analysis or interpretation, no matter how full, can exhaust the affective or intellectual significance of a major literary text. There are various approximate readings of varying degrees of acceptability, various competent or "good" readings, not just one single "right" reading.

Anyone who has heard two accomplished musicians faithfully perform the same work, playing all the "same" notes; or anyone who has seen two performances of *Hamlet*, will recognize how "interpretations" can be both correct and different. You might try to get hold of several recordings of one or more of Hamlet's soliloquies—by John Barrymore, Sir John Gielgud, Richard Burton, Sir Laurence Olivier, or Mel Gibson, for example—and notice how each of these actors lends to identical passages his own emphasis, pacing, tone, color, his own effect, and so, ultimately, his own meaning. These actors reading the identical words are, in effect, "copying." They are not paraphrasing or putting Shakespeare's Elizabethan poetry into modern American prose, not "interpreting" as we have defined it, or putting his play into their own words. If merely performing or reading the words aloud generates significant differences in interpretation, it is no wonder that when you write an interpretive essay about litera-ture, when you give your conception of the meaning and effect of the literary text in your own words, your interpretation will differ from other interpreta-tions, even when each of the different interpretations is competent and "cor-rect."

Any communication, even a work of literature, is refracted—that is, inter-preted and modified—by the recipient. In one sense, it is not complete until it is received, just as, in a sense, a musical score is not "music" until it is played. Philip Roth reported, not too long ago, how perturbed he was by what the crit-ics and other readers said of his first novel—that was not at all what he intended, what the novel really was, he thought at first. But then he realized that once he had had his say in the novel, it was "out there," and each reader had to understand it within the limits and range of his or her own perspectives and literary and life experiences. His novel, once in print, was no longer merely "his," and rightly so.

That quite different interpretations may be "correct" is not to say, with Alice's Humpty-Dumpty, that a word or a work "means just what I choose it to mean." Though there may not be one "right" reading, some readings are more appropriate and convincing than others and some readings are demonstrably wrong.

What would you say about this reading of *Hamlet*?

> The play is about the hero's sexual love for his mother. He sees his father's "ghost" because he feels guilty, somehow responsible for his father's death, more than likely because he had often wished his father dead. To free himself from this feeling of guilt, he imagines that he sees his father's ghost and that the ghost tells him that his uncle murdered his father. He focuses upon his uncle because he is fiercely jealous that it is his uncle, not himself, who has replaced his father in his mother's bed. He so resents his mother's choice of so unworthy a mate, he attributes it not to love but to mere lust, clearly a projection of his own lust for his mother, which he calls love. His mother's lust so disgusts him that he hates all women now, even Ophelia. When his father was alive he could be fond of Ophelia, for his sexual feeling for his mother was deflected by his father-the-king's powerful presence. Now, however, he must alienate Ophelia not only because of his new hatred of women but because he has a chance of winning his mother, especially if he can get rid of Claudius, his uncle.

Such a reading explains more or less convincingly certain details in the play, but it wrenches some out of context and it leaves a good deal out and a good deal unexplained: why, for example, do others see the ghost of Hamlet's father if it is just a figment of his imagination? What are Horatio and Fortinbras and the political elements doing in the play? *If* you accept certain Freudian premises about human psychology and see life in Freudian terms; *if* you see literary texts as the *author's* psychic fantasy stimulating your own psychic fantasies and believe that interpretation of *Hamlet* is not merely a reading of the play itself but an analysis of Shakespeare's psyche, you may find this reading somewhat convincing. You will perhaps explain away some of the details of the play that do not seem to fit your Freudian reading as a cover-up, an attempt by Shakespeare to disguise the true but hidden meaning of his dramatic fantasy from others—and from himself. Such a reading is probably neither right nor wrong but only a way of interpreting *Hamlet* based on certain assumptions about psychology and about the way literature *means* and so it could seem "right" or acceptable to those who share those assumptions.

Suppose one of your ingenious classmates were to argue that the real subject of *Hamlet* is that the hero has tuberculosis. This would explain, your classmate would say, the hero's moodiness, his pretended madness that sometimes seems real, his rejection of Ophelia (he wouldn't want their children to suffer from the disease), his father's ghost (he, too, died of consumption), his anger at his uncle (who carries the disease, of course) for marrying Hamlet's mother, and so on. Your classmate might even argue that the text of the play is flawed, that it was just copied down during a performance by someone in the audience or was printed from an actor's imperfect copy. Therefore, "O that this too too *solid flesh*" should read "*sullied flesh*," as many scholars have argued (and might not "sullied flesh" suggest tuberculosis?). And, therefore, isn't it quite possible that the most famous soliloquy in the play really began or was meant to begin, "TB or not TB"? "No way!" we'd say. We would be reasonably sure that this is not just "not proved" but just plain *wrong*. It might be interesting and illuminating to rebut that reading in a paper of your own and to notice what kinds of evidence you bring to bear on an interpretive argument.

Reader and Text

If it is difficult to say exactly what a piece of literature *says*, it is usually not because it is vague or meaning*less* but because it is too specific and meaning*ful* to paraphrase satisfactorily in any language other than its own. Since no two human beings are identical and no two people can inhabit the same space at the same time, no two people can see exactly the same reality from the same angle and vantage point. Most of us get around this awkward truth by saying that we see what we are "supposed" to see, a generalized, common-sense approximation of reality. We are all, in effect, like Polonius in the third act of

Hamlet, who sees in a cloud, a camel, a weasel, a whale—whatever Hamlet tells him he sees.

Some individuals struggle to see things as fully and clearly as possible from their own unique vantage point and to communicate to others their particular—even peculiar—vision. But here too we are individuated, for though we speak of our "common language," we each speak a unique language, made up of "dialects" that are not only regional and ethnic but also conditioned by our age group, our profession, our education, travel, reading—all our experiences. Yet if we want to express our unique vision to others who have different visions and different "languages," we have to find some medium that is both true to ourselves and understandable to others.

There is for these individuals—these writers of literature—a constant tug-of-war between the uniqueness of their individual visions and the generalizing nature of language. The battle does not always result in sheer loss, however. Often, in the very struggle to get their own perceptions into language, writers sharpen those perceptions or discover what they themselves did not know when they began to write. You have probably made similar discoveries in the process of writing a letter or an assigned paper. But writers also find that what they have written does not perfectly embody what they meant it to, just as you perhaps have found that your finished papers have been not quite so brilliant as your original idea.

"Understanding" is not a passive reception of a text but an active reaching out from our own experiences toward the text. At least at first we need to do so by meeting the author on the ground of a common or general language and set of conventions—things that everybody "knows." The first task of the reader, therefore, is to get not to the author's intention, but to the general statement that the work itself makes—that is, its theme or thesis. After a few readings we can usually make a stab at articulating the theme of a text. What a work says in the way of a general theme, however, is not necessarily its full or ultimate meaning; otherwise we would read theme summaries and not stories. The theme is the meaning accessible to all through close reading of the text and common to all, but a literary text is not all statement. There are often cloudy areas in the text where we cannot be sure what is **implication**, the suggestion of the text, and what is our **inference**, or interpretation, of the text. Why does Doris Lessing's Judith prefer having a tomcat put to death to having him neutered but does not suggest that the female kitten who has been ruined for procreation be put death? Does this suggest that males, including human males, exist only to fertilize eggs, but that females have other functions as well? Or, at least, that this is what Judith believes? Does this give us more insight into

Judith's life, her singleness, her refusal to marry the Greek professor, her ultimate flight from Luigi? The story does not *say* this, but many readers will find this inference convincing. If accepted, this changes the meaning of the story to some degree. Still, it need not be accepted; the story does not, will never say. The meaning of the story for the reader who is convinced will differ from the meaning for the reader who is not convinced.

The full meaning of a work for you is not only in its stated theme, one that everyone can agree on, but in the meaning you derive by bringing together that generalized theme, the precise language of the text, and your own response and experiences—including reading experience—and imagination. That "meaning" is not the total meaning of the work, not what the author originally perceived and "meant to say"; it is the vision of the author as embodied in the work *and re-viewed from your own angle of vision.*

Your role in producing a meaning from the text does not free you from paying very close attention to the precise language of the text, the words and their meanings, their order, the syntax of the sentences, and even such mundane details as punctuation. You cannot impose a meaning on the text, no matter how sincerely and intensely you feel it, in defiance of the rules of grammar and the nature of the language.

Still, the reader has to be an artist too, trying to experience the reality of the work as the author experienced reality, and with the same reverence and sense of responsibility for the original. To write about literature you need to embody your reading experience—or interpretation—of the work in language. Alas, writing about literature, using words about words, is not as easy as it sounds at first. But it is more exciting, giving you a chance to see with another's eyes, to explore another's perceptions or experiences, and to explore and more fully understand your own in the process, thus expanding the horizon of your experience, perception, consciousness.

When some rich works of literature, like *Hamlet,* seem to have more than one meaning or no entirely satisfactory meaning or universally agreed upon single theme, it is not that they are not saying something, and saying something very specific, but that what they are saying is too specific, and complex, and profound (and true, perhaps) to be generalized or paraphrased in a few dozen words. The literary work is meaning*ful*—that is, full of meaning or meanings; but it is the reader who produces each particular meaning from the work, using the work itself, the language of the community and of the work, and his or her own language, experience, and imagination.

As a reader trying to understand the unique perception and language of the author, you should try to translate the text as best you can into terms you can understand. Do your best to approach the text with an open, receptive mind.

An interpretation, then, is not a clarification of what the writer "was trying to say"; it is a process that itself says, in effect, "The way I am trying to understand this work is . . . ."

CRITICAL APPROACHES

The way you read and talk about a literary text depends on your assumptions, usually unconscious or unarticulated, about what a work of literature is, what is it supposed to do, and what makes it good. Literary critics, however, often define their assumptions about literature and the proper way to go about reading it and writing about it. The results are critical theories or critical approaches. Looking at a few of these, you may recognize some of your own assumptions, see new and exciting ways of looking at literature, or, at the very least, become aware of your own critical premises and prejudices.

Objectivism

We might begin by asking just what, quite literally, a work of literature *is*. There are critics who think of it as a fixed and freestanding object made up of words on a page. It is "freestanding" in that it has no connection on the one hand with the author or his or her intention or life, or, on the other hand, with the historical or cultural context of the author or the reader. These we might call **objectivist** critics; they believe that a text is an independent object, free from the subjectivity of author and reader.

Formalism

Among the objectivist critics are the **formalists.** One common formalist conception is that a work is **autotelic,** that is, complete in itself, written for its own sake, and unified by its form—that which makes it a work of art. Content is less important than form. Literature involves a special kind of language that sets it apart from merely utilitarian writing; the formal strategies that organize and animate that language elevate literature and give it a special, almost religious character.

NEW CRITICISM   One group of formalists, the **New Critics,** dominated literary criticism in the middle of the twentieth century, and New Criticism remains an important influence today. Their critical practice is to demonstrate formal unity by showing how every part of a work—every word, every image, every element—contributes to a central unifying theme. Because the details of the work relate to a theme or idea, they are generally treated as *symbolic*, as figurative or allegorical, representations of that central, unifying idea. The kind of unity thus demonstrated, in which every part is related to the whole and the whole is reflected in each part, is called **organic unity.** The New Critics differentiate organic unity from (and much prefer it to) **mechanical unity,** the external, preconceived structure or rules that do not arise from the individuality of the work but from the type or genre. New Critical analysis, or **explication of the text,** is especially effective in the critical reading of lyric poetry. It has become so universally accepted as *at least the first step* in the understanding of literature that it is almost everywhere the critical approach taught in introductory literature courses, even in those that do not share its fundamental autotelic assumption. It is, indeed, the basic approach of the "Understanding the Text" sections in *The Norton Introduction to Literature.*

The New Critics' focus on theme or meaning as well as form signifies that for them literature is **referential:** it points to something outside itself, things in the real, external world or in human experience—a tree, a sound wave, love. The New Critics, in general, do not question the reality of the phenomenal world or the ability of language to represent it.

Structuralism

For many formalists, however, literature is not referential. The words in a story, poem, or play no longer point outward to the things, people, or world they are supposed to denote, as they might do in ordinary, "nonliterary" discourse, but point inward to each other and to the formal system they create. The critic still focuses on interrelatedness but is less concerned with "meaning"; words are treated not as referential symbols but as natural numbers; poetry is likened to mathematics or music.

Structuralism focuses on the text as an independent aesthetic object and also tends to detach literature from history and social and political implications, but (much more than New Criticism) structuralism emphasizes systematic analysis, aspiring to make literary criticism a branch of scientific inquiry. It sees every literary work as a separate "system" and seeks to discover the principles or general laws that govern the interaction of parts within the system. Structuralism has its roots in modern linguistic theory; it looks especially to the work of Ferdinand de Saussure (1857–1913), who founded structural linguistics early in the twentieth century. Structuralism in criticism did not, however, flourish internationally until the early 1960s, when a combination of space-age preoccupation with science and cold-war fear of implication led to a view of literature as intellectually challenging yet socially and politically noncontroversial.

Although based on linguistic theory, structuralism tries to extend newly discovered principles about language to other aspects of literature. Drawing on the **semiotic** principle that a vast and intricate system of signs enables human beings to communicate through language, structuralism asks readers to consider the way that other kinds of sign systems within a work—structures all—combine to produce meaning. Language and its characteristic habits are important to structuralists, but it is not enough to consider any single part of a work or any single kind of sign—linguistic or otherwise—within it. Structuralism aspires to elucidate the meaning of a work of literature by seeing the way all of its parts work relationally toward some wholeness of structure and meaning. Like formalism, it shows little interest in the creative process as such and has virtually no interest in authors, their intentions, or the circumstances or contexts of creation. It takes texts to represent interactions of words and ideas apart from individual human identities or sociopolitical commitments, and concentrates its analytical attention on what can be said about how different elements or processes in a text operate in relation to one another. Structuralists are less likely than formalists to concentrate their attention on some single all-explaining characteristic of literature (such as Cleanth Brooks's "tension" or William Empson's "ambiguity") and its practitioners are less likely to privilege a particular text for its revelation or authority. Structuralism may be seen as a sort of secular equivalent of formalism; it is less mysterious and authoritarian, and it has both the advantage and disadvantage of seeming to be less arbitrary and more "objectively" reliable. But in some ways it seems to promise too much for method and "objectivity," and by the 1970s its insights into the ways of language were already beginning to be used against it to attack the certitudes it appeared to promise and to emphasize instead the uncertainties and indeterminateness of texts.

Post-Structuralism

Post-Structuralism is the broad term used to designate the several directions of literary criticism that, while depending crucially on the insights of science-based theory, attack the very idea that any kind of certitude can exist about the meaning, understandability, or sharability of texts. Post-structuralists, disturbed at the optimism of positivist philosophy in suggesting that the world is knowable and explainable, ultimately doubt the possibility of certainties of any kind, and they see language as especially elusive and unfaithful. Much of post-structuralism involves undoing; the best-known variety of post-structuralism, **deconstruction,** suggests as much in its very name.

DECONSTRUCTION Deconstruction takes the observations of structuralism to their logical conclusion, arguing that the elaborate web of semiotic differentiations created by the principle of difference in language means that no text can ultimately have any stable, definite, or discoverable meaning.

For the deconstructionist, language consists just in black marks on a page that repeat or differ from each other and the reader is the only author, one who can find whatever can be found in, or be made to appear in, those detached, isolated marks. The deconstructionist conception of literature is thus very broad—almost any writing will do. While this may seem "subjective," in that the critical reader has great freedom, it is the object—the black marks on the blank page—that is the sole subject/object of intention/attention.

As practiced by its most famous proponent, the French philosopher Jacques Derrida (b. 1930), deconstruction endeavors to trace the way texts challenge or cancel their explicit meanings and wrestle themselves into stasis or neutrality. Many deconstructionists have strong radical political commitments (it is possible to argue that the radical counterculture of the 1960s and especially the political events in Paris of 1968 are the crucial context for understanding the origins of deconstructionism), but the retreat from meaning and denial of clear signification that characterizes deconstruction also has affinities with formalism and structuralism, particularly as deconstruction is practiced by American critics. Rather than emphasizing form over content, however, deconstruction tries to deny the possibility of content and places value instead on verbal play as a characteristic outlet of a fertile, adroit, and supple human mind. Like structuralism, it lives almost completely in a self-referential verbal world rather than a world in which texts represent some larger or other reality, but unlike structuralism it denies that the verbal world adds up to anything coherent, consistent, or meaningful in itself. Deconstruction also influences other varieties of post-structuralism with different kinds of interests in history and ideology. Michel Foucault (1926–1984), Julia Kristeva (b. 1941), and Jacques Lacan (1901–1981), though their disciplinary interests are in social history, feminist philosophy, and psychoanalysis, respectively, all come out of deconstructionist assumptions and carry the indeterminacies of post-structuralism (and of post-modernism more generally) into kinds of literary criticism with interests fundamentally different from those of structuralism.

Subjectivism

Opposed to objectivism is what might be called **subjectivism**. This loose term can be used to embrace many forms of psychological and self-, subject-, or reader-centered criticism.

Psychological Criticism

The assumption is that literature is the expression of the author's psyche, often his or her unconscious, and, like dreams, needs to be interpreted.

FREUDIAN CRITICISM   The dominant school is the **Freudian**, based on the work of Sigmund Freud (1856–1939). Many of its practitioners assert that the meaning of a literary work does not lie on its surface but in the psyche (some would even claim, in the neuroses) of the author. The value of the work, then, lies in how powerfully and convincingly it expresses the author's unconscious and how universal the psychological elements are. A well-known Freudian reading of *Hamlet*, for example, insists that Hamlet is upset because he is jealous of his uncle, for he, *like all male children*, unconsciously wants to go to bed with his mother. The ghost may then be a manifestation of Hamlet's unconscious desire; his madness is not just acting but is the result of this frustrated desire; his cruelly gross mistreatment of Ophelia is a deflection of his disgust at his mother's being "lecherous," "unfaithful" in her love for him. A Freudian critic may assume then that Hamlet is suffering from an Oedipus complex, a Freudian term for the desire of the son for his mother, its name derived from the Greek myth that is the basis of Sophocles' play *Oedipus the King*.

Some Freudian critics stress the author's psyche and find *Hamlet* the expression of Shakespeare's own Oedipus complex. Others stress the effect on the reader, the work having a purgative or cleansing effect by expressing in socially and morally acceptable ways unconscious desires that would be unacceptable if expressed directly.

LACANIAN CRITICISM   As it absorbs the indeterminacies of post-structuralism under the influence of thinkers such as Jacques Lacan, psychological criticism has become increasingly complex. Accepting the Oedipal paradigm and the unconscious as the realm of repressed desire, Lacanian psychology (and the critical theory that comes from that psychology) conflates these concepts with the deconstructionist emphasis on language as expressing absence—you use a word to represent an absent object but you cannot make it present. The word, then, like the unconscious desire, is something that cannot be fulfilled. Language, reaching out with one word after the other, striving for but never reaching its object, is the arena of desire.

JUNGIAN CRITICISM Just as a Freudian assumes that human psyches have similar histories and structures, the **Jungian** critic assumes that we all share a universal or **collective unconscious** (as well as having a racial and individual unconscious). According to Carl Gustav Jung (1875–1961) and his followers, in the collective and in our individual unconscious are universal images, patterns, and forms of human experiences or **archetypes.** These archetypes can never be known directly, but they surface in art in an imperfect, shadowy way, taking the form of **archetypal images**—the snake with its tail in its mouth, rebirth, mother, the double, the descent into Hell. To get a sense of the archetype beneath the archetypal images or shadows in the characters, plot, language, and images of a work, to bring these together in an archetypal interpretation, is the function of the Jungian critic. He is guided by his belief that there is a central myth common to all literature. Just as, for the Freudian literary critic, the "family romance," out of which the Oedipus story comes, is central, so the Jungian assumes there is a **monomyth** that underlies the archetypal images and gives a clue as to how they can be related to suggest the archetypes themselves. The myth is that of the quest. In that all-encompassing myth the hero struggles to free himself (the gender of the pronoun is specific and significant) from the Great Mother, to become a separate, self-sufficient being who is then rewarded by union with his ideal other, the feminine *anima.*

Phenomenological Criticism

Another kind of subjectivist criticism is **phenomenology,** especially as it is practiced by **critics of consciousness.** They consider all the writings of an author—shopping lists and letters as well as lyrics—as the expression of his or her mindset or way of looking at reality. Such a critic looks for repeated or obsessive use of certain key words, incidents, patterns, and angles of vision, and, using these, maps out thereby the inner world of the writer.

Reader-Response Criticism

The formalists focus on the text. Though the psychological critics focus most frequently on the author, their assumptions about the similarity or universality of the human mind make them consider as well the role of the reader. There is another approach that, though not psychological in the usual sense of the word, also focuses on the reception of the text, on **reader response.** The conventional notion of reading is that a writer or speaker has an "idea," **encodes** it—that is, turns it into words—and the reader or listener **decodes** it, deriving, when successful, the writer/speaker's "idea." What the reader-response critic assumes, however, is that such equivalency between sender and receiver is impossible. The literary **work** therefore does *not* exist on the page; that is only the **text.** The text becomes a work only when it is read, just as a score becomes music only when it is played. And just as every musical performance, even of exactly the same notes, is somewhat different, a different "interpretation," so no two readers read or perform exactly the same work from identical texts. Besides the individual differences of readers, space is made for different readings or interpretations by **gaps** in a text itself. Some of these are temporary—such as the withholding of the name of the murderer until the end—and are closed by the text sooner or later, though each reader will in the meantime fill them differently. But others are permanent, and can never be filled with certainty; the result is a degree of uncertainty or **indeterminacy** in the text.

The reader-response critic's focus on the reading process is especially useful in the study of long works such as novels. The critic follows the text sequentially, observing what **expectations** are being aroused, how they are being satisfied or modified, how the reader recapitulates "evidence" from the portion of the text he has read to project forward a **configuration,** a tentative assumption of what the work as a whole will be and mean once it is done. The expectations are in part built by the text and in part by the repertoire of the reader, i.e., the reader's reading experience plus his or her social and cultural knowledge.

Historical Criticism

Dialogism

Another critical approach that gives a significant role to the reader and is particularly useful for long fiction is **dialogism,** largely identified with the work of Mikhail Bakhtin (1895–1975). The dialogic critic bases the study of language and literature on the individual utterance, taking into account the specific time, the place, the speaker, and the listener or reader. Such critics thus see language as a continuous dialogue, each utterance being a reply to what has gone before. Even thought, which they define as inner speech, is a dialogue between utterances that you have taken in. Even your own language (and thus thought) is itself dialogic, for it is made up of the dialogue in which you are engaged, that which you have heard from parents and peers, teachers and television, all kinds of social and professional discourse and reading. Indeed, you speak many "languages"—those of your ethnic, social, economic, national, professional, gender, and other identities. Your individual language consists in the combination of those languages. The literary form in which the dialogic is most interesting, complex, and significant is the novel, for there you have the languages not only of the characters (as you do in drama), but also that of a mediator or narrator and passages of description or analysis or information that seem to come from other voices—newspapers, whaling manuals, legal cases, and so on. Because the world is growing more interrelated and we have multiple voices rather than one dominant voice or language, the novel has become the most appropriate form for the representation of that world.

Because the dialogic sees utterances, including literary utterances or works, as specific to a time and place, one of its dimensions, unlike formalist, structuralist, or psychological criticism, is *historical*. Nineteenth-century **historical criticism** took the obvious fact that a work is created in a specific historical and cultural context and that the author is a part of that context in order to treat literature as a product of the culture. Formalists and others emphasizing the **aesthetic** value of literature saw this as reducing the literary work to the status of a mere historical document and the abandonment of literary study to history. The dialogic critic sees the work in relation to its host context, a part of the dialogue of the culture. The work in turn helps to create the context for other utterances, literary and otherwise. Some consider dialogic criticism a form of sociological criticism.

SOCIOLOGICAL CRITICISM More recently, as scientists from psychology to physics recognized the role of the perceiver in perception, historians realized that they were not only discovering and looking at facts but were finding what they were looking for, selecting facts to fit preconceived views or interpretations. Literary historians or historical critics began to see literature not as a mere passive product of "history" but a contributor and even creator of history. An early form of this kind of historicism was **sociological criticism,** in which literature is seen as one aspect of the larger processes of history, especially those processes involving people acting in social groups or as members of social institutions or movements. Much sociological criticism uses literary texts to illustrate social attitudes and tendencies—and therefore has been strongly resisted by formalists, structuralists, and other "objectivist" critics as not being properly literary—but sociological criticism also attempts to relate what happens in texts to social events and patterns and is as concerned about the effects of texts on human events as about the effects of historical events on texts. Sociological criticism assumes that the most significant aspects of human beings are social and that the most important functions of literature thus involve the way that literature both portrays and influences human interactions. Much sociological criticism centers its attention on contemporary life and texts, seeking to affect both societal directions and literary ones in the present, but some sociological criticism is historical, concerned with differences in different times and places and anxious to interpret directions of literature in terms of historical emphases and patterns.

MARXIST CRITICISM　　The most insistent and vigorous historicism through most of the twentieth century has been **Marxism,** based on the work of Karl Marx (1818–1883). Marxist criticism, like other historical critical methods in the nineteenth century, treated literature as a passive product of the culture, specifically of the economic aspect, and therefore of class warfare. Economics, the underlying cause of history, was thus the *base,* and culture, including literature and the other arts, the *superstructure.* Viewed from the Marxist perspective, the literary works of a period would, then, reveal the state of the struggle between classes in the historical place and moment.

　　Marxist critics, however, early on recognized the role of perception. They insisted that all use of language, including literary and critical language, is **ideological,** that is, that it derives from and expresses preconceived ideas, particularly economic or class values. Criticism is thus not just the product of the culture but part of the discourse or "conversation" that we call history. Formalism and even the extreme apolitical position of **aestheticism,** "art for art's sake," by placing art in a realm above the grubbiness of everyday life—above such mundane things as politics and money—removes art from having any importance in that life. According to Marxists, this "bourgeois mystification of art" tends to support the class in power. Marxism has traditionally been sensitive to and articulate about power politics in both life and literature, and both its social and literary analyses have often been based on an explicit or implicit political agenda, though many Marxist critics are motivated more by theoretical than practical aims. In recent years, especially in the wake of post-structuralism and the psychoanalytical criticism of the 1970s and 1980s, Marxist criticism has become increasingly theoretical and less doctrinaire politically. Critics such as Raymond Williams, Fredric Jameson, Terry Eagleton, Pierre

Macherey, Walter Benjamin, and Louis Althusser have gained wide audiences among readers with a variety of political and literary commitments. Over the course of the century, it has been Marxism that has most often and most consistently raised referential and historical issues about literature, and those readers who have been interested in the interactive relationship between literature and life have most often turned for their guidance on such issues to Marxist analysts, whether or not they share their philosophical or political assumptions. In the past decade, however, two other critical schools with strong commitments to historical and cultural issues have become very powerful intellectually and have attracted many practitioners and adherents. These two, feminism and new historicism, have (along with Marxism and, in its way, dialogism) turned critical attention powerfully toward historical and representational issues, and since the mid-1980s they have set the dominant directions in literary criticism.

FEMINIST CRITICISM   Like Marxist criticism, feminist criticism derives from firm political and ideological commitments and insists that literature both reflects and influences human behavior in the larger world. Feminist criticism often, too, has practical and political aims. Strongly conscious that most of recorded history has given grossly disproportionate attention to the interests, thoughts, and actions of men, feminist thought endeavors both to extend contemporary attention to distinctively female concerns, ideas, and accomplishments and to recover the largely unrecorded and unknown history of women in earlier times. Not all directions of feminist criticism are historical; feminism has, in fact, taken many different directions and forms in recent years, and it has many different concerns. French feminist criticism, for example, has been deeply influenced by psychoanalysis, especially Lacanian psychoanalysis, and by French post-structuralist emphasis on language. Beyond their common aim of explicating and furthering specifically female interests, feminist critics may differ substantially in their assumptions and emphases. Like Marxism, feminism draws creatively on various other approaches and theories for its several methodologies. The most common historical directions of American feminism in particular involve the recovery of neglected or forgotten texts written by women in earlier times, the redrawing of literary values to include forms of writing (letters and autobiography, for example) that women were able to create when more public and accepted forms were denied to them, the discovery of the roles (positive and negative) that reading played in the lives and consciousnesses of women when they were unable to pursue more "active" and "public" courses, and the sorting out of cultural values implicit in the way women are represented in the texts of particular times and places.

New Historicism

New historicism has less obvious ideological commitments than Marxism or feminism, but it shares their interest in the investigation of how power is distributed and used in different cultures. Drawing on the insights of modern anthropology (and especially on the work of Clifford Geertz), new historicism wishes to isolate the fundamental values in texts and cultures, and it regards texts both as evidence of basic cultural patterns and as forces in cultural and social change. Many of the most influential practitioners of the new historicism come out of the ranks of Marxism and feminism, and new historicists are usually knowledgeable about most varieties of literary theory. Like Marxists and feminists, they are anxious to uncover the ideological commitments in texts, and they care deeply about historical and cultural difference and the way texts represent it. But personal commitments and specific political agendas usually are less important—at least explicitly—to new historicists, and one of the main contentions between feminists and new historicists—or between Marxists and new historicists—involves disagreement about the role that one's own politics should play in the practice of criticism. Many observers regard new historicism as politically to the left in its analysis of traditional cultural values, but critics on the left are suspicious of new historicism, especially of its reluctance to state its premises openly, and they generally regard its assumptions as conservative. Whatever its fundamental political commitments, however (or whether its commitments can be fairly described as having a consistent and specifiable bias), new historicism is far more interested than any other literary approach in social groups generally ignored by literary historians, and it refuses to privilege "literature" over other printed, oral, or material texts. "Popular literature" often gets major attention in the work of new historicists, who see all texts in a culture as somehow expressive of its values and directions and thus as equally useful in determining the larger intellectual, epistemological, and ethical system of which any text is a part. Texts here are thus seen as less specifically individual and distinctive than in most objectivist criticisms, and although new historicists are sometimes interested in the psychology of authors or readers their main concern is with the prevailing tendencies shared across a culture and thus shared across all kinds of texts, whatever their class status, literary value, or political aim.

Pluralism

These classifications are not pigeonholes, and you will notice that many of the approaches overlap: many feminists, especially French feminist critics, are Lacanian or post-structuralist as well, while British feminists often lean toward sociological, especially Marxist, criticism; dialogic critics accept many of the starting points and methods of reader-response and sociological critics, and so on. These crossovers or combinations are generally enriching; they cause problems only when the critic seems to be operating out of contradictory assumptions.

There is a lively debate among critics and theorists at present involving the question of whether readers should bring together the insights and methods of different schools (practitioners of the mixing of methods are usually called **pluralists**) or whether they should commit themselves wholeheartedly to a single system. Pluralists contend that they make use of promising insights or methods wherever they find them and argue that putting together the values of different approaches leads to a more fair and balanced view of texts and their uses. Opponents—those who insist on a consistency of ideological commitment— argue that pluralists are simply unwilling to state or admit their real commitments, and that any mixing of methods leads to confusion, uncertainty, and inconsistency rather than fairness. Readers, conscious or not of their assumptions and their methods, make this basic choice—to follow one lead or many—and the kind of reading they do and the conclusions they come to depend not only on this basic choice but many others suggested by the dominant strands of recent criticism that have been described here. Not all critics are aware of their assumptions, methodologies, or values, and some would even deny that they begin with any particular assumptions or biases, but is is often useful, especially to readers newly learning to practice literary criticism, to sort out their own beliefs carefully and see exactly what kind of difference it makes in the way they read literature and ask questions of it.

Further Reading on Critical Approaches

For good introductions to the issues discussed here, see the following books from which we have drawn in our discussion and definitions:

Robert Alter, *The Pleasures of Reading in an Ideological Age*, New York, 1989

Jonathan Culler, *The Pursuit of Signs*, London, 1981

Jonathan Culler, *On Deconstruction*, London, 1983

Robert Con Davis and Ronald Schleifer, *Contemporary Literary Criticism*, 2d ed., New York, 1989

Mary Eagleton (ed.), *Feminist Literary Theory: A Reader*, Oxford, 1986

Terry Eagleton, *Literary Theory: An Introduction*, Minneapolis, 1983

Nannerl Keohane, Michelle Z. Rosaldo, and Barbara C. Gelpi (eds.), *Feminist Theory: A Critique of Ideology*, Chicago, 1982

Dominick LaCapra, *History and Criticism*, Ithaca, N.Y., 1985

Frank Lentricchia, *After the New Criticism*, Chicago, 1980

Frank Lentricchia and Thomas McLaughlin (eds.), *Critical Terms for Literary Study*, Chicago, 1990

Richard Macksey and Eugenio Donato (eds.), *The Structuralist Controversy: The Languages of Criticism and the Sciences of Man*, Baltimore, 1972

Toril Moi, *Sexual-Textual Politics*, New York, 1985

Jean Piaget (translated by Chanihan Maschler), *Structuralism*, New York, 1970

Tzvetan Todorov, *Mikhail Bakhtin: The Dialogic Principle*, Minneapolis, 1984

WRITING ABOUT FICTION,
POETRY, DRAMA

So far we have been discussing writing about literature in general, rather than writing about a story, a poem, or a play in particular, though we have used specific works as examples. There are topics, such as a study of imagery, symbol, or theme, that are equally applicable to all three genres: you can write a paper on the images or symbols in or the theme of a story, a poem, or a play. Indeed, you can write an essay comparing imagery, say, in a story, poem, and play—comparing the water imagery in James Baldwin's story "Sonny's Blues," for example, with the air or wind imagery in Shelley's "Ode to the West Wind," and the fire or burning imagery in Ibsen's *Hedda Gabler*. Fiction and drama also have action and character in common, so that you can not only choose to write on the plot of a story or play or on characters or characterization in a particular story or play, but you can compare, for example, a character in a story with a character in a play—Lessing's Judith with Ibsen's Hedda perhaps.

Narrative

A story has not only elements common to all three genres, such as plot and character; it also has something special—a narrator, someone who tells the story. Everything in fiction—action, character, theme, structure, even the language—is mediated: everything comes to us through an intervening mind or voice; we often see the story from a particular vantage point or several vantage points (*focus*) and always are told the story by someone, whether that someone is identified or is merely a disembodied *voice*. We must be aware of the narration, the means by which the story comes to us. We must be aware that the action, characters, all the elements in a story, are always mediated (there is someone between us and the story), and that the mediation contributes greatly to the meaning, structure, and effect of the story. Who is telling us the story of "The Lame Shall Enter First"? What is the physical and emotional relationship of the narrator of that story to its characters? How would you describe the language or voice of the narration? These are essential questions to ask about

Flannery O'Connor's superb story, and in answering them you may want to write a paper called "The Narrator in 'The Lame Shall Enter First' " (or, if you want to be more dramatic, "The Ghostly Reporter of 'The Lame Shall Enter First.' " A story is told *to* someone as well as by someone, and you might want to ask yourself what the relationship is supposed to be between us—the audience—and the narrator. To what kind of audience is the narrator of "Our Friend Judith" telling her story? How do we, as readers, differ from that audience? What impression of the narrator do we form that she does not intend? Such questions might lead to an analysis of the tone of that story—and a paper we might sardonically call "With Friends Like Judith's . . . ." These are the kinds of questions raised by the simple but central fact that stories do not come to us directly but are narrated; these are therefore the kinds of questions of special importance to readers of fiction and the kinds of questions writing about fiction frequently centers upon.

Even the conventional past tense in fiction that we take for granted implies a narrator. Since the story is not happening "now," in the present, is not being enacted before us but is over with, having already happened in the past, it is being recalled, and someone must be recalling it, someone who knows what happened and how it all came out. That someone is the narrator. Knowing the end, the narrator has been able to select and shape the events and details. For that reason everything in a well-constructed story is relevant and significant.

Even narrative time is purposefully structured. Stories, unlike actual time as we know it, have beginnings and endings, but they do not have to begin at the beginning and proceed in a uniform direction at a uniform pace toward the end. They can be told from end to beginning, or even from middle to beginning to end, as in "Sonny's Blues." In a story an hour, day, or decade can be skipped or condensed into a narrative moment (a phrase or sentence), or a moment can be expanded to fill pages. Since this manipulation of time affects the meaning and effect of the story, we must pay close attention to it and question its significance. For example, the beginning of the third section of "An Occurrence at Owl Creek Bridge" follows immediately from the end of the first section, so why is the second section there at all? Why does the first section cover only a few minutes of action but the third, only a little longer, cover what seems to be a whole day? Can you explain why—in terms of meaning and effect—each of the lengthy scenes in "The Lady with the Dog" is dwelled upon? why other, longer periods are briefly summarized or skipped? Why do some stories, such as "Her First Ball," cover only a very short period of time, while other, such as "A Rose for Emily" cover years and years? Why are stories such as "Her First Ball" presented largely through dialogue, while others, such as "A Rose for Emily," are "told" rather than presented, with few dramatized scenes and little dialogue?

Dramatization

Scenes presented more or less immediately (that is, without mediation) through dialogue and action, taking place over a short period of time, are said to be *dramatized*. Though there may be gaps of time *between* the scenes or acts of a play, once the action begins it takes exactly as much time on the stage as it would in actuality: the actors speak and move in "real" time. Though there is, of course, a playwright who knew how it would all come out and has shaped the play accordingly, the language of the play that we respond to is in the present tense, the dialogue and action are happening in the present, right before our eyes. And though the playwright has written all the lines, his or her voice is not directly heard: only the characters speak. Neither the playwright nor a surrogate in the form of a narrator stands at your elbow to tell you who are the good guys and who the bad, what each character is like or whether what is being said is true, distorted, false. Only very rarely—as in the Shakespearean soliloquy or aside—do we know what a character is thinking. In plays such as *Oedipus the King* and even *Hamlet*, there are only very brief indications of setting, costume, movement of characters, tone of voice, if they are present at all. Such stage directions—which may be as elaborate as the detailed description of setting and costumes and the instructions for action and tone in *Hedda Gabler*—are not, in a sense, purely dramatic. Watching a play being performed on a stage, we do not see or hear these words at all. On the page, they are usually distinguished from the text of the play by italics or some other typographical device, so as we read we register—or are supposed to register—them as separate from "the play itself." They seem to belong to some other dimension and clearly belong to a voice other than that of any character.

When we read a play we tend to imagine it—in the literal sense of putting it into images—in our minds as if it were being performed on a stage. We act, as it were, as our own directors; if we were to put into words all that would be necessary to stage the play as we see it in our minds, we would be writing the stage directions, or narrative, of the play. The relative absence of such narrative in drama makes our part in the imaging or staging of a play as we read more crucial than it is in reading fiction. How you would stage a play or a scene in order to bring out its full meaning and effect as you imagined it can serve as a significant topic for writing about drama. You might ask yourself such questions as, What instructions would I give the actors for speaking the apparently banal lines of *The Black and White* and what effect would I strive for? What scene or passage would I use as the best example of how the play should be read? How would I costume Oedipus in the first and last scenes in order to bring out the main movement and theme of the play? How can I, in the early scenes, subtly reveal that Oedipus has an injured ankle without detracting from the power and majesty of his presence at that time . . . In the middle of his stage directions describing the set for *Hedda Gabler*, Ibsen specifies that on the rear wall of the smaller room there "hangs the portrait of a handsome old man in general's uniform." What, precisely, should this portrait look like? What expression should be on the general's face? How prominent should the picture be in the set as a whole?

Though you may wish to write on the theme, characters, action, imagery, or language of a play from time to time, one central element you will certainly want to write about sooner or later is the staging, or dramatization—the set, costumes, acting, moving of characters about on the stage, even lighting—and how this can enhance the effect and meaning of the play on the page.

Words

Some plays, like *Hamlet*, are written partly or entirely in verse. Though we may be able to make a distinction between poetry and verse, it is reasonable to say that as the term is generally used, poetry itself is not so much a literary genre as it is a medium. It might be more logical to break literature down into "prose" and "poetry" rather than into "fiction," "drama," and "poetry." For besides poetic dramas like *Hamlet*, there are also dramatic poems, such as Browning's "My Last Duchess" and John Donne's "The Flea," poems in which a distinguishable character speaks in a definable, almost "stageable" situation. There are also narrative poems, those that tell a story through a narrator, such as "Sir Patrick Spens" or *Paradise Lost*. What these and other poems—lyrics, for example—have in common is rhythmical language (and, some people would add, highly figurative language).

All literature is embodied in words, of course, but poetry uses words most intensely, most fully. It uses not only the statements words make, what they signify or *denote*, using them with great precision; not only what words suggest or *connote*, usually with wide-ranging sensitivity and inclusiveness; but the very sounds of the words themselves. Not all poems have highly patterned or very regular meter, but almost all poetry is more highly patterned than almost any prose. Not all poems rhyme, but it seems safe to say that all extensively rhymed works are poems. So much writing about poetry concentrates on the words themselves: some treats the patterns of sounds, the rhythms or rhymes, some the precision or suggestiveness of the language, and some the relation of sounds to shades of meaning. This is not to say that excellent papers may not be written on the themes, characters, settings of poems. There are many excellent topics as well for comparative papers; the themes of a poem and a story may be compared—"Dover Beach" and "The Lady with the Dog," for example—or of a poem and a play—"Harlem (A Dream Deferred)" and *Fences*, perhaps. But in writing about poetry, even when discussing theme or other elements, at some point one usually comes to concentrate on the medium itself, the sound, precision, suggestiveness of the language. The sample paper on Sharon Olds's "The Victims" (p. 861) is an example of how one writes about this central element of poetry, words.

Sample Topics and Titles

We have been stressing, on the one hand, writing about the most characteristic elements of stories, plays, and poems—narration, dramatization, and words—and on the other hand, writing about the elements common to all three genres, like theme or symbols. For further hints about likely topics you might look at the chapter headings in the table of contents of this volume and read the introductory material to the chapter, or chapters, that looks most interesting or most promising for your immediate purpose. You might look, too, at the "Writing Suggestions" at the end of each chapter, the sample student papers, and at the list of sample topics that follows, not so much for the topic that you will actually come to write on but as a trigger for your own imagination and ideas.

Fiction

1. A Plotless Story about Plot: Grace Paley's "A Conversation with My Father"
2. The Selection and Ordering of the Scenes in "The Country Husband"
3. What does the voice in "Love Medicine" contribute to the story's structure, tone, and effect?

4. Who Am I? The Nature of the Narrator in "Our Friend Judith"
5. The Self-Characterization of Montresor in "The Cask of Amontillado"
6. Sonny's Brother's Character
7. Another Ending to "Happy Endings"
8. The Image and Import of the Sea in "The Lady with the Dog"
9. "Only a Girl": The Theme of "Boys and Girls"
10. What is the theme of "The Rocking-Horse Winner," and how does it relate to the title of the story?

Poetry

1. Attitudes toward Authority in "Sir Patrick Spens"
2. Scene, Sequence, and Time in "Sir Patrick Spens"
3. Sir Patrick Spens as a Tragic Hero
4. Why "Facts" Are Missing in "Western Wind"
5. Birth and Death Imagery in "The Death of the Ball Turret Gunner"
6. Varieties of Violence in Frost's "Range-Finding"
7. The Characterization of God in "Channel Firing"
8. The Idea of Flight in "Ode to a Nightingale"
9. Attitudes toward the Past in "Mr. Flood's Party" and "They Flee from Me"
10. Satire of Distinctive American Traits in "Boom," "Dirge," and "What the Motorcycle Said"

Drama

1. What is the conflict and what is the reversal (peripety) in *The Bear*?
2. What is the effect on the reader or audience of having so much of the major actions of *Hedda Gabler* (or *Oedipus*) happen offstage?
3. Rosencrantz and Guildenstern as Half-Men in *Hamlet*
4. The Past Recaptured: What We Know (or Can Infer) about Blanche's Life in *A Streetcar Named Desire*
5. Varieties of Verbal Wit as a Device of Characterization in *The Importance of Being Earnest*
6. Realistic Drama versus Comedy: Love and Marriage in *Hedda Gabler* and *The Importance of Being Earnest*
7. Staging Polonius: Language and Cliché as Guides to Gestures, Facial Expression, and Character in *Hamlet*
8. How important is the visual impression that Hedda makes in *Hedda Gabler*? How would you stage her appearance? How would you clothe

her? What gestures would you give her? How would you instruct the actress playing her to speak? What textual clues lead you to your decisions?

Intergeneric Topics

1. Motivation in *Hedda Gabler* and "Aunt Jennifer's Tigers"
2. The Functions of Spare Language in "A Very Short Story" and "On My First Son"
3. The Uses of Fantasy in "Araby" and "Wild Nights—Wild Nights!"
4. The Disillusioned Lovers in Joyce's "Araby" and Wyatt's "They Flee from Me"
5. The Loyalty of the Survivor: Maupassant's "The Jewelry" and Chekhov's *The Bear*
6. Francis Weed and Henry Higgins: A Comparison
7. The Murderer Confesses: Browning's Duke of Ferrara and Poe's Montresor
8. Remembering Grandmother: Pat Mora's "Gentle Communion" and Mordecai Richler's "The Summer My Grandmother Was Supposed to Die"

Creative Topics

1. The speaker in "My Last Duchess" has been charged with the murder of his last duchess. On the basis on his words in the poem, prepare a case for the prosecution.
2. Write a "reply" to the speaker of "To His Coy Mistress," declining his invitation and picking out the flaws in his argument.
3. Write a soliloquy for Gertrude (*Hamlet*) in which she defends herself against the most serious charges made against her motives and conduct.
4. Reconstruct the events and sentiments in "Dover Beach" as a short mood play by writing dialogue and stage directions for a scene between the speaker and the woman.
5. Retell (in poetry or prose) the story in "Cherrylog Road" from the point of view of the woman who is looking back on the experience twenty years later.
6. Using "Fern Hill" as a model, write the kind of imaginary reverie Hedda Gabler might have written about her childhood.
7. What would happen in your neighborhood (town) if one morning there appeared a very old man with enormous wings?

8. Select three scenes for a one-act play called "The Rocking-Horse Winner."

9. Choose a story from *Reading More Fiction* that you have not read before, read to a crucial point or a pause marked by the author, and describe your expectations of how the story will develop and conclude.

DECIDING WHAT TO
WRITE ABOUT

Having Something to Say

Deciding what to write about—what approach to use, which questions to ask—seems like the first step in the process of writing a paper about a work of literature. It isn't. Before that, you have to have confidence that you have something to say. If you are a beginner at this kind of writing, you are likely to have deep doubts about that. Developing confidence is not, at first, easy. You may feel as if you can *never* begin and want to put off the paper forever, or you may want to plunge in fast and get it over with. Either of these approaches, though common and tempting, is a mistake: the best way is to begin preparing for the paper as soon as possible—the moment you know you have one to write—but not to hurry into the writing itself.

The first step is to get close enough to the work to feel comfortable with it. Before you can tell anyone else about what you have read—and writing about literature is just another form of talking about literature, although a more formal and organized one—you need to "know" the work, to have a sure sense of what the work itself is like, how its parts function, what ideas it expresses, how it creates particular effects, and what your responses are. And the only way you will get to know the work is to spend time with it, reading it carefully and thoughtfully and turning it over in your mind. There is no substitute for reading, several times and with care, the work you are going to write about *before* you pick up a pen and prepare to write. And let your reading be of the *work itself*, not of something *about* that work, at least at first; later, your instructor may steer you to background materials or to critical readings about the work, but at first you should encounter the work alone and become aware of your own private responses to it.

Begin, then, by reading, several times, the work you are going to write about. The first time, read it straight through at one sitting: read slowly, pausing at its natural divisions—between paragraphs or stanzas, or at the ends of scenes—to consider how you are responding to the work. Later, when your knowledge of the work is more nearly complete and when you have the "feel" of the whole, you can compare your early responses with your more considered thoughts, in effect "correcting" your first impressions in whatever way seems necessary on the basis of new and better knowledge. But if you are noncommittal at first, refusing to notice what you think and feel, you will have nothing to correct, and you may cut yourself off from the most direct routes of response. Feelings are not always reliable—about literature any more than about people—but they are always the first point of contact with a literary work: you feel before you think. Try to start with your mind open, as if it were a blank sheet of paper ready to receive an impression from what you read.

When you have finished a first reading, think about your first impressions. Think about how the work began, how it gained your interest, how it generated expectations, how its conflicts and issues were resolved, how it ended, how it made you feel from beginning to end. Write down any phrases or events that you remember especially vividly, anything you are afraid you might forget. Look back at any parts that puzzled you at first. Write down in one sentence what you think the story, poem, or play is about. Then read it again, this time much more slowly, making notes as you go on any passages that seem especially significant and pausing over any features or passages that puzzle you. Then write a longer statement—three or four sentences—summarizing the work and suggesting more fully what it seems to be about. Try to write the kind of summary described above on pages 2109–2111. If you get stuck, try brainstorming all of your ideas about the work for fifteen minutes, and then write the summary.

Stop. Do something else for a while, something as different as possible—see a movie, do math problems, ride a bicycle, listen to music, have a meal, take a nap, mow the lawn, build a loft. Do NOT do some other reading you have been meaning to do. When you go back to the work and finish reading it for the third time—rapidly and straight through—write down in a sentence the most important thing you would want to tell someone else who was about to read it for the first time: not just whether you liked it or not, but what exactly you liked, how the whole thing seems to have worked.

Now you are ready to choose a topic.

Choosing a Topic

Once you are ready to choose a topic, the chances are that you have already—quietly and unconsciously—chosen one. The clue is in the last statement you wrote. The desire to tell someone about a work of literature is a wonderful place to begin. Good papers almost always grow out of a desire to communicate. Desire is not enough, of course—the substance (and most of the work, sentence by sentence) is still ahead of you; but desire will get you started. Chances are that what you wrote down as the one thing you most wanted to say is close to the heart of the central issue in the work you are going to write about. Your statement will become, perhaps, in somewhat revised form, your thesis.

The next step is to convert your personal feelings and desire to communicate into a sentence or two that states your purpose—into an "objective" statement about the work, a statement that will mean something to someone else. This will be your thesis. Again, you may already be further along than you realize. Look at the "summary" you wrote after your second reading. The summary will probably sound factual, objective, and general about the work; the personal statement you wrote after the third reading will be more emotional, subjective, and particular about some aspect of the work. In combining the two successfully lies the key to a good paper: what you need to do is to write persuasively an elaboration and explanation of the last statement so that your reader comes to share the "objective" view of the whole work that your summary expresses. The summary you have written will, in short, be implicit in the whole essay; your total essay will suggest to your reader the wholeness of the work you are writing about, but it will do so by focusing its attention on some particular aspect of the work—on a part that leads to, or suggests, or represents the whole. What you want to do is build an essay on the basis of your first statement, taking a firm hold on the handle you have found. The summary is your limit and guide: it reminds you of where you will come out. Any good topic ultimately leads back to the crucial perceptions involved in a summary. Ultimately, any good writing about literature leads to a full and resonant sense of the central thrust of the work, but the most effective way to find that center is by discovering a pathway that particularly interests you. The best writing about literature presents a clear—and well-argued—thesis about a work or works and presents it from the perspective of personal, individual perception. But the thesis should clarify the central thrust of the work, helping it to open itself up to readers more completely and more satisfyingly.

Topics often suggest themselves after a second or third reading, simply because one feature or problem stands out so prominently that it almost demands to be talked about. What is real in "The Real Thing"? Will the love between Gurov and the lady with the dog last? Sometimes you may be lucky: your instructor may *assign* a topic instead of asking you to choose your own. At first glance, that may not seem like a good break: it often feels confining to follow specific directions or to have to operate within limits and rules prescribed by someone else. The advantage is that it may save a lot of time and prevent floundering around. If your instructor assigns a topic, it is almost certain to be one that will work, one that has a payoff if you approach it creatively and without too much resentment at being directed so closely and precisely. It is time-consuming, even when you have tentatively picked a topic, to think through its implications and be sure it works. And an instructor's directions, especially if they are detailed and call attention to particular questions or passages, may aid greatly in helping you focus on particular issues or in leading you to evidence crucial to the topic.

If your instructor does *not* give you a topic and if no topic suggests itself to you after you have read a particular work three or four times, you may sometimes have to settle for the kind of topic that will—more or less—be safe for any literary work. Some topics are almost all-purpose. You can always analyze devices of characterization in a story, showing how descriptive detail, dialogue, and the reactions of other people in the story combine to present a particular character and evoke the reader's response to him or her; with a poem you can almost always write an adequate paper analyzing rhythm, or verse form, or imagery, or the connotations of key words. Such "fall-back" topics are, however, best used only as last resorts, when your instincts have failed you in a particular instance. When choice is free, a more lively and committed paper is likely to begin from a particular insight or question, something that grabs you and makes you want to say something, or solve a problem, or formulate a thesis. The best papers are usually very personal in origin; even when a topic is set by the assignment, the best papers come from a sense of having personally found an answer to a significant question. To turn a promising idea into a good paper, however, personal responses usually need to be supported by a considerable mass of evidence; the process often resembles the testing of "evidence" in a laboratory or the formulation of hypotheses and arguments in a law case. You may need to narrow your topic so that your thesis is focused and can be supported by examples from throughout the text. If your topic is too broad, your paper will likely become long, unweildy, and overly general.

Considering Your Audience

Thinking of your paper as an argument or an explanation will also help with one of the most sensitive issues in writing about literature. The issue: To whom are you writing? Who is your audience? The obvious answer is, your instructor, but in an important sense, that is the wrong answer. It is wrong because, although it could literally be true that your instructor will be the only person (besides you) who will ever read your paper, your object in writing about literature is to learn to write for an audience of peers, people a lot like yourself who are sensible, pretty well educated, and need to have something (in this case a literary work) explained to them so that they will be able to understand it more fully. Picture your ideal reader as someone about your own age and with about the same educational background. Assume that the person is intelligent and has some idea of what literature is like and how it works, but that he or she has just read this particular literary work for the first time and has not yet had a chance to think about it carefully. Don't be insulting and explain the obvious, but don't assume either that your reader has noticed and considered every detail. The object is to inform and convince your reader, not to try to impress.

Should you, then, altogether ignore the obvious fact that it is an instructor—probably with a master's degree or Ph.D. in literature—who is your actual reader? Not altogether: you don't want to get so carried away with speaking to people of your own age and interests that you slip into slang, or feel the need to explain what a stanza is, or leave an allusion to a rock star unexplained, and you do want to learn from the kind of advice your instructor has given in class or from comments he or she may have made on other papers you have written. But don't become preoccupied with the idea that you are writing for someone in "authority" or someone you need to please. Most of all, don't think of yourself as writing for a captive audience, for a reader who *has* to read what you write. It is not always easy to know exactly who your audience is or how interested your readers may be, so you have to make the most of every single word. It is your job to get the reader's attention. And you will have to do it subtly, making conscious assumptions about what your reader already knows and what he or she can readily understand. The tone of your paper should be serious and straightforward and its attitude respectful toward the reader, as well as toward the literary work. But its approach and vocabulary, while formal enough for academic writing, should be readily understandable by someone with your own background and reading experience. And it should be lively enough to interest someone like you. Try to imagine, as your ideal reader, the person in your class whom you most respect. Write to get, and hold, that person's serious attention. Try to communicate, try to teach.

FROM TOPIC TO ROUGH DRAFT

Writing about literature is very much like talking about literature. But there is one important difference. When we talk, we organize as we go—trying to get a handle, experimenting, working toward an understanding. And the early stages of preparing a paper—the notetaking, the outlining, the rough drafts—are much like that. A "finished" paper, however, has the uncertainties and tentativeness worked out and presents an argument that moves carefully and compellingly toward a conclusion. How does one get from here to there?

Once you have decided on a topic, the process of planning is fairly straightforward, but it can be time consuming and (often) frustrating. There are three basic steps in the planning process: first you gather the evidence, then you sort it into order, and (finally) you develop it into a convincing argument. The easiest way is to take these steps one by one.

Gathering Evidence

The first step involves accumulating evidence that supports the statement you have decided to make about your topic (that is, your thesis), and that takes you back to the text. But before you read the text again, look over the notes you have already made in the margin of that text or on separate pieces of paper. Which of them have something to do with the topic you have now defined? Which of them say something about your main point? Which ones can you now set aside as irrelevant to your topic?

Reading over the notes you have already made is a good preparation for re-reading the work again, for this time as you read it you will be looking at it in a new and quite specific, looking for all the things in it that relate to the topic you have decided on. This time you will, in effect, be flagging everything—words, phrases, structural devices, changes of tone, anything—that bears upon your topic. As you read—very slowly and single-mindedly, with your topic always in mind—keep your pen constantly poised to mark useful points. Be ready to say something about the points as you come upon them; it's a good idea to write down, immediately, any sentences that occur to you as you reread this time. Some of these sentences will turn out to be useful when you actually begin to write your paper. Some will be incorporated in your paper; but some will not: you will find that a lot of the notes you take, like a lot of the footage shot in making a film, will end up on the cutting room floor.

No one can tell you exactly how to take notes but there are some general guidelines that may be useful. The notes you will need to take and how you take them will depend on the particulars of the paper you are about to write. Here are five hints toward successful notetaking.

1. Keep your topic and your thesis about your topic constantly in mind as you reread and take notes. Mark all passages in the text that bear on your topic, and for each one write on a note card a single sentence that describes how the passage relates to your topic and thesis. Add a "key" word that identifies the note at the top of the card to help you to organize the cards into clusters later in the process. Then indicate, for each passage, the specific location in the text—by page or paragraph number if you are working on a story; by line number if you are writing about a poem; by act, scene, and line number if you are writing about a play. If you are taking notes on a computer, put page breaks between each one, so that when you print them out, there will be one note per page.

2. Keep rereading and taking notes until one of five things happens:
   a. You get too tired and lose your concentration. (If that happens, stop and then start again later, preferably the next day.)
   b. You stop finding relevant passages or perceive a noticeable drying up of your ideas. (Again, time to pause; give the work at least one more reading later when your mind is fresh and see whether the juices start anew. If they don't, you may be ready to outline and write.)
   c. You begin to find yourself annotating every single sentence or line, and the evidence all begins to run together into a single blob. (If this happens, your thesis is probably too broad. Try simplifying and narrowing it so that you don't try to include everything. Then go back to your notetaking and discriminate more carefully between what actually is important to your thesis and what only relates at some distance.)
   d. You become impatient with your notetaking and can't wait to get started writing. (Start writing. Use scrap paper, and be prepared to go back to systematic notetaking if your ideas or your energy fades. The

chances are that the prose passages you write this way will find a
place in your paper, but they may not belong exactly where you think
they do when you first write them down.)

    e. You find that there is insufficient evidence for your thesis, that the evi-
dence points in another direction, or that the evidence contradicts
your thesis. (Revise your topic to reflect the evidence, and begin rereading once more.)

    3. When you think you have finished your notetaking, read all your note
cards over slowly, one by one, and jot down any further ideas as they occur to
you, each one on a separate note card. Computer users can either read the file
on screen and add notes as they wish, or print out all of the notes and read
through them on paper. (Sometimes it will seem as if note cards beget note
cards. Too much is better than too little at the notetaking stage: you can always
discard them before the final draft. Don't worry if you seem to have too many
notes and too much material. But later, when you boil down to essentials, you
will have to be ruthless and omit some of your favorite ideas.)

    4. Transfer all of your notes to pieces of paper—or note cards—that are all
the same size, one note on each. It is easier to sort them this way when you get
ready to organize and outline. If you like to write notes in the margin of your
text (or on the backs of envelopes, or on dinner napkins, or shirtsleeves), systematically transfer every note to uniform sheets of paper or cards before you
begin to outline. Having everything easily recorded on sortable cards that can
be moved from one pile to another makes organizing easier later, especially
when you change your mind (as you will) and decide to move a point from
one part of your paper to another. Index cards—either 3 × 5, if you write
small and make economical notes, or 4 × 6, if you need more space—are
ideal for notetaking and sorting.

    5. When you think you are done taking notes (because you are out of ideas,
or out of time, or getting beyond a manageable number of pieces of evidence),
read through the whole pile one more time, again letting any new ideas—or
ideas that take on a fresh look because you combine them in a new way—
spawn new sentences for new note cards.

    How many times should you read a story, poem, or play before you stop tak-
ing notes? There is no right answer. If you have read the work three times
before settling on a topic, two more readings may do. But it could take several
more. Common sense, endurance, and deadlines will all have an effect on
how many rereadings you do. Let your conscience, your judgment, and your
clock be your guides.

Organizing Your Notes

The notes you have taken will become, in the next few hours, almost the whole content of your paper. The task remaining is to give that content the form and shape that will make it appealing and persuasive. But it is not an easy task: the best content in the world isn't worth much if it isn't effectively presented. The key to the task is getting all your ideas into the right order, that is, into a sequence that will allow them to argue your thesis most persuasively.

In order to put your notes into a proper order, you will need (ironically) to get a little distance from your notes. (The key to good planning and writing—and to many other pursuits—is in knowing when to back away and get some perspective.) Set your notes aside, but not too far away. On a fresh sheet of paper, write down all the major points you want to be sure to make. Write them down randomly, as they occur to you. Now read quickly through your pack of note cards and add to your list any important points you have left out. Then decide which ideas should go first, which should go second, and so on.

Putting your points in order is something of a guess at this point. You may well want to reorder them before you begin to write—or later when you are writing a first (or even later) draft. But make your best guess. The easiest way to try out an order is to take your random list and put a 1 in front of the point you will probably begin with, a 2 before the probable second point, and so on. Then copy the list, in numerical order, onto a clean sheet of paper, revising (if you need to) as you go. Do not be surprised if later you have to revise your list further. Your next task is to match up your note cards (and the examples they contain) with the points on your outline. If you've added "key" words to the top of each card, you can make a "rough cut" according to these words.

Putting things in a particular order is a spatial problem, and by having your notes on cards or pieces of paper of a uniform size you can do much of your organizing physically. Do your sorting on a large table or sit in the middle of the floor. Prepare a title card for each point in your outline, writing on it the point and its probable place in your paper, then line them up on the table or floor in order before you begin writing. If you're using your computer, you can use the search function to find each instance of a key word, phrase, or name, and arrange your electronic "cards" under the headings on your list by blocking and moving your "cards" to new parts of the document.

Two-thirds of this exercise is quite easy: most examples and ideas you have written down will match quite easily with a particular point. But some cards will resist classification. Some cards will seem to belong in two or more places;

others will not seem to belong at all. If a card seems to belong to more than one point, put it in the pile with the lowest number (but write on it the number or numbers of other possible locations). If, for example, a card might belong in point 2 but could also belong in point 6 or 9, put it in the pile of 2's and write "maybe 6 or 9" on the card; if you don't use it in writing about point 2 move it to pile 6; if you don't use it in 6, move it to 9. Remember that you will work your way through the piles in numerical order, so that you have a safety system for notes that don't seem to belong where you first thought but that still belong somewhere in your paper. Move them to a possible later point, or put them in a special file (marked "?" or "use in revised draft") and, once you have completed a first draft on your paper, go through this file, carefully looking for places in your paper where these ideas may belong. Almost never will everything fit neatly into your first draft. If everything does seem to fit exactly as you had originally planned, you have either done an incredible job of planning and guessing about the organization of your paper, or you are forcing things into inappropriate places.

Don't be surprised if you have a large number of leftover note cards, that is, cards whose ideas you haven't yet used, after you have written your first draft. You will probably find places for many of these ideas later, but some just won't fit and won't be needed for the paper you ultimately write, no matter how good the ideas are. No paper will do everything it could do. Writing a paper is a *human* project; it has limits.

Before you actually start writing, you may want to develop a more elaborate outline, incorporating your examples and including topic sentences for each paragraph, or you may wish to work from your sketchy outline and the accompanying packs of cards. Do the more detailed outline if it seems right to you, but don't delay the writing too long. You are probably ready right now, and any exercises you invent to delay writing are probably just excuses.

Developing an Argument

Once you have decided on your major points and assembled your evidence, you have to decide how you are going to present your argument and how you are going to present *yourself*. What you say is, of course, more important than how you say it, but your manner of presentation can make a world of difference. Putting your evidence together effectively—in a coherent and logical order so that your readers' curiosities and questions are answered systematically and fully—is half the task in developing a persuasive argument. The other half involves your choice of a voice and tone that will make readers want to read on—and make them favorably disposed toward what you say.

The tone of your paper is the basis of your relationship with your reader. "I will be just *me*," you may say, "and write naturally." But writing is not a "natural" act, any more than swinging a tennis racket, carrying a football, or dancing a pirouette. The "me" you choose to present is only one of several possible me's; you will project a certain mood, a certain attitude toward your subject, a certain confidence. How do you want your readers to feel about you and your argument? Being too positive can make your readers fell stupid and inadequate and can turn them into defensive, resistant readers who will rebel at your every point. Friendship with your reader is better than an adversary relationship. Sounding like a nice person who is talking reasonably and sensibly is not enough if in fact you don't make sense or have nothing to say, but the purpose of the tone you choose is to make your reader receptive to your content, not hostile. The rest of the job depends on the argument itself.

It has been said that all good papers should be organized in the same way:

1. Tell 'em what you're going to tell 'em.
2. Tell 'em.
3. Tell 'em what you told 'em.

That description fits—in pretty general terms—the most common kind of organization, which includes an introduction, a body of argument, and a conclusion, but if it is followed too simplistically it can lead to a paper that sounds simple-minded. The beginning does need to introduce the subject, sort out the essential issues, and suggest what your perspective will be, and the conclusion does need to sum up what you have said in the main part of your paper, but the first paragraph shouldn't give *everything* away, nor should the final one simply repeat what is already clear. Lead into your subject clearly but with a little subtlety; arrange your main points in the most effective manner you can think of, building a logical argument and supporting your general points with clear textual evidence, concisely phrased and presented, and at the end *show how* your argument has added up—don't just *say* that it did.

There are, of course, other ways to organize than the basic Tell-3 method, but the imagination and originality that can be exercised in a straightforward Tell-3 paper are practically unlimited.

Writing the First Draft

It is now time to set pen to paper or fingers to keyboard. No one can help you much now for a while. The main thing is to get started right, with a clear first sentence that expresses your sense of direction and arrests the attention of your readers. (If you can't think of a good first sentence, don't pause over it too long. Write down a paraphrase of what you want it to say—something like the statement you wrote down after your third reading—and go on to start writing about your main points. Your "first" sentence may sometimes be the last one you will write.) And then you inch along, word by word and sentence by sentence, as you follow your outline from one paragraph to another. Keep at it. Struggle. Stare into space. Bite your pen when you feel like it. Get up and stride about the room. Scratch your head. Sharpen a pencil. Run your fingers through your hair. Groan. Snap your fingers. But keep writing.

It is often frustrating as you search for the right word or struggle to decide how the next sentence begins, but it is satisfying when you get it right. If you get stuck, try working out your ideas on a separate piece of paper or free writing for a while inside your computer document. Sometimes, working out an idea, away from your draft, can be helpful. Stay with your draft until you're reasonably satisfied with it. Write "The End" at the bottom and set it aside. Breathe a sigh of relief and put it away until tomorrow.

FROM ROUGH DRAFT TO
COMPLETED PAPER

Revising

This final stage of the process is the most important of all, and it is the easiest one to mismanage. There is a world of difference between a bunch of ideas that present a decent interpretation of a work of literature and a cogent, coherent, persuasive essay that will stir your readers to a nod of agreement and shared pleasure in a moment of insight. If you haven't done good literary analysis and sorted out your insights earlier, nothing you do at this stage will help much, but if what you have done so far is satisfactory, this is the stage that can turn your paper into something special.

The important thing is not to allow yourself to be too easily satisfied. If you have struggled with earlier stages, it may be tempting to think you are finished when you have put a period to the last sentence in your first draft. It will often feel as if you are done: you may feel drained, tired of the subject, anxious to get on to other things, such as sleep or food or friends or another project. And it *is* a good idea to take a break once you've finished a draft and let what you have done settle for a few hours, preferably overnight. (The Roman poet and critic Horace suggested putting a draft aside for nine years, but most instructors won't wait that long.) Rereading it "cold" may be discouraging, though: all those sentences that felt so good when you wrote them often seem flat and stale, or even worthless, when a little time has elapsed. The biggest struggle in moving from a first draft to a second one is to keep from throwing what you have written into a wastebasket. You've spent a lot of time on this already, and with some more work, you'll have a paper you can be proud of.

It may take *several* more drafts to produce your best work. Often it is tempting to cut corners—to smooth out a troublesome paragraph by obscuring the issue or by omitting the difficult point altogether instead of confronting it, or to ask a roommate or friend for help in figuring out what is wrong with a particular passage. But you will learn more in the long run—and probably do better in the short run as well—if you make yourself struggle a bit. When a particular word or phrase you have used turns out to be imprecise, or misleading, or ambiguous, search until you find the *right* word or phrase. (At the least put a big X in the margin so that you will come back and fix it later.) If a paragraph is incomplete or poorly organized, fill it out or reorganize it. If a transition from one point to another does not work, look again at your outline and see if another way of ordering your points would help. *Never* decide that the problem can best be solved by hoping that your reader will not notice. The satisfaction of finally solving the problem will build your confidence and sooner or later make your writing easier and better.

Reviewing Your Work and Revising Again

Precisely how you move from one draft to another is up to you and will depend on the ways you work best; the key is to find all the things that bother you (and that *should* bother you) and then gradually correct them, moving toward a better paper with each succeeding draft. Here are some things to watch for.

Thesis and central thrust: Is it clear what your main point is? Do you state it clearly, effectively, and early? Do you make clear what the work is about? Are you fair to the spirit and emphasis of the work? Do you make clear the relationship between your thesis and the central thrust of the work? Do you explain *how* the work creates its effect rather than just asserting it?

Organization: Does your paper move logically from beginning to end? Does your first paragraph set up the main issue you are going to discuss and suggest the direction of your discussion? Do your paragraphs follow each other in a coherent and logical order? Does the first sentence of each paragraph accurately suggest what that paragraph will contain? Does your final paragraph draw a conclusion that follows from the body of your paper? Do you resolve the issues you say you resolve?

Use of evidence: Do you use enough examples? Too many? Does each example prove what you say it does? Do you explain each example fully enough? Are the examples sufficiently varied? Are any of them labored, or over-explained, or made to bear more weight than they can stand? Have you left out any examples useful to your thesis? Do you include any gratuitous ones just because you like them? Have you achieved a good balance between examples and generalizations?

Tone: How does your voice sound in the paper? Confident? Does it show off too much? Is it too timid or self-effacing? Do you ever sound smug? Too tentative? Too dogmatic? Would a neutral reader be put off by any of your assertions? By your way of arguing? By your choice of examples? By the language you use?

Sentences: Does each sentence read clearly and crisply? Have you rethought and rewritten any sentences you can't explain? Is the first sentence of your paper a strong, clear one likely to gain the interest of a neutral reader? Is the first sentence of each paragraph an especially vigorous one? Are your sentences varied enough? Do you avoid the passive voice and "there is/there are" sentences?

Word Choice: Have you used any words whose meaning you are not sure of? In any cases in which you were not sure of what word to use, did you stay with the problem until you found the exact word? Do your metaphors and figures of speech make literal sense? Are all the idioms used correctly? Is your terminology correct? Are your key words always used to mean *exactly* the same thing? Have you avoided sounding repetitive by varying your sentences rather than using several different terms to mean precisely the same thing?

Conciseness: Have you eliminated all the padding you put in when you didn't think your paper would be long enough? Have you gone through your paper, sentence by sentence, to eliminate all the unnecessary words and phrases? Have you looked for sentences (or even paragraphs) that essentially repeat what you have already said—and eliminated all repetition? Have you checked for multiple examples and pared down to the best and most vivid ones? Have you got rid of all inflated phrasing calculated to impress readers? Have you eliminated all roundabout phrases and rewritten long, complicated, or confusing sentences into shorter, clearer ones? Are you convinced that you have trimmed every possible bit of excess and that you cannot say what you have to say any more economically?

Punctuation and mechanics: Have you checked the syntax in each *separate* sentence? Have you checked the spelling of any words that you are not sure of or that look funny? Have you examined each sentence separately for punctuation? Have you checked every quotation word by word against the original? Have you given proper credit for all material—written or oral—that you have borrowed from others? Have you followed the directions your instructor gave you for citations, footnotes, and form?

As you begin to revise it's a good idea to look first at the larger issues (your thesis, organization, and supporting evidence) to make sure you find and solve any major problems early on. Then, you're in a better position to work on your tone, sentences, choice of words, and punctuation and mechanics. In the final stages, the most effective way to revise is to read through your paper looking for one problem at a time, that is, to go through it once looking at paragraphing, another time looking at individual sentences, still another for word choice or problems of grammar. It is almost impossible to check too many things too often—although you can get so absorbed with little things that you overlook larger matters. With practice, you will learn to watch carefully for the kinds of mistakes you are most prone to. Everyone has individual weaknesses and flaws. Here are some of the most common stumbling blocks for beginning writers:

1. Haste. (Don't start too late, or finish too soon after you begin.)
2. Pretentiousness. (Don't use words you don't understand, tackle problems that are too big for you, or write sentences you can't explain; it is more important to make sense than to make a big, empty impression.)
3. Boredom. (The quickest way to bore others is to be bored yourself. If you think your paper will be a drag, you are probably right. It is hard to fake interest in something you can't get excited about; keep at it until you find a spark.)
4. Randomness. (Don't try to string together half a dozen unrelated ideas or insights and con yourself into thinking that you have written a paper.)
5. Imprecision. (Don't settle for approximation, either in words or ideas; something that is 50 percent right is also 50 percent wrong.)
6. Universalism. (Don't try to be a philosopher and make grand statements about life; stick to what is in the work you are writing about.)
7. Vagueness. (Don't settle for a general "sense" of the work you are talking about; get it detailed, get it right.)
8. Wandering. (Don't lose track of your subject or the work that you are talking about.)
9. Sloppiness. (Don't sabotage all your hard work on analysis and writing by failing to notice misspelled words, grammatical mistakes, misquotations, incorrect citations or references, or typographical errors. Little oversights make readers suspicious.)
10. Impatience. (Don't be too anxious to get done. Enjoy the experience; savor the process. Have fun watching yourself learn.)

Being flexible—being willing to rethink your ideas and reorder your argument as you go—is crucial to success in writing, especially in writing about literature. You will find different (and better) ways to express your ideas and feelings as you struggle with revisions, and you will also find that—in the course of analyzing the work, preparing to write, writing, and rewriting—your response to the work itself will have grown and shifted somewhat. Part of the reason is that you will have become more knowledgeable as a result of the time and effort you have spent, and you will have a more subtle understanding of the work. But part of the reason will also be that the work itself will not be exactly the same. Just as a work is a little different for every reader, it is also a little different with every successive reading by the *same* reader, and what you will be capturing in your words is some of the subtlety of the work, its capacity to produce effects that are alive and that are therefore always changing just slightly. You need not, therefore, feel that you must say the final word about the work you are writing about—but you do want to say whatever word you have to say in the best possible way.

You can turn all this into a full-time job, of course, but you needn't. It is hard work, and at first the learning seems slow and the payoff questionable. A basketball novice watching the magic of Michael Jordan may find it hard to see the point of practicing lay-ups, but even creative geniuses have to go through those awful moments of sitting down and putting pen to paper (and then crossing out and rewriting again and again). But that's the way you learn to make it seem easy. Art is mostly craft, and craft means methodical work.

It *will* come more easily with practice. But you needn't aspire to professional writing to take pleasure in what you accomplish. Learning to write well about literature will help you with all sorts of tasks, some of them having little to do with writing. Writing trains the mind, creates habits, teaches you procedures that will have all kinds of long-range effects that you may not immediately recognize or be able to predict. And ultimately it is very satisfying, even if it is not easy, to be able to stand back and say, "That is mine. Those are my words. I know what I'm talking about. I understand, and I can make someone else understand."

One final bit of advice: do not follow, too rigidly or too closely, anyone's advice, including ours. We have suggested some general strategies and listed some common pitfalls. But writing is a very personal experience, and you will have talents (and faults) that are a little different from anyone else's. Learn to play to your own strengths and avoid the weaknesses that you are especially prone to. Pay attention to your instructor's comments; learn from your own mistakes.

A SUMMARY OF THE PROCESS

Here, briefly, is a summary, step by step, of the stages we have suggested you move through in preparing a paper about literature.

Stage One: Deciding what to write about

- Read the work straight through, thoughtfully. Make notes at the end on any points that caught your special attention.
- Read the work again more slowly, pausing to think through all the parts you don't understand. When you finish, write a three- or four-sentence summary.
- Read the work again, carefully but quite quickly. Decide what you feel most strongly about in the work, and write down the one thing you would most want to explain to a friend about how the story, poem, or play works, or (if the work still puzzles you) the one question you would most like to be able to answer.
- Decide how the statement you made at the end of your third reading relates to the summary you wrote down after the second reading.
- Write a one-paragraph "promise" of what your paper is going to argue.

Stage Two: Planning and drafting your paper

- Read the work at least twice more and make notes on anything that relates to your thesis.
- Read through all your notes so far, and for each write a sentence articulating how it relates to your thesis.
- Transfer all your notes to note cards of uniform size.
- Read through all your notes again and record any new observations or ideas on additional note cards.
- Set aside your note cards for the moment, and make a brief outline of the major points you intend to make.
- Sort the note cards into piles corresponding to the major points in your outline. Sort the cards in each separate pile into the most likely order of their use in the paper.
- Make a more detailed outline (including the most significant examples) from your pile of note cards on each point.

- Reconsider your order of presentation and make any necessary adjustments.
- Write a first draft.

Stage Three: Rewriting

- Go over your writing, word by word, sentence by sentence, and paragraph by paragraph, in draft after draft until your paper expresses your ideas clearly and concisely.

Stage Four: Final preparation

- If you have not been working on a computer, type or word-process your paper.
- Proofread carefully for errors of all kinds—spelling, typing, etc.
- Proofread again. Find your mistakes before someone else does.
- Congratulate yourself on a job well done.

BIOGRAPHICAL SKETCHES[1]

AI (b. 1947)

Born to parents of Asian, African, and Native American heritage, Ai earned a B.A. in Oriental Studies from the University of Arizona and an M.F.A. from the University of California at Irvine. Her first collection of poetry, *Cruelty*, appeared in 1973. Notable for its dramatic monologues, Ai's subsequent collection, *Killing Floor* (1979), received the Lamont Poetry Prize. Her narrative poetry, most recently *Fate* (1991) and *Greed* (1993), invokes graphic images and defiant characters.

RUDOLFO ANAYA (b. 1937)

Born in Pastura, New Mexico, Anaya studied at the University of New Mexico, where he now directs the creative writing program. He also serves as the editor for the *Blue Mesa Review*. Anaya is the recipient of many literary awards, including an NEA Fellowship and the prestigious Premio Quinto Sol in 1972 for his novel *Bless Me Ultima*. His many publications include *Heart of Aztlan* (1976), *Tortuga* (1979), *A Chicano in China* (1986), *Lord of Dawn* (1987), and *Albuquerque* (1992).

MARGARET ATWOOD (b. 1939)

Atwood spent her first eleven years in sparsely populated areas of northern Ontario and Quebec, where her father worked as an entomologist. After her education at the University of Toronto and Harvard, she held various jobs in Canada, America, England, and Italy. Atwood published her first poem when she was just nineteen, and she has won numerous prizes for her poetry as well as her fiction, which has become increasingly political over the years. Her novels include *The Edible Woman* (1969), *Surfacing* (1972), *Lady Oracle* (1976), *Life Before Man* (1979), *Bodily Harm* (1982), *The Handmaid's Tale* (1985), *Cat's Eye* (1988), and *Robber Bride* (1993). Many of her stories have been collected in *Dancing Girls and Other Stories* (1978), *Murder in the Dark* (1983), *Bluebeard's Egg* (1983), and *Wilderness Tips* (1991).

W. H. AUDEN (1907–1973)

A prolific writer of poems, plays, essays, and criticism, Wystan Hugh Auden was born in York, England, to a medical officer and a nurse. Auden studied at Oxford and taught at various universities in the United States, where he became a naturalized citizen in 1946. He won the Pulitzer Prize in 1948 for his collection of poems, *Age of Anxiety*, and is regarded as a poet of political and intellectual conscience. His long-term relationship with poet Chester Kallman has been the subject of several recent biographies.

JAMES BALDWIN (1924–1987)

Baldwin was for some time a leading literary spokesman for black Americans. Born in Harlem, long a resident of France, he first attracted critical attention with two extraordi-

---

1. Biographical sketches are included for all fiction writers and playwrights, and for poets represented by two or more poems.

nary novels, *Go Tell It on the Mountain* (1953) and *Giovanni's Room* (1956), which dealt, somewhat autobiographically, with religious awakening (Baldwin was a minister at fourteen but later left his church) and the anguish of being black and homosexual in a white and heterosexual society. Baldwin was also a dramatist and an outstanding essayist, his best-known nonfiction prose being *Notes of a Native Son* (1955), *Nobody Knows My Name* (1961), and *The Fire Next Time* (1963), aimed at unraveling the repressive myths of white society and at healing the disastrous estrangement he found in the lives of black people in America. His stories are collected in *Going to Meet the Man* (1965), from which "Sonny's Blues" is taken.

TONI CADE BAMBARA (b. 1939–1995)

Born in New York City, Bambara grew up in Harlem and Bedford-Stuyvesant, two of its poorest neighborhoods. She began writing while still a child. After graduating from Queens College, she worked at various jobs while studying for her M.A. at the City College of New York, writing fiction all the while in "the predawn in-betweens." Bambara began to publish her stories in 1962. She has also been a dancer, teacher, editor, and critic, and has worked in psychiatric and drug therapy, youth organizing, and settlement houses. Her work includes two anthologies, *The Black Woman* (1970) and *Stories for Black Folks* (1971), and two collections of stories, *Gorilla My Love* (1972) and *The Sea Birds Are Still Alive* (1977). She has also written two novels, *The Salt Eaters* (1980) and *If Blessing Comes* (1987).

CHARLES BAXTER (b. 1947)

Baxter was born in Minneapolis and teaches at the University of Michigan in Ann Arbor. His short story collections include *Harmony of the World* (1984) and *A Relative Stranger* (1990), and his novels are *First Light* (1987) and *Shadow Play* (1993).

ANN BEATTIE (b. 1947)

Beattie grew up in the Washington suburb of Chevy Chase, Maryland. She received a B.A. from American University and went on to the University of Connecticut as a graduate student in English literature. Beattie's first published story, "A Rose for Judy Garland's Casket," appeared in 1972, and after many rejections she began publishing in the *New Yorker* shortly thereafter. Beattie's stories have made her a spokesperson for a generation that came of age in the 1960s as they adapt to or are baffled and worn out by the oncoming years. Many of them have been collected in *Distortions* (1976), *Secrets and Surprises* (1979), *Jacklighting* (1981), *The Burning House* (1982), *Where You'll Find Me* (1986), and *What Was Mine: Stories* (1990). Her novels are *Chilly Scenes of Winter* (1976), *Falling In Place* (1980), *Love Always* (1985), and *Picturing Will* (1990).

AMBROSE BIERCE (1842–1914?)

The tenth child of a poor Ohio family, Bierce rose during the Civil War to the rank of major, was twice wounded and cited fifteen times for bravery. He stayed in the army for a time after the war, then was a journalist in California and London, where his boisterous western mannerisms and savage wit made him a celebrity and earned him the name "Bitter Bierce." He published *Tales of Soldiers and Civilians* (later called *In the Midst of Life*) (1891) and another volume of short stories, *Can Such Things Be?* (1893). The death of his two sons in 1889 and 1901, along with his divorce in 1891, might well have led him to Mexico, where he reportedly rode with Pancho Villa's revolutionaries. He disappeared and is presumed to have died there. Bierce is well known as the author of *The Cynic's*

Wordbook (later called *The Devil's Dictionary*) (1906), but his short stories are his finest achievement.

ELIZABETH BISHOP (1911–1979)

Born in Worcester, Massachusetts, Bishop endured the death of her father before she was a year old and the institutionalization of her mother when she was five. Bishop was raised by her maternal grandmother in Nova Scotia, then by her paternal grandparents back in Worcester. Bishop attended Vassar College and met the poet Marianne Moore, who encouraged her to give up plans for medical school to pursue the life of a poet. Bishop traveled through Canada, Europe, and South America, finally settling in Rio de Janeiro, where she lived for nearly twenty years. Bishop produced only four volumes of poetry: *North and South* (1946); *A Cold Spring* (1955), which won the Pulitzer Prize; *Questions of Travel* (1965); and *Geography III* (1976), which won the National Book Critics' Circle Award.

WILLIAM BLAKE (1757–1828)

In defense of his unorthodox and original work, Blake once said: "That which can be made Explicit to the Idiot . . . is not worth my care." The son of a London haberdasher, he studied drawing at ten and at fourteen was apprenticed to an engraver for seven years. After a first book of poems, *Poetical Sketches* (1783), he began experimenting with what he called "illuminated printing"—the words and pictures of each page were engraved in relief on copper and the printed sheets partly colored by hand—a laborious and time-consuming process that resulted in books of singular beauty, no two of which were exactly alike. His great *Songs of Innocence* (1789) and *Songs of Experience* (1794) were printed in this manner, as were his increasingly mythic and prophetic books, which include *The Marriage of Heaven and Hell* (1793), *The Four Zoas* (1803), *Milton* (1804), and *Jerusalem* (1809). Blake devoted his later life to pictorial art, illustrating *The Canterbury Tales*, the Book of Job, and *The Divine Comedy*, on which he was hard at work when he died.

ROO BORSON (b. 1952)

While considered a Canadian poet, Ruth Elizabeth Borson was born in Berkeley, California. She later attended the University of California at Santa Barbara and earned her B.A. in 1973 from Gordon College. Four years later, she published her first collection of poetry, *Landfall*, in addition to receiving her M.F.A. from the University of British Columbia, where she was awarded the Macmillan Prize for Poetry. Borson's poetry suggests what she calls the "intricacy of the physical world" as it recognizes the powers of sensuality and memory. She has published a number of collections, including *The Whole Night Coming Home* (1984) and *Intent, or the Weight of the World* (1989).

GWENDOLYN BROOKS (b. 1917)

Brooks was born in Topeka, Kansas, and was raised in Chicago, where she began writing poetry at the age of seven. Her formal training began at the Southside Community Art Center, and she produced her first book of poems, *A Street in Bronzeville*, shortly after, in 1945. Her second book of poems, *Annie Allen* (1949), won Brooks the distinction of being the first African American to win the Pulitzer Prize for Poetry. Brooks's early poetry concentrated on what Langston Hughes called the "ordinary aspects of black life," but her work was transformed in the 1960s and Brooks became a passionate advocate for African American consciousness and activism.

ROBERT BROWNING (1812–1889)

Born in London, Browning was an aspiring but unknown poet and playwright when he met the already-famous poet, Elizabeth Barrett. After their elopement in 1846, the Brownings moved to Italy, where Elizabeth Barrett Browning authored the chronicle of their love, *Sonnets from the Portuguese* (1850). Browning wrote most of his great poems during this period, and after his wife's death in 1861, he returned to England and began to establish his own literary reputation for his fine dramatic monologues.

ANGELA CARTER (1940–1992)

Born in Eastbourne, Sussex, England, Carter chose to take a job in journalism rather than attend Oxford University, though she later enrolled at the University of Bristol and studied medieval literature. Her early novels were *Honeybuzzard* (1967), *The Magic Toyshop* (1967), and *Several Perceptions* (1968), which won the Somerset Maugham Award in 1969. Her later novels included *The Infernal Desire Machines of Dr. Hoffman* (1972), *The Passion of New Eve* (1977), and *Wise Children* (1991). "A Souvenir of Japan" is from her 1974 short story volume, *Fireworks*. Carter's writing gained widespread popularity after the release of the film *The Company of Wolves* (1984), which was based on a story from *The Bloody Chamber* (1979), a collection of macabre and erotic retellings of fairy tales. Her chief nonfiction work was *The Sadeian Woman: An Exercise in Cultural History* (1979).

DENISE CHÁVEZ (b. 1948)

Actor, playwright, and novelist, Chávez was born in Las Cruces, New Mexico, and educated at the University of New Mexico. She served as writer-in-residence at many colleges until she was appointed professor of drama at the University of Houston. Chávez has written many plays as well as two books of fiction, *The Last of the Menu Girls* (1986) and *Face of an Angel* (1993).

JOHN CHEEVER (1912–1982)

Cheever was born in Quincy, Massachusetts. His formal education ended when he was expelled from Thayer Academy at the age of seventeen; thereafter he devoted himself completely to fiction writing, except for brief interludes of teaching at Barnard College and the University of Iowa, and script-writing for television. Cheever published his first story when he was sixteen, and until his first novel, *The Wapshot Chronicle*, won the National Book Award in 1958, he was known primarily as a superb and prolific writer of short stories. Built around a strong moral core and tinged with melancholy nostalgia for the past, they form a running commentary on the tensions, manners, and crippled aspirations of urban and suburban life. Many have won awards, including the O. Henry Award in 1956 for "The Country Husband." *The Stories of John Cheever* (1978) won the Pulitzer Prize.

ANTON CHEKHOV (1860–1904)

Chekhov was born in Taganrog, a small town in southern Russia. After attending medical school at Moscow University, he began practicing medicine in 1884, while writing short stories, jokes, and plays to support his family. His writing was well-received, and he left medicine to write full time. Stanislavsky was the first to direct Chekhov's *The Seagull* (1896) and *The Cherry Orchard* (1903), which he adapted as a tragedy though Chekhov considered it a comedy. Along with these plays, he wrote a number of other realistic dramas dealing with turn of the century Russian life, including *The Three Sisters* (1901).

KATE CHOPIN (1851–1904)

Born Katherine O'Flaherty in St. Louis, Missouri, Chopin moved to Louisiana when she married Oscar Chopin in 1870. She did not begin writing until after her husband's death, but produced many short stories, collected in *Bayou Folk* (1894) and *A Night in Acadie* (1897), and the now-classic novel *The Awakening* (1899).

CARYL CHURCHILL (b. 1938)

Born in London, Churchill's family moved to Montreal, Canada, during World War II. While earning her B.A. in English literature from Oxford, she wrote and produced a few plays. Since 1970, Churchill has been associated with the Royal Court Theatre in London, and her drama is often satirical in its socialist and feminist directions. She won an Obie Award for *Top Girls*, and her play, *Fen*, won the Blackburn Prize in 1984. She continues to write for radio and television as well as for the stage. Her most recent work is *Mad Forest: A Play from Romania* (1990).

JUDITH ORTIZ COFER (b. 1952)

Born in 1952 in Hormigueros, Puerto Rico, Cofer spent her childhood between Puerto Rico and Patterson, New Jersey, where her father's family lived. This bicultural childhood is a common theme in both her poems and fiction. Cofer attended Augusta College in Georgia and received her M.A. in English from Florida Atlantic University. She received a fellowship to study at Oxford and subsequent scholarships to the Bread Loaf Writers' Conference, where she taught for a number of years. Her first collection of poetry, *Peregrina* (1985), won the Riverstone International Poetry Competition, and in 1989 Cofer was a National Endowment for the Arts Fellow in Poetry. Her novel, *The Line of the Sun* was published in 1989, and her most recent work, a collection of poetry and essays, is titled *The Latin Deli* (1993).

SAMUEL TAYLOR COLERIDGE (1772–1834)

Born in the small town of Ottery St. Mary, in rural Devonshire, England, Coleridge was one of the greatest and most original of the nineteenth-century Romantic poets. He wrote three of the most haunting poems in the English tradition—*The Rime of the Ancient Mariner* (1798), *Christabel* (1816), and *Kubla Khan* (1816)—as well as immensely influential literary criticism and a revolutionary treatise on biology, *Hints Towards the Formation of a More Comprehensive Theory of Life*. In 1795, in the midst of a failed experiment to establish a "Pantisocracy" (his form of ideal community), he met William Wordsworth, and in 1798 they published together their *Lyrical Ballads*, which was to influence the course of English Romanticism for decades to come. Coleridge's physical ailments, addiction to opium, and profound sense of despair have to this day shaped our sense of the poet suffering for the sake of art.

RICHARD CONNELL (1893–1949)

Connell, like Ernest Hemingway, began his writing career as a journalist. At the age of sixteen, he was city editor of his native *Poughkeepsie News-Press*; later he was editor of both the *Crimson* and the *Lampoon* at Harvard, from which he graduated in 1915. After World War I, he left his New York job as an advertising editor to become a freelance writer, traveling to Paris and London and finally settling in Beverly Hills, California. His works include volumes of short stories—*Apes and Angels* (1924), *The Sin of Monsieur Pettipon* (1925), *Variety* (1925), and *Ironies* (1930)—and novels: *Mad Lover* (1927), *Murder at Sea* (1929), *Playboy* (1936), and *What Ho!* (1937).

JOSEPH CONRAD (1857–1924)

Jozeph Teodor Konrad Nalecz Korzeniowski was born in Berdyczew, Polish Ukraine. At five he accompanied his parents into exile in northern Russia and later near Kiev; he was left an orphan at eleven. Before he was seventeen he was off to Marseilles, making several trips to the West Indies as an apprentice seaman. After some veiled troubles in France, involving gambling debts and an apparent suicide attempt, he sailed on a British ship, landed in England in 1878, and spent the next sixteen years in the British merchant service, rising to master in 1886, the year he became a British subject. In 1890, he worked on a boat that sailed up the Congo, the inspiration for *Heart of Darkness* (1899). He began writing in 1889 but did not publish his first novel, *Almayer's Folly*, until 1896. Though a successful writer, he was not truly popular or financially independent until the publication of *Chance* in 1912–13. Among his major novels are *The Nigger of the "Narcissus"* (1897), *Lord Jim* (1900), *Nostromo* (1904), *Under Western Eyes* (1910), and *Victory* (1915). His short-story collections include *Tales of Unrest* (1898), *Typhoon and Other Stories* (1903), *'Twixt Land and Sea* (1912), from which "The Secret Sharer" is taken, and *Within the Tides: Tales* (1915).

WENDY COPE (b. 1945)

Born in Kent, England, Cope studied history and learned to play the guitar at Oxford University. While working as a primary school teacher, she began writing poetry. Her first volume, *Making Cocoa for Kingsley Amis*, was published in 1986, and the following year, she received a Cholmondeley Award for Poetry. Her most recent collection, *Serious Concerns* (1992), includes her trademark optimistic and witty verses. Cope has also published a children's book and a narrative poem, *The River Girl* (1991), commissioned for performance.

JULIO CORTÁZAR (1914–1984)

Born in Brussels to Argentinian parents, Cortázar was raised in Argentina and moved to Paris in 1952. A poet, translator, and amateur musician, as well as a fiction writer, Cortázar's publications include *The Winners, Hopscotch, Blow-Up and Other Stories, 62: A Model Kit, All Fires the Fire and Other Stories, A Manual for Manuel, A Change of Light, We Love Glenda So Much,* and *A Certain Lucas.*

HART CRANE (1899–1932)

Crane's vision of modernist poetry refused the popular pessimism of T. S. Eliot's *The Waste Land*, and called for "a more positive, or . . . ecstatic goal." Born in Garretsville, Ohio, Harold Hart Crane spent his childhood in Cleveland, and after adolescent visits to Cuba, Paris, and New York, he opted to leave high school and move to Greenwich Village. In spite of the artistic intensity of the Village, Crane was unable to support himself financially, and moved back to Cleveland to work for his father. While back in Ohio, Crane published a number of poems, and in 1923 he again moved to New York City, where he wrote extensively and published his first collection, *White Buildings*, in 1926. At the same time, he was working on his epic poem, *The Bridge*, which received *Poetry Magazine*'s annual award. Crane was awarded a Guggenheim Fellowship in 1931, but a year later he took his own life.

E. E. CUMMINGS (1894–1962)

Cummings's variety of modernism was distinguished by its playful sense of humor, its formal experimentation, its lyrical directness, and above all by its celebration of the individual against mass society. Born in Cambridge, Massachusetts, the son of a Congregationalist minister, Edward Estlin Cummings attended Harvard University, where he wrote poetry in the Pre-Raphaelite and Metaphysical traditions. He joined the ambulance corps in France the day after the United States entered World War I and was imprisoned by his own side for his outspoken letters and disdain for bureaucracy; he transmuted the experience into his first literary success, *The Enormous Room* (1922). After the war, Cummings established himself as a poet and artist in Greenwich Village, made frequent trips to France and New Hampshire, and showed little interest in wealth or his growing celebrity.

JAMES DICKEY (b. 1923)

Dickey did not become seriously interested in poetry until he joined the Air Force in 1942. When he returned from World War II, he earned a B.A. and an M.A. at Vanderbilt University, publishing his first poem in *Sewanee Review* his senior year. Since the publication of his first book of poems, *Into the Stone* (1960), Dickey, while primarily a poet, has engaged in diverse careers ranging from advertising writer and novelist to poetry teacher at various universities. His 1965 collection, *Buckdancer's Choice*, received the National Book Award, and from 1967 to 1969 Dickey was Consultant in Poetry to the Library of Congress. He is more popularly known for his best-selling novel, *Deliverance* (1970), which he later adapted for Hollywood. Most recently, he has published *The Whole Motion: Collected Poems 1949–1992* (1992) and a novel, *The White Sea* (1993).

EMILY DICKINSON (1830–1886)

From childhood on, Dickinson's life was sequestered and obscure. Yet her verse had a power and influence that has traveled far beyond the cultured yet relatively circumscribed environment in which she lived her life: her room, her father's house, her family, a few close friends, and the small town of Amherst, Massachusetts. Indeed, along with Walt Whitman, her far more public contemporary, she all but invented American poetry. Born in Amherst, the daughter of a respected lawyer and revered father ("His heart was pure and terrible," she once wrote), Dickinson studied for less than a year at the Mount Holyoke Female Seminary, returning permanently to Amherst. In later life she became more and more of a recluse, dressing in white, seeing no visitors, yet working without stint at her poems—nearly eighteen hundred in all, only a few of which were published during her lifetime.

RICHARD DOKEY

A native of Stockton, California, and a graduate of the University of California, Berkeley, Dokey has worked as a laborer on a railroad, in a shipyard, for a soft drink bottling company, and for an ink factory, but he now teaches philosophy at San Joachin Delta Community College in Stockton, California. His works include *August Heat* (1982), *Funeral: A Play* (1982), and *Sánchez and Other Stories* (1981). His novel, *The Adidas Kid*, was published in 1993.

JOHN DONNE (1572–1631)

The first and greatest of what came to be known as the "Metaphysical" school of poets, Donne wrote in a style, revolutionary at the time, that combined highly intellectual conceits with complex, compressed phrasing. Born into an old Roman Catholic family at a time when Catholics were subject to constant harassment, Donne quietly abandoned his religion and had a brilliant early career until a politically disastrous marriage ruined his worldly hopes and forced him to struggle for years to support a large and growing family; impoverished and despairing, he even wrote a treatise (*Biathanatos*) on the lawfulness of suicide. King James (who had ambitions for him as a preacher) eventually forced Donne to take Anglican orders in 1615, and indeed he became one of the great sermonizers of his day, rising to dean of St. Paul's Cathedral in 1621. Donne's private devotions were published in 1624, and he continued to write sacred poetry until a few years before his death.

RITA DOVE (b. 1952)

When Dove won the 1987 Pulitzer Prize for Poetry for *Thomas and Beulah* (1986), she became only the second African American poet (after Gwendolyn Brooks in 1950) to receive such high recognition. A native of Akron, Ohio, Dove attended Miami University in Ohio, studied for a year in West Germany as a Fulbright scholar, and received an M.F.A. in creative writing from the University of Iowa. She taught creative writing at Arizona State University and is now a professor of English at the University of Virginia as well as an associate editor of *Callaloo*, the journal of African-American and African arts and letters. Dove's books include *The Yellow House on the Corner* (1980), *Museum* (1983), and *Grace Notes* (1989). In 1993, Dove published *Selected Poems* and was appointed Poet Laureate of the United States by the Library of Congress.

JOHN DRYDEN (1631–1700)

Called "the father of English criticism" by Samuel Johnson, Dryden was a prolific poet and dramatist. He attended Trinity College, Cambridge, where he took his A.B. in 1654, and for most of his career, Dryden wrote nondramatic, occasional, and public poems, celebrating historical moments. In 1667 he wrote "Annus Mirabilis," which celebrated England's "year of wonders." During his middle years, Dryden focused mostly on creating popular drama and literary criticism. In 1677, he adapted Shakespeare's *Antony and Cleopatra* into a play called *All for Love*, and in "An Essay of Dramatic Poesy" (1668), he outlined new theoretical principles for drama. That same year he was named England's Poet Laureate. Later in his career, Dryden became known for his political satires, like the scathing mock-heroic, "MacFlecknoe" (1682) and "Absalom and Achitophel" (1681).

T. S. ELIOT (1888–1965)

Thomas Stearns Eliot—from his formally experimental and oblique writings to his brilliant arguments in defense of "orthodoxy" and "tradition"—dominated the world of English poetry between the world wars. Born in St. Louis, Missouri, of New England stock, Eliot studied literature and philosophy at Harvard, and later in France and Germany. He came to England in 1914, read Greek philosophy at Oxford, and published his first major poem, "The Love Song of J. Alfred Prufrock," the next year. In 1922, with the help of his great supporter and adviser, Ezra Pound, Eliot published his long poem, *The Waste Land* (1922), which would profoundly influence a whole generation of poets. In his later work, particularly the *Four Quartets* (completed in 1945), Eliot explored religious questions in a quieter, more controlled idiom. He was awarded the Nobel Prize for Literature in 1948.

LOUISE ERDRICH (b. 1954)

Born in Little Falls, Minnesota, of German-American and Chippewa descent, Erdrich grew up in Wahpeton, North Dakota, as a member of the Turtle Mountain Band of Chippewa, and attended Dartmouth College. After graduation, she returned to teach in

North Dakota's Poetry in the Schools Program. She received an M.A. in creative writing from Johns Hopkins University in 1979. In the same year, *Jacklight*, a collection of poetry, was published. Her first novel, *Love Medicine* (1984), has been praised as a landmark work in its depiction of the lives of contemporary Native Americans, and was the winner of the National Book Critics' Circle Award for Fiction. An expanded version was published in 1993. Erdrich has also published another collection of poetry, *Baptism of Desire* (1989), several novels in the North American series that includes *Love Medicine*, *The Beet Queen* (1986), *Tracks* (1988), and *The Bingo Palace* (1993), and jointly authored *The Crown of Columbus* (1991) with her husband Michael Dorris.

WILLIAM FAULKNER (1897–1962)

Faulkner spent almost his entire life in his native state of Mississippi. He left high school without graduating, joined the Royal Canadian Air Force in 1918, and in the mid-1920s lived briefly in New Orleans, where he was encouraged by Sherwood Anderson. He then spent a few miserable months as a clerk in a New York bookstore, published a collection of poems, *The Marble Faun*, in 1924, and took a long walking tour of Europe in 1925. In later years he made several visits to Hollywood, writing a screenplay for *The Big Sleep*, among others, and spent his last years in Charlottesville, Virginia. With the publication of *Sartoris* in 1929, Faulkner began a cycle of works interrelated by his fictional Yoknapatawpha County and the reappearance of characters or families from work to work. These include *As I Lay Dying* (1930), *Light in August* (1932), *Absalom, Absalom!* (1936), *The Unvanquished* (1939), *The Hamlet* (1940), and *Go Down, Moses* (1942). His short fiction can be found in *The Collected Stories of William Faulkner* (1950). He received the Nobel Prize for Literature in 1950.

CAROLYN FORCHÉ (b. 1950)

Born in Detroit, Michigan, Forché studied creative writing and international relations at Michigan State University and did graduate study at Bowling Green State University. Her first book of poetry, *Gathering the Tribes* (1976), won the Yale Series of Younger Poets Award. Forché was a journalist for Amnesty International in El Salvador and Beirut correspondent for National Public Radio's "All Things Considered." She has taught at many universities and has published several volumes of poetry, including *The Country Between Us* (1981).

RICHARD FORD (b. 1944)

Ford was born in Jackson, Mississippi, attended Michigan State University, and received an M.F.A. in creative writing from the University of California. Since that time he has been awarded a Guggenheim Foundation Fellowship and lived in western Montana, New York, Mississippi, and currently New Orleans. His first novel, *A Piece of My Heart*, was published in 1976. He has published three more novels, *The Ultimate Good Luck* (1981), *The Sportswriter* (1986), and *Wildlife* (1990), and a volume of short stories, *Rock Springs* (1987).

ROBERT FROST (1874–1963)

Though his poetry forever identified Frost with rural New England, he was born and lived to the age of eleven in San Francisco. Coming to New England after his father's death, Frost studied classics in high school, entered and dropped out of both Dartmouth and Harvard, and spent difficult years as an unrecognized poet before his first book, *A Boy's Will* (1913), was accepted and published in England. Frost's character was full of contradiction—he held "that we get forward as much by hating as by loving"—yet by the end of his long life he was one of the most honored poets of his time. In 1961, two years before his death, he was invited to read a poem at John F. Kennedy's presidential inauguration ceremony.

GABRIEL GARCÍA MÁRQUEZ (b. 1928)

Born in Aracataca, a remote town in Magdalena province near the Caribbean coast of Colombia, García Márquez studied law at the University of Bogotá and then worked as a journalist in Latin America, Europe, and the United States. In 1967 he took up permanent residence in Barcelona, Spain. His first published book, *Leaf Storm* (1955, translated 1972), in which "A Very Old Man with Enormous Wings" appears, is set in the fictional small town of Macondo, based on the myths and legends of his childhood home. His most famous novel, *One Hundred Years of Solitude* (1967, translated 1970) presents six generations of one family in Macondo, fusing magic, reality, fable, and fantasy in a way that also allows the town to serve as a microcosm of many of the social, political, and economic problems of Latin America. Among his works are *The Autumn of the Patriarch* (1975, translated 1976), *Innocent Eréndira and Other Stories* (1972, translated 1978), *Chronicle of a Death Foretold* (1981, translated 1982), and *Love in the Time of Cholera* (1987, translated 1988). García Márquez won the Nobel Prize for Literature in 1982.

JOHN GAY (1685–1732)

After attending school in Devon, Gay moved to London to work as an apprentice; within five years he was involved in contemporary literary circles as well as the publishing world. Known for both his playfulness and his serious social commentary, Gay, with Pope, Swift, and Arbuthnot, founded the Scriblerus Club, which became famous for its literary satires and practical jokes. In addition to poems like "The Shepherd's Week" (1714) and "Trivia, or the Art of Walking the Streets of London" (1716), Gay wrote *The Beggar's Opera* (1728), a ballad-opera that satirized contemporary political corruption.

CHARLOTTE PERKINS GILMAN (1860–1935)

Charlotte Anna Perkins was born in Hartford, Connecticut. After a painful, lonely childhood and several years supporting herself as a governess, art teacher, and designer of greeting cards, Charlotte Perkins married the artist Charles Stetson. Following several extended periods of depression, she was put by her husband into the hands of Dr. S. Weir Mitchell, who "sent me home with the solemn advice to 'live as domestic a life as . . . possible,' to 'have but two hours' intellectual life a day,' and 'never to touch pen, brush, or pencil again' as long as I lived." Three months of this, ending "near the borderline of utter mortal ruin," became the inspiration for "The Yellow Wallpaper." In 1900 she married George Houghton Gilman, having divorced Stetson in 1892. Her nonfiction works, which placed her at the center of the early women's movement, include *Women and Economics* (1898) and *Man-Made World* (1911). She also wrote several utopian novels, including *Moving the Mountain* (1911) and *Herland* (1915).

SUSAN GLASPELL (1882–1948)

Born and raised in Davenport, Iowa, Glaspell graduated from Drake University and worked on the staff of the *Des Moines Daily News* until her stories began appearing in magazines such as *Harper's* and the *Ladies' Home Journal*. In 1911, Glaspell moved to New York City, where, two years later, she married George Cram Cook, a talented director. In 1915 they founded the Provincetown Playhouse on Cape Cod, an extraordinary gathering of actors, directors, and playwrights, including Eugene O'Neill, Edna St. Vincent Millay, and John Reed. She spent the last part of her life in Provincetown, devoting herself to writing novels. Glaspell's plays include *The Verge* (1921) and *Alison's House* (1930). Among her novels are *The Visionary* (1911), *Fidelity* (1915), and *The Morning Is Near Us* (1939).

THOMAS HARDY (1840–1928)

In a preface dated 1901, Hardy called his poems "unadjusted impressions," which nevertheless might, by "humbly recording diverse readings of phenomena as they are forced upon us by chance and change," lead to a philosophy. Indeed, though he was essentially retrospective in his outlook, Hardy anticipated the concerns of modern poetry by treating the craft as an awkward, often skeptical means of penetrating the facade of language. Born at Upper Bockhampton in Dorset, England, the son of a master mason, Hardy began to write while in the midst of an architectural career. After a long and successful career as a novelist, he turned exclusively to poetry; he died in the midst of preparing his last book, *Winter Words* (1929), for publication.

NATHANIEL HAWTHORNE (1804–1864)

Hawthorne was born in Salem, Massachusetts, a descendant of Puritan immigrants; one ancestor had been a judge in the Salem witchcraft trials. Educated at Bowdoin College, he was agonizingly slow in winning acclaim for his work, and supported himself from time to time in government service—working in the custom houses of Boston and Salem and serving as the United States consul in Liverpool. His early collections of stories, *Twice-Told Tales* (1837) and *Mosses from an Old Manse* (1846), in which "Young Goodman Brown" appears, did not sell well, and it was not until the publication in 1850 of his most famous novel, *The Scarlet Letter*, that his fame spread beyond a discerning few. His other novels include *The House of the Seven Gables* (1851) and *The Blithedale Romance* (1852).

ROBERT HAYDEN (1913–1980)

Hayden was born in Detroit, Michigan, and studied at Wayne State University and the University of Michigan. He taught at Fisk University for over twenty years and at the University of Michigan for more than ten. Although Hayden produced ten volumes of poetry he did not receive acclaim until late in life. In the 1960s, Hayden resisted pressure to express the militancy some African Americans wanted, and thus alienated himself from a growing body of African American literary tradition.

H.D. (HILDA DOOLITTLE) (1886–1961)

The only surviving daughter in a prominent family that included five sons, Hilda Doolittle grew up in Pennsylvania. She moved to London in 1911, in the footsteps of her friend and one-time fiancé Ezra Pound, who helped her begin her poetic career. Her first book of poems, *Sea Garden*, was published in 1916, followed by *Hymen* (1921), *Heliodora and Other Poems* (1924), *Collected Poems* (1925), and *Red Roses for Bronze* (1931), among others. After surviving the bombings of London in World War II, she wrote two major epics about war, *Trilogy* (1944–1946) and *Helen in Egypt* (1961). In 1960, she was given the Award of Merit Medal for Poetry from the American Academy of Arts and Letters.

LILLIAN HELLMAN (1907–1984)

Hellman's toughness and pragmatism allowed her to stretch the rigid conventions of the Broadway stage to explore unconventional subjects and to stand up to Senator Joseph McCarthy during a period when most writers were terrified to speak out. Born into a Jewish family in New Orleans, Hellman moved to New York, where she attended New York and Columbia universities and worked briefly in publishing. Her first successful play, *The Children's Hour* (1934), explored the pain of two women accused of lesbianism at a rigidly conventional private school. During the McCarthy period, Hellman was blacklisted for her "left-wing" politics. Nevertheless she refused to inform on other writers, explaining that "to hurt innocent people whom I knew many years ago in order to save myself is, to me, inhuman and indecent and dishonorable." After the death of the writer Dashiell Hammett, her companion for many years, Hellman began work on her memoirs, which were published in three volumes, *An Unfinished Woman* (1969), *Pentimento*, and *Scoundrel Time* (1976).

ERNEST HEMINGWAY (1899–1961)

Born in Oak Park, Illinois, Hemingway was first a reporter, then an ambulance-service volunteer in France and infantryman in Italy in 1918, when he was wounded and decorated for valor. After the war and more reporting, he settled for a time in Paris, where he knew Gertrude Stein and Ezra Pound, among others. From 1925 to 1935 he published two volumes of stories, *In Our Time* (1925) and *Death in the Afternoon* (1932), and two major novels, *The Sun Also Rises* (1926) and *A Farewell to Arms* (1929), which established his international reputation. Hemingway helped the Loyalists in the Spanish Civil War, the subject of *For Whom the Bell Tolls* (1940), served as a war correspondent in the Second World War, and from 1950 to 1962 lived in Cuba. *The Old Man and the Sea* was published in 1952, winning a Pulitzer Prize. Hemingway was awarded the Nobel Prize for Literature in 1954. He committed suicide in 1961.

GEORGE HERBERT (1593–1633)

After the early death of his Welsh father, Herbert was raised by his mother, a literary patron of John Donne. Herbert graduated with honors from Cambridge and was subsequently elected public orator at the University. He twice served as a member of Parliament in the 1620s, but his political career never flourished. Instead, he began to work for the church in 1626, married, and took holy orders in 1630. While living in Bemerton, he became known as "Holy Mr. Herbert" for his diligent care of the members of his ministry. He died of consumption in 1633, and his most famous poetry collection, *The Temple*, was published posthumously by a friend.

ROBERT HERRICK (1591–1674)

The son of a London goldsmith, Herrick would have liked nothing better than to live a life of leisured study, discussing literature and drinking sack with his hero, Ben Jonson. For a number of reasons, though, he decided to take religious orders and moved to a parish in Devonshire. Herrick eventually made himself at home there, inventing dozens of imaginary mistresses with exotic names (his housekeeper was prosaically named Prudence) and practicing, half-seriously, his own peculiar form of paganism. When the Puritans came to power, Herrick was driven from his post to London where, in 1648, he published a volume of over fourteen hundred poems with two titles, *Hesperides* for the secular poems and *Noble Numbers* for those with sacred subjects. Though they did not survive the harsh atmosphere of Puritanism and were virtually forgotten until the nineteenth century, Herrick was eventually restored to his post in Devonshire where he lived out his last years quietly.

JOHN HOLLANDER (b. 1929)

Known for his originality, wit, and keen perception of language, Hollander plays with words and shapes in his poetry. Hollander was born in New York City and later attended Columbia University, earning a B.A. in 1950 and an M.A. in 1952. He received his Ph.D. from Indiana University after serving as a Junior Fellow in the Society of Fellows at Harvard and teaching there. He now teaches at Yale. While he is most widely known as a poet, he has also written extensive criticism and created several children's books. His first book, *A Crackling of Thorns* (1958) was introduced by W. H. Auden as the 1958 volume in the Yale Series of Younger Poets. Hollander received the Bollingen Prize for Poetry in 1963, and his subsequent collections include *Types of Shape* (1969) and *Powers of Thirteen* (1983). In 1990, Hollander was made a Fellow of the MacArthur Foundation. He has two recent volumes, *Tessarae and Other Poems* and *Selected Poetry*; both were published in 1993.

SPENCER HOLST (b. 1926)

Well known in the literary underground, Holst has published his short stories and poetry in numerous periodicals such as *Mademoiselle* and *Oui*. He has translated the work of German poet Vera Lachmann and published several volumes of his own writing, including two volumes of short stories, *The Language of Cats and Other Stories* (1971) and *Spencer Holst Stories* (1976), a collection of imaginative and humorous fables that play with reality and fantasy.

GERARD MANLEY HOPKINS (1844–1889)

Hopkins's verse, in all its superbly controlled tension, strong rhythm, and sheer exuberance, has been championed by a number of modern poets—yet he made few attempts to publish what many of his contemporaries found nearly incomprehensible, and he was all but unknown until long after his death. Born the eldest of eight children of a marine-insurance adjuster (shipwrecks later figured in his poetry, particularly *The Wreck of the Deutschland*) Hopkins attended Oxford, where his ambition was to become a painter—until he was converted to Catholicism. He taught for a time, decided to become a Jesuit, burnt all his early poetry as too worldly, and was ordained in 1877. Near the end of his life Hopkins was appointed professor of Greek at University College, Dublin. Out of place and miserable, he died there of typhoid at the age of forty-four.

LANGSTON HUGHES (1902–1967)

Hughes, born in Joplin, Missouri, was a major figure of the intellectual and literary movement called the Harlem Renaissance. A graduate of Lincoln University in 1929, Hughes traveled through the world as a correspondent and columnist. He also founded theaters and produced plays, as well as authoring poems and novels. His works include *The Weary Blues* (1926), *Montage of a Dream Deferred* (1951), and *The Panther and the Lash: Poems of Our Time* (1961). Hughes has recently been incorporated into the gay literary canon and has been the subject of the film *Looking for Langston*.

HENRIK IBSEN (1828–1906)

Ibsen was the foremost playwright of his time; his work is both a culmination of nineteenth-century "bourgeois" drama and a precursor of social realist and symbolist theater.

Born in Skien, Norway, Ibsen was apprenticed to an apothecary until 1850, when he left for Oslo and published his first play, *Catilina*, under a pseudonym. Two of his early works, written in Rome, were in verse—*Brand* (1866) and *Peer Gynt* (1867). During the course of his career, he turned to more realistic plays—including *Ghosts* (1881) and *An Enemy of the People* (1882)—that explored contemporary social problems; they won him a reputation throughout Europe as a controversial and outspoken advocate of moral and social reform. Near the end of his life, Ibsen explored the human condition in the symbolic terms of *The Master Builder* (1892) and *When We Dead Awaken* (1899), plays that anticipated many of the concerns of twentieth-century drama.

HENRY JAMES (1843–1916)

Son of a writer and religious philosopher, brother of the philosopher William James, Henry James was born in New York and entered Harvard Law School in 1862, after private study, art school, and study and residence abroad. Thereafter his American home was in Cambridge, Massachusetts, but he lived in England from 1876 until his death forty years later, having become a British subject in 1915. James's fiction often centers on the confrontation of Americans with Europe or Europeans; he treats the two as moral or value systems as much as geographical entities. His practice and theory of fiction, set forth mainly in the prefaces to his novels, dominated fiction criticism for generations. Among his works are *The American* (1877), *Daisy Miller* (1879), *Portrait of a Lady* (1881), *The Turn of the Screw* (1898), *The Wings of the Dove* (1902), *The Ambassadors* (1903), and *The Golden Bowl* (1904).

HA JIN (b. 1956)

Ha Jin grew up in mainland China. From the age of fourteen to eighteen he served in the People's Army; he then worked in a railroad company for three years. He has degrees from Heilongjiang and Shandong universities in China and a doctorate from Brandeis. After the Tiananmen massacre, he decided to emigrate and write in English. He has published a book of poems, *Between Silences* (1990) and two books of short fiction, *Ocean of Worlds: Army Stories* and *Man to Be: Country Stories* from which "In Broad Daylight" is taken. He teaches creative writing at Emory University.

BEN JONSON (1572?–1637)

Poet, playwright, actor, scholar, critic, translator, and leader, for the first time in English, of a literary "school" (the "Cavalier" poets), Jonson was born the posthumous son of a clergyman and stepson to a master bricklayer of Westminster. He had an eventful early career, going to war against the Spanish, working as an actor and killing an associate in a duel, and converting to Catholicism (which made him an object of deep suspicion after the Gunpowder Plot of Guy Fawkes in 1605). Jonson wrote a number of plays in the midst of all this, including *Every Man in His Humor* (in which Shakespeare acted a leading role), *Volpone* (1606), and *The Alchemist* (1610). He spent the latter part of his life at the center of a vast literary circle. When in 1616 he published his collected works, *The Works of Benjamin Jonson*, it was the first time an English author had been so presumptuous as to consider writing a profession.

JAMES JOYCE (1882–1941)

In 1902, after graduating from University College, Dublin, Joyce left his native city for Paris, only to return in April 1903 to teach school. In the spring of 1904 he lived at the Martello Tower, Sandycove, a site made famous by his great novel, *Ulysses* (1921). In

October 1904 he eloped with Nora Barnacle and left Ireland again, this time for Trieste, where he taught English for the Berlitz school. Though he lived abroad the rest of his life, that first abortive trip proved symbolic: in his fiction the expatriate could never leave Dublin. Joyce had more than his share of difficulties with publication and censorship. His volume of short stories, *Dubliners* (in which "Araby" appears), completed in 1905, was not published until 1914. His *Portrait of the Artist as a Young Man*, dated "Dublin 1904, Trieste 1914," appeared first in America, in 1916. *Ulysses* was banned for a dozen years in the United States and as long or longer elsewhere. Though he published a play, *Exiles*, and poetry, the three works mentioned and the monumental, experimental, and puzzling *Finnegans Wake* (1939) are the basis of his reputation.

FRANZ KAFKA (1883–1924)

Born in Prague of a middle-class Jewish family, Kafka earned a doctorate in law from the German University in that city and held an inconspicuous position in the civil service for many years. Emotionally and physically ill for the last seven or eight years of his short life, he died of tuberculosis in Vienna, never having married (though he was twice engaged to the same woman and lived with an actress in Berlin for some time before he died) and not having published his three major novels, *The Trial* (1925), *The Castle* (1926), and *Amerika* (1927). Indeed, he ordered his friend Max Brod to destroy them and other works he had left in manuscript. Fortunately, Brod did not, and not long after his death, Kafka's work was world famous and widely influential. His stories in English translation can be found in *The Great Wall of China* (1933), *The Penal Colony* (1948), and *The Complete Stories* (1976).

YASUNARI KAWABATA (1899–1972)

Born in Osaka, Japan, Kawabata graduated from Tokyo Imperial University in 1924 and made his literary debut with the semiautobiographical *The Izu Dancer* (1926). He was a cofounder of what was called the Neosensualist group, which shared much in common with the European literary movements of Dadaism, Expressionism, and Cubism. His best-known novels include *Snow Country* (1948), *Thousand Cranes*, and *The Sound of the Mountain* (1954). "The Grasshopper and the Cricket" is from his collection *Palm-of-the-Hand Stories*, translated in 1988. Kawabata was awarded the Nobel Prize for Literature in 1968.

X. J. KENNEDY (b. 1929)

Kennedy's *Nude Descending a Staircase* (1961) is a *tour de force* performance, one of the most remarkable first volumes of poetry written in this century. Its range, from elegy to lyric to song to light verse, encompasses a great variety of tones and poetic kinds. Born Joseph Charles Kennedy in Dover, New Jersey, he was educated at Seton Hall College in New Jersey, Columbia University, and the Sorbonne in Paris. After serving in the U.S. Navy, he taught at several colleges and universities, was poetry editor of *Paris Review*, and edited anthologies of poetry, fiction, and essays. At present he works as a free-lance writer. His most recent volume, with Dorothy M. Kennedy, is *Talking Like the Rain: A First Book of Poems* (1992).

JAMAICA KINCAID (b. 1949)

Born in St. John's, Antigua (an island in the West Indies north of Guadeloupe), Kincaid now lives in New York, where she is a staff writer for the *New Yorker*. She is the author of a volume of short stories, *At the Bottom of the River* (1984), and two novels, *Annie John*

(1985) and *Lucy* (1990). Although Kincaid left her native island as a teenager, a deeply felt—and richly evocative—sense of place pervades her work.

GALWAY KINNELL (b. 1927)

Born in Providence, Rhode Island, Kinnell writes poetry that calls attention to humanity's deep connection with nature. After earning a B.A. from Princeton in 1948 and an M.A. from the University of Rochester, he was a journalist, a civil rights field worker, and a teacher at numerous colleges and universities. With a keen sense of combining personal and national historical events, Kinnell's 1969 collection *Body Rags* calls upon the civil rights movement and, more recently, *The Past* (1985) speculates on the Hiroshima and Nagasaki bombings. His early poetry, collected in *What a Kingdom It Was* (1960) and *First Poems 1946–1954* (1970), is highly formal; his more recent work, however, invokes a more colloquial style. His *Selected Poems* (1982) received both a Pulitzer Prize and the American Book Award. Currently teaching creative writing at New York University, Kinnell has recently published a compilation of earlier work, *Three Books: Body Rags, Mortal Acts, Mortal Words, The Past* (1993).

ARCHIBALD LAMPMAN (1861–1899)

Born in Ontario to German parents, Lampman, as the son of a clergyman, was headed for the Anglican ministry. After graduating from the University of Toronto in 1882 with honors in languages, however, he went into the civil service where he worked as a clerk until the end of his life. Along with Duncan Campbell Scott and William Wilfred Campbell, Lampman was a member of the Confederation group, a number of Canadian nature poets who have been praised for their efforts to articulate a Canadian national literature. Inspired by music, Lampman wrote poetry as a peaceful mode of self-expression, and he published his first volume, *Among the Millet*, in 1888. Two subsequent collections appeared after his death, *Lyrics of Earth: Sonnets and Ballads* (1925) and *At the Long Sault and Other New Poems* (1943).

MARGARET LAURENCE (1926–1987)

Laurence was born in Neepwa, Manitoba, which reappeared as the fictional town of Manawaka in many of her novels and short stories, including *The Stone Angel* (1964), *A Jest of God* (1966), and the collection *A Bird in the House* (1970). *This Side of Jordan* (1960), her first novel, was set in Africa during the 1950s rather than in her native Canada, but reflected a similar concern with the oppression of native peoples that characterizes her later work.

D. H. LAWRENCE (1885–1930)

Son of a coal miner and a middle-class schoolteacher, Lawrence won a scholarship to Nottingham High School at thirteen but had to leave a few years later when his elder brother died. He worked for a surgical appliance manufacturer, attended Nottingham University College, and taught school in Croydon, near London. In 1911, when his first novel, *The White Peacock*, was published, he left teaching to devote his time to writing, though it was not until the publication of *Sons and Lovers* (1913) that he was established as a major literary figure. In 1912 he eloped to the Continent with Frieda von Richthofen, and in 1914, after her divorce, they were married. During World War I, both his novels and the fact that his wife was German gave him trouble: *The Rainbow* was published in September 1915 and suppressed in November. In November 1919 the Lawrences left England and their years of wandering began: first Italy, then Ceylon and Australia, Mexico and New Mexico, then back to England and Italy. *Women in Love* was published in

New York in 1920, and *Lady Chatterley's Lover,* his most sexually explicit and controversial novel, eight years later. Through it all he suffered from tuberculosis, the disease from which he finally died, in France. Lawrence's stories are available in a three-volume edition, first published in 1961.

IRVING LAYTON (b. 1912)

Considered Canada's most prolific poet, Layton was born to Jewish parents in Romania in 1912. One year later, his family emigrated to Canada. After a series of unrelated jobs, Layton earned a degree in agriculture before embarking on a career writing poetry. He was critical of both literary tradition and the most representative modernist poetry like that of T. S. Eliot. Pivotal in rethinking the boundaries of poetic conventions, Layton has served on the editorial boards of a number of literary magazines, most prominently the *Black Mountain Review.* His irreverent career is collected in numerous volumes of poetry. Two recent works, *The Gucci Bag* (1983) and *A Spider Danced a Cozy Jig* (1984), highlight Layton's unique sense of humor.

DORIS LESSING (b. 1919)

Born in Persia, Lessing lived for twenty-five years in Southern Rhodesia (now Zimbabwe) before moving to England, where soon thereafter her first novel, *The Grass Is Singing* (1950), was published. She has since published voluminously. Her books include *The Golden Notebook* (1962), the five Martha Quest novels, *Children of Violence,* published between 1952 and 1969, *Briefing for a Descent into Hell* (1971), *The Summer Before the Dark* (1973), and *The Good Terrorist* (1985). She has also published eight volumes of short fiction, including *A Man and Two Women* (1963) and *The Memoirs of a Survivor* (1975), and has written plays, television plays, poetry, and essays. Her work is known for its range and variety, some of it set in Africa, a significant portion of it political (she was once a Communist), much of it examining inner lives of women in modern society, and some of it lately reflecting her interest in extrasensory perception. Lessing published a five-volume science fiction collection under the collective title *Caopus in Argos: Archives* between 1979 and 1983, and tried her hand at satire with *The Good Terrorist* (1985). *Particularly Cats . . . and Rufus* (1991) is a reflection on various pets in Lessing's life, and *African Lands* (1992) is based on her recent visit to Zimbabwe.

AUDRE LORDE (1934–1992)

Born in New York City, Lorde grew up in Harlem and attended Hunter College and Columbia University. She later returned to Hunter College in 1980 as a professor of English. Lorde raised a son and a daughter in an interracial lesbian relationship and helped to start Kitchen Table: Women of Color Press. Her poetry publications include *The First Cities* (1968), *The Black Unicorn* (1987), and *Undersong: Chosen Poems Old and New* (1993). Lorde has also published two volumes of essays, *Sister Outsider* (1983) and *Burst of Light* (1988), as well as an autobiograhical novel, *Zami* (1980).

CLAUDE MCKAY (1890–1948)

Born in Sunny Ville, Jamaica, McKay became one of the most prominent figures of the Harlem Renaissance—the oldest as well as the first to publish. Always politically active, he was attracted to Communism and in 1922 met Lenin and Trotsky in Moscow, though he later repudiated this commitment with his 1942 conversion to Catholicism. "[To] have a religion," he wrote, "is very much like falling in love with a woman. You love her for her . . . beauty, which cannot be defined." McKay's conception of black experience, infused with social reform and a consciousness of ethnic vitality, made him a catalytic poet for his generation. His works include *If We Must Die* (1919), *Home to Harlem* (1928), and *A Long Way from Home* (1937).

REGINALD MCKNIGHT (b. 1956)

McKnight teaches writing at Carnegie-Mellon University in Pittsburgh and has earned such prizes for his writing as the O. Henry Award for Short Stories and the Kenyon Review New Fiction Prize. McKnight has published two collections of short stories, *Moustapha's Eclipse* (1988) and *The Kind of Light That Shines on Texas* (1992), and a novel, *I Get on the Bus* (1990).

KATHERINE MANSFIELD (1888–1923)

Born in New Zealand, Mansfield studied music at Queen's College, London, and was an accomplished cellist. She published three major volumes of short stories during her short life: *Bliss* (1920), which established her reputation, *The Garden-Party* (1922), and *The Dove's Nest* (1923). With John Middleton Murry and D. H. Lawrence she founded an influential literary review, *The Signature*. She died of tuberculosis in France, and a final volume of stories, *Something Childish* (1924), appeared shortly after her death. Her *Collected Stories* were published in 1945.

MARTIAL (40?–104?)

Known for his witty epigrams, Marcus Valerius Martialis was born in Northeast Spain to Roman colonists in about 40 A.D. He received an excellent education and moved to Rome, discovering that he could find and keep patrons by writing compliments in verse. Early in his career, Martial performed his epigrams in private presentations, but after the spectacular inauguration at the Colosseum (80 A.D.), he published *Liber de Speactaculis (The Book of the Shows)*; he continued to write and publish until 96 A.D.

ANDREW MARVELL (1621–1678)

Marvell was born in Yorkshire, England and educated at Cambridge. He was a supporter of the Puritans and a member of the British Parliament. Marvell was known in his day for his satires in prose and verse, but today is better known for his less public poems.

BOBBIE ANN MASON (b. 1940)

Mason, who grew up on a farm near Mayfield, Kentucky, has written for *Movie Stars, Movie Life,* and *T.V. Star Parade.* The *New Yorker* published her first story in 1980. Since then, she has been awarded a Guggenheim Foundation Fellowship, has had stories in *Best American Short Stories* in 1981 and 1983, and won the Pushcart Prize for Fiction in 1983. *Shiloh and Other Stories* (1982), her first collection, won the Ernest Hemingway Foundation Award. She has also written two novels, *In Country* (1985) and *Feather Crowns* (1993), a short novel, *Spence and Lila* (1988), and a second collection of stories, *Love Life* (1989). "The people I write about," she says "either want to get away from home, get away from town, see the world, or they want to stay home, and they're afraid to leave, so they accommodate. . . . I'm interested in that tension between longing to stay and longing to go."

GUY DE MAUPASSANT (1850–1893)

Born Henri René Albert in Normandy, France, at sixteen Maupassant was expelled from a Rouen seminary and finished his education in a public high school. After serving in the Franco-Prussian War, he was for ten years a government clerk in Paris. A protégé of Flaubert, during the 1880s he published some three hundred stories, a half-dozen novels, and plays. The short stories, which appeared regularly in popular periodicals, sampled military and peasant life, the decadent world of politics and journalism, prostitution, the supernatural, and the hypocrisies of solid citizens. With Chekhov, he may be said to have created the modern short story; his reliance on plot, plot twists, and sometimes heavy irony became facile in the hands of his followers and has somewhat diminished his own reputation the past quarter-century and more. His life ended somewhat like one of his own stories: he died in an asylum, of syphilis. His novels include *Une Vie* (*A Life*, 1883), *Bel Ami* (*Handsome Friend*, 1885), and *Pierre et Jean* (1888). His stories are most readily available in his *Collected Works*.

EDNA ST. VINCENT MILLAY (1892–1950)

Winner of the 1923 Pulitzer Prize for Poetry, Millay was born in Maine and educated at Vassar. After college, with her reputation as a poet already established, Millay moved to Greenwich Village in New York and became notorious for her bohemian life and passionate love affairs.

ARTHUR MILLER (b. 1915)

Born and raised in New York City, Miller studied journalism at the University of Michigan, began writing plays, and went to work—in the middle of the Depression—with the Federal Theatre Project, a fertile proving ground for some of the best playwrights of the period. He had his first Broadway success, *All My Sons*, in 1947, followed only two years later by his masterpiece, *Death of a Salesman*. With McCarthy's Communist "witch-hunts" of the early 1950s as his inspiration, Miller fashioned another modern parable, basing *The Crucible* (1953) on the seventeenth-century Salem witch trials. His work has provoked much theoretical discussion over whether real tragedy is possible in a modern context. In 1984, Miller was given the John F. Kennedy Award for Lifetime Achievement. His most recent play, *Broken Glass*, was published in 1994.

JOHN MILTON (1608–1674)

Born in London, the elder son of a self-made businessman, Milton exhibited unusual literary and scholarly gifts at an early age; before entering Cambridge University, he was already adept at Latin and Greek and was well on his way to mastering Hebrew and most of the European languages. After graduation, he spent six more years reading, day and night, just about everything of importance written in English, Italian, Latin, and Greek—after which his father sent him abroad for another year of travel and study. Returning to England, Milton immediately embroiled himself in political controversy, writing pamphlets defending everything from free speech to the execution of Charles I by Cromwell and his followers. In the midst of this feverish activity, the monarchy was restored, and Milton was imprisoned and his property confiscated—but worst of all he lost his sight. Blind, impoverished, and isolated, he set about writing the great works of his later years: *Paradise Lost* (1667), *Paradise Regained* (1671), and *Samson Agonistes* (1671).

MARIANNE MOORE (1887–1972)

Of poetry, Moore self-consciously wrote, "I, too, dislike it"; the phrase captures her fascinating character. Born in Kirkwood, Missouri, near St. Louis, Moore's family moved to Pennsylvania, where she earned a degree from Bryn Mawr College in 1909. In 1918, she and her mother moved to Brooklyn, New York, where Moore became an avid Brooklyn

Dodgers fan. While she began to write and publish poetry in college, she did not immediately devote herself to it full time. Instead, she studied business science, taught stenography, and eventually worked as branch librarian at the New York Public Library from 1921 to 1925. In addition to writing poetry, Moore was a prolific critic and served as the editor of the *Dial* from 1926 to 1929. Her *Collected Poems* (1951) were honored with the Bollingen, Pulitzer, and National Book awards. Her *Complete Poems* (1967), while hardly complete, reveal a poet whose constant revisions showed her changing relationship to both nature and language.

PAT MORA (b. 1942)

Born to Mexican-American parents in El Paso, Texas, Mora earned both her B.A. and M.A. from the University of Texas, El Paso. Her first two collections of poetry, *Chants* (1985) and *Borders* (1986), won Southwest Book Awards. Along with these books, her most recent volume of poetry, *Communion* (1991), reflects and addresses her Chicana and Southwestern background. She has recently compiled a collection of essays called *Nepantla: Essays from the Land in the Middle* (1993).

BHARATI MUKHERJEE (b. 1940)

Brought up in an upper-class Bengali family of the Brahmin caste, Mukherjee attended private schools in India, London, and Switzerland before a business disaster wiped out the family fortune. She won a scholarship in 1961 to the University of Iowa Writer's Workshop, and has since lived with her husband (also a writer) and two children in Canada, India, and the United States, supporting herself through teaching and other jobs, and writing in the small hours of the morning. In 1971 her critically acclaimed first novel, *The Tiger's Daughter*, appeared; her other novels are *Wife* (1975) and *Jasmine* (1989). Mukherjee's short fiction collections are *Darkness* (1985), stories of South Asian immigrants, and *The Middleman* (1988), which includes characters and voices from various countries and social strata: "Mine is not minimalism, which strips away, but compression, which reflects many layers of meaning."

ALICE MUNRO (b. 1931)

Munro grew up on a farm near Lake Huron in Ontario and attended the University of Western Ontario, where she began publishing short stories. Much of her fiction grows out of her childhood memories of rural family life: "I write about places where your roots are and most people don't live that kind of life anymore at all." Her first book, a collection of stories entitled *Dance of the Happy Shades* (1968) in which "Boys and Girls" appears, won a Governor General's Award. Munro has written a novel, *Lives of Girls and Women* (1971), and six other short-story collections, *Something I've Been Meaning to Tell You* (1974), *Who Do You Think You Are?* (1978, published in the United States as *The Beggar Maid* in 1979), *The Moons of Jupiter* (1983), *The Progress of Love* (1986), *Friend of My Youth* (1990), and *Open Secrets* (1994).

SUSAN MUSGRAVE (b. 1951)

Born in Santa Cruz, California in 1951, Musgrave now resides in Canada. *Songs of the Sea-Witch* (1970), her first collection, invokes nightmares and darkness where the speakers live on the border of madness. She was the writer-in-residence at the University of Waterloo in Ontario from 1983 until 1985, when she published *Cocktails at the Mausoleum*. Her work, most recently *The Embalmer's Art* (1991), includes many personal moments, and their explicitness invites confrontation. Musgrave has also written plays, novels, and poetry for children.

HOWARD NEMEROV (1920–1991)

Nemerov once called his poems "bad jokes, and even terrible jokes, emerging from the nature of things as well as from my propensity for coming at things a touch subversively, and from the blind side, or the dark side, the side everyone concerned with 'values' would just as soon forget." The resonance of his poetry may lie in his ability to balance this subversive, wayward imagination with lucid, precise language and traditional verse forms. Born in New York City, Nemerov graduated from Harvard University, served in the Air Force during World War II, and returned to New York to complete his first book, *The Image and the Law* (1948). He taught at a number of colleges and universities and published books of poetry, plays, short stories, novels, and essays. His *Collected Poems* won the Pulitzer Prize and the National Book Award in 1978. In addition, he served as Poet Laureate of the United States from 1988 to 1990. *Trying Conclusions: New and Selected Poems 1961–1991* was published in 1991.

MARSHA NORMAN (b. 1947)

Norman grew up in Louisville, Kentucky, and now makes her home in New York City. Her work with disturbed teenagers in a Kentucky state hospital sparked the story behind Norman's first play, *Getting Out* (1977), which had its first performance at the Actors' Theatre in New York. Since then, she has written a number of plays, including *'night, Mother* (1983), for which she won the Pulitzer Prize, *Traveler in the Dark* (1984), and the script for the Broadway musical, *The Secret Garden* (1990).

FLANNERY O'CONNOR (1925–1964)

O'Connor was born in Savannah, Georgia, studied at the Georgia State College for Women, and won a fellowship to the Writer's Workshop of the University of Iowa, where she received an M.F.A. degree. Her first novel, *Wise Blood*, was published in 1952, and her first collection of stories, *A Good Man Is Hard to Find*, in 1955. She was able to complete only one more novel, *The Violent Bear It Away* (1960), and a second collection of stories, *Everything That Rises Must Converge* (1965), before dying of an incurable illness in Milledgeville, Georgia. Her reputation has grown steadily since her untimely death. A collection of letters, edited by Sally Fitzgerald under the title *The Habit of Being*, appeared in 1979.

SHARON OLDS (b. 1942)

Olds's poems might well be compared with those of the "confessional" poets (particularly Plath and Sexton) in their intense focus on and preoccupation with sexual and family relationships. Born in San Francisco, Olds studied at Stanford and Columbia universities, settling afterwards in New York City, where she teaches creative writing at New York University and the Goldwater Hospital (a public facility for the severely physically disabled). Olds's books include *Satan Says* (1980), *The Dead and the Living* (1983; National Book Critics Circle Award), and *The Gold Cell* (1987). She has received a National Endowment for the Arts Grant and a Guggenheim Fellowship. Her most recent volume, *The Father*, appeared in 1992.

GRACE PALEY (b. 1922)

Born to Russian immigrants in New York, Paley never finished college because she was too busy reading and writing. Her short stories are collected in *The Little Disturbances of Man: Stories of Men and Women at Love* (1959), *Enormous Changes at the Last Minute* (1974), and *Later the Same Day* (1985). Her poetry has been published in *New and*

Collected Poems (1992). Paley has been conferred an honorary doctorate and most recently has taught at Dartmouth University.

DOROTHY PARKER (1893–1967)

Parker satirized the literary, social, and sexual pieties of her time with a sharp eye and sardonic exuberance. If "Brevity is the soul of Lingerie," as she announced in a *Vogue* advertisement, it is also the heart of her wit. There are a number of "Parkerisms"—brief, witty aphorisms—still in circulation. Parker was born in New York City and was friendly with several other prominent writers and humorists of the 1920s and 1930s, including Harold Ross, founder of the *New Yorker*. Author of poetry, criticism, screenplays, and short stories, she published a number of collections, including *Enough Rope* (1926), *Sunset Gun* (1928), *Death and Taxes* (1931), and *Not So Deep as a Well* (1936).

LINDA PASTAN (b. 1932)

Author of more than half a dozen volumes of poetry, Pastan was born in New York City and attended Radcliffe College and Brandeis University before settling in suburban Washington, D.C. Her books include *A Perfect Circle of Sun* (1971), *The Five Stages of Grief* (1978), *A Fraction of Darkness* (1985), and *The Imperfect Paradise* (1988). *PM / AM: New and Selected Poems* (1982) was nominated for the American Book Award. Her latest collection, *Heroes in Disguise*, was published in 1991.

MARGE PIERCY (b. 1936)

Piercy's earlier poetry examined the complex interplay between personal relationships and political forces, at the same time voicing the rage of women who have for so long been dominated and overwhelmed by men ("I imagine that I speak for a constituency, living and dead," she writes). Her later work, particularly the poems in *Stone, Paper, Knife* (1983), expresses also a sense of inclusiveness, of interconnection with all living things. Born in Detroit, Piercy studied at the University of Michigan and Northwestern University and taught for some time before the success of her novels allowed her to live a semirural life on Cape Cod. Her books of poetry include *Living in the Open* (1976), *The Moon Is Always Female* (1980), and *Available Light* (1988). In 1990 Piercy received the Golden Rose Award. Her most recent book of poetry, *Mars and Her Children*, was published in 1992.

HAROLD PINTER (b. 1930)

Born and educated in East London, Pinter acted in a repertory company under the stage name of David Baron until his first play, *The Room*, was produced in 1957. This was followed immediately by *The Dumb Waiter*, *The Birthday Party*, and, in 1960, *The Caretaker*, which established his reputation as a writer of disturbing and often absurd "realist" drama, as well as a master of pauses, double-entendres, and silences that communicate a secondary level of meaning beneath the surface textures of everyday speech. More recently, Pinter has worked on screenplays for filmed versions of John Fowles's *The French Lieutenant's Woman*, F. Scott Fitzgerald's *The Last Tycoon*, Marcel Proust's *A la Recherche du Temps Perdu*, Franz Kafka's *The Trial*, and Margaret Atwood's *The Handmaid's Tale*.

SYLVIA PLATH (1932–1963)

Plath has attained the status of a cult figure as much for the splendid and beautiful agony of her poems as for her "martyrdom" to art. Her life, in all its outer banality and inner tragedy, might be seen as a confirmation that poetry is a dangerous vocation. Born the daughter of a Polish immigrant who died in 1940, Plath's early years were a vision of conventional success, including poetry prizes, scholarships at Smith College, and a *summa cum laude* graduation. She won a Fulbright Scholarship to Cambridge University, where she met and married the English poet, Ted Hughes, with whom she had two children. Yet beneath it all was a woman whose acute perceptions and intolerable pain led her to produce a novel, *The Bell Jar* (1963), and three volumes of poetry—and to commit suicide at the age of thirty.

EDGAR ALLAN POE (1809–1849)

Poe's actor father deserted his wife and son when Edgar was less than a year old. His mother died before he was three, and he and his younger sister were separated and taken into different families. The Allans (who gave Poe his middle name) moved, in 1815, to England, where Edgar had his early schooling. He studied briefly at the University of Virginia and in 1827 paid to have a volume of poems published in Boston (his birthplace); a second volume appeared in 1829 in Baltimore (where he was to die twenty years later). Having served for two years in the army, he was appointed to West Point in 1830 but apparently managed to have himself expelled within the year for cutting classes. Living in Baltimore with his grandmother, aunt, and cousin Virginia (whom he married in 1835 when she was thirteen), Poe began to attract critical attention but made very little money. For the twelve years of his bizarre marriage, he wrote, worked as journalist and editor, and drank. Not long after his wife died in 1847 he seemed to be straightening himself out when, on election day—October 3—he was found semiconscious near a polling place and died four days later without fully regaining consciousness. It is testimony to the continuing fame of his works that they need not be named here.

SHARON POLLOCK (b. 1936)

Pollock began her association with the theater as an actor and director in the mid-1960s, first in her native New Brunswick and then in Calgary as a member of Prairie Players, a touring company. Her first works for radio and theater date from the early 1970s; since then she has written several major stage plays and a number of children's works and radio scripts. She has taught at the University of Alberta, was playwright-in-residence at A.T.P., Calgary, and has been head of the Playwright's Colony at Banff. Her plays include *The Komagata Maru Incident* (1976), *One Tiger to a Hill* (1980), and *Generations* (1980). Her most recent play, *Doc*, was first produced in Calgary in 1984.

ALEXANDER POPE (1688–1744)

Born near London, Pope was delicate as a child and deformed early on by tuberculosis of the spine. He nevertheless was encouraged to read widely and exhibited a precocious talent for poetry; his first successes were the *Essay on Criticism* (1711) and *The Rape of the Lock* (1712 and 1714). Pope's Catholicism, which precluded him from attending a university, voting, holding public office, or receiving the sort of patronage commonly bestowed on writers of his generation, led him to embark on translations of Homer's *Iliad* and *Odyssey* in 1713, the success of which would eventually make him the only important writer of his generation to make his living solely by his craft. Pope's extraordinary career resulted in works as diverse as the *Dunciad* (1728 and 1743), his great verse satire, and the *Essay on Man* (1733–34), his exploration of ethics and philosophy.

EZRA POUND (1885–1972)

Pound's tremendous ambition—to succeed in his own work and to influence the development of poetry and Western culture in general—led him to found the Imagist school of poetry, to advise and assist a galaxy of great writers (Eliot, Joyce, Williams, Frost, and Hemingway, to name a few), and to write a number of highly influential critical works. It also led him to a charge of treason (Pound served as a propagandist for Mussolini during World War II), a diagnosis of insanity, and twelve years at St. Elizabeth's, an institution for the criminally insane. Born in Hailey, Idaho, Ezra Loomis Pound studied at the University of Pennsylvania and Hamilton College before traveling to Europe in 1908. He remained there, living in Ireland, England, France, and Italy, for much of his life. Pound's verse is collected in *Personae: The Collected Poems* (1949) and *The Cantos* (1976).

SIR WALTER RALEGH (1552–1618)

Clearly a man of immense versatility, Ralegh undertook a variety of adventures in his tumultuous life. Born in Devonshire, England, he briefly attended Oxford but withdrew to fight in the army. He is credited with bringing the potato to Ireland and tobacco to Europe, and through his many explorations, he became an investor in the North American colonies. He was knighted and named a member of Parliament, but after offending the Queen, Ralegh was imprisoned in the Tower of London. After his release in 1595, he charted a failed expedition to Guiana, and in 1603 he was again imprisoned on trumped-up treason charges. In prison, he began his unfinished *History of the World*. After another unsuccessful trip to Guiana, he was again imprisoned and executed on the orders of James I. His writings include the popular "The Nymph's Reply to the Shepherd," a response to Marlowe's "Passionate Shepherd," and some extensive writings on his findings in Guiana.

ISHMAEL REED (b. 1938)

Born in Chattanooga, Tennessee, Reed attended the University of Buffalo. Considered a writer of the 1960s and 1970s counterculture, Reed, through his novels, essays, plays, songs, and poems, calls attention to the marginalization of nonwhite cultures and traditions in mainstream America. While he is probably best known for his satirical novel, *Mumbo Jumbo* (1972), Reed is a prolific poet. His first volume, *Catechism of D NeoAmerican Hoodoo Church*, was published in 1970. His most recent work is a novel, *Japanese by Spring* (1993). Reed has taught at a variety of colleges and universities; he currently teaches at the University of California, Berkeley.

MORDECAI RICHLER (b. 1931)

Richler was born in Montreal, the son of working-class Jewish parents; *The Street* (1975) is a loosely autobiographical depiction of his childhood. Richler attended Sir George Williams University for two years and worked as a freelance writer in Paris and London from 1952, returning to live in his native Quebec only in 1980. His writing is varied and includes short stories, essays, screenplays, and novels. His *Cocksure* (1968) and *St. Urbain's Horseman* (1971) won the Governor General's Award, and his own screen adaptation of his novel *The Apprenticeship of Duddy Kravitz* (1959) was nominated for an Academy Award in 1974. His novels include *Joshua Then and Now* (1980) and *Solomon Gursky Was Here* (1990).

ALBERTO ALVARO RÍOS (b. 1952)

Ríos was born in Nogales, Arizona, to a British mother and a Mexican father. He graduated from the University of Arizona and teaches at Arizona State University. He has recieved an NEA Fellowship and the 1981 Academy of American Poets Walt Whitman's

Award for his collection of poems entitled *Whispering to Fool the Wind*. His other publications include three books of poetry, *Five Indiscretions* (1985), *The Lime Orchard Woman* (1988), and *Teodoro Luna's Two Kisses* (1990), as well as a collection of short stories, *The Iguana Killer: Twelve Stories of the Heart* (1984).

THEODORE ROETHKE (1908–1963)

Born in Saginaw, Michigan, Roethke grew up around his father's twenty-five-acre greenhouse complex—its associations with nurture and growth became an important subject in his later poetry. He worked for a time at Lafayette College, where he was professor of English and tennis coach, and later at the University of Washington, which appointed him poet-in-residence one year before he died. Roethke was an unhappy man, suffering from periodic mental breakdowns, yet the best of his poetry, with its reverence for and fear of the physical world, its quest for an ecstatic union with nature, seems destined to last. Roethke's books include *Open House* (1942), *Praise to the End!* (1951), and *The Far Field* (1964), which received a posthumous National Book Award.

MURIEL RUKEYSER (1913–1980)

Born in New York City, Rukeyser later attended Vassar College and Columbia University. Uncomfortable with her family's wealth, Rukeyser associated herself with more radical issues, namely the labor movement of the 1920s and 1930s. Her first collection of poetry, *Theory of Flight* (1935) was apparently inspired by her attendance at the Roosevelt Aviation School. In the 1940s Rukeyser wrote poetry highlighting the destruction of World War II. She later protested against U.S. involvement in Korea and Vietnam, and in the 1970s, she addressed feminist issues in her art. *The Collected Poems of Muriel Rukeyser* was published in 1978.

ANNE SEXTON (1928–1974)

Born in Newton, Massachusetts, Anne (Harvey) Sexton interrupted her attendance at Garland Junior College to marry. She wrote poetry as a child, abandoned it, and, on the advice of her doctors, began writing again after suffering a nervous breakdown. Sexton attended Boston University with fellow student Sylvia Plath, and she studied poetry with Robert Lowell. Published in 1960, her first book of poems, *To Bedlam and Part Way Back*, recounted her mental collapse and subsequent recovery period. A "confessional" poet, Sexton received many awards, most notably the Pulitzer Prize for *Live or Die* (1966). She committed suicide in 1974. That same year, she had published *Death Notebooks*; a posthumous volume, *The Awful Rowing toward God*, appeared in 1975.

WILLIAM SHAKESPEARE (1554–1616)

Considering the great and deserved fame of his work, surprisingly little is known of Shakespeare's life. We do know that between 1585 and 1592 he left his birthplace of Stratford for London to begin a career as playwright and actor. No dates of his professional career are recorded, however, nor can we be certain of the order in which he composed his plays and poetry. By 1594 he had established himself as a poet with two long works—*Venus and Adonis* and *The Rape of Lucrece*—but it was in the theater that he made his strongest reputation. Shakespeare produced perhaps thirty-five plays in twenty-five years, proving himself a master of many genres in works such as *Macbeth*, *King Lear*, *Othello*, and *Antony and Cleopatra* (tragedy); *Richard III* and *Henry IV* (historical drama); *Twelfth Night* and *As You Like It* (comedy); and *The Tempest* (romance). His more than one hundred fifty sonnets are supreme expressions of the form.

BERNARD SHAW (1856–1950)

Like Chekhov, Shaw's dramas address the turn of the century in a comic and realistic way. Shaw's frequent use of satire enabled him to confront idealistic and romantic notions about love and war. Like Swift, Shaw was born in Dublin to English parents and moved to London when he was nineteen. He worked as a witty music and drama critic for various London newspapers while at the same time promoting socialism in England. His first play, *Widowers' Houses*, was produced in 1891. Addressing the issue of prostitution, his second play, *Mrs. Warren's Profession* (1893), was banned. His more popular works, all of which highlight hypocrisy, include *Man and Superman* (1904), *Major Barbara* (1907), *Pygmalion* (1912), *Heartbreak House* (1919), and *Saint Joan* (1923).

PERCY BYSSHE SHELLEY (1792–1822)

Born in Sussex to a wealthy member of Parliament, Shelley attended Eton and Oxford. An unconventional young man, Shelley was expelled from Oxford during his first year for collaborating with a friend, Thomas Jefferson Hogg, on a pamphlet entitled "The Necessity of Atheism" (1811). That same year, Shelley eloped with Harriet Westbrook, but within three years, he left her to be with Mary Wollstonecraft Godwin. After Harriet's suicide, Shelley married Mary and the couple and their children moved permanently to Italy. The death of their two children, coupled with financial difficulties, left Shelley in despair, and it was at this time (1819) that he wrote his most memorable poetry, namely "Prometheus Unbound" and "Ode to the West Wind." Shelley's important critical essay, "A Defence of Poetry," was published posthumously in 1840.

STEVIE SMITH (1902–1971)

Because of her small size, Florence Margaret Smith earned her nickname from a famous jockey, Steve Donoghue. At a young age, her family moved to a London suburb, and later Smith worked as a secretary at a publishing company and as a writer and broadcaster for the BBC. In the 1930s, she began publishing fiction and poetry, which she often illustrated. Her first novel, *Novel on Yellow Paper*, appeared in 1936, followed by her first collection of poetry, *A Good Time Was Had By All* (1937). Her fascination with death was collected in verse in a volume called *Not Waving But Drowning* (1957) in which she maintains her consistently witty voice. In 1966 she was given the Cholmondely Award, and in 1969, she received the Queen's Gold Medal for Poetry. Both her *Collected Poems* (1976) and *Me Again: The Uncollected Writings* (1981) were published after her death.

SOPHOCLES (496?–406? B.C.)

Sophocles lived at a time when Athens and Greek civilization had reached the peak of their power and influence. He not only served as a general under Pericles and played a prominent role in the city's affairs but was also arguably the greatest of the Greek tragic playwrights, an innovator who fundamentally changed the form of dramatic performance and the model Aristotle turned to when he discussed the nature of tragedy in his *Poetics*. Today only seven of Sophocles' tragedies survive—the Oedipus Trilogy (*Oedipus the King*, *Oedipus at Colonus*, and *Antigone*), *Philoctetes*, *Ajax*, *Trachiniae*, and *Electra*— though records suggest that his output may have amounted to over 120 plays.

WALLACE STEVENS (1879–1955)

"I believe that with a bucket of sand and a wishing lamp I could create a world in half a second that would make this one look like a hunk of mud," Stevens once remarked to his wife. One of the great imaginative forces of this century, he was nevertheless an extraordinarily self-effacing public man, working for much of his adult life as an executive of the Hartford Accident and Indemnity Company while recreating the world at night in the "supreme fiction" of poetry. Born in Reading, Pennsylvania, Stevens attended Harvard University and New York Law School; his first book of poems, *Harmonium*, appeared in 1923. Stevens's poetry and prose can be found in *The Palm at the End of the Mind* (1971) and *The Necessary Angel: Essays on Reality and Imagination* (1951).

JONATHAN SWIFT (1667–1745)

Born to English parents in Dublin, Ireland, Swift later attended Trinity College. In 1689, he moved to England in the service of Sir William Temple. Swift later received an M.A. from Oxford, and in 1695 he took orders to become an Anglican clergyman. He became known for his scathing religious and political satires, and after writing "A Tale of a Tub" and "The Battle of the Books," he returned to Ireland and was named dean of Saint Patrick's Cathedral in Dublin. In his later years, Swift suffered from senility and was removed from his post. He is most popularly known for his 1726 book, *Gulliver's Travels*. His poetry, too, is masterfully satiric.

ELIZABETH TALLENT (b. 1954)

Tallent studied anthropology at the University of Illinois before turning to writing. Best known for her stories, she has won the Pushcart Prize and has had work published in the *New Yorker*, the *Paris Review*, *Esquire*, and *Grand Street*. Tallent makes her home in both Little River and Davis, California, where she teaches at the University of California. Her published books include the story collections *In Constant Flight* (1983), *Time with Children* (1987), and *Honey: Stories* (1993), as well as the novel *Museum Pieces* (1985).

AMY TAN (b. 1952)

Tan was born in Oakland, California, just two and a half years after her parents immigrated there from China. She has worked as a consultant to programs for disabled children and as a freelance writer. In 1987 she visited China for the first time—"As soon as my feet touched China, I became Chinese"—and returned to write her first book, *The Joy Luck Club* (1989). Tan has since published a second book, *The Kitchen God's Wife* (1991), and co-authored the screenplay for the film adaptation of *The Joy Luck Club*.

ALFRED, LORD TENNYSON (1809–1892)

Perhaps the most important and certainly the most popular of the Victorian poets, Tennyson demonstrated his talents at an early age; he published his first volume in 1827. Encouraged to devote his life to poetry by a group of undergraduates at Cambridge University known as the "Apostles," Tennyson was particularly close to Arthur Hallam, whose sudden death in 1833 inspired the long elegy, *In Memoriam* (1850). With that poem he achieved lasting fame and recognition; he was appointed Poet Laureate the year of its publication. Whatever the popularity of his "journalistic" poetry—"The Charge of the Light Brigade" (1854) is perhaps his best known—Tennyson's great theme was always the past, both personal (*In the Valley of Cauteretz*, 1864) and national (*Idylls of the King*, 1869).

DYLAN THOMAS (1914–1953)

In a note to his *Collected Poems* (1952), Thomas wrote: "These poems, with all their crudities, doubts, and confusions, are written for the love of Man and in praise of God, and I'd be a damn fool if they weren't." Given their somber undertones and often wrenching awareness of death, his poems are also rich verbal and visual celebrations of life and its sweetness. Born in Swansea, Wales, into what he called "the smug darkness of a provincial town," Thomas published his first book, *18 Poems* (1934), at the age of twenty. Thereafter he had a successful, though turbulent, career publishing poetry, short stories, and plays, including the highly successful *Under Milk Wood* (1954). In his last years he supported himself with lecture tours and poetry readings in the United States, but his extravagant drinking caught up with him and he died in New York City of chronic alcoholism.

LEO TOLSTOY (1828–1910)

Tolstoy's life would have made a fitting subject for one of his novels. Born into a noble Russian family, orphaned before he was ten, he studied Oriental languages, then law, then settled on the family estate where he tried to improve the lot of his serfs though they treated him with suspicion. He served in the army, returned home to found a school, married, and wrote two monumental novels, his masterpieces *War and Peace* (1863–69) and *Anna Karenina* (1873–76). But he wasn't satisfied; he found his life, in his own words, "absurd . . . a stupid and spiteful joke," and was converted, first to his national religion, then to a kind of "primitive" Christianity. He opposed the military, capital punishment, persecution of the Jews; he gave up alcohol, meat, and as much of his property as his family would allow. In the end he fled from home—where his wife was trying to have him declared incompetent—intending to enter a monastery, but died in a railway station en route. His works, after his conversion, include *The Death of Iván Ilyich* (1886), "How Much Land Does a Man Need?" and many other stories, parables, and novels.

JEAN TOOMER (1894–1967)

Born in Washington, D.C., Toomer later briefly attended a number of colleges and universities. He published poetry and fiction in a variety of small magazines, in addition to African American publications like *Crisis* and *Opportunity*. A crucial text of the Harlem Renaissance, Toomer's landmark, *Cane*, was published in 1923. *Cane* combines a variety of genres, and Toomer's juxtapositions of poetry, drama, and prose foreground his comparisons between rural and urban life for African Americans. After *Cane*, Toomer was unable to publish his work, and he primarily wrote for himself. In 1980, his previously unpublished works appeared in a volume called *The Wayward and the Seeking*.

GUY VANDERHAEGHE (b. 1951)

A native of Saskatchewan, Canada, Vanderhaeghe worked as an archivist and teacher until the early 1980s. He has published collections of short stories, including *Man Descending* (1982), which won the Governor General's Award for Fiction, *The Trouble with Heroes* (1983), and *Things As They Are* (1992), as well as two novels, *My Present Age* (1984) and *Homesick* (1989).

EUDORA WELTY (b. 1909)

Welty, a prolific and highly acclaimed southern writer, was born in Jackson, Mississippi, attended Mississippi State College for Women, and earned a B.A. from the University of Wisconsin. She has earned two Guggenheim Fellowships, three O. Henry Awards, a Pulitzer Prize, the National Medal for Literature, and the Presidential Medal of Freedom. Although Welty has authored many novels, including *The Robber Bridegroom* (1942), *The Optimist's Daughter* (1972), and the autobiographical *One Writer's Beginnings* (1984), she is best known for her short stories, many of which have been published in *The Collected Stories of Eudora Welty* (1980).

WALT WHITMAN (1819–1892)

Born on a farm in West Hills, Long Island, to a British father and a Dutch mother, Whitman eventually worked as a journalist throughout New York for many years. After teaching for a while, he founded his own newspaper, *The Long Islander* in 1838, but he left journalism to work on *Leaves of Grass*, which was originally intended as a poetic treatise on American democratic idealism. Published privately in multiple editions from 1855 to 1874, the book originally failed to reach a mass audience. In 1881 Boston's Osgood and Company published another edition of *Leaves of Grass*, which sold well until the district attorney called it "obscene literature" and stipulated that Whitman remove certain poems and phrases. He refused, and many years later, his works were published in Philadelphia. Whitman's poetry creates tension between the self-conscious and political, the romantic and realistic, the mundane and mystical, and the collective and individual.

OSCAR WILDE (1854–1900)

Born and raised in Dublin, Wilde later majored in classical studies at Trinity College and went on to take his degree from Oxford in 1878. While at Oxford he was influenced by the "aesthetic movement" as theorized by John Ruskin and Walter Pater. Upon graduation, he moved to London to write and became a major proponent of the "art for art's sake" school. In addition to drama, Wilde wrote criticism, poetry, and fiction, most notably *The Picture of Dorian Gray* (1891). However, he is most remembered for his comic dramas, especially *The Importance of Being Ernest*, which was performed in 1895. That same year, Wilde was accused of homosexuality, and while he sued for libel, he lost the case and was imprisoned. Public sentiment in England and America was unsupportive, and during his two years in jail, Wilde's writing became more serious. Upon his release, he emigrated to France under an assumed name. He is buried in Paris.

LYNNA WILLIAMS (b. 1951)

Born in Waco, Texas, Williams attended the University of Missouri School of Journalism and earned a Master's in Fine Arts at George Mason University. She currently teaches creative writing at Emory University in Atlanta. Her short fiction has been published in *Atlantic Monthly* and *Lear's*, and has earned Williams the Dobie-Pisano Fellowship from the Texas Institute of Letters and a nomination for the Townsend Prize. A collection of short stories, *Things Not Seen and Other Stories*, was published in 1992, and Williams is currently at work on her first novel, which follows the protagonist of "Personal Testimony" into adulthood.

TENNESSEE WILLIAMS (1911–1983)

Born in Columbus, Mississippi, Thomas Lanier Williams moved to St. Louis with his family at the age of seven. Williams's father was a violent drinker, his mother was ill, and his sister, Rose, suffered from a variety of mental illnesses. Each of them became a model for the domineering men and genteel women of his plays. He attended college at the University of Missouri and Washington University in St. Louis, but he did not earn his degree until he was in his mid-twenties. While earning his B.A. from the University of Iowa, Williams won prizes for his fiction and began writing plays. From this time until his death, he created an extensive body of work. His plays confront issues usually marginalized by society: adultery, homosexuality, incest, and mental illness. In 1944, his drama *The Glass Menagerie* won the New York Drama Critics' Circle Award. He earned his first Pulitzer Prize with *A Streetcar Named Desire* in 1948, and the play was made into a film in 1951. Williams's second Pulitzer Prize was awarded for his 1955 *Cat on a Hot Tin Roof*. His other dramas include *Suddenly Last Summer* (1958) and *The Night of the Iguana* (1961). His last Broadway play, *Clothes for a Summer Hotel*, failed in 1980.

WILLIAM CARLOS WILLIAMS (1883–1963)

Williams influenced a generation of American poets—many of them still living—▮ bringing to poetry the sense that "life is above all things else at any moment subversi▮ of life as it was the moment before—always new, irregular." Born in Rutherford, Ne▮ Jersey, Williams attended school in Switzerland and New York, and studied medicine ▮ the University of Pennsylvania, where he met Hilda Doolittle (H.D.) and Ezra Poun▮ Thereafter he spent most of his life in Rutherford, practicing medicine and crafting ▮ poetry of palpable immediacy, written in vital, local language. His long poem, Paters▮ (completed in 1963), vividly expresses what lies at the heart of his work: "No ideas but ▮ things."

AUGUST WILSON (b. 1945)

Born in Pittsburgh, Wilson grew up in poverty and dropped out of school at sixteen. ▮ was then, while working at low-paying jobs, that he started to write poetry. In 1968 ▮ founded the Black Horizons Theatre Company of St. Paul, Minnesota, but he bega▮ writing plays only in the 1980s. His first play, Jitney (1982), was produced in Pittsburg▮ Since then he has crafted several major works chronicling the black experience ▮ America, all of which have opened on Broadway after initial productions at the Ya▮ Repertory Theatre and on tour. Two of them, Fences and The Piano Lesson (1990), ha▮ won Pulitzer Prizes. His most recent play, Two Trains Running, opened in 1990 at th▮ Yale Repertory Theatre.

WILLIAM WORDSWORTH (1770–1850)

Born in Cockermouth in the sparsely populated English Lake District (which Coleridg▮ and he would immortalize), Wordsworth spent his early years "drinking in" (to use ▮ favorite metaphor) a rural environment that would provide material for much of his lat▮ poetry. After study at Cambridge University, he spent a year in France, hoping to witne▮ first-hand the French Revolution's "glorious renovation." Remarkably, he was able ▮ establish "a saving intercourse with my true self"—and to write some of his fine▮ poetry—after a love affair with a French woman whose sympathies were Royalist, h▮ own disillusionment at the Revolution, a forced return to England, and near emotion▮ collapse. Perhaps because he was, above all, a poet of remembrance (of "emotion reco▮ lected in tranquility"), and his own early experience was not an inexhaustible resourc▮ Wordsworth had written most of his great work—including his masterpiece, The Pr▮ lude—by the time he was forty.

WILLIAM BUTLER YEATS (1865–1939)

Perhaps the greatest twentieth-century poet in English, Yeats was born in Dubli▮ attended art school for a time, and left to devote himself to poetry (at the start of h▮ career, a self-consciously romantic poetry, dreamy and ethereal). Yeats's reading ▮ Nietzsche, his involvement with the Nationalist cause, and his desperate love for th▮ actress (and Nationalist) Maud Gonne led to a tighter, more actively passionate verse an▮ a number of innovative dramatic works. Bitter and disillusioned at the results of revolu▮ tion and the rise of the Irish middle class, Yeats later withdrew from contemporary even▮ to "Thoor Ballylee," his Norman Tower in the country, there to construct an elaborat▮ mythology and to write poetry, at once realist, symbolist, and metaphysical, whic▮ explored what were, for Yeats, fundamental questions of history and identity. Of th▮ progress of his life, Yeats once said: "Man can embody truth but cannot know it."

RUDOLFO ANAYA: "The Water People," Chapter 11 from *Bless Me Ultima* by Rudolfo Anaya. Copyright © 1972 by Rudolfo Anaya. Reprinted by permission of the author.

MARGARET ATWOOD: "Happy Endings" by Margaret Atwood. Originally published in *Murder in the Dark* (Coach House Press). Reprinted by permission of the author.

JAMES BALDWIN: "Sonny's Blues" from *Going to Meet the Man*. Copyright © 1948, 1951, 1957, 1958, 1960, 1965 by James Baldwin. Reprinted by Doubleday, a division of Bantam, Doubleday, Dell Publishing Group, Inc.

TONI CADE BAMBARA: "Gorilla, My Love" from *Gorilla, My Love* by Toni Cade Bambara. Copyright © 1972 by Toni Cade Bambara. Reprinted by permission of Random House, Inc.

CHARLES BAXTER: "Fenstad's Mother" reprinted from *A Relative Stranger, Stories* by Charles Baxter, by permission of W. W. Norton & Company, Inc. Copyright © 1990 by Charles Baxter.

ANN BEATTIE: "Janus" from *Where You'll Find Me*. Copyright © 1986 by Irony & Pity. Reprinted with permission of Simon & Schuster, Inc.

ANGELA CARTER: "A Souvenir from Japan" from *Fireworks*. Copyright © 1974 by Angela Carter. Reprinted by permission of HarperCollins Publishers, Inc., and Rogers, Coleridge & White, Ltd.

DENISE CHÁVEZ: "The Last of the Menu Girls" from *The Last of the Menu Girls* by Denise Chávez. Copyright © 1987 by Denise Chávez. Reprinted by permission from Arte Publico Press, University of Houston.

JOHN CHEEVER: "The Country Husband" from *The Stories of John Cheever* by John Cheever. Copyright 1954 by John Cheever. Reprinted by permission of Alfred A. Knopf, Inc.

ANTON CHEKHOV: "The Lady with the Dog" reprinted from *The Russian Master and Other Stories* by Anton Chekhov, translated by Ronald Hingley (Worlds Classics, 1984), from *The Oxford Chekhov, Vol. 9* (1975) by permission of Oxford University Press.

RICHARD CONNELL: "The Most Dangerous Game" by Richard Connell. Copyright © 1924 by Richard Connell. Copyright renewed © 1965 by Louise Fox Connell. Reprinted by permission of Brandt & Brandt.

JULIO CORTÁZAR: "Blow-Up" from *End of the Game and Other Stories* by Julio Cortázar, translated by Paul Blackburn. Copyright © 1967 by Random House, Inc. Reprinted by permission of Pantheon Books, a Division of Random House, Inc.

RICHARD DOKEY: "Sánchez," by Richard Dokey. Copyright © 1967. This story first appeared in *Southwest Review*. Reprinted by permission of the author.

LOUISE ERDRICH: "Love Medicine" from *Love Medicine* by Louise Erdrich. Copyright © 1984, 1993 Louise Erdrich. Reprinted by permission of Henry Holt and Co., Inc. Revised and expanded edition.

WILLIAM FAULKNER: "Barn Burning" and "A Rose for Emily" from *The Collected Stories of William Faulkner*. Copyright 1939 and renewed 1967 by Estelle Faulkner and Jill Faulkner Summers. Copyright 1930 and renewed 1958 by William Faulkner.

RICHARD FORD: "Great Falls" from *Rock Springs*. Copyright © 1987 by Richard Ford. Used by permission of Grove/Atlantic, Inc.

HA JIN: "In Broad Daylight." First published in *The Kenyon Review*—New Series, Summer 1993, vol. XV, no. 3, Copyright © 1993 by Kenyon College. Reprinted with permission by *The Kenyon Review*.

ERNEST HEMINGWAY: "A Very Short Story" from *In Our Time* by Ernest Hemingway. Copyright 1925 by Charles Scribner's Sons. Copyright renewed 1953 by Ernest Hemingway. Reprinted with permission of Scribner's, an imprint of Simon & Schuster, Inc.

SPENCER HOLST: "The Zebra Storyteller" © 1971. Reprinted with permission of the author. *The Zebra Storyteller: Collected Stories of Spencer Holst/93*. Station Hill Press, Barrytown, New York 12507.

FRANZ KAFKA: "A Hunger Artist" from *Franz Kafka: The Complete Stories* by Franz Kafka, edited by Nahum N. Glatzer. Copyright 1946, 1947, 1948, 1954, 1958, 1971 by Schoken Books, Inc. Reprinted by permission of Schoken Books, published by Pantheon Books, a Division of Random House, Inc.

YASUNARI KAWABATA: "The Grasshopper and the Bell Cricket" from *Palm-of-the-Hand Stories* by Yasunari Kawabata. Copyright by Yasunari Kawabata. Reprinted with permission from Farrar, Straus & Giroux, Inc.

EUDORA WELTY: "Why I Live at the P.O." from *A Curtain of Green and Other Stories*, copyright © 1941 and renewed 1969 by Eudora Welty, reprinted by permission of Harcourt Brace and Company.

LYNNA WILLIAMS: "Personal Testimony" from *Things Not Seen and Other Stories* by Lynna Williams. Copyright © 1992 by Lynna Williams. Reprinted by permission of Little, Brown & Company.

DIANE ACKERMAN: "Sweep Me Through Your Many-Chambered Heart" from *Jaguar of Sweet Laughter: New and Selected Poems* by Diane Ackerman. Copyright © 1991 by Diane Ackerman. Reprinted by permission of Random House, Inc.

FRANKLIN P. ADAMS: "Composed in the Composing Room" from *By and Large* by Franklin P. Adams. Copyright © 1914 by Franklin P. Adams. Reprinted by permission from Bantam Doubleday Dell.

AI: "Twenty-year Marriage" from *Cruelty* by Ai. Copyright © 1970, 1973 by Ai. Reprinted by permission from Houghton Mifflin Company. All rights reserved. "Riot Act, April 29, 1992" reprinted from *Greed* by Ai, by permission of W. W. Norton & Company, Inc. Copyright © 1993 by Ai. In *Greed*, the dramatic monologues are 100 percent fiction and are merely characters created by the poet. Some of them project the names of "real" public figures onto made-up characters in made-up circumstances. Where the names of corporate, media, or public or political figures are used in the monologues, those names are meant only to denote figures, images, the stuff of imagination; they do not denote or pretend to private information about actual persons, living, dead, or otherwise.

ELIZABETH ALEXANDER: "Boston Year" from *The Venus Hottentot*, edited by Charles Rowell. Copyright © 1990 by Elizabeth Alexander. Reprinted by permission of the University Press of Virginia.

AGHA SHAHID ALI: "The Dacca Gauzes" reprinted from *The Half-Inch Himalayas*, copyright © 1987 by Agha Shahid Ali, Wesleyan University Press. By permission of University Press of New England.

A. R. AMMONS: "Needs" reprinted from *Collected Poems, 1951–1971* by A. R. Ammons, by permission of W. W. Norton & Company, Inc. Copyright © 1972 by A. R. Ammons.

MAYA ANGELOU: "Africa" from *Oh Pray My Wings Are Gonna Fit Me Well* by Maya Angelou. Copyright © 1975 by Maya Angelou. Reprinted by permission of Random House, Inc.

RICHARD ARMOUR: "Hiding Place" from *Light Armour*. Copyright © 1954 by Richard Armour. Reprinted by permission of John Hawkins & Associates, Inc.

MARGARET ATWOOD: "Death of a Young Son by Drowning" from *The Journals of Susanna Moodie* by Margaret Atwood, © 1970 by Oxford University Press Canada. "Siren Song" from *You Are Happy*, © 1978 by Margaret Atwood. Reprinted by permission of Oxford University Press Canada and Houghton Mifflin Company.

W. H. AUDEN: "Musée des Beaux Arts" and "In Memory of W. B. Yeats" from *Collected Poems* by W. H. Auden, edited by Edward Mendelson. Copyright © 1940 W. H. Auden. Reprinted by permission of Faber & Faber Ltd. and Random House, Inc.

REGINA BARRECA: "Nighttime Fires" by Regina Barreca, from *The Minnesota Review*, Fall 1986. Reprinted by permission of the author and The Minnesota Review.

APRIL BERNARD: "Praise Palm of the City-Dweller" from *Psalms* by April Bernard, by permission of W. W. Norton & Company, Inc. Copyright © 1993 by April Bernard.

JOHN BETJEMAN: "In Westminster Abbey" from *Collected Poems* by John Betjeman. Reprinted by permission of the author and John Murray (Publishers) Ltd.

EARLE BIRNEY: "Anglosaxon Street" from *The Collected Poems of Earle Birney*. Used by permission of the Canadian Publishers, McClelland & Stewart, Toronto.

ELIZABETH BISHOP: "Sestina" and "The Armadillo" from *The Complete Poems 1927–1979* by Elizabeth Bishop. Copyright © 1979, 1983 by Alice Helen Methfessel. Reprinted by permission of Farrar, Straus & Giroux, Inc.

LOUISE BOGAN: "Cartography" from *The Blue Estuaries* by Louise Bogan. Copyright © 1968 by Louise Bogan. Reprinted by permission of Farrar, Straus & Giroux, Inc.

ROO BORSON: "After a Death" and "Save Us From" from *Intent, or the Weight of the World* by Roo Borson. Used by permission of the Canadian Publishers, McClelland & Stewart, Toronto.

ROBERT BRINGHURST: "For the Bones of Joseph Mengele, Disinterred June 1985," copyright © 1986 by Robert Bringhurst, reprinted from *Pieces of Map, Pieces of Music*, by permission of McClelland & Stewart Ltd. and the author.

GWENDOLYN BROOKS: "We Real Cool," "Queen of the Blues," and "First Fight. Then Fiddle" from *Blacks*, by Gwendolyn Brooks. Copyright © 1991 by Third World Press, Chicago. Reprinted by permission from Gwendolyn Brooks.

HELEN CHASIN: "Joy Sonnet in a Random Verse" and "The Word *Plum*" from *Coming Close and Other Poems* by Helen Chasin. Copyright © 1968 by Helen Chasin. Reprinted by permission of Yale University Press.

MARILYN CHIN: "Aubade" from Dwarf Bamboo by Marilyn Chin. Reprinted by permission of Greenfield Review Press, Greenfield Review Literary Ctr.

JUDITH ORTIZ COFER: "How to Get a Baby" from *The Latin Deli* by Judith Ortiz Cofer. Reprinted by permission of the University of Georgia Press. "The Changling" and "Unspoken" from *Prairie Schooner*, Fall 1992, vol. 66, no. 3, pp. 28–29. Reprinted by permission of the University of Nebraska Press. Copyright © 1992 by the University of Nebraska Press.

WENDY COPE: "Emily Dickinson," "From Strugnell's Sonnets IV, 'Not only marble, but the plastic toys'" and "From Strugnell's Sonnets I, 'The expense of spirits is a crying shame'" from *Making Cocoa for Kingsley Amis* by Wendy Cope. "Another Christmas Poem" from *Serious Concerns* by Wendy Cope. Reprinted by permission of Faber & Faber, Ltd.

FRANCES CORNFORD: "Parting in Wartime" from *Collected Poems* by Frances Cornford. Reprinted by permission from Random House U.K. Limited.

HART CRANE: "Exile," "Forgetfulness," "Episode of Hands," "To Emily Dickinson" reprinted from *Complete Poems of Hart Crane*, edited by Marc Simon, by permission of Liveright Publishing Corporation. Copyright © 1933, 1958, 1966 by Liveright Publishing Corporation. Copyright © 1986 by Marc Simon.

COUNTEE CULLEN: "For a Lady I Know" from *Color* by Countee Cullen. Copyright © 1925 by Harper & Brothers; copyright renewed 1953 by Ida M. Cullen. Reprinted by permission of GRM Associates, Inc., Agents for the Estate of Ida M. Cullen.

E. E. CUMMINGS: "in Just-," "Buffalo Bill's," "l(a," "(ponder,darling,these busted statues," "anyone lived in a pretty how town" reprinted from *Complete Poems, 1904–1962* by E. E. Cummings, edited by George J. Firmage, by permission of Liveright Publishing Corporation. Copyright © 1923, 1926, 1940, 1951, 1954, 1958, 1968, 1986, 1991 by the Trustees for the E. E. Cummings Trust. Copyright © 1976, 1985 by George James Firmage.

WARING CUNEY: "No Images" by Waring Cuney. We have made diligent efforts to contact the copyright holder to obtain permission to reprint this selection. If you have information that would help us, please write W. W. Norton & Company, 500 Fifth Avenue, New York, NY 10110.

J. V. CUNNINGHAM: "History of Ideas" from *Collected Poems and Epigrams of J. V. Cunningham*. Reprinted by permission of Jessie C. Cunningham.

NORA DAUENHAUER: "Tlingit Concrete Poem" from *The Droning Shaman*. Copyright © 1988 by Nora Dauenhauer. Reprinted by permission of the author.

PETER DE VRIES: "To His Importunate Mistress" by Peter De Vries, originally published in *The New Yorker*. Reprinted by permission of the Watkins/Loomis Agency.

JAMES DICKEY: "Cherrylog Road" and "The Leap" reprinted from *Poems, 1957–1967*. Copyright © 1967 by James Dickey, Wesleyan University Press. Reprinted by permission of University Press of New England.

EMILY DICKINSON: "After great pain, a formal feeling comes—" "I dwell in Possibility—" "My Life had stood—a Loaded Gun—" "The Brain—is Wider than the Sky—" "I reckon—when I count it all—" "We do not play on Graves—" "She dealt her pretty words like blades—" "The Wind begun to knead the Grass" reprinted by permission of the publishers and the Trustees of Amherst College from *The Poems of Emily Dickinson*, Thomas H. Johnson, ed., Cambridge, Mass.: The Belknap Press of Harvard University Press. Copyright © 1951, 1955, 1983 by the President and Fellows of Harvard College. From *The Complete Works of Emily Dickinson*, edited by Thomas

GEOFFREY HILL: "In Memory of Jane Fraser" from *Collected Poems* by Geoffrey Hill. Copyright © 1985 by Geoffrey Hill. Reprinted by permission of Oxford University Press, Inc.

JOHN HOLLANDER: "Adam's Task" from *Selected Poetry* by John Hollander. Copyright © 1993 by John Hollander. Reprinted by permission of Alfred A. Knopf, Inc. "A State of Nature" from *Types of Shape*. Copyright © 1967 by John Hollander. Reprinted by permission of Yale University Press.

ROBERT HOLLANDER: "You Too? Me Too—Why Not? Soda Pop" from *The Massachusetts Review*, vol. 9, no. 3. Copyright © 1968 by Robert Hollander. Reprinted with permission by The Massachusetts Review.

BARBARA HOWES: "Mirror Image: Port-au-Prince" reprinted from *Light and Dark*. Copyright © 1959 by Barbara Howes, Wesleyan University Press. By permission of University Press of New England.

LANGSTON HUGHES: "Theme for English B" from *Montage of a Dream Deferred*. Copyright © 1951 by Langston Hughes. Copyright renewed 1979 by George Houston Bass. Reprinted by permission from Harold Ober Associates, Inc. "The Negro Speaks of Rivers" from *Selected Poems of Langston Hughes* by Langston Hughes. Copyright © 1926 by Alfred A. Knopf, Inc. and renewed by Langston Hughes. "Harlem (A Dream Deferred)" from *The Panther and the Lash* by Langston Hughes. Copyright © 1951 by Langston Hughes. Reprinted by permission of Alfred A. Knopf, Inc.

RANDALL JARRELL: "The Death of the Ball Turret Gunner" from *The Complete Poems* by Randall Jarrell. Copyright © 1945, 1969 by Mrs. Randall Jarrell. Reprinted by permission from Farrar, Straus & Giroux, Inc.

ELIZABETH JENNINGS: "Delay" from *Collected Poems* by Elizabeth Jennings. Reprinted with permission from David Higham Associates, Inc.

PAULETTE JILES: "Paper Matches" from *Cousins* by Paulette Jiles. Copyright © 1992 by Paulette Jiles. Reprinted by permission of Alfred A. Knopf, Inc.

HELENE JOHNSON: "Sonnet to a Negro in Harlem" by Helene Johnson. We have made diligent efforts to contact the copyright holder to obtain permission to reprint this selection. If you have information that could help us, please write to W. W. Norton & Company, 500 Fifth Avenue, New York, NY 10110.

ERICA JONG: "Penis Envy" from *Loveroot* by Erica Jong. Copyright © 1968, 1969, 1973, 1974, 1975 by Erica Mann Jong. Reprinted by permission of Henry Holt and Company, Inc.

JUNE JORDAN: "Something Like a Sonnet for Phillis Miracle Wheatley" from *Naming Our Destiny* by June Jordan. Copyright © 1989 by June Jordan. Used by permission of the publisher, Thunder's Mouth Press.

X. J. KENNEDY: "Epitaph for a Postal Clerk" and "In a Prominent Bar in Secaucus One Day" from *Nude Descending a Staircase*. Copyright © 1961 by X. J. Kennedy. Reprinted by permission of Curtis Brown, Ltd.

GALWAY KINNELL: "Blackberry Eating," and "After Making Love We Hear Footsteps" from *Mortal Acts, Mortal Wounds* by Galway Kinnell. Copyright © 1980 by Galway Kinnell. Reprinted by permission of Houghton Mifflin Company. All rights reserved.

A. M. KLEIN: "Heirloom," from *Complete Poems* by A. M. Klein, edited by Zailig Pollock. Copyright © 1990. Reprinted by permission of University of Toronto Press Incorporated.

ETHERIDGE KNIGHT: "Hard Rock Returns to Prison from the Hospital from the Criminal Insane" from *Poems From Prison*. Copyright © 1968 by Etheridge Knight. Reprinted by permission of Broadside Press.

KENNETH KOCH: "Variations on a Theme by William Carlos Williams" from *Thank You and Other Poems*. Copyright © 1962 by Kenneth Koch. Reprinted by permission of the author.

MAXINE KUMIN: "Woodchucks," copyright © 1971 by Maxine Kumin, from *Our Ground Time Here Will Be Brief* by Maxine Kumin. Used by permission of Viking Penguin, a division of Penguin Books USA Inc.

PHILIP LARKIN: "Church Going" by Philip Larkin, reprinted from *The Less Deceived* by permission of The Marvell Press, England and Australia.

IRVING LAYTON: "The Way the World Ends," "From Colony to Nation," "Street Funeral" from *Collected Poems* by Irving Layton. Used by permission of the Canadian Publishers, McClelland & Stewart, Toronto.

LI-YOUNG LEE: "Persimmons" from *Rose* by Li-Young Lee. Copyright © 1986 by Li-Young Lee. Reprinted by permission of BOA Editions, Ltd., 92 Park Avenue, Brockport, NY 14420.

DOROTHY LIVESAY: "Green Rain" by Dorothy Livesay. We have made diligent efforts to contact the copyright holder to obtain permission to reprint this selection. If you have information that would help us, please write W. W. Norton & Company, 500 Fifth Avenue, New York, NY 10110.

AUDRE LORDE: "Hanging Fire" and "Recreation" reprinted from *The Black Unicorn, Poems* by Audre Lorde, by permission of W. W. Norton & Company, Inc. Copyright © 1978 by Audre Lorde.

ROBERT LOWELL: "Skunk Hour" from *Life Studies* by Robert Lowell. Copyright © 1956, 1959 by Robert Lowell. Copyright renewed © 1987 by Harriet Lowell. Reprinted by permission of Farrar, Straus & Giroux, Inc.

ARCHIBALD MACLEISH: "Ars Poetica" from *Collected Poems 1917–1982* by Archibald MacLeish. Copyright © 1985 by the Estate of Archibald MacLeish. Reprinted by permission of Houghton Mifflin Company. All rights reserved.

WALTER DE LA MARE: "Slim Cunning Hands" from *Walter de la Mare: Slim Cunning Hands* by Walter de la Mare. Reprinted by permission of The Literary Trustees of Walter de la Mare, and The Society of Authors as their representative.

CLAUDE MCKAY: "The Harlem Dancer," "The White House," and "America" from *Selected Poems of Claude McKay*. Copyright © 1981 by Harcourt Brace. Reprinted by permission of the Archives of Claude McKay, Carl Cowl Administrator.

EDNA ST. VINCENT MILLAY: "I, being born a woman and distressed," "What lips my lips have kissed, and where, and why," "Women have loved before as I love now," "An Ancient Gesture," "First Fig," and "Second Fig" by Edna St. Vincent Millay. From *Collected Poems*, HarperCollins. Copyright © 1923, 1931, 1951, 1954, 1958, 1982 by Edna St. Vincent Millay and Norma Millay Ellis. Reprinted by permission of Elizabeth Barnett, literary executor.

MARIANNE MOORE: "Poetry" from *Collected Poems of Marianne Moore*. Copyright 1935 by Marianne Moore, renewed 1963 by Marianne Moore and T. S. Eliot. Reprinted with permission of Simon & Schuster. "Love in America," from *The Complete Poems of Marianne Moore* by Marianne Moore. Copyright © 1981 by Clive E. Driver, Literary Executor of the Estate of Marianne C. Moore. Used by permission of Viking Penguin, a division of Penguin Books USA Inc.

PAT MORA: "Gentle Communion," and "Sonrisas" by Pat Mora are printed with permission from the publishers of *Borders* (Houston: Arte Publico Press—University of Houston, 1986).

ERIN MOURÉ: "Thirteen Years" from *Furious* by Erin Mouré. Reprinted by permission of the author and Stoddart Publishing Co. Limited, Don Mills, Ontario.

SUSAN MUSGRAVE: "I Am Not a Conspiracy" from *Cocktails at the Mausoleum*, "Hidden Meaning" and "You Didn't Fit" from *Embalmer's Art*, both by Susan Musgrave. Reprinted by permission of the author.

HOWARD NEMEROV: "A Way of Life," "Epigram: Political Reflexion," "Boom!" "The Vacuum," "The Goose Fish," and "The Town Dump" from *The Collected Poems of Howard Nemerov*. Copyright © 1977 by Howard Nemerov. Reprinted with permission of the Howard Nemerov Trust and Margaret Nemerov.

SHARON OLDS: "Leningrad Cemetery, Winter of 1941" by Sharon Olds from *The New Yorker*, December 31, 1979. Reprinted by permission © 1979 of The New Yorker Magazine, Inc. "The Glass" and "The Lifting" from *The Father* by Sharon Olds. Copyright © 1992 by Sharon Olds. "Sex Without Love," "The Victims," and "The Elder Sister" from *The Dead and the Living* by Sharon Olds. Copyright © 1975, 1978, 1979, 1980, 1981, 1982, 1983 by Sharon Olds. Reprinted by permission of Alfred A. Knopf, Inc.

MICHAEL ONDAATJE: "King Kong Meets Wallace Stevens" from *The Cinnamon Peeler* by Michael Ondaatje. Copyright © 1989 by Michael Ondaatje. Reprinted by permission of the Canadian Publishers, McClelland & Stewart, Toronto and Alfred A. Knopf, Inc.

WILFRED OWEN: "Dulce et Decorum Est" from *Collected Poems of Wildred Owen*. Copyright © 1963 by Chatto & Windus, Ltd. Reprinted by permission of New Directions Publishing Corporation.

DOROTHY PARKER: "Comment," copyright 1926, renewed © 1954 by Dorothy Parker; "Indian Summer," copyright 1926, renewed © 1954 by Dorothy Parker; "One Perfect Rose," copyright 1929, renewed © 1957 by Dorothy Parker; "A Certain Lady," copyright 1928, renewed © 1956 by Dorothy Parker, from *The Portable Dorothy Parker* by Dorothy Parker, Introduction by Brendan Gill.

Used by permission of Viking Penguin, a division of Penguin Books USA Inc.

LINDA PASTAN: "Marks" reprinted from *PM/AM, New and Selected Poems*, by Linda Pastan, by permission of W. W. Norton & Company, Inc. Copyright © 1982 by Linda Pastan. "To a Daughter Leaving Home" and "love poem" from *The Imperfect Paradise, Poems* by Linda Pastan, by permission of W. W. Norton & Company, Inc. Copyright © 1988 by Linda Pastan.

RAYMOND R. PATTERSON: "You Are the Brave" from *26 Ways of Looking at a Black Man* by Raymond R. Patterson. Copyright by Raymond Patterson. Reprinted with permission from Ayer Company Publishers, Inc.

RICARDO PAU-LLOSA: "Foreign Language" from *Bread of the Imagined* by Ricardo Pau-Llosa (Tempe: Bilingual Press, Arizona State University, 1992), originally appeared in *Kayak*, no. 64, May 1984. Reprinted with permission from the author.

MARGE PIERCY: "Barbie Doll" from *Circles on the Water* by Marge Piercy. Copyright © 1982 by Marge Piercy. "To Have Without Holding" from *The Moon Is Always Female* by Marge Piercy. Copyright © 1979 by Marge Piercy. "What's That Smell in the Kitchen?" from *Stone, Paper, Knife* by Marge Piercy. Copyright © 1980 by Marge Piercy. Reprinted by permission of Alfred A. Knopf, Inc.

SYLVIA PLATH: "Point Shirley" from *The Collossus and Other Poems*. Copyright © 1959 by Sylvia Plath. Reprinted by permission of Alfred A. Knopf, Inc. and Faber & Faber Ltd. "Daddy," "Black Rook in Rainy Weather," "Lady Lazarus," "Morning Song," and "Mirror," (originally appeared in *The New Yorker*) from *Collected Poems* by Sylvia Plath, edited by Ted Hughes. Reprinted with permission of Faber & Faber Ltd. and HarperCollins Publishers, Inc.

KATHA POLLITT: "Two Fish" from *Antarctic Traveller* by Katha Pollitt. Copyright © 1972 by Katha Pollitt. Reprinted by permission of Alfred A. Knopf, Inc.

EZRA POUND: "The River-Merchant's Wife: A Letter," "The Garden," "In a Station of the Metro" from *Personae* by Ezra Pound. Copyright © 1926 by Ezra Pound. Reprinted by permission of New Directions Publishing Corporation.

JAROLD RAMSEY: "The Tally Stick" by Jarold Ramsey. Reprinted by permission of the author.

DUDLEY RANDALL: "Ballad of Birmingham" from *Poem Counter Poem* by Dudley Randall. Reprinted by permission of the Broadside Press.

JOHN CROWE RANSOM: "Bells for John Whiteside's Daughter" from *Selected Poems* by John Crowe Ransom. Copyright © 1924 by John Crowe Ransom. Reprinted by permission of Alfred A. Knopf, Inc.

HENRY REED: "Lessons of the War: Judging Distances," from *Henry Reed: Collected Poems*, edited by Jon Stallworthy (1991). Copyright © The Executor of Henry Reed's Estate. Reprinted by permission of Oxford University Press.

ISHMAEL REED: "beware: do not read this poem" and "I Am a Cowboy in the Boat of Ra" by Ishmael Reed. Copyright © 1972 by Ishmael Reed. Reprinted by permission of author and Whitman Breed Abbott & Morgan.

ADRIENNE RICH: "Origins and History of Consciousness" reprinted from *The Dream of a Common Language, Poems 1974–1977* by Adrienne Rich. "Walking Down the Road" and "Letters in the Family" reprinted from *Time's Power, Poems 1985–1988* by Adrienne Rich. Part 3, "My mouth hovers across your breasts," from *Contradictions: Tracking Poems*, reprinted from *Your Native Land, Your Life, Poems* by Adrienne Rich. "Dialogue," Delta," "Power," "Living in Sin," "Leaflets," "Planetarium," "Aunt Jennifer's Tigers," "At a Bach Concert," "Storm Warnings," and "Snapshots of a Daughter-in-Law," "Orion," "Diving into the Wreck," "Two Songs," and "For the Record" all reprinted from *The Fact of a Doorframe, Poems Selected and New, 1950–1984*, by Adrienne Rich. "How does a poet put bread on the table?" and an excerpt from "A communal poetry" reprinted from *What Is Found There, Notebooks on Poetry and Politics*, by Adrienne Rich. Excerpt from "When We Dead Awaken: Writing as Re-Vision" reprinted from *On Lies, Secrets, and Silence, Selected Prose 1966–1978* by Adrienne Rich, by permission of W. W. Norton & Company, Inc. Copyright © 1978 by W. W. Norton & Company, Inc. "Talking with Adrienne Rich," an interview with Wayne Dodd and Stanley Plumly, from *The Ohio Review*, no. 1. Used by permission of The Ohio Review.

ALBERTO RÍOS: "Advice to a First Cousin" from *Five Indiscretions* by Alberto Ríos. Copyright © 1985 The Sheep Meadow Press. Reprinted by permission. Riverdale-on-Hudson, New York.

EDWIN ARLINGTON ROBINSON: "Mr. Flood's Party" from *Collected Poems of Edwin Arlington Robinson*. Copyright © 1921 by Edwin Arlington Robinson, renewed 1949 by Ruth Nivision. Reprinted with permission of Simon & Schuster, Inc.

THEODORE ROETHKE: "My Papa's Waltz," copyright 1942 by Hearst Magazines, Inc. "The Dream," copyright © 1955 by Theodore Roethke. "The Waking," copyright 1948 by Theodore Roethke. "I Knew a Woman," copyright 1954 by Theodore Roethke. Used by permission of Doubleday, a division of Bantam Doubleday Dell Publishing Group, Inc.

LIZ ROSENBERG: "Married Love" reprinted from *The Fire Music* by Liz Rosenberg, by permission of the University of Pittsburgh Press. Copyright © 1986 by Liz Rosenberg.

MURIEL RUKEYSER: "Reading Time : 1 Minute 26 Seconds" and "Myth" by Muriel Rukeyser. Reprinted by permission of William L. Rukeyser.

MARY JO SALTER: "Welcome to Hiroshima" from *Henry Purcell in Japan*, by Mary Jo Salter. Copyright © 1984 by Mary Jo Salter. Reprinted by permission of Alfred A. Knopf, Inc.

DUNCAN CAMPBELL SCOTT: "The Onondaga Madonna" from *Selected Poems of Duncan Campbell Scott* by Duncan Campbell Scott. Reprinted by permission of John G. Aylen.

ANNE SEXTON: "The Fury of Overshoes" from *The Death Notebooks* by Anne Sexton. Copyright © 1974 by Anne Sexton. "With Mercy for the Greedy" from *All My Pretty Ones* by Anne Sexton. Copyright © 1962 by Anne Sexton, renewed © 1990 by Linda G. Sexton. Reprinted by permission from Houghton Mifflin Company, 215 Park Avenue South, New York. All rights reserved.

KARL SHAPIRO: "Auto Wreck," copyright © 1941, 1987 Karl Shapiro by arrangement with Wieser & Weiser, Inc. New York. Reprinted by permission of Wieser & Weiser, Inc.

DESMOND SKIRROW: "Ode on a Grecian Urn Summarized" by Desmond Skirrow. Reprinted by permission of The New Statesman, Foundation House, Perserverance Works, London, England.

KAY SMITH: "Annunciations" by Kay Smith. Reprinted by permission of the author.

STEVIE SMITH: "Our Bog is Dood," "The Jungle Husband," and 'I Remember' from *Collected Poems of Stevie Smith*. Copyright © 1972 by Stevie Smith. Reprinted with permission of New Directions Publishing Corporation.

W. D. SNODGRASS: "Leaving the Motel" by W. D. Snodgrass. Reprinted by permission of the author.

RICHARD SNYDER: "A Mongoloid Child Handling Shells on the Beach" from *Practicing Our Sighs: The Collected Poems of Richard Snyder*, edited by Mary Snyder and Robert McGovern. Copyright © 1989 by Richard Snyder. Reprinted with permission of The Ashland Poetry Press, Ashland University.

CATHY SONG: "A Mehinaku Girl in Seclusion" reprinted from *Frameless Windows, Squares of Light, Poems* by Cathy Song, by permission of W. W. Norton & Company, Inc. Copyright © 1988 by Cathy Song.

WILLIAM STAFFORD: "At the Bomb Testing Site" from *The Rescued Year* by William Stafford. Copyright © 1960. Reprinted by permission of the estate of William Stafford.

WALLACE STEVENS: "Anecdote of the Jar," "The Emperor of Ice-Cream," and "Sunday Morning" from *The Collected Poems of Wallace Stevens* by Wallace Stevens. Copyright © 1923 and renewed 1951 by Wallace Stevens. Reprinted by permission of Alfred A. Knopf, Inc.

DYLAN THOMAS: "Fern Hill," "In My Craft or Sullen Art," and "Do Not Go Gentle into That Good Night" from *The Poems* by Dylan Thomas. Copyright © 1939 by Dylan Thomas. Reprinted with permission of David Higham Associates, Ltd., and New Directions Publishing Corporation.

JEAN TOOMER: "Reapers" and "Song of the Son" reprinted from *Cane* by Jean Toomer, by permission of Liveright Publishing Corporation. Copyright © 1923 by Boni & Liveright. Copyright renewed 1951 by Jean Toomer.

MONA VAN DUYN: "What the Motorcycle Said" from *If It Be Not I* by Mona Van Duyn. Copyright © 1993 by Mona Van Duyn. Reprinted by permission of Alfred A. Knopf, Inc.

MIRIAM WADDINGTON: "Ulysses Embroidered" from *The Last Landscape* by Miriam Waddington. Copyright © 1992 by Miriam Waddington. Reprinted by permission of Oxford University Press Canada.

DAVID WAGONER: "My Father's Garden" from *Through the Forest*. Copyright © 1987 by David Wagoner. Used by permission of Grove/Atlantic, Inc.

DIANE WAKOSKI: "A Poet Recognizing the Echo of the Voice" by Diane Wakoski. Copyright © 1970 by Diane Wakoski. Reprinted by permission of the author.

DEREK WALCOTT: "A Far Cry from Africa" from *Collected Poems 1948–1984* by Derek Walcott. Copyright © 1986 by Derek Walcott. Reprinted by permission of Farrar, Straus & Giroux, Inc.

TOM WAYMAN: "Wayman in Love" by Tom Wayman. Reprinted by permission of Harbour Publishing Company, Limited.

RICHARD WILBUR: "Love Calls Us to the Things of This World" from *Things of This World*, copyright © 1956 and renewed by Richard Wilbur, reprinted by permission of Harcourt Brace & Company.

WILLIAM CARLOS WILLIAMS: "The Red Wheelbarrow" and "This Is Just to Say" from *Collected Poems 1909–1939, Vol. I*. Copyright © 1938 by New Directions Corporation. "Raleigh Was Right," "The Dance," and "Poem" from *Collected Poems 1939–1962, Vol. II*. Copyright © 1944, 1948, 1962 by William Carlos Williams. Reprinted by permission of New Directions Publishing Corporation.

YVOR WINTERS: "At the San Francisco Airport" from *The Collected Poems of Yvor Winters* (Ohio University Press/Swallow Press, 1980).

JAMES WRIGHT: "Arrangements with Earth for Three Dead Friends" reprinted from *Collected Poems* by James Wright. Copyright © 1971 by James Wright, Wesleyan University Press. By permission of University Press of New England.

JUDITH WRIGHT: " 'Dove-Love' " from *Collected Poems 1942–1970* by Judith Wright. Reprinted by kind permission of Angus & Robertson Publishers.

W. B. YEATS: "Byzantium," copyright 1933 by Macmillan Publishing Company, renewed 1961 by Bertha Georgie Yeats. "Leda and the Swan," "Sailing to Byzantium," and "Among School Children," copyright 1928 by Macmillan Publishing Company, renewed 1956 by Georgie Yeats. "Easter 1916," "The Second Coming," copyright 1924 by Macmillan Publishing Company, renewed 1952 by Bertha Georgie Yeats. From *The Poems of W. B. Yeats: A New Edition*.

ANTON CHEKHOV: "The Bear" from *Twelve Plays* by Anton Chekhov, translated by Ronald Hingley (World Classics, 1992). Copyright © 1968 by Ronald Hingley. "The Cherry Orchard" from *Five Plays* by Anton Chekhov, translated by Ronald Hingley, copyright © 1965 by Ronald Hingley. Originally published in *The Oxford Chekhov*. Reprinted by permission of Oxford University Press. Excerpts from Chekhov's letters, translated by Ralph E. Matlaw, are reprinted from *Anton Chekhov's Short Stories*, A Norton Critical Edition, selected and edited by Ralph E. Matlaw, by permission of W. W. Norton & Company, Inc. Copyright © 1979 by W. W. Norton & Company, Inc. "On the Injurious Effects of Tobacco" reprinted from *Anton Chekhov's Plays*, A Norton Critical Edition, translated and edited by Eugene K. Bristow, by permission of W. W. Norton & Company, Inc. Copyright © 1977 by W. W. Norton & Company, Inc.

CARYL CHURCHILL: "Top Girls" by Caryl Churchill. Copyright © 1982 by Caryl Churchill. Reprinted by permission of Reed Consumer Books.

SUSAN GLASPELL: "Trifles" by Susan Glaspell. Copyright © 1951 by Walter H. Baker Company. Reprinted by arrangement with Baker's Plays, 100 Chauncy Street, Boston, MA 02111.

LILLIAN HELLMAN: "The Little Foxes" by Lillian Hellman. Copyright © 1939 and renewed 1967 by Lillian Hellman. Reprinted by permission of Random House, Inc.

HENRIK IBSEN: "Hedda Gabler," translated by Michael Meyer, published in *The Plays of Ibsen, Vol. II* by Washington Square Press. Copyright © 1962, 1974 by Michael Meyer. Reprinted with permission from Harold Ober Associates Incorporated.

ARTHUR MILLER: "Death of a Salesman" by Arthur Miller. Copyright © 1949, renewed © 1977 by Arthur Miller. Used by permission of Viking Penguin, a division of Penguin Books USA Inc.

MARSHA NORMAN: "Getting Out" from *Four Plays* by Marsha Norman. Copyright © 1978, 1979 by Marsha Norman. Reprinted by permission of Theatre Communications Group.

HAROLD PINTER: "The Black and the White" from *A Slight Ache and Other Plays*. Copyright © 1966 by Harold Pinter. Reprinted by permission of Faber & Faber Ltd. and Grove/Atlantic, Inc.

SHARON POLLOCK: "Blood Relations" from *Blood Relations and Other Plays* by Sharon Pollock. Copyright © 1981 by Sharon Pollock. Reprinted by permission of NeWest Publishers Ltd., Edmonton, Alberta, Canada.

WILLIAM SHAKESPEARE: "A Midsummer Night's Dream" from *The Complete Works of Shakespeare*, edited by David Bevington. Copyright © 1980, 1973, 1961, 1951 by Scott, Foresman and Company. Reprinted by permission of HarperCollins College Publishers.

BERNARD SHAW: "Pygmalion" from *The Collected Plays of George Bernard Shaw* by Bernard Shaw. Copyright © 1913, 1914, 1916, 1930, 1941 by George Bernard Shaw. Copyright © 1957 by The Public Trustee as Executor of the Estate of Bernard Shaw. Reprinted by permission of The Society of Authors on behalf of the Estate of Bernard Shaw.

SOPHOCLES: "Antigone" and "Oedipus the King" from *Complete Greek Tragedies*, translated by D. Grene. Copyright © 1942 by The University of Chicago. Reprinted by permission of the University of Chicago Press.

TENNESSEE WILLIAMS: "A Streetcar Named Desire" by Tennessee Williams. Copyright © 1947 by Tennessee Williams. Reprinted by permission of New Directions Publishing Corporation.

AUGUST WILSON: "Fences" by August Wilson. Copyright © 1986 by August Wilson. Used by permission of Dutton Signet, a division of Penguin Books USA Inc.

INDEX OF AUTHORS

INDEX OF TITLES AND FIRST LINES

INDEX OF LITERARY TERMS